MUSIC SINCE 1900

SIXTH EDITION

MUSIC SINCE 1900

SIXTH EDITION

NICOLAS SLONIMSKY

with updates by
LAURA KUHN

SCHIRMER REFERENCE

GALE GROUP

THOMSON LEARNING

New York • Detroit • San Diego • San Francisco
Boston • New Haven, Conn. • Waterville, Maine
London • Munich

Sixth Edition

Copyright © 2001 by Schirmer Reference, an imprint of the Gale Group

Fifth edition copyright © 1994 by Nicolas Slonimsky
Fourth edition copyright © 1971 by Nicolas Slonimsky
Copyright © 1937, 1938, 1949 by Charles Scribner's Sons
Renewal copyright © 1965, 1966, 1977 by Nicolas Slonimsky

Schirmer Reference
1633 Broadway
New York, New York 10019

Gale Group
27500 Drake Road
Farmington Hills, Michigan 48331-3535

Printed in the United States of America

Printing number
2 3 4 5 6 7 8 9 10

Library of Congress Cataloging-in-Publication Data

Slonimsky, Nicolas, 1894-
    Music since 1900 / Nicolas Slonimsky ; with updates by Laura Kuhn.—
6th ed.
        p. cm.
Includes index.
  ISBN 0-02-864787-4 (alk. paper)
    1. Music—20th century—History and criticism. 2. Music—20th
century—Chronology. I. Kuhn, Laura Diane. II. Title.
  ML197.S634 2001
  780'.9'04—dc21   2001020636

This paper meets the requirements of ANSI/NISO Z39.48-1992 (Permanence of Paper).

To all, ex post facto,
who contributed to the advancement of music
written after 1900

PREFACE TO THE SIXTH EDITION

There are any number of stories to tell about Nicolas Slonimsky, our beloved, legendary Russian-born American musicologist of manifold endeavors, but the one that comes most quickly to mind with respect to music of the twentieth century is his oft-expressed opinion that nothing really new had occurred by the end of the century that hadn't occurred prior to the end of its first half. Indeed, he asserted that nothing really new could be said to have happened after the extraordinary achievements of Charles Ives, the inventive American composer whose works Nicolas himself had ardently championed during his remarkable, if lamentably short-lived, career as a conductor in the 1920s and 1930s.

From Nicolas's nearly centenarian vantage point, such a bold (and argumentative!) opinion wasn't arbitrary, but inevitable, given his quirky, uncanny powers of observation. I remember once, in the late 1980s, taking him to a concert of modern music at Los Angeles's Dorothy Chandler Pavilion, at the outset of which he promptly fell asleep, snoring peacefully throughout the evening's three long works. At the concert's close, with the onset of modest audience applause, he finally stirred, sat up squarely in his seat, and promptly made the most pithy, astute comments about each work that had been played.

Knowing too well Nicolas's penchant for tricks, and not wishing to be duped yet again, I pressed him further during our drive home, testing the limits of what appeared to be his extraordinary subliminal absorption. What did he think of the use of the brass in the last piece? How about that odd transition into the development section in the second movement of the opening work? Didn't he think the composer's use of percussion wasn't a bit heavy handed in the second piece? And could he discern, as I did, an affinity between the third composer's penchant for ornamentation and Schubert's late tendencies? Each question was carefully considered and met with a quite reasoned answer, ostensibly from one who had been thoroughly attentive to, indeed deeply enraptured by, the evening's fare.

How could this be, I finally blurted out, since he had slept through the entire concert?! He was matter-of-fact in his explanation, which had nothing to do with magical powers in the realm of somnambulist divination. He calmly explained to me that after so many decades of listening to music, he was simply able to accurately project, upon hearing a few strains at the start of any given work, how that work was most likely to unfold and end.

There were a few exceptions to his summary dismissal of what was purportedly "contemporary" in newly composed works, and those exceptions were clearly what had sustained his lifelong interest in music of his own time. The ideas and compositions of the iconoclastic American composer John Cage, for example, never failed to delight him, and the experiments with the spatial dis-tribution of instruments by the lively American composer Henry Brant were of genuine interest. He also found much of real value in virtually all of the work of the formidable French composer Pierre Boulez. I remember, too, his fascination with particular pieces by other, younger contemporary composers: Charles Amirkhanian's tetraphallic *Mooga Pook* (1967), for example, Daniel Lentz's patently coital *Love and Conception* (1968–69), and, later, Ingram Marshall's *Fog Tropes* (1982), with its beautiful use of electronically manipulated taped sounds gathered around the San Francisco Bay, including foghorns and the falsetto keenings of seagulls. And as a quick read of his prefaces to earlier editions of *Music Since 1900* reveals, he also found something to say about virtually anyone willing to do patently audacious, even ridiculous, things in concert settings, above and beyond what might be called their purely "musical" merit.

But from where we sit today, barely five years after Nicolas's death on Christmas Day 1995, it would appear that much is observably new in new music, and it is literally breathtaking to reflect upon the fact that all of this has come to pass in just five years' time. Granted, the most noteworthy innovations are being most fully exploited in more popular realms, but they are not entirely foreign to contemporary classical composers: intoned speech or even lip sync in place of previously sung texts; performers who confine their compositional efforts exclusively to the rhythmic manipulation of LPs and turntables; a pervasive, virtually assimilated use of electronics across the board; the use of sound samples in place of traditional musical materials; a seamless integration of styles and genres in one and the same work, including elements of diverse world music as well as the incorporation of instruments known earlier only within pop, rock, and jazz; the design and implementation, via high-speed computers, of "automatic" compositional systems; an unbelievably realistic simulation of sounds through computer synthesis and the concomitant rise of "virtual" instruments—all of this and more at work in a field that is at the same time exploring radically new, wider, and easier means of dissemination via television, the Internet, and, one can be sure, the as-yet-unimaginable beyond. Democratic self-sufficiency is the overriding catchphrase at the turn of the twenty-first century— MIDI technology; high-speed, multimedia computers; sophisticated electronic instruments; fiber-optic technology—all contributing to a situation wherein composers are better able to self-produce, self-promote, and self-publish, affecting all the while the way compositions are being made and performed.

But as the present, sixth edition of *Music Since 1900* shows, such radical, innovative practices, while clearly reflective of grand societal changes at large, are not yet the common practice of classical composers of our time. Indeed, as the latest entries updating the last decade of the twentieth century reveal, the nearly 1,000 composers represented therein, in the main, still mostly compose works in a nineteenth-century tradition, utilizing the compositional means and materials as well as the instruments common to several centuries past. They also, in the main, compose exclusively for what are fast becoming what might reasonably be called "historical" modes of public delivery and consumption. But, just as Nicolas was able to observe exceptions in his view, there are exceptions in ours: Boulez and Cage remain in the avant-garde, with staunch competition from such colleagues as Robert Ashley, Mikel Rouse, and William Duckworth, to name just a few. We are also witness to extraordinary and unprecedented collaborations with the most modern of music in the sister arts, prominent among them being the works of the enfant terrible of theater, director Robert Wilson, and of the now-legendary choreographer Merce Cunningham. And it is not insignificant to note that in the year 1999, the Academy Award for Best Original Score was given, for the first time, to a composer well known in the world of purely classical composition, John (Paul) Corigliano, for his *Chaconne* for violin and orchestra (1997), put to such effective use in François Girard's highly acclaimed film *The Red Violin* (1998).

It is clearly, as Charles Dickens said, both the best and worst of times, at least insofar as classical music is concerned. The diminishing of both government and corporate sponsorship, the virtual death of independent recording labels, the lack of adequately equipped and acoustically responsive performance spaces, a general rise of what might be called moral conservatism are just a few of the most unhappy developments and tenaciously enduring situations of the past decade that have affected, and are continuing to affect, classical music and musicians. But, as noted, in other ways the final years of the twentieth century were very kind to the arts, and particularly to serious music, with technology, and perhaps especially the Internet, affording composers and performers alike far greater options as to how music might be made and disseminated. I, for one, greatly look forward to the decade or two just ahead, since changes and advances, at the present moment, are coming fast and furious. In the meantime, it is my hope that the present, final, twentieth-century edition of *Music Since 1900* will amuse and enlighten its readers with regard to classical music for centuries to come.

LAURA KUHN
New York City
April 2001

PREFACE TO THE FIFTH EDITION

The first edition of *Music Since 1900* appeared in 1937, under the imprint of W. W. Norton. A second edition was issued in 1938; it included but a few additions to the chronology. A substantial third edition was published in 1949 by Coleman-Ross Company. In addition to its three basic parts—Descriptive Chronology, Explanation of Terms, and Letters and Documents—that edition also introduced a Tabular View of Stylistic Trends in music: Increasing Grandiosity (1900–1914), Retrogressive Neo-Classicism (1915–1939), and Search for New Style (1939–48). Each of these divisions had several subdivisions: Impressionism, Expressionism, Futurism, Neo-Primitivism, Neo-Romanticism, Neo-Nationalism, Neo-Utilitarianism, Sophisticated Folk Music, etc. Specific compositions were listed under each category, with additional descriptions of each, for example, "austere religionism," "exotic imagism," "impassionate megasymphonism," "operatic pathetism," etc. But this Tabular View proved so inflated in trying to extend it further in time that, with some pangs of regret, I had to drop it in the fourth edition published by Scribner's in 1971. In that edition, the Descriptive Chronology was brought up to the year 1969, and its Letters and Documents section was greatly increased. The Dictionary of Terms was enlarged to include a detailed analysis of modern techniques.

In 1986, a *Supplement to Music Since 1900* appeared, also published by Scribner's, and also comprised of three sections: a continuation of Descriptive Chronology from 1970 to 1985, additional items as well as amplifications and rectifications of errors in the basic Chronology of 1900 to 1969, and several new documents. The Index covered names and subjects of the Supplement. In the present, fifth edition of *Music Since 1900*, the 1986 *Supplement* has been rolled together with the 1971 Fourth Edition; new materials comprise a continuation of Descriptive Chronology from 1985 to 1991 and additional items as well as amplifications and rectifications of errors in the *Supplement* Chronology of 1970 to 1985.

I vividly remember the opening line of the review of the first edition of *Music Since 1900* appearing in the *Musical Times* of London, which began "... like *everyone* I have been reading Slonimsky's astounding book!" This review, and others like it, astonished me. What was so remarkable in my compilation and analyses of catalogue titles that marked the opening of the new century? In thinking about what the present compilation represents, I was drawn back to the materials comprising the Letters and Documents portion of that first edition. There was, for example, a reply to a query I addressed to George Bernard Shaw explaining the reason why he regarded the opening of the new century as of basic importance for composers, performers, and theorists. Another arresting quotation in my little compendium was an account of "Music of the Future" as envisaged by the Italian Futurists. And from the theological front, there was an explication of the historical transition from medieval to modern music. Perhaps the most important contribution, however, was a signal statement by Arnold Schoenberg, in which he explained the origin and psychological underpinning of his epoch-making introduction of the technique of composition in twelve related tones. Schoenberg's proclamation of the supremacy of atonal composition was prophetic, for the most important technical concern of 20th-century composers has been the abolition of the concept of dissonance. Music in the modern concept equates to logic; what makes musical sense becomes ipso facto music. Dissonance is, in this definition, equatable to music, which of course means that the concept of dissonance itself is a kind of self-negation.

The radical change in both practice and taste from the last decades of the 19th century to the first of the 20th is vividly illustrated by a remark of Richard Strauss with reference to his song *Wenn*, composed in 1895. With a typical sense of late 19th-century humor, he suggested that performers who chose to sing this song in the late 19th century should use the previous tonality while performers who chose to sing it in the early 20th century should feel free to use the new.

The "new" tonality was, of course, marked by a decisive liberation of dissonant chords, and modern composers tended to avoid major triads and their inversions. Schoenberg himself explained, in a sort of historiographic sense, that triadic formations had been so abused in Classical and Romantic music that it was necessary to avoid them in modern times. In his own works, and in those of countless composers in his wake, the major seventh assumed the function of the perfect octave, while the forbidden tritone, the augmented fourth, assumed the function of the perfect fifth. It was as though the major triad (the seemingly unshakable foundation of music) had been squeezed so as to reduce all intervals of the tempered scale by a minor second.

With the emancipation of dissonant chords also came an end to the need for consonant resolution, and indeed many early 20th-century composers experimented with the practice of concluding their works in harmonies not immediately related to the original key. There was an occasional appearance of an augmented triad in final cadences, as well as of major sixths and ninths, as in certain piano pieces by Debussy or in American ragtime.

It is important to note, however, that what were formerly held to be the forbidden intervals, and what were so freely used by early 20th-century composers in their final cadences, are in actuality acoustically natural overtones of the fundamental. A high A placed over a C major chord, for example, forms not only the "dissonant" interval of a minor sixth but also the 27th natural overtone of the fundamental C. An even more striking dissonance, often employed in ragtime, is formed by adding the 15th overtone to the fundamental chord tone, forming the interval of a major seventh. Thus the chord C-E-G-B becomes, in ragtime as elsewhere, a new concord. Even the proverbial "devil" of modal harmony, the augmented fourth (diminished fifth), can be reduced to an overtone; high F-sharp placed over the fundamental C forms the 45th overtone of the fundamental. This curious relationship may be at the root of the frequent bitonality of C major and F-sharp major as seen in modern works by Debussy, Ravel, and Stravinsky, often employed in piano pieces which combine the two using the black keys in the treble over the white keys in the bass.

Even more remarkable is the fact that while all formerly dissonant tones are in fact members of the natural overtone series, the hallowed interval known as the perfect fourth—formed by an F over the bass fundamental C—does not partake of the overtone series. This may explain why composers of the first half of the 20th century rarely if ever attempted to incorporate the interval of the perfect fourth in their cadential formulas, while freely using all other intervals. An examination of modern compositions by such composers as Debussy, Ravel, Casella, and Malipiero bears this out, as does the practice of ragtime players and their successors in jazz and rock.

It is true enough that all dissonances, however difficult to absorb by a classically trained ear, are now easily tolerated in modern harmony. Indeed, the most complex of melodies, harmonies, and rhythms all take part in modern music in the most embracing manner; virtually every item among the hundreds comprising the present text exemplifies some form of novel harmony or of an orchestral ensemble of distinctly modern employment. And, further, there is room for not only a diversity of techniques and applications, but for the negation of specific applications, exemplified in the extreme by the silent music of John Cage. It would appear that at the end of the second millennium, the absence of music has itself become the essence of musical invention.

At the conclusion of this exordium, words of great warmth and thanks must be extended to several marvelous people, each of whom uniquely, unselfishly, and intelligently provided assistance in completing the present work. First, a word of praise for Steve Ellis, a Glenview, Illinois-based music editor with an eagle eye for errors and inconsistencies and a talent for information gathering that is *non pareil*. Thanks, too, to the Indianapolis-based musicological sleuth Dennis McIntire for his contributions of important last-minute premieres. Particular praise must go to the extraordinary Laura Kuhn who, as coordinating editor of the present volume, helped me to prepare and then organize its literally hundreds of new entries. And, finally, praise mixed with the sincerest personal affection for Karen Murphy, who watched lovingly and faithfully over me during the final stages of my work.

NICOLAS SLONIMSKY
Los Angeles

PREFACE TO THE FOURTH EDITION

"This is a book in the first place of materials, in the second of evaluation. The main body of the book, a Descriptive Chronology, is intended to be a sort of newsreel reflecting the 'inner headlines' of musical events that may not be at the moment of their occurrence of any significance, and yet contain elements of evolutionary power that subtly but surely influence the entire future of music. Thus, the date of completion of *Le Sacre du Printemps* or of *Pierrot Lunaire*, while quite unnoticed by the music world at large, is an inner headline of extreme importance; such dates, when ascertainable, are given particular attention. . . . Spectacular performers, great singers, big impresarios have been left out of the picture almost entirely, although their power in the musical world and their hold on the outer headlines are incomparably superior to that of a composer-inventor.

"Descriptive Chronology is here unrolled without national subdivisions. An event of musical interest may happen today in America, tomorrow in Russia; it is their contiguity in time alone that places them one after another. This method has the disadvantage of lumping together unrelated phenomena, but so has every chronology.

"A history of the modern musical idiom is yet to be written. Here we may cautiously draw a general outline of musical evolution since 1900, and post its milestones. We must remember that all musical innovation, no matter how extreme, is useful in that it indicates potentialities heretofore overlooked. Thus, composers thoroughly averse to the spirit of the twelve-tone technique may find its methods of great value within the tonal framework. The exploration of quarter-tone music may be an isolated phenomenon, and yet it subtilizes our perception of chromatic harmony.

"Selection of landmarks in modern music is perforce arbitrary, but no more so than the designation of historical eras. It was not announced in Rome in A.D. 476 that the Middle Ages had then and there begun; yet historians accept this date as a convenient chronological landmark. Similarly, we are justified in selecting an important event in 20th-century music as a chronological symbol of esthetic evolution. The first performance of Debussy's *Pelléas et Mélisande*, on 30 April 1902, may be considered such a symbol, signalizing the advent of impressionist opera. The outbreak of World War I brought about a musico-psychological re-alignment, with the romance of the machine replacing the romance of sentiment. The era of machine music came abruptly to an end with the economic collapse of 1929, when musicians abandoned the cult of the discredited machine and turned to composing pure music in a neo-classical manner. As if by general consent, pictorial and descriptive titles disappeared from the pages of musical scores. Honegger's first 'mouvement symphonique,' composed in December 1923, was subtitled *Pacific 231*, and was intended to glori-

fy the American locomotive of that designation; his second 'mouvement' was *Rugby,* written in 1928 as a musical picture of a fashionable game; but his third work in the same genre, composed between October 1932 and January 1933, is entitled simply *Mouvement Symphonique.*

"The process of forming a new technique is illuminated in a remarkable letter from Arnold Schoenberg (in the section Letters and Documents) regarding the origin of his method of composition with twelve tones related only to one another. This letter shows how an idea latent in a musician's mind crystallizes, by the logic of true intuition, into a definite formula, at a definite point in time."

The foregoing paragraphs are extracted, with minor alterations, from the introduction to the first edition of *Music Since 1900*, published in 1937. There was a second printing in 1938 and an enlarged edition in 1949. An eventful third of a century has passed since this introduction was written. *Music Since 1900* was designed as a history of the future, a future which has now come to pass. Schlegel has said: "Der Historiker ist ein rückwärts gekehrter Prophet." What events are memorable enough to be included in such a prophetic history? I have established a simple criterion: when in doubt, do not delete. Better to have a hundred bits of musical flotsam and jetsam in circulation than to omit a single potentially important event. The fear of leaving out an interesting work has even invaded my dreams. One particularly vivid nightmare was that I had overlooked a really sensational item—the "Red Army Symphony" by Brahms, written in 1938 and dedicated by him to Marshal Voroshilov. Commenting on the perishable quality of new works commissioned by the New York Philharmonic on the occasion of its quasisesquicentennial, a British music critic wryly observed that these pieces "may well disappear into that impeccably kept graveyard of our century—*Music Since 1900*." The burial may be premature. The composers interred herein may yet arise in glory at the sound of the last trump. *Et exspecto resurrectionem mortuorum,* etc.

Many ghosts of these pale *morituri,* opaque luminaries of music, are gathered on these pages from all over the world, including the *partes infidelium* not often visited by music historians—Rumania, Bulgaria, even Albania. Nearer the center of musical culture, virtually all opera of Siegfried Wagner, "the little son of a great father," are recorded here with a brief summary of content for each. The dates of completion and first performances of all 27 symphonies of Miaskovsky are faithfully tabulated. He fell into the habit in his later years of notifying me in regular succession of the progress made in adding yet another symphony to his enormous catalogue of works. Miaskovsky's Soviet biographers report that when he was hard pressed for information, he would tell them, only half-facetiously, to write Slonimsky in America for details. It would be unchivalrous not to make full use of these data.

A perspicacious, and on the whole sympathetic critic, reviewing the third edition of *Music Since 1900*, detected a streak of sensationalism in its choice of material. When, he wondered, had I eliminated the entry on the natural death of an American music critic from the earlier editions, but retained that of his colleague who died by a self-inflicted gunshot wound in the mouth? Why did I quote a personal letter from Percy A. Scholes in which he frankly admits his role in the suicide of Arthur Eaglefield Hull? "Hull's suicide was the result of my exposure of his thefts in his book," Scholes wrote. "He threw himself under a train." But why shouldn't I have? This book is a historical study of factual romanticism, and violence and tragedy are part of the romance of our times.

Admittedly, some entries are frivolous—endurance records for piano-fortitude, underwater harp playing, a competition of singing canary birds, the timetable of the Chopin Express between Vienna and Warsaw, a horoscope of Scriabin, the arrest of a Rumanian diva for spying during World War I, etc., etc., etc. But these are passing sights and sounds of the general musicorama of the period, and as such are of illustrative value.

The scenes unreeled in Descriptive Chronology are so expansive that concision of technical analysis of each individual item becomes an economic necessity. A program annotator of the Boston Symphony Orchestra nodded approval of my summary description of the last movement of Béla Bartók's *Music for Strings, Percussion and Celesta* as a "paradoxical rondo with a non-recurrent subject." But he also cautioned the reader to beware of my loquacity when upon occasion I am prolix rather than terse, discursive rather than curt, rhetorical rather than pert. To illustrate the point he quoted a non-stop sentence purporting to describe another movement of the same Bartók piece—a sentence which I, most reluctantly, had to leave out in the present edition for the simple reason that, upon examination, I could not justify it on technical grounds.

"Brevitate moderni gaudent," is a frequent incipit in medieval treatises on music. Brevity still remains a desideratum, but no one has ever approached the utmost succinctness of expression of two fabled Renaissance scholiasts tied in a contest for the briefest possible non-nonsensical statement—in Latin, of course. "Eo rus," wrote one, tersely announcing his decision to depart for the country. "I," replied the other in a magnificently vertical imperative of the Latin verb "ire," to go, winning the match.

A measure of prolixity is inherent in the format of Descriptive Chronology, inasmuch as each entry is arranged in the form of a continuous paragraph without intermediate full stops, ramifying autogenetically, with subsidiary excrescences and efflorescences, into a network of ancillary clauses (a stylistic idiosyncrasy which I developed in the first edition of the book in order to achieve a would-be Aristotelean unity of place, time and action within each item, and which necessitates frequent recourse to long parenthetical enclaves so as to secure clear articulation of separate rubrics without dislocating the grammatical succession of substantives and predicates with their adverbial modifiers), all this further ornamented by hyphenated appositions, creating at times a veritable ziggurat of interdependent verbal structures with topical gradients traversing historical, biographical, analytical, and proleptic matters, consciously invoking alliteration's artful aid in a plasma of seemingly untenable paronomasia (if not incontinent logorrhea), while striving to preserve a technically correct syntactical arrangement so as to make it possible for the constituent parts of speech to be retrieved and placed in proper perspective in the pervasive quagmire of quaquaversal qualifiers.

Errors and misprints can make a fortune for a lucky philatelist who chances upon an airmail stamp with an inverted airplane. But to a lexicographer, they are so many poltergeists—furtive, diabolically inventive, grimacing with self-contented malice while going about their mischievous business. Still one can't deny a certain appositeness to such typographical accidents as Charminade for Cécile Chaminade (caught in time and purged of the intrusive *r*), orbits for obits (inspired perhaps by a master mortician's plan to dispose of a surplus of cadavers by shooting them into outer space), or loverlooking for overlooking (positively inspirational). The first prize must go to the poltergeist who caused the author of a book dealing with the preparation of a manuscript for publication to express his gratitude to his secretary for her careful reading of the. . . *poofs!*

Far more menacing than these playful sprites are doublegangers, the chronological revenants that, thanks to an inadvertent substitution of a digit, stage a reappearance a year or several years later on the same day of the month. Most of these chimeras have been exorcised. Let us hope that none will slip through the crack of time to haunt the distraught chronicler.

Alfred Einstein, who had a plentiful share of his own Sisyphean struggle for accuracy, wrote me once, wondering whether we—"und natürlich vor allem Sie"—would receive our just reward in Heaven for having cleansed the world of some lexicographical *Ungenauigkeiten*. Would fain that the present edition of *Music Since 1900* would merit such a heavenly accolade. I should like to be able to emulate with some confidence the wording of the festooned banner on my favorite 17th-century map, which proudly proclaims itself "Orbis Terrarum Nova et Accuratissima Tabula." But even in this "most accurate chart," California is detached from the North American continent and sent drifting off into the Pacific, and Hollandia Nova—not yet Australia—is allowed to fade away into the terra incognita of the Antarctic. My fond hope is that no such peninsular islands or insular isthmuses will be encountered in my own "Orbis Musicae Modernae Nova et Accuratissima Tabula."

Most entries in Descriptive Chronology are world premières of significant works, even if they take place inconspicuously in some small town prior to a gala vernissage in a metropolitan center. American musical comedies are usually tried out in Boston, Philadelphia or some other perfectly respectable but not very glamorous spot. Soviet operas and symphonies are often performed first in Leningrad before coming to Moscow for a grand opening. In each case, it is the *prima assoluta* that is recorded here.

The dating of opera premières poses a problem. In European opera houses, particularly in Paris, two *pre-*

mieères auditions are usually presented—one a *répétition générale* for the élite and the press, and one for the paying public. It is the press première that is given chronological priority in this book.

Any attempt at rational chronology crumbles in reporting the manifestations of the avant-garde of the last third of the 20th century. Some composers blithely advise the performer that the duration of this or that composition is a matter of personal discretion; it may last a day or a minute, a year or a chiliad, a hebdomad of lustra, a quadrillion of milliseconds, a sextillion of nanoseconds, or a quindecillion of non-zero moments—all these temporal segments to be fragmented, quadrated or quaquadrated at will. And how are we to date a work of duration zero? Unheard for the first time? Here we reach the Ultima Thule of uncertainty and passivity. The experience of the Greek philosopher Cratylus comes to mind: he passed days and nights moving his forefinger to and fro in front of his nose to demonstrate the only verity of the world. Another precursor of 20th-century modernism was St. Simeon the Stylite who spent 68 years in the sixth century perched on a number of successively taller pillars, the last one being 66 feet in elevation. His career could provide a fitting subject for a symphonic poem with leitmotifs based on a series of gradually increasing intervals.

Verbalization without musical notation as it is practiced by the avant-garde is almost Hesychastic in its contemplative solipsism. The title itself becomes a composition. Karlheinz Stockhausen draws a parabolic curve with this inscription: "Sound a note. Continue sounding it as long as you please. It is your prerogative." John Cage has made verbalization a cardinal discipline in his aleatory scores. In the coalition of music with theater, motion pictures, art, literature, and drama that constitutes the program of the contemporary avant garde, every action, every "happening," becomes a musical event. Nam June Paik gives explicit instructions for the performance of his piece entitled *Playing Music:* "Cut your left arm very slowly with a razor (more than 10 centimeters)." This has been executed. Philip Corner issues a simple command: "One anti-personnel type CBU (Cluster Bomb Unit) will be thrown into the audience." This composition has not been performed.

Then there are musical non-events that may be described by the term *Unwasity,* something that never was. A historical instance of such an unwasity was the announced first performance of Prokofiev's *Scythian Suite* at a Koussevitzky concert in Moscow in December 1916, which was cancelled because of wartime conditions. This did not deter the Russian critic Leonid Sabaneiev from publishing a scathing review of the piece, going so far in his reporting of an unwasity as to mention that Prokofiev himself conducted the work with "barbaric abandon."

The period of time covered in Descriptive Chronology traverses the biblical span of three score and ten. Actuarial statistics make it almost inevitable that total lifetimes of several 20th-century composers should be encompassed within these years. Dates of birth and death are here given in local time. When Schoenberg died in Los Angeles late at night on the 13th of July of 1951, it was past midnight in New York and early morn-

ing of the next day in Europe. As a result, Schoenberg's death was reported in European newspapers as having taken place on the 14th. Yet in Schoenberg's case, local time is of dramatic import, for he was seriously afflicted with triskaidecaphobia, and feared number 13 with grave apprehension. He thought it was an evil omen that he was born on the 13th of the month of September in 1874. When he reached his 76th birthday, his last, he fell to brooding on the numerological fact that the sum of the digits of 76 is 13. During the last conscious hours of his life he remarked that all would be well if he would survive the fatefully numbered day. But he died 13 minutes before midnight on that 13th day of July of 1951.

The famous prima donna Melba died in Australia on 23 February 1931, but her death was reported in New York newspapers dated the previous day! This preposthumous calendarization was the consequence of Australia's position on the other side of the International Dateline. Melba died while the Western Hemisphere was still rotating under the sun of the preceding day—hence the anachronological paradox.

All Russian musical events between March 1900 and 1918, when the Soviet government adopted the Western calendar, have been adjusted by adding 13 days to equalize the Julian and the Gregorian styles. The difference between the two calendars increased from 12 to 13 days in 1900 because of the intercalation of 29 February in 1900, a bissextile year in Russia, but not in the West.

Spelling of names poses a knotty problem. Not infrequently, changes are made in the first or last names of persons during their lifetimes. Before Schoenberg came to America he spelled his last name with an umlaut, Schönberg, which is still the form used in German reference books. For uniformity's sake, the later spelling Schoenberg has been adopted throughout. Sibelius signed his first name Jean, and this form has been adopted in the present edition, not Jan as in the earlier editions and in some biographical sources. The baptismal name of Varèse was Edgard. He dropped the final *d* early in his career, and all original additions of his scores are signed Edgar Varèse, but about 1950 he restored the missing letter. However, I decided to retain the more familiar *d*-less form. Even in America, Varèse kept the grave accent in the middle of his last name, but his close contemporary and friend Carlos Salzedo, whose last name originally had an *accent aigu* on *e*, removed it in the process of Americanization.

Eugen Zádor jettisoned his tonic Hungarian accent and anglicized his first name to Eugene in his American avatar. In this case I made a compromise, listing his works first performed in Europe under the Hungarian cognomen, and those produced in America in the naturalized spelling. For some reason Leoncavallo's forename is commonly spelled Ruggiero, whereas the offical Italian form is Ruggero. The latter form is adopted here.

The transliteration of Russian names is as insoluble a proposition as the squaring of the circle, because of the non-correspondence of the sounds represented by the letters of the Cyrillic alphabet and those of the Latin vocables. Since Russian music was first published in Germany, Russian composers became embedded in

Germanic matrices. Tchaikovsky was Tschaikowsky in American concert halls, even though the initial Russian consonant of his name has the exact phonetic equivalent in the English diphthong "ch." Even more intractable is the Cyrillic symbol for the sound "shch." To locate Shcherbachev in a German music lexicon one must start with the acervulus of seven consonants, Schtsch. It was thanks to the former premier of the Soviet Union Nikita Khrushchev that the phonetically accurate transliteration of the Russian "shch" sound became finally crystallized in American and British usage.

The introductory "T" persists in the common American spelling of Tchaikovsky, even though most library catalogues list him under "Ch." But familiarity breeds respect, and Chaikovsky looks queer. A similar ambivalence exists in the spelling of Tcherepnin. On the other hand, the adequate "ch" is gradually superseding the nimiety of "tch" in the middle and at the end of Russian names. Shostakovich is no longer Shostakovitch, as he was in the early editions of *Music Since 1900*. The former Khatchaturian has been slenderized into Khachaturian. But considerations of preeminent usage dictate the retention of the supererogatory "t" in Gretchaninoff. Igor Markevitch, though born in Russia, made his professional career as composer and conductor in Paris. He signs his name in the form containing "tch," and there is no reason for tampering with it.

It is most unfortunate that the English alphabet has no symbol for the German guttural sound "ch" or the Spanish "j" (as in José). No difficulty exists in spelling the name of the Soviet composer Tikhon Khrennikov in German (Tichon Chrennikow) or in Spanish (Tijon Jrennikov). The Spanish spelling Jachaturian for Khachaturian is an exact phonetic equivalent of the Russian sound. Conceivably, the spelling Hrennikov and Hachaturian could be proposed in English, but the visual aspect of such a rendering would be forbidding.

There are musical Russian names whose spelling is sanctified by usage and cannot be altered without giving offense. Rachmaninoff is Rachmaninoff is Rachmaninoff. This is the way he invariably signed his name, and this is the spelling retained in this book. To adopt the phonetically consistent but repulsively unmusical spelling Rakhamaninov would be as unnatural as calling Rachmaninoff's C-sharp minor Prelude D-flat minor.

Objections have been raised, principally by British music editors, to the spelling of Koussevitzky, on the ground that it is a mixture of French and German. But this is the way Koussevitzky used to sign his name, and this is the way it is preserved in this book. Besides, I acquired the habit of spelling it this way during the years of my service as Koussevitzky's personal secretary.

As a matter of common sense, names of Russian composers of French or German origin retain their ancestral spelling. It is César Cui, not the ridiculous Tsezar Kyui. It is Maximilian Steinberg, not the abnormal Shteinberg. In their determination to square the Cyrillic circle the catologuers of the Library of Congress went so far as to retransliterate the names of classical composers in the titles of Russian publications, resulting in such monstrosities as Shooman, Shoobert, Dzhyakomo Poochchi-

ni, and even Bethkoven. No person of healthy constitution can stomach any of these.

As a natural corollary of the commanding lead that America is beginning to assume in the world of music, increasing representation of works by American composers has been given in the present edition of *Music Since 1900*. A contributing factor to this enhancement is the massive migration of European composers to the United States during the period between wars and revolutions. The list of names is imposing: Rachmaninoff, Stravinsky, Schoenberg, Hindemith, Toch, Krenk, Kurt Weill, all of whom became naturalized if not totally Americanized. Béla Bartók wrote some of his most significant scores during his few years in America before his death in 1945. At the same time, native American composers began to impress themselves on the surprised world. As late as 1948, *Le Guide du Concert* of Paris could declare with an air of pompous condescension: "L'Amérique n'est plus une nation a-musicale: elle compte une cinquantaine de compositeurs de talent." Soon Europe discovered the greatness of Charles Ives. It is with understandable pride that I am including in Descriptive Chronology the programs of my European concerts at which I conducted works by Ives and other American composers for the first time on the continent.

Even a history of the future must have a temporal finis. I have resolved to mark it by the romantically realistic landing of men on the moon. But what, one may ask, is the connection between the soundless moon and music? The Harmony of the Spheres, of course. This Pythagorean link provides a perfect ending.

In the first edition of *Music Since 1900* I introduced the term of my own invention, Pandiatonicism, intended to describe the free use in melody and harmony of all seven degrees of the diatonic scale. The term has since been widely adopted, and its success encouraged me to follow up with additional neologisms that may prove useful. As a result, the modest glossary of terms of earlier editions has grown into a propaedeutical compendium of rather formidable dimensions. For good measure, I threw in some parerga—or perhaps offal (awful offal?)—of my purely linguistic elucubrations. The modus operandi in making up new terms is simple. I first determine in my mind the area to be covered. Then, in the best tradition of scientific logodaedaly, I put together a Graeco-Latin compound corresponding to the nascent concept. I have felt, for instance, the necessity of a term to describe modern idioms peculiar to the 20th century, and I hit upon the word Vigesimosecular, which would supplement such crescively vaguescent descriptions as Modern, New, Contemporary, Advanced, Avant-Garde, Ultramodern, etc., and which by the ponderous sound of its sesquipedalian Latinity would suggest progressive modernism. Among other functional terms in the present glossary are Asomatous Variations (variations without a theme), Aud Music (an auditory analogy of Op Art), Demotic Music (a generic rubric covering vernacular, urban, and country music), and Icositetraphonic Harmony (relating to quarter-tones).

Much new material has been added to the last section of the book, Letters and Documents. The text of the dramatic interrogation of Hanns Eisler by the House of Representatives Committee on Un-American Activities has been extracted from the official transcript of the hearings. A comical pendant to this grim inquisition is the Resolution of the Fire and Police Research Association of Los Angeles, urging Congress to ban folk music festivals as hotbeds of Communist activity, and the hilarious debate that followed in the Senate, proving that legislators can display upon occasion an exquisite sense of the ridiculous. On the more serious side, there is a message addressed to the Subcommittee on the Environment by that tireless ecological gadfly Ralph Nader, sounding alarm at the noise pollution generated by Rock 'n' Roll bands. One of the most important documents in this section is the Charter of the Union of Soviet Composers, setting forth the guiding principles for the desirable type of Soviet composition. Also included is an ideological article in *Peking Review*, dealing with the correct application of Chairman Mao's thoughts to the domain of fine arts and music.

Not without some hesitation, I have decided to publish the letters I received through the years from Charles Ives. My scruples arise from his extreme praise of me as a person and as a conductor. There is something inexpressibly poignant in what he writes about my courage in "ferreting out a nonentity." In his last letter he congratulates me on the publication of the first edition of *Music Since 1900*. He wrote all his letters to me in his seismic handwriting—his muscular coordination was badly affected by chronic diabetes. But Charles Ives is a great spirit of the age and a towering genius of American music. This correspondence, so personal in its expression, offers a revealing glance into his heart and mind. As such it must be made known.

Quite different in tone are the letters from Varèse, also included in the last section of the book. They demonstrate a sense of unflinching purpose, a firm confidence in the validity of his musical ideals in the face of disheartening hostility towards his music on the part of the press and the public. A single letter from Anton von Webern betrays his crying need for sympathy.

My list of acknowledgments will be brief but global. I am deeply grateful to a legion of anonymous (for their signatures are usually illegible) archivists, librarians, embassy officials and municipal clerks in many parts of the world for their willingness to search musty files on dusty shelves in damp basements for some chronological minutiae essential in the preparation of this book. Along more personal lines, the overwhelming share of my overflowing gratitude goes to Wayne Shirley of the Music Division in the Library of Congress, whose instant and multilingual erudition has saved me from many an embarrassing imbroglio. He is also an *acharné* collector of musical and literary curiosa, and last but not least, a born grammarian—inestimable qualities of a true editorial mind. Viva Wayne Shirley!

Help came also from the 6'3", 130 lbs. astronomer and meteorologist David Cloud, a cumulus of non-nebulous data, teeming with a lot o' news, not only about the square of the hypotenuse, but about a fantastic amount of things musical.

On an entirely different level, untutored in the niceties and technicalities of the subject, Joyce Knapp, a California blonde, born in Hollywood in 1946, lent decisive support by typing, retyping and overtyping, albeit defiantly and often petulantly, the harrowing immensity of the continually fluctuating text of the manuscript, spotting a duplication here and a pleonasm there, pointing out unwarranted unintelligibilities and suggesting workable substitutions for inordinately involved auxiliary clauses. For this I owe her a sempiternal debt of gratitude.

Then came Teri, or to spell her out in full, Mary Thérèse Friedrichs, who entered the scene on her 21st birthday during the semifinals in the assembly of "insticks" (a Swedish word I adopted for last-minute inserts) in the manuscript. She applied herself to this task with a devotion to the cause that would have given credit to the "little flower" from whom she received her middle name. Thanks, Teri. (You're welcome, Nicolas.)

NICOLAS SLONIMSKY
December 1970

DESCRIPTIVE CHRONOLOGY

1.1.1900 — 12.14.2000

1900

1 JANUARY 1900

The first volume of the collected works of Hector BERLIOZ, true precursor of 20th-century music, whose grandeur of design and subjective programmaticism engendered new and fertile non-classical forms marked by an associative thematic development and an expansive inflation of symphonic sonorities, is issued by Breitkopf & Härtel, on the symbolic day when the 1900's begin. (The 20th century proper did not open until January 1901.)

1 JANUARY 1900

Chris and the Wonderful Lamp, opera by the American March King John Philip SOUSA, based on the epic tales of the *Arabian Nights*, is performed for the first time in New York.

13 JANUARY 1900

Hiawatha, overture by Rubin GOLDMARK, American-born nephew of the grand master of Central European romanticism Carl Goldmark, inspired by Longfellow's famous poem of Indian lore, and couched in a Germanically effusive style with occasional pentatonic themes to depict the redskins, is performed for the first time by the Boston Symphony Orchestra, Wilhelm Gericke conducting.

14 JANUARY 1900

At the Costanzi Theater in Rome the world première is given of *Tosca*, opera in three acts by Giacomo PUCCINI, after Victorien Sardou's poignant melodrama *La Tosca* (the definite article is used in the title of the French play but not in the title of the opera); wherein a voluptuously desirable Italian songstress Floria Tosca, mistress of an artist member of a Napoleonic conspiracy of June 1800 at the time of Napoleon's surprising victory at Marengo, slays the lecherous, treacherous chief of Roman police at a private dinner as she feigns a willingness to submit to his desires as a price to save her lover, but is posthumously outwitted by him when the secret order of execution is carried out, and in despair throws herself to her death from a high parapet, the score couched in the most effective manner of Italian Verismo, containing such harmonic innovations as systematic progressions of parallel triads, parallel progressions of inverted seventh-chords, and ominously sounding whole-tone scales.

Last evening at the Costanzi Theater the first performance of Puccini's new opera was given before an immense audience, the largest that ever filled that theater. Early in the evening the crowd began to assemble. Every seat and every ticket had been sold for days previous, so that when the curtain rose, the house was packed from top to bottom to its fullest capacity, even standing room being at a premium. The boxes were filled with a dazzling array of richly dressed women, while celebrities of all kinds—the court, diplomats, artists, literary men, critics, clerics, army and navy men, musicians—were seen on every side. Never has such interest been shown any first representation as upon this occasion. . . . After the close of the first act the composer was called out eight times in response to the demands of the audience. (*The Musical Courier*, New York, 31 January 1900)

The great musical event of the New Year in Rome is over, and Giacomo Puccini, the young composer, has launched a new opera. . . . The general opinion seems to be that the story is somewhat too dramatic for an opera, that the music is lost in the general interest of the development of the plot. However, difficult as the situations are from a musical standpoint, the "maestro" has handled them in a masterly manner. (*Pall Mall Gazette*, London, February 1900)

Signor Puccini's opera *Tosca* is a typical example of the proclivity of Italian composers to seek inspiration in the crudest forms of elemental passion, and of their apparent inability to perceive that ignoble sentiment is a fatal bar to the creation of noble music. In *Tosca* another degradation has certainly been put on music by seeking to make it express physical torture. Although the music consists of little more than growls and screams from the orchestra and declamatory passages of little meaning from the soloists, the gruesomeness of this portion of the play is invested with peculiar objectionableness by force of contrast. (An unidentified London newspaper, February 1900)

Those who were present at the performance of Puccini's opera *Tosca* were little prepared for the revolting effects produced by musically illustrating the torture and murder scenes of Sardou's play. The alliance of a pure art with scenes so essentially brutal and demoralizing . . . produced a feeling of nausea. . . . What has music to do with a lustful man chasing a defenseless woman or the dying kicks of a murdered scoundrel? (A London newspaper, 13 July 1900)

Tosca is a melodrama in the truest sense. The music is almost entirely subordinated to the drama. . . . The parlando is employed continually. It is as if a broken mirror was made to reflect and distort bits of sunlight; both eye and ear are often offended by the consecutive fifths, raw harmonic progressions and alterations of the tawdry with the solemn. . . . Indeed, the short bursts of sustained melody are generally formless. Here is the Wagner theory skeletonized, almost reduced to an absurdity. (New York *Sun*, 5 February 1901)

At the first hearing, much, perhaps most, of Puccini's *Tosca* sounds exceedingly, even ingeniously ugly. Every now and then one comes across the most ear-flaying succession of chords. . . . To my ear, the most complex dissonant harmonies of Wagner or Richard Strauss—"chords" (so-called) of six or seven notes perhaps—have not half the rasp that some perfectly consonant triad progressions have. (W. F. Apthorp, Boston *Evening Transcript*, 12 April 1901)

18 JANUARY 1900

Thyl Uylenspiegel, opera in three acts by the Flemish composer Jan BLOCKX, dealing with the Dutch rebellion against the Spanish rule in the Netherlands in 1568–1573 and the patriotic role of the legendary jester Till Eulenspiegel, set to music in an opulently Wagneromantic

3

vein, with refreshing interludes of Flemish folk dances, is produced in Brussels.

20 JANUARY 1900

Raquel, opera in four acts by the Spanish composer Tomás BRETÓN, after Grillparzer's play *Die Jüdin von Toledo,* dealing with the loves and tragedies of a Toledan Jewess and set in a fastidiously dramatic musical idiom, is produced in Madrid.

22 JANUARY 1900

Es war einmal, three-act opera by the 28-year-old Vienna-born composer of Polish origin, Alexander ZEMLINSKY, based on a triptych of Danish folk tales of pastoral imprint with grim overtones, set to music in a freshly Wagnerized fluent idiom, is produced at the Vienna Opera, Gustav Mahler conducting.

27 JANUARY 1900

The final volume of the monumental edition of the collected works of Johann Sebastian BACH is published by Breitkopf & Härtel under the auspices of the Bach-Gesellschaft, which was founded on 28 July 1850, the centennial of Bach's death.

2 FEBRUARY 1900

Adonais, elegiac overture by the Boston composer George Whitefield CHADWICK, inspired by Shelley's threnody to the memory of Keats, "The Pard-like spirit, beautiful and swift," and composed in a fine Germanic manner acquired by Chadwick during his apprentice years in Leipzig, is performed for the first time by the Boston Symphony Orchestra.

2 FEBRUARY 1900

Louise, "roman musical" in four acts by Gustave CHARPENTIER, his first opera, to his own libretto (his mistress at the time was also named Louise and, like the heroine, was employed in a dressmaking shop), portraying with sensuous melodiousness and sentimental harmoniousness the pleasures of Paris, "cité de lumitère, cité d'amour," amid lovable nyctophiliacs, amorous artists, grisettes, soubrettes and midinettes, alive with city noises and precisely notated cries of vegetable vendors, is produced at the Opéra-Comique in Paris, destined to become the most popular French opera of the 1900's and the first successful example of French operatic naturalism.

7 FEBRUARY 1900

Lancelot du lac, lyric drama in four acts by the French composer Victorin de JONCIÈRES, to a libretto dealing with Sir Lancelot of the Lake and his love for Queen Guinevere, with a conventional musical score in the style of Gounod, is performed for the first time at the Paris Opéra.

9 FEBRUARY 1900

Der Bärenhäuter, opera in three acts by Arnold MENDELSSOHN, son of a cousin of Felix Mendelssohn, to a libretto derived from a grim Grimm brothers' tale wherein a handsome German soldier is turned by the devil into a repellent monster covered by a bearskin (hence the title *The Bearskinned*), and is saved from his ursine deformation by the love of a maiden to whom he cleaves despite the repeated attempts of a succession of seductive she-devils to abduct him, is produced in Berlin.

10 FEBRUARY 1900

Riccardo DRIGO, Italian conductor of the Russian Imperial Ballet, conducts at the Hermitage Theater in St. Petersburg the first performance of his most successful ballet *Les Millions d'Arlequin,* which includes the perennially popular *Sérénade d'Arlequin* fashioned in the finest Italian vein for a soulful solo by the cello.

16 FEBRUARY 1900

Vasa SUK, Czech composer of the romantic school, conducts in Kharkov, Russia, during his sojourn there as an operatic director and teacher, the first performance of his opera *The Forest King* dealing with the bold adventures of an endearing bandit chief and containing effective dances in the Slavic vein. (The first performance to the original libretto in the Czech language took place in Prague on 5 April 1903, the composer conducting.)

17 FEBRUARY 1900

Kain, one-act opera by Eugen D'ALBERT, to the biblical story of the first human murder, in which Abel is slain to the ominous sounds of chromatically heaving diminished seventh-chords, with the voice of avenging Jehovah represented by a mighty chorus in unison, is produced in Berlin.

17 FEBRUARY 1900

Anton, opera in three acts by the 27-year-old Italian composer Cesare GALEOTTI, wherein a young Libyan, whose pagan mistress slays his early Christian concubine known as the "Flower of the Catacombs," flees to the Egyptian desert, suppresses his sensuous memories, resists a series of diabolically contrived temptations and becomes sanctified as Saint Anthony, to a musical score gushing out crimson floods of curvilinear melos, is produced at La Scala, Milan.

18 FEBRUARY 1900

Charles Russell DAY, English soldier who was gazetted to Light Infantry in India in 1882 and became an authority on Hindu music, is killed in the battle of Paardeberg in South Africa during the Boer War.

22 FEBRUARY 1900

Cenerentola, opera in three acts by the 24-year-old half-German half-Italian composer Ermanno WOLF-FERRARI, recounting in harmonious tones the ever-inspiring tale of a lowly maid who rises from domestic cinders to princely incense, is produced in Venice with some cuts necessitated by the enormous length (1007 manuscript pages) of the original score.

2 MARCH 1900

Kurt WEILL, composer of highly functional theater music throbbing with modern rhythms in energizing march time alternating with ruefully nostalgic waltzes against a dissonant but tonally stable harmonic background, is born in Dessau, Germany.

6 MARCH 1900

Carl BECHSTEIN, founder of the piano manufacturing company bearing his name, whose handsomely wing-shaped Flugel are distinguished by a velvet-like tone and resilient key action, dies in Berlin in his 74th year.

10 MARCH 1900

Atahualpa, grand opera in four acts by the Italian composer Ferruccio CATTELANI (1867–1932) who settled in South America in 1886, to a libretto about the last king of the Incas betrayed by the conquistadores and garroted on 29 August 1533, is produced in Buenos Aires.

10 MARCH 1900

Johann Peter Emilius HARTMANN, patriarch of Danish opera composers and the last representative of the Hartmann musical dynasty in Denmark, the son of August Wilhelm Hartmann and grandson of Johann Ernest Hartmann, dies in his native Copenhagen at the age of 94 years, 9 months and 25 days.

10 MARCH 1900

Ballet music from the opera *Azara* by James Knowles PAINE, learned Bostonian composer and first chairman of the music department at Harvard University, to his own scenario after the medieval French tale *Aucassin et Nicolette* (in this version Nicolette is Azara, a daughter of a Saracen chieftain), is performed for the first time by the Boston Symphony Orchestra. (A concert performance of the entire opera, with considerable cuts, was given at Symphony Hall in Boston on 9 April 1907, almost a year after Paine's death.)

12 MARCH 1900

Lady Jane Douglas SCOTT, who in 1834 wrote the air *Annie Laurie*, the most famous song of nostalgic loyalty among British and American swains, dies at her estate at Spottiswode, Berwickshire, at the age of 90.

17 MARCH 1900

Norwegische Hochzeit, opera in two acts by the Norwegian composer Gerhard SCHJELDERUP, to his own libretto in German dealing with a Norwegian wedding, is performed for the first time in Prague.

19 MARCH 1900

Charles-Louis HANON, French composer and pedagogue whose books of piano exercises are second in ubiquitous immortality only to Czerny's, and who, like Czerny, remained a childless célibataire, dies at Boulogne-sur-Mer at the age of 81.

(Hanon was born at Rénescure, district of Dunkerque, Département du Nord, on 2 July 1819, according to a certificate of birth obtained by the author from the Mairie of Rénescure. All dictionaries and reference works give wrong date and wrong place of Hanon's birth.)

22 MARCH 1900

Samuel COLERIDGE-TAYLOR, Afro-British composer, conducts at the Royal Choral Society in London the first performance of *Hiawatha's Departure*, his choral work with orchestra, the third of his trilogy on the life of the legendary Indian.

6 APRIL 1900

Piano Concerto by the 32-year-old American composer Mrs. H.H.A. BEACH is performed for the first time by the Boston Symphony Orchestra with the composer as soloist.

11 APRIL 1900

Le Juif polonais, opera in three acts by Camille ERLANGER, after a ghostly novella from Erckmann-Chatrian's tales, detailing the murder in an Alsatian inn of a transient Jew who comes back to torment his murderer in a realistic posthumous appearance, is produced at the Opéra-Comique in Paris.

15 APRIL 1900

The 1900 Exposition Universelle opens in Paris, offering among its attractions the spectacles, dances and music of Cambodia, Annam, Java, Japan and China, bringing to Europe a cornucopia of exotic scales and asymmetrical rhythms deeply impressive to the impressionable impressionists.

29 APRIL 1900

Vikingeblod (*Viking Blood*), last opera in four acts by the Danish composer Peter Erasmus LANGE-MÜLLER (1850–1926), is produced in Copenhagen.

1 MAY 1900

Mazeppa, grand opera in four acts by the Polish composer Adam MINHEJMER (1831–1904), based on the dramatic story of the Ukrainian chieftain who fought a losing battle against Peter the Great, receives its belated production in Warsaw a quarter of a century after its composition.

7 MAY 1900

A century has passed since the death in Paris of Niccolò PICCINNI who went down into oblivion as a hapless rival of Gluck in their contest for Parisian favors, but who was a knowledgeable opera composer in his own right.

15 MAY 1900

The Paderewski Fund of $10,000 is established in New York by Ignace PADEREWSKI, universally idolized Polish genius of the piano, to award annual prizes to American composers for the best orchestral works.

22 MAY 1900

Edwin S. VOTEY patents a "pneumatic piano attachment" constituting the basic principle of the Pianola. (Patent filed in Washington on 25 January 1897; renewed application on 5 February 1900; patent granted on 22 May 1900. Dates in the official Gazette of the U.S. Patent office of 22 May 1900, No. 650,285, p. 1572)

28 MAY 1900

Sir George GROVE, grand seigneur of British musical scholarship, the begetter, with the aid of continental contributors, of the monumentally famous *Dictionary of Music and Musicians,* dies in his native London eleven weeks before his 80th birthday.

30 JUNE 1900

The Schweizerischer Tonkünstlerverein is formally organized in Zürich by Joseph LAUBER, Carl VOGLER and other Swiss composers, with the object of promoting the cause of national music in Switzerland.

1 JULY 1900

The music publishing firm of Breitkopf & Härtel issues the first volume of the collection *Denkmäler der Tonkunst in Bayern,* devoted to the publication of works by composers of Bavaria. (Date of the preface)

2 JULY 1900

Finlandia, patriotic symphonic poem by Jean SIBELIUS, proclaiming in forcefully somber melodies and granitically noble harmonies the right of Finland to national independence, profoundly expressive of the spiritual essence of the Finnish people, is performed for the first time in Helsingfors, under its original title *Suomi* (Finnish for Finland), with Robert Kajanus conducting.

2 JULY 1900

Second Symphony, op. 115, by the Swiss composer Hans HUBER, composed in 1897 under the impression of an exhibition of Böcklin's paintings and for that reason known as Böcklinsinfonie, in four movements, of which the last is a theme with eight variations each named after a Böcklin picture, written in an expansive Wagneromantic manner within a formal Brahmsogenic framework, is performed for the first time at the first Swiss Music Festival in Zürich. (The Symphony was tentatively scheduled for performance in Basel on 20 March 1898, but was withdrawn by the composer after one rehearsal for further revisions.)

4 JULY 1900

Louis ARMSTRONG, the Great Satchmo (i.e., Satchel Mouth), trumpeter extraordinary who was to cut a powerful swath through decades of hot jazz and swing and whose unlearned art combined spontaneity of expressive performance and fantastic technical prowess (he set a record by hitting High C 280 times in succession) with an immediacy of popular appeal characteristic of Dixieland Negro music, is born in New Orleans on Independence Day.

8 JULY 1900

George ANTHEIL, self-styled "Bad Boy of Music," whose *Ballet mécanique* glorified the spirit of the machine age with magnificently contrived acousma, is born in Trenton, New Jersey.

14 JULY 1900

On Bastille Day the Opéra-Comique presents in Paris a patriotic opera by Lucien LAMBERT entitled *La Marseil-*laise, melodramatically depicting the scene purported to have taken place in Strasbourg on the night of 24 April 1792 when Rouget de l'Isle is supposed to have improvised the famous tune of the French National Anthem. (It is almost certain that Rouget de l'Isle was the author of only the text, not the music.)

22 JULY 1900

I due fratelli, opera by the Greek composer Denis LAVRANGAS, to an Italian libretto, is produced for the first time by an Italian opera company in Athens.

23 AUGUST 1900

Ernst KRENEK, whose versatile musical talent epitomizes the mutations of the 20th-century style in composition, ranging from satire in jazz to the mathematically involved complexities of the dodecaphonic technique and integral serialism, is born in Vienna.

25 AUGUST 1900

Friedrich NIETZSCHE, whose scant musical production lacks the proud virility that his philosophy glorifies, dies in Weimar at the age of 55 in a pathetic state of dementia praecox consequent upon syphilitic infection contracted by him during his student days.

26 AUGUST 1900

Prométhée, "tragedie lyrique" in three acts by Gabriel FAURÉ, his first opera, wherein Prometheus (who has only a spoken part) deters Pandora from opening her baleful box, thus assuring a temporary tranquility in a strife-torn world, set to an austerely economic score in neo-Grecian modalities, is performed for the first time in the ancient Roman Arena at Béziers.

15 SEPTEMBER 1900

Princessen paa Aerten, one-act opera by the Danish composer August ENNA (1860–1939), after Hans Christian Andersen's fairy-tale about a royal princess who proves her highborn supersensitivity by sensing the presence of a pea under a score of fluffy mattresses on her ample bed and thus qualifies for marriage to the heir-apparent of a neighboring kingdom, is performed for the first time at the opening of the new municipal theater in Aarhus.

28 SEPTEMBER 1900

Asya, opera in three acts by Mikhail IPPOLITOV-IVANOV, after Turgenev's story of a short-lived but profoundly felt summer romance in a pastoral German town blossoming forth between a vacationing Russian student and an expatriate Russian girl named Asya, set to an emotionally heaving score in a Tchaikovskian manner, is performed for the first time in Moscow.

3 OCTOBER 1900

The Dream of Gerontius, sacred oratorio in two parts by Edward ELGAR (completed on 7 June 1900), to Cardinal Newman's devoutly Catholic poem, wherein the dying Gerontius (i.e., oldster) prays in English and Latin for divine intercession against the "sour and uncouth dissonance" of chromatically vocal demons, and after an agonizingly protracted suspension of a minor thirteenth-chord ("for one moment must every instrument exert its full force") arrives at a D-major apotheosis, with harps arpeggiating, the organ pealing and the celestially confident chorus saying Amen, is performed for the first time at the Birmingham Festival, Hans Richter conducting.

What every connoisseur of orchestration must have said at the first hearing of Elgar's *Gerontius* (among other things) was, "What a devil of a fortissimo." Here was no literary paper instrumentation, no muddle, no noise, but an absolutely new energy given to the band by a consummate knowledge of what it could do and how it could do it. (George Bernard Shaw, *Music and Literature*, 1920)

4 OCTOBER 1900

Janek, opera in two acts by the 63-year-old Polish composer Wladislaw ZELEŃSKI, is produced in Lwów.

6 OCTOBER 1900

Three centuries have passed since the production of the earliest opera of which the music is extant, *Euridice* by Jacopo PERI, presented at the Pitti Palace in Florence at the wedding feast of Maria de'r Medici and King Henri IV of France, with Peri himself singing the part of Orpheus. (Peri was also the composer of the musical drama *Dafne*, produced at the Palazzo Corsi in Florence during the carnival of 1597; its music is lost.)

15 OCTOBER 1900

Symphony Hall, acoustically one of the finest concert auditoriums in the world, along with Carnegie Hall, Musik-Verein-Saal in Vienna and Concertgebouw in Amsterdam, is formally inaugurated in Boston as the permanent home of the Boston Symphony Orchestra.

Musical Boston has lost its real music hall forever, and Symphony Hall is its la-di-da substitute. But why not Nocturne Hall, or Kapellmeister Hall, or Sostenuto Hall, or, in fact, why not Oratorio Hall? These titles are no sillier than Symphony Hall. (From a column signed *Chatterer* in the Boston *Herald*, 16 September 1900, before the official inauguration)

You have proved here that the Science of Acoustics certainly exists in a definite form. (From a letter to the architect Wallace Sabine from Major Lee Higginson, founder of the Boston Symphony Orchestra)

15 OCTOBER 1900

Zdeněk FIBICH, Czech composer of 376 works, among them a trilogy of music dramas and a number of highly playable concert pieces for the violin, of which the *Romance* (composed in 1879) became a perennial favorite, dies in Prague at the age of 49.

1 NOVEMBER 1900

Petru Rareş, opera in three acts by the Rumanian composer Eduard CAUDELLA, wherein a heroic bastard son of a 16th-century Moldavian voyevoda regains his ancestral throne and frees his beloved from the villainous clutches of a wily gospodar, set to music in an Italianate Wagneromantic manner retouched with colorful Balkanized orientalisms, is produced in Bucharest.

2 NOVEMBER 1900

Vincent D'INDY reads his Inauguration Speech as new President of the Schola Cantorum in Paris.

Where shall we find the quickening life that will give us fresh forms and formulas? The source is not difficult to discover. Do not seek it anywhere but in the decorative art of the plainsong singers, in the architectural art of the age of Palestrina, and in the expressive art of the great Italians of the seventeenth century. It is there, and there alone, that we shall find melodic craft, rhythmic cadences, and a harmonic magnificence that is really new—if our modern spirit can only learn how to absorb their nutritious essence. And so I prescribe for all pupils in the School the careful study of classic forms, because they alone are able to give the elements of a new life to our music, which will be founded on principles that are sane, serious and trustworthy. (Quoted from *Tribune de Saint-Gervais*, November 1900, by Romain Rolland in his *Musiciens d'aujourd'r hui*)

3 NOVEMBER 1900

Sémiramis, "*scène lyrique*" by Florent SCHMITT, which won him the Premier Prix de Rome, dedicated "*à mes chers Maîtres Massenet et Fauré*" is performed for the first time in Paris.

I had to compete five times for the Prix de Rome to win it once. And if in the end I was not left out in the cold, it was thanks to Gabriel Fauré, my much lamented teacher, who managed to gather for me enough votes among sculptors and painters to counterbalance the animosity of musicians, who, with the exception of Massenet, Reyer and Saint-Saëns, turned thumbs down on me. So it was not really a music prize. But I have no shame for all that, for the other musicians among committee members were Paladilhe, Dubois and Lenepveu. The important thing was the thirty thousand gold francs. (Florent Schmitt, in *Cinquante ans de musique française*, Paris, 1925, vol. II p.51)

3 NOVEMBER 1900

The Tale of Tsar Saltan, opera in four acts with a prologue by RIMSKY-KORSAKOV (completed on 31 January 1900), after Pushkin's poem, wherein the heir to the throne of a mythical kingdom exiled by a camarilla led by his mother's sisters, learns magic, turns into a bumblebee, revisits his native land and in buzzingly painful chromatics repeatedly stings his perfidious aunts, and eventually regains his rightful throne accompanied by a beautiful swan-bride whose life he had saved from a predatory falcon, is performed for the first time in Moscow, Ippolitov-Ivanov conducting.

9 NOVEMBER 1900

Pád Arkuna (Fall of Arcona), opera by Zdeněk FIBICH in the Czech language, relating the royally dramatic love of Dargun and Helga in 1168 A.D., is posthumously produced in Prague, 25 days after Fibich's death.

9 NOVEMBER 1900

Atzimba, opera in three acts by the 36-year-old Mexican composer Ricardo CASTRO, dealing with the depredations of the Spanish conquistadores in Mexico, is produced in Mexico City.

10 NOVEMBER 1900

Zazà, lyric comedy in four acts by Ruggero LEON-CAV-ALLO, dealing with a Parisian chanteuse whose yearning for matrimonial respectability is shattered by the revelation that her lover is a married man and a father, with a score in an effective veristic manner redolent of melorhythmic patterns of his famous opera *Pagliacci*, is produced in Milan, Arturo Toscanini conducting.

14 NOVEMBER 1900

Aaron COPLAND, American composer who has set a new norm for an integrated national style of 20th-century composition, widely varied in technical resources, ranging from jazzy asymmetries to symphonic serenity, from ethnic melorhythms to dodecaphonic serialism and from triadic pandiatonicism to polyharmonic quadritonality, is born in Brooklyn.

16 NOVEMBER 1900

The Philadelphia Orchestra presents its inaugural concert under the direction of Fritz SCHEEL in a program of symphonic favorites including Beethoven's *Fifth Symphony*, with the participation of the 22-year-old Russian pianist Ossip GABRILOWITSCH playing Tchaikovsky's *First Piano Concerto*.

17 NOVEMBER 1900

Medio Evo Latino, operatic triptych by the 25-year-old Argentine composer Ettore PANIZZA, in which the action takes place in three Latin countries in medieval times, is performed in a world première at Genoa.

20 NOVEMBER 1900

The House of Ice, opera in four acts by the Russian composer Arseny KORESHCHENKO, to a libretto based on a horrendous tale about an 18th-century Russian landlord who punishes a recalcitrant serf by pouring water on his naked body in midwinter until he becomes a human icicle, with a musical score imitative of Tchaikovsky, is produced for the first time in Moscow.

22 NOVEMBER 1900

Edward ELGAR is awarded the honorary degree of Doctor in Music by the University of Cambridge, England.

22 NOVEMBER 1900

Sir Arthur SULLIVAN, English composer of superb mock-Italian operettas to the exhilarating quasi-Shake-spearean texts of Sir William Gilbert, as well as of two imperishable vocal favorites, *The Lost Chord* and *Onward, Christian Soldiers*, dies in London at the age of 58.

The death of Sir Arthur Sullivan may be said without hyperbole to have plunged the whole of the Empire in gloom; for many years he has ranked with the most distinguished personages rather than with ordinary musicians. Never in the history of the art has a position such as his been held by a composer. For all the English-speaking races, with the exception of a very small and, possibly, unimportant class, Sullivan's name stood as a synonym for music in England. (*The Times*, London, 23 November 1900)

24 NOVEMBER 1900

First Symphony in E major by Alexander SCRIABIN, couched in a Russianized Wagnerian idiom presaging the proclamatory style of his later music, is performed, without its sixth choral movement, at the Russian Symphony Concerts in St. Petersburg, under the direction of Anatoli Liadov. (A complete performance, including the last choral movement, entitled *Hymn to Art*, was given in Moscow on 29 March 1901.)

9 DECEMBER 1900

The first two sections of the symphonic suite *Nocturnes* by Claude DEBUSSY, *Nuages*, an impressionistic evocation containing only 102 bars, diaphanously set for divided strings and paired woodwinds, and *Fêtes*, an animated movement in ternary form, evanescently concluding until nothing remains of the festal sound but a faintly percussive rhythm, are performed for the first time at the Concerts Lamoureux in Paris, Camille Chevillard conducting.

21 DECEMBER 1900

Festival of Pan, the first of the three symphonic romances by the efficaciously competent American composer Frederick S. CONVERSE, suggested by *Endymion* of Keats, a romantically fluent musical score infused with Wagneromorphic ninth-chords and augmented triads, is performed for the first time by the Boston Symphony Orchestra, Wilhelm Gericke conducting.

26 DECEMBER 1900

Ollanta, by José Mariá VALLE-RIESTRA, the first truly national Peruvian opera by a native composer, dealing with the rebellion of an Inca general against the emperor whose daughter he loves, and employing authentic pentatonic chants of pre-Columbian times, is produced in Lima.

1901

11 JANUARY 1901

Vassili KALINNIKOV, Russian composer of melodious symphonic and other works, imitative of Borodin and Tchaikovsky but breathing a lyrical sentiment of individual grace, dies at Yalta in the Crimea, succumbing to tuberculosis two days before his 35th birthday.

17 JANUARY 1901

Le Maschere, opera in three acts by Pietro MASCAGNI (originally dedicated "to myself, with my distinguished consideration and unaltering esteem"), wherein the familiar characters of the commedia dell'arte are embroiled in conflicting emotions, culminating in a wedding feast when Arlecchino weds his Colombina, with a musical setting in a traditional Italian manner, is produced in a sextuple première on the same day in Milan, Venice, Turin, Genoa, Verona and Rome (where Mascagni himself conducted the performance).

18 JANUARY 1901

Victor HERBERT conducts the Pittsburgh Symphony Orchestra in the first performance of his symphonic poem *Hero and Leander*, inspired by the classical legend about a Greek youth swimming the Hellespont every night to visit Hero, a vestal of Venus. (Lord Byron duplicated Leander's feat in 1810 in one hour and ten minutes.)

27 JANUARY 1901

Giuseppe VERDI, great Italian operatic composer whose 26 operas range from Bellinian simplicity to symphonic drama, dies in Milan at the age of 87 years, 3 months and 17 days.

Signor Verdi died at Milan today, 27 January, at 2:50 A.M. . . . The Senate was specially convoked this afternoon in order to commemorate the great musician to whom it was decided to grant the same honors as those paid in 1873 to Alessandro Manoni—namely, a State funeral, and the execution of a bust of Verdi for the Senate.

In person Verdi was the ideal of a well-bred Italian: the finely-cut features, the piercing black eyes, and the expressive face which are familiar to all, were associated with a figure of a height unusual among his countrymen and a bearing of the utmost dignity. (*The Times*, London, 28 January 1901)

The maestro is dead. He carried away with him a great quantity of light and vital warmth. We had all basked in the sun of his Olympian old age. He died magnificently like a fighter redoubtable and mute. This silence of death fell on him a week before he died. With his head bent, his eyebrows set, he seemed to measure with half-shut eyes an unknown and formidable adversary, calculating in his mind the force that he could summon up in opposition. Thus he put up a heroic resistance. The breathing of his great chest sustained him for four days and three nights; on the fourth night the sound of his breathing still filled the room; but what a struggle, poor Maestro! How magnificently he fought up to the last moment! (Giuseppe Giacosa, quoted by Francis Toye, in *Giuseppe Verdi and His Works*, New York, 1931)

29 JANUARY 1901

Divertissement espagnol by the Alsatian-born Americanized composer Charles Martin LOEFFLER for orchestra with alto saxophone obbligato, written in the form of a rhapsody based on a hispanoid rhythmic theme, is performed for the first time in Boston by the Orchestral Club of 75 amateur musicians "from select social circles, at least half of them being attractive young women," with Georges Longy, prime oboist of the Boston Symphony Orchestra, conducting.

31 JANUARY 1901

El Náufrago, opera by the Cuban composer Eduardo SÁNCHEZ DE FUENTES, to a libretto from Tennyson's *Enoch Arden*, wherein a shipwrecked sailor given up for dead returns home only to find his supposed widow married to another, and nobly goes back to sea, is produced in Havana.

2 FEBRUARY 1901

Jascha HEIFETZ (properly Jacob, Jascha being a diminutive form used in application to children), one of the few child prodigies who, having taken up the violin in early infancy, achieved merited fame as a virtuoso of the modern school of "cold tonal beauty," is born in Vilna, the Polish-Lithuanian town which by some arcane magic spawned a disproportionate number of Jewish violinists.

3 FEBRUARY 1901

Pelléas et Mélisande, orchestral suite by Gabriel FAURÉ drawn from his incidental music to Maeterlinck's drama, in three movements: (1) *Prélude*, depicting in a serenely modal idiom the finding of Mélisande by Golaud; (2) *Fileuse*, where Mélisande weaves a gentle fabric of unwarped woof in sextuple semiquavers; (3) *Molto Adagio*, a somber threnody as her life ebbs slowly away from grievous wounds inflicted in a jealous rage by Golaud after he has slain his half-brother Pelléas, is performed for the first time at the Concerts Lamoureux in Paris.

7 FEBRUARY 1901

Chansons de Bilitis by Claude DEBUSSY (a different work from his songs on the same poems of Pierre Louÿs), scored for two flutes, two harps and celesta, is performed for the first time in the Salon of *Le Journal* in Paris, in the form of a mimo-melodrama, with the poems read to music while a mime interprets in eloquently symbolic gestures the sensual content of the verses. (The musical material of this score was incorporated later in Debussy's *Six Épigraphes antiques* for piano duo.)

15 FEBRUARY 1901

Astarté, opera in four acts by Xavier LEROUX, depicting in Gallically Wagnerian colors the story of the Lydian queen Omphale, the worshipper of the moon-goddess Astarte, who subjects Hercules to humiliatingly effeminate work at her spinning wheel while she struts girt in a lionskin as lady paramount, is produced at the Paris Opéra.

The score is one of the noisiest ever heard. From the first note to the last it rattles along a ceaseless interminable flow of earsplitting clangor and hullabaloo, thundering, clanking, jangling, without a single moment of respite or instant's pause in the deafening clatter. Then the subject is repugnant, indecent. (*Era,* London, 23 February 1901)

17 FEBRUARY 1901

Gustav MAHLER conducts the Vienna Philharmonic in the first performance of his youthful cantata *Das klagende Lied,* completed in 1880, to his own text after a harrowing fairy-tale by Ludwig Bechstein, in which the male heir to the throne murders his brother to remove a rival in royal succession, a crime that comes to haunt him horrifyingly when a shepherd fashions a flute out of one of the victim's extant bones which miraculously sings out the tale, set to music in a Wagneromantic spirit but illuminated by proleptic Mahlerian flashes.

17 FEBRUARY 1901

Ethelbert NEVIN, American composer of melodious songs of great sentimental appeal, of which *The Rosary* attained extraordinary popularity, and of harmonious piano pieces, of which the melliferous *Narcissus* is a perfect specimen, dies of apoplexy in New Haven, Connecticut, at the age of 38.

20 FEBRUARY 1901

La Fille de Tabarin, lyric comedy in three acts by Gabriel PIERNÉ, dealing with the amours and heartbreaks of the daughter of a celebrated 17th-century mountebank, is performed for the first time at the Opéra-Comique in Paris.

23 FEBRUARY 1901

Picarol, zarzuela by Enrique GRANADOS, is produced in Barcelona.

3 MARCH 1901

Der polnische Jude, opera in two acts by the Bohemian composer Karel WEIS, his most successful work, to a libretto from Erckmann-Chatrian's tale of the robbery and murder of a rich Polish Jew by an Alsatian innkeeper, avenged fifteen years later on a wintry Candlemas day in 1833 when another rich Polish Jew arrives at the inn, inducing in the murderer a fatal nightmare, the curtain falling as the reincarnated Polish Jew gazes meaningfully at the dead body, is performed for the first time at the German Opera in Prague.

4 MARCH 1901

Gugeline, opera in five acts by the German composer Ludwig THUILLE, set in an expansive Wagneromorphic idiom depicting the happy romance of a rustic damsel with a democratic prince who rejects three potential royal-blooded mates in her favor, is produced in Bremen.

6 MARCH 1901

Charlotte Corday, music drama in three acts by Alexandre GEORGES, portraying the stabbing in the bathtub of the "*ami du peuple*" Marat by aristocratic Charlotte Corday, after she declines the honorable attentions of Count de Lux, and culminating in her death on the guillotine, is produced at the Opéra-Populaire in Paris. (The title page of the printed score gives a premature date, 16 February 1901. The correct date is given in *Le Ménestrel* of 10 March 1901.)

8 MARCH 1901

Peter BENOIT, ardent cultivator of Flemish music in Belgium, whose durable and endurable operas and cantatas to original Flemish texts are written in a chromaticized musical idiom of Gounod and César Franck, but are enlivened by the use of authentic melorhythms of his native Flanders, dies in Antwerp at the age of 66.

14 MARCH 1901

Herzog Wildfang, second opera in three acts by Siegfried WAGNER, to his own libretto wherein an 18th-century German girl accidentally wounded by a young duke during a deer hunt recovers in his castle and promises her heart to the fastest runner in a local foot race, which is won by her former sweetheart, whereupon the disappointed duke returns to his profitable trade of supplying Hessian mercenaries for use against American colonists in the Revolutionary War, set to a filially faithful Wagneromantic score, is produced in Munich.

20 MARCH 1901

Nausikaa, opera in three acts with a prologue by the German composer August BUNGERT to his own libretto, constituting the second part of his ambitious Homeric tetralogy covering the Mediterranean travels of Ulysses, is produced in Dresden.

23 MARCH 1901

Herzog Wildfang, opera in three acts by the industrious son of a great father, Siegfried WAGNER, to his own libretto, is performed for the first time in Munich.

31 MARCH 1901

Rusalka, lyric folk tale in three acts by Antonín DVOŘÁK, wherein a mermaid, miraculously turned into a complete girl and subsequently debauched by a young profligate, gives him the lethal kiss of a nix and then returns to her undine home in a central European lake, with a score permeated by bittersweet melodiousness of Slavic folksongs, is produced in Prague.

1 APRIL 1901

Claude DEBUSSY publishes in the Paris journal *La Revue Blanche* his first article on music under the nom de plume Monsieur Croche (i.e., Mr. Quaver, or Mr. Eighth-Note).

13 APRIL 1901

Lorenzo, opera in three acts by the Italian opera conductor Edoardo MASCHERONI, is produced in Rome.

26 APRIL 1901

Le Roi de Paris, grand opera in three acts by Georges HÜE, dealing with the abortive rebellion of the Duc de Guise against Henri III of France (at the end of the opera, the king delivers his historic *mot* as he looks down upon the prostrate body of the assassinated duke: "*Il ne m'r a jamais paru si grand*"), is performed for the first time at the Paris Opéra. (Date on the title page of the printed score, confirmed by the cable dispatch to the *New York Herald.*)

29 APRIL 1901

L'Ouragan, lyric drama in four acts by Alfred BRUNEAU, to a libretto from Emile Zola's stormy tale of raging passions on a French island in the tempestuous English Channel, wherein a 40-year-old seaman, loved by his 25-year-old sister-in-law and her 35-year-old sister, sails away from them for the French West Indies with his tropical 15-year-old shipmate Lulu, the music heaving in tidal waves of Gallic recitative supported by the pillars of major ninth-chords and anchored deep in sustaining pedal points, is produced at the Opéra-Comique in Paris.

3 MAY 1901

On his fifteenth birthday the precocious French organist Marcel DUPRÉ plays the organ part in the domestic first performance in his parental home in Rouen of his oratorio *La Vision de Jacob* (with a fugal treatment of the celestial stairway), his father leading a local choral society named *L'Accord Parfait,* and his mother filling in the requisite harmonies at the piano.

17 MAY 1901

Pope Leo XIII publicly commends the erudite Benedictine monks of Solesmes for their reconstitution of Gregorian modes by diligent collation and intelligent summation of authentic manuscripts.

17 MAY 1901

Werner EGK, German composer whose compact operas and ballets contributed to the formulation of the modern style of utilitarian musical theater, is born in Auchsesheim, in Bavaria. (The story circulated in the 1950's that Egk's name was an arrogantly self-aggrandizing pseudonym formed by the acronym *Echt grosser künstler* is a scurrilous canard, confuted by Egk's birth certificate obtained by the author, which proves that Egk's family name was Egk.)

29 MAY 1901

Manru, tragic opera in three acts by Ignace PADEREWSKI, wherein an adventurous gypsy named Manru shares his leisure with a wife in the Tatra Mountains and a belle in a village, culminating in his wife's suicide and his own death at the hands of the belle's suitor, set to a competently synthetic score with undertones by Chopin and overtones by Wagner, and containing several boisterous Gypsy dances for orchestra, is produced in a German version at the Dresden Opera.

30 MAY 1901

Much Ado About Nothing, opera in four acts after Shakespeare by Charles Villiers STANFORD, written in a melodious and harmonious manner with some humorous touches, but otherwise steeped in a plasma of traditional music, is produced at Covent Garden in London.

Much Ado About Nothing was strangled at birth. It was given twice in all at Covent Garden and then withdrawn. Judged on its merits, this was a rank injustice. Full of the loveliest tunes, sparkling with humour, beautifully scored, and sung and acted by a splendid cast, it made a great hit. I was there and can testify to this. (Harry Plunket Greene, *Charles Villiers Stanford,* London, 1935)

1 JUNE 1901

Universal Edition, music publishing firm dedicated in a truly universal spirit to the support and encouragement of modern music, in Austria and anywhere, is formally established at the constitutional assembly of its founders in Vienna.

From C major to the *Mutterakkord,* containing all the 12 different notes and all the different intervals, runs the range of works published by Universal Edition. (Alban Berg in *Die Musik,* Berlin, November 1929)

19 JUNE 1901

The German Ministry of Justice promulgates a law of literary and musical property, in which Article 13 expressly forbids "the utilization in musical works of a recognizable melody from another work, taken as a base of a new musical composition."

20 JUNE 1901

Edward ELGAR conducts the London Philharmonic in the world première of his concert-overture *Cockaigne (In London Town),* set in a descriptive sonata form, the first subject reflecting London gaiety, the second a London romance; the development projecting loud fanfares in artful antiphony with a church service, the recapitulation and coda resounding with Cockney hubbub (Cockaigne being the name of a mythical country, connected with the Cockneys only through whimsical alliteration).

23 JUNE 1901

Vivre Aimer, symphonic diptych by the 20-year-old Swiss composer Ernest BLOCH, dedicated to his teacher Jaques-Dalcroze, consisting of two large sections, *La vie* and *L'Amour,* developed thematically in a Lisztian manner, is performed for the first time during the Second Festival of Swiss music in his native Geneva.

30 JUNE 1901

The Académie des Beaux-Arts, composed of Saint-Saëns, J. P. Lourens, Reyer, Massenet, Paladilhe, Théodore Dubois, with Duvernoy, Hillemacher, Lefevre, Fauré and Widor as supplementary judges, awards, after one hour of deliberation at their annual session in Paris, the "deuxiéme second" Prix de Rome to Maurice RAVEL for the composition of the cantata *Myrrha* (the assigned subject), while the first Grand Prix goes to André Caplet, and the "premier second" to Gabriel Dupont.

(*Le Temps* of 1 July 1901 states that the deliberation proceeded in the "ultra-Senegalian heat, of which the hot-air furnace can give only a slight approximation." Yet, from the meteorological bulletin in the same issue, it appears that the Paris temperature on 30 June 1901 stood at 24° centigrade, only 6° above normal, so that the passing-up of Ravel in favor of Caplet cannot be excused on the grounds of thermal debilitation of the jury.)

4 JULY 1901

Dona Mecia, "lyrical novelette" in two acts by the 31-year-old Portuguese pianist-composer Oscar DA SILVA, is performed for the first and last time in Lisbon.

28 JULY 1901

Rudy VALLÉE (*recte* Hubert Prior Vallée), American prototypal protagonist of the fine art of crooning, i.e., singing in head-tones in approximate pitch while maintaining a blandly suggestive expression without a perceptible movement of facial muscles, is born in Vermont.

17 AUGUST 1901

Edmond AUDRAN, French composer of gay and popular Parisian operettas, of which *La mascotte* was performed about 2000 times in twenty years since its production in 1880, whose funeral march on the death of Meyerbeer provoked, according to plausible reports, a winged bon mot of Rossini ("it would have been better if he had died and Meyerbeer had written a funeral march"), dies in Tierceville at the age of 61.

20 SEPTEMBER 1901

Die Musik, an illustrated bi-monthly, begins publication in Berlin, the first issue containing 104 pages.

Our publication was born out of a clear consciousness of the fact that there is lacking, in the art of Music to which hundreds of thousands pledge their devotion, an organ that might favorably compare with the foremost magazines of literature, pictorial and applied arts. (From the "Praeludium" in the first issue)

20 SEPTEMBER 1901

Os Saldunes, opera in three acts by the Brazilian composer Leopoldo MIGUEZ (1850–1902), to a libretto romantically elaborated from Caesar's *De bello gallico* and relating the noble sufferings of a group of Roman soldiers in Gallia (*saldunes*, i.e., comrades) banded together in a pact of mutual fidelity in life, in war, and in death, with a servilely Wagneromorphic musical setting, is performed for the first time in Rio de Janeiro.

26 SEPTEMBER 1901

Judith, lyric drama in three acts by George Whitefield CHADWICK, after the biblical story of a heroic Hebraic widow who enters the tent of the Assyrian chieftain Holofernes laying siege on her home town of Bethulia in 656 B.C., and, after making him drunk with lust and wine, decapitates him with his own sword, returning in triumph to her people with the bearded head of the foe concealed under her mantle, to a musical score competently imitative of the best varieties of European biblical operas, is performed for the first time in concert form at the Worcester, Massachusetts, Music Festival.

19 OCTOBER 1901

The first two of the five imposingly imperialistic symphonic marches by the uncrowned musical laureate of Great Britain, Edward ELGAR, united under the Shakespearean title *Pomp and Circumstance* (in Othello's farewell speech), are performed for the first time in Liverpool.

23 OCTOBER 1901

Les Barbares, lyric drama in three acts with a prologue by Camille SAINT-SAËNS, dealing with the assault upon the last refuge of the vestal Virgins during the siege of Orange in southern Gaul by the Cimbri and Teutones in 105 B.C., wherein the conquering chieftain takes the priestess as his wife, but is in the last act stabbed to death by the widow of the fallen Roman commander, with the musical score harmoniously arranged in a series of dramatic scenes and lyrical arias, is produced at the Paris Opéra.

26 OCTOBER 1901

Toussaint L'Ouverture, concert-overture by the mulatto composer Samuel COLERIDGE-TAYLOR, inspired by the career of the mulatto Haitian leader who assumed the name L'Ouverture to celebrate his military coup in forcing an opening (ouverture) in the French camp during the island war of liberation in 1796, is performed for the first time in London.

27 OCTOBER 1901

The first integral performance of DEBUSSY's symphonic triptych, *Nocturnes* (composition completed at 3:00 A.M. on 15 December 1899), with a third movement, *Sirènes*, presenting a mistily mystical tonal painting in impressionistically modulative aquamarine colors including a wordless chorus of alluring female voices intercalated with instrumental cascades of whole-tone scales, is given by the Lamoureux Orchestra in Paris under the direction of Camille Chevillard who was also the conductor of the first performance of the initial two movements of *Nocturnes* on 9 December 1900.

1 NOVEMBER 1901

Priscilla; or, the Maid of Plymouth by Francesco Rogers FANCIULLI, based on Longfellow's *The Courtship of Miles Standish*, is produced in Norfolk, Virginia.

3 NOVEMBER 1901

One hundred years have elapsed since the birth in Catania of Vincenzo BELLINI, composer of dramatically songful operas, of which *Norma* and *La Sonnambula* have become perennial favorites.

(Exact date of birth is deduced from his baptismal certificate, a copy of which was obtained by the author from the registry of birth in Catania. The baptism certificate is dated 4 November 1801, and contains the notation by the priest: "Infantem *hieri natum* baptisavi," "born yesterday," i.e., on 3 November 1801.)

4 NOVEMBER 1901

Maid Marian, comic opera in three acts by the American composer Reginald de KOVEN, being a sequel to his 19th-century opera *Robin Hood,* wherein the champion of the poor embarks on a Crusade to the Holy Land, but eventually returns to England and his bride Marian, is produced in Philadelphia.

9 NOVEMBER 1901

Seven months and eight days after his 28th birthday, Serge RACHMANINOFF plays at a Moscow Philharmonic concert, with his cousin Alexander Siloti conducting, the solo part in the first complete performance of his *Second Piano Concerto* in C minor, dedicated to Dr. Nicholas Dahl in gratitude for the cure by neuropsychotherapy of a nervous tremor in his fingers, a work destined to become the new century's most celebrated piano concerto, set in three equilibrated movements:

(1) *Allegro,* in C minor, opening with spacious chordal formations rooted in the deepest subdominant, and plagally passing to a series of broadly rolling arpeggios in the tonic and the dominant, while the orchestra intones a ruminating theme, growing in expansive harmonic waves and leading to a soaring second theme in the relative major key, then hastening on to a rhythmically pulsating coda; (2) *Andante,* in E major, with the piano monodically chanting a nostalgic lament, presently gathering momentum and spreading through the entire range of the keyboard in precipitous diatonic cascades; (3) *Finale,* in restive festive C major, undimmed in its luminous élan by the constant flatting of the submediant, in a peculiarly Russian, inexorably wistful harmonic major mode, and culminating in a sky-high display of C major jubilation.

(A partial performance of the *Second Piano Concerto,* without the first movement, which was written after the second and third movements, was given by Rachmaninoff in Moscow on 15 December 1900 at a special concert organized by the Moscow Prison Philanthropic Committee.)

9 NOVEMBER 1901

Hans PFITZNER conducts in Elberfeld the world première of his romantic opera *Die Rose vom Liebesgarten,* a modern German fairy-tale in two acts with a prologue and an epilogue, in which the rose from the garden of love grows amid starmaidens, sunchildren, little woodwomen, giants, elves, mossmen, marshmen, minnesingers, as well as some incorporeal mystical abstractions, with a musical setting suggesting woodsy murmurings, watery drippings, aerial meanderings and cosmic maunderings in a polythematically allusive idiom of deep Wagneromantic colors. (A shortened version was produced in Frankfurt on 5 May 1939.)

14 NOVEMBER 1901

Ib and Little Christina, opera in three acts by Franco LEONI, to a libretto from Hans Christian Andersen, is produced in London.

17 NOVEMBER 1901

Fantaisie for piano and orchestra by Louis AUBERT, set in an impressionistically florid style in which tangential modalities and tonalities serve as asymptotes for a series of thematic fragments, is performed for the first time by the Colonne Orchestra in Paris, with Aubert's teacher Louis Diémer conducting.

20 NOVEMBER 1901

Grisélidis, opera in three acts by Jules MASSENET, derived from Boccaccio's whimsical tale about a submissively acquiescent woman whose sadistically pietistic husband subjects her to a series of calculated humiliations to test her uxorial devotion, with a musical score abounding in melodiously florid and harmoniously dramatic scenes, is performed for the first time at the Opéra-Comique in Paris.

21 NOVEMBER 1901

Richard STRAUSS conducts at the Dresden Opera the first performance of his third opera *Feuersnot* (completed on 22 May 1901), with a libretto derived from a poem by Ernst von Wolzogen dealing with a preternatural deprivation of phlogiston in medieval Munich, relieved when a virginal town belle accedes to a Tristanesque tryst with the local magus whose philosophy is that only a warm young woman's body can give light, with the promise fulfilled in a tremendous climax in an instrumental interlude building up into a single silent post-coital measure at which moment all the fires—the pyres before the doors, the lanterns of the townsfolk, the torches of the men of armor, the lamps in the house—flare up simultaneously, set to music marked by Wagneromantic fervor, with a sly intent to berate the Munich society, which disdained Richard I (Wagner) and failed to appreciate Richard II (Strauss).

24 NOVEMBER 1901

A Feast in Time of Plague, one-act opera in an effective lyrico-dramatic style by César CUI, the least mighty of the "Mighty Five" of Russia, to the text of Pushkin's play derived from John Wilson's tragedy *The City of the Plague* which describes the London pestilence of 1665, is performed for the first time in Moscow.

25 NOVEMBER 1901

Gustav MAHLER conducts in Munich the world première of his *Fourth Symphony* in G major, scored for a large orchestra with the significant omission of trombones, in four movements, each bearing descriptive indications of tempo and mood, with the inclusion of a soprano solo in the finale to the text from the old German collection of folk poems *Des Knaben Wunderhorn:*

(1) *Bedächtig Nicht eilen,* in G major, in 4/4 time, opening in presumptive B minor with an exaltation of a quartet of resonant flutes, heterophonically joined by the clarinet, and gently accompanied by a rhythmic tinkling of sleigh-bells (a vignette that is to recur in the final movement) followed by the appearance of a bright vernal melody, "as inconspicuous as a dewdrop on the petals of a flower before sunrise," in Mahler's own words, "but breaking out in a thousand luminous colors in every pearl of the dew as the first rays of the sun fall on the field so that a sea of sunbeams greets us in reflection"; (2) *In gemächlicher Bewegung, ohne Hast* in C minor, in 3/8 time, comprising three scherzo-like expositions and two trio-like interludes separating them, set in the measure of a melancholy *Ländler,* introduced by a surrealistic violin *scordatura* with all four strings raised a whole tone up "so that it

would sound strong and raw, as if Death herself struck the tune," the entire movement conjuring up "a kaleidoscopic tourbillion of a myriad sparkling gems, like so many dancing, changing drops of the rainbow," occasionally disrupted by staccato points of wandering *ignis fatuus* "that will make your hair stand on end with horror"; (3) *Ruhevoll*, in 4/4, in G major, designed as a set of variations that "vary thoroughly as true variations ought to do, with the entire movement pervaded by a divinely merry and profoundly mournful melody, so that one can only laugh and weep listening to it," comprising so many radical changes of tempo that "the movement could be marked *Andante, Adagio, Allegro,* or *Presto,* in the most diversified mixture of instrumental colors ever devised, resulting in the type of sound that is spherical, in an almost ecclesiastically Catholic spirit"; (4) *Sehr behaglich,* a vocal ballad, originally entitled *Das himmlische Leben,* envisioned by Mahler as "an undifferentiated expanse of cerulean sky color," with a soprano solo limning the life in Heaven in terms of a prosperous Bavarian home, with St. Peter as the celestial majordomo looking down bemusedly upon a fiddle-riddled firmament, St. Martha serving as cook and St. Cecilia taking charge of the heavenly music in Gregorian organum-like polyphony arranged in bare consecutive fifths, and containing such innovations as glissandi in the cellos, finally subsiding in a solemn hymnal incantation in E major, significantly remote from the principal key of the symphony, G major, thus making a definite departure from the cyclical Aristotelian unity of symphonic tonalities. (The earliest case of symphonic heterotonality was probably that of the *First Symphony* by Carl Nielsen, composed in 1892.)

(Originally, Mahler entitled the Fourth Symphony *Humoresque,* and planned it in six movements: (1) *Die Welt als ewiges Jetztsein (The World as Eternal Now),* in G major (2) *Das irdische Leben (Earth Life),* in E-flat minor (3) *Caritas (Love),* in B major (4) *Morgenglocken (Morning Bells),* in F major (5) *Die Welt ohne Schwere (The World Without Trouble),* in D major (6) *Das himmlische Leben (Heavenly Life),* in G major.)

Those who hoped that with his Fourth Symphony Mahler would return to a healthier musical idiom, to the prime sources of all art and natural expression, must have been disappointed. There is no spontaneity, no original ideas, no individual feeling, not even genuine colors for artificial tonal images. Everything is technique, calculation and inner falseness, a morbid tasteless supermusic. The budding weeds of Mahler's Third Symphony, which has some of his better qualities, are grown in this new work to thorny tares. Everywhere the exploitation of all possible orchestral devices to dress up a formless stylistic monster made up of superficial details indiscriminately thrown together. (Theodor Kroyer, *Die Musik,* Berlin, December 1901)

Richard Strauss hat die Gegenwart, Mahler die Zukunft. (Ernst Otto Nodnagel in his account of Mahler's *Fourth Symphony* in *Jenseits von Wagner und Liszt,* Königsberg, 1902, pp. 185–192)

It is not fair to the readers of *The Musical Courier* to take up their time with a detailed description of that musical monstrosity which masquerades under the title of Gustav Mahler's *Fourth Symphony.* There is nothing in the design, content or execution of the work to impress the musician, except its grotesquerie. . . . The writer of the present review frankly admits that to him it was one hour or more of the most painful musical torture to which he has been compelled to submit. (*The Musical Courier,* New York, 9 November 1904)

25 NOVEMBER 1901

Chopin, opera arranged from Chopin's piano works by Giacomo OREFICE, depicting in four acts the four great loves of Chopin (who sings in tenor voice), from his ado-

lescence to his death in the arms of the first and the fourth, is produced in Milan.

25 NOVEMBER 1901

Josef RHEINBERGER, German musician of superhuman industry, accomplished composer and famous piano teacher whose career was never marred by a worldly setback from the time when he as a mere child was church organist in his native Vaduz, capital of the Duchy of Liechtenstein, dies in Munich at the age of 62 after a protracted decline of his health and an even more precipitous caducity of his symphonies, chamber music, and innumerable piano pieces.

30 NOVEMBER 1901

De Bruid der Zee (The Bride of the Sea), Flemish national opera in three acts by Jan BLOCKX, foremost representative of operatic modernism of the Belgian Flanders, depicting the tempestuous passions among shrimp fishermen, crayfish fisherwomen and adolescent catchers of marine macruran decapod crustaceans, wherein a brawny prawn monger vanishes on a fishing expedition to Iceland, and his betrothed, hearing his disembodied voice from a fog bank, leaps into the sea, while her rejected suitor plunges a knife into the heart of an importunate lobster girl who proffers herself as a substitute for the "bride of the sea," the arpeggiated Wagnerian ocean waves engulfing the scene in a score in which dramatic events are ingratiatingly alternated with authentic Flemish melorhythms, is produced at the Flemish Opera in Antwerp.

5 DECEMBER 1901

Walt DISNEY, originator of the animated cinematic cartoons *Silly Symphonies,* of which the polyscopic *Fantasia* of 1940 is the silliest, is born in Chicago.

11 DECEMBER 1901

The first transatlantic radio signal is transmitted by Guglielmo MARCONI from Poldhu, Cornwall, to St. John's, Newfoundland.

On Monday 9 December 1901, Marconi cabled the Poldhu station to begin sending signals at 3 P.M. daily, and to continue them until 6 P.M., these hours being, respectively, 11:30 A.M. to 1:30 P.M. St. John's time. During these hours Wednesday, 11 December, Signor Marconi elevated a kite with an aerial wire, by means of which signals are sent or received. He remained at the recorder attached to the receiving apparatus, and to his profound satisfaction, signals were received by him at intervals, according to the programme arranged previously with the operator at Poldhu. These signals consisted of repeating at intervals the letter S, which, in Marconi's code, is made by three dots or quick strokes. (New York *Tribune* in the story headlined: "Signor Marconi's Triumph. Wireless Messages Flashed Over the Ocean From Cornwall to Newfoundland. Most Wonderful Achievement of the Electric Age," published in the issue of 15 December 1901, and reprinted in the centennial issue of the New York *Herald Tribune* of 13 April 1941.)

20 DECEMBER 1901

On the 30th birthday of Henry HADLEY, his *Second Symphony,* subtitled *The Four Seasons:* (1) *Winter* "deflowering

Nature's grassy robe" in coldly self-confident, intervalically masculine tonal strides, (2) *Spring,* marking the reappearance of diatonically ambulating ants and chromatically busy bees, (3) *Summer,* projecting pentatonic Indian madrigals in a pastoral scene with birdcalls of the flutes and gurgling brooks in the strings, (4) *Autumn,* heralded by invigorated hunting horns against the seasonally deciduous violins, is performed for the first time as the

winner of the 1901 Paderewski Prize, by the New York Philharmonic, Emil Paur conducting.

26 DECEMBER 1901

Georgy RIMSKY-KORSAKOV, grandson of the great Rimsky from whose legacy he deviated far afield to become a foremost Russian exponent of quarter-tone music, is born in St. Petersburg.

1902

4 JANUARY 1902

I Pirenei, first part of an operatic trilogy by the "Spanish Wagner" Felipe PEDRELL (the second part, *La Celestina* and the third, *Raimundo,* remaining unperformed), dealing with the feudal feuds between France and Aragon (separated by the Pyrenees, hence the title) in the 13th century, in three historic scenes, *Il Conde de Foix* (1218), *Rayo de Luna* (1245) and *La Jornada de Panissares* (1285), eloquently projected in a Wagneromorphically Iberomantic manner of a music drama, with thematic motives descriptive of people and places identifiable also by vivid folkloristic allusions in hispanistic dances and eclectically ecclesiastical chants, is produced in Barcelona in an Italian version of the original Catalan libretto.

12 JANUARY 1902

Till Eulenspiegel, opera in two parts with an epilogue by Emil von REZNIČEK, to his own libretto about the roguish but lovable transgressor of medieval mores, is performed for the first time in Karlsruhe.

17 JANUARY 1902

Les Guelfes, grand opera by Benjamin GODARD, to the story of political strife between the Guelfs and the Ghibellines in medieval Italy, is produced posthumously in Rouen.

18 JANUARY 1902

Filippo MARCHETTI, Italian composer of grandiose operas in which the gentle afflatus of Gounod is Italianized in the spirit of Mercadante, whose transitory art of lyric invocation and dramatic concitation had its luster of popular success, and who as Director of the Liceo Musicale in Rome was the appreciated teacher of a generation of aspiring Italian musicians, dies in Rome at the age of 70.

25 JANUARY 1902

First Symphony by the 27-year-old Austrian composer Franz SCHMIDT, completed in 1899, in the romantic key of E major, in four Brahmsogenic movements with

Wagnerophiliac excrescences, is performed for the first time in Vienna.

25 JANUARY 1902

Second Symphony in C minor by Alexander SCRIABIN, in five movements, the idiom of which is characterized by irresolutions of amplified ninth-chords and ecstatic upward leaps of sensuous melody premonitory. of the "jeux divins" and the orgiastic yearnings of his ultimate symphonic style, is performed for the first time at the Russian Symphony Concerts in St. Petersburg, Anatoli Liadov conducting.

Some Symphony! The Devil knows what it is! Scriabin may well join hands with Richard Strauss. God, what happened to music?! Decadents crawl in from every hole. Holy Saints, help!! Police!!! I am all beaten up, like Don Quixote by the shepherds. Next to Scriabin, Wagner is just a suckling babe in the arms mumbling sweet nothings. I am going crazy! Where can I flee from such music? Help! (Liadov in an apparently jocular letter to Belaieff after receiving the score of Scriabin's Second Symphony which he was assigned to conduct)

The Russian Symphony Society put on the program of its last concert the Second Symphony by Scriabin. I believe that it was a gross typographical error; instead of Symphony the program should have read Cacophony, because in this so-called Symphony there seem to be no consonances whatsoever. The peace is disturbed for 30 or 40 minutes by dissonances piled up one upon another with no sense at all. I cannot understand why Liadov consented to perform such an absurdity. I went to hear it only to amuse myself. Glazunov never showed up. Rimsky-Korsakov, whom I asked what he thought of it, said that he could not understand why any composer should want to depreciate consonances to such an extent as Scriabin. (From a letter by Anton Arensky to Sergei Taneyev, written shortly after the concert)

Scriabin deliberately flaunts dissonances at the public and they saturate his Second Symphony to the point that the music offends the ear. (From a review in the *Russian Musical Gazette,* St. Petersburg, 1 February 1902)

1 FEBRUARY 1902

Salomon JADASSOHN, learned German music pedagogue, nicknamed "musical Krupp" (he wrote canons, Krupp made cannons), dies in Leipzig at the age of 70.

9 FEBRUARY 1902

Hans HUBER conducts in Basel the first performance of his *Third Symphony*, surnamed *Heroische*, but set in the key of C major, thus differing in tonality from a similarly surnamed and identically numbered Beethoven symphony, with the funeral movement *Totentanz* being third of the four, whereas Beethoven put a corresponding movement second.

15 FEBRUARY 1902

Orestes, opera by the German conductor Felix WEINGARTNER in three acts, to a text from the trilogy of Aeschylus, is produced in Leipzig.

18 FEBRUARY 1902

Le Jongleur de Notre-Dame, a miracle play in three acts by Jules MASSENET, from a medieval fable about a monk who, having nothing of material value to offer on the altar of the Virgin, sings and dances before her statue which comes to life and blesses him whereupon he dies of ecstasy, is performed for the first time at Monte Carlo.

22 FEBRUARY 1902

La Pompadour, first opera in two acts by the Hungarian composer Emanuel MOÓR, after Alfred de Musset's poem about the politically powerful mistress of Louis XV, written in an effective pseudo-classical settecento style, is performed in a German version for the first time in Cologne.

25 FEBRUARY 1902

Der Improvisator, opera by Eugen D'ALBERT, to a libretto from 16th-century Italy wherein a minstrel, accidentally sentenced to death for treason, turns out to be a nobleman who saved Padua from Venetian domination, is liberated and marries the Paduan podesta's daughter, is performed for the first time in Berlin.

1 MARCH 1902

The Legend of the Great City of Kitezh and the Calm Lake Svetoyar, dramatic cantata by Sergei VASSILENKO, after an ancient Russian tale of a city which saves itself from the invading Tatar hordes by submerging in a lake, tolling the church bells underwater, is performed for the first time in Moscow.

(An operatic version of the cantata was produced in Moscow on 3 March 1903; a famous opera on the same subject by Rimsky-Korsakov was brought out in St. Petersburg on 20 February 1907.)

8 MARCH 1902

Jean SIBELIUS conducts in Helsingfors the first performances of his early *Overture* in A minor and of his lofty masterpiece, the tumultuously serene and rhapsodically lyric *Second Symphony* in D major, in four movements:

(1) *Allegretto*, progressing in mounting waves of string sonorities antiphonally contrasted with independent parts for wind instruments and reaching a harmonious coalition in a final dynamic recession; (2) *Tempo andante, ma rubato*, with a pair of lugubrious bassoons initiating a rhythmically excited motion of melodic phrases built at singularly angular thematic intervals; (3) *Vivacissimo*, a fugal gigue with lyrical interludes; (4)

Finale, Allegro moderato, wherein a simple progression in D major is exalted by dint of relentless repetition in varying registers to a dramatic proclamation of extraordinary power, concluding on a vibrant plagal cadence.

9 MARCH 1902

Gustav MAHLER, 41 years old, marries Alma Maria Schindler, 23, ten weeks after the premarital consummation of their union. (Alma Schindler wrote on 4 January 1902: "Wonne über Wonne!")

10 MARCH 1902

Bucolic Suite for orchestra by Ralph VAUGHAN WILLIAMS, in four movements imbued with English folksong inflections, is performed for the first time in Bournemouth.

11 MARCH 1902

Germania, lyric drama in two acts by the 41-year-old German-educated Italian composer Baron Alberto FRANCHETTI, wherein a German girl, seduced by a university student, marries his comrade in an atmosphere of continued seething rivalry, and in the epilogue conciliates them as they lie dying of patriotic wounds on the battleground of Leipzig on 19 October 1813, to a Wagneromantic setting strongly impregnated with a Tristanesque fluid, is produced at La Scala in Milan.

18 MARCH 1902

Verklärte Nacht, string sextet for two violins, two violas and two cellos by Arnold SCHOENBERG, completed by him on 1 December 1899 at the age of 25, and inspired by a poem of Richard Dehmel—a rare example of a chamber music work with a definite literary link—wherein a woman confesses to her beloved in a walk through a darkened forest that she is with child which is not by him (the words "Ich trag ein Kind, und nicht von dir" fit precisely into the melorhythmic figure of a corresponding motive in the music, and further identification is suggested by the notation "mit schmerzlichem Ausdruck" and "wild, leidenschaftlich"), to which he serenely replies (and the score contains the expression marks "weich, zart, warm" to depict his soft tenderness towards her, marked by a passionate flow into the illumined key of F-sharp major, in perfect prosodical concordance with the words of the poem, "Das Kind das Du empfangen hast sei deiner Seele keine Last") that the warmth within him will transfigure the alien child within her to become his own, with the music rooted in the profoundest intimacy of twilit romanticism, from the opening measures in sad D minor almost literally suggestive of two people walking, to the spiritual conciliation in the "transfigured night" of the title, concluding in pendulously swaying harmonious arpeggios in the lucent key of D major, is performed for the first time in Vienna by the Rose String Quartet and two players from the Vienna Philharmonic. (All books on Schoenberg and all music dictionaries give the erroneous year 1903 for the first performance.)

Lieber Herr Schönberg! Last night I heard *Verklärte Nacht*, and I would be guilty of the sin of omission were I not to send you a word of thanks for your wonderful sextet. I expected to peruse the motives of my poem in your composition, but I soon forgot about it, so bewitched was I by your music . . . Ein Wörtlein Dank—o schönster Schall: des Schöpferwortes Widerhall . . . (From Richard Dehmel's letter from Hamburg dated 12 December 1912)

25 MARCH 1902

Urvasi, opera in two acts by the 45-year-old Polish-born composer Erasmus DLUSSKI, wherein a Hindu princess loves a disembodied but exceedingly handsome spirit and is turned into a morning star with her astral soul enjoying an orbital Nirvana, to a score saturated with tangible recollections from Tchaikovsky and Rimsky-Korsakov, is performed for the first and last time at a charity performance at the Imperial Opera in St. Petersburg.

29 MARCH 1902

William Turner WALTON, English composer of grandiloquent symphonies and romantic overtures, with an incisive satirical strain in lighter works, is born in Oldham, Lancashire.

31 MARCH 1902

Paul LINCKE conducts in Berlin the first performance of his two-act operetta *Lysistrata*, after Aristophanes, suggesting an effective anti-war deterrent by a female strike against marital relations during wartime, the score containing the famous *Glühwürmchen (Glow-Worm)* song.

2 APRIL 1902

Merrie England, operetta in two acts by Edward GERMAN, lightly picturing the affairs of Sir Walter Raleigh, Queen Elizabeth et al., is produced in London.

5 APRIL 1902

Jeux d'eau by Maurice RAVEL, a historically significant piano piece forcefully written in a new technique of massed sonorities, harmonically based on the principle of counter-position of two mutually exclusive scales, heptatonic (white keys) and pentatonic (black keys), equitably distributed over the entire range of the keyboard (the nonexistent G-sharp in the lowest bass register in the black-key avalanche of the cadenza is replaced by its acoustical approximation A), is performed for the first time by the Spanish pianist Ricardo Viñes at a concert of the Société Nationale de Musique in Paris.

9 APRIL 1902

Der Wald, one-act music drama by the English composeress Ethel SMYTH, to her own libretto in German, dealing with an unholy passion of a feudal lady for a young forester whom she orders to be shot as a trespasser when he scorns her ardor in favor of the love of a peasant girl (who dies with him in the attempt to protect him with her interposed body), with mystical hamadryads drenched in Wagnerian fluid in the role of a Grecian chorus, is performed for the first time at the Royal Opera in Berlin, Karl Muck conducting.

At the final rehearsal, Dr. Muck laid down his baton and uttered the ominous words: "So geht's nicht!" His Majesty Emperor William II, however, insisted upon a production of the work at the Royal Opera House, where his wish, of course, is command. Who, however, is Miss Smyth that she could prevail upon the Emperor so as to have her opera produced? She is a prim, neat and cold-looking spinster, high in the thirty-nine, as they say. Her sister is first lady-in-waiting upon the present Queen of England. Be that as it may, Miss Smyth's influence must be a very potent one, and she used it for her own discomfort, for she brought upon her virginal head a fiasco the like of which I have never witnessed. (*The Musical Courier*, New York, 14 April 1902)

11 APRIL 1902

Chonchette, opéra-bouffe in one act by the 35-year-old French composer Claude TERRASSE, dealing with a ravishing Parisian laundress and her multiple swains, including a whistled arioso, the first of its kind in any opera, is produced in Paris.

14 APRIL 1902

Two weeks before the dress rehearsal of Claude DEBUSSY's opera *Pelléas et Mélisande*, the Paris daily *Le Figaro* publishes an open letter from Maurice Maeterlinck, author of the drama, sharply denouncing both Carré's libretto and Debussy's setting and expressing a wish that the production should result in a "prompt and resounding failure," his wrath aroused because Debussy preferred Mary Garden in the title role to Georgette Leblanc, Maeterlinck's common-law wife.

Paris 13 April 1902

Dear Sir: The direction of the Opéra-Comique announces the impending performance of *Pelléas et Mélisande*. This performance will take place against my will, for Messrs. Carré and Debussy have ignored my legitimate rights.

I should have solved this difference in the courts, which would probably rule once more that a poem belongs to the poet, if a particular circumstance had not altered the espèce as they say in the courts.

Indeed, Monsieur Debussy, having first agreed with me on the choice of the interpreter whom I judged the sole person capable of creating the role of Mélisande in conformity with my intentions and desires, decided, when confronted with unjustifiable opposition to this choice on the part of Monsieur Carré, to deny me the right of intervention in the casting, by taking advantage of an all-too-confident letter I wrote him more than six years ago.

Bizarre practices followed this inelegant gesture, as proved by the receipt record of the work, manifestly antedated in an attempt to establish that my protests had been tardy.

Thus, they managed to oust me from my own work, and thenceforth it has been treated as conquered territory. Arbitrary and absurd cuts have been made in the play, rendering it incomprehensible; on the other hand, they have left intact the parts that I intended to delete or improve as I did in a booklet just published, and from which one can see how much the text adopted by the Opéra-Comique differs from the authentic text.

In a word, the *Pelléas* under discussion is a piece which has become an almost enemy alien to me. Barred from all control of my work, I am compelled to wish that its failure should be resounding and prompt.

I beg you, dear Sir, to accept the expression of my highest regard.

MAURICE MAETERLINCK

18 APRIL 1902

The Celestial Country, cantata by Charles IVES, scored for chorus, string quartet, trumpet, euphonium, timpani and organ, in seven sections, is performed for the first time at Central Presbyterian Church in New York, where Ives served as organist.

28 APRIL 1902

A public rehearsal is held at the Opéra-Comique in Paris of DEBUSSY's sublime masterpiece, *Pellés et Mélisande*, lyric drama in five acts and twelve tableaux, portraying with translucent penetration the peripeteia of Maeterlinck's poignantly symbolic play, from the mysterious finding of Mélisande forlorn in a medieval forest to the insensate murder by the jealously deluded Golaud of his young half-brother Pelleas, and to the serene death of Mélisande in childbirth, with a musical setting of startling originality and concentrated power of latent expressiveness, the voices singing the poetic lines according to the inflections of natural speech following every nuance of sentiment in a continuously diversified declamation, the melodic curves tending towards their harmonic asymptotes in tangential proximity and forming chords of quasi-bitonal consistency, the modal intervalic progressions with their concomitant cadential plagalities imparting a nostalgically archaic sound to the music, the frequent parallel motion of triadic units, seventh-chords and ninth-chords providing instant modulatory shifts, extensive vertical edifices in fourths and fifths reposing on deeply anchored pedal-points giving stability in fluidity, while the attenuated orchestra becomes a multicellular organism in which the instrumental solos are projected with pellucid distinction echoing the text in allusive symbolism (when light is mentioned, the strings are luminously tremulous; for water, harps respond), and the psychologically adumbrative motives reflect the appearances of dramatic characters in graphically imprecise identifications. (Composition begun in August 1893; the score completed in August 1895, but revised; the second version finished in 1898, reorchestrated in December 1901; some symphonic interludes written shortly before the first performance, in 1902.)

The theater programs that the noisy boys are in the habit of peddling at the entrance usually expatiate on the merits of the production. Yesterday, at the rehearsal at the Opéra-Comique, those privileged to attend the first audition of Claude Debussy's work were not a little astonished at reading the program sold at the door which contained an ironic description of Maeterlinck's work. This little drama is a chef-d'oeuvre, and Maeterlinck is a genius. At least, they say so. Is it a mystification? Is there anything behind this? There was a great deal of talk about this and very singular stories have been heard with great curiosity in the lobby. Some propose to call the play Pelléas et Médisances. (*Le Figaro*, Paris, 29 April 1902)

The copyist was conscientious but very inexperienced; he wrote sharps for flats so that Debussy himself could not make out which was which; frequently the change of clef or time-signature after a rest was left out. Result: exasperating rehearsals; impossible to proceed; every time a stop. "Is this a sharp?" . . . A first-desk player declares that the music makes no sense, but after the twenty-first rehearsal admits that the enthusiasts were right. The trombone player, speaking for the brass section, opines: "We have little to play here, but what we do play is great!" . . . To gain time, the scenery is entrusted to two great specialists, Jusseaume and Ronsin. Catastrophe! *Pellés* demands thirteen changes of scenery, but it is impossible to accomplish in the hall. The stage technicians swear a thousand oaths, and, to save the situation, Debussy sits down to compose, between two rehearsals, the necessary interludes; it is a miracle that the stitches do not show. . . . After the end, the assistant secretary of the Ministry of Education demands the deletion of fifteen bars on account of the portion of the dialogue inadmissible on the stage of a subsidized theater:

"Golaud: Et . . . et le lit? Sont-ils près du lit?
Yniold: Le lit, petit père? Je ne vois pas le lit."
(Robert Jardillier, *Pellés*, Paris, 1927)

Here is a work of art outside the beaten path, a new impression, a subtle expression, in which the critics, to their joy, found no imitation of Wagner, Gounod or Massenet. In our times such works are not daily occurrences. The music of *Pelléas et Mélisande* possesses originality so specialized that it would be strange if it would not encounter its detractors. Since the right to deny merit to a musical work is an absolute right, and since in this particular case impression is everything, one should not be particularly surprised that the remarkable score of Debussy should suffer the destiny that pursued long ago the masterpieces of Wagner or *Carmen* of Bizet. We are not trying to establish any comparison between Wagner and Bizet with Debussy. We simply wish to remind ourselves that works debated at their first appearance are apt to become most pleasing to the connoisseurs and to the general public later on. While we find it quite natural that not everybody relishes the exquisite savor of Debussy's music, while we can explain very well that the noble allure and the unusual terms of the lyric drama presented yesterday might exasperate and annoy some listeners, while we concede that we must above all respect the opinion of everyone, we humbly demand for ourselves the liberty to be charmed by this curious, delicious, poetic music of Debussy. It does not resemble anything we have ever heard. You would look in vain in the 283 pages of the score for a piece that can be extracted for separate performance. There are no arias so greatly favored. The personages on the stage avoid singing. They declaim in a sort of melodic speech, summarily notated, what they have to say, and the task of expressing and of communicating their sentiments is left entirely to the orchestra.

The changes of scenes do not interrupt the musical current. Instrumental playing ceases only at the end of an act. The orchestra, in which the images rise and vanish, where clear visions and troubling apparitions pass with a light touch, murmurs of the breeze, fluttering of wings, sound of waves, the pallor of the moon, the crimson of the twilight, the tenderness, the impatience, the timidity, the spasms of passion, the malaise, the fragrance of the roses, the lure, the contained impulses, the freshness of dew, the agonies of light, the bluish reflections and the indecisive movement, this atmosphere is created in the orchestra which bathes the action in a sonorous vapor exquisitely tinted with the most elusive nuances. The souls of the actors seem to float like fine dreams on a sea of harmony.

One should not conclude, however, that the score of *Pelléas et Mélisande*, in which melody, at least what one generally understands as melody, is absent, and in which the rhythm disappears in intentionally imprecise harmonic aggregations, is devoid of character or shape. From the initial prelude, the delicately poetic music is invested with an adorably remote color and leaves in the ear an evanescent echo of faraway things . . . for Debussy's music constantly floats above the realities of life. Its emotion is poetic, and its suffering is without a human outcry. This dream music never escapes the world of reverie. (André Corneau, in *Le Matin*, Paris, 1 May 1902)

Debussy has imparted to Maeterlinck's tragic legend his own musical atmosphere. He was not preoccupied with the musical expression which formulates with precision, rhythm and movement the psychological states which are devoid of action. One would seek in vain in *Pelléas et Mélisande* either the arias with their time-honored strophes and refrains or the Wagnerian leitmotif and its transformations. In his orchestral commentary, which is rich and sonorous, the composer creates, we repeat, an atmosphere of the drama and its characters. This word, atmosphere, is the only one which fits the fluidity of this music. It does not resemble in any of its parts a configuration, an ordonnance, a development. The composer understands the alliance of music with the words as a color that is applied to a point in order to make it come out with greater emphasis, or, better still, as a light placed behind an object or drawing to illuminate a detail with greater clarity. It remains to be seen whether in this system of "spoken music" the art does not lose all it has to offer by absorbing itself in another art. We believe, on our part, that it is a dangerous system. Others may find it excellent, but they will refuse to imitate it. (Montcornet, *Le Petit Parisien*, 1 May 1902)

Pelléas c'est encore de la musique à écouter la figure dans les mains. Toute musique à écouter dans les mains est suspecte. Wagner c'est le type de la musique qui s'écoute dans les mains. (Jean Cocteau, *Coq et l' Arlequin*, Paris, 1918)

Claude Debussy is a representative of the most advanced school of music. His *Nocturnes* and particularly a prelude entitled *L'Aprés-midi d' un faune* indicate a very extensive knowledge of the orchestra, but also an absolute disdain for all the rules transmitted to us by musical masters. M. Debussy has a horror of the perfect triad, and if by chance he uses one, it is almost always in an antitonal progression, as if to say "This is a perfect triad, to be sure, but you must admit that it does not look it!" Besides, M. Debussy covers with gauze his coarsest passages. The use of a mute and of pianissimo allow him to take greater risks for the good reason that one hears less. . . . The production of *Pelléas et Mélisande* proves once more that the world of music is divided into two camps, on the one hand a group of *arrivistes* who have noisy friends determined to defend them in spite of everything, and on the other, a company of fervent devotees of art who believe that music is a Holy Trinity whose three parts, melody, harmony and rhythm, are regulated by laws which cannot be continually infringed to the detriment of reason and of the ear. . . . *Pelléas et Mélisande* marks the limit that, I believe, can not be transgressed, and it certainly merits a place, as a curiosity, in all music libraries. (Eugene d'Harcourt, in *Le Figaro*, Paris, 1 May 1902)

M. Debussy's score defies description, being such a refined concatenation of sounds that not the faintest impression is made on the ear. The composer's system is to ignore melody altogether, and his personages do not sing, but talk in a sort of lilting voice to a vague musical accompaniment of the text. No solo, no detached phrase ever breaks the interminable flow of commonplace sound. The effect is quite bewildering, almost amusing in its absurdity. (Paris dispatch in *Era*, London, 1 May 1902)

The public is tired of hearing music which is not music; it is weary of this heavy, continuous declamation, without air and light; it is sated with this unsupportable abuse of chromatics, thanks to which all sense of tonality disappears along with the melodic sense. . . . Rhythm, melody, tonality—these are three things that are unknown to M. Debussy. His music is vague, without color or nuance, without motion, without life. It is not even declamation, but a continual dolorous melopocia, without vitality or vigor, deliberately shunning all semblance of precision. . . . And what a delightful series of false relations! What adorable progressions of consecutive triads, with the inevitably resulting fifths and octaves! What a collection

of dissonances, sevenths and ninths, ascending even by disjunct intervals! I recommend to music lovers a ninth-chord on page ten of the full score, where the voice sings the fifth of that ninth, so that only one note is missing to complete the scale in this chord. Very pretty! No, I will never have anything to do with these musical anarchists! (Arthur Pougin, in *Le Ménestrel*, Paris, 4 May 1902)

The music is such as one could expect from the composer of *L'Aprés-midi d' un faune*, *Damoiselle élue*, *Trois Nocturnes*, etc., i.e. indefinite, strange, escaping, full of harmonic hardness, particularly in the preludes and postludes of the orchestra. . . . We know too well that one shouldn't be scandalized by notes not in the harmony, for examples of such attempts one might find in the works of the greatest masters. But, with them, it is an exception, and the ear relishes their bold innovations as long as they are tempered by tonalities pure of all accidents. With Debussy, it is exactly the reverse: harmonic simplicity is a rare thing in his score. (H. Imbert, in *Le Guide musical*, Paris, 4 May 1902)

Music is the final religion of these last centuries without faith. The disciples of Wagner were at least sincere. They were recruited from all classes of society, and the poverty of their dress, the ugliness, sometimes sublime, of their drawn faces, bore witness to the fervor and fury of their faith. The religion of Mr. Claude Debussy has more elegance. The neophytes affect especially the orchestra fauteuils, the first boxes, the orchestra stalls; they are found by the side of the young blonde girls, too delicate, too white, too blonde, in evident imitation of the type to which Mary Garden belongs.

"Je regardais Lucie, elle était pâle et blonde." And turning over with a lazy hand the score placed on the rail of the box there is a whole class of beautiful young men (nearly all the Debussyites are young, O, so young), ephebes with long hair cunningly brought in stringy locks over the forehead, with dull, smug faces, with deep-sunken eyes. Their dress coats have a velvet collar and puffed sleeves; their frock coats are a little too pinched in the waist; their satin cravats are mussy over the neck or they float loosely, tied carelessly to the turnover collar when the Debussyite is "en veston." They all wear on their little fingers (for they all have pretty hands) precious rings of Egypt or Byzantium, rings of turquoise or of twisted greenish gold. Thus adorned, they go in couples. Orestes and Pylades commune together, or the model son accompanies his mother. They are archangels with visionary eyes, and under the spell of an impression they whisper in each other's ears, and their whispers go to the lowest depths of the soul. "The Pelléastres!" (Jean Lorrain, in *Le Journal*, Paris, May 1902)

Not the least originality of M. Debussy is his ability to write a whole musical composition without a single melodic phrase, without a single measure of melody. . . . In *Pelléas et Mélisande* there are no leitmotifs for the good reason that it has no motifs of any kind. . . . Rhythm is no less detestable to him. In his doubly formless art, the abolition of rhythm corresponds to the suppression of melody. . . . M. Debussy's orchestration appears sickly and gaunt. When it intends to caress, it scratches and bruises. *Il fait peu de bruit, je l' accorde, mais un vilain petit bruit.* No one is more qualified than the author of *Pelléas et Mélisande* to preside over the decomposition of our art. . . . M. Debussy's music contains the seed not of life and progress but of decadence and death. (Camille Bellaigue, in *Revue des Deux Mondes*, Paris, 15 May 1902)

A work of singular novelty and beauty has been presented at the Opéra-Comique, and it was received, naturally, with surprise, scandal, mockery and hostility. . . . The play that M. Claude Debussy set to music was not an adaptation for the stage, but the actual text of Maurice Maeterlinck. Only a few scenes were cut from it. . . . One might have feared that the opera would appear disjointed, divided into small episodes, agreeable and brilliant, but disparate. To the contrary it possesses a style, a consistency, a continuity, a unity quite out of the ordinary, a line of admirable simplicity and purity . . . a sobriety, a limpidity of a classical art. . . . M. Claude Debussy is a poet; all is poetry and all is music in his work; and all of his music is poetry. (Pierre Lalo, in *Le Temps,* Paris, 20 May 1902)

The vocal parts are written without any attention being paid to the characteristics of the singing voices. In fact, the singers recite their roles to notes without the composer's having cared as to whether the sequence of these notes shall prove agreeable to the ear. Of melody there is not the slightest pretension. In fact, the same results would be obtained exactly if the singers were to declaim their parts instead of singing them, provided they kept the pitch of the voice quite distinct from the tonality of the orchestra. (*The Musical Courier,* New York, 28 May 1902)

Through the intellectual refinement of a crazy pursuit for novelty, Debussy has arrived at the greatest negation of every doctrine. He disowns melody and its development, and despises the symphony with all its resources. The opinion of the best musical critics is unanimous in declaring *Pelléas et Mélisande* a work of musical decline. . . . France may be still congratulated upon possessing Reyer, Massenet, Saint-Saëns and Charpentier. They cannot certainly prevent the decline of the musical art; but they will delay it for a while. (S. Marchesi, *Monthly Musical Record,* London, 1 June 1902)

In Debussy's opera consecutive fifths, octaves, ninths and sevenths abound in flocks, and not only by pairs but in whole passages of such inharmonious chords. . . . Such progressions sound awful, and as they come out in the strings one gives an involuntary start, as when the dentist touches the nerve of a sensitive tooth. (Arthur Bles, *The Musical Courier,* New York, 16 July 1902)

I met Debussy at the Café Riche the other night and was struck by the unique ugliness of the man. His face is flat, the top of his head is flat, his eyes are prominent, the expression veiled and somber, and, altogether, with his long hair, unkempt beard, uncouth clothing and soft hat, he looked more like a Bohemian, a Croat, a Hun, than a Gaul. His high, prominent cheek bones lend a Mongolian aspect to his face. The head is brachycephalic, the hair black. . . . Debussy is not a stylist, but an impressionist. Like Claude Monet he seems to delight in giving us the complementary hue of every tone. There are no purples on his palette—no blacks. His colors occasionally screech, so "high" are they, and their vibrations never cease. If the Western World ever adopted Eastern tonalities, Claude Debussy would be the one composer who would manage its system, with its quarter-tones and split quarters. . . . The music to Maeterlinck's *Pelléas et Mélisande* is so absolutely incidental that as music *qua* music it is unthinkable. At first hearing you set the composer as lacking ear. But Richard Strauss via the music of Wagner, Liszt and Berlioz has set the pace for the cacophonists. Since his *Don Quixote* there has been nothing new devised—outside of China—to split the ears of diatonic lovers. . . . *Pelléas* is a perfect specimen of decomposition. The musical phrase is dislocated; the rhythms are decomposed: the harmonic structure is pulled to pieces, melts before our eyes, or ears; is resolved into its constituent parts. And his themes are often developed in opposition to all laws of musical syntax. . . . His future should be viewed with suspicion from all the critical watchtowers. (James Gibbons Huneker, in the New York *Sun,* 19 July 1903)

In *Pelléas et Mélisande* Debussy has come closer than most artists to the goal of all conscious art, be it in words or tones, in line or in color—the nearly perfect fusion of the manner of utterance with the thing to be uttered. (H. T. Parker, in the Boston *Evening Transcript,* 8 April 1909)

30 APRIL 1902

DEBUSSY's opera *Pelléas et Mélisande* is presented at the Opéra-Comique in Paris, in an official première, with the Scottish soprano Mary Garden singing the part of Mélisande betraying a strong English accent, supported by a cast of French singers conducted by André Messager to whom the work is dedicated.

7 MAY 1902

Circe, opera in three acts by the Spanish composer Ruperto CHAPÍ, dealing with the enchantress of the island of Aeaea who holds Ulysses in sensual thrall after turning his shipmates into swine, is produced at the inaugural spectacle of the Teatro Lirico in Madrid.

21 MAY 1902

Orsola, lyric drama in three acts by P. L. (initials of two Prix-de-Rome-winning brothers Paul and Lucien) HILLEMACHER, dealing with a Venetian courtesan Orsola who induces her lover to kill the reigning Doge and is in the end stabbed to death herself by the assassin who is led to the execution block in the choral finale, set to a turbulently chromatic score densely inseminated with concatenations of dramatic diminished seventh-chords, is produced at the Paris Opéra.

25 MAY 1902

Consuelo, prologue in three acts by the 49-year-old Italian composer Alfonso RENDANO, to a libretto after a novel of the same name by George Sand, depicting the life of an opera singer resembling the career of Pauline Viardot (1821–1910), is produced in Turin.

30 MAY 1902

La Troupe Jolicœur, "comédie musicale" in three acts, the last stage work by Arthur COQUARD, completed by him on Christmas Day 1899, to his own libretto involving a quadrangular love triangle, wherein the strongman and the clown in an itinerant circus headed by a kind-hearted Mme Jolicœur courting a pretty street singer lose out to a composer who teaches her elementary solfeggio, is produced at the Opéra-Comique in Paris.

9 JUNE 1902

Twenty-eight days before his forty-second birthday, Gustav MAHLER conducts in Krefeld the first complete performance of his *Third Symphony,* composed in 1893–1896, subtitled in the original manuscript *Ein Sommermorgentraum,* and designated "F-dur" (rather than D minor, as stated in most analytical notes), in six principal sections with an introduction, bearing programmatic descriptions in the original manuscript but not in the printed score:

Introduction: *Pan erwacht,* announcing the awakening of Pan, with eight horns in unison; I. *Der Sommer marschiert ein,* a dramatic pastorale full of Dionysiac outbursts in emphatic major seventh-chords, alternating with episodes of intense serenity; II. *Was mir die Blumen auf der Wiese erzählen,* a minuet in the most ingratiating Viennese manner, elaborated by four variations; III. *Was mir die Thiere im Walde erzählen*, presenting in rondo form a fairly naturalistic para-Wagnerian forest idyll with bird-like flutes and wolf-like barks and howls, until a posthorn signalizes the end of the outing; IV. *Was mir der Mensch erzählt*, with a dark, deep and sonorous contralto voice intoning the *Nachtwanderers Lied* from Nietzsche's *Also sprach Zarathustra*, warning transients to beware of ineffable woe; V. *Was mir die Engel erzählen*, for contralto, women's chorus and boys' chorus, to a text from the German anthology of children's verses *Des Knaben Wunderhorn*, with chimes characterizing the angelic advice to those who innocently break the Ten Commandments; VI. *Was mir die Liebe erzählt*, peacefully advancing to full-throated sound, scaling the heights and plumbing the depths of pantheistic joy.

10 JUNE 1902

Horatio PARKER is awarded the honorary degree of Doctor in Music by the University of Cambridge, England. (Date and information received from the Registrar of the University of Cambridge.)

20 JUNE 1902

Kryse, lyric drama in four acts by the 40-year-old Argentinian composer Arturo BERUTI, to a libretto dealing with a virtuous courtesan who flourished in Alexandria in 60 B.C., set in Wagneromorphic harmonies with Verdian melodies, is produced in the Italian language in Buenos Aires.

1 AUGUST 1902

Oscar SONNECK, American music scholar, is appointed to organize a Music Division at the Library of Congress in Washington.

17 AUGUST 1902

Parysatis, incidental music of operatic proportions by Camille SAINT-SAËNS, to a play taking place in Persia in 401 B.C. dealing with the Persian Queen Parysatis and the struggle between her son Artaxerxes and her grandson Darius for love of the Greek concubine of her slain son Cyrus, is performed for the first time at the Grand Roman Arena in Beziers, France, by a grandiose ensemble of 450 orchestra players plus 20 harps, 15 trumpets, 12 cornets, 250 choristers and 60 dancers.

6 OCTOBER 1902

Das war ich, a "village idyll" in one act by Leo BLECH, after Boccaccio's tale of an amorous farmer making love to a milkmaid in the barnyard and to a neighbor's wife in the house, using both affairs as alibis against each other, is performed for the first time at the Dresden Opera House.

6 OCTOBER 1902

When Johnny Comes Marching Home, "spectacular military opera in 3 acts" by Julian EDWARDS, from the time of the Civil War, wherein a Southerner steals important documents from a Northern general during a vocal quintet, Negro slaves sing spirituals, while twelve Southern belles try to undermine the vigilance of twelve federal officers, and though the latter succumb en masse, the North wins the war to the strains of a final chorus *My Own United States*, is produced in Detroit.

14 OCTOBER 1902

Rymond, opera by the 18-year-old Polish piano prodigy Raul KOCZALSKI, dealing with a Lithuanian chieftain converted to Christianity during the crusade of 1217 through the love of a well-born lady, is performed for the first time at Elberfeld.

14 OCTOBER 1902

Servilia, opera in five acts by RIMSKY-KORSAKOV, completed on 12 June 1901, one of the four of his stage works not on Russian subjects (the others being *Mozart and Salieri*, *Mlada*, and *Pan Voyevoda*), wherein a beauteous maiden's love for a noble tribune in Nero's Rome is thwarted by a wily centurion, causing her to die of a broken heart, is performed for the first time at the Imperial Opera in St. Petersburg.

21 OCTOBER 1902

Tor AULIN conducts the inaugural concert of the Stockholm Symphony Orchestra, *Konsertfoerening*, incorporated on 27 May 1902. (Dates from *Stockholms Konsertfoerening, 1902–1927*, a 25-year anniversary booklet, Stockholm, 1927.)

22 OCTOBER 1902

A century has elapsed since the death in London of Samuel ARNOLD, English composer of stately oratorios and sedate operas, and learned editor of the collected works of Handel.

O shade rever'd! Our nation's loss and pride! For mute was harmony when Arnold died! (From a poem engraved on a plaque near the tombstone of Arnold in Westminster Abbey)

1 NOVEMBER 1902

The Philadelphia Orchestra Association is incorporated "to exist perpetually" with the aim of encouraging performances of first-class orchestral music in Philadelphia. (Date from Appendix A, in F. Wister's *Twenty-Five Years of the Philadelphia Orchestra, 1900–1925*.)

2 NOVEMBER 1902

En Saga (A Legend), tone poem by the eminent Finnish composer Jean SIBELIUS (1865–1957), expressively written to an unspecified program displaying the composer's genius for variation forms and based on the cumulative growth of a basic theme with effective contrapuntal embellishments, is premiered in its final revised form in Helsinki. (Composed in 1892–93 and premiered in Helsinki on 16 Febuary 1893, the original *En Saga* was withdrawn by a dissatisfied Sibelius after just a few performances and extensively revised just prior to its 1902 reintroduction.)

6 NOVEMBER 1902

Adriana Lecouvreur, lyric drama in four acts by Francesco CILÉA, his most celebrated work, to a libretto dealing in a highly dramatized manner with the life and the loves of the French actress Adrienne Lecouvreur (1692–1730), who undergoes a series of misadventures including mistaken identities, misdirected letters, mislaid jewels, and misfired amourettes, and dies from the fumes of poisoned violets sent to her by a jealous rival (the real Adrienne died of an internal hemorrhage), with a musical setting luxuriating in sonorous cantilena and throbbing with melodramatic diminished seventh-chords, is produced at the Teatro Lirico in Milan.

9 NOVEMBER 1902

Andreas Hofer, opera in two acts by the Hungarian composer Emanuel MOÓR, to his own German libretto dealing with the Tyrolese patriot Andreas Hofer who valiantly opposed Napoleon in the interests of the Austrian cause and then was betrayed into the hands of the French and executed in Mantua in 1810, is produced in Cologne.

12 NOVEMBER 1902

Dornröschen (Sleeping Beauty), short opera by Engelbert HUMPERDINCK, written in the ingratiating manner of his fairy-tale classic *Hänsel und Gratel* and similarly Wagneromantic in its style, is produced in Frankfurt.

21 NOVEMBER 1902

Wiener Frauen (Der Klavierstimmer), operetta in three acts by Franz LEHÁR, dealing with a versatile piano tuner who instructs his exclusively female pupils in both music and love, is produced in Vienna, with an overture artfully reproducing the tuning in fifths of a grand piano.

27 NOVEMBER 1902

Theodore Körner, opera in four acts by the 23-year-old Sicilian composer Stefano DONAUDY, to a libretto by his brother dealing with the short, dramatic, and lyric life of the German poet Karl Theodore Körner who fell on the field of battle in Schwerin in 1813 at the age of twenty-one, is performed for the first time in Hamburg in the German version of its originally Italian libretto.

28 NOVEMBER 1902

Saul og David, first opera in four acts by the 37-year-old Danish composer Carl NIELSEN, conceived in a grandly oratorical manner and articulated into a series of symphonically designed dramatic tableaux, in which the biblical characters of Saul and David assume a veristic psychological coloration, is produced in Copenhagen.

1 DECEMBER 1902

Carl NIELSEN conducts in Copenhagen the first performance of his *Second Symphony,* subtitled *The Four Temperaments,* and reflecting in its four movements the four putative humors (yellow bile, phlegm, black bile, blood): (1) *Allegro collerico,* wherein the eruptive choleric mood is mitigated by gently lyric interludes; (2) *Allegro comodo e flemmatico,* based on a phlegmatic two-note motive; (3) *Andante malincolico,* in which the pervading melancholy is expressed by unstable intervalic maundering; (4) *Allegro sanguineo,* marching in sanguine major keys through ostentatious syncopation to an optimistic conclusion.

4 DECEMBER 1902

Feodor Ignatievich STRAVINSKY, father of Igor Stravinsky, Russian operatic bass of velvety vocal magnificence and dramatic grandiloquence, dies in St. Petersburg, the scene of his many operatic triumphs, at the age of 59. (Previous editions of *Music Since 1900* mistakenly give the place of Feodor Stravinsky's death as Wildungen, Germany, where he lived during the summer of 1902 and whence he was brought *in extremis* to St. Petersburg on 28 October 1902.)

My father died on 21 November (old style, 4 December new style) 1902. After death, the body was frozen like a piece of meat, dressed in evening clothes, and photographed. The funeral procession started from our house on an unseasonably humid day. The artists and directors of the Maryinsky Theater were present, and Rimsky-Korsakov stood by my mother. (Igor Stravinsky & Robert Craft, *Expositions and Developments,* New York, 1962, p. 56)

9 DECEMBER 1902

Francesca da Rimini, after Dante, the last opera, in four acts, by the famous Russian conductor Eduard NAPRAVNIK, is produced in St. Petersburg.

16 DECEMBER 1902

Götz von Berlichingen, opera in five acts by Karl GOLDMARK, based on Goethe's famous story, is produced in a Hungarian version in Budapest.

16 DECEMBER 1902

Potemkin Holiday, opera in four acts by Mikhail IVANOV, Russian music critic of ultraconservative tendencies, to a libretto by the reactionary editor of a right-wing St. Petersburg newspaper, descriptive of the celebration in 1791 of Fieldmarshal Potemkin's victories, and set to music in abecedarian harmonies, is produced in St. Petersburg.

16 DECEMBER 1902

La Carmélite, opera in four acts by the Venezuelan-born French composer Reynaldo HAHN, to a libretto by Catulle Mendès patterned after the life of Madame de la Vallière, the country girl who became the favorite mistress of Louis XIV, but was eventually replaced by the more worldly Madame de Montespan, and in her chagrin joined the decalced order of Carmelites, the musical score written in the manner of Massenet with some pleasing neo-Lullyan dance music in the ballet interludes, and employing rhythmed speech in the religious scene in the last act, is performed for the first time at the Opéra-Comique in Paris.

The taking of the veil was reproduced with such fidelity on the stage of the Opéra-Comique that it wounded the religious scruples of many spectators, and one or two critics expressed in vigorous language their objections to such a masquerade. The immediate result has been that the director has cut out the first part of the last act, which in the future will commence after Madame de la Vallière has taken the veil, the objectionable mimicry being thus suppressed. (*Era,* London, December 1902)

25 DECEMBER 1902

Kashchey the Immortal, "little autumn tale" in one act and three tableaux by RIMSKY-KORSAKOV (composition begun in St. Petersburg on 9 July 1901 and completed there on 1 April 1902), wherein a beauteous Russian princess kept in oppressive durance by a malevolent white-bearded wizard is rescued by the fair-headed princely youth Ivan, written in a harmonic idiom rich in surprising innovations such as "cross-relations formed by consecutive major thirds, deceptive cadences on unresolved dissonances and a multitude of passing chords" (as Rimsky-Korsakov himself characterized the modernism of the score), is performed for the first time in Moscow, Ippolitov-Ivanov conducting.

1903

1 JANUARY 1903

Claude DEBUSSY receives the Cross of Chevalier de la légion d'honneur, through the efforts of the musicographer Jules Combarieu, an official of the French government.

2 JANUARY 1903

Victor HERBERT conducts the Pittsburgh Symphony Orchestra in the first performance of his symphonic sketch *Columbus*.

3 JANUARY 1903

Jane FOSTER, Stephen Foster's wife who inspired the song *Jeanie with the Light Brown Hair*, composed during their period of separation, but published in June of 1854 after their reconciliation, dies in Pittsburgh as Mrs. Matthew D. Wiley (she remarried in 1879).

3 JANUARY 1903

Alexander GLAZUNOV conducts at the second of the annual series of Russian Symphony Concerts in St. Petersburg the world premières of two of his works: *Seventh Symphony* in F major (completed on 16 July 1902) in four movements, *Allegro moderato, Andante, Scherzo, Finale*, couched in a combined sonata-variation form, and distinguished by soaringly songful lyricism, deep-grounded and opulent harmonies, ingenious contrapuntal interplay of thematic elements, and majestic modality in the epic Russian manner, with an ending on a festive fanfare with clanging bells; and an orchestral suite *From the Middle Ages* (completed 3 October 1902), in four parts: *Prelude, Scherzo, Serenade of a Troubadour,* and *The Crusaders,* written in a proclamatory style of nearly operatic eloquence.

7 JANUARY 1903

L'Étranger, "action musicale" in two acts by Vincent ĎINDY, to his own libretto from an ancient French legend about a shipwrecked mariner who exercises mystical attractive power on an affianced local maiden and sails away with her on his miraculously navigable shipwreck as the awed villagers sing *De Profundis*, with a setting in which Wagnerian harmonies are veiled in an impressionistic mist and thematic materials are enriched by Gallic virelais, is performed for the first time at the Théâtre de la Monnaie in Brussels.

L'Étranger is what dogmatic people call an example of pure and lofty art, but in my humble opinion it is more than that. It is the working out of formulas which are admittedly pure and lofty, but which have the coldness, blueness, delicacy, and hardness of steel. Beautiful music is there, but it is, as it were, cloaked; and the mastery is so amazing that one hardly ventures to feel anything so incongruous as emotion. Say what you will, Wagner's influence on Vincent d'Indy was never really profound. If *Fervaal* owes something to the influence of the Wagnerian tradition, it is protected from it by its conscientious scorn of the grandiloquent hysteria which ravages the Wagnerian heroes. (Debussy, *Monsieur Croche, Anti-Dilettante*)

16 JANUARY 1903

First Symphony in E-flat major by Reinhold GLIÉRE, Russian composer of remote Belgian extraction, in four movements, *Andante, Allegro molto vivace, Andante,* and *Finale*, conceived in a grand epic manner with the application of a totality of favorite Russian melodic, rhythmic, harmonic and instrumental devices, short folk-like refrains within the compass of a pentachord, a major hexachord with a lowered submediant, drones on the dominant, deep pedal-points, and symmetrically compounded meters, is performed for the first time in Moscow.

19 JANUARY 1903

Het Eerekruis (The Cross of Honor), one act opera by the Dutch composer Cornelis DOPPER, is produced in Amsterdam.

19 JANUARY 1903

Boris BLACHER, composer of abstract chamber operas and concrete instrumental music, who was to identify himself with the cause of German modernism, is born in Newchwang, China, of Russian-bred ethnically Estonian-German parents.

22 JANUARY 1903

Oceana, short opera by Antonio SMAREGLIA, 48-year-old Italian composer who lost his eyesight in 1900 but continued to compose Wagneromantic Italianate music by dictating it note by note while improvising at the piano, is performed for the first time at La Scala in Milan.

27 JANUARY 1903

La Botte secrète, opéra-bouffe in one act by Claude TERRASSE, in which a pair of shoes serves as evidence to trap the blackguard who kicked an aristocratic customer's derrière, set to music with Gallic elegance, is produced in Paris, on the composer's 36th birthday.

28 JANUARY 1903

Four French musicians die on the same day: Augusta Mary HOLMÈS, Parisian-Irish composer and pupil of César Franck, pianistic wonder-child of the Second Empire, in Paris in her fifty-sixth year; Robert PLANQUETTE, composer of celebrated operettas, among them *Les Cloches de Corneville*, in his native Paris in his fifty-fifth year; Edmond NEUKOMM, writer on music, in Paris in his sixty-third year; and one AUGEUZ, a singer in his fifty-sixth year.

"Funereal, indeed, is this week, which had brought the news on the same day, Wednesday, of the death of four artists meriting recognition! Our poor friend Augusta Holmes is gone. . . . She was older than it was believed. The year 1854 was given for her birth. But, it was in 1847 that she was born. I am absolutely certain of this. . . . It is quite a distance to the author of *Cloches de Corneville*. They rejuvenated him, too, making him appear in this world in 1850. The truth is, he was born on 31 July 1848. . . . I must also give the final farewell to my old comrade, Edmond Neukomm, who was nephew of the two Haydns. . . . His most curious and original work is the one he will not see accomplished: *Le Tour de France en musique*. . . . He was a gentleman and an artist of rare talent, this excellent Auguez. . . . Ah! If only his voice had equalled his talent!" (Arthur Pougin in *Le Ménestrel*, Paris, 1 February 1903)

7 FEBRUARY 1903

Two symphonic poems, *Minnehaha* and *Hiawatha*, by the German composer Hugo KAUN (1863–1932), a tribute to America where he dwelt from 1887 to 1902, was cherished by German friends and made happy by Theodore Thomas and Frederick Stock who loyally conducted his competently fashioned sub-Wagnerian post-Mendelssohnian symphonies with the Chicago Symphony Orchestra, are performed for the first time in Chicago.

11 FEBRUARY 1903

Six years and four months after the death of the great Austrian symphonist Anton BRUCKNER, his unfinished *Ninth Symphony* in d minor, dedicated "An meinem lieben Gott," is performed for the first time in Vienna under the direction of Bruckner's devoted friend and disciple Ferdinand Loewe, considerably edited, altered and reorchestrated by him, with the substitution for the unfinished finale of Bruckner's *Te Deum*, in three movements:

(1) *Feierlich*, hurling anguished defiance at the dedicatee, the "lieber Gott," with 8 horns blasting heavenwards in challenging octave leaps, while the violins voice their lament in lan-

guorous chromatics, the commotion ultimately subsiding in ascetic hollow fifths and meek minor thirds; (2) *Bewegt, lebhaft*, a sensuous septuagenarian fantasy in the spirit of a lambent Scherzo, with fluvial flutes, clarion clarinets and bacchanalian bassoons indulging in insouciant dalliance; (3) *Sehr langsam, feierlich*, a solemn *Adagio*, in which the rebellious spirit of theomachy is revealed in mounting minor ninths and tortured minor seconds, ending in a harmonious conciliation with the Deity in a poignant motive marked "Abschied vom Leben." (On 2 April 1932 the original version of the three extant movements was performed for the first time in Munich before an invited audience under the direction of Siegmund von Hausegger; a public performance of these movements was first given in Vienna under the direction of Clemens Kraus on 23 October 1932. Hans Redlich and Robert Simpson assembled and organized Bruckner's sketches for the finale, and had the synthetic result performed in London on 17 September 1948.)

14 FEBRUARY 1903

Le Tasse, opera in three acts by the French composer-nobleman Count Eugene ĐHARCOURT, dealing with the fateful passion of tbe famous poet Torquato Tasso for the duchess Leonora d'Este, which drove him to self-imposed celibacy in a monastery and her to a loveless marriage and an early death, with an appropriately emotional but harmonically static and dramatically constricted score, is produced in Monte Carlo.

16 FEBRUARY 1903

Tapu, opera by the New Zealand composer Alfred HILL, to his own libretto having to do with rituals of the Maori Indians, is performed for the first time in Wellington, New Zealand, with the composer conducting.

20 FEBRUARY 1903

Bruder Straubinger, operetta in three acts by Edmund EYSLER, wherein a virginal child of nature in a sinful Teutonic town is unwittingly procured by a dissimulating panderer to satisfy the perverted lust of a licentious landgrave but is rescued from debauched perdition by a young peasant impersonating his own 114-year-old grandfather who volunteers to marry her, ostensibly to provide matrimonial cover, is produced in Vienna.

21 FEBRUARY 1903

Moharózsa (Moss-Rose), after Ouida's fairly tale *Two Little Wooden Shoes*, opera in four acts by the famous Hungarian violinist Jenö HUBAY, is produced in Budapest.

22 FEBRUARY 1903

Hugo WOLF, the Wagner of the Lied, who was to the last quarter of the 19th century what Schubert was to the first quarter, and who developed the art of accompanied song into a polyphonic form wherein the voice becomes a contrapuntal strand in the highly chromaticized tonal fabric and the piano part is a harmonic determinant, dies 19 days before his 43rd birthday in an insane asylum in Vienna where he was kept with some intermissive remissions from 20 September 1897.

4 MARCH 1903

Jean-Michel, opera in four acts by the Belgian composer Albert DUPUIS, is produced in Brussels.

8 MARCH 1903

Gheorge ENESCU (who to acclimatize himself in Europe adopted the French form of his name Georges ENESCO), prodigiously gifted 21-year-old Rumanian violinist and composer, conducts in Bucharest the first performances anywhere of his *First Suite* for orchestra in C major and his two *Rumanian Rhapsodies*, the first (which was to become his most famous work) based on the popular tunes *Am un leu si vreau să-l beau* (I have a leu and I want to buy a drink), *La moara* (At a Mill), a "hora," *Ciocilia* (A Lark) and *Banu Mărăcine* (a quick dance in alternating tones and semitones) and the second being an essay in Balkan orientalism pregnant with sesquitonal melismas. (Date from actual program in the Georges Enesco Museum in Bucharest, 23 February 1903 according to old-style calendar then valid in Rumania.)

18 MARCH 1903

Muguette, opera in four acts by the French composer Edmond MISSA, after Ouida's tale *Two Little Wooden Shoes*, wherein a flower girl, poetically nicknamed after the lily of the valley and seasonally blossoming in Flanders in May 1810, succumbs to the savoir-faire of a French painter for whom she poses, and when he acquires another model in Paris, trudges in her two little wooden shoes to join him there, and surprisingly achieves an emotional reunion with wedding overtones (in Ouida's original story she dies), with an unassuming musical setting in the manner of Missa's teacher Massenet, gaining much by the ingratiating infusion of authentic Flemish folksongs, is performed for the first time at the Opéra-Comique in Paris.

21 MARCH 1903

La Vita Nuova, oratorio after Dante by Ermanno WOLF-FERRARI, is performed for the first time in Munich.

3 APRIL 1903

President Theodore ROOSEVELT inaugurates East Room Musicales in the White House, with a special concert given by Paderewski.

9 APRIL 1903

Endymion's narrative, the second of the two symphonic romances by Frederick S. CONVERSE, suggested by the allegorical poem of Keats, wherein the solo violin narrates to a mildly Wagnerian orchestral accompaniment the sad tale of the legendary Greek youth loved for one terrestrial night by the goddess of the moon and thenceforth doomed to dream of her as a thing of beauty without attainment in a magically induced sleep, is performed for the first time by the Boston Symphony Orchestra, Wilhelm Gericke conducting.

16 APRIL 1903

Le sire de vergy, opera in three acts by the French composer Claude TERRASSE, to a story of a trusting Provençal crusader who hands the key to his wife's corselet of chastity to his best friend before going to the wars, and having found out that his friend betrayed him and misused the key, serves his wife a slice of calf's liver, pretending it was the cooked heart of her lover, and yet himself picks up a comely medieval midinette from Paris, is performed for the first time at the Théâtre des Variétés in Paris.

17 APRIL 1903

Nicolas NABOKOV, Russian composer of operas, ballets and instrumental works of euphonious facture, embellished with prudential dissonant counterpoint, is born in an ancient castle, near Lubcha, in the Minsk region, ancestral seat of his family, tracing his genealogy back to a Russian concubine of Genghis Khan.

19 APRIL 1903

Edvard GRIEG conducts the Colonne Orchestra in Paris in a program of his works at his first appearance in France since his angry rejection of Colonne's invitation in 1899 accompanied by a denunciation of French justice in the Dreyfus Affair (Dreyfus had in the meantime been released from his detention at Devil's Island).

Did you read about my concert with the Colonne Orchestra in Paris? Never in my life did I experience anything like that. When I appeared on the stage, there were hisses and boos. But I had my full revenge, for my artistic victory was as great as I could have desired. (From Grieg's letter to Alexander Siloti, dated Paris, 30 April 1903, and published in *A. Siloti, Letters and Documents*, Leningrad, 1963)

1 MAY 1903

Luigi ARDITI, Italian composer of celebrated arias of which the vocal waltz *Il bacio* is an imperishable favorite, and who eventually settled in England, dies in Hove, Sussex, at the age of 80.

5 MAY 1903

Gino MARINUZZI, 21-year-old Italian composer, conducts in his native Palermo the first performance of his first opera *Barberina* in three acts.

6 JUNE 1903

Aram KHACHATURIAN, Armenian composer of orientally inflected and rhythmically bubbling music in all genres, is born in Tiflis.

7 JUNE 1903

Ilsebill, "dramatic symphony" in five operatic scenes by the German composer Friedrich KLOSE, to a tale by the brothers Grimm about an overweeningly ambitious fisherwoman whose outrecuidance leads her to proclaim herself divine and demand absolute obedience to her wishes until the whole presumption collapses as in a dream, written in a faithfully Wagneromorphic idiom in resonant harmonies, with the oceanographic key of E major as the guiding tonality, is performed for the first time in Klose's native town of Karlsruhe. (The date, 29 October 1905, given in some reference works as absolute première is the first Munich production.)

17 JUNE 1903

Babes in Toyland, musical extravaganza in three acts by Victor HERBERT, populated with familiar characters from Mother Goose, who aid and abet the rebellion of toys in the nursery against the toymaker, is performed for the first time in Chicago.

27 JUNE 1903

Académie des Beaux-Arts in Paris awards the first Grand Prix de Rome to Raoul LAPARRA, from six contestants admitted to the finals, passing up Ravel, who applied for the second time, having received the Deuxième Second Prix de Rome in 1901.

30 JUNE 1903

Harry Lawrence FREEMAN, American Negro composer, conducts in Chicago the first performance of his opera *African Kraal*, with an all-Negro cast.

14 JULY 1903

Viy, short opera by the Czech composer Karel MOOR, after Gogol's horrifying tale of a nightmarish monster preying on human blood to sustain his posthumous existence, is performed for the first time in Prague.

20 JULY 1903

Maguelone, lyric drama in one act by the facile French composer Edmond MISSA, wherein a superbly desirable orphan girl in a fishing village of southern France, irrationally infatuated with a nefarious but masculine shipwrecker, enters on a shameful bargain with a sleuthing customs official ("ton corps pour le sauver," he sings), but is saved by her lover who stabs him in the back at the critical moment and lets her accept the blame as acting in self-defense, with a songful but unoriginal score pleasingly interspersed with endearing Provençal airs, is performed for the first time on any stage at Covent Garden in London.

24 JULY 1903

At the centennial celebration of the birth of Charles-Adolphe ADAM, his melodious opera *Le Postillon de Lonjumeau*, dealing with the adventures of the post coach-man whose vocal prowess in announcing arrivals and departures led to his engagement by Louis XV at the court opera, is performed for the first time in Longjumeau itself. (The spelling of the town's name as it appears on the title page of the opera is Lonjumeau, but it is Longjumeau in French geography books.)

3 AUGUST 1903

Sarrona; or the Indian Slave, one-act opera by the American composer William Legrand HOWLAND to his own libretto, wherein the queen of a kingdom on the Ganges River, preparing to plunge a dagger into the dissipated flesh of her treacherous royal husband embroiled with a Greek dancer, is prevented in her design by a slave who demands carnal gratification as a price for his silence but, deterred by her reminder of his untouchability to a person of her caste, stabs himself to death, is performed for the first time on any stage in Bruges, Belgium, in an Italian version.

25 AUGUST 1903

Second Symphony by the 23-year-old English composer Cyril SCOTT is performed for the first time in London, at a Promenade Concert conducted by Henry Wood. (It was subsequently converted into *Three Symphonic Dances*—Gavotte, Eastern Dance, English Dance—and ceased to exist as a separate work.)

1 SEPTEMBER 1903

Erik SATIE writes a piece for piano four hands entitled *3 Morceaux en Forme de Poire avec une Manière de Commencement, une Prolongation du même et un en plus suivi d'une Redite*, caricaturing the pedantry of musical terminology and of impressionistic preciosity.

Impressionist composers cut a pear in twelve pieces and gave each of them the title of a poem. Then Satie composed twelve poems and entitled the whole: *Morceaux en Forme de poire*. (Jean Cocteau, *Le Rappel à l'ordre*, Paris, 1926)

This title, Satie explained, had been given to them because Debussy had declared them shapeless: "So I called them 'pear-shaped'—and *that* ought to show him and everybody that they are *not* shapeless." (M. D. Calvocoressi, *Musicians' Gallery*, London, 1935)

9 SEPTEMBER 1903

The Afro-British composer Samuel COLERIDGE-TAYLOR conducts at the Hereford Festival the first performance of his cantata *The Atonement*.

1 OCTOBER 1903

Alpenkönig und Menschenfeind, opera in three acts by Leo BLECH, is produced in Dresden. (It was revived in a new version under the title *Rappelkopf* in Berlin on 2 October 1917.)

8 OCTOBER 1903

Carl NIELSEN conducts in Copenhagen the first performance of his concert-overture *Helios*, inspired by the sunset over the Aegean Sea, and completed during his visit in Athens on 23 April 1903, when, as he wrote in a letter to a friend, "Helios burned all day long."

10 OCTOBER 1903

Prinses Zonneschijn, Flemish opera in four acts by the Belgian composer Paul GILSON, to the libretto from an old German legend of a lovely princess radiating sunshine in the darkest feudal forests, loved by a young Teutonic commoner, with the path to their union strewn with necessary royal cadavers, to a mildly Wagnerian setting full of foreboding horn calls, mystical reverberations among the flutes, and muted tremolos in the strings, is performed for the first time at the Flemish Opera in Antwerp.

14 OCTOBER 1903

The Apostles, oratorio by Edward ELGAR, to the text depicting the apostolic missions at the birth of Christianity, and the establishment of the church among the Gentiles, making use of an authentic Hebrew melody set to traditional Western harmonies, is performed for the first time at the Birmingham Festival.

17 OCTOBER 1903

The Vagabond and the Princess, the first opera, in one act, by the Hungarian composer Ede POLDINI, after Hans Christian Andersen's fairy tale, is produced in a Hungarian version translated from the original German libretto, at the Royal Opera in Budapest.

17 OCTOBER 1903

The Duchess of Dantzic, operetta in three acts by Ivan CARYLL (1861–1921), prolific Belgian-born British-bred American composer, to a libretto based on Sardou's play *Madame Sans-Gêne* dealing with an ambitious laundress who marries into nobility and becomes an influential intrigante at Napoleon's court, is performed for the first time in London.

27 OCTOBER 1903

Dobrinya Nikititch, opera in three acts by Alexandre GRETCHANINOFF, depicting in a grandiloquently Russian manner the daring exploits and ardent loves of a fabled figure of Russian folklore, is produced in Moscow.

30 OCTOBER 1903

Odysseus' Tod, the last part of the operatic tetralogy *Homerische Welt* by the Wagneromantic German composer August BUNGERT, to his own libretto from *The Odyssey,* in three acts with a prologue, is produced in Dresden.

1 NOVEMBER 1903

The Christmas Tree, one-act opera by the 37-year-old Russian composer Vladimir REBIKOV, to a libretto from various sources depicting the heart-rending misery of an orphan girl deprived of Christmas joys, with a musical setting boldly applying novel devices, such as whole-tone scales, pentatonic scales, nefarious parallel fifths and progressions of unresolved dissonances, ending defiantly on an augmented triad, but containing several pleasing arias and a Chopinesquely Tchaikovskyan waltz (which later became popular), is performed for the first time in Moscow, on the same bill with his earlier opera entitled *In the Storm.*

5 NOVEMBER 1903

The Minneapolis Symphony Orchestra makes its first appearance as a permanent organization under the direction of Emil OBERHOFFER, the conductor of the parent Philharmonic Club, or, as it was formerly called, Philharmonic Choral Society.

7 NOVEMBER 1903

Liebeswogen, "spoken opera" in one act by Theodor GERLACH, after Heinrich Heine's poem, with some singing passages and short choruses, all in an asthmatically post-Wagnerian vein, is produced in Bremen.

15 NOVEMBER 1903

Tiefland, lyric drama in three acts by the Scottish-born but self-Germanized composer Eugen D'ALBERT, to a libretto drawn from the play *Terra Baixa (Lowlands)* by the Catalan writer Angel Guimerá, wherein a young shepherd descends from his mountain pastures into the valley to marry a village maiden only to find that she is his master's mistress, a revelation that drives him to such homicidal fury that he strangles her seducer as he once strangled a prowling wolf, and carries his bride to the highlands where they can breathe the unpolluted air and enjoy unviolated love, set to music in an effective Wagneromantic style in which the contrapuntal woof is thematically enlaced with chromatic warp in the dramatically tense scenes that take place in the iniquitous lowlands while the episodes in the highlands are exalted in the spacious intervals of the natural scale, a contrast that made the opera a durable product despite the derivativeness of its eclectic idiom of composition, is produced at the German Opera House in Prague.

17 NOVEMBER 1903

Mam'zelle Fifi, one-act opera by César CUI, after a celebrated novelette by Maupassant in which a Prussian lieutenant, nicknamed Mam'zelle Fifi for his ephebic beardlessness, stationed with an occupational squad near Rouen in 1871, is stabbed to death by a patriotic fille de joie when he dares to speak slightingly of France, is performed for the first time in Moscow.

17 NOVEMBER 1903

Storia d'amore, opera in three acts by the Greek composer Spiro SAMARA, is performed for the first time in Milan. (It was produced under a changed title *La Biondinetta,* in Gotha, on 1 April 1906.)

22 NOVEMBER 1903

Pope PIUS X issues the epoch-making encyclic *Motu proprio,* in which he sets down the basic precepts for the interpretation and performance of Gregorian chant in the light of the findings by the Benedictine monks of Solesmes. (Full text in Letters and Documents.)

As regards the reforms of the Pontiff, in brief, all this seems very wonderful to me in substance, but not realizable in practice. This return to primordial purity of Gregorian Chant seems very difficult to me. Who can define essentially the difference between sacred and secular styles? Why proscribe the cymbals and the drums when angels play them in the old paintings? In all this I see words, phrases of excellent effect, but not much else. The world will go on as before. (Camille Saint-Saëns in *Le Figaro,* Paris, 1905, quoted by Arthur Dandelot, in *La Vie et l'œuvre de Saint-Saëns,* Paris, 1930)

27 NOVEMBER 1903

Le donne curiose, musical comedy in three acts by Ermanno WOLF-FERRARI, whose name hyphenates that of his German father and his Italian mother, with a libretto drawn from a play by Carlo Goldoni, wherein a bevy of inquisitive Venetian wives intent upon discovering the agenda of an exclusive men's club where their husbands habitually congregate, enter it by ruse only to find that, contrary, to their suspicions, the club is indeed womanless, written in a merry settecento vein with Wagneromimic simulation, is performed for the first time in Munich, in a German version under the title *Die neugierigen Frauen.*

30 NOVEMBER 1903

Le Roi Arthurs, opera by Ernest CHAUSSON, to his own libretto based on the life of the legendary King Arthur, is performed posthumously for the first time in Brussels.

3 DECEMBER 1903

Acté, opera in four acts by the Catalan violinist Joan MANÉN, to his own libretto in the Catalan language, wherein a Christian maiden, coveted by Nero, defies and scorns him, whereupon he burns Rome to the accompaniment of a lyre and accuses her of complicity, with an Italianate setting utilizing stylized Greek modalities to depict early Christian rites, is performed for the first time in Barcelona. (A new version to a libretto in German was produced on 3 February 1928 in Karlsruhe, under the title *Nero und Akté.*)

7 DECEMBER 1903

Muirgheis, Irish opera in three acts by O'Brien BUTLER (1870–1915), the first to be written to a libretto in the Gaelic language, is produced in Dublin.

8 DECEMBER 1903

In a pontifical letter to Cardinal Respighi, Pope PIUS X expresses his apostolic disapproval of "endless musical compositions to the words of the Psalms . . . in a traditional theatrical manner, which are of so little artistic value that they would not be acceptable even at mediocre secular concerts," and urges the return to a proper musical treatment of sacred texts.

11 DECEMBER 1903

A century has passed since the birth of Hector BERLIOZ.

14 DECEMBER 1903

The Presbyterian Churches of Chicago adopt a resolution condemning the announced production of Wagner's *Parsifal* in New York as contributing to the promotion of a blasphemous work.

16 DECEMBER 1903

The Richard Wagner Society of America issues a protest against the intended production of *Parsifal* by the Metropolitan Opera of New York for audiences to whom "the essential character of Wagnerian art has never been and probably never will be revealed."

19 DECEMBER 1903

At the Teatro alla Scala in Milan, a gala première is given of *Siberia,* opera in three acts by the 36-year-old Italian composer Umberto GIORDANO, dealing with the deepest passions in darkest Tsarist Russia, wherein the lover of the mistress of a St. Petersburg nobleman nearly kills him in a duel and is dispatched to Siberia, whither she follows him and stabs herself to death after a failure to engineer his escape, the musical setting constituting a veritable anthology of Russian songs and dances wherein the doleful Volga Boatmen's song ungeographically serves as a Siberian motto and a complete rendition of the Tsarist national anthem is given by a police band during the hero's arrest, while the composer's own contribution is limited to Italianate mimicry of Russian sentimental ballads and to instrumental interludes such as a chromatic blizzard in the Siberian "Hungry Steppes."

20 DECEMBER 1903

Taras Bulba, opera in five acts by Nicolai LISSENKO, the "Ukrainian Glinka," to a libretto in the Ukrainian language based on Gogol's epical novel, wherein an unflinchingly stern Cossack leader embroiled in a 17th-century fight against Poland shoots down his own son treasonably infatuated with a Polish beauty, receives its belated first production in Kiev, a dozen years after its composition.

20 DECEMBER 1903

Zlatorog (Russian word for *Goat with Golden Horns*), fairy-tale opera in five acts by the 59-year-old German composer Georg RAUCHENECKER, is produced in Elberfeld.

24 DECEMBER 1903

The first performance of WAGNER'S *Parsifal* outside Bayreuth is given by the Metropolitan Opera in New York despite the formal objections of Cosima and Siegfried Wagner made through their New York attorneys, asserting that no production of the opera can be given under the German copyright law until fifty years after Wagner's death, i.e., before 13 February 1913.

No one can deny that the production of *Parsifal* under the circumstances will justify the condemnation that will be uttered against us, and the efforts of all those to restore to us an opinion favorable to our character will now go for naught. This full-blooded American stock will point to the fact that those who have been engaged in the name of the people of the United States in committing this offense against ethics are chiefly foreigners. . . . Taking the opera house personnel we would find that the men who conducted the stage work were foreigners; that the orchestra consists of foreigners or their children; that the conductor was a foreigner; that the manager was foreign born; that his assistants were, to a great extent, foreign born, or the children of foreigners in the first generation. The whole scheme is essentially anti-American . . . and the newspapers of Germany which have denounced this production so vehemently should not forget to mention the names of those people who were identified with it, and those names will disclose the origin and the character of the people who are called American "Parsifalites." (*The Musical Courier,* New York, 30 December 1903)

27 DECEMBER 1903

Sweet Addine, "echo song" by Henry ARMSTRONG, beloved by Manhattan inebriates as they travel from bar to bar banded in small groups, leaning mutually to maintain an unstable equilibrium, the title derived from the great Adelina Patti, is launched on its glorious career at the Sure Pops Sunday Nights in New York.

28 DECEMBER 1903

La Reine Fiammette, opera in four acts by Xavier LEROUX, French composer of Italian extraction on the maternal side, to a semidemihistorical novel of Catulle Mendès, wherein a young monk is induced by a wily secular cardinal in medieval Bologna to assassinate the local reigning queen for dynastic reasons, but upon penetrating into her chambers recognizes in her his hebdomadal inamorata of a suburban convent and falls into her passionate embrace, whereupon a more reliable hired killer slays them both at the crucial moment, with a musical setting in the lyrico-dramatic manner of Leroux's master, Jules Massenet, is produced at the Opéra-Comique in Paris.

1904

2 JANUARY 1904

Stanislav BINICKI, 31-year-old Serbian composer, conducts in Belgrade the first performance of his one-act opera, *Na uranku (At Dawn),* the first national opera to a libretto in the Serbian language, dealing with a Balkan love rivalry between a Turk and a Serbian under Ottoman rule, ending tragically when the girl of their choice throws herself in the path of the slow but lethal Turkish bullet to protect her lover, with the score vitalized by Balkanized orientalisms and native rhythmic asymmetries within a German harmonic framework.

2 JANUARY 1904

Peter JURGENSON, German-born founder of the Russian music publishing firm bearing his name, enlightened publisher and true friend of Tchaikovsky and a pleiad of other Russian composers, dies in Moscow at the age of 67.

8 JANUARY 1904

In a decree of the Congregation of Rites, Pope PIUS X sanctions the *cantus traditionalis* according to the restored texts transcribed by the Benedictine monks of Solesmes, in preference to the reformed Gregorian chant.

9 JANUARY 1904

The Spanish pianist Ricardo VIÑES gives the first performance at the Société Nationale de Musique in Paris of *Estampes* by DEBUSSY, a suite in three movements: *Pagodes,* an impressionistic distillation of Cambodian pentatonicism ornamented with Orientalistic tintinnabulations; *Soirée dans Grenade,* in a refined hispanistic idiom; and *Jardins sous la pluie,* an alliteratively pluvious tableau with raindrops in the treble watering the flower roots of the pedal points.

10 JANUARY 1904

Mitrofan Petrovich BELAIEFF, Maecenas of national Russian music, founder and munificent supporter of the Belaieff publishing firm, which printed in its Leipzig shop a series of magnificently engraved operas, symphonies, chamber music, piano pieces and songs by a galaxy of Russian luminaries of varying magnitudes, among them Balakirev, Borodin, Glière, Liadov, Gretchaninoff, Scriabin, Taneyev, Liapunov, Maximilian Steinberg, Wihtol, Nicolas Tcherepnin and his son Alexander, as well as a number of resplendent obscurities—Akimenko, Alferaki, Amani, Artzibushev, Kalafati and Zolotarev—dies in his native St. Petersburg, where his father made a fortune in lumber export, at the age of 67.

13 JANUARY 1904

Kossuth, first truly symphonic work by the 22-year-old Béla BARTÓK, in ten tableaux glorifying the leader of the Hungarian uprising against Austria in 1848 with a mockingly atonalized version of Haydn's Austrian anthem *Gott, erhalte Franz den Kaiser* is performed for the first time in Budapest.

15 JANUARY 1904

Eduard LASSEN, Danish-born, Belgian-trained, German-domesticated conductor, and himself composer of competent operas and symphonies, dies at the age of 73 in Weimar, where he settled as Court Music Director in 1858, and where he led important operatic premières including the first performance of *Samson et Dalila* of Saint-Saëns.

21 JANUARY 1904

Jeji Pastorkyna (Her Foster Daughter; also known as *Jenufa),* opera in three acts by Leoš JANÁČEK, in which young Jenufa, loved by two brothers, is made pregnant by one whom she loves but who refuses to marry her, and knifed by the other whose true love she rejects but who remains loyal to her even when her infant is found drowned in a nearby lake and she is accused of infanticide until her adoptive mother confesses guilt, to a musical setting richly imbued with modally Slavic melorhythms plastically adapted to depict transient joy, black melancholy, and stark tragedy, is performed for the first time in Brno.

28 JANUARY 1904

Modest ALTSCHULER conducts the first concert, at Cooper Union Hall in New York City, of the Russian Symphony Orchestra founded by him in America to promote the cause of Russian symphonic music.

29 JANUARY 1904

Der Kobold, opera in three acts by Siegfried WAGNER, to his own libretto dealing with sprites and fays, nymphs and sylphs, dryads and hamadryads, oreads and limoniads, kobolds, gnomes and other elfenfolk puckishly intervening in the otherwise realistic events taking place in a small German town early in the 19th century, with the paternal ghost of the composer's great father determining the shaping of musical themes and the formation of harmonies, is performed for the first time in Hamburg.

I am well aware that of the applause bestowed upon my *Kobold* only 20% is due me, and 80% due my father. If my name were not Siegfried Wagner, but Müller or Schulz, this distinguished assembly would not be gathered here. (Siegfried Wagner's remark at a banquet given in his honor after the production of *Der Kobold* in Graz on 3 December 1904)

The tragedy of sons of great fathers is not that they lack talent but precisely because they possess a talent. (Julius Korngold, *Neue Freie Presse*, 20 January 1905, after the Vienna production of *Der Kobold*)

1 FEBRUARY 1904

Enrico CARUSO makes his first phonograph recording in America for the Victor Company, singing the aria *Vesti la giubba* from *Pagliacci*, which he made famous by the application of the "Caruso sob," known technically as *Coup de Glotte*.

3 FEBRUARY 1904

Luigi DALLAPICCOLA, whose inventive skill and stylistic flexibility has enabled him to integrate the dodecaphonic technique into a neoclassical Italian framework in his instrumental and vocal compositions, is born in Pisino, Italy.

4 FEBRUARY 1904

La Cigale, ballet by Jules MASSENET, wherein the improvident grasshopper of La Fontaine's fable is transformed into a Parisian coquette and the industrious ant into a bourgeois matron, with the moral propounded by a bank clerk, is produced at the Opéra-Comique in Paris.

8 FEBRUARY 1904

Jean SIBELIUS conducts in Helsingfors, with Victor NOVÁČEK as soloist, the first performance of his *Violin Concerto* in three movements, *Allegro moderato, Adagio di molto*, and *Allegro ma non tanto*, rooted in the German romantic tradition, treating the violin with a philosophical disregard for self-propelled virtuoso play, yet constantly maintaining interest by relentlessly propulsive rhythms and somberly colorful instrumentation. (A revised final version of the Violin Concerto was performed for the first time in Berlin, Carl Halir soloist, on 19 October 1905.)

All the heights of the violin are furiously scaled in this new concerto of Sibelius, and all its most lugubrious depths explored. There are few opportunities for the violin to speak in tones of beauty while the accompaniment is for the greater part either a mutter or a growl. Solo instrument and orchestra do not love each other in this new work. (New York *Tribune*, 1 December 1906)

13 FEBRUARY 1904

Edward MACDOWELL addresses the following letter to Felix Mottl on the status of American composers:

I see by the morning papers a so-called American Composers' Concert advertised for tomorrow evening at the Opera House. I have for years taken a strong stand against such affairs, and though I have not seen the program, fearing there might be some thing of mine in it, I write to protest earnestly and strongly against the lumping together of American composers. Unless we are worthy of being put on programs with other composers, to stand or fall, leave us alone. By giving such a concert, you tacitly admit that we are too inferior to stand comparison with composers of Europe. If my name is on the program and it is too late to have new ones made, I beg of you to have a line put through the number, crossing it off the programs. If necessary, I will pay the expense of having this done. (Quoted by Alfred Frankenstein in the *Juilliard Review*, New York, Winter, 1955–56)

16 FEBRUARY 1904

Marya, opera in three acts by the Polish composer Henryk MELCER, is produced in Warsaw.

17 FEBRUARY 1904

At the Teatro alla Scala in Milan, the world première (unsuccessful to the point of a resounding fiasco) is given of *Madama Butterfly*, "Japanese tragedy" by Giacomo PUCCINI, in two acts (the second subdivided into two parts), to a libretto by Giacosa and Illica, after an American play by David Belasco, based on a short story by John Luther Long purported to be derived from an actual event but seemingly influenced by the French novelette Madame Chrysanthème, telling the piteous tale of a 15-year-old Nagasaki geisha married in a ceremony of dubious legality (for a consideration of 100 yen) to a U.S. Navy lieutenant Francis Blummy Pinkerton (thus in the original libretto; later changed to Benjamin Franklin Pinkerton; yet even in the revised editions, Butterfly herself refers to him as F. B., rather than B. F., Pinkerton; in German productions, the name invariably appears as Linkerton in order to avoid the urinary associations of the verb *pinkeln*), with the tragically predictable harakiri ensuing when Pinkerton revisits Japan with his American wife, the curtain falling upon the self-eviscerated body of his ephemeral Butterfly as their Nipponese-American infant stands uncomprehendingly by, holding a tiny American flag, the musical score abounding in authentic Japanese songs (including the Imperial Anthem) in pentatonic and para-Phrygian modes, while the American side is represented by snatches from *The Star-Spangled Banner* to which Pinkerton sings in English, "America Forever!" —all this enveloped in soaringly passionate Puccinian melos accoutred in harmonies often moving in parallel formations and consolidated in powerful unisons at dramatically climactic points.

Growls, roars, laughter, animal noises, giggling, such was the reception that the audience of La Scala gave to the new work of Maestro Puccini. This performance in the hall seemed as well organized as the one on the stage, for it started precisely as the opera began. It had an air of actuality, as if the Russians, in serried battalions, attacked to rout Puccini's Japanese from the stage. Afterwards, Puccini, Giacosa, Illica, in agreement with the publisher Ricordi, withdrew *Madama Butterfly* and reimbursed the management of the theater for the amount of the rights of performance. (Giulio Ricordi, in *Musica e Musicisti*, March 1940)

Fiasco . . . but good lord, how can anyone expect to set to music episodes which have no lyric substance? The personality of Puccini sins on the side of uniformity. The heroes and heroines of his musical dramas do not present variety of type or sentiment. Almost all of them resemble each other. *Butterfly* is a replica of *La Bohème*, but with less freshness. . . . Instead, there is exaggerated emphasis and musical fragmentation. (Gian Battista Nappi, *Perseveranza*, February 1904)

A long, too long, first act was received coldly. After the first stage call for the singers, Maestro Puccini, leaning on a cane (he broke his leg during an automobile accident on 25 February 1903) appeared twice in front of the curtain. The public, gathered in the theater in the expectation of a new victory by a favorite composer, changed its mood from excessive approbation to harsh condemnation. . . . Even Butterfly's aria *Un bel di vedremo*, which possesses a fine romantic quality, ended amid protests. . . . Yet it is a page of most delicate texture and of immediate effectiveness. . . . I persist in believing that the opera, condensed and lightened up, will come back to life. (Giovanni Pozza, in *Corriere della Sera*, 19 February 1904)

Butterfly is coated with Japanese lacquer amalgamated with American rubber. . . . It is Japanese more in appearance than in substance. . . . Puccini resorts to the Parisianism of *La Bohème*, to Romanism of *Tosca*, to Franco-Americanism of *Manon*, making use of his favorite musical phrases. He obtains local color by allusions and patterns of the singing line, and by quotations of Japanese songs. But these elements are merely photographic, and do not convey the true essence. (*La Lombardia*, 19 February 1904)

A terrible evening. The failure of *Madama Butterfly* struck me deeply, for it was totally unexpected. But I met this rebuke with a sense of rebellion. . . . On that night of sorrow, I had the pride of protest, but the next morning I felt annihilated, and this feeling was deepened by endless humiliation. It was not the labor of three years that I mourned, but the destruction of my hopes. It was the sorrow of seeing this poetic dream, which I cherished with so much love, crushed. For a while it seemed to me that I would never again be able to write a single note. On that morning, the newsboys passing under my windows in the vicinity of La Scala shouted: "Il fiasco del Maestro Puccini" For two weeks I did not want to go out of the house. I was ashamed. (Puccini's words of recollection quoted by Amaldo Fraccaroli in his *La vita di Giacomo Puccini*, Milan, 1925)

The press and the public can say whatever they want, they can hurl at me all their darts as at St. Stephen, but they will not bury me and destroy my Butterfly. She will rise again, alive and well. . . . You shall see if I am telling the truth. (Puccini's letter to Alfredo Vandini, 21 February 1904)

(Puccini's faith was justified. On 28 May 1904, a slightly revised version of the opera was given in Brescia, with triumphant success; seven numbers were encored.)

All the telegrams which I have received, accord faithfully and exactly with the colossal, clamorous and genuine success. It is only right that today it is our turn to laugh a little! And it is just that the enemy horde should be compelled to swallow the rust of their casseroles and of their fury. In the meantime: Viva Butterfly forever! (Puccini's letter to Giulio Ricordi, 2 June 1904)

18 FEBRUARY 1904

Hélène, lyric poem in one act and four tableaux by Camille SAINT-SAËNS, to his own libretto in rhymed verse detachedly detailing the fateful flight of Helen and Paris in a boat propelled by the "double caresse des zéphires et des baisers" undeterred by the monitory and minatory vision of burning Troy conjured up by Pallas Athena, who sides with the forces of conjugal fidelity against Aphrodite's aphrodisiac proddings, the music bathed in impeccably fluid harmonies, is performed for the first time at Monte Carlo, as a commissioned work dedicated "to His Serenest Highness Prince Albert I of Monaco."

18 FEBRUARY 1904

Second Symphony in B-flat major by the master of Gallic neo-classicism, Vincent D'INDY, in four movements: (1) *Extrêment lent—Très vif*, (2) *Modérément lent*, (3) *Modéré—Très animé*, (4) *Lent—Fugue et Final*, in a cyclic construction with passages in whole-tone scales, consecutive major ninth-chords, instantaneous modulations by means of parallel motion, and other modernistic paraphernalia contrasted with folkloric references to regional songs of France, is performed for the first time in Paris.

29 FEBRUARY 1904

An orchestral *Scherzo* by Béla BARTÓK, composed in 1902 at the age of 20, is performed for the first time in Budapest.

5 MARCH 1904

String Quartet in F by Maurice RAVEL, in four movements: (1) *Allegro moderato—Très doux*, (2) *Assez vif—Très rythmé*, (3) *Très lent*, (4) *Vif et agité*, monothematic in substance but polyharmonic and allorhythmic in variations, with widely ranging technical resources, from modal pandiatonicism to chordal parallelism and opulent Andalusian cadences wherein a descending Phrygian tetrachord is harmonized in major triads, concluding in an ascending series of major six-four chords along a sesquitonal root progression, is performed for the first time at a concert of the Société Nationale de Musique in Paris.

12 MARCH 1904

Thirteen centuries have elapsed since the death of Pope GREGORY THE GREAT, organizer of sacred music of the church into a great code known as gregorian chant.

16 MARCH 1904

La Fille de Roland, "tragédie musicale" in four acts by Henri RABAUD, wherein a young warrior in Charlemagne's ranks loves the daughter of the great paladin Roland, unaware that it was his own father who betrayed his beloved's father to the infidels at the battle of Roncesvalles in 778 A.D., with a musical score set in two-dimensional heterophony to impart the feeling of the period but exploding in ample arpeggios in the scenes of passion, is performed for the first time at the Opéra-Comique in Paris. (The title page of the printed score gives the date of the first performance as 15 March 1904, but the account of the production in *Le Ménestrel* gives 16 March 1904.)

16 MARCH 1904

Edward ELGAR conducts the Hallé Orchestra of Manchester, england, in the first performance of his orchestral work *In the South*.

18 MARCH 1904

Baba-Yaga, symphonic poem by Anatoly LIADOV, picturing in uninterrupted presto motion the flight through the air of a fabulous Russian witch Baba-Yaga in a mortar propelled by a pestle and navigated with a broom, taking off in a whirlwind of whole-tone scales and disappearing beyond the horizon in a chromatic pianissimo, is performed for the first time in St. Petersburg.

21 MARCH 1904

On his first visit to the United States, Richard STRAUSS conducts in New York a concert of his music with the Wetzler Symphony Orchestra, in a program including *Don Juan, Also Sprach Zarathustra*, and the world première of his enormously protracted *Symphonia Domestica* (completed by him in Charlottenburg on the last day of 1903), scored for a huge orchestra and dedicated "to my beloved wife and our young one," presenting a systematic chronological account of 24 hours of domestic felicity, the psychomusical material containing 67 distinct but tonally interrelated motives in constant mutation and mutual adaptation through inversion, augmentation, diminution, canon and fugue, the whole work articulated into four sections:

Introduction, presenting the four principal aspects of the composer himself (genial, dreamy, sullen, fiery), three sides of his wife's nature (graceful, angry, gay), and, intoned by the oboe d'amore accompanied by the softest violins, the entirely lovable child, whose countenance is commented upon by the aunts (muted trumpets and assorted clarinets in unison), "Ganz der Papa!" and by the uncles (oboes, oboe d'amore, English horn, muted horn and muted bass trombone), "Ganz die Mama!" (the words are written out in the score); *Scherzo*, in which the child's theme is accelerated four-fold and intertwined with the father's bugle-like motive in inversion, until the infantile lallation subsides, as the old-fashioned clock's peal in glockenspiel announces the time for the evening bath with 7 strokes; *Adagio*, with an emotional upsurge of marital love through the night in artfully connubial braces of complementary leitmotivs and harmonious contrapuntal osculation, culminating in a soaring fortissimo after which the flutes, out of breath, the whispering harps, and the moan of stifled violins *suponticello* veil the domestic scene; the clock's peal in glockenspiel is heard again at 7 o'clock in the morning, ushering in the *Finale* with a new day's vigor, with all the 67 motives in all their mutations, and the parental themes merging into a mighty double fugue, with the child's motive trumpeted for the full-blown coda.

I see no reason why I should not write a symphony about myself. I find the subject as interesting as Napoleon or Alexander the Great. (Richard Strauss quoted in Romain Rolland's *Musique française et Musique allemande* in *Richard Strauss et Romain Rolland,* Paris, 1951)

The Symphonia Domestica—Home Sweet Home as Written by Richard Strauss—Papa and Mama and Baby Celebrated in a Huge Conglomeration of Orchestral Music. (Headlines in the New York *Sun*, 22 March 1904)

In the whole of the *Domestic Symphony* there is only one particularly individual melody, the one which represents the baby; and even that is rather commonplace. It is developed and orchestrated with much skill, and towards the end it is built up into a climax which suggests a megalosaurian monster rather than a Bavarian baby. . . . So far as there is any relation between music and subject, the *Domestic Symphony* might be called quite as appropriately A Trip to Constantinople or A Day at Vladivostok. . . . The whole thing is either a deplorable aberration of taste or else a clever method of courting publicity. (Henry T. Finck, in the New York *Evening Post*, 22 March 1904)

It is not every family which has double fugues for breakfast, but this Strauss family is a peculiar one. If *Symphonia Domestica* were a true biographical sketch, we fancy that the wife would be portrayed on trombones and tubas while the husband would be pictured on the second violin. (Louis C. Elson, in the Boston *Daily Advertiser*, 12 January 1917)

25 MARCH 1904

Armida, the last opera by Antonin DVOŘÁK (begun on 11 April 1902 and completed on 29 June 1903), in four acts, derived from Tasso's *La Gerusalemme liberata*, wherein the crusader Rinaldo, held in voluptuous thrall by the magically seductive daughter of the infidel commander, mortally wounds her as she meets him in combat incognito accoutred in a black cuirass, to a dramatically effective score replete with chromatically moving diminished seventh-chords, and closing with a chorale as Armida is baptized by Rinaldo before expiring in his arms, is produced in the original Czech version in Prague.

30 MARCH 1904

Koanga, opera in three acts by Frederick DELIUS, recounting the story of a royal African prince Koanga abducted from his proud equatorial domain and sold into slavery in 18th-century Louisiana under the Spanish rule, of his ardently reciprocated love for the mulatto half-sister of the planter's wife, his death in a futile uprising and the consequent suicide of his beloved, to a score brightened by authentic creole rhythms and pentatonically stylized Negro tunes, with an ensemble of banjos integrated into the orchestra, while the harmonic setting adheres to the conventional German-Italian formula in its chromaticized idiom, is performed for the first time anywhere, in Elberfeld, to a German translation of the originally English libretto.

20 APRIL 1904

Le Fils de l'Étoile, music drama in five acts by Camille ERLANGER, to a libretto of Catulle Mendès, wherein the legendary "son of the star" leading the hebrews in their last rebellion against the Roman rule becomes entangled with the malignantly passionate imprecatrix Lilith and loses the battle, set to a Wagneromantically luxuriant score, is produced at the Paris Opéra.

25 APRIL 1904

Jean SIBELIUS conducts in Helsingfors the first performance of the chamber-orchestra version of his perennial favorite *Valse Triste*. (In the original score of incidental music to Järnefelt's play *The Death*, *Valse Triste* was orchestrated for strings only.)

1 MAY 1904

Antonin DVOŘÁK, great Czech composer, the Verdi of Bohemia, who by his consummate art of harmonic universalization of natural melodic resources of his native land contributed to the creation of a national school of Czech music, and who was the first European to write an American symphony, *From the New World*, in which he made use of melorhythms adumbrative of the Negro spirituals, dies suddenly at the dinner table in his home in Prague, at the age of 62 years, 7 months, and 3 weeks.

10 MAY 1904

Hugo ALFVÉN, 32-year-old Swedish composer of romantically suffused music, conducts in Stockholm the first performance of his symphonic work, *Midsommarvaka (Midsummer Vigil)*, subtitled *Swedish Rhapsody No. 1*, thematically derived from Swedish folk tunes with the addition of two sub-Scandinavian melodies from Schleswig-Holstein, representing a rustic revelry during the summer solstice festival of St. John's Eve. (The score was choreographed by the Ballet Suedois and produced under the French title *Le Nuit de Saint-Jean* in Paris on 25 October 1920.)

15 MAY 1904

Manuel Menendez, one-act opera by Lorenzo FILIASI, is produced in Milan.

15 MAY 1904

Rübezahl und der Sackpfeifer von Neisse, opera in four acts by the 66-year-old German composer Hans SOMMER, is produced in Brunswick.

16 MAY 1904

Exactly one month before "Bloomsday" proclaimed by James JOYCE in his novel *Ulysses*, replete with musical anamneses, he enters a contest at the Dublin *Feis Ceoil* judged by Luigi Denza, the composer of *Funiculi-Funicula*, and sings adequately in a tenorized baritone voice the two test pieces (*Come Ye Children* by Arthur Sullivan and the Irish air *A Long Farewell*), but refuses to try his unconsummate skill at sight reading, and so loses the potential gold medal, although he obtains a second prize when its original winner is in turn disqualified.

17 MAY 1904

At a concert of the Société Nationale de Musique in Paris the first performance is given of *Shéhérazade*, song cycle for voice and orchestra, by the 29-year-old Maurice RAVEL, to the texts of three exotic poems of Tristan Klingsor: (1) *Asie*, breathlessly exhaling puffs of Gallically perfumed Orientalistic vapors, apostrophizing in hypnotic glossolalia the distant "Asie, Asie, vieux pays merveilleux," enticing by its very longuinquity, tonally illustrated by rapid melismatic arabesques and delicately dissonant instrumental couplings against a deeply resonant foundation of open fifths; (2) *La Flûte enchantée*, depicting a timeless girl standing immobile listening as the sounds of a flute fall on her cheek with the intangible caress of a wafted kiss; (3) *L'indifférent*, a fleeting image of an effeminate youth whose lips shape the vocables of an alien language ("comme une musique fausse") intimated by a linear discord in false modality, and terminating on a pandiatonically extended triad with a major ninth. (At the same concert, Albert ROUSSEL'S symphonic prelude *Résurrection*, his first orchestral work, inspired by Tolstoy's moralistic novel of that name and written in a congenially religious mood concluding with a liturgical chorale from the Catholic Easter service, is performed for the first time anywhere.)

17 MAY 1904

La Cabrera, opera in two acts by the 26-year-old French composer Gabriel DUPONT, to a libretto wherein a Spanish cabrera (i.e., goatherdess), seduced and left pregnant by a dissolute villager and rejected by her betrothed upon his return from the Cuban front in the Spanish-American war of 1898, leaves her village and goes into the mountains with her child which dies of inanition, and she dies, too, as the two men in her life tardily try to console her, to a somewhat Italianate setting enlivened by the inclusion of authentic Basque dances in asymmetrical meters, is performed for the first time at the Teatro Lirico in Milan as the prize-winning opera (50,000 Italian lire in gold) in the International Competition of the Italian music publisher Sonzogno, selected among 237 entries in 1902, the last of the series of these competitions, the first of which, held in 1889, propelled into world fame Mascagni's opera *Cavalleria rusticana*.

17 MAY 1904

Choral varié for saxophone and orchestra by Vincent D'INDY, one of the earliest examples of the use of the saxophone as a solo instrument, is performed for the first time in Paris.

27 MAY 1904

Der Bundschuh, opera by the 37-year-old German composer Waldemar VON BAUSZNERN, based on an episode in the peasant rebellion in southern Germany in 1525, led by a revolutionary group named Der Bundschuh (The Council Boot), is performed for the first time in Frankfurt.

9 JUNE 1904

The London Symphony Orchestra, organized by dissident members of the Queen's Hall Orchestra on a democratic basis as a "commonwealth" with players sharing financial risks but controlling the artistic policy, presents its inaugural concert under the direction of the bearded Hungarian master Hans RICHTER.

14 JUNE 1904

Sergeant Brue, a musical farce by Liza LEHMANN, English-born soprano of german extraction, dealing with a London policeman's desperate stratagems to get promoted to inspector in order to satisfy the terms of a whimsically conditioned bequest of a fortune, is produced in London.

15 JUNE 1904

Otto NUSSBAUMER makes the first transmission by wireless telegraphy of music and speech from Salzburg. (Date and claim on the plaque on the municipal building in Mozartplatz, Salzburg.)

16 JUNE 1904

Leopold BLOOM, Irish-Jewish Ulysses of James Joyce's novel of that name, fulfills in a single Bloomsday the exagminations round his factification for incamination as a Dublin newspaper advertisement canvasser, in the course of which he experiences a number of musical impressions, viz. (1) hears a barmaid intone a tune from the vaudeville show *Florodora;* (2) befriends a blind piano tuner; (3) overhears a Jesuit priest sing Lionel's aria *M'appari* from Flotow's opera *Martha;* (4) hears a bass "barreltone" render a ballad in native Doric; (5) punningly recollects his wife's chamber music ("empty vessels make most noise, and the resonance . . . is equal to the law of falling water, like those rhapsodies of Liszt's Hungarian, gypsy-eyed diddle-iddle-addle"), follows "chordsdark lumpmusic" harping slower, paronomastically muses that "tenors get women by the score"; (6) attends a gathering to bid farewell to Hungarian printers as a band of Irish pipers strikes up *Come Back to Erin* and the *Rákóczy March;* (7) chants medieval Latin hymns in church; (8) listens attentively to a recurrent playing of Ponchielli's *Dance of the Hours* on a pianola in a local brothel in the drunken belief that the clanking timepieces are his parcae.

22 JUNE 1904

At the close of a performance in the courtyard of the Schola Cantorum at Rue Saint-Jacques, Paris, of Rameau's pastorale *Guirlande,* Claude DEBUSSY suddenly rises from his seat and cries, "Vive Rameau! A bas Gluck!"

28 JUNE 1904

Daniel Decatur EMMETT, the Northerner whose song *Dixie* became the fighting hymn of the Confederacy during the Civil War, dies in his native Mount Vernon, Ohio, at the age of 88.

4 JULY 1904

Charles E. IVES sketches a *March 1776* (later incorporated in the second movement of his symphonic suite *Three Places in New England,* an amazingly proleptic leap into the musical future, illustrating the coming together of two marching bands in a New England village playing march tunes at two different speeds, polymetrically constructed in the ratio of velocities of 4:3, resulting in a fantastic imbroglio of fractional rhythms and heterotonal harmonies. (Date in the manuscript lent by Ives to the author.)

5 JULY 1904

Edward ELGAR is knighted at the King's investiture.

When he was a small boy at school he was asked a question and to his reply the master said: "What is your name?" "Edward Elgar," said the boy. "Say Sir" said the master. "Sir Edward Elgar," said the boy. (W. H. Reed, *Elgar,* London, 1939)

14 JULY 1904

Rosalie ("Lily") TEXIER, the first wife of Debussy whom he deserted for the more socially desirable and financially prosperous matron Madame Bardac, shoots herself in Paris, inflicting a grave but not fatal wound in the heart.

Debussy loved few women. Each brought him what he needed spiritually at the moment of their meeting. In Lily Texier, Debussy loved her ravishing beauty, boyish vivacity, ardor of devotion. This midinette was, according to the opinion of those who had known her, a model of patience, tact, discretion. When Debussy seemed perturbed and preoccupied, she always managed to divert him with a pleasantry and never spared an effort to bring him cheer. Nonetheless Lily Texier's spirit of a petite Parisienne could not make up for the almost complete absence of culture. Very soon Debussy began to suffer from her lack of refinement and intellectual poverty. . . . Against his will, he ceased to love her. Her voice became repulsive to him to the point that his blood congealed in his veins when he heard it. It was in this state of mind that he met the woman who was to become the second Madame Debussy. She was an accomplished femme du monde, brilliant conversationalist, a singer of compelling talent. She presented a complete contrast to Lily. . . . As Debussy would leave the salon of Madame Bardac to join Lily, silent and brooding, suspicious, ready to burst into the violent passions of a woman of the people that she always remained, he could measure the chasm that separated them. He hesitated a long time. Several times he left her and then came back, until he finally decided to abandon his ruined household forever. For those who have followed this psychological crisis there cannot be any question of cold calculation on Debussy's part. It is beyond doubt that he suffered cruelly even as he made suffer. (Henry Prunières, in an article *Autour de Debussy* in *La Revue Musicale,* Paris, May 1934)

6 AUGUST 1904

Eduard HANSLICK, Austrian music critic who earned an unenviable fame through his venomous assaults on the moderns of his day, and above all on Wagner (the name of Beckmesser, the giftless caviller of *Die Meistersinger,* was originally Hans Lick) but whose esthetic treatise *Vom Musikalisch-Schönen,* published in 1854, had tremendous reverberations in musical philosophy despite its dogmatic formalism, dies in Vienna at the age of 78.

7 SEPTEMBER 1904

The Love that Casteth Out Fear, "sinfonia sacra" for contralto, bass, semi-chorus and orchestra by the professorial English composer Sir Hubert PARRY, to his own hermeneutically evangelical text descriptive of the Passion of Christ, set to music in a grand and lofty Handelian style, is performed for the first time at the Gloucester Musical Festival.

14 SEPTEMBER 1904

Filenis, two-act opera by the Polish composer Roman STATKOWSKI (1859–1925), is produced in Warsaw.

21 SEPTEMBER 1904

Edward GERMAN (whose real name was Edward German JONES) conducts at the Cardiff Music Festival the first performance of his *Welsh Rhapsody,* an amalgam of gay Welsh tunes calculated to find eager response in Celtic hearts.

When the last bar of the *Welsh Rhapsody* had been played, there was an outburst of applause. Women waved their handkerchiefs and the men shouted lustily. . . . Three times was the composer recalled to acknowledge the enthusiastic cheers of the crowded assembly. (From a Cardiff paper, 22 September 1904)

29 SEPTEMBER 1904

Sigurd LIE, Norwegian composer of precocious and versatile gifts who wrote Grieg-like music, occasionally elaborated by contrapuntal artifice, a facility he acquired during his apprentice days in Leipzig, dies in Drammen at an early age of 33.

10 OCTOBER 1904

The *Sho-Gun,* comic opera in two acts by the 38-year-old German-born American composer Gustav LUDERS, wherein a mythical Korean island is invaded by an American chewing-gum salesman who is accidentally appointed the Sho-Gun of Korea, but is rescued from his high office by the U.S. Marines, is produced in New York.

14 OCTOBER 1904

Pan Voyevoda, opera in four acts by the Russian titan of Russian operatic art, RIMSKY-KORSAKOV, to a libretto dealing with a feudal Polish lord who captures a comely peasant maiden while hunting wild animals in a forest, and decides to marry her, but is poisoned in the last act by the rejected lover of his former favorite, with a score written in a conventionally effective manner including several symphonic Polish dances, is produced in St. Petersburg.

15 OCTOBER 1904

Zeevolk, Flemish opera in two acts by the Belgian composer Paul GILSON, to a libretto drawn from Victor Hugo's tale of poverty and passion among mariners, *Les pauvres Gens,* is performed for the first time in Antwerp.

18 OCTOBER 1904

Gustav MAHLER conducts in Cologne the first performance of his *Fifth Symphony,* known as *The Giant,* for indeed it is a sprawlingly extensive body of music comprising three principal parts but alternatively divisible into five distinct movements, each one in turn constituting a multicellular organism of many interlocking functions, opening in a mournful C-sharp minor and ending heterotonally in a resounding D major, with every major and minor key explicitly employed between the outer termini, and every key signature from zero to six flats or sharps explicitly staved, while evading the quintal consecution of adjacent modulatory sections and similarly avoiding the use of enharmonism, a calculated distributive pantonality of symphonic design of a decisive philosophical and musico-theoretical significance:

(1) *In gemessenem Schritt. Streng. Wie ein Kondukt—Plötzlich schneller. Leidenschaftlich. Wild,* opening with a solemnly somber trumpet solo and proceeding "in measured steps, rigorously, like a funeral procession," quickly accumulating sonorous energy and suddenly accelerating in an impassioned display of controlled wildness eventually subsiding in percussive pianissimo. (2) *Stürmisch bewegt—Mit grösster Vehemenz,* stormily entering with utmost vehemence in triple forte on a clonic motivic convulsion, rending the tonal firmament with protracted anguished implorations in tormented suspensions of falling semitones in a series of modulatorily unrelated keys with A minor paramount. (3) *Scherzo—Kräftig, nicht zu schnell,* an enormously expanded (fully 800 bars) movement occasionally relaxing in ironic waltzing but otherwise powerfully self-assertive, formally constructed in concentric annular triptychs, circumscribing one another, with some tangential excrescences, and terminating abruptly in a volcanically explosive cadence. (4) *Adagietto,* a poetic invocation in a pastoral key of F major, scored only for harp and strings, with thematic material related to Mahler's tragic *Kindertotenlieder* of 1902. (5) *Rondo-Finale,* a series of resonant rounds, rotundly rotated, with forceful fugues separating chorale-like proclamations and concluding, after a torrential rush of whole-tone scales, on a triumphantly unisonal D.

Mahler is in the noblest sense of the word a tone poet. . . . Yet to believe that he intends to set down specific and narrowly circumscribed ideas in his works is to misinterpret him completely. . . . For Mahler is an enemy of programmatic descriptions and painstaking analytical studies. The following episode is singularly indicative of his train of thought. In October 1900, after a concert which he conducted in Munich, an illustrious company of artists, men of learning, and writers gathered together in a joyful circle to spend the rest of the evening with him. The conversation touched on the subject of program annotations. Suddenly, like a bolt of lightning on a hot and sunny day, Mahler's eyes lightened up, his countenance rose, he sprang excitedly from the table, and cried out: "Away with program notes that generate false ideas! The concertgoers must be allowed to form their own opinions about the music! They should not be urged to read during the concert and to be prejudiced by what they read. If a composer succeeds in impressing upon the listeners the sensations that went through his own mind when he wrote his music then he will have attained his goal. The language of tones will then have come close to words, but it will have infinitely more to communicate than words." . . . Then Mahler raised his glass and emptied it exclaiming, "*Pereant the program books!*" And all of us exchanged meaningful glances. (Ludwig Schiedermair, *Gustav Mahler, biographisch-kritische Würdigung,* Leipzig, 1900)

It is a matter of extreme difficulty to detect tangible themes in the second movement of Mahler's Fifth Symphony, and it is an almost impossible task to follow them through the tortuous mazes of their formal and contrapuntal development. One has to cling by one's teeth, so to speak, to a shred of theme here and there, which appears for an occasional instant above the heavy masses of tone, only to be jumped upon immediately by the whole angry horde of instruments and stamped down into the very thick of the orchestral fray. The fighting grows so furious toward the finish that one is compelled to unclose one's teeth on a morsel of themes and lo and behold! it is seized upon, hurled through the screaming and frenzied ranks of the combatants, and that is the last seen or heard of the poor little rag of a theme. (*The Musical Courier,* New York, 21 February 1906)

Mahler had not much to say in his Fifth Symphony and occupied a wondrous time in saying it. His manner is ponderous, his matter imponderable. (New York *Sun,* 5 December 1913)

2 NOVEMBER 1904

Monsieur de la Palisse, operetta in three acts by Claude TERRASSE, dealing with a French aristocrat so deeply engrossed in advancing his career in diplomacy that he totally neglects his desirable wife and tardily begins to appreciate her attractions only after she irretrievably plunges into an illicit liaison, is performed for the first time at the Théâtre des Variétés in Paris.

10 NOVEMBER 1904

Ferruccio BUSONI plays in Berlin with an orchestra conducted by Karl Muck, the solo part in the first performance of his *Piano Concerto* (completed on 3 August 1904, with the title page of his own design, showing three buildings, Greek, Egyptian and Assyrian, a miraculous mythical flower, a bird, Mt. Vesuvius and a group of cypress trees), in five movements conceived as an architectonic pentacle, with the odd-numbered movements symbolizing the apexes of spirituality, while the second movement, a scherzo, and the fourth, a tarantella, represent terrestrial transience, with a hidden chorus intoning a *Hymn to Allah* for an ending, the music gravid with Lisztian fustian but often illumined by felicitous transparencies in the finest Busonian manner.

During the five movements of Busoni's *Piano Concerto* we were submerged in a flood of cacophony; a *pezzo giocoso* painted the joys of barbarians lusting in war, and a tarantella, the orgies of absinthe drinkers and of harlots. (*Die Tägliche Rundschau*, Berlin, 12 November 1904)

12 NOVEMBER 1904

Die lustigen Nibelungen, a gaily irreverent operetta by Oskar STRAUS, wherein the Teutonic divinities of Valhalla frolic in a most unseemly manner hurling portentous Wagnerian quotations in the brass, is produced in Vienna.

13 NOVEMBER 1904

Caprice andalou for violin and orchestra, a musical souvenir of a visit in Andalusia by Camille SAINT-SAËNS, is performed for the first time in Paris.

16 NOVEMBER 1904

At the invitation of the Coleridge-Taylor Society of Washington, Samuel COLERIDGE-TAYLOR, 28-year-old London-born composer whose father was a native of Sierra Leone and whose mother was an English-woman, conducts in Washington, D.C., the first integral performance of his choral trilogy *Hiawatha*, after Longfellow's classic Amerindian poem, with a cast of Negro singers.

21 NOVEMBER 1904

It Happened in Nordland, comic opera in two acts by Victor HERBERT, wherein an American ambassadress to an operettically mythical court is compelled to impersonate the queen whom she physically resembles to save Nordland from scandal when the real queen stages a disappearance, is performed for the first time in Harrisburg, Pennsylvania, preliminary to the New York opening two weeks hence.

29 NOVEMBER 1904

Ernst von DOHNÁNYI plays in Vienna the first performances of his four *Rhapsodies* for piano solo.

30 NOVEMBER 1904

Risurrezione, opera in three acts by Franco ALFANO, after Tolstoy's moralistic tale wherein an inoffensive Russian orphan girl, seduced on a wintry Easter day by a young city wastrel and abandoned by him in a railroad station, is driven by despair to further degradation through drink and petty crime, and is marched off to Siberia after rejecting the offer of honorable marriage by her now penitent seducer so as to expiate her fall by condign suffering, the score adhering to the esthetics of the Italian verismo in a traditional idiom sprinkled with a few whole-tone scales at dramatically tense moments, a slightly altered Russian church hymn serving as an identifying national motto, is performed for the first time in Turin.

2 DECEMBER 1904

Le réveil de Bouddha, a Hindu mystery by the 46-year-old English composer Isadore DE LARA (whose real name was Isadore Cohen), is performed for the first time, to a French libretto, in Ghent, Belgium.

7 DECEMBER 1904

Byron, symphonic poem by the 26-year-old English composer Josef HOLBROOKE, with a choral ending to the words of Keats, "Byron, how sweetly sad thy melody . . .," is performed for the first time at the Leeds Festival.

10 DECEMBER 1904

The first distribution of the Glinka Prizes from the income of the basic capital of 75,000 rubles willed by the publisher Belaieff for annual prizes to best compositions by Russian composers, is held on the exact anniversary of the productions of Glinka's operas, *Life for the Tsar* (produced on 10 December 1836) and *Russlan and Ludmila* (10 December 1842) with prizes awarded by Rimsky-Korsakov, Liadov, and Glazunov, as executors of the Belaieff fund, to Anton ARENSKY for his *Piano Trio*, op. 32 (500 rubles), to Sergei LIAPUNOV for his *Piano Concerto* (500 rubles), to Serge RACHMANINOFF for his *Second Piano Concerto* (500 rubles), to Alexander SCRIABIN for his *Third* and *Fourth Piano Sonatas* (500 rubles) and to Sergei TANEYEV for his *Symphony*, op. 12 (1000 rubles).

13 DECEMBER 1904

Der Roland von Berlin, opera in four acts by Ruggero LEONCAVALLO, the subject of which, relating to the strife among burghers and knights in medieval Berlin, was suggested to him by Emperor Wilhelm II himself, the musical substance and treatment remaining incongruously Italianate, is produced at a gala performance in Berlin.

14 DECEMBER 1904

Vlasty Skon (The Death of Vlasta), the first opera, in three acts, by Otakar OSTRČIL, dealing with a women's rebellion in medieval Bohemia whose leader Vlasta is treacherously slain by a male assassin, is performed for the first time in Prague.

19 DECEMBER 1904

Il re si annoia, opera by Ausonio de LORENZI-FABRIS, is produced in Trieste.

19 DECEMBER 1904

Cristo Alla Festa di Purim, one-act opera by the Neapolitan composer Giovanni GIANNETTI, who settled in Brazil, is produced in Rio de Janeiro.

31 DECEMBER 1904

Die Dorfmusikanten, a gay fable with singing and dancing by the Czechoslovak composer Karel WEIS, dealing with a village fifer traveling around to finance his wedding to a girl at home and in the process curing a congenitally unsmiling royal princess from perennial melancholy, entertaining ghosts, phantoms and other disembodied creatures by playing rhythmic Slavic dance tunes, is performed for the first time at the German Theater in Prague.

1905

2 JANUARY 1905

Michael TIPPETT, English composer of nobly designed choral and instrumental music, whose pacifistic passions led him to prison during World War II but did not prevent him from being knighted in 1966, is born in London.

4 JANUARY 1905

Theodore THOMAS, American conductor, founder in 1891 of the Chicago Symphony Orchestra, who was taken to the United States from his native Hannover at the age of ten, toured the Southern states as a precocious violinist advertising himself in handwritten posters as "The Prodigy" went on to play chamber music in New York, and eventually achieved fame as a competent, conscientious and circumspect conductor, dies in Chicago at the age of 69.

8 JANUARY 1905

Le Palais hanté, symphonic poem by Florent SCHMITT, effectively conjuring up the "vast forms that move fantastically to a discordant melody" in the haunted palace of Edgar Allan Poe's eerie tale of horror by means of tritone-compassed motives coursing and recoursing through somberly sonorous corridors echoing with impressionistic harmonies, is performed for the first time at the Concerts Lamoureax in Paris.

8 JANUARY 1905

Irrlicht, the only opera by the Austrian composer of successful operettas, Leo FALL, relating in three acts the melancholy tale of a lad's love for a lass who turns out to be his illegitimate half-sister thus making their amorous intimacy but a will-o'-the-wisp (hence the title), set to an emotionally Wagneromorphic score, is produced in Mannheim.

18 JANUARY 1905

La Croisade des Enfants, "légende musicale" by Gabriel PIERNÉ for soli, children's chorus and orchestra, depicting in an effective oratorio style the semi-legendary crusade of 1212 when thousands of children fled their homes in Flanders, embarked in unseaworthy ships for the Holy Land and perished in a storm, is performed for the first time in Paris, with a chorus of 200 school children, under the direction of Edouard Colonne.

26 JANUARY 1905

Arnold SCHOENBERG conducts in Vienna the first performance of his symphonic poem *Pelleas und Melisande* (completed in Berlin on 28 February 1903; sketches begun on 4 July 1902), inwardly and expressionistically rather than explicitly and impressionistically paralleling the peripeteia of Maeterlinck's poignant drama, conceived in a quadripartite form approximating that of a sonata, couched in a highly chromaticized idiom without abandoning the tonal system (the principal key is D minor, and appropriate key signatures are used in modulatory, sections), forming a complex contrapuntal web of para-Wagnerian leitmotivs, and using novel instrumental sound colors (including the first instance of trombone glissandos to express the horror and the pity of the fate befalling the innocent lovers).

Schoenberg's *Pelleas und Melisande* is not just filled with discords, in the sense that *Don Quixote* by Strauss is, but constitutes in itself a protracted discord lasting fifty minutes. This is to be taken literally. What else might be concealed behind this cacophony is impossible to guess. (Ludwig Karpath, *Signale für die musikalische Welt*, Berlin, 1 March 1905)

28 JANUARY 1905

Giovanni Gallurese, historic melodrama in three acts by Italo MONTEMEZZI, portraying in glowing colors with a quasi-Wagnerian emphasis the noble career of a Sardinian patriot from the province of Gallura who in 1662 repeatedly rescues his beloved from the evil clutches of a Catalan bravo during the seething warfare against the alien Spanish rule, only to die in an ambush in the end, is produced in Turin.

2 FEBRUARY 1905

Robert EITNER, scholarly and persistent German archivist who spent a lifetime in the dusty recesses of German and other European libraries compiling a gigantic list of music manuscripts and published the results in a monumental ten-volume edition, *Biographisch-Bibliographisches Quellenlexikon der Musiker und Musikgelehrten*, which in spite of laughable errors (phantom composers are spontaneously generated, e.g., Berger, Ungay, whose name was formed from a *Chanson d'un gai berger* and L'Auberge, Isolée, similarly conjured up from a *Chanson de l'auberge isolée*) is of unique documentary value, dies in Templin at the age of 72.

5 FEBRUARY 1905

Second Concerto for cello and orchestra by Camille SAINT-SAÉNS in four distinct sections combined into two parts, is performed for the first time in Paris.

13 FEBRUARY 1905

Les Dragons de l'Impératrice, comic opera in three acts by André MESSAGER, detailing in exhilarating Offenbachian tunes the multiplex imbroglio wherein a resplendently uniformed captain of the guards of the Third Empire steals the affections of the mistress of a captain of the dragoons, and the latter avenges himself twelvefold by seducing a dozen of his rival's former mistresses, with a conciliatory ending when a chorus of seducers, adulteresses and cuckolds chant a hymn to love in perfect harmony, is performed for the first time at the Théâtre des Variétés in Paris.

14 FEBRUARY 1905

Chérubin, "comédie chantée" in three acts by Jules MASSENET, depicting in euphonious harmonies the light-hearted adventures of a youthful amorist who makes love in quick succession to an ingenue, a countess, a baroness and a famous Spanish ballerina, with an allusive quotation from Mozart's *Don Giovanni* in the finale, is performed for the first time at Monte Carlo.

15 FEBRUARY 1905

RIMSKY-KORSAKOV, RACHMANINOFF, TANEYEV, GRETCHANINOFF, GLIÉRE, CHALIAPIN, SILOTI and 25 other Russian musicians sign a declaration protesting against the political oppression of the Tsar's government.

When life itself is in chains, art cannot be free. When there is no freedom of thought, of religion, of expression, of the press, artistic ideals of the nation are also repressed and creative art withers. The title of "free artist" (conferred on Conservatory graduates) becomes a bitter mockery. We are not free artists but victims of the present abnormal situation. Along with the rest of the Russian population we are deprived of our civil rights. There is but one way out of this impasse for Russia, namely, a program of radical political reforms. (Quoted from the *Russian Musical Gazette*, St. Petersburg, No. 7, 1905)

23 FEBRUARY 1905

Amid vast revolutionary tremors in Russia, the general assembly of St. Petersburg Conservatory students votes 451 to 146 to discontinue attendance of classes for the remainder of the academic year, and adopts the following resolution: "We reject the false doctrine of the separation of art from political life. Believing that the continuation of classes is incompatible with our civic and human dignity under present conditions, we resolve not to return to the Conservatory until the demands of the Russian people for political liberty are satisfied by the government."

I implore you not to reveal the names of Conservatory students who attended their meeting to the Board of Education. Police measures have no place in a temple of art. What can be accomplished by handing lists of names to those bemedaled and beribboned generals who preside over the board? This would ruin the careers of many talented students. The Jews would particularly suffer, for they would probably be subjected to much harsher reprisals than the Christians. Eventually the Conservatory would have to be placed under administrative authority in which case many of its best teachers would probably resign. (From a letter addressed by Glazunov on 25 February 1905 to the administrative director of the St. Petersburg Conservatory, A. R. Bernhardt)

25 FEBRUARY 1905

Serge KOUSSEVITSKY plays the double-bass solo in the first performance in Moscow of his *Concerto for Double-Bass and Orchestra* in F-sharp minor, dedicated to his recent wife Natalie Ouchkoff, in three movements, *Allegro, Andante, Allegro*, with thematic materials (betraying obvious derivation from Dvořák and Tchaikovsky) organized, developed, harmonized and orchestrated by Reinhold Glière.

27 FEBRUARY 1905

The Knights of the Road, operetta by Sir Alexander Campbell MACKENZIE, is produced in London.

3 MARCH 1905

Martylle, opera by Albert DUPUIS, is performed for the first time in Brussels.

3 MARCH 1905

The Mystic Trumpeter, symphonic fantasy by Frederick S. CONVERSE, inspired by Walt Whitman's poetic vision of a strange musician hovering unseen in the air, vibrating capricious tunes, incarnating haply some dead composer in whom musical oceans chaotically surge, the musical score articulated, like Whitman's poem itself, into five distinct sections—serene, amorous, warlike, sullen, joyful—with the solo trumpet carrying the mystic message, is performed for the first time by the Philadelphia Orchestra, Fritz Scheel conducting.

3 MARCH 1905

L'Enfant-Roi, lyric comedy in five acts by Alfred BRUNEAU, after a posthumous novelette of Emile Zola, wherein a Paris baker, wondering where his wife goes every Tuesday, follows her to a clandestine rendezvous with a young man who turns out to be her pre-maritally conceived natural son and magnanimously agrees to adopt him, to a musical setting in a veristic Gallic vein containing an interestingly syncopated bread-baking episode ("C'est Paris qui toujours mange"), is performed for the first time at the Opéra-Comique in Paris.

4 MARCH 1905

Alexander GLAZUNOV conducts in St. Petersburg the first performance of his *Violin Concerto* in A, with Leopold Auer, to whom it is dedicated, as soloist, the violin entering in the very first bar on a germinal theme out of which a songful subject is artfully evolved through the mechanism of intervalically precise inversions, the two themes presently interlocked in a contrapuntal mesh until a rhythmically propulsive violin cadenza breaks into the open, leading to a clarion fanfare in the orchestra, and, after momentary divagations into major keys situated at the right angles in the circle of scales in relation to the principal tonality of A major, concluding with a triumphant finale. (Mischa Elman's performance of the Concerto in London on 17 October 1905 is erroneously cited in most reference works as its world première.)

8 MARCH 1905

Edward ELGAR conducts the London Symphony Orchestra in a program of his works, including the first performances of his Welsh-inspired *Introduction and Allegro* for string quartet and string orchestra, with a fugato ending, and of his imperial march *Pomp and Circumstance* No. 3.

12 MARCH 1905

Re Enzo, first opera by Ottorino RESPIGHI, in three acts, presenting in a droll manner of the commedia dell' arte the otherwise tragic episode from the turbulent times of 13th-century Italy, is performed for the first time in Bologna, where the real Enzo, poet and nominal Emperor of Sardinia, was imprisoned after losing a battle.

12 MARCH 1905

Fischer und Kalif, opera by Felix DRAESEKE, is produced in Prague.

16 MARCH 1905

Amica, opera by Pietro MASCAGNI, in two acts separated by an orchestral intermezzo, to a French libretto recounting a torridly Mediterranean tale wherein a young married woman pursues her brutish lover through a precipitous mountain pass, stumbles and, oblivious to her loyal husband's anguished pleas, perishes in a torrent, to a musical setting in a dramatic manner of the Italian verismo foreshadowed in his famous *Cavalleria rusticana,* is performed for the first time in Monte Carlo.

18 MARCH 1905

Two operas by the prodigiously precocious 17-year-old Italian composer Renzo BIANCHI, *In Umbria,* in two acts, and *Il Canto di Francesca,* in one act, written in flamboyantly inflatable Italianate harmonies, are produced in Pavia.

25 MARCH 1905

Les Girondins, lyric tragedy in four acts by Fernand LE BORNE, dealing with sanguinary events in Paris in 1793, with several interpolated pieces of the period (e.g., Gossec's *Hymn to Nature* and *Hymn to Liberty*), concluding with the singing of the *Marseillaise* by the chorus of doomed moderates from the province of La Gironde with the bloodthirsty women of the people supplying a cunningly elaborate motet *Ça ira, ça ira, aristocrates à la lanterne,* is produced in Lyon.

30 MARCH 1905

Emil Nikolaus REZNIČEK, 44-year-old Vienna-born composer, conducts the Berlin Philharmonic in the first performance of his *Symphonietta* in B flat major, in four movements, later subtitled by him *Ironische Symphonie,* with reference to some innocuous whimsicalities contained in the Scherzo.

30 MARCH 1905

Nemo, the second part of an ambitious operatic trilogy by Géza ZICHY on the life of the famous Magyar patriot Rákóczy, is produced in Budapest (the first and the third parts were staged, also in Budapest, respectively on 30 January 1909 and 20 March 1912).

1 APRIL 1905

RIMSKY-KORSAKOV is discharged from his professorship at the St. Petersburg Conservatory as a disciplinary measure for his public protest made in a letter to the newspaper *Russia* on 19 March 1905 against the reprisals of the Tsarist-appointed Directorate of the Conservatory in the affair of the student strike.

14 APRIL 1905

Die Heirat wider Willen, comic opera in three acts by Engelbert HUMPERDINCK, to a libretto by Frau Humperdinck freely adapted from *Les Demoiselles de Saint-Cyr* by Alexandre Dumas, wherein two young men are forced to marry two inmates in a nunnery whom they were visiting and after the initial consternation find marriage a desirable condition, with a musical score containing elements of ribald burlesque, is performed for the first time at the Royal Opera in Berlin.

15 APRIL 1905

The first public demonstration of Eurhythmics, a method developed by Émile JAQUES-DALCROZE "to create with the help of rhythm a rapid and regular current of communication between brain and body" is given at the Conservatory of Geneva. (See Letters and Documents for the history of the Dalcroze method.)

16 APRIL 1905

Jessica, an opera in three acts by the prime Czech opera composer Josef Bohuslav FOERSTER (after Shakespeare's *The Merchant of Venice*) is produced in Prague.

27 APRIL 1905

On his eleventh birthday Sol MYSNIK stages, in the recreation hall of High School No. 11 in St. Petersburg, in which he is a student, the world première of his politico-revolutionary opera in eleven scenes, *The X-Ray Vindicator,* scored for three countertenors, basso profondo, piano, balalaika, toy pistol and a static electricity generator, the action dealing with a young scientist confined in the dreaded Peter-and-Paul Fortress for advocating the extermination of the Tsar and the termination of the Russo-Japanese war, who escapes by directing a stream of Röntgen rays at himself from a hidden cathode tube as a Secret Police officer enters his cell to question him, putting him to flight in superstitious horror by appearing as a skeleton, and then calmly walking through the open gate to resume his terroristic propaganda, with petty-bourgeoisie characterized by insipid arpeggios on the balalaika and the playing of the waltz *On the Dunes of Manchuria* on the phonograph, revolutionary fervor by the songs "The Sun Goes Up, the Sun Goes Down, I Wish the Tsar Would Lose his Crown" and "We Fell as Martyrs to Our Cause Because We Scorned the Tsarist Laws," the X-rays by chromatically advancing sequences of diminished seventh-chords, and "Freedom through Terror" by blazingly incandescent C major.

(Sol Mysnik is an obvious anagram of the last name of the author of the present volume, who indeed turned eleven on that date. *The X-Ray Vindicator* is a fantasy generated in the corpus callosum, medulla oblongata or some other part of his inchoate cerebellum long after his eleventh birthday. No such opera ever existed on paper, on the piano keyboard or on the balalaika.)

2 MAY 1905

On his third and last attempt to qualify for the Grand Prix de Rome before the age limit of thirty, Maurice RAVEL fails to pass even the preliminary test of admission at the Académie des Beaux-Arts, all six winning entries being by students of Lenepveu, an influential professor at the Paris Conservatory.

14 MAY 1905

Danze piemontesi, suite of two symphonic dances by Leone SINIGAGLIA, artfully fashioned from folksongs of his native Piedmont in a bouquet of florid melodies harmoniously scented with finely distilled perfumery and wafted from colorfully assembled instrumental solos, is performed for the first time in Turin, under the direction of Arturo Toscanini.

20, 21, & 22 MAY 1905

A three-day Music Festival of Alsace-Lorraine, the first of its kind under German government, is held in Strasbourg, presenting programs of German and French music as a token of reconciliation between the two national elements of the region wrested from France in 1871, with Richard STRAUSS conducting his autobiographical *Symphonia Domestica* and Gustav MAHLER his cyclopean *Fifth Symphony* in C-sharp minor (the orchestra paid tribute to Mahler by playing a congratulatory *Tusch* in D major, the concluding tonality of the symphony), Camille CHEVILLARD conducting César FRANCK 's *Les Béatitudes* and Gustave CHARPENTIER his *Impressions d' Italie,* the Festival closing with Beethoven's *Ninth Symphony* under Mahler's direction, with a pointed political stress on the line "Alle Menschen werden Brüder" in the choral finale.

Music accomplishes its highest mission when it serves as a link between nations, races and governments. . . . In such festivals as this there can be no pursuit of victory of one esthetic tendency over another. The purpose is to assemble all that is great, noble and ageless in the art of different epochs and different nations. (From a program note of the Festival)

It was a noble design to inaugurate these Olympic Games of Europe in Alsace, that perpetual battlefield of nations. In actual fact, this congress became a contest on the musical ground between two civilizations and two arts; French and German. And it is right, for these two arts represent at this time all that is truly vital in the music of Europe. (Romain Rolland, in *Musique Française et musique allemande,* reprinted in his *Musiciens d' aujourd' hui*)

25 MAY 1905

Onkel Dazumal, one-act opera by Émile JAQUES-DAL-CROZE to a German libretto after a French play *Le Bonhomme Jadis,* is produced in Cologne.

29 MAY 1905

Third Symphony by Alexander SCRIABIN, *Poème Divin,* his first orchestral work of mystical connotations, in three linked movements bearing pregnantly meaningful subtitles in French: *Luttes,* opening with a brass proclamation of tremendous majesty and then proceeding to develop within the framework of sonata form, the second subject soaring heavenwards in the trumpets; *Voluptés,* replete with caressing trills and thrills; and *Jeu Divin,* marked "avec une joie éclatante," inexorably moving towards immarcessible, immaculately virginal, divinely white tonality of C major, with a harmonically figurated plagal cadence ending on a sustained and concentrated unison, is performed for the first time in Paris, Arthur Nikisch conducting.

31 MAY 1905

Franz STRAUSS, one of the greatest players upon the French horn, whose heroic *Eroica* tones, nocturnal poesy of *Tristan* solos, and the glowing lyrical quality of romantic horn passages in German symphonic music aroused universal admiration, father of Richard Strauss (he was too old to essay the acrobatic horn part in *Till Eulenspiegel*), himself a composer of ten trios for Bavarian postillion horns and other estimable pieces, dies in Munich at the age of 83.

26 JUNE 1905

Gabriel FAURÉ is appointed Director of the Paris Conservatory to succeed Théodore DUBOIS, its Director since 6 May 1896.

28 JUNE 1905

L 'Oracolo, opera in one long act by Franco LEONI, Italian composer resident in London, to a libretto based on the short story *The Cat and the Cherub* by C. B. Fernald, dealing with multiplex villainy in San Francisco's Chinatown, wherein a wily opium-den keeper kidnaps the child of the uncle of a girl he covets, kills her young lover, and is in the end strangled by the latter's father (a passing policeman mistakes his death rattle for Chinese talk), with a local astrologer delivering remarkably accurate oracles, an Italianate musical score tinkling with tiny bells, booming with deep gongs, and bubbling with orientalistic pentatonicisms, is performed for the first time at Covent Garden, London.

2 JULY 1905

Having eliminated Maurice RAVEL in the preparatory test, the French Académie des Beaux-Arts selects winners of the Prix de Rome from the number of six young composers, awarding two Premier Grand Prix (to make up for the 1904 defection of composer Pech who broke the celibacy clause by getting married), and two Second Grand Prix to the following men, all pupils of Professor Lenepveu, influential member of the Academy: Premier Grand Prix, Victor-Léon GALLOIS; Premier Grand Prix (vacated by Pech) to Marcel-Auguste SAMUEL-ROUSSEAU; Premier-Second Prix to Philippe GAUBERT; Deuxième-Second Grand Prix to Charles-Louis DUMAS.

It is not against the law to be an imbecile, for this is a congenital affliction, but when people suffer from it, they are treated by psychotherapy which has made considerable progress thanks to the new techniques of trepan and thyroid serum. (Jean Marnold, commenting on the members of the jury in his article *Le Scandale du Prix de Rome,* in *Le Mercure Musical,* Paris, June 1905)

The competition for the Prix de Rome is preceded by a preparatory test which serves to eliminate students insufficiently prepared. The jury for this test is formed by the music section of the Académie des Beaux-Arts, which coopts several composers who are not members of the Academy. Teachers of competing students cannot be members of the jury unless they are members of the Institut de France as well, in which case they are jury members by virtue of their status. There are three professors of composition. One is Fauré who has in the meantime become Director of the Conservatory, and who is one of the most original and fine artists of our time. The second is Widor, admirable organist and learned composer. Neither of the two is a member of the Institute. The third is a poor musician, author of a few worthless compositions; without ideas, or art: but he is a member of the Institute; it is unnecessary to mention him by name. Each of these three professors presented for the preliminary test their best pupils. But the first two, not being members of the jury, could not defend the interests of their students, while the third protected his pupils well, which was amply repaid by the outcome. As if by coincidence, his pupils were the only ones to be admitted at the final competition, from which it naturally follows that they divided all the prizes, and that their class would get all the honors of the competition and their professor would derive a great luster from it. Inasmuch as the poor musician in question schemed at the time to obtain the directorship of the Conservatory, he counted on this glory so acquired to be designated as the choice of the administration, a profound calculation which was upset by the events. This story is in itself rather extraordinary; but certain details make it scandalous. Among students who were not passed in the preliminaries there was Ravel, pupil of Fauré, and Mademoiselle Fleury, pupil of Widor, who not only were admitted to the finals in previous years, but who were each awarded a second Grand Prix. But this is not all. Mlle Fleury's adventure is painful; but Ravel's is even more so. Mlle Fleury can compete again in the future; but Ravel will not be able to do so for he has reached the age limit this year. Then, whatever are the qualities of Mlle Fleury, she has not heretofore disclosed exceptional talents, while Ravel, through a singular and deplorable coincidence for the Institute, is one of two or three young men on whom French music can rightfully put her highest hopes. (Pierre Lalo, *Le Temps,* Paris, 11 July 1905)

In 1901 Ravel obtained the second Prix de Rome; but since then the Institute has refused him not only the prize but even the entry, to the finals. Hence, the scandal, resignation of Theodore Dubois, utter ruin of the hopes of another official hack, and the arrival at the director's post at the Conservatory of Gabriel Fauré. (M. D. Calvocoressi, in *Le Courier Musical,* Paris, 1 March 1907)

11 AUGUST 1905

The Sacred Congregation of the Rites of the Vatican issues a decree approving the Vatican edition of Gregorian chant.

15 AUGUST 1905

Gustave-Adolphe KOÉLLA, the youngest of the four precocious Swiss brothers who, under the aegis of their covetous and tyrannous father, toured Europe from 1829 (when their respective ages were 12, 11, 10 and 7) until 1834 as the Koëlla String Quartet, gathered ducats from ducal courts and were graciously commended by Paganini, dies at the Nestorian age of eighty-three in Lausanne, where he founded in 1861 the prestigious Institut de Musique.

27 AUGUST 1905

Les Hérétiques, opera in three acts by Charles LEVADÉ, dealing with the struggle of Albigensian antisacerdotalists and Catharist anticonsubstantialists against the sanguinary crusader Monfort, set to a melodramatically exploding score, generously sprinkled with multiple drops of whole-tone scales, is produced in the open-air Arena of Béziers in southern France, the town where the action of the opera itself evolved seven centuries before.

31 AUGUST 1905

Miss Dolly Dollars, Victor HERBERT's operetta lightheartedly detailing the losing contest of a dollar-laden American canned-soup heiress with an Aristotle-quoting stenographer for the love of a semi-intellectual male, is produced in Rochester, New York.

13 SEPTEMBER 1905

Lilia, first opera by the future futurist Francesco Balilia PRATELLA, still safely embedded in the traditional Italianate songfulness, is produced at Lugo, the composer's birthplace.

29 SEPTEMBER 1905

Cleopatra, symphonic poem by the Boston composer George Whitefield CHADWICK, focused on the story of Cleopatra's dalliance with Anthony, and written in a luscious Wagneromantic idiom, is performed for the first time at the Worcester, Massachusetts, Music Festival.

7 OCTOBER 1905

Mlle Modiste, comic opera by Victor HERBERT, wherein a Paris hat shop model is launched on a singing career by an American millionaire, and surprisingly becomes a prima donna, thus qualifying for the marriage with a French nobleman, the score containing the perennially popular waltz *Kiss Me Again,* is performed for the first time in Trenton, New Jersey, preliminary to the New York opening on Christmas Day of 1905.

8 OCTOBER 1905

Sinfonietta in A major, op. 90, by Max REGER, set in a post-classical idiom heavily romanticized by harmonic suspensions and contrapuntal elaborations, is performed for the first time in Essen, Felix Mottl conducting.

I shall make music, and only music. . . . My *Sinfonietta* ought to prove most resoundingly that the classical form is not obsolete. And since my technical demands are quite modest compared to Richard Strauss, no one can say that the music suffers the malady of unplayability. (Max Reger in a letter to Karl Straube of 2 May 1905)

In this discordantly hatched tonal pap of Reger's *Sinfonietta* there is not a single distinct theme, not a single melodically compact idea, but only thematic fragments of astounding aridity and poverty of invention. (Carl Krebs, *Der Tag*, Berlin, 12 November 1905)

Reger has manifestly wished to be simple. But it remained only a wish; he has been unable to carry out this intention. . . . The *Sinfonietta* is not inherently a significant work; its tonal langnage depends mainly on conjuring up the illusion of significance by a thousand contrapuntal tricks. (Rudolph Louis, in *Münchener Neueste Nachrichten*, 7 February 1906)

I am sitting in the smallest room of my house. I have your review before me. In a moment it will be behind me. (From Max Reger's letter to Rudolph Louis)

13 OCTOBER 1905

Bruder Lustig, opera in three acts by Siegfried WAGNER, to his own libretto from a 10th-century German legend with a historical background, wherein a Frankish knight nicknamed Brother Lusty for his virile joy of life desecrates the person of King Otto by pulling his red beard, communes with witches and nixes and takes one of them for a bride, then makes peace with the King, helps him to capture an important Rhenish town, and in the last act of lustful generosity gives his soldiers the freedom of all unattached local women and maidens; with a musical setting in a ripe style of *Die Meistersinger* from its C-major overture to its C-major ending, and 88 leading motives serving to identify the characters and concepts, is produced in Hamburg.

15 OCTOBER 1905

Camille Chevillard conducts the Lamoureux Orchestra in Paris in the first performance from manuscript of DEBUSSY'S impressionistic masterpiecc *La Mer,* "trois esquisses symphoniques" (completed at six o'clock in the evening of 5 March 1905), a triptych of symphonic aquatints etched with the finest precision of tonal craftsmanship suggesting the minutissimic equilibration of Japanese prints (Hokusai's blue wave delicately suspended on the rim of white foam like an unresolved major ninth-chord serves as the cover of the published score of *La Mer,*) each of the three symphonic sketches illustrating a marine scene:

(1) *De l'aube à midi sur la mer,* compressing the six hours from dawn to noon into a relatively few minutes, with a somberly susurrant seascape, pierced by an insistent rhythmic wavelet, then suddenly erupting into a multicolored aquatic musicorama of concerted instrumental splendors, while pentatonic melodies soar high above anchored basses; (2) *Jeux de vagues,* with submarine tritones serving as prickly mainstays of the

harmonic structure through which whole-tone chords softly glide in swift cascades, while aquamarine melodies undulate on the surface and luminescent animalcules of the cymbals and the fatuous lights of the flutes flicker in the interplay of randomly colliding wavering waves; (3) *Dialogue du vent et de la mer,* with windy gusts stirring up chromatic wails while the oceanic motto is sounded in whole-tone steps, ending in a sonorous apotheosis in the parent D-flat major tonality.

One would seek in vain in these "three symphonic sketches" not only an appearance of an inner structure but an idea, a clearly outlined design. The composer, by a preconceived notion, avoids all that might resemble a melody, a leading theme, however short; rather, he superposes and intermingles an infinity of designs so as to form a sort of sonorous complex which the ear is incapable of disentangling. (J. Jemain, *Le Ménestrel*, Paris, 29 October 1905)

21 OCTOBER 1905

Ferruccio BUSONI conducts in Berlin the first performance of an orchestral suite in eight movements arranged from his incidental music to the play *Turandot* by Gozzi, making use of stylized Asian melorhythms, both of the pentatonic and ultra-chromatic variety, to tell the story of a beautiful but inscrutable Chinese princess whose eager suitors are given a chance to possess her orientally desirable self, with death as an alternative should they fail to supply correct answers to three preposterous riddles.

22 OCTOBER 1905

Hjoerdis, opera in four acts by the Czech composer Karel MOOR, is produced in Prague.

7 NOVEMBER 1905

Miarka, opera in four acts by Alexandre GEORGES, after Jean Richepin's novel about a nomadic girl, strangely born in a Gypsy camp in medieval Picardy without a mother but with a grandmother, who upon reaching the flower of eager nubility dreams prophetically of becoming the Queen of Rumanian Gypsies, and after repulsing the inopportune advances of a locally amorous peasant, marches eastward as her grandmother dies on the dusty roadway within sight of royal glory heralded by slightly orientalized fanfares, the score incorporating primitivistic hymns to the sun, to the clouds, to the running water, to love and to other natural things, set in unisonal or quintal harmonies (these hymns were originally published by the composer in a successful song album), is staged at the Opéra-Comique in Paris.

9 NOVEMBER 1905

Mademoiselle de Belle-Isle, opera in three acts by the Greek composer Spiro SAMARA, after Alexandre Dumas, is produced in Genoa, with an Italian libretto.

12 NOVEMBER 1905

Flauto solo, one-act musical "lustspiel" by the Scottish-born self-Germanized composer Eugen D'ALBERT whose father was a Frenchman and mother a Scotchwoman, to a whimsical play by the Wagnerian theorist Hans von Wolzogen, wherein a flute-playing Francophile Prussian Prince (obviously the future Frederick the Great) holds a contest of skill in composition with participants from France, Italy, and Germany in order to prove the superiority of French art, but is compelled to give the palm of greatness to Germany as represented by Dr. Pepusch, with a score containing imitations of various national styles to illustrate the story, is performed for the first time at the German Opera in Prague.

14 NOVEMBER 1905

A Tigris (The Tiger), one-act opera by the Hungarian composer Peter Lazar STOJANOVITS, is produced in Budapest.

22 NOVEMBER 1905

Fourth Symphony, subtitled *Easter Eve*, by the Czech romanticist Josef Bohuslav FOERSTER, in four movements, purporting to express the philosophical and religious implications of the eschatological doctrine of bodily resurrection, and containing appropriately devout hymnal sections, is performed for the first time in Prague.

1 DECEMBER 1905

Zenobia, grand opera in three acts by Louis Adolphe COERNE, American composer of German extraction, wherein Queen Zenobia of the Syrian city of Palmyra is defeated by the Roman Emperor Aurelian in 272 A.D., and dies in the arms of her Greek lover, scorning Aurelian's offer of freedom and imperial status as his consort, to a score steeped in Wagneromantic harmonies, is produced in a world première in Bremen, Germany, the first opera by a native American to be staged in Europe.

3 DECEMBER 1905

L'Albatro, "northern legend" in two acts by the 28-year-old Italian composer Ubaldo PACCHIEROTTI, is produced in Milan.

3 DECEMBER 1905

An appeal to unionize Russian musicians is launched in St. Petersburg, with unauthorized signatures of many prominent musicians, among them RIMSKY-KORSAKOV, GLAZUNOV and SILOTI:

COMREDES! Now that workers in many fields are organized to protect their rights, only we, musicians, remain without protection. We are not free servants of our art but slaves of our daily bread. We are serfs of managers and contractors. Not so long ago musicians were treated like chattel. A bourgeois landlord, in his desire to achieve importance, used to keep horses, hounds and musicians. And now, when all Russia is engaged in a struggle for a happier future, many of us are thrown out of work and are starving. Organization is imperative. Let this day, the third of December 1905, be a historic day, the day of decision for St. Petersburg musicians to unite and organize the nucleus of the first all-Russian Musicians' Union. We appeal to you, our comrades, to join us in this undertaking. (Text in the *Russian Musical Gazette*, St. Petersburg, No. 7–8, 1906)

5 DECEMBER 1905

Cassandra, opera in two parts with a prologue by the 29-year-old Italian composer Vittorio GNECCHI, telling the classical tale of the prophetically minded Trojan princess in Greek captivity, culminating in the murder of Agamem-

non predicted by her, the score luxuriating in exclamatory incandescence of spasmodic dissonance in a concentrated post-Wagnerian un-Italian style, is performed for the first time in Bologna, Arturo Toscanini conducting.

The opera obtained a dubious success and would have been quickly forgotten had it not become at a later date the subject of a widespread controversy. A few months after the first performance of *Elektra* by Richard Strauss, the well-known critic Tebaldini published an essay with a comparative table of musical examples, demonstrating a very close analogy between the themes and motives of *Elektra* and those of *Cassandra*. The curious coincidence, or whatever else it might have been, was elusively described by Tebaldini as a case of musical telepathy (cf. his two articles in No. 2 and No. 3, 1909, of the *Rivista Musicale Italiana: Telepatia musicale; a proposito dell' Elettra di R. Strauss*, and *Telepatia musicale? Sempre a proposito*, etc.) which aroused great interest in European musical circles and provoked peremptory defense of Strauss by numerous critics. Despite the unquestionable chronological precedence of Gnecchi's opera over *Elektra*, and the fact that Gnecchi presented to Strauss a copy of his score already in 1905 during their meeting in Turin, American newspapers openly accused Gnecchi of plagiarism. But apart from these misadventures, Gnecchi did not succeed in his ambitious project to evoke the tragic Aeschylean atmosphere, even though he resorted to Greek modes to attain an austere style, agitated here and there by "modern violence." (*Enciclopedia dello Spettacolo*, vol. V, 1958)

5 DECEMBER 1905

The Flonzaley Quartet, organized in 1903 by Edward J. de Coppet of New York City, the name derived from the Villa Flonzaley, his summer home in Switzerland, where the quartet was first assembled (the word "Flonzaley" means little river in the local Swiss dialect), with the original personnel comprising Adolfo Betti, Alfred Pochon, Ugo Ara and Ivan d'Archambeau, presents its first American concert in Carnegie Chamber Music Hall, New York City.

9 DECEMBER 1905

At the Dresden Opera, the world première is given of *Salome*, one-act opera by Richard STRAUSS (completed by him in Berlin on 20 June 1905), to a German libretto drawn from Oscar Wilde's French play, exhibiting with horrendous naturalism Salome's immund passion for the imprisoned John the Baptist who curses her variously and powerfully when she implores him to let her kiss his mouth, with murderous vengeance swiftly forthcoming as she prevails upon her stepfather Herod, the tetrarch of Judea, who covets her himself to deliver to her, as a pledged reward for dancing before him a voluptuous dance of the seven veils during which she casts off one cover after another from her body (a ballerina actually performing the dance by adroit substitution on the stage), the severed head of the prophet, which she proceeds to kiss avidly after it is brought in on a silver platter, sinking her teeth into the dead mouth "as into a ripe fruit" in an ecstasy so hideous that Herod, appalled and frustrated in his own lust, orders his soldiers to slay her, with the score embodying all the resources of the modern orchestra (a newly constructed baritone oboe, the Heckelphone, is here used for the first time), scaling the heights and plumbing the depths of vocal expression in a Wagnerogenic psycho-musical identification of characters (the prophet vociferating in piously wrathful monody, Herod raising his voice in whole-tone steps, Salome writhing in anguishedly languishing, lasciviously languorous orientalistic chromatics), with acervative polyharmony reaching its maximal embroilment in a well-nigh unresolvable tonal tangle of five unsympathetic Jews, and eventually leading, through a plethora of labyrinthine peripeteia, to a long-deferred catharsis in a magniloquently protracted cadence.

For a long time no work has been awaited here with such expectancy as Strauss's *Salome*. It has been an open secret that the censor's prohibition in Vienna has only served as a cloak wherewith to hide the real reason for abandoning the performance—i.e. the refusal of the singers to devote themselves to its insane difficulties. It was expected that a similar condition might arise here even at the eleventh hour, but no obstacle intervened and everything went off in perfect order. The singers and orchestral musicians who accomplished almost supernatural deeds received full reward. First, the public accorded them an ovation that lasted ten minutes by actual count, and culminated in twenty recalls, and secondly, the triumph was witnessed by all the managers of Germany's largest opera houses and by the most representative audience, intellectually, that could be gathered together in this country. There is no doubt that all the leading opera houses in Germany will give *Salome*. The public will be fascinated and awed. Men of the world and tender virgins, in unanimous accord, will applaud until the palms of their hands ache. In spite of the unwillingness with which I say it, I feel impelled to point out that it is a sign of the most dangerous decadence that such a work is able to achieve a success so complete. Strauss and his school have reached the limit of this kind of music, and further progress in the same direction must end in the destruction of all musical law and order, where tonal anarchy reigns supreme, where cacophony, ugliness and dissonance become a sport, and where everything that has been regarded as beautiful, true, poetical, artistically satisfying and uplifting must be left behind. The musicians in the orchestra say that in *Salome* they themselves often are not sure whether they are playing correctly or not. Some of the orchestral sections play unconcernedly in keys that are a semitone removed from the tonality used at the same time by other groups. At one place the orchestra plays B-flat major while Salome sings insistently in B natural. (Paul Pfitzner, *Musikalisches Wochenblatt*, Berlin, 15 December 1905)

Seldom has the première of a new opera been expected more eagerly than the first performance of Richard Strauss's *Salome* at the Dresden Royal Opera. It was considered almost certain that the intelligent and educated Dresden public, accustomed as it is to the best in art, would protest angrily and loudly at an opera whose story exceeds in gruesomeness and perverted degeneracy anything that has been offered in a musical work for the stage. These fears were not realized, for the opera had a thunderous, stormy and unanimous success. The public would not rest until the composer and the officiating conductor had come before the curtain and bowed their thanks at least a dozen times. This proves that the most perverted, the most degrading and revolting vice that was ever conceived by human mind and put into an art form, can be presented on the stage today. Merely to bring the severed head on the stage was not suggestive and grim enough for Oscar Wilde; he felt the need of presenting the public with a new and extraordinarily stimulating nerve sensation. Salome, who has been instructed in all the ways of sexual vice by her mother, saw in the white body of the innocent young prophet

a new gratification of her lustful instincts. As he repulses her, there ripens in her a devilish plan, and she nurses her lewd imagination with the thought at once bestial and voluptuous that if she may not kiss the living man, then at least she shall satisfy her desires with the quivering head of her decapitated victim. To this story Strauss has composed music which fascinates one not so much with the importance of its themes as through the masterful manner in which he uses his thematic material and the glittering brilliancy of its orchestral dress. One of the phenomenal gifts possessed by Strauss is his faculty for imitating the sounds of nature and picturing external occurrences. For instance, when Salome, attracted by the voice of the prophet, looks into the pit where he is imprisoned, the double basses play the notes C, E-flat, F-sharp, and G, mysteriously and pianissimo, while the rest of the strings play an insistent tremolo on E-flat *sul ponticello*. This remarkable combination of tones conveys the feeling of the gruesome atmosphere of the underground prison. Even more impressive is the ghastly quiet when Salome, shortly before the end of the opera, looks into the pit once more to assure herself that the executioner has done his bloody deed. There are short staccato sounds which suggest, for all the world, the falling of drops of blood. (Arno Kleffel, *Allgemeine Musik-Zeitung*, Berlin, 15 December 1905)

The chromatics in *Salome* begin with the second note of the score. At times we find the bass in a flat key and the other harmonies in sharps. All rhythms are interwoven with a strong predilection for 5/4 and 7/4. As regards tonality, it is utterly unnecessary for Strauss to give any key signature to his music. It is impossible to know whether one is playing true or false, and misprints could not be detected by any known musical rule. The libretto is a compound of lust, stifling perfumes and blood, and cannot be read by any woman or fully understood by anyone but a physician. (Louis C. Elson, Boston *Advertiser*, 27 February 1906)

Salome is a real work of genius which belongs to the most important productions of our time! There labors and lives under a lot of rubbish a volcano, a subterranean fire—not mere fireworks! And it is so with the whole personality of Strauss! That is why it is so difficult to separate wheat from chaff in him. But I have gained enormous respect for this entire phenomenon. (From a letter from Gustav Mahler to Alma Mahler, after he heard a performance of *Salome* in January 1907)

16 DECEMBER 1905

Lucullus, opera-burlesque in three acts by the 44-year-old Russian-born ethnically German composer Erik MEYER-HELMUND, to his own libretto depicting the extravagant orgies of a Roman epicurean of that name who flourished in the first century before the Christian era, is produced, in German, in Riga.

17 DECEMBER 1905

At the first meeting of the Autonomous Artistic Council of the St. Petersburg Conservatory, organized as a result of concessions on the part of the Tsarist-appointed directorate, RIMSKY-KORSAKOV is asked to rejoin the faculty from which he was expelled on 1 April 1905, and Alexander GLAZUNOV is unanimously elected Director of the Conservatory.

26 DECEMBER 1905

Les Pêcheurs de Saint-Jean, opera in four acts by Charles-Marie WIDOR, portraying the turbulent scenes among mariners at Saint-Jean-de-Luz, in the course of which the young suitor of a local belle spurned by her imperious father unselfishly rushes into a stormy Bay of Biscay to save him and thus wins the girl, with a musical score swimming in the majestic waves of resonant arpeggios and basking in well-proportioned melodic curves, is produced at the Opéra-Comique in Paris.

28 DECEMBER 1905

La Mort de Tintagiles, lyric drama in three acts by Jean NOUGUÈS, after the poem of Maeterlinck, written in neo-medieval modalities and depicting the horror of a lit-

tle boy's death at the hands of unknown malefactors, is produced in Paris.

28 DECEMBER 1905

Die lustige Witwe, famous operetta by Franz LEHÀR, that embodies, in a series of rollicking, nostalgic, sentimental, and eminently waltzable or polkable tunes, the Weltanschauung of the irrepressibly cozy world of glory and pleasure, dealing with a free-loving prince of a mythical kingdom gallivanting in Paris and eventually finding stable happiness with a rich and merry widow, is performed for the first time in Vienna.

1906

6 JANUARY 1906

Černé Jezéro (The Black Lake), opera in three acts by the Czech composer Josef Richard ROZKOŠNÝ, is produced in Prague.

20 JANUARY 1906

Emporium, opera in three acts by the Catalan composer Enrique MORERA, in which a fugitive male slave is purchased by a benevolent Roman philosopher as a gift to his favorite concubine, with a romance growing between them interrupted by the slave's legitimate wife arriving unexpectedly from the country of his origin, all this drenched in Wagnerian harmonies, is produced in Barcelona.

21 JANUARY 1906

First Symphony in E-flat major by the Rumanian composer Georges ENESCO, in three movements, *Assez vif et rythmé* (in marching waltz time opening with proclamatory brass), *Lent* (permeated with chromaticized melismas of Balkanized orientalism, with muted strings and fluent harps), and *Vif et vigoureux* (in propulsive rhythms rising excelsiorly to a fiery plagal conclusion), is performed for the first time in Paris, at a Colonne concert, with Colonne himself conducting. (The first Rumanian performance of the Symphony took place under Enesco's own direction in Bucharest on 19 January 1908.)

People are puzzled and annoyed because they cannot classify me, for my musical education was not confined to one locality. I was born in Rumania; studied in Vienna, then went to Paris, and absorbed French influence which, combined with German ingredients, imparted a novel quality to my Rumanian music. (Enesco quoted in a contemporary interview)

24 JANUARY 1906

Serge RACHMANINOFF conducts in Moscow the world première of his two short operas, *The Miserly Knight,* after

Pushkin, dealing with a morbidly avaricious baron who refuses to help even his own son, and dies in his dingy cellar stingily guarding his purposeless gold; and *Francesca da Rimini,* after Dante, telling the piteous tale of Paolo and Francesca slain by her jealous husband, the music of both operas throbbing with Tchaikovskian anxiety in somberly suspenseful harmonies.

26 JANUARY 1906

William Ratcliff, opera by the French composer Xavier LEROUX, disciple of Massenet, to a libretto drawn from a sanguinary ballad of the same title by Heinrich Heine, wherein a medieval Scottish knight slays a succession of suitors of his beloved, and after a licentious explosion of illicit passion, stabs her to death (so that she would belong to no one else), murders her father and then kills himself, is produced for the first time in Nice.

27 JANUARY 1906

Ernest BLOCH conducts in Geneva the world première of his symphonic diptych *Hiver-Printemps,* composed in 1905 as a study in contrasts between hibernal somberness and vernal exultation, and concluding on a resolutely unresolved E major tonic seventh-chord, symbolic of heliotropic elliptical turn in the Northern hemisphere after solstice. (The date 16 October 1916, cited in reference works as the world première, was the first performance in America, conducted by Bloch in New York.)

31 JANUARY 1906

The Pipe of Desire, "romantic grand opera" in one act by Frederick S. CONVERSE, to a diffusely symbolic libretto dealing with an old man with a magical pipe ruling over a forestful of sylphs, a riverful of undines and a swampful of salamanders, who wreaks dire punishment upon a defiant shepherd who seizes the pipe (corno di bassetto) and by playing tunes disastrously harmonized by inverted major seventh-chords and augmented triads, inadvertently causes his young bride to wither and die of malaria, set to an ambitiously Wagnerian score, is performed for the first time in Boston. (This was also the first opera by an American composer to be produced by the Metropolitan Opera Company, in New York, on 18 March 1910.)

4 FEBRUARY 1906

Slovácká Suite for orchestra by the 35-year-old Czech composer Vítězslav NOVÁK, based on Slovak songs, is performed for the first time in Prague.

5 FEBRUARY 1906

In a letter addressed to Pierre Lalo, music critic of *Le Temps*, Maurice RAVEL affirms his priority in evolving new functional techniques of writing for the modern piano:

You have commented at great length upon a rather special method of writing for piano, the invention of which you attribute to Debussy. I wish to point out that my *Jeux d'eau* appeared early in 1902, when there were no piano works by Debussy except his three pieces *Pour le Piano*, which I admire very much but which contain nothing new from the pianistic point of view. (Quoted from *Le Temps*, Paris, 9 April 1907)

6 FEBRUARY 1906

Concert Overture, by the 23-year-old Polish composer Karol SZYMANOWSKI, based on two contrasting themes with much chromatic involution, is performed for the first time in Warsaw, Gregor Fitelberg conducting.

11 FEBRUARY 1906

Fifth Symphony by Hans HUBER, subtitled *Romantische*, with an important violin solo, making it practically a concerto (another subtitle describes it as *Der Geiger von Gmünd*,) is performed for the first time in Basel.

14 FEBRUARY 1906

President Theodore ROOSEVELT receives at the White House a delegation of Negro students from the Industrial Institute of Manassas, Virginia, and declares, after hearing them perform some songs for him, that "gradually out of the capacity for melody that the Negro race has, America shall develop some school of national music." (President Says Negro Makes American Music—May Furnish the Foundation of the True National Music—captions in the New York *Times*, 15 February 1906)

18 FEBRUARY 1906

Jour d'Été à la Montagne, symphonic triptych by Vincent D'INDY, an impressionistic evocation of a day in the Cevennes Mountains, wherein chromatic violins and joyful trumpets mark the progress of *Aurore* from mistily mystical C minor to sun-drenched B major; the advent of *Jour* under the pine trees is portrayed in cool E major with tarantellic rhythms punctuated by drumbeats and the *Soir* reverses the auroral modulating scheme falling from the cinquefoil of invigorating B major into a crepuscular C minor, introducing partly inverted themes of *Aurore*, is performed for the first time at a Colonne concert in Paris.

21 FEBRUARY 1906

Benvenuto Cellini, opera in three acts by the 33-year-old Apulian composer Angelo TUBI, based on the autobiographical adventures of the famous Florentine artist and multifutuent lover, is produced in Parma.

21 FEBRUARY 1906

Sanga, lyric drama in three acts by Isidor de LARA wherein a vindictive village girl in Savoy prays for the Alpine glaciers to melt and flood her inconstant lover's farm, but illogically rushes to his rescue when her prayer is answered, resulting in the death of both in the darkly churning waters to the accompaniment of Valkyrian augmented triads, is produced in Nice.

24 FEBRUARY 1906

L'Ancêtre, lyric drama in three acts by Camille SAINT-SAËNS, dealing with a family vendetta in Corsica circa 1810, wherein the implacable grandmother of a feuding clan takes aim to kill the youthful slayer of her grandson, but misses and fatally wounds her own granddaughter, set to a luxuriantly prolix score ingratiatingly adorned with Corsican melodies, is produced in Monte Carlo.

25 FEBRUARY 1906

Anton ARENSKY, Russian composer of wistful songs and brilliant piano pieces, limner of twilight moods in minor keys, poet of nostalgic indetermination, dies at the melancholy age of 44, in Terijoki, a Finnish resort near St. Petersburg.

Arensky was a student of mine. After graduating from the St. Petersburg Conservatory, he became a professor of the Conservatory of Moscow. . . . His life was spent in dissipation, drunkenness and gambling. . . . At one time he became mentally ill. . . . He languished for a time in Nice, and died of tuberculosis in Finland. . . . In his youth he was somewhat influenced by my music, and later by Tchaikovsky. He will be forgotten soon . . . (Rimsky-Korsakov, *The Chronicle of My Musical Life*, St. Petersburg, 1909)

1 MARCH 1906

Greysteel, or *The Bearsarks Come to Surnadale*, first opera in one act by the English composer Nicholas Comyn GATTY, to his brother's libretto, wherein an Icelandic carl defeats, with the aid of his trusted runic sword Greysteel, the fierce Bearsarks and restores the rule of the gentle Princess of Soursop, is produced in London.

7 MARCH 1906

Concerto for cello and orchestra by Ernst von DOHNÁNYI is performed for the first time by Hugo Becker and the Budapest Philharmonic, under the direction of the composer.

10 MARCH 1906

Hugdietrichs Brautfahrt, operetta in three acts by Oscar STRAUS, dealing with a Byzantine potentate in search of an adequate wife who is helped in his pursuit by various preternatural personages, is produced in Vienna.

10 MARCH 1906

Don Procopio, an early opera in two acts by Georges BIZET, written by him in 1858 to an Italian libretto, receives its first performance, in a French version, at Monte Carlo.

11 MARCH 1906

Russian Fantasy, by Alexander GLAZUNOV, scored for an ensemble of balalaikas, and composed especially for the Great-Russian Orchestra founded and conducted by the virtuoso balalaikist Vasily Andreyev, is performed for the first time at his concert in St. Petersburg.

19 MARCH 1906

I Quattro Rusteghi, opera buffa in three acts by Ermanno WOLF-FERRARI, after Goldoni's comedy dealing with four brutish Venetians who try putting obstacles into the course of love between the son of one of them and a daughter of another, but are outwitted by their more humane wives, with a hedonistic score in the manner of the Italian baroque, is performed for the first time anywhere in Munich, in a German version under the title *Die vier Grobiane.*

22 MARCH 1906

Martin WEGELIUS, German-trained grandmaster of Finnish music, composer of competent symphonic works and esteemed pedagogue who counted Sibelius among his students, dies in his native Helsingfors at the age of 59.

26 MARCH 1906

The Free Lance, comic opera by the American "March King" John Philip SOUSA, to a story wherein the Prince of Graftiana and the Princess of Braggadocia, slated for a diplomatically convenient marriage sight unseen, run away from their palaces in peasant dress to escape the forced wedding, meet accidentally and fall in love incognito, thus arranging things to universal satisfaction, is performed for the first time in Springfield, Massachusetts.

27 MARCH 1906

Aphrodite, music drama in six tableaux by Camille ERLANGER, after a novella by Pierre Louÿs, set in humid Alexandria in 57 B.C., wherein a Greek sculptor forsakes Cleopatra's older sister in favor of a Hebrew enchantress who is put to death for abstracting sacred objects from the temple of Aphrodite, with a musical setting full of opulent Wagnerian sonorities, is produced at the Opéra-Comique in Paris.

29 MARCH 1906

La Figlia di Jorio, opera in three acts by Alberto FRANCHETTII, to a libretto drawn from the pastoral tragedy by Gabriele d'Annunzio, wherein a mystical virgin, seeking protection from a group of sensually inflamed harvesters at the home of a young affianced villager, is taken by him to an Apennine cave, where he kills his own father when the latter in an unexpected intrusion tries to possess her by force, and is condemned to death but is replaced at the burning stake by the heroine who

dies exclaiming appreciatively, "La fiamma è bella!", all this set to a facile Italianate score in which ecclesiastical chants and folk tunes of the Abruzzi mountains are freely intermingled, is produced at La Scala in Milan.

3 APRIL 1906

Déidamia, the first opera, in four acts, by the Belgian composer François RASSE, to a libretto drawn from Alfred de Musset's poem *La Coupe et les lèvres,* wherein the multifutuent vagabond lover of a chaste Alpine girl claims her for a bride, and is stabbed to death by a former mistress on his wedding night, is performed for the first time at the Théâtre de la Monnaie in Brussels.

6 APRIL 1906

Chopiniana, ballet in one act, music by CHOPIN, orchestrated by various hands, is performed for the first time at the Imperial Opera House in St. Petersburg. (*Chopiniana* was produced under the title *Les Sylphides* by Diaghilev's Ballet Russe in Paris on 2 June 1909.)

8 APRIL 1906

Medea, opera in three acts by Vincenzo TOMMASINI, to his own libretto, is produced in Trieste.

10 APRIL 1906

Tess, opera in four acts by Frédéric D'ERLANGER after Thomas Hardy's *Tess of the d'Urbervilles,* is produced in an Italian version in Naples.

14 APRIL 1906

Hans, le Joueur de flûte, comic opera in three acts by Louis GANNE, wherein a medieval Flemish piper arranges the marriage of a loving couple against the opposition of their parents by threatening to lure away all cats in town and let the local mice proliferate unimpeded, is produced in Monte Carlo.

17 APRIL 1906

On the eve of the San Francisco earthquake and fire that destroyed its opera house, the Metropolitan Opera Company gives its second and, by fatal inevitability, last production of its San Francisco season, playing *Carmen,* with Enrico Caruso as Don José, to a packed house.

The fact that Caruso was announced packed the building on the second night, and it is terrible to contemplate the awful results had the earthquake surprised the community during the operatic performance. The loss of the Metropolitan Company was not as great as may be expected. The two houses brought in about $15,000, if not more. . . . In sixteen performances the company should have taken in $160,000. . . . There has been considerable talk about contributing the advance sale to the relief fund, but this is all nonsense. The money must be returned to the purchasers of tickets, who need the funds more than the city at large. The purchasers of opera tickets are in far more distress than the poorer classes of people, who are no strangers to adversity. So it is certain that the money will be returned to the purchasers of tickets. Notwithstanding his $1,200 performance, Caruso had to sleep in Golden Gate Park on Wednesday and Thursday nights, April 18 and 19. (*The Musical Courier,* New York, 9 May 1906)

25 APRIL 1906

John Knowles PAINE, American composer, chairman of the first American faculty of music at Harvard University, whose own music was exquisitely Mendelssohnian in its flowing harmonies (he studied in Berlin), dies in Cambridge, Massachusetts, at the age of 67.

1 MAY 1906

At the graduation exercises of the Bucharest Conservatory, 17-year-old Rumanian violinist Grigoras DINICU plays as an encore for a regular academic program his newly composed, contagiously rhythmical *Hora Staccato,* a stylized rustic dance in a gypsified Mixolydian mode, destined to become a perennial prestidigital violinistic favorite.

8 MAY 1906

Le Roi aveugle, opera in two acts by Henry FÉVRIER, wherein a Nordic princess, abducted in front of her blind father, falls in love with her ravisher and sails away with him in his kayak, set to a musical score which justifies the dedication of the opera to Février's teacher Gabriel Fauré (there are freely flowing modalities, consecutive melodic fourths and other Fauréisms as well as some incongruous whole-tone progressions), is produced at the Opéra-Comique in Paris.

24 MAY 1906

Sea Drift, coloristic rhapsody by Frederick DELIUS, set for baritone solo, chorus and orchestra to Walt Whitman's impressionistically autobiographical poem of the sea, sea birds and sea bird tragedy, is performed for the first time at the Music Festival in Essen, Germany.

27 MAY 1906

Six weeks before his 46th birthday, Gustav MAHLER conducts in Essen the first performance of his autobiographically tragic *Sixth Symphony,* with a symbolic motto heralded by an A-major triad, which is depressed into A minor by a pessimistic lowering of the mediant, in four clearly delineated movements:

(1) *Allegro energico,* treading in heavy marching steps, slowly mounting the diatonic ladder to the sounds of a metronomical drum, until the sonorous climax is reached in the triadic metamorphosis from major to minor, followed by a fleeting relaxation before returning to the original somber mood; (2) *Scherzo,* a rapid succession of powerfully stressed rhythmic figures, apocopated by the alternation of the metrical compasses of 3/8 and 4/8, relieved by smiling interludes of gracefully acknowledged irony, but ineluctably striving for a restatement of the major-minor chiaroscuro motto, falling by consecutive triadic steps into the profundity of the tonic A minor; (3) *Andante moderato,* in an outspoken optimistic mood established by the alternation of the resonant major keys of E and E-flat, with horn calls and cowbells painting a pastoral scene; (4) *Finale,* constituting the antithesis of the first three movements, equalling their combined length and overshadowing them in elemental power generated by a Berliozian orchestra, and culminating in a fateful stroke of a heavy hammer.

The classical form is not abandoned; the traditional number of movements is retained. And an allegro is really an allegro, the andante is an andante, the scherzo is a scherzo, and the finale a finale. Only in the orchestra is there an innovation; percussion is employed with a completeness hitherto unheard of, and constitutes an organized invasion of rhythmic noises into the symphonic field. A hammer clashes in the last movement which has a duration of 30 minutes. A colossal structure is built up in a thoroughly thematic style, and at the same time in a strict unity of sentiment. This sentiment Mahler designates as a tragic one. The new symphony surpasses its predecessors in the solidity of structure but also in its realism and nerve-wracking intensity. It operates like an alarm. Friend and foe rush to arms. (Julius Korngold, *Neue Freie Presse,* Vienna, 30 May 1906)

Mahler's *Sixth Symphony* contains not one original thought of moment. Its themes, when they are Mahler's own, are commonplace and banal, and nearly always in march time. And as to reminiscences, the Symphony is full of them. One hears a few notes of Goldmark's *Sakuntala Overture,* of the Liszt E flat and Tchaikovsky B flat minor concertos, of *Carmen,* of Spohr, of the *Faust Overture* by Wagner. Mahler's weakness is his lack of continuity in style; and he patches together these stray scraps from ancient and modern music with a conventional thread or two of his own, making a heterogeneous crazyquilt of music. (Arthur M. Abell, *The Musical Courier,* New York, 20 June 1906)

28 MAY 1906

Snow Man, musical fairy tale in one act by César CUI written for school children, receives its first performance in Yalta.

29 MAY 1906

Edvard GRIEG receives the degree of Doctor of Music *honoris causa* from Oxford University.

14 JUNE 1906

Samuel COLERIDGE-TAYLOR, British mulatto composer, conducts in London the first performance of his symphonic *Variations on an African Air,* in which he makes use of ancestral tetraphonic themes.

1 JULY 1906

Manuel GARCÍA, member of a singing Spanish family, brother of the fabulous María Malibran and of Pauline Viardot-García, teacher of Jenny Lind, and the inventor of the laryngoscope enabling him to look into the human larynx and, if need be, pharynx, to see what might be wrong with the vocal cords of an imperfect prima donna, dies in London, where he settled in 1848, at the incredible age of 101 years, 3 months and 14 days.

1 JULY 1906

New Music for an Old World, article by Ray Stannard BAKER, describing a Dynamophone, "an extraordinary electrical invention for producing scientifically perfect music," constructed by Dr. Thaddeus CAHILL at the cost of 200 dollars, is published by McClure's Magazine in New York.

Dr. Cahill's new invention suggests a complete change in the system by which a comparatively few rich people enjoy the best music to the exclusion of all others. Instead of bringing the people to music, the new method sends music to the people. The instrument itself produces no music; it merely gives out electrical waves of various sorts which are carried over wires like a telegraph message. Highly skilled musicians, located in a quiet room distant from the whir of the machinery, regulate the production of these waves by playing upon keyboards similar to those of the pipe-organ. Connected with the central plant, cables are laid in the streets, from which wires may be run into your house or mine, or into restaurants, theaters, churches, schools, or wherever music is desired. Upon our table, or attached to the wall, we have an ordinary telephone receiver with a funnel attached. By opening a switch we may 'turn on' the music. . . . You and I may sit in our homes on Easter morning and hear the same music that is being produced in the churches, or in the evening, dining at the restaurant, we may enjoy identical selections given in the opera house or the theater. It is the dream of the inventor that in the future we may be awakened by appropriate music in the morning, and go to bed at night with lullabies. (Extract from the article)

(The machine was patented as No. 580.035 on 6 April 1897, under the name of "Art of an apparatus for generating and distributing music electrically." The briefer description is given in the *Official Gazette*, vol. 79, pp. 32–42; the full description in the volume of *Specifications*, April, 1906, Part I, pp. 155–200, and the drawings are appended at the end of Part II, volume of the *Specifications* for the same month on pp. 34–36.)

29 JULY 1906

Alexandre LUIGINI, French composer of the popular pseudo-oriental *Ballet égyptien* and of numerous other attractive symphonic confections, dies in Paris at the age of 56.

2 AUGUST 1906

Zino-Zina, ballet-pantomime in two acts by the 43-year-old French composer Paul VIDAL, written in an elegant Gallic idiom, dealing with an 18th-century Calabrian poet Zino who kills himself for the love of a socially impregnable and physically insurmountable Signora, and is avenged by his sister Zina who seduces and marries the lady's royal lover, is produced in Paris.

23 AUGUST 1906

Norfolk Rhapsody No. 1 in E minor by Ralph VAUGHAN WILLIAMS, thematically based on five Norfolk tunes, contrapuntally elaborated, fugued and intervalically dislocated, with a pentatonically piping clarinet for a bucolic motto, is performed for the first time at a Promenade Concert in London. (*Norfolk Rhapsody No. 2* and ditto No. 3 were first performed at the Cardiff Festival, on 27 September 1907, but later were discarded by the composer.)

24 AUGUST 1906

Josef HOLBROOKE conducts the Kursaal Orchestra at Ostend in the first performance of his symphonic poem *Dreamland*. (The performance at the Three Choirs Festival of 12 September 1906 is erroneously listed as the absolute première in the official Festival history.)

3 SEPTEMBER 1906

The Red Mill, comic opera in two acts by Victor HERBERT, telling a tale of two American youths staying at a Dutch inn named The Sign of the Red Mill who help the burgomaster's daughter escape via a revolving wing of a windmill from her room where she was locked by her irascible father intent on keeping her away from her chosen mate, with a desired consummation vouchsafed by the discovery that the bridegroom is heir to a vast fortune, is performed for the first time in Buffalo. (The New York production followed on 24 September 1906.)

4 SEPTEMBER 1906

RIMSKY-KORSAKOV completes the manuscript of his *Chronicle of My Musical Life*, with the following confession: "The chronicle of my musical life is now at its end. It is disorganized, uneven in details, badly written, and frequently too dry; but it tells the truth, and this alone justifies the reader's interest."

25 SEPTEMBER 1906

Dmitri SHOSTAKOVICH, prime composer of the Soviet period of Russian music, whose many symphonies, profoundly spiritual in their philosophical overtones but grandly Russian in the broad vistas of their thematic landscape, have contributed powerfully to the formation of a characteristically national and yet distinctly individual type of Soviet music, is born in St. Petersburg.

10 OCTOBER 1906

On his first American tour Ruggero LEONCAVALLO conducts in New York a concert of his own music, concluding with a march *Viva l'America*, dedicated to President Theodore Roosevelt, and consisting of varied repetitions of *Yankee Doodle* and *Dixie*.

10 OCTOBER 1906

Joseph GUTTOVEGGIO, American composer of Italian parentage, who adopted the name Paul CRESTON after a high-school nickname as an Anglo-Saxon assonance of Crespino, a role he acted in a play, and whose many instrumental works are distinguished by rational dissonances in the framework of basic tonality, is born in New York City.

23 OCTOBER 1906

Vladimir STASOV, white-bearded Russian music critic, grandiloquent champion of enlightened nationalism in art, whose winged phrase in a newspaper article in 1867 affixed the honoring appellation "The Mighty Five of Russian Music" to Balakirev, Borodin, Cui, Mussorgsky and Rimsky-Korsakov, dies at St. Petersburg at the patriarchal age of 82.

27 OCTOBER 1906

Gaziel, zarzuela by Enrique GRANADOS, is produced in Barcelona.

31 OCTOBER 1906

Ariane, opera in five acts by Jules MASSENET, to a libretto by Catulle Mendès, wherein the familiar story of a helpful Cretan girl abandoned by an ungrateful Greek hero is expanded to include his island romance with her sister and Ariadne's death in the sea, with the music flowing unimpeded through waves of melodious passion, is produced at the Paris Opéra.

6 NOVEMBER 1906

Birute, melodrama in two acts by the Lithuanian composer Mikas PETRAUSKAS, constituting the first attempt in Lithuanian to create a national opera, is produced in Vilna. (An expanded version was produced in Kaunas on 16 February 1921.)

8 NOVEMBER 1906

La Légende de Rudel, opera in three episodes and 12 scenes by the Mexican composer Ricardo CASTRO, dealing with the medieval Provençal troubadour who deserts a devoted French maiden for a futile crusade and dies at the feet of a haughty Countess of Tripoli after a shipwreck, written in a conventional melodramatic idiom embellished by orientalistic arabesques, is produced for the first time in Mexico City, in an Italian version of the original French libretto, in the presence of the permanent president dictator Porfirio Diaz.

8 NOVEMBER 1906

Les Armaillis, dramatic legend in two acts by the Swiss composer Gustave DORET, recounting the tragic story of an Alpine "armailli" (shepherd) who pushes a friend to his death down a precipice to secure for himself a shepherdess they both love, but is driven to suicide by remorse and jumps into the same chasm that swallowed his rival, is produced for the first time anywhere at the Opéra-Comique in Paris.

8 NOVEMBER 1906

Hermes, opera in three acts by the 32-year-old Italian composer Attilio PARELLI, to a mythological libretto about the messenger of the Olympian gods, is performed for the first time in Genoa.

10 NOVEMBER 1906

The world première is given at the Leipzig Opera of a German version of the three-act opera *The Wreckers* (*Strandrecht* in German, which means "salvage rights"), composed by the mannish English suffragette Ethel SMYTH, after the original French drama *Les Naufrageurs* by Henry Brewster, wherein a youth and a maid who light fires to warn off mariners on stormy nights in a Cornish seacoast village are left to die in a cave at high tide by looters of wrecked ships, with a score full of Wagnerian sound and fury. (An English version was first performed in London in concert form, on 30 May 1908, and on the stage on 22 June 1909; a revised version was produced at Sadler's Wells, London, on 19 April 1939.)

11 NOVEMBER 1906

Carl NIELSEN conducts at the Danish Royal Opera House in Copenhagen the première of his opera in three acts, *Maskarade,* wherein a young man betrothed by parental decision to a young lady he has never met falls in love with a girl behind a mask at a masked ball, and proceeds to arrange a series of illicit meetings with her, only to find that, happily, she is his chosen fiancée.

11 NOVEMBER 1906

Third Symphony by the bearded Breton composer Guy ROPARTZ, for soli, choruses and orchestra, in three Wagneromantically pantheistic movements, depicting the sunlit serenity of nature, the gloom of men and the philosophic synthesis of life and humanity through love, is performed for the first time at the Paris Conservatory.

12 NOVEMBER 1906

The Vicar of Wakefield, a romantic light opera by Liza LEHMANN, London-born soprano of German extraction, to Goldsmith's classical novel dealing with a commendably equanimous Dr. Primrose who unostentatiously rescues his venturesome daughter from the primrose path of dalliance with an unscrupulous squire by proving to him that he cannot escape legal marriage, and judiciously arranges his other daughter's marriage to the squire's uncle, is produced in London.

13 NOVEMBER 1906

Christmas Overture by Cyril SCOTT, with a choral ending a cappella, is performed for the first time by the London Symphony Orchestra.

13 NOVEMBER 1906

Il Battista, "azione sacra" in three acts by Giocondo FINO, depicting the holy life and decapitation of John the Baptist, is produced in Turin.

23 NOVEMBER 1906

Enrico CARUSO is found guilty of molesting a woman in the monkey house in the Central Park Zoo in New York City by touching her left forearm with his right elbow, and is fined ten dollars in a New York City Municipal Court. (Caruso cabled his father in Italy after the verdict: "I swear upon thy white hair that I am innocent.")

1 DECEMBER 1906

Vendetta, opera in three acts by Emilio PIZZI, is produced in Cologne, with a German libretto. (It was performed in Italian as *Ivania* at Bergamo on 14 September 1926.)

3 DECEMBER 1906

Oscar HAMMERSTEIN, 60-year-old German born operatic impresario, opens in New York the first season of his ambitious Manhattan Opera House, with a roster of celebrated *prime donne* in his company, and with an avowed intention to offer bold commercial competition to the Metropolitan Opera. (He sold the Manhattan Opera House to the Metropolitan Opera Company in April 1910 for $1,200,000.)

8 DECEMBER 1906

Moloch, musical tragedy in three acts by Max von SCHILLINGS, to a libretto dealing with a priest of the Moloch cult in Carthage who leaves the ruins of his city destroyed by the Romans and goes to Ultima Thule where he instructs the sub-arctic natives in agriculture, viniculture and apiculture, but, frustrated in his attempt to organize a local army against Roman rule, leaps from a cliff into the cold North Sea, with a score of viscously Wagneromantic music, is produced in Dresden.

14 DECEMBER 1906

The French Chamber of Deputies votes against the taxation of private motor cars, but instead imposes special taxes on privately owned pianos as being more numerous than automobiles and therefore more productive of revenue.

22 DECEMBER 1906

Alexander GLAZUNOV conducts in St. Petersburg the first performance of his *Eighth* (and last) *Symphony* in E-flat major, set as usual in four movements (*Allegro moderato, Mesto, Scherzo, Finale*) with stately oscillations between two contrasting musicosophical ideals (it has been described as his Ormuzd-Ahriman symphony), harmonically rich without inordinate turgidity, diatonic in its melos and somberly chromatic in its labyrinthine polyphony. (The Symphony was begun on 12 August 1905 and completed on 13 November 1906.)

26 DECEMBER 1906

The Bohemian Club, dedicated to the promotion of good music, is organized in New York City, the founding members being benefactors of great wealth and important social figures.

27 DECEMBER 1906

Psalm XLVII by Florent SCHMITT for orchestra, chorus and organ, remarkably proleptic in its innovating techniques, with asymmetrical meters and unresolved dissonant structures and starkly primitivistic vocal lines, is performed for the first time at a concert of Prix de Rome winners in Paris.

The *Psalm XLVII* holds a singular place in the history of modern music. . . . We are in the presence of a grandiose work. Certainly, this score of 120 orchestral pages, notated on 32 staves generously blackened with notes, has not been filled with music by means of a dropper. The performers have no time to read their newspapers between two passages in forte, and the Women of Israel must not spare their high B's. But all this edifice is so neat and so well balanced that it should not frighten anybody. (Emile Vuillermoz, *Musiques d'aujourd'hui,* pp. 111–112, Paris, 1923)

29 DECEMBER 1906

Three weeks after his 41st birthday Jean SIBELIUS conducts in St. Petersburg, at one of the Siloti concerts, the first performance anywhere of his symphonic fantasy *Pohjola's Daughter,* based, as so many of his works are, on the Finnish epic *Kalevala,* painting in majestically modal melodies and granitically stable harmonies the rune of mighty. Väinämöinen on his ride through northernmost Lapland (in smoothly gliding rhythmic passages in the strings), who is struck by the arctic beauty of the Virgin of the Air, Daughter of the North, as she spins reclining on the rainbow (in spirally involuted melismas), and asks her to come down and share his sled with him (jingling the sleighbells by instantaneous grace notes in the wind), to which she agrees on condition that he split a horsehair for her (by chromatically halving the diatonic steps), tie an egg in knots (by involuting arpeggiated augmented triads), peel a stone (by enharmonic compression of brass chords) and build a boat out of her spindle, which latter he fails to accomplish, only bruising his fingers against prickly wholetone scales, and sadly slides away under the midnight sun foreglimpsing perhaps her hideous end when the Finnish Zeus Kullervo lets loose a pack of wolves on her, and she is devoured.

(Date, 16 December 1906 old style, corresponding to 29 December 1906 new style, is taken from the original program of the Siloti concert at which Sibelius appeared as guest conductor. That this performance was indeed the world première is corroborated by Karl Ekman in his biography of Sibelius, published in Helsinki in 1935, stating that *Pohjola's Daughter* was completed in the autumn of 1906, and that Sibelius conducted its first performance in St. Petersburg "shortly before Christmas," referring of course to old-style calendar.)

1907

3 JANUARY 1907

The first Bulgarian symphonic work of European stature, the overture *Ivailo* by the Bulgarian composer Dobry KHRISTOV, who studied in Prague with Dvořák, inspired by the heroic tale of a medieval Balkan peasant who wrested the power from Byzantine usurpers and ascended his rightful throne as Tsar of Bulgaria, is performed for the first time in Sofia.

5 JANUARY 1907

Mytislaw der Moderne, operetta by Franz LEHÁR with the background of amorous intrigue among modernized Slavs, is produced in Vienna.

12 JANUARY 1907

Histoires naturelles, song cycle by Maurice RAVEL to a set of animal fables of Jules Renard, depicting in anthropomorphic imagery the idiosyncrasies of the peacock (panpentatonically preening himself for a wedding ceremony that never takes place), the cricket (grinding its extremities in high frequency over chords of the thirteenth), the swan (diving under the surface of the lake, with resonant ninth-chords reposing on deep submarine pedal points), the kingfisher (insouciantly alighting on a fishing rod with piscivorous expectations on sustained upper notes and volatile arpeggios underneath), the guinea hen (neurotically clucking in semitones and nearly suffocating in rapid pianissimos), is performed for the first time at a concert of the Société Nationale de Musique in Paris, eliciting indignant animal noises from the conservative sections of the audience.

The Société Nationale de Musique played a useful part in French music, but after 1900 it fell under the influence of Vincent D'Indy so completely that compositions by mediocre students of the Schola Cantorum, which he headed, were constantly performed while works of real value were often rejected. Even Ravel's music was regarded with suspicion, and the whole clan of the Schola expressed its hostility to the point of discourtesy at its performances. (From a 1936 letter to the author from Charles Koechlin, one of the secessionists who left the Société Nationale de Musique and organized the more open-minded Société Indépendante de Musique)

There are few subjects more alien to music than these *Histoires naturelles*.... M. Ravel furnished them with appropriate settings, laborious, affected and dry, almost devoid of real essence, a collection of diligently worked-out curiosities.... When M. Ravel encounters in the texts a particularly important point or a word, the piano ceases to play, the complex harmonies disappear and the solo voice presents the narrative. After a while the piano resumes with a succession of altered chords. It makes one think of the café-concert, a café-concert with a ninth-chord. But I should be inclined in favor of the café-concert pure and simple. (Pierre Lalo, *Le Temps*, Paris, 19 March 1907)

22 JANUARY 1907

Salome, notoriously famous opera by Richard STRAUSS, after Oscar Wilde's French play, is performed for the first time in America by the Metropolitan Opera Company in New York, precipitating a moralistic explosion among the wealthy, the proper and the self-righteous members of New York society.

4000 Survive The Most Appalling Tragedy Ever Shown on the Mimic Stage—Composer Who Out-Herods Richard Wagner Conquers Every Hearer of His Incomparable Score—The Last Touch of Genius that Germany's Tone-Poet Achieves by the Dramatic Dynamite of Britain's Unforgiven Oscar Wilde Such a Rehabilitation as No Music Ever Gave a Poet Before—And in a Half-Hour Horror of Death's-Head Embrace the Young American Star, Olive Fremstad, Wins Her Place Among the Greatest Dramatic Singers in the World (Subheadlines in the New York *Sun*, 23 January 1907)

A reviewer... should be an embodied conscience stung into righteous fury by the moral stench with which *Salome* fills the nostrils of humanity, but, though it makes him retch, he should be sufficiently judicial in his temperament calmly to look at the drama in all its aspects and determine whether or not as a whole it is an instinctive note on the life and culture of the times and whether or not this exudation from the diseased and polluted will and imagination of the authors marks a real advance in artistic expression.... There is a vast deal of ugly music in *Salome*—music that offends the ear and rasps the nerves like fiddlestrings played on by a coarse file....

There is not a whiff of fresh and healthy air blowing through *Salome* except that which exhales from the cistern.... The orchestra shrieked its final horror and left the listeners staring at each other with smarting eyeballs and wrecked nerves. (H. E. Krehbiel, New York *Tribune*, 23 January 1907)

Strauss has a mania for writing ugly music; a modern harpy, he cannot touch anything without besmearing it with dissonance. What more natural then that he should cast about for a subject which imperatively demands hideous din to correspond with and justify his concatenated discords? And what more natural than that the noisome Salome should seem an ideal companion for his noisy music? The presentation of such a story is ethically a crime; Richard Strauss's music is esthetically criminal or at least extremely coarse and ill-mannered. His music often suggests a man who comes to a social reception unkempt, with hands unwashed, cigar in mouth, hat on, and who sits down and puts his feet on the table. No boor ever violated all the laws of etiquette as Strauss violates all the laws of musical composition. There is one consolation. Thanks to the prevailing dissonance, nobody knows—or cares—whether the singers sing the right notes—that is, the notes assigned to them—or not. Who can fail to see the stupendous originality of Richard Strauss? What composer before him has been so clever as to be able to write music in which it makes no difference whether or not you sing or play correctly? (W. J. Henderson, New York *Sun*, 23 January 1907)

I am a man of middle life who has devoted upwards of twenty years to the practice of a profession that necessitates a daily intimacy with degenerates. I say after deliberation that *Salome* is a detailed and explicit exposition of the most horrible, disgusting, revolting and unmentionable features of degeneracy that I have ever heard, read of or imagined. (From a physician's letter, New York *Times*, 24 January 1907)

Mr. Clemens has never been able to sit through any production of grand opera. He is very fond of good acting and of good music, but he wants the one divorced from the other. The spectacle of a beautiful singer trying to earn a large salary as an actor while he or she is getting good pay as a musician, he says, has always made him nervous.... (Statement by Mark Twain's secretary in the New York *Herald*, 24 January 1907)

I know an old lady in Germany who has heard *Salome* twenty-seven times, and she likes it very much. It never did her any harm. (An unidentified statement in the New York *Times*, 25 January 1907)

25 JANUARY 1907

Hesperia, one-act opera by Juan Lamote de GRIGNON, is produced in Barcelona.

27 JANUARY 1907

Yielding to the protests of the Board of Directors of the Metropolitan Opera and Real Estate Company of New York City (among them such notables as J. P. Morgan, William K. Vanderbilt and A. D. Juilliard), the Executive Committee of the Metropolitan Opera Company takes *Salome* off the repertory and makes arrangements to refund the tickets already bought for the three scheduled performances.

Salome Not Immoral Says Its Composer—Strauss Amazed at the Opposition to his Play in New York (Headlines in the Boston *Advertiser*, 28 January 1907)

Shaw, Praising Salome, Says People Don't Understand Him or Wilde (Headline in the Boston *Post*, 28 January 1907)

28 JANUARY 1907

The New England Watch and Ward Society launches an investigation with a view of ascertaining the degree of obscenity in the text and the music of *Salome* so as to forestall attempts to present the opera in Boston.

Boston Anxious to Hear Salome—Salome Named an Indecent Opera—The Rev. McElveen Condemns Music Which Appeals to Beast in Man—Clergy Opposed to Salome—Strauss's Opera Disgrace to Civilization Is View—Dragging Sacred Things Down to Mire—Mayor Intimates That Show May Not Come—Doubts If Theater Will Do Anything Offensive to Public Opinion—No Salome for Boston—Too Many Stumbling Blocks Stop Presentation (Assorted headlines in Boston newspapers of 29 January 1907)

29 JANUARY 1907

Mayor John F. FITZGERALD of Boston (grandfather of President John F. Kennedy), in reply to the petition of the New England Watch and Ward Society seeking to prevent possible performances of *Salome* in Boston, issues the following statement:

The Mayor's office does not interfere as a rule with the productions in the Boston theaters. Licenses are issued under such conditions as the office makes, and we insist at all times that the productions be up to the proper standard. If any theater violates public decency by the presentation of anything offensive, we can revoke the license. If the people of Boston do not want the opera *Salome* presented and give expression to that view, I do not think that the opera will be given. No theater manager will fly in the face of public opinion.

2 FEBRUARY 1907

Naïs Micoulin, opera in two acts by Alfred BRUNEAU, after Zola's novelette *La Douleur de Toine*, wherein a Marseille fisherman's daughter, infatuated with a Parisian wastrel, is unrequitedly admired by an honest toiler of the sea and embraces virtue in the end by pushing the former off a precipitous cliff and marrying the latter, set in effectively gallicized Wagneromantic harmonies, is performed for the first time at Monte Carlo.

3 FEBRUARY 1907

Asrael, second symphony, in C minor, by Dvořák's son-in-law Josef SUK, dedicated to the memory of his wife and of Dvořák himself, set in five movements of funereally fatalistic music, with themes consisting of mournfully falling fifths and sobbingly suspended semitones in minor keys, intermittently utilizing passages in whole tones suggestive of facelessly untonal horrors, and progressing mostly in slow motion except for the central scherzo despairingly waltzing around the skeletons of tritones, is performed for the first time in Prague.

Dvořák criticized his son-in-law severely for attempting to erect this pentagonal monument of a symphony. "God gave us five fingers," he said, "not four or six. Beethoven gave four movements to a symphony. Three is too few; five is too many." (William Ritter, in *Mercure Musical et S.I.M.*, Paris, 15 January 1907)

3 FEBRUARY 1907

Une Barque sur l'Océan, Maurice RAVEL's orchestral version of a movement from his piano suite *Miroirs*, is per-

formed for the first time at a Concert Colonne in Paris, Gabriel Pierné conducting.

Une Barque sur l'Océan presents, one might say, a number of lessons in orchestration, demonstrating various methods of altering the original instrumental color. In Ravel's orchestra no instrument keeps its natural sound; to him there are no trumpets but muted trumpets. Despite all this, Ravel fails to evoke an impression of nature. There is no boat, no ocean; there are only notes and instruments; there is nothing suggesting the sea. (Pierre Lalo in *Le Temps*, Paris, 19 March 1907)

Ravel has fallen upon this defenseless city ere now with piano music of the decayed school, but never before did he launch at us such extraordinary roulades of false notes as in his *Barque sur l'Océan*. For a time it sounded as if the upper half of the piano had suddenly gone out of tune with the lower half, but it was only a progressive composer being "intensely modern" and writing in two keys at the same time. The little boat—such a tiny bark—was groaning at every seam, bravely battling the discordant gale, but eventually fell apart, and all on board were lost. The composer unfortunately did not sail on the ship. (W. J. Henderson, the New York *Sun*, 9 November 1907)

5 FEBRUARY 1907

Cavalleria rusticana, one-act opera by Domenico MONLEONE, to a libretto by his brother Giovanni Monleone derived from the same play by Verga as the celebrated opera of Mascagni, is performed for the first time in Amsterdam.

(Mascagni and his publishers sued Monleone for infringement of copyright and succeeded in preventing further performances, but not before a production in London took place under the disputed title; eventually a new libretto was provided by Giovanni Monleone, and the opera was produced in Florence on 18 February 1914 as *La Giostra dei Falchi*.)

Although the outlines of the two libretti and most of the details are identical, the text is not quite the same, and one or two small points are slightly modified. Still, in spite of these differences and the absence of any obvious telepathic communications on the matter of themes between the two composers, it all comes very much to the same thing in the end. In both operas the melodies are either laden with sugar or torn to the usual shreds with the usual passion, and in both operas the orchestration is the conventional mixture of harp and muted strings and very unmuted brass. (London *Times*, 11 May 1910)

5 FEBRUARY 1907

Ludwig THUILLE, Tyrolean-born German-bred composer of Wagneromantic operas and of some durable chamber music, master pedagogue whose composition classes at the Munich School of Music have attracted aspiring apprentices from many lands, dies in Munich at the age of 45.

7 FEBRUARY 1907

Thérèse, music drama in two acts by Jules MASSENET, expertly put together in his most effective style, to a libretto drawn from the events of the French Revolution, wherein the heroine's loyalty is torn between her husband, a Girondin, and her pre-nuptial lover, a royalist, both of whom are seized as the tide of terror rises in 1793, and greet her as their open cart passes under her window on the way to the guillotine whereupon she shouts "Vive le Roi!" to provoke arrest, and joins them in death, is produced at Monte Carlo.

8 FEBRUARY 1907

Kammersymphonie, for 15 solo instruments, op. 9, by Arnold SCHOENBERG, completed on 25 July 1906, and constituting the turning point in his methodical evolution from explicit tonality to implicit atonality, with a key signature still firmly impaled on the staff, its four sharps designating the principal key of E major, but with melodic and harmonic elements built horizontally and vertically in fourths and fifths connoting a departure from the traditional tertian system and the abundant whole-tone scales utilized structurally rather than coloristically, while each instrument is treated as a soloist in the contrapuntal matrix of thematic tissues, is performed for the first time in Vienna.

15 FEBRUARY 1907

String Quartet No. 1, in D minor, op. 7, by Arnold SCHOENBERG (completed on 26 September 1905), set entirely within a tonal framework as the explicit designation of the key indicates, comprising a single continuous movement, sonatically divisible into at least four well-demarcated sections, including a simulacrum of a scherzo and a slow lyric episode, and ending, after a series of intensely emotional chromatically involved stresses and interstitial precipitations of whole-tone scales, in unequivocal D major, is performed for the first time in Vienna.

20 FEBRUARY 1907

Legend of the Invisible City of Kitezh and of the Maiden Fevronia, opera in four acts by RIMSKY-KORSAKOV, to a libretto from ancient Russian chronicles telling the tale of a Russian city that disappears under the surface of a lake in the year 6751 after the Creation to save itself from Tatar invasion while the saintly maiden Fevronia is taken prisoner, with an apotheosis in which she joins her slain bridegroom in a transfigured eternal Kitezh, with church bells pealing majestically, the score rich in Wagnerian undertones (which caused it to be described as the Russian *Parsifal*), employing the scale of alternating tones and semitones to depict the Mongolian horde in a symphonic interlude, asymmetrically divided meters in modal chants, and a highly colorful orchestration, is produced at the Imperial Theater in St. Petersburg.

21 FEBRUARY 1907

A Village Romeo and Juliet, fourth and the most important opera by Frederick DELIUS, in three acts with a prologue, after a story (based on an actual event that occurred in Germany in 1847) dealing with two neighboring children of opposite sexes forbidden by their feuding parents to intermingle, who hold secret trysts and, upon maturity become lovers and elope on a stolen river barge but, perturbed by the wickedness of their unsanctified bliss, scuttle it and in the last ecstatic embrace float to their chilly deaths, the score presenting a musicorama of romantic nature painting contrasted with the brooding quality of human peripeteia elaborated with the aid of para-Wagnerian thematic identifications and tesselated with artful canonic developments, is

performed for the first time in a German version by Mrs. Jelka Delius (translated from a discarded English version made by a friend of Delius) under the title *Romeo und Julia auf dem Dorfe* at the Kroll Opera House in Berlin.

22 FEBRUARY 1907

Introduction et Allegro by Maurice RAVEL, for harp solo, string quartet, flute and clarinet, wherein contrasting sonorities float atmospherically suspended in an exquisitely incorporeal equilibrium, with the principal tonality of six flats assuming pentatonic or modal guises by facile tonal elision, while thematic phrases waft over the columnar shafts of ninth-chords, is performed for the first time at the Cercle Musical in Paris.

1 MARCH 1907

DEBUSSY'S *La Mer* receives its first American performance as the impeccably Germanic Dr. Karl Muck courageously conducts it with the Boston Symphony Orchestra for an audience of easily discomfited dowagers, quiet academically minded New England music lovers, and irascible music critics. (The first New York performance of *La Mer* took place on 21 March 1907, given also by Dr. Muck with the Boston Symphony.)

When we read the title of the first of the sea sketches Debussy—*From Dawn till Noon*—we feared that we were to have a movement seven hours long. It was not so long, but it was terrible while it lasted . . .. Frenchmen are notoriously bad sailors, and a Gallic picture of the sea is apt to run more to stewards and basins and lemons than to wild majesty of Poseidon. We clung like a drowning man to a few fragments of the tonal wreck, a bit of a theme here, and a comprehensible figure there, but finally this muted-horn sea overwhelmed us. If this be Music, we would much prefer to leave the Heavenly Maid until she has got over her hysterics. (Louis C. Elson, Boston *Daily Advertiser,* 4 March 1907)

The Sea is persistently ugly. . . . It is prosaic in its reiteration of inert formulas. Debussy fails to give any impression of the sea. . . . There is more of barnyard cackle in it than anything else. (New York *Times,* 22 March 1907)

The Sea of Debussy does not call for many words of comment. The three parts of which it is composed are entitled *From Dawn till Noon, Play of the Waves* and *Dialogue of the Wind and the Sea,* but as far as any pictorial suggestiveness is concerned, they might as well have been entitled *On the Flatiron Building, Slumming in the Bowery* and *A Glimpse of Chinatown During a Raid.* Debussy's music is the dreariest kind of rubbish. Does anybody for a moment doubt that Debussy would not write such chaotic, meaningless, cacophonous, ungrammatical stuff, if he could invent a melody? . . . Even his orchestration is not particularly remarkable. M. Loeffler of Boston is far more original from this point of view. (New York *Post,* 22 March 1907)

New York heard a new composition called *The Sea,* and New York is probably still wondering why. The work is by the most modern of modern Frenchmen, Debussy. . . . Compared with this, the most abstruse compositions of Richard Strauss are as primer stories to hear and to comprehend. (New York *World,* 22 March 1907)

We believe that Shakespeare means Debussy's ocean when he speaks of taking up arms against a sea of troubles. It may be possible, however, that in the transit to America the title of this work has been changed. It is possible that Debussy did not intend to call it *La Mer,* but *Le Mal de Mer,* which would at once make the tone-picture as clear as day. It is a series of symphonic pictures of seasickness. The first movement is *Headache*. The second is *Doubt*, picturing moments of dread suspense, whether or no! The third movement, with its explosions and rumblings, has now a self-evident purpose. The hero is endeavoring to throw up his boot-heels! (Louis C. Elson, Boston *Daily Advertiser*, 22 April 1907)

1 MARCH 1907

La Faute de l' Abbé Mouret, "pièce avec musique" in four acts by Alfred BRUNEAU, set for spoken dialogue accompanied by orchestra, to his own libretto from Zola's novelette of the same name, wherein a young unbeneficed secular ecclesiastic in Provence, seduced by flesh in the person of a 16-year-old parishioner, suffers agonies of spirit before rebounding to his prelapsarian prelature, with a score illustratively contrasting the two sundering forces in tumescently sonorous harmonies and ascetically repressive monodies, is performed for the first time in Paris.

2 MARCH 1907

Ein Walzertraum, operetta in three acts by Oskar STRAUS, dealing with the foundering marriage of the princess of Snobia happily salvaged after she takes a course of exotic *ars amandi* from her husband's Gypsy mistress, is produced in Vienna.

2 MARCH 1907

Monna Vanna, opera in three acts by Emil ABRÁNYI, after the play by Maeterlinck, is produced in Budapest.

2 MARCH 1907

O Amor e Perdicão (Love and Perdition), opera in three acts by João Marcelino ARROYO, Minister of Education and Fine Arts in the cabinet of the last King of Portugal Manuel, composed in a Wagneromantically Tristanomorphic parachromatic idiom, is produced in Lisbon.

5 MARCH 1907

Lee DE FOREST, the American wizard of the cathode rays, succeeds in transmitting by wireless a performance of Rossini's *William Tell* overture from Telharmonic Hall in New York to the Brooklyn Navy Yard, marking the first broadcast of a musical composition.

There's music in the air about the roof of the Hotel Normandie these days. A good deal of it is being collected by wireless telephone ready for distribution to possible purchasers. (New York *Tribune*, 7 March 1907)

9 MARCH 1907

Arnold SCHOENBERG finishes the composition of *Friede auf Erden*, a Christmas ballad for chorus a cappella set in dissonantly harsh harmonies obliquely tending towards ultimate tonality and depicting the peace on earth of the title by explicit key signatures.

14 MARCH 1907

Stara Baśń (An Old Tale), opera by the 69-year-old Polish composer Wladislaw ZELEŃSKI, is produced in Lwów.

17 MARCH 1907

Théodora, music drama in three acts by Xavier LE-ROUX, to a libretto dealing with the adventurous life of the 6th-century Empress Regnant of Byzantium, with a musical setting rich in allusive orientalisms, is produced in Monte Carlo.

19 MARCH 1907

Edward ELGAR, the Edwardian English composer of marvelously outspoken and hearty symphonic and choral music, makes his first American appearance conducting the Oratorio Society of New York City in a performance of his reverentially reverberant oratorio *The Apostles*. (This was not Elgar's first American appearance, but his third; previous appearances were in 1905 and 1906.)

19 MARCH 1907

Das ewige Feuer, one-act opera by Richard WETZ, is produced in Düsseldorf.

22 MARCH 1907

Second Symphony by the Norwegian composer Christian SINDING is performed for the first time in Berlin.

12 APRIL 1907

Salome, tone poem by Henry HADLEY, inspired by Oscar Wilde's play and composed in 1905 before the production of Strauss's famous opera, wherein Salome moans concupiscently in quasi-oriental but neatly arranged arabesques, the prophet curses her in trombones, Herod enters with heraldic fanfares, and the decapitation is accomplished with shocked pauses, is performed for the first time by the Boston Symphony Orchestra, Karl Muck conducting.

13 APRIL 1907

Les Enfants à Bethléem, Christmas oratorio by Gabriel PIERNÉ, to a poetic story of children guided by a soprano-voiced star to the manger where the Christ Child, pale and underweight, is tenderly tended by a devout ox (tenor) and a perspicacious ass (baritone) exhaling animal warmth in the December chill, the musical idiom eclectically combining quasi-Gallic folksong melos with solemn organum-like harmony, is performed for the first time in Amsterdam.

15 APRIL 1907

Gloria, lyric drama in three acts by Francesco CILÈA, dealing with the internecine strife in 14th-century Siena, ending in a double tragedy when Gloria's young husband is slain and she kills herself, is produced at La Scala in Milan.

17 APRIL 1907

Circe, lyric drama in three acts by P. L. HILLE-MACHER (actually two brothers, Paul and Lucien, both former Prix de Rome winners), a conventional operatic portrait of the Homeric enchantress from whose dehumanizing magic Ulysses was protected by a fabulous herb, receives its belated first production, ten years after its composition, at the Opéra-Comique in Paris on the same bill with *La*

Légende du point d'Argentan, one-act opera by the 27-year-old French composer Félix FOURDRAIN, to a story about a poor lacewoman trying to win a prize for needle point such as was practiced in Argentan (hence the title) supernaturally helped by a chorus of angels who weave a divinely inspired mantle under the instructions of a Gothic Madonna descended from a Fra Angelico fresco.

17 APRIL 1907

Tom Jones, comic opera by Edward GERMAN after the celebrated novel by Fielding, *The History of Tom Jones, a Foundling*, in which the multifutuent hero turns out to be the natural son of the sister of a highly puritanical moralist, the libretto and the musical setting couched in the style made familiar in the operettas of Gilbert and Sullivan, is produced at the Apollo Theater in London.

20 APRIL 1907

Souvenirs, symphonic threnody by Vincent D'INDY in memory of his wife, the *bien aimée* of the dedication, with the principal theme (taken from his youthful *Poème des Montagnes*) intoned by a griefstricken English horn, followed by an agitated section characterizing Madame d'Indy's vitality in life, and concluded with a solo on a muted small trumpet, is performed for the first time at a concert of the Société Nationale in Paris.

27 APRIL 1907

First Symphony by Igor STRAVINSKY, dedicated "to my dear teacher Nicolai Andreyevich Rimsky-Korsakov," in E-flat major, set in four traditional movements: (1) *Allegro moderato*, in 4/4 time in strict sonata form, (2) *Scherzo*, in 2/4 time, with a trio section very Russian in melody, somewhat akin to the folksong *Down the Street*, utilized in *Petrushka*, (3) *Largo*, in 2/4 time in G-sharp minor, and (4) *Finale, Allegro molto*, with a triumphant ending in glorious E-flat major, in the style of Glazunov, is performed for the first time in St. Petersburg, at a private concert of the orchestra of the Imperial Chapel. (The first public performance was given by the same orchestra on 5 February 1908.)

27 APRIL 1907

Sperduti nel buio (Lost in the Dark), opera in three acts by the 28-year-old Sicilian composer Stefano DONAUDY (who had his first opera performed at the age of 13) is produced in Palermo.

9 MAY 1907

Two centuries have passed since the death in Lübeck of Dietrich BUXTEHUDE, the great organist of Danish extraction, whom to hear Handel and Bach made arduous journeys.

10 MAY 1907

The first performance is given at the Opéra-Comique in Paris of *Ariane et Barbe-bleue*, fairy tale in three acts by Paul DUKAS, depicting in liquescent sonorities the elusively symbolic drama of Maurice Maeterlinck, wherein Ariane, the sixth wife of Bluebeard, opens not only the five doors behind which she finds sparkling jewels, but also the forbidden sixth door which leads to a darksome casement where Bluebeard's five former wives are kept, and sets them free, emaciated but alive (among them one named Mélisande whose appearance is signalized by a quotation from Debussy's *Pelléas et Mélisande*, Act I, Scene III), while the crowd outside assaults Bluebeard who is brought bleeding into the castle, arousing unexpected pity among his abused wives who elect to stay with him and let Ariane depart alone from the scene of the "délivrance inutile" (the original subtitle of the play), to a symphonically conceived setting, with voices singing in prosodically measured recitative, their delicate melorhythms gliding radiantly across the columnar supports of ninth-chords and of finely equilibrated pandiatonic structures while opulent whole-tone scales flow alongside in recurrent streams.

The Maeterlinck drama might perhaps dispense with a musical commentary, but these personages in *Ariane et Barbe-bleue* move about in a somewhat imprecise atmosphere and express themselves in a rather remote manner. The music of Paul Dukas, so strong, so precise, so eloquent, does it not shed a little light that enables us to gain better grasp of their nature, does it not bring us closer to their actions and make their utterances more vibrant and more articulate? In a dreamy world, conjured up by the poet, what marvelous aid is this pictorial music! What magical sonorities, what variety, what invention in this phantasmagoria of precious stones falling in a cataract of emeralds, sapphires, pearls, rubies!. . . . How I rejoice in seeing our music enriched by such a gem! (Gabriel Fauré in *Le Figaro*, Paris, 11 May 1907)

The score of Paul Dukas is very significant from the standpoint of the present state of mind. Written with rare technical ability, it floats between two opposite tendencies: here and there, classical in the noble sense of the word, it is subject to influences of the current fashion that one could call *modern style*. In what does it consist? First of all, and particularly, in one characteristic fact: an absolute exclusion of melody. Note that the question does not concern those sugary vocalizations that one justly despises. No, we speak of the expressive and inspired melody, such as was understood by Rameau and Gluck, Beethoven and Schumann, as well as César Franck and Wagner. And by what is it replaced? It is a grave question, because the entire future of music is at stake. I am not praising, I am not condemning. I merely expound the situation. (Arthur Coquard, *Echo de Paris*, 11 May 1907)

16 MAY 1907

Miller R. HUTCHISON files at the U.S. Patent Office the original application for his invention, a motor-driven Diaphragm Actuated Horn and Resonator, for use as a signal in automobiles, which under the trade name Klaxon became a musical instrument used in various orchestral scores of the automobile age, including Gershwin's symphonic tableau *An American in Paris*. (The patent was granted on 3 May 1910; it was subsequently acquired by F. Hallett Lovell, manufacturer and distributor, who died on 19 May 1962 at the age of 94.)

16 MAY 1907

Under the auspices of the Société des Grandes Auditions Musicales de France, Serge DIAGHILEV presents in Paris the first of the five "historic concerts" of Russian music, with RIMSKY-KORSAKOV and GLAZUNOV conducting their own works, RACHMANINOFF playing his *Second Piano Concerto*, Arthur Nikisch and Camille Chevillard conducting orchestral and operatic excerpts by Glinka, Borodin, Balakirev, Mussorgsky, Cui, Tchaikovsky, Scriabin, Liapunov, Liadov and Alexander Taneyev (uncle of Sergei Taneyev and holder of an influential position at the Tsarist Court who obtained a subsidy of 70,000 rubles in gold for the concerts), and featuring the first appearance in Paris of Feodor Chaliapin. (The other four concerts took place on 19, 23, 26 and 30 May 1907.)

Chaliapin made such an impression at the opening concert that the audience, containing many Russians, insisted upon endless recalls. Nikisch finally emerged and, mounting the podium, awaited an opportunity to begin the closing number. But he was not permitted to make a start. Finally, with a gesture of despair, he descended from the podium and beckoned the orchestra to leave. (*The Musical Courier,* New York, 5 June 1907)

In May 1907 Richard Strauss conducted in Paris several performances of his opera *Salome;* Rimsky-Korsakov attended one of them. He met Strauss at a reception, but their personal acquaintance did not go beyond an exchange of a few chance remarks. For Rimsky-Korsakov knew Strauss's comments on Russian music: "We are no longer children." (Annotations to the Russian Edition of Rimsky-Korsakov's *Chronicle of My Life,* Moscow, 1935, by Andrei Rimsky-Korsakov)

Our American composers, if they had as good an opportunity at home as have Russians who are supported financially and morally by the government, by society, by the Court, and by the people, would produce as good and palatable music. . . . The Russians have said au revoir, but the Russian music has said good-bye; it is gone never to return to Paris. (*The Musical Courier,* New York, 19 June 1907)

24 MAY 1907

La Catalane, lyric drama in four acts by the Belgian-born Paris-educated 45-year-old composer Fernand LE BORNE, after the celebrated Catalan play *Terra Baixa* by Angel Guimerá (which also supplied the libretto for Eugen d'Albert's opera *Tiefland*) wherein a simple-minded mountain shepherd who innocently marries the discarded mistress of a rich farmer in the valley avenges her dishonor by strangling him to death, set to music in an effective lyrico-dramatic manner of the composer's master Massenet, is produced at the Paris Opéra.

26 MAY 1907

The Bach Museum is formally dedicated in the house where he was born in Eisenach on 21 March 1685, the permanent collection containing the old clavichord on which Bach played, contemporary portraits, manuscripts, letters and other pertinent documents.

4 JUNE 1907

Otho Visconti, opera in three acts by the German-bred American composer Frederick Grant GLEASON, to his own libretto dealing with the monstrous "viper of Milan" who founded in the 13th century the politically powerful Visconti family, with a score dramatically luxuriating in the uncoagulated plasma of Germanic romanticism, is performed for the first and last time, two and a half years after his death, in Chicago where he dwelt as a respected pedagogue from 1876. (According to the terms of his will, other operas left among his manuscripts were not to be studied or performed until fifty years after his death, which occurred in Chicago on 6 December 1903.)

5 JUNE 1907

Fortunio, "comédie musicale" in five acts by André MESSAGER, after Alfred de Musset's play *Le Chandelier,* dealing with gallant intrigues among 18th-century immoralists, wherein a clerk in the office of a middle-aged notary serves as a candle carrier to light the way for clandestine meetings between his employer's young wife and a dashing army captain, with Fortunio's fortune brightened when he becomes the lover and the captain the chandelier, to an appropriately gay setting abounding in grandiloquently humorous arias and vocal ensembles, is produced at the Opéra-Comique in Paris.

12 JUNE 1907

Alexander GLAZUNOV is awarded the honorary degree of Doctor in Music by the University of Cambridge, England.

Gaudium nostrum cumulavit hodie vir in arte musica insignis, qui Russorum in imperio maximo iam per annos quinque et viginti in luce publica versatus, primum abhinc annos decem Britanniae innotuit. Argumenta magna vir magnus aggressus, popularium suorum artis musicae hodiernae in "Raymonda" praesertim documentum splendidum protulisse dicitur. Inter peritos vero constat, "nympham pulchram dormientem" illiam a Tschaikovskio, doctore olim nostro, musicis modis accommodatam, quasi statuarum elegantissimarum ordinem effingere; viri huius autem "Raymondam" figuris potius ex aere fusis immensis comparari. Iuvat nunc iterum ex imperio Russorum ad nos advectum salutare magistrorum in arte musica magnorum aemulum, qui artis suae genus pulchrum, genus severum et sobrium repraesentat, patriaeque cantus populares non minus fideliter quam feliciter exprimit. (Text of the speech delivered by the Public Orator in presenting to the Chancellor the recipient of the honorary degree of Doctor in Music)

18 JUNE 1907

Alexander GLAZUNOV is awarded the honorary degree of Doctor in Music by Oxford University.

26 JUNE 1907

Camille SAINT-SAËNS is awarded the honorary degree of Doctor in Music by Oxford University.

1 JULY 1907

KALEIDOSKOP: ORIGINAL THEME AND VARIATIONS for orchestra by the Austrian-born composer Heinrich NOREN, with the last variation, dedicated "to a celebrated contemporary," making use of the themes of the hero and the antagonists from *Ein Heldenleben* by Richard Strauss, is performed for the first time in Dresden. (Although Strauss graciously accepted the homage, his publishers sued Noren for infringement of copyright, but lost when the Royal Court of Dresden ruled that the Strauss motives represent "a conscious negation of melody" and therefore cannot be construed as recognizable musical materials subject to protection by copyright.)

27 JULY 1907

Der fidele Bauer, operetta in two acts by Leo FALL, in which an inhibited German professor tries to conceal his peasant origin but is freed from his acquired snobbishness when his semi-aristocratic wife welcomes his demi-rustic relatives as equals, is produced in Mannheim.

15 AUGUST 1907

Joseph JOACHIM, Hungarian violin virtuoso, one of the greatest interpreters of classical music, whose playing, according to the acoustical measurements made by Helmholtz, was more precise in just intonation than any other's, the founder in Berlin in 1869 of the superlative Joachim Quartet, devoted friend of Brahms who dedicated his violin concerto to him, and teacher of two generations of ascending violinists, dies in Berlin at the age of 76 years, one month and 18 days.

22 AUGUST 1907

La Princesse Maleine, symphonic poem by Cyril SCOTT, inspired by the poignant drama of Maurice Maeterlinck, set in impressionistic harmonies interspersed with neo-archaic modalities (the organ enters in open fifths when the Beguines begin their sermon), evolving into a polychromatic tempest and concluding with a matutinal cockcrow solo, is performed for the first time in London.

24 AUGUST 1907

Pomp and Circumstance No. 4, the most famous of the grandly imperial orchestral marches by the sublimely British composer Edward ELGAR, containing the stirring middle section, later adapted to the rousing text, *Song of Freedom* by A. P. Herbert, is performed for the first time in London.

4 SEPTEMBER 1907

Edvard GRIEG, "Chopin of the North," whose strikingly colorful and romantically saturated piano pieces, songs and symphonic suites reflect and enhance the lyric poetry and rhythmic vivacity of Norwegian folk songs and dances, and who made the characteristic cadential fall from the leading tone to the fifth in a minor key the true hallmark of Scandinavian modality, dies in his native Bergen at the age of 64.

Mr. Grieg stayed at the Hotel Norge in Bergen during the last few days, and intended to leave for Christiania yesterday; his luggage had already been taken on board. At noon, however, he complained of feeling ill, and, as the symptoms appeared to be serious, was removed to the hospital. His wife was with him all night, and at half-past three in the morning he passed away peacefully. (London *Times*, 5 September 1907)

25 SEPTEMBER 1907

Jean SIBELIUS conducts in Helsingfors the first performance of his *Third Symphony* (composed in 1904–1907), concisely set in three compact movements, with the principal key of C major:

(1) *Allegro moderato*, with a foreboding motto in low register, gathering strength in proclamatory brass while the strings are engaged in rhythmed propulsion, ending with a plagally cadenced chorale; (2) *Andantino con moto quasi Allegretto*, in G-sharp minor, a somberly questioning, modally inflected musical essay; (3) *Allegro*, with dramatically crisscrossing chains of parallel thirds and sixths in oblique modalities teleologically tending towards the ultimate catharsis of immaculate C major.

27 SEPTEMBER 1907

Ralph VAUGHAN WILLIAMS conducts at the Cardiff Festival the world premières of his *Norfolk Rhapsody No. 2*, in D minor, and *Norfolk Rhapsody No. 3* in G minor. (Both works were subsequently discarded by Vaughan Williams, and remained unpublished.)

8 OCTOBER 1907

For Valor, concert overture by the 31-year-old English composer Havergal BRIAN, composed in 1902 and inspired by a passage from Walt Whitman's *Drum Taps*, is performed for the first time in London, Henry Wood conducting.

15 OCTOBER 1907

Variationen und Fuge über ein lustiges Thema von Johann Adam Hiller (the inviting adjective "lustiges" was added by the publisher to original title), op. 100, by Max REGER, a series of eleven variations elaborating an unassuming folk-like tune from a singspiel written by Hiller in 1771 to a maximum of polyphonic density through canonic imitation, thematic augmentation, contrapuntal permutation and harmonic inspissation, concluding with a magisterial double fugue, is performed for the first time in Cologne.

15 OCTOBER 1907

Gustav MAHLER conducts his last performance at the Vienna Opera as its Music Director, before departure for America as conductor of the New York Metropolitan Opera Orchestra.

The hour has come marking the end of our work together. I am now taking leave of a place that has become dear to me. . . . Not always have my efforts been crowned with success. No one bears greater responsibility for the overcoming the resistance of the material and attaining a treacherously elusive objective than a practicing artist. . . . I have done my best to subordinate my person to the task at hand and my inclinations to my duty. I have not spared myself, and I felt that I could demand also from others that they exert their strength to the utmost. Under the pressure of the battle, in the heat of the moment, neither you nor I have escaped injuries and errors. But the work has been done and the task has been fulfilled. (From Mahler's letter addressed to the orchestra of the Vienna Opera, published in *Signale für die musikalische Welt*, Berlin, 18 December 1907)

26 OCTOBER 1907

Die Role Gret, first opera in three acts by the Vienna composer Julius BITTNER, to his own libretto derived from an Austrian folk tale, is produced in Frankfurt.

29 OCTOBER 1907

Shafras, lyric drama by the Argentine composer Constantino GAITO to an Italian libretto, the central character Shafras being a heroic Gypsy during the repression of the tribe in the Ottoman Empire, is produced in Buenos Aires.

1 NOVEMBER 1907

RIMSKY-KORSAKOV completes the composition of his orchestral piece *Neapolitan Song*, a fantasy on the celebrated ballad *Funiculi, funicula* by Luigi Denza, mistaken for a genuine anonymous folksong, as it was also mistaken by Richard Strauss in an early symphonic poem *Aus Italien*. (*Neapolitan Song* was put in rehearsal at a concert conducted by Siloti in St. Petersburg on 10 December 1907, but Rimsky-Korsakov found the piece unsatisfactory and cancelled its performance.)

2 NOVEMBER 1907

Die Dollarprinzessin, operetta by Leo FALL, exhilaratingly propounding the legend of the Plenipotential Dollar, personified by a Chicago heiress who regards European nobility as a purchasable commodity but in the end marries an untitled German for love, while her widowed father enters matrimony with a moderately voluptuous Russian songstress, is produced in Vienna.

6 NOVEMBER 1907

Le Chemineau, lyric drama in four acts by Xavier LEROUX, after a poem by Jean Richepin, wherein a rootless wayfarer seduces a farm girl in a Burgundian village, leaves her pregnant, but exhibits sudden paternal interest in his son while passing through the same village twenty years later and succeeds in mending the latter's broken romance with a girl whose family discovers the young man's bastardy, to a dramatically effective score with some lyrically pleasing arias, is produced at the Opéra-Comique in Paris.

7 NOVEMBER 1907

Piano Quintet by Anton von WEBERN is performed for the first time in Vienna at a concert of works by students of Arnold Schoenberg.

9 NOVEMBER 1907

Marcella, opera by Umberto GIORDANO, in three episodes bearing descriptive subtitles: (1) *Trovata*, wherein a disillusioned artist's model is found in a Paris café-chantant by a young expatriate painter; (2) *Amata*, wherein she is loved by him; (3) *Abandonnata*, wherein she is abandoned by her lover who confesses that he is no painter but the legitimate heir to a distant Slavic throne to which he is summoned by his oppressed people to wrest the reins of the reign from the imbecilic hands of his senile father fallen under the sway of greedy and cruel ministers, with a musical setting expertly synthesizing the Parisian music of other Italian operas, from *La Traviata* to *La Bohème,* is produced at La Scala in Milan.

9 NOVEMBER 1907

Tragédie de Salomé, "mute drama" by Florent SCHMITT, in five symphonic episodes (*Prelude, Danses de perles, Les enchantements sur la mer, Danse des éclairs, Danse de l'effroi*) with serpentine melismas and asymmetrical rhythms illustrating the fibrillar spasms of Salome's body as she strives to please Herod with her voluptuous whirlings, and culminating in the horror of the decapitation of John the Baptist portrayed in a "dance of fear" in an asymmetric time signature notated 3 + 1/2/4, and savagely dissonant harmonies, is performed for the first time in Paris in a version for chamber orchestra. (A performance for large orchestra took place in Paris at a Colonne concert on 8 January 1911.)

11 NOVEMBER 1907

Paolo e Francesca, one-act opera by Luigi MANCI-NELLI, after Dante's tale of the two unfortunate lovers, is produced in Bologna.

21 NOVEMBER 1907

Gaetano BRAGA, Italian composer of eight operas and of the perennially nostalgic song *Angel's Serenade*, dies in Milan at the age of 78.

22 NOVEMBER 1907

A Pagan Poem for orchestra and piano obbligato by the Alsatian-born American composer Charles Martin LOEFFLER, inspired by the 8th Eclogue of Virgil written in 39 B.C., wherein a country girl sings magic songs to bring her truant lover back from the city (three trumpets off stage represent the imploration, "Ducite ab urbe domum, mea carmina, ducite Daphnim"), the pagan timelessness being conjured up by the inclusion of a pair of antique cymbals and tam-tam in the orchestra, while the spirit of the young 20th century is sustained by impressionistically fluid streams of arpeggios in the piano part and intermittent precipitation of whole-tone scales elsewhere, with columnar ninth-chords resonantly placed to attain temporary harmonic stability and interstitial chromatics supplying the needs of greater cohesion within a basically tonal framework bearing a permanent key signature of two flats, is performed for the first time by the Boston Symphony Orchestra, Karl Muck conducting. (Originally written for a chamber group in 1901, and first performed at the home of Isabella Stewart Gardner in Boston on 13 April 1903.)

We consider *A Pagan Poem* to be Mr. Loeffler's greatest work. Its mastery of orchestration is wonderful, and its ingenuity of figure development equally phenomenal. Surely, if the modern school becomes permanent, Mr. Loeffler will be reckoned among its greatest exponents. He is not so purely cerebral as the bitter Vincent d'Indy nor as romantic as the fawning Debussy. He is as great as either of them—or greater. (Louis C. Elson, Boston *Advertiser,* 27 November 1907)

Mr. Loeffler's music will not stale with many repetitions for in substance and in expression *A Pagan Poem* is a masterpiece of musical eloquence. Mr. Loeffler before this has composed music of indisputable originality. With it, he has risen to a still greater height, and at the same time he has sounded a still more emotional depth—a composer of true genius. (Philip Hale, the Boston *Herald,* 15 March 1908)

The text of Mr. Loeffler's *Pagan Poem* ran: "Fetch water forth and twine the altars here with the soft fillet and burn resinous twigs and male frankincense that I may try by magic rites to turn my lover's sense from sanity" from Virgil's 8th Eclogue; that is to say, something uncanny was happening, and this was emphasized by the ominous sound of trumpets in three-part harmonies. It was an effort to listen for nearly half an hour. (London *Times,* October 1917)

24 NOVEMBER 1907

Lady Godiva, overture by the Czech composer Vítězslav NOVÁK, celebrating in luscious romantic tones the legendary English noblewoman who ignored the trombone threats of her 11th-century feudal husband and took a noontime ride through the streets of Coventry totally denuded, caressed by four solo violins and bathed in the coda in warm E major, pianissimo, to win the human rights and freedom from excessive taxation for her vassals, is performed for the first time in Prague.

25 NOVEMBER 1907

Le Pavillion d'Armide, ballet by Nicolas TCHEREPNIN, after Théophile Gautier's poem *Omphale*, in which a French viscount dreams of a Gobelin tapestry in his bedroom coming to life and imagines himself to be the crusader Rinaldo held in a delectably oriental subjection at the pavilion of the seductive Armida, as Hercules was held by Omphale, to a musical score full of agreeable Franco-Russian sounds, is performed for the first time in St. Petersburg.

1 DECEMBER 1907

Two centuries have elapsed since the death by his own hand of Jeremiah CLARKE, English composer, and real author of the celebrated *Trumpet Voluntary* whose authorship was long ascribed to Purcell.

3 DECEMBER 1907

Tragaldabas (Der geborgte Ehemann), one-act opera by the Germanized Scottish-born composer Eugen D'ALBERT, wherein a professional pauper hired to pose socially as a wealthy lady's husband, is dismissed when he becomes unduly familiar with her, and is given the job to impersonate a recently deceased ape in a circus, is produced in Hamburg.

7 DECEMBER 1907

V Tatrach (In the Tatras), symphonic poem by the Czech composer Vítězslav NOVÁK, painting in romantically dramatic Smetanesque tones the beauty and the eerie mystery of the Tatra mountains of the Carpathian range (Novák was an ardent Alpinist), is performed for the first time in Prague.

14 DECEMBER 1907

The Wand of Youth, subtitled *Music to a Child's Play*, symphonic suite in seven movements by Edward ELGAR, originally composed by him for piano at the age of twelve and orchestrated 37 years later, is performed for the first time in London.

19 DECEMBER 1907

Soléa, lyric drama in four acts by Isidore DE LARA, London-born composer whose original name was Cohen, to a libretto by Jean Richepin, set in the island of Rhodes in 1522, wherein a proudly virginal Gypsy girl single-handedly foils a local traitor in dramatic recitative, slays a spy to the accompaniment of muted trumpets, fires a fairly effective cannon shot at the besieging Turkish flotilla to the roll of a bass drum, inspires a transitory naval victory in a symphonic interlude bristling with syncopated Ottoman melodies, and in the last act blows up an enemy magazine in a loud explosion of descending chromatic scales while locked in a harmonious embrace with a noble Greek-born Knight Hospitaller of St. John of Jerusalem, is produced with a German libretto in Cologne.

27 DECEMBER 1907

Henry HADLEY conducts the Berlin Philharmonic Orchestra in the first performance anywhere of his *Third Symphony* in B minor (completed in Munich on 1 August 1906), conceived in an exuberantly Germanic vein, in four movements: *Moderato e maestoso*, *Andante* (in the spirit of an Angelus, with three large church bells in the orchestra), *Scherzo*, and *Allegro*.

27 DECEMBER 1907

Matteo Falcone, dramatic scene by César CUI, after a novella of Prosper Mérimée, dealing with the passions and perils among Corsican contrabandists during Napoleonic wars, is produced in Moscow.

1908

1 JANUARY 1908

Gustav MAHLER makes his first appearance in the United States, conducting *Tristan und Isolde* at the Metropolitan Opera in New York.

2 JANUARY 1908

At the aristocratic Paris salon of Armande de Polignac, patroness of arts, the avant-garde pianist Blanche SELVA, plays for the first time the three pieces of the third book from the piano suite *Iberia* by Isaac ALBÉNIZ, *El Albaicín*, *El Polo* and *Lavapiés*.

In *El Albaicín* one finds the atmosphere of those Spanish nights that radiate the fragrance of carnation and aguardiente. . . . It is like the muffled sounds of a guitar complaining in the night. (Claude Debussy, in the *Bulletin français de la Société Indépendante de Musique*, Paris, 1 December 1913)

18 JANUARY 1908

Brigg Fair, "English Rhapsody" for orchestra by Frederick DELIUS, in variation form, with some interstitial unrelated materials, based on a Lincolnshire country tune in lilting pastoral time, in a Dorian mode with a characteristic cadential plagal subtonic, dedicated to Percy Grainger who originally notated the song (the title of the piece being derived from the line in the refrain, "Unto Brigg Fair I did repair"), is performed for the first time in Liverpool, Granville Bantock conducting.

(Sir Thomas Beecham in his biography of Delius, New York, 1960, states, on p. 149, that *Brigg Fair* was first performed at Basel, Switzerland, in January 1908, by Hermann Suter, preceding its initial English performances. This is in error, for Hermann Suter, who was conductor of the Basel concert series from 1902, did not produce *Brigg Fair* until 13 November 1910; the original program of that concert states that it was the first local performance in Basel of the piece. Perhaps Beecham confused *Brigg Fair* with another work by Delius, *Dance Rhapsody,* written in 1908, which was dedicated to Hermann Suter.)

20 JANUARY 1908

DEBUSSY marries the affluent and socially influential divorcée Mme Bardac after divorcing the poor and socially inadequate Rosalie Texier, who was his mistress and subsequently wife during the years of composition of *Pelléas et Mélisande.*

21 JANUARY 1908

Der Mann mit den drei Frauen, operetta by Franz LEHÁR, positing in gayly waltzing and polkaing rhythms the horns of the modern trilemma of de facto trigamy among philogynous men, is produced in Vienna.

21 JANUARY 1908

Sternengebot (The Stars' Command), opera in three acts by Siegfried WAGNER, son of Richard Wagner and grandson of Liszt, to his own libretto dealing with the power struggle among the Ripuarian Franks of the 10th century, wherein a German ruler, informed by an astrologer that the house of his chief tribal rival is to inherit his throne, orders the whole enemy clan slain but lets a youngling inadvertently escape only to discover that he is his own bastard son, the score presenting a weird simulacrum of the composer's father's music dramas and his grandfather's mystical rhapsodism, is performed for the first time in Hamburg.

23 JANUARY 1908

At his debut as conductor outside Russia, Serge KOUSSEVITSKY presents in Berlin an orchestral concert of Russian music including the world première of the *Second Symphony* of Reinhold GLIÈRE, conceived in an epical style, with occasional orientalisms imparting an exotic touch to the broadly diatonic Russian melodies, in four movements:

(1) *Allegro pesante,* in 4/4 time, in majestically flowing C minor; (2) *Allegro giocoso,* a scherzo in 2/4 time in G minor; (3) *Andante con variazoni,* in F minor, in 3/4 time, with a fugally propulsive last variation; (4) *Allegro vivace,* returning to the initial C minor, in 12/8 time, presenting a sonorous panorama of Russian laetification.

23 JANUARY 1908

Edward MACDOWELL, the first truly national composer of America, whose talent, fostered in German institutions of musical learning, retained nonetheless the spirit of free American rhythmic song, but whose mind collapsed, reducing him to a pathetic state of second infancy, dies in New York at the age of 46 years, one month and 5 days.

E. A. MacDowell Dead—Noted Composer and Pianist Passes Away at Home Here.—Dr. Edward A. MacDowell, the composer and pianist, died about 8 o'clock last night in his apartment at the Westminster Hotel, Irving Place and 16th Street, following a long illness. . . . In the spring of 1905 overwork and insomnia brought on what eminent medical specialists pronounced to be a hopeless case of cerebral collapse. This it proved to be. Under the devoted care of his wife, he lived on, spending the summer months at Peterboro, New Hampshire, the winter at his apartment in the Westminster Hotel, in New York, oblivious to all the things which had once occupied a peculiarly active and sensitive mind. (New York *Tribune,* 24 January, 1908)

25 JANUARY 1908

Baldie, lyric drama in three acts in Flemish by the Belgian composer Jean BLOCKX, wherein an unscrupulous but prosperous 18th-century Flemish farmer named Baldie insidiously abuses the innocence of a village belle during the temporary absence of her artistic fiancé (he sculpts), plunging her into melancholy, inappetence and terminal inanition, with condign punishment meted out to him by her sister who stabs him to death with a kitchen knife during a colorful kermess, set to tumultuous music enlivened by Netherlandish dance tunes, is performed for the first time in Antwerp.

(A completely revised version of the story which replaces the violation of chastity by an honest rivalry between two suitors of unimpeachable integrity culminating in a bloodless duel with bows and arrows and a subsequent triumph of selective love, with the musical score essentially unaltered, was staged for the first time under the title *Liefdelied,* i.e., *Song of Love,* in Antwerp, on 14 January 1912.)

25 JANUARY 1908

Leili and Medzhnun, first opera by the 23-year-old Shusha-born Azerbaijan composer Uzeir GADZHIBEKOV, to his own libretto, after an ancient Caucasian legend dealing with the tragic love of a fearless warrior for a beauteous mountain maiden, written in a homophonic style making use of native instruments in the orchestra, is produced in Baku, the heroine's part being sung by a man in deference to the Moslem customs forbidding the appearance of women on the stage, and conducted by an amateur musician ignorant of written notes.

1 FEBRUARY 1908

Claude DEBUSSY conducts, in Queen's Hall, London, his *Prélude à l'Après-midi d' un Faune* and *La Mer.*

With all the wealth of picturesque orchestration and piquant harmony and rhythm, we are inclined to doubt whether a second hearing of *La Mer* pieces would make us feel that they are the equal to the Prelude in imaginative impression. . . . The breath of freshness that came with Schubert's "Unfinished" Symphony, which Mr. Wood conducted immediately after Mr. Debussy's work, was a tribute to older methods of expression, and showed up one defect at any rate in the French composer's music, its monotonous orchestral coloring. (An unidentified London paper—not The *Times*—3 February 1908)

7 FEBRUARY 1908

The first complete performance is given by the Boston Symphony Orchestra, Karl Muck conducting, of *Symphonic Sketches* by George Whitefield CHADWICK, in four movements: *Jubilee* (with a "Juba" horn call imitating a Southern plantation Negro "breakdown"), *Noël* (a simple Christmas offering), *Hobgoblin* (a quasi-Mendelssohnian scherzo), and *A Vagrom Ballad* ("a tale of tramps and railway ties, of old clay pipes and rum") which includes an irreverent quotation from Bach's great G-minor organ fugue. (The first performances of two separate movements, *Jubilee* and *A Vagrom Ballad*, were conducted by Chadwick himself at a Chickering Production concert in Boston on 23 March 1904.)

8 FEBRUARY 1908

RACHMANINOFF conducts the orchestra of the Moscow Philharmonic Society in the first performance of his *Second Symphony* in E minor, completed by him in Dresden in January, 1908 in four movements all in 4/4 or 2/2 time:

(1) *Largo*, a mournful lamentation enhanced in its pessimism by recurrent lapses into the homonymous Phrygian mode, reluctantly rising from its fatalistic depths to an *Allegro moderato* marked by a strongly symmetric rhythmic pulse, entering the bright landscape of E major, and concluding abruptly in a chordal cadence; (2) *Allegro molto*, in A minor, suggesting in its animated motion *alla breve* a modified scherzo, with the middle section fugally developed; (3) *Adagio*, in A major, with ascending suspensions against plagally somber harmonies; (4) *Allegro vivace*, in optimistic E major qualified by characteristically Russian declination of the submediant while the glockenspiel dispiritedly tolls its intermittent chimes, but recovering its primal strength in richly sonorous harmonies supported by resonant pedal points.

13 FEBRUARY 1908

Espada, Spanish ballet by Jules MASSENET, forming a concentration of sword dances (espadas), card dances, Marches of toreros, a bolero, a corrida, a fandango, etc., is performed for the first time at Monte Carlo.

15 FEBRUARY 1908

Giuseppe MARTUCCI conducts the dedicatory program at the inauguration of a new concert series at the Augusteo in Rome.

16 FEBRUARY 1908

Eliána, opera in three acts by the Hungarian composer Ödön MIHALOVICH, his last stage work, after Tennyson's *Idylls of the King*, is produced in Budapest.

19 FEBRUARY 1908

DEBUSSY's *Pelléas et Mélisande* is performed for the first time in America at the Manhattan Opera House in New York.

Lyric Drama Dazes New York—Debussy's Opera Exquisite But Creepy Characters Do Not Sing, They Intone to Wonderful and Mystic Harmonies. (Headlines in the New York *American*)

Preraphaelite Opera—Pelléas et Mélisande a Study in Glooms—A Mass of Shifting and Inessential Details— The Fundamentals of Music Left Out of Account. (Headlines in the New York *Sun*)

26 FEBRUARY 1908

La Habanera, lyric drama in three acts by Raoul LAPARRA, 31-year-old composer of Hispanic antecedents (he was destined to be killed in an Allied air raid on a Paris suburb on 4 April 1943), to his own libretto wherein an insanely jealous young Castillian stabs to death his own brother for the love of a woman as a habanera is danced by the populace, is haunted by its tune and by the hallucinatorily realistic form of his victim on each anniversary of the murder, and, when in the last act he finds their beloved lying dead on his brother's grave, goes mad, to a musical setting abounding in Spanish and Basque refrains, with moderately modern *fin-de-siècle* harmonies and appropriately colorful orchestration, is performed for the first time at the Opéra-Comique in Paris.

In my opera, singing must not be aimed to produce conventional effects, but must depend intimately on the prosody and expression. Therefore, the roles must be declaimed, and the vocalization must be made part of this declamation. . . . All soft sonorities must be excluded from the orchestra. The power and the accents must be conveyed with the energy of the dance itself that seems to circumscribe the entire Spanish character. (From *Quelques opinions de l'auteur sur la manière d'interpréter son œuvre*, printed in the score)

M. Raoul Laparra's opera *La Habanera* has much in common with the half-hour shockers at the Grand Guignol in Paris. From the first strenuous phase of the prelude to the final drum tap the chief aim of the composer seems to be hair-raising. . . . The melodramatic plot of *La Habanera* might have excused the employment of the most villainous discords, but the author-composer in moments of the greatest hurly-burly contents himself with discords that pass into good resolutions and in some of the most exciting situations he uses the orchestra with reticence and a powerful effect little short of genius. (From a review of the production of *La Habanera* at Covent Garden, London, published in *Referee*, 24 July 1910)

How the management could present such a horrible piece of dilettante workmanship at the Royal Opera in Berlin must ever remain a conundrum. Where the audience were intended to be impressed with horror, they roared with laughter. (From a review of the Berlin production of *La Habanera*, in *Era*, London, 10 December 1908)

27 FEBRUARY 1908

Eidelberga Mia!, an operatic tribute in three acts by a romantic Italian composer Ubaldo PACCHIEROTTI (1877–1916) to the glories of the old German university town of Heidelberg, is produced in Genoa.

29 FEBRUARY 1908

Le Faune et la Bergèe, suite of three songs for mezzo soprano and orchestra by 25-year-old Igor STRAVINSKY, to poems by Pushkin: (1) *The Shepherdess*, depicting in pneumatically triadic harmonies and curvilinear melodies the post-adolescent flowering of an ancient

Greek maiden; (2) The *Faun*, wherein the lusty hircine creature disports himself in his sylvan retreat in characteristically Russian tritonal capers with occasional excursions into whole-tone configurations; (3) *The River*, an operatically dramatic scene wherein the incensed faun pursues the shepherdess in precipitate syncopated rhythms and chromatically rising diminished seventh-chords enharmonically resolving into beatific aqueous harmonies in the finest manner of Stravinsky's teacher Rimsky-Korsakov to illustrate the protective waters of the river whither the maiden hastens to plunge, is performed for the first time in public at a concert of the Russian Symphony Society in St. Petersburg. (A semi-private performance was given in 1907 in St. Petersburg by the Imperial Court Orchestra.)

I received your letter containing the most delightful and joyful news that *Le Faune et la Bergère* is to be performed by the Russian Symphony Society. I rejoice, and mentally I bow low before my benefactors, and especially before you, my dear Nicolay Andreyevitch. You say in your letter in regard to the progress of *Le Coq d'or* that in old age work goes rather slowly. Would that I, in my young age, could work as fast as you do! How wonderful it would be! (From Stravinsky's letter to Rimsky-Korsakov written in July 1907)

13 MARCH 1908

Nikita BALIEV inaugurates, in a house next to the Church of Christ the Savior in Moscow, his intimate cabaret, later to be known in Western Europe as *Le Chauve-Souris*, devoted to verbal and musical persifiage of self-important social and literary figures.

15 MARCH 1908

Rapsodie espagnole, symphonic suite by Maurice RAVEL in four contrasting movements: (1) *Prélude à a Nuit*, in 3/4 time, based on a hauntingly recurrent descending motive of four notes, F, E, D, C-sharp, in a nocturnal setting in which muted instruments predominate; (2) *Malagueña*, an infectiously rhythmic Spanish dance in very rapid 3/4 time, artfully presented in a continuous crescendo from an accentuated susurrus in the low register to a multicolored orchestral fireworks display; (3) *Habanera* (originally written for two pianos in 1895), a hesitatingly sensuous Hispano-Cuban air acidulated by softly discordant minor seconds in the pendulously swinging accompaniment; (4) *Feria*, spectacular tableau of a Spanish fiesta in a typical dual meter of 6/8 and 3/4, with a cornucopia of Iberian drums and shakers, and the use of novel coloristic instrumental devices, such as tangent glissandos *sul ponticello* and the unprecedented glissandos on natural harmonics in the viola and cello, is performed for the first time at a Colonne concert in Paris, the near-septuagenarian Edouard Colonne himself ineffectually leading the orchestra.

The work received a courteous welcome from the audience, which turned to enthusiasm at the end of the *Malagueña*, encored at a request from the upper gallery. This encore was followed by certain ironical murmurs from the orchestra stalls. It was then that the thunderous voice of Florent Schmitt asked from the top of the gallery for a second encore "just once more, for the gentlemen below who haven't been able to understand." (Roland-Manuel, *Maurice Ravel*, London, 1947)

Not mere impressionism, but "pointillisme" in music is Mr. Maurice Ravel's *Spanish Rhapsody*. Even Mr. Claude Debussy's musical poem *La Mer* is painted in broader strokes. Mr. Ravel throws tiny little dabs of color in showers upon his canvas. There is not an outline nor an expanse in the sketch; everything is in spots. In the third part, a fête, the first violins, literally mewing like a rather deep-voiced tom-cat, brought laughs from the audience. (From the Paris dispatch in *Era*, London, 21 December 1909)

22 MARCH 1908

First Symphony by Albert ROUSSEL, subtitled *Le Poème de la Forêt*, in four descriptive movements corresponding to the four seasons (*Forêt d'Hiver, Renouveau, Soir d'été, Faunes et Dryades*, evoking a winter forest, the rebirth of nature in the spring, a pastoral summer evening and an autumnal frolic of sylvan divinities) is performed for the first time in Brussels.

23 MARCH 1908

Ferruccio BUSONI plays in Berlin the solo part in the world première of the *Ukrainian Rhapsody* for piano and orchestra by the Russian composer Sergei LIAPUNOV, written in an expansive Lisztian manner without loss of the lyric and rhythmic flavor of the Ukrainian songs used as basic material.

30 MARCH 1908

Les Jumeaux de Bergame, two-act opera by the prophet of eurhythmics, Émile JAQUES-DALCROZE, his last stage work, is produced in Brussels.

5 APRIL 1908

Toman a lesní panna (Toman and the Forest Nymph), symphonic poem by the romantic Czech composer Vítězslav NOVÁK, inspired by an absorbingly horrifying folk tale of murder by massive osculation, wherein a faithless lover is kissed to death by a congregation of forest nymphs to avenge his kissing betrayal of one of their trusting sisters, set to an ingratiatingly titillating score punctuated by bradyseismic rhythms, is performed for the first time in Prague.

11 APRIL 1908

Rhea, opera in three acts by the Greek composer Spiro SAMARA, to an Italian libretto recounting the tale of multilateral passion, bilateral jealousy, intentional adultery, murder, suicide and general human turbulence, projected against the paradisiac scenery of the fabled Greek island Chio, wrested in 1346 from the infidel Saracens by an Apollo-like Greek warrior in the service of the podestà of Genoa, who is loved by the podestà's young Greek wife Rhea and is affianced to her stepdaughter, with the tragic denouement as an envious love rival stabs him to death, and Rhea, falling on his lifeless body, takes a potently poisonous potion contained in her votive ring, to a singingly Italianate score saturated with dramatic chromatics occasionally relieved by ethnically Grecian, orientally florid arabesques, is produced in Florence.

17 APRIL 1908

Piano Concerto in D-flat major by Emanuel MOÓR is performed in a world première by Harold Bauer and the Boston Symphony Orchestra.

Emanuel Moór, a Hungarian by birth, married a Miss Burke, the daughter of the famous bottler of ale, and has thus been enabled to write music at his leisure. Whether it would not have been as profitable for him to tipple his ale in the shade is a question for posterity to decide. (Philip Hale, Boston *Herald*, 19 April 1908)

I played Moór's piano concerto with the Boston Symphony Orchestra while Karl Muck was the conductor. "Es klingt," he said to me, screwing up his face in that Mephistophelian manner for which he was famous. (Harold Bauer, *His Book*, New York, 1948) (Muck did not conduct the Concerto, however, but delegated the task to his assistant Carl Wendling.)

1 MAY 1908

Frühlingsnacht, one-act opera by the Germanically educated Norwegian composer Gerhard SCHJELDERUP, to his own German libretto romantically descriptive of gentle love on a spring night, set in warmly Mendelssohnian harmonies, is performed for the first time in Dresden. (Expanded to three acts, it was produced in Lübeck on 18 October 1934 under the more explicit title *Liebesnächte*.)

4 MAY 1908

The Garden of Death, symphonic poem by Sergei VASSILENKO, tonalizing Oscar Wilde's story of a disenchanted phantom with orientalistically twisted scales conjuring up an air of ultramundane mysteries and promises of millennial tranquility, is performed for the first time in Moscow.

10 MAY 1908

Arthur LEMBA, 22-year-old Estonian graduate of the St. Petersburg Conservatory under Rimsky-Korsakov, conducts in Tartu the first performance of his Estonian opera *Lembitu Tütar (Lembitu's Daughter)*, in which the valorous daughter of the commander of pagan but noble Estonians resists to the death the wiles of the victorious leader of the well-caparisoned crusaders of the Teutonic Order of the Knights of the Sword intent on converting her after Lembitu himself falls on the field of honor in 1217.

1 JUNE 1908

Overture to Heine's drama of Scottish passion, *William Ratcliffe* by the Swiss composer Othmar SCHOECK, a work of abecedarian Mendelssohnian harmonies and Meyerbeerish foudroyance, is performed for the first time in Dresden.

4 JUNE 1908

Flagellantenzug, symphonic poem by the German composer Karl BLEYLE, depicting in Marching rhythms the scenes of massive self-flagellation of medieval penitents, men, women and children, perambulating the German city streets in long processions in double file and scourging themselves with leathern thongs to exorcise the pestilence on earth and perdition in afterlife, is performed for the first time in Munich.

13 JUNE 1908

BLIND TOM, American Negro slave who amazed the world as a musical child prodigy playing whole concerts of piano pieces of moderate difficulty (a brochure, *Le merveilleux prodigue musical Tom l'Aveugle*, published in Paris in 1867, adequately glorified his achievements), dies at the age of 59, in Hoboken, New Jersey, in the family home of Colonel Bethune to whom he was originally sold as a suckling.

Tom was born in Georgia, owned by a man named Jones. He was an idiot from birth. His father and mother were offered for sale. "Price: $1,500 without Tom, $1,200 with him." (Dwight's *Journal of Music*, ca. 1880)

15 JUNE 1908

Erik SATIE, the eccentric genius of Parisian musical sophistication, belatedly determined to acquire an academic education, obtains at the age of 42 a certificate of the satisfactory completion of a course in counter-point at the Schola Cantorum in Paris, with a notation by his professor Albert Roussel, "très bien."

17 JUNE 1908

On Igor STRAVINSKY's twenty-sixth birthday, his symphonic *Fireworks*, realistically descriptive of Roman candles, pinwheels and other pyrotechnical devices, for a large orchestra luxuriating in the contrasted sonorities of flutes, harps, bells and individualized strings playing high harmonies, and dedicated to Maximilian Steinberg and RimskyKorsakov's daughter Nadezhda, is performed in St. Petersburg, a few hours after their marriage in a village church near Kritzi.

The modern tonal coruscations and explosions entitled *Fireworks* seemed unartistic enough. One could hear the flashes and (very decidedly) the final bombs. What some of the brass dissonances meant we could not imagine unless the man who lit the pieces had burned his fingers and made a few resultant remarks. (Louis C. Elson, the Boston *Advertiser*, 1914)

Arthur Brock, the head of a firm of pyrotechnics, was invited to hear Igor Stravinsky's *Fireworks* performed in London on 28 February 1914. He made the following comments: "It was a wonderful impressionistic rendering of pyrotechnic effects, in beautiful colors, sparkling scintillations, graceful forms and movements, leading up to the Grande Mêlée and an impressive Final Bouquet. As a pyrotechnist, I am grateful to Stravinsky as the first musical composer to recognize the absorbing beauties of the pyrotechnic art." (London *Observer*, 1 March 1914)

20 JUNE 1908

Federico CHUECA, prolific and popular Spanish composer, described as "the barrel-organ of his generation," among whose penetratingly infectious zarzuelas *La Gran Vía* attained enormous success, and whose patriotic March from the operetta *Cádiz* became in the 1880's an unofficial national anthem of Spain, dies in his native Madrid at the age of 62.

21 JUNE 1908

RIMSKY-KORSAKOV, the professorial tone poet of Russian music, whose epically designed operatic spectacles reflect with civilized definition the grandeur of Russian history and legend, who enriched the technical vocabulary of musical resources by some extraordinary innovations such as the scale of alternating whole-tones and semitones (in Russia it came to be known as the Rimsky scale), venerated teacher of two generations of Russian composers, dies of angina pectoris at his summer home in Lubensk in the vicinity of St. Petersburg, the capital where he spent his life in domestic tranquility and social respectability, at the age of 64 years, 3 months and 3 days.

1 JULY 1908

Max REGER receives an honorary degree of Doctor of Music from the University of Vienna, presented to him as "modorum musicorum inventori novorum cultissimo . . . qui Joannis Sebastiani Bach divinis vestigiis ingressus Artis organariae fines inopino successu propagavit," giving an academic imprimatur to Hugo Riemann's declaration that Reger could become the Bach of the twentieth century.

7 JULY 1908

Horrida Nox, one-act opera by the 46-year-old Argentinian composer Arturo BERUTI, the first opera by a native composer to a libretto in Spanish to be publicly performed in Argentina, in which a rebel patriot dies in the arms of his beloved after his escape from the dungeon where he was held by henchmen of the tyrannical South American dictator Rosas, is performed for the first time in Buenos Aires.

2 AUGUST 1908

Hochzeitsglocken, one-act opera by the Hungarian pianist and composer Emanuel MOÓR, in which the felicitous wedding bells chime incessantly, is produced in Kassel.

5 SEPTEMBER 1908

Ettore PANIZZA, Argentine-born composer of Italian extraction, conducts at the inauguration of the renovated Teatro Colón in Buenos Aires the first performance of his patriotic opera *Aurora*, in three acts, expressly commissioned for the occasion by the Argentine government and competently written in an effective Italian idiom, to a libretto wherein Aurora, daughter of the Spanish Governor of Argentina, enamored of a young rebel imprisoned by her father during the war of liberation in 1810, is fatally shot in a pre-auroral encounter and dies in her temporarily unchained lover's arms, pointing at the rubescent horizon symbolically incarnadined by her blood as the harbinger of national independence (the initial strains of the Argentine National Anthem are here sounded in the orchestra).

12 SEPTEMBER 1908

Uku and Vanemujne, opera by the Estonian composer Karl August HERMAN (1851–1908), based on Estonian mythology, is produced in Tartu.

19 SEPTEMBER 1908

Gustav MAHLER conducts in Prague the first performance of his *Seventh Symphony*, written during the summers of 1904 and 1905, but revised and refurbished in detail many times, variously designated by unauthorized exegeticists as "Song of the Night," "Romantic Symphony," etc., in five movements, of which the two outer ones, connoting the diurnal states of pessimistic introspection and pantheistic convection, spherically encycle the nocturnally romantic inner three, the heterotonal embrasures of the entire work being the initial indeterminate E minor and the ultimate triumphant C major:

(1) *Langsam—Allegro con fuoco*, the slow exordium optically suggesting a funeral March, interrupted by an impulsive attack of four fiery horns joined by trumpets apostrophizing in fanfares of calculated tonal obliquity in quartal and tritonal ascents; (2) *Nachtmusik—Allegro moderato*, a bucolic tone poem with flutey birdcalls and resonant cowbells, converging tonally on a philosophically homonymous C, in minor and in major; (3) *Schattenhaft—Fliessend aber nicht schnell*, a crepuscular scherzo, with emotional implosions so intense that at one point the cellos and the doublebasses are explicitly exhorted to snap the strings in quintuple forte to cause them to rebound forcibly against the fingerboard; (4) *Nachtmsik—Andante amoroso*, an idyllic serenade, with a guitar and a mandolin suggesting the amorous dalliance of the *amoroso* section, the principal key being the traditionally pastoral F major; (5) *Rondo-Finale—Allegro ordinario*, with kettledrums introducing a series of exultant fanfares ascending along the entire scale of harmonic tones and driving in impatient exaltation towards a self-assertive apotheosis in the pantheistically foudroyant key of C major.

20 SEPTEMBER 1908

Pablo SARASATE, grandly artistic Spanish violinist who for nearly half a century fascinated all of Europe by the brilliance of his technique and the beauty of his singing tone, composer of numerous prestidigital concert pieces for the violin, of which the Gypsy dance known under the German title *Zigeunerweisen* has become a perennial favorite, dies in his villa at Biarritz at the age of 64.

4 OCTOBER 1908

Durchs Fenster, opera by Iwan KNORR, is produced in Karlsruhe.

8 OCTOBER 1908

Olav Trygvason, unfinished early opera by Edvard GRIEG, his only attempted work for the musical theater, dealing with the first Christian king of Norway who after many heroic exploits perished in a naval battle in 1000, is produced in Christiania.

13 OCTOBER 1908

Max REGER's hour-long *Violin Concerto* in A major, op. 101, thickeningly vortical in its labyrinthine polyphony, in three movements, the outer two fast and the inner slow, with a formidable cadenza at the end of the first movement, is performed for the first time by Henri Marteau with the Gewandhaus Orchestra of Leipzig conducted by Arthur Nikisch.

Your concerto is of the highest significance to our violin literature; it is simply *kolossal*. (Henri Marteau in a letter to Reger)

In his powerful presentation of polyphonic forms and in the expressive mobility of his melismatic writing, Reger appears as the blessed inheritor of Bach's treasure. Through the confluence of the richest sources of the musical past and present his music streams towards a sea of sounds which will perhaps be the musical ocean of the future. (*Leipziger Zeitung,* 16 October 1908)

24 OCTOBER 1908

Lamia, symphonic poem by Edward MACDOWELL (after Keats), depicting in chromatic harmony, laden with successive diminished seventh-chords, the enchantress who lures a youth to her magical palace and then reverts to her original form of a serpent, shocking him to death, is performed posthumously for the first time by the Boston Symphony Orchestra.

Lamia was written in 1888. When we came to America, we ran up against the fact that it would be impossible to get an orchestra to try over a composition in a rehearsal. In Germany it would have been a simple and easy thing to accomplish. I can see, as if it were yesterday, the kindly faces of the members of different orchestras in Wiesbaden, Darmstadt, Frankfurt, so willing to help out the young American. The only grumble I ever heard was over the parts. I copied most of them, and the early ones must have been awful. I can hear an old musician say under his breath: "Schrecklich copiert." (From a letter of Mrs. Edward MacDowell to Philip Hale, editor of the Boston Symphony Program Notes)

30 OCTOBER 1908

Antoine MARIOTTE conducts in Lyon the first production of his lyric tragedy in one act, *Salomé,* to the original text of Oscar Wilde's French play (its composition was begun before Mariotte knew that Richard Strauss was writing an opera on the same libretto), a dramatically inflated score strewn with whole-tone scales and their concomitant augmented triads to convey a sense of horror, with pseudo-oriental jangle accompanying Salomé's septuple dance, suggesting orectic aprosexia rather than erotic parorexia.

4 NOVEMBER 1908

Versiegelt, one-act comic opera by Leo BLECH, to a Falstaffian story of a jolly widow who conceals a philandering burgomaster in a cupboard containing her friend's wardrobe subject to confiscation for debts, and when the bailiffs have it sealed (hence the title) uses his discomfiture to force his consent to the marriage of his daughter to a disapproved swain, is produced in Hamburg.

4 NOVEMBER 1908

Anton von WEBERN conducts the Tonküinstlerverein Orchester in Vienna in the first performance of his *Passacaglia for Orchestra,* marked op. 1, scored for woodwinds, four horns, three trombones, bass tuba, timpani, percussion, harp and strings, in which the subject in D minor, in duple meter, undergoes twenty-three variations. *See* 10 June 1921.

14 NOVEMBER 1908

Der tapfere Soldat, operetta in three acts by Oskar STRAUS, fashioned from George Bernard Shaw's Voltairean play *Arms and the Man,* cynically glorifying a reluctant soldier who prefers chocolates to bayonets (in England and America the operetta became famous as *The Chocolate Soldier*) is produced in Vienna.

16 NOVEMBER 1908

Arturo TOSCANINI makes his first American appearance, conducting *Aida* at the Metropolitan Opera House in New York City.

25 NOVEMBER 1908

Kunálovy ocj (Kunala's Eyes), opera in three acts by the Czech composer Otakar OSTRČIL, to a libretto from an old Indian legend dealing with the incestuous passion of a queen for her stepson whom she blinds by magic when he rejects her overtures but who regains his eyesight through countermagic, is produced in Prague.

28 NOVEMBER 1908

Il Grillo del focolare, first opera in three acts by Riccardo ZANDONAI, to a libretto freely adapted from the Dickens tale *The Cricket on the Hearth,* is produced in Turin.

3 DECEMBER 1908

Hero and Leander, tone poem by the 32-year-old English composer Havergal BRIAN, inspired by Leander's fabled trans-Hellespontine non-stop swimming trek to see his beloved across the strait (Byron duplicated this mythological feat to prove it could be done), is performed for the first time in London conducted by Thomas Beecham. (The score and parts disappeared after this performance without a trace.)

3 DECEMBER 1908

Hans RICHTER conducts in Manchester, England, the premiere of the *First Symphony* in A-flat major by Edward ELGAR, dedicated to him as "a true artist and true friend" and set in four movements:

Andante nobilmente e semplice leading to the main *Allegro* moving along in energetic para-Brahmsian melorhythms towards a climactic *Grandioso,* then receding, idiosyncratically for Elgar, to a soft ending; *Allegro molto* in a remote key of F-sharp minor, in effect a scherzo, bearing a curious time signature 1/2, debouching into an *Adagio* in D major, the very slow initial theme of which is identical with the initial 24 notes of the rapidly evolving motto of the preceding movement, but aurally is beyond recognition owing to rhythmic deformation and harmonic dislocation; *Lento,* in D minor, opening with an ominously distant roll of the bass drum as a prelude to an agitated *Allegro,* leading, after many an artful modulatory exploration, to the main key of the work and, aided and abetted by beatific sonorities of the arpeggiating harps, reaching the final *Grandioso* and a powerful chordal ending.

10 DECEMBER 1908

Olivier MESSIAEN, "compositeur de musique et rythmicien," is born in Avignon to Cécile Sauvage, the poetess, who immediately wrote the poem *L' Aime en bourgeon,* dedicated to the infant's "burgeoning soul."

10 DECEMBER 1908

The Russian Symphony Orchestra of New York City, under the direction of its founder Modest ALTSCHULER gives the first performance anywhere of SCRIABIN's Fourth Symphony, *Le Poème de l'Extase,* completed in Lausanne in the summer of 1907, reflecting in a solipsistically erotic and pantheistically expansive continuous movement the mystic intent to "possess the Cosmos as a man possesses a woman," the music traversing eight initially passive but progressively active states of ecstasy—languor, yearning, volitation, emergent creativeness, anxiety, volition, postulation of self, challenge—symbolized by thematic figures mutually combining in augmentation, diminution, truncation, apocopation, intervalic torsion and rhythmic contortion in an ambience of tonal obliquity yet adhering to fundamental tonality with a purposive predominance of major triads and cohering in the formal symmetry of cyclic unity, bearing the following designations of tempo and sentiment:

Andante, Languido, wherein the temporary passivity of the dormant spirit is suggested by a symmetrically rotated theme, and the nascent activity by melodic nutation and rhythmic libration; *Lento, Soavemente,* in which the clarinet yearns for the ineffable in quartal ascension over a tonically dominant pedal point, forming an altered chord of the major 13th; *Allegro volando,* flying at asymptotic tangents from the tonal coordinates in volitient volitation; *Lento, Allegro non troppo,* wherein the imperious trumpet postulates "avec une noble et douce majesté" the primacy of self; *Moderato,* "avec délice," intensifying and torrefying the senses in egocentric rhythmic implosions and spastic melodic exhalations, oriented "avec une ivresse toujours croissante, presque en délire" towards a delectable goal of consciously savored self-intoxication; *Allegro drammatico, Tragico, Tempestoso,* with the trumpet, ever the protagonist, resuming its spasmodically mounting calls "avec une noble et joyeuse émotion" as a prelude to a grand recapitulation of languorously passive, sensuously sinuous, volantly exultant declarations, and after an episode marked *Charmé* and a transitory *Scherzando* leading to the majestic consummation of the final *Maestoso,* with the French horns chanting orgiastically holding their infundibula aloft, the powerful organ entering in majesty followed by the sonorous large campana, with a tremendous tension sustained over an undeviatingly powerful deep C for 53 long measures, erecting a compound plagal cadential structure before dissolving in ultimate ecstasy in the purest of triadic harmonies in cosmically apocalyptic C major.

The nerves of the audience were worn and racked as nerves are seldom assailed even in these days. Scriabin's *Poème de l'Extase* was the cause. This composition was heralded as a foster child of theosophy. Certainly it conveyed a sense of eeriness and uncanny connotation. Most of the time, the violins were whimpering and wailing like lost souls, while strange, undulating and formless melodies roved about in the woodwinds. A solo violin spoke occasionally, growing more and more plaintive, and finally being swallowed in a chaos of acid harmonies with violins screaming in agony overhead. There were three such climaxes in the composition, all built upon a basis of cymbals, drums and inchoate blarings of the brass. It all seemed far more like several other things than ecstasy. (W. J. Henderson, New York *Sun,* 11 December 1908)

(The première of *Le Poème de l'Extase* was scheduled by the Russian Symphony Concert Society for its concert of 29 February 1908, but was cancelled for ambiguously stated reasons that the parts had not arrived in time. The first performance of the work in Russia took place on 1 February 1909 by the Court Orchestra in St. Petersburg.)

The ultra-moderns all resemble each other. When one of these extreme gentlemen comes at you with a *Poem of Ecstasy,* you may be sure of one thing, he is going to use every known instrument. Some of this ecstasy was extremely bitter, while some of it reminded of the ecstasy of the too convivial gentleman who thought that the air was filled with green monkeys

with crimson eyes and sparkling tails, a kind of ecstasy that is sold in Russia at two rubles a bottle. (Louis C. Elson, Boston *Daily Advertiser,* 22 October 1910)

In Paris, in May 1907, when concerts of Russian music were presented, Scriabin played on the piano some excerpts from his *Poème de l'Extase,* in the presence of Rimsky-Korsakov and others. This music impressed Rimsky-Korsakov as morbid eroticism. "Is he losing his mind?" he remarked half-facetiously. (From annotations by Andrei Rimsky-Korsakov in his edition of his father's *Chronicles of My Life,* Moscow, 1935)

Le Poème de l'Extase is the Joy of Liberated Action. The Cosmos, i.e. Spirit, is Eternal Creation without External Motivation, a Divine Play with Worlds. The Creative Spirit, i.e. the Universe at Play, is not conscious of the Absoluteness of its creativeness, having subordinated itself to a Finality and made creativity a means towards an end. The stronger the pulse beat of life and the more rapid the precipitation of rhythms, the more clearly the awareness comes to the Spirit that it is consubstantial with creativity, immanent within itself, and that its life is a play. When the Spirit has attained the supreme culmination of its activity and has been torn away from the embraces of teleology and relativity, when it has exhausted completely its substance and its liberated active energy, the Time of Ecstasy shall then arrive. (From a program note of a concert of Scriabin's music given in Moscow by the Imperial Russian Music Society on 6 March 1909)

11 DECEMBER 1908

Elliott CARTER, American composer who has developed a masterly modern style of composition by imaginative hyperclassical and serial methods, is born in New York City.

11 DECEMBER 1908

Frederick DELIUS conducts the London Philharmonic in the first performance of his symphonic poemette *In a Summer Garden,* dedicated to his wife Jelka Rosen, and justifying by its unpretentious musical setting, with simple symmetric tunes of folksong lilt and flowery melismas in the frequent instrumental solos, the insertion of a motto from Rossetti in the printed score: "All are my blooms; and all sweet blooms of love/To thee I gave while spring and summer sang."

Very much may happen in a summer garden, and, truth to tell, the presence of 3 bassoons, 3 tenor trombones, chromatic timpani and 3 tubular bells led me to expect a summer thunderstorm; but the prevailing tone color was somber and suggested an autumn rather than a summer atmosphere. (*Referee,* London, 12 December 1908)

As there is no organic idea in the piece, no thematic germ of any consequence, *In a Summer Garden* is a little like a play in which there is nothing but scenery and limelight, or like the efforts of an unimaginative country organist who is obliged to extemporize until the clergyman is ready to begin the service. . . . The list of extra instruments in the program leads ordinary hearers to wonder what is the object of employing so many players to say so very little. (*The Times,* London, 12 December 1908)

18 DECEMBER 1908

Harold BAUER gives the first performance, at the Cercle Musical in Paris, of Debussy's *Children's Corner,* "petite suite pour piano seul" composed in July 1908, and touchingly dedicated to his small daughter "a ma chère petite Chouchou avec des tendres excuses de son père pour ce qui va suivre" (Chouchou was not destined to live beyond adolescence), in six movements furnished with English titles (Chouchou had an English governess):

(1) *Doctor Gradus ad Parnassum*, an ironically affectionate stylization of Clementi's famous didactic studies set in sterling C major acidulated by pandiatonic mixtures, with a meditative middle section in melodic augmentation; (2) *Jimbo's Lullaby* (Chouchou's elephant toy Jumbo, mispronounced Jimbo with nasal French semi-vowel), marked "doux et un peu gauche," stepping awkwardly but cautiously in secundal harmonies on pachydermatous pentatonic basses, with a mock-exotic interlude in whole-tone scales; (3) *Serenade of the Doll*, musical aquatint of a porcelaneously delicate, orientally slant-eyed idol inaudibly nodding in quartal harmonies on pentatonically black keys reposing on the tonic-dominant pedal point in E major; (4) *The Snow Is Dancing*, an animated pantomime of rhythmically cadent snowflakes with fleeting whole-tone images passing softly and sadly by over the thematic phrase of a Phrygian tetrachord; (5) *The Little Shepherd*, a modally inflected Grecian air in tenuously bucolic harmonies; (6) *Golliwogg's Cake Walk*, a gently syncopated piece of ragtime inspired by the American dance popular in Paris vaudeville theaters, with a sly interpolation of the opening motive of *Tristan und Isolde*, irreverently disharmonized in a modern lilting rhythm sarcastically marked "avec une grande émotion" and followed by a sardonic un-Wagnerian cachinnation.

(Golliwoggs are children's dolls, extremely popular early in the twentieth century, inspired by the series of "golliwogg" books by the American-born British writer Florence Upton, who published her first Golliwogg story in collaboration with her mother, Mrs. Bertha Upton, in London in 1895, at the age of 22; the word itself is Welsh in its phonetical make-up, but it was invented by Florence Upton. Golliwogg dolls manufactured in England were usually dark-skinned to provide "exotic" color. Debussy's daughter apparently had such a colored Golliwogg, which led Debussy to use the rhythms of a Negro dance in his *Golliwogg's Cake Walk*.)

After I played the last piece, *Golliwogg's Cake Walk*, Debussy remarked: "You don't seem to object today to the manner in which I treat Wagner." I had not the slightest idea what he meant, and asked him to explain. He then pointed out the pitiless caricature of the first measures of *Tristan und Isolde* that he had introduced in the middle of the *Cake Walk*. It had completely escaped me. I laughed heartily. (Harold Bauer: *His Book*, New York, 1948) (Léon Vallas asserts in his biography of Debussy that Harold Bauer learned about the Tristan quotation in 1932, after reading the biography, an implausible assertion in the light of Harold Bauer's story.)

21 DECEMBER 1908

String Quartet No. 2, op. 10, in F-sharp minor, by Arnold SCHOENBERG (begun 9 March 1907 and completed on 11 July 1908), the last of his works designated with an express key signature in the title, apart from some didactic compositions, in four movements: (1) *Moderato*, embalmed in a dissolvent chromatic fluid with condoling convergences into cadential triads and set in a discernible sonata form; (2) *Sehr rasch*, a rash tourbillon of perturbing

sonorities off center of the 16 strings of the quartet suddenly interrupted by a macabre strain of disharmonized Viennese tune "Ach du lieber Augustin, alles ist hin!"; (3) *Litanei*, with a soprano part singing the introspective verses of the Viennese poet Stefan George, rising to the highest range of plaintive agony, with Hebraistic semitone sighs in the instrumental interludes; (4) *Entrückung*, with a soprano solo intoning an extra-terrestrial poem by Stefan George ("I feel the air of other planets") set to a nostalgically Tristanesque accompaniment, leading to a serene conclusion on a submissive major tonic triad, is performed for the first time in Vienna.

It was a veritable *Katzenmusik*. Nevertheless the audience kept quiet. After the end of the first movement, there were heard some signs of approval. This gave a signal for a regular *scandale*, which increased like an avalanche, subsided, again grew in force, and finally reached fortissimo. . . . Someone said: "Now they will play Beethoven, so let us first ventilate the hall!" (*Wiener Tageszeitung*, Vienna, 23 December 1908)

During the performance of a new string quartet by the ultraviolet musical secessionist Arnold Schoenberg, there was some booing and laughter. Suddenly the music critic Karpath rose and cried out, "Stop it! Enough!" His colleague Specht countered by shouting, "Quiet! Continue to play!" The majority of the public was against the music. Some discords made elegantly dressed ladies cringe under the painful impact on their delicate ears, and elderly gentlemen were at the point of tears from fury. In the middle of all this tumult stood the figure of the composer who gestured towards the performers in an expression of gratitude and encouragement. (Richard Batka, *Prager Zeitung*, 28 December 1908)

25 DECEMBER 1908

Eva WAGNER, Wagner's natural daughter born to Cosima Liszt, the then undivorced wife of Hans von Bülow, marries the Germanized British Wagnerite and proponent of the doctrine of Teutonic racial supremacy, Houston Stewart CHAMBERLAIN.

31 DECEMBER 1908

Sergei PROKOFIEV makes his first public appearance at the age of 17, as a pianist and composer at a concert of the Society for Contemporary Music in St. Petersburg, playing seven short piano pieces of his own, including the provocatively dissonant and rhythmically impulsive *Suggestions diaboliques*, earning for himself the sobriquet of the *enfant terrible* of modern Russian music.

Young Prokofiev belongs to the extreme radical wing of modernism, and in his boldness and originality goes even farther than contemporary French modernists. (*Slovo*, St. Petersburg, 2 January 1909)

Suggestions diaboliques ought to have a more concrete title. I suggest *Wild Pandemonium of Dirty Devils in Hell*, or *Savage Fight of Two Infuriated Gorillas*. (*Novy Den*, St. Petersburg, 2 January 1909)

1909

13 JANUARY 1909

Monna Vanna, lyric drama in four acts by Henry FÉVRIER, to a play by Maurice Maeterlinck set in 15th-century Italy, wherein the virtuous wife of the defender of Pisa offers herself to the commander of the besieging forces as the price of the city's relief, but is spared defilement as the latter recognizes in her his childhood sweetheart and she decides to remain with him, set to a resonantly throbbing score in which the elements of French romanticism and Italian verismo are touched with impressionistic colorism, is produced at the Paris Opéra.

14 JANUARY 1909

Bon-Bon Suite, cantata for baritone, chorus and orchestra in six movements by the British mulatto composer Samuel COLERIDGE-TAYLOR, confected in an infantiloquent idiom, is performed for the first time in its complete orchestral version at the Brighton Music Festival. (An arrangement for voices with two pianos was played previously on 9 December 1908 at the Hampstead Conservatoire.)

15 JANUARY 1909

Ernest REYER, French composer who added "er" to his real name Rey out of Wagnerolatrous devotion and whose Nordic opera *Sigurd* remains a Nibelungian homunculus of singular incongruity, dies at Le Lavandou, Hyères, at the age of 85.

21 JANUARY 1909

Ein Herbstmanöver, first operetta in three acts by the 26-year-old Hungarian composer Emmerich KÁLMÁN, portraying in coyly waltzing Vindobonic melodies the smiling dalliance of the Austrian Hussars with the obliging countryside damsels during the time of autumn maneuvers (hence the title), is performed for the first time in Vienna. (Originally, it was performed in Budapest in the Hungarian language, under the title *Tatárjárás,* on 22 February 1908.)

25 JANUARY 1909

The world première is given at the Dresden Royal Opera House of *Elektra,* opera in one act by Richard STRAUSS, scored for a huge orchestra including the Heckelphone, a bass oboe specially constructed by Heckel, to a libretto by Hugo von Hofmannsthal, marking their first collaboration, in which the terrifying story of the daughter's vengeance for the assassination of her father through the murder, with the aid of her brother, Orestes, of their guilty mother and her lover, is told in terms not of inexorable fate but of personal will, pervaded by unremitting and unresolved dissonances, set in a network of identifying motives, characterizing Elektra's hatred by a ven-

omously disfigured fanfare of royal pride, the bloody footsteps by inspissatedly clotted chromatic progressions of hissingly discordant bitonalities, her resolve of matricide by a stately ascent along the major scale stumbling midway into chromatic blocks, her dance of joy by maniacally triumphant battology, and her sudden collapse by an abrupt chordal spasm; Klytemnestra's remembered misdeed by an atonally rising syncopated figure, her imperiousness by dark successions of unrelated triadic harmonies, her tinkling jewelry by futile flights of flutes against incongruously broken chords, her spiritual decay by cadential dejections into exhausted minor heteroharmonies in low register, and her fear of death by tense, prolonged and discordant suspensions; the revelation that Orestes lives by rapid knocks along the notes of major triads, and the virginal virtue of Elektra's sister Chrysothemis by concordantly harmonized implorations.

Elektra was produced for the first time on any stage before a brilliant international audience at the Saxon Royal Opera tonight. . . . With one act lasting an hour and forty minutes and 122 players in the orchestra, for thrilling histrionic vocal and orchestral effects *Elektra* outrivals *Salome.* It is a prodigious orchestral orgy, with nothing that can be called music in the score, and makes superhuman demands upon the physical and mental powers of the singers and players. . . . The marvelous imitative effects of the orchestra are bloodcurdling, drastic and gruesome to the last degree. It is fortunate for hearers the piece is no longer for it would else be too nerve-racking. (From the cable dispatch from Dresden by H. E. Krehbiel, in the New York *Times* of 26 January 1909)

Violent, Lurid *Elektra*—First Impressions of Richard Strauss's New Opera—A Remarkable Work Whatever May Be Thought of the Theme—Gruesome Expressions in Music of Mysterious Moments of Horror. (Headlines in the New York *Sun,* 26 January 1909)

Elektra has known for some time that her papa was killed by mamma's gentleman friend. . . . She screams and then gets down and digs up out of the dirt the axe her papa was killed with. . . . Her mother is afraid of her. Elektra keeps on howling. . . . The orchestra breaks into strange and unearthly noises. . . . Muted trumpets, woodwinds in the lowest register and strings leaping in intervals of ninths and sevenths mingle in a medley of sounds which gives the idea of a snarling frightened animal. In the great scene in which Elektra accuses her mother of murdering her father, the music ends with a long shrill whistle like that of a locomotive entering a tunnel. Elsewhere the music reproduces sounds of smashing glass and china, the bursting of bottles, the clashing of shovels and tongs, the groaning and creaking of rusty hinges and stubborn doors, avalanches in the mountains, the crying of babies, the squealing of rats, the grunting of pigs, the bellowing of cattle, the howling of cats and the roaring of wild beasts. . . . I didn't pick out a tune that I should imagine would be later on included in "Gems from the Opera for the Parlor Organ." (Dispatch from New York City in the Boston *Herald,* 31 January 1910)

In *Elektra* Strauss lets loose an orchestral riot that suggests a murder scene in a Chinese theater. He has a constitutional aversion to what sounds beautiful. . . . If the reader who has not heard *Elektra* desires to witness something that looks as its orchestral score sounds, let him poke a stick into an ant hill and watch the black insects darting, angry and bewildered, biting and clawing in a thousand directions at once. (H. T. Finck in the New York *Post*, 2 February 1910)

Is it progress to use the human voice as Strauss does? Madame Schumann-Heink, who is noted for her big robust voice, found the strain of singing Klytemnestra in Dresden so great that she resigned after the first performance. She has related how, at the rehearsals, when Conductor Schuch, out of regard for the singers, moderated the orchestral din, Strauss declared: "But, my dear Schuch, louder, louder the orchestra; I can still hear the voice of Frau Heink!" (H. T. Finck, *Richard Strauss*, Boston, 1917)

In *Elektra* of Strauss, jarring discords, the desperate battle of dissonances in one key against dissonances in another, settle themselves down into total delineation of shrieks and groans, of tortures physical in the clear definition and audible in their gross realism. Can you conceive of the inward scream of a conscience in the flames of the inferno being translated into the polyphonic utterances of instruments writhing in a counterpoint no longer required to be the composition of two or more melodies which shall harmonize with one another but of melodies which shall spit and scratch and claw at each other, like enraged panthers? Snarling of stopped trumpets, barking of trombones, moaning of bassoons and squealing of violins are but elementary factors in the musical system of Richard Strauss. (W. J. Henderson, New York *Sun*, 2 February 1910)

30 JANUARY 1909

Vampuka, African Bride, Exemplary in all Respects, one-act opera-parody with text and music by V. ERENBERG, ridiculing the preposterous type of exotic operatic libretti, is performed for the first time at the cabaret "Crooked Mirror" in St. Petersburg.

3 FEBRUARY 1909

A century has passed since the birth in Hamburg of Felix MENDELSSOHN, the felicitously facile genius of Romantic music, endowed with a superb melodic gift, a natural sense of mellifluous harmony, a penetrating musical intelligence and an unfailing mastery of the art of composition in all its aspects.

3 FEBRUARY 1909

Il Principe Zilah, opera by Franco ALFANO in two acts, with a prologue and an epilogue, is produced in Genoa.

3 FEBRUARY 1909

Hircus Nocturnus, symphonic poem by Sergei VASSILENKO, inspired by an episode in Dmitri Merezhkovsky's novel *The Resurrected Gods*, wherein the nocturnal goat suddenly throws off his animal vesture and, brandishing a thyrsus and a cluster of grapes, reveals himself as Dionysius, the orgiastic god of vinous revelry, and flies away surrounded by a nymphomaniacal swarm of witches whirling under the full moon, to a score written in the fine tradition of Russian musical demonism with ominously syncopated thematic pronouncements intervalically based on the "diabolus in musica" of medieval lore, the tritone, is performed for the first time in Moscow.

6 FEBRUARY 1909

Scherzo fantastique by Igor STRAVINSKY, scored for a luxuriant orchestra including three harps and a celesta, suggesting by its entomologically buzzing chromatics the intense activity of a beehive, the nuptial flight of the queen bee in the soaring piccolos, the death of her discarded mate in sonorously Wagnerian augmented triads, and the return of the cycle of life and death in tremulous diminished seventh-chord harmonies, is performed for the first time in St. Petersburg, Alexander Siloti conducting.

The composer recounted of this work:

I had for quite some time an idea to write a symphonic Scherzo, but I had no program for it. But now I happened to read *La Vie des Abeilles* by Maeterlinck, a partly philosophical, partly literary work, which completely captivated me. I had thought of selecting quotations from the book as a programmatic element of the music. However, I realized that it was impractical because the scientific language in it is linked too closely with the literary passages. So I decided to follow a definite programmatic plan without actual quotations, and to entitle my score simply *Bees* (after Maeterlinck), *a fantastic scherzo*. (From Stravinsky's letter to Rimsky-Korsakov, dated July 1907.)

Some bad literature about bees was published on the flyleaf of my *Scherzo*, to satisfy my publisher who thought it would help to sell the music. (Conversations with Igor Stravinsky by Robert Craft, New York, 1959.)

8 FEBRUARY 1909

Mieczyslaw KARLOWICZ, Polish composer of romantically inspired choral and symphonic pieces written in a consciously national manner closely associated with authentic folk melodies, perishes in a snowy avalanche while mountain climbing in Zakopane, Galicia, at the age of 32.

9 FEBRUARY 1909

Quo Vadis?, opera in five acts by Jean NOUGUÈS, after the celebrated historical novel from Nero's time by Henryk Sienkiewicz, panoramically depicting with a fine sense of dramatic theatricality and an easily accessible inventory of effective melodies, resonant harmonies and nicely calculated vocal effusions and instrumental colorations, the immoral Roman ways, the burning of Rome while Nero sings to the accompaniment of an anachronistic lute, the martyrdom of the Christians and the salvation of a young maiden loved by a Roman patrician whom she has converted to Christianity, as her giant of a slave slays the bull to whose back she was tied as a bait for carnivorous beasts in the Coliseum, with the central episode recounted by Apostle Peter—his vision of Jesus returning to Rome to be crucified again to whom he poses the famous question of the title—all these varied scenes fittingly characterized by hymnal harmonies, ominous progressions of chromatically ascending diminished seventh-chords and reservedly orgiastic wide-ranging arpeggios, is performed for the first time anywhere in Nice.

11 FEBRUARY 1909

Boleslaw Smialy, the first opera, in three acts, by Ludomir RÓZYCKI, relating in majestically romantic Wagneromorphic tones the turbulent events in the life of the 11th-century King of Poland, Boleslaw the Bold, grandson of

Boleslaw the Brave, who tried to impose his will on the Russians in Kiev and on the clergy in Cracow, and who was excommunicated by Pope Gregory VII for the murder of a bishop during a solemn mass, is produced in Lwów.

12 FEBRUARY 1909

At a concert of the Boston Symphony Orchestra conducted by Max Fiedler, Ignace PADEREWSKI plays the *Fourth Concerto* for piano and orchestra by Saint-Saëns and hears the first performances anywhere of his *Symphony* in B minor expressing his grief for the extinction of Poland's sovereignty but voicing his faith that, in the words of the patriotic air sung at the time of the third partition of Poland in 1795 "jeszcze Polska nie zginela" (this hope that Poland had not yet perished was to be vindicated eight years after the performance of the symphony when Paderewski himself became Prime Minister of the resurrected Polish Republic), set in three movements:

(1) *Adagio maestoso*, serving as a somber introduction to the main section *Allegro vivace e molto appassionato* invoking in a well-calibrated sonata form the past glories of Poland, and ending with a solemn chorale played by the organ solo; (2) *Andante con moto*, a lyric dedication to the Polish people in B-flat minor; (3) *Vivace*, in B minor, an impassioned commemoration of the heroically ineffectual Polish uprising of 1863, with courageous fanfares and optimistic tambourines crushed by assembled sarrusophones marching in heavy Russian steps, while distant thunder of resistance is heard in the foudroyant tonitruones, specially constructed at Paderewski's instructions, ending in a grand finale wherein the patriotic Polish hymn, disfigured and debilitated by intervalic alterations, emerges in all its autonomous power.

Great is Paderewski's New Symphony—It will Insure Piano Virtuoso Fame as a Composer (Headlines in the Boston *Globe* of 13 February 1909)

Paderewski's Symphony—The Disappointment That It Brought and a Lukewarm Reception For It—The Monotony of Mood and Color and the Lack of Vital Emotional Appeal (Headlines in the Boston *Evening Transcript* of 13 February 1909)

12 FEBRUARY 1909

F. T. MARINETTI, Italian protagonist of *Futurismo*, publishes in the Paris newspaper *Le Figaro* his First Futurist Manifesto promulgating the militant ideals of futurist drama, literature, art and music—irrealistic, irrational, illogical, intuitive, improvisatory, autocephalous, synthetic, abstract, fantasmic, cerebral, unpredictably fulminating and stupefying. (See Letters and Documents for full text.)

13 FEBRUARY 1909

Le vieil Aigle, lyric drama in one act by the Rumanian-born French impresario Raoul GUNSBOURG, to his own libretto from the tumultuous history of the Tatar khanate in 14th-century Crimea, wherein the Khan throws his favorite concubine into the Black Sea when he discovers his son's infatuation for her, and as he belatedly realizes that by this impetuous act he has alienated his son's affections, he plunges into the dark waters himself, is produced at the Monte Carlo Opera under Gunsbourg's own management, in an arrangement from disparate musical materials supplied by the nominal composer, made by Leon Jehin, and with Chaliapin in the title role of the "old eagle."

(Loewenberg in his *Annals of Opera*, Grove's *Dictionary of Music and Musicians*, Baker's *Biographical Dictionary of Musicians* edited by Nicolas Slonimsky, and *Die Musik in Geschichte und Gegenwart,* all incorrectly state that the libretto is taken from a story by Maxim Gorky.)

16 FEBRUARY 1909

Le Cobzar, one-act lyric drama by Gabrielle FERRARI, a pupil of Gounod and one of the very few female composers of opera in France, depicting a Rumanian itinerant musician whose strumming on his four-stringed backbent-necked *cobza* fascinates a local matron so irresistibly that she kills her husband and follows the Cobzar to hard labor in the salt mines whither he has been sent for the previous murder of his Gypsy mistress, with both going blind from the reflected white light of the saline rocks while their hypersalinated bodies disintegrate into painful compounds of flesh, to a musical setting in a competently imitative style with some coloristic Rumanian dances appearing in a symphonic intermezzo, is produced in Monte Carlo.

19 FEBRUARY 1909

Arnold SCHOENBERG composes the first piece of *Drei Klavierstücke*, op. 11, which marks the historic departure from tonality and the inception of conscious atonality, leading eventually to the new method of composition with twelve tones related only to one another.

I am striving towards a goal that seems to be a certainty, and I already feel the opposition that I shall have to overcome. . . . It is not any lack of invention, of technical skill, or the knowledge of postulates of other contemporary systems of esthetics that has impelled me in this direction. . . . I am following an inner compulsion that is stronger than my education, stronger than my artistic training. (Arnold Schoenberg in a program note) (Date, from Josef Rufer's *Das Werk Arnold Schoenbergs*, Kassel, 1959, refers to the first manuscript, in pencil; the date of 19 March 1909, given in previous editions of *Music Since 1900*, is that of a final copy.)

21 FEBRUARY 1909

Enchanted Lake, "fable-tableau" by Anatoli LIADOV, a concentrically symmetric symphonic cinquefoil, in which the serene surface of the water is gently agitated by a summer wind on a starlit Russian night, calling forth a lyrical round of romantic Russian mermaids, with fleeting thematic motives following a tertian modulatory scheme shifting either by minor or major thirds in the characteristic manner of Rimsky-Korsakov's marine music, and rich harmonies of ninth-chords supported by deeply anchored pedal points, scored for an orchestra vibrant with airy harps, celesta raindrops and fluid flute figurations, is performed for the first time in St. Petersburg, Nicolas Tcherepnin conducting.

Ah, how I love my Enchanted Lake! How picturesque it is, how clear, with its stars and mystery in its depths! (From Liadov's letter to a friend written during the composition of the work in 1908)

22 FEBRUARY 1909

Arnold SCHOENBERG composes the second piece of *Drei Klavierstücke*, op. 11, with a vestigial basso ostinato remaining as the unsevered umbilical link with the tonal past. (Date from the manuscript in pencil, without expression marks and tempo indications, as given in Josef Rufer's *Das Werk Schoenbergs*, Kassel, 1959; the date 20 February 1909, given in previous editions of *Music Since 1900*, is apparently less substantiated.)

22 FEBRUARY 1909

In the Fen Country, symphonic impression by Ralph VAUGHAN WILLIAMS, composed in 1904, written in a folk-like English fashion, is performed for the first time in London at a concert conducted by Sir Thomas Beecham.

24 FEBRUARY 1909

Margarita la Tornera, last opera, in three acts, by Ruperto CHAPÍ is produced in Madrid.

27 FEBRUARY 1909

Katharina, dramatic legend in three acts by the Belgian composer Edgar TINEL, dealing with the life and death of Saint Catherine, the Egyptian virgin of Alexandria converted to Christianity in 307 A.D., who became so steadfast in her new faith that she confuted the court philosophers charged with her repaganization (she is the tutelary saint of philosophers) and rejected the passionate proposal of the Emperor Maximinus to be his concubine, whereupon he ordered her to be drawn and quartered on a specially constructed wheel (she is the patron saint of wheelwrights), and when the wheel was providentially split by a bolt of lightning, had to resort to decollation, and in despair took poison himself, the score being constructed in the style of a religious oratorio, with the martyred saint's ecstasy illustrated by harp arpeggios and the Emperor's anger by trumpet fanfares, the Christian spirit being reflected in noble triadic harmonies imitative of *Tannhäuser* and *Parsifal*, and paganism represented by a fugal counterpoint derivative of *Die Meistersinger*, is produced in Brussels.

28 FEBRUARY 1909

Suite Française for orchestra by ROGER-DUCASSE, in four movements, *Ouverture, Bourrée, Récitatif et Air, Menuet vif*, an elegant stylization of 18th-century French dances, is performed for the first time at the Concerts Colonne in Paris.

1 MARCH 1909

Giovanni TEBALDINI publishes in the *Rivista Musicale Italiana* an article sarcastically entitled *Telepatia Musicale* purporting to prove, by tabulating some fifty musical examples, that Richard Strauss made use in his opera *Elektra* of a number of thematic patterns and harmonic progressions from the opera *Cassandra* by Vittorio GNECCHI produced three years and one and a half months before *Elektra*.

What should I do? Is there a better way to combat hatred and envy than noble silence? You know the story of Hercules and the hydra. I had already decided not to make any reply even before I had read the article of Tebaldini in which he makes publicity in behalf of Gnecchi. Now that I have read it, I am even more determined to remain silent. This whole affair is too silly to discuss, not to mention the chauvinistic undertones distinctly noticeable in these attacks. . . . (From a letter dated 5 May 1909 from Richard Strauss to Romain Rolland,

published in a French translation in *Richard Strauss et Romain Rolland*, Paris, 1951)

6 MARCH 1909

Et Bryllup i Katakomberne (The Wedding in the Catacombs), opera in three acts by the Danish composer Georg HOEBERG, is produced in Copenhagen.

9 MARCH 1909

Sinfonischer Prolog zu einer Tragödie by Max REGER, his op. 108, a rhapsodically sprawling overture to an unnamed and unimplied tragedy, is performed for the first time in Cologne.

The whole vapid *Prologue to a Tragedy*, overladen with the ballast of laborious counterpoint and overheated by straining after tragic pathos, is utterly artificial. It lacks, as does all of Reger's music, the warm rays of a more genuine, greater and simpler art. (Walter Niernann, *Leipziger neueste Nachrichten*, April 1909)

16 MARCH 1909

Serge KOUSSEVITSKY and his wife Natalie establish in Moscow, with branches in Germany and France, the Russian Music Publishing House (*Editions Russes de Musique, Russischer Musikverlag*), with a capital of 1,250,000 French francs in gold currency, founded for the purpose of publishing works by important Russian composers. (Scriabin's *Prometheus*, Stravinsky's *Pétrouchka, Le Sacre du Printemps*, and *Symphonie de Psaumes*, Prokofiev's *Classical Symphony* were among its publications.)

17 MARCH 1909

Hellera, opera in three acts by Italo MONTEMEZZI, is produced in Turin.

25 MARCH 1909

Prinzessin Brambilla, first opera in two acts by the German composer Walter BRAUNFELS, after a whimsical tale of E. T. A. Hoffmann in which European royalty and characters from the commedia dell'arte commingle, set to a thoroughly conventional musical score, with some metrical asymmetries as a token of modernity, is produced in Stuttgart.

25 MARCH 1909

Ruperto CHAPÌ, Spanish composer of 168 zarzuelas and some operas in a grander manner, dies in Madrid two days before his 58th birthday.

26 MARCH 1909

First Symphony in F minor by Karol SZYMANOWSKI is performed for the first time by the Warsaw Philharmonic Orchestra, Gregor Fitelberg conducting.

2 APRIL 1909

Mayor Hibbard of Boston bans the announced local production by the Manhattan Opera Company of *Salome* by Richard STRAUSS, giving for a reason a telephone call from a woman acquaintance who had heard the opera in

New York, was shocked by it, and declared that its presentation would endanger Boston morality.

4 APRIL 1909
Henry HADLEY conducts in Maine (where he held the post of Kapellmeister) the first, and last, performance of his one-act opera *Safié* to a German libretto dealing with a Persian princess poisoned by the court magician after she refuses to submit to the amorous blandishments of his son, with a musical score comprising sinuous oriental melismas and exotic colorisms set in Wagnerian harmonies.

9 APRIL 1909
In a historic first wireless transmission of the human voice Enrico CARUSO's singing is broadcast from the Metropolitan Opera House in New York through two microphones placed in the footlights of the stage to the home of Lee DE FOREST, inventor of the Audion, three-element vacuum tube which made radio possible.

9 APRIL 1909
DEBUSSY conducts at the Concerts Colonne in Paris the first performance of his *Trois chansons de Charles d'Orléans*, for a chorus a cappella, conceived in a medievally restrained idiom with a revealing infusion of bleakly heterophonic elements.

10 APRIL 1909
The Beauty Spot, a musical play by Reginald DEKOVEN, revolving around a revealing birthmark on the knee of a Paris model married to a Tsarist envoy General Samovar who spends a fortune tracking down her portraits showing the compromising feature, is produced in New York City.

19 APRIL 1909
Dido, opera by the Greek composer Denis LAVRANGES, derived from Virgil's *Aeneid* and depicting in effective Italianate cantilena the self-immolation of the Carthaginian Queen abandoned by Aeneas, is produced in Athens.

23 APRIL 1909
Second Symphony, in D minor, by the sage dean of the Russian Mighty Five, Mily BALAKIREV, written at the age of 70, and set in four movements: (1) *Allegro ma non troppo*, lively and direct in its classical symmetry, (2) *Scherzo alla Cosacca*, containing quotations from Ukrainian dance tunes, (3) *Romanza*, frankly romantic in its Schumannesque inspiration, and (4) *Finale*, marked *Tempo di Polacca*, a vigorous orchestral polonaise, is performed for the first time in St. Petersburg, Sergei Liapunov conducting.

24 APRIL 1909
La Perugina, last opera by Edoardo MASCHERONI, in four acts, is produced in Naples.

26 APRIL 1909
Samson et Dalila, celebrated opera of Camille SAINT-SAËNS, is at long last presented on an English stage, at Covent Garden, London, after the Lord Chamberlain at a special request of Queen Alexandra rescinds the ban imposed on theatrical plays and operas portraying biblical characters.

1 MAY 1909
Serge RACHMANINOFF conducts in Moscow the first performance of his symphonic poem *The Island of the Dead* (completed on 17 April 1909), inspired by Böcklin's tenebrous painting in which shrouded human figures cross in a somber boat the Stygian waters to a cypress-lined island resembling one of the Ponza Islands north of the Gulf of Naples ("It must produce a stillness such that one would be awed by a knock at the door," Böcklin once said), set in a pantheistic A minor with asymmetrical rhythms within the meter of 5/8, softly eddying in the strings until the minatory tones of Dies Irae are heard, and after a tide of inexorable mortuary waves of diminished-seventh chords, lapsing into the cadential caducity of the sempiternal tonic A.

5 MAY 1909
Bacchus, opera in four acts by Jules MASSENET, to a libretto after Catulle Mendès in which Bacchus takes Ariadne to India where a local queen tries to seduce him with the aid of holy monkeys but is fulminated down by Zeus, and Bacchus with Ariadne are apotheosized on Olympus, with both the Greek and Indian mythological figures characterized uniformly by ecclesiastic plainchant melos, is produced at the Paris Opéra.

5 MAY 1909
Robin's Ende, first opera, in two acts, by the German composer Eduard KÜNNEKE, is produced in Mannheim.

15 MAY 1909
Zoraide, opera by the Argentinian composer Juan Bautista MASSA, is produced in Buenos Aires.

15 MAY 1909
Giuseppe BLANC, 23-year-old Italian student, composes the song *Giovinezza*, destined to become the official anthem of the Fascists.

On the 15th of May 1909, we students were to have a farewell dinner before graduation, and on that morning several students came to me and said: "You must write a song for the dinner tonight." I said I would if somebody would write the words. Nino Oxilia volunteered, and in five minutes completed the verse. It took me no longer than that to write the music. (From an interview with Giuseppe Blanc in the New York *Times* of 10 October 1934; the story is corroborated in the article on Blanc in *Dizionario dei musicisti* by Alberto de Angelis, 3rd edition, Rome, 1930)

18 MAY 1909
Isaac ALBÉNIZ, Spanish composer, the first among his countrymen to develop a national style of composition in which the festive spirit of the dance and the nocturnal poetry of the land are transmuted in all their variety into the virtuoso idiom of modern piano music, dies in Cambo-les-Bains, in the French Pyrenees, eleven days before reaching his 49th birthday.

21 MAY 1909

Wassili LEPS, 39-year-old Russian pianist, conducts the Philadelphia Operatic Society in the first performance of his grand Japanese opera *Hoshi-San*, in three acts, with the action evolving in 1688 and dealing with a dancing girl of the Buddhist temple who is imprisoned without food or water because of her love for a desecrator of shrines, but whose prayer-dance redeems her soul and permits her to rejoin him in a hill of skulls, to a musical score presenting an amalgam of pentatonic orientalisms with Russian-style harmonies.

22 MAY 1909

Richard H. STEIN completes, in a brochure meaningfully dated "am Geburtstage Richard Wagners 1909" (i.e., 22 May 1909), a detailed exposition of his system of composition in quarter-tones, elaborating the introduction to his *Zwei Konzertstücke* of 1906, for cello and piano, the first composition containing quarter-tones ever to be published.

23 MAY 1909

Fourth Symphony by the Swiss composer Hans HUBER, subtitled *Akademische*, in four movements couched in the form of a concerto grosso for string orchestra, is performed for the first time in Basel. (A revised version, for two string orchestras, organ and piano, was first performed in Zurich on 3 February 1919.)

30 MAY 1909

Benny David GOODMAN, "The King of Swing," magnetic killer-diller on the "licorice stick" (clarinet), by his art capable of moving cats and jitterbugs of the 1930's to ritualistic frenzy, is born in Chicago.

1 JUNE 1909

Giuseppe MARTUCCI, Italian pianist, conductor and educator, one of the most ardent adherents to the cause of German music in Italy, the composer of Wagneromantic symphonies and chamber music, dies in Naples, at the age of 53.

2 JUNE 1909

Lucien HILLEMACHER, French composer who amalgamated his musical personality with that of his brother Paul, both being Prix de Rome winners, and wrote passable operas in fraternal collaboration under the name P. L. Hillemacher, dies in his native Paris eight days before reaching 49 years of age, destined to be survived by his older brother by 24 years.

7 JUNE 1909

A Mass of Life, grandiose oratorio for soloists, chorus and large orchestra by Frederick DELIUS, pagan rather than Christian in its pantheism, written to selected passages from Nietzsche's *Also sprach Zarathustra*, and couched in a solemn romantic style with occasional modernistic discordancies, is performed for the first time in its entirety in London, under the direction of Thomas Beecham. (The second part only of *A Mass of Life* was performed in Munich on 4 June 1908.)

Mr. Delius was not happy in naming his work *A Mass of Life*, for the composition refers neither to the ritual of the Church of Rome nor to any particular seething mass of vitality. Its essence is the personality of Nietzsche, who, it may be added, died in a lunatic asylum. (*Referee*, London, 13 June 1909)

The ear in listening to the choral climaxes in *A Mass of Life* is bewildered that any man should consider this ugly featureless noise as music. (Glasgow *Herald*, 9 June 1909)

(In his book *Frederick Delius*, New York, 1960, Sir Thomas Beecham writes [p. 155]: "The climax in the crescendo of interest was attained in the performance at Queen's Hall on June 10th of *A Mass of Life*; this being the first time the complete work had been given anywhere." The date is in error, for an extensive account of the concert of 7 June 1909 at which *A Mass of Life* was performed for the first time is found in *The Times*, London, 8 June 1909, concluding as follows: "There was a fairly large and appreciative audience and Mr. Delius was called to the platform and heartily applauded.")

9 JUNE 1909

Ode to Discord, "a chimerical bombination in four bursts" by Charles Villiers STANFORD, dedicated to the Amalgamated Society of Boiler Makers, for voices and a large orchestra which includes a hydrophone and a dreadnaught drum, with all kinds of modernities such as the whole-tone scale and ninth-chords strewn over the score, and featuring the aria, "Hence, loathed Melody!—Divine Cacophony, assume—The rightful overlordship in her room—And with Percussion's stimulating aid—Expel the Heavenly but no longer youthful Maid!" is performed for the first time in London.

1 JULY 1909

United States Copyright Law, securing exclusive rights to composers and/or publishers to print, publish, copy, vend, arrange, record by means of a gramophone or any other mechanical device, and perform publicly for profit original musical compositions, and affording protection against infringement for a period of 28 years and a renewal period of the same length, enacted by Congress on 4 March 1909, comes into force (information and wording from *The Copyright Law of the United States of America*).

4 JULY 1909

Erik SATIE is presented an honorary academic degree at Arcueil-Cachan, a suburb of Paris, for his services to the cause of local musical education, and, presaging the formation of a mythically realistic École d' Arcueil, to which Milhaud, Poulenc, Auric and many other young musical rebels subsequently flocked, adopts the long-winded title of *Président d'Honneur du Comité de Pupilles Artistes et Directeur du Service Intérieur du Patronage Laïque*.

13 JULY 1909

Elegy for orchestra by Edward ELGAR, written in memory of a junior warden of the English Worshipful Company of Musicians, is performed for the first time in London.

15 JULY 1909

The name of Igor STRAVINSKY appears for the first time in a European press review, in a dispatch from St. Petersburg, published in the *Bulletin français de la Société Indépendante Musicale*:

The young Stravinsky was a private pupil of Rimsky-Korsakov. He is the composer of a symphony in E-flat major and of a suite *La Bergère et le Faune*. This suite contains interesting pages of music, and it will draw attention to its young composer whose talent will develop still further.

3 AUGUST 1909

Eithne, "romantic opera" in two acts by Robert O'DWYER, founded on the Irish folk story *Ean an Ceoil Binn*, the first opera to words in the Erse language, dealing with the king of Eirinn whose heir is unjustly accused of killing the royal hound, but is exonerated, meets a mysterious princess named Eithne, fights a tournament with his step-brothers for her possession, defeats them, marries her and is crowned when the old ruler dies, written in an unpretentious style of folk-like balladry, with occasional thematic uses of the Celtic pentatonic scale, is produced by the Irish Company of the Oireachtas in Dublin. (Date communicated by the composer. The date given in Loewenberg's *Annals of Opera* refers to a later production at the Gaiety Theatre in Dublin on 16 May 1910, which is also cited in the printed score of the opera.)

7 AUGUST 1909

Arnold SCHOENBERG composes the third of *Drei Klavierstücke*, op. 11, completing the suite of three piano pieces marked by a conspicuous absence of a key signature and a decisive recession from tonality.

12 AUGUST 1909

Maïda, first opera by the 36-year-old French composer André BLOCH, is performed for the first time at Aix-les-Bains.

7 SEPTEMBER 1909

Frederick DELIUS conducts at the Hereford Music Festival the first performance of his *Dance Rhapsody No. 1*, derived in its thematic material from English countryside tunes, and scored for a colorful orchestral ensemble, including the novel baritone oboe, the Heckelphone.

The *Dance Rhapsody* is an extremely brilliant piece. . . . Although it is the work of a thoroughly modern composer, it was warmly applauded, and Mr. Delius, who conducted, had repeatedly to bow his acknowledgements to the audience. (*Manchester Guardian*, 8 September 1909)

The performance of the *Dance Rhapsody* by Frederick Delius under the composer's direction only served to impress the mind with the second-rate and second-hand character of the tunes. The duet between the English horn and the Heckelphone (a kind of bass oboe) at the beginning was robbed of its misty atmospheric effect by the fact that the player had to struggle with the Heckelphone to produce the notes in any way possible. Then the prosaic dance tune and the still more commonplace pendant to it were emphasized without a gleam of humor or rhythmic lightness. It is really unkind to allow a composer to dissect his score in public. (*The Times*, London, 8 September 1909)

Mr. Percy Grainger believes that Delius is the greatest living composer. . . . He was not heated by wine when he made this statement, for he is a total abstainer. . . . Delius is a strange apparition in the musical world, not easily classified. Take this *Dance Rhapsody*, for instance. The chief theme is of a jig-like nature; this is repeated in a scrappy fashion, and then suddenly we are in the East, and there is the thought of Russians waiting for languorous dancing girls. What, pray, has the little introduction to do with what follows? We have yet to be persuaded that Delius warrants Mr. Grainger's perfervid admiration. (Philip Hale, Boston *Herald*, 25 February 1916)

11 SEPTEMBER 1909

Bacchus triomphant, opera by Camille ERLANGER, is produced in Bordeaux.

14 SEPTEMBER 1909

Sergei PROKOFIEV graduates from the St. Petersburg Conservatory in the classes of pianoforte (with Anna Essipova) and composition (with Rimsky-Korsakov, Wihtol and Liadov), and receives a diploma as a "free artist." (Date communicated to the author in 1936 by Maximilian Steinberg, professor of the St. Petersburg Conservatory, and later its director.)

6 OCTOBER 1909

Dudley BUCK, American organist, pianist and composer of competent organ music and impressively sounding cantatas, who, like so many serious American musicians of his generation, went to Leipzig for his training, and upon return taught younger Americans the Germanic science of music, dies in Orange, New Jersey, at the age of 70.

7 OCTOBER 1909

A posthumous production is given in Moscow of RIMSKY-KORSAKOV'S last opera *Le Coq d'or (The Golden Cockerel)*, subtitled "impersonated fable," after Pushkin's versified tale, in three acts:

(1) wherein a gluttonous and somnolent tsar withdraws his armies from the horders to the immediate vicinity of the capital and for security obtains from the court astrologer a magically alert weathervane in the shape of a cock who would crow an alarm in a gaily fanfarous trumpet call of a major triad soaring into a lamentably unrelated key the moment the enemy attacks; (2) wherein the tsar arrives too late on the battlefield strewn with the corpses of his soldiers, the stillness and the corruption of death signalized by the creeping motion of diminished seventh-chords colliding in strident dissonance with a procession of augmented triads moving in the opposite direction, while inverted whole-tone scales stride in the basses in gigantic steps of minor sevenths and mournful progressions of alternating semitones and sesquitones enhance the tonal ambiguity of the music, when suddenly an oriental queen makes an appearance and sings a radiant hymn to the sun embroidered with serpentine melismas of such seductive power that the tsar forgets his disasters and takes her home for a bride; (3) wherein the wedding march combining the intervalic obliquity of orientalistic melos with sonorous Russian harmonies heterophonically embedded in well-lined pedal points is rudely interrupted by the astrologer who demands as his payment for the golden cockerel the cession of the bride herself, so infuriating the tsar that he slays him with a baton, whereupon the cock flies off his perch and administers a fatal peck at the tsar's occipital fissure.

17 OCTOBER 1909

Nicola SPINELLI, Italian composer of melodramatic operas, a minor master of the Verismo who explored the rustic chivalries and the caustic rivalries among passionate Sicilians in search of inspiration, dies in Rome at the age of 44, a victim of dementia praecox induced by youthful incontinence and intemperance.

19 OCTOBER 1909

William Ratcliff, last opera in two acts by the Dutch composer Cornelis DOPPER, after Heine's melodramatic ballad detailing the gory murders in a Scottish family, is produced in Weimar.

4 NOVEMBER 1909

Serge RACHMANINOFF makes his first appearance in the United States as a pianist, in a recital at Smith College, Northampton, Massachusetts.

6 NOVEMBER 1909

Izeÿl, music drama in three acts by the Germanized Scottish-born composer Eugen D'ALBERT, dealing with a venomously mouthed Hindu princess of 600 B.C., who implants a kiss of death on the lips of her suitors but perishes of her own labiodental poison when she attempts to seduce an osculatorily immune stranger, set to an artificially flavored orientalistic musical score inspissated with Wagneromantic harmonies, is produced in Hamburg.

8 NOVEMBER 1909

The Boston Opera House, erected in the fashionable Fenway Park section of the town, opens under the management of Henry Russell, with a gala performance of Ponchielli's *La Gioconda.*

10 NOVEMBER 1909

Ludvig SCHYTTE, German-trained Danish pianist, whose ingratiatingly pianistic pieces with programmatic titles are eminently suitable for teaching purposes, dies in Berlin at the age of 61.

11 NOVEMBER 1909

Pierrot and Pierrette, allegorical fantasy in two scenes by the English composer Josef HOLBROOKE, wherein Pierrot, incited by the devil, temporarily plunges into the vice-ridden tourbillon of urban life, but remorsefully returns to his irreproachable and unreproaching Pierrette, is produced in London, under the direction of the composer.

12 NOVEMBER 1909

Der Graf von Luxemburg, operetta in two acts by Franz LEHÁR, wherein a Russian Grand Duke, infatuated with a complaisant girl in a European spa, engages an accommodating local count to marry her incognito so that after a quick divorce she would, as a titled lady, be eligible to marry his royal self, but is frustrated as the count and the lady unpremeditatedly fall in love at a masked ball, with a musical score rich in singingly swinging waltz tunes, is performed for the first time in Vienna.

15 NOVEMBER 1909

On Wenlock Edge, suite in six sections for tenor, piano and string quartet by Ralph VAUGHAN WILLIAMS, after A. E. Housman's poem *A Shropshire Lad,* reflecting thoughts on life, love and death, set to music in spacious modalities of English country folksongs, is performed for the first time in London.

22 NOVEMBER 1909

Second Suite for small orchestra by Béla BARTÓK, based on Hungarian rural dance tunes, is performed for the first time in Budapest. (A two-piano arrangement made 30 years later was performed by Bartók and his wife in Chicago on 6 January 1942.)

26 NOVEMBER 1909

The Wasps, incidental music to a play by Aristophanes, by Ralph VAUGHAN WILLIAMS, scored for tenor, baritone, male quartet and orchestra, is performed for the first time at the University of Cambridge, England. (A symphonic suite was drawn from this score in 1912, and first performed in London on 23 July 1912, under the composer's direction.)

28 NOVEMBER 1909

During his first tour of the United States, Serge RACHMANINOFF gives in New York the first performance anywhere, with the New York Symphony Orchestra conducted by Walter Damrosch, of his *Third Piano Concerto,* in D minor, in three movements, composed in Moscow between June and October 1909:

(1) *Allegro ma non tanto,* in 4/4 time, opening with a contemplative alternation of the tonic and the supertonic, in homophonically lyric tones, efflorescing into garlands of arpeggios leading to an exuberant cadenza covering the entire range of the keyboard, then returning to the initial mood in a philosophical recapitulation; (2) *Intermezzo,* 3/4, ostensibly in A major with a characteristically Russian chromatic declination of the submediant tending towards the basic D minor, then evolving into a magniloquent D-flat harmonic major and finally, through enharmonic change, returning to A major and D minor, concluding on a plagal cadence; (3) *Finale,* attacked without pause, set in *alla breve* time, in the initial key of D minor, palpitating in rhythms similar to the opening, then digressing into C major, and ending with a typical rhythmic figure of one long, two short and one long note in fortissimo, identical with the melorhythmic ending of the *Second Piano Concerto.*

The title Fantasy would seem to suit Rachmaninoff's *Third Piano Concerto* better. It is rambling in texture and unstereotyped in its makeup.... The first movement is neither long nor brilliant.... A wailing Russian note pervades not only this movement but the other two. Mr. Rachmaninoff has labeled the second movement an Intermezzo. It is in several tonalities and several tempos, and leads into the finale, which is the longest and the most brilliant movement of the work. When the composer had finished, he received a well-deserved ovation from the audience, and it is likely that the concerto will be heard soon again. (New York *Times,* 29 November 1909)

30 NOVEMBER 1909

Sheikh Senan, opera in four acts by the 24-year-old Tatar composer Uzeir GADZHIBEKOV, to his own libretto dealing with a muezzin's love for a beautiful Georgian maiden inconveniently betrothed to a local prince, is performed for the first time in Baku, the composer conducting.

1 DECEMBER 1909

Zeppelins grosse Fahrt, dramatic symphony by the 64-year-old German composer August BUNGERT, subtitled *Genius triumphans*, and depicting in grandiosely Wagnero-mantic tones the proud flight of an early dirigible airship, with engines working in fugal counterpoint, the propeller whirring in the kettledrums, and the lyrical Zeppelin leitmotiv soaring over Germany until the landing at Echterdingen where it is torn asunder at its mooring mast by a sudden gust of ascending chromatic thirds, is performed for the first time in Coblenz.

4 DECEMBER 1909

La Sina d'Vargöun, opera in three acts by the vocal spokesman of Italian Futurism, Francesco Balilla PRATELLA, to his own libretto depicting the amorous turbulences in the life of Rosselina dei Vergoni (whose name in the Romagnese dialect is represented by the title of the opera), written in a realistic manner of the Italian Verismo (the heroine stabs her unfaithful lover to death in church during his wedding to her successor), the score abounding in folk melodies, in a harmonic idiom, utterly non-Futurist and non-antimelodic, closely emulating that of Mascagni, is produced in Bologna, as the winner of the Baruzzi prize.

A year ago, a jury composed of Pietro Mascagni, Giacomo Orefice, Guglielmo Mattioli, Rodolfo Ferrari, and the critic Gian Battista Nappi, selected my futurist opera *La Sina d'Vargöun*, to my own libretto in free verse, as the winner in a competition for the prize of 10,000 lire, willed by the Bologna Citizen Cincinnato Baruzzi to cover the expenses of production of a superior and worthy operatic work. The performance that took place in December 1909 at the Teatro Comunale in Bologna brought me a success, marked by stupid and despicable criticisms, generous defense by friends and unknowns, honors and a host of enemies. Having thus made my entrance in triumph upon the Italian musical scene, and placed in contact with the public, music publishers and critics, I could judge with utmost composure the intellectual mediocrity, the mercantile baseness and misoneism which reduce Italian music to a single immutable form of vulgar melodrama, placing Italy in the position of absolute inferiority in the futurist evolution of music among nations. (Francesco Balilla Pratella in his *Manifesto dei Musicisti Futuristi*, issued in Milan on 11 October 1910)

4 DECEMBER 1909

Il Segreto di Susanna, one-act musical comedietta, or Intermezzo, by Ermanno WOLF-FERRARI (the horrifying secret being that Suzanne indulged in smoking—a dreadful offense to the morality of the 1900's), with music written in a pleasantly neo-classical Italian style, is produced for the first time in Munich, under the German title *Susannens Geheimnis*.

5 DECEMBER 1909

Ebenezer PROUT, English music theorist, author of detailed and magnificently ponderous tomes dealing with harmony, counterpoint, form and orchestration, himself the composer of symphonic and chamber music in which no academic rule is ever broken, dies in London at the age of 74.

8 DECEMBER 1909

Le Cœur du Moulin, "pièce lyrique" in two acts by the aristocratic French composer Déodat DE SÉVERAC (he descended from the kings of Aragon), to a libretto dealing with an 18th-century villager in Languedoc who leaves home and a fiancée in quest of better fortunes and upon return tries to win her back from his friend who in the meantime has honorably married her, but is dissuaded from his treacherous design by the miraculously audible voices emanating from the heart of the local mill (hence the title), to a musical setting in which the intrinsic operatic monotony is relieved by the intercalation of melodic refrains from old French songs, is produced at the Opéra-Comique in Paris.

10 DECEMBER 1909

Aino, opera by the Finnish composer Erkki MELARTIN, his only stage work, inspired by an episode in the *Kalevala*, is produced in Helsingfors.

12 DECEMBER 1909

Kikimora, fantastic scherzo for orchestra by Anatoly LIADOV, depicting the posthumous pranks of an unbaptized infant girl, in two sections, a poetic *Adagio* wherein the kikimora is incubated in a crystal carriage tended by a cat, in gently swinging feline cradle rhythms, and a demoniacal tritone-laden *Presto*, representing her emergence into a life of mischief, is performed for the first time in St. Petersburg, Alexander Siloti conducting.

15 DECEMBER 1909

Francisco TÁRREGA, the Spanish guitarist who elevated the guitar to the stature of a classical instrument by writing for it works of formal elegance, dies in Barcelona at the age of 57.

16 DECEMBER 1909

Duke or Devil, a farcical opera in one act by the English composer Nicholas Comyn GATTY, dealing with a ruling duke of 15th-century Bologna mistaken for the devil because of his black cloak and nearly put to death, is produced in Manchester.

23 DECEMBER 1909

Das Tal der Liebe, a musical comedy in three acts by Oskar STRAUS, set in 1770, wherein a stern Prussian Markgraf announces a contest for the best wet nurse for his newly born son, thus giving a chance for a young bride to join her soldier husband in a valley of love (hence the title), is produced in Vienna.

26 DECEMBER 1909

Den Lille Havfrue, ballet by the Danish composer Fini Valdemar HENRIQUES, after Hans Christian Andersen's melancholy tale about a little mermaid who had her fishtail bifurcated for the love of a riparian prince but returns to her native aquatic element when she realizes that she can never be more than an unsexual companion, is produced in Copenhagen.

(The ballet provided the inspiration for the famous bronze statue The Little Mermaid in Copenhagen harbor, made by the sculptor Edvard Eriksen, for which Ellen Price, the original prima ballerina of the ballet, was the model until she became pregnant, and Eriksen's wife finished the modeling. The statue was installed on a rock in Copenhagen harbor in August 1913. On the night of 25 April 1964, the statue was mysteriously decapitated by vandals, but a new head was cast from the plaster original, with the neck reinforced with an extra layer of bronze to prevent a recurrence of vandalism, and the completed statue reinstalled on 1 June 1964.)

26 DECEMBER 1909

Kôsçak YAMADA, 23-year-old Japanese composer, conducts in Tokyo the first performance of his oratorio *The Star of Promise*.

The Star of Promise is the first attempt to render a dramatic theme musically by a Japanese composer by means of a Japanese orchestra, chorus and soloists. (Japan *Advertiser*, Tokyo, 28 December 1909)

1910

8 JANUARY 1910

Zigeunerliebe, operetta in three acts by Franz LEHÁR, wherein a Gypsy girl tempted by a vagrant guitar strummer in a Hungarian camp is saved from perdition through a prophetic dream exposing her lover's future perfidy, richly spangled with Csárdás melorhythms and cymbalom clangs, is performed for the first time in Vienna.

10 JANUARY 1910

Rumanian Symphony for piano and orchestra by the Paris-educated Rumanian composer Stan GOLESTAN is performed for the first time in Bucharest, with Georges Enesco playing the piano part.

13 JANUARY 1910

The first radio broadcast of operatic selections is made from the stage of the Metropolitan Opera House in New York, with Caruso singing arias from *Cavalleria Rusticana* and *Pagliacci*, "trapped and magnified by the dictograph directly from the stage and borne by wireless Hertzian waves."

15 JANUARY 1910

Maia, lyric drama in three acts by Ruggero LEONCAVALLO, to a melodramatic libretto by his French publisher Paul Choudens, culminating in a fatal encounter between two competitors for Maia's favors on the island of Cainargtle and her suicide by drowning in the delta of the Rhône River, with an undistinguished musical score palely reminiscent of his striking *Pagliacci*, is produced in Rome, with Pietro Mascagni conducting.

17 JANUARY 1910

Fritz Stein conducts in Jena the first performance of the so-called *Jena Symphony* in C major, attributed to BEETHOVEN in an old inscription in the orchestral parts copied by an unknown hand and found in the archives of the College of Music in Jena, in four movements, *Adagio-Allegro vivace*, *Adagio cantabile*, *Menuetto* and *Finale*, in a style about 75% Haydn, 20% Mozart and 5% early Beethoven. (The symphony proved to be the work of Beethoven's close contemporary Friedrich Witt when C. Robbins Landon discovered in 1956 the original manuscript signed by Witt.)

19 JANUARY 1910

Malbruk, comic fantasy in three acts by Ruggero LEONCAVALLO after a story from Boccaccio, dealing with a semi-legendary king of Lower Navarra who woos the Damsel of the White Goose but is diverted into a crusade and ends up as the master of a Turkish harem with 49 odalisques, is produced in Rome.

22 JANUARY 1910

Der Schleier der Pierrette, pantomime in three scenes by the Hungarian composer Ernst von DOHNÁNYI, to the bittersweet story of modern Vienna in terms of a fairy tale by Arthur Schnitzler, is performed for the first time at the Dresden Opera, conducted by Ernst von Schuch.

23 JANUARY 1910

Banadietrich, opera in three acts by Siegfried WAGNER, to his own libretto wherein a Germanic youth (Banadietrich means Dietrich of Bern in the Wendish language) trades away to a realistically East Prussian devil his true devotion to a swan-white undine Schwanweiss but is redeemed in the end and joins her in the waters of her native river, the score genetically derived from the musical substance of his father Richard Wagner and his grandfather Franz Liszt, exhaling dramatic valor and exuding lyric emotion from the deepest recesses of major ninth-chords, is performed for the first time in Karlsruhe.

When one bears the name of Wagner, a certain degree of diffidence attends one's efforts, and one has greater difficulties to overcome than other musical composers. I hope, however, that in the course of time this distrust of my own efforts will disappear. (Siegfried Wagner's statement at the Vienna production of *Banadietrich* on 15 May 1912)

24 JANUARY 1910

La Glu, musical drama in four acts by the 31-year-old French composer Gabriel DUPONT, to a highly melodramatic libretto wherein a Parisian cocotte, the Glu, glues herself nefariously to the only son of a pious widowed lady in a heretofore sinless seacoast village in Brittany and in the last act is slain by her with an axe while a local doctor rushing in to lend tardy medical aid is revealed as the Glu's separated husband, set to a suitably emotive musical score in the manner of Dupont's teacher Massenet, with symphonic interludes painting the desolate landscape in bleakly vacuous fifths, is performed for the first time in Nice.

3 FEBRUARY 1910

Endymion's Dream, cantata by the British mulatto composer Samuel COLERIDGE-TAYLOR, for women's voices, chorus and orchestra, to the words of Keats dealing with the selenophilic infatuation of a Greek youth kissed by the moon goddess, is performed for the first time in Brighton, England.

(Date from *The Times*, London, 4 February 1910. W. C. Berwick Sayers, in his monograph on Coleridge-Taylor, published in 1915, gives the correct date on p. 229, 4 February 1910 on p. 318, and 5 February 1910 on p. 231. The list of works appended to the memoir on Coleridge-Taylor by his widow gives the erroneous 4 February.)

8 FEBRUARY 1910

Fünf Sätze für Streichquartett, op. 5, by Anton von WEBERN, is performed for the first time in Vienna.

16 FEBRUARY 1910

Piemonte, symphonic suite by Leone SINIGAGLIA, based on authentic tunes of his native Piedmont, in four colorful movements: a countryside idyll with violins and harp sustaining the pastoral mood; a rustic ballet throbbing with delicate vulgarity; a religious intermezzo in which an old chant sacred to the Madonna is heard; and a fast festive fair with piercing trumpets and punctuating drums, is performed for the first time anywhere in Utrecht, Holland.

16 FEBRUARY 1910

La Fête chez Thérèse, ballet-pantomime by Reynaldo HAHN, Venezuelan-born Parisian composer, to a story from the world of haut monde and haute couture in Paris in the 1840's, where duchesses, seamstresses, grisettes and ballerinas jealously pullulate, with Carlotta Grisi dancing the *Valse de Giselle* by Friedrich BURGMÜLLER (which Adam actually incorporated in his famous ballet created by her in 1841), to a musical score of high hedonistic piquancy, is performed for the first time at the Grand Opéra in Paris.

19 FEBRUARY 1910

Don Quichotte, "heroic comedy" in five acts by Jules MASSENET, written in a floridly melodious style, wherein Dulcinea disports herself in melismatic coloratura, while guitars, tambourines and castanets strum, jangle and clap, and the harmonies luxuriate in pseudo-Iberian Phrygian cadences, is produced in Monte Carlo, with Chaliapin in the title role providing the tragic idealism absent in the music.

(Date on the printed score is 24 February 1910, but *Le Ménestrel* of 26 February 1910 gives the date 19 February, which is also the date accepted by Loewenberg in his *Annals of Opera*.)

20 FEBRUARY 1910

At a Colonne concert in Paris, under the direction of Gabriel Pierné, the world première is given of DEBUSSY's *Iberia*, second of his three orchestral works under the general title *Images* (the first being *Gigues*, the third *Rondes de Printemps*), completed on 25 December 1908, and consisting of three sections evoking the sights, the odors, and the sounds of Spain:

(1) *Par les rues et par les chemins*, animated walk through the Spanish countryside in whole tones peculiar of Debussy's general musical vocabulary; (2) *Les Parfums de la nuit*, a stilled *tableau odorant*, with the ethereal oil of divided and muted strings dissolving in the rhythms of nocturnal tambourines and flowery melismas adorned in fragrantly soft harmonies; (3) *Le Matin d'un jour de fête*, a joyful festival of Iberian sound, in gentle march time sonorous with chimes and castanets and overflowing with incipient whole-tone scales, reaching an internal climax when the violinists are instructed to hold their instruments under the arms and strum four-part chords like guitar players.

The Iberia of M. Debussy is no longer the Spain of Bizet or Chabrier! What fog! Can there be a typographical error in the program? But surely! The first letter of the title must have fallen out. It should be Siberia! Then everything becomes clear. (René Brancour, *Le Ménestrel*, Paris, 28 June 1913)

21 FEBRUARY 1910

L'Auberge Rouge, lyric novella in two acts by Jean NOUGÈS, after a story by Balzac dealing with a French soldier stationed at Andernach on the Rhine in 1806 who is accused and summarily executed for a murder he did not commit (the killer was his German companion), to a melodramatically effective score (the murder is illustrated by a series of augmented triads), is performed for the first time in Nice.

21 FEBRUARY 1910

Ernst von DOHNÁNYI, 32-year-old Hungarian romanticist, conducts in Budapest the first performance Of his *Suite for Orchestra* in F sharp minor, in four movements:

(1) *Andante con variazioni*, on a modally infected theme with six amiably confected Brahmsophiliac variations; (2) *Scherzo*, wafting pulverized Mendelssohnophonic molecules of euphonious dust, with paired harps providing the gossamer environment; (3) *Romanza*, a Schumannonymous interlude; (4) *Ronda*, a vigorous Brahmsonorous finale.

23 FEBRUARY 1910

Max REGER conducts at Chemnitz the first complete performance of his *Psalm 100* for chorus and orchestra, dedicated to the University of Jena on the occasion of three and a half centuries of its existence.

1 MARCH 1910

The Superior Court of Boston orders the management of the Lenox Hotel to desist from using the name of the Russian prima donna Lydia Lipkovska in the chef Niccolo Sabattini's special "soufflé de fraises à la Lipkovska," charging $2 for it à la carte.

1 MARCH 1910

A century has passed since the birth in Zelazowa Wola, a village near Warsaw, of Fredryk CHOPIN, supreme poet of piano music, originator of a mode of technical expression that in its melismatic complexity borders on polytonality of polar keys in the tritone relationship (as in the B-minor Sonata), atonality (as in the E-minor Prelude) and polyrhythmy (as in *Fantaisie Impromptu*).

(Chopin's baptism certificate of 23 April 1810 gives his date of birth as 22 February 1810, but it is in all probability an error, perhaps through confusion with the day and month of birth of his godfather Fryderyk Skarbek. Chopin's mother always celebrated his birthday on 1 March, and Chopin himself gives this date in his letter of acceptance of membership in the Polish Literary Society in Paris, dated 16 January 1833.)

2 MARCH 1910

DEBUSSY conducts in Paris, at the third of the four Concerts de Musique Française, organized by the French publisher Durand, the first performance of *Rondes de Printemps*, third movement of his orchestral suite *Images*.

These are real pictures in which the composer has endeavored to convey aurally the impressions received by the eye. He attempts to blend the two forms of sensory perception in order to intensify them. The melody, with its infinitely varied rhythms, corresponds to the multiplicity of lines in drawing; the orchestra represents a large palette where each instrument supplies its own color. Just as a painter delights in contrasts of colors, in the interplay of light and shade, so the musician takes pleasure in the shock of unexpected dissonances and the fusion of unusual timbres; he wants us to visualize what he intends us to hear, and the pen he holds in his fingers becomes a brush. This is musical impressionism of a very special kind and of a very rare quality. (From a program note by Charles Malherbe written for this concert)

M. Claude Debussy conducted a new *Image* of his suite in three parts. *Rondes de Printemps* is a relatively short composition, luminous and colorful, always free in form and imprecise in its design, according to the familiar procedure of the composer. However, an ingenious use of the popular round "Nous n'irons plus au bois" lends to this piece some cohesion and unity. (J. Jemain, *Le Ménestrel*, Paris, 12 March 1910)

6 MARCH 1910

Symphonie française, an academically Gallic work by the professorial Théodore DUBOIS, in four movements with allusions to the *Marseillaise* in the Finale, is performed for the first time at the Concerts Colonne in Paris.

7 MARCH 1910

Éros Vainqueur, lyric fairy tale in three acts by Pierre DE BRÉVILLE, wherein Eros, vagabonding in search of unprobed hearts, kidnaps two out of three well-guarded princesses but releases them after instructing them in the art of love while the third princess dies of emotional inanition, to a semi-Wagnerian demi-Debussyan hemi-Straussian musical score containing a ballet wherein nymphs and aegypans descend from a medieval tapestry in a dream and participate in the action, is produced in Brussels.

7 MARCH 1910

Léone, lyric drama in four acts by Samuel ROUSSEAU, wherein a Corsican bandit so fascinates the daughter of a local voltigeur that when he is arrested by her father she falls into deep melancholy and dies of vulvar atrophy, set to music in a harmoniously dramatic vein with a patina of Tristanesque chromaticization, is performed posthumously at the Opéra-Comique in Paris, five and a half years after the composer's death. (Rousseau died on 1 October 1904.)

9 MARCH 1910

Samuel BARBER, American composer whose symphonic, vocal and chamber music is fired by a powerful romantic imagination sustained by a consummate mastery of modern technical means, is born in West Chester, Pennsylvania.

11 MARCH 1910

Malířský Nápad (A Painter's Whim), one-act opera buffa by the Czech composer Otakar ZICH, dealing with life in Bohemia, is produced in Prague.

17 MARCH 1910

Mese mariano (Mary's month, i.e., *May),* one-act opera by Umberto GIORDANO, to a libretto describing the pathetic life of inmates in an orphan asylum, is performed for the first time in Palermo, Sicily.

26 MARCH 1910

Finnish Fantasy for orchestra by Alexander GLAZUNOV, derived thematically from authentic Finnish sources and accoutred in sonorous Russian harmonies, is performed for the first time in St. Petersburg.

27 MARCH 1910

Franz MIKOREY, Munich composer and conductor of the Opera of Dessau, conducts there the first performance of his musical fable in two acts, *Der König von Samarkand,* wherein a young bridegroom dreams of taking possession of the Samarkand throne through fraud, murder and royal marriage, but awakens happily in his native Caucasus and, having exorcised the sinister side of his nature symbolized by the blackness of the skin of his blameless Negro helper, marries his appointed bride and forgets the illusive Orient.

28 MARCH 1910

Édouard COLONNE, French conductor, founder of the renowned series of concerts hospitable to French composers in search of performances, dies in Paris at the age of 71.

6 APRIL 1910

A Somerset Rhapsody by Gustav HOLST, founded on three folksongs, a pastoral tune played by an oboe, a march with trumpets and drums, and a love song introduced by the cello, ending softly, is performed for the first time in London.

10 APRIL 1910

Madame Sherry, musical comedy in three acts by the Bohemian-born naturalized American composer Karl HOSCHNA, dealing with a profligate nephew of an eccentric American millionaire who feigns an Irish marriage to induce his ethnically Gaelic uncle to will him his fortune, featuring a vivacious *Dublin Rag,* is produced in Chicago.

12 APRIL 1910

Der Musikant, a Wagneromantic opera in two acts by Julius BITTNER to his own libretto in which a musician in 1780 loses his favorite coloratura soprano to a petty duke, but quickly finds a less temperamental replacement, is produced in Vienna.

13 APRIL 1910

Arnljot, opera in three acts by the 43-year-old Swedish composer Wilhelm PETERSON-BERGER, to his own libretto, is produced in Stockholm.

13 APRIL 1910

Julius Ferdinand BLÜTHNER, founder of the German piano manufacturing company bearing his name and patent holder of the Aliquot system of stringing in which sympathetic strings are added above the strings in the upper register to increase resonance, dies in Leipzig at the age of 86.

14 APRIL 1910

Boure (The Tempest), cantata by the Czech composer Vítězslav NOVÁK, depicting in turbulent Wagnerian tones the sinking of a slave ship in mid-Atlantic with one of the abducted Africans himself abducting the slave trader's woman, is performed for the first time in Brno.

15 APRIL 1910

Daniel Hjört, opera in five acts by the Finnish composer Selim PALMGREN, to his own libretto in Swedish dealing with the Finnish attack on a Swedish castle in the 16th century complicated by a Swedish officer's love for a rebel daughter of the Finnish chief, is produced in Abo. (First production in the Finnish language took place in Helsinki on 20 February 1929.)

17 APRIL 1910

Gustav MAHLER makes his first appearance in Paris, conducting the orchestra of Concerts Colonne in a performance of his *Second Symphony.*

18 APRIL 1910

La Dorise, lyric drama in three acts by Cesare GALEOTTI, 37-year-old Italian composer permanently resident in Paris, with a libretto wherein a chanteuse at a Paris café-concert uses her immoral earnings to bring up her daughter as an honorable bourgeoise and who poisons herself when her double status is disclosed by her former customer, the uncle of her respectable son-in-law, to a musical score turbulent with chromatic harmonies obstructing the flow of Italianate arias, is produced in Brussels.

18 APRIL 1910

Margherita, opera in four acts by the 37-year-old German composer Alfred BRÜGGEMANN, to a libretto adapted from Goethe's *Faust* and constituting the second part of an unperformed Faustian trilogy, is produced at La Scala in Milan.

20 APRIL 1910

At the first concert of the secessionist Société Musicale Indépendante in Paris, founded by a group of dissident members of the academically disposed Société Nationale de Musique, two female infants, Christine Verger, age six, and Germaine Durant, age ten, give the first performance of the original version for piano four hands of Maurice RAVEL's suite *Ma mère l'Oye,* "cinq pieces enfantines":

(1) *Pavane da le Belle au bois dormant,* a gently drawn pastel evoking in the Aeolian mode the dormant belle awaiting in the woods the arrival of her Prince Charming; (2) *Petit Poucet,* a lightfooted promenade of Tom Thumb melodiously scattering thematic bread crumbs across the keyboard to guide him on his way back unsuspecting that the birds discanting in melismatic twirls in the treble would pick them up, and completing his promenade on a self-contented third of Picardy in the candidly white key of C major; (3) *Laideronnette, Impératrice des pagodes,* wherein the unbeautiful (*laide*) Empress of China pentatonically arrays her china, shaped like male and female pagodas, on the black keys in euphonious tertian, quartal and quintal counterpoint; (4) *Les Entretiens de la Belle et da le Bête,* a dialogue in gentle waltz time between the Belle in dulcet treble and the beast in the saturnine bass; (5) *Le Jardin féérique,* wherein the dormant belle of the first piece is awakened by her Prince Charming in gladsomely pandiatonic C major, and other characters of Mother Goose join them in quiet jubilation.

21 APRIL 1910

Daniel Hjort, opera in five acts by the 32-year-old Finnish composer Selim PALMGREN, dealing with a patriotic son of the slain leader of the peasant rebellion against the feudal power of the Catholic church in Sweden in 1599, who sides with the victorious future King Charles IX, is produced in Turku, to a libretto in Swedish. (A production in a Finnish translation took place in Helsinki on 20 February 1929; a second redaction, again in Finnish, was produced in Helsinki on 27 February 1938.)

23 APRIL 1910

Alfredo CASELLA, 26-year-old Italian composer, conducts in Paris a concert of his orchestral works, all performed for the first time: *Second Symphony* in C minor, *Suite* in C major in three movements (*Prelude, Sarabande, Bourrée*) and a symphonic rhapsody entitled simply

Italia, employing various Sicilian and Neapolitan airs, a lover's exhortation, a lament of a pulmonary sulphur miner, Mario Costa's *Lariula,* Paolo Tosti's *A Marechiare,* and Luigi Denza's perennially popular *Funiculi-Funicula,* glorifying the funicular train of Mt. Vesuvius.

23 APRIL 1910

At the Royal Opera of Berlin the world première is given of the three-act Indian opera *Poia* (in a German version) by the 39-year-old American composer Arthur NEVIN, the first opera by an American to be staged in Berlin, and dealing with an American Blackfoot Indian who journeys to the court of the Sun God to cure himself of an evil scar which renders him ineligible for the hand of a beautiful squaw, is made clean in his sleep by the magical intercession of The Four Seasons, but loses his bride who is slain by a rival's arrow aimed at Poia himself, the score strewn with authenticated pentatonic tunes in sterilized Wagnerian harmonies.

(*Poia* had four performances in Berlin; none in the United States, except in excerpts presented by the Pittsburgh Symphony Orchestra on 15 January 1906, and at a White House reception on 23 April 1907 in the presence of President Theodore Roosevelt, with the composer at the piano in lieu of an orchestra.)

23 APRIL 1910

La Dolorosa, opera in two acts by the Cuban composer Eduardo SÁNCHEZ DE FUENTES, to a melodramatically religious libretto depicting the symbolic transsubstantiation of an ailing peasant girl into Virgin Mary, is performed for the first time in Havana.

1 MAY 1910

Das Gelöbnis (The Pledge), two-act opera by the Berlin-rooted Java-born Dutch composeress Cornelie van OOSTERZEE (1863–1943), to a libretto dealing with an Italian girl briefly flourishing circa 1800, whose bandit lover kills her rich bridegroom on their wedding night well before the consummation of their marriage, who unwittingly betrays him to the police, and after he is executed joins him in death in his open grave, written in a thoroughly Germanic idiom relieved by sporadic tarantellas, is produced in Weimar.

4 MAY 1910

Le Mariage de Télémaque, lyrical comedy in five acts by Claude TERRASSE, wherein Ulysses forces his son smitten with adulterous love for Helen of Troy to marry Nausicaa, the princess who had saved Ulysses when he was shipwrecked on her father's island, to a musical score in a candidly Offenbachian vein, is produced at the Opéra-Comique in Paris.

5 MAY 1910

Alba eroica, opera by Domenico MONLEONE, to a libretto by his brother Giovanni Monleone dealing with the heroic struggle against Austrian rule led by the brothers Attilio and Emilio Bandiera who were captured and executed in 1844, is performed for the first time in Genoa, in commemoration of half a century of the sailing from Genoa of Garibaldi's liberating force.

9 MAY 1910

Serge KOUSSEVITZKY opens in Tver a month-long tour of the Volga River traveling in a specially chartered steamer, conducting 19 concerts of old and new music in eleven towns, with an orchestra of 65 musicians mostly from the personnel of the Bolshoi Theater of Moscow (where he himself played the double-bass earlier in his career), and Scriabin as composer-soloist in his own *Piano Concerto.*

18 MAY 1910

Pauline VIARDOT-GARCÍA, French mezzo-Soprano, daughter of the famous Spanish operatic singer and impresario Manuel del Popolo Vicente García, sister of the fabulous Maria Malibran and of the centenarian laryngoscopist Manuel García, wife of the French impresario Louis Viardot whom she married in 1841, and intimate friend of the Russian novelist Turgenev, dies in her native Paris at the age of 88 years and 10 months.

21 MAY 1910

Mendi Mendiyan, lyric pastorale by the 23-year-old Basque composer José María USANDIZAGA, to a libretto in Spanish dealing veristically with life among the Basques, with a tragic denouement as rural passions collide, is produced in Bilbao.

25 MAY 1910

Claude DEBUSSY plays at a concert of the Société Musical Indépendante in Paris a group of pieces from his newly completed first book of piano *Préludes:*

Danseuses de Delphes, a sybillic evocation of the Grecian sacred dance through a series of archaically homophonic triadic parallelisms with a strong pedal support for the slow motion of the vestal virgins; *Voiles,* an impressionistic tableau of a congregation of slender sailboats gently balanced in a light breeze on the crest of whole-tone waves in parallel major thirds, with a brief pentatonic interlude providing for black-key glissandos; and *La Cathédrale engloutie,* inspired by an old legend of an Armorican city submerged after a princess, out of suicidal jealousy for her sister's successful romance, lets the enemy open the dykes, the music reverberating with marble echoes over the gothically sustained ostinatos creating a stained-glass texture of pandiatonic mosaics; and *Puck,* a mischievously light Shakespearean scherzo.

29 MAY 1910

Mily BALAKIREV, dean of the Russian National School, the most venerable of the Mighty Five, teacher of Rimsky-Korsakov, mentor of Moussorgsky, initiator of the peculiar type of Russian symphonic poem, protagonist of Russian orientalism with its melismatic fiorituras accoutred in opulent harmonies, dies in St. Petersburg at the age of 73.

30 MAY 1910

Gabriel PIERNÉ conducts at the Opéra-Comique in Paris the première of his lyric comedy in three acts, *On ne badine pas avec l'amour,* after Alfred de Musset's story of true love that by excess of sensual passion literally kills its object, with a musical score in a fine Gallic manner of harmonious hedonism.

4 JUNE 1910

Percy GRAINGER completes the piano version (begun on 19 May 1908) of his dance *Mock Morris*, one of the series of "Room-Music Tit-Bits," to be played at "fast jog-trotting speed." (Dates on Grainger's manuscripts in the British Museum.)

No folk-music tune-stuffs at all are used herein. The rhythmic cast of the piece is Morris-like, but neither the build of the tunes nor the general lay-out of the form keep to the Morris dance shape. (Grainger's remarks on the manuscript)

8 JUNE 1910

A century has passed since the birth in the Saxon town of Zwickau of Robert SCHUMANN, generator of romantic music in its most subjective form, who was driven into the world of total insanity in his last years of life.

12 JUNE 1910

Bamboula Rhapsodic Dance by the Afro-British composer Samuel COLERIDGE-TAYLOR, based on Indian folk songs, is performed for the first time in Litchfield, Connecticut.

25 JUNE 1910

A week after STRAVINSKY's 28th birthday, his first ballet *The Firebird*, "conte dansé en 2 tableaux" completed on 18 May 1910 and dedicated to Rimsky-Korsakov's son Andrei, to a libretto fashioned from a familiar Russian folk tale by Michel Fokine, the balletmaster, wherein Ivan Tsarevitch armed with a magic feather from the flaming plumage of the Firebird liberates his beloved Princess Never-To-Be-Looked-Enough-At Beauty from the enchanted domain of Kashchei the Immortal by breaking the mysterious egg holding the secret of his perennial vitality in its yolk, is produced in a world première by Serge DIAGHILEV's splendorous company, Ballet Russe, at the Grand Opéra in Paris, the coruscating score subdivided into the following tableaux:

(1) *Introduction*, opening with an eerie ostinato within the compass of a tritone, the *diabolus in musica* of medieval musical theology; (2) the *Magic Garden of Kashchei*, an orientalistic tonal painting with a striking novel effect of glissandos on natural harmonics in the strings over the range of 12 overtones; (3) *Appearance of the Firebird pursued by Ivan Tsarevitch*, a cornucopia of dazzling luminous colors in rhythmic scintillation with a broadly Russian theme for Ivan; (4) *Dance of the Firebird*, marked *Allegro rapace* (for the Firebird is of a rapacious nature), with a dramatic precipitation of tritone-pivoted scales over a colonnade of firmly anchored ninth-chords; (5) *Capture of the Firebird by Ivan Tsarevitch*, a brief interlude of contrasting character; (6) *Supplication of the Firebird*, a poignantly chromaticized plaint embellished with melismatic bird songs, her release and her gift of the magic feather to Ivan in a descending progression of two semitones, a major third, two semitones, and a major third again in tritonal harmonic formation; (7) *Appearance of Thirteen Enchanted Princesses*, in a quiet narrative exposition; (8) *The Princesses' Game With Golden Apples*, a resilient melorhythmic saltation in aurific instrumental sonorities; (9) *Sudden Appearance of Ivan Tsarevitch*, an expressively Russian interlude in the Aeolian mode;

(10) *Round Dance of the Princesses*, a poetic Russian melodic figure canonically treated; (11) *Dawn of the New Day;* (12) *Magic Carillon*, with paganized chimes in spiraling centripetal and centrifugal intervals; (13) *Apparition of the Monster Guardians of Kashchei*, with such abominations as unbaptized female infants— the Kikimoras, midget Russian homunculi— the Boliboshki, bicephalous abortions, etc., accompanied by grossly tritonal brass figures in bleakly homophonic harmonies; (14) *Capture of Ivan Tsarevitch;* (15) *Entrance of Kashchei the Immortal*, marked by ominous progressions in the lowest bass leading to an explosion of demoniac power in triple forte; (16) *Dialogue with Ivan;* (17) *Intercession of the Princesses in Ivan's Behalf*, with futile but melodious entreaties; (18) *Appearance of the Firebird* with her appanage of vermilion colors; (19) *Dance of Kashchei's Henchmen Bewitched by the Firebird*, pounding discordant tonal groups; (20) *Infernal Dance of Kashchei's Kingdom*, a savagely syncopated orgy in triple time with an intervalic thrust of the thematic tritone; (21) *Berceuse of the Firebird*, a plumed cadent melodic strain in a minor key; (22) *Death of Kashchei*, a monstrously malformed threnody as the egg yolk of his soul oozes out in slowly diverging melodic particles with outer darkness ensuing as the polar tonalities of C and F sharp major approximate a conjunction; (23) *Coming Back to Life of Petrified Knights*, a powerful revival of vital forces from their dormant state; (24) *Universal Joy* in a hymnal Russian song reaching a stretto and concluding on a coda in asymmetrical septuple time.

29 JUNE 1910

Aloys OBRIST, 53-year-old custodian of the Liszt Museum in Weimar, kills the singer Anna Sutter in a fit of jealous passion, and then lays a violent hand upon himself.

4 JULY 1910

Louis BOURGAULT-DUCOUDRAY, French composer and enlightened aesthetician, one of the earliest Western theorists to make a first-hand study of non-European music and demand recognition for "all possible modes, old or new, European or exotic," dies in Paris in his 71st year.

23 JULY 1910

A Summer Night, one-act opera by the English composer George H. CLUTSAM, is produced in London.

4 AUGUST 1910

William SCHUMAN, American composer of tense but basically hedonistic music in various genres is born in New York City.

17 AUGUST 1910

Comedy Overture on Negro Themes by Henry F. GILBERT, an enthusiastic pioneer of autochthonous American music, containing a fugue based on the tune *Old Ship of Zion*, is performed for the first time by the Municipal Symphony Orchestra of New York in an open-air concert in Central Park.

21 AUGUST 1910

Héliogabale, lyric tragedy in three acts by Déodat DE SÉVERAC, the action taking place during the brief rule (218–222 A.D.) of the profligate Roman Emperor who assumed the name of the Syrian sun-god Elagabalus whom he worshipped and who was slain by his praetorian guard as the Christians whom he persecuted passed by singing Alleluia, with a musical score containing amid operatic banalities some interesting ballet numbers, in the oriental style, and incorporating the twelve instruments (reeds, drums, trumpets) of the Catalan cobla of deep antiquity in the orchestra, is performed for the first time at the Théâtre des Arènes, itself going back to the Roman times, in Béziers.

27 AUGUST 1910

Aura, first opera by the 37-year-old Italian composer Amilcare ZANELLA, in three acts, after an ancient fable of incarnated atmospheric phenomena, is produced in Pesaro, where Zanella succeeded Mascagni as director of the Liceo Rossini.

29 AUGUST 1910

Pietro FLORIDIA, 50-year-old Italian composer who migrated to America in 1904, conducts in Cincinnati the first performance of his grand opera in four acts, *Paoletta,* completed 19 days before its production, commissioned by the City of Cincinnati on the occasion of the Ohio Valley Exposition to a non-Ohioan story of a necromancer infatuated with the daughter of the King of Castile, who drinks from a fountain of youth to woo her hilt is reduced to his primordial debility when a concave sacred mirror focuses sunrays on his body and shrinks it, whereupon princess Paoletta marries a genuinely youthful don, to an Italianate score of such mellowness as to evoke 48 curtain calls for the singers.

31 AUGUST 1910

Pierre AUBRY, French musicologist and paleographer, collector of folksongs and codifier of oriental modes, dies in Dieppe as a result of a fencing accident, at the age of 36.

6 SEPTEMBER 1910

Ralph VAUGHAN WILLIAMS conducts in the Gloucester Cathedral in the course of the Gloucester, England, Music Festival, the first performance of his *Fantasia on a Theme by Thomas Tallis,* "father of English Cathedral Music," who flourished in the reign of Elizabeth I, set for double stringed orchestra in homophonically sonorous intermodal progressions antiphonally opposed to a melismatically contrapuntal section, the theme being the third of the eight written in 1567, and characterized as "raging and braying" in a contemporary verse: "The first is meeke, devout to see; the second sad in majesty; the third doth rage and roughly brayeth. . . ."

12 SEPTEMBER 1910

Two months and five days after his 50th birthday, Gustav MAHLER conducts at the Exposition Concert Hall in Munich the world première of his *Eighth Symphony,* announced as the Symphony of a Thousand, and indeed employing 1003 performers (146 orchestral players, two mixed choruses of 250 voices each, a children's choir of 350, and seven vocal soloists, with 5 harps, organ, piano, harmonium, mandolin, bells, tam-tam and four kettledrums in the score) set in two parts:

(1) *Veni, creator spiritus,* on a Latin ninth-century hymn for two combined choruses and orchestra, in clear E-flat major,

and (2) Concluding Scene from Goethe's *Faust,* conceived as a symphonic poem with chorus, opening in E-flat minor and ending in E-flat major, very diatonic throughout, on a consciously reduced modulatory plan, with a magniloquently sonorous chorale to the philosophical and enigmatic words of Goethe, "All that passes is a parable, all that is unattainable is a true event; the eternal feminine draws us near."

This is the greatest work that I have produced so far, and so unique in content and form that it is impossible to describe it. You must imagine that the Universe itself is set to sound and to song. These are no longer voices of man, but of orbiting planets and suns. (Mahler in a letter to Willem Mengelberg, 1910)

This symphony is a gift to the nation. All my previous works are but preludes to this. In other works there is still present a subjective tragic quality, but this one is a grand dispenser of joy. (Mahler in a conversation with Richard Specht, 1910)

Flames seemed to dart from Mahler as he conducted; a thousand wills obeyed his will. (*Neue Freie Presse,* Vienna, 13 September 1910)

The Damascus blade matched with 1000 fencing spears. (*Frankfurter Zeitung,* 13 September 1910)

Eight trumpeters and 4 trombone players stood up in a row at the top of the platform and blew for all they were worth into the faces of the audience. . . . A faithful Achates, busy with tinkling triangles, ringing bells and banging big drums, would drop his own work, sprint 20 feet across the platform, never once upsetting a music desk, snatch up a pair of sticks and let loose on the kettledrums. There was also a gentleman who played on a large concert grand piano. He was very industrious. I know it because I saw him. Unfortunately, in the general clamor, none of his notes even got as far as my ear. Max Reger was there and Richard Strauss, who sat in the front of a box and read the piano score—through a lorgnette! (*The Musical Courier,* New York, 28 September 1910)

12 SEPTEMBER 1910

Antonio MARTELLO pleads guilty in a New York court to playing a guitar and singing Neapolitan ballads to women in the Bronx, and is sentenced to serve 20 days in the workhouse as a common nuisance.

18 SEPTEMBER 1910

Richard STRAUSS issues a declaration asserting that the stipulation in his contracts with opera houses wishing to produce his highly desirable new opera *Der Rosenkavalier* must guarantee the production of his less desirable operas *Salome* and *Elektra* four times annually for ten years is not motivated by financial considerations but by a morally compelling reason to give a composer a fair chance to promote all his works. (The Dresden Opera Company notified Richard Strauss on 7 September 1910 of its refusal to produce *Der Rosenkavalier* on such terms.)

18 SEPTEMBER 1910

Liebelei, opera in three acts by the Czech-born composer Franz NEUMANN, to a play by the Viennese writer Arthur Schnitzler dealing with a pleasant lovelet indulged in by a reasonably congenial couple, is produced in Frankfurt in the presence of Schnitzler himself.

20 SEPTEMBER 1910

The Veil, oratorio by Sir Frederic Hymen COWEN, is performed for the first time at the Cardiff Festival.

24 SEPTEMBER 1910

La Maja de Rumbo, grand opera by the Spanish composer Emilio SERRANO (1850–1939), dealing with an 18th-century Madrid damsel, liberal in love, charity and hope-giving conduct, is produced at the Teatro Colón in Buenos Aires.

25 SEPTEMBER 1910

Askepot (Cinderella), ballet by the Danish composer Otto MALLING, is performed for the first time in Copenhagen.

2 OCTOBER 1910

Kleider machen Leute (Clothes Make the Man [lit., people]), comic opera in three acts by the greatly significant 38-year-old Viennese composer Alexander von ZEMLINSKY, deriding the moral hypocrisy of the bourgeoisie who judge people by the clothes they wear, is produced in Vienna.

3 OCTOBER 1910

JAQUES-DALCROZE, creator of eurhythmics, as a revival in a modern form of Grecian gymnopaedia, contributing to musical education through graceful bodily motion in coordinated rhythms, leaves Geneva with fifteen of his best disciples for Hellerau, Germany, to establish an Institute of Eurhythmics there. (Date obtained from the Secretariat of the Dalcroze School in Geneva. See history of the Dalcroze movement in the section Letters and Documents.)

4 OCTOBER 1910

Der Schneemann, pantomime by the prodigiously precocious musically mature adolescent Erich Wolfgang KORNGOLD, written by him in piano score at the age of eleven and orchestrated by his teacher Alexander Zemlinsky, to a story wherein Pierrot paints himself white, stands as a snowman in front of the house of Pantalon who keeps his beloved Colombine in durance vile, horrifies him into submission as he suddenly begins to move, and captures the enraptured Colombine, is produced at the Vienna Opera, with Franz Schalk conducting.

The music to the pantomime *The Snow Man*, young Korngold wrote as a piano solo when he was eleven years old. . . . When it had received a most favorable reception at some aristocratic houses here, the authorities of the Imperial Opera resolved to have it performed. Till then Dr. Korngold (father of Erich, musical critic at the Vienna *Neue Freie Presse*, successor of Hanslick) had purposely kept a knowledge of his prodigy from the public. Finally he came to the conclusion that he had no right any longer to conceal his son's marvelous achievements. . . . So extraordinary are they that they have been made the subject of theoretical study at the Berlin University, and Professor Arthur Seidl has lectured on them at the Leipzig Conservatoire (Vienna dispatch in the *Musical Standard*, London, 5 November 1910)

8 OCTOBER 1910

An exhibition of paintings by Arnold SCHOENBERG, marked by expressionist intensity of geometric forms and opulence of color, opens at the Heller Bookstore in Vienna. (Date from an announcement in the *Neue Freie Presse*, Vienna, 2 October 1910)

What Schoenberg represents in his paintings are not impressions of so-called reality, but its reflections on a higher psychic plane. These paintings are the realizations of completely transcendental phenomena made perceptible through outer senses. (Anton von Webern, *Rheinische Musik- und Theater-Zeitung*, 24 February 1912, reprinted by Willi Reich in *Melos*, January 1969)

When Schoenberg paints he does not intend to produce a "pretty" or an "attractive" picture. Scorning the objective result he seeks only to fix his own subjective "apperception" and therefore needs only such means as appear to him indispensable at the moment. Not every professional painter can boast of such a creative method! In his painting, as in his music, Schoenberg avoids the superfluous, that is, detrimental, and takes the direct path to the essential, that is, necessary. (Wassily Kandinsky, 1912)

11 OCTOBER 1910

Francesco Balilla PRATELLA issues in Milan a *Manifesto dei Musicisti Futuristi*, in which he makes an appeal to young composers to desert music schools, conservatories and academies, to combat with assiduous contempt the venal and ignorant critics, to abstain from the participation in any competition that requires payment of fees for admission, to denounce publicly the incompetence of contest juries usually composed of idiots and senile mental defectives, to stay aloof from academic circles, preferring a modest life to rich profits from art for sale, to condemn loathsome Neapolitan ballads and sacred music which has no reason for existence now that faith has declined, and which has become the monopoly of impotent conservatory directors and unordained priests, to exalt all that is original and revolutionary in music, and to regard the insults and the sarcasms of the moribund reactionaries and opportunists as a signal honor. (See complete text in Letters and Documents.)

12 OCTOBER 1910

Max REGER receives the honorary degree Dr. med. from the Faculty of Medicine at the University of Berlin in appreciation of the fact that "the harmoniousness of his music raises the spirits of those stricken with melancholy and heals sick minds."

12 OCTOBER 1910

Ralph VAUGHAN WILLIAMS conducts at the Leeds Festival the first performance of his *Sea Symphony (First Symphony)*, scored for soprano, baritone, mixed chorus and orchestra, to texts from poems of Walt Whitman, set to music in an elevated narrative style mirroring the varying aspects of the sea and the human characteristics of the intrepid sea-farers, in four movements: (1) *A Song for All Seas, all Ships, Moderato maestoso*; (2) *On the Beach at Night Alone, Largo sostenuto*; (3) *The Waves*, a scherzo, *Allegro brillante*; (4) *The Explorers, Grave e molto adagio*. (A revised version of the score was first performed in London on 4 February 1913.)

15 OCTOBER 1910

Lord Giorgio Byron, opera in three acts by the 42-year-old Italian composer Luigi Stefano GIARDA, is performed for the first time in Santiago, Chile.

20 OCTOBER 1910

Ivan le Terrible, opera in three acts by the Bucharest-born French impresario Raoul GUNSBOURG, to his own gory story wherein the depraved Russian ruler orders the daughter of an impenitent boyar dissenter to be deflowered in the presence of her father who then blurts out the terrible secret that she is the tsar's own daughter produced as a result of a violation of the boyar's wife's hospitality sixteen years before, the horrifying revelation followed by the strangling of the girl's fiancé by the tsar's henchmen, her death of a broken heart and the tsar's collapse in the mortal throes of tardy repentance, is produced in Brussels.

23 OCTOBER 1910

The Orquesta Sinfónica of Barcelona, Spain, gives its inaugural concert.

24 OCTOBER 1910

Naughty Marietta, light opera in two acts by Victor HERBERT in which a boyishly exuberant French "Casket Girl" named Marietta, sent to New Orleans in mid-18th century, nearly weds a pirate but ultimately finds her true love in the person of an upright young American captain, offering such musically communicative airs as *Ah, Sweet Mystery of Life!, Tramp, Tramp, Tramp, Naughty Marietta* and the *Italian Street Song*, is performed for the first time in Syracuse, New York.

10 NOVEMBER 1910

Concerto for Violin and Orchestra by Edward ELGAR, with an enigmatic epigraph from Le Sage's *Gil Bias*, "aquí está encerrada el alma de . . ." in three movements, *Allegro, Andante,* and *Allegro molto,* all in 4/4 time, but in varied moods, from stately contemplation to dignified hedonism, and some novel effects, such as pizzicato tremolando, is performed for the first time in London by Fritz KREISLER to whom the *Concerto* is dedicated, with Elgar himself conducting the London Philharmonic.

12 NOVEMBER 1910

Gabriel FAURIÉ appears as guest conductor in a concert of his orchestral works in St. Petersburg, on his first visit to Russia.

17 NOVEMBER 1910

Piano Trio in D major, op. 1, by the 13-year-old Vienna prodigy Erich Wolfgang KORNGOLD, composed between December 1909 and April 1910, marked by a modern quasi-Straussian idiom, is performed for the first time anywhere by the Margulies Trio in New York.

Maybe his papa is trying to bring him up to be a real modern composer, but if he is not, then something ought to be done. If we had a little boy of 12 who preferred writing this sort of music to hearing a good folk tune or going out and playing in the park, we should consult a specialist. (W. J. Henderson, New York *Sun*, 18 November 1910)

17 NOVEMBER 1910

Elinan Surma (Elina's Death), opera by the Finnish composer Oskar MERIKANTO, is produced in Helsingfors.

19 NOVEMBER 1910

Der Talisman, opera in four acts by the 44-year-old English composeress Adela MADDISON, is produced in Leipzig.

20 NOVEMBER 1910

Semirama, lyric tragedy in three acts by Ottorino RESPIGHI, is performed for the first time in Bologna.

25 NOVEMBER 1910

Stella Maris, opera in three acts by the Belgian composer Alfred KAISER (who changed his name to De Kevser during World War I to dispel the odium attached to the Kaiser) is produced in Düsseldorf in a German version.

25 NOVEMBER 1910

Liturgy of St. John Chrysostom, for chorus a cappella, by Serge RACHMANINOFF, is performed for the first time in Moscow.

30 NOVEMBER 1910

Macbeth, the only opera by Ernest BLOCH, composed in 1902, preserving the most essential parts of Shakespeare's tragedy, in an expressively illustrative modernistic idiom, using harsh secundal dissonances to describe the murder, augmented triads and combinative whole-tone chords to express the horror of premonition, naturalistic applosive rhythms to characterize Lady Macbeth's attempts to take the damned spot off her hands, and sinister tritone-laden progressions for the appearance of Banquo's ghost, is produced at the Opéra-Comique in Paris.

New Opera is Called Barbaric—Composer of Macbeth is Accused of Sacrificing Art to Brutal Sincerity (Wireless dispatch published in the New York *Sunday Herald* of 3 December 1910)

This music is an indecipherable rebus, rhythmically as well as tonally, and I wonder how the singers and the orchestra found their way through it. As for the rhythm, it is not only capricious but downright incoherent as a result of incessant changes of meter. Judge for yourself. In one place in the score I find this succession of time signatures: 3/4, 4/4, 3/4, 4/4, 6/4, 4/4; in another I find a measure of 4/4, followed by 5/4, 6/4 and 4/4. What becomes of rhythmic unity, and how can accuracy of performance be secured under such circumstances? As for harmonic progressions, they are no less extraordinary, and one can only qualify them as savage. . . . It is noise for the sake of noise, and the abuse of trumpets would break the sturdiest ear drums. (Arthur Pougin, in *Le Ménestrel*, Paris, 3 December 1910)

2 DECEMBER 1910

Kleider machen Leute, opera in three acts by Alexander ZEMLINSKY, with a satirical point that all men are created equal, but that different clothes make them unequal in society, is produced in Vienna.

4 DECEMBER 1910

Claude DEBUSSY conducts a concert of his works in Budapest.

5 DECEMBER 1910

At a student concert of the St. Petersburg Conservatory, 19-year-old Sergei PROKOFIEV conducts the first performance of his symphonic poem *Dreams* and plays his first *Piano Sonata* in F minor.

10 DECEMBER 1910

The world première of PUCCINI's opera in three acts, *La Fanciulla del West*, after a play by David Belasco, *The Girl of the Golden West*, wherein a golden-hearted and brave Western girl, working in a California mining town in 1849, wins the life of her reformed robber-lover from a duty-conscious but love-smitten sheriff in a game of poker during which she produces an extra pair of aces from her stocking, and who subsequently persuades the uncouth but noble-minded miners not to hang him on a tree, finally departing with him sadly singing "addio, mia California," with a musical score full of dramatic progressions of augmented triads and their concomitant whole-tone scales, harmonious pandiatonic sequences and emotionally suspended ninth-chords, including also some velvet-toned Italianate arias and love duets, with the American motives represented by pentatonic tunes and ragtime rhythms, is given at the Metropolitan Opera House in New York, with Arturo Toscanini conducting, and Caruso singing the lover's part.

Great Welcome for New Opera—Brilliant Audience Wildly Applauds Puccini's Girl of the Golden West— Composer, Originator and Conductor Have a Triumph After Each Act— The Opera House Thronged—Ticket Speculators Got Some Seats But Had to Sell Out at Less Than Cost (New York *Times*, 11 December 1910)

An International Premiere—America Proud of The Girl of the Golden West—Under Two Flags, a $22,000 House Riots Over Puccini, the Opera Directors Send a Silver Wreath to the Stage—Caruso Looks and Acts His Best— Emmy Destinn Sings Heroically the Most Powerful Woman's Role in Recent Melodrama—Sheriff Pasquale Amato Shares the Big Scene Where the Composer Gives Native Playwright a Free Hand—Fifty Curtain Calls and a Forest of Flowers Too. (New York *Sun*, 12 December 1910)

The Girl of the Golden West is an apotheosis of the barroom and of gambling. The play caters to a depraved taste, and the music is without any appeal beyond that of emphasizing the meretricious elements in the libretto. Puccini's harmonic scheme is extremely limited and consists of intervals studiously made unconventional and tonal succession arbitrarily distorted to titillate the senses. . . . Of course, there is nothing American about the music. Puccini had no models to go to when he undertook to make music to this American play, for not even the composers who were born in this country have ever written any music different from the music of Europe. (*The Musical Courier*, New York, 14 December 1910)

10 DECEMBER 1910

Leif Erickson, three-act opera set in Vineland (America) and Greenland in 1001 B.C. by Gerard TONNING, with a Norwegian text by C. M. Thuland, is produced for the first time, in its original language, in Seattle, Washington.

15 DECEMBER 1910

Bourgogne, a symphonic poem by the 26-year-old French composer Edgar VARÈSE, temporarily residing in Berlin, written in a flamboyantly romantic vein, with some ethnic allusions to folk songs of Bourgogne, is performed for the first time in Berlin, under the direction of Josef Stransky.

Varèse wants to say everything at once, and gets so confused in the process that it is impossible to discover even a single clear idea in this work. (*Signale für die musikalische Welt*, Berlin, 21 December 1910)

15 DECEMBER 1910

Concerto for Piano and Orchestra in F minor, op. 114, by Max REGER, in three movements, *Allegro moderato*, *Largo* and *Allegretto con spirito*, completed on 16 July 1910, and written in a luxuriant romantic manner of high viscosity, is performed for the first time by the Gewandhaus Orchestra in Leipzig, Arthur Nikisch conducting, Frieda Kwast-Hodapp soloist.

The Piano Concerto is another abortion of Reger's Muse degenerated through constant inbreeding. (*Leipzig Tageblatt*, 16 December 1910)

In his latest work, the Piano Concerto, op. 114, Professor, Dr. phil. h. c. and Dr. med. h. c. Max Reger demonstrates that the painful complication of asthmatic invention and dropsical swelling of facture of which he is known to have suffered for a long time, has now become chronic. In the first movement, amid the familiar commotion there stare at us some thematic fragments reminiscent of Brahms, Liszt and Grieg. . . . In the Finale, an insane army of churlish tonality-free chords blunder into a somewhat more amiable kobold of a fugato and trample underfoot a frightened little elf of a melody which becomes somehow entangled in all this. (Arthur Smolian, *Signale für die musikalische Welt*, Berlin, 21 December 1910)

28 DECEMBER 1910

Königskinder, an operatic version in three acts of incidental music by Engelbert HUMPERDINCK to a play by Ernst Rosmer (pseudonym of the wife of a Munich lawyer, Dr. Max Bernstein, originally produced on 23 January 1897), to a grim Grimm-like fairy tale wherein a goose girl, who is really a royal princess, held in durance vile by a witch, is rescued by a swineherd, who is really a royal prince, but both die in the cold night most piteously when they fail to persuade the authorities that they are indeed of royal blood, to a Wagnerian score of great chromatic intensity, is produced for the first time on any stage at the Metropolitan Opera House in New York.

30 DECEMBER 1910

Le Miracle, lyric drama by Georges HÜE, to the story of a medieval courtesan who saves a besieged city by bewitching the besieger, poses for a statue of St. Agnes, becomes enamored of the young sculptor, kills an unwelcome suitor, petulantly strikes the statue and falls dead at its feet, whereupon the statue changes miraculously into a real likeness of St. Agnes, is produced at the Grand Opéra in Paris.

1911

4 JANUARY 1911

Pocahontas, opera by the 57-year-old American composer Willard PATTON, relating the story of the Indian princess, daughter of a powerful inter-tribal leader, who according to legend saved the life of the founder of the Jamestown Colony, Capt. John Smith, was converted to Christianity and died of smallpox in 1617, is performed for the first time in concert form in Minneapolis.

16 JANUARY 1911

Maurice RAVEL performs at the Société Musicale Indépendante de Paris three piano pieces by Erik SATIE, written in 1888, as an act of homage to (in Ravel's words) "a precursor of genius whose music astounds by its prescience of the modern vocabulary and by the almost prophetic character of its harmonic innovations."

19 JANUARY 1911

As the Tsar Nicholas II of All the Russias enters the imperial box during a performance of Mussorgsky's opera BORIS GODUNOV at the Imperial Opera House in St. Petersburg, the great Russian bass singer Feodor CHALI-APIN, as Boris, in a sudden frenzy of patriotic fervor, falls to his knees and begins to sing *God Save the Tsar.*

You rose from the depths of democracy, and you were to us a symbol of the growing creative forces of that democracy. You have now sullied the name of Chaliapin by the dust on your knees, when you prostrated yourself before the Tsar. (From a letter addressed to Chaliapin by a group of Russian workers)

Let me tell you that my soul and my heart did not take part in what happened on that occasion. I am guilty only on two counts: (1) that I became distracted (2) that I was employed in an organization in which, unfortunately, such surprises as crawling on one's knees are always possible. (From Chali-apin's letter to Maxim Gorky dated July 1911)

19 JANUARY 1911

Knez Ivo od Semberije (Count Ivo of Semberija), one-act opera by the Serbian composer Isidor BAJIĆ, dealing with a Bosnian patriot who purchases Slav slaves from Turks during the Ottoman domination of Serbia and sets them free, selling even the family icon to raise funds, which shocks his pious mother so much that she dies of a cardiac arrest, is performed for the first time in Belgrade under the direction of the composer.

25 JANUARY 1911

La Vendetta, lyric drama in three acts by the 35-year-old French romantic opera composer Jean NOUGUÈS, deal-ing with a bitter family vendetta in Italy and culminating in the murder of a woman who challenged the warring factions, is produced in Marseilles.

25 JANUARY 1911

Poupĕ (The Bud), one-act opera by the Czech com-poser Otakar OSTRČIL, dealing with a neurotical-ly reluctant bride, is produced in Prague.

26 JANUARY 1911

Der Rosenkavalier, "Komödie für Musik" in three acts by Richard STRAUSS (completed on 26 September 1910; begun on 1 May 1909), full of sophisticated waltzes and ironically sentimental arias, to Hugo von Hof-mannsthal's tale placed in 18th-century Vienna, in which a conniving dowager designates her young lover as the bearer of a symbolic silver rose sent from her aging cousin to a young coquette in proposing marriage, with a characteristic reversal of roles as the cavalier of the rose woos and wins her after many a transvestiture (in the third act the Rosenkavalier, a mezzo-soprano, is dis-guised as a maid, thus reverting to her natural sex), the score containing 118 identifiable leitmotivs, according to officious exegetes, is produced at the Dresden Opera, Ernst Schuch conducting.

12 FEBRUARY 1911

On the eve of the 28th anniversary of WAGNER's death, his youthful *Symphony in C Major,* written at the age of 19 in a prevalent idiom of early 19th-century music, is pub-lished for the first time in Leipzig.

21 FEBRUARY 1911

Gustav MAHLER conducts the New York Philharmonic Orchestra for the last time, twelve weeks before his death.

21 FEBRUARY 1911

From Shakespeare, symphonic suite by the Germanic Czech composer Josef Bohuslav FOERSTER, illustrating five Shakespearean characters in a proleptic prelude and four movements (*Perdita, Viola, Lady Macbeth, Katharine* and *Petruchio*), is performed for the first time in Prague.

25 FEBRUARY 1911

Natoma, opera by Victor HERBERT in three acts, dealing with amorous entanglements in the wilds of Spanish Cal-ifornia in 1820 wherein an Indian princess, nurturing self-sacrificial love for an American lieutenant, kills the Spanish suitor of the girl he loves and then enters a con-vent, is performed for the first time in Philadelphia.

Natoma Performed—A dull Text Set to Mediocre Music— The Comparative Failure of the First Performance in Philadelphia in Spite of the Able Cast and Thorough Prepara-tion—An Antiquated "Book" Written in Stilted Speech and Silly Verse That Contains Neither Operatic Drama nor Oper-atic Characters—The Mediocrity and the Dull Commonplace of Mr. Herbert's Music Except Where It Approximates

Operetta—Its Undramatic and Untheatrical Quality (Headlines in the Boston *Evening Transcript*, 27 February 1911)

26 FEBRUARY 1911

Aux Étoiles, the second and last orchestral piece by Henri DUPARC, written in the atmospheric manner of his evocative songs, is performed for the first time at a Lamoureux concert in Paris.

27 FEBRUARY 1911

The Captain's Daughter, opera in four acts by César CUI, after Pushkin's tale dealing with the peasant rebellion against Catherine the Great (who sings mezzosoprano), is produced in St. Petersburg.

3 MARCH 1911

The Sacrifice, opera in three acts by Frederick S. CONVERSE, to his own melodramatic libretto, wherein the commander of an invading U.S. detachment becomes deeply enamored of a beauteous señorita in a desecrated Mexican Mission in Southern California in 1846, but lets himself be stabbed to death by an intruding bravo when he realizes that the interloper is his inamorata's prior lover, is produced in Boston.

3 MARCH 1911

On the fiftieth anniversary of the liberation of Russian serfs, a cantata by Alexandre GRETCHANINOFF entitled *19 February 1861* (the date of the issuance of the Tsar's manifesto of emancipation, according to old-style calendar) is performed for the first time in St. Petersburg.

4 MARCH 1911

Borislav, opera in three acts by the Italian-trained 28-year-old Bulgarian composer Georgy ATANASOV, written in a verdantly Verdian manner, and dealing with a medieval Bulgarian commander's patriotic love for the Bulgarian Tsar's daughter, is produced in Sofia.

11 MARCH 1911

Francesco Balilla PRATELLA issues in Milan a "Manifesto Tecnico della Musica Futurista" in which he advocates the creation of new music that would synthesize melody and harmony in a chromaticized continuum, confidently predicting the eventual victory for an ideal enharmonic mode to be discovered by true harbingers of the future and a universal emergence of a "futurist melody" similar to an ideal line formed by the "incessant flowering of thousands of ocean waves." (Full text in Letters and Documents)

11 MARCH 1911

Enrique GRANADOS plays in Barcelona the first performance of his piano suite *Goyescas*, magically congenial translations of Goya's paintings into rhythms and melodies of Spain, and comprising two books of colorfully descriptive pieces: *Los Requiebros, Coloquio en la reja, El Fandango del Candil, Quejas, o la Maja y el Ruisenor, El Amor y la Muerte* and *La Serenada del espectro*.

In *Goyescas*, I tried to convey a personal note, a mixture of bitterness and grace, of rhythm, color and life that are typically Spanish, of a sentiment at once amorous, passionate, dramatic and tragic, such as can be perceived in Goya's works. (Granados quoted by Henri Collet in *Albéniz et Granados*, Paris, 1926)

13 MARCH 1911

The Pink Lady, operetta by the Belgian-born American composer Ivan CARYLL, dealing with a dandy who takes his sweetheart to a restaurant and there runs into his current fiancée, containing the famous waltz *My Beautiful Lady*, is produced in New York.

14 MARCH 1911

Déjanire, opera in four acts by Camille SAINT-SAËNS, expanded from incidental music to a tragedy by Louis Gallet (first performed at Béziers on 25 August 1898), dealing with the hapless wife of Hercules induced by the centaur Nessus to give his bloody shirt to Hercules to wear as an aphrodisiac, thus poisoning him, is performed for the first time in its full-fledged operatic form in Monte Carlo.

15 MARCH 1911

Alexandre SCRIABIN plays the piano part, with Serge Koussevitzky conducting, in the world première in Moscow of his tremendous symphonic work *Promethée, Poème du Feu*, his fifth symphony, scored for a large orchestra, piano, organ, voices, and a special instrument of light, Luce, or *clavier à lumières*, designed to immerse the concert hall in a kaleidoscopic scintillation of multicolored lights, reflecting the inner progress of the music, with the harmonic and melodic content derived from a basic "mystic chord" (C, F-sharp, B-flat, E, A, D), corresponding to the high ethereal primary tones of the harmonic series (1, 45, 7, 5, 27, 9), in a single continuous movement symbolizing five quintessences (Will, Movement, Anxiety, Contemplation, Mystery) in a series of constantly contrasting moods, all furnished with ecstatic expression marks in French:

Lent, brumeux, with an oriflamme of French horns announcing a Promethean motto drawn from the "mystic chord," epitomizing the idea of a "creative principle" emerging from a "cosmic mist," clearing the way to the entrance of piano solo marked *impérieux*, exemplifying will-power, followed by a variety of spiritual states and sensual materializations: *voluptueux, presque avec douleur, avec délice, avec un intense désir, avec émotion et ravissement, voilé, mystérieux, avec enthousiasme, limpide, sourd, menaçant, étrange, charmé* giving rise to a Promethean uplift in the piano part, in a crescendo of esthetic concepts and their emotional incarnation, *soudain très doux et joyeux, avec un effroi contenu, avec défi belliqueux, orageux, avec un splendide éclat, déchirant, comme un cri*, vesuviating in a spasmodic outburst of instrumental colors in thrice triple time, driving to the coda by a cumulative assault, frustrated by sudden relapses into a debilitating softness, indicated by the expression marks, *extatique, étincelant, de plus en plus large, avec un éclat éblouissant ailé, dansant, flot lumineux, dans un vertige*, accomplishing the mystical synthesis of Self and All and the incorporation of human ideals and cosmic laws into the perfect musical form of a sphere yielding a maximum of volume with a minimum of surface in bright-blue F-sharp major, a color associated with this tonality in Scriabin's chromotonal scheme. (Because of technical difficulties, the part of *Luce* was not included in the performance.)

20 MARCH 1911

Russia promulgates its first copyright law, extending the protection of composers and authors in all countries previously bound by an international copyright treaty.

22 MARCH 1911

Symphonie antique by the prime French organist Charles-Marie WIDOR, inspired by the poem of Sophocles written on the night of the Greek Victory over the Persians at Salamis in 480 B.C., in four grandiloquent movements, concluding with a choral *Te Deum*, with thematic materials set in Grecian modes, is performed for the first time in Paris.

23 MARCH 1911

At a meeting of militant English Suffragettes in Albert Hall in London, a *March of the Women*, written by Ethel SMYTH for the cause, with its main tune derived from an Italian folksong she heard in Abruzzi, is intoned by the Suffragette Choir, aided and abetted by a cornet and organ, to keep them in tune.

25 MARCH 1911

Claude DEBUSSY conducts in Paris the orchestral version of his piano suite *Children's Corner* arranged by André CAPLET, and first performed by Caplet in New York a year earlier.

29 MARCH 1911

Alexandre GUILMANT, French organist, co-founder with Charles Bordes and Vincent d'Indy of the Schola Cantorum of Paris on 6 June 1894, dies at Meudon at the age of 74.

1 APRIL 1911

The word "dodecafonia" is used for the first time to describe synthetic chords of 12 chromatic degrees, in an article by the Italian theorist and composer Domenico ALALEONA, entitled *L'armonia modernissima*, published in *Rivista musicale italiana*, in which he advances the idea of a "neutral" tonality, effected by an "art of stupefaction" by means of consecutive diminished seventh-chords.

2 APRIL 1911

In anticipation of a complete ballet performance of *Daphnis et Chloé* by Maurice RAVEL, Gabriel Pierné conducts a Colonne Concert in Paris in the first performance of the first suite drawn from the score, in three sections:

Nocturne, set in nebulously quartal harmonies reposing on resonant pedal points while a wordless chorus intones Grecian chants with lips closed, in the first tremor of love as Daphnis meets Chloé; *Interlude*, with ominously piercing fanfares introducing a savage *Danse guerrière* bristling with prickly tritones and asymmetrical rhythms as alien invaders abduct Chloé, who is rescued as a company of fawning fauns fights feral foes to the accompaniment of Pan's panpentatonic panpipes delectably simulated by reedy roulades in the woodwinds.

The score of the first suite from Ravel's *Daphnis et Chloé* has strength, rhythm, brilliance. Voices mingle with the instruments, mysterious and fervid voices. . . . The freedom of form and of texture surpasses imagination. Harmonic and polytonic anarchy here reign supreme, and I must confess that I cannot accept this music without hesitation. (Alfred Bruneau, *Le Matin*, Paris, 3 April 1911)

The *Nocturne*, with its multiple *divisi* of various instrumental groups produces a curious effect of transparence and dreamlike atmosphere; the *Interlude* with its chorus placed backstage sounding with great tenderness, its trumpet calls and an adroitly wrought gradation leading to a barbarically rhythmed *Danse guerrière*, are pages of unusual music which must astonish, attract and please the public. (*Le Ménestrel*, Paris, 2 April 1911)

Ravel's suite from *Daphnis and Chloé* is a series of what the Futurists might call rhythmic pictures. There is no characterization and no drama, but the score pulsates with a life that is now sensitive and subtle, now vigorous and wild. (London *Times*, 3 August 1912)

3 APRIL 1911

Jean SIBELIUS conducts a concert of his music in Helsingfors, including the first performance of his *Fourth Symphony*, his most modernistic work, in four movements:

(1) *Tempo molto moderato, quasi adagio*, opening with brooding somberness in low strings and bassoons in a characteristic Lydian mode accentuating its thematic tritone, leading to a main subject in A minor, and after six dynamic implosions and an interlude for soft strings, vanishing towards a unisonal A; (2) *Allegro molto vivace*, maintaining the tritone emphasis, soaring dancingly in ascending strophes towards a claritonal cadence; (3) *Il Tempo Largo*, a poetic nocturne with characteristically Sibelian solos of the woodwinds, containing a considerable incidence of whole-tone scales with their concomitant tritones, ending in a pianissimo unison on C; (4) *Allegro*, reviewing and reassessing the thematic materials of the previous movements in a tersely brusque manner, with slowly rising dynamics in the strings leading towards a sonorous climax, then subsiding into nothingness and concluding on eight funereal A minor chords in the strings.

6 APRIL 1911

Mot Nordpolen (To the North Pole), opera in three acts by the Norwegian composer Johan HALVORSEN, is produced in Christiania.

7 APRIL 1911

The first performance is given in Warsaw of *Second Symphony* in B-flat major by Karol SZYMANOWSKI, in three long, connected movements:

(1) *Allegro moderato*, in contrapuntal harmonies progressing along disparate paths, with a multiplicity of appoggiatured stresses and constant tonal deviations, reaching telestically for a plagal cadence; (2) *Lento*, a chromatically involuted theme with six variations leading to a magistrally projected quintuple fugue: (3) *Allegro moderato molto energico*, cyclically reverting to the principal theme of the first movement and, after an eloquent development, concluding on a triumphal tonic chord.

19 APRIL 1911

Le Spectre de la Rose, choreographic tableau from a poem by Théophile Gautier, to the music of Carl Maria Weber's *Invitation to the Waltz*, wherein the spectre of the rose, in a sensuously roseate contact with a sleeping maiden vanishes with her dream, is mimed by Nijinsky who performs a leap through the window with a preternatural power of levitation, is produced for the first time by Diaghilev's Ballet Russe in Monte Carlo.

He upsets the law of gravitation. He seems to be painted on the ceiling. He reclines softly in space, he makes a thousand little assaults on the sky, and his dancing has the appearance of beautiful poems written in capital letters. (Jean Cocteau on Nijinski, *Comœdia Illustré*, Paris, 1911)

24 APRIL 1911

String Quartet, op. 3, by Alban BERG is performed for the first time in Vienna.

26 APRIL 1911

The cornerstone of the JAQUES-DALCROZ INSTITUTE is laid at Hellerau-Dresden, the "garden city" of eurhythmic education.

26 APRIL 1911

La Jota, lyric opera in two acts by the 34-year-old French composer Raoul LAPARRA, a sequel to his opera *La Habanera*, to his own libretto wherein a young soldier and his fiancée, torn apart by conflicting allegiances during the Aragon-Navarre clash of 1835, are reunited in a ruined church and dance a sanguinary jota in a mortal embrace as a renegade priest monstrously lusting after the bride is nailed by the invading soldiery to a life-size crucifix from which the figure of Christ has been wrested by an explosion, is produced for the first time at the Opéra-Comique in Paris, on the same program with the first performance of *Le Voile du Bonheur*, a lyric scene in two acts by the 40-year-old Charles Pons, to a libretto from a play by the French statesman Georges Clemenceau.

26 APRIL 1911

Narcisse, choreographic tone poem to music by Nicolas TCHEREPNIN, portraying in melodious Russian modalities the melancholy tale of Narcissus, infatuated with his own image in the waters and oblivious to the anguished appeals of the forlorn nymph Echo, with the poetic justice of Greek mythology transforming him into a bulbous amaryllidaceous flower with a fluffy corona, while the hapless nymph is reduced to a disembodied sound, is

produced by Diaghilev's Ballet Russe in Monte Carlo, with the composer conducting the orchestra.

30 APRIL 1911

Monsieur Bonaparte, opera-farce by the 52-year-old Silesian composer Bogmil ZEPLER, to a libretto dealing with a fashionable Paris tailor who looks like Napoleon, is produced in Leipzig.

5 MAY 1911

James BLAND, Negro minstrel composer of the famous song *Carry Me Back to Old Virginny*, dies in Philadelphia at the age of 56.

8 MAY 1911

Two weeks before the scheduled production of Claude DEBUSSY's musical setting of Gabriele d'Annunzio's mystery play *Le Martyre de Saint-Sébastien*, the Archbishop of Paris enjoins Catholics to refrain from attending a spectacle in which Ida Rubinstein, an Israelite, is to take the part of the perforated Saint, an injunction causing many pious customers to ask for refunds of purchased tickets, and the refusal of the critic Camille Bellaigue to review the performance.

In his recent edict, the Archbishop of Paris ill-advisedly attacked our work, with which he is unfamiliar. We wish to express our regret over this strange attitude undeserved by us, and we affirm upon our honor and upon the honor of all who are acquainted with the score and the scenario of *Le Martyre de Saint-Sébastien* that this work is deeply religious in spirit and is the lyric glorification not only of the admirable "athlete of Christ," but of all Christian heroism. (From a joint declaration signed by Gabriele d'Annunzio and Debussy)

9 MAY 1911

Concert des auteurs anonymes, with the audience playing the game of guessing the names of the composers, is given by the Société Indépendante de Musique in Paris, with the intention of probing the stylistic understanding of cultivated audiences.

The outcome of this referendum was appalling. Professional critics cautiously abstained from voting, and failed to publish a single line about this concert, which must have been so dis-

Titles and True Names of Composers	Majority Opinion	Other Guesses
1st Vocal Quartet (Leo Sachs)	Dubois, Sachs	Labey, Charpentier
2nd Vocal Quartet (Leo Sachs)	Sachs, Schmitt, Debussy	Labey, Chausson, Samazeuilh
3 Poèmes (Ingelbrecht)	Ingelbrecht, Debussy	Dupin, Philippe, Delage
Valses nobles et sentimentales (Ravel)	Ravel, Satie, Kodály	Blanche Selva, Szánto, Salomon
Poème de pitié (Mariotte)	Hutŕ, Wurmser, Sachs	Leroux, Chabrier, Roussel, Max d'Ollone
J'aime l'âne (Fraggi)	Ravel, Koechlin	Botrel, Saint-Saëns, Teriasse, Messager, Bruneau, Vincent d'Indy
Vocal Quartet (Büsser)	Auber, Saint-Saëns, Hahn	Caussade, Lalo, Pillois, Caplet
Vocal Quartet (Mignan)	Locard, Duparc, Debussy	Widor, Delage, Gaubert
Deux Rondels (Wurmser)	Wurmser, Ravel	Madame de Polignac Dalcroze, Dubois
Concert (Couperin)	Rameau, Casella	Schmitt, Enesco, Dubois
(Date and table from *Le Courier Musical*, Paris, 15 May 1911, p. 365)		

concerting to them. As for the rest of the audience, they naively ascribed works, in which personality of our extreme modernists was clearly reflected, to Mozart, Schumann, Chopin, Gounod, Wagner or Mendelssohn. And not one of those present discerned the hand of Ravel in a succession of waltzes, which bear so clearly Ravel's distinctive imprint. (Emile Vuillermoz, in *Maurice Ravel par quelques-uns de ses familiers*, Paris, 1939. Vuillermoz's memory was inexact, as is apparent from the above chart of guesses, which were not so wide of the mark.)

Ravel was in a loge in the midst of a group of society dilettantes who habitually swooned when they heard even a few bars of Ravel's music. Heroically faithful to his oath of a conspirator, the composer of *Valses nobles et sentimentales* had not forewarned them that his unpublished work was included in the program. When they heard this composition played with an imperturbably serious mien by Louis Aubert, the composer's sycophantic companions began to jeer, hoping to give Ravel pleasure by assailing ferociously these "ridiculous pages." Stoically, but no doubt somewhat bitterly, Ravel accepted these remarks in silence. (*ibidem*)

The title *Valses nobles et sentimentales* is a sufficient indication that my intention was to compose a chain of waltzes following the example of Schubert. *Valses nobles et sentimentales* were performed for the first time, amidst protests and booing, at the concert without the names of composers given by the Société Indépendante de Musique. The listeners voted for the authorship of each piece. The paternity of the *Valses* was correctly attributed to me, but by a weak majority. (From Ravel's autobiographical sketch, written in 1928 and published in the memorial Ravel issue of *La Revue musicale*, Paris, December 1938)

17 MAY 1911

Joseph STRANSKY is appointed conductor of the New York Philharmonic Orchestra, succeeding Gustav Mahler.

18 MAY 1911

Gustav MAHLER, the last of the great romantic composers of Vienna, who strove to translate his inner spiritual struggles into symphonic works of cosmic grandeur, dies in Vienna at 11:05 in the evening, of heart disease complicated by septic poisoning resulting from inflammation of the throat and pneumonia, 50 days before his 51st birthday.

WORRIED BY NEW YORK WOMEN.—Mahler was taken gravely ill in Paris and went to a sanitarium in Neuilly. When an American correspondent called there on the 4th of May he met Madame Mahler, who said that she attributed her husband's illness to nervous prostration and its consequences caused by his unfortunate relations with the Philharmonic Society of New York. "You cannot imagine," she said, "what he has suffered. In Vienna my husband was all-powerful. Even the Emperor did not dictate to him. But in New York, to his amazement, he had ten women ordering him about like a puppet. He hoped, however, by hard work and success to rid himself of his tormentors. Meanwhile he lost health and strength. Then, after an excursion to Springfield, he contracted angina pectoris. At his last concert in New York, rather than disappoint the public, he conducted while he was in a high fever. (New York *American*, 20 May 1911)

It was generally understood that Mr. Mahler had frequent struggles with the women managers of the New York Philharmonic Orchestra who assembled the large guarantee fund which was needed to cover the deficits of the orchestra. His physical breakdown was said to be the result of these disagreements although this has been denied even by the conductor himself. His wife, however, repeated the charges when it was thought that Mr. Mahler was about to die in a Paris sanitarium. (New York *Sun*, 20 May 1911)

"It is easy to kill a man through witchcraft, provided it be helped out with a little arsenic." So said Voltaire. "Nobody dies of a broken heart," say we, unconvinced when we are not able to find the germ or "bug." There were some expressions of derision when it was reported that Gustav Mahler, late of this city, was dying in Europe of "worry." His wife was the authority for the statement. Mahler, Tchaikovsky, Dvořák and Richard Strauss were the most distinguished men to conduct in our Carnegie Hall. Perhaps if the first had had some amiable peculiarities, if he had used no baton in conducting, or had had a huge family, or had gone to afternoon teas, he would have been more popular, and would be alive today. (Editorial in the New York *Evening Sun*, 20 May 1911)

He was looked upon as a great artist, and possibly he was one, but he failed to convince the people of New York of the fact, and therefore his American career was not a success. . . . In his treatment of the simple melodies of his symphonies (some of them borrowed without acknowledgment) he was utterly inconsiderate of their essence. . . . We cannot see how any of his music can long survive him. (New York *Tribune*, 21 May 1911)

The extremity which plunged us into the deepest mourning, no longer to possess the revered Gustav Mahler, has still left for our lives the imperishable ideal of his art and his living work. (Arnold Schoenberg's inscription on the wreath he brought to Mahler's funeral in Vienna on 21 May 1911)

19 MAY 1911

L'Heure Espagnole, one-act opera by Maurice RAVEL, after a play of Franc-Nohain of that name, wherein a vivacious Spanish señora in 18th-century Toledo conceals two of her lovers in the clock cabinets in the shop of her horologist husband, and when they are discovered by him, explains that they are customers interested in the workings of the mechanism and, while he is preoccupied with making a sale, takes a muscular muleteer to her upstairs chamber for an interlude of amours, set to music with horological precision, wherein the tiniest rhythmic wheels transmit melodic motion to the metrical cogs in nicely calculated kinetic impulses, with spacious tertian harmonies integrating in the chord of the 13th, and human voices declaiming in finely inflected prosody imparting the sense of continuous action, is produced at the Opéra-Comique in Paris.

L'Heure Espagnole is a curious and peculiar work. Its humor, precious, dry and stiff, does not relax for a single moment. Its characters lack vitality. Their declamation, strangely stressed, compressed and savored, possesses inflections and intervals peculiar to *Pelléas et Mélisande* but it has none of the fluidity, vivacity and suppleness of M. Debussy's musical language. It sounds like *Pelléas* played on a phonograph at a greatly reduced speed. This increases the resemblance of M. Ravel's characters to speaking and singing automatons. Everything is congealed and glacial; all elements are small, minuscule, narrow, foreshortened—the stature, the manner, the gestures, the words themselves and their intonation. They are cabinet puppets, figurines of a music clock. As for musical materials, chord progressions and harmonic subtleties, it is obvious that M. Ravel owes much to M. Debussy. But the soul of his music and of his art is absolutely different. M. Debussy is all sensibility, M. Ravel, all insensibility. (Pierre Lalo, *Le Temps*, Paris, 28 May 1911)

We find ourselves in the presence of pure music in the "chorus of little voices" of the horlogerie, this delectable prelude where the singing soul of familiar objects is harmoniously exhaled, where the whole childish mystery, the secret and distant poetry of minute organisms of steel is enriched by the power of the musical talisman possessed by the suave sorcerer Ravel. (Emile Vuillermoz, *La Revue Musicale*, Paris, 15 June 1911)

20 MAY 1911

Two short symphonic pieces by the 38-year-old French composer Déodat DE SÉVERAC, *Fête des Vendanges* and *Danse des Treilles et du Chevalet*, the latter being a ballet number from his opera *Cœur du Moulin*, are performed for the first time at the Société Nationale de Musique in Paris.

22 MAY 1911

The world première is given in Paris of *Le Martyre de Saint-Sébastien*, mystery play by Gabriele d'Annunzio, set to music by Claude DEBUSSY, with Ida Rubinstein miming the part of the punctured saint, in five parts:

(1) *The Court of the Lilies*, in which Saint Sebastian sends an arrow into infinity and performs an ecstatic dance on burning coals, accompanied by lambent strings pizzicato and incandescent woodwinds around a median C-sharp; (2) *Magic Chamber*, wherein Christian maidens are exquisitely tortured in the Roman Coliseum by parallel augmented triads, with the thematic C-sharp providing a focal rack; (3) *The Council of False Gods*, with triadic fanfares announcing a sinister pagan theme, yielding to the Christian tonal center on C-sharp; (4) *The Wounded Laurel Tree*, in which the master archer Sebastian becomes a passive target for whole-tone missiles; (5) *Paradise*, wherein Sebastian's perforated body is carried away by lamenting women, with the lethal arrows remaining miraculously affixed to the trunk of the laurel tree sacred to Apollo, while the portals of Paradise are thrown wide open as choruses of virgins, Apostles and angels intone reverential chants in Gregorian modalities.

No matter what the opinion of the critics and the public may be of my play, I am convinced that all will recognize in the score of Debussy the most divine source of emotion. (Gabriele d'Annunzio in a summation of the production)

Ida Rubinstein is beneath the level of being merely repellent. She even failed to present a plastic composition of her role. She offered a series of unconnected poses, lacking in continuity. (Henri Bidou, *Journal des Débats*, Paris, 29 May 1911)

Ida Rubinstein makes one think of a miraculously animated stained-glass window whose image is full of immobile memory, mute, translucid and sacred. (Jean Cocteau, *Comœdia*, Paris, 1 June 1911)

Debussy's score is characteristic in its expression of religious respect, discretion, mystic contemplation. It seems that it disappointed certain "Debussyites." They expected infinite subtleties of nuance, curious sonorous refinements, morbid search for rare effects. But Debussy is not a slave to formula. His style is always the same, but here it is amplified, matured, ennobled. It expands gloriously in the orchestra, flows in powerful waves in the voices. (Special issue of *Le Théâtre*, Paris, June 1911)

Le Martyre de Saint-Sébastien represents barbarism, all the more dangerous because it wears the Mediterranean mask of beauty. (Henri Ghéon, *Nouvelle Revue française*, Paris, July, 1911)

24 MAY 1911

Edward ELGAR conducts at the London Music Festival the first performance of his *Second Symphony* in E-flat major, dedicated "to the memory of His Late Majesty King Edward VII" and consisting of four movements:

(1) *Allegro vivace e nobilmente*, eloquently Brahmsogenic in its contrapuntal rigor, vigor and fervent nobility, with a brace of vivacious harps providing a confection of dulcet arpeggios; (2) *Larghetto*, a solemn march punctuated by mortuary strokes of the bass drum, gradually rising to the altitude of predictable grandeur "nobilmente e semplice"; (3) *Rondo—Presto*, in an invigorating triple measure; (4) *Moderato e maestoso*, arriving through a series of well-equilibrated climaxes to a soft finish.

24 MAY 1911

Granville BANTOCK conducts in Glasgow the first performance of his symphonic poem *Dante and Beatrice*, opening with three bars solo on three kettledrums, then embarking on a romantically flowing course in Lisztogenic harmonies towards a pianissimo conclusion.

24 MAY 1911

Americanesque, a symphonic movement by Henry F. GILBERT, based on three Negro minstrel tunes, is performed for the first time at a concert of the Boston Pops.

Numerous scraps of melody and of rhythm are at present drifting about in the musical atmosphere of America. Without inquiring too closely into their origin, I have tried to bind a few such scraps together into an art form. It may easily be said: that is not necessarily American music which merely uses American tunes as themes on which to build. But America itself was not discovered unpremeditatively. Its ultimate discovery was the result of many attempts. So it will undoubtedly be with American music. And when real American music does arrive, it will be the result of many attempts to write it, each of which considered by itself may be far afield, but all of which, taken together, will form the soil from which it must spring. (From Gilbert's statement, quoted in *Musical America*, New York, 3 June 1911)

29 MAY 1911

Sir William S. GILBERT, the satirical disestablishmentarian whose marvelously versified lines in the comic operas of the unheavenly twins Gilbert & Sullivan poked irreverent fun at the most formidably dignified and impregnable Victorian institutions, including the House of the Lords and even Windsor Castle itself, dies at the age of 74 of a cardiac syncope induced by an excessive exertion in assisting an inexpert girl swimmer in the artificial lake on his estate in Harrow Weald, Middlesex.

2 JUNE 1911

Isabeau, opera in three acts by Pietro MASCAGNI, to a libretto based on a modified version of the famous horseback ride of the medieval Lady Godiva, wherein the daughter of a tyrannical feudal lord parades through town mounted on a white horse completely naked to protest against being forced into a physically and morally abhorrent marriage, and when a fervent swain who throws roses on her unclad figure from a balcony is condemned to death at the stake, leaps into the flames herself on a sudden impulse, set to music full of incandescent Italianate emotionalism, is produced at the Teatro Colón in Buenos Aires.

We intended to have Isabeau appear naked, but not every soprano would consent to this. Besides, she might catch a cold. (Mascagni in an interview with an American correspondent in November 1911)

On his arrival in Buenos Aires, Mascagni was met at the pier by a crowd of 50,000 people. Women threw flowers at him, and he threw kisses in return—another portable commodity no Italian composer or prima donna can afford to travel without. Seventy-five banquets were arranged in his honor. "If my Isabeau is a success, I am a dead man—dead of indigestion" was Mascagni's despairing cry. (*Musical America*, New York, July 1911)

6 JUNE 1911

Henry, HADLEY conducts at the Norfolk, Connecticut, Music Festival the world première of his *Fourth Symphony*, subtitled *North, East, South, West*, wherein the North blows arctic blasts in brass while frigid strings moan, the Orient is lavish with exotic flutes, the American South fiddles away in ragtime rhythms, and the West exhibits a parade of pentatonic Indians attired in Wagneromorphic augmented triads.

13 JUNE 1911

Silence, a romantic symphonic poem by the 30-year-old Russian composer Nicolai MIASKOVSKY, inspired by the poetry of Edgar Allan Poe, is performed for the first time in Moscow. (Composition completed on 20 February 1910; date communicated by the composer.)

13 JUNE 1911

Four days before Igor STRAVINSKY's 29th birthday, his ballet *Pétrouchka* (completed by him in Rome on 26 May 1911) glorifying the pathetic Russian puppet (Pétrouchka is the French spelling of the rustic Russian diminutive of Peter, Petrushka), subtitled "Scènes burlesques en 4 tableaux," to the scenario of Alexandre Benois in collaboration with Stravinsky himself, is produced by Serge Diaghilev's Ballet Russe at the Théâtre du Châtelet in Paris, with Pétrouchka mimed by Nijinsky, and the orchestra conducted by Pierre Monteux.

BRIGHT WINTER DAY IN ADMIRALTY SQUARE IN ST. PETERSBURG IN THE 1830'S. At the height of Shrovetide, a puppeteer of an oriental cast of countenance presents an exhibition of his animated puppets, Pétrouchka, a Ballerina and a Moor, who perform a frenetic dance before an astounded public. The puppeteer's art imbues the puppets with the sentiments and passions of real people. Pétrouchka is so strongly endowed with these qualities that he feels more deeply than the Ballerina and the Moor. He bitterly resents the cruelty of the puppeteer, and his own subjection to him, his separation from the outside world, his ungainly and ludicrous appearance. He seeks solace in his love for the Ballerina, and he imagines that in her heart she reciprocates his sentiments, while in reality she is frightened by his strange behavior and avoids him. The life of the stupid and malevolent Moor presents a complete contrast to Pétrouchka's existence. The Ballerina likes the Moor and seeks to allure him in various ways. She finally succeeds, but Pétrouchka is furiously jealous and interrupts their rendezvous. The Moor, enraged by the intrusion, throws him out. The gaiety of the fair reaches its height. A merchant makes merry with Gypsy girls and

throws coins to the crowd; the coachmen of the court dance with fashionably attired nurses; an animal trainer enters with a dancing bear; a band of maskers appears and the crowd follows them in a wild dance. At the climactic moment, screams are heard from the theater booth. The contest between the Moor and Pétrouchka reaches its critical point. The animated puppets run out into the street. The Moor cuts Pétrouchka with his saber, and he dies pitifully in the snow amid the crowd of celebrants. The puppeteer is summoned by a guard to calm the crowd. At his hands Pétrouchka becomes once more a puppet. The crowd sees that his broken skull is made of wood and his torso is filled with sawdust, and disperses. But the affair is not over for the wily puppeteer. To his horror, the ghost of Pétrouchka appears over his booth making threatening gestures at his tormentor and mocks the people who believed in his magic tricks. (Translation by Nicolas Slonimsky from the Russian text of the scenario printed in the score.)

FIRST SCENE: *Popular Festivities at Shrovetide Fair*, with the thematic four notes D-E-G-A dominating the scene and establishing the elements of the tonic (D-A) and the dominant (E-G) in a cardiac diastolic-systolic accordion-like dominant-tonic pulsation within the triadic spectrum of D major. *Intoxicated Revelers Pass Dancingly*, in consecutive triads, in inebriated duple time. *The Old Man of the Fair* entertains the crowd from his theater booth in asymmetrically propulsive 5/8 time within a heavily accented Dorian mode. *Organ Grinder and a Street Dancer*, marking time with a triangle, presently competing with another street dancer singing a sentimental romance. *Gay Revelers Return*, recapitulating the accordion music in consecutive triads, in constantly changing meters of 2/8, 3/8, 4/8 and 5/8 time. *The Puppeteer Plays the Flute*, wherein Pétrouchka, the Moor and the Ballerina come to life as the puppeteer touches them with his flute during the *fermate* of a luxuriant cadenza, while *flautando* violins, inwardly spiralling within a narrow compass produce a highly concentrated series of 12 different notes out of a group of 14, canonically distributed in sequential cellular figures. *Russian Dance*, with Pétrouchka, the Moor and the Ballerina gloriously bursting out into an overwhelmingly vitalistic symmetric step in accordion-like dominant-tonic pulsations rooted in a deep dominant pedal G, the piano prancing, leaping and thumping pandiatonically on white keys, the dance presently modulating up a whole tone, producing some acidulated accidentals and dashing off a fistful of Russian refrains before returning to pandiatonically embroidered C major festivities and ending on a tonic chord enriched by a major sixth.

SECOND SCENE: *At Pétrouchka's*, a torturous succession of spasmodic outcries, during which a bitonal chord combining C major and F-sharp major is outlined in closely overlapping arpeggios in the paired clarinets and in the piano cadenza, constituting the earliest use in music history of overt bitonality of two major triads whose tonics are related by a tritone. *Adagietto*, wailing in spiral convolutions as Pétrouchka's unrequited love for the Ballerina drives him to distraction, presently erupting in furibund malediction of bitonally copulated muted trumpets and muted cornets, vociferating imprecations in the top register of a maddened clarinet, and finally collapsing on a fatalistic plagal cadence.

THIRD SCENE: *At the Moor's*, wherein the Moor, attired in a sumptuous oriental gown, juggles coconuts to exotically ornate susurrations, presently joined by the Ballerina introduced by a flourish on a cornet, whereupon they indulge in a hypersentimental display of ostentatious pseudo-vulgarity to a stylized salon waltz. *Appearance of Pétrouchka and His Quarrel with the Moor*, with Pétrouchka restraining his desperation in depressing minor arpeggios in the muted trumpets, growing into open conflict at the ominous entrance of bitonally arpeggiated trombones, causing the Ballerina to faint.

FOURTH SCENE: *Popular Festivities at Shrovetide*, returning to the initial merry-making, with the four principal thematic tones D-E-G-A again forming the dominant-tonic complex suggesting the diastolic-systolic accordion rhythms. *Dance of the Nurses*, with their sentimental singing of the Russian urban tunes "Down the Street" and "Oh, my gates, my brand-new gates" in stimulatingly discordant harmonies. *Muzhik with a Dancing Bear*, lumbering to the accompaniment of a ponderous tuba in whole-tone progressions within the compass of a tritone. *A Merchant Carousing*, squeezing a gay accordion with two Gypsy girls. *Dance of the Coachmen and Stable Boys*, accentuated by heavy brass in a Mixolydian mode and crude syncopation. *Dance of Nurses and Coachmen*, with sentimental ballad tunes tenderly nursed against the rudely masculine encroachments of the male menials. *The Maskers*, in an animated asymmetrical march movement, leading to uninhibited revelry in 5/8 time. *General Dance*, once more returning to the spirit of the initial scene, with its thematic 4-note motto, while foreboding chromatics rise from the depths presaging disaster, as Pétrouchka runs out of the theater booth screaming bitonally in his attempt to evade the pursuing Moor, who overtakes him and smites him down with his Ottoman scimitar, cracking Pétrouchka's skull to the accompaniment of a dull thud of a tambourine dropped on the floor in the orchestra pit, and followed by a stifled bitonal spasm of the piccolos. *Pétrouchka's Death*, as sawdust oozes out of his wooden head to a pathetic dirge of a dulcet clarinet and a dolorous bassoon, expiring in residual bitonalities; the puppeteer appears and shakes Pétrouchka to the shivering sound of *spiccato* violins, and, as the crowd disperses, drags the cadaver away, but flees in horror when Pétrouchka's ghost materializes over the theater booth and thumbs his nose in a caducous tritone.

In my unbounded admiration for the unquestionable genius of Stravinsky's music, I was quite willing to minimize my own part in the creation of *Pétrouchka*. The subject of the ballet was entirely Stravinsky's idea, and I only helped him to organize it in a concrete dramatic form. But the libretto, the cast of characters, the plot and the denouement of the action, as well as a number of other details, were almost wholly mine. My share in the production, however, seems trivial in comparison with Stravinsky's music. I do not know a single work which flows in such an uninterrupted current (or rather in continuous cascades, jets and rivulets) as this. The collision of Pétrouchka's lonely soul with the mass of humanity is linked and intertwined with a sense of profound inevitability, and therein lies its tragic quality. All this does not follow from the words of the scenario but from the essence of the music itself. In fact, it is quite impossible to translate this drama into words; its meaning can be expressed only in music. When at a rehearsal Stravinsky asked me who should be listed as the author of *Pétrouchka*, I replied without a moment's hesitation, "You, of course." Stravinsky objected to this verdict and insisted that I should be named as the actual author of the libretto. Our *combat de générosité* was resolved by putting both our names on the program as co-authors, but I succeeded in having Stravinsky's name placed first, despite my alphabetical precedence. Still, my name appears twice in the score, because Stravinsky decided to dedicate Pétrouchka to me, which touched me infinitely . . . From my earliest childhood I carried the vivid memories of the riotous turmoil and merrymaking of the "plain people" of St. Petersburg at the Shrovetide, the peepshows and the excitement of the street fair, where my friends used to come "to learn what Russia really is like." These unforgettable scenes of a vanishing world remain dear and near to me in many ways. Some will say that these memories are colored by the remoteness of my childhood, and that in reality it was just dirt, brawling and lust. Naturally, these street fairs were not idyllic events conforming with the bittersweet ideals of virtue so dear to our temperance societies. But no matter how much drunkenness, how much crudity there was in these scenes, the street life had its own rights, and set its own rules of conduct and its own code of decency. (Alexandre Benois, *Rech*, St. Petersburg, 17 August 1911)

Pétrouchka is a marvel. The scenario of these "scènes burlesques" is of no consequence. The important thing is what the composer, co-author with Benois of this scenario, has retained of it. It does not seem possible to achieve a stronger, richer, and more intense evocation of the story. It is simply astonishing. Apart from an abundance of musical themes, original and "classical" and a profusion of fantastic rhythms, Igor Stravinsky's orchestral scoring is extraordinary. Instrumental timbres flow in a stream in a most novel fashion. These sonorities engender among the audience a sense of inexpressible exhilaration. Not a single measure remains indifferent. And what boldness in the handling of the instruments! What eloquence! What life! What youthfulness! (*Comœdia*, Paris, 14 June 1911)

14 JUNE 1911

Johan SVENDSEN, Norwegian composer of romantic music with ingratiating Scandinavian inflections, including the ubiquitous *Romance* for violin, dies in Copenhagen, where he was court conductor, at the age of 70.

22 JUNE 1911

At the conclusion of the coronation of King George V and Queen Mary, Edward ELGAR's *Coronation March*, expressly written for the occasion, is performed for the first time.

1 JULY 1911

Arnold SCHOENBERG completes in Vienna his significant pedagogical work, *Harmonielehre*, dedicated to the memory of Gustav Mahler.

No art has been so hindered in its development by its teachers as music. For no one watches more jealously over his property than that man who knows that, strictly speaking, it does not belong to him. (From the opening chapter of *Harmonielehre*.)

2 JULY 1911

Felix MOTTL, Austrian conductor whose knowledgeable devotion to Wagner (he took part in the preparatory work of the first Wagner Festival in Bayreuth) elevated him to the highest rank among conductors of Wagner's music dramas and whose congenial orchestral transcriptions of ballet music by Lully, Rameau, Grétry and Gluck have contributed greatly to the popularity of these works, dies in Munich at the age of 54.

3 JULY 1911

Madeline SCHILLER, London-born American pianist of German extraction, once so fresh of flesh and comely of countenance, who made musicological history by playing the world première of Tchaikovsky's *Second Piano Concerto* with the New York Philharmonic on 12 November 1881, six months before its Russian performance, and whose artistic appearances spanned all English-speaking countries, dies of a piteously unesthetic uterine cancer at the wrinkled age of 65.

7 JULY 1911

Gian Carlo MENOTTI, composer of expertly made operatic melodramas to his own librettos in the English language, is born in Cadegliano, Italy. (He has retained faithfully his Italian citizenship during his long and successful career in America.)

19 JULY 1911

Anton von WEBERN composes in Vienna the shortest piece of orchestral literature, the fourth of his *Five Pieces for Orchestra*, op. 10, scored for clarinet, trumpet, trombone, mandolin, celesta, harp, small drum, violin and viola, containing 6 1/3 measures in 3/4 time lasting 19 seconds according to the metronome mark. (The date of composition of No. 1 of the *Five Pieces* is 28 June 1911; of No. 2, 13 September 1913; of No. 3, 8 September 1913; of No. 5, 6 October 1913. All these dates communicated by Anton von Webern himself in a personal letter to the author.)

1 AUGUST 1911

Autumn, symphonic tableau by 20-year-old Sergei PROKOFIEV, is performed for the first time in Moscow.

5 AUGUST 1911

A century has passed since the birth in Metz of Ambroise THOMAS, French composer of the Gallic operatic classic *Mignon* and of other mellifluous music for the stage.

27 AUGUST 1911

Three centuries have elapsed since the death in Madrid of Tomás Luis de VICTORIA, great Spanish composer of the Renaissance, whose masses, motets, hymns, psalms, antiphons, canticles, and other sacred vocal works are, in grandeur, spiritual elevation, and polyphonic virtuosity, all but equal to the sublime creations of his contemporary Palestrina.

25 SEPTEMBER 1911

The Little Millionaire, musical comedy with book, lyrics and music by George M. COHAN, dealing with the predicament of an heir to a fortune who has to make sure that his fiancée loves him for his physical and mental distinctions and not for his gold, is produced and staged by George M. Cohan at the Cohan Theater in New York, with George M. Cohan starring in the title role.

14 OCTOBER 1911

Conchita, opera in four acts by Riccardo ZANDONAI, written to a story adapted from the erotic novella, *La Femme et le Pantin* by Pierre Louÿs, in which a Carmen-like girl, employed in a Seville cigar factory, taunts her wealthy admirer into a rage of unconsummated passion, is produced in Milan.

22 OCTOBER 1911

A century has passed since the birth of Franz LISZT, titanic pianist and fantastically productive composer whose expansive romanticism bore a seed of futurity in the bold projections of his musical speculations revealed in the polytonal and atonal usages in his post-humous keyboard pieces.

1 NOVEMBER 1911

At a benefit performance of Massenet's opera *Cendrillon* by the Chicago Opera Company, Mary GARDEN, the Prince Charming of the cast, sells kisses to young men for charity.

Mary Garden's kiss lasts a long time and makes the world look sort of different. Mary looks squarely in your eyes, and, believe me, she is some kisser! (From a testimonial report by "Tough" Darnum, one of the seven men who bought Mary Garden's kisses)

4 NOVEMBER 1911

E. H. CRUMP is reelected Mayor of Memphis, Tennessee, after an arduous campaign, helped along by a song *Mr. Crump* especially composed for him by the Negro balladeer W. C. Handy, and later renamed *Memphis Blues*, which created a new style of American popular music technically distinguished by a flatted "blue" seventh and a flatted "blue" third in a major key.

(The following statement from Mr. Crump's secretary obtained by Mrs. Frances Fink at the author's request seems to contradict the story of *Memphis Blues:* "Mr. Crump did not use Handy's song in either of his elections. The song was written a couple of years after Mr. Crump was elected Mayor the first time. . . . He was elected the second time in November 1911, and again in November 1915. I do not think Handy wrote the song as a campaign song, but simply used Mr. Crump's name in the composition of same." But from Mr. W. C. Handy comes a rejoinder: "I did not write the *Memphis Blues* as a campaign song for Mr. Crump but wrote *Mr. Crump* as a campaign song for Mr. Crump and then changed the title for publication to the *Memphis Blues* and published it in 1912 myself . . . I then followed that with the *St. Louis Blues*, copyrighted on 14 September 1914.")

4 NOVEMBER 1911

Symphony in G by Walford DAVIES, renowned English musical educationist, is performed for the first time in London. (The originally scheduled performance on 15 May 1911, with Arthur Nikisch conducting the London Symphony Orchestra, was cancelled.)

9 NOVEMBER 1911

Der Bergsee, Wagneromantic opera in two acts with a prelude by the Austrian composer Julius BITTNER, to his own libretto in the Austrian dialect, from the time of peasant uprisings in the Austrial Tyrol, wherein a frustrated maiden crushes the wall of a dam with an axe to drown her uncertain lover and herself in a flood of augmented triads, is performed for the first time at the Vienna Opera.

11 NOVEMBER 1911

The AEROPHOR, a tone-sustaining instrument, consisting of a rubber bulb with a tube appliance, enabling the player on a wind instrument to hold a note indefinitely, is given its first demonstration by the inventor, Bernard Samuels, in Berlin.

12 NOVEMBER 1911

La Vendetta, opera by the 36-year-old French composer Jean NOUGÈS, melodramatically portraying vengeful mores among the Mediterranean coast villagers, is performed for the first time in Marseilles.

19 NOVEMBER 1911

Sixth Symphony by the Swiss composer Hans HUBER is performed for the first time in Basel.

20 NOVEMBER 1911

Thor kører til Jotunheim (Thor Drives to Jotunheim Mountains), orchestral fantasy by the Danish composer Hakon BØRRESEN, his first and most successful work, written at the age of 19 in 1895, reaches its belated first performance in Copenhagen.

20 NOVEMBER 1911

Six months and two days after the death of Gustav MAHLER, Bruno Walter conducts in Munich the first performance of his pantheistic song-symphony *Das Lied von der Erde*, in six sections, scored for tenor, contralto and orchestra, to texts of a German translation of 8th-century Chinese poems, with the basic tetraphonic motto, A,G,E,C, undergoing motivic metamorphosis through augmentation, diminution, inversion, rhythmic alteration, permutation and, in the final chord integration into a vertical complex rooted in deep C:

(1) *Das Trinklied vom Jammer der Erde (Drinking Song of Earthly Anguish)*, for tenor and orchestra with a pentatonic horn call of the ageless Song of the Earth intoned in fatalistic A minor, achieving antinomial catharsis by enharmonic equivocation of modal structure; (2) *Der Einsame im Herbst (Solitary Soul in Autumn)*, for contralto and orchestra, a resigned plaint in philosophical D minor with caducous cadences in the Phrygian mode; (3) *Von der Jugend (Of Youth)*, for tenor and orchestra, an exhilarating interlude set in optimistic B-flat major mitigated by the pentatonicism of its melodic structure to avoid the inexorable finality of the leading tone; (4) *Von der Schönheit (Of Beauty)* for contralto and orchestra, set in mundane G major with pentatonic melos outlined in the thematic pattern E, G, A, B, D, in the orchestra; (5) *Der Trunkene im Frühling (The Drunkard in Springtime)*, for tenor and orchestra, a bittersweet soliloquy in ostentatiously cheerful A major, descriptive of the dual intoxication by wine and singing birds; (6) *Der Abschied (The Farewell)*, for contralto and orchestra, a symphonic concept abounding in instrumental flourishes, melismatically centered on the pessimistic C minor, and slowly progressing in the direction of the redemptive tonality of C major, with the ultimate 90° turn from the horizontal melody to the vertical harmony in the chord of the unresolved tonic sixth.

"Is it safe to have this music performed? Will not the people, after hearing my work, go out in the streets and kill themselves?" (Mahler's question reportedly addressed to a friend)

23 NOVEMBER 1911

Kuhreigen, seventh opera by the Austrian composer Wilhelm KIENZL, dealing with a Swiss soldier in the service of Louis XVI, condemned to death for singing the associatively subversive nationalistic Alpine air *Kuhreigen*, but pardoned thanks to the intercession of a humanistic marquise (to whom he subsequently offers consolation after

the French Revolution, when she herself goes to the guillotine), is produced in Vienna.

24 NOVEMBER 1911

Eva, operetta in three acts by Franz LEHÁR, to a story of a Paris factory girl who acquires sophistication from an experienced soubrette, fascinates a grand duke and eventually marries her young industrialist employer, is produced in Vienna.

27 NOVEMBER 1911

Esvelia, the first opera in one act by the 27-year-old Italian composer Iginio ROBBIANI, after a poem by Heinrich Heine, is performed for the first time in Rome.

6 DECEMBER 1911

A Tale of Old Japan, an orientalistic cantata by Samuel COLERIDGE-TAYLOR, employing a simulacrum of pentatonic modalities of Japanese court dances, is performed for the first time in London.

8 DECEMBER 1911

The San Francisco Symphony Orchestra, established as a "permanent orchestral body along the lines of those maintained by the larger cities of Europe and the East," opens its first season of six concerts, in a program of works by Wagner, Tchaikovsky, Haydn and Liszt, under the direction of Henry Hadley, the first American to head a major symphony orchestra.

14 DECEMBER 1911

Schauspiel Ouvertüre, op. 4, by the remarkably precocious 14-year-old Austrian composer Erich Wolfgang KORNGOLD, whose Mozartomorphic middle name was given to him by his father, eminent Vienna music critic, is performed for the first time at the prestigious Gewandhaus (so named because it was originally a warehouse), in Leipzig, under the direction of Arthur Nikisch.

Mozart and Korngold are two geniuses who began to write music in their earliest childhood. Why does Mozart spontaneously lisp music in the simple idiom of his own day, while Korngold lisps in the complex idiom of his? Korngold can hardly have derived his harmonic system from the study of other composers, for in what composer's work could he have found it? It is the spontaneous product of a most subtly organized brain that at the first span embraces practically all we know and feel today in the way of harmonic relation. (Ernest Newman, in *The Nation*, London, quoted in *Musical America*, 5 October 1912)

Korngold's *Overture* deserves an honorable place in the Museum of Infant Prodigies. If Master Korngold could make such a noise at fourteen, what will he not do when he is twenty-eight? The thought is appalling. (Philip Hale, Boston *Herald*, 16 February 1914)

15 DECEMBER 1911

Bérénice, "tragedy in music" in three acts by Albéric MAGNARD, to his own libretto fashioned from Racine's play about the Jewish concubine of the Roman Emperor Titus, who, like the legendary Egyptian queen of the same name, surrenders her luxuriant tresses to Aphrodite in exchange for an aphrodisiac potion she desperately needs to lure back an errant lover, set to music, according to Magnard's own admission, "dans le style wagnérien," but containing some enticing illustrative inventions such as canons in the octave to illustrate a consummated amour, is produced at the Opéra-Comique in Paris.

19 DECEMBER 1911

At a gala spectacle staged at the Paris Opéra under the auspices of the Aero-Club de France, Camille ERLANGER conducts the première of a mimed "épopée lyrique" *Icare*, glorifying the pioneer of man-powered winged flight, competently arranged by Erlanger from raw materials contributed by a wealthy amateur musician named Henri Deutsch de la Meurthe.

23 DECEMBER 1911

The Miracle, a Catholic mystery play to a scenario by Max Reinhardt in two acts and an intermezzo, with music by Engelbert HUMPERDINCK to a libretto derived from medieval Marian cult poems, dealing with an excitable nun who runs away with a knight errant, whereupon the Virgin descends from her altar to fill the vacancy created by her sinful trespass, is performed for the first time in London, calling forth street demonstrations of Protestant groups brandishing placards proclaiming NO POPERY.

23 DECEMBER 1911

I Gioielli della Madonna, tragic opera in three acts by the paternally Bavarian and maternally Venetian composer Ermanno WOLF-FERRARI, to a highly charged melodramatic story of his own invention wherein a maddened lover lays the jewels stolen from the Madonna's altar at the feet of his beloved, who thereupon surrenders herself to him, but jumps into the Bay of Naples when she realizes the enormity of the sacrilege, and her suitor stabs himself to death, is performed for the first time anywhere at the Berlin Opera, in a German version under the title *Der Schmuck der Madonna*.

29 DECEMBER 1911

L'Aube rouge, lyric drama in four acts by Camille ERLANGER, dealing with a group of romantic Russians on the French Riviera idealistically plotting to liquidate an Imperial Grand Duke to advance the "red dawn" in Russia over the objections of a girl conspirator enamored of the appointed assassin (he dutifully throws his bomb in Moscow, and is shot down by the Tsarist police), set to an appropriately dynamitic score, with some incidental Russianisms such as Greek Orthodox church hymns and asymmetrical meters of 7/4, is performed for the first time anywhere in Rouen.

1912

8 JANUARY 1912

A century has passed since the birth in Geneva of Sigismond THALBERG, piano virtuoso and composer of brilliant waltzes and études, whose steely octaves, meteoric chromatics and gurgling trills captivated the salons of Europe.

(Date of birth, 8 January 1812, obtained from the registry of births in Geneva, certifying that Thalberg was a legitimate son of Joseph Thalberg, and not an illegitimate offspring of a titled nobleman as stated in most reference works, and as Thalberg himself chose to proclaim.)

10 JANUARY 1912

First Symphony by the prime Swedish symphonist Kurt ATTERBERG is performed for the first time in Stockholm.

18 JANUARY 1912

Oberst Chabert, opera in three acts by the 29-year-old German composer Hermann von WALTERSHAUSEN, to a libretto from a novella by Balzac wherein a Napoleonic colonel given up for dead after the wars returns to Paris only to shoot himself after he finds that his wife is married to another is produced in Frankfurt.

21 JANUARY 1912

Ma Mère l'Oye, orchestral version of RAVEL's suite of children's pieces (first performed in the original setting for piano 4 hands in Paris on 20 April 1910), distinguished by a delicate equilibrium of instrumental forces, and featuring a uniquely expressive solo by the double-bassoon as the shy Beast who becomes a princely youth when the flute, as Beauty, accepts his love, is presented for the first time in Paris.

26 JANUARY 1912

Ormazd, symphonic poem by Frederick S. CONVERSE, depicting in Wagneromantic colors Ormazd's victory over the forces of evil, is performed for the first time by the St. Louis Symphony Orchestra, Max Zach conducting.

1 FEBRUARY 1912

Le Pays, opera in three acts by the French composer Guy ROPARTZ, wherein a French fisherman married to an Icelandic girl pines for his native Brittany and in the end plunges to his death into the arctic waters to the accompaniment of Wagneromantic brass, is produced in Nancy, conducted by the composer, the director of the local conservatory of music.

2 FEBRUARY 1912

L'Aigle, "lyric epic" in three acts by Jean NOUGUÈS, an illustrated musical chronicle of revolutionary events in France, from the thunderous fall of Robespierre in 1794 to the death of Napoleon in 1821, with quotations from suitable popular tunes, is produced in Rouen.

3 FEBRUARY 1912

Der liebe Augustin, operetta in three acts by the Austrian composer Leo FALL, involving an accidental exchange of two female babies, one of them of princely birth, who when grown fall in love with their music teacher Augustin, who marries the presumptive princess who turns out to be of lowly birth, is produced in Berlin.

6 FEBRUARY 1912

Die verschenkte Frau, comic opera in three acts by Eugen D'ALBERT, in which a susceptible 18th-century Italian innkeeper finds his wife acting a loving columbine with a harlequin in a company of visiting comedians, explodes in fury and offers her to him in perpetuity, but relents as he realizes that it was all a play, set to music in an automatized abecedarian idiom of the opera buffa, is produced in Vienna.

6 FEBRUARY 1912

Die Geburt des Herrn, first part of the triple oratorio *Christus* by the 76-year-old German composer Felix DRAESEKE, traversing the life of Jesus in three subdivisions, composed between 1896 and 1899 in a grandiosely Germanic and lutulently pietistic manner, is performed for the first time in Berlin. (The second part of the trilogy, *Christus der Prophet,* was first performed in Berlin on 13 February 1912; the third, *Tod und Sieg des Herrn,* on 20 February 1912.)

7 FEBRUARY 1912

La Lépreuse, opera in three acts by the Tyrol-born French composer of Italian extraction Sylvio LAZZARI, wherein a beauteous yet piteously leprous girl contaminates her vacillating lover to secure his fidelity and settles with him on an isolated mountain retreat conducted thither by a Wagneromantic chorus of monks, nuns and peasants in a triadically harmonized procession, is produced at the Opéra-Comique in Paris.

7 FEBRUARY 1912

Jaufré Rudel, one-act opera by the 23-year-old Italian composer Pasquale SAYA, dealing with a legendary trouvère of Provence who sang of his eternal love for a distant fair lady, is produced in Messina.

11 FEBRUARY 1912

Second Symphony by the foremost Swedish symphonist Kurt ATTERBERG is performed for the first time in Stockholm.

15 FEBRUARY 1912

Rhéna, opera in four acts by the Belgian composer Jean Baptiste van der EEDEN, is produced in Brussels.

17 FEBRUARY 1912

Roma, opera in five acts by Jules MASSENET, set in Rome in 216 B.C. and focused on the tragic fate of a vestal virgin who becomes the concubine of a legionnaire and is doomed to die just as the Roman soldiers return after their victory over Carthage, is produced in Monte Carlo.

22 FEBRUARY 1912

Der Simplicius, opera in three acts by the Swiss composer Hans HUBER, written in 1899, to a libretto dealing with a noble simpleton who pacifies the rebellious Westphalian peasantry in 1640 and marries his feudal lord's daughter, set to music in a turbulent Wagnerogenic idiom, receives its belated first performance in Basel.

24 FEBRUARY 1912

Les trois masques, opera in four acts by Isidore de LARA, is produced in Marseilles.

28 FEBRUARY 1912

Carl NIELSEN conducts in Copenhagen the first performance of his *Third Symphony,* subtitled *Sinfonia Espansiva* (completed on 30 April 1911), comprising four movements, *Allegro espansivo, Andante pastorale, Allegretto non troppo* and *Allegro pomposo,* written in an expansively romantic idiom replete with impatient modulations, sudden inturgescences of orchestral sonorities, and sequential detumescences of harmonic substance; and on the same program, the first performance of his *Violin Concerto* (completed on 13 December 1911) in two connected movements, *Praeludium* and *Poco Adagio* and an appended *Rondo,* with Nielsen's son-in-law Emil Telmányi as soloist.

29 FEBRUARY 1912

Lelia, first opera in four acts by the 33-year-old Swedish composer Natanael BERG, after Byron's exotic poem *The Giaour* is produced in Stockholm.

1 MARCH 1912

Sangre y sol, opera by the French composer Alexandre GEORGES, is produced in Nice.

6 MARCH 1912

I Dispettosi Amanti, one-act opera by the 37-year-old Italian composer Attilio PARELLI (whose real name at birth was Paparella), is produced in Philadelphia.

7 MARCH 1912

Édénie, opera in three acts by the Belgian composer Léon DU BOIS, his last, is produced at Antwerp with a Flemish version of the original French libretto.

11 MARCH 1912

The Crown of India, an "imperial masque" with music by Edward ELGAR, written to celebrate the visit to India by King George V, is performed for the first time at the London Coliseum.

14 MARCH 1912

Mona, opera in three acts by Horatio PARKER, the winning work in a competition for the Metropolitan Opera Prize of $10,000, to a gory libretto wherein an early British noblemaiden stabs her Roman lover to death in 99 A.D. when he meddles in her druidic rites, set to a Wagneromantic score chockful of suspended ninth-chords and anguished chromatics, is produced at the Metropolitan Opera House in New York, destined to vanish from the repertory after only four performances.

One device which I have used in *Mona* is that of associating the different personalities of the drama with definite tonalities. For instance, Gwynn, the hero, is associated with the key of B major. With Mona herself I carried the idea still further, assigning separate keys to the two distinct aspects of her personality. In her character of a Druid priestess she is associated with the key of E minor, while in her character as a woman she is assigned to the key of E-flat major. (Horatio Parker in a statement to the press)

17 MARCH 1912

Gabriel Pierné conducts in Paris the first performance of the symphonic picture *Thèbes* by Ernest FANELLI, a music copyist and drummer, written in 1883, which anticipates in a tentative manner some impressionistic devices of tone painting, such as progressions of ninth-chords and whole-tone scales.

21 MARCH 1912

La Farce du Cuvier, opera in two acts by the French composer Gabriel DUPONT based on a 15th-century mystery play, is produced in Brussels.

23 MARCH 1912

Ilya Murometz, third symphony by the Russian composer Reinhold GLIÈRE, illustrating in epically grandiloquent four movements the four phases in the legendary career of the 11th-century giant of Russian folklore, (1) *Ilya Murometz's Confrontation with a Rival*, (2) *The Highwayman named Nightingale*, (3) *At the Court of the Sun Prince Vladimir*, (4) *Heroic Exploits of Ilya and his Petrification* (introduced by ominous tritone progressions), is performed for the first time in Moscow.

29 MARCH 1912

Útok na Mlýn, opera in three acts by the 50-year-old Czech composer Karel WEIS, after Emile Zola's novel *L'Attaque du Moulin*, is produced in the Czech version in Prague.

6 APRIL 1912

Pompeii, opera in four acts by Marziano PEROSI, after Bulwer Lytton's historic novel, is produced in Vienna.

6 APRIL 1912

A thousand years have elapsed since the death of NOTKER (BALBULUS), the St. Gall monk who was one of the earliest church musicians to develop the ecclesiastical sequence.

11 APRIL 1912

Oudelette, opera in three acts by the Belgian composer Charles RADOUX, is produced in Brussels.

12 APRIL 1912

Cyrano de Bergerac, symphonic poem for horn and orchestra by the 25-year-old Belgian composer Robert HERBERIGS, in three movements picturing Cyrano as frondeur, lover and warrior, is performed for the first time in Brussels.

13 APRIL 1912

Die Brautwahl, opera in three acts with an epilogue by Ferruccio BUSONI (completed by him in Berlin on 8 October 1911) after a fantastic tale by E.T.A. Hoffmann, scored in an opulent polyphonic idiom in which the choice of the bride becomes entangled in invertible counterpoint, is performed for the first time in Hamburg.

Die Brautwahl is suffering from constipation, like the composer himself. (Busoni, in a letter quoted in Edward J. Dent's *Ferruccio Busoni, A Biography*, London, 1933)

15 APRIL 1912

Eight British musicians, W. Hartley, J. Hume, P.C. Taylor, J.W. Woodward, R. Bricoux, F. Clarke, G. Krius and W.T. Brailey, members of the ship's band on the White Star liner, S.S. *Titanic*, go down with the iceberg-ripped ship playing *Nearer My God to Thee*.

15 APRIL 1912

Hoffmann, opera in three acts by the Italian composer Guido LACCETTI, dealing with the life and literary productions of E.T.A. Hoffmann, is produced in Naples.

16 APRIL 1912

La Baronessa di Carini, one-act opera by Giuseppe *Mulè*, his first, is produced in Palermo.

22 APRIL 1912

Mary Carr MOORE conducts in Seattle the first performance of her four-act opera *Narcissa*, to the libretto by her mother, detailing the missionary exploits of Marcus Whitman in the American Northwest culminating in his and his wife Narcissa's murder on 29 November 1847 at the hands of Oregon Indians armed with authentic-sounding pentatonic war cries when they suspect that an outbreak of measles is the result of the white man's pale-faced sorcery.

22 APRIL 1912

Four French composers conduct their own works in Paris at a dance recital of the Russian ballerina Natacha Trouhanova: (1) Paul DUKAS, the first performance of his symphonic poem *La Péri*, a score of rarefied exoticism with a fluid enharmonic modulatory chord employed as a sonorous "block"; (2) Vincent D'INDY, his orientalistic symphonic variations *Istar;* (3) Florent SCHMITT, his barbaric ballet *La Tragédie de Salomé;* (4) Maurice RAVEL, the first performance of *Adélaïde, ou le Langage des fleurs*, a delicate orchestral version of his *Valses nobles et sentimentales*.

22 APRIL 1912

Naïl, lyric drama in three acts by the English-Parisian composer Isidor de LARA, dealing with an Algerian nautch-girl enamored of an anti-French guerrilla fighter, resisting to the death the lewd advances of a multi-futuent Moroccan emir, written in a rhapsodically expansive manner with a melismatic patina of orientalistic arabesques and containing a hymn to Allah in the whole-tone scale, is produced in Paris.

1 MAY 1912

Beni Mora, oriental suite in three movements for orchestra by Gustav HOLST, inspired by a 4-note motive he heard played on a bamboo flute in Algeria for two and a half hours without stopping, and which he incorporated verbatim for 163 bars, taking only 5 minutes and 26 seconds to play, in the third movements of the suite, is performed for the first time in London.

3 MAY 1912

Vasksenje (Resurrection), by the Serbian composer Stevan HRISTIĆ, to a romantically interpreted biblical story, is performed for the first time in Belgrade.

14 MAY 1912

Le Dieu bleu, Hindu ballet in one act with music by the Venezuelan-born Parisian composer Reynaldo HAHN, is produced by Diaghilev's Ballet Russe in Paris.

18 MAY 1912

Évocations, symphonic suite in three movements by Albert ROUSSEL, evoking in impressionistic colors the sights and sounds of India which he visited in 1909, is performed for the first time in Paris:

(1) *Les Dieux dans l'ombre des cavernes*, painting in tones the feral aspects of the murderous gods carved in the rock, their animal joy and their passions; (2) *La Ville rose*, portraying the festive noises of a sundrenched Hindu village; (3) *Aux Bords du fleuve sacré*, reflecting the scenes of ritual ablutions in the Ganges River, with a chorus glorifying the aromatic spirits of human love.

26 MAY 1912

Jean BLOCKX, Flemish composer of romantic operas, choruses and songs perfused with the melorhythms of Flemish folkways, dies in his native Antwerp in his 62nd year.

29 MAY 1912

The choreographic tableau *L'Aprés-midi d'un Faune*, to the music of DEBUSSY, is presented for the first time by Diaghilev's Ballet Russe in Paris.

4 JUNE 1912

Aphrodite, symphonic fantasy by the Boston romanticist George Whitefield CHADWICK, inspired by the contemplation of the head of Aphrodite in the Boston Museum of Fine Arts, in nine well-defined sections, with foamy harps, humid strings, and zephyr-wafted woodwinds assaulted by Wagnerophallic trombones and mating trumpets before coming to a plagally pastoral F-major cadence, is performed for the first time at the Norfolk, Connecticut, Music Festival.

8 JUNE 1912

Three centuries have passed since the death of Hans Leo HASSLER, German composer who was the first to apply the polyphonic style of Italian madrigals to works derived from German folk music.

8 JUNE 1912

Daphnis et Chloé, ballet in one act and three tableaux by Maurice RAVEL, with a scenario fashioned after a Greek erotic tale of pastoral love, wherein Daphnis plays the alto flute to lure Chloé, as Pan once lured Syrinx, and leopard-skinned Bacchantes burst out in a corybantic dance in rapid quintuple meters while delicate drums and poetic harps suffuse the scene in a translucid neo-archaic gauze, suspended in an aerostatically euphonious equilibrium above deep-rooted pedal points, is produced by Diaghilev's Ballet Russe in Paris.

14 JUNE 1912

The first solo performance on a PIANOLA is given in London playing Grieg's *Piano Concerto*, manipulated by Easthope MARTIN, and accompanied by Arthur Nikisch with the London Symphony Orchestra.

15 JUNE 1912

The Children of Don, opera in three acts with a prologue by the 33-year-old English composer Josef HOLBROOKE, constituting the first part of his Wagneromorphic Welsh trilogy *The Cauldron of Annwyn*, wherein the children of the earth goddess wrest a magical cauldron from the Druids to bring about a millennium, is performed for the first time in London. (The second part, *Dylan, Son of the Wave*, was produced in London on 4 July 1914; the third part, *Bronwen*, on 1 February 1929.)

20 JUNE 1912

Twenty-five days after his 19th birthday, Eugene GOOSSENS, London-born composer, son of Eugene Goossens, French-born operatic conductor, grandson of Eugene Goossens, Belgian-born operatic conductor, conducts at a students' concert at the Royal College of Music in London the first performance of his first orchestral composition, *Variations on a Chinese Theme*, with a pentatonic melodic figure accoutred in an exotically impressionistic harmonic garb.

24 JUNE 1912

La Reginetta delle Rose (The Little Rose Queen), operetta in three acts by Ruggero LEONCAVALLO, to a libretto opaquely allusive to the events of the Portuguese Revolution of 1910, wherein the heir to the throne of a transparently named Kingdom of Portowa plots to depose himself and marry an English flower girl, is produced simultaneously in Rome and in Naples, but fails to arouse interest even remotely comparable to the spontaneous success of Leoncavallo's youthful opera *Pagliacci*.

26 JUNE 1912

A year, a month and eight days after the death of Gustav MAHLER, Bruno Walter conducts in Vienna the first performance of Mahler's posthumous *Ninth Symphony*, in four movements, the outermost two pantheistically contemplative, the inner two choreographic, with a significantly heterogeneous tonal relationship between the first movement in D major and the last movement in D-flat major:

(1) *Andante comodo*, opening with a foreboding pianissimo on the unison A in the low register, then introducing the seminal theme of three notes, building up towards multiple climaxes with recurrent outcries of dynamic pulsation at shorter and shorter intervals of time forming a "dynamic stretto," and concluding on a unison D, thus encasing the whole movement in a dominant-tonic clause: (2) *Im Tempo eines gemächlichen Ländlers*, a scherzo in the form of a chain of angularly anamorphosed and ostentatiously vulgarized waltzes wandering through many keys but converging on the central C major; (3) *Rondo. Burlesque*, a restless concatenation of polkas and marches around an axial tritone; (4) *Adagio*, an impassioned invocation holding on faithfully to the principal key of D-flat major, soaring to resonant heights, then subsiding into the softest triadic ending.

5 JULY 1912

In the presence of qualified witnesses in a photographer's studio at 42nd Street and Sixth Avenue, New York City, Professor Charles MUNTER hypnotizes an admittedly inept vocal student Marian Graham into performing a series of thrillingly Trilbyesque trills.

18 JULY 1912

In Milan, Francesco Balilla PRATELLA issues a manifesto entitled *Destruction of Quadrature*, inveighing against the hegemony of binary meters and postulating the liberating principle of a "new musical order of disorder."

23 JULY 1912

Ethel SMYTH, English composeress and militant suffragette, is arrested in London on a charge of complicity in an attempt, made on 13 July 1912 during a suffragist demonstration, to burn the historic country house of Lewis V. Harcourt, Secretary of State for the Colonies.

24 JULY 1912

Second Symphony by Nicolai MIASKOVSKY, set in the melancholy Russian key of C-sharp minor, in three movements (completed on 22 December 1911), is performed for the first time in Moscow.

All my works of this period bear the imprint of deep pessimism. It is difficult for me to analyze the reason for it. (Miaskovsky in his *Autobiographical Notes*, published in *Sovietskaya Musica*, No. 6, 1936)

7 AUGUST 1912

Sergei PROKOFIEV appears in Moscow as soloist in the first performance of his *First Piano Concerto* in D-flat major, in a single movement marked by rhapsodically explosive energy with an intimately lyric middle section. (He played this Concerto also at the commencement at the St. Petersburg Conservatory on 24 May 1914, and won the Rubinstein Prize, a grand piano, for his performance.)

This energetically rhythmed concerto, coarse and crude, primitive and cacophonic, scarcely merits its honorable title. The composer, in his quest of novelty, but lacking it in the depth of his nature, has apparently contorted himself to the ultimate limit. This sort of thing does not happen with real talents. (Leonid Sabaneyev, *Voice of Moscow*, No. 173, 1912)

10 AUGUST 1912

Under the auspices of the Bohemian Club of San Francisco, Henry HADLEY conducts, amidst the millennial trees of the Redwood Grove in northern California, the first performance of his music drama in three scenes, *The Atonement of Pan*, in which Pan expiates the wickedness of his past deeds by fostering the romance of Zephyr and Flora and overcoming the sinister quintal harmonies of the harpies by the Arcadian pastorality of panpipe music.

13 AUGUST 1912

Jules MASSENET, French composer of melodious and harmonious operas usually centering on an attractive though sinful feminine figure lyrically outpouring her amorous distresses while dramatic events bearing on her ultimate fate are ominously suggested in perilously concatenated diminished seventh-chords and violent orchestral strokes (his father was the inventor of a steel hammer), dies in Paris, the scene of his many triumphs, three months and a day after his 70th birthday.

"... Mais aussi, Massenet, tu
tiens le violon
Dans l'orchestre divin où
Mozart tient la flûte ..."

(From a sonnet by Edmond Rostand read at a celebration in Massenet's honor at the Paris Opëra on 11 November 1911)

17 AUGUST 1912

Anush, opera in four acts by the Armenian composer Armen TIGRANIAN (1879–1950), dealing with a bloody feud in an Armenian village, leading to a lover's murder and his betrothed's suicide in a precipitous mountain river, is produced in Alexandropol.

18 AUGUST 1912

Der ferne Klang, first opera, in three acts, by the Monaco-born Austrian composer Franz SCHREKER (his real name was Schrecker but he excised the letter C before K to exorcise the frightening spectre of Schreck) to his own libretto, dealing with a beautiful girl, who, after a temporary stay in a Venetian bordello, joins her musician lover at the production of his unsuccessful opera *Die Harfe*, during which he expires in her arms to the thematic "far clang" of whole-tone clusters suspended in a sonorous cloud formed by high violins, tambourine and celesta, is produced in Frankfurt.

23 AUGUST 1912

Erik SATIE completes the composition of his cycle of three piano pieces entitled *Véritables Préludes flasques*, with a subtitle "*pour un chien*," in barless notation. (The first piece was written on 12 August 1912; the second on 17 August 1912.)

1 SEPTEMBER 1912

Samuel COLERIDGE-TAYLOR, son of a West African Negro and his white English wife, and named after the English poet Samuel Taylor Coleridge, dies at Croydon, 16 days after his 37th birthday.

2 SEPTEMBER 1912

Caio Petronio, "Roman scenes" in three acts by the 34-year-old Argentine composer Constantino GAITO, glorifying Gaius Petronius, *arbiter elegantiarum* of Nero's time and the author of *Satyricon,* is produced at the Teatro Colón in Buenos Aires.

3 SEPTEMBER 1912

Arnold SCHOENBERG's epoch-making score *Fünf Orchesterstücke,* op. 16 (completed on 11 August 1909), receives its world première in London, conducted by Sir Henry Wood:

(1) *Vorgefühle,* forefeelings of unnamed but fearful events in a tonifugal hyperchromatic idiom laden with horizontally arrayed heterotonal tritones within quartal and quintal harmonies; (2) *Vergangenes,* looking back in time with serene recollection of faces seen and emotions experienced; (3) *Der wechselnde Akkord,* centering on a thematically static chord in quartal structure surrounded by kaleidoscopically changing spectral tone colors in subtle dynamic shades never rising above *mezzo piano,* with a notice in the score warning that "the change of harmonies should occur gently, without emphasis on instrumental entries, so that only the difference in color is perceived"; (4) *Peripetie,* marked *Sehr rasch,* rashly exposing a series of vertiginous peripeteia charged with secundal progressions and periodically detonating in bright explosions; (5) *Das obligate Recitativ,* wherein paired mirror-imaged symbols are introduced for the first time in musical notation to designate principal and secondary themes thus outlining intellectually the emotionally inventive melodies.

(In an entry in his diary of 27 January 1912 Schoenberg states that the titles were added at the request of the publisher C. F. Peters for business reasons: "I will probably give in, for I have found titles that at least are plausible. But otherwise, the idea does not appeal to me. For music is wonderful in that one can express in it everything that one wishes to express, so that the knowing will understand all. Yet it has its mysteries which ought not to be revealed. Titles are too garrulous. Music has already said what was to be said. Why add words? Were words needed, they would have been used. Art says more than words. Titles, which I may use in my pieces, communicate without betraying, for they are partly obscure, partly technical: (1) *Vorgefühle* (everyone has premonitions); (2) *Vergangenes* (everyone has a past, too); (3) *Akkordfärbungen* (chord colors; technical); (4) *Peripetie* (common enough); (5) *Das obligate* (perhaps better said 'ausgeführte' or 'unendings') *Recitativ.* But in any case, all this with an annotation that this is a publishing technicality, and not a suggestion of 'poetic' content.")

(In a new version of the score, 1950, for a reduced orchestra, the third piece was retitled *Sommermorgen an einem See (Summer Morning by the Lake);* other movements retained their original titles.)

The greatest difficulty in performing these pieces is that this time it is really impossible to read the score. It would be almost imperative to perform them through blind faith. I can

promise you something really colossal, especially in sound and mood. For that is what they are all about— completely unsymphonic, devoid of architecture or construction, just an uninterrupted change of colors, rhythms and moods. (Schoenberg's letter to Richard Strauss, dated 14 July 1909, relating to the *Fünf Orchesterstücke,* translated from the original in the Strauss-Archive in Garmisch)

This music seeks to express all that swells in us subconsciously like a dream; which is a great fluctuant power, and is built upon none of the lines that are familiar to us; which has a rhythm, as blood has its pulsating rhythm, as all life in us has its rhythm; which has a tonality, but only as the sea or the storm has its tonality; which has harmonies, though we cannot grasp or analyze them nor can we trace its themes. All its technical craft is submerged, made one and indivisible with the content of the work. (From a program note for the first performance)

It was like a poem in Tibetan; not one single soul could possibly have understood it at a first hearing. We can, after all, only progress from the known to the unknown; and as the program writer, who had every reason to know, said, there was not a single consonance from beginning to end. Under such circumstances the listener was like a dweller in Flatland straining his mind to understand the ways of that mysterious occupant of three dimensions, man. . . . At the conclusion half the audience hissed. That seems a too decisive judgment, for after all they may turn out to be wrong; the other half applauded more vehemently than the case warranted, for it could hardly have been from understanding. (London *Times,* 4 September 1912)

The program of last Tuesday's Promenade Concert included *Five Orchestral Pieces,* op. 16, by Arnold Schoenberg, who evidently revels in the bizarre. According to Dr. Anton von Webern, his music "contains the experience of his emotional life," and that experience must have been of a strange, not to say unpleasant character. . . . Is it really honest music or merely a pose? We are inclined to think the latter. If music at all, it is music of the future, and we hope, of a distant one. There is plenty of interesting and noble music to enjoy. Why, then, should the ears of the Promenade audience be tortured with scrappy sounds and perpetual discord? (London *Daily Mail,* 7 September 1912)

Imagine the scene of the bleating of sheep in *Don Quixote,* the sacrificial procession in *Elektra,* and the scene of the opponents in *Heldenleben,* all played together, and you will have a faint idea of Schoenberg's idea of orchestral color and harmony. As to theme or subject, it must be supposed that he would consider it an insult to be told that he has any traffic with such things. . . . The pieces have no program or poetic basis. We must be content with the composer's own assertion that he has depicted his own experiences, for which he has our heartfelt sympathy. (London *Daily News,* 4 September 1912)

Schoenberg's music is a return to an elemental condition. It is a collection of sounds without relation to one another. It is the reproduction of the sounds of nature in their crudest form. Modern intellect has advanced beyond mere elementary noise: Schoenberg has not. If the mind of man is superior to that of beast, then it should be able to improve and not rest content with imitation. The course adopted by Schoenberg is retrograde. (*Morning Post,* London, 4 September 1912)

It is impossible to give an idea of the music. The endless discords, the constant succession of unnatural sounds from the extreme notes of every instrument, and the complete absence of any kind of idea, which, at one hearing at least, one can get hold of, baffle description. Herr Schoenberg, in short, is to Strauss at his wildest what Strauss is to Mozart, and he is never for a bare space normal. He does not even end his pieces with recognizable chords. He is a Futurist painter, and he scores as he paints. (*Manchester Guardian*, 5 September 1912)

It is not often that an English audience hisses the music it does not like; but a good third of the people the other day permitted themselves that luxury after the performance of the five orchestral pieces of Schoenberg. Another third of the audience was not hissing because it was laughing, and the remaining third seemed too puzzled either to laugh or to hiss. . . .. Nevertheless, I take leave to suggest that Schoenberg is not the mere fool or madman that he is generally supposed to be. . . .. May it not be that the new composer sees a logic in certain tonal relations that to the rest of us seem chaos at present, but the coherence of which may be clear enough to us all some day? (Ernest Newman, *Nation*, London, September 1912)

5 SEPTEMBER 1912

John CAGE, revolutionary American composer and experimenter, pioneer of the concept of "total music" embracing not only tonal parameters but also environmental acoustical phenomena, incidental noises, and other aleatory elements, inventor of the "prepared piano" in which the tone color is altered by placing screws, bolts, coins and other unpianistic objects on the strings, is born in Los Angeles.

5 SEPTEMBER 1912

Music Pictures, symphonic suite by the 31-year-old English theorist and composer John FOULDS, in four movements, inspired by the paintings of William Blake and others, significant because the second movement makes use, perhaps before any other orchestral work, of quarter-tones, is performed for the first time at the Promenade Concerts in London.

In the year 1898 I had tentatively experimented in a string quartet with smaller divisions than usual of the intervals known to musicians. In 1912, having set myself to paraphrase in music the sensations received from certain pictures, I again found it necessary to call upon this item in my musical vocabulary. I was forced over the old borderlines and produced a piece described as *Study in Whole-Tones, Half-Tones, and Quarter-Tones*, No. 2 of *Music Pictures*. (*Music Today* by John Foulds, London, 1934)

8 SEPTEMBER 1912

Bernhard ZIEHN, German-American music theorist who developed some original ideas about harmonic relations in modern music, and who taught two generations of American musicians, dies at the age of 67 in Chicago, his home since 1868.

16 SEPTEMBER 1912

Zingari, opera in two acts by Ruggero LEONCAVALLO, after Pushkin's poem depicting the ardors and internecine passions of a Bessarabian Gypsy camp, is produced for the first time in London.

24 SEPTEMBER 1912

The Sea, suite for orchestra by Frank BRIDGE, enlightened and progressive-minded English professor of music, in four impressionistic movements, *Seascape*, *Seafoam*, *Moonlight* and *Storm*, containing a distillation of

Debussyan aquamarine harmonies, is performed for the first time in London, Sir Henry Wood conducting.

4 OCTOBER 1912

Konzert im alten Stil for orchestra, op. 123, by Max REGER, in three sections marked by considerable contrapuntal commotion, in the manner of a concerto grosso, with a lyrical middle movement, is performed for the first time in Frankfurt, Willem Mengelberg conducting.

11 OCTOBER 1912

Romantische Suite for orchestra by Max REGER, op. 125, in three evocative movements, *Notturno*, *Scherzo* and *Finale*, set in intricate polyphonic patterns, blossoming forth unexpectedly into impressionistic floridity, and including sonorous progressions in whole-tone scales, is performed for the first time in Dresden.

11 OCTOBER 1912

Leopold STOKOWSKI, 30-year-old London-born organist, son of an émigré Polish cabinetmaker and a Scottishwoman, leads the opening concert of the season of the Philadelphia Orchestra as its new music director.

Every seat was taken and the extra chairs had been placed within the orchestra rail. There was much enthusiasm, manifesting itself at the beginning in prolonged applause as Stokowski came forward with bowed head, evidently pondering the content of his musical message. Those who went forth to see a hirsute eccentric were disappointed. They beheld a surprisingly boyish and thoroughly business-like figure, who was sure of himself, yet free from conceit, who dispensed with the score by virtue of infallible memory, and held his men and his audience from first note to last firmly in his grasp. (*Public Ledger*, Philadelphia, 12 October 1912)

14 OCTOBER 1912

The Firefly, operetta by Rudolf FRIML, dealing with an Italian street singer who gets a job as a cabin boy on a yachting trip to Bermuda to be near a young man with whom she is secretly in love, and two years later suddenly emerges as a prima donna, finally capturing her beloved, is performed for the first time in Syracuse, New York. (Date on the title page of the score; first New York performance was given on 2 December 1912.)

15 OCTOBER 1912

The Dove of Peace, "a satire on the dream of universal peace," with music by Walter DAMROSCH, with scenes taking place in Portsmouth, New Hampshire, where the Russo-Japanese peace treaty was signed, in the United States Senate Chamber, and on Guam Island during the Spanish-American war, is produced, unsuccessfully, at Philadelphia.

16 OCTOBER 1912

After forty rehearsals, Arnold SCHOENBERG's *Pierrot Lunaire*, "cycle of thrice seven melodramas," opus (significantly!) 21, to texts by the Belgian poet Albert Giraud, rendered into German by Otto Erich Hartleben, "set to tones" (*vertont*) for a spoken voice (*Sprechstimme*), piano, flute (interchangeable with piccolo), clarinet (or bass clarinet), violin (or viola) and cello, containing in its three septule parts $(39 + 41 + 31 + 18 + 44 + 24 + 27 = 224) + (26 + 20 + 20 + 29 + 13 + 36 + 22 = 166) + (31 + 27 + 32 + 19 + 53 + 30 + 30 = 222) = 612$ measures, in quarternote meters 2/4, 3/4, 4/4, 6/4 (with the exception of No. 20 which is in 6/8) written in a supremely expressionistic, articulately crystalline, dissonantly atonal idiom, replete with mutually precipitating canonic devices crowned by a magistrally symbolistic retrograde canon in No. 18, *Der Mondfleck*, mirroringly halved in the paired groups of clarinet with piccolo, and violin with cello, to paint the inerasable reflection of the bright moon on the back of the lunar Pierrot's black jacket, is performed for the first time in Berlin, with Albertine Zehme, to whom the score is dedicated "in heartfelt friendship," as the speakingly singing recitalist, the individual 21 "melodramas" bearing the following titles and completed on the following dates in 1912, according to the original manuscript in the Library of Congress (the dates in the printed edition are erroneously listed according to the sequence of the titles rather than the non-consecutive chronology of actual times of composition):

(1) *Mondestrunken* (29 March) (2) *Colombine* (20 April) (3) *Der Dandy* (2 April) (4) *Eine blasse Wäscherin* (5) *Valse de Chopin* (7 May) (6) *Madonna* (9 May) (7) *Der kranke Mond* (18 April) (8) *Nacht* (21 May) (9) *Gebet an Pierrot* (12 March) (10) *Rauh* (9 May) (11) *Rote Messe* (24 April) (12) *Galgenlied* (12 May) (13) *Enthauptung* (23 May) (14) *Die Kreuze* (9 July) (15) *Heimweh* (22 May) (16) *Gemeinheit* (6 June) (17) *Parodie* (4 May) (18) *Der Mondfleck* (28 May) (19) *Serenade* (25 April) (20) *Heimfahrt* (9 May) (21) *O alter Duft* (30 May).

Hermann Helmholtz speaks somewhere about so-called "metamathematical spaces," that is, spaces wherein the known axioms of Euclid's geometry are not valid. I think of these remarkable spaces when I tread on the tone-space of the latest Schoenberg: I feel translated into "metamusical" spaces. To breathe in this new atmosphere one must leave behind all that is considered axiomatic in things musical. One must first learn the new alphabet to approach this new frightful Schoenberg, to get the bearings of this "Prose of Music," as Herr von Webern calls it. (*Signale für die musikalische Welt*, Berlin, 2 November 1912)

To arouse any kind of a sensation in these days is of itself an extraordinary feat. Arnold Schoenberg may he either crazy as a loon, or he may be a very clever trickster who is apparently determined to cause a sensation by writing music that in its hideousness and illogical ear-splitting ugliness defies description . . . His music to Albert Giraud's poems entitled *Pierrot Lunaire* is the last word in cacophony and musical anarchy. Some day it may be pointed out as of historical interest, because it represents the turning point, for the outraged muse surely can endure no more of this; such noise must drive even the moonstruck Pierrot back to the realm of real music. Albertine Zehme, a well-known Berlin actress, dressed in a Pierrot costume, recited the "Three Times Seven" poems, as the program announced, while a musical, or rather unmusical, ensemble, consisting of a piano, violin, viola, cello, piccolo and clarinet, stationed behind a black screen and invisible to the audience, discoursed the most ear-splitting combinations of tones that ever desecrated the walls of a Berlin music hall. Schoenberg has thrown overboard all of the sheet anchors of the art of music. Melody he eschews in every form; tonality he knows not and such a word as harmony is not in his vocabulary. The remarkable part of the whole farce is that Schoenberg is taken seriously . . . The critics have written columns about Schoenberg. To be sure, they condemn him almost to a

man, but they give him space—from four to five times the space that other more deserving composers get, and they do this for the same reason that I am now doing it, because there is an element of interest for the readers . . . Schoenberg even has adherents who rally round his standard and swear by his muse, declaring that this is music of the future. Otto Taubmann, the critic of the *Börsen Courier* expressed the feelings of all sane musicians when he wrote, "If this is music of the future, then I pray my Creator not to let me live to hear it again." (Arthur M. Abell, *The Musical Courier*, New York, 6 November 1912)

What is Arnold Schoenberg? An Altruist Laboring for the Second and Third Generations or a Colossal Joker? A Berlin Hearing of His *Pierrot Lunaire* Fails to Shed Light on the Problem (Headlines in *Musical America*, New York, 16 November 1912)

25 OCTOBER 1912

Richard STRAUSS conducts in Stuttgart the world première of his incidental music to Molière's *Le Bourgeois Gentilhomme*, with a one-act opera *Ariadne auf Naxos* as a play within a play (composition completed on 24 April 1912), to the text by Hugo yon Hofmannstahl, wherein Ariadne, abandoned on an Aegean island, is revitalized by Bacchus, set in a neo-archaic homophonic idiom for a small ensemble of 39 highly individualized instruments, while the Molière comedy, representing the nouveau-riche society in quest of theatrical entertainment, is characterized by burlesqued polyphony.

25 OCTOBER 1912

On the 48th birthday of Alexandre GRETCHANINOFF, his three-act opera *Soeur Béatrice*, after Maeterlinck's play, is produced in Moscow, followed by an outcry in the monarchist press about the blasphemy of the theme, and resulting in the opera's suppression after three performances.

The Moscow newspapers report a new affront against our religious feelings. On the same stage where naked women disport themselves night after night, there will appear—it is horrible to utter!—the image of the Purest Virgin, More Glorious than the Seraphim. . . . As if this were not enough, the Purest Virgin will be represented on the stage by a godless and depraved actress. . . . What is Moscow coming to? Is it being transformed into a dissolute Babylon, invoking the wrath of God upon Holy Russia? (From an article in the monarchist daily *Kolokol*, quoted in Gretchaninoff's *My Life*, New York, 1952)

25 OCTOBER 1912

Radda, one-act opera by the 47-year-old Italian composer Giacomo OREFICE, to a libretto based on Maxim Gorky's tale *Makar Chudra*, dealing with a proudly beauteous Ukrainian maiden Radda who is stabbed to death by a passion-inflamed Gypsy fiddler who is in turn fatally knifed by Radda's father, is produced in Milan.

26 OCTOBER 1912

Meduza, opera in three acts by the 28-year-old Polish composer Ludomir RÓŻYCKI, dealing with episodes in the life of Leonardo da Vinci, is produced in Warsaw.

29 OCTOBER 1912

La Danseuse de Pompei, opera-ballet in five acts by the French composer Jean NOUGES, depicting the destruction of Pompeii, is produced at the Opéra-Comique in Paris.

1 NOVEMBER 1912

Holland announces its adherence to the international copyright law guaranteeing performance and publication rights to composers.

6 NOVEMBER 1912

Nikolai LISSENKO, a Ukrainian composer of several operas to Gogol's tales (*Taras Bulba, Night Before Christmas, The May Night*), and an ardent collector of Ukrainian folksongs, which he harmonized in congenial arrangements, dies in Kiev at the age of 70.

7 NOVEMBER 1912

La Dubarry, an opera by Ezio CAMUSSE, dealing with the famous courtesan and influential mistress of Louis XV, in three acts and with an epilogue of her death on the guillotine on 7 December 1793, is produced in Milan.

10 NOVEMBER 1912

Nattergallen (The Nightingale), opera in three acts by the Danish composer August ENNA, after Hans Christian Andersen's tale, is produced in Copenhagen.

12 NOVEMBER 1912

Liebesketten, ninth opera by the self-Germanized English-born composer Eugen D'ALBERT, wherein the tangled chains of adulterous love among fisherfolk of Brittany are tragically resolved by the brown-skinned castaway maiden who dies of stab wounds protecting her lover from the cuckolded husband of his former mistress, is produced in Vienna.

13 NOVEMBER 1912

Melenis, third opera in three acts by Riccardo ZANDONAI, to a gory story dealing with a Greek courtesan who kills herself when her gladiator lover marries another, is produced in Milan.

15 NOVEMBER 1912

Lebenstanz, tone-poem by Frederick DELIUS, known in England as *Life's Dance* and constituting a revision of his French-titled work *La Ronde se déroule*, composed in 1900, and revealing traits of vague impressionism superimposed on a Germanically conceived program piece, receives its belated first performance in Berlin.

17 NOVEMBER 1912

Suffering from an excruciating toothache, exactly five months after his 30th birthday, Igor STRAVINSKY completes in Clarens, Switzerland, the composition of *Le Sacre du Printemps*, in piano score, with indications as to instrumentation.

(Date and description from Stravinsky's own contemporary notation in the manuscript title page reproduced in facsimile in *Melos*, June 1962, and reading, in Russian "Today, 4/17 XI 1912, Sunday, while having an excruciating toothache, finished the music of *Le Sacre*. Igor Stravinsky, Clarens," The scoring was completed on 8 March 1913.)

17 NOVEMBER 1912

Der Schneider von Malta, comic opera by the 39-year-old German composer Waldemar WENDLAND, dealing with a Maltese tailor who became involved in a conspiracy against the governor of Malta in 1850, is performed for the first time in Leipzig.

30 NOVEMBER 1912

Chrysis, ballet by the romantic nationalist of Russian music Reinhold GLIÈRE, inspired by an exotically erotic tale by Pierre Louÿs, set to music replete with luscious orientalistic modalities, is produced in Moscow.

5 DECEMBER 1912

Sir Charles Hubert Hastings PARRY, eminent British academician of music, conducts in London the first performance of his *Symphony-Fantasy* in B minor, couched in a Germanically tumescent romantic idiom, in four linked movements, with psychological subtitles: (1) *Stress* (2) *Love* (3) *Play* (4) *Now!*

8 DECEMBER 1912

From the Apocalypse, last symphonic poem by the Russian composer of evocative symphonic poems, Anatoli LIADOV, written in an exalted neo-ecclesiastical manner, opening with a descending double major tetrachord with tritonally related roots, followed by modally harmonized Russian hymns, and ending with seven thunderclaps of grandisonant apocalyptic sounds in the brass and drums, raising aloft the oriflamme of Russianized Revelation, is performed for the first time in St. Petersburg, conducted by Alexander Siloti.

11 DECEMBER 1912

Isabelle et Pantalon, opera buffa by the 21-year-old French composer Alexis ROLAND-MANUEL (whose real name was Roland Alexis Manuel Levy), to a modernized commedia dell'arte libretto in which the old Doctor Pantalon keeps his young ward Isabelle isolated in a hydrotherapeutic intitution, whence she in spite of all precautions is abducted by Arlequin, is performed for the first time in Paris.

12 DECEMBER 1912

Harald SAEVERUD, precocious 15-year-old Norwegian composer, conducts in Bergen a concert consisting entirely of his symphonic works.

18 DECEMBER 1912

La Sorcière, opera in four acts by Camille ERLANGER, is performed for the first time at the Opéra-Comique in Paris.

21 DECEMBER 1912

During his first and only Russian tour, Arnold SCHOEN-BERG conducts in St. Petersburg the first local performance of his romantic symphonic poem *Pelleas und Melisande,* composed in 1903.

22 DECEMBER 1912

Le Chant de la Cloche, dramatic legend by Vincent D'INDY, to Schiller's text, in seven scenes with a pro-logue, is performed for the first time as a stage work in Brussels. (A concert version was first played at a Lamoureux concert in Paris on 25 February 1886.)

28 DECEMBER 1912

Megae, first opera in three scenes to a libretto from an old Japanese legend, by Adam Tadeusz WIENIAWSKI, Polish composer of romantic music, nephew of the famous violinist Wieniawski, is produced in Warsaw.

1913

3 JANUARY 1913

Doctor Merryheart, comedy overture by the 36-year-old English composer Havergal BRIAN, an extended piece of program music constructed as a set of symphonic variations, is performed for the first time in Birmingham as part of the Annual Conference of the Incorporated Society of Musicians.

7 JANUARY 1913

La Forêt bleue, opera in three acts by the 35-year-old French composer Louis AUBERT, to a libretto in which several characters from fairy tales of Perrault meet in social intercourse, set to music in an ingratiatingly harmonious vein, is performed for the first time in Geneva, Switzerland.

11 JANUARY 1913

Camille SAINT-SAËNS receives the Grande Croix of the Légion d'Honneur, the highest decoration of the Order.

15 JANUARY 1913

Gala Placidia, lyric drama by the Catalan composer Jaime PAHISSA, dealing with a heterogenetic passion of a patrician Roman matron for a chieftain of the barbarian Goths, symbolizing the conflict between Mediterranean and Teutonic cultures, with a musical setting in a sumptuous modernistic idiom, is produced in Barcelona. (*Gala Placidia* is named for a Roman matron captured by the Visigoths in A.D. 410 during the sack of Rome. After being carried to Catalonia, she ignites the passions in the Teutonic heart of King Ataulfo, marries him and, upon his assassination, returns to Italy, marries a future Roman emperor and, upon his death, becomes regent for their son.)

20 JANUARY 1913

Tante Simona, comic opera in one act by the 35-year-old Hungarian composer Ernst von DOHNÁNYI, wherein a misandronous Italian spinster keeps her innocent niece from treacherous heterosexual contacts, but undergoes a psychological rejuvenation when an ancient beau appears after a lapse of decades and offers her his superannuated heart, set to music in a conventional Germanic manner, is performed for the first time in Dresden.

29 JANUARY 1913

La Festa dei Fiori, "idyllic operetta" by the 26-year-old Italian composer Giuseppe BLANC (the future author of the Fascist hymn *Giovinezza*), is produced in Rome.

10 FEBRUARY 1913

Hamilton HARTY conducts in London the first performance of his *Variations on an Irish Folk Tune,* for violin and orchestra, with Paul Kochanski as soloist.

10 FEBRUARY 1913

The Days of Our Life, opera by the 37-year-old Russian composer Alexei GLUKHOVTZEV, after a play of that title by the famous Russian writer Leonid Andreyev, inspired by the popular Russian student song "The Days of Our Life flow fast, like ocean waves" and focused on the life of a student whose family name is coincidentally the same as that of the composer, is produced in Kiev.

12 FEBRUARY 1913

Madame Roland, opera by Félix FOURDRAIN, is produced in Rouen.

20 FEBRUARY 1913

Uguale Fortuna, an opera buffa by the 34-year-old Italian composer Vincenzo TOMMASINI, centered on a pair of aspiring balladeers serenading a widow under her balcony, only to lose out to a stranger already embedded in her room, is produced as a prize-winning work in the Verdi Contest, in Rome.

20 FEBRUARY 1913

The Sun Dance, Indian opera in five acts by the 25-year-old American composer William HANSON, who spent his youth among the Sioux Indians where he became known under the nickname Ampa-o-Luta, meaning "the first light at the red dawn," or more intimately as "Big Elm," is first performed in Vernal, Utah.

21 FEBRUARY 1913

Sinfonia della Vita by the Italian Futurist composer Francesco Balilla PRATELLA, is performed for the first time at a Futurist exposition in Rome, with the futuristic element represented by whole-tone scales.

22 FEBRUARY 1913

Kaatje, opera in three acts by the 45-year-old Belgian composer Victor BUFFIN, to a libretto dealing with the patriotic struggle in Flanders against Spanish rulers in the 16th century, is produced in Brussels.

23 FEBRUARY 1913

Fifteen and a half months after the completion of Arnold SCHOENBERG'S vocal cycle *Gurre-Lieder* which occupied his creative energies from March 1900 until May 1901, to the text of the German translations of poems by the Danish poet Jens Peter Jacobsen written by him in 1868 at the age of 21, traversing the tragic events in the life of King Waldemar IV of Denmark, his eternal love for a commoner Tove who waits for him at the Gurre Castle on the Esrom Sea in North Zealand, his anguish when he learns of her death and his mystical expectation of her resurrection, set in richly resonant harmonies and progressing along chromatically unwinding Wagneromorphic paths leading to an apotheosis in diatonic splendor, scored for 5 solo voices, a speaking voice, 3 male choirs, a mixed chorus of 8 parts and a tremendously expanded orchestra (Schoenberg had to order special manuscript paper of 48 staves to accommodate the instrumental parts), including a large iron chain to be shaken with concussive effect, and introducing for the first time a trombone glissando, is performed for the first time in Vienna, Franz Schreker conducting, the work subdivided into three parts:

PART I, opening with an E-flat major chord enriched by an upper sixth, from which the thematic elements unfold in fanfare-like tones, comprising nine arias sung in dialogue by Waldemar and Tove, and concluding with the song of a woodland dove announcing in mournfully chromaticized melismas the death of Tove.—PART II, wherein Waldemar hurls defiant imprecations at the cruel god of death.— PART III, *Die wilde Jagd,* an episode of a satanically wild chase, the choruses lamenting lost peace, but ultimately finding diatonic solace in a joyous hymn to the ever-returning sun, leading to a 28-bar coda in which the thematic sixth on the C-major triad resolves after an eon of suspensions into a revitalized, immaculately white C major.

24 FEBRUARY 1913

Carmosine, "conte romanesque" in four acts by Henry FÉVRIER, after Alfred de Musset's poem dealing with a 13th-century girl who suffers pernicious anemia as a result of her love for King Pedro of Aragon, but is saved from ultimate inanition by her appointment as a lady-in-waiting at the palace where she is enabled to observe her royal idol in daily proximity, and by a subsequent marriage to her old admirer willing to act as a vicarious substitute, set to music in harmonious sonorities, is produced at the Théâtre-Lyrique in Paris.

26 FEBRUARY 1913

Deux images, symphonic diptych by Béla BARTÓK, the first titled *En pleine fleur* representing the rebirth of nature in late spring with flowery inuted strings and trilling avian flutes, the second, *Danse campagnarde,* robustly rhythmical in a propulsive Hungarian manner, is performed for the first time in Budapest.

26 FEBRUARY 1913

Felix DRAESEKE, German composer of grandly academic instrumental music, dies in Dresden at the age of 77.

27 FEBRUARY 1913

Cyrano de Bergerac, opera in four acts by the German-American conductor Walter DAMROSCH, to a libretto fashioned from the famous play of Edmond Rostand dealing with the nasute 17th-century poet and soldier whose long nose makes him repugnant to the lady of his adoration but who wins her love for an inarticulate friend by writing eloquent letters to her in his behalf, set to an amiably melodious score fatally handicapped by a lack of verve, is performed for the first and preantepenultimate time by the Metropolitan Opera Company in New York.

28 FEBRUARY 1913

Coco-Chéri, operetta in one act with music by Erik SATIE, is performed for the first time in Monte Carlo.

2 MARCH 1913

La Leggenda delle sette torri, one-act opera by the Italian music critic and occasional composer Alberto GASCO (1879–1938), inspired by two pre-Raphaelite paintings of Dante Gabriel Rossetti, *The Tune of Seven Towers* and *Bonifacio's Mistress,* is performed for the first time in Rome.

3 MARCH 1913

Elektra by Richard STRAUSS is produced for the first time in St. Petersburg, evoking a vehement denunciation in the monarchist newspaper *Novoye Vremya:* "It is inadmissible that in this year when Russia celebrated the 300th anniversary of the ruling Romanov dynasty, the Imperial Opera House should produce an opera in which royal personages are brutally slain."

4 MARCH 1913

Pénélope, opera in three acts by Gabriel FAURÉ, presenting in quasi-Grecian modalities the Homeric episode of the virtuous wife of Ulysses, his homecoming in the disguise of an ancient mendicant and his victory over her intrusive suitors, with a serenely dolorous theme for Pénélope and a heroically valorous theme for Ulysses forming the principal materials, and ending in marble-white C major, is performed for the first time at the Opera of Monte Carlo, in the principality of Monaco.

6 MARCH 1913

The word JAZZ appears in print for the first time as a synonym for pep, in the San Francisco *Bulletin,* in a sports column written by "Scoop" Gleeson. (See complete text in Letters and Documents.)

11 MARCH 1913

Luigi RUSSOLO, Italian futurist musician and painter, issues in Milan a defiant manifesto legislating the fundamental tenets of Art of Noises. (See full text in Letters and Documents.)

15 MARCH 1913

Das Spielwerk und die Prinzessin, opera by the Monegasque-born German composer Franz SCHREKER, in two acts with a prologue, wherein an ailing princess perishes in a conflagration when a maddened suitor destroys a specially constructed therapeutic music box designed to warn her of dangerous body symptoms, set to a Wagneromantic score, diversified by archaizing modalities and impressionistic nebulosities, is produced simultaneously in Frankfurt and Vienna. (A revised version in one act was produced in Munich on 30 October 1920, in the form of a mystery play, under the shortened title *Das Spielwerk.*)

20 MARCH 1913

Le Carillonneur, lyric opera in four acts by Xavier LEROUX, depicting the turbulent life of an ambitious bell ringer who wins a prize in a professional contest but suffers emotional failures in his personal life, is produced at the Opéra-Comique in Paris.

24 MARCH 1913

Sweethearts, romantic opera in two acts by Victor HERBERT, dealing with a Neapolitan damsel adopted by a 15th-century laundress with six daughters of her own who discovers that royal blood courses in her veins and opportunely marries the heir-presumptive to the throne of Zilania, containing the melodious duet *The Angelus* and the irresistibly harmonious waltz tune *Sweethearts,* is produced in Baltimore. (Its first New York performance took place on 8 September 1913.)

28 MARCH 1913

Le Château de la Bretèche, lyric drama in four acts by the Belgian composer Albert DUPUIS, after the lugubrious novella by Balzac, wherein a cuckolded husband immures his wife's paramour in his castle, set to music in an egalitarian harmonic idiom using conventional resources of Gallic operatic art, is produced in Nice.

30 MARCH 1913

La Procesión del Rocío, symphonic poem by Joaquín TURINA in two sections, descriptive of Triana, the colorful suburb of Seville, and the Procession of the Dew carrying the image of the Virgin in an ox-driven cart, set to music in typically Iberian melorhythms, with alternating isotopic meters 3/4 and 6/8, is performed for the first time in Madrid.

31 MARCH 1913

The Academic Society for Literature and Music in Vienna presents a concert of advanced music, Arnold SCHOENBERG conducting, comprising the following:

(1) *6 Stücke für Orchester* by Anton von Webern, the "dynamic psychographer" of new music, dedicated "in greatest love" to Arnold Schoenberg, "teacher and friend," written in 1910 and anticipating the serialistic code of non-repetition of thematic tones (the opening melody is composed of nine different notes in atonally oriented intervals) and of non-recurrence of instrumental colors; (2) *Four Songs* for voice and orchestra to poems of Maeterlinck by Schoenberg's teacher and brother-in-law Alexander Zemlinsky; (3) *Kammersymphonie* by Schoenberg himself, in one continuous movement, written in 1906 and still well within the tonal framework despite the quartal harmonic structure; (4) Two songs out of *5 Orchesterlieder* by Alban Berg, to text by the Vienna café poet Peter Altenberg jotted by him on the back of picture postcards, and therefore referred to sometimes as "postcard songs."

A certain section of the audience attended the concert for the sake of sensation seeking and with the obvious intention of provoking a scandal. There were present, for instance, some operetta composers who usually stay away from performances of new music. Already during the playing of Webern's orchestral pieces and Schoenberg's *Kammersinfonie* there were clashes between the enthusiastically applauding young students and individuals who tried to interfere with the music by hissing and shouting "Pfui!" During the performance of Alban Berg's songs the noise became so deafening that it was impossible to hear anything . . . The whole thing ended in a wild melée which found its sequel in court. There, a well-known operetta composer summoned as a witness, declared to the judge: "I, too, laughed, and why shouldn't I laugh when something really comic is going on?" Another, a physician by profession, asserted that the effect of this type of music is "unnerving for a major part of the public and therefore harmful to the nervous system, so that many among those who attend such concerts show outward symptoms of profound mental depression." (Egon Wellesz, *Arnold Schoenberg*, Vienna, 1921)

The Grosser Musikverein-Saal audience has an air of expectancy. Vienna prides itself on being "advanced," and this is no joke either. There are more things possible with the modern orchestra, so we find out, than Strauss ever dreamed of. These strange whimpers and sighs, the growls of the basses underneath the peculiar wheezes which the clarinet can produce by pressing the lower lip in a certain way—can they be the birth pangs of a new art, these zoological expressions that would make a real menagerie seek cover with drooping tails and ears in their general disgust at nature's provision to them of such inadequate vocal talents? As for the key, gracious! people wrote in "keys" far back in 1910. We thought we knew all the discords which human ingenuity could devise, but here even the wisest can learn something. It is without doubt "original" music. It is, to be specific, the music of some of Schoenberg's pupils being performed under the auspices of the Akademischer Verband für Literatur and Musik, with the master himself conducting. They may be called "Ultraists," though by any other name they could by no means lose any of their fragrance. If this concert was intended to be a "memorable occasion" it surely succeeded, for it occasioned the greatest uproar which has occurred in a Vienna concert hall in the memory of the oldest critics. Laughter, hisses and applause continued throughout a great part of the actual performance of the disputed pieces. After the Berg songs the dispute became almost a riot. The police were called and the only officer who could be found actually threw out of the gallery one noisemaker who persisted in blowing on a key for a whistle. But this policeman could not prevent one of the composers from appearing in a box and yelling to the crowd, "Heraus mit der Baggage!" ("Out with the trash!"), whereat the uproar increased. Members of the orchestra descended from the stage and entered into spirited controversy with the audience. And finally the president of the Akademischer Verband came and boxed the ears of a man who had insulted him while he was making an announcement. (Vienna dispatch in *The Musical Courier*, New York, 23 April 1913)

1 APRIL 1913

La Vida breve, lyric drama in two acts by Manuel DE FALLA, dealing with the pathetically brief life of a Gypsy girl in Granada who dies of a broken heart after denouncing the perfidy of her seducer on the day of his marriage to a street vendor, to a score vibrant with Andalusian modalities, fandango rhrthms and orientalistically chromaticized arabesques, against the background of strumming guitars, clapping castanets and outcries of "Olé," is performed for the first time in Nice.

2 APRIL 1913

Maurice RAVEL completes the orchestration of the piano part of the first of his *Trois Poemés* to Maltarmé's texts, *Soupir*, for two flutes, two clarinets, piano and strings, in ethereally delicate sonorities. (The second song was orchestrated in May 1913; the third in August 1913. Dates at the end of each song in the printed score.)

J'ai pris à peu près pour cette œuvre l'appareil instrumental du *Pierrot Lunaire* de Schoenberg. (Ravel in his autobiographical sketch, in *Le Ménestrel*, Paris, 26 May 1939)

It was with special interest that I marked the dates given in *Music Since 1900* for Schoenberg's *Pierrot Lunaire* . . . It has been said that Ravel's *Trois Poemés de Mallarmé* (1913) were composed under the influence of this work, an allegation against which I have already protested. *Pierrot Lunaire* was not given outside Germany and Austria until after the war, and Ravel visited neither country in 1912–1913 . . . I had questioned Ravel before this piece of information came to me, and his reply was that he had not heard or read Schoenberg's work at the time, but only heard of it (probably through Stravinsky, who attended the Berlin performance). On the other hand, he knew the *Kammersymphonie* and this knowledge coupled with the information about *Pierrot Lunaire* gave rise to the idea of composing the *Trois Poemés* for voice and nine instruments. (M. D. Calvocoressi in his review of the first edition of *Music Since 1900*, in *Musical Opinion*, London, June 1938)

3 APRIL 1913

Le Festin de l'Araignée ballet-pantomime by Albert ROUSSEL, an arachnoid drama wherein an inhumanly voracious spider lures a multicolored butterfly into his net by deceptively ingratiating melodies wrapped in a gauze of impressionistic harmonies but, as he prepares his cannibalistic feast, is killed in turn by a vigilant praying mantis attacking in dramatically detonating dissonant chords, is performed for the first time in Paris, two days before Roussel's 44th birthday.

10 APRIL 1913

L'Amore dei tre re, opera in three acts by Italo MONTEMEZZI, set in 10th-century Italy, wherein a blind barbarian king strangles his daughter-in-law whom he rightly suspects of infidelity to his son, and puts poison on her dead lips so that when her princely lover kisses her in her crypt, he dies, as does her husband who kisses her too, leaving the old man alone with three cadavers, set to music in the style of Italian Verismo in opulent Wagneromorphic harmonies, is produced at La Scala, in Milan.

14 APRIL 1913

Mimi Pinson, lyric comedy in four acts by Ruggero LEONCAVALLO, a new version of his 1897 opera *La Bohème*, is produced in Palermo, under a new title in order to disassociate it from Puccini's famous homonymous opera.

18 APRIL 1913

Au Jardin de Marguerite, symphonic poem with chorus by the French romantic composer ROGER-DUCASSE, written in 1901–1905, describing Faust's visit, in his second old age, to Marguerite's garden, where the scent of fragrant flowers excites his debile flesh with aphrodisiac memories, while gentle marguerites envelop him in their chaste petals, set to florid impressionistic music, is performed for the first time in Paris.

18 APRIL 1913

Merlin, music drama in three acts by the German composer Felix DRAESEKE (completed on 13 May 1905), wherein Satan begets Merlin by a celestial virgin but is foiled in his design to use his hybrid offspring in the service of his anti-Christian crusade, despite the contributory seduction of Merlin by King Arthur's sister-in-law, set in a turbulent Wagnerolatrous idiom, is produced posthumously in Gotha. (Date from *Signale für die Musikalische Welt*, Berlin, of 30 April 1913; in his worshipful Nazigenic biography of Draeseke published in Berlin in 1937, Erich Roeder gives the erroneous date 10 May 1913.)

25 APRIL 1913

Panurge, "high musical farce" in four acts by Jules MASSENET, retailing the licentious adventures, tempered by philosophical divinations, of the gay rogue Panurge, devious and cunning companion of the hirsute and multifutuent giant Pantagruel in the celebrated satirical chronicle by Rabelais, is performed posthumously in Paris.

26 APRIL 1913

Three weeks before his forty-seventh birthday Erik SATIE composes *Sur un Casque*, the third and last piece of his piano suite *Descriptions automatiques*, in barless notation, interspersed with self-congratulatory marginal remarks such as *C'est magnifique!* and nonsensically mocking exhortations such as *Léger comme un œuf*.

(The first piece, *Sur un vaisseau*, written on 21 April 1913, contains this annotation: *Le Captiaine dit: Très beau voyage;* the second, composed on 22 April 1913, entitled *Sur une lanterne*, warns the player: *N'allumez pas encore: vous avez le temps!*)

The public is shocked by the charming mockery of the titles and expression marks used by Erik Satie, but it has respect for the formidable nonsense of the *Parsifal* libretto. The same public accepts the craziest titles of François Couperin: *Le tic-tic choc on Les Maillotins, Les Culbutes JXCXBXNXS, Les Coucous bénévoles, Calotins et Calotines ou la Pièce à tretous, Les Vieux galants, Les Trésorières surannées.* (Jean Cocteau, *Le Rappel à l'ordre*, Paris, 1926)

27 APRIL 1913

Arianna, musical intermezzo by Benedetto MARCELLO, written by him in 1727 and rediscovered in 1885, is performed for the first time in concert form at the Liceo Benedetto Marcello in Venice.

15 MAY 1913

The first set of *Impressioni dal Vero*, a symphonic triptych by Gian Francesco MALIPIERO, in three sections, illustrating the sound of a warbler, a woodpecker (repeatedly pecking at a high F-sharp), and an owl (represented by an intermittent hoot in the low register of the flute), in impressionistically succulent harmonies, is performed for the first time in Milan.

15 MAY 1913

Jeux, ballet by Claude DEBUSSY, representing a tennis match during which a ball bouncing off the grass court gives the pretext for a country lad to chase girls running after the ball, written in a rhythmically hedonistic manner with brief explosive motives suggesting the action, is performed for the first time by Diaghilev's Ballet Russe in Paris, with Nijinsky as the principal dancer and choreographer.

22 MAY 1913

A century, has passed since the birth in Leipzig of Richard WAGNER, originator of music drama in which the orchestra is elevated to symphonic significance and a network of leitmotivs is established to characterize personages, objects and even abstract concepts.

29 MAY 1913

Diaghilev's Ballet Russe presents in Paris the world première of Igor STRAVINSKY's epoch-making ballet *Le Sacre du Printemps* (in the original Russian, *Vesna Sviashchennaya*, i.e., Spring the Sacred), "scenes of pagan Russia" (completed in piano score on 17 November 1912; orchestration finished on 8 March 1913), with choreography by Nijinsky, in two parts:

Part I: THE KISS OF THE EARTH. opening with a bassoon solo in the uppermost reaches of its range; *Fortune-Telling in the Spring* in stamping duple time; *Dance of Smartly-Dressed Young Women*, with the melodies confined within the compass of a perfect fifth, characteristic of very old Russian folksongs; *The Game of Abduction*, primitivistic and brusque with truncated meters, pullulating rhythmic patterns and asymmetric chordal ejaculations; *Spring Rounds*, a syncopated march, opening and closing with six bars of serene folk refrains; *Game of Two Camps*, a polytonal and polyrhythmic display of primitive strength in a millennial bowling game; *Procession of the Oldest and Wisest Chieftain*, stupefyingly persistent in crutch-pounding in the low brass; *Dance of the Earth*, with a stolid terrestrial solo in triple time, accompanied by seismic activities

throwing out enormous boulders of blunt sonorities into the instrumental stratosphere, with a subterranean motto on the primeval pedal point C. Part II: THE GREAT SACRIFICE, opening with a polyharmonic reedy murmuration in volatile timbres; *Secret Rites and Rounds of Young Maidens*, in a major-minor bitonal complex, ending with a series of eleven identical bitonal chords; *The Glorification of the Chosen Maiden*, in constantly changing meters, with the eighth-note as the lowest common metrical denominator, dynamically and rhythmically vitalized into a frenzied dance; *Appeal to the Ancestors*, a turgidly treading, ominously austere vision of stony menidols; *Rites of Old Men, Human Forebears*, with D as the keynote, projecting a sinuously chromatic solo of the English horn against a rhythmic duple-time figure, culminating in a cadential petrification; *The Great Sacred Dance* in ternary form, with a 16th-note as the lowest common denominator in the first and third sections, and the eighth-note in the middle section; *Sostenuto e Maestoso*, with a quarter-note as the main unit, in triplets or duplets, reverting to the *Great Sacred Dance* in constantly changing meters of 1, 2, 3, 4 and 5 16th notes in a measure, until, after a scratch on a Cuban guiro (used here for the first time in European orchestral music) and a fertilizing seminal ejaculation from the piccolos and flutes, the music comes to a stop on the keynote D, topped by the tritone G-sharp in the highest register, acoustically constituting the 45th overtone.

Does Stravinsky really believe that a melody would become more intense and eloquent if it is doubled for 50 bars by a second above it, a second below it, or both? The innovations embodied in the score of *Le Sacre du Printemps* are mostly of this type. (H. Quttard, *Le Figaro*, Paris, 31 May 1913)

The most important distinction achieved by *Le Sacre du Printemps* is its claim to be the most discordant composition ever written. Never has the cult of the wrong note been applied with such industry, zeal and ferocity. From the first measure to the last, whatever note one expects is never the one that comes, but the nearest one to it; whatever harmony is suggested by a preceding chord, it is always another chord that is heard; and this chord and this note are used deliberately to produce the sensation of acute and almost cruel dissonance. When two melodies are superimposed, far be it from the composer's mind to use those that fit together; quite to the contrary, he selects them so that their superposition should produce the most irritating friction and squeaking that can be imagined. (Pierre Lalo, *Le Temps*, Paris, 3 June 1913)

Igor Stravinsky is displeased. The audience of the Ballets Russes reacted to his new work *Le Sacre du Printemps* with discordant outcries and laughter, interrupted by the applause of a few initiates. But in all fairness I must say that the composer was not very much upset and did not fulminate too violently against his detractors when we interviewed him yesterday.

Stravinsky is small in stature, but looks tall because he holds his forehead high, so that he dominates his interlocutor; he speaks from an elevation, and his eyes rove over objects and people with a mobility that engulfs them like a sudden shower.

"That my music could not be immediately accepted, I quite understand," he declared backstage at the Théâtre des Champs-Elysées. "What is unjustifiable, however, is the lack of good will on the part of the audience. It seems to me that they should have waited for the end of the performance to express their disapproval. This would have been courteous and honest. I gave them something new, and I fully expected that those who had applauded *Pétrouchka* and *The Firebird* would be somewhat dismayed, but I also expected an understanding attitude. I have acted in good faith; my previous works which have been well received were a guarantee of my sincerity, and should have proved that I had no intention whatsoever of making fun of the public. During the première, when the commotion made it impossible for the dancers to hear the music, we all were quite unhappy, not only because of our own pride, but because we feared that we would not be able to go on with the show. And this was the reward for 130 rehearsals and of a year of work!"

"Nijinsky was criticised for his choreography; some said it was alien to the music.

"They were wrong. Nijinsky is an admirable artist. He is capable of revolutionizing the art of ballet. He is not only a marvelous dancer, but he is able to create something new. His contribution to *Le Sacre du Printemps* was very important. However, I am confident that some day, perhaps soon, my music will be fully understood. An unexpected novelty disconcerts Paris, but Paris knows how to regain its composure and forget its bad humor."

Paris, which admires Nijinsky as a dancer, does not admire him at all as a choreographer. It is regrettable, but it is a fact. Recall his staging of *L'Après-midi d'un Faune* and *Jeux*, when Debussy went through some pretty bad moments, watching the spectacle in silence, philosophically and prudently. Let Nijinsky dance, for he dances like a young god. But for the sake of all of us, poor French art lovers, he must stop trying to direct the dancing of others, interpreting poetic texts and transforming *Le Sacre* into a *Massacre du Printemps*. (Henri Postel du Mas, *Gil Blas*, Paris, 4 June, 1913)

The music of *Le Sacre du Printemps* baffles verbal description. To say that much of it is hideous as sound is a mild description. There is certainly an impelling rhythm traceable. Practically, it has no relation to music at all as most of us understand the word. (*The Musical Times*, London, 1 August 1913)

The Paleozoic Crawl turned into tone with all the resources of the modern orchestra . . . the primitive run riot, almost formless and without definite tonality, save for insistently beating rhythms that made the tom-tom melodies of the gentle Congo tribes seem super-sophisticated in comparison . . . Without description or program, *Le Sacre du Printemps* might have suggested a New Year's Eve rally of moonshine addicts and the simple pastimes of early youths and maidens, circumspectly attired in a fig leaf apiece. (Philadelphia *North American*, 4 March 1922)

The public played the role that it had to play. It laughed, spat, hissed, imitated animal cries. They might have eventually tired themselves of that if it had not been for the crowd of esthetes and a few musicians who, carried by excess of zeal, insulted and even pushed the occupants of the loges. The riot degenerated into a fight. Standing in her box, her diadem askew, the old Comtesse de Pourtalès brandished her fan and shouted: "It is the first time in sixty years that anyone has dared to make a fool of me!" The good lady was sincere. She really thought it was a mystification. (Jean Cocteau, *Le Rappel a l'ordre*, Paris, 1926)

2 JUNE 1913

Luigi RUSSOLO, 28-year-old Italian Futurist musician and painter, presents in Modena for the first time in public his ensemble of noise-makers, *Intonarumore*, invented by him and constructed in collaboration with Ugo Piatti.

2 JUNE 1913

Julien, or *La Vie du Poète*, opera in four acts with a prologue by Gustave CHARPENTIER, a sequel to his masterwork *Louise*, to his own libretto depicting in naturalistic colors the decline, despair and ultimate dissolution of a philosophically disposed artist, marked by ethereal mysticism and eclectic pantheism (a bearded priest discourses in a Temple of Beauty, Julien challenges Nature

on a Hungarian plain, an artistic festival is held in Montmartre), is presented at the Opéra-Comique in Paris in a special public rehearsal. (The official world première took place on 4 June 1913.)

Paris Sees Charpentier's *Julien*—Enthusiasm Evoked by Sheer Beauty and Lyric Passion of the Music and Superb Stage Setting—Long Expected Continuation of *Louise* Is a Success—Critics Disappointed, However, by the Failure of the Composer to Produce Any Really New Note (Headlines in the New York *Sun*, 3 June 1913)

3 JUNE 1913

Edgar Stillman KELLEY conducts at the Norfolk, Connecticut, Music Festival the first performance of his *Second Symphony*, subtitled *New England*, 24 years before the first performance of his *First Symphony*.

5 JUNE 1913

Henry F. GILBERT, American composer, ardent champion of musical Americanism, conducts the New York Philharmonic at the 25th Meeting of the Litchfield County Choral Union in Norfolk, Connecticut, in the first performance of his *Negro Rhapsody*, subtitled *Shout*, inspired by the exalted outcries at Negro religious gatherings and making use of themes from Negro spirituals.

7 JUNE 1913

First Symphony by Josef Matthias HAUER, subtitled *Nomos*, in seven movements for 2 pianos 4 hands, derived from the putative law (nomos) of Terpandros, Greek philosopher who flourished circa 700 B.C., is performed for the first time in Sankt Pölten, Austria.

10 JUNE 1913

Tikhon KHRENNIKOV, Russian composer whose healthy diatonic style represents the optimistic philosophy underlying the Soviet doctrine of Socialist Realism unobscured by pre-revolutionary ambiguities and ambivalences, is born in Eletz.

19 JUNE 1913

A concert of music by Claude DEBUSSY, prefaced by a lecture "Claude Debussy et la Pensée contemporaine" by Emile Vuillermoz, takes place in Paris, with Debussy at the piano playing the first performances in public of three pieces from his newly completed second book of *Préludes: Canope*, inspired by the Grecian urn in his workroom ("canope" is the cover of a funerary receptacle), in which mortuary outcries interrupt stately progressions of parallel triads; *La Terrasse des audiences du clair de lune*, an impressionistic evocation of the tenaced approaches to a moonlit Buddhist temple in Indo-China; and *Hommage à Pickwick, Esq.*, opening with the strains of *God Save the King* in the bass and progressing through a series of portentously portly harmonies, with incidental discords suggesting the risible gaucheries of Pickwick's figure.

30 JUNE 1913

Abul, opera on a biblical subject by the Brazilian composer Alberto NEPOMUCENO, is produced for the first time at the Teatro Colón in Buenos Aires.

30 JUNE 1913

Erik SATIE composes *Holothurie*, the first of his three piano pieces under the general title *Desiccated Embryos*, in barless notation, urging the player to perform "comme un rossignol qui aurait mal aux dents" in order to adequately paint in tones the ossicles and the spicules of the echinodermic sea cucumber.

1 JULY 1913

Erik SATIE composes *Edriophthalmia*, the second piano piece of his suite *Desiccated Embryos*, portraying a group of crustaceans with sessile eyes, with a quotation from Chopin's Funeral March waggishly labeled "*citation de la célèbre mazurka de Schubert.*"

4 JULY 1913

Erik SATIE writes the third and last number of his piano suite *Desiccated Embryos*, entitled *Podophthalmia*, in barless notation, purported to represent the order of malaeostracan crustaceans with eyes supported on movable stalks, in humorously trite F-major arpeggios.

6 JULY 1913

At the annual audition of works submitted for the Prix de Rome, the Académie des Beaux-Arts in Paris awards the Premier Grand Prix de Rome to Lili BOULANGER, nineteen years and ten and a half months old, the first woman to receive this high award.

The Academy of Fine Arts assembled yesterday for the final audition of cantatas submitted for the Prix de Rome in music. The contestants, five in number, were to set to music the text *Faust and Helen* after Goethe. Upon the requisite drawing of lots, the cantata by Claude Delvincourt was heard first; the cantata by Marc Delmas followed. Mademoiselle Lili Boulanger, a pupil of Paul Vidal, came next. Her cantata was accompanied by her sister Nadia Boulanger. Then cantatas of Marcel Dupré and Edouard Mignan were performed. After a long deliberation, the Academy adjudged the Grand Prix de Rome, by 31 votes to 5, to Mlle Lili Boulanger and the Second Grand Prix to Claude Delvincourt by 29 votes to 7. Marc Delmas received the first Second Grand Prix. The result was greeted by a long ovation. Mlle Boulanger, who is not quite twenty, is the first woman to be awarded the Grand Prix in music. Her elder sister, Nadia Boulanger, had also entered the competition for the Grand Prix. She obtained the Second Grand Prix in 1908, but was less fortunate than her younger sister and did not succeed in carrying the Grand Prix in 1909. (*Le Temps*, Paris, 7 July 1913)

18 JULY 1913

Nine centuries have passed since the birth of Hermannus CONTRACTUS (nicknamed "contracted" because he was a hunchback), enlightened musical scientist and inventor of a system of intervalic notation that anticipated equal temperament.

7 AUGUST 1913

David POPPER, Prague-born virtuoso cellist and composer of numerous celebrated pieces for his instrument, dies in Baden at the age of 70.

25 AUGUST 1913

Erik SATIE composes Españaña, the third and last of the series of piano pieces in barless notation under the general title *Croquis et Agaceries d'un gros Bonhomme en Bois*, a sarcastic bisyllabilization of *España*, containing anamorphosed quotations from Chabrier's famous *España*.

(The first number of the series, heteroethnically entitled *Tyrolienne turque*, was written on 28 July 1913; the second, *Danse maigre*, a quasi-homonymous phonetic variant of *Danse nère*, was written on 2 June 1913.)

5 SEPTEMBER 1913

At a summer concert in Pavlovsk, a suburb of St. Petersburg, 22-year-old Sergei PROKOFIEV plays the solo part in the first performance of his *Second Concerto* in G minor for piano and orchestra, in four movements, alternatively lyric and energetic, marked by widely leaping melodic intervals in resonant harmonies and instantaneous modulations into keys a semitone off the principal tonic, resulting in a playful barbarization of the classical modalities, and culminating in the finale in overt polyharmony. (A revised version of the *Second Concerto* was first performed by Prokofiev on 8 May 1924 in Paris, at a concert conducted by Serge Koussevitzky.)

The debut of the pianistic cubist and futurist Prokofiev has brought excitement in the public. In the train going to Pavlovsk, one hears on all sides: "Prokofiev, Prokofiev, Prokofiev . . . a new star of the piano!" A youngster appears on the podium. It is Sergei Prokofiev. He sits at the piano and proceeds to make motions as though he were dusting the keys or tuning the instrument. All this he does with a sharp dry touch. The audience is puzzled. Some are outraged. A couple leaves and runs for the exit: "This kind of music will drive you crazy!" "What is this? A deliberate persiflage?!" After the first exits, other listeners begin to leave their seats. Prokofiev is now playing the second movement of his Concerto. Once more, a rhythmic jumble of sounds. The more audacious members of the audience begin to hiss. The hall is gradually emptying. Finally, with a mercilessly dissonant combination of brass instruments, the young artist concludes his Concerto. Most listeners react by booing. Prokofiev bows defiantly, then plays an encore. The public flees. On all sides one hears, "To the devil with this futurist music! My cat can play like that!" Prokofiev's Concerto is cacophony which has nothing to do with cultural music. His cadenzas are insufferable. The Concerto is filled to overflow with musical mud, produced, one may imagine, by accidental spilling of ink on music paper. (St. Petersburg *Gazetta*, 7 September 1913)

Young Prokofiev outdid the "man of wisdom and light" Scriabin. His Concerto is a torrent of muddy water. (*Novove Vremya*, St. Petersburg, 7 September 1913) The audience hissed. This is in the order of things. Some ten years from now it will expiate these hisses by unanimous applause for Sergei Prokofiev, famous composer with a European reputation. (*Rech*, St. Petersburg, 7 September 1913)

2 OCTOBER 1913

Edward ELGAR conducts at the Leeds Festival the first performance of his "symphonic study in C minor with two interludes in A minor" titled *Falstaff*, an affectionate tonal portrait of Shakespeare's amiable fat hero whose pomposity is epitomized in a bassoon cadenza marked "full tone, coarse" bestriding in large awkward intervals the entire range of the instrument, and his tragedy in repudiation and death signalized by a puny solo on the small side-drum.

2 OCTOBER 1913

A *Shropshire Lad*, orchestral rhapsody by the 28-year-old English composer George BUTTERWORTH, expanded from his song *The Cherry Tree*, to the words of A. E. Housman, poetically reflecting the brooding meditations of a rustic lad away from his native place, in a tranquil modal manner with occasional outbursts of quasi-impressionistic harmonies, is performed for the first time at the Leeds Festival, Arthur Nikisch conducting.

2 OCTOBER 1913

Two pastoral symphonic pieces by Frederick DELIUS, *On Hearing the First Cuckoo in Spring* and *Summer Night on the River*, permeated with the folkloric spirit of English song and set in euphonious Germanic harmonies, are performed for the first time anywhere in Leipzig.

(The first English performance of both pieces took place on 20 January 1914, played by the London Philharmonic Orchestra, under the direction of Willem Mengelberg.)

8 OCTOBER 1913

The Fair at Sorotchintzy, unfinished opera by MUSSORGSKY, after Gogol's tale depicting the lusty merriment of a Ukrainian market day, supplemented by music from other works of Mussorgsky, and arranged by various hands, is performed for the first time in Moscow in a three-act version. (Another version, by César Cui, was produced in Petrograd on 26 October 1917; still another, edited by Vissarion Shebalin, using only Mussorgsky's own materials, was first performed in Leningrad on 21 December 1931; a version with supplementary materials by Shebalin, was brought out in Moscow on 13 March 1952.)

12 OCTOBER 1913

The Gesellschaft der Musikfreunde of Donaueschingen (organized on 18 September 1913) presents its first concert of an annual series intended to foster general interest in modern music, and destined to continue, with some interruptions by wars and political upheavals, for more than half a century.

12 OCTOBER 1913

Max REGER conducts in Essen the world première of his *4 Tondichtungen nach Arnold Böcklin*:

(1) *Der geigende Eremit*, picturing in folk-like tones a violin-playing hermit before the statue of the Madonna; (2) *Im Spiel der Wellen*, a waltztime seascape representing Böcklin's picture of mermaids and merlads porpoising purposefully amid gentle waves; (3) *Die Toteninsel*, a thanatological evocation of Böcklin's volcanic island lined with funereal cypress trees, with the horns sounding a sepulchral fanfare; (4) *Bacchanal*, a riotous dance of vinous Romans.

19 OCTOBER 1913

Festliches Præludium by Richard STRAUSS (completed on 11 May 1913) for orchestra and chorus, making use of the novel device Aerophor, helping to sustain breath playing long notes in the brass instruments, is performed for the first time at the inauguration of the Konzert-Haus in Vienna, for which occasion the work was commissioned.

19 OCTOBER 1913

Moscou, third symphony by Charles TOURNEMIRE, is performed for the first time anywhere in Amsterdam.

25 OCTOBER 1913

Polenblut, operetta by the 39-year-old Czech composer Oskar NEDBAL, outlining a love quadrangle wherein an impoverished Polish count disdains an eager heiress who thereupon therapeutically dons peasant skirts and approaches him incognito stirring his Polish blood (hence the title) sufficiently to lure him into marriage, is produced in Vienna.

26 OCTOBER 1913

Erik SATIE composes three piano pieces in one day, under the general title *Peccadilles importunes*, with a self-deprecating marginal note in the manuscript "Si le bon Dieu voit cela il sera furieux."

30 OCTOBER 1913

Der Abenteurer, musical play in four acts by the 39-year-old Austrian composer Julius BITTNER, to his own libretto dealing with a semi-legendary adventurer named Jerome de Montfleury in which he makes use of a psychological "tendency motive" serving as a monothematic melorhythmic motto of the entire score, is performed for the first time in Cologne.

1 NOVEMBER 1913

Are you there?, musical farce in three acts by Ruggero LEONCAVALLO, to an English text, is produced in London.

5 NOVEMBER 1913

Men on the Line, cantata by the 30-year-old English operetta composer Hubert BATH, containing in the score some onomatopeic sounds descriptive of the bustle and commotion of a large railway in operation, is performed for the first time by the Great Eastern Railway Musical Society in London.

22 NOVEMBER 1913

Benjamin BRITTEN, magus of modern English music, whose operas, symphonies, oratorios and chamber music are imbued with the imperishable spirit of musical Englishry and marked by technical expertise, astutely incorporating the most viable elements of cosmopolitan modernism, is born in Lowestoft.

22 NOVEMBER 1913

Shylock, opera in three acts by the Belgian composer Flor ALPAERTS, to a libretto after Shakespeare in the Flemish language, is produced in Antwerp.

28 NOVEMBER 1913

Sinfonietta by the 16-year-old Viennese wonder boy Erich KORNGOLD, a score of Straussian complexity with a "motive of the cheerful heart" built on ascending fourths as a thematic nucleus, is performed for the first time in Vienna, Felix Weingartner conducting.

Occasion: the third Philharmonic concert. Scene: the great concert hall of the Musikverein in Vienna. Prophets to the right, prophets to the left, and the wonder child, young Korngold, in the middle. . ... His *Sinfonietta* performed for the first time before what is perhaps the most critical audience in the world went the way of most productions destined to outlive the praise or blame of the day: it evoked storms of applause and protests. (*The Musical Courier,* New York, 7 January 1914)

3 DECEMBER 1913

Second Symphony by the 38-year-old Austrian romantic composer Franz SCHMIDT, in the heroic key of E flat major, in three movements, the middle one being a theme with ten variations, and the Finale containing a magisterial fugue, is performed for the first time in Vienna.

3 DECEMBER 1913

Victory Over the Sun, futuristic extravaganza to a text in surrealistic language made up from unwieldy Russian vocables by the poet Kruchenykh, with a prologue by another lingual surrealist Khlebnikov, and stage and costume designs by the chief of the Suprematist school of abstract painting Kazimir Malevich, set to a rude and crude musical score by Mikhail MATIUSHIN, is performed for the first time at the Luna Park Theater in St. Petersburg.

4 DECEMBER 1913

L'Amore Medico, opera in two acts by the German-Italian composer Ermanno WOLF-FERRARI, after Molière's comedy *L'Amour médecin,* is performed for the first time in Dresden, in the German version under the title *Der Liebhaber als Arzt.*

9 DECEMBER 1913

Der Rosenkavalier by Richard STRAUSS is presented for the first time in America by the Metropolitan Opera in New York.

Richard Strauss Turns His Hand to a Comedy Opera— Von Hofmannsthal's Sprightly Libretto Filled with Music Which is Mozartian in Terms of the Modern Orchestra— The Altogether New and Different Strauss of This Score—Its Waltz Tunes Not Distinguished—Its Humor Often Exaggerated, but Remarkable in His Union of Intricacy and Simplicity. (Headlines in the Boston *Evening Transcript,* 10 December 1913)

Rosenkavalier at Metropolitan—A Vapid and Salacious Comedy Given with Great Earnestness—From Necrophilism to Lubricity—The Policy of Such a Production at the Opera Questioned (Headlines in the New York *Tribune,* 10 December 1913)

9 DECEMBER 1913

Franz KULLAK, German piano pedagogue and highly conscientious and competent editor of piano classics, son of Theodor KULLAK, nephew of Adolf KULLAK, first cousin of Ernst KULLAK, respectively respectable pianists and teachers, dies in Berlin in his 70th year.

10 DECEMBER 1913

Morton GOULD, American composer of modernistic symphonies, concertos and chamber music, as well as inventive pieces in a popular vein, is born in New York City.

10 DECEMBER 1913

In his first appearance in Russia as a symphonic conductor, Claude DEBUSSY leads Serge Koussevitzky's orchestra in Moscow in a program of his works, including *Nocturnes, Clarinet Rhapsody, La Mer, L'Aprèsmidi d'cun Faune, Images* and *Marche écossaise.*

13 DECEMBER 1913

Serge RACHMANINOFF conducts in St. Petersburg the first performance of his choral symphonic poem *Kolokola (The Bells),* completed by him on 9 August 1913, to the text of Edgar Allan Poe's onomatopoeic ode to tintinnabulating bells translated into Russian, in four movements: a merrily jangling *Allegro,* an epithalamian *Lento* adorned by caressing orientalistic melismas, a *Presto,* ringing the chimes of alarums, and a sepulchrally funereal *Lento lugubre.*

15 DECEMBER 1913

Parisina, opera in four acts by Pietro MASCAGNI, to a libretto by Gabriele d'Annunzio, wherein the Duke of Ferrara orders his natural son to be beheaded when he learns that his favorite concubine Parisina was his son's clandestine inamorata, set to an emotionally Italianate score in the Verismo manner, scaling the operatic heights and plumbing dramatic depths, is performed for the first time at La Scala, Milan.

19 DECEMBER 1913

Flup!, the first and the most popular operetta in three acts by Jósef Zygmunt SZULC, 38-year-old Warsaw-born Parisianised composer of light music, with action taking place in Ceylon in May 1913, wherein a British Duke exchanges identities with a waterfront porter known under the quasi-canine appellation Flup (the exclamation point in the title indicates the vocative case suitable to Flup's profession) in order to win by proxy the hand of the British Colonial Resident's daughter, a royalty-hating militant suffragette, is produced in Brussels.

1914

9 JANUARY 1914

The King of the Jews, mystery play by the Russian Grand Duke Konstantin Romanov, with incidental music by Alexander GLAZUNOV, is performed for the first time by the Imperial Russian Court Orchestra, Hugo Warlich conducting, at the Hermitage at St. Petersburg.

14 JANUARY 1914

Three Poems from the Japanese by Igor STRAVINSKY, scored for soprano, 2 flutes, 2 clarinets, piano and string quartet are performed for the first time in Paris.

17 JANUARY 1914

Erik SATIE composes a *Choral hypocrite* for violin and piano, ten bars in length, set in acerbic harmonies, with a verbal declaration, "My chorales are equal to those of Bach, with this difference that they are fewer and less pretentious," this being the first of his three violin pieces, under the general title *Choses vues à Droite et à Gauche (Sans Lunettes)* calculated to present a monocular view of bars dexter and bars sinister.

(The second piece, *Fugue à tâtons*, a tentative fugue on a French nursery tune, bears the date of 21 January 1914; the third, *Fantaisie musculaire*, consisting of a series of flexed arpeggios and debile trills, with a pompously inane violin cadenza ending "very contritely" on a succession of 13 low G's, is dated 30 January 1914.)

17 JANUARY 1914

At his first appearance in London as composer-conductor, Arnold SCHOENBERG conducts his *5 Orchesterstücke*.

London Baffled by Schoenberg's Orchestral Pieces—Composer Himself Conducts and He at Least Is Pleased—Reminiscent of a Nightmare (Headlines in *Musical America*, New York, 14 February 1914)

To one critic, the music of Schoenberg's *Five Orchestral Pieces* suggested feeding time at the zoo; also a farmyard in great activity while pigs are being ringed and geese strangled. On another the identical section of the work produced the impression of a village fair with possibly a blind clarinetist playing at random. The same listener heard sounds as of sawing steel and the distant noise of an approaching train alternately with the musical sobs of a dynamo. (*Daily Telegraph*, London, 24 January 1914)

Sir: Any one acquainted with music history would find little cause for surprise at the incoherent criticism following on the performance of Schoenberg's *Five Orchestral Pieces*. The vulgarity of the writer who stated that "long hair used to be indispensable but now has been superseded by the bald head" (an obvious and disgraceful attack on the personality of Herr Schoenberg) and the even more stupid remark of the other person who wrote that "they (the Schoenberg pieces) were so ridiculous in their chaotic formlessness that the orchestra sometimes laughed down their instruments instead

of blowing down them," may be dismissed as examples of ignorance and lack of decency. It is, however, surprising to find this bewilderment on the part of our most sincere critics. May I venture to suggest that it is a lack of constructive vision in regard to musical psychology? (Letter to the Editor of the *Daily Telegraph*, London, by Leigh Henry, 17 February 1914)

In January 1914 we repeated Schoenberg's *Five Orchestral Pieces* with Schoenberg conducting. The performance drew a large and appreciative audience who may or may not have been surprised by the following notice in the programme: "Herr Arnold Schoenberg has promised his cooperation at today's concert on condition that during the performance of his *Orchestral Pieces* perfect silence is maintained." (Henry J. Wood, *My Life in Music*, London, 1938)

24 JANUARY 1914

Canossa, musical scene by Gian Francesco MALIPIERO, based on the episode of the Emperor Henry IV's genuflected submission to the Pope in Canossa in 1077, is given its first and last performance in Rome, after which Malipiero destroyed the manuscript.

24 JANUARY 1914

Madeleine, lyric opera in one act by Victor HERBERT, dealing with a temperamental prima donna whose friends insist on spending New Year's day with their mothers, is produced at the Metropolitan Opera in New York, with considerable acclaim and 16 curtain calls.

26 JANUARY 1914

Postolar od Delfta (The Cobbler of Delft), fantastic opera by the 40-year-old Serbo-Croatian composer Blagoje BERSA, to a libretto in the Serbo-Croatian language translated from the original German text *Der Schuster von Delft*, from a story derived from the fairy tale *Lykkens kalosker (Lucky Galoshes)* by Hans Christian Andersen, is performed for the first time in Zagreb. (The German version was given for the first time in Vienna on 7 November 1918.)

31 JANUARY 1914

Orphée, lyric mimodrama in three acts by the 50-year-old French composer Jean-Jules Aimable ROGER-DUCASSE, for orchestra, solo voices and choruses, depicting Orpheus as a virtuous virtuoso on the lyre, who is dismembered by furibond mænads when he scorns their nymphomaniacal advances, set in an evocatively neo-archaic manner, with explosive rhythmic asymmetries, is performed for the first time, without choreography, in St. Petersburg, Alexander Siloti conducting. (First stage performance of *Orphée* as a ballet was given at the Paris Opéra on 11 June 1926.)

4 FEBRUARY 1914

Las Golondrinas (The Swallows), opera in three acts by the 26-year-old Basque composer José María USANDIZAGA, dealing with passionate turbulence among members of a traveling circus, and culminating in the murder of a fickle equestrienne by the director of the troupe, set to music in a pleasingly Italianate idiom, seasoned with stimulating Pyrenean melorhythms, is produced in Madrid, less than two years before Usandizaga's untimely death.

6 FEBRUARY 1914

A year after the death of the Germanic romantic composer Felix DRAESEKE, his last symphony, completed on 22 August 1912, and entitled *Symphonia comica*, in four movements, the humor of which reaches its high point in an episode called *Fliegenkrieg*, with flies battling chromatically against a background of buzzing tremolos, is performed for the first and last time from manuscript, in Dresden.

A musician's lot in Germany is a canto missing in Dante's *Inferno*. But I did not allow my sense of humor to be ruined, as I proved in my latest opus. (From Draeseke's letter written in June, 1912, to a friendly symphonic conductor)

10 FEBRUARY 1914

Abisso, last opera in three acts by the 59-year-old blind Italian composer Antonio SMAREGLIA, couched in a Wagnerophylic idiom refreshed by sprays of florid Mediterranean melos, is produced at La Scala, Milan.

12 FEBRUARY 1914

Estrellita, nostalgic song by the 31-year-old Mexican composer Manuel PONCE, so authentically Latin in its expansive melorhythmic expression that it became mistakenly identified as a folk song, is published in Mexico City.

13 FEBRUARY 1914

The American Society of Composers, Authors and Publishers (ASCAP), established to protect performing rights and to distribute annual fees to members according to the frequency of performance of their music, is formally organized at a dinner meeting in the Hotel Claridge in New York under the directorship of Victor HERBERT.

14 FEBRUARY 1914

La Chanson d'Halewyn, musical legend by the Belgian composer Albert DUPUIS, depicting in Wagneromantic tones a series of mystical events in a medieval castle, is produced in the Flemish language, under the title *Det Lied van Heer Halewyn*. (It was first produced as a cantata for which Dupuis won the Prix de Rome, in Brussels, on 25 November 1903; the printed score gives the apparently premature date of 6 December 1913 for the performance of the operatic version.)

17 FEBRUARY 1914

Ernst von DOHNÁNYI, 36-year-old hungarian composer and pianist, plays in Berlin the solo piano part in the first performance of his *Variationen über ein Kinderlied (Variations on a Nursery Song)*, dedicated "to the enjoyment of lovers of humor and to the annoyance of others," containing eleven variations on the 18th-century French air *Ah, Vous dirai-je, maman*, introduced by the theme played bidigitally on the piano solo, and replete with polychromatic pianistic pyrotechnics in a Brahmsogenetic vein.

Dohnányi's *Variations* must rank high among the modern classics in one of the severest of art forms. (Sir Donald Tovey, *Essays in Musical Analysis*, vol. 3, London, 1939)

Dohnányi's wit can be very ponderous, as in the *Variations on a Nursery Song*, where the comic effect of the deliberately portentous introduction, followed by the thin, schoolgirlish delivery of the theme by the soloist, has no more subtlety than the mountain delivering the ridiculous mouse. (Eric Blom, in the article on Dohnányi in the Fifth Edition of *Grove's Dictionary of Music and Musicians*, London, 1954)

19 FEBRUARY 1914

Francesca da Rimini, fourth and most successful opera in four acts by Riccardo ZANDONAI, to a libretto after a tragedy by Gabriele d'Annunzio, inspired by the famous episode in Dante's *Inferno*, is produced in Turin.

23 FEBRUARY 1914

Cléopâtre, "drame passionel," last opera by Jules MASSENET, in four acts, to a libretto introducing a historically undocumented emancipated Greek slave as Cleopatra's last lover, is produced posthumously in Monte Carlo.

23 FEBRUARY 1914

The Midnight Girl, first American operetta by the 26-year-old Hungarian-born composer Sigmund ROMBERG, is produced in New York.

5 MARCH 1914

On the day after his fifteenth birthday Henry COWELL presents at the San Francisco Music Club the first demonstration of his "tone-clusters," pandiatonic and panpentatonic, played on the white or on the black keys of the piano keyboard with fists or forearms. (In a remarkable synchronization of invention the Russian composer Vladimir REBIKOV published in 1912 a *Hymn to the Sun* for piano, in special columnar notation, indicating that the conglomeration of keys are to be encompassed with the edge of the palm of the hand.)

10 MARCH 1914

La Fille de Figaro, operetta in three acts by Xavier LEROUX, is performed for the first time in Paris.

11 MARCH 1914

Hashish, symphonic poem by the Russian composer Sergei LIAPUNOV, illustrating the vividly sensual visions of lissome oriental beauties seductively disporting themselves in serpentine chromatics induced by the smoking of hashish, is performed for the first time in St. Petersburg.

11 MARCH 1914

At Carnegie Hall, New York, Jim EUROPE conducts a Negro symphony orchestra in an instrumental ensemble anticipatory of jazz bands, sans oboes, bassoons or second violins, but with a cornucopia of clarinets, trumpets, trombones, banjos, a set of drums and a phalanx of ten pianos.

12 MARCH 1914

Ferruccio BUSONI appears as soloist in Berlin in the first performance of his *Indianische Fantasie* for piano and orchestra, written in an expansively rhapsodic vein with extensive cadences covering the entire range of the piano keyboard, and making use of authentically pentatonic American Indian melodies in opulent harmonic dressing.

17 MARCH 1914

I Mori di Valenza, opera by Amilcare PONCHIELLI, written by him in 1879, and rediscovered in 1902, is performed for the first time at Monte Carlo.

20 MARCH 1914

The Banks of Green Willows, orchestral idyll by the English composer George BUTTERWORTH with melodic materials inspired by English countryside tunes, is performed for the first time in London.

27 MARCH 1914

The world première is given in London of *A London Symphony* by Ralph VAUGHAN WILLIAMS, his *Second Symphony*, descriptive of the sights and sounds of London, scored for a very large orchestra with an extensive set of percussion including tam-tam and a pod of jingles, in four movements:

(1) *Lento; Allegro risoluto*, opening at dawn on the Thames River with the solemn sound of the Big Ben leading to the busy London day, newspaper boys shouting the headlines, costermongers singing their refrains, clerks whistling confidently, while the residential section of the town remains dreamily lyrical and tonally relaxed; (2) *Lento*, a Bloomsbury vigil in November fog, an old fiddler playing in front of a pub, the distant voice of a lavender vendor forming an antiphonal contrast, concluding in a modally inflected diatonic mist; (3) *Scherzo (Nocturne): Allegro vivace*, a Saturday night near the Houses of Parliament, with the sounds of muted merriment wafted by a slow wind from the other side of the Thames, coster girls dancing a double-shuffle jig accompanied by a mouth harmonica, a hurdy-gurdy grinding its ballads, until the sempiternal London fog lowers its veil upon the scene; (4) *Andante con moto, Maestoso alla Marcia. Epilogue: Andante sostenuto*, revealing the London of the lower classes, still struggling against economic oppression, with the strains of a "Hunger March" colliding with the crowds in the wealthy districts of the city, gradually resolving into silence, in which the philosophical sound of the Westminster Chimes is heard again.

The title might run *A Symphony by a Londoner*. Various sights and sounds of London may have influenced the composer, but . . . if the hearers recognize a few suggestions of such things as the Westminster chimes, or the lavender cry, these must be treated as accidents and not essentials of the music. (Vaughan Williams in a statement)

The composer of the *London Symphony* understood that music begins where realistic noise leaves off. If his thoughts are not all pleasant or all hopeful individually, in their relations to one another he builds up something which is beautiful in its entirety. (London *Times*, 28 March 1914)

29 MARCH 1914

Alfredo CASELLA conducts the orchestra of the Concerts Colonne in Paris in the first performance of his *Notte di Maggio* for voice and orchestra, in which his "second style" of composition, polytonal and polymodal, is definitely established. (In his review of *Notte di Maggio* in *Comœdia*, Paris, on 30 March 1914, Emile Vuillermoz suggested that the term "polyharmony" might be advantageously used in place of polytonality to describe the superposition of two or more chords or melodic figures in different keys.)

29 MARCH 1914

Variations for Orchestra, the first important work by the 32-year-old Dutch composer Sem DRESDEN, is performed for the first time by the Concertgebouw Orchestra in Amsterdam, Willem Mengelberg conducting.

1 APRIL 1914

Madame Roland, lyric drama in three acts by Felix FOURDRAIN, to the dramatic story of the French lady of progressive views who perished on the guillotine on 8 November 1793, ending with her famous cry "Oh Liberty, how many crimes are committed in your name," is produced in Paris.

1 APRIL 1914

Notre Dame, opera in two acts by Franz SCHMIDT, to a libretto from Victor Hugo's famous novel, is performed for the first time in Vienna. (An orchestral suite from the opera, characteristically titled *Zwischenspiel aus einer unvollständigen romantischen Oper*, was first performed in Vienna on 6 December 1903.)

2 APRIL 1914

Five months before his tragic death, Albéric MAGNARD conducts, at a concert of the Union des Femmes Professeurs et Compositeurs in Paris, the first performance of his magnum opus, the resplendently expansive *Fourth Symphony*, in C-sharp minor, in four movements: (1) *Modéré*, with an oriflamme of fanfaric calls against the rumble of multidivisional harmonic figurations; (2) *Vif*, a scherzo in 1/2 time in F minor; (3) *Sans lenteur et nuancé* in E major; (4) *Animé*, homonymically passing from the basic key of C-sharp minor to the eloquent tonality of D-flat major.

2 APRIL 1914

L'Ombra di Don Giovanni, opera in three acts by Franco ALFANO, is produced in Milan.

5 APRIL 1914

STRAVINSKY's *Le Sacre du Printemps* receives its first performance as a symphonic composition without stage action, at the Casino de Paris, conducted by Pierre Monteux.

12 APRIL 1914

A century has elapsed since the death of the great English music historian Charles BURNEY.

Full of years and full of virtues, the pride of his family, the delight of society, the unrivalled chief and scientific HISTORIAN of his tuneful Art! Beloved, revered, regretted, breathed in Chelsea College his last sigh! Leaving to posterity a fame unblemished, raised on the noble basis of intellectual attainments. High principles and pure benevolence, goodness with gaiety, talents with taste, were of his gifted mind the blended attributes; while the genial hilarity of his airy spirits animated or softened his every earthly toil; and a conscience without reproach prepared in the whole tenour of his mortal life, through the meditation of our Lord Jesus Christ his soul for heaven. Amen. Born April 7th Old Style 1726. Died April 12th 1814. (From the inscription on Burney's tombstone in Westminster Abbey)

19 APRIL 1914

Der Heilige Berg, the only opera by the Norwegian composer Christian SINDING, in two acts with a prologue, is produced, in a German version, in Dessau.

21 APRIL 1914

Luigi RUSSOLO, Futurist composer, inventor of *Intonarumori* (intonators of noises), presents in Milan the first performance of his bruitistic *Networks of Noises*. (The first public demonstration of *Intonarumori* as an instrumental medium was given by Russolo in Modena on 2 June 1913.)

The program of the first concert of *4 Networks of Noises* comprised the following works: (1) *The Awakening of the Capital;* (2) *A Meeting of Automobiles and Airplanes; (3) A Dinner on the Terrace of the Casino; (4) A Skirmish in an Oasis.* Russolo conducted the orchestra composed of 19 bruiteurs:

3 bumblers	2 exploders	2 gurglers
3 thunderers	3 whistlers	2 rufflers
1 fracasseur	2 stridors	1 snorer

There was an enormous crowd. Boxes, the orchestra and balcony seats were filled to capacity. A deafening uproar of "passéistes" greeted us. They arrived with the express purpose of interrupting the concert at all costs. For an hour, the Futurists offered passive resistance. But an extraordinary thing happened just at the start of *Network of Noise No. 4:* five Futurists—Boccioni, Carra, Amando Mazza, Piatti and myself—descended from the stage, crossed the orchestra pit, and, right in the center of the hall, using their fists and canes, attacked the "passéistes," who appeared to be stultified and intoxicated with reactionary rage. The battle lasted fully half an hour. During all this time Luigi Russolo continued to conduct imperturbably the nineteen bruiteurs on the stage. It was a display of an amazing harmonic arrangement of bloody faces and dissonances, an infernal mêlée. Our previous battles took place in the streets or backstage after the performance. For the first time on this occasion the performing artists were suddenly divided into two groups: one group continued to play, while the other went down into the hall to combat the hostile and rioting audience. It is thus that an escort in the desert protects the caravan against the Touaregs. It is thus that the infantry sharpshooters provide cover for the construction of a military pontoon. Our skill in boxing and our fighting spirit enabled us to emerge from the skirmish with but a few bruises. But the "passéistes" suffered eleven wounded, who had to be taken to a first-aid station for treatment. (F. T. Marinetti, *L'Intransigeant*, Paris, 29 April 1914)

Real battles took place during my concerts. The incomprehension of the very serious principles underlying my music on the part of the public and the critics was exasperating. Only a few musicians of stature—among them Ravel and Stravinsky—understood the value of my innovations, as yet realized only in part. The financial impossibility to do my research compelled me to discontinue my work several years ago. I regret that I did not have an occasion to give a demonstration of my instruments when I had the pleasure of meeting you in Paris, at the time you conducted concerts of modern American music there. (Letter to Nicolas Slonimsky from Luigi Russolo, dated 24 August 1934)

23 APRIL 1914

Madelon, song by Camille ROBERT glorifying an amiable, accommodating and cooperative French barmaid, destined to become the most popular ballad of the battle-scarred poilus of World War I, is performed for the first time at the café-concert Eldorado in Paris.

6 MAY 1914

Scemo, lyric drama in five acts by Alfred BACHELET, his first opera, written in a mild Wagneromorphic idiom, dealing with a Corsican village idiot (*scemo* is a mental defective in a local dialect) who inspires a perverted passion in the bosom of a young matron in spite of his reputation as a *jettatore* (evil-eye), is produced at the Paris Opéra.

Composers of M. Bachelet's ilk are in my view the most savage enemies of music, who would inevitably lead it to total perdition if they were allowed to go on without a protest against their criminal activities. . . . The most complex difficulties of Wagner's music are nothing in comparison with obstacles posed at every step in M. Bachelet's score. (Arthur Pougin, *Le Ménestrel*, Paris, 9 May 1914)

9 MAY 1914

A "Moderner Musikabend" is given in Wiener-Neustadt, with a program including the first performance of the *Third Symphony* by Josef Matthias HAUER.

10 MAY 1914

Lillian NORTON, American soprano, who was given a euphonious operatic name Giglia Nordica (Lily of the North) by her Italian teacher, possessor of a resonant Wagnerian voice and solid femininity (her first husband Frederick A. Gower vanished in a balloon flight over the English Channel), *diva assoluta* of prideful temperament (she once told the Boston Symphony Orchestra men that they played like a Kalamazoo band, thus alienating the affections of both Boston and Kalamazoo) and an authority on international cuisine (she baptized a delicacy, Chicken à la Nordica), dies at the age of 56 in Batavia, Java, on a concert tour around the world.

10 MAY 1914

Die Marketenderin, opera by Engelbert HUMPERDINCK, is produced in Cologne.

11 MAY 1914

Don Juans Letztes Abenteuer, opera in three acts by Paul GRAENER, depicting Don Juan's final affair with a Venetian patrician's young daughter, and postulating the supremacy of carnal love in chromatically Wagnerophallic harmonies is produced in Leipzig.

14 MAY 1914

Richard STRAUSS conducts, at Diaghilev's Ballet Russe in Paris, the first performance of his ballet in one act *Josephs Legende*, to the biblical story of Joseph's virtuous rejection of Potiphar's wife, set to music in the characteristic idiom of his tone poems, with stolid virtue painted in cerulean major tonalities and strident polyharmonies depicting the abomination of carnality.

15 MAY 1914

Marouf, Savetier du Caire, opera in four acts by the French romanticist Henri RABAUD, generally regarded as his chef d'coeuvre, after the Arabian tale wherein a poor Cairo cobbler marries the Sultan's daughter under false pretenses, but makes his prevarication come true when, at the behest of a sympathetic genie, a caravan he boasted of owning materializes in time to save him from the execution block, is performed for the first time at the Opéra-Comique in Paris.

15 MAY 1914

Erik SATIE composes (in the morning, before breakfast) his dyspeptic *Choral inappétisant* set in regurgitating modalities with ecclesiastical borborygmuses, concluding on a cathartic C major cadence, serving as a postlude to a series of short piano pieces under the general title *Sports et Divertissements*.

(The other pieces of the suite are, in the chronological order of composition: *La Pêhe*, 14 March 1914; *La Pieuvre*, 17 March 1914; *Le Yachting*, 22 March 1914; *Les Courses*, 26 March 1914; *Le Flirt*, 29 March 1914; *La Balcançoire*, 31 March 1914; *Le Carneval*, 3 April 1914; *Le Feu d'artifice*, 6 April 1914; *La Chasse*, 7 April 1914; *La Bain de mer*, 11 April 1914; *Le Water-Chute*, 14 April 1914; *Le Pique-Nique*, 19 April 1914; *Les Quatre Coins*, 24 April 1914; *La Comédie italienne*, 29 April 1914; *Le Tennis*, 21 April 1914; *Colin-Maillard*, 27 April 1914; *Le Traineau*, 2 May 1914; *Le Tango*, 5 May 1914; *Le Réveil de la Mariée*, 16 May 1914; *Le Golf*, 20 May 1914.)

17 MAY 1914

Kain und Abel, one-act opera by the prestigious German conductor Felix WEINGARTNER, to his own libretto presenting a romantically dramatic version of the biblical story dealing with the first murder committed on earth, is produced in Darmstadt.

26 MAY 1914

Le Rossignol, opera-ballet in three tableaux by Igor STRAVINSKY, after the tale of Hans Christian Andersen, in which a manically depressed Emperor of China, mortified by the metallic tintinnabulations of a mechanical nightingale made in Japan, with its Nipponese pentatonicism polluted by chromatic impurities, is restored to life by the thrilling trills and therapeutically euphonious atonal melismata of a sinologically authentic philomel brought back from the woods whither he fled from his insular rival, written in a dissonantly bitonal idiom rooted in quartal harmonies superimposed on structures of major sevenths and tritones, is produced in Paris by Diaghilev's Ballet Russe, with the orchestra under the direction of Pierre Monteux. (A symphonic poem extracted from *Le Rossignol* was first performed, under the title *Le Chant du Rossignol*, by the Orchestre de la Suisse Romande in Geneva, conducted by Ernest Ansermet on 6 December 1919. It was given as a ballet in Paris on 2 February 1920.)

One recalls the scandalous spectacle of *Le Sacre du Printemps*—or rather *Massacre du Printemps*—a year ago. Never were human ears assailed more defiantly. One cannot say that *Le Rossignol* is quite as outrageous as that. Apart from some croaking of frogs and the mooing of a young cow, the music holds together, more or less. One finds in it quite as many offensive dissonances as in *Le Sacre*, but they are presented in a more dissimulated manner, more shamefacedly, without conviction, as if the composer in his embarrassment wished to apologize but had no strength to repudiate them. But all is changed in the second act, where we enter the new manner of Mr. Stravinsky. There reigns insufferable cacophony, an accumulation of bizarre chords which succeed one another without rhythm or justification; it seems like a wager that one can make the gullible public and the snobs swallow anything at all in our concert halls. We will say nothing about the delirium of some enthusiasts lodged on top of the gallery who cried out loudly for the author, but the latter had the good sense not to appear. (H. Moreno, *Le Ménestrel*, Paris, 6 June 1914)

28 MAY 1914

Maruxa, lyric eclogue in two acts by the prolific Spanish composer of light opera Amadeo M. VIVES, to a story of tumescent rustic passions, wherein a farmer's daughter covets a simple-minded shepherd while her male cousin cozens the shepherd's favorite shepherdess, all this vitalized by a cornucopia of Iberian melorhythms, is produced in Madrid.

1 JUNE 1914

The fifth, and last, Congress of the International Music Society is held in Paris, two months before the outbreak of World War I puts an end to it as to many other international cultural enterprises, so auspiciously flourishing during a century of major peace since the Congress of Vienna.

2 JUNE 1914

First Symphony by the foremost Russian symphonist Nicolai MIASKOVSKY in G minor (completed on 21 September 1908), in three contrasting movements representing the formation of his early romantic style of composition, is performed for the first time at a summer concert in Pavlovsk, near St. Petersburg.

The summer of 1908 brought the First Symphony and earned me a scholarship at the St. Petersburg Conservatory. Were it not for this scholarship, I would have been forced to leave the Conservatory for I could not afford the annual tuition of 250 rubles. The composition of the First Symphony determined my future, for prior to that time I was afraid to tackle orchestral writing. And I was never interested in composing operas or ballets. (From Miaskovsky's *Biographical Notes*, published in *Sovietskaya Musica*, June 1936)

4 JUNE 1914

On his first visit to America, Jan SIBELIUS conducts at the 28th meeting of the Litchfield County Choral Union, held at Norfolk, Connecticut, a concert of his orchestral works, including *Pohjola's Daughter, Christian II, The Swan of Tuonela* and *Oceanides*, the last being a world première.

14 JUNE 1914

Seven weeks before the outbreak of Franco-German hostilities, the French government confers the order of Chevalier of the Légion d'Honneur on Richard STRAUSS.

17 JUNE 1914

The degree of Doctor of Music is conferred upon Jean SIBELIUS by Yale University, with the following summary of his position:

By his music, intensely national in inspiration, and yet in sympathy with the mood of the West, Doctor Jan Sibelius long since captured Finland, Germany and England, and on coming to America to conduct a symphony concert found that his fame had already preceded him also. Still in the prime of life, he has become, by the power and originality of his work, one of the most distinguished of living composers. What Wagner did with Teutonic legend, Dr. Sibelius has done in his own impressible way with the legends of Finland as embodied in her national epic. He has translated the Kalevala into the universal language of music, remarkable for its breadth, large simplicity, and the infusion of a deeply poetic personality.

19 JUNE 1914

The Bavarian Civil Court rejects the suit brought by Isolde Beidler against her mother Cosima Wagner seeking legal recognition of her status as a natural daughter of Richard WAGNER, and an equal share with her brother Siegfried and her sister Eva in the proceeds from Wagner's estate.

(Isolde was born on 10 April 1865, and was registered as a legitimate daughter of Hans von Bülow, then legal husband of Cosima Wagner. The court found no proof that Cosima had not carnally cohabited with Von Bülow between the dates of 12 June and 12 October 1864, the limits for conception of a child born on 10 April 1865, according to Bavarian law, and that consequently Isolde might have been a legitimate issue. This period corresponds to the time when Wagner was a guest of Hans and Cosima von Bülow at Villa Pellet in Starnberg. Isolde's husband, Franz Beidler, acting as her lawyer, published on 26 May 1914 a report citing contemporary accounts tending to establish Wagner's intimacy with Cosima at the time, including a neighbor's report that von Bülow, returning one evening to his villa from Munich, found Wagner's bedroom locked with Cosima inside, became despondent, began to shriek, banged on the furniture and rolled on the floor. Beidler also proposed phrenological and hemological tests of Isolde and Siegfried to establish their total consanguinity.)

24 JUNE 1914

Three hundred years have passed since the completion of the first music encyclopedia, *Syntagma Musicum* by Michael PRAETORIUS, planned in four volumes, of which only three were published.

(Date of the preface of the first volume, in Latin, dealing with sacred music, is 24 June 1614. The second volume, in German, was published in 1619, and has the subtitle, *De Organographia*, dealing with organ playing and construction. The preface is curiously dated: "in the year after Christ, *stylo Vulgari*, 1616, but, according to exact calculation, 1621; since the creation of the world, 5568; since the exodus from Egypt, 3116; since the foundation of Rome, 2371; in the 599 Olympiad." The third volume, also in German, has the date 14 May 1619 in the preface and contains an explanation of French and Italian terms, description of dances, and numerous musical examples.)

25 JUNE 1914

Erik SATIE composes *Obstacles vénimeux*, the first number in his suite of three barless piano pieces bearing the oxymoronic title *Heures séculaires et instantanées*, with the following text accompanying the music:

This vast part of the world is inhabited by a single man, a Negro. He is bored to the point of dying of laughter. The shadow of millennial trees marks 9:17 o'clock. [The time of the day is indicated in the music by 9 chords in the bass for the hours, and 17 notes in the treble for the minutes]. The toads call each other by name. For better cogitation the Negro holds his cerebellum in his outstretched right hand. From a distance he looks like a distinguished physiologist. Four anonymous serpents hold him captive, suspended on the tails of his uniform, deformed by suffering and loneliness. An old mangrove tree slowly bathes its repulsively filthy roots at the riverside. It is not the hour of the shepherd. (A footnote reads: To Whom it May Concern: I forbid to recite the text aloud during the musical performance. Failure to comply will cause justified indignation on my part against the transgressor.)

2 JULY 1914

Two centuries have passed since the birth at Erasbach of Christoph Willibald GLUCK, audacious reformer of operatic traditions, who put dramatic ideals above vocal virtuosity and vindicated the poetic essence in theatrical music.

3 JULY 1914

Erik SATIE composes *Crépuscule matinal (de midi)*, the second piece of his oxymoronic piano suite, entitled *Heures séculaires et instantanées*, to ridicule the impressionistic fashion of musical landscape painting, with the following text in the music:

The sun rose early, in good humor. The temperature is expected to be above normal, for this is an antediluvian sunrise. The sun is now high in the sky and it looks like a nice fellow. But do not trust the sun. It may burn the harvest or administer a stroke: a sun-stroke. Behind the hangar a bull gorges himself on fodder to the point of nausea.

(The third piece, entitled *Affolements granitiques*, wherein some noxious miasmata disport themselves in heteronymous pseudo-bitonalities of E-sharp and F major while the clock strikes metachronistic 13, bears no date of composition in the printed edition.)

4 JULY 1914

Dylan, Son of the Wave, opera by the British composer Josef HOLBROOKE, being the second part of his Wagneromorphic trilogy, wherein the hero is slain by a blackguard uncle, who perishes in turn, as the ocean waves invade his moated castle to avenge the death of his kith and kin, is produced in London.

10 JULY 1914

Piano Concerto in C minor by the 21-year-old English composer Herbert HOWELLS is performed for the first time in London, with Arthur Benjamin as soloist.

2 AUGUST 1914

Gabriel DUPONT, French composer of youthful promise and great expectations, dies at the age of 36 in war-oppressed Paris.

15 AUGUST 1914

The annual series of Promenade Concerts opens its first war season in London with the playing of national hymns of the Allied powers, in a changed program substituting ELGAR's *sospiri* for strings, harp and organ and TCHAIKOVSKY's *Italian Capriccio* for the previously scheduled performance of the symphonic poem *Don*

Juan by Richard STRAUSS, removed from the program in agreement with the general wartime concert policy in England to ban music by living German composers.

17 AUGUST 1914

A program of French and Russian music is substituted for the announced all-Wagner evening at the Promenade Concerts in London.

The taboo of Wagner is much to be regretted. Apparently, the directors of the Queen's Hall and of the Orchestra feared a demonstration by non-musical super-patriots. (*Musical Times*, London, September 1914)

In London during August 1914 the usual cheap evening orchestral concerts, so-called Promenade Concerts, were announced in a patriotic manner, with the comment that no German musician would be represented on the program. Everybody applauded this announcement, but nobody attended the concert. A week later a program of Beethoven, Wagner and Richard Strauss was announced. Everybody was indignant and everybody went to hear it. It was a complete and decisive German victory without a single man being killed. (From George Bernard Shaw's letter to a friend in Vienna, published in the *Frankfurter Zeitung* of 21 April 1915 and reprinted in the New York *Times* of May 1915)

17 AUGUST 1914

Edward ELGAR volunteers to serve in the Hampstead Special Constabulary, and is sworn in, receiving an armlet and a heavy baton as the symbol of authority.

26 AUGUST 1914

The Immortal Hour, opera in two acts by the 36-year-old English composer Rutland BOUGHTON, to a libretto from Irish legendary tradition, wherein the King of Shadows arranges for the young King of Ireland to meet his immortal bride from the Land of Youth and Heart's Desire only to lose her and be left with the Dream of Death at an Immortal Hour, set to music of Celtic provenance, thematically derived from ancient pentatonic modalities, yet bleak and stark in facture, is performed for the first time at Glastonbury.

28 AUGUST 1914

Anatoly LIADOV, Russian composer of miniature symphonic poems inspired by Russian folklore, distinguished by an imaginative melodic and harmonic presentation, dies at his family estate, near the ancient Russian capital of Novgorod, at the age of 59.

3 SEPTEMBER 1914

Albéric MAGNARD, French composer of four symphonies, three operas and other works conceived in a rhapsodically grandiloquent style representing the French counterpart of Wagnerianism, perishes in his house on the Marne, in the act of armed resistance to the advancing Germans.

At 9:45 in the morning, the Germans appeared at my place and told me that there was a sniper in the village. It was Albéric Magnard, who killed a hussard and wounded another. The Germans threatened to burn the village in reprisal and to shoot down any inhabitants who would try to flee. At 11:40 A.M., they took me to Magnard's villa and set it on fire. As the smoke began to rise, we heard a shot inside the house. A German officer remarked: "He chose the best way out." (From the testimony of F. J. Robert, notary at Baron, given on 28 January 1915, and quoted in Gaston Garraud, *La Vie et la Mort d'Albéric Magnard,* Paris, 1921, pp. 284–285)

I swear to tell the truth. On 3 September I was returning to our house at Baron, when I noticed a detachment of German soldiers on the terrace. Approaching the house, they shouted: "Komm heraus! Einmal, zweimal, dreimal!" At that moment my father-in-law fired two shots through the blinds of the window in the first floor. Two Germans fell in the garden, some five meters from where I stood. Thereupon the soldiers fired at the house. A superior officer was called, and he ordered the house burned. It was set afire by grenades. While the house was burning I heard a shot, and my impression was that my father-in-law had killed himself. He had said before that he had four bullets for the enemy and one for himself. (Testimony of R. Creston, son-in-law of Magnard, given in Paris on 6 February 1915, and quoted in Garraud's book, pp. 285–286)

On 4 October 1914 I went to Baron to try to find the remains of my poor husband in the ruins of our house, of which only a pile of rubble within the four walls was left. The position in which I found his remains makes it possible for me to state that he was standing behind the window when he died. I am convinced, therefore, that he was killed by the Germans. I also found, near his body, the blackened and burned pages of the manuscript of his opera *Bérénice.* (Testimony of Mme Magnard, given in Paris on 3 November 1914, and quoted in Carraud's book, pp. 287–288)

10 SEPTEMBER 1914

Two centuries have passed since the birth in Aversa, near Naples, of Niccolo JOMMELLI, "the Italian Gluck."

19 SEPTEMBER 1914

Camille SAINT-SAËNS publishes in *l'écho de paris* the first of a series of articles denouncing German art and music under the title *Germanophilie,* vehemently denouncing Wagner (whom he knew in Paris and who admired Saint-Saëns) and urging a total ban on Wagner's operas in France.

What Hohenzollernian fly has stung Saint-Saëns? Was it perhaps during his recent trip to Berlin, after which an inscribed photograph of the Kaiser was seen adorning his piano? We can explain his present Wagnerophobia only by senile debility. (Jean Marnold, *Le Cas Wagner,* Paris, 1920)

27 SEPTEMBER 1914

Frédéric Masson of the French Academy publishes in *L'Écho de Paris* an article, *L'art sans patrie,* ferociously attacking WAGNER, "the composer of that miserable rhapsody, *Die Meistersinger*" and urges Frenchmen to banish Wagner from French musical life "by law, by persuasion, by force, or even by violence if need be."

29 SEPTEMBER 1914

Stevan MOKRANJÁC, Serbian composer of fine church music, including a devotional *Serbian Liturgy,* dies in Skoplje at the age of 58.

30 SEPTEMBER 1914

The German publishing house of BREITKOPF & HÄRTEL announces the dissolution of the International

Music Society because of the wartime breakdown of international cooperation.

10 OCTOBER 1914

Margot, lyric comedy by Joaquín TURINA, is produced in Madrid.

12 OCTOBER 1914

The Berlin Philharmonic Orchestra opens its first wartime season in a program of Beethoven and Brahms conducted by Arthur Nikisch.

13 OCTOBER 1914

Perseus, second symphonic work by the 21-year-old English composer Eugene GOOSSENS, is performed for the first time at the Promenade Concerts in London.

14 OCTOBER 1914

Walford DAVIES, 45-year-old English composer and educationist, plays at the Promenade Concerts in London the piano part in the first performance of his *Conversations* for piano and orchestra, in four movements, fancifully labelled *Genial Company, A Passing Moment, Intimate Friends* and *Playmates.*

22 OCTOBER 1914

Britain's War March, patriotic orchestral piece by Cyril SCOTT, is performed for the first time at the Promenade Concerts in London.

27 OCTOBER 1914

Richard HEUBERGER, Austrian composer of numerous respectable musical works in the manner of Brahms (whose worshipful friend he was), who achieved his more or less durable fame mainly with an operetta *Das Opernball,* dies in Vienna at the age of 64.

3 NOVEMBER 1914

Thomas Beecham conducts in London the Royal Philharmonic Orchestra in the first performance of *Two Passacaglias* by Cyril SCOTT, the first based on the pentatonic *Irish Famine Song,* the second on the medievally lugubrious tetratonic tune *Poor Irish Boy,* liberally bestrewn by whole-tone scales, and lavishly orchestrated, reaching an exalted climax with massed sonorities of gliding harps, crashing piano chords, drums, violins glissando along the natural series of overtones, and the organ in a grandly resonant C-major peal.

1 DECEMBER 1914

Hunold der Spielmann (Hunold the Player), folk opera by the 58-year-old German composer Hermann GENSS, to his own libretto, is produced in German in San Francisco.

6 DECEMBER 1914

Middle-aged French musicians, members of the Lamoureux and Colonne orchestras in Paris, who are not subject to military service, combine forces to present their initial concert in wartime Paris under the auspices of both orchestras.

7 DECEMBER 1914

Carillon for voice and orchestra by Edward ELGAR, to patriotic words by a Belgian poet, is performed for the first time at the Promenade Concerts in London.

8 DECEMBER 1914

Watch Your Step, "a syncopated musical show" by Irving BERLIN, in which Giuseppe Verdi appears on the stage to protest against the syncopation of his arias, but is eventually won over to the novel zip of ragtime, is produced in New York.

14 DECEMBER 1914

Giovanni SGAMBATI, Italian composer, pianist and renowned pedagogue, dies in his native Rome at the age of 73.

16 DECEMBER 1914

Giovanni von ZAYTZ, whose real name was Ivan Zajc, Croatian composer of about 1200 works of all kinds and author of the first Croatian national opera, *Nikola Šbrič Zrinski* (1876), dies in Zagreb at the age of 83.

27 DECEMBER 1914

The Academy of Santa Cecilia in Rome confers honorary membership on Vincent D'INDY.

1915

1 JANUARY 1915

The first issue of *The Musical Quarterly,* devoted to both the human and theoretical aspects of music, is published in New York by G. Schirmer, Inc., under the editorship of Oscar George SONNECK, Chief of the Music Division of the Library of Congress.

Publisher and editor are agreed not to throttle *The Musical Quarterly* at birth with a "program." . . . The policy of the magazine? That may best be defined by this subtle alteration of a good, old doctrine: *Audietur et altera pars.* The foundations of this magazine were laid months before the European War broke out. Since then many foreign collaborators have been called to the colors, and the editor suddenly found himself under the necessity of changing the distribution of his forces and of adjusting his plans to unwelcome circumstances. While the war lasts, of necessity, articles by continental contributors will be fewer than were solicited and promised. Indeed, the editor fears that the pen of more than one valued contributor rests forever. (From the preface to the first issue)

1 JANUARY 1915

Florent SCHMITT conducts his *Chant de Guerre* for tenor, chorus and orchestra at a patriotic matineae; in Toul, given for the wounded French soldiers, early victims of the first few months of the great senseless war between civilized nations.

2 JANUARY 1915

Karl GOLDMARK, Austrian composer of effective orchestral and operatic music, in a romantic idiom midway between Mendelssohn and Wagner, dies in Vienna in his 85th year.

4 JANUARY 1915

I Didn't Raise My Boy to Be a Soldier, sentimentally pacifistic tune by Al PIANTADOSI, to the words by A. Bryan, challenging, in quick-step time, anyone to place a musket on his shoulder and to make him shoot some other mother's darling boy, with a garish cover representing a gray-haired American mother babying a boy about twenty years old and protecting him with an upraised hand from bombs exploding in an alien war on a transatlantic continent, is copyrighted by Leo Feist, publishers, bearing a dedication "respectfully to every mother everywhere." (650,000 copies were sold in the first three months of 1915.)

After America's entry into World War I in 1917, numerous sequels were published reflecting the changing sentiment toward war; dates in parentheses are copyright dates: *I Didn't Raise My Dog to Be a Sausage* (21 April 1915); *I Did Not Rear My Boy to Be a Coward* (18 October 1915); *I Did Not Raise My Girl to Be a Soldier's Bride* (24 June 1916); *I Didn't Raise My Boy to Be a Soldier, I'll Send My Girl to Be a Nurse* (17 January 1917); *America, Here's My Boy* (16 February 1917); *I'm Glad I Raised My Boy to Be a Soldier* (14 April 1917); *I'm Raising My Boy to Be a Soldier to Fight for the U.S.A.* (28 April 1917); *I Didn't Raise* *My Boy to Be a Molly-Coddle* (4 May 1917); *I Want to Be a Soldier Boy* (11 May 1917); *I'm Raising My Boy for a Soldier* (15 May 1917); *I'll Give My Boy to My Country* (7 June 1917); *I Raised My Boy to Be a Soldier,* (12 June 1917); *I Didn't Raise My Boy to Be a Soldier, But He'll Fight for the U.S.A.* (13 June 1917); *I Didn't Raise My Boy to Be a Slacker* (13 July 1917); *I Did Give My Boy to Uncle Sammy* (31 December 1917); *I Raised You For a Soldier Lad* (13 June 1918); *I Didn't Raise My Boy to Be a Soldier, But!* (10 August 1918); *I Wish I Had a Thousand Sons to Fight for U.S.A.* (6 September 1918); *I Raised My Darling Boy to Be a Soldier* (21 October 1918).

14 JANUARY 1915

Notte di Leggenda, one-act opera by Alberto FRANCHETTI, is produced at La Scala, in Milan.

24 JANUARY 1915

Sinfonia drammatica by Ottorino RESPIGHI, in three movements of intensive tone painting, ranging in mood from muted premonitions to sonorous implosions, is performed for the first time in Rome.

25 JANUARY 1915

Madame Sans-Gêne, opera by Umberto GIORDANO in three acts, taking place respectively, on 10 August 1792 in the laundering establishment of Madame Sans-Gêne in turbulent revolutionary Paris, at Compiègne in September 1811, and finally in the private quarters of Napoleon whose temporary mistress she had become, the musical score containing a number of inserted dances in the French *style galant,* while the harmonic and orchestral idiom follows the precepts of Italian Verismo in the manner of Giordano's preceding opera from the period of the French Revolution, *Andrea Chénier,* is produced at the Metropolitan Opera in New York for the first time anywhere, Arturo Toscanini conducting.

5 FEBRUARY 1915

Max REGER conducts in Berlin the first performances of his *Variationen und Fuge über ein Thema von Mozart,* op. 132, for orchestra, wherein the ingenuous theme of Mozart's piano sonata in A major, itself in the form of variations, is subjected to torturous melodic anamorphoses, contrapuntal contortion, canonic dislocation, rhythmic incrustation and harmonic inspissation, and of *Eine vaterländische Ouvertüre,* dedicated to the German Army, then in the flush of its initial successes in World War I, with the German national anthem *Deutschland, Deutschland über alles* and the patriotic song *Die Wacht am Rhein* trumpeted mightily against polyphonic countercurrents.

6 FEBRUARY 1915

La Candidata, operetta by Ruggero LEONCAVALLO, is produced in Rome.

8 FEBRUARY 1915

The Birth of a Nation, ultra-patriotic film produced by the egomaniacal cinemagus D. W. GRIFFITH (called during its first engagement *The Clansman* after the Negrophobic novel by Thomas Dixon on which it was based), with a special score for orchestra and chorus nominally supplied by the American composer Joseph Carl Breil, but actually constituting a medley of popular classical and semi-classical selections in the established tradition of the silent cinema accompaniment, with the heroic Klan Call taken bodily from *The Ride of the Valkyries* by Richard Wagner, opens a successful run across the United States.

8 FEBRUARY 1915

Sociedad Nacional de Música, formed in Madrid for the purpose of promoting native music, presents its first concert with works by Manuel de FALLA, Enrique GRANADOS and Joaquín TURINA.

11 FEBRUARY 1915

The New York District Court grants but suspends an injunction of sales to Charles T. Boosey, publisher of the song *I Hear You Calling Me,* against the Empire Music Company, Inc., publishers of the song *Tennessee, I Hear You Calling Me,* for infringement of copyright, in the following ruling:

The composition which plaintiffs own is of a dignified character, has been sung by a distinguished singer, and has at its basic theme a living person standing on the grave of his dead loved one and hearing her voice. The composition owned by defendant is in syncopated time (familiarly known as rag-time), has been sung by a master of that art, and expresses the desire of a Negro to go back to his old home in Tennessee. The two compositions are considerably different, both in theme and execution, except as to this phrase *I hear you calling me,* and, as to that, there is a marked similarity. . . . The words *I hear you calling me* and the music accompanying those words are practically identical in both compositions, and the real controversy in the case is whether the use of this similar phraseology and the similar bars of music is sufficient to warrant the charge of piracy and infringement of copyright. I have had someone, indifferent to the controversy, play both songs for me, and the sentiment of one song is about the same as the other.

16 FEBRUARY 1915

Emil WALDTEUFEL, Alsatian-born waltz composer, who became a successful dance director at the court of Napoleon III, dies in Paris, his adoptive home, at the age of 77.

19 FEBRUARY 1915

Jules ÉCORCHEVILLE, 42-year-old French musicologist, editor of the music catalogue of the Bibliothèque Nationale de Paris, falls in combat at Perthes-les-Hurlus in Champagne while leading his company against the advancing Germans.

27 FEBRUARY 1915

Third Symphony in A minor by Nicolai MIASKOVSKY, in two movements, composed in 1914, and couched in a brooding Russian style characteristic of his romantic inspiration, is performed for the first time in Moscow.

10 MARCH 1915

Vesper Mass for chorus a cappella by Serge RACHMANINOFF is performed for the first time in Moscow.

15 MARCH 1915

Alexander GLAZUNOV conducts at the Petrograd Conservatory the second "Patriotic Concert" of a series inaugurated during the first season of wartime, giving the first performance of his orchestral *Paraphrases of the National Anthems of the Allied Nations,* including those of Russia, Serbia, Montenegro, France, England, Belgium and Japan.

19 MARCH 1915

Adventures in a Perambulator, orchestral suite by the American composer and railroad industrialist John Alden CARPENTER, describing in modernistic modalities with a vocabulary of the impressionist palette six typical scenes as seen and heard from the vantage point of a baby carriage, *En voiture!, The Policeman, The Hurdy-Gurdy, The Lake, Dogs,* and *Dreams,* is performed for the first time by the Chicago Symphony Orchestra.

20 MARCH 1915

The Russian Symphony Orchestra of New York, directed by its founder and conductor Modest ALTSCHULER, gives the first American performance of Scriabin's symphonic poem *Prometheus,* including the part of *Luce* (light) ineffectively executed on a rudimentary "color organ" projecting blurred color images on the screen.

20 MARCH 1915

Fedra, the first opera in three acts by the 34-year-old Italian composer Ildebrando PIZZETTI, to a libretto by Gabriele d'Annunzio, depicting the heroine's unnatural passion for her stepson that leads to tragic death for both, set to music with a novel technique of non-Wagnerian melosomatic psychomotives, Fedra herself being characterized by an involuted chromatic theme, recitatives austerely drawn in a luminescent musical prosody, opulent pedal points supporting the aerostatically buoyant upper harmonies, the whole marking a significantly new type of modern Italian music drama, is produced at La Scala in Milan.

In the score of *Fedra* not a single note is at variance with the spontaneous rhythm that marks every line. Indeed, each note makes the rhythmic group of words with which it is associated more expressive, without dislocating or distorting it. (Gabriele d'Annunzio on *Fedra,* quoted in Guido M. Gatti, *Ildebrando Pizzetti,* London, 1951)

28 MARCH 1915

Georges ENESCO, 33-year-old Rumanian composer, conducts in Bucharest the first performance of his *Second Symphony* in A major, couched in a Gallic romantic manner along neo-baroque lines, with rural melorhythms of his native Rumania providing a welcome local color.

3 APRIL 1915

Fedra, "tragic rhapsody" in one act by the Italian composer Romano ROMANI on the classical subject of quasi-incestuous love, is produced in Rome.

8 APRIL 1915

Evangelio, symphonic poem by the Spanish romantic composer Joaquín TURINA, is performed for the first time in Madrid.

9 APRIL 1915

La Chasse aux Boches, patriotic French operetta by F. PER-PIGNAN showing the brave French poilus chasing the panicked boches, is staged at the Folies-Bergère in Paris.

14 APRIL 1915

Upon Reading the Psalms, cantata by Sergei TANEYEV, his last work (completed on 12 January 1915), inspired by the modes of the Russian liturgy and accoutred in fine 19th-century harmonies, is performed for the first time in Moscow, Serge Koussevitzky conducting in the presence of the composer.

15 APRIL 1915

El Amor Brujo (Love the Sorcerer), ballet-pantomime with voices by Manuel de FALLA, based on an old Andalusian tale wherein the courtship of a young widow by an ardent swain is systematically interrupted by the ghostly apparition of her husband claiming posthumous marital rights, which his harassed widow finally provides by proxy in the warming flesh of a Gypsy girl, set to music with a profusion of Spanish melorhythms, and reaching its greatest impact in the *Ritual Fire Dance*, destined to become one of the most popular numbers in orchestral literature, is produced in Madrid.

15 APRIL 1915

Twelve days before his death, Alexander SCRIABIN plays at the Petrograd Conservatory his last piano recital in a program of his works, including his last composition, the hauntingly atonal and polytonal *5 Préludes*, op. 74.

27 APRIL 1915

Alexander SCRIABIN, Russian composer who sought to create new music of pantheistic universality and who believed himself to be an instrument of divine will whose works are steeped in deep solipsistic theosophy and bear titles expressive of these associations—*Divine Poem, Poem of Ecstasy, Satanic Poem*—who constructed a six-note "Mystic Chord" as a medium of preternatural harmonies and who evolved a unique piano technique of resonant power and subtly equilibrated dynamics, dies in Moscow from a fulminatingly rapid blood infection (which could be, thirty years later, unfailingly remedied by the administration of sulfa drugs), at the lamentable age of 43 years, 3 months, 20 days, 17 hours and 55 minutes.

I treasure the devotion you feel for the One who dwells within me. You have faith in Him, because He is great, even though I myself am often meek, small, weak and exhausted. I am not yet He, but I will soon become that which is He! . . . I am carried aloft to extraordinary heights by the immense wave of my inspiration! I suffocate! I am in a state of blessedness! I write music that is divine! (From Scriabin's letter to his common-law wife Tatiana Schloezer)

On 20 April Scriabin was forced to stay in bed as he developed a small furunculus on the upper lip. This caused no alarm at first, particularly since he had suffered a similar infection a year before and it disappeared without ill effects. On 26 April the swelling diminished somewhat and Scriabin felt better. But towards noon he began to complain of pain in the chest and his doctor diagnosed symptoms of pleurisy. At one o'clock the following night Scriabin began to lose consciousness. At three o'clock he was given the last Sacrament, and on 27 April, at 8:05 in the morning, he died. (Y. Engel, *Musical Contemporary*, Moscow, December 1915) (Scriabin's exact age at the time of his death can be established because it is known that he was born at 2:10 P.M. on Christmas Day 1871, according to old style calendar; he attached considerable significance to the fact that he was born on the day of Nativity.)

Scriabin's life and death can be analyzed astrologically with great accuracy. He is known to have been born at 2:10 P.M. local Moscow time, when the mystic star Betelgeuse was in ascendance in the zodiacal sign of Gemini, and Mars almost exactly at the zenith. His was a difficult birth chart to live up to: great tensions, great power, very poor health, home tragedies, a most difficult marriage with the sign of inevitable separation. A weaker soul would have broken down at once. His mother's sickness before his birth is found as sowing seeds of ill health, probably through glandular disturbances. Strong series of blood poisoning are shown, anemia and digestive difficulties. His life was sustained entirely by faith and inner inspiration. His death closes a cycle begun as he entered the Moscow Conservatory in 1888. As he died, Uranus was exactly at the zenith point of his birth chart, Saturn exactly at the Eastern horizon point. His was indeed a mystic's death, a token of personal immortality. (Horoscope of Scriabin drawn at the author's request in 1937 by Dane Rudhyar, French-born American composer, mystic and astrologer)

5 MAY 1915

The German music weekly *Signale für die musikalische Welt* publishes an editorial appeal to extreme German patriots to heed Bismarck's dictum, *quieta non movere*, not to disturb quiescent objects, and stop advocating the forcible Germanization of Italian musical terminology as long as Italy remains neutral. (Italy declared war on Germany and Austria 18 days after the publication of this article.)

7 MAY 1915

O'Brien BUTLER, composer of the first Irish opera with Gaelic words, *Muirgheis*, perishes on the S.S. *Lusitania*, torpedoed by a German submarine not far from the coast of Kerry, where the first act of *Muirgheis* is laid.

7 MAY 1915

A group of commuters waiting at the Hanover Square Station of New York's Third Avenue Elevated Railroad, moved by the news of the sinking of the S.S. *Lusitania* by a German submarine, and prompted by the sound of a hurdy-gurdy playing *In the Sweet Bye and Bye*, begins spontaneously singing the song in memory of the dead, causing Charles IVES, one of the commuters, to commemorate the incident in the last movement of his *Second Orchestral Set*, entitled *From Hanover Square North at the End of a Tragic Day the Voice of the People Again Arose*.

10 MAY 1915

Two one-act operas by the 30-year-old Italian composer Adriano LUALDI, *La Rosa di Saaron (Rose of Sharon)* and *Le furie di Arlecchino,* an "intermezzo giocoso," are performed for the first time at the Teatro Carcano in Milan.

(Loewenberg in his *Annals of Opera* gives a much later date for the production of *Le Furie d'Arlecchino,* 19 June 1924, in Buenos Aires, and adds: "Stated sometimes to have been produced at the T. Carcano, Milan, as early as 1915, a statement which I could not verify." *Encyclopedia dello Spettacolo* lists the exact dates of first performances of both operas.)

14 MAY 1915

The Boston Symphony Orchestra, under the direction of Karl MUCK, presents the first of thirteen daily concerts at the Panama-Pacific International Exposition in San Francisco in programs of music of all nations.

15 MAY 1915

Cyril SCOTT plays with the Royal Philharmonic Orchestra in London, Thomas Beecham conducting, the piano part in the world première of his *Piano Concerto* in C major, in three contrasting movements, *Allegro maestoso, Adagio* and *Allegro poco moderato,* couched in an eclectic para-modernistic style, containing elements of neoclassical formalism, impressionistic rhapsodism and exotic pentatonicism, described by one listener as "impressions of Bach taken while on a supposed journey to China."

Cyril Scott's music has passed through many phases and exhibited almost every kind of inchoate experiment, but in his piano concerto he seems to have entirely emerged from the experimental stage. The untiring vitality of his own playing, of course, helped it immensely. (London *Times,* 17 May 1915)

29 MAY 1915

The Lewisohn Stadium, gift to the College of the City of New York by Adolph LEWISOHN, is dedicated and officially opened. (The regular summer symphony concerts were inaugurated in 1917 with an eight-week season.)

2 JUNE 1915

Botho SIGWARD, Count of Eulenburg, German composer of orchestral and vocal music in a romantic vein, is killed in Galicia during the retreat of the Austrian and German armies before a temporary Russian offensive.

9 JUNE 1915

The Italian composer Riccardo ZANDONAI, born in Tyrol as an Austrian subject, is accused of high treason by the Austrian Governor of the province of Trieste for composing and circulating a student hymn calling for the return of the lost provinces of *Italia irredenta.*

19 JUNE 1915

Sergei TANEYEV, Russian composer, theorist and pedagogue, teacher of 135 students at the Moscow Conservatory and at his home (he never accepted payment from private pupils), whose vocal and instrumental works possess an architectural solidity of design in a fine classical tradition barely touched by Russian folk element, compiler of an imposingly scientific tome *Mobile Counterpoint in*

Strict Style, dies on his estate in the village of Dyudkovo in the Zvenigorod District, near Moscow, at the age of 58.

19 JUNE 1915

Camille SAINT-SAËNS conducts in San Francisco, as an invited guest at the Panama-Pacific International Exposition, the first performance of his orchestral ode composed for the occasion, *Hail, California!*

1 JULY 1915

Fairyland, allegorical opera by Horatio PARKER, winner of the $10,000 prize of the National Federation of Women's Clubs (his second large prize, the first being for *Mona,* produced by the Metropolitan Opera on 14 March 1912), to a story of a medieval novitiate nun who contrary to ecclesiastical regulations took unto herself a lover (albeit a supernatural fairy), is condemned to be burned at the stake, but is saved when the faggots are miraculously extinguished and all witnesses become fairies, set to music in magniloquently Wagneromorphic tones, is performed for the first, and practically last, time in Los Angeles.

It may be that many men—perhaps some of genius (if you won't admit that all are geniuses)—have been started on the downward path of subsidy by trying to write a thousand-dollar prize poem or a ten-thousand-dollar prize opera. . . . If a bishop should offer a "prize living" to the curate who will love God the hardest for fifteen days, whoever gets the prize would love God the least. (Charles Ives, from *Essays Before a Sonata,* New York, 1920)

6 JULY 1915

Polonia, symphonic poem by Edward ELGAR written especially for the benefit of the Polish Relief Fund, is performed for the first time in London.

15 JULY 1915

The West Virginia Folklore Society is organized with the purpose of ascertaining the possible derivation of Negro spirituals from the songs of mountain white folks.

21 JULY 1915

Four centuries have elapsed since the birth of St. Philip NERI whose Christian piety was so intense that during one of his penitential implorations his heart became supernaturally dilated and broke two ribs in his thoracic cavity, whose place in music history was secured because he was the spiritual father of the Oratorio, so named after the place of religious meetings accompanied by singing which Neri organized in 1558 in a chapel (*oratorio,* prayer room).

5 AUGUST 1915

The Blue Paradise, operetta by the 28-year-old Hungarian composer Sigmund ROMBERG, who settled in the United States in 1909, with additional music by the Viennese composer Edmund EYSLER, to a libretto wherein an Americanized native revisits Vienna in quest of nostalgic memories centered on a flower girl whom he first met at the café called The Blue Paradise, and featuring one of Romberg's most popular songs, *Auf Wiederseh'n,* is produced for the first time in New York.

15 AUGUST 1915

Concerto for cello and orchestra by the Chilean composer Humberto ALLENDE, containing some impressionistic touches in the general framework of classical form, is performed for the first time in Santiago, Chile.

18 AUGUST 1915

Anfion y Zeto, opera by the Italian-born Argentine composer Pascual de ROGATIS, to a libretto dealing with the twin brothers Amphion (the lyre-player) and Zethus (the shepherd) who capture the town of Thebes and fortify it telekinetically by charming the stones into place by music, is produced in Buenos Aires.

23 AUGUST 1915

Erik SATIE writes *Idylle, à Debussy*, first of three piano pieces in barless notation in the suite under the general title *Avant-dernières pensées*, with an affectionately derisive text mockingly imitative of impressionistic verbal imagery:

What do I see? The rivulet is all wet and the woods are inflammable like matches. But my heart is very small. The trees resemble crooked combs and the sun has attractively gilded rays. But my heart has a cold in its back. The moon has quarreled with her neighbors and the rivulet is wet to the bone.

(On 3 October 1915 Satie wrote an *Aubade, à Paul Dukas*, with some marginal notes such as *Do not sleep, Sleeping Beauty;* on 6 October 1915 he wrote *Méditation, à Albert Roussel*.)

1 SEPTEMBER 1915

Igor STRAVINSKY composes a militantly anti-German piano piece, *Souvenir d'une Marche Boche*, as a protest against the "unheard-of barbarism of the German hordes," for *The Book of the Homeless*, published in London in 1916 for the benefit of Belgian war orphans.

25 SEPTEMBER 1915

Fritz JÜRGENS, 27-year-old German composer of songs in a lyrico-dramatic Wagneromantic manner, is killed in action on the Champagne front.

26 SEPTEMBER 1915

Max von SCHILLINGS conducts in Stuttgart the first performance of his two-act opera *Mona Lisa*, composed in the Wagnerian system of contrapuntal leitmotifs, the most important of which is that of the mysterious smile of Madonna Lisa del Giocondo, which appears on her lips only as the altermath or the foretaste of a gratifying love experience, a phenomenon which enables her husband, del Giocondo, to trap one of her lovers in a casemate of his Florentine palazzo, where he himself becomes immured after La Gioconda tricks him into entering it, with an epilogue taking place four centuries later, in which a woman tourist stops at Leonardo da Vinci's famous portrait in the Louvre in Paris and pays a guide to say a prayer for the salvation of Mona Lisa's soul and then departs wearing a mysterious smile on her lips.

29 SEPTEMBER 1915

Rudi STEPHAN, 28-year-old German composer of neo-classical music, is killed on the Russian front, near Tarnopol.

5 OCTOBER 1915

José Mafía USANDIZAGA, Basque composer of sensitive vocal music redolent of Iberian melorhythms, dies in Yanti of tuberculosis at the age of 28.

10 OCTOBER 1915

Zvíkovský Rarášek (Der Burgkobold, or *The Imp of Zvíkov*), the first opera by Vítězslav NOVÁK, in one act, to a story about a poet who in 1585 attempted a disloyal seduction of the wife of his best friend in the town of Zvíkov, but was foiled in his hazardous undertaking by her precociously perspicacious son, is produced in Prague.

12 OCTOBER 1915

After the closure, due to the exigencies of war, of the Jaques-Dalcroze Institute for Eurhythmics in its original site of Hellerau, Germany, it transfers its activity to neutral Geneva.

24 OCTOBER 1915

Berceuse Héroïque for small orchestra, a musical tribute to King Albert of Belgium by Claude DEBUSSY, is performed for the first time in Paris.

26 OCTOBER 1915

August BUNGERT, German composer of a turgidly Wagnerolatrous teratological tetralogy based on the *Odyssey* and a similarly monstrous trilogy on the *Iliad*, dies disillusioned and unappreciated in Leutesdorf, at the age of seventy, the biblical span of life vouchsafed also to his idol Wagner.

28 OCTOBER 1915

Richard STRAUSS conducts the Berlin Philharmonic Orchestra in the first performance of his *Alpensinfonie*, "a hundred days' symphony," for it had taken Strauss exactly that time to complete this Baedeker in tones (the date at the end of the score is 9 February 1915), the most literal piece of program music in orchestral literature, embanked within one continuous movement and subdivided into the following illustrative episodes:

(1) *Night,* a peaceful descent along the B-flat minor scale over the entire bassoon range, while the strings slide slowly in pandiatonic tone-clusters; (2) *Sunrise,* in crimson-faced brass sonorities rooted in a deep pedal point on A; (3) *Ascent,* a glorified fanfare in the foothills sounded in the natural harmonics of E-flat major; (4) *Entrance in the Forest,* in romantically sylvan C minor; (5) *Wandering by the Brook,* in a shimmering display of colors in A-flat major; (6) *At the Waterfall,* with a flourish of trumpets in oxygenated D major; (7) *Apparition,* a sudden lapse into a dramatic series of diminished seventh-chords, with the violins in a state of commotion resorting to glissando; (8) *On Blossoming Meadows,* with snow-white edelweiss springing up staccato in the wood-wind section; (9) *On Mountain Pastures,* wherein the postillion horns announce a halt in E-flat major; (10) *Through Thicket and Underbrush, on the Wrong Way,* with angular melodic intervals in heterotonally baleful harmonies; (11) *On the Glacier*

in cycloramically sunlit D minor; (12) *Perilous Moments*, with chromatic avalanches leaving behind them a conglomerate of fused semitones; (13) *On the Summit*, set in pastoral F major leading in plagal triumph to the apotheosis in the heretofore unapproached, sublimely Alpine and virginally immaculate, sharpless and flatless C major; (14) *Vision*, with illusionistic trills and harmoniously arpeggiated harps; (15) *Rising Mists*, an inchoate agitation of darksomely low tones in the primordial key of B-flat minor; (16) *Gradual Darkening of the Sun*, in premonitory tritones against a rumblingly muted instrumental ground; (17) *Elegy*, in the romantic key of F-sharp minor; (18) *Stillness Before the Storm*, recalling the thematically descending B-flat minor scale with foreboding large drops of pizzicato strings and cohesive pandiatonic clusters forming in the increasingly sharp wind section; (19) *Thunderstorm and Descent*, wherein a novel wind machine and a roaring thunder machine are introduced for naturalistic effect, with flutes flutter-tonguing in cascades rushing towards the home key of B-flat minor but resolving deceptively into the opaque submediant G-flat major; (20) *Sunset*, with scattered thematic fragments clashing in a clatter of dissonant counterpoint; (21) *Ausklang*, sounding out in unadulterated E-flat major; (22) *Night*, descending along the path of the parent B-flat minor scale forming opulent pandiatonic clusters consolidated in the final seven-note chord.

A work like the Alpine Symphony could be created only in a German land. Its place in history will be for posterity to evaluate. For us it is at present the first and the only towering musical monument from the great era in which we live. (Leopold Schmidt, *Berliner Tageblatt*, 29 October 1915)

5 NOVEMBER 1915

The Sociedad Nacional de Música is inaugurated in Buenos Aires with a concert of chamber music by composers of Argentina.

10 NOVEMBER 1915

Marguerite LONG gives at the Société Nationale de Musique in Paris the first performance of DEBUSSY's piano études, among them *Les Arpèges composées*, *Pour les Sonorités opposées* and *Pour les cinq doigts*, ranging in technical application from five-finger exercises, "according to Monsieur Czerny" (in which the left hand mischievously crosses over into the treble to place a discordant A-flat amid the snow-white landscape of C major), to prestidigital double-thirds, double-fourths, double-sixths, chromatics, rapidly repeated notes, altered arpeggios, and antiphonally distributed massive harmonic aggregations.

13 NOVEMBER 1915

Die Czardasfürstin, operetta by Emmerich KÁLMÁN dealing with a dancing chanteuse who marries a prince and is nicknamed the *Czardas Princess*, is produced in Vienna.

13 NOVEMBER 1915

Heitor VILLA-LOBOS, 28-year-old Brazilian composer, presents in Rio de Janeiro the first concert of his instrumental and vocal pieces, including a piano trio, a cello sonata and several songs.

13 NOVEMBER 1915

Leo FEIST, commercial American music publisher, still making money from the sales of the anti-war song *I Didn't Raise My Boy to Be a Soldier*, copyrights the patriotic song *Don't Bite the Hand That's Feeding You*, with words by Thomas Hoier and music by Jimmie Morgan, counseling foreign-born residents of the United States that "if you don't like your Uncle Sammy, then go back to your home o'er the sea" and, by implication, advising them to cease their pacifist agitation.

14 NOVEMBER 1915

Theodor LESCHETIZKY, Polish-born great man of piano pedagogy, originator of the *Kugelhand* (arched hand) method of piano playing, pupil of Czerny, and through him a grand-pupil of Beethoven (with whom Czerny studied), teacher of Paderewski and of a multitude of other celebrities of the piano, composer of virtuosistic piano studies, and successive husband of four of his female pupils, dies in Dresden at the age of 85.

20 NOVEMBER 1915

In conformity with the decree of the Imperial Government of Russia banning performances of works by German and Austrian composers during the war, Alexander SILOTI is compelled to replace works of Bach, technically an enemy alien, he was to conduct in Petrograd by a program of orchestral music by Russian composers. (On a later date Siloti was forced to cancel a performance of Beethoven's *Seventh Symphony*.)

21 NOVEMBER 1915

Piano Concerto by Vítězslav NOVÁK, in one movement subdivided into three sections (fast, slow, fast), richly arpeggiated and solemnly cadenced in a characteristic virtuoso manner of central European music, is performed for the first time in Prague.

26 NOVEMBER 1915

Kudeyar, ballad opera in five acts by the Russian composer Alexander OLENIN, to his own libretto dealing with an imaginative and attractive bandit who flourished in 17th-century Russia, conquered feminine hearts and befriended ambitious youths, to a musical score flowingly rolling with Russian folksong material, is produced in Moscow.

30 NOVEMBER 1915

Die Geschwister, opera by Ludwig ROTTENBERG, father-in-law of Paul Hindemith, is produced in Frankfurt.

1 DECEMBER 1915

The American inventor Lee DE FOREST publishes an article entitled *Audion Bulbs as Producers of Pure Musical Tones* in *The Electrical Experimenter*, in which he refers for the first time to music produced by vacuum tubes:

In my laboratory there are a number of small spherical incandescent bulbs, from which I am able to obtain a succession of musical notes, clear and sweet, of surprising volume, the pitch and timbre of which can be varied almost at will to imitate any musical tone of an orchestra. Here, then, in the laboratory we have for the first time the Music of the Lamps.

(The term Electronic Music was used for the first time in print in an article by Hugo Gernsback in *Radio-Craft*, March 1933.)

2 DECEMBER 1915

Katinka (Russian diminutive of Catherine), musical comedy by Rudolf FRIML, to a story dealing with a pompous Tsarist ambassador who loses his flighty fiancée to a younger Russian, is produced in Morristown, New Jersey. (The New York performance followed on 23 December 1915.)

8 DECEMBER 1915

On his fiftieth birthday, the great Finnish composer Jean SIBELIUS conducts in Helsingfors a concert of his orchestral music, including two *Serenades*, the symphonic poem *Oceanides*, and the first performance of his *Fifth Symphony* in E-flat major, marked by the cumulative thematic grandeur of its form and granitic poetry of his national sentiment, in three movements:

(1) *Tempo molto moderato; Allegro moderato*, beginning with a four-note phrase as a formative nucleus amid a variety of scattered themes, cast in somber hues and favoring the low registers of the instrumental range; (2) *Andante mosso, quasi Allegretto*, a scherzo evolving from the first movement by thematic links, with the profusion of fluvial flutes and clarion clarinets in aquamarine harmonies; (3) *Allegro molto; un pochettino largamente*, building up tension through persuasive iteration of a sharply contoured melody appearing in multiple instrumental guises, until the cumulative thematic drive attains a critical saturation, leading to a series of spasmodic chords in the simplest terms of the dominant and the tonic, and concluding in a blaze of tonal brass. (The Symphony was revised considerably, and the new version was conducted by Sibelius for the first time in Helsingfors on 14 December 1916.)

11 DECEMBER 1915

Willem PIJPER, 21-year-old Dutch composer of impressionistic proclivities, plays the solo part in the first performance, in Utrecht, of his *Piano Concerto* in one movement.

25 DECEMBER 1915

Les Cadeaux de Noël, opera in one act by the 52-year-old French composer Xavier LEROUX, described as a "heroic tale" and dedicated to his son, a French army soldier, is performed, fittingly so, on Christmas Day at the Opéra-Comique in Paris.

28 DECEMBER 1915

Bethlehem, choral drama by Rutland BOUGHTON based on the Coventry Nativity Play, is produced at an annual Christmas Festival he inaugurated in the town of Glastonbury in Southwest England in the forlorn hope of establishing there a Bayreuth-like Wagnerian site for his grandiose music dramas.

28 DECEMBER 1915

Everyman, an ancient morality play set to a blandly homophonic score by the British singer Liza LEHMANN, in which a pious Everyman is advised by a bevy of personified abstractions such as Good Deeds, Knowledge, Discretion, Strength, and Riches to reconcile himself to Death, and is ultimately led by a chorus of his sinless cousins to a sanctified grave, is produced in London.

31 DECEMBER 1915

Impressions from an Artist's Life in Form of Variations on an Original Theme for piano and orchestra by Ernest SCHELLING, with 21 variations marked by initials of his famous friends, Karl Muck, Hans Pfitzner, Paderewski, Mahler, Kreisler, Anna Pavlova, Mengelberg, and others, is performed for the first time by the Boston Symphony Orchestra, Karl Muck conducting, with Schelling playing the piano part.

1916

11 JANUARY 1916

On his 60th birthday, Christian SINDING is awarded by the Norwegian government a purse of 30,000 crowns in appreciation of his services to Norwegian music as "the greatest national composer since Grieg."

14 JANUARY 1916

Der Sterngucker (The Star Gazer), operetta by Franz LEHÁR, is produced in Vienna.

14 JANUARY 1916

Le Poilu, a military operetta in two acts by Maurice JACQUET, glorifying the courage of the French *poilu* (the "hairy one," in the affectionate argot of World War I for French soldiers), is produced in Paris.

14 JANUARY 1916

The Critic, or an Opera Rehearsed, a comic opera in two acts by Charles Villiers STANFORD, after Sheridan's play (but Sheridan's subtitle was "a tragedy rehearsed"), wherein the author Puff and critic Sneer engage in a deep philosophical discourse on the meaning of art, with a Spanish soldier Don Whiskerandos providing exotic color, is produced in London, conducted by Eugene Goossens (who is himself included in the cast of characters, pretending that something has gone wrong with the music.)

15 JANUARY 1916

Das Dreimäderlhaus (The House of Three Maidens), operetta by the Hungarian composer Heinrich BERTÉ, a pasticcio of Schubert's melodies to a romanticized tale of his emotional frustrations in a Vienna cottage inhabited by three coquettish girls named Hederl, Haiderl and Hannerl, none of whom would yield to Schubert's amorous importunities (he sings tenor), is performed for the first time in Vienna, becoming Berté's most popular stage work, destined to achieve fame in England and America under the title *Lilac Time* (first produced in that particular version in London on 22 December 1922).

15 JANUARY 1916

Modest TCHAIKOVSKY, loyal biographer of his famous brother, the librettist of *The Queen of Spades* and a competent dramatist in his own right, dies in Moscow at the age of 65.

15 JANUARY 1916

The Lover's Knot, opera with action taking place in post-bellum Norfolk, Virginia, by the Russian-born American composer Simon BUCHAROFF, is produced by the Chicago Opera.

17 JANUARY 1916

Ferruccio BUSONI appears as soloist in Zürich in the performance of his *Indianische Fantasie* for piano and orchestra, written in an expansively rhapsodic vein with extensive cadenzas covering the entire range of the piano keyboard, and making use of authentically pentatonic American Indian melodies in opulently harmonic dressing.

17 JANUARY 1916

Hebridean Symphony by Granville BANTOCK (completed on 23 November 1915) in four linked movements, depicting in stark pentatonic melodies embanked within chromaticized Wagneromimic harmonies the romantically bleak landscape of the islands off the coast of western Scotland, with a rare sunny day portrayed by 40 bars of cloudless C major, is performed for the first time in Glasgow.

19 JANUARY 1916

At a meeting of the Russian cult of Abstainers in Vyritza, near Petrograd, twenty phonographs and several recordings of Bach and Beethoven are solemnly burned in a bonfire as products of "German abomination." (Date and circumstances found in the weekly *Russian Musical Gazette*, St. Petersburg, No. 3, 1916, p. 78.)

20 JANUARY 1916

Le Tambour, a brief lyric poem by Alfred BRUNEAU, nostalgically depicting in ballad-like tones the outbreak of war and the conscription of sons and husbands into the French army, with the military drum beating ominously repetitious rhythms, is produced at the Opéra-Comique in Paris.

22 JANUARY 1916

Iwan KNORR, Prussian-born composer who spent many years in Russia and absorbed some Slavic inflections in his melodic writing, champion of invertible counterpoint, assiduous scholar and teacher of a generation of composers, dies in Frankfurt, at the age of 63.

28 JANUARY 1916

Goyescas, one-act opera by Enrique GRANADOS, to a libretto inspired by scenes from Goya's paintings wherein a young captain of the Royal Guards of the Spanish Court is killed by a bull fighter over the affections of an aristocratically desirable young lady, the music derived from Granados's suite of piano pieces *Goyescas* and containing the popular aria *La Maja y el Ruiseñor (The Lady and the Nightingale),* is produced for the first time anywhere by the Metropolitan Opera in New York.

Goyescas Seen for First Time—Standing Room at Premium—If Applause Counts for Aught, Latest Production Will Be Palpable Hit (Headlines in the New York *Times*)

Opera in Spanish First Sung Fails to Impress—*Goyescas* a Series of Tapestry Pictures Lacking in True Character and Without Real Consistency (Headlines in the New York *World*)

28 JANUARY 1916

The Boatswain's Mate, two-act opera by England's most prominent woman composer, Ethel SMYTH, to her own libretto dealing with an ex-boatswain who asks a friend to fake a burglary of a pub owned by a comely widow, intending to pose as her rescuer and thus impress her into marrying him, the plot miscarrying when she surprises the pretended burglar and decides to marry him instead, is performed for the first time in London.

29 JANUARY 1916

Sergei PROKOFIEV conducts in Petrograd the first performance of his *Scythian Suite,* subtitled *Ala and Lolli,* originally intended for a ballet wherein an ancient Slav warrior saves the sun-god Ala from the spirit of darkness, in four movements depicting Scythian sun-worshipping rites (in primitivistic rhythmic iteration), the dance of evil spirits (in bleak quartal harmonies), a nocturnal scene (in sonorous pandiatonic complexes) and the sunrise (in magnificently swelling brass sonorities in solar B-flat major), and his Conservatory teacher Nicolas TCHEREPNIN leads the orchestra in the première of his own choreographic poem *The Masque of the Red Death,* after the horror story of Edgar Allan Poe (the ominous pendulum swings at the regular human pulse rate, while the chimes are illustrated by an eerie ensemble of gusli, mandolines and zithers).

It is probable that our remote ancestors would have accepted Prokofiev's *Scythian Suite* as their very own for the music is really wild . . . It produces some kind of aggressive, crude sound which expresses nothing but infinite braggadoccio. (*Petrograd Listok,* 30 January 1916)

1 FEBRUARY 1916

Carl NIELSEN conducts in Copenhagen the first performance of his *Fourth Symphony,* completed on 14 January 1916, subtitled *The Inextinguishable,* in four linked movements (*Allegro, Poco allegretto, Poco adagio* and *Allegro*), the title being a subjective expression of the inextinguishability of life in its evolutionary process, the struggle for survival reflected in fluctuating tonalities, with portentous beats of the kettledrums significantly tuned at the interval of the tritone, the medieval "diabolus in musica."

4 FEBRUARY 1916

The Paris periodical *La Renaissance* publishes a symposium of opinions by musicians and artists on the question whether the music by Richard WAGNER should be performed in France after the war, with five in favor and 16 against Wagner, including the sculptor Rodin, who wrote, "Wagner a été trop mêlé à nos affaires."

8 FEBRUARY 1916

Tristan TZARA invents the word DADA expressive of utter mental nihilism in the domains of art, literature and music.

Dada is something newer, different, a bewilderment that affected the art world of Europe for a few shell-shocked years during and immediately after the War. The object of Dadaism was a conscious attack on reason, a complete negation of everything, the loudest and silliest expression of post-War cynicism. "I affirm," wrote early Dadaist Hans Arp, "that Tristan Tzara discovered the word Dada on the 8th of February, 1916, at 6 o'clock in the evening in the Terrace Café in Zürich. I was there with my twelve children when Tzara pronounced for the first time this word, which aroused a legitimate enthusiasm in all of us." Later, Dadaist Richard Hülsenbeck claimed: "It was I who pronounced the word Dada (hobby-horse) for the first time." In moments of Harmony and Logic which they affected to despise, Dadaists admitted that their object was "to spit in the eye of the world." (*Time*, 14 December 1936)

10 FEBRUARY 1916

First Symphony by the Finnish composer Leevi MADETOJA, written in an intelligent Sibelian manner, is performed for the first time in Helsingfors.

11 FEBRUARY 1916

The Baltimore Symphony Orchestra gives its inaugural concert in Baltimore, under the direction of its permanent conductor, the German musician Gustav STRUBE.

18 FEBRUARY 1916

First Symphony in C minor by the American composer Daniel Gregory MASON, in three cyclic movements "conceived dramatically in the interplay of musical ideas and emotions," stating its three principal themes in the slow introduction, and distinguished by a stolid solidity of Brahmsogenic polyphony with frequent outbursts of Wagneromorphic fanfares, is performed for the first time by the Philadelphia Orchestra. (The Symphony was subsequently revised, and first performed in its new version in New York on 1 December 1922.)

23 FEBRUARY 1916

Dame Kobold, opera in three acts by Felix WEINGARTNER, to his own libretto after Calderón, is produced in Darmstadt.

24 FEBRUARY 1916

L'Ultimo dei Mohicani, grand opera in five acts by the Bostonian composer Paul ALLEN, written in an eloquent Italianate style with an admixture of Indian pentatonic elements to characterize the action of the libretto after James Fenimore Cooper's famous novel, is produced in Florence.

26 FEBRUARY 1916

The word DADA, eloquently meaningless slogan of the anti-esthetical nihilistic movement arising from cumulative frustrations of the immobile trench war and stagnation in belles-lettres, beaux-arts and music, appears for the first time in print in a poster exhibited at the Cabaret Voltaire in Zürich, the cradle of Dadaism.

Grande soirée—Poème simultané 3 langues protestations bruit musique nègre Hoosenlatz Hoosenlatz piano Tipperary Lanterna magica démonstration proclamation dernière!! Invention dialogue!! DADA!! Dernière nouveauté!!! Syncope bourgeoise, musique BRUITISTE, dernier cri, chanson Tzara, danse, protestations—la grosse caisse—lumière rouge, policemen—chansons tableaux cubistes, cartes postales, chanson Cabaret Voltaire—poème simultané breveté Tzara Hoosenlatz et van Hoddis Hülsenbeck Hoosenlatz tourbillon Arp-two-step réclame alcool fument vers les cloches—on chuchote! arrogance—silence Mme Hennings, Janco déclaration, l'art transatlantique—peuple se réjouit, étoile projetée sur la danse cubiste en grelots.— Collaborateurs: Apollinaire, Picasso, Modigliani, Arp, Tzara, van Hoddis, Hülsenbeck, Kandinsky, Marinetti, Cangiulio, Van Rees, Slodky, Ball, Hennings, Janco, Cendrars, etc. Dialogue DaDaDa dada dadadadadada—la vie nouvelle—contient un poème simultané—la critique carnivore nous plaça platoniquement dans la maison des vertiges de génies trop mûrs, Évite l'appendicite éponge l'intestin. J'ai constaté que les attaques venaient de moins en moins et qui veut rester jeune évite les rhumatismes (From *Dada Almanach*, Berlin, 1920)

5 MARCH 1916

Die toten Augen (Sightless Eyes), opera in one act with a prologue by the self-Germanized Scottish-born composer Eugen D'ALBERT, his most successful production (composition completed on 20 August 1913), wherein a blind woman of Corinth is cured by Jesus on Palm Sunday A.D. 29, through a persistent application of curative C major, and when her sightless eyes are opened, impulsively embraces a handsome Roman centurion mistaking him for her malformed husband, whereupon the latter kills the former in blind rage and the woman commits oculocide by deliberately staring at the incandescent sun to make the outside world black again, set to music in an eloquent Wagneromantic style, seasoned by modernistic whole-tone progressions, impressionistic triadic parallelisms and occasionally unresolved prudential discords, is performed for the first time in Dresden.

10 MARCH 1916

Concertino for piano and orchestra by John Alden CARPENTER, designed as a "light-hearted conversation between piano and orchestra as between two friends," is performed for the first time by Percy Grainger with the Chicago Symphony Orchestra.

13 MARCH 1916

Frank BRIDGE conducts in London the first performance of his tone-poem *Summer.*

24 MARCH 1916

Enrique GRANADOS perishes with his wife at sea as the S.S. *Sussex* is sunk by a German submarine between Folkestone and Dieppe, at three o'clock in the afternoon.

Abandon Hope for *Goyescas* Composer—Sr. and Sra. Granados Lost in Sussex Disaster, Friends fear—No Trace of Either—When Last Seen Sr. and Sra. Granados Were Clinging to a Small Raft Which, It Is Thought, Was Unable to Weather the Heavy Sea or the Couple Was Washed Overboard to Drown (Headlines in the London *Morning Telegraph,* 28 March 1916)

24 MARCH 1916

Protomastoras (Master-Builder), musical drama in two acts by Manolis KALOMIRIS, first opera by a Greek composer on a Hellenic subject, dealing with an architect who relinquishes the love of a young bride to devote his life to the building of a Bridge of Arts, is produced in Athens.

28 MARCH 1916

Two one-act operas by the 18-year-old Vienna *wunderkind* Erich Wolfgang KORNGOLD are produced in a single evening in Munich:

(1) *Violanta,* wherein a young Venetian matron intent on avenging the violation of her sister's chastity, arranges a clandestine assignation with its perpetrator and asks her husband to come, too, and slay him with impunity vouchsafed by the Venetian adultery law, but is overcome at the critical moment by an overwhelming sexual desire for the seducer and throws herself between him and her husband, receiving a mortal dagger blow, set to music replete with vibrant dissonances and suspended melodic resolutions; (2) *Der Ring des Polykrates,* inspired by Schiller's ballad about the tyrant of Samos whose ill-starred ring which he throws into the ocean returns to him inside a fish he caught, with the action transferred to Saxony in 1797 and centered on a married kapellmeister, his drummer and an attractive maidservant embroiled in an imbroglio of triangular emotions, with a musical setting of the type of neo-Mozartean rococo.

1 APRIL 1916

Die drei Schneider von Schönau (Three Tailors of Schönau), comic opera in three acts by the 47-year-old Dutch composer Jan BRANDTS-BUYS, is produced in Dresden.

2 APRIL 1916

Die schöne Bellinda, romantic opera in three acts by the Swiss composer Hans HUBER, is performed for the first time in Bern.

9 APRIL 1916

Noches en los jardines de España, symphonic suite for piano and orchestra by Manuel DE FALLA, in three sections—(1) *En el Generalife,* unveiling in atmospheric harmonies the panorama of the hillside gardens in Generalife near the Alhambra in Granada, with Andalusian melorhythms palpitating in brief motivic themes and pyrotechnically exploding in piano cadenzas; (2) *Danza lejana,* with a serpentine Moorish dance tune sounded at a distance; (3)

En los jardines de la Sierra de Córdoba, an enfilade of Andalusian cantillation abutting in Phrygian cadences on the major dominant—is performed for the first time by the Orquesta Filarmónica of Madrid, Enrique Fernández Arbos conducting, José Cubiles pianist.

11 APRIL 1916

Alberto GINASTERA, Argentinian composer of operas, ballets, symphonic and vocal music in a hypermodern style, employing serial techniques and nostalgic melorhythms nurtured on native ethnic resources, is born in Buenos Aires.

27 APRIL 1916

Goffredo Mameli, one-act opera by Ruggero LEONCAVALLO, is produced in Genoa.

27 APRIL 1916

Suite Brève for orchestra by the 39-year-old French composer Louis AUBERT, in three movements, *Menuet, Berceuse* and *Air de Ballet,* is performed for the first time in Paris.

11 MAY 1916

Max REGER, formidably industrious and prolific German composer and master organist whose extraordinary polyphonic prowess caused his teacher Hugo Riemann to earnestly opine that Reger was the Bach of the 20th century and whose palindromic name suggested an invertible versatility, but whose aridity of imagination and infertility of invention made his massive music lifeless, is found dead at the age of 43, in a hotel room in Leipzig, with his spectacles still in position and an evening newspaper of the day before in his rigid hands.

(Reger went to his hotel in Leipzig, where he was on a visit, at 10:30 P.M. on the night of 10 May 1916, after complaining to friends of an indisposition, and must have died of a sudden heart failure, during the night, i.e., on 11 May 1916.)

23 MAY 1916

Learned HAND, United States District Judge in New York City, rules in favor of the plaintiff Harry Haas who claimed that the tune of the popular song *I Didn't Raise My Boy to Be a Soldier* was plagiarized by its supposed composer Al Piantadosi from a previously published song by Haas, *You Will Never Know How Much I Really Cared.*

The defendant Feist has a large publishing house in the city of New York, and employed the defendant Piantadosi as a casual composer of melodies, though he has small knowledge of musical notation and small skill in playing. His custom was, when he composed a song, to play it over to some other employee of Feist, who took down the simple theme upon a "lead sheet" as it is called, and afterwards worked it up into so much musical form as was necessary. Piantadosi's piracy of the chorus seems to me sufficiently established . . . .. I am aware that in such simple and trivial themes as these it is dangerous to go too far upon suggestions of similarity. For example, nearly the whole of the leading theme of Piantadosi's song is repeated literally from a chorus of *Pinafore,* though there is not the slightest reason to suppose that the plaintiff ever heard of the opera . . . .. It is said that such similarities are of constant occurrence in music and that little inference is permissible. . ... Nevertheless, between (the) two choruses in question (by Piantadosi and by Haas), there is a parallelism which seems to my ear to pass the bounds of mere accident.

(However, Judge Learned Hand, upon a re-hearing on 8 June 1916, ruled for the defendant on a technicality, since the plaintiff's publishing firm was not properly incorporated and hence not legally entitled to seek damages.)

28 MAY 1916

Albert LAVIGNAC, French musical encyclopedist and popularizer, editor of the voluminous *Encyclopédie de la musique et Dictionnaire du Conservatoire,* which started publication on 30 May 1913, dies in his native Paris at the age of 70.

7 JUNE 1916

In a letter to the Ligne Nationale pour la Défense de la Musique Française, Maurice RAVEL, employed by the French Army as a military camion driver, voices his repugnance towards the current campaign in France against performances of contemporary German and Austrian music.

I do not believe that it is necessary to ban public performances in France of works by contemporary German and Austrian composers in order to protect the French artistic commonwealth. It would be dangerous for French composers to ignore systematically the production of their foreign colleagues and to create a national coterie of the arts. Our music, so rich now, would then degenerate into stereotyped formulas. It matters little to me that Schoenberg is an Austrian. He is a musician of high merit whose interesting experiments exercise a healthy influence on composers of the allied nations, and on us. I am glad that Bartók, Kodály and their followers are Hungarian nationalists, and that they show this adherence with such excellent taste in their music. (From Ravel's letter quoted in *La Revue Musicale,* Paris, December 1938)

8 JUNE 1916

At the Litchfield County Choral Union Festival in Norfolk, Connecticut, Percy GRAINGER plays the piano part in the world première of his suite *In a Nutshell* scored for orchestra, wood and steel marimbas and a synthetic Nabimba (a marimba with an admixture of clarinet timbre), in four movements: (1) *Arrival Platform Humlet* (inspired by Grainger's travel between the Liverpool Street and Victoria stations of the London railway system on 2 February 1908 and his humming a "humlet"); (2) *Gay but Wistful,* inspired by contradictory moods induced by riding a train in America; (3) *Pastoral;* (4) *The Gum Suckers' March* (gum suckers being Australian slang for natives of Victoria, Grainger's home state).

7 JULY 1916

Jules COMBARIEU, eminent French music historian, dies in Paris at the age of 57.

14 JULY 1916

The Dadaists present in Zürich their first public show.

Pour la première fois dans tout le monde DADA-SOIRÉE (Musique, Danses, Théories, Manifeste, Poèmes, Tableaux, Costumes, Masques)

Devant une foule compacte Tzara manifeste, nous voulons nous voulons nous voulons pisser en couleurs diverses, Hülsenbeck manifeste, Ball manifeste, Arp Erklärung, Janco meine Bilder, Heusser eigene Kompositionen—Les chiens hurlent et la dissection du Panama sur piano et embarcadère—Poème crié—on crie dans la salle, on se bat, premier rang approuve, deuxième rang se déclare incompétant, le reste crie, qui est plus fort, on apporte la grosse caisse, Hülsenbeck contre 200, Hoosenlatz accentué par la très grosse caisse et les grelots au pied gauche—on proteste, on crie, on casse les vitres, on se tue, on démolit, on se bat, la police interruption.

Reprise du boxe: Danse cubiste, costumes de Janco, chacun sa grosse caisse sur la tête, bruits, musique nègre— trabatgea bonooooooo oooooo—5 expériences littéraires: Tzara en frac explique devant le rideau, sec sobre pour les animaux, la nouvelle esthétique: poème gymnastique, concert de voyelles, pòme bruitiste, poème statique, arrangement chimique des notions, Biribum Biribum saust der Ochs im Kreis herum (Hülsenbeck), poème de voyelles a a o, i e o, a i i, nouvelle interprétation, la folie subjective des artères, la danse du cœur sur les incendies et l'acrobatic des spectateurs. De nouveau cris, la grosse caisse, piano et canons impuissants, on se déchire les costumes de carton, le public se jette dans la fièvre puerpérale interomprrrre. Les journaux, mécontents, poème simultané à 300 idiotisés définitivs (From multilingual and heterotypographical *Dada Almanach,* Berlin, 1920)

15 JULY 1916

Gott strafe England, German hymn of hate for England, is published in Leipzig.

22 JULY 1916

Huémac, one-act opera to the story of the Toltecs of ancient Mexico by the Italian-born naturalized Argentinian composer Pascual DE ROGATIS, is produced at the Teatro Colón in Buenos Aires.

27 JULY 1916

Karl KLINDWORTH, German pianist, conductor, pedagogue, erudite musical scholar, renowned editor of piano literature, arranger of Wagner's *Ring des Niebelungen* in piano score, dies at Stolpe at the age of 85.

5 AUGUST 1916

George BUTTERWORTH, 31-year-old English composer of evocative instrumental pieces imbued with the melorhythms of the English countryside, is killed in action near Pozières on the Somme, after successfully capturing a German trench.

21 AUGUST 1916

The Happy Ending, a play with music by Eugene HAILE, wherein a girl summons at a spiritual séance the ghost of her aviator lover fallen in aerial combat and is told that he did not suffer when he was shot down because "life was instantaneous," a "spoken opera" in which words are accompanied by the orchestra, with the melodic line calculated to follow the rhythmic verbal inflections, is produced in New York City.

31 AUGUST 1916

Arturo TOSCANINI conducts a military band on the hilltop of Monte Santo after its capture by Italian soldiers, and is subsequently awarded a medal of valor for courage under fire.

2 SEPTEMBER 1916

Prestami tua moglie, operetta by Ruggero LEONCAVALLO, is produced in Montecatini.

9 OCTOBER 1916

Incensed by his anti-German feelings, Pierre MONTEUX refuses to conduct *Till Eulenspiegel* by Richard Strauss at the Ballet Russe presentation at the Manhattan Opera House in New York, and the German conductor Anselm Goetz takes his place at the podium. (Monteux conducted the rest of the program consisting of works by Russian composers.)

10 OCTOBER 1916

K-K-K-Ka—ty, Beautiful Katy, stuttering and stammering ballad by Geoffrey O'Hara, inspired by a lady named Katy Richardson, is copyrighted in Washington. (A pedicular parody on this song, dedicated to the typhoid carrier, *C-C-C-Coo—tie, Horrible Cootie, you're the only B-B-B—Bug that I Abhor,* dedicated to the typhoid carrying *parasita vestimenti,* became popular in the American Expeditionary. Force in 1918.)

17 OCTOBER 1916

Violin Concerto by Ernest SCHELLING, in one movement subdivided into several autonomous sections, interludes and variations (some of them borrowed and rearranged from his own *Impressions from an Artist's Life* for piano and orchestra), traversing through classical, romantic, Scottish and Spanish moods, with an occasional application of asymmetric meters, and fertilized by non-toxic dissonances, is performed for the first time at a concert by the Boston Symphony Orchestra in Providence, Rhode Island, with Fritz Kreisler (to whom the Concerto is dedicated) as soloist.

27 OCTOBER 1916

The earliest mention in print of jazz bands (spelled jass band) is made in *Variety.*

Chicago has added another innovation to its list of discoveries in the so-called *Jass Bands.* The *Jass Band* is composed of three or more instruments and seldom plays regulated music. The College Inn and practically all the other high-class places of entertainment have a *Jass Band* featured, while the low cost makes it possible for all the smaller places to carry their *Jass* orchestra. (*Variety,* 27 October 1916, p. 18)

Re the Original Dixieland Jazz Band. This band was organized in New Orleans about the year 1912 and played under the name Dixieland Band and the word Jazz was not added until after we played in Chicago in 1914 for Harry James at the Booster Club. He billed us as The Original Dixieland Jazz Band coming to Reisenweber's in New York City in 1916 to 1918 . . . Re any information you wish I am the man that can give you same, being the leader and manager for this band till we disbanded in 1927 in New York City. (From a letter from D. Jas. La Rocca dated 6 April 1936)

The Original Dixieland Jazz Band was the first band in the world to be called a Jazz Band. Our first billing was in the year of 1914, month of March, place Booster Club, Chicago, Illinois, Manager Harry James. It occurred one night while we played for dancers, one frenzied couple kept yelling for more jazz. Mr. James, hearing them call out "play some more jazz" or "jazz it up!" gave him the idea to bill us as such a band . . . The word Jazz is of northern origin. We never before had heard this word Jazz down south. It was used in the theatrical profession, meaning various things, one meaning to pep or excite one . . . The word was not known widely until the release of our Victor Records around the latter part of 1916 or first part of 1917. Our records sold in the millions. (From a subsequent letter from La Rocca dated 19 April 1936)

(Inquiries from the Victor Company established that the first jazz record was issued in March 1917. The Columbia Phonograph Company issued their first jazz record at a later date. The following letter from Mr. A. W. Toos, of the Columbia Phonograph company, written in reply to the author's inquiries, and dated 11 March 1937, stated in part: "In the Columbia record catalog issued October 1st, 1918, the following record is listed, and it was not included in the previously issued catalog dated January 1st, 1918, and accordingly, was released during that interval. Columbia 10-inch Record A-2297 *Darktown Strutters Ball* (Brooks)—Fox Trot, coupled with *Indiana* (Hanley)—One-Step, played by the Original Dixieland Jass Band. . .. In the October 1st, 1919, Columbia catalog, that is the next following complete catalog, the spelling of the artist for Record A-2297 is changed to Original Dixieland Jazz Band. In that 1918 catalog and in many other places we have many uses of the word Jazz but never any other of Jass. . .. I have carefully examined our record catalogs for 1914, 1915, 1916 and 1917, but find no use of the word Jass or Jazz before the entry of Record A-2297, evidently released by us about the middle of 1918.")

29 OCTOBER 1916

Two Indian Dances for orchestra by Charles Sanford SKILTON, based on American Indian melodies, and comprising Part I of his *Suite Primeval* (Part II was first performed in Minneapolis on 13 November 1921), is performed for the first time in Minneapolis.

30 OCTOBER 1916

Silas Gamaliel PRATT, eccentric American composer who in his heyday produced a series of patriotic musical spectacles, but who is chiefly remembered by his probably apocryphal remark to Richard Wagner, "Herr Wagner, you are the Silas G. Pratt of Germany," dies in Pittsburgh at the age of 70.

11 NOVEMBER 1916

LILIUOKALANI, Queen of the Sandwich Islands, author of the Hawaiian national anthem *Aloha Oe,* who claimed English blood "because my grandfather ate Captain Cook," dies in Honolulu, her quondam capital, at the age of 78. (She was born on 2 September 1838.)

13 NOVEMBER 1916

Frederick Septimus KELLY, Australian composer of versatile gifts, a popular athlete and a prize-winning oarsman, is killed in action at Beaucourt, on the Ancre, France, at the age of 35.

18 NOVEMBER 1916

Karlštejn, comic opera in three acts by the Czech composer Vítězslav NOVAK, to a libretto about Emperor Carl IV who forbade women to enter his castle only to be outwitted by his Queen who gains entrance in a man's attire to make sure that she is the only one whom he really loves, is performed for the first time in Prague.

18 NOVEMBER 1916

Arcady DUBENSKY, 26-year-old Russian composer, conducts in Moscow the first performance of his one-act opera *A Romance with a Contrabass*, after Chekhov's story wherein a Russian girl takes a swim in the nude, cannot find her clothes when she emerges from the water, and takes shelter in a string-bass case which is picked up by her fiancé, a clarinet player, with ensuing imbroglios reflected in a duet of clarinet and string bass in the orchestra.

19 NOVEMBER 1916

During the playing of *Siegfried's Funeral Music* from *Götterdämmerung* in Rome under Toscanini's direction, an Italian soldier shouts from the balcony: "In memory of our battalions!" an incident that leads to the prohibition of performance of German music in Italy for the duration of the war. (Information and date obtained from Alfredo Casella.)

21 NOVEMBER 1916

Ole from Nordland, opera in four acts by the Russian composer Mikhail IPPOLITOV-IVANOV, to a story about a young Norwegian fisherman whose unsuccessful love rival kills him on the eve of his wedding, is produced in Moscow.

23 NOVEMBER 1916

Eduard NAPRAVNIK, Russianized Czech composer of operas in a lyrically Tchaikovskian vein, and from 1869 chief conductor of the Imperial Opera Theater in St. Petersburg, where he acquired fame as a fanatical disciplinarian intolerant of the slightest deviation from fidelity of pitch and rhythm (in *The Brothers Karamazov* Dostoevsky uses his name, which in Slavic languages suggests directive authority, as a synonym for instructor), dies in St. Petersburg at the age of 77.

24 NOVEMBER 1916

Josef HOFMANN plays with the Cincinnati Symphony Orchestra the piano part in the world première of his pseudonymous *Chromaticon*, programmed as a work by Michel Dvorsky (Dvor is Russian for Hof which is German for courtyard), described in the program notes as a "semi-Polish composer born in France in 1890."

24 NOVEMBER 1916

Klara Militch, opera in four acts by the 60-year-old Russian composer Alexander KASTALSKY, to his own libretto after a novel of that name by Turgenev, inspired by the fate of Russian singer Eulalia Kadmina who committed suicide at the age of twenty-eight in 1881, is produced in Moscow.

28 NOVEMBER 1916

Third Symphony by the Swedish composer Kurt ATTERBERG is performed for the first time in Stockholm.

2 DECEMBER 1916

Die Rose von Stambul, operetta in three acts by Leo FALL, dealing with a pasha's daughter who discovers to her delight that her family-imposed Turkish fiancé is the novelist with a French nom de plume with whom she has conducted an amorous correspondence, is produced in Vienna.

5 DECEMBER 1916

Sāvitri, one-act opera by Gustav HOLST, based on an episode from the Hindu epic poem *Mahabharata*, with Death singing an introductory solo and a hidden female chorus vocalizing on the symbolic vowel "U," is performed for the first time in London.

5 DECEMBER 1916

Hans RICHTER, monumentally corpulent and luxuriantly bearded Hungarian-born conductor, a benevolent autocrat of the baton, dies at the age of 73 in Bayreuth where he led the rehearsals and the productions of Wagner's music dramas during the first Wagnet Festival of 1876.

6 DECEMBER 1916

Elga, opera in seven scenes by Erwin LENDVAI, to a libretto from Gerhart Hauptmann's play of the same name, is produced in Mannheim.

6 DECEMBER 1916

Das Testament, opera by Wilhelm KIENZL, is produced in Vienna.

10 DECEMBER 1916

A concert of music by Sergei PROKOFIEV is given in St. Petersburg, featuring the first performance of his narrative ballad for voice and piano *The Ugly Duckling*, telling the story, after Hans Christian Andersen, of a swan hatched by a duck and regarded as ugly by anatine standards (Maxim Gorky, hearing the piece, said: "Prokofiev meant himself in this music!") and *Humorous Scherzo* for a quartet for bassoons.

15 DECEMBER 1916

American Negro Suite by the Danish composer Thorvald OTTERSTRÖM, dwelling in Chicago from 1892, consisting of a group of instrumental pieces based on Negro spirituals, is performed for the first time by the Chicago Symphony Orchestra.

25 DECEMBER 1916

Les Quatre Journées, opera in four acts by Alfred BRUNEAU, to his own libretto inspired by a story by Émile Zola, is produced at the Opéra-Comique in Paris, in which each act is represented by a season of the year, projecting the calendar far into the future:

(1) *Spring 1914*, picturing pastoral life in Provence rumbling with undertones of the imminent war; (2) *Summer 1920*, with

war unprophetically scheduled as still continuing, and describing the encounter after a battle between a French farmer-soldier and an Alsatian in a German uniform who become friends; (3) *Autumn 1938,* portraying peace and growing families; (4) *Winter 1956,* painting in tones a disastrous flood overtaking an aging family, with only two friends and a small child surviving.

25 DECEMBER 1916

Leonid Sabaneyev, Russian music critic, publishes in the Moscow newspaper *News of the Season* a devastating review of the *Scythian Suite,* by Sergei PROKOFIEV, originally scheduled for performance at a Koussevitzky concert on 12 December 1916 in Moscow, but cancelled owing to the dispersion of orchestral musicians conscripted into the army.

At a current Koussevitzky concert one of the main attractions was the first performance of the *Scythian Suite* by a young composer Prokofiev, under his own direction. . ... If one says that this music is bad, that it is cacophonous, that a listener with a well differentiated auditory organ cannot tolerate it, people will say "but this is supposed to be barbaric music." And the critic is forced to retreat in shame. So I will not condemn this music. Quite to the contrary, I shall say that it is magnificently barbaric, the world's best barbaric music. But if I am asked whether this music gives me pleasure or artistic satisfaction, if it produces a profound impression, I must categorically say no. The composer himself conducted with barbaric abandon. (Excerpts from Sabaneyev's review)

In the preliminary announcement of Koussevitzky's concerts my *Scythian Suite* was programmed for the 12th of December 1916, under my direction. In view of the impossibility to assemble a large orchestra in wartime, the performance was cancelled. Nevertheless, the Moscow periodical *News of the Season,* whose music department is headed by Leonid Sabaneyev, published a review signed L.S. I hereby state (1) that I have never appeared as conductor in Moscow (2) that my *Scythian Suite* has never been performed in Moscow (3) that the critic could not possibly acquaint himself with the music because the only manuscript score of the work is in my possession. (From Prokofiev's statement published in *Musikalny Sovremennik,* Petrograd, 30 January 1917)

29 DECEMBER 1916

Concerto for Two Pianos and Orchestra by the 78-year-old German composer Max BRUCH is performed, in a drastically revised version, for the first time by the sibling American piano team Ottilie and Rose Sutro with the Philadelphia Orchestra under the direction of Leopold Stokowski. (In 1971 the authentic version was discovered in Berlin. It was given its first performance by Nathan Twining and Mer Berkofsky with the London Symphony, Antal Dorati conducting, on 6 May 1974.)

1917

1 JANUARY 1917

Eileen, romantic comic opera in three acts by Victor HERBERT, dealing with the Irish agitation for home rule in 1798, and including a miscegenating romance between an English lady and an Irish rebel, generating in the process a lot of fine Irish tunes (*My Little Irish Rose, Too-re-loo-re, In Erin's Isle*), concluding with the prophetic proclamation, *When Ireland Stands Among the Nations of the World,* is performed for the first time in Cleveland under the original title *Hearts of Erin.*

5 JANUARY 1917

Variety marks the progress of JAZZ (spelled JAZ) in Chicago's night clubs.

The most popular attractions in Chicago cabarets are now the Jaz Bands or Orchestras, and every cabaret, regardless of its size has a Jaz aggregation. Bert Kelly is credited with the introduction of the Jaz Orchestra in and around Chicago, Kelly featuring his own organization at the College Inn. The College Inn Jaz combination is probably the best of the local outfits, with Kelly at the banjo and Gus Mueller playing the saxophone. At Harry James' Casino on the North Side, the Jaz Band is also a big drawing card, but James has strengthened his amusement end there with a so-called Jug-Band. The Jug-Band is a Jaz Band with a "Juggist" blowing bass notes into an ordinary whiskey jug. The tone resulting resembles the music of a bass viol.

17 JANUARY 1917

Leo SOWERBY, 21-year-old composer from Grand Rapids, Michigan, presents in Chicago a program of his works, billed "Leo Sowerby: His Music" including the world premières of the concert overture *Comes Autumn Time,* an orchestral scherzo entitled *The Irish Washerwoman,* a cello concerto, and a piano concerto with a soprano obbligato, with the composer at the piano, Eric De Lamarter conducting.

I took the advice of a not-too-friendly critic, stole out one dark night and deposited the cello concerto in an ashcan. (From a letter by Leo Sowerby to the author dated 22 June 1961)

(The piano concerto, condensed and exuviated of its ectoplasmic soprano part was performed by Sowerby for the first time in the new version with the Chicago Symphony Orchestra on 5 March 1920.)

17 JANUARY 1917

The ORIGINAL DIXIELAND JAZZ BAND, the first ensemble to make use of the word Jazz, consisting of cornet played by the leader James (Nick) LAROCCA, trombone, clarinet, piano and drums, billed as "Creators of Jazz," opens at Reisenweber's Restaurant at 8th Avenue and 58th Street in New York.

20 JANUARY 1917

Der Eiserne Heiland, opera in three acts by Max von OBERLEITHNER, is produced in Vienna.

21 JANUARY 1917

Elegia Eroica by Alfredo CASELLA, a symphonic tribute to the soldiers of the Allied Armies, is performed for the first time in Rome.

22 JANUARY 1917

In a historic decision, Victor Herbert vs. the Shanley Co., Justice Oliver Wendell HOLMES of the United States Supreme Court rules that "the performance in a restaurant or hotel of a copyrighted musical composition, for the entertainment of patrons without charge for admission to hear it, infringes the exclusive right of the owner of a copyright under the act of 4 March 1909, to perform the work publicly for profit."

The plaintiff owns the copyright on a lyric comedy in which is a march called *From Maine to Georgia.* The defendant hotel company caused this march to be performed in the dining room of the Vanderbilt Hotel for the entertainment of guests during meal times, in the way now common, by an orchestra employed and paid by the company. It was held by the circuit court of appeals, reversing the decision of the district court, that this was not a performance for profit within the meaning of the act. If the rights under the copyright are infringed only by a performance where money is taken at the door, they are imperfectly protected. Performances not different in kind from those of the defendants could be given that might compete with and even destroy the success of the monopoly that the law intends the plaintiffs to have. It is enough to say that there is no need to construe the statute so narrowly. The defendant's performances are not eleemosynary. They are part of a total for which the public pays, and the fact that the price of the whole is attributed to a particular item which those present are expected to order is not important. It is true that the music is not the sole object, but neither is the food, which probably could be got cheaper elsewhere. The object is a repast in surroundings that to people having limited powers of conversation or disliking the rival noise give a luxurious pleasure not to be had from eating a silent meal.

26 JANUARY 1917

The DIXIE JASS BAND (so spelled) of New Orleans opens at Reisenweber's Cabaret in Chicago.

(Date and facts from *Variety* of 2 February 1917, p. 8: "The Dixie Jass Band, five pieces, is at Reisenweber's, brought on by Max Hart. The band opened last Friday. It is said to have come from New Orleans.")

30 JANUARY 1917

Eine florentinische Tragödie, one-act opera by Alexander ZEMLINSKY, to a libretto after Oscar Wilde, is performed for the first time in Stuttgart.

2 FEBRUARY 1917

I Love the Neutral U.S.A., a pacifistic song reflecting the lingering isolationist spirit on the eve of America's entry into World War I, is copyrighted in Washington. (Another pacifistic song, *It is the Mothers Who Pay the Price of War,* was copyrighted on 13 June 1917, when America was already in the war.)

2 FEBRUARY 1917

The first full-fledged JAZZ BAND makes its first appearance in New York City.

The Jazz Band has hit New York at last, but just how popular it will become here is a matter that is going to be entirely in the hands of certain authorities that look after the public welfare. There is one thing that is certain, and that is that the melodies as played by the Jazz organization at Reisenweber's are quite conducive to making the dancers on the floor loosen up and go the limit in their stepping. Last Saturday night the Jazz musicians furnished the bigger part of the music for dancing at the 400 Club, and the rather "mixed" crowd that was present seemed to like it, judging from the encores that were demanded, and from the manner in which the dancers roughened up their stepping. The band carries its strongest punches in the trombone and the piccolo, the latter hitting all the blues. (*Variety,* 2 February 1917)

9 FEBRUARY 1917

Walter DAMROSCH, German-born conductor of the New York Symphony Orchestra, whose acquired Americanism was the product of his sincere devotion to the cause of democracy, lectures his mostly Germanic players at a rehearsal on the necessity of being loyal to their adoptive country.

I gave the men a lecture . . . on their patriotic duties toward the country in which they made their living. The last was necessary because a few German members objected to being made to play *America* so often, "as if they were an American orchestra." I told them plainly that that was just what we were. (From Damrosch's letter to his wife, in the archives of the Library of Congress)

10 FEBRUARY 1917

Emile-Louis-Fortuné PESSARD, amiable French harmony teacher and Prix de Rome winner, composer of pleasingly pre-Impressionistic songs, one of which (*Chanson d'un fou*) was copied by Debussy when he was a student at the Paris Conservatory, the manuscript in Debussy's handwriting being published erroneously as Debussy's own work, dies in Paris at the age of 73.

10 FEBRUARY 1917

The Kairn of Koridwen, dance-drama by Charles T. GRIFFES, dealing with a druidess who defies the moon goddess Koridwen in her kairn by refusing to slay an intruding non-druidical Gaul and is forced to take poison from the sacred caldron brewing deadly belladonna, with an impressionistic score colorfully arranged for five wind instruments, celesta, harp and piano, is performed for the first time in New York.

25 FEBRUARY 1917

Lazare SAMINSKY, 34-year-old Russian composer, conducts in Petrograd the first performance of his *First Sym-*

phony, surnamed *Symphony of the Great Rivers*, and designated as being in the key of *E-frimoll* (free E minor).

28 FEBRUARY 1917

Kullervo, opera in three acts by the Finnish composer Armas LAUNIS, after the *Kalevala*, is produced in Helsinki.

7 MARCH 1917

The world's first jazz recording is issued by the Victor Company, with *Livery Stable Blues* on one side and *Dixieland Jazz Band One-Step* on the other.

7 MARCH 1917

Antonina Ivanovna TCHAIKOVSKAYA, née Milyukova, widow of Tchaikovsky, from whom she was never divorced (their nominal cohabitation lasted only six weeks in the summer of 1877 before Tchaikovsky fled from unconsummated heterosexual horrors) and who had two surviving sons, fruits of a liaison with her solicitor, dies in a psychiatric clinic in Petrograd where she was confined in 1896.

8 MARCH 1917

The Canterbury Pilgrims, opera in four acts by the American composer Reginald DE KOVEN, after Chaucer, the action taking place in the late afternoon of 16 April 1387, with the musical score commenting lightly on the characters including Chaucer himself, is produced by the Metropolitan Opera in New York.

(Five performances only were given; during the fifth performance an announcement was made from the stage of America's entry into the war, whereupon the German soprano cast as the Wife of Bath fainted and could not go on; other German members became similarly distracted, and as a result further performances of the opera had to be cancelled.)

10 MARCH 1917

Eros und Psyche, opera in five acts by the Polish composer Ludomir RÓŻYCKI, his most successful stage work, is performed for the first time in Breslau, in the German version translated from the Polish original.

11 MARCH 1917

Fontane di Roma, symphonic poem by Ottorino RESPIGHI, descriptive of four contrastingly inspiring Roman fountains, at dawn, in the morning, at midday and at sunset, is performed for the first time at the Augusteo in Rome:

(1) *La Fontana di Valle Giulia all'alba*, a pastoral scene at dawn, opening with an oboe solo in the Phrygian mode and developing into a cycloramic tableau with atmospheric changes at dawn reflected in tremulously rising warm air in the strings and gentle drops of rain in the celesta; (2) *La Fontana del Tritone al mattino*, in which the marine demigod blows his conch shell in a mighty unison of four French horns and summons a school of naiads riding on sea-horses; (3) *La Fontana di Trevi al meriggio*, with declaratory trumpet calls and proclamatory trombone announcements, followed by poetic effusions in the harps and strings; (4) *La Fontana di Villa Medici al Tramonto*, pensive and archaic, as befits a fountain in

the vicinity of a museum, marking the sunset in attenuated sonorities.

(Date of first performance obtained from the Augusteo in Rome. The performance conducted in Rome by Arturo Toscanini on 10 February 1918 is often erroneously given as the première.)

11 MARCH 1917

Second part of *Impressioni dal Vero* by Gian Francesco MALIPIERO, a triptych of musical cameos: (1) *Colloquio di Campane*, an intimate confabulation of tintinnabulating carillons; (2) *I Cipressi e il Vento*, a study of stately cypresses wafted gently by the zephyr; (3) *Baldoria campestre*, a festive scene of rustic laetification, is performed for the first time in Rome.

17 MARCH 1917

La Société Française de Musicologie is founded in Paris, with Lionel de La Laurencie as its first President. (Exact date obtained from the Secretary of the Society.)

17 MARCH 1917

The world's first jazz phonograph record is advertised in the catalogue of Victor Records: "Spell it Jass, Jas, Jaz or Jazz—nothing can spoil a Jass band."

22 MARCH 1917

Four centuries have passed since the birth in Chioggia of Gioseffo ZARLINO, grandmaster of the Venetian school of composition and influential teacher of a multitude of disciples who flocked to him from many lands.

23 MARCH 1917

Ernest BLOCH conducts the Boston Symphony Orchestra in the first performance of his *Trois Poèmes juifs*, dedicated to the memory of his father:

(1) *Danse*, a somberly distant rhythmic evocation of the Jewish spirit of dance, devoid of literal melismatic Hebraicisms and set in modal harmonies; (2) *Rite*, a solemn ceremonial service in emotionally insistent melodic sequences interrupted by sudden anguished outcries; (3) *Cortège funèbre*, in mournfully vacant organum-like quartal and quintal harmonies with trumpeted theomachian imprecations.

Strange and Signal Music of Ernest Bloch—Three Jewish Poems That Evoke a Composer of Remarkable Idiom and Procedure, Invention, Imagination and Power—Pieces of a Singing Vehemence (H. T. Parker's headlines in the Boston *Evening Transcript*, 24 March 1917)

27 MARCH 1917

La Rondine, "lyric comedy" in three acts by Giacomo PUCCINI, dealing with a Parisian grisette flourishing circa 1860 who fascinates and captivates a decent provincial youth but, overcome by scruples, rejects his offer of marriage and flies away, like a swallow—*la rondine*—back to her natural demi-monde, the musical score approaching light opera in its popular dance style, but retaining the characteristically Puccinian modalities and chordal parallelisms, is produced in Monte Carlo.

The production of Puccini's opera *La Rondine* was accompanied by fierce political polemics, as a result of an article by

Léon Daudet in *L'Action française,* in which he asserted that the idea of the opera was suggested to Puccini by a Vienna editor and that the libretto was written by another Viennese, and demanded that the producer of the opera Raoul Guns-bourg be indicted for unlawful commerce with the enemy. The controversy ended in the courts, where Daudet's accusation was found unjustified. From an artistic point of view the work was criticized as an uncertain compromise between grand opera and operetta and for its numerous lapses into the waltz-type of light opera of Lehár and his followers. (Alberto de Angelis, *Dizionario dei musicisti,* Rome, 1918)

30 MARCH 1917

Il Macigno, opera in two acts by Victor DE SABATA, is performed for the first time at La Scala, in Milan. (A new version was produced under the title *Driada,* in Turin, on 12 November 1935.)

1 APRIL 1917

Scott JOPLIN, creator of throbbing ragtime pieces such as *The Maple Leaf Rag,* dies in New York at the age of 48, of a stroke aggravated by tertiary syphilis.

3 APRIL 1917

Arthur HONEGGER, 25-year-old French modernist, and a student in Vincent d'Indy's orchestration class, conducts at the Paris Conservatoire his first symphonic work, *Aglavaine et Sélisette,* an overture to Maeterlinck's drama of that name.

4 APRIL 1917

At a "metachoreographic" dance recital of abstract miming in New York, the modernistic French choreographer Valentine de Saint-Point presents the first orchestral works of Daniel CHENNEVIÈRE, 22-year-old French-born American composer, theosophist and astrologer, later known under his adopted astral name Dane RUDH-YAR, *Poèmes ironiques* and *Vision végètale,* influenced by the impressionistically nihilistic manner of Parisian sophisticates and touched by the rhythmic dynamism of primitivistic Russian ballets, with Pierre Monteux conducting the orchestra.

6 APRIL 1917

On the day of the declaration of war on Germany by the United States, George M. COHAN composes the famous song *Over There,* based on the three notes of the bugle call. (The song was copyrighted by Leo Feist, publishers, on 1 June 1917; Cohan received a check for $25,000 from the publishers on 31 October 1917 in full payment for the song; this money he gave to soldiers' funds and civic charities.)

7 APRIL 1917

El Corregider y la Molinera (The Governor and the Miller's Wife), "mimic farce" with music by Manuel de FALLA, the scenario derived from *El Sombrero de tres picos* by Alarcón, dealing with a philandering local governor whose emblem of authority is the three-cornered hat, and whose amorous entanglement with a miller's wife leads to adulterous imbroglios, with the fate motive from Beethoven's *Fifth Symphony* quoted ominously as the miller knocks at the door during their assignation, is performed for the first time in Madrid. (In the final version of the score, the ballet was produced under the English title *The Three-Cornered Hat* by Diaghilev's Ballet Russe in London on 22 July 1919.)

9 APRIL 1917

At a gala performance of Diaghilev's Ballet Russe in Rome, given for the benefit of the Italian Red Cross, Igor STRAVINSKY'S orchestral arrangement of the *Volga Boatmen's Song,* especially made as a substitute for the Russian Imperial National Anthem rendered obsolete by the Revolution, is played for the first time, conducted by Ernest Ansermet. (Date from *Il Giornale d'Italia,* Rome, 10 April 1917)

9 APRIL 1917

Tabu, comic opera in three acts by the Polish composer Lucjan KAMIEŃSKI, is produced in Königsberg.

12 APRIL 1917

Les Femmes de Bonne Humeur, choreographic comedy after Carlo Goldoni, to the music of Domenico Scarlatti, arranged and orchestrated by Vincenzo TOMMASINI, is produced by Diaghilev's Ballet Russe in Rome.

15 APRIL 1917

Gloria Arsena, opera in four acts by the Danish composer August ENNA (after Alexandre Dumas), is produced in Copenhagen.

17 APRIL 1917

Das Höllische Gold, a "German Singspiel" in one act by the Austrian composer Julius BITTNER, his most successful opera, to his own libretto after a medieval fairy tale of Hans Sachs, centered on a simple-minded dev-ilkin sent from the nether regions to the surface of the earth with a mission to corrupt a virtuous couple by gold, but becoming converted himself by their purity of soul, written in the manner of a folk play with simple illustrative motives forming its thematic substance, is performed for the first time in Vienna.

25 APRIL 1917

Ženidba Miloša Obilića or *Vilin Veo (The Wedding of Miloš Obilić* or *The Fairy's Cloak),* opera in three acts by the foremost Serbian composer Petar KONJOVIĆ, to a story inspired by a popular ballad wherein Miloš invades a fairy dance and pulls the magic cloak off one of the doll-like creatures who is then instantly transformed into an earthly maiden and eagerly accepts his offer in marriage, the music following the early models of German romantic operas, against the pastoral background of Slavic folk-wise inflections, in a normal harmonic setting, is produced in Agram (Zagreb).

(The original title of the opera centering on the name of a folk hero of Serbian folklore was changed to the neutral description *The Fairy's Cloak* at the demands of the wartime Austrian authorities to suppress any ethnic sentiments among the people in Croatia, then a part of the Austro-Hungarian Empire.)

28 APRIL 1917

Where Do We Go From Here, a patriotic American song by Howard JOHNSON and Percy WENRICH, with the boast to "slip a pill to Kaiser Bill and make him shed a tear," is published in New York.

30 APRIL 1917

Lodoletta (Little Skylark), lyric drama by Pietro MASCAGNI, his third opera, in three acts, after Ouida's sentimental tale of an innocent Dutch girl who is seduced by a Parisian painter and when, seized by scruples, he goes to Holland to find her, she is dead and her native wooden shoes are all that is left for him, written in an effectively Italian manner but falling short of his unsurpassed *Cavalleria rusticana* despite attempts at modernization by means of whole-tone scales and augmented triads, is produced in Rome.

3 MAY 1917

The New York Society of the Friends of Music presents a concert of orchestral works by Ernest BLOCH, with Bloch himself conducting two movements of his *Israel* symphony, the rest of the program (led by Artur Bodanzky) including *Three Jewish Poems, Three Psalms* for solo voices and orchestra, and the world première of *Schelomo* (Solomon), "Hebrew rhapsody" for cello and orchestra composed in Geneva in February 1916 and inspired by the wax sculpture by Catherine Barjansky (to whom the score is dedicated), the cello representing King Solomon as a songful monarch and the orchestra as his collective concubines submissively attentive to the constantly fluctuating moods of the music, nostalgic in its orientalized scale passages, despairing and defiant in its wide intervalic leaps, fearfully palpitating in the *saltando* violins and tapping drums, fatalistically bleak in open fifths and fourths, poetically meditative in arpeggiating harps, and sorrowfully gay in dance-like interludes.

It is not my purpose, not my desire, to attempt a reconstitution of Jewish music. . . . It is the Jewish soul that interests me, the complex, glowing, agitated soul that I feel vibrating throughout the Bible. It is this that I endeavor to hear in myself and to transcribe in my music: the venerable emotion of the race. (From Ernest Bloch's letter to Philip Hale published in Philip Hale's Boston Symphony Program Notes, New York, 1935)

Mr. Bloch's ideal of the Jewish music of the future is apparently the grotesque, hideous, cackling dispute of the Seven Jews in Richard Strauss's *Salome* . . . Nearly all of Bloch's music is hot in the mouth with curry, ginger and cayenne, even where one has a right to expect vanilla and whipped cream . . . Even the mellifluous Mozart can be made to sound like Bloch or Schoenberg by simply changing all flats to sharps and all sharps to flats. Mr. Bloch seems to be really in need of such a method . . . An interminably long "Hebrew rhapsody" called *Solomon (Schelomo)* does not reveal that monarch in all his glory. (New York *Evening Post*, 4 May 1917)

5 MAY 1917

In his last public appearance in Paris, Claude DEBUSSY, already ravaged by cancer, plays the piano part with Gaston Poulet as violinist in the first performance of his *Violin Sonata*, completed by him on 14 April 1917.

8 MAY 1917

The Provisional Government of Russia, headed by Alexander Kerensky, offers to Serge KOUSSEVITZKY the position of musical director and conductor of the former Imperial Court Orchestra in Petrograd, which he accepts.

11 MAY 1917

Two short operas by Ferruccio BUSONI to his own libretti are produced in Zürich:

(1) *Turandot*, in two acts derived from his incidental music for Max Reinhardt's production of Carlo Gozzi's play of that name in Berlin on 27 October 1911, and dealing with the cruelly nubile Chinese lady whose condition for marrying is that the suitor should give correct answers to three ambiguously worded riddles on arcane subjects, but who relents at the sight of a nameless young pretender who successfully passes his examination, with a passionately rhapsodic score including orientalistic pentatonic progressions; (2) *Arlecchino*, "a theatrical capriccio" set in Bergamo in the 19th century; in four connected scenes wherein Harlequin appears in four different guises, as adventurer, soldier, family man and army general.

11 MAY 1917

Gloemenkind, fairy-tale opera by the Dutch composer Frits Adriaan KOEBERG, is performed for the first time in Amsterdam.

12 MAY 1917

A fából faragott királyfi (Tale of the Wooden Prince), ballet in one act by Béla BARTÓK, dealing with a xylophilic young lady, who fetishistically caresses an invultuated wooden simulacrum of her beloved prince and a malevolent melanoptic forest sprite who shakes the trees to prevent the prince from reaching her chamber, set to music palpitating with strong asymmetrical rhythms and weighed down with knotted secundal chord formations but resolving into a seamlessly planed two-dimensional C major as the heroine surrenders herself to carnal delights, is performed for the first time in Budapest.

18 MAY 1917

Serge Diaghilev's Ballet Russe presents in Paris the first performance of "ballet réaliste" *Parade* by Erik SATIE, to a surrealist scenario by Jean Cocteau, wherein three frantic American managers advertise their rival shows, featuring a Chinese prestidigitator, a girl dancing ragtime, two acrobats passing "in parade" before the public, and a battery of American-made typewriters in the orchestra pit, with a cubistic curtain by Pablo Picasso, set to music in an ostentatiously "dépouillé" style, as a reaction against both the luxuriant impressionism of Debussy and the primitivistic *fauvisme* of Stravinsky.

Paris is an enfant terrible. Parisians always break the toys given to them. But *Parade* is an unbreakable toy. In 1917, the haste, the turmoil, the defective lighting prevented us from giving to the audience a spectacle planned by us. As a result, the public judged us through a misunderstanding: it mistook its own *scandale* for the show and its own noisy demonstration for the music. That is why even fairminded critics spoke of the orchestral sound as a charivari, because it had the audacity of being simple, of dispensing with stuffing, with musical surplus, with harmonic tinsel and the pulverized gold of impressionism. Satie's orchestra is a false straw-man. Don't break *Parade* to find out what is inside. There is nothing. It does not conceal anything. *Parade* has no meaning. *Parade* is a parade. *Parade* contains no symbols. *Parade* is as simple as bonjour, as frank as gold, as fresh as a rose, as free as air. After a performance of *Parade*, with a fight going on in the audience, I heard a man say to a friend: "If I knew it was so silly, I would have taken the children along!" This was the best tribute. (Jean Cocteau, *Paris-Midi*, 21 December 1920)

It was a *scandale*. All Paris was there and rioted. Satie was delighted: they fought on account of him! . . . The press was charming: Satie, Cocteau and Picasso were called "boches." One review provoked Satie to such an extent that he sent an insulting postcard to the critic. Dragged to court, the author of *Parade* was sentenced to eight days in jail for "public insults and defamation of character." (P. D. Templier, *Erik Satie*, Paris, 1932. The critic was Jean Poueigh. The text of Satie's letter contained but a single sentence: "Vous n'êtes qu'un cul, mais un cul sans musique." Satie never served the imposed sentence)

31 MAY 1917

We're Going to Take the Germ from Germany, the first of the punning jingo songs of the war is copyrighted in Washington. Others using the same pun are *When we Take the Germ out of Germany* (26 September 1917), *We're Going to Take the Germ out of Germany* (7 November 1917), *When the Yanks Yank the Germ out of Germany* (23 July 1918), *Our Yankee Boys Have Yanked the Germ out of Germany* (7 October 1918) and finally, *There'll Be no Germ in Germany*, copyrighted on 23 November 1918.

7 JUNE 1917

Ardid de Amor, lyric comedy in one act by the Uruguayan composer Carlos PEDRELL, nephew of the "Spanish Wagner" Felipe Pedrell, to a story of conquering love in 19th-century Spain, is produced in Buenos Aires.

7 JUNE 1917

We Are Out for the Scalp of Mister Kaiser Man, the first of a series of 88 American Kaiser-hanging war songs, is copyrighted in Washington, to be followed by such titles as *We Will Make the Kaiser Wiser* (copyrighted 25 August 1917; several other songs used the same rhyme); *We're Going to Hang the Kaiser Under the Linden Tree* (1 October 1917); *We're Going to Whip the Kaiser* (12 November 1917); *We're Truly on Our Way to Can the Kaiser* (19 December 1917); *We're Going to Show the Kaiser the Way to Cut Up Sauerkraut* (14 March 1918); *We'll Lick the Kaiser If It Takes Us Twenty Years* (2 April 1918); *Ropin' the Kaiser* (11 April 1918); *We All Want a Separate Piece of Kaiser Bill* (16 April 1918); *I'd Like to See the Kaiser with a Lily in His Hand* (8 May 1918); *We'll Give the Stars and Stripes to the Kaiser* (15 May 1918); *We're Going to Kick the Hell Out of Will-Hell-em* (15 May 1918); *I'd Kill the Kaiser for You* (15 July 1918); *If I Only Had My Razor Under the Kaiser's Chin* (20 July 1918); *We'll Take the I Out of Kaiser* (24 July 1918); *Shoot the Kaiser* (3 August 1918); *We'll Yank the Kaiser's Moustache Down* (19 August 1918); *When We've Taken the Kaiser's Scalp* (22 August 1918); *The Kaiser's Pants Afire* (14 September 1918); *We'll Swat the Kaiser for Uncle Sam* (30 September 1918); *If I Catch That Kaiser in de Chicken Coop* (16 October

1918); and— after the Armistice—*Hang the Kaiser to a Sour Apple Tree* (23 November 1918); and *Kaiser Now Is Wiser* (16 December 1918).

(The Kaiser died, unscalped and unhung, of a heart attack in his exile home in Doorn, Holland, at 11:30 A.M. on 4 June 1941, in territory occupied by Hitler's armies.)

9 JUNE 1917

Seventh Symphony, surnamed *Schweizerische*, by Switzerland's foremost symphonist Hans HUBER, based on melodic materials from Swiss folksongs, with particular distinction given to *Ranz des vaches*, a national air dating back to 1710 and used by Liszt in his nostalgic piano piece *Le mal du pays* from *Années de pèlerinage*, first series, devoted to reminiscences of his travels in Switzerland, is performed for the first time in Basel.

11 JUNE 1917

Der liebe Augustin, "scenes from the life of a Vienna talent" in four acts by the Austrian composer Julius BITTNER, to his own libretto centered on the amorous adventures of Augustin, the mythical hero of the famous popular song of unknown origin, is performed for the first time in Vienna.

12 JUNE 1917

Palestrina, "musical legend" in three acts by Hans PFITZNER, to his own libretto related to the dramatic twenty-two days in Palestrina's life in 1563 when the Council of Trent ruled that his florid type of polyphonic composition was unsuitable for liturgy (Palestrina's vindication came with his *Missa Papae Marcelli*, the theme of which was sung to him by an angel in a dream), with intrinsic allusions identifying Palestrina's strife with Pfitzner's own artistic discomfitures, the musical score written with an application of modernized ecclesiastical modes, is performed for the first time in Munich, Bruno Walter conducting.

12 JUNE 1917

Teresa CARREÑO, Venezuelan-born "Valkyrie of the Pianoforte," so nicknamed because of her massive personal appearance and powerful chordal technique, dies in New York at the age of 63.

16 JUNE 1917

We'll Soon Be in Old Berlin, the first of a series of Berlin-capturing songs, is copyrighted in Washington, to be followed by numerous similar titles: *We'll Take Old Berlin or Bust* (copyrighted 26 October 1917); *We'll Go A-Whirling to Berlin in an Airship Built for Two* (18 March 1918); *We're Going to Get to Berlin Through the Air* (2 April 1918); *Berlin or Bust* (21 October 1918); *A Hot Time Down in Old Berlin* (18 November 1918) and finally, as an accomplished fact but without reference to forcible physical capture, *Berlin Has Fallen* (29 November 1918).

19 JUNE 1917

Two centuries have passed since the birth in Deutsch-Brod, Bohemia, of Johann STAMITZ, grandmaster of the Mannheim School, whose 74 symphonies stabilized the form of sonata in orchestral music, thus anticipating and strengthening the direction taken by Haydn and Mozart.

19 JUNE 1917

Gergana, opera by the 36-year-old Bulgarian composer Georgi ATANASOV, dealing with the trials and tribulations of the Bulgarian girl Gergana nicknamed "white-legged" in consideration of the incandescent immaculacy of her habitually naked nether limbs, is produced in Sofia. (A revised version was first performed in Stara Zagora on 1 July 1925.)

2 JULY 1917

Rapsodia Satanica for orchestra by Pietro MASCAGNI, arranged from music written to accompany a motion picture, is performed for the first time in Rome.

5 JULY 1917

Ghismonda, lyric tragedy in two acts with a sexual intermezzo entitled *Incubus*, by the 30-year-old Italian composer Renzo BIANCHI, in which a beauteous medieval damsel falls into the dark powers of demoniac debauchery, is produced in Rome.

15 JULY 1917

Erik SATIE composes in Paris a *Sonatine bureaucratique* for piano, depicting an office bureaucrat who hums "an old Peruvian air which he picked up from a deaf-mute in Lower Brittany" while a pianist next door practices a Clementi sonata.

16 JULY 1917

Philipp SCHARWENKA, Polish-born but thoroughly Germanized composer and pedagogue, whose romantic piano pieces provided eupeptic pabulum for sentimental piano teachers, co-founder with his younger brother Franz Xaver Scharwenka, of the once-renowned Scharwenka Conservatory in Berlin, dies at Bad Nauheim at the age of 70.

16 AUGUST 1917

Maytime, operetta in four acts by Sigmund ROMBERG, dealing with two youthful lovers who married unloved mates in 1840, after burying a valuable property deed near Washington Square in New York, and its accidental discovery two generations later by her granddaughter and his grandson, who fall in love and get married thus gaining happiness denied to their respective grandparents, the score containing the famous love duet *Will You Remember?* sung transchronically by both couples separated by two generations, is performed for the first time in New York City.

25 AUGUST 1917

Schwarzwaldmädel, operetta by Leon JESSEL, set in early 20th century wherein an ardent maiden from Schwarzwald pursues a vacillating musician whose tastes are for chambermaids, is produced in Berlin.

28 AUGUST 1917

Leave It to Jane, musical comedy by Jerome KERN, in which a co-ed induces a college football quarterback to remain in the college of her choice and then seduces him into marriage, featuring the songs *Cleopatterer, Just You Watch My Step*, and *Leave It to Jane*, is produced in New York.

18 SEPTEMBER 1917

The UKULELE is patented by the Honolulu Ad Club as "a musical instrument made in Hawaii." (Date from the U.S. Patent Bureau, Washington, D.C.)

25 SEPTEMBER 1917

Three Pieces for Cello and Piano, op. 8, by the 21-year-old German composer Paul HINDEMITH, his first printed work, is published by Breitkopf & Härtel in Leipzig. (Information and date obtained from the publishers)

13 OCTOBER 1917

The Board of Education of New York City rules that operas by German composers, being products of enemy provenance, are not to be used as subjects for school and college lectures under its jurisdiction.

25 OCTOBER 1917

In a speech before the opening concert of the New York Symphony Society, the German-born but sincerely Americanized conductor and composer Walter DAMROSCH voices an earnest plea that Bach, Beethoven and Brahms should not be treated like enemy aliens and that their music should be allowed to be heard in America.

26 OCTOBER 1917

The Fair of Sorochintzy, the unfinished opera by MUSSORGSKY, inspired by an episode from Gogol's Ukrainian tale *Evenings on a Farm Near Dykanka*, abounding in fine melodies and infectious dancing rhythms (the Hopak has become famous as an independent dance number), with musical interstices filled in by César Cui, Mussorgsky's comrade-in-arms in the group of Mighty Five, is performed for the first time in Petrograd.

27 OCTOBER 1917

Jascha HEIFETZ, 16-year-old Russian-Jewish prodigy of the violin, makes his first appearance in America in his concert at Carnegie Hall, New York, producing a sensation by the virtuosity and maturity of his playing.

(During the intermission, Mischa Elman, a whilom *Wunderkind* himself, remarked to Leopold Godowsky, the sharp-witted pianist, that it was hot in the hall, to which Godowsky replied "Not for pianists." The accuracy of this story was confirmed to the author by Godowsky himself.)

1 NOVEMBER 1917

Elena TEODORINI, Rumanian prima donna, is arrested on a steamer en route from Buenos Aires to France, as it neared Cadiz, by a boarding party of British officers on suspicion of pro-German espionage, is transferred to a British destroyer, stripped by a female attendant and immersed in a chemical bath to verify an informer's report that a message in invisible ink was tattooed on her bare shoulders.

You know already about the adventure, both painful and grotesque, that I went through on the boat last year. Fortunately, after being held for 24 hours, I was finally permitted to continue my voyage and enter France. But the rival professional clique in Buenos Aires hastened to take advantage of this incident to fill the local newspapers with all sorts of lies, even saying that I was in a Paris jail and was going to be . . . executed! (From Elena Teodorini's private letter dated 30 November 1918 and preserved in the archives of the Rumanian Academy in Bucharest)

I certify that the accusation that Madame Elena Teodorini was involved in espionage is absolutely false, an infamous calumny made out of whole cloth by her enemies in Buenos Aires. (Statement signed on 12 December 1921 by the Rumanian consul in Rio de Janeiro, preserved in the archives of the Rumanian Academy in Bucharest, manuscript No. 5,366, p. 56)

3 NOVEMBER 1917

Lanzelot und Elaine, opera in four acts by the German conductor Walter COURVOISIER (after Tennyson), is produced in Munich.

9 NOVEMBER 1917

The management of the Philadelphia Orchestra announces that it is "heartily in accord with any movement directed by patriotic motives" and will "conform with pleasure" to the request of the Pittsburgh Orchestra Association to eliminate German music from the program of its Pittsburgh concert of 19 November 1917, and will devote it entirely to works by American composers.

11 NOVEMBER 1917

Alexander GLAZUNOV conducts in revolutionary Petrograd a matinée concert at the Conservatory, in a program including the first performance of his *Second Piano Concerto* in B major (the nucleus of which originated in 1894), in a single movement, built on a cyclical model and couched in a network of erudite polyphony.

14 NOVEMBER 1917

Šumařovo dítě (Fiddler's Child), symphonic poem by Leoš JANÁČEK, foremost composer of Czechoslovakia, is performed for the first time in Prague.

17 NOVEMBER 1917

At a war benefit performance of the Chicago Opera Company, a German named Reinhold Faust rolls a bomb down the aisle from his seat in Row K in the hall as a demonstration against America's entry into the war. (The bomb failed to go off; four more bombs were found in Faust's safe in the National Safe Deposit Company during another German war, 22 years later, in 1939.)

24 NOVEMBER 1917

The Spirit of England, a choral triptych by Sir Edward ELGAR to the text from three patriotic ballads connected with the war—*The Fourth of August, To Women* and *For the Fallen*—is given for the first time in its entirety in London.

6 DECEMBER 1917

An allem ist Hütchen Schuld, opera in three acts by Siegfried WAGNER, the "little son of a great father," to his own libretto, containing a spoken scene in which Jakob Grimm, the fabulist, complains to the composer (or his Thespian simulacrum) that the abstruse events going on in the opera constitute an inexcusable falsification of his simple fairy tale, is produced in Stuttgart.

7 DECEMBER 1917

Alois MINKUS, Austrian composer of ballets who went to Russia in 1853 as leader of the unique serf orchestras organized by Prince Yusupov and later wrote music for a number of ballets for the Imperial Theaters in Moscow and St. Petersburg, of which *Don Quixote* and *La Bayadère* suited the popular Russian tastes by their unsophisticated tunes and cosmopolitan dance rhythms so well that they became perennial favorites of Russian audiences through both the Czarist and Bolshevik regimes, dies in his native Vienna whither he returned in 1891, at the venerable but totally oblivious age of 91.

8 DECEMBER 1917

Ernst KUNWALD, German conductor of the Cincinnati Symphony Orchestra, is arrested as an enemy alien and immediately freed on bail and even allowed to conduct concerts before internment. (Kunwald conducted two more weekly concerts and rehearsals and then was asked to resign.)

(An announcement appeared in the Cincinnati Symphony program book of 16–17 November 1917, with a waving American flag in color on the cover, that the American National Anthem would be played at the beginning of each concert, and Kunwald complied with this requirement.)

10 DECEMBER 1917

The Vatican issues a decree, signed by the Secretary of the Consistorial Congregation, enjoining Catholics against dancing the tango and the maxixe, at home, in public, in the daytime or at night.

11 DECEMBER 1917

Rapsodie nègre by the 18-year-old French composer Francis POULENC, scored for piano, string quartet, flute, clarinet and baritone voice, in five movements: (1) *Prélude;* (2) *Ronde;* (3) *Honoloulou ("le chant sans nuances")* syllabilizing pseudo-Hawaiian words *Patata, Bananalou,* etc.; (4) *Pastorale;* and (5) *Final*, based on pentatonic progressions in saccadic rhythms, is performed for the first time in Paris, with Poulenc himself being forced to sing the vocal solo in *Honoloulou,* after the scheduled singer refused to appear.

11 DECEMBER 1917

Das Christ-Elflein, Christmas opera in two acts by Hans PFITZNER (derived from his incidental music to a play produced exactly 11 years before, on 11 December 1906, in Munich), to a story combining elements of pagan Germanic magic and the Christian concept of divinity, wherein the Christ Child befriends an elfin scion of an old fir tree, and together they fetch a Christmas tree to bring cheer to an ailing girl, set to music in a pleasingly harmonious style, is performed for the first time in Dresden.

13 DECEMBER 1917

Sortilegi, symphonic poem for piano and orchestra by the 35-year-old Bohemian-born Italian composer Riccardo PICK-MANGIAGALLI, with the spirit of sortilege illustrated by the lambent saltation of igneous instrumental colors, is performed for the first time in Milan.

26 DECEMBER 1917

Henry HADLEY conducts in Chicago the first performance of his opera *Azora, Daughter of Montezuma,* in three acts wherein an Aztec princess, condemned to death with her lover, is saved when Cortez rides on a white charger into the Aztec temple where she awaits her fate, and the conquistadores intone *Gloria in Excelsis Deo,* set to music in an effective melodramatic style with a modicum of pentatonic progressions to illustrate the Indian modalities.

1918

5 JANUARY 1918

A Daughter of the Forest, one-act opera by the American composer Arthur Finley NEVIN, brother of the song composer Ethelbert Nevin, dealing with the life of animal trappers in Pennsylvania at the time of the Civil War, with tragedy ensuing when the daughter of one of them becomes illegitimately pregnant and kills herself, whereupon her lover joins the Federal troops to seek death in combat, is produced in Chicago.

5 JANUARY 1918

Serge RACHMANINOFF leaves Russia, never to return.

14 JANUARY 1918

Der Eroberer (The Conqueror), comic opera in two acts by the 49-year-old Dutch composer Jan BRANDTSBUYS, is produced in Dresden.

15 JANUARY 1918

An auspicious public presentation of music by the "nouveaux jeunes" of France is made at an intimate concert in Paris under the benevolent tutelage of Erik Satie, in a program of music by 26-year-old ROLAND-MANUEL, 25-year-old Arthur HONEGGER, 25-year-old Germaine TAILLEFERRE, 19-year-old Francis POULENC and 18-year-old Georges AURIC.

19 JANUARY 1918

Sylvio LAZZARI, 60-year-old French composer born in Tyrol of Italian parents, conducts the Chicago Opera in the world première of his three-act opera *Le Sauteriot,* an epic of life among lowly Lithuanians, in which an illegitimately conceived girl surnamed *sauteriot* (grasshopper) for her saltatory amours, commits suicide by poison when her desirable beau, after spending a night with her, joins his regular mistress in the morning, set to music in a Wagnerogenically Gallic vein, with some exotic supplements such as a Lithuanian Bear Dance.

21 JANUARY 1918

The directors of the Philharmonic Society of New York issue a public statement banning all works by living German composers from its programs.

22 JANUARY 1918

Mrs. William Jay, superpatriotic Boston dowager, dispatches the following letter to Major Henry Lee Higginson, founder and director of the board of trustees of the Boston Symphony Orchestra, protesting against the continuance of Karl Muck's tenure as conductor of the orchestra:

As a result of the intense feeling regarding a man who bears the German Emperor's decoration and whose sympathies are most palpably opposed to the United States, the Boston Symphony concerts in New York have become a gathering place for everyone who hopes for a defeat of Allied arms. In our opinion even art must stand aside so that every possible influence can be brought to bear to terminate the war with an Allied victory. To this end, there seems no swifter means of emphasizing the whole-heartedness of the United States than by terminating the German influence in musical affairs. (Higginson replied on 30 January 1918 as follows: "Dr. Muck is probably German in feeling, but he has done nothing wrong. He has been eminently satisfactory to me as a conductor and as a man. His industry, knowledge and power are great, and his place cannot be supplied in this country." Mrs. Jay retorted in a letter dated 25 February 1918, demanding the removal of "the last tentacle of the German octopus" from American musical life.)

23 JANUARY 1918

François CASADESUS conducts at the Opéra-Comique in Paris the first performance of his "evocation dramatique et lyrique" entitled *Au beau jardin de France.*

24 JANUARY 1918

Gottfried Von EINEM, Austrian composer of operas in a modern romantic vein, is born in Bern, Switzerland, the son of an attaché at the Austrian Embassy.

25 JANUARY 1918

Peintures, a set of three impressionistic sketches for orchestra (*Portrait d'une jeune fille*, *Le Jardin de Nuit*, *La Fête*), by the English-born violinist Felix BOROWSKI is performed for the first time by the Chicago Symphony Orchestra, Frederick Stock conducting.

27 JANUARY 1918

The first part of *Pause del Silenzio*, "seven symphonic expressions" by Gian Francesco MALIPIERO, portraying in eloquent sonorities the spirit of softness, crudity, melancholy, gaiety, mystery, war, and savagery, concluding on a thematic pause of silence, is performed for the first time in Rome.

George Moore knew in his sojourn in Paris a strange musician, poor, but wearing silk shirts . . . He should be remembered by a remark he made: "To express silence in music I should need at least three brass bands." There were moments when one might be pardoned for thinking that Malipiero had pondered that theory. (Philip Hale, *Boston Herald*, 5 April 1919)

1 FEBRUARY 1918

Wo die Lerche singt, operetta in three acts by Franz LEHÁR, dealing with a morally unstable painter whose picture of an Austrian *milchmädel* wins him a prestigious prize but who loses her as a model and as a prospective inamorata after his promiscuous dalliance with a sexually experienced actress, is produced in Budapest.

7 FEBRUARY 1918

Doreya, opera by the Cuban composer Eduardo SÁNCHEZ DE FUENTES, to a libretto from the life and legend of pre-Columbian Indians in Spanish America, containing authentic pentatonic material from ancient tribal chants, is produced in Havana.

11 FEBRUARY 1918

Pan and Syrinx, symphonic poem by the Danish composer Carl NIELSEN, depicting in romantic tonalities the poetic Greek myth of an Arcadian nymph who changed into a reed to escape the pursuit of Pan and whose hollow stem Pan fashioned into a panpipe, is performed for the first time in Copenhagen.

14 FEBRUARY 1918

Swanee, the first successful song by the 19-year-old American composer George GERSHWIN, is performed for the first time as a number in the revue *Sinbad*, produced in New York.

17 FEBRUARY 1918

A Child's Garden of Verses, symphonic suite by the American composer Edward Burlingame HILL, inspired by Robert Louis Stevenson's cycle of poems, in four sections: (1) *March*, a merry procession with some chromatic acerbities; (2) *The Land of Nod*, a sophisticated lullaby ornamented by resolvable discords; (3) *Where Go the Boats*, a stylized tarantella; (4) *The Unseen Playmate*, a romantic reverie, is performed for the first time by the New York Symphony under the direction of its permanent conductor Walter Damrosch.

20 FEBRUARY 1918

Schaaban, opera in three acts by Vittorio RADEGLIA, who was the composer of the Turkish national anthem, is produced in Vienna, to a German libretto translated from an original text in Turkish.

10 MARCH 1918

Der Stier von Olivera, opera in three acts by the deracinated Germanized English-born composer Eugen D'ALBERT, is produced in Leipzig.

10 MARCH 1918

Ritorna Vincitor, opera in Italian by the Philippine composer Antonio J. MOLINA, is performed for the first time in Manila, the composer conducting.

14 MARCH 1918

Karl MUCK conducts the Boston Symphony Orchestra in Carnegie Hall, New York, despite the frenetic efforts of ultra-patriots to prevent his appearance.

City Is Confident Ban Will Be Put on Doktor Muck—Loyal Foes of Prussian Direktor Expect Action Today—Trinity Rector Writes Concert Should Be Prohibited—Condemns Tolerance—Mrs. William Jay Moves to Stop Muck's Concerts—Patronage of Boston Symphony Is Largely Pro-German, She Says, Moving to Silence Orchestra—Muck and His Enemy Aliens Here Tonight—Patriotic Societies and Loyal Citizens by Thousands Protest in Vain—Kaiser's Direktor and Band Reach City—Carnegie Hall Swings Wide Its Doors to German Doktor—Nine Austrians in Orchestra—Muck Plays Here Guarded by Police—Only Subscribers Admitted to Concert Which Was Not Interrupted—Opens With Our Anthem—New York Bows Head in Shame as Muck Leads—Germans Applaud Their Hero Loudly (Assorted consecutive headlines in the New York newspapers of March 1918).

15 MARCH 1918

Lili BOULANGER, first woman composer ever to receive the Premier Grand Prix de Rome annually awarded by the lofty Institut de France, whose delicate vocal and instrumental works were cast in a fine impressionistic manner of the *fin de siècle*, dies in her native Paris at the lamentably unfulfilled age of 24 years, 6 months and 3 weeks, only 4 years, 8 months and 9 days after receipt of the prize.

23 MARCH 1918

A century has passed since the death in Paris of Nicolò ISOUARD, Malta-born composer of many melodious and harmonious operas to fanciful French libretti, often set in exotic lands.

23 MARCH 1918

John POWELL, 35-year-old American composer, plays with the Russian Symphony Orchestra in New York the solo part in the world première of his *Rapsodie nègre* for piano and orchestra, inspired by Joseph Conrad's novel *Heart of Darkness*.

23 MARCH 1918

The Paris Opéra cancels the evening performance of *Rigoletto* and *Coppélia* owing to the bombardment of Paris by the German long-range gun, manufactured by the Krupp Company and known as "the Big Bertha" with an affectionate allusion to Frau Bertha Krupp, the matriarch of the Krupp family.

23 MARCH 1918

Two new American works are performed for the first time at tbe Metropolitan Opera in New York:

Shanewis, or The Robin Woman, opera by Charles Wakefield CADMAN, in two acts, dealing with a beautiful Indian girl brought up in an aristocratic Californian home, whose American lover follows her to an Indian Reservation in Oklahoma where he is killed by a poisoned arrow shot by her brother after it becomes clear that he could not marry Shanewis because of laws and customs against miscegenation, set to music in an effectively melodious and harmonious vein, abounding in pentatonically stylized arias and duets; and *The Dance in Place Congo,* ballet-pantomime by Henry F. GILBERT, evoking in stark ethnic colors the tribal Negro festivals in Place Congo in ante-bellum New Orleans and making thematic use of French Creole songs of the period.

24 MARCH 1918

Despite daily bombardment, the Paris Opéra opens its doors with the performance of Gounod's *Faust,* taking in 8,262 francs 10 centimes at the box office. (Information from *Cinquante ans de musique française,* Paris, 1926)

25 MARCH 1918

Claude DEBUSSY, sublime poet of new French music, originator of a distinctive style of composition that came to be called Impressionism, even though he himself deprecated the term, dies of cancer in war-saddened Paris, as cannons thunder, at ten o'clock at night, having lived 55 years, 7 months and 3 days.

Il est mort, Claude de France, l'Orphée des songes interrompus. *Le miel mélodieux ne coule plus des alvéoles* . . . (Gabriele d'Annunzio's lines upon learning of Debussy's death)

25 MARCH 1918

Karl MUCK, German conductor of the Boston Symphony Orchestra, is arrested in Boston as an enemy alien.

Dr. Karl Muck Arrested as Alien Enemy—Symphony Conductor Taken As He Leaves Motor Car at His Home—Locked Up in Back Bay Police Station—Federal Authorities Silent Regarding Possible Recent Evidence.

Dr. Karl Muck, director of the Boston Symphony Orchestra, was arrested at his home, 50 Fenway, at 11:30 o'clock last night, by policemen and agents of the Department of Justice. . . . The arrest was decided upon late last evening. Policemen and Department of Justice agents kept vigil on the Fenway residence from about 8:30 until 11:30. Dr. Muck, they learned, was either at a play or at some social affair. Immediately upon the arrival of his limousine at his home a policeman stepped to his side, identified him, and told him he was under arrest. (Boston *Herald,* 26 March 1918)

It is evident that the federal authorities view Dr. Muck as an important prisoner. They consider it established that his Boston residence was part of the Kaiser's policy of some years ago of "planting" musicians, college professors and other men of great accomplishments and culture in various countries as part of his gorgeous scheme of eventual world-wide conquest. Dr. Muck, claiming Swiss citizenship, was "loaned" by the

Kaiser to the Boston Symphony Orchestra and constantly expressed his pride in the fact that his orchestra was composed almost wholly of Germans and Austrians. (Boston *Herald,* 28 March 1918)

26 MARCH 1918

César CUI, the last surviving and least mighty of the Mighty Five of Russia, composer of poetic miniatures of which *Orientale* is a paradigm, whose father, a French officer in Napoleon's army taken prisoner in 1812 married a Russian woman, and who was himself a general in the Tsarist Army and instructor in the science of military fortification to the last Russian Tsar Nicholas II, dies in Petrograd at the age of 83, surviving Balakirev by nearly 8 years, Rimsky-Korsakov by nearly 10, Borodin by 31 and Mussorgsky by 37 years.

(24 March 1918 was cited erroneously as the date of Cui's death in the previous editions of *Music Since 1900,* in *Baker's Biographical Dictionary of Music and Musicians, Fifth Edition,* edited by Nicolas Slonimsky, in *Die Musik in Geschichte und Gegenwart,* in *Grove's Dictionary of Music and Musicians* and *Enciclopedia dello Spettacolo.* The correct date, 26 March 1918, is verified by obituaries in the Petrograd newspapers and published announcements by the family.)

27 MARCH 1918

If He Can Fight Like He Can Love, Good Night, Germany, a jingoistic popular song, with a suggestive erotic angle, is copyrighted in Washington, D.C.

4 APRIL 1918

Kjartan und Gudrun, opera in three acts by the German composer Paul von KLENAU, is produced in Mannheim.

6 APRIL 1918

1814, opera by Xavier LEROUX, to a libretto depicting the decline and fall of Napoleon, is produced in Monte Carlo.

7 APRIL 1918

Karl MUCK is interned as an enemy alien at Fort Oglethorpe, Georgia, for the duration of the war.

Dr. Muck's Boast in Berlin His Undoing—Letters Show His Propaganda Connection and Contempt for America and Boston—Written to a Young Boston Woman He Deceived by Promise of Marriage—Complete Wireless Outfit in Muck's House—Muck Active German Spy Many Years—Boston People Gave Cash to Dr. Muck to Help Germany in War—Dr. Muck Was Audacious in Use of Cipher—Complained Code was Muddled by Telegraph Co.—Listed Women with Phone Calls—Kept Record of Names and Activities in German Cause (Assorted headlines in the Boston *Post*).

21 APRIL 1918

Two days before his 27th birthday Sergei PROKOFIEV conducts in Petrograd the first performance of his *Classical Symphony* in D major (completed on 23 September 1917), ostentatiously classical in form but unorthodox in its wide melodic leaps, curt plagal cadences, asymmetrical rhythms and modulatory detours, in four movements:

(1) *Allegro,* in energetic sonata form, with the recapitulation in the lateral tonality of C major; (2) *Larghetto,* in A major, with a songful theme in the violin projected upon the murmurations

and susurrations of the rest of the ensemble; (3) *Gavotte*, a courtly dance in D major, with a Musette in G major, a delicate rococo creation, suggesting a Parisian music box in its fragile sonorities, but providing a sharply scented snuff in deceptive cadences thumbing the nose at the classics; (4) *Finale*, in D major, a spirited mobile rondo.

When you appeared on the podium to conduct your sunlit symphony, a ray of sun illuminated your dear features. Was it a smile of sympathy towards your kindred element? I cannot tell, but I believe it might be. (From a note in Prokofiev's album by Nicolas Tcherepnin, his teacher of conducting, inscribed on 20 April 1918 after the final rehearsal of the *Classical Symphony*)

23 APRIL 1918

First Symphony by the 23-year-old Dutch modernist Willem PIJPER (completed on 14 October 1917), in four movements: (1) *Allegro burlesca*, set in a rustically rhythmic idiom; (2) *Lento*, a neo-romantic nocturnal intermezzo; (3) *Giocoso*, in the manner of a modern minuet; and (4) *Andante maestoso*, an animistic representation of Pan's funeral procession, is performed for the first time by the Concertgebouw Orchestra in Amsterdam, Willem Mengelberg conducting.

25 APRIL 1918

Die Gezeichneten (The Stigmatized), opera in three acts by Franz SCHREKER, to his own libretto dealing with an unconsummated passion of a cripple with a beautiful soul for a girl with a beautiful body in 16th-century Genoa, set to music in a tensely dramatic expressionistic idiom presaging the emancipated chromatic syle of the immediate future, is produced in Frankfurt.

27 APRIL 1918

Russian Rag, ragged version of RACHMANINOFF's famous C-sharp minor *Prelude*, one of the earliest examples of jazzification of respectable music, perpetrated by George L. Cobb, is copyrighted in Washington, D.C.

7 MAY 1918

What General Pershing Will Do to Germany Is Just What Dewey Did at Manila Bay, a patriotic song, is copyrighted in Washington.

18 MAY 1918

Toivo KUULA, Finnish composer of music based on East-Bothnian melodic resources organized within Western contrapuntal and harmonic confines, is murdered in a tavern brawl in Vyborg, seven weeks before his 35th birthday, and three weeks after the brief occupation of the city by the White Finnish Army fighting the Bolsheviks.

22 MAY 1918

Grab a Gun, Put the Hun on the Run, one of the many anti-Hun songs of World War I, is copyrighted in Washington.

24 MAY 1918

A Kékszkállú Herceg Vára (Duke Bluebeard's Castle), one-act opera by the foremost modern composer of Hungary Béla BARTÓK, written in 1911, and depicting the fabled polygamist and his inquisitive fourth wife who opens the forbidden seventh door where she finds Bluebeard's previous three wives kept in an anabiotic state, set to a tortuously dramatic score with strident discords stressing the cumulatively melodramatic peripeteia, is performed for the first time at the Budapest Opera.

Bluebeard's Castle is for Hungarians what Pélléas is for the French . . . The seven doors, opened one after another, give occasion for as many musical images, not through external characterization but by means of intimate sentiment . . . Bartók's opera may be called a "symphonie à tableaux," or a drama with symphonic accompaniment, but what is certain is that the combination is a masterpiece, a musical geyser of sixty minutes of compressed tragedy. (Zoltán Kodály in *La Revue Musicale*, Paris, March 1921)

1 JUNE 1918

Jaroslav NOVOTNÝ, Czech composer of impressionistic songs in the French manner, is killed at the age of 32 in the Ural mountains during a skirmish between the Red Army and former Austrian prisoners of war of Bohemian extraction forming a unit in the anti-Soviet White Army.

5 JUNE 1918

Theophano, opera in three acts by the German composer Paul GRAENER, dealing with the illicit passion of Theophano, twin sister of the Roman Emperor in Byzantium, for his trusted aide, with the lovers saved from execution for immorality by the intercession of the people of the country, written in a lutulent Wagneromimic idiom, fertilized by non-toxic dissonances, is performed for the first time in Munich. (A new version, under the title *Byzanz*, was produced in Leipzig on 22 April 1922.)

10 JUNE 1918

Arrigo BOITO, Italian opera composer and librettist, himself a poet of superior literary gifts, dies in Milan at the age of 76.

17 JUNE 1918

A century has passed since the birth of Charles GOUNOD, the lyric genius of the French musical theater.

23 JUNE 1918

The New York Philharmonic Orchestra inaugurates an annual series of summer concerts in open air financed by Adolph Lewisohn, and presented in a stadium that was to bear his name.

29 JUNE 1918

Tucumán, opera by the Argentine composer Felipe BOERO, based on an episode of the South American war of independence in the town of Tucumán, set to music in a conventional Italian manner, brightened by the injection of authentic folk dance rhythms, is produced at the Teatro Colón in Buenos Aires.

6 JULY 1918

On his way from Russia via Siberia to the United States, Sergei PROKOFIEV presents in Tokyo a recital of his piano music, introduced in the English-language program as "The Gigantic Russian Composer & Pianist Virtuoso, The Another Prizz Winner."

12 JULY 1918
By decree of the Soviet of People's Commisars, the conservatories of Petrograd and Moscow are nationalized and put under the authority of the Department of Education.

27 JULY 1918
Gustav KOBBÉ, 61-year-old New York music critic and compiler of books on opera, is killed in his sailboat by a Navy seaplane maneuvering in the bay near Babylon, Long Island, New York.

11 AUGUST 1918
Gino MARINUZZI conducts in Buenos Aires the first performance of his opera in three acts, *Jacquerie*, on the subject of the bloody peasant rebellion in 14th-century France.

18 AUGUST 1918
Fernando, opera written by Franz SCHUBERT in 1815, has its first stage performance 103 years later, in Magdeburg.

19 AUGUST 1918
Yip, Yip, Yaphank, revue with book, music and lyrics by the 30-year-old Russian-born musician Irving BERLIN, is performed for the first time in Camp Upton, New York, with Berlin himself taking the part of a reluctant recruit singing *Oh, How I Hate to Get Up in the Morning* and voicing homicidal intentions towards the army bugler who sounds the reveille, and including also the inspirational hymn *God Bless America*, destined to achieve immense patriotic popularity.

25 AUGUST 1918
Leonard BERNSTEIN, uniquely versatile pianist-composer-conductor, destined to be as successful in the domain of exalted music-making at the helm of a great orchestra as in the composition of melodiously rhythmic and harmoniously stimulating Broadway shows, is born in Lawrence, Massachusetts, to a family of second-generation Jewish immigrants from Russia.

28 AUGUST 1918
Shanghai, operetta in two acts by Isidore WITMARK, picturing in a conventional stylized form the life in imperial China, with a couple of American characters, Flash Pansy (female) and Pete Dark (male), indulging in some crooked deals, is performed for the first time in London.

9 SEPTEMBER 1918
Caramurú, symphonic poem by the 21-year-old Brazilian composer Francisco MIGNONE, descriptive of the anthropophagic rites of the Brazilian Indians, is performed for the first time in São Paulo, conducted by Mignone's father.

15 SEPTEMBER 1918
Meister Guido, comic opera in three acts by the German composer Hermann NOETZEL, dealing with a poor music teacher who wins the hand of a Florentine lady by assuming the air of a nobleman dabbling in arts, is produced in Karlsruhe.

16 SEPTEMBER 1918
One thousand, nine hundred and twenty-five years after the death of Gaius Maecenas, Mrs. Elizabeth Sprague COOLIDGE, American encourager of the arts, opens on her estate in the Berkshires, near Pittsfield, Massachusetts, a Temple of Music dedicated to concerts of classical and modern music by American and European composers.

18 SEPTEMBER 1918
Sergei PROKOFIEV arrives in New York from Petrograd via Japan and declares that Russian musicians keep working despite intolerable conditions of famine and civil dislocation.

18 SEPTEMBER 1918
Ernest Bristow FARRAR, 33-year-old English composer of fine-textured music in a neo-Elizabethan manner, is killed during the Battle of the Somme.

18 SEPTEMBER 1918
Carillon magico, mimo-symphonic comedy by the 36-year-old Bohemian-born Italian composer Riccardo PICK-MANGIAGALLI, to his own libretto, is produced at La Scala, Milan.

19 SEPTEMBER 1918
Liza LEHMANN, English singer and accomplished composer whose melodious song cycle *In a Persian Garden*, a setting for 4 voices and piano of assorted verses from the *Rubaiyát* of Omar Khayyam, has become a favorite of easily satisfied lovers of semi-classical music, its antepenultimate movement, *Ah Moon of My Delight*, possessing the deepest emotional appeal to tenors of all descriptions, dies in her native London at the age of 56.

28 SEPTEMBER 1918
The first performance is given in Lausanne under the direction of Ernest Ansermet of Igor STRAVINSKY's ballet with narration, *L'Histoire du Soldat*, a morality play to the text of C. F. Ramuz, "to be read, played and danced," centering on a demoralized soldier who gives away his violin to the benevolent-looking devil in exchange for wisdom, loses his soul in a card game, and after many an adventure returns home to surrender himself to the devil, with a speaker accompanied by an ensemble of seven instruments selected so as to achieve a maximum efficiency with a minimum of means and yet to cover the entire useful range in a given timbre, namely, two string instruments (violin and contrabass), two woodwinds (clarinet and bassoon), two brasses (cornet and trombone), and a monticule of percussion manned by a single player, the work having the following distinctive parts:

(1) *Soldier's March*, a polymetric grotesque with the contrabass maintaining an unchanging four-note *ostinato* while the melody parts are variously apocopated, generating cross-rhythms and shift of stress; (2) *Soldier's Violin*, a musette-like intermezzo with a steady drone on the dominant, simulating an untutored

fiddler's dance tune, while the narrator queries querulously: "Where is he going?"; (3) *Pastorale*, a serene interlude of philosophical contemplation in statically sonorous harmonies; (4) *Royal March*, a discordant asymmetrical military march in which the trumpet and the trombone perform melodic acrobatics against a persistent march-time rhythm; (5) *Little Concert*, using the entire available ensemble, and marked by distinctly Russian melodic and rhythmic inflections; (6) *Tango*, for violin, clarinet and percussion, a nostalgically discordant modern dance; (7) *Waltz*, a caricature of an old-fashioned dance in mock-serious blanched, bland and blank C major; (8) *Ragtime*, an Americanized syncopated number played by a ragged violin accompanied by agitated drums; (9) *Devil's Dance*, recalling the *Soldier's March* and his violin, and foreshadowing the Devil's triumph; (10) *Little Chorale*, an osculatory intermezzo, accompanying the soldier's silent embrace with a princess; (11) *The Devil's Song*, a melodrama in denuded thumping rhythms as background for the spoken text; (12) *Grand Chorale*, replete with multi-cadential *fermate*, a majestically Gothic and statically chordal presentation; (13) *Triumphal March of the Devil*, in which artful disharmonies serve to express the satanic lure of profitable evil, ending with a protracted solo for percussion, in constantly changing meters, in rapid tempo, varying from 2 to 6 eighth-notes to a bar.

L'Histoire du Soldat was born of opportunistic preoccupations. The war was still continuing; no one could foretell when it would end. The Ballet Russe had suspended its productions; the theaters were virtually inactive. I myself was in difficult circumstances because of my inability to find what is known commercially as an outlet. I recall that one day, rather naively, Stravinsky and I wondered: Why not write something simple, something that would not require a large theater or a large audience to produce? It may be a piece for a few instruments with two or three actors on the stage. Since the theaters were no longer available, we could create a theater of our own, with scenery which could be set up anywhere, even in the open air. We would then resume the tradition of itinerant players. . . . *L'Histoire du Soldat* was the outcome of these practical ideas. As for the scenario, all we had to do was to peruse a few volumes of an enormous collection of fairy tales by a famous Russian folklorist. Among a multitude of stories, in which the devil seemed to play the dominating part, we selected one about a soldier and his violin, perhaps for the very reason that it was so completely incoherent. (C. F. Ramuz, *Souvenirs sur Igor Stravinsky*, Paris, 1929)

7 OCTOBER 1918

Sir Hubert PARRY, English composer of an enormous quantity of music written in a culturally romantic and academically competent style, author of books and erudite scholar, dies at Rustington at the age of 70.

18 OCTOBER 1918

Henry HADLEY conducts in New York the first performance of his one-act opera *Bianca*, to a libretto based on Carlo Goldoni's comedy *La Locandiera*, taking place in Florence in 1760 and dealing with the desirable proprietess of an inn where two cavaliers, fighting a duel over her favors, are stopped by a brave interloper who strikes their swords out of their hands with Bianca's ironing board and wins her love for his resourceful action.

20 OCTOBER 1918

Joseph BOULNOIS, 34-year-old French composer of melodious and harmonious songs and instrumental pieces, is killed in battle at Chalaines.

22 OCTOBER 1918

All music publishing firms of the Russian Soviet republic are nationalized and declared State property.

24 OCTOBER 1918

Charles LECOCQ, French composer of the celebrated operettas *Giroflé-Girofla* and *La Fille de Madame Angot*, dies in Paris at the age of 86.

30 OCTOBER 1918

The word GEBRAUCHSOPER (practical opera) is used for the first time in an article by the composer Heinrich Noren in the Berlin music periodical *Signale für die musikalische Welt*.

30 OCTOBER 1918

Zrání, symphonic poem by the Czech composer Josef SUK, is performed for the first time in Prague.

1 NOVEMBER 1918

The VEREIN FÜR MUSIKALISCHE PRIVATAUFFÜHRUNGEN, a society for private performances from which newspaper critics were excluded and where applause was forbidden, is formed in Vienna, with Arnold SCHOENBERG as president. (See Declaration of the Society in Letters and Documents section.)

1 NOVEMBER 1918

La Nave, opera by Italo MONTEMEZZI, consisting of a prologue and three episodes, to Gabriele d'Annunzio's poem, the action taking place in Venice in A.D. 552, centering on a fearless girl who takes vengeance on the murderous Venetian tyrant for having gouged the eyes of her parents and brothers by arousing in him the sensation of unappeasable lust for her but in the end suffers horrible death when he affixes her alive to the prow of his proud ship (hence the title) as its figurehead, the music illustrating the hideous plot by hyper-dramatic vocalization and explosively rising waves of orchestral sonorities, is produced at La Scala in Milan.

4 NOVEMBER 1918

One of a series of army love songs, *She's Teaching Me to Parlez-Vous Français, and I'm Learning More and More Each Day*, is copyrighted in Washington, on the same day with the song *Let Us Make the World Safe for Democracy*.

5 NOVEMBER 1918

Schwarzschwanenreich, Wagnerofilial opera in three acts by Siegfried WAGNER, describing a legendary land of black swans, is performed for the first time in Karlsruhe.

11 NOVEMBER 1918

On the morning of the Armistice, Igor STRAVINSKY completes in neutral Morges, Switzerland, the composition of his *Ragtime*, scored for eleven instruments, including the cimbalom (a Hungarian dulcimer used in Gypsy bands), a symbolic recognition of the growing spread of American syncopated music and the post-war necessity for economy in orchestration. (The first performance of

Ragtime was given in London on 27 April 1920, Arthur Bliss conducting.)

14 NOVEMBER 1918

A Provisional Central Musical Council is formed in Berlin after the German revolution and assumes the jurisdictional authority over musical affairs of the German Republic.

15 NOVEMBER 1918

Russians, a cycle of five songs with orchestra by Daniel Gregory MASON, to verses by Witter Bynner, characterizing in imitatively Mussorgskian models a group of supposedly typical Russians—a drunkard (on diluted vodka), an accordion player (apparently on a foreign-made instrument), a revolutionist (mystically self-doubting), a boy (prematurely debile) and a prophet (balefully proclamatory)—is performed for the first time by Reinald Werrenrath (to whom the cycle is dedicated) with the Chicago Symphony Orchestra.

16 NOVEMBER 1918

ALFVÉN's *Fourth Symphony* in C minor is performed for the first time in Stockholm.

17 NOVEMBER 1918

An American jazz band under the direction of Harry PILCER appears for the first time in Europe, playing in Paris at the Casino de Paris. (Date communicated by the management of the Casino de Paris.)

In 1918 the first jazz band arrived from New York. . . . I recall the shock, the sudden awakening that its staggering rhythm and its new sonorities brought to France. . . . This influence from North America has given us the *Ragtime du Paquebot* in Satie's *Parade,* and *Adieu New York* by Georges Auric. In these compositions we have a portrait of a ragtime and of a foxtrot seen through a symphonic glass. (Darius Milhaud, *Études,* Paris, 1927)

20 NOVEMBER 1918

Sergei PROKOFIEV makes his American debut as pianist-composer in New York in a program of his own works.

New ears for new music! The new ears were necessary to appreciate the new music made by Sergei Prokofiev in his first pianoforte recital at Aeolian Hall yesterday afternoon. He is younger looking than his years, which are patriarchal, twenty-seven. He is blond, slender, modest as a musician, and his impassibility contrasted with the volcanic eruptions he produced on the keyboard. We have already one musical anarch here, Leo Omstein, but that youth's *Wild Man's Dance* is a mere exercise in euphony, a piece positively Mozartian, in comparison with the astounding disharmonies gentle Sergei extorted from his suffering pianoforte. The young man's style is orchestral, and the instruments of percussion rule in his Scythian brains. His fingers are steel, his wrists steel, his biceps and triceps steel, his scapula steel . . . As a composer he is cerebral. His music is volitional and essentially cold, as are all cerebral composers . . . The finale of his second sonata evoked visions of a charge of mammoths on some vast immemorial Asiatic plateau. Rebikov seems a miniaturist after this. Prokofiev uses, like Arnold Schoenberg, the entire modern harmonies. He is a psychologist of the uglier emotions—hatred, contempt, rage—above all rage— disgust, despair, mockery, and defiance . . . His scale scheme is omniton-

ic—or is it omphalic? But now and then we get a glimpse of a recondite region, a No Man's Land wherein wander enigmatic and fascinating figures, an unearthly landscape, an atmosphere, murky and ominous, but painted in bold feverish strokes. (Richard Aldrich, New York *Times,* 21 November 1918)

21 NOVEMBER 1918

Mr. Wilson, You're a Wonderful Man, a tuneful tribute to the wartime President, is copyrighted ten days after the Armistice.

24 NOVEMBER 1918

Frutta di Mare, opera in three acts by the Swiss composer Hans HUBER is produced in Basel.

27 NOVEMBER 1918

Four centuries have elapsed since the publication of the musical treatise *De Harmonia musicorum instrumentorum* by the Italian music theorist Franchinus GAFURIUS.

29 NOVEMBER 1918

Booze, Booze, Booze, the first song of the Prohibition era, is copyrighted in Washington.

30 NOVEMBER 1918

The Société de l'Orchestre de la Suisse Romande gives its inaugural concert in Geneva under the direction of Ernest ANSERMET.

2 DECEMBER 1918

Le Dit des Jeux du Monde, incidental music by Arthur HONEGGER to Paul Meral's play, in the form of a suite of ten dances, two interludes and a coda, is performed for the first time in Paris.

5 DECEMBER 1918

Malvolio, opera in three acts by the 44-year-old British composer Fritz HART, after Shakespeare's comedy *Twelfth Night,* is performed for the first time in Melbourne by local conservatory students.

11 DECEMBER 1918

Das heisse Eisen, one-act opera by the 26-year-old Swiss composer Werner WEHRLI, to a text from a play by Hans Sachs, is produced in Bern.

14 DECEMBER 1918

The Metropolitan Opera of New York presents the absolute world première of three one-act operas by Giacomo PUCCINI, *Il Tabarro, Suor Angelica* and *Gianni Schicchi,* often described as *Il Trittico* despite Puccini's specific and emphatic disavowal of such collective title inasmuch as there is no common theme uniting the three:

Il Tabarro (The Cloak), inspired by a play from the Paris Grand Guignol, taking place on a barge on the Seine, where its owner strangles the trespassing lover of his wife and then invites her to lie down under the cloak hiding the body, set to music in a characteristically melodramatic style, marked by resonant modal harmonies and ingratiating melorhythmic sequences.

Suor Angelica, dealing with a formerly noble young lady of Florence flourishing circa 1600 whose loss of chastity induces her family to send her to a convent, and who takes poison when she learns that her illegitimate child is dead, prays to the Virgin to save her soul while discordant carillon tolls, is rewarded by the vision of the Mother of God leading a blond boy—her child—and dies in peace while the angels sing a hymn of salvation in virginally immaculate C major.

Gianni Schicchi, whose name appears in the tenth chasm of Dante's *Inferno* as a cunning deceiver, a Florentine peasant active in 1299 who helps his daughter and her young suitor to unite by posing as the latter's rich relative and dictating a will leaving most of his estate to himself but later handing the illicit patrimony to the happy lovers, stylistically treated as a traditional Italian opera buffa, with modernistic polytriadic harmonies revealing its vigesimosecular provenance.

15 DECEMBER 1918

Hieroglyphs by the Dutch modernist Daniel RUYNEMAN, scored for a sonorously uncommon group of three flutes, celesta, harp, piano, two mandolines, two guitars and a series of chromatically tuned, hemispherical cup-bells with a compass of 2 1/2 octaves specially made in England according to the composer's specifications, set in an exotically hieroglyphic style calculated to evoke the pictorial writing of ancient Egypt, making liberal use of tin-

klingly disparate whole-tone progressions and atonal melismas, is performed for the first time in Amsterdam on the same program with Ruyneman's choral work *De Roep (The Call)* for a "color scale of mixed voices" a cappella, in a polyphony of contrasting vowels with occasional consonants to intensify the plastic accent.

17 DECEMBER 1918

Second Symphony by the Finnish composer Leevi MADETOJA, written in somber colors and couched in Sibelian harmonies, is performed for the first time in Helsinki.

19 DECEMBER 1918

Nepřemoženi (The Invincibles), opera in four acts by the Czech composer Josef Bohuslav FOERSTER, to his own libretto in which an ailing musician nurses an insurmountable passion for an unattainable countess, is produced in Prague.

24 DECEMBER 1918

Le Cochon qui sommeile, operetta by Claude TERRASSE, is produced in Paris.

1919

11 JANUARY 1919

Eventyr (Once Upon a Time), a symphonic poem by Frederick DELIUS, inspired by Norwegian fairy tales and couched in a Grieg-like manner, with Impressionistic harmonies coloring the unassuming thematic substance, is performed for the first time at the London Promenade Concerts, Sir Henry Wood conducting.

14 JANUARY 1919

Gismonda, lyric drama in three acts by Henry FÉVRIER, to a play by Victorien Sardou, wherein the Florentine duchess, ruler of Athens in 1451, impelled by anti-pagan zeal, orders the destruction (to a whole-tone scale) of a newly found ancient statue of Aphrodite and is condemned by the outraged goddess to submit to a falconer (whom she however learns to love after a preliminary night), to a score of Wagneromorphic resplendence, rich in grandiosely arpeggiated sonorities and cascading chromatic scales (one of them going fully five octaves down to illustrate the falling into a lion's den), is produced for the first time anywhere by the Chicago Opera Company as a commissioned work, with Mary Garden, the current directress of the enterprise, in the title role.

17 JANUARY 1919

Ignace PADEREWSKI becomes Premier of Poland, the first musician to head a modern state.

26 JANUARY 1919

After two years of a ludicrously chauvinistic ban on German music in Italy, Beethoven's *Egmont* Overture is performed in Rome without incident.

26 JANUARY 1919

Poème de la Maison, oratorio by the French composer Georges Martin WITKOWSKI, written in a neo-Renaissance polyphonic idiom, is performed for the first time in Lyons, France.

30 JANUARY 1919

Requiem, suggested by Lincoln's Gettysburg Address, by the New York-born German-trained 46-year-old romantic composer Rubin GOLDMARK, in five connected sections, appropriately opening with a trumpet solo, and concluding with an assertive peroration in the militant key of E-flat major subliminally alluding to Beethoven's *Eroica,* is performed for the first, and antepenultimate, time by the New York Philharmonic Orchestra.

30 JANUARY 1919

Ferhuda, opera in one act by the Italian composer Francesco SANTOLIQUIDO, based on a North African tale of passionate violence, is performed for the first time in Tunis, where the composer himself has long dwelt.

2 FEBRUARY 1919

Xavier LEROUX, French composer of melodramatic operas in a competent traditional style, pupil of Massenet, teacher of Alfredo Casella and other modern composers, dies in Paris at the age of 55.

5 FEBRUARY 1919

Legend of Shota Rustaveli, opera in four acts by the Georgian composer Dmitri ARAKISHVILI, after the medieval Georgian epic, is produced in Tiflis.

15 FEBRUARY 1919

Carl NIELSEN conducts in Copenhagen the first performance of his symphonic suite *Aladdin,* in five movements inspired by the Arabian Nights: (1) *Oriental Festival March;* (2) *Aladdin's Dream and Dance of the Morning Mists;* (3) *Dance of the Captives;* (4) *Market Place in Ispahan;* and (5) *Negro Dance.*

18 FEBRUARY 1919

Through the Looking Glass, suite for small orchestra by Deems TAYLOR, after the classic tale of Lewis Carroll, written in a pleasingly Gallic vein and vividly orchestrated (the clarinet paints the brillig afternoon in *Jabberwocky,* and the vorpal blade of a xylophone snickersnacks the Jabberwock in the bassoon) is performed for the first time by the New York Chamber Music Society. (The suite was subsequently revised for full orchestra; the first performance in this amplified version took place in New York on 10 March 1923, with Walter Damrosch conducting the New York Symphony Society Orchestra.)

21 FEBRUARY 1919

Abesalom e Etheri, opera in four acts by the Georgian composer Zakhar PALIASHVILL, to an Italian libretto dealing with a dynastic struggle in ancient Georgia, wherein the heir to the throne becomes involved in a morganatic liaison with the king's adopted daughter, is produced in Tiflis.

3 MARCH 1919

Passa la Ronda!, one-act opera by Renzo BOSSI, is produced in Milan.

8 MARCH 1919

Three pieces for orchestra, *Chinoiserie, Valse sentimentale* and *Cossack Dance* by Lord BERNERS, the Satie of England, set in a characteristically British ironic manner seasoned with acrid harmonies, pungent rhythms and cultivated exoticisms, are performed for the first time in Manchester.

8 MARCH 1919

El Avapiés, opera in three acts, written in collaboration by the Spanish composers Angel BARRIOS and Conrado del CAMPO, with the action taking place in the densely populated district around the Calle de Lavapiés (colloquially transmogrified into El Avapiés) in Madrid, around 1800, with thematic materials assembled from old street airs, is produced in Madrid.

12 MARCH 1919

The Metropolitan Opera produces in New York two American one-act operas:

(1) *The Legend* by the 48-year-old composer Joseph Carl BREIL, with action evolving in a mythical Balkan country Muscovadia where a brave girl, defending her bandit father, stabs to death her affianced police officer and is shot down herself as the curtain falls rapidly while the orchestra plays a rousing finale; (2) *The Temple Dancer* by the 46-year-old Connecticut composer John Adam HUGO, to a story of a Hindu priestess who steals the jewels of a monstrously cruel idol originally purchased at the price of her carnal abasement, but is struck by lightning as she undulates with a holy snake around her waist to the accompaniment of sinuously serpentine orientalistic scales.

14 MARCH 1919

Gabriel FAURÉ conducts in Paris the first performance of his *Ballade* for piano and orchestra, with Alfred Cortot as soloist.

18 MARCH 1919

Gaudeamus, "scenes from German student life" by Engelbert HUMPERDINCK, with the famous hedonistic Latin student song providing a resonant climax, is performed for the first time in Darmstadt.

22 MARCH 1919

Habanera, symphonic dance in the Spanish vein by Louis AUBERT, set in Parisian harmonies of bitonal implications, is performed for the first time in Paris.

27 MARCH 1919

Fourth Symphony by Kurt ATTERBERG is performed for the first time in Stockholm.

5 APRIL 1919

Das Dorf ohne Gloke (The Village Without a Bell), sing-spiel by the German operetta composer Eduard KÜNNEKE, is performed for the first time in Berlin.

7 APRIL 1919

André MESSAGER conducts in Birmingham, England, the world première of his three-act opera *Monsieur Beaucaire,* in an English version translated from the original French libretto derived from a story by the American writer Newton Booth Tarkington, dealing with a cousin of Louis XV masquerading as a barber during an incognito visit to England, contemptuously rebuked by an English noblewoman who is subsequently dismayed when he is re-introduced to her as the Duke of Orleans, to a score full of musical galanteries characterizing the variously animated peripeteia of the action.

8 APRIL 1919

At the 8th Soirée Dada in Zürich, Tristan TZARA, the inventor of both the word and the concept of DADA, issues his *Proclamation sans prétention,* in which he launches the destructive exhortation, "Musiciens, Cassez Vos Instruments Aveugles Sur la Scène," and asseverates his thesis that Dada is but a natural process of urinal relief: "J'écris parce que c'est naturel comme je pisse."

10 APRIL 1919

Nausicaa, opera in two acts by the Venezuelan-born Parisian composer Reynaldo HAHN, to the story of the Homeric princess who befriends Odysseus on her father's Aegean island, set in a pleasingly perfumed idiom with a proliferation of sonorously marshalled ninth-chords, is produced in Monte Carlo, on the same bill with the first performance of Gabriel FAURÉ's "divertissement lyrique" in one act *Masques et Bergamasques,* the title alluding to the alliterative line from a poem of Paul Verlaine.

13 APRIL 1919

Starý král (The Old King), opera after Rémy de Gourmont's play by the Czech composer Jaroslav JEREMIAŠ, who died on 19 January 1919 at the age of 29, is produced posthumously in Prague.

16 APRIL 1919

Don Ranudo de Colibrados, comic opera in four acts by the Swiss composer Othmar SCHOECK, to a libretto from a Danish play by Ludwig Holberg, dealing with a fatuous Spanish grandee who indignantly rebukes a colored aspirant for his daughter's hand, only to find that the latter is a Royal Ethiopian prince, which makes him accept his offer with supine obsequiousness, set to music in a Wagneromantic manner with a profusion of flamboyant sonorities, is produced in Zürich.

18 APRIL 1919

A century has passed since the birth in Spalato, Dalmatia, of Franz von SUPPÉ, an aristocrat of Germanic-Italian descent whose full name was Francesco Ezechiele Ermenegildo SUPPÉ-DEMELLI, composer of ingratiatingly melodious light operas, whose harmonious overture *Poet and Peasant* has become permanently embedded in the popular orchestra repertory.

24 APRIL 1919

Camille ERLANGER, French composer of several effective operas, of which *Le Juif polonais* has proved viable, dies in Paris at the age of 55.

25 APRIL 1919

Augustus D. JUILLIARD, self-made millionaire and generous supporter of the arts, dies in New York six days after reaching his 83rd birthday (he was born at sea in a sailing vessel in which his French Huguenot parents embarked on their way to America), leaving the bulk of his great estate for the establishment of a Juilliard Music Foundation, "to aid all worthy students of music."

29 APRIL 1919

Blodwen (White Flower), Welsh opera in three acts by Joseph PARRY (1841–1903), first performed in concert form in Swansea, Wales, on 20 June 1878, dealing with the abortive attempt of the Welsh to gain independence from England in the 14th century, wherein Blodwen, the daughter of a Welsh patriot, is reunited with her imprisoned lover to the triumphant strains of a Welsh national march, receives its first stage performance in Colwyn Bay, with the original libretto in the Welsh language.

30 APRIL 1919

Anti-Symphonie, subtitled *Musikalische Kreisguillotine,* by the Ukrainian emigrant composer Jef GOLYSCHEFF, an early exponent of serial tonal techniques, in several sections surrealistically entitled "Provocational Injections," "Chaotic Oral Cavity, or Submarine Aircraft" and "Clapping in Hyper F-sharp Major," is performed for the first time at a Dada exhibition in Berlin.

6 MAY 1919

Notturno e Rondo fantastico, a diptych for piano and orchestra by Riccardo PICK-MANGIAGALLI, is performed for the first time in Milan.

8 MAY 1919

Ihre Hoheitdie Tänzerin, popular operetta by the German composer Walter W. GOETZE, is produced in Stettin.

9 MAY 1919

Jim EUROPE, Negro leader of the jazz band "Hell Fighters," is mortally stabbed at 9:15 P.M. in his dressing room at Mechanics Hall, Boston, by the drummer of his band, and dies two hours later in a Boston hospital.

11 MAY 1919

Thirteen and a half months after DEBUSSY's death, his *Rhapsody* for saxophone, sketched out at the behest of Mrs. Elisa Hall of Boston in 1903, receives its first performance at a concert of the Société Nationale de Musique in Paris, in a version completed and orchestrated by Roger-Ducasse.

12 MAY 1919

The Royal Opera of London resumes its regular season at Covent Garden, after its closure during the war.

14 MAY 1919

Fantaisie, op. 111, for piano and orchestra by Gabriel FAURÉ, in a single movement, opening with a piano solo, in the key of G major, with characteristic excursions into plagal modalities, is performed for the first time at the Société Nationale de Musique in Paris, with Alfred Cortot, to whom the score is dedicated, at the piano.

20 MAY 1919

Sœur Béatrice, opera in three acts by the 23-year-old Greek composer and conductor Dimitri MITROPOULOS, written by him at the age of 19, after

Maeterlinck's religious play, and set in impressionistic colors, is produced in Athens.

25 MAY 1919

Georges ENESCO conducts in Bucharest the first performance of his *Third Symphony* in C major, scored for organ, piano, wordless chorus and orchestra, in three movements portraying three periods of the first two decades of the 20th century—the ephemeral nearly warless world before 1914, the advent of the war, with men of different nations marching mindlessly to their deaths; and the ultimate arrival of precarious peace. (The Paris performance on 26 February 1921 is erroneously listed in some reference works as the world première.)

29 MAY 1919

Xenia, opera by Alexander SAVIN, Belgrade-born naturalized American conductor, written to his own Serbian libretto, is performed for the first time anywhere in Zürich, in a German version, with his wife, the American soprano Lillian Blauvelt, in the title role.

5 JUNE 1919

La Boutique fantasque, ballet in one act on themes from Rossini's posthumous piano pieces, assembled and prismatically orchestrated by Ottorino RESPIGHI in an attractively heterogeneous "fantastic shop" is produced in London by Diaghilev's Ballet Russe.

15 JUNE 1919

Poland issues a 20-pfenning postage stamp (1/5 of a zloty) with the head of Premier PADEREWSKI. (Date obtained in 1936 from the Philatelic Division of the Post Office in Warsaw.)

15 JUNE 1919

Les Choéphores, musical tragedy after Aeschylus and Paul Claudel by Darius MILHAUD, is performed for the first time in concert form in Paris. (The first stage performance was given in Brussels on 27 March 1935.)

16 JUNE 1919

The 1919 edition of The Ziegfeld Follies, introducing Irving BERLIN's famous song *A Pretty Girl Is Like a Melody*, is produced in New York.

20 JUNE 1919

A century has elapsed since the birth in Cologne of Jacques OFFENBACH, the gayest spirit of the comic opera during the Second Empire in Paris.

22 JUNE 1919

The White Peacock, first of the four pieces in the piano suite *Roman Sketches* by the American composer Charles Tomlinson GRIFFES, depicting in fine Impressionistic harmonies the exotic bird of Southeast Asia displaying its multicolored tail in a luxuriant kaleidoscope of ninth-chords, is performed for the first time in an orchestral version as a ballet, in New York. (The first concert performance of *The White Peacock* was given by Leopold

Stokowski conducting the Philadelphia Orchestra on 19 December 1919.)

22 JUNE 1919

Julian SCRIABIN, 11-year-old son of Alexander Scriabin, who as a student of Glière, wrote several preludes (later published in Moscow) in a terse and tense quasi-atonal manner suggestive of the last opus numbers of his father, drowns during an outing in the Dnieper River at Kiev.

5 JULY 1919

Balada de Carnaval, one-act opera by Amadeo VIVES, is produced in Madrid.

7 JULY 1919

Samuel GARDNER, Russian-born violinist and composer, conducts at a concert in New York City the first performance of his symphonic poem *New Russia*.

10 JULY 1919

Hugo RIEMANN, German music scholar and illustrious pedagogue, author of books on harmony, counterpoint, fugue, orchestration and form, compiler of the redoubtably compendious *Musik-Lexikon*, firm believer in the uniqueness of solutions of all musical problems according to strict Hegelian modes, so that music history could be interpreted as a coalition of opposing premises, dies in Leipzig, where he taught a generation of worshipful students, 8 days before reaching the Biblical span of 70 years of age.

14 JULY 1919

CHOUCHOU, Debussy's 14-year-old daughter to whom he tenderly dedicated his *Children's Corner*, succumbs to diphtheria in Paris, after the failure of a desperate attempt to relieve her pulmonary congestion by tracheotomy.

20 JULY 1919

Guillermo URIBE-HOLGUÍN, prime composer of Colombia, who acquired a fine impressionistic flair as a student of Vincent d'Indy in Paris, conducts in Bogotá the first performance of his harmonious *First Symphony*.

22 JULY 1919

The first complete performance of Manuel de FALLA's ballet *El Sombrero de Tres Picos*, is presented in London by Diaghilev's Ballet Russe, under the English title, *The Three-Cornered Hat*. (Absolute world première of the work in its original version was given in Madrid on 7 April 1917 under the title *El Corregidor y la Molinera*.)

27 JULY 1919

La Via della finestra, fifth opera in three acts by the Italian veristic composer Riccardo ZANDONAI, is produced at Pesaro. (A revised version, compressed into two acts, was produced in Trieste on 18 January 1923.)

9 AUGUST 1919

Ruggero LEONCAVALLO, pioneer of Italian Verismo, who cultivated dramatic verisimilitude in operatic libretti and musical characterization, and who as a young man wrote an immortal opera *Pagliacci,* but could never duplicate this success in his many subsequent theatrical works, dies at Montecatini at the age of 62.

20 AUGUST 1919

MANA-ZUCCA (née Augusta Zuckermann), 28-year-old American pianist, soprano and composeress, plays the solo part in the first performance of her *Piano Concerto* in New York.

22 AUGUST 1919

The Academy of Santa Cecilia in Rome is "regificated," and is renamed Regio Conservatorio Musicale di Santa Cecilia.

23 AUGUST 1919

Los Heroes, grand opera in three acts by the 57-year-old Argentine composer Arturo BERUTI, to an Italian libretto glorifying the heroic march over the Andes of the patriotic armies of San Martín during the war of Liberation of Spanish America in 1810 (the composer's grandfather fought in their ranks), making use of native melorhythms in an Italianate setting, is produced at the Teatro Colón in Buenos Aires.

29 AUGUST 1919

Josef Matthias HAUER completes in Vienna the first of his series of *Nomos* for piano, in which his self-promulgated law (nomos) that each theme should consist of 12 different tones, subdivided into symmetrical tropes, is applied for the first time, without, however, attaining the integrality of Schoenberg's method of composition with 12 tones related only to one another.

2 SEPTEMBER 1919

Caio Petronio, an effectively Italianate opera in three acts by the Argentinian composer Constantino GAITO, to a libretto centering on the fate of the *arbiter elegantiarum* Petronius who was ordered to commit suicide by Nero in 66 A.D., is produced at the Teatro Colón in Buenos Aires.

27 SEPTEMBER 1919

Adelina PATTI, fabulous Spanish-born coloratura soprano, the *prima donna assoluta* who moved audiences to frenzied raptures by her thrilling trills and enchanting bel canto, and who continued to inspire adulation on her multiple farewell tours in both hemispheres, dies at the age of 76 at Brecknock, Wales, where she was married to her third husband.

29 SEPTEMBER 1919

Härvard Harpolekare (Härvard the Potter), first opera in two acts by the 31-year-old Swedish composer Kurt Atterberg, is produced in Stockholm. (A revised version, with a new third act, was produced in Linz, Austria, on 14 June 1952.)

10 OCTOBER 1919

Die Frau ohne Schatten, opera in three acts by Richard STRAUSS, to a mystically symbolic libretto of Hugo von Hofmannsthal, wherein a supernatural queen of a group of mythical islands, reincarnated from a white gazelle, casts no shadow and is therefore unable to bear offspring, since progeny is an umbilically umbral projection, but who becomes fertile after she demonstrates her superior humanity by refusing to purchase a shadow from a poor woman at the price of her perdition, and is saluted by a chorus of their unborn children, is produced in Vienna.

16 OCTOBER 1919

A *chi la giarettiera?,* operetta by Ruggero LEONCAVALLO, centered on an anonymous garter of unidentified provenance and possibly adulterous implications, is produced posthumously in Rome.

21 OCTOBER 1919

Kronburden, opera in four acts by the Swedish composer Ture RANGSTRÖM, after Strindberg's play, is produced for the first time, in a German version, under the title *Die Kronbraut (The Crown Bride),* in Stuttgart.

21 OCTOBER 1919

Fennimore und Gerda, the last opera by Frederick DELIUS, completed in 1910, in two individually separable acts, to a libretto after a psychological novel by the Danish writer Jens Peter Jacobsen, detailing the passionate contention between a poet and a painter for a girl named Fennimore, happily resolved when the poet finds solace with his childhood sweetheart Gerda, set to music in a characteristically Deliusian manner, ingenuously combining German neo-romanticism with Gallic quasi-impressionism, is performed for the first time in Frankfurt, to a German libretto by the composer.

24 OCTOBER 1919

The newly formed Los Angeles Philharmonic Orchestra gives its initial concert under the direction of Walter Rothwell.

26 OCTOBER 1919

Revolutionshochzeit, opera in three acts by the Germanized English-born composer Eugen D'ALBERT, the action taking place near Conde in France in April 1793, focused on the self-sacrifice of the one-night bride of an unjustly condemned young Jacobin, who throws herself in front of the firing squad set to execute him, and both perish, with the score containing some innovations (a speaking chorus, realistic instrumental onomatopeia of string glissandi to illustrate the consummation of wedded love), is produced in Leipzig.

27 OCTOBER 1919

Edward ELGAR, the prime Edwardian romanticist of English music, conducts in London the first performance of his *Concerto for Violoncello and Orchestra,* in E minor, with Felix Salmond as soloist, in four discursive movements:

(1) *Adagio—Moderato,* where the cello plays a pensive soliloquy, leading to a slow jig in a bland Aeolian mode; (2) *Lento—*

Allegro molto, erupting after some artful vacillation into a coruscating *perpetuum mobile;* (3) *Adagio,* a spirited romanza with decorative undulating convolutions in the solo part; (4) *Allegro,* featuring a rhapsodic recitative in the cello, followed by a decisive *Allegro molto,* in dancing steps with propulsively symmetric rhythms, ending with gentlemanly gentility in peaceful E minor.

28 OCTOBER 1919

The Star Opera Company of New York City, organized with the intention of presenting German operas in the German language, voluntarily cancels its season after a series of violent ultrapatriotic demonstrations organized by the American Legion.

The Star Opera Co. has retired, egg-stained, from the lyric stage of America, and the attempt of German propagandists to storm the fortress of American post-bellum opinion is a thing of the past. The genial insolence of the Star Opera Co. and its Teutonic associates in testing American tolerance gave New York a series of thrills. Even the New York Supreme Court became interested—to the final regret of Fritz, the uncomprehending and still dazed personification of Germanism. The season opened on 20 October 1919 despite adverse public opinion. On 21 October Mayor Hyland exercised police power to keep the theater closed, but he was overruled by a temporary injunction of the New York Supreme Court and Lortzing's opera *Czar und Zimmermann* was given. Only 150 persons had dared to run the gauntlet of the street. A pitched battle between police and patriots ebbed and flowed down Lexington Avenue. Although the former were supported by Cavalry, the latter sent out a motor truck, preceded by a barrage of milk bottles. Next night rioting was renewed. On 25 October the Star Opera abandoned its plan to sing German opera. (*The Musical Leader,* Chicago, 30 October 1919)

1 NOVEMBER 1919

L'Invasion, opera in three bloody acts with a victorious epilogue by the 31-year-old Belgian composer Fernand BRUMAGNE, whose house and musical manuscripts were burned by the invading Germans in 1914, is performed for the first time at the Théâtre de la Monnaie in Brussels.

8 NOVEMBER 1919

Three days before the first anniversary of the Armistice, WAGNER is played again in Paris for the first time by the Pasdeloup Orchestra, after a vote taken in the audience gives 4,983 in favor of re-Wagnerization of the French musical theater and only 213 for de-Wagnerization.

12 NOVEMBER 1919

Ein Fest zu Haderslev, opera by the 33-year-old Alsatian composer Robert HEGER, is produced in Nuremberg.

15 NOVEMBER 1919

Den Kongelige Gast (The Royal Guest), one-act opera by the Danish composer Hakon BÖRRESEN, is produced in Copenhagen.

15 NOVEMBER 1919

Henry Lee HIGGINSON, munificent founder of the Boston Symphony Orchestra, dies in Boston, three days before his 85th birthday.

16 NOVEMBER 1919

Poem for flute and orchestra by the American composer Charles Tomlinson GRIFFES, written in a delicately Impressionistic manner, is performed for the first time in New York, with Georges Barrère as soloist.

18 NOVEMBER 1919

Irene, musical comedy by Harry TIERNEY on a tale of a modern Cinderella who makes her nonchalant way from the slums of Ninth Avenue in New York to the plush mansions of Long Island, is produced in New York.

22 NOVEMBER 1919

Taras Bulba, opera in five acts by the French composer Marcel SAMUEL-ROUSSEAU, son of Samuel Rousseau whose first name he subjoined to his last, to a libretto from Gogol's powerful novel dealing with a fiercely patriotic Ukrainian Cossack who fought the invading Poles so intransigently that he had no hesitation to shoot his own son for having become infatuated with a Polish beauty, is produced in Paris.

23 NOVEMBER 1919

Grajek (The Player), opera in two acts by the Polish composer Tadeusz JOTEYKO, dealing with the life of a dedicated church organ player, is produced in Warsaw.

25 NOVEMBER 1919

Boudour, ballet-pantomime in one act by the 47-year-old English-born American composer Felix BOROWSKI relating the story of intermingled infidelity and mutual poisoning, with a caliph's concubine named Boudour plotting his overthrow in complot with a muscular male slave, is performed for the first time by the Chicago Opera Company. (An instrumental suite drawn from the ballet was first performed by the Chicago Symphony Orchestra on 14 February 1919.)

27 NOVEMBER 1919

After ten months and ten days in office Ignace PADEREWSKI resigns as Premier of Poland.

28 NOVEMBER 1919

The Pleasure Dome of Kubla Khan, symphonic poem for orchestra by Charles Tomlinson GRIFFES, inspired by the celebrated verses of Coleridge, and depicting the sacred river flowing "through caverns measureless to man down to a sunless sea" in characteristically bleak tone colors, changing to prismatic fountain music with sounds of dancing merriment heard from the Pleasure Dome "decreed" by the mighty monarch, and returning to the somber evocation of "caves of ice" once more overwhelmed by Mongolian revelry, is performed for the first time by the Boston Symphony Orchestra, Pierre Monteux conducting.

30 NOVEMBER 1919

La Mafia, sanguinary opera in two acts by Georges de SEYNES, in which a member of the Sicilian Mafia gouges out the eyes of a suspected traitor and nails his wife's right hand to the table whereupon the blinded victim knifes the killer to death, is produced in Paris.

2 DECEMBER 1919

The former Imperial Opera House in Petrograd announces the discontinuance of further performances owing to extreme winter cold and the utter impossibility to obtain fuel in the disruption of communications during the raging civil war.

13 DECEMBER 1919

Sì, operetta in three acts by Pietro MASCAGNI, described as a "duetto americano" and caricaturing the modern dances of transatlantic provenance, with the purported aim of "safeguarding light Italian music from the enslavement by alien fashions," is produced in Rome.

14 DECEMBER 1919

Sinfonia brevis de Bello Gallico (Third Symphony) by Vincent D'INDY, written during World War I (hence the title), in four movements (thus not very "brevis") abounding in rhapsodically contrasting episodes, and ending in a victorious fanfare, is performed for the first time at the Société Nationale de Musique in Paris.

Premier mouvement—la mobilisation, la Marne; *Scherzo*—la gaîté au front; *Andante*, l'art latin et l'art boche; *Finale*, la victoire avec l'hymne de Saint-Michel comme peroraison. . . . *La Symphonie de Bello Gallico* n'a rien de Stravinsky—tant pis! (From Vincent d'Indy's letter to Guy Ropartz, dated 4 January 1918)

18 DECEMBER 1919

Horatio PARKER, American composer of a series of works distinguished by an impressive Germanic technique, whose pedagogical gift brought profound satisfaction to a generation of grateful students at Yale University where he was a long-term professor of music, dies at Cedarhurst, New York, at the unfulfilled age of 56.

20 DECEMBER 1919

La Boîte à joujoux, "ballet pour enfants" by Claude DEBUSSY, written in 1913 in piano score and subsequently arranged for orchestra by his intimate collaborator André Caplet, to a scenario in which a wooden soldier parades to the burlesqued sounds of the military march from Gounod's *Faust*, woos and wins a handsome doll in mortal combat with the wily Polichinelle, set to music of diaphonous infantiloquy and harmonized in gently archaic open fifths and translucently fragile ninth-chords, with the application of whole-tone scales and chromatically moving consecutive major seconds to depict scenes of infantile terror, and incorporating an exotic episode based on an authentic Hindu elephant-training chant in 5/4 time, is performed posthumously for the first time in Paris, under the direction of André Caplet.

23 DECEMBER 1919

The Birthday of the Infanta, ballet-pantomime by the Chicago composer and railroad man John Alden CARPENTER, after the short story by Oscar Wilde, depicting the tragedy of a Spanish court dwarf who is horrified as he accidentally sees himself in the mirror and, after a grotesque dance that pleases the young princess at her birthday party, drops dead at her feet from exhaustion, is performed for the first time in Chicago.

27 DECEMBER 1919

Albert WOLFF conducts at the Metropolitan Opera House in New York the world première of his opera *L'Oiseau Bleu*, in four acts, after Maeterlinck's play about mystical children yearning for a bluebird of happiness and fulfillment.

29 DECEMBER 1919

The Council of People's Commissars of the Russian Soviet Socialist Republic issues an order to close all vaudeville and light music theaters as detrimental to the educational needs of the proletarian masses.

1920

1 JANUARY 1920

Music and Letters, a quarterly publication devoted impartially and equally to problems of musical todays and yesterdays, begins publication in London, under the editorship of Arthur Henry Fox-Strangways.

It is just six years over the century since the first musical quarterly in the English language was born and six since the last one died. Between these there have been half a dozen, but their united ages have amounted to a bare fifty years. So that a musical quarterly may have a merry life but is evidently a thing that people get tired of in time. (From the editorial in the first issue)

2 JANUARY 1920

Rip Van Winkle, opera in three acts by Reginald DE KOVEN, to a libretto derived from a colonial American legend made famous by Washington Irving, wherein a narcoleptic Dutch villager in the Catskills of 1750 hunts for a magic flask in possession of the phantom of Hendrik Hudson, discoverer of the Hudson River, and falls asleep for twenty years, but returns to marry his old sweetheart, is produced by the Chicago Opera Company, two weeks before DE KOVEN's sudden death.

2 JANUARY 1920

La Veglia, one-act opera by Arrigo PEDROLLO based on J. M. Synge's *The Shadow of the Glen,* is produced in Milan.

3 JANUARY 1920

Le Chant de Nigamon, symphonic poem by Arthur HONEGGER, descriptive of the internecine war between Indian tribes, in which the victorious Huron warrior issues the order to burn the defeated Iroquois alive, but listens in awe as their chief Nigamon intones his own funeral chant, making use in the score of authentic war songs in the pentatonic mode interspersed with agonizingly wistful chromatic laments, and ending on a minor chord with added major sixth and major seventh, is performed for the first rime in Paris.

10 JANUARY 1920

La Terra del sogno, opera by Franco LEONI, is produced in Milan.

12 JANUARY 1920

La Rôtisserie de la Reine Pédauque, opera in four acts by Charles LEVADÉ, after Anatole France's story of convivial encounters in a popular refectory, is produced at the Opéra-Comique in Paris.

13 JANUARY 1920

Quentin Durward, opera in three acts after Walter Scott by the unappreciated but honorable English composer Alexander Morvaren (known mostly as Alick) MACLEAN, is produced in its second (revised) version at Newcastle-on-Tyne (the first version, unproduced, was written in 1892).

16 JANUARY 1920

Reginald DE KOVEN, 60-year-old American composer of several lively operettas, whose immortality was secured by a single song *Oh, Promise Me,* dies suddenly of an apoplectic stroke, after a banquet given in his honor by Mrs. Joseph Fish, patroness of art, in her South Side mansion in Chicago.

16 JANUARY 1920

Henri COLLET writes in the Paris theatrical daily newspaper *Comœdia* a historic article *Les Cinq Russes, Les Six Français et Erik Satie,* drawing an esthetic and numerical parallel between the Russian Mighty Five and a group of six young French composers—Darius MILHAUD, Louis DUREY, Georges AURIC, Arthur HONEGGER, Francis POULENC and Germaine TAILLEFERRE.

"I want a French music for France," writes Jean Cocteau in his remarkable little volume *Le Coq et l' Arlequin.* We are happy that he did write that, for it is precisely what we preach ourselves in our tribune of *Comœdia.* "Music that is not national does not exist," writes Rimsky-Korsakov in *My Musical Life,* and continues: "Indeed, all music that is regarded as universal is in fact national." Jean Cocteau and Rimsky-Korsakov tell us what no conservatory can teach: it is necessary to belong to a nation and to unite with compatriots. Russian music, cultivated by the illustrious Five—Balakirev, Cui, Borodin, Mussorgsky, Rimsky-Korsakov—was united in its aims and became the object of universal admiration because these composers appreciated the initiative of Glinka. The Six Frenchmen, Darius Milhaud, Louis Durey, Georges Auric, Arthur Honegger, Francis Poulenc and Germaine Tailleferre, henceforth inseparable as it was demonstrated by an interesting collection of their compositions as Le Groupe de Six, have by their splendid decision to return to simplicity, brought about a renaissance of French music, because they appreciated the phenomenon of Erik Satie and because they followed the precepts, so lucid, of Jean Cocteau. The above-mentioned album of Le Groupe de Six is a suite of six pieces: *Prélude* by Georges Auric, *Romance sans paroles* by Louis Durey, *Sarabande* by Arthur Honegger, *Mazurka* by Darius Milhaud, *Valse* by Francis Poulenc and *Pastorale* by Germaine Tailleferre. The different temperaments of these six composers clash without conflict, and their works, individual and distinctive, reveal a unity of approach to art that conforms to the ideas of the spokesman of Le Groupe de Six: Jean Cocteau. (Excerpts from Collet's article)

17 JANUARY 1920

Maurice RAVEL refuses to accept his nomination as a Chevalier of the Légion d'Honneur.

What a ridiculous proposition! Who could have played such a joke on me? . . . Members of the Légion d'Honneur are like morphine addicts who would use trickery to force others to share their passion, perhaps to justify it in their own eyes. (From Ravel's letter to Roland-Manuel)

17 JANUARY 1920

Fantasy Scenes from an Eastern Romance for orchestra by Hamilton HARTY is performed for the first time at Leeds.

21 JANUARY 1920

Der Schatzgräber (The Treasure Digger), opera in four acts by Franz SCHREKER to his own libretto from the realm of German fable, in which a minstrel, guided by a sensitive lute which raises its pitch and accelerates the tempo in the vicinity of gold, locates a treasure-trove and presents it to his Queen who graciously commutes his long-standing death sentence and enables him to rejoin his bride who, however, succumbs to anemia, set to music with Wagneromantic fervor, with an inventory of seminal motives immersed in sebaceously pregnant sonorities, is produced in Frankfurt.

24 JANUARY 1920

Il Monaco nero, opera in one act by the Spanish composer Joaquín CASSADÓ, dealing with the "black monk" Schwartz who invented gunpowder in 1340 and blew up the house of his faithless inamorata, killing her and himself, is produced in Barcelona in an Italian version of the original Spanish libretto.

26 JANUARY 1920

Overture on Hebrew Themes by Sergei PROKOFIEV for piano, clarinet and string quartet, based on authentic Jewish folk songs and arranged in a characteristic Russian manner with plagal cadences and agitated trochaic rhythms, is performed for the first time anywhere in New York by a Jewish-American group of former students of the St. Petersburg Conservatory, which supplied Prokofiev with the thematic material for the work.

27 JANUARY 1920

On his American visit, Maurice MAETERLINCK hears DEBUSSY's *Pelléas et Mélisande* for the first time, in a performance by the Chicago Opera Company at the Lexington Theater in New York, with Mary Garden as Mélisande, 17 years and 9 months after the original production in Paris, which Maeterlinck opposed so strongly and which he believed to be a travesty of his play, an additional annoyance to him being the refusal of the management of the Opéra-Comique to cast his mistress Georgette Blanc as Mélisande.

29 JANUARY 1920

Ritter Blaubart, opera in three acts by Emil REZNIČEK, to a libretto dealing with the uxoricidal bluebeard, set in an effectively synthetic idiom of German folk romance, Italian Verismo and Gallic Impressionism, is produced in Darmstadt.

30 JANUARY 1920

Regina von Emmeritz, the last opera, in five acts, by the Finnish composer Oskar MERIKANTO, is produced in Helsinki.

30 JANUARY 1920

Second Symphony by the American composer Frederick S. CONVERSE, set in an academically solid cosmopolitan romantic style, is performed for the first time by the Boston Symphony Orchestra.

31 JANUARY 1920

Cleopatra's Night, opera in two acts by the American composer Henry HADLEY, adapted from Théophile Gautier's story *Une Nuit de Cléopâtre*, wherein Cleopatra grants a night of Egyptian delights to a muscular freeman on condition that it will be his last, whereupon her favorite maid who loves him stabs herself to death and is thrown to the crocodiles, and her lover dutifully drinks a flask of venom as Anthony arrives to join Cleopatra, seasoned with pseudo-exotic whole-tone progressions and serpentine orientalistic arabesques and supported by bombastic Wagneromantic harmonies, is produced at the Metropolitan Opera in New York.

1 FEBRUARY 1920

Melos, fortnightly German magazine devoted to modern music, starts publication in Berlin under the general editorship of the modern-minded conductor Hermann SCHERCHEN, shortly after his return from Russia where he was interned as an enemy alien during World War I.

2 FEBRUARY 1920

Le Chant du Rossignol, ballet in one act adapted from the opera *Le Rossignol* by Igor STRAVINSKY, is produced by Diaghilev's Ballet Russe in Paris.

5 FEBRUARY 1920

Leopold GODOWSKY, the scholarly pianist of prodigiously prestidigital powers, completes the composition in New York of his piano cycle of thirty pieces *Triakontameron*, so named by analogy with Boccaccio's *Decameron*, each piece having been written on a single day, containing his most popular piece, the perennial light classic *Alt Wien*.

7 FEBRUARY 1920

Der türkisenblaue Garten, "a play of love and death" in one act by the 35-year-old Hungarian composer Aladar SZENDREI, taking place amid vermillion pillows and sensuous Persian rugs in a turquoise blue garden wherein the Shah's young wife restores the life of her poisoned lover by a protracted oriental kiss to the accompaniment of chromatic Wagneromantic roulades, is produced in Leipzig.

14 FEBRUARY 1920

Nocturne de Printemps, symphonic poem by the 46-year-old French composer ROGER-DUCASSE, contrasting the exterior impressions of a spring night with the interior emotions of two conjointed human beings, set to music in impressionistic colors, is performed for the first time in Paris.

14 FEBRUARY 1920

Socrate, "symphonic drama" by Erik SATIE, scored for four sopranos and orchestra, set in an artfully archaic, gymnopedically Hellenistic idiom stripped of all melismatic ornamentation, is performed for the first time at the Société Nationale de Musique in Paris in a version for voices and piano. (A complete orchestral performance was first given in Paris on 7 June 1920.)

Those who fail to understand *Socrate* are asked by me to observe a most respectful silence and to manifest an attitude of total obsequiousness and inferiority. (Satie's inscription under the beard of his drawing of Socrates reproduced on the cover of *Le Guide du Concert*, Paris, 15 February 1920)

Satie gestated *Socrate* and beat the bass drum around it. The score is strung together in a succession of melodic fragments of two or four bars each, in the manner of salon chatter. Impotence would not be too harsh a word to characterize the nullity of the whole thing. (Jean Marnold, *Le Mercure de France*, Paris, March 1920) Dans *Socrate*, du génie. (Charles Koechlin)

21 FEBRUARY 1920

A program of modern ballet performances by the "nouveaux jeunes" of French music is presented at the Comédie des Champs-Elysées in Paris, comprising the first performances of the following productions:

Le Bœuf sur le Toit (The Bull on the Roof) by the 27-year-old Darius MILHAUD, completed by him on 21 December 1919, and subtitled, in the original English, "The Nothing Doing Bar," a "cinéma-fantaisie, imagined and arranged by Jean Cocteau," with an appropriately cinematic variety of choreographic and musical materials, including a Brazilian scene (Milhaud served as an attaché at the French Embassy in Rio de Janeiro during the last year of World War I), a policeman's dance in waltz time, a sketch ridiculing the follies of American Prohibition (a bartender hangs out a sign, "Only Milk is Served Here"), couched in an advanced technical idiom, including the first systematic use of bitonality in a section entirely written in the synchronized triadic harmonies of C major and F sharp major, and an authentically sounding excursion into early American jazz (art influenced life when the proprietor of a Paris bistro renamed his establishment, with Milhaud's permission, "e Bœuf sur le Toit"); *Cocarde* by the 21-year-old Francis Poulenc; *Foxtrot* by 21-year-old Georges Auric, and *Trois petites pièces montées* by the perpetual vieux-jeune Erik Satie.

23 FEBRUARY 1920

Der Fremde, opera in four scenes by the German composer Hugo KAUN, after Grimm's grim tale *Gevatter Tod*, in which death plays the role of Godfather, is produced in Dresden.

24 FEBRUARY 1920

Poèmes bouddhiques by the Siamese-born Parisian composer Eugène GRASSE, an oriental triptych of impressionistic tableaux, *Les Oiseaux inspirés*, *La Procession* and *Le Réveil des Bouddhos*, is performed for the first time at the Concerts Colonne in Paris. (The last movement was performed previously in Paris on 20 February, 1920.)

28 FEBRUARY 1920

Le Tombeau de Couperin by Maurice RAVEL, an orchestral suite arranged from four of Ravel's six piano pieces, *Prélude*, *Forlane*, *Rigaudon* and *Menuet*, a stylized tribute to Couperin's Gallic muse set in pandiatonically enriched harmonies, is performed for the first time by the Pasdeloup Orchestra in Paris.

6 MARCH 1920

L'Uomo che ride, opera by Arrigo PEDROLLO (after Victor Hugo's *LHomme qui rit*), is produced in Rome.

8 MARCH 1920

Erik SATIE presents at the Galéries Barbezanges in Paris his provocative *Musique d'Ameublement* dedicated to the proposition that music should be regarded as a utilitarian object of immediate environment, like furniture (hence the title), a potpourri of unrelated tunes performed by musicians stationed in separate parts of the hall so as to enable the public to hear the playing of individual instruments while walking.

10 MARCH 1920

Fifth Symphony, subtitled *Dans les Alpes*, by the French organist Charles TOURNEMIRE, is performed for the first time anywhere at The Hague.

21 MARCH 1920

Balada blanická (The Ballad of Blaník), symphonic poem by Leoš JANÁČEK, is performed for the first time in Brno.

31 MARCH 1920

Mirra, opera in two acts by the Italian modernist Domenico ALALEONA, wherein a young woman of Cyprus, possessed by incestuous love for her young father, neglects her ardent husband causing him to wither in utter inanition in gymnosophistical naked fifths, while her father curses her in highly chromaticized dissonances, driving her to suicide by stabbing herself with the aid of perpendicularly integrated columns of whole-tone scales, making use also of nontempered "pentafonia" dividing the octave into five equal intervals, is produced in Rome.

8 APRIL 1920

Komedianter, opera in three acts by the Danish composer August ENNA, after Victor Hugo's story *Lhomme qui rit*, is produced in Copenhagen.

8 APRIL 1920

Charles Tomlinson GRIFFES, American composer of Impressionistically flavored music with delicately poetic invocations of distant lands and exotic creatures, written in a style directly influenced by Debussy and Ravel, but containing elements of individual tonal perceptivity, dies in New York at the age of 35.

11 APRIL 1920

Ballata delle Gnomidi, symphonic poem by Ottorino RESPIGHI, written in his characteristic picturesque style, is performed for the first time at the Augusteo in Rome, Bernadino Molinari conducting.

17 APRIL 1920

Marche française, symphonic poem by ROGER-DUCASSE, descriptive of peace, summons to arms, and victorious marching, written during World War I and dedicated to Georges Clemenceau and Marshal Foch, is performed for the first time at the Pasdeloup Concerts in Paris.

23 APRIL 1920

Výlety páně Broučkovy (Flights of Mr. Brouček), opera in two acts by Leoš JANÁČEK, to a satirical libretto ridiculing the extraterrestrial fantasies of a central European burgher, who in a state of inebriation imagines trips both through time to the 15th century and through space to the moon, reaching it a full 49 years before the actual lunar landing of 20 July 1969, vigorously set to music pulsating with asymmetrical rhythms and stimulatingly angular melodies, is produced in Prague.

24 APRIL 1920

Amy Robsart, opera in three acts by the Argentine composer Alfredo SCHIUMA, to a libretto from Walter Scott's historical novel *Kenilworth*, focused on the unhappy fate of Lady Leicester whose husband murdered her in the hope of marrying Queen Elizabeth, is produced at the Teatro Colón in Buenos Aires.

24 APRIL 1920

Isabella Orsini, lyric tragedy in four acts by the Italian composer Renato BROGI, dealing with the internecine struggle between powerful family groups in medieval Tuscany, is produced in Florence.

27 APRIL 1920

Ragtime for eleven instruments, including cimbalom, by Igor STRAVINSKY is performed for the first time in London.

28 APRIL 1920

Schirin und Gertraude, opera in four acts by Paul GRAENER, dealing with a German feudal lord who imports a Turkish odalisque from a Crusade and persuades his wife to acquiesce in a triangular concubinage, set to music in a luxuriantly Wagneromorphic vein in ponderous harmonies inspissated with gravid dissonant combinations, is produced in Dresden.

13 MAY 1920

Two one-act operas by the German conductor Felix WEINGARTNER, *Die Dorfschule* and *Meister Andrea*, are produced in Vienna.

15 MAY 1920

Pulcinella, "ballet avec chant" by Igor STRAVINSKY, based on the musical materials of various instrumental pieces attributed to Pergolesi (but in fact suspected to be works by other Italian 18th-century composers), is produced at the Paris Opéra by Diaghilev's Ballet Russe, with a scenario centering on the famous character of Neapolitan commedia dell'arte, who perseveres in his pursuit of a girl he fancies above all others, with the musical score following the form of a classical dance suite:

(1) *Overture*, set in a strict manner of the Italian Baroque, in a major mode; (2) *Serenata* (a tenor solo); (3) *Scherzino*, leading to *Allegro*, followed by *Andantino*, *Allegro* and *Presto;* (4) *Allegretto* with soprano solo, *Allegro assai*, followed by *Allegro* with a bass solo, *Largo*, *Allegro*, with a duet for soprano and tenor, *Presto* with a tenor solo, *Allegro*, *Andantino* with a soprano solo and *Allegro;* (5) *Gavotte* with two variations; (6) *Vivo*, *Minuetto* and *Finale*, concluding on a sumptuously emblazoned, triumphantly festive, pandiatonically enriched, fiercely white C major.

19 MAY 1920

Lorenzaccio, opera in four acts by the French composer Ernest MORET, based on the play by Alfred de Musset depicting a life of debauchery and murder in 16th-century. Florence, centering on the dissolute member of the Medici family Lorenzaccio (a contemptuous Italian diminutive for Lorenzo), whose misdeeds included the slaying of the first Medici who claimed the title of Duke, is produced at the Opéra-Comique in Paris.

20 MAY 1920

A festival of music by Camille SAINT-SAËNS opens in Athens, with the participation of the 84-year-old composer as pianist and conductor. (Three more concerts were given on 22, 28 and 29 May 1920.)

22 MAY 1920

Amaya, opera in three acts by Jesús GURIDI, the first ever written in the Basque language, dealing with the conflict of pagan and Christian doctrines and mores in the Pyrenees, with dance interludes set in characteristic dual meters, 3/4 and 6/8, is produced in Bilbao.

24 MAY 1920

Pablo PICASSO makes a three-quarter drawing of Igor STRAVINSKY showing him as a seated figure, with hands enlarged by natural perspective and left forefinger hooked around the right middle finger. (Picasso drew Stravinsky in profile on 31 December 1920.)

24 MAY 1920

The British Music Society adopts the standard pitch A = 435.4 vibrations per second at 59° Fahrenheit.

28 MAY 1920

Die blaue Mazur, operetta by Franz LEHÁR, in which a virginal Austrian damsel is compelled to marry a dissolute Polish count after she accepts the invitation to dance the matrimonially binding blue mazurka with him at an aristocratic ball, but flees in horror from their bridal chamber when it is invaded by a procession of ci-devant concubines, returning to him only when he solemnly abjures recidival pluralistic fornication, is produced in Vienna.

29 MAY 1920

Banjuta, opera in four acts by Alfreds KALNIŅŠ, the first national Latvian opera to a libretto from medieval Livonian life, involving rape, murder and the bereaved woman's sudden passion for the killer of her husband, is produced at the newly opened (inaugurated on 2 December 1919) Latvian National Opera House in Riga.

6 JUNE 1920

The Austrian Government adopts a new national anthem to replace the old Imperial hymn written in 1797 by Haydn, with the text by Austria's Chancellor Karl Renner and music by Wilhelm KIENZL. (On 13 December 1929, the Haydn melody was reinstated with a different set of words eliminating imperial references.)

6 JUNE 1920

La Légende de Saint Christophe, sacred drama by Vincent D'INDY, set in the form of a triple triptych, containing three acts of three scenes each, depicting the conversion of Christopher by the Infant Jesus whom he carried across a stream (hence the name Christopher, Christ-Bearer), his temptation in a prison cell by the Queen of Lust (who becomes herself converted as her pagan whole-tone motto is transmuted into an ecclesiastical mode), his uninflammability (the flames are diverted by celestially pure medieval harmonies at the stake), his invulnerability (diatonic arrows rebound from his skin) and his ultimate martyrdom, is performed for the first time at the Paris Opéra, with the omission of an episode in which Satan stages a procession of false savants, Jews, socialists and composers of ultra-modern music. (Date from the review in *Le Ménestrel;* the same date is given in Loewenberg's *Annals of Opera*. But the printed score of the work cites 8 June 1920 for the first performance, as does Grove's *Dictionary of Music and Musicians*.)

6 JUNE 1920

Lešetínský Kovář (The Blacksmith of Lešetín), opera by the Czech composer Karel WEIS, is produced in Prague.

1 JULY 1920

Die ersten Menschen, two-act opera by Rudi STEPHAN, German composer killed on the Russian front on 29 September 1915, is produced in Frankfurt.

7 JULY 1920

De Triomfeerende Min (Love's Triumph) in one act, first opera in the Dutch language, written and published in 1680, by Carolus HACQUART, is performed in a newly rearranged version by P.A. van Westhreen, in Arnheim.

18 JULY 1920

Fifth Symphony in D major by Nicolai MIASKOVSKY, completed in the summer of 1918, in four classically outlined movements, written in a more objectively optimistic style than his somberer works of previous years, and showing a preponderance of major keys, is performed for the first time in Moscow.

20 JULY 1920

The first experiment in broadcasting music by wireless telephony from a ship is made during the passage from England to Canada of the S.S. *Victoria.*

21 JULY 1920

Saika, operatic fairy tale by the Argentine composer Floro UGARTE, to his own libretto, similar to the story of *Hänsel und Gretel,* in which two children are lured into an enchanted forest by the witch Saika, and are saved from immolation by angelic intercession, is produced at the Teatro Colón in Buenos Aires.

4 AUGUST 1920

Vladimir REBIKOV, Russian composer and experimenter, who introduced such innovations as systematic sequences of unresolved discords, chordal integration of whole-tone scales (as in his piano piece *Les Démons s'amusent*), counterpoint in open fourths and fifths, and pandiatonic matrices of sound (as in his *Hymn to the Sun,* for piano solo composed in 1912 synchronously with Henry Cowell's experiments in tone-clusters, and using identical notation as Cowell), dies in Yalta, Crimea, of a brain hemorrhage, at the age of 54.

(Date according to the death certificate in the Russian Orthodox Church of Autka, Yalta; the date 1 December 1920, given in the previous editions of *Music Since 1900* and in all music dictionaries is wrong.)

5 AUGUST 1920

Leon THEREMIN, 23-year-old Russian electrical engineer, presents at the Physico-Technical Institute in Petrograd an experimental demonstration of his historic invention, AETHEROPHONE (later renamed THEREMINOVOX, and known in America simply as THEREMIN), the first musical instrument to produce musical tones by electronic impulses, effected by the interaction of two ultra-sonic circuits passing through a set of oscillating radio tubes, one circuit operating at a constant frequency, the other being altered by the movement of the player's hand through the air in front of an antenna, with the resulting differential tones falling in the audible range.

5 AUGUST 1920

Ariana y Dionisios, opera by the Argentine composer Felipe BOERO, relating Ariadna's peripeteia after she is abandoned by Theseus and restored to life by Dionysus, is produced at the Teatro Colón in Buenos Aires.

20 AUGUST 1920

The first commercial radio broadcast featuring musical numbers is made by the Detroit Station WWJ.

On the night of 20 August 1920, the first commercial radio broadcast station in all the world was opened. And every night and every day since that momentous beginning WWJ has maintained this service. . . . Not until eleven weeks after its founding did WWJ share the channels of the air with a rival broadcasting station. The honor of being second fell to KDKA of Pittsburgh . . . and, though it has erroneously claimed and been credited with priority among broadcasters, it is still entitled to a place of distinction. (From an announcement by Lee de Forest, American inventor and pioneer of broadcasting, on the occasion of the 16th anniversary of the initial broadcast, on 20 August 1936)

23 AUGUST 1920

The Sunset Trail, Indian music drama by Charles Wakefield CADMAN, is produced for the first time by the California Theater Ensemble at San Diego, California.

4 SEPTEMBER 1920

L'Aviatore Dro, "futurist opera" by the Italian composer Francesco Balilla PRATELLA, to his own libretto in which the aviator Dro abandons his beauteous mistress to be alone with his beloved biplane, and flies aloft to merge with the universe, with a motorcycle engine included in the score to illustrate the revving up of an airplane, is performed for the first time in the composer's native town of Lugo.

5 SEPTEMBER 1920

Peter Racine FRICKER, English composer of symphonic and chamber music in a lyrically dramatic modernistic style verging on atonal melos and polytonal harmonies, with a fine texture of non-toxic dissonance, is born in London.

11 SEPTEMBER 1920

Sinfonía sevillana by Joaquín TURINA, a symphonic integration of Andalusian melorhythms, is performed for the first time at San Sebastian, Spain, under its original title *Sevilla,* with Fernandez Arbos conducting.

1 OCTOBER 1920

Henri RABAUD is appointed Director of the Paris Conservatory.

2 OCTOBER 1920

Max BRUCH, industrious and competent German composer whose *Kol Nidrei,* a romance for violin and orchestra, written in 1880 for a Jewish community of Liverpool, is so intimately impregnated with the spirit of Hebrew cantillation that he was mistakenly listed as a Jew in the early editions of Grove's *Dictionary* and other reference books, and whose *Violin Concerto* in G minor is still cherished by romantically inclined virtuosos, dies in Berlin at the age of 82.

19 OCTOBER 1920

Anatoly LUNACHARSKY, People's Commissar of Education of the Russian Soviet Socialist Republic, declares the continued maintenance of the Petrograd Philharmonic Orchestra to be of national importance:

I herewith serve notice that the Philharmonic Orchestra of Petrograd is the only exemplary symphonic institution of the Republic. Any attempt at the disorganization of its activities is a criminal offense. The Petrograd Philharmonic must remain intact as an institution of prime national importance. All musicians who were included in the orchestra personnel before 1 January 1919 are to be regarded as original members whose principal obligation is to the Philharmonic, and employment elsewhere is to be allowed only as an inevitable concession to the prevailing conditions of our time. (Date and text from *The Leningrad Philharmonic*, Leningrad, 1935)

24 OCTOBER 1920

At a Colonne concert in Paris, the first performance is given of Darius MILHAUD's *Second Orchestral Suite*, from the materials of his incidental music to Paul Claudel's play *Protée*, comprising the following movements:

(1) *Overture*, in a protean bitonal idiom, with D major serving as an axis and an anchor; (2) *Prelude and Fugue*, based on a grotesquely iterative figure originating in the low wind instrument register; (3) *Pastorale*, set in the compound meter of 8/8 separated into asymmetrical groups of 3, 3 and 2 eighth-notes, alternating with simple 3/4 time; (4) *Nocturne*, in a propulsively steady 5/8 time; (5) *Finale*, in square time, with polytonal excursions, reverting in the end to a concentrated, unisonally assertive C.

29 OCTOBER 1920

The Garden of Fand by Arnold BAX, his best-known and valid symphonic poem, written in 1913 and illustrating the Irish legend of an enchanted garden on a mid-Atlantic island, ruled by a beautiful Irish girl, who captures an enthralled boat crew and causes the island to submerge amid dance and sensuous revelry under the aquamarine waves of impressionistic ninth-chords, amethyst triadic inversions and pearly arpeggios on the celesta, is performed for the first time anywhere by the Chicago Symphony Orchestra.

1 NOVEMBER 1920

La Revue Musicale, "Revue mensuelle internationale d'art musical ancien et moderne," starts publication in Paris, edited by Henry PRUNIÈRES, inaugurating a fruitful period of informative and elegant musical journalism.

2 NOVEMBER 1920

Des Kaisers Dichter, opera in three acts by Clemens von FRANCKENSTEIN, to a libretto dealing with the life of the Chinese poet Li Tai Po, is produced in Hamburg.

4 NOVEMBER 1920

Zeelandia, symphonic poem descriptive of the lowlands of Holland by the Dutch composer Frits Adriaan KOEBERG, is performed for the first time in Amsterdam.

5 NOVEMBER 1920

On his first visit to the United States, Cyril SCOTT appears as soloist with the Philadelphia Orchestra conducted by Leopold Stokowski in the first American performance of his *Piano Concerto*, and also conducts his two orchestral *Passacaglias*.

5 NOVEMBER 1920

Suite for viola and orchestra by Ernest BLOCH, an orchestral version of his suite for viola and piano, in four movements—(1) *Lento-Allegro*, (2) *Allegro ironico*, (3) *Lento*, (4) *Molto vivo*—with the music redolent of quasi-Oriental exoticism in its melismatic arabesques, is performed for the first time in New York.

7 NOVEMBER 1920

On the third anniversary of the Soviet Revolution, *The Conquest of the Winter Palace*, spectacle with music, is enacted with a cast of thousands in Winter Palace Square in Petrograd.

15 NOVEMBER 1920

The first complete public performance of the astrological symphonic suite *The Planets* by the English composer Gustav HOLST (he studied astrology assiduously in 1913) takes place in London under the direction of Albert Coates (a private performance of *The Planets* was first given in London on 29 September 1918):

Mars, the Bringer of War with hollow chords portraying the vacuous inexorability of martial endeavor against the restless agitation of the strings in asymmetrical 5/4 time; *Venus, the Bringer of Peace,* with a tender violin solo introduced by a pacific harp, and some contention between rival factions manifested by clashing seventhchords; *Mercury, the Winged Messenger* in dual meters of 6/8 and 3/4 alternating with choreographic agility; *Jupiter, the Bringer of Jollity*, projecting a powerful high-gravity central theme in ponderously sententious harmonies; *Saturn, the Bringer of Old Age*, a debile progression of emasculated quintal harmonies; *Uranus, the Magician*, opening with a passage of catarrhal bassoons, developing non-thematically into a sonorous bubble, and, after an organ glissando, exploding into the solar whiteness of februated C major before subsiding into inaudible timelessness; *Neptune, the Mystic*, an impressionistic study with discursive arpeggios rolling along over the angular intersections of 5/4 time while a wordless chorus of female voices intones measured syllables of expressionless communication.

18 NOVEMBER 1920

El Greco, ballet by the French conductor and composer Désiré Émile INGHELBRECHT, to a scenario on the life and art of the great Greco-Hispanic painter whose ascetically limned saints and somberly contemplative landscapes presage the expressionistic configurations of the modern era, set to music incorporating elements of Spanish and ecclesiastical modalities, is produced by the Ballets Suédois in Paris.

23 NOVEMBER 1920

Pilgrim Vision by John Alden CARPENTER, a symphonic poem written to celebrate the tercentenary of the landing of the Pilgrims at Plymouth, Massachusetts, is performed for the first time by the Philadelphia Orchestra.

27 NOVEMBER 1920

Scherzo veneziano, choreographic comedy by Ottorino RESPIGHI, is performed for the first time in Rome.

1 DECEMBER 1920

Le Roi Candaule, lyric comedy in four acts by Alfred BRUNEAU, wherein a dissolute ruler of the rich kingdom of Lydia is assassinated by his prime minister who then marries his queen giving rise to the last Lydian dynasty, set to music in a pseudo-exotic manner brightened by naturalistic dramatic touches, such as a quasi-Debussyan croaking of frogs in sharply accentuated secundal counterpoint, and impressionistic chordal parallelisms, is produced at the Opéra-Comique in Paris.

4 DECEMBER 1920

Die Vögel, opera in two acts by the German composer Walter BRAUNFELS, after Aristophanes, is produced in Munich.

4 DECEMBER 1920

Die tote Stadt, opera in three acts by the 23-year-old Austrian composer Erich Wolfgang KORNGOLD, after Rodenbach's novel *Bruges-la-Morte*, wherein a grieving widower meets a ballerina who resembles his wife in every respect but the quality of virtue, and in a reverie strangles her with his wife's golden tresses preserved in a crystal container, to the accompaniment of a baleful "hair motive" in the trombones, whereupon he wakes up and decides to leave the "city of the dead," is produced on the same night in Hamburg and Cologne.

6 DECEMBER 1920

Karel KOVAŘOVIC, Czech composer, conductor of the National Opera in Prague, who wrote operas on historical subjects in an effective dramatic manner slightly touched by Wagneromantic effluvia, dies in Prague, three days before reaching his 58th birthday.

12 DECEMBER 1920

La Valse, "choreographic poem for orchestra in the tempo of the Viennese waltz" by Maurice RAVEL, presenting a nostalgic panorama of old Vienna, opening with fragments of waltz tunes and developed with calculated hesitation into a flamboyant ball, richly supported by deeply anchored pedal points and gothic columns of ninth-chords, and suggesting a gauze-covered painting in muted colors, is performed for the first time in Paris, by the Lamoureux orchestra, Camille Chevillard conducting.

Whirling clouds give glimpses, through rifts, of couples waltzing. The clouds scatter little by little. One sees an immense hall peopled with a twirling crowd. The scene is gradually illuminated. The light of the chandeliers burst forth in fortissimo. An Imperial Court about 1855. (From the description in the printed score)

13 DECEMBER 1920

Edipo rè, posthumous one-act opera, after Sophocles, by Ruggero LEONCAVALLO, is produced for the first time anywhere in Chicago.

21 DECEMBER 1920

Sally, musical comedy by Jerome KERN, in which a waitress crashes a society party in Long Island pretending to be a Russian ballet dancer, and using her meretricious snob appeal lures a gullible millionaire into matrimony, containing the hit songs *Sally*, *Look for the Silver Lining* and *The Little Church Around the Corner*, is produced by Florenz Ziegfeld in New York.

28 DECEMBER 1920

Arturo TOSCANINI conducts in New York the first concert of his American tour with the orchestra of La Scala, Milan.

31 DECEMBER 1920

The Lithuanian National Opera is organized in Kaunas, the capital of the Lithuanian Republic.

1 JANUARY 1921

Fritz KLEIN completes the score of his symphonic poem for chamber orchestra *Die Maschine, Eine extonale Selbstsatire;* signing it *Heautontimorumenos (Self-tormentor)*, containing nine innovating musico-mathematical devices: (1) a 12-note rhythm; (2) a 12-note modal theme; (3) a chord containing 12 different intervals, from a minor second to an octave; (4) a "neutral" scale of alternating minor and major seconds; (5) a theme composed of the three preceding intervalic arrangements; (6) a Pyramid Chord constructed of 12 intervals in an arithmetical progression; (7) *Mutterakkord*, containing 12 different notes and 11 different intervals; (8) a mirror reflection of a symmetrically arranged chord-theme; (9) a contrapuntally combined development of all themes and intervalic arrangements of the piece.

2 JANUARY 1921

Das Wandbild, scene and pantomime by the foremost lyric composer of Switzerland, Othmar SCHOECK, to a story by Ferruccio Busoni, wherein a youthful swain pursues an oriental girl in a picture on the wall in a Paris shop into the land of erotogenic delights set to music in Wagneromantic harmonies, is performed for the first time in Halle.

2 JANUARY 1921

For the first time, a complete radio broadcast is made of a church service from Calvary Church in Pittsburgh. (The date is commemorated on the plaque at the entrance of Calvalry Church.)

5 JANUARY 1921

For the first time since the war, the Paris Opéra presents a Wagner music drama, *Die Walküre*, collecting the unprecedented sum of 35,977 francs at the box office.

10 JANUARY 1921

By order of municipal authorities of Zion City, Illinois, the playing of jazz music is forbidden in all public places.

10 JANUARY 1921

Third Symphony by the Norwegian composer Christian SINDING is performed for the first time anywhere in Berlin.

19 JANUARY 1921

Nemici, opera in three acts by Guido GUERRINI, to his own libretto, is produced in Bologna.

28 JANUARY 1921

The Federal Court of New York City orders an injunction restraining J. H. Remick & Co., music publishers, from selling copies of *Avalon*, a popular song about a beautiful ocean island of the Arthurian romances, set to music identical with Cavaradossi's anguished lines *O dolci baci, o languide carezze*, from the aria *E lucevan le stelle* in Puccini's *Tosca* (with the line "I found my love in Avalon" hideously altered to a major key), and imposes a fine of $25,000 for damages in favor of the plaintiff, G. Ricordi & Co., owners of the copyright.

9 FEBRUARY 1921

James Gibbons HUNEKER, American author of brilliant essays on music, self-confessed "old fogey" (the expression which he applied to himself in the title of one of his books), believer in an absolute standard of esthetics, urbane demolitionist of ultra-modern composers, such as Debussy and Strauss, dies in Brooklyn nine days after his 61st birthday.

11 FEBRUARY 1921

Fanfulla, tragicomedy in three acts by the 46-year-old Italian composer Attilio PARELLI, to a libretto dealing with the heroic sixteenth-century Italian warrior Giovanni Bartolomeo Fanfulla, is performed for the first time in Trieste.

12 FEBRUARY 1921

Pastorale d'été, Arcadian evocation for a small ensemble of instruments by Arthur HONEGGER, is performed for the first time in Paris.

13 FEBRUARY 1921

Per una Favola cavalleresca, "symphonic illustration of legendary love scenes, tournaments and battles" by Gian Francesco MALIPIERO, written in a characteristic dual idiom of Italian musical modernism, affecting archaic forms in pandiatonic harmonies, is performed for the first time in Rome.

3 MARCH 1921

Les Trois Mousquetaires, opera in six scenes by the Anglo-French composer Isidore DE LARA, after the famous novel of flamboyant adventure of Alexandre Dumas, is produced in Cannes.

4 MARCH 1921

Indian Sketches, orchestral suite by the American composer Henry F. GILBERT, making use of authentic Indian tunes, is performed for the first time by the Boston Symphony Orchestra, Pierre Monteux conducting.

5 MARCH 1921

Violin Concerto in three movements by the 21-year-old Bulgarian composer Pantcho VLADIGEROV, written in an expansively romantic melodious manner powdered with Balkanized rhythmic asymmetries, is performed for the first time by his older nonidentical twin brother Luben with the Berlin Philharmonic, under the direction of Fritz Reiner. (Luben was born in Zürich, whither Mother Vladigerov sped before parturition mistrustful of Bulgarian obstetrical skill in multiple birth cases, late on 12 March 1899, with Pantcho following into the world 16 hours later on 13 March 1899; these dates have been obtained by the author from the registries of birth in Zürich.)

12 MARCH 1921

The Rebel Maid, light opera by the 35-year-old English organist and harmony teacher Montague PHILLIPS, dealing with a militant girl supporter of William of Orange on his landing in England on 5 November 1688, who witnesses him crowned as King of England in joint sovereignty with his wife Mary, written in a melodiously harmonious academic manner, is produced in London.

14 MARCH 1921

Antar, "heroic narrative" in four acts by the French composer Gabriel DUPONT (1878–1914), to a libretto in which a desert sheik's nomadic marriage is rescinded when he is struck down by an arrow shot by a blinded love rival whose guidance in archery was made possible by an accurate vectorial measurement of his foe's loud voice, set to music contrasting the cerulean brilliance of the aquamarine colors of the Mediterranean melorhythms with the sandy monotony of the orientalistically oriented chants of the Sahara, is posthumously produced at the Paris Opéra.

16 MARCH 1921

Kaddara, opera by the Danish composer Hakon BÖRRENSEN, to a libretto set in Greenland, wherein Kaddara, an intransigent Arctic housewife, locks out her whaling husband when he comes home without booty, whereupon he reembarks in his kayak, harpoons a giant whale and takes it to a local widow whose daughter bites his shoulder according to the ancient Greenlandian welcoming ritual, which fails to fascinate him, and he returns to his igloo, as his wife sings a lullaby for their child and the sun appears on the horizon after a long polar night, set to music with the application of authentic modes of Eskimo songs, is performed for the first time in Copenhagen.

17 MARCH 1921

Pantcho VLADIGEROV, 22-year-old Bulgarian composer, plays the solo part with the Berlin Philharmonic in the first performance of his *First Piano Concerto*, written in a romantic manner with injections of typical Bulgarian melorhythms.

17 MARCH 1921

Ramuntcho, lyric drama in four acts by the 42-year-old Sicilian composer Stefano DONAUDY, is performed for the first time in Milan.

19 MARCH 1921

Two and a half centuries have passed since the opening of the first public opera theater in Paris by the poet Pierre PERRIN and the court musician Robert CAMBERT.

21 MARCH 1921

La Colombe de Bouddha, one-act opera by the Venezuelan-born Parisian composer Reynaldo HAHN, to a libretto dealing with the sacred dove of the Buddha, is performed for the first time in Cannes.

24 MARCH 1921

Déodat DE SÉVERAC, French composer of delicately wrought impressionistic music in various forms, dies of chronic albuminuria, at Céret in the Pyrenees, at the age of 48. (He was born on 20 July 1872, as proved by his birth certificate, not on 20 July 1873 as he liked to believe.)

27 MARCH 1921

Kyra Frossini, opera by the Greek composer George SKLAVOS, is performed for the first time in Athens.

29 MARCH 1921

La Jane, one-act opera by the Belgian composer Armand MARSICK, to a story of a piteously seduced damsel who avenges herself by killing her corrupter on the day of his marriage to another, is produced in Liège.

5 APRIL 1921

Alfons DIEPENBROCK, Dutch composer, ardent polyphonist and guardian of the old Flemish tradition, dies in his native Amsterdam at the age of 58.

9 APRIL 1921

Die Kohlhaymerin (Kohlhaymer's Spouse), opera in four acts by the Austrian composer Julius BITTNER, to his own libretto, focused on a well-preserved Viennese widow who flourished in 1810, with an element of fantasy intruding as her deceased husband steps out of the frame of his portrait to the accompaniment of ominous progressions in whole-tone scales to warn her against a predatory local Don Juan, is produced in Vienna.

15 APRIL 1921

Anima allegra, lyric comedy in three acts by the Italian composer Franco VITTADINI, in which a girl from Granada, the "merry soul" of the title, invades circa 1830 the dank premises of her suburban aunt's home, introduces her male cousin to a Gypsy camp, and eventually marries him, the score set in a conventional Mediterranean style with the insertion of Andalusian dance episodes, is produced in Rome.

15 APRIL 1921

Der Vetter aus Dingsda (The Cousin from Dingsda), light opera by Eduard KÜNNEKE, is performed for the first time in Berlin.

22 APRIL 1921

Serge KOUSSEVITZKY inaugurates in Paris the annual series of Concerts Koussevitzky.

28 APRIL 1921

Die Krähen (The Crows), "Lustspiel" in one act by the German conductor Walter COURVOISIER, to a libretto from Benvenuto Cellini's autobiography, portraying a gathering of young artists and their "crows" (female friends) at the height of the plague in Rome in the early 16th century, at which Cellini brings a male apprentice dressed as a woman to mock the unjustified jealousy of his suspicious inamorata, is performed for the first time in Munich.

2 MAY 1921

Pietro MASCAGNI conducts in Rome the first performance of his three-act opera *Il piccolo Marat*, in which a young French nobleman infiltrates the ranks of terrorists in Arras about 1793 so successfully that he earns the sobriquet "Little Marat," and in the last act rescues his widowed mother from the Revolutionary sans-culottes and elopes with the niece of the dreaded chairman of the local Committee of Public Safety, ending in an aristocratic display of royally immaculate C major.

7 MAY 1921

Il Mistero, opera by Domenico MONLEONE, is performed for the first time in Venice.

9 MAY 1921

Pan Twardowski, ballet by the Polish composer Ludomir RÓZICKI, after the classical poem of Adam Mickiewicz, is performed for the first time in Warsaw.

11 MAY 1921

Middelalderig (The Middle Ages), opera by the 36-year-old Swedish composer Ture RANGSTRÖM, is produced in Stockholm.

15 MAY 1921

Die Prinzessin Girnara, first opera, in two acts, by Egon WELLESZ of Vienna, to a mystical play by Jakob Wassermann in which the real and symbolic characters intermingle in somnial ambulation, set to music in nervously implosive dissonant harmonies, is performed for the first time in Hannover. (A revised version was produced in Mannheim on 2 September 1928.)

The opera is blatant nonsense of unspeakable hideousness. We must refuse to tolerate in the future such criminal assaults in art and on the public. (Richard Ohlekopf, *Signale für die musikalische Welt*, Berlin, 25 May 1921.)

16 MAY 1921

Sirocco, opera in three acts by Eugen D'ALBERT, wherein a Parisian cocotte, nicknamed after the devastating desert wind, demoralizes the stalwart soldiers of fortune in North Africa and is ultimately throttled by a member of the French Foreign Legion, set to a synthetic score, incestuously combining elements of German romanticism and Italian Verismo, is performed for the first time anywhere in Darmstadt.

17 MAY 1921

Diaghilev's Ballet Russe presents in Paris the first performance of *Chout* (French spelling of the Russian word for Buffoon) by the 30-year-old Sergei PROKOFIEV, derived from a medieval Russian folk tale, *The Buffoon Who Outwitted Seven Other Buffoons*, set to a grotesquely agitated musical score bristling with asymmetrical rhythms against a steady marching beat and diversified by the interpolation of ironically lyric episodes, in six compact scenes interlarded with five symphonic interludes:

(1) *Buffoon's Room*, in brusque bombastic rhythms and melodies set in pandiatonic harmonies; (2) *At the House of Seven Buffoons*, a boisterously discordant burlesque in which the buffoons slaughter their wives trusting their colleague's assurances that it would improve their character after they are brought back to life with the aid of his magic wand; (3) *In the Backyard*, illustrating the onset of doubt and anxiety on the part of the bereaved buffoons in a nervously chromaticized idiom, changing to a furious diatonic *prestissimo* and concluding on an *Andante innocente;* (4) *Reception Room*, with a polka-like dance of the seven daughters of the seven buffoons; (5) *Merchant's Bedroom*, wherein the scoundrel buffoon in a woman's clothes is taken to the merchant's quarters, accompanied by a sentimental ballad, but at the crucial moment substitutes a she-goat with whom the merchant dances an animated cossack step; (6) *Merchant's Garden*, in which the she-goat, succumbing to the exhaustion of the dance, is buried to the strains of a dissonant funeral march, interrupted by the invasion of the seven buffoons starting a frenzied dance, abruptly ending on a unisonal C.

20 MAY 1921

La Voz de las Calles, symphonic poem by the foremost modern composer of Chile, Humberto ALLENDE, in which he employs authentic melodies of street vendors as thematic material, thus justifying the title, *The Voice of the Streets*, is performed for the first time in Santiago.

21 MAY 1921

Prince Ferelon, or *The Princess's Suitors*, one-act musical extravaganza by the English composer Nicholas Comyn GATTY, to his own libretto in which a wandering minstrel enters a contest for the hand of the princess in the guise of a musician, dress designer and a dancer, and after being rejected in all three assumed identities, succeeds when he reveals his true self, is produced in London.

24 MAY 1921

Le Piège de Méduse, lyric comedy in one act by Erik SATIE, with dance interludes, to his own libretto, composed in 1913, and facetiously scored for a surrealist ensemble of two piston flutes, two slide clarinets, a siphon in C, three keyboard trombones, a group of "cephalophones" with a range of 30 octaves, interspersed with such expression marks as "silencieusement, je vous prie," is performed for the first time in a modest arrangement for realistic musical instruments, in Paris.

26 MAY 1921

Uguns un Nakts (Fire and Night), opera in four acts by the Latvian composer Jānis MEDINŠ, is produced in Riga.

27 MAY 1921

The Society for Private Musical Performances presents in Vienna a special concert of waltzes by Johann STRAUSS, arranged for string quartet, piano and harmonium in a program including, among others, *Wine, Women and Song* arranged by Alban BERG and *Treasure Waltz* from *The Gypsy Baron* arranged by Arnold SCHOENBERG, the performers being Schoenberg and Rudolf Kolisch as violinists, Anton von Webern as cellist, Alban Berg at the harmonium and Eduard Steuermann at the piano.

31 MAY 1921

Edgar VARÈSE organizes in New York the International Composers' Guild with the purpose of promoting the cause of 20th-century music. (The date of the charter.)

The composer is the only one of the creators of today who is denied direct contact with the public. When his work is done, he is thrust aside, and the interpreter enters, not to try to understand the composition but impertinently to judge it. Not finding in it any trace of the conventions to which he is accustomed, he banishes it from his programs, denouncing it as incoherent and unintelligible . . . In every other field, the creator comes into some form of direct contact with his public. The poet and novelist enjoy the medium of the printed page; the painter and sculptor the open doors of a gallery; the dramatist the free scope of the stage. The composer must depend upon an intermediary, the interpreter . . . . It is true that in response to public demand, our official organizations occasionally place on their programs a new work surrounded by established names. But such a work is carefully chosen from the most timid and anemic of contemporary productions, leaving absolutely unheard the composers who represent the true spirit of our times . . . . Dying is the privilege of the weary. The present day composers refuse to die. They have realized the necessity of banding together and fighting for the right of each individual to secure a fair and free presentation of his work. It is out of such a collective will that the International Composers' Guild was born . . . . Its aim is to centralize the works of the day, to group them in programs intelligently and organically constructed, and, with the disinterested help of singers and instrumentalists, to present these works in such a way as to reveal their fundamental spirit. . . . It refuses to admit any limitation, either of volition or action . . . disapproves of all "isms"; denies the existence of schools; recognizes only the individual. (From the Manifesto of the International Composers' Guild)

4 JUNE 1921

Two one-act operas by Paul HINDEMITH are produced for the first time in Stuttgart:

(1) *Mörder, Hoffnung der Frauen*, a duodrama involving a nameless Man and an equally nameless Woman, developing the thesis that only by murder can women achieve self-fulfillment, set to a grindingly dissonant score; (2) *Das Nusch-Nuschi*, a musical play for Burmese marionettes in which a monster born of a giant rat and an alligator assumes the role of deus ex machina, while the King, the Crown Prince, the Hangman, a falsetto-singing Eunuch and assorted bayaderes disport themselves in an astutely discordant musical setting with the interpolation of some parodistic elements (King Mark's motive from *Tristan und Isolde* makes its appearance in the orchestra when the King of Burma finds out that his aide-de-camp has seduced four of his wives).

6 JUNE 1921

La Esclava, opera by the Cuban composer José MAURI (1856–1937), to a libretto dealing with a mulatto girl imported into Cuba as a slave in 1860, set to music replete with Afro-Cuban melorhythms within the har-monic framework of Italian operatic convention, is produced in Havana.

6 JUNE 1921

L'Homme et son désir, surrealist ballet by Darius MILHAUD, to a scenario fashioned from Paul Claudel's "plastic poem," picturing a symbolic modern man debilitated by ineffectual fantasies of half-materialized nudes, scored for a multifarious ensemble, including iron castanets and a wooden plank struck with a hammer, with the stereophonic placement of instruments in five quasi-autonomous groups, is produced in Paris.

L'Homme et son désir was the fruit of the collaboration of three friends in 1917 who exchanged ideas about music and art on the heights of the Serra which dominates Rio de Janeiro. This "plastic drama" drew out of the ambiance of the Brazilian jungle forest in which we were, so to say, submerged. (Paul Claudel in *La Danse,* Paris, June 1921)

10 JUNE 1921

Symphonies d'instruments à vent by Igor STRAVINSKY, dedicated to the memory of Debussy, in which the word symphony denotes a polyphonic ensemble of instrumental voices, set in static and placid harmonies with its central idea formed by a reverential chorale, is performed for the first time at Koussevitzky's third concert of Russian music given in London.

To us, the *Symphonies of Wind Instruments* spelt nothing but senseless ugliness. (*The Times,* London, 12 June 1921)

10 JUNE 1921

Passacaglia for orchestra, op. 1, by Anton von WEBERN, written in 1908 in a firmly tonal idiom in the explicitly indicated key of D minor, but already containing the foretaste of the atonal principle of nonrepetition of thematic notes in the subject (D, C-sharp, B-flat, A-flat, F, E, A, D) has its first German performance at Bochum, Germany, at a concert of modern Austrian music.

After Schoenberg's more or less tolerable *Verklärte Nacht* and Erich Korngold's music of real genius to *Much Ado About Nothing,* Anton von Webern's *Passacaglia* seemed like an evil spirit, not to say a bad joke and wretched pretentiousness. (Joseph Schwermann, *Signale für die musikalische Welt,* Berlin, 27 July 1921)

11 JUNE 1921

Le Roi David, symphonic psalm by Arthur HONEGGER (begun on 25 February 1921 and completed on 28 April 1921), in three parts, after the drama of René Morax, scored for chamber orchestra, chorus, soloists and a narrator, in the manner of a modern oratorio, making free use of stridently frictional harmonies and atonally oriented melodies while remaining within the framework of basic tonality, tracing King David's career from the smiting of Goliath, through the defeat of discordantly marching Philistines and to the point of death on a pandiatonic major chord, is performed for the first time at Jorat, Switzerland.

14 JUNE 1921

The British Music Society gives its inaugural concert of symphonic music in London, presenting *The Planets* by

Gustave HOLST, the overture to the opera *The Children of Don* by Josef HOLBROOKE, *The Eternal Rhythm* by Eugene GOOSSENS, *Piano Concerto* by Cyril SCOTT and *The Lark Ascending* by Ralph VAUGHAN WILLIAMS.

16 JUNE 1921

Legenda z Erinu (The Legend of Erin), opera by the Czech composer Otakar OSTRČIL, to a story dealing with an Irish king's bride who flees from matrimony to join her former lover, with retribution vouchsafed to them when the king refuses to save his mortally wounded rival by the miraculous powers of the imposition of royal hands and lets him die, whereupon the distracted girl kills herself, is produced in Brno.

18 JUNE 1921

Luigi RUSSOLO, Italian musician and painter, conducts in Paris a concert of Futurist music with a noise orchestra, consisting of Thunderclappers, Exploders, Crashers, Splashers, Bellowers, Whistlers, Hissers, Snorters, Whisperers, Murmurers, Mutterers, Bustlers, Gurglers, Screamers, Screechers, Rustlers, Buzzers, Cracklers, Shouters, Shriekers, Groaners, Howlers, Laughers, Wheezers, and Sobbers.

19 JUNE 1921

Les Mariés de la Tour Eiffel, a synthetic spectacle devised by Jean COCTEAU, combining drama, comedy, vaudeville, pantomime and opera, in two scenes, *Marche Nuptiale* and *Fugue du Massacre*, with the music by five of the French Six (HONEGGER, MILHAUD, AURIC, POULENC, TAILLEFERRE), is presented by the Ballets Suédois in Paris.

24 JUNE 1921

The American Conservatory of Music is established at Fontainebleau, near Paris, to serve the growing needs of American music students gravitating towards France after the twilight of the German musical gods during the First World War.

7 JULY 1921

El Caminante, lyric drama in one act, on a religious theme, by the Cuban composer Eduardo SÁNCHEZ DE FUENTES, is produced in Havana.

20 JULY 1921

A pageant to commemorate the tercentenary of the Pilgrims' landing is given in Plymouth, Massachusetts, with music provided by George CHADWICK, Henry F. GILBERT, Frederick S. CONVERSE, Arthur FOOTE, Edward Burlingame HILL, Edgar Stillman KELLEY, John POWELL, Leo SOWERBY and Chalmers CLIFTON.

31 JULY 1921

The first Festival for Promotion of Contemporary Music opens in Donaueschingen, Germany, with the following programs:

(1) Morning concert: first performance of *String Quartet No. 4* by the Czech pioneer of fractional music Alois HÁBA; piano pieces by the Austrian modernist Wilhelm GROSZ played by himself; first performance of *Serenade* for clarinet and string quartet by the 20-year-old Viennese composer, thenceforth destined for fame, Ernst KRENEK. (2) Evening concert: *Piano Quartet* by the German neo-romanticist Franz PHILIPP; *Lieder* by the Austrian atonalist Karl HORWITZ; *Six Fugues* for piano by the German neo-classical composer Arthur WILLNER; *String Quartet* by the French-born Catalonian composer active mainly in Germany, Philipp JARNACH.

While there exists today a lively debate regarding the innovations in plastic arts, prose, poetry and drama, young composers must struggle against overwhelming odds to secure a public hearing of their works. Interpreters and publishers, on whom composers depend for self-expression, usually refuse to aid unknown talents. Considering the situation, the Gesellschaft der Musikfreunde of Donaueschingen decided to contribute its modest effort to the promotion of the creative work of the young generation of composers ... When a series of chamber music concerts was organized in this little Schwarzwald town of Donaueschingen, it was not an artificially planted seed in an uncultivated soil, but a continuation of a long and fine tradition established through 150 years of the Dukedom ... The programs are arranged without partisan bias. Only the inner worth of each work and its craftsmanship were the determining factors for acceptance. Emphasis is laid, however, on giving priority to unknown or little known names; mature works by established composers may be passed over in favor of music by younger men struggling for recognition, even if their efforts show for the time being more ardor than accomplishment. (From the declaration of the Donaueschingen Committee for the Promotion of Contemporary Music, published in the *Neue Musik Zeitung*, 21 July 1921)

1 AUGUST 1921

At the third concert of the first Donaueschingen Music Festival, three chamber-music works are performed for the first time: *Sonata* for violin and piano by the 19-year-old German composer Rudolf PETERS, with him playing the piano part; *Piano Sonata* by Schoenberg's disciple Alban BERG, his opus No. 1, written in 1908, and first performed in Vienna on 24 April 1911, in a single movement, in classical form, but intervalically emancipated and tending to wide distribution of thematic notes in quartal, tritonal and quintal leaps; and *String Quartet No. 3* by the 25-year-old master of German neoclassicism Paul HINDEMITH. (Information from the original programs, obtained from the Secretariat of the Gesellschaft der Musikfreunde in Donaueschingen.)

2 AUGUST 1921

Enrico CARUSO, the most celebrated Italian tenor of all time, whose art of bel canto moved audiences to a frenzy of adulation, and whose notorious "coup de glotte," known as the "Caruso sob," became his throatmark, who was also a gifted caricaturist, a gastronomic gourmet (a brand of macaroni was named after him), a lover of women, and despite his corpulence, an agile and convivial celebrant of good living, dies at the age of 48 years, five months and one week, at 9 o'clock in the morning at the Hotel Vesuvius in his native Naples, a victim of a combination of ailments, which first manifested themselves when he suffered a throat hemorrhage during a performance at the Brooklyn Academy of Music on 11 December 1920.

8 AUGUST 1921

Arthur POUGIN, scholarly French music critic, inveterate denouncer of modern ways in music, who hurled jovian thunderbolts against Debussy and all those who broke the inviolable rules of traditional music, dies in Paris two days after his 87th birthday.

27 AUGUST 1921

Four centuries have passed since the death of Josquin DES PREZ, great precursor of modern polyphony. (The spelling Des Prez appears in a contemporary. acrostic, and must therefore be regarded as authentic, although the spellings Des Pres and Despres are encountered in various sources.)

14 SEPTEMBER 1921

Six centuries have passed since the formation of the first musicians' union, when 29 minstrels and 8 female jugglers banded together in Paris on 14 September 1321.

25 SEPTEMBER 1921

A State Institute of Musical Science is organized in Moscow.

27 SEPTEMBER 1921

Engelbert HUMPERDINCK, German composer whose fairy-tale opera *Hänsel und Gretel* is a dramatic projection of Wagner's methods into musical infantiloquy, dies at Neustrelitz at the age of 67.

29 SEPTEMBER 1921

Blossom Time, operetta by Sigmund ROMBERG, adapted from *Das Dreimäderlhaus*, a romanticized story of Schubert's life, made up of Schubert's tunes, with the hit number *Song of Love* set to the famous cello tune in the *Unfinished Symphony*, is produced in New York.

4 OCTOBER 1921

The American Academy in Rome is founded and grants its first fellowship in musical composition to Leo SOWERBY.

9 OCTOBER 1921

Taras Bulba, symphonic rhapsody by Leoš JANÁČEK, after Gogol's tragic tale from the period of savage struggle between the Cossacks of the Dnieper and the Poles in the early 17th century, in three movements, describing the death of two sons of Taras—Andrei, slain by Taras for betraying the Cossack cause for the sake of a beautiful Polish girl, and Ostap, captured by the Poles and executed after torture in Warsaw—and finally Taras himself, crucified and burned alive, written in a tense quasi-modern idiom, irrigated by streams of Slavic melorhythms, is performed for the first time in Brno. (The first Prague performance on 9 November 1924 is erroneously listed in reference works as the world première.)

13 OCTOBER 1921

Study for Pianola by Igor STRAVINSKY is performed for the first time in London from the pianola roll recorded expressly by him for the Aeolian Company.

16 OCTOBER 1921

Three centuries have elapsed since the death of Jan Pieterszoon (i.e., Peter's son) SWEELINCK (or Swellinck; 24 variants of his name are known, and he himself used three), superb organist of the Old Church in Amsterdam, teacher of a generation of North European organists, composer of exalted vocal and instrumental music in the superlative manner of autochtonous Flemish florid counterpoint, independent of the dominant Venetian School (contrary to a persistent error, Sweelinck never went to Venice).

> *M. Joannes Petri Swellingus Amstelo-batavus*
> *Musicus et Organista toto orbe celeberrimus*
> *Vir singulari modestia ac pietate cum in vita*
> *Tum in morte omnibus suspiciendus*

(Inscription on a copper engraving by Joh. Müller made in 1624, three years after Sweelinck's death)

28 OCTOBER 1921

Alfredo CASELLA makes his first American appearance with the Philadelphia Orchestra, in the triple capacity of composer, conductor and pianist.

29 OCTOBER 1921

Eighth Symphony by the 69-year-old Swiss composer Hans HUBER, being an orchestral arrangement of his only string quartet, is performed for the first time in Basel, eight weeks before his death.

29 OCTOBER 1921

Pour une Fête de Printemps, symphonic poem by Albert ROUSSEL, formed out of the materials originally intended for a scherzo of his *Second Symphony*, written in the vernal spirit of Gallic modernism and harmonically based on the euphonious bitonality of major triads at a tritone's distance, is performed for the first time at a Colonne concert in Paris under the direction of Gabriel Pierné.

30 OCTOBER 1921

Horace Victorieux, "mimed symphony" by Arthur HONEGGER, depicting in starkly dissonant tones the legendary encounter between the three Horatii and three Curiatii, in which the surviving Horatius slays all three of the Curiatii and then smites, in thunderous anger spouted by the maximal discord formed by two contiguous diminished seventh-chords, his own sister who loved a Curatius, is performed for the first time in Lausanne, Ernest Ansermet conducting.

17 NOVEMBER 1921

Henry HADLEY conducts the New York Philharmonic Orchestra in the first performance of his symphonic poem *The Ocean*, with the syncopated waves of chromatics in the strings lashing at Wagneroaring brasses while the chant of the high wind instruments is counterposed by the sustained foghorn of the nethermost tuba.

20 NOVEMBER 1921

Mon Lac, symphonic poem for piano and orchestra by Georges Martin WITKOWSKI, 54-year-old Algerian-born

French composer of remote Polish origin, a romantically illustrative impression, in three sections, of a provincial lake Paladru, near Lyons, is performed for the first time in Lyons.

23 NOVEMBER 1921

Katá Kabanová, opera in three acts by Leoš JANÁČEK, after Ostrovsky's play *The Storm,* depicting the illicit love affair of a married mid-19th-century Russian woman repressed by her tyrannical mother-in-law, her voluntary confession and her suicide in the waters of the Volga River, set to a romantically saturated score, with strong melodic and rhythmic inflections of Russian folk music (the cadential falling fourth in a minor mode is thematically manifest), is produced in Brno. (Date from the actual program, confirmed by a newspaper review; 23 October 1921 is erroneously given in Loewenberg's *Annals of Opera.*)

26 NOVEMBER 1921

Third Symphony by Karol SZYMANOWSKI, subtitled *Song of the Night,* in three connected movements for orchestra, chorus and tenor solo, to the words of the mystical divan by the Persian poet Jalal al-Din Rumi (1207–1273), with an orientalistic ambience suggested by serpentine melodic arabesques, alternating with whole-tone progressions and pedal-pointed bitonalities, ultimately reaching the firmament of celestially cerulean C major, with glissandi along the overtone series in the cellos and violas leading to a semipiternal moment of vibrant silence, is performed for the first time in London, conducted by Albert Coates, the chorus replaced by the organ and the tenor solo by cello. The first completely authentic performance, with chorus, took place in Lwów in 1928.

1 DECEMBER 1921

Vincent D'INDY conducts the New York Symphony in the world première of his symphonic suite *Poème des rivages,* dedicated to his second wife whom he married in 1918, and set in four geographic movements recalling his travels with her: (1) *Agay,* a poetic view of the coastal line; (2) *Majorca,* a glorification of the cerulean waters of the Mediterranean; (3) *Falconara,* with an audibly puffing Italian train; (4) *Gascogne,* an expansive cyclorama of the Basque country in Gascogne.

7 DECEMBER 1921

Dans l' ombre de Cathédrale, lyric drama in three acts by Georges HÜE, after a mystically realistic story of Blasco Ibañez wherein the guardian of the jewels of the Madonna in the cathedral of Toledo is killed by his former revolutionary associates when he, seized by sudden loyalty, resists their planned expropriation, is produced at the Opéra-Comique in Paris.

8 DECEMBER 1921

On his first American tour, the prime French organist Marcel DUPRÉ improvises at the Wanamaker organ in Philadelphia a complete *Symphonie-Passion* in four movements, on six themes offered by musicians in the audience. (The improvisation was subsequently written down and performed in a definitive form at Westminster Abbey, London, on 9 October 1924.)

10 DECEMBER 1921

La Leggenda di Sakuntala, opera in three acts by Franco ALFANO, to a libretto from the 5th-century play by Kalidasa, the Shakespeare of India, centered on a marine girl searching for the father of her child, finding it was the King and becoming the Queen, to a conventionally orientalized score with serpentine melodies and free rhythms within the framework of modernistic harmonies, is performed for the first time in Bologna.

16 DECEMBER 1921

Sergei PROKOFIEV appears as soloist with the Chicago Symphony Orchestra in the world première of his *Third Piano Concerto* in C Major, in three movements:

(1) *Andante—Allegro* opening with a very Russian songful theme and then suddenly attacking the keyboard in a vehement exercise of the whitest C major scales and arpeggios with a maximum of cumulative effect; (2) *Theme and Variations,* based on a lyric melody notated in 1913, lending itself to flowing and translucid transformations; (3) *Allegro ma non troppo,* a precipitous rondo charged with animal vitality alternating with romantically colored thematic episodes and ending in an irresistibly rhythmical display of optimistically impeccable C major, Prokofiev's favorite pianistic tonality.

16 DECEMBER 1921

Camille SAINT-SAËNS, French composer, the Victor Hugo of music, apostle of clarity and immediacy of communication, prolific creator of operas, symphonies, concertos and other works that endure in posterity despite their essentially neutral esthetic quality, universal musician, virtuoso pianist and organist, cultured writer and occasional poet, dies at his winter home at Hôtel de l'Oasis in Algiers, at the age of 86.

Il est possible d'être aussi musicien que Saint-Saëns, mais il est impossible de l'aftre davantage. (Liszt)

23 DECEMBER 1921

Krazy Kat, an orchestral Suite from the "jazz pantomime" by John Alden CARPENTER, inspired by the famous newspaper comic strip, in which the misspelled cat, "Don Quixote and Parsifal rolled into one," is driven to madness by a bouquet of catnip presented with malice aforethought by an impudently aggressive mouse, set to music replete with jazzy inflections, constituting the first such jazzification of a piece of concert music, is performed for the first time by the Chicago Symphony Orchestra, Frederick Stock conducting.

25 DECEMBER 1921

Hans HUBER, foremost Swiss symphonist of Switzerland, music educator and teacher of a generation of Swiss musicians, dies in Locarno at the age of 69.

26 DECEMBER 1921

La Scala of Milan, closed since 1917, reopens with a performance of Verdi's *Falstaff* conducted by Arturo TOSCANINI.

30 DECEMBER 1921

Sergei PROKOFIEV conducts in Chicago the world première of his opera in four acts *The Love for Three Oranges*, fashioned after the 18th-century comedy of Carlo Gozzi wherein a hypochondriac prince is doomed to fall in love with three gigantic oranges which he pursues to the end of the earth and in one of them finds a beautiful princess, the dream of his life since infancy, whom, after many a tragicomic peripeteia, in which the spectators placed in a loge participate, he happily marries, set to a musical score compactly filled with energetic grotes-

queries alternating with moments of lyric exuberance, and containing a march destined to become Prokofiev's most popular creation, ending on an assertively positivistic C major triad.

The music of Love for Three Oranges is, I fear, too much for this generation. After intensive study and close observation at rehearsals and performances, I detected the beginnings of two tunes.. . . For the rest of it, Mr. Prokofiev might well have loaded up a shotgun with several thousand notes of varying lengths and discharged them against the side of a blank wall. (Edward Moore, *The Chicago Tribune*, 31 December 1921)

1922

9 JANUARY 1922

Four Orchestral Pieces, a suite by Béla BARTÓK, in four movements, *Preludio, Scherzo Intermezzo* and *Marcia funebre*, composed in 1912 and orchestrated in 1921, is performed for the first time by the Philharmonic Society in Budapest, under tbe direction of Ernst von Dohnányi.

10 JANUARY 1922

Thomas WILFRED presents in New York the first demonstration of his CLAVILUX, an instrument which throws colors on a screen according to the key struck on the keyboard, thus correlating the visual and auditory sensations.

17 JANUARY 1922

Ferruccio BUSONI addresses an open letter to the editor of the modern-minded German magazine *Melos*, expressing his strong views against excesses in modern music:

When a physician recommends wine to a patient, he does not intend to make him drunk. Anarchy is not liberty. Liberality must not become libertinism, and free love must not be turned into prostitution. An attractive idea does not constitute a work of art; a talented person does not become a master at once; a seed, however vigorous and fertile, is not the harvest. I do not wish to deprecate the use of novel effects in art, but I believe that such effects should be applied esthetically, with proper regard for balance and rhythm, with sonorities achieved through skill, so that a musical work in whatever idiom it is written is raised to the level of classical art in the original sense of the word as ultimate perfection.

20 JANUARY 1922

Skating Rink, "danced poem" by Arthur HONEGGER, of strongly bitonal consistency reflecting the sensual anxiety of mutual attraction and revulsion, and proceeding through a series of angularly pirouetted melorhythms to a climax when the patineur captures his patineuse "like a holocaust consuming all the beauty and intoxication of

life," is performed for the first time by the Ballets Suédois in Paris.

23 JANUARY 1922

Arthur NIKISCH, whose passionate interpretation of German symphonic masterpieces in finely controlled performance earned for him an exalted position among conductors, dies in Leipzig at the age of 66.

24 JANUARY 1922

Nine days after the completion of the score, Carl NIELSEN, prime modernist of Denmark, conducts in Copenhagen the first performance of his *Fifth Symphony*, in two movements:

(1) *Tempo giusto*, opening with a viola tremulating on two successive notes, A and C, upon which the conjugated wind instruments engender heterophonic patterns, leading to a pacification of emotions in *Adagio*, with a snare-drum part "to be played in its own rhythm as though intended at all costs to disrupt the music," followed by a cadenza drummed independently of the steady flow of the music elsewhere "in complete freedom and in all possible rhythmic figures with occasional fermatas," the movement finally disintegrating into a *sotto voce* dialogue between the clarinet and the sempiternal drum; (2) *Allegro*, marked by angular intervalic patterns, subsiding into an *Andante poco tranquillo*, and then returning to the initial tempo and ending in an eloquently rhetorical E-flat major epilogue.

26 JANUARY 1922

Luigi DENZA, Italian composer of some 500 songs and ballads, among which *Funiculi-Funicula* written to celebrate the opening of the funicular railway on Mt. Vesuvius, attained universal popularity, dies in London, where he made his home in 1879, at the age of 75.

26 JANUARY 1922

The first performance is given in London, under the direction of Adrian Boult, of *Pastoral Symphony (Third*

Symphony) by Ralph VAUGHAN WILLIAMS (completed on 25 November 1921) in four movements:

(1) *Molto moderato,* with dulcet woodwinds and a bucolic harp setting the mood while the divided strings move in parallel triadic harmonies; (2) *Lento moderato,* an idyllic scene of quiet contemplation, containing solo passages by a natural trumpet in E flat and a natural French horn using non-tempered 7th and 9th partials of the harmonic series; (3) *Moderato pesante,* an optimistic jig; (4) *Lento,* with a wordlessly distant voice in a hexatonically transparent melodic line opening and closing the movement.

30 JANUARY 1922

La Megère apprivoisée, opera in four acts by the French composer Charles SILVER, to a libretto from Shakespeare's play *The Taming of the Shrew,* is produced at the Paris Opéra.

4 FEBRUARY 1922

L'Amour en quatrième vitesse, operetta by H. MORISSON, glorifying the automotive sport combined with love in fourth gear (overdrive), is produced at the Variétés Parisiennes, in Paris.

5 FEBRUARY 1922

Concerto gregoriano for violin and orchestra by Ottorino RESPIGHI in three movements—(1) *Andante tranquillo-Allegro molto moderato;* (2) *Andante espressivo e sostenuto;* (3) *Allegro energico,* with the solo violin symbolizing the cantor and the orchestra the congregation, concluding on a universal Alleluia in the spirit of medieval jubilation—is performed for the first time in Rome.

5 FEBRUARY 1922

Herbstsymphonie in E major by the Viennese composer Joseph MARX, in three movements exuding the aroma of tardigrade romanticism, is performed for the first time in Vienna, Felix Weingartner conducting.

8 FEBRUARY 1922

Ciottolino, musical fable in two acts by Luigi FERRARI-TRECATE, is produced by the Teatro dei Piccoli in Rome.

13 FEBRUARY 1922

PERSYMFANS (PERVYI SYMPHONICHESKY ENSEMBLE), first conductorless ensemble, opens its initial season in Moscow in a program of Beethoven music, intent on demonstrating that in a proletarian state orchestra men do not need a musical dictator.

(The Persymfans received the nomination of an Honored Collective of the Russian Socialist Soviet Republic awarded by the Soviet Government in 1927 and continued its leaderless activities for another lustrum sans lustre, until it fell into a state of innocuous desuetude, languished and finally was discontinued in 1932, the year when militant opposition to all guidance ceased to be regarded as ideologically correct, and when once more conductors, wearing full dress and white ties, assumed their imperious attitudes and privileges on the podium.)

14 FEBRUARY 1922

Giulietta e Romeo, opera in three acts by Riccardo ZANDONAI, to Shakespeare's tragedy, supplemented by interpolations from Italian versions of the story, set in a harmoniously euphonious manner, replete with chromatic progressions of diminished seventh-chords, the "accorde di stupefazione" of the Italian operatic stage, is produced in Rome.

14 FEBRUARY 1922

The Two Sisters, opera in three acts by the English composer Cyril ROOTHAM, based on the Scottish ballad *The Twa Sisters o' Binnorie,* telling the bleak tale of a maid of the moors who drowns her sister to take possession of her fiancé, but goes mad at her wedding when a minstrel plays a threnody on a harp strung with the dead girl's hair, is produced in Cambridge.

25 FEBRUARY 1922

Carnaval des Animaux, "grande fantaisie zoologique" by Camille SAINT-SAËNS, scored for two pianos, strings, flute, clarinet, harmonium, xylophone and celesta, in 14 colorful tableaux illustrating the lions, hens and a rooster, hémiones, turtles (portrayed by Offenbach's cancan in multiple augmentation), elephants (pachydermic borborygmuses in the basses derived from *La Valse des Sylphes* of Berlioz), kangaroos, an aquarium, a "personage with, long ears," a cuckoo, an aviary, pianists (treated as an animal species in a run of mindless scales), fossiles, and the cellifluous swan, followed by a rollicking finale, originally composed in 1886, receives the first public hearing in its entirety at the Concerts Colonne in Paris, under the direction of Gabriel Pierné, two months and nine days after the composer's death. (Saint-Saëns forbade public performances of the *Carnaval des Animaux* during his lifetime, with the sole exception of *The Swan.*)

4 MARCH 1922

Symphonie en Si bémol, second symphony by Albert ROUSSEL, in three movements: *Introduction et Allegro, Scherzo, Adagio et final,* suggesting the three stages of man—youthful aspirations, emotional gaiety and disillusioned age—and set in a neo-classical idiom, with tritonally oriented melodies within quartal and quintal harmonies propelled by asymmetric syncopation, is performed for the first time in Paris.

7 MARCH 1922

The Rose of Stamboul, operetta in three acts by the Austrian composer Leo FALL, with additional songs by Sigmund Romberg, depicting in rousing melodies the adventures of a companionate international girl on the banks of the Bosporus, is performed for the first time in New York City.

9 MARCH 1922

Olivier le Simple, lyric drama in three acts by the Belgian composer Victor VREULS, his first opera, to a libretto in which the simple-minded knight Olivier is bewitched by the oriental charms of a captive girl brought back by the crusaders in the 13th century, and, against the insistent advice of his family and his fiancée, flees with her to her distant home in the mysterious East, set to music in a dramatically Gallic manner with a patina of conventional exoticisms, is produced in Brussels.

14 MARCH 1922

Vina (Guilt), opera in three acts by the Czech composer Otakar ZICH, is produced in Prague.

16 MARCH 1922

English Suite No. 3 by the 46-year-old English composer Havergal BRIAN, in five folkloric movements (*Ye Ancient Village, Morris Dance, Postillions, The Stone-Breaker, The Merry Peasant*), written in a modernistically Straussian vein flaunting its incongruity with English dance rhythms, is performed for the first time in Bournemouth, England.

18 MARCH 1922

La Figlia del Rè, opera in three acts by Adriano LUALDI, to his own libretto depicting the mystical and amorous career of a Hindu princess and abounding in episodes of exotic color set in effective Italianate forms, is produced in Turin.

19 MARCH 1922

A Vajda Tornya (The Tower of the Voivod), opera in three acts by the Hungarian composer Ernst von DOHNÁNYI, to the subject of a clash between a powerful Valachian chieftain and the oppressed masses of the countryside, is produced in Budapest.

23 MARCH 1922

Requiem for chorus and orchestra by Frederick DELIUS, composed in 1914–1916 "to the memory of all young artists fallen in the war" to a text in German, with Latin interpolations from Ecclesiastes, set to music in an effective romantic idiom, with spacious harmonies in minor modes projected against austerely receding chromatic bases forming terse dissonances, comes to a belated first performance in London.

26 MARCH 1922

Selim PALMGREN, Finnish composer in the tradition of Grieg and Sibelius, plays the piano part in the world première of his *Metamorphoses (Third Piano Concerto)* with the Minneapolis Symphony Orchestra.

26 MARCH 1922

Sancta Susanna, one-act opera by Paul HINDEMITH, for two large singing roles (and a minuscule third), two speaking parts, a female chorus and orchestra, to a mystical libretto wherein a youthful nun, known as Saint Susan for her constant piety, strips the loincloth from the figure on a Crucifix as a spider crawls down her neck and reveals herself as the spiritual sister of another nun who was immured in a corner of the cathedral for a similar offense long before, set to music in a neo-ecclesiastical vein making use of authentic Gregorian chants in dissonant counterpoint, with flutes offstage and celesta limn-

ing the intoxicating sensuality of the secular world outside while a sustained C-sharp in the organ part suggests the singleness of the nun's idolatrous obsession, is produced for the first time in Frankfurt.

27 MARCH 1922

The Flaming Arrow, one-act opera by the abecedarian American composeress Mary Carr MOORE, is produced in San Francisco.

29 MARCH 1922

San Francesco d' Assisi, mystery play by Gian Francesco MALIPIERO, for solo voices, chorus, and orchestra, completed on 25 May 1921, in four linked sections illustrative of the life of St. Francis, set in a translucidly diatonic idiom, symbolic of his vows of animistic asceticism, with deep pedal points expressive of the profundity of his religious conscience, is performed for the first time anywhere in New York.

1 APRIL 1922

Amadis, opera in four acts by Jules MASSENET, dealing with a cenobite knight who dreams about a distant Saxon princess, flees his monastic cell to contend in a tournament for her hand, and after mortally wounding his opponent recognizes in him his long-lost twin brother, but marries the princess and participates in the repulsion of Danish invaders from the British coast, is produced posthumously in Monte Carlo.

1 APRIL 1922

The Benedictine monks of Solesmes, restorers of authentic Gregorian usage in French ecclesiastical practice, return to their Solesmes home after twenty-one years of virtual exile on the Isle of Wight.

1 APRIL 1922

Ta Bouche, operetta by Maurice YVAIN, centering on a rich American tourist who could submit dispassionately to any feminine enchantments, but could not remain indifferent to French kisses on the mouth, is produced in Paris.

7 APRIL 1922

First Symphony by the 26-year-old American composer Leo SOWERBY, in three movements marked *With Restless Energy, With Quiet Languor* and *With Triumphal Sweep*, is performed for the first time by the Chicago Symphony Orchestra, Frederick Stock conducting.

8 APRIL 1922

Glauco, opera in three acts by the 61-year-old Italian composer Alberto FRANCHETTI, wherein Glauco, the protective god of sailors and fishermen, falls in love with the nymph Scylla, arousing the murderous jealousy of the proprietary temptress Circe, who transforms Scylla into a hexacephalous monster and assigns her to guard the Strait of Messina opposite another monster, Charybdis, is performed for the first time in Naples.

11 APRIL 1922

The New York Philharmonic Orchestra makes its first recording for the Victor Co., with Willem Mengelberg conducting Beethoven's *Coriolan* Overture on two 12-inch single-faced discs.

13 APRIL 1922

La bella addormentata nel bosco, operatic fairy tale for marionettes, by Ottorino RESPIGHI, to the perennially alluring subject of a beauty sleeping in the woods, is produced in Rome by the imaginative puppeteer Vittorio Podrecca and his Teatro dei Piccoli, with the singers off stage.

21 APRIL 1922

Third Symphony by the American composer Frederick S. CONVERSE, written in a consolidated Brahmsogenic idiom, in three competent movements expressive of "suffering, resolute defiance and solace in hope," is performed for the first time by the Boston Symphony Orchestra.

21 APRIL 1922

Alessandro MORESCHI, the last of the castrati, whose voice was of such celestial purity that he became known as *l'Angelo di Roma*, dies in Rome at the age of 63.

24 APRIL 1922

The Austrian Post Office issues a series of stamps with portraits of BEETHOVEN (7 1/2 kronen), BRUCKNER (25 kronen), HAYDN (2 1/2 kronen), MOZART (5 kronen), SCHUBERT (10 kronen), Johann STRAUSS (50 kronen) and Hugo WOLF (100 kronen.)

25 APRIL 1922

La Fiamminga, last opera, in one act, by 43-year-old Italian composer Stefano DONAUDY, is performed for the first time in Naples.

29 APRIL 1922

First Symphony by Georges MIGOT, subtitled *Agrestides* and extolling the pleasures of rural life, is performed for the first time in Paris.

4 MAY 1922

At its convention in Rochester, New York, the Society of St. Gregory of America issues a "Black List" of music regarded as unsuitable for performances at sacred services of the Catholic Church. (See complete Index Expurgatorius in Letters and Documents section.)

6 MAY 1922

Leila, opera by the 31-year-old Georgian composer Victor DOLIDZE, dealing with a girl of the Lezgin tribe, is produced in Tbilisi in the Georgian language.

9 MAY 1922

Hagoromo, choreographic symphony by Georges MIGOT is performed for the first time in Monte Carlo.

10 MAY 1922

Othmar SCHOECK, foremost lyric composer of Switzerland, conducts in Zürich the first performance of his three-act opera *Venus*, after a tale of Prosper Merimée set in Paris in 1820, wherein a newly unearthed ancient statue of Venus materializes as an ectoplasmic apparition between the bridegroom and his bride on their wedding night effectively preventing the consummation of their marriage, and crushes him to death in her marmoreal embrace, set to music in a lyrico-dramatic vein of romantic opera.

12 MAY 1922

Scaramouche, "tragic pantomime" by Jan SIBELIUS, composed in 1913, to a scenario in which Scaramouche is stabbed by Blondelaine, the dancing wife of a cardiac sufferer who dies of emotional upset, as does Blondelaine herself, is performed for the first time in Copenhagen.

13 MAY 1922

Hagith, one-act opera by the prime modernist of Poland Karol SZYMANOWSKI, to a dramatic libretto paralleling the Biblical story of David and his last untouched concubine Abishag, wherein a young country damsel, summoned to the royal palace to give the dying King the comfort of her bodily warmth, becomes enamored of the heir to the throne and lets the old King die, in consequence of which impiety she is stoned to death at the orders of the priests, set to music in turbulent modernistic harmonies and coloristic orchestration, is performed for the first time in Warsaw.

18 MAY 1922

Renard, "a fable about a fox, a rooster, a cat and a ram, a merry spectacle with singing and music after popular Russian fairy tales" by Igor STRAVINSKY (completed by him in Morges, Switzerland, on 1 August 1916, "at noon, under cloudless skies"), in which the proverbially wily fox is outfoxed and garroted with his own tail by animals it has tried to trap, with dancers and jugglers miming the action, while the parts for the four animals are sung in the orchestra pit by two tenors and two basses, set to music in astringent dissonant harmonies, apocopated meters and angular rhythms, profoundly Russian in intervalic construction within a hexachordal diatonic range, is performed for the first time by Diaghilev's Ballet Russe in Paris. (In the earlier editions of *Music Since 1900*, the date of the first performance of *Renard* is given as 3 June 1922; and the same erroneous date is cited in Stravinsky's *Autobiography*, in Loewenberg's *Annals of Opera*, and in a number of other reference works.)

19 MAY 1922

Dr. Eisenbart, comic opera in three acts by the 52-year-old Viennese composer Rolf RUEFF, dealing with the devious career of a settecentesco trumpeter and medical quack, Quirin (who actually existed), nicknamed Eisenbart (literally, Iron Beard), is performed for the first time in Kiel. Two days later another opera on the same subject, *Doktor Eisenbart*, by Hermann ZILCHER was premièred in two cities, Leipzig and Mannheim.

20 MAY 1922

Staerstikkeren, opera by the Danish composer Fini Valdemar HENRIQUES, is produced in Copenhagen.

21 MAY 1922

Doktor Eisenbart (Doctor Iron Beard), opera in three acts by the German composer Hermann ZILCHER, dealing with a medical charlatan who guarantees the birth of a male heir to a childless ducal couple in Germany circa 1680, and is sentenced to hang when no pregnancy results from his ministrations, but is saved from the gallows when the duchess reveals that her gestation period is elephantine in duration, set to music in an infra-modern idiom containing a modicum of prophylactic dissonances, is performed in a double première on the same day in Leipzig and Mannheim.

23 MAY 1922

Deevi un Cilveki (Gods and Men), opera in four acts on a subject from Egyptian mythology by the foremost Latvian composer Jānis MEDIŅŠ, is produced in Riga in the Latvian language.

27 MAY 1922

A century has passed since the birth of Joseph Joachim RAFF, once-revered German composer of expertly manufactured symphonies exuding the romantic spirit from every contrapuntal pore.

28 MAY 1922

Der Zwerg, one-act opera by Alexander ZEMLINSKY, after Oscar Wilde's story *The Birthday of the Infanta,* in which the court dwarf dances himself to death to please the Infanta on her 16th birthday, is produced in Cologne.

3 JUNE 1922

Mavra, comic opera in one act by Igor STRAVINSKY after Pushkin's poem *A House in Colomna,* dealing with an amorous hussar who disguises himself as a *cuisinière* and is hired by his sweetheart's mother, with a catastrophic denouement when he is surprised while shaving and thus exposed as an intruding transvestite, set to music in a typical Stravinskian neo-Russian manner, marked by lyrical ariosos in compact pandiatonic harmonies with off-base basses, is produced by the Diaghilev Ballet Russe in Paris, on the same bill with *Renard, Pétrouchka* and *Le Sacre du Printemps.* (A private performance of *Mavra* was first presented at the Hotel Continental in Paris on 29 May 1922.)

6 JUNE 1922

Smrt majke Jugovića (Death of the Mother of the Brothers Jugović), symphonic poem by the Yugoslav composer Miloje MILOJEVIĆ (1884–1946), inspired by a legend of the savage battle of Kosovo Pole in 1389 in which the Turks slew countless Slavs, and its aftermath when the mother of nine Serbian soldiers finds their bodies, with a grisly addendum as two black ravens bring her the hands of her youngest son, causing her death from supernumerary horror, all this immersed in a plasma of chronic chromatics mitigated by scoriaceous and vesicular diatonic cavities and interspersed with thematic leading motives, is performed for the first time in Belgrade.

13 JUNE 1922

A two-day festival of *Cante Hondo,* or *Canto Jondo,* or Flamenco (literally, "Flemish"), or gypsified music, of southern Spain, with its characteristically deciduous Phrygian cadences, accompanied by the onomatopeic ejaculation "Olé" (corrupted from Allah, indicative of Moorish influence), organized by the Spanish poet Federico GARCÍA LORCA and Manuel DE FALLA, opens in the Alhambra, in Granada.

11 JULY 1922

The Hollywood Bowl, open-air auditorium built in a natural canyon in the Los Angeles area, is inaugurated with a symphonic concert conducted by the bearded German conductor Alfred HERTZ.

11 JULY 1922

The Shepherds of the Delectable Mountains, "pastoral episode" by Ralph VAUGHAN WILLIAMS, his first operatic work, after John Bunyan's classic *The Pilgrim's Progress,* is performed for the first time in London. (The music was later incorporated in his full-scale opera *The Pilgrim's Progress,* produced in London on 26 April 1951.)

30 JULY 1922

The Second Chamber Music Festival for the Promotion of Contemporary Music, organized by the Gesellschaft der Musikfreunde in Donaueschingen, presents two Sunday concerts consisting of first performances of works by young composers:

Morning concert: *Symphonic Music for 9 Solo Instruments* in an abstract formalistic idiom with masterly technique by 21-year-old Ernst KRENEK; *Michelangelo Lieder* by the German composer Edmund SCHRÖDER; *Fuga Grotesca* for string quartet by the German composer Rudolf DINKEL; *Quintet* in a Reger-like linear idiom, by the German composer Richard ZÖLLNER; and *Trio-Sonata* for violin, viola and piano in a competent contrapuntal style by the Austrian-born Reger disciple Hermann GRABNER.

Evening concert: *String Quartet* by Bernard VAN DIEREN, philosophical Dutchman living in London, set in a neo-Flemish polyphonic style; *Clarinet Sonata* by the 28-year-old Swiss-Italian composer Reinhold LAGUAI; *Lieder* by the Prussian, composer Hans VON DER WENSE, and *Sextet* for clarinet, string quartet and piano, in one condensed movement, rhythmically and atonally advanced in the direction of Schoenberg's ideals by the Viennese composer Felix PETYREK.

31 JULY 1922

On the second day of concerts of the Chamber Music Festival at Donaueschingen, the following program of new chamber music works is given:

Quintet for oboe, clarinet, violin, viola and cello by the German composer Max BUTTING, set in a polyphonically elaborate neo-classical style; *String Quartet* by the Bohemian-born German-influenced polyphonist Fidelio FINKE; and the first performance of the thematically concise, contrapuntally heterotonal *Kammmermusik No. 1* for chamber orchestra by the

26-year-old master of modern German music, Paul HIN-DEMITH. (Programs and dates from the Donaueschingen issue of the *Neue Musik-Zeitung* of 20 July 1922)

3 AUGUST 1922

The first artificially contrived sound effect on radio is introduced at Station WGY in Schenectady with the aid of two strips of wood slapped together to imitate a door slammed in anger. (Date from an article by Lucille Fletcher in *The New Yorker*, 13 April 1940.)

3 AUGUST 1922

Flor de Nieve, opera by the Argentine composer Constantino GAITO, to the story of a 16-year-old Italian Gypsy girl, nicknamed a snow flower, who is accused by the villagers of ruining the harvest by black magic, and is stoned to death, expiring in the arms of her faithful suitor, is produced at the Teatro Colón in Buenos Aires.

7 AUGUST 1922

The First International Festival of Contemporary Music opens in Salzburg with the following program:

Five Songs by Richard STRAUSS; a militantly hedonistic polytonal *Sonata* for flute, oboe, clarinet and piano by the 29-year-old Darius MILHAUD; a *Lied,* with flute and piano, by the Austrian composer Joseph MARX, set in a traditional neo-romantic idiom; a neo-classical pandiatonic *Passacaglia* for piano by the Austrian composer Felix PETYREK; *Rout,* a linguistically modernistic futuristic piece by Arthur BLISS for soprano and ten instruments to a text consisting of meaningless but phonetically sonorous syllables; and *Sonata No. 1* for violin and piano by Béla BARTÓK, in three movements, a rhapsodically oriented *Allegro appassionato,* a speculative *Adagio* with a long atonal recitative by the solo violin, and the stormy *Allegro molto,* in stamping Hungarian rural rhythms, percussively accentuated and heterotonally harmonized.

8 AUGUST 1922

Two concerts of modern chamber music take place in the course of the First Festival of Contemporary Music in Salzburg:

In the morning concert: *Quintet* for woodwind and piano by Albéric MAGNARD, performed in commemoration of his tragic death eight years before at the outset of World War I; songs by Gian Francesco MALIPIERO, Ildebrando PIZZETTI and Mario CASTELNUOVO-TEDESCO; *Six Impromptus* for piano by 23-year-old French modernist Francis POULENC, played by the composer himself; *Piano Rag Music* by Igor STRAVINSKY (composed on 28 June 1919), a stylized piece of American pre-jazz syncopation; *Syrinx,* DEBUSSY's heretofore unpublished composition for unaccompanied flute rhapsodically reciting in Grecian modalities, billed on the program under the title *La Flûte de Pan* (it was Pan who invented the musical pipe of seven reeds which he named Syrinx in memory of the nymph of that name whom he loved and who was changed into a reed to help her escape him); *Sonata* for two flutes by the master composer of France Charles KOECHLIN, set in a Baroque manner; three songs from RAVEL's cycle *Mélodies populaires grecques;* five songs by Manuel DE FALLA and *Rapsodie* for two flutes, clarinet and piano by Arthur HONEGGER, written in a lyrically expansive idiom marked by broad cantilena, acrid harmonies and propulsive rhythm.

In the evening concert: *Sonata* for violin and piano by the Danish neo-romanticist Carl NIELSEN; four songs by the Swedish composer Ture RANGSTRÖM; *Gaspard de la Nuit,* piano suite by Maurice RAVEL, in three movements of extraordinary illustrative brilliance and impressionistic evocation, entitled *Ondine, Le Gibet* and *Scarbo; Sonatina* for piano by Ferruccio BUSONI; *Tantris le bouffon* for piano by the Polish modernist Karol SZYMANOWSKI; *String Quartet* by Schoenberg's disciple Egon WELLESZ; a pleasing burlesque for piano, entitled *Marionettes,* by Fidelio FINKE; *5 Sätze für Streichquartett,* op. 5, by Anton von WEBERN, composed in 1909, a set of aphoristic and laconic essays for string quartet (the middle piece, a *Scherzo,* takes only 35 seconds to play), in a sharply atonalized idiom in which the generating chromaticism is inverted so as to form intervalic progressions in major sevenths, and dynamic range extended from the faintest pianissimo to the most thundering triple forte, while the technical applications include swiftly changing effects of virtuoso performance; and a poetically impressionistic *Sonata* for violin and piano by the Dutch composer Willem PIJPER.

Anton von Webern appears. I never saw an angrier man; he is about 35, dry and thin, as though pickled in perennial fury, and erect as a ramrod. It was amusing to see him face up to each of the four executants of his five pieces for string quartet, as if he were going to kill them, then relent, wring his hands bitterly, glare defiance at the audience, and rush off stiffly into the artists' room. Thereupon, one suddenly became aware of the sixth furious man (who I subsequently learned was an architect and stone-deaf), passionately reproaching the audience, and more especially a certain Kapellmeister there present, for laughing and spoiling everything. Most ungrateful, since but for those ever-recurring scenes, the school, whom no one takes seriously except Schoenberg, would have fizzled out long ago. Webern's five pieces follow his very subjective formula. One long-drawn note on the bridge of the first violin (pause); a tiny scramble for viola solo (pause); a pizzicato note on the cello. Then another pause, after which the four players get up very quietly, steal away and the thing is over. And now, snorts and laughter are heard in the audience, while four furious admirers clap and yell amid not ill-natured giggles. (*Daily Telegraph,* London, 9 September 1922)

9 AUGUST 1922

A "Viennese Matinée" is given in the course of the Salzburg Festival of Contemporary. Music in a program of songs and chamber music by the modernists of Vienna: Walter KLEIN, Ernst KANITZ, Hugo KAUDER, Egon LUSTGARTEN, Carl HORWITZ, Karl ALWIN, Wilhelm GROSZ and Karl WEIGL, all writing in an idiom marked by neo-romantic subjectivism, retaining the native predilection for ternary form and waltzing rhythms.

9 AUGUST 1922

At the evening concert of the Salzburg Festival for Contemporary Music, the following program of chamber music is presented:

Piano music by Joseph MARX, Adolfo SALAZAR, Manuel DE FALLA and Egon KORNAUTH; *Odelette* by Dame Ethel SMYTH; Ernest BLOCH's *Schelomo* for cello, played with piano accompaniment, since an orchestra could not be had; *Second String Quartet* in three movements—*Allegro, Lento, Vivace*—by 26-year-old Paul HINDEMITH, written in an acutely chromaticized melodic idiom but maintaining a translucidly diatonic triadic substratum; and *Violin Sonata* in three movements by Ernest BLOCH, written in 1920, and set in a highly personal, strongly rhythmic and tangentially bitonal idiom combining the tonics of two polar major triads at a tritone's distance.

10 AUGUST 1922

The Salzburg Festival of Contemporary Music concludes with two concerts of modern chamber music, in the morning and in the evening:

Morning concert: *Serenade* for two violins and viola by the foremost master of national Hungarian music Zoltán KODÁLY; four songs with violin obbligato by Gustav HOLST; a song by the English composer Gerrard WILLIAMS; three songs by Arnold BAX; *Sonata* for violin and piano by the American composer Leo SOWERBY; two songs by the Danish neo-romantic composer Poul SCHIERBECK; *Summer,* a song by the Danish neoclassicist Ebbe HAMERIK; *Nod,* for voice with string quartet by the English composer Armstrong GIBBS, performed coincidentally on his 33rd birthday; and two songs with string quartet by Eugene GOOSSENS.

Evening concert: *Variations and Fugue on a Theme by Schumann* for piano by the German contrapuntist Guido BAGIER; *Molly on the Shore,* a stylized dance tune by the Australian composer Percy GRAINGER, arranged for string quartet; six songs by the Austrian composer of vanguard ideas, Rudolf RETI; three songs for voice and string quartet by the scholarly Viennese modernist Paul A. PISK; songs by the Czech composers Jaroslav KŘIČKA and Ladislav VYCPÁLEK; and *Second String Quartet* by Arnold SCHOENBERG.

It seems almost incredible that one can have heard so much music in four days, but the programs are there to vouch for it: Fifty-four composers of fifteen different nationalities! If we include Strauss who arrived later to conduct the Mozart operas, there were more than twenty composers present. Beginning at 7 o'clock, not any of the evening concerts were over before ten, and the matinees, at the unearthly hour of half past ten, made it difficult to keep luncheon appointments at one. Twenty hours of music! (Edwin Evans, *Musical Times,* London, September 1922)

11 AUGUST 1922

At a meeting held after the conclusion of the Salzburg Festival of Contemporary music, a resolution was unanimously brought out to organize a permanent body for the promotion of modern music, to be named International Society for New Music, with the central office in London and branches in all musical capitals of the world, with Edward J. Dent as President.

The plan is that in each country either an existing body, or one to be created for the purpose, shall draw all those interested in new music, that is to say contemporary music, regardless of tendency. These national organizations pledge themselves to mutual aid by the transmission of information, of books and music, of programs, and of anything further that appears likely to spread the knowledge of contemporary music. Each of them will elect a delegate to the committee of the International Society for New Music as the new concern is to be called. There will be an annual Festival, provisionally at Salzburg. Wherever it takes place, it will be under the control of the International, which will, however, delegate to the local section the duty of technical organization. (Edwin Evans, *Musical Times,* London, September 1922)

12 AUGUST 1922

Escenas Argentinas, symphonic suite by the Argentinian composer Carlos LOPEZ-BUCHARDO, consisting of three authentically ethnic native soundscapes *Día de Fiesta, El Arroyo,* and *La Campera,* is conducted in a world première by Felix Weingartner in Buenos Aires.

15 AUGUST 1922

Lukas Fuchs, later destined to gain modernistic fame in America and the world under the anglicized name FOSS, is born in Berlin.

19 AUGUST 1922

Felipe PEDRELL, the "Spanish Wagner" who entertained Wagnerian ideas of music drama and who attempted to compose an operatic cycle of Nibelungan dimensions, enlightened music scholar and pioneer of theoretical Spanish nationalism in his conviction that all true art ought to derive its essential inspiration from folk music, teacher of Manuel de Falla and Isaac Albéniz, who brilliantly carried out his lofty ideals, dies in Barcelona at the age of 81.

26 AUGUST 1922

Alkestis, opera after Euripides, by Rutland BOUGHTON, is produced in Glastonbury, England, at a theater founded by himself in the forlorn hope of establishing a British Bayreuth.

7 SEPTEMBER 1922

Arthur BLISS conducts at the Three Choirs' Festival in Gloucester, England, the first performance of his *Colour Symphony,* in four sections representing four heraldic colors:

(1) *Purple,* the color of amethysts, pageantry, royalty, and death, proudly imperial in its neo-Handelian mantle, parading sonorously in triadic harmonies; (2) *Red,* the color of rubies, wine, revelry, furnaces, courage, and magic, compulsively discordant, then subsiding into pastoral contemplation; (3) *Blue,* the color of sapphires, deep water, skies, loyalty, and melancholy, aquatically impressionistic, containing a Falstaffian marching waltz; (4) *Green,* the color of emeralds, hope, joy, youth, spring, and victory, melorhythmically involute in the spiral patterns of the music, with rich basses descending chromatically towards the ultimate synthesis of the complementary colors of the preceding movements, the color of White, symbolized by the unpigmented key of C major, and ending triumphantly on the parapandiatonically lucid chord of the tonic sixth.

15 SEPTEMBER 1922

Pierozzo, lyric poem in two parts by Luigi FERRARI-TRECATE, is produced in Alexandria.

11 OCTOBER 1922

Il Barbiere di Siviglia, lyric comedy in three acts by the Italian composer Leopoldo CASSONE, an attempt to create a new version of the famous Beaumarchais comedy according to the principles of the school of Verismo, is performed for the first and last time in Turin.

13 OCTOBER 1922

Sedlak Jakub, opera by the Czech composer and conductor Oskar NEDBAL, is performed for the first time in Brno.

19 OCTOBER 1922

Serge KOUSSEVITZKY conducts in Paris the first performance of MUSSORGSKY's graphic *Pictures at an Exhibition* in the orchestration of Ravel, specially commissioned by Koussevitzky for the sum of 10,000 francs, magically scored with coruscating aptness, as exemplified by the use of a lumbering tuba solo to represent a slow-moving Polish horse-wagon, and rising to a climax of sonorous magnificence in the bell-filled finale The Great Gate of Kiev. (3 May 1923 given in the earlier editions of *Music Since 1900* was not the date of the first performance.)

22 OCTOBER 1922

Ballade de la geôle de Reading, first significant orchestral work by the 32-year-old French composer Jacques IBERT, in three interconnected sections, inspired by Oscar Wilde's anguished poem written during his imprisonment, and set in a correspondingly dark impressionistic idiom, in astringent harmonies chained to immovable pedal points, and leading to the desperate conclusion that "each man kills the thing he loves" in the dim central key of F-sharp minor, is performed for the first time at the Concerts-Colonne in Paris, Gabriel Pierné conducting.

23 OCTOBER 1922

Mayor Curlery of Boston bars Isadora DUNCAN from further appearanccs on the Boston stage on the grounds of immorality (she wore a transparent Grecian dress) and political outrage (she addressed the audience at Symphony Hall the night before, praising the Soviet regime and her Soviet husband, the poet Sergei Essenin).

2 NOVEMBER 1922

Second Symphony by the prime Dutch modernist Willem PIJPER (completed on 18 August 1921), in two movements separated by sixty seconds of silence: a polyharmonically tense *Allegro maestoso,* punctuated by persistent ictus of a varied monothematic motto, and *Lento molto rubato,* with chromatic convolutions in secundal harmonies, ending in an abrupt rhythmic figure, is performed for the first time by the Concertgebouw Orchestra in Amsterdam, Willem Mengelberg conducting.

3 NOVEMBER 1922

Jacques BIZET, son of Georges Bizet, shoots himself dead in Paris in consequence of hopeless frustrations in art, literature, music and multiple loves, succeeding only in automobilism (he was instrumental in building the first small French car, named Zèbra.)

3 NOVEMBER 1922

The Société des Compositeurs in France issues a protest against the attempts of visiting American jazz bands to jazz up Chopin's *Funeral March.*

6 NOVEMBER 1922

Quand la cloche sonnera, one-act opera by the French composer Alfred BACHELET, centering on the tragic dilemma of a Russian bellringer's daughter whose soldier friend waits for her on a bridge over the Niemen River which is to be blown up to stop Napoleon's invading army in 1812 at a signal given by the bell rung by her father, whose tone, a low E, becomes the crucial motto of the opera, is performed for the first time at the Opéra-Comique in Paris.

7 NOVEMBER 1922

On the fifth anniversary of the Soviet Revolution, "Symphony for Factory Whistles" is performed for the first time in Baku with the participation of the foghorns of the entire Caspian Fleet, all local factory sirens, two batteries of artillery, several infantry regiments, a machine-gun section, real hydroplanes, and finally choirs, with participation of spectators.

11 NOVEMBER 1922

The British Broadcasting Corporation commences the transmission of musical programs by wireless telephony.

16 NOVEMBER 1922

Second Symphony by Lazare SAMINSKY, subtitled *Symphony of the Summits,* and designated as being in the key of H-fridur (free major tonality on B), is performed for the first and last time by the Concertgebouw Orchestra in Amsterdam, under the direction of Willem Mengelberg.

21 NOVEMBER 1922

Zingareska, orchestral suite by the 22-year-old American composer George ANTHEIL, is performed for the first time in Berlin.

23 NOVEMBER 1922

After eighteen years of intermittent litigation between the two brothers Pierre and Adolphe DEGEYTER over the authorship of the music to the *Internationale,* the song of the rising proletarian masses written in 1888, the Appellate Court in Paris decides in favor of Pierre. (Date and information from Alexandre Zévaés, *Chants révolutionnaires, l'Internationale, ses auteurs, son histoire,* in *Le Monde,* Paris, 27 April 1929.)

23 NOVEMBER 1922

La Tempesta, opera by Felice LATTUADA in three acts with a prologue to a libretto from Shakespeare's play *The Tempest,* is performed for the first time in Milan.

4 DECEMBER 1922

First Symphony in E-flat major by the English composer Arnold BAX, scored for a very large orchestra, which includes the heckelphone and a sarrusophone, in three movements cast in a neo-Celtic mood and opaque harmonies, subjectively related to the horrors of war and laden with naked tritones in the thematic structure, in three movements, *Allegro moderato e feroce, Lento solenne* and *Allegro maestoso,* all set in 4/4 time with momentary excursions into other meters, is performed for the first time in London.

7 DECEMBER 1922

Two Chorale Preludes by BACH, *Schmücke dich, O liebe Seele* and *Komm, Gott, Schöpfer, Geist* arranged by Arnold

SCHOENBERG for large orchestra, including a triangle, celesta and glockenspiel, faithfully preserving Bach's original melody and harmony, are performed for the first time, from the manuscript, by the New York Philharmonic, Josef Stransky conducting.

10 DECEMBER 1922

A century has passed since the birth in Liège of César FRANCK, grandmaster of French romanticism, whose works, few in number but impeccable in the purity of style and cleanliness of harmonies maintaining a fluid course amid constant enharmonic modulations, whose influence on the French musicians maturing at the *fin de siècle* felicitously counterbalanced the Wagnerian wave, virtuoso organist and teacher of several generations of composers gathered in his classes from many lands.

11 DECEMBER 1922

Isabelle et Pantalon, two-act opera by the French composer ROLAND-MANUEL (Roland Alexis Manuel Lévy), inspired by the familiar characters and situations of the commedia dell'arte, is produced in Paris.

15 DECEMBER 1922

Fantasia dos Movimentos Mixtos for violin and orchestra by the prime composer of Brazil, Heitor VILLA-LOBOS, in three movements subtitled *Serenity, Butterfly in Sunlight* and *Contentment,* set in an impressionistic but highly individual idiom, is performed for the first time in Rio de Janeiro. (In a later version the first movement was renamed *Convulsed Soul; Serenity* was shifted to second place, a permutation which partly accounts for the general title *Fantasy of Mixed Movements.*)

16 DECEMBER 1922

Dèbora e Jaele, three-act opera by Ildebrando PIZZETTI, constituting the first part of an operatic triptych (the second and the third are *Fra Gherardo* and *Lo Straniero*), written to the biblical story dealing with a patriotic maiden who seduces the hostile chieftain to ruin him but learns to love him unto death, is produced at La Scala in Milan.

19 DECEMBER 1922

Fredigundis, opera in three acts by the Austrian romantic composer Franz SCHMIDT, dealing with the mistress of a sixth-century king of the Merovingian dynasty whom she inadvertently poisons with a potion prepared by her for the queen and perishes as her golden tresses become enmeshed in the lid of his coffin, dying in the arms of her previous lover, a bishop, is produced in Berlin.

29 DECEMBER 1922

Polyphème, lyric drama in four acts by the French composer and a captain in the French Navy, Jean CRAS, in which cyclopean amourettes are developed against the oceanic sonorities of the orchestra and each situation is assigned a protoplasmic musical motto, is produced at the Opéra-Comique in Paris.

1923

4 JANUARY 1923

The first radio network program is given when the Boston station WNAC transmits the radio program of the New York station WEAF.

6 JANUARY 1923

Fifth Symphony by Kurt ATTERBERG is performed for the first time in Stockholm.

8 JANUARY 1923

MOZART's opera *The Magic Flute* is broadcast direct from a London concert hall by the British Broadcasting Corporation, marking the first wireless transmission of a complete opera.

15 JANUARY 1923

Odalise et le Chèvre-pied, ballet by Gabriel PIERNIÉ, after a tale of Rémy de Goncourt, in which a young demigod demi-goat strays away from the herd and falls in love with an 18th-century damsel, is performed for the first time at the Paris Opéra.

18 JANUARY 1923

Negro Rhapsody by the 50-year-old New York-born Germanic composer Rubin GOLDMARK, based on seven Negro Spiritual themes, developed in the manner of a romantic prelude, is performed for the first time by the New York Philharmonic, Josef Stransky conducting.

24 JANUARY 1923

Il Principe e Nuredho, one-act opera by Guido BIANCHINI, is produced in Venice.

3 FEBRUARY 1923

Ballade for piano and orchestra by the only female member of Les Six, Germaine TAILLEFERRE (the other five were Georges Auric, Louis Durey, Arthur Honegger, Darius Milhaud and Francis Poulenc), is performed for the first time by Ricardo Viñes at the Concerts Pasdeloup in Paris.

7 FEBRUARY 1923

Wildflower, musical comedy by Vincent YOUMANS, wherein a richly promiscuous heiress is restrained by the terms of the inheritance from all sexual activity for six months before the probate, is produced in New york.

9 FEBRUARY 1923

Die gelbe Jacke, romantic operetta in three acts by Franz LEHÁR, dealing with a Viennese girl of 1912 who goes to China to marry a technically polygamous mandarin, but soon becomes disenchanted with exotic living, obtains an instant oriental divorce and weds her original Viennese suitor, lieutenant of the Imperial Hussars, set to music with pseudo-Sinological pentatonic melodic patterns lending local color to a typically Viennese score, is performed for the first time in Vienna. (The operetta was revised and produced under the title *Das Land des Lächelns* in Berlin on 10 October 1929.)

15 FEBRUARY 1923

L'Amour masqué, operetta by André MESSAGER, in which a Parisian amourette is unmasked at a masquerade, is produced in Paris.

16 FEBRUARY 1923

Bessie SMITH, archetypal blues singer, makes her first recording, *Downhearted Blues,* for Columbia Records.

17 FEBRUARY 1923

La Monacella della Fontana, one-act opera by Giuseppe MULÉ, is produced in Trieste.

18 FEBRUARY 1923

Germelshausen, fantastic opera by the 37-year-old German composer Hans GRIMM, recounting the tale of the village of Germelshausen, obliterated from the face of the earth by a vengeful deity for its unspeakable sins, with a merciful amendment allowing it to revive in its pristine hypostasis for twenty-four hours once in a hundred years, is produced in Augsburg.

19 FEBRUARY 1923

Jean SIBELIUS conducts in Helsinki the first performance of his *Sixth Symphony,* op. 104, in four movements:

(1) *Allegro molto moderato,* set in steady motion of thematic molecules, placidly diatonic in its Dorian mode (there is only one accidental in 62 bars), developing by simple doubling of voices paired in characteristically Sibelian thirds; (2) *Allegretto moderato,* a syncopated scherzo in an increasing rhythmic frequency of 3, 6, 9 and 12 notes to a 3/4 measure; (3) *Poco vivace* in the rhythm of a jig; (4) *Allegro molto,* a modal rondo, in vigorous duple time, ending softly on the tonic D minor.

My *Sixth Symphony* is wild and impassioned in character, somber in its pastoral contrasts . . . The orchestra rises in a menacing roar, in which the main theme is completely drowned. (From a letter dated 20 May 1918, long before its composition was actually begun, sent by Sibelius to a friend and quoted in Karl Ekman's biography of Sibelius published in 1935)

22 FEBRUARY 1923

The Juilliard Musical Foundation of New York City receives a $10,000,000 fund bequeathed by Frederick A. JUILLIARD for furtherance of music education in the United States.

23 FEBRUARY 1923

A Victory Ball, fantasy for orchestra, after the poem of Alfred Noyes, by the American composer Ernest SCHELLING, "a vision of troops marching on irresistibly, inexorably . . . to victory or disaster," dedicated "to the memory of an American soldier," a macabre musicorama traversing a tragic military march, a languid tango and a mortuary, waltz, with the organ "playing as many notes as possible with flat hands and arms" at the climactic point, and concluding on a distant trumpet call, is performed for the first time by the Philadelphia Orchestra, under the direction of Leopold Stokowski.

2 MARCH 1923

Madame Pompadour, operetta by Leo FALL, presenting the gay Paris of Louis XV and his legendary, mistress in a rollicking Viennese manner, is produced in Vienna.

4 MARCH 1923

La Primavera, cantata for soloists, chorus and orchestra by Ottorino RESPIGHI, is performed for the first time in Rome.

4 MARCH 1923

Hyperprism by Edgar VARÉSE, 39-year-old Frenchborn genius of new music, illustrating in abstractly expressionistic musical terms the geometric projection of a prism into the fourth dimension, athematically composed as a matrix of "organized sound" in a totality of dissonant counterpoint, scored for 9 wind instruments and 18 percussion devices and exploring extreme registers of the instrumental range, ending in fortissississimo, is performed for the first time at a concert of the International Composers Guild in New York.

6 MARCH 1923

Jardín de Oriente, opera by Joaquín TURINA, written in a brilliant Hispanic style, is produced in Madrid.

9 MARCH 1923

Le Hulla, lyric oriental tale in four acts by the 40-year-old French composer Marcel SAMUEL-ROUSSEAU, in which a Persian polygamist dismisses his favorite wife and gives her to a *hulla,* a nominally anonymous transitional husband, who unexpectedly develops a sensual attachment for her and is sentenced to death for his failure to live up to his pledge of continence, but is saved from the gallows by the shah in plain clothes and awarded the disputed wife in permanent possession, while the original husband becomes himself a *hulla,* with flutes purring serpentine oriental melismas and drums providing an exotic ambiance, is produced at the Opéra-Comique in Paris.

18 MARCH 1923

Das Rosengärtlein, opera to his own libretto by the 48-year-old Austrian composer Julius BITTNER, with the action taking place on the banks of the Danube in the 13th century, wherein a Turkish odalisque occupying a castle on the Danube under the Ottoman Imperial rule loses her love match for the heart of the feudal castellan to a fishmaiden, is produced in Mannheim.

18 MARCH 1923

Sixty years after its composition, Anton BRUCKNER's *Symphony in F minor* is performed for the first time in Klosterneuburg, Germany.

20 MARCH 1923

Mahit, symphonic ballet with voices by the 40-year-old Bohemian-born Italian composer Riccardo PICK-MAN-GIAGALLI, is produced at La Scala in Milan.

31 MARCH 1923

Marianela, opera in three acts by the Catalan composer Jaime PAHISSA, to the story of a blind man who miraculously recovers his sight, is produced in Barcelona.

31 MARCH 1923

Zapustialata Vodenitza (Abandoned Watermill), opera in two acts by the 41-year-old Bulgarian composer Georgi ATANASOV, is produced in Sofia.

7 APRIL 1923

Ciboulette, light opera by the Venezuelan-born Parisian composer Reynaldo HAHN, dealing with a milkmaid nicknamed *ciboulette* ("little garlic girl") working in the Halles, "the belly of Paris" in 1867, who becomes an actress and wins the love of a young aristocrat of the Second Empire, set to music in an Offenbachian vein, replete with hedonistic melorhythms, is produced in Paris.

10 APRIL 1923

I Compagnazzi (Companions), opera in one act by the 47-year-old Italian composer Primo RICCITELLI, with the action set in 15th-century Florence, wherein a company of determined young men preaching the doctrine of free sensuous love confute the obscurantic monastic penitents led by the fanatical ascetic Savonarola, written in a harmonious Italian vein contrasted with ecclesiastical chants in parsimonious counterpoint, is produced in Rome.

11 APRIL 1923

A group of American composers secedes from the International Composers Guild of New York to form a League of Composers in order to gain equal representation to moderate as well as radical tendencies of modern music.

The presentation in America of contemporary music is an undertaking that has rapidly outgrown the capacities of existing musical organizations. The media recently formed to promote modern music have been adequate only to offer a special phase of the whole movement. No organization exists today which proposes to bring the entire range of modern tendencies before the public . . . . It is for this purpose that the League of Composers has been organized. It believes not only that the creative artist needs contact with the public, but that the public is willing to give him a hearing . . . . The League intends to encourage and give support to the production of new and significant works. It will promote the publication of new music. It will effect cooperation between composers of all nations, and it will give well planned performances of new music selected from every school. (From the *Foreword to the Season of 1923–1924* issued by the League of Composers)

22 APRIL 1923

Poéme symphonique sur le nom de Gabriel Fauré by ROGER-DUCASSE, dedicated "à mon Maître Gabriel Faurè" and based on the three musical notes in Fauré's name, F-A-E, with an insertion of G for U and D for R, is performed for the first time in Paris.

26 APRIL 1923

Belfagor, lyric comedy in two acts with a prologue and epilogue by Ottorino RESPIGHI, wherein the archdemon Belfagor, fittingly characterized in the score by the leading motive of the tritone, the medieval "diabolus in musica," is sent to earth to test the theory that wives make marriage a living hell, and flees to real hell to escape impending matrimony, with a setting of functional modernity, periodically relaxing into Italianate neo-classicism, is performed for the first time at La Scala in Milan.

26 APRIL 1923

The White Buffalo Maiden, "a Western music-play" in one act by the 34-year-old American composer Eugene Farmer, dealing with the life of Sioux Indians, is produced for the first time in Boise, Idaho.

27 APRIL 1923

Maria, opera in three acts written in 1904 by the Polish composer Henryk OPIEŃSKI, is produced in Poznan.

29 APRIL 1923

Die Heilige Ente, opera in three acts by the 32-year-old Austrian composer Hans GÁL, is produced in Düsseldorf.

29 APRIL 1923

Il primo bacio, one-act opera by Ruggero LEONCA-VALLO, treating lightly the solemn subject of the first kiss, is produced posthumously in Montecatini.

3 MAY 1923

Chant de joie, symphonic movement for orchestra by Arthur HONEGGER, in three sections, the first and the third vigorous and joyful, the middle one meditative and lyrical, is performed for the first time in Paris, under the direction of Serge Koussevitzky.

3 MAY 1923

Casanova, opera in three acts by the 39-year-old Polish composer Ludomir RÓZYCKI, dealing with Casanova's abduction of the Algerian Bey's favorite concubine and his subsequent affair with the mistress of the chief of police in Venice, set in a melodiously Italianate manner, is produced in Warsaw.

5 MAY 1923

Society of Quarter-Tone Music is organized in Petrograd under the direction of Georg RIMSKY-KORSAKOV, grandson of the composer, to promote icositetraphony in Russia.

13 MAY 1923

Lucerna (The Lantern), musical legend in four acts by the Czech composer of the modern romantic school VÍTĚSLAV NOVÁK, in which a lantern lit by a linden tree, a symbol of the feudal vassalage of a local miller, is destroyed by a pair of sympathetic male water sprites, who subsequently force the landlord to surrender his fief, set to music in a vivacious Bohemian vein, is produced in Prague.

14 MAY 1923

The Perfect Fool, one-act opera by Gustav HOLST, wherein a maleficently thaumaturgic wizard standing on top of a Stonehenge trilithon brews a potion to make himself irresistible to women, but is outwitted by a mentally retarded narcoleptic youth who drinks it first and marries a nubile princess, with two secondary characters, a Troubadour singing a Verdian aria and a Traveler intoning baleful Wagnerogenic incantations, is produced at Covent Garden in London. (A symphonic suite from *The Perfect Fool* was performed at a London concert on 11 December 1921.)

The Characters of this opera (excepting the Troubadour and Traveler whose origins are obvious) belong to no particular country or period. The author asks that the spirit of high comedy shall be maintained throughout. (Gustav Holst's prefatory note in the printed score)

17 MAY 1923

Peter MENNIN, American composer of symphonies and oratorios written in a civilized neo-classical idiom with the application of prudential dissonances, is born in Erie, Pennsylvania, of Italian parents. (His real name was Mennini.)

21 MAY 1923

Ninna nanna della bambola, children's opera by the futuristically minded Italian composer Francesco Balilla PRATELLA, is produced in Milan.

30 MAY 1923

Howard HANSON, 26-year-old American composer, conducts in Rome, during his residence there as holder of the American Rome Prize, the first performance anywhere of his *First Symphony* in E minor, surnamed *Nordic Symphony,* expressive of his intimate sentiment for the Scandinavian North of his ancestors, "its solemnity, austerity and grandeur, its restlessness and surging and strife, its somberness and melancholy," with a predilection, Sibelius-like, for the lowest reaches of the instrumental compass, in three movements: a philosophical *Andante solenne* leading to a dramatic *Allegro con fuoco,* a

tenderly simple *Andante* (dedicated to his mother), and an energetic *Finale* (dedicated to his father). (The first American performance, conducted by Hanson with the Rochester Philharmonic on 19 March 1924 was erroneously listed in the previous editions of *Music Since 1900* as an absolute first performance.)

30 MAY 1923

Camille CHEVILLARD, French conductor, son-in-law of Charles Lamoureux and his successor as permanent conductor of the famed Lamoureux concerts in Paris, dies in his native Paris at the age of 63.

1 JUNE 1923

Padmâvatî, opera-ballet in two acts by Albert ROUSSEL, to a libretto based on the story of the legendary 13th-century Hindu queen who refuses to submit to the desires of a conquering Mongol khan (the instructions in the text specify that the role of Padmâvatî demands "une grande beaute physique"), stabs the wounded King to death and dies with him, ascending his funeral pyre as the frustrated invader enters the temple, set to music in acrid modern harmonies without ostentatious orientalization, is produced at the Paris Opéra.

4 JUNE 1923

Fête galante, operatic "dance dream" in one act by the foremost musical suffragette of England Dame Ethel SMYTH, is produced in Birmingham.

5 JUNE 1923

Old King Cole, ballet for orchestra and chorus by Ralph VAUGHAN WILLIAMS, to a scenario dealing with the Saxon King of Colchester whose daughter became a Roman empress and organized a music contest, is performed for the first time in Cambridge, England.

12 JUNE 1923

Façade, "an entertainment for reciting voice and instruments" by the 21-year-old English composer William WALTON, to the texts of syntactically nonsensical but syllabically meaningful blank verses by Edith Sitwell, is performed for the first time in London, with Edith Sitwell herself speaking her lines through the "sengerphone," a decorated megaphone protruding through the mouth of a monstrous head painted on the curtain. (A private performance of *Façade* was given first in the London home of Sir Osbert Sitwell, brother of Edith Sitwell, on 24 January 1922; the title *Façade* was an intrafamilial joke, Edith Sitwell being described as clever, but "only a façade.")

13 JUNE 1923

Serge Diaghilev's Ballet Russe presents in Paris the first performance of *Les Noces,* "choreographic scenes with singing and music" by Igor STRAVINSKY (completed in Monaco on 6 April 1923), scored for chorus, vocal soloists, four pianos and 17 percussion instruments, a stylized portrayal of a Russian village wedding, to a text garnered from authentic peasant locutions, marked by asymmetrical rhythms within changing meters united by a constant mutual beat, and set in pandiatonically extended modalities in desiccated sonorities, containing two principal parts and four tableaux:

(1) *In the Bride's Room,* a ritual lamentation for the maiden about to become a bride, interrupted by other maidens proffering gratuitous encouragement in angular melodic intervals and syncopated rhythms, with the eighth-note as a metrical constant; (2) *In the Bridegroom's Room,* an ode in starkly bland counterpoint suggesting a modernized organum in quartal and quintal harmonies, followed by the parental lament, in a triadic compass, with an ambivalent mediant of a fluctuating major-minor third, succeeded by a rudely intoned choral chant; (3) *The Bride's Farewell,* an intense static epithalamium set against an ostinato within the range of a minor ninth; (4) *The Wedding Repast,* a hocket in stridently dissonant counterpoint, with the metrical invariant of an eighth-note, brutalized into rhythmic speech and followed by an instrumental postlude in slow, bell-like sounds of widely spaced chords on the piano-forte.

14 JUNE 1923

The "École d'Arcueil" is formally organized and in all seriousness announced by Erik SATIE, a resident of Arcueil, a placid sub-Parisian village, at a Paris concert of his young admirers, Henri CLIQUET-PLEYEL, Roger DÉSORMIÈRE, Maxim JACOB and Henri SAUGUET, founding members of the new sodality dedicated to Satie's esthetic ideals.

J'ai toujours fait crédit à le jeunesse. (Satie's declaration at the occasion)

They chose the name "School of Arcueil" because of their affection for an old inhabitant of that suburban locality. I shall not discuss their merits, being happily neither a sycophant nor a professional critic. The public must be their critic, for it is the public that has real powers to pass judgment upon them. Personally, I am happy at the arrival of the School of Arcueil in the musical arena. They will replace the Group of Six, some of whom have already won a reputation despite the absurd attacks on them by parlor artists, envious second-raters and criticasters. (From Erik Satie's letter to Rolf de Mare, director of the Ballets Suédois in Paris)

17 JUNE 1923

In the course of the Third Festival of Modern Chamber Music at Donaueschingen, the first performance is given of *Das Marienleben,* cycle of 15 songs for voice and piano by 27-year-old Paul HINDEMITH, to the poems of Rainer Maria Rilke, depicting the life of Virgin Mary in diatonically lucid melodic lines against dissonant contrapuntal progressions in the piano part, conjuring up an attractive neo-medieval ambience but revealing emotional intensity beneath the austere surface of the music.

24 JUNE 1923

Die Chinesische Flöte, a chamber symphony in six sections for 14 solo instruments and soprano by Ernst TOCH, to a German version of ancient Chinese poetry, wherein Buddhist monks intone a polytonal chorale and Confucius introduces a series of aphorisms in an ascending progression of whole-tone scales, is performed for the first time in Frankfurt.

25 JUNE 1923

In the Paris salon of the Princesse de Polignac, the first stage production is given of the marionette opera *El*

Retablo de Maese Pedro by Manuel DE FALLA, after an episode in *Don Quixote* where the errant knight wrecks a little theater trying to save a noble damsel from a pack of maleficent puppet Moors, realistically including spoken parts for the director of the theater and a singing role for Don Quixote seated in the orchestra, the music palpitating with Andalusian melorhythms in a gibbous tonality astutely maintained by recurrent Phrygian cadences on a major dominant. (The first concert performance was given in Seville on 23 March 1923.)

25 JUNE 1923

Raquela, one-act opera by the 39-year-old Argentine composer Felipe BOERO, is produced in Buenos Aires.

4 JULY 1923

English Folk Song Suite by Ralph VAUGHAN WILLIAMS, scored for military, band, in three movements of fanciful variations on popular English ditties, *Seventeen Come Sunday, Pretty Caroline, Dives and Lazarus, My Bonny Boy, Green Bushes, Blow Away the Morning Dew, High Germany, The Tree so High* and *John Barleycorn,* is performed for the first time in London as a commissioned work by the Royal Military School of Music.

4 JULY 1923

Three hundred years have passed since the death of the great Elizabethan madrigalist William BYRD.

13 JULY 1923

Asger HAMERIK, Danish composer of seven symphonies, four operas, two choral trilogies and other music in a respectable romantic idiom, who for 26 years (1872–1898) was director of the Peabody Conservatory of Baltimore, brother of the music historian Angul Hammerich (which is the original Germanic family surname), dies at Frederiksberg at the age of 80.

13 JULY 1923

Ilse, opera by the Argentine composer Gilardo GILARDI, to a story of a Bavarian maiden fatefully involved in a melodramatic romance with an improvident painter, is produced at the Teatro Colón in Buenos Aires.

25 JULY 1923

Sruth na Maoile (The Sea of Moyle), one-act opera by the 40-year-old English-born Irishman Geoffrey PALMER, to a libretto founded on the Irish saga *The Children of Lir,* is produced in Dublin with the original libretto in the Gaelic language.

2 AUGUST 1923

The First Festival of the International Society for Contemporary Music (first, because the parent 1922 Salzburg Festival took place before the formation of the Society) opens in Salzburg with the following program of chamber music:

String Quartet by Alban BERG, written in 1910 in an anamnestically Wagnerian and consciously Mahlerophiliac manner and revised in 1920 under the impact of the Schoenbergian concepts, emancipated in its use of unresolved chords and independent from central tonality; Arnold SCHOEN-BERG's cycle of 15 songs *Das Buch der hängenden Gärten* for voice and piano, to poems by the Viennese expressionistic poet Stefan George, written in 1909 and representing the inception of the atonal period, free from key-signatures, consistently dissonant in harmonic complexes, ending on unresolved chords, and favoring the acoustically inharmonious intervals of major sevenths and tritones while avoiding all triadic implications; and *Second Violin Sonata* by Béla BARTÓK, composed in 1922, in two movements in which the melodic structure is based on the technique of octave displacement so that the semitones of the chromatic scale become intervalic leaps of major sevenths, but concluding paradoxically on a candid and purified C-major triad.

3 AUGUST 1923

At the second concert of the First Festival of the International Society for Contemporary Music in Salzburg, the following program of chamber music is given:

Sonate libre en deux parties enchaînées (ad modum clementis aquae) for violin and piano by Florent SCHMITT (so titled with reference to Clemenceau's newspaper originally appearing as *l'Homme Libre* and later, when censorship began to intervene, *L'Homme Enchaîné*), in two movements separated in their principal tonalities by the "diabolus in musica," the first being in C-sharp minor, the second in D minor, symbolically reflecting the diabolical horrors of the war of 1914–1918 during which it was partly written, the harmonic idiom marked by a considerable incidence of polytonality, sharpened by polyrhythmic asymmetry and melodic angularity; *Hafislieder,* a cycle of five songs by the foremost Swiss lyric composer Othmar SCHOECK, inspired by Persian poetry but devoid of ostentatious musical orientalism, performed with the composer at the piano; *Sonata for Violin Solo* by the Latvian-born Germaneducated romantic composer Eduard ERDMANN; songs by Yrjö KILPINEN, the "Hugo Wolf of Finland"; and *Third String Quartet* by the 22-year-old Viennese modernist Ernst KRENEK.

4 AUGUST 1923

At the third concert of the First Festival of the International Society for Contemporary Music in Salzburg, the following program of chamber music is presented:

Overture on Hebrew Themes for clarinet, string quartet and piano by Sergei PROKOFIEV, based on authentic modern Jewish songs and first performed in New York on 26 January 1920; *Délie,* a cycle of three songs by ROLAND-MANUEL; *Eine Reiterburlesque* for piano by the Czechborn German composer of lyric music, Fidelio FINKE; *2 Hafis Songs* by Karol SZYMANOWSKI, inspired by Persian legends; 2 Songs by Manuel DE FALLA; *Duo* for violin and cello by RAVEL; *Sonatina* for flute and piano by the French-born half-German half-Catalan composer Philipp JARNACH; *2 Sacred Songs* for voice and organ by the Viennese composer Paul A. PISK; and *First String Quartet,* written in an ingratiatingly hedonistic neo-classical idiom by the 21-year-old English composer William WALTON.

5 AUGUST 1923

At the fourth concert of the First Festival of the International Society for Contemporary Music in Salzburg, the following program of chamber music is presented:

Austere and somber *Sonata* for violin and piano by the foremost Czech romanticist Leoš JANÁČEK; colorful *Rhapsody* by Arthur BLISS, a nonet for soprano, tenor, flute, English

horn, two violins, viola, cello and doublebass, set in an Arcadian mood with two voices vocalizing on an open syllable "Ah"; *Divertissement* for flute, oboe, clarinet, bassoon, French horn and piano by Albert ROUSSEL, written in 1906, ingeniously intertwining rhythmic strains in a kaleidoscopic variety of melodic turns in semi-impressionistic harmonies; *Sonata* for flute and harp by the Dutch composer Sere DRESDEN, in three movements inspired by folk-like melorhythms and accoutred in Debussyan harmonies, performed with the composer at the piano replacing the harp; *Valses bourgeoises* for two pianos by the British musical wit Lord BERNERS; *New York Days and Nights* for piano solo by the American composer Emerson WHITHORNE, descriptive of the turmoil of the great city of skyscrapers with the Woolworth Building, the tallest in the world, towering over the populace riding in the new model T Ford automobiles; *Il Raggio verde* for piano by the Italian lyric composer Mario CASTELNUOVO-TEDESCO; *Three Pieces for String Quartet* by Igor STRAVINSKY, composed in 1914, and based on brief Russian-like refrains in apocopated meters, with triadic melodic conformations; and Stravinsky's *Concertino for String Quartet*, written in 1920, in one monolithic but not monothematic compressed movement, with open quartal and quintal melodic progressions set in neolithically crude harmonies.

6 AUGUST 1923

At the fifth concert of the First Festival of the International Society for Contemporary Music in Salzburg, the following program of chamber music is presented:

Sonata for viola and piano by Arthur HONEGGER; *2 Sonetti del Berni* for soprano and piano by Gian Francesco MALIPIERO; *Second String Quartet* in quarter-tones by Alois HÁBA, the Czech icositetraphonic pioneer, making use not only of quarter-tones, but also of 3/4-tones, 5/4-tones, etc., and notated with the aid of specially designed symbols; *Sonata* for violin and cello by Maurice RAVEL, in four movements, cyclically conceived and monothematically centered on an intervalic sequence of major or minor sevenths constituting the melodic inversion of consecutive notes in the chromatic and diatonic scales; and the first performance of the two-piano version of Ferruccio BUSONI's monumental *Fantasia contrappuntistica*, originally written for piano solo during his American tour of 1910 in emulation of Bach's *Kunst der Fuge*, set in 12 interdependent sections, and architectonically designed as a grandiose triptych of fugues, variations and intermezzi, extending the resources of the keyboard technique to the utmost neo-classical limits, while remaining within the larger confines of conceptual tonality.

7 AUGUST 1923

At the sixth concert of the First Festival of the International Society for Contemporary Music in Salzburg, the following program is presented:

Fourth String Quartet by Darius MILHAUD, written in an Arcadian pastoral mood, with the bucolic melodies translucidly attired in polytonal harmonies; *Promenades* for piano by Francis POULENC; *Piano Sonata* by Charles KOECHLIN; *Five Songs* by the neo-romantic German musician Manfred GURLITT for voice with chamber orchestra, the composer conducting; *Sonata* for cello solo by Zoltán KODÁLY, a tour de force of modern instrumental writing, with an ingenious and esthetically justified application of *scordatura*, with the C and C strings lowered a semitone to provide a B-minor tonic chord for basic harmony; and *Quintet* for clarinet and string quartet by Paul HINDEMITH, in five movements, of which the last is a free retrograde canon of the first.

10 SEPTEMBER 1923

The Ajanta Frescoes, ballet by Alexander TCHEREPNIN portraying the Buddha's renunciation of the world as depicted in the mural paintings in the caves of Ajanta, India, is performed for the first time in London, with Anna Pavlova in the role of the princess.

29 SEPTEMBER 1923

Schwanenweiss, opera in three acts by the German composer Julius WEISMANN, to a libretto from a play by August Strindberg, is produced in Duisburg.

17 OCTOBER 1923

Doña Francisquita, opera in three acts by the Spanish composer Amadeo VIVES, based on Lopez de Vega's comedy *La discreta enamorada*, is produced in Madrid.

18 OCTOBER 1923

Two world premières are given at a Koussevitzky concert in Paris:

Octet by Igor STRAVINSKY (conducted by him), scored for flute, clarinet, 2 bassoons, 2 trumpets and 2 trombones, marking a new turn in his creative evolution in the neo-classical direction of parsimonious economy of means, with a dynamic scheme of chiaroscuro precision, limited to stark contrasts of annunciatory forte and antiphonal piano, set in three movements of great frugality of expression and flaming frigidity of consequential exposition: (1) *Sinfonia*, opening with a reserved *Lento*, leading to a decisively styled *Allegro moderato*; (2) *Tema con variazioni*, a carefully equilibrated study in controlled variants of a robust melorhythmic statement; (3) *Finale*, a sturdy piece of polyphonic sonification with a terminal C major chord in second inversion; *First Violin Concerto* in D major by Sergei PROKOFIEV (performed by Marcel Darrieux, with Koussevitzky conducting), written in Russia in 1917, in three movements: (1) *Andantino*, commencing with a lyrically inflected theme for solo violin and developed with structural and emotional logic along rhapsodically drawn lines; (2) *Scherzo*, constituting a characteristic display of Prokofiev's rhythmic verve and restrained irony in the intervalic saltation of the melody; (3) *Moderato*, a nostalgic meditation, reverting to the elegiac mood of the initial movement and concluding with a poetic peroration.

19 OCTOBER 1923

Der Hochzeiter (The Bridegroom), comic opera in two acts by the 43-year-old German composer Karl BLEYLE, to his own libretto derived from the novella *Aus dem Regen in die Traufe (Out of the Rain into the Gutter)*, is performed for the first time in this version, the original being titled *Hannele und Sannele*, in Rostock.

25 OCTOBER 1923

La Création du Monde, ballet by Darius MILHAUD, to a scenario depicting the creation of the world by three Central African gods and the fashioning of primitive men out of hairy primates, the first symphonic work based on jazz rhythms and melodic inflections of the Blues, anticipating Gershwin's symphonic jazz, is produced by the Ballets Suédois in Paris.

25 OCTOBER 1923

Third part of *Impressioni dal Vero* by Gian Francesco MALIPIERO in three divisions—(1) *Festa in Val d' Inferno*, a bolero-like multicolored bacchanale; (2) *I Galli*, a barnyard scene, with gallivanting roosters strutting in descending consecutive minor triads and nervous hens emitting explosive hockets; and (3) *La Tarantella a Capri*, symphonic exteriorization of a Dionysiac dance once believed to possess curative powers against the venomous bite of the tarantula— is performed for the first time in Amsterdam, Alfredo Casella conducting.

27 OCTOBER 1923

Holofernes, biblical opera in two acts by Emil Nikolaus von REZNIČEK, depicting the bloody deed of Judith in the decapitation of the enemy commander, is produced in Berlin.

31 OCTOBER 1923

Le Jardin du Paradis, lyric tale in four acts by Alfred BRUNEAU, fashioned after a tale by Hans Christian Andersen, dealing with a young prince whose beloved tests his faith in her by confessing untruthfully that she has once been inadvertently kissed and shocks him to such an extent that he goes to the garden of Eden to avenge his disgrace on Eve as the source of the original sin, but finds that Eve is identical with his beloved who finally consoles him by admitting her absolute immaculacy, is produced at the Paris Opéra.

31 OCTOBER 1923

Mareike von Nymwegen, opera by Eugen D'ALBERT, to a subject from a medieval Dutch folk tale, is produced in Hamburg.

1 NOVEMBER 1923

Hugo GERNSBACK, Luxembourg-born inventor and science fiction writer, gives a demonstration over Radio Station WJZ in New York unveiling his STACCATO-PHONE, an electronic piano with vacuum tubes instead of strings, capable of producing the pitch of all 88 notes of the keyboard.

10 NOVEMBER 1923

Anna Karenina, opera in three acts by the Hungarian violinist Jenö HUBAY, based on Tolstoy's novel of sin and retribution and ending in the heroine's suicidal death under the wheels of a locomotive, set to a dramatically Wagnerogenic score with an injection of Russianized melodies as *couleur locale*, is produced in Budapest.

11 NOVEMBER 1923

At the inaugural concert in New York of the League of Composers, the first performance is given of Ernest BLOCH's *Quintet* for piano and string quartet, in three movements, *Agitato, Andante mistico* and *Allegro energico*, introducing quarter-tones used as "affective" devices to enhance the emotional elements of individual melodic tones, without consecutive icositetraphonic progressions, but in the manner of instantaneously close appoggiaturas, while the main thematic material is grounded in expressive cantillation and deep pedal-points.

11 NOVEMBER 1923

The 43-year-old English composer and conductor John FOULDS leads, on Armistice Day in London, the first performance of his oratorio *A World Requiem*, written in an aridly reverential spirit to commemorate those fallen in World War I.

12 NOVEMBER 1923

Vendetta, grand opera by the American Negro composer Harry Lawrence FREEMAN, is produced in New York.

15 NOVEMBER 1923

Srdce (The Heart), opera in two acts by the Czech composer of German extraction Josef Bohuslav FOERSTER, to his own libretto dealing with an actor who decides to devote his life to helping the poor after an unrequited love affair with a frigid-hearted young lady, is produced in Prague.

19 NOVEMBER 1923

On the occasion of the 50th anniversary of the union of the twin cities of Buda and Pest, three specially commissioned works by three eminent Hungarian composers are performed for the first time in Budapest:

(1) *Festival Overture* by the Hungarian academic romanticist Ernst von DOHNÁNYI; (2) *Psalmus Hungaricus* for tenor, mixed chorus, children's chorus and orchestra by Zoltán KODÁLY to an old Hungarian text adapted from the Penitential Psalms, with a pentatonic unison chant in the ancient Magyar manner as a choral ritornello, developing by cumulative accretion of contrapuntal and harmonic elements and reaching a grandiloquent expansion of astutely applied modern harmonies; (3) *Five Dances* by Béla BARTÓK, composed in a folksong idiom on original themes melorhythmically derived from various national elements of southeastern Europe: oriental motives in the first and fourth dances, Magyar inflections in the second and third dances, and Gypsy refrains in the fifth dance, building a multi-colored sonic quincunx.

26 NOVEMBER 1923

Bubbles, one-act opera by the Irish composer Hubert BATH, a farce in which the bubbles of gossip are burst when a farm hand presumed to have been slain as a victim of adulterous fornication appears in the court room where his rustic inamorata is being tried for his murder, in a jigful Irish setting, is performed for the first time in Belfast, Ireland, conducted by the composer.

26 NOVEMBER 1923

The American barefoot dancer Isadora DUNCAN presents in Moscow a ceremonious choreographic monodrama to the music of Schubert's *Ave Maria* to celebrate the civil christening of a Communist baby girl, with the matriarch of German Communism Klara Zetkin acting as an atheistic godmother and the Soviet theorist Bukharin, who was to be shot by Stalin in 1938, as a dialectical godfather.

10 DECEMBER 1923

La Brebis égarée, "roman musical" in three acts by Darius MILHAUD, wherein the wayward wife of a lenient hus-

band contritely returns home, like the lost sheep of the biblical parable, after a disillusioning affair with an insubstantial bravo in Spain, during which she has to undergo a prosaic operation of appendectomy, is performed for the first time at the Opéra-Comique in Paris.

16 DECEMBER 1923

Der Schmied von Marienburg, opera in three acts by Siegfried WAGNER, glorifying the exploits of Teutonic German knights fighting the Poles at one of the many medieval encounters at Marienburg during which a brave local smith excels in love and war, the actions depicted in resonant fanfares of loyally filial Wagneromantic colors, is produced in Rostock.

18 DECEMBER 1923

Scarecrow Sketches, symphonic suite by the American composer Frederick S. CONVERSE, assembled from materials of his "photo-music-drama" *Puritan Passions*, is performed for the first time in Boston.

19 DECEMBER 1923

Daisi (Twilight), opera in three acts by the Georgian composer Zachar PALIASHVILI, dealing with the struggle for national independence in the Caucasian dukedom of Georgia in the 18th century, and making use of old native folk rhythms harmonized in the framework of Russian orientalism, is produced in Tiflis.

22 DECEMBER 1923

La Dame en décolleté, operetta in three acts by Maurice YVAIN, is produced in Paris.

22 DECEMBER 1923

Diana, one-act opera by the 29-year-old Hungarian composer Eugen ZÁDOR, wherein a gruesome medieval knight slays his wife's lover and then serves her a glass of his coagulated blood as a mockery of the wine of the Eucharist, is produced in Budapest.

28 DECEMBER 1923

The first Hebrew opera house is opened in Tel Aviv with the intention of launching a series of classical and romantic operas in the Hebrew language.

29 DECEMBER 1923

Epiphanie for cello and orchestra in three movements, *Cortège, Prière de Melchior, Danse des petits nègres*, by the French conductor and master orchestrator André CAPLET, who had helped Debussy in putting together his ballet scores and who himself was impressionistically inclined in his symphonic inspirations, is performed for the first time at the Concerts Colonne in Paris, Maurice Maréchal soloist, Gabriel Pierné conducting.

31 DECEMBER 1923

Kid Boots, American musical comedy by Harry TIERNEY, dealing with a gifted crook and featuring (by interpolation) the famous song *Dinah* sung by Eddie Cantor, is produced in New York.

1924

5 JANUARY 1924

Faust en ménage, operetta by Claude TERRASSE, a sequel to Gounod's opera, in which Faust marries and becomes a becalmed bourgeois, is produced in Paris.

6 JANUARY 1924

Les Biches, "ballet avec chant" by Francis POULENC, in which a bevy of human does and roes presents a succession of stylized dances, classical and new, pure and hybrid (such as Rag-Mazurka), in a musical idiom eclectically combining elements of Scarlatti, Delibes and Stravinsky, is produced in Monte Carlo by the Ballet Russe on the eve of Poulenc's 25th birthday.

6 JANUARY 1924

Escales, symphonic suite by Jacques IBERT, in three movements descriptive of his Mediterranean cruise as a winner of the Prix de Rome, with stops at three ports of call—not specifically mentioned in the printed score, but presumed to be (1) Palermo, marked *Calme-Assez animé* suggesting a poetically humid and warmly fragrant atmosphere of Sicily followed by a sudden outburst of dancing energy; (2) Tunis, *Modéré, très rythmé*, with a solitary oboe on a high minaret broadcasting his prayerful message to the faithful while drums beat distantly; (3) Valencia, *Animé*, an exulting fandango full of Mauretanian vigor. and Andalusian vivacity, vibrating with impressionistic colors—is performed for the first time at the Concerts Lamoureux in Paris.

11 JANUARY 1924

La plus forte, opera in four acts by Xavier LEROUX, wherein a passionate woman of the people, married to a harried tiller of the soil, engages in an affair with a sensuously supercharged youth, who turns out to be her own stepson, whereupon she hurls herself into the sea, while father and son return to their fertile earth, the "stronger one" of the title, is produced posthumously at the Opéra-Comique in Paris, in a version completed and orchestrated by Henri Busser.

13 JANUARY 1924

Octandre (meaning a flower having eight stamens) by Edgar VARÈSE, scored for flute, clarinet, oboe, bassoon, horn, trumpet, trombone and double-bass, constructed in a typical Varèsian manner and moving in harmonic blocks supported by deep sonorous layers, is performed for the first time in New York.

14 JANUARY 1924

Count Géza ZICHY, Hungarian pianist who at the age of fourteen lost his right arm in a hunting accident, and subsequently became a virtuoso left-hand pianist, composed sinistro-manual piano pieces and performed a three-hand arrangement of Liszt's Rakóczy March with Liszt himself playing the other two hands, dies in Budapest at the age of 74.

19 JANUARY 1924

Les Fâcheux, ballet after Molière's comedy, with the music by the youngest of the French Six, 24-year-old Georges AURIC, in the form of a dance suite, classical in movement and rhythm, modernistically bitonal or pandiatonic in harmony, is produced by Diaghilev's Ballet Russe in Monte Carlo. (Exact date obtained from the management of the Monte Carlo Opera.)

26 JANUARY 1924

Alexander TCHEREPNIN plays at the Société Nationale de Musique in Paris the solo part in the first performance of his *Second Piano Concerto*, with Nadia Boulanger conducting.

28 JANUARY 1924

Das verfemte Lachen (The Forbidden Laughter), comic opera by the 45-year-old German composer Fritz COR-TOLEZIS, based on a historical episode in the life of the Danish crown prince who became King Christian VI of Denmark and Norway and who issued an order in 1722 forbidding laughter in or around his hunting lodge, is produced in Rostock.

2 FEBRUARY 1924

The sinistro-manual *Concertante Variationen über ein Thema von Beethoven* for left-hand piano and orchestra by the Austrian composer Franz SCHMIDT, based on the theme of the Scherzo from Beethoven's F-major Violin Sonata, with its pointed syncopation, is performed for the first time in Vienna, with the amputated Viennese pianist Paul Wittgenstein, for whom the work was written, as soloist. (The work was subsequently arranged in a bimanual version, and first performed in Wuppertal on 12 April 1940.)

9 FEBRUARY 1924

Le Petit Elfe Ferme-l'Œil, "une semaine dansée" by Florent SCHMITT, after Hans Christian Andersen's fairy tale, traversing seven days in a child's life and dealing with the poetic image of a little elf who closes the eyes of good children going to sleep and puts an imaginative assortment of pleasant dreams under their eyelids—mice getting married, armored knights fighting wooden soldiers, the alphabet staging a dance—but lets bad children go dreamless, to a score saturated with impressionistically opulent sonorities, is produced at the Opéra-Comique in Paris. (A concert performance was given earlier, on 1 December 1923, at the Concerts Colonne in Paris.)

10 FEBRUARY 1924

Věčný Návrat (Eternal Return), "poem in music" for orchestra by the Czech romantic composer Villém PETRŽELKA, is performed for the first time in Brno.

12 FEBRUARY 1924

George GERSHWIN, 25-year-old Brooklyn-born composer of inspired popular songs in an authentically modern American style, appears as piano soloist in the first performance, at a concert conducted by Paul Whiteman in Aeolian Hall in New York, of his epoch-making *Rhapsody in Blue,* completed by him in piano score on 7 January 1924, and arranged for piano and a jazz-type ensemble by Ferde Grofé, the title indicating its derivation from the soulful "blues" of urban American melos, and permeated with the spirit of nostalgic Negritude, comprising the following subdivisions:

Molto Moderato, opening with an acrobatic clarinet climb from low F to the stratospheric B-flat, stating the principal "blue" subject in a Mixolydian mode with a lowered sixth; *Moderato assai,* with the piano presenting the principal theme in a hedonistically optimistic and virtuosistically Lisztian manner in three keys whose tonics are distanced by minor thirds—G-flat major, A major and C major—succeeded by the exposition of two new themes; *Meno Mosso e poco scherzando,* with a jazzily dancing chromatic arabesque; a recapitulation in which the principal subject appears successively in G, C and E-flat major, with a new rhapsodic theme in a hypo-Ionian hexachord, soon jazzed up along the successive degrees of the whole-tone scale; *Agitato e misterioso,* in which the 2/4 meter is subdivided into asymmetrical groups of 3/16, 3/16 and 2/16 producing an effect of natural syncopation; *Molto slendando,* insistently stressing the songful C-major theme; *Grandioso,* in an expansively Lisztian manner in which the *scherzando* motive appears in diminution, concluding with the final triumphant enunciation of the primary subject in the original key of B-flat major, with a "blue" seventh converting the major scale into a Mixolydian mode.

The audience was stirred, and many a hardened concert-goer excited with the sensation of a new talent finding its voice, and likely to say something personally and racially important to the world. A talent and an idiom, also rich in possibilities for that generally exhausted and outworn form of the classic piano concerto (Olin Downes, New York *Times,* 13 February 1924)

This music is only half alive. Its gorgeous vitality of rhythm and of instrumental color is impaired by melodic and harmonic anemia of the most pernicious kind . . . . How trite and feeble and conventional the tunes are, how sentimental and vapid the harmonic treatment, under the disguise of fussy and futile counterpoint! (Lawrence Gilman, New York *Tribune,* 17 February 1924)

He is a link between the jazz camp and the intellectuals. His *Rhapsody* had all the faults one might expect from an experimental work. . . . It was crude, but it hinted at something new, something that has not hitherto been said in music. Mr. Gershwin will bear watching; he may yet bring jazz out of the kitchen. (Deems Taylor, New York *World,* 17 February 1924)

There had been so much chatter about the limitations of jazz. . . . Jazz, they said, had to be in strict time. It had to cling to dance rhythms. I resolved, if possible, to kill that misconception with one sturdy blow. Inspired by this aim, I set to work composing with unwonted rapidity. No set plan was in my mind, no structure to which my music would conform. The *Rhapsody,* as you see, began as a purpose, not a plan. At this stage of the piece, I was summoned to Boston for the première of *Sweet Little Devil.* I had already done some work on the *Rhapsody.* It was on the train with its steely rhythms, its rattlety-bang that is so stimulating to a composer. . . . I frequently hear music in the very heart of noise. And then I suddenly heard— and even saw on paper—the complete construction of the *Rhapsody,* from beginning to end . . . as a sort of musical kaleidoscope of America. (Gershwin quoted in Isaac Goldberg's book, *George Gershwin, a Study in American Music,* New York, 1931)

14 FEBRUARY 1924

Thomas l'Agnelet, Gentilhomme de Fortune, opera in four acts by the Belgian composer Lèon JONGEN, to a story of adventure wherein a corsair in the employ of Louis XIV during the Franco-Spanish war, frustrated by the refusal of a captive Spanish beauty to reciprocate his ardor, kills all male members of her family whereupon she decides to seduce him to gain an opportunity to slay him, when his conscience unexpectedly compels him to confess his misdeeds to the authorities with the result that he is sentenced to hang on the mast of his own depredatory frigate, all these peripeteia set to sonorously Wagneromantic music, is produced in Brussels.

16 FEBRUARY 1924

Farsangi Lakodalom (Carnival Wedding), comic opera in three acts by the Hungarian composer Ede POLDINI, is produced in Budapest.

21 FEBRUARY 1924

Sandha, one-act opera by the Italian composer Felice LATTUADA, depicting the tragedy of an Indian woman compelled to abide by the humiliating customs of her caste, as an untouchable Pariah, an object of animal male concupiscence, is produced in Genoa.

25 FEBRUARY 1924

The first number of the quarterly *The League of Composers' Review,* later renamed *Modern Music,* is issued in New York as the official organ of the League of Composers.

28 FEBRUARY 1924

Gräfin Mariza, operetta in three acts by Emmerich KÁLMAN, Hungarian composer of light music, with the action taking place in Hungary in 1922, wherein a nubile countess is shocked by the amorous advances of her own majordomo, but acquiesces when he turns out to be an impoverished but titled nobleman, is produced in Vienna.

1 MARCH 1924

Tycho Brahes Dröm, ballet by the Danish composer Hakon BÖRRESEN, wherein the Danish astronomer Tycho Brahe (1546–1601) achieves his cherished dream in building the famous Uranienborg observatory, is produced in Copenhagen.

2 MARCH 1924

A century has passed since the birth in Leitomischl of Bedřich SMETANA, great nationalist composer of Bohemia and musical innovator in his use of modal melodies and asymmetrical rhythms redolent of authentic music of his people.

6 MARCH 1924

The White Bird, one-act opera by the American composer Ernest CARTER, wherein a forester passionately involved with his employer's wife shoots her by accident mistaking the white scarf around her bosom for a low-flying white bird, and in desperate fury strangles the husband, making use of American songs peculiar to the scene in upper New York State, arranged in abecedarian harmonies, is performed for the first time in Chicago.

8 MARCH 1924

Clo-clo, musical farce in three acts by Franz LEHÁR, dealing with a temperamental star of the Folies-Bergère in Paris sexually pursued by her piano teacher, a provincial sexagenarian politician, and other libidinously inclined gentlemen, who eventually finds a congenial soul and adequate physique in the person of a cultured French nobleman, is produced in Vienna.

17 MARCH 1924

Yugoslav Symphony by the Serbian composer Milenko PAUNOVIĆ, in three movements thematically based on native melorhythms and unified by a "motive of fate", esthetically derived from Bruckner and Dvořák, is performed for the first time in Ljubljana, shortly before the composer's death at the age of 35.

18 MARCH 1924

August FOERSTER, German piano manufacturer, receives the patent for his quarter-tone piano, the first ever issued for such an instrument. (Exact date communicated to the author by Foerster.)

19 MARCH 1924

Les Dieux sont morts, opera in two acts by the French organist Charles TOURNEMIRE, composed in 1912, based on a mystic concept that Pan and other poetically attractive pagan gods died when Christ was born, is produced at the Paris Opéra, on the same program with *Siang-Sin,* ballet-pantomime by Georges HÜE, wherein an old king of magical powers punishes a recalcitrant concubine by inducing a case of accelerated senescence in her body, but reverses the process when she promises to satisfy his exotic proclivities in amorous congress.

20 MARCH 1924

Alkestis, one-act opera after Euripides by Egon WELLESZ, is produced in Mannheim.

24 MARCH 1924

Jean SIBELIUS conducts in Stockholm the world première of his *Seventh Symphony,* op. 105, his last, completed on 2 March 1924, in a single compressed movement containing four contrasting sections, crystalizing in it the stylistic and musico-philosophical ideals of his entire creative life, set within the tonal confines of serene C major, opening with a kettle-drum on the dominant, picking up an ascending scale in the strings in a measured procession of quarter-notes, maintaining this configuration with remarkable consistency, the scales ascending, reaching upper range, dropping a few octaves and ascending again, while ever new melodies spring up in solo instruments, the enharmonic modulations leading to remote keys, the rhythmic pulse being tripled in further developments, and dynamic levels abruptly shifted, Beethoven-like, with the rhythmic agitation reaching its maximum frequency in strings tremolando in 1/128-notes, and finally coming to rest on a long appoggiatura on the sensible leading tone and its consequent catharsis on the tonically pure, self-sufficient C.

On the 2nd of March 1924, at night, as I entered it in my diary, I completed the composition of my *Fantasia sinfonica*—the title that I had thought of giving my one-movement *Seventh Symphony.* (Sibelius, quoted by Ekman, in his biography of Sibelius, Helsinki, 1936)

27 MARCH 1924

Irrelohe, opera in three acts by Franz SCHREKER, to his own libretto centering on the curse of the house of Irrelohe (etymologically divisible into Irre Lohe, errant flame) continuing through the centuries and involving lycanthropy, with a deadly rivalry developing between two half-brothers for the possession of a maidenly guest until a general conflagration engulfs their ancestral castle leaving only her and the better of the two brothers alive, set to music with Wagnerogenic fervor, is produced in Cologne.

29 MARCH 1924

Sir Charles Villiers STANFORD, English composer of seven operas, seven symphonies, six Irish rhapsodies, and many other works in a spirited academic manner, full of workable but easily forgettable musical ideas, dies in London at the age of 71, after a stroke suffered twelve days before.

29 MARCH 1924

Noc letnia (Summer Night), comic opera by the Polish conductor and composer Emil MLYNARSKI, is produced in Warsaw.

10 APRIL 1924

L'Appel de la Mer, one-act opera by Henri RABAUD, fashioned from J. M. Synge's drama *Riders to the Sea,* depicting the tragic loss of young men to the cruel ocean on a desolate island west of Ireland, set in naked vocalization and bleak harmonies, relieved by occasional injection of Irish jig rhythms, and ending on a tormented unresolved chord of the thirteenth, is produced at the Opéra-Comique in Paris.

16 APRIL 1924

Saint John's Eve, one-act opera by the 76-year-old Scotch composer and educator Sir Alexander Campbell MACKENZIE, a dream story in which a tinker and a poacher both dream concomitant dreams of a seductive wood nymph making her home in a tree and a nixie dwelling in the River Severn, is produced in Liverpool.

21 APRIL 1924

No No Nanette, musical comedy by Vincent YOUMANS, in which a compiler of hymn anthologies with an insecure penchant for semi-pregnant young girls, finds himself enmeshed with three abandoned damsels and a jealous wife, but extricates himself thanks to a cunning lawyer, containing the famous songs *Tea for Two* and *I Want to Be Happy,* is produced for the first time in Detroit; it was next staged in Chicago on 5 May 1924 and after nearly a year was produced in London on 11 March 1925, finally reaching Broadway on 16 September 1925.

24 APRIL 1924

Le Carrosse du Saint-Sacrement, one-act opera by Lord BERNERS, to a story from Mérimée, is produced in Paris.

26 APRIL 1924

At a concert of RAVEL's music in London, Jelly d'Arányi, Hungarian violinist, presents the first performance of *Tzigane* for violin and piano with Ravel himself playing the accompaniment on the "lutheal," a hybrid keyboard instrument with an organ attachment, composed for her and completed only two days before the performance, and written in an unabashed bravura style with just a half-smile behind the violinistic pyrotechnics, ending abruptly after many a rhapsodic episode, in a vertiginous dash of 488 sixteenth-notes.

To hear a whole program of Ravel's works is like watching some midget pygmy doing clever but very small things within a limited scope. Moreover, the almost reptilian cold-bloodedness, which one suspects of having been consciously cultivated, of most of M. Ravel's music is almost repulsive when heard in bulk; even its beauties are like the markings on snakes and lizards . . . . In *Tzigane* one is puzzled to understand what M. Ravel is at. Either the work is a parody of all the Liszt-Brahms-Joachim school of Hungarian violin music, or it is an attempt to infuse into his work a little of that warm blood it needs. But in neither case does it greatly matter. (London *Times,* April 28, 1924)

1 MAY 1924

Arturo Toscanini conducts at La Scala, Milan, the posthumous world première of *Nerone,* opera in four acts by Arrigo BOITO, to his own libretto depicting the persecution of the Christians under the Emperor Nero, with the emotional interest centered on a Roman girl of dual allegiance as a pagan Vestal and a devout Christian, who is absolved of sin in the end as she is carried into the solarium, mangled by pagan lions in the Coliseum, while Rome burns. (Boito began the composition of *Nerone* in 1879, but left the music unfinished at his death in 1918; the score was completed and partly orchestrated by Vincenzo Tommasini and Arturo Toscanini.)

1 MAY 1924

Miroir de Jésus, chamber oratorio by André CAPLET, in fifteen religious tableaux, is performed for the first time in Paris.

2 MAY 1924

Symphonic Mystery by the Soviet composer Andrei PASHCHENKO, scored for the Thereminovox and orchestra, the first symphonic work ever written for an electronic instrument as soloist, is performed for the first time in Leningrad.

3 MAY 1924

Panie Kochanku, comic opera in three acts by the Polish composer Mieczyslaw SOLTYS, is produced in Lwów.

4 MAY 1924

The first performance is given in Moscow of the *Sixth Symphony* by the polysymphonic Soviet composer Nicolai MIASKOVSKY, completed on 3 July 1923, one of his most significant works from the esthetic and technical standpoint, set in the symphonically rare key of E-flat minor, reflecting his individual conception of the Russian Revolution as a martyrdom, and set in four movements:

(1) *Poco largamente, Allegro feroce,* in 4/4 time, replete with chromatic lamentations; (2) *Presto tenebroso,* a tenebrous scherzo employing explicit bitonality of C major combined with G-flat major; (3) *Andante appassionato,* a lyrical confession of inner turmoil; (4) *Allegro vivace,* making use of the French revolutionary songs *Carmagnole* and *Ça ira,* and the medieval hymn of Doomsday *Dies irae,* concluding with an ancient Russian religious chant, "The parting of the soul from the body," with chorus ad libitum.

In spite of my instinctively correct ideological orientation, the absence of a theoretically firm and rational philosophy of life has generated in my mind a neurotic and submissive attitude towards the Revolution, not uncommon among the Russian intelligentsia. This attitude affected the embryo of my *Sixth Symphony. . . .* The first stimulus for its composition was provided by an accidental hearing of the French revolutionary songs *Ça ira* and the *Carmagnole* sung by a French artist. When I began work on my *Sixth Symphony* in 1922, these melodies came back to me. My somewhat confused state of mind at that time made me think of a program, which now seems strange to me, involving a "sacrificial offering," the "parting of the soul from the body" and some sort of apotheosis of eternal salvation at the end. Still, it seems to be capable of stirring the listener, as I can judge from its frequent performances abroad, particularly in America. (From Miaskovsky's *Autobiographical Notes* published in *Sovietskaya Musica,* Moscow, June, 1936)

6 MAY 1924

Anna Karenina, melodrama in four acts by the 40-year-old Italian composer Iginio ROBBIANI, his most successful opera, to a libretto after Tolstoy's famous novel dealing with an obsolescently dramatic carnal passion, adulterous imbroglio, anguished compunction, moral retribution and pathetic suicide as the guilty woman throws herself under the wheels of a slowly puffing Russian train, set to music with an Italianate flamboyance and incorporating some ethnic elements from Russian folksongs, is produced in Rome.

8 MAY 1924

Angel MENCHACA, Paraguayan-born music theorist who invented a keyboard with the black keys sloping towards the white keys so as to make the playing of chromatic scales more comfortable, and who also devised a system of musical notation to make sight reading more uncomfortable, dies in Buenos Aires, where he served as an emigration officer, at the age of 69.

8 MAY 1924

Pacific 231, "symphonic movement" by Arthur HONEGGER, rhapsodically glorifying the robust energy of the great American locomotive (the digits 2–3–1 stand for 2 front trucks, 3 pairs of driving wheels and 1 rear truck), "an intelligent monster, a joyous giant," is performed for the first time in Paris by Serge Koussevitzky and his specially assembled orchestra, the music traversing the following stages from start to full speed and to the final stop:

The friction of the wheels against the rails is demonstrated by playing *sul ponticello* on the upper strings against the trilled dominant G-sharp in the bass, with the flutes assisting by artful flutter-tonguing, the engine slowly starting in rhythmic pulsations, first in whole-notes, then, in measured acceleration, in dotted half-notes, undotted half-notes, half-notes in triplets, quarter-notes, eighth-notes, eighth-notes in triplets, finally reaching full speed in 16th-notes while the trumpets and the horns intone the chant of the rails and the switches in angular melodies, bursting into a fugato of telegraph poles, while the solemn trombones roar warnings to the unwary at the top of their muscular range, the piccolos emit continuous steam whistles and the violins haw and yaw sideways in wide jerking intervals, until the whole orchestra begins to throb with the steady beat of the piston engine, the restraining brakes are applied and the rhythmic pulsations retard from 16th-notes to eighth-notes in triplets to eighth-notes in duplets to quarter-notes in triplets to quarter notes in duplets to half-notes to dotted half-notes, pulling into the terminal station in whole-notes and coming to a full stop on the tonic unison of C-sharp, forming a cyclic design from the initial presumed dominant to the tonic of the implied key of C-sharp minor in the absence of a key signature.

I have always loved locomotives passionately. For me they are living beings whom I love as others love women or horses. What I sought to achieve in *Pacific 231* was not the imitation of the noises of the locomotive but the translation of a visual impression and of physical enjoyment through a musical construction. It opens with an objective observation, the calm respiration of the machine at rest, the effort of the start, a gradual increase in speed, ultimately attaining the lyric stage, the pathos of a train 300 tons in weight launched in the dark of night at 120 kilometers an hour. For my subject I selected a locomotive of the Pacific type, bearing the number 231. (From Honegger's interview published in the Geneva magazine *Dissonances* and reproduced in the printed score)

9 MAY 1924

Richard STRAUSS conducts in Vienna the first performance of his *Schlagobers*, "gay Viennese ballet in two acts," completed by him on 16 October 1922, a series of adventures in a Vienna pastry shop under the guidance of Schlagobers (whipped cream liberally laid on Viennese desserts) presented as gauze-clad girls, with chocolate creams, ginger cookies, pralines and other delectable confections waltzing dreamily, and exotic liqueurs dancing in French, Russian and Polish rhythms, blissfully unaware that the proletarian buns, Vienna batons and matzos conspire to overturn the hegemony of the upper baking classes.

17 MAY 1924

Salade, "ballet chanté" by Darius MILHAUD (composed between 5 and 20 February 1924), a gay salad of miscellaneous ingredients seasoned with sophisticatedly vulgarized exotic condiments, is presented for the first time, in the form of a "contrepoint choréographique" in Paris.

21 MAY 1924

Léontine Sœurs, "comédie musicale" in three acts by the French composer Antoine MARIOTTE, dealing with a patriotic manicurist who poses as the King's daughter when a dastardly republican conspiracy to kidnap her is discovered, thus enabling the royal family to take a vacation in Norway unmolested, is produced in Paris.

22 MAY 1924

Igor STRAVINSKY appears as piano soloist at a concert with Serge Koussevitzky's orchestra in Paris, in the world première of his *Concerto* for piano, wind instruments and double-basses, written in his newly promulgated neo-Baroque style of composition, in three classically balanced movements:

(1) *Largo,* an austere exordium leading to *Allegro* in a pellucid manner of the Italian settecento; (2) *Larghissimo,* a fantasia, with cadenzas in successively astringent diminutions; (3) *Allegro,* couched in pandiatonic harmonies and marked by asymmetric rhythmic patterns punctuated by recurrent bradyseismic implosions.

25 MAY 1924

The first concert of Latin American music to be given a radio performance is broadcast from Washington under the auspices of the Pan American Union.

26 MAY 1924

Victor HERBERT, 65-year-old Irish-born creator of the special genre of American sentimental light opera possessing an immediacy of communication as certain as its continental counterparts, dies in New York at 4 P.M., of heart disease while climbing the stairs of his doctor's apartment at 57 East 77th Street.

Instead of sending for his doctor, he decided that he was well enough to go there himself. He left his automobile unassisted, but weighing over 250 pounds, the extra effort of walking up the stairs caused him to collapse. (New York *Times,* 27 May 1924)

27 MAY 1924

From the Northland, orchestral suite by Leo SOWERBY, composed in Italy in 1922–1923, but recording earlier impressions of the Lake Superior country in Canada, in four movements (*Forest Voices, Cascades, Burnt Rock Pool, The Shining Big-Sea Water*), pleasingly neo-Romantic, Sibelian, sylvan, pastoral or rhapsodically hydropathic, with some harsh dissonances mitigated by deep-seated pedal points, is performed for the first time at the Accademia Americana in Rome, Howard Hanson conducting.

29 MAY 1924

Memories of My Childhood, symphonic poem by Charles Martin LOEFFLER, a rhapsody of reminiscences of a small town in Russia where the composer spent his childhood, is performed for the first time at the North Shore Festival in Evanston, Illinois.

29 MAY 1924

Alexandre GRETCHANINOFF conducts in Kiev the first performance of his *Symphony in E major (Third Sympho-*

ny), op. 100, written in a broad Russian manner, with epic, lyric and dramatic episodes neatly balanced and effectively orchestrated.

29 MAY 1924

Seven Are They, "Chaldean incantation" for tenor solo, chorus and orchestra by Sergei PROKOFIEV, composed in Russia in 1918, to words by the symbolist Russian poet Constantin Balmont, an apocalyptic vision of seven giant deities commanding the world, set in eight contrasting episodes with thundering silences and mute explosions, and abounding in special effects, such as a whispering chorus *glissando*, the whole constituting the most extremely modernistic work in Prokofiev's creative evolution, is performed for the first time in Paris, under the direction of Serge Koussevitzky.

31 MAY 1924

The Second Festival of the International Society for Contemporary Music opens in Prague with the following program of symphonic music:

Introduction and Polonaise from the unfinished opera, *The Carnival of Prague* by SMETANA, written during his last torturous years of deafness and creeping madness, performed here to mark the centennial of his birth; *Sinfonietta* by the Czech neo-romantic composer and violinist Otakar OSTRČIL, belying its diminutive title by its inordinate symphonic length; a cycle of songs by the Austrian Schoenberg disciple Carl HORWITZ who had the misfortune of losing his hearing shortly before the Festival; *Concerto* for wind quintet and orchestra, a lively neo-classical piece in the pandiatonic technique by the Italian composer Vittorio RIETI, a disciple of Casella; the passionate *22nd Psalm* by Ernest BLOCH, revealing his deep consciousness of racial and religious participation in the eternal spiritual life of the Jews through the millennia; Bacchanale from Florent SCHMITT'S score of incidental music to Shakespeare's play *Anthony and Cleopatra*, produced in Paris in André Gide's version on 14 June 1920; and Arthur HONEGGER's kinetic locomotive piece *Pacific 231.*

1 JUNE 1924

At the second concert of the Second Festival of the International Society for Contemporary Music in Prague, the following program of orchestral works is presented:

Second Symphony by the Latvian-born German-educated composer Eduard ERDMANN, written in a ponderous polyphonic and moderately discordant idiom; *First Violin Concerto* by Sergei PROKOFIEV, composed in 1917 and first performed in Paris on 18 October 1923; *Le Chant du Rossignol*, symphonic poem by Igor STRAVINSKY, first performed in Geneva, on 6 December 1919; and the emotive, impassioned and somewhat Russianized *First Symphony* by Arnold BAX.

2 JUNE 1924

At the third concert of the Second Festival of the International Society for Contemporary Music in Prague, the following program of symphonic music is performed:

Zrání (Maturity), a romantically autobiographic symphonic poem by Josef SUK, son-in-law of Dvořák, descriptive of the provincial life of a contented middle-aged musician; *First Violin Concerto* by Poland's foremost modern composer Karol SZYMANOWSKI, in a single movement written in the spirit of virtuoso display, articulated into three sections—fast, slow,

fast—and written in a richly ornamental melorhythmic idiom, with harmonies tending towards bitonality of major keys whose tonics are set at a tritone's distance from each other; the third suite of *Impressioni dal Vero* by Gian Francesco MALIPIERO; and Albert ROUSSEL's austere and masterly *Symphonie en Si bémol.*

6 JUNE 1924

Erwartung, monodrama in four scenes by Arnold SCHOENBERG, his first stage work, and the first opera ever written for a single character, a woman, to a poem by Marie Pappenheim, depicting the protagonist wandering in a dark forest in a state of surrealistic irrationality, expressionistically exteriorized in an *Angsttraum* (as Schoenberg himself described it) until she stumbles and falls over the body of her lover whom she had gone to meet, with a score of anguished atonality, containing an early adumbration of dodecaphony, is performed for the first time at the Prague Festival of the International Society for Contemporary Music, almost fifteen years after the completion of the work (composition begun 27 August 1909 and completed on 12 September 1909).

8 JUNE 1924

The Orquesta Filarmónica of Havana, Cuba, opens its first season under the direction of Pedro SANJUÁN, Spanish conductor and composer.

9 JUNE 1924

Der Sprung über den Schatten, comic opera in three acts and ten episodes by the 23-year-old Vienna-born composer Ernst KRENEK, to his own libretto, written in the sophisticated manner of a modern detective story, with a musical setting in an amalgamated neo-classical and constructivistic idiom, encompassing a variety of forms, from passacaglia to foxtrot, is produced in Frankfurt.

This is a comic opera partly with a satirical tendency directed against the aberrations of modern society (corruption, occultism, snobbism, dance craze, etc.), musically combining seriously treated atonal elements with deliberate banality. (From Krenek's statement in a letter to the author dated 5 February 1938)

10 JUNE 1924

Fra Angelico, "tableau musical" by Paul HILLEMACHER, the surviving member of the composing team of two French brothers who produced their many stage works under the composite name P. L. Hillemacher, is performed for the first time at the Opéra-Comique in Paris.

15 JUNE 1924

Mercure, "poses plastiques" in three tableaux and 12 scenes by Erik SATIE, in which various Grecian deities playfully disport themselves to the accompaniment of modern dance rhythms, Mercury steals pearls from the Three Graces during their ablutions and is chased by the three-headed dog Cerberus in ragtime, and Pluto abducts Persephone to the strains of a jazzy march, is produced in Paris.

17 JUNE 1924

Abenteuer des Casanova, opera in four acts by the Swiss conductor Volkmar ANDREAE, depicting four of Casanova's international amourettes, taking place in Italy, France, Spain and Germany, is performed for the first time in Dresden.

18 JUNE 1924

George White's Scandals of 1924 is produced in New York, with a score by George GERSHWIN, including the celebrated song *Somebody Loves Me.*

19 JUNE 1924

Nazdah, opera by the Argentine composer Athos PALMA, to the story of a devoted Hindu nurse who defeats the treacherous scheme of a wily courtier to kidnap the heir to the throne by substituting her own child for him and stabs herself to death after the child is found murdered, is produced at the Teatro Colón in Buenos Aires.

20 JUNE 1924

Le Train bleu, "operette dansée" by Darius MILHAUD, named after the "blue train" that carried the rich and the idle from Paris to the Riviera, illustrating in a harmonious and melodious manner the confused inaction on the beach, with *poules*, gigolos, sailors and elderly lechers milling around (Picasso's curtain design showed two enormous females fleeing from invisible pursuers), is produced in Paris by Diaghilev's Ballet Russe.

1 JULY 1924

Nicolas OBOUHOV, 32-year-old Russian expatriate, "Nicolas l'Illuminé" as he liked to be called, completes in Paris the full score of his mystical magnum opus *Le Livre de Vie*, some 2,000 pages long, in the composer's own notation of 12 notes named after syllables found in Guido d'Arezzo's original hymn, Do-Lo-Re-Te-Mi-Fa-Ra-Sol-Tu-La-Bi-Si, with expression marks marked in red in his own blood as a symbol of the blood shed in the Russian Revolution.

Nicolas Obouhov m'a fait entendre des fragments du *Livre de Vie;* j'ai été frappé par la force pathétique géniale, à vrai dire, de cette œuvre singulière. Sans doute l'idéá conductrice en est bien loin des miennes, aussi bien que la mystique russe peut l'être du sensualisme français, mais je ne dois tenir compte ici que des qualités musicales qui sont d'une profondeur et d'une élévation des plus rares. (From Maurice Ravel's letter to Nicolas Slonimsky written in 1928 at his request to help raise some money for Obouhov in his desperate financial situation; about $250 was collected and sent to him in Paris by the author)

4 JULY 1924

Hugh the Drover, ballad opera by Ralph VAUGHAN WILLIAMS, to a story of true love opposed by the girl's father who favors a rival John the Butcher, with Hugh the Drover winning out in a boxing match between them, set in England in the year 1812 (political overtones are superinduced when Hugh is unjustly accused of being in Napoleon's pay as a spy), is performed for the first time at the Royal College of Music in London. (The first public performance took place at His Majesty's Theater, London, on 14 July 1924.)

19 JULY 1924

Six Bagatelles for string quartet, op. 9, by Anton von WEBERN, is performed for the first time at the Donaueschingen Festival of New Music, lasting only two minutes in all.

20 JULY 1924

In the course of the Fourth Festival of Chamber Music in Donaueschingen the first public performance is given of the historic *Serenade*, op. 24, by Arnold SCHOENBERG, for baritone, violin, cello, clarinet, bass clarinet, mandolin and guitar, the first work in which the method of composition with 12 tones was definitely established, in seven sections:

(1) *March;* (2) *Minuet;* (3) *Variations;* (4) *Sonett 217* of Petrarca, in which the row of 12 different notes appears for the first time, horizontally in the vocal line, the work having been completed on 16 April 1923; (5) *Tanzszene;* (6) *Lied ohne Worte;* (7) *Finale,* a modified recapitulation of the introductory *March.*

22 JULY 1924

After ten years of Wagnerian "Götterdämmerung" caused by war and revolution, the Bayreuth Festival House opens its doors with a performance of *Die Meistersinger von Nürnberg.*

24 JULY 1924

On the occasion of the quadricentennial of the founding of Guatemala City, *Quiché Vinák*, opera by the Guatemalan composer Jesús CASTILLO, after the legend of an Indian *brujo* who foretells the ruin of the Quiché empire at the hands of European invaders, with a liberal application in the score of authentic Indian melodies, is produced in Guatemala City. (Date and description communicated by Jesús Castillo.)

27 JULY 1924

Ferruccio BUSONI, Italian composer, pianist and teacher, who introduced a new symphonic dimension into piano playing simulating the sonorities of orchestral instruments by an infinitely sensitive use of the 18 possible gradations of sound on the keyboard and an ingenious application of the pedals, who aggrandized Bach's works into grandiose pianistic cycloramas, and himself composed music of rare romantic consciousness, postulated on a sui generis esthetic philosophy, dies in Berlin, where he spent most of his later years, of chronic inflammation of the cardiac muscles, at the age of 58.

At the time of Busoni's death and for some years previously so many unfounded rumors were in circulation as to his alleged intemperance that it is necessary to give a medical account of his last illness on the authority of his physician, Dr. Hans Meyer of Berlin. It was commonly reported in Switzerland that Busoni was taken home every night from the station restaurant at Zürich in a state of complete intoxication. Directly after his death, Italian papers asserted that he had died of *delirium tremens* in an inebriates' home. It cannot be too emphatically stated that these stories were utterly untrue. Busoni was Italian by birth and breeding; he was naturally brought up from infancy to regard wine as his normal beverage. He was always fond of wine and appreciated wines of fine quality, but he never drank to excess at any time of his life. The disease of which Busoni died was chronic inflammation of the kidneys together with chronic inflammation of the muscles of the heart. (Edward J. Dent, *Ferruccio Busoni*, London, 1933)

6 AUGUST 1924

A supplementary Festival of the International Society for Contemporary Music opens in Salzburg, with the following program of chamber music:

Viola Sonata by Arnold BAX, in three movements, written in a surprisingly energetic manner, with one episode, *feroce*, and the concluding bars marked by eruptive power; *Cello Sonata* by Ildebrando PIZZETTI, an instrumental litany comprising two adagios interrupted by an agitated movement, with bitonalities accumulating in dramatic interludes; *Drei geistliche Lieder* for voice, clarinet and violin, by the German lyric polyphonist Heinrich KAMINSKI, set in stylized ecclesiastical modalities; *Frauentanz* for soprano, viola, flute, clarinet, horn and bassoon by Kurt WEILL, German composer of palpitatingly vital music, elemental in the directness of its impact; a group of songs by the Viennese neo-romantic composer Ernst KANITZ; songs by the Czech composer Ladislav VYCPÁLEK; and *Fourth String Quartet* by Ernst KRENEK.

7 AUGUST 1924

At the second concert of the supplementary Festival of the International Society for Contemporary Music in Salzburg the following program of chamber music is presented:

Septet for flute, oboe, clarinet, horn, double-bass and piano by Willem PIJPER, Dutch composer of impressionistically colored romantic music suspended on the brink of atonality and polytonality, favoring especially the scale of alternating whole-tones and semitones (which his disciples termed Pijper's scale, unaware that Rimsky-Korsakov used it in the 19th century); *The Curlew*, a song by Philip HESELTINE, English musician who adopted the characteristically witching nom de plume Peter Warlock; *On Wenlock Edge*, song with string quartet accompaniment by Ralph VAUGHAN WILLIAMS; *Duo for Violin and Cello* by the Hungarian master of modern music Zoltán KODÁLY, in four contrasting movements making artful use of the available sonorities, wherein broad lyrical episodes of pentatonic spaciousness alternate with dance-like moments in asymmetric rhythms; a song by the Russian composer Alexander SHENSHIN; and *String Trio* by the 28-year-old master of modern German polyphony Paul HINDEMITH, containing instances of natural polytonality and polyrhythmy and a highly complex fugue applying a variety of learned devices of canonic writing.

8 AUGUST 1924

At the third concert of the supplementary Festival of the International Society for Contemporary Music in Salzburg the following program of chamber music is presented:

Second String Quartet subtitled *Stornelli e Ballate* by Gian Francesco MALIPIERO, comprising a theme and 14 stanzas derived in spirit from the popular types of Italian ritornello and danced ballads; *Socrate*, symphonic drama by Erik SATIE written in ostentatiously arid modalities, making use in the vocal part of monotonously scanned speech rhythms; *4 Pieces* for string quartet by the Czech composer Erwin SCHUL-HOFF, written in a pleasingly modernistic vein; *Sonata* for clarinet and bassoon by Francis POULENC, composed in a hedonistic Parisian vein of facile *contrepoint sans peine* and dispensing attractively confected puerilities of the Satiesque *art dépouillé; 12 Etudes* for piano by Karol SZYMANOWSKI,

written in a trans-Lisztian virtuoso technique; *Sonata* for cello and piano, in three movements, by the English composer John IRELAND, conceived in a broadly melodic manner, but dramatically departing from strict tonal procedures; and *Gaselen*, a song cycle for baritone, flute, oboe, bass clarinet, trumpet, percussion and piano by the neo-romantic Swiss composer Othmar SCHOECK.

9 AUGUST 1924

At the fourth concert of the supplementary Festival of the International Society for Contemporary Music in Salzburg, the following program of chamber music is given:

String Quartet by the French-born German-Catalan composer Philipp JARNACH, highly contrapuntal in texture and relentlessly developed from homuncular motives; piano pieces by Boleslav VOMÁČKA and Karl Boleslav JIRÁK of Czechoslovakia, and by Francis POULENC; *Catalogue de Fleurs* for voice and piano by Darius MILHAUD, a surrealistic florilegium with melodious characterizations of seven flowers, set to music with a fine Parisian flair; *Short Suite* for seven instruments by the Viennese modernist Egon WELLESZ; songs by Mario CASTELNUOVO-TEDESCO; and Igor STRAVINSKY's neo-Baroque *Octet* for wind instruments, first performed under Stravinsky's direction in Paris on October 18, 1923.

21 AUGUST 1924

The Queen of Cornwall, opera in two acts by the English composer Rutland BOUGHTON, after Thomas Hardy's play on the subject, is performed for the first time in Glastonbury.

2 SEPTEMBER 1924

Rose Marie, musical play in two acts by the Prague-born American-rooted operetta composer Rudolf FRIML, dealing with an irresistibly attractive French-Canadian damsel who cuts the swath of adoration in male hearts from Vancouver to Quebec, containing the famous songs *Rose Marie, I Love You* and the somewhat chromaticized but still authentically pentatonic *Indian Love Call*, is produced in New York.

4 SEPTEMBER 1924

A century has passed since the birth in Ansfelden, Austria, of Anton BRUCKNER, the "Wagner of the Symphony," whose music, grandiose in design and supremely romantic in its essence, marked the summit of the heroic esthetics of the 19th century.

19 SEPTEMBER 1924

PUCCINI's opera *Tosca* is produced at the Mamont (MAstershop of MONumental Theater) in Leningrad, with a new libretto fashioned by the Moscow stage director Nikolai Vinogradov, entitled *Struggle for the Commune*, in which the action is transferred from 1800 to 1871, Tosca is metamorphosed into a Russian revolutionary émigrée, Cavaradossi into a leader of the Communards, and Scarpia into the anti-Commune General Gallifet, duly murdered by Tosca in the second act. (The real General Gallifet died peacefully in his bed on 8 July 1909 and not murdered in 1871. There were only 14 performances of *Struggle for the Commune;* on 25 May 1929 *Tosca* reappeared on the Leningrad stage in its original Puccinian form.)

20 SEPTEMBER 1924

Contractador dos Diamantes, first opera by the 27-year-old Brazilian composer Francisco MIGNONE, dealing with the gay adventures of a diamond merchant in 18th-century colonial Brazil and containing the rousing Brazilian dance *Congada* often performed as a separate symphonic piece, is produced in Rio de Janeiro.

22 SEPTEMBER 1924

Piano Concerto for left hand alone in one movement by Erich Wolfgang KORNGOLD written in an engagingly romantic manner but bristling with technical formidabilities that would challenge even a two-armed soloist, is performed for the first time in Vienna by Paul WITTGENSTEIN, the Austrian pianist who lost his right arm on the preposterous Russian front in World War I and who made a career by commissioning famous composers to write left-handed concertos. (Korngold himself conducted the orchestral accompaniment.)

27 SEPTEMBER 1924

The Seal Woman, opera in two long acts by the English composer Granville BANTOCK, wherein a Celtic islander catches a beautiful female seal, skins her, attires her in woman's clothes and marries her in church, with their domestic tranquility unhappily interrupted by her septennial estrous calls to the sea until she dons her exuviated sealskin kept in the attic and swims away in the bay, is produced in Birmingham.

1 OCTOBER 1924

Paul Schwers, editor-in-chief of the *Allgemeine musikalische Zeitung*, is found guilty in a Berlin court of having defamed Eugen D'ALBERT in print by erroneously asserting that he was writing an operetta on the subject of a polygamous nobleman (Eugen d'Albert had at least eight successive wives), and is fined 500 gold marks, with an alternative of 15 days in jail.

9 OCTOBER 1924

Anton von WEBERN conducts the first performance in Vienna of his *Five Sacred Songs* for soprano, flute, clarinet, bass clarinet, trumpet, harp, violin and viola.

10 OCTOBER 1924

Two and a half months after his 50th birthday, Serge KOUSSEVITZKY leads the initial concert of the season as permanent conductor of the Boston Symphony Orchestra.

Four-fold Comes New Conductor to Boston Stage—The Quality and the Rank of Mr. Koussevitzky—Master of Line, Color, Tone, and Characterization in Music—The new conductor somewhat belies report oral, textual, pictorial. He is in the flower of middle years; but no lingering aura of youth seems to gild them; while to one pair of eyes he was less romantic presence than twentieth-century musician in unglamored practice of his profession. . . . Koussevitzky Superbus, as the old Romans might have written; but Koussevitzky passioning for his music—not for himself. (H. T. Parker, *Boston Evening Transcript*, 11 October 1924)

11 OCTOBER 1924

Ilseino Srdce (Else's Heart), lyric comedy in three acts by the Czech composer Rudolf KAREL, is produced in Prague.

12 OCTOBER 1924

Anton BRUCKNER's early symphony in D minor, composed in 1864 and revised in 1869, which he designated as *Symphony No. Zero*, is brought out for the first time in public performance in Klosterneuburg, Germany.

12 OCTOBER 1924

Gustav MAHLER's unfinished *Tenth Symphony*, faithfully and intelligently edited by Ernst Krenek, in two movements: *Adagio*, (a slowly developing musical peroration culminating on the chord of the diminished 19th (C-sharp, G-sharp, B, D, F, A, C, E-flat, G) and *Purgatorio* haunted by the spectre of death (the manuscript contains this inscription in Mahler's handwriting: "Madness seizes me, annihilates me so that I cease to exist"), is performed in Vienna for the first time, Franz Schalk conducting.

13 OCTOBER 1924

Fire Flies, comedy of masks in one act by the 59-year-old English composer Philip Napier MILES, is produced in Clifton, near Bristol, on the same program with his dramatic sketch *Markheim*, after a novella by Stevenson.

14 OCTOBER 1924

Die glückliche Hand drama with music by Arnold SCHOENBERG, in one brief act to his own words, in which a symbolic Man vainly struggles for the possession of a symbolic Woman who rejects him definitively by kicking a large rock down a ravine at the bottom of which he lies prostrate (her role is songless and wordless), set to music of extreme anguish, integrally dissonant and atonal, beginning with a discord of seven different notes and ending on a discord of ten different notes, with the application of a unique expressionistic effect of "color crescendo" accompanying the scene in which the Man emerges from a tenebrous grotto brandishing a bloodied sword as a chromatic wind begins to blow and the illumination changes from rubiginous to grayish blue, to violet, to deep red, which becomes brighter until it reaches crimson, and then subsides to yellow and serenely cerulean blue, is brought to public performance in Vienna almost eleven years after the completion of the work.

16 OCTOBER 1924

Zwingburg, scenic cantata in one act by the 24-year-old Austrian modernist Ernst KRENEK, to a story by Franz Werfel, in which a tyrannical lord, invisibly ruling the populace (only his hideous laughter betrays his presence in the castle), is overthrown by a revolutionary coup, but ironically the new masters establish the same regime of inaccessibility and absolute power, set to music in incisively dissonant harmonies, is produced in Berlin.

Zwingburg is an essay in "social" opera without a concrete political tendency. Its theme is the separation of the masses from the individual; there is a large choral participation—hence the title of a scenic cantata. A revival of *Zwingburg* was planned in the later 1920's in Stuttgart, but was cancelled because of its supposed "revolutionary" character. At the same time it was also rejected in Russia on account of its "reactionary" tendency. (Krenek's statement in a letter to the author dated 5 February 1938)

20 OCTOBER 1924

Guillermo URIBE-HOLGUÍN, prime composer of Colombia, conducts in Bogotá the first performance of his *Second Symphony*.

20 OCTOBER 1924

The newly organized Society of Rumanian Composers opens its active program by a concert honoring Béla BARTÓK who appears as pianist in his *Second Violin Sonata* with Georges Enesco as violinist.

The Society of Rumanian Composers begins its activities inspired by high ideals. The concerts organized by the Society will give an opportunity to all gifted Rumanian composers to acquaint the public with their works. Responding to a long-felt need the Society will also establish a music publishing press as soon as it becomes financially possible. The Society of Rumanian Composers intends to develop and strengthen friendly ties with foreign musicians, endeavoring to spread the knowledge of Rumanian music abroad. The Society expresses its firm assurance that its efforts in the direction of promoting national music will find support among music lovers of the land. (Declaration signed by Georges Enesco, Mihail Jora, Alfons Castaldi, George Enacovici, Ion Brediceanu, Ion Vidu, Alfred Alessandrescu, Dmitri Kiriac, Filip Laxar and Ion Nonna-Ottescu)

23 OCTOBER 1924

Third Symphony in one movement by the 36-year-old German composer Max TRAPP, is performed for the first time by the Gewandhaus Orchestra in Leipzig, Furtwängler conducting.

25 OCTOBER 1924

Pohjalaisia, folk opera by the Finnish composer Leevi MADETOJA (1887–1947) from the life of the Finnish peasantry, with action evolving, circa 1850, in the northernmost land of Pohjola (hence the title), wherein an impetuous bridegroom kills a friend for making objectionable remarks about the bride but escapes with the aid of her brother, set to music in a Sibelian style, with technical devices largely derived from Rimsky-Korsakov's operas, is produced in Helsinki.

27 OCTOBER 1924

Nerto, lyric drama in four acts by the dean of French organists Charles-Marie WIDOR, dealing with a medieval maiden who seeks the intercession of the dissident Pope of Avignon to save her soul sold to the devil by her father, but is unexpectedly pursued by the Pope's lecherous nephew, and flees to the convent where she perishes resisting Satan's claims on her, set to music with Gallic savoir-faire and some originality as manifested in the quaint quodlibets in the medieval celebration of the Advent of the Ass, is produced at the Paris Opéra.

29 OCTOBER 1924

The Red Whirlwind, ballet by the Soviet composer Vladimir DESHEVOV, subtitled "a synthetic poem in two processes," the first process being a choreographic representation of growing revolutionary consciousness, and the second depicting a proletarian unification of working men and women, is produced in Leningrad.

29 OCTOBER 1924

John Reed, opera in four acts by the 26-year-old Soviet composer Vladimir KASHNITSKY, depicting the life and experiences of the American reporter John Reed who witnessed the Soviet Revolution and wrote *Ten Days That Shook the World*, died in Russia, and was buried in the Kremlin, is produced in Leningrad.

4 NOVEMBER 1924

Intermezzo, "domestic comedy with symphonic interludes" by Richard STRAUSS, in two acts (completed in Buenos Aires on 21 August 1923 during his South American journey), to his own libretto with transparent autobiographical allusions, wherein the court conductor named Robert Storch gets into trouble when a love letter addressed to his colleague named Stroh is mistakenly delivered at his home and is intercepted by Frau Storch, is performed for the first time in Dresden.

4 NOVEMBER 1924

Gabriel FAURÉ, French composer of poetic music profoundly national in the source of its inspiration, creator of a new transitional style of neo-archaic modal harmony, touched with pre-impressionistic imagery, great educator and teacher of two generations of French musicians, dies in Paris at the age of 79.

6 NOVEMBER 1924

Příhody Lišky Bystroušky (Cunning Little Vixen), comic opera in three acts by Leoš JANÁČEK to his own libretto in the form of an animal parable, in which a schoolmaster and a parson contend for the love of a Gypsy girl while a vixen entices hens to rebellion and is finally shot by the forester who fashions from its skin a fox muff for his wife, with an epilogue in which the vixen's progeny symbolizes the renewal of the life cycle, set to music in vivid melorhythms of the Bohemian countryside, is produced for the first time in Brno.

8 NOVEMBER 1924

Sergei LIAPUNOV, Russian composer, worthy epigone of the national school of composition, whose brilliant piano pieces are almost Lisztian in virtuosity of technical writing, dies as an emigré in Paris at the age of 64.

13 NOVEMBER 1924

Irish Symphony by Sir Hamilton HARTY is performed in Manchester for the first time in its final version, after several revisions. The original version premiered in Dublin on 18 May 1904.

14 NOVEMBER 1924

Le Miracle des loups, a French film with a musical score specially composed by Henri RABAUD to accompany the action on the screen, showing an attack on travelers by wolf packs in the snow, is presented at the Paris Opéra, the first demonstration of a motion picture with music ever to be given in an opera house.

14 NOVEMBER 1924

First Symphony, subtitled *Assyrian*, by the American composer Frederick JACOBI is performed for the first time in San Francisco.

15 NOVEMBER 1924

Don Gil von den grünen Hosen, comic opera in three acts by Walter BRAUNFELS, after a play by Tirso de Molina, is produced in Munich.

15 NOVEMBER 1924

Khamma, "légende dansée" by Claude DEBUSSY, originally written for piano in 1912 and orchestrated by Charles Koechlin, dealing with an ancient Egyptian virgin who dances to propitiate a cruel stone god and to invoke his aid against the enemy besieging the city, and is struck dead by the carnally aroused idol as it begins to melt from unexpected passion, couched in a characteristically Debussyan idiom of exotic Impressionism, is performed for the first time in Paris.

16 NOVEMBER 1924

Ernst von DOHNÁNYI conducts in Budapest the first performance of his symphonic suite, *Ruralia Hungarica*, in five sections, arranged from his piano pieces, and reflecting the changing melorhythms of rural Hungarian songs, making use of Gypsy scales with their characteristic ambiguity of the supertonic placed either a major or a minor second above the tonic and their abundance of augmented seconds, harmonized with the application of occasional circumspect dissonances.

16 NOVEMBER 1924

Die Burger von Krähwinkel, comic opera in three acts by the 38-year-old German composer Kuno STIERLIN, after a comedy *Die deutschen Kleinstädter* by Kotzebue ridiculing the provincial mores of the inhabitants of a mythical little German town named Krähwinkel (literally, crow corner), is performed for the first time in Osnabrück.

19 NOVEMBER 1924

La Giara, "choreographic comedy" by Alfredo CASELLA, after Pirandello's Sicilian tale about a hunchback who crawls inside a large jar to repair it and becomes caught in it so that he has to break the jar again in order to get out, set to music with the idea of creating a "modern synthesis of the old type of Neapolitan comedy with the elements of Italian folklore," and written in the refreshing idiom of modernistically elaborated Italian Baroque, is performed for the first time at the Ballets Suedois in Paris.

28 NOVEMBER 1924

A Baltic Legend, opera by the 47-year-old Polish composer Felix NOWOWIEJSKI, is produced in Poznań.

29 NOVEMBER 1924

Relâche, "ballet instantanéiste" by Erik SATIE, in two acts (the title means "release," i.e., no performance) with an ostentatiously vulgarized musical score illustrating the irrational behavior of the characters on the stage, including a cinematographic entr'acte by René Clair in which Satie is shown by trick photography firing a cannon from the roof of the theater, is produced in Paris by the Ballets Suédois, with the curtain bearing the inscription: "Erik Satie est le plus grand musicien du monde."

29 NOVEMBER 1924

Giacomo PUCCINI, Italian genius of operatic craft, creator of striking melodramas destined to become immortal masterpieces of the musical theater, who was not averse to experimentation and who used modern devices in his operas, including whole-tone scales, parallel progressions of massed chords, and instantaneous modulatory procedures, dies in Brussels of cancer of the throat at the age of 65.

29 NOVEMBER 1924

Typhoon, opera in three acts by the Hungarian pianist and composer Theodor SZÁNTÓ, dealing with the tragic devastation brought upon a Japanese village by the destructive forces of the wind and the sea, and making use of authentic Japanese melorhythms, is performed for the first time in Mannheim.

30 NOVEMBER 1924

Stepan, "revolutionary" opera in three acts by the 26-year-old Danish composer Ebbe HAMERIK, in which a band of atheist Ukrainians crucifies a lapsed Bolshevik on a cross made of liquidated furniture from the comfortably appointed hut of a local kulak, to the accompaniment of a semi-dissonant pseudo-proletarian march, is produced in a German version in Mainz.

1 DECEMBER 1924

Lady Be Good, musical by George GERSHWIN with lyrics by Ira Gershwin, containing one of his most important, musicologically speaking, songs, *Fascinating Rhythm*, in which an apocopated 7/8 theme generates off-beat ictuses as it overlaps the barlines in 4/4 time, is produced in New York.

2 DECEMBER 1924

The Student Prince, operetta in four acts by Sigmund ROMBERG, based on Mansfield's play *Old Heidelberg*, a bittersweet story of the heir to a small throne, who, while studying and drinking beer at Heidelberg University, loses his heart to the maid of the inn, but unexpectedly becomes King, and weds a staid princess, with a score containing some of Romberg's most memorable songs (*Golden Days, Deep in My Heart, Dear, Serenade* and *Drink, Drink, Drink*), is performed for the first time in New York.

2 DECEMBER 1924

Drei kleine Stücke for cello and piano, op. 11, by Anton von WEBERN, is performed for the first time in Mainz.

3 DECEMBER 1924

For the Hammer and the Sickle, a revised Soviet version of the opera *A Life for the Tsar* by GLINKA, wherein a Communist peasant scarifices his life to lead astray a gang of Polish spies sent to assassinate Lenin during the undeclared Soviet-Polish war of 1921, is performed for the first and last time in Odessa.

(Glinka's classical opera was revived after the Revolution at the Bolshoi Theater in Moscow on 21 February 1939, under the title *Ivan Susanin*, after the hero's name in the original opera, which had indeed been the original title, changed by Glinka to please the Tsar Nicholas I.)

7 DECEMBER 1924

Men and Mountains, symphonic suite by the nonconformist individualistic 48-year-old New Englander Carl RUGGLES, with a motto from William Blake, "Great things are done when men and mountains meet," in three movements—(1) *Men*, a succession of monumental unisons unshaken by the sky-rending discords; (2) *Lilacs*, a cameo of melodic color for strings alone; (3) *Marching Mountains*, growing more discordant with every bar, scaling heights, plumbing depths, proclaiming polysyllabical millennia—is performed for the first time in New York.

8 DECEMBER 1924

Franz Xaver SCHARWENKA, Polish-born German pianist and pedagogue, co-founder with his older brother Philipp Scharwenka of the prestigious Scharwenka Conservatory in Berlin, author of numerous fingerbuilding and octave-mastering exercises in a hyper-Czernian style, and composer of a plethora of technically effective and melodically pleasing piano pieces, among which his early *Polish Dance* became the rage in both hemispheres in the last quarter of the 19th century, dies in Berlin at the age of 74.

10 DECEMBER 1924

American Symphonic Suite by the 48-year-old St. Louis-born composer Walter STOCKHOFF, an orchestral version of his piano suite *In the Mountains: Seven Impressions*, is performed for the first time in Frankfurt, Germany, Hermann Scherchen conducting.

Stockhoff is America's most original composer. A distinct and genuine American note is sounded in his *Seven Impressions* for pianoforte. A European hearkens spellbound, forgets the tra-

ditions of his schooling and his art, and is enthralled by the virginal quality and authenticity of this language. (From the testimonial given to Stockhoff by Ferruccio Busoni in 1915 upon hearing him play the *Seven Impressions*)

14 DECEMBER 1924

Pini di Roma, symphonic poem by the foremost master of Italian Impressionism Ottorino RESPIGHI, limning the inspiring vistas of nobly erect colonnades of pine trees in the gardens and roads of Rome, with the inclusion in the score of six ancient crooked horns, *buccinae*, and, for a naturalistic touch, a phonograph record of a real nightingale, listed in the catalogue of the Concert Record Gramophone Co. under No. 6,105 as *Il canto dell' usignuolo*, is performed in Rome for the first time, conducted by Bernardino Molinari, and comprising the following four tableaux:

(1) *I Pini di Villa Borghese*, with children disporting themselves happily in the park near the famous Renaissance villa, singing popular nursery songs accompanied by harps in crisscrossing *glissandos*, strings *saltando*, wind instruments *tremolando*, self-important brass and exuberant drums; (2) *Pini presso una catatacomba*, in a devotional Hypodorian mode set in arid organum-like counterpoint, recalling the Christian vigils near the catacombs and gradually rising in religious fervor until a state of ecstatic exultation is reached; (3) *I Pini del Gianicolo*, a crepuscular idyl, in which, for the first time in orchestral literature, a phonograph record is introduced singing the song of a nightingale against faint muted strings and a distant clarinet; (4) *I Pini di Via Appia*, a march starting in the deep recesses of the somber low region of the instrumental range, and mounting in measured steps to a rousing triumph of militant national pride recalling the glories of the Roman consular army ascending the Capitoline Hill and, by historic association, the successful march on Rome of Benito Mussolini's Fascist legions.

20 DECEMBER 1924

La Cena delle Beffe (The Feast of the Jests), opera in four acts by Umberto GIORDANO, dealing with a tubercular poet scorned by a fishmonger's daughter in favor of a muscular army captain, with the grim operatic jest delivered in the last scene when the captain kills his own brother, believing him, to be the poet lurking in the bride's room, is produced at La Scala, Milan, Arturo Toscanini conducting.

24 DECEMBER 1924

L'Arlequin lyric comedy in five acts by the French composer Max D'OLLONE, dealing with an actor who arouses the passion of a young heiress from the Fortunate Isle but decides to send her back to her parents, whereupon she languishes and dies, and he accepts the offer to become the successor to the ruler of the now Unfortunate Isle, is produced at the Opéra-Comique in Paris.

1925

1 JANUARY 1925

Fritz KLEIN publishes a significant article in *Die Musik,* entitled *Frontiers of the Semitone World,* suggesting new ways of combining tones and intervals, as part of his theory of "musical statics," applied in his piece *Die Maschine* of 1921 and giving the formula for the construction of a *Mutterakkord,* which includes all 12 different notes and all 12 different intervals, forming an invertible series of 11, 8, 9, 10, 7, 6, 5, 2, 3, 4, 1 semitones. (Klein's Mutterakkord is not the only matrix; several other "mother chords" are given in the *Thesaurus of Scales and Melodic Patterns* by Nicolas Slonimsky.)

Although I saw Mr. Klein's 12-tone composition about 1919, 1920, or 1921, I am not an imitator of him. I wrote a melody for a scherzo which was composed of 12 tones. This was in 1915, as Webern knows. It was planned as a movement of a long symphony, the finale of which was part of what became later *Jakobsleiter.* Besides, I wrote piano pieces, op. 23, which I called "composing with the tones of the basic motif." In these pieces I used a technique which is certainly a first step towards composing with 12 tones. Besides, you will find that in the first edition of my *Harmonielehre* (1911) there is a description of the new harmonies and their application, which has probably influenced all these men who now want to become my models. At least I know that Hauer used it almost literally in the first edition of his book and eliminated it later. It states the reasons that led me to this new technique in these words: "The repetition of a tone produces the danger of lending it the importance of a *Grundton,* which ought to be avoided." I have not much interest in originality, and that is why I never objected to misstatements. (Schoenberg's letter, in English, to the author dated Los Angeles, 2 January 1940)

8 JANUARY 1925

Igor STRAVINSKY makes his first appearance in America as conductor with the Philharmonic Orchestra of New York, in a program of his works.

11 JANUARY 1925

Symphony for organ and orchestra by the 24-year-old Brooklyn-born composer Aaron COPLAND, in three movements, *Prelude, Scherzo,* and *Finale,* cast in a declarative diatonic idiom, with widely ambulant melodic intervals and assertive melismas around strategic points, static tonal harmonies in chorale-like episodes, and incisive asymmetrical rhythms with ragtime-like syncopation in dance-like sections, is performed for the first time by the New York Symphony, Walter Damrosch conducting, with Nadia Boulanger, Copland's teacher during his Parisian period of apprenticeship, at the organ. (The score, dedicated "with admiration" to Nadia Boulanger, was revised in 1928, and the organ part absorbed into the new orchestration.)

Mr. Copland is a child of his time. Naturally enough, his speech is the atonal, polytonal speech of today. Why anyone should expect him or his fellows to write in any other idiom than that which is characteristic of 1925, is more than we can understand. Let us get used to the fact that it is as normal for the youth of 1925 to write in two keys simultaneously as it was for the youth of 1825 to confine himself frugally to one. . . . Mr. Damrosch, hearing some hisses at the end of the piece, remarked to his audience that a youth who could write such a symphony at twenty-four would be capable some day of murder. That was a bit rough on Mr. Copland. He does not strike us as one of the murderous kind. (Lawrence Gilman, New York *Herald Tribune,* 12 January 1925)

23 JANUARY 1925

Bäckahästen (The River Horse), opera in four acts by the foremost Swedish symphonist Kurt ATTERBERG, is produced in Stockholm.

23 JANUARY 1925

Igor STRAVINSKY makes his first American appearance as pianist, in the first American performance of his neobaroque *Piano Concerto,* with the Boston Symphony Orchestra, Serge Koussevitzky conducting. (The absolute first performance took place at a Koussevitzky concert in Paris on 22 May 1924)

31 JANUARY 1925

A suite of three pieces of Jacques IBERT, orchestrated by him from *Les Rencontres: petite suite en forme de ballet:* (1) *Les Bouquetières,* a gracefully stylized evocation of flower girls in peppery harmonies and jogging rhythms; (2) *Créoles,* in tango-like see-saw manner; (3) *Les Bavardes,* in quick quintuple time, is performed for the first time in Paris.

31 JANUARY 1925

Zéphyr et Flore, the first ballet by the 21-year-old Russian composer Vladimir DUKELSKY, written in a pleasingly stylized bucolic manner of neo-Baroque dance music, is performed for the first time, for an invited audience, by Diaghilev's Ballet Russe in Monte Carlo.

31 JANUARY 1925

Alladina a Palomid, opera by the 31-year-old Czech composer Osvald CHLUBNA, after Maeterlinck's drama dealing with a passionate encounter of the fiancé of a royal princess and her Greek slave maid servant, is produced in Brno in the Czech translation, on the same evening with the ballet *Kdo je na světě najmocnější? (Who Is the Most Powerful Person in the World?)* by Bohuslav MARTINŮ.

7 FEBRUARY 1925

Il Convento veneziano, "choreographic comedy" by Alfredo CASELLA, composed in 1912, has its first stage performance at La Scala, Milan. (A symphonic suite extracted from this score was first performed under the title *Le couvent sur l'eau,* in Paris on 23 April 1914, Casella conducting.)

8 FEBRUARY 1925

Two symphonies by Russia's most prolific symphonist Nicolai MIASKOVSKY, the *Fourth*, in E minor, subjective and somber albeit with an optimistic ending, in three contrasting movements (composed in 1918), and the *Seventh*, in B minor (composed in 1922), animated and extrovert, and more harmoniously adhering to the Soviet ideals of healthy music, are performed at the same concert for the first time in Moscow.

13 FEBRUARY 1925

Leo ORNSTEIN, 32-year-old Russian-born modernistically minded composer, experimenter in metapianistic sonorities, plays the first performance with the Philadelphia Orchestra, Leopold Stokowski conducting, of his *First Piano Concerto*, arranged from his earlier sonata for two pianos of 1921, its modernity expressed by the absence of key signature and the abundance of metrical shifts, the finale pursuing its course in rapid 5/8 time.

13 FEBRUARY 1925

Le Mariage de Rosine, comic opera after Beaumarchais by the Belgian composer Robert HERBERIGS, is produced in Ghent.

14 FEBRUARY 1925

Giuseppe DONATI DE BUDRIO, the inventor (in 1867) of the ocarina, the bird-shaped (ocarina means, literally, a little goose) hollow-sounding whistleflute, known in U.S. parlance as "sweet potato," dies in poverty in Milan, at the age of eighty-eight (he was born on 2 December 1836), with part of his ocarina glory usurped by Luigi Silvestri, who even got himself nicknamed "papa dell' ocarina."

(Luigi Silvestri died at an even more advanced age, well over ninety, at Camisano, on 1 March 1927. Information from the article by Mario Sandri, *Storia dell' ocarina di Budrio* in *Gazetta del Popolo*, Turin, 25 April 1927.)

15 FEBRUARY 1925

Preludio a Cristóbal Colón, overture to an unwritten opera on Christopher Columbus by Julián CARRILLO, Mexican pioneer of music in fractional intervals, scored for a quarter-tone soprano and orchestra playing in quarter-tones, eighth-tones and 16th-tones, is performed for the first time in Mexico City.

18 FEBRUARY 1925

Pas sur la bouche, operetta by Maurice YVAIN, dealing with a middle-aged American businessman gallivanting in Paris in quest of exotic amours, who stoutly resists the implantation of specialized French kisses on the mouth which render him helpless against nuptial inducements, the score containing a delectably explicit song detailing the mechanism of male sexual response by a young Frenchman, "Je fais ça machinalement sans savoir comment," is produced in Paris.

19 FEBRUARY 1925

Gli Amanti Sposi, opera in three acts by Ermanno WOLF-FERRARI, after Goldoni's comedy *Il Ventaglio*, is produced in Venice.

20 FEBRUARY 1925

Enrico BOSSI, 63-year-old Italian composer of operas and oratorios in a fine Verdian manner, dies on board the S.S. *De Graisse* on his return from an American tour. (Date from a letter to the author from the Compagnie Générale Transatlantique: "Marco Enrico Bossi, de nationalité italienne, né le 25 avril 1861, est décédé à bord du *De Grasse* le 20 février 1925, à 13 heures G.M.T.)

28 FEBRUARY 1925

Violin Concerto in E minor by the 64-year-old romantic Austrian composer Emil Nikolaus von REZNIČEK, in three movements, patently patterned after Mendelssohn's famous concerto in the same minor key and containing further borrowing from Cherubini's melodious legacy, is performed for the first time in Berlin.

1 MARCH 1925

Intégrales by Edgar VARÈSE, a captivating piece of "organized sound," scored for eleven winds and seventeen percussion instruments integrated in a magnificent tonal symmetry with a germinal motive in the center of ever-expanding spiral melody, is performed for the first time in New York.

If it be music to . . . make sounds like an injured dog's cry of pain or a cat's yell of midnight rage . . . then this is the real thing. (W. J. Henderson, *New York Sun,* 2 March 1925.)

Varèse's *Intégrales* sounded a good deal like a combination of early morning in the Mott Haven freight yard, feeding time at the zoo and a Sixth Avenue trolley rounding a curve, with an intoxicated woodpecker thrown in for good measure. (Ernest Newman, *New York Evening Post,* 2 March 1925.)

3 MARCH 1925

Joseph the Beautiful, ballet with music by Sergei VASILENKO, based on the biblical story of the aborted seduction of the beautiful Jewish lad Joseph by the lecherous queen of Egypt, is performed for the first time at the Experimental Theater in Moscow.

4 MARCH 1925

Moritz MOSZKOWSKI, silesian-born virtuoso pianist, composer of the perennial piano favorites *Spanish Dances* and *Serenata*, and numberless pieces of romantically spiced salon music, dies of stomach cancer in Paris, at the age of 70.

7 MARCH 1925

I Cavalieri di Ekebù, seventh opera by Riccardo ZANDONAI, to a libretto from Selma Lagerlöf's novel *Gösta Berling*, focused on the turbulent passion of a disorganized youth who eventually marries a divorced countess, is produced at La Scala, Milan, conducted by Arturo Toscanini.

10 MARCH 1925

Thermidor, opera in four acts by the Apulian composer Angelo TUBI, focusing on the overthrow of Robespierre on the 9th of Thermidor (27 July 1793), is produced in Cagliari, Sardinia.

21 MARCH 1925

The world première is given at Monte Carlo of *L'Enfant et les Sortilèges*, opera in two parts by Maurice RAVEL, to a tale based on a "fantaisie lyrique" by Colette, with animated characters of house furniture, in which a mischievous six-year-old boy smashes the Chinese mezzo-contralto cup, pulls the pendulum off the baritone horloge, breaks the tenor teapot, rips the bass armchair, and pulls the tail of the mezzo-soprano cat, set to music in an asymmetrically rhythmic idiom, reaching the climax when the crockery accompanied by a sofa, the ottoman and the wicker chair, joined by exercises from his torn arithmetic book, engage themselves in all kinds of baleful sortileges, aided and abetted by an amorous duo of the baritone tomcat under the window meowing in nasal glissandos in ascending intervals and the female domestic cat responding in feline glissandos in descending intervals, the whole score attaining the illustrative quality of a children's picture book in its imaginative and poetic infantiloquy.

26 MARCH 1925

Pierre BOULEZ, French composer of abstract constructivist music based on serial principles and exploring the ultimate of structural potentialities in the tempered scale, is born in Montbrison.

29 MARCH 1925

Le Marchand de Venise, opera by Reynaldo HAHN, after Shakespeare, is performed for the first time at the Paris Opéra.

30 MARCH 1925

Trio for violin, viola and cello, by the Russian expatriate composer Jef GOLYSCHEFF, in four movements indicating the dynamic values as serialistic entities—(1) *Mezzoforte*; (2) *Fortissimo*; (3) *Piano*; (4) *Pianissimo*, and written according to a *sui generis* system of twelve non-repeated thematic tones, termed by him *12 Tondauer-Musik*—is published in Berlin a year after the promulgation, on 1 March 1924, of Schoenberg's epoch-making dodecaphonic *Serenade*, op. 24, but elaborated independently.

(Herbert Eimert states in his *Atonale Musiklehre*, Leipzig, 1924, that Golyscheff experimented in dodecaphonic composition as early as 1914, but gives no proof; Golyscheff himself became a painter, and in 1968 was living in Brazil.)

1 APRIL 1925

Three Soviet composers, Alexander DAVIDENKO, Boris SCHECHTER and Victor BYELY, organize in Moscow a Society for Promotion of Proletarian Music, Production Collective (PROCOLL).

3 APRIL 1925

At the Boar's Head, one-act opera by Gustav HOLST, to his own libretto arranged from Shakespeare's play *King Henry IV*, musically derived from old English melorhythms and accoutred in circumspect dissonances, is produced in Manchester, England.

21 APRIL 1925

Il Diavolo nel Campanile, one-act opera by the 40-year-old Italian composer Adriano LUALDI, to a libretto from Edgar Allan Poe's fantastic tale *The Devil in the Belfry*, is produced in La Scala, Milan.

22 APRIL 1925

André CAPLET, French composer of impressionistic pieces of chamber music, sensitive conductor of opera and symphony, an intimate friend and collaborator of Debussy, dies in Paris at the age of 46.

24 APRIL 1925

For Red Petrograd, opera in three acts by Arseny GLADKOVSKY and Eugene PRUSSAK, the first opera ever written on a Soviet subject dealing with the defense of Petrograd in October 1919 against the massive assault of the White Army, which is characterized in the score by an eerie progression of ominous whole-tone scales, is produced in Leningrad. (A revised version, in four acts, under the title *Front and Rear*, was produced in Leningrad on 7 November 1930.)

30 APRIL 1925

The Traveling Companion, posthumous four-act opera by Charles Villiers STANFORD, to a libretto from Hans Christian Andersen's fairy, tale, is produced in Liverpool by an amateur group in a makeshift orchestration, with a piano filling in the missing instrumental parts. (The first tolerably professional performance was given in Bristol on 25 October 1926.)

30 APRIL 1925

Howard HANSON, newly appointed as Director of the Eastman, School of Music in Rochester, New York, conducts the first of an annual series of concerts devoted exclusively to American music.

1 MAY 1925

Scie Musicale, a musical saw capable of sounding melodies in tempered or non-tempered scales in the range of three octaves, is demonstrated for the first time at the Gervex Pavilion at the Paris Exposition.

4 MAY 1925

Esther, Princesse d'Israël, opera in three acts by Antoine MARIOTTE, to a libretto dealing with the resourceful biblical damsel who makes herself so desirable to the oppressive king Ahasuerus that he delivers into her hands his murderously antisemitic minister Haman, is produced at the Paris Opéra.

7 MAY 1925

A century has passed since the death, insane, of Antonio SALIERI, fine Italian craftsman of great musical expertise, author of many melodious and harmonious operas, whose destiny was to be unjustly accused of poisoning Mozart.

9 MAY 1925

Four centuries have elapsed since the birth of Giovanni Pierluigi PALESTRINA, the "Saviour of Liturgical Music," founder of modern counterpoint, universalizer of modern polyphony.

(The date of Palestrina's birth, 9 May 1525, is derived from his inscription in a manuscript music book, "Libro de' ricordi scritto da me, Giovanni Pierluigi da Palestrina, commenzato a dì 19 di settembre 1578, per memoria da Iginio mio figliuolo, di età de' 53 anni, mesi 4, giorni 10, perconto de' stampe de' Messe con messer Dorico," cited by Raffaele Casimir, in *Noto d'Archivio* of March 1924.)

10 MAY 1925

All records for precocious musical wunderkindism are broken by the 2 1/4-year-old Spanish girl Giocasta CORMA (born in Barcelona on 4 February 1923), at her public concert in a program of ten classical pieces in the Salle Mozart in Barcelona. (Dates from *Diccionario de la Música Ilustrado*, Barcelona, 1930.)

15 MAY 1925

The Third Festival of the International Society for Contemporary Music opens in Prague with the following program:

Ferruccio BUSONI's early *Serenata* for cello and piano, composed in 1892; *5 Pieces for Chamber Orchestra* by Ernst TOCH, lyrically modal in its slow episodes, boisterously chromatic in rapid passages, astringently rhythmed and diaphanously orchestrated; *Tempo di Ballo*, a Gallic pastiche by ROLAND-MANUEL; a symphonic suite from the ballet *Noah's Ark* by the Italian composer Vittorio RIETI, representing a panorama of vivacious animal scenes; *Demon*, a somberly conceived symphonic poem by the Czech composer Rudolf KAREL; and *Concerto Grosso* for double orchestra by the German master of polytechnical polyphony Heinrich KAMINSKI.

17 MAY 1925

At the second concert of the Third Festival of the International Society for Contemporary Music in Prague, the following program of orchestral music is presented:

A neo-classical *Partita* by Paul A. PISK of Vienna, dissonant and complex in its polyphonic texture; *6 Pieces for Orchestra* by the Hungarian composer Georg KÓSA, with expressionistically pessimistic titles, such as *Seul, Prière sceptique* and *Sans Espoir;* a formalistic *Concertino* for piano and orchestra by the Serbian-born Austrian composer and theorist Rudolf RETI; *Les Adieux,* for soloists and orchestra, by the Czech-born German-educated romantic composer Fidelio FINKE; *Half-Time,* a symphonic impression of a soccer game by the Czech composer Bohuslav MARTINU, written in his Parisian style of hedonistic constructivism; and *Pastoral Symphony* by Ralph VAUGHAN WILLIAMS (first performed in London on 26 January 1922.)

19 MAY 1925

At the third concert of the Third Festival of the International Society for Contemporary Music in Prague, the following program of orchestral music is given:

Concerto Grosso by Ernst KRENEK, written in a modernistic neo-Baroque style; *Voriazioni senza tema* for piano and orchestra by Gian Francesco MALIPIERO (completed by him on 29 July 1923), the title being selected "not for the sake of a paradox, but because the component parts of this work actually possess the character of variations on an absent theme"; *Toman a lesní panna (Toman and the Forest Nymph),* symphonic poem by the Czech romanticist Vítězslav NOVÁK (first performed in Prague on 5 April 1908); *Protée,* symphonic suite by Darius MILHAUD, from incidental music to Paul Claudel's play; and the infectiously rhythmogenic *Dance Suite,* by Béla BARTÓK, consisting of five movements linked by ritornels, on original themes patterned on Slavic, Hungarian and Rumanian melorhythms.

19 MAY 1925

Jacob chez Laban, biblical pastoral in one act by Charles KOECHLIN, dealing with the mutual deception practiced by Laban (who contrary to his covenant with Jacob placed an older daughter in the bridal bed of Jacob instead of the younger one) and Jacob (who schemed to secure a majority of speckled cattle by holding crossed rods in front of copulating animals, in the belief that this would alter their genes so as to produce striped offspring which were to be his by a previous agreement), all this set to music with the application of audacious dissonances, is performed for the first time in Paris, many years after its composition.

21 MAY 1925

Nine months and three weeks after the death of Ferruccio BUSONI, his unfinished opera *Doktor Faust,* in six scenes, to his own text, drawn from an old marionette play, in which Mephistopheles appears in six different hypostasies—a man clad in black, a chaplain, a monk, a messenger, a courier and a night watchman—all these encounters projected against the realistic background of 16th-century German student life (the actual Dr. Faustus was a university alchemist), is performed for the first time at the Dresden Opera, in a version completed by Busoni's pupil, French-born half-Catalan half-German composer Philipp Jarnach.

23 MAY 1925

Concertino for piano and orchestra by Arthur HONEGGER, a hedonistic modernistic piece in three movements, *Allegro molto moderato,* an antiphonal interplay with fugal developments, *Larghetto sostenuto,* a bucolic air with variations, and *Allegro,* containing some infectious Gallic jazz, is performed for the first time in Paris at a concert directed by Serge Koussevitzky, with Honegger's fiancée, Andrée Vaurabourg, at the piano.

28 MAY 1925

Der Alchimist, opera in three scenes by Cyril SCOTT, 45-year-old English composer educated in Germany, to his own text focused on a young alchemist in the pursuit of the *lapis philosophorum,* who is compelled to count the hairs on his head to summon a cooperative demon, set to music in romantic colors, is performed for the first time in Essen, in a German version of the original English libretto.

30 MAY 1925

Germaine TAILLEFERRE, French composer, the only woman in the group *Les Six,* appears as soloist with Serge

Koussevitzky and his orchestra in Paris in the first performance of her *Piano Concerto*, written in a lively French style.

1 JUNE 1925

Ernest BLOCH conducts in Cleveland the first performance of his *Concerto Grosso* for piano obbligato and string orchestra, composed in a neo-Baroque idiom as a didactic piece for his students at the Cleveland School of Music during the last year of his directorship there, in four contrasting movements:

(1) *Prelude*, set in energetically massive chordal complexes with bitonal ramifications; (2) *Dirge*, a solemn invocation in plagal modes; (3) *Pastorale and Rustic Dances*, a bucolic essay followed by a controlled outburst of feral rural rhythms; (4) *Fugue*, a modernistic exercise in bitonal polyphony.

5 JUNE 1925

Eric DELAMARTER, 45-year-old American composer, conducts at John Wanamaker's store in Philadelphia the first performance of his *Second Symphony*, set in conventional modalities vivified by jazzy American balladry, in three movements inspired by lines from Walt Whitman: (1) *I Sound My Barbaric Yawp;* (2) *Glistening Perfumed South;* (3) *Robust, Friendly, Singing With Open Mouths.*

6 JUNE 1925

Second Symphony by Sergei PROKOFIEV, in D minor, in two movements—(1) *Allegro ben articolato*, set in metallic tones of primitivistic constructivism; (2) *Tema con variazioni*, marked by melodic saltation, trochaic rhythms and progressively dense harmonic concentrations in septuple counterpoint, with a thematic recapitulation after six variations, concluding on a structure of three minor triads suspended over the fundamental D in pianissimo—is performed for the first time in Paris by Serge Koussevitzky and his orchestra.

My *Second Symphony* sounded overloaded. Although one critic commended my septuple counterpoint, my friends preserved an embarrassed silence. (Prokofiev, in his *Autobiography;* he planned to rewrite the work, as op. 136, during the last year of his life in 1953, but the project remained incomplete.)

11 JUNE 1925

Arthur HONEGGER conducts in Mezières, Switzerland, the first performance of his incidental music to *Judith*, a play by René Morax, telling the famous biblical story of a Jewish widow of "goodly countenance" who penetrated the camp of the besieging Assyrians as a refugee, captivated and inebriated their chief Holofernes, decapitated him with his own falchion, packed the severed head in her maidservant's meat bag, returned in triumph to her people and lived in total chastity until the age of 105, set to music of anguished intensity in starkly dissonant polyphony. (*Judith* was produced as an "opéra sérieux" in an amplified version, in Monte Carlo on 13 February 1926.)

14 JUNE 1925

Alexander LÁSZLÓ, 29-year-old Hungarian composer, gives at the Music Festival in Kiel the first public demonstration of his specially constructed "color pianoforte" (Farblichtklavier) as an experiment in controlled subjectivism of sensory impressions of synchronized light and sound.

15 JUNE 1925

On the occasion of the 60th birthday of Paul GILSON, Belgian composer and esteemed pedagogue, eight of his pupils—René BERNIER, Gaston BRENTA, Francis de BOURGUIGNON, Théo de JONCKER, Robert OTLET, Marcel POOT, Maurice SCHOEMAKER and Jules STRENS—proclaim their esthetical credo in conformity with their teacher's ideals, and designate themselves as SYNTHÉTISTES whose aim is to "couler dans les formes bien définies tous les apports de la musique actuelle" and to abandon "les longs développements, les froides et pédantes rhétoriques au profit d'un art clair et vivant." (Quotations from a speech by Brenta at a concert of the Synthétistes broadcast by Radio-Belgique on 1 October 1930.)

17 JUNE 1925

Les Matelots, ballet by the 26-year-old French composer Georges *Auric*, is produced by Diaghilev's Ballet Russe in Paris, depicting in five concise tableaux, set to hedonistically facile music, the story of a sailor and his girl:

(1) *Engagement and Departure*, a hornpipe frolic; (2) *Solitude*, the girl's lament; (3) *Return*, a sensuous waltz during which the sailor and his two friends try to seduce the bride as a test of her fidelity; (4) *Temptation*, in which the sailors fail to induce the girl to have a drink with them; (5) *Finale*, the scene of recognition and reconciliation between the lovers in jig-time.

17 JUNE 1925

La Forêt païenne, ballet by Charles KOECHLIN, is presented for the first time, in concert performance, in Paris.

17 JUNE 1925

Concerto for cello and chamber orchestra by Ernst TOCH, in four movements marked by a hyperchromatic tension and devoid of key signature, but with a clearly sensed barycenter on B, is performed for the first time in Kiel.

26 JUNE 1925

La maschera nuda, three-act operetta arranged by Salvatore ALLEGRA from posthumous fragments of an unfinished opera by Ruggero LEONCAVALLO, is performed for the first time in Naples.

27 JUNE 1925

Sous-marine, constructivistic ballet by Arthur HONEGGER, is produced at the Opéra-Comique in Paris.

1 JULY 1925

La Naissance de la Lyre, "conte lyrique" in one act and three scenes by Albert ROUSSEL (completed by him on 14 September 1923), to a subject from the writings of the French Hellenist Théodore Reinach, based on a recently discovered play by Sophocles, *The Bloodhounds*, dealing with the invention of the lyre by Hermes from the guts and horns of sheep stolen by him from Apollo and its appropriation by Apollo in exchange for his entire flock, set to music in neo-Grecian modalities, is produced at the Paris Opéra.

1 JULY 1925

Erik SATIE, French composer whose life, like his art, was a carefully calculated series of aphorisms and paradoxes, but who in spite of the lack of substance in his music exercised an incommensurately great influence on the 20th-century generation of French composers, dies in Paris in his 60th year. (Date communicated by the Saint-Joseph Hospital in Paris where he was confined.)

1 JULY 1925

Gergana, opera in three acts by the pioneer Bulgarian composer Georgi ATANASOV, wherein a 19th-century Bulgarian maiden, obsessed by the fear that a Turkish overlord might force her into his harem, dies of inanition in the temporary absence of her faithful suitor, who, upon learning of her death, succumbs himself to shock and grief, written in a facile Italianate manner, is produced in Stara Zagora, Bulgaria.

25 JULY 1925

Concerto for orchestra with oboe, bassoon and violin soli, by Paul HINDEMITH, is performed for the first time in Duisburg.

6 AUGUST 1925

Tabaré opera by the Argentine composer Alfredo SCHIUMA, in a setting from the time of the Conquistadores, dealing with the story of a mestizo named Tabaré who is loved by the sister of a Spanish captain, and expires in her arms in the last act, is produced at the Teatro Colón in Buenos Aires.

24 AUGUST 1925

Arnold DOLMETSCH, English musician and manufacturer of replicas of obsolete old instruments, inaugurates his first Festival of Old Music in his home town of Haslemere.

3 SEPTEMBER 1925

A supplementary Chamber Music Festival of the International Society for Contemporary. Music opens in Venice with the following program:

String Quartet by the Czech composer of Schoenbergian music, Erwin SCHULHOFF; *L'Horizon chimérique,* a song cycle by Gabriel FAURÉ performed to commemorate his death ten months before; *Nocturnal Impressions of Peking* and *Korean Sketch,* for chamber orchestra by the 55-year-old American traveler and collector of oriental instruments, Henry EICHHEIM; *Jassband* for violin and piano, a Central European version of American syncopated music by the Austrian composer Wilhelm GROSZ; songs by the prime Brazilian composer Heitor VILLA-LOBOS; and *Concerto,* op. 36, No. 1, for pianoforte and 12 instruments by Paul HINDEMITH, in four movements of propulsively rhythmical neo-classicism, with the eighth-notes as metrical constants.

4 SEPTEMBER 1925

At the second concert of the supplementary Chamber Music Festival of the International Society for Contemporary Music in Venice, the following program is presented:

Sonata for cello and piano by the Catalan cello virtuoso Gaspar CASSADÓ; a Scriabinesque *Piano Sonata* by the Russian composer Samuel FEINBERG; *Sonata* for unaccompanied violin by the Hungarian musician Zoltán SZÉKELY; *5 Pieces* by the German composer Max BUTTING; *Songs* by the Czech composer Ladislav VYCPÁLEK; *Duo* for violin and cello by Hanns EISLER, a disciple of Schoenberg whose proletarian political predilections have deterred him from wholehearted adoption of total dodecaphony; and *String Quartet* by the grandmaster of Czech music, LEOŠ JANÁČEK.

5 SEPTEMBER 1925

At the third concert of the supplementary Chamber Music Festival of the International Society for Contemporary Music in Venice, the following program is given:

String Quartet by the whilom *Wunderkind,* now 28 years old, Erich KORNGOLD; *2 Mouvements* for two flutes, clarinet and bassoon by Jacques IBERT; *Sonata* for cello and piano by Arthur HONEGGER in his most felicitous lyrico-dramatic style combined with an artfully applied modern instrumental technique; *Joueurs de Flûte* for flute and piano by Albert ROUSSEL, in four movements evoking the images of Pan, Virgil, Krishna and a literary personage, set in a stylized quasi-exotic manner; *Tzigane* for violin and piano by RAVEL, a virtuosistic vision of Gypsy vitality; and *Sonata* for piano, flute, oboe and bassoon by Vittorio RIETI.

7 SEPTEMBER 1925

At the fourth concert of the supplementary Chamber Music Festival of the International Society for Contemporary Music in Venice, the following program is given:

String Quartet in A minor by Mario LABROCA, pupil of Respighi and Malipiero, in three movements, conventionally but pleasingly written; *Piano Sonata* by the celebrated pianist Arthur SCHNABEL composed in a surprisingly advanced quasi-atonal idiom; *Merciless Beauty,* three rondels for tenor and strings by VAUGHAN WILLIAMS; and *Serenade* for clarinet, bass clarinet, mandolin, guitar, violin, viola, cello and bass voice by Arnold SCHOENBERG, op. 24, the historic work which establishes within the confines of a classical suite a new style and technique of organized method of composition in twelve tones.

8 SEPTEMBER 1925

At the fifth and last concert of the supplementary Chamber Music Festival of the International Society for Contemporary Music in Venice, the following program is performed:

String Quartet by Karol SZYMANOWSKI in three movements, written in a lyrico-dramatic style with passing allusions to Polish folksongs, concluding with an uncompromisingly polytonal movement *Scherzando alla burlesca,* with the key signatures of A major, C-sharp major, E-flat major and C major in the four string instruments; *Le Stagioni italiche,* cycle of four songs for soprano and piano by Gian Francesco MALIPIERO, traversing four contrasting moods of Italian lyric poetry; *Angels* for six trumpets by the self-taught and aggressively individual American composer Carl RUGGLES, opening in angelically soft dissonances but fissioning forthwith into raucous atonalities; *Piano Sonata* by STRAVINSKY, his second work of purposive neo-classicism, played by himself; and *Daniel Jazz* by the Russian-born American composer Louis GRUENBERG, a stylized essay in jazzification for a Negro voice, string quartet, trumpet, piano and percussion, first performed in New York on 22 February 1925.

14 SEPTEMBER 1925

Tango Jalousie by the Danish composer Jacob GADE, inspired by an actual drama of passion with a fatal outcome that took place in Denmark in 1925, a tune destined to become celebrated all over the world, is performed for the first time at the Paladsteatret in Copenhagen, in connection with the showing of the Douglas Fairbanks film *Don Q.*

15 SEPTEMBER 1925

Leo FALL, Austrian composer of numerous operettas, among them the celebrated *Dollar Princess*, poking fun at America's cult of the Almighty Dollar, dies in Vienna at the age of 52.

21 SEPTEMBER 1925

The Vagabond King, musical play in two acts by the Czech-born American composer Rudolf FRIML, after Justin Huntly McCarthy's novel *If I Were King,* inspired by the legend of the medieval French poet François Villon who was made king for a day by Louis XI and was ordered to generate love in the frigid bosom of a stolid lady-in-waiting, under penalty of death in case of failure, set to music with abundant élan, including in the score such perennial favorites as *Love Me Tonight, Some Day, Waltz Huguette, Only a Rose,* and the *Song of the Vagabonds,* is produced in New York.

22 SEPTEMBER 1925

Sunny, musical comedy by Jerome KERN, in which Sunny, a comely British lass employed as a horseback rider in a circus, marries, divorces and remarries an American doughboy, featuring a popular duet *Who?* is produced in New York.

7 OCTOBER 1925

Choral Symphony by Gustav HOLST for soprano, chorus and orchestra, to poems of Keats, is performed for the first time at the Leeds Festival.

11 OCTOBER 1925

Two jazz pieces for orchestra by Leo SOWERBY, *Monotony* and *Syncopata,* are performed for the first time in Chicago, Paul Whiteman conducting.

12 OCTOBER 1925

Monodía for orchestra by the Catalan composer Jaime PAHISSA, written exclusively in unisons, octaves, and multiple octaves, but creating an impression of intricate polyphony through the ingenious use of contrary motion, atonal melodic lines, asymmetrical rhythms and quick transitions from one instrument to another, is performed for the first time in Barcelona by the Casals Orchestra.

16 OCTOBER 1925

Paul WITTGENSTEIN, amputated Austrian pianist who lost his right arm on the Russian front during World War I, plays in Dresden the world première of *Parergon zur Symphonia Domestica* by Richard STRAUSS, for left-hand piano and orchestra, dedicated to Wittgenstein and commissioned by him, the thematic materials being by-products (parergon) of the *Symphonia Domestica.* (Date from *Signale für die musikalische Welt,* Berlin, 21 October 1925, p. 1622. The performance in Leipzig on 29 October 1925, given in the article on Strauss in Nicolas Slonimsky's edition of Baker's *Biographical Dictionary of Musicians,* 1958, was not the first.)

19 OCTOBER 1925

Flos Campi, suite for viola, small chorus and small orchestra by Ralph VAUGHAN WILLIAMS, suggested by lines from the Song of Solomon, which are entered into the score as captions but are not sung, the chorus being wordless, is performed for the first time in London.

25 OCTOBER 1925

La Nuit de Saint-Jean, ballet by the Swedish composer Hugo ALFVÉN, to the music of his most popular symphonic work *Midsommarvaka* written in 1904, is produced by the Ballets Suédois in Paris.

25 OCTOBER 1925

The centennial anniversary of the birth of Johann STRAUSS, the splendidly mustachioed Waltz King, is observed in Vienna by a gala performance of his operetta *Der Zigeunerbaron.*

28 OCTOBER 1925

The first Festival of Chamber Music opens at the Library of Congress in Washington under the auspices of the Elizabeth Sprague Coolidge Foundation, in a program containing the first performances of three specially commissioned works by American composers:

Canticle of the Sun for voice and chamber orchestra by Charles Martin LOEFFLER of Boston; *Rhapsodic Fantasy* for chamber orchestra by Frederick A. STOCK, conductor of the Chicago Symphony Orchestra; and *Two Assyrian Prayers* for voice and chamber orchestra by Frederick JACOBI.

29 OCTOBER 1925

Menandra, opera in three acts by the German composer Hugo KAUN, is produced in Brunswick, Kiel, Osnabrück and Rostock, all on the same night.

30 OCTOBER 1925

Paganini, light opera by Franz LEHÁR in which Nicolò Paganini, singing in tenor voice, pursues an ardent love affair with Napoleon's sister Maria-Anna-Elisa, Duchess of Lucca, but abandons her in the end to devote himself to his violin, is performed for the first time in Vienna.

5 NOVEMBER 1925

L'Orfeide, opera in three parts to his own texts by Gian Francesco MALIPIERO—(1) *La Morte delle Maschere* (completed 15 January 1922), in which the old masks of the ancient drama are taken out of a trunk to revitalize the artificial modern art; (2) *Sette Canzoni,* seven "dramatic expressions" (completed in February 1919) gathered from Malipiero's personal observations; (3) *Orfeo*, "musical representation in one act" (completed 14 June 1920), a philosophical continuation of the *Sette Canzoni*—is performed for the first time in its entirety in Düsseldorf. (*Sette Canzoni* was performed separately in Paris on 14 July 1920.)

6 NOVEMBER 1925

Concerto accademico in D minor for violin and string orchestra by Ralph VAUGHAN WILLIAMS, in three movements, *Allegro pesante, Adagio, Presto,* systematically flaunting a series of flagrantly unacademic consecutive fifths in a highly unorthodox modulatory scheme, and ending with a violin cadenza presenting an ostentatious display of tonal ambiguity of homonymous major and minor thirds, is performed for the first time in London, with the modernistically minded Hungarian violinist Jelly d'Arányi, to whom the work is dedicated, as soloist.

7 NOVEMBER 1925

Eagles in Revolt, opera in five acts by the Soviet composer Andrei PASHCHENKO, to a libretto based on the historic Volga Cossack rebellion against Catherine the Great, is produced in Leningrad.

11 NOVEMBER 1925

Šárka, opera in three acts by Leoš JANÁČEK, written in 1887, is belatedly brought to performance in Brno, after many revisions of the original score.

13 NOVEMBER 1925

Volpino il Calderaio, one-act opera by Renzo Bossi, son of Enrico Bossi, after Shakespeare's play *The Taming of the Shrew,* is produced in Milan.

20 NOVEMBER 1925

Music for the Theatre, suite for small orchestra with piano by the 25-year-old American composer Aaron COPLAND, in five imaginative movements (*Prologue, Dance, Interlude, Burlesque, Epilogue*), a fine study in contrasts, almost austere in its classical formulation and making use of jazz rhythms in the *Dance,* is performed for the first time in Boston, conducted by Serge Koussevitzky to whom the score is dedicated.

21 NOVEMBER 1925

La Fête chez la Bergère by Georges Migot, orchestral version of his *3 Epigrammes* for piano, is performed for the first time at a Pasdeloup concert in Paris.

21 NOVEMBER 1925

L'Île désenchantée, comic opera in two acts by Henry FÉVRIER, is produced in Paris.

24 NOVEMBER 1925

The Asra, one-act opera by the American composer Joseph Carl BREIL, to his own libretto after Heine's orientalistic poem *Der Asra,* wherein a low-caste musician is seized with a strangling paroxysm during an illicit embrace with a high-caste damsel and gives up the ghost, is performed for the first and last time in Los Angeles, two months before the composer's death precipitated by acute neurasthenia.

26 NOVEMBER 1925

Suton (Twilight), music drama in one act by the Croatian composer Stevan HRISTIĆ, focused on a Dalmatian girl of 1830 who enters a convent after she is prevented by her class-conscious aristocratic mother from marrying a soldier of her heart's desire, is produced in Belgrade.

28 NOVEMBER 1925

"Grand Ole Opry," a series of Saturday night broadcasts lasting 4 hours each and embodying a medley of cowboy tunes, country ballads, and rustic jazz, is inaugurated in Nashville, Tennessee, on Radio Station WSM, under its initial appellation "Barn Dance."

2 DECEMBER 1925

Mozart, "musical comedy" by Sacha Guitry with a Mozartian musical score by the Venezuelan-born Parisian composer Reynaldo HAHN, depicting Mozart's imaginary amourettes during his sojourn in Paris as a youth of 22, with a variety of women from the former mistress of Rousseau to a chambermaid, is performed for the first time in Paris.

3 DECEMBER 1925

George GERSHWIN appears as soloist with the New York Symphony Orchestra, under the direction of Walter Damrosch, in the world première of his *Concerto in F* for piano and orchestra, in three movements of classical formulation, but deeply American in the blue chromaticism of the music and asymmetrical rhythms within square meters:

(1) *Allegro,* opening with a jazzy motive contrasted with a rousing emotional theme; (2) *Adagio,* serving as an introduction to an elegiac *Andante con moto,* building up to a sonorous climax and then subsiding to a harmonious ending; (3) *Allegro con brio,* with the most conspicuous theme of the initial movement returning in Tchaikovskian splendor for a brilliant ending.

6 DECEMBER 1925

Féerique, symphonic poem by Jacques IBERT, an artful evocation of the Ravelesque phantasmagoria in a fine form of "petit art," is performed for the first time at the Concerts Colonne in Paris, Gabriel Pierné conducting.

11 DECEMBER 1925

Barabau, ballet in one act with chorus by Vittorio RIETI, is performed for the first time by Diaghilev's Ballet Russe in London.

11 DECEMBER 1925

Carl NIELSEN, prime Danish modernist, conducts in Copenhagen the first performance of his *Sixth Symphony,* entitled *Sinfonia semplice,* completed barely six days before the performance, in four classically designed movements: (1) *Tempo giusto,* (2) *Humoresca,* (3) *Proposta seria,* (4) *Tema con variazioni,* set in nutritious triadic harmonies, with some surprisingly audacious excursions into the realm of emancipated dissonances, suggesting that the simplicity proclaimed in the subtitle may have been an irony.

11 DECEMBER 1925

Namiko-San, lyric drama in one act by the naturalized American Italian-born composer Aldo FRANCHETTI, to his own libretto in English from a French translation of an ancient Japanese tale, wherein an adolescent geisha in the household of a warrior prince in the valley of Fujiyama is slain by him when he surprises her in the company of a young itinerant monk, is produced by the Chicago Civic Opera, with the composer conducting.

13 DECEMBER 1925

Rustic Symphony by Alexander KASTALSKY, written in a Russian folk-song manner, is performed for the first time in Moscow.

14 DECEMBER 1925

After one hundred and thirty-seven rehearsals, the State Opera in Berlin presents the world première of Alban BERG's expressionistic masterpiece *Wozzeck,* opera in three acts to the libretto from a play by the early 19th-century romantic German writer Georg Büchner (his original spelling of the name of the protagonist was *Woyzeck*), focused on a private soldier whose mistress Marie has a child by him but keeps company with a swashbuckling drum major, a situation leading to a fateful dénouement when the desperate Wozzeck stabs her to death and then accidentally drowns while trying to retrieve his bloody murder weapon from a pond, with a poignant epilogue in which their uncomprehending child rocks on a hobby-horse urging it on with infantiloquent interjections, set to music in a style of emancipated melody and harmony, employing both atonal and tonal media in a free flow of the sonic liquid, unified by a conscious formal scheme of classical organization in a Baroque-like triptych, evolving in these peripeteia:

ACT I. EXPOSITION, portraying Wozzeck's relationship to his environment, in five scenes: (1) *Classical Suite,* comprising Prelude, Pavane, Gigue, Gavotte, Air, and a recapitulation of the Prelude, partly in retrograde motion; (2) *Fantasy* on three thematic chords; (3) *March and Berceuse;* (4) *Passacaglia,* based on a 12-tone series, and containing 21 variations; (5) *Rondo.* ACT II. DEVELOPMENT, a symphony descriptive of Wozzeck's torments, in five sections: (1) *Sonata,* cast in a strict classical form with a repeat of the exposition; (2) *Prelude and Triple Fugue;* (3) *Adagio,* scored for chamber orchestra using the same instrumentation as Schoenberg's *Kammersymphonie,* and intended as homage to Berg's revered master; (4) *Scherzo,* illustrating Wozzeck's distress as he sees Marie dallying with the drum major; (5) *Rondo,* wherein Wozzeck is taunted by his successful rival. ACT III. CATASTROPHE, in the form of a suite of six Inventions: (1) *Theme and Variations;* (2) Invention on a single note, B natural, alphabetically alluding, in German notation, to the initial letter of the word *Hilfe,* which Marie sings out, crying for help to ward off the knife-wielding Wozzeck; (3) Invention on a rhythm, a realistically constructed improvisation, with a deliberately mistuned pianino on the stage suggesting the irony, pity and horror of Wozzeck's fate; (4) Invention on a 6-note chord; (5) Invention on a key, in the traditionally romantic tonality of D minor, culminating in a 12-tone conglomerate formed by three contiguous diminished-seventh chords; (6) *Moto perpetuo,* marked by a precipitation of rapid triplet eighth-notes in continuous motion and terminating with a serene catharsis symbolic of the eternal cycle of life.

Opera of Noisy Dissonance Gets Composer Called a genius.—The State Opera at Berlin has become a storm center of musical discussion through its production of the opera *Wozzeck* by Alban Berg, which breaks all records for dissonance and cacophony. The composer is acclaimed by critics in terms varying from "musical mountebank" to "inspired genius." Not content with having the orchestra attack the ears with noises so inharmonious that some listeners aver they suffer physical pain, the composer prescribes that the tin-pan piano used in one of the scenes must be out of tune and that the singers must sing off key (Associated Press dispatch in the New York *Times,* 15 December 1925)

Splitting the convulsively inflated larynx of the Muse, Alban Berg produces tortured and mistuned cackling, a pandemonium of dismembered orchestral sounds, mishandled men's throats, bestial outcries, bellowing, rattling, and all sorts of other hideous noises . . . Berg is the poisoner of the fountainhead of German music. (*Germania,* Berlin, 15 December 1925)

As I left the State Opera last night I had a sensation not of leaving a public institution, but an insane asylum. On the stage, in the orchestra, in the hall, everywhere, plain madmen. Among them, in defiant squadrons, the shock troops of atonalistis, the dervishes of Arnold Schoenberg. *Wozzeck* by Alban Berg was the battle cry. It is a work by a Chinaman from Vienna. For with European music and music history this massive assault of instrumental sounds has nothing in common. In Berg's music there is not a trace of melody. There are only scraps, shreds, spasms, snorts. Harmonically, the work is beyond debate, for everything in it sounds wrong. The perpetrator of this opera counts with assurance on the stupidity and human kindness of his fellow-men, and relies for the rest on God Almighty and the Universal Edition of Vienna. I regard Alban Berg as a musical swindler, one who represents a musical danger to the community. I might go even further. Unprecedented occurrences demand new steps. We must in all seriousness pose the question as to what extent the profession of music may be criminal. We are confronted here, in the field of music, with a capital offense. (Paul Zschorlich, *Deutsche Zeitung,* Berlin, 15 December 1925)

One cannot imagine without having lived through the dissonant orgy of *Wozzeck* the murderous demands made on the voice, the torture to which the ears of the poor singers and members of the State Opera Orchestra were subjected during the rehearsals of the opera. (Adolf Diesterweg, *Die Zeitschrift für Music,* Berlin, January 1926)

Alban Berg is the creator of sounds which horrify the ear accustomed as it is to all manner of excesses. . . . Dissonance has been elevated to the point of principle in this music. Forms resolve into a continuous flow, colors coalesce, but the result is something that, by its constant fluctuation and nebulous substance, is the kind of music that justifies the transformation of *Wozzeck* into an opera. (Max Marschalk, *Die Vossische Zeitung,* Berlin, 15 December 1925)

Alban Berg's *Wozzeck,* born of his tragic consciousness of the reality of life, and grown out of the expressionistic transformation of the living tissue, reflecting the hopelessness of human suffering in the clutches of the monstrous and inhuman capitalist society, reveals the helplessness of the Western European petty-bourgeois intelligentsia before the imminent Fascist assault, proving that Europe is going through a crisis not alone in the individual consciousness of a Western European bourgeois composer, but in its general music culture. (Boris Asafiev, *Sovietskaya Musica,* Moscow, 1934)

23 DECEMBER 1925

Reinhold GLIÈRE conducts in Odessa the first performance of his symphonic tableau *The Cossacks of Zaporozh*, inspired by the famous painting of Repin showing the indomitable Cossacks dictating to a scribe an insulting letter to the Turkish Sultan Mahomet IV in reply to his demand to submit to his rule.

24 DECEMBER 1925

Le Joueur de Viole, opera in four acts by Raoul LAPARRA, to his own libretto focused on a philosophical player on a magical viol who strives to fulfill his destiny by harmonizing the vibrations of the four strings of his instrument with the four seasons of the year and the four dominant human events—love, glory, sorrow and death—is produced at the Opéra-Comique in Paris.

26 DECEMBER 1925

The Decembrists, opera in four acts by the Russian composer Vasily ZOLOTAREV, is produced in Moscow to mark the centennial of the abortive revolt of the "Decembrists" against the incumbent Tsar Nicholas I in December 1825, led by a group, subsequently hanged, of liberal officers and literary men.

26 DECEMBER 1925

A Light From St. Agnes, "lyric tragedy" in one act by the 38-year-old American composer William Franke HARLING, to a libretto dealing with sacrilegious desecration of a church in Louisiana, theft of a crucifix and murder, set to a score making use of saxophones and banjos for local color, is produced in Chicago.

31 DECEMBER 1925

Ottorino RESPIGHI appears as soloist with the New York Philharmonic Orchestra in the world première of his *Concerto in modo misolidio* for piano and orchestra, a stylized neo-archaic work set in the consistently employed Mixolydian mode.

31 DECEMBER 1925

Arnold SCHOENBERG completes the composition of the second of a group of three satires, entitled *Vielseitigkeit*, for chorus a cappella, set in the form of invertible retrograde canon (symmetrical in relation to its axis so that, allowance made for the position of sharps and flats, it is identical when read upside-down, from the last bar to the first) to his own text deriding a transparently pseudonymous contemporary, "der kleine Modernsky" who wears "authentic false hair" and looks quite like "der Papa Bach."

I wrote these satires when I was very angry over the attacks against me by some of my younger contemporaries. I wanted to warn them that it does not pay to tangle with me. (From Schoenberg's letter dated 13 May 1949, quoted in Josef Rufer's *Das Werk Schoenbergs*, 1959)

Immediately after the war I received some very cordial letters from Schoenberg. . . . Then, in 1925, he wrote a very nasty verse about me (though I almost forgive him for setting it to such a remarkable mirror canon). I do not know what had happened in between. (*Conversations with Igor Stravinsky* by Igor Stravinsky and Robert Craft, New York, 1959)

1926

1 JANUARY 1926

An Association for Contemporary Music is founded in Leningrad, stating the following theses and beliefs:

(1) That during the transitional period of Socialist construction contemporary music can play a socially organizing role along with other arts. (2) That our music should utilize all technical and formal attainments of modern music in the West in order to achieve the fullest musical expression and the greatest technical mastery. (3) That the absorption of serious Western music must be effected by means of a critical selection of products of practical value. Tendencies that are purely esthetical and decadent are strongly opposed by the Association. . . . With these reservations, contemporary music may become a powerful factor of Socialist culture and a fitting medium of self-expression of the class responsible for that culture. (From the Declaration of Aims of the Association for Contemporary Music published in S. Korev, *Disposition of Class Forces on the Musical Front*, Moscow, 1930)

8 JANUARY 1926

Émile PALADILHE, French composer and educator who began his musical career as a child prodigy amazingly endowed by the external gifts of absolute pitch, retentive memory, and precocious facility for composition, won the Prix de Rome at the age of sixteen, and then lapsed into didactic mediocrity and became an unimaginative professor at the Paris Conservatory, dies in Paris at the unenviable age of 81.

15 JANUARY 1926

Enrico TOSELLI, Italian composer of the celebrated *Serenade*, by which he is solely remembered, dies in Florence at the age of 42.

16 JANUARY 1926

Dĕduv Odkaz (Old Man's Bequest), opera in three acts by the Czech composer Vítězslav NOVÁK, dealing with a village fiddler married to a wood nymph who flees from him after he offends her chastity, but endows him with a charismatic virtuosity on the violin so that he becomes famous, is produced in Brno.

16 JANUARY 1926

Passionnément, musical comedy by André MESSAGER dealing with an American lady who finds romance in Paris, divorces her uninteresting American husband, and marries a passionate Frenchman, is produced in Paris.

30 JANUARY 1926

The Prefect of Police in Paris decrees a ban on jazzing up the *Marseillaise* by dance hall bands.

30 JANUARY 1926

Aeroplane, symphonic movement by the American composer Emerson WHITHORNE, the first orchestral composition on an aeronautical subject, arranged from his piano piece of the same title written in 1921, is performed for the first time anywhere in Birmingham, England, Adrian Boult conducting.

31 JANUARY 1926

Concerto Italiano, for violin and orchestra, by Mario CASTELNUOVO-TEDESCO, is performed for the first time in Rome.

5 FEBRUARY 1926

André GEDALGE, French theorist and pedagogue, author of the prestigious *Traité de fugue,* dies in Paris at the age of 69.

6 FEBRUARY 1926

Quodlibet, eine Unterhaltungsmusik by Kurt WEILL, a modern counterpart of the medieval improvisatory quodlibet (literally, "what pleases"), and in this sense constituting true *Unterhaltung* (entertainment), is performed for the first time in Coburg, Germany, signalizing a significant advance in the generic concept of *Gebrauchsmusik* (utilitarian music).

10 FEBRUARY 1926

Salinieki (The Islanders), patriotic opera in four acts by the Latvian composer Alfred KANIŅŠ, to a Latvian libretto, is performed for the first time in Riga. (A revised version of the opera, retitled *Dzimtenes Atmoda,* i.e., *The Awakening of Fatherland,* was produced in Riga on 9 September 1926. Loewenberg, in his *Annals of Opera,* gives a much later date, 9 September 1933, as that of the première.)

11 FEBRUARY 1926

Mr. Pepys, ballad-opera in three acts by the English composer Martin SHAW, to a libretto based on the famous 17th-century diary of Samuel Pepys, is produced in London.

13 FEBRUARY 1926

Arthur HONEGGER conducts at the Monte Carlo Opéra the first performance of his three-act opera *Judith,* "opéra sérieux" expanded from the incidental music he wrote for a play by René Morax, first performed nine months and two days before.

16 FEBRUARY 1926

Concertino for piano, two violins, viola, clarinet, bassoon and horn by Leoš JANÁČEK, completed by him on 29 April 1925 at the age of seventy, in four contrasting movements, written in a modernistic manner, without key signatures, and yet tonally gravid, marked by brusque asymmetric rhythms and an artful intervalic nutation in heterotonal counterpoint, accoutred in audacious dissonances, and permeated by national Moravian melorhythms, is performed for the first time in Brno.

19 FEBRUARY 1926

Skyscrapers, "ballet of modern American life" by the 49-year-old American composer John Alden CARPENTER, polyrhythmically reflecting in agitated motion the sights and sounds of megalopolitan New York City, vibrating in nervous foxtrot time, seeking oblivion in narcoleptic Broadway ballads, submerging in the ceaseless rattle of subways and puffing flivvers, scored for a large orchestra with the inclusion of such vernacular instruments as banjo and saxophones, is performed for the first time by the Metropolitan Opera Company in New York.

25 FEBRUARY 1926

Die zehn Küsse (Ten Kisses), "merry, opera" in four acts by the 53-year-old German composer Bernhard SEKLES, after Hans Christian Andersen's tale *Svinedrengen (Swineherd),* is produced in Frankfurt.

28 FEBRUARY 1926

Concerto for cello and wind instruments by Jacques IBERT is performed for the first time in Paris.

3 MARCH 1926

Général d'Amour, operetta in a pseudo-Parisian manner by the Austrian composer Julius BITTNER, is produced in Vienna.

13 MARCH 1926

Saturday's Child, "an episode in color" for mezzo-soprano, tenor and chamber orchestra by the 41-year-old American composer Emerson WHITHORNE, to the texts from *Color* by the Negro poet Countee Cullen, with reference to the nursery rhyme predicting children's careers according to the day of the week of their births ("Saturday's child works hard for its living"), with melorhythmic materials freely fashioned from Negro spirituals, ragtime and the Blues, is performed for the first time at a concert given by the League of Composers in New York.

17 MARCH 1926

The Girl Friend, musical comedy by Richard RODGERS, in which a gambler's attempt to fix a bicycle race is foiled by a prime contestant whose rectitude receives its award when he wins first prize and the heart of his favorite girl, featuring besides the title song, an ingratiating ballad *The Blue Room*, is produced in New York.

20 MARCH 1926

La Bella e il Mostro, fairy tale opera by the 41-year-old Italian composer Luigi FERRARI-TRECATE, to the age-old story of the dramatic confrontation between a beauty and an ostensible monster (who is transmuted into an aristocratic youth as soon as she pledges her love for him), is produced at La Scala, Milan.

21 MARCH 1926

Foules, symphonic poem by the 26-year-old French composer Pierre Octave FERROUD, marked by a systematic application of the scale in alternating tones and semitones to represent an animated movement of city crowds, is performed for the first time in Paris.

24 MARCH 1926

Tre Commedie goldoniane, three one-act operas by Gian Francesco MALIPIERO, to plays by Goldoni: *La bottega da Caffè, Sior Todaro Brontolon* and *Le Baruffe Chiozzotte*, evoking the atmosphere of old Venice, with considerable additions and alterations made by Malipiero in the original texts, and making liberal use of *parlando*, are performed for the first time anywhere in Darmstadt.

26 MARCH 1926

Die Zirkusprinzessin, operetta by Emmerich KÁLMÁN, is produced in Vienna.

26 MARCH 1926

Franz KNEISEL, Rumanian-born violinist, who organized in 1885 the prestigious Kneisel Quartet responsible for first performances of numerous works by European and American composers, dies in New York at the age of 61.

27 MARCH 1926

Der Protagonist, one-act opera by Kurt WEILL, in which the protagonist in a drama being performed at a duke's palace in Elizabethan England kills the leading actress out of jealousy while the spectators admire the realism of the acting, is staged for the first time in Dresden.

3 APRIL 1926

Rapsodie grecque for piano and orchestra by the Greek composer Manolis KALOMIRIS, orchestrated by Gabriel Pierné is performed for the first time in Paris, Pierné conducting.

6 APRIL 1926

Tamar Tsbieri (Perfidious Tamar,) opera in three acts by the 63-year-old Georgian composer Meliton BAL-ANTCHIVADZE, in which an imperious 17th-century Georgian queen throws a reluctant young folk poet, who rejects her advances, into a dungeon, and then takes poison, is produced in Tiflis.

8 APRIL 1926

Third Symphony by the Finnish composer Leevi MADETOJA (1887–1947), conceived in a Sibelian manner, with folklike melodies enveloped in bleakly static harmonies, is performed for the first time in Helsinki.

9 APRIL 1926

Amériques, symphonic poem by the French-American composer Edgar VARÈSE, titled in plural to embrace all Americas, abstract and concrete, present and future, scored for a huge orchestra and set in dissonant harmonic counterpoint built of functional thematic molecules, proceeding by successive crystallizations in the sonorous mass of organized sound, is performed for the first time anywhere by the Philadelphia Orchestra, Leopold Stokowski conducting.

10 APRIL 1926

Die Opferung des Gefangenen (The Sacrifice of the Captive), sectarian drama from Aztec life for voices and dance in one act by the learned Austrian composer Egon WELLESZ, is produced in Cologne.

15 APRIL 1926

Pageant of P. T. Barnum, symphonic suite by Douglas MOORE, delineating Barnum's fantastically successful career as promoter of "the greatest show on earth," in five illustrative episodes—(1) *A Boyhood at Bethel*; (2) *Joyce Heth, 161-year-old Negress*; (3) *General and Mrs. Tom Thumb*, in the rhythm of a midget march; (4) *Jenny Lind*, with the flute reaching high A for which Jenny Lind was famous; (5) *Circus Parade*—is performed for the first time by the Cleveland Orchestra.

22 APRIL 1926

Four months after the production of Alban BERG's sensational opera *Wozzeck*, another *Wozzeck* to the same play by Büchner, composed independently and synchronously by Manfred GURLITT, comprising 18 scenes with an epilogue and couched in a modernistic but not radically atonal style, is produced in Bremen.

24 APRIL 1926

Das Lied der Nacht, opera by Hans GÁL, is produced in Breslau.

25 APRIL 1926

PUCCINI's three-act opera *Turandot*, left unfinished at his death, completed by Franco Alfano who added the last duet and the brief final scene, dealing with a cruelly beautiful Chinese princess who, to avenge the abusive treatment of her ancestress at the hands of male invaders, rules that all suitors unable to solve the three riddles of her invention ("What is it that is born at night and dies during the day?"—*Hope*; "What is it that blazes like a fever and grows cold at death?"—*Blood*; "What is the ice that sets you on fire?"—*Turandot*) are to be executed, but who is herself challenged by a heroically astute youth to guess his name after he has successfully answered the riddles, replies "*Amore*" and succumbs to his charms, to a score filled with ultra-modernistic usages, such as frank bitonalities, concatenations of unresolved discords, angularly atonal melodic deviations and asymmetric rhythms, is performed for the first time at La Scala, Milan, conducted by Arturo Toscanini, up to the last measure written by Puccini himself, omitting Alfano's ending.

29 APRIL 1926

Castle Agrazant, opera in three acts by the American composer Ralph LYFORD (1882–1927), to his own libretto dealing with a noble crusader whose beautiful wife is forcibly abducted with vile intent by a former suitor, but who returns to his castle from his holy mission disguised as a monkish minstrel and slays the blackguard, the bride herself being mortally wounded when she tries to intervene and dies as he sings in Wagneromimic tones of the land of eternal sunshine, is produced in Cincinnati under the composer's direction and at a cost of $15,000 raised by the American Opera Foundation there.

4 MAY 1926

La Mandragola, opera in three acts by the 31-year-old Italian composer Mario CASTELNUOVO-TEDESCO, to a libretto fashioned from a story by Machiavelli wherein a licentious bravo seduces a pudent, prudent matron by immobilizing her with a potent potion of narcotic mandragora administered to her under the pretext that it would cure her barrenness, is produced in Venice.

4 MAY 1926

Romeo and Juliet, the first ballet by the 20-year-old English composer Constant LAMBERT, is produced by Diaghilev's Ballet Russe in Monte Carlo.

7 MAY 1926

Sancta Civitas, oratorio by Ralph VAUGHAN WILLIAMS, to a text from the Revelation of St. John, scored for tenor, baritone, mixed chorus, semi-chorus and distant chorus, is performed for the first time in Oxford.

7 MAY 1926

Les Malheurs d'Orphée, short opera by Darius MILHAUD, in three minuscule acts, with Orpheus pictured as "having long hair and wearing a sheepskin cloak" and Eurydice presented as a "jeune Bohémienne," is performed for the first time anywhere in Brussels.

12 MAY 1926

The Leningrad Philharmonic, under the direction of Nikolai Malko, gives the first performance of the *First Symphony*, in F minor, by the 19-year-old Soviet composer Dmitri SHOSTAKOVICH, written by him as his graduation work at the Leningrad Conservatory in 1925, and marked by motoric vivacity, contemplative lyricism and relentless rhythmic drive within a classical consistency of formal structures, in four movements:

(1) *Moderato*, opening with a muted trumpet solo, gradually gathering momentum and developing to a high climax before returning to the initial lyric sentiment; (2) *Allegretto*, an animated succession of thematically related motives; (3) *Lento*, a reflective elegy with instrumental solos against the shimmer-

ing strings; (4) *Allegro molto* prefaced by a slow meditation, accumulating latent energy and pressing sonorously towards an electrically charged finale.

(On the same program, a *March of the Orient* for large orchestra by scientifically-minded Joseph SCHILLINGER, and a symphonic cantata *The Twelve* by Julia WEISSBERG, wife of Rimsky-Korsakov's son Andrei, to the poem by Alexander Blok likening a patrol of twelve Red Army soldiers to twelve apostles, were performed.)

A bright outstanding creative talent. There is a great deal of imagination and invention in his music. . . . His *First Symphony* is accepted as graduation work for a diploma. (From the transcript of remarks adjudging Shostakovich's qualifications for graduation made in 1926 by Alexander Glazunov, Director of the Leningrad Conservatory of Music)

15 MAY 1926

Four symphonic pieces by the Greek composer Petro PETRIDIS based on authentic Greek melorhythms, *Danse de Kleftes*, *Prélude de Zemfira*, *Berceuse* and *Le petit vaisseau*, are performed for the first time at the Concerts Colonne in Paris, Gabriel Pierné conducting.

20 MAY 1926

Leonora Christina, opera in four acts to a Danish libretto by the 41-year-old Danish composer of German-Jewish origin Siegfried SALOMON, dealing with the tragic seventeenth-century Danish princess who spent twenty-two years in the Blue Tower of the Copenhagen Prison as wife of the traitor Count Ulfelt, is produced in Copenhagen.

23 MAY 1926

Eighth Symphony in A major by Nicolai MIASKOVSKY, conceived as an objective reflection of Russian life and containing melorhythmic formations peculiar to Russian folksongs of the Volga region, in four movements, *Andante*, *Allegro risoluto e con spirito*, *Adagio* and *Allegro deciso* (completed on 29 June 1925) is performed for the first time in Moscow.

23 MAY 1926

Hypatia, opera in three acts by the 54-year-old Italian composer Roffredo CAETANI, dealing with the death on the Ides of March in A.D. 415 of the philosopher and astronomer Hypatia (370–415), who was torn limb from limb by a mob of Christian fanatics instigated by Bishop Cyril of Alexandria, is performed for the first time, in a German translation of the original Italian libretto, in Weimar.

26 MAY 1926

La Pastorale, ballet by Georges AURIC, to a scenario in which a messenger boy falls asleep after a swim and is caught in the camera-grinding turmoil when a cinema company moves in, with a happy ending provided by a starlet who rides off with him on his bicycle, is produced by Diaghilev's Ballet Russe in Paris.

27 MAY 1926

Alexandre TANSMAN, 28-year-old Parisianized Polish composer, plays with the Koussevitzky Orchestra in Paris the first performance of his *First Piano Concerto,* in four movements, *Allegro molto, Lento, Intermezzo* and *Finale,* written in a neo-classical form, with harmonies enhanced by pandiatonic quartal excrescences and bitonal superimpositions on resonantly spaced triadic basses, and distinguished by authentically inflected Polish dance melorhythms. (The date 27 May 1925 given in previous editions of *Music Since 1900* is in error.)

29 MAY 1926

Masquerade, "American rhapsody for orchestra" by the 30-year-old American composer Carl MCKINLEY, is performed for the first time at the Chicago North Shore Festival.

3 JUNE 1926

Préface au Livre de Vie, the initial fragment of the pantheistic *Livre de Vie* by the Russian expatriate Nicolas OBOUHOV, scored for orchestra, two pianos and four soloists, making use of shrieking and hissing sounds to express religious ecstasy, is performed for the first time in public, at a Koussevitzky concert in Paris, with the composer and Nicolas Slonimsky playing the piano parts.

"I suggest that, for your own safety, you'd better put up a sign, 'I am not the composer.'" (A remark made to Nicolas Slonimsky at the concert)

5 JUNE 1926

A century has passed since the death in London of the protagonist of German operatic romanticism, Carl Maria von WEBER.

11 JUNE 1926

Orphée, lyric mimodrama in three acts by ROGER-DUCASSE, written in 1913, depicting the classical story of the divine singer, culminating in the horrifying spectacle of the Bacchantes tearing his body limb from limb when he refuses to satisfy their carnal desires (in the final scene his head floats in the water on a luminous lyre), the score adhering to the principle of identifying leading motives in a synthetic Wagnerian manner, is performed for the first time at the Paris Opéra. (The first concert performance of *Orphée* took place on 31 January 1914, in St. Petersburg, at one of Siloti's concerts.)

18 JUNE 1926

The Fourth Festival of the International Society for Contemporary Music opens in Zürich with the performances of two modern oratorios: Zoltán KODÁLY's *Psalmus Hungaricus* and Arthur HONEGGER's *King David.*

19 JUNE 1926

Ballet Mécanique by the 25-year-old Parisian-American avant-garde composer George ANTHEIL, originally written for an abstract motion picture by Léger, scored for eight pianos, a player piano and assorted percussion, is presented for the first time anywhere in Paris, Vladimir Golschmann conducting, on the same program with the first performance of his unassumingly tonal, triadically nurtured, academically titled *Symphony in F.*

If America has given or is to give anything to general esthetics, it is presumably an esthetic of machinery. . . . Antheil has made a beginning; that is in writing music that couldn't have been written before. His musical world is a world of steel bars, not of old stone and ivy. With the performance of the *Ballet Mécanique* one can conceive the possibility of organizing the sounds of a factory, let us say, of boiler plate or any other clangorous noisiness, the actual sounds of the labor, the various tones of the grindings, according to the needs of the work. (Ezra Pound, *George Antheil and Harmony,* 1927)

19 JUNE 1926

At the second concert of the Fourth Festival of the International Society for Contemporary Music in Zürich the following program of chamber music is presented:

String Trio by the Swiss composer Walther GEISER, cast in a neo-Baroque idiom; Arnold SCHOENBERG's *Quintet,* op. 26, for flute, oboe, clarinet, bassoon and horn (began on 21 April 1923 and completed on 26 July 1924), hard on untutored ears because here the relentless logic of the method of composition with 12 tones attains its intellectual perfection; and *String Quartet* making use of authentic Indian themes by the American composer Frederick JACOBI.

19 JUNE 1926

Król Roger, opera in three acts by Karol SZYMANOWSKI, dealing with the 12th-century Norman king of Italy, and involving the participation of supernatural forces in the historic events, set to an expansively sonorous lyrico-dramatic score rich in dissonant content, is produced in Warsaw.

21 JUNE 1926

At the Fourth Festival of the International Society for Contemporary Music in Zürich, two choral works are given:

Le Miroir de Jésus, a fervently religious work in an austere neo-medieval setting by the French composer André CAPLET commemorating his death 14 months before; *Litanies* by the Czech composer Felix PETYREK, scored for a boys' chorus, singing in their low register, accompanied by two trumpets, two harps and percussion.

22 JUNE 1926

At the Fourth Festival of the International Society for Contemporary Music in Zürich the following program of orchestral music is given:

World première of *Portsmouth Point,* pictorial overture by William WALTON, inspired by an 18th-century print of Thomas Rowlandson representing the quayside of Portsmouth in a state of great animation in varied modalities, with a finale in an unpigmented key of C; *Concerto for Orchestra* by Paul HINDEMITH, in a neo-classical idiom revitalized by propulsive rhythm; *Partita* for piano and orchestra in a neo-baroque manner, by Alfredo CASELLA; the long, and grandiose *Fifth Symphony* for violin, trumpet and orchestra by the Swiss composer Ernst LÉVY, written in an obsolescent but erudite idiom; *Foules,* symphonic movement by the French composer Pierre Octave FERROUD, couched in a utilitarian impressionistic style; and *Danse de la Sorcière,* a ballet suite in attractive quartal harmonies by the Parisian-Polish composer Alexandre TANSMAN.

23 JUNE 1926

At the Fourth Festival of the International Society for Contemporary Music in Zürich the following program is presented:

Fourth Piano Sonata, in C minor, in three movements, by the Russian romanticist Nicolai MIASKOVSKY; *Septet* for soprano, flute, piano and strings written in a Ravelesque manner by the Parisian Belgian music critic and composer Arthur HOERÉE; the charismatic *Fünf Stücke für Orchester* op. 10, by the Viennese master Anton von WEBERN, composed in 1911–1913, consisting of five miniatures containing only 12 + 14 + 11 1/2 + 6 1/3 + 32 = 75 5/6 measures, scored for most uncommon instrumental combinations, including a harmonium, a mandolin, a guitar, sheep bells besides the ordinary orchestral instruments, written in a pointillistic manner, each instrument playing mostly alone, all essence of counterpoint, sequence or harmony being practically eliminated, while the changing timbres acquire a new melodic significance (Schoenberg writes about this "timbre-melody": "subtle, indeed, are the senses that can differentiate between these elements; fine is the mind that is capable of finding pleasure in things so recondite"); *Concerto* by the 26-year-old German composer Kurt WEILL, for violin, woodwinds, doublebass and percussion in three neo-classical movements: (1) *Andante con moto,* with the violin solo of an atonal design, sparked by asymmetrical rhythms and agitated dissonant counterpoint; (2) *Notturno-Cadenza-Serenata,* an unromantic interlude replete with syncopated pulsations; (3) *Allegro,* a spirited tarantella, coming to an end with dominant-tonic postscripts in the timpani; and *Pastorale and March,* set in dispirited dissonant counterpoint, by the Czech composer Hans KRÁSA.

29 JUNE 1926

Sinfonietta by Leoš JANÁČEK, Czech national composer, written by him at the age of 72, in five movements, originally subtitled *Fanfares, The City, The Cloister of the Empress, The Street* and *City Hall* (the subtitles were removed in the published edition), a colorful cinquefoil of illustrative musical vignettes perfused by whole-tone scales and asymmetrical rhythms, is performed for the first time in Prague under the title *Sokol-Sinfonietta,* at a festive concert in honor of the Czechoslovak Sokol (Eagle) Youth Society.

1 JULY 1926

Hans Werner HENZE, German composer of symbolistically realistic stage works and instrumental pieces couched in a modern idiom within a free network of rational dissonances, is born in Gütersloh.

4 JULY 1926

A century has passed since the birth in Lawrenceville, Pennsylvania, on the 50th anniversary of the Declaration of Independence, of Stephen Collins FOSTER, creator of songs glorifying in words and music the spirit of antebellum America, its masculine men, its lovely women and its contented Negro slaves.

17 JULY 1926

First Symphony by the 29-year-old Danish composer Knudaage RIISAGER, in three movements, is performed for the first time in Copenhagen.

23 JULY 1926

Ollantay, grand opera by the Argentine composer Constantino GAITO, dealing with the heroic rebel Ollantay who leads a patriotic struggle against the tyrannical king of the Incas whose daughter he adores, is produced at the Teatro Colón in Buenos Aires.

25 JULY 1926

The SPHÄROPHON, electronic musical instrument constructed by Jörg MAGER and named with reference to the mystical "music of the spheres," is demonstrated for the first time at the Donaueschingen Festival of New Music.

30 JULY 1926

At the Sesquicentennial International Exposition in Philadelphia, the first complete performance is given of the orchestral suite *New York Days and Nights* by Emerson WHITHORNE (originally written for piano and performed at the First Festival of the International Society for Contemporary Music in Salzburg on 5 August 1923), in five movements:

(1) *On the Ferry,* an early morning scene picturing a daily voyage to Manhattan from across the East River in clangily dissonant harmonies; (2) *The Chimes of Saint Patrick,* with the bell sonorities represented by a progression of parallel minor ninth-chords, the organ intoning the melody of *Dies Irae;* (3) *Pell Street (Chinatown),* set in the pentatonic scale making use of an authentic old Chinese tune *The Fifteen Bunches of Blossoms;* (4) *A Greenwich Village Tragedy,* depicting an idyllic love affair beginning *fervente* and *con esaltazione* in rhapsodically expansive tones and ending on a hateful discord in grindingly incompatible frictional disharmonies; (5) *Times Square,* megalopolitan apotheosis of the Great White Way with its electric signs and the mass of moving flivvers and flappers, the tumult illustrated by chromatic rows of dominant seventh-chords on a pedal tone. (A partial performance, of the 2nd, 3rd and 5th movements, was given in Paris on 24 June 1923.)

6 AUGUST 1926

The first "100% sound motion picture," *Don Juan,* made by the Vitaphone Company and featuring Henry HADLEY, American composer and conductor, leading the New York Philharmonic Orchestra, is shown for the first time in New York City. (An invitation performance was given at the Warner Theater, New York, on 5 August 1926.)

15 SEPTEMBER 1926

Jelly Roll MORTON and his RED HOT PEPPERS (George Mitchell, cornet; Kid Ory, trombone; Omer Simeon, clarinet; Johnny St. Cyr, banjo; John Lindsay, bass; Andrew Hilaire, drums) hold their first recording session in Chicago for R.C.A. Victor, cutting among other pieces their famous *Black Bottom Stomp,* whose rollicking swing beat artfully conceals the total absence of the tonic chord in the entire opening section.

18 SEPTEMBER 1926

Deep River, "native opera with jazz" by the American composer W. Franke HARLING, in three acts focusing on a New Orleans ball in 1830, at which a lovely quadroon girl tries to bewitch a wealthy plantation owner with the aid of a voodoo amulet, set to a Puccinian score filled with pseudo-exotic effusions, is produced for the first time anywhere at Lancaster, Pennsylvania.

19 SEPTEMBER 1926

Sturmvogel, opera by the Germanized Norwegian composer Gerhard SCHJELDERUP, is produced in Schwerin.

20 SEPTEMBER 1926

Corimayo, grand opera by the Argentine composer Enrique CASELLA to a libretto from the time of the Incas is produced at the Teatro Colón in Buenos Aires.

1 OCTOBER 1926

The German Post Office issues stamps with portraits of Bach at 50 pfennigs and of Beethoven at 20 pfennigs.

8 OCTOBER 1926

First Piano Concerto by Ernst TOCH, in three movements, *Allegro, Adagio, Rondo disturbato*, set in a modernistic and richly rhythmical style in fluid tonality, is performed for the first time in Düsseldorf.

15 OCTOBER 1926

The Leper's Flute, one-act opera by the English composer Ernest BRYSON, to a grim South African tale in which a flutist avenges himself on his perfidious fiancée through whose machinations he has been placed in a leprosarium by passing a leprosy-riddled flute to her new flutist lover, resulting in her contamination through labial contact in defiance of medical opinion that leprosy is not a contagious disease, set to music in a coloristic manner of abecedarian impressionism containing a plethora of fluvial flute airs, is performed for the first time in Glasgow. (A concert performance of the work was given in the spring of 1926 at Golder's Green Hippodrome in London.)

16 OCTOBER 1926

Háry János, opera by Zoltán KODÁLY, relating in a brilliant musicorama the imaginary exploits of a fabulous Hungarian folk liar whose wild tales of royal love and martial glory are introduced by a dynamic sneeze, a traditional Hungarian indication that the tale to follow is absolutely true, illustrated by a chromatic ascension in the woodwinds and a sternutatory glissando in the horns, is performed for the first time in Budapest.

20 OCTOBER 1926

Entente Cordiale, a "post-war comedy" by England's suffragette composer Ethel SMYTH, dealing with a group of British soldiers taking leave of France, one of whom gets married to a French girl through a linguistic misunderstanding when he asks for a poule instead of a poulet, the entente cordiale being restored when a horde of British wives descend on the port of disembarcation to claim their lawful husbands, is produced in Bristol.

21 OCTOBER 1926

Concerto for flute and orchestra by the prime Danish composer Carl NIELSEN, in two movements: *Allegro Moderato* and quadripartite *Allegretto* (with an intervening *Adagio* and the final *Tempo di marcia*), is performed for the first time in Paris, 20 days after the completion of the score. (Nielsen arranged another ending after this first

performance, and the revised score was first heard in Oslo on 9 November 1926.)

24 OCTOBER 1926

Suite Intertonal in four movements by the 46-year-old Catalan composer Jaime PAHISSA, written (with the exception of the third movement) according to the "intertonal" system of pure "di-sonancy" (di-sonant, twice-sounded), is performed for the first time by the Casals Orchestra in Barcelona.

28 OCTOBER 1926

Third Symphony by the 32-year-old Dutch composer Willem PIJPER in four movements—a persistently rhythmic *Allegro*, an atonally attenuated *Molto Adagio*, a rustically saltatory *Scherzo* and a vigorously polyrhythmic *Molto Allegro*—written in a somberly heroic mood, the philosophical intent summarized in the appended motto from the Aeneid, "Flectere si neque superos, Acheronta movebo," conceding the inability to deflect the gods, but trying instead to move the Acheron, thematically symbolized by aggressive descending fourths harmonically amalgamated into quartal harmonies and further enriched by sonorous bitonalities, is performed for the first time by the Concergebouw Orchestra in Amsterdam, Pierre Monteux, to whom the score is dedicated, conducting.

29 OCTOBER 1926

Tzigane, symphonic poem by the Parisian-Rumanian composer Filip LAZAR, based on Gypsy melorhythms of Southeast Europe, is performed for the first time by the Boston Symphony Orchestra, Serge Koussevitzky conducting.

1 NOVEMBER 1926

Der Krämerspiegel, a self-satirizing musical pastiche written for the amusement of friends by Richard STRAUSS, in which themes and phrases from his symphonic and operatic works collide and recoil in witty counterpoint, to a set of texts attacking various music publishers for their mercenary attitude towards composers (hence the title, *A Mirror for Merchants*), is performed for the first time at a semi-private gathering in Berlin.

5 NOVEMBER 1926

Eighteen days before his 50th birthday Manuel DE FALLA conducts in Barcelona the first performance of his neo-classical *Concerto* for harpsichord, flute, oboe, clarinet, violin and cello, with Wanda Landowska at whose suggestion the work was written and to whom the score is dedicated taking part at the harpsichord, in three movements:

(1) *Allegro*, in a vigorous Baroque manner with asymmetrically propulsive rhythms in a laconic sonata form; (2) *Lento (giubiloso ed energico)*, containing a long old-style cadenza for the harpsichord; (3) *Vivace (flessibile, scherzando)*, in the dual Spanish meters of 3/4 and 6/8, proceeding relentlessly toward a sonorous conclusion in D major.

8 NOVEMBER 1926

Oh Kay, musical comedy by George GERSHWIN, which includes the celebrated tunes *Clap Yo' Hands* and *Do, Do,*

Do, What You Done, Done, Done, Before, Baby, is produced in New York.

9 NOVEMBER 1926

Cardillac, opera in three acts by Paul HINDEMITH, after the horrendous tale of E. T. A. Hoffman, dealing with an insanely possessive Paris goldsmith named Cardillac who murders his customers in order to get back the jewels he sold them, until his daughter's fiancé buys a necklace for her and valiantly resists Cardillac's attempt to murder him too, so that a mob gathers and slays the chronic slayer, set to music in a neo-classical form of 18 discrete numbers (indicating a rejection of the Wagnerian esthetic of "thorough composition"), written in a satirically dissonant polyphonic idiom, is produced at the Dresden Opera, a week before Hindemith's 31st birthday.

11 NOVEMBER 1926

Winona, three-act opera by the 44-year-old Italian-born American composer Alberto BIMBONI, dealing with the dramatic peripeteia of an Indian girl named Winona (which means first-born) who, thwarted by the stern chief Red Hat in her love for a brave youth from another tribe, in despair jumps from a cliff into a lake below, the score replete with genuine Indian motifs, is produced in Portland, Oregon, the composer conducting.

13 NOVEMBER 1926

Two new works by Soviet composers are performed for the first time in Leningrad: *Symphony in F minor* by the 24-year-old Vissarion SHEBALIN and *Revolutionary Episode,* symphonic poem by the 27-year-old Lev KNIPPER.

14 NOVEMBER 1926

Der Golem, music drama in three acts by the self-Germanized English-born composer Eugen D'ALBERT, to a fantastic tale of a 17th-century rabbi of Prague, who builds with the aid of black magic an android figure (called a Golem in Hebrew folklore), and in his exultation and pride of God-like powers, tells his daughter to teach him to express himself in an artificial language sung syllabically in consecutive tritones and whole-tone scales, with a tragic dénouement when she dies of a ghostly infection and the Golem is turned into stone, is performed for the first time in Frankfurt.

15 NOVEMBER 1926

The first chain broadcast over the newly organized National Broadcasting Company network is inaugurated in New York, with a concert by the New York Symphony Orchestra conducted by Walter DAMROSCH, the New York Oratorio Society led by Albert STOESSEL, and the Goldman Band directed by its founder Edwin Franko GOLDMAN.

16 NOVEMBER 1926

Delitto e castigo, opera in three acts by the 47-year-old Italian composer Arrigo PEDROLLO, after Dostoyevsky's novel *Crime and Punishment,* written in the melodramatic style of the Italian Verismo, is produced in Milan.

27 NOVEMBER 1926

The Miraculous Mandarin, pantomime by Béla BARTÓK, composed in 1918, dealing with a prostitute who lures an inexhaustible Chinese *homo libidinus* into a den of iniquity where he is set upon by her accomplices, robbed, suffocated by cushions, thrice stabbed by a rusty knife and hanged from a collapsible lamp hook, but rebounds each time with renewed chromatic inturgescence and tremulous tremolos in artfully copulated intussusceptions in dissonant double counterpoint, with the emphasis on the angst-ridden intervals of the tritone and major sevenths, in a relentlessly monistic élan, culminating in a series of monstrous orgasms *fortissimo,* followed by a labile sonic detumescence in trombones and strings glissando, is performed for the first time in Cologne. (An orchestral suite extracted from the score was first performed on 1 April 1927 by the Cincinnati Symphony Orchestra under the direction of Fritz Reiner.)

27 NOVEMBER 1926

The Creation, a "Negro Sermon" for voice, clarinet, flute, bassoon, horn, trumpet, percussion, viola and piano, by the Russian-born American composer Louis GRUENBERG, to the text by James Weldon Johnson, presenting an ingenuous picture of the Creator ("I'm lonely, I'll make me a world"), set to music in an intellectualized jazz idiom, arranged in euphonious dissonant harmonies, is performed for the first time at a concert of the League of Composers in New York.

27 NOVEMBER 1926

Don Pistacchio, a newly-exhumed comic opera by Luigi CHERUBINI, is produced for the first time in Dresden.

28 NOVEMBER 1926

Darker America, by the American Negro composer William Grant STILL, a litany of racial sorrow expressed in the melodious modalities of Negro spirituals, is performed for the first time in New York.

29 NOVEMBER 1926

La Tisseuse d'Orties, lyric drama in four acts by the Swiss composer Gustave DORET, wherein the concubine of a royal prince usurps the throne during his absence and denounces him upon his return, with a mystical dénouement when a beauteous webster of polygamous apetalous urticaceous flower tissues rescues him after he assents to submit to the purgatory of carnal love, is produced at the Opéra-Comique in Paris during Doret's brief tenure of its directorate.

29 NOVEMBER 1926

The municipal authorities of Prague ban further performances of Alban BERG's opera *Wozzeck* to forestall the repetition of disturbances that attended the first Prague performance of the Czech version of the opera on 11 November 1926.

30 NOVEMBER 1926

The Desert Song, operetta in two acts by Sigmund ROMBERG, set in the locale of the Riff War in North Africa in 1925, wherein a mustachioed Riff chieftain clandestinely romances with a highborn French beauty, whom he eventually weds as war actions subside, containing a number of rousing tunes, among them the swashbuckling *Riff Song,* the masculine *Sabre Song* and the rhapsodic title song, is produced in New York City.

3 DECEMBER 1926

The Triumph of Neptune, "English pantomime in ten tableaux" by Lord BERNERS, to a scenario by Sacheverell Sitwell, with Britannia dancing the hornpipe, shipwrecks occurring to the accompaniment of a wind machine and a battery of drums, and a suddenly materialized inebriated singer drunkenly intoning *The Last Rose of Summer* culminating in a pandiatonically white C-major apotheosis of Neptune, is produced in London.

5 DECEMBER 1926

Diptyque méditeranéen by Vincent D'INDY, a symphonic impression of sunrise and sunset on the Mediterranean, is performed for the first time in Paris.

8 DECEMBER 1926

A Witch of Salem, one-act opera by Charles Wakefield CADMAN, to a story of the Puritan struggle against the prevalence of witches in Salem of 1682, in which a local maiden accuses her love rival of witchcraft on the evidence of a blood-red cross on her breast, but confesses her perjury as the other is brought to the gallows, and is stoned to death by the infuriated populace cheated of the hanging spectacle, written in a melodious and harmonious style with a considerable display of dramatic chromatic progressions of diminished seventh-chords, is produced by the Chicago Civic Opera Company.

9 DECEMBER 1926

Darius MILHAUD plays the piano part in the world première of his hedonistic piece of sophisticated urban music *Le Carnaval d'Aix* on themes from his ballet *Salade* (he was born in Aix-en-Provence), with the New York Philharmonic, Willem Mengelberg conducting.

15 DECEMBER 1926

Chôros No. 10 by Heitor VILLA-LOBOS, for mixed chorus and orchestra, subtitled *Rasga o Coracão,* is performed for the first time in Rio de Janeiro.

18 DECEMBER 1926

Věc Makropulos, opera in three acts by the 72-year-old grandmaster of modern Czech music, Leoš JANÁČEK (begun 11 November 1923 and completed 12 November 1925) after a play by Čapek, *The Makropulos Affair,* centering on a litigation involving Elina Makropulos, 342 years of age, whose father, the court alchemist to the Emperor Rudolf II, gave her an elixir of indefinite longevity, and who became a famous singer in the 20th century, set to a musical score of pointed modernity in its thematic brevity, rhythmic asymmetry and dramatic precipitation, is performed for the first time in Brno.

26 DECEMBER 1926

Tapiola, symphonic poem by Jean SIBELIUS (composed between March and May 1926), the title relating to the forest god of Finnish demonology, Tapio, set in the somber and austere tones of Nordland, somnolent but dreaming savage dreams within a monothematic structure in which variety is achieved by a constant fluctuation of instrumental colors and occasional insertions of whole-tone passages, culminating in a chromatic rise in a 56-bar crescendo of cumulative string sonorities, is performed for the first time anywhere as a commissioned work by Walter Damrosch and the New York Symphony Society Orchestra.

1927

8 JANUARY 1927

Penthesilea, one-act melodrama by Othmar SCHOECK, after Kleist's play wherein the Amazon queen captured by Achilles is engaged in a game of hostile passion with him and after Achilles is slain to the sound of an excurciatingly dissonant polychord, falls dead on his body while secundal disharmonies clash, is performed for the first time in Dresden.

8 JANUARY 1927

The first performance is given in Vienna by the Kolisch String Quartet of *Lyrische Suite* by Alban BERG, written in a distinctive individual style, wherein the Schoenbergian method of 12-tone composition is applied in alternation with non-dodecaphonic, tonal and even triadic procedures, melodically and harmonically anchored on additive intervalic complexes of fourths and tritones summing up to major sevenths, and fifths and tritones summing up to minor ninths, in six movements:

(1) *Allegretto giovale*, a hedonistic dodecaphonic essay, concluding with a canon of two mutually exclusive major hexachords at distances of minor thirds and tritones, resulting in a surprising melodramatic precipitation of consecutive diminished-seventh chords; (2) *Andante amoroso*, in a free lyrico-dramatic vein; (3) *Allegro misterioso*, containing a *Trio estatico* with a dodecaphonic episode of mutually exclusive whole-tone scales; (4) *Adagio appassionato*, with a melodic quotation from the *Lyrische Symphonie* by Alexander von Zemlinsky, Schoenberg's teacher and brother-in-law, to whom the score is dedicated; (5) *Presto delirando*, a scherzo employing diamond-shaped notes to indicate sustained tones; (6) *Largo desolato*, withthe insertion of the initial motive from *Tristan und Isolde*, terminating in a series of despondent tertian oscillations in one instrument after another, trailing off into inaudibility. (Berg subsequently arranged three movements of the *Lyrische Suite* for chamber orchestra; the first performance of this version took place in Berlin on 21 January 1929.)

Berg's *Lyric Suite* contains a germinal four-note motive H, F, A, B (German notation for B, F, A, B♭), the initials of Hanna Fuchs-Robettin (Berg's secret love), with metronome markings and bar numbers throughout the score being multiples of 23 (Alban Berg's mystic number, embodied in a Vienna publication entitled 23) and 10, Hanna's astrological numeral.

9 JANUARY 1927

Houston Stewart CHAMBERLAIN, English-born Wagnerite who married Wagner's daughter Eva and who expanded Wagner's pan-Teutonic philosophy into a political doctrine, dies in his spiritual home, Bayreuth, at the age of 71, only six years before the advent of the Wagnerogenic Nazi millennium.

15 JANUARY 1927

Iñes de Castro, opera in three acts by the prime Portuguese opera composer Ruy COELHO, to a libretto presenting a melodramatized story of the mistress of the Emperor Pedro I of Portugal, put to death in 1355 by a coterie of perfidious courtiers but posthumously rehabilitated in her martyrdom in a grisly scene of the coronation of her exhumed cadaver, set to music in an expansive Italianate vein, is produced in Lisbon in the original Portuguese version. (An Italian version was produced in Lisbon on 27 April 1951.)

16 JANUARY 1927

Fonctionnaire MCMXII: *Inaction en Musique*, symphonic skit by Florent SCHMITT, deriding old-fashioned bureaucracy of the 1912 vintage whose slogan was "never do today what you can make someone else do tomorrow," is performed for the first time in Paris.

21 JANUARY 1927

Suite en fa for orchestra by Albert ROUSSEL, his first work written in a neo-classical manner, in three movements, *Prélude*, *Sarabande* and *Gigue*, completed on 21 August 1926, is performed for the first time anywhere by the Boston Symphony Orchestra, under the direction of Serge Koussevitzky to whom it is dedicated.

22 JANUARY 1927

Scarlattiana, a divertimento based on 88 themes from 545 sonatas of Domenico Scarlatti by Alfredo CASELLA, for piano and chamber orchestra, is performed for the first time anywhere by the New York Philharmonic Orchestra, conducted by Otto Klemperer, with the composer at the piano.

28 JANUARY 1927

Aaron COPLAND, 26-year-old Brooklyn-born composer, appears as soloist with the Boston Symphony Orchestra, Serge Koussevitzky conducting, in the first performance of his *Piano Concerto*, in two connected movements, evolving, after an elegiac exordium, into a boldly polyrhythmic essay in jazz, with the nervously syncopating melody set against a steady ostinato in the manner of the Blues, then erupting in a series of angular intervalic leaps, while maintaining a clearly identifiable classical sonata form.

Copland's Piano Concerto shows a shocking lack of taste, of proportion. After thunderous, blaring measures in which one brass instrument vies with another in arrogant announcement, there are gentle purposeless measures for the piano, which is struck by fingers apparently directed at random, as a child amuses itself by making noises when it is restless in the room. (Philip Hale, Boston *Herald*, 29 January 1927)

If there exists anywhere in the world a stranger concatenation of meaninglessly ugly sounds and distorted rhythms than Mr. Copland's *Piano Concerto*, Boston has been spared it. (Warren Storey Smith, Boston *Post*, 29 January 1927)

From all Copland Concertos and others of the same sort, Good Lord deliver us. . . . Last Saturday night the generous audience politely laughed. It ought to have been a case of tears rather than laughter. I fear that the listeners didn't appreciate how insulting the piece was. We hear so much about prohibition nowadays; let us have a little prohibition against the awful sounds made sometimes in the name of music. (Letter to the Editor of the Boston *Herald*, 2 February 1927, signed by Clayton Johns, a Boston musician and composer of songs)

Mr. Copland, for aught anyone can affirm, may be the merest freak or a composer of eminence in embryo. A serene and distant future, not a clamoring present, will give judgment. Meanwhile, he speaks for a "chapel" of young American composers, for a new and experimental sort of American music. . . . Not prejudice, but perception, will reduce Mr. Copland to his level. (H. T. Parker, Boston *Evening Transcript*, 4 February 1927)

All sorts of things are said about the Boston Symphony Orchestra's performance of an extraordinary piano concerto by Aaron Copland—among them that Mr. Koussevitzky, as a cynical foreigner, is seeking only to satirize American music, to bring it into contempt, by the production of such a musical monstrosity. . . . The Listener acquits Mr. Koussevitzky of cynicism, but he finds no music at all in the Copland composition. To him, it is a harrowing horror from beginning to end. . . . There is no rhythm in the so-called concerto. The piano part is not played, but merely happened upon at random, as it might be if the performer struck the keyboard with his elbows instead of his fingers. At least that is the way the piece impressed persons in the audience who have welcomed and enjoyed the newer developments that have come since Strauss, Debussy and Stravinsky dawned on the world. The Listener believes that the Boston Symphony audiences are tolerant to the point of docility; but this performance was too much for them. (The Listener, in a column in the Boston *Evening Transcript*, 5 February 1927)

Dear Kolya—You're a darling to have sent all those delightful write-ups. After reading them I went to the mirror to see if I could recognize myself. How flattering it was to read that the 'Listener' can understand Strauss, Debussy, Stravinsky—but not poor me. How instructive to learn that there is 'no rhythm' in this 'so-called concerto!' Only one thing got my nanny: how dare H. T. Parker talk of *reducing* me to my level, while I am waiting to be *raised* to my level. And all that really worries me is whether or not the Maestro will ever again have sufficient courage to perform me anywhere. When the Concerto is played again (O horrid thought!) we must see if we can't get the police to raid the concert hall to give a little added interest to this 'horrible' experiment.—Till Soon, Aaron. (Letter to Nicolas Slonimsky from Aaron Copland, dated New York, 10 February, 1927)

28 JANUARY 1927

Angélique, musical farce in one act by Jacques IBERT, dealing with a shrew whom not even the devil himself could tame, set to a modernistic score with the inclusion of a jazzy interlude to portray the ethnological consciousness of a voodooistic tribal chief in the African interior, is performed for the first time in Paris.

29 JANUARY 1927

Herrn Dürers Bild, opera in three acts by the Czechborn German-educated composer Joseph Gustav MRACZECK, in which a Nuremberg girl infatuated with Albrecht Dürer who painted her portrait in 1520 is mortally wounded by her blind father as he seeks to kill the painter, set to a romantically expansive musical score, is produced in Hanover.

29 JANUARY 1927

Second movement of the *Fourth Symphony,* a work of prophetic modernity by the New England composer of genius Charles E. IVES, set in a polymetrical notation comprising improvisational instrumental parts, forming a monumental counterpoint of two symphonic units, independent in concept and design but coalescing into a dual entity, while the harmonic complications arising therefrom exemplify a complete emancipation of dissonance, is performed for the first time in New York, Eugene Goossens conducting.

30 JANUARY 1927

Beatrix Cenci, tragic opera in five acts by the Polish composer Ludomir RÓŻYCKI, dealing with the beautiful Roman gentlewoman executed in 1599 as an accomplice in the murder of her father, is performed for the first time in Warsaw.

2 FEBRUARY 1927

Rio Rita, vivacious musical comedy by Harry TIERNEY, dealing with a Texas Ranger in hot pursuit of a Mexican bandit, gaining a girl in the process, is produced in New York.

6 FEBRUARY 1927

Kolo, symphonic dance by the Croatian composer Jakov GOTOVAC, set in propulsively asymmetric rhythms peculiar to the Slavic Balkan regions, is performed for the first time in Zagreb.

9 FEBRUARY 1927

Variations on a Hungarian Folksong, orchestral suite by the 32-year-old Hungarian composer Eugen ZÁDOR, based on a Hungarian army song popular during World War I, is performed for the first time in Vienna.

10 FEBRUARY 1927

Jonny Spielt Auf, opera in two acts and eleven scenes by the 26-year-old Viennese composer Ernst KRENEK (completed 19 June 1926), to his own libretto portraying in an astutely dissonant idiom, liberally spiced with jazzified polyrhythms, the adventures of the Negro jazzband leader Jonny, indulging in miscegenating amourettes with an accessible prima donna and a Paris chambermaid, appropriating a Stradivarius from an anachronistically long-haired violin virtuoso, entering into a lucrative business relationship with a euphoric American concert manager, set against the background of mystically humanized nature, singing glaciers and other supernatural phenomena, employing the scientific marvels of radio loudspeakers, and culminating in Jonny's apotheosis as he triumphantly straddles a revolving terrestrial globe, dancing jazz on top of the world, is performed for the first time at the Leipzig Opera House.

The main idea of *Jonny Spielt Auf* is the split between the historically overburdened and brooding European, and especially central European, spirit and the fresh life-asserting mentality of the West symbolized by America. At the time, this conflict appeared to me in such a simple formulation. I used jazz elements only by way of quotation to characterize a certain sphere of action, and jazz affects the entire opera only in passing. Naturally, it never occurred to me to call it a "jazz opera." While in Europe it was often held as an offensive glorification of Americanism, many Americans took it as a contemptuous criticism of their own country. (Ernst Krenek's statement in a letter to the author dated 5 February 1938)

12 FEBRUARY 1927

La Rosiera, "tragic idyll" in three acts by Vittorio GNECCHI, after Alfred de Musset's play *On ne badine pas avec l'amour,* telling the piteous tale of a country girl who kills herself with a scythe after her defilement and betrayal by a philandering feudal baron, the music seasoned with opulent modernities, with occasional quarter-tones to express erotic anxiety, is performed for the first time, sixteen years after its composition, in a German version, in Gera. (The first performance in Italian was given in Trieste, on 24 January 1931.)

17 FEBRUARY 1927

The King's Henchman, first opera, in three acts, by the American composer Deems TAYLOR, to the text of Edna St. Vincent Millay, from a Tristanesque legend of Eadgar, King of England who incautiously entrusts his foster brother with the task of bringing the ineffably beautiful Aelfrida of Devon to be his consort, with a mellifluously Wagneromantic score, is produced by the Metropolitan Opera House in New York, bringing in $15,504 at the box office, the only opera by an American composer to retain its place in its repertory for three consecutive seasons before vanishing into limbo.

17 FEBRUARY 1927

Hanneles Himmelfahrt, opera in two acts by the 55-year-old German composer Paul GRAENER, to a libretto drawn from a play by Gerhart Hauptmann, relating the mystical story of an ailing girl who succumbs in a plasma of Wagnerogenic chromatic harmonies, undergoes a diatonic transfiguration and is carried to heaven in celestial D major, is produced simultaneously in Dresden and Breslau.

21 FEBRUARY 1927

Le Poirier de Misère, a musical fable in three acts by the French composer Marcel DELANNOY, in which the pear tree shelters personified Misery, which captures everyone that climbs on it, trapping Death itself in its fruit-laden branches and releasing it only at the demand of the human *morituri* desperate at the prospect of ineluctable immortality, is produced at the Opéra-Comique in Paris.

21 FEBRUARY 1927

Der Zarewitsch, light opera in three acts by Franz LEHÁR, in which the Russian Tsarevich's dalliance with a complaisant damsel in Naples is unhappily broken when the Tsar dies, and the Tsarevich obeys the call of duty and returns to St. Petersburg to ascend the Russian throne, set to music in a vivacious Viennese manner, with interludes of balalaika music supplying local color, is produced in Berlin.

21 FEBRUARY 1927

Sophie Arnould, lyric comedy in one act by Gabriel PIERNÉ based on apocryphal anecdotes about the stormy life of the Paris soprano Sophie Arnould (1740–1802), is performed for the first time at the Opéra-Comique in Paris.

25 FEBRUARY 1927

Vetrate di Chiesa, four impressions for orchestra by Ottorino RESPIGHI, inspired by stained-glass windows in Italian churches—(1) *La Fuga in Egitto,* depicting in reverently illustrative tones the flight of the Holy Family into Egypt; (2) *San Michele Arcangelo,* a trumpetingly wrathful inovcation of the Archangel Michael smiting the legions of the rebellious ex-angel Lucifer; (3) *Il Mattutino di Santa Chiara,* a poetic elegy suggested by the contemplation of a morning in the life of Saint Clara (1191–1212); (4) *San Gregorio Magno,* the apotheosis of Gregory the Great blessing the crowds—is performed for the first time anywhere by the Boston Symphony Orchestra, Serge Koussevitzky conducting.

27 FEBRUARY 1927

Adils och Elisiv, opera in three acts by the Swedish composer Wilhelm PETERSON-BERGER, is produced in Stockholm on his sixtieth birthday.

1 MARCH 1927

Poland issues a CHOPIN commemorative stamp with his portrait of the denomination of 40 groschen.

2 MARCH 1927

Royal Palace, one-act opera by Kurt WEILL, dealing with an international charmer named Deianira (symbolically identified with the wife of Hercules whom she inadvertently poisoned with the blood of the centaur slain by him) who holds in sensuous thrall three men of her past, present and future on vacation at the Royal Palace Hotel on a South Pacific island, to a score in a satiric idiom vibrating with derisive syncopation and stylized balladry, is produced in Berlin.

3 MARCH 1927

Basi e Bote, comic opera in three acts by the Bohemian-born Italian composer Riccardo PICK-MANGIAGALLI, to a libretto, in the Venetian dialect, by Arrigo Boito, with characters of old commedia dell'arte depicted in a mellifluous Donizettian score orchestrated with Wagneromantic lusciousness, is produced in Rome.

4 MARCH 1927

Concertino by the 52-year-old Mexican composer Julián CARRILLO, written for special instruments capable of producing fractional tones (quarter-tones, eighth-tones, sixteenth-tones), is performed for the first time anywhere by the Philadelphia Orchestra, Leopold Stokowski conducting.

5 MARCH 1927

Concerto for violin, horn and orchestra by the foremost English composeress Ethel SMYTH, is performed for the first time in London, Henry Wood conducting, Jelly d' Arányi and Aubrey Brain soloists.

5 MARCH 1927

Second Symphony in one movement by the Danish composer Knudaage RIISAGER is performed for the first time in Copenhagen, on the eve of his 30th birthday.

9 MARCH 1927

Madama di Challant, opera in three acts by the 33-year-old Italian composer Carmine GUARINO, is produced at La Scala in Milan.

11 MARCH 1927

On his fourth American tour, Alfredo CASELLA conducts at the Wanamaker department store in New York the first performance anywhere of his *Concerto Romano* for organ, brass, percussion and strings, commissioned by the manager of the store and set in a neo-Baroque style intended to recreate in music the plastic monumentality of classical Roman architecture.

13 MARCH 1927

Nikolai MEDTNER appears as soloist in the first performance in Moscow of his *Second Piano Concerto* in C minor.

17 MARCH 1927

Shah-Senem, opera in four acts by Reinhold GLIÈRE, commissioned by the Soviet Socialist Republic of Azerbaijan, to a legend dealing with the love of a beautiful Caucasian maiden for a young folksinger who arrives on a white charger to claim her at the last moment before the expiration of a seven-years' test period granted to Shah-Senem by her father intent on giving her in marriage to a feudal lord, set to an astutely orientalistic score glowing with serpentine fiorituras and based on original native folksongs, is performed for the first time to a Russian libretto in Baku.

(Date from *The Worker of Baku* of 18 March 1927; a new version, to a libretto in the Tatar language, was produced in Baku on 4 May 1934. Previous editions of *Music Since 1900*, Loewenberg's *Annals of Opera* and Baker's *Biographical Dictionary of Musicians*, 5th Edition, 1958, edited by Nicolas Slonimsky, all give the date of the revised version.)

18 MARCH 1927

Serge RACHMANINOFF appears as soloist with the Philadelphia Orchestra, Leopold Stokowski conducting, in the first performance of his *Fourth Piano Concerto*, in G minor (begun in Russia in 1914, and completed on 25 August 1926 in New York), dedicated to his spiritually and esthetically close friend Nikolai Medtner, in three movements:

(1) *Allegro vivace (alla breve)*, with a spacious opening gradually increasing in rhythmic frequencies per metric unit and expanding in pianistic virtuosity; (2) *Largo*, in C major, with a mournfully flatted submediant, set in a pessimistically elegiac mood, and leading directly to the finale; (3) *Allegro vivace*, a rondo in 3/4 time, moving energetically along its foreseeable course, and ending in the assertive G major.

(The Finale was totally revised in 1941, with the first two movements reorchestrated, and the new version performed by Rachmaninoff with the Philadelphia Orchestra, Eugene Ormandy conducting, on 12 October 1941)

18 MARCH 1927

Third Symphony by the Chicago composer Arne OLDBERG, written in a competent Germanic manner, in three movements, is performed for the first and last time by the Chicago Symphony Orchestra, Frederick Stock conducting.

18 MARCH 1927

First Symphony in A minor by Alexandre TANSMAN, in four contrasting movements, set in a romantically classical style, with acrid bitonalities in its harmonic structure and a suggestion of incisive Polish rhythms, is performed for the first time anywhere by the Boston Symphony Orchestra, under the direction of Serge Koussevitzky to whom the score is dedicated.

20 MARCH 1927

Kammerkonzert for piano, violin and 13 wind instruments by Alban BERG, completed on 23 July 1925, thematically based on the modified musical letters, in German notation, present in the names of his friend and teacher Arnold Schoenberg (ArnolD SCHönBErG, where S = Es = E-flat), to whom the score is dedicated, Anton Webern

(Anton wEBErn) and his own (AlBAn BErG), wherein the coincidence of the initial letters in their first names creates a simulacrum of a tonal center in an otherwise atonal matrix, cast in three movements, each naturally divisible into three sections (the figure 3 acquires here a magical significance)—*Thema scherzoso con variazioni*, scored for piano and wind instruments, *Adagio* for violin and wind instruments, and *Rondo ritmico con Introduzione*, for all fifteen instruments as a Hegelian synthesis of thesis and antithesis—is performed for the first time in Berlin, Hermann Scherchen conducting.

20 MARCH 1927

From the Black Belt, a suite of character pieces for small orchestra by the American Negro composer William Grant STILL, in seven sections—(1) *Lil' Scamp*, lasting only eight measures; (2) *Honeysuckle*, in dulcet melodies and facile rhythms; (3) *Dance*; (4) *Mah Bones Is Creakin'* wherein an old man bemoans his rheumatic pain in rattling syncopation; (5) *Blue*, in the style of Negro spirituals; (6) *Brown Girl*, a musical tribute to a handsome mulatto; (7) *Clap Yo' Han's*, with musicians clapping their hands rhythmically as in a children's game—is performed for the first time by the Barrère Little Symphony in New York.

22 MARCH 1927

Canto a Sevilla, poem for voice and orchestra by Joaquín TURINA, is performed for the first time in Madrid.

26 MARCH 1927

A century has passed since the death of BEETHOVEN.

31 MARCH 1927

Lilacs, poem for orchestra (after Amy Lowell) by Edward Burlingame HILL, written in a cerulean impressionistic manner marked by intertonal freedom but free of chromatic complexities, is performed for the first time by the Boston Symphony Orchestra, Serge Koussevitzky conducting.

1 APRIL 1927

The world première of the second part of *Pause del Silenzio*, "five symphonic expressions" by Gian Francesco MALIPIERO, is given by the Philadelphia Orchestra, Leopold Stokowski conducting.

(The score was published under the title *L'esilio dell'eroe*, suggested by Gabriele d'Annunzio, and later renamed by the composer *Sul fiume del tempo*, and again renamed *Il grillo cantarino*, eventually reverting to its original title *Pause del Silenzio*, none of which renaming helped the fortunes of the piece, which, as Malipiero remarked in 1952, should have perhaps been titled *Silenzio senza pause*.)

2 APRIL 1927

Concerto for piano, flute, cello and string orchestra by Vincent D'INDY, is performed for the first time in Paris.

7 APRIL 1927

Naïla, opera in three acts by Philippe GAUBERT, is produced at the Paris Opéra, under the direction of the composer, chief conductor there from 1920.

8 APRIL 1927

Arcana, symphonic poem by Edgar VARÈSE, French-American builder of "organized sound," inspired by the hermetic philosophy of Paracelsus in probing the arcane essence of the arts, designed as a macrocosmic passacaglia developing through an athematic concatenation of melorhythmic molecules, wherein melody (in spacious atonally oriented intervalic progressions), rhythm (precise in its complexity within variable meters), harmony and counterpoint (dissonant with the exception of two measures of pure C-G fifths inserted to achieve the paradoxical effect of maximal discordance) and instrumental color (exploiting extreme ranges) are integral parts of the formal matrix, scored for a tremendously large orchestra including 40 percussion instruments, is performed for the first time by the Philadelphia Orchestra, under the direction of Leopold Stokowski.

Varèse's *Arcana* plunged the listener into morasses of sound which seemingly had little relation to music. . . . There was no mercy in its disharmony, no pity in its successions of screaming, clashing, clangorous discords. . . . A series of gunpowder explosions might similarly overawe the ear. . . . but their musical quality would he open to question. (Oscar Thompson, *Musical America*, New York, 23 April 1927)

10 APRIL 1927

Shortly after his return from Europe, George ANTHEIL presents at Carnegie Hall, New York, a program of his works which includes a *Jazz Symphony*, a *String Quartet*, a *Sonata* for violin, piano and drums, and his monumental *Ballet Mécanique*.

Antheil Art Bursts on Startled Ears—First Performance of Ballet Mécanique in This Country Draws Varied Response-Hisses, Cheers Greet Him—Concatenation of Anvils, Bells, Horns, Buzzsaws Deafens Some Pleases Others. (Headlines in the New York *Times*, 11 April 1927)

I personally consider that the *Ballet Mécanique* was important in one particular and that it was conceived in a new form, that form specifically being the filling out of a certain time canvas with musical abstractions and sound material composed and contrasted against one another with the thought of time values rather than tonal values. . . . In the *Ballet Mécanique* I used time as Picasso might have used the blank spaces of his canvas. I did not hesitate, for instance, to repeat one measure one hundred times; I did not hesitate to have absolutely nothing on my pianola rolls for sixty-two bars; I did not hesitate to ring a bell against a certain given section of time or indeed to do whatever I pleased to do with this time canvas as long as each part of it stood up against the other. My ideas were the most abstract of the abstract. Still I was totally misunderstood by the morons who listened to the *Ballet Mécanique* in 1926. Although I had *very clearly* published exactly what I had intended way back in 1923 and 1924 in many *avant-garde* magazines, practically all of the *dumbbells* in New York went to listen to the *Ballet Mécanique* expecting to see me grind out pictures of the machine age! Some imbeciles expected to see a kind of Buck Rogers fantasy of the future. I was totally misunderstood, so deeply misunderstood that I have never made any attempt whatever of explanation what I was after in America. I realized that it was hopeless. Today, almost ten years afterwards I am making my first explanation to you. (From Antheil's letter to Nicolas Slonimsky, dated 21 July 1936)

15 APRIL 1927

Flivver 10,000,000, a Joyous Epic: Fantasy for Orchestra Inspired by the Familiar Legend The Ten Millionth Ford Is Now Serving Its Owner by Frederick S. CONVERSE, the main stops in the course of the music being Dawn in Detroit, The Call to Labor, Birth of the Hero (in a whole-tone trumpet fanfare), Trying His Metal, May Night by the Roadside (America's romance), The Joy Riders (America's Frolic) and The Collision (America's Tragedy), with frictional secundal harmonies illustrating the close call, concluding on an apotheosis, Phoenix Americanus, with the Hero recovering from the shock of the accident proceeding on his way "with redoubled energy, typical of the indomitable American spirit," the music set in a modestly modernistic vein, and the score including the wind machine and the Ford auto horn, is performed for the first time by the Boston Symphony Orchestra, Serge Koussevitzky conducting.

16 APRIL 1927

Agamemnon, musical play after Aeschylus and Paul Claudel by Darius MILHAUD, is performed for the first time in Paris.

17 APRIL 1927

Carlos SALZEDO plays the harp in the first performance in New York of his *Concerto* for harp and seven wind instruments, introducing novel effects, such as percussive taps on the frame, glissandi obtained by means of the pedals and xylophonic sounds.

21 APRIL 1927

Veste di cielo, opera by Ermanno WOLF-FERRARI, is performed for the first time in Munich, in a German version entitled *Das Himmelskleid*.

22 APRIL 1927

Symphony in E minor by the 30-year-old American composer Roger SESSIONS (completed in Florence on 31 January 1927) in three neo-classical movements—(1) *Giusto* with eighth-notes as invariables through a succession of changing meters, in the manner of a symphonic toccata; (2) *Largo*, in pandiatonically expanded modalities; (3) *Allegro vivace* in synocopated polyphony, in the homonymous initial key of E major—is performed for the first time by the Boston Symphony Orchestra, Serge Koussevitzky conducting.

23 APRIL 1927

Three centuries have passed since the production of the first opera by a German composer, *Dafne* by Heinrich SCHÜTZ (its music is lost), presented at the wedding of Princess Sophie of Saxony at Hartenfels Castle in Torgau, to a text from the same play by Rinuccini which served as the libretto for the first opera ever written, *La Dafne* by Jacopo PERI, composed in 1597, the music of which is also lost.

25 APRIL 1927

Hit the Deck, musical comedy by Vincent YOUMANS, dealing with the circumnavigatory passion of a wealthy society lady from Newport, Rhode Island, for a sailor, containing the famous sailor's chorus *Hallelujah* and the love duet *Sometimes I'm Happy*, is produced in New York.

27 APRIL 1927

Švanda Dudák (Schwanda the Bagpiper), comic opera in two acts by the 31-year-old Czech composer Jaromír WEINBERGER, to a libretto from a folk tale dealing with a minstrel who falsely assures his wife that he has never kissed the queen at a court entertainment, is dispatched to Hell for perfidy and throws the local devils into a choreographic pandemonium by the infectious virtuosity of his bagpipe playing, redeeming his soul and returning to the earth for a life of domestic tranquility, is produced in Prague in the Czech language obtaining the greatest acclaim accorded to any native opera of the 20th century, and marking a start of world-wide successes.

28 APRIL 1927

The first Russian Jazz Band ever to perform in public is introduced in a program of miscellaneous jazz numbers in Leningrad.

30 APRIL 1927

La Chatte, ballet by Henri SAUGUET, wherein a felinophilic youth, whose favorite kitten, happily metamorphosed into a young girl, reverts to her atavistic instincts when she sees a mouse, is produced in Monte Carlo.

5 MAY 1927

Madonna Imperia, comic opera in one act by Franco ALFANO, to a libretto derived from Balzac's tale, dealing with a young man enamored of a noblewoman at the Council of Constance in 414 A.D. who encounters two rivals, a bishop and a cardinal, in her boudoir (although clerical continence was decreed in 386 A.D., concubinage among ordained priests of the Church was not formally prohibited until the twelfth century), but wins her love through intellectual cunning, set to music in a passionately Italianate and luxuriantly sonorous manner, is produced in Turin, with a chancellor and an ambassador substituted for the parts of bishop and cardinal.

15 MAY 1927

La Fata Malerba, opera by Vittorio GUI, is produced in Turin.

20 MAY 1927

The Nicaraguan composer Luis A. DELGADILLO conducts in Caracas the first performance of his *Sinfonia Incaica*, based on ancient Peruvian themes.

21 MAY 1927

Der Sprung über den Schatten by Ernst KRENEK, the first modern European opera to be given on the Soviet stage, is presented in Leningrad.

With Mozart-like power of observation, nonchalance, and directness, Krenek portrays an astutely chosen group of people who have lost the healthy attitude towards life, and are seeking sensuous excitement at any price. . . . Krenek is a master of the stage and a musician who has succeeded in returning the opera to healthy Mozartean traditions. (Igor Glebov in *Krasnaya Gazeta*, Leningrad, 20 May 1927, reproduced in Bogdanov-Berezovsky's *Soviet Opera*, Leningrad, 1940, p. 82).

Krenek's opera is rather confused in its plot, and it is in this respect a perfect counterpart of contemporary European culture, which is incapable of creating anything of the least value. (Lunatcharsky, Soviet Commissar of Education, in *Krasnaya Gazeta*, Leningrad, 7 March 1928, quoted in Bogdanov-Berezovsky's *Soviet Opera*, Leningrad, 1940, p. 83)

30 MAY 1927

Maurice RAVEL plays the piano part, with Georges Enesco as violinist, in the first performance, in Paris, of his *Sonata* for violin and piano, in three movements:

(1) *Allegretto*, in which a quasi-pentatonic theme is tensed by acrid major sevenths; (2) *Blues*, a nervously syncopated melody with a "blue" flatted mediant in a major key; (3) *Allegro*, a waltzed summary of melorhythmic materials of the first two movements, with a precipitate *perpetuum mobile* of scale passages against a harmonic background of secundal and septimal dissonance.

30 MAY 1927

Igor STRAVINSKY conducts in Paris for Diaghilev's Ballet Russe the world première of the concert version of his opera-oratorio *Œdipus Rex* (completed in vocal score on 14 March 1927; orchestration finished on 10 May 1927, at 4 o'clock in the morning), in two acts, to the text (in French) by Jean Cocteau, after Sophocles, translated into impersonal Latin (in order to make the drama stand out as timeless and nongeographic) by J. Danielou, the action explained to the audience by a Speaker in the vernacular (French in the original score) without musical accompaniment, providing a connective tissue between the successive episodes, from the supplication of the people to save them from the plague to the final revelation of the enormity of the King's guilt in killing his father and marrying his mother, with the music suggesting the atmosphere of a medieval mystery play along the precepts of *Ars Antiqua*, replete with recurrent thematic statements in stark, bleak harmonies stripped of all accoutrements of modernity, aridly dissonant in their open intervalic spaces and proleptic canonic progressions, cast in Gothic sonorities creating the impression of passionate immobility.

7 JUNE 1927

Le Pas d'Acier, ballet by Sergei PROKOFIEV, a choreographic interpretation of the "Leap of Steel" in industrialized new Russia, with hydraulic hammers illustrated by moving pillars of dissonant harmonies, sailors gallivanting on the stage to the strains of revolutionary songs, a former countess selling her garments at a flea market to the tune of a sentimental ballad, boys peddling cigarettes in polka time, and commissars orating in marching rhetorics, conjuring up a panorama of Bolshevistic exhilaration in an urbanistically constructivist vein, is produced by Diaghilev's Ballet Russe in Paris.

The tense, dramatic struggle, rich in great deeds of heroism and examples of supreme sacrifice, has apparently failed to impress Prokofiev's consciousness. . . . The musical characterizations in his ballet *Leap of Steel* are so monotonously similar, so completely submerged in buffoonery and persiflage that it is difficult to distinguish among them. . . . In the eyes of the bourgeoisie, Soviet Russia appears as a backward, half-civilized country populated by idiots, and its Bolshevik inhabitants as crude barbarians living according to pre-historic morals and customs. Consciously or unconsciously, Prokofiev adopts this hostile attitude in his musical descriptions of Soviet types. (Yuri Keldysh, *The Proletarian Musician*, Moscow, June 1929)

Q. Why is the last scene of *Leap of Steel* so saturated with mechanical, machine-like rhythms? A. Because machines are more attractive than people. Q. Is the factory represented in your ballet a capitalistic factory where workers are slaves, or a Soviet factory where the worker is master? If it was your intention to represent a Soviet factory, where and when did you study its operations, seeing that you lived abroad since 1918 and visited Soviet Russia for the first time in 1927, and then only for two weeks? A. This is a political and not a musical question, and I will not answer it. (Questions and answers during an interview with Prokofiev in the spring of 1929 in Moscow arranged by the Association of Proletarian Musicians and reported in *The Proletarian Musician*, Moscow, June 1929)

10 JUNE 1927

Le Rêve de Cyniras, lyric comedy in three acts by Vincent D'INDY, is produced in Paris.

12 JUNE 1927

Piccola Suite for orchestra by Riccardo PICK-MANGIA-GALLI, in three minuscule movements—*I piccoli soldati*, *Berceuse* and *La Danza d'Olaf*—is performed for the first time in Milan.

14 JUNE 1927

The Red Poppy, ballet in three acts by Reinhold GLIÈRE, focused on a gallant Soviet crew at a Chinese port of call, featuring an infectious sailors' dance in the polka rhythms of the popular Soviet song *Little Apple*, which inspires the downtrodden coolies to break the chains of oppressive minor seconds and rise in rebellion in the ascending fourths of the *Internationale*, containing a lyric episode of a beautiful proletarian cabaret singer who sacrifices her life to foil a counter-revolutionary plot against a valiant Soviet army captain, with the apotheosis proclaiming the victory of the Chinese people over the feudal lords and their imperialist allies and an unbreakable fraternal friendship with Soviet Russia, is produced with an appropriate socialist enthusiasm at the Bolshoi Theater in Moscow.

23 JUNE 1927

Igor STRAVINSKY presents in Paris a performance on the specially constructed "piano pneumatique" of the four-hand piano arrangement of his ballet score *Le Sacre du Printemps*, amplified by the PANOTROPE, "le plus fort phonographe du monde."

30 JUNE 1927

The Fifth Festival of the International Society for Contemporary Music opens in Frankfurt with the following program of chamber music:

String Quartet in an optimistically polyphonic manner by the Soviet composer Alexander MOSSOLOV; a subtly impressionistic *Flute Sonata* by the Dutch modernist Willem PIJPER; *Concertino* for piano and six instruments by the 72-year-old grandmaster of Czech music Leoš JANÁČEK, first performed in Brno on 16 February 1926, cast in a hedonistically modernistic form; *Le Danze del Re David*, a Hebraic suite for piano in a stylized neo-paleographic idiom by the Italian neo-romanticist Mario CASTEL-NUOVO-TEDESCO.

1 JULY 1927

The second concert of the Fifth Festival of the International Society of Contemporary Music in Frankfurt presents the following program of symphonic music:

Dance in Place Congo, a symphonic panorama of a Negro and Creole street festival in New Orleans by the New England composer Henry F. GILBERT, the "Ur-Amerikaner," as a German critic has described him; *Seventh Suite* by the Viennese theorist and dodecaphonic pioneer Josef Matthias HAUER, based on a series of two mutually exclusive six-note tropes; the world première of the *First Piano Concerto* by Béla BARTÓK, completed by him on 12 November 1926, played by Bartok himself with Wilhelm Furtwängler conducting the orchestra, distinguished by barbaric rhythmic power and couched in dissonant counterpoint, with the major seventh becoming a substitute for the octave, within a modal framework in which E and C-sharp assume the function of strong barycenters, and making use of tone-clusters (borrowed by personal permission from Henry Cowell's pianistic innovation), in three movements: (1) *Allegro moderato*, marked by cumulative kinetic energy, with the eighth-note as the least common denominator within the matrix of changing meters, in a dissonant idiom intensified by the process of gradual accretion of non-harmonic notes; (2) *Andante*, a colloquy between the piano and a consortium of drumlets in the manner of an antiphonal concertino, with the strings conspicuously absent and wind instruments arriving at the very end; (3) *Allegro molto*, an essay in spontaneous motility, with distinctive thematic molecules passing back and forth between the piano and the orchestra, concluding with a terse, crisp and sharp coda, accentuated by hard desiccated strokes of sonic matter; *Fifth Symphony* by the Danish neo-romantic composer Carl NIELSEN (first performed in Copenhagen on 24 January 1922).

2 JULY 1927

The third concert of the Fifth Festival of the International Society for Contemporary Music in Frankfurt presents the following program of chamber music:

Third String Quartet by the Swiss neo-classicist Conrad BECK; *String Quartet* by the Russian-born German-educated romantic modernist Wladimir VOGEL; the logical, austere, and yet emotionally intense *Kammerkonzert* by Alban BERG, first performed in Berlin on 20 March 1927; and the neo-ecclesiastical *Magnificat* by the German master of choral polyphony Heinrich *Kaminski*.

3 JULY 1927

Two concerts are presented during the course of the Fifth Festival of the International Society for Contemporary Music held in Frankfurt, in the morning and in the evening:

Morning concert: a Slavic oratorio by the Croatian composer Božidar ŠIROLA, *The Lives and Remembrance of the Holy Brethren and Apostles to the Slavs, Cyril and Methodius*.

Evening concert: *Offrande à Siva*, choreographic poem with pleasingly orientalistic music expressing in artful arabesques the spirit of Hindu rituals, by the French composer Claude DELVINCOURT; *I Cantico del Sole*, to the poem of St. Francis, by the Parisian composer Raymond PETIT; the dynamic and transcendentally modernistic *Piano Concerto* by Ernst TOCH; and the academically competent *Second Symphony* by the Czech composer Emil AXMAN.

3 JULY 1927

Wanda LANDOWSKA, superbly endowed modern mistress of the harpsichord, inaugurates at her summer home in St.-Leu-la-Forêt near Paris, a series of concerts of old music performed on the replicas of ancient instruments manufactured under her supervision, with splicitous regard for authenticity of tone production.

4 JULY 1927

The Fifth Festival of the International Society for Contemporary Music in Frankfurt concludes with the following program of chamber works:

Fourth String Quartet, in a neo-Flemish contrapuntal manner by the Dutch-born London resident Bernard van DIEREN; *Sonatina* for flute, clarinet and bassoon by the romantically disposed Danish composer Jörgen BENTZON, a pupil of Carl Nielsen; an attractive *Trio* for piano, violin and cello by the Spanish composer Joaquín TURINA; *Psalm 139*, for chorus a cappella by the English composer William WHITTAK-ER; the consistently atonal *Sonata* for violin and piano by the Hungarian composer Alexander JEMNITZ; and *Music for the Theater*, an energetic and poetic suite for chamber orchestra by the 26-year-old American composer Aaron COPLAND, first performed in Boston on 20 November 1925.

17 JULY 1927

Four short modern chamber operas are produced in the course of a Festival of New Music in Baden-Baden:

World première of *Hin und Zurück* by Paul HINDEMITH, a "film sketch" in which the action proceeds in a crab canon after reaching the middle (hence the title, "forth and back"): an adulteress is killed by her husband, returns to life, the attending physician backs out of the door, the husband pockets the revolver and the scene reverts to the *status quo ante*; *Mahagonny*, a satirical skit by Kurt WEILL, picturing the degradation in an imaginary capitalist city named Mahagonny with specifications suggesting Florida; first performance of *Die Prinzessin auf der Erbse*, fable after Hans Christian Andersen by Ernst TOCH, picturing a highly sensitive princess who could feel a pea through twenty layers of mattresses; and the world première of *L'Enlèvement d'Europe*, "opéra-minute" by Darius MILHAUD, to Paul Claudel's imaginative libretto wherein Europa prefers the company of cattle to that of men, taking particular fancy to a bull, who is Jupiter in disguise, with a happy ending secured as she elopes with him while the chorus sings encouragingly in thematic ascending sevenths and ninths.

11 AUGUST 1927

Study in Sonority for ten violins, an atonal essay in polyphonic writing by the scholarly American composer Wallingford RIEGGER, written as a school exercise, is performed for the first time by the student orchestra of Ithaca Conservatory, New York, where Riegger served as a member of the faculty. (Leopold Stokowski quadru-pled the number of violins and performed the work with the Philadelphia Orchestra on 30 March 1929.)

12 AUGUST 1927

Half a century has passed since the day that Thomas Alva EDISON patented the phonograph.

14 AUGUST 1927

Two centuries have passed since the English organist William CROFT, composer of pious hymn music, "at cælum demigravit chorum praesentior angelorum concentibus suum additurus Hallelujah" as his entry into Heaven is phrased on his tombstone in Westminster Abbey in London.

24 AUGUST 1927

The Soviet Government deprives the famous Russian bass singer Fedor CHALIAPIN of his honorary title as a People's Artist for his anti-Soviet declarations in the émigré circles.

27 AUGUST 1927

We, symphonic poem by the American composer James DUNN, celebrating Lindbergh's transatlantic flight (the first person plural of the title refers to Lindbergh's collective identification with his plane, the Spirit of St. Louis), is performed for the first time by the New York Philharmonic.

3 SEPTEMBER 1927

T-DOXC, "poème mécanique" for orchestra by the 30-year-old Danish composer Knudaage RIISAGER, is performed for the first time in Copenhagen.

9 SEPTEMBER 1927

Pomona, ballet by Constant LAMBERT, a bucolic idyll depicting the courtship of Pomona, the goddess of fruit, by the god Vertumnus, is produced in Buenos Aires.

12 SEPTEMBER 1927

My Maryland, operetta in three acts by Sigmund ROMBERG, in which Barbara Frietchie, rejuvenated from Whittier's poetic image of her as "bowed with her fourscore years and ten" to a luxuriant and sensuous Southern Rebelle who captivates the Yankee captain of the Union troops that captured her town, is produced in New York.

19 SEPTEMBER 1927

Third String Quartet by Arnold SCHOENBERG, op. 30, completed on 8 March 1927, cast in a consciously elaborated method of composition with 12 tones, in four classically correlated movements—(1) *Moderato*, (2) *Adagio*, (3) *Intermezzo*, *Allegro moderato*, (4) *Rondo*, *Molto moderato*—is performed for the first time by the Kolisch String Quartet in Vienna.

30 SEPTEMBER 1927

A new International Musicological Society is formed in Basel under the honorary chairmanship of Guido Adler to supplant the International Music Society dissolved at the outbreak of the war in 1914. (The first issue of the trilingual Bulletin of the International Musicological Society was published on 1 October 1928)

6 OCTOBER 1927

The Jazz Singer, first film with a synchronized optical sound track, starring Al JOLSON, opens at the Warner Brothers' Theater in New York. (This was only partly a sound film; the first motion picture with sound throughout, also starring Al Jolson and titled *The Singing Fool,* opened in New York on 19 September 1928.)

7 OCTOBER 1927

Das Wunder der Heliane, opera-mystery in three acts by the once wonder boy of modern music Erich Wolfgang KORNGOLD of Vienna, now 30 years old, wherein the angelic Heliane enrolls the aid of an archangelic stranger to combat the sinister designs of a Lucifer-like demon, set to music of mystically Wagneromantic effusiveness replete with Straussian harmonic protuberances, is produced in Hamburg.

15 OCTOBER 1927

New Music, a quarterly for publication of ultra-modern American music, edited by Henry COWELL, publishes its first issue, the full score of *Men and Mountains,* 'symphonic ensemble' in a poignantly atonal idiom by Carl RUGGLES, rugged individualist from Vermont.

New Music affords a means of publication of ultra-modern works, and also insures their distribution among its subscribers. It publishes works for orchestra, piano, voice, violin, chamber music, etc., specializing in the music of Americans, but not excluding occasional foreign works. It is not a profit-making plan, and any profits which may accrue will be equitably divided among the contributing composers. (From the publisher's statement in the first issue)

24 OCTOBER 1927

Chôros No. 8 for large orchestra and two pianos by Brazil's foremost composer Heitor VILLALOBOS, is performed for the first time anywhere in Paris.

29 OCTOBER 1927

First Symphony by the 28-year-old Russian composer Alexander TCHEREPNIN, marked "en Mi," but lacking a key signature, in four well-balanced movements, of which the second, *Vivace,* scored for pitchless percussion instruments, reinforced by gentle taps with the bow on the body of violins, violas, cellos, and double-basses, constitutes the earliest known example of an integral percussive movement in a symphony, and the third, *Andante,* exemplifies Tcherepnin's personal technique of *Interpunctus,* leading to a finale, *Allegretto con anima,* concluding on a coagulated major-minor triad on E, and making consistent use of the "Tcherepnin Scale" of nine notes in a variety of permutations, is performed for the first time in Paris.

3 NOVEMBER 1927

A Connecticut Yankee, musical comedy, fashioned after Mark Twain's story, by Richard RODGERS, wherein a skeptical American anachronistically blunders into King Arthur's court in Camelot, and decides to modernize the place by introducing the telephone and radio, featuring the popular songs *My Heart Stood Still* and *Thou Swell,* is produced in New York.

5 NOVEMBER 1927

Salle PLEYEL, the largest concert hall in Paris, is officially opened to the public.

6 NOVEMBER 1927

To October, Second Symphony in one movement by 21-year-old Dmitri SHOSTAKOVICH, "a symphonic dedication," concluding with a choral ode to the Soviet Revolution "the herald of the awaited Sun, the will of the centuries in revolt, the happiness of fields and work benches and the banner of living generations containing numerous instrumental and technical innovations—(1) a factory whistle, (2) polyrhythmic counterpoint combining 2, 3, 4, 5, and 6 notes to a beat, (3) chromatic canon in the major seventh in nine parts, resulting in the progression of chords comprising nine different chromatic tones—is performed for the first time in Leningrad, at the Festival on the occasion of the tenth anniversary of the Soviet Revolution, on the same program with the cantata *October* by Nicolas ROSLAVETZ and an orchestral suite from the ballet *Zavod (The Iron Foundry)* by Alexander MOSSOLOV, which includes in its orchestration a sheet of steel to simulate the sound produced by industrial machines at work.

13 NOVEMBER 1927

Komödie für Orchester by Ernst TOCH is performed for the first time by the Berlin Philharmonic Orchestra, Furtwängler conducting.

18 NOVEMBER 1927

La Campana sommersa, opera in four acts by Ottorino RESPIGHI, after the drama of Gerhart Hauptmann, dealing with a bell maker whose masterpiece, a large church bell, falls accidentally into a lake, and who is lured to follow it beneath the waters by a mysterious mountain maiden, is produced, in a German version, in Hamburg.

18 NOVEMBER 1927

La Bagarre, symphonic rondo by Bohuslav MARTINU, illustrating in realistically impressionistic tones the emotional commotion that greeted Lindbergh at his landing at Le Bourget airport after his transatlantic flight, is performed for the first time anywhere by the Boston Symphony Orchestra, Serge Koussevitzky conducting.

22 NOVEMBER 1927

Funny Face, musical comedy with a score by George GERSHWIN, featuring among others the celebrated song *'S Wonderful,* is produced in New York.

23 NOVEMBER 1927

Zuluméar (The Tyrant), opera in three acts by the Serbian composer Petar KRSTIĆ, based on rustic life in

Ottoman-dominated Bosnia, is performed for the first time in Belgrade.

27 NOVEMBER 1927

Les Euménides, opera in three acts by Darius MILHAUD, the third of the three parts of his operatic trilogy after Aeschylus' *Oresteia* (the first two being *Agamemnon* and *Les Choephores*) dealing with Orestes pursued by the furies, Erinys, to punish him for the murder of his mother committed by him to avenge the murder at her hands of his father Agamemnon, but protected by Athena and Apollo, and declared innocent by the people of Athens by reason of justifiable matricide, whereupon the Erinys change their name to Eumenides (meaning benevolent ones), is performed for the first time in Antwerp.

4 DECEMBER 1927

Satuala, opera in three acts by Emil von REZNIČEK, involving a fair-skinned Hawaiian girl-spy who lures a captain of the landing American forces in Sandwich Islands in 1893 in order to delay the operation but becomes enamored of him in earnest and stabs herself to death as he, realizing his delinquency, shoots himself to the strains of the *Star-Spangled Banner,* in an effective theatrical setting including a hula-hula ballet accompanied by secundal harmonies and syncopated rhythms, is produced in Leipzig.

5 DECEMBER 1927

Somdet Phra Chao Yu Hua Bhumibol Adulyadej, King ANANDA of Siam, composer of American jazz tunes, among them *Blue Night* to lyrics by the Royal Chamberlain, is born in the Grand Palace in Bangkok.

5 DECEMBER 1927

Le Bon Roi Dagobert, opera in four acts by Marcel SAMUEL-ROUSSEAU, after the old French fable about the good old King Dagobert, who loves his queen in the daytime but fails to notice that another woman plays the succuba at night, and when he finds out, cannot decide which one he prefers, is produced at the Opéra-Comique in Paris.

5 DECEMBER 1927

Glagolithic Mass (Slavonic Mass), the last work of the Czech grandmaster Leoš JANÁČEK, completed by him on 15 October 1926 at the age of 72, to the orthodox text in old Slavonic, scored for soloists, chorus, organ and orchestra (thus violating the tradition of the Eastern Church admitting only a cappella singing), making use of undiatonic melodies in whole-tone scales and occasional polytonalities, with the rhythmic line often in asymmetric patterns, comprising eight sections, five of which are choral, with a final apotheosis consisting of an organ solo and an instrumental envoi, is performed for the first time in Brno.

10 DECEMBER 1927

Fantaisie basque for violin and orchestra by Gabriel PIERNÉ is performed for the first time in Paris, with Jacques Thibaud as soloist and the composer conducting.

11 DECEMBER 1927

La Principessa di Perepepé, musical comedy by the Italian composer Mario LABROCA, is produced in Rome.

13 DECEMBER 1927

The Bromberg Jazz Orchestra in Warsaw, Poland, establishes the world's endurance record by playing thirty-three hours and ten minutes, with only forty-five seconds' intermission between the numbers, bettering the previous record by two hours.

15 DECEMBER 1927

Arthur SHEPHERD conducts the Cleveland Orchestra in the first performance of his first symphony, *Horizons,* in four movements representing four geographically psychological scenes of the American West: (1) *Westward;* (2) *The Lone Prairie,* with the song *The Dying Cowboy* played by a saxophone; (3) *The Old Chisholm Trail,* making use of the old tune of that name; (4) *Canyons,* painting a spacious musicorama of a famous Western landmark.

16 DECEMBER 1927

Le Pauvre Matelot, "a complaint in three acts" in the form of an opera, by Darius MILHAUD (completed on 7 September 1926), to a libretto by Jean Cocteau, wherein a sailor returning home after many years at sea represents himself to his wife as a stranger to test her fidelity and is murdered by her for his money which she hopes to save for his return, is produced at the Opéra-Comique in Paris.

21 DECEMBER 1927

Jakub lutnista (Jacob the Lutenist), opera by the 57-year-old Polish composer Henryk OPIENSKI, is produced in Poznan.

22 DECEMBER 1927

Willem PIJPER, 33-year-old Dutch modernist, plays the piano solo with the Concertgebouw Orchestra in Amsterdam, Pierre Monteux conducting, in the first performance of his *Piano Concerto* (completed on 26 August 1927), consisting of four symphonic pieces with piano obbligato separated by three unaccompanied piano solo sections.

(This was originally Pijper's *Second Piano Concerto;* the *Orkeststuk* for piano and orchestra, first performed by Pijper in Utrecht on 11 December 1915, was *Piano Concerto No. 1,* but the numeral was subsequently removed and the erstwhile *Second* was redesignated simply *Piano Concerto.*)

27 DECEMBER 1927

Show Boat, musical play by Jerome KERN, his masterpiece of the American musical theater, with book and lyrics by Oscar Hammerstein II, based on the novel by Edna Ferber of the same name, presenting a romantic story of events on a Mississippi showboat in the 1880's, wherein the captain's daughter elopes with a gambler, featuring one of the most authentically inspired songs in American popular music, the hymnal *Ol' Man River* conceived in the tones of a Negro spiritual, is performed for the first time in New York, produced by Florenz Ziegfeld.

28 DECEMBER 1927

Dinara, comic opera in three acts by the 54-year-old Georgian composer Dmitri ARAKISHVILI, to a libretto in the Georgian language, after the Arabian tale *Caliph for an Hour*, is produced in Tbilisi.

28 DECEMBER 1927

Antigone, "musical tragedy" by Arthur HONEGGER, to a libretto by Jean Cocteau after Sophocles, couched in a stylized neo-Grecian idiom, vitalized by astringent secundal discords, is produced in Brussels.

29 DECEMBER 1927

Sly, opera in three acts by Ermanno WOLF-FERRARI, founded on the prologue to Shakespeare's *The Taming of the Shrew*, descriptive of the drunken sot named Sly, is produced at La Scala in Milan.

29 DECEMBER 1927

Alexandre TANSMAN, 30-year-old Polish-Parisian composer, appears as soloist with the Boston Symphony Orchestra, Serge Koussevitzky conducting, in the world première of his *Second Piano Concerto*, in three movements, of which the last opens with a *Berceuse* set in nostalgic Polish inflections and then erupts into a rhythmic finale.

1928

1 JANUARY 1928

Legend, symphonic poem by the totally blind Bulgarian composer Petko STAINOV, dealing with a medieval maiden who is passionately importuned by an incontinent monk but is appropriated by a brutal Tatar, set to music in purple colors redolent of Russian orientalisms, is produced in Sofia.

9 JANUARY 1928

Jean Eugène Gaston LEMAIRE, Paris composer of light theater music, commits suicide at the age of 73 by jumping into the Seine.

16 JANUARY 1928

Angelo, Tyran de Padoue, opera in five acts by Alfred BRUNEAU, after Victor Hugo's drama wherein a tyrannical podestà of Padua orders his wife to be poisoned on suspicion of adultery, but is circumvented when she drinks a sleeping potion instead, and upon awakening flees with the knight of her desire, set to a melodramatic score in the best tradition of French theatrical realism, is produced at the Opéra-Comique, in Paris.

16 JANUARY 1928

La Tour de Feu, opera in three acts by the Tyrol-born composer of Italian extraction Sylvio LAZZARI, to his own libretto wherein the passion-ridden wife of the lighthouse keeper in a small island off the coast of Brittany, whose Portuguese seaman lover is shipwrecked when her husband extinguishes the guiding beacon in a stormy night, jumps to her death in the raging waters and he sets the lighthouse afire and perishes in the "tower of fire," set to a musical score of effective melodramatic power, is produced for the first time at the Paris Opéra.

27 JANUARY 1928

Violin Concerto by Cyril SCOTT, in one movement, marked by a considerable interjection of unresolved dissonances with polytonal implications employed in chromatic blocks in the orchestral accompaniment, while the violin part moves along exotic scales, is performed for the first time in Birmingham, May Harrison soloist, Sir Adrian Boult conducting.

29 JANUARY 1928

Traumwandel, opera in two acts by the Swiss composer Karl Heinrich DAVID (based on a story by Turgenev), is produced in Zürich.

31 JANUARY 1928

Ol-Ol, opera in three acts by Alexander TCHEREPNIN, after a drama by Leonid Andreyev depicting the mores of prerevolutionary Russian students, with the heroine Olga (nicknamed Ol-Ol) representing the element of intellectual love, is produced in Weimar.

12 FEBRUARY 1928

Egdon Heath, symphonic poem by Gustav HOLST, inspired by Thomas Hardy's description of it as "a place perfectly accordant with man's nature... singularly colossal and mysterious in its swarthy monotony," is performed for the first time by the New York Symphony Orchestra under the direction of Walter Damrosch who commissioned the work.

16 FEBRUARY 1928

More than 58 years after MUSSORGSKY completed the full score of *Boris Godunov* on 15 December 1869 according to old-style calendar, the opera is performed in

Leningrad for the first time in its original form, without Rimsky-Korsakov's mellificent alterations.

18 FEBRUARY 1928

Der Zar lässt sich photographieren, one-act opera buffa by Kurt WEILL, in which a tsar vacationing in Paris visits a photographer's studio and is charmed by its female operator who, on orders from a revolutionary group, shoots him dead with a gun concealed in her camera, is produced in Leipzig.

26 FEBRUARY 1928

Violin Concerto by the Venezuelan-born Parisian composer Reynaldo HAHN is performed for the first time in Paris with the composer conducting.

28 FEBRUARY 1928

The THEREMINOVOX, electronic apparatus generating musical sounds by rheostatic regulation of the electric current through the motion of a hand in front of an antenna, is patented in Washington by its inventor, the Russian engineer Leo THEREMIN.

2 MARCH 1928

Capriccio by Leoš JANÁČEK, for piano-left hand, flute, two trumpets, three trombones and tuba, written for the Czech pianist Otakar Hollmann whose right hand was badly mutilated in World War I, is performed for the first time by him and an instrumental ensemble in Prague.

3 MARCH 1928

The Government of Cuba rescinds its prohibition of the jungle drum BONGO used by Afro-Cuban villagers for communication and potential clarion calls for a rebellion.

8 MARCH 1928

Il Finto Arlecchino, opera buffa in two acts by Gian Francesco MALIPIERO, constituting the second part of the trilogy *Il mistero di Venezia*, is produced separately in Mainz, to a German libretto.

11 MARCH 1928

Lied der Sturmkolonnen, Hitlerite storm troop song, to the tune of the *Internationale*, is sung for the first time at a Nazi rally in Bernau, with a new set of words extolling Hitler's love of freedom, his solicitude for workers and determination to end unemployment. (Date and information from *Die Musik*, Berlin, December 1936, p. 174.)

11 MARCH 1928

Preludio e Fuga for orchestra by Riccardo PICK-MAN-GIA-GALLI (the fugue theme being a monorhythmic ascending C major scale) is performed for the first time in Milan.

14 MARCH 1928

Dafni, opera in three acts by Giuseppe MULÈ, a "pastoral poem" recounting the flight of Daphné from Apollo, is produced in Rome.

16 MARCH 1928

Latavra, opera in three acts by the 57-year-old Georgian composer Zakhar PALIASHVILI, is performed for the first time in Tiflis, in the Georgian language.

18 MARCH 1928

Žena a Bůh (A Woman and God), one-act opera by the 37-year-old Czech composer Karel Boleslav JIRÁK entered on a neo-Pythagorean philosopher of the first century A.D. named Apollo of Tyan, who was reputed to be a miracle worker, is performed for the first time in Brno.

20 MARCH 1928

Chirurgie, one-act opera by Pierre Octave FERROUD, to Chekhov's play about painful Russian dentistry, with a musical score illustrating abortive tooth extraction in a naturalistic Mussorgskyan manner, is performed for the first time at Monte Carlo.

21 MARCH 1928

A group of conscientious objectors to modern music and jazz hurl a stink bomb in the Budapest Opera Theater during the Hungarian premiere of the opera *Jonny spielt auf* by Ernst KRENEK.

23 MARCH 1928

Symphonic Piece by the Boston classicist Walter PISTON, written in an "absolute idiom" of modern polyphony with a justifiable admixture of tolerable dissonance, is performed for the first time by the Boston Symphony Orchestra, on the same program with the first performance of a similarly conceived but quite differently executed piece, *Music for an Orchestra* by the Rumanian composer Filip LAZAR.

24 MARCH 1928

Beatrix, Flemish opera in three acts by the 30-year-old Flemish composer Ignaz LILIEN, is produced in Antwerp.

25 MARCH 1928

At a festival of Bulgarian music in Prague, the first performance is given of *Vardar*, symphonic rhapsody by the 29-year-old Bulgarian composer Pantcho VLADIGEROV, with thematic materials derived from authentic popular songs of the Vardar River valley.

27 MARCH 1928

Armand GIVELET, Vice-President of the French Radio Club gives the first public demonstration in Paris of a heterodyne instrument capable of producing musical tones of definite pitch by the movement of the hand, similar to the principle of the Thereminovox, but securing greater accuracy of intonation within the tempered scale.

27 MARCH 1928

Leslie STUART (real name T. A. Barrett), English composer of light operas, of which *Florodora* (a fancied name of a tropical island), featuring a famous sexy sextet of Victorian girls, has attained enormous success, dies in

London at the age of 64. (The statement in previous editions of *Music Since 1900* that Leslie Stuart was the author of the song *It's a Long Long Way to Tipperary* is erroneous; its composer and lyricist were respectively Jack Judge and Harry Williams.)

29 MARCH 1928

A new harp model perfected by the French-American master harpist Carlos SALZEDO (in comparison with which the old harp was said to be "as an ox to an airplane") is demonstrated for the first time in public at the eighth annual National Harp Festival in Philadelphia.

29 MARCH 1928

A Holtak Szigete (The Isle of Death), two-act opera by the 33-year-old Hungarian composer Eugen ZÁDOR, inspired by the famous painting of Arnold Böcklin, wherein Böcklin himself is taken to the funereal cypress-lined isle of death by the jealous lover of his beloved, whither she follows him in a rowboat on a stormy afternoon and is dashed to her death against the rocky shore, is produced in Budapest.

30 MARCH 1928

The Philharmonic Society of New York is merged with the New York Symphony Society, forming the New York Philharmonic-Symphony Society, with Arturo Toscanini as the principal conductor and Walter Damrosch, former music director of the New York Symphony, as guest conductor.

30 MARCH 1928

Symphony, by the American composer Edward Burlingame HILL, in three movements, *Allegro moderato, Moderato maestoso* and *Allegro brioso,* written "with no descriptive basis, no dramatic conflict or spiritual crisis" in the cerulean key of B-flat major, with excursions into the impressionistic regions of enhanced tonality, is performed for the first time by the Boston Symphony Orchestra under the direction of Serge Koussevitzky, to whom the score is dedicated.

31 MARCH 1928

Filomela e l'Infatuato, music drama in three parts by Gian Francesco MALIPIERO (completed on 22 June 1925), to a libretto dealing with a man infatuated with a human philomel whose thrilling trilling fascinates him, is produced in Prague.

4 APRIL 1928

MUSSORGSKY's piano suite *Pictures at an Exhibition* is presented in Dessau as an abstract ballet, with a highly stylized, surrealistic decor by the Russian painter Wassily Kandinsky, wherein *Gnomus* is symbolized by a cellular circle surrounded by triangular hemoglobins, the *Old Castle* is built on superimposed spherical segments, and the *Great Gate of Kiev* is represented by a heavenward-reaching tower flanked by a lunar crescent and an eclipsed sun.

Mussorgsky's work is not program music merely because it was inspired by pictures. If this music mirrors anything at all, it is not the painted image but some inner experiences of Mussorgsky himself, which rise much higher than the subject of the actual paintings and are expressed in pure musical forms. With the exception of the sketch portraying Samuel Goldenberg and Schmuyle and that of the Market of Limoge, my entire décor is abstract. (Wassily Kandinsky in *Kunstblatt* August 1930)

5 APRIL 1928

Danças Africanas, orchestral suite by Brazil's prime composer Heitor VILLA-LOBOS, subtitled *Danças dos Indios mestisos do Brasil* and based on the melorhythmic figurations of the Brazilian jungle songs, in three sections—(1) *Farrapos,* a dance of youths; (2) *Kankikis,* a dance of old men; and (3) *Kankukus,* a children's dance—all set in 2/4 time in asymmetric rhythms, with a liberal infusion of whole-tone scales, but differing in tempo and kinetic energy, is performed for the first time in Paris.

5 APRIL 1928

Die Herzogin von Chicago, operetta by Emmerich KÁLMÁN, dealing with the wilful daughter of a Chicago sausage magnate who gives a $5,000 tip to a Budapest Gypsy band to play Charleston for her dance with a jazz-hating crown prince of Sylvaria and wins a million-dollar bet from the Young Ladies' Eccentric Club of New York for this achievement, is made a Duchess of Chicago by the aged King of Sylvaria so as to enable the crown prince to marry her without demeaning his royal status, and is contracted by Fox Films of New York to act out her princely romance on the screen, is produced in Vienna.

6 APRIL 1928

California, "festival scenes" by Frederick S. CONVERSE, is performed for the first time by the Boston Symphony Orchestra.

7 APRIL 1928

Tenth Symphony by Russia's most prolific symphonist Nicolai MIASKOVSKY, in F minor, completed by him on 29 December 1927, in one movement consisting of two sections, *Un poco sostenuto* and *Allegro tumultuoso,* inspired by Pushkin's poem *The Bronze Knight,* descriptive of the mad challenge to the bronze statue of Peter the Great hurled by a humble clerk whose betrothed perished in the 1824 inundation in St. Petersburg, the town which Peter built, is performed for the first time in Moscow.

9 APRIL 1928

Thien-Hoa (Fior di cieto), opera in three acts, to a pseudo-Sinological libretto, by the 42-year-old Italian composer Guido BIANCHINI, is produced at La Scala, in Milan.

12 APRIL 1928

Six Symphonic Epigrams, orchestral suite by the foremost Dutch modernist Willem PIJPER, written for the 40th anniversary of the Concertgebouw Orchestra in Amsterdam and inspired by Shakespeare's line, "Brevity is the soul of wit" (the entire suite lasts less than five minutes when played at the proper tempo), is performed for the first time in Amsterdam.

14 APRIL 1928

Frühlings Erwachen, opera in three acts by Max ETTINGER, to a libretto based on Frank Wedekind's vivid story of torments of adolescent sexuality, is produced in Leipzig.

20 APRIL 1928

Two "minute operas" by Darius MILHAUD, *La Délivrance de Thesée*, depicting the deliverance of Theseus with the help of Ariadne, from the labyrinth of Minotaur in Crete, and *L'Abandon d'Ariane*, illustrating the abandonment of Ariadne by Theseus on the island of Naxos, are produced in Wiesbaden.

20 APRIL 1928

ONDES MUSICALES, electronic musical instrument, invented by the French musician and engineer Maurice MARTENOT, known also as ONDES MARTENOT, is demonstrated for the first time in Paris. (The instrument was patented in Paris on 30 March 1929.)

25 APRIL 1928

René BERTRAND gives in Paris a demonstration of an orchestra of six dynaphones, producing sounds by heterodynamic frequencies, the first instance of multiple employment of electronic instruments.

26 APRIL 1928

Present Arms, musical comedy by Richard RODGERS, in which an American Marine in Hawaii, dishonorably discharged for impersonating an officer, salvages a British yacht and wins the hand of a peer's daughter, featuring the song *You Took Advantage of Me*, is produced in New York.

27 APRIL 1928

Apollon Musagète, ballet in two scenes by Igor STRAVINSKY for string orchestra, written in a gymnosophistical, Delphically austere, stately neo-Baroque style, with meaningful pauses at the points of harmonic congeries when dissonant chords are ominously suspended, with a motto-chord C, F, B, D, F-sharp symbolizing Apollo, set in a highly choreographable rhythmic design, depicting Apollo as the leader of the muses of poetry, mimic action, and dance, is performed for the first time at the Library of Congress in Washington, D.C., as a work commissioned by the Elizabeth Sprague Coolidge Foundation.

29 APRIL 1928

Ninth Symphony, in E minor, by Nicolai MIASKOVSKY (completed 21 July 1927), in four movements, *Andante sostenuto*, *Presto*, *Lento molto*, and *Allegro con grazia*, conceived as a lyric and contemplative work, is performed for the first time in Moscow, three weeks and a day after the performance of his *Tenth Symphony*.

3 MAY 1928

Tam-Man-Nacup, opera based on Indian spring chants by the 40-year-old American composer William F. HANSON, is produced for the first time in Provo, Utah.

6 MAY 1928

At a festival of modern music in Wiesbaden, three satirical one-act operas by Ernst KRENEK, to his own texts, are given for the first time:

(1) *Der Diktator*, wherein a woman, trying to murder a Mussolini-type modern dictator, suddenly asks him to kiss her and is accidentally killed by a bullet fired at him by his wife; (2) *Das geheime Königreich*, wherein a coloratura singer becomes the queen of a Utopian kingdom and falls in love with a political dissenter planning the king's assassination, with a happy ending ensuing when the rebel returns to his revolutionary comrades and the queen reconciles herself to monarchy; (3) *Schwergewicht, oder die Ehre der Nation* (completed on 14 June 1927), a burlesque inspired by the contemplation of the adulation extended to sport figures and a German statesman's declaration that "a prize fighter or a channel swimmer does more for the glory of the nation than all the artists and scientists put together," the story evolving around a muscular heavyweight champion loved by a habitual adulteress and an erratic medical student who disguises herself as a boxing trainee and to her great delight is knocked out by him in a gym.

For some time I pursued the stylistic direction of *Jonny Spielt Auf*. The three one-act operas that I wrote immediately afterwards may be regarded as a kind of marginal observation to it. *Der Diktator* treated a bloody episode from the private life of a Duce type character. *Das geheime Königreich* was a fairy tale which was to demonstrate that all worldly might was a *vanitas vanitatum* and recommended a return to innocent nature. *Schwergewicht, oder die Ehre der Nation*, was a satirical operetta, which attacked hero worship in the field of sports, exposing a heavyweight world champion as a helpless idiot despite an honorary doctor's degree bestowed upon him by the department of philosophy in a university. (Ernst Krenek, in *Selbstdarstellung*, Zürich, 1948)

6 MAY 1928

Die Freunde von Salamanca, opera written by Franz SCHUBERT in 1815, is produced posthumously in Halle.

9 MAY 1928

Sarati le Terrible, opera in four acts by the 37-year-old French composer Francis BOUSQUET, dealing with an Algerian coal merchant named Sarati, incestuously infatuated with his young niece, who kills himself after she marries a mysterious young stranger, is produced at the Opéra-Comique in Paris.

9 MAY 1928

Blackbirds of 1928, an all-Negro revue by Jimmy MCHUGH, with a locale placed in Harlem, and containing the celebrated song *I Can't Give You Anything But Love, Baby*, is produced in New York.

10 MAY 1928

Anathema, opera in three acts by Alfred TOFFT (founded on a story by Mérimée), his second and last opera, is produced in Copenhagen.

12 MAY 1928

Il Patto dei tre, comic opera in three acts by the 53-year-old Italian composer Domenico MONLEONE, dealing with three friends who formed a pact of eternal faith symbolized by a rock in the form of a large bell, is produced in the Genoese dialect in Genoa.

15 MAY 1928

Napasta (Disaster), opera in three acts by the 33-year-old Rumanian composer Sabin DRAGOI, written in a passionately romantic manner and depicting the horrors of a hidden murder when the second husband of a rural widow is revealed as the killer of her first husband, a crime for which an innocuous village idiot was unjustly convicted, is produced in Bucharest.

16 MAY 1928

Fra Gherardo, opera in three acts by Ildebrando PIZZETTI, to his own text dealing with an actual flagellant friar burned at the stake for heresy about 1260 in Parma, with fictional additions involving a local girl seduced and abandoned by him, and in the end stoned as a witch, to a musical score artfully applying elements of authentic medieval modalities, with empty fifths illustrating monastic asceticism, recurrent rhythmic strokes in dissonant harmonies suggesting penitential self-flagellation, and luxuriant Italianate outbursts of flowing melodies depicting the incontinence of earthly passions, is produced at La Scala, Milan, Arturo Toscanini conducting.

19 MAY 1928

Henry F. GILBERT, American composer of native-conscious philosophy, a primordial American who refused to regard American music as a colonial by-product of the art of Europe, and whose own instrumental and vocal works draw amply upon Indian, Negro and Creole resources for thematic material, dies in Cambridge, Massachusetts, at 3:42 A.M. of cerebral hemorrhage (he was born as a "blue baby" with imperfect cardiac walls) at the age of 59.

25 MAY 1928

The new building of the Teatro Colón is opened in Buenos Aires.

6 JUNE 1928

Die Ägyptische Helena, opera in two acts by Richard STRAUSS, to a libretto by Hugo von Hofmannsthal, wherein the cuckolded King Menelaus intends to kill Helen after the destruction of Troy, but is given to drink a potion of oblivion which makes him believe that she was not with Paris in Troy but in Egypt waiting for a marital reunion, making it possible for them to return to Sparta together after some additional complications when he drinks a potion of remembrance, with a musical score much less complex than the highly charged *Salome* and *Elektra*, but still revealing the familiar Straussian flights into empyrean harmonies, is produced in Dresden.

6 JUNE 1928

Ode, or Meditation at Night on the Majesty of God as Revealed by the Aurora Borealis, ballet-cantata by the 25-year-old Russian émigré composer Nicolas NABOKOV, to the text of a poem by the Russian scientist-poet Mikhail Lomonosov written by him on the occasion of the coronation of Empress Elizabeth, daughter of Peter the Great, is produced in Paris by the Ballet Russe directed by Serge Diaghilev, great-great-grand-son of one of Elizabeth's several illegitimate children.

7 JUNE 1928

Concerto for piano and orchestra by Albert ROUSSEL, in three movements, a propulsive *Allegro molto*, a contemplatively somber *Adagio* and a precipitate *Allegro con spirito* in the form of a rondo with variations, is performed for the first time at a Koussevitzky concert in Paris, with Alexander Borovsky as piano soloist.

9 JUNE 1928

Belkis, biblical opera by the Portuguese composer Ruy COELHO, is produced in Lisbon.

13 JUNE 1928

Wolfgang GRAESER, youthful Swiss composer and able music scholar, editor of *Die Kunst der Fuge* in the *Neue Bach-Gesellschaft* edition, kills himself in Berlin at the age of 21.

15 JUNE 1928

Alexander GLAZUNOV leaves Leningrad for Vienna as a delegate to the Schubert Centennial, never to return. (Exact date of Glazunov's departure obtained from Maximilian Steinberg, Glazunov's successor as Director of the Leningrad Conservatory.)

16 JUNE 1928

During his Brazilian tour Ottorino RESPIGHI conducts in São Paulo the first performance of his newly composed symphonic suite *Impressioni Brasiliane*, in three sections:

(1) *Notte tropicale*, an impressionistic tableau of a tropical night with humidly sliding chord blocks and violins glissando as an atmospheric background for a soft echo of a Brazilian carnival song; (2) *Butantan*, a tonal painting of a snake garden in Butantan near São Paulo, with a bassoon introducing a serpentine tune, the clarinet responding in colubrine arabesques and sibilant violins in sforzando puffs, ending on a hissing solo in the bass clarinet; (3) *Canzone e Danza*, a stylization of popular Brazilian rhythms subtly accompanied by syncopated drumbeats, without specifically Brazilian percussion instruments, and concluding on a pizzicato chord in A major in the strings. (The performance was first announced for 9 June 1928, but was postponed until a week later. Information received from the Music Section of the Biblioteca Nacional in Rio de Janeiro.)

19 JUNE 1928

Frenos, four-act opera by the Argentine composer Raul ESPOILE, dealing with a reincarnated Greek philosopher Frenos (from *phrenos*, mind) working in a biological laboratory in Argentina, and becoming involved intellectually with a reincarnated Sappho and carnally with a reincarnated Helen of Troy, with a score set in lush Pucciniesque harmonies, is performed for the first time at the Teatro Colón in Buenos Aires.

28 JUNE 1928

Louis ARMSTRONG and his Hot Five record *West End Blues*, a milestone in the history of Jazz.

14 JULY 1928

Actualités, suite for a small orchestra by Darius MIL-HAUD, subtitled 'Musique de film,' a series of stylized musical pictures of a newsreel—an official reception for aviators, a boxer, industrial application of water, a murder attempt in a train, the Derby horse race—is performed for the first time at a music festival in Baden-Baden.

15 JULY 1928

The Hero, satirical opera in one act by the Soviet composer Alexander MOSSOLOV, to his own text ridiculing bourgeois hero worship in capitalist Germany, is produced for the first time anywhere in Baden-Baden, unique occasion of the world première of a Soviet work outside of the Soviet Union.

1 AUGUST 1928

Detvan, opera by the Slovak composer Viliam FIGUŠBYSTRÝ, the first stage work to a text in the Slovak language on a subject from Slovak folklore, is produced in Bratislava.

5 AUGUST 1928

Aphrodite, grand opera by the Italian-born Argentine composer Arturo LUZZATTI, with a French libretto based on the aphrodisiac novel by Pierre Louys, is produced at the Teatro Colón in Buenos Aires.

9 AUGUST 1928

Percy GRAINGER marries the Swedish poet and painter Ella Viola Ström in a public ceremony performed by a Swedish Lutheran minister, at the Hollywood Bowl, with a lighted cross atop a nearby mountain illuminating the amphitheater, and conducts for an audience of 22,000 his orchestral dedication *To a Nordic Princess.*

10 AUGUST 1928

In a public address Mustafa KEMAL PASHA, the founder of modern Turkey, urges the adoption of Western dances and jazz to relieve the traditional homophony and rhythmic indeterminacy of Turkish folk music.

12 AUGUST 1928

Leoš JANÁČEK, modern grand master of Czech music, great animator of native musical culture whose works are built on the realistic concept of melody as spoken music, and harmony as a product of moving voices, dies at Ostrava at the age of 74.

31 AUGUST 1928

Die Dreigroschenoper, ballad-opera in eight scenes with an epilogue by the 28-year-old German composer Kurt WEILL, modeled after *The Beggar's Opera* of John Gay (produced 200 years, 7 months, and 2 days before, in London—Dr. Johnson remarked to Boswell after attending a performance: "Sir, there is in it such a labefaction of all principles that it may be injurious to morality"), to a libretto by Bertolt Brecht, with the action transferred to the year of Queen Victoria's coronation, 1837, telling a story of Mackie Messer (Mack the Knife) and his girl friend from a low London bordello, and his rise to social eminence and prosperity with the connivance of corrupt officials, set to music vibrating with the honky-tonk melorhythms of Americanized popular tunes (the song *Mack the Knife* was to become a world hit), ending with a mock-solemn chorale propounding the cynical moral "Combat the wrong, but not too strong," is produced for the first time in Berlin.

5 SEPTEMBER 1928

L'Innocente, second opera by the Brazilian composer Francisco MIGNONE, written to an Italian libretto, is produced in Rio de Janeiro.

7 SEPTEMBER 1928

Królowa Jadwiga (Queen Jadwiga), opera by the Polish composer Tadeusz JOTEYKO, is produced in Warsaw.

8 SEPTEMBER 1928

Vikerlased (The Vikings), national opera in three acts by the 28-year-old Estonian composer Evald AAV, dealing with the Estonian resistance to the invading Scandinavians in the twelfth century, and focusing on the love of an Estonian youth for a patriotic Estonian maiden who is lustfully coveted by an overweening Swede, to a musical score thoroughly marinated in Wagneromantic fluids, is produced in the Estonian language in Tallinn.

10 SEPTEMBER 1928

Harry Lawrence FREEMAN, American Negro composer, conducts in New York the first performance, with an all-Negro cast, of his opera *Voodoo,* to the story of a Louisiana snake-cult queen who kidnaps her rival for the affections of a Creole lover, and is about to put her to death in a voodoo orgy when the lover arrives, rescues the victim and slays the prospective murderess, set to music compounded of Negro spirituals, barn dance tunes and jazz, with recitatives in southern dialect.

10 SEPTEMBER 1928

The Sixth Festival of the International Society for Contemporary Music opens at Siena, Italy, under the auspices of its Italian branch, CORPORAZIONE DELLE NUOVE MUSICHE, in a program of old Italian music under the direction of Bernardino Molinari.

11 SEPTEMBER 1928

At the Sixth Festival of the International Society for Contemporary Music in Siena, the following program of chamber music is given:

String Quartet by the Italian neo-classicist Vincenzo TOMMASINI; a neo-romantic *Flute Sonata* by Karel HÁBA, brother of the pioneer of quarter-tone music Alois Hába; *Suite* for piano by Paul HINDEMITH; *Violin Sonata* by RAVEL, with a slow movement, *Blues,* emulating American ballad modalities; and a *String Quartet* by the rightfully venerated Austrian composer Alexander ZEMLINSKY.

12 SEPTEMBER 1928

In the course of the Sixth Festival of the International Society for Contemporary Music in Siena, Emil František BURI-

AN of Prague presents his "Voice Band" in wordless vocalization, accompanied by piano and drums, and creating harmonic effects by adroit combinations of vowels (treated as consonances) and consonants (treated as dissonances).

13 SEPTEMBER 1928

The Sixth Festival of the International Society for Contemporary Music in Siena presents the following program of chamber music:

Third String Quartet by the English romantic composer Frank BRIDGE, originally commissioned by the Elizabeth Sprague Coolidge Foundation and first performed in Washington on 17 September 1927, in three movements, with an elegiac quasi-atonal *Andante* flanked by two kinetic *Allegros; Duo* for violin and piano by the German composer of Wagnerogenic music Heinz TIESSEN; *String Trio,* op. 20 by Anton von WEBERN, in two movements, his first instrumental work integrally planned according to the Schoenbergian method of composition with 12 tones related only to one another, with the basic tone-row thematically stressing the interval of minor second, the music evolving in the classical forms of sonata and rondo, wherein the principle of variation form is extended to the ultimate in the aspects of metrical asymmetry, rhythmical diminution and augmentation, melodic inversion, octave translocation, retrograde movement and thematically construed pauses of silence; *Concerto* for harpsichord, flute, oboe, violin and cello by Manuel DE FALLA, with the composer at the harpsichord, its performance greatly delayed in view of the turbulence in the audience, aroused by the hearing of Webern's Trio, so that Manuel de Falla openly voiced his apprehension at the possibility of a physical attack on composers, whether guilty or innocent of dodecaphony or cacophony, and hesitated to appear on the podium until assured that the passions had subsided; and *Music for Eight Instruments* by the Swiss composer Robert BLUM.

After the performance of Anton von Webern's *String Trio* there was a disturbance, hisses and boos. The correspondent of the Milan newspaper *Popolo d'Italia* roared: "This is the music of the savages!" (*Breslauer Neueste Nachrichten,* Breslau, 15 September 1928)

14 SEPTEMBER 1928

In the course of the Sixth Festival of the International Society for Contemporary Music in Siena, Alfredo CASELLA conducts, in the morning, two consecutive performances of *Façade* by William WALTON, and, in the afternoon, his own *Serenata* for five instruments and STRAVINSKY's scenic cantata depicting the Russian wedding ritual, *Les Noces.*

14 SEPTEMBER 1928

Concerto for clarinet and orchestra by the Danish grandmaster Carl NIELSEN (completed on 15 August 1928), in four sections (*Allegretto un poco, Poco Adagio, Allegro non troppo* and *Allegro vivace*) set in a quasi-modernistic idiom, stressing the dichotomy of the polar tonalities at a tritone's distance, while thematic melorhythms remain well within the traditional forms, is performed for the first time in Humblebaeck.

15 SEPTEMBER 1928

At the last concert of the Sixth Festival of the International Society for Contemporary Music in Siena, the following program of chamber music was given:

Second String Quartet by the master polyphonist of Czech music Bohuslav MARTINU; a florid *Cello Sonata* by the Italian composer Franco ALFANO; and *Piano Quintet* (with affective quarter-tones) by Ernest BLOCH. (Prokofiev's *Quintet* for oboe, clarinet, bassoon, viola and double-bass was announced in the program, but could not be performed because the instrumental parts failed to arrive in time.)

19 SEPTEMBER 1928

The first "100% all-talking, all-singing" motion picture, *The Singing Fool,* with the title role performed by Al Jolson in blackface, and an animated cartoon *Steamboat Willie* by Walt Disney, introducing Mickey Mouse, both with a newly perfected synchronized musical sound track, are shown for the first time in New York City.

19 SEPTEMBER 1928

The New Moon, musical romance in two acts by Sigmund ROMBERG, wherein a young revolutionary arrested by the French Royal authorities of New Orleans in 1788 and taken aboard the French ship *New Moon,* escapes detention and establishes a settlement on a small West Indies island with his sweetheart and a group of comrades-in-arms until the French Revolution liberates them, with a musical score containing the popular osculatory ballads *One Kiss* and *Lover, Come Back to Me,* the masculine chorus *Stout-Hearted Men* and the mutually optative duet *Wanting You,* is produced in New York.

28 SEPTEMBER 1928

Coups de roulis, operetta in three acts by the 74-year-old French composer André MESSAGER, is produced in Paris.

1 OCTOBER 1928

Mariette, gay operetta in an Offenbachian manner by Oscar STRAUS, to a libretto by Sacha Guitry, dealing with a fictional story of a young enchantress (acted by Yvonne Printemps, Sacha Guitry's wife) who captivates Prince Louis Napoleon (acted by Sacha Guitry), only to lose his love when he becomes Emperor Napoleon III, is produced in Paris.

4 OCTOBER 1928

Friederike, operetta in three acts by Franz LEHÁR based on an episode in Goethe's life, when as a law student in Strassburg in 1771 he formed a deep attachment for a village pastor's daughter actually named Friederike, and revisited her eight years after going through three more romances, with some of his tenor arias in waltz time set to his poems actually inspired by Friederike, is performed for the first time in Berlin.

8 OCTOBER 1928

Brothers Karamazov, opera in five acts, after Dostoyevsky's famous novel, by the Czech composer Otakar JEREMIÁŠ, is produced in Prague.

8 OCTOBER 1928

Concerto in A minor for violin and orchestra by Alfredo CASELLA, a work representing a concession to the romantic trends in modern music, is performed for the first time anywhere by the conductorless orchestra in Moscow, Josef Szigeti soloist.

8 OCTOBER 1928

Bratři Karamazovi, opera in three acts by the Czech composer Otakar JEREMÍÁŠ, in which the drama of the Karamazov brothers depicted in Dostoyevsky's psychological novel receives a romantic interpretation, is produced in Prague.

10 OCTOBER 1928

L'Eau du Nil, the first French "film sonore" with a synchronized sound track, is demonstrated in Paris.

10 OCTOBER 1928

Hold Everything, a musical comedy by Ray HENDERSON, wherein a welterweight champion dejected by a psychological misunderstanding with his girl friend is sufficiently aroused by jealousy against the challenger to knock him out in the prize ring, featuring the perennially alluring song *You're the Cream in My Coffee*, is produced in New York.

14 OCTOBER 1928

Wakuta, opera in four acts by the 53-year-old American composer E. Bruce KNOWLTON to the composer's own libretto on an Indian subject, is produced in Portland, Oregon.

14 OCTOBER 1928

Tyll, opera in three acts by the 26-year-old German composer Mark LOTHAR, detailing the adventures of the legendary character Ulenspiegel, is produced in Weimar.

15 OCTOBER 1928

Symphony in C Major by the Swedish composer Kurt ATTERBERG, winner of the $10,000 Schubert Memorial Prize offered by the Columbia Phonograph Company of New York awarded to him on 17 August 1928 by an International Grand Jury of eminent composers and scholars—Franz Schalk, Donald Francis Tovey, Alfred Bruneau, Max von Schillings, Franco Alfano, Emil Mlynarski, Alexander Glazunov, Carl Nielsen, Adolfo Salazar and Walter Damrosch—as the best work conceived in the spirit of the lyrical genius of Schubert, written to commemorate the centennial of his death, is performed for the first time in Cologne.

Every one was busy spotting reminiscences in the Symphony; and it can not be denied that they are plentiful and obvious. Atterberg may have looked down the list of judges, and slyly made up his mind that he would put in a bit of something that would appeal to each of them in turn—a bit of *Scheherazade* for the Russian Glazunov, a bit of *Cockaigne* for Mr. Tovey, a bit of the *New World Symphony* for Mr. Damrosch, a bit of *Pétrouchka* for the modernist Alfano, a bit of Granados for Salaxar. . . . But I wonder if there may not be another explanation. . . . Atterberg is not merely a composer. He is a musical critic. . . . Suppose he looked round with the cynical smile that, as all the world knows, all critics wear, and decided to pull the world's leg? (Ernest Newman, Sunday *Times*, London, 18 November 1928)

(Kurt Atterberg published an article in the *Musical Digest*, Chicago, February 1920, entitled *How I Fooled the Music World*, admitting that his symphony was a satirical challenge to Schubert worshippers.)

19 OCTOBER 1928

The Orchestre Symphonique de Paris gives its inaugural concert in Paris, in a program comprising the world première of the "symphonic movement" *Rugby*, by Arthur HONEGGER descriptive of the restless animation of the game. (*Rugby* was subsequently performed during the intermission of the International Rugby Match between France and England on 31 December 1928)

20 OCTOBER 1928

The French Academy rules that celibacy is to be no longer a *conditio sine qua non* for applicants for the Prix de Rome.

20 OCTOBER 1928

Suite Canadienne for orchestra and chorus by the 37-year-old Canadian composer Claude CHAMPAGNE is performed for the first time in Paris.

25 OCTOBER 1928

Joaquín TURINA conducts in Barcelona the first performance of his orchestral choreographic fantasy *Rítmos*.

25 OCTOBER 1928

Tuhotulva (Deluge), opera in three acts by the Finnish musicologist Ilmari KROHN, is produced in Helsinki.

27 OCTOBER 1928

El Giravolt de Maig (Round Dance of May), one-act opera in the Catalan language by Eduardo TOLDRÁ, is produced in Barcelona.

1 NOVEMBER 1928

The National Opera House is inaugurated in Tashkent, capital of the Uzbek Soviet Republic in Central Asia.

4 NOVEMBER 1928

Dr. Arthur Eaglefield HULL, English musicologist, champion of Scriabin and modern music in general, dies in London at the age of 52, in consequence of the injuries sustained in his suicide attempt (fractured ribs and amnesia) on 18 September 1928 when he jumped under the train at the Huddersfield Railway Station, driven to this desperate act by the public exposure of extensive plagiarism perpetrated in his book *Music, Classical, Romantic and Modern*, published by J. M. Dent & Sons, Ltd., on 8 April 1927 and withdrawn from its catalogue on 28 August 1928 after the evidence of Hull's literary expropriations became irrefutable.

Hull's suicide was the result of my exposure of his thefts in his book *Music, Classical Romantic and Modern*. He threw himself under a train. (Percy A. Scholes in a letter to the author dated 21 March 1948)

4 NOVEMBER 1928

Carlos CHÁVEZ conducts in Mexico City the first performance of his ballet *El fuego nuevo*, in the form of a suite of four dances, the action of which unfolds around an Aztec pyramid, making use of primitive Mexican instruments of percussion in the score.

10 NOVEMBER 1928

Los Hijos del Sol, opera by the Argentine composer Athos PALMA, based on a story of the Inca priests, "Sons of the Sun," in an appropriately pentatonic melodic setting, is produced at the Teatro Colón in Buenos Aires.

13 NOVEMBER 1928

Mondnacht, opera in three acts by Julius BITTNER, to his own libretto, dealing with a lieutenant of the German Army, in love with a somnambulist, who steals and sells a portfolio containing information pertaining to the military plans of 1865, is apprehended and ordered to commit suicide, with the sound of the shot on a moonlit night upsetting the equilibrium of his beloved walking precariously on a ledge who falls to her death, is produced in Berlin.

16 NOVEMBER 1928

Igor STRAVINSKY conducts the Orchestre Symphonique in Paris in the first performance of the orchestral version of his *Étude* for pianola composed in 1917.

19 NOVEMBER 1928

A century has passed since Franz SCHUBERT, genius of the German lied and youthful creator of immortal symphonies, dies at his brother's house in Vienna, at the age of 31.

22 NOVEMBER 1928

Ida Rubinstein presents at her dance recital at the Paris Opéra the world première of *Boléro* by Maurice RAVEL, specially written for her, a fantastically varied rondo comprising eighteen recurrences of a binary subject of a Hispanic melorhythmic nature, the first section in pure C major, the second in the Mixolydian mode on C, culminating in a fulminant digression into E major in the coda, with triadic harmonies in parallel motion (in one variation the high harmonics create an overtone complex that forcibly changes the color of the solo instrument), scored for a large and diversified orchestra including an oboe d'amore, three saxophones and an important percussion ensemble.

Boléro is an experiment in a very special and limited direction . . . a piece lasting seventeen minutes and consisting entirely of orchestral fabric without music, of one long, very gradual crescendo. There are no contrasts, and practically no inventive ideas except in the design and manner of execution. The themes are impersonal folk-like melodies of the common Spanish-Arabian sort. (From Ravel's statement to M. D. Calvocoressi, published in the *Daily Telegraph,* London, 16 July 1931, and reprinted in the article *Ravel's Letters to Calvocoressi* in *The Musical Quarterly* of January 1941)

23 NOVEMBER 1928

Chanticleer, festival overture by Daniel Gregory MASON, with a motto from Thoreau's *Walden:* "I do not propose to write an ode to dejection but to brag as lustily as Chanticleer in the morning," faithfully portraying a rooster crowing on the notes of an arpeggio, then yielding to the chromatic cackling of a hen, is performed for the first time by the Cincinnati Symphony Orchestra.

23 NOVEMBER 1928

Pilgrim's Progress, oratorio by Sir Granville BANTOCK, written in commemoration of Bunyan's tercentenary, illustrating the scenes of Bunyan's moralistic dream in luxuriantly Wagneromantic tones, is performed for the first time in London.

27 NOVEMBER 1928

Ida Rubinstein stages at the Paris Opéra the world première of the allegorical ballet in four tableaux *Le Baiser de la Fée* by Igor STRAVINSKY, dedicated "to the memory of Tchaikovsky, identifying his Muse with the Fairy whose genius has marked his music with a magic kiss," the subject being inspired by Hans Christian Andersen's fairy tale *The Snow Maiden,* with the thematic material built on songs and piano pieces by Tchaikovsky, masculated and invigorated by converting his feminine phrase endings into monosyllabic rhythmic thrusts.

27 NOVEMBER 1928

Jazz Poem for piano and orchestra by Randall THOMPSON, is performed for the first time by the Rochester Philharmonic, Howard Hanson conducting, and Thompson himself playing the solo part.

30 NOVEMBER 1928

A Union of Young Composers is organized at the Central House of Art Workers in Moscow "to collectively guide the young unorganized creative talents, to eradicate by means of comradely advice any undesirable aberrations and to create artistically valid musical works that would reflect the Soviet scene and are suitable for mass audiences."

1 DECEMBER 1928

Die schwarze Orchidee, opera-grotesque in three acts by Eugen D'ALBERT, focused on a gentleman-thief who customarily leaves a rare black orchid in apartments he robs in New York, then suddenly inherits an English estate and a title of nobility, and marries an eccentric American lady whose house, situated on Fiftieth Avenue, No. 5, he has once burglarized, the cast of characters including "Tanzgirls" dancing the "Eros Foxtrot" at the Mount Everest Bar, a reporter named Schmuckele and an ensemble of "Jazz-Neger" playing syncopated banjo music, all this immersed in a heterogeneous compost of pre-fabricated discords and whole-tone scales, is produced in Leipzig.

1 DECEMBER 1928

Moschopulos, opera in three tableaux by the 25-year-old German composer Rudolf WAGNER-RÉGENY, to his own libretto dealing with a malevolent Oriental magician, is produced in Gera, on the same program with his opera after Hans Christian Andersen's tale *Der nackte König (The Emperor's New Clothes).*

2 DECEMBER 1928

Variationen für Orchester, op. 31, by Arnold SCHOENBERG (completed on 20 September 1928), his first orchestral work written according to his method of composing in twelve tones related only to one another, with the thematic series (B-flat, F-flat, G-flat, E-flat, F, A, D, C-sharp, G, G-sharp, B, C) treated in 48 different configurations (melodic inversion, retrograde, inversion of the retrograde, besides the original basic form), and integrated vertically and diagonally in canon, polyphonic imitations, harmonic combinations, with the barycenter on the initial note of the series, B-flat, producing a simulacrum of tonality, even though no triads or triadic melodic progressions ever occur and the emancipation of dissonance is complete, the orchestral score including exotic instruments (mandolin, flexaton, etc.), is performed for the first time by the Berlin Philharmonic, Wilhelm Furtwängler conducting.

The majority of the audience remained silent, but two excitable minorities engaged in combat. The exchange of remarks for and against the Schoenberg Variations soon assumed a more violent form than we ever experienced even at a Schoenberg première, and we are accustomed to almost anything. (Max Marschalk, *Die Vossische Zeitung,* Berlin, 4 December 1928)

Arnold Schoenberg's work, *Variations* for orchestra, is calculated and excogitated musical mathematics, dictated by the intellect of someone who is obsessed with a fixed idea. I have a complete understanding of the stubborn and almost tragic determination with which Schoenberg undeviatingly pursues his path. And yet I cannot take him and his music seriously, for its logic must lead to nonsense because its premises are false. (Fritz Ohrmann, *Signale für die musikalische Welt,* Berlin, 12 December 1928)

Straying from the main road, Schoenberg goes along his lost pathways a lonesome figure, a fanatic, a martyr of his intellectual eccentricity; one who is lost in himself, a madman, if you will, but still a character. I therefore do not laugh when I hear these unnatural sounds; rather am impressed by the tragedy of a man who deliberately chooses the road to oblivion, which will probably overtake him still during his lifetime . . . . His music, insofar as these tonal combinations excogitated by their own laws can be described as such, creates a world of sounds which are inaccessible to our ears and our brains . . . . At the public rehearsal and at the concert itself the playing of Schoenberg's *Variations* led to a mighty uproar. The public begins to protect itself against assaults on its better nature. Such incidents are to be deplored, but they are understandable in the light of the torture inflicted on the nervous system. For Schoenberg and the few faithful beneficiaries of his speculations the performance of his *Variations* was a catastrophe . . . . I am sorry for him, and yet I must pose a serious question: How long can the untenable situation be tolerated whereby a person like Arnold Schoenberg, lost to the world of music, continues to lead a master class in composition in a State-supported academic institution where he may cause incalculable harm to innocently trustful youth? When will an energetic interpellation be finally submitted to the Prussian Ministry of Education demanding steps to prevent such cultural damage in the future? Let Schoenberg be given a decent financial settlement, or a state pension, but let us, for God's sake, remove him, and very soon, from his teaching post. (Paul Schwers, *Allgemeine Musikzeitung,* Berlin, 7 December 1928)

2 DECEMBER 1928

Anacaona, symphonic poem by the Cuban composer Sáchez DE FUENTES, inspired by the melodramatic self-sacrifice of a patriotic 16th-century Indian queen, is performed for the first time in Havana.

2 DECEMBER 1928

Third Symphony by the 53-year-old Austrian composer Franz SCHMIDT in the youthful key of A major, in four movements written in a Schubertogenic romantic manner, is performed for the first time in Vienna as winner of the Schubert Centennial Prize for the Austrian Section awarded by the Columbia Phonograph Company of New York, on the same program with the *Sixth Symphony* by the Swedish composer Kurt ATTERBERG, the absolute winner of the contest.

9 DECEMBER 1928

First Piano Concerto by Mario CASTELNUOVO-TEDESCO is performed for the first time in Rome.

10 DECEMBER 1928

Der singende Teufel, opera in four acts by Franz SCHREK-ER, to his own libretto dealing with a magister organum in darkly medieval Germany passionately attached to an inconvertibly pagan Frankish maiden who destroys his organ as a singing devil, written in the *al fresco* manner of an archaically stylized static counterpoint of Hucbaldian aridity, is produced in Berlin.

11 DECEMBER 1928

The Society of Friends of Music is founded at the Library of Congress, Washington, D.C., "to provide a link among serious lovers of music in our country by associating them, through the National Library, in musical activities devoted to artistic and educational ends."

(Date from the stenographic report of the first meeting of the Society; but the Society's brochure of 1930 gives the date of the foundation as 16 December 1928.)

13 DECEMBER 1928

An American in Paris, an "orchestral tone poem" by George GERSHWIN (completed on 18 November 1928), a touristic musicorama, with identifiable "walking themes" of nostalgic, wistful, joyful, nonchalant and amorous (when a solo violin approaches the tourist in a suggestively inviting manner) implications and illustrative quotations such as the Paris vaudeville tune *La Sorella,* with four Paris taxi horns for realistic effect, is performed for the first time by the Philharmonic-Symphony Society of New York, Walter Damrosch conducting.

The honks have it. Four automobile horns, vociferously assisted by three saxophones, two tom-toms, rattle, xylophone, wire brush, wood blocks, and an ensemble not otherwise innocent of brass and percussion blew or thumped the lid off in Carnegie Hall when *An American in Paris* by George Gershwin had its first performance. . . . For those not too deeply concerned with any apparently outmoded niceties of art, it was an amusing occasion. . . . To conceive of a symphonic audience listening to it with any degree of pleasure or patience twenty years from now, when whoopee is no longer even a word, is another matter. Then . . . there will still be Franck with his outmoded spirituality. (Oscar Thompson, New York *Evening Post,* 14 December 1928)

An American in Paris is nauseous claptrap, so dull, patchy, thin, vulgar, long-winded and inane, that the average movie audience would be bored by it. . . . This cheap and silly affair seemed pitifully futile and inept. (Herbert F. Peyser, New York *Telegram*, 14 December 1928)

14 DECEMBER 1928

La Symphonie by Bohuslav MARTINU, written in memory of the occasion when the first national Czechoslovak flag was presented to the first Czech regiment at Darney, France, in June 1918, and conceived as a jubilant, but lyrical procession of musical colors, is performed for the first time anywhere by the Boston Symphony Orchestra, Koussevitzky conducting, on the same program with *Two Pieces for String Orchestra* by Aaron COPLAND (originally written for string quartet), in two movements, *Lento molto* and *Rondino*, which latter is based on a theme derived (as far as alphabetically possible) from the name of Gabriel Fauré.

20 DECEMBER 1928

On the occasion of the ninth centenary of the coming of Guido d'Arezzo to Rome and his reception by Pope John XIX, Pope PIUS XI issues the Apostolic Constitution, *Divini Cultus Sanctitatem*, establishing the laws of performance of the Liturgy and other sacred music, and confirming the principles laid down in the papal decree of 22 November 1903, *Motu Proprio*.

20 DECEMBER 1928

America, 'an epic rhapsody in three parts' for orchestra, a national American musicorama by the Swiss-American composer Ernest BLOCH, winner of the prize offered by the magazine *Musical America* for the best symphonic work glorifying the ideals of the United States, tracing the history of the land beginning with serene pentatonic chants of the Indian aborigines through the landing of the Pilgrims to the auspicious advent of the Machine Age in the 1920's and culminating with an anthem,

"America! America! Thy Name is in my Heart!" is performed by the New York Philharmonic for the first time anywhere. (Performances by the Boston, Philadelphia, Chicago and San Francisco Symphony orchestras were given simultaneously on 21 December 1928.)

21 DECEMBER 1928

Riquet à la Houppe, musical comedy in three acts by Georges HÜE, after the fable of Perrault dealing with an ugly prince who becomes beautiful when a beauteous princess, ignoring his temporarily repulsive exterior, accepts his love, is produced at the Opéra-Comique in Paris.

23 DECEMBER 1928

Maurice MARTENOT appears as a soloist on his electronic keyboard instrument ONDES MARTENOT at a Pasdeloup concert in Paris, in the first performance of a work specially written for this instrument by the Parisian-Greek composer Dimitri LEVIDIS, entitled *Poème symphonique pour solo d'Ondes Musicales et Orchestre*.

28 DECEMBER 1928

Domenico ALALEONA, Italian composer and music theorist whose ideas of potential new techniques in composition were vindicated by the rapidly advancing future, dies in his native town of Montegiorgio, at the age of 47.

29 DECEMBER 1928

Kejserens nye Klaeder (The Emperor's New Clothes), first opera, in three scenes, by the 29-year-old Danish composer Finn HÖFFDING, after the famous skeptical tale of Hans Christian Andersen in which a court tailor makes a suit of clothes for his Emperor of the finest possible material, as thin as air, thus exposing the essential nakedness of his body and soul to the populace, deceiving everyone except an innocent child who cries out that the Emperor has no clothes on, is produced in Copenhagen.

1929

1 JANUARY 1929

The Proletarian Musician, a monthly journal of the Russian Association of Proletarian Musicians (RAPM), dedicated to the militant propaganda of a constrictive ideology of utilitarian musical optimism in major keys, coercing Soviet composers to relinquish their freedom of creative self-expression in favor of a peremptory dogma, begins publication in Moscow.

The Marxist ideology of the Association of Proletarian Musicians and the necessity of pursuing ideological propaganda on the musical front make it imperative to create a special publication

for these purposes . . . . *The Proletarian Musician* will (1) oppose the influence of decadent bourgeois music among young Soviet musicians (2) impress on them the necessity of absorbing the best, the healthiest and the most acceptable ideological elements of the musical legacy of the past (3) prepare the ground for the creation of a new specifically proletarian type of music. (From the declaration of policy in the first issue of *The Proletarian Musician*)

6 JANUARY 1929

Ernesto LECUONA, the Cuban composer of dance melodies, writes four songs destined to become popular hits, all in one day: *Blue Night, Siboney, Say Si Si* and *Two Hearts That Pass in the Night.*

8 JANUARY 1929

First Symphony by the Russian-born composer of neoclassically melodious and modernistically stimulating music, Nicolai LOPATNIKOFF, is performed for the first time in Karlsruhe.

11 JANUARY 1929

The Golden Goose, choral ballet by Gustav HOLST, based on a German folk tale by the Grimm Brothers, is performed for the first time in Liverpool.

12 JANUARY 1929

Il Rè, one-act opera by Umberto GIORDANO, the Italian composer of the Veristic school, is produced at La Scala, Milan.

14 JANUARY 1929

Strike Up the Band, satirical musical comedy by George GERSHWIN, focused on American ultrapatriots striking up the band in their campaign for war on Switzerland over the issue of chocolate imports, featuring the ballad *Soon,* is produced in New York.

17 JANUARY 1929

The Red Army Ensemble is founded in Moscow to stimulate spontaneous musical activities among soldiers, with a nucleus of twelve army men, among them performers on the balalaika, accordion and mandolin, under the direction of Alexander Alexandrov.

18 JANUARY 1929

The Path of October, the first collective symphonic work by nine Soviet composers: Victor BIELY, Henrik BRUCK, Alexander DAVIDENKO, Marian KOVAL, Zara LEVINA, Sergei RIAUSOV, Vladimir TARNOPOLSKY, Nicolai TCHEMBERDZHI and Boris SCHEKHTER, all members of the Production Collective (Procoll), is performed for the first time in Moscow.

19 JANUARY 1929

Ernst KRENEK's "jazz opera" *Jonny Spielt Auf* is produced in English for the first time at the Metropolitan Opera in New York, with the role of the miscegenating Negro bandleader performed by a black-faced white singer in deference to the segregationist susceptibilities of patrons from the southern states.

19 JANUARY 1929

Casanova a Venezia, "choreographic action" by the 46-year-old half-Bohemian half-Italian composer Riccardo PICK-MANGIAGALLI, portraying in eight scenes the multifutuent lover's carnival of Venetian amours and amourettes in an appropriately hedonistic style fertilized by aphrodisiacally syncopated rhythms, is produced at La Scala, Milan. (An orchestral suite drawn from it was first performed under the title *Scene carnevalesche* in Milan on 6 February 1931.)

25 JANUARY 1929

Balkanofonia, orchestral suite by the 32-year-old Serbian composer Josip SLAVENSKI, in seven parts, an artful Balkanophonic stylization of Serbian, Albanian, Turkish, Greek, Rumanian, Istrian and Bulgarian melorhythms, is performed for the first time in Berlin. (The date 18 November 1929, cited in K. Kovačević's authoritative volume *Hrvatski Kompozitori i njikova djela,* published in Zagreb in 1960, is that of the first Zagreb performance.)

25 JANUARY 1929

Cello Concerto by Frederick STOCK, in three movements, written in an eclectically romantic idiom, with Spanish melorhythms accoutred in Germanic harmonies, is performed for the first time by the Chicago Symphony Orchestra, with Alfred Wallenstein, first cellist of the orchestra, as soloist under the direction of the composer, as permanent conductor of the Orchestra.

1 FEBRUARY 1929

Bronwen, Daughter of Llyr, opera in three acts by the English composer Josef HOLBROOKE, third part of his Wagneromorphic Celtic trilogy *The Cauldron of Annwyn,* wherein a Siegfried-like blond hero named Dylan, reincarnated as a son of Bronwen, perishes in the final battle between the British and Irish human divinities, is performed for the first time at Huddersfield. (Part I was produced on 15 June 1912; part II, on 4 July 1914.)

9 FEBRUARY 1929

Der Tenor, opera in three acts by Ernst DOHNÁNYI, to a libretto dealing with a provincial German tenor who captivates multiple feminine hearts but fails to achieve artistic success, is produced in German in Budapest.

9 FEBRUARY 1929

Le Preziose Ridicole, one-act opera by the 47-year-old Italian composer Felice LATTUADA, after Molière, is produced at La Scala in Milan.

21 FEBRUARY 1929

Feste Romane, symphonic poem in four movements by Ottorino RESPIGHI, illustrating four festive actions in Rome—(1) *Circenses,* the great spectacles in the Circus Maximus; (2) *Il Giubileo,* a jubilee celebration; (3) *L'ottobrata,* an excursion to Roman suburbs; (4) *La befana,* the Feast of Epiphany, the manifestation of a benevolent sorceress—the musical score drawing upon a variety of resources, from ancient Greco-Roman modalities to highly chromaticized dissonances, is performed for the first time by the New York Philharmonic Orchestra, conducted by Arturo Toscanini.

22 FEBRUARY 1929

Bunte Suite for orchestra by the 41-year-old Viennese composer Ernst TOCH, in six unamalgamated movements (hence the title), *Marschtempo, Intermezzo, Adagio espressivo, Marionetten-Tanz, Galante Passacaglia, Karussel,* set to music in a characteristic hedonistic manner of lyrical grotesquerie, is performed for the first time in Frankfurt.

24 FEBRUARY 1929

André MESSAGER, French composer of comic operas in the best Gallic tradition, brilliant symphonic and operatic conductor and a tolerant interpreter of modernistic works, dies in Paris at the age of 75.

24 FEBRUARY 1929

Živí Mrtvým (The Living to the Dead), oratorio by the Czech composer Boleslav VOMÁČKA, is performed for the first time in Prague.

28 FEBRUARY 1929

Concerto dell' Estate (Summer Concerto) by Ildebrando PIZZETTI, a symphonic triptych—(1) *Mattutino*, a joyful matutinal overture; (2) *Notturno*, a pensive nocturnal eclogue in 5/4 time; (3) *Gagliarda*, a rustic round in vivacious triple time—is performed for the first time by the New York Philharmonic Orchestra under the direction of Arturo Toscanini. (The first Italian performance of the work took place in Rome on 10 November 1929.)

1 MARCH 1929

Frederick DELIUS, paralyzed and blind, is made a Companion of Honour by Royal decree "for conspicuous national service," the only musician among the forty members of this British order instituted in 1917, whose motto is "in action faithful and in honour clear."

4 MARCH 1929

L'Éventail de Jeanne (Jeanne's Fan), a tenfold symphonic offering to the Parisian hostess Mme Jeanne Dubost by ten French composers—Florent SCHMITT, Albert ROUSSEL, Maurice RAVEL, Jacques IBERT, ROLAND-MANUEL, Darius MILHAUD, Marcel DELANNOY, Francis POULENC, Georges AURIC, and Pierre Octave FERROUD—each contributing an elegant Gallic dance as a souvenir of musical congregations in her salon, is performed for the first time as a ballet at the Paris Opéra. (The first performance of the suite in its original form for piano took place in Mme Dubost's Paris salon on 16 June 1927; it was then that the idea came to name the collection *Jeanne's Fan*, each dance by each composer being an individual "plait" of her *éventail*.)

11 MARCH 1929

Concerto for piano and wind octet by the 27-year-old Canadian composer Colin MCPHEE, is performed for the first time in Boston.

20 MARCH 1929

Der verlorene Sohn, one-act opera by the 28-year-old German composer Hermann REUTTER, to Rainer Maria Rilke's story adapted from André Gide's novelette *Le Retour*, is produced in Reutter's native town, Stuttgart. (A later version in the form of a chamber oratorio, *Die Rückkehr des verlorenen Sohnes*, was performed for the first time in Munich on 15 February 1952.)

21 MARCH 1929

Sir John in Love, opera in four acts by Ralph VAUGHAN WILLIAMS, after Shakespeare's play *The Merry Wives of Windsor* focused on the incongruity of Falstaff's image as a lover and making liberal use of English folk-tunes in the process, with *Greensleeves* (specifically mentioned by Shakespeare) as a recurrent motive, is produced at the Royal College of Music in London. (*A Fantasia on Greensleeves*, adapted by Vaughan Williams from *Sir John in Love*, became a highly popular symphonic piece.)

22 MARCH 1929

Jazz Suite for orchestra by the American composer Louis GRUENBERG, in four movements—(1) *Fox-Trot Tempo*, (2) *Boston Waltz-Tempo*, (3) *Blues Tempo, Slow Drag* and (4) *One-step Tempo*—is performed for the first time by the Cincinnati Symphony Orchestra.

23 MARCH 1929

La Femme nue, lyric drama in four acts by the 53-year-old French composer Henry FÉVRIER, to a play written in 1908 by Henri Bataille, wherein a Paris midinette, modeling for her lover's painting "La Femme nue," shoots herself in the breast after he decides to marry a rich femme du monde (precisely as Debussy's mistress Lily did on 14 July 1904 when he deserted her for Madame Bardac), but recovers from her carnal and spiritual wounds and marries her old sweetheart, also a painter, set to a melodious score laden with dramatically suspenseful ninth-chord harmonies, is produced in Monte Carlo.

24 MARCH 1929

Tupeyny Khudozhnik (Toupée Artist, i.e., master barber), opera in four acts by the Soviet composer Ivan SHISHOV, depicting a fanciful episode from the era of Russian serfdom about 1820, wherein a serf wig maker elopes with a serf actress, is produced in Moscow.

29 MARCH 1929

Second Symphony, in B minor, in three movements, by the 33-year-old American composer Leo SOWERBY, is performed for the first time in Chicago.

3 APRIL 1929

Le Mas, opera in three acts by the 49-year-old French composer Joseph CANTELOUBE (who added the name of his ancestral family estate Malaret to his patronymic, making it Canteloube de Malaret), written in 1910–1913, dealing with the grandson of a wealthy farmer who abandons his Parisian fiancée in favor of a more rustic and uncomplicated provincial cousin, set to music redolent of the melorhythms of the composer's native Auvergne and arranged in tasteful quasi-impressionistic harmonies, is performed for the first time in Paris.

4 APRIL 1929

The Woodsman, opera in three acts by the 53-year-old American composer Bruce KNOWLTON to his libretto dealing with love, infidelity, bastardy and murder among frontier woodsmen, is produced by the composer's own Bruce Knowlton Opera Company, in Portland, Oregon.

6 APRIL 1929

The Seventh Festival of the International Society for Contemporary Music opens in Geneva with the following program of orchestral music:

Symphony in E minor by Roger SESSIONS, written in a neo-classical vein, the first symphony by an American to be performed by the International Society for Contemporary Music; *Concertino* for piano and orchestra by the Dutch composeress Henriette BOSMANS, set in a refined idiom of Dutch impressionism; *Le Fou de la Dame*, ballet-cantata by Marcel DELANNOY, an animated tableau of a chess game conceived in the manner of a medieval "chanson de geste," with the white Queen's Bishop (*fou* in French chess terminology) falling lifeless at her feet after fighting a valiant combat in her name along the musical diagonal; and *Rythmes*, an ingenious study in asymmetric linear counterpoint and vertical polyharmonies by the Swiss composer Frank MARTIN.

6 APRIL 1929

Edison DENISOV, Soviet composer of avant-garde leanings whose works compass a large spectrum of modernistic devices, from neo-medieval homophony to post-impressionistic colorism and coruscating sonorism, whose first name was given to him by his electrical engineer father in homage to the great American inventor Edison, and which incidentally formed a 6/7 anagram of his last name, is born in Tomsk, Siberia.

7 APRIL 1929

At the Seventh Festival of the International Society for Contemporary Music in Geneva, the following program of chamber music is presented:

String Quartet in one slow movement by the Viennese composer Julius SCHLOSS; *Piano Sonatina* by the English composer John IRELAND, played by himself; *Songs to the Virgin Mary* by the Parisian Russian composer Nicolas NABOKOV; *Five Variations and a Double Fugue on a Theme by Schoenberg* for chamber orchestra by Schoenberg's disciple Viktor ULLMAN; and a neo-romantic *Violin Sonata* by the Czech composer Erwin SCHULHOFF.

(In the afternoon of the same day, choral works by Karl MARX of Germany, and Krsto ODÁK and Leoš JANÁČEK of Czechoslovakia were performed.)

8 APRIL 1929

At the Seventh Festival of the International Society for Contemporary Music in Geneva, the following program is given:

Serenade for violin, viola, and cello by the Hungarian composer Alexander JEMNITZ, written in a highly economical (maximum sonority with minimum of means) atonal idiom; *Sonatina* for two violins and piano by the Parisian composer Manuel ROSENTHAL, conceived in a neo-classical manner with an injection of euphoniously pleasurable dissonances; *Piano Sonata* by Berthold GOLDSCHMIDT of Germany; 7 Haï-Kaïs, a song cycle by Maurice DELAGE, to the texts of laconic Japanese tristichs, written in a reticent orientalistic manner; and *Second String Quartet* by the Polish composer Jerzy FITELBERG, set in a pellucid neo-classical style. (In the evening of the same day, vocal works of MONTEVERDI, CIMAROSA and Adriano LUALDI were given.)

9 APRIL 1929

The Seventh Festival of the International Society for Contemporary Music in Geneva concludes with the following concert of orchestral music:

Flos Campi, suite for viola solo, wordless chorus and orchestra by Ralph VAUGHAN WILLIAMS, inspired by the Song of Songs, and written in a neo-medieval polyphonic style with impressionistic touches; *Concerto* for piano and chamber orchestra by the German operetta composer Johannes MÜLLER; *Dance* for clarinet and orchestra by the Dutch lady composer Emmy HEIL-FRENSEL-WEGENER; and a ponderous *Third Symphony* by Max BUTTING of Germany.

12 APRIL 1929

Bérengère, opera written in 1912 by the French composer Marcel LABEY, is performed for the first time in Le Havre.

13 APRIL 1929

Maschinist Hopkins, opera in three acts with a prologue by the Austrian composer Max BRAND, to his own libretto, with the action taking place in factories and nightclubs in New York, wherein a cuckolding libertine pushes the husband of his mistress to his death in the cogs of a monstrous machine and strangles her when he finds out that she has become a promiscuous prostitute, whereupon the foreman, Machinist Hopkins, dismisses him from his job ostensibly for inefficiency, set to a polytonally jazzy score, is produced in Duisburg, Germany.

24 APRIL 1929

La Peau de chagrin, "comédic lyrique" in four acts by Charles LEVADÉ, after Balzac's fantastic tale dealing with a young Paris poet bent on suicide who acquires in a curiosity shop a magic piece of leather which carries out his wishes but shrinks with every fulfillment and concomitantly diminishes his days of life until he dies of consumption at the feet of his beloved whom he has thoughtlessly neglected in favor of a mundane noblewoman, with a score written in a functionally romantic style, is produced at the Opéra-Comique in Paris.

27 APRIL 1929

Jürg Jenatsch, drama with music in six scenes by the German composer Heinrich KAMINSKI, to a story from the period of the Thirty Years' War, focused on the tragic dilemma of a soldier-politician named Jürg Jenatsch who is given the order to kill the father of a woman he loves, set to music in a sharply dissonant idiom containing spoken recitative and a Greek-like chorus commenting on the action, is performed for the first time in Dresden.

29 APRIL 1929

The Gambler, opera in four acts by Sergei PROKOFIEV, composed in 1916 and revised in 1927, after Dostoyevsky's novel of that name, dealing with an imperious Russian grandmother who, to the horror of her descendants, gambles away the family fortune in European spas, written in a lyrico-dramatic vein, and containing a realistic tonal illustration of the roulette wheel in a dissonant counterpoint of minor seconds, is performed for the first time at the Théâtre Royal de la Monnaie in Brussels.

3 MAY 1929

Concert champêtre for harpsichord and orchestra by Francis POULENC, in three movements, *Allegro, Andante* and *Finale,* set in a hedonistically pastoral manner of the French "style galant," with asymmetric rhythmic figurations pleasingly stimulating the senses, is performed for the first time by the Orchestre Symphonique de Paris, under the direction of Pierre Monteux, with Wanda Landowska, to whom the score is dedicated, as soloist on a clavecin manufactured according to her instructions.

4 MAY 1929

Il Gobbo del califfo, one-act opera by the formerly futuristic Italian composer Franco CASAVOLA, portraying the misadventures of a hunchbacked Caliph in the manner of an opera buffa, the sole manifestation of futuristic modernity being an occasional use of whole-tone scales, is produced in Rome as the winner of a municipal prize.

7 MAY 1929

German students, members of Hitler's brownshirted Nazi gang, hurl stink bombs during the performance of *Dreigroschenoper* by Kurt WEILL at the Berlin State Opera to express their olfactory reaction to modern music by Jewish composers.

15 MAY 1929

Persée et Andromède ou le plus heureux des trois, opera in two acts by Jacques IBERT with Andromeda modernized as a Parisian cocotte who subdues her monster captor and frustrates her destined rescuer Perseus, is produced at the Paris Opéra on the same program with the ballet *L'Écran des jeunes filles* by ROLAND-MANUEL, in which an itinerant movie actor induces a schoolmistress to let him give a demonstration of his films at her school and then, with other actors, materializes from the screen and joins the delighted schoolgirls in a frenzied dance.

17 MAY 1929

Third Symphony by Sergei PROKOFIEV, in four movements, *Moderato, Andante, Allegro agitato (Scherzo), Andante mosso,* with most of the thematic material taken from his opera *The Flaming Angel,* so that the heroine's chromatic anguish and her diatonic love for the Flaming Angel form the contrasting subjects of the first movement, the scene in the convent contributes its archaically stylized harmonies to the second movement, the demonological orgy of the opera is incorporated in the Scherzo and the apocalyptic medieval visions of pandemonium provide the inspiration for the finale, is performed for the first time by the Orchestre Symphonique de Paris, Pierre Monteux conducting.

20 MAY 1929

Sergi PROKOFIEV conducts at Diaghilev's Ballet Russe in Paris the first performance of his ballet *The Prodigal Son,* after the biblical parable, traversing the scenes of the prodigal son's departure from his home, his polyrhythmic meeting with dubious wayfarers, a polytonally organized robbery, a quasi-atonal drinking orgy, a diatonic romance, and an ascetically harmonized penitent home-coming.

21 MAY 1929

Les Enchantements d'Alcine, ballet by Georges AURIC, picturing Alcina as the personification of carnal delights in Ariosto's epic poem *Orlando Furioso,* with the terrifying prospect that Orlando, like other beneficiaries of her enchantments, might be turned to stone, set to music in neo-medieval quartal and quintal harmonies, is produced at the Paris Opéra by Ida Rubinstein and her dance group.

23 MAY 1929

Sergei VASSILENKO conducts the world première in Moscow of his grand opera *Son of the Sun,* in four acts, with the action taking place during the Boxer Rebellion of 1900 in Pekin, wherein a Chinese scientist nicknamed "Son of the Sun" successfully counters the diplomatic representations of the British ambassador, American Navy, German Army officers and a bevy of sanctimonious missionaries, with the score employing authentically pentatonic Chinese-style themes.

25 MAY 1929

Knez od Zete (Duke of Montenegro) music drama in four acts by the prime romantic composer of Yugoslavia Petar KONJOVIĆ, to a fictional historic episode concerning the marriage arranged for political reasons between the daughter of the Doge of Venice and a Montenegrin duke, ending in a tragedy as the bride-groom deformed by smallpox asks his friend to act as his proxy and the double suicide of the bride and groom, incorporating in the score the ethnic elements of the Adriatic Montenegrin mountain songs, is produced in Belgrade.

30 MAY 1929

Amazonas by the prime Brazilian composer Heitor VILLA-LOBOS, a symphonic poem to a story by his father, depicting primeval life in the Amazon River basin in Brazil, wherein an Indian virgin is pursued by the monsters of the jungle, written in luxuriantly tropical harmonies, with the application of novel orchestral effects such as playing on string instruments below the bridge, is performed for the first time in Paris.

8 JUNE 1929

Neues vom Tage, journalistic "Gebrauchsoper" in three acts by Paul HINDEMITH, wherein a married couple performs a Hate Duet, the chorus sings a Divorce March, and, in the second act, the wife takes a naked bath in her hotel room in the presence of witnesses and a detective impersonating a lover to establish a case of adultery, with a number of other news items, including stenographers taking atonal dictation in dissonant counterpoint, typewriters clicking in asymmetric rhythms, etc., is performed for the first time in Berlin.

18 JUNE 1929

Francis POULENC plays the solo piano part in the first performance of his *Aubade,* "concerto choréographique," at the Opéra-Comique in Paris.

19 JUNE 1929

Aubade, a "choreographic concerto for piano and 18 instruments" by Francis POULENC, is performed for the first time at the Paris home of the Vicomtesse de Noailles, to whom the work is dedicated.

25 JUNE 1929

Eugene GOOSSENS conducts at Covent Garden in London the first performance of his one-act opera *Judith*, to a libretto based on the biblical novel by Arnold Bennett, composed in a bold modernistic idiom (the opening motto contains ten different notes) and set in dissonant counterpoint, without resorting to pseudoexotic melodic effects.

12 JULY 1929

El Matrero, dramatic legend in three acts by the Argentinian composer Felipe BOERO, to a story dealing with a nomad gaucho enamored of the daughter of a village elder, is produced at the Teatro Colón in Buenos Aires.

28 JULY 1929

At the concluding concert of the *Musiktage* in Baden-Baden, a Hörspiel ("hearing play," i.e., a radio cantata), entitled *Lindberghflug*, with music by Kurt WEILL and Paul HINDEMITH, to the text by Bertolt Brecht, is performed for the first time, illustrating the realistic and surrealistic aspects of Lindbergh's transatlantic solo flight of 21 May 1927:

The voice of the ocean (monodically); Lindbergh's thoughts (in the syncopated manner of the Blues); New York radio stations urging ships to report sighting of Lindbergh's plane (canonically); the formation of fog (in nebulously opaque, somberly static harmonies); inventory of equipment (flashlight, food rations, etc.); a dialogue with the clouds (in Baroque counterpoint); the waltz of falling snow (a soft scherzo); Erlkönig-like cajolery of the elements lulling Lindbergh to sleep, chanting in bass voice, "Schlaf, Charlie . . . ,"; sensation-mongering American reporters (in jazz accents); the French newspapermen (an anxious chorus a cappella); Lindbergh's apostrophe to the sputtering motor (*tremolando*, in asymmetric rhythms); sighting of the plane by Scottish fishermen (in jig-time); waiting crowd at Le Bourget airport at night (in agitated foxtrot time); the landing (a triumphant hymn-like march); epilogue (Lindbergh's philosophical musings on the "unattainable" that has been attained).

(In 1930 Brecht revised the text of his play as *Der Flug der Lindberghs*, i.e., Flight of the Lindberghs, treating the flyer as a representative of the general species of *Homo volans*. In 1950 he changed the title to the impersonal description *Der Ozeanflug*, eliminating Lindbergh's name as politically repugnant. The radio performance included musical numbers contributed by Paul Hindemith; his name appeared in the program as cocomposer, but he withdrew his music shortly afterwards, and at the first concert performance of the score, which took place in Berlin on 5 December 1929, under the direction of Otto Klemperer, Kurt Weill only was named as the composer of the work.)

11 AUGUST 1929

Leo SOWERBY conducts at Interlochen, Michigan, the first performance of his symphonic poem *Prairie*, inspired by Carl Sandburg's vision of the great open American spaces.

19 AUGUST 1929

Serge DIAGHILEV, magister elegantiarum of the world of modern dance, sophisticated, cultured and imaginative animator of choreographers, dancers, mimes, composers, artists and stage directors, creator of the great Ballet Russe that received its artistic baptism in Paris and influenced profoundly the evolution of the modern Terpsichorean art, under whose tutelage, marked by an impeccable taste, Stravinsky, Prokofiev and a host of others contributed some of their most significant works for the stage, great-great-great-great grandson, through an illegitimate line, of Peter the Great whom he resembled physically, dies in Venice at the age of 57.

21 AUGUST 1929

Bitter Sweet, operetta in three acts, with words and music by the English playwright Noel COWARD, in which a sophisticated lady helps her inexperienced niece to engage in free love with a sexually competent and potent band leader, is produced in London.

25 AUGUST 1929

Chapultepec, symphonic triptych by Manuel PONCE, first Mexican composer of the advanced modern school, in three contrasting movements, *Primavera*, *Nocturno Romántico* and *Canto y Danza*, written in an impressionistic style, but profoundly Mexican in thematic substance (the title refers to the historic suburb of Mexico City), is performed for the first time in Mexico City, conducted by Carlos Chávez, who was one of Ponce's many Mexican pupils. (A new, radically revised version, was first performed by Chavez in Mexico on 24 August 1934.)

2 SEPTEMBER 1929

Sweet Adeline, a musical romance by Jerome KERN, dealing with a chorus girl in a beer garden during the Spanish-American War who sincerely lends her charms to a succession of male admirers, is produced in New York.

21 SEPTEMBER 1929

Engelbrekt, opera in four acts by the Swedish composer Natanael BERG, to his own libretto, is produced in Stockholm.

25 SEPTEMBER 1929

The Woman Who Laughed at Faery, fantastic opera in one act by the 55-year-old English composer Fritz HART, is produced in Melbourne, Australia.

3 OCTOBER 1929

Viola Concerto by William WALTON, in three movements, *Andante comodo*, *Vivo* and *Allegro moderato*, neo-classically diversified by asymmetrical rhythmicalities and accoutred in polyharmonic dress, is performed for the first time in London, with Paul Hindemith playing the viola solo part. (The work was revised for a smaller orchestra, with an added harp part, and was first performed in the new version in London on 18 January 1962.)

10 OCTOBER 1929

Il Carnevale di Venezia, symphonic poem by Vincenzo TOMMASINI, is performed for the first time anywhere by the New York Philharmonic under the direction of Arturo Toscanini.

12 OCTOBER 1929

A festival of music by Frederick DELIUS opens in London, with Sir Thomas Beecham conducting the London Symphony Orchestra in the following program: *Brigg Fair, A Late Lark* for tenor and orchestra (first performance), *Dance Rhapsody No. 2, Sea Drift, In a Summer Garden,* and an excerpt from the opera *A Village Romeo and Juliet.*

Delius, blind and helpless though he was, was determined to be present. The distance to be traveled from France, where he lived, was 400 miles, and included a long car journey and a sea crossing . . . He was carried in his invalid chair, propped up with cushions, down the gangway to a waiting ambulance. (Glare Delius, *Frederick Delius, Memories of My Brother,* London, 1935)

Delius had suffered a heavy blow in the defection of his favorite goddess Aphrodite Pandemos who had returned his devotions with an affliction which, although temporarily alleviated, was to break out again incurably some twenty-five years later. (Sir Thomas Beecham, *Frederick Delius,* New York, 1959, p. 119)

(The second concert of Delius' music, on 16 October 1929, comprised the first performance of his *Air and Dance* for string orchestra; the third concert, on 18 October 1929, included the first performance of *Cynara* for baritone and orchestra; a revised version of his *Piano Concerto;* Norwegian-inspired symphonic ballad *Eventyr; Arabesque* for baritone, chorus and orchestra; and *Appalachia,* variations on an old Negro song for chorus and orchestra, named after the extinct Indian tribe of northwestern Florida where Delius briefly sojourned in 1884; the fourth concert, on 23 October 1929, included a performance of his *String Quartet,* songs and choruses; the fifth concert, on 24 October 1929, programmed the orchestral *Dance Rhapsody No. 1;* two scenes from the opera *Fennimore and Gerda; Songs of Sunset* for orchestra; *Violin Concerto;* and the symphonic suite *North Country Sketches.*)

25 OCTOBER 1929

Jungle, symphonic movement by the Alsatian-born American composer Werner JOSTEN, inspired by Henri Rousseau's primitivistic painting *Forêt exotique,* using a rich fauna of African drums and a lion's roar (a drum with a rosined cord drawn through the drumhead), is performed for the first time by the Boston Symphony Orchestra, Serge Koussevitzky conducting.

1 NOVEMBER 1929

The London Festival of music by Frederick DELIUS concludes with a performance of *A Mass of Life,* Sir Thomas Beecham conducting, followed by the composer's brief word of leave-taking from his invalid chair.

The strength and weakness of Delius is his solitariness. He belongs to no school, follows no tradition, and is like no other composer in the form, content, or style of his music . . . This spiritual isolation is reflected in his technique. Variation form offers endless scope for reflecting on a subject without getting any farther. Delius is not happy in his use of sonata form, which demands progressive development of the thought; his use of variations is masterly. Other symptoms of his lack of vigour are a rhythmic languor and the absence of counterpoint. His harmony, moreover, is curiously static; it belongs to a world from which time and movement have been banished. (*A Retrospect* editorial in *The Times,* London, 2 November 1929)

4 NOVEMBER 1929

A new building for the Chicago Opera is inaugurated by Samuel INSULL, utility magnate.

12 NOVEMBER 1929

Violin Concerto in one movement by Josef Matthias HAUER, subtitled *Zwölftonmusik for Orchestra with a Solo Instrument,* with 112 derivative tone-rows formed by permutations of the original dodecaphonic series, and ending on a typical Hauerian seventh-chord B-D-sharp-F-sharp-B-flat, is performed for the first time in Berlin.

20 NOVEMBER 1929

Fifth Symphony in D minor, op. 141, by the 69-year-old Czech composer of German extraction Josef Bohuslav FOERSTER, in four movements, the first of which, *Moderato solenne,* is derived from the musical acrostic on the four letters (AFED) in the name of his only son Alfred who died at the age of fifteen in 1921, is performed for the first time in Prague.

21 NOVEMBER 1929

Alexander GLAZUNOV makes his first American appearance as conductor leading his *Sixth Symphony* with the Detroit Symphony Orchestra.

27 NOVEMBER 1929

Fifty Million Frenchmen, musical comedy by Cole PORTER, in which an American playboy woos and wins a footloose American girl in Paris against the formidable competition of an expatriated Russian Grand Duke, is produced in New York.

27 NOVEMBER 1929

Bilý Pán (Gentleman in White), opera in two acts by the Czech composer Jaroslav KŘIČKA, to a libretto derived from Oscar Wilde's story *The Canterville Ghost,* wherein Mr. and Mrs. Hollywood of U.S.A. rent a haunted castle in Bohemia and, intent on capturing a local ghost for the museum of their midwestern home town, instruct their daughter to kiss the apparition, which turns out to be the prankish owner of the castle dressed in ghostly white, with a happy dénouement vouchsafed to both when the ci-devant phantom marries the girl, is produced in Brno. (A revised version in German, entitled *Spuk im Schloss, oder Böse Zeiten für Gespenster,* was produced in Breslau on 14 November 1931.)

28 NOVEMBER 1929

The First Airphonic Suite by Joseph SCHILLINGER, written for the electronic instrument Thereminovox and orchestra, is performed for the first time anywhere in Cleveland, with its Russian inventor Leon Theremin, as the soloist, manipulating the instrument by the wave of the hand, to and fro, thus changing the heterodyne frequency and producing the desired tone.

28 NOVEMBER 1929

A century has elapsed since the birth in a small village, Vikhvotinetz, in Southwestern Russia, of Anton RUBINSTEIN, great pianist of the romantic school, composer of grandiloquent operas and virtuoso piano pieces.

(Rubinstein was born a Jew but was baptized, along with thirty other members of the Rubinstein family, on 6 August 1831; the act of Baptism was published in the *Russian Musical Gazette*, No. 45, 1909. Altmann's *Künstlermusikcion*, 1936, erroneously states that Rubinstein was a Siberian of Aryan extraction.)

29 NOVEMBER 1929

The Stephen Foster Society is organized in New York City with the aim of collecting and publishing American folksongs.

3 DECEMBER 1929

The Depraved Heavenly Maid, opera written in 1908 by the Japanese composer Kôsçak YAMADA, is produced in Tokyo.

3 DECEMBER 1929

Lara, "musical fresco" in three acts by the 52-year-old Belgian composer Armand MARSICK, to a Flemish libretto after Byron's poem by that name dealing with the leader of rebellious peasants, is produced in Antwerp.

6 DECEMBER 1929

Igor STRAVINSKY plays the solo part with the Orchestre Symphonique de Paris, under the direction of Ernest Ansermet, in the first performance of his *Capriccio* for piano and orchestra, set in the "style galant" of the French Baroque, in three well-demarcated movements, *Presto*, *Andante rapsodico* and *Allegro capriccioso*, wherein episodes in varied genres are arrayed in free succession with capricious logic.

11 DECEMBER 1929

Atsumori, one-act Japanese opera by Charles W. LAWRENCE is performed for the first time, in concert form, in Seattle. (First stage performance, in the Japanese language, took place in Tokyo, on 9 December 1950.)

12 DECEMBER 1929

Constant LAMBERT, 24-year-old English composer, conducts in Manchester, England, the first performance of his symphonic cantata *The Rio Grande*, scored for piano, mixed chorus, strings, brass and five percussion sections, to the poem by Sacheverell Sitwell, glorifying the tropical luxuriance of the great Rio Grande of Brazil ("By the Rio Grande they dance no sarabande"), in artful jazzy rhythms.

13 DECEMBER 1929

Second Symphony by Arnold BAX, designated as being in E minor and C, in three movements—(1) *Molto moderato*,

set in arid Celtic fifths and abounding in consecutive triadic progressions, exploding "riotously" into great rhapsodic turbulence; (2) *Andante*, in B major, with alternating meters of 3/4 and 4/4, lyric, mystical, mounting rebelliously in sonorous waves of symphonic color; (3) *Poco largamente*, leading to *Allegro feroce*, with the ferocity of angular melodies and apoplectic rhythms mitigated by the deep pedal points of the organ—the entire work being unified by a thematically pregnant three-note figure, is performed for the first time by the Boston Symphony Orchestra under the direction of Serge Koussevitzky, to whom the score is dedicated.

14 DECEMBER 1929

Ijola, opera by the 45-year-old Polish composer Piotr RYTEL, to his own libretto, is produced in Warsaw.

15 DECEMBER 1929

La Légende de Bebek, symphonic poem by the Turkish composer Djemal RECHID, after a gruesome Turkish fairy tale about a young mother whose infant child falls from a camel and is devoured by vultures, is performed for the first time in Paris.

15 DECEMBER 1929

Viola Concerto in four movements by Darius MILHAUD is performed for the first time by the Concertgebouw Orchestra in Amsterdam, with Paul Hindemith playing the solo part and Pierre Monteux conducting.

18 DECEMBER 1929

Symphonie, op. 21, by Anton Von WEBERN, written in the sylleptically polyphonic, canonic, palindromic, dodecaphonic techniques, thematically derived from the guiding series A, F-sharp, G, A-flat, E, F, B, B-flat, D, C-sharp, C, E-flat consisting of two mutually reflexive groups of six notes each, in which the second is formed by the transposed inversion of the first, the central interval being the tritone and the equidistant intervals from it (first and last, second and penultimate, third and antepenultimate, fourth and preantepenultimate, fifth and quasipreantepenultimate) standing also in the relationship of a tritone, in two movements—(1) *Ruhig schreitend*, opening with great liberality of dodecaphonic legalities, so that the 12-tone series is not assembled until 23 notes are distributed among the instruments of the orchestra; (2) *Variationen*, comprising a theme with seven variations, each constructed quasipalindromically, with the central fourth variation being a self-reflecting longitudinally broken mirror, all these elements arrayed in pointillistically propulsive rhythms, the entire work presenting a paradigm of dodecaphonic chirality, is performed for the first time as a commissioned work by the League of Composers in New York.

In Goethe's primordial plant the root is no different from the stalk, the stalk from the leaf, the leaf from the flower—these are all variations of the same idea. . . . The same law is valid for all living things. Variations on a theme represent a primordial form which underlies everything, something that is apparently something else, and yet always the same. . . . In my *Symphonie* the second movement is the crab form, of the first. . . . There are therefore only 24 forms, because each pair represents one unit. The accompaniment of the theme is also a crab form. The first variation is a double canon. No greater intimacy of relationship can be imagined. Even the Flemish polyphonists never achieved such union. The fourth Variation is a mirror reflection. It is the middle point of the entire movement, after which the music turns backwards again, so that it becomes itself a double canon in crab motion! (Anton von Webern, *Der Weg zur neuen Musik*, Vienna, 1960)

Symphonie for Chamber Orchestra of Schoenberg's pupil Anton von Webern is one of those whispering, clucking, picking little pieces which Webern composes when, he whittles away at small and futile ideas, until he has achieved the perfect fruition of futility. . . . Webern's little orchestra suggested nothing so much as a cat that, arching its back, glared and bristled its fur, and moaned or growled or spat. . . . Yells of laughter came from all over the hall and nearly drowned the sounds of Webern's whimpering orchestra. (Olin Downes, *New York Times*, 19 December 1929)

Mr. Webern's Symphony was composed of fractional sounds uttered at night by the sleeping inhabitants of a zoo. (Samuel Chotzinoff, New York *World*, 19 December 1929)

21 DECEMBER 1929

Samuel Pepys, one-act opera by Albert COATES, depicting in an astutely stylized manner the times and the mores of the famous London diarist, with topical citations from 17th-century English songs, is performed for the first time with a German libretto, in Munich.

22 DECEMBER 1929

Sergei PROKOFIEV conducts in Paris the first performance of his symphonic *Divertissement* in four movements, *Moderato, Nocturne, Dance, Epilogue*, of which the first and the third were salvaged from the discarded music of the ballet *Trapeze* written in 1925.

My *Divertissement* was called "a little abstract." Why? I think now that it was my new conception of melody which caused the impression of abstraction. (Prokofiev quoted by Olin Downes in the New York *Times*, 2 February 1930)

1930

10 JANUARY 1930

Cuauhtémoc, symphonic poem by the Mexican composer José ROLÓN, inspired by the historic legend of the last Indian Emperor of Mexico, is performed for the first time by the Orquesta Sinfónica de Mexico, Carlos Chávez conducting, in Mexico City.

12 JANUARY 1930

The Nose, the first opera by 23-year-old Dmitri SHOSTAKOVICH, in three acts, scored for large orchestra, chorus and 78 singing and speaking personages, after Gogol's fantastic tale about a humble government clerk whose nose vanishes from his face to be reincarnated as an important official, set to music of great comic impact, including an octet of janitors in dissonant canonic counterpoint, a sentimental romance with a deliberately incompatible accompaniment, and a thunderous orchestral sneeze, in the realistically grotesque tradition of Mussorgsky, solicitously safeguarding the natural inflections of common Russian speech, is produced in Leningrad.

I took Gogol's story for my opera because I believe that classical literature possesses a sense of actuality. As a satire on the era of Tsar Nicolas I, *The Nose* is one of Gogol's strongest works. But my music does not exaggerate the parody. Gogol reports his comic episodes in a very serious tone. Similarly, my music does not indulge in deliberate witticisms. (Shostakovich in his declaration, *Why the Nose?*, published in the original program book for the première)

15 JANUARY 1930

Le Roi d'Yvetot, comic opera in four acts by Jacques IBERT, dealing with an insouciant king who loses a war but preserves the affection of his people and marries his favorite concubine, is performed for the first time at the Opéra-Comique in Paris.

19 JANUARY 1930

Leben des Orest, opera in five acts by the 29-year-old Austrian modernist Ernst KRENEK, to his own version of the famous story of the infamous Atridae, in which the lover of Klytemnestra, mother of Elektra and Orestes, gives a cup of venomous potion to Elektra who unwittingly tenders it to her father Agamemnon, is caged for her involuntary deed, retaliates by inciting Orestes to kill Klytemnestra and is subsequently slain herself by an outraged mob, is produced in Leipzig.

21 JANUARY 1930

Third Symphony, subtitled *May First*, by the 23-year-old Soviet composer Dmitri SHOSTAKOVICH, in a single exuberant movement, set in an optimistic idiom rooted in major modalities and maintaining a proletarian marching rhythm, with a choral ending to an anonymous text celebrating in confident revolutionary terms the annual Day of International Labor, accompanied by an oriflamme of French horns, an ovation of trumpets and proclamatory trombones, with an industrious sibilation of the piccolos, is performed for the first time in the

Leningrad House of Culture by the Leningrad Philharmonic, conducted by Alexander Gauk.

(A second performance of the *Third Symphony* was given on the following day in Leningrad for a special audience of Communist Youth groups; the earlier editions of *Music Since 1900* cite a much later production that took place in Leningrad on 6 November 1931, on the 14th anniversary of the Soviet Revolution, as the first; the same date is given in most Soviet reference works. The *Third Symphony* was judged ideologically inadequate to its theme and was allowed to lie fallow for 34 years until its revival in Leningrad on 12 May 1964.)

May First! Burning in the whistle of bullets, in the bayonets and rifles leading assault on the Tsar's Winter Palace! Our turn has come! Listen, proletarian masses, to the voice of our factories! Burn the old! Ignite the flames of new reality! With the sun emblazoned on our uplifted banners, let our march thunder in the ears of the world! Revolution, stamp the march of the millions! (From the text of the chorus in the finale of the *Third Symphony*)

26 JANUARY 1930

A series of concerts for the proletariat, with admission free, is inaugurated by the Orquesta Sinfónica in Mexico City.

26 JANUARY 1930

Galatea, Greek opera in one act by the 47-year-old German composer Walter BRAUNFELS, to his own libretto after Ovid, in which Galatea, a water nymph, loves a shepherd who is slain out of jealousy by the cyclops Polyphemus, but who joins her beloved in her natural element when his blood becomes a river, is performed for the first time in Cologne.

1 FEBRUARY 1930

Von Heute auf Morgen, one-act opera by Arnold SCHOEN-BERG (completed at 3:15 P.M. on 1 January 1929), scored for voices and orchestra including two saxophones, mandolin, guitar and flexaton, limning a modern mismarriage, wherein the husband indulges in a mental flirtation with a seductive soprano and his wife dissimulates as a potential mistress of a tenor, with both abandoning their fantasies in favor of life "from day to day," set in an anguished dissonant idiom, with the thematic materials based on a dodecaphonic series, is performed for the first time in Frankfurt. (Schoenberg remarked to the orchestra after the performance: "Gentlemen, the difference between what you played tonight and what I actually wrote in my score would make a new opera.")

6 FEBRUARY 1930

Petite Suite for orchestra by Albert ROUSSEL, in three movements, *Aubade*, *Pastorale* and *Mascarade*, in the "style galant" of the rococo period, is performed for the first time in Paris.

15 FEBRUARY 1930

Çançunik (phonetic transcription of the French traffic sign *Sens unique*, one-way street), a humorous symphonic sketch by Florent SCHMITT, is performed for the first time in Paris.

16 FEBRUARY 1930

Symphonie lyrique by the 26-year-old expatriate Russian composer Nicolas NABOKOV, in three classically designed movements, *Allegro, Largo, Allegro*, is performed for the first time in Paris by the Orchestre Symphonique de Paris, Pierre Monteux conducting.

20 FEBRUARY 1930

First Symphony by the 26-year-old American composer Randall THOMPSON (completed by him on 29 December 1929) is performed for the first time by the Rochester Philharmonic, under the direction of Howard Hanson.

23 FEBRUARY 1930

Horst WESSEL, "martyred poet" of the Nazi cause, author of the text of the Storm Troopers' marching song, set to music plagiarized from a Hamburg waterfront ballad, which as the *Horst-Wessel-Lied* became a Nazi anthem, extolling in lofty syllables the glories of the sanguinary SA (one version had a stanza "When Jewish blood drips off your trusted penknife/ We march ahead with twice as steady step"), dies at the age of 22 in a Berlin hospital, of blood poisoning resulting from a revolver wound suffered by him on the night of 14 January 1930, in a Berlin street brawl over the favors of a "Lucie of Alexanderplatz."

(Sol Epstein, a painter, Peter Stoll, a tailor, and Hans Ziegler, a barber, sentenced to prison terms by the Republican German court as accomplices in the murder, were later retried by the Nazi court, which, on 15 June 1934, sentenced Epstein and Ziegler to death, and Peter Stoll to 7 1/2 years of hard labor. Epstein and Ziegler were decapitated on 10 April 1935.)

25 FEBRUARY 1930

John Hays HAMMOND, JR., American musical inventor, presents in New York the first demonstration of his CREA-TONE, a pianoforte capable of sustaining and increasing the strength of a tone.

27 FEBRUARY 1930

Rondo veneziano for orchestra by the foremost proponent of Italian tradition in modern music Ildebrando PIZZETTI, is performed for the first time anywhere by the New York Philharmonic, Arturo Toscanini conducting. (It was staged in the form of a ballet at La Scala, Milan, on 8 January 1931.)

9 MARCH 1930

Aufstieg und Fall der Stadt Mahagonny (*Rise and Fall of the City of Mahagonny*), opera in three acts by Kurt WEILL, to a libretto by the fiery denunciator of inequities and iniquities of modern life, Bertolt Brecht, expanded from the one-act *Singspiel* originally produced at the Baden-Baden Music Festival on 17 July 1927 under the title *Mahagonny,* and portraying scenes of rapacious capitalist society in a Miami-like American town, ruled by three loan sharks to whom financial irregularities are graver crimes than murder, but whose order to execute a citizen for non-payment of a bill precipitates popular revolt, with an apotheosis in which Mahagonny goes up in flames like a modern Sodom, set to a musical score flaunting its ostentatiously sophisticated vulgarity and polytonally harmonized jazz ballads to texts in pseudo-American English ("Oh Moon of Alabama, We now must say goodbye, We've lost our good old Mamma, And must have whiskey, oh you know why!"), is performed for the first time in Leipzig, accompanied by shouts from the audience: "Es stinkt!" and "Schweinerei!"

13 MARCH 1930

Fantasia on Sussex for violoncello and orchestra by Ralph VAUGHAN WILLIAMS, based on the hymn-tune *Sussex*, is performed for the first time in London, with Pablo Casals as soloist with the Royal Philharmonic Orchestra, conducted by Sir John Barbirolli.

14 MARCH 1930

Third Symphony by Arnold BAX, couched in somber Northern colors of static turbulence, in three movements with an epilogue—(1) *Lento moderato*, with a motto proffered by a sad bassoon, erupting suddenly in the energetically controlled *Allegro moderato*; (2) *Lento dolcissimo*, in which a brooding horn solo is accompanied by plucked muted strings; (3) *Moderato*, leading to a slow *Epilogue* and ending on a pietistically white C-major triad, "the basic idea of the music being adumbrated as through a dark haze"—is performed for the first time in London, Sir Henry Wood conducting.

15 MARCH 1930

Boruta, opera by the 56-year-old Polish composer Witold MALISZEWSKI, is produced in Warsaw.

19 MARCH 1930

Georges Dandin, one-act opera by Max D'OLLONE, after Molière's comedy of manners in which a merchant marries above his social status and has to supply money to his aristocratic in-laws, is produced at the Opéra-Comique in Paris, on the same program with another short opera after Molière, *Le Sicilien ou l'amour peintre*, by Omer LETOREY.

26 MARCH 1930

The Golden Hoop, music drama in four acts by the Ukrainian composer Boris LIATOSHINSKY, dealing with the struggle for liberation of mountain tribes in the Caucasus during the Mongol invasion of 1241, is produced in Odessa.

28 MARCH 1930

Walter PISTON conducts the Boston Symphony Orchestra in the first performance of his *Suite for Orchestra*, in three movements, derived from old forms of absolute music, but containing an American section with a syncopated blues-type tune over an ostinato suggesting the popular type of ragtime accompaniment.

29 MARCH 1930

The Music Supervisors National Conference, held in Chicago, unanimously adopts the following resolution opposing the bill pending in Congress for the nomination of *The Star-Spangled Banner* as the National Anthem of the United States:

WHEREAS, this Conference is informed that a bill is to be considered by Congress which would make *The Star-Spangled Banner* our national anthem, and

WHEREAS, the approval of this bill would signify to our people and to the people of the world at large a unique endorsement of this song as embodying the ideals of our nation, and

WHEREAS, the text of this song is largely the reflection of a single war-time event which cannot fully represent the spirit of a nation committed to peace and good will, and

WHEREAS, the music of this song, while thrilling and effective when well sung on occasions of high patriotic fervor, is not suitable for frequent singing in school rooms and assemblages of many kinds where a national anthem is needed;

THEREFORE, the Music Supervisors National Conference, with a membership of 7,500 and with the support of the great body of music educators who direct the musical activities of millions of children in our schools and deeply affect spiritual values in our communities, does hereby

RESOLVE, that while recognizing the legitimate place of *The Star-Spangled Banner* as one of our historic patriotic songs, the Conference still vigorously opposes its adoption as our national anthem.

29 MARCH 1930

Meine Schwester und ich, operetta by Ralph BENATZKY, wherein a music librarian inadvertently marries a French heiress who poses as her own non-existent sister, becomes inhibited by their social disparity but eventually overcomes his inferiority complex and consummates the marriage, is produced in Berlin.

30 MARCH 1930

The Football Players, ballet by the 30-year-old Soviet composer Victor ORANSKY (whose real name was Gershov), a choreographic social tract contrasting the healthy Soviet love of a football player for a proletarian scrubwoman with the degenerate romance between an unliquidated bourgeois individual and an obsolete noblewoman, is produced in Moscow.

31 MARCH 1930

North Wind, tragic opera in three acts by the Soviet composer Lev KNIPPER, dealing with the historic episode of the execution in 1918 of a group of Soviet commissars by the British occupation army in the "windy city" of Baku on the Caspian Sea, is performed for the first time in Moscow.

1 APRIL 1930

Cosima WAGNER, imperious matriarch of Wagner's musical domain, daughter of Franz Liszt and former wife of Hans von Bülow whom she left for Wagner, dies in her Bayreuth domain at the age of ninety-two, surviving Wagner by forty-seven years and one and a half months.

3 APRIL 1930

Summer Evening, symphonic poem by the Hungarian master Zoltán KODÁLY, reorchestrated and remodeled from his early graduation piece of 1906, scored for a soft orchestra, sans trumpets or trombones, thematically derived from spaciously pentatonic melorhythms redolent of the folk patterns of immemorial Pannonia, and including a vivacious fugato in the Dorian mode touched by Magyar syncopation in felicitously diaphonous contrapuntal harmonies, is performed for the first time by the New York Philharmonic, Arturo Toscanini conducting.

3 APRIL 1930

The violinistic Hungarian sisters Adila Fachiri and Jelly d'Aranyi give in London the first performance of *Double Concerto* for two violins and orchestra, by Gustav HOLST, written especially for them.

9 APRIL 1930

Variazioni sinfoniche, a set of orchestral variations by Mario CASTELNUOVO-TEDESCO, in forms and idioms ranging from the Renaissance to vigesimosecular America, comprising four sections—(1) *Chaconne e Corrente*, (2) *Minuetto e Pastorale*, (3) *Notturno*, (4) *Foxtrot ed Epilogo*—is performed for the first time by the New York Philharmonic Orchestra, Arturo Toscanini conducting.

12 APRIL 1930

Z mrtvého domu, last opera, in three acts, by Leoš JANÁČEK, to his own libretto after Dostoyevsky's semi-autobiographical novel *From the House of the Dead*, describing the horrors of life in a Tsarist Siberian prison camp, set to music in an expressionistic idiom with tangential allusions to Russian folksong modalities, and concluding with an ode to freedom, is produced posthumously in Brno, a year and eight months after Janáček's death.

14 APRIL 1930

The first complete performance of the final version of *Drei Orchesterstücke*, op. 6, by Alban BERG, bearing the dedication "To my teacher and friend Arnold Schoenberg in immeasurable gratitude and love," conceived as a symphony, in which the first section, *Präludium*, which opens with a consortium of pitchless drumlets, tam-tams and cymbals, presenting a rich assortment of varied atonal themes in opulent polyphonic treatment, corresponds to the first movement; the second, *Reigen*, has the combined function of Scherzo and a slow movement; and the finale, *Marsch*, is a grotesque stylization of a Prussian military tune, concluding on a pyramidal tritone consisting of low E's and high B-flats fortississississimo with a chasm of three and a half octaves in between, is performed for the first time in Oldenburg. (The score was completed on 23 August 1914, and revised in 1929; the first two sections, *Präludium* and *Reigen*, were performed previously in Berlin on 5 June 1923.)

17 APRIL 1930

The Sun Bride, one-act opera to a libretto derived from American Indian folklore, by Charles Sanford SKILTON, the most industrious cultivator among American composers of Indian-inspired theatrical and orchestral music, receives its world première in a radio performance in New York.

19 APRIL 1930

L'Ultimo Lord, opera in three acts by Franco ALFANO, is produced in Naples.

26 APRIL 1930

La Sagredo, opera in three acts by the 46-year-old Italian composer Franco VITTADINI, is produced at La Scala, Milan.

29 APRIL 1930

Lo Straniero, opera in two acts by Ildebrando PIZZETTI, the third part of his operatic triptych, of which *Dèbora e Jaele* and *Fra Gherardo* are the first two, wherein an Oedipus-like parricide, the Stranger of the title, is doomed to travel through the deadly desert pursued by the Furies, but finds spiritual support in the company of a shepherd's young daughter who follows him through his fateful journey to the end, set in the manner of a Greek tragedy, with the chorus commenting on the events and their meaning, and with a candidly melodious and harmonious musical score in the emotive Italian tradition, is performed for the first time in Rome.

5 MAY 1930

Christophe Colomb, opera by Darius MILHAUD, to a text by Paul Claudel, in two parts, containing 27 scenes, with elements of Greek drama (in the moralistic use of a suasive chorus), mystery play (in allegorical parables), music drama (in the use of identifying though non-Wagnerian musical phrases), surrealist projection (Columbus conversing with his second self), modern realism (through insertion of cinematic sequences) and symbolistic allusions (doves are released on the stage, the name of Columbus in French being almost identical with *colombe*, a dove), set to music in an eloquently rhetorical style, with passing quotations of Spanish refrains, is produced for the first time at the Berlin Opera, in a German version.

7 MAY 1930

Die Richterin (The Woman Judge), opera in three acts by the 44-year-old Austrian composer Hermann GRABNER, is produced in Wuppertal.

15 MAY 1930

Ice and Steel, opera in four acts by the 41-year-old Soviet composer Vladimir DESHEVOV, dealing with the 1921 rebellion of a politically immature contingent of the Red Fleet against the Soviet government, with much incidental action descriptive of the life in Petrograd at the time—commotion on the black market illustrated by a rapid tarantella on a 12-tone theme, an obsolete lady-in-waiting begging alms in French in the intonations of a sentimental romance, a disfranchised officer of the liquidated Tsarist Army playing a bourgeois guitar number, a former courtier selling the anachronistic trousers of his abolished uniform—with a grand climax picturing the victorious assault on the dissident citadel of Kronstadt across the frozen surface of the Gulf of Finland led by the class-conscious proletariat to the accompaniment of stridently dissonant music reinforced by acervative tone-clusters played on the piano with the forearms (a technical device demonstrated by Henry Cowell during his tour of Russia in 1928) is produced in Leningrad.

24 MAY 1930

X-mal Rembrandt, opera-burlesque by the Hungarian composer Eugen ZÁDOR, dealing with a painter copying a self-portrait of Rembrandt in a German museum, and then substituting his copy for the original, only to discover that the supposed original was also a fake placed on exhibition by the museum director after selling the original to an American lady, and that even that was a fake supplied years back by an old man, who chants philosophically: "One time Rembrandt, two times Rembrandt, X times Rembrandt" (hence the title of the opera), is performed for the first time in Gera.

25 MAY 1930

Transatlantic, opera in three acts by George ANTHEIL, subtitled *The People's Choice*, depicting the turbulent events during an American presidential campaign, with the president-elect attempting to strangle a promiscuous lady friend, set to music against the background of jazz and booze, flappers and flivvers, is produced in Frankfurt, Germany.

In general, the story of *Transatlantic* is one of political corruption in the U.S.A.; a character something like J. P. Morgan (basso) who backs a presidential candidate only to have this candidate turn traitor to the powers of blackness. There is, of course, a love story, too: J. P. Morgan (let us say) uses a woman, a very beautiful one, to try and induce our hero to come along to his way of thinking. But she loves our president-to-be and turns coat to J. P. Morgan, too. The whole thing shows the horrible whirlwind of 1927 in the U.S.A.; a Happy End is practically posted on the opera to make it even more ironic; I wanted to have rose petals falling all over the stage at the end. A satire, and the first modern political opera. (From George Antheil's letter to the author, dated 21 July 1936)

29 MAY 1930

Zagmuk, oriental opera in four acts by Alexander KREIN, dealing with the struggle of Babylonian slaves against their Assyrian oppressors in 703 B.C., is presented for the first time in Moscow.

2 JUNE 1930

Rayon de soieries, comic opera in one act by Manuel ROSENTHAL, wherein a young silk hosiery salesman is temporarily deflected from his constant girlfriend by the munificent matronage of the Queen of the Island of Aloha who appoints him her exclusive purveyor of silk garments in the "rayon de soieries," of a Paris department store, is produced at the Opéra-Comique in Paris, on the same bill with the first stage performance of *Le Fou de la Dame*, ballet-cantata by Marcel DELANNOY, a neo-medieval allegory in the framework of a chess game in which the queen's bishop (*fou de la dame*) makes a supreme sacrifice for his sovereign, originally performed in concert form at the Geneva Festival of the International Society for Contemporary Music on 6 April 1929.

4 JUNE 1930

Der Wein, concert aria for voice and orchestra by Alban BERG, to the words of three poems by Baudelaire

(*L'acÂme du vin, Le vin des amants*, and *Le vin du solitaire*) in German translations by Stefan George, written in a dodecaphonic idiom, is performed for the first time in Königsberg.

8 JUNE 1930

Der Fächer (*The Fan*), opera-capriccio in three acts by Ernst TOCH, to a whimsical story dealing with a Chinese widow who swears a binding oath to remain chaste as long as the earth covering her old husband's grave retains moisture, and then speeds up the drying process by ventilating it with a magically efficient fan so as to be able to yield herself to a cinemactor during a radio performance of Toch's own opera *Die Prinzessin auf der Erbse*, while China is in the throes of revolutionary disorders, with a finale in which the rebels and the dispossessed classes dance a universal foxtrot in the spirit of syncopated solidarity, to an ingeniously contrived musical setting containing quasipentatonic chinoiseries, is performed for the first time at the festival of the Allgemeiner Deutscher Musikverein in Königsberg.

17 JUNE 1930

A modern music festival, *Fest der neuen Musik*, opens in Berlin, with the professed aim of exploring various forms of utilitarian music, mechanically produced (by phonograph recording, radio transmission, electronically generated by heterodynamic frequency modulation) and socially applied (*Hausmusik*, community music, amateur music, school music, *Sprechstimme*,) featuring the first performances of *Sabinchen*, a "Hörspiel" by Paul HINDEMITH and *Fuge aus der Geographie* for chorus a cappella, and a piece of "Gesprochene Musik" by Ernst TOCH, articulating in syllabic counterpoint a number of names of exotic geographical places.

18 JUNE 1930

Das Wasser, a "Lehrstück" by Ernst TOCH for a speaker and chorus reciting a disquisition on the chemical and physiological virtues of H_2O, is performed for the first time during the course of the *Fest der neuen Musik in Berlin*.

19 JUNE 1930

Ombre Russe, grand opera by the Neopolitan-born American composer Cesare SODERO, written in 1909 when he was 23 years old, and dealing with the dramatic dilemma of a Russian nihilist student assigned to assassinate the Tsarist chief of police with whose daughter he is in love (he accidentally kills her taking aim at her father and goes mad in the final act), set to music in a passionately inflated Italianate manner, is produced in Venice.

Cesare Sodero Acclaimed as Composer of Genius.—Success was great and affirms the genius of the composer. There were 30 recalls. The applause was delirious. (Dispatch from Sodero's manager to *The Musical Courier*, New York, 28 June 1930)

20 JUNE 1930

A millennium has elapsed since the death of the Benedictine monk HUCBALD who codified and amplified the Gregorian modes and warned church composers against the explicit or implied use of the tritone, the "diabolus in musica," credited also with the invention of a system of notation with 18 lines.

21 JUNE 1930

Wir bauen eine Stadt, children's opera by Paul HINDEMITH, a modernistic piece of utilitarian music with a simple story about building a city, recited in an infantiloquent vein to a neo-Baroque accompaniment in clearly separated tonal pictures containing just a modicum of acescent dissonance and asymmetric rhythms, is performed for the first time in Berlin.

23 JUNE 1930

Almast, opera in four acts by the foremost Armenian composer Alexander SPENDIAROV, to the legend of the 18th-century Armenian princess Almast who betrays her people to the besieging Persians in the hope of becoming the Persian queen, but is captured, placed in the royal harem, and is killed when she tries to stab the libidinous shah, set to music in an orientalistic manner, replete with serpentine augmented seconds and helical melismas, is posthumously produced in Moscow.

30 JUNE 1930

Der Jasager, school opera in two acts by Kurt WEILL, to a libretto by Bertolt Brecht derived from an ancient Japanese tale of fatalistic feudalism, wherein a young boy crossing the mountains into a valley in quest of a miraculously curative herb to combat an epidemic, falls ill himself and, according to a pre-arranged ritual does not resist when his companions push him into the precipice (hence the title, *The Yea-Sayer*), so as to enable them to accomplish their laudable purpose, set to music in a relentless rhythmic style, with grimacing discords stressing the irony of the action, is performed for the first time in the course of the *Fest der neuen Musik* in Berlin, by schoolchildren seemingly undeterred by the grimness of the subject.

(When the pupils of the Karl Marx Schule in Berlin pointed out to Brecht that the death of the boy in obedience to a feudal custom is against socialist humanity, he rewrote the play as *Der Neinsager,* in which the boy refuses to die, proclaims the necessity of a new way of thinking, and is taken safely home. The new version of the play was subsequently performed by the same schoolchildren in the same Berlin school.)

6 JULY 1930

First Symphony by the Dutch composer Henk BADINGS is performed for the first time in Amsterdam.

15 JULY 1930

Leopold AUER, celebrated Hungarian-born violin teacher, trainer of a flock of *Wunderkinder* including Mischa Elman and Jascha Heifetz, for many years the mainstay of the violin master class at the St. Petersburg Conservatory, a virtuoso in his own right, to whom Tchaikovsky dedicated his violin concerto (Auer criticized it and Tchaikovsky dejectedly took back the dedication), dies in Loschwitz, near Dresden, at the age of 85.

> When we began, our notes were sour
> Until a man, Professor Auer,

> Set out to show us, one and all
> How to pack 'em in the Carnegie Hall.

[Initial quatrain from George Gershwin's song, *Mischa, Jascha, Toscha, Sascha*]

22 JULY 1930

Carlos CHÁVEZ conducts in Mexico City the world première of his ballet *Los Cuatros Soles,* derived from the Mexican cosmogony, in four ages of the sun (of fire, of air, of water, of earth), with the music presenting a symphonic reflection of the austere and yet expressive nature of the people of Mexico.

4 AUGUST 1930

Siegfried WAGNER, "Little son of a Great Father," whose birth Wagner celebrated by writing his passionate *Siegfried Idyll,* dies in the shrine of the Wagner cult, Bayreuth, at the age of 61, surviving his mother by four months and three days.

1 SEPTEMBER 1930

The Eighth Festival of the International Society for Contemporary Music opens in Liège with a concert of band music played by the First Regiment of Les Guides, in the following program:

Fanfare pour une Corrida by the Belgian composer Raymond MOULAERT; *Spiel* by Ernst TOCH; *Konzertmusik* in military march rhythms, by Paul HINDEMITH; *Pièce symphonique* for piano and band by the Belgian composer and pedagogue Joseph JONGEN; *Dionysiaques,* a symphonic bacchanale by Florent SCHMITT; *Symphonies d'instruments à vent à la mémoire de Claude-Achille Debussy* by STRAVINSKY; *Danse funambulesque* by the Belgian composer Jules STRENS; and *Feu d'artifice* by the Flemish-Belgian composer Maurice SCHOEMAKER.

2 SEPTEMBER 1930

At the second concert of the Eighth Festival of the International Society for Contemporary Music in Liège, the following program of chamber music is presented:

Musique pour Piano by the German-Czech composer Erhard MICHEL; *Septet* for violin, clarinet, viola, horn, cello, bassoon and piano by Karel HÁBA, semi-atonal brother of the quarter-tonalist Czech modernist Alois Hába; *Chansons Françaises,* in an ingratiating neo-Lullyan vein, by the sole lady composer of the Group of Six, Germaine TAILLEFERRE; a neo-romantic *Sonata* for two pianos by Arnold BAX; and *Second String Quartet* by the Belgian neo-classical polyphonist Albert HUYBRECHTS.

3 SEPTEMBER 1930

At the third concert of the Eighth Festival of the International Society for Contemporary Music in Liège, the following program of chamber music is presented:

Quintet for wind instruments by the Czech polyphonist Karel Boleslav JIRÁK. K; *Moralités non légendaires* for voice and divers instruments, set in a satirically dadaistic vein, by the Belgian composer Fernand QUINET; *Trio* for flute, viola and cello by Albert ROUSSEL, in three movements, marked by his customary expertise and elegance; *Quintet* for saxophone and string quartet by Karl STIMMER of Germany; and the precisely fashioned *Serenata* for clarinet, bassoon, trumpet, violin and cello by Alfredo CASELLA, written in a fine style of Italian neo-Baroque.

4 SEPTEMBER 1930

At the fourth concert of the Eighth Festival of the International Society for Contemporary Music in Liège, the following program of orchestral music is given:

Music for Orchestra by the Swiss conductor-composer Volkmar ANDREAE, set in a neo-Straussian vein, the non-programmatic title of the work concealing a variety of illustrative allusions; *Sinfonietta* by the Dutch-born American composer Bernard WAGENAAR, in a neo-Beethovenian idiom, vigorous and dramatic; *Concerto for Viola and Orchestra* by the brilliant representative of the English neo-Baroque school, William WALTON; *Sinfonia Italiana* in a rhapsodically conceived Mediterranean style by Antonio VERETTI; *Rondo Burlesque* by Florent SCHMITT; and *Poème de l'Espace*, a modernistically dissonant and rhythmically propulsive ode to transatlantic fliers by the Belgian composer Marcel POOT.

6 SEPTEMBER 1930

At the fifth and last concert of the Eighth Festival of the International Society for Contemporary Music in Liège, the following program of symphonic music is given:

Praeludium, a neo-Bachian piece of *Augenmusik* by the German constructivist composer Ernst PEPPING; *Start*, a "symphonic Allegro" descriptive of a sports event by the Czech urbanistic composer Pavel BOŘKOVEC; *Chant funèbre* by the French composer of new music in old forms Jean RIVIER; *Temptation*, a Gaelic marching piece by Henry GIBSON; *Violin Concerto* by the Viennese atonalist Josef Matthias HAUER, built on a dodecaphonic series of two mutually exclusive six-tone tropes, a method of composition initiated by him in parallel development with Schoenberg's ideas; a hedonistically utilitarian symphonic *Suite* by the Polish-born German-educated composer Karol RATHAUS; *Fantaisie* by the Parisian-Rumanian composer Marcel MIHALOVICI; and the stupendous *Steel Foundry* by the Soviet enfant terrible Alexander MOSSOLOV, including in the score a metal sheet shaken longitudinally for realistic onomatopoeia.

20 SEPTEMBER 1930

The fifth and last march of the orchestral series *Pomp and Circumstance* by Edward ELGAR is performed for the first time in London.

24 SEPTEMBER 1930

Henry HADLEY conducts in Tokyo the world première of his symphonic suite *Streets of Pekin* in seven touristic movements, illustrating Great Stone Men's Street, Sweet Rain Street, Ricksha Boy No. 309, Jade Street, Shoemaker Street, Sleeping Lotuses, and The Forbidden City, replete with simulated orientalisms, pentatonic tintinnabulations, sinuous sinologicalities and various other auricular bombilations accoutred in Germanic harmonies.

2 OCTOBER 1930

Concerto for piano and orchestra by the 51-year-old English composer John IRELAND, written in the rejuvenating tonality of E-flat major, in two movements, *In tempo moderato* and *Lento espressivo*, of highly romantic music barely tinged with amiable modernities, maintaining an almost unvarying, dreamily waltzing, 3/4 time through-

out, leading to an optimistic finale, *Allegretto giocoso*, and concluding in an embracing unison, is performed for the first time in London by Ireland's pupil, 20-year-old pianist Helen Perkin, for whom the work was written. (The dedication to Helen Perkin was removed by the composer in 1950, long after she married another.)

3 OCTOBER 1930

Vom Fischer un seiner Fru, operatic fantasy by the Swiss composer Othmar SCHOECK, to his own libretto in the *plattdeutsch* dialect, after a fairy tale by the Grimm brothers, dealing with the overweening wife of a fisherman, who in seven consecutive scenes asks the demiurgical flounder her husband has befriended to fulfill her increasingly presumptuous wishes—a new hut, a castle, a kingdom, an empire, the papacy, and finally divinity—until her sacrilegious outrecuidance impels the outraged fish to take away from her all her acquisitions and to send her back to her dilapidated waterfront shack to the sounds of a magisterial double fugue with a symbolically inverted second subject in the *stretto*, is performed for the first time in Dresden.

10 OCTOBER 1930

Sir George HENSCHEL, first conductor of the Boston Symphony Orchestra, leads the Boston Symphony Orchestra at the opening concert of its 50th season in a program almost identical with the one he gave on its inaugural concert on 22 October 1881, with the exception of Weber's *Jubel Overture*, replaced by the Prelude to Wagner's opera *Die Meistersinger von Nürnberg*.

14 OCTOBER 1930

Girl Crazy, musical comedy by George GERSHWIN, dealing with a Park Avenue playboy sent by his rich father to a desert town in Arizona, which he promptly transforms into a den of iniquity, although he later renounces vice and marries the local postmistress, containing a number of syncopatingly stimulating songs, one of which, *I Got Rhythm*, presents a fascinating study in infra-metrical asymmetry (measures in 4/4 time are subdivided into the rhythmic molecules of 2/16, 3/16, 3/16, 3/16, 3/16, 2/16), is produced in New York.

15 OCTOBER 1930

Three's a Crowd, an "intimate revue," by Arthur SCHWARTZ, with additional songs by Vernon Duke and others, featuring some mildly scabrous sketches (a young lady inadvertently stumbles into the bathroom while a gentleman performs ablutions in the tub and by instant observation of his intimate anatomy recognizes him as an old sexual acquaintance), is produced in New York.

16 OCTOBER 1930

Second Piano Concerto, in three movements, a propulsive *Allegro energico*, an angularly lyrical *Andantino*, and a neo-Baroque *Allegro molto*, by Nikolai LOPATNIKOFF, premiers in Düsseldorf with Walter Frey as soloist.

20 OCTOBER 1930

In a Berlin court, Kurt WEILL wins a lawsuit brought against the Nero Film Company to prevent it from altering the musical score for a screen version of his *Dreigro-schenoper,* at the same session at which Bertolt Brecht, the author of the play, is denied the right to restore the anti-capitalist ending of his original in which the villain-hero Mack the Knife becomes a bank president.

20 OCTOBER 1930

Hitlerite students throw stink bombs during the perfor-mance of the opera *Mahagonny* by Kurt WEILL at the Frankfurt Opera House, as a gesture of protest against the alleged immorality of its plot and the racial impurity of its Jewish composer, with a post-theatrical fracas resulting in the killing of a Communist student by a Nazi-operated beer stein.

22 OCTOBER 1930

Morning Heroes, symphony for orator, chorus and orches-tra by Arthur BLISS, dedicated to the memory of the composer's brother "and all other comrades killed in bat-tle," in six sections—(1) *Hector's Farewell to Andromache* from Homer's *Iliad;* (2) *The City Arming,* after Walt Whit-man; (3) *The Bivouac's Flame,* after Walt Whitman; (4) *Achilles Goes Forth to Battle;* (5) *Spring Offensive,* after Wil-fred Owen, English poet killed in battle; (6) *Dawn on the Somme,* after Robert Nichols, English poet killed in bat-tle—is performed for the first time at the Norwich Festi-val in England.

24 OCTOBER 1930

Symphony in G minor by Albert ROUSSEL, his *Third,* com-pleted on 29 March 1930, in four movements, *Allegro vivo, Adagio, Vivace* and *Allegro con spirito,* a "symphony of energy" suffused with an *élan vital* and evolving along lucidly Gallic lines, with a central motive of five notes as a guiding musical idea, is performed for the first time by the Boston Symphony Orchestra, as a commissioned work for its 50th anniversary, under the direction of Serge Koussevitzky, to whom the score is dedicated.

25 OCTOBER 1930

Missa in Dedicatione Ecclesiae by Ernst von DOHNÁNYI, for soloists, chorus and orchestra, is performed for the first time at the consecration of the Cathedral of Szeged.

26 OCTOBER 1930

The Age of Gold, ballet by the 24-year-old Soviet composer Dmitri SHOSTAKOVICH, is produced in Leningrad, to a satirical scenario picturing the capitalist way of life in the West, with the cast of characters including a racist referee discriminating against a Negro challenger in a prize fight, an immoral operatic diva, an imperialist *agent-provocateur* and—on the virtuous side of the ledger—a young girl Communist, a downtrodden shoeshine boy, and a host of oppressed proletarians, with a discordant polka portray-ing the international disarmament conference in Geneva, and an optimistic finale projecting a *Solidarity Dance* of Soviet and Western workers.

31 OCTOBER 1930

Serge KOUSSEVITZKY conducts the Boston Symphony Orchestra in the first performance of his *Overture,* mod-

estly listed in the program book as a work by an unknown composer, written in an apologetically unpro-fessional manner and concluding with a slightly modified finale of Glinka's opera *A Life for the Tsar.*

6 NOVEMBER 1930

Begleitungsmusik zu einer Lichtspielszene, op. 34, by Arnold SCHOENBERG (completed in Berlin on 14 February 1930), designed as the musical score for a typical cinemat-ic scene, in three expressive sections—*Drohende Gefahr, Angst, Katastrophe*—with mounting dynamic tension indi-cating the transition from an objective imminent danger through subjective anxiety to the ultimate catastrophe, written according to Schoenberg's method of composition with twelve tones related only to one another, the basic tone-row being E-flat, G-flat, D, E, C-sharp, C, A, B, B-flat, A-flat, G, F, which is developed both melodically and harmonically with classical clarity of structure, is per-formed for the first time in Berlin, Otto Klemperer con-ducting the orchestra of the Berlin State Opera.

Whether Schoenberg's score is to be regarded as an accompa-niment to an imaginary motion picture or as absolute music is entirely immaterial. This is absolute Unmusic. (Walter Her-schberg, in an article published in *Signale für die musikalische Welt,* Berlin, 12 November 1930)

7 NOVEMBER 1930

Metamorphoseon, Modi XII, orchestral theme and varia-tions by Ottorino RESPIGHI, set in neo-medieval modal-ities, is performed for the first time by the Boston Sym-phony Orchestra as a commissioned work for the 50th anniversary of its founding, under the direction of Serge Koussevitzky.

7 NOVEMBER 1930

4 Etudes by Igor STRAVINSKY, orchestral arrangements made by him in 1928 of his *Three Pieces for String Quartet* (composed in 1914 and first performed in New York on 30 November 1915 by the Flonzaley Quartet) and a *Study for Pianola* (composed in 1917 and first performed on a piano roll in London on 13 October 1921), to which he appended descriptive titles—*Dance, Excentrique* (inspired by the spastic miming of the English dancer Little Tich), *Cantique* and *Madrid* (a souvenir of Stravin-sky's visit to Spain in 1916)—are performed for the first time in Berlin.

7 NOVEMBER 1930

Second Symphony in A major by the dean of the American academic school of composition Daniel Gregory MASON, written in a competent Brahmsogenic manner, is per-formed for the first time by the Cincinnati Symphony Orchestra, Fritz Reiner conducting.

8 NOVEMBER 1930

Im weissen Rössl, operetta in three acts by the Bohemian-born composer Ralph BENATZKY, focused on the durable landlady of a hostelry called "The White Stal-lion," at an Austrian summer resort circa 1900, whose middle-aged passion for a lawyer who courts a lingerie manufacturer's daughter whose eligible fiancé prefers the company of an impoverished professor's daughter, creates a multilateral interamorous imbroglio resolved by a deus ex machina in the person of Emperor Franz Joseph who visits the inn and advises its proprietress to marry her faithful headwaiter, and helps to pair off the other two couples according to their emotional choices, set to a hedonistic score abounding in romantic waltzes, erotic tangos and virile foxtrots, is produced in Berlin.

9 NOVEMBER 1930

Soldaten, opera in three acts by the German composer Manfred GURLITT, to his own libretto, is produced in Düsseldorf.

11 NOVEMBER 1930

Lord Spleen, comic opera by the 28-year-old German composer Mark LOTHAR, freely adapted from Ben Jonson's play *Epicine, or the Silent Woman,* wherein the main character, whose family name is Morose, is nicknamed Lord Spleen, is produced in Dresden, on the same bill with the première of Emil Nikolaus von REZNIČEK's one-act opera *Spiel oder Ernst? (In Play or in Earnest?).*

11 NOVEMBER 1930

Spiel oder Ernst? by Emil von REZNIČEK, one-act comic opera with the action taking place during a rehearsal of Rossini's opera *Otello,* dealing with a dishonorable pianist-répétiteur, who, lusting after the soprano who sings the part of Desdemona and who is in private life the wife of the tenor who sings Otello, insinuates that she is cuckolding him with the bass who sings Iago, but is exposed and dismissed from his job, is produced in Dresden.

14 NOVEMBER 1930

Serge Koussevitzky conducts the Boston Symphony Orchestra in the first performance of the *Fourth Symphony* in C major by Sergei PROKOFIEV, in four movements, with considerable portions of its materials taken from Prokofiev's unsuccessful ballet *L'Enfant prodigue* of 1929, in four movements:

(1) *Andante,* drawn in epically spacious modalities in a heroic mold, with a ballad-like contrasting theme, and ending with an impetuous march-toccata; (2) *Andante tranquillo,* a pastoral episode in which a bucolic chant alternates with ominous proclamations in the somber bass register; (3) *Moderato quasi allegretto,* a lyrical scherzo with characteristic passages of intervalic saltation; (4) *Allegro risoluto,* a rondo finale, animated by propulsive motion culminating in a sonorous apotheosis in the whitest sound of C major.

28 NOVEMBER 1930

Second Symphony by the 34-year-old American composer Howard HANSON, subtitled *Romantic* as a candid declaration of faith, but employing masculine melodic configurations in angular rhythms and bold bitonal superpositions of major triads related by a tritone and written in an enlightened modernistic manner, in three movements— (1) *Adagio—Allegro Moderato,* opening with a gentle recitation, leading to the epical annunciation of the main theme; (2) *Andante con tenerezza,* a bucolic eclogue in tones of tender gentility; (3) *Allegro con brio,* an energetic exposition of romantic ideals with triumphant sonorous fanfares—is performed for the first time by the Boston Symphony Orchestra, Serge Koussevitzky conducting, as a commissioned work for its 50th anniversary.

28 NOVEMBER 1930

Dances of Marosszék, symphonic rondo with variations by Zoltán KODÁLY, based on folksong materials collected by him in the Marosszék region of Transylvania, some of them couched in the millennial modes of immemorial Pannonia, characterized by the ambiguous major-minor modes with raised subdominants and lowered submediants, is performed for the first time in Dresden.

29 NOVEMBER 1930

Morana, national romantic opera by the 35-year-old Croatian composer Jakov GOTOVAC, to a libretto centered on rural lovers who flee into the hills and settle in healthy concubinage to elude the perfidious machinations of their avaricious relatives scheming to marry them off into advantageously affluent families, set to music pregnant with asymmetric Slavic melorhythms and gravid with ponderous harmonic layers, is produced in Brno. (The first performance in Yugoslavia took place on 3 October 1931 in Zagreb.)

30 NOVEMBER 1930

Divertissement, symphonic suite by Jacques IBERT, extracted from his score of incidental music for a farce, *Le Chapeau de paille d'Italie,* produced in Paris in 1929, in six sections—(1) *Introduction,* (2) *Cortège,* a discordantly vulgarized march with a sudden irruption of Mendelssohn's *Wedding March,* (3) *Nocturne,* (4) *Valse,* containing an episodic allusion to *The Blue Danube Waltz,* (5) *Parade,* (6) *Finale,* a stimulatingly noisy cancan—is performed for the first time in Paris.

1 DECEMBER 1930

Kaikhosru SORABJI, 38-year-old English-born composer of Parsi and Spanish extraction, whose real baptismal names are Leon Dudley, plays in Glasgow, under the auspices of the Active Society for the Propagation of Contemporary Music, the first performance of his monumental *Opus Clavicembalisticum* (completed by him on 25 June 1930), written in a fantastically complex polyphonic idiom, in three parts and twelve subdivisions, two of which have 44 and 81 variations respectively, the printed score containing 252 pages, making it the longest individual piano composition ever written, and bearing a dedication "to the everlasting glory of those few men blessed and sanctified in the curses and execrations of those many whose praise is eternal damnation."

I am of Parsi, i.e., Persian, and Spanish-Sicilian descent. . . . Do not dare to call me an *Indian* composer. We Parsis repudiate that description indignantly. We are *not* Indians, we are Persians. . . . *My Opus Clavicembalisticum* has been described as the greatest and most important work for piano since the *Art of Fugue,* the *Forty-Eight,* or the *Diabelli Variations,* as indeed it is. I have no false modesty nor mock humility in my make-up, so do not be surprised at the calm way in which I recognize the importance of my own work!! (From Sorabji's letter to Nicolas Slonimsky, dated 23 March 1933)

5 DECEMBER 1930

Concerto for percussion and chamber orchestra by Darius MILHAUD, in two contrasting movements, is performed for the first time in Paris.

5 DECEMBER 1930

The Black Maskers, symphonic suite by Roger SESSIONS from his incidental music to Leonid Andreyev's symbolistic play of that name (written for the production of the play at Smith College, Northampton, Mass., in June 1923), in four movements, *Dance, Scene, Dirge, Finale,* with the black maskers invading a man's castle symbolic of his soul, culminating in a general conflagration in which he finds his death and redemption, set to music with great romantic fervor, in a contrapuntally dissonant but firmly tonal idiom, is performed for the first time by the Cincinnati Symphony Orchestra, Fritz Reiner conducting.

9 DECEMBER 1930

Námořník Mikuláš (Mariner Nicholas), symphonic drama by the 41-year-old Czech composer Vilém PETRŽELKA, dealing with a romantic sailor, his faithful dog and his unfaithful wife, scored for narrator, chorus, organ, orchestra and jazz band, with occasional passages in quarter-tones to express anxiety, is performed for the first time in Brno.

10 DECEMBER 1930

Camille, opera in three acts by the 29-year-old American composer Hamilton FORREST, to his own libretto, based on *La Dame aux Camélias,* the play used by Verdi in *La Traviata,* but brought up to date by placing the action in a dual plane of 1850 and 1930, containing passages in half-sung half-spoken recitative, with interludes in the rhythms of foxtrot, Charleston and other modern dances, is performed for the first time by the Chicago Civic Opera Company, with Mary Garden, who commissioned the score, in the title role, to a French version of the original English libretto.

10 DECEMBER 1930

Fremde Erde, first opera in four acts by the 35-year-old Polish-born composer Karol RATHAUS, portraying a group of Russian immigrants on board a ship bound for America inspired by false hopes of making a fortune, written in a modernistically dissonant Central European idiom, and seasoned with the rhythms of ragtime and blues, is produced in Berlin.

12 DECEMBER 1930

Les Aventures du Roi Pausole, the first operetta by Arthur HONEGGER, after a novel by Pierre Louÿs, dealing with extra-marital adventures of the leader of a nudist kingdom who has 365 queens of high fidelity, and a supernumerary bissextile queen whom he can use only once in a quadrennium on 29 February, and whose daughter reared in utter innocence elopes with a trousered danseuse unaware of her technical gender, is performed for the first time in Paris.

13 DECEMBER 1930

Symphonie de Psaumes by Igor STRAVINSKY (completed on 15 August 1930), "composed for the glory of God and dedicated to the Boston Symphony Orchestra on the occasion of the 50th anniversary of its existence," scored for chorus and orchestra without violins and violas, using the Latin text of the Psalms, is performed for the first time in Brussels, six days before its production by the Boston Symphony Orchestra (a chronological displacement owing to the illness of the conductor Serge Koussevitzky, forcing the postponement of the scheduled performance from 12 December to 19 December 1930, in three sections originally designated *Prélude, Double Fugue* and *Allegro symphonique* but changed in the published edition to impersonal metronomic markings:

(1) *quarter-note = 92,* an accompanied chorale paragraphed by powerful columns of E-minor chords and couched in a devotional neo-ecclesiastical style in Baroque techniques, with groups of repeated eighth-notes followed by a precipitation of 16th-notes; (2) *eighth-note = 60,* a magisterial four-part double fugue, in C minor, with the first subject in oscillating major sixths and the second subject based on a motive of two disjunct minor thirds confined within the compass of a perfect fifth; (3) *quarter-note = 48,* opening with a devotional Alleluia in humbly dissonant counterpoint, the tempo accelerating to 80 half-notes per minute and the contrapuntal design traversing the heterophony of the second species, the Baroque mobility of the third species, the syncopated agility of the fourth species and culminating in the florid quaquaversality of the fifth species, at 48 half-notes per minute, crowned with a medievally canonized solemn coda in seraphic C major.

13 DECEMBER 1930

Die Massnahme (The Measures Taken), didactic play for tenor, three speakers, chorus and orchestra by the 32-year-old German composer of music of social significance, Hanns EISLER, to words by Bertolt Brecht, a series of songs for the agitation and propaganda section of the German Communist Party, set in strong proletarian marching rhythms invigorated by belligerent discords, is performed for the first time in Berlin.

The singers must strive to perform *Die Massnahme* without expression or sympathetic insight as in a love song; rather the music must be treated only for its reference values, in the manner of a militant progress report at a mass meeting, cool, sharp, and incisive. Each singer must fully understand the political import of the text. (From an instruction supplied by Hanns Eisler for performances of *Die Massnahme.*)

Here is at least an ideologically mature and artistically perfect choral work for workers. There is no musical grasshopping here, no mechanical game of leitmotivs, but a vigorous appeal to revolutionary action. (*Die rote Fahne,* Berlin, 20 January 1931.)

14 DECEMBER 1930

Leggenda sinfonica, tone poem by the 30-year-old Boston-born composer Alexander STEINERT, written in an impressionistic style replete with luscious minor ninth-chords and neo-archaic modalities, is performed for the first time anywhere in Rome, Howard Hanson conducting.

17 DECEMBER 1930

Philip HESELTINE, 36-year-old English composer and writer on music, brilliant exponent of hedonistic modernity in the arts, who had selected the nom de plume Peter Warlock to indicate the subliminal witchery of his motivations, is found dead in his London apartment, suffocated by escaping gas. (Although suicide was widely suspected, it was not conclusively proved.)

22 DECEMBER 1930

Franco ALFANO conducts in Caracas, Venezuela, the world première of his *Hymn to Bolívar,* as part of the centennial commemoration of the death of the liberator of South America Simon Bolívar.

23 DECEMBER 1930

Victoria und ihr Hussar, operetta in three acts by Paul ABRAHAM, in which Victoria's hussar husband, given up for dead in World War I, suddenly turns up in Tokyo after escaping from a Siberian prisoner camp and confronts his wife who in the meantime has mistakenly married an American diplomat stationed there, with the marital status quo eventually restored to all concerned, is produced in Vienna.

24 DECEMBER 1930

Oscar NEDBAL, Czech composer and conductor, commits suicide by defenestration, jumping to his death from the third floor of the National Theater in Zagreb.

26 DECEMBER 1930

Benzin, industrial ballet by the 33-year-old Danish composer Knudaage RIISAGER, is performed for the first time in Copenhagen.

28 DECEMBER 1930

Henry COWELL plays with the Havana Philharmonic the first complete performance of his *Piano Concerto* in three movements, *Polyharmony, Tone Cluster* and *Counter Rhythm,* in which tone clusters, invented and named by him, are produced by pounding the keys with the fists, plastering them with the palms of the hands, and loudly depressing them with extended forearms, pandiatonically covering two octaves on the white keys or, panpentatonically, two octaves on the black keys. (A squad of Cuban policemen guarded the hall to forestall threatened disturbances by local anti-modernists.)

(A performance of the first two movements with a repetition of the first serving as a finale was given by the Conductorless Orchestra in New York on 26 April 1930, with the composer at the piano.)

1931

2 JANUARY 1931

Sonido 13, a fantasy by the Mexican pioneer of fractional music Julián CARRILLO (*Sonido 13* denotes the domain beyond the twelve notes of the chromatic scale), scored for violin, horn, guitar, piccolo, cello and harp, tuned to play quartertones, eighth-tones and (for the harp) sixteenth-tones, is performed for the first time in Mexico City, Leopold Stokowski conducting.

4 JANUARY 1931

The Bruckner Society of America is founded in New York with the expressed purpose "to develop in the Public an appreciation of the music of Bruckner, Mahler, and other moderns."

7 JANUARY 1931

Virginie, lyric comedy in three acts by Alfred BRUNREAU, 73-year-old French composer of the realistic operatic school, depicting an episode from the life of the French actress and singer Virginie Déjazet who left, in 1825, a gallant lover to form a more profitable liaison with his courtier father, set to music with eclectic savoir-faire, is produced at the Paris Opéra.

10 JANUARY 1931

The absolute world première is given in New York by Nicolas SLONIMSKY, conducting his Chamber Orchestra of Boston, of *Three Places in New England* by the prophetic genius of American music Charles E. IVES, limning three tonal images of historic American sites, landscapes and monuments, written between 1906 and 1914 but never performed heretofore, anticipating by many years such novel usages as emancipated harmony, atonal extensions of essentially triadic structures, asymmetrical rhythms and polymetrical superpositions, and palimpsests of folksongs, creating a sense of pantechnical freedom in an individual style of national expression:

(1) *Colonel Shaw and his Colored Regiment,* evoked by the famous basrelief on Boston Common, opening with a lyric recollection of the Civil War victory song, *Marching Through Georgia* with its refrain, "Hurrah! Hurrah! We Bring the Jubilee!" in a polyharmonic setting, gradually growing into a rousing march, then subsiding into a memory and an echo; (2) *Putnam's Camp,* suggested by martial relics of the American Revolution, making ingenious use of old songs and march tunes refracted into angular atonal configurations in a polymetric arrangement making it imperative for the conductor to beat four bars in *alla breve* time with his left hand against

three bars in 4/4 time in the right hand to illustrate the episode in which two marching bands meet in a village square while playing tunes at two different tempi; (3) *The Housatonic at Stockbridge*, painting the majestic flow of the great New England river in polymetric designs of great complexity, mathematically precise as to rhythmic values and yet spacious and free in its poetic progress, with the main motto formed by Zeuner's *Missionary Chant* and the "Fate motive" of Beethoven's Fifth Symphony, annexing in its course a number of old American tunes, expanding into a fantastic panoply of simultaneous melodies and polytriadic harmonies, and after a thunderous climax ending suddenly in a residual hymnal chorale, a unique effect of colorful sonority.

16 JANUARY 1931

Perkin, "legende basque" in three acts by the French composer Jean POUEIGH, is performed for the first time in Bordeaux.

20 JANUARY 1931

Brummel, operetta in three acts by the Parisianized Venezuela-born composer Reynaldo HAHN, dealing with the life of the London dandy George Bryan Brummel (1778–1840) whose Byronic adventures and effeminate beauty earned him the sobriquet Beau Brummel, is produced in Paris.

31 JANUARY 1931

La Notte di Zoraima, tragic opera in one act by Italo MONTEMEZZI, dealing with a 16th-century Inca princess who offers her body to the commander of the besieging Spanish forces in Peru in exchange for the safe conduct of her wounded lover, and when the bargain is carried out by the enamored conquistador, she stabs herself to death, set to music with Italianate eloquence, is produced at La Scala, in Milan.

4 FEBRUARY 1931

Piano Concerto by the Venezuela-born Parisian composer Reynaldo HAHN is performed for the first time in Paris, with Magda Tagliaferro soloist under the direction of the composer.

5 FEBRUARY 1931

Evocation by the Alsatian-American composer Charles Martin LOEFFLER, scored for speaker, women's chorus and orchestra, descriptive of the erection of a temple of the Muses, and illustrating in neo-archaic tones Pan's playing on the syrinx for his beloved naiad Syrinx, echoed by his favorite nymph Echo, is performed for the first time as a dedication piece at the inauguration of Severance Hall, the permanent home for the Cleveland Orchestra, named after a local philanthropist who financed the building project.

7 FEBRUARY 1931

Peter Ibbetson, lyric drama in three acts by the American composer Deems TAYLOR, to a libretto after George du Maurier's novel of the same name, dealing with a young London architect "dreaming true" of a childhood sweetheart whom he meets years later when she, as an influential Duchess, saves his life by securing the commutation of his death sentence to life imprisonment for killing his adoptive uncle with a stroke of his cane, with a final dream scene in Elysian Fields suggestive of the garden in Paris where he grew up, to a musical setting of turbulent sentimentality and harmoniously consistent spissitude, is performed for the first time at the Metropolitan Opera in New York, culminating in 36 curtain calls.

9 FEBRUARY 1931

Cantegril, comic opera in four acts by ROGER-DUCASSE dealing with a shrewd villager Cantegril around 1880 in the French Pyrenees who lures the temporary fiancée of a rich local boy into a compromising situation in his bed and wins her over as his wife, with a musical score sprinkled with Pyrenean rhythms and colored with quasi-impressionist harmonies, is performed for the first time at the Opéra-Comique in Paris.

9 FEBRUARY 1931

Kleine Theater-Suite for orchestra by Ernst TOCH, in five movements suggesting five theatrical situations—*Overture, Timid Approach, Dance, Night, Finale*—is performed for the first time by the Berlin Philharmonic, Wilhelm Furtwängler conducting.

12 FEBRUARY 1931

La Bisbetica Domata, opera in four acts by Mario PERSICO, after Shakespeare's play *The Taming of the Shrew*, is produced in Rome.

13 FEBRUARY 1931

Marcel DUPRÉ improvises in Brussels an organ symphony, *Le Chemin de la Croix* (he performed it in a definitive version in Paris, 18 March 1932).

13 FEBRUARY 1931

Symphonie by Arthur HONEGGER (his *First Symphony*), without a key signature, but with the tonal barycenter audibly sensed as C for the first movement, *Allegro marcato;* F-sharp for the second, *Adagio;* and C again for the last, *Presto*, with the thematic structure largely derived from the inversion of the chromatic scale into an intervalic series of major sevenths, is performed for the first time by the Boston Symphony Orchestra, Serge Koussevitzky conducting, as a commissioned work for the 50th anniversary of its existence.

16 FEBRUARY 1931

L'illustre Fregona, opera in three acts by Raoul LAPARRA, to his own libretto derived from a story by Cervantes, is produced in Paris.

19 FEBRUARY 1931

Les Offrandes oubliées by the 22-year-old French composer Olivier MESSIAEN, a "symphonic meditation" on the "forgotten offerings" to Jesus on the cross, is performed for the first time in Paris.

21 FEBRUARY 1931

Młyn diabelski (*The Diabolical Mill*), opera in six scenes by the Polish composer Ludomir RÓŻYCKI, is produced in Poznan.

23 FEBRUARY 1931

Nellie MELBA, grand prima donna whose sonorous voice and queenly presence enthralled opera audiences all over the world, holder of the imposing title of a Dame Commander of the British Empire, whose fame reached even the realm of gastronomy in the shape of *Peach Melba* and *Melba Toast*, and whose consecutive farewell tours in England and America continued until 1926, dies in Sydney in her native Australia, at the age of 69.

26 FEBRUARY 1931

Az Álarc (*The Mask*), last opera, in three acts, by the Hungarian violinist Jenö HUBAY, is produced in Budapest.

27 FEBRUARY 1931

Second Symphony in C major by Edward Burlingame HILL in four movements (composition completed 11 February 1930) is performed for the first time by the Boston Symphony Orchestra, Serge Koussevitzky conducting.

28 FEBRUARY 1931

Sonatine transatlantique by Alexandre TANSMAN, in three sections (*Fox-Trot, Spiritual et Blues, Charleston*), inspired by his American journeys, and reflecting the genre of sophisticated Parisian jazz, set in succulent bitonal harmonies, is performed for the first time in its orchestral version at the Concerts Pasdeloup in Paris, Rhené-Baton conducting. (The first performance of the original version for piano solo was given by José Iturbi in Boston on 10 November 1930. The music was used by Kurt Jooss in his ballet *Impressions of a Big City*, first performed in Cologne on 21 November 1932.)

28 FEBRUARY 1931

Die geliebte Stimme, opera in three acts by Jaromír WEINBERGER, dealing with a Balkan belle fascinated by a lovable singing voice she hears from afar, who devotes three acts to trace its possessor only to discover that the singer is her family-appointed fiancé whom she has repeatedly spurned, set to music in a felicitous vein, rich in folklike asymmetrical meters, is produced in Munich, with a German libretto translated from the Czech original by the composer, derived from a contemporary German novel.

1 MARCH 1931

Igor MARKEVITCH, 18-year-old Russian-born pianist, composer and conductor, plays the solo part with the Orchestre Symphonique de Paris, Pierre Monteux conducting, in the performance of his *Piano Concerto* in three vivaciously lyric movements, written in a Gallic neo-Baroque manner. An earlier performance of Markevitch's *Piano Concerto* was given in London on 15 July 1929. *The Times* of London in its review characterized the music as "Bach gone wrong."

3 MARCH 1931

A bill designating *The Star-Spangled Banner* as the national anthem of the United States of America is passed by the Senate, and sent to President Hoover for his signature, thus sanctioning the *de facto* status of the hymn written by lawyer Francis Scott Key on 12 September 1814, and sung to an old English drinking tune.

4 MARCH 1931

Piér li Houïeu (*Peter the Collier*), one-act opera in the Walloon dialect by the famous Belgian violinist Eugène YSAŸE, is produced in Liège, in the presence of the composer *in extremis*, brought in to attend the performance in an invalid chair, suffering from diabetes which necessitated the amputation of his left foot and led to his death eleven weeks after the presentation of this opera.

5 MARCH 1931

La Vedova scaltra, comic opera in three acts by Ermanno WOLF-FERRARI, after Goldoni's comedy dealing with a shrewd widow who maneuvers skillfully to her advantage, among four suitors, a phlegmatic Englishman, an incontinently passionate Spaniard, an ebullient Frenchman and a scheming Italian of low birth but high virility, is performed for the first time in Rome.

8 MARCH 1931

Symphonie en La by Pierre-Octave FERROUD, in three well-constructed movements, astutely varying moments of lyricism with explosions of drama in a placidly romantic manner, is performed for the first time by the Orchestre Symphonique de Paris, Pierre Monteux conducting.

19 MARCH 1931

The Canterbury Pilgrims, oratorio for chorus, soloists and orchestra by George DYSON, depicting in harmoniously melodious tones the pilgrimage of the travelers from the Prologue to Chaucer's *Canterbury Tales* to the grave of the sainted Archbishop of Canterbury Thomas à Becket, is performed for the first time in Winchester, England, a few miles from the scene of Becket's assassination.

26 MARCH 1931

Moineau, best-known operetta by the French composer Louis BEYDTS, wherein an unscrupulously immoral Paris painter attracts his consecutive mistresses by displaying suggestive exhibits of his art in an open window of his Montmartre apartment, baiting passing girls into conversation and subsequent intimacy, like so many sparrows (hence the title) with crumbs of bread, but who eventually is trapped by one of them into a solidified marriage, thus becoming himself a moineau, is produced in Paris.

3 APRIL 1931

Konzertmusik for string orchestra (with the two violin sections coalesced into one) and brass instruments by Paul HINDEMITH (completed on 27 December 1930) in two compound parts, the antiphony of the participating choirs being the philosophical idea animating the music, set in a grandly rhetorical Baroque style, with a tonal barycenter firmly established on C-sharp (D-flat), while the ambiguity of major and minor thirds creates a fluid modulatory atmosphere, is performed for the first time by the Boston Symphony Orchestra under the direction of Serge Koussevitzky.

4 APRIL 1931

George Whitefield CHADWICK, American composer of symphonic music of a grand romantic design containing occasional Americanisms in thematic sources, director of the New England Conservatory of Music, educator of a generation of American musicians, dies in Boston at the age of 76.

4 APRIL 1931

Corradino lo Svevo, lyric drama in two acts by the 23-year-old Italian composer Pino DONATI, dealing with the youthful prince Conradin, Duke of Swabia, the last of the Hohenstaufens, who following an abortive attempt to wrest the crown of the Kingdom of the Two Sicilies from the usurper Charles d'Anjou, was captured and beheaded in 1268 at the age of sixteen, set to music in the elevated modalities suitable to the solemnity of the story, is produced in Verona.

5 APRIL 1931

Comedians, ballet by Reinhold GLIÈRE, freely after the play *La Fuente ovejuna* of Lopez de Vega, wherein a feudal lord who takes advantage of the medieval *jus primae noctis* forcing young brides of his fief to spend their virginal night with him at the castle, is foiled by a troupe of comedians who mimic the revoltingly immoral practice so realistically that the populace rises, slays the violator and liberates the captive maidens, with local color furnished by a number of Spanish-accented dances, is produced in Moscow.

8 APRIL 1931

In the Captivity of Apple Trees, opera in five acts by the Ukrainian composer Oles TCHISHKO, with the action taking place during the multilateral civil war in 1918–19, involving the Red Army, the White Army, and the Green Army of anarchistic Ukrainian nationalists, is produced in Odessa.

8 APRIL 1931

Three Chinese Pieces (originally written for piano) by Abram CHASINS (*A Shanghai Tragedy, Flirtation in a Chinese Garden* and *Rush Hour in Hong Kong*), set in a pentatonically tintinnabulating vein, is performed in an orchestral version by the New York Philharmonic under the direction of Arturo Toscanini.

8 APRIL 1931

Bolt, "choreographic spectacle" in three acts and seven scenes by the 24-year-old Soviet composer Dmitri SHOSTAKOVICH, to a scenario dealing with attempted sabotage by an anti-Soviet worker who sticks a bolt into a vital piece of machinery but is foiled by the vigilant Communist Youth Brigade, with an *Enthusiasm Dance* concluding the ballet, is produced in Leningrad.

16 APRIL 1931

Koštana, folk opera in three acts by the Serbian composer Petar KONJOVIĆ, wherein a Gypsy girl in Ottoman-ruled Serbia in 1870 inflames the passions of a youthful Turk, his aging father and sundry local dignitaries, creating an emotional commotion of such sexual dimensions that the mayor orders her to marry a deaf mute from her own tribe to pacify the local male population, set to music in a vivaciously ethnic vein and containing a number of orientalized Balkan dances in asymmetrical rhythmic sequences, is produced in Zagreb.

17 APRIL 1931

Sinfonia Dialectica, first symphony by the Russian esthetician Arthur LOURIÉ, cast in an ascetic neoscholastic style of vacuous musical rhetoric, is performed for the first time by the Philadelphia Orchestra.

18 APRIL 1931

Dornröschens Erwachen, fairy opera in two acts by the Hungarian composer Eugen ZÁDOR, a variant of the story of *Sleeping Beauty*, is performed for the first time in Saarbrucken.

19 APRIL 1931

Das Ziel (The Goal), opera in four tableaux by Otto KLEMPERER, to his own libretto, is performed for the first time in a concert version, conducted by Klemperer himself, in Berlin.

24 APRIL 1931

Guercœur, posthumous opera in three acts by Alberic MAGNARD, to his own libretto, dealing with a valiant fighter for liberty who dies in combat, goes to Heaven where he communes with divine personages, returns to earth to visit his mistress who has in the meantime joined a popular dictator, leads a crusade for freedom for the second time and is slain once more, achieving the highest order of celestial beatitude, with a romantic score restored and rescored by Guy Ropartz from the partially preserved drafts of the manuscript charred by fire when the Germans burned down Maguard's house and killed him on 3 September 1914, is produced at the Paris Opéra.

5 MAY 1931

Bacco in Toscana, dithyramb in one act, for voices, chorus and ballet by Mario CASTELNUOVO-TEDESCO, dealing with the myth of Ariadne who, after being abandoned by Theseus, is restored to life and temporary ecstasy by Bacchus, is performed for the first time at La Scala in Milan.

12 MAY 1931

Eugène YSAŸE, Belgian violinist who elevated the art of violin playing to an intellectually contained display of emotional powers, to whom César Franck dedicated his famous violin sonata, dies in Brussels at the age of 72, after a long struggle with diabetes, which necessitated the amputation of his left foot.

14 MAY 1931

A young Fascist strikes TOSCANINI in Bologna for his refusal to conduct the Fascist song *Giovinezza* before his symphonic concert. (On 18 May 1931 the Musicians' Syndicate of Bologna condemned Toscanini's refusal to conduct *Giovinezza* as "absurd and unpatriotic.")

15 MAY 1931

Torneo Notturno, music drama by Gian Francesco MALIPIERO (completed by him on 10 December 1929), set in the form of a septuple nocturnal tournament, depicting seven psychologically connected scenes, landscapes and moods, with symphonic portions alternating with singing episodes, *Le Serenate, La Tormenta, La Foresta, La Taverna del Buon Tempo, Il Focolare spento, Il Castello della Noia,* and *La Prigione*, is performed for the first time in Munich, in a German version, under the title *Komödie des Todes.*

17 MAY 1931

Die Mutter, opera in ten scenes by Alois HÁBA, the first stage work making systematic use of quarter-tones and their multiples, dealing with a self-denying second wife of a Czech peasant whose children of the first marriage are hostile to the new children and to her, is produced for the first time in Munich. (The original Czech version was produced in Prague on 23 May 1947.)

My first quarter-tone opera *Die Mutter* proves that it is humanly possible to build large musical forms on an athematical principle. Harmonically, I have used combinations ranging from two to 24 different sounds. Melodically, I have applied multiples of quarter-tones (3/4-tones and 5/4-tones), as well as neutral thirds, sixths, fourths and sevenths. This may be described as diatonic music in the quarter-tone system. For the first performance of my opera in Munich, the piano manufacturer August Förster has built a special quarter-tone piano, Kohlert has constructed two new clarinets in quarter-tones, and Heckel has furnished two quarter-tone trumpets. (Alois Hába, *Anbruch*, Vienna, May 1931)

18 MAY 1931

Count Alexander Dmitrievitch SHEREMETIEV, founder and conductor of a series of symphonic concerts of Russian music in St. Petersburg in the heyday of the Russian autocracy, when money and noble blood could buy fame, dies at the age of 72 in exile in a Russian charity home at Ste-Geneviève-des Bois, near Paris.

19 MAY 1931

Wagadus Untergang durch die Eitelkeit, oratorio for three solo voices, singing and speaking chorus, and five saxophones by the Moscow-born half-German half-Russian composer Vladimir VOGEL, inspired by a North African legend of the decline and fall of a proud Berber kingdom, is performed for the first time in Munich.

22 MAY 1931

Sahdji, ballet by the American Negro composer William Grant STILL, with chorus singing comments on the action and a bass voice reciting African proverbs, to a scenario dealing with an adulterous favorite wife of an ancient central-African chieftain punished for her sins by the jungle deities beating the ritual drums, is performed for the first time in Rochester, New York.

22 MAY 1931

Bacchus et Ariane, ballet in two acts by Albert ROUSSEL, dealing with Theseus's abandonment of Ariadne (who had saved him from the Minotaur) on the island of Naxos, where she finds solace in the arms of Bacchus, and takes part in a Bacchanale, is performed for the first time at the Paris Opéra.

22 MAY 1931

The Marriage of Aude, one-act opera by the American composer Bernard ROGERS, is produced in Rochester, New York.

2 JUNE 1931

Cris du monde, stage oratorio by Arthur HONEGGER, portraying a peaceful recluse trying to elude the modern world chanting in propulsively dissonant harmonies of its urban accessories, the twinkling electric signs, the automobiles, the Métro, "Join us! Join us!" is performed for the first time in Paris.

3 JUNE 1931

Deep Forest, prelude for chamber orchestra by the 52-year-old American composeress Mabel DANIELS, who enjoyed the benefit of German musical training under the tutelage of Thuille, thus becoming the most erudite among American women composers of her generation, written in a romantic vein with some impressionistic daubs of color, is performed for the first time in New York.

3 JUNE 1931

The Band Wagon, a musical revue by Arthur SCHWARTZ, featuring the celebrated song *Dancing in the Dark,* is produced in New York.

6 JUNE 1931

Under the auspices of the Pan American Association of Composers, Nicolas SLONIMSKY conducts in Paris the first of his two concerts of modern American music:

American Life, an overture by the Baltimore-born American composer Adolph WEISS, written in a lively but erudite manner, combining jazzy inflections of the American life in the first quarter of the century with atonal and parado-decaphonic devices of his master Arnold Schoenberg; *Three Places in New England* by the greatest musical genius of modern America Charles E. IVES, composed between 1906 and 1914, but not performed until Nicolas Slonimsky conducted it in New York on 10 January 1931; *Men and Mountains,* symphonic poem by the individualistically intractable Vermont composer Carl RUGGLES, set in an uncompromisingly severe tonal, polytonal and atonal style (one of the viola players in the Paris orchestra added the words *Il* before *viola* in his part and *la musique* after the word *viola,* to record his opinion that Ruggles has violated music); the world première of *Synchrony,* a study in functional simultaneity of tones, timbres and rhythms by the indomitable innovator Henry COWELL, with the application of symphonic tone-clusters in chromatic compacts of homogeneous instrumental elements; and *La Rebambaramba,* a multicolored musicorama by the fiery

Cuban mulatto composer Amadeo ROLDÁN, depicting an Afro-Cuban fiesta in a gorgeous display of Caribbean melorhythms, with the participation of a multifarious fauna of native percussion effects, including a polydental glissando on the jawbone of an ass.

It seems that polyrhythmic and polyharmonic experiments are conducted in America in a spirit more sane, more candid, and more youthful than here. One needs to possess a certain amount of savagery to march with easy steps in this new kind of music administered by hammer blows. With us, in Europe, a burdensome artistic heritage takes away the element of joyous insouciance from this spontaneous display. (Emile Vuillermoz, *Excelsior*, Paris, 8 June 1931)

Nicolas Slonimsky of Boston, indefatigable in furthering the cause of the extreme radical composers, has brought out in Paris orchestral compositions by Americans who are looked on by our conservatives as wild-eyed anarchists. He thus purposed to acquaint Parisians with contemporaneous American music. But the composers represented were not those who are regarded by their fellow-countrymen as leaders in the art, nor have they all been so considered by the conductors of our great orchestras. If Mr. Slonimsky had chosen a composition by Loeffler, Hill, one of Deems Taylor's suites, Foote's suite, or music by some who, working along traditional lines, have nevertheless shown taste, technical skill and a suggestion at least of individuality, his audience in Paris would now have a fairer idea of what Americans are doing in the art. Are these Parisians to be blamed if they say that the American composers thus made known to them are restless experimenters, or followers of Europeans whose position in the musical world is not yet determined, men who show ingenuity chiefly by their rhythmic inventions and orchestral tricks; men who apparently have no melodic gift, or, having it, disdain it for the tiresome repetition and transformation of an insignificant pattern; who neglect the sensuous charm of stringed instruments and put their trust for startling effects in combinations of wind and percussion choirs? (Philip Hale, in an editorial entitled *Mr. Slonimsky in Paris*, in the Boston *Herald*, 7 July 1931)

The Paris concerts given by Slonimsky were better received than I expected they would be; the only unfavorable comment which I saw was by a Prof. Pruniéries—it wasn't so unfavorable as unfair or weak-eared. He says that I "know my Schoenberg"—interesting information to me as I have never heard nor seen a note of Schoenberg's music. Then he says that I haven't applied the lessons as well as I might. This statement shows almost human intelligence. It's funny how many men, when they see another man put the breechin' under a horse's tail, wrong or right, think that he must be influenced by someone in Siberia or Neurasthenia. No one man invented the barber's itch. But one thing about the concerts that everyone felt was that Slonimsky was a great conductor. (Letter from Charles Ives to Robert E. Schmitz, dated 10 August 1931)

11 JUNE 1931

Nicolas SLONIMSKY conducts in Paris his second concert of American music in the following program of works for chamber orchestra:

Sones de Castilla, suite by the Spanish-Cuban composer Pedro SANJUÁN, in expansive melodic forms of Castillian songs and dances modernized by Stravinskian rhythms; the first performance anywhere of *Energía* by the Mexican composer Carlos CHÁVEZ, primitivistically virile in its rejection of common esthetics; *Préambule et Jeux* for harp and nine instruments by the Franco-American innovator Carlos SALZEDO; *Bembé*, Afro-Cuban movement in powerfully asymmetrical rhythms and discordant harmonies by the 25-year-old Cuban composer Alejandro CATURLA; *Three Canons* in dissonant counterpoint by the American modern polyphonist Wallingford RIEGGER; and *Intégrales* for wind instruments, doublebass and percussion by Edgar VARÈSE, an essay in organized sound expressing in the abstract terms of condensed and static emotion the concept of integral calculus.

14 JUNE 1931

The Black Cliff, opera in four acts by Andrei PASHCHENKO, to a story dealing with the civil war raging in 1919 in Central Asia, couched in a homophonic idiom with abundant melorhythmic allusions to Kirghiz folksongs, is produced in Leningrad.

20 JUNE 1931

Die Bakchantinnen, opera in two acts by Egon WELLESZ, after the last play of Euripides, *The Bacchae*, dealing with the hideous vengeance of Bacchus upon the townspeople of Thebes for their rejection of the bacchanals and persecution of the maenads, is performed for the first time in Vienna.

23 JUNE 1931

Amphion, scenic melodrama in one act by Arthur HONEGGER to a text by Paul Valéry wherein Apollo orders Amphion to invent music, which he does by creating a scale of two major tetrachords disjunct by a semitone, thus dividing the octave bitonally into tritones, and playing a fugue on the lyre so powerfully that stones are moved telekinetically to erect a temple to Apollo in Thebes, is produced at the Paris Opéra, with Ida Rubinstein miming Amphion.

5 JULY 1931

Job, "masque for dancing" by Ralph VAUGHAN WILLIAMS, inspired by William Blake's illustrations to the Book of Job and delineating the increasingly dramatic tests of faith administered by the implacable God of the Old Testament, set to music in old modalities, with Satan's irruptions of cachinnating rhythms, is performed for the first time in London.

21 JULY 1931

Hans BARTH registers the patent for his quarter-tone piano.

This instrument has two keyboards of 88 notes each and appears to be much larger than the present-day piano. The upper keyboard is tuned to the regular international pitch and has the usual five black keys and seven white keys. The other keyboard is a quarter-tone lower and has five blue keys and seven red keys. The A, a quarter-tone lower than the regular 440 pitch, is 427 1/2 pitch. The music written for this instrument sounds weird at first to the average listener, but after a while it gives one a new feeling of tone color never experienced before. (From a letter to the author by Hans Barth, 1936)

23 JULY 1931

The ninth annual Festival of the International Society for Contemporary Music opens at Oxford, England, with the following program of symphonic music:

Lyric Suite for small orchestra in the classical four movements by the Soviet composer Lev KNIPPER, written in a Scriabinesque manner and subtilized instrumentation; *Piano Sonata* in a continuous four-segmented movement, marked by a cumulatively rising dissonant tension, by the American neoclassicist Roger SESSIONS; *String Trio* in an atonally constructivistic idiom by the Polish composer Jozef KOFFLER; *Âme en peine* for unaccompanied chorus by the French composer Jean HURÉ, who died a year and a half before this performance; 3 *Choruses a cappella* by Schoenberg's disciple and Byzantine scholar Egon WELLESZ, couched in an austerely dissonant polyphonic idiom; *4 Japanese Songs* for voice and orchestra, set in the "Tokyo scale" (with quarter-tones) by the Polish composer Jan MAKLAKIEWICZ; and *Sinfonietta* in three movements in a hedonistic neo-Rococo manner by the 26-year-old Spanish composer Ernesto HALFFTER.

24 JULY 1931

At the second concert of the Ninth Festival of the International Society for Contemporary Music in Oxford, the following program of choreographic music is given:

Orchestral suite from *Pomona* by Constant LAMBERT, conducted by the composer; *La Somnambule*, a grotesque dance by the Prague-born atonal neo-classicist Erwin SCHULHOFF, designed as an absolute piece of music with an abstract expressionist scenario, conducted by the composer; and *Job*, "being Blake's vision of the Book of Job," by Ralph VAUGHAN WILLIAMS, arranged for theater orchestra by Constant Lambert and conducted by him.

24 JULY 1931

Die Blume von Hawaii, operetta by Paul ABRAHAM dealing with the exotic shenanigans of a jazz singer named Jim Boy, and taking place in Honolulu and Monte Carlo, is performed for the first time in Leipzig.

25 JULY 1931

During the Ninth Festival of the International Society for Contemporary Music in Oxford, a musical play for children by Paul HINDEMITH, *Wir bauen eine Stadt*, his most characteristic piece of *Gebrauchsmusik*, with simple stage action and a neo-Baroque score seasoned with temperate discords, is presented in the afternoon, and the following program of chamber music is given at the evening concert:

String Quartet in four descriptive movements (*Calme, Rythmique, Douloureux, Rigaudon*) by Marcel DELANNOY, French impressionist composer turning towards neo-classicism; *Sonatina* for piano in three movements by Otto JOKL of Vienna, in a light neo-classically polytonal vein; *Sonatina* for flute and clarinet by the young French composer Jean CARTAN, in a concise utilitarian manner of Gallic neo-classicism; the ultrachromatic, harmonically tense and dynamically explosive *Second Sonata* for violin and piano by Eugene GOOSSENS; and a discursive *Piano Quintet* by the Italian composer Mario PILATI.

27 JULY 1931

As part of the Ninth Festival of the International Society for Contemporary Music, with its principal site at Oxford, a concert of symphonic music is given at Queen's Hall in London with the following program:

Symphonic Music in an ostentatiously nonprogrammatic absolute style by the Polish composer Roman PALESTER;

Symphony for chamber orchestra, op. 21, by Anton von WEBERN (first performed in New York on 18 December 1929), built on a series of twelve different notes in two mutually exclusive and symmetrically disposed tropes related by a tritone; a neo-romantic *Rapsodia* by the Italian composer Virgilio MORTARI; *Second Symphony* by the cosmopolitan Russian composer Vladimir DUKELSKY (first performed in Boston on 25 April 1930), in three classically outlined movements with the subject matter approximating a stylization of Glinka's melodic concepts; *Music for Orchestra*, nonprogrammatic in its neo-classical orthodoxy, by Constant LAMBERT, conducted by the composer; and *An American in Paris*, a nostalgic piece of symphonic tourism by George GERSHWIN.

28 JULY 1931

At the Ninth Festival of the International Society for Contemporary Music in London, the following program of symphonic and choral works is given:

3 Symphonic Pieces by the Argentinian composer Juan José CASTRO; *3 Symphonic Movements* by the Belgian composer Fernand QUINET; *Polish Songs* for chorus a cappella by Karol SZYMANOWSKI; *Songs of the Wolves* for chorus a cappella by the Hungarian composer Ferencz SZABÓ; *Benedicite* for soprano solo, chorus and orchestra by VAUGHAN WILLIAMS; *2 Studies for Orchestra* (*Ritmica funebre, Ritmica scherzosa*) by the Russian-born German-bred neo-romanticist Vladimir VOGEL, written in an expansively sonorous musical language; and *Psalm 80* for chorus and orchestra by Albert ROUSSEL.

15 AUGUST 1931

The first annual Festival of Mountain White Folk Music ("White Top Folk") is held at Marion, Virginia.

30 AUGUST 1931

Cinderella, ballet by Marcel DELANNOY, is performed for the first time anywhere in Chicago. (A revised version was first performed in Paris on 14 May 1935, under the title *Pantoufle de vair*, i.e., *Fur Slipper*, the probably correct title of Perrot's classical tale, the word *vair* having been misspelled through the centuries as *verre*, leading to the popular misinterpretation of Cinderella's being shod in glass rather than in a much more likely material, fur.)

3 SEPTEMBER 1931

Washington's Birthday by Charles IVES, an orchestral potpourri of a popular gathering on Washington's birthday, is performed for the first time in San Francisco.

10 SEPTEMBER 1931

Los Rubios, opera depicting in abecedarian harmonies the early history of Los Angeles by the 58-year-old American composer Mary Carr MOORE, is produced in Los Angeles.

17 SEPTEMBER 1931

A Song of Summer, orchestral piece by blind and bedridden Frederick DELIUS, dictated by him to his musical amanuensis, Eric Fenby, who wrote it down note by note, is performed for the first time at a concert of Delius's music in London, the composer listening in by radio from his retreat in Grez, in France.

3 OCTOBER 1931

Armastus ja surm (*Love and Death*), opera in three acts by the Russian-educated Estonian composer Arthur LEMBA, with the action taking place on a Baltic island where a wrecked seaman finds local love interrupted by sea death, is produced in Reval (Tallin), capital of Estonia.

3 OCTOBER 1931

Carl NIELSEN, prime modernist of Denmark, whose romantically impassioned symphonies with mystically inspired programmatic designs written, in a singularly peninsular manner, half-detached from the musical continent, half-surrounded by an impressionistic sea, yet distinctly of the twentieth century in the austerities and asperities of the idiom, dies in Copenhagen at the age of 66.

10 OCTOBER 1931

Belshazzar's Feast, neo-Handelian oratorio for baritone, chorus and orchestra by William WALTON, to a text arranged from Biblical sources by Osbert Sitwell, beginning with the shattering prophecy by Isaiah and ending with the Babylonian king's death and jubilation by the captives, is performed for the first time at the Leeds Festival in England.

15 OCTOBER 1931

The Cat and the Fiddle, musical comedy by Jerome KERN, to the story of a chorus girl who marries a Rumanian opera composer to the tune *The Night Was Made for Love*, is produced in New York.

20 OCTOBER 1931

Emanuel MOÓR, Hungarian pianist, composer, inventor of the Duplex Pianoforte with two keyboards, the upper sounding an octave above the lower, with a coupler uniting both keyboards so as to enable a pianist to play octave passages with unisonal dexterity, dies at Mont-Pelerin, near Vevey, Switzerland, at the age of 68.

(All music dictionaries give the erroneous date of Moór's death as 21 October 1931; Max Pirani, in his monograph on Moór, published in London in 1959, states that he died shortly after 5:00 P.M. on 20 October 1931, and this date has been confirmed by Moór's niece from documentary evidence.)

23 OCTOBER 1931

The American composer Harold MORRIS plays the solo part in the first performance with the Boston Symphony Orchestra, Serge Koussevitzky conducting, of his ultraromantic infra-modern *Piano Concerto*, in three movements, *Allegro-Andante, Variations on the Negro Pilgrim Song* and *Rondo*, distinguished by a somberly evocative quasi-impressionistic style, with an enchorial sentiment in the melorhythmic configurations of thematic content.

23 OCTOBER 1931

Igor STRAVINSKY conducts in Berlin the first performance, with Samuel Dushkin as soloist, of his *Concerto en Ré* for violin and orchestra, in four movements, *Toccata, Aria I, Aria II,* and *Capriccio,* set in an austere neo-

Baroque idiom, with pandiatonic harmonies adding resonance to the ascetically shaped spacious melodies.

24 OCTOBER 1931

Au Béguinage, symphonic tableau by the 58-year-old French composer André BLOCH, suffused with the tropical scents of the island of Martinique, with its native dance, the béguine, providing the vitalizing spark to his conventionally designed score, is performed for the first time in Paris.

25 OCTOBER 1931

L'ospite inatteso, lyrical opera buffa in one act by the Bohemian-born 49-year-old Italian composer Riccardo PICKMANGIAGALLI to a libretto describing the emotional and social imbroglios created by an unexpected visitor, is performed for the first time on the Milan-Turin-Genoa radio network, the first opera to be premièred on the radio.

29 OCTOBER 1931

Afro-American Symphony by William Grant STILL, in four movements depicting in melodious and harmonious tones the authentically racial musical world of the black people of America, is performed for the first time by the Rochester Philharmonic Orchestra, Howard Hanson conducting.

29 OCTOBER 1931

Der Gondoliere des Dogen, opera in one act by Emil Nikolaus von REZNIČEK, is produced in Stuttgart.

1 NOVEMBER 1931

The first piece in *Klavarskribo* notation, based on the tablature principle with the position of each note indicated on the diagram of the piano keyboard, is published in Slikkerveer, near Rotterdam, Holland.

(Klavarskribo is the Esperanto word for piano writing. The idea was worked out by C. Pot between 1905 and 1931, and copyrighted on 6 September 1933. A similar method was proposed earlier by Gustave Neuhaus in his book *Zur Einführung in die Neuhaussche Notenschrift Natürliches Notensystem*, published in Nuremberg in 1906. Richard Zeiler published several works in this notation in 1906.)

10 NOVEMBER 1931

Der Freikolporal, opera in three acts by Georg VOLLERTHUN, is produced in Hannover.

12 NOVEMBER 1931

Das Herz, music drama in three acts by Hans PFITZNER to a supernatural story of cadaverous and astral heart transplants, suggested by Pfitzner himself and elaborated by his pupil Hans Mahner-Mons, dealing with a 17th-century German doctor, who successfully transplants a healthy heart from a corpse he saw in a dream into the body of a prince with a hopelessly damaged heart, only to discover that the heart he so recklessly used was his wife's (she dies, and her heart in the prince's body dies too, precipitating his death and the doctor's political downfall), with a happy ending provided by her astral body with the heart restored, carrying him into the realm of heavenly dreamland, is produced for the first time simultaneously in Berlin and Munich.

13 NOVEMBER 1931

Five Picture Studies, a symphonic arrangement by Ottorino RESPIGHI of five *Etudes-Tableaux* by RACHMANINOFF, with gratuitous fortuitous descriptive titles attached to each (*The Sea and the Gulls, The Fair, Funeral March, Red Riding-Hood and the Wolf, March*), is performed for the first time by the Boston Symphony Orchestra, Serge Koussevitzky conducting.

13 NOVEMBER 1931

Friedemann Bach, opera in three acts by Paul GRAENER, depicting in ostentatiously Bachian polyphony the hedonistic Dresden years of Bach's profligate eldest son Wilhelm Friedemann, after his appointment as court organist in Saxony in 1733, is produced in Schwerin.

19 NOVEMBER 1931

Jack and the Beanstalk, "a fairy opera for the childlike" by the 47-year-old Russian-born American-bred composer Louis GRUENBERG, to the book by John Erskine, with a modernistic musical setting imparting a surrealist touch to the old nursery tale, in which the cow sings tenor, and the giant countertenor in falsetto, while golden eggs are laid in impressionistic harmonies, is performed for the first time at the Juilliard School of Music in New York.

21 NOVEMBER 1931

Das Unaufhörliche, oratorio by Paul HINDEMITH to the text of a mystically idealistic poem by Gottfried Benn, written in a neo-medieval manner, modal in its melodic teleology, compact in its intricate polyphony, and starkly pandiatonic in harmony, is performed for the first time in Berlin.

22 NOVEMBER 1931

Grand Canyon Suite, a rotating musicorama by Ferde GROFÉ, presenting in vivid orchestral colors the changing tableaux: *Sunrise, Painted Desert, On the Trail, Sunset* and *Cloudburst*, is performed for the first time by Paul Whiteman and his orchestra in Chicago.

25 NOVEMBER 1931

Sonata for chamber choir by the Dutch composer and innovator Daniel RUYNEMAN, with vocal instrumentation built on the differentiation of tone-color of vowels, is performed for the first time in Vienna.

25 NOVEMBER 1931

Die Heilige aus U.S.A., a play by Ilse LANGNER dealing with the life of the founder of Christian Science, Mary Baker Eddy, presenting her career as the commercial undertaking by a made-in-America "saint" with incidental music by Ernst TOCH, applying discordant hymnal harmonies to characterize the building of The Mother Church in Boston, jazz rhythms for the prying reporters,

and a grand fugue for the symbolic confrontation with Mark Twain and other early critics of Christian Science, is produced in Berlin.

27 NOVEMBER 1931

Paul WITTGENSTEIN, one-armed Austrian pianist (his right arm was amputated in a Russian hospital where he was a prisoner of war during World War I), plays in Vienna the first performance anywhere of RAVEL's *Piano Concerto for the Left Hand* and orchestra, specially written for him, in a triune movement:

Lento, majestic and sonorous, covering the entire range of the keyboard creating aurally an impression of bimanual technique reaching a climax in a deceptively dexterous quinquedigital cadenza; *Allegro*, a curiously hybrid blues episode with a Hispanic motto akin to that of Ravel's *Boléro* in which the third and the seventh of the major scale are lowered while the major harmony is maintained elsewhere, shifting to a merrier jazzy idiom; *Lento*, in an improvisatory mood, first lyrical then rushing towards a precipitate ending in full orchestral and pianistic sonority.

In a work of this kind, it is essential to give the impression of a texture no thinner than that of a part written for both hands. For the same reason, I resorted to a style that is much nearer to that of the more solemn kind of traditional concerto. A special feature is that after the first section in this traditional style a sudden change occurs and the jazz music begins. Only later does it become manifest that the jazz music is built on the same theme as the opening part. (Ravel's statement to M. D. Calvocoressi, published in the *Daily Telegraph*, London, on 16 July 1931, and reprinted in the article *Ravel's Letters to Calvocoressi* in *The Musical Quarterly*, New York, January 1941)

1 DECEMBER 1931

The Devil Take Her, a farcical musical comedy in one act with a prologue by the 38-year-old Australian-born English composer Arthur BENJAMIN, is performed for the first time in London.

2 DECEMBER 1931

Vincent D'INDY, grand master of French music, whose academically pure musical language is a model of clarity while conveying evocative images of landscapes and moods through astute use of folksong inflections, dies in his native Paris at the age of 80.

8 DECEMBER 1931

The Blonde Donna, or The Fiesta of Santa Barbara, opera in three acts by the 65-year-old American composer Ernest CARTER, first performed in concert form in New York in February 1912, to his own libretto involving an uprising of Mission Indians in Santa Barbara, California, in 1824, against the obtusely beneficent Padres, with the Blonde Donna of the title persuading the rebels to desist and take part in a general dance, receives its first complete stage production in Brooklyn.

11 DECEMBER 1931

Dmitri KABALEVSKY, 26-year-old Soviet composer, plays the solo part in the world première in Moscow of his *First Piano Concerto* in A minor in three movements, written in a lyrico-heroic manner, with recurrent eruptions of kinetic energy in an optimistic tonal ambience, vitalized by prudential and temperate dissonances.

15 DECEMBER 1931

Igor MARKEVITCH, 19-year-old Russian-born Parisian composer, conducts the Orchestre Symphonique de Paris in the first performance of his ballet suite *Rebus*, dedicated to the memory of Serge Diaghilev, in six neo-Rococo movements: *Prélude, Danse, Gigue, Variations, Fugue* and *Parade de vices*. (The solution of the rebus is the Russian proverb "Poverty is not a vice.")

20 DECEMBER 1931

Rotative, symphonic poem by the 26-year-old Italian composer Giacinto SCELZI, inspired by the phrase from a poem by Rupert Brooke: "the keen impassioned beauty of a great machine" and written in a mechanistically romantic manner to portray the transformation of the reciprocating motion of the piston into a continuous rotary motion of a steam engine, with the rhythmic pulsation humanly faulted by occasional asymmetrical meters, is performed for the first time by the Orchestre Symphonique de Paris, Pierre Monteux conducting.

21 DECEMBER 1931

Schön ist die Welt (The World Is Beautiful), optimistic operetta by Franz LEHÁR, is produced in Vienna.

26 DECEMBER 1931

Of Thee I Sing, a musical comedy with book by Morrie Ryskind and George Kaufman, lyrics by Ira Gershwin and music by George GERSHWIN, describing in tones of supreme persiflage the presidential campaign of Wintergreen and Throttlebottom running on the platform of Love, with embarrassing problems ensuing when the President-elect jilts his fiancée of Imperial lineage, being the illegitimate granddaughter of an illegitimate nephew of Napoleon, and marries a country girl who can cook, so that it devolves upon the Vice-President to marry his chief's former fiancée, is produced in New York.

Of Thee I Sing is funnier than the government, and not nearly so dangerous (Brooks Atkinson, New York *Times*, 27 December 1931)

1932

4 JANUARY 1932

Maximilien, opera in three acts by Darius MILHAUD, after Franz Werfel's play *Juarez und Maximilien*, portraying the sad fate of the unfortunate Archduke of Austria set up as Emperor of Mexico by Napoleon III and executed by the forces of the Mexican popular leader Juárez in 1867, with a turbulently dramatic score rich in topical rhythmic materials arranged in intensely dissonant harmonies, is produced by the Paris Opéra.

9 JANUARY 1932

La Jungle, a "polyphonie" for organ and orchestra by Georges MIGOT, is performed for the first time in Paris.

10 JANUARY 1932

A year and three weeks before Hitler's advent to power, the National Socialist Symphony Orchestra, organized by Nazi party members, gives its inaugural concert at a Munich circus, not far from the beer cellar where Hitler embarked on his road to infamy.

14 JANUARY 1932

Maurice RAVEL conducts in Paris a concert of his music; including the world première, with Marguerite Long as soloist, of his *Concerto* in G major for piano and orchestra, for both hands (composed before its left-handed companion which was performed on 27 November 1931), in three movements:

(1) *Allegramente*, in which the basically pentatonic melodic line is embanked in polytonal arpeggios, with the second tonality, F-sharp major, gaining ascendancy and, ultimately, supremacy; (2) *Adagio assai*, in a poetically Chopinesque vein; and (3) *Presto*, set in pandiatonic harmonies and containing elements of jazzy syncopation in energetic motion.

14 JANUARY 1932

Innominata, symphonic movement by the 30-year-old Swiss composer Conrad BECK, so named to emphasize the namelessness of its musical form and content, written in an austerely dissonant idiom without a key signature, but with tangibly set tonal barycenters, is performed for the first time in Geneva by the Orchestre de la Suisse Romande, Ernest Ansermet conducting.

23 JANUARY 1932

Belkis, regina di Saba, "choreographic spectacle with musical illustrations" by Ottorino RESPIGHI, written in a resplendently eclectic style, with orientalistically undulant arabesques characterizing the Queen of Sheba and pentatonic scales depicting the populace, is produced at La Scala, in Milan.

27 JANUARY 1932

Plameny (Flames), opera in two acts by the Czech composer Erwin SCHULHOFF, is produced in Brno.

28 JANUARY 1932

Lady Dean PAUL, Brussels-born posthumous daughter of the Polish pianist Henryk Wieniawski, composeress, under the pen-name Poldowski, of impressionistic songs to French texts and of innocuous piano miniatures, dies in London at the age of 52.

29 JANUARY 1932

George GERSHWIN plays the solo part with the Boston Symphony Orchestra, Serge Koussevitzky conducting, in the world première of his *Second Rhapsody* for piano and orchestra, commissioned for the 50th anniversary of the Boston Symphony and picturing in polyrhythmic constructivist sonorities diversified by lyric interludes in rutilant hues, the "eternal tattoo" of the skyscraper riveters of Manhattan erecting the tallest buildings in the world, the nucleus of thematic inspiration being derived from his score for the motion picture *Delishious*.

I wanted to write a serious composition and found the opportunity in California to do it. Nearly everybody comes back from California with a Western tan and a pocketful of moving-picture money. I decided to come back with both those things, and a serious composition—if the climate would let me. (From Gershwin's letter of 30 June 1931 to Philip Hale, program annotator of the Boston Symphony Orchestra.)

11 FEBRUARY 1932

Krieg über Sonja, "musical stage poem" in three acts by the 47-year-old German composer Horst PLATEN, to a libretto dealing with the conflicting loves of two German soldiers for a Russian girl named Sonia during the First World War, is produced in Hamburg.

12 FEBRUARY 1932

Rip van Winkle, opera by the 57-year-old American composer Edward MANNING to a libretto prepared by the composer, after the famous tale by Washington Irving dealing with the predicament of a man who slept for many years to awake in an entirely different society, is produced in New York.

14 FEBRUARY 1932

Cemal Reshid REY, 27-year-old Turkish composer, conducts in Paris the first performance of his *Karagueuz*, a symphonic suite in 12 movements illustrating 12 tableaux of Turkish shadow silhouette marionettes (*karaguez* means black eyes).

14 FEBRUARY 1932

Der Gewaltige Hahnrei, opera in three acts by the 29-year-old German composer Berthold GOLDSCHMIDT, extolling the virtues and generosities of a "powerful cuckold," is produced in Mannheim.

18 FEBRUARY 1932

Helvetia, the Land of Mountains and its People, a symphonic fresco by Ernest BLOCH, composed intermittently between 1900 and 1929, with the multinational diversity of his native Switzerland exemplified by some thirty motives derived from Helvetian folksongs, is performed for the first time anywhere by the Chicago Symphony Orchestra, Frederick Stock conducting, as the winning work of one-fifth of a prize of $25,000 offered by the Victor Talking Machine Company, shared with four other works submitted for this contest.

18 FEBRUARY 1932

Tragödie in Arezzo, a melodramatic opera in three acts with a prologue and epilogue by the Dutch-born American composer Richard HAGEMAN, after Robert Browning's poem *The Ring and the Book*, dealing with the trial for murder, conviction and execution of a uxoricidal nobleman of Arezzo who in 1698 slew his wife whom he suspected of carnal intercourse with the young priest named Caponsacchi, is performed for the first time at Freiburg-im-Breisgau, in a German translation, with 25 curtain calls for the composer. (The opera was produced in the original version in English, under the title *Caponsacchi*, by the Metropolitan Opera in New York on 4 February 1937, conducted by the composer.)

19 FEBRUARY 1932

Symphonic Ode by Aaron COPLAND, with thematic materials drawn from an earlier *Nocturne* for violin and piano, is performed for the first time by the Boston Symphony Orchestra as a commissioned work for its 50th anniversary, Serge Koussevitzky conducting.

21 FEBRUARY 1932

Jazz Music by the Belgian composer Marcel POOT, a symphonic movement with a saxophone and a trombone syncopating in American rhythms, is performed for the first time in Brussels.

25 FEBRUARY 1932

Sun-Treader, symphonic poem by Carl RUGGLES, 55-year-old rugged American individualist, inspired by Robert Browning's line, "Sun-treader, life and light be thine forever," written in a tense atonal idiom, in unrelentingly driven march time from the initial drumbeats to the final solar illumination in revelatory C major (Browning spoke of "the C major of life"), with powerful tonal protuberances forming a pandiatonic corona, is performed for the first time anywhere, by the Orchestre Symphonique de Paris conducted by Nicolas Slonimsky.

3 MARCH 1932

Eugen D'ALBERT, Scottish-born pianist and composer, who renounced his insular birthright to return to the land of his German ancestors, dies in Riga, Latvia, during one of his many tours, at the age of 67.

6 MARCH 1932

John Philip SOUSA, American March King, Washington-born son of a Portuguese father and a Bavarian mother, whose marching tune *Stars and Stripes Forever* provided a vitalizing bio-musical stimulus to generations of American soldiers, dies in Reading, Pennsylvania, at the age of seventy-seven, forty years after the first concert of the Sousa Band which he led in Plainfield, New Jersey, on 26 September 1892. (The story, generated by an unknown mythologist, that SOUSA is an acrostic for SUPER OMNES USA, is a fantasy.)

10 MARCH 1932

Die Bürgscaft (The Pledge), musical play in three acts with a prologue by Kurt WEILL, wherein an abandoned cache of gold bullion is appropriated by the state to finance an aggressive war, scored for voices, two electrically amplified pianos and a jazz band, is produced in Berlin.

12 MARCH 1932

The Vatican Congregation of the Council issues a warning against the singing and playing in Catholic churches of sacred music written in the modern idiom, and forbidding such performances altogether in case royalties are to be paid to the composer.

14 MARCH 1932

A Congress of Arab musicians opens in Cairo to discuss the adoption of a uniform method of musical notation capable of indicating with precision the non-tempered intervals in oriental scales.

14 MARCH 1932

George EASTMAN, inventor of Kodak (he coined the word himself), munificent patron of music, although tone-deaf himself, founder of the Eastman School of Music in Rochester, New York, commits suicide by shooting himself, because of incurable cancer.

16 MARCH 1932

Fourth Symphony by Arnold BAX, in E-flat, in three movements—(1) *Allegro moderato*, marked by an energetically fanfarous sound with epically narrative undertones; (2) *Lento moderato*, in a pentatonically Celtic melodic structure, suggesting by its muted colors a mystically distant realm of thought; (3) *Allegro*, a cyclic return to the initial mood of affirmation through doubt—is performed for the first time anywhere by the San Francisco Symphony Orchestra under the direction of the English conductor Basil Cameron.

16 MARCH 1932

Ottorino RESPIGHI conducts in New York the world première of his mystery play *Maria Egiziaca*, a neo-medieval triptych relating an old legend of Mary of Egypt, first a dissolute woman in sinful Alexandria, then a penitent, and finally a devout Christian, cleansed of her sins by baptismal ablutions in the river Jordan, set to music in an appropriately Gothic manner, in archaic modalities of naked fifths and palpitant rhythms.

17 MARCH 1932

Alfredo CASELLA conducts in Rome the world première of his first opera *La Donna Serpente*, in three acts (begun on 16 October 1928 and completed on 22 October 1931), to a fantastic play by Carlo Gozzi wherein a fairy donna is turned into a serpent for a period of 200 years as punishment for carnal intercourse with a mortal, but is transformed into a human female when a lover divines her true self, set to music in a pandiatonically translucid and energetically rhythmic style.

The audience was full of beautiful half-naked women, but there was perfidy and menace in the air. A stage box was occupied by a "madmen's gang" intent on sabotaging the opera. I was aware of their presence and had a group of muscular young friends placed in their vicinity. My appearance on the podium was greeted by applause, interrupted by catcalls. For a composer making his debut as an opera conductor at the age of forty-nine the performance presented a real endurance test, but it was concluded in an atmosphere of cordiality. (Alfredo Casella, *I Segreti della Giara*, Florence 1941)

(In his monograph on Casella, published in Genoa in 1936, Luigi Cortese gives on p. 120 the erroneous year, 1931, for the first performance of the opera.)

17 MARCH 1932

On the Market Place, ballet by the 40-year-old Rumanian composer Mihail JORA, who despite his training with Max Reger in Leipzig succeeded in preserving his Balkan rhythmic vivacity, wherein vendors of oriental sweets are depicted by melismatic arabesques, knife sharpeners by strident trumpets, junk dealers by heavy brass and inebriates by slippery bassoons, with flower girls tempting casual military men by the promissory floridity of their orientalistic modalities, with harsh heterophony characterizing the crowds, is produced in Bucharest.

17 MARCH 1932

Il Favorito del Rè, first opera, in three acts, by the 32-year-old Italian composer Antonio VERETTI, wherein the king's favorite courtier and his wife feign their own deaths in order to collect funeral expenses, set to music in a modern opera buffa manner, incorporating a jazz episode, is produced at La Scala, in Milan. (A compressed version, in one act, was produced in Rome on 29 January 1955 under the title *Burlesca*.)

23 MARCH 1932

Pietro MASCAGNI conducts in San Remo the first performance of his youthful two-act opera *Pinotta*, written in 1880, the manuscript of which was lost for fifty years and recovered by chance, on the same bill with the 13,000th performance of his perennial favorite, *Cavalleria Rusticana*.

24 MARCH 1932

Second Symphony by the 32-year-old American composer Randall THOMPSON (completed by him in Switzerland on 6 September 1931), in four contrasting movements—(1) *Allegro*, in a forceful motoric drive; (2) *Largo*, set in spaciously pentatonic modalities; (3) *Vivace*, containing fugal episodes in asymmetric rhythms; (4) *Andante moderato*, leading to *Allegro con spirito*, marked by frenzied jazzy ejaculations—is performed for the first time by the Rochester Philharmonic Orchestra under the direction of Howard Hanson.

24 MARCH 1932

Hop! Signor, lyric drama in three acts by the French composer Manuel ROSENTHAL, to a libretto dealing with a medieval woman who sends her crippled husband to his death to save him from lifelong torment, is performed for the first time in Toulouse.

31 MARCH 1932

Caballos de Vapor, or *H.P. (Horsepower),* constructivistic ballet of the modern age by the prime composer of Mexico Carlos CHÁVEZ, drawing a sharp contrast between the industrialized, capitalistic society of the United States and the pauperized but primitivistically vigorous Americas to the south, constructed in the form of a symphony, in four movements, with the northern foxtrot expressing the technological drive of advanced civilizations, and the southern huapango and tango depicting the languorous but purposeful ontology of homogenized tropical populations, set to music in an emancipated dissonant idiom, with harmonies anchored in focal tonalities, is performed for the first time anywhere, in Philadelphia, under the direction of Leopold Stokowski.

31 MARCH 1932

Two centuries have passed since the birth at Rohrau of Joseph HAYDN, whose intuitive genius for musical organization made the 18th century the era of the instrumental Sonata, the String Quartet and their orchestral counterpart, the Symphony, the forms brought by him to the summit of perfection.

2 APRIL 1932

Three completed movements of the posthumous *Ninth Symphony,* by Anton BRUCKNER, in their original version cleansed of the gratuitous emendations made by Ferdinand Loewe (who conducted his adulterated edition of the work in Vienna on 11 February 1903), are performed for the first time before an invited audience in Munich under the direction of Siegmund von Hausegger.

(The first public performance of these three authentic movements took place in Vienna on 23 October 1932, conducted by Clemens Kraus. The finale of the *Ninth Symphony,* assembled and synthesized by Hans Redlich and Robert Simpson from materials contained in the 184 manuscript pages on which Bruckner worked until the very day of his death on 11 October 1896, was performed for the first time in London, on 17 September 1948.)

2 APRIL 1932

Hugo KAUN, German composer of highly respectable operas and other romantically colored music, dies in his native Berlin at the age of 69.

4 APRIL 1932

Jascha HEIFETZ performs for the first time in Vienna his brilliant violin arrangement of *Hora Staccato,* a dance tune written in 1906 by the 17-year-old Rumanian violinist Grigoraş DINICU.

5 APRIL 1932

Gino MARINUZZI, 50-year-old Italian composer, conducts at La Scala in Milan the first performance of his opera in three acts, *Palla de' Mozzi,* dealing with the leader of the Black Band in 16th-century Siena whose son falls in love with the daughter of a castellan imprisoned by him, and who, horrified by this act of filial disloyalty, kills himself, set to music in a quasi-impressionistic idiom with a considerable admixture of hard chromaticized disharmonies.

8 APRIL 1932

Der Bettler Namenlos, opera in three acts by the Austrian composer Robert HEGER, to a Homeromorphic story of the return of Odysseus to his native island of Ithaca as a nameless beggar, set in grandisonous Wagneromantic harmonies, is performed for the first time in Munich, under the composer's direction.

15 APRIL 1932

Philharmonisches Konzert (Variationen für Orchester) by Paul HINDEMITH, written in a euphonious manner of neoclassical stylization, is performed for the first time by the Berlin Philharmonic Orchestra, under the direction of Wilhelm Furtwängler, as a commissioned work on the occasion of its 50th anniversary.

23 APRIL 1932

The Central Committee of the Council of People's Commissars of the Russian Soviet Socialist Republic announces the dissolution of the RUSSIAN ASSOCIATION OF PROLETARIAN MUSICIANS (RAPM), along with related organizations in literature and art, as factional, divisive and detrimental to progressive ideology in Soviet culture.

April twenty-third 1932. Seven o'clock in the evening. An air of expectancy reigns in the hall of the Collegium of the People's Commissariat for Education. . . . Different generations and different trends of creative musical craft are represented, from Ippolitov-Ivanov to the leaders of the RAPM. . . . On the serious faces, there is a question: what is going to happen? It is apparent that something very unusual is in the air, perhaps a decisive battle. . . . The Commissar for Education, Comrade Bubnov, opens the discussion dealing with problems of Soviet culture. . . . He asks for a frank debate. The floodgates are open. Those present take the floor one after another, attacking the RAPM with extraordinary vehemence. Its theoretical, creative, tactical attitudes are under fire. In some speeches there is bitterness; theoretical contentions give way to echoes of recent squabbles. Personal feelings run high. It becomes clear that the RAPM by its policies, limiting the sphere of creative musical activity, has caused unhealthy conditions for the development of Soviet music. It is clear also that these conditions cannot be allowed to continue. On the 24th of April, the Moscow newspapers publish the decree of the Central Committee announcing the dissolution of all Proletarian Art Associations. The announcement is laconic and unexpected. It is read and discussed everywhere. A new responsibility is given to all. A new path has been opened for creative work. (*Sovietskaya Musica,* Moscow, No. 3, 1933, p. 132. See also the Declaration of Aims of the RAPM in the section Letters and Documents.)

24 APRIL 1932

Székely Fonó (The Spinning Room of the Szeklers), operatic ballad by Zoltán KODÁLY, composed of a series of 27 connected authentic songs of Transylvanian Szeklers (known, in Magyar, as Székely, descendants of Atilla's Huns or of Black Ugrians), to the texts of madrigal-like salutes to love as a socially liberating force, scored for chorus and orchestra applying Kodály's favorite device of "Hungarian counterpoint" wherein two different songs are combined canonically, is performed for the first time in Budapest.

25 APRIL 1932

The Bride of Dionysus, mythological opera in three acts by the erudite British musicologist Sir Donald TOVEY, is produced in Edinburgh.

30 APRIL 1932

The First Festival of Contemporary American Music opens at Yaddo (the name being derived in memory of a child's palatalized pronunciation of "shadow"), private estate near Saratoga Springs, New York, presenting 18 chamber works on two consecutive evenings and one afternoon:

Piano Variations by Aaron COPLAND, played by himself, written in a maximally economical and sparse idiom of reflexive dissonant counterpoint, with variations formed by the interpolations of non-thematic elements thus generating new melodic configurations; *Sonata* for flute and piano in a compact neo-Baroque idiom by Walter PISTON; a song with string quartet accompaniment by Virgil THOMSON; seven songs by Charles IVES, ranging from the obliquely romantic *Serenity* to the highly dissonant swashbuickling Western ballad *Charlie Rutlage;* songs by Paul BOWLES written in a subtilized quasi-impressionistic vein; songs with string quartet accompaniment by Robert Russell BENNETT; a polyphonically designed and economically worked out *Piano Sonata* by Roger SESSIONS; the tersely individualistic *Piano Sonata* by Roy HARRIS; *Unidad* and *36* for piano by the prime Mexican composer Carlos CHÁVEZ, written in a constructivistic percussive idiom; *Suite* for unaccompanied flute by Wallingford RIEGGER, in four movements, the last of which contains a group of 36 different notes as a triple dodecaphonic series; *Four Diversions* for string quartet by Louis GRUENBERG; *String Quartet* by Nicolai BEREZOWSKY; *String Quartet* by Marc BLITZSTEIN; *String Quartet* by Israel CITKOWITZ; a dissonantly racial *String Quartet* by the Mexican composer Silvestre REVUELTAS; and piano pieces by Vivian FINE, Oscar LEVANT and Henry BRANT.

1 MAY 1932

Five winning orchestral works by five American composers, Philip JAMES, Max WALD, Carl EPPERT, Florence GALAJIKIAN and Nicolai BEREZOWSKY, selected from 573 manuscripts in a contest for the best American compositions organized by the National Broadcasting Company, are broadcast under the direction of Eugene Goossens, and the prize of $5,000 is awarded to James for his topical score *Station WGZBX*, in four movements, *In the Lobby, Interference, A Slumber Hour, Mikestruck. (Traffic,* a movement from *Symphony of a City* by Carl EPPERT, composed in 1929 while he was working in a Cleveland cigar store observing the vehicular traffic in the street, received the third prize.)

2 MAY 1932

The Pulitzer Committee of Columbia University announces the award of its annual prize to George KAUF-MAN and George GERSHWIN for their political musical extravaganza *Of Thee I Sing*, the first such distinction bestowed on a musical comedy.

This award may seem unusual, but the play is unusual. Its effect on the stage promises to be very considerable, because musical plays are always popular, and by injecting genuine satire and point into them, a very large public is reached. (From the statement issued by the Pulitzer Committee)

4 MAY 1932

Striženo-Košeno (Cut-Mown), opera in three acts by the 37-year-old Croatian composer Krešimir BARANOVIĆ, dealing with a quarrelsome couple who argue interminably whether it is more proper to say that grass is cut or mown, finally bringing the philological discussion to the attention of the court, set to an appropriately humorous musical score with numerous allusions to popular songs of Serbo-Croatia, is produced in Zagreb.

26 MAY 1932

David Rizzio, opera in two acts by the abecedarian American composeress Mary Carr MOORE, active in women's clubs, is produced in Los Angeles.

26 MAY 1932

Sinfonia Technica, industrial symphony by the 37-year-old Hungarian composer Eugen ZÁDOR, in four illustrative sections—(1) *The Bridge*, thematically constructed on spacious fourths and fifths unruffled by disequilibrating rhythmic syncopation but reasserting its stability on the final D-minor chord with an added ninth fortississimo; (2) *The Telegraph Pole*, with fluted birds reposing nonchalantly on wires chromatically buzzing with important messages in divided string instrument parts, finishing off pianississimo; (3) *Water Works*, wherein the cluttered trombones, glissando strings and trilling woodwinds create hydraulic power; (4) *The Factory*, getting to production in dissonantly clashing brass and culminating in a sonorous A minor—is performed for the first time in Paris, conducted by Ivan Boutnikoff.

1 JUNE 1932

Twelfth Symphony in G minor by the most prolific Russian symphonist of all time, Nicolai MIASKOVSKY, completed on 31 January 1932, known popularly as "Collective Farm Symphony," reflecting in its three movements, *Andante, Presto agitato* and *Allegro festivo*, the three stages of the process of agricultural collectivization—its beginnings, the high point of rural struggle and the successful abolition of individual ownership—making use of folksong materials for realistic representation, is performed for the first time in Moscow.

16 JUNE 1932

The 10th Festival of the International Society for Contemporary Music opens in Vienna with the following program of orchestral music:

Innominata, neo-classical work in dissonant counterpoint by the Swiss composer Conrad BECK, performed by coincidence on his 31st birthday; *Piano Concerto* in a vigorously diatonic and rhythmically propulsive manner by the Russian-educated composer Nicolai LOPATNIKOFF; *Overture to an Ancient Tragedy* by Miroslav PONC of Czechoslovakia, based on the Greek enharmonic mode, which includes quarter-tones in the upper degrees of tetrachords; *Violin Concerto* by Karel HÁBA, brother of the quartertone pioneer Alois Hába, set in a discursive instrumental idiom without recourse to fractional intervals; *Melodies of Catalonia* by Roberto GERHARD of Barcelona; and an impressionistically romantic score, *Bal Vénitien*, by the French composer Claude DELVINCOURT.

17 JUNE 1932

At the second concert of the 10th Festival of the International Society for Contemporary Music in Vienna, the following program of chamber music is presented:

Cantàri alla Madrigalesca, third string quartet by Gian Francesco MALIPIERO, so named to indicate that the participating string instruments sing in the melodic madrigal manner without development; *Flute Sonata* by the Czech-born German composer Fidelio FINKE; *Viola Sonata* by Walter LEIGH of England; *Piano Sonata* by the Austrian composer Julius SCHLOSS, set in an eclectic style embodying elements of Liszt's rhapsodism in Americanistic jazz rhythms; *Children's Cantata*, in modernized ecclesiastical modes by the Polish composer and pianist Boleslaw WOYTOWICZ; and *Quintet* for wind instruments, a piece of abstraction in counterpoint, by the Croatian composer Josef MANDIĆ.

20 JUNE 1932

At the third concert of the 10th Festival of the International Society for Contemporary Music in Vienna, the following program of orchestral music is presented:

Serenade for small orchestra by the Latvian-born German-bred composer Eduard ERDMANN, in a melodious neo-classical vein touched with dissonance; *Piano Concerto* in a percussive modernistic manner by the German composer Norbert von HANNENHEIM; a vigorously accented neo-Baroque *Violin Concerto* by the Polish composer Jerzy FITELBERG, son of the conductor Gregor Fitelberg; *Durch die Nacht*, a song cycle in a post-romantic Mahlerian mood by Ernst KRENEK; and a *Symphony for Brass* in a slightly jazzified manner by the Vienna atonalist Hans JELINEK.

21 JUNE 1932

At the fourth, and last, concert of the 10th Festival of the International Society for Contemporary Music in Vienna, the following program of chamber music is given:

Quintet for oboe and strings in a lyric neo-Elizabethan manner by the English modernistic romanticist Arthur BLISS; a percussively discordant *Kleine Sonate* for piano by the not quite 22-year-old Czech composer Karel REINER; *Serenata* by the Italian composer of neo-classical music Vittorio RIETI; *String Trio* in academically worked out five movements by the Austrian composer Leopold SPINNER; *8 Bagatelles* for string quartet and piano by the 20-year-old Parisian hedonist Jean FRANÇAIX; and *Nonet* for flute, oboe, clarinet, bassoon, horn and string quartet by the Hungarian-Parisian composer Tibor HARSÀNYI. (On the same day, Anton von Webern conducted the Workers' Orchestra of Vienna, the Arbeiter-Sinfonie, in a program containing works by Mahler, Schoenberg and Berg.)

3 JULY 1932

The Green Table, "dance of death in eight scenes" by the German choreographer Kurt JOOSS, with music by Fritz COHEN, depicting scenes at the diplomats' green table, recruits' departure from sweethearts and wives, military brothels, and survivors' recessional, is produced at the Théâtre des Champs-Elysées in Paris, as a prize-winning ballet (25,000 francs) in a competition of the *Archives Internationales de la Danse* in Paris.

16 AUGUST 1932

Cuban Overture by George GERSHWIN, in three distinct sections, the first in propulsive rhumba rhythms, the second in an elegiac manner, and the third in an explosive outburst of Caribbean colors brought to the point of sonic saturation by the use of Cuban percussion instruments, is performed for the first time at an all-Gershwin concert at the Lewisohn Stadium in New York, Albert Coates conducting, under its original title, *Rhumba*.

(Gershwin renamed the piece *Cuban Overture* for a performance at a benefit concert of the Metropolitan Opera in New York on 1 November 1932, in order to avoid the association with the popular type of Cuban music manufactured on Broadway. The first performance of the *Cuban Overture* in Cuba was conducted by Nicolas Slonimsky in Havana on 10 April 1933.)

17 AUGUST 1932

La Sangre de las Guitarras, opera by the Argentine composer Constantino GAITO, to a libretto based on the internal struggles in Argentina in 1840, with the "blood of the guitars" luxuriantly blended with the dulcet wine of the Italianate score, is produced in Buenos Aires.

28 AUGUST 1932

The management of the Philadelphia Orchestra issues a statement to the effect that "debatable" new works will be severely rationed in future concert programs so as not to antagonize those among its patrons who prefer approved music of a melodious nature.

5 SEPTEMBER 1932

Concerto for two pianos and orchestra by Francis POULENC, written in a sybaritically hedonistic manner, in three movements, *Allegro ma non troppo*, *Larghetto* and *Finale*, the stylistic pendulum swinging nonchalantly from mandatory urbanity to pseudosophisticated sentimentality with a fashionable admixture of acrid polytonalities, is performed for the first time at the Venice Festival, with the composer and Jacques Février as dual soloists.

6 SEPTEMBER 1932

Two short operatic works are performed for the first time at the Fifth Music Festival in Venice: *La Favola di Orfeo*, in one act, by Alfredo CASELLA, a classically proportioned score in a homophonic monochrome, to the mythological play by Poliziano, first produced with incidental music at the ducal court of Mantua on 18 July 1472; and *Pantea*, symphonic drama by Gian Francesco MALIPIERO, for a ballerina solo, baritone, chorus and orchestra.

8 SEPTEMBER 1932

Golem, orchestral suite by Joseph ACHRON, in which the last movement is the exact reversal of the first movement, note by note, and in the same orchestration, symbolizing the making and the destruction of the Golem, the mechanical monster of the medieval Jewish legend, is performed for the first time anywhere in Venice, Fritz Reiner conducting.

12 SEPTEMBER 1932

Bachianas Brasileiras No. 1, scored for an orchestra of violoncellos by Heitor VILLA-LOBOS, the first of his nine works in which Brazilian thematics are subjected to Bachian treatment, in three movements with classical titles (*Prelude, Aria* and *Fugue*) and Brazilian subtitles (*Embolada, Modinha* and *Conversa*), is performed for the first time by the Philharmonic Orchestra of Rio de Janeiro, conducted by Burle Marx, to whom the work is dedicated. (Villa-Lobos conducted the work in Rio de Janeiro ten days later on 22 September 1932.)

15 SEPTEMBER 1932

Paris, a suite for chamber orchestra by Jacques IBERT arranged from his incidental music to *Donogoo*, a play by Jules Romains, is performed for the first time in Venice.

25 SEPTEMBER 1932

Romanticismo, opera in three acts by the 48-year-old Italian composer Iginio ROBBIANI, the first part of his "Trittico lirico italiano," is performed for the first time in concert form, on the Italian Radio. (The first stage performance took place in Venice on 10 January 1933.)

29 SEPTEMBER 1932

Leo Blech conducts in Dresden the posthumous first performance of an unfinished opera by Eugen D'ALBERT, *Mister Wu* (in Blech's own completed version), dealing with a vengeful mandarin who beheads his own daughter when she admits having been innocently dishonored by an Englishman, and then kidnaps the seducer's mother to wreak a corresponding abuse on her in retaliation, his plot failing when she puts poison into his tea, set to vapidly romantic music scented with pentatonic themes and sprinkled with a Chinese shower of gong sonorities.

10 OCTOBER 1932

Quartet for Strings and Orchestra by Bohuslav MARTINU, scored for the string quartet as a quadruple soloist with orchestra, in three movements, in a luminously lyrical mood, is performed for the first time anywhere as a commissioned work in London by the Pro Arte String Quartet with the London Philharmonic, Malcolm Sargent conducting.

10 OCTOBER 1932

Symphonie Concertante (Fourth Symphony) by Karol SZYMANOWSKI, for piano and orchestra, in three movements, *Moderato, Andante molto sostenuto* and *Allegro non troppo*, with thematic materials derived from Polish songs and dances of the Tatra Mountains region, treated in asymmetric rhythms and accoutred in bitonal harmonies, is performed for the first time in Poznan, Gregor Fitelberg conducting, with Szymanowski as soloist.

21 OCTOBER 1932

John Alden CARPENTER plays the piano part in the first performance by the Boston Symphony Orchestra, Serge Koussevitzky conducting, of his *Patterns* for piano and orchestra, in one movement of eclectic hedonism, comprising waltzes, jazzy discursions and bits of Spanish dances.

23 OCTOBER 1932

Wilhelm Hintze, the banker husband of the 38-year-old Wagnerian soprano Gertrud BINDERNAGEL, exasperated by true and false reports of her systematic infidelities, shoots her fatally in the kidney at the Charlottenburg Opera House in Berlin after a performance of *Siegfried*, in which she sang the part of Brünnhilde. (She died of her wounds on 3 November 1932.)

28 OCTOBER 1932

At a radio concert in Berlin, Igor STRAVINSKY plays the piano part, with Samuel Dushkin as violinist, in the first performance of his *Duo Concertant* (completed on 15 July 1932), in five movements in the decorative style of the French Rococo, inspired by the classical serenity of ancient bucolic poetry.

29 OCTOBER 1932

Der Schmied von Gent, fairy opera in three acts by Franz SCHREKER, to his own libretto (based on a story by the Belgian writer Charles de Coster, *Smeetse Smee*, from his anthology of *Les légendes flamandes*) dealing with a Ghent blacksmith who sells his soul to the devil to save himself from political persecution by the Spanish authorities of the Netherlands in the late Middle Ages, but refuses to carry out his bargain and instead opens a restaurant at the heavenly gates, ingratiating himself by his culinary art with St. Peter and the Holy Family, until he is finally granted admission to Heaven, is produced in Berlin.

31 OCTOBER 1932

Sergei PROKOFIEV appears as soloist with the Berlin Philharmonic under the direction of Wilhelm Furtwängler, in the world première of his *Fifth Piano Concerto* in G major, in five movements: *Allegro con brio, Moderato ben accentuato, Allegro con fuoco (Toccata), Larghetto* and *Vivo*, written in a classically modernistic manner saturated with euphonious discords in a grand manner of percussive virtuosity alternating with passages permeated by lyric irony.

1 NOVEMBER 1932

Charles MUNCH (original spelling, Münch), Alsatian-born violinist, makes his first appearance as conductor in Paris at the unusually advanced age of 41.

3 NOVEMBER 1932

Un Jardin sur l'Oronte, lyric drama in four acts by the French composer Alfred BACHELET, after a melodramatic novel by Maurice Barrès, in which a devout Christian crusader is ensorceled by a sultry sultana and dies entrammeled in her arms in a garden on the Syrian river Oronto, under siege by his former comrades-in-arms, is produced at the Paris Opéra.

6 NOVEMBER 1932

Symphonie by the 20-year-old French composer Jean FRANÇAIX, in four movements, written in a neo-Rococo "style galant" seasoned with melodic angularities, harmonic asperities and rhythmic asymmetries, is performed for the first time by the Orchestre Symphonique de Paris, Pierre Monteux conducting, with two interruptions by booing and hissing conscientious objectors to dissonant counterpoint, using housekeys as resonators, and causing Monteux to plead with them for the freedom of modernistic musical expression.

7 NOVEMBER 1932

The Flames of Paris, ballet in four acts by the Russian musicologist and composer Boris ASAFIEV, to a scenario from the French Revolution, focused on a dramatic episode wherein an obsolete Marquis is slain by the brother of a peasant gift whose virtue he tried to corrupt, with topical quotations from the *Marseillaise, La Carmagnole* and other popular songs of the time, is produced in Leningrad, on the 15th anniversary of the Soviet Revolution.

8 NOVEMBER 1932

Music in the Air, musical comedy by Jerome KERN, featuring a turbulent romance between a Bavarian music master and an aspiring comic opera songstress, is produced in New York.

9 NOVEMBER 1932

First Symphony, in C-sharp minor, by Dmitri KABALEVSKY, originally conceived as a historical cantata representing the contrast between Tsarist and Soviet Russia, but ultimately crystallized as an instrumental work in two parts, the somberly oppressed tone picture of "the crown and the knout" (*Andante molto sostenuto*) and the optomistic *Allegro molto agitato,* symbolizing the struggle for freedom and better life, with a ballad about Lenin forming a finale, is performed for the first time in Moscow.

9 NOVEMBER 1932

Concerto for string quartet and wind instruments by the 38-year-old Czech composer Envin SCHULHOFF, in three movements, *Allegro moderato, Largo,* and *Allegro con brio,* composed in the manner of a Baroque concerto grosso, with a vitalizing intrusion of fugal jazzification, is performed for the first time in Prague.

19 NOVEMBER 1932

Lazaro, lyric drama in one act by the Argentine composer Constantino GAITO, the first opera to incorporate a tango, is produced at the Teatro Colón in Buenos Aires.

19 NOVEMBER 1932

Lidé z Pokerflatu (The Outcasts of Poker Flat), opera in five acts by Jaromir WEINBERGER, after the Californian tale of adventure and love by Bret Harte, with local color introduced in the form of old-fashioned American dance rhythms, is produced in Brno.

24 NOVEMBER 1932

Resan till Amerika (The Journey to America), comic opera by the Swedish composer Hilding ROSENBERG, is produced in Stockholm.

25 NOVEMBER 1932

On his first and only American tour, Florent SCHMITT appears as pianist, playing the solo part in the first performance of his SYMPHONIE CONCERTANTE for piano and orchestra, with the Boston Symphony Orchestra, Serge Koussevitzky conducting, as a commissioned work on its 50th anniversary, written in a highly congested polyphonic idiom in three contrasted movements:

(1) *Assez animé,* a polyharmonic essay in modernity, with the major seventh as the thematic interval; (2) *Lent,* in a pensively elegiac mood, gaining momentum in a series of pianistically varied scale passages; (3) *Animé,* with an energetic fugato containing quasi-improvisatory trilled cadenzas in asymmetrical meters, gravitating towards the tonal barycenter of G.

28 NOVEMBER 1932

Three centuries have elapsed since the birth of Jean-Baptise LULLY, the Florentine master of French ballet and opera.

(*Notice historique* in the authorized edition of Lully's complete works states erroneously that Lully was born on Monday, 29 November 1632, at 9 o'clock in the morning, which was the day and hour of Lully's baptism. He was born on the day before, 28 November 1632, at 4 o'clock in the afternoon, as testified by the following document obtained by the author from the registries of the births and baptisms in Florence: "'anno 1632 a di 29 del mese di Novembre è stato battezzato Gio. Battista di Lorenzo di Nalolo Lulli e di Caterina di Gabriello del Sera. Nato il dì 28 Novembre 1632 a ore 16:30 nel popolo di St. Lucia sul Prato." All new editions of music dictionaries have amended the date accordingly after the publication of Lully's birth certificate by Nicolas Slonimsky in *Le Guide Musical,* Paris, 1 February 1952.)

29 NOVEMBER 1932

Two days after the 65th birthday of the venerably bearded, orally admired but seldom performed French master of modern composition, Charles KOECHLIN, a concert of his music is given by the Orchestre Symphonique de Paris, under the direction of Roger Desormière, in a program containing first performances of his *Trois Poèmes du Livre de la Jungle,* for voices and orchestra, composed in 1899–1910, inspired by Rudyard Kipling's *Jungle Book, Cinq Chorals dans les modes du moyen-âge* and *Fugue symphonique,* both written in 1932.

29 NOVEMBER 1932

The Gay Divorcee, a musical comedy by Cole PORTER, in which a divorce-bound actress enters a collusion with a professional corespondent who falls in love with her after faking a scene of adultery, containing Cole Porter's greatest song, *Night and Day,* is produced in New York.

7 DECEMBER 1932

Walk a Little Faster, a revue by Vernon DUKE (né Vladimir Dukelsky), containing the nostalgic and sinuously sensuous song *April in Paris,* is produced in New York.

11 DECEMBER 1932

The English Folk-Dance Society and the Folk Song Society are amalgamated in London under the combined name English Folk-Dance and Song Society.

15 DECEMBER 1932

Il Mistero di Venezia, trilogy by Gian Francesco MALIPIERO, is produced for the first time in its totality in Coburg, in a German version under the title *Mysterium Venedigs*, comprising the following individual three parts:

Le Aquile di Aquileia (completed on 12 May 1928), a music drama in three episodes glorifying the heroic origins of Venice as the home of eagles in their aerie; *Il Finto Arlecchino*, musical comedy in two parts (completed on 15 December 1925, and first performed separately in a German version in Mainz on 8 March 1928); and *I Corvi di San Marco*, music drama in pantomime without words (completed on 23 December 1928), depicting the decline and fall of Venice's greatness under the symbolic image of the ravens of San Marco Square.

16 DECEMBER 1932

TRITON, Paris society dedicated to the propagation of modern chamber music, the name referring both to the sea demigod whose attribute is a trumpet made of a conch shell with which he raises or calms the waves, and to the interval of the augmented fourth, basic to atonal melody and bitonal harmony, presents its first concert comprising the first performances of the *Third String Quartet* by the Hungarian-Parisian composer László LAJTHA and *Sonatine* for violin and cello by Arthur HONEGGER, the first Paris performance of a *String Quartet* by Albert ROUSSEL, and the non-premières of FAURÉ's song cycle *L'Horizon chimérique* and PROKOFIEV's *Sonata* for two violins, in his favorite key of C major, originally performed in Moscow on 27 November 1932.

(The *Triton* concerts continued for seven seasons, until World War II stopped them. Complete programs of all concerts are reproduced in Claude Rostand's *L'œuvre de Pierre-Octave Ferroud*—who was one of the founders of *Triton*—published in Paris in the form of a catalogue in 1957.)

16 DECEMBER 1932

Sur le Borysthène, ballet by Sergei PROKOFIEV, to a love story on the banks of the Dnieper (Borysthène is the old Greek name of the river inserted because no Frenchman could pronounce its Slavic name Dnyepr), wherein a soldier wins back his beloved after a fight at her wedding with another, is produced unsuccessfully by the choreographer Serge Lifar at the Paris Opéra.

(Prokofiev sued Lifar to collect the remaining sum of 30,000 francs out of the total fee of 100,000 francs for the composition and exclusive rights, when the latter refused to pay it claiming that the music was inferior and that the production failed because of this, and on 5 January 1937 won his suit, the Paris court ruling that "any person acquiring a musical work puts faith in the composer's talent, since there is no dependable criterion for the evaluation of the quality of a work of art, which is received according to individual tastes, history teaching us that the public is often mistaken.")

17 DECEMBER 1932

Ten Italian composers, two of them eminent, Ottorino RESPIGHI, Giuseppe MULÈ, Ildebrando PIZZETTI, Riccardo ZANDONAI, Alberto GASCO, Alceo TONI, Riccardo PICK-MANGIAGALLI, Guido GUERRINI, Gennaro NAPOLI and Guido ZUFFENATO issue a manifesto deploring the cerebrality of modern music.

We take the stand against this art which cannot have and does not possess any human content and tends to be only a mechanical experiment and a cerebral conundrum. In the musical world today there reigns the biblical Babel. For twenty years the most diverse and disparate trends have been consolidated in an uninterrupted revolutionary chaos. . . . A logical connection must bind the past with the future, and the romanticism of yesterday must become the romanticism of tomorrow. (From the manifesto, as quoted in the New York *Times* of 7 January 1933)

28 DECEMBER 1932

The United States District Court in New York City rules that George GERSHWIN's musical comedy *Of Thee I Sing* does not infringe on the copyright issued on 17 February 1930 to the authors of the musical revue *U.S.A. with Music*, and that the similarity in the political plot between them is purely coincidental and in no way constitutes an act of plagiarism.

29 DECEMBER 1932

Two children's operas by the Czech composer Jaroslav KŘIČKA, *Tlustý Pradědeček (Fat Great-grandfather)* and *Lupici a Detektyvove (Robbers and Detectives)*, are performed for the first time in Prague.

1933

6 JANUARY 1933

Vladimir de PACHMANN, eccentric Russian pianist, who charmed world audiences by his poetic renditions of Chopin and stormy interpretations of Beethoven, and unnerved them by looking for wrong notes under the piano, applauding himself, or grimacing (James Gibbons Huneker called him Chopinzee), dies in Rome at the age of 84.

7 JANUARY 1933

The Emperor Jones, opera in two acts with a prologue and an interlude by Louis GRUENBERG, to his own libretto after Eugene O'Neill's play, centered on a former Pullman porter wanted for murder during a dice game who becomes an imperial potentate on a Caribbean island but is forced to flee into the jungle as his people rebel against his rule, and sends a magical silver bullet into his heart when the cumulative crescendo of voodooistic drums leaves him no escape, with a highly dissonant but basically homophonic setting, is produced at the Metropolitan Opera House in New York.

The Emperor Jones Triumphs as Opera—World Première of Gruenberg's Version of O'Neill's Play Hailed at Metropolitan—Drama Swift, Tense, Emotional, with Fantastical Music, and Spectacular Finale (Headlines in the New York *Times*, 8 January 1933)

16 JANUARY 1933

Eleventh Symphony by Nicolai MIASKOVSKY, completed on 19 March 1932, in three movements—(1) *Lento-Allegro agitato;* (2) *Andante-Adagio;* (3) *Precipitato-Allegro*, set in the "Russian" key of E minor, alternating with its tritonal apotone, B-flat minor, thus producing an intermittent rotatory polarization in the modulatory scheme conjuring up a sense of ineffable melancholy, but reaching a more optimistic relationship of major modes in the finale—is performed for the first time in Moscow.

19 JANUARY 1933

Rudolf GANZ conducts the Detroit Symphony Orchestra in the first performance of his symphonic suite, *Animal Pictures,* with onomatopoeic zoological effects in the orchestra.

23 JANUARY 1933

Béla BARTÓK plays in Frankfurt the solo part in the first performance of his *Second Piano Concerto*, in three classically molded movements: (1) *Allegro* (for piano, wind instruments and percussion); (2) *Adagio*, opening with a chorale-like prelude, suddenly bursting out in *Presto*, and then returning to a pacific *Adagio;* and (3) *Allegro molto*, exploding with untamed energy, with the piano and the kettledrums engaged in a percussive antiphony.

29 JANUARY 1933

First Symphony by the French composer Jean RIVIER, in three movements, with an impetuously energetic finale, is performed for the first time by the Orchestre Symphonique de Paris under the direction of Pierre Monteux.

1 FEBRUARY 1933

Piano Concerto in C major by Ralph VAUGHAN WILLIAMS, in four movements—(1) *Toccata*, in 7/8 time, a kinesthetic essay in a free rhapsodic vein, containing a luxuriantly arpeggiated cadenza; (2) *Romanza*, set in a serenely monodic idiom, in which a central tone effloresces into a songful instrumental arioso; (3) *Fuga cromatica*, based on an involuted chromatic subject with a clear tonal epicenter; (4) *Finale alla tedesca*, a rhythmic German dance in rondo form—is performed for the first time in London by the BBC Symphony Orchestra conducted by Sir Adrian Boult, with Harriet Cohen as soloist. (A quotation from the *Third Symphony* by Arnold Bax, incorporated in the *Finale* after a cadenza, as a friendly gesture to an admired colleague, was eliminated after the first performance for reasons of esthetical congruity.)

3 FEBRUARY 1933

The first performance is given in Brno of *Smrt Kmotřička (Godmother Death)*, opera in three acts by the Czech composer Rudolf KAREL, wherein a fecund musician invites Death to be godmother of his thirteenth child, a boy, to promote his career as a doctor by her infallible medical prognosis (she would stand at the patient's feet as a signal of recovery, and at the head if the disease is fatal), who circumvents the scheme when Death takes the stand at the head of the sick girl he loves by turning the bed around.

5 FEBRUARY 1933

Alexander TCHEREPNIN plays in Paris the piano part in the first performance of his *Third Piano Concerto* in three movements, with the principal motive derived from a song of Egyptian oarsmen on the Nile and other motives inspired by Eurasian chants, while the fugue in the second movement is derived from Tcherepnin's own technique of Interpunctus, in which coupled voices enter the intussusception between two other voices placed at extreme registers so as to avoid overlapping.

5 FEBRUARY 1933

Vocero, symphonic poem by the 31-year-old Corsican composer Henri TOMASI, depicting a professional mourner who intones a vociferous VOCERO at the funeral of a vendetta victim, is performed for the first time in Paris under the composer's direction.

275

6 FEBRUARY 1933

Angels and Devils by the American composer Henry BRANT, scored for seventy-six flutes, alternatively angelic (represented by avian tunes in bucolic diatonic fashion) and demonic (depicted by double and triple tonguing in jazzy syncopation), is performed for the first time in New York, directed by the supreme French pan-pipist Georges Barrère.

11 FEBRUARY 1933

Il Galante tiratore, "choreographic action" by the 32-year-old Italian composer Antonio VERETTI, is performed for the first time in San Remo.

11 FEBRUARY 1933

Rossknecht, one-act opera by the 27-year-old German composer Winfried ZILLIG, dealing with a hippophilic maniac who murders a tractor dealer to deter him from undermining the rural rule of horsepower by machinery, set to a constructivistically satirical musical score, is produced for the first time in Düsseldorf.

12 FEBRUARY 1933

Lev KNIPPER conducts in Moscow the first performance of his *Third Symphony* for orchestra, chorus and military band, written in a socialistically optimistic mood, mostly in major keys, with thematic elements partly derived from Siberian folksongs, and patriotically dedicated to the Soviet Army of the Far East having continuous skirmishes on the Manchurian frontier with the encroaching Japanese.

12 FEBRUARY 1933

Henri DUPARC, French composer of pre-impressionistic songs of historic interest since they represent the earliest examples of a truly symphonic treatment of piano parts, dies in Paris at the age of 85, nearly half a century after he stopped composing any music.

12 FEBRUARY 1933

Le Tombeau resplendissant, a thanatological symphonic poem by Olivier MESSIAEN, is performed for the first time in Paris.

16 FEBRUARY 1933

Gražina, opera in four acts by the Lithuanian composer Jurgio KARNEVIČIUS, with the action focused on the 15th-century Lithuanian queen who dons the armor of her effeminate husband to fight the German Knights, falls in battle and is cremated on a solemn pyre, to a musical score replete with folk refrains, is produced in Kaunas on the occasion of the 15th anniversary of the independence of Lithuania.

17 FEBRUARY 1933

At a concert of modern music in Vienna, a man in the fifth row who shouted after the performance of a work by Josef Matthias HAUER, "Das ist Musik! Pfui Mozart!," is promptly arrested for interfering with a public function and disturbing the peace.

21 FEBRUARY 1933

La Berceuse, ballet by Riccardo PICK-MANGIAGALLI, to a story from the time of Louis XV, in which a handsome marchioness plays an adulterous practical joke on her somnolent husband (hence the sly title), is performed for the first time in San Remo.

22 FEBRUARY 1933

La Farsa amorosa, opera in three acts, five scenes and three comic interludes by Riccardo ZANDONAI, to the Spanish tale by Alarcón dealing with a town official who wears a three-cornered hat as a symbol of authority, indulges in an unsuccessful attempt to seduce a miller's wife and misplaces his evidential hat in the process, is performed for the first time in Rome.

23 FEBRUARY 1933

The first issue of the monthly *Sovietskaya Musica,* serving not only professional interests but helping to build the ideological foundations of Soviet music, examining, dissecting and interpreting every quiddity and every haecceity of the dogma and the pragma of Socialist Realism to provide correct guidance to Soviet composers, theorists and historians, swerving neither to the left in the direction of the discredited and abolished Russian Association of Proletarian Musicians, nor to the right of the Western orientation with its tantalizing decadence and ultimate laissez-faire, is published in Moscow under the dateline January–February 1933. (Date of the actual release.)

Our periodical starts publication at a time of extraordinary significance. Our Soviet land, under the guidance of the Party, its Central Committee, and the leader of the world proletariat Comrade Stalin, has completed the first 5-year plan in 4 years, and is now entering its second 5-year plan. . . . We will fight relentlessly against the danger of the rightist interpretation of the decree of 23 April 1932 in the sense that the Central Committee has "amnestied" all bourgeois idealistic theories. Under the pretense of studying Western European techniques, the rightist musicians are trying to smuggle in the ideological baggage of the rotting bourgeois world, "atonalities," jazz harmonies, etc. . . . But with equal determination our periodical will fight "leftist" distortions of Marxism-Leninism, vulgarization and pseudo-simplification, which was the practice and theory of the now liquidated Russian Association of Proletarian Musicians. (From an editorial statement of aims published in the first issue of *Sovietskaya Musica*)

2 MARCH 1933

At a concert of works by Lev KNIPPER, given at the Moscow Conservatory, his *Fourth Symphony,* subtitled *Four Etudes for Orchestra: Improvisation, March, Aria, Finale,* is performed for the first time.

(Knipper subsequently destroyed the manuscript of the *Fourth Symphony,* and wrote a new symphony, *Ballad about a Komsomol Fighter,* designating it as his Fourth; it is in that new *Fourth Symphony,* first performed on the Moscow Radio on 23 February 1934, that the famous song *Polyushko-Polye* [*Meadowland*] appears in the choral finale.)

5 MARCH 1933

Violin Concerto by Gian Francesco MALIPIERO, completed on 10 March 1932, in three movements, in which "rhetorical virtuosity is avoided like a contagious disease," technically based on pandiatonic concepts, in which the seven notes of the heptatonic scale are superimposed freely over a functional bass (thus the opening chordal complex is C-G-E-A-D-G-B, with the semantical value of a C-major triad), is performed for the first time in Amsterdam, Viola Mitchell soloist, Pierre Monteux leading the Concertgebouw Orchestra.

6 MARCH 1933

Ionisation, epoch-making work by Edgar VARÈSE, scored for instruments of percussion, friction and sibilation, all of indeterminate pitch (kettledrums being excluded), completed by him on 13 November 1931 in Paris and portraying in a recognizably classical sonata form the process of atomic change as electrons are liberated and molecules are ionized, the main subject suggesting a cosmic-ray bombardment introduced by an extra-terrestrial rhythmic figure on the tambour militaire while two sirens slide in contrary motion over the whole spectrum of audible frequencies, much in the manner of harp glissando, the second subject, of an ominously lyrical nature, reflecting in palpitating rhythms the asymmetrical interference pattern of heterodyne frequencies, the development section being marked by the appearance of heavy nuclear particles in the metal group (anvils, gongs, tam-tams), as contrasted with the penetrating but light wood-and-membrane sonoritics of the exposition, and after an artfully abridged recapitulation arriving at a magistral coda, with tubular chimes ringing as new atomic polymers are created and the residual thermal energy of vigorous tone-clusters on the piano keyboard serving as a cadential ostinato, is performed for the first time anywhere at a concert of the Pan American Association of Composers in New York, with Nicolas Slonimsky (to whom the score of *Ionisation* was eventually dedicated) conducting an ensemble of fourteen professional composers and innate rhythmicians manning 41 multifarious instruments, among them Carlos Salzedo playing the Chinese blocks, Henry Cowell pounding the tone-clusters on the piano, Paul Creston striking the gongs and William Schuman pulling the cord of the lion's roar.

7 MARCH 1933

Lili Spiewać, comic opera in three acts by the Polish composer Ludomir RÓZICKI, is produced in Poznan.

11 MARCH 1933

Rapsodia sinfónica for piano and string orchestra by the Spanish composer Joaquín TURINA, discursively ambling through sonorous passes and impasses of Mediterranean melorhythms, with whole-tone scales floating in a plasma of impressionistic harmonies, is performed for the first time in Madrid.

11 MARCH 1933

Carl EBERT, director of the Berlin Municipal Opera, and Fritz STIEDRY, its conductor, are summarily removed from their posts by the Ministry of Propaganda of the Nazi government as non-Aryans. Carl Ebert had in fact pure Aryan blood flowing in his Teutonic veins and arteries; he was dismissed from his post as director of the Berlin Municipal Opera for having polluted his racial and cultural purity by an association with avowed and even possibly Jewish modernists abominated by the stolid Nazi establishment; he left Germany voluntarily.

12 MARCH 1933

Cemal Reşid REY, 28-year-old Turkish composer, plays the solo part of his *Concerto chromatique* for piano and orchestra, with the Orchestre Symphonique de Paris, Dmitri Mitropoulos conducting.

15 MARCH 1933

The Berlin Radio issues an absolute ban on broadcasting of "Negro Jazz."

16 MARCH 1933

The municipal authorities in Leipzig cancel a scheduled symphony concert under the direction of Bruno WALTER, on the grounds that the appearance of a Jew on the podium might create public disturbances.

17 MARCH 1933

Die Hochzeit der Sobeide, opera in three acts by the 34-year-old Russian composer Alexander TCHEREPNIN, to the play by Hugo von Hofmannstahl, wherein the beautiful Sobeide, married to an elderly merchant, elopes with a virile youth, and in the despondence of guilty feeling jumps from the garden tower, expiring in her loving husband's arms, set to music thematically derived from Tcherepnin's favorite scale of nine notes, with dramatic points marked by tolerable dissonance, is produced in Vienna.

24 MARCH 1933

Music for a Scene from Shelley for orchestra by the 25-year-old American composer Samuel BARBER, written in a poetic neo-romantic idiom, is performed for the first time by the New York Philharmonic.

25 MARCH 1933

Guido del Popolo, a megadramatic lyric tragedy in four acts by the 48-year-old Italian composer Iginio ROBBIANI, a second part of his "Trittico lirico italiano," to his own libretto from the times of medieval strife in Italy, is produced at La Scala, in Milan.

27 MARCH 1933

Mouvement symphonique No. 3 by Arthur HONEGGER, significantly lacking a programmatic subtitle (its predecessors were the pointedly illustrative *Pacific 231* and *Rugby*), signalizing his transition from programmatic to absolute music, is performed for the first time anywhere by the Berlin Philharmonic, Wilhelm Furtwängler conducting.

1 APRIL 1933

Arturo TOSCANINI, Walter DAMROSCH, Frank DAMROSCH, Serge KOUSSEVITZKY, Arthur BODANZKY, Alfred HERTZ, Fritz REINER, Ossip GABRILOWITSCH, Harold BAUER, Charles Martin LOEFFLER and Rubin

GOLDMARK dispatch the following cable to Adolf Hitler, newly elevated chancellor of Germany, urging him to cease racial persecution:

The undersigned artists who live and execute their art in the United States of America feel the moral obligation to appeal to your Excellency to put a stop to the persecution of their colleagues in Germany for political or religious reasons. We beg you to consider that the artist all over the world is esteemed for his talent alone and not for his national or religious convictions. . . . We are convinced that such persecutions as take place in Germany at present are not based on your instructions, and that it cannot possibly be your desire to damage the high cultural esteem Germany, until now, has been enjoying in the eyes of the whole civilized world. Hoping that our appeal in behalf of our colleagues will not be allowed to pass unheard, we are, respectfully yours, etc. (signatures follow)

I am not enchanted over the idea of addressing as "your Excellency" a man for whom I have not the slightest respect, nor do I think it quite truthful to say, "We are convinced that such persecutions as take place in Germany at present are not based on your instructions," whereas in reality I am thoroughly convinced that Hitler is personally responsible for all that is going on in Germany at the present time. I also want to make it clear that I am not in the least bit afraid to add my signature. (From a letter by Ossip Gabrilowitsch, New York *Times*, 2 April 1933)

2 APRIL 1933

Kaa, symphonic poem by the 60-year-old French composer André BLOCH, portraying the sly serpent of Kipling's *Jungle Book* in a sinuously undulating saxophone solo and the threatened monkeys by nervous jazz rhythms, is performed for the first time in Paris.

4 APRIL 1933

The Nazi director of the Berlin Radio issues the following order in connection with the protest of American musicians against the racial German policies:

According to newspaper reports, several conductors and musicians in the United States have lodged a complaint with the Chancellor because of the rejection of certain Jewish and Marxist fellow-musicians in Germany. . . . Pending clarification of this matter I direct that the compositions and recordings of these gentlemen shall no longer find a place on the programs of German broadcasting stations and that no musical performance in which they have a part in any capacity shall be transmitted from concert halls.

6 APRIL 1933

Inni (*Hymns*), symphonic piece by Gian Francesco MALIPIERO, completed on 14 May 1932, marking his turn from rhetorical romanticism towards a linear style of absolute music in a classical Italian manner, is performed for the first time in Rome.

9 APRIL 1933

Sigfrid KARG-ELERT, German organist and composer of versatile pieces, some touched with un-German impressionistic colors (his real name was simply Karg, but he added the hyphenated second name to dispel the unpleasant connotations of the word which suggests covetousness and avidity), dies in Leipzig at the age of fifty-five.

10 APRIL 1933

Dr. Goebbels, Nazi Minister of Propaganda, rejects the appeal by Wilhelm Furtwängler, conductor of the Berlin Philharmonic, not to exclude Jewish musicians and artists, specifically Max Reinhardt, Otto Klemperer and Bruno Walter, from German cultural life.

12 APRIL 1933

Second Violin Concerto by Mario CASTELNUOVO-TEDESCO, subtitled *The Prophets*, in three movements that purport to give musical characterizations of Isaiah, Jeremiah and Elijah, is performed for the first time by Jascha Heifetz and the New York Philharmonic under the direction of Arturo Toscanini.

24 APRIL 1933

Momus, symphonic scherzo by the Brazilian composer Francisco MIGNONE, depicting a Brazilian carnival character Momus named after the Greek god of satire, and abounding in typical rhythms of Brazilian dances, is performed for the first time in Rio de Janeiro, Villa-Lobos conducting.

27 APRIL 1933

At the initiative of the International Music Bureau, the Moscow Radio presents its first broadcast dedicated to the international revolutionary musical movement, with a program consisting of two works by the Hungarian Communist composer Ferenc SZABÓ: a symphonic poem significantly entitled *Class Struggle*, and a chorus a cappella, *November Seventh*, the day of the Soviet Revolution according to the Western calendar.

27 APRIL 1933

Jeunesse, ballet by Pierre-Octave FERROUD, wherein amorous young men meet casual young girls in bars and dancing halls in a Riviera resort, uniting after initial comedies of error in recognition, set to easily choreographable music with a touch of dissonant sophistication, is produced at the Paris Opéra.

2 MAY 1933

Bootleggers, satirical operetta by Manuel ROSENTHAL, to a story from the period of American Prohibition, in which a group of thespian bootleggers organize a theatrical company in Canada to import liquor into the dry United States, is performed for the first time in Paris.

5 MAY 1933

La Guiablesse, ballet by William Grant STILL, with the action taking place on the island of Martinique, in which the demoniac guiablesse (meaning she-devil in local patois) lures a young lover away from his beloved and frightens him to death in the mountain abyss when she reverts to her original hideous exterior, to a score based on authentic Creole refrains of the West Indies, is performed for the first time in Rochester, New York.

7 MAY 1933

A century has elapsed since the birth in Hamburg of Johannes BRAHMS, the epigonic genius of German classical music, the third B of the trinity Bach, Beethoven, Brahms, as nominated by his staunch admirer Hans von Bülow (the B's in Bülow's canonized witticism referred not to the second letter of the alphabet, but to the colloquial German designation for a flat; in his opinion, Büllow said, the greatest work was the *Eroica* Symphony with its three B's—*Be'en*—in the key signature, for Bach, Beethoven and Brahms.)

11 MAY 1933

Symphony by Yuri SHAPORIN, in four movements with chorus, portraying the confrontation of a human being with the demands of a great social upheaval—(1) *The Past*, a non-lamenting recollection of obsolete society and the implantation of the revolutionary seed in the form of the popular song, "Little Apple, where are you going? If you go too far, you will never come back," treated in tragic tones; (2) *Dance*, a realistic festival of latent dynamism of the people; (3) *Lullaby*, representing the eternally feminine aspect of life; (4) *March*, symbolizing the revolution as energy transformed into action—is performed for the first time in Moscow.

18 MAY 1933

Verlobung im Traum, opera by the Czech composer Hans KRÁSA, after Dostoyevsky's short story *Uncle's Dream*, is performed for the first time in a German version in Prague.

25 MAY 1933

The Three Little Pigs, famous "Silly Symphony" of a series of cinematic animated cartoons created by Walt DISNEY, containing the greatly popular song "Who's Afraid of the Big Bad Wolf?," is shown for the first time in New York.

26 MAY 1933

The Fugitive, opera in four acts by the Soviet composer Nicolai STRELNIKOV, after Leo Tolstoy's short story *What For?* depicting the escape of a political prisoner from Siberia in 1830, is performed for the first time in Leningrad.

30 MAY 1933

Arnold SCHOENBERG and Franz SCHREKER are dismissed from the faculty of the Prussian Academy of Arts in Berlin, as unfit to teach music in Nazi Germany.

31 MAY 1933

Twenty-nine American composers band together in a Composers' Protective Society and issue a militant statement protesting against the inferior social position in which composers in America find themselves vis-à-vis conductors and instrumentalists, citing the following obstacles in the path to a better future:

(1) The attitude which has reduced the composer to a minor position in the modern musical world; (2) The usurpation of the dominant position in modern musical life by interpreters—instrumentalists, singers, conductors; (3) The consequently unhealthy atmosphere for the nurturing of new music—the apathy of the public, the limitations of the press, the lack of organized encouragement of new music; (4) The concentration of power in the hands of an average conductor,

a self-confessed autocrat at whose mercy the average composer invariably is; (5) The exaggerated attention bestowed upon a new reading of a familiar masterpiece, as compared with the grudging, inadequate notice of a new work; (6) The operation of petty prejudices in directorial circles and nationalistic loyalties on the part of conductors, resulting frequently in the performance of inferior works which reflect discredit on the whole of modern music; (7) The familiar practice of conductors and virtuosi in making up their season's repertoire while abroad during the summer months, with the result that the American composer is deprived of the opportunity of acquainting the public with his works via the programs of these artists who provide the bulk of our musical activity during the winter; (8) The lack of opportunity for the composer (unless he is also an interpreter) to earn a living through the serious pursuit of his profession; (9) The paucity of informed discussion of new works in the periodical press as compared with the attention devoted to new literature and painting. (New York *Times*, 1 June 1933)

5 JUNE 1933

Arturo TOSCANINI cancels his engagement to conduct at the Bayreuth Festival as a protest against Nazi persecution of Jewish musicians.

9 JUNE 1933

The 11th Festival of the International Society for Contemporary Music opens in Amsterdam with the following program of orchestral works:

Symphonic Suite by the 32-year-old Alsatian composer Leo Justinus KAUFFMANN, written in a neo-Baroque manner; *15 Variations* for strings by the 35-year-old Polish composer Josef KOFFLER, derived from a governing 12-tone series; *Piano Concerto* by the 29-year-old Hungarian neo-romanticist Paul KADOSA, set in a propulsively percussive manner, consanguineous with the music of Béla Bartók, with Kadosa at the piano; *First Symphony* by the Dutch composer Guillaume LANDRÉ, composed along neo-Flemish polyphonic lines; and a *Symphonic Suite* by the Czech composer František BARTÓŠ.

10 JUNE 1933

In the course of the 11th Festival of the International Society for Contemporary Music in Amsterdam, the Catalan composer Roberto GERHARD conducts the following program of choral and orchestral music:

Gerhard's own *Passacaglia and Chorale*, from his cantata derived thematically from a 14-note figure which serves alternatively as a cantus firmus or an ostinato; *Pater Noster* for chorus a cappella by Jean CARTAN, French composer who died young the year before; and *Belshazzar's Feast*, powerful neo-Handelian cantata by William WALTON.

11 JUNE 1933

At the 11th Festival of the International Society for Contemporary Music in Amsterdam, a concert of choral music a cappella by Dutch composers is given, including works by the great polyphonists of the Renaissance, Obrecht, Orlando Lasso, Jan Tollins and Sweelinck, and by modern composers Bernhard van den SIGTENHORST-MEYER, J. N. MUL and Willem PIJPER.

12 JUNE 1933

Die Sieben Todsünden der Kleinbürger (The Seven Mortal Sins of the Petty-Bourgeois), ballet by Kurt WEILL, with song lyrics and spoken dialogue by Bertolt Brecht, depicting an unselfish Louisiana girl who successfully plies her utilitarian profession in order to provide her backwoods family with a decent home but is reviled by petty-bourgeois townspeople for alleged immorality, is performed for the first time in Paris, where both Brecht and Weill fled after Hitler's accession to power in their native Germany.

13 JUNE 1933

The world première is given in Amsterdam of *Halewijn*, symphonic drama in nine scenes by the prime Dutch modernist Willem PIJPER, to a libretto in Dutch, dealing with a preternaturally macrophallic and diabolically multifutuent demigod-like archdemon who is symbolically emasculated by an imperious princess after he refuses to sing his magic song for her except at the price of complete carnal submission, set to music in a coloristically vigesimo-secular style intensified by chromatic torques and transintervalic saltation.

My symphonic drama is not synonymous with music drama. The music is here completely self-contained, with all problems of a psychological, metaphysical or esthetic nature already solved in the music. I would call *Halewijn* a monothematic work. The germinal cell is the principal motive consisting of a perfect fourth containing in it a minor third (F, B-flat, A-flat) and its melodic inversion G, D, E. There are also present some melodies derived from Dutch folksongs. (Willem Pijper, in his article published in *De Telegraaf*, Amsterdam, 11 June 1933)

13 JUNE 1933

The 31-year-old French composer Henri TOMASI conducts in Paris the first performance of his orientalistic symphonic poem *Tam-tam*.

13 JUNE 1933

At the 11th Festival of the International Society for Contemporary Music in Amsterdam, the following program of symphonic music is given:

Second Symphony, a brief work in a pleonastically polyphonic manner by the Dutch composer Bertus VAN LIER; *5 Orchesterstücke*, set in a neo-Baroque manner supercharged with dissonant counterpoint by the 27-year-old German composer Edmund VON BORCK, destined to die in war a decade later; *Concertino* for piano and orchestra by the half-French half-Russian composeress Marcelle DE MANZIARLY, with herself at the piano; *Partita* by the Italian modernist Goffredo PETRASSI, in a neo-classical manner characteristic of the young school of composers in Italy; and *Theme and Variations* for orchestra by the Scottish composer Erik CHISHOLM.

15 JUNE 1933

At the last concert of the 11th Festival of the International Society for Contemporary Music in Amsterdam, the following program of chamber music is presented:

Tense, terse and sparse *Piano Variations* by Aaron COPLAND; *Sonatina* for flute and clarinet by Juan Carlos PAZ of Buenos Aires; *Sonatina* for clarinet and piano by the Czech neo-romanticist Isa KREJČI; *Lieder* by Ernst KRENEK; *Three Songs* by the modernistically minded American composer Ruth CRAWFORD, to Carl Sandburg's three surrealistic poems: *Rat Riddles* ("*Why do you sneeze on Tuesdays?*" to the accompaniment of a bass drum), *Prayers of Steel* and *Tall Grass;* and a remarkably involute but molecularly coherent

Quintet for wind instmments by the 24-year-old Croatian girl composer Ljubica MARIĆ.

25 JUNE 1933

L'Envoi d'Icare, ballet by the 21-year-old Russian-born Parisian composer Igor MARKEVITCH, depicting in cerulean melodies and airy harmonies the fateful flight of Icarus, is performed for the first time in Paris.

26 JUNE 1933

Vercingétorix, lyric drama in four acts by Joseph CANTELOUBE, poignantly descriptive of the heroic saga of the great Gaul defeated by Caesar and carried off in ignominy to Rome, set to music in austere harmonies, with the application for the first time in an opera of the electronic instrument *Ondes Musicales* to limn the ethereal mysteries of the Druid cult, is produced at the Paris Opéra.

1 JULY 1933

Arabella, lyric comedy in three acts by Richard STRAUSS, to a libretto by Hugo von Hofmannstahl, with the action taking place in Vienna circa 1860, in which Arabella's sister, dressed in boy's clothes, plays Cupid on Arabella's behalf to a youth and becomes enamored of him herself, the confusion being compounded by Arabella's sudden passion for an exotic Slav, with a finale in which the couples are paired according to their altered tastes, to a lissome musical setting in the waltzingly tuneful manner of *Der Rosenkavalier* is produced in Dresden.

13 JULY 1933

Columbus, radio opera by Werner EGK, is produced in Frankfurt. (Its first stage presentation took place in Frankfurt on 13 January 1942.)

24 JULY 1933

At a ceremony in a Paris synagogue, Arnold SCHOENBERG returns to the Hebrew faith which he abandoned in 1921 when he became converted to Catholicism.

24 JULY 1933

Max von SCHILLINGS, German composer whose operas absorbed the Wagneromorphic doctrines of music drama, with features of the Italian Verismo, dies in Berlin at the age of 65.

29 JULY 1933

Gerhard SCHJELDERUP, Norwegian composer of romantic operas, symphonic pieces, songs, and instrumental mtisic, competently manufactured in an unadventurous Germanic vein, dies at the age of 83 at Benediktbeuren in Bavaria, his home for many years.

30 JULY 1933

A Wagner museum is opened at Triebschen, Switzerland, in a villa occupied by Wagner when he wrote *Tristan und Isolde*.

13 AUGUST 1933

Paul HILLEMACHER, the older of the two Hillemacher brothers who wrote collective operas under the joint initials P. L. (for Paul and Lucien), dies in Versailles, at the age of 80, having survived his younger brother by more than 24 years.

17 AUGUST 1933

Godiva, second opera in three acts by the German composer Ludwig ROSELIUS, depicting in a Wagneromantic manner with an admixture of Straussian melodramatic ecstasies, Pfitznerian austerity and Schrekerian colorism, the legendary naked ride of the medieval British housewife on a propaganda mission against high taxes, is produced in Nuremberg.

30 AUGUST 1933

The School for Scandal, overture after Sheridan's play by the 23-year-old American composer Samuel BARBER, written in a blithely Baroque manner suitable for the 18th-century subject of the music, is performed for the first time at a summer concert of the Philadelphia Orchestra in Robin Hood Dell.

13 SEPTEMBER 1933

In reply to Wilhelm FURTWÄNGLER's invitation to resume his concert appearances in Germany, Bronislaw HUBERMANN sends him a reasoned refusal:

My dear friend, you write that "someone must make a beginning to break down the wall that separates us!" Oh, if it were only a wall in a concert hall! The question is not just of giving violin recitals; it is not a question concerning the Jews as such. No, the issue touches on the elementary pre-conditions of our European culture, of freedom of personal expression regardless of class or race.

15 SEPTEMBER 1933

Kamarinsky Muzhik, opera by Valery ZHELOBINSKY, dealing with the rebellion of the fugitive serf Bolotnikov against the provisional Tsar Shuisky during the troubled times in Russia in 1607, with mass scenes à la Mussorgsky, and some comic episodes such as a quartet of princes to the accompaniment of four double-basses, is produced in Leningrad.

19 SEPTEMBER 1933

Špaliček, cycle of folksongs, games and enacted fables with miming and dancing for orchestra and women's chorus, by Bohuslav MARTINU, derived principally from Czech melorhythmic patterns and diversified by acrid but invariably tonal harmonies, is performed for the first time in Prague.

28 SEPTEMBER 1933

In Terra di Leggenda, opera in three acts by the Italian composer Lodovico ROCCA, wherein a maiden in a legendary land, given in marriage to an overbearing overlord, succumbs to acute anaphrodisia after her youthful lover is caught during their illicit meeting and cruelly put to death, is performed for the first time in concert form, in Milan. (The first stage production of the opera was given in Bergamo on 1 October 1936.)

30 SEPTEMBER 1933

Zwei Herzen im 3/4 Takt, subtitled *Der verlorene Walzer*, operetta in three acts by the Austrian composer Robert STOLZ, wherein an operetta composer suffers waltzing amnesia when the source of his inspiration, a singer named Fee Florabella, vanishes from his horizon and the production of his operetta is held up until she suddenly reappears, sings the lost waltz, their hearts beat together again in perfect 3/4 time, while the tune is written down by an arranger (the composer being illiterate), and, after the tremendous success of the piece, they are happily united in matrimony, is produced for the first time in Zürich.

30 SEPTEMBER 1933

As Thousands Cheer, a topical revue with book by Moss Hart and music by Irving BERLIN, darting slings and arrows at political and social figures of the day, and containing an imperishable song *Easter Parade* (unsuccessfully used by Irving Berlin in 1917 with different words, *Smile and Show Your Dimple*), is produced in New York.

3 OCTOBER 1933

Idyll by Frederick DELIUS for soprano, baritone and orchestra, after Walt Whitman ("I once passed through a populous city"), is performed for the first time at the London Promenade Concerts, Sir Henry Wood conducting.

5 OCTOBER 1933

O mon bel inconnu, musical comedy in three acts by Reynaldo HAHN, to a libretto by the Paris actor Sacha Guitry, is performed for the first time in Paris.

5 OCTOBER 1933

Second Symphony by Henk BADINGS is performed for the first time in Amsterdam.

6 OCTOBER 1933

Second Violin Concerto by Karol SZYMANOWSKI in one movement embodying varied musical materials, archaically modal, orientalistically chromatic and rhythmically resilient, with fleeting motives appearing, vanishing, and reappearing in assorted instrumental solos, set in the key of A minor but departing from it to the remotest tonalities and bitonalities, and resonantly supported by pedal points, is performed for the first time by Paul Kochanski (to whom the concerto is dedicated, and who wrote a virtuosistic cadenza for it), with Gregor Fitelberg conducting the Warsaw Philharmonic Orchestra.

14 OCTOBER 1933

Der Kreidekreis, opera in three acts by Alexander ZEMLINSKY, to his own libretto after a vertistically modernized Chinese tale of a mystical "chalk circle" circumscribing the murderous events in the Manchurian court, to a musical setting in which perfunctory pentatonicisms are presented in quasi-atonal quartal and secundal harmonies, is performed for the first time in Zürich, as a musical drama with spoken dialogue and mimo-plastic interludes.

14 OCTOBER 1933

Alexander GLAZUNOV conducts in Paris the first performance of his *Concerto-Ballata* for cello and orchestra, with Maurice Eisenberg as soloist.

15 OCTOBER 1933

Twenty days after his 27th birthday, Dmitri SHOSTAKOVICH plays the piano part with the Leningrad Philharmonic in the first performance of his *First Concerto* for piano, solo trumpet and strings, in four contrasting movements: an optimistic *Allegro Moderato*, a meditative *Lento*, a short transitional *Moderato*, and a rollicking *Allegro con brio*, ending endlessly in an unceasing display (*style pompier*) of trumpeted C major.

21 OCTOBER 1933

Let 'em Eat Cake, a musical comedy by George GERSHWIN, titled after Marie-Antoinette's famous but spurious saying, "Qu'ils mangent de la brioche," when told that her people had no bread (Rousseau quotes a similar remark in his *Confessions,* published before the unfortunate Queen of France was born), brought up to date as a sequel to Gershwin's *Of Thee I Sing* with a proletarian dictatorship established in New York and shaggy revolutionists singing "Down with music by Stravinsky! Down with shows except by Minsky!," is produced in New York.

21 OCTOBER 1933

Madame Liselotte, opera in three acts by Ottmar GERSTER, dealing, in a melodiously harmonious folklike manner, with the patriotic princess of Pfalz (1652–1721) who marries a brother of Louis XIV but remains German at heart despite her French adhesions, is produced in Essen.

23 OCTOBER 1933

Hermann Göring March, composed by Horst GERLACH, in the martial key of E-flat major, with a self-complacent *Trio* in A-flat, a grandiose Coda, and a subtitle, *Hakenkreuz stets voran (The Swastika ever onward!)*, is published in the Third Reich.

31 OCTOBER 1933

Arnold SCHOENBERG arrives in the United States, leaving Germany forever.

4 NOVEMBER 1933

Michael Kohlhaas, opera in three acts by the Danish-born but completely Germanized composer Paul von KLENAU, to his own libretto after Heinrich von Kleist's novel dealing with oppression of common people in medieval Germany, to a musical score of a singularly angular structure, opening with a thematically important 12-tone motto, containing passages of *Sprechstimme*, and concluding in B minor, the favorite key of German romantic composers, is produced in Stuttgart. (A revised version was produced at the Berlin Opera on 7 March 1934.)

5 NOVEMBER 1933

Aurora, opera written in 1811 by the great fabulist E. T. A. HOFFMANN, who was also a fairly competent composer, the manuscript of which was discovered in 1907, is performed for the first time in Bamberg in a slightly refurbished version.

12 NOVEMBER 1933

A century has passed since the birth in St. Petersburg of Alexander BORODIN, registered officially as a son of the serf butler named Boroda (The Beard), but in fact the illegitimate son of the 62-year-old Georgian prince Luke Gedeonov and his 25-year-old mistress, a physician's wife named Avdotia Antonova, the child so procreated destined to become one of the Mighty Five of the Russian National School of composition.

13 NOVEMBER 1933

Corsaresca (Lady Pirate), "tragic spectacle" (*visione tragica*) by the 53-year-old Italian composer Pasquale LA ROTELLA, is produced in Rome. (It was first performed as an oratorio in Milan on 24 September 1933.)

15 NOVEMBER 1933

A revised version of *Donna Diana*, the best known opera by Emile-Nicolas von REZNIČEK, originally produced in Prague on 16 December 1894, and dealing with a coquettish Spanish damsel playing a double game with a shrewd torero, who finally overcomes her wiles by the simple expedient of exciting her jealousy, is produced in Wuppertal.

15 NOVEMBER 1933

The Reichsmusikkammer, affiliated with the German Ministry of Propaganda, is organized in Berlin by Dr. Joseph Goebbels, to supervise the esthetic and racial problems of German music, and the following officers are named: President, Richard STRAUSS; Vice-President, Paul GRAENER; General Music Director, Wilhelm FURTWÄNGLER; members, Fritz STEIN, Gustav HAVEMANN; Secretary, Heinz IHLERT.

(The general Reichkulturkammergesetz, a decree empowering the Ministry of Propaganda to establish six Reich Culture Chambers for literature, press, radio, theater, music and fine arts, was signed by Hitler on 22 September 1933; the provisional Filmkammer for the cinema industry was established on 14 July 1933. The text of the general decree, along with other regulations relating to musical activities in the Third Reich, was contained in *Musikrecht*, compiled by Karl Friedrich Schrieber and Karl Heinz Wachenfeld, and published in Berlin in 1936.)

15 NOVEMBER 1933

1929, A Satire, symphonic sketch by David Stanley SMITH, Dean of the Yale School of Music, depicting with gentle professorial humor the emotions preceding and following the disastrous stock market crash, is performed in New York for the first time.

17 NOVEMBER 1933

Concerto for piano, violin, cello and orchestra by Alfredo CASELLA is performed for the first time in Berlin.

18 NOVEMBER 1933

Roberta, musical comedy by Jerome KERN, dealing with an American football player who takes over the management of a Paris dress shop owned by his Aunt Roberta, and falls in love with a model who turns out to be a Russian Princess, featuring the famous ballad *Smoke Gets in Your Eyes*, is produced in New York.

20 NOVEMBER 1933

Värmlandsrhapsodie for orchestra by Kurt ATTERBERG, based on the folk music of Värmland, the northern region glorified in the novels of Selma Lagerlöf, is performed on the Swedish radio for the first time as a tribute on her 75th birthday.

22 NOVEMBER 1933

Three Dance Movements by the 28-year-old American composer William RUSSELL, scored for expanded and ameliorated piano, with tone clusters and piano strings activated by a fork, a cymbal played by drawing the teeth of a saw across its edge, and a bottle to be broken at the climax, is performed for the first time in New York.

30 NOVEMBER 1933

Sea-Drift, symphonic poem after Walt Whitman, by the American industrialist-composer John Alden CARPENTER, is performed for the first time by the Chicago Symphony Orchestra, Frederick Stock conducting.

30 NOVEMBER 1933

Feier der neuen Front, a cycle of four choral movements a cappella by Richard TRUNK, professor of the Musikhochschule in Cologne, titled *Hitler, Des Führers Wächter, O Land*, and *Horst Wessel*, to the text by the youth leader of the Third Reich, Baldur von Schirach, is performed for the first time in Berlin.

A folklike penetrating melos which comes unmistakably from the heart, the working out of specific sonorous materials that is wholly admirable, make this composition of Richard Trunk, written in February and March 1932, a worthy tribute to the Führer and serves as the mirror of his spirit and his deeds. (Arthur Egidi, *Musik im Zeitbewusstsein*, 16 December 1933)

In that turbulent year 1933 many German poets and composers contributed, quite spontaneously, occasional pieces which can be understood only in the light of the political reality of the time. That a weird error was thus committed was realized sooner or later by everyone. (From a letter by Richard Trunk to Fred K. Prieberg, dated 7 November 1961)

2 DECEMBER 1933

La giornata di Marcellina (Marcellina's Day), "merry opera" in two acts by the 59-year-old Italian composer Attilio PARELLI, is performed for the first time on the Turin Radio. (A stage performance took place in San Remo on 24 February 1940.)

2 DECEMBER 1933

Maximilian STEINBERG, Russian composer and teacher, son-in-law of Rimsky-Korsakov, conducts the Leningrad Philharmonic in the first performance of his *Fourth Symphony*, surnamed *Truksib*, glorifying in a rhapsodically heroic style the construction of the Turkestan-Siberian railroad.

6 DECEMBER 1933

Münchhausen, opera in three acts by Mark LOTHAR, depicting the career of the famous liar in a sympathetic light, leaning towards the conclusion that imaginative falsehoods are the essence of great art, set to music in the style of old Italian opera buffa is produced in Dresden.

12 DECEMBER 1933

Theodore MOSES-TOBANI, American song writer who wrote the celebrated ballad *Hearts and Flowers* in 1893, which reflects with florid cordiality the sentiments of the era, dies in New York of apoplexy at the age of 78.

15 DECEMBER 1933

Carlos CHÁVEZ, prime composer of Mexico, conducts in Mexico City the first performance of his *Sinfónia de Antígona*, inspired by Greek mythology, but paradoxically redolent of Mexican melorhythms in the framework of austere quasi-Grecian modalities.

15 DECEMBER 1933

Moon Trail, suite of four symphonic sketches by Emerson WHITHORNE (completed 26 April 1933) depicting in impressionistic colors the western American landscape, is performed for the first time by the Boston Symphony Orchestra, Serge Koussevitzky conducting.

16 DECEMBER 1933

Der Heidenkönig, opera in three acts by Siegfried WAGNER, dealing with the pagan king of East Prussia during the Polish invasion in the 12th century whose queen, unfaithful with a Christian, is fatally stabbed by her brother-in-law for her un-pagan attitude, with Christianity winning over when a miraculous monk dispels a choreographic pandemonium, is posthumously produced in Cologne, with a musical score marked by harmonic chromaticism and orchestral sonorities characteristic of Wagner-père.

31 DECEMBER 1933

An anti-jazz parade is held at Mohall, Ireland, with banners proclaiming "Down with Jazz and Paganism."

1934

1 JANUARY 1934

The German State Philharmonic Orchestra of the German Soviet Republic of the Volga basin is established by a Soviet decree.

5 JANUARY 1934

First Symphony by Ernst BACON is performed for the first time by the San Francisco Symphony Orchestra, Issay Dobrowen conducting.

6 JANUARY 1934

Ralph VAUGHAN WILLIAMS conducts at the National Folk Dance Festival in London the first performance of his orchestral work, *The Running Set*, based on traditional dance tunes.

10 JANUARY 1934

Le Astuzie di Bertoldo, opera in three acts by the Italian composer Luigi FERRARI-TRECATE, set in a neo-Baroque manner, modernized by polytonal rococo harmonies, is produced in Genoa.

10 JANUARY 1934

Fourth Symphony in C major by the 59-year-old Austrian composer Franz SCHMIDT, his last, opening and closing with a pessimistic trumpet solo funereally matted by flatting the supertonic, mediant and submediant, inspired by the death of his only daughter, and therefore also known as *Requiem Symphony*, in four movements—*Allegro molto moderato, Adagio, Molto vivace* and *Poco sostenuto*—unified by an integrated sonatomorphic design in which the first movement is the exposition, the two middle movements represent the development, and the last movement corresponds to the recapitulation, is performed for the first time in Vienna, conducted by Oswald Kabasta, to whom the score is dedicated.

12 JANUARY 1934

First Symphony by the American composer Emerson WHITHORNE is performed for the first time by the Cincinnati Symphony Orchestra.

12 JANUARY 1934

Ernest BLOCH conducts in Turin, Italy, the world première of his *Sacred Service*, in five movements, inspired by the Hebrew cantillation of the old ritual, but set in modern harmonies.

13 JANUARY 1934

La Favola del Figlio Cambiato, opera in three acts by Gian Francesco MALIPIERO, to Pirandello's play dealing with a dynastic switch wherein a mentally defective heir to the throne is replaced by a normal but non-royal young man, is performed for the first time in Brunswick, Germany, in a German version as *Die Legende vom vertauschten Sohn*.

14 JANUARY 1934

George GERSHWIN plays the solo piano part, with the Leo Reisman Orchestra in Boston, in the first performance of his *Variations on "I Got Rhythm"* for piano and orchestra, derived from the song of that name in his revue *Girl Crazy*, and built on a palindromic tetratonic rhythmic figure of four dotted eighth-notes flanked by two eighth-note rests in square time, with variations traversing the entire spectrum of ethnic American expression, from propulsive aggressiveness to poignant melancholy of the Blues.

15 JANUARY 1934

Madrisa, folk opera in three acts by the Swiss composer Hans HAUG, is performed for the first time in Basel.

15 JANUARY 1934

Fifth Symphony by Arnold BAX, revealing a selective consanguinity to Sibelius, to whom the score is dedicated, in its tenebrous harmonies and self-generating rhythmic motives, in three romantic movements—(1) *Poco lento*, followed by an ignescent *Allegro con fuoco* vesuviating in an eruption of tonal lava before subsiding into C-sharp minor; (2) *Poco lento*, again, a rhapsodically contemplative essay, focused on B-flat minor, containing a whimsical solo of the muted bass tuba, disparting itself in a rude rustic manner; (3) *Poco moderato*, in pregnant unisons in strong strings, leading to a dancing *Allegro*, potently exhibiting an array of muscular rhythms, with brass and drums supplying the generative power for polythematically cyclic development until a coda on a plagally approached unison D-flat in fortissimo—is performed for the first time by the London Philharmonic, Sir Thomas Beecham conducting.

17 JANUARY 1934

Albert EINSTEIN makes his American debut as a violinist in the New York home of the financier and music patron Adolph Lewisohn, at a private concert for the benefit of Jewish and other scientists in Nazified Berlin, with Einstein playing the second violin in Bach's *Concerto* for two violins and in a Mozart *Quartet*.

18 JANUARY 1934

Otakar ŠEVČÍK, Czech violinist and pedagogue, compiler of famous manuals of violin playing, who taught some five thousand aspiring violinists in Prague, Vienna, London and New York, dies at the age of 81 in the small Bohemian town of Písek, in retirement from his Herculean labors in cleansing the Augean stables of the four fiddle strings.

20 JANUARY 1934

Giuditta, operetta by Franz LEHÁR, dealing with the depredations inflicted by the irresistible titular heroine on male Mediterranean hearts, set to music in a grandiloquently emotional style, is performed for the first time in Vienna.

21 JANUARY 1934

To commemorate the tenth anniversary of the death of Vladimir Lenin, *Lenin,* dramatic symphony with narrator and chorus by Vissarion SHEBALIN, to texts of Vladimir Mayakovsky, opening with a fugal movement symbolizing the cumulative impact of the Revolution, followed by a threnody mourning Lenin's death, and ending with a choral shout "Lenin!," is performed for the first time in Leningrad. (A partial performance of the work was given in Moscow on 21 January 1933.)

21 JANUARY 1934

Third Symphony, the "Lenin Symphony" by Dmitri KABALEVSKY (completed on 26 December 1933 before his *Second Symphony*), in two conjunct movements *Allegro impetuoso* and *Andante marciale lugubre,* written in the somber tones befitting the subject, and concluding with a dirge for "one who fell silent, but who is more alive than ever," is performed for the first time in Moscow, on the tenth anniversary of Lenin's death.

22 JANUARY 1934

Lady Macbeth of the District of Mzensk, opera in four acts by the 27-year-old Soviet composer Dmitri SHOSTAKOVICH, to the libretto from a short story of that name by the 19th-century Russian writer Leskov, dealing with an emotionally frustrated Russian woman who murders her merchant husband in a complot with her lover, goes to Siberia with him for their crime and stabs him to death when he leaves her for another murderess, set to music in a powerful dramatic style, rich in satirical grotesquerie, including a naturalistic symphonic interlude illustrating, with realistic slide trombone glissandos, sexual intercourse on the marital bed behind the curtains on an open stage, is performed for the first time in Leningrad.

I have tried to make the musical language of my opera as simple as possible. I do not agree with the once fashionable theory that the operatic vocal line should be nothing more than recitation with accented inflection. An opera is by definition a vocal work. Accordingly, the voice parts in my opera are built on broad cantilena, making use of all available resources of the human voice, which is the richest musical instrument we have. The musical development of the opera follows a symphonic plan, proceeding in a continuous flow. Musical interludes between the scenes form a part of this continuous flow; they serve the purpose of developing basic musical ideas and illustrating the action. (Shostakovich in an article published in the program book of the first performance of his opera)

Shostakovich reveals himself in his opera as a powerful satirist. He exposes the bestiality of the merchant class of all Russia, the stupidity of the priests, the crudity of the soldiery, the greed of the bourgeoisie, the corruption of the lackeys of the aristocracy. He applies the method of vulgarizing his musical material to characterize social phenomena. The scene at the police station, for instance, is illustrated by a deafening march. The coarseness of such intentionally blatant music

reveals the animalistic nature of the repellent bourgeoisie of Old Russia. (A. Ostretzov, in an article in the program book of the first performance of the opera)

Lady Macbeth of the District of Mzensk, later renamed *Katerina Izmailova,* after the name of the heroine, held me spellbound when I first heard it at my home with Shostakovich playing it at the piano. All those present understood at once that we were witnessing the birth of a work of the highest creative caliber. The silence that followed after he stopped playing lasted several minutes and expressed the depth of our emotional response. No one wished to indulge in easy words of praise. (Boris Mordvinov, director of the first production of the opera, in an article published in the program book)

23 JANUARY 1934

La Fiamma, musical melodrama in three acts by Ottorino RESPIGHI, dealing with the flaming passion of a woman for her young stepson, set to music in the manner of "ritorno all'antico" making use of ancient modes in modern pandiatonic dress, is performed for the first time in Rome.

24 JANUARY 1934

L'Alba della Rinascità, opera by the 47-year-old Italian composer Nino CATTOZZO (real name Cattozzo Luigi), is produced at La Scala, in Milan.

26 JANUARY 1934

First Symphony, subtitled *1933,* by the 35-year-old American composer Roy HARRIS, in three movements, portraying respectively the moods of "adventure and physical exuberance, the pathos underlying human existence and a positive will to power and action," is performed for the first time by the Boston Symphony Orchestra, Serge Koussevitzky conducting.

27 JANUARY 1934

Fanal, opera in three acts by the Swedish composer Kurt ATTERBERG, to a romantic subject from Heine's ballad *Der Schelm von Bergen,* is produced in Stockholm.

5 FEBRUARY 1934

Four centuries have elapsed since the birth in Florence of Giovanni de' BARDI, founder of the Florentine Camerata whose gatherings at his palatial home led to the formation of the art of opera.

8 FEBRUARY 1934

Four Saints in Three Acts, surrealist opera by the 37-year-old American composer Virgil THOMSON, to Gertrude Stein's ostentatiously simplicistic book replete with inventive incongruities (there are in the cast sixteen, not four, saints, two hypostases of Ste. Theresa, and the number of acts is four, not three), with the high point of magnificent inanity reached in the choral lament "Pigeons on the grass—Alas!" set to music in a congenially coy, triadically sophisticated style, is performed for the first time anywhere in Hartford, Connecticut, by a Negro cast wearing cellophane clothes, and presented under the auspices of the Society of Friends and Enemies of Modern Music.

Gertrude Stein loved these saints because they were Spanish, and I loved them because they were saints. (Virgil Thomson in *This Week*, New York, 28 April 1952)

10 FEBRUARY 1934

First Symphony by Louis GRUENBERG, composed in 1919 and revised in 1929, set in orthodox four movements, reaches a belated first performance at a Boston Symphony concert, Serge Koussevitzky conducting.

10 FEBRUARY 1934

Merry Mount, opera in four acts by Howard HANSON, after Hawthorne's tale *The Maypole of Merry Mount*, dealing with the Puritan leader of colonial Massachusetts, immolated in fiery death with the woman infidel who corrupted him to ungodly practices at the pagan rites of the Maypole, set to music in colorful contrasts of religious chants artfully spiked by the tritone, the "diabolus in musica" of medieval demonology, with hedonistic songs and paganistic dances marked by acute but euphonious discordancies and vitalized by rhythmic asymmetries, ending hyperplagally in a tritonally cadenced E major, is produced by the Metropolitan Opera Company in New York.

(The first performance of the opera, in concert form, took place at the University of Michigan, Ann Arbor, on 20 May 1933.)

14 FEBRUARY 1934

El castillo de Almodovar, three symphonic impressions by the Spanish composer Joaquín TURINA, orchestrated by him from his three piano pieces bearing the same title, is performed for the first time in Madrid.

15 FEBRUARY 1934

Cecilia, "sacred action" in three episodes by Licinio REFICE, dealing with the life and martyrdom of Santa Cecilia, patron saint of music, ending in sonorous B-flat major in the apotheosis, is performed for the first time in Rome.

16 FEBRUARY 1934

Second Symphony by the Russian-born American composer Nicolai BEREZOWSKY, neo-romantic in essence but modernistic in substance (he forgoes the key signature), is performed for the first time by the Boston Symphony Orchestra, Richard Burgin conducting.

23 FEBRUARY 1934

Sir Edward ELGAR, uncrowned laureate of English music, creator of a powerful national style of composition, supremely British in its stately pomp and its dignified humor, and expressed in a technically impeccable, romantically inspired idiom, dies in Worcester at the age of 76.

23 FEBRUARY 1934

Ballad about a Komsomol Fighter by Lev KNIPPER, his Fifth Symphony, renumbered No. 4 (after he destroyed the manuscript of the original *Fourth Symphony* first performed in Moscow on 2 March 1933), containing the famous song *Polyushko-Polye (Meadowland)*, is performed for the first time on the Moscow Radio.

23 FEBRUARY 1934

Jánošík, opera in three acts by the Czech modernist Karel HÁBA, brother of the famous ultra-modernist Alois Hába, dealing with a rebellion led by the historic Jánošík against the feudal lords of medieval Bohemia, ending in a victorious defeat as he is treacherously slain after he has enriched the poor by expropriating the rich, is produced for the first time in Prague.

25 FEBRUARY 1934

Georges ENESCO conducts in Bucharest the first performance of his *Symphony in D minor*, written by him in 1896 when he was 14 years old.

25 FEBRUARY 1934

Concerto for flute and orchestra by Jacques IBERT, in three flautogenic movements set in impressionistic harmonies, is performed for the first time in Paris.

28 FEBRUARY 1934

Helen Retires, opera in three acts by George ANTHEIL, freely derived from John Erskine's novel *The Private Life of Helen of Troy*, wherein Helen announces her retirement from erotic activities after seducing Achilles in the Elysian Fields, but breaks her vow when she meets a virile youth, set to music in an appropriately sophisticated idiom, ranging from mock-classicism to jazz, is produced at the Juilliard School of Music in New York.

6 MARCH 1934

Walter PISTON conducts the Boston Symphony Orchestra at a concert in Cambridge in the first performance of his *Concerto for Orchestra*, in three movements, marked by neo-Baroque effervescence with an admixture of stimulatingly tolerable dissonances.

11 MARCH 1934

Sergei PROKOFIEV conducts in Paris the first performance of his symphonic suite *Sur le Borysthène*, derived from his ballet of the same name and picturing pagan Russian scenes on the banks of the Dnieper River.

12 MARCH 1934

Mathis der Maler, symphony by Paul HINDEMITH, in three movements formed from the materials of his future opera of that name inspired by the altar triptych of the 16th-century painter Mathias Grünewald in the Alsatian town of Isenheim, in three movements—(1) *Engelkonzert*, written in an austerely open diatonic idiom, with the old German folk theme *Es sungen drei Engel* as a permeating motto; (2) *Grablegung*, brief threnody in agonized muted discords ending on a fatalistic major triad; (3) *Versuchung des Heiligen Antonius*, opening with a rhapsodic invocation in polymodal unisons and free measure, leading through a tense section of high motility to the victorious chorales *Lauda Sion Salvatorem* and *Alleluia* in broad chordal harmonies concluding on the thematic tonic of D-flat major—is performed for the first time by the Berlin Philharmonic, Wilhelm Furtwängler conducting. (A partial performance of the symphony was conducted by Paul Hindemith with the British Broadcasting Company in London on 21 December 1933.)

15 MARCH 1934

Elga, opera in five scenes, with a prologue and an epilogue, by the Russian-trained Estonian composer Arthur LEMBA, after the homonymous drama by Gerhart Hauptmann, with the action taking place in Poland in the 17th century, is performed for the first time in Tallin.

15 MARCH 1934

First Symphony by the French composer Marcel DELANNOY is performed for the first time in Paris.

16 MARCH 1934

Arnold SCHOENBERG makes his first American appearance as conductor with the Boston Symphony Orchestra, in a program limited to his early works.

(Schoenberg was scheduled to conduct the Boston Symphony Orchestra in a program of his works on 12 and 13 January 1934, but was unable to appear on account of a severe cold.)

20 MARCH 1934

Uzbekistan, symphonic suite on native themes by the Russian nationalist composer Mikhail IPPOLITOV-IVANOV, is performed for the first time at the inauguration of the Uzbek Symphony Orchestra in Tashkent.

21 MARCH 1934

Franz SCHREKER, Monaco-born Vienna-bred German composer of expressionistic music dramas of meaningful literary and musical content (he wrote his own libretti) and influential teacher of a generation of modernists, dies in Berlin two days before his 56th birthday.

22 MARCH 1934

Giration, choreographic divertissement by Gabriel PIERNIÉ, with the participation of talking machines in the stage action, is performed for the first time in Paris.

24 MARCH 1934

Il Dibuk, opera in three acts by the Italian composer Lodovico ROCCA, inspired by the mystically realistic Jewish tale of a girl possessed by the mental complex of her suicidal suitor to such an extent that she absorbs his mentality and dies herself, is produced at La Scala, Milan.

26 MARCH 1934

On the occasion of the semicentennial of the death of the national Bohemian composer Bedřich SMETANA, the government of Czechoslovakia issues a commemorative postage stamp of 50 kronen.

26 MARCH 1934

La Princess lointaine, opera in four acts by the 67-year-old French composer of remote Polish extraction Georges-Martin WITKOWSKI, to a libretto after Rostand's play in which an aging crusader undertakes an arduous voyage to Tripoli to meet his appointed young bride but expires from cardiac arrest induced by her first embrace, while his loyal henchman suppresses his own hidden passion for her and continues on his way to Jerusalem, is performed for the first time in Paris.

26 MARCH 1934

Two days after the Rome production of the opera *La Favola del figlio cambiato* by Gian Francesco MALIPIERO, first performed in Brunswick on 13 January 1934, the Fascist government forbids its further representations by an express order of Mussolini for reasons of "moral incongruity" of the Pirandello play on which the libretto is based.

2 APRIL 1934

The 12th Festival of the International Society for Contemporary Music opens in Florence with the following program of Italian orchestral music, arranged by its Italian branch, the Corporazione delle Musiche Nuove:

Second Symphony by the romantic composer Franco ALFANO, written in the characteristically expansive and grandiloquent idiom of his operas; *Partita* by the 30-year-old Luigi DALLAPICCOLA, marking a tonal trend toward neo-Casellan Scarlattianism; the world première of the *First Symphony* by Gian Francesco MALIPIERO, subtitled "in quattro tempi come le quattro stagioni" (in four movements like four seasons): (1) *Quasi andante, sereno* (Spring), (2) *Allegro* (Summer), (3) *Lento ma non troppo* (Autumn), (4) *Allegro quasi allegretto* (Winter), conceived in a refined ottocento style with pandiatonically enriched Italianisms and seasoned with spicy percussion effects; *Two Sicilian Songs* by Giuseppe MULÈ; and the neo-Baroque *Introduction, Aria,* and *Toccata* by Alfredo CASELLA.

3 APRIL 1934

At the second concert of the 12th Festival of the International Society for Contemporary. Music in Florence, the following program of chamber music is presented:

String Quartet in a somewhat impressionistic manner by the French composer Henri MARTELLI; *Suite* for trumpet (mostly muted), bass clarinet, saxophone and piano by Rudolf HOLZMANN, 24-year-old German expatriate composer, written in a sophisticated *style pompier* (this piece replaced a work by Hindemith withdrawn by him from performance to avoid the aggravation of his situation in Nazi Germany); *Four Songs* on national themes by the Yugoslav composer Slavko OSTERC; a vigorous and loud *Piano Sonata* by the young Dane, Knudaage RIISAGER; Alban BERG's *Lyric Suite* for string quartet, written in a technique largely within the system of 12-tone composition; and *Sonata* for two violins and cello in a neo-classical vein by a typical *jeune français* Jean FRANÇAIX.

4 APRIL 1934

At the third concert of the 12th Festival of the International Society for Contemporary Music in Florence, the following program of orchestral music is presented:

Arthur HONEGGER's *Mouvement Symphonique No. 3* (sequel to his *Pacific 231* and *Rugby*, respectively Symphonic Movements No. 1 and No. 2), devoid of a descriptive subtitle and representing Honegger's renunciation of programmatic composition in favor of neo-classical conceptions; RAVEL's *Concerto* for left hand alone with orchestra, commissioned by the one-armed Austrian pianist Paul Wittgenstein, and performed by him; *Rhapsody* for violin and orchestra by Béla BARTÓK; *Psalm* for soprano and orchestra by the 21-year-old Russian-born Paris-bred composer Igor MARKEVITCH, written in a strident neo-diatonic idiom, conducted by the composer himself, and shocking the audience into shouts of esthetic indignation; *Turkmenia*, symphonic suite on Central Asian themes by the Soviet composer Boris SCHECHTER.

5 APRIL 1934

At the fourth concert of the 12th Festival of the International Society for Contemporary Music in Florence, the following program of chamber music is given:

Phantasy Quartet for oboe, violin, viola and cello, Op. 2, by Benjamin BRITTEN, written by him at the age of 19 in 1932 in a rhapsodically cyclic form of symmetrically positioned imaginative variations, his first work to attract attention at an international gathering of musicians; PIANO TRIO by the Hungarian composer Heinrich NEUGEBOREN; *Quartettino* for strings by the Austrian composer Leopold SPINNER, written in an expressionistically introspective quasi-atonal manner; explosively percussive *Sonata* for violin and piano by the Czech composer Jaroslav JEŽEK; *5 Lyric Pieces* by the Viennese composer Hans Erich APOSTEL, couched in a neo-romantic style with an injection of bland atonalities; *Cantata* for mezzo-soprano, flute, oboe d'amore, lute, viola d'amore, viola da gamba and cello in a neo-archaic modal idiom by the Swiss composer Richard STÜRZENEGGER; and the neo-classically burnished *Sinfonietta* by the Swedish composer Lars-Erik LARSSON.

5 APRIL 1934

Little Women, two-act opera by Eleanor Everest FREER, based on Louisa May Alcott's novel of the same name, is performed for the first time in Chicago.

6 APRIL 1934

Union Pacific, ballet by Nicolas NABOKOV, 30-year-old Russian composer newly resident in America, depicting in rhythmically impulsive and lyrically discursive diatonic images the completion of the transcontinental railroad and making occasional use of American western tunes for local color, is produced for the first time by the Monte Carlo Ballet in Philadelphia.

7 APRIL 1934

At the fifth and last concert of the 12th Festival of the International Society for Contemporary Music in Florence, the following program of Italian chamber music is given:

Second Quartet by Mario LABROCA, in an unpretentious tonal manner; *Concertino* for wind instruments, percussion, and piano, in a hedonistic urban style, by the 20-year-old Venetian Gino GORINI; *Songs* by the Italian romanticist Mario CASTELNUOVO-TEDESCO; *Divertimento* for string trio, clarinet, bassoon and trumpet, by Riccardo NIELSEN of Bologna; and the poetically dramatic *String Quartet in D* by the grandmaster of the modern Italian school of composition, Ildebrando PIZZETTI.

12 APRIL 1934

Thaddeus CAHILL, American inventor of the futuristic-looking machine called Telharmonium, patented by him early in the century, and capable of generating sounds by electro-magnetic induction which he proposed to broadcast by telephone, whose eccentrically prophetic notions earned for him an admiring mention in Busoni's book on new musical esthetics, dies in New York at the age of 67.

12 APRIL 1934

Macbeth, Shakespearean opera in three acts by the English composer Lawrence Arthur COLLINGWOOD, is performed for the first time in London.

14 APRIL 1934

Symphonic Song by Sergei PROKOFIEV, written after his return to Russia from Paris, and despite the compulsory demodernization of Soviet music still betraying in its idiom the acuity and acridity of his naturally aggressive manner, is performed for the first time in Moscow.

15 APRIL 1934

Ecuatorial, symphonic poem for bass voice, brass ensemble, percussion and Thereminovox by Edgar VARÈSE, to texts from the sacred book of the Mayan priests of Mexico, describing the horrifying tribulations of a group of mountain people lost on their way to the City of Abundance, is performed for the first time in New York, under the direction of Nicolas Slonimsky.

22 APRIL 1934

By a decree of the Nazi government, all German singing societies are incorporated into the national Sängerbund, to which the practical policy of using music as a tool of racial propaganda is arrogated.

30 APRIL 1934

Igor STRAVINSKY conducts in Paris the first performance of his *Perséphone,* ballet-melodrama in three parts to the text by André Gide, dealing allegorically with the abduction of Perséphone by Pluto, scored for orchestra, tenor, chorus and a children's choir, and set in a gymnosophistical idiom marked by an austere polyphonic design, with Ida Rubinstein appearing in the title role as dancer and speaker. (On the same program, the first performance took place of *Diane de Poitiers,* ballet by Jacques IBERT, hedonistically depicting the royal pastimes of a favorite concubine of Louis XIV, with musical interludes of exotic Russian and Peruvian dances.)

Inasmuch as I have been asked to present my own attitude towards my ballet *Perséphone,* I should like to call the attention of the public to a word that summarizes my entire program: Syllable. This comprises everything that I intend to communicate in *Perséphone:* beautiful strong syllables, and action. Music is not thinking. I do not exteriorize. The function of music is, in my view, something entirely different from what it is to others. The art of music is given to us with the purpose of putting things in order, arranging them in an organized state of perfect consciousness that insures vitality and durability. . . . When one becomes conscious of an emotion, it is already cold. It becomes like lava, converted to trivial substance used to manufacture souvenirs sold in the foothills of Mt. Vesuvius. . . . I abhor instrumental effects used solely for the sake of color. In *Perséphone* the listener should not expect to be dazzled by seductive sonorities, for I have long ago realized the futility of *brio.* I recoil from the idea of courting the public. It embarrasses me. Let those who make a profession of this honorable practice, in composing as well as in conducting, indulge in it to the point of complete saturation. The public expects the artist to disembowel himself and to exhibit his entrails. This action is regarded as the noblest expression of art, and is termed variously as Personality, Individuality, or Temperament. My score to *Perséphone* must remain in the musical annals of our era as I conceived it. *Perséphone* forms an indissoluble link with my ideas expressed in my previous works. It follows *Oedipus Rex, Symphonie de Psalmes, Capriccio, Violin Concerto* and *Duo Concertant* as a sequel of a series, and my abstention from spectacular effects in these works does not diminish in the least the autonomous life of the music. Things that are felt and things that are true are susceptible to projections on an enormous scale. I follow a very definite path, which cannot be the subject of a debate or criticism. One does not criticize somebody, or something, that functions. The nose is not manufactured. The nose is. So is my art. (Igor Stravinsky, in *Excelsior*, Paris, 29 April 1934, reprinted in *Le Monde Musical*, Paris, 31 May 1934)

M. Stravinsky warns us that his way in art is not to be debated or criticized. Such self-assurance is probably without precedent in music history. Bach, Mozart, Beethoven, Wagner, Debussy, Fauré, were all conscious of the validity of their art, but none of them presumed to guarantee the vitality and the durability of their works. Curiously, it is not as the composer of such scores as *Petrouchka, L'Oiseau de feu, Le Rossignol* or *Le Sacre du Printemps*, which have earned him world renown, that Stravinsky aspires to enter the Pantheon. No, it is his works which even his most fervent admirers hesitate to glorify, works written during the period of his "return to Bach," that he regards as "enormous projections." At its first performance, *Perséphone* received meager signs of appreciation from the audience. During the last scene, in which Persephone descends into Hell for the second time, someone was heard to whisper: "Let's hope she stays there." (A. Mangeot, *Le Monde Musical*, Paris, 31 May 1934)

3 MAY 1934

Popieliny, opera in two acts by the 31-year-old Russian-born Polish composer Michal KONDRACKI, freely arranged after the Polish medieval mysterium *Marcholt gruby a sprośny (Fat and Obscene Marcholt)*, is performed for the first time in Warsaw.

7 MAY 1934

Kykunkor, the Witch, African opera by Asadata Dafora HORTON of Sierra Leone, derived from West African songs and dances, is produced for the first time at the Unity Theatre Studio in New York, with a Negro cast, accompanied by an instrumental ensemble including a large section of African percussion instruments.

11 MAY 1934

Sémiramis, ballet by Arthur HONEGGER, to Paul Valéry's dramatic poem, dealing with the fabulous queen of Babylon who orders the execution of a captive king because he has failed to satisfy her orgiastic expectations, and then exposes herself to the murderous rays of the sun after consulting a quartet of astrologers, to the mystically sounding vibrations of the Ondes Martenot in the orchestra, is performed for the first time at the Paris Opéra, with Ida Rubinstein, the Parisian Terpsichore who also mimed St. Sebastian in Debussy's mystery play, Ravel's *Boléro* and Stravinsky's *Perséphone*, in the title role.

11 MAY 1934

Çemal ERKIN, 28-year-old Turkish composer, conducts in Ankara the first performance of his symphonic poem *Bairam*, depicting the whirling dervish dances of the Moslem holiday.

15 MAY 1934

Nicolas OBOUHOV, Russian expatriate composer and religious mystic, who has adopted the signature "Nicolas l'Illuminé," presents in Paris the first demonstration of the *Croix Sonore*, an electronic musical instrument in the form of a cross, in a program of his works designed to accomplish a theosophic synthesis of divinity by means of demiurgic aggregations of twelve chromatic notes in a non-dodecaphonic order and to achieve instant communication on a telepathic musical wavelength with the extra-terrestrial intelligences of the Spiritus Mundi.

M. Obouhov has no other pretensions except to let us hear True Music, the Music of the Inspired, which crowns the Divine Spirit and guides mankind to the eternal abyss on the mystical accents of Verity. (*Le Ménestrel*, Paris, 1 June 1934)

25 MAY 1934

Gustav HOLST, English composer of romantically elevated symphonic and choral pieces, whose real name was Gustavus Theodore von Holst (he was of Swedish extraction) but who removed the embarrassing Germanic nobiliary particle after the outbreak of World War I, dies in London in his 60th year.

25 MAY 1934

Cantata Profana for chorus and orchestra by Béla BARTÓK (completed in Budapest on 8 September 1930), to the text relating the fantasmagoria of nine enchanted stags, set to music in a neo-primitivistic percussive idiom, is performed for the first time in London.

26 MAY 1934

Honzovo Královstvi (Ivan's Kingdom), opera in seven scenes by the 55-year-old Czech composer Otakar OSTRČIL, after Tolstoy's fairy tale in which a simple peasant succeeds in curing an incurable princess, accedes to the throne and distributes land to indigent workers of the soil, following the precepts of Tolstoy's favorite American economist Henry George, advocate of a single tax, is produced in Brno.

28 MAY 1934

Rolande et le mauvais garçon, opera in five acts by the French composer Henri RABAUD, dealing with a mythical Mediterranean queen who is embroiled in a passionate affair with a lowly "mauvais garçon," loses all interest in him when she discovers that the philosophically inclined king openly condones her affair, and returns to her queenly chores in the royal garden, set to music in a mellifluously harmonious and melodious Gallic manner, is produced at the Paris Opéra.

1 JUNE 1934

Belgium issues a postage stamp for 75 Belgian francs in honor of the national Flemish composer Peter BENOÎT on the centennial of his birth.

2 JUNE 1934

The first performance is given in Belgrade of *Oriental Symphony*, subtitled *Religiofonia*, by the 38-year-old Serbian composer Josip SLAVENSKI, scored for soloists, chorus and orchestra, in seven movements intended to represent five religions of the East and two other socio-historical categories:

(1) *The Pagans*, or *Musica Ritmica*, derived from a primitive motive of three notes, C, D and F, in widely varied rhythmic patterns, with singers intoning the exhortatory syllable "Ha"; (2) *The Hebrews*, or *Musica Coloristica*, representing a stylized version of the Hebrew chant of death, *Kaddish;* (3) *The Buddhists*, or *Musica Architectonica*, set in the conventionally oriental pentatonic scale subjected to canonic treatment; (4) *The Christians*, or *Musica Melodica*, a solemn consecration with melodic references to medieval religious hymns; (5) *The Moslems*, or *Musica Articulatiae*, illustrated by a muezzin's anguished laments in the orientalistic scale of anfractuous semitones and sesquitones; (6) *Musica Poliphonia*, set in dissonant counterpoint, recapitulating the principal motive, C, D, F, in quadruple canonic treatment; (7) *Pjesma Radu (Song of the Popular Assembly)*, or *Musica Harmoniae*, an ode to socialistic joy and realistic comradeship, concluding with a sonorously optimistic jubilation.

3 JUNE 1934

The American Musicological Society is organized and formally incorporated in New York City, with Carleton Sprague Smith as chairman.

7 JUNE 1934

Oratorio über die Sprüche des Angelus Silesius by the 32-year-old Swiss composer Conrad BECK, to the texts gathered from the pantheistic aphorisms of Johannes Scheffler, 17th-century gnomic poet from Silesia, who assumed the name Angelus Silesius (Messenger from Silesia) when he was ordained to priesthood, is performed for the first time by the Basel Chamber Orchestra, Paul Sacher conducting.

9 JUNE 1934

Maschinenmensch, ballet by the 39-year-old Hungarian composer Eugen ZÁDOR, dealing with a superhumanly efficient robot who, at his inventor's command, kidnaps a famous violinist's mistress, written in an ostentatiously mechanistic style in polytonal harmonies bristling with asymmetric rhythms, culminating in a grandly copulative C major chord, is performed for the first time in Braunschweig, Germany.

10 JUNE 1934

Frederick DELIUS, English composer of German extraction, whose pictorial symphonic essays are marked by a unique combination of sentimental Germanic romanticism, Gallic impressionism and English folklorism, with a modicum of modernistic devices such as whole-tone scales and consecutive major ninth-chords, dies in his French retreat near Fontainebleau, at the age of 72, after a long period of paresis, blindness and pathetic inanition.

10 JUNE 1934

Igor STRAVINSKY becomes a French citizen by decree of the French Ministry of Justice. (Date from *Le Journal officiel* for 1934, p. 5769, col. 3.)

11 JUNE 1934

On his 70th birthday, Richard STRAUSS receives from Hitler his framed picture with the inscription: "Dem grossen Komponisten Richard Strauss in aufrichtiger Verehrung, Adolf Hitler" and a framed photograph of the Nazi Minister of Propaganda Goebbels, inscribed: "Dem grossen Meister der Töne in dankbarer Verehrung zum 70. Geburtstag."

15 JUNE 1934

Alfred BRUNEAU, prolific French composer, initiator of a realistic operatic Gallic style, dies in Paris at the age of 77.

1 AUGUST 1934

Merlino mastro d'organi, musical drama in two parts by the Italian master of the national modern style of composition Gian Francesco MALIPIERO, dealing with a malevolent organist who kills his unfaithful inamorata by lethal vibrations of his powerful organ, and is killed in turn by a deaf mendicant impervious to sonic impact, is performed for the first time in Rome.

10 AUGUST 1934

Rock and Roll, with a score by Richard WHITING and lyrics by Sidney CLARE, the first musical composition bearing a title that was to generate the most powerful form of American popular music, originally designed for use in the motion picture *Transatlantic Merry-Go-Round*, with the key words indicating the rolling and rocking movement of an ocean liner, is copyrighted in Washington, D.C. (It was published on 8 October 1934 by the Irving Berlin Corporation.)

20 AUGUST 1934

Self-exiled from Germany after its Hitlerization, Ernst TOCH, in London on his way to America, plays the piano solo part in the world première of his *Symphony* for piano and orchestra.

31 AUGUST 1934

A century has passed since the birth of the Italian composer Amilcare PONCHIELLI, whose opera *La Gioconda*, with its sempiternally popular ballet interlude *The Dance of the Hours*, has never lost its appeal.

4 SEPTEMBER 1934

The Music Therapy Project, the first of its kind since the tarantella was played to cure tarantula bites in Taranto, is inaugurated at the Veterans' Administration Hospital in Lyons, New Jersey, with the establishment of a 24-piece band under the direction of W. J. Borland, himself seeking melosomatic medication to cure his own neurosis which he developed during his service as a psychological interrogator in the United States Army.

10 SEPTEMBER 1934

Sir George HENSCHEL, German conductor, who began his career as a singer and was the first conductor of the Boston Symphony Orchestra in 1881, became naturalized in England in 1890 and was knighted on the eve of the war against his fatherland in 1914, dies in Aviemore in Scotland at the age of 84.

10 SEPTEMBER 1934

The Lily Maid, opera in two acts by the romantic English composer Rutland BOUGHTON, to his own libretto centered on Elaine, the "lily maid" of the Arthurian romance, is performed for the first time in Stroud, Gloucester. (The first London production took place on 12 January 1937.)

11 SEPTEMBER 1934

Concerto for cello and orchestra by Ildebrando PIZZETTI, written in a songful Italian style emblazoned in kaleidoscopic instrumental colors, is performed for the first time in Venice.

27 SEPTEMBER 1934

Ralph VAUGHAN WILLIAMS conducts the BBC Symphony Orchestra in London in the first concert performance of his *Fantasia on Greensleeves* for strings and harp, adapted from his opera *Sir John in Love,* and based on an old Shakespearean tune, twice mentioned in *The Merry Wives of Windsor,* set in euphoniously flowing triadic modalities, with an interpolation of another folk melody, of newer provenance, *Lovely Joan,* and then returning to the dulcet rusticity of *Greensleeves* to form a perfect symmetry of ternary design.

28 SEPTEMBER 1934

The Council of People's Commissars of the Union of Soviet Socialist Republics issues a list of ratings of payment for musical composition: 10,000 to 12,000 rubles for an opera, 6,000 to 8,000 rubles for a symphony, 3,000 to 5,000 rubles for a piece of chamber music and 500 to 1,000 rubles for a chorus.

28 SEPTEMBER 1934

The Fountain of Bakhchisarai, ballet after Pushkin's poem by the Russian music scholar and composer Boris ASAFIEV, marked by an abundance of anfractuously orientalized melodies and languorous rhythms characteristic of the Tatar folk music in the Crimea, where the action of the ballet takes place, is produced in Leningrad.

29 SEPTEMBER 1934

The Nazi Ministry of Propaganda issues an order prohibiting the use by musicians of foreign-sounding pseudonyms, setting the date 31 October 1934 as final for restoring original German names of such users.

29 SEPTEMBER 1934

Carlos CHÁVEZ conducts in Mexico City the first performance of his *Llamadas (Calls),* subtitled *Sinfonía Proletaria,* scored for chorus and small orchestra and written in a virile proletarian manner marked by alternating duple and triple meters and terse harmonic formations.

1 OCTOBER 1934

The Mutual Broadcasting System, the third American Radio network, is inaugurated in New York City. (It was extended to a coast-to-coast network on 29 December 1936.)

3 OCTOBER 1934

Pacat Boieresc (The Boyar's Sin), opera by the 41-year-old Rumanian composer Martian NEGREA, wherein a vicious Balkan overlord villainously dishonors a villager's wife and daughter and is ultimately slain by the aroused populace, in a musical setting in an ingenuously indigenous manner vitalized by asymmetrical Balkan rhythms, is produced in Cluj.

11 OCTOBER 1934

Second Symphony by Kurt WEILL, written in a euphoniously modernistic manner in three movements— (1) *Sostenuto,* 4/4, with a somber introduction emerging into a pantonal waltz; (2) *Largo,* 4/4, a romanza on a funereal march rhythm; (3) *Allegro vivace,* a neo-romantic rondo in 2/4 followed by a hedonistic tarantella—is performed for the first time by the Concertgebouw Orchestra in Amsterdam, Bruno Walter conducting.

13 OCTOBER 1934

Theodore BAKER, German-educated American musicologist, who compiled in 1900 the original edition of the prestigious *Baker's Biographical Dictionary of Musicians,* which listed a number of Americans theretofore not accorded lexicographical honors, and who was also the author of a pioneer work on American Indian music in the German language, dies in Dresden at the age of 83.

15 OCTOBER 1934

The Pageant of Labour opens at Crystal Palace in London, presenting a Marxist ballet in Six scenes: (1) *Capital Enslaves the Worker,* (2) *Martyrdom of the Children,* (3) *Consolation of Philanthropy and Religion,* (4) *London Receives the Chartists,* (5) *The Triumph of the Trade Unions,* (6) *Fletcher Family, 1900,* set to music in a properly socialistic idiom by Alan BUSH, member of the left wing of the Labour Party, based on a system of leading motives, each characterizing a personage or a political idea.

16 OCTOBER 1934

Thirteenth Symphony by Nicolai MIASKOVSKY, in B-flat minor (completed on 20 October 1933), in three continuous movements, *Andante moderato, Agitato molto tenebroso* and *Andante nostalgico,* abounding in somber tonal fluxions with tritone-laden melodies asymptotically approaching the acknowledged tonal focus, is performed for the first time by the Musikkollegium in Winterthur,

Switzerland, Hermann Scherchen conducting. (Exact date obtained from the Musikkolegium in Winterthur. The date 15 November 1934, given in previous editions of *Music Since 1900* and other reference works as the world première, is that of the first American performance in Chicago.)

17 OCTOBER 1934

Fragonard, comic opera by Gabriel PIERNIÉ, depicting the ambience of 18th-century France, as reflected in the rococo art of Jean-Honoré Fragonard, is produced at the Opéra-Comique in Paris.

20 OCTOBER 1934

Lucedia, opera in three acts by the 31-year-old American composer Vittorio GIANNINI, telling in harmoniously melodramatic tones the story of a vestal virgin who violates her oath of chastity and is sent to her death in a leaking boat, is produced in Munich, with a German version of the original Italian libretto.

25 OCTOBER 1934

La Leyende de Urutaú, opera by the 45-year-old Argentinian composer Gilardo GILARDI, with action taking place at the time of the Spanish conquest of South America, written in a competent ethnomusical manner, making use of authentic Inca and Spanish melorhythms, is produced in Buenos Aires.

1 NOVEMBER 1934

The German monthly *Die Musik* discloses that the National-Socialist Kulturgemeinde has, through its leader Dr. Walter Strang, commissioned from the impeccably Aryan German composers Rudolf WAGNERRÉGENY and Julius WEISMANN new musical settings for Shakespeare's *A Midsummer Night's Dream* to replace the racially tainted Mendelssohn's score. (These new scores came to performance respectively on 6 and 11 June 1935, during the Reichstagung of the National-Socialist Kulturgemeinde at Düsseldorf.)

The National-Socialist Kulturgemeinde has discharged an important obligation of the National-Socialist Revolution in commissioning a new score for *A Midsummer Night's Dream* of Shakespeare. Mendelssohn's music is inadmissible in the Third Reich, where the unalienable laws of racial purity must be uncompromisingly maintained. (Wilhelm Herzog in *Die Musik,* 1 November 1934)

6 NOVEMBER 1934

Iernin, Celtic saga-opera in three acts by the 21-year-old Welsh composer George LLOYD, to his father's libretto wherein a benevolent Faery of the Shining People of the Hills helps a brave youth to win a beauteous maiden away from the sinister blandishments of a hideous seventh-century Saxon overlord, is produced in Penzance.

7 NOVEMBER 1934

Kyz-Zhibek, the first national opera of Kazakhstan by the 28-year-old Soviet composer Evgeny BRUSILOVSKY, in four acts, to the story of the suicide of a beautiful medieval Central Asian lass named Kyz-Zhibek, who leaps to her death into a lake from a cliff after her lover, a proletarianized son of a khan, is slain in jealous rage by a feudal Mongolian knight, set to music in abecedarian but ethnomusicologically authentic monody vivified by a rhythmical whine, plink and plunk of assorted native instruments, is produced in Alma-Ata, capital of Kazakhstan, on the 17th anniversary of the Soviet Revolution.

7 NOVEMBER 1934

Serge RACHMANINOFF plays at a concert of the Philadelphia Orchestra in Baltimore, conducted by Leopold Stokowski, the piano part in the first performance anywhere of his *Rhapsody on a Theme by Paganini,* composed between 3 July and 24 August 1934, in A minor, consisting of 24 variations on Paganini's *Caprice No. 24* (the same that Brahms used for his piano variations), written in a superlative virtuoso manner, covering the entire range of the keyboard, with the 18th variation presenting an ingenious inversion of the subject, so that the ascending minor phrase becomes the descending major motive, curiously resulting in a Slavic-flavored ballad-like melody, the whole work culminating in a grandiose invocation of the thematically related medieval hymn *Dies Irae* which had already been introduced in the piano part of the 7th variation. (The theme of the eighteenth variation of the *Rhapsody on a Theme by Paganini* is the precise reproduction of a passage from William Byrd's *Credo* in the Mass for three voices with the words "non erit finis," which Rachmaninoff happened to have heard in March 1934.)

8 NOVEMBER 1934

Arctic Symphony by the Russian composer Sergei VASSILENKO, his fourth symphony, glorifying in its five chronologically programmatic movements the Arctic explorations of Soviet scientists, is performed for the first time in Moscow.

10 NOVEMBER 1934

Czechoslovakia issues a commemorative stamp at 50 kronen for Antonín DVOŘÁK.

12 NOVEMBER 1934

Suite for viola and small orchestra by Ralph VAUGHAN WILLIAMS, comprising three groups of stylized English dances, is performed for the first time in London, with Lionel Tertis as soloist.

16 NOVEMBER 1934

First Symphony by the American composer Harl MCDONALD, subtitled *The Santa Fe Trail,* illustrating in pleasingly harmonious tones his impressions of the Western desert, the mountains, and the pioneer explorations in the American West, is performed for the first time by the Philadelphia Orchestra, Leopold Stokowski conducting.

21 NOVEMBER 1934

Anything Goes, musical comedy by Cole PORTER, with the action taking place on a transatlantic ship, marshalling a multiplicity of incompatible international characters involved in a puzzling web of incongruous events, including in its score the rollicking tunes *Blow, Gabriel Blow; You're the Top; I Get a Kick Out of You*, is produced in New York.

22 NOVEMBER 1934

Pablo Casals gives the first performance of the affably competent *Cello Concerto* by the erudite Sir Donald Francis TOVEY, with the composer conducting the Reid Symphony Orchestra in Edinburgh.

Le 22 novembre 1934 sera la plus importante date de ma vie de musicien. Joachim a dû ressentir la même joie et l'honneur le jour qu'il a remis sur pied le concerto pour violon de Beethoven et celui de la première audition du concerto de Brahms. (From a letter by Casals to Tovey written on the eve of the performance, and quoted in the original French in Mary Grierson's monograph on Tovey, London, 1952, p. 181)

23 NOVEMBER 1934

First Concerto for piano and orchestra by Darius MILHAUD, in three movements—(1) *Très vif*, marked by euphonious bitonalities; (2) *Barcarolle*, a harmonious aquatic piece set in furfuraceous chromatic harmonies; (3) *Finale*, a hedonistic rondo—is performed for the first time in Paris, with the modernistically minded French pianist Marguerite Long as soloist.

25 NOVEMBER 1934

Concerto for Saxophone, op. 109, by the venerable classicist of the Russian National School Alexander GLAZUNOV, his last work, written in the spring of 1934, in E flat major, in a single movement articulated into three sections, an *Allegro*, an *Andante* with a florid cadenza, and a concise *Fugato*, is performed for the first time anywhere with a local orchestra in an old church in Nyköping, Sweden, by the Danish saxophone virtuoso Sigurd Rascher, to whom the work is dedicated.

I met Glazunov in Paris early in 1934 and went to visit him at his home. . . . "Alors, jouez!" he said. I played, soft, loud, in cascades and ripples. "Merveilleux!" Glazunov exclaimed. I timidly explored the idea of his composing a saxophone concerto for me. He looked benevolent, shook the ashes off his cigar and asked me to come again. When I saw him next, the Concerto was almost ready. For a whole wonderful afternoon, and late into the evening, we worked together on the score, changing a note here and a note there, and fixing the cadenza. Thanks to his patience I had the opportunity of receiving his instructions on every point in the Concerto. It was one of the greatest lessons I had ever had. (Sigurd Rascher in a letter to the author, dated 29 December 1960)

25 NOVEMBER 1934

Short Symphony by the prime American composer Aaron COPLAND, a magnetic piece of pulsing rhythms and lyric invocations, opulent in thematic intercommunications, and reaching its climax in a jazzified celebration of the American spirit, is performed for the first time in Mexico City, conducted by Carlos Chávez. (A chamber music version of the *Short Symphony* was made by Copland in 1937 in the form of a sextet for string quartet, clarinet and piano.)

30 NOVEMBER 1934

Symphonic Suite from the unfinished opera *Lulu* by Alban BERG to Frank Wedekind's plays, *Erdgeist* and *Die Büchse der Pandora*, dealing with an inflammable seductress whose three husbands and a lesbian admirer all meet violent death, and who herself is disemboweled in London in 1889 by Jack the Ripper to the harrowing sound of a dodecaphonic chord symbolizing the tearing of her entrails in the duodenum measuring 12 fingerbreadths between the stomach and the jejunum, the entire score deriving from a basic 12-tone series, is performed for the first time in Berlin under the direction of Erich Kleiber.

The accounts of the performance of Alban Berg's symphonic suite from his opera *Lulu* demonstrate the ideological confusion and lack of artistic understanding of the majority of Berlin critics. It is significant that one of the most degraded foreign yellow newspapers, the *Neues Wiener Journal,* was able to quote several Berlin reviews which seemed favorably inclined toward the émigré *Musikjuden.* . . . Such reviews are inadmissible in our age of directed public opinion, for they befuddle the mind and hinder the rebuilding of our culture. The National Association of the German Press would do well to reexamine basically the fitness of these reviewers for their jobs. (*Die Musik*, Berlin, January 1935)

1 DECEMBER 1934

Don Quichotte à Dulcinée, three songs with orchestral accompaniment by Maurice RAVEL, his last work written before the onset of his final illness, characterized by apraxia and aphasia, is performed for the first time in Paris, in the vacuous presence of the semi-amnesiac composer.

4 DECEMBER 1934

Wilhelm FURTWÄNGLER resigns as conductor of the Berlin Philharmonic, Deputy President of the Reichsmusikkammer and as Director of the Berlin State Opera, as a result of his failure to establish a modus vivendi with the Nazi regime, and specifically because of his objections to the Nazi drive to exclude Paul Hindemith from German musical life as a *Kulturbolschevist*.

State Counsellor Dr. Wilhelm Furtwängler has asked the Minister of the Reich Dr. Goebbels to relieve him from his duties as Deputy President of the Reichsmusikkammer and conductor of the Berlin Philharmonic Orchestra. At the same time he requested the Prussian First Minister to release him from the post of Director at the Berlin State Opera. Both ministers have granted his requests. (From an official statement)

The Hindemith Case has broadened itself into a Furtwängler Case. In this problem we are faced with two conflicting ideologies. One of them regards everything in the light of pure artistic pursuit. The other, represented by National Socialism, realizes that an artist reflects a political situation. So when a man like Hindemith, after a few German beginnings, lives and works for fourteen years among Jews and feels himself at ease in such company, consorts almost exclusively with Jews, and is loved by them; when he, following the ideology of the Weimar Republic, commits the foulest perversions of German music, we have a right to reject him and his environment. The accomplishments of such a person under the Weimar Republic, and the laurels bestowed upon him by that now overthrown regime are of no value to our movement. . . . It is a great pity that so great an artist as Dr. Wilhelm Furtwängler entered this controversy, and chose to identify himself with Hindemith's cause. Herr

Furtwängler clings to his 19th-century ideas and has manifestly lost all sense of the national struggle of our times. (Excerpts from the article *Esthetics or National Struggle?* by Alfred Rosenberg, foremost theorist of National Socialism, in *Die Musik*, Berlin, January 1935)

6 DECEMBER 1934

Dr. GOEBBELS, Minister of Propaganda of the Third Reich, delivers a thunderous denunciation of the "moral decay of atonal composers" with specific reference to the bathtub aria in Hindemith's opera *Neues vom Tage.*

Technical mastery is not an excuse but an obligation. To misuse it for meaningless musical trifles is to besmirch true genius. Opportunity creates not only thieves but also atonal musicians, who in their eagerness to make a sensation exhibit naked women in the bathtub on the stage in the most disgusting and obscene situations and further befoul such scenes by the most atrocious dissonance of musical impotence. (Excerpt from the statement by Goebbels)

6 DECEMBER 1934

Almos, opera by the pioneer Hungarian composer Mihály MOSONYI, composed in 1862, is performed for the first time in Budapest, sixty-four years after Mosonyi's death.

8 DECEMBER 1934

Das Veilchen, two-act opera by the 60-year-old Austrian composer Julius BITTNER, is produced in Vienna.

15 DECEMBER 1934

While conducting a rehearsal of the musical comedy *Feodoro* at the Rio de Janeiro Opera Theater, the Italian conductor Franco PAOLANTONIO is shot to death by a disgruntled orchestra musician.

15 DECEMBER 1934

Jean FRANÇAIX, precocious 22-year-old French composer (he published a piano piece at the age of nine) plays the piano part in the first performance in Paris of his *Concertino* for piano and orchestra, in four movements animated by the spirit of the Gallic rococo, *Presto leggiero, Lento, Allegretto, Rondo.*

15 DECEMBER 1934

Hester Prynne, three-act opera by Avery CLAFLIN based on Nathaniel Hawthorne's *The Scarlet Letter,* is produced in an abridged version in Hartford, Connecticut.

17 DECEMBER 1934

Eleven days after losing his position as musical director of Radio Station WTIC, Christian KRIENS, Dutch-born violinist and composer, who had a precocious career in Holland, shoots himself to death in a fit of despondency, in Hartford, Connecticut.

No wealth, no friends, no influence, Christian Kriens, composer, tells how he made his way despite handicaps—Advantages of America over Europe—Mr. Kriens is not only optimistic, he is enthusiastic, and his enthusiasm is upheld by an activity that bids well for his own future. (Unprophetic headlines in an interview with Christian Kriens published upon his arrival in the United States, in *Musical America*, New York, 19 November 1910)

18 DECEMBER 1934

Podzimní Symfonie (Autumn Symphony) by the 64-year-old Czech composer Vítězslav NOVÁK, for tenor, chorus and orchestra, in three movements, each ending on a pandiatonically amplified triad, and portraying the sadness, the joy and the wisdom of autumn, is performed for the first time in Prague.

19 DECEMBER 1934

Francis PLANTÉ, eccentric French pianist (in 1915 he gave a concert in Paris hidden from the audience by a screen, in conformance with his solemn vow "never to be seen again in public"), dies at St. Avit, near Mont-de-Marsan, at the age of 95.

20 DECEMBER 1934

Big Ben, fantasy with variations on the melody of the Westminster chimes, by the 47-year-old Vienna-born romantic composer Ernst TOCH, now resident of America, written in a sophistically elaborated neo-romantic idiom, is performed for the first time anywhere at a concert of the Boston Symphony Orchestra in Cambridge, Massachusetts, Richard Burgin conducting.

25 DECEMBER 1934

Second Symphony by the 29-year-old Soviet composer Dmitri KABALEVSKY (completed on 8 November 1934, after he finished his *Third Symphony*), in the key of C minor, in three movements—(1) *Allegro,* built on an artful contrast of dramatic and lyric moods; (2) *Andante,* an eloquently serene elegy; and (3) *Prestissimo,* an optimistically dynamic Russian finale—is performed for the first time in Moscow, with the Russian-born Englishman Albert Coates conducting.

26 DECEMBER 1934

Klein Dorrit, singspiel by the 49-year-old German operetta composer Eduard KÜNNEKE, making use of story material of *Little Dorrit* by Dickens, is produced in Oberhausen.

27 DECEMBER 1934

Bayönder, one-act opera by the 26-year-old Turkish composer Necil KÂZIM AKSES, and *Taşbebek,* one-act opera by the 27-year-old Turkish composer Ahmed Adnan SAYGUN, are produced in Ankara.

31 DECEMBER 1934

GOUNOD's *Faust* is given at the Paris Opéra for the 2,000th time.

1935

1 JANUARY 1935

SWING appears in print for the first time in the American monthly *Down Beat*, defined as "a musician's term for perfect rhythm," with pragmatic connotations as a free improvisation on a clarinet or a jazz trumpet, accompanied by steady square beat in the piano and drums.

8 JANUARY 1935

Mount Mihara, the Suicide Volcano, symphonic poem by the Kansas-born composer Claude LAPHAM, inspired by suicides of Japanese lovers jumping into the mouth of Mihara, is performed for the first time by the Tokyo Symphony Orchestra under the direction of Klaus Pringsheim, German musician long resident of Japan.

13 JANUARY 1935

When Johnny Comes Marching Home, overture by Roy HARRIS, in the form of variations of the famous Civil War tune, is performed for the first time in its definitive version, by the Minneapolis Symphony Orchestra, Eugene Ormandy conducting. (An earlier version, entitled *Overture from the Gayety and Sadness of the American Scene*, was first performed by Nicolas Slonimsky conducting the Los Angeles Philharmonic Orchestra on 29 December 1932.)

14 JANUARY 1935

Heinrich SCHENKER, Polish-born Austrian music theorist, originator of the analytical concept of *Urlinie*, according to which the essence and the substance of every composition can be reduced to a melorhythmic prototype, dies in Vienna at the age of 66.

16 JANUARY 1935

Pietro MASCAGNI conducts at La Scala in Milan the first performance of his opera *Nerone*, traversing in three acts the imperial career of Nero amid scenes of Roman debauchery and meretricious artistry, set to music throbbing with melodramatic flamboyance and exuberant bel canto.

23 JANUARY 1935

A concert of music from Iceland is broadcast by the Danish Radio in Copenhagen, featuring *Icelandic Dances* for orchestra and an overture *Iceland* by Jón LEIFS, German-bred prime Icelandic composer, written in an appropriately glacial pentatonic idiom harmonized by slow processions of naked fifths.

24 JANUARY 1935

Eroii de la Rovine, grand opera by the 47-year-old Rumanian composer Nicolae BRETAN, to his own libretto glorifying the heroic victory of the Walachian warriors against the invading Ottoman Turks at the battle of Rovine in 1394, is performed for the first time in Cluj.

24 JANUARY 1935

In the Pasha's Garden, one-act opera by the American composer John Laurence SEYMOUR, his ninth in chronological order, the previous eight remaining unperformed, to the story of a Turkish effendi who correctly surmises that the large coffer in his beautiful French wife's chamber is used as the hiding place for her lover, and gleefully buries it, with the adulterer inside, in his garden, to the accompaniment of whole-tone scale runs, with some exotically inflected arias providing local color, is performed for the first and last time by the Metropolitan Opera House in New York.

26 JANUARY 1935

Second Piano Concerto by Ernst TOCH, in four movements—*Allegro, Lebhaft, Adagio* and *Cyclus variabilis*— is performed for the first time in Frankfurt, at a concert of the *Kulturbund deutscher Juden* (according to Nazi racial laws, Toch, as a Jew, could not be represented on any programs except those given by explicitly designated Jewish cultural organizations in Germany), by Heida Hermanns, pianist, Wilhelm (William) Steinberg conducting, in the absence of the composer, emigrated to the United States.

28 JANUARY 1935

Mikhail IPPOLITOV-IVANOV, Russian composer of operas and orchestral works couched in an expansively romantic Russian style saturated with folkloric melorhythms, dies in Moscow in his sleep (he was found dead in his bed by his wife at 2:30 A.M.) at the age of 75.

31 JANUARY 1935

The first American performance of the opera *Lady Macbeth of the District of Mzensk* by Dmitri SHOSTAKOVICH is given in Cleveland, conducted by Artur Rodzinsky.

31 JANUARY 1935

Concerto for violoncello and orchestra by the 39-year-old Italian composer Mario CASTELNUOVO-TEDESCO, written in a melodious and harmonious Mediterranean idiom, is performed for the first time by Gregor Piatigorsky with the New York Philharmonic conducted by Arturo Toscanini.

31 JANUARY 1935

Primavera, concert overture by the 37-year-old Danish composer Knudaage RIISAGER, portraying the season of spring in a resounding aviary of woodwind instruments in secundal formations of atonally arrayed melodies, is performed for the first time in Copenhagen.

1 FEBRUARY 1935

Ungarisches Capriccio, symphonic sketch in the Hungarian style by the 40-year-old Hungarian composer Eugen ZÁDOR, is performed for the first time in Budapest.

2 FEBRUARY 1935

Liola, lyrico-comic opera in three acts by the Italian composer Giuseppe MULÈ, after Luigi Pirandello's play dealing with a young Sicilian peasant Liola whose pregnant mistress marries a rich old man who takes pride in rumors that the prospective child is his own, is performed for the first time in Naples. (Pirandello disowned the opera because of its licentious departures from the symbolic theme of his original play.)

7 FEBRUARY 1935

In reply to a query from Olin Downes, the music critic of the New York *Times*, Fritz KREISLER admits in a cable from Venice that the violin pieces published as his purported arrangements of works by various 18th-century composers are in fact his own original compositions.

The entire series labelled classical manuscripts are my original compositions, with the sole exception of the first eight bars from the Chanson Louis XIII, taken from a traditional melody. Necessity forced this course on me thirty years ago when I was desirous of enlarging my programs. I found it inexpedient and tactless to repeat my name endlessly on the programs. (From Kreisler's cable to Olin Downes)

10 FEBRUARY 1935

Second Piano Concerto in E flat major for left-hand piano and orchestra by the Austrian composer Franz SCHMIDT, in three movements, with the vivacious finale containing a virtuosistic sinistromanual cadenza, is performed for the first time in Vienna by Paul Wittgenstein, the amputated Viennese pianist for whom it was written, with the composer conducting the orchestra. (The work was subsequently arranged in a bimanual version, which was performed for the first time in Vienna on 5 February 1940.)

13 FEBRUARY 1935

Gargantua, opera in four acts by the 59-year-old French composer Antoine MARIOTTE, subtitled "abelaisian scenes" and traversing in conventionally lyrico-dramatic terms the story of the fantastic adventures of the gigantically dissolute Gargantua, is produced in Paris.

17 FEBRUARY 1935

Juha, opera by the Finnish composer Leevi MADETOJA, to his own libretto inspired by Finnish sagas, is produced in Helsinki.

20 FEBRUARY 1935

Der Günstling, opera in three acts by the German composer Rudolf WAGNER-RÉGENY, subtitled *Die letzten Tage des grossen Hernn Fabiani*, derived from Victor Hugo's play *Marie Tudor* and dealing with the stormy career of the Italian adventurer Fabiano at the court of Bloody Mary in 16th-century England, is produced in Dresden.

23 FEBRUARY 1935

Prologue to the operatic cycle in four acts *Hri o Marii (Deeds of Mary)* by the prime Czech composer Bohuslav MARTINU, based on medieval sacred dramas, in the Czech text by Martinu, is performed for the first time in Brno. (The four parts of the cycle, unperformed, are *Wise and Unwise Maidens, Mariken of Neurnegen, Nativity* and *Sister Pascalina.*)

24 FEBRUARY 1935

Fourteenth Symphony by the prime Russian symphonist Nicolai MIASKOVSKY (completed on 11 October 1933), in five movements of varied moods and rhythms, resolutely set in the optimistic and socialistically realistic key of C major, in contrast to his previous symphonies, twelve of which are in minor keys, is performed for the first time in Moscow.

26 FEBRUARY 1935

The youthful *First Symphony* by Georges BIZET, in four classically proportioned movements, set in the primordial key of C major, written by him at the age of 17 but discarded as naive, is performed for the first time anywhere, 80 years after its composition, in Basel, Switzerland, conducted by Felix Weingartner from a copy of the manuscript kept in the Paris Conservatory. (The date 26 February 1933 given in the earlier editions of *Music Since 1900* is erroneous.)

2 MARCH 1935

A Milói Vénusz (Venus of Milo), romantic opera by the Hungarian violinist Jenö HUBAY, is produced in Budapest.

7 MARCH 1935

In a campaign against street noise, Mayor WALKER of New York City cancels licenses of all local organ-grinders.

14 MARCH 1935

Der Prinz von Homburg opera in four acts by the 63-year-old German composer Paul GRAENER, to Heinrich von Kleist's story dealing with a Prussian princeling who achieves a military victory by defying the judgment of his general staff and wins the hand of a gallant lady, written in the style of a "dialogue opera" immersed in Regeromantically lutulent Prussianized polyphony, is produced in Berlin.

16 MARCH 1935

Orfeo, opera by Claudio MONTEVERDI, arranged in a discreetly modernized style by Ottorino Respighi, is performed for the first time at La Scala in Milan.

24 MARCH 1935

Concerto Grosso by the 33-year-old Soviet composer Mikhail STAROKADOMSKY, one of the few Soviet works written in a neo-classical idiom, is performed for the first time in Moscow.

24 MARCH 1935

Das kalte Herz, radio opera by the 32-year-old German composer Mark LOTHAR, after a fairy tale dealing with a greedy miser who trades his own warm heart for a magician's cold heart, is produced in Berlin.

25 MARCH 1935

Le Marchand de Venise, opera in three acts by the Venezuelan-born Parisianized composer Reynaldo HAHN, set in an elegant Gallic style, to a libretto modelled very freely after Shakespeare, ending with a septet of three happy couples joined by the Merchant of Venice himself, is produced at the Paris Opéra, on the same day with the dress rehearsal at the Paris theater Gaîté-Lyrique, of Hahn's operetta *Malvina*, depicting the gay Paris life of the eve of the Revolution of 1830, which overthrew the last of the Bourbon dynasty.

26 MARCH 1935

Her Name Day, opera in three acts by the 22-year-old Soviet composer Valery ZHELOBINSKY, in which an emancipated Russian serf kills himself after he is rejected by his former owner's daughter on her name day, is performed for the first time in Leningrad.

2 APRIL 1935

Second Concerto for violoncello and orchestra by the 39-year-old American composer Leo SOWERBY, is performed for the first time in New York.

3 APRIL 1935

First Piano Concerto by Gian Francesco MALIPIERO, in a continuous movement in three distinct sections, with the piano treated in a translucent Baroque idiom enlivened by modernistically percussive effects, is performed for the first time in Rome.

4 APRIL 1935

The Limpid Stream, ballet by Dmitri SHOSTAKOVICH, depicting in optimistic tones the scenes of Soviet life on a collective farm named Limpid Stream and situated on the Kuban River in North Caucasus, is performed for the first time in Leningrad.

In the ballet by Shostakovich, the characters are tinsel puppets who pretend to be enjoying a dance, but whose activities have nothing to do with authentic folk dances on the Kuban River or any other place. (From an article *Choreographic Misrepresentation*, in *Pravda*, 6 February 1936)

8 APRIL 1935

Maria Malibran, opera in three acts by the American composer Robert Russell BENNETT, inspired by the life story of the young Spanish singer María García (1808–1836) who was forced to marry an elderly New York merchant named Malibran to save her family from ruin is produced in New York.

10 APRIL 1935

Fourth Symphony in F minor by the dean of English composers Ralph VAUGHAN WILLIAMS, in four movements—(1) *Allegro*, a rhapsodically free essay built on a tensely chromaticized theme alternating with spacious diatonic progressions; (2) *Andante moderato*, marked by a moderate cornucopia of folk-like themes, with a concluding flute solo set in dolorous accents redolent of muezzin-like arabesques; (3) *Scherzo*, a highly syncopated jig in rapidly modulating keys; (4) *Finale, con epilogo fugato*, a coruscating mosaic of artfully varied folk-like themes, culminating in a magisterial fugal epilogue and concluding on the focal F—is performed for the first time in London by the British Broadcasting Corporation Symphony, Sir Adrian Boult conducting.

13 APRIL 1935

Variazioni coreografiche, ballet by the Italian composer Riccardo PICK-MANGIAGALLI, is performed for the first time at San Remo.

16 APRIL 1935

Petar STOJANOVÍC, Hungarian-born Serbian composer, conducts in Belgrade the first performance of his symphonic poem *Sava*, an ethnic musicorama of Serbia's great river, from its source in the Triglav mountains to its confluence with the mighty Danube.

25 APRIL 1935

As a result of a temporary reconciliation with the Nazi Government of Germany, Wilhelm FURTWÄNGLER is allowed to resume his post as conductor and music director of the Berlin Philharmonic.

28 APRIL 1935

Riccardo ZANDONAI, minor master of the Italian Verismo, composer of grand operas throbbing with exuberant melodrama, regarded by some as a legitimate successor to Puccini, is awarded the Mussolini Prize from the Royal Academy of Rome.

Riccardo Zandonai has glorified the lyric Italian theater in which he has maintained its sacred traditions in a modern design. (From Respighi's valedictory speech on the occasion of the presentation of the Prize)

2 MAY 1935

Third Symphony by the modern Dutch composer Henk BADINGS is performed for the first time in Amsterdam.

5 MAY 1935

Orsèolo, opera in three acts by the Italian composer Ildebrando PIZZETTI, to a libretto depicting the emotional conflict between the Venetian doge Orsèolo and a young nobleman who courts his daughter, is performed for the first time in Florence.

11 MAY 1935

Harnasie, ballet in three tableaux by the romantic Polish composer Karol SZYMANOWSKI dealing with the picaresque leader of "harnasies," the patriotically inspired Polish brigands active in the igneous chain of Central Carpathian Mountains, who elopes with a villager's bride on her scheduled wedding day, with authentic regional melorhythms set to sonorous bitonal harmonies and anchored in deeply rooted pedal points, is performed for the first time anywhere in Prague.

14 MAY 1935

La Pantoufle de vair, "conte dansé" by the French composer Marcel DELANNOY, after the famous fairy tale of Charles Perrault, in which Prince Charming recognizes his Cinderella by her dainty slipper made of fur (*vair,* not *verre,* as commonly misinterpreted, a fur slipper being aristocratic whereas a glass slipper is unwearable), is produced at the Opéra-Comique, as an expanded version of Delannoy's ballet *Cinderella,* originally produced in Chicago on 30 August 1931.

17 MAY 1935

Paul DUKAS, "Degas of Music," French composer of impressionistically rarefied symphonic works, master of illustrative evocation revealed in full power in his celebrated orchestral scherzo *L'Apprenti Sorcier,* dies in Paris in his 70th year, having destroyed in his last lucid moments all his unpublished manuscripts, including a violin sonata, an overture, and an unfinished work commissioned by the Boston Symphony Orchestra.

18 MAY 1935

Suite for String Orchestra, by Arnold SCHOENBERG (originally titled *Suite im alten Stile für Streichorchester*), completed in Hollywood on 26 December 1934, and bearing, for the first time since his *Second String Quartet* of 1908, a definite key signature, in five movements—(1) *Ouverture* in G major, (2) *Adagio* in E minor, (3) *Minuet* in G major, (4) *Gavotte* in B-flat major, and (5) *Gigue* in G major—is performed for the first time by the Los Angeles Philharmonic, Otto Klemperer conducting.

The spots in this score are Klemperer's drops of perspiration. (Schoenberg's inscription on the title page of the original manuscript)

I have become convinced that every modern composer, and particularly myself, ought to be interested in satisfying the demands of American high school orchestra in these respects: Without momentarily exposing the student to the "poison of atonality" to build the foundation of a modern technique leading to modern sensitivities, in fingering, articulation, form, counterpoint and phrase structure so as to enable him to acquire gradually a feeling for something more than the primitive symmetric construction, the unvaried and undeveloped melody, which give pleasure to mediocrities of all lands and peoples. Even in this music there should be room for higher forms which belong to a higher species of art not only from a technical but also from a spiritual standpoint. (From Schoenberg's foreword, translated from German)

19 MAY 1935

Charles Martin LOEFFLER, Alsatian-born American composer, whose art of sensitive decalcomania in reproducing the coloristic images of cultured French impressionism made him a minor master of American modernism, dies in Medfield, near Boston, at the age of 74.

20 MAY 1935

Die Zaubergeige, opera in three acts by the 34-year-old German composer Werner EGK, to a libretto derived from a Bavarian folk tale dealing with a farmhand who receives a magic violin from the Prince of the Elements, becomes an instant virtuoso, is entrammeled in an affair with an aristocratic belle, and finally returns to the peaceful life with his plain peasant wife, set to music in Germanically stolid harmonies, is produced in Frankfurt.

20 MAY 1935

The Rake's Progress, ballet by the 33-year-old Scottish singer Gavin GORDON, inspired by Hogarth's moralistic drawings, is produced in London.

25 MAY 1935

Uirapurú, symphonic poem by the prime Brazilian composer Heitor VILLA-LOBOS, in which the Brazilian jungle bird Uirapurú (*Levolepis modulator*), incarnated in an Amazon Indian playing the nose flute, reverts to its ornithological prototype after the Indian is slain by a youth, the latter being himself a product of reincarnation induced by a non-metamorphosed jungle maiden, written in an idiom saturated with tropical melorhythms, against which Uirapurú intones a pentatonic cantus firmus, is performed for the first time in Buenos Aires.

29 MAY 1935

Josef SUK, Czech composer, son-in-law of Dvořák and continuator of his musical heritage, dies at Benešovo at the age of 61.

2 JUNE 1935

Henry HADLEY conducts at the Norfolk, Connecticut, Festival, the world première of his *Fifth Symphony,* commemorating the tercentenary of the State of Connecticut and depicting in its three movements the three centennial landmarks in its history: *A.D. 1635,* with pentatonic allusions to aboriginal Indians; *A.D. 1735,* portraying in pastoral tones the agricultural period of the colonial settlement; and *A.D. 1935,* a musicorama of modern Connecticut vivified by jazzy rhythms.

9–10 JUNE 1935

First Labor Olympiad is held in Strasbourg, with concerts of orchestral and choral music given by proletarian groups from Switzerland, Holland, England, Czechoslovakia and France, and sponsored by radical-minded composers and writers of Europe and America.

13 JUNE 1935

La Novia del Hereje (Heretic's Bride), opera in three acts by the 54-year-old Italian-born Argentinian composer Pascual de ROGATIS, written in a melodramatically Italianate operatic idiom, is performed for the first time in Buenos Aires.

17 JUNE 1935

Holland issues a postage stamp of 5 centimes in honor of the national Flemish composer Alfons DIEPENBROCK (1862–1921).

19 JUNE 1935

Training, ballet by the 36-year-old Russian composer Alexander TCHEREPNIN, symphonically and choreographically illustrating the training of sportsmen, is performed for the first time in Vienna.

20 JUNE 1935

Holland issues a postage stamp of 12 1/2 centimes in honor of the great Dutch organist and composer Jan Pieterszoon SWEELINCK (1562–1621), whose works mark a historic advance in polyphonic instrumental writing.

24 JUNE 1935

Die schweigsame Frau, eleventh opera by Richard STRAUSS (completed by him on 20 October 1934 at the age of seventy), in three acts, to a libretto by Stefan Zweig, based on Ben Jonson's comedy *Epicene,* wherein a retired mariner, oversensitive to noise, is tricked by a designing nephew into a fraudulent marriage to an ostensibly silent woman who is actually the nephew's own wife, and who stages at once a wild charivari, driving the victim to distraction, set to music full of effervescent badinage, containing sly quotations from *Rigoletto* and *Tannhäuser* with a happy ending vouchsafed to all in idyllic E-flat major when true identities are revealed, is produced in Dresden.

13 JULY 1935

Richard STRAUSS resigns his post as President of the Reichsmusikkammer, ostensibly on account of lack of time and advanced age, but reportedly because of profound distaste for Nazi interference in artistic life and reluctance to part with his favorite Jewish librettist Stefan Zweig. (Peter Raabe was appointed to succeed Richard Strauss.)

17 JULY 1935

Emile RIADIS, "the Greek Ravel," whose instrumental music preserves the modal ethos of eternal Hellas under the glitter of impressionistic coloristic devices, dies in Saloniki at the age of 45.

31 JULY 1935

Aeneas, ballet with chorus by Albert ROUSSEL, after Virgil's epic poem *The Aeneid* is performed for the first time in Brussels.

1 AUGUST 1935

The Federal Music Project is organized in Washington as a branch of the Emergency Relief Bureau to provide work for unemployed American musicians.

2 AUGUST 1935

Mikola KOLIADA, 28-year-old Ukrainian Soviet composer, whose symphonic poem *Assault on Tractorstroy* provided a classical specimen of Socialist Realism in its optimistic portrayal of agricultural industrialization, perishes in a fall in the Caucasus during a mountain climbing trip.

30 AUGUST 1935

The Nazi Reichsmusikkammer issues a decree forbidding Jews and other non-Aryans to play in German orchestras.

1 SEPTEMBER 1935

The 13th Festival of the International Society for Contemporary Music opens in Prague with the following program of orchestral music:

Miserae by Karl Amadeus HARTMANN of Germany, set in a brooding introspective mood and marked by atonal melos; *Piano Concerto* by the Yugoslav composer Slavko OSTERC, in three movements, written in a modernistically percussive style, enlivened by asymmetric Balkan rhythms; *Variations* for orchestra, op. 31, by Arnold SCHOENBERG, a masterpiece of logical construction as instructive in its application of the method of composition with 12 tones as Bach's *Kunst der Fuge* is for Baroque counterpoint; *Cello Concerto* by the Prague composer Karel HÁBA, brother of the quarter-tone pioneer Alois Hába, written in an athematic modern idiom and governed solely by contrasts of adhesive mood-motifs; and *Second Symphony* by the Soviet composer Vissarion SHEBALIN, set in an expansive rhapsodic style, instinct with broad Russian melos.

2 SEPTEMBER 1935

At the second concert of the 13th Festival of the International Society for Contemporary Music in Prague, the following program of chamber music is presented:

Sonata for violin and piano by the Dutch composer Henk BADINGS, in a motoristically modernistic and lyrically implosive idiom; *Berceuse* for voice, flute, clarinet, and harp by the Polish composer Boleslaw WOYTOWICZ, written in a dramatic neo-Mussorgskyan vein; *Four Songs* for voice and string quartet by H. W. SUESSKIND of Czechoslovakia, conceived in a fresh lyric manner; *Concertino* for two pianos by the German composer Fidelio FINKE, in three characteristically archaizing neo-classical movements, *Alla Marcia, Nocturno* and *Quodlibet; Dialectic* for string quartet by the English composer Alan BUSH, written in a lucid polythematic vein; *Divertimento in Four Studies* for soprano, flute, oboe, clarinet, viola and cello by the Italian modernist Luigi DALLAPICCOLA, set in a rationally pantonal style, depicting four basic tempers— melancholy, gaiety, joy, despair—of the medieval system of four humors; and *Fantasy* for string orchestra by the Swiss composer Willy BURKHARD, in a neo-classical setting.

4 SEPTEMBER 1935

At the third concert of the 13th Festival of the International Society for Contemporary Music in Prague, the following program of chamber music is presented:

String Quartet by Sándor VERESS of Hungary, in a synthetic style set in the matrix of Bartók and Kodály; *Introduction and Allegro* for violin and eleven instruments by the Italian modernist Goffredo PETRASSI, in a hedonistic neo-Scarlattian style, performed under the composer's direction; *String Quartet* by the Belgian composer Raymond CHEVREUILLE, written according to the expressionistic concordance of harmony-moods; *Concerto* for 9 instruments by Anton von WEBERN, op. 24, dedicated to Arnold Schoenberg on his 60th birthday, and based on a dodecaphonic series of four 3-note segments, related to one another by reversion, inversion and reversed inversion, with the minor second and its inversion, the major seventh, as cybernetical intervals governing the melodic and harmonic formations, in linear and vertical dimensions, arranged in a characteristically subtilized instrumentation of maximum expressive power achieved by a minimum of sonorous means; *Sonata for Harp* by Alexander JEMNITZ of Hungary, set in an atonal manner marked by the minutest discrimination of dynamic elements; *Prelude, Interlude and Fugue* for two violins by the Scottish composeress Elizabeth MACONCHY, in a neo-Bachian style; *Chaconne* and *Etude-Toccata* for piano by Vladimir VOGEL, of Moscow and Berlin, written in a neo-Baroque style trammeled with neo-Busonian polyphony; and *Wind Quintet* in a hedonistically utilitarian vein by Alexander MOYZES of Czechoslovakia.

6 SEPTEMBER 1935

At the fourth concert of the 13th Festival of the International Society for Contemporary Music in Prague, the following program of symphonic music is given:

Poème héroique by Jef van DURME of Belgium, set in a neo-romantic pseudo-programmatic vein owing occasional excursions into harmonic modernities; *Symphony in A Major* by the French neo-romanticist Pierre Octave FERROUD, performed less than a year before his tragic death, written in a polyphonically imbricated, harmonically dense style influenced by his teacher Florent Schmitt; *Piano Concerto* by Pavel BORKOVEC of Czechoslovakia, in a modernistic virtuoso style of the Prokofiev type; *Symphonic Suite* from the opera *Lulu* by Alban BERG, played less than four months before his untimely death; and *Česta života (The Road of Life)*, symphonic fantasy in seven connected sections by Alois HÁBA of Prague, atonal and athematic in structure, set in a densely polyphonic dissonant idiom, and portraying in varying intervallic formations the three dominant anthroposophic figures of the universe, Christ (the most diatonic), Lucifer (the most atonal) and Ahriman (the most compressed).

12 SEPTEMBER 1935

A century has elapsed since the bass tuba was patented by Wilhelm WIEPRECHT, Director of the Berlin Gardes du Corps-Musik.

30 SEPTEMBER 1935

Porgy and Bess, folk opera in three acts by George GERSHWIN, his last major work (completed by him on 2 September 1935), to the libretto by his brother Ira Gershwin drawn from the play *Porgy* by Du Bose and Dorothy Heyward, portraying in nostalgic blues and neurotically vibrant jazz modalities the dark peripeteia of Negro life in Catfish Row in Charleston, South Carolina, focusing on the cripple Porgy who kills the former lover of his beloved Bess but loses her in the end when she goes off to New York with a character called Sportin' Life, containing such perennial classics as *Summertime, I Got Plenty of Nuttin'* and the skeptical exposure of biblical tales, *It Ain't Necessarily So*, is performed for the first time in Boston. (The first New York production took place on 10 October 1935. The European première took place in Copenhagen, in Nazi-infested Denmark, on 27 March 1943.)

4 OCTOBER 1935

Second Symphony by the 36-year-old American composer Harl MCDONALD, subtitled *Reflections of an Era of Turmoil*, with a *Rumba* movement replacing the conventional scherzo, is performed for the first time by the Philadelphia Orchestra, Leopold Stokowski conducting.

10 OCTOBER 1935

First Symphony in B-flat minor by the 22-year-old Soviet composer Tikhon KHRENNIKOV, his graduation piece at the Moscow Conservatory, in three movements, *Allegro, Adagio,* and *Molto Allegro,* set in an enticingly melodious, ingratiatingly harmonious and exuberantly rhythmic vein, in commendable accord with the symphonic precepts of Socialist Realism, is performed for the first time in Moscow.

12 OCTOBER 1935

Eugen HADAMOWSKI, director of the Nazi Radio Network issues the order to ban jazz music from the German air waves in order to "eliminate the last vestige of Jewish Kultur-Bolschewismus."

13 OCTOBER 1935

Klaus PRINGSHEIM, German conductor long resident in Japan conducts in Tokyo the first performance of his *Piano Concerto* in C major, employing Japanese pentatonic melodies set in accommodating Western harmonies.

15 OCTOBER 1935

On the approximate centennial of the death in France of the great Italian opera composer Vincenzo BELLINI, the Italian post office issues a series of postage stamps in his honor, at 20, 30, 50, 125, and 275 lire and at six denominations of airmail stamps.

18 OCTOBER 1935

Carlos CHÁVEZ conducts in Mexico City the first performance of his *Obertura Republicana*, making thematic use of three revolutionary Mexican songs of the 19th-century—*Marcha Zacatecas, Club Verde* and *La Adelita*.

19 OCTOBER 1935

Radio-Panoramique, symphonic sketch by Arthur HONEGGER, a mechanistic radiorama burlesquing the multi-channeled versatility of the radio, switching stations from symphony to jazz, from Viennese waltzes to sacred music in kaleidophonic profusion, is performed for the first time in public in Paris. (The first radio broadcast of *Radio-Panoramique* was given by Radio-Geneva as a commissioned work in March 1935.)

19 OCTOBER 1935

Fourth Symphony in A major by Albert ROUSSEL, in four classically contrasted movements: an incisive *Allegro con brio;* a wistfully pensive *Lento molto;* a tersely mobile *Allegro scherzando;* and a graceful *Finale,* marking a historical turn away from obsolescent Impressionism in the direction of enlightened Gallic neo-classicism, with sparkling polytonalities projected on the clear surfaces of tonal writing, is performed for the first time in Paris.

22 OCTOBER 1935

Quiet Flows the Don, opera in four acts by the 27-year-old Soviet composer Ivan DZERZHINSKY, after the novel of Mikhail Sholokhov, detailing the dramatic events in the Don basin during the turbulent early months of the Revolution, written in an esthetically proper idiom with ethnic undertones, in accordance with the tenets of Socialist Realism, diversified by euphonious dissonances and stark progressions in consecutive triads, is performed for the first time in Leningrad. (The title is usually given in English as *Quiet Flows the Don;* the Russian title, *Tikhy Don,* is literally *Pacific Don.*)

The success of Dzerzhinsky's opera is explained by the fact that its dramatic backbone is constructed firmly and effectively. There is no unnecessary psychologizing, no annoying digging into the hero's soul, no leftist oversimplification in the portrayal of significant social phenomena. Striving towards the realistic tenth, Dzerzhinsky remains uncontaminated by the extremes of musical expressionism with its morbid exposure of psychic aberrations. He does not ignore individual heroic personages to put emphasis solely on mass action, as some Soviet composers are apt to do. *Don, the Pacific* is superior as a historical opera to the propaganda type of certain other Soviet operas. One of its great advantages is the accessibility of its musical language. The score is distinguished by simplicity, expressive vigor and fine characterization of action. The composer does not resort to musical quotations from revolutionary songs, but rather endeavors to recreate the revolutionary genre in accordance with historical tenth. The folksong intonations in the opera are products of complex transformations of materials underlying the melos of popular songs and dances. Naturalistic ethnology and artificial folksiness are alien to the realistic method of Ivan Dzerzhinsky. (A. Ostretzov in the program book for the performance of the opera at The Bolshoi Theater in Moscow in 1936)

25 OCTOBER 1935

Constantin Bríncoveanu, opera by the 41-year-old Rumanian composer Sabin DRĂGOI, to a libretto in Rumanian dealing with the ruler of Valachia (1654–1714) of that name, is produced in Bucharest.

26 OCTOBER 1935

O noapte furtunoasa, comic opera by the 26-year-old Rumanian composer Paul CONSTANTINESCU, based on a modern Rumanian farce, wherein a gallant beau inadvertently enters the darkened bedroom of a policeman's wife instead of that of her sister with whom he had a nocturnal assignation, written in a vivacious Gallic manner seasoned with native gitanesque rhythms, is produced in Bucharest.

28 OCTOBER 1935

Fifteenth Symphony in D minor by the most prolific Russian symphonist Nicolai MIASKOVSKY, in four movements (completed on 29 November 1934), exhaling an optimistic air with relatively few introspective digressions, ostentatiously Russian in its rhapsodic expanse, but free from explicit folkloric references, is performed for the first time by the Moscow Radio Orchestra.

Many praise my *Fifteenth Symphony* for its optimism and lyricism. But this is not the proper language in order to express the feelings of an artist of the present day. I do not know what this language ought to be, and I possess no recipe for its formation. Neither folksong patterns nor city ballads can be the exclusive ingredients of the musical language of Socialist Realism. (Nicolas Miaskovsky, *Autobiographical Notes,* in *Sovietskaya Musica,* No. 6, 1936)

28 OCTOBER 1935

Two one-act operas by the 62-year-old English-born South African composer William Henry BELL, *The Pillow of Kantan,* inspired by the Japanese Noh theater, and *The Wandering Scholar,* are produced in Capetown.

30 OCTOBER 1935

The Composers' Forum-Laboratory, a branch of the Federal Music Project, designed to provide a pragmatic outlet for creative activities of American composers in the depths of economic and moral depression, opens in New York with a program of compositions by Roy HARRIS.

Here music expressive of every shade of thought and feeling peculiar to this movement in history will have a hearing. The purpose of these Forums is to provide an opportunity for serious composers residing in America, both known and unknown, to hear their own compositions and to test audience reaction. (From the statement of aims of the Composers' Forum-Laboratory)

2 NOVEMBER 1935

Ero s onoga Svijeta (A Rogue from the World Beyond), comic opera in three acts by the 40-year-old Croatian composer Jacov GOTOVAC, wherein a playful revenant causes posthumous mischief in his native village, is produced in Zagreb.

6 NOVEMBER 1935

The first complete performance is given by the British Broadcasting Corporation Symphony Orchestra in London, with Sir Hamilton Harty conducting, of the *First Symphony* by the 33-year-old English composer William WALTON, in four classically delineated movements, marked by the conspicuous absence of a key signature, but with the music firmly rooted in tonal foundations:

(1) *Allegro assai,* opening and closing on B flat in unison, moving gently along a swift Baroque current of kinetic energy, with a dynamic design following the logarithmic curve ranging from pianissimo to fortissimo; (2) *Presto, con malizia,* focused on a unison E, an ironic scherzo in rustic modalities, with the "malice" of the title implied by an episodic use of obsolete diminished-seventh chords and obsolescent whole-tone progressions and the ostentatious employment of the tritone, the "diabolus in musica" of the medieval theorists, the dynamic curve being that of a catenary; (3) *Andante con malinconia,* opening and closing on C sharp in unison, a stylized eclogue permeated by unpessimistic melancholy, the dynamic design following the outline of the arching "Witch of Agnesi" oscillating between piano and forte; (4) *Maestoso,* opening and closing on B flat in unison, coming to a standstill on a pause, then plunging into a precipitous *Brioso ed ardentemente,* culminating in a pyrotechnical fugue on a subject built on ascending fourths, the dynamic design being that of a catenary extending from fortissimo to fortississimo. (The first three movements, without the Finale, were first performed in London by the BBC Orchestra, Sir Hamilton Harty conducting, on 3 December 1934.)

14 NOVEMBER 1935

Gwalia, a Welsh Rhapsody for orchestra by the 45-year-old American composer Philip JAMES is performed for the first time in New York.

14 NOVEMBER 1935

Paul HINDEMITH plays the solo viola part with the Concertgebouw Orchestra in Amsterdam, Willem Mengelberg conducting, in the world première of his concerto for viola and orchestra, entitled *Der Schwanendreher.*

16 NOVEMBER 1935

Jumbo, American musical comedy by Richard RODGERS, in which the circus elephant Jumbo becomes the object of contention between two rival impresarios, featuring also the non-pachydermic songs *The Most Beautiful Girl in the World* and *My Romance,* is produced in New York.

21 NOVEMBER 1935

Sixth Symphony by the English neo-romantic composer Arnold BAX, in three movements: (1) *Moderato,* set in opulent secundal harmonies over deep pedal-points, (2) *Lento molto espressivo,* marked by a cornucopia of crepuscular melismas in tenebrous polyphony with a plethora of sepulchral cadences, (3) *Introduction, Scherzo and Trio, Epilogue,* successively pensive, somberly exulting, and funereally festive, is performed for the first time by the London Philharmonic Orchestra, Sir Hamilton Harty conducting.

21 NOVEMBER 1935

Igor STRAVINSKY plays in Paris, with his son Sviatoslav Soulima-Stravinsky, the first performance of his *Concerto for Two Pianos,* without orchestral accompaniment, couched in a terse neo-Baroque idiom, in four movements: (1) *Con moto,* focused on the tonic E in the pandiatonic matrix of a toccata; (2) *Notturno,* a neo-Scarlattian eclogue; (3) *Quattro Variazioni,* in a pellucid percussive manner; (4) *Preludio e Fuga,* set in sharply clashing tonalities, with a magistral coda concluding on a tonic seventh E major chord.

21 NOVEMBER 1935

Malaisie, symphonic triptych by the 50-year-old neo-romantic Belgian composer Léon JONGEN, reporting in exotically coloristic tones the impressions of his travels in Malaya, is performed for the first time in Brussels.

21 NOVEMBER 1935

Third Symphony by the 38-year-old Danish composer Knudaage RIISAGER, in three vehement movements, *Feroce, Violente e fantastico, Tumultuoso,* is performed for the first time in Copenhagen.

23 NOVEMBER 1935

Ethel LEGINSKA, English-born Americanized composeress and conductoress (who added a feminine Slavic ending *ka* to her unappealingly Anglo-Saxon name Liggins, and also modulated the initial vowel, in the hope of having a better chance for a career in a music world riddled with Polish-Russian aspirants) conducts in Chicago the first performance of her opera in two scenes *Gale,* subtitled *The Haunting,* dealing with a sailor named Gale who drowns his brother in a pool to secure his part in the family fortune, but is lured by his victim's ghost to his death in the same watery grave.

28 NOVEMBER 1935

The Italian Ministry of Propaganda issues a decree forbidding performances in Italy of works by authors and composers of nations, members of the Council of the League of Nations, which have voted punitive sanctions against Italy for its aggressive war on Ethiopia.

The Ministry of Propaganda has issued precise instructions to all its branches to define the proper attitude in the field of artistic activities adopted by Italy towards nations which have voted sanctions against it. On the basis of these instructions, plays by the nationals of the sanctionist powers are to be excluded from the repertory of Italian theaters, with the exception of Shakespeare and George Bernard Shaw. Special provisions have been made in regard to French drama, in consideration of the respectful attitude towards Italy taken by the majority of French intellectuals. Italian opera companies are to cancel productions of works by composers belonging to the sanctionist nations, except for French operas, with a reduced number of presentations. . . . In the concert field, music by composers of the sanctionist nations is to be eliminated entirely from the programs with the exception of a limited number of symphonic and chamber works by French and Spanish composers. In the field of light music, however, all works by representatives of sanctionist countries are to be taken off the repertory. Prohibitions and limitations will also be imposed on the activities in Italy of artists from the sanctionist nations. Performers of vaudeville, musical revues, operettas, operas, dancers, concert artists and conductors will no longer be allowed to appear in Italy, with some exceptions of individual French artists. The production of works by all expatriate living Russian authors who carry White Russian passports, is allowed without any restrictions, and Russian artists traveling on such passports are free to engage in professional activities in Italy. In the field of radio, Italian music and the music of nations that are nor signatories to the sanctions against Italy are the only works allowed to be broadcast, although a limited quantity of French music may be included. Regulations similar to those applied to radio programs will be enforced also to cinema orchestras and public functions in general. (Excerpts from the order of the Italian Ministry for the Press and Propaganda obtained by the author in 1936)

1 DECEMBER 1935

Second Violin Concerto in G minor by Sergei PROKOFIEV (completed in Baku on 16 August 1935) in three movements: an impulsively exuberant *Allegro Moderato,* set in sonata form, with lyrical discursions imparting a characteristic touch of poetic irony; *Andante assai,* an eclogue, in which an artfully exfoliating melody in the violin solo is accompanied by rhythmic figurations, and a waltzing Finale, *Allegro ben marcato,* is performed in Madrid, Spain, for the first time anywhere.

5 DECEMBER 1935

May Wine, musical play by Sigmund ROMBERG, exploring in uninhibitedly enticing accents the psychoanalytic aspects of marital infidelity, is produced in New York.

8 DECEMBER 1935

Pamir, a geographically scenic symphonic suite by the French composer Claude DELVINCOURT, extracted from his film score *La Croisièare jaune*, and depicting in its four movements the alpestrine Central Asian mountains of Pamir, known as "Top of the World," a caravan ascending the snow-covered trails, the nomadic Kirghiz horsemen, and the Great Wall of China, is performed for the first time in Paris. (Another symphonic suite from the same film score entitled *Films d'Asie*, was first performed in Paris on 16 January, 1937.)

12 DECEMBER 1935

La Spirale, a group of modern-minded French composers, organized to promote French music, presents its initial concert at the Schola Cantorum in Paris, in a program of chamber music by Claire DELBOS, André JOLIVET, Paul LE FLEM, Jules LEFEBVRE, Édouard SCIORTINO, Georges MIGOT, DANIELLESUR, and Olivier MESSIAEN.

La Spirale does not limit itself to first performances but will rather strive to give repeated hearings of significant works. The name *La Spirale* was adopted because a spiral is infinite and symbolizes the spirit of progress, being constantly attached to its point of origin and yet tracing a new path at its every turn. (From the declaration of the organizational committee of *La Spirale* printed in the program book of its inaugural concert)

15 DECEMBER 1935

La Passione, oratorio for soloists, chorus and orchestra by Gian Francesco MALIPIERO, to the text of the second part of the 16th-century mystery play by Pierrozzo Castellani, *Rappresentazione della Cena e Passione*, written in a deliberately archaic two-dimensional monodic perspective, in the manner of a religious fresco, is performed for the first time in Rome.

16 DECEMBER 1935

The Metropolitan Opera Company of New York issues a ruling banning the paid claque and forbidding its singers to hire claqueurs, and a fortiori, hissers and booers of rival artists.

21 DECEMBER 1935

Divertissement for chamber orchestra by the 23-year-old "jeune français" Jean FRANÇAIX, written in a hedonistic neo-rococo manner of Gallic modernism, is performed for the first time in Paris.

24 DECEMBER 1935

Nerghiz, opera in four acts by the 50-year-old Azerbaijan composer Muslim MAGOMATEV, relating in epical tones and ethnically Caucasian accents the story of a native village girl named Nerghiz, who fights in the Bolshevik ranks against the imperialist forces operating in the Caucasus in 1919, shoots to death a lecherous landlord who tries to lure her to his capitalistic habitat and subvert her proletarian consciousness, and liberates her shepherd lover, as the Red Army batters down the last bastion of the enemy's defense, is produced in Baku. (A new version, orchestrated by Reinhold Glièare, was produced at the Festival of Azerbaijan Music in Moscow on 11 April 1938.)

24 DECEMBER 1935

Alban BERG, Austrian composer whose expressionistic music penetrates deeply into the subliminal recesses of the human consciousness and at whose hands the twelve-tone method of composition promulgated by his teacher Arnold Schoenberg has become the emotional language of modern man, dies in Vienna of blood poisoning at the age of fifty.

In the first days of September 1935, Alban Berg had to cancel his trip to Prague to participate in the Festival of the International Society for Contemporary Music on account of an abscess on his back. The abscess was removed by surgical means and soon healed, but it proved to be the beginning of a fatal illness. On 17 December 1935 he was taken to the hospital; a blood transfusion brought about a slight improvement. He expressed a wish to thank the blood donor personally. After he saw him—it was a young Viennese boy—he turned to me and observed with an ineffable expression, "I only hope that his blood will not make an operetta composer out of me!" On 22 December the illness took a catastrophic turn: the heart refused to function. On 24 December 1935, 15 minutes after one o'clock, Alban Berg died in the arms of his wife. (Willi Reich, *Alban Berg*, Vienna, 1937)

25 DECEMBER 1935

Salmhofer's opera *Dame im Traum* was first performed on 26 December (not 25 December) 1935; the other two operas, *Das almächtige Gold* and *Harba* (not *Harla*), were never produced.

26 DECEMBER 1935

The opera *Dame in Traum*, by Franz SALMHOFER, is produced in Vienna.

1936

3 JANUARY 1936

Third Symphony by the 36-year-old American composer Harl MCDONALD, subtitled *Lamentations of Fu Hsuan,* for soprano solo, chorus and orchestra, is performed for the first time by the Philadelphia Orchestra.

11 JANUARY 1936

On the eightieth birthday of the Norwegian composer Christian SINDING, his *Fourth Symphony,* subtitled *Winter and War,* is performed for the first time in Oslo, as a tribute to his earnest achievements in advancing the cause of Norwegian music.

12 JANUARY 1936

Theodore METZ, American composer of the celebrated inebriating song hit *There'll Be a Hot Time in the Old Town Tonight,* dies in New York in his 89th year.

19 JANUARY 1936

At the dedication ceremony of the Theodore Roosevelt Memorial at the American Museum of Natural History in New York, Vittorio GIANNINI, 32-year-old American composer of Italian parentage, conducts the first performance of his symphonic work commissioned for the occasion, entitled *In Memoriam: Theodore Roosevelt.*

22 JANUARY 1936

Cyrano de Bergerac, opera in four acts by the 59-year-old Italian composer Franco ALFANO, to a libretto fashioned after Edmond Rostand's dramatic play dealing with the nasute poet's vicarious romance as an epistolary alter ego of an untutored but sexually balanced army soldier, is produced in Rome.

22 JANUARY 1936

Two days after the death of King George V of England, Paul HINDEMITH plays in London the solo part in the first performance of his *Funeral Music* for viola and string orchestra, written on the day before as a tribute to the innocuous old British sovereign.

22 JANUARY 1936

Quadruple Concerto for woodwind quartet and orchestra by the "jeune français" Jean FRANÇAIX is performed for the first time in Paris.

23 JANUARY 1936

Carlos CHÁVEZ conducts the Columbia Broadcasting Symphony Orchestra in New York in the first performance of his *Sinfonia India,* his second symphony, employing a large array of primitive Mexican percussion instruments (Yaqui drums, water gourd, a string of desic-cated butterfly cocoons, a chain of deer hooves, two teponaxtles, a huehuetl, claves, maracas, guïro, etc., interchangeable, if necessary, with more common drums and rattles), in one continuous movement, making use of three authentic pentatonic Mexican, tunes, in a treatment abounding in changing meters, but with the eighth-note as the least common denominator maintaining a uniform beat, with a coda of 125 bars of relentless reiteration of a tune from the island of Tiburon in the gulf of Baja California over the firm pedal-point on tonic F, and concluding on a pandiatonic chord.

24 JANUARY 1936

The Nations of the Soviet Land, "vocal symphony" by the 36-year-old Soviet composer Klimenty KORCH-MAREV, in five choral movements, each representing an ethnic section of the Soviet Union, *Sonata* (Kazakhstan), *Andante* (Russian), *Scherzo* (Jewish), *Canzona* (Ukrainian) and *Danza-Finale* (Moldavian), is performed for the first time in Moscow.

28 JANUARY 1936

An ominously anonymous article entitled *Confusion Instead of Music,* bearing all the signs of a centrally inspired authoritative declaration of policy, is published in *Pravda,* organ of the Communist Party of the USSR, condemning SHOSTAKOVICH's opera *Lady Macbeth of the District of Mzensk* as the product of Western-oriented un-Soviet activities in the field of music.

As culture continues to advance in our land, there has been an increasing demand for good music. Never in history have composers enjoyed such public support as in our country. Popular masses are eager to hear new songs, instrumental works, good operas. . . . Several Soviet theaters have presented the opera *Lady Macbeth of the District of Mzensk* by Dmitri Shostakovich. Officious music critics have praised the opera to the skies, spreading its fame far and wide. But audiences were bewildered by a stream of deliberately discordant sounds in the music. Melodic fragments, bits of musical phrases popped up on the surface here and there but were immediately drowned, emerging only to disappear once more in the general uproar. To follow this sort of music is difficult, and to enjoy it is impossible. . . . Singing is replaced by screaming. If by some lucky chance the composer happens to hit upon an attractive melodious tune, he hastens, as though horrified by such a calamity, to plunge back into the jungle of musical confusion, at times degenerating into complete cacophony. . . . All this is done not because of the composer's lack of talent, not because of his inability to express simple and profound emotions in musical tones. No, his music is distorted deliberately, so as to obliterate all resemblance to classical opera, all connection with natural musical speech. The fundamental concept of this music is a total negation of opera, by analogy with the ideas dominating leftist drama which rejects simplicity and realism in the theater, and scorns imagery and the normal sounds of human speech. It transfers

the most pernicious methods of Meyerhold's theatrical productions into the field of music. It is a leftist bedlam instead
of human music. The inspiring quality of good music is sacrificed in favor of petty-bourgeois formalist cerebration, with
pretense at originality by cheap clowning. This game may
end badly. . . . The peril of such distortion for Soviet music is
clear. Leftist monstrosities in the opera are derived from the
same sources as leftist monstrosities in art, in poetry, in pedagogy and in science. The petty-bourgeois "innovations" lead
to the renunciation of true art, true science, true literature. . . .
While our press and our music critics swear by the ideas of
Socialist Realism, the musical theater serves us in
Shostakovich's opera the coarsest kind of naturalism. Land-
lords and workers are painted in the same color, emphasizing
their most bestial aspects. The predatory merchantwoman
who gains a fortune and power through murder is represented
as a victim of the bourgeois state. . . . The orchestra squeals,
grunts, growls, and chokes itself to express love scenes as
realistically as possible. This "love" is smeared all over the
opera in the most vulgar manner imaginable. The merchant
bed occupies the center of the stage, and on it all "problems"
are solved. . . . The composer apparently is not interested in
the wishes and expectations of the Soviet public. He scram-
bles his notes together in order to appeal to formalistic
esthetes who have lost all taste for good art long ago. . . .
Some critics call this glorification of merchant lust a satire.
But there are no satirical elements in the opera. The composer is trying to involve his audience in the lurid and vulgar passions and actions of the merchantwoman, making use of the
entire arsenal of his musical and dramatic resources. . . . *Lady
Macbeth* is highly successful with the bourgeois audiences
abroad. It may be that this success is owing to the fact that
Shostakovich's opera is utterly devoid of all political meaning,
and that it titillates the perverted tastes of the bourgeoisie
with its fidgeting, screaming, neurasthenic music. (From the
Pravda article)

28 JANUARY 1936

Astuzie d' Amore, opera in three acts by the 44-year-old
Italian composer Franco CASAVOLA, is produced in Bari.

2 FEBRUARY 1936

Farhad and Shirin, music drama in four acts by the Russian composer Victor USPENSKY (1879–1949), to a romantic libretto dealing with the tribulations of a loving couple in Central Asia, written with a declared purpose of
promoting ethnological music, and including numerous
native instruments in the score, is produced in Tashkent.
(The second enlarged version was staged for the first
time in Tashkent on 22 March 1937.)

4 FEBRUARY 1936

The plenary meeting of the Union of Soviet Composers
unanimously votes to expel Alexander MOSSOLOV for
staging drunken brawls in public places, beating up a
waiter in a restaurant and generally behaving "in the glorious old Russian manner" utterly unbecoming to a citizen of a Socialist country.

Having heard the testimony by several comrades revealing a
picture of civil and moral decay of Alexander Mossolov, and
considering that his disgraceful conduct in the Press Building
restaurant on the night of 31 January 1936 was not an isolated
instance, but one of numerous episodes that corroborate the
above estimate of his character, the plenum of the Union of
Soviet Composers, regarding Mossolov's actions as incompatible with the honorable status of a Soviet composer and inadmis-

sible for a Soviet musician, unanimously resolves to expel him
from the Union. (*Sovietskaya Musica*, Moscow, March 1936)

8 FEBRUARY 1936

Giulio Cesare, opera in three acts by Gian Francesco
MALIPIERO, to his own libretto after Shakespeare's play,
is produced in Genoa.

9 FEBRUARY 1936

Genoveva, opera by the 32-year-old German composer
Alexander ECKLEBE, dealing with the virtuous
Genevieve of Brabant, unjustly accused of infidelity by
her suspicious husband, the margrave of Trier, is produced
in a radio broadcast in Berlin. (The first stage performance
took place at Hagen, Westphalia, on 22 April 1937.)

10 FEBRUARY 1936

The Italian Ministry of Propaganda rescinds its ban
against the authors and composers of nations, members
of the League of Nations, which have voted for the
application of sanctions against Italy for its invasion of
Ethiopia, but leaves in force the prohibition of appearances by artists from such nations.

Effective on 10 February 1936, provisions regarding the foreign plays and operas promulgated on 28 November 1935 are
abrogated. . . . Performances of all foreign works may take
place if they are approved by the censor's office and receive
special authorization issued by the Italian Society of Authors
and Publishers. The provision regarding performing artists
remains unchanged. (From the text of the order of the Italian
Ministry of Propaganda)

12 FEBRUARY 1936

Il Campiello (The Intersection), comic opera in three acts by
the German-Italian composer Ermanno WOLF-FER-
RARI, after a comedy by Carlo Goldoni, detailing a triv-
ially triangular contention among three girls in a three-
way intersection for the favors of a handsome stranger, is
produced in Milan.

15 FEBRUARY 1936

Asra, one-act opera by the 41-year-old Hungarian composer Eugen ŽADOR, wherein the sociologically inadmissible passion of a young soldier of Yemen for the
Caliph's daughter is unexpectedly requited, precipitating a dual cardiac palpitation of such amplitude that they
both die, is produced in Budapest.

17 FEBRUARY 1936

Sixth Symphony by the Soviet composer Lev KNIPPER is
performed for the first time in Moscow.

17 FEBRUARY 1936

Hamlets (Latvian for *Hamlet*), Shakespearean opera in
three acts by the Latvian composer Janis KALNINŠ, to a
libretto in the Latvian language, is produced in Riga.

18 FEBRUARY 1936

Das Gesicht Jesajas (Isaiah's Vision,) biblical oratorio by the
35-year-old Swiss composer Willy BURKHARD, set in a

grand Handelian manner with a discreet admixture of euphonious discords, is performed for the first time by the Chamber Orchestra of Basel, under the direction of its founder Paul Sacher.

21 FEBRUARY 1936

A century has passed since the birth of Léo DELIBES, French master of delectably harmonious ballets and appealingly melodious operas.

22 FEBRUARY 1936

Judith, biblical opera in five acts by the 57-year-old romantic Swedish composer Natanael BERG, is produced in Stockholm.

25 FEBRUARY 1936

Bakhtrioni, opera by the 33-year-old Georgian composer Grigori KILADZI, in the Georgian language, based on the legendary defense of the ancient castle Bakhtrioni in the Caucasian mountain country against invaders, is produced in Tbilisi (Tiflis).

26 FEBRUARY 1936

Farhad and Shirin, first national Uzbek operatic drama, notated and organized from genuine native motives for a choral ensemble singing chants in unison and orchestrated for indigenous instruments by the Russian composer and ethnomusicologist Victor USPENSKY, to a libretto dealing with the exotic love match of the Chinese prince Farhad and Armenian maiden Shirin, is produced in Tashkent.

27 FEBRUARY 1936

Fourth Symphony in B-flat major by the 33-year-old Soviet composer Vissarion SHEBALIN, in two movements scored for orchestra and military band, couched in the expansive modalities of Slavic melos and dedicated to the heroes of the Russian Civil war of 1918–1920, is performed for the first time in Moscow.

28 FEBRUARY 1936

Bloud (*The Simpleton*), opera in three acts by the dean of Czech composers Josef Bohuslav FOERSTER, to his own libretto after Tolstoy's moralistic tale, contrasting the pharisaical ostentation of two sanctimoniously eleemosynary mendicants with the sincere goodness of a simple youth who comes to the aid of a blind girl with a sick grandmother, is performed for the first time in Prague.

28 FEBRUARY 1936

Two new works by the 38-year-old American composer Roy HARRIS are performed for the first time on the same day, one in Boston and one in Philadelphia: *Second Symphony* in three movements, presented by the Boston Symphony Orchestra, Richard Burgin conducting; and *Prelude and Fugue* for string orchestra, played by the Philadelphia Orchestra, Werner Janssen conducting.

1 MARCH 1936

Guignol, opéra-bouffe by the 63-year-old French composer André BLOCH, is produced in Lyon.

1 MARCH 1936

The once respectable German music monthly, *Die Musik*, now designated as the official organ of the Nazi Cultural Community, issues a special anti-Semitic number featuring articles on such repulsive subjects as *Der Jude als Musik-Fabrikant*, illustrated by portraits and photographs of MENDELSSOHN, MEYERBEER, OFFENBACH, MAHLER, SCHOENBERG, TOCH, WEILL and KLEMPERER, retouched to make their facial expressions appear sinister, with the pupils of their eyes dilated darkly, prefaced by quotations in bold Gothic type from Adolf Hitler's utterances, e.g., "The Jew possesses no culture-building power whatsoever," and quoting also, without documentation, the statement of the long-dead German composer Felix Draeseke, "Our sole salvation lies in anti-Semitism."

6 MARCH 1936

Rubin GOLDMARK, New York-born nephew of the Austrian composer Karl Goldmark, and himself the composer of a considerable number of competently fashioned romantic pieces for orchestra, renowned chiefly as a useful pedagogue and compassionate teacher of a generation of American composers, dies in New York, where he settled in 1891, at the age of 63.

8 MARCH 1936

Pagan Symphony by the 67-year-old romantically inclined British composer Granville BANTOCK, with a motto "Et ego in Arcadia vixi," implying his consanguinity with the world of pre-Christian innocence, completed on 20 June 1928, in a single movement in four sections, a tranquil exordium in denuded harmonies of bare fifths, a scherzoid "dance of satyrs" for frolicking wood-wind instruments, a fast episode with a lot of drum thrumming and a finale concluding in a resonantly unpagan C major, is performed for the first time by the BBC Orchestra in London, conducted by Sir Adrian Boult.

10 MARCH 1936

Œdipe, lyrical tragedy in four acts by the prime Rumanian composer Georges ENESCO, traversing the tragic peripeteia in the life of Oedipus and the consummated prophecy of parricide and incest, written in a grand romantic style, diversified by numerous modernistic effects, including a brief passage in quarter-tones in the strings to illustrate the psychotomic anguish of the king, with instrumental interludes serving as philosophical commentary on events, is produced at the Paris Opéra.

14 MARCH 1936

In consequence of a storm of protest in the United States against the announced engagement of Wilhelm FURTWÄNGLER as conductor of the New York Philharmonic for the season 1936–1937, aroused by his ambiguous relationship with the Nazis and his willingness, however reluctant, to continue his artistic activities in Germany, he releases the management of the New York Philharmonic from its contract in the following cablegram from Luxor, Egypt:

Political controversies disagreeable to me/am not politician but exponent of German music which belongs to all humanity regardless of politics/propose postpone my season in the interests of Philharmonic society and music until the public realizes that politics and music are apart.

18 MARCH 1936

The Theater of People's Art, organized for the purpose of promoting musical activities of European and Asian nations, members of the Union of Soviet Socialist Republics, is established in Moscow.

21 MARCH 1936

Alexander GLAZUNOV, last great symphonist of old Russia, who wrote his first symphony at the age of sixteen, heir to the glorious national traditions of Balakirev, Borodin and Rimsky-Korsakov, grand master of the arts of counterpoint, harmony and orchestration, noble defender of time-honored musical precepts of beauty, euphony and formal perfection, for many years beloved director of the St. Petersburg Conservatory, and teacher of a pleiad of Russian composers, dies at the age of 70 in Paris where he settled after leaving Russia on 15 June 1928.

26 MARCH 1936

A Decade (ten days) of Music for National Defense, organized at the initiative of the Political Council of the Union of Soviet Composers, concludes in Moscow its series of four public concerts and three radio broadcasts, in programs of works by 37 composers, each portraying an event of the Soviet Revolution, the Civil War, a phase of domestic economic policy, or a signal achievement in Soviet industry.

27 MARCH 1936

Rossini in Neapel, light opera in three acts by the 48-year-old Austrian conductor Bernhard PAUMGARTNER on the subject of Rossini's purported amorous adventures in Naples, couched in a congenially songful Neapolitan manner, is performed for the first time in Zürich.

3 APRIL 1936

The International Music Festival in Baden-Baden is inaugurated by the Reichsmusikkammer of Nazi Germany to compete with the racially impure International Society for Contemporary Music, in programs of works by composers of untainted Aryan blood, representing eight nations.

4 APRIL 1936

Thirteen centuries have elapsed since the death of the Spanish musician and theologian ISIDOR of Seville who said that musical sounds could never be reproduced on paper in precise notation (*scribi non possunt*).

9 APRIL 1936

American Guild of Musical Artists (AGMA) is incorporated in New York, the first of its kind in the United States, empowered to act as a bargaining agent for musical performers, on the basis of equality with all labor unions.

11 APRIL 1936

On Your Toes, musical comedy by Richard RODGERS with book and lyrics by Lorenz Hart, incorporating a jazz ballet *Slaughter on Tenth Avenue,* featuring a love duet *There's a Small Hotel* and a mock-classical number, *The Three B's,* is produced in New York.

18 APRIL 1936

Ottorino RESPIGHI, Italian composer of flamboyantly colorful symphonic poems, whose tonal portrayals of the Roman landscape, the pines of its ancient roadways, the fountains of Rome and the stained glass paintings of its churches, coruscate with an almost panoptical brilliance, dies in Rome at 6:10 A.M. at the age of 56.

19 APRIL 1936

The 14th Festival of the International Society for Contemporary Music opens in Barcelona, presenting two concerts, one in the morning and one in the evening, with the following programs:

Three Symphonic Movements (*Pastorale, Dance, Nuptial*) for wind instruments by the Catalan composer Josep M. RUERA, set in a neo-archaic style, making use of ancient Greek modes; *Devise* by the Moscow-born German resident composer Wladimir VOGEL, based on a pentaphonic motto-device and a marching tune, the two subjects uniting in the Finale in sextuple counterpoint; *Joan of Os,* symphonic legend for solo singers, chorus and wind instruments by the director of the Municipal Band of Barcelona, Ricard LAMOTE DE GRIGNON, written in a frugal neo-medieval style; and *Dionysiaques,* corybantically turbulent symphonic poem by Florent SCHMITT.

Prelude and *Fugue* by the German neo-classical composer Edmund von BORCK (fated to be killed on 16 February 1944 on the German front in Italy); *Ariel,* ballet suite by the Catalan composer Roberto GERHARD, subdivided into four sections, expressing the four moods of the Shakespearean sprite of *The Tempest;* three fragments from the historical opera *Karl V* by Ernst KRENEK, his first work in the 12-tone style; and the world première of the *Violin Concerto* by Alban BERG, completed by him on 11 August 1935 shortly before his death, and dedicated "to the memory of an angel" (Manon Gropius, 18-year-old daughter of Alma Mahler and her second husband, the architect Gropius), in two bipartite movements, *Andante*/*Allegretto* and *Allegro*/*Adagio,* based on a remarkably tonal 12-tone series—G, B-flat, D, F-sharp, A, C, E, G-sharp, B, C-sharp, E-flat, F—representing four conjunct alternating minor and major triads ending with a succession of three whole tones, undergoing a variety of transformations in retrograde and inverted forms, the concluding section being a set of variations on Bach's chorale *Es ist genug* from the cantata *O Ewigkeit, du Donnerwort,* which opens with three whole tones, thus corresponding to the ending of the 12-tone series in the work, played by the American violinist Louis Krasner, who commissioned the concerto, and conducted by Hermann Scherchen replacing Anton von Webern who in his dogmatic insistence on perfection spent several hours rehearsing the introductory measures of the work, and had to resign from his task; and three fragments from Berg's opera *Wozzeck.*

19 APRIL 1936

Meredith WILLSON conducts in San Francisco the first performance of his *First Symphony* on the thirtieth anniversary of the San Francisco earthquake.

20 APRIL 1936

In the course of the 14th Festival of the International Society for Contemporary Music in Barcelona, the following program of chamber music is given:

Piano Sonata, Op. 1, in one tripartite movement by the Viennese dodecaphonist Ludwig ZENK; *Four Psalms* for soprano and chamber orchestra by the Swiss neo-classicist Robert BLUM; *Two Movements for String Quartet*, Op. 1, by the 34-year-old New York composer Mark BRUNSWICK, set in a neo-classical idiom; *5 Berceuses* by the Slovak composer Václav KAPRÁL, inspired by memories of cradle songs his mother sang for him and for his eleven brothers and sisters; and *Concertino da Camera* for alto saxophone and small orchestra by the master of French tone-painting Jacques IBERT, in three movements in the compact manner of modern rococo, with explosive cross-accents punctuating the asymmetrically juxtaposed thematic phrases.

20 APRIL 1936

Tsar Kaloyan, opera in four acts by the 37-year-old Bulgarian composer Pantcho VLADIGEROV, to the story of the Bulgarian 13th-century tsar who slays the non-Bulgarian seducer of the tsarina who thereupon kills herself, in a musical setting enlivened by the influx of asymmetrical Balkan polyrhythms and titivated by Italianate melodic fioriture, is produced in Sofia.

21 APRIL 1936

In the course of the 14th Festival of the International Society for Contemporary Music in Barcelona, the following program of chamber music is given:

Sonata for flute and piano by the American master contrapuntist Walter PISTON in three classically contrasted movements, written in a rationally lucid, rhythmically virile melodic style; *5 Sonnets of Elizabeth Browning* by the erudite Vienna composer Egon WELLESZ, for soprano and string quartet set in the style of an instrumental Lied; *Suite* for violin and piano by the rising 22-year-old Englishman Benjamin BRITTEN, in four movements, *March, Moto Perpetuo, Lullaby*, and *Waltz*, based on a thematic 4-note motto; *Quelques Airs de Clarisse Juranville* for soprano, string quartet and piano by the Belgian composer André SOURIS, couched in a surrealistic but tonal style of "kinesthetic action"; *Les Ombres perennes* for piano by the Catalan composer Manuel BLANCAFORT, in three neoclassical movements; and *String Quartet No. 5* by Béla BARTÓK in sharply contrasted five movements permeated with resiliently asymmetrical Transylvanian rhythms, composed in a month between 6 August and 6 September 1934 as a commission by Elizabeth Sprague Coolidge, and first performed on 8 April 1935 at the Coolidge Festival, at the Library of Congress in Washington.

22 APRIL 1936

At the 14th Festival of the International Society for Contemporary Music in Barcelona, the following program of orchestral music is given:

Sun-Treader by the American composer Carl RUGGLES, with a motto from Robert Browning, written in an intensely emotional, dissonant atonal style (first performed in Paris on 25 February 1932); *Fourth Symphony* by Albert ROUSSEL, in four movements written in a translucid neo-classical style; *Concerto* for piano and orchestra by the Swiss composer Frank MARTIN, in a contained romantic style marked by propulsive rhythms; *Don Lindo de Almería*, choreographic tone poem

by the 35-year-old Spanish modernist Rodolfo HALFFTER; *Concerto quasi una Fantasia* for violin and orchestra by the Parisianized Rumanian, Marcel MIHALOVICI; and *Danse Polonaise*, based on Carpathian melorhythms, by the Polish composer Roman PALESTER.

23 APRIL 1936

In the course of the 14th Festival of the International Society for Contemporary Music in Barcelona, the following program of orchestral music is presented:

Overture, a piece of abstract theatrical music by the 32-year-old Englishman Lennox BERKELEY, written in the pandiatonic technique of freely intermingled and superimposed tones of the major scale resulting in a cornucopia of multitriadic harmonies; *Symphony* in two movements by the Austrian composer Karl Alfred DEUTSCH, resident in Paris, set in a melodiously atonal idiom; *Second Concerto* for violin and orchestra by the prime composer of modern Poland, Karol SZYMANOWSKI, thematically derived from Carpathian folk songs; *Sinfonía* with piano concertante by the Manila-born Spanish composer, Federico ELIZALDE, in four movements bristling with Hispanic melorhythms; and a neo-classical *Overture* by the 27-year-old Swedish composer Lars-Erik LARSSON.

25 APRIL 1936

Notturno romantico, lyric drama by the Italian composer Riccardo PICK-MANGIAGALLI, is produced in Rome.

25 APRIL 1936

The 14th Festival of the International Society for Contemporary Music in Barcelona concludes with a concert of modern Spanish music in the following program:

La Nochebuena del Diablo, cantata by the prime Spanish romanticist Oscar ESPLÁ, to a text derived from a popular children's story dealing with the prowling devil at Christmas time; *Sonatina*, in the form of a ballet by the 31-year-old Spanish composer Ernesto HALFFTER, brother of Rodolfo Halffter; three dances from the ballet *Sombrero de las Tres Picos* by Manuel de FALLA; *Bailada* for piano and orchestra by the 37-year-old Spanish composer Salvador BACARISSE; *Por el Rio Guadalquivir* by the Spanish colorist Joaquín TURINA; *Triana* by Isaac ALBÉNIZ, orchestrated by Fernández ARBOS; *Iniciación* from *Liturgía Negra* by the 49-year-old Spanish composer Pedro SANJUÁN, inspired by the Afro-Cuban ritual; *Sardana* by the Catalan composer Juli GARRETA (1875–1925); fragments from *Goyescas* by Enrique GRANADOS; and *El Comte Arnau*, lyric poem for voices, chorus and orchestra by the founder of Spanish ethnomusicology Felipe PEDRELL.

1 MAY 1936

The Soviet *Wind Massive*, instrumental ensemble of 3,150 wind and percussion players, gives its inaugural performance in Leningrad in celebration of May Day.

2 MAY 1936

At a children's concert of the Moscow Philharmonic, the first performance is given of *Peter and the Wolf*, symphonic fairy tale by Sergei PROKOFIEV, with a speaker recounting the ingenuous story, set to music in an euphoniously infantiloquent style with acrid dissonances at dramatic points, wherein each character is portrayed by a musical instrument: Peter by the violins, his grouchy grandfather by the bassoon, the predatory wolf by three massed horns, the bird, which helps Peter to fling the rope around the wolf's head and capture him, by the flute, the hapless duck, temporarily swallowed by the wolf, by the oboe, the unreliable cat by the clarinet in the low register, and the hunters by the kettledrums and the bass drum. (First sketches were completed on 15 April 1936; full score was finished on 24 April 1936; these dates were communicated to the author by Prokofiev in 1938.)

7 MAY 1936

The first flying piano recital is given by the German pianist Franz WAGNER of Dresden, who presents a program of romantic music on the aluminum grand piano installed in the German dirigible *Hindenburg* during its first transatlantic crossing from Hamburg to New York.

12 MAY 1936

Second Piano Concerto in G minor, by the Soviet composer Dmitri KABALEVSKY, in three movements, an optimistic *Allegro moderato*, a philosophical *Andante semplice* and a tempestuous *Allegro molto*, written in an idiom gravitating towards the conjugate foci of tonality, but making use also of 20th-century devices such as concatenations of consecutive triads, instant modulation and juxtapositions of unresolved dissonances, is performed for the first time in Moscow.

12 MAY 1936

The Poisoned Kiss, or *The Empress and the Necromancer*, romantic extravaganza in three acts by Ralph VAUGHAN WILLIAMS, to a libretto drawn from Richard Garnett's story *The Poison Maid*, wherein a magician's daughter named Tormentilla, who is inured to poisons but whose veneniferous kiss is lethal to ad mirers, is decontaminated by the antitoxic love of the son of the Empress, is produced in Cambridge, England.

13 MAY 1936

The last concert is given at the Teatro Augusteo in Rome before its demolition to uncover the tomb of the Emperor Augustus presumed to lie under the site of the hall. (1,935 concerts had been given at the Teatro Augusteo, producing 940 works by Italian composers, of which 531 were first performances, and 1,492 non-Italian compositions.)

26 MAY 1936

Doktor Johannes Faust, opera by the 35-year-old German composer Hermann REUTTER, to a libretto in which the devil guarantees to Faust 24 years of uninhibited fulfillment of all his desires, is produced in Frankfurt.

27 MAY 1936

The Orquesta Sinfónica Nacional of Bogotá is formally established by the Colombian government, with Guillermo ESPINOSA as its conductor.

29 MAY 1936

Igor MARKEVITCH, 23-year-old Russian-born Parisian composer and conductor, leads in Paris the first perfor-mance of his oratorio *Paradis Perdu*, inspired by Milton's classic poem, in two parts, of which the first portrays the fall of Adam and Eve in tumultuously discordant harmonies and the second depicts their redemption in relatively euphonious tones.

3 JUNE 1936

La Jeune France, a group of young French composers, united in their determination to promote modern French music, presents in Paris a program of orchestral compositions, by its founding members, Olivier MESSIAEN, DANIEL-LESUR, Yves BAUDRIER, André JOLIVET, and, in a matripotestal capacity, Germaine TAILLE-FERRE, a member of the young French group of a previous generation, Les Six.

As life becomes increasingly strenuous, mechanized and impersonal, musicians ought to endeavor to contribute spiritual excitement to music lovers. *La Jeune France*, reviving the name once used by Berlioz, sets out on the intransigent course taken by him long ago. Its membership consists of four young French composers working in friendly association: Olivier Messiaen, Daniel-Lesur, Yves Baudrier, and André Jolivet. The aim of the group is to promote performances of musical works which are youthful and free, standing aloof from revolutionary slogans or academic formulas. . . . The personal tendencies of the members of the group are diverse; their common agreement lies in their desire to cultivate sincerity, generosity and artistic good faith. . . . The society intends to encourage performances of new French works which suffer from neglect through the indifference of official institutions, or lack of funds, and to continue in this century the tradition of the great composers of the past who have made French music one of the purest gems of civilization. (From the manifesto of *La Jeune France* printed in the program of its inaugural concert)

15 JUNE 1936

Le Roi nu, ballet with music by the young Gallic musical hedonist Jean FRANÇAIX, after the celebrated ironic tale by Hans Christian Andersen about a vain king wearing invisible clothes, is performed for the first time in Paris.

29 JUNE 1936

The Congress of the United States presents a gold medal to George M. COHAN in recognition of his meritorious service as the composer of the rousing World War I song *Over There* and of the patriotic ballad *You're a Grand Old Flag*.

11 JULY 1936

On the occasion of the centennial of the birth of the Brazilian national composer Antonio Carlos GOMES, the Brazilian Post Office issues a series of stamps with musical quotations from his works, marking the first use of musical notation in philatelic history.

14 JULY 1936

On the French national holiday, two plays by Romain Rolland, *Danton* and *Le 14 Juillet* are presented in public performance at the Paris Arena, with incidental music especially written for the occasion by Albert ROUSSEL, Arthur HONEGGER, Jacques IBERT, Daniel LAZARUS, Darius MILHAUD, Georges AURIC, and Charles KOECHLIN.

17 JULY 1936

La Ciudad roja, patriotic opera in three acts by the Argentinian composer Raúl ESPOILE, dealing with the blockade of the littoral of Argentina by the French fleet in 1840, ending on a major triad with an added sixth as a symbol of victory, is produced at the Teatro Colón in Buenos Aires.

17 JULY 1936

Nie ER, 23-year-old Chinese Communist composer of the revolutionary song *Along the Yangtze River*, accidentally drowns in the Sea of Japan.

12 AUGUST 1936

The great Polish pianist and statesman Ignace PADEREWSKI appears for the first time in a cinematic performance, with sound, playing Beethoven's *Moonlight Sonata* in a London film studio.

16 AUGUST 1936

At the Olympiad in Berlin, first performances are given of the following works by certified Aryan composers belonging to the German-Italian political axis, prizewinners of the Olympic competition, organized by the Nazi Ministry of Propaganda with the aid of the subservient Reichsmusikkammer.

Olympic Hymn by Richard STRAUSS, based on the leading motive "Olympia"; *Il Vincitore* by the 34-year-old Italian composer Lino LIVIABELLA, written in an amplified Respighian manner; *Olympic Cantata* 1936 by the 32-year-old German composer Kurt THOMAS, based on chants from Protestant hymnology; *Olympic Festival Music* by the 35-year-old German composer Werner EGK, written in an appropriately exuberant marching vein; and *Olympic Pledge* by Paul HOEFFER, set in officiously hymnal Handelian harmonies.

17 AUGUST 1936

Pierre-Octave FERROUD, 36-year-old French composer of symphonic and chamber music written in a sophisticated modernistic idiom, is killed while motoring near Debrecen, Hungary.

29 AUGUST 1936

The National Bureau of Standards in Washington starts broadcasting the 440-cycle standard A for tuning purposes. (The broadcast continued until 11:40 A.M., 13 September 1936.)

4 SEPTEMBER 1936

Second Symphony by the Mexican composer of Indian extraction Candelario HUÍZAR, subtitled *Ochpaniztli* (the ancient name for the month of October), in three movements, *Sacrificial Dance, Dance of Birds and Butterflies* and *Mask Dance*, set in stark primitivistic modalities, is performed for the first time in Mexico City by the Orquesta Sinfónica de Mexico under the direction of Carlos Chávez.

11 SEPTEMBER 1936

Te Deum of Budavár by Zoltán KODÁLY, thanksgiving hymn for soloists, chorus and orchestra, written for the celebration of the 250th anniversary of the successful defense of the city of Buda against the Turks, opening with an exultant fanfare of victory to the majestic Latin lines of the ancient Christian hymn *Te Deum laudamus*, combining the pentatonic modes of immemorial Pannonia with devotional ecclesiastical tropes set in freely modulating triadic harmonies, is performed for the first time in Budapest.

14 SEPTEMBER 1936

The first music typewriter is patented in Berlin under the trade name *Nototyp Rundstatler*, possessing 44 keys in four rows: (1) upper row: clefs, numeral for time signatures, sharps, flats and bar lines; (2) second row: notes on the staff up to the third line; (3) third row: notes above the middle line; (4) lowest row: stems. (Rests, dots, crescendo, diminuendo, etc. are distributed among all four rows.)

The work on which I am now engaged would have been finished long ago, were it not for the fact that my hand gets weary of putting notes on paper. I wish that some ingenious person would invent a machine enabling tired composers to write music faster and less laboriously. (From Haydn's letter to a friend, quoted in the article *Die Sonate auf der Schreibmaschine*, published in the *Hamburger Fremdenblatt* of 13 September 1936)

14 SEPTEMBER 1936

Ossip GABRILOWITSCH, 58-year-old Russian-born pianist of the golden age of virtuosistic exuberance, and since 1918 conductor of the Detroit Symphony Orchestra, dies of cancer in Detroit.

15 SEPTEMBER 1936

The Federal Music Project of the Works Progress Administration in Washington announces the figures of attendance for the period from 1 January to 15 September 1936: 15 WPA orchestras gave concerts throughout the United States with an estimated attendance of 32 million people; the grand total of 10,797 performances were given before audiences aggregating 11,167,173 persons in July and August 1936.

22 SEPTEMBER 1936

L'acAmante in Trappola, one-act opera by the 57-year-old Italian composer Arrigo PEDROLLO, is performed for the first time in Verona.

25 SEPTEMBER 1936

At the 34th Norwich Triennial Festival Ralph VAUGHAN WILLIAMS conducts the first performance of his choral suite, *Five Tudor Portraits*, for soloists, chorus and orchestra, to the text by John Skelton. (The printed program listed Dr. Heathcote Statham as the conductor, but he only prepared the chorus; Vaughan Williams conducted the actual concert.)

4 OCTOBER 1936

The Bells of Zlonitz, an early unnumbered symphony by Antonin DVOŘÁK, the manuscript of which was discovered in the Prague archives, is performed for the first time by the Czechoslovak State Radio Orchestra in Prague.

8 OCTOBER 1936

First Symphony in D minor by the dean of Canadian composers Healey WILLAN is performed for the first time in Toronto.

15 OCTOBER 1936

Die schwarze Spinne, radio opera in one act by the 26-year-old Swiss composer Heinrich SUTERMEISTER, to a horrendous Swiss folk tale of arachnoid deviltry, in which a woman is forced to give birth to a litter of black spiders, is performed for the first time in Bern. (First stage production of the opera took place in St. Gall, Switzerland, on 2 March 1949.)

16 OCTOBER 1936

Concertino for piano, violin, cello and orchestra by the 45-year-old Czech composer Bohuslav MARTINU, written in a neo-Baroque style with the thematic elements permeated by vigorous Bohemian melorhythms, is performed for the first time in Basel.

18 OCTOBER 1936

Le Jeu sentimental for orchestra by the 24-year-old French composer Jean FRANÇAIX, a symphonic stylization of 19th-century salon music, is performed for the first time in Paris.

20 OCTOBER 1936

First Symphony by the 26-year-old American composer William SCHUMAN is performed for the first time by the Gotham Symphony Orchestra in New York.

22 OCTOBER 1936

Partita for orchestra by the 40-year-old Austrian composer Johann Nepomuk DAVID, in six movements, based on a single subject in four interrelated forms (direct, specular reflection, retrograde and reflected specular retrograde), is performed for the first time in Leipzig.

24 OCTOBER 1936

Sixteenth Symphony in F major by the prime Russian symphonist Nicolai MIASKOVSKY (completed on 5 April 1936), dedicated to the Soviet Air Force, and reflecting in its four movements (1) social optimism and faith in progress, (2) gaiety of youth, (3) sorrow at the loss of the giant Soviet plane *Maxim Gorky* during its inaugural flight, (4) contemplation of Russia's greatness as revealed in folk music, is performed for the first time in Moscow.

29 OCTOBER 1936

Russian Overture by Sergei PROKOFIEV (completed on 25 September 1936), based on three contrasting Russian melodies, a dance, a city ballad and a lyric chant, and emulating in its orchestration the sound of Russian folk instruments (balalaika, domra, accordion), is performed for the first time in Moscow.

29 OCTOBER 1936

Bogatyri (Giants), operatic pasticcio with music put together by BORODIN in 1867, consisting of 22 numbers partially borrowed from Meyerbeer, Rossini, Offenbach, Verdi and Serov, and first performed in Moscow on 18 November 1867, is produced in Moscow with a new militantly atheistic text by the proletarian Soviet poet Demian Biedny, burlesquing the Christianization of Russia in 988.

6 NOVEMBER 1936

Third Symphony in A minor by Serge RACHMANINOFF (completed on 30 June 1936), in three movements— (1) *Allegro moderato,* in a characteristic Russian style with a three-note motto; (2) *Adagio ma non troppo,* a set of discreet variations on a slow theme, gradually increasing in mobility, then subsiding and reiterating the three-note motto of the first movement; (3) *Allegro,* a vivacious Russian dance in triumphant A major with a tritonally cadenced ending—is performed for the first time by the Philadelphia Orchestra, Leopold Stokowski conducting.

8 NOVEMBER 1936

Enoch Arden, opera in three acts by the 39-year-old German composer Ottmar GERSTER, after Tennyson's poem about a sailor shipwrecked on a desert island, who returns to his native village after many years to find his wife married to another, and decides to go away without revealing his identity, set to a Wagneromorphic score with leading motives assigned to each character and subject, is performed for the first time in Düsseldorf.

8 NOVEMBER 1936

Jean FRANČAIX, 24-year-old French composer, appears as piano soloist with the Berlin Philharmonic in the world première of his elegantly hedonistic *Piano Concerto,* set in the fashionable neo-classical vein, in four movements distinguished by glittering melodic surfaces adorned with asymmetric rhythmic designs.

11 NOVEMBER 1936

Edward GERMAN, English composer of effective light operas, whose real name was Edward German Jones, dies in London at the age of 74.

12 NOVEMBER 1936

Das Opfer, opera by the 31-year-old German composer Winfried ZILLIG, written in an advanced Wagneromantic style, but embodying some daring dodecaphonic structures, with the tone row vertically integrated in the form of four mutually exclusive triads, is produced in Hamburg.

14 NOVEMBER 1936

Le Testament de la Tante Caroline, comic opera in three acts by Albert ROUSSEL, in which an eccentric aunt wills her considerable fortune to the first of her three nieces to bear a child, starting a trilateral pregnancy race during which a barren niece unsuccessfully tries to pass an adopted child for her own, and another niece has a furious affair with her chauffeur endowed with an exceptional spermatozoic fertility who turns out to be the missing natural son of the third niece who, upon verification of her maternity, gains the entire contested estate, is produced for the first time in Olomouc, Czechoslovakia, in a Czech version. (The first French production of the opera took place at the Opéra-Comique in Paris on 11 March 1937.)

14 NOVEMBER 1936

The Council of People's Commissars of the Union of Soviet Socialist Republics cancels all performances of the opera *Bogotyri*, based on music of BORODIN, produced in Moscow on 29 October 1936, on the grounds that the abusive attitude in the libretto by the proletarian Soviet poet Demian BIEDNY towards the objectively progressive conversion of Russia to Christianity in 988 is ideologically incorrect.

Considering that the opera-farce *Bogatyri* by Demian Biedny making use of music by Borodin (1) glorifies the bandit chiefs of Kiev as positive revolutionary characters, falsifying the historical truth and propagating erroneous political views (2) tarnishes the image of Russian epic heroes, *Bogatyri*, who personify in the popular imagination the inherent traits of the people of Russia (3) gives an unhistoric and offensive interpretation of the conversion of Russia to Christianity, which was in fact a positive factor of Russian history and which contributed to cultural relations of Slavic nations with other countries of superior civilizations . . . the Committee for the Arts at the Council of People's Commissars resolves that the opera shall be removed from the theatrical repertory as inimical to the ideals of Soviet art. (*Pravda*, Moscow, 14 November 1936)

16 NOVEMBER 1936

France issues a BERLIOZ postage stamp valued at 40 francs.

19 NOVEMBER 1936

Johnny Johnson, a fable with music by Kurt WEILL, his first theatrical score written in America, dealing with a helplessly pacifistic American soldier who feeds laughing gas to his superior officers to deter them from making war, and is eventually sent to an insane asylum for his bizarre behavior, is produced in New York.

20 NOVEMBER 1936

Pickwick, opera in three acts, after Dickens, by the English conductor Albert COATES, written in an engagingly vivacious style, with clever topical quotations from contemporary English balladry, is produced in London.

22 NOVEMBER 1936

Concerto for cello and orchestra by Holland's prime modernist Willem PIJPER (completed on 27 October 1936), with the Latin motto "Vulnerant omnes, ultima necat," suggesting an increasing vulnerability of man, culminating in the ultimate mortal wound, in five movements played without pause, employing polycentric tonalities in resonant superposition, and embroidering the thematic quasi-atonal melodies with coloristic arabesques, is performed for the first time in Amsterdam.

24 NOVEMBER 1936

The Astrology of Personality by Dane RUDHYAR, French-born American composer who changed his original name Daniel Chennevière to a more theosophic cognomen, is published in New York, the first book on astrology ever written by a professional musician.

The Astrology of Personality is said to be for the future of astrology what Ptolemy's *Tetrabiblos* has been for astrology of the past. It reveals a new philosophy of Creative Time, of an Algebra of Life. (The appraisal of Rudhyar's publisher, made shortly after the publication of the book)

25 NOVEMBER 1936

Slaraffenland (*Fool's Paradise*), ballet by the 39-year-old Danish composer Knudaage RIISAGER, dealing with a fatuous boy who ventures into the land of King Sauce where he gets indigestion from immoderate consuming of condiments, is produced in Copenhagen.

27 NOVEMBER 1936

The German Minister of Propaganda Dr. Joseph Goebbels issues a circular letter to newspaper reviewers with an injunction to confine themselves to factual accounts of artistic events, eschewing excessive praise or sharp criticism, and establishing a minimum age of thirty to qualify as purveyors of directed opinion in the Third Reich.

Among professional critics who write their reviews objectively in a business-like manner and who regard their function as that of intermediaries between the performing artists and the public, the order of Dr. Goebbels to replace criticism by an observation of art (*Kunstbetrachtung*) ought to meet with full agreement. Germany of today enables artists and critics to be comrades again, united in the service of a common cause and workers for a common purpose. (Richard Ohlekopf in *Signale für die Musikalische Welt*, Berlin, 9 December 1936)

What are the present conditions of literary, artistic and theatrical criticism in Germany? What was the motive that impelled the German government to forbid young men less than thirty years of age to be employed as critics? Italy whose national song is *Giovinezza* would never exclude the young. . . . In a country where art thrives on polemical discussion, it would be quite impossible to replace a critical review by an "objective account." We are told in school that every sentence, even such as "This beefsteak is good" or "The yolk of an egg is yellow," is a judgment expressed in words. This is fully corroborated when we consider that to a vegetarian, beefsteak is not good, and that to Italians the yolk of an egg is *rosso* (red) but to the French it is *jaune* (yellow). (From the article *Abolire la critica?* in *La Tribuna*, Rome, 3 December 1936)

30 NOVEMBER 1936

Second Piano Concerto by the 41-year-old American composer Leo SOWERBY is performed for the first time by the Boston Symphony Orchestra, with Serge Koussevitzky conducting.

1 DECEMBER 1936

To mark the centennial of the death of the Swiss composer Hans Georg NÄGELI, the Swiss post office issues a 5-franc postage stamp with his romanticized portrait.

8 DECEMBER 1936

The Nazi Ministry of Propaganda issues a directive limiting all outdoor performances of Gottfried SONNTAG's *Nibelungen-Marsch*, based on motives from Wagner's *Ring* cycle, only to important meetings under the aegis of the Nazi party. (A supplementary order, signed by Hitler himself on 6 July 1937, made the playing of the march compulsory at all *Parteitage*.)

10 DECEMBER 1936

Pinocchio, "a merry overture" by Ernst TOCH, his first orchestral work written after he settled in California, inspired by the beguiling children's fable of Carlo Collodi about a mendacious pine-ocular fibber whose nasal longitude grew proportionately to the enormity of each tale told, set to music in relaxed march time vivified by fugal imbroglios in a slightly disoriented tonality, is performed for the first time by the Los Angeles Philharmonic under the direction of Otto Klemperer.

13 DECEMBER 1936

First Symphony by the 26-year-old American composer Samuel BARBER, in a single pluralistic movement, with a tarantella forming a vivacious interlude between the dramatic first section and the lyrically rhapsodic finale, converging from quasi-atonal approaches onto a resonant E-minor coda, is performed for the first time in Rome, Bernardino Molinari conducting. (First American performance of the work was given by the Cleveland Orchestra on 21 January 1937.)

15 DECEMBER 1936

The Dream of Wei Lien, Chinese ballet by the Chinarooted expatriate Russian composer Aaron AVSHALOMOV,

making use of pentatonic Chinese melodies in Russianized harmonies and Germanized counterpoint, is produced in Shanghai with a Chinese cast.

19 DECEMBER 1936

Joseph ACHRON plays the solo part in the first performance of his *Second Violin Concerto* with the Los Angeles Philharmonic, under the direction of Otto Klemperer.

20 DECEMBER 1936

Bret Harte, symphonic overture by the 46-year-old American composer Philip JAMES, inspired by Bret Harte's tales of adventure, is performed for the first time by the New York Philharmonic.

26 DECEMBER 1936

The newly organized Palestine Symphony Orchestra, consisting mainly of refugees from Nazi Germany, presents it inaugural concert at Tel Aviv, under the direction of Arturo Toscanini, in a program of German classics and Rossini.

Toscanini refused any remuneration, not even traveling expenses. He said that at the time when dark forces were seeking the destruction of the Jewish people he felt it his duty to prove his sympathy with the Jews within his own domain of music. (New York *Times*, 27 December 1936)

31 DECEMBER 1936

First Symphony by the Cyprus-born American composer Anis FULEIHAN is performed for the first time by the New York Philharmonic.

1937

2 JANUARY 1937

A century has passed since the birth in Nizhny-Novgorod, on the Volga River, of Mily BALAKIREV, the genial Amphitryon of the Russian National School of Composers and friendly mentor of Mussorgsky and Rimsky-Korsakov.

21 JANUARY 1937

A Voice in the Wilderness, symphonic poem in six movements for orchestra and cello obbligato by Ernest BLOCH with the sections "bound together by a barely perceptible thematic relationship or reminiscence" wherein the cello has "an aggressive role without endless displays of virtuosity, like the character in a drama," written in Bloch's

typical expansive harmonic vocabulary of contrasting polar tonalities distanced by a tritone, is performed for the first time by the Los Angeles Philharmonic, Otto Klemperer conducting.

(The well-known passage in Isaiah 40:3, from which the title is taken is actually a mistranslation; correct meaning is found in Powis Smith's "American Translation" of the Bible: "Hark! one calls: In the wilderness clear the way of the Lord.")

21 JANUARY 1937

The Chamber Orchestra of Basel, Switzerland, under the direction of its founder Paul Sacher, gives the world première of *Music for Strings, Percussion and Celesta* (containing also harp and piano) by Béla BARTÓK (completed on 7 September 1936), in four movements:

(1) *Andante tranquillo*, a fugue on a highly chromaticized subject centering on A, in propulsive asymmetrical rhythms firmly maintaining the common denominator of an eighth-note; (2) *Allegro*, wherein the strings are subdivided in two groups operating in antiphonal variations, coalescing in vigorous, rigorous polyphony, with glissandos in the strings, harp and piano, imparting an exotic ambiguity to the strong tonality gravitating towards the focal C; (3) *Adagio*, with a xylophone chiming on a single high F introducing a chromaticized subject related to that of the initial movement, and followed by a spectacular panpentatonic exhibition on the black keys of the piano accompanied by similar exhibitions in the celesta and the harp, leading to a restatement of the chromatic subjects with an epitaph on the high F of the xylophone; (4) *Allegro molto*, a paradoxical rondo, with a non-recurrent theme leading to a magisterial coda in which the chromatic fugal subject of the first movement is conformally expanded into a diatonic statement, concluding with a Lydian cadence in fortissimo.

21 JANUARY 1937

Third Symphony in three movements by the 36-year-old Siberian-born American composer Nicolai BEREZOWSKY, written in a brightly tonal idiom marked by perceptible Russianisms, is performed for the first time in Rochester.

23 JANUARY 1937

Rembrandt van Rijn, opera in four acts by the Germanized Danish-born composer Paul von KLENAU, to his own libretto, relating the story of Rembrandt's marital sorrows, financial troubles and other misfortunes, set to music of multiple resources, including polyharmony and quasi-dodecaphonic atonalities, with episodes of spoken commentary to attenuated orchestral accompaniment, is performed for the first time, simultaneously in Berlin and Stuttgart.

24 JANUARY 1937

Divertissement pour une fête de nuit for piano and orchestra by Reynaldo HAHN is performed for the first time in Paris.

25 JANUARY 1937

Ivan WYSCHNEGRADSKY, expatriate Russian composer of experimental music, conducts in Paris a concert of his works in quarter-tones: *Symphonic Fragments*, in an arrangement for four pianos, two of which are tuned a quarter-tone higher than the others; *Thus Spake Zarathustra*, in a similar arrangement for four pianos; *Etude en forme de Scherzo* for two pianos tuned a quarter-tone apart; and *Preludes* in quarter-tones.

25 JANUARY 1937

Second Symphony by Gian Francesco MALIPIERO, subtitled *Elegiaca*, in four movements, an energetic *Allegro non troppo*, a meditative *Lento*, a brisk *Mosso* and an elegiac *Finale*, is performed for the first time as a commissioned work by the Seattle Symphony Orchestra, under the direction of Basil Cameron.

I wrote my *Elegiaca* in the anxious and tragic months of 1936, a year full of sadness. I wish to point out that the word *Elegia-*

ca does not signify an intention to write program music. (From Malipiero's note in the program book of the Seattle Symphony Orchestra)

26 JANUARY 1937

The Brazilian Parliament patriotically votes a bill stipulating that "musical programs performed in Brazil shall include compulsory works by Brazilian-born composers."

6 FEBRUARY 1937

Concertino for cello and orchestra by the French master Albert ROUSSEL, in three movements, *Allegro moderato*, *Adagio*, *Allegro molto*, following the classical models but imbued with the Gallic spirit of vigorous hedonism, is performed for the first time in Paris.

8 FEBRUARY 1937

Tanzsymphonie by Eugen ZÁDOR is performed for the first time in Budapest.

20 FEBRUARY 1937

Mirjana, opera in three acts by Josef MANDIĆ, Croatian composer active in Prague as a prosperous lawyer, to the macabre story of a young man's visit to his dead fiancée's grave on the day of his marriage to another girl, his subsequent disappearance for a hundred years and his adventure with Mirjana rediviva as a noblewoman with whom he circumnavigates the world, is performed for the first time at Olmütz.

20 FEBRUARY 1937

Sergei PROKOFIEV conducts in Paris the first performance of his symphonic suite *Lieutenant Kijé* from film music of that name, dealing with a mythical army officer whose last name was the product of the accidental typographical coupling of two Russian verbal particles, disgorging a cornucopia of wittily dislocated marching tunes and mock-sentimental ballads.

22 FEBRUARY 1937

Fernando del Nonsensico, operatic satire in three acts by the English-born 64-year-old Chicago composer Felix BOROWSKI, with its shafts aimed at the absurdities of Italian opera, containing distorted quotations from Bellini and Verdi and ending with the death of all participants, is presented for the first time in Los Angeles.

24 FEBRUARY 1937

Garrick, opera in three acts by the 42-year-old American composer Albert STOESSEL, to a libretto recounting the professional and amorous ventures of the Shakespearean actor David Garrick, is performed for the first time by the Opera Department of the Juilliard School of Music in New York, conducted by the composer.

24 FEBRUARY 1937

Lucrezia, one-act opera by Ottorino RESPIGHI, to a libretto recounting the sad story of Lucretia who killed herself in 508 B.C. after she was ravished by an unscrupulous princeling, is performed posthumously for the first time in Rome, in a version completed and edited by Respighi's widow, Elsa Olivieri Respighi.

28 FEBRUARY 1937

Scènes Ibériennes, symphonic suite by the Hispanically inclined French composer Raoul LAPARRA, is performed for the first time in Paris.

2 MARCH 1937

Massimila Doni, opera in four acts by the 50-year-old Swiss composer Othmar SCHOECK, after Balzac's novelette of that name, wherein a Venetian lady conducts in 1830 an intellectualized love affair with an emotional man from Genoa, set in a Wagneromorphic style of composition with identifying motivs and the inclusion of spoken song to gently orchestrated accompaniment, is produced for the first time at the Dresden Opera.

2 MARCH 1937

Le Rossignol en Amour, chamber opera by the 46-year-old French composer Georges MIGOT, is performed for the first time in Geneva.

5 MARCH 1937

The Headless Horseman, one-act operetta by Douglas MOORE, after *A Legend of Sleepy Hollow* by Washington Irving, is performed for the first time at Bronxville, New York.

11 MARCH 1937

L'Aiglon, opera in five acts after Edmond Rostand's nostalgic play about Napoleon's tubercular son, "the eaglet," with music by Arthur HONEGGER (Acts II, III, and IV) and Jacques IBERT (Acts I and V), written in a style midway between post-Wagnerian expansiveness and ante-Debussyan colorism, is produced at the Opera of Monte Carlo.

12 MARCH 1937

Charles-Marie WIDOR, Nestor of French music, last surviving pupil of Rossini, master organist, composer of operas, symphonies, and organ works, teacher of three generations of French composers, dies in Paris 19 days after his 93rd birthday.

18 MARCH 1937

Veselohrz na mostě, one-act opera by the prime Czech composer Bohuslav MARTINU, after an old Czech parable dealing with a group of civilians trapped on a bridge between two opposing armies, with the resulting stalemate giving an opportunity for social satire and amorous gunplay, is performed for the first time on the Prague radio. (The opera was performed with an English libretto under the title *Comedy on the Bridge*, at Hunter College in New York on 28 May 1951.)

19 MARCH 1937

Oedipus Rex, tragedy by Sophocles, with music arranged from works of the great Venetian madrigalist Andrea Gabrieli by Fernando LIUZZI (1884–1940), is performed for the first time in Sabratha, Libya, at the inauguration of the Teatro Romano, reconstructed from the ruins of an ancient Roman coliseum.

19 MARCH 1937

Second Symphony by the modernistic American composer Emerson WHITHORNE, is performed for the first time by the Cincinnati Symphony Orchestra, Eugene Goossens conducting.

24 MARCH 1937

Violin Concerto by the 21-year-old American composer David DIAMOND, written in a romantically flavored classical style, is performed for the first time in New York with Nicolai Berezowsky as soloist, the composer conducting.

28 MARCH 1937

Karol SZYMANOWSKI, "20th-century Chopin," whose music, written in the modern manner, employs with discrimination the valid devices of polyharmony and dissonant counterpoint while faithfully retaining the melorhythmic elements of ancestral Polish songs and dances, dies near Lausanne, Switzerland, at the age of 54.

1 APRIL 1937

Amelia Goes to the Ball, one-act opera-buffa by the 25-year-old Italian-born American composer Gian Carlo MENOTTI, to his own Italian libretto *Amelia al Ballo*, dealing with social tourbillions at the cotillions of Milan at the turn of the century, with a score written in a dynamically propulsive and expansively Italianate manner, is performed for the first time, in an English version, at the Philadelphia Academy of Music, Fritz Reiner conducting.

7 APRIL 1937

The Bleeding Heart of Timpanogos, Indian opera by the 50-year-old American composer William HANSON, to a libretto based on a legend that a stalactite in the shape of a human heart in a cave in Mount Timpanogos melts away in bloody tears at tragic moments in the lives of a local Indian tribe, is produced at Brigham Young University in Provo, Utah.

8 APRIL 1937

Arthur FOOTE, American composer of instrumental and vocal music of a fine-textured romantic quality, dies in Boston at the age of 84.

It is difficult to realize that Arthur Foote is no longer among us with his sunny smile and cheerful manner . . . He always made everyone happy and at case in his presence—the hallmark of a true gentleman. This broad humility appeared in his compositions which struck a note not likely to be duplicated. (Walter R. Spalding, in a letter published in the Boston *Evening Transcript,* 13 April 1937)

9 APRIL 1937

Five days before the 80th birthday of the American composer Edgar Stillman KELLEY, his symphony *Gulliver* traversing in its four movements Gulliver's first voyage, his visit to the land of Lilliput and his return, set to music in an unpretentious romantic manner, is performed for the first time by the Cincinnati Symphony Orchestra, Eugene Goossens conducting.

10 APRIL 1937

Algernon ASHTON, English composer of 24 elaborate string quartets in all 24 major and minor keys, known to the British public mainly as an inveterate writer of letters on every conceivable topic to the editors of London newspapers, with an especial fondness for the subject of neglected tombstones, dies in London at the age of 77.

10 APRIL 1937

Paul HINDEMITH makes his first appearance in America at the 8th Festival of Chamber Music given at the Library of Congress in Washington, under the auspices of the Elizabeth Sprague Coolidge Foundation playing his own *Sonata* for viola solo.

13 APRIL 1937

Music for strings in 1/6 tones and other fractional intervals by the Czech pioneer of microtonal composition Alois HÁBA and his pupils is presented in Prague by the modern music society *Pritomnost* (*The Present*).

14 APRIL 1937

Babes in Arms, musical comedy by Richard RODGERS, with book and lyrics by Lorenz Hart, dealing with a gang of abandoned children who make good as producers of adolescent ballets, the score including the perennially popular songs *My Funny Valentine* and *The Lady Is a Tramp*, as well as *Where or When* and *Johnny One-Note*, is produced in New York.

14 APRIL 1937

The Bleeding Heart of Timpanogos, opera in three acts by William F. HANSON, professor of music at Brigham Young University, Utah, dealing with the sacrifice of an Indian virgin made in order to induce the rain god Timpanogos to end the draught, momentarily delayed when the virgin's lover impersonates the god but is exposed and mortally wounded by the medicine woman of the tribe as the virgin leaps to her death from a high cliff and the rain begins to fall, the score teeming with Indian pentatonicisms and supernumerary whole-tone scales, is performed for the first time in Provo, Utah, conducted by the composer.

19 APRIL 1937

Five Incapacitated Preludes, a symphonic suite by the 35-year-old Canadian-born American Byron ARNOLD, is performed in Rochester, Howard Hanson conducting, with the following specifications:

(1) *For a One-Armed Man* (the conductor to lead with his left arm only); (2) *For a Blind Man* (to be conducted gropingly with arms extended full length); (3) *For a Cross-Eyed Man* (crossing the baton with the left arm); (4) *For a Deaf Man* (the players to simulate the motions of playing from the notes actually written out, without making any sounds); (5) *For a Lame Man* (the conductor being instructed to limp on the downbeat).

21 APRIL 1937

The Second Hurricane, school opera by Aaron COPLAND, designed for performance by boys and girls between the ages of 8 and 18, to a libretto dealing with a rescue team of high-school students flying in a chartered airplane to help victims of a hurricane in the Ohio Valley, who become stranded there themselves as a second hurricane strikes, so that another airplane has to be sent to bring them back, set to music with deceptive simplicity in abecedarian triadic harmonies fertilized by incisive asymmetric rhythms, is performed for the first time by a cast of 150 children at the Henry Street Music School in New York, Lehman Engel conducting.

24 APRIL 1937

La Morte di Frine, one-act opera, subtitled *Leggenda tragica*, by the 41-year-old Italian composer Lodovico ROCCA, to the legend of a famous courtesan Phryne, on trial in Athens for the profanation of Eleusinian mysteries, who presented her own defense by taking off her robe to show that her beauty was sufficient justification for her act, is performed for the first time on the stage of La Scala, Milan. (A radio performance of *La Morte di Frine* was given in Turin on 31 May 1936.)

27 APRIL 1937

Igor STRAVINSKY conducts at the Metropolitan Opera House in New York the world première of his ballet *Jeu de Cartes*, representing three deals of straight poker (of which Stravinsky is a devotee), with the situation complicated in each deal "by the endless guiles of the perfidious Joker who believes himself invincible because of his ability to become any desired card":

(1) First Deal: *Introduction, Pas d'action, Dance of the Joker, Little Waltz* (one player is out; two remain in the game, both holding straights); (2) Second Deal: *Introduction, March, Variations of the Four Queens, Variations of the Jack of Hearts and Coda, March and Ensemble* (three aces and a joker beat four queens); (3) Third Deal: *Introduction, Waltz-Minuet, Combat between Spades and Hearts, Triumph of the Hearts* (climactic gamble with each player holding a flush, culminating in a monumental duel in which the joker heading a straight in spades is defeated by a royal flush in hearts), each of the deals opening with a neo-baroque exordium, and the entire score possessing an elastic quality of eclectic classicism, containing latent quotations from Rossini, Delibes and Johann Strauss, all this vitalized by constant rhythmic mobility, at times suggesting the syncopation of early ragtime.

30 APRIL 1937

Uzeir GADZHIBEKOV, prime composer of Azerbaijan, conducts in Baku the first performance of his three-act opera *Kyor-Oglu* (*A Blind Man's Son*), dealing with a 17th-century uprising of the Tatar population in the region of the Caspian Sea against their Turkish overlord, the brutal perpetrator of the monstrous act of blinding Kyor-Oglu's father, set to music in a simple ethnic style, making use of the authentic pentatonic and chromatically angular folk tunes.

(The present date is verified by the original program and contemporary reviews in the Baku newspapers. The date 13 January 1937 given in the previous editions of *Music Since 1900* is erroneous.)

30 APRIL 1937

First Symphony by the 35-year-old English composer Edmund RUBBRA, in three classically contrasted movements—(1) *Allegro moderato e tempestoso*, written in a sharply dissonant emotionally charged style; (2) *Perigourdine*, a set of variations marked *Allegro bucolico e giocoso*, on a French tune taken from an old Paris anthology; (3) *Lento*, leading to a magistral fugue, and ending on a resonant coda—is performed for the first time in London.

6 MAY 1937

On the eve of the first anniversary of the proclamation by the Fascist government of the Italian Empire, *Il Deserto tentato*, opera in one act by Alfredo CASELLA, presenting a mystical interpretation of Mussolini's conquest of Ethiopia, is performed for the first time at the May Festival in Florence.

Il Deserto tentato is a mystery play in one act, in the manner of a secular oratorio in which both poet and composer have tried to invoke the Ethiopian war into a totally unreal arid mythical plane. . . . It exalts, in the elevated language of poetry, the humanitarian mission of a great nation in taking possession, thanks to the exploits of her aviators, of a barren desert, carrying to it the fruits of civilization it has been waiting for since time immemorial. The music, at least in appearance, is simple, monumental and severe, with important choruses. I should like to add that in my opinion this opera is my best work. (From Alfredo Casella's letter to the author, dated Rome, 1 June 1937)

7 MAY 1937

The Ordering of Moses, biblical oratorio by the Negro composer Robert Nathaniel DETT, is performed for the first time in Cincinnati.

The Moses here depicted is not the Moses familiarized to us by the other arts, especially by the work of Michelangelo, whose statue of the patriarch has become symbolic. At the time of this "ordering" Moses was a shepherd, undoubtedly a young man, which explains the part being assigned to a tenor voice. (Composer's foreword to the printed score)

9 MAY 1937

Crown Imperial, coronation march by William WALTON, inspired by William Dunbar's poem "In beawtie beryng the crone imperiall," marked *Allegro real* and set in a royally festive honi-soit-qui-mal-y-pense key of C major, is performed for the first time by the British Broadcasting Corporation in anticipation of the actual ceremony on the day of coronation of George VI, 12 May 1937, in Westminster Abbey, when the march was repeated.

12 MAY 1937

Walter DAMROSCH, 75-year-old German-born American conductor and composer, conducts at the Metropolitan Opera House in New York, where he made his debut as conductor 52 years before, the world première of his grand opera in two acts, *The Man without a Country*, to Edward Everett Hale's famous story of an American Navy lieutenant involved in Aaron Burr's imperial conspiracy, who insolently damns the United States, and is sent away on maritime exile on the high seas with an injunction to everyone in his entourage never to mention America in his presence, his redemption coming at last when he is allowed to participate in military action against the Berber pirates and is mortally wounded, while the feminine voice of a woman who took pity on him sings an unseen lullaby, in a commensurately emotional musical setting in a lushly Wagneromantic manner.

12 MAY 1937

At the end of the ceremonies in the coronation of King George VI and Queen Elizabeth of Great Britain, the first performance of the *Festival Te Deum*, specially written for the occasion by Ralph VAUGHAN WILLIAMS, is given in the Abbey Church of St. Peter Westminster in London.

20 MAY 1937

Third Symphony by the unappreciated but significant American composer John BECKER, subtitled *Symphonia Brevis*, is performed for the first time in Minneapolis.

23 MAY 1937

Lenox Avenue, symphonic musicorama of life in the Negro district of Harlem in New York, by the Negro composer William Grant STILL, is given its first performance in a radio broadcast by the Columbia Broadcasting System in New York.

24 MAY 1937

The International Society for Promoting Cooperation among Composers, created in 1933 under the presidency of Richard Strauss to replace the International Society for Contemporary Music from which Nazi Germany withdrew, opens a Music Festival of its own in Dresden, with works by hematologically unadulterated Aryan composers from 18 nations, among them Henk BADINGS of Holland, Hugo ALFVÉN of Sweden, Carl NIELSEN of Denmark, Paul GRAENER of Germany, Jón LEIFS of Iceland, Leevi MADETOJA of Finland, Božidar KUNC of Czechoslovakia, Joseph HAAS of Austria, Adriano LUALDI of Italy, Jean RIVIER of France, Béla BARTÓK of Hungary, and, by special dispensation, the half-Jewish half-German Pantcho VLADIGEROV of Bulgaria.

26 MAY 1937

Requiem by the Philadelphia-born composer Vittorio GIANNINI, written in memory of his mother, is given its first performance anywhere in Vienna, with the composer's sister Dusolina Giannini as soprano soloist.

30 MAY 1937

The Moscow State Radio broadcasts a special concert of salutatory music on a directional short wavelength for the Soviet polar party of scientists slowly floating on an ice floe in the vicinity of the North Pole.

2 JUNE 1937

Louis VIERNE, 66-year-old French master organist and composer of melodious and harmonious music for his instrument, collapses and dies while playing his *Stèle pour un enfant défunt* at Notre Dame de Paris, where he was organist since 1900.

2 JUNE 1937

Two acts and two fragments of the third act of Alban BERG's unfinished opera *Lulu*, to his own libretto after Frank Wedekind's macabre plays of rapine, perversion, lust and crime, *Erdgeist* and *Die Büchse der Pandora*, in which Lulu ends up in a London garret abdominally ripped by Jack the Ripper in 1889 to the accompaniment of an eviscerating dodecaphonic chord made up of minor seconds and perfect fourths, the music derived from a 12-tone matrix and yet allowing for liberal employment of tonality (Frank Wedekind's own folk-like tune in C major is used as a theme for a set of variations) and of uniform chromatic progressions (Lulu kills her third husband by five consecutive bullets on the ascending chromatic scale, C-sharp, D, E-flat, E and F), the entire score being cast in ostentatiously classical forms (Sonata, Rondo, Variations), with the central Ostinato, marked *Filmmusik*, forming a strict cancrizans outlining Lulu's arrest and imprisonment and, in the retrograde section, her escape, are given for the first time in Zürich, Switzerland. (A symphonic suite for *Lulu* was first performed in Berlin prior to the stage production, on 30 November 1934.)

5 JUNE 1937

The British Broadcasting Corporation gives the first successful demonstration of televising opera, transmitting the entire third act of Gounod's *Faust* to a television receiver in its London studio.

This was not a special television production but rather a presentation by television of a regular performance. The first opera to be televised in its entirety was *La Serva Padrona* by Pergolesi on 23 December 1937. In the case of *Hänsel und Gretel*, the experiment was tried for the first time with two casts. The singers were not seen, the acting casts were silent, and their movements consisted largely of miming specially devised for the music of the opera. The next special television production, again with two casts, was Act II of *Tristan* on 25 January 1938. (From a letter to the author from the Assistant Director of Television of the BBC)

5 JUNE 1937

W. J. HENDERSON, American "reporter with a specialty, music," as he liked to style himself, commits suicide in New York at the age of 81, by shooting himself in the mouth with his old 38-caliber army pistol which he carried as a soldier in the Spanish-American war of 1898.

8 JUNE 1937

Carmina Burana for soloists, choruses, orchestra and a battery of percussion by the 41-year-old German composer Carl ORFF, the first of a trilogy of "scenic cantatas" under the collective title *Trionfi*, with the Latin subtitle, *Cantiones profanae cantoribus et choris cantandae comitantibus instrumentis atque imaginibus magicis*, to the texts in vulgar Latin, French and Bavarian dialects in a macaronic linguistic mixture, drawn from a book of ribald medieval student songs discovered in 1803 at the Bavarian monastery of Benediktbeuren (the adjective Burana is from the Latin name of the town), in three parts relating to springtime, drinking and love, set to music in an amalgam of heterogeneous neo-medieval, ecclesiastical, ethnic and popular melodic and rhythmic elements, accou-

tred in bland modalities and marked by a hypnotically repetitive asymmetrical cantillation alternating with monometrical ululation and syncopated hockets, is performed for the first time in Frankfurt.

8 JUNE 1937

Jeanne d'Arc, "symphonie concertante" for soprano and orchestra by Maurice JAUBERT, 37-year-old French composer fated to be killed in combat on 19 June 1940, in three parts depicting three principal stages of Joan's life—*Domrémy, Les Batailles, Rouen*— set to music in a severely reverential idiom in which the voice assumes the role of a chronicler, is performed for the first time in Paris.

8 JUNE 1937

Georges ENESCO, prime composer of Rumania, conducts in Paris a concert of Rumanian symphonic music, including the first performance of *Caprice roumain* by the Parisianized Rumanian composer Marcel MIHALOVICI.

10 JUNE 1937

Georges ENESCO conducts in Paris a second concert of Rumanian symphonic music, including the first performance of an elegantly proportioned *Divertissement* by the precocious 20-year-old Rumanian pianist Dinu LIPATTI.

12 JUNE 1937

MANETO (acronym for Manifestatie Van Nederlandsche Tookunst), organized in Holland as the "manifestation of Netherlandish tonal art," presents in Amsterdam its first concert of Dutch music featuring works by Johan WAGENAAR, Henk BADINGS, Bertus van LIER and Guillaume LANDRÉ.

12 JUNE 1937

The German Tonkünstler Verein, founded by Liszt, is dissolved after its 68th Annual Music Festival held in Darmstadt and Frankfurt, in silent protest against the imposition of the doctrine of *Gleichschaltung* by the Nazi Ministry of Propaganda leveling all musical activities to the arbitrary norms of racist nationalism.

15 JUNE 1937

Checkmate, dramatic ballet in one scene and prologue by the English composer Arthur BLISS, to his own scenario suggesting the Vienna opening of the chess game, in six moves, Dance of the Four Knights, Entry of the Black Queen, The Red Knight, Ceremony of the Red Bishops, Death of the Red Knight and Checkmate, and set in a lyrico-dramatic neo-Baroque idiom, is produced in Paris by the visiting opera and ballet company of Sadler's Wells of London.

16 JUNE 1937

Tá Mar, opera by the Portuguese composer Ruy COELHO, is produced in Lisbon. The title *Tá Mar* is a dialect expression used by Portuguese fishermen in Estremadura for "O mare esta bravo" (the sea is rising).

16 JUNE 1937

The Cradle Will Rock, proletarian opera in two acts by Marc BLITZSTEIN, to his own libretto, picturing class warfare between a rapacious capitalist Mr. Mister and a group of workers trying to organize a union in Steeltown, U.S.A., the score consisting of a series of vernacular ballads, such as *Croon-Spoon*, or *The Nickel under the Foot*, is given its first performance in New York in a makeshift production, without scenery or costumes, with Blitzstein himself at the piano and singers stationed in the hall, to circumvent the ban imposed by the Federal Theater, branch of the Works Progress Administration, on account of the radical nature of the play. (It was finally presented as an opera in a Broadway theater in New York on 27 December 1947, and later by the New York City Opera, on 11 February 1960.)

17 JUNE 1937

Emek (*The Valley*), symphonic poem by the 33-year-old Latvian-born Palestinian composer Marc LAVRY, descriptive of pioneer work in cultivating the agricultural resources of the Jezreel Valley in the Gilboa Mountains, in the form of variations on an authentic Emek folksong, culminating in an agitated Hora dance, is performed for the first time in Tel-Aviv.

20 JUNE 1937

Walter PISTON conducts the first performance, broadcast from New York over the CBS network, of his *Concertino* for piano and chamber orchestra, "an adventure of a musical idea," as he characterized it in his introductory speech.

21 JUNE 1937

Dreadnaught Potemkin, realistic opera in four acts by the Soviet composer Oles TCHISHKO, to a libretto from the historical naval mutiny during the abortive Russian revolution of 1905, containing such naturalistic lines as "Our borsht is full of vermin," set to music according to the Soviet doctrine of Socialist Realism, in broad Russian harmonies, is performed for the first time in Leningrad. (An amplified version, with a sharpened political point, in which the part of a wily Menshevik has been introduced into the libretto, was produced in Leningrad on 30 December 1955.)

21 JUNE 1937

The 15th Festival of the International Society for Contemporary Music opens in conjunction with the Paris Exposition of 1937, presenting the following program of chamber music:

Second String Quartet by Arthur HONEGGER; *La voix de Yamato* for soprano, two flutes, clarinet, bassoon and cello by the Japanese woman composer Michigo TOYAMA; *Nonet* by the young Czech composer Karel REINER; *Duo* for flute and clarinet by the Catalan composer Joaquín HOMS; *Morceau de Concert* for cello and piano by the English leftist composer Alan BUSH, calculated to secure compositional accessibility of its idioms; and *Suite en Rocaille* for flute, violin, viola, cello and harp in an elegant rococo style by the dean of French modernists, Florent SCHMITT.

22 JUNE 1937

At the second concert of the 15th Festival of the International Society for Contemporary Music in Paris, the following program of orchestral music is presented:

Symphonie Concertante by Karol SZYMANOWSKI of Poland (his fourth symphony) for piano and orchestra, written in an opulent quasi-impressionistic manner (it was first performed in Poznan on 9 October 1932); *Concerto for Orchestra* in a vigorous neo-classical idiom by the Soviet composer Mikhail STAROKADOMSKY; *Fantasy* for string orchestra by Norbert von HANNENHEIM, who represented Republican Germany at the Vienna Festival of 1932, but changed his allegiance to Rumania after the Nazification of German music; *Second Violin Concerto* by the young Polish neo-classicist Jerzy FITELBERG, conducted by his father Gregor Fitelberg; *Hommage à Babeuf* for wind instruments and percussion by the Belgian modernist André SOURIS; *Symphonie Concertante* by the Swedish neo-romantic composer Hilding ROSENBERG; and *Second Symphony*, subtitled *Elegiaca*, in four movements, by Gian Francesco MALIPIERO.

23 JUNE 1937

At the third concert of the 15th Festival of the International Society for Contemporary Music in Paris, the band of the Garde Républicaine de Paris presents a concert with the following program:

Prélude from the *Suite in F* by Albert ROUSSEL, written in a neo-classical Gallic manner, in which clarity and logic are paramount; *Canción y Movimiento* by the Spanish composer Ernesto LOVREGLIO; *Gulliver au pays de Lilliput*, a Swiftian intermezzo by Gabriel PIERNIÉ; and *Chorale and March* by the foremost master of Italian modern music Alfredo CASELLA.

24 JUNE 1937

Don Juan de Mañara, second opera by Eugene GOOSSENS, in four acts, after Arnold Bennett's story dealing with the 17th-century sensualist Miguel de Mañara to whom "the alcove was the altar," composed in an eminently cohesive modernistic idiom with some naturalistic touches (Don Juan's sexual excitement is illustrated by asymmetrical staccato beats), is produced in London.

24 JUNE 1937

At the fourth concert of the 15th Festival of the International Society for Contemporary Music in Paris, the following program of chamber music is given:

Second String Quartet by the Hungarian composer Sándor VERESS; *Ninth String Quartet* by Darius MILHAUD; *Four Melodies* by the Austrian atonalist Hans Erich APOSTEL; *Trio* for piano, violin and cello by the Dutch neo-classicist Henk BADINGS. (*Two Pieces* for clarinet and piano by the German composer Peter SCHACHT were scheduled for performance on this program, but withdrawn at the last moment by the composer in deference to the official opposition by the Nazi Ministry of Propaganda to the International Society for Contemporary Music.)

25 JUNE 1937

At the fifth concert of the 15th Festival of the International Society for Contemporary Music in Paris, the following program of orchestral music is presented:

Overture from the opera *Nova Zeme* (*New Land*) by the Czech modernist Alois HÁBA, a political music drama expressing unlimited faith in the ability of collective labor to build a happy future, with the injection of fragments of the *Internationale; Concerto* for piano and orchestra by the *jeune français* Jean FRANÇAIX, written in the newly fashionable style of neo-classical mannerism; *Passacaglia* by Juan Carlos PAZ of Argentina, written in the 12-tone technique; two movements from *German Symphony* by Hanns EISLER, a politically and musically radical disciple of Schoenberg; *Concerto* for string quartet and orchestra by the Catalan composer Josep VALLS; and *Toccata* by the Serbian neo-classical composer Demetrij ZEBRE.

25 JUNE 1937

La Samaritaine, lyric drama by Max d'OLLONE, depicting in three tableaux the meeting of Christ with the Samaritan woman at the well, composed in an orthodox style, with some orientally serpentine melodies for local color, is produced at the Paris Opéra.

26 JUNE 1937

The 15th Festival of the International Society for Contemporary Music closes with its sixth concert, presenting the following program of chamber music:

Second String Quartet by Elizabeth MACONCHY of England, written in an advanced modernistic idiom tending towards integral atonality; *Grimaces rythmiques* for piano by the Serbian impressionist Miloje MILOJEVIĆ, written with considerable Parisian verve; *Musica per tre pianoforti*, hymns with the motto "Il paradiso è all'ombra delle spade," by the 33-year-old Italian modernist Luigi DALLAPICCOLA; and *Divertimento* for chamber orchestra by the Swedish neo-classicist Lars-Erik LARSSON.

1 JULY 1937

Scaramouche, suite for two pianos by Darius MILHAUD, in three movements, *Vif*, *Modéré* and *Brasileira*, abounding in tropical melorhythms set in bitonal harmonies, is performed for the first time in Paris.

5 JULY 1937

Piano Concerto by the 34-year-old Soviet Armenian composer Aram KHACHATURIAN, in three movements, *Allegro ma non troppo e maestoso*, *Andante con anima* and *Allegro brillante*, abounding in quasi-oriental melismatic adornments and sonorous cadenzas of an improvisatory nature, set in acrid harmonies of major and minor seconds, and ending with a triumphant Caucasian dance, is performed for the first time in Leningrad.

11 JULY 1937

George GERSHWIN, American genius of jazz, whose epoch-making *Rhapsody in Blue*, written at the age of 24, has become an American classic, whose folk opera *Porgy and Bess* has set a new mark in the American musical theater, whose songs embody with piercing vividness the sadness and gladness of the American scene and whose polyrhythmic syncopation has caught the American musical pulse beat, dies in Hollywood at 10:35 A.M., following an operation on a cystic brain tumor, at the age of 38.

Music was to George Gershwin not a mere matter of ability. It was the air he breathed, the dream he dreamed. I grieve over the deplorable loss of music, for there is no doubt that he was a great composer. (Arnold Schoenberg in a radio broadcast from Hollywood at the Gershwin memorial service at 9 P.M. on 12 July 1937)

17 JULY 1937

Mekhano, mechanical ballet by the modern Argentinian composer Juan José CASTRO, featuring a dance of the hammer, a dance of seduction, and a realistic transfusion of blood to a robot (illustrated by runs of whole-tone scales), is produced at the Teatro Colón in Buenos Aires, conducted by the composer.

17 JULY 1937

Gabriel PIERNIÉ, French composer of elegant music in various genres, distinguished also as an opera conductor, dies in Ploujean, Brittany, at the age of 73.

25 JULY 1937

Music for Radio by Aaron COPLAND is performed for the first time as a commissioned work by the Columbia Broadcasting System Orchestra. (A national contest for a descriptive title of *Music for Radio* was held after the initial performance, and *Saga of the Prairie* was selected as the most fitting title, reflecting the melodic expansiveness, metrical tranquility and triadic resonance of the music.)

27 JULY 1937

Igor STRAVINSKY is awarded by a Paris tribunal the token sum of one French franc in compensation for the "moral damage" sustained by him through the illicit use of his music in Warner Brothers' motion picture *The Firebird*, in which a virtuous girl is systematically ruined by a roué while under the aphrodisiac influence of the playing of a phonograph recording of the syncopated pagan dance of the immund teratological creatures from the finale of Stravinsky's ballet of the same title.

"Mais, Monsieur Stravinsky c'est le plus grand compliment du monde pour un compositeur!" (Purported comment by the Paris judge on the moral issue involved in the use of Stravinsky's music as an instrument of seduction)

The musician Stravinsky claimed damages of 300,000 francs from a motion picture company which has incorporated in its film *The Firebird* a few musical fragments taken from Stravinsky's ballet of that name. Among the various complaints in the suit only one was considered valid by the Tribunal de la Seine, namely that Stravinsky's music was preceded without explanation by a Viennese waltz. The judge found in this a regrettable incomprehension of the music by a great artist and adjudged to him the damages for the sum of one French franc as a mark of their disapproval. (Tribunal Civil de la Seine, 27 July 1937, Stravinsky v. Société Warner Bros., reproduced in *La Semaine juridique*, Paris, 1937, p. 392) (The date 3 February 1938, given in the previous editions of *Music Since 1900*, is erroneous, taken from a delayed report in the American press.)

1 AUGUST 1937

Anti-Fascist Symphony for orchestra, chorus and military band by 28-year-old Soviet composer Boris MOKROUSOV, a sharp symphonic warning to the Nazis and

Fascists not to underestimate the musical and military strength of the Soviet Union, counterposing in the score a powerful expansion of Russian folksong modalities to the mechanical themes of the Nazi machine, is performed for the first time in Moscow, less than four years before the Hitlerized hordes moved madly into Russia.

17 AUGUST 1937

A *London Overture* by John IRELAND, with a rhythmic motto inspired by a bus conductor's cry "Piccadilly!" and containing other topical allusions to the melodious turmoil of London streets, set to music in an unpretentiously harmonious manner, is performed for the first time at the Promenade Concerts in London, Sir Henry Wood conducting.

23 AUGUST 1937

The Works Progress Administration announces in Washington that the Federal Music Project under its aegis gave 4,360 musical presentations for audiences aggregating to 4,346,705 listeners during the month of July 1937, and that the highest monthly attendance was reached in August 1936 with a total of 6,178,093 listeners.

23 AUGUST 1937

Albert ROUSSEL, French master composer of nobly conceived and expertly realized instrumental and vocal works, whose early evocations of the Orient where he travelled as a marine officer and his symphonies set in classical forms have contributed to the formation of a peculiarly identifiable modern French style of composition, in which elements of impressionism, romanticism and neo-classicism coalesce in a fine synthesis, dies in Royan at the age of 68.

On 28 July 1937 Albert Roussel went to Royan in quest of much needed rest. On 13 August he was compelled to take to bed, interrupting the composition of his Trio for oboe, clarinet and bassoon. Of this Trio, only the middle section was completed; it is a stirring swan song. He bore valiantly the terrible suffering caused by a heart attack. On Monday, 23 August 1937, shortly before 4 o'clock in the afternoon, the great composer died. (Arthur Hoérée, *Albert Roussel,* Paris, 1938)

27 AUGUST 1937

El Salón Mexico, symphonic sketch by Aaron COPLAND named after a popular night club in Mexico City, thematically based on authentic Mexican ballads and dance tunes set in astute juxtaposition, with apocopated melorhythms emphasizing the polymetric nature of Mexican folk music, unobtrusively harmonized and orchestrated with congenial economic coloration, is performed for the first time by the Orquesta Sinfónica de Mexico, Carlos Chávez conducting.

6 SEPTEMBER 1937

Henry HADLEY, American composer of operas and symphonies, on programmatic subjects of geographical categories, ranging from the state of Connecticut to the deep Orient depicted in median Germanized harmonies, conductor of various orchestras, including a term with the New York Philharmonic, dies in New York at the age of 65.

8 SEPTEMBER 1937

Mizú, operetta by the Brazilian composer Francisco MIGNONE, is produced in Rio de Janeiro.

9 SEPTEMBER 1937

Maria d'Alessandria, opera in three acts by the 45-year-old Italian composer Georgio Federico GHEDINI, centered on a historically authentic demi-vierge of Alexandria, Egypt, whose perverse delight was to inflame dark passions in the guarded groins of minifutuent pilgrims passing through on their way to the Holy Land, but who repented in holy horror after a monk corrupted by her was struck down by a punitive bolt of lightning, is produced in Bergamo.

12 SEPTEMBER 1937

Partisan Days, ballet in three acts by the Russian music scholar and imitative composer Boris ASAFIEV, dealing with the civil war in the Caucasus in 1919–1920, centering on the heroism of a Bolshevik girl guerrilla captured by a squad of White Army officers, is produced in Leningrad.

12 SEPTEMBER 1937

Darius MILHAUD conducts in Venice the first performance of his *Suite Provençale,* a tasteful symphonic confection of Mediterranean melorhythms in a bouillabaisse of spicy bitonalities.

14 SEPTEMBER 1937

The Marriage, unfinished comic opera by MUSSORGSKY, completed and orchestrated by Alexander TCHEREPNIN, is performed for the first time in this version in Essen, Germany.

19 SEPTEMBER 1937

Yanina's Nine Brothers, opera in four acts by the Bulgarian composer Lubomir PIPKOV, to a libretto from Bulgarian rustic life, abounding in asymmetric dancing rhythms of Balkan folkways in a euphonious solution of nutritious triadic harmonies, is produced in Sofia.

19 SEPTEMBER 1937

Howard HANSON conducts the orchestra of the Columbia Broadcasting System in New York in the first performance of three movements—(1) *Andante lamentando-Agitato,* (2) *Andante tranquillo,* (3) *Tempo scherzando* (without the finale)—of his *Third Symphony,* written in commemoration of the 300th anniversary of the first Swedish settlement on the shores of Delaware in 1638, and conceived as a tribute to the epic qualities of the Swedish pioneers in America (of which Hanson himself was a descendant), with their "rugged and turbulent character alternating with a religious mysticism." (The Finale, *Largamente e pesante,* was added to the symphony later, and the work was performed in its entirety in a broadcast of the NBC Symphony Orchestra on 26 March 1938, the composer conducting. First concert performance was conducted by Hanson with the Boston Symphony Orchestra on 3 November 1939.)

22 SEPTEMBER 1937

Silvestre REVUELTAS, Mexican composer of impassioned music in which his innate Mexicanism harmonizes with the modern techniques of polyharmony and polyrhythmy, conducts in Madrid, under siege by the Franco forces, his orchestral *Homenaje a Federico García Lorca*, an homage to the great Spanish poet executed by the Falangists.

26 SEPTEMBER 1937

Refused admission to a white hospital after being gravely injured in an automobile accident, Bessie SMITH, the greatest of blues singers, dies in Clarksville, Mississippi, before the arrival of a properly segregated Negritudinal ambulance.

1 OCTOBER 1937

Eighteenth Symphony by the prime Soviet symphonist Nicolai MIASKOVSKY, in three movements, *Allegro*, *Lento* and *Allegro giocoso*, written for the celebration of the 20th anniversary of the October Revolution, and completed during the night of 7–8 September 1937, set in the optimistic and socially realistic key of C major, with thematic material derived from the intervalic and rhythmic elements of national Russian songs and dances, is performed for the first time in Moscow, nearly three months before the first performance of Miaskovsky's earlier *Seventeenth Symphony*.

1 OCTOBER 1937

Orači (Harvesters), "symphonic meditation" by the Croatian composer Jacov GOTOVAC, is performed for the first time in Zagreb.

6 OCTOBER 1937

In Honour of the City of London for chorus and orchestra by William WALTON, set in variation form, to the words of William Dunbar, is performed for the first time at the Leeds Festival.

7 OCTOBER 1937

The Society of Recorder Players is incorporated in London, England, with the purpose to revive the vertical flute of the Renaissance, with Arnold DOLMETSCH, inventor of the modern recorder, as president, and his son Carl as musical director.

17 OCTOBER 1937

Green Mansions, "non-visual radio opera" by the American composer Louis GRUENBERG, after a novel of the same name by W. H. Hudson, dealing with a South American explorer whose malarial hallucinations include the voice of a jungle girl calling to him in the language of the birds (her voice is represented by a solo on the musical saw, the first such use in an opera), as well as the voices of trees, insects and the hisses of snakes, is performed for the first time over the Columbia Broadcasting System in New York.

23 OCTOBER 1937

Soil Upturned, second opera, in four acts, by the 28-year-old Soviet composer Ivan DZERZHINSKY, a sequel to his first opera *Quiet Flows the Don*, after the epic novel by Mikhail Sholokhov, depicting in sonorously moving modalities the roaring rural rumbles during the collectivization of agriculture in the Don basin in 1930, is performed for the first time at the Bolshoi Theater in Moscow.

25 OCTOBER 1937

Italy issues two postage stamps in honor of PERGOLESI, at 30 and 75 centesimi, and two stamps in honor of SPONTINI, at 10 centesimi and 1 lire 75 centesimi.

27 OCTOBER 1937

Third Symphony by Bernard ROGERS, the American composer, set in four contrasting movements, is performed for the first time in Rochester, Howard Hanson conducting.

1 NOVEMBER 1937

The Central Committee on Arts of the Council of People's Commissars of the Union of Soviet Socialist Republics issues a tabulation of fees to be paid to concert artists, ranging from 50 to 600 rubles per concert according to four categories of merit.

2 NOVEMBER 1937

I'd Rather Be Right, musical comedy by Richard RODGERS, in which a couple cannot afford to marry until the national budget is balanced and the groom receives a salary raise, is produced in New York.

4 NOVEMBER 1937

First Symphony in A minor by the 24-year-old American composer Gardner READ, set in four movements in cyclic relationship, wherein the three principal themes explicitly stated in the first movement are restated by virtually every instrument, with an ending on a chord of muted cellos and basses in the low register, is performed for the first time by the New York Philharmonic, John Barbirolli conducting, as the winner of a $1000 prize of the New York Philharmonic Society.

4 NOVEMBER 1937

After many a weary month of research, international correspondence and painful collation of divergent data culled from purportedly authoritative reference works, the first edition of *Music Since 1900* by Nicolas SLONIMSKY, a chronological panorama of musical events since the turn of the century, is published in New York by W. W. Norton Co.

6 NOVEMBER 1937

Il Festino, comic opera in one act by Gian Francesco MALIPIERO, is performed for the first time in concert form over the Turin Radio.

15 NOVEMBER 1937

Das Opfer (The Sacrifice), opera in three acts by the 32-year-old German composer Winfried ZILLIG, depicting the tragic Antarctic expedition of 1912, is produced in Hamburg.

17 NOVEMBER 1937

A *Lincoln Symphony* by Daniel Gregory MASON, dean of American academic symphonists, set in four musico-biographic movements, in the historiosophic key of B-flat major unified by a stolid fugue—(1) *The Candidate from Springfield*, in syncopated quadrille tempo; (2) *Massa Linkum*, a Negro lament voiced by the English horn; (3) *Old Abe's Yarns*, in playful waltz time; (4) *1865, Lento serioso*, in *tempo di marcia funebre*, in the key of Chopin's funeral march, B-flat minor, ending with a memorial trumpet fanfare—is performed for the first time by the New York Philharmonic, John Barbirolli conducting.

18 NOVEMBER 1937

Violin Concerto by the American composer John Alden CARPENTER, in a single movement articulated into several contrasting sections, couched in a conventional style of instrumental writing, with occasional excursions into modernistic bitonalities, and ending on a naked tritone, is performed for the first time by the Chicago Symphony Orchestra, Zlatko Baloković soloist.

This is the Concerto of a gentleman. (Oscar Thompson, New York *Sun*, 10 March 1939)

18 NOVEMBER 1937

Wallenstein, fourth opera by the Czech composer Jaromir WEINBERGER, in six episodes, after Schiller's play, focused on the dramatic career of Wallenstein, the valiant Austrian general assassinated in 1634 during the Thirty Years' War, and dedicated to the Austrian Chancellor Schuschnigg, in allegorical reference to his continued resistance to the encroaching Nazis, is produced in Vienna in a German version translated from the original Czech libretto.

21 NOVEMBER 1937

The Leningrad Philharmonic presents the first performance of the *Fifth Symphony* by Dmitri SHOSTAKOVICH, his first publicly performed work after the denunciation of his music by *Pravda* on 28 January 1936, approved in advance by the Union of Soviet Composers and sanctioned by Soviet spokesmen as a sincere manifestation of his redemption in the spirit of Socialist Realism, set, as most of his symphonies, in four classically disposed movements:

(1) *Moderato*, opening with majestic Beethoven-like tones, and then embarking on a vibrantly agitated *Allegro non troppo*, in steady 4/4 time, reverting to a slower tempo for a soft ending in D minor; (2) *Allegretto*, a vivaciously dissonant scherzo, with constant shifts of tonal epicenters, and stentorian trumpets proclaiming an optimistic credo; (3) *Largo*, a dramatic soliloquy, dynamically ranging from expressive pianissimo to grandiloquent fortissississimo, concluding on a moribundly muted F-sharp major chord; (4) *Allegro non troppo*, a triumphant peroration on a determined course culminating in a magistral coda, with the brass blaring blatant D major fanfares against 251 eighth-notes on the dominant A in the high strings and woodwinds.

The subject of my *Fifth Symphony* is the evolution of an individual. The music is conceived in a lyrical vein. The finale resolves on an optimistic plane the tragic tension of the first three movements. The question is sometimes asked whether tragedy should have a place in Soviet art at all; but tragedy is not to be confused with hopelessness and pessimism. It is my belief that Soviet tragedy is entirely valid as a genre. But its essence must be suffused with a positive ideal, as in the life-asserting pathos of Shakespeare's tragic plays. (From Shostakovich's statement *My Creative Reply*, published in *Vetchernaya Moskva*, Moscow, 25 January 1938)

Shostakovich's *Fifth Symphony* consists of four movements, each presenting a clear formulation of psychological moods. At the same time, the work is an artistic monolith. . . . There is a feeling of joy, of happiness bubbling in the orchestra, and spreading throughout the concert hall like a spring breeze. The audience feels the sense of gratitude to the composer whose music has the sound of truth. The Soviet listener rejects decadent, somber or pessimistic art, but he responds enthusiastically to joyful, optimistic, self-asserting artistic declarations. The artistic optimism of Shostakovich's *Fifth Symphony* was communicated to and unreservedly accepted by the public. (Alexei Tolstoy in *Izvestia*, Moscow, 23 November 1937)

24 NOVEMBER 1937

Tobias Wunderlich, opera in three acts by the 58-year-old German composer Joseph HAAS, dealing with a Bavarian cobbler and town councilman who refuses to agree to the sale of a wooden church figurine of Santa Barbara to an American tourist for half a million dollars, and is rewarded for his devotion when the Gothic saint descends from her wall and offers her services to him as a Mädchen für alles, gets back on the wall when he incautiously reveals her identity to the council, but returns to his household to alleviate his sincere distress while the American millionaire assuages his financial troubles by an annual order of 10,000 wooden shoes, set to music in Regeromantic harmonies with an infusion of pietetic modalities and dietetic dissonances, is produced in Kassel.

26 NOVEMBER 1937

Three days after the 75th birthday of the dean of Argentinian composers Alberto WILLIAMS, whose English patronymic was derived from his grandfather Benjamin Williams of Exeter, England, a concert of his works, including the first performances of his *Sixth Symphony*, surnamed *Death of the Comet* and *Seventh Symphony, Eternal Repose*, written in an expansive romantic style, marked by sonorous chromaticism redolent of the mannerisms of César Franck who was his teacher, is presented in Buenos Aires.

26 NOVEMBER 1937

Schumann's *Violin Concerto*, written by him between 21 September and 3 October 1853, as he was struggling against the Stygian darkness of mental disease, unperformed hereto because of the stipulation in the will of the violinist Joseph Joachim, who owned the manuscript, barring its performance before the expiration of 100 years after Schumann's death, is brought to performance in Berlin 19 years in advance of that centennial term.

Before the performance of Schumann's *Violin Concerto* takes place, a remarkable book will have been published and reviewed, *Horizons of Immortality* by Baron Erik Palmstierna. The last pages of this book contain a detailed account of spirit messages that have been conveyed to Miss Jelly d'Aranyi expressing Schumann's personal wish that this Concerto should be produced. . . . I assert my positive conviction that the spirit of Schumann is inspiring Jelly d'Aranyi's production of Schumann's posthumous *Violin Concerto*. (Donald Tovey in a letter to the London *Times*, 24 September 1937. But Schumann's spirit, which spoke to his communicant in a peculiarly ungrammatical German, had apparently failed to impress the Nazis, and the revival of the concerto was entrusted not to Jelly d'Aranyi but to an obscure violinist, a member of the Nazi Party.)

27 NOVEMBER 1937

Vikings by the 53-year-old Belgian composer Arthur MEULEMANS, to a libretto in the Flemish language, is performed for the first time in Antwerp.

30 NOVEMBER 1937

Riders to the Sea, one-act opera by Ralph VAUGHAN WILLIAMS, to a play by J. M. Synge, depicting the recurrent tragedies of seamen lost off the coast of Ireland, set in recitative following natural inflections of normal human speech, economically harmonized, but resorting, when dramatically expedient, to harsh bitonalities, with the inclusion of a wordless female chorus, is produced in London.

3 DECEMBER 1937

Third Symphony in G major by Edward Burlingame HILL, in three movements, completed on 19 February 1937, "with no descriptive background, but aiming merely to present musical ideas according to the traditional forms," is performed for the first time by the Boston Symphony Orchestra under the direction of Serge Koussevitzky.

6 DECEMBER 1937

Concertante Musik for orchestra by the China-born Russo-Estonian composer Boris BLACHER, domiciled in Berlin, written in an economic polyphonic idiom with strong asymmetrical rhythmic beats, is performed for the first time in Berlin.

16 DECEMBER 1937

Lambeth Walk, jaunty cockney dance in which the participants are instructed to slap their knees, point thumbs over their shoulders while loudly shouting "Hoy!" and strut in an uninhibited manner of the lower classes of society, makes its sensational appearance in the London musical comedy *Me and My Girl*, with the score by Noel GAY. (1,065 performances were given in a continuous run until 2 September 1939 when all London theaters were closed at the outbreak of World War II.)

17 DECEMBER 1937

Vodník (Water Spirit), opera in three acts by the Czech composer Boleslav VOMÁČKA, to the popular legend about a man from the river who lures a village girl to his watery domain, allows her to come up to the dry surface for a visit, and kills their submarine child when she refuses to rejoin him, set to music in the manner of Smetana, with realistic Czech tunes and folk rhythms, is produced in Prague.

17 DECEMBER 1937

Seventeenth Symphony by Nicolai MIASKOVSKY, in the mournful tonality of G-sharp minor (completed on 25 June 1937), set in the orthodox four movements in contrasting moods, is performed for the first time in Moscow, several weeks after the première of his *Eighteenth Symphony*, given on 1 October 1937.

18 DECEMBER 1937

Two centuries have passed since the death in Cremona, at the age of 92, of the mirific reifier of ideal violins, Antonio STRADIVARI.

18 DECEMBER 1937

An exhibition of 39 paintings by George GERSHWIN opens in New York.

George had a way of regarding his painting and music as almost interchangeable phenomena. They sprang, he felt, from the same Freudian elements in him—one emerging as sight, the other as sound. . . . There were, indeed, periods when the palette almost weaned him from the piano; when he willingly stopped composing to paint, and only grudgingly stopped painting to compose. (From the introductory article by Frank Crowningshield in the catalogue of the Gershwin Memorial Exhibition)

19 DECEMBER 1937

Forty-eight representative American composers assemble in New York with the purpose of establishing the new protective organization, American Composers' Alliance, protecting the performing rights of composers who are not members of the American Society of Composers, Authors and Publishers.

19 DECEMBER 1937

Second Symphony by the 42-year-old American composer William Grant STILL is performed for the first time by the Philadelphia Orchestra under the direction of Leopold Stokowski.

21 DECEMBER 1937

A Boy Was Born, choral set of six variations by the 24-year-old English composer Benjamin BRITTEN, is broadcast for the first time by the British Broadcasting Corporation in London.

21 DECEMBER 1937

The German *Reichsmusikkammer* forms a board of examiners to weed out phonograph recordings made wholly or partly by Jewish and Negro musicians in order to protect the racial purity and mental integrity of true Aryans in the Nazi Reich.

25 DECEMBER 1937

The first concert of the newly formed National Broadcasting Company Symphony Orchestra, with Arturo

TOSCANINI as music director, is broadcast by the National Broadcasting Company in New York.

28 DECEMBER 1937

Transatlantic radio transmission of a musical score is successfully made when, in consequence of the loss in the mails of the string parts of *Origin of Fire* by SIBELIUS, scheduled for performance by the Boston Symphony Orchestra, its management arranges with Breitkopf and Härtel, publishers, to transmit the missing parts from Leipzig by radio photo.

28 DECEMBER 1937

Maurice RAVEL, great French composer, supreme artificer of tonal art whose masterly precision in handling exquisitely molded melodies and fine-textured impressionistic harmonies has created a magic world of translucently oscillating rhythmic images suffused with the prismatic light of instrumental coloration, described in the citation of the honorary degree of Doctor of Music conferred upon him by the Oxford University as "Musarum interpretes modorum daedalus Mauritius Ravellus," dies in Paris at the age of sixty-two, nine days after brain surgery made necessary by an acute state of apraxia and dysphasia.

The perfection of Ravel's art may be likened to that of Chopin, Mozart or Bach. Ravel recalls particularly the composer of *Le Nozze di Figaro* by his astounding combination of a child's simplicity of soul with a musical technique of such completeness that it would be no exaggeration to call it magical. (Alfredo Casella in the memorial Ravel issue of *La Revue Musicale*, Paris, December 1938)

From the political and cultural standpoint, Hungary has for centuries suffered from the immediate proximity of Germany. But young Hungarian musicians since the turn of this century have been directing themselves towards the culture of France. And that is the reason, from our Hungarian point of view, that the genius of Ravel, along with that of Debussy, has such significance for us. (Béla Bartók; *ibidem*)

Maurice Ravel was one of those rare creative artists who possessed the power of revolutionizing the very foundations of his art while remaining faithful to its immutable laws. . . . Among the many reasons for our admiration for Ravel in Greece, that makes his memory sacred, is that one of our best composers, Emil Riadis, prematurely taken from us, was a fervent disciple and admirer of Ravel. (Manolis Kalomiris, director of the Conservatory of Athens, Greece; *ibidem*)

The great respect that I have for Ravel's art increases my regret that I am not sufficiently informed about the particulars of his life to write a tribute that would do justice to the stature of this great composer. (Richard Strauss; *ibidem*)

It has been said more than once in the present publication that Albert Roussel is much closer to the spirit of the French people than Ravel, and no wonder, for we learn from a reliable source that Maurice Ravel, whose real name was Rawelowitsch, was a descendant from a family that had emigrated from the Near East, and so cannot be regarded as *urfranzösisch. (Signale für die musikalische Welt,* Berlin, 9 March 1938)

Ravex, Ravez and Ravet are fairly current in Savoie. The form Ravel probably originated in a misreading of the final *t*. The hypothesis that the name can be traced back to the Jewish patronymic Rabbele is unfounded. Ravel's mother, née Marie Délouart, was born in 1840 in the Bassess-Pyrénées, France, the descendant of a Basque family whose name was Deluarte or Eluarte. (M.D. Calvocoressi, in the 1940 Supplement to Grove's *Dictionary of Music and Musicians*)

France loses in Ravel one of its great musicians whose prestige is recognized in the entire world. History will assure for him the glorious place in the domain of music which he has earned with such great courage and such firm conviction. (Igor Stravinsky in *Instransigeant*, Paris, 29 December 1937)

1938

1 JANUARY 1938

Margherita da Cortona, lyric drama in three acts by the 54-year-old Italian composer Licinio REFICE, dealing with a 13th-century woman in Umbria who expiates her carnal sins by inducing the seductive murderer of her former lover to join the Holy Land Crusade, is produced in La Scala, Milan.

5 JANUARY 1938

Songs of Our Day, a set of nine choral pieces with orchestra by Sergei PROKOFIEV, written in a socialistically realistic idiom fertilized by felicitous harmonic acer-bities, to texts from Soviet poems, including a solemn piece about Stalin, is performed for the first time in Moscow.

6 JANUARY 1938

Filling Station, automobilistic ballet by Virgil THOMSON, wherein a courteous filling station attendant welcomes passing motorists in an immaculately clean gasoline palace, set to a vernacular score, with thematic elements "like all the familiar tunes, though there is no direct quotation," is performed for the first time in Hartford, Connecticut.

7 JANUARY 1938

Oriane et le Prince d'Amour, choral ballet by the 67-year-old dean of French modernists Florent SCHMITT, dealing with a polyandrous Renaissance lady who successively seduces a poet, a Mongol merchant and a Prince of Love, but perishes when she dances at a masked ball with Death, in a musical setting saturated with polyharmonies and marked by incisive asymmetrical rhythms, is produced at the Paris Opéra.

(The original title of the work was *Oriane la Sans-Égale;* it was changed to *Oriane et le Prince d'Amour* at the suggestion of Serge Lifar, the choreographer of the Paris Opéra. An orchestral suite drawn from the ballet was first performed in Paris on 12 February 1937. Florent Schmitt's "tragédie dansee" entitled simply *Oriane,* and containing materials later used in the present ballet, was first performed at a dance recital of Ida Rubinstein in Paris on 11 May 1934.)

13 JANUARY 1938

Symphony in G Minor by the 43-year-old English composer of Irish descent Ernest John MOERAN, in four movements closely adhering to the romantic formulae, but enlivened by melodic elements of Irish and East Anglian origin, is performed for the first time in London.

13 JANUARY 1938

Maurice MARTENOT takes out the patent No. 841,128 for a microtonal keyboard of his electronic instrument ONDES MUSICALES, which can produce 1/12 tones, constructed especially to approximate the intervallic scale of the Hindu *ragas.*

16 JANUARY 1938

Béla BARTÓK and his wife Ditta play in Basel, Switzerland, the solo parts in the first performance of his *Sonata for Two Pianos and Percussion,* in three movements: (1) *Assai lento—Allegro molto,* (2) *Lento ma non troppo,* (3) *Allegro non troppo,* written in a tersely economic, scintillatingly dissonant idiom, attaining the utmost degree of subtilization in the coloristic employment of percussion instruments, and containing extensive xylophone solos, with the pianos themselves treated as specialized percussion media.

(Bartók made an orchestral arrangement of his sonata in 1940, and renamed it *Concerto for Two Pianos, Percussion and Orchestra.* The first performance of this version took place in London on 14 November 1942, with the London Philharmonic Orchestra, Sir Adrian Boult conducting; the pianists were Louis Kentner and Llona Kabos. The first American performance of the *Concerto* was given by the New York Philharmonic, Fritz Reiner conducting, on 21 January 1943, with Béla Bartók and his wife as soloists; it is erroneously listed as the *Uraufführung* in the authoritative edition, *Béla Bartók, Weg und Werk, Schriften und Briefe* by Bence Szabolcsi, published in Budapest in 1957.)

18 JANUARY 1938

Un Drame sous Philippe II, historical opera in three acts by the 60-year-old Belgian composer Albert DUPUIS, written in the grandiloquent manner of Wagneromantic music drama, is produced for the first time in Brussels.

27 JANUARY 1938

Horoscope, ballet by the urbanely mundane 32-year-old English composer Constant LAMBERT, to a scenario dealing with an astrologically incompatible love of a boy, born under the sign of Leo, for a zodiacally divergent girl born under the sign of Virgo, with a happy ending provided by their discovery of a mutual selenological congruence since both were born with the moon in Gemini, set to music in an eclectically modernistic manner, is produced in London. (An orchestral suite from *Horoscope* was performed for the first time in London under Lambert's direction on 8 August 1938.)

29 JANUARY 1938

Suite sans esprit de suite, a whimsical orchestral-sketch by Florent SCHMITT, written in an anti-baroque manner, is performed for the first time in Paris.

30 JANUARY 1938

Darius MILHAUD conducts in Paris the world première of his choreographic poem *L'Oiseau.*

30 JANUARY 1938

Ocean, ballet by the Japanese composer Shiro FUKAI, is performed for the first time in Tokyo.

2 FEBRUARY 1938

Le Cantique des cantiques, ballet by Arthur HONEGGER, is produced at the Paris Opéra.

10 FEBRUARY 1938

Die Wirtin von Pinsk, opera in three acts by the 33-year-old German composer Richard MOHAUPT, to the story of a clever hostess of an inn in Pinsk during its occupation by Napoleon's retreating armies in 1812, modeled after Goldoni's play *Mirandolina,* to a musical setting in an effective polyharmonic idiom fertilized by strong asymmetrical rhythms, is performed for the first (and last) time at the Dresden Opera.

For some time I have been attacked on account of the fact that my wife is Jewish. The sensational success of my opera *Die Wirtin von Pinsk* in Dresden was followed by protests against its further performances. The opera was immediately banned, and a few months later an official directive was issued by the Nazi authorities forbidding performances of any of my works. (From Mohaupt's letter to the author, dated Berlin, 28 June 1938)

11 FEBRUARY 1938

Evocations, orchestral suite by Ernest BLOCH, composed between 1930 and 1937, written in an effectively exotic style, in three tableaux: a buddhistically serene *Contemplation;* a pentatonically vibrant tone poem *Houang-Ti, God of War;* and an onomatopeically tintinnabulating musicorama of San Francisco's Chinatown, *Renouveau-Spring,* is performed for the first time by the San Francisco Symphony Orchestra, Pierre Monteux conducting.

13 FEBRUARY 1938

While listening to the radio broadcast of Tchaikovsky's *Fourth Symphony* by the New York Philharmonic, Nicolas SLONIMSKY suddenly discovers, at 4:30 P.M., the formula for the "Grossmutterakkord," containing all twelve tones (C, B, D-flat, B-flat, D, A, E-flat, A-flat, E, G, F and C-flat, in this order) and eleven different intervals, the equidistant intervals from the central interval being inversions of one another, and the central interval, the tritone, being the inversion of itself, with even-numbered intervals forming an increasing arithmetical progression, and the odd-numbered intervals forming a decreasing arithmetical progression, with a semitone as a unit.

(The melodic version of the "Grossmutterakkord" is the principal motto of the interplanetary opera *Aniara* by Karl-Birger Blomdahl; it also appears in other dodecaphonic works of the 1950's and 1960's. It is known among American dodecaphonists as the "screw row" because of its spiral winding out and in towards its axis.)

I wish great prosperity and more progeny to the "Grossmutterakkord." (Paul Hindemith in a guest album of Nicolas Slonimsky, 1938)

To the devil with Grandmother! Let us write real music! (Sergei Prokofiev, *ibid.*)

15 FEBRUARY 1938

The ashes of Teresa CARREÑO, Venezuelan pianist who died in New York in 1917, are repatriated in Caracas by the government of Venezuela.

19 FEBRUARY 1938

Bruno Walter conducts the Vienna Philharmonic for the last time before the infamous Nazi *Anschluss* of Austria, in a program comprising the original version of *Fourth Symphony* by Anton BRUCKNER and the world première of *Prosperos Beschwörung*, symphonic poem after Shakespeare's play *The Tempest* by Egon WELLESZ, in the presence of the composer, also destined soon to leave Nazified Austria.

20 FEBRUARY 1938

Les Petites Cardinal, light opera in two acts composed jointly by Arthur HONEGGER and Jacques IBERT, is performed for the first time in Paris.

21 FEBRUARY 1938

Ulysse et les Sirènes, symphonic poem with female voices by the French impressionist composer Jean-Jules Aimable ROGER-DUCASSE, with the sirens weaving seductive chromatic arabesques around a focal D-flat symbolizing the firm course of the ship, while Ulysses struggles diatonically to free himself from self-imposed restraining pentatonic ropes, ignoring the warnings of anxious trumpets, is performed for the first time in Paris.

22 FEBRUARY 1938

Colas Breugnon, opera in three acts by the Soviet composer Dmitri KABALEVSKY, after Romain Rolland's novel *Le Maître de Clamecy*, dealing with a French wood carver, a man of the people who rebels against a feudal lord who fails to appreciate humble folk art, written in a socialistically realistic idiom marked by lucid tonalities and clear symmetric rhythms and incorporating quotations from authentic old French melodies, is performed for the first time in Leningrad.

I received the vocal score of your opera *Le Maître de Clamecy* and played it over several times with great pleasure. You have succeeded very well in your treatment of the French folk songs; you have absorbed their essence and recreated it in your music. My ear of a Frenchman has caught these songs without difficulty in your lively tableaux. Your opera is one of the best works for the stage I know in new Russian music. (From Romain Rolland's letter to Kabalevsky, dated 27 November 1937)

28 FEBRUARY 1938

Ramona (renamed *The Captive*), opera in three acts by the German-American composer Gustave STRUBE, is produced in Baltimore.

4 MARCH 1938

Alan BUSH, 37-year-old English composer, plays the solo part in the first performance in London of his *Piano Concerto*, in four movements of resolutely diatonic, rhythmically propulsive music, with a choral ending containing a triadic message of social significance in major keys.

9 MARCH 1938

Ivan Sergejewitsch Tarassenko, lyric drama in two acts by the Viennese composer Franz SALMHOFER, to a sentimental libretto from Russian life, is produced in Vienna.

15 MARCH 1938

Chansons populaires juives, a "collectivistic distillation" for orchestra of seven East-European Jewish songs by the 30-year-old Palestinian composer Uriah BOSCOVICH, is performed for the first time by the Palestine Symphony Orchestra in Haifa.

16 MARCH 1938

Julietta, fantastic opera in three acts by Bohuslav MARTINU, to a libretto wherein a young man exteriorizes his three dreams about an ethereally beauteous maiden amid oneiristically fluctuating scenes involving Arabian camel riders, pawnbrokers and blind souvenir vendors, in a musical setting full of languorous polyharmonies, is performed for the first time in Prague.

17 MARCH 1938

Ernst KRENEK plays the piano part in the first performance, with the Concertgebouw Orchestra in Amsterdam, under the direction of Bruno Walter, of his *Second Piano Concerto* (composed between 25 May and 22 August 1937) in four movements without pause, written according to the 12-tone system of composition, adopted by Krenek in 1931 as a method which "by the nature of its historical development has supplanted the harmonic scaffolding of tonality by a new unifying force."

"Conditions in Europe must be dreadful." (Comments of a Boston lady after Krenek's performance of his *Concerto* with the Boston Symphony Orchestra on 4 November 1938, overheard and reported by H. W. Heinsheimer in his *Menagerie in F Sharp*, New York, 1947)

18 MARCH 1938

Cyril ROOTHAM, English composer of sonorous symphonic music in a stately Elgarian vein, dies in Cambridge at the age of 62, leaving behind an unorchestrated manuscript of his *Second Symphony*, which he, stricken with paralysis, had dictated to his friends and pupils, note by note, instrument by instrument. (Rootham's *Second Symphony* was orchestrated by Patrick Hadley and performed for the first time in London on the eve of the first anniversary of Rootham's death, on 17 March 1939.)

23 MARCH 1938

Proserpina, opera in three acts by the 52-year-old Italian composer Renzo BIANCHI, is produced at La Scala in Milan.

24 MARCH 1938

De Snoek (The Pike), comic opera in one act by Guillaume LANDRÉ, 33-year-old Dutch composer, son and namesake of the 63-year-old dean of Dutch composers Guillaume (or Willem) Landré, dealing with the fishing trip of an inmate in a modern penological institution, and couched in an appropriately progressive harmonic idiom, with some atonal discursions in the vocal parts, is produced in Amsterdam.

24 MARCH 1938

Grossdeutschland zum 10. April, hymn-fanfare by the Nazi composer Paul WINTER, urging the Austrian populace in the grip of the Hitlerian Anschluss to vote on 10 April 1938 for the incorporation of Hitler's native Austria in the Third Reich, is performed for the first time on the Vienna Radio.

I was the happy witness of the Führer's first journey through his liberated fatherland. I watched the indescribable and tumultuous jubilation of the enthusiastic Austrians. As I drove back to Linz from Vienna, the day after the Führer's arrival in the Austrian capital, I suddenly decided to write a fanfare as an expression of my profound joy inspired by the events and the magnificent consummation of Greater Germany. (Paul Winter, *Die Musik*, Berlin, May 1938)

2 APRIL 1938

Quincy PORTER, 41-year-old American composer, conducts the New York Philharmonic in the first performance of his *First Symphony* in three movements, "an attempt to find expression for feelings and emotions which the composer knew no other way of setting down," written in an aggressively rhythmic, opulently massive harmony, but lyrical in melodic outline and impressionistically colorful in instrumentation.

8 APRIL 1938

Walter PISTON conducts the Boston Symphony Orchestra in the first performance of his *First Symphony* (completed on 25 September 1937), in three movements constituting an essay in absolute forms, "devoid of any pictorial, narrative, political or philosophical intent," revolving around a focal theme and ending with its sonorous restatement in the euphoniously euphorious key of C major.

8 APRIL 1938

Fourth Symphony by the 38-year-old American composer Harl MCDONALD is performed for the first time by the Philadelphia Orchestra under the direction of Eugene Ormandy.

11 APRIL 1938

Society for the Preservation and Encouragement of Barbershop Quartet Singing in America is organized in Tulsa, Oklahoma, by the oil millionaire O. C. CASH.

For a year or more, I have been collecting words to all the old barbershop favorites. I decided to have a meeting of twelve men who on occasion had been caught in the throes of a barbershop chord. Much to my surprise, 35 men showed up instead of twelve. . . . Attendance doubled for the next three or four meetings. . . . Within two months chapters were formed all the way from Hollywood, with Bing Crosby as President, to New York, Mayor La Guardia, President. (From a letter to the author from O. C. Cash, dated 11 April 1940)

(A barbershop quartet contest was held in July 1940 at the New York World's Fair, with the first prize, consisting of radio receivers and phonograph recording machines, awarded by Mayor La Guardia, President of the New York chapter of the SPEBSQSA, to the Flat Four, a police team. Other contestants were Melody Maulers, Frog Hollow Four, Chromatic Canaries, and Phillip's 6 Barflies.)

12 APRIL 1938

Feodor CHALIAPIN, great Russian bass whose fabulous career, from peasant beginnings to world glory, embraced half a century of singing, and whose portrayal of Boris Godunov constitutes, in its dramatic power, one of the greatest achievements of operatic art, dies in Paris at the age of 65.

Chaliapin suffered from chronic diabetes aggravated by acute anemia. His doctors recommended blood transfusion. The first was given by his wife, the second by his youngest daughter. The third transfusion was given by a professional blood donor whose name was Chien. Chaliapin joked: "Since his name is Dog, I am afraid I will be barking tomorrow." But the transfusions were futile. In the morning of 12 April 1938 he became delirious. He kept asking, "Where am I? In a theater in Russia? To sing, I must breathe, but I cannot . . ." At 5:15 P.M. he died. (*Les Dernières Nouvelles*, Russian Émigré Newspaper, Paris, 13 April 1918)

Chaliapin betrayed his people and sold his fatherland for petty cash. Having lost contact with his native soil, he failed to create a single new character on the stage during his stay abroad. His great talent faded long ago. He left nothing behind him after his death. (*Izvestia*, Moscow, 14 April 1938)

Only those are really dead who are forgotten. . . . I read this inscription on a tombstone somewhere. If so, then Chaliapin will never die. He cannot die! For this amazing artist, who had a truly fabulous talent, is unforgettable. Forty-one years ago, almost at the beginning of his career, the development of which I witnessed myself, he had stood on a pedestal, from which he had never come down, never even stumbled. Chaliapin was a giant. To future generations he will be a legend. (Rachmaninoff, in *Les Dernières Nouvelles*, Paris, 17 April 1938)

14 APRIL 1938

The Captive of the Caucasus, ballet by the erudite 53-year-old Russian music scholar and prolific composer of theatrical music, Boris ASAFIEV, after a poem by Pushkin, dealing with a prisoner's passion for a Circassian girl, whom he encounters while serving in the Russian army during periodical skirmishes with bellicose Caucasian tribes, is produced in Leningrad.

22 APRIL 1938

Concerto for Organ and Orchestra by the 42-year-old American composer Leo SOWERBY, in three contrasting movements, ending in a triumphantly academic C-major finale, is performed for the first time by the Boston Symphony Orchestra, under the direction of Serge Koussevitzky, with E. Power Biggs as organ soloist.

27 APRIL 1938

The French master organist Marcel DUPRÉ plays the organ solo in the first performance of his *Concerto* for organ and orchestra in Groningen, Holland. (The first Paris performance of the *Concerto* took place on 27 October 1938.)

1 MAY 1938

The REICHSMUSIKKAMMER, the governing organ of Nazified German music, issues a directive ruling that no Aryan music instructors are to be allowed to teach Jewish pupils.

2 MAY 1938

Second Symphony for strings by the 41-year-old French composer Jean RIVIER is performed for the first time in Paris.

4 MAY 1938

Antonio e Cleopatra, opera in three acts by Gian Francesco MALIPIERO (completed on 2 April 1937) to his own libretto after Shakespeare, written in a pandiatonically enriched harmonic style, is performed for the first time at the May Festival in Florence.

6 MAY 1938

To celebrate Hitler's state visit to Mussolini in Rome, the Italian opera composer Gino MARINUZZI conducts an open air concert with a Fascist ensemble comprising an orchestra of 900 players, 45 military bands and 111 choruses, aggregating to 10,000 performers.

8 MAY 1938

Dumbarton Oaks for chamber orchestra by Igor STRAVINSKY, named after the estate of the American music patron Robert Woods Bliss, in three neo-classical movements, characteristically reviving the Baroque custom of dedicating works to munificent patrons, is performed for the first time in Dumbarton Oaks, Washington, D.C., under the direction of Nadia Boulanger. (At the first Paris performance on 16 June 1938 the piece was programmed under the title *Concerto*, without reference to Dumbarton Oaks.)

Stravinsky's *Concerto* sounds strangely dull. It abounds in scholastic clichés and banalities. Every vestige of imaginative effect is systematically eliminated. This type of music may signify its final decline, its mortal illness, unless it is the radical reincarnation and rejuvenation of the art. There is no other alternative. (Boris Schloezer in *Les Dernières Nouvelles*, Russian émigré paper, Paris, 21 June 1938)

11 MAY 1938

I Married an Angel, musical comedy by Richard RODGERS with lyrics by Lorenz Hart dealing with a mystical count who vows never to marry except an angel, actually finds one but experiences trouble when she proves to be angelically truthful with people, thus causing him embarrassment, presenting, besides the attractive title number, a lovely duet, *Spring Is Here*, is produced in New York.

12 MAY 1938

Jeanne d'Arc au Bûcher, dramatic oratorio by Arthur HONEGGER (completed on 30 August 1935) and conceived as a modern *chanson de geste*, to the text by Paul Claudel, set to music of high tension and dissonant consistency, including spoken dialogue, with Joan of Arc tied to the stake throughout the play, is performed for the first time in concert form by the Chamber Orchestra of Basel, Switzerland, with Paul Sacher, its founder, conducting, and with Ida Rubinstein in the role of Joan.

12 MAY 1938

Schneider Wibbel, comic opera in four acts by the 35-year-old German composer Mark LOTHAR, is produced in Berlin.

16 MAY 1938

Uprising, opera in three acts by the Azerbaijan composer Lev KHODZHA-EINATOV, dealing with social upheavals during the civil war in Central Asia in 1920, written in the idiom of socialist realism and containing musical quotations from indigenous melodies, is produced in Leningrad.

22 MAY 1938

Emil GILELS, 21-year-old Odessa-born Soviet pianist, wins the first prize of 50,000 Belgian francs at the Concours Ysaÿe in Brussels, an international competition of 95 pianists from 23 countries, the *pièce de résistance* among the 12 finalists being a new piano concerto by the Belgian composer Jean ABSIL, in three contrasting movements, written in a moderately modern, rhythmically intricate and harmonically opulent idiom, handed to the contestants only seven days before the public performance with an orchestra, for study in isolated rooms of a suburban castle. (Second prize was awarded to Mary JOHNSTON of England; third prize to Jacob FLIER of Russia.)

Gilels literally fought his way through the impasse of Absil's piano Concerto. He and Flier were particularly at a disadvantage since they had no experience in performing modernistic music, or even listening to such music. The atonal constructions of Absil's concerto, with its constant rhythmic changes, appeared to them absolutely devoid of meaning. Gilels wrote to his teacher in Moscow: "I am completely isolated from the outside world. They handed me a tremendously difficult concerto. I am working on it six or seven hours every day. Very difficult!" (S. Hentova, *Emil Gilels*, Moscow, 1959)

22 MAY 1938

An exhibition of ENTARTETE MUSIK (Debased Music) opens in Düsseldorf under the auspices of the Nazi Ministry of Propaganda, with the declared aim to forestall the proliferation of "microbes of musical decomposition, Marxist, Bolshevist, Jewish and other un-German tendencies, such as atonal music and jazz," with special alcoves containing phonograph recordings of modernistic music and published scores by such "cultural Bolsheviks" as Stravinsky, Paul Hindemith, Franz Schreker, Arnold Schoenberg, Alban Berg, Josef Matthias Hauer, Ernst Toch, Ernest Bloch, Ernst Krenek, Kurt Weill and Hanns Eisler, as well as books and articles by Schoenberg, Hindemith, Alfred Einstein, Hermann Scherchen, and other Aryan and non-Aryan proponents of alleged *Kulturbolschewismus.*

22 MAY 1938

Ostmark-Overture by the German composer Otto BESCH, a nationalistic piece written to celebrate the nazification and annexation of Austria, now renamed Ostmark, by the Third German Reich, is performed for the first time at the opening of a Nazi music festival in Düsseldorf.

25 MAY 1938

Second Symphony by the 27-year-old American composer William SCHUMAN is performed for the first time by the Greenwich Orchestra in New York.

28 MAY 1938

The first air-conditioned opera theater opens at Dessau, Germany, enabling singers and audience to act and react in a purified atmosphere at comfortable temperatures.

28 MAY 1938

Mathis der Maler, opera in seven scenes by Paul HINDEMITH, to his own libretto inspired by the triptych painting of the altar piece in Isenheim, Alsace, by Mathis Grünewald (1470–1531), with symphonic and choral tableaux limning the three thematic scenes—*Angels' Concert, Entombment* and *Temptation of St. Anthony* (in which Mathis dreams of himself being tempted by seductive visions)—set against the realistic background of peasant rebellion in Germany, which Mathis led, with the musical score in a tense contrapuntal idiom, culminating in a theodicy in grandiloquent triadic harmonies, is produced in Zürich, Switzerland, after Hindemith had been declared a persona non grata in Nazi Germany. (Symphony *Mathis der Maler,* incorporating the interludes from the opera, was first performed in Berlin on 12 March 1934.)

30 MAY 1938

Lusabatzin (At Dawn,) opera in five acts by the 41-year-old Armenian composer Aro STEPANIAN, with the action taking place during the civil war in Armenia in 1920, illustrating in socialistically realistic tones the Bol-

shevik magnanimity, Menshevik pusillanimity, and bourgeois parvanimity, is produced in Erevan.

30 MAY 1938

The Incredible Flutist, ballet by Walter PISTON, to a story about a circus player who could charm not only snakes but also snake charmers, in an uninhibited hedonistic medium in luxuriant orchestration ranging from pseudosentimental to ostentatiously romantic, at one point inserting a dodecaphonic tune (recording of a barking dog has been sanctioned by the composer at some performances), is played for the first time by the Boston Pops Orchestra, Arthur Fiedler conducting.

2 JUNE 1938

Hans von WOLZOGEN, fervent Wagnerophile who popularized the term *Leitmotiv* to designate the identifying leading motifs in Wagner's music dramas (Wagner's own term was *Grundthema*), dies in his beloved Bayreuth in his 90th year.

2 JUNE 1938

La Femme à Barbe, pogonological musical farce by the 50-year-old French composer Claude DELVINCOURT, recounting the transsexual adventures of a bearded woman, is performed for the first time in Versailles.

2 JUNE 1938

The Scarlet Letter, opera in two acts, after Hawthorne's classic tale, by the 34-year-old Philadelphia-born composer Vittorio GIANNINI, to his own libretto in Italian, is produced for the first time at the State Opera of Hamburg, in the German version as *Das Brandmal,* with the composer's sister Dusolina Giannini in the role of the young matron of Salem, Massachusetts, whose unhallowed affair with a Puritan clergyman was stigmatized with the embroidered initial A for Adulteress on her dress, set to music in an impassionate dramatic manner, with ingratiating modernities within the matrix of the Italianate operatic idiom.

12 JUNE 1938

Venezuela issues a 25-centavo postage stamp to commemorate the Venezuelan pianist Teresa CARREÑO, "the Valkyrie of the piano."

15 JUNE 1938

Das Buch mit Sieben Siegeln, oratorio by the Austrian romantic composer Franz SCHMIDT, his last and most ambitious work, to the text from the Revelation of St. John, in two parts, culminating in the opening of the seventh seal and revealing the awesome panorama of the Last Judgment with horrendous explosions of dissonant tonite, is performed for the first time in Vienna.

15 JUNE 1938

Karl V, allegorical historical music drama in two parts by Ernst KRENEK, in which the dying Emperor of the Holy Roman Empire is questioned by God speaking to him from Titian's painting *La Gloria,* while his mundane enemies—Martin Luther, King Francis I of France, the Sultan and the Pope—offer philosophical comments, Krenek's first work written entirely according to the method of composition with 12 tones, completed by him on 24 May 1933, and embodying some non-dodecaphonic illustrative devices, including a naturalistic quartet of preternatural voices and pendulum clocks, is performed for the first time in Prague, in the absence of Krenek himself, who could not take the risk of flying over Hitler's Germany from London where he was staying as an exile from Nazi-infested Austria.

The story of my opera embraces the entire life of Emperor Charles V, who first took America under his rule, fought the Turks and got in trouble with the Pope. The scenes of his life appear on a second stage. Musical recitative is often interrupted by spoken dialogue. *Karl V* is my first composition in the 12-tone system. (From Ernst Krenek's letter to the author, dated 5 February 1938)

17 JUNE 1938

Zadig, opera in four acts by the French composer Jean DUPÉRIER, after Voltaire's novel of that name, is produced at the Paris Opéra-Comique.

17 JUNE 1938

The 16th Festival of the International Society for Contemporary Music opens in London with the following program of orchestral works:

Military Symphonietta by Vítězslava KAPRÁLOVÁ, 23-year-old daughter of the Czech composer Vaclav Kaprál, conducted by herself, and dedicated to the President of Czechoslovakia Beneš, with a notation that the word "military" in the title "is not an appeal for war but rather a conscious defensive posture in mobilizing physical sensations and the determination to preserve the national independence of one's own country"; *Third Symphony,* in four classically designed movements by the Polish modernist Józef KOFFLER, who was to perish tragically five years hence, killed by the Nazis with his wife and child; *Domini est Terra,* a psalm for chorus and orchestra, by the 35-year-old English neo-classicist Lennox BERKELEY, written in neo-ecclesiastical modalities; *Das Augenlicht* for mixed chorus and orchestra by Anton von WEBERN, with a seemingly conventional four-part harmonic setting ingeniously made up of three statements of the fundamental 12-tone row and its inversion, replete with characteristically Webernian major sevenths, the total creating an impression of hierophantic solemnity; *Jeanne d'Arc,* symphonic suite in five movements by the nearly 34-year-old French composer Manuel ROSENTHAL, a hedonistically anachronistic evocation of the canonized virgin-whore, concluding with a contorted version of the *Marseillaise* (the third movement was omitted at this performance); *Tres Ciudades* for voice and orchestra by the 37-year-old Spanish composer Julián BAUTISTA, to the text by Federico García Lorca, the radical poet murdered by the Falangists during the Spanish Civil War; and *Le Nouvel Âge,* "symphonie concertante" by the Russian-born Parisian composer and conductor Igor MARKEVITCH, conceived in a neo-classical idiom, in clear tonalities with pandiatonic incrustations.

18 JUNE 1938

At the second concert of the 16th Festival of the International Society for Contemporary Music in London, the following program of chamber music is presented:

Quintet for flute, clarinet, violin, viola and cello by the Swedish composer Franz SYBERG; *String Quartet* by the German neo-classical composer Karl Amadeus HARTMANN, written in the neo-baroque technique of dissonant counterpoint; *Theme and Variations* for two violins by the 33-year-old English composer Alan RAWSTHORNE (the festival program book states: "The composer is convinced that the theme appears in each variation"); *String Quartet* by the 40-year-old Polish composer Karol RATHAUS, written in a Schoenbergian atonal idiom; *Violin Sonata,* by the 53-year-old German-born American composer Werner JOSTEN, in an academically effective neo-romantic style; *String Quartet* by the 40-year-old Austrian composer Viktor ULLMAN; and *Pianoforte Quintet* by the Berlin-born Spanish-Cuban composer Joaquín NÍN-CUL-MELL, couched in a neo-classical Hispanic idiom.

19 JUNE 1938

At the third concert of the 16th Festival of the International Society for Contemporary Music in London, two old English operas are presented: *Venus and Adonis* by Dr. John BLOW (1649–1708), newly arranged by Anthony Lewis, and *The Ephesian Matron* by Charles DIBDIN (1745–1814).

20 JUNE 1938

At the fourth concert of the 16th Festival of the International Society for Contemporary Music in London, the following program is given:

Suite for strings and piano by the dean of Dutch composers Willem LANDRÉ; two movements from *Suite* for female voices, oboe and strings by the 25-year-old Australian neo-classical composeress Peggy GLANVILLE-HICKS; *Variations on a Theme of Frank Bridge* for string orchestra by the 24-year-old English composer Benjamin BRITTEN, a set of ten imaginative metamorphoses on a melodious subject by Britten's revered teacher, replete with whimsical allusions to Italian operatic arias and Viennese waltzes; *Music for Radio* by František BARTOŠ of Czechoslovakia; *Concerto for Trumpet and Strings* by the Danish neo-classicist Knudaage RIISAGER; *Cantata* for soprano, chorus and piano by Ernst KRENEK; and *Sonata for Two Pianos and Percussion* by Béla BARTÓK, first performed by him and his wife in Basel on 16 January 1938.

22 JUNE 1938

At the fifth concert of the 16th Festival of the International Society for Contemporary Music in London, the following program of chamber music is presented:

Two pieces from *La Nativité du Seigneur* for organ by the 29-year-old French composer Olivier MESSIAEN, set in a stark neo-medieval idiom, played by the composer himself; three movements from *Nonet* by the 31-year-old Lithuanian composer Jeronimas KAČINKAS, written in a neo-classical manner with some impressionistic touches; *Nachtklänge,* a set of songs for voice and wind quintet by the Czech composer Isa KREJČI; *Little Suite* for violin and piano by the Dutch composer Bertus VAN LIER; *Racconto* for flute, saxophone, bassoon and doublebass by the 41-year-old Danish neo-classicist Jörgen BENTZON; *Two Songs* for soprano, oboe, clarinet and bassoon by the 27-year-old Serbian composer Vojislav VUČKOVIĆ, fated to be murdered by the Nazis on Christmas Day four years hence; *Composition* for violin and viola by the Swedish composer Sten BROMAN, written in a deliberate two-dimensional idiom, in strict two-part counterpoint without double-stops for either instrument; and *Suite dans le goût espagnol* for oboe, bassoon, trumpet and harpsichord by the French composer ROLAND-MANUEL, with profusion of coloristic Hispanic melorhythms.

24 JUNE 1938

The 16th Festival of the International Society for Contemporary Music in London presents its last concert in the following program of orchestral music:

Concerto for Orchestra by the Italian modernist Riccardo NIELSEN set in a neo-classical style with atonal excrescences; *Mouvement Symphonique* by the Serbian composer Slavko OSTERC, written in a highly chromaticized idiom, thematically diversified with an express avoidance of repetitious melodic patterns and sequences; *El Salón Mexico*, a brilliant Latin American pasticcio by Aaron COPLAND, first performed in Mexico City on 27 August 1937; *Aubade, Interlude and Dance* by the 41-year-old Catalan composer Roberto GERHARD; excerpts from the opera *Mathis der Maler* by Paul HINDEMITH; *Danses* by the Swiss composer Jean BINET; fragments from the oratorio *Das Gesicht Jesajas* by the Swiss composer Willy BURKHARD, written in a linear neo-classical style of vigesimosecular dissonant counterpoint.

24 JUNE 1938

Zadig, musical comedy by the 52-year-old Swiss composer Jean DUPÉRIER, after Voltaire's Oriental tale *Zadig, ou la destinée*, with the central character being a youth named Zadig, is produced in Paris.

21 JULY 1938

St. Francis, choreographic legend for orchestra by Paul HINDEMITH, on the life and the natural philosophy of St. Francis of Assisi, set in a stark neo-medieval idiom in sinewy linear counterpoint, is performed for the first time in London by the Ballet Russe of Monte Carlo. (A suite for orchestra drawn from this ballet, in three movements, is catalogued under the title *Nobilissima Visione*.)

24 JULY 1938

Friedenstag, one-act opera by Richard STRAUSS, with its action taking place on 24 October 1648, the day of the conclusion of the Westphalian Peace Treaty ending the Thirty Years' War, illustrated in the finale by a militantly concordant display of demonstratively peaceful C major, is produced in Munich before an international audience, with 16 curtain calls for the composer, but in the conspicuous absence of Nazi officials. (In his speech of 30 January 1940, Hitler described the Westphalian Peace Treaty, which dismembered Germany into a number of small royal and ducal states, as treasonable.)

28 JULY 1938

Jack JUDGE, a music hall singer, whose popular song *Tipperary*, written jointly with Harry J. Williams in 1912, became a favorite of the British Tommies in World War I, dies at West Bromwich at the age of 60.

31 JULY 1938

Morton GOULD, 24-year-old American composer, conducts the New York Philharmonic at the Lewisohn Stadium in the first performance of his *Second American Symphonette*, "entertainment music attempting to utilize the elements of American swing in the classical form of the sinfonietta," in three movements, the second of which, entitled *Pavanne*, fuses elements of jazz in swing time with the form of a classical court dance.

I know that the spelling *Pavanne* is incorrect, but at the time I wrote the piece, the *Pavanne* was not a well-known word. Those who knew Ravel's *Pavane* could spell the name right, but the people who knew mine had difficulty in pronouncing the title. Among the misspellings were "Pavayne," "Puvunie," and even "Parvenu," and I decided to use two n's to give at least some idea of what the phonetic sounds were. (Morton Gould in a letter to the author dated 26 July 1961, in reply to an orthographic inquiry)

31 JULY 1938

A century has elapsed since the death, on board the brig *Otis* bound from the West Indies to the United States, of Johannes Nepomuk MAELZEL, eccentric inventor of the useful metronome and of the futuristic Panharmonicon (for which Beethoven wrote his *Wellington's Victory*) and the perpetrator of the Chess Automaton Hoax, which he promoted in both hemispheres with the aid of a midget chess master hidden inside among pieces of collapsible machinery, and moving the magnetized chessmen from beneath the board.

18 AUGUST 1938

Benjamin BRITTEN, 24-year-old English composer, plays the piano part in the first performance of his *Piano Concerto* in four movements, *Toccata, Waltz, Recitative and Aria* (replaced in 1945 by an *Impromptu*) and *March* (consisting of a series of march tunes, played, in the words of the composer, "full of confidence by the pianoforte and then by the orchestra"), at the Promenade Concerts in London, Sir Henry Wood conducting.

The Concerto was conceived with the idea of exploiting various important characteristics of the pianoforte, such as its enormous compass, its percussive quality, and its suitability for figuration; so that it is not by any means a symphony with pianoforte, but rather a bravura concerto with orchestra. (From Britten's annotations in the program book of the concert)

1 SEPTEMBER 1938

Shchors, opera in five acts by the 43-year-old Ukrainian composer Boris LIATOSHINSKY, with the action taking place during the civil war in the Ukraine in 1918, centering on the heroic figure of Nicolai Shchors, commander of the partisan group fighting against the troops of the Hetman, the German army of occupation and the nationalist Ukrainian bands, couched in the heroic tones of socialist realism with a liberal utilization of Ukrainian folksongs, is performed for the first time in Kiev.

3 SEPTEMBER 1938

At the opening concert of the Nordic Music Festival in Copenhagen, Jón LEIFS, prime composer of Iceland, conducts the first performance of the orchestra suite from his music to the drama *Loftr*.

3 SEPTEMBER 1938

Conquest of the Air, symphonic suite from incidental music for the London Films Production, by the English modernist Arthur BLISS, in six illustrative movements, *The*

Wind, The Vision of Leonardo da Vinci, Stunting, Over the Arctic, Gliding and *March*, is performed for the first time in London, the composer conducting.

7 SEPTEMBER 1938

Los Amos del Barrio, a "sainete" (burlesque) by the 48-year-old Spanish violinist Manuel QUIROGA, is performed for the first time in Madrid.

23 SEPTEMBER 1938

Aurelio GIORNI, Italian-born American composer, vanishes at 6:30 P.M. near the Housatonic River in Western Massachusetts (his body was recovered) in a state of profound depression, induced by exceedingly bad reviews of his symphony, at its first performance in New York on 25 April 1938.

23 SEPTEMBER 1938

Phonograph recordings and full orchestral scores of *Finlandia* by SIBELIUS, *Stars and Stripes Forever* by John Philip SOUSA, and a swing piece *Flat Foot Floogie*, are deposited, along with other memorabilia of 20th-century civilization, in a Time Capsule, encased in an indestructible metal tube, buried underground in the area of the New York World's Fair, with engraved instructions to posterity to open it in A.D. 6938.

25 SEPTEMBER 1938

Eugenie SCHUMANN, last surviving daughter of Robert Schumann, dies in Bern, Switzerland, five weeks before her 87th birthday.

26 SEPTEMBER 1938

Knickerbocker Holiday, operetta in two acts by Kurt WEILL, 38-year-old German composer of bimusical talent, excelling both in modern symphonic and light theatrical genres, with the book and lyrics by Maxwell Anderson, after Washington Irving's chronicle *Father Knickerbocker's History of New York*, wherein the Dutch Governor Peter Stuyvesant appears as a proto-Fascist, including among many melodious arias, the celebrated *September Song*, is produced for the first time at Hartford, Connecticut. (The first New York performance took place on 19 October 1938.)

1 OCTOBER 1938

Walter KAUFMANN, 31-year-old Czech composer, conducts in Bombay, India, where he found temporary employment after flight from Czechoslovakia overhung by the dark cloud of Nazi menace, the first performance of his radio opera *Anasuya*, on the subject of an Indian maiden struggling in a world of multidirectional perils.

2 OCTOBER 1938

Lancillotto del Lago, opera in three acts by the 31-year-old Italian composer Pino DONATI, telling the eternally fascinating story of Lancelot of the Lake, knight of King Arthur's Round Table, and set to music in an unpretentiously abecedarian triadic idiom, is performed for the first time in Bergamo.

5 OCTOBER 1938

Serenade to Music by Ralph VAUGHAN WILLIAMS, scored for vocal soloists, chorus and orchestra, to the text from Shakespeare's play *The Merchant of Venice* ("Soft stillness and the night become the touches of sweet harmony"), set to music in sonorously resonant triadic harmonies, is performed for the first time at the Promenade Concerts in London, under the direction of Sir Henry Wood.

10 OCTOBER 1938

Trepak, ballet by the 39-year-old Russian modernist composer Alexander TCHEREPNIN, is performed for the first time anywhere by the Mordkin Russian Ballet in Richmond, Virginia.

15 OCTOBER 1938

Daphne, bucolic tragedy in one act by Richard STRAUSS (completed in Taormina, Italy, on 24 December 1937), derived from the Greek myth of Daphne's metamorphosis into a laurel tree (Daphne means laurel in Greek), to escape Apollo's amorous pursuit, and ending with Daphne's voice heard from the branches of the tree, set in characteristically Straussian harmonic sonorities mellowed by a high incidence of triadic consonances, is performed for the first time at the Dresden Opera House, on the same program with his opera, *Friedenstag*, first produced in Munich on 24 July 1938.

16 OCTOBER 1938

Billy the Kid, ballet in one act by Aaron COPLAND, to a scenario by Lincoln Kirstein, nostalgically depicting the short life of William H. Bonney, picaresque badman of the Old West who was trapped and killed in 1881, permeated with incisive American frontier melorhythms and incorporating several authentic cowboy songs, among them *Git Along Little Dogie, Old Chisolm Trail* and *O Bury Me Not on the Lone Prairie*, traversing the Kid's life beginning with his killing, at the age of 12, of the murderers of his mother, through episodes of card games with his outlaw friends, his jailing and his escape from prison, and finally his death after a posse led by his former friend tracks him down as he rests in the desert with his girl, is produced by Ballet Caravan in Chicago. (A symphonic suite in 7 sections, *The Open Prairie, Street in a Frontier Town, Card Came at Night, Gun Battle, Celebration Dance, Billy's Death*, the *Open Prairie Again*, was performed for the first time on 9 November 1940 in New York by the NBC Symphony under the direction of William Steinberg.)

20 OCTOBER 1938

The Serf, opera in three acts by the 25-year-old English composer George LLOYD, to his father's libretto, dealing with the tragic love of a Saxon vassal youth for a Saxon maiden in 11th-century Britain, who discover to their incestuous horror that they are both natural children of the old Norman King, is produced in London.

22 OCTOBER 1938

Preludio e Scherzo Sinfonico by the 56-year-old Czechborn Italian composer Riccardo PICK-MANGIAGALLI, written in a propulsively rhythmic idiom, is performed for the first time in Milan.

24 OCTOBER 1938

THE BACH SOCIETY of New Jersey sends a letter of protest to the Federal Communications Commission in Washington against the practice of jazzing up the classics by swing bands on the radio.

Recently we heard a jazz orchestra giving a rendition of Bach's *Toccata in D Minor*. All the beautiful fugue effects were destroyed by the savage slurring of the saxophone and the jungled discords of the clarinet. As a group interested in bringing the best music to the people in our state, we must protest against the jazzing of Bach. (An excerpt from the letter of the Bach Society)

Why should the jazzing of Bach's music be any more profane than the mundane treatment it receives at the hands of theater orchestra arrangers? I dare say that the well-fed, salty, beerdrinking, begetting Bach might have delighted in some of the glamorous virtuoso performances of our American jazz transcriptions. (Roy Harris in an open letter to the Bach Society of New Jersey)

25 OCTOBER 1938

A century has elapsed since the birth in Paris of Georges BIZET, whose sunny Mediterranean music enchanted the world and captivated even the tenebrous mind of ruminant Friedrich Nietzsche as an antidote to the octopus-like embrace of Wagner's Teutonic genius.

5 NOVEMBER 1938

Arturo Toscanini conducts the Orchestra of the National Broadcasting Company in New York in the first performances of two works by the 28-year-old American composer Samuel BARBER: *First Essay for Orchestra*, a romantically compact narrative in poetically inflected musical paragraphs, forming a compound of three contrasting sections, *Andante sostenuto, Allegro molto, Scherzando;* and *Adagio for Strings*, an orchestral version of the slow movement from Barber's early *String Quartet* written in an austerely eloquent manner of a polyphonic chorale, destined to become one of the most frequently performed American works, particularly favored on funereal occasions (it was played on the radio after the official announcement of President Roosevelt's death on 14 April 1945).

9 NOVEMBER 1938

Leave It to Me, a musical comedy by the harmonious tunesmith Cole PORTER, dealing with a bumptious American correspondent stationed in Moscow who constantly gets in trouble with both Russians and Americans, featuring the famous song *My Heart Belongs to Daddy*, and the pseudo-political ditties *I'm Taking the Steppes to Russia* and *From U.S.A. to U.S.S.R.*, is produced in New York.

11 NOVEMBER 1938

Violin Concerto by Edward Burlingame HILL, a cultured New Englander, an enlightened Harvardman of music, wrought in an expert manner imbued with an impressionistic aura, is performed for the first time by the Boston Symphony Orchestra, Serge Koussevitzky conducting, with Ruth Posselt as soloist.

11 NOVEMBER 1938

On the 20th anniversary of the end of World War I, Kate SMITH, the voluminous songstress of the radio, broadcasts Irving BERLIN'S anthem-like song *God Bless America*, originally composed in 1918 for the musical revue *Yip Yip Yaphank* at Camp Upton, New York, where he served as a draft sergeant, but never performed in public.

(On 29 November 1940, an octogenarian song writer Alfred M. Aarons filed a lawsuit in Los Angeles against Irving Berlin and Kate Smith charging plagiarism from his own song *America, My Home So Fair*, copyrighted in 1918 and allegedly similar in melody and rhythm with Berlin's song, but lost the case.)

14 NOVEMBER 1938

Violin Concerto in D minor by Nicolai MIASKOVSKY, in three movements (completed on 20 July 1938), couched in a lyrico-dramatic style, with luscious melodies in the solo instrument harmoniously supported by a resonant orchestra, is performed for the first time in Leningrad.

21 NOVEMBER 1938

Leopold GODOWSKY, fabulously endowed Polish-born pianist virtuoso, composer of transcendentally difficult piano pieces and polypianistic arrangements, such as an ambidextrous palimpsest of Chopin's *Black-Key Etude* in the left hand and the *Butterfly Etude* in the right hand, whose aphoristic verbal wit matched his digital agility, dies in New York at the age of 68.

21 NOVEMBER 1938

Ruby HELDER, American woman-tenor with vocal cords masculine in size and resonant power, capable of singing an octave lower than a normal soprano, dies in Hollywood at the age of 48.

23 NOVEMBER 1938

The Boys from Syracuse, musical comedy by Richard RODGERS, derived from Shakespeare's play *A Comedy of Errors*, wherein the mistaken identities of the translocated twins result in fortuitous adultery, including in the score the popular waltz tune *Falling in Love with Love* and the ballad *This Can't Be Love*, is produced in New York.

24 NOVEMBER 1938

Beauty and the Beast, one-act opera by Vittorio GIANNINI, is produced in concert form on the CBS radio. (The first stage performance took place in Hartford, Connecticut, on 14 February 1946.)

24 NOVEMBER 1938

Werner EGK, 37-year-old German composer, conducts at the Berlin State Opera the first performance of his opera in three acts, *Peer Gynt*, to a libretto amplified from Ibsen's dramatic allegory, including an episodic voyage to America, set to music in a fairly modernistic manner, boldly challenging the supremacy of Grieg's celebrated score from incidental music written for the same Ibsen play.

The Nazi press made an assault upon *Peer Gynt* by Werner Egk, and declared it to be unfit for the Nationalist Socialist outlook on the world. Then something quite unexpected occurred: at one of the more recent presentations of the opera in Berlin, there appeared—a *deus ex machina*, so to speak—Führer Adolf Hitler himself. The work pleased him extremely. He asked to have the composer introduced, and is said to have made the statement that he was happy to have met such talent. The direct result of this was the proposal of the opera to the executive board of the Reich Music Festival (and thereby the prospect of numerous productions throughout the Reich) and also the bestowal upon Egk of a government prize of 10,000 marks for the composition of a new opera. (From a Düsseldorf dispatch in the *Christian Science Monitor* of 15 July 1939)

26 NOVEMBER 1938

Concerto for cello and orchestra in E minor by Sergei PROKOFIEV, sketched in Paris in 1934 and completed in Moscow on 18 September 1938, in three movements, *Andante, Allegro giusto* and *Reminescenza,* the finale being a later addition, a thematic metempsychosis, containing a "reminiscence" of the first two movements, the music being of an expressively tonal and rhythmically propulsive facture, is performed for the first time in Moscow by Mstislav Rostropovich.

(Prokofiev incorporated the materials of this concerto in his Second Cello Concerto, which he entitled *Symphony-Concerto for Violoncello and Orchestra,* and which was performed for the first time by Mstislav Rostropovich in Moscow on 18 February 1952.)

28 NOVEMBER 1938

The State Jazz Orchestra of the Union of Soviet Socialist Republics is inaugurated in Moscow, signalizing official Soviet acceptance of jazz as legitimate popular art, in a program of jazzified pieces by Tchaikovsky and Rachmaninoff, and a suite for jazz orchestra expressly written for the occasion by Dmitri SHOSTAKOVICH.

28 NOVEMBER 1938

Vano MURADELI, 30-year-old Georgian Soviet composer, conducts in Moscow the first performance of his *First Symphony,* dedicated to the memory of Sergei Kirov (whose real name was Kostrikov), the Soviet leader assassinated in 1934, who was in his pre-revolutionary past a theater critic and had a pleasing tenor voice.

29 NOVEMBER 1938

A *Poem about Stalin,* symphonic dedication by Aram KHACHATURIAN, set in a loyally devotional lyrico-dramatic manner, with thematic allusions to the native melorhythms of Georgia in the Caucasus, where both Stalin and Khachaturian were born, is performed for the first time at the Second Festival of Soviet Music, in Moscow, with a choral ending to the words of the Caucasian folk poet Ashug Mirza:

Leader of our land! Higher than the mountain rises your glory among nations! Like the sun itself you spread your light through space! The entire globe will soon open its eyes and raise your banner! Ashug Mirza knows that it is true, and that is why he sings so freely! With a song of joyous labor the open pathways will resound! Your name will be our banner forever, O Comrade Stalin!

2 DECEMBER 1938

First Piano Concerto by Darius MILHAUD, composed in 1933, in three contrasting movements, marked *Très Vif, Mouvement de Barcarolle* and *Final,* is performed for the first time by the Minneapolis Symphony Orchestra, with Dimitri Mitropoulos acting in the dual capacity as piano soloist and conductor. (The première took place on 23 November 1934, in Paris.)

4 DECEMBER 1938

The Bishop of the Fejervar Diocese in Hungary issues a directive forbidding the playing of the wedding marches from *Lohengrin* and *A Midsummer Night's Dream* in the Catholic churches under his jurisdiction, reminding his parishioners that Wagner's march is a prelude to adultery and that Mendelssohn's music illustrates the transformation of the bridegroom into a jackass.

10 DECEMBER 1938

Alfred, "heroic opera" by Antonin DVOŘÁK glorifying the reign of Anglo-Saxon King Alfred the Great, translated from the original German libretto used by Dvořák in 1870 when he wrote the opera, is produced in a Czech translation for the first time in Olomouc, thirty-four years after Dvořák's death.

11 DECEMBER 1938

President Franklin Delano ROOSEVELT gives an official sanction to the placing of a new Steinway grand piano in the East Room of the White House to replace the old-fashioned gold-cased instrument installed in 1903 by Theodore Roosevelt, and voicing the hope that future Presidents would make actual use of it. (His successor, Harry Truman, was the first President since Jefferson able to play the piano.)

11 DECEMBER 1938

Orquesta Sinfónica Nacional, the first Peruvian orchestra capable of playing the entire repertory of classical works is inaugurated in Lima, with the Austrian musician Theo Buchwald as conductor and music director.

15 DECEMBER 1938

Sensemayá, "indigenous incantation to kill a snake" for voice and orchestra by the great Mexican composer Silvestre REVUELTAS, to the text of the Afro-Cuban poet Nicolas Guillen, full of voodoo words (Mayombé, Bembé, Mayombé!), with a bumbling bass tuba giving the main theme, is performed for the first time in Mexico City.

15 DECEMBER 1938

Violin Concerto by Ernest BLOCH, in three movements—(1) *Allegro deciso,* in which a broad pentatonic foundation is ornamented with melisinatic arabesques; (2) *Andante,* a rhapsodic cantillation in Hebraic plagal modes; (3) *Deciso-Allegro moderato,* harmonically rooted in stark naked parallel fifths, and concluding on a pandiatonic A minor chord—is performed for the first time by Joseph Szigeti and the Cleveland Orchestra conducted by Dimitri Mitropoulos.

16 DECEMBER 1938

Dédicaces by Vladimir DUKELSKY, for piano, orchestra and soprano, in five pleasingly concatenated movements, is performed for the first time by the Boston Symphony Orchestra, Serge Koussevitzky conducting.

16 DECEMBER 1938

Second Symphony by the 37-year-old English composer Edmund RUBBRA, in four movements, *Lento, Scherzo, Adagio tranquillo* and *Rondo*, written in a classically designed and modernistically accoutred idiom, with an ending in unobstructed D major, is performed for the first time in London.

16 DECEMBER 1938

An Outdoor Overture, a functional orchestral piece by Aaron COPLAND, written in an ozonically spacious pandiatonic idiom, designed for painless musicalization by school orchestra, "optimistic in tone" and calculated to "appeal to the adolescent youth in the country," is performed for the first time at the High School of Music and Art in New York.

23 DECEMBER 1938

Boogie-Woogie, a new way of "swinging the 88" (that is, disporting oneself freely on the 88 keys of the piano keyboard), with a "walking bass" following the rigid metro-harmonic formula—Tonic, Subdominant, Tonic, Dominant—while the right hand promenades along the keys in rhythmically diversified improvisations, is given its first public demonstration at Carnegie Hall, New York, in a historical exposition "from Spiritual to Swing."

The originator of boogie-woogie was Pine Top SMITH of Chicago, who died a few years ago after a barroom brawl. We don't know where his name came from, but the music's name is based on an old phrase, 'pitch a boogie,' which simply meant 'throw a party.' It was at 'house-parties' in the prohibition days that boogie-woogie flourished; a crowd would gather around while the boogie-woogie boys, who bore such names as Crippled Clarence and Toothpick, held a little cutting session. (Maybe we ought to explain that cutting means trying to outplay your predecessor.) (*The New Yorker*, 31 December 1938)

Boogie-woogie is a kind of blues piano playing in which the left hand drones a set bass phrase over and over, while the right hand goes to town with whatever variations the player can think up. Its form is identical with that of the classical *passacaglia*, a kind of dance music (of Spanish origin) that was old stuff to Bach's grandfather. Though boogie-woogie's mournful thump and clatter has long been heard in the humbler dives of New Orleans and Chicago, it was not taken up by the connoisseurs until 1938. In Manhattan, the temple of boogie-woogie has been a subterranean leftist cabaret in Greenwich Village called *Café Society*. Its high priests: Negroes Albert Ammons, Pete Johnson, Meade Lux Lewis. (*Time*, 4 March 1940)

1939

5 JANUARY 1939

VODER (vo-coder, i.e., voice-coder), the first machine ever to produce the sound of the human voice electronically synthesized from primary sibilant and buzzing elements, is demonstrated publicly for the first time at the Franklin Institute in Philadelphia.

5 JANUARY 1939

Horus, opera in four acts by the 60-year-old Hungarian-American composer Baron Gabriel WAJDITSCH VERBOVAC VON DÖNHOFF, to his own libretto, in which the Egyptian god Horus incarnates himself to make love to a beautiful woman, written in a fairly dissonant quasi-impressionistic monodic manner, is performed for the first time by the Philadelphia-LaScala Opera Company at the composer's own expense ($7,500), Fritz Mahler conducting.

The music (if it may justly be called that) of *Horus* was discordant from beginning to end, with an occasional consonant chord occurring so rarely that it seemed as though the composer had made a mistake. He showed an ability bordering upon genius for selecting orchestral combinations which entirely drowned the voices, for there is no chorus in *Horus*. (Samuel L. Laciar, Philadelphia *Record*, 6 January 1939)

It was a shoemaker's performance. The orchestra was too small. But my *Horus* is really a modern opera, not like one by Stravinsky, who knows very little, and is an imitator of Strauss. I have little respect for him. (Baron Gabriel Wajditsch von Dönhoff in a letter to the author, dated 17 November 1963)

9 JANUARY 1939

Béla BARTÓK plays in New York the piano part in the first performance of his *Contrasts* for violin, clarinet and piano (completed in Budapest on 24 September 1938), assisted by Josef Szigeti, violinist, and Benny Goodman, jazz clarinetist, in three movements derived from Hungarian folk melorhythms, the first being the Hungarian recruiting dance *Verbunkos*, the second a slow lyrical piece, and the third a fast rondo, with the violinist making use in its opening bars of an extra violin in *scordatura* tuning, G-sharp, D, A and E-flat calculated to facilitate the playing of open-string tritones, fundamental to Bartók's Lydian modalities and polarized tonalities.

10 JANUARY 1939

The Darvaz Pass, opera in four acts by the 30-year-old Soviet composer Lev STEPANOV, subtitled *The Border Guards*, to his own libretto, dealing with class struggle in pre-revolutionary Central Asia, in which hirelings of feudal Tadzhik overlords unnecessarily murder a non-political girl on her wedding day, thus precipitating a popular revolt, is performed for the first time in Moscow.

10 JANUARY 1939

Julius BITTNER, Austrian composer of neo-romantic operas, dies in Vienna at the age of sixty-four, after the amputation of both legs due to varicose veins.

19 JANUARY 1939

David VAN VACTOR, 32-year-old American composer, conducts the New York Philharmonic in the first performance of his *Symphony in D*, winner of the $1,000 prize of the American Composers' Contest.

20 JANUARY 1939

John Kirkpatrick gives in New York the first complete performance of the *Second Pianoforte Sonata*, entitled *Concord, Mass. 1840–1860*, by the great American individualist Charles IVES, a work of transcendental music in the philosophical conception of the word, constituting a new type of impressionism in which ideas and convictions, even politics, are used as programmatic and descriptive elements, written between 1909 and 1915 and anticipating, in a flash of genius, the musical developments of the future years, published by Ives himself and distributed gratis to anyone with a companion volume, *Essays before a Sonata*, dedicating it "to those who can't stand his music," dedicating the music "to those who can't stand the essays," and "respectfully dedicating" both "to those who can't stand either," in four immensely varied and yet dialectically cohesive movements, each named after a Concord writer:

(1) *Emerson*, with the material derived from a projected "Emerson Piano Concerto," transcendentally complex in texture, with tremendous dissonances enveloped in the lyric substance of cerulean transparency; (2) *Hawthorne*, "trying to suggest some of his wilder, fantastical adventures into the half-childlike, half-fairylike phantasmal realms," in which for the first time in piano literature, clusters of notes are played by pressing a strip of board, 14 3/4 inches long, on the keyboard to convey the idea of Hawthorne's dream of a celestial railroad; (3) *The Alcotts*, a gentle pastorale incorporating the thematic four notes of the "Fate" motive from Beethoven's Fifth Symphony as though played on "the little old spinet-piano Sophia Thoreau gave to the Alcott children"; (4) *Thoreau*, embodying "a transcendental tune of Concord," with an optional flute part, for Thoreau "much prefers to hear the flute over Walden."

This Sonata is exceptionally great music—it is, indeed, the greatest music composed by an American, and the most deeply and essentially American in impulse and implication. (Lawrence Gilman, the New York *Herald Tribune*, 21 January 1939)

23 JANUARY 1939

Alt-Danzig, orchestral suite by the 62-year-old German composer Georg VOLLERTHUN, written with the nationalistic purpose of extolling the spirit of German Danzig, and making use of a number of local German songs, is broadcast for the first time in Berlin as part of the Nazi propaganda campaign to annex the Free City of Danzig.

26 JANUARY 1939

Re Hassan, opera in three acts by the 46-year-old Italian composer Giorgio Federico GHEDINI, to a libretto dealing with the fall of the last Moorish bastion in Granada at the time when the Moorish King Hassan arranged his son's alliance with Spain, in a musical setting containing verisimilitudinarian Mauretanian arabesques, is performed for the first time in Venice.

28 JANUARY 1939

Die Bürger von Calais, opera in three acts by the 35-year-old German composer Rudolf WAGNER-RÉGENY, to a libretto concerning the siege of Calais by the English in 1347, wherein a group of prominent citizens volunteer to be executed as hostages in exchange for the permit to import food for 6,000 inhabitants of the town to save them from starvation, is performed for the first time in Berlin.

31 JANUARY 1939

Cello Concerto by Gian Francesco MALIPIERO is performed for the first time anywhere in Belgrade, Yugoslavia.

1 FEBRUARY 1939

La Dama boba, comic opera in three acts by Ermanno WOLF-FERRARI, subtitled *La Ragazza sciorca (The Foolish Girl)*, after Lope de Vega's comedy of old Spanish mores and amores, written in the manner of the Italian Baroque, is produced at La Scala in Milan.

2 FEBRUARY 1939

NOVACHORD, an electronic musical instrument invented by Laurens HAMMOND, capable of reproducing the timbre of any instrument, from the Hawaiian ukulele to the clavichord, from the piccolo to the trombone, from the violin to the double-bass, is given the first public demonstration in Washington.

3 FEBRUARY 1939

Cotillon, a suite of symphonic dances by the Australian-born composer Arthur BENJAMIN, derived from melodies in the old collection, *The Dancing Master* (London 1719), in nine dancing figures—(1) *Lord Hereford's Delight*, (2) *Daphne's Delight*, (3) *Marlborough's Victory*, (4) *Love's Triumph*, (5) *Jig It*, (6) *The Charmer*, (7) *Nymph Divine*, (8) *The Tattler*, (9) *Argyle*—is performed for the first time in London.

5 FEBRUARY 1939

Der Mond, "theatrical macrocosm" in three acts by the 43-year-old German composer Carl ORFF, to a libretto adapted from a tale of Brothers Grimm about four village boys who capture the moon for the private illumination of their lodgings and take it underground after their deaths, waking up neighboring corpses by lunar luminosity, until St. Peter retrieves the satellite by dispatching a supersonic comet to reinstate it in the firmament to the accompaniment of a zither solo, scored for a modernistically economic instrumental ensemble vivified and rhythmically enriched by a diversified flora and fauna of exotic percussion, is produced in Munich.

11 FEBRUARY 1939

Franz SCHMIDT, romantic Austrian composer of rhapsodically impassioned symphonies and oratorios, dies in Perchtoldsdorf, near Vienna, at the age of 64, largely ignored by an unappreciative musical world.

11 FEBRUARY 1939

Nuptiae Catulli, cantata by the 31-year-old German composer Wolfgang FORTNER after poems by Catullus, is performed for the first time by the Basel Chamber Orchestra.

11 FEBRUARY 1939

Die pfiffige Magd (A Sly Maid), comic opera in three acts by the 59-year-old German composer Julius WEISMANN, is produced in Leipzig.

15 FEBRUARY 1939

Nineteenth Symphony by the prime Soviet symphonist Nicolai MIASKOVSKY, composed between 3 and 26 January 1939, and scored for military band in the optimistic key of E-flat major, in four movements suggesting, respectively, a folk dance, a symphonized waltz, a lyric meditation and constructive rejoicing, is performed for the first time at the Comintern Radio Station in Moscow.

16 FEBRUARY 1939

Wiktor LABUNSKI, 43-year-old Polish-American composer, plays the solo part with the Kansas Symphony Orchestra in the first performance of his *Piano Concerto,* in three movements, *Krakowiak, Nocturne* and *Mazurek,* inspired by Polish dance forms.

16 FEBRUARY 1939

Cynthia Parker, short opera by the American composeress Julia SMITH, relating the story of an American girl kidnapped by the Indians in Old Texas who marries an Indian chief and becomes completely Indianized, with local color supplied by stylized pentatonic songs and dances, is produced at North Texas State Teachers' College in Denton, Texas.

20 FEBRUARY 1939

Two Choric Dances, symphonic diptych in a neo-Grecian manner by the 32-year-old American composer Paul CRESTON, scored for orchestra, piano and tomtom, with the first dance being slow and stately, and the second impulsive and precipitous, is performed for the first time by the Cleveland Federal Orchestra, Arthur Shepherd

conducting. (Originally, the work was scored for chamber orchestra, and performed at the Yaddo Festival in Saratoga Springs, New York, in 1938.)

24 FEBRUARY 1939

Third Symphony by Roy HARRIS, set in a single continuous movement articulated into five contrasting sections, with the first section incorporating materials from an aborted violin concerto written for Jascha Heifetz but rejected by him for lack of violinisticality, opening with a spacious melody in the concerted cellos autogenetically evolving through translucid mazes of contrapuntal configurations, pausing for a pastoral episode with woodwinds pollinating the receptive strings in synchronized motion, reaching a grandiloquent climax in the magisterial fugue in the clarion key of D major (although no key signature is used in any part of the work), and concluding on a somberly powerful G-minor chord, is performed for the first time by the Boston Symphony Orchestra, under the direction of Serge Koussevitzky.

The *Third Symphony* by Harris is America's most successful work in that form.... It is earnest, clumsy, pretentious, imaginative, and terribly sincere. (Virgil Thomson, New York *Herald Tribune,* 17 January 1949)

Let's not kid ourselves. My *Third Symphony* happened to come along when it was needed. The first season it was greeted with the same boos and bravos as have been all my works. Then *Time* magazine hailed it as the most important American symphony, and the Third Symphony was in. (Roy Harris in a statement to the author in 1951)

26 FEBRUARY 1939

Aaron COPLAND's *Sextet* for clarinet, piano and string quartet (arranged from his *Short Symphony*), is performed for the first time in New York.

26 FEBRUARY 1939

On his 20th tour of the United States, Ignace Jan PADEREWSKI gives his first radio recital at Radio City in New York, playing Beethoven's *Moonlight Sonata,* a group of works by Chopin and his own compositions. (The program was printed on silk to prevent audible rustling by the studio audience during the broadcast.)

27 FEBRUARY 1939

Mrs. Eleanor ROOSEVELT resigns her membership in the society of Daughters of the American Revolution in protest against the refusal of the patriotic society, proprietor of Constitution Hall in Washington, to lease it to Marian ANDERSON, Negro contralto, for a public concert.

(Marian Anderson gave an Easter Sunday open-air concert in Lincoln Memorial Park in Washington on 9 April 1939, with 75,000 people in attendance. Eventually she succeeded in overcoming the resistance of the reactionary elements among the membership of the society, and was enabled to sing in Constitution Hall on 7 January 1943.)

27 FEBRUARY 1939

A Life for the Tsar, GLINKA's epoch-making national Russian opera is performed in Moscow for the first time after the Revolution, under the title *Ivan Susanin,* the name of the peasant hero of the opera, who led a group of Polish men bent upon the assassination of the newly elected Tsar Mikhail Romanov in 1606 into an impassable wintry forest and sacrificed his own life by so doing.

(The text of the final chorus, "Glory be to our Russian Tsar," was demonarchized into an acceptably patriotic "Glory be to our Russian land." A preview of *Ivan Susanin* was given on 21 February 1939 in Moscow for a select audience and another special presentation took place in Moscow on 24 February 1939 for the members of the Red Army and Navy.)

28 FEBRUARY 1939

Qarrtsiluni, symphonic poem on Eskimo themes by the 41-year-old Danish composer Knudaage RIISAGER, is performed for the first time in Copenhagen. (A ballet version of *Qarrtsiluni* was first produced in Copenhagen on 21 February 1942.)

1 MARCH 1939

Hamilton HARTY conducts in London the first performance of his symphonic poem *The Children of Lir*, inspired by the ancient Irish saga in which two pairs of twins are transformed into swans by their malevolent stepmother, but are restored to human shape by the sound of a church bell, enabling them to die a Christian death at 1,000 years of age, written in an ambitiously modernistic idiom full of augmented triads and their concomitant whole-tone scales, and including a wordlessly distant soprano voice intoning a pentatonic Celtic chant.

2 MARCH 1939

Amadeo ROLDÁN, Cuban mulatto composer of Afro-Cuban music, including the ballet *La Rebambaramba*, productive of tremendous kinesthetic energy, dies of cancer in Havana, at the age of 38.

6 MARCH 1939

Second Piano Concerto by Gian Francesco MALIPIERO is performed for the first time in Duisburg.

8 MARCH 1939

Third Symphony by the Czech composer and conductor Karel Boleslav JIRÁK is performed for the first time in Prague.

11 MARCH 1939

Die Komödie der Irrungen, opera in two acts after Shakespeare's play *The Comedy of Errors*, by the German composer Carl LORENZ, is produced in Stettin sixteen years after Lorenz's death.

11 MARCH 1939

Pogromes, symphonic poem by the French composeress Elsa BARRAINE, depicting in vivid colors the horrors of anti-Semitic outrages in Tsarist Russia, is performed for the first time in Paris.

16 MARCH 1939

La Chartreuse de Parme, first opera in four acts by the 37-year-old French composer Henri SAUGUET, after Stend-

hal's famous novel, dealing with a young adventurer roaming Italy in 1815, who escapes after imprisonment for murder, rejoins his faithful inamorata but eventually withdraws into the Carthusian monastery in Parma, set to music in a modernistically renovated Italianate idiom, is produced at the Paris Opéra.

21 MARCH 1939

A century has passed since the birth of Modest MUSSORGSKY, the mightiest of the Mighty Five of Russia, who introduced in his operas and songs a true realistic style of melodic expression, faithful to the prosody of Russian speech.

22 MARCH 1939

Laurencia, ballet by the Soviet composer Alexander KREIN, after Lopez de Vega's play *Fuente Ovejuna*, dealing with a 15th-century peasant girl who leads a rebellion against a local feudal lord, making use of genuine Spanish folk songs in an epically rhapsodic and romantically sonorous musical setting, is performed for the first time in Leningrad, as a tribute to the defeated republican cause in the Spanish Civil War of 1936–1939.

23 MARCH 1939

Violin Concerto by Béla BARTÓK, completed by him on 31 December 1938, is performed for the first time by Zoltán Székely in Amsterdam, with Willem Mengelberg conducting the Concertgebouw Orchestra, in three movements:

(1) *Allegro non troppo*, written in a varied sonata form, based on a spacious theme centering on B and developing by cumulative ornamentation into a colorful tapestry of chromatic designs, including a theme of 12 different notes in the solo part without an overt dodecaphonic treatment and some incidental quarter-tones in the recapitulation; (2) *Andante tranquillo*, a set of six variations on a Transylvanian-shaped tune focused on G, subjected to artful translocations and intervallic contractions and expansions, with a fugal episode leading to a tonal pacification, and the violin solo restating the main theme at the end; (3) *Allegro molto*, a precipitous Rondo, wherein a folklike subject is topologically dislocated, followed by a fanfaric canon in proclamatory fourths accumulating vertically in quartal pillars, and after a tremendous crescendo leading to a coda with an epicenter on the tonic B colliding with an avalanche of C's, and culminating in an unobstructed terminal B major triad.

25 MARCH 1939

Heitor VILLA-LOBOS conducts in Rio de Janeiro the first performance of his *Bachianas Brasileiras No. 5*, scored for voice and eight (or any multiple of eight) cellos.

29 MARCH 1939

REICHSMUSIKPRÜFSTELLE, a Nazi agency in charge of musical policy, declares the American ballad *Frankie and Johnny* and all music by Ignace Paderewski inadmissible for performance in Germany.

29 MARCH 1939

The EARL OF CLARENDON, Lord Chamberlain and Supervisor of the London stage, bans the song *Even Hitler Had a Mother* scheduled for first performance in a musical revue opening in London on 20 April 1939, as discourteous to the head of a foreign nation. (The ban was lifted after the outbreak of World War II in September 1939.)

29 MARCH 1939

Elisabeth von England, opera in four acts by the Danish-born German composer Paul von KLENAU, to his own libretto picturing the Queen torn between love for power and love for Essex, written in a sui generis 12-tone idiom with a high incidence of dissonance and the application of *Sprechgesang* is performed for the first time in Kassel. (After the outbreak of World War II, the title was changed to the non-committal designation *Die Königin.*)

31 MARCH 1939

A 50-schilling stamp, bearing the portrait of Josef RHEINBERGER, the estimable German composer and teacher who was born in Vaduz, capital of Liechtenstein, on 17 March 1839, is issued by the government of Liechtenstein to commemorate, with a fortnight's delay, the centennial of his birth. (A large souvenir sheet of 20 multicolored Rheinberger stamps was issued as an accompanying collection.)

1 APRIL 1939

A Festival of Music for the People opens in London with the professed intention of mobilizing music in the service of peace, freedom and labor, featuring a pageant in ten episodes, with the participation of 500 singers, 100 dancers and the People's Festival Wind Band, in performances of works especially written by pacifically inclined English composers, among them Frederic AUSTIN, Alan BUSH, Erik CHISHOLM, Arnold COOKE, Christian DARNTON, Norman DEMUTH, Elizabeth LUTYENS, Elizabeth MACONCHY, Alan RAWSTHORNE, Edmund RUBBRA, Victor YATES and Ralph VAUGHAN WILLIAMS.

3 APRIL 1939

L'Intransigeant Pluton, one-act opera by the 40-year-old Parisian Rumanian composer Marcel MIHALOVICI, is performed for the first time in Paris.

3 APRIL 1939

The second concert of the Festival of Music for the People is given in London with the following program:

Two English Folk Songs by Ralph VAUGHAN WILLIAMS; *British Folk-Music Settings* by Percy GRAINGER; *Matra,* a set of Hungarian folksongs by Zoltán KODÁLY; a militantly satirical suite for voice and instruments by the expatriated leftist Austrian composer Hanns EISLER, in three movements: (1) *News from Vienna, 1938,* (2) *Cantata of Exile,* (3) *Prison House; Friede auf Erden* by Arnold SCHOENBERG for chorus a cappella, composed in 1907; and *Popular Tunes of the Day in USSR* by several Soviet composers arranged for an ensemble of balalaikas.

5 APRIL 1939

The third concert of the Festival of Music for the People in London presents the following program:

BEETHOVEN's *Egmont Overture,* as a symbol of popular struggle for national freedom; the first performance of Benjamin BRITTEN's *Ballad of Heroes* for tenor, chorus and orchestra, composed as a tribute to the men of the British Battalion of the International Brigade, killed while fighting Fascism during the Spanish Civil War; *Lento and Finale* from the *Concerto* for piano and orchestra, baritone and male chorus, by the leftist member of the British Parliament Alan BUSH, ending with a chorus of social significance, with the composer at the piano; and an optimistically eschatological cantata, *These Things Shall Be* by John IRELAND.

5 APRIL 1939

Ferruccio BURCO, precocious boy maestro who, barely out of diapers and into velvet pants, was to conduct professional orchestras, is born in Milan, destined to die in an automobile crash on 27 April 1965.

5 APRIL 1939

Fifth Symphony by the 74-year-old Russian composer Alexandre GRETCHANINOV is performed for the first time by the Philadelphia Orchestra, Leopold Stokowski conducting.

6 APRIL 1939

Symphonie by the 26-Year-old Polish composer Witold LUTOSLAWSKI, written in a neo-classical idiom, is performed for the first time by the Radio Orchestra of Katowice, Gregor Fitelberg conducting.

9 APRIL 1939

Concerto a tre for violin, cello, piano and orchestra, by Gian Francesco MALIPIERO, is performed for the first time in Florence.

14 APRIL 1939

Four and a half months before the Nazi attack on Poland, the 17th Festival of the International Society for Contemporary Music opens in Warsaw, with the following program of orchestral music:

Symphony by the 35-year-old Catalan composer Josep VALLS, written in polyrhythmically vitalized asymmetrical meters (the finale is a dance in 7/8); *5 Orchestral Pieces* by the English composer Christian DARNTON, all extremely short, lasting an average time of 96 seconds each; *Epic Legend* by the Belgian composer Marcel POOT, designed as a modern version of an old-fashioned romantic ballad; *Passacaglia-Chorale* by the Serbian neo-classicist Slavko OSTERC; Scherzo and Finale from the *Violin Concerto* by the Moscow-born half-German, half-Russian composer Wladimir VOGEL, based on a 24-tone theme derived from a 12-tone series and its melodic inversion, culminating with a double fugue, advisedly modeled with a declared intention after Mozart's overture to *Die Zauberflöte;* and *First Symphony* in D major by the French composer Jean RIVIER.

15 APRIL 1939

The first national Kirghiz opera *Aytchurek* composed by Abdylas MALDYBAYEV with the aid of two Russian ethnomusicologists Vladimir VLASOV and Vladimir FERE, to a libretto from an old Kirghiz folk tale concerned with a young maiden nicknamed Lunar Beauty and her beloved fighting for a better life in their benighted land, with the application of genuine melorhythms of the Mongolian tribes of Kirghizstan, is produced in Frunze.

15 APRIL 1939

At the second concert of the 17th Festival of the International Society for Contemporary Music in Warsaw, the following program is presented:

Chamber Cantata by the Swiss neo-classicist Conrad BECK; *Concertino* for saxophone and chamber orchestra by the Danish composer Knudaage RIISAGER; *Mass in G Major* for chorus a cappella by the quadrigenarian member of the once youthful Groupe des Six, Francis POULENC; *Suite* for four trombones in quarter-tones by the Serbian composer Milan RISTIĆ; *Tre Laudi* for voice and chamber orchestra by the Italian modernist Luigi DALLAPICCOLA; *Rengaines* for wind quintet by the Belgian musical surrealist André SOURIS; and *Five Etudes* for piano and orchestra by the Dutch composer Robert DE ROOS.

16 APRIL 1939

Two ancient Egyptian trumpets, one 22 1/2 inches in length made of silver and gold, and one 19 1/2 inches in length made of copper, found in the sarcophagus of King Tutankhamen, are sounded on a world-wide radio broadcast from Cairo after a silence of 3,297 years.

16 APRIL 1939

At the third concert of the 17th Festival of the International Society for Contemporary Music in Warsaw, the following program of choral music by Polish composers is given: *Cantate Romantique* by Stanislaw WIECHOWICZ; *Cantata Ecclesiastica* by Michal KONDRACKI; and *Stabat Mater* by Karol SZYMANOWSKI.

17 APRIL 1939

At the fourth concert of the 17th Festival of the International Society for Contemporary Music in Warsaw, the following program of chamber music is presented:

String Quartet by the English atonal composeress Elizabeth LUTYENS; *Sonatina* for violin and piano by the Czech neo-romanticist Eugen SUCHOŇ; *String Quartet*, Op. 28, by Anton von WEBERN, commissioned by the Elizabeth Sprague Coolidge Foundation, and first performed at the Berkshire Festival of Chamber Music in Pittsfield, Massachusetts, on 22 September 1938, in three movements, with the fundamental series derived from the intervallic figure BACH, its inversion and its transposition; *String Quartet* by the Japanese composer Kojiro KOBUNE; *Coplas Sefardies* for voice and piano by Alberto HEMSI of Egypt; *Two Songs* by Honorio SICCARDI of Argentina; and *String Quartet* by the Dutch composer Henk BADINGS.

19 APRIL 1939

Zvezdoliki (The Star-Faced), cantata by Igor STRAVINSKY, usually catalogued under the French title *Le Roi des Etoiles*, written in 1911–12, to words by the Russian poet Constantin Balmont from his cycle *The Vigil of the White Doves*, wherein a Nietzschean superman arises in Apocalyptic glory to lead mankind towards a mystical consummation of faith, set to music in subtilized sonorities using special effects such as glissandos on harmonics in the divided strings, and ending on a dissonant chord of an augmented eleventh, is performed for the first time anywhere in Brussels, 27 years after its composition, by the Belgian State Radio Orchestra and male chorus, on the date of the solar eclipse (partial in Belgium).

(*Zvezdoliki* was announced for performance in the printed program of the Philadelphia Orchestra, under the direction of Leopold Stokowski, for 9–10 December 1932, but the performance was canceled at the last moment owing to the difficulty in obtaining clearance of performance rights.)

20 APRIL 1939

At the fifth concert of the 17th Festival of the International Society for Contemporary Music in Warsaw, the following program of chamber music is presented:

String Quartet by the Polish composer Jerzy FITELBERG; *Trois Poèmes Lyriques* for violin and piano by the Yugoslav composer Demetrij ZEBRE; *String Quartet* by the Catalan composer Joaquín HOMS; *Petite Suite* for violin and piano by the Czech composer Jozef ZAVÁDIL; *Fugue* for piano by the Dutch composer Piet KETTING; *String Quartet* by the Czech composer Vladímir POLÍVKA.

21 APRIL 1939

The 17th Festival of the International Society for Contemporary Music concludes in Warsaw with the following program of orchestral works:

20 Variations in Symphonic Form by the Polish composer Boleslaw WOYTOWICZ, based on the principle of cumulative accretion of thematic material, each variation containing added components of the gradually integrated subject; *Le Savetier et le Financier*, aria for baritone and orchestra by Gaston BRENTA of Belgium; *Ostinato* for orchestra by Lars-Erik LARSSON of Sweden; *Prélude et Invention* for string orchestra by the Parisianized Rumanian composer Marcel MIHALOVICI; *Symphonic Studies* by the English composer Alan RAWSTHORNE; and *Overture* by the Polish composer Antoni SZALOWSKI.

22 APRIL 1939

The Old Maid and the Thief, grotesque opera by Gian Carlo MENOTTI, to his own libretto in English, depicting in 14 episodes in merry Rossinian tones, the picaresque adventures of a sexy intruder in the bedroom of an American spinster who becomes fascinated by his physique ("tall and burly, black hair and curly, light complexion, Southern inflection") and joins him in his kleptophilic profession, is performed for the first time in concert form by the National Broadcasting Company in New York. (First stage performance was given by the Philadelphia Opera Company on 11 February 1941.)

28 APRIL 1939

Paul Bunyan, ballet for puppets and solo dancers by the 18-year-old American composer William BERGSMA, is performed for the first time in Rochester, New York.

29 APRIL 1939

Gudrun, ballad opera in two acts by the 36-year-old German composer Ludwig ROSELIUS, is performed for the first time in Graz.

30 APRIL 1939

The New York World's Fair inaugurates its Music Hall, with Olin DOWNES, the music critic of the New York

Times, as its director. (He resigned on 24 May 1939 after the administration of the fair announced a new policy of presenting only popular musical programs.)

2 MAY 1939

Suite variée for symphony orchestra by the American composer Ernest SCHELLING, in six descriptive movements couched in a romantically old-fashioned idiom—*Catalonian Evocation* (written in memory of Enrique Granados), *The Fountains of Garengo* (a tonal impression of Shelling's estate in Switzerland), *Cradle Song for a Sick Child, Tarantella* (for strings only), *Irlandaise* (a musical portrait of a vivacious Irishwoman) and *The Last Flight*, subtitled *Aviation Field, October 10, 1918* (commemorating the fatal flight of an aviator friend over Verdun at the end of World War I)—is performed for the first time by the San Francisco Symphony Orchestra, Pierre Monteux conducting.

12 MAY 1939

Luis A. DELGADILLO, prime composer of Nicaragua, conducts in Managua the intermittently active Orquesta Sinfónica de Nicaragua in the first performances of his colorful symphonic suites, *Escenas Pastoriles* and *Los Tincos,* based on Nicaraguan folk melodies.

17 MAY 1939

Sergei PROKOFIEV conducts in Moscow the world première of his cantata *Alexander Nevsky,* completed by him on 7 February 1939, with the music expanded from the material of his film score of the same name, in seven sections:

(1) *Russia under the Mongolian Yoke,* written in an ostentatiously static Asiatic melismatic style; (2) *Song about Alexander Nevsky,* commemorating the Russian victory against Sweden on the banks of the River Neva, which gave Alexander his honorary surname Nevsky; (3) *Teutonic Knights in Pskov,* a medieval Latin chant in mock-Gregorian monotone; (4) *Arise, Russian People,* a patriotic marching song with characteristic folksong inflections and plagal cadences; (5) *Battle on Ice,* a triumphant proclamation of the Russian victory over the Teutonic knights on the frozen surface of Lake Peipus on 5 April 1242, constituting a meaningful reminder to the latter-day Nazi Teutons not to venture into Russia; (6) *The Field of the Dead,* a lyrical lament in gently modulated minor tonalities; (7) *Alexander's Entry in Pskov,* a grandiloquent celebration of the victory by ringing church bells and singing Russian songs.

18 MAY 1939

The Devil and Daniel Webster, American folk opera in one act by Douglas MOORE, to a libretto by Stephen Vincent Benét, wherein a young New England farmer incautiously signs a contract selling his soul to the Devil incarnated in the affable shape of a Boston lawyer named Scratch, but is saved from perdition by the forensic eloquence of the great Webster, who proves the Devil legally wrong, set to music in an artfully simplicistic melodious and harmonious manner, is produced in New York.

19 MAY 1939

Under the auspices of the Society of Friends and Enemies of Modern Music of Hartford, Connecticut, Ernst KRENEK conducts his first major work written in America, *Eight-Column Line,* a newspaper ballet in the 12-tone technique, with the principal tone-row emblematic of the pressure in meeting the daily deadline.

24 MAY 1939

München Walzer, orchestral suite of nostalgic waltzes by Richard STRAUSS, composed on 3 January 1939 for a film about Munich, is performed for the first time at a Munich municipal ball.

(The film itself was never shown. The second version of the music was completed by Strauss on 24 February 1945, with the inclusion of a supplementary section in G minor marked "trauernd einverlebt" as a mourning *Gedächtniswalzer* after the devastating fire air raid on Munich by the Allied Air Force. This second version was performed for the first time in Vienna on 31 March 1951.)

24 MAY 1939

Pocahontas, ballet-legend in one act by the 30-year-old American composer Elliott CARTER, dealing with the Indian maiden of that name (1595–1617) who reportedly saved the valiant Virginian settler John Smith from death at the hands of her segregationist anti-miscegenating father, is performed for the first time in New York.

2 JUNE 1939

Josef REITER, Austrian composer, sadly remembered as one who wrote a *Festgesang an den Führer des deutschen Volkes,* dedicated to Hitler, and published by the Nazi-dominated Universal Edition, but never performed, dies in Vienna at the age of 77.

5 JUNE 1939

Two stamps at 10 and 70 centimes with portraits of Claude DEBUSSY are issued by the French Post Office.

9 JUNE 1939

The British Week at the New York World's Fair is inaugurated with a concert by the New York Philharmonic conducted by Sir Adrian Boult, featuring the world première of the *Seventh Symphony* in A-flat by the English romantic composer Arnold BAX, dedicated to the American people, in three movements, alternatingly muscular, lymphatic and melancholic, along with the first American performance of the *Concerto* for Oboe and Orchestra by Eugene GOOSSENS, with the composer's brother Leon playing the solo part (first performed by him in London on 2 October 1930).

10 JUNE 1939

Sir Adrian Boult conducts the New York Philharmonic in the second concert under the auspices of the British Council for the British Week at the New York World's Fair, featuring the world première of the *Piano Concerto* by Arthur BLISS, dedicated "to the people of the United States of America," in three movements, *Allegro con brio, Adagietto* and *Andante maestoso,* written in a grandly pianistic manner, chromatically opulent but firmly anchored in tonality, with sonorous explosions mitigated by lyric interludes; and the world première of *Five Variants on Dives and Lazarus* for string orchestra by Ralph VAUGHAN WILLIAMS.

11 JUNE 1939

On his 27th birthday, Mukhtar ASHRAFI, Bukharaborn Soviet composer, conducts in Tashkent the first performance of the first national Uzbek opera *Buran*, in five acts, written with the help of his teacher Sergei Vassilenko, to a libretto dealing with the Uzbek rebellion against Tsarist rule in Central Asia in 1916 led by an indigent proletarian named Buran and his son whose young wife, violated by the soldiery, goes insane.

17 JUNE 1939

Variations Symphoniques by the 26-year-old Polish composer Witold LUTOSLAWSKI with a theme in E major of Chopinesque facture evolving in its variations into complex configurations adorned by neo-Baroque frills and trills, long scales with migratory tonics and tritone-terraced canons, ending on a major seventh tonic chord, is performed for the first time in Cracow.

17 JUNE 1939

Katchkyn (The Fugitive), opera by the 28-year-old Tatar composer Nazib ZHIGANOV, first national Tatar opera, in three acts, to a libretto in the Tatar language, dealing with Pugatchov's rebellion against Catherine the Great, is produced at the opening of the National Tatar Opera House in Kazan, once the main stronghold of the Golden Horde of the conquering Mongols to whom Russia paid tribute for centuries.

20 JUNE 1939

Las Vírgenes del Sol, opera by the Argentine composer Alfredo SCHIUMA, in three acts, glorifying in sonorous Italianate tones the desperate stand of the Sun Virgins in an Inca temple in Peru in 1532, during the final assault of the Conquistadores, is produced at the Teatro Colón in Buenos Aires.

23 JUNE 1939

By the order of the War Department in Washington, the marching cadence of the United States Army is reduced from 128 to 120 steps per minute, effective as of September 1939.

24 JUNE 1939

H_2O, symphonic poem by the 31-year-old Belgian composer Robert ROUSSEAU, winner of the competition for the best aquatic composition for the Exposition Internationale de l'Eau at Liège, written in a scientifically illustrative idiom, in a fine fluvial vein, with melodious hydrogen atoms and harmonious oxygen particles combining in double counterpoint in an effective chemical reaction producing a molecule of water, is performed for the first time at the inaugural of the Liège Exposition.

18 JULY 1939

The Spanish composer Manuel PALAU conducts the inaugural concert of the newly established Orquesta de Falange Española Tradicionalista in Valencia, organized and supported by the Falangist party.

24 JULY 1939

The Nazified municipality of Vienna expropriates the personal estate and royalties of the family of Johann STRAUSS in order to deprive his non-Aryan stepdaughter of her rights to the inheritance, overruling her claim that she was an illegitimate daughter of Johann Strauss himself, and therefore an Aryan in good standing.

8 AUGUST 1939

The Fascist Department of Education issues in Rome a directive aimed at the elimination of French musical terminology, arguing that "just as omelette can be replaced by the Italian word *frittata*," so the French form *Ouverture* can and ought to be changed to *Introduzione*, and *Suite* to *Sequenza*.

28 AUGUST 1939

Chasca, lyric opera by the Argentinian composer Enrique M. CASELLA, with an orchestra of native wind and percussion instruments concealed behind the scenery, is produced at Tucumán.

28 AUGUST 1939

Drygva (Woodland Thicket), national Byelorussian opera in four acts by the 26-year-old Vitebsk-born composer Anatoly BOGATYREV, to a libretto in the Byelorussian (White Russian) language, portraying in socialistically realistic tones the partisan resistance of Byelorussian peasants against the Polish occupation army during the civil war of 1919, with an ending paralleling that of Glinka's opera *A Life for the Tsar* as the peasant hero dies chanting "Voroshilov leads us forward," is performed for the first time in Minsk, the capital of Byelorussia.

11 SEPTEMBER 1939

The song writers Jimmy KENNEDY and Michael CARR of London compose the first British World War II marching song *We're Gonna Hang Out the Washing on the Siegfried Line, If the Siegfried Line's Still There*, with a traditional 32-bar refrain. (As fate would have it, the Siegfried Line wasn't there, militarily speaking, when the Allied armies reached it during the last weeks of the war in 1945.)

27 SEPTEMBER 1939

The initial eleven notes of CHOPIN's *Military Polonaise*, serving as signature of the Warsaw State Radio, are sounded on the xylophone for the last time before the final occupation of the burning Polish capital by the Nazi war machine.

6 OCTOBER 1939

American Festival Overture by the 29-year-old American composer William SCHUMAN, an animated musical fresco of modern American life, with the initial three notes imitating the teenage call of New York streets, evolving into a tetrahedron of quadruple counterpoint punctured by explosive polyrhythms, is performed for the first time by the Boston Symphony Orchestra, Serge Koussevitzky conducting, at a special concert "in honor of the American composer" on the same program with George

GERSHWIN's *Piano Concerto*, Randall THOMPSON's *Second Symphony* and the *Third Symphony* of Roy HARRIS.

7 OCTOBER 1939

Médée, opera in three scenes, after Euripides, by Darius MILHAUD, portraying in ominous bitonalities and tragically translocated asymmetric rhythms the terrorizing story of the mythological Greek mother avenging herself on her perfidious husband by killing her children, is produced for the first time in Antwerp.

7 OCTOBER 1939

Die Kathrin, opera in three acts by Erich Wolfgang KORNGOLD, erstwhile musical prodigy from Vienna, forced to go into exile in Hollywood, to a libretto dealing with the amorous military life in a garrison town in Southern France, is produced in Stockholm, after its planned first performance in Vienna scheduled for spring 1938 was canceled by the invading Nazis as a work by a Jewish composer.

8 OCTOBER 1939

Columbus, one-act opera by Eugen ZÁDOR, 44-year-old Hungarian composer, who arrived in the United States as war clouds began to gather in Europe in the spring of 1939, written originally to a Hungarian libretto by Archduke Joseph Franz of Hungary, grandson of the Emperor Franz Joseph, depicting in five episodes the successive stages leading to the discovery of America, receives its world première in an English version, over the National Broadcasting Company Network in New York.

8 OCTOBER 1939

Unwilling to continue to live in Spain conquered by the Falangist regime, Manuel DE FALLA arrives in Buenos Aires after a sea voyage of 16 days, destined to remain in Argentina until his death.

10 OCTOBER 1939

During the Storm, opera in four acts by the 26-year-old Soviet composer Tikhon KHRENNIKOV, dealing with the turbulent events during the communization of agriculture in the Tambov region in 1919–1921, incorporating a romantic love story between two militant young collectivists, with the epicenter occupied, for the first time in Soviet opera, by the vigilant but benevolent figure of Lenin in his Kremlin office, couched in a socialistically realistic, melodious and harmonious idiom, is produced in Moscow. (A second version of this opera was produced in Moscow on 12 October 1952.)

12 OCTOBER 1939

Variations and Fugue by the expatriate Czech composer Jaromir WEINBERGER, on the melody *Under the Spreading Chestnut Tree* by William Sterndale Bennett (1816–1875), made newly popular by King George VI who sang it at a boys' camp in London shortly after the outbreak of World War II, is performed for the first time by the New York Philharmonic, John Barbirolli conducting.

14 OCTOBER 1939

The new American musical protective society, BROADCAST MUSICAL INC., is organized in New York City, "pursuant to a resolution to carry out the building of an alternate source of music suitable for broadcasting," thereby entering competition with the hitherto practically monopolistic American Society of Composers, Authors and Publishers (ASCAP), established in 1914.

21 OCTOBER 1939

Die Nacht, symphonic suite written in a lyrical Germanic idiom by the expatriate octogenarian American composer George Templeton STRONG, who took up permanent residence in Switzerland in 1892 as a gesture of protest against the neglect of American music in the United States, is performed for the first time anywhere by the NBC Symphony Orchestra in New York conducted by Arturo Toscanini.

24 OCTOBER 1939

Third Symphony for string orchestra by the French composer Jean RIVIER, in four movements of gallantly Gallic music elegantly projecting nostalgic, vivacious, ruminant and declarative moods, is performed for the first time at Hartford, Connecticut, Leon Barzin conducting. (The French première of the work took place in Paris on 25 September 1940.)

28 OCTOBER 1939

Concerto in D for guitar and orchestra by the 44-year-old Italian composer Mario CASTELNUOVO-TEDESCO is performed for the first time by Andrés Segovia in Montevideo, Uruguay.

30 OCTOBER 1939

San Juan Capistrano, two nocturnes for orchestra by the 40-year-old American composer Harl MCDONALD, subtitled *The Mission* and *The Fiesta,* is performed for the first time by the Boston Symphony Orchestra, Serge Koussevitzky conducting.

31 OCTOBER 1939

Overture by the Soviet composer Lev KNIPPER, written to celebrate "the liberation of the Western Ukraine and Byelorussia," heretofore Eastern Polish provinces, by the Red Army, is performed for the first time on the Moscow Radio.

2 NOVEMBER 1939

Mario CASTELNUOVO-TEDESCO, Italian composer who was compelled to leave Italy in 1939 when the Fascist officialdom under pressure from Hitler adopted discriminatory measures against Jews, plays the solo part with the New York Philharmonic conducted by John Barbirolli, in the world première of his *Second Piano Concerto*, in three contrasting movements, *Vivo, Romanza* and *Vivo e impetuoso*, written in an effective manner of the modern Italian Baroque.

2 NOVEMBER 1939

Blennerhassett, radio opera by the 36-year-old American composer Vittorio GIANNINI, written in a flowingly melodious and ingratiatingly harmonious idiom, dealing with the seditious ruminations of the imperial-minded Vice President of the United States Aaron Burr on the island of Blennerhassett on the Ohio River, is performed for the first time by the Columbia Broadcasting Company in New York.

5 NOVEMBER 1939

Sixth Symphony by Dmitri SHOSTAKOVITCH, in three movements—(1) *Largo,* proceeding from a unisonal opening through contrapuntal involvements and pastoral discursions to a quiet ending in D minor; (2) *Allegro,* a scherzo in 3/8 time, neatly symmetrical in outline, marked by an incessant rhythmic propulsion and ending in a pianississississimo in D major; (3) *Presto,* a perpetually self-generating rondo in socialistically realistic 4/4 time, with an interlude in 3/4, ending in a sonorous D major—is performed for the first time in Leningrad.

9 NOVEMBER 1939

The Palestine Symphony Orchestra inaugurates in Haifa a series of conductorless concerts under the motto "The Orchestra Conducts Itself," in a program of classical works.

17 NOVEMBER 1939

Kleine Sinfonie for strings, woodwinds, trumpet, harp and cymbals, by the aging conservative German composer Hans PFITZNER, written in an engagingly old-fashioned romantic manner, is performed for the first time in Hamburg.

18 NOVEMBER 1939

Upon his arrival in Argentina from Spain, Manuel DE FALLA conducts at the Teatro Colón in Buenos Aires the first complete performance of his *Homenajes,* a symphonic suite of four homages: *Pour le Tombeau de Debussy* (originally composed for guitar in 1920); *Fanfare pour Arbós* (written in 1933 as a friendly offering to the Spanish conductor Enrique Fernández Arbós); *Pour le Tombeau de Paul Dukas* (originally a piano piece written as an elegy on the death of Dukas in 1935); and *Pedrelliana,* a dedication to the Spanish composer and folklorist Felipe Pedrell, composed in 1938.

18 NOVEMBER 1939

The Third Soviet Music Festival opens in Moscow with the first performances of the symphony-cantata *On the Field of Kulikovo* by the 52-year-old Soviet composer Yury SHAPORIN, glorifying in grandly resonant harmonies the Russian victory over the entrenched Mongols in 1380, and dedicated to the ideal of "immortal national heroism and eternal all-conquering patriotic love of the Russian people for our fatherland," and of a *Harp Concerto* by Alexander MOSSOLOV, regenerated Soviet ex-modernist, chastened into a frame of mind suitable for composing music for the harp.

20 NOVEMBER 1939

Lev KNIPPER, 40-year-old Soviet symphonist, conducts in Moscow the first performance of his *Seventh Symphony,* subtitled *Military Symphony,* signalizing "the readiness of the Soviet people to answer, blow for blow, the agitation of the warmongers," and presenting in its three movements a series of musical episodes in the life of the Red Army, on the same program with a similarly monitory cantata *Alexander Nevsky* by Sergei PROKOFIEV.

20 NOVEMBER 1939

Désiré PÂQUE, Belgian composer of eight symphonies and a number of pieces of chamber music, inventive excogitator of the athematic method of composition, "adjonction constante" who wrote the first atonal pieces for children dies in Bessencourt, France, at the age of 72.

23 NOVEMBER 1939

Peacock Variations for orchestra by Zoltán KODÁLY, a set of sixteen very short pieces in various forms, meters and rhythms, all derived melodically from the pentatonic Hungarian folk song *Fly, Peacock, Fly,* prefaced with an Introduction and capped by a Finale, arranged in brilliant instrumental colors, is performed for the first time by the Concertgebouw Orchestra in Amsterdam as a commissioned work for its 50th anniversary, with Willem Mengelberg conducting.

25 NOVEMBER 1939

Emelian Pugatchov, historical oratorio by the Soviet composer Marian KOVAL, glorifying the Russian cossack who led a rebellion against Catherine the Great, and even taunted her by impersonating her husband Peter III, assassinated by a band of her lovers, but who was eventually cornered, drawn and quartered in Moscow on 11 January 1779, set to music in appropriately heroic tones, with dramatic plagal cadences and resonant Russian harmonies, is performed for the first time at the Moscow Festival.

6 DECEMBER 1939

Du Barry Was a Lady, musical comedy by Cole PORTER, in which an American washroom attendant dreams of being Louis XIV, in hot pursuit of Madame Du Barry (who appears to him as the incarnation of a nightclub entertainer after whom he lusts) and is shot in the groin by the Dauphin, is produced in New York.

7 DECEMBER 1939

Violin Concerto by the 37-year-old English composer William WALTON, in three movements, *Andante tranquillo, Presto capriccioso alla napolitana* and *Vivace,* written in a resonant cosmopolitan, inframodern idiom, with firm tonal epicenters reposing above the modulatory lyric turbulence, is performed for the first time by Jascha Heifetz, by whom it was commissioned, with the Cleveland Orchestra, Artur Rodzinski conducting.

8 DECEMBER 1939

Ernest SCHELLING, American erstwhile child prodigy of the piano, and in his maturity a successful conductor of concerts for children, composer of urbane albeit unnecessary symphonic pieces, dies in New York at the age of 63.

9 DECEMBER 1939

Imaginary Landscape No. 1, first of a series of surrealistic compositions by the 27-year-old Californian apostle of the musical avant-garde, John CAGE, scored for two phonograph turntables, muted piano and a suspended cymbal, comprising four 15-bar sections, each divided into three equal parts, alternating with three interludes, respectively one, two and three bars in length, is performed for the first time in Seattle, Washington.

16 DECEMBER 1939

Fascinated by the rhythmically scanned injunction on a cautionary paper sign in a Harvard University men's room, "Do Not Throw Paper Towels in Toilets," Igor STRAVINSKY rips it off and jots down a fitting melody in duple time marked *Andante 2/4*: efD, ddd, (cd), e, d#C (capital letters represent quarter notes; small letters represent eighth notes; run-together letters represent sixteenth notes; letters in parentheses are to be sung on a single syllable).

21 DECEMBER 1939

Zdravitza (Health Toast), salutatory cantata by Sergei PROKOFIEV composed for Stalin's 60th birthday, to words in the Russian, Ukrainian, Byelorussian, Kurd, Mari and Mordva languages, is performed for the first time in Moscow, on the same program with a *Birthday Overture* by Nicolai MIASKOVSKY, also written for Stalin, and cast in the appropriately optimistic, socialistically realistic, flatless and sharpless key of C major.

22 DECEMBER 1939

Second Symphony by the 36-year-old Russian-American composer Nikolai LOPATNIKOFF, written in a cheerfully neo-classical manner, in the traditional four movements, is performed for the first time by the Boston Symphony Orchestra, Serge Koussevitzky conducting.

23 DECEMBER 1939

Monte Ivnor, opera in three acts by the 44-year-old Italian composer Lodovico ROCCA, to a libretto derived from Franz Werfel's novel *Die vierzig Tage des Mussa Dagh*, wherein a tribal group ensconced in the caves of an impregnable Caucasian mountain defends itself for forty days against a fearful enemy assault, set to music in a bleak homophonic idiom inspissated by drops of dissonant blobs, is performed for the first time in Rome.

1940

2 JANUARY 1940

Jacques HEUGEL, descendant of the founder of the French music publishing firm Heugel, publishes an editorial in *Le Ménestrel* cautioning Frenchmen against emotional Wagnerophobia justified by Hitler's annexation of Wagner's racial notions, and urging the detractors of "le grand Saxon" to devote their patriotic energies to the safeguarding of the Rhine frontier (here two lines were deleted in the magazine by the French military censor) and to the fight against Bolshevism.

5 JANUARY 1940

The linking of radio stations by short wave is successfully demonstrated by an experimental connection between the local radio station in Worcester, Massachusetts, and New York City, using frequency modulation techniques developed by Major Edwin H. Armstrong, effectively eliminating background noises produced by static electricity.

7 JANUARY 1940

Effie Canning CARLTON, American lady who wrote in 1886, when she was 15, the famous berceuse *Rock-a-Bye,*

Baby, whose somnific cadences lulled generations of American children to restful sleep, dies in Boston at the age of 69.

7 JANUARY 1940

Violin Concerto by the Dutch modernist Willem PIJPER (completed on 8 February 1939), in three movements, monothematically designed and polyharmonically evolved, ending on a bitonal chord with D as epicenter, is performed for the first time in Amsterdam.

8 JANUARY 1940

Violin Concerto by the 43-year-old American composer Roger SESSIONS, rationally neo-classical in form, imaginatively dissonant in contrapuntal harmony, fundamentally tonal in its centripetal mobility and asymmetrically kinesthetic in rhythmic patterns, cast in four movements, *Largo e tranquillo, Scherzo, Romanza* and *Molto vivace,* is performed for the first time in Chicago.

9 JANUARY 1940

La Rosa rossa, opera by Renzo BOSSI, after Oscar Wilde's tale of a mysteriously potent red rose, is performed for the first time in Parma.

11 JANUARY 1940

The Great American Goof, ballet by the 26-year-old American composer Henry BRANT, is performed for the first time in New York.

11 JANUARY 1940

Romeo and Juliet, ballet by Sergei PROKOFIEV, in three acts and 13 tableaux, with a prologue and epilogue, wherein the multiple aspects of Shakespeare's play are reflected in a musical mirror resplendent with lyrical sentiment, dramatic tension and tragic somberness, and presented in an infinite variety of artful melodious settings, vitalized by a propulsive current of vivacious rhythms and colorful instrumentation, is produced in Leningrad. (Three orchestral suites, drawn from the ballet score, were performed respectively in Moscow on 24 November 1936, in Leningrad on 15 April 1937 and in Moscow on 8 March 1946.)

20 JANUARY 1940

Joan von Zarissa, ballet by the 38-year-old German composer Werner EGK, is produced in Berlin.

27 JANUARY 1940

After playing a piano recital in Town Hall, New York City, in a program consisting exclusively of works in minor keys, and concluding with *Totentanz* by Liszt, Alexander KELBERINE, 36-year-old Russian-born American pianist, takes a lethal overdose of sleeping drugs to end a life made intolerable by financial troubles and marital disharmony (his wife, Jeanne Behrend, was also a pianist). (His body was found in his New York apartment on 30 January 1940.)

There were distortions in rhythmic patterns, blurred pedal effects and exaggeration of inner voices. . . . A psychic turmoil seemed to be reflected in Mr. Kelberine's performances. (Robert Lawrence in the New York *Herald Tribune,* 28 January 1940)

Kelberine Suicide After Recital That Revealed Psychic Turmoil—Pianist's Condition Noted in Critic's Review. (Headlines in the New York *Herald Tribune,* 31 January 1940)

30 JANUARY 1940

Les Illuminations, suite of ten pieces for high voice and string orchestra by the 26-year-old English composer Benjamin BRITTEN (completed on 25 October 1939 in Amityville, New York, where he was staying, having left England as a conscientious objector to the war), to French poems by Arthur Rimbaud, set in delicately luminous tonal transparencies, is performed for the first time in London.

1 FEBRUARY 1940

The first issue of the British magazine *The Music Review,* intended to provide a forum for the free expression of every shade of critical opinion, exclusive of patent prejudice or blatant vulgarity, is published in Cambridge, England, under the editorship of Geoffrey Sharp.

2 FEBRUARY 1940

Dance Symphony for orchestra and women's chorus by the 55-year-old Flemish composer Arthur MEULEMANS, is performed for the first time in Brussels.

4 FEBRUARY 1940

Ghirlino, fairy-tale opera by the 55-year-old Italian composer Luigi FERRARI-TRECATE, in two acts, dealing with an adolescent hero who slays the monster kidnapper of his sister and of other little girls, is produced in Milan.

4 FEBRUARY 1940

The Ballad of Magna Carta, cantata by Kurt WEILL, foremost proponent of European political theater music, now living in the United States, to the text by Maxwell Anderson, relating in rhythmic speech and vocal narration the events accompanying the signing of the Magna Carta by King John of England in 1215 A.D., marking the advent of modern democratic concepts, set to music in marching and waltzing motion, in triadic harmonies seeded with pandiatonic dissonance, is performed for the first time on the Pursuit of Happiness Radio Program of the Columbia Broadcasting System in New York, as an expression of concerted determination of free nations to oppose European dictators.

5 FEBRUARY 1940

Second Symphony by Ernst BACON is performed for the first time in Chicago.

6 FEBRUARY 1940

Barbershop Ballad for orchestra by the American composer Ross Lee FINNEY, a sophisticated medley of enticingly vulgar tunes beloved by the mustachioed celebrants of the gay nineties, is performed for the first time on a Columbia Broadcasting System radio program in New York.

9 FEBRUARY 1940

Double Concerto for two string orchestras, piano and timpani by the prime Czech composer Bohuslav MARTINU, completed by him in Switzerland on 29 September 1938, the day on which his country was dismembered at the appeasement conference in Munich, written in a neo-Baroque style, with searching atonal melodic leaps, impatient and yet restrained rhythmic pulse, basically tonal and bitonal, triadic in harmony, though key signature is never applied, in three movements, *Poco Allegro, Largo, Allegro,* the first two ending on major triads, the last on an agonizingly polytonal chord, is performed for the first time as a commissioned work by the Chamber Orchestra of Basel, Paul Sacher conducting.

With anguish we listened every day to the news bulletins on the radio. During this time I was at work on my *Double oncerto;* but all my thoughts were constantly with my endangered country . . . It is a work written under terrible circumstances, but the emotions it voices are not those of despair, but rather of revolt, courage and unshakable faith in the future . . . The foreboding of approaching tragedy anticipated the character of the whole composition, like a warning against unleashed destructive elements, as if it were in my power to hold them back. (Martinu's words quoted in the article *Music and War* by Gerald Larner in *The Listener,* London, 17 March 1966)

15 FEBRUARY 1940

La Pulce d'Oro, opera buffa in one act and three scenes by the 47-year-old Italian composer Giorgio Federico GHE-

DINI, dealing with an aurific flea with a Midas touch whose bite produces a golden pimple on the thigh of an innkeeper's daughter, whereupon the flea's owner asks the girl's hand in marriage, and departs with her and the flea, is produced in Genoa.

20 FEBRUARY 1940

Il Revisore, comic opera by Amilcare ZANELLA, after Gogol's comedy descriptive of civic corruption and official subservience in a provincial Russian town early in the 19th century, is produced in Trieste.

24 FEBRUARY 1940

Irek (Freedom), opera in four acts by the 29-year-old Soviet composer Nazib ZHIGANOV, to a libretto in the Tatar language, dealing with the revolutionary events of 1917 in the Tatar villages on the Volga, is produced in Kazan.

28 FEBRUARY 1940

Arnold DOLMETSCH, "Musical Confucius," restorer of old instruments and scholarly interpreter of Baroque music (in medieval German, Dolmetsch means interpreter), founder of the Haslemere Festivals presenting concerts of new music specially composed for his instruments, dies in Surrey, England, four days after his 82nd birthday.

1 MARCH 1940

La Danse des Morts, dramatic oratorio for solo voices, chorus and orchestra, by Arthur HONEGGER to the text by Paul Claudel, inspired by Holbein's drawings of macabre skeleton dances, fusing choral polyphony and spoken psalmody in eschatological pageantry, in which the majestic voice of Jehovah thunders sepulchral reminders of man's mortality, and the tune of the French song *Sous le Pont d'Avignon* is interwoven with the strains of the revolutionary ballad *La Carmagnole* and the ominous sounds of *Dies Irae* in a pandemoniac *quodlibet,* is performed for the first time by the Chamber Orchestra of Basel, Paul Sacher conducting.

3 MARCH 1940

Karl MUCK, imperious and authoritative German conductor (Philip Hale described him as "calm, undemonstrative, graceful, elegant, aristocratic") whose interpretations of German symphonic masterpieces were marked by strict fidelity to the composer's score, dies in Stuttgart at the age of 80.

7 MARCH 1940

Arthur SHEPHERD, 60-year-old Idaho-born composer, conducts the Cleveland Orchestra in the first performance of his *Second Symphony,* in four classically organized movements, interspersed with a few American tunes.

7 MARCH 1940

Pennsylvania Symphony by the American romanticist Charles Wakefield CADMAN, depicting in a vast musicorama the history of Pennsylvania, from its founding by William Penn in the sylvan wilds of the American Atlantic Coast to the dawn of the industrial age (illustrated by banging on an iron plate in the orchestra), is performed for the first time by the Los Angeles Philharmonic, Albert Coates conducting.

10 MARCH 1940

The first American television broadcast of an operatic work takes place in New York, presenting a condensed version of Leoncavallo's opera *Pagliacci* performed by members of the Metropolitan Opera Company.

10 MARCH 1940

Paul PARAY conducts in Paris a concert of the combined orchestras of Concerts Colonne and Lamoureux, composed of musicians not drafted into the French Army, in a program of works by Berlioz, Debussy and Ravel, and, despite a general clamor against performances of Wagner's music in wartime France, including also the overture to Wagner's opera *Tannhäuser.*

(The concert was originally announced as a Berlioz-Wagner Festival, but the program was changed on the advice of the French Minister of Finance, replacing three Wagner selections by works of Debussy and Ravel, and retaining only the Overture to *Tannhäuser* as a gesture of artistic impartiality, reasoning that the annexation of Wagner by Hitler should not impair the intrinsic value of Wagner's art.)

14 MARCH 1940

Dame Kobold, comic opera by the Latvian-born German composer Kurt von WOLFURT, written in a fairly modernistic vigesimosecular idiom, is performed for the first time in Kassel.

14 MARCH 1940

Violin Concerto by Paul HINDEMITH, in three movements, marked *Mässig bewegte Halbe, Langsam* and *Lebhaft,* written in free tonality, with spacious quartal melodies contracting into tense chromatics in the development, is performed for the first time by the Concertgebouw Orchestra in Amsterdam, under the direction of Willem Mengelberg.

16 MARCH 1940

Singoalla, opera by the 31-year-old Swedish composer Gunnar de FRUMERIE, is performed for the first time in Stockholm.

18 MARCH 1940

Violin Concerto by the American master of neo-classical composition, Walter PISTON, in three movements, an acidly energetic *Allegro,* a reticently modal *Andantino* and a spirited *Allegro,* cast in ternary tonality (D major, F minor, D major) is performed for the first time in New York, with Ruth Posselt as soloist.

20 MARCH 1940

The German music periodical *Signale für die musikalische Welt* publishes the article *Angst vor Richard Wagner* deploring the "fear of Wagner" in France during the period of so-called "phony war" on the Western front when neither the French nor the Germans initiated aggressive military action as though observing a tacit armistice:

In the absence of military activity at the West Wall (our adversaries call it the Siegfried Line), the French government has opened an offensive against German art and issued orders against playing Wagner's music. The strange association between the Siegfried Line and Wagner is explained in the Paris daily *Le Jour*: "Wagner's art is a mirror of the brutal and rapacious German soul. Now that the front line, where our sons may be fighting tomorrow, bears the name of Siegfried, it seems hardly fitting for us to participate in Wagner's glorification."

23 MARCH 1940

ANNA, veteran white mare of the Metropolitan Opera House in New York, an honored member of the cast, distinguished particularly for her supporting role in *Aida*, and once mounted by Caruso himself, dies of old age at the Pegasus Club in Rockleigh, New Jersey.

24 MARCH 1940

Edouard BRANLY, French inventor of the coherer, an essential element in wireless telegraphy, who sent the first radio signals from one room to another (he reported his experiment to the Paris Académie des Sciences on 24 November 1890), dies in war-darkened Paris at the age of 95.

3 APRIL 1940

Masao OKI, 38-year-old Japanese composer, conducts in Tokyo the first performance of his symphonic ballet suite *Hagoromo* inspired by an old Japanese legend.

6 APRIL 1940

Heitor VILLA-LOBOS conducts in Rio de Janeiro the first complete performance of his opera *Izaht*, to the story of an American Indian girl in Paris who unselfishly saves the life of the bride of the French viscount she loves, incidentally revealing the fact that the winning bride is the natural daughter of an Apache chieftain, set to a harmonious score enlivened by heteroousian Brazilian rhythms.

7 APRIL 1940

New York Skyline, "symphonic millimetrization" scientifically contrived by Heitor VILLA-LOBOS, with its melorhythmic shape derived from the diagram of a photograph of the New York skyline, is broadcast from Rio de Janeiro to New York on the occasion of the opening of the Brazilian Pavilion at the New York World's Fair.

9 APRIL 1940

Stereophonic reproduction of recorded music from sound film, producing an illusion of multidirectional lifelike performance and three-dimensional listening, is demonstrated in public for the first time by the Bell Telephone Laboratories in Carnegie Hall in New York.

11 APRIL 1940

Moby Dick, dramatic cantata by the 29-year-old American composer Bernard HERRMANN, a sonorous characteriza-

tion of the cetacean hero of Melville's famous novel, employing an appropriately leviathanic orchestra, including a set of radio thunder drums, is performed for the first time by the New York Philharmonic, John Barbirolli conducting.

12 APRIL 1940

A Tale About the Land, ballet by the 33-year-old American composer Paul CRESTON, is performed for the first time in Philadelphia.

12 APRIL 1940

Eugene GOOSSENS conducts the Cincinnati Symphony Orchestra, of which he is the music director, in the world première of his *First Symphony* in four movements, written in a characteristically cosmopolitan modern manner, brightened by a cornucopia of colors from his impressionistic palette, and dedicated to "my colleagues of the Cincinnati Symphony Orchestra."

13 APRIL 1940

Romeo and Julia, opera in two acts, after Shakespeare, by the 29-year-old Swiss composer Heinrich SUTERMEISTER, is produced in Dresden.

16 APRIL 1940

Aotearoa, overture on the themes of the aboriginal Maori tribes by the 24-year-old New Zealand composer Douglas LILBURN, is performed for the first time in London.

17 APRIL 1940

Suite Georgienne by the 41-year-old expatriate Russian composer Alexander TCHEREPNIN, in four movements, a symphonic evocation of the mountainous landscape of Georgia in the Caucasus, is performed for the first time in Paris, Charles Munch conducting.

17 APRIL 1940

Christophe Colomb, radio drama by Arthur HONEGGER, portraying in philosophical terms the search by Columbus of the way to the Indies, is performed for the first time by the Radio Lausanne, under the direction of Ernest Ansermet.

18 APRIL 1940

Pravo Horo, symphonic dance by the 28-year-old Bulgarian-born American composer Boris KREMENLIEV, employing asymmetrical meters peculiar to Balkan music, and utilizing a battery of native percussion, is performed for the first time in Rochester, New York, Howard Hanson conducting.

19 APRIL 1940

Concertino for string orchestra by the Boston composer Edward Burlingame HILL, in three balanced movements, the last being in the form of a quadruple concerto, is performed for the first time by the Boston Symphony Orchestra, Serge Koussevitzky conducting.

23 APRIL 1940

A Stopwatch and an Ordnance Map, a realistic piece of wartime music by Samuel BARBER, scored for men's chorus and kettledrums, is performed for the first time in Philadelphia.

24 APRIL 1940

The Wise Virgins, ballet by the English composer William WALTON, to a scenario from the parable of ten virgins in the New Testament, making use of themes from Bach's cantatas, is performed for the first time in London.

25 APRIL 1940

America Was Promises, cantata by the 37-year-old Russian-born American composer Nicolas NABOKOV, to a text by Archibald MacLeish, with the application of rhythmic speech, is performed for the first time on the radio in New York.

28 APRIL 1940

Luisa TETRAZZINI, Italian prima donna, voluminous of torso and mighty of lungs, who could pick up a carnation from a bouquet on the floor while singing a high C without losing power, and whose turbulent life story included a provisional marriage to a professional gigolo, dies in Milan at the age of 68.

29 APRIL 1940

Concertino for marimba and orchestra by the American composer Paul CRESTON is performed for the first time in New York.

3 MAY 1940

As part of the American Composers' series, a one-cent Stephen FOSTER stamp and a two-cent John Philip SOUSA stamp are issued by the United States Post Office.

7 MAY 1940

A century has elapsed since the birth of Peter Ilytch TCHAIKOVSKY, great Russian melodist whose contagious emotionalism flowing in the harmonious streams of his symphonies, concertos and songs has endeared him to Old and New Russia alike, and made his music a perennial art. (The Soviet government commemorated the Tchaikovsky centennial by renaming a Moscow street Tchaikovsky Boulevard, and by issuing a series of postage stamps with Tchaikovsky's portraits.)

7 MAY 1940

The New York Song Writers Protective Association overwhelmingly adopts a vote of censure against commercial exploitation of pornography in popular American music, and orders the expulsion of all members purveying lewd, lascivious, licentious and libidinous songs for juke boxes, but reserves judgment on sophisticated songs with an optional double meaning, such as *She Had to Go and Lose It at the Astor,* or *I Don't Know How He Does It But He Does It.*

9 MAY 1940

Two centuries have passed since the birth in Taranto of Giovanni PAISIELLO, Italian composer of melodious operas who enjoyed a fine success not only in Italy but in Russia, whither he went at the invitation of Catherine the Great, and whose setting of *Le Barbier de Séville* enjoyed considerable popularity until displaced by Rossini's masterpiece on the same subject.

11 MAY 1940

Kleopatra, opera in two acts by the Yugoslav composer Danilo SVARA, depicting the familiar tragedy of the Egyptian Queen, is produced in Ljubljana.

13 MAY 1940

As part of the American Composers Postage Stamps Series, 2,200,000 Victor HERBERT 3-cent stamps are placed on sale in New York, and the same number of 5-cent Edward MACDOWELL stamps are issued at the MacDowell Colony in Peterborough, New Hampshire.

16 MAY 1940

Carlos CHÁVEZ conducts at the Museum of Modern Art in New York an ensemble of Mexican musicians in a program of modern Mexican music, including the first performance of his piece for percussion orchestra *Xochipili-Macuilxochitl*, named after the Aztec god of music.

17 MAY 1940

Marie Grubbe, opera by the Danish composer Ebbe HAMERIK, to a libretto based on the life story of a cunning Danish intrigante who wrought havoc in the dynastic affairs of Scandinavia in the second half of the 17th century, is produced in Copenhagen.

18 MAY 1940

Volo di Notte, one-act opera by the Italian composer Luigi DALLAPICCOLA (completed on 18 April 1939), to a libretto after *Vol de nuit* by the French aviator Antoine de Saint-Exupéry, describing a dramatic night flight over the Andes, fighting the winds and the cold in a single-engine fabric monoplane, written in a tense atonal idiom, with incidental dodecaphonic passages (a wordless voice speaks to the pilot in 12-tone phrases) and spoken dialogue, is performed for the first time in Florence.

27 MAY 1940

Amerindia, ballet by the foremost Bolivian composer José María VELASCO MAIDANA, glorifying "the new Indian of tomorrow," is produced in La Paz, an event described by the President of Bolivia as "of transcendent significance in the history of Bolivia's artistic culture."

27 MAY 1940

Adrian LEVERKÜHN, the fictional inventor of the 12-tone method of composition in Thomas Mann's novel *Doktor Faustus*, dies in Munich at the age of forty-four, after suffering a catatonic seizure while giving a lecture on his symphonic cantata *The Lamentation of Dr. Faustus*, written in the 12-tone system of composition, with a mystical fundamental verbal tone-row containing 12 syllables, "Denn ich sterbe als ein böser und guter Christ," set to a melody consisting of 12 different notes and all different intervals between successive tones, with numberless ramifications in which "the ordering of basic materials becomes total," so that "there is no longer a free note," concluding on a high G *pianissimo*.

27 MAY 1940

A century has passed since the death in Nice of Niccolò PAGANINI, the Mephistophelean wizard of the violin.

30 MAY 1940

Rosas de Todo o Ano, opera by the Portuguese composer Ruy COELHO, is produced in Lisbon.

31 MAY 1940

Arturo TOSCANINI and the National Broadcasting Company Symphony Orchestra sail from New York on the S.S. *Brasil* on a good-will tour of South America, with the first concert stop in Rio de Janeiro, where Toscanini made his debut as opera conductor in 1886 at the age of 19.

7 JUNE 1940

Král Lávra (King Laurence), opera by the Czech composer Jaroslav KŘIČKA, is produced in Prague.

10 JUNE 1940

As part of the American Composers' postage stamp series, the United States Post Office issues a ten-cent stamp for Ethelbert NEVIN.

11 JUNE 1940

Genug ist nicht genug, cantata for mixed chorus, string orchestra, two trumpets and kettledrums by the Swiss composer Willy BURKHARD, written in an effective neo-ecclesiastical vein, is performed for the first time by the Chamber Orchestra of Basel, Paul Sacher conducting.

11 JUNE 1940

Divertimento for string orchestra by Béla BARTÓK, in three movements, *Allegro non troppo*, *Molto adagio*, and *Allegro assai*, written in an ebullient neo-Baroque vein, with an insistent rapid pulse in triple meters governing the outer, fast movements and the slow middle part marked by rhythmic fibrillation in dissonant secundal harmonies, is performed for the first time by the Chamber Orchestra of Basel, Paul Sachet conducting.

12 JUNE 1940

Durad Branković, music drama in five scenes by the Serbian composer Svetomir NASTASIJEVIĆ, to a libretto depicting the misfortunes of a medieval Balkan maiden abducted by the Turkish Sultan for his harem, is produced in Belgrade.

19 JUNE 1940

Maurice JAUBERT, French composer of theater music for cinema and dance, is killed leading a company of soldiers at Azérailles, near Baccarat, during the last days of fighting on the Western front, before the French capitulation to the overpowering Nazi might.

20 JUNE 1940

Jéhan ALAIN, 29-year-old French composer of 127 organ pieces, a young keeper of the ornate Franckian tradition, is killed a few days before the end of hostilities in France while leading a motorcycle patrol near Saumur.

21 JUNE 1940

Jean VUILLERMOZ, 33-year-old French composer, is killed during the last hours of military action before the surrender of France, while on patrol duty at Lobsonn, Alsace.

23 JUNE 1940

Semyon Kotko, opera in five acts by Sergei PROKOFIEV, to a libretto dealing with the dramatic events of the Civil War in the Ukraine in 1918–1920, written in a heroically realistic manner thematically imbued with native melorhythms, in a framework of typical Prokofievian harmonies, is produced in Moscow.

25 JUNE 1940

Three American works: *And They Lynched Him on a Tree*, cantata by the Negro composer William Grant STILL; *1940* by Roy HARRIS, a choral work to the text of the Preamble of the Constitution of the United States; and *Ballad for Americans*, "a statement of democracy" for voice and orchestra by Earl ROBINSON, are performed for the first time in public by the New York Philharmonic at the Lewisohn Stadium in New York, Artur Rodzinski conducting. (*Ballad for Americans* had a previous radio performance on 5 November 1939.)

1 JULY 1940

A lawsuit brought by Jack DARRELL against the authors and publishers of the popular song *It Happened on the Beach at Bali Bali* charging infringment of copyright of his tune, *Does Anybody Want a Kew Pie?* is dismissed by the United States Circuit Court of Appeals on the ground that "the infantile demands of the popular ear" reduce the choice of available combinations of tones to a very low number, and that apparent plagiarism is easily explicable by a probable coincidence.

5 JULY 1940

This Is Our Time, cantata of social consciousness by the 29-year-old American composer William SCHUMAN is performed for the first time at the Lewisohn Stadium in New York by the New York Philharmonic, assisted by the workers' chorus of the People's Philharmonic Choral Society, composed of members of many trades, among them house painters, carpenters, laundrymen, and furriers, with Artur Rodzinski conducting. (The performance was originally scheduled for Independence Day, 4th of July, but had to be postponed on account of rain.)

8 JULY 1940

The Berkshire Music Center opens its first academic summer session at Lenox, Massachusetts, with Serge

Koussevitzky as its founder and director, as the out-growth of the annual Berkshire Music Festivals, established by him in 1934.

10 JULY 1940

Sir Donald TOVEY, hyper-cultured British musical essayist, master of elegant English prose, and incidentally a composer of romantic pieces of all descriptions, able conductor and a pianist, dies in Edinburgh a week before his 65th birthday.

12 JULY 1940

Panambí, ballet by the 24-year-old Argentine composer Alberto GINASTERA, written in a modemistically stylized Latin American idiom, bristling with asymmetrical rhythms projected against steady meters, is performed for the first time in Buenos Aires. (A symphonic suite from *Panambí* was performed in Buenos Aires for the first time on 27 November 1937.)

26 JULY 1940

Ernst TOCH becomes an American citizen.

4 AUGUST 1940

Twenty days after his arrival in New York from subjugated France, Darius MILHAUD conducts the first performance, broadcast over the Columbia network, of his orchestral elegy, *Le Cortège funèbre*, written by him in his native Aix-en-Provence shortly before the French surrender to the overwhelming Nazi forces.

4 AUGUST 1940

Charles NAGINSKI, 31-year-old Egyptian-born American-Jewish composer of brilliant eclectic music, drowns himself in the Housatonic River near Lenox, Massachusetts, in a fit of despondency over his inability to meet the strict contrapuntal test in Paul Hindemith's composition class at the Berkshire Music Center.

9 AUGUST 1940

Ferial, symphonic divertimento by the Mexican composer Manuel PONCE, bearing the simple dedication "A México," and depicting the colorful commotion of a Mexican fiesta, introduced by a reverent church scene, is performed for the first time in Mexico City, under the direction of Carlos Chávez.

16 AUGUST 1940

As a result of a statistical survey conducted by the Parliamentary Secretary to the Ministry of Information of Great Britain, regarding the catalytic property of suitable music in wartime factory work, it is announced in London that the playing of music by Chopin and Rachmaninoff produces an increase of the munitions output from 6 to 12 percent.

27 AUGUST 1940

Meredith WILLSON, 38-year-old American composer of popular music, conducts the San Francisco Symphony Orchestra on Treasure Island, California, in the world première of his *Prelude to The Great Dictator*, arranged by him from the background music of Chaplin's motion picture *The Great Dictator*, the thematic material of which was "composed," by whistling and humming, by Charlie Chaplin himself, and set on paper, organized and harmonized by Hanns Eisler and others, with Hynkel (Hitler) represented by a hoarse trumpet. (The program included also Willson's own *Second Symphony*, subtitled *The Missions of California*.)

11 SEPTEMBER 1940

Hold On to Your Hats, a musical comedy by Burton LANE, centered on a radio singer who goes off to Mexico to capture a bandit as an advertising stunt, the score containing the popular song *There's a Great Day Coming Mañna*, is produced in New York.

15 SEPTEMBER 1940

Stabat Mater, a newly discovered work by Domenico SCARLATTI, scored for a ten-part chorus, a rare example of a truly polyphonic work in his catalogue, is performed for the first time at the opening of the Musical Festival in Siena.

19 SEPTEMBER 1940

De Två Kungadöttrarna (Two Princesses), radio opera by the Swedish composer Hilding ROSENBERG, is performed for the first time in Stockholm.

1 OCTOBER 1940

Nadezhda PLEVITSKAYA, Russian singer of folk ballads, who once sang for the Tsar and who had appeared at a concert in New York with Rachmaninoff at the piano as an accompanist, dies in a prison cell in Rennes, France, where she was confined for her involvement in a conspiracy to kidnap and murder an expatriate Russian general in Paris.

6 OCTOBER 1940

Silvestre REVUELTAS, jovial 40-year-old Mexican composer (he was born on the last day of the 1800's), fervent believer in the political function of music (his posthumous ballet *La Coronela* centers on a female colonel leading the Mexican revolution against the dictatorial President Diaz), dies in Mexico City of pneumonia, aggravated by chronic alcoholism, at ten minutes after midnight (and thus, technically speaking, on 6 October), on the night of the performance of his last completed ballet *El Renacuajo Paseador (Promenading Pollywog)*.

7 OCTOBER 1940

Guslar, symphonic poem by the Croatian composer Jacov GOTOVAC, a tonal biography of a player on the Balkan instrument *gusla*, depicting the peripeteia of his life and concluding in an ethnic catharsis, is performed for the first time in Zagreb.

10 OCTOBER 1940

The Jubilee season of the Chicago Symphony Orchestra, celebrating its 50th anniversary, is inaugurated by its

German-born music director and conductor Frederick STOCK with the first performance of his own *Festival Fanfare* scored for a vociferous ensemble including the Schellenbaum, a luxuriantly ornamented percussion and concussion instrument, known also as Turkish Crescent, Chinese Pavilion, or Jingling Johnny, used in Turkish Janizary music and introduced into European military bands to provide visual and auditory exotic effects.

17 OCTOBER 1940

Darius MILHAUD conducts the Chicago Symphony Orchestra in the world première of his *First Symphony* in neatly articulated four movements, completed on 19 December 1939 in his native Aix-en-Provence, and conceived in a broadly rhapsodic style, based on native melorhythms.

17 OCTOBER 1940

Nele Dooryn, lyric opera in three acts by the 64-year-old French composer Antoine MARIOTTE, is produced at the Opéra-Comique in Paris.

20 OCTOBER 1940

At the opening of a ten-day festival of Buriat-Mongol music in Moscow, two four-act operas in the Buriat language are given for the first time:

Enkhe-Bulat-Bator (Enkhe, the Steel Giant), first national opera of the Buriat-Mongol Republic, written on native themes by the Byelorussian-born composer Markian FROLOV (1892–1944), dealing with the overthrow of a repressive Siberian Khan by his adopted son of proletarian parentage, whose perilous struggle is diversified by his lyrical love for the daughter of a downtrodden blacksmith; and *Bair* by the 40-year-old Soviet composer Pavel BERLINSKY, centering on the heroic rescue of a beauteous peasant girl kept in a golden cage in the expectation of her transportation to the harem of a Mongol warlord. (*Bair* was first performed in the form of incidental music to a play in Ulan-Ude on 3 July 1938.)

22 OCTOBER 1940

A revised version of *Guntram* by Richard STRAUSS, his first opera, to a medieval story of the chivalrous love of the German knight Guntram, a member of the Holy Society of Peace, for a duke's daughter, is performed for the first time in Weimar, where it was originally staged on 10 May 1894.

24 OCTOBER 1940

Fourth Symphony subtitled *Sinfonia gaia*, by the 43-year-old Danish composer Knudaage RIISAGER, in three hedonistic movements, is performed for the first time in Copenhagen.

24 OCTOBER 1940

Symphony in C by the American composer and successful railroad executive John Alden CARPENTER, a single movement of romantic inspiration, articulated in sections, with occasional excursions into the colorful realm of impressionistic tone painting, is performed for the first time by the Chicago Symphony Orchestra as a commissioned work for its golden anniversary.

25 OCTOBER 1940

Cipressi, a symphonic suite by the 45-year-old Italian composer Mario CASTELNUOVO-TEDESCO, an orchestrated version of his romantically colored dendrological piano suite written in 1921, is performed for the first time by the Boston Symphony Orchestra, Serge Koussevitzky conducting.

25 OCTOBER 1940

Cabin in the Sky, musical fantasy by Vernon DUKE (né Vladimir Dukelsky), containing among its tunes the memorable ballad *Taking a Chance on Love*, is produced in New York.

26 OCTOBER 1940

Gherman, symphonic poem by the Bulgarian composer Filip KUTEV, a ritual prayer for rain during which a stone idol nicknamed Gherman is mourned to the refrain "Gherman died of drought, send a drop of water, o God," melorhythmically derived from orientalized Balkan motives in asymmetrical rhythms, is performed for the first time in Sofia.

27 OCTOBER 1940

Festmusik by Richard STRAUSS, composed on the occasion of the 2,600 years of the Imperial dynasty of Japan, is performed for the first time in Tokyo. (Strauss completed the score on 22 April 1940 and handed it over to the Japanese Ambassador in Berlin on 11 June 1940 as an act of solidarity to an ally in the political Axis of Germany, Italy and Japan.)

28 OCTOBER 1940

Hamlet, Shakespearean symphonic poem by the Manchurian-born German composer Boris BLACHER, is performed for the first time by the Berlin Philharmonic Orchestra.

29 OCTOBER 1940

Violin Concerto by the Soviet master of instrumental music Vissarion SHEBALIN, in three movements, *Introduction and Fugue*, *Aria* and *Rondo*, is performed for the first time in Leningrad.

30 OCTOBER 1940

Panama Hattie, a musical comedy by Cole PORTER, in which an American diplomat shocks society by marrying a Panama nightclub hatcheck girl but proves the wisdom of his choice when she foils an anarchist plot to blow up the Panama Canal, is produced in New York.

6 NOVEMBER 1940

After an arduous journey from Switzerland through Nazi-occupied France and Falangist Spain, in a flight from the "unbearable moral atmosphere of the European continent," the grand old man of Polish music Ignace PADEREWSKI lands in New York on the S.S. *Excambion* from Lisbon, Portugal.

7 NOVEMBER 1940

Sixth Symphony, by the New England composer of Wagneromantic orchestral music Frederick S. CONVERSE (1871–1940), is performed posthumously for the first time by the Indianapolis Symphony Orchestra, Fabien Sevitzky conducting.

7 NOVEMBER 1940

Igor STRAVINSKY conducts the Chicago Symphony Orchestra in the world première of his *Symphony in C*, completed by him in Beverly Hills, California, on 19 August 1940, commissioned by the Chicago Symphony Orchestra to mark its semicentennial, bearing a dedication identical in wording with Stravinsky's dedication of the *Symphony for Psalms* to the Boston Symphony Orchestra ten years before: "This Symphony, composed for the glory of God, is dedicated to the Chicago Symphony Orchestra on the occasion of the 50th anniversary of its existence," in four movements:

(1) *Moderato alla breve*, set in a classical bithematical form of a sonata, in pandiatonic tonality; (2) *Larghetto concertante*, an aria, "simple, clear and tranquil"; (3) *Allegretto*, "white music," in Stravinsky's words, comprising the neoclassical counterparts of a *Minuet*, a *Passepied* and a *Fugue*; (4) *Largo, Tempo giusto*, distributed in spacious harmonies, and concluding on a medievally oblique cadence, coming to rest on a pandiatonic complex, with a G-major triad superimposed on the C-major sixth-chord.

9 NOVEMBER 1940

Concierto de Aranjuéz for guitar and orchestra by the blind Spanish composer Joaquín RODRIGO, in three movements, *Allegro con spirito, Adagio, Allegro gentile*, painting the fragrant ambience of the streets and plazas of the town of Aranjuéz in the fertile plain near Madrid in an artlessly harmonious and melodious manner, rich in an authentic feeling for Spanish folkways, and distinguished by virtuoso cadenzas for the guitar, is performed for the first time in Barcelona.

12 NOVEMBER 1940

Alejandro García CATURLA, Cuban composer of aggressively modernistic music of Afro-Cuban inspiration, saturated with primitivistic rhythms of the jungle in a modernistic setting of sonorously dissonant harmonies, is assassinated with two bullets fired in his chest, by a petty criminal about to be sentenced to a prison term by Caturla acting as district judge of his native town of Remedios.

12 NOVEMBER 1940

The French Post Office issues two DEBUSSY stamps, at 10 and 80 centimes.

13 NOVEMBER 1940

Fantasia, a cosmogonic "silly symphony" contrived for the motion picture screen in full color by Walt Disney, opens its presentations at the Broadway Theater in New York with special "fantasound" equipment creating the illusion of a realistically stereophonic sound, conducted by Leopold Stokowski (whose coattails are occasionally pulled by Mickey Mouse), with Deems Taylor supplying urbane comments, set to a musical score zeugmatically arranged from the following sources:

Abstract animation for Bach's *Toccata and Fugue;* vesuviating mushroom dance for Tchaikovsky's *Nutcracker Suite;* Mickey Mouse as *Sorcerer Appretice* for Paul Dukas's symphonic scherzo; mesozoic monsters disporting themselves in the primordial slime for Stravinsky's *Le Sacre du Printemps* (with an anachronism of some 90,000,000 years occurring in the animation, in which a giant Tyrannosaurus Rex of the Cretaceous period is locked in combat with a Stegosaurus of the Jurassic period); flirting centaurs and centaurettes for excerpts from Beethoven's *Pastoral Symphony;* alligators and hippopotamuses choreographically cavorting to the music of Amilcare Ponchielli's *Dance of the Hours;* a nocturnal sortilege to Mussorgsky's symphonic tableau *Night on the Bald Mountain;* and an angelic apotheosis in a sonorously amplified and flamboyantly devotional rendition of Schubert's *Ave Maria*.

16 NOVEMBER 1940

At the Moscow Festival of Soviet Music in Moscow, three new works are performed for the first time:

Twenty-First Symphony in F-sharp minor by Nicolai MIASKOVSKY (composed between 28 May and 1 July 1940), a lyrico-dramatic work in one cyclic movement, with distinct subdivisions marked by contrasting moods (which was performed, as a commissioned work, by the Chicago Symphony Orchestra on a later date, 26 December 1940, under the title *Symphonie-Fantaisie*); *Violin Concerto* by Aram KHACHATURIAN, in three movements, *Allegro con fermezza, Andante sostenuto* and *Allegro vivace*, embodying orientalistic elements of Caucasian melorhythms, ultrachromatic in nostalgic lyrical episodes, diatonic in volitional dramatic passages and orgiastic in the dancing finale; and excerpts from the unfinished opera *The Decembrists* by Yury SHAPORIN.

17 NOVEMBER 1940

Gualicho, one-act opera by the Italian-Argentinian composer Alfredo PINTO, is produced in Buenos Aires.

21 NOVEMBER 1940

Die Walküre is brilliantly staged at the Moscow Opera House, marking the first Russian performance of a WAGNER opera since 6 December 1925, staged as a conciliatory gesture towards Wagnerophilic Germany, in harmony with the non-aggression and rapprochement pact, concluded by the Union of Soviet Socialist Republics with the Third Reich on the eve of World War II in August, 1939.

23 NOVEMBER 1940

At the Moscow Festival of Soviet Music, Dmitri SHOSTAKOVICH plays the piano part in the world première of his *Quintet* for piano and strings (which was to win for him a Stalin prize of 100,000 rubles), in five movements:

(1) *Prelude*, with a slow introduction leading to an infectiously rhythmic gigue, and cyclically reverting to the slow statement: (2) *Fugue*, a stately projection, entirely orthodox in the tonal imitation of the subject: (3) *Scherzo*, in a boisterously furfuraceous spirit; (4) *Intermezzo*, gaunt in its philosophic rumination; (5) *Finale*, in the manner of toccata, with whimsically percussive episodes, concluding with an exuberant circus-like march tune.

24 NOVEMBER 1940

Toktogul, opera in four acts by the 41-year-old Soviet composer Aleksander VEPRIK, to a libretto in the Kirgiz language glorifying a pioneer of national Kirgiz arts named Toktogul Satylganov (1864–1933), is performed for the first time in Frunze, capital of the Kirgiz Soviet Socialist Republic.

25 NOVEMBER 1940

Third Symphony for string orchestra by the French romantic composer Jean RIVIER, set in four movements in classical forms and marked by impressionistic procedures, is performed for the first time in Paris.

28 NOVEMBER 1940

Twentieth Symphony by Nicolai MIASKOVSKY, in E major (completed on 20 September 1940), in three contrasting movements, is performed for the first time in Moscow, twelve days after the first performance of his *Twenty-first Symphony.*

1 DECEMBER 1940

Don João IV, opera by the Portuguese composer Ruy COELHO, is produced in Lisbon.

5 DECEMBER 1940

Jan KUBELÍK, Czech violin virtuoso, raven-locked darling of feminine audiences of the early years of the century, dies in Nazified Prague at the age of 60.

6 DECEMBER 1940

The world première is given by Louis Krasner, soloist, with the Philadelphia Orchestra, Leopold Stokowski conducting, of the *Violin Concerto* by Arnold SCHOEN-BERG, completed by him in Hollywood on 23 September 1936, and written according to the method of composition with 12 tones related only to one another, carried out with classical lucidity and precision, with the basic tone row, A, B-flat, E-flat, B, E, F-sharp, C, D-flat, G, A-flat, D and F, containing in its configuration three significantly consecutive tritones, in three movements:

(1) *Poco Allegro,* rich in isorhythmic thematic phrases, gaining momentum as incidence of notes per time unit increases, while the basic tone row is solidified in vertical formations, culminating in a flowery violin cadenza, before subsiding into a euphonious coda; (2) *Andante* grazioso, gently swaying in waltzing Viennese rhythms, with characteristically Schoenbergian choriambic sighs, while sternly maintaining the unrelentingly dissonant harmonies and steadfastly evading any tonal connotations; (3) *Allegro,* marked by an extraordinary prevalence of dry drum rolls, giving rise to passionate discords and eventuating in a stentorian restatement of the original tone row.

Schoenberg: I believe that in my Violin Concerto I have created the necessity for a new kind of violinist.

José Rodriguez: A virtuoso recently told me that the concerto is unplayable until vionists can grow a new fourth finger especially adapted to play on the same string at the same stop as three other fingers.

Schoenberg (laughing like a pleased child): Yes, yes, that will be fine. The Concerto is extremely difficult, just as much for

the head as for the hands. I am delighted to add another unplayable work to the repertoire. I want the Concerto to be difficult and I want the little finger to become longer. I can wait. (From a dialogue between José Rodriguez and Schoenberg in the anthology *Arnold Schoenberg,* edited by Merle Armitage, New York, 1937)

The new Violin Concerto by Arnold Schoenberg combines the best sound effects of a hen yard at feeding time, a brisk morning in Chinatown, and practice hour at a busy music conservatory. The effect on the vast majority of hearers is that of a lecture on the fourth dimension delivered in Chinese. (Edwin H. Schloss, Philadelphia *Record,* 7 December 1940)

The violinist slithers his bow around, apparently at random, pauses to pluck at a string here and poke at another three there. While this is going on, the orchestra is busy playing a game that sounds like every man for himself. (Philadelphia *Inquirer,* 7 December 1940)

For thirty years, bald, parchment-faced, Austrian-born composer Arnold Schoenberg has written music so complicated that only he and a couple other fellows understand what it is all about. This music, which sounds to the uninitiated not only queer, but accidental, has been enjoyed by very few. But it has thrown the world of music into a Kilkenny cat fight. One cat camp maintains that Schoenberg's music, like Einstein's theory, sounds queer because it is way over the average man's head; opponents swear that Schoenberg is pulling everybody's leg, including his own, and that his miscalled music is a gibberish of wrong notes. Gibberish or no, Arnold Schoenberg's music is fearfully difficult to play. The main difficulty is to get all of Schoenberg's wrong notes in the right places. (*Time,* 26 December 1940)

15 DECEMBER 1940

Third Symphony by the English composer Edmund RUBBRA, in four classically contrasted movements, with its academic substance enriched by sonorous polyharmonies and colorful instrumentation, is performed for the first time in Manchester. (Its first performance, announced for 23 September 1940 in London, was cancelled on account of German air raids.)

15 DECEMBER 1940

Chamber Symphony No. 2, op. 38, by Arnold SCHOEN-BERG, marking a deliberate regression to his tonal past, in two movements—(1) *Adagio,* in 2/4 time, with a key signature of six flats centered on E-flat minor (originally sketched out in Vienna in 1906; radically revised in 1939 and completed in Los Angeles on 16 August 1939), and (2) *Con fuoco,* in 6/8 time, with a key signature of one sharp in the clear ambience of G major, reverting in a subsequent *Molto Adagio* to the tonality and the spiritual atmosphere of the initial movement and terminating on an E-flat minor triadic configuration (composition completed in Los Angeles on 21 October 1939)—is performed for the first time by the New Friends of Music in New York under the direction of Fritz Stiedry.

The difficulties that Schoenberg faced were enormous. As he had meanwhile advanced to an entirely different level, he found that his personal contact with his work had been disrupted: it was remote from him from the point of view both of time and style. He solved his task in a brilliant way: he finished the *Kammersymphonie* in his former style, but with his new technique developed by his compositions based on the chromatic scale. He used all his knowledge of musical development and orchestration he had acquired in recent years. So the work underwent a reformation more far reaching than, for instance, a classical work does when it is orchestrated by a modern composer. It was *Schoenberg interpreted by Schoenberg*. (From a program note written by Schoenberg's pupil and son-in-law Felix Greissle)

24 DECEMBER 1940

On the second Christmas Eve of World War II, the British Broadcasting Corporation broadcasts a program of Christmas carols from Coventry Cathedral reduced to ruins by Nazi air raids.

25 DECEMBER 1940

Pal Joey, musical comedy by Richard RODGERS, based on stories by John O'Hara, revolving around an amiably tough Chicago character, who sacrifices love for cash, the most popular number being *Bewitched, Bothered and Bewildered*, is produced in New York.

26 DECEMBER 1940

Folk-Song Symphony for chorus and orchestra by Roy HARRIS, his fourth symphony, with thematic material of its seven sections derived from American country tunes, is performed for the first time in its entirety by the Cleveland Orchestra.

(Four choral movements from the *Folk-Song Symphony* were performed for the first time at the American Spring Festival in Rochester on 25 April 1940, Howard Hanson conducting. On 9 March 1941 the New York Philharmonic performed the two orchestral *Interludes* from the *Folk-Song Symphony* plus an extra *Interlude*.)

30 DECEMBER 1940

Mergen, opera in five acts by the 65-year-old Soviet ethnomusicologist Anton EICHENWALD, to a libretto in the Bashkir language depicting the great national deed of an ethnically conscious patriot by the name of Mergen, is produced in Ufa, capital of the Bashkir Autonomous Soviet Socialist Republic.

1941

1 JANUARY 1941

As a result of a disagreement between ASCAP (American Society of Composers, Authors and Publishers) and the radio networks, a trained canary named Cheerio whose repertoire included an arrangement of *Yankee Doodle*, copyrighted by ASCAP, and Sharkey, the trained seal who has learned to play the tune *Where the River Shannon Flows* on the mouth harmonica, also an ASCAP property, are barred from appearances as guest artists on the radio.

2 JANUARY 1941

Sinfonia Biblica by Nicolas NABOKOV, 37-year-old Russian composer living in the United States, in four movements—(1) *Ecclesiasticus* (Wisdom), (2) *Solomon* (Love), (3) *Absolom* (Fear), (4) *Hosannah* (Praise), intended as "a piece of music first of all, the Old Testament being the stimulus," with principal subjects thematically interrelated (e.g., the motive of Absalom's flight is a rhythmically accelerated intervallic inversion of the theme of Wisdom)—is performed for the first time by the New York Philharmonic, Dimitri Mitropoulos conducting.

3 JANUARY 1941

Symphonic Dances, a suite by Serge RACHMANINOFF, originally planned as a triptych describing the passage of twelve hours of the day, *Midday*, *Twilight* and *Midnight*, with germinal materials taken from his unfinished ballet

The Scythians of 1915, is performed for the first time by the Philadelphia Orchestra, under the direction of Eugene Ormandy to whom the score is dedicated.

5 JANUARY 1941

No for an Answer, second opera of social significance by the American composer Marc BLITZSTEIN (Blitzstein means lightning-stone), to his own libretto dealing with the attempts of a group of unemployed Greek waiters to organize a union, whose leader is murdered by the police and whose gathering place, the Diogenes Social Club, is burned down by hired arsonists, is performed for the first time in New York City, with Blitzstein acting as a one-man orchestra at the piano and simultaneously conducting the singers on the stage.

No for an Answer is a labor drama leaning so far to the left that it is practically horizontal. (Brooks Atkinson in the New York *Times*, 6 January 1941)

10 JANUARY 1941

Frank BRIDGE, cultured English composer of romantically colored pieces in various genres, gently touched with tantalizing atonalities, dies in Eastborne at the age of 61.

10 JANUARY 1941

Concerto for two pianos and orchestra by the 40-year-old Cyprus-born American composer Anis FULEIHAN is performed for the first time in Hempstead, New York.

11 JANUARY 1941

Ecuba, tragic opera by Gian Francesco MALIPIERO, in three acts after Euripides, dealing with the dreadful misfortunes of Hecuba, the Queen of Troy, written in the neo-Renaissance manner of accompanied monody, is produced in Rome.

11 JANUARY 1941

Alexandru Lapuşneanu, sociological opera by the Rumanian composer Alexandru ZIRRA, dealing with the leader of a 16th-century Balkan rebellion against the Turks, written in a strong dramatic style influenced by Mussorgsky's national realism, is produced in Bucharest in its final revision. (The early version was performed in Bucharest in 1934.)

12 JANUARY 1941

The Virgin of Sparta, short opera with spoken dialogue by the dean of Greek composers Manolis KALOMIRIS, is performed for the first time in Athens.

15 JANUARY 1941

Quatuor pour la fin du temps by the 32-year-old French composer Olivier MESSIAEN, scored for violin, cello, clarinet and piano, in eight movements, inspired by the Apocalypse, is performed for the first time at the German prisoners' camp, Stalag VIII-A in Görlitz, with Messiaen, himself a prisoner of war, playing the piano part.

19 JANUARY 1941

Architectura, a symphonic concerto in seven connected movements by the 48-year-old Italian composer Giorgio Federico GHEDINI, so named to emphasize the architectonic evolution of the basic themes of the piece, is performed for the first time in Rome.

19 JANUARY 1941

Mukhtar ASHRAFI, Bukhara-born Soviet composer, conducts in Tashkent the first performance of his opera *The Great Canal*, in five acts, in the Uzbek language, composed in collaboration with his teacher Sergei Vassilenko, with the action taking place in 1939 during the building of the great Fergana Canal in Uzbekistan.

23 JANUARY 1941

Lady in the Dark, musical play by Kurt WEILL, in which a lady magazine editor goes through the torments and absurdities of a psychoanalytic treatment, is produced in New York.

24 JANUARY 1941

Albert EINSTEIN plays a program of violin music at the Present Day Club in Princeton, New Jersey, at a benefit concert to raise funds for the American Friends Service Committee for Refugee Children in England, in a program including the E minor *Sonata* of Mozart and first performances of two pieces by Frida S. Bucky of New York, *Old Indian Song* and *Russian Dance*.

25 JANUARY 1941

Iver HOLTER, Nestor of Norwegian composers, dies in Oslo six weeks after his 90th birthday.

28 JANUARY 1941

Quiet City, instrumental suite by Aaron COPLAND, scored for trumpet, English horn and string orchestra, arranged from incidental music to a play of that name, conjuring up a fine tonal picture of urban serenity, is presented by the Saidenberg Little Symphony in New York.

1 FEBRUARY 1941

Under the megadollar threat of a lawsuit for the infringement of copyright, Western Union and Postal Telegraph discontinue the use of the song *Happy Birthday to You* in their telephoned "singing telegrams," upon the disconcerting discovery that the tune, with the original words *Good Morning Dear Teacher*, is taken from *Song Stories for the Kindergarten* by the sisters Patty S. and Mildred J. HILL, copyrighted by Clayton F. Summy Publishing Company of Chicago.

1 FEBRUARY 1941

Gli Orazi, one-act opera by the 31-year-old Italian composer Ennio PORRINO, on the subject of the legendary combat between three heroic Roman Horatii and three equally valorous Albanian Curiatii, is produced at La Scala, Milan.

5 FEBRUARY 1941

Fürstin Tarakanowa, opera in three acts by the 38-year-old Manchurian-born German composer of Russian-Estonian parentage Boris BLACHER, on the subject of the hideous death of the Russian Countess Tarakanova, imprisoned for political opposition, who perished in a rat-riddled dungeon during the 1824 flood in St. Petersburg, is performed for the first time in Wuppertal, Germany.

6 FEBRUARY 1941

Concerto for Orchestra by Zoltán KODÁLY, commissioned by the Chicago Symphony Orchestra for its 50th anniversary, with thematic materials derived isochronically from pentatonic modes of immemorial Pannonia and popular Magyar dance rhythms, while preserving the Baroque form of a classical concerto in antiphonal structure, is performed for the first time by that orchestra, with Frederick Stock conducting.

7 FEBRUARY 1941

Violin Concerto by the 30-year-old American composer Samuel BARBER, in three movements—(1) *Allegro molto moderato*, introducing a broad narrative theme in the solo violin, developed in a free rhapsodic form with a cornucopia of contrasting melodies, with tension subsiding in a metempsychosis of the initial theme; (2) *Andante sostenuto*, a bucolic sarabande; (3) *Presto, in moto perpetuo*, an impetuous tarantella with the rhythmic stimulus provided by the unaccompanied kettledrums—is performed for the first time by the Philadelphia Orchestra, Albert Spalding soloist, Eugene Ormandy conducting.

7 FEBRUARY 1941

Concerto for Violoncello and Orchestra by Paul HINDEMITH, his first major work written in America (completed in Tanglewood, Massachusetts, on 9 September 1940), in three classically framed movements—(1) *Moderato*, opening with an assertive G major chord but oscillating widely in tonality, rhythm and mood; (2) *Andante con moto*, an elegy in meditative E major; (3) *Allegro marciale*, a hedonistic finale containing a set of variations on an old march tune and concluding in the focal tonality of G major—is performed for the first time by Gregor Piatigorsky and the Boston Symphony Orchestra, Serge Koussevitzky conducting.

9 FEBRUARY 1941

Morton GOULD conducts in New York the first performance of his *Spirituals for String Choir and Orchestra*, in five movements, *Proclamation, Sermon, A Little Bit of Sin, Protest* and *Jubilee*, reflecting the entire gamut of American Negro music, from devotional hymns to secular jazz.

15 FEBRUARY 1941

Guido ADLER, eminent Austrian musicologist, mercifully allowed by fate to draw his earthly days to a natural close without the lethal catalysis of a Nazi extermination camp for Jews, dies in Nazi-infested Vienna at the age of 85.

15 FEBRUARY 1941

Tata Vasco, opera in five acts by the Mexican composer Bernal JIMÉNEZ, written on the occasion of the quadricentennial of the arrival in Michoacán of Vasco de Quiroga, to a libretto based on the turbulent events of the time of the conquistadores, with the music fusing the disparate elements of Indian pentatonic modes and Spanish hymnal liturgy, is performed at Patzcuaro, Mexico, on the eve of the composer's 31st birthday.

19 FEBRUARY 1941

Sir Hamilton HARTY, English conductor of eloquent powers, cultured keeper of British traditions in music, dies in Brighton at the age of 61.

20 FEBRUARY 1941

Rudolph GANZ plays with the Chicago Symphony Orchestra, under the direction of Frederick Stock, the piano part in the world première of his *Piano Concerto*, set in four romantically inspired movements, with the two subjects of the *Scherzo* intervallically derived from the numbers of Ganz's automobile licenses for 1940 (280893, in A minor) and for 1941 (501127, in A major).

21 FEBRUARY 1941

Eugene Goossens conducts the Cincinnati Symphony Orchestra in the world première of the *First Symphony* by the Manila-born 31-year-old American composer John HAUSSERMANN, in four movements, of which the third, an elegy, is inspired by the mournful news of the death of Maurice Ravel.

22 FEBRUARY 1941

The National Youth Administration Symphony Orchestra presents in Brooklyn, under the direction of Fritz Mahler, nephew of Gustav Mahler, a program of first performances of American symphonic works, including the following:

First Symphony by the 34-year-old American composer Paul CRESTON (whose real name was Joseph Guttoveggio, and who adopted the name Creston by assonance with Crespino, a role he acted in a high school performance, which his schoolmates simplified to Crest), in four movements, marked *With Majesty,* in free sonata-allegro form; *With Humor,* a lyrically animated scherzo; *With Serenity,* in which the muted strings sustain a tranquil mood; *With Gayety,* a hedonistic rondo in a rhapsodic manner; *Ballad of a Railroad Man* for chorus and orchestra by Roy HARRIS; *Violin Concerto* by Henry BRANT; and *Latin American Symphonette* by Morton GOULD, in four dance movements, *Rumba, Tango, Guaracha* and *Conga.* (*Jazz Poem* for orchestra by Randall THOMPSON, first performed in Rochester on 27 November 1928, was also included in the program.)

23 FEBRUARY 1941

Rebus by the romantic English composer Frank BRIDGE, a symphonic movement illustrating the murmuration of a rumor in which an explicitly stated subject becomes metamorphosed into a number of remote shapes, a sort of variations *ad absurdum,* is given a posthumous first performance by the London Philharmonic Orchestra under the direction of Sir Henry. Wood.

25 FEBRUARY 1941

Der Uhrmacher von Strassburg, opera in three acts by the 36-year-old German composer Hans BREHME, is produced in Kassel.

1 MARCH 1941

Seth FLINT, the bugler who played the bugle call marking the end of the Civil War, at Appomattox on 9 April 1865, dies at Worcester, New York, at the age of 93.

4 MARCH 1941

Wesley LA VIOLETTE conducts the San Francisco Symphony Orchestra in the first performance of his symphonic poem *Music from the High Sierras,* melorhythmically derived from the old Spanish chants of the mountains.

5 MARCH 1941

Kristoffer Columbus, opera by the 41-year-old Danish composer Finn HÖFFDING, is produced in Copenhagen.

6 MARCH 1941

Third Symphony by the 45-year-old American composer Leo SOWERBY, in three movements marked (1) *With Vigor and Drive* (2) *Slowly, with Warmth of Expression* (3) *Fast and with Fiery Energy,* is performed for the first time by the Chicago Symphony Orchestra under the direction of Frederick Stock.

7 MARCH 1941

Camargo GUARNIERI, a leading composer of modern Brazil, conducts in São Paulo the first performance of his incisive symphonic *Dansa Brasileira,* a coruscating modern realization of the tropically rhythmed Brazilian samba.

11 MARCH 1941

Sir Henry Walford DAVIES, the 20th keeper of the office of Master of the King's Musick since its creation by Charles II in 1660, whose duties comprised the arrangement of musical programs for royal weddings, coronations and funerals, composer in his own right of a variety of symphonic and vocal works written in an impeccably British academic idiom, and, in his later years, wireless lecturer on school music with "a perfect radio voice," dies at his home near Bristol at the age of 71.

18 MARCH 1941

Aladdin, opera in three acts by Kurt ATTERBERG, is produced in Stockholm.

20 MARCH 1941

Ferghana Holiday, symphonic poem by Reinhold GLIÉRE, inspired by the building of the Ferghana Canal and based on authentic nomad tunes of Central Asia, is performed for the first time anywhere by the Chicago Symphony Orchestra as a commissioned work for its semicentennial.

23 MARCH 1941

Fantaisie Portugaise for orchestra, by the half-German, half-Spanish composer Ernesto HALFFTER, long resident of Portugal, is performed for the first time in Paris.

27 MARCH 1941

Third Symphony by Alfredo CASELLA (completed by him in Siena on 24 August 1940), in four neo-classically conceived movements, is performed for the first time anywhere by the Chicago Symphony Orchestra as a commissioned work, with Frederick Stock conducting.

29 MARCH 1941

Sinfonia da Requiem by the 27-year-old English composer Benjamin BRITTEN, originally commissioned in 1939 by the Japanese Government as a jubilee piece for the 2600th anniversary of the reigning dynasty of Japan, but rejected as being excessively Christian in nature, written by him under the impression of the death of his father during his stay in the as yet neutral United States as a pacifist and conscientious objector to all war however righteous, in three parts—(1) *Lacrymosa* "a slow marching lament in a persistent 6/8 rhythm with a strong tonal center on D"; (2) *Dies Irae,* "a form of dance of death, with occasional moments of quiet marching rhythm"; (3) *Requiem Aeternam,* a devotional imploration for eternal peace after righteous death—is performed for the first time by the New York Philharmonic, under the direction of John Barbirolli.

3 APRIL 1941

Scapino, comedy overture by William WALTON, inspired by a 1622 etching of Jacques Callot depicting the mischievous character of the Italian commedia dell'arte, composed in a correspondingly hedonistic manner with a lot of drumfire in the orchestra, and ending in a triumphantly self-righteous unison C, is performed for the first time by the Chicago Symphony Orchestra as a commissioned work for its semi-centennial, Frederick Stock conducting.

4 APRIL 1941

Johanna Balk, opera in three acts by the 37-year-old German composer Rudolf WAGNER-RÉGENY, dealing with a pacific 17th-century German matron who succeeds in bringing peace among feuding households, is produced in Vienna.

11 APRIL 1941

Arnold SCHOENBERG becomes an American citizen.

17 APRIL 1941

The first national Tadzhik ballet, *Two Roses,* by the 31-year-old Soviet composer Alexander LENSKY, dealing with the revolutionary struggle of the Tadzhik people against feudal overlords, is staged in Moscow.

20 APRIL 1941

Igor MARKEVITCH, 28-year-old Russian-born Parisian composer and conductor, whose precocious gifts as composer caused some of his incautious admirers to call him Igor the Second (the first being, of course, Stravinsky), conducts in Rome the first performance of his historic oratorio *Lorenzo the Magnificent.*

5 MAY 1941

Paul Bunyan, "a choral operetta" in five scenes by Benjamin BRITTEN, to the text by W. H. Auden, conceived in a whimsically modernistic vein, updating the legendary lumberjack of American folkways who blares his sylvan ballads through a radio loud-speaker, while a Western Union messenger rides by on a bicycle, is performed for the first time at Columbia University in New York City.

10 MAY 1941

Queen's Hall, the historic London theater, is destroyed by incendiary bombs dropped by the Nazi Luftwaffe during a night air raid.

At 10 o'clock in the morning of Sunday, May 11, 1941, the members of the London Philharmonic Orchestra arrived for the rehearsal. They found clouds of smoke pouring from the ruined building and "water, water everywhere." Many of them had left their instruments there overnight. Arrangements were then made to transfer the concert to the Duke's Hall of the Royal Academy of Music, and an emergency box-office was established at a table outside the wrecked building. At 3 o'clock that afternoon the concert was given as advertised, but unrehearsed and largely with borrowed instruments. Queen's Hall was gone; music carried on. (From *Queen's Hall, 1893–1941,* by Robert Elkin, London, 1943)

10 MAY 1941

Robert WARD, 23-year-old American composer of versatile gifts, conducts the Juilliard Graduate School Orchestra in New York in the first performance of his *First Symphony*, in three movements, written in a concise and compact neo-Baroque idiom, vitalized by asymmetrical American rhythms and occasional pandiatonic bitonalities.

11 MAY 1941

Tales of the Countryside, suite for piano and orchestra by Henry COWELL, in four movements, each written in a different state of the Union, *Deep Tides* (in California), *Exultation* (in New York), *The Harp of Life* (in Iowa cornfields) and *Country Reel* (on a Kansas farm), conceived in a pleasingly folk-like manner, with the application of Cowell's tone-clusters (pandiatonic and panpentatonic columns of notes, played respectively on white and on black keys), arranged from original piano pieces of c. 1920, is performed for the first time by the All-American Youth Orchestra, organized and conducted by Leopold Stokowski, at its inaugural concert in Atlantic City, New Jersey, with Cowell himself at the piano.

12 MAY 1941

Die Windsbraut, opera in three scenes by the 36-year-old German composer Winfried ZILLIG, to a story of sylvan elves and the Wind Bride, daughter of Storm, written in a fundamentally Wagnerogenic but rationally dissonant idiom, containing tangential dodecaphonic passages and other atonal approximations, but concluding in an unambiguously tonal F-sharp major, is produced in Leipzig.

13 MAY 1941

Tarquin, "a new opera for the modern stage" in two acts, with a prologue and epilogue, by Ernst KRENEK (completed by him in Hollywood on 13 September 1940) to a libretto in English, is produced by the Experimental Theater at Vassar College, Poughkeepsie, New York, with the composer, as member of the faculty, playing the piano part of the reduced version, originally scored for four vocal soloists, four speakers, clarinet, trumpet, violin, percussion and two pianos. (A complete stage performance of *Tarquin* was given in Cologne on 16 July 1950.)

16 MAY 1941

A Symphony in D for the Dodgers by the 46-year-old American composer Robert Russell BENNETT, in four movements, entitled (1) *Allegro con brio: Brooklyn Wins* (2) *Andante lamentoso: Brooklyn Loses* (3) *Scherzo* (4) *Finale: The Giants Come to Town*, with a choral finale glorifying the composer's favorite baseball team, is played for the first time in a radio performance in New York.

17 MAY 1941

The 18th Festival of the International Society for Contemporary Music, blacked out of war-torn Europe, opens in New York with a broadcast of modern chamber music over the Columbia Broadcasting System, in a program including *Three Sonnets from Shakespeare* for voice and piano by Piet KETTING of Holland, and the miniaturistically brief *Third String Quartet* by Antoni SZALOWSKI of Poland.

18 MAY 1941

In the course of the 18th Festival of the International Society for Contemporary Music, the following program is presented by the Columbia Broadcasting System in New York:

Prelude to a Tragedy by Henk BADINGS of Holland, for string orchestra, written in a rationalized neoclassical idiom, with fugal elements animating the musical action; *Les Illuminations* by Benjamin BRITTEN for high voice and string orchestra to texts from ten poems by Arthur Rimbaud (first performed in London on 30 January 1940).

19 MAY 1941

In the course of the 18th Festival of the International Society for Contemporary Music, the following program of chamber music is given at Columbia University in New York:

Second String Quartet by Paul KADOSA of Hungary, written in a neo-classical idiom; *Psalm 54* for voice and piano by the German atonal composer Stefan WOLPE, who settled in New York after the advent of the Nazis; *Second Piano Sonata* by René LEIBOWITZ, leading French modernist of the Schoenbergian persuasion; *Divertimento* for solo flute by the British composer William ALWYN; and *Fourth String Quartet* by the Polish neo-classicist Jerzy FITELBERG, resident in New York City.

20 MAY 1941

In the course of the 18th Festival of the International Society for Contemporary Music, at Columbia University, Bernard WAGENAAR, Dutch-born American composer of neo-Baroque music, conducts a broadcast performance of his *Triple Concerto* for flute, cello, harp, and orchestra. The absolute first performance of Wagenaar's *Triple Concerto* took place in Philadelphia on 18 March 1938, with Georges Barrère, Carlos Salzedo and Horace Britt as soloists. The New York première followed four days later, on 22 March 1938.

21 MAY 1941

In the course of the 18th Festival for the International Society for Contemporary Music, the following program of chamber music is presented at the New York Public Library:

Second String Quartet by the 36-year-old Hungarian composer Mátyás SEIBER, now resident of London, couched in a neo-classical idiom with high incidence of atonal dissonance; *Piano Sonata* by the 43-year-old Austrian composer Viktor ULLMAN; *String Quartet* op. 28, by Anton VON WEBERN (described in the program book as "independent" but still living in Nazified Vienna despite his being blacklisted as a Kultur-Bolschewik in the Nazi brochure *Entartete Musik*), originally commissioned by the Elizabeth Sprague Coolidge Foundation and first performed at the Berkshire Chamber Music Festival in Pittsfield, Massachusetts, on 22 September 1938, in three movements, based on a 12-tone row of the intervallic pattern of BACH appearing in inversion, several transpositions and retrograde forms; *Les Voix de Paul Verlaineà Anatole France* by Paul DESSAU, a German refugee living in New York, scored for voice, two pianos and percussion, and written in a sharply dissonant quasi-dodecaphonic idiom; and atonally inflected Regeromantic *Piano Pieces in Seven Parts*, by the renowned pianist Artur SCHNABEL.

22 MAY 1941

During the 18th Festival of the International Society for Contemporary Music held in New York, *Tre Ricercari* for orchestra by Bohuslav MARTINU and *Saga of the Prairie* for orchestra by Aaron COPLAND are broadcast by Radio Station WOR.

23 MAY 1941

In the course of the 18th Festival of the International Society for Contemporary Music, a concert of chamber music by American and Latin American composers is presented at the Museum of Modern Art in New York, in the following program:

Theme with Variations and Finale for violin and piano, by the 24-year-old composer Edward T. CONE, from North Carolina, written in a stable neo-classical style with a modicum of atonal digressions; *Three Songs* by Russel G. HARRIS; *Piece for String Quartet* by the Mexican composer Salvador CONTRERAS; *Theme and Variations* for cello and piano by Paul NORDOFF; *String Quartet* by Emil KOEHLER; *Music for Trio* (clarinet, saxophone and trumpet), by the Argentinian modernist Juan Carlos PAZ, written in the orthodox 12-tone technique; and *Música de Feria* for string quartet, a posthumous work by the Mexican composer Silvestre REVUELTAS.

24 MAY 1941

As part of the 18th Festival of the International Society for Contemporary Music in New York, two works by Hungarian composers, *Concerto for String Quartet* by Edmund PARTOS and *Second String Quartet* by Zoltán KODÁLY, are broadcast by the Columbia Broadcasting System.

25 MAY 1941

At the 18th Festival of the International Society for Contemporary Music in New York, three orchestral works are broadcast over the Columbia Broadcasting System:

Little Overture by Roman PALESTER of Poland, written in an optimistically bland neo-Baroque idiom; *Obertura Concertante* by Rodolfo HALFFTER, Spanish composer settled in Mexico after the defeat of the anti-Fascist forces in Spain; and *Hymnus, Der Tag und Die Nacht* by the Swiss composer Willy BURKHARD, set in a hymnally devotional style.

27 MAY 1941

Bal vénitien, ballet by the French composer Claude DELVINCOURT, is produced at the Opéra-Comique in Paris.

27 MAY 1941

At the conclusion of the 18th Festival of the International Society for Contemporary Music in New York, the National Broadcasting Company Orchestra presents a posthumous performance of *Sinfonietta* by Charles NAGINSKI, who suicidally drowned himself in the Housatonic River on 4 August 1940, and *Two Preludes* for orchestra by the Mexican composer Blas GALINDO.

5 JUNE 1941

Paul BEN-HAIM, 43-year-old Palestinian composer (who changed his real name, Frankenburger, when he fled the Nazis), conducts in Tel-Aviv the first performance of his

First Symphony, opening with a lament depicting the despair of Nazi victims, but concluding with an optimistic tarantella expressive of the faith in the victory against the ideological and military menace of Fascism.

8 JUNE 1941

Nine-minute Overture by the 21-year-old American composer Harold SHAPERO, written in a propulsive neo-Baroque manner, is performed for the first time by the Columbia Broadcasting Symphony Orchestra.

10 JUNE 1941

Concerto for organ, strings, and kettledrums by the most hedonistic of the French Six, Francis POULENC, in one quadripartite movement, based on a melorhythmic motto of four notes, written in an uninhibitedly synthetic idiom freely combining old-fashioned salon music with suggestive modernities and aggravated by a periodically tumescent organ part, is performed for the first time in Paris, Charles Munch conducting.

12 JUNE 1941

On the occasion of the official birthday of King George VI of Great Britain (his real birthday was 14 December), the pianist Myra HESS is named Dame Commander of the British Empire for her musical service in wartime.

13 JUNE 1941

Sunčanica (Sunflower), opera in three acts by the 35-year-old German-born Croatian composer of Greek origin, Boris PAPANDOPULO, relating the pathetic peripeteia of a Serbian girl nicknamed Little Sunflower, recruited for the Sultan's harem at the time of the Turkish domination of the Balkans, written in a nostalgically dramatic idiom combining elements of Slavonic folksongs and colubrine Oriental melorhythms, is produced in Zagreb.

27 JUNE 1941

The British Broadcasting Company urges the subjugated populations of France, Holland, Belgium, Luxembourg, Denmark, Norway and other countries submerged under the Nazi military occupation, to adopt the Morse signal for the letter V for Victory (three short taps and one long) or whistle the opening motive of Beethoven's *Fifth Symphony*, rhythmically corresponding to the V code word, whenever Nazi soldiers are around.

(On 8 July 1941 the British Press Service reported that the radio station at Hilversum in occupied Holland pointedly substituted a recording of Beethoven's *Fifth Symphony* for a previously scheduled work. The day of 20 July 1941 was proclaimed by Winston Churchill to be a symbolic V Day in Nazified Europe. The Nazis retaliated by adopting the symbol themselves and advertising the V sign as the initial letter of the German nonce word Viktoria, and persistently featured broadcasts of the first four notes of Beethoven's *Fifth Symphony*. The same four notes were added to the hours of the Westminster chimes in London.)

28 JUNE 1941

Francisco MIGNONE conducts in São Paolo the first performance of his orchestral suite *Sonho de um Menino Trav-*

esso (Dream of a Spoiled Child), in four movements descriptive of the pranks of an inventively mischievous infant.

29 JUNE 1941

Ignace Jan PADEREWSKI, grand seigneur of the piano whose romantic genius and the magnificence of personal stature inflamed the hearts of millions in Europe and America, composer of celebrated piano pieces, Polish patriot and statesman, who briefly served as Prime Minister of Poland after its resurrection in 1918, dies in New York at the age of eighty during the dark days of a new subjugation of his native country. (At President Roosevelt's orders, Paderewski's body was laid to rest under the mast of the battleship *Maine* in Arlington Cemetery pending its return to Poland after its liberation from the Nazis.)

4 JULY 1941

Jean SIBELIUS sends an impassionate appeal to the government and the people of the United States imploring for assistance in Finland's unequal fight against the Red Army seeking to prevent the military occupation of Finland by the Nazis:

In 1939 my country was attacked by the Bolsheviks. The enlightened American opinion realized then that we were fighting not only for our national freedom, but for Western civilization itself, and they gave us valued assistance. Now once more the barbaric hordes from the East are attacking us in their attempt to bolshevize Europe. I am convinced that freedom-loving and intelligent Americans will understand and judge the present situation correctly, and will oppose the bolshevization of Europe which would annihilate freedom and civilization on the entire continent.

5 JULY 1941

Lorin MAAZEL, 11-year-old boy wonder, "a chubby little chap with a big shock of black hair and a round, earnest face," born of American parents at Neuilly, France, on 5 March 1930, actually conducts from memory a concert of the National Broadcasting Symphony Orchestra in an adult program, including a complete Mendelssohn symphony, and succeeds in maintaining a steady tempo throughout the performance.

6 JULY 1941

Two weeks after the German invasion of Russia, Reinhold GLIÈRE addresses the following message to American musicians:

In this portentous hour, when savage Fascist bands are attacking my native land, I wish to send my greetings to my colleagues beyond the ocean who are supporting the Soviet people in its struggle for human rights. We, Soviet composers, in common with the entire nation, are using the medium of our art to help the Red Army carry on its fight against the brutal enemy. Like the rest of the country, we have put ourselves on a war footing. I have already written a marching song to the words, *Hitler's End Will Come.*

10 JULY 1941

Tango, orchestral version of a piano piece of Igor STRAVINSKY by a professional arranger is performed for the first time at the Robin Hood Dell Concerts in Philadelphia, under the direction of the "King of Swing"

Benny Goodman, beating time with a pencil. (Stravinsky made his own orchestration of the *Tango* in 1953, and it was first performed in Los Angeles on 19 October 1953 under the direction of Robert Craft.)

12 JULY 1941

Altyntchetch (The Golden-Haired), opera in four acts by the 30-year-old Tatar composer Nazib ZHIGANOV, in the Tatar language, to a story from the time of the Mongol invasion of the Volga region in the 13th century, wherein a golden-tressed native maiden magically sprouts wings to flee the lecherous pursuit of a predatory Mongol warlord, and summons a flock of golden-winged swans to strike him down and to liberate the land from his rapacious depredations, is performed for the first time in Kazan, the capital of the Tatar Soviet Socialist Republic.

18 JULY 1941

Concierto Argentino for piano and orchestra by the 25-year-old Argentinian composer Alberto GINASTERA, written in classical form with the thematic use of indigenous melorhythms, is performed for the first time in Montevideo.

27 JULY 1941

Two orchestral works by the 34-year-old American composer Paul CRESTON, *Prelude and Dance* and *A Rumor,* are performed for the first time in New York.

28 JULY 1941

"Defense Swing," a new ballroom dance in which the male makes a covertly libidinous advance towards the female who parries him off with the crook of her elbow, is accepted as a legitimate dance form at the sixth Annual Convention of the Dance Educators of America.

29 JULY 1941

El Indio, a group of dance tunes by the untutored Peruvian composer Daniel Alomía ROBLES (1871–1942), arranged in the form of a symphonic suite by Rudolf Holzmann, German conductor resident in Peru, is performed for the first time by the Orquesta Sinfónica Nacional of Lima, under Holzmann's direction.

4 AUGUST 1941

Eleven years after Siegfried WAGNER's death, his *Symphony in C Major,* completed in 1927, in four movements couched in a loyally filial Wagnerogenic style, with additive Weberomantic and Brahmsomorphic turns, is performed for the first time in the baronial site of Wagnerocracy, the medievally Germanic town of Bayreuth.

8 AUGUST 1941

Lin-Calel, one-act opera by the Italian composer Arnaldo D'ESPOSITO resident in Argentina, to a libretto dealing with a legendary Indian Queen of the Andes, is produced at the Teatro Colón in Buenos Aires.

10 AUGUST 1941

Dean DIXON, 26-year-old Negro musician, first member of his race to lead a major American orchestra, conducts a concert of the New York Philharmonic during its summer season at the Lewisohn Stadium in a program of works by Brahms, Berlioz and Liszt.

25 AUGUST 1941

In anticipation of the centennial of the birth of Antonin DVOŘÁK, the government of Czechoslovakia issues two commemorative postage stamps of 60 hellers and 1 krone 20 hellers.

7 SEPTEMBER 1941

Eleazar de CARVALHO, 29-year-old Brazilian conductor of Dutch-Indian extraction, conducts in Rio de Janeiro the first performance of his opera *Tiradentes (The Tooth Puller)*, dealing with a revolutionary dentist during Brazil's war for independence from Portuguese rule, written in a national Brazilian style and containing orchestral interludes onomatopoeically evoking the heterotonally jumbled sounds of the jungle.

13 SEPTEMBER 1941

Franz IPPISCH, Austrian composer who settled in Guatemala after the seizure of Austria by the Nazis in 1938, conducts in Guatemala City the first performance of his *Sinfonía Guatemalteca*, composed as a tribute to his adoptive country and based on the folksongs of Guatemala, organized in an expectedly academic Germanic manner.

15 SEPTEMBER 1941

Festival of Insects, ballet by the 31-year-old Japanese composer Kozaburo HIRAI, is produced in Tokyo.

28 SEPTEMBER 1941

Goffredo PETRASSI conducts in Venice the first performance of his dramatic madrigal *Coro di Morti*, for male voices, brass instruments, three pianos, doublebasses and percussion, to the text of the pessimistic Italan poet Giacomo Leopardi, proclaiming that the dead fear life as much as those living fear death, set to music in suitably asomatous monodic harmonies, to depict the chants of the dead and an instrumental fugue to reflect the mechanical mobility of biological existence.

30 SEPTEMBER 1941

The Brazilian composer Oscar Lorenzo FERNANDEZ, described as the "brasileirissimo" for the authenticity of his native inspiration, conducts in Rio de Janeiro the world première of his five-act opera *Malazarte*, to the story of a legendary Master of the Evil Arts (Malazarte = Malas artes) active in colonial Brazil, written according to a sui generis system of motivic themes, identifying the principal moods—Destiny, Seduction, Love, Death—and thematically derived from authentic Brazilian melorhythms.

1 OCTOBER 1941

Dmitri SHOSTAKOVICH, his wife, son and daughter, fly to Moscow from besieged Leningrad over the Nazi lines encircling the city.

3 OCTOBER 1941

Wilhelm KIENZL, Austrian composer of Wagneromantic operas and lyric songs, author of the short-lived Austrian National Anthem, officially adopted in 1920 and relinquished in 1929, appreciated for the rectitude of his musical intentions and honored by his intimates, dies in Nazi-depressed Vienna at the age of 84, having long outlived his ephemeral fame.

4 OCTOBER 1941

Manuel PONCE, pioneer of modern music in Mexico, conducts in Montevideo, Uruguay, the world première of his *Concierto del Sur (Concerto of the South)* for guitar and orchestra, with Andrés Segovia, to whom the work is dedicated, as soloist.

9 OCTOBER 1941

De profundis, symphonic poem by the Czech composer Vítězslav NOVÁK, expressive of national hope amid misery in his subjugated fatherland under Nazi occupation, is performed for the first time in Brno.

11 OCTOBER 1941

Die Hexe von Passau (The Witch of Passau), opera in four acts by Ottmar GERSTER, to a verisimilitudinarian story wherein an inspired woman of mantic powers induces the pious mayor of Passau to join her in leading the German peasant rebellion of 1489, is performed for the first time in Düsseldorf.

11 OCTOBER 1941

Nicolai BEREZOWSKY, Russian-American composer of romantic music, plays the viola part with the Columbia Broadcasting Symphony Orchestra in New York in the first performance of his *Concerto* for viola and orchestra.

17 OCTOBER 1941

Third Symphony by the 31-year-old American composer William SCHUMAN (completed on 11 January 1941), conceived in an energetically neo-classical idiom, with the component structures oscillating axially in the vicinity of variable tonal asymptotes, in two parts, (1) *Passacaglia*, adhering to its basic formula in stating the dominating subject as the cantus firmus of an enfilade of variations, leading to a *Fugue*, marked by ingeniously contrived canonic unisons (2) *Chorale*, a stately hymnal utterance, and *Toccata*, in a furfuraceous flux of string sonorities, is performed for the first time by the Boston Symphony Orchestra, Serge Koussevitzky conducting.

17 OCTOBER 1941

The Lincoln Symphony by Jaromir WEINBERGER, Czech composer of the famous comic opera Schwanda, who settled in the United States after the Nazi occupation of Czechoslovakia in 1938, in four biographically arranged movements—(1) *The Hand on the Plough*, (2) *Scherzo Heroïque*, (3) *O Captain!, My Captain!*, (4) *Deep River*—is performed for the first time by the Cincinnati Symphony Orchestra, Eugene Goossens conducting.

19 OCTOBER 1941

Baal Shem (so named after the Jewish-Polish founder of the religious sect of Hassids) by Ernest BLOCH, for violin and orchestra, is performed for the first time by Joseph Szigeti and the Works Progress Administration Orchestra in New York.

21 OCTOBER 1941

Aaron COPLAND plays in Buenos Aires the world première of his *Piano Sonata* in three movements, based on the principle of evolving melodic and rhythmic patterns, an architectonic study of balanced sonorities and interrelated formal divisions, in austerely contrapuntal textures with widely spaced chordal axes marking moments of tonal rarefaction.

23 OCTOBER 1941

Scenario, tone poem by Jerome KERN based on the thematic material of his great song "Ol' Man River" from his musical *Show Boat,* is performed for the first time by the Cleveland Orchestra, Artur Rodzinski conducting.

28 OCTOBER 1941

Roma dei Cesari, opera in four acts by the 57-year-old Italian composer Iginio ROBBIANI, the third part of his "Trittico lirico italiano," is performed for the first time in Rome.

29 OCTOBER 1941

Let's Face It, a musical comedy by Cole PORTER, dealing with three Army wives who acquire gigolos for sexual congress in retaliation of the libertine ways of their philandering husbands, is produced in New York.

31 OCTOBER 1941

Nicolas SLONIMSKY conducts in Buenos Aires the world premiere of his instrumental *Suite,* written according to a system of integral consonant counterpoint in mutually exclusive pentatonic and heptatonic tonal matrices, in 8 movements: *Jazzelette, Penny for Your Thoughts, Happy Farmer, Fugato, Anatomy of Melancholy* (originally scored for a domestic cat solo whose tail is pulled to induce high-register meows, or a small lion's roar if a cat is unobtainable, or if local police regulations forbid the abuse of animals in musical performance on the stage), *Bitonal March, Valse très sentimentale* and *Typographical Errors* with a typewriter solo.

5 NOVEMBER 1941

Czech Rhapsody for orchestra by the 45-year-old Bohemian composer Jaromir WEINBERGER, now making his home in America, is performed for the first time by the National Symphony Orchestra in Washington.

7 NOVEMBER 1941

Second Symphony, subtitled *Kormtchaya* (stochastic, goal-directed, teleological, leading), by the 49-year-old Russian composer Arthur LOURIÉ, consisting of ten variations without a theme and couched in an austerely modal manner, is performed for the first time by the Boston Symphony Orchestra under the direction of Serge Koussevitzky.

13 NOVEMBER 1941

A Bird's Opera, symphonic fantasy by Jaromir WEINBERGER, depicting in illustrative tunes and rhythms the animal life in a barnyard, in four movements: *Overture, Nuptial Ceremonies, Junior Reception* and *Fugue on Many Subjects* "with undue interference by a dog," is performed for the first time in Detroit.

14 NOVEMBER 1941

Rapsodie Polonaise by Alexandre TANSMAN, dedicated to the defenders of Warsaw, set in propulsive rhythms of the Polonaise and Mazurka and containing thematic allusions to the Polish national anthem, "Poland has not perished yet," is performed for the first time by the St. Louis Symphony, Vladimir Golschmann conducting.

14 NOVEMBER 1941

Concerto Grosso for chamber orchestra, in three movements, *Allegro non troppo, Lento, Allegretto,* by Bohuslav MARTINU, originally scheduled to be played in Vienna in 1938, but canceled after the Anschluss; later announced for a performance in Prague but taken off the program after the Nazi invasion of Czechoslovakia; subsequently scheduled for a performance in Paris in May 1940, only to be called off once more as the Nazis invaded Belgium and Holland, is finally performed for the first time anywhere by the Boston Symphony Orchestra, under the direction of Serge Koussevitzky.

17 NOVEMBER 1941

Second Symphony by Virgil THOMSON in three movements—(1) *Allegro militaire,* (2) *Andante,* (3) *Allegro,* based on a continuous transformation of the musical materials of the opening statement—is performed for the first time in its entirety by the Seattle Symphony Orchestra under the direction of Sir Thomas Beecham.

21 NOVEMBER 1941

Symphony in E-flat by Paul HINDEMITH (completed by him in New Haven on 15 December 1940), in four classically contoured movements marked *Sehr lebhaft, Sehr langsam, Lebhaft, Mässig schnell Halbe,* devoid of key signature except for the indication of the tonic in the title, but concluding on a full-blooded E-flat major chord, written in a propulsive rhythmic idiom, with lyrical episodes providing some elegiac digressions, and combining in its melodic structure triadic elements and spacious quartal leaps, while the harmonic fabric preserves its essential diatonicism, is performed for the first time by the Minneapolis Symphony Orchestra, Dimitri Mitropoulos conducting.

25 NOVEMBER 1941

Wiener Symphonie by the 69-year-old German composer Paul GRAENER, in three movements written in an eclectic Viennese style, traversing the idioms from Haydn to Johann Strauss, and ending in the affirmative key of C major, is performed for the first time by the Berlin Philharmonic.

28 NOVEMBER 1941

Scottish Ballad for two pianos and orchestra by Benjamin BRITTEN, in three linked sections thematically derived from old Scottish tunes, *Lento, Adagio* and *Allegro*, in which the strains of *Dundee* are heard, leading to a lament for the Scottish soldiers who fell in the battle of Flodden, based on a funereal song *The Flowers of the Forest*, and concluding with a lively *Scottish Reel* (after funerals in Scotland, a merry military tune is often played), is performed for the first time by the Cincinnati Symphony Orchestra, under the direction of Eugene Goossens, with Ethel Bartlett and Rae Robertson as piano soloists.

28 NOVEMBER 1941

Ballade for flute, string orchestra and piano by the Swiss composer Frank MARTIN is performed for the first time by the Basel Chamber Orchestra, Paul Sacher conducting.

3 DECEMBER 1941

Christian SINDING, Norwegian romantic composer, whose piano piece *Rustles of Spring* has become a perennial favorite, dies in Oslo at the age of 85.

6 DECEMBER 1941

Alan BUSH, 40-year-old English composer, ardent anti-Fascist, conducts the London String Orchestra in the first performance of his *Meditation on a German Song of 1848*, symbolic of the ancient revolutionary spirit of Germany as contrasted with the Nazi savagery of the day.

9 DECEMBER 1941

For the first time since the Russian Revolution, TCHAIKOVSKY's *1812 Overture*, expressive of the patriotic dedication to eternal Russia, brandishing the glorious oriflamme of sonorous brasses as the symbol of victory over the invader, is performed in the famine-stricken city of Leningrad under Nazi siege as a symphonic pledge that Hitler would suffer the fate of Napoleon, in an arrangement made by the Soviet composer Vissarion SHEBALIN, with the chorus from GLINKA's opera *Ivan Sussanin* (originally titled *A Life for the Tsar*) isoharmonically substituted for the unacceptable Tsarist national hymn in Tchaikovsky's score.

11 DECEMBER 1941

Canti di Prigionia, vocal cycle by the 37-year-old Italian composer Luigi DALLAPICCOLA, scored for chorus, two pianos, two harps and a phalanx of percussion, in three tableaux depicting with vigesimosecular Angst the agonies of three exalted personages put to death at three points of history, and set to Latin texts—(1) *Prayer of Mary Stuart*, (2) *Invocation of Boethius*, (3) *Farewell of Savonarola*,—is performed for the first time in its entirety in Rome, on the day when Mussolini declared war on the United States. (*Prayer of Mary Stuart* was performed separately in Brussels for the first time anywhere on 10 April 1940.)

15 DECEMBER 1941

The Red Army recaptures the town of Klin, near Moscow, and proceeds to repair the depredations committed by the Nazis in the Tchaikovsky Museum there.

A pack of mad swine could not have befouled the house of Tchaikovsky as much as the Germans did. They tore off the wall panels and used them for fuel, even though there was plenty of wood in the backyard. Fortunately, Tchaikovsky's manuscripts, his library, his favorite piano, his writing desk, all had been previously evacuated. I saw with my own eyes a Beethoven portrait torn down from the wall and carelessly thrown on a chair. Near this chair, the German soldiers excreted on the floor. The German army men made a latrine next to an excellent portrait of Beethoven! (Eugene Petrov in *Izvestia*, Moscow, 17 December 1941)

18 DECEMBER 1941

Darius MILHAUD plays with the Chicago Symphony Orchestra the piano part in the world première of his *Second Concerto* for piano and orchestra, in three contrasting movements, *Animé, Romance* and *Bien modérément animé*, with the finale suggesting the rhythms of the rumba.

21 DECEMBER 1941

First Symphony by the 26-year-old American composer David DIAMOND, in three movements, based on a motto of three notes constituting the thematic nucleus of the entire work, is performed for the first time by the New York Philharmonic, conducted by Dimitri Mitropoulos.

1942

1 JANUARY 1942

Piano Concerto by the foremost Mexican composer Carlos CHÁVEZ, written in a kinetically energetic idiom, economically compact in its flinty parallelisms of strident bitonalities, with lyrical statements of quasi-monastic austerity and occasional glimpses of Mexican folkways, in three movements—(1) *Largo non troppo,* leading to *Allegro agitato,* (2) *Molto lento,* (3) *Allegro non troppo*—is performed for the first time by the New York Philharmonic under the direction of Dimitri Mitropoulos, with Eugene List as soloist.

4 JANUARY 1942

Schwanhild, lyric opera in three acts by the German composer Paul GRAENER, to a libretto after a German folk tale, in which a young maiden, moved by religious fervor, flies to the Holy See using the aerodynamic attachment of a swan's wings and fuselage, only to be shot down by a misguided bürgher on her way home, set in a Regeromantic idiom, expressionistically enhanced by atonal angularities, is performed for the first time in Cologne, a week before the composer's 70th birthday.

4 JANUARY 1942

Nestenarka, ballet on national Bulgarian themes by the 33-year-old Bulgarian composer Marin GOLEMINOV, is produced in Sofia.

6 JANUARY 1942

Eight Etudes for Orchestra by the American composer Robert Russell BENNETT, intended to provide "specific problems to overcome, in the same way that etudes for solo instruments present technical difficulties to the performer or student," is performed for the first time at a concert of the Philadelphia Orchestra in New York.

7 JANUARY 1942

Statements for Orchestra, a symphonic suite by Aaron COPLAND, in six brief sections, *Militant, Cryptic, Dogmatic, Subjective, Jingo, Prophetic,* with the descriptive titles intended "as a help to the public in understanding what the composer had in mind when writing these pieces," is performed for the first time in its entirety by the New York Philharmonic, Dimitri Mitropoulos conducting.

9 JANUARY 1942

O Espantalho (*Scarecrow*), symphonic essay by the 44-year-old Brazilian composer Francisco MIGNONE, making use of a train whistle and a police siren in the score, is performed for the first time in São Paolo.

10 JANUARY 1942

La Dispute des Orgues for chorus and orchestra by the Belgian composer Raymond CHEVREUILLE is performed for the first time in Brussels.

12 JANUARY 1942

Twenty Second Symphony (subtitled *Symphonie-Ballade*), in B minor, by the prime Soviet symphonist Nicolai MIASKOVSKY, written in Naltchik, Caucasus, where Miaskovsky betook himself, as the Nazi armies drove relentlessly toward the Caucasian mountain range, in three movements, with thematic material largely derived from Caucasian folk melodies, is performed for the first time in Tbilisi, capital of Georgia.

13 JANUARY 1942

Kilderejsen, opera by the Danish composer Finn HÖFFDING, is produced in Copenhagen.

14 JANUARY 1942

Fred FISHER, 66-year-old composer and lyricist, author of an early aeronautical courtship song *Come Josephine in My Flying Machine,* a man of the world who served in the German Navy and in the French Foreign Legion, hangs himself in New York.

16 JANUARY 1942

Paul WITTGENSTEIN, left-handed, amputated Austrian pianist who lost his right arm on the Russian front in World War I, plays the solo part with the Philadelphia Orchestra under the direction of Eugene Ormandy, in the first performance anywhere of *Diversions on a Theme* by Benjamin BRITTEN, written especially for him, and consisting of eleven variations on a simple musical theme.

21 JANUARY 1942

Blood of the People, one-act opera by the Soviet composer Ivan DZERZHINSKY, extolling the heroism of a Soviet girl guerrilla captured and hanged by the Nazis in 1941, with the concluding chorus chanting "Rise, Soviet People, defend your native land! Never will our people be captives of the Fascist foe!" is produced in the town of Tchkalov (formerly Orenburg), in the Ural region, by the Leningrad Opera Company, moved there from the besieged city of Leningrad.

21 JANUARY 1942

La Doncella Ixquic, ballet suite by the Guatemalan composer Ricardo CASTILLO, a "mythological tragedy" revolving around an Indian maiden pursued by beastly creatures, is performed for the first time in Guatemala City, Nicolas Slonimsky conducting.

21 JANUARY 1942

Jamaican Rumba by the 48-year-old Australian-born English composer Arthur BENJAMIN, a rollicking stylization of the infectious Caribbean dance, is performed for the first time anywhere by the WOR Radio Orchestra in New York, under the direction of Alfred Wallenstein.

22 JANUARY 1942

Fourth Symphony by the 31-year-old American composer William SCHUMAN (completed on 17 August 1941), in three movements, with a strong axial tonality diversified by chromatic episodes and vitalized by jazz rhythms, is performed for the first time by the Cleveland Orchestra, Artur Rodzinski conducting.

23 JANUARY 1942

Concerto da camera, in F minor, by Bohuslav MARTINU, for violin and string orchestra, with piano and timpani, in three movements of a classical consistency—(1) *Moderato, poco Allegro*, (2) *Adagio*, (3) *Poco Allegro*, with a motivic character redolent of Czech melorhythms—is performed for the first time in Basel, with Gertrude Flügel as soloist, and Paul Sacher conducting the Basel Chamber Orchestra.

28 JANUARY 1942

Enriquillo, symphonic poem by the Dominican composer José CERÓN, portraying in pentatonic melodies the story of an Indian chief in the Caribbean converted to Catholicism, is performed for the first time by the Orquesta Sinfónica Nacional in Ciudad Trujillo, Casal Chapí conducting.

8 FEBRUARY 1942

Igor STRAVINSKY conducts the Janssen Symphony Orchestra in Los Angeles in the first performance anywhere of his *Danses Concertantes* (completed on 13 January 1942 in Los Angeles), in five movements, with the introductory march identically repeated in the last movement, the second movement being a *Pas d'Action*, the third a theme with variations, and the fourth a *Pas de Deux*, written in an elegant manner of the French galanterie, with coquettish musical Gallicisms, neo-classical mannerisms and choreographic affectation of measured rhythmic steps.

10 FEBRUARY 1942

Felix POWELL, English composer of the optimistic war song *Pack Up Your Troubles in Your Old Kit Bag and Smile, Smile, Smile*, pessimistically shoots himself to death in Brighton.

10 FEBRUARY 1942

Ramuntcho, fourth opera by the American composer Deems TAYLOR, in three acts, to a libretto from the picaresque tale of Pierre Loti dealing with a Basque smuggler Ramuntcho whose patrician fiancée becomes a nun, set to music in an urbanely craftsman-like style, with snatches from Basque folk songs lending an aura of authenticity to the score, is produced for the first time in Philadelphia. (A public dress rehearsal of *Ramuntcho* was given on 7 February 1942 for an invited audience.)

17 FEBRUARY 1942

Oscar LEVANT, American pianist, composer, causeur and raconteur, author of a self-deprecating autobiogra-phy, *A Smattering on Ignorance*, plays the piano part in the world premiere in New York of his impressively competent *Concerto in One Movement*, with the National Broadcasting Company Symphony Orchestra, Alfred Wallenstein conducting.

19 FEBRUARY 1942

Das Jahr, oratorio by the 41-year-old Swiss composer Willy BURKHARD, is performed for the first time by Paul Sacher and his Chamber Orchestra of Basel.

20 FEBRUARY 1942

The Island God, one-act opera by the 30-year-old Italian-born American composer Gian Carlo MENOTTI, to his own libretto, dealing with a married couple marooned on a Mediterranean island during World War II and a young fisherman who seduces the wife, starting a tumult and rousing an obsolescent Greek god from his musty antiquity in a ruined temple, who hurls an Olympian thunderbolt at the offenders, but loses so much electric potential by this violent discharge that he lapses into an ontologically primordial nihility, is produced by the Metropolitan Opera Company in New York.

20 FEBRUARY 1942

Philatelie, chamber cantata by the 48-year-old Belgian composer Jean ABSIL, in five movements, passing in review the philatelic rarities of Europe, Asia, Africa, America and Oceania, scored for a vocal quartet and small orchestra, with a variety of exotic-sounding instruments of percussion, friction and sibilation, including a siren, is performed for the first time in Brussels.

21 FEBRUARY 1942

Suvorov, opera in four acts by Sergei VASILENKO, written in a grand Russian national style, patriotically glorifying the generalissimo who fought Napoleon in the Italian Alps, subtly drawing the inference that Russians cannot be defeated by Napoleon or Hitler, is performed for the first time in Sverdlovsk.

26 FEBRUARY 1942

David VAN VACTOR, 35-year-old American composer, conducts the Chicago Symphony Orchestra in the first performance of his *Gothic Impressions*, a set of twelve variations on an "aggressive" theme.

1 MARCH 1942

The first performance is given in Kuibischev on the Volga (formerly called Samara) of the *Seventh Symphony* by Dmitri SHOSTAKOVICH, glorifying the heroic city of Leningrad, where he was born, and partly composed under Nazi siege, in four movements:

(1) *Allegretto* (completed in Leningrad on 3 September 1941), depicting in lyrically majestic C major the socialist labor in Soviet Russia ominously menaced by the distant drumbeat of the invasion, with an insipid marching tune of the Nazi hordes growing into a monstrous machine, but held back by the irrepressible counterflow of Russian melos, and eventually reduced to a pathetic metric relic; (2) *Moderato* (completed in Leningrad on 17 September 1941), an elegiac scherzo reflecting the peace-

ful life before the June solstice of 1941 when the Nazis struck; (3) *Adagio* (completed in Leningrad on 29 September 1941), an agonizing chronicle of suffering and death, in a slow rhythmic step; (4) *Allegro non troppo* (completed on 27 December 1941 in Kuibischev), marking the growing glorious tide of Russian might struggling through a field of minor keys towards the apotheosis of victorious C major.

My *Seventh Symphony* is inspired by the great events of our patriotic war, but it is not battle music. The first movement is dedicated to the struggle and the fourth to victory. . . . No more noble mission can be conceived than our fight against the dark powers of Hitlerism. That is why the roar of the cannon does not keep the muse of our people from lifting their powerful voice. (From Shostakovich's statement of March, 1942)

1 MARCH 1942

John CAGE, 29-year-old American experimenter in rhythmed sounds, conducts in Chicago the first performance of his metamusical *Imaginary Landscape No. 3*, scored for an electric oscillator, buzzers of variable frequency, Balinese gongs, generator whine, tin cans, plucked coil and a marimbula.

10 MARCH 1942

Caribbean Concerto for mouth harmonica and orchestra, the first of its kind, by the 32-year-old German-born American composer Jean BERGER, is performed for the first time by Larry Adler, harmonica virtuoso, with the St. Louis Symphony Orchestra.

12 MARCH 1942

Das Märchen vom Aschenbrödel, ballet on the subject of Cinderella by the Swiss composer Frank MARTIN, is produced in Basel.

15 MARCH 1942

King John, Shakespearean overture by the Italian composer Mario CASTELNUOVO-TEDESCO, now living in America, is performed for the first time anywhere by the New York Philharmonic, John Barbirolli conducting.

16 MARCH 1942

Alexander VON ZEMLINSKY, Austrian composer of fervently romantic music in a progressive Viennese tradition, first teacher of Schoenberg, who came to America in 1938 after the Nazi Anschluss, dies in musical oblivion, in Larchmont, New York, at the age of 70.

(Zemlinsky was born in Vienna on 14 October 1871, according to the irrefutable evidence of the registries of birth in Vienna and in the Jewish Cultural Community there, not on 4 October 1872 as stated in all reference works)

The one to whom I owe most of my knowledge of the technique and the problems of composing was Alexander von Zemlinsky. I have always thought and still believe that he was a great composer. I do not know one composer after Wagner who could satisfy the demands of the theater with better musical substance than he. His ideas, his forms, his sonorities, sprang directly from the action, from the scenery, and from the singers' voices, with a naturalness and distinction of supreme quality. (Arnold Schoenberg, *My Evolution*, in *The Musical Quarterly*, October 1952)

16 MARCH 1942

Sinfonietta giocosa by Bohuslav MARTINU, Czech composer now making his home in America, is performed for the first time in New York.

26 MARCH 1942

Le Vin herbé, oratorio in three parts, with a prologue and an epilogue, by the 51-year-old Swiss composer Frank MARTIN, to the text from the perpetually moving legend of Tristan and Iseut whose nefarious passion is inflamed by a potent wine philter filtered through a compost of aphrodisiac herbs, set to music in the austere narrative manner of a mystery play, with a chorus commenting on the passing events, and sustained by the compact texture of neo-medieval polyphony, is performed for the first time in Zürich, Switzerland.

28 MARCH 1942

During an Allied air raid on Lübeck, a bomb falls on the Marienkirche destroying the great organ on which Buxtehude gave his concerts and Bach played in 1705.

29 MARCH 1942

Solomon and Balkis, one-act opera by the 42-year-old American composer Randall THOMPSON, to a libretto adapted from Kipling's story *The Butterfly That Stamped*, dealing with a magical butterfly that stamped its feet with great uproar to deter Solomon's 999 wives from quarreling, set to music in a mockheroic Handelian manner, with sinuously orientalistic arabesques characterizing Balkis, the Queen of Sheba, is performed for the first time over the radio in New York. (The first stage performance of the opera was given at Harvard University, Cambridge, Massachusetts, on 14 April 1942.)

8 APRIL 1942

Two and a half centuries have passed since the birth of Giuseppe TARTINI, great violin virtuoso and composer of numerous violin pieces, including the vertiginous *Trillo del Diavolo*, inspired by a tune played by Satan in Tartini's dream.

9 APRIL 1942

Fourth Symphony by Alexandre GRETCHANINOV, Russian composer of deeply felt national roots now dwelling in New York, dedicated to the memory of Tchaikovsky, in four movements each containing quotations from Tchaikovsky's works, is performed for the first time by the New York Philharmonic, John Barbirolli conducting.

12 APRIL 1942

Hymne Védique, cantata by the 78-year-old French composer Alfred BACHELET, to the text by Leconte de Lisle invoking the ancient Vedic ritual of the sun, set to music in an exotically melodious idiom in fluid Wagneromorphic harmonies, is performed for the first time in Paris.

13 APRIL 1942

Two centuries have passed since the first performance in Dublin, Ireland, of HANDEL's *Messiah*.

16 APRIL 1942

Second Essay for Orchestra by the 32-year-old American composer Samuel BARBER, a miniature symphonic drama, opening with a spacious Celtic theme accompanied by an ominous rumble of the bass drum, erupting into an impetuous tarantella, and concluding with a solemn chorale, is performed for the first time by the New York Philharmonic, Bruno Walter conducting.

17 APRIL 1942

Violin Concerto by Nikolai LOPATNIKOFF, Russian-born, German-educated, American composer, in three movements of neo-classical proportions, is performed for the first time by Richard Burgin with the Boston Symphony Orchestra, under the direction of Serge Koussevitzky.

22 APRIL 1942

On his tour of the United States, the Brazilian composer Francisco MIGNONE conducts the National Broadcasting Company Symphony Orchestra in New York in the first performance of his symphonic suite *Festa das Igrejas* (*A Festival of Churches*), portraying in its four movements the impressions of four Brazilian cathedrals.

30 APRIL 1942

Concerto for violoncello and orchestra by the 26-year-old American composer David DIAMOND, written in an expansively rhapsodic, tensely modernistic manner, with aggressive discords stridently striding across the score, is performed for the first time in Rochester, New York, by Luigi Silva, with Howard Hanson conducting the orchestra.

1 MAY 1942

Gold and the Señor Commandante, ballet by the 21-year-old American composer William BERGSMA, is performed for the first time in Rochester, New York.

2 MAY 1942

Ernst BACON, 43-year-old American composer, conducts in Spartanburg, South Carolina, the first performance of his opera in four scenes, *A Tree on the Plains*, to a libretto by Paul Horgan, dealing with an emotionally disturbed family in the American Southwest during a drought and abounding in authentic Americanisms, including a hitch-hiking call and a chewing-gum ballad, culminating in a hymn of praise in the final scene, as the eagerly awaited rainfall refreshes the thirsty land.

3 MAY 1942

Twelve Tribes of Israel, symphonic poem by the 50-year-old Jewish-German composer Erich Walter STERNBERG, is performed for the first tmne by the Palestine Symphony Orchestra in Tel Aviv.

5 MAY 1942

Le Rossignol de Saint-Malo, one-act opera by the French composer Paul LE FLEM, is produced in Paris.

12 MAY 1942

Sinfonía Porteña (that is, Symphony of the port of Buenos Aires) by the 26-year-old Argentine composer Alberto GINASTERA is performed for the first time in Buenos Aires.

14 MAY 1942

Lincoln Portrait, symphonic poem by Aaron COPLAND for speaker and orchestra (completed on 16 April 1942), to texts from Lincoln's sayings, linked by the recurring phrase "This is what Abe Lincoln said," making use of melodies from two contemporary songs, *Camptown Races* and *The Pesky Sarpent*, set in a compact tonal idiom with pandiatonic connotations, is performed for the first time as a commissioned work by the Cincinnati Symphony Orchestra, André Kostelanetz conducting, on the same program with symphonic portraits of other great Americans, *Mark Twain* by Jerome KERN, and *The Mayor La Guardia Waltzes* by Virgil THOMSON.

(The printed program of the first performance had an indefinite article prefacing the title; most symphony programs designate the work as *A Lincoln Portrait*, but the published score omits the article. In a letter to the author dated 20 August 1960, Aaron Copland confirms that the title should be *Lincoln Portrait*.)

The composition is roughly divided into three sections. In the opening section I wanted to suggest something of the mysterious sense of fatality that surrounds Lincoln's personality. Also, near the end of that section, something of his gentleness and simplicity of spirit. The quick middle section briefly sketches in the background of the times he lived in. This merges into the concluding section where my sole purpose was to draw a simple but impressive frame about the words of Lincoln himself. (Copland's statement in the program book)

18 MAY 1942

The French government issues two postage stamps, of 2 and 3 francs, in honor of Emmanuel CHABRIER, in a belated commemoration of the centennial of his birth on 18 January 1841.

23 MAY 1942

Second Symphony by Arthur HONEGGER, scored for string orchestra, is performed for the first time by the Chamber Orchestra of Basel, Switzerland, Paul Sacher conducting, in three movements:

(1) *Molto moderato*, opening in somber tones and leading to an energetic atonal fugato; (2) *Adagio mesto*, a chromatic lamentation yielding to a diatonic chant; (3) *Vivace non troppo*, a discordant gigue, bitonally notated with 6 sharps in the first violins and none in the other string instruments, concluding on a devotional chorale, reinforced by an optional trumpet and coming to rest on a pandiatonically enriched D-major chord.

25 MAY 1942

Salomon, grand opera by the Italian-Argentinian composer Arturo LUZZATTI, to the biblical story of King Solomon's multiple concubines, is produced in Buenos Aires.

2 JUNE 1942

By Jupiter, musical comedy by Richard RODGERS and Lorenz HART, the last product of their fruitful collaboration, with the action taking place in prehistoric Asia Minor at the time when the roles of the sexes were reversed, with women making war, and men keeping house, is produced in New York.

6 JUNE 1942

Heitor VILLA-LOBOS conducts in New York the first performance of his *Bachianas Brasileiras No. 4* for orchestra, in four movements reflecting the duality of the music, Brazilian in essence and Bachian in substance: *Preludio, Aria, Coral* (in which a recurrent B-flat in high treble is intended to reproduce the jungle cry of the Brazilian bird arapunga) and *Dança*.

11 JUNE 1942

L'Apocalypse, oratorio by Jean FRANCAIX, written in 1939, is performed for the first time in Nazi-oppressed Paris.

12 JUNE 1942

On the centennial of the birth of the Norwegian composer Rikard NORDRAAK, who during his very short life gave a vital impetus towards the formation of truly national Norwegian music, and who wrote the Norwegian National Anthem, the government of Norway issues a series of stamps in his honor, of 10, 15, 20, and 30 øre.

12 JUNE 1942

Yusup and Akhmed, heroic opera in four acts by the Soviet composer Boris SHEKHTER, to a libretto from a 12th-century Mongolian epic, in which a young romance flowers among the downtrodden Central Asian masses who rise in rebellion against their feudal overlords, is produced in Ashkhabad, the capital of Turkmenistan.

12 JUNE 1942

Walter LEIGH, English composer of tasteful instrumental and choral music written in an urbanely diatonic idiom, is killed in combat near Tobruk, Libya, during a tank encounter with the Nazi forces.

14 JUNE 1942

A *Ceremony of Carols* by Benjamin BRITTEN, scored for a chorus of adolescent boys, tenderly accompanied by a gentle harp, to texts from medieval poetry, set in a restrained, but polyphonically strong idiom, is performed for the first time in Aldeburgh.

15 JUNE 1942

Cinq Danses rituelles, suite for orchestra by the 36-year-old French composer André JOLIVET, a founder of the optimistically self-proclaimed group "La Jeune France," dedicated to the propaganda of French music young in spirit, is performed for the first time in Paris.

20 JUNE 1942

Die Geschichte vom schönen Annerl, opera in nine scenes, to a libretto from a German folk tale, by the 40-year-old Alsatian composer Leo Justinus KAUFFMANN, his last, for he was destined to be killed in an Allied air raid on Strasbourg on 25 September 1944, is performed for the first time in Strasbourg, now occupied by Germany.

22 JUNE 1942

Kabelia, last opera by the Cuban composer Eduardo SÁNCHEZ DE FUENTES, to a libretto from Hindu mythology, set to music in an Italianate manner with the infusion of some orientalistic melismas, is performed for the first time in Havana.

22 JUNE 1942

On the occasion of the centennial of the birth of the supremely melodious and sublimely harmonious French master of mellifiuous operas Jules MASSENET, the French government issues a commemorative 4-franc postage stamp bearing his portrait.

26 JUNE 1942

Violin Concerto in four movements by the Spanish composer Rodolfo HALFFTER, resident in Mexico since the defeat of the Spanish anti-Fascist forces in 1939, is performed for the first time by Samuel Dushkin with the Orquesta Sinfónica de México under the direction of Carlos Chávez.

3 JULY 1942

Haft MCDONALD, manager of the Philadelphia Orchestra and a symphonic composer in his own right, conducts the National Symphony Orchestra in Washington in the first performance of his symphonic poem *Bataan*, illustrating in cinematically vivid tones, the dramatic retreat of Americans on Bataan Peninusla in the Philippines before the overpowering Japanese pressure.

14 JULY 1942

My Toy Balloon, a set of symphonic variations of a Brazilian folk song by Nicolas SLONIMSKY, scored for a regular orchestra supplemented by one hundred multicolored toy balloons to be perforated with hatpins at the final *sforzando*, is performed for the first time by the Boston Pops Orchestra, Arthur Fiedler conducting.

14 JULY 1942

Newsreel, symphonic suite "in five shots" by the 31-year-old American composer William SCHUMAN, illustrating in cinematic modalities a prestipedal *Horse Race*, a sentimentally waltzing *Fashion Show*, a primitivistic *Tribal Dance*, syncopatingly grimacing *Monkeys at the Zoo*, and a plangently circensian *Parade*, is performed for the first time in New York City.

15 JULY 1942

Heitor VILLA-LOBOS conducts in Rio de Janeiro the first performances of three of his orchestral *Chôros*: No. 6, No. 9 and No. 11, exhaling the rhythms, the perfumes and the colors of the Brazilian scene, with tropical birds exotically chanting in the woodwinds against the measured beats of jungle drums.

20 JULY 1942

Twenty-Third Symphony by the prime Soviet symphonist Nicolai MIASKOVSKY, composed by him in Tbilisi, Georgia, in three movements based on ten folk melodies of the Caucasus, is performed for the first time in Moscow.

24 JULY 1942

Alan BUSH conducts the London Philharmonic in the first performance of his *First Symphony*, set in the firmly proletarian key of C major as a symbol of social directness and popular action, in harmony with the dialectical philosophy of his socialistic convictions.

25 JULY 1942

Ginevra, comic opera by Marcel DELANNOY, to a libretto after Boccaccio, is produced in Paris.

31 JULY 1942

First Symphony by the 42-year-old Mexican composer Eduardo HERNÁNDEZ MONCADA, in four movements containing melorhythmic allusions to the huapango and other Mexican folk dances, is performed for the first time by the Orquesta Sinfónica de México under the direction of Dimitri Mitropoulos.

1 AUGUST 1942

Bridegroom from the Embassy, political operetta by the Soviet composer Vissarion SHEBALIN, is produced in Sverdlovsk.

1 AUGUST 1942

The American Federation of Musicians enjoins its members to boycott radio stations and recording companies that refuse to respect the performing rights of American composers. (The Government of the United States instituted a suit against the American Federation of Musicians, its members and its president James C. Petrillo for violation of the Anti-Trust Act, but its suit was dismissed by the Chicago Federal District Court on 12 October 1942.)

1 AUGUST 1942

The 19th Festival of the International Society for Contemporary Music opens in Berkeley, California, representing 34 composers from thirteen nations, including those subjugated by the Nazis, in the following program of orchestral music:

Divertimento for string orchestra by Béla BARTÓK; *Viola Concerto* by Nicolai BEREZOWSKY (first performed by him in New York on 11 October 1941); *Canon and Fugue* for string orchestra by the progressive American composer Wallingford RIEGGER; the world première of the *Piano Concerto* by the Polish composer Karol RATHAUS, now making his home in America; and *Symphonic Sketch on Three American Folk Tunes* by the American composer Arthur KREUTZ.

2 AUGUST 1942

At the second concert of the 19th Festival of the International Society for Contemporary Music at Berkeley, California, the following program of orchestral music is presented:

Concerto for small orchestra by the 27-year-old American composer Robert PALMER; *Sinfonietta* by the English composer Stanley BATE, temporarily residing in the United States; *Sinfonietta* by Nikolai LOPATNIKOFF; and *Suite for String Orchestra* by Felix LABUNSKI.

3 AUGUST 1942

At the third concert of the 19th Festival of the International Society for Contemporary Music at Berkeley, California, the following program of music for string quartet is presented:

Introduction and Scherzo by the 37-year-old English composer Norman SUCKLING; *Informal Music* by the 36-year-old American composer Normand LOCKWOOD; *Divertimento* by the Hungarian composer Frederic BALAZS; and *Fifth String Quartet* by the Polish-born Parisian composer, temporarily in the United States, Alexandre TANSMAN.

5 AUGUST 1942

At the fourth session of the 19th Festival of the International Society for Contemporary Music at Berkeley, California, Darius MILHAUD presents an informal talk dealing with the French Six, of whom he was an important representative, with musical illustrations from his ballet *Le Bœuf sur le toit* and the *Concerto for Two Pianos* by Francis POULENC.

6 AUGUST 1942

At the fifth concert of the 19th Festival of the International Society for Contemporary Music at Berkeley, California, the following program of chamber music is presented:

Sonata for oboe and piano by the Russian-born Argentinian composer Jacobo FICHER; *Sonata de Primavera* for piano by the Argentinian composer José María CASTRO, written in an ingratiatingly vernal pianistic idiom with a stimulating infusion of euphonious dissonances; *Prelude, Allegro* and *Pastorale* for clarinet and viola by the English violist Rebecca CLARKE; *Three Songs* by the Yugoslav-born composer André SINGER; and *Sonatina* for oboe, clarinet and piano by the 23-year-old pupil of Darius Milhaud, Donald FULLER.

7 AUGUST 1942

At the sixth concert of the 19th Festival of the International Society for Contemporary Music at Berkeley, California, the following program of chamber music is presented:

Sonatina for violin and piano by Charles JONES, 30-year-old American student of Darius Milhaud; *6 kleine Klavierstücke*, op. 19, by Arnold SCHOENBERG, written in 1911, in which the organization of the tonal material and dynamic nuances presages the imminent dodecaphonic future and the coming age of serial composition; *Poems of the Sea* for piano and *Piano Sonata* by Ernest BLOCH; *Three Songs* by Carlos CHÁVEZ of Mexico; *Música para niños*, a piano suite for sophisticated infants by the Argentinian composer Luis GIANNEO; *7 Miniatures on Brazilian Folk Themes*, a set of colorful piano pieces by the Brazilian composer Fructuoso VIANNA, written in delicately scented tropical modalities in an appealingly romantic manner; and *Toccata* for piano by Jacques de MENASCE, 36-year-old Austrian disciple of Alban Berg, resident of New York from 1941.

8 AUGUST 1942

Les Animaux modèles, ballet in six scenes by Francis POULENC, inspired by six fables of La Fontaine, wherein distinctive animal characteristics serve as masks of human types, set to music in a neo-archaic manner with a modernistic patina barely covering the rococo surface of old Gallic dance music, is performed at the Paris Opéra.

8 AUGUST 1942

At the seventh concert of the 19th Festival of the International Society for Contemporary Music at Berkeley, California, the following program of orchestral music is performed:

Fanfare, Chorale and Finale for brass by the 29-year-old English composer Godfrey TURNER (fated to kill himself in New York on 7 December 1948 for the love of a woman); *Sinfonia da Requiem* by Benjamin BRITTEN (first performed by the New York Philharmonic on 29 March 1941); *Concerto du Loup* by the Italian composer Vittorio RIETI (Loup in the title being a French river, not a wolf); *Folk Tunes of Castille* by Pedro SAN-JUÁN, Spanish composer domiciled in Cuba, coloristically portraying the scenes of eternal Spain; and a *Concerto for Orchestra* by the 26-year-old Chicago composer Ellis KOHS.

9 AUGUST 1942

At the eighth and last concert of the 19th Festival of the International Society for Contemporary Music at Berkeley, California, the following program of orchestral music is given:

Prelude to a Holiday by Arthur BENJAMIN, Australian-born composer of hedonistic and optimistic music; *Symphony in E-Flat* by Paul HINDEMITH, now professor of music at Yale University, set in a didactically classical vein; *Concerto for Chamber Orchestra* by the 27-year-old American composer David DIAMOND, written in a tense neo-classical technique; and *Allegro Symphonique* by the Belgian composer Marcel POOT, a founder in Brussels of the modernistic group Synthesistes dedicated to enlightened eclecticism.

11 AUGUST 1942

Richard Heinrich STEIN, German music theorist and composer who was the first to publish a work containing quarter-tones in 1906, and who built a quarter-tone clarinet, dies at the age of 60 at Santa Brigida in the Canary Islands, whither he fled from Nazified Germany.

13 AUGUST 1942

Musiques liliputiennes for four flutes (hence the diminutive title) by the Belgian composer Raymond CHEVREUILLE, is performed for the first time in Brussels.

14 AUGUST 1942

Fourth Symphony by the 41-year-old English composer Edmund RUBBRA, in three movements—(1) *Con moto*, characterized by impulsive melorhythmic anapests in a dissonant atmosphere of clashing bitonalities mitigated by moments of candid lyricism; (2) *Intermezzo*, a graceful scherzo in measured waltz time; (3) *Grave e molto calmo*, leading to an impetuous *Allegro Maestoso*, and ending on a forceful E major chord is performed for the first time in London.

18 AUGUST 1942

Erwin SCHULHOFF, Austrian composer of expressionistic music, author of a cantata to the text of the Communist Manifesto, dies at the age of 48 in a German concentration camp in Wülzburg. (Date communicated by his widow.)

8 SEPTEMBER 1942

João GOMES DE ARAUJO, Nestor of Brazilian composers, whose Italianate operas were favorably received in Italy at the time when Verdi and Wagner still flourished, dies in São Paulo at the age of 96.

20 SEPTEMBER 1942

Violin Concerto by the 35-year-old Brazilian composer Camargo GUARNIERI is performed for the first time in Rio de Janeiro.

20 SEPTEMBER 1942

Napoleon, opera by the 36-year-old German composer Edmund von BORCK, destined to be killed in combat in Italy in 1944, is performed for the first time in Gera.

4 OCTOBER 1942

Festliche Toccata for orchestra by the 45-year-old German composer Ottmar GERSTER is performed for the first time in Düsseldorf.

7 OCTOBER 1942

Odysseus, opera in three acts by the 42-year-old German composer Hermann REUTTER, is produced in Frankfurt.

15 OCTOBER 1942

Leningrad, suite for chorus and orchestra by Dmitri SHOSTAKOVICH, written as a tribute to the courage of the citizens of Leningrad during the still continuing siege of their city, is performed for the first time in Moscow.

16 OCTOBER 1942

Rodeo, or *The Courting at Burnt Ranch*, one-act ballet by Aaron COPLAND, a lyrico-dramatic musical stereopticon of the American west, in which a cowbelle outdoes the cowboys in bronco busting, and wins her favorite roper at a ranch house dance, utilizing in the score two western ballads and two square-dance tunes, is produced, as a commissioned work, by the Ballet Russe de Monte Carlo in New York. (An orchestral suite drawn from *Rodeo*, in four dancing movements, was first performed on 28 May 1932, by the Boston Pops Orchestra, with Arthur Fiedler conducting.)

18 OCTOBER 1942

Concerto for String Orchestra by the 39-year-old Chinese-born Estonian-German composer Boris BLACHER, is performed for the first time in Hamburg.

22 OCTOBER 1942

Second Symphony by the American composer John Alden CARPENTER, in three movements—*Allegro Andante, Allegro*—with some allusions to Algerian tunes among its themes (Carpenter had visited Algiers upon his retirement as Vice-President of the Carpenter Railway and

Ship Supplies Co.), is performed for the first time by the New York Philharmonic conducted by Bruno Walter.

22 OCTOBER 1942

Ankara Castle, symphonic suite by the Turkish composer Necil KAZIM AKSES, is performed for the first time in Ankara.

24 OCTOBER 1942

I Capricci di Callot, comic opera in three acts by Gian Francesco MALIPIERO, inspired by the carnavelesque masques in the etchings of Jacques Callot (1592–1635) as transmuted in Hoffmann's tales, is produced in Rome.

28 OCTOBER 1942

Capriccio, opera in one act by Richard STRAUSS (completed on 3 August 1941) to a libretto by Clemens Krauss and the composer, set as a conversation piece in Paris of 1775, debating the problem of relative importance of words and music in an opera, with interpolations of anachronistic musical quotations—including passages from Strauss's own operas, specifically *Ariadne auf Naxos*—is produced in war-darkened Munich.

28 OCTOBER 1942

La Tentation dernière, cantata by André JOLIVET, depicting the trial of Joan of Arc, is performed for the first time in Paris.

30 OCTOBER 1942

Die Zauberinsel, opera in two acts by the Swiss composer Heinrich SUTERMEISTER, after Shakespeare's play *The Tempest* is performed for the first time in Dresden.

1 NOVEMBER 1942

Hugo DISTLER, 36-year-old German composer of an imposing array of cantatas, oratorios, motets and organ works, written in a massive polyphonic manner of neoclassical rhetoric, commits suicide in Berlin.

1 NOVEMBER 1942

A Lincoln Legend, symphonic paragraph by Morton GOULD, ambidextrous American composer of serious and popular music, is performed for the first time by the National Broadcasting Company Symphony Orchestra in New York.

3 NOVEMBER 1942

Walter DAMROSCH, 80-year-old German-born American composer and conductor, leads in New York the first performance of his one-act opera *The Opera Cloak*, to a fanciful libretto by his daughter, dealing with a sad seamstress languishing in New York in 1915, who finds vicarious enjoyment in reading a passionate love letter inadvertently left in the pocket of an opera cloak given to her for repairs, accidentally rings a fire alarm and is rescued from loneliness by a handsome fireman who takes her to a dance, written in a synthetically competent operatic idiom replete with subliminal recollections of fragments from Wagner, Verdi and Puccini, galvanized in some scenes by ragtime rhythms.

5 NOVEMBER 1942

George M. COHAN, American song and dance man, the "Yankee Doodle Dandy" of the vaudeville stage, who wrote the rousing popular song of World War I, *Over There*, dies of cancer in New York at the age of 64. (A motion picture portraying his life, with James Cagney cast as Cohan, was shown to him in New York five months before his death.)

7 NOVEMBER 1942

At the Approaches to Moscow, opera in four acts by the 37-year-old Soviet composer Dmitri KABALEVSKY, to a libretto dealing with the Soviet counteroffensive against the Nazis in the suburbs of Moscow in December 1941, written in a militantly patriotic manner, is produced in Moscow less than a year after the events depicted in the score, and coincidentally celebrating the 25th anniversary of the Soviet Revolution. (The second version of the opera was produced for the first time in Moscow under the title *Under Fire* on 19 September 1943.)

7 NOVEMBER 1942

Ildar, opera in four acts by the 31-year-old Soviet composer Nazib ZHIGANOV, dealing with the earnest love pact between a tractor driver and a collective farm milkmaid in the midst of Nazi war, is performed for the first time, in the Tatar language, in Kazan, former stronghold of the Tatar kingdom crushed by Ivan the Terrible in 1582.

7 NOVEMBER 1942

Emelian Pugatchov, opera in five acts by the Soviet composer Marian KOVAL, depicting in heroic Russian harmonies the bold rebellion led against Catherine the Great by the ambitious Ural cossack Pugatchov, who eventually was caught, and publicly drawn and quartered in Moscow, is performed for the first time in the Ural town of Perm by an opera group moved from besieged Leningrad.

13 NOVEMBER 1942

First Symphony by Bohuslav MARTINU, in four movements, *Moderato, Allegro, Largo, Allegro vivace*, notated without key signatures but teleologically directed towards the tonal centers of B and B-flat, with the neoclassical idiom enriched by the intussusception of secundal harmonies, while deep-rooted pedal points provide basses for euphonious bitonalities, and ending in sonorous B-flat major, is performed for the first time by the Boston Symphony Orchestra, Serge Koussevitzky conducting.

13 NOVEMBER 1942

Concerto for two pianos and orchestra by Darius MILHAUD, in three movements, *Animé, Funèbre, Vif et précis*, is performed for the first time by the Pittsburgh Symphony Orchestra, Fritz Reiner conducting, with Vitya Vronsky and Victor Babin as soloists.

14 NOVEMBER 1942

Marco Takes a Walk, a set of symphonic variations by Deems TAYLOR, depicting a child's walk through a busy street, transforming the passing scene in his fantasies into a world of fabulous creatures, set to music in an affectionately coloristic idiom, is performed for the first time by the New York Philharmonic.

18 NOVEMBER 1942

A millennium has elapsed since the death of Odo DE CLUGNY, the Benedictine monk who expanded the hexachordal system of the ancients into a continuous diatonic scale from A to G, and formulated the distinction between B-flat (*b rotundum*, so named from its shape, and later developed into the modern flat sign) and B natural (*b quadratum* which evolved into the modern natural sign).

19 NOVEMBER 1942

Minnie la Candida, opera by Riccardo MALIPIERO, nephew of Gian Francesco Malipiero, is performed for the first time in Parma, Italy.

20 NOVEMBER 1942

The General Government of Poland, under Nazi occupation, issues a postage stamp of 50 Groschen honoring the memory of Chopin's teacher Joseph Xaver ELSNER.

23 NOVEMBER 1942

The Italian Government issues four postage stamps at 25, 30, and 50 centesimi and one lira, belatedly commemorating the sesquicentennial year of the birth of ROSSINI, who was born on 29 February 1792.

27 NOVEMBER 1942

Cantata de los Rios de Chile for chorus and orchestra by the prime Chilean modernist Domingo SANTA CRUZ, descriptive of the great mountain stream Maipo and Mt. Aconcagua, written in a grand polyphonic idiom, with occasional topical allusions to the Chilean scene, such as the imitation of a policeman's whistle by the oboe, is performed for the first time in Santiago.

27 NOVEMBER 1942

A *Fanfare for Paratroopers* by Paul CRESTON is performed by the Cincinnati Symphony Orchestra, under the direction of Eugene Goossens, as one of several musical salutations by American composers to the United States Armed Forces.

3 DECEMBER 1942

The Boston Symphony Orchestra, the last surviving nonunion orchestra in the United States, joins the American Federation of Musicians under the pressure of a virtual boycott by all union-controlled institutions and recording companies.

4 DECEMBER 1942

Concierto sinfónico for violin and orchestra by the Chilean composer Humberto ALLENDE, set in three contrasting movements within a neo-classical framework, is performed for the first time in Santiago.

9 DECEMBER 1942

Gayane, ballet by Aram KHACHATURIAN, in which a class-conscious Armenian girl worker on a Soviet collective farm foils the insidious machinations of her anti-Soviet husband, and after he is liquidated, marries his valorous executioner, with a series of orientalistic Caucasian dances in the score (of which the *Saber Dance,* with its sinuous melorhythms, has become universally popular), is produced in the town of Molotov, renamed in honor of the Soviet Minister of Foreign Affairs from its ancient name of Perm, in the Ural region.

11 DECEMBER 1942

Fanfare de la Liberté, a brief symphonic tribute by Darius MILHAUD to the undaunted spirit of France under Nazi occupation, is played for the first time by the Cincinnati Symphony Orchestra, Eugene Goossens conducting.

25 DECEMBER 1942

Vojislav VUČKOVIĆ, Croatian composer of mass songs, among them *Chorus of 10,000 Strikers,* author of scholarly monographs on Marxism in music, is shot by the Nazi police as he emerges from his secret hiding place in occupied Belgrade, dying a few hours later, on the same day that his wife was captured and tortured to death in another Gestapo dungeon.

28 DECEMBER 1942

Stronger than Death, opera in three acts by the 37-year-old Soviet composer Victor VOLOSHINOV, depicting the heroism of Soviet men and women in a Nazi-occupied village in 1941, is produced in Orenburg.

31 DECEMBER 1942

Yakob ORLANSKY, Russian accordion player, who in 1905 designed the BAYAN, so named after the legendary Russian minstrel, destined to become universally popular in Russia under that name, manufactured according to his instructions by the Russian instrument builder Peter Sterligov, and completed after two years of experimentation in August 1907, consisting of 58 spade-shaped keys chromatically arranged in three manuals for the right hand and four groups of buttons regulating triads and dominant-seventh-chord harmonies in the left hand, is found dead in his apartment in besieged, famine-stricken Leningrad.

1943

7 JANUARY 1943

Something for the Boys, a musical comedy by Cole PORTER, in which two nightclub songstresses and a New York street vendor unexpectedly inherit a Texas ranch, with intermingled love affairs entering their financial squabbles, further diversified by the discovery that one of the trio is a human radio receiver through the carborundum fillings in her bridgework, featuring besides the title song a popular ditty *Hey, Good Looking*, is produced in New York.

10 JANUARY 1943

Second Symphony in C minor by Tikhon KHRENNIKOV, expressing "the irresistible will to defeat the Fascist foe," and depicting in its four movements the purposeful Socialist labor of the Soviet man, a lament for the victims of the Nazi aggression, the undaunted spirit of young Soviet soldiers and the victorious military impetus, culminating in a triumph, in gloriously shining C major, over the Nazi war machine, is performed for the first time in Moscow. (The *Finale* was later revised, and the new version performed in Moscow on 9 June 1944.)

13 JANUARY 1943

Concerto for piano and small orchestra by William SCHU-MAN (completed by him on 18 July 1942) is performed for the first time in New York.

15 JANUARY 1943

Fanfare for France by Virgil THOMSON is performed by the Cincinnati Symphony Orchestra.

19 JANUARY 1943

The Shoestring Opera Company, a non-profit corporation formed "to demonstrate that artistic, dramatic music can be presented without the prohibitive cost of present-day grand opera," opens its first season with a performance of *Tales of Hoffmann*, at Hunter College in New York.

"*Shoestring*. Colloq. a very small amount of money or capital used to start or carry on an enterprise or business." (*The American College Dictionary*)

21 JANUARY 1943

1941, a symphonic suite by Sergei PROKOFIEV in three movements, *Battle*, *At Night*, and *For the Brotherhood of Nations*, depicting the anxieties of the Nazi invasion, the determination to win the war, and the hope for the creation of a new world of universal peace, is performed for the first time at Sverdlovsk.

22 JANUARY 1943

Fanfare for Freedom by Morton GOULD is sounded by the Cincinnati Symphony Orchestra.

31 JANUARY 1943

Divertimento for chamber orchestra by Richard STRAUSS, on the themes from piano pieces by François Couperin (the score completed on 12 September 1941), is performed for the first time in Vienna.

1 FEBRUARY 1943

Serge RACHMANINOFF becomes an American citizen.

2 FEBRUARY 1943

Alexandre TANSMAN, 45-year-old Parisian Polish composer, a musical refugee in America during the Nazi occupation of France, conducts the National Symphony Orchestra of Washington at its concert in Baltimore, in the first performance of his *Fifth Symphony* in D minor, in four classically outlined movements: (1) *Lento, Allegro con moto* in simple harmonious polyphony; (2) *Intermezzo*, a bucolic eclogue; (3) *Vivo*, a scherzo palpitating with jazzy rhythms in asymmetrical meters; (4) *Lento, Allegro con moto*, coming to an assertive ending in the tonic major.

13 FEBRUARY 1943

Prayer in the Time of War for orchestra by William SCHU-MAN is performed for the first time in Pittsburgh.

14 FEBRUARY 1943

Seventh Symphony, surnamed *Sinfonia Romantica*, by the prime symphonist of Sweden, Kurt ATTERBERG, is performed for the first time in Frankfurt.

18 FEBRUARY 1943

Die Kluge, "a story of the King and the wise woman," in six scenes by the 47-year-old German composer Carl ORFF, to his own text derived from Grimm's fairy tale *Die kluge Bauerntochter* and synthesized with tales from China and Afghanistan, in which a rural damsel cunningly solves three crucial riddles propounded by a simple-minded king, written in a characteristically denuded soli-tonic melologue employing rhythmed speech, spoken song and singing melody, replete with obstinate ostinati and ostentatious repetition of ostensibly monothematic motives symbolizing the rough-shod wisdom of German peasantry, containing whimsical quotations in orchestral ritornelli from Mozart's *Entführung aus dem Serail*, is performed for the first time in Frankfurt.

23 FEBRUARY 1943

Tania, opera in one act by the 32-year-old Soviet composer Vasily DEKHTEREV, depicting the heroism of a Soviet girl guerrilla during the Nazi invasion of Russia in 1941, is produced in Moscow.

23 FEBRUARY 1943

Violin Concerto by the Dutch modernist Daniel RUYNE-MAN is performed for the first time at a concert of the Concertgebouw Orchestra in Amsterdam.

26 FEBRUARY 1943

Fifth Symphony by Roy HARRIS, in three classically formal movements, *Prelude, Chorale* and *Fugue,* dedicated "to the heroic and freedom-loving people of our great ally, the Union of Soviet Socialist Republics, as a tribute to their strength in war, their staunch idealism for world peace, their ability to cope with stark materialistic problems of world order without losing a passionate belief in the fundamental importance of the arts," is performed for the first time by the Boston Symphony Orchestra, conducted by Serge Koussevitzky.

28 FEBRUARY 1943

Complaintes du Soldat, a melancholy triptych for voice and orchestra by André JOLIVET, is performed in Nazi-oppressed Paris.

28 FEBRUARY 1943

Michelangelo, oratorio by the 42-year-old Swiss composer Hans HAUGW, is performed for the first time at Solothurn, Switzerland.

1 MARCH 1943

Three centuries have passed since the death in Rome of the great contrapuntist and master organist Girolamo FRESCOBALDI.

3 MARCH 1943

Variationen für Orchester, op. 30 by Anton von WEBERN, comprising a theme with six variations, based on a symmetric 12-tone series, divisible into three segments of four notes each, of which the middle tetrad is identically self-invertible and self-reversible, while the outer tetrads are mutually invertible in their intervallic structure, the entire series consisting of two six-note intervallically mirrorable tropes, all these materials being treated in augmentation, diminution, canonic imitation and chordal integration of dodecaphonic ingredients, is performed for the first time in Winterthur, Switzerland, under the direction of Hermann Scherchen. (Exact date obtained from the Municipality of Winterthur.)

Imagine this: six tones are given in a basic form, which is determined in respect to successive ordering and rhythm, and what follows is nothing but this same basic form over and over again!!! Goethe says about the "Primal Phenomenon" that it is "Ideal, because it is the last we can know/Real, because we know it/Symbolic, since it comprises all events/Identical with all events." This is also the essence of my *Variations.* (Anton von Webern, in a letter written in 1943)

5 MARCH 1943

Morton GOULD, 29-year-old American composer of symphonic and light music, conducts the Pittsburgh Symphony Orchestra in the first performance of his *First Symphony.*

11 MARCH 1943

Capriccio for orchestra by the 25-year-old Austrian composer Gottfried VON EINEM is performed for the first time by the Berlin Philharmonic Orchestra.

12 MARCH 1943

Fanfare for the Common Man by Aaron COPLAND is sonorously heralded by the Cincinnati Symphony Orchestra.

23 MARCH 1943

Joseph SCHILLINGER, Russian musical scientist and composer, who devised a leviathanic Schillinger System of Composition, in which music is treated as a technology of sound, and proposed to train composers like mechanical engineers, dies in New York at the age of 47, at the peak of an astonishingly successful teaching career during which a whole pleiad of Broadway composers, including George Gershwin, flocked to his gadget-filled studio-laboratory in quest of instant musical knowledge.

26 MARCH 1943

A *Free Song,* secular cantata by William SCHUMAN (completed on 16 October 1942), to the text from Walt Whitman, couched in a propulsive rhythmic style as a 20th-century counterpart of old Handelian forms, is performed for the first time by the Boston Symphony Orchestra, Serge Koussevitzky conducting.

28 MARCH 1943

Serge RACHMANINOFF, last giant of the golden age of Russian music, great virtuoso pianist, composer of emotionally stirring, supremely pianistic concertos and preludes imperishable in their romantic appeal to successive generations of music lovers all over the world, dies of cancer and terminal pneumonia, at Beverly Hills, California, at 1:30 A.M. four days before his 70th birthday.

31 MARCH 1943

Oklahoma!, a musical play by Richard RODGERS, with book and lyrics by Oscar HAMMERSTEIN, based on the play *Green Grow the Lilacs* by Lynn Riggs, depicting with ineffable nostalgia the rustic joys of 1900 in the virgin countryside of Oklahoma, containing such perennial favorites of the American musical theater as the bucolic opening number *Oh, What a Beautiful Mornin',* and *The Surrey with the Fringe on Top,* is produced in New York. (Its run of 5 years and 9 weeks established a record for any Broadway musical play; prior to the New York production it was given a try-out in New Haven, under the title *Away We Go,* on 11 March 1943, and in Boston, under the same title, on 15 March 1943; it was only in New York that it acquired its permanent title with an exclamation point at the end.)

1 APRIL 1943

Das Schloss Dürande, opera in four acts by the lyrical Swiss composer Othmar SCHOECK, to a romantic libretto from the time of the French Revolution, wherein a young Jacobin sets a royalist castle on fire circa 1790 to avenge his sister's ruin by its aristocratic owner, but realizes that their love was reciprocal and joins them in the holocaust himself, is performed for the first time at the Staatsoper in Berlin.

4 APRIL 1943

Raoul LAPARRA, 66-year-old French composer of romantic operas and Spanish-flavored symphonic music, is killed in an American air raid upon the Renault works near Paris.

13 APRIL 1943

The Testament of Freedom by Randall THOMPSON, for men's voices and orchestra, written for the 200th anniversary of Thomas Jefferson's birth, to a text from the writings of Jefferson, with a musical score conceived in the spirit of simplicity, leaving not a discord untamed in its prevalent C major, is presented for the first time by the Virginia Glee Club, with the composer at the piano.

17 APRIL 1943

Le Nozze di Haura, one-act opera by Adriano LUALDI, is performed for the first time in Rome, 35 years after its composition. (A radio performance of the opera was given in Rome on 19 October 1939.)

12 MAY 1943

Concerto for coloratura soprano and orchestra by Reinhold GLIÈRE, in two movements of singable vocalization and considerable lyrical power without words, the first full-fledged vocal concerto of this genre, is performed for the first time in Moscow.

12 MAY 1943

Albert STOESSEL, 48-year-old American conductor and composer, collapses and dies of heart failure while conducting the ballad-poem *Dunkirk* by Walter Damrosch at the National Institute of Arts and Letters in New York, scored for baritone solo, solo chorus, piano and chamber orchestra, and dedicated to the heroes of the evacuation of Dunkirk by the British, with Walter Damrosch himself at the piano. (The world première of *Dunkirk* was given by the NBC Symphony Orchestra under the direction of the composer on 2 May 1943.)

18 MAY 1943

José ARDÉVOL, 32-year-old Spanish-born Cuban composer, conducts in Havana the first performance of his choral ballet *Forma*, inspired by a solipsistic concept of an ego in flux, and arranged in a formal classical instrumental suite of court dances.

22 MAY 1943

To commemorate the 130th anniversary of WAGNER'S birth, the Nazi occupation authorities of Bohemia and Moravia issue three commemorative postage stamps, with Wagner's portraits, in the denominations of 60 hellers, one krone 20 hellers and 2 kronen 50 hellers.

27 MAY 1943

The 46-year-old Norwegian composer Harald SAEVERUD conducts in Bergen the first performance of his *Sixth Symphony*, subtitled *Sinfonia Dolorosa*, in a single movement conceived in a national Scandinavian vein, with drums and bells marking the fortissimo ending.

1 JUNE 1943

To circumvent the prohibition by the Nazi authorities in occupied Paris to play music by Darius MILHAUD as a non-Aryan Frenchman making his home in America, Milhaud's *Scaramouche* for two pianos is performed by two Aryan French pianists at the École Normale de Musique in Paris, anagrammatically programmed as Mous-Arechac by Hamid-al-Usurid.

2 JUNE 1943

The Brazilian composer Camargo GUARNIERI conducts in São Paulo the first performance of his *Aber tura concertante*, an orchestral overture in a baroque style seasoned with Brazilian melorhythms.

12 JUNE 1943

The American Army Task Force presents at Kiriwina Island in the Pacific, captured from the Japanese, the first concert of military band music, terrifying the natives by the jazzy sounds of brass instruments shining in the tropical sun.

15 JUNE 1943

To commemorate the centennial of the birth of Edvard GRIEG, the Nazi-dominated Quisling government of Norway issues a series of special stamps in the denominations of 10, 20, 40 and 60 øre.

21 JUNE 1943

Michael TIPPETT, 38-year-old English composer, director of music at Morley College, London, and a militant pacifist, is sentenced to three months' imprisonment in Wormwood Scrubs, Surrey, for violation of terms of his registration as a conscientious objector, and for failing to perform farm labor tasks assigned to him by the British Army.

24 JUNE 1943

VAUGHAN WILLIAMS conducts at the London Promenade Concerts the first performance of his *Fifth Symphony* in D major, dedicated "in sincere flattery" to Sibelius, marked by a somber serenity of musical utterance and developed by measured accretion of thematic substance, concomitant with cumulative rise and recession in dynamic strength, in four classically conceived movements: *Preludio, Scherzo, Romanza* (bearing an epigraph from Bunyan's *Pilgrim's Progress*, and using some thematic material from the subsequent opera of that title) and *Passacaglia*.

30 JUNE 1943

La Vita è Sogno, three-act opera, after Calderón, by Gian Francesco MALIPIERO, is performed for the first time anywhere in a German version, in Breslau.

5 JULY 1943

Gli Dei a Tebe, opera in three acts by the half-German half-Italian composer Ermanno WOLF-FERRARI, based on a Greek myth wherein Hera grants to Zeus a night of love with Amphitryon's wife, until the cuckoo in the Temple sacred to Hera signalizes the coming of dawn, is performed for the first time in Hannover, Germany, in the German version, under the title *Der Kukuck von Theben.*

8 JULY 1943

Lennox BERKELEY, 40-year-old English composer, conducts in London the first performance of his *First Symphony,* in four classically designed movements.

13 JULY 1943

The German ethnomusicologist Kurt HUBER, distinguished by his profound and valuable research in the field of German folk music, is beheaded by the Nazi executioner in Munich, on the charge of participation in student demonstrations and circulating anti-Hitlerian proclamations. (Exact date obtained from the Oberbürgermeister of Munich. Riemann's *Musiklexikon* gives the erroneous date 13 May 1943.)

11 AUGUST 1943

Second Concerto for French horn and orchestra by Richard STRAUSS (completed on 28 November 1942) is performed for the first time in Salzburg.

15 AUGUST 1943

Tivoli-Tivoli, orchestral suite by the modern Danish composer Knudaage RIISAGER, a musical tribute to the famous central park Tivoli Gardens in Copenhagen, is performed for the first time at the summer concert series in the Tivoli Gardens in Copenhagen.

16 AUGUST 1943

During an Allied air attack on the industrial installations of Milan, a direct bomb hit is made on the Teatro alla Scala, destroying the auditorium, but, thanks to the protection of the steel curtain, leaving the stage intact. (The theater was restored after the war; the first post-war season was inaugurated on 11 May 1946, with Arturo Toscanini conducting.)

19 AUGUST 1943

Ernest John MOERAN, 48-year-old English composer, plays at the London Promenade Concerts the solo part in the first performance of his *Rhapsody* for piano and orchestra.

20 AUGUST 1943

Concerto for violin and orchestra by the Mexican composer Manuel PONCE, in three movements, which incorporates his famous song *Estrellita* in the slow second movement, is performed for the first time in Mexico City, under the direction of Carlos Chávez.

25 AUGUST 1943

Morton GOULD conducts the first performance in New York of his *Interplay* for piano and orchestra, with José Iturbi as soloist, in four movements designated *With drive and vigor, Gavotte, Blues,* and *With verse and gusto,* written in a jaunty jazzy idiom replete with brave atonalities and saturated with non-harmonic additives (a section in the *Blues* is marked "Slow and dirty").

5 SEPTEMBER 1943

The Automatic Pistol, chorus by Ellis KOHS to text from the U.S. Army Weapons Manual, is performed for the first time by the Army Music Chorus in Washington, D.C., William Strickland conducting.

8 SEPTEMBER 1943

Nadezhda Svetlova, lyric opera in three acts by the Soviet composer Ivan DZERZHINSKY to his own libretto dealing with the heroism of a surgeon and his daughter, an art student, in besieged Leningrad in 1941, is produced in Orenburg by members of the evacuated staff of the Leningrad Opera.

15 SEPTEMBER 1943

Hans HUMPERT, 42-year-old German composer of romantic symphonies and choral music, is killed in combat at Salerno, Italy, fighting in the German ranks against the American landing forces.

26 SEPTEMBER 1943

Brébeuf and His Brethren, historical musical pageant by the Canadian composer Healey WILLAN, scored for speaker, chorus and orchestra, is performed for the first time in Toronto as a commissioned work by the Canadian Broadcasting Corporation.

26 SEPTEMBER 1943

The Four Freedoms, symphonic suite by the American composer Robert Russell BENNETT, inspired by the famous speech of President Roosevelt, with Freedom of Speech exemplified by a tonal portrait of a street orator; Freedom of Worship by a stately anthem; Freedom from Want illustrated by a prosperous dance tune; and Freedom from Fear by a confident cradle song gradually evolving into a happy march, is performed for the first time in New York by the National Broadcasting Company Symphony Orchestra.

28 SEPTEMBER 1943

Freedom Morning, symphonic poem by the 38-year-old American composer Marc BLITZSTEIN for orchestra, tenor and chorus, dedicated to "all Negro troops in the service of the United States" and containing Negro spirituals in its thematic material, is performed for the first time at an Anglo-American concert in London with the participation of the London Symphony Orchestra, the Negro tenor Roland Hayes, and a Negro chorus of 200 members of aviation engineering units stationed in England.

7 OCTOBER 1943

One Touch of Venus, musical comedy by Kurt WEILL, dealing with a jesting New York barber who puts an engagement ring on the finger of a statue of Venus, whose marmoreal body thereupon changes to warm flesh, and who becomes his statuesque companion for life, is produced in New York.

8 OCTOBER 1943

Ode by Igor STRAVINSKY, in three parts *Eulogy, Eclogue, Epitaph*, "an elegiac chant" dedicated to the memory of Natalie Koussevitzky, wife of Serge Koussevitzky, as "an appreciation of her spiritual contribution to the art of the eminent conductor, in which the second part is a kind of concert champêtre, suggesting out-of-door music, an idea cherished by Natalie Koussevitzky," is performed for the first time by the Boston Symphony Orchestra, Serge Koussevitzky conducting.

9 OCTOBER 1943

Italo MONTEMEZZI conducts in New York the first performance of his opera *L'Incantesimo* (*Enchantment*), in a radio broadcast over the network of the National Broadcasting Company.

10 OCTOBER 1943

Barbe-Bleue, comic opera by Jacques IBERT in which the fabled uxoricide (he painted his beard blue) is outwitted by his six wives and is reduced in the end to the humiliating status of the head of a bourgeois household with his seventh bride, is performed for the first time on the radio in Lausanne.

14 OCTOBER 1943

Frontiers, a symphonic musicorama in three tableaux by Paul CRESTON, depicting in rhapsodic tones "the westward American migration achieved through the vision, constancy and indomitable spirit of the pioneers," is performed for the first time by the Toronto Symphony Orchestra, André Kostelanetz conducting.

15 OCTOBER 1943

Serenade for tenor voice, horn solo and string orchestra by Benjamin BRITTEN, to poems of Ben Jonson, Blake, Keats, Tennyson and others, is performed for the first time in London.

15 OCTOBER 1943

The Prairie, orchestral suite by the 21-year-old Berlin-born American composer Lukas FOSS, extracted from his cantata to the poem of Carl Sandburg of the same name, suggesting "vast open landscapes, and lots of fresh air," is performed for the first time by the Boston Symphony Orchestra, Serge Koussevitzky conducting. (The entire cantata was performed for the first time in New York on 15 May 1944 by the Collegiate Chorale, Robert Shaw conducting.)

17 OCTOBER 1943

Invasion, symphonic sketch by Bernard ROGERS, portraying the hope and anxiety of the expectation of the imminent landing by the Allied forces in Nazi-infested Europe, cast in ominously somber harmonies, is performed for the first time by the New York Philharmonic, Artur Rodzinski conducting.

18 OCTOBER 1943

The National Theater of Munich, housing the Staatsoper built in 1818, is destroyed during an incendiary bomb attack by the Allied air forces.

18 OCTOBER 1943

Symphony by the 30-year-old American composer Jerome MOROSS, in four movements, the third being based on the hobo song "Midnight Special," is performed for the first time by the Seattle Symphony under the direction of Thomas Beecham.

22 OCTOBER 1943

Nicolai BEREZOWSKY, 43-year-old Russian-born American composer of euphoniously modernistic instrumental music, conducts the Boston Symphony Orchestra in the first performance of his *Fourth Symphony*, in four movements of cyclic design, with well-planned thematic retrospection at strategic musical points.

28 OCTOBER 1943

On the 25th anniversary of the establishment of Czechoslovakia as an independent republic after World War I, two orchestral works by the prime Czech composer Bohuslav MARTINU, making his temporary home in America, are given their world premières on the same day: *Memorial to Lidice*, a symphonic tribute to the martyrs of the Czech village destroyed by the Nazis, performed by the New York Philharmonic under the direction of Artur Rodzinski; and *Second Symphony* (composed between 29 June and 24 July 1943), played by the Cleveland Orchestra, Erich Leinsdorf conducting.

29 OCTOBER 1943

Cupid and Psyche, ballet overture by Paul HINDEMITH, inspired by an old Roman fresco, is performed for the first time by the Philadelphia Orchestra, Eugene Ormandy conducting.

29 OCTOBER 1943

Commando March by Samuel BARBER, originally written for military band and used on American shortwave broadcasts throughout the world, is performed for the first time in its symphonic form by the Boston Symphony Orchestra, Serge Koussevitzky conducting.

29 OCTOBER 1943

Percy GOETSCHIUS, grand old man of American musical education, confirmed believer in the imminent goodness of Germanic academic classicism (he used to call the C-major scale "God's own scale"), dies in Manchester, New Hampshire, at the patriarchal age of 90.

4 NOVEMBER 1943

Eighth Symphony by Dmitri SHOSTAKOVICH, conceived as a symphonic tragedy and reflecting the growing hope of liberation from the dark power of Nazi Germany, in five movements, of which the last three are played without pause—(1) *Adagio*, a demanding challenge to humanity locked in a mortal struggle, leading to a vigorous *Allegro* charged with kinetic energy in a fugally developed motion; (2) *Allegretto*, a rondo in five distinct sections, throbbing with militant energy; (3) *Allegro non troppo*, based on a persistent triadic motive achieving tremendous power, with the kettledrums repeating it 29 times and eventually subsiding to an echo of a military drum; (4) *Largo*, a philosophical passacaglia; and (5) *Finale*, set in resolutely optimistic C major—is performed for the first time in Leningrad conducted by Evgeny Mravinsky.

5 NOVEMBER 1943

Concerto for Two Pianos and Orchestra by Bohuslav MARTINU (composed in New York between 3 January and 23 February 1943), evocative of the poignant melorhythms of Moravian folk music, in three movements in the contrasting styles of brisk toccata, lyrical contemplation and propulsive rondo form, with lengthy cadenzas for each of the two pianos, is performed for the first time by the Philadelphia Orchestra under the direction of Eugene Ormandy, with Pierre Luboshutz and Genia Nemenoff as soloists.

6 NOVEMBER 1943

Catulli Carmina, scenic cantata to Latin texts from the poems of Catullus, by Carl ORFF, scored for voices, 4 pianos and percussion, with a cast of characters that includes Catullus himself, his beloved Lesbia, his friend Caelius (who surreptitiously takes Lesbia's place in the slumbering poet's bed), and assorted courtesans, couched in a percussively modernistic manner, with protracted iteration of single notes accompanied by polytonal harmonies, is performed for the first time in Leipzig.

12 NOVEMBER 1943

Symphony for Strings by William SCHUMAN, his *Fifth Symphony*, set in three movements—(1) *Molto agitato ed energico*, evolving from a theme played in unison by violins on the G string; (2) *Larghissimo*, set in bitonal harmonies, and employing a novel effect of fortissimo on muted strings; (3) *Presto leggiero*, written in a sophisticated jazz manner— is performed for the first time by the Boston Symphony Orchestra, Serge Koussevitzky conducting.

13 NOVEMBER 1943

On the 75th anniversary of the death of ROSSINI (whose acute triskaidekaphobia was aggravated by a superstitious fear of Fridays, and who died on 13 November 1868 which was a Friday), the Italian government issues a series of four postage stamps in his honor, in denominations of 25, 30 and 50 centesimi and one lira.

14 NOVEMBER 1943

Leonard BERNSTEIN, 25-year-old native of Lawrence, Massachusetts, youthful disciple of Serge Koussevitzky, makes a spectacular debut as associate conductor of the New York Philharmonic when he is called upon short notice as a substitute for the ailing Bruno Walter, and acquits himself sensationally in a challenging program including *Don Quixote* of Richard STRAUSS and an artfully intricate set of *Variations on a Hungarian Peasant Song* by the Hollywoodized Hungarian composer Miklós RÓZSA.

There are many variations of one of the six best stories in the world: the young corporal takes over the platoon when all the officers are down; the captain, with the dead admiral at his side, signals the fleet to go ahead; the young actress, fresh from Corinth or Ashtabula, steps into the star's role; the junior clerk, alone in the office, makes the instantaneous decision that saves the firm from ruin. The adventure of Leonard Bernstein, 25-year-old assistant conductor of the Philharmonic, who blithely mounted the podium at Carnegie Hall Sunday afternoon when Conductor Bruno Walter became ill, belongs in the list. The corporals and captains must be brave, the young actress beautiful and talented, the clerk quick on his feet. Likewise, Mr. Bernstein had to have something approaching genius to make full use of his opportunity. It's a good American success story. The warm, friendly triumph of it filled Carnegie Hall and spread far over the air waves. (*A Story Old and Ever New*, Editorial in the New York *Times*, 16 November 1943)

15 NOVEMBER 1943

With the German Army in full retreat only a few miles away, the San Carlo Opera House in Naples reopens its season after the theater is cleaned up and the bomb damage repaired.

17 NOVEMBER 1943

The Anxious Bugler, orchestral sketch by the American composer-industrialist John Alden CARPENTER, depicting in folksy tones the emotions of "any boy anywhere, who finds himself a soldier," is performed for the first time by the New York Philharmonic, Artur Rodzinski conducting.

24 NOVEMBER 1943

Symphonie de danses by André JOLIVET is performed for the first time in Paris.

25 NOVEMBER 1943

Fredlös (*The Outlaw*), opera by the 56-year-old Swedish composer Oskar LINDBERG, after a short story by Selma Lagerlöf, is produced in Stockholm.

26 NOVEMBER 1943

Gardner READ, 30-year-old American composer, conducts the Boston Symphony Orchestra in the first performance of his *Second Symphony* in three movements, cast in impressively somber, somewhat Nordic, sonorities in the manner of Sibelius, with concealed rhythmic energies periodically released in frenetic eruptions.

29 NOVEMBER 1943

Three centuries have passed since the death in Venice of Claudio MONTEVERDI, initiator of the true operatic style of stage music as a glorified elaboration of the dramatic madrigal achieving an inspired coalescence of instrumental polyphony with vocal monody.

2 DECEMBER 1943

Carmen Jones, a Negro version of Bizet's *Carmen,* to a new Americanized libretto by Oscar HAMMERSTEIN II, with the score reorchestrated by Robert Russell BENNETT, and the scene of action transferred from Seville to an American parachute factory during World War II, in which Carmen is employed, Don José is a military guard who goes AWOL for her sake, and the toreador a prize fighter, is produced in New York with an all-Negro cast.

3 DECEMBER 1943

Howard HANSON conducts the Boston Symphony Orchestra in the first performance of his *Fourth Symphony,* subtitled *Requiem,* dedicated to the memory of his father and written in a fervid devotional style, in four movements named after the parts of the Latin service for the dead, *Kyrie, Requiescat, Dies Irae* and *Lux Aeterna,* and ending softly on a mysteriously inconclusive first inversion of the C-major triad as a pledge of faith in an eventual conversion to the eternal tonic.

4 DECEMBER 1943

The stockrooms and the building of the historic German publishing firm Brietkopf & Härtel are destroyed in an Allied air raid on Leipzig, cremating many engraved treasures of past musical glories, with only a few copper plates of the works by great composers recovered from the ashes. (Manuscripts and precious memorabilia had been saved from destruction through the heroic efforts of employees who had deposited them in rural air-raid shelters.)

5 DECEMBER 1943

Das Werbekleid, "merry opera in three acts" by the 46-year-old Viennese composer Franz SALMHOFER, to his own libretto wherein an ambitious Tyrolean villager spurns a hefty local milkmaid for a slender-legged city damsel, a happy ending vouchsafed when the abandoned maiden dons a "Werbekleid," a lucky ancestral attire which had helped many of its previous wearers to win back a fickle lover, the whole thing set to music in an engagingly waltzing manner, is produced in Salzburg.

6 DECEMBER 1943

Opus Americanum, a symphonic tribute to America by Darius MILHAUD in gratitude for American hospitality to him in a temporary refuge from subjugated France, is performed for the first time by the San Francisco Symphony Orchestra, Pierre Monteux conducting.

8 DECEMBER 1943

Twenty-Fourth Symphony by the most prolific 20th-century symphonist Nicolai MIASKOVSKY (completed on 3 September 1943), in F minor, in three movements, written in a lyrical Russian style contrasted with dramatic episodes in fanfare-like sonorities, is performed for the first time in Moscow.

10 DECEMBER 1943

Biblical Scenes, triptych for orchestra by the Hungarian-American composer Eugene ZÁDOR, with three sections portraying Joseph as the symbol of innocence, David as a symbol of victory over superior forces and Paul in his dual role as Saul, persecutor of Christ, and as Paul, Christ's great disciple, is performed for the first time by the Chicago Symphony.

16 DECEMBER 1943

Bernard HERRMANN, 32-year-old American composer, conducts the New York Philharmonic in the first performance of his symphonic elegy *For the Fallen,* "a berceuse for those who lie asleep on the many alien battlefields," with a consolatory quotation from Handel's *Messiah* in the coda.

30 DECEMBER 1943

The first performance is given in Moscow of the *Second Symphony* by the 40-year-old Soviet Armenian composer Aram KHACHATURIAN, described as *Symphony of Bells* by some Soviet commentators on account of the introduction of large church bells in the score suggesting the impact of bombs on bronze, a war-generated work in four movements:

(1) *Adante maestoso,* in which the "bell motive" dominates the musical scene alternating with a songful theme, and ending in a resolute march; (2) *Allegro risoluto,* a somber dance with macabre overtones relieved briefly by lyric interludes; (3) *Andante sostenuto,* a tragic elegy reflecting the immense sufferings of the Soviet people inflicted by the brutal Nazi war machine, with the ominous tones of *Dies irae* rising from the depths as a universal motive of death and lamentation; (4) *Andante mosso; Allegro sostenuto,* voicing the faith in ultimate triumph over the dark enemy forces in sonorous fanfares and culminating in a grand declaration of expected victory raising the oriflamme of the confident brass to the sound of great church bells symbolic of eternal impregnable and holy Russia.

31 DECEMBER 1943

Concerto for violin and orchestra by Bohuslav MARTINU in three movements—(1) *Andante; Allegro,* (2) *Poco moderato,* (3) *Poco allegro*—cast in a lyrico-dramatic vein, alternating between classically terse and rhapsodically emotional moods, tonally lucid but occasionally ramifying into euphonious bitonalities, is performed for the first time by Mischa Elman, for whom it was written, and the Boston Symphony Orchestra, under the direction of Serge Koussevitzky.

1944

5 JANUARY 1944

In Memoriam: The Colored Soldiers Who Died for Democracy, symphonic paragraph by William Grant STILL, the American Negro composer, one of a series of works commissioned by the League of Composers of New York in dedication to an aspect of World War II, is performed for the first time by the New York Philharmonic, Artur Rodzinski conducting.

13 JANUARY 1944

Igor STRAVINSKY conducts the Boston Symphony Orchestra in Cambridge, Massachusetts, the first performances of his symphonic suite *Four Norwegian Moods* (originally designed for a motion picture about Norway), written "without any assumption of ethnological authenticity," and making use of Norwegian folk tunes "only as a rhythmic and melodic basis," and the orchestral version of his *Circus Polka*, written in Hollywood on 15 February 1942 for the elephant dance commissioned by the Ringling Brothers Circus, and devised in the manner of sophisticated grotesquerie with the insertion of a quotation from Schubert's *March Militaire* in a polyharmonic arrangement, prefacing the concert with his own version of *The Star-Spangled Banner* containing an unorthodox modulation into the subdominant in the cadence, thereby running afoul of a Massachusetts statute forbidding any tampering with the national anthem.

Searching about for a vehicle through which I might best express my gratitude at becoming an American citizen, I chose to harmonize and orchestrate as a national chorale the beautiful sacred anthem The Star-Spangled Banner. It is a desire to do my bit in these grievous times toward fostering and preserving the spirit of patriotism in this country that inspires me to tender this, my humble work, to the American people. (Stravinsky's statement in English, upon completing his arrangement on 4 July 1941)

Mr. Stravinsky's harmonies seemed a little queer to the New Englanders of today. In response to complaints, Boston Police Commissioner Thomas F. Sullivan and Police Captain Thomas F. Harvey appeared at the Saturday concert, 15 January 1944, flanked by six members of the "radical squad" prepared to sign a complaint charging Mr. Stravinsky with violation of chapter 264, Section 9, of the Massachusetts laws which forbids rearrangement of the national anthem and provides a penalty of $100. But the performance of the new version was cancelled, the police refrained from taking action, and quiet was restored to the banks of the Charles. (*Musical America*, New York, January, 1944)

20 JANUARY 1944

Symphonic Metamorphoses on Themes of Carl Maria von Weber by Paul HINDEMITH, in four movements—(1) *Allegro*, an astute variation derived from four-hand piano music of Weber; (2) *Turandot-Scherzo*, with thematic material taken from Weber's score of incidental music to Schiller's play of that name, titivated by percussive chinoiserie, and containing a jazzy fugue launched by the trombones in unison; (3) *Andantino*, an artful transmogrification of an innocent Weber piece for piano duet; (4) *March*, a magnisonant fanfaronade of vigesimosecular polyphony—is performed for the first time by the New York Philharmonic under the direction of Artur Rodzinski.

21 JANUARY 1944

André JOLIVET conducts in Nazi-held Paris the first performance of his first "radiophonic legend" *La Queste de Lancelot*, inspired by Arthurian legends.

27 JANUARY 1944

Concerto for Saxophone and Orchestra by Paul CRESTON, in three movements designated (1) *Energetic*, (2) *Meditative*, (3) *Rhythmic*, is performed for the first time by the New York Philharmonic with Vincent Abato as soloist and William Steinberg conducting.

28 JANUARY 1944

Mexican Hayride, musical comedy by Cole PORTER, in which an American female bullfighter, sensationally successful in Mexico, abandons her New York gangster lover in favor of a well-mannered American diplomat, set to music in an ingratiating Mexican-flavored style, is produced in New York.

28 JANUARY 1944

Leonard BERNSTEIN, 25-year-old American composer and conductor, leads the Pittsburgh Symphony Orchestra in the première of his *First Symphony* entitled *Jeremiah*, in three movements, *Prophecy, Profanation, Lamentation*, intended "to parallel in feeling the intensity of the prophet's pleas with his people," embodying in its thematic content both the ritualistically devotional and primitivistically orgiastic elements of Hebrew music, with the voice of the prophet in the finale intoning sacred verses in the original Hebrew.

30 JANUARY 1944

Summer Rhapsody, by the 46-year-old Danish composer Knudaage RIISAGER, based on Danish folksongs, is performed for the first time in Copenhagen.

2 FEBRUARY 1944

Yvette GUILBERT, Paris chanteuse who was erotically immortalized by Toulouse-Lautrec in his flamboyant posters depicting her with flying petticoats and multi-plumed chapeaux, dies in Aix-en-Provence at the age of 77.

5 FEBRUARY 1944

Prinzessin Turandot, ballet by the 26-year-old Austrian composer Gottfried VON EINEM, on the subject of a cruel Chinese princess who put to death a number of unlucky suitors, is performed for the first time in Dresden.

6 FEBRUARY 1944

Piano Concerto by Arnold SCHOENBERG, op. 42 (completed in Hollywood on 30 December 1942), in a single movement articulated into four classically contrasted sections, containing distinct elements of an introduction, a scherzo, a slow interlude and a rondo, thematically built on a unifying 12-tone series, E-flat, B-flat, D, F, E, C, F-sharp, G-sharp, C-sharp, A, B, G, and displaying despite its strict dodecaphonic organization a surprising liberality towards tonality and even triadic permissiveness, terminating with an incandescently white major seventh-chord anchored in deep C, is performed for the first time in New York with Eduard Steuermann as soloist and Leopold Stokowski conducting the Orchestra of the National Broadcasting Company.

7 FEBRUARY 1944

Lina CAVALIERI, Italian lyric soprano, renowned at the turn of the century as "la donna più bella del mondo," and whose first three husbands were a Russian prince, an American millionaire and a French tenor, perishes tragically with her fourth husband, an Italian nobleman, when a bomb falls on her villa near Florence during an American air raid.

8 FEBRUARY 1944

Violin Concerto by the Soviet composer Lev KNIPPER is performed for the first time in Moscow.

11 FEBRUARY 1944

Third Symphony by the Soviet composer Vissarion SHEBALIN, in four classically symmetric movements, culminating in a magisterial fugue in the optimistic key of C major, is performed for the first time in Moscow.

13 FEBRUARY 1944

Fourth Symphony by the 43-year-old American composer George ANTHEIL, erstwhile *enfant terrible* of music, cast in his newly adopted un-modern idiom, adhering to explicit tonality and rhythmically symmetric, concluding on a jubilant E-flat major triad, is performed for the first time in New York, with Leopold Stokowski conducting the Symphony Orchestra of the National Broadcasting Company.

15 FEBRUARY 1944

Ludus Tonalis, piano suite by Paul HINDEMITH, subtitled "Studies in Counterpoint, Tonal Organization and Piano Playing," a "tonal game" without key signatures, east in dissonant linear counterpoint, with the Prelude and the Postlude being upside-down retrograde conjugates of each other (allowing for non-retroactive accidentals), is performed for the first time at the University of Chicago.

16 FEBRUARY 1944

Edmund VON BORCK, German composer of neo-classical instrumental music, is killed in the ranks of the German Army during the fighting in Italy near Nettuno, six days before his 38th birthday.

17 FEBRUARY 1944

William Billings Overture by William SCHUMAN, built on themes from three choral works by "America's first professional composer, William Billings," is performed for the first time by the New York Philharmonic, Artur Rodzinski conducting.

19 FEBRUARY 1944

Nicolai MEDTNER, 64-year-old romantic Russian pianist and composer, expatriated in England since the Revolution deprived him of his native habitat, plays, with the London Philharmonic under the direction of Sir Adrian Boult, the solo part in the first performance of his *Third Piano Concerto* in E minor, subtitled *Ballade*, dedicated to the Maharaja of Mysore "with deep gratitude for the appreciation and furtherance of my work" (the Maharaja, like a Rex ex machina manifested himself at a most critical moment of Medtner's financial distress and gave him munificent support), conceived in an ascetically restrained contrapuntal idiom, in three movements:

(1) *Con moto largamente*, freely modulating from austere hexatonic modalities into keys situated in chromatic propinquity, and spreading copious pianistic cadenzas across the breadth of the keyboard; (2) *Interludium*, a diptych of variations on previously stated themes; (3) *Finale: Allegro molto, svegliando eroico*, in rondo form, culminating in a heroically rhetorical declaration of musical faith in E major.

19 FEBRUARY 1944

Burnet TUTHILL conducts the St. Louis Symphony Orchestra in the first performance of his orchestral rhapsody *Come Seven*, intended not as "a musical description of the well-known gutter game," but reflecting "an attempt to compose in seven rhythm," with 11/8 ending, emblematic of the consummation of the ardent wishes of all players of crap, "seven, come eleven."

21 FEBRUARY 1944

Ballad of a Boy Who Remained Unknown, cantata by Sergei PROKOFIEV, inspired by the real story of a young Soviet partisan who blew up the Nazi staff automobile in a Nazi-occupied Russian village where his mother and sister were murdered by the invaders, is performed for the first time in Moscow.

23 FEBRUARY 1944

Ode to the Red Army, cantata by Sir Arnold BAX, to a poem by John Masefield, British Poet Laureate, written in homage to Soviet soldiers ("Though flanks were turned and center gone/ You stood for home and struggled on/ And now you reap reward; the line/ Comes west again; the foes decline"), is performed in London as a tribute to the Red Army on the 26th anniversary of its founding.

25 FEBRUARY 1944

Missa Oecumenica for soil, chorus, organ and orchestra by Alexandre GRETCHANINOFF, 79-year-old Russian expatriate composer living in New York, "inspired by the idea of the ecumenic significance of the church," set to the Latin words of the Mass and containing the characteristics of both the Russian orthodox church and the Roman Catholic ritual, is performed for the first time by the Boston Symphony Orchestra, Serge Koussevitzky conducting.

1 MARCH 1944

Hans KRÁSA, 44-year-old Prague-born Jewish composer of finely wrought music sensitized by anguished atonalities, perishes in the Nazi concentration camp at Auschwitz.

1 MARCH 1944

Hudson River Legend, ballet by the 44-year-old American composer Joseph WAGNER, to a scenario after Washington Irving's story of supernatural phenomena in colonial America, with a moderately modernistic score featuring among other things a Geometry Dance, is performed by the Boston Civic Symphony Orchestra, Arthur Fiedler conducting.

3 MARCH 1944

Second Symphony by Samuel BARBER, in three movements gravitating towards the focal tonic F-sharp—(1) *Allegro ma non troppo*, (2) *Andante un poco mosso*, (3) *Presto*—dedicated to the U.S. Army Air Forces and incorporating in the second movement an electrical tone generator simulating the rhythmic radio signal code, with a spirally mounting melody in the finale expressing the rapid ascent in flight, is performed for the first time by the Boston Symphony Orchestra, Serge Koussevitzky conducting.

(The Symphony was revised in 1947, eliminating all navigational allusions, and first performed in this new demilitarized version at the Curtis Institute of Music in Philadelphia on 5 January 1949, and publicly by the Philadelphia Orchestra on 21 January 1949.)

5 MARCH 1944

Second Symphony by Walter PISTON in three movements, a bithematically classical *Moderato*, a candidly lyrical *Adagio*, and a trithematical *Allegro*, with some Americanisms audible despite the composer's rejection of conscious musical nationalism ("Is the Dust Bowl more American than, say, a corner in the Boston Athenaeum? . . . The composer cannot afford the wild-goose chase of trying to be more American than he is"), is performed for the first time, as a commissioned work, by the National Symphony Orchestra in Washington, Hans Kindler conducting.

13 MARCH 1944

VILLA-LOBOS conducts in Rio de Janeiro the first performance of his *Bachianas Brasilieras No. 7* for string orchestra, designed to express his fervid Brazilianism in terms of Bach's polyphony, in four sections, with Bachian titles, *Prelude, Gigue, Tocatta, Fugue*, and Brazilian subtitles, *Ponteio, Quadrilha, Desafio, Conversa*.

15 MARCH 1944

Hymn of the Bolshevik Party by Alexander ALEXANDROV, conductor of the Red Army Band, with a new set of words stressing the national rather than the political point, is adopted by the Soviet Government as the official anthem of the Union of Soviet Socialist Republics to replace the Internationale, reserved only for purely Communistic functions.

18 MARCH 1944

A century has passed since the birth in Tikhvin, at 4:53 P.M., local time, of Nicolas RIMSKY-KORSAKOV, supreme artificer of gorgeously painted Russian musicscapes limned in luminously bright orchestral colors.

19 MARCH 1944

A Child of our Time, oratorio for chorus and orchestra by the 39-year-old English composer Michael TIPPETT, to his own libretto, inspired by the act of a young Jewish boy who shot a German diplomat in Paris in November 1938, in three parts symbolizing (1) General state of the world as it affects nations, societies and individuals; (2) Conflict between personal destiny and overwhelming social forces; (3) Synthesis of a man's shadow with a man's light, with a musical setting of multiple derivations, incorporating five Negro spirituals in the score as symbols of inhumane persecution, is performed for the first time at Morley College, London, under the direction of the expatriate German conductor Walter Goehr.

13 APRIL 1944

Cécile CHAMINADE, French composeress of ingratiatingly harmonious piano pieces adorned with endearingly sentimental titles, possessing a perennial appeal to frustrated spinsters and emotional piano teachers, dies in war-darkened Monte Carlo at the hopeless age of 86.

14 APRIL 1944

Sixth Symphony by Roy HARRIS, in four movements subtitled *Awakening, Conflict, Dedication, Affirmation*, symbolizing the four states of Abraham Lincoln's mind during the Civil War (the score was completed on Lincoln's birthday, 12 February 1944, which also was the composer's 46th birthday), set in the appropriate tones of civic exaltation, with tense bitonal harmonies expressing moods of expectation, strife, devotion and faith, is performed for the first time by the Boston Symphony Orchestra, Serge Koussevitzky conducting.

14 APRIL 1944

Führerworte, oratorio by the 29-year-old German composer Gottfried MÜLLER, dedicated to the "heroes of the German fight of destiny" to texts reverently selected from Hitler's speeches, with the Führer's applosive sentences nearly submerged in a magma of neo-gothic polyphony, with a brassy ending in the key of C major intended to symbolize the purity of Nazi ideals, is performed for the first time in Dresden.

18 APRIL 1944

Leonard BERNSTEIN, 25-year-old American-born conductor and composer, conducts at the Metropolitan Opera House in New York the première of his one-act ballet *Fancy Free*, written in a popular Broadway manner, with a scenario in which three sailors, with only two girls on their hands, play a romantic American roulette for their favors and in the end set off to chase after a third girl.

18 APRIL 1944

Tale of the Battle for the Russian Land, a patriotic cantata in twelve scenes by the Soviet composer Yury SHAPORIN— (1) *A Spring Day,* (2) *Invasion,* (3) *Women's Lament,* (4) *An Old Man's Word,* (5) *Red Army Singing,* (6) *Letter to a Friend,* (7) *Battle Of the Partisans,* (8) *On the Banks of the Volga River,* (9) *On the Steppes of the Don River,* (10) *Eternal Glory,* (11) *The Oath,* (12) *The Return of Spring*—picturing in heroic Russian modalities the awesome chronology of the Nazi invasion of Russia in 1941, the crucial battles of 1942 and the turn of the tide in 1943, is performed for the first time in Moscow.

24 APRIL 1944

P. Kilian KIRCHHOFF, learned German analyst of Byzantine hymnography, translator of the complete Kanons and Stichera of the Byzantine Triodion and Pentekostarion, is beheaded by the Nazi executioner in Brandenburg for his militant opposition to the infamous deeds of the Nazi government.

26 APRIL 1944

Arctic Forest, symphonic poem by the Japanese composer Akira IFUKUBE, is performed for the first time in Chungchung, in Japanese-occupied China.

27 APRIL 1944

Night Flight, tone poem by the 31-year-old American composer Gardner READ, depicting in impressionistic harmonies and coloristic instrumentation the flight of Antoine de St.-Exupéry, is performed for the first time in Rochester, New York, under the direction of Howard Hanson, on the same program with the *First Symphony* by the 35-year-old American composer Elliott CARTER, in three movements designated *Moderately and Wistfully, Andante serioso, Rondo,* and inspired by "the characteristic beauties of Cape Cod" where the work was written.

29 APRIL 1944

Guignol et Pandoré, surrealist ballet in one act by André JOLIVET, in which Guignol, the director of a puppet theater, himself becomes a marionette, culminating in the seduction of Guignol's wife by one of the puppets named Pandore, is produced in Nazi-occupied Paris.

6 MAY 1944

Carl ENGEL, Paris-born American writer of urbanc musical prose, librarian, editor, bibliographer, dies in New York at the age of 60.

8 MAY 1944

Dame Ethel Mary SMYTH, British composeress who was periodically gaoled as a militant suffragette, and whose Wagneromantic operas reflected her distinctly mannish personality, dies in Woking, Surrey, at the purposeless age of 86.

12 MAY 1944

The Passion, oratorio by the American composer Bernard ROGERS, aiming at expressionistic realism (non-tempered scales are employed in the prayer on the Cross), with an ending on an integral quintal tonal pillar containing all the 12 notes of the cycle of fifths from low C to high F, is performed for the first time at the May Festival in Cincinnati, under the direction Eugene Goossens.

12 MAY 1944

Obertura para el Fausto Criollo, symphonic overture by the 28-year-old Argentinian composer Alberto GINASTERA, portraying the strange sensations of a gaucho from the pampas attending a production of Gounod's *Faust* at the Teatro Colón in Buenos Aires, is performed for the first time anywhere in Santiago, Chile.

12 MAY 1944

To commemorate the 60th anniversary of the death of the national Czech composer Bedřich SMETANA, the Nazi-controlled government of Bohemia and Moravia issues a series of postage stamps with his portrait at the denominations of 60 hellers, one krone 40 hellers, one krone 70 hellers and 3 kronen 80 hellers.

30 MAY 1944

To commemorate the centennial of the birth of RIMSKY-KORSAKOV, the Soviet government issues a series of postage stamps at the denominations of 30 kopecks, 60 kopecks, one ruble and 3 rubles.

4 JUNE 1944

Symphony on Marching Tunes by Morton GOULD, composed in celebration of the centennial of the Young Men's Christian Association, in four movements, *March Variations, Bivouac, Quickstep, Memorial,* derived mainly from Civil War campfire ballads and fast dances, is performed for the first time by the New York Philharmonic, during its summer concerts in New York.

5 JUNE 1944

Riccardo ZANDONAI, Italian composer of romantically flamboyant operas in the tradition of modern Verismo, dies in Pesaro at the age of 61.

11 JUNE 1944

On his 80th birthday, Richard STRAUSS conducts the Vienna Philharmonic in a program of his works in the afternoon and attends a broadcast performance of his opera *Ariadne auf Naxos* at the Vienna Staatsoper in the evening.

18 JUNE 1944

Sylvio LAZZARI, French composer of Wagneromorphic operas to melodramatic librettos from contemporary life, glossed over with a fine impressionistic patina, dies in Nazi-infested Paris at the superannuated age of 86.

18 JUNE 1944

Sonatina No. 1 for 16 wind instruments by Richard STRAUSS (completed by him on 22 July 1943) is performed for the first time in war-darkened Dresden.

30 JUNE 1944

As the twilight of the Nazi gods draws near, WAGNER's *Götterdämmerung* is performed at the Vienna Opera House, marking with symbolic irony the conclusion of the last wartime season in that glorious edifice of obsolete Austrian splendor before its utter destruction during the Allied air raid of 12 March 1945.

2 JULY 1944

A few days before the closure of all theaters in Germany as a war measure, the comic opera *Die Hochzeit des Jobs* in four acts by the academically romantic German composer Joseph HAAS, dealing with a German university student who fails in his examination in Roman law in 1800 but wins the hand of his landlady's daughter, is produced in Dresden.

3 JULY 1944

The Song of Norway, a musical pastiche of Grieg's music, macerated by Robert Wright and George Forrest to make it accessible to public taste, with Grieg's *Piano Concerto* serving as the motto, wherein Grieg himself appears as a romantic hero saved from the immoral clutches of a scheming Italian prima donna by the constructive devotion of his future wife, is produced in San Francisco. (The first New York production took place on 21 August 1944.)

4 JULY 1944

La Gageure imprévue, one-act comic opera by the 43-year-old French composer Henri SAUGUET, is produced at the Opéra-Comique in Paris.

22 JULY 1944

Berlenhemd, opera in two acts by the Alsatian composer Leo Justinus KAUFFMANN, is produced in Strasbourg, during the German occupation.

29 JULY 1944

Of New Horizons, overture by the 27-year-old Arizona-born American Negro composer Ulysses S. KAY, written in an optimistic Americanistic manner maintaining a hedonistic momentum of positivistic 4/4 time throughout the work, opening and ending in clear D major, but devoid of an explicit key signature to allow freedom of modulatory action, is performed for the first time by the New York Philharmonic at the Lewisohn Stadium in New York.

19 AUGUST 1944

Sir Henry WOOD, English symphonic and choral conductor, indefatigable champion of British music, who in the words of Arnold Bax "purified and enriched the musical taste of at least two geneiations," dies in Hitchin, Hertshire, at the age of 75.

23 AUGUST 1944

Nicolai ROSLAVETZ, Russian composer who early in the century wrote atonal music and was subsequently hounded by the reactionary Association of Proletarian Musicians for his progressive musical ideas, dies in obscurity in Moscow at the age of 63.

3 SEPTEMBER 1944

Theme and Variations According to the Four Temperaments by Paul HINDEMITH, scored for string orchestra and piano, depicting in spacious neo-Baroque modalities the four "humors" of medieval biology—melancholy (in muted violins, followed by a manic-depressive march), sanguine (a hedonistic waltz), phlegmatic (in turgid motion), and choleric (in vigorously impassioned rhythms)—is performed for the first time in Boston under the direction of Richard Burgin.

25 SEPTEMBER 1944

Leo Justinus KAUFFMANN, 43-year-old German composer and professor of the Strasbourg Conservatory under the Nazi regime since the German occupation of the city in 1940, is killed in Strasbourg at noon during an Allied air raid.

30 SEPTEMBER 1944

Concerto in A minor for oboe and string orchestra by Ralph VAUGHAN WILLIAMS in three movements, *Rondo pastorale*, *Minuet* and *Finale-Scherzo*, is performed for the first time by Leon Goossens, to whom it is dedicated, with the Liverpool Philharmonic Orchestra conducted by Malcolm Sargent.

8 OCTOBER 1944

Capricorn Concerto for flute, oboe, trumpet and strings by Samuel BARBER, so named after the composer's house at Mt. Kisco, New York, is performed for the first time in New York.

13 OCTOBER 1944

Second Symphony by David DIAMOND, in four movements—*Adagio funebre*, *Allegro vivo* (*Scherzo*), *Andante espressivo quasi adagio*, *Allegro vigoroso*—traversing the moods of elegiac lyricism, mocking gayety, somber reflection and optimistic expectation, making use of atonally inclined melodies in trenchantly multitonal harmonies vivified by aggressively tilted rhythms, is performed for the first time by the Boston Symphony Orchestra, Serge Koussevitzky conducting.

It was in no way my intention to have the musical substance represent specific emotional reactions or to conjure up programmatic fantasies. I have a horror of anything as prosaic as that. My emotional life and reactions to certain events and situations have worked hand in hand with purely abstract musical conception and manipulation of material; and it was always the material that remained foremostly important to me in my working stages. (From David Diamond's declaration in the Boston Symphony program book)

16 OCTOBER 1944

The first version of the opera *War and Peace* by Sergei PROKOFIEV after Tolstoy's epic novel, in eleven scenes, to his own libretto written in a collaboration with his second wife Myra Mendelson, set to music in a heroic Russian style, with grandly developed panoramic musical tableaux in strongly tonal but constantly fluctuating harmonies, containing arias in an expansively melodic idiom, vitalized by vibrant rhythmic flow, is produced in Moscow.

(Composition began on 15 August 1941 in Nalchik, Caucasus, where Prokofiev stayed as the Nazis approached Moscow; vocal score completed in Tbilisi on 13 April 1942; orchestration finished in Alma-Ata, Turkmenia, in April 1943. The number of scenes was subsequently extended to 13, with a symmetrical division of subject matter, the first 6 scenes describing the period of peace and emphasizing the lyric, personal and psychological qualities in arias, duets and vocal ensembles; the middle scene representing transition to war, and the last six scenes portraying the war itself in its dramatic, social and national aspects, mainly in massive choral episodes. Part I, comprising eight scenes, was performed for the first time in Leningrad on 12 June 1946, forming a nucleus of the second version, which was completed in 1947; the third and final version, calculated to compress the entire opera into a single evening, was completed in 1952; it preserves the original 13 scenes with many cuts in secondary episodes; the cast of characters numbers 72 dramatis personae.)

17 OCTOBER 1944

Letter from Home by Aaron COPLAND, an unpretentious symphonic recitative for chamber orchestra, reflecting the emotions associated with the receipt of reassuring news, is performed for the first time by Paul Whiteman and the Philco Radio Orchestra in New York. (A version for full orchestra was first performed by the Cleveland Symphony Orchestra, on 27 February 1947, under the direction of George Szell.)

19 OCTOBER 1944

First Symphony, by the 44-year-old American composer Joseph WAGNER, in three cyclic movements, is performed for the first time in Rochester, Howard Hanson conducting.

20 OCTOBER 1944

Theme and Variations for Orchestra, op. 43b (op. 43a is scored for band) by Arnold SCHOENBERG, bearing the explicit key signature of G major, and constituting his second reversion to tonal writing in ten years (the first was his *Suite for String Orchestra*, also in G major, composed in 1934), with a march-like subject non-atonally transfigured in seven variations, and the Finale "using motival and harmonic features of the themes, this producing new themes of contrasting character and mood," is performed for the first time by the Boston Symphony Orchestra, Serge Koussevitzky conducting.

When I had finished my first *Kammersymphonie*, op. 9, I told my friends: "Now I have established my style. I know now how I have to compose." But my next work showed a great deviation from this style; it was a first step toward my present style. My destiny had forced me in this direction—I was not destined to continue in the manner of *Verklärte Nacht or Gurre-lieder* or even *Pelléas and Mélisande*. The Supreme Commander had ordered me on a harder road. But a longing to return to the older style was always vigorous in me; and from time to time I had to yield to that urge. This is how and why I sometimes write tonal music. To me stylistic differences of this nature are not of special importance. I do not know which of my compositions are better; I like them all, because I liked them when I wrote them. (From Schoenberg's article *One Always Returns* in the New York *Times*, 19 December 1948)

21 OCTOBER 1944

Fugue on a Victory Tune by Walter PISTON, one of a long series of wartime pieces commissioned by the League of Composers of New York, is performed for the first time by the New York Philharmonic, Artur Rodzinski conducting.

22 OCTOBER 1944

Chant de Libération for baritone, chorus and orchestra by Arthur HONEGGER, composed in German-occupied Paris in 1942, is performed for the first time in liberated Paris.

24 OCTOBER 1944

A Stopwatch and an Ordnance Map, a realistic piece of wartime music by Samuel BARBER, scored for men's chorus and kettledrums, is performed in Columbus, Ohio.

26 OCTOBER 1944

Miracle in the Gorbals, ballet by Sir Arthur BLISS, dealing with the miraculous resuscitation of a completely dead suicide wrought by a mysterious stranger in the Gorbals slums of Glasgow, is produced in London.

30 OCTOBER 1944

Martha Graham and her dance group give in Washington the first performance of *Appalachian Spring*, "ballet for Martha" by Aaron COPLAND, named after the title of a poem by Hart Crane (though unrelated to its content), a vivid musicorama in seven scenes depicting in tonally pellucid harmonies equipped with unequivocal key signatures the time of spring in the Appalachian foothills in early 19th-century Pennsylvania, around a farmhouse built for a newly married couple, with the groom, the bride and a counselling old neighbor in the cast of characters, and concluding in a hymnal jubilation of the pious sect of Shakers, shaking before the Lord and chanting their ancient song, "When true simplicity is gained/To bow and to bend we shan't be ashamed/ To turn, turn will be our delight/ Till by turning, twining we come round right," set in the immaculate white key of C major. (The ballet version was scored for 13 instruments; Copland later arranged it for full orchestra as a symphonic suite, which was first performed by the New York Philharmonic on 4 October 1945, and on the next day by the Boston Symphony Orchestra and the Cleveland Orchestra.)

31 OCTOBER 1944

Sebastian, ballet by the 33-year-old Italian-born composer Gian Carlo MENOTTI, is produced for the first time in New York.

1 NOVEMBER 1944

Manuel ROSENTHAL, 40-year-old French composer, conducts in Paris the first performance of his oratorio *Saint Francis d'Assisi*, with the inclusion in the orchestra of the electronic musical instrument Ondes Martenot.

11 NOVEMBER 1944

Ozark Set for orchestra by the 35-year-old American composer Elie SIEGMEISTER, in four movements, *Morning in the Hills, Camp Meeting, Lazy Afternoon* and *Saturday Night*, portraying the folkways of the Ozark mountain people of Missouri and Arkansas and employing authentic American melorhythms set in rational harmonies spiced with endurable dissonances, is performed for the first time by the Minneapolis Symphony Orchestra, Dimitri Mitropoulos conducting.

13 NOVEMBER 1944

Paul GRAENER, one of the few German composers who cultivated an impressionistic manner of harmony and orchestration and whose operas reveal a modern expressionistic character with an occasional earnest utilization of dodecaphonic methods, dies in the war-depressed Mozartean town of Salzburg at the age of 72.

17 NOVEMBER 1944

Virgil THOMSON conducts the Philadelphia Orchestra in the first performance of a symphonic suite from his *Portraits*, composed by him with the subject sitting for his likeness as he would for a painter, featuring among them *Bugles and Birds* for Picasso, *Tango Lullaby* for a young girl, and *Percussion Piece* for a California lady.

22 NOVEMBER 1944

The first annual Day of Music, established by a decree of General Trujillo, self-styled permanent President and benefactor of the Dominican Republic before his final assassination, is celebrated throughout the land, on the feast day of St. Cecilia, patron saint of music.

23 NOVEMBER 1944

Ode to Napoleon Buonaparte, op. 41 by Arnold SCHOENBERG, for string orchestra, piano and speaker, to Byron's poem ruefully reflecting on the fall of Napoleon, written according to a novel version of Schoenberg's method of composition for 12 tones, enhanced by an allegorical code of intervallic semantics, wherein the motto of an ascending fourth and a descending minor second, thrice repeated, symbolizes presumptuous dictators of any historic period, ending in an unobstructed chord of E-flat major, as an emblem of eventual liberation, is performed for the first time by the New York Philharmonic, Artur Rodzinski conducting.

24 NOVEMBER 1944

Rounds for string orchestra by the 29-year-old American composer David DIAMOND, a "spherical" work in three movements played without pause, with the middle section *Adagio* "acting as a resting point between the two fast movements," is performed for the first time by the Minneapolis Symphony Orchestra, Dimitri Mitropoulos conducting.

24 NOVEMBER 1944

Ernst VON DOHNÁNYI flees Budapest as the Russian Army penetrates its environs.

30 NOVEMBER 1944

Antoine MARIOTTE, French composer of romantic operas, dies in Izieux, Loire at the age of 68.

1 DECEMBER 1944

The Boston Symphony Orchestra, under the direction of Serge Koussevitzky, gives the world première of *Concerto for Orchestra* by Béla BARTÓK, his last symphonic work, composed between 15 August and 8 October 1943 in New York during recuperation from his next-to-last illness, in five movements bearing Italian titles:

(1) *Introduzione,* opening with sylvan murmuration of strings and flutes and developing like a scherzo in rondo form; (2) *Giuoco delle Coppie,* a game of couples, so named because the wind instruments are copulated at specific intervals, the bassoons in sixths, the oboes in thirds, the clarinets in sevenths, the flutes in fifths, the muted trumpets in major seconds, while the time signature, 2/4, represents still another couple; (3) *Elegia,* a sepulchral threnody, almost oriental in its profusion of melorhythmic arabesques; (4) *Intermezzo interrotto,* derived from two asymmetrical subjects, the interruption being a sly intrusion of a refrain from the Nazi theme in the *Seventh Symphony* by Shostakovich which Bartók heard on the radio in obsessive quantity; (5) *Finale,* based on a persistently repetitive fugal subject, developed in single, double and triple augmentation, single, double and triple diminution and multiple stretti in quadruple counterpoint, culminating in a magisterial coda in an oriflamme of brass sonorities.

1 DECEMBER 1944

Violin Concerto by the American composer Louis GRUENBERG, in three movements—(1) *Rhapsody,* (2) *With Simplicity and Warmth,* (3) *Lively and With Good Humor*—derived in its thematic contents from Negro spirituals and rustic American songs, is performed for the first time by Jascha Heifetz, who commissioned the work, with the Philadelphia Orchestra.

2 DECEMBER 1944

Josef LHÉVINNE, Russian pianist of formidable technical powers and lyrically romantic Musikanschauung, dies in New York, eleven days before his 70th birthday.

5 DECEMBER 1944

Cinq danses rituelles, orchestral suite by André JOLIVET, which received the Prix de l'État in 1942, is performed for the first time in a Paris now cleansed of Nazi infestation.

7 DECEMBER 1944

The Seven Lively Arts, revue produced by Billy Rose, containing parts of a score he commissioned to Igor STRAVINSKY for a fee of $5,000 (the material of which was later utilized by Stravinsky in his *Scènes de Ballet* conducted by him with the New York Philharmonic on 3 February 1945), opens in New York.

(The preview took place in Philadelphia a few days earlier; after the opening night there, Billy Rose telegraphed to Stravinsky: YOUR MUSIC GREAT SUCCESS STOP COULD BE SENSATIONAL SUCCESS IF YOU WOULD AUTHORIZE ROBERT RUSSELL BENNETT RETOUCH ORCHESTRATION STOP BENNETT ORCHESTRATES EVEN THE WORKS OF COLE PORTER. Stravinsky wired back: SATISFIED WITH GREAT SUCCESS.)

7 DECEMBER 1944

Poem for Orchestra by the American Negro composer William Grant STILL, expressing the despair of humanity "on the rim of a desolate world," is performed for the first time by the Cleveland Orchestra.

10 DECEMBER 1944

Nocturne by George ANTHEIL, a movement from his symphonic suite *Decatur at Algiers*, reflecting an American boy's vision of an American hero, illustrated by a profusion of orientalistic inflections, is performed for the first time by the St. Louis Symphony Orchestra, under the direction of Vladimir Golschmann.

15 DECEMBER 1944

Saturnalia, opera by the 47-year-old Danish composer Jorgen BENTZON, to a libretto inspired by the erotic epic, *The Golden Ass* of Apuleius, is produced in Copenhagen.

16 DECEMBER 1944

Sinfonia Tripartita by the Italian composer Vittorio RIETI, now resident in New York, his fourth symphony, dedicated to Igor Stravinsky, and set in an austere neo-Baroque idiom, is performed for the first time by the St. Louis Symphony Orchestra, Vladimir Golschmann conducting.

20 DECEMBER 1944

Il Giuoco del Barone, opera by the Italian composer Valentino BUCCHI, is performed for the first time in Florence.

25 DECEMBER 1944

Burevesnik (Stormy Petrel), symphonic poem after Maxim Gorky by the Serbian composer Vojislav VUČKOVIĆ, is performed for the first time in liberated Belgrade exactly two years after the composer's death at the hands of the Nazis.

28 DECEMBER 1944

On the Town, musical comedy by Leonard BERNSTEIN, to a libretto suggested by the scenario of his ballet *Fancy Free,* in which three sailors, engaged in the pursuit of happiness in New York City, find gratification by pairing off with a female taxi driver, an anthropology student and a dancer, set to music with a rollicking hedonistic élan, is produced in New York.

30 DECEMBER 1944

Romain ROLLAND, French novelist and inspired writer on music, whose serial novel *Jean-Christophe* was the first literary work ever written in which the central character is a professional composer, dies at his home in Vézelay, France, at the age of 78.

31 DECEMBER 1944

Alesia, opera in four acts by the 51-year-old Byelorussian composer Evgeny TIKOTSKY, dealing with a heroic Byelorussian girl who inspired the fight against the invading Nazis in 1941, is produced in Minsk, capital of Byelorussia, shortly after the expulsion of Nazi troops from Byelorussia by the Red Army.

1945

1 JANUARY 1945

Vít NEJEDLÝ, 32-year-old Czech composer, son of the musicologist Zdenek Nejedlý (who was appointed Minister of Education of Czechoslovakia in 1948), dies of typhoid fever near Dukla, in the ranks of the Liberation army advancing with the Soviet Red Army into Slovakia.

13 JANUARY 1945

Sergei PROKOFIEV conducts in Moscow a concert of his orchestral music, including the first performance of his *Fifth Symphony,* op. 100, "a symphony about the spirit of man," composed during the Summer of 1944, set in the victoriously optimistic key of B-flat major, in four movements exuding fervid Russian lyricism and rhythmic energy:

(1) *Andante,* in B-flat major, in 3/4, opening with a soaring Russian melody in thematically controlled variations with fugal excrescences scaling the heights of sonorous exuberance, and then receding to the depths of a dramatic envoi, anchored on the pedal point in the bass; (2) *Allegro marcato,* in D minor, in 4/4 time, a scherzo maintaining its relentless momentum with a drumfire beat evoking the recent memories of war and tragedy, changing to a more affective 3/4 time, and then returning to the initial

square beats, culminating in a tremendous explosion of vital forces; (3) *Adagio*, a somber elegy in 3/4 time, in F major, with dotted rhythms emphasizing the inner tension within a steady metrical division; (4) *Allegro giocoso*, in B-flat major in 2/2 time, depicting a scene of pastoral contentment, in anticipation of a victory over the brutality of Fascism, now within a few months of achievement, in an apotheosis, marked by an ovation of trumpets, an irresistible advance of trombones and the brandished oriflamme of horns reinforced by a cotillion of drums, and nailed down by a triumphant beat of the bass drum.

24 JANUARY 1945

Ernst KRENEK becomes a citizen of the United States.

26 JANUARY 1945

Violin Concerto by the Swiss neo-classical composer Willy BURKHARD is performed for the first time in Zürich.

26 JANUARY 1945

First Symphony by the 28-year-old Swedish modernist Karl-Birger BLOMDAHL is performed for the first time in Stockholm.

26 JANUARY 1945

Concerto for doublebass and orchestra by the expatriate Russian composer Thomas DE HARTMANN is performed for the first time in Paris.

27 JANUARY 1945

Up in Central Park, musical play in two acts by Sigmund ROMBERG, dealing with the real-life exploit of a New York *Times* reporter who in 1870 exposed the sinister machinations of Tammany Hall and married the widow of a slain crook, with the song *Close as Pages in a Book* serving as a romantic motto, is produced in New York.

1 FEBRUARY 1945

Lycksalighetens (*Isle of Felicity*), opera by the 52-year-old Swedish composer Hilding ROSENBERG, is performed for the first time in Stockholm.

1 FEBRUARY 1945

Concerto for Orchestra by Morton GOULD, in three American-flavored movements, with a boogie-woogie finale, is performed for the first time by the Cleveland Orchestra.

3 FEBRUARY 1945

Igor STRAVINSKY conducts the New York Philharmonic in the first performance of his *Scènes de Ballet* for orchestra, consisting of eleven terpsichorean poses proffered in the elegant manner of the gallant era of French choreography, "patterned after the forms of the classical dance, free of any given literary or dramatic argument."

(The work was originally written for Billy Rose's production *The Seven Lively Arts*, which opened in New York on 7 December 1944, but was not presented in its entirety; the score was subsequently revised and adjusted for concert performance.)

4 FEBRUARY 1945

Lukas FOSS, 22-year-old Berlin-born (his original surname was Fuchs) American pianist and composer, conducts the Pittsburgh Symphony Orchestra in the first performance of his romantically inspired and pleasurably eclectic *Symphony in G*, written in a variety of styles ranging from Handelian harmony to prudential jazzification.

5 FEBRUARY 1945

Takhir and Zukhra, opera in four acts by the Soviet composer Alexander LENSKY, dealing with a dramatic romance of a Tadzhik couple in medieval Central Asia, is performed for the first time at the Tadzhik Opera House in Stalinabad.

9 FEBRUARY 1945

Eighth Symphony by the prime symphonist of Sweden Kurt ATTERBERG is performed for the first time in Helsinki.

11 FEBRUARY 1945

Leonora Tellez, opera by the Portuguese statesman and amateur musician João Marcelino ARROYO, is produced posthumously in Lisbon.

15 FEBRUARY 1945

Second Symphony by the American composer Paul CRESTON, "conceived as an apotheosis of the two foundations of all music: song and dance," in two movements— (1) *Introduction and Song*, (2) *Interlude and Dance*—is performed for the first time by the New York Philharmonic, under the direction of Artur Rodzinski.

17 FEBRUARY 1945

Marc LAVRY, Latvian-born Palestinian composer, conducts the world première in Tel Aviv of his Hebrew opera *Dan the Guard*, to Max Brod's libretto dealing with the kibbutz movement of Palestinian settlers working towards the goal of building a national Jewish state.

21 FEBRUARY 1945

Heitor VILLA-LOBOS conducts the Boston Symphony Orchestra in the first performance anywhere of his *Chôros No. 12*, scored for a gargantuan orchestra with a large assortment of Brazilian drums and shakers to suggest the popular impression of a *chôros*, a "sui generis form of musical composition in which are synthesized the different modalities of Brazilian, Indian and modern popular music."

22 FEBRUARY 1945

Virgil THOMSON conducts the New York Philharmonic in the first performance of his *Symphony on a Hymn Tune*, derived from two pentatonic hymns of the Southern Baptists, in four movements:

(1) *Introduction*, "a conversational passage for solo instruments and pairs of instruments followed by a statement of the hymn tune in half-in and half-out-of-focus harmonization," leading to *Allegro*, "a succession (and superposition) of dance-like passages derived from the main theme," ending with a

heteroousian cadenza for piccolo, violin, cello and trombone; (2) *Andante*, a series of variations with a simulated locomotive whistle alliterated by a total glissando of all brass instruments; (3) *Allegretto*, "a passacaglia of marked rhythmic character on the hymn-tune bass;" (4) *Finale*, "a canzona on a part of the main theme."

26 FEBRUARY 1945

Concerto for the Thereminovox, electronic musical instrument invented by the Russian engineer Leon Theremin, and orchestra by the Cyprus-born American composer Anis FULEIHAN, is performed for the first time by the New York City Symphony Orchestra, Leopold Stokowski conducting, with Clara Rockmore at the Thereminovox, producing the alteration of pitch by wafting her hand to and fro thus altering the heterodynamic field, resulting in a differential frequency within the audible range.

5 MARCH 1945

Rudolf KAREL, 64-year-old Czech composer of folkloristically inspired music, dies in a Nazi concentration camp at Teresin near Prague.

12 MARCH 1945

During an air raid on Vienna by American bombers, five bombs fall on the Vienna Opera House, three of them destroying the iron curtain separating the stage from the orchestra, one exploding above the right proscenium box, and one bursting in the adjacent street Operngasse, opening a gap of 120 square yards in the left side of the building and reducing it to a heap of twisted debris.

17 MARCH 1945

Cello Concerto in C minor by Nicolai MIASKOVSKY, in two movements, *Lento ma non troppo* and *Allegro vivace*, written in an elegiac lyric manner, with moments of rhythmic tension creating a dramatic contrast, is performed for the first time in Moscow.

22 MARCH 1945

Concerto for string orchestra, piano and percussion by Alfredo CASELLA is performed for the first time in Basel, Switzerland.

22 MARCH 1945

First Symphony, subtitled *Sinfonia pastorale*, by the Swedish composer Hilding HALLNÄS, is performed for the first time in Göteborg.

25 MARCH 1945

Figure Humaine, cantata for double chorus a cappella by Francis POULENC, written by him in Paris in 1943 under Nazi occupation, to the text by Paul Eluard, expressing the silent wrath of a subjugated people yearning for liberty, is performed for the first time by the British Broadcasting Company in London, whose wartime broadcasts to France were, in Poulenc's words, "the unfailing source of hope during the German occupation."

26 MARCH 1945

Symphony of the Brave Young Men, a patriotic piece by the dean of Greek composers Manuel KALOMIRIS, is performed for the first time in Athens.

6 APRIL 1945

Gunther SCHULLER, 19-year-old first horn player of the Cincinnati Symphony Orchestra, plays the solo part in the world première of his *Concerto for Horn and Orchestra*, in two movements, *Rhapsody* and *Scherzo*.

8 APRIL 1945

At the approach of the final hour of Nazidämmerung, the Austrian conductor Leopold REICHWEIN, one of the few musicians who was lured by the opportunities for individual and racial aggrandizement offered by the Nazi doctrine, kills himself in Vienna.

10 APRIL 1945

Undertow, a suite of choreographic psychological episodes for orchestra by the 34-year-old American composer William SCHUMAN, traversing the "emotional development of a transgressor" from a Freudian infancy through the anxiety-riddled period of puberty, reflected in a sonorously discordant, angularly rhythmed music, is performed for the first time in New York.

12 APRIL 1945

Peter RAABE, German esthetician and music theorist, who in 1935 succeeded Richard Strauss as President of the inglorious Reichsmusikkammer, dies in Weimar at the age of 72, on the day of the entry of American troops into the town.

Peter Raabe did not commit suicide, as was rumored; he was ill for weeks, perhaps for years, distressed by his long struggle against the regime which was imposed upon him and whose views were alien to him. . . . I myself was present at his sickbed a few days before his death, and I spoke at his funeral. (From a letter to the author, dated 24 July 1947, from Prof. Dr. Wahl, Director of the Goethe Museum in Weimar)

15 APRIL 1945

The Polish Music Publishing Society is founded in Cracow, shortly after the liberation of the city from the Nazis.

16 APRIL 1945

The Canticle of the Sun for chorus and orchestra by the 40-year-old American composer Leo SOWERBY, to the text of the hymn by St. Francis, is performed for the first time in New York.

19 APRIL 1945

Carousel, a musical play by Richard RODGERS, with book and lyrics by Oscar HAMMERSTEIN II, to an Americanized story from Ferenc Molnár's play *Liliom*, with the original Hungarian locale transferred to the New England of 1873, wherein the circus barker Liliom becomes Billy Bigelow, is involved in a robbery, kills himself, but is given a pass to Heaven to fetch a star for his small daughter on earth, containing the hit tunes *June is Bustin' Out All Over* and *You'll Never Walk Alone,* is produced in New York.

21 APRIL 1945

Trois petites de la Présence Divine by Olivier MESSIAEN, for female chorus in unison and instruments, to his own texts on subjects from theology, botany, geology and astronomy, scored for "a Europeanized Hindu or Balinese ensemble," including celesta, vibraphone, maracas, Chinese cymbals, gong, piano, Ondes Martenot and strings, and couched in Messiaen's individual polymodal and polyrhythmic language, is performed for the first time in Paris.

1 MAY 1945

Deda da Shvili (*Mother and Son*), opera in two acts by the 31-year-old Georgian composer Alexei MACHAVARIANI, is performed for the first time in Tbilisi.

2 MAY 1945

Monte Carlo, ballet by the 30-year-old Spanish composer Carlos SURINACH, depicting in humorous tones the aleatory alternations of fortunes and misfortunes at the gambling tables of the Casino in Monte Carlo, is produced in Barcelona.

7 MAY 1945

In terra Pax, oratorio by Frank MARTIN, is performed for the first time in Geneva.

8 MAY 1945

Thanksgiving for Victory by Ralph VAUGHAN WILLIAMS, scored for speaker, soprano, chorus and orchestra, to texts from Shakespeare's *Henry V,* the Bible and patriotic poems of Kipling, is performed for the first time by the British Broadcasting Corporation on the day of victory over Nazi Germany.

8 MAY 1945

Veten (*Fatherland*), opera in four acts by the Azerbaijan composers Dzhevdet GADZHIEV and Kara KARAEV, to a patriotic libretto in the Tatar language dealing with the desperate struggle against the Nazi invasion of Azerbaijan in 1943, is produced in Baku.

9 MAY 1945

The Scarecrow, one-act opera by the American composer Normand LOCKWOOD, in which Beelzebub transforms a scarecrow in a 17th-century New England village into a man and commands him to corrupt a Puritan maiden, but is foiled when true love blossoms forth between them, is performed for the first time in New York.

12 MAY 1945

The First Annual Festival of Contemporary American Music opens at Columbia University in New York in a program including *Rounds for Strings* by David DIAMOND, *Fourth Symphony* by Howard HANSON, *Saxophone Concerto* by Henry BRANT and *Second Symphony* by Walter PISTON.

7 JUNE 1945

Peter Grimes, opera in three acts by England's prime 20th-century composer Benjamin BRITTEN, to a libretto from Crabbe's poem *The Borough* (1810), wherein a young Suffolk fisherman, suspected of murder after the successive but accidental drownings of his two apprentices, sails away to a certain death in his small boat to escape the vengeance of the villagers, written in a tense expressionistic idiom, with tonal harmonies drowned in tempestuous waves of chromatic dissonances, relieved only by realistic "sea interludes" of stormy winds and crying gulls, with uninhibited use in the libretto of such hitherto unoperatic vocables as "bitch" and "hell," is performed for the first time at the opening of the first postwar season at the Sadler's Wells Theatre in London. (Five orchestral tableaux from *Peter Grimes*—*Passacaglia, Dawn, Sunday Morning, Moonlight, The Storm*—forming a symphonic suite, were performed for the first time under Britten's direction in Cheltenham on 13 June 1945.)

13 JUNE 1945

Suite Française for band by Darius MILHAUD, a pentaptych of musical picture postcards depicting five typical French provinces—Normandy, Brittany, Ilede-France, Alsace-Lorraine and Provence—is performed for the first time in New York.

21 JUNE 1945

Tuleelegid (*Flames of Vengeance*), Estonian opera in five scenes by Eugen KAPP, dealing with the historic rebellion of Estonian patriots against Teutonic Crusaders on the night of 23 April 1343, after a young village bride is ravished by a brutal Teuton, whereupon the people storm his castle and slay him and his henchmen, and once the flames of vengeance are lit, go forth to the final battle for liberation from the feudal yoke, set to music in flamboyantly rousing modalities with an influx of lyric Estonian strains to depict the sorrows of oppression and the sempiternity of the patriotic fervor, is produced in Tallin.

24 JUNE 1945

Tulyak, opera in five scenes, in the Tatar language, by the 34-year-old Soviet composer Nazib ZHIGANOV, dealing with the bloody events of the Mongol invasion of Central Asia in the 12th century, is produced in Kazan.

3 JULY 1945

As a gesture of good will toward America, the State Symphony Orchestra of Moscow presents a concert of modern American symphonic music in a program including *Ode to Friendship* by Roy HARRIS, *March in Memoriam* by Wallingford RIEGGER, *First Essay for Orchestra* by Samuel BARBER, *Ozark Set* by Elie SIEGMEISTER and *Rhapsody in Blue* by George GERSHWIN.

9 JULY 1945

L'appel de la montagne, ballet in three tableaux by Arthur HONEGGER, dealing with a Scotsman who loves a Swiss lass but loses her to a Swiss shepherd and in his despair climbs an inaccessible Swiss mountain, falling into a moderately precipitous abyss where droll trolls mock him until he is rescued by the Virgin of the Fairies, is produced in Paris.

14 JULY 1945

The Allied Occupation Authorities in Germany issue an order forbidding playing military music or singing Nazi songs.

27 JULY 1945

Alan BUSH, 44-year-old English composer of socially significant music and a left-wing member of Parliament, conducts the London Symphony Orchestra in the world première of his orchestral *Fantasia on Soviet Themes.*

31 JULY 1945

Ralph VAUGHAN WILLIAMS conducts in London the first performance of his symphonic suite *The Story of a Flemish Farm*, drawn from incidental music to a film about a group of patriotic Belgian airplane pilots escaping to England after the German occupation of Belgium.

2 AUGUST 1945

Pietro MASCAGNI, Italian opera composer whose *Cavalleria Rusticana*, written in his early youth, earned him an enduring place in music history as a Pioneer of Verismo and operatic realism, but whose honor was tarnished by his willful association with Mussolini's Fascists, dies in Rome at the age of 81.

2 AUGUST 1945

Emil Nikolaus VON REZNIČEK, 85-year-old Austrian-born composer of romantic operas, succumbs in devastated Berlin to typhoid fever aggravated by starvation.

No coffins were available in Berlin when Rezniček died, and his body remained unburied for four days in the upper story of a tenement house in Charlottenburg; finally a coffin was procured; Rezniček was buried on the day the atom bomb fell on Japan. (From a memoir of Rezniček's daughter, *Gegen den Strom, Leben und Werk von E. N. Reznicek*, Vienna, 1960)

17 AUGUST 1945

Gino MARINUZZI, 63-year-old Italian conductor and composer of Wagneromorphic operas and of a jubilee piece on the occasion of Hitler's meeting with Mussolini, dies of hepatitis.

23 AUGUST 1945

Leo BORCHARD, conductor of the Berlin Philharmonic Orchestra, is accidentally shot and killed by an American sentry in Berlin when the driver of the car in which he is riding ignores the order to stop.

1 SEPTEMBER 1945

Grünewald, patriotic symphonic poem by the Polish composer Jan MAKLAKIEWICZ glorifying the battle of 1410 in which the presumptuous Teutonic Knights were routed by the Polish Army on the fields of Grünewald, is performed for the first time in Cracow, to mark the liberation of Poland from Nazi occupation.

3 SEPTEMBER 1945

The Union of Polish Composers is organized in Warsaw.

15 SEPTEMBER 1945

Anton VON WEBERN, 61-year-old Austrian composer of music so subtle and succinct that not only notes, but intervals, dynamic marks and durations assume thematic significance, philosopher-musician and pioneer of integral serialism as an expansion of the dodecaphonic concept formulated by his master Arnold Schoenberg, is accidentally shot and killed by an American soldier of the army of occupation in Mittersill, near Salzburg, in the house of his son-in-law suspected of black market speculation. (Webern's son-in-law was subsequently sentenced to one year's imprisonment; Raymond Bell, the unwitting killer of Anton von Webern, though cleared of blame, died on 3 September 1955 of acute alcoholism induced by remorse. He had been a cook in the U.S. Army.)

16 SEPTEMBER 1945

John MCCORMACK, golden-voiced Irish tenor whose emotional ballad-singing made the hearts of millions in Europe and America beat faster, dies near Dublin at the age of 61.

17 SEPTEMBER 1945

The heart of CHOPIN, hidden during the war in the Polish provincial town of Milanowek, is returned to its sanctified place in the wall of the Holy Cross Cathedral in Warsaw, with a plaque bearing, the inscription in French: "Où se trouve mon trésor, là se trouve mon cœur."

26 SEPTEMBER 1945

Béla BARTÓK, great composer of modern Hungary, explorer in his symphonic and chamber music of the outermost frontiers of tones, rhythms and dynamic nuances, indefatigable collector and codifier of ethnically diversified folksongs and dances of his native Transylvania, dies of leukemia in New York, where he settled after fleeing Fascist-infested Europe in 1940, at the age of 64.

The man whose music had elemental sweep, barbaric rhythm and penetrating force, never weighed more than 116 pounds and sometimes as little as 90. His constant battle with ill health started as a youth when he had lung trouble. His body remained delicate, and other difficulties—asthma, skin trouble, stomach disorders and fever—made their appearance. The fever increased and in the spring of 1944 it was diagnosed as leukemia. In September 1945 there was an abrupt rise in his white cell count, and the doctors knew he was near the end. He died on 26 September 1945, shortly before noon. ASCAP paid the funeral expenses, for, following the tradition set by so many other great composers, Bartók left no estate save the boundless wealth of his music. (Ernö Balogh in *Musical Digest*, Chicago, September 1947)

(Bartók's body was cremated and the ashes kept in parcel No. 470 of the Ferncliff Cemetery near Hartsdale, N.Y., sans headstone, sans marker, sans everything. Not until the third anniversary of Bartók's death was this mortuary anonymity broken and a memorial tablet placed on his grave.)

4 OCTOBER 1945

First Symphony by the 39-year-old Norwegian composer Klaus EGGE (completed on 17 May 1942), dedicated to Norwegian sailors who served in World War II, set in his personalized key of E minor (the score is signed in musical letters E-G-G-E) and immersed in romantically dulcet modalities, is performed for the first time in Oslo.

12 OCTOBER 1945

Third Symphony by Bohuslav MARTINŮ, in three movements—(1) *Allegro poco moderato*, (2) *Largo*, (3) *Allegro-Andante*—with literal recapitulations in each movement, ending pianissimo, is performed for the first time by the Boston Symphony Orchestra, Serge Koussevitzky conducting.

14 OCTOBER 1945

Prière pour les condamnés à mort, a tragic evocation of the victims of the Nazi executions, for narrator and orchestra, by the Belgian composer Raymond CHEVREUILLE, is performed for the first time in Brussels.

19 OCTOBER 1945

Put u pobedu (*The Road to Victory*), symphonic poem by the 45-year-old Serbian composer Mihailo VUKDRAG-OVIĆ, depicting in heroic triadic harmonies the partisan struggle in occupied Yugoslavia against the Nazis during World War II, culminating in the singing of the triumphant socialist song, the Internationale, is performed for the first time in Belgrade, under the direction of the composer.

23 OCTOBER 1945

Vincent PERSICHETTI plays the solo part, with the Eastman Orchestra in Rochester, under the direction of Howard Hanson, of his *First Piano Concerto*, in one movement, written in a prudential neo-classical idiom, spiced with judiciously cultivated dissonant counterpoint.

26 OCTOBER 1945

Suite Symphonique by Ernest BLOCH in three movements—(1) *Overture*, (2) *Passacaglia*, (3) *Finale*—culminating in "a grotesque sardonic fugue," is performed for the first time by the Philadelphia Orchestra, conducted by Pierre Monteux.

27 OCTOBER 1945

Harvest for harp, vibraphone and strings by Morton GOULD, employing chordal counterpoint leading to agreeable polytonality, with American-flavored melodic materials of a cheerful nature suitable for singing at harvest time, is performed for the first time by the St. Louis Symphony Orchestra, Vladimir Golschmann conducting.

28 OCTOBER 1945

Neustupujte (*Do Not Yield!*) cantata of resistance the Czech composer Miloslav KABELÁČ, written on the eve of Hitler's invasion of Czechoslovakia in the spring of 1939, is performed for the first time in liberated Prague.

30 OCTOBER 1945

Victory, overture by Reinhold GLIÈRE, written to commemorate the final rout of Fascism in all its forms, is performed for the first time in Moscow.

2 NOVEMBER 1945

Piano Concerto by the 34-year-old Italian-born American composer Gian Carlo MENOTTI, in F major, in three movements: *Allegro, Lento, Allegro moderato*, exuding the baroque aura of the Italian classical period, is performed for the first time by the Boston Symphony Orchestra, Rudolf Firkušny soloist, Richard Burgin conducting.

3 NOVEMBER 1945

Ninth Symphony by Dmitri SHOSTAKOVICH (completed on 30 August 1945), designated as being in E-flat major, and indeed adhering more closely to the principal key than an average classical symphony, in five movements, *Allegro, Moderato* (a waltz), *Presto, Largo* (a very brief meditation) and *Allegretto* (a symmetric rondo), a varicolored musicorama ranging in mood from philosophical lyricism to quasi-choreographic rapture, conceived as a joyous postlude to a devastating but ultimately victorious war, is performed for the first time in Leningrad.

4 NOVEMBER 1945

Third Symphony by Gian Francesco MALIPIERO, completed on 14 February 1945, subtitled *Delle Campane* (*Of the Bells*), in four movements, *Allegro moderato, Andante molto moderato, Vivace,* and *Lento*, is performed for the first time in Florence.

War refuses to live in peace, even with itself. The composition of my *Third Symphony* relates to that ominous day, 8 September 1943, when Mussolini was rescued by the Nazis and set up a new Fascist government in Northern Italy. The bells of San Marco in Venice rang at sunset but they could not deceive those who knew their true voice. They tolled not for peace but for new torments, new horrors. (Malipiero in a statement quoted in *L'Opera di Gian Francesco Malipiero*, Treviso, 1952)

10 NOVEMBER 1945

Ode to the End of the War by Sergei PROKOFIEV, scored for a victoriously grandiose orchestra comprising woodwinds, brass, percussion, four pianos, eight harps and 16 doublebasses, but no violins, violas or cellos, is performed for the first time in Moscow.

10 NOVEMBER 1945

Ivan VYSHNEGRADSKY, Russian pioneer of quartertone music, conducts in Paris the first performance of his symphonic poem *Cosmos* for four pianos, two of which are tuned a quarter-tone higher than the other two, his mimodrama *Linnite* and *5 Variations* on the single note C.

10 NOVEMBER 1945

First Symphony by the English composer Sir Michael TIPPETT, written in an extremely self-contained contrapuntal idiom, with a double fugue in the finale concluding on a chord of the eleventh which dissolves into a unison on E, is performed for the first time in Liverpool.

11 NOVEMBER 1945

Jerome KERN, American composer of melodious operettas and musical revues, among them the classic of the American musical theater, *Show Boat*, dies in New York at the age of 60.

16 NOVEMBER 1945

Suite for Violin and Orchestra by Darius MILHAUD, in three sections, *Gigues, Sailor Song* and *Hornpipes*, with thematic materials taken from popular 18th-century English tunes, is performed for the first time by Zino Francescatti as violin soloist with the Philadelphia Orchestra under the direction of Eugene Ormandy.

18 NOVEMBER 1945

Genesis for narrator and orchestra, a suite of seven scenes by seven composers—(1) Arnold SCHOENBERG: *Prelude;* (2) Nathaniel SHILKRET: *Creation;* (3) Alexandre TANSMAN: *Adam and Eve;* (4) Darius MILHAUD: *Cain and Abel;* (5) Mario CASTELNUOVO-TEDESCO: *Noah's Ark;* (6) Ernst TOCH: *The Covenant;* (7) Igor STRAVINSKY: *The Tower of Babel*—is performed for the first time by the Janssen Symphony in Los Angeles, under the direction of its founder Werner Janssen.

The Prelude to *Genesis* was by Arnold Schoenberg, the text for which was "The Earth was without form, and void." This reviewer has never heard music that had less form or was more nearly void than Mr. Schoenberg's contribution. It was simply a succession of ugly sounds bearing no relation whatsoever to the thing generally known as music ... Stravinsky's *Babel* vindicated this writer's belief that except when Stravinsky uses borrowed thematic material he has not composed anything of real value since *The Firebird.* Truly this was Babel to the nth degree ... *Creation* was one of the very engaging sections of the work; it was composed by Nathaniel Shilkret, who commissioned the entire work. (*Pacific Coast Musician*, Los Angeles, 15 December 1945) (The first performance of *Genesis* was originally scheduled for 21 October 1945, but was postponed until 18 November 1945; the date 15 December 1947 given in the 3rd edition of *Music Since 1900* is that of a later performance.)

21 NOVEMBER 1945

Cinderella, opera-ballet by Sergei PROKOFIEV, completed in 1943, an earthy Russian version of the classic wish-fulfilling fairy tale, in which a mysophiliac Russian girl Mascha Chernushka (literally, "Dirty Black Little Mary," the name for Cinderella used in Russian children's books), wins her prince charming, scored in the traditional manner of Russian classical ballet, featuring a *pas de deux*, a mazurka, waltzes, etc., with twenty arias interspersed between choreographic numbers, is performed for the first time in Moscow.

21 NOVEMBER 1945

Two hundred and fifty years have passed since the death of the great English composer Henry PURCELL.

23 NOVEMBER 1945

Symphonie des Souvenirs for voices, narrator and orchestra by the Belgian composer Raymond CHEVREUILLE, written in a cultured vigesimosecular manner, is performed for the first time in Brussels.

25 NOVEMBER 1945

Arturo Toscanini conducts the National Broadcasting Symphony Orchestra in the world première of *Western Suite* by the 36-year-old American composer Elie SIEGMEISTER, in five descriptive Americanistic movements, *Prairie Morning, Round-up, Night-Herding, Buckaroo,* and *Riding Home,* hippophiliac in content and ostentatiously folkloric in derivation containing quotations from a number of authentic prairie songs, stylized in fertilizingly non-toxic harmonies.

26 NOVEMBER 1945

Aaron AVSHALOMOV, Russian-American composer of Chinese-inspired works, conducts in Shanghai the first performance of his music drama in five acts *The Great Wall*, dealing with the tragedy of a young woman tortured to death at the Great Wall on orders of the Chinese Emperor whose celestial lechery she has imprudently spurned.

27 NOVEMBER 1945

Second Symphony by the 22-year-old American composer Peter MENNIN (his real surname was Mennini; he was of Italian parentage) is performed for the first time at the Eastman School of Music in Rochester, New York.

29 NOVEMBER 1945

The Seven Ages, symphonic suite by John Alden CARPENTER, inspired by the famous lines spoken by Jaques in Shakespeare's *As You Like It,* in seven musical episodes, ending with "sans eyes, sans teeth, sans everything," is performed for the first time by the New York Philharmonic, Artur Rodzinski conducting.

30 NOVEMBER 1945

Fourth Symphony by the expatriate Czech composer Bohuslav MARTINU, temporarily making his home in the United States, written without a key signature but strongly gravitating towards tonal centers, in four movements—(1) *Poco moderato,* calibrated in the mercurial melorhythms of a Siciliana; (2) *Allegro vivo,* in the spirit of a tarantella, with a lyrical middle part; (3) *Largo,* a moribund dumka erupting into a furibund furiant; (4) *Poco Allegro,* a vigorous finale ending in a victorious display of unencumbered C major—is performed for the first time by the Philadelphia Orchestra, Eugene Ormandy conducting.

2 DECEMBER 1945

Hans HENKEMANS, 31-year-old Dutch composer, plays in Amsterdam the piano part in the first performance of his neo-classical *Passacaglia and Gigue* for piano and orchestra, with the Concertgebouw Orchestra under the direction of Eduard van Beinum.

5 DECEMBER 1945

Majova Symphonie by the Czech composer Vítězslav NOVÁK, for chorus and orchestra, in three movements, begun under the Nazi Occupation in 1943, and completed after the liberation of Czechoslovakia in May, 1945 by the

Soviet armies, and for this reason named *Majova* (i.e. of the month of May), graphically portraying the historic event by the quotation of the Volga Boatmen's song which reduces the Nazi brawling Host Wessel tune and the pan-Germanic hymn *Deutschland über alles* to pathetic shreds in a minor key alternating with an apocalyptic chant of Dies Irae, is performed for the first time in Prague.

6 DECEMBER 1945

Darius MILHAUD conducts the New York Philharmonic in the world première of his Caribbean diptych *La Bal Martiniquais*, in two divisions, *Chanson Créole* and *Biguine*, inspired by the creole rhythms of the French-governed island of Martinique, with the thematic material derived from Milhaud's *La Libération des Antilles*, for voice and piano, a setting of poems by the islanders expressing their joy at the liberation of the French West Indies from the repugnant regime of Vichy.

8 DECEMBER 1945

On the 80th birthday of Jean SIBELIUS, Finland issues a postage stamp of five marks with his portrait, a unique philatelic honor for a living composer.

8 DECEMBER 1945

Alexander SILOTI, Russian pianist and conductor, keeper of the best traditions of the Russian performing arts, a pupil of Liszt, teacher and first cousin of Rachmaninoff, dies in New York at the age of 82.

9 DECEMBER 1945

Violin Concerto by Ildebrando PIZZETTI, in three movements—(1) *Molto mosso e appassionato*, an impassionately lambent lament with lachrymally cadent semitones

forming the principal thematic figures; (2) *Aria*, a frugal baroque theme with rococo variations; (3) *Andante largo*, on the subject from Pizzetti's choral work *Recordare*—written in the spirit of devout imploration, is performed for the first time in Rome.

14 DECEMBER 1945

The Hungarian Ministry of Justice removes the name of Ernst VON DOHNÁNYI from the list of war criminals and exonerates him from the charge that he was a member of the pro-Nazi Hungarian Arrow-Cross Party. (The Communist Budapest newspaper *Az Ember* of 15 March 1947 revived the charge, but it was decisively refuted by a number of Hungarian refugees in America, some of them of Jewish extraction, who would be the first to militate against anyone tainted with Nazi affiliations.)

19 DECEMBER 1945

Concerto for flute and orchestra by the Dutch composer Marius FLOTHUIS, floatingly fluvial in flute passages, is performed for the first time in Utrecht.

19 DECEMBER 1945

Thunderbolt P-45, orchestral scherzo by Bohuslav MARTINU is performed for the first time in Washington.

28 DECEMBER 1945

Igor STRAVINSKY becomes an American citizen, renouncing his previous allegiance to France whose citizen he had become on 10 June 1934.

30 DECEMBER 1945

The Enchanted Kiss, one-act radio opera by Robert Russell BENNETT, is performed for the first time in New York.

1946

5 JANUARY 1946

Rejsekammeraten, opera by the 46-year-old Danish composer Ebbe HAMERIK, to a libretto after Hans Christian Andersen, is produced in Copenhagen.

10 JANUARY 1946

Harry von TILZER, American composer of sentimental ballads (his real name was Harry Gumm), purported originator of the expression "Tin Pan Alley" (he used to put strips of paper on the strings of a grand piano, making it sound like a tin pan), dies a lonely death in a New York hotel at the age of 73.

23 JANUARY 1946

Dark Meadow, ballet choreographed by Martha Graham to the score of *Hija de Cólquide* by Carlos CHÁVEZ, is produced by her dance group in New York.

24 JANUARY 1946

Igor STRAVINSKY conducts the New York Philharmonic Orchestra in the first performance of his *Symphony in Three Movements* (parenthetically directed in the program book to be played without a pause, but actually containing a double-bar at the end of the first movement automatically requiring a stop), with its three sections evolving in the following forms:

(1) *Symphony-Overture* (so titled in the program book, but replaced in the printed score by a scholastic metronomic tempo indication of 160 quarter-notes per minute), set in a propulsive neo-Baroque style, in 4/4 time, punctuated by frequent rhetorical aposiopeses causing the metrical bars to collapse into irregular units, with thematic groupings rotating around the migratory tonal foci of G, A and C, the entire melorhythmic momentum having been suggested to Stravinsky by viewing a newsreel of the Japanese invasion of China, and after multiple instrumental monologues and dialogues terminating on a spacious chord of a major seventh anchored on deep C; (2) *Andante*, a terse concertino, thematically utilizing the flotsam and jetsam from Stravinsky's unrealized score for the motion picture of Franz Werfel's *Song of Bernadette;* (3) *Con moto*, a rondo, reverting to Stravinsky's primitivistic avatar with its volcanically disequilibrated meters, convulsive silences and quaquaversal quick quivers of asymmetrical rhythms, culminating with a magisterial fugue suggested to Stravinsky by the films of the Allies' victorious march into Germany, and concluding with a gloriously grandisonant D-flat major chord pandiatonically enriched by an added sixth and an added ninth and spread in the orchestra upon a range of six octaves and a fifth.

Each episode in the Symphony is linked in my imagination with a specific cinematographic impression of the war. But the Symphony is not programmatic. Composers combine notes—that is all. How and in what form the things of this world are impressed upon their music is not for them to say. (Stravinsky in his annotations for a recording of the *Symphony in Three Movements*, issued by Columbia Phonograph Records)

25 JANUARY 1946

Metamorphosen for 23 solo string instruments by Richard STRAUSS, composed between 13 March and 12 April 1945, in the dying throes of the great German Reich, inscribed *In Memoriam* and containing thematic quotations from Beethoven's Funeral March of the *Eroica*, is performed for the first time in Zürich, Switzerland, where Strauss took refuge after the final German debacle.

29 JANUARY 1946

Sidney JONES, English composer of light music, whose operetta *The Geisha* portraying the accessible delights of Japanese femininity as judged by British visitors, produced in 1896, became a world favorite, dies in his native city of London at the age of 84.

30 JANUARY 1946

Concerto for clarinet and orchestra by Darius MILHAUD, in four contrasting movements marked *Animé, Très décidé, Lent, Animé,* is performed for the first time at the Marine Barracks in Washington.

2 FEBRUARY 1946

Ballad for harp and orchestra by the 42-year-old Odessa-born Palestinian composer Joseph KAMINSKI, is performed for the first time by the Palestine Symphony Orchestra in Tel Aviv.

6 FEBRUARY 1946

Oswald KABASTA, 49-year-old Austrian conductor who without circumspection or prescience joined the Austrian Nazi party during its early suppuration, kills himself in Munich, as retribution and professional disgrace became imminent.

8 FEBRUARY 1946

Third Concerto for piano and orchestra by Béla BARTÓK, his last work, completed by him with the exception of the final 17 bars which had to be deciphered from sketches by his friend Tibor Serly (Bartók wrote *Vege* in the last bar of the *Concerto*, a Hungarian word meaning End, which he had never used before in his music), conceived in a surprisingly simplified idiom, replete with baroque sequences and symmetrically arrayed cadences, in three movements, *Allegretto, Adagio religioso* and *Allegro vivace*, which form a satisfying neo-Baroque triptych, is performed posthumously for the first time by György Sándor with the Philadelphia Orchestra, Eugene Ormandy conducting.

13 FEBRUARY 1946

Edge of the World, symphonic poem by the 32-year-old Canadian composer John WEINZWEIG, is performed for the first time in Toronto.

15 FEBRUARY 1946

Makar Čudra, symphonic poem for bass voice and orchestra by the Croatian composer Petar KONJOVIĆ, inspired by the novella of Maxim Gorky, dealing with the passion of a Gypsy singer for a proud Russian beauty, whom he stabs when she rebukes his professions of love, and then is himself killed by her father, written in a melodramatically romantic idiom with occasional adumbrations of Russian folk songs, is performed for the first time in Belgrade.

17 FEBRUARY 1946

Danzón Cubano by Aaron COPLAND, a symphonic movement derived from the asymmetrical rhythms of popular Afro-Cuban dances, maintaining a steady beat as a common denominator of constantly shifting meters, is performed for the first time by the Baltimore Symphony Orchestra, Reginald Stewart conducting. (In its original form for two pianos, *Danzón Cubano* was first performed by Aaron Copland and Leonard Bernstein on 17 December 1942, at a concert of the League of Composers in New York.)

18 FEBRUARY 1946

Four centuries have passed since the death of the great religious reformer and composer of hymns Martin LUTHER, who created the German Protestant chorale, the *Kirchenlied*, in the vernacular, to justify his apocryphal dictum that the devil should not have all the best tunes.

25 FEBRUARY 1946

Legend of Tariel, opera in four acts to a libretto in the Georgian language by the 41-year-old Georgian composer Shalva MSHVELIDZE, after the classical epic of the Georgian 12th-century poet Shota Rustaveli, dealing with the return of the warrior Tariel on the wedding day of his beloved to a tribal chieftain, whom he manfully slays to regain her, is produced in Tbilisi.

26 FEBRUARY 1946

Concerto for oboe and chamber orchestra by Richard STRAUSS, completed by him on 25 October 1945 in Switzerland, in three classically equilibrated movements, *Allegro, Andante, Rondo,* is performed for the first time in Zürich, in the presence of Strauss himself.

6 MARCH 1946

Second Symphony by the Dutch composer Guillaume LANDRÉ is performed for the first time in The Hague.

7 MARCH 1946

Halsey STEVENS, 37-year-old American composer, conducts in San Francisco the first performance of his *First Symphony.* (A revised version of the work was first performed in Los Angeles on 3 March 1950, under the composer's direction.)

9 MARCH 1946

Les Amours de Jupiter, a hedonistically mythological ballet by Jacques IBERT, is performed for the first time in Paris.

22 MARCH 1946

Igor STRAVINSKY conducts the San Francisco Symphony Orchestra in the first performance of the version for full orchestra of his *Scherzo à la Russe,* a symphonic pasticcio on popular Russian refrains, originally written for Paul Whiteman's band and performed by him on the radio in 1944.

23 MARCH 1946

Airborne, symphony for narrator, singers and orchestra, by the American composer Marc BLITZSTEIN, depicting in twelve vivid musical tableaux the history of human flight from Icarus to the fighting airmen of World War II, with brassy detonations punctuating the terse declarative prose of the narration, is performed for the first time by the New York City Symphony Orchestra, Leonard Bernstein conducting.

25 MARCH 1946

Edward LA VINE, popular vaudeville actor, whose performance in Paris in 1910 inspired DEBUSSY to write his prelude, *General Lavine-Eccentric,* dies at the desert town of Twenty-Nine Palms in California.

25 MARCH 1946

Sonatina No. 2 for 16 wind instruments by Richard STRAUSS (completed by him on 22 June 1945) is performed for the first time in Winterthur, Switzerland.

25 MARCH 1946

Ebony Concerto by Igor STRAVINSKY, scored for "ebony stick" (swing term for clarinet) and band, written in a highly stylized but not condescendingly sophisticated jazz idiom, with fitful instrumental sternutations creating a stimulatingly neurotic ambience, while the harmony remains parsimoniously austere in its tonal foundations within a classical form of three movements, is performed for the first time by Woody Herman and his band as a commissioned work, in Carnegie Hall, New York.

1 APRIL 1946

Arlequin Radiophile, chamber opera by the 47-year-old French composer Marcel DELANNOY, combining the spirit of commedia dell'arte with the 20th century, is performed for the first time in Paris.

5 APRIL 1946

Forty-two years after its composition, the first performance is given by the Little Symphony of New York, Lou Harrison conducting, of the *Third Symphony* by Charles IVES, in three movements bearing titles of remembered American events:

(1) *Old Folks Gatherin',* opening with an original hymnal tune of a devotional pentatonic structure, leading to the prime thematic mover, *Azmon* (commonly sung to the words "O For a Thousand Tongues to Sing"), constituting, with its characteristic falling thirds, the main motivic material of the movement, the second subject being *Erie* by Charles Crozat Converse (1832–1918), widely known by the incipit "What a Friend We Have in Jesus," used as countersubject to the original theme and to *Azmon;* (2) *Children's Day,* a tender memory of childhood in the 1880's with the hymnal tune *Naomi* as a guiding cantus firmus combined with Lowell Mason's pentatonically constructed melody *Fountain* ("There is a Fountain Filled with Blood"), switching to a march-like anthem *Happy Land,* also pentatonic in strvcture, popular among children of several generations with parody words, "There is a Boarding-House Far, Far Away Where They Have Ham and Beans Three Times a Day/Oh, How Those Boarders Yell/When They Hear That Dinner Bell!" harmonized in audacious polytonalities, but returning in the end to the serenity of children's tranquil joys; (3) *Communion,* based principally on the tune known as *Woodworth* identifiable by the incipit "Just as I Am, Without One Plea," written by an actress named Charlotte Elliott after a personally experienced epiphany, and ever since used as the standard closing anthem at revival meetings, the movement concluding with falling minor thirds in the cello solo, as though evoking the voice repeating, "I Come, I Come . . ." (On 5 May 1947, Ives was notified that the Pulitzer Prize was awarded to him for his *Third Symphony;* he accepted, but murmured a demurrer: "Prizes are for boys—I'm grown up!")

5 APRIL 1946

Cello Concerto by the 36-year-old American composer Samuel BARBER, written in a rhapsodically discursive manner with an astute injection of jazzy rhythms, in three movements, *Allegro moderato, Andante sostenuto, Molto allegro e appassionato,* evolving along a centripetal melodic spiral with a tritone as the focal interval, and ending on a unison A, is performed for the first time by Raya Garbousova with the Boston Symphony Orchestra, Serge Koussevitzky conducting.

5 APRIL 1946

Vincent YOUMANS, American composer of musical comedies, whose *Tea for Two* became a perennial favorite, dies of tuberculosis in Denver at the age of 47.

8 APRIL 1946

The first *Concerto portugues* for piano and orchestra by the Portuguese composer Ivo CRUZ, is performed for the first time in Lisbon. (The second *Concerto portugues* was first performed in Lisbon on 16 December 1946.)

8 APRIL 1946

Adam Zero, choreographic spectacle in 16 scenes by the 54-year-old English composer Arthur BLISS, in which the life cycle of a symbolic Adam is traced, from birth to death, adding up to Zero, which God, personified by a stage director, marks on a blackboard, with the creation of Adam illustrated by agonizingly chromaticized harmonies and his illicit acquisition of the knowledge of good and evil by jazzy percolation of thematic fragments, is produced in London.

9 APRIL 1946

August LUDWIG, German composer and journalist who attained dubious fame by completing Schubert's *Unfinished Symphony*, adding two movements, entitled *Philosopher's Scherzo* and *March of Fate* (it had its first and last performance at the concert of the Berlin Philharmonic on 8 December 1892), dies in Dresden at the age of 81.

10 APRIL 1946

The Government of Rumania issues a series of stamps at 10, 20, 55, 80 and 160 lei in homage to the Bucharest Philharmonic and two large souvenir sheets with music from George ENESCO's *Second Rumanian Rhapsody* (the initial three notes of which were erroneously reproduced on the stamps as B, D, D, instead of A, B, C).

2O APRIL 1946

Deirdre, first Canadian grand opera, dealing with a Celtic love triangle in Ulster in A.D. 1, composed by Healey WILLAN, himself an Ulster Celt, is performed for the first time, in concert form, by the Canadian Broadcasting Corporation in Toronto.

26 APRIL 1946

The Bells, symphonic suite by Darius MILHAUD, in five movements, *Overture, Silver Bells, Golden Bells, Brazen Bells* and *Iron Bells*, inspired by the versicular tintinnabulations of Edgar Allan Poe's celebrated alliterative poem, is performed for the first time in Chicago.

2 MAY 1946

Equinox, opera by Marjan KOZINA, 38-year-old Slovenian composer, to a libretto dealing with a love contest in 1860 at a Dalmatian port town between a native youth and an American visitor, both infatuated with the same Slovenian girl, is produced in Ljubljana.

5 MAY 1946

Second Symphony in A major by the American composer Douglas MOORE, in four movements, (1) *Andante con moto, Allegro giusto*, (2) *Andante quieto e semplice*, (3) *Allegretto*, (4) *Allegro con spirito*, written in an "objective modified classical style, with emphasis on rhythmic and melodic momentum," is performed for the first time in Paris. (The first American performance of the work took place in Los Angeles on 16 January, 1947.)

5 MAY 1946

L'Homme à la Peau de Léopard, ballet in three acts based on the famous epic by the 12th-century Georgian poet Shota Rustaveli, with music collectively written by Arthur HONEGGER (first act), Alexander TCHEREPNIN (second act), and Tibor HARSÁNYI (third act), is produced in Monte Carlo.

5 MAY 1946

From These States by Ernst BACON, a "cycle of people's songs" presented as a symphonic reflection of geographic, demographic and psychological aspects of America, is performed for the first time in New York.

8 MAY 1946

The Medium, opera in two acts by the 34-year-old Italian-American composer Gian Carlo MENOTTI, to his own libretto in English, dealing with a fraudulent spiritualist who falls victim to her own deception when she begins to experience tactile hallucinations and in her terror murders her deaf-mute boy assistant believing him to be a ghost, set to music in a highly dramatic manner enhanced by artful modernistic devices safeguarding a basic tonal design, is produced in New York. (The National Spiritualist Association protested against a Chicago production of *The Medium* in January 1948 as an attempt "to discredit honest and sincere mediums of the Spiritualist Religion at the time of its 100th birthday.")

8 MAY 1946

Boris PAPANDOPULO, German-born Croatian composer of Greek origin, conducts in Zagreb the first performance of his *Second Symphony*, in five movements depicting five states of his own mind: optimistic, resigned, hallucinatory, lyrical and libertarian, combining neo-romantic traits with earthy asymmetrical Balkan rhythms.

10 MAY 1946

The Serpent Heart, ballet by Samuel BARBER to a Freudianized story of Medea's possessive and destructive love "which feeds upon itself like a Serpent heart," with the principal characters designated as One Like Medea and One Like Jason, set to music applying both archaic modal patterns and modern idioms, with agonizing dramatic tension achieved by the thematic use of atonally arrayed major sevenths and colubrine sinuosities of the melodic line, is produced at the opening presentation of the Second Annual Festival of Contemporary American Music at Columbia University, with choreography by Martha Graham.

(Barber revised the ballet, and it was produced under the title *Cave of the Heart*, with choreography again by Martha Graham, in New York on 27 February 1947. A symphonic suite in 7 movements from this version was first performed by the Philadelphia Orchestra. Eugene Ormandy conducting, on 5 December 1947. Finally, a scoring for large orchestra was made of sections from the ballet and published under the title *Medea's Meditation and Dance of Vengeance*. This final version was first performed by the New York Philharmonic Orchestra under the direction of Dimitri Mitropoulos on 2 February 1956.)

11 MAY 1946

At the Teatro alla Scala in Milan, restored after the aerial bombardment of 16 August 1943, with its six candelabra and a huge central chandelier of Bohemian glass comprising 365 electric bulbs installed in the hall, Arturo TOSCANINI conducts the music of Rossini, Verdi, Boito and Puccini. (The official reopening took place on 26 December 1946, with Tullio Serafin conducting *Nabucco* of Verdi.)

11 MAY 1946

Koreanisches Märchen (*A Korean Fairy-Tale*), one-act opera by the German composer Waldemar WENDLAND, is produced in Altenburg.

12 MAY 1946

Phoenix, mythological ballet by the Danish composer Knudaage RIISAGER, is performed for the first time in Copenhagen.

14 MAY 1946

When Lilacs Last in the Dooryard Bloom'd, "American Requiem" by Paul HINDEMITH for soprano, contralto, baritone, chorus and orchestra, written under the impression of the sudden death of President Roosevelt on 14 April 1945, to the words of Walt Whitman's threnody on Abraham Lincoln, in four sections, couched in a stately polyphonic idiom, is performed for the first time in New York by The Collegiate Chorale under the direction of its founder Robert Shaw.

16 MAY 1946

Annie Get Your Gun, musical comedy in three acts by Irving BERLIN, dealing with Annie Oakley, sharpshooting star of Buffalo Bill's Wild West Show, who falls in love with an even sharper shooter of a rival show, with a score including the suggestive ballad *Doin' What Comes Natually*, and many other infectious songs (*The Girl That I Marry, You Can't Get a Man with a Gun, Anything You Can Do I Can Do Better*) culminating in the apotheosis of the American theater, *There's No Business Like Show Business*, is produced in New York.

17 MAY 1946

Petite Symphonie Concertante for harp, harpsichord, piano and two string orchestras by the 55-year-old Swiss composer Frank MARTIN, in four movements, set in an elegant neo-classical style with momentary episodes in the 12-tone technique, embellished by coloristic daubs of the impressionistic palette is performed for the first time as a commissioned work by the Basel Chamber Orchestra in Zürich, Paul Sacher conducting.

21 MAY 1946

Central Park in the Dark by Charles IVES, written in 1906, is performed for the first time at Columbia University, New York. It is in three-part form, with strings maintaining the dreamy shimmering of the dark, in intervallic columns, first in major thirds (forming whole-tone harmonies), then in quartal structures, then in tritones overlapped by fifths, then in pure quintal harmonies, while the middle section erupts in shrill sounds of the youthful revelry contrasted with the still continuing lyric reverie. (A forgotten performance of the piece was given about 1907. Ives wrote in a hasty note: "Central Park was played between the acts in a downtown theater in New York, in 1906 or 1907. The players had a hard time with it—the piano player got mad, stopped in the middle, and kicked in the bass drum. However it would be hardly fair to those old fellers who stood up for a dangerous job to say this was the first performance. The present 1946 performance was the first." An alternative title was *A Contemplation of Nothing Serious, or Central Park in the Dark in the Good Old Summer Time*.)

25 MAY 1946

The Turkish composer Ahmet Adnan SAYGUN conducts the Presidential Philharmonic Orchestra and chorus in Ankara in the first performance of his oratorio *Yunus Emre*.

26 MAY 1946

Third Piano Concerto by Darius MILHAUD, in three contrasting movements, is performed for the first time at the Spring Festival in Prague.

31 MAY 1946

Sinfonia Elegiaca by the 30-year-old Argentinian composer Alberto GINASTERA, in one movement divided into four sections, depicting the state of serenity in coruscatingly colorful harmonies, is performed for the first time in Buenos Aires.

1 JUNE 1946

Leo SLEZAK, great Austrian tenor, famous also for his brilliant wit (when the mechanical swan in the last act of *Lohengrin* swam away ahead of schedule, Slezak inquired of a stage hand, "When does the next swan leave?"), dies on his estate in Egern on the Tegernsee at the age of 72.

16 JUNE 1946

Miloje MILOJEVIĆ, Serbian composer of agreeably impressionistic piano pieces, dies in his native Belgrade at the age of 61.

21 JUNE 1946

Vergilii Aeneis, heroic symphony by Gian Francesco MALIPIERO for voices and orchestra, inspired by Virgil's *Aeneid*, is performed for the first time in Turin.

22 JUNE 1946

A century has passed since the patenting of the saxophone, invented by the French instrument-maker Adolphe SAX, and named after him.

22 JUNE 1946

Niobe, monodrama in two acts for soprano, double chorus, orchestra and dancers by the Swiss composer Heinrich SUTERMEISTER, depicting the tragic story of Niobe who lost her 14 children when her defiant boasting of fecundity aroused the lethal wrath of the relatively infertile Leto, mother of Apollo and Artemis, is produced in Zürich.

7 JULY 1946

After four years of inactivity during World War II, the International Society for Contemporary Music resumes the presentation of its annual festivals, inaugurating its 20th Festival in London in the following program of symphonic music:

Stadtpfeiffermusik by the German composer Richard MOHAUPT, a hedonistic utilitarian score stylizing the merry music-making of old German town fifers; *Three Symphonic Preludes* by the quadrigenarian English composeress Elizabeth LUTYENS, written in a neo-classical idiom; *Piano Concerto* by the 39-year-old Dutch composer Robert de ROOS; *Second Symphony* by the 36-year-old French composeress Elsa BARRAINE; and *Ode to the End of the War* by Sergei PROKOFIEV.

8 JULY 1946

The second concert of the 20th Festival of the International Society for Contemporary Music is given in London, presenting the following program of chamber music:

Fifth String Quartet by the Polish composer Jerzy FITELBERG resident in New York; *Sonatina* for clarinet and piano by the Swiss impressionist composer Albert MOESCHINGER; *Canti di Prigionia* for chorus, two pianos, two harps and percussion by the prime Italian modernist Luigi DALLAPICCOLA, first performed in Rome on 11 December 1941, and written in the idiom of expressionistic atonality; *Sonata for Two Pianos* by Igor STRAVINSKY, written in a compact and concise neo-classical idiom, first performed on 8 August 1944 at a "Concert with Commentaries" given by Nadia Boulanger at the University of Indiana in Bloomington; and *String Quartet* in E-flat by Paul HINDEMITH.

10 JULY 1946

The third concert of the 20th Festival of the International Society for Contemporary Music in London presents the following program of chamber music:

String Quartet No. 7 by Ernst KRENEK; *Suite* for violin and piano by Jozef ZAVADIL of Czechoslovakia; *Quatour pour la Fin du Temps* for violin, clarinet, cello and piano by Olivier MESSIAEN (originally performed, with the composer at the piano, on 15 January 1941 in a German prisoner-of-war camp in Silesia); and *Ode to Napoleon Buonaparte* for string quartet, piano and reciter by Arnold SCHOENBERG (first performed in a version with a string orchestra in New York on 23 November 1944).

12 JULY 1946

The fourth concert of the 20th Festival of the International Society for Contemporary Music is presented in London with the following program:

Symphony for Strings by the 35-year-old American composer William SCHUMAN, his fifth symphony (originally performed by the Boston Symphony Orchestra on 12 November 1943); *5 Folk Tunes* for childrens' voices and instruments by the 31-year-old Polish composer Andrzej PANUFNIK; *First Cantata*, op. 29, for soprano, chorus and orchestra by Anton von WEBERN, composed in 1939, in three movements, conceived as an exercise in Hegelian dialectics in music, with the melodic thesis opposed by antithesis, resolving in thematic synthesis, derived from a bisected 12-tone series, in which the second half is the retrograde inversion of the first; and *Divertimento No. 2* for string orchestra and solo trumpet by the 48-year-old Hungarian-Parisian composer Tibor HARSÁNYI.

12 JULY 1946

The Rape of Lucretia, opera in two acts by Great Britain's glorified composer, 32-year-old Benjamin BRITTEN, based on a French play derived from Shakespeare's poem dealing with the monstrous rape in 509 B.C. of the virtuous Roman matron, who kills herself after her ordeal, scored for an economical ensemble of 8 singers and 17 solo instruments, wherein atonal elements are polarized by pedal-pointed polyharmonies, and dramatic impact is attained by strong and spacious rhythmic dispositions while the text itself flaunts such erotically realistic lines as "let me rise to my first sepulchre, which is your thighs," is produced at the Glyndebourne Festival in England.

14 JULY 1946

The fifth concert of the 20th Festival of the International Society for Contemporary Music is presented in London in the following program of symphonic music:

Cortèges by the British composer Alan RAWSTHORNE; *Nocturne* by Raymond LOUCHEUR of France; *Violi Concerto* by Roman PALESTER of Poland; *Concerto for Orchestra* by Béla BARTÓK.

19 JULY 1946

Puhajarv (*Holy Lake*), opera in three acts by the 37-year-old Estonian composer Gustav ERNESAKS, to a libretto in the Estonian language, dealing with the Estonian peasant rebellion against German feudal lords in 1840, is performed for the first time in Tallin, as a parabolic allusion to the Nazi invasion of Estonia in 1941.

12 AUGUST 1946

The Mikado, comic opera by GILBERT and SULLIVAN, making flippant fun of Japanese Emperor worship and heretofore banned in Japan for its disrespectful treatment of the Emperor, is produced for the first time in Tokyo by the Special Services Detachment of General Headquarters of the American Army of Occupation, with a new overture on oriental themes especially written by Klaus PRINGSHEIM, German musician long resident of Japan. (The production, originally scheduled for 22 July 1946, was postponed until 12 August 1946 on account of extremely hot weather which made the wearing of heavy ceremonial robes uncomfortable.)

There was considerable discussion as to the propriety of doing *The Mikado* in Japan. Permission was finally obtained and production began in May 1946. The principals were all members of the United States Armed Forces, with the exception of the women's roles which were sung by the Civilian Actress Technicians, American Women employed in the Special Services Soldier Show Program.... The Corps de Ballet was entirely Japanese ... At no time was any performance open to the Japanese public. However, on 11 August 1946 a dress rehearsal was held and passes were issued to 111 Japanese artists, singers, theater producers, newspaper editors and columnists. These were the only Japanese authorized at any time to see *The Mikado*. (From a letter to the author, dated 14 May 1948, from Gerald J. Cameron, Executive Officer of the Entertainment & Recreation Branch of the United States Army)

17 AUGUST 1946

Symphonie Liturgique by Arthur HONEGGER, his *Third Symphony*, in three movements—(1) *Dies Irae*, evoking the apocalyptic vision of an atonal Doomsday; (2) *De Pro-fundis clamavi*, tortuously rising from the somber depths of the bass register and scaling the heights of desperate clamor in chromatic anxiety; (3) *Dona Nobis Pacem*, an imploration for peace against the distant drumfire of war, with diatonic aspirations gradually overcoming the chromatic waves of despair—is performed for the first time in Zürich under the direction of Charles Munch to whom the score is dedicated.

18 AUGUST 1946

Corrobboree, ballet suite by the 42-year-old Australian composer John ANTILL, depicting in primitivistically modernistic modalities the traditional festival of Australian aborigines—(1) *Welcome Ceremony*, (2) *Dance to the Evening Star*, (3) *Rain Dance*, (4) *Procession of Totems and Fire Ceremony*—is performed for the first time in Sydney.

3 SEPTEMBER 1946

Moriz ROSENTHAL, "little giant" of the piano, one of the two remaining pupils of Liszt (the last survivor being the Portuguese pianist José Vianna Da Motta), whose wit matched his digital dexterity (asked for biographical information, he wrote: "I was born at an early age and sang a chromatic scale when I was one hour old. I am never nervous when I play in public, but pianists in the audience usually are"), dies in New York at the age of 83.

27 SEPTEMBER 1946

First performances of two symphonic works by Polish composers are given by the Cracow Philharmonic:

Concerto for string orchestra by 42-year-old Tadeusz KAS-SERN, written in a neo-Polonian manner of classical constructivism; *Second Symphony* by 46-year-old Boleslaw WOY-TOWICZ, dedicated to his stepson killed in the Warsaw uprising of 1944, in four movements: (1) *Disaster*, growing out of an embryo motive of three notes, C-D-F, rising to great exertions but soon receding into forced passivity; (2) *Insurrection*, an energetic scherzo, quoting a Polish resistance tune of 1863; (3) *Contra spem spero*, a double fugue, containing rhythmic allusions to the radio signals for help sent to the Allies in the "hope against hope" as Poland was being crushed by the Nazi war machine in September 1939; (4) *Jubilation*, a polymetric rondo in Krakowiak rhythms, ending with a bitonal chord of F-sharp major superimposed on F major, symbolic of victory against impossible odds.

7 OCTOBER 1946

Two centuries have elapsed since the birth in Boston of William BILLINGS, the first professional American composer who created a *sui generis* type of American "fuguing tunes" (which gave rise through an imaginative misspelling, to "fudging" tunes of the hill country in Kentucky and Tennessee.)

8 OCTOBER 1946

RCA Victor releases its billionth recording: John Philip SOUSA's perennial patriotic favorite, the march *Stars and Stripes Forever*.

10 OCTOBER 1946

Musique de Table, symphonic suite by the French composer Manuel ROSENTHAL, composed in 1942 in France as a salivating gastronomic fantasy relishing the then unobtainable products of the French cuisine, with a menu of eight dishes in eight movements: *Salade russe*, *Eels in Red Wine*, *Quenelles*, *Beef Tenderloin*, *Mixed Fresh Vegetables*, *Loin of Venison*, *Salade de saison* and *Fromage de montagne*, set to music in an appetizingly hedonistic manner of tonal gourmandise, is performed for the first time in America by the New York Philharmonic, Artur Rodzinski conducting.

16 OCTOBER 1946

Sir Granville BANTOCK, English composer of impeccable gentility and stately competence, whose oratorios and symphonic pieces command admiration for their irreproachable academic solidity, dies in London at the age of 78.

18 OCTOBER 1946

Third Symphony by Aaron COPLAND, in four movements—(1) *Molto moderato*, containing three principal themes and presented in an unambiguous tonal setting; (2) *Allegro Molto*, in the form of a classical cyclic scherzo; (3) *Andantino quasi Allegretto*, a set of three variations; (4) *Molto deliberato*, the longest movement of the work, containing a quotation from Copland's *Fanfare for the Common Man*, and set in sonata form— the whole work revealing proclamatory lyricism, alternating with nervously asymmetric rhythms creating the impression of jazzy turbulence under its finely equilibrated surface, is performed for the first time by the Boston Symphony Orchestra, Serge Koussevitzky conducting.

22 OCTOBER 1946

After 28 years of vacillation and violent political peripeteia, the government of Austria adopts a melody from Mozart's *Little Masonic Cantata* as its new national anthem, with words by Paul Preradovic, *Land der Berge, Land am Strome*, selected in a special contest.

(The original Austrian anthem was Haydn's *Gott erhalte unsern Kaiser*, adopted in 1797. From 1920 until 1929 an anthem with words by Karl Renner, prime minister of Austria, and music by Wilhelm Kienzl was in use; on 13 December 1929, the Haydn tune was reinstated with a different set of words, and was current in that form until 1946.)

22 OCTOBER 1946

Sinfonietta by the 45-year-old Belgian composer Marcel POOT, a member of Synthétistes, a group promoting music as a synthesized product of classical forms and modern content, is performed for the first time by the Chicago Symphony Orchestra, under the direction of the Belgian conductor Désiré Defauw.

24 OCTOBER 1946

Leonard BERNSTEIN conducts in New York the first performance of his ballet *Facsimile*, set to music in a rambunctiously modernistic manner, with an existentialist scenario dealing with the intersected passions of two men contending for the favors of one woman.

30 OCTOBER 1946

Cello Concerto in E major by Aram KHACHATURIAN, in three classically proportioned movements, *Allegro moder-*

ato, Andante sostenuto and *Allegro a battuta,* written in an attractively coloristic manner, with orientalistic arabesques set in luxuriant harmonies, is performed for the first time in Moscow.

3 NOVEMBER 1946

Betrothal in a Convent, opera in four acts by Sergei PROKOFIEV, to a libretto by Prokofiev's second wife Myra Mendelson, after Sheridan's comedy *The Duenna,* dealing with intersected amours, mistaken identities and various other embroilments of 18th-century Seville, set to music in a hedonistic lyrico-dramatic manner, with sharp rhythmic thrusts perforating the tonal surface of vocal and instrumental fabric, is produced in Leningrad.

12 NOVEMBER 1946

Les Sirènes, ballet by Lord BERNERS, depicting in modulatory fluxions and asymmetric rhythms an encounter of two mermaids with a group of masculine human swimmers on a beach in 1910 "when spirits were high and skirts were low," is produced in London.

14 NOVEMBER 1946

Manuel DE FALLA, great spanish composer whose ballets and operas are vibrant with the melorhythms of rural and urban Spain set in resonant modern harmonies, dies nine days before his 70th birthday at Alta Gracia, Argentina, where he went in 1938 leaving Spain torn asunder by civil war.

14 NOVEMBER 1946

Fifth Symphony by Guy ROPARTZ, 82-year-old French composer of melodious and harmonious music in the tradition of Cesar Franck, is performed for the first time in Paris, Charles Munch conducting.

15 NOVEMBER 1946

On his first visit to the United States, Zoltán KODÁLY, foremost living composer of Hungary, conducts the Pittsburgh Symphony Orchestra in a performance of his symphonic *Dances of Galánta* composed in 1933, inspired by the memories of his childhood spent in the polyethnic western Hungarian village of Galanta, set in characteristically amygdaline Magyar modalities.

22 NOVEMBER 1946

Third Piano Concerto by Ernst KRENEK, in five movements, written in a basically tonal idiom, with the application of some special effects (at one point the soloist silently presses down the keys while playing glissandi on the strings inside the grand piano), is performed for the first time by Dimitri Mitropoulos with the Minneapolis Symphony Orchestra, playing and conducting simultaneously from memory.

28 NOVEMBER 1946

Sevastopoltzy, opera in four acts by the Soviet composer Marian KOVAL, extolling the courage of Sebastopol guerrilla fighters during the invasion of the Crimea by the Nazis in 1942, is produced in Molotov (Perm).

28 NOVEMBER 1946

Second Concerto for violoncello and orchestra by Darius MILHAUD, in three movements, marked *Gai, Tendre* and *Alerte,* is performed for the first time by the New York Philharmonic, Artur Rodzinski conducting.

29 NOVEMBER 1946

Instruments of the Orchestra, educational English film with music by Benjamin BRITTEN, from which he has fashioned an instrumental suite *The Young Person's Guide to the Orchestra,* is produced for the first time in London.

29 NOVEMBER 1946

Camargo Mozart GUARNIERI, Brazilian composer, who usually omits his given middle name out of modesty, conducts the Boston Symphony Orchestra in the world première of his *Symphony* in three movements marked *Rude, Profundos, Radioso,* set in classical form but containing colorful references to Brazilian dance rhythms.

11 DECEMBER 1946

Sérénade à Angélique by Arthur HONEGGER, a fanciful symphonic scherzo, wherein the trombone's stentorian passion is pipingly rebuked by a flute-like Angélique, is performed for the first time in Paris.

13 DECEMBER 1946

First Symphony by the internationally renowned pianist and pedagogue Artur SCHNABEL, in four traditional movements cast in an uncompromising idiom of dissonant counterpoint, with the principal decaphonic and hendecaphonic themes on the verge of dodecaphonic extension, is performed for the first time by the Minneapolis Symphony Orchestra, Dimitri Mitropoulos conducting, preceded, to assuage the tonal feelings of the audience in advance, by Schnabel's exuberantly romantic rendition of Beethoven's chaste *Fourth Piano Concerto,*

13 DECEMBER 1946

Three Cyprus Serenades, symphonic triptych by the Cyprus-born American composer Anis FULEIHAN, marked by luxuriantly expressive Mediterranean arabesques but without "too much mustard," is performed for the first time by the Philadelphia Orchestra, Eugene Ormandy conducting.

14 DECEMBER 1946

As part of musical festivities marking the 800th anniversary of the foundation of the city of Moscow, *Moscow,* patriotic cantata by Vissarion SHEBALIN, glorifying in five movements the city and its people ("7 times 7 roads, 7 times 7 blue rivers . . . all lead to the wonderful town of Moscow"), with a magnivocal climax in grandiose Russian homophony accompanied by an aggregation of pealing church bells, is performed for the first time in Moscow.

15 DECEMBER 1946

Les Saisons et les Jours, "allegoric symphony" by Henri SAUGUET, is performed for the first time in Paris.

17 DECEMBER 1946

At a session of the Berlin Tribunal charged with denazification proceedings in the field of art and music, Wilhelm FURTWÄNGLER, former conductor of the Berlin Philharmonic, is found not guilty of passive participation in the criminal activities of the Nazi regime.

What made me remain in Germany was my anxious desire to preserve the integrity of German music. When Thomas Mann asks, "How can Beethoven be played in Himmler's Germany?" I answer, "When was the music of Beethoven more needed than in Himmler's Germany?" I could not therefore leave Germany in her hour of greatest need, and I have no regrets for having stayed at my post. (From Furtwängler's statement to the world press)

17 DECEMBER 1946

Kamenik, opera by the Yugoslav composer Jacov GOTOVAC, is performed for the first time in Zagreb.

19 DECEMBER 1946

Norman DELLO JOIO, 33-year-old American composer of Neapolitan extraction, plays the solo part, with the New York Philharmonic under the direction of George Szell, in the first performance of his *Ricercari* for piano and orchestra, written in a Baroque idiom vitalized by melorhythmic asymmetries.

20 DECEMBER 1946

Die Flut, one-act chamber opera by Boris BLACHER, to a libretto fashioned after a short story by Guy de Maupassant, *Mademoiselle Henriette*, in which a group of travelers becomes stranded on a sandbar at high tide, a young man murders and robs a banker and runs away with his mistress, with a chorus supplying a moralistically cynical commentary, set to music in stark lines of direct action in hard polytriadic harmonies, is performed for the first time on the Berlin Radio. (First stage performance took place in Dresden on 4 March 1947.)

20 DECEMBER 1946

Darius MILHAUD conducts the Boston Symphony Orchestra in the first performance of his *Second Sympho-*ny, in five movements: (1) *Paisible*, pacific, despite some bellicose outbursts of the trumpet and the piccolo; (2) *Mystérieux*, with arcane atonalities in the high register of the violins; (3) *Douloureux*, a dolorous manifestation in roaring fortissississimo; (4) *Avec Sérénité* wherein serenity is portrayed in jig time; (5) *Allélouia*, a fugal laetification in modernistic psalmody.

21 DECEMBER 1946

Minstrel Show by the 33-year-old American composer Morton GOULD, "a musical impression of the old minstrel tunes," scored in a coloristic folksy manner, with the application of special effects such as sandpaper blocks imitating the shuffling sound of the soft-shoe dance, is performed for the first time by the Indianapolis Symphony Orchestra, Fabien Sevitzky conducting.

27 DECEMBER 1946

Charles MUNCH, Alsatian-born, German-educated French conductor makes his American debut with the Boston Symphony Orchestra, of which he was to become the conductor and Music Director in 1949–1962, in a program of French music, featuring a *Sonata a due* by Maurice JAUBERT, killed at the front on 19 June 1940, during the last days of French military resistance to the Nazis.

28 DECEMBER 1946

Carrie Jacobs BOND, whose ultra-sentimental tunes such as *The End of a Perfect Day*, which she published herself on borrowed money, stirred millions of American hearts and sold millions of copies, dies in Glendale, California, at the age of 84, and is buried in the Forest Lawn Memorial Court of Honor, Hollywood's Westminster Abbey.

30 DECEMBER 1946

Charles Wakefield CADMAN, American composer of melodious and harmonious songs, among them *At Dawning*, rejected by 14 publishers before it became a perennial best seller, dies in Los Angeles at the age of 65.

1947

2 JANUARY 1947

L'Oro, music drama in three acts by the prime Italian romantic modernist Ildebrando PIZZETTI, to his own libretto, dealing with the idealistic mayor of a medieval Italian village who refuses to reveal the location of a hidden gold treasure lest sudden prosperity should undermine the morality of its heretofore frugal inhabitants, is produced at La Scala, Milan.

4 JANUARY 1947

Dolores, opera-buffa in one act by André JOLIVET, subtitled *Miracle de la Femme laide,* in which a repellently ugly woman conquers men by irresistible subcutaneous attractions, is performed for the first time on the Paris Radio.

9 JANUARY 1947

Street Scene, dramatic folk opera by Kurt WEILL, after the play of the same name by Elmer Rice, portraying in idiomatically functional tones the drab life in a New York tenement district tragically disrupted when a jealous husband kills his wife and her milkman lover, is produced in New York.

9 JANUARY 1947

Second Symphony by the 50-year-old American composer Roger SESSIONS, in four movements—(1) *Molto agitato; Tranquillo e misterioso; Molto agitato,* (2) *Allegretto capriccioso,* (3) *Adagio, tranquillo ed espressivo,* (4) *Allegramente*—dedicated to the memory of President Roosevelt, written in a highly dissonant polyphonic idiom within a classical formal scheme, is performed for the first time by the San Francisco Symphony Orchestra, Pierre Monteux conducting.

10 JANUARY 1947

Finian's Rainbow, a fantastic musical play by Burton LANE, involving mysterious Irishmen, a leprechaun, Southern racists and Negro sharecroppers, and including the hit songs *How Are Things in Glocca Morra?* and *Look to the Rainbow,* is produced in New York.

11 JANUARY 1947

The Warrior, opera by Bernard ROGERS, "a drama in which the characters speak musically," to the biblical story of Samson and Delilah, cast in an advanced non-operatic style midway between colorful Parisian impressionism and somber Viennese expressionism, is produced at the Metropolitan Opera in New York.

16 JANUARY 1947

Violin Concerto by the Parisian-Hungarian composer Tibor HARSÁNYI is performed for the first time in Paris.

17 JANUARY 1947

First Symphony by the 30-year-old Finnish composer Einar ENGLUND is performed for the first time by the Helsinki Philharmonic, Leo Funtek conducting.

18 JANUARY 1947

Prairie Legend, "a midwestern set" for orchestra by the American composer Elie SIEGMEISTER, "inspired by the quietness and simple beauty of endless fields and the black earth," is performed for the first time in its entirety by the New York Philharmonic, Leopold Stokowski conducting. (The second part, *Harvest Evening,* was performed separately on 29 December 1946 by Stokowski and the New York Philharmonic.)

21 JANUARY 1947

Paul Sacher conducts the Basel Chamber Orchestra in the world premières of three works written to mark its twentieth anniversary:

Toccata e due Canzoni by Bohuslav MARTINU; *Concerto in D* for string orchestra by Igor STRAVINSKY, in three movements, *Vivace, Arioso, Rondo,* set in an austere chiaroscuro manner of the modern baroque; *Fourth Symphony* by Arthur HONEGGER, subtitled, to honor the Swiss city for which it was written, *Deliciae Basilienses,* in three movements: (1) *Lento e misterioso—Allegro,* a lyrically discursive instrumental confabulation expressing a relish and a delight of the artistic ambience of Switzerland; (2) *Larghetto,* built on the old Basel tune "Z'Basel an mim Rhy"; and (3) *Allegro-Finale,* a tripartite Rondo, Passacaglia and Fugue, intoning a fife fanfare on the tune *Basler Morgenstreich* and concluding with a Lutheran chorale and a brief coda.

26 JANUARY 1947

Grace MOORE, American opera star, perishes in an airplane crash, two minutes after taking off from Copenhagen for Stockholm on a concert tour.

28 JANUARY 1947

Reynaldo HAHN, Venezuelan-born Parisian composer of urbane theater music, mundane entertainment pieces, and daintily cadenced, lavender-scented chansons, who was the slender model of the delicately perfumed, sensitively capricious character of Vinteul in Proust's *À la recherche du temps perdu,* dies in Paris at the age of 72.

28 JANUARY 1947

The Birthday of Infanta, symphonic suite in seven sections after Oscar Wilde, by the Italian neo-romantic composer Mario CASTELNUOVO-TEDESCO, who settled in Hollywood in 1939, is performed for the first time in New Orleans.

31 JANUARY 1947

Third Symphony for string orchestra by the 42-year-old Soviet composer Gavriil POPOV, based on Spanish themes, written in homage of the heroic resistance of the Loyalist forces to the overwhelming Fascist bands of the Falange in the Spanish Civil War of 1936–1939, is performed for the first time in Moscow.

1 FEBRUARY 1947

Symphonia Serena by Paul HINDEMITH, in four movements of glorified *Hausmusik*—(1) *Moderately fast*, a neo-classical essay set in energetic rhythms; (2) *Geschwind-marsch by Beethoven*, a paraphrase of a Beethoven military march; (3) *Colloquy*, in which two groups of strings engage in an antiphonal exchange of sentiments, containing a recitative for violin solo played backstage; (4) *Gay*, a polythematic finale—is performed for the first time by the Dallas Symphony Orchestra, under the direction of Antal Dorati.

3 FEBRUARY 1947

Artur RODZINSKI resigns from his post as conductor of the New York Philharmonic in protest against the monopolistic policies of the manager Arthur Judson, and shortly afterwards accepts an appointment as conductor and music director of the Chicago Symphony Orchestra, without signing a legally binding contract.

4 FEBRUARY 1947

Luigi RUSSOLO, far-seeing Italian futurist, imaginative pioneer of the Art of Noises, signatory along with four futurist painters of the original Futurist Manifesto of 11 February 1910, and himself the painter of flamboyant surrealistic canvasses under such fantastically phrased titles as *The Solidity of Fog* and *Plastic Synthesis of the Actions of a Woman*, dies at Cerro di Laveno on Lago Maggiore at the age of 61.

8 FEBRUARY 1947

Le Malade Imaginaire, comic opera after Molière by the Swiss composer Hans HAUG, is produced in Zürich.

9 FEBRUARY 1947

Concerto in D for violin and orchestra by the reformed *enfant terrible* of American music, 46-year-old George ANTHEIL, written in a socially acceptable melodious idiom, perfused with the nutritious extract of triadic harmonies, is performed for the first time in Dallas.

15 FEBRUARY 1947

Violin Concerto in D major, in 3 movements, by the 49-year-old Vienna-born composer Erich Wolfgang KORN-GOLD, once hailed as a 20th-century Mozart (his given name Wolfgang underlining the kinship), but now living in un-Mozartean Hollywood, is performed for the first time by Jascha Heifetz who commissioned the work, with the St. Louis Symphony Orchestra, Vladimir Golschmann conducting.

The work was contemplated for a Caruso of the violin rather than for a Paganini. It is needless to say how delighted I am to have my Concerto performed by Caruso and Paganini in one person: Jascha Heifetz. (From a statement by Erich Wolfgang Korngold)

In this Concerto there was more corn than gold. (Irving Kolodin in the *Saturday Review of Literature*, after the New York performance of the work)

16 FEBRUARY 1947

Morton GOULD, 33-year-old American composer of popular semi-classical pieces as well as impressive symphonic works, conducts the Dallas Symphony Orchestra in the first performance of his *Third Symphony* (completed on 27 January 1947) in four movements, stylistically ranging from rhapsodic romanticism to fugal frugality. (The last movement was revised in the form of a passacaglia, and a new version performed for the first time on 28 October 1948 by the New York Philharmonic, Dimitri Mitropoulos conducting.)

18 FEBRUARY 1947

Gian Carlo MENOTTI, 35-year-old Italian-born composer, conducts in New York the first performance of his one-act opera *The Telephone*, to his own libretto in English, bearing the subtitle *L'Amour à trois* (the third member of the amorous equilateral triangle being the telephone whose raucous ring keeps interrupting the timorous suitor until he goes out and uses his rival, the telephone, to propose to his beloved), set to music in a humorously melodious idiom peppered with euphonious dissonances, together with a revised version of his opera *The Medium*, which was originally produced in New York on 8 May 1946.

19 FEBRUARY 1947

Heitor VILLA-LOBOS conducts the orchestra of the Columbia Broadcasting System in New York in the first performance of his *Bachianas Brasileiras No. 3* for piano and orchestra, which artfully combines Brazilian musical folkways with baroque devices of Bachian polyphony.

21 FEBRUARY 1947

André JOLIVET conducts the Paris Radio Orchestra in the world première of his second "radiophonic legend" *Le Livre de Christophe Colomb*, to the text from a poem of Paul Claudel.

27 FEBRUARY 1947

Third Symphony by the 23-year-old American composer Peter MENNIN, in three movements, *Allegro robusto, Andante moderato, Allegro assai,* with the energetic first and precipitous third movements contrasted with lyrical "voice-weaving" in the slow middle movement, is performed for the first time by the New York Philharmonic, with Walter Hendl conducting.

27 FEBRUARY 1947

Concerto for Piano and Orchestra by Paul HINDEMITH (completed on 29 November 1945), in three movements, *Moderately fast, Slow, Medley on the Medieval Dance Tre Fontane,* the latter consisting of a canzone for solo piano developing into a non-medieval march and a romantic waltz, written in a neo-classical idiom, tonal at its core but resonantly amplified by chromatic counterpoint, is performed for the first time by Jesús María Sanromá with the Cleveland Orchestra under the direction of George Szell.

5 MARCH 1947

Alfredo CASELLA, scholarly animator of new Italian music, civilized composer of astutely calibrated symphonic and chamber music, operas and ballets, perspicacious observer of the contemporary musical scene, dies of cancer in Rome, at the age of 63.

5 MARCH 1947

Folk Symphony by MAHLER-KALKSTEIN, 39-year-old Jewish-Polish composer (he later changed his German-sounding name to its near-Hebrew equivalent Menahem Avidom), in six movements with thematic material derived from Palestinian dance rhythms, is performed for the first time by the Palestine Symphony Orchestra in Tel Aviv.

6 MARCH 1947

Twenty-Fifth Symphony by Nicolai MIASKOVSKY, in D-flat major, set in three symmetrically contrasting movements, *Adagio, Moderato* and *Allegro impetuoso*, is performed for the first time in Moscow.

7 MARCH 1947

The Song of Songs, biblical solo cantata by the 24-year-old Berlin-born American composer Lukas FOSS (whose original name was Fuchs), in four sections, written in an appropriately Solomonesque manner of devotional sensuality, is performed for the first time by the Boston Symphony Orchestra, Serge Koussevitzky conducting, Ellabelle Davis, Negro soprano, to whom the work is dedicated, soloist.

13 MARCH 1947

Brigadoon, whimsical musical fantasy by the Viennese-born American operetta composer Frederick LOEWE, set in a mythical village in Scotland, which magically vanishes in 1747 to escape a plague of witches, but reappears once in a century for twenty-four hours, leading to a fantastic situation when an American tourist anachronistically wanders into it during its periodical time corridor in 1947 and falls in love with a ravishing bicentennial Scottish lass, is produced in New York.

14 MARCH 1947

Lestenitza, one-act opera by the 58-year-old Greek composer George SKLAVOS, is performed for the first time in Athens.

14 MARCH 1947

Habeyssée (whimsical phonetic homonym of ABC, pronounced in French) for violin and orchestra by the venerable French modernist Florent SCHMITT, is performed for the first time in Paris.

18 MARCH 1947

Willem PIJPER, Dutch composer of atmospheric symphonies, coloristic chamber music and impressionistic chansons, whose persistent use of the scale of alternating whole tones and semitones caused it to be known in Holland as the "Pijper scale" (Rimsky-Korsakov had a long established priority on it, and in Russia it is known as the "Rimsky-Korsakov scale"), dies at Leidschendam at the age of 52.

26 MARCH 1947

The Minotaur, ballet by the 38-year-old American composer Elliott CARTER, depicting in somberly dramatic tones the classical horrors of the gluttonously carnivorous Cretan bull, with Ariadne unwinding her qua-quaversally labyrinthine thread to lead the heroic but ungentlemanly tauricide Theseus out to safety, is performed for the first time by the New York Ballet Society.

26 MARCH 1947

Khamma, "légende dansée" by Claude DEBUSSY in the orchestration of Charles Koechlin, is produced for the first time as a ballet at the Opéra-Comique in Paris. (Its first concert performance took place at the Concerts-Colonne in Paris, on 15 November 1924.)

28 MARCH 1947

Tic-Tac, operetta by the Swiss composer Paul BURKHARD, is performed for the first time in Zürich.

1 APRIL 1947

Europa und der Stier, opera by the synthetic composer Siegfried SITZPLATZ, conjured up by synchronous playing of several different phonograph records in heteroousian disharmony interspersed with unauthentic singing commercials, is broadcast on April Fool's Day over radio station WQXR in New York, for the delectation of the cognoscenti and consternation among the untutored radio masses.

11 APRIL 1947

Ernst KRENEK conducts at the University of Chicago the first performance of his choral work a cappella, *The Sante Fe Time Table*, to the text from the timetable of the Santa Fe Railroad, covering all stops between Albuquerque and Los Angeles.

12 APRIL 1947

La follia di Orlando, ballet by the 42-year-old Italian modernist Goffredo PETRASSI, is given for the first time at La Scala, Milan.

16 APRIL 1947

Marion, ou la Belle au Tricorne, radio opera by the 31-year-old Swiss composer Pierre WISSMER, is performed for the first time in Geneva.

16 APRIL 1947

Fourth Symphony by the 56-year-old Czech composer Karel Boleslav JIRÁK is performed for the first time in Prague.

18 APRIL 1947

The Trial of Lucullus, opera in one act by Roger SESSIONS, to the radio play written in 1939 by Bertolt Brecht, an anti-Hitler allegory involving a predatory Roman general brought to trial before the tribunal of common people at the entrance to the Elysian Fields, and condemned for his crimes against humanity despite his proud claims of having dethroned seven kings and destroyed 53 cities, set to music in a structurally compact, texturally dissonant, melodically atonal and rhythmically asymmetric idiom, is performed for the first time at the Berkeley Campus of the University of California.

19 APRIL 1947

Rachel, one-act opera by Reinhold GLIÈRE, after Guy de Maupassant's short story *Mademoiselle Fifi*, dealing with the assassination by a patriotic French tart of an obnoxious Prussian lieutenant nicknamed Mademoiselle Fifi during the occupation of Rouen in 1871 by the Prussian Army (who are characterized in the score by a grotesquely dislocated Austrian tune *Ach du lieber Augustin*), receives its first stage performance in Moscow. (A radio performance of *Rachel* was given in Moscow in 1943 as a propaganda production at the height of the Soviet-Nazi war.)

19 APRIL 1947

Veronika, opera by the 32-year-old Czech composer-conductor Rafael KUBELÍK, son of the once idolized violin virtuoso Jan Kubelík, is produced in Brno.

23 APRIL 1947

Symphony in A by the American composer John POWELL, in four movements, reflecting four different genres of American folkways—*Country Dance, Folksong, Ballad, Ritual Dance*—as "a synthesis of American folk music tradition" is performed for the first time by the Detroit Symphony Orchestra.

24 APRIL 1947

Two Rustic Dances, symphonic set by the 62-year-old German-Czech novelist, playwright, philosopher and occasional composer Max BROD, who immigrated into Palestine in 1939, is performed for the first time in Tel Aviv, with Charles Munch conducting the Palestine Symphony Orchestra.

1 MAY 1947

A three-day Symposium on Music Criticism intended "to help the new army of listeners by providing them with a greater number of competent guides," and "to initiate a fundamental reexamination of the principles of music criticism," opens at Harvard University in Cambridge, Massachusetts with introductory remarks by various musicologists, followed by first performances of specially commissioned works: *Third String Quartet* by Walter PISTON, professor of composition at Harvard University; *String Trio*, op. 45, by Arnold SCHOENBERG, in one movement divided into three sections by two intervening "episodes" providing formal and stylistic contrasts; and *Sixth String Quartet* by Bohuslav MARTINU.

2 MAY 1947

On the second day of the Harvard Symposium on Music Criticism, three choral works commissioned for the occasion are performed for the first time: *Apparebit repentina Dies* for mixed chorus and brasses by Paul HINDEMITH, to the text of a medieval hymn; *La Terra* for chorus and organ by Gian Francesco MALIPIERO, to words from Virgil's *Georgics;* and *In the Beginning* by Aaron COPLAND for mezzo-soprano and chorus, to words from the opening chapters of *Genesis*.

3 MAY 1947

The Harvard Symposium of Music Criticism concludes with the first performance by Martha Graham and her dance group of *Night Journey*, obstetrical ballet by William SCHUMAN, in which an allegorical umbilical cord is tangled up prior to parturition in a discordant coil of atonal filaments and spasmodically jactitating rhythms within an amniotic sac of constantly colliding acrid bitonalities.

7 MAY 1947

The Mother of Us All, opera in three acts by the subtle symphonizer of sophisticated simplicities Virgil THOMSON, to words by Gertrude Stein (before a single note was put on paper, she called it "the greatest American tragic opera"), dealing with the story of the American pioneer of women's suffrage Susan B. Anthony, and introducing such historic figures as Ulysses S. Grant, Daniel Webster and Lillian Russell, as well as Gertrude S. and Virgil T. "to supply comment and interpretation," set to music in an ostentatiously triadic idiom with allusive old American melodic turns ("jamais de banalité, le plus possible de lieux communs," as the composer put it in French), is produced at Columbia University in New York.

12 MAY 1947

At the opening concert of the Third Annual Festival of Contemporary American Music given at Columbia University in New York, the 46-year-old Russian-American composer Nicolai BEREZOWSKY conducts the first performance of his oratorio *Gilgamesh*, relating the proud chronicle of King Gilgamesh of Babylon who in 1750 B.C. refused to submit to a Sumerian tyrant, set to music in an effective blend of archaic and modern devices.

13 MAY 1947

The Seasons, ballet by the 34-year-old American musical experimentalist John CAGE, reflecting the traditional view of the seasons of the year as quiescence (winter), creation (spring), preservation (summer) and decay (autumn), with thematic components arranged serially in single tones, intervals and chords, is performed for the first time in New York.

27 MAY 1947

Fifth Symphony by Bohuslav MARTINU, in three movements—(1) *Adagio-Allegro-Adagio-Allegro-Adagio*, shimmeringly dissonant and bitonal, set in nervously asymmetrical rhythms; (2) *Larghetto*, a study in serenely nostalgic modalities; (3) *Lento*, a Moravian dumka—is performed for the first time in Prague under the direction of Rafael Kubelík.

28 MAY 1947

Larry ADLER, American virtuoso performer on the oral harmonica, gives the world première in Paris of the *Suite for Harmonica and Orchestra* by Darius MILHAUD, in three dance-like movements: *Gigues, Sailors Song, Hornpipes.* (The *Suite* was originally performed in Philadelphia on 16 November 1945, in a version for violin and orchestra, by Zino Francescati with the Philadelphia Orchestra, Eugene Ormandy conducting.)

29 MAY 1947

The 21st Festival of the International Society for Contemporary Music opens in Copenhagen with the following program of symphonic music:

Fifth Symphony by the 37-year-old Danish composer Vagn HOLMBOE; *Variations symphoniques* by the 53-year-old Belgian composer Jean ABSIL, conceived monothematically, in three parts with 12 variations; *Concerto for String Orchestra* by Sweden's most prolific composer Hilding ROSENBERG; *De Profundis* for chorus and orchestra by the Slovak composer Vítězslav NOVÁK (first performed in Brno on 20 November 1941 as a mute litany of Czechoslovakia under the Nazi domination); and *Galdreslätten*, symphonic dance by the Norwegian nationalistic modernist Harald SAEVERUD, inspired by a perdurable childhood memory of his great-grandfather who was a village fiddler and maker of fiddles.

31 MAY 1947

At the second concert of the 21st Festival of the International Society for Contemporary Music in Copenhagen, the following program of chamber music is given:

Second String Quartet in one movement by the neo-classical Swiss composer Willy BURKHARD; *Toccata* for two pianos by the 23-year-old Austrian composer Anton HEILLER; *Trio* for two violins and viola by György KÓSA of Hungary; *Piano Sonata* by Jan KAPR of Czechoslovakia, written in an atonally inflected neo-classical idiom; and *Sextet* for wind instruments and piano by Herman KOPPEL of Denmark.

1 JUNE 1947

At the third concert of the 21st Festival of the International Society for Contemporary Music in Copenhagen, the following program of chamber music is presented:

Trio for string instruments by the 30-year-old Swedish composer Karl-Birger BLOMDAHL; *Piano Sonata* by Aaron COPLAND, a meticulously calculated study in thematic patterns and percussively pianistic sonorities, in three movements of austerely passionate music (first performed in Buenos Aires on 21 October 1941); *Second Violin Sonata* by Sergei PROKOFIEV, written in a characteristic, ironically lyrical vein (in a postcard of 3 February 1948, addressed to the *Musical Digest* of Chicago, George Bernard Shaw describes this Sonata as "a humorous masterpiece of authentic violin music," unaware of the fact that Prokofiev originally composed it for flute and piano, later arranging it for violin); *Partita* for piano by the 27-year-old Dane Niels Viggo BENTZON, couched in a peculiarly Hindemithish neo-classical idiom; and *Second String Quartet* by the 41-year-old English composer Benjamin FRANKEL.

2 JUNE 1947

At the fourth concert of the 21st Festival of the International Society for Contemporary Music in Copenhagen, the following program of instrumental music is given:

Serenades for piano and chamber orchestra by David van de WOESTYNE of Belgium; *Concerto* for clarinet and strings by the modernistic 40-year-old neo-Elizabethan Elizabeth MACONCHY of England; *Duae fugae novem compositae sonis quattuor sine nomine vocibus* by Adone ZECCHI of Italy, based on a 9-note subject and scored for four anonymous instrumental or vocal parts; *Sonetto di Michelangelo* for chamber orchestra by the Norwegian modernist Fartein VALEN; *Concerto* for bassoon and orchestra by Michal SPISAK of Poland; and *Préludes joyeux* by Camille SCHMIT of Belgium.

2 JUNE 1947

Herman DAREWSKI, Russian-born pianist, inventor of Kiddie Music Notation, in which the notes of the scale are designated by animal names, who used this method as music instructor of Princess Elizabeth, later Queen Elizabeth II of England, dies in London at the age of 64.

3 JUNE 1947

At the fifth concert of the 21st Festival of the International Society for Contemporary Music in Copenhagen the following program of chamber music is presented:

Arcana Musae Dona by the 35-year-old Dutch composer Rudolf ESCHER, combining urbane impressionism with conscious neo-medieval modalities; *Trio* for oboe, clarinet and bassoon by Klement SLAVICKÝ of Czechoslovakia; *Second String Quartet* by Ernest BLOCH, marked by passionate expressiveness with modernistically acerbic departures from tonality; *Piano Sonata* by André JOLIVET, 41-year-old representative of the group "a jeune France"; and three sacred choruses, *Cade la sera, Ululate* and *Recordare Domine* by the Italian master of neoecclesiastic modern music Ildebrando PIZZETTI.

3 JUNE 1947

Les Mamelles de Tirésias, opéra bouffe in two acts by the 48-year-old French modernist Francis POULENC, after the surrealist play by Guillaume Apollinaire, wherein a lady's *mamelles* are detached and float away in the form of inflated mammary balloons, exploding when ignited, which induces her to assume a male identity under the name of Tirésias, whereupon her outraged husband retaliates by effecting a transsexual change of his own, leading to such embroilment in a series of incongruous peripeteia that both decide to resume their original sexual denominations and functions to the strains of a "metamorphosis waltz" and address a fervent plea to the audience to multiply freely for the glory of France ("Faites des enfants . . ."), announcing proudly that in his female avatar, the husband produced from his womb fully 40,000 offspring, is performed for the first time at the Opéra-Comique in Paris. (Date from the announcement in *Le Figaro*, Paris, of the date of the première, 3 June 1947; the date of the répétition générale, 31 May 1947, is given in some reference works as the première.)

4 JUNE 1947

At the sixth and last concert of the 21st Festival of the International Society for Contemporary Music in Copenhagen the following program is presented:

Sinfonia breve, in five neo-classical movements by the 56-year-old Swedish composer Gösta NYSTROEM; *Spoon River Anthology*, oratorio for soloists, chorus and orchestra by Gino

NEGRI of Italy, to the text from the American modern classic by Edgar Lee MASTERS; *Petite Symphonie Concertante* for harp, harpsichord, piano and two string orchestras by the 56-year-old Swiss composer Frank MARTIN (first performed in Zürich on 17 May 1946); and a symphonic suite from the ballet *Don Quixote* by Roberto GERHARD, Catalan expatriate modernist now living in London.

8 JUNE 1947

Fourth Symphony by the Austrian composer Max BUTTING is performed for the first time in Berlin.

12 JUNE 1947

Nina MAKAROVA, wife of Aram Khachaturian, and composeress in her own right, conducts in Moscow the first performance of her optimistically feminine *First Symphony*.

15 JUNE 1947

Die Bernauerin, folk opera in two parts and seven scenes by the German composer Carl ORFF, dedicated to the memory of Kurt Huber, German ethno-musicologist executed by the Nazis on 13 July 1943, to a libretto revolving around the Bavarian duchess of low birth, Agnes Bernauer, known as die Bernauerin, who was set upon and drowned by her tyrannical father-in-law in 1435, set to music of maundering monodies, scored for a stringless orchestra floating despondently in a pond of quintal homophony (the bass voices are programmed to sing la-la-la on a single note 75 times), is produced in Stuttgart.

20 JUNE 1947

Benjamin BRITTEN conducts at the Glyndebourne Festival in England the first performance of his fourth opera *Albert Herring* in three acts, to a libretto after Guy de Maupassant's story *Le Rosier de Madame Husson*, with its locale transferred to an English town, wherein a shy and over-chaste citizen named Albert Herring is crowned as May King as the sole virginal person in the area, but is declassified when he undergoes a scandalous deterioration in his character after drinking an alcoholic potion (a *Tristan* chord is sounded in the orchestra at this point) under the impression that it was lemonade.

20 JUNE 1947

LEMONADE OPERA, a cooperative enterprise, so named after the beverage served during theater intermissions, opens in New York its first and last season with a tepid production of Mozart's *Don Giovanni*.

25 JUNE 1947

Symphony No.5 1/2 by the Democritically cachinnigenous Missourian Don GILLIS, so named because it was written between his 5th and 6th symphonies, subtitled *Symphony for Fun*, in four movements, *Perpetual Emotion*, *Spiritual Scherzophrenia* and *Conclusion*, is performed for the first time by the Boston Pops Orchestra, Arthur Fiedler conducting.

2 JULY 1947

In the Denazification Court in Bayreuth, Winifred WAGNER, widow of Wagner's son Siegfried, is declared guilty of willing participation in the criminal actions of Hitler's Third Reich. (60% of her personal property, including shares in the Bayreuth Festival Company, was ordered to be confiscated, but the ruling was rescinded in March 1949 by the Bavarian Bureau for Political Exoneration.)

9 JULY 1947

Two hundred years have passed since the death in Vienna, in abject poverty, of Giovanni BONONCINI, the Italian rival of Handel for operatic supremacy in London, who was exalted in a contemporary jingle, "Some say, compared to Bononcini/That Mein Herr Handel's but a ninny."

6 AUGUST 1947

Heitor VILLA-LOBOS conducts in Rome the first performance of his orchestral *Bachianas Brasileiras No. 8*, in four movements combining the baroque techniques of Bach with the native melorhythms of Brazil, *Preludio*, *Aria* (*Modinha*), *Toccata* (*Catira Batida*) and *Fuga*.

6 AUGUST 1947

Dantons Tod, opera in two acts by the 29-year-old Swiss-born Austrian composer Gottfried von EINEM, to a libretto by the Manchurian-born half-Estonian, half-German composer Boris Blacher, after a play by the short-lived German romanticist Georg Büchner (1813–1837), expressive of human futility and individual ineluctability during major historical upheavals, such as the French Revolution, with a score of two-dimensional monody in opaquely discordant harmonies and statically coalescent polyphony, marking Danton's death on the guillotine by impassive choral commentary, and concluding with a philosophical stroke of a tam-tam, is produced in Salzburg. (Waggish tongues commented, with reference to the eclectic nature of the music, "Nicht von Einem sondern von vielen.")

20 AUGUST 1947

Song of The Antipodes, symphonic poem by the 31-year-old New Zealand composer Douglas LILBURN, is performed for the first time in Wellington, New Zealand.

22 AUGUST 1947

The Free Wind, operetta by the Soviet composer Isaak DUNAYEVSKY dealing with an Italian anti-Fascist resistance member during World War II, who is persecuted again, after Allied victory, by the American occupation army in Italy as a Communist, with a happy ending as he joins his proletarian girl companion, is produced in Moscow.

27 AUGUST 1947

Heimferd, opera by the Norwegian composer Ludvig Irgens JENSEN, is produced in Oslo.

20 SEPTEMBER 1947

El Salvador issues a commemorative stamp of 12 centavos to honor Felipe SOTO, native bandleader who composed the music of the Salvadorean national anthem.

28 SEPTEMBER 1947

Great Friendship, opera in four acts by the Georgian composer Vano MURADELI, depicting in luxuriantly orientalistic tones the turmoil of the Civil War in North Caucasus in 1919, is produced in Stalino (Donetz).

(It was produced under the title *Friendship of Peoples* in Perm on 24 October 1947, and under the original title in Leningrad on 5 November 1947; and on 7 November 1947, on the 30th anniversary of the Soviet Revolution, simultaneously in Moscow, Gorky, Novosibirsk and Saratov. These productions led to the denunciation of the opera for the erroneous interpretation of the role of Caucasian ethnic groups, for the modernistically simplicistic musical characterizations and the fallaciously formalistic technical treatment. See complete text of the denunciation in the section LETTERS AND DOCUMENTS.)

9 OCTOBER 1947

High Button Shoes, musical comedy by Jule STYNE, dealing with a couple of imaginative crooks in the pacific world of 1913, containing a song *Papa, Won't You Dance with Me?*, is produced in New York City.

10 OCTOBER 1947

Allegro, a musical play by Richard RODGERS with book and lyrics by Oscar HAMMERSTEIN II, dealing with a small-town doctor who rises to social eminence in Chicago, but becomes disillusioned and returns to his point of origin and humble but honest practice, containing the popular number *The Gentleman Is a Dope*, and including extended excursions into the domain of grand opera in ensembles written for chorus, soloists and orchestra, is produced in New York.

10 OCTOBER 1947

Sixth Symphony by Sergei PROKOFIEV, set in the explicitly designated and symphonically rare key of E-flat minor, in three movements—(1) *Allegro moderato*, lyrically austere but propulsively energetic; (2) *Largo*, a songfully bright and harmoniously contemplative elegy; (3) *Vivace*, cyclically reminiscent of the first movement, precipitating into a cataract of major keys—is performed for the first time in Leningrad. (The first Moscow performance, on 25 December 1947, is erroneously listed as the absolute first hearing in the Third Edition of *Music Since 1900*.)

13 OCTOBER 1947

Fourth Symphony by the Dutch composer Henk BADINGS is performed for the first time in Rotterdam.

20 OCTOBER 1947

Thomas K. SCHERMAN inaugurates in New York a series of concerts of the Little Orchestra Society, founded and conducted by him, with the aim of providing a convenient outlet for contemporary composers and opaque luminaries of the Baroque past, presenting during its first season the première of music for *Romeo and Juliet* by David DIAMOND; a brisk neo-classical *Concerto* for harp and orchestra by Norman DELLO JOIO; *farm journal*, a suite by the smiling philosopher of American music Douglas MOORE, which includes such pastoral symphonic tableaux as *Up Early, Sunday Clothes, Lamplight* and *Harvest Song;* and sundry pieces by Georges ENESCO, Ferruccio BUSONI and others.

21 OCTOBER 1947

First Symphony by the 32-year-old American composer Vincent PERSICHETTI, in one movement, written in 1942, and set in a humanistically deployed neoclassical idiom with discreetly discrete dissonances and emanations of chromatic vapors liberated by diatonic vesicles in nutritious polytriadic harmonies, is performed for the first time in Rochester, New York, under the direction of Howard Hanson.

24 OCTOBER 1947

Short Symphony by Henry COWELL, his fourth, in four movements—(1) *Hymn*, (2) *Ballad*, (3) *Dance*, (4) *Fuguing Tune*—oriented towards American melodic and rhythmic materials and concluding with a stylization of fuguing tunes developed from the shaped-note style of *Southern Harmony* (1854), is performed for the first time by the Boston Symphony Orchestra, Richard Burgin conducting.

24 OCTOBER 1947

Seventh Symphony by the 50-year-old Polish-born Parisian composer Alexandre TANSMAN, in four linked movements, opening with a slow meditative introduction, followed by an energetic main portion, and, after an *Andante cantabile* connecting with a scherzo, ending cyclically with a reversion to the initial movement, is performed for the first time by the St. Louis Symphony Orchestra, Vladimir Golschmann conducting.

25 OCTOBER 1947

Genoveva, opera in three acts by the Swedish composer Natanael BERG, to the Germanic legend (previously used by Schumann for his identically named opera) of a crusader's immaculately chaste bride monstrously charged with inconceivable adultery by a scheming henchman coveting her with licentious lust, aided and abetted by a diabolical magus who conjures up lascivious visual tableaux calculated to incense his lecherous fantasies, with virtue triumphant at the end and the collusive villains foiled, set to music in constantly tumescent Straussian harmonies, is produced in Stockholm.

29 OCTOBER 1947

Beautiful Season, symphonic poem by the Japanese composer Hisaharu WATANABE, is performed for the first time in Tokyo.

30 OCTOBER 1947

Third Symphony by Darius MILHAUD, subtitled *Hymnus Ambrosianus*, in four movements, concluding with a *Te Deum*, is performed for the first time in Paris. (Although *Te Deum* is commonly ascribed to St. Ambrose, and is often called Ambrosian Hymn, it was probably the work of the Bishop of Remesiana; Milhaud followed the general assumption in subtitling his symphony *Ambrosianus*.)

30 OCTOBER 1947

First Symphony by the 38-year-old American composer Elie SIEGMEISTER, in four movements, *Andante, Vivace brioso, Moderato cantibile, Maestoso,* expressive of "the Spirit, the struggle and the hope of man," permeated by the American melos without actual quotations from folk tunes, is performed for the first time by the New York Philharmonic, Leopold Stokowski conducting.

31 OCTOBER 1947

Toccata for Percussion Instruments by Carlos CHÁVEZ, in three movements: *Allegro* for drums only; *Largo* for metallic instruments and a xylophone; and *Allegro un poco marziale* for small drums, maracas, claves and glockenspiel, is performed for the first time in Mexico City.

3 NOVEMBER 1947

Fifth Symphony by Gian Francesco MALIPIERO (completed on 25 September 1947), subtitled *Concertante, in eco* (with reference to two conspicuous piano parts echoing each other and "dominating the music like a dual spinal column of the instrumental organism"), without a key signature, but with clear tonal intent, in four sections, *Allegro agitato* (in traditional sonata form), *Lento* (projecting a series of bell-like chords in the piano parts), *Allegro vivace* (opening with a consortium of drumlets accompanied by a triangle) and *Lento ma non troppo* (ending in an evanescently pandiatonic chord), is performed for the first time by the orchestra of the British Broadcasting Corporation in London.

7 NOVEMBER 1947

The Young Guard, opera in four acts by the Ukrainian composer Yuli MEITUS, depicting in epic Russian modalities the heroic resistance against the brutal Nazi occupation by a group of young boys and girls in a mining locality in the Don basin in 1943, who perish with the name of Stalin on their lips as the red dawn heralds liberation, is produced in the Ukrainian language in Kiev, on the 30th anniversary of the Soviet Revolution.

8 NOVEMBER 1947

The first Estonian ballet, *Kalevipoeg,* by the Estonian composer Eugen KAPP, to a scenario derived from the medieval Estonian tale of a peasant girl abducted by a demon who in turn is destroyed by a benevolent Estonian god, while the girl is transformed into a stone image, is performed for the first time in Tallin.

9 NOVEMBER 1947

Les Douze, cantata by Alexander TCHEREPNIN, for narrator, strings, harp, piano and percussion, to the text of the religiously revolutionary ballad by the Russian poet Alexandre Blok, in which twelve Red Army Guards are likened to the Twelve Apostles led by Jesus Christ, is performed for the first time in Paris.

9 NOVEMBER 1947

During the radio festival of Slavic music in Cracow, Andrzej PANUFNIK, 33-year-old Polish composer, con-

ducts the first performance of his *Berceuse,* scored for 29 string instruments and two harps, and making use of icositetraphonic harmonies in quarter-tones.

17 NOVEMBER 1947

Cosmogonie, symphonic prelude by André JOLIVET, is performed for the first time, nine years after it was composed, by the Paris Radio Orchestra.

20 NOVEMBER 1947

Mediator Dei, encyclical letter by Pope PIUS XII, is issued at the Vatican, promulgating a new and more liberal view (as compared with *Motu Proprio* of 1903) regarding the use of secular music in Catholic liturgy and allowing the inclusion in church services of "modern music and singing . . . if such is not profane and does not spring from a desire of achieving extraordinary and unusual effects," while reaffirming the supremacy of the Gregorian chant, "which the Roman Catholic Church considers her own as handed down from antiquity and kept under her close tutelage," and further urging "that the faithful take part in the sacred ceremonies, alternating their voices with the priest and the choir, according to the prescribed norms" (Full text is given in the section Letters and Documents.)

21 NOVEMBER 1947

Third Symphony by the 32-year-old American composer Vincent PERSICHETTI, in four movements bearing subtitles expressive of mood and tempo—(1) *Somber,* built on two dotted-note figures and ending on a 12-tone chord; (2) *Spirited,* in a dancing mode; (3) *Singing,* centered on a sustained melody in the English horn; (4) *Fast and Brilliant,* an exuberant exposition of varied themes, concluding with a chorale—is performed for the first time by the Philadelphia Orchestra, Eugene Ormandy conducting.

25 NOVEMBER 1947

A waterproof Irish harp, manufactured by Melville CLARK of Syracuse, New York, strung with pre-shrunk nylon strings, is given its first public demonstration in New York by a mermaid-shaped harpist enclosed in a glass tank filled with water, in a fluvially fluent demonstration of marine arpeggios, underwater glissandos and aquatic passages of enharmonic liquidity.

27 NOVEMBER 1947

Fourth Symphony by Ernst KRENEK, in three movements, the inner meaning of which is the materialization of an ideal detached from reality and the victory of that ideal over the menace of disruptive forces, written in the 12-tone technique to secure a "very high amount of logical coherence and intelligible significance," within the framework of classical divisions, the first movement following a sonata-allegro form, the second, an *Adagio,* being a dual variation and the last, a triune *Allegro* constituting an abstract rondo, is performed for the first time by the New York Philharmonic, Dimitri Mitropoulos conducting.

27 NOVEMBER 1947

Variation for Orchestra on a Theme by Paganini, a set of 16 variations by the 44-year-old Manchurian-born Russian-bred, genetically Estonian-German composer Boris BLACHER, using the same theme as the famous variations of Brahms and Rachmaninoff, each variation posing a distinct structural problem in which the melorhythmic parameters are arranged in different arithmetical proportions, with the exploitation of sophisticated crudity to dispel the illusion of euphony, is performed for the first time in Leipzig.

29 NOVEMBER 1947

The Legend of Ohrid, ballet in four acts by the 62-year-old Serbian composer Stevan HRISTIĆ, depicting the abduction of a Serbian bride by Turkish janissaries for the Sultan's harem and her liberation as she is magically transformed into a turtle dove, with a colorful score making use of asymmetrical Balkan melorhythms, is performed for the first time in Belgrade, under the composer's direction.

30 NOVEMBER 1947

On the day of the official proclamation at the United Nations of the independence of Israel, Avner CARMI, a Jewish piano technician, completes his repair work on the so-called Siena Piano, the sounding board of which, according to legend, contained wood from King David's harp (thus fulfilling the prophecy that Israel would be reborn when David's harp is sounded again in the land), which became part of the two pillars, known as Joachim and Boaz, of King Solomon's Temple, was carried away from Jerusalem by Roman soldiers after the destruction of the Temple in 70 A.D., subsequently used as material for a Roman Caesarian sanctuary, and after its destruction by an earthquake eventually found its way to Italy and was embedded in the Siena Piano constructed in the 18th century.

1 DECEMBER 1947

The Spanish Government issues a series of postage stamps at 15, 20, 25, and 80 centavos, honoring Manuel DE FALLA, great Spanish composer who died in Argentina in exile on 14 November 1946.

3 DECEMBER 1947

Ernst von DOHNÁNYI, Nestor of Hungarian composers, plays in Sheffield, England, the piano part in the first performance of his *Second Piano Concerto* in B minor, with Thomas Beecham conducting the orchestra.

4 DECEMBER 1947

Song of the Dead Proletarians, cantata by the 36-year-old Slovenian composer Ivan RUPNIK, glorifying in sonorous triadic modalities the heroism of Yugoslav partisans during the Nazi occupation, is performed for the first time in Belgrade, conducted by the composer.

11 DECEMBER 1947

Trilogy by the 50-year-old American composer Leroy ROBERTSON, a symphonic poem inspired by the ambience of the high plateaus of his native Utah where he tended sheep as a youth, and written in an effective abecedarian idiom, vitalized by some realistic onomatopoeia, such as the sound of male tobacco expectorations into brass spittoons, winner of the $25,000 prize for the best symphonic work by an American composer donated by the chemical magnate Henry Reichhold (Robertson submitted his score under the nom de plume Nostrebor, i.e., Robertson spelled backwards), is performed for the first time by the Detroit Symphony Orchestra.

14 DECEMBER 1947

Exodus, biblical choreographic poem for baritone solo and orchestra by the 37-year-old Polish-born composer Josef GRÜNTHAL (who later abbreviated his name to Tal), is performed for the first time by the Palestine Symphony Orchestra in Tel Aviv.

15 DECEMBER 1947

Les Mirages, choreographic fairy tale for symphony orchestra by the 46-year-old French composer Henri SAUGUET, to a scenario in which a youth invades the palace of the moon and rouses the ethereal maidens of the night only to find that his mirage of love is the image of death, is produced at the Paris Opéra.

18 DECEMBER 1947

Rosa de Papel, opera by the Portuguese composer Ruy COELHO, is produced in Lisbon.

21 DECEMBER 1947

Saul, opera in five scenes by the German composer Hermann REUTTER, to the biblical story of a tortured superstitious king of the Hebrews, punctuated by Handelian trumpet calls and tinctured by modern Angst, expressed by tumid dissonances and corrosive orientalistic chromatics, is produced in its third version by the Hamburg State Opera. The original work, in one act, was first performed in Baden-Baden on 15 July 1928; the second version was produced in Düsseldorf on 18 November 1928.

29 DECEMBER 1947

Militza, heroic ballet by the Russian composer Boris ASAFIEV, written in 1942 to glorify the name of a Serbian girl guerrilla, leader of the resistance movement against the Nazi occupation troops in Yugoslavia, with the authenticity of the music enhanced by the use of Serbian dance tunes, is performed for the first time in Leningrad.

1948

1 JANUARY 1948

Buduj Vlast, Posíliš mír (Build Your Nation, and You Will Strengthen Peace), cantata by the Czech composer Václav DOBIÁŠ, suffused with patriotically socialistic sentiments in the virile rhythms of Bohemian rustic dances, is performed for the first time in Prague.

9 JANUARY 1948

Third Symphony in E by Walter PISTON, in four movements—(1) *Andantino*, (2) *Allegro*, (3) *Adagio*, (4) *Allegro*—designated respectively as being in Tonality C, Tonality F, Tonality G and Tonality C and constructed on a network of interdependent thematic "phrases" is performed for the first time by the Boston Symphony Orchestra, Serge Koussevitzky conducting.

10 JANUARY 1948

El Mozo que casó con mujer brava, one-act comic opera by the Spanish composer Carlos SURINACH, is produced in Barcelona.

13 JANUARY 1948

The board of trustees of the Chicago Symphony Orchestra peremptorily dismisses its conductor and music director Artur RODZINSKI in the middle of his first season, charging him with "last-minute program changes causing confusion in rehearsals, staging of operatic productions in place of regular concerts, exceeding the budget by $30,000 and attempting to secure a three-year contract."

15 JANUARY 1948

Étude, ballet by the Danish composer Knudaage RIISAGER, with the music based on Czerny's celebrated finger exercises, is performed for the first time in Copenhagen.

21 JANUARY 1948

Ermanno WOLF-FERRARI, Italian opera composer whose *Il Segreto di Susanna* (the secret is Suzanne's shocking indulgence in cigarette smoking) has created a new type of comic *verismo*, dies in Venice at the age of 72.

21 JANUARY 1948

The Austrian Government issues a 20-groschen postage stamp in honor of Karl Michael ZIEHRER (1843–1922), Austrian band leader and composer of a myriad of Viennese waltzes.

23 JANUARY 1948

Fourth Symphony by the 32-year-old American composer David DIAMOND, his "smallest large symphony," in three movements—(1) *Allegretto*, symbolizing a state of uninterrupted sleep; (2) *Andante*, illustrative of the transition from sleep to wakefulness; and (3) *Allegro*, signifying eternal awakening in death—is performed for the first time by the Boston Symphony Orchestra, Leonard Bernstein conducting.

23 JANUARY 1948

Mandu-Carará, symphonic poem by Heitor VILLA-LOBOS, scored for two pianos, percussion, mixed choir and children's chorus, inspired by a Brazilian legend of two resourceful Indian children who, like their European analogues Hänsel and Gretel, kill the malevolent ogress while her ogre husband goes into the jungle in search of two fat monkeys, is performed in a world première in New York.

25 JANUARY 1948

Second Symphony by the 30-year-old American composer Robert WARD, intended to demonstrate the validity of music "in older forms treated in a new way," in three movements, (1) *Fast and energetic*, (2) *Slowly*, (3) *Fast*, is performed for the first time by the National Symphony Orchestra in Washington, Hans Kindler conducting.

30 JANUARY 1948

Symphony for Classical Orchestra by the 27-year-old American composer Harold SHAPERO, premeditatedly cast in the traditional four movements, set in the proclamatory key of B-flat major, the natural tonality of the bugle, and ending in a display of tonic major triads, is performed for the first time by the Boston Symphony Orchestra, Leonard Bernstein conducting.

30 JANUARY 1948

First Symphony in B-flat major by the American composer Henry BRANT, inspired by the jazzy ambience of modern America, in four movements, *Sermon*, *Ballad*, *Skit* and *Procession*, is performed for the first time by the Cincinnati Symphony Orchestra, Thor Johnson conducting.

2 FEBRUARY 1948

Second Symphony by the 50-year-old Palestinian composer paul BEN-HAIM (paul frankenburger) who adopted his Hebraic name after leaving Hitlerized Germany in 1933, in four movements, is performed for the first time by the Palestine Symphony Orchestra in Tel Aviv.

8 FEBRUARY 1948

Symphonie expiatoire by the 46-year-old French composer Henri SAUGUET, written at the end of World War II as an act of expiation of the unconscious guilt in the national apathy and helplessness during the Nazi subjugation of France, in four movements, concluding with a "berceuse des morts," is performed for the first time in Paris.

10 FEBRUARY 1948

The Central Committee of the Communist Party of the Union of Soviet Socialist Republics issues a resolution condemning "decadent formalism" (i.e. formulism, adherence to cerebral formulas in art) in Soviet music, naming SHOSTAKOVICH, PROKOFIEV and KHACHATURIAN as the principal culprits, and MIASKOVSKY and SHEBALIN as conscious inculcators of inharmonious music at the Moscow Conservatory. (Full text in the section Letters and Documents.)

11 FEBRUARY 1948

Fifth Symphony by the German composer Hermann ZILCHER, who died on 1 January 1948, is performed posthumously for the first time in Hamburg.

12 FEBRUARY 1948

Fantasy for trombone and orchestra by the 41-year-old American composer Paul CRESTON, in one continuous movement esthetically articulated in three sections (lively, lyric and fugally agitated), is performed for the first time by the Los Angeles Philharmonic.

20 FEBRUARY 1948

L'Âme heureuse, ballet by the 80-year-old patriarch of French modern music Charles KOECHLIN, is performed for the first time in Paris.

21 FEBRUARY 1948

Mosquito Serenade, an orchestral scherzo by the American composer Arthur KREUTZ, onomatopoeically imitating the enervating buzz of the *Culex pipiens,* is performed for the first time by the New York Philharmonic.

22 FEBRUARY 1948

Le Baccanti, opera in three acts, after Euripides, by the 55-year-old Italian composer Giorgio Federico GHEDINI, is produced at La Scala, Milan.

22 FEBRUARY 1948

Wilhelm FURTWÄNGLER conducts with the Berlin Philharmonic the first performance of his own exuberantly romantic *Second Symphony,* modelled after the German symphonic masterpieces of the 19th century, and set in a formally cohesive and academically competent manner.

24 FEBRUARY 1948

The Seine at Night, symphonic poem by the trans-sequanic Missourian Virgil THOMSON, the "Lutecian Maro" who (as he himself phrased it) "wrote in Paris music that was always, in one way or another, about Kansas City," is performed for the first time by the Kansas City Philharmonic.

25 FEBRUARY 1948

Les Malheurs de Sophie, ballet by the 35-year-old "jeune français" Jean FRANÇAIX, to a scenario after the French children's classic detailing a series of misfortunes that ultimately bring a fortune to a peculiarly susceptible young girl, written in an insouciantly hedonistic manner, is produced at the Paris Opéra.

25 FEBRUARY 1948

Die Nachtschwalbe, "dramatic nocturne" in one act by the 45-year-old Manchurian-born German-Estonian composer Boris BLACHER, to a libretto centered on a company of pimply pimps and putative putains in a small German town, during which the head of the vice squad finds out that one of the "night swallows" is his orphaned daughter, set to music in poignant dissonant harmonies and asymmetrically angular rhythms, is produced in Leipzig.

27 FEBRUARY 1948

Fourth Symphony (In Memoriam) by Gian Francesco MALIPIERO, in four movements, all ending in minor keys, the first, *Allegro moderato,* and the third, *Allegro,* expressive of a timid hope; the second, *Lento funèbre,* lamenting the loss of friends in the war, and the fourth, *Lento,* being a set of six variations on a funereal enfilade of chimes of church bells, written in an idiom in which "the musical dissonance is linear, developed with the spontaneous logic of Italian classicism" is performed for the first time by the Boston Symphony Orchestra, under the direction of Serge Koussevitzky, as a commissioned work written for the Koussevitzky Foundation, and dedicated to the memory of Mrs. Natalie Koussevitzky.

29 FEBRUARY 1948

First Violin Concerto by the 32-year-old American composer David DIAMOND is performed for the first time in Vancouver.

2 MARCH 1948

An orchestral suite of stage music for Ibsen's *Peer Gynt* by the 50-year-old Norwegian composer Harald SAEVERUD, boldly departing from Grieg's sanctified treatment of the same subject, is performed for the first time in Oslo.

4 MARCH 1948

Second Symphony, subtitled *Sinfonia notturna,* by the Swedish composer Hilding HALLNÄS, is performed for the first time in Göteborg.

13 MARCH 1948

Third Symphony by the American composer Harold MORRIS, subtitled *Amaranth,* after a poem of that name by Edwin A. Robinson relating to a perennially blossoming flower, in four movements, expressive of (1) joy and freedom, (2) play and humor, (3) exaltation and (4) triumph, written without key signatures, but centripetally gravitating towards the terminal albification of C major, the alpha and the omega of the work, is performed for the first time in Houston, Texas.

15 MARCH 1948

Czinka Panna, one-act opera by the prime Hungarian composer Zoltán KODÁLY, to the story of a Gypsy girl who inspired Rákóczi's fighting men in the Hungarian struggle against the Austrians in 1703, featuring an originally conceived Magyar-rhythmed *Rákóczi March*, is performed for the first time at the Budapest Opera. (On the same day, Kodály was awarded the newly-instituted Kossuth Prize "for signal services in the arts.")

18 MARCH 1948

Posledni Hejtman (*The Last Captain*), opera by the Czech composer Miroslav KREJČÍ, is produced in Prague.

20 MARCH 1948

Piano Concerto by Boris BLACHER is performed for the first time in Göttingen.

20 MARCH 1948

Five days before his 81st birthday, Arturo TOSCANINI conducts the Symphony Orchestra of the National Broadcasting Company in New York in a program of Wagner's music, televised by a network including Washington, Philadelphia, Schenectady and Buffalo.

(This was to be the first television broadcast of a major symphony orchestra, but it was anticipated by one hour by the Columbia Broadcasting System in a televised concert of the Philadelphia Orchestra, Eugene Ormandy conducting, transmitted from Philadelphia to New York by the newly-laid coaxial cable.)

23 MARCH 1948

Hilding ROSENBERG, prolific Swedish composer of vocal music, conducts in Stockholm the first performance of the last portion of his eight-hour-long oper-oratorio *Joseph and His Brethren*, after Thomas Mann's biblical novel.

26 MARCH 1948

Hanns EISLER, German composer of atonal symphonies and optimistically triadic proletarian songs, who came to the United States in 1933, leaves America as a "voluntary deportee," after the House of Representatives Committee on Un-American Activities, in its campaign directed mainly against Eleanor Roosevelt and other liberals who helped to save Eisler's life by obtaining an American visa for him, uncovers the fact of his brief membership in the German Communist Party in 1926, and thunders that "he has perjured his way in and out of the United Sates at will, going to Soviet Russia and other countries when he pleased." (See extracts from *Hearings Regarding Hanns Eisler* in Letters and Documents.)

I recall reading in a French newspaper in 1933 that Hitler put a price on my head. I was not surprised. But I never dreamed that I would experience the same sort of thing in the United States, a country that I love. (Eisler's statement in Los Angeles upon posting $1,000 bail for himself and $500 for his wife pending a hearing with the Commissioner of Immigration to answer charges of perjury.)

1 APRIL 1948

First Symphony by the 35-year-old Polish composer Witold LUTOSLAWSKI is performed for the first time in Katowice.

2 APRIL 1948

The newly erected State Opera in Ankara, Turkey, is inaugurated with a concert of Turkish music including *Symphony* by Cemal REŞID REY, *Violin Concerto* by Ulvi CEMAL ERKIN, *Ballade* by Necil KAZIM AKSES and a fragment from the opera *Kerem* by Ahmed Adham SAYGUN. (The first complete performance of *Kerem* was given in Ankara on 1 March 1953.)

2 APRIL 1948

Fourth Symphony for strings by the foremost German polyphonist Karl Amadeus HARTMANN, in three movements written in a tense dramatic idiom marked by tremendous melorhythmic peripeteia—(1) *Lento assai, con passione*, (2) *Allegro di molto, risoluto* (3) *Adagio apassionato*, the latter exfoliating in an explicit dodecaphonic statement, and ending in a precipitous dynamic descent, from *fortississississimo* to *pianississimo*—is performed for the first time in Munich.

4 APRIL 1948

Fifth Symphony in one movement by the German composer Max BUTTING is performed for the first time in Berlin.

4 APRIL 1948

Vision dramatique, symphonic movement by the Polish composer Karol RATHAUS, is performed for the first time by the Palestine Symphony Orchestra in Tel Aviv.

4 APRIL 1948

Duett-Concertino for clarinet, bassoon, string orchestra and a harp, by Richard STRAUSS, written by him in Switzerland where he went after the German debacle, and built upon the contrast between the "gay clarinet" and the "sad bassoon," is performed for the first time over the network of the Radio-Swizzera Italiana.

9 APRIL 1948

Knoxville: Summer of 1915 for soprano and orchestra by Samuel BARBER, to the text of the prose poem in the novel *A Death in the Family* by James Agee, bearing the legend: "We are talking now of summer evenings in Knoxville, Tennessee, at the time when I lived there so successfully disguised to myself as a child," metempsychotically conjuring up the simple life of the obsolescent American past in a musical idiom combining elements of folkloric melodiousness with poignant atonalities and realistic details, as in illustrating the electric sparks of a streetcar antenna by pizzicati glissando in the lower strings, is performed for the first time by Eleanor Steber with the Boston Symphony Orchestra, Serge Koussevitzky conducting.

9 APRIL 1948

Saga of the Mississippi, tone poem by the 48-year-old American composer Haft MCDONALD, in two parts, *Prehistoric Mississippi* and *Father of Waters*, is performed for the first time by the Philadelphia Orchestra, Eugene Ormandy conducting.

15 APRIL 1948

Pierre SCHAEFFER, French radio engineer, conjures up the concept of *Musique Concrète*, a phono-montage of recordings of random sounds, including speech, heterogeneous noises and bits of music.

Pour la musique classique un *do* est un *do* quelle que soit sa situation dans sa tessiture. Pour la musique concrète, un *son* est un *son* (qu'il soit put ou complexe) et il est inséparable de sa situation dans le spectre sonore.

MUSIQUE HABITUELLE (dite *abstraite*)	MUSIQUE NOUVELLE (dite *concrète*)
Phase I. Conception (*mentale*)	Phase I. Composition (*matérielle*)
Phase II. Expression *chiffrée*	Phase II. Esquisses (*experimentation*)
Phase III. Exécution (*fabrication*)	Phase III. Matériaux (*instrumentale*)
(de l'abstrait au concret)	(du concret à 'abstrait)

(*Introduction a la Musique Concrète* by Pierre Schaeffer, *Polyphonie*, Paris, 1950)

21 APRIL 1948

Sixth Symphony by the 75-year-old dean of British composers ralph VAUGHAN WILLIAMS, in four movements, interconnected so that "each of the first three has its tail attached to the head of its neighbor"—(1) *Allegro*, (2) *Moderato*, (3) *Scherzo*, (4) *Epilogue*—opulently magniloquent in its triadic sonorities, revitalized by energetic syncopation and tonally subordinated to tbe commanding unity of the key of E minor despite numerous excursions into the penumbra of atonality (the fugue in the scherzo is built on a series of disjunct tritones), is performed for the first time by the Royal Philharmonic in London, Sir Adrian Boult conducting.

22 APRIL 1948

Morton GOULD conducts in New York the first performance of his ballet *Fall River Legend* after the celebrated Lizzie Borden parricide case ("Lizzie Borden took an axe and gave her mother forty whacks; when she saw what she had done, she gave her father forty-one"), with thematic materials ranging from New England hymnody to stylized social dances and balladry. (A symphonic suite from the ballet was performed for the first time on 6 January, 1949 by the San Francisco Symphony, under the direction of Pierre Monteux.)

23 APRIL 1948

Concerto for Ondes Martenot and Orchestra by the 42-year-old French composer André JOLIVET, scored for large orchestra with a substantial percussion section, in three movements, *Allegro moderato*, *Allegro vivace* and *Largo Cantabile*, with an extended cadenza for the Ondes Martenot, is performed for the first time anywhere in Vienna.

24 APRIL 1948

Manuel PONCE, pioneer of Mexican modern music, composer of ephemeral symphonic works imbued with the spirit of *Mexicanismo*, whose song *Estrellita* achieved universal popularity (he never collected royalties on it owing to a faulty copyright registration), dies in Mexico City at the age of sixty-five.

(Ponce gave his date of birth as 8 December 1886, but he was in fact born at 11:45 P.M. on 8 December 1882, and baptized on 12 December 1882, as proved by Jesús Romero in his solidly documented calendar of Ponce's life, *Efemérides de Mauel M. Ponce* in the periodical *Nuestra Música*, Mexico City, No. 2, 1950.)

24 APRIL 1948

Momtchil, opera in three acts by the 43-year-old Bulgarian composer Lubomir PIPKOV, to a libretto dealing with a 14th-century rebellion of Balkan peasants against their feudal oppressors, romanticized by the gratuitous episode of a requited passion of the rebel leader for the overlord's virginal daughter, written in an emphatic national idiom making artful use of Balkan asymmetrical dance rhythms, is produced in Sofia.

24 APRIL 1948

Joseph WIHTOL (or, in Latvian, Vitols), foremost Latvian composer, who taught at the St. Petersburg Conservatory (among his pupils were Prokofiev and Miaskovsky), went after the Russian Revolution to Riga, where he established a Latvian Conservatory, and fled Riga for Germany at the approach of the Soviet Armies in 1944, dies in Lübeck at the age of 84.

25 APRIL 1948

Wonsik LIM conducts the Korean Symphony Orchestra in Seoul in the first performance of his *Korean Dance Fantasy*.

28 APRIL 1948

Orpheus, choreographic poem by Igor STRAVINSKY, cast in a Hellenistic idiom of static monody ornamented by melodious mannerisms of the baroque era and irrigated by warm streams of Tchaikovskian sentiment with a somberly inharmonious G sharp protruding in the bass through an A-minor triad in the opaque peroration, culminating in an overwhelming vesuviation of the Bacchantes as they set upon Orpheus to tear him apart in their nymphomaniacal fury, is performed for the first time in New York.

30 APRIL 1948

Inside U.S.A., a revue by Arthur SCHWARTZ, a wildly whimsical musical show in which a Broadway mermaid is melodically wooed by Chopin, Liszt and Tchaikovsky, who lavish their famous tunes on her, is produced in New York.

4 MAY 1948

Fourth Symphony in four movements by the American composer Bernard ROGERS, written in 1945 "to trace a line leading from darkness and despair to affirmation," is performed for the first time by the Rochester Philharmonic Orchestra, Howard Hanson conducting.

5 MAY 1948

At thc opening of the Fourth Annual Festival of Contemporary Music at Columbia University, New York, Otto LUENING conducts the belated world première of his three-act opera *Evangeline*, written 16 years previously after Longfellow's celebrated poem, embodying in the score a variety of thematic elements pertaining to the life in early New England, including church anthems and Indian war cries.

7 MAY 1948

Gli Incantenati, one-act opera, with three characters, by the 61-year-old Italian composer Renzo BIANCHI, to his own libretto, is performed for the first time at La Scala, Milan.

9 MAY 1948

The Experimental Theater in New York presents the first performance of *Ballet Ballads*, a novel synthetic art show, with lyrics by John LATOUCHE and music by Jerome MOROSS, esemplastically fusing instruments and voices, dance and lighting effects, into a recognizably Americanoid product, in three tableaux:

(1) *Susanna and the Elders*, a folkloristic fresco exposing under a biblical guise the lechery and treachery in the deep South; (2) *Willie the Weeper* "12-tone Willie with his sexy sax" dreaming terpsichorean marijuana dreams; (3) *The Eccentricities of Davy Crockett*, a musical portrait of the popular American hero who fishes a mercurial mermaid out of the Tennessee River, catches Halley's Comet by the tail, goes to Congress, and returns to Texas to suffer martyrdom in the Alamo massacre.

9 MAY 1948

Jugoslovenska partizanska rapsodija (*Yugoslav Partisan Rhapsody*), cantata on Yugoslav guerrilla songs by the Yugoslav composer Jovan BANDUR (1899–1956), is performed for the first time in Belgrade, on the same program with his *Poem 1941* for bass solo, chorus and orchestra, lamenting the massacre of patriotic schoolboys by the Nazis in occupied Serbia in 1941.

12 MAY 1948

La Roi de Camargue, opera by the 72-year-old French composer Jean POUEIGH, is performed for the first time in Marseilles.

13 MAY 1948

The Hospital, musico-medical suite for orchestra by Dr. Herman M. PARRIS of Philadelphia, portraying a young woman's appendectomy in ten prophylactic vivisections, introducing a smiling nurse (*Allegro e amabile*), anxious intensive care (*Andantino*), the operating room (*Allegro*, realistically followed by *Molto agitato*) and anesthesia (*Presto*), set to music in an impartially bland idiom, imitative of Handel, Tchaikovsky and Gershwin, is performed for the first time by the Doctors' Orchestral Society in New York.

16 MAY 1948

Third Symphony by the progressive American composer Wallingford RIEGGER, in four movements, *Moderato*, *Andante affettuoso*, *Moderato*, *Passacaglia and Fugue*, employing modified dodecaphonic techniques, each movement containing a fugal development, and ending with a resonant array of thematic forces, is performed for the first time by the Columbia Broadcasting System Symphony Orchestra in New York, Dean Dixon conduct-

ing, on the same program with the first performance of *Concerto* for viola and orchestra, in four movements, by Quincy PORTER.

20 MAY 1948

Darius MILHAUD conducts in Paris the first performance of his *Fourth Symphony*, subtitled *1848*, in four movements marked *Insurrection, To the Dead of the Republic, The Peaceful Joys of Liberty Regained* and *Commemoration 1948*, commissioned by the French government to commemorate the 1848 revolution against King Louis Philippe, making use of fragments of French revolutionary songs and marches of the time, with the notation at the end of the score reflecting Milhaud's geographical mobility: "Pacific Ocean, Atlantic Ocean, August–September, 1947; orchestrated at Genval and Aix-en-Provence, October–December, 1947."

20 MAY 1948

Les Demoiselles de la nuit, dramatic ballet in three scenes by Jean FRANÇAIX, a fantasy about a female cat which for one *nuit d'amour* becomes a human girl, but, disgusted by the physical crudity of men's love, goes back to prowl on rooftops with her pliable feline companions, is produced in Paris.

24 MAY 1948

Benjamin BRITTEN conducts in Cambridge, England, the first performance of his modernized version of John Gay's *Beggar's Opera*, with the 200-year-old tunes of its first harmonizer, the Prussian musician Johann Christoph Pepusch, pepped up and contrapuntally rejuvenated.

28 MAY 1948

First Symphony by the 35-year-old Polish composeress Grazyna BACEWICZ is performed for the first time in Cracow.

29 MAY 1948

The Second International Congress of Composers and Musicologists, assembled in Prague, issues a declaration of aims of contemporary composers of the Socialist bloc and its sympathizers, urging the adoption of a program of conciliation and coordination of creative effort in the art of music, aiming at its accessibility to the masses. (Complete text in the section Letters and Documents.)

2 JUNE 1948

Le Carrosse du Saint Sacrement, one-act lyric comedy by Henri BÜSSER, is produced at the Opera-Comique in Paris.

5 JUNE 1948

Saint Nicholas, cantata by Benjamin BRITTEN (completed on 31 May 1948), scored for tenor solo, mixed chorus, two pianos, strings, percussion and organ, in nine movements, to the text by Eric Crozier, traversing in devotional but urbane tones, not devoid of secular gaiety, the career of the Saint, his birth, his dedication, his pilgrimages, his bishopric, his imprisonment, the miraculous resuscitation of the butchered "pickled" boys, his piety, his death and his sainthood in glorious D major, making artful use of old English tunes to create an atmosphere of familiarity and intimacy, is performed for the first time in the course of the Aldeburgh Music Festival. (The cantata was written for the Centenary celebration of Lancing College, Sussex, where it was performed on 24 July 1948, but the absolute priority of the world première was pre-empted in Aldeburgh.)

5 JUNE 1948

The 22nd Festival of the International Society for Contemporary Music opens in Amsterdam with the following program of symphonic music:

Concerto for Orchestra by Raymond CHEVREUILLE of Belgium, in four movements, written in a neo-baroque idiom with sporadic atonal discursions; *Second Violin Concerto* by the Dutch composer Sem DRESDEN; and *Fifth Symphony*, subtitled *Concertante, in eco,* by Gian Francesco MALIPIERO, in four movements set in an emotionally romanticized Vivaldian style, first performed in London on 3 November 1947. (*Second Symphony* by Miloslav KABELÁČ of Czechoslovakia was programmed but not performed.)

6 JUNE 1948

In the course of the 22nd Festival of the International Society for Contemporary Music in Amsterdam two works by Hendrik ANDRIESSEN of Holland are presented: *Christus Rex* for double choir and organ and the first part of a *Sinfonia* for organ solo.

6 JUNE 1948

Abraxas, ballet by Werner EGK, to a scenario derived from a pre-Goethean representation of Faust as a magus in possession of the abracadabramorphic charm abraxas, receives its first stage performance in Munich. (A concert performance was first given on the Baden-Baden radio on 7 December 1947.)

7 JUNE 1948

At the 22nd Festival of the International Society for Contemporary Music in Amsterdam the following program of orchestral music by modern Dutch composers is presented:

Little Suite on the notes E–F by Willem LANDRÉ (1874–1948), written in a tensely chromatic idiom and first performed in Rotterdam on 11 June 1943; *Sinfonia Sacra In Memoriam Patris* by Willem Landré's son Guillaume LANDRÉ, composed as a tribute of filial devotion shortly after the elder Landré's death on 1 January 1948; *Sinfonia piccola* by Léon ORTHEL, cast in an energetically polyrhythmic idiom, in six interconnected sections, first performed in Rotterdam on 31 October 1941; *Six Symphonic Epigrams* by Willem PIJPER (1894–1947), a set of variations on a 16th-century Dutch song; and *Symphonic Variations* by Henk BADINGS, set in a modernistic neoclassical idiom of melorhythmically angular intervallic facture. (Daniel RUYNEMAN's *Amphitryon Overture* was programmed but not performed.)

8 JUNE 1948

In the course of the 22nd Festival of the International Society for Contemporary. Music in Amsterdam the following program of chamber music is presented:

Trio in four movements by Klaus EGGE, Norwegian composer of tightly knit polyphonic music; *Put Away the Flutes* for tenor, flute, oboe, and string quartet by Humphrey SEARLE of England, to a poem by the Irish poet W. R. Rogers, written during World War II as an ironic sermon of psychological renunciation in wartime: "Put away the flutes into their careful clefts, and cut the violins that like ivy climb flat to their very roots"; *Sonata* for two pianos by Hans HENKEMANS of Holland; *Sonatina* for oboe and piano by Antoni SZALOWSKI of Poland; *Eight Poems by Michelangelo* by the Swiss cellist Richard STURZENEGGER, designed as "a group of musical sculptures"; and *Quintet* for wind instruments by Finn HØFFDING of Denmark.

8 JUNE 1948

At a Denazification Court in Munich Richard STRAUSS is officially absolved of the taint of his passive collaboration with the Nazi regime in Germany.

9 JUNE 1948

At the 22nd Festival of the International Society for Contemporary Music in Amsterdam the following program of orchestral music is given:

Second Symphony by Roger SESSIONS, in four movements of tensely wrought polyphony; *Violin Concerto* by Karl-Birger BLOMDAHL of Sweden; *Symphonic Etudes* for piano and orchestra by the Polish composer Artur MALAWSKI (first performed on 30 April 1948, in Sopot, Poland), in six sections cast in a luscious quasi-Rachmaninoffian virtuoso manner; and *Musique pour l'Esprit en Deuil,* a somber threnody dramatized by xylophone and drums by the Dutch composer Rudolf ESCHER, written during the war years but not given its mournful title until 1945, and first performed in Amsterdam on 19 January 1947.

9 JUNE 1948

Six hundred and sixty-four years after the mass abduction of children by the fabled Pied Piper of Hamelin, the British Broadcasting Corporation broadcasts an audition of a flute, manufactured by John HEYWOOD, imitating the mating call of rats, making use of rodent sex appeal to lure them into an electric death trap, but unlike the flute used by the Pied Piper in 1284, having no harmful effect on impressionable children.

10 JUNE 1948

In the course of the 22nd Festival of the International Society for Contemporary Music in Amsterdam, the following program of chamber music is given:

Three Songs for soprano and piano by Sándor JEMNITZ, Hungarian composer of atonally inflected music; *Concerto da Camera* for flute, clarinet, bassoon and piano by the Australian composeress Peggy GLANVILLE-HICKS; *4 Poemas Gallegos* for voice and chamber orchestra by Julián BAUTISTA, Spanish composer living in Argentina; and *Quintet* for wind instruments by Stepan LUCKÝ of Czechoslovakia, a survivor of a Nazi concentration camp, and an enlightened experimentalist in icositetraphonic structures. (*Primavera* for harp, flute and strings by the French grandmaster of modern music Charles KŒCHLIN was included in the printed program but not played owing to lack of rehearsal time.)

12 JUNE 1948

At the concluding concert of the 22nd Festival of the International Society for Contemporary Music in Amsterdam the following program of symphonic music is given:

40th May, heterochronistically titled symphonic suite in three movements by the Austrian composer Alexander SPITZMUELLER, living in Paris, written ostensibly for a "birthday of a beloved friend," and set in an imbricatingly complex polyphonic idiom with a proliferation of palindromic canons; *Lullaby* for 29 string instruments and two harps by Andrzej PANUFNIK of Poland, derived from a folk tune fragmentized by a prevalence of singultation and hockets and punctuated by icositetraphonic glissandos; *Violin Concerto* in one movement by the atonally tense Norwegian composer Fartein VALEN whose early years were spent in tropical Madagascar; *Horn Concerto* by Elizabeth LUTYENS of England; and *Sinfonietta* in three movements by Walter PISTON, first performed in Boston on 10 May 1941.

14 JUNE 1948

La Femme et son Ombre, ballet by the Russian-Parisian composer Alexander TCHEREPNIN, is performed for the first time in Paris.

18 JUNE 1948

Columbia Records, jointly with the Columbia Broadcasting System and Philco, presents in New York the first public demonstration for the press of LP (long playing) Microgroove, a non-breakable 12-inch vinylite disc, capable of playing recorded music for 45 minutes, perfected by Dr. Peter GOLDMARK, Director of CBS Engineering Research and Development Laboratories.

24 JUNE 1948

La Farce du Maître Pathelin, one-act comic opera by Henry BARRAUD, is produced at the Opéra-Comique in Paris.

27 JUNE 1948

George Templeton STRONG, cantankerous American composer who, discouraged by the general lack of interest in native music in America, settled in 1892 in Switzerland where he took up watercolor painting, dies in Geneva at the patriarchal age of 92.

30 JUNE 1948

First Symphony by the Australian composer Arthur BENJAMIN, written "to reflect the feelings, the hopes and despairs of the times," and cast in an appropriately ambivalent mood, is performed for the first time at the Cheltenham Festival of Contemporary British Music, John Barbirolli conducting.

1 JULY 1948

Violin Concerto, by the 43-year-old English composer Alan RAWSTHORNE, in two movements, is performed for the first time at the Cheltenham Festival.

14 JULY 1948

Down in the Valley, folk opera, named after a Kentucky mountain song, by the Americanized German expressionist Kurt WEILL, to a libretto dealing with a condemned murderer who kills his old sweetheart's new beau, is produced at the University of Indiana at Bloomington.

26 JULY 1948

Patriarch ALEXEI of the Russian Orthodox Church in Moscow issues an edict condemning the "worldliness" in Russian church music and urging the appointment of a religious censor to preserve the purity of Russian church singing and to prevent performances of modern or uneuphonious choral works at the services.

26 JULY 1948

MAGDALENA, "a musical adventure" for the stage by Heitor VILLA-LOBOS, dealing with the amours of an equatorial dictator and a Parisian cocotte on the banks of the Colombian river Magdalena, involving the theft of a statue of the Holy Virgin by the heathen Indian fiancé of a Christian native girl, set to music in languorously tropical modalities and humid harmonies, diversified by mechanistic effects (a broken-down pianola accompanies a frenetic jungle dance; an old Ford motor car is cranked up to raucously polytonal harmonies) is given its world première in Los Angeles.

29 JULY 1948

Igor STRAVINSKY files in Los Angeles a lawsuit for $250,000 against the Leeds Music Corporation of New York for using his name as the composer of *Summer Moon*, a denatured version of a theme from Stravinsky's uncopyrighted score of *The Firebird*, equipped with mawkish lyrics, thereby damaging his standing as "world famous composer of serious and sincere music."

(The suit was dismissed by the Superior Court of Los Angeles on 9 March 1949, with a finding that Stravinsky had voluntarily entered into a valid contract with the defendant corporation in full knowledge that the tune would be used for commercial purposes in the form of a popular song.)

9 AUGUST 1948

Shur and *Kurdy-Ovshary*, a symphonic diptych by the 25-year-old Azerbaijan composer Fikret AMIROV, based on Caucasian ballad forms and consisting of an integrated series of coloristic dances, is performed for the first time in Baku.

13 AUGUST 1948

At the opening of the American Dance Festival on the campus of Connecticut College in New London, Martha Graham presents the first performance of *Wilderness Stair*, ballet by norman DELLO JOIO, subtitled *Diversion of Angels*, cupidophilously portraying "games, flights, fancies, configurations of the lover's intention" in its choreography, and neo-classically hedonistic in its musical score.

19 AUGUST 1948

Eloise, symphonic poem by Ernest Clyde SALISBURY, former inmate of the Wayne County General Hospital in the town of Eloise, Michigan (after which the piece was named), where he was treated for chronic alcoholism and manic depression by the musical therapist Dr. Ira M. Altshuler, who also helped him in supplying maudlin Tchaikovskian themes as material for his work, is performed for the first time by the Detroit Symphony Orchestra, as a demonstration of confidence in mental therapy which, in the ineffable composer's own words, "done me good."

25 AUGUST 1948

First Symphony by the 21-year-old German composer Hans Werner HENZE is performed for the first time in its entirety at Bad Pyrmont. (A revised version was first performed in Berlin on 9 April 1964.)

26 AUGUST 1948

Oscar Lorenzo FERNANDEZ, 50-year-old Brazilian composer of nostalgically poetic, tropically languorous music in all genres and forms, described as "Brasileirissimo" for his intimate communication of the spirit of "Brasilidad," dies during sleep in his native Rio de Janeiro.

8 SEPTEMBER 1948

Concerto for string orchestra "alla memoria di Béla BARTÓK," by the Italian composer Guido TURCHI, is performed for the first time in Venice.

9 SEPTEMBER 1948

Marsia, ballet in one act by the 44-year-old Italian modernist Luigi DALLAPICCOLA, in three parts—(1) *La presentazione di Marsia*; (2) *Dramma di Marsia*, including a Magic Dance, a Dance of Apollo and Last Dance of Marsia; (3) *La Morte di Marsia*, depicting the fate of a legendary satyr, who dared to challenge Apollo in a music contest and was put to death after he lost—is performed for the first time at the Venice Music Festival.

12 SEPTEMBER 1948

L'Incubo, opera by the Italian dodecaphonic composer Riccardo NIELSEN, is performed for the first time in Venice.

13 SEPTEMBER 1948

Oboe Concerto by Cyril SCOTT is performed for the first time in London.

30 SEPTEMBER 1948

In compliance with the will of the Italian-born violinist Louisa TERZI of Los Angeles, her Stradivarius violin, which she won at a contest in Milan in 1888, is buried with her in her coffin.

3 OCTOBER 1948

Third Symphony, subtitled *Little Symphony*, by the Swedish composer Hilding HALLNÄS, is performed for the first time in Göteborg.

5 OCTOBER 1948

The first *Concert de bruit*, in five sections arranged by the inventor of *Musique concrète* Pierre SCHAEFFER by simultaneous playing of several phonograph records selected at random—a recitation of Sacha Guitry, incidental coughing in the studio, a harmonica solo, Balinese ritual music, acoustically denatured piano—is broadcast by the Paris radio.

11 OCTOBER 1948

Where's Charley?, a musical comedy by Frank LOESSER after Brandon Thomas' farce, *Charley's Aunt*, in which a youth impersonates his mythical aunt, acts as a chaperon for couples in love in Oxford, England, and eventually remasculinizes himself to woo a British college girl, is produced in New York.

14 OCTOBER 1948

The Orchestre National de France, under the direction of Charles MUNCH, conductor-elect of the Boston Symphony Orchestra, presents the first concert its first American tour (and first by any French orchestra since 1919), at Bridgeport, Connecticut, in a program of French music plus a specially written American work, a terse symphonic *Toccata* by Walter PISTON.

14 OCTOBER 1948

Raskolnikoff, music drama in two acts by the Swiss composer Heinrich SUTERMEISTER, after Dostoyevsky's psychological novel *Crime and Punishment*, is performed for the first time in Stockholm.

22 OCTOBER 1948

Suite delphique by the French modernist André JOLIVET, scored for wind instruments, harp, Ondes Martinot and percussion, is performed for the first time anywhere in Vienna.

23 OCTOBER 1948

Two Mexican one-act operas, *Carlota* by Luis SANDI and *La Mulata de Córdoba* by Pablo MONCAYO, are performed for the first time in Mexico City.

24 OCTOBER 1948

Sinfonietta by Francis POULENC, written in his newly adopted neo-classical vein, is performed for the first time anywhere by the British Broadcasting Corporation Orchestra in London.

24 OCTOBER 1948

Franz LÉHAR, 78-year-old Austrian composer, melodious fashioner of elegant Viennese operettas extolling the light amours and innocent intrigues of merry widows, Gypsy lovers and Balkan princes expensively romancing in plush Paris, dies in Bad Ischl, at 2:45 P.M., of the combined effects of cancer, double pneumonia, gastric ulcers and heart disease.

27 OCTOBER 1948

Mass according to the Catholic ritual by Igor STRAVINSKY, comprising *Kyrie, Gloria, Credo, Sanctus* and *Agnus Dei*, for a chorus of treble and alto voices (sung by children), tenors and basses (sung by adults), and a double wind quintet (5 woodwind instruments and 5 brasses), set in archaically austere gymnosophistical harmonies with rosary-like melorhythmic iteration, is performed for the first time in Milan, Ernest Ansermet conducting.

28 OCTOBER 1948

Tři Vlasy Děda Vševěda (*Three Hairs of Old Wise Man*), musical fairy tale by the Czech composer Rudolf KAREL (his last work, written in a concentration camp, where he died), receives its posthumous first performance in Prague.

29 OCTOBER 1948

Violin Concerto by the Soviet composer Dmitri KABALEVSKY, the first of a "trilogy of concertos" dedicated to the Soviet youth (the second being a cello concerto, the third a piano concerto), in three movements, *Allegro Molto, Andantino cantabile* and *Vivace giocoso,* alternatively lyric and boisterous, evolved in strong melodic structures with bitonally enriched triadic formations, is performed in a double première in Leningrad and Moscow.

4 NOVEMBER 1948

A Survivor of Warsaw, cantata by Arnold SCHOENBERG, scored for narrator, men's chorus and orchestra, to a text in English by Schoenberg himself, with chillingly realistic interpolations of shouted Nazi commands in brutal German slang making a count of the decimated remnants of Warsaw ghetto Jews to be sent to the gas chambers, written in an expressively inflected *Sprechstimme,* and concluding with a shatteringly dramatic chorus intoning a Hebrew prayer, with the entire work couched according to Schoenberg's method of composition with twelve tones, symbolic in its chromatic dispersal of the diaspora of the twelve tribes of Israel, is performed for the first time by the Albuquerque Civic Symphony Orchestra, Kurt Frederick conducting.

7 NOVEMBER 1948

Second Violin Concerto by Darius MILHAUD (composed at Mills College, Oakland, California, in ten days between 6 February and 16 February 1946), in three movements—*Dramatique, Lent et sombre, Emporté*—is performed for the first time in Paris.

12 NOVEMBER 1948

Umberto GIORDANO, Italian composer who at the age of 28 wrote his only successful opera *Andrea Chenier,* veristically dramatizing the tragic life of the guillotined French poet, dies in Milan at the age of 81.

13 NOVEMBER 1948

Arnold SCHOENBERG addresses an indignant letter to the editors of the *Saturday Review of Literature* protesting against the unlicensed use of his method of composition with twelve tones related only to one another, in Thomas Mann's musicosophical novel *Doctor Faustus* featuring a mythical German composer of 12-tone music, Adrian Leverkühn (1885–1940), who wrote dissonances to express hope and gladness and used consonant triadic harmonies to portray deep anguish.

In his novel *Doctor Faustus,* Thomas Mann has taken advantage of my literary property. He has produced a fictitious composer as the hero of his book; and in order to lend him qualities a hero needs to arouse people's interest, he made him the creator of what one erroneously calls my "system of twelve tones," which I call "method of composing with twelve tones."

He did this without my permission and even without my knowledge. In other words, he borrowed it in the absence of the proprietor. The supposition of one reviewer, that he obtained information about this technique from Bruno Walter and Stravinsky, is probably wrong; because Walter does not know anything of composition with twelve tones, and Stravinsky does not take any interest in it.

I have still not read the book itself, though in the meantime Mann had sent me a German copy, with a handwritten dedication, "To A. Schoenberg, dem Eigentlichen." As one need not tell me that I am an "Eigentlicher," a real one, it was clear that he wanted to tell me that his Leverkühn is an impersonation of myself.

Leverkühn is depicted, from beginning to end, as a lunatic. I am seventy-four and I am not yet insane, and I have never acquired the disease from which this insanity stems. I consider this an insult.

When Mrs. Mahler-Werfel discovered this misuse of my property, she told Mann that this was my theory, whereupon he said: "Oh, does one notice that? Then perhaps Mr. Schoenberg will be angry!" This proves that he was conscious of his guilt, and knew it was a violation of an author's right.

Finally I sent him a letter and showed him the possible consequences of ascribing my creation to another person which, in spite of being fictitious, is represented like a living man, whose biography is told by his friend Serenus Zeitblom.

One knows the superficiality and monomania of some historians who ignore facts if they do not fit in their hypotheses. Thus I quoted from an encyclopedia of the year 2060, a little article in which my theory was attributed to Thomas Mann, because of his Leverkühn.

Much pressure by Mrs. Mahler-Werfel had still to be exerted to make Mann promise that every forthcoming copy of *Doctor Faustus* will carry a note giving me credit for the twelve-notes composition. I was satisfied by this promise, because I wanted to be noble to a man who was awarded the Nobel Prize. "But Mr. Mann was not as generous as I, who had given him good chance to free himself from the ugly aspect of a pirate. He gave an explanation: a few lines which he hid at the end of the book on a place on a page where no one ever would see it. Besides, he added a new crime to his first, in the attempt to belittle me: He calls me '*a* (a!) *contemporary* composer and theoretician.' Of course, in two or three decades, one will know which of the two was the other's contemporary." (From Schoenberg's letter, published in the *Saturday Review of Literature,* New York, 1 January 1949)

Arnold Schoenberg's letter both astonished and grieved me. If his acquaintance with the book were not based exclusively on the gossip of meddling scandal mongers, he would know that my efforts to give the central figure of the novel "qualities a hero needs to arouse people's interest" were neither limited to the transfer of Schoenberg's "method of composing with twelve tones," nor was this characteristic the most important one.

It is quite untrue that it required 'much pressure' to induce me to give him due credit. As soon as I understood his concern I gave instructions to include in all translations, as well as in the German original, the statement which now appears in the English edition of *Doctor Faustus.* The statement does not raise the question who is whose contemporary. If Schoenberg wishes, we shall, all of us, consider it our greatest and proudest claim to be his contemporaries.

Instead of accepting my book with a satisfied smile as a piece of contemporary literature that testifies to his tremendous influence upon the musical culture of the era, Schoenberg regards it as an act of rape and insult. It is a sad spectacle to see a man of great worth, whose all-too-understandable hypersensitivity grows out of a life suspended between glorification and neglect, almost wilfully yield to delusions of persecution and of being robbed, and involve himself in rancorous bickering. It is my sincere hope and wish that he may rise above bitterness and suspicion and that he may find peace in the assurance of his greatness and glory! (From Thomas Mann's reply to Schoenberg in the *Saturday Review of Literature*, 1 January 1949)

14 NOVEMBER 1948

Suite palestinienne for cello and orchestra by the 75-year-old French composer André BLOCH, based on Jewish and Arabian tunes of Palestine, is performed for the first time in Paris.

20 NOVEMBER 1948

Shunko-Den, opera by the Japanese composer Toroko TAKAGI, to a melodramatic libretto in which a virtuous 18th-century Korean geisha, enamored of a virginal nobleman, suffers a cardiac collapse as a result of his persistent respect for her chastity, set to music built on pentatonic patterns of oriental folk melodies, is produced in Tokyo.

23 NOVEMBER 1948

Second Symphony in E major by Ernst von DOHNÁNYI, distinguished by a flow of Brahmsogenic exuberance, is given its world première by the Chelsea Symphony Orchestra in London, Norman Del Mar conducting.

25 NOVEMBER 1948

In Praise of Peace, symphonic poem by the 28-year-old Japanese composer Shin-ichi TAKATA, written in turgid Straussian harmonies, is performed for the first time in Tokyo.

26 NOVEMBER 1948

Suite for Orchestra from incidental music for the film Louisiana Story by Virgil THOMSON in four sections—(1) *Pastoral—The Bayou and the Marsh Buggy*, (2) *Chorale—The Derrick Arrives*, (3) *Passacaglio—Robbing the Alligator's Nest*, (4) *Fugue—Boy Fights Alligator*— with local color provided by verisimilitudinarian regional melorhythms organized in vigesimosecular counterpoint with occasional application of tonal dodecaphony in serial groups of four mutually exclusive triads, is performed for the first time by the Philadelphia Orchestra, Eugene Ormandy conducting.

29 NOVEMBER 1948

The British-made film, *Scott of the Antarctic*, with a musical score by ralph VAUGHAN WILLIAMS in 23 sections depicting "the terror and fascination of the South Pole," reflected in the diaries of Robert Falcon Scott who perished on his return from the South Pole in 1912, is demonstrated for the first time in London.

7 DECEMBER 1948

Godfrey TURNER, 35-year-old English-born composer of sanely euphonious, optimistic and even hedonistic symphonic and chamber music, driven to the depths of despondency by the agony of unrequited love, shoots himself to death in New York City.

7 DECEMBER 1948

Virgil THOMSON conducts the Louisville Orchestra in the world première of his "landscape piece," *Wheat Field at Noon*, conceived as a series of free variations on a theme containing all twelve tones of the chromatic scale arranged in four mutually exclusive triads (C minor, F-sharp minor, B-flat major, and E major).

8 DECEMBER 1948

Lucifer, cantata-mimodrama by the 60-year-old French composer Claude DELVINCOURT, in which the mutely mimed stage action is sententiously commented upon by a chorus seated in the orchestra pit, to a scenario dealing with the mighty fall of dissident angels and incidentally with the first human murder (the original title of the opera was *Le Mystère de Caïn*), is produced in Paris.

8 DECEMBER 1948

Istrian Suite for orchestra by the 34-year-old Croatian composer Natko DEVČÍČ, in four movements, arranged in the style of Istrian folk songs and dances, and marked by characteristic asymmetric meters mitigated by Italianate mellowness, is performed for the first time in Zagreb.

12 DECEMBER 1948

Violin Concerto by the 22-year-old German composer Hans Werner HENZE is performed for the first time in Baden-Baden.

18 DECEMBER 1948

Werner EGK, 47-year-old German composer, conducts in Berlin the first performance of his opera *Circe* in three acts, after the Homeric story dealing with the seductive siren who perfidiously lured the fascinated Greek sailors to her island and perdition.

18 DECEMBER 1948

The Austrian government issues a postage stamp of 60 groschen in honor of Franz Xaver GRUBER, the author of the perennially popular Christmas song *Stille Nacht, Heilige Nacht*.

28 DECEMBER 1948

Twenty-Sixth Symphony on Russian themes by the prime Soviet symphonist Nicolai MIASKOVSKY (completed on 2 October 1948), set in the socialistically realistic key of C major calculated to eliminate all formalistic impurities in the totality of tonal albification, so as to satisfy the demands of the edict of the Central Committee of the Communist Party of the USSR promulgated on 10 February 1948, in three movements—(1) *Adagio sosenuto-Allegro*, (2) *Andante quasi lento*, (3) *Adagio maestoso*—is performed for the first time in Moscow.

29 DECEMBER 1948

The Union of Soviet Composers completes in Moscow a nine-day Plenum on Soviet Music, commending some composers for proper application of the principles of Socialist Realism in their music, condemning others for unregenerate formalism, and concluding with this pronouncement: "Only Bolshevik art, the mighty lever of our national enlightenment in the spirit of Communism is capable of truthfully reflecting the greatness of the Leninist-Stalinist era."

The works by composers mentioned in the Resolution of the Central Committee of the All-Union Soviet Communist Party (Bolsheviks) of 10 February 1948 as representatives of the formalistic trend, naturally attracted the attention of the Plenum of the Union of Soviet Composers. Among recent works by these composers the most successful were the score for the film *Young Guard* by SHOSTAKOVICH and some choruses by MURADELI. The effort to enter the path of realistic creativeness and its partial success are demonstrated in Khachaturian's score for the film about V. I. Lenin, MIASKOVSKY's *Symphony on Russian Themes* and SHEBALIN's *Seventh String Quartet*. The Plenum concedes that the creative reorientation of these composers is proceeding at a very slow pace, as shown by the presence of some unliquidated formalistic elements in their music. Defeated ideologically, formalism still lingers in Soviet music. This is demonstrated by the new opera of PROKOFIEV, *Tale of a Real Man*. In the modernistic, antimelodic music of this opera, in its treatment of the Soviet characters, the composer perseveres in his old positions, condemned by the Party and by the Soviet public. The spiritual world of the Soviet man who performs miracles of valor and heroism for the love of his Fatherland, fails to attract the composer's attention. He is still interested only in the external sharpness of stage action and in naturalistic details. (Tikhon Khrennikov, Secretary General of the Union of Soviet Composers, in his article, *Soviet Music in Its New Period*, in *Pravda*, Moscow, 4 January 1949)

30 DECEMBER 1948

Kiss Me Kate, a musical comedy by Cole PORTER, dealing with an estranged couple who regain their mutual love after acting in a musical version of Shakespeare's comedy *The Taming of the Shrew*, and containing in the score an ingratiatingly tuneful waltz in a continental manner, *Wunderbar*, is produced in New York.

30 DECEMBER 1948

Curtain Raiser to an American Play, symphonic appetizer in a fugal style with a lyric interlude, by the Constantinople-born half-Austrian Americanized 45-year-old composer Frederick PIKET, is performed for the first time by the Minneapolis Symphony Orchestra, Dimitri Mitropoulos conducting.

31 DECEMBER 1948

Howard HANSON conducts the Boston Symphony Orchestra in the first performance of his *Piano Concerto*, in four brief movements, with Rudolf Firkušny as soloist, and Lukas FOSS conducts the first performance of his symphonic threnody *Recordare*, dedicated to the memory, of Mahatma Gandhi.

31 DECEMBER 1948

Fifth Symphony by the 48-year-old whilom *enfant terrible* of American music George ANTHEIL, subtitled "Joyous," and voicing in its three well-contrasted movements the spirit of euphonious euphoria in triadic laetification, is performed for the first time by the Philadelphia Orchestra, Eugene Ormandy conducting.

1949

2 JANUARY 1949

Dynam-Victor FUMET, French organist and composer, whose flamboyant career as a dynamic fumer (he was once arrested for making bombs for anarchist purposes) carried him from the piano bench of a café chantant to the console of a church organ, and who wrote a number of multifarious pieces in various genres couched in a Gallicized Wagneromantic vein, dies in Paris at the age of 81.

3 JANUARY 1949

The first performance of a work announced as the *21st Symphony* by an early 19th-century composer Dmitri OVSIANNIKO-KULIKOVSKY, with the finale in the rhythms of a Ukrainian dance, but in reality a stunning fabrication perpetrated by the Soviet violinist and composer Michael Goldstein whose original works have been

systematically rejected for performance or publication in the Soviet Union, is played for the first time in Odessa.

4 JANUARY 1949

Kentuckiana, a symphonic divertimento on twenty Kentucky airs by Darius MILHAUD, is performed in a world première by the Louisville Orchestra.

5 JANUARY 1949

Fifth Symphony by Henry COWELL is performed for the first time in Washington.

7 JANUARY 1949

Fourth Symphony by the 53-year-old American composer Leo SOWERBY, in three movements marked: *Fast and*

Violently; Slowly and Wistfully; Agitated, expressive of "the excitement and gusto, noise and glamour of a big city, sprawling and youthful—perhaps Chicago," is performed for the first time by the Boston Symphony Orchestra, Serge Koussevitzky conducting.

14 JANUARY 1949

Joaquín TURINA, Spanish composer of colorful symphonic pieces throbbing with languorously applosive Iberian rhythms and accoutred in luxuriant inframodern harmonies, dies in Madrid at the age of 66.

16 JANUARY 1949

Mirandolina, ballet by the venerable 76-year-old master of Russian romantic music, Sergei VASSILENKO, based on Carlo Goldoni's comedy *La Locandiera (The Mistress of the Inn,))* is produced in Moscow.

26 JANUARY 1949

Fifth Symphony in B-flat minor by the 47-year-old English composer Edmund RUBBRA, in four movements: a sepulchrally lugubrious *Adagio* leading to a turbidly kinetic *Allegro energetico;* a bucolic *Allegro moderato;* a stately passacaglia , *Grave;* and an *Allegro vivo,* is performed for the first time in London.

27 JANUARY 1949

Boris ASAFIEV, Russian composer of neo-romantic operas, and author, under the nom de plume of Igor Glebov, of voluminous tomes on musical esthetics, dies in Moscow at the age of 64.

29 JANUARY 1949

Puck, fairy opera by the 50-year-old French composer Marcel DELANNOY, after Shakespeare's play *A Midsummer Night's Dream,* is performed for the first time in Strasbourg.

4 FEBRUARY 1949

Second Symphony by the 34-year-old American composer Cecil EFFINGER is performed for the first time in Cincinnati.

9 FEBRUARY 1949

White Wings, chamber opera by the 55-year-old American composer Douglas MOORE, to a libretto concerning an incompatible romance blossoming up in 1900 in the fetid fragrance of unpaved New York streets between a sanitation department worker assigned to the removal of equine merde (the title *White Wings* refers to the antiseptic uniform of the corps), and the daughter of an automobile manufacturer whose horseless carriages threaten the abolition of his job, written in a sophisticated simplicistic idiom combining elements of mock-grand opera, ragtime rhythms, and sentimental balladry, with a patina of euphoniously pandiatonic non-odoriferous dissonant counterpoint, is performed for the first time in Hartford, Connecticut.

10 FEBRUARY 1949

Sixth Symphony, by the 48-year-old American whilom modernist George ANTHEIL, written in a candidly tonal idiom sprinkled with non-toxic dissonances, in three romantically sociological movements, the first *Maestoso,* inspired by the painting of Delacroix, "Liberty Leading the People," depicting in tones "the smoke of battle, courage, despair and hope, all marching into the future;" the second, *Larghetto,* being a "breath of Autumn;" and the third, *Allegro,* "a triumph of joy," set in ozonized triadic harmonies, is performed for the first time by the San Francisco Symphony Orchestra, Pierre Monteux conducting.

11 FEBRUARY 1949

Sixth Symphony (degli archi)) by Gian Francesco MALIPIERO, scored for strings only in the manner of a Concerto Grosso, and set in the classical four movements, *Allegro, Piuttosto Lento, Allegro vivo* and *Lento ma non troppo,* ending on a wistfully vanishing dissonant chord, is performed for the first time in Basel, Paul Sacher conducting.

12 FEBRUARY 1949

Concerto for marimba, vibraphone and orchestra by Darius MILHAUD is performed for the first time by the St. Louis Symphony Orchestra.

19 FEBRUARY 1949

The Emperor's New Clothes, opera by Douglas MOORE, based on the famous fairy tale by Hans Christian Andersen about a naked king, who was attired in garments so fine as to be invisible, a tailoring finesse dispelled by a child's outcry of astonishment at royal nakedness, set to music in an appropriately grand mock-imperial manner, is performed for the first time, in concert form, by the New York Philharmonic.

19 FEBRUARY 1949

Movements, symphonic suite for orchestra by the 22-year-old Israeli composer Ben-Zion ORGAD, is performed for the first time by the Israel Philharmonic Orchestra in Tel Aviv.

23 FEBRUARY 1949

Prima Donna, one-act opera by Arthur BENJAMIN, set in 18th-century Venice, and featuring a singing contest between rival prima donnas, is produced in London.

25 FEBRUARY 1949

Symphony in B major by the Brazilian composer Oscar Lorenzo FERNANDEZ (1897–1948), in four movements, suffused with Brazilian melorhythms, is performed posthumously for the first time by the Boston Symphony Orchestra, Eleazar de Carvalho conducting.

27 FEBRUARY 1949

Sixth Symphony by the 38-year-old American composer William SCHUMAN, in one movement divided into six sections, the initial and the final sections being in slow tempo, with atonal, quasi-dodecaphonic themes developed in passacaglia-like variations, is performed for the first time by the Dallas Symphony Orchestra, Antal Dorati conducting.

2 MARCH 1949

Red Ear of Corn, ballet by the 35-year-old Canadian composer John WEINZWEIG, is performed for the first time in Toronto.

2 MARCH 1949

Die Schwarze Spinne, one-act opera by the Swiss composer Heinrich SUTERMEISTER, after a chimerical Swiss tale in which the devil, trying to obtain an unbaptized child for his diabolical ritual, transforms a local woman into a black spider, with poisonous arachnids pouring forth out of her defiled womb, is produced for the first time in St. Gall, Switzerland.

6 MARCH 1949

Sosi for violin, piano, percussion and strings, by the half-Armenian, half-Scottish American composer Alan HOVHANESS, is performed for the first time in New York, two days before his 38th birthday.

8 MARCH 1949

Third Piano Concerto by Gian Francesco MALIPIERO, in three linked sections, *Allegro*, *Lento*, and *Allegro agitato*, couched in a transparent contrapuntal manner of the Italian settecento, is performed for the first time, as a commissioned work, by the Louisville Orchestra.

14 MARCH 1949

The Bronze Knight, ballet in four acts by Reinhold GLIÈRE, after Pushkin's poem centering on a St. Petersburg youth driven to despair when his beloved perishes in the catastrophic inundation of the river Neva in 1824, and who hurls imprecations at the equestrian statue of Peter the Great, the founder of the city, whereupon the bronze giant chases him down the streets to his death, is produced in Leningrad.

15 MARCH 1949

Concerto for cello and orchestra in G minor by Dmitri KABALEVSKY, the second of his "trilogy of concertos," and like the other two (the *Violin Concerto* and the *Third Piano Concerto*) set in three cyclic movements (fast, slow, very fast), designed for performances by young players and rooted in the modal variations of major and minor thirds in homonymic triads, nostalgically poetic in slow interludes, impetuously alert in rapid passages, is performed for the first time, in Moscow.

17 MARCH 1949

Regina Uliva, opera in three acts by the 42-year-old Italian composer Giulio Cesare SONZOGNO, to a libretto from the history of Castille, is produced at La Scala, in Milan.

18 MARCH 1949

Fourth Symphony, subtitled *The Cycle*, for chorus and orchestra by the 25-year-old American composer Peter MENNIN, is performed for the first time in New York.

24 MARCH 1949

Tragic Overture by the 34-year-old Polish composer Andrzej PANUFNIK, written in memory of the victims of the Warsaw uprising of 1943, is performed for the first time in New York.

31 MARCH 1949

The Troubled Island, opera in three acts by the 53-year-old American Negro composer William Grant STILL, to a libretto from the time of the Haitian struggle for independence against Napoleonic France, is produced at the New York City Center of Music and Drama.

3 APRIL 1949

First Symphony, subtitled *Jean de la Peur*, by the 34-year-old French composer Marcel LANDOWSKI, in three movements of deep mystical content descriptive of the pious individual Jean's struggle against fear in his soul, is performed for the first time in Paris.

5 APRIL 1949

Roy HARRIS conducts the Louisville Orchestra in the first performance of his symphonic scherzo *Kentucky Spring*, reflecting the "soft air of Kentucky, filled with bird song, and earth clothed in a riot of colors," and containing thematic references to Stephen Foster's song *My Old Kentucky Home*.

7 APRIL 1949

South Pacific, musical play by Richard RODGERS, with lyrics by Oscar HAMMERSTEIN II, based on James A. Michener's *Tales of the South Pacific*, wherein a French planter dwelling in paradisiac contentment on a south Pacific island sires two Polynesian children, performs other deeds of valor during World War II, and subsequently woos and wins an American girl in marriage, containing the ineffably mellifluous tropical songs *Bali Ha'i, Happy Talk, I'm in Love with a Wonderful Guy, Younger Than Springtime*, and *There Is Nothing Like a Dame*, is produced in New York.

8 APRIL 1949

Leonard BERNSTEIN, 30-year-old pianist, conductor and composer, plays the piano part with the Boston Symphony Orchestra, Serge Koussevitzky conducting, in the world première of his *Second Symphony*, subtitled *The Age of Anxiety*, for piano and orchestra, inspired by W. H. Auden's poem *The Age of Anxiety: a Baroque Eclogue*, "a dream-odyssey through common experience and alcohol," couched in an omnimusical syncretic idiom, from existentialistic melologues to urbanistic jazz, containing also a dodecaphonic episode, in six sections: (1) *Prologue*, a merry scene in a New York bar; (2) *The Seven Ages*, in seven athematic variations; (3) *The Seven Stages*, with seven variations making "an inner and highly symbolic journey,"; (4) *The Dirge*, a dodecaphonic lamentation of three men and a girl in a taxicab, voicing their need of a protective father figure, the "colossal Dad"; (5) *The Masque*, "a fantastic piano-jazz" in the form of a scherzo; (6) *Epilogue*, wherein the entire orchestra makes "a positive statement of the newly-recognized faith."

22 APRIL 1949

The 23rd Festival of the International Society for Contemporary Music opens in Palermo, Sicily, with a performance of the opera *King Roger* by Karol SZYMANOWSKI (first produced in Warsaw on 19 June 1926), to a libretto from the time when King Roger the Norman (1093–1154) ruled Sicily.

23 APRIL 1949

At the 23rd Festival of the International Society for Contemporary Music in Palermo the following program is given:

String Quartet in one neo-classical movement by the 28-year-old Swiss composer Armin SCHIBLER; *Piano Sonata* by the 33-year-old French composer Henri DUTILLEUX; *Fifth String Quartet* by the prime Dutch impressionist Willem PIJPER (1894–1947); *Canti di Morte* for chorus by the 42-year-old Italian composer Gino CONTILLI; and *14 Different Ways of Describing Rain* for speaker and chamber orchestra by the German disciple of Schoenberg Hanns EISLER, written in 1944 in honor of Schoenberg's 70th birthday, based on a 12-tone series, and scored for the same ensemble as Schoenberg's *Pierrot Lunaire.*

24 APRIL 1949

At the 23rd Festival of the International Society for Contemporary Music in Palermo the following program of stage music is presented:

La Favola d'Orfeo, opera in one act by Alfred CASELLA (first performed in Venice on 6 September 1932); *Le Diable boiteux*, a musical dialogue for two male voices by Jean FRANÇAIX (first performed in the Paris salon of Princess Polignac in 1937): *The Pit*. a dramatic scene for tenor and bass by the English composeress Elisabeth LUTYENS, to the story of a coal mine disaster; and *Qarrtsiluni*, ballet from Eskimo life by the Danish composer Knudaage RIISAGER (*Qarrtsiluni* is an Eskimo word expressing the mysterious moment of apprehensive silence before disaster strikes), first performed in Copenhagen on 21 February 1942.

24 APRIL 1949

The Inn Hostess, comic opera in three acts by the 41-year-old Odessa-born Russian composer of Italian parentage Antonio SPADAVECCHIA, after Carlo Goldoni's play *La Locandiera*, with the music couched in an appropriate style of the Italian settecento, is produced in Moscow.

25 APRIL 1949

At the 23rd Festival of the International Society for Contemporary Music in Palermo, the following program of chamber music is presented:

Fourth String Quartet by the 54-year-old Czech composer Pavel BOŘKOVEC (first performed by the League of Composers in New York on 11 April 1948); *3 Pieces* for Ondes Martenot, voice and percussion by the Algerian-born French composeress Yvette GRIMAUD, making use of quarter-tone polyphony in icositetraphonic harmonies; *String Quartet* by the 48-year-old Austrian composer Hans Erich APOSTEL; *Sonetto a Dallapiccola* for piano by the 46-year-old Russian-born Belgian composer Wladimir WORONOW, written according to his own system of "polyvariations"; *Noctures* for contralto and string quartet by the 33-year-old German-Brazilian dodecaphonic composer Hans Joachim KOELLRE-

ITTER; and *Primavera* for five instruments by the patriarch of French modern music Charles KŒCHLIN, composed in 1936, and couched in bitonal harmony.

26 APRIL 1949

The following program of orchestral music is presented at the 23rd Festival of the International Society for Contemporary Music in Palermo:

Fuga giocosa by the 33-year-old English composer Humphrey SEARLE; *Concerto* for piano and orchestra in three movements by the 45-year-old English composer Lennox BERKELEY; *Second Suite* from the oratorio *Thyl Claes* (after the medieval folk-tale about Till Eulenspiegel) by the 52-year-old Russian-born Swiss composer Wladimir VOGEL; and *Second Symphony* by the 40-year-old Czech composer Miloslav KABELÁČ (first performed in Prague on 17 April 1947), in three movements opening with a funereal dirge as a memorial of the Nazi occupation of Czechoslovakia, and concluding with an optimistic finale.

27 APRIL 1949

The following program of Italian music is presented at the 23rd Festival of the International Society for Contemporary Music in Palermo:

Concerto for string orchestra in three movements by Vincenzo TOMMASINI; suite from the ballet *Ritratto di Don Chisciotte* by Goffredo PETRASSI; *Tre tempi* from *Musica d'Archi* by 41-year-old Riccardo NIELSEN; and *Concerto dell'albatro* in five movements by Giorgio Federico GHEDINI, scored for a narrator, violin, cello, piano and small orchestra. (Alfredo CASELLA's *Paganiniana*, originally programmed for this concert, was not performed.)

28 APRIL 1949

The following program is presented at the 23rd Festival of the International Society for Contemporary Music in Palermo:

Variations for brass and string instruments by the 50-year-old Rumanian-French composer Marcel MIHALOVICI; *Fourth Symphony* for string orchestra, in three movements, *Lento con passione, Allegro di molto (Schrezo)* and *Adagio appassionato*, by the 43-year-old German master of modern polyphony Karl Amadeus HARTMANN; *Miniature Symphony* in four short movements by the 33-year-old Belgian composer Victor LEGLEY; and *Symphonic Suite* from the ballet *Orphée* by the French composer Jean Louis MARTINET.

29 APRIL 1949

The first concert of a newly formed *Groupe du Zodiaque*, dedicated to "the defense of the freedom of the musical language from all sorts of tyrannical esthetics," is presented in Paris.

29 APRIL 1949

At the 23rd Festival of the International Society for Contemporary Music held at the Teatro Greco-Romano in Taormina, a performance is given of *The Cyclops* by Euripides, with stage music and choruses by Giuseppe MULÈ. (It was at Taormina that, according to Homer's *Odyssey*, Ulysses met and smote the Cyclops Polyphemus.)

29 APRIL 1949

Golgotha, oratorio by Frank MARTIN, to the text of St. Augustine, with a neo-baroque musical score based on a three-note motto evolving into triadic harmonies in luminous hymn-like tones, is performed for the first time in Geneva.

30 APRIL 1949

The 23rd Festival of the International Society for Contemporary Music concludes with a concert in Taormina, presenting the following program:

Fantasia concertante for violin solo and string accompaniment by the 43-year-old expatriate Hungarian composer Mátyás SEIBER, resident in England since 1935, written in an expressionistic paradodecaphonistic idiom; *Canciones castellanas* for soprano and 8 instruments by the 30-year-old Chilean composer Juán ORREGO SALAS; Variations for piano and 10 instruments, in classical forms of dodecaphonic content, by the 24-year-old French composer Serge NIGG (first performed in Paris on 29 January 1947); *6 Canzoni* for tenor, strings, and piano by the 55-year-old Swiss composer Jean BINET; and *Concerto* for two pianos with chamber orchestra, in three movements, in a neo-baroque manner, by the 29-year-old Italian conductor and composer Bruno MADERNA.

4 MAY 1949

Ildebrando PIZZETTI conducts in Florence his music drama, *Vanna Lupa,* in three acts, to his own libretto garnered from Florentine chronicles of the 14th century, focused on a widowed lady alienated from her sons because of political and social disparity, written in an eloquently dramatic Italian manner with a tropism towards post-Verdian cantilena.

7 MAY 1949

Das Wundertheater, operatic melodrama by the 22-year-old German composer Hans Werner HENZE, to a libretto from Cervantes, written in an exuberantly rubicund rhythmic style, with an artfully disoriented vocal line accoutred in acerb but non-corrosive harmonies and orchestrated in the hedonistic manner of the utilitarian German musical theater, is produced in Heidelberg.

8 MAY 1949

Sinfonia by the 35-year-old Rumanian composer Ion DUMITRESCU is performed for the first time in Bucharest.

9 MAY 1949

Don't We All, one-act opera by Burrill PHILLIPS, is produced in Rochester, New York.

9 MAY 1949

A Drumlin Legend, opera in three acts by Ernst BACON, is performed for the first time, in concert form, at Columbia University in New York.

12 MAY 1949

Il Cordovano, one-act opera buffa by the 44-year-old Italian modernist Goffredo PETRASSI, to a libretto from Cer-vantes, in which a bravo intrudes into the chambers of a respectable matron by pretending to be a vendor of tanned goatskins (*cordovano*), is produced at La Scala in Milan.

13 MAY 1949

Till Eulenspiegel, opera by the 56-year-old Czech composer Otakar JEREMIÁŠ, is produced in Prague.

13 MAY 1949

Paris-Magie, ballet in one act by the only woman member of the group of the French Six Germaine TAILLE-FERRE, is produced at the Opéra-Comique in Paris.

13 MAY 1949

Andrzej PANUFNIK, 34-year-old Polish composer, conducts in Warsaw the world première of his *Sinfonia Rustica,* in four movements: *Con tenerezza, Con grazia, Con espressione, Con vigore,* scored for a small orchestra with the strings divided into two groups, couched in an optimistic diatonic idiom, with a recurring chromatic motive serving as a nostalgic counterfoil.

15 MAY 1949

Third Symphony in A minor by the 50-year-old American composer Randall THOMPSON, in four movements—(1) *Largo elegiaco,* suffused with nostalgic modalities; (2) *Allegro appassionato,* in rondo form inspired by a sense of tonal defiance, but collapsing in desolate wistfulness in an episode entitled *Calmato ma triste assai;* (3) *Lento tranquillo,* a bucolic eclogue; (4) *Allegro vivace,* in which the somber introspection of the preceding movements is dispelled by exuberant extroversion of triadic jubilation—is performed for the first time as part of the American Music Festival in New York.

17 MAY 1949

The First Congress of Dodecaphonic Music opens a four-day session in Milan, presenting (with the telegraphic blessing from Arnold Schoenberg who sent this message: "Proudly I greet my companions who aim to present musical ideas with new tools of musical logic—good luck!") works by Arnold SCHOENBERG (*Piano Suite,* op. 25); Ernst KRENEK (*Kafka Lieder*); Hans Erich APOSTEL (*Quartet* for flute, clarinet, horn and bassoon); Wallingford RIEGGER (*Third Symphony*); Luigi DAL-LAPICCOLA (5 *Fragments from Sappho* for voice and orchestra); and *Zwölftonmusik* for orchestra by Josef Matthias HAUER.

18 MAY 1949

Darius MILHAUD conducts at Temple Emanuel in San Francisco the world première of his *Sabbath Morning Service,* written according to a free Hebrew ritual, without precise quotations of liturgical chants.

22 MAY 1949

Hans PFITZNER, romantic German composer of operas and instrumental music wrought with masterly art but lacking vitality, dies in Salzburg, at 6:30 in the morning, 17 days after his 80th birthday.

27 MAY 1949

Ulysses, cantata for tenor solo, mixed chorus and orchestra, by the 44-year-old expatriate Hungarian composer, now residing in London, Mátyás SEIBER, to the text from the famous surrealist novel by James Joyce, reaching climactic heights in the fugue: "our system plunging towards the constellation of Hercules," with an atonally oriented setting (the first two chords from Schoenberg's *Klavierstück,* op. 19, No. 6, are quoted in the score), is performed for the first time in London.

28 MAY 1949

Die schwarze Spinne, opera in two acts by the Swiss composer Willy BURKHARD, after a nightmarish little tale by the Swiss cleric Albert Bitzius (1797–1854), wherein a village woman, preternaturally impregnated by the devil, procreating a pack of poisonous black spiders is redeemed from perdition by a normally gravid maiden who exorcises the monstrous arachneous progeny at the time of her own parturition, is performed for the first time in Zürich. (The same story was used in Heinrich Sutermeister's identically named opera, produced in St. Gall on 2 March 1949, and by Josef Matthias Hauer in his opera produced in Vienna on 23 May 1966.)

10 JUNE 1949

Ouanga, three-act opera by the American Negro composer Clarence Cameron WHITE, to a libretto dealing with a Haitian voodoo priestess who refuses to surrender her fetish *ouanga* (hence the title) to a presidential usurper, is performed by an all-Negro cast in South Bend, Indiana.

14 JUNE 1949

Let's Make an Opera, an "entertainment for young people" by Benjamin BRITTEN, incorporating a miniature opera *The Little Sweep,* dealing with a child chimney sweep, a pathetic victim of the inhuman exploitation of little boys in England early in the 19th century used as living brushes to go through the chimney and clean the soot with their small bodies, is performed for the first time at the Aldeburgh Music Festival, with the audience invited to participate in singing a few simple songs "rehearsed" in the first part of the play.

15 JUNE 1949

Die Bremer Stadtmusikanten, opera by the 44-year-old German composer Richard MOHAUPT, is produced in Bremen.

18 JUNE 1949

Fourth Symphony, subtitled *Metamorphoses*, by the 29-year-old Danish composer Niels Viggo BENTZON, is performed for the first time in Copenhagen.

20 JUNE 1949

Stradivario, "a choreographic fantasy of instruments that dance" for orchestra, by Gian Francesco MALIPIERO, picturing the telekinetic conduct of antique instruments at the Palazzo Pisani in Venice, which attack an old beggar who attempts to steal a Stradivarius violin, is performed for the first time at the Maggio Musicale in Florence.

21 JUNE 1949

Le Oui des Jeunes Filles, lyric comedy in three acts by Reynaldo HAHN, is produced posthumously at the Opéra-Comique in Paris, with the last act orchestrated by Henri Büsser.

25 JUNE 1949

Das verzauberte Ich, comic opera by the 51-year-old German composer Ottmar GERSTER, is performed for the first time in Wuppertal.

27 JUNE 1949

Second Symphony by the 48-year-old English composer Alan BUSH, *The Nottingham*, in four movements, subtitled *Sherwood Forest, Clifton Grove, Castle Rock* and *Goose Fair,* glorifying the liberating movement of Robin Hood, is performed at Nottingham, England, to mark the city's semimillennium.

28 JUNE 1949

Illusion, radio opera by the Parisianized Hungarian composer Tibor HARSÁNYI, is performed for the first time in Paris.

30 JUNE 1949

The Bärenreiter Verlag in Kassel launches the publication of the most voluminous encyclopedia of music ever undertaken, *Die Musik in Geschichte und Gegenwart*, edited by Friedrich Blume. (The article on Bach was not to be reached until column No. 962.)

8 JULY 1949

Riccardo PICK-MANGIAGALLI, Bohemian-born Italian composer of effective ballets and lyrical instrumental pieces, dies in Milan two days before his 67th birthday.

14 JULY 1949

Spring Symphony by Benjamin BRITTEN, for soprano, alto, tenor, mixed chorus and orchestra, consisting of twelve vocal numbers, to vernal texts by English poets from the 13th to the 20th century, is performed in a world première at the Holland Festival in Amsterdam.

15 JULY 1949

Francisco MIGNONE, 51-year-old Brazilian composer, conducts in Rio de Janeiro the first performances of his ballet suite *Quadros Amazonicos* and his oratorio *Allerias de Nossa Senhora.*

18 JULY 1949

Vítězslav NOVÁK, Bohemian composer, pupil of Dvořák and teacher of a generation of Czechoslovak musicians, whose own operatic and symphonic music is suffused with national thematic materials on a flow of romantic harmonies, dies in Skuteč Slovakia, at the age of 78.

22 JULY 1949

Rapsodie provençale by the 53-year-old French composer Jean RIVIER, an unpretentious piece of pastoral symphonic music, is performed for the first time at the International Festival in Aix-en-Provence.

2 AUGUST 1949

Paw i dziewczyna (*The Peacock and the Maiden*), ballet by the 52-year-old Polish composer Tadeusz SZELIGOW-SKI, is produced in Wroclaw (Breslau).

9 AUGUST 1949

Antigonae, musical play by the 54-year-old German composer Carl ORFF, with the text adapted from Sophocles, relating the tragic story of a loyal sister who violated her father's order and gave a decent burial to her brother who fought and fell in the enemy camp during the siege of Thebes, in the German version by the poet Friedrich Hölderlin, scored for a modernistically primitivistic ensemble of six pianos (to be played also on their insides, hitting the strings by mallets of various sizes), four harps, African drums, ten Javanese gongs, several large xylophones, an anvil and vocalists, assigned cephalotriptic singlenote parts (in one scene the watchman has 174 consecutive D's before interrupting his solipsistic iteration) is performed for the first time in Salzburg.

10 AUGUST 1949

String Octet in three movements: *Animé, Modéré, Vif,* by Darius MILHAUD, an ingenious musical palimpsest of his 14th and 15th string quartets (which can also be played separately), is performed for the first time at Mills College, California, Milhaud's principal American teaching place, by the combined Budapest and Paganini Quartets.

15 AUGUST 1949

Prayer for Peace, choral symphonic poem by the Japanese composer Shiro FUKAI, is performed for the first time in Tokyo.

27 AUGUST 1949

The Government of the Federal German Republic commemorates the centennial of the death of the German opera composer Konradin KREUTZER by issuing a postage stamp of 10 marks with his picture.

2 SEPTEMBER 1949

On the centenary of CHOPIN's death, Paulina CZERNIC-KA, a middle-aged Polish lady pathologically obsessed with the image of Chopin, who manufactured and circulated a number of letters purportedly written by Chopin to Delfina Potocka, which represented him as a pornographic sensualist using anachronistic verbal vulgarity (some obscene Polish slang found in the letters were of World War I vintage), kills herself by taking an overdose of sleeping pills in Warsaw. (In October 1961 the Chopin Institute in Warsaw officially declared the correspondence to be a forgery.)

3 SEPTEMBER 1949

Charles KELLOGG, "California Nature Singer," reputed to be able to reproduce the song of any bird, thanks to his congenitally ornithomorphic syrinx in addition to the normal larynx (his tessitura encompassed 12 1/2 octaves, reaching into the ultrasonic range beyond 14,000 cycles), dies at the age of 80 at Morgan Hill, California. (On 6 September 1926 he broadcast a shrill note over radio station KGO, which extinguished a candle in Hawaii and a chemical flame on the Berkeley campus of the University of California, where the test was made.)

3 SEPTEMBER 1949

At the Edinburgh Music Festival, Ernest BLOCH conducts the BBC Scottish Orchestra in the world première of his *Concerto Symphonique* for piano and orchestra in three movements: *Pesante* (chime-like unison progressions); *Allegro Vivace* (a scherzo with a contrasting songful section); and *Allegro deciso* (rhapsodic and energetic).

3 SEPTEMBER 1949

On the eve of the 125th anniversary of the birth of Anton BRUCKNER, the Austrian Government issues a commemorative stamp of 40 groschen in his honor.

7 SEPTEMBER 1949

Billy Budd, one-act opera by the Italian veristic composer Giorgio Federico GHEDINI, after Melville's tragic tale of an unjustly hanged seaman, is produced in Venice. (Benjamin Britten's opera on the same subject was produced in London on 1 December 1951.)

8 SEPTEMBER 1949

Richard STRAUSS, "Richard the Second" (so nicknamed by Hans von Bülow to dub him the inheritor of Wagner's mantle), the last of the titans of German musical romanticism, creator of the sui generis philosophical tone poem, daring explorer of the extreme regions of tonality, dies in his home at Garmisch-Partenkirchen, at the age of 85.

11 SEPTEMBER 1949

Henri RABAUD, French composer of effective operas and symphonic poems (of which *La Procession Nocturne* for orchestra was a transitory favorite), dies in Paris in his 76th year.

15 SEPTEMBER 1949

King's Rhapsody, operetta by the 56-year-old English composer Ivor NOVELLO, in which a modern-minded prince marries a conventional Scandinavian princess but carries on an illicit affair with a Riviera temptress with such flagrant nonchalance that he is forced to abdicate, is produced in London.

18 SEPTEMBER 1949

Naši furianti (*Our Wild Ones*), opera in three acts by the Czech composer Rudolf KUBÍN, is produced at Ostrava.

19 SEPTEMBER 1949

Nikos SKALKOTTAS, Greek composer, disciple of Schoenberg who elaborated the 12-tone method in an imaginatively personal manner in his numerous instrumental works, dies in Athens at the age of 45.

19 SEPTEMBER 1949

Stormen, opera by the dean of Swedish composers Kurt ATTERBERG, after Shakespeare's play *The Tempest*, is performed for the first time in Stockholm.

24 SEPTEMBER 1949

On the eve of the centennial of the death of Johann STRAUSS, SR., "Father of the Waltz," the government of Austria issues a commemorative 30-groschen stamp in his honor.

29 SEPTEMBER 1949

Tormida Rand (*Stormy Coast*), opera in five acts by the 40-year-old Estonian composer Gustav ERNESAKS, to a libretto dealing with the oppression of 19th-century Estonian fishermen by a feudal landlord who deliberately sets false signals to ships on stormy nights to lure them to destruction and then rob the wreckage, but is eventually hurled over a cliff into the sea by a shipwrecked Russian sailor, is produced in Talinn.

29 SEPTEMBER 1949

The Olympians, fanciful opera in three acts by the urbane English modernist Arthur BLISS, to a story about a couple of lovers whose happiness is arranged by the intercession of Jupiter, Venus, Mars, Mercury, Bacchus and other Greek deities convivially gamboling in an English seaport in 1810, in the guise of travelling players, returning to Mt. Olympus one night every year, is produced in London.

30 SEPTEMBER 1949

Fourth Symphony by the 61-year-old Dutch romantic composer Matthijs VERMEULEN is performed for the first time in Rotterdam.

4 OCTOBER 1949

Edmund EYSLER, Austrian composer of vivacious operettas, dies in his native city of Vienna at the age of 75.

11 OCTOBER 1949

Regina, musical drama in three acts by the American composer Marc BLITZSTEIN, to his own libretto based on Lillian Hellman's play *The Little Foxes*, focused on a vulpine covey of contentious siblings of an ante-bellum Southern family torn by avarice and pride, with Regina outfoxing the other little foxes in obtaining the largest share in a lucrative contract for building a cotton mill, set to music in a diversified but distinctly vigesimosecular idiom with a lively influx of antique ragtime, is produced in Boston. (The first New York performance of *Regina* took place on 30 October 1949.)

13 OCTOBER 1949

Fourth Symphony by the 53-year-old Austrian composer Johann Nepomuk DAVID, in four movements, *Adagio*, *Allegro moderato*, *Scherzo* and *Finale*, monothematically conceived but pluralistically carried out, so that the basic intervallic ascent increases from the second to a third, a fourth, a fifth and a sixth, reaching the ultimate expansion in the tumescent finale, is performed for the first time in Leipzig.

16 OCTOBER 1949

Carl Emil SEASHORE, Swedish-born American psychologist who devised the "Seashore Test," a method for rating musical ability by measuring instruments of his own invention, such as audiometer, tonoscope, and chronograph, dies in Lewiston, Idaho, at the age of 83.

20 OCTOBER 1949

Des Simplicius Simplicissimus Jugend, "scenes from German destiny," by Karl Amadeus HARTMANN, in three parts, to an allegorical scenario from the time of the Thirty Years' War (1618–1648), in which a young wanderer Simplicius voices his incomprehension of internecine carnage, stumbles into the governor's palace during an orgy, and survives because "he is not worth a bullet," scored for speaking and singing voices, ten instruments and percussion, and marked by a stark rhythmic pattern of atonal melodies, with episodic Germanic folksongs in triadic harmonies pandiatonically amplified, and distinguished in the text by occasional scatological similes ("this young lady has hair as yellow as a small child's excrement"), is produced in Cologne. (A performance of the work in concert form was presented in Cologne on 23 October 1948.)

24 OCTOBER 1949

Joaquin NÍN Y CASTELLANOS, Spanish pianist and composer of sensitive Hispanic piano pieces and subtle arrangements of old Spanish songs, dies in his native Havana at the age of 70.

25 OCTOBER 1949

Concerto for seven instruments, percussion and strings by the 59-year-old Swiss composer Frank MARTIN, in three movements, *Allegro*, *Adagietto*, *Allegro vivace*, each commencing with the same syncopated theme, which is successively introduced by oboe, clarinet, horn, trumpet, trombone, bassoon and flute, is performed for the first time in Bern.

28 OCTOBER 1949

Ginette NEVEU, 30-year-old French violinist whose technical perfection and masculine energy in performance earned her the renown of the greatest woman violin virtuoso of the first half of the 20th century, perishes in an airplane accident near the Azores on her way from France to the United States, carrying her Stradivarius violin with her to flaming destruction.

29 OCTOBER 1949

Ollantay, symphonic triptych by the 33-year-old Argentinian composer Alberto GINASTERA, dealing with an

Inca soldier who violates the priest's daughter in the temple of the virgins and is slain by the celestial army of the Sun God, in a somberly tense setting in a resonant dissonant idiom overlaying the basic pentatonic melos of pre-Columbian America, is produced in Buenos Aires.

3 NOVEMBER 1949

Seventh Symphony by Gian Francesco MALIPIERO in four movements (*Allegro, Lento, Allegro impetuoso,* and *Lento*), subtitled *Dellecanzoni* because it evokes the impressions of imagined old songs inaudibly streaming from distant hills, is performed for the first time in Milan.

6 NOVEMBER 1949

Alan BUSH, member of the left wing of the British Labor Party, conducts the Massed Choirs and Orchestra of the Workers' Music Association in London in the first performance of his *Song of Friendship* for bass, chorus and band, dedicated to the ideal of international cooperation with the socialist countries of Europe and Asia.

15 NOVEMBER 1949

Song of the Forests, ontario for tenor, bass, boys' chorus, mixed chorus and symphony orchestra by Dmitri SHOSTAKOVICH, in seven sections, glorifying in heroic triadic stanzas the Soviet reforestation plan, composed according to the tenets of Socialist Realism, with the text voicing the optimistic expectations of the time when young trees will rise majestically on the banks of Russian rivers, and concluding with a perfervid expression of faith in the Leninist Party and in the limitless wisdom of sagacious Stalin, is performed for the first time in Leningrad.

16 NOVEMBER 1949

Le Peintre et son Modèle, ballet by Georges AURIC, in which a modern Pygmalion emulates in marble the carnal perfection of a living Parisian model, is produced in Paris.

19 NOVEMBER 1949

The Enormous Room, symphonic poem by the 34-year-old American composer David DIAMOND, after the novel of that name by e. e. cummings, descriptive of an actual "enormous room" in a French military camp, with 40 mattresses, 40 urinal cans and 40 multiracial suspects, in which cummings was detained himself for two months in 1917, set to music in the manner of an "unfolding song" expressive of the mood of "a new and beautiful darkness," in a starkly dissonant idiom, is performed for the first time by the Cincinnati Symphony Orchestra under the direction of Thor Johnson.

20 NOVEMBER 1949

Third Concerto for piano and orchestra by the Czech composer Bohuslav MARTINU, in three movements, *Allegro, Andante poco moderato* and *Moderato,* written in a neo-classical manner, is performed for the first time by Rudolf Firkušny with the Dallas Symphony Orchestra, Walter Hendl conducting.

22 NOVEMBER 1949

Guillermo URIBE-HOLGUÍN, dean of Colombian composers, conducts in Bogotá the first performance of his *Sinfonieta campesina.*

22 NOVEMBER 1949

Hindustani Concerto for piano and orchestra by the 45-year-old Scottish composer Erik CHISHOLM, presenting an artful fusion of Hindu ragas with modern harmonies, is played for the first time in a world première in Capetown, South Africa, where Chisholm was a resident composer and teacher.

25 NOVEMBER 1949

Apocalypse, oratorio by the 42-year-old Dutch composer Henk BADINGS, in two parts and seven chapters, scored for chorus, orchestra and a vocal quartet representing the four apocalyptic beasts, is performed for the first time in Rotterdam.

1 DECEMBER 1949

David Symphony by the 41-year-old Polish-born Israeli composer Menahem AVIDOM (who Hebraized his original Germanic cognomen Mahler-Kalkstein), is performed for the first time by the Israel Philharmonic Orchestra in Tel Aviv.

1 DECEMBER 1949

Hans Werner HENZE, 23-year-old German composer, conducts in Stuttgart the first performance of his *Second Symphony,* in three movements, cast in a proclamatory dramatic manner, with peals of distant drums and fanfares of declarative trumpets leading to a conglomerate of thundering polyharmonies and taciturn but eloquent silences, chromatic torsion of polythematic compaction and polyglot fugues in judiciously copulated invertible counterpoint, terminating in a magma of heteroousian sounds relentlessly increasing in saturation and finally erupting in an abrasive discord.

2 DECEMBER 1949

Turangalîla (Hindu word meaning love song), an expansive mystical symphony in ten movements by Olivier MESSIAEN (composed between 17 July 1946 and 29 November 1948), scored for piano, Ondes Martenot and large orchestra with an augmented percussion section, and abounding in sonorities redolent of the music of Bali and Java, with melorhythmic lines derived from Messiaen's theory of melodic and rhythmic modes as expounded in his musico-philosophical treatise *Technique de mon langage musical,* is performed for the first time anywhere by the Boston Symphony Orchestra, Leonard Bernstein conducting. (Three movements of *Turangalîla* were first performed under the title *Trois Talas* in Paris on 15 February 1948.)

2 DECEMBER 1949

Viola Concerto by Béla BARTÓK, in three movements, *Moderato, Adagio religioso, Allegro vivace,* connected by interludes, left in incomplete sketches after his death on

25 September 1945, reconstructed and orchestrated by his friend Tibor Serly, is performed for the first time by William Primrose, at whose behest the work was originally planned, with the Minneapolis Symphony Orchestra, under the direction of Antal Dorati.

6 DECEMBER 1949

Huddie LEDBETTER, known as LEADBELLY, Louisiana-born Negro balladeer who was a cotton picker on southern plantations, was jailed for felonious assault, but won a pardon from the Louisiana State Prison in 1934 after he sang for the Governor, and got into jail again in New York in 1939 for stabbing, albeit unfatally, another man, dies in New York at the age of 60.

7 DECEMBER 1949

Fifth Symphony by the 42-year-old Dutch modernist Henk BADINGS is performed for the first time by the Concertgebouw Orchestra in Amsterdam.

8 DECEMBER 1949

Gentlemen Prefer Blondes, musical comedy by Jule STYNE, after the exhilarating book of that title by Anita Loos, dealing with an acquisitive American blonde who latches herself onto a substantial sugar daddy, embodying her credo in the declarative song *Diamonds Are a Girl's Best Friend*, is produced in New York.

10 DECEMBER 1949

Krútňava (Whirlpool), opera in six scenes by the 41-year-old Slovak composer Eugen SUCHOŇ, a folk drama in which the bride of a slain Slovak peasant reluctantly marries his slayer who is tormented by the memories of the as yet undiscovered crime and is impelled to confess when he begins to suspect that his putative child is in reality the pre-marital offspring of his victim, set to music within the framework of traditional Slavonic melos with a patina of mellow Wagneromorphic harmonies, is produced in Bratislava.

16 DECEMBER 1949

Bernard WAGENAAR, 55-year-old Dutch-born American composer, conducts the Boston Symphony Orchestra in the world première of his *Fourth Symphony* in five movements, couched in a prophylactic neo-classical idiom covered by lyrical emulsions and invigorated by mobile counterpoint.

17 DECEMBER 1949

Two centuries have passed since the birth in Aversa, near Naples, of Domenico CIMAROSA, the composer of harmonious melodramatic operas in the finest tradition of the Italian Baroque. (To commemorate Cimarosa's bicentennial the Italian Government issued a postage stamp of 20 lire with his portrait.)

20 DECEMBER 1949

Enchanted Citadel, ballet by the Japanese composer Akira IFUKUBE, is performed for the first time in Tokyo.

22 DECEMBER 1949

Ricercari for orchestra by the 52-year-old Parisianized Polish composer Alexandre TANSMAN, consisting of four classical movements (*Notturno, Scherzo, Intermezzo, Toccata*) and one unclassical section *(Study in Boogie-Woogie)* is performed for the first time by the St. Louis Symphony Orchestra, Vladimir Golschmann conducting.

23 DECEMBER 1949

Juan José CASTRO, 54-year-old Argentinian composer, conducts in Montevideo the world première of his two-act opera *La Zapatera prodigiosa*, after the story by Federico García Lorca.

31 DECEMBER 1949

To commemorate the 50th anniversary of the death of the famous Viennese operetta composer Karl MILLÖCKER, the Austrian Government issues a postage stamp of one schilling bearing his portrait.

1950

4 JANUARY 1950

Judith, choreographic poem for orchestra by the 39-year-old American composer William SCHU-MAN, to the biblical story of the valorous Hebrew damsel who penetrated the camp of the Assyrian general Holofernes besieging her city and expertly decapitated him during his sleep, interpreted as "an ancient fertility ritual of rebirth, in which the woman casts off the garment of mourning and puts on her garments of gladness symbolic of her femininity thereby defeating the enemy, death," composed in a severely dissonant polyphonic idiom, rhythmically vivified by raucous outcries of triumph as Judith exhibits the bearded head of Holofernes for the delectation of the populace, is performed for the first time by Martha Graham and her dance group with the Louisville, Kentucky, Orchestra.

6 JANUARY 1950

Francis POULENC plays the solo part with the Boston Symphony Orchestra, Charles Munch conducting, in the world première of his *Piano Concerto*, set in a gallant Gallic style, in three mundane movements: (1) *Allegretto*, a hedonistically lyric essay in rococo harmonies; (2) *Andante con moto*, a pastoral interlude in salubrious march time; (3) *Rondeau à la française*, on the theme of an old French song "À la claire fontaine."

7 JANUARY 1950

Susanne, opera buffa by the Danish composer Knudaage RIISAGER is produced in Copenhagen.

11 JANUARY 1950

Piano Concerto by the 43-year-old American composer Paul CRESTON, in three movements—(1) *Allegretto maestoso*, in a vigorously lyric and coherently rhapsodic tonal idiom; (2) *Andante tranquillo*, a bucolic presentation of tranquil modalities; and (3) *Presto*, in the rhythmic scheme of a tarantella—is performed for the first time in Washington.

12 JANUARY 1950

Mondi celesti e infernali, opera in three acts "con 7 donne" by Gian Francesco MALIPIERO, written in the style of a baroque Italian madrigal suite, is produced in concert form on the Turin Radio (The first stage performance took place in Venice on 2 February 1961.)

15 JANUARY 1950

Auto da Barca do Inferno, opera by the Portuguese composer Ruy COELHO, is produced in Lisbon.

17 JANUARY 1950

4 Mouvements Symphoniques by the 44-year-old Dutch composer Guillaume LANDRÉ are performed for the first time in The Hague.

18 JANUARY 1950

The Barrier, two-act opera on the subject of race relations in Georgia by Jan MEYEROWITZ, to a libretto by Langston Hughes based on his *Mulatto* and *Father and Son*, is produced for the first time at Columbia University in New York.

21 JANUARY 1950

On the 60th anniversary of his first public appearance as a violinist at the age of eight, Georges ENESCO, prime Rumanian musician of the 20th century, gives his last American concert in New York in the multiple capacity of violinist, pianist, conductor and composer, in a program comprising Bach's concerto for two violins (as a dual soloist, with his pupil Yehudi Menuhin), his violin sonata (as pianist, with Menuhin), his *Second Suite* for orchestra in C major and his *First Rumanian Rhapsody* (as conductor).

22 JANUARY 1950

Chiarina, ballet-grotesque by Boris BLACHER, is produced in Berlin.

26 JANUARY 1950

Carlos SURINACH, 34-year-old Spanish composer, conducts in Paris the first performance of his *Second Symphony*.

27 JANUARY 1950

Four Transylvanian Dances for string orchestra by the 42-year-old Transylvanian composer Sándor VERESS is performed for the first time in Basel.

28 JANUARY 1950

Französische Suite for orchestra by Werner EGK, on themes by Rameau, is performed for the first time in Munich. (It was first performed as a ballet in Hamburg on 1 February 1952.)

29 JANUARY 1950

Das Spiel vom König Aphelius, music drama for narrator and orchestra by Heinrich KAMINSKI, is performed posthumously for the first time in Göttingen.

30 JANUARY 1950

The widow of Camille SAINT-SAËNS (separated from him in 1881, but never legally divorced) dies in Bordeaux at the age of 95.

1 FEBRUARY 1950

Timon of Athens, a symphonic portrait after Shakespeare, by the 34-year-old American composer David DIAMOND, is performed for the first time by the Louisville Orchestra.

1 FEBRUARY 1950

Concerto for piano and orchestra by the 52-year-old German-born Israeli composer Paul BEN-HAIM, in three movements, subtitled *Vision, Voices in the Night* and *Dance*, reflecting respectively a romantic image, a Mediterranean landscape and an Oriental festival, is performed for the first time in Tel Aviv.

5 FEBRUARY 1950

Concerto for violin and orchestra by the 53-year-old French composer Jean RIVIER, written in a virtuoso idiom of modern France, is performed for the first time by the Société des Concerts du Conservatoire in Paris.

7 FEBRUARY 1950

The Enchanted Pear Tree, one-act radio opera by Hall OVERTON, is produced in New York.

8 FEBRUARY 1950

L'Orso Re, musical fable in three acts the 65-year-old Italian composer Luigi FERRARI-TRECATE, dealing with an ensorcelled King who assumes an ursine form and rules a nation of bears, but is restored to the human species after the sorcerer's invultuation loses its magic, set to music replete with atonal acerbities and polytonal acridities and ending on a chord of eight different notes, is produced at La Scala in Milan.

8 FEBRUARY 1950

The German Democratic Republic formally adopts the musical setting by Hanns EISLER of the socialist hymn of Johannes R. Becher, "Auferstanden aus Ruinen und der Zukunft zugewandt" (composed by Eisler during a visit to Warsaw in 1949 and played by him for the first time on Chopin's piano in the house where Chopin was born), as its national anthem.

10 FEBRUARY 1950

Third Symphony by the 44-year-old German master contrapuntist Karl Amadeus HARTMANN, in three movements, "rooted in the spiritual landscape of Alban Berg," with a magistral fugue flanked by two slow movements—a *Largo* for strings and an "ecstatically hymnal" *Adagio*, is performed for the first time in Munich.

10 FEBRUARY 1950

Violin Concerto by the 39-year-old American composer William SCHUMAN, in two movements—(1) *Allegro risoluto*, set in bitonal major-minor triadic harmonies in which the mediant is ambivalent, ending on the E major-minor chord; (2) *Introduzione Adagio, Poco più mosso, Presto subito, Allegretto*, in stark quintal-quartal counterpoint, resulting in organum-like sonorities and ending on a unison—is played for the first time by Isaac Stern with the Boston Symphony Orchestra, Charles Munch conducting.

12 FEBRUARY 1950

Die Füsse im Feuer and *Fingerhütchen*, two ballad operas by the Swiss composer Heinrich SUTERMEISTER, are performed for the first time in Berlin.

19 FEBRUARY 1950

Concerto for flute and string orchestra by André JOLIVET, in four contrasting movements, is performed for the first time in Paris under the composer's direction, with Jean Pierre Rampal as soloist.

20 FEBRUARY 1950

Don Quixote, ballet by the Spanish composer Roberto GERHARD, resident in England, is produced in London.

24 FEBRUARY 1950

Frol Skobeyev, comic opera in four acts by the 36-year-old Soviet composer Tikhon KHRENNIKOV, dealing with a liberal Russian nobleman of the 17th century who buys off and frees the serfs of the father of his beloved, is produced in Moscow.

1 MARCH 1950

The Consul, musical drama in three acts by Gian Carlo MENOTTI, to his own libretto depicting the agonizing peril of an anti-Fascist couple in an anonymous European country trying desperately to obtain a salutary visa from the consul of an unnamed great nation, set to music with intense lyrico-dramatic expressiveness, rivalling Puccini in theatrical power, in a distinctly personal cosmopolitan idiom with a judicious application of vigesimosecular technical media, is produced in Philadelphia, staged by Menotti himself. (The first New York production took place on 15 March 1950.)

1 MARCH 1950

Paul HINDEMITH conducts the Louisville Orchestra in the world première of his *Sinfonietta in E*, in four movements, conceived as a 20th-century replica of an 18th-century entertainment piece, and abounding in lively contrapuntal gambados.

3 MARCH 1950

Fourth Piano Concerto by Darius MILHAUD, in three movements conceived in contrasting meditative and joyous moods, and reaching polytonal polyphony at recurring climaxes, is performed for the first time by Zadel Skolovsky with the Boston Symphony Orchestra, Charles Munch conducting.

7 MARCH 1950

Violin Concerto by the 34-year-old Canadian composer Alexander BROTT is performed for the first time in Montreal.

10 MARCH 1950

Lukas FOSS, 27-year-old Berlin-born American composer conducts the Boston Symphony Orchestra in the world première of his *Song of Anguish*, biblical solo cantata for baritone and orchestra to the text freely arranged from the Book of Isaiah: "Woe unto them that call evil good and good evil!"

16 MARCH 1950

Fifth Symphony by Ernst KRENEK, in five linked movements, written in a free dodecaphonic idiom, is performed for the first time by the Albuquerque Symphony Orchestra.

18 MARCH 1950

A concert of "Musique Concrète," glorifying the "dialectic of the fortuitous" fructified by "esthetic volition," and compiled of aleatory combinations of recorded noises and unrelated fragments of speech and melodies, played at different speeds and sometimes in reverse, is presented at the École Normale de Musique in Paris, by Pierre SCHAEFFER and Pierre HENRY in a program of synthetic pieces entitled *Symphonie pour un homme seul*, *Bidule en ut*, and *Concerto des ambiguités*.

24 MARCH 1950

Cello Concerto by Virgil THOMSON in three movements, subtitled *Rider on the Plains*, *Variations on a Southern Hymn Tune*, and *Children's Games*, employing simple parallel major triads for straight harmonization, and mutually exclusive pairs of major and minor triads, with some bitonal, pentatonic, and hexatonic excrescences for more complex developments, is performed for the first time by the Philadelphia Orchestra.

31 MARCH 1950

The First Waltz, operetta by the 80-year-old Viennese composer Oskar STRAUS is performed for the first time in Munich, in the presence of the composer, with 28 curtain calls saluting him at the end.

31 MARCH 1950

Metaphor, ballet by Niels Viggo BENTZON, 30-year-old Danish composer, is performed for the first time in Copenhagen.

2 APRIL 1950

Fifth Symphony by the 26-year-old American composer Peter MENNIN is performed for the first time by the Dallas Symphony Orchestra, Walter Hendl conducting.

3 APRIL 1950

Kurt WEILL, German composer, creator of a new type of modern opera, in which simple melodies are set in the framework of complex and often raspingly dissonant harmonies, dies at the age of 50 in New York, at the height of his new American career as the composer of successful stage music in a witty, folk-wise American manner.

9 APRIL 1950

Der spanische Rosenstock, opera in three acts by the 29-year-old Swiss composer Armin SCHIBLER, is performed for the first time in Bern, Switzerland.

19 APRIL 1950

LORD BERNERS (originally Gerald Tyrwhitt), aristocratic English composer of humorous modernistic pieces, dies in London at the age of 66.

19 APRIL 1950

L'Inconnue, ballet by the French modernist André JOLIVET, is produced in Paris.

4 MAY 1950

Concerto de mai for piano and orchestra by the 51-year-old French composer Marcel DELANNOY, so named because it was begun in May 1949 and its orchestration completed in May 1950, barely in time for performance, is performed in Paris by the Société des Jeunesses Musicales de France.

4 MAY 1950

L'Allegra brigata, "six novellas in one drama of three acts" with words and music by Gian Francesco MALIPIERO, six stories of zealous love and dark jealousy, narrated by six members of the "merry brigade," culminating in the murder of one of them, is produced at La Scala, Milan.

5 MAY 1950

Le Chevalier Errant, ballet with chorus by Jacques IBERT, musically miming the more salient sallies of the "Knight Errant" Don Quixote, is performed for the first time in Paris. (A symphonic suite in four movements from this ballet was first performed in Paris on 22 February 1952.)

7 MAY 1950

La Main de Gloire, "macaronic history of an enchanted hand," opera in four acts by Jean FRANÇAIX, to the fantastic story by Gérard de Nerval about a duelist who by artful magic makes his right hand unerringly effective in killing his rival in love, but who subsequently loses control over the "glorious hand" and is led by it, against his will, to crime and eventually to self-destruction, is produced in Bordeaux.

9 MAY 1950

The Triumph of St. Joan, chamber opera by the 37-year-old American composer Norman DELLO JOIO, is performed for the first time at Sarah Lawrence College, Bronxville, New York. (The musical material of the opera was subsequently used by Dello Joio in an orchestral work *The Triumph of St. Joan Symphony*, first performed in Louisville, Kentucky, as a ballet on 5 December 1951. With an entirely different score, *The Triumph of St. Joan* was produced as an opera in New York on 16 April 1959.)

11 MAY 1950

Rapsodia banateana by the Rumanian composer Zeno VANCEA, based on the themes of the Banat region is performed for the first time in Bucharest.

12 MAY 1950

Pohádka máje (*Romance in May*), opera in three acts by the Czech composer Jaroslav KVAPIL, is produced in Pragne.

12 MAY 1950

Bolivar, opera in three acts by Darius MILHAUD (completed at Mills College, California, on 3 June 1943), symbolically representing the struggles and the victory of the

Spanish-American Liberator, with a musical score full of polytonal tension and vibrating with tropical rhythms, is performed for the first time at the Paris Opéra.

13 MAY 1950

De Nachtwacht, opera by the Dutch composer Henk BADINGS, inspired by the famous painting by Rembrandt representing a company of soldiers enveloped in nocturnal shadows dappled with light, is performed for the first time in Antwerp.

17 MAY 1950

Nine centuries have passed since the death in Pomposa of GUIDO D'AREZZO, the initiator of musical pedagogy by means of the syllabic vocalization on Ut, Re, Mi, Fa, Sol, La.

17 MAY 1950

Eduardo FABINI, Uruguayan composer of impressionistic music imbued with Latin American melorhythms, dies in Montevideo on the eve of his 67th birthday.

18 MAY 1950

The Jumping Frog of Calaveras County, opera in two scenes by the 27-year-old Berlin-born American composer, Lukas FOSS, after Mark Twain's famous story of a frog race, is performed for the first time at Indiana University in Bloomington, during the week in May when actual jumping frog contests are held annually in Calaveras County, California.

18 MAY 1950

Second Symphony in C minor by the dean of Canadian composers Healey WILLAN, is performed for the first time in Toronto.

20 MAY 1950

First Symphony by the 29-year-old American composer William BERGSMA is performed for the first time on a radio broadcast from New York.

20 MAY 1950

Il Prigioniero, one-act opera with a prologue by the 46-year-old Italian modernist Luigi DALLAPICCOLA, to a libretto based on *La Torture par l'Espérance* from *Nouveaux Contes cruels* by Villiers de l'Isle-Adam and Charles de Coster's *La Légende d' Ulenspiegel* dealing with a prisoner of Philip II in Saragossa provoked and aided in his escape by a guard who turns out to be the Grand Inquisitor in person (the prisoner exclaims: "La speranza, l'ultima tortura!"), with musical materials based on three dodecaphonic themes, symbolizing prayer, hope and freedom (with a choral finale of four mutually exclusive triads, thus equating tonality with liberty), is produced at the May Festival in Florence. (The first concert performance of the work was given on the Turin Radio, 4 December 1949.)

22 MAY 1950

Vier Letzte Lieder for soprano and orchestra by Richard STRAUSS, written in 1948, are posthumously performed for the first time in London by Kirsten Flagstad, with Wilhelm Furtwängler conducting.

26 MAY 1950

Third Symphony by the 46-year-old Japanese composer Saburo MOROI is presented for the first time in Tokyo.

27 MAY 1950

Jan Hus, opera by the Czech composer Karel HORKÝ, dealing with the life of the religious Czech martyr, is produced in Brno.

8 JUNE 1950

Concerto for French horn and orchestra by Paul HINDEMITH is performed for the first time in Baden-Baden.

11 JUNE 1950

Ein Sommertag, ballet by Werner EGK, is performed for the first time in Berlin.

11 JUNE 1950

Don Juan und Faust, opera by the 49-year-old German composer Hermann REUTTER, is performed for the first time in Stuttgart.

12 JUNE 1950

Manuel ROSENTHAL conducts the orchestra of Radiodiffusion Française in Paris in the world première of his *Sinfonia in Do*, in three classically shaped movements of French provincial life, including realistic animal cries, and carrying a carillon motto in percurration throughout the work.

15 JUNE 1950

Il Nazzareno, opera by the Italian religious composer Lorenzo PEROSI, is produced at La Scala, Milan.

23 JUNE 1950

Philomela, opera in seven scenes by the 57-year-old Dutch composer Hendrik ANDRIESSEN, to a libretto from the Greek myth of a tyrannical king who carnally violates the chastity of his sister-in-law Philomela and cuts out her tongue to prevent her from reporting the outrage to others, but suffers grim retribution when Philomela kills his child and serves its roasted body at the royal feast, for which deed she is metamorphosed into a nightingale, is performed for the first time at the Holland Festival in Amsterdam.

23 JUNE 1950

La Pierre enchantée, ballet by Georges AURIC, is performed for the first time in Paris.

23 JUNE 1950

The 24th Festival of the International Society for Contemporary Music opens in Brussels presenting the following program:

Chamber Symphony in five movements by Schoenberg's disciple Hanns EISLER; *Concerto* for piano and chamber orchestra by the 35-year-old Dutch composer Marius FLOTHUIS; *Concerto for String Orchestra* by the 45-year-old English composer Alan RAWSTHORNE; and *Second Cantata*, op. 31, by Anton von WEBERN, for soprano, bass, chorus and orchestra, in six sections based on a single 12-tone series, two divisions of which are so fashioned that each division states each of the 48 avatars of the series once and once only.

24 JUNE 1950

The 24th International Society for Contemporary Music Festival in Brussels presents the following program of chamber music:

String Quartet in one movement by the 29-year-old English composer Peter Racine FRICKER; *Psalm CXXVII* for three voices, violin, viola and cello, by the 27-year-old Italian composer Camillo TOGNI; *String Quartet* in three movements by the 43-year-old Russian-born, ethnically Polish, Swiss resident composer Constantin REGAMEY; *Hommage à Schoenberg* by the 35-year-old Brazilian composeress Eunice CATUNDA, scored for clarinet, bass clarinet, viola, cello and piano, with Latin American rhythms punctuating the dodecaphonic thematic material; *Sonata for Cello and Piano* by the 42-year-old German composer Wolfgang FORTNER; and *String Quartet* by the 34-year-old South African Arnold Van WIJCK (who sometimes spells his name simply WYK).

25 JUNE 1950

At the 24th International Society for Contemporary Music Festival in Brussels, the following program of Belgian music is presented:

James Ensor, orchestral suite in four movements, *L'entrée du Christ à Bruxelles, Aquelettes se disputant un pendu, Jardin d'amour, Cortège infernal,* by the 73-year-old composer Florent ALPAERTS, inspired by the lugubrious paintings of the Belgian artist Ensor (1860–1949); *Allegro Symphonique* by the 49-year-old neo-classicist Marcel POOT; *3 mouvements Symphoniques* by the 52-year-old neo-romanticist Fernand QUINET; *Chant d'angoisse* for cello and orchestra by Albert HUYBRECHTS (1899–1938); and *Second Symphony* in three movements by the 56-year-old modernist Jean ABSIL.

25 JUNE 1950

Namus (*Honor*), opera by the 39-year-old Soviet composer Nazib ZHIGANOV, to a patriotic libretto in the Tatar language, is produced in Kazan, which was the seat of the Tatar Golden Horde that subjugated Russia before Kazan was stormed by Ivan the Terrible in 1572.

27 JUNE 1950

The following program is presented at the International Society for Contemporary Music Festival in Brussels:

Hai-kai de Basho for chamber orchestra by the 54-year-old Japanese composer Shukichi MITSUKURI, in ten aphoristic sections inspired by the three-line Japanese verses; *Laudi,* a neo-medieval unaccompanied chorus by the 29-year-old Swedish composer Ingvar LIDHOLM; *5 Comptines* (children's counting nursery rhymes) for voice and 11 instruments by the 36-year-old Belgian composer Pierre FROIDEBISE; *3 Lieder* for six wind instruments by the 27-year-old Belgian composer Karel GOEYVAERTS; *L'Explication des Métaphores* for speaker, two pianos, harp and percussion by the apostle of dodecaphonic music, René LEIBOWITZ, conducted by the composer, and *Cantata of the Vistula River* by the 42-year-old Polish composer Roman PALESTER.

28 JUNE 1950

The following program of orchestral music is presented at the 24th International Society for Contemporary Music Festival in Brussels:

Sinfonia giocosa in three movements by the 43-year-old Norwegian composer Klaus EGGE; *Toccata and Fugue* for piano and orchestra by the 45-year-old Polish composer Artur MALAWSKY; *Psyché*, symphonic movement by the French modernist André JOLIVET; and *La Naissance du Verbe* for chorus and orchestra by the 45-year-old Italian composer Giacinto SCELSI, which contains a polytonal canon in 48 parts written in 12 different keys.

29 JUNE 1950

The following program is presented at the 24th International Society for Contemporary Music Festival in Brussels:

String Quartet by the 47-year-old Swedish composer Hilding HALLNÄS; *Second Sonatina* for violin and piano by the 49-year-old Swiss composer Conrad BECK; *Quintet* for wind instruments by the 34-year-old Belgian composer Marcel QUINET; *Les Rêves de Jacob,* choreographic suite for oboe, violin, viola, cello and doublebass, by Darius MILHAUD; and *String Quartet* by the 28-year-old Czech neo-classicist Karel HUSA.

30 JUNE 1950

The 24th Festival of the International Society for Contemporary Music in Brussels concludes with a concert of orchestral music consisting of the following compositions:

Fourth Symphony for string orchestra, by the German master-contrapuntist Karl Amadeus HARTMANN, in three well-demarcated movements: *Lento con passione, Allegro di molto* (*Scherzo*), *Adagio appassionato*, written in an expressionistic manner of a quasi-serial nature, and related to the usages of Alban Berg; *Concerto* for flute and orchestra by the 36-year-old Dutch composer Hans HENKEMANS; *Concerto* for 3 pianos and 8 instruments by the 30-year-old Danish neo-romanticist Niels Viggo BENTZON; and *Fifth Symphony* by Harald SAEVERUD of Norway.

1 JULY 1950

Émile JAQUES-DALCROZE, creator of Eurhythmics and composer of lyric pieces of an ethnomusicological nature, dies in Geneva five days before his 85th birthday.

3 JULY 1950

Concertante for piano left hand and orchestra by the British composer Arnold BAX, in three movements, written in a classical idiom, economically designed in its harmonic and contrapuntal techniques, is performed for the first time at the Cheltenham Festival, England, by Harriet Cohen, for whom it was written after she fell carrying a tray of glass dishes into the kitchen of her London home in 1948 and cut the wrist of her right hand damaging the nerve and causing it to wither. (Initially, the work was called a *Concerto,* but in view of the slenderness of the piano part limited to the left hand, its designation was changed to *Concertante.*)

5 JULY 1950

First Symphony by the 29-year-old English composer Peter Racine FRICKER, in four movements making use of a variety of modern devices, including dodecaphonic approximations, devoid of a key signature but tonocentric in its teleological design, is performed for the first time at the Cheltenham Festival in England, Sir John Barbirolli conducting.

9 JULY 1950

Hans CHEMIN-PETIT, 47-year-old Potsdam-born composer whose Germanic first name and French patronymic are reflected in the duality of his semi-Teutonic demi-Gallic style of composition, conducts in Potsdam (where he remained through the years of wartime devastation) the first performance of his *Second Symphony,* set in the bland key of C major.

12 JULY 1950

Concerto for French Horn and Orchestra by the 48-year-old Belgian composer Raymond CHEVREUILLE, is performed for the first time in Brussels.

18 JULY 1950

Josef KRIPS, Austrian conductor, is forced to fly back to Vienna from New York two days after landing, when the immigration officials refuse to honor his valid American visa, owing to undisclosed information regarding his alleged leftist associations.

20 JULY 1950

The first Estonian opera on a Soviet theme, *Vabaduse laulik* (*The Singer of Freedom*), by the 42-year-old Volga-born Estonian composer Eugen KAPP, dealing with turbulent years of the Nazi invasion of Soviet Estonia in 1941, the heroic death of the patriotic bride of the hero, and ending with the expulsion of the invaders by the victorious Red Army in the last act, is produced in Tallin.

28 JULY 1950

On the bicentennial of the death of BACH, the Government of the Federal German Republic issues two stamps, at 12 and 23 pfennigs, bearing his image.

29 JULY 1950

To commemorate the 900th anniversary since the death on 17 May 1050 of the initiator of modern musical notation GUIDO D'AREZZO, the Italian Government issues a stamp of 20 lire bearing his likeness.

8 AUGUST 1950

Nicolai MIASKOVSKY, Russian composer of 27 symphonies, the greatest number written by anyone since Haydn, and teacher of a generation of Soviet composers, dies in Moscow of an inoperable intestinal cancer, at the age of 69.

5 SEPTEMBER 1950

The Australian composer Arthur BENJAMIN plays the solo part in the first performance of his *Piano Concerto* with the Sydney Symphony Orchestra under the direction of Eugene Goossens.

8 SEPTEMBER 1950

An organ based on the division of the octave into 31 unequal degrees, originally proposed for acoustical reasons by the celebrated Dutch astronomer Christiaan HUYGENS (1629–1695) in his *Nouveau Cycle Harmonique,* in which the smallest interval is 1/5 of a tone, a system which permits sounds to be produced in pure Pythagorean intonation as well as in the traditional scales of tempered semitones, is demonstrated for the first time in Rotterdam.

10 SEPTEMBER 1950

Second Symphony by the 45-year-old German composer Karl Amadeus HARTMANN, in a single movement, *Adagio,* with a median contrasting section *Allegro,* cyclically evolved from a guiding germinal theme through multiple variations in a series of terraced dynamic arches, is performed for the first time at the annual festival of modern music in Donaueschingen. (Hartmann's *Third Symphony* and his *Fourth* were performed prior to the *Second.*)

18 SEPTEMBER 1950

Saga-Symphony by the prime Icelandic composer Jón LEIFS, set in bleak pentatonic modalities arrayed in glacially immobile harmonies and arranged in arctically gelid instrumentation, is performed for the first time in Helsinki.

19 SEPTEMBER 1950

Son of a Clown, operetta by the Soviet composer Isaak DUNAYEVSKY, a satire exposing the unsocialistic conduct of a popular Soviet circus artist, with a happy ending as he yields to the power of dialectical persuasion by his proper colleagues and returns to the path of Communist virtue, is produced in Moscow.

20 SEPTEMBER 1950

Rosaura, romantic opera after Goldoni by the learned Danish music theorist Knud JEPPESEN, is produced in Copenhagen.

22 SEPTEMBER 1950

Ballade for orchestra by the 43-year-old Java-born Dutch composer Henk BADINGS is performed for the first time in Maastricht.

4 OCTOBER 1950

Ekvinocij (*Equinox*), music drama in three acts by the 43-year-old Croatian composer Ivan BRKANOVIĆ, wherein a rich American immigrant returning to his native Dalmatia on June 21, 1867, is confronted by the abandoned mother of his illegitimate Dalmatian son who is in love with the ship captain's young daughter coveted by his natural father as well, with a tragic retribution meted out when the mother kills the American by a well-aimed stone so as to enable their son to marry the captain's daughter, set to music in a melodramatic idiom, modernistically titivated by polytriadic harmonies and non-corrosive dissonances, is produced in Zagreb.

12 OCTOBER 1950

Call Me Madam, musical comedy by Irving BERLIN, inspired by the appointment of Perle Mesta, the Washington "hostess with the mostest" as the American envoy to Luxemburg, wherein the American ambassadress to a tiny European republic promises a billion-dollar American subsidy to its prime minister and gains his personal affection, the score containing the politically shrewd song by three vocal Congressmen, *They Like Ike,* destined to play a historic role in overcoming Eisenhower's reluctance to enter the presidential campaign and resulting in his election in 1952, is performed for the first time in New York.

15 OCTOBER 1950

On the 50th anniversary of the death of the Czech composer Zdenko FIBICH, the Czechoslovak post office issues two commemorative stamps in the denominations of 3 and 8 kronen bearing his image.

24 OCTOBER 1950

La Morte dell' Aria, opera by the 46-year-old Italian composer Goffredo PETRASSI, is produced in Rome.

27 OCTOBER 1950

Third Symphony, by the 44-year-old American composer Paul CRESTON, subtitled *Three Mysteries,* with its three movements, *The Nativity, The Crucifixion,* and *The Resurrection,* thematically derived from Gregorian chants, developed in an austerely lyrical manner, is performed for the first time by the Philadelphia Orchestra, Eugene Ormandy conducting, at the Worcester, Massachusetts Music Festival.

29 OCTOBER 1950

Quartet for piano and strings by Aaron COPLAND, commissioned by the Elizabeth Sprague Coolidge Foundation, his first work in an overtly serial method of composition, with the opening theme constituting a hendecaphonic tone-row, and the second theme being its retrograde, containing also some jazzy inflections, in three movements, *Adagio serioso, Allegro giusto, Non troppo lento,* is performed for the first time at the Coolidge Festival at the Library of Congress in Washington.

31 OCTOBER 1950

Octavio PINTO, Brazilian composer of attractive piano pieces, husband of pianist Guiomar Novaẽs, dies in his native town of São Paulo, three days before his 60th birthday.

31 OCTOBER 1950

Job, "sacra rappresentazione" by the 46-year-old Italian modernist Luigi DALLAPICCOLA, written in a consistent dodecaphonic idiom eschewed only in the solemn triadic harmonies to accompany the Lord's climactic peroration, is performed for the first time in Rome.

2 NOVEMBER 1950

George Bernard SHAW, great Irish dramatist who during his meteoric interlude as a London music critic in the 1880's initiated a new journalistic treatment of musical events, coloring his reviews with brilliant personal prejudices, dies at 4:59 in the morning at his home at Ayot-St.-Lawrence, at the age of ninety-four, leaving stern instructions that no cross "or any other instrument of torture" be erected on his grave and that his body be cremated and ashes strewn in the garden.

3 NOVEMBER 1950

Third Symphony by the 35-year-old American composer David DIAMOND, dedicated to his parents, in five sections, alternatingly fast and slow, unified by two basic motives which appear in augmentation, diminution, and retrograde movement, is performed for the first time by the Boston Symphony Orchestra, Charles Munch conducting. (Diamond's *Fourth Symphony* was performed before the *Third* at a Boston Symphony concert on 23 January 1948.)

6 NOVEMBER 1950

Concerto for clarinet, string orchestra, harp and piano by Aaron COPLAND, in two sections marked *Slowly and Expressively* and *Rather Fast,* linked by a flamboyant jazz cadenza for the clarinet, is performed for the first time by Benny Goodman, "King of Swing" who commissioned the work, with the NBC Symphony Orchestra in New York, conducted by Fritz Reiner.

7 NOVEMBER 1950

The Family of Taras, opera in four acts by the 45-year-old Soviet composer Dmitri KABALEVSKY, to a libretto dealing with the heroic family of a metal worker whose two sons and daughter join the partisans to fight the Nazi occupation army in the Ukraine in 1942, with thematic materials derived from popular Soviet songs, is produced in Leningrad.

(The first version of the opera was given in Moscow on 2 November 1947; both versions included some material from a previous opera by Kabalevsky, *In the Fire,* produced in Moscow on 7 November 1947, which in turn was a revised version of the opera *At Moscow,* produced in Moscow on 28 November 1943.)

I transferred some thematic materials from the opera *In the Fire* into *The Family of Taras,* namely the theme of the enemy, the motive of the mother, and some other melodic elements, but not a great quantity in all. The longest episode among these borrowed materials is the chorus of Russian women driven away into Fascist slavery. This episode remained without change in the subject and the text, but was modified only in some details of the orchestral scoring. (From a letter to the author from Kabalevsky, dated Moscow, 28 January 1960)

12 NOVEMBER 1950

Concerto for Koto and Orchestra (the koto is a Japanese zither) by the 40-year-old Japanese composer Kozaburo HIRAI is performed for the first time in Tokyo.

18 NOVEMBER 1950

Concerto Grosso by Ralph VAUGHAN WILLIAMS, in five movements, scored for string orchestra subdivided into three groups to be played by amateurs of various grades of skill, written in a melodious, harmonious, generally euphonious, sophisticatedly abecedarian musical language fortified by a plasma of nutritious triadic harmonies, and including a part in which only open strings are used, is performed for the first time by a massed ensemble of 400 semi-professional and manually unskilled members of the Rural Music Schools Association in London, under the direction of Sir Adrian Boult.

19 NOVEMBER 1950

Hamlet, ballet by Boris BLACHER, is produced in Munich.

20 NOVEMBER 1950

Francesco CILÈA, Italian composer of melodramatic operas in the tradition of Verismo, of which *Adriana Lecouvreur* became a repertory piece, dies in Varazza at the age of 84.

21 NOVEMBER 1950

Fifth Symphony by the 53-year-old Danish composer Knudaage RIISAGER, subtitled *Sinfonia serena*, in four movements, *Allegro ardito, Vivace ilare, Lamentoso, Allegro spregiudicato*, set in a style of tempestuous tranquility, traversing the moods of defiance, vivacious hilarity, lament and unprejudiced merriment, without overflowing the banks of tonality, is performed for the first time in Copenhagen.

23 NOVEMBER 1950

Short Symphony by the 41-year-old Negro composer Howard SWANSON, is performed for the first time by the New York Philharmonic Orchestra, Dimitri Mitropoulos conducting.

23 NOVEMBER 1950

A Japanese musical group HAKUTOKAI (WHITE WAVE SOCIETY), formed with the aim of "reworking traditional Japanese music into a thing to be proud of on the international level," presents in Tokyo its inaugural concert consisting of works by modern Japanese composers.

24 NOVEMBER 1950

Guys and Dolls, "a musical fable of Broadway," by Frank LOESSER, based on tales by Damon Runyon, with various picturesque characters milling around a Manhattan nightclub, into which blunders a starry-eyed Salvation Army lass, idiomatically set to music in the colorful lingo of Tin Pan Alley, including among its hit tunes the melosomatic ballad, *Adelaide's Lament* marked by onomatopoeic tonal sternutations caused by amorous frustra-tions, *If I were a Bell, A Bushel and a Peck*, and a three-part *Fugue for Tinhorns*, is produced in New York.

29 NOVEMBER 1950

Catharsis, symphonic ballet by the 44-year-old Dutch composer Bertus van LIER, to a scenario in which mysterious intruders terrorize a married couple, their two children and a pregnant woman, is performed for the first time in Utrecht.

1 DECEMBER 1950

Ernest John MOERAN, 55-year-old Irish composer of pleasantly lilted instrumental music permeated by authentically inflected melodic patterns of Irish and East Anglian folk tunes, is found drowned in the Kenmare River, County Kerry, Ireland, possibly a victim of a sudden suicidal impulse.

2 DECEMBER 1950

Facanapas, opera written in 1935 by the Greek composer Denis LAVRANGAS, is produced in Athens, nine years after the composer's death.

2 DECEMBER 1950

Ernest BLOCH conducts the first performance with the Chicago Symphony Orchestra of his *Schrezo Fantasque* for piano and orchestra.

2 DECEMBER 1950

Dinu LIPATTI, Rumanian pianist whose frail physique and lapidary pianism made him a Chopinesque figure, dies in Geneva of lymphogranulomatosis, at the lamentable age of 33.

3 DECEMBER 1950

Symphonie de Numance by the 50-year-old French composer Henry BARRAUD, inspired by a play of Cervantes about the capture of the Spanish town of Numantia by the Roman armies of General Scipio in 133 B.C. is produced in Baden-Baden. (An opera by Henry Barraud expanded from the materials of *Symphonie de Numance* was produced at the Opéra-Comique in Paris on 15 April 1955.)

6 DECEMBER 1950

President TRUMAN, infuriated by the disparaging review by Paul HUME in the Washington *Post* of a song recital by Truman's daughter Margaret, dispatches a letter to him written in longhand on White House stationery, as follows: "Mr. Hume: I have just read your lousy review of Margaret's concert. I've come to the conclusion that you are an eight-ulcer man on four-ulcer pay . . . Some day I hope to meet you. When that happens, you'll need a new nose, a lot of beefsteak for black eyes, and perhaps a supporter below."

8 DECEMBER 1950

Sinfonia concertante for violin, oboe, bassoon, cello and orchestra by Bohuslav MARTINU is performed for the first time in Basel.

9 DECEMBER 1950

Twenty-Seventh Symphony, in C minor, the last of a long series by the most prolific symphonist of the 20th century, Nicolai MIASKOVSKY (completed by him on 2 November 1949), in three cyclically bound movements—(1) *Adagio-Allegro animato*, (2) *Adagio-Molto elevato*, (3) *Presto*—distinguished by a sense of symphonic dramaturgy following the Aristotelian dialectic of catharsis through tragedy and pity and couched in lyrical Russian modalities, is performed for the first time in Moscow, four months after Miaskovsky's death.

11 DECEMBER 1950

Clarinet Concerto by Paul HINDEMITH, in four neo-classically balanced movements, *Ziemlich schnell, Schnell, Ruhig, Heiter,* reflecting the moods of hedonism, optimism, lyricism, and gaiety, written in a translucent polyphonic idiom with a generous application of temperate dissonances, is performed for the first time by the Philadelphia Orchestra, Eugene Ormandy conducting, with the whilom killer-diller on the licorice stick, Benny Goodman, to whom the score is dedicated, as soloist.

12 DECEMBER 1950

Ninth Symphony by the foremost Swiss symphonist Fritz BRUN, in five movements, subtitled *Einleitung, Serenade, Liebesruf, Lob der Freundschaft* and *Lob Gottes und der Natur,* is performed for the first time in Zürich.

14 DECEMBER 1950

Moldavian Suite for orchestra by the 34-year-old Moscow-born composer Nicolai PEYKO, based on folk themes of Moldavia, a region newly incorporated into the Union of Soviet Socialist Republics, is performed for the first time in Moscow.

18 DECEMBER 1950

Max und Moritz, dance-burlesque by the 46-year-old German composer Richard MOHAUPT, inspired by the fairy tales of Wilhelm Busch retailing in gaily rhymed verses the unspeakable outrages wrought by two sadistically inventive small boys, is performed for the first time in Karlsruhe.

19 DECEMBER 1950

On Guard for Peace, cantata by Sergei PROKOFIEV, in ten sections, to texts by the foremost Soviet writer of children's verse Samuel Marshak, inveighing against the American militarists importing "one hundred thousand tons worth of death" to Europe, is performed for the first time in Moscow.

20 DECEMBER 1950

First Symphony by the 63-year-old Austrian composer Ernst TOCH, bearing the epigraph from Martin Luther's anacoluthic oath "Und wenn die Welt voll Teufel wär . . .," containing the thematic use of tritones, the *diabolus in musica* of medieval theorists, in four movements—(1) *Molto tranquillo*, (2) *Allegro molto*, (3) *Langsam, zart*, (4) *Allegro non troppo,* concluding on a hymnal D major chord—is performed for the first time in Vienna.

22 DECEMBER 1950

Walter DAMROSCH, German-born American musician, who conducted a great many American premières of famous works, dies in New York at the age of 88.

23 DECEMBER 1950

Vincenzo TOMMASINI, Italian composer of neo-romantic symphonic pieces touched with impressionistic color, dies in his native Rome at the age of 72.

31 DECEMBER 1950

Charles KOECHLIN, the bearded patriarch of French music, composer of numerous pieces of symphonic and vocal music in a highly personal idiom marked by brilliant eruptions of instrumental colors, dies in his villa, Le Canadel, in the province of Var, in Southern France, at the age of 83.

1951

6 JANUARY 1951

The Shadowy Waters, opera by the 67-year-old dean of the traditional school of Greek composers Manolis KALOMIRIS, to a libretto drawn from an Irish tale of W. B. Yeats, is produced in Athens.

16 JANUARY 1951

From the Bottom of My Heart, opera in three acts by the 37-year-old Ukrainian composer Herman ZHUKOVSKY, with action taking place on a Ukrainian collective farm, wherein an unsocialistically individualistic youth is won over to the collectivistic way of life by his proletarian bride and together they attend the unveiling of an electric power station, set to music modeled after Mussorgsky's realistic style, is produced at the Bolshoi Theater in Moscow.

Our nation expects Soviet composers to produce operas realistically reflecting the contemporary scene, in which the beauty and spiritual power of our people are revealed in full measure. Performances of new Soviet operas are eagerly awaited by the public. Great interest was aroused by the production at the Bolshoi Theater of the opera by Herman Zhukovsky, *From the Bottom of My Heart*, devoted to an important subject, the life on our collective farms, the Kolkhozs. But the authors of the opera and its producers failed to examine closely the Kolkhoz way of life. They failed to portray it adequately, in vivid artistic imagery, accompanied by colorful realistic music. The opera proved to be a feeble production marked by serious errors. Its melodic materials are largely deficient in characterization. The dramatic episodes are musically faceless. One has the impression of listening to essentially the same melodies over and over again. As a result, there is no realistic representation of our heroes of labor at the Kolkhoz. . . . The composer's exclusive preoccupation with sentimental whimsicalities leads to incongruities. In the scene of the conference of the praesidium of the Kolkhoz, the contradiction between the action on the stage and the music becomes particularly obvious. Completely unnatural is also the ballad music in the scene in the tavern, which has nothing to do with the words of the aria about new man, about Communism. . . . Herman Zhukovsky's score, weak from a professional standpoint, compounds the ideological falsity of the libretto in its portrayal of the Soviet people as devoid of all individuality. In this respect the authors reveal their inability to achieve fidelity to life. (*Pravda*, Moscow, 19 April 1951)

The article in *Pravda* of 19 April 1951, regarding the opera *From the Bottom of My Heart*, contains alongside some correct critical judgments of the music and the libretto of the opera, some instances of exaggerations and prejudice. . . . Its evaluation of the opera is incorrect and one-sided. (From the statement of the Central Committee of the Communist Party of the Soviet Union, published in *Pravda*, 8 June 1958)

19 JANUARY 1951

Le Rire de Nils Halerius, "lyric and choreographic legend" by the French composer Marcel LANDOWSKI is performed for the first time at Mulhouse, Alsace.

20 JANUARY 1951

Dimnjiaci Uz Jadran (*The Chimneys of the Adriatic Coast*), opera in five acts by the 55-year-old Croatian composer Ivo TIJARDOVIĆ, to a Story of mortal strife between Yugoslav partisans and Fascists on the Dalmatian coast in 1943, is produced in Zagreb.

22 JANUARY 1951

Ernst von DOHNÁNYI appears as soloist in the first American performance with the Florida State Symphony Orchestra in Tallahassee (where he made his home in 1949 as professor of music at Florida State College) of his *Second Piano Concerto* in B minor, written in Austria in 1947.

24 JANUARY 1951

A century has passed since the death of Gasparo SPONTINI, Italian composer whose opera *La Vestale* was the rage of Napoleonic France, but whose fame declined to a historical footnote in the annals of grand opera.

25 JANUARY 1951

Volpone by the 52-year-old French composer Marcel DELANNOY, a symphonic suite of four scenes from the musical score to a film after the novel of Stefan Zweig, derived from the famous play of Ben Jonson, is performed for the first time on the Lyons Radio.

26 JANUARY 1951

Fourth Piano Concerto by Gian Francesco MALIPIERO, in three movements, a *Lento* flanked by two *Allegros*, written in a compact neo-baroque style, is performed for the first time in Turin.

27 JANUARY 1951

To mark the 50th anniversary of the death of Giuseppe VERDI, Toscanini conducts in New York a performance of Verdi's *Manzoni Requiem*.

29 JANUARY 1951

Bogdan Khmelnitzky, opera in four acts by the Ukrainian composer Konstantin DANKEVICH, centering on the 17th-century Cossack chieftain who fought against the Polish invaders, is produced in Kiev, evoking an outraged condemnation in *Pravda* on 20 July 1951, after its performance at the Ukrainian Music Festival in Moscow, for its erroneous treatment of historic realities in the relationship between the Russians and Ukrainians and its inadequate musical characterization. (The libretto of the opera was radically revised, the motive of Ukrainian separatism softened and the patriotic element of struggle against the Polish feudal imperialism strengthened, with the finale depicting the joy of the reunion of the Ukraine and Great Russia announced on 8 January 1654; this revised version was first performed, with the musical score essentially unchanged, in Kiev on 21 June 1953.)

3 FEBRUARY 1951

The CANADIAN LEAGUE OF COMPOSERS is formed in Toronto, with John Weinzweig as chairman.

6 FEBRUARY 1951

Concerto for French horn and string orchestra by the Swiss composer Othmar SCHOECK, written in a neo-Schubertian lyrical manner, is performed for the first time in Winterthur.

11 FEBRUARY 1951

Lady Hamilton, opera by the 64-year-old German composer Robert HEGER, dealing with Lord Nelson's Mediterranean romance, is produced in Nuremberg.

22 FEBRUARY 1951

Second Symphony by Charles IVES, composed between 1897 and 1901, in five movements: *Andante moderato, Allegro, Adagio cantabile, Lento maestoso, Allegro molto vivace*, expressing "the musical feelings of the Connecticut country in the 1890's" and embodying an extraordinary variety of thematic resources, including a mockingly distorted quotation of a chromatic passage from the *Third Symphony* of Brahms, all this immersed in an ocean of American tunes, jigs, gallops, reels and ragtime, culminating with the orifiamme of brass, vociferating *Columbia, The Gem of the Ocean*, is performed for the first time, half a century after its composition, by the New York Philharmonic, Leonard Bernstein conducting.

23 FEBRUARY 1951

Symphonie concertante for oboe and string orchestra by Jacques IBERT is performed for the first time in Basel.

28 FEBRUARY 1951

Suite Archaïque by Arthur HONEGGER, in four movements, *Ouverture, Pantomime, Ritournelle et Serenade, Processional,* written in architecturally proportioned measures of the French rococo, is performed for the first time by the Louisville Orchestra.

1 MARCH 1951

Auto Accident by the American composer Harold G. DAVIDSON, inspired by the magazine article "And Sudden Death" (whose author himself died in an automobile accident), scored for percussion, a siren, and glass plates to be smashed at the climax, is performed for the first time at the University of Illinois School of Music, in Urbana.

2 MARCH 1951

La Vita Nuova for voices and orchestra by the 47-year-old Russian-American composer Nicolas NABOKOV, inspired by Dante, is performed for the first time by the Boston Symphony Orchestra, Charles Munch conducting.

9 MARCH 1951

Il était un petit Navire, satirical opera in three acts by Germaine TAILLEFERRE, the only woman member of the French Six, based on the popular French children's song of that name, is performed for the first time at the Opéra-Comique in Paris.

9 MARCH 1951

Fifth Symphony by Arthur HONEGGER, completed in Paris on 10 November 1950, subtitled *Di tre re* (because each of its three movements, *Grave, Allegretto, Allegro marcato,* terminates on an unadorned *Re* in the lower strings and timpani), devoid of a key signature and marked by atonal intervallic saltation, is performed for the first time as a commissioned work, by the Boston Symphony Orchestra, Charles Munch conducting.

13 MARCH 1951

Amphitryon, a neo-classical opera by the Swiss composer Robert OBOUSSIER, to a libretto based on the classical Greek myth of Zeus making a visitation of Amphitryon's wife in the guise of Amphitryon himself and inadvertently procreating Heracles, is performed for the first time in Berlin.

17 MARCH 1951

Das Verhör des Lukullus, opera by the German composer Paul DESSAU, to a radio play by Bertolt Brecht, originally broadcast by a Swiss station in 1939, representing the trial of the Roman General Lucullus (c.110–56 B.C.) in Hades, by the victims of his aggressive wars, is per-formed for the first and last time at the German Opera in East Berlin, and then banned by the authorities of the German Democratic Republic as ideologically false in its libretto and decadently discordant in its music.

The world peace camp with its 800 million people, led by the Soviet Union, is not a court presided over by ghosts, but one wielding realistic power to put war criminals on trial down on earth. What at the outbreak of Hitler's war may have been an expression of the uncertain political stand on the part of an exiled anti-Fascist dramatist, such as Brecht, registers in our minds in 1951 as a relapse into doubt and weakness. . . . As for the music, it follows Igor Stravinsky, a composer resident in the U.S.A., who is a fanatical destroyer of all European musical traditions. Paul Dessau has missed the opportunity to arouse the spirit of the masses against a new war of conquest. A musical work that drowns the listener in a flood of dissonances and intellectualistic tricks lends support to reactionary groups in the audience and is repugnant to the progressive elements of our society. (*Neues Deutschland,* East Berlin, 22 March 1951)

Look at the orchestra of *Das Verhör des Lukullus.* There are no violins. This most noble of all instruments, capable of producing the most beautiful tonal designs is missing from the score. Instead, there is a piano doctored with drawing-pins set up on the strings and nine different kinds of percussion instruments, among them metal sheets struck by rocks. (ibid., as quoted in *Deutsche Zeitung,* Berlin, 1 January 1953)

(A revised version of the opera, under the more explicit title *Die Verurteilung des Lukullus,* i.e. condemnation, rather than a mere trial, was produced in East Berlin on 12 October 1951, with a notation in the program stating that the verdict of the dead is to be interpreted as the judgment of posterity, and that the more objectionable modernistic devices were removed from the score, dissonances replaced whenever possible by consonances, and *Sprechgesang* changed to arias.)

18 MARCH 1951

Fourth Symphony, subtitled *Autochthonous,* by William Grant STILL, in four movements, representing the optimistic, the pensive, the humorous and the humanistic aspects of the American character, is performed for the first time by the Oklahoma City Symphony Orchestra, Victor Alessandro conducting.

19 MARCH 1951

Croquis Egyptiens, orchestral suite by the Egyptian composer Alberto HEMSI, is performed for the first time by the Alexandria Symphony Orchestra.

21 MARCH 1951

Eighth Symphony by Gian Francesco MALIPIERO, subtitled *Di un tempo* to indicate that the work should be played without pause between clearly demarcated movements connected by transitional passages, is performed for the first time in Rome.

21 MARCH 1951

Willem MENGELBERG, Dutch conductor, who excelled in performances of Beethoven, Mahler and Strauss (the score of *Ein Heldenleben* is dedicated to him), dies in Chur, Switzerland, an exile from his native Holland, where he was barred from conducting for his cultural collaboration with the Nazis during the Hitlerian occupation.

26 MARCH 1951

Fourth Symphony by the Japanese composer Saburo MOROI is performed for the first time by the Nippon Symphony Orchestra in Tokyo.

28 MARCH 1951

Giants in the Earth, opera in three acts by Douglas MOORE, to a story of Norwegian pioneers in the Dakota Territory in 1873, is produced by the Columbia University Opera Workshop in New York.

29 MARCH 1951

The King and I, a musical play by Richard RODGERS, with book and lyrics by Oscar HAMMERSTEIN II, based on the historically true account of a Victorian lady engaged by the King of Siam to teach Western amenities to his multiple children by his many wives and concubines, written in a cosmopolitan idiom flavored with Westernized orientalisms and stylized pentatonicisms, the most famous numbers being *Getting to Know You, I Whistle a Happy Tune, Hello, Young Lovers* and *Shall We Dance?*, is produced in New York.

30 MARCH 1951

Fourth Symphony by the 57-year-old American composer Walter PISTON, commissioned by the University of Minnesota on the occasion of its centennial, in four movements: *Piacevole, Ballando, Contemplativo* and *Energetico*, written in a compact neo-classical manner calculated to solve "the problem of balance between expression and formal design," is performed for the first time by the Minneapolis Symphony Orchestra, Antal Dorati conducting.

31 MARCH 1951

München: ein Gedächtniswalzer for orchestra by Richard STRAUSS, a nostalgic reminiscence of waltz time in old Munich, revised in 1945 from a film score of 1939, is performed for the first time in Vienna.

2 APRIL 1951

The Russian pianist Simon BARIÈRE collapses and dies on the stage of Carnegie Hall in New York, while playing Grieg's *Piano Concerto*.

4 APRIL 1951

Kállai Kettós (Kálló Double) by Zoltán KODÁLY, scored for chorus, three clarinets, two cimbaloms and strings, with occasional humming effects in the voice parts, based on a Hungarian tune from the locality of Kálló, usually danced by a couple (*Kettós*, double, in the title), is performed for the first time by the Hungarian People's Ensemble in Budapest.

4 APRIL 1951

Ballade for cello and orchestra by the Swiss composer Frank MARTIN is performed for the first time in Geneva.

6 APRIL 1951

Kerkeb, opera by the 68-year-old French composer Marcel SAMUEL-ROUSSEAU, is produced at the Opéra-Comique in Paris.

6 APRIL 1951

Sinfonia in one movement by the 47-year-old American composer Vittorio GIANNINI, dedicated to the memory of his mother who taught him the violin (his father was a singer from Florence, Italy), built on an autogenetic theme ramified into four derivative subjects, culminating in a magistral quadruple fugue and vanishing in *pianississississimo* in immaculately white C major, is performed for the first time by the Cincinnati Symphony Orchestra, Thor Johnson conducting.

10 APRIL 1951

Violin Concerto by the 44-year-old American composer David VAN VACTOR is performed for the first time in Knoxville, Tennessee.

12 APRIL 1951

On the sesquicentennial of the birth of Joseph LANNER, Austrian pioneer in the art of the waltz, the Austrian Government issues a 60-groschen stamp bearing his likeness.

14 APRIL 1951

Zeybek, Interlude and *Horon*, three national orchestral dances by the Turkish composer Ahmed Adnan SAYGUN are performed for the first time in Ankara.

20 APRIL 1951

Petite Suite for orchestra by the Polish composer Witold LUTOSLAWSKI, his most successful piece, is performed for the first time by the Radio Orchestra in Warsaw.

21 APRIL 1951

Olive FREMSTAD, Swedish prima donna of ample pectoral powers, who sang the title role in the first American performance of *Salomé* by Richard Strauss, dies in Irvington-on-Hudson, New York, at the age of 80.

21 APRIL 1951

Fifth Symphonie (Symphonie Concertante) by the 45-year-old German polyphonist Karl Amadeus HARTMANN, scored for wind instruments, cellos and doublebasses, in three movements, a kinetically functional *Toccata*, a tonally parsimonious *Melodie*, subtitled *Hommage à Stravinsky*, and a *Rondo*, is performed for the first time in Stuttgart.

21 APRIL 1951

Alexander KREIN, Russian-Jewish composer of operatic and symphonic music, much of it based on traditional Hebrew chants, dies in Moscow at the age of 67.

22 APRIL 1951

Commemorating the sesquicentennial of the birth of the German opera composer Albert LORTZING, the Government of the Federal German Republic issues a 20-pfennig stamp in his honor.

26 APRIL 1951

The Pilgrim's Progress, a "morality," in four acts, prologue and epilogue by Ralph VAUGHAN WILLIAMS, with his own libretto adapted from John Bunyan's famous Christian allegory, being an expansion and amplification of his one-act pastoral *The Shepherds of the Delectable Mountains,* first performed in London on 11 July 1922, with the additions of the episodes of the City of Destruction, the Valley of Humiliation, and the climactic Celestial City, set to music in illustrative neo-medieval modalities, associating valor with pentatonic trumpet calls, temptation with claudicant atonal steps, and sin with strident counterpoint, is produced at Covent Garden in London.

26 APRIL 1951

John Alden CARPENTER, American railroad shipping magnate and composer of ballets and instrumental music in a distinctive modernistic manner (the score of his jazzified ballet *Skyscrapers,* one of the earliest examples of American urbanistic music, was deposited in the cornerstone of Hampshire House, a forty-story New York skyscraper erected in 1931, as a symbol of the jazz age), dies in Chicago, the site of his gratifying financial successes, at the age of 75.

28 APRIL 1951

Die weisse Rose, ballet by the 43-year-old German composer Wolfgang FORTNER, after Oscar Wilde's story *Birthday of the Infanta,* interpreted on two planes, realistic and surrealistic, in which the Infanta dances boogie-woogie in the sensual fantasy of the court dwarf enamored of her, is performed for the first time at the State Opera in Berlin.

1 MAY 1951

Camargo GUARNIERI, 44-year-old Brazilian composer, conducts in Rio de Janeiro the first performance of his orchestral suite *Brasiliana,* in three movements: *Entrada, Moda, Dansa.*

2 MAY 1951

Dark Waters, one-act opera by Ernst KRENEK, to his own libretto in English, dealing with a neurotic heiress who runs away from her wealthy parents in quest of adventure and meets accidental death of a gunshot wound in a river barge in the American South, is performed for the first time by the Opera Workshop at the University of Southern California School of Music in Los Angeles.

2 MAY 1951

Symphony in E by the 34-year-old American Negro composer Ulysses KAY, in three classically constructed movements, is performed for the first time in Rochester, Howard Hanson conducting.

4 MAY 1951

Ildebrando PIZZETTI conducts in Florence the first stage performance of his one-act opera *Ifigenia,* to the story of the immolation of Agamemnon's daughter to placate the goddess Artemis. (The opera was performed for the first time in concert form over the Italian Radio on 3 October 1950.)

6 MAY 1951

The Sons of Light, cantata by Ralph VAUGHAN WILLIAMS, is performed in London for the first time by a chorus of 1000 school children and the London Philharmonic Orchestra.

8 MAY 1951

Das Vokaltuch der Sängerin, ballet-pantomime by the 24-year-old German composer Hans Werner HENZE, is performed for the first time, in concert form, in West Berlin.

12 MAY 1951

First Symphony, by the 35-year-old New Zealand composer Douglas LILBURN, is performed for the first time at Wellington, New Zealand.

12 MAY 1951

Krěsimir BARANOVIĆ, eminent Croatian composer, conducts the first performance of his comic opera *Nevjesta od Cedtingrada (The Bride from Cedtingrad)* in Belgrade.

15 MAY 1951

In observance of the centennial of the birth of Vincent D'INDY, the French Post Office issues a 25-franc stamp with his likeness.

15 MAY 1951

John Socman, opera by the 37-year-old English composer George LLOYD, to his father's libretto dealing with an unscrupulous 15th-century British magistrate, active amid a plethora of yeomen, bowmen, gleemen, friars and lollards, who tries to entice a farmer's daughter into marriage but yields her to her beloved archer, hero of the battle of Agincourt, when a wandering glee-maiden reveals herself as the magistrate's undivorced French wife, written in an abecedarian operatic idiom in which dramatic tension is created by an antiphony of brassy bombast and meretricious melodrama, is produced in Bristol.

15 MAY 1951

Felix Robert MENDELSSOHN, German cellist, great-grandnephew of Felix Mendelssohn, collapses and dies on the stage during his recital in Baltimore while playing a piece by Ernst von Dohnányi.

25 MAY 1951

Symfonia Pokoju (Symphony of Peace) for chorus and orchestra by the 36-year-old Polish composer Andrzej PANUFNIK in three sections—(1) *Lamentoso,* with a folk melody intoned amid the bins of European cities; (2) *Drammatico,* an agonizing appeal for world peace accentuated by purposefully concentrated syncopation; (3) *Solenne,* an impassioned declaration that peace must be enforced by the will of the people, with an ending on a promissory chord of E major—is performed for the first time in Warsaw.

27 MAY 1951

Theodor ROGALSKI, 50-year-old Rumanian composer, conducts in Bucharest the first performance of his most successful work, *Three Dances for Orchestra*: (1) *Dansure Rominesti*, based on a Transylvanian melody; (2) *Gayda*, a Macedonian slow dance, with a trumpet making "wa-wa" sounds by muting it intermittently with the hand; (3) *Hora*, a rapid Balkan dance.

29 MAY 1951

Josef Bohuslav FOERSTER, Nestor of Czech music, composer of numerous operas and symphonic works imbued with Bohemian melorhythms, within the matrix of Germanic operatic arts, dies in Nový Vestec at the venerable age of 91.

30 MAY 1951

On the occasion of the inauguration of the First International Music Festival "Pražske Jaro" (Prague Spring), Czechoslovakia issues four commemorative postage stamps with the portraits of the founding fathers of Czech music, Bedřich SMETANA (1.50 and 3 kronen) and Antonín DVOŘÁK (1 and 2 kronen).

30 MAY 1951

Dimitri LEVIDIS, Greek composer of impressionistically flavored instrumental and vocal music, the first to use electronic instruments in symphonic works, dies in Athens at the age of 65.

1 JUNE 1951

Madame Bovary, opera in three acts by the 52-year-old French composer Emmanuel BONDEVILLE, after Flaubert's famous novel of provincial adultery, is performed for the first time at the Opéra-Comique in Paris.

1 JUNE 1951

Two days after the death of the Moldavian composer Stepan NIAGA, his oratorio *The Song of Rebirth*, in eight sections traversing the history of Moldavia, from the period of Ottoman subjugation through Fascist domination and final liberation by the Soviet Army, is performed for the first time in Kishinev, capital of the Soviet Socialist Republic of Moldavia.

2 JUNE 1951

The Soviet Government issues two stamps, at 40 kopecks and one ruble, to honor the Viennese composer of ballets Leon MINKUS who spent most of his life in Russia.

2 JUNE 1951

Festlicher Hymnus for orchestra by the dean of Swiss composers Othmar SCHOECK, based on the tune of an Alpine shepherd's horn which develops into a Gregorian cantus firmus, ending on a resonant C, is performed for the first time in Grossmünster, on the occasion of the 600th anniversary of the entry of Zürich into the confederation of Swiss towns.

4 JUNE 1951

Serge KOUSSEVITZKY, Grand Seigneur of the baton, who ardently promoted the cause of modern music in Moscow, Paris and Boston, founder of the Edition Russe de Musique which published a series of works by Russian composers, including those of Scriabin, Stravinsky and Prokofiev, and who commissioned a whole generation of American composers to write symphonic works for him which he faithfully brought out during the quarter of a century of his conductorship of the Boston Symphony Orchestra (1924–1949), dies in Boston at the age of 76.

7 JUNE 1951

Symphonie by the 35-year-old French composer Henri DUTILLEUX, in four movements, *Passacaglia, Scherzo, Intermezzo, Finale*, each developing autogenetically from thematic structures derived from the intervals of the major seventh and the tritone, making use of bitonal harmonies and frequently resorting to powerful ostinato figures, is performed for the first time by the Orchestre National in Paris, under the direction of Roger Desormière.

11 JUNE 1951

Belgrade, symphonic poem by the Serbian composer Dragutin GOSTUSKI, a historical musicorama of Belgrade, resolutely preserving its national Slavic aspects through centuries of invasion, subjugation and exploitation, is performed for the first time in Belgrade.

12 JUNE 1951

Monopartita by Arthur HONEGGER, in eight linked movements, indicating its antinomy of structure, the unifying aspect expressed by the prefix *mono*, and the divisive element implicit in the word *partita*, is performed for the first time in Zürich as a commissioned work on the occasion of the 600th anniversary of the entrance of the Canton of Zürich into the Helvetic Confederation.

13 JUNE 1951

Stabat Mater, a polyptych of intercessionary prayers by Francis POULENC, austerely scored for soprano solo, mixed choir and orchestra, is performed for the first time at the Music Festival in Strasbourg.

16 JUNE 1951

Third Symphony by the 46-year-old Dutch composer Guillaume LANDRÉ is performed for the first time by the Concertgebouw Orchestra in Amsterdam, Rafael Kubelik conducting.

17 JUNE 1951

Second Piano Concerto by the 46-year-old neo-classical English composer Alan RAWSTHORNE, in four movements—(1) *Allegro piacevole*, (2) *Allegro molto*, (3) *Adagio semplice—Poco Allegro*, (4) *Allegro*—traversing in classical modalities a variety of moods creating an equilibrium of contrasting themes, firmly adhering to the triadic idiom, and concluding with a fugato building up into a jubilant oriflamme of exclamatory fanfares, is performed for the first time by Clifford Curzon and the London Symphony conducted by Sir Malcolm Sargent, as a commissioned work for the Festival of Great Britain of 1951.

19 JUNE 1951

André JOLIVET conducts in Strasbourg the first performance with Lucette Descaves as piano soloist of his *Piano Concerto,* subtitled *Equatoriales,* evoking in its three movements the statically placid, humidly erotic and pacifically contemplative geographical regions lying on the equator, Central Africa, the East Indies and Polynesia, making colorful use of drums, bells, shakers, vibrators, and other indigenous percussion instruments.

22 JUNE 1951

The 25th Festival of the International Society for Contemporary Music opens in Frankfurt, presenting the following program of works by modern German composers:

Third Symphony in three movements by Karl Amadeus HARTMANN (first performed in Munich on 10 February 1950); *Catulli Carmina* for two solo voices and mixed choir by Carl ORFF (first performed in Leipzig on 6 November 1943); *Concerto* for two pianos and orchestra in one movement by Hermann REUTTER, written in a free diatonic idiom, with an influx of polytonal harmonies; and *Sonata for Orchestra* by Werner EGK, the title emphasizing the neo-classical aspect of the work.

23 JUNE 1951

The 25th Festival of the International Society for Contemporary Music in Frankfurt presents two concerts:

Morning program: *Chant funèbre à la mémoire des jeunes femmes défuntes* for mixed choir, orchestra and organ, by the veteran French modernist Charles KOECHLIN, to the Latin words of the Requiem; and *D'un diable de briquet* by the 49-year-old Belgian composer Raymond CHEVREUILLE, a "radiophonic tale after Hans Christian Andersen," incorporating an imitation of a phonograph record played at 33 revolutions a minute, abruptly switching to 78 revolutions a minute, resulting in an effect of rhythmic diminution.

Evening program: *First Symphony* by Ernst TOCH (first performed in Vienna on 20 December 1950), in four movements unified by a thematic parabolic "ballistic curve"; *6 Chants* for chorus and orchestra by the 34-year-old French composer Jean-Louis MARTINET, written in the manner of medieval madrigals; *Coro di Morti,* dramatic madrigal for men's voices, three pianos, brass instruments, doublebasses and percussion, by Goffredo PETRASSI, written in 1941, to a text by the Italian romantic poet Leopardi, expressing the notion that to the dead the land of the living is as mysterious and horrifying as the dead are to those who are alive; *Symphonic Fragments* from the ballet *L'Auberge ensorcelée* by the 44-year-old Polish composer Antoni SZALOWSKI, written in a neo-classical manner.

24 JUNE 1951

Fifth Symphony by the 54-year-old French composer Jean RIVIER is performed for the first time in Strasbourg.

24 JUNE 1951

The 25th Festival of the International Society for Contemporary Music in Frankfurt presents the following program of symphonic music:

Third Symphony by the 34-year-old Swedish composer Karl Birger BLOMDAHL, subtitled *Facets* to indicate the pluralistic appearance of its five movements within a monistic entity; *Piccola Sinfonia giocosa* in four movements by the 51-year-old Swiss composer Willy BURKHARD; *Spiritual Chants* for mixed choir and organ by the 44-year-old Corsican composer Leo PREGER, written in emulation of medieval chants; and *Four Symphonic Movements* by the 46-year-old Dutch composer Guillaume LANDRÉ, in which thematic unity is maintained by periodic recurrence of the principal motive.

25 JUNE 1951

At the 25th Festival of the International Society for Contemporary Music in Frankfurt, the following program of chamber music is given:

String Quartet in six contrasting movements by the 26-year-old English composer Robert CRAWFORD; *Four Ancient Greek Poems* by the 26-year-old Brazilian composeress Nininha GREGORI, for soprano, woodwind quartet and celesta, conceived as an essay of ethnomusicological fidelity, but allowing some atonal discursions; *String Quartet* by the 25-year-old German composer Giselher KLEBE, in six short movements, based on the idea of "permanent variation," verging on dodecaphony without rigidity; *Sphenogramme* by the 22-year-old Japanese composer Toshiro MAYUZUMI, for contralto, flute, saxophone, marimba, violin, violoncello and piano, in five movements of widely contrasting materials, from Hindu liturgy to Bebop; and a neo-classical *Sextet* for woodwind instruments by the 30-year-old English composer John ADDISON.

26 JUNE 1951

At the 25th Festival of the International Society for Contemporary Music in Frankfurt the following program is presented:

Concerto for string orchestra in two movements by the 40-year-old German composer Helmut DEGEN; *5 Rechants* for 12 voices by the 42-year-old French composer Olivier MESSIAEN (*Rechant* being the 16th-century French word for *Refrain*), conceived in a neo-medieval style, with an admixture of Hindu rhythms; *Variations on a Haydn Theme* by the 50-year-old Austrian composer Hans Erich APOSTEL, in which the innocuous theme from the slow movement of Haydn's *Pauken-Symphonie* is subjected to intervallic translocations, procrustean melodic elongations and dodecaphonic torsions; and *Sonata for Violin and Orchestra* by the 36-year-old Polish composer Michal SPISAK.

27 JUNE 1951

As part of the 25th Festival of the Society for Contemporary Music in Frankfurt, the world première of the opera *The Duenna,* after Sheridan's play, by the Spanish composer Roberto GERHARD, resident in England, is given at the State Opera Theater in Wiesbaden.

28 JUNE 1951

The following works are presented at the 25th Festival of the International Society for Contemporary Music in Frankfurt:

Das hohe Lied for soprano and orchestra by the 27-year-old Polish composer and conductor Stanislaw SKROWACZEWSKI, in four sections, to the biblical text relating to King Solomon's young Shulamite concubine; *Piano Concerto* in four movements by the 46-year-old German composer Richard MOHAUPT; symphonic poem *La Isla de las Calmas* by the 63-year-old Norwegian composer Fartein VALEN, written in a tense atonal idiom within an impressionistic framework;

Nocturne for Orchestra by the Polish-American composer Jerzy FITELBERG (1903–1951), in the form of a theme with four variations; and *Three Psalms of King David* for tenor, chorus and orchestra by the 42-year-old Danish composer Herman KOPPEL, dedicated to the memory of the sufferings endured by humanity during World War II.

29 JUNE 1951

The following program is presented at the 25th Festival of the International Society for Contemporary Music in Frankfurt:

String Quartet in three movements by the 41-year-old Danish composer Vagn HOLMBOE, illustrating the dialectical principle of antithetical motivic development in the first two movements and their synthesis in the third movement; *Gethsemane* for women's voices and a string trio by the 59-year-old Austrian composer Felix PETYREK, conceived as a 20th-century replica of a medieval religious play; *String Quartet* in four movements by the 35-year-old Argentinian composer Alberto GINASTERA, couched in the baroque idiom vivified by an injection of Argentinian melorhythms; and *Quintet* for wind instruments by the 39-year-old French composer Jean FRANÇAIX, written in a hedonistically Gallic manner.

29 JUNE 1951

On the 1,900th anniversary of St. Paul's arrival in Athens, the 58-year-old Greek composer Petro PETRIDIS conducts in Athens the first performance of his oratorio *St. Paul.*

30 JUNE 1951

At the 25th Festival of the International Society for Contemporary Music in Frankfurt, the following works are performed:

Ulysses, cantata after James Joyce's novel of that name by the 46-year-old Hungarian composer, resident of England, Mátyás SEIBER (first performed in London on 27 May 1949), and *Il Prigioniero,* opera by Luigi DALLAPICCOLA (first performed in a concert version, on Radio Turin, 4 December 1949 and on the stage in Florence on 20 May 1950)

1 JULY 1951

L'Apostrophe, comic opera in one act by Jean FRANÇAIX, to a libretto from Balzac's *Contes drôlatiques,* dealing with a hunchback's fateful infatuation with a married belle, is performed on the stage for the first time, in Amsterdam, in the course of the Holland Music Festival.

1 JULY 1951

A program of contemporary German works is presented at the 25th Festival of the International Society for Contemporary Music in Frankfurt:

Orchestral Vacations on a Paganini Theme by the 48-year-old Manchuria-born German-Estonian composer Boris BLACHER, in which the variations develop only the basic tonal elements of the theme, derived from Paganini's *Capriccio,* op. 28; *Violin Concerto* in four movements by the German composer Hans Werner HENZE (the performance took place on his 25th birthday), written in a discursively rhapsodic style, abandoning his youthful dodecaphony; *Fantasy on the Theme of B-A-C-H* for two pianos and orchestra by the 43-year-old neo-classicist Wolfgang FORTNER, where the Bach motive is construed as part of a 12-tone series; and the *Symphonic Dances* in four sections by Paul HINDEMITH, written in 1937.

(The Festival concluded on the evening of July 1951 with the stage performance of the five-act opera *The Life of Orestes* by Ernst KRENEK.)

2 JULY 1951

The Soviet Government issues a series of stamps with pictures of the Bolshoi Theater and portraits of GLINKA, TCHAIKOVSKY, MUSSORGSKY, RIMSKY-KORSAKOV and BORODIN.

6 JULY 1951

Malcolm ARNOLD conducts at the Cheltenham Festival the first performance of his *First Symphony,* in three movements, *Allegro, Andantino* and *Vivace con fuoco,* written in an aggressively vitalistic and ostentatiously extrovert idiom, with a fugal finale marked by a proliferation of *stretti,* and punctuated by loud drum beats.

7 JULY 1951

Terres du Rhône, festive symphonic suite by the 50-year-old Swiss composer Hans HAUG, depicting in ethnomusicological modalities the glories of the river Rhône, flowing from the Alps through the Lake of Geneva into the Mediterranean, is performed for the first time under the composer's direction during the course of the Swiss Athletic Festival in Basel.

13 JULY 1951

Arnold SCHOENBERG, revolutionary genius, creator of the epoch-making method of composition with twelve tones related only to one another that has profoundly influenced a whole generation of composers in all parts of the world, dies at the age of seventy-six in Los Angeles, his American home from 1935. (Profoundly affected by triskaidekaphobia, Schoenberg regarded the date of his birth, 13th of September, as inauspicious; fearfully aware that the sum of the digits of 76, his age at his last birthday, was 13, he observed during his terminal illness in July 1951, that should he survive the fateful 13th of the month, all would be well, but he died on that day at 13 minutes before midnight.)

14 JULY 1951

Bunt Zakow (Rebellion of Clerks), opera by the Polish composer Tadeusz SZELIGOWSKI, with the action evolving in Cracow in 1549, after the accession to the throne of King Sigismund II of Poland and his conflict with the powerful scribes of the state, employing some Gregorian canticles in the score to characterize the Catholic priesthood and the general harmonic scheme in the Mussorgsky style, is performed for the first time at Wroclaw.

21 JULY 1951

Kappa, ballet by the Japanese composer Yasushi AKUTAGAWA, symphonic poem depicting a Japanese mermaid, is performed for the first time by the Tokyo Philharmonic Orchestra.

26 JULY 1951

Second Symphony by the 30-year-old English composer Peter Racine FRICKER, in three movements, in an astutely synthetic idiom, frugal in sonorities and expressionistic in melodic atonality, is performed for the first time by the Liverpool Philharmonic Orchestra.

1 AUGUST 1951

The Great Campaign, opera by the Chinese woman composer Lee BO-CHAO, portraying in monodic tones the impressions of the 7,000-mile military trek of the Chinese Red Army in which she participated in 1935, is performed for the first time in Peking.

10 AUGUST 1951

La Cuarterona, opera by the Argentinian composer Juan García ESTRADA, to a libretto telling the story of a beautiful quadroon slave girl beset by amorous vicissitudes in colonial Argentina, is produced at the Teatro Colón, in Buenos Aires.

15 AUGUST 1951

Artur SCHNABEL, Austrian pianist and renowned pedagogue whose interpretations of German classics established a tradition among generations of his disciples and pupils of his disciples, who also wrote works in an extremely advanced atonal and polytonal idiom, dies in Axenstein, Switzerland, at the age of 69.

21 AUGUST 1951

Constant LAMBERT, English composer of sophisticated modern pieces, conductor, and writer of provocative essays, dies in London two days before his 46th birthday.

24 AUGUST 1951

MODERN JAZZ QUARTET is founded in new york by John LEWIS (pianist), Milt JACKSON (vibraphonist), Percy HEATH (bassist) and Kenny CLARKE (drummer), with the aim of establishing a fruitful coalition of classical music and jazz. (The official beginning of the Modern Jazz Quartet is reckoned from their first recording session of 22 December 1952.)

26 AUGUST 1951

Fifth Symphony in four movements by the Chicago resident Czech composer Karel Boleslav JIRÁK, "an autobiographical work expressing the feelings of a human being who, after the tribulations of the great war has finally found a secure haven," is performed for the first time at the Edinburgh International Festival.

28 AUGUST 1951

The Soviet Government issues two commemorative musical postage stamps of 40 kopecks each, to mark the centennial of the death of the Russian song composer Alexander ALIABIEV bearing a musical quotation from his most famous song *The Nightingale,* and the 50th anniversary of the death of the symphonic composer Vassili KALINNIKOV.

5 SEPTEMBER 1951

Heroic Oratorio by Vojislav VUCKOVIĆ, Serbian composer who fell victim to the Nazis in 1942, melorhythmically derived from native folksongs, is performed for the first time, posthumously, in Cetinje, in an orchestration completed by Alexander Obradović.

11 SEPTEMBER 1951

Igor STRAVINSKY conducts in Venice the world première of his opera in three acts, subdivided into nine scenes, *The Rake's Progress,* to the text of W. H. Auden and Chester Kallman, after Hogarth's eight engravings dealing with a profligate young man who concludes a pact with a gentleman-like Beelzelbub, is tempted by him to marry a bearded lady, then gambles for the price of his soul, eventually landing in Bedlam, the whole summarized in a moral in the Epilogue, "For idle hearts and hands and minds the Devil finds a work to do," set to music in a mannered neo-baroque idiom, with rhythmic and melodic formulas reverting to the Italian settecento, artfully seasoned with pandiatonic spice.

23 SEPTEMBER 1951

Third Symphony by the 55-year-old Latvian-born, German pianist and composer Eduard ERDMANN, is performed for the first time in Essen.

30 SEPTEMBER 1951

Lysistrata, ballet by Boris BLACHER (after the comedy by Aristophanes, in which the heroine stops the Pelopopesian War by inducing the women of Athens to refuse marital favors to their soldier husbands unless peace is promptly made), is performed for the first time in Berlin.

1 OCTOBER 1951

Herbert EIMERT broadcasts a lecture, *Die Klangwelt der elektronischen Musik,* over the radio network Nordwestdeutscher Rundfunk, in which he makes use of the term "electronic music," coined by him, for the first time.

3 OCTOBER 1951

To commemorate the tenth anniversary of the death of the Austrian composer Wilhelm KIENZL, who wrote the first National Anthem of the Austrian Republic in 1920, the Austrian Government issues a stamp of one and a half schillings bearing his portrait.

4 OCTOBER 1951

The Dybbuk, opera by the American composer David TAMKIN, to the play by Ansky based on a medieval Jewish legend in which the spirit of a dead bridegroom invades the mind of his bride, is produced in New York.

6 OCTOBER 1951

Five world premières are presented at the opening day of the Donaueschingen Festival of Contemporary Music:

Double Concerto for violin, piano and small orchestra, in seven short movements, by Ernst KRENEK; *Piano Sonata* by the 40-year-old Swiss composer, Rolf LIEBERMANN; *Polyphonie X* for 17 solo instruments by the 26-year-old French composer Pierre BOULEZ, in three movements, set in a highly dissonant idiom (the audience reacted violently, and one outraged woman blew a police whistle, described by a reporter as "a nice, clean sound"); *Der himmlische Vagant*, a lyrical portrait of François Villon, for two voices and instruments, by the 51-year-old German composer Hermann REUTTER; and *Etude* in two parts for piano, wind instruments and percussion by the 52-year-old Rumanian-French composer Marcel MIHALOVICI.

7 OCTOBER 1951

Lukas FOSS, 29-year-old Berlin-born American composer plays in Venice the solo piano part in the world premiere of his *Second Piano Concerto* in three movements, written in the manner of a 19th-century virtuoso piece, in extended tonality with the final C-major chord encrusted with a supplementary D, warranted here as the acoustically consonant ninth overtone.

7 OCTOBER 1951

The second and last concert of the Donaueschingen Music Festival presents the following works:

Piccolo Concerto Notturno in five movements by the Italian composer Guido TURCHI; *Konzertstück* for piano and orchestra in two movements by the Hungarian-Parisian composer Tibor HARSÁNYI; *Symphonia Brevis* in four movements by the Austrian composer Hanns JELINEK written in a neo-baroque idiom with superinduced atonalities; *Fifth Symphony* by Arthur HONEGGER; and the first performance of *Third Symphony* by the 25-year-old German composer Hans Werner HENZE, conducted by him, written in a turbulent idiom, saturated with atonal plaints, noxious dissonances and containing unconsummated fugatos, erupting at points of critical tensions into a multitude of incorporeal tintinnabulations out of which a jazz orgy is spontaneously generated, ultimately coming to rest on a pacific concord.

7 OCTOBER 1951

For the first time in nineteen centuries the Colosseum in Rome is used for a public spectacle, with selections from VERDI's operas performed by the orchestra and the chorus of the Opera House of Rome.

10 OCTOBER 1951

JIYU SAKKYOKUKA (free composers association) is formed in Japan.

The Association of Free Composers is trying to create a new music to suit the modern taste. It does not subscribe to the philosophy of destruction and rejection for their own sake. Instead, it tries to foster a firm belief in the free will of creation. (From the inaugural statement of the Association)

11 OCTOBER 1951

Violin Concerto in two movements by the 54-year-old Danish composer Knudaage RIISAGER is performed for the first time in Copenhagen.

11 OCTOBER 1951

Il Principe felice, opera after Oscar Wilde, by the Italian composer Renzo BOSSI, is performed for the first time in concert form on the Milan Radio.

12 OCTOBER 1951

Ivan le Terrible, opera in four acts by Georges BIZET, the score of which, believed to have been destroyed by Bizet in 1865, was discovered intact among the possessions of the family of the nephew of the second husband of Bizet's widow, is given a world première in Bordeaux.

14 OCTOBER 1951

Pablo CASALS conducts in Zürich an all-violoncello orchestra comprising of 123 French, German, Italian, English and Belgian violoncellists, male and female, in a program including the world première of his multicellistic score *La Sardana*.

18 OCTOBER 1951

Seventh Symphony by the 41-year-old Danish composer Vagn HOLMBOE, in four movements separated by three intermezzi, is performed for the first time in Copenhagen.

19 OCTOBER 1951

Apocalypse, symphonic poem by the 40-year-old Italian-born American composer Gian Carlo MENOTTI, is performed for the first time in Pittsburgh.

23 OCTOBER 1951

Romantic Overture by the 52-year-old Russian composer Alexander TCHEREPNIN, domiciled in America, inspired by "the sound of horses' hooves on the pavement" evoking "the romantic era to which it belongs," written in the virtually unobstructed key of C major and surcharged with equine kinetic energy, is performed for the first time in Kansas City.

25 OCTOBER 1951

Manuel ROSENTHAL, French composer and conductor, is summarily dismissed as music director of the Seattle Symphony Orchestra for moral turpitude in his unsanctified cohabitation with Claudine Pillard Verneuil, French singer whom he engaged as a soloist featured as Mme. Rosenthal, disregarding the existence of his undivorced wife in Paris.

2 NOVEMBER 1951

Bonampak, ballet by the 46-year-old Mexican composer Luis SANDI, inspired by the archaeological discovery in 1949 of Mayan frescoes in the jungle village of Bonampak, is performed for the first time in Tuxtla Gutiérrez, in the province of Chiapas, where Bonampak is situated.

5 NOVEMBER 1951

Virginia Symphony by the 69-year-old Virginian composer John POWELL is performed for the first time in Richmond, Virginia, and the day is declared by Governor John S. Battle of Virginia as John Powell Day, in appreciation of Powell's achievement as composer and as a valiant champion of white race supremacy. (Powell was a chief sponsor of Virginia's Racial Integrity Act of 1924 which barred the marriage of a white person and a person having a single platelet of Negro blood or more than one-sixth of Indian blood, all of which does not alter the fact that the only piece he is known for is *Rapsodie nègre*.)

7 NOVEMBER 1951

Erosion, or *The Origin of the Amazon River*, symphonic poem by Heitor VILLA-LOBOS, is performed for the first time by the Louisville Orchestra.

8 NOVEMBER 1951

Theme and Variations for orchestra by the 37-year-old American composer Charles MILLS is performed for the first time by the New York Philharmonic Orchestra, Dimitri Mitropoulos conducting.

9 NOVEMBER 1951

Sigmund ROMBERG, 64-year-old Hungarian-born American composer of 78 Operettas to English libretti, among them such perennial favorites as *The Student Prince* and *The Desert Song*, dies suddenly of cerebral hemorrhage at 11:15 P.M. in his hotel room in New York, a week after he arrived there from his residence in California.

10 NOVEMBER 1951

Le Voyage de Magellan, symphonic suite by the Parisianized Polish composer Alexandre TANSMAN, drawn from an unperformed opera of the same title, tracing the semicircumnavigation of Magellan in six colorful episodes, ending in the Philippine Islands which he inadvertently discovered and where he was butchered and devoured by the xenophagic aborigines, is performed for the first time by the St. Louis Symphony Orchestra, Vladimir Golschmann conducting, 430 years after Magellan's death.

13 NOVEMBER 1951

Nicolai MEDTNER, Russian composer of expressive piano pieces fashioned with exquisite lapidary care, convinced believer in the eternal verities of music as a profoundly humanistic art (he was of German extraction, and his brother was a philosopher of mystical orientation), dies at 4:50 A.M., at the age of 71, in London where he settled after the debacle in the turmoil of the Russian Revolution of everything he held dear.

13 NOVEMBER 1951

Hugo LEICHTENTRITT, German-born scholar educated at Harvard University, author of a standard book on motets, biographer of Handel, and an unfortunate composer of Regeromantic instrumental pieces, dies in Cambridge, Massachusetts, at the age of 77.

14 NOVEMBER 1951

Blanche Neige, ballet by the French operetta composer Maurice YVAIN, is produced at the Paris Opéra.

15 NOVEMBER 1951

The Government of Poland issues stamps at 45 and 90 groschen, honoring CHOPIN and MONIUSZKO.

16 NOVEMBER 1951

Eastward in Eden, opera in four acts by the Czech-born American composer Jan MEYEROWITZ, is produced in Detroit.

17 NOVEMBER 1951

Marion, La Belle au tricorne, comic opera in three acts by the 36-year-old Swiss composer Pierre WISSMER, is produced at the Opéra-Comique in Paris.

19 NOVEMBER 1951

To mark the semicentennial of the death of Giuseppe VERDI, the Italian Government issues three stamps, at 10, 25 and 60 lire, bearing his likeness.

22 NOVEMBER 1951

Der rote Stiefel, "picture book for music" in two parts by the Swiss composer Heinrich SUTERMEISTER (with an invisible vocal quartet substituted for the customary chorus), is performed for the first time, with a Swedish libretto, at the Stockholm Royal Opera.

23 NOVEMBER 1951

Henri COLLET, French music critic who coined the title "Les Six Français," dies in Paris at the age of 66.

28 NOVEMBER 1951

Le Cercle Culturel du Conservatoire de Paris presents a concert of advanced music, featuring quarter-tone compositions by Ivan WYSCHNEGRADSKY, Russian émigré resident in Paris, for two and four pianos tuned a quarter-tone apart; three melodies "en langue imaginaire" by Marina SCRIABIN, daughter of Alexander Scriabin; *Suite monodique* for piano by Jéhan ALAIN, French composer and organist killed in France in June, 1940; and *Prelude and fugue* by Jean-Louis MARTINET.

29 NOVEMBER 1951

Ein Landarzt, radio cantata by the 25-year-old German composer Hans Werner HENZE, written in a free dodecaphonic idiom, after Kafka's story of a surrealistic country doctor's life, with symptomatic atonal vocalization to hemorrhagingly discordant harmonies and polyrhythmic chorea in syncopated singultation accentuating the neurasthenic malaise of the music, is performed for the first time on the Hamburg Radio.

30 NOVEMBER 1951

Horizontes by the Mexican pioneer of fractional tonalities Julian CARRILLO, scored for violin and cello in quarter-tones, a specially constructed zither-harp tuned in 16th-tones, and an accompanying normal orchestra playing mostly in semitones, is performed for the first time by the Pittsburgh Symphony Orchestra, Leopold Stokowski conducting.

30 NOVEMBER 1951

Ugrum-Reka (River Ugrum), opera in four acts by the 45-year-old Soviet composer Daniel FRENKEL, with its action set in Tsarist Siberia in 1910, wherein a mine owner strangles his bride when he finds out that she is a member of the Bolshevik party, and is driven to suicide by the outraged proletarian masses, set to music in a socialistically realistic style rooted in Russian melorhythms, is performed for the first time in Leningrad.

1 DECEMBER 1951

Felix PETYREK, Brno-born composer of progressively modernistic music who consistently employed a scale of alternating whole-tones and semitones in the conviction that this scale, cultivated by Rimsky-Korsakov, was his own invention, dies in Vienna, at the age of 59.

1 DECEMBER 1951

Billy Budd, opera in four acts by Benjamin BRITTEN, after the posthumously published novel of Herman Melville depicting the hanging of a young sailor on an 18th-century British man-of-war in 1797, scored for men's voices only, with orchestra, and set in emphatic triadic harmony (the pronouncement of the death sentence is illustrated in the orchestra by a succession of 34 triads, related only by the presence in each of them of at least one note of the F major triad), is produced in London.

5 DECEMBER 1951

Incognita, opera by Egon WELLESZ, 66-year-old Viennese composer and music scholar, to a libretto after Congreve, dealing with a masked lady (the *Incognita* of the title) in a man's attire who is saved from a male annoyant by her fiancé unaware of her identity, set to music in neoarchaic modalities acidulated by Viennese atonalities, is performed for the first time in Oxford, England, where he settled in 1938 after the Nazi Anschluss of Austria.

7 DECEMBER 1951

Concerto for Two Pianos and Orchestra by the 48-year-old Russian-American composer Nikolai LOPATNI-KOFF, in three movements, set in a percussively neo-baroque style, is performed for the first time by Victor Babin and his wife Vitya Vronsky as soloists, with the Pittsburgh Symphony Orchestra.

13 DECEMBER 1951

Selim PALMGREN, Finnish composer of impressionistic miniatures permeated by Suomian melorhythms, dies in Helsinki at the age of 73.

14 DECEMBER 1951

Sinfonia Giocosa in two movements by the Parisianized Rumanian composer Marcel MIHALOVICI, set in a hedonistically bland melodious and harmonious idiom, is performed for the first time by the Chamber Orchestra of Basel, Paul Sacher conducting.

14 DECEMBER 1951

Pedro SANJUÁN conducts the St. Louis Symphony Orchestra in the world première of his "ritual symphony" *La Macumba* derived from Afro-Cuban rhythms and chants.

22 DECEMBER 1951

Huszti kaland (*Adventure in Huszt*), comic opera in two acts by the 48-year-old Hungarian composer Pál KADOSA, dealing with a Magyar 17th-century student who captures a Hapsburg general in a castle in Huszt and as a reward gains the hand of his professor's daughter, is produced in Budapest.

24 DECEMBER 1951

Amahl and the Night Visitors, opera in one act by the 40-year-old Italian-American composer Gian Carlo MENOTTI, the first opera especially written for television, to his own libretto, inspired by the painting by Hieronymus Bosch, "The Adoration of the Magi," wherein a poor Arab boy whose dwelling is visited by the three Kings on their way to see the Infant Jesus, is cured of his lameness, set to music with a poignant sense of melodramatic tension and lyric expression, containing some implosive modernities under the tonal surface of Puccinian melos, is produced by the National Broadcasting Company as a special Christmas offering, becoming an annual event to be repeated every Christmas Eve during the second half of the twentieth century, as long as television exercises its lure.

29 DECEMBER 1951

Drums of Japan, ballet by the Japanese composer Akira IFUKUBE, is performed for the first time in Tokyo.

1952

11 JANUARY 1952

Second Symphony by Ernst TOCH in four movements, dedicated to Albert Schweitzer, as "the only victor in a world of victims," and presenting a musicorama of romantic moods passing through impassioned assertion of religious faith (*Allegro fanatico*), skeptical philosophy (*Sehr leicht, huschend, schattenhaft*), an introspective *Adagio*, and a proclamatory *Allegro*, in a tonal idiom with islands of dramatic dissonance in transit, is performed for the first time in Vienna.

14 JANUARY 1952

Violin Concerto by the 37-year-old Dutch composer Marius FLOTHUIS is performed for the first time in Utrecht.

17 JANUARY 1952

The Cowherd and the Sky Maiden, opera in one act by John VERRALL, is produced in Seattle.

20 JANUARY 1952

Arthur FARWELL, American composer of ethnomusicologically inspired instrumental pieces and songs, a fervent champion of musical Americanism, dies in New York at the age of 79.

23 JANUARY 1952

Sinfonia dello Zodiaco by Gian Francesco MALIPIERO, completed by him on 8 November 1951, subtitled "della Primavera all'Invierno," in four parts, beginning in a vernal pentatonic manner in the oxygenated key of C, and ending on a damp and gelid hibernal dissonance, is performed for the first time in Lausanne. (The work bears no numerical index; a symphony designated by Malipiero as "Ottava sinfonia" was written in 1964; there is therefore no justification to classify the present symphony as his ninth, as in some music reference books.)

23 JANUARY 1952

Two centuries have elapsed since the birth in Rome, of an Italian father and a German mother (née Kaiser), of Muzio CLEMENTI, the sagacious reformer and innovator of pianistic techniques, whose *Gradus ad Parnassum* has become an emblem of excellence for young pianists aspiring to perform a gradual ascent to the summit of the mountain of the Muses.

(Clementi's baptismal certificate obtained by the author from the Archivio Segreto Vaticano bears the date 24 January 1752 and states "infantem hieri natum baptizavi" thus establishing 23 January 1752 as Clementi's true date of birth; the date 24 January 1752 encountered in some music dictionaries is tardy.)

24 JANUARY 1952

On the occasion of the 25th anniversary of the Kammerorchester of Basel, its founder and conductor Paul Sacher presents a program of world premières:

Die Harmonie der Welt, a symphony in three movements by Paul HINDEMITH, drawn from the orchestral portions of his opera on the life of the astronomer Johannes Kepler: (1) *Musica Instrumentalis* (not in the sense of instrumental music but as a category in the philosophy of Boethius indicating the instrumentality of art in the relationship between man and God); (2) *Musica humana*, expressing the harmony between the spiritual and the material aspects of man; (3) *Musica mundana*, world harmony, depicting the concord of the planetary spheres: *Violin Concerto* by the 61-year-old Swiss composer Frank MARTIN, in three movements, *Allegro, Andante, Presto*, in a *sui generis* tonal idiom, in which octaves are excluded in melodic and harmonic structures, thus asymptotically approaching dodecaphony; and *Second Concerto for Orchestra* by Goffredo PETRASSI.

26 JANUARY 1952

Second Violin Concerto by the self-exiled Hungarian master of romantic music Ernst von DOHNÁNYI (completed on 7 January 1950, in Tallahassee, Florida) in C minor, in four movements, scored for orchestra without violins, is performed for the first time in San Antonio, Texas.

26 JANUARY 1952

Reinhold GLIÈRE conducts in Moscow the first performance of his *Concerto* for horn and orchestra.

27 JANUARY 1952

The Pulitzer Prize-winning *Symphonie concertante* for piano, viola, trumpet and orchestra by the 37-year-old American composer Gail KUBIK is performed for the first time in New York.

30 JANUARY 1952

Yuzuru, romantic opera by the 27-year-old Japanese composer Ikuma DAN, to a libretto from the ancient Japanese legend about a crane flying home in the twilight, with singsong melodies in Nipponese modes accoutred in European harmonies, is produced in Tokyo.

30 JANUARY 1952

Fourth Symphony by the 45-year-old American composer Paul CRESTON in four well-contrasted movements—(1) *Maestoso*, leading to a spirited *Allegro*; (2) *Andante pastorale*, in a cyclic triune form, with a dancing episode as the middle section; (3) *Allegretto giocoso*, a hedonistic scherzo; (4) *Vivace saltellante*, a tarantella-like finale—is performed for the first time by the National Symphony Orchestra in Washington, Howard Mitchell conducting.

31 JANUARY 1952

Sinfonia by the 33-year-old American composer Leon KIRCHNER is performed for the first time by the New York Philharmonic.

1 FEBRUARY 1952

Rondo vom goldenen Kalb, ballet "in three night pieces" by the 34-year-old Austrian composer Gottfried VON EINEM, to the biblical story of the worship of the golden calf, is performed for the first time in Hamburg.

5 FEBRUARY 1952

Symphony in D by the 49-year-old American composer John VINCENT is performed for the first time in its initial version by the Louisville Orchestra, Robert Whitney conducting. (In its revised version it was performed for the first time by the Philadelphia Orchestra, Eugene Ormandy conducting on 12 April 1957.)

7 FEBRUARY 1952

Přehedra Socialismu (*Overture to Socialism*) by Emil Frantíšek BURIAN, Czech composer of modernistically colored choral and instrumental music, composed in 1949 to salute the advent of the Communist government in Czechoslovakia, and containing quotations from the Soviet National Anthem, is performed for the first time in Prague.

8 FEBRUARY 1952

String Quartet in D major by Arnold SCHOENBERG, composed in 1897, the score of which was regarded as lost, is performed for the first time in the 20th century, after a hiatus of 55 years, at the Library of Congress in Washington.

This is the first publicly performed work of Schoenberg... played in Vienna during the season 1897–98. Grove and Leibowitz erroneously state that the score has been lost! In fact not only the score, but also the parts (written by Schoenberg himself) are preserved. (From a note by Schoenberg, in English, using third person singular, accompanying the manuscript of the score and parts of the *String Quartet* in D, which he offered for sale to the Library of Congress, and which was purchased shortly before his death)

8 FEBRUARY 1952

L'Uragano, opera in three acts by the 56-year-old Italian composer Lodovico ROCCA, after Ostrovsky's somber Russian play about a 19th-century merchant woman Katia Kabanova, whose drinking husband and oppressive mother-in-law drive her to suicide, is produced at La Scala in Milan.

11 FEBRUARY 1952

Hugo WEISGALL, 39-year-old Czech-born American composer, conducts in Baltimore the first performance of his short opera *The Tenor*, to a libretto drawn from the novella *Der Kammersänger* by Franz Wedekind, dealing with a self-centered tenor who steps over the dead body of one of his multitudinous mistresses in his haste to get to the opera theater in time to sing Tristan, set to music in a tense style between a narrative ballad and atonal expressionism, with several quotations from *Tristan und Isolde*.

13 FEBRUARY 1952

Alfred EINSTEIN, eminent German music scholar and lexicographer, dies in his California retreat at El Cerrito, at the age of 71. Alfred and Albert Einstein were friends and came from the same part of Germany. Although they themselves believed that they were related, a thorough search through birth and death registers for many generations failed to discover a common ancestor.

17 FEBRUARY 1952

Boulevard Solitude, lyric drama in seven scenes by the 25-year-old German composer Hans Werner HENZE, to the story of Manon Lescaut interpreted in an existentialistically surrealistic manner, written in an expressionistically synthetic idiom, ranging from triadic constructions in plain C major to overt dodecaphony, a conception radically different from the melodramatic lyricism of the operas by Massenet and Puccini on the same subject, is performed for the first time in Hannover.

18 FEBRUARY 1952

Mstislav Rostropovich, prime Soviet cellist, plays the first performance in Moscow of *Symphonie Concertante in E minor* for cello and orchestra, by Sergei PROKOFIEV, written especially for him and dedicated to him, with much thematic material taken from Prokofiev's *First Cello Concerto* of 1938, and combining in its score the most felicitous qualities of Prokofiev's energetically lyrical and dramatically individual style, with flashes of irony illuminating the music, in three movements:

(1) *Andante*, in 2/4 time, in E minor, intoning, after a thunderous orchestral introduction, a spacious melody in the solo cello part, soon reaching a maximal saturation of sonorous matter, with the cello scaling the heights of its range before subsiding to a lyrical ending; (2) *Allegro giusto*, in 4/4 time, in C major, in the manner of a toccata, with tennis-like tossing of chordal balls across the contrapuntal net, and basic tonality enhanced by particles of chromatic dust clinging to strategic points; (3) *Andante con moto*, in 3/2 time, in E major, beginning with a chorale-like recitative, then embarking on a kinesthetic *Vivace* in 3/4 time, erupting in asymmetrical blasts of brass, and coming to rest on a unison E.

21 FEBRUARY 1952

The South African Musical Festival, celebrating the tricentennial of the Boer settlement, opens at Cape Town with a program of ballet music, including a world première of *Legend of Princess Vlei* by the 24-year-old South African composer John JOUBERT.

22 FEBRUARY 1952

The Meeting of the Volga with the Don River, festive overture by Sergei PROKOFIEV, written to celebrate the completion of the Volga-Don Canal, is performed for the first time on the Moscow radio.

22 FEBRUARY 1952

Violin Concerto by the 50-year-old Russian-born American composer Boris KOUTZEN, in three movements, written in a traditional 19th-century manner, with the employment of some hidden contrapuntal devices such as the superposition of a theme on its alter ego in reverse progression, is performed in a world première by Koutzen's daughter Nadia with the Philadelphia Orchestra, Eugene Ormandy conducting.

29 FEBRUARY 1952

Carlos CHÁVEZ conducts in Mexico City the world pre-mière of his *Violin Concerto,* with Viviane Bertolami as soloist, in eight linked movements of which the last four, separated from the first four by a florid violin cadenza, recapitulate in reverse the basic four movements, so that the entire work becomes an equilibrated specular octad possessing a perfect chirality.

3 MARCH 1952

The Austrian Government issues a stamp for 1 1/2 schillings in honor of the Viennese violinist and organizer of a popular quartet of two violins, guitar and accordion, Johann SCHRAMMEL (1850–1893).

3 MARCH 1952

Seljaci (The Peasants), comic opera in three acts by the Croatian composer Petar KONJOVIĆ, picturing rustic life, love and drama in a Serbian village at the end of the 19th century, written in a socialist realistic tradition with copious quotations of ethnic elements in Balkanized asymmetrical melorhythms, is produced in Belgrade.

4 MARCH 1952

Tartiniana for violin and orchestra by the 48-year-old Italian modernist Luigi DALLAPICCOLA, based on themes of Giuseppe Tartini, the initiator of the virtuoso school of Italian violin playing, is performed for the first time in Bern, Switzerland.

7 MARCH 1952

Albert COATES, Russian-born English composer-conductor resident in South Africa conducts at Cape Town the first performance of his opera *Tafelberg se Kleed (Van Hunks and the Devil),* to a libretto in the Afrikaans language, drawn from a native legend of a Dutchman holding a smoking contest with the devil on top of 3,550-foot Table Mountain near Cape Town, causing violent winds and interfering with navigation in the harbor, set to music in an intelligently ethnomusicological idiom, with a generous application of rational dissonances.

7 MARCH 1952

Twelth Symphony, with a choral ending, by the 56-year-old Swiss-American composer Ernst LÉVY, written in an austerely sonorous, frugally romantic style, is performed for the first time in Chicago under the composer's direction.

14 MARCH 1952

Second Symphony by the Hawaiian composer Dai-Keong LEE is performed for the first time in San Francisco.

14 MARCH 1952

Harry PARTCH, 50-year-old Californian composer, presents at Mills College, Oakland, his musical score to *King Oedipus* of Sophocles (in the version by William Butler Yeats), built on a 43-note scale in nontempered pitch and employing specially constructed instruments: a modernized kithara with 72 strings, a Harmonic Canon with 44 strings, each of which is a freely tunable monochord;

Marimba Eroica; Bass Marimba; two altered guitars; two flexible saxophones; microtonal string bass; microtonal violoncello and a set of Cloud Chamber Bowls, borrowed from the atomic laboratory of the University of California.

17 MARCH 1952

Juan José CASTRO, 56-year-old Argentinian composer, conducts at La Scala in Milan the world premiere of his opera *Proserpina e lo Straniero,* awarded the first prize of 4 million lire in a contest on the occasion of the semicentennial of Verdi's death, to an Italian libretto translated from the original Spanish, a modern rendition of the classical myth, wherein Proserpina appears as a Buenos Aires prostitute, and Pluto, the "stranger" of the title, is transferred from the nether to the upper regions, as an aviator in World War II who is compelled to lead an air raid on a monastery in which his own wife had taken shelter, kills her, and expiates his crime by being himself killed by one of Proserpina's lovers, set to music in a tense melodramatic style, vitalized by South American melorhythms.

18 MARCH 1952

At the South African Festival in Cape Town, Szymon Goldberg plays the first performance of the *Violin Concerto* by the resident Scottish composer Erik CHISHOLM, in four substantial movements, inspired by Hindu modes, but clothed in a modern technique.

19 MARCH 1952

Overture for the Dedication of a Nuclear Reactor by the atomic physicist Arthur ROBERTS, in four movements representing the design, construction, and modus operandi of a nuclear reactor, derived from the motto A-E-C (for Atomic Energy Commission) with subsidiary parameters indicating specific weights in the periodical table of elements, C-12 (graphite or carbon), U-235 (uranium) and Pu-239 (plutonium), wherein the numbers represent intervals from the tonic, undergoing transmutation in a jazzified scherzo until the theme of the Atomic Energy Commission ominously cautions the operators to keep the reactor under control, is performed for the first time at Oak Ridge, Tennessee, the atomic research center. (The score itself was designated as not musically or atomically classified and conveying no secret diatonic, pandiatonic or dodecaphonic information.)

20 MARCH 1952

Second Symphony by the 53-year-old Russian composer Alexander TCHEREPNIN, in four movements, written in 1945–1951 as a musical memorial of his father Nicolas Tcherepnin who died in Paris in 1945, is performed for the first time by the Chicago Symphony Orchestra, Rafael Kubelik conducting.

22 MARCH 1952

To mark the centennial of the birth of the notable Bohemian violinist and famous teacher, Ottakar ŠEVČÍK, the Czechoslovak government issues postage stamps for 2 and 3 kronen.

25 MARCH 1952

Leonore 40/45, opera in two acts and eight scenes by the Swiss composer Rolf LIEBERMANN, to a libretto drawn from the true story of a love affair between a German soldier and a French girl during the Nazi occupation of Paris and their separation after the liberation in August 1944 (the title alludes to the crucial years 1940–1945, and the name Leonore connotes fidelity, as in Beethoven's opera *Fidelio*), is performed for the first time in Basel.

26 MARCH 1952

To mark the 125th anniversary of BEETHOVEN's death, both West Germany and East Germany issue a series of stamps with his portrait.

27 MARCH 1952

The world première of the ballet *Chemin de Lumière* by Georges AURIC, to an existentialist human scenario in which love triumphs over death, in a symbolic setting designated as "somewhere in the world," is given in Munich.

28 MARCH 1952

Walt Whitman, symphonic essay by Paul CRESTON, is performed for the first time in Cincinnati.

30 MARCH 1952

Don Perlimplin, one-act opera by the 54-year-old Italian composer Vittorio RIETI, making his home in America, after the poem by Francisco García Lorca, is performed for the first time at the University of Illinois in Urbana.

1 APRIL 1952

Atlanta, symphonic suite by the American composer and arranger Don GILLIS, in six topographical movements descriptive of the historic landmarks of Atlanta, Georgia, is performed for the first time by the Atlanta Symphony Orchestra.

3 APRIL 1952

Wat Tyler, socio-historical opera by the left-wing member of the British Labour Party Alan BUSH, glorifying the leader of the peasant uprising in England in 1381, set to music steeped in English folk rhythms, is performed for the first time in a broadcast production in East Berlin.

3 APRIL 1952

Cemal REŞID REY, Turkish composer, conducts in Paris the first performance of his symphonic poem *L'Appel*.

3 APRIL 1952

Third Symphony by the American composer Roger GOEB is performed for the first time by the CBS Symphony under the direction of Leopold Stokowski.

5 APRIL 1952

Inês Pereira, opera by the Portuguese composer Ruy COELHO, is produced in Lisbon.

6 APRIL 1952

First Concerto for String Orchestra by the 40-year-old Swedish composer Allan PETTERSSON is performed for the first time on the Swedish Radio in Stockholm.

13 APRIL 1952

Morton GOULD conducts the United States Military Academy Band at West Point in the world première of his *Fourth Symphony*, written for the sesquicentennial of West Point, in two movements, *Epitaphs*, an elagiac fantasy about absent femininity, and *Marches*, a virile fanfaronade, hoisting a brassy orifiamme in the Army regulation time of 132 steps a minute, metronomed by a "Marching machine."

17 APRIL 1952

Fourth Symphony, subtitled *Metamorfose Sinfonische,* by the Swedish composer Hilding HALLNÄS, is performed for the first time in Göteborg.

22 APRIL 1952

The Brazilian Government issues a postage stamp of 60 milreis to mark the centennial of the birth of the Brazilian composer Henrique OSWALD.

30 APRIL 1952

Fifth Symphony in A minor by the dean of Swedish composers Hugo ALFVÉN is performed for the first time in Stockholm.

2 MAY 1952

Water Music by the leader of the musical avant-garde John CAGE, scored for a pianist, who also uses a radio, whistles, water containers and a deck of cards, with thematic elements drawn from the *I-Ching*, a Chinese book of oracles, is performed for the first time by David Tudor in New York.

Unlike Handel's, it actually splashes. (From a letter of invitation to the author to attend a performance of *Water Music*)

3 MAY 1952

During a televised tour of the White House, President TRUMAN, acting as an amiable guide, obligingly plays a few bars from MOZART's *Ninth Sonata in A major* on the Steinway piano (installed in the White House on 11 December 1938), then goes over to the second piano (a Baldwin) to improvise a series of harmonious chords (boldly modulating from C major to D-flat major), adding for color a series of chromatically ascending diminished seventh-chords.

3 MAY 1952

Romance in D-flat for harmonica, string orchestra and piano by Ralph VAUGHAN WILLIAMS, in three contrasting movements, is performed for the first time by the American mouth harmonica virtuoso Larry Adler with the Little Symphony Orchestra in New York. (The first English performance of the *Romance* took place in Liverpool on 16 June 1952.)

3 MAY 1952

Fifth Symphony by the 56-year-old Austrian composer Johann Nepomuk DAVID is performed for the first time in Stuttgart.

5 MAY 1952

Rítmo Jondo for clarinet, trumpet, xylophone, and percussion by the Catalan-American composer Carlos SURINACH, based on *Canto flamenco* rhythms, is performed for the first time in New York. (An extended version, in ballet form, was produced in New York under the title *Deep Rhythm* on 15 April 1953.)

5 MAY 1952

President Theodor Heuss of West Germany sanctions the restoration of the HAYDN melody of the Emperor's Hymn, used during the pan-Germanic period from Wilhelm II to Hitler as the vehicle of the geophagous anthem *Deutschland über alles* (it was originally written by Professor August Hoffmann von Fallersleben about 1840, with the intended meaning *Germany before all else,* rather than the imperialistic *Germany above all,* and expressing a patriotic feeling for the unification of individual German states), to a revised text eliminating the ambiguous words.

6 MAY 1952

The Boston Symphony Orchestra makes its first appearance abroad, with Charles Munch conducting it at the opening concert of the Paris Festival of 20th-century Music, sponsored by the Congress for Cultural Freedom, in a program listing DEBUSSY'S *La Mer;* RAVEL's *Daphnis et Chloé* (second suite), HONEGGER's *Second Symphony,* Samuel BARBER's mellifluously neo-classical *Overture to the School for Scandal,* and the tersely contrapuntal *Toccata* by Walter PISTON.

7 MAY 1952

Cordélia, ballet by Henri SAUGUET, to the story of a little girl's daylight nightmare in which she is pursued by a man with a whip and a woman with a cudgel, is performed for the first time at the Paris Festival of 20th-century Music, on the same program with the première of a ballet by Georges AURIC, *Coup de feu,* in which two lovers literally set each others' hearts on fire which rages until a torrential rain extinguishes them, and the lovers return to a life of controlled amours.

7 MAY 1952

Acres of Sky, ballad opera by the 45-year-old American composer Arthur KREUTZ, dealing with subnormal rural family life in Arkansas, set to music in a sophisticatedly simplicistic ballad manner, is performed for the first time at Columbia University in New York.

11 MAY 1952

The Revelation of the Fifth Seal, apocalyptic symphonic poem by the Greek composer Yorgo SICILIANOS, is performed for the first time in Athens.

13 MAY 1952

Cantata from Proverbs by Darius MILHAUD, scored for women's chorus, oboe, cello and harp, in three movements—(1) *Who crieth "Woe"?,* an emotional exhortation against the use of stimulants, dramatically underlined by the warning "Thine eyes shall behold strange things"; (2) *The Woman Folly,* a pandiatonic portrait of females circa 1,000 B.C.; (3) *A Woman of Valor,* extolling the virtues of a righteous and submissive housewife in orthodox society—is performed for the first time by the United Temple Chorus of Lawrence, Long Island, Isadore Freed conducting.

15 MAY 1952

Italo MONTEMEZZI, Italian composer of operas, among which *L'Amore dei tre re* became a perennial favorite, dies in Vigasio at the age of 76.

18 MAY 1952

Mila Gojsalića, opera by the Croatian composer Jakov GOTOVAC, is performed for the first time in Zagreb.

18 MAY 1952

KING FREDERICK of Denmark, an amateur musician and pupil in conducting of Nikolai Malko, conducts the Danish State Radio Orchestra in an adequate performance of the *Second Symphony* by Sibelius, deferentially helped along by his faithful subjects in the orchestra, whenever he falters in beating time.

19 MAY 1952

Josef Matthias HAUER, the bearded Viennese prophet of 12-tone music, makes public in Vienna his *Zwölftonspiel-Manifest* proclaiming, with a defiant display of unsophrosyne hubris, his priority and supremacy as the only begetter of 12-tone music, "der geistiger Urheber und trotz vielen schlechten Nachahmern immer noch der einziger Kenner und Könner der Zwölftonmusik."

The Builder of the Universe created Absolute Music in final fulfillment, once and for all. We, sons of men, have endeavored for eons of time to learn this divine primordial language. *Zwölftonspiel* regulates the physiological premises of pure intuition which alone enables us to perceive immutable Absolute Music as the revelation of the world order in all eternity. Tones with their overtones are suns with their planets. Solar systems temper one another. Their intervals are ordered with cogent necessity in the Harmony of the Spheres. *Zwölftonspiel* performs the functions of galaxies and constitutes the formative dynamic centers of organic processes. The language of the Builder of the Universe, with its 479,001,600 vocables, the Art of the Arts, the Science of Sciences, the Most Holy, the Most Spiritual, the Most Exalted in the world, is Music. But this Music must be distinguished from mere music-mongering, such as tone-paintings and symphonic poems, and suchlike "new" modern cultural dung heaps. Absolute Music is the link with Eternity, Religion, Spiritual Reality, different from various parochial denominations, philosophical systems and political ideologies. Music is of prime importance in directing the people along the right path. . . . You, 12-tone ignoramuses, learn the Tropes! (Text of Hauer's manifesto, translated from Hermann Frogner's book *Die Zwölfordnung der Töne,* Vienna, 1953, pp. 231–232)

23 MAY 1952

On the 80th anniversary of his first public appearance as a child prodigy, Gustave L. BECKER, 91-year-old American pianist and composer presents at Steinway Hall in New York a concert in a program including Beethoven's *Appassionata*, Chopin's *Polonaise* in A-flat, and five innocuous pieces by Becker himself: *Fugue* in G major, *Gavotte-Humoresque*, *Étude mélodique*, *Rondo-Scherzino* and *Flight of the Swallows*.

24 MAY 1952

Defender of the Peace, pacifist symphonic essay by the English composer Alan BUSH, is performed for the first time on the Vienna Radio.

26 MAY 1952

Second Piano Concerto by the 50-year-old Belgian composer Raymond CHEVREUILLE, is performed for the first time in Brussels.

30 MAY 1952

On the occasion of its sesquicentennial, the United States Military Academy Band, assisted by the Dialectic Society of the Corps of Cadets, presents at West Point, New York, a program of specially commissioned works for band, including *Fantasy* by Henry COWELL, derived in its thematic contents from separate segments of the Alma Mater melody; *West Point Suite* in three movements by Darius MILHAUD; and *Symphony in One Movement* for wind instruments by Roy HARRIS, expressive of the "idealism which has motivated the fighting men of our nation" and ending with a fugal dance.

2 JUNE 1952

Aucassin et Nicolette, marionette play by Mario CASTELNUOVO-TEDESCO, to the story of the medieval love of Aucassin, a nobleman, for the Saracen girl Nicolette captured during a Crusade, who is revealed as daughter of the King of Carthage, scored for soprano and 11 instruments, with a mimodrama enacted by marionettes on the stage, is performed for the first time, 14 years after its composition, at the Festival Maggio fiorentino, in Florence.

4 JUNE 1952

Travesti, comic ballet by the French composer Marcel DELANNOY is performed for the first time at Enghien-les-Bains.

7 JUNE 1952

Merlijn, symphonic drama in three scenes by Willem PIJPER, left unfinished after his death (only six episodes were completed, corresponding to six of the twelve signs of the Zodiac), inspired by the magician Merlin of King Arthur's legend, is performed posthumously for the first time in Rotterdam.

12 JUNE 1952

At the opening of the Festival of Creative Arts at Brandeis University in Waltham, Massachusetts, Leonard BERNSTEIN conducts the world première of his one-act opera *Trouble in Tahiti*, written in a modernistically titivated jazz idiom, to his own libretto descriptive of a marital collision in a suburban American home with mutual recriminations appeased when the married couple attends a motion picture depicting the delights of simple life on the pacific Pacific Island of Tahiti.

14 JUNE 1952

An Americanized version of Kurt WEILL's *Dreigroschenoper* set in a slangy dialogue by Marc Blitzstein, under the title *The Three-penny Opera*, is given in a world première, on the same program with a ballet, *Symphonie pour un homme seul*, acoustically compiled by the creator of "musique concrète" Pierre SCHAEFFER, at the Festival of Creative Arts at Brandeis University.

14 JUNE 1952

A nine-day festival of choral music opens at Aldeburgh, England, with Benjamin BRITTEN conducting a visiting Boys' Choir from Copenhagen in his *Ceremony of Carols*, and presenting modern arrangements of 18th-century music made by the 25-year-old Englishman Arthur Oldham, France's "jeune Français" Jean Françaix and others.

16 JUNE 1952

The German pianist Heinz ARNTZ sets a world record of continuous piano playing in a Düsseldorf restaurant by completing a keyboard marathon of 224 hours, allowing a minimal amount of time each day for dormition, micturition, defecation and ingestion of food.

17 JUNE 1952

Alberto WILLIAMS, cultured and prolific Argentinian composer (his grandfather was an Englishman), a student of César Franck in Paris, who upon return to Argentina made Buenos Aires a veritable Conservatoriopolis by opening several music schools there, writing nine romantic symphonies and hundreds of piano pieces inspired by Argentinian melorhythms, and publishing them all in his own publishing house, dies in his native city of Buenos Aires in his 90th year.

20 JUNE 1952

The 26th Festival of the International Society for Contemporary Music opens in Salzburg (where it was founded in 1923) in a program of orchestral works by German composers:

Symphony in three movements by Wolfgang FORTNER, in a neo-baroque style with tangential atonalities, conducted by the composer; *Fifth Symphony* by Karl Amadeus HARTMANN, in three movements of neo-classical inspiration; a *Choral Fantasy* by the 47-year-old Schoenberg disciple Winfried ZILLIG, written in a determined dodecaphonic technique; *Allegria*, by the 51-year-old German composer Werner EGK, in the form of a classical suite, conducted by the composer.

20 JUNE 1952

Paul HINDEMITH conducts in Zürich a revised version of his opera *Cardillac*, with a completely revised libretto drawn from E. T. A. Hoffman's story, *Madame de Scuderi*, containing new episodes, including the insertion of a

Lully opera segment, expertly Hindemithized in scoring and harmonization.

21 JUNE 1952

At the second concert of the 26th Festival of the International Society for Contemporary Music in Salzburg, the following works are presented:

Sixth Symphony by the Swiss neo-classicist Conrad BECK, in five movements, of which two pairs are linked reducing the whole to three larger movements; *Phantasie* for clarinet, piano and orchestra by the Vienna dodecaphonist Hanns JELINEK, paying homage to classicism by including the B-A-C-H motive in the introduction and at the conclusion; *Mythological Figurines* by the 49-year-old German composer Rudolf WAGNER-RÉGENY, in three sections, *Ceres, Amphitrite*, and *Diana*, designed in a free dodecaphonic idiom in variable meters, intended to unify archaic modes, asymmetric rhythms and euphonious dissonances; tripartite *Concertino* for oboe, bassoon and orchestra by the Vienna-born 47-year-old composer Paul CSONKA, introduced as a representative of Cuba, whither he emigrated in 1938, after the Austrian Anschluss; and *Three Pieces for Orchestra* by the 37-year-old Belgian composer Marcel QUINET, written in an eclectic neo-romantic vein daubed with impressionistic colors.

22 JUNE 1952

A concert of music by Arnold SCHOENBERG is given as part of the 26th Festival of the International Society for Contemporary Music in Salzburg, presenting his *Five Orchestra Pieces*, the monodrama *Erwartung* and *Variations for Orchestra*.

23 JUNE 1952

The following program of chamber music is presented at the 26th Festival of the International Society for Contemporary Music in Salzburg:

Violin Sonata by the Posen-born 41-year-old Israeli composer Josef TAL, based on Jewish melodies; *Three Invocations* for voice and piano by the Rumanian-born 32-year-old Italian composer Roman VLAD, couched in a neo-ecclesiastical modal idiom; *Sonata* for clarinet and violoncello by the 41-year-old British composeress Phyllis TATE, set in a pleasantly feminine neo-classic manner; *Variations* for piano by the 39-year-old Chilean composer Alfonso LETELIER; *Duo* for violin and violoncello by the 28-year-old Australian composer Don BANKS, written in a motoric modernistic style; *Sonata* for trumpet and piano by the 51-year-old Icelandic composer Karl Otto RUNOLFSSON, in a candidly classical idiom; and *String Quartet* by the 42-year-old French composer Jean MARTINON, set in the classical matrix with impressionistic discursions.

24 JUNE 1952

The following program is presented at the 26th Festival of the International Society for Contemporary Music in Salzburg:

Canto de amor e paz by the 32-year-old former dodecaphonist Claudio SANTORO of Brazil, couched in an Italianate neo-romantic manner; *Sextet* for wind instruments by the 45-year-old Finnish composer Nils Erik RINGBOM, in three movements disposed in an academic form, with fugal developments and concatenated variations; *Poem* for 22 string instruments by the 36-year-old British composer Humphrey SEARLE, written in a vertically-horizontal dodecaphonic manner, with the thematic 12-note chords melodically terraced in the develop-

ment; *Piano Concerto* by the 45-year-old Norwegian composer Klaus EGGE, in a single compact movement with the accompaniment of string instruments only, couched in the form of seven variations on a folk-like Norwegian theme; *Variations* for wind instruments by the 44-year-old Swiss composer Edward STAEMPFLI, in a free dodecaphonic style in which the seventh and last variation is the mirror of the first; and *Sinfonia serena* for string instruments and kettledrums by the 55-year-old Danish composer Knudaage RIISAGER, in four movements of neo-classical inspiration.

24 JUNE 1952

Lodewijk MORTELMANS, Belgian composer, whose congenital Wagnerophilia did not deter him from viable utilization of folk music and lyric settings of Flemish poems, dies in his native city of Antwerp, at the age of 84.

25 JUNE 1952

Third Symphony by the half-a-century-old Belgian composer Raymond CHEVREUILLE, is performed for the first time in Brussels.

25 JUNE 1952

The following program of chamber music is presented at the 26th Festival of the International Society for Contemporary Music in Salzburg:

Piano Sonata by the 34-year-old Sumatra-born naturalized American composer Claus ADAM; *Music* for clarinet, trumpet and viola by the 36-year-old Hungarian-born Viennese composer Karl SCHISKE, in a cosmopolitan neo-classical idiom; *Theme and Variations* for two violins, an essay in double counterpoint by the 29-year-old New Zealander Ronald TREMAIN; *Three Religious Chants* for soprano and string trio by the 22-year-old Belgian composer Henri POUSSEUR, to Latin texts in ecclesiastical modes encased in a dodecaphonic matrix; *Sonata* for unaccompanied violin by the 53-year-old Parisianized Rumanian composer Marcel MIHALOVICI, in four brief divisions in a neo-classical mold; *Three Piano Pieces* by the 29-year-old South African composer Stefans GROVÉ, in a neo-classical idiom; *Duo* for flute and harp by the 32-year-old Dutch composer Lex van DELDEN, in three classically inspired sections; and *String Trio* by the 37-year-old Austrian-born Argentinian composer Guillermo GRAETZER.

26 JUNE 1952

At the 26th Festival of the International Society for Contemporary Music in Salzburg, the following program of orchestral music is presented:

Symphony in C major by the 53-year-old Hungarian-born Parisian composer Tibor HARSÁNYI, written in a cosmopolitan classical style; *Violin Concerto* by the 34-year-old German composer Bernd Alois ZIMMERMANN, in the spiritual manner of instrumental classicism with the thematic interpolation of *Dies Irae* in the middle movement; *Piano Concerto* by the Italian composer Mario PERAGALLO, classical in form and modernistically atonal in content; and *Le Soleil des Eaux* for voices and orchestra by the 27-year-old French radical composer Pierre BOULEZ, conceived in an agglutinatory motivic manner, in which each phrase is split into sections consecutively sung or played by different voices or instruments.

28 JUNE 1952

While conducting the third of the *Three Little Orchestra Pieces* by Wilhelm Heubner in a program of modern Austrian music at the 26th Festival of the International Society for Contemporary Music in Salzburg, Herbert HAEFNER, 46-year-old Austrian conductor collapses and dies on the podium.

(The scheduled program included a *Suite* for two flutes and string orchestra by Georg GRUBER, *Piano Concerto* by Cesar BRESGEN, *Three Little Orchestra Pieces* by Wilhelm HUEBNER, *Violin Concerto* by S. C. ECKHARDT-GRAMATTE, and *Hymn* for chorus, alto solo and orchestra by Gottfried von EINEM; the concert was interrupted after Haefner's dramatic death, and the last two works of the program remained unperformed.)

29 JUNE 1952

The 26th International Society for Contemporary Music Festival in Salzburg concludes with a concert of orchestral music in the following program:

Symphonic Antithesis by the 55-year-old Yugoslav composer Matija BRAVNIČAR (first heard in Ljubljana on 9 February 1948) based on two antithetical concepts, sacred and profane, in native folk music, set in canonic and fugal forms with variations; *Theme and Variations* by the 45-year-old Japanese composer Yoritsune MATSUDAIRA, derived from old Japanese modes, and varying in melodic content from pentatonicism to dodecaphony, and in rhythm from asymmetrical Japanese meters to syncopated patterns of jazz and boogie-woogie; *Hymns to Beauty* for chorus and orchestra by the 32-year-old Swedish composer Göte CARLID, to Baudelaire's poems on the subject of debilitude of man, set to music of impressionistic colors; *Violin Concerto* by the 37-year-old Dutch composer Marius FLOTHUIS, in three parts, in a neo-classical vein; and *Canzoni* by the 60-year-old Italian composer Giorgio Federico GHEDINI, a neo-Renaissance essay in old Italian forms.

11 JULY 1952

A three-day Festival of national Swiss music opens at St. Gall, featuring concerts on long Alpine horns, and a yodeling contest with 2,800 participants, 95 of them receiving silver buttons for excellence.

17 JULY 1952

A Provincial Episode; or, Gay Little World, chamber opera in one act and one scene by Max WALD, to a libretto by the composer, is produced for the first time, with two-piano accompaniment, at Ohio University in Athens, Ohio.

22 JULY 1952

Tankred und Cantylene, ballet by the 26-year-old German composer Hans Werner HENZE, is performed for the first time in Munich.

22 JULY 1952

Pas de cœur, ballet by the Austrian composer Gottfried von EINEM, is produced in Munich.

22 JULY 1952

Don Fortunio, one-act opera by the American composer Hamilton FORREST, is produced at Interlochen, Michigan.

27 JULY 1952

Uvertura bohaterska (*Heroic Overture*) by the 37-year-old Polish composer Andrzej PANUFNIK, written in an optimistic, socialist realistic style, with brass and drums accentuating the import of the theme, and ending on the heroic chord of E-flat major, consanguine to the key of Beethoven's *Eroica*, is performed for the first time during the International Olympic Games in Helsinki, conducted by the composer.

9 AUGUST 1952

Hugo WEISGALL, Bohemian-born 39-year-old American composer, conducts in Westport, Connecticut, the first performance of his one-act opera *The Stronger*, after Strindberg's play in which a provincial matron taunts a former matrimonial rival about her inability to find a husband, while the other silently fixes her gaze on the audience with a meaningful smile suggesting that she is the stronger one, set to music in an expressionistically atonal idiom with jazzy interpolations illustrating the surrealistic mysteries of life.

13 AUGUST 1952

The Farmer and the Fairy, whimsical opera by Alexander TCHEREPNIN, dealing with a preternaturally promiscuous female whiling away twenty years of human cohabitation with a terrestrial farmer before returning to the phantom world, with the pentatonic scale used to express the simplicity of the tale, is performed for the first time at the Music Festival in Aspen, Colorado.

14 AUGUST 1952

Die Liebe der Danae, opera in three acts by Richard STRAUSS, portraying in a "psychological counterpoint" the Milesian tale of a concupiscent Zeus who descends upon the virginal Danaë in the form of a rain of gold, is produced posthumously in Salzburg.

(Strauss completed the score on 28 June 1940; the opera was initially scheduled for performance in Salzburg in August 1944, and the final rehearsal took place on 16 August 1944, when the Nazis closed all German and Austrian theaters.)

18 AUGUST 1952

Henry EXPERT, expert French music scholar, who spent much of his life editing and publishing French and Flemish music of the 15th and 16th centuries, dies in Tourettes-sur-Loup in the Alpes-Maritimes, in his 90th year.

19 AUGUST 1952

Estancia, ballet by the prime modern composer of Argentina, Alberto GINASTERA, illustrating a day spent on a farm in the pampas, set to music in vivid subtropical colors, is performed for the first time in its entirety in Buenos Aires.

29 AUGUST 1952

4'33" by John CAGE, for piano, two pianos, or any instrument, or any combination of instruments, in three movements *tacet*, with no sounds intentionally produced, the length of time for each non-performed and unheard movement determined by chance, is unplayed on the piano by his loyal famulus David Tudor, at Maverick Concert Hall in Woodstock, New York.

The difficulty to judge John Cage's *4'33"* is that it is impossible to tell what music has not been played. (From an unidentified newspaper report of a New York non-performance of *4'33"* of 14 April 1956)

1 SEPTEMBER 1952

Der Idiot, ballet-pantomime after Dostoyevsky, by the 26-year-old German composer Hans Werner HENZE, is performed for the first time in Berlin.

14 SEPTEMBER 1952

Concerto for harpsichord and orchestra by the prime Swiss modernist Frank MARTIN is performed for the first time at the International Festival of Contemporary Music in Venice.

15 SEPTEMBER 1952

Second Piano Concerto by the Manchurian-born half-Estonian half-German composer Boris BLACHER, in three movements, based on the concept of form-rhythm, so that metric formulas based on the arithmetic progressions (e.g. 1,2,3,4,5,4,3,2,1,), and summation series (1,2,3,5,8,13, etc.) determine the melodic and rhythmic pattern, is performed for the first time in Berlin.

17 SEPTEMBER 1952

Die Witwe von Ephesus, one-act chamber opera by the 44-year-old German composer Wolfgang FORTNER, is performed for the first time in Berlin.

23 SEPTEMBER 1952

Preussisches Märchen, ballet-opera by Boris BLACHER, after a famous play *Captain of Koepenick*, wherein a humble and frustrated government clerk successfully impersonates a captain of the guard and arrests the mayor of his home town for corruption, set to music in an appropriately comic, harmonically crude manner, with military rhythms subjected to asymmetrical dislocation, is performed for the first time at the Municipal Opera in West Berlin as part of a month-long Music Festival.

4 OCTOBER 1952

Noctambulation for orchestra by the 26-year-old American composer Lee HOIBY is performed for the first time in New York.

11 OCTOBER 1952

Seventh Symphony by Sergei PROKOFIEV, in C sharp minor, his last (completed on 5 July 1952), stylistically summarizing the entire course of his musical esthetics, declaratively lucid, ironically optimistic, tonally firm despite constant modulatory translocations, animated by irresistible rhythms, and humanized by pervasive lyric sentiment, in four classically designed movements: *Moderato, Allegretto, Andante expressivo* and *Vivace*, with an expansive, very Russian finale, is performed for the first time in Moscow.

Prokofiev's *Seventh Symphony* is full of joy of life, lyricism. It arouses admiration by its lucid and luminous material and its uncommonly fresh harmonic language. (Dmitri Shostakovich, in *Sovietskaye Iskusstvo*, Moscow, 12 November 1952)

11 OCTOBER 1952

The Danish State Symphony Orchestra arrives in New York for an American tour of 38 concerts.

12 OCTOBER 1952

Concerto for harp and chamber orchestra by André JOLIVET in three cyclic movements is performed for the first time at the Donaueschingen Festival.

15 OCTOBER 1952

Symphonic Etude by the 60-year-old Dutch composer Hendrik ANDRIESSEN, in four movements based on a 12-tone series consisting of converging groups of chromatic intervals, is performed for the first time by The Hague Philharmonic Orchestra, Willem van Otterloo conducting.

18 OCTOBER 1952

The French Government issues two stamps, for 4 francs and 15 francs, in honor of Camille SAINT-SAËNS.

20 OCTOBER 1952

Concertato for Orchestra by the 29-year-old American composer Peter MENNIN (ńe Mennini), subtitled *Moby Dick* (its musical materials were to form the skeleton of an inchoate cetacean opera inspired by Melville's famous novel), is performed for the first time in the town of Mennin's birth, Erie, Pennsylvania.

20 OCTOBER 1952

Erik CHISHOLM, 48-year-old Scottish composer, conducts at the University of Capetown, South Africa, the first performance of his monodrama *Dark Sonnet*, in 14 sections, corresponding to the 14 lines of a sonnet, to the scenario suggested by Eugene O'Neill's playlet *Before Breakfast*, in which a nagging housewife drives her adulterous poet-husband to suicide (he cuts his throat, while shaving, in the 14th movement), scored for two pianos and chamber orchestra and written in highly dissonant harmonies.

22 OCTOBER 1952

Lord Inferno, "harmonious comedy" in one act by the 60-year-old Italian composer Giorgio Federico GHEDINI, to a libretto after *The Happy Hypocrite* of Max Beerbohm, is performed for the first time in concert form over the Italian Radio. (A stage production of the opera was first given by La Scala in Milan on 10 March 1956, under a more precisely translated title *L'Ipocrita felice*.)

26 OCTOBER 1952

Richard COBURN (whose real name was Frank De Long), American songwriter who wrote the hit tune *Whispering* dies in Los Angeles at the age of 66.

27 OCTOBER 1952

My Darlin' Aida, musical play by Charles FRIEDMAN, in which Guiseppe VERDI's Aida is transferred from Memphis, Egypt, to Memphis, Tennessee, A.D. 1861, and becomes a Negro slave, while Radames, whose name is transmogrified into Raymond Demarest, is reincarnated as a dashing confederate officer, with the famous aria *Celeste Aida* colloquially rendered "My Darlin' Aida," is produced in New York.

28 OCTOBER 1952

The first public concert of tape recorder music in the United States takes place at the Museum of Modern Art in New York, featuring *Sonic Contours* by the 40-year-old American composer Vladimir USSACHEVSKY, and three pieces by the 52-year-old American composer Otto LUENING: *Low Speed* and *Invention* for tape, and *Fantasy in Space* for flute solo and tape on which Luening himself was recorded, by a sound-on-sound method, playing four different flute parts, and which in turns accompanies Luening as live soloist.

2 NOVEMBER 1952

Ein Sommernachtstraum, musical play after Shakespeare's *A Midsummer Night's Dream* by Carl ORFF, is performed for the first time in Darmstadt.

4 NOVEMBER 1952

Jadranski Kapričo (*Adriatic Capriccio*) for violin and orchestra by the Croatian composer Petar KONJOVIĆ, in three movements making use of euphonious Dalmation folk melodies, is performed for the first time in Belgrade.

5 NOVEMBER 1952

Cagliostro, radiophonic drama in four acts by Ildebrando PIZZETTI, to his own libretto depicting in resonantly eloquent tonalities the adventures of the famous Sicilian charlatan who captivated the court of Marie Antoinette, is produced by the Italian Radio. (The first stage performance as an opera was given at La Scala, Milan, on 24 January 1953.)

7 NOVEMBER 1952

Dolores, "roman musical" in three acts by Michel-Maurice LÉVY (who gained popularity as a comic artist "Betove," i.e., Beethoven), is produced at the Opéra-Comique in Paris.

9 NOVEMBER 1952

Capitaine Bruno, comic opera by the Swiss composer Pierre WISSMER, is performed for the first time in Geneva.

11 NOVEMBER 1952

Igor STRAVINSKY conducts in Los Angeles the world première of his *Cantata* for soprano, tenor, female chorus and five instruments, to the texts of four anonymous English poems of the 15th and 16th centuries, artfully set in a gentle archaizing manner, in a melodically modal and harmonically pandiatonic idiom, interspersed in its interstices with a multiplicity of canonic devices including the cancrizans heretofore shunned by Stravinsky.

16 NOVEMBER 1952

Morton GOULD conducts in Rochester, New York, the first performance of his *Concerto for Tap Dancer and Orchestra*, in four movements, *Toccata, Pantomime, Minuet* and *Rondo*, with pedal percussion of the solo tap dancer on a resonant floorboard, variegated by shoe shuffling and heel glissando.

16 NOVEMBER 1952

20th Century Folk Mass ("Jazz Mass") for cantor and congregation by the Rev. Geoffrey BEAUMONT, M.A., M.B.E., Vicar and Warden of Trinity College Mission, Cambridge, England, based on mundanely American jazz rhythms (the composer warns expressly against "ecclesiasticising" his unchurchly hymns), is performed for the first time at St. Luke's Church, Chesterton, Cambridge, as part of a Sunday service.

20 NOVEMBER 1952

Gilgamesj opera by Ture RANGSTRÖM (1884–1947), Swedish composer of somberly turbulent romantic music (left incomplete at his death and orchestrated by John Fernström), based on the Babylonian epic of King Gilgamesh's quest in the world of the dead for his dearest enemy Enkidu, a lion-muscled man tamed by a lithesome temple maiden, is produced in Stockholm.

20 NOVEMBER 1952

The first version of the *Seventh Symphony* by Roy HARRIS, in a single movement, constituting a passacaglia with five variations couched in a clear tonal idiom with polyharmonic extensions, is performed for the first time by the Chicago Symphony Orchestra, Rafael Kubelik conducting. (A new and more compact version eliminating some of the complexities of the original, was first performed on 15 September 1955 by the Philadelphia Orchestra, Eugene Ormandy conducting, in Copenhagen, during its European tour.)

22 NOVEMBER 1952

The Government of the Federal German Republic issues a stamp for 4 marks in honor of Carl Friedrich ZELTER (1758–1832), the master of the Lied.

25 NOVEMBER 1952

Seventh Symphony for chamber orchestra by Henry COWELL, in four movements, is performed for the first time in Baltimore.

29 NOVEMBER 1952

Concerto for piano four hands by the 37-year-old American composer Vincent PERSICHETTI is performed for the first time in Pittsburgh.

5 DECEMBER 1952

The Polish Government issues a series of stamps at 45 and 60 groschen commemorating the romantic Polish violinist and composer Henryk WIENIAWSKI.

5 DECEMBER 1952

Violin Concerto by Gian Carlo MENOTTI is performed for the first time by Efrem Zimbalist and the Philadelphia Orchestra.

10 DECEMBER 1952

Sea Piece with Birds for orchestra by Virgil THOMSON, a portrait of "the undertow of the sea, the surface tension of waves, and the flight of birds as they sail back and forth," with trumpet calls imitating the cries of seagulls, engulfed in a sea of whole-tone scales and mutually exclusive augmented triads, is performed for the first time in Dallas.

11 DECEMBER 1952

For the first time in history, a regularly scheduled opera performance is televised on the screens of 31 movie houses in 27 cities in the United States, when the Metropolitan Opera broadcasts the complete performance of *Carmen* over a closed television circuit not yet reachable in private homes.

11 DECEMBER 1952

The Toronto Symphony presents at the Commonwealth Arts Festival in Toronto, a program of orchestral music, including the first performance of *Suite* for harp and chamber orchestra by Harry SOMERS of Canada.

12 DECEMBER 1952

Second Symphony by the Swedish modernist Karl-Birger BLOMDAHL is performed for the first time in Stockholm.

14 DECEMBER 1952

Fartein VALEN, Norwegian composer of symphonies, symphonic poems and other works written in a highly individual manner, employing a dissonant idiom of atonal polyphony, and yet redolent of characteristically Scandinavian romanticism, dies at Haugesund at the age of 65.

23 DECEMBER 1952

Second Symphony, subtitled *Victory*, by the American composer Harold MORRIS is performed for the first time in Chicago.

25 DECEMBER 1952

Bernardino MOLINARI, Italian conductor who brought out many works by modern Italian composers, including Respighi and Malipiero, dies in his native city Rome at the age of 72.

28 DECEMBER 1952

Pope Pius XII attends, for the first time as Pontiff, a concert at the Vatican to hear the 80-year-old Master of the Pope's music Lorenzo PEROSI conduct his oratorio *Il Natale del Rendentore* (*The Birth of the Redeemer*), first performed in Como on 12 September 1899.

1953

1 JANUARY 1953

Suite Hebraïque for viola and orchestra by Ernest BLOCH is performed for the first time by the Chicago Symphony Orchestra, Rafael Kubelik conducting.

1 JANUARY 1953

THREE MEN'S CLUB to promote modern music is organized in Tokyo.

By intimate contact with each other, the three men of the Club, Ikuma DAN, Yasuki AKUTAGAWA and Toshiro MAYUZUMI, different in tendencies, try to stimulate each other into fuller fruition in their objectives. The three men are in honor bound to act in unison against the present-day commercialism. (From the statute of the Three Men's Club.)

7 JANUARY 1953

Symphony for 42 String Instruments by the 27-year-old German composer Gishelher KLEBE is performed for the first time in Hamburg.

9 JANUARY 1953

Volpone, opera in three acts by George ANTHEIL, freely adapted from the famous play of Ben Jonson dealing with a foxy old man who deludes his expectant heirs, is performed for the first time at the University of Southern California, Los Angeles.

14 JANUARY 1953

Sir John Barbirolli conducts the Hallé Orchestra in Manchester in the world première of *Seventh Symphony*, subtitled *Sinfonia Antartica*, by Ralph VAUGHAN WILLIAMS, derived from his music for the film *Scott of the Antarctic*, which opened in London on 30 December 1948, as an homage to Sir Robert Scott who perished with his group of Antarctic explorers on his return from the South Pole in 1912, in five movements:

(1) *Prelude* (*Andante Maestoso*), bearing a motto from Shelley's *Prometheus Unbound*, moving in stately progressions of alternating whole-tones and semitones harmonized by unrelated major and minor triads and, after a chromatic constriction, rarefied

into pentatonic patterns, projecting ominous wordless voices and pouring cascades of purlingly pearly tintinnabulations on the celesta and Glockenspiel; crashing into fortississimo, and concluding on a congealed oblique cadence; (2) *Scherzo (Moderato)*, in pendulously barcarolling lolling rhythms in pentatonic and hexatonic scale patterns with shifting dominants and yet gravitationally tonal, ending in pianississississimo; (3) *Landscape (Lento)*, with a motto from Coleridge's *Hymn Before Sunrise*, pictorializing the "motionless torrents" and "silent cataracts" in glacial triadic harmonies, static unisons and tritone-bound scales, ending on a tremulous cymbal receding into inaudibility; (4) *Intermezzo (Andante sostenuto* in an oscillating major and minor tonalities with hymnal tunes made austere by frigid Phrygian modalities; (5) *Epilogue (Alla marcia moderato)*, with a motto from Captain Scott's last entry in his journal, in which he noted, before his frozen death, his serene acceptance of it, testified by brave trumpet calls in boldly ascending perfect fourths, and, as the gelid respiration of the Antarctic blizzard is registered in the accelerating turns of the wind machine, the wordless chorus intones its crying cryogenic semitones and the music freezes on a glacier-like minor sixth, in soundless *niente*.

17 JANUARY 1953

La Capanna dello zio Tom, opera in three acts by the Italian composer Luigi FERRARI-TRECATE, freely adapted from the famous abolitionist novel of Harriet Beecher Stowe, depicting the piteous state of Negro slaves in ante-bellum Kentucky, wherein the malevolent Signor Legree roars in impervious basso profundo and Zio Tom expatiates in tenor bel canto, is produced in Parma.

18 JANUARY 1953

The scheduled performance of Aaron COPLAND's *Lincoln Protrait* at the concert by the National Symphony in Washington for Eisenhower's inauguration as President, is cancelled at the instigation of Congressman Fred E. Busbey, Republican of Illinois, on the ground of Copland's alleged association with subversive political organizations.

There are many patriotic composers available without the long record of questionable affiliations of Copland. The Republican Party would have been ridiculed from one end of the United States to the other if Copland's music had been played at the inaugural of a President elected to fight Communism, among other things. (From Busbey's statement)

No American composer, living or dead has done more for American music and the growth of the reputation of American culture throughout the civilized world than Aaron Copland. To bar from the Inaugural Concert his music, and especially music about Abraham Lincoln, will be the worst kind of blunder and will hold us up as a nation to universal ridicule. (Statement by the League of Composers of New York City)

18 JANUARY 1953

Louise Nguyen VAN TY, Indo-Chinese composeress, plays the piano part in the first performance with the Lamoureux Orchestra of Paris, of her coloristic work *La Fête du Têt*, celebrating the lunar calendar holiday by an artful code of instrumental symbolism (trombone representing a tiger, bass drum a dragon, etc.) and nativistic pentatonicism.

25 JANUARY 1953

Concerto for Kettledrums and Orchestra by the 36-year-old French composer Gabriel Pierre BERLIOZ (no relation to Hector Berlioz) is performed for the first time by the Lamoureux Orchestra, Jean Martinon conducting.

29 JANUARY 1953

La Luna dei Caraibi, one-act opera by the 67-year-old Italian composer Adriano LUALDI to the libretto based on Eugene O'Neill's drama *The Moon of the Caribbees*, with an Italianate score Americanized by the presence of syncopating saxophones and tropical West Indian drums, is performed for the first time in Rome.

31 JANUARY 1953

The Taming of the Shrew, Shakespearean opera by the 49-year-old American composer Vittorio GIANNINI, an opulent Italianate score generously endowed with an attractive melodic curvature encompassed by sensuously carnal harmonies in a Wagneroverdian general idiom, is performed for the first time in concert form in Cincinnati.

(A color television production of this opera, the first of its kind, was broadcast by the National Broadcasting Company from New York on 13 March 1954.)

1 FEBRUARY 1953

Dmitri KABALEVSKY conducts in Moscow the first performance of his *Third Piano Concerto* in D major, with Vladimir Ashkenazy as soloist, the last of a "trilogy of concertos" and, like the other two (for violin and for cello), set in three movements, fast, slow, very fast, full of accessible musical virtues, predictable melodic sequences, rhythmic vivacity and formal cohesiveness, sharpened by modulatory saltation from one tonal orbit into another in its chromatic proximity, creating a sense of pleasing disequilibrium.

7 FEBRUARY 1953

Ralph VAUGHAN WILLIAMS, recently widowed octogenarian dean of English composers marries his secretary, Mrs. Ursula Wood, a World War II widow.

7 FEBRUARY 1953

The Marriage, one-act television opera by Bohuslav MARTINU, to an English libretto after Gogol's play dealing with a hesitant bridegroom who jumps out of a ground-level window to escape matrimony, with a veristically Mussorgskian vocal dialogue in a vigorous rhythmic style, is performed for the first time by the National Broadcasting Company Television Network in New York.

11 FEBRUARY 1953

Carlos CHÁVEZ, prime Mexican composer, conducts the Louisville Orchestra in the first performance of his *Fourth Symphony*, subtitled *Sinfonia romantica* in three movements: *Allegro, Molto lento, Vivo*, with the melodic line dominated by the tritone, imparting to the music a stark Lydian color, and harmonized with pragmatic economy of means.

13 FEBRUARY 1953

Trionfo di Afrodite, "scenic concerto" by Carl ORFF, to poems by Catullus (in Latin), Sappho and Euripides (in

Greek), scored for a large orchestra of strings, winds and percussion, and realized in a typical Orphean Orffian manner, with a motionless melody ornamented by a floridly antiquarian melisma (the "Hymn to Hymen" is represented by an unchangeable major third repeated 235 times in succession) and an immobile harmony barely stuffing its gears (the Nuptial Cortège consists of a pattern of two chromatically expanding and contracting three-note chords, repeated 80 times before moving elsewhere), is produced in Milan.

(Orff designated this work ex post facto as the third part of a trilogy under the general title *Trionfi di Afrodite*, the first being *Carmina Burana*, a secularly profane medieval ode to the goddess of love, the second, *Catulli Carmina*, a classically Roman and sensuously personal dedication to Aphrodite's simulacra on earth.)

17 FEBRUARY 1953

Three centuries have passed since the birth at Fusignano, Imola, of Arcangelo CORELLI, the initiator of the modern school of violin playing, himself a virtuoso of great powers, teacher of many other virtuosos, and a composer of numerous works for string instruments in the purest Italian style. (To commemorate the Corelli tercentenary, the Italian Government issued on 30 May 1953 a 25-lire stamp bearing Corelli's likeness.)

18 FEBRUARY 1953

The Book of Mormon, oratorio by Leroy ROBERTSON, Utah-born composer, is performed for the first time at the Mormon Tabernacle in Salt Lake City.

19 FEBRUARY 1953

Rhapsody-Concerto for Viola and Orchestra by Bohuslav MARTINU in two principal movements, *Moderato* and *Molto Adagio*, with a cadenza introducing a subsidiary *Allegro* and ending in an *Andante molto tranquillo*, is performed for the first time in Cleveland.

21 FEBRUARY 1953

On the eve of the 50th anniversary of the death of Hugo WOLF, the Austrian Government issues a commemorative stamp for one and a half schillings bearing his portrait.

21 FEBRUARY 1953

Babar the Elephant, children's opera by the Russian-American composer, Nicolai BEREZOWSKY, is performed for the first time in New York.

25 FEBRUARY 1953

Wonderful Town, second musical comedy by Leonard BERNSTEIN based on the play *My Sister Eileen* and dealing with two ambitious sisters who come to New York from Ohio and get involved with a variety of dubious characters, including a whole contingent of the visiting Brazilian navy, set to music saturated with happy nostalgia and desperate merriment, is performed for the first time in New York.

1 MARCH 1953

Guadia Mundana, a "secularly joyful oratorio" by the 32-year-old German composer Johannes DRIESSLER, is performed for the first time in Frankfurt.

1 MARCH 1953

Eighth Symphony by Henry COWELL, in four movements, with a mixed chorus singing nonsensical syllables, but blossoming forth in the finale into a typically Cowellian recreation of a fuguing tune to the text "Behold a voice angelic sounds," is performed for the first time at Wilmington, Ohio.

5 MARCH 1953

Sergei PROKOFIEV, Russian composer whose music, capable of a great variety of expression—mercurial, martial, jovial, saturnine—has brought new vigor to twentieth-century composition, whose musical language is marked by elastic tonality, plastic rhythmology, tensile polyphony and ductile harmony, within the ambience of euphonious dissonance, without losing its profound Russian quality, dies of a cerebral hemorrhage at 9 o'clock in the evening, in his home in Moscow, at the age of sixty-one, less than an hour before Stalin, whose reactionary views on music contributed to Prokofiev's harassment.

5 MARCH 1953

Midas, ballet in two acts by Jean FRANÇAIX, is performed for the first time in its orchestral version by the Paris Radio Orchestra.

11 MARCH 1953

First Symphony by the 25-year-old Serbian composer Aleksander OBRADOVIĆ, in two movements, the first depicting the sacrifice of Yugoslav men and women in their heroic struggle against the Nazis and the second expressing their joy at the ultimate victory, is performed for the first time in Belgrade.

11 MARCH 1953

Johannes Faustus, opera by the proletarian-minded 54-year-old German composer Hanns EISLER, in which the legendary island of Atlantis is raised from the ocean by the 16th-century alchemist Dr. Faustus, is produced in East Berlin, arousing sharp criticism in the Communist press for the characterization of the utopian life of Atlantis resembling the urban culture of capitalist America.

11 MARCH 1953

A Parable of Death, cantata for narrator, tenor and chorus by the 30-year-old Berlin-born American composer Lukas FOSS, in six sections, to a text from thanatological poems and stories of Rainer Maria Rilke, set to music in neo-ecclesiastical modalities in starkly dissonant counterpoint, is performed for the first time in Louisville, Kentucky.

13 MARCH 1953

Medea for contralto and orchestra by Ernst KRENEK, an expressionistic cantata recounting in anguished dodecaphonic figurations the Greek tragedy of demented infanticide, is performed for the first time by the Philadelphia Orchestra.

17 MARCH 1953

Le Loup, ballet by the 37-year-old French composer Henri DUTILLEUX, a choreographic fantasy to a scenario in which a wolf abducts a young bride on her wedding night and inflames her with animalistic passion so that the hunters are forced to kill them both as they are locked in a bestial embrace, is produced in Paris.

22 MARCH 1953

Joseph ORECCHIO, Italian bootmaker who was the chief of the claque at the Metropolitan Opera House for twenty seasons (1915–1935) until a ban was put on such catalytic practices, dies in New York at the age of 72.

27 MARCH 1953

Narciso GARAY, the first educated composer of the Republic of Panama, author of a treatise on native music, and formerly Minister of Foreign Affairs of the Republic, dies in Panama City at the age of 73.

6 APRIL 1953

Gerard VICTORY, 31-year-old Irish composer, conducts the first performance in Dublin of his opera *An Fear a Phós Balbhín* (*The Silent Wife*), dealing with a deaf-mute woman who spectacularly regains her power of speech and drives her husband to distraction by her continuous vociferation, whereupon he forces the physician who has cured her to restore her to her erstwhile blissful state of muteness.

9 APRIL 1953

The Temptation of St. Anthony, "dance symphony" by the 40-year-old american composer gardner READ, containing a prelude and four scenes, portraying a series of temptations, culminating in a sinuously seductive, sensually serpentine dance of the Queen of Sheba, set to music marked by concentric implosions of increasingly dissonant conglomerations of sound, with a bitonal chord of two minor triads distanced by a tritone serving as a harmonic motto, is performed for the first time by the Chicago Symphony Orchestra.

11 APRIL 1953

Two new works by Ernest BLOCH are performed for the first time by the BBC Symphony Orchestra, Sir Malcolm Sargeant conducting:

Sinfonia Breve (completed in Oregon on 3 December 1952) in four movements: (1) *Moderato,* written in an anxious tritone-laden dramatic manner, with atonal melodic protrusions; (2) *Andante,* an elegiac eclogue; (3) *Allegro molto,* in a dissonantly chromatic idiom, with an emphasis on major ninths in contrapuntal texture; (4) *Allegro deciso,* ending on a pallid C major in pianissimo.

Second Concerto Grosso for strings, in G minor, designed in a neo-baroque style, in three sections, *Maestoso, Andante, Allegro,* ending in rubicund B major.

11 APRIL 1953

Ideas of Order for orchestra by the 40-year-old American composer Arthur BERGER, inspired by poems of Wallace Stevens, is performed for the first time by the New York Philharmonic, Dimitri Mitropoulos conducting.

16 APRIL 1953

McNair ILGENFRITZ, wealthy amateur musician, holder for decades of Box 1 at the Metropolitan Opera House, dies in New York, bequeathing the bulk of his estate (about $150,000) to the Metropolitan Opera on condition that it should produce within two years of his death one of his two unorchestrated operas, *Phèdre,* in three acts, or *Le Passant,* in one act, the piano scores of which he submitted to the management in 1943. (Upon examination of the music, the Board of Trustees of the Metropolitan Opera House declined the posthumous offer.)

17 APRIL 1953

Tràghadh na Taoide (*Ebbtide*), Irish opera by Tomás O'COILEAIN, is performed for the first time in Dublin.

17 APRIL 1953

A Tale of Two Cities, "romantic melodrama" in six scenes by Arthur BENJAMIN (completed by him in London on 17 February 1950), to a libretto after the famous biurban novel of Dickens with its violent action taking place between 1783 and 1790 in revolutionary Paris and apprehensive London, with the inclusion of topical quotations from contemporary songs, such as *Ça ira* and *La Carmagnole,* concluding with a dramatic cadenza on the drum as the heroic Englishman, sacrificing his own life for his beloved Frenchwoman, ascends the guillotine, is performed for the first time in concert form, in London, by the British Broadcasting Corporation Symphony Orchestra and soloists.

17 APRIL 1953

Jascha HEIFETZ is slugged on his right hand with an iron bar by an unidentified Jewish assailant in Jerusalem after his performance of the *Violin Sonata* by Richard STRAUSS, objectionable to Israelis on account of the composer's dubious associations with the Nazi regime.

21 APRIL 1953

Seventh Symphony by the Danish composer Niels Viggo BENTZON is performed for the first time in Copenhagen.

24 APRIL 1953

Sixth Symphony by the 47-year-old German master polyphonist Karl Amadeus HARTMANN, in two movements, an expressionistic *Adagio* presenting a shimmering interplay of somber sonorities rising to fiery *Allegro moderato con fuoco,* receding to pianississimo and reverting to *Adagio;* and *Presto,* comprising three fugues forming a terraced sequence of dynamic and rhythmic elements, each fugue opening in *pianississimo* and ending in *fortississimo,* is performed for the first time in Munich.

27 APRIL 1953

Second Symphony by the 29-year-old Vienna-born composer Robert STARER, now a citizen of Israel, is performed for the first time, in Tel Aviv, Erich Leinsdorf conducting.

28 APRIL 1953

The pianist Robert SERGIL completes a stretch of nonstop piano playing of 255 hours in Le Havre, France, beating by 31 hours the record of pianofortitude established by Heinz Arntz on 16 June 1952.

4 MAY 1953

Sixty years after its composition, *Irmelin,* posthumous opera in three acts by Frederick DELIUS, to his own libretto, dealing with a romantic princess who keeps vigil for an ideal lover and meets a swineherd who follows a silver stream in the hope of finding true love, is performed for the first time anywhere in Oxford, under the direction of Sir Thomas Beecham.

4 MAY 1953

The Mighty Casey, baseball opera by the 42-year-old American composer William SCHUMAN, dealing with the legendary pitcher for the Phillies who on 21 August 1887 struck out in the ninth inning in a game with the New York Giants, thus inspiring Ernest L. Thayer to write his poem *Casey at the Bat* ("Oh! Somewhere in this favored land the sun is shining bright . . . But there is no joy in Mudville—Mighty Casey has struck out!"), is performed for the first time at Hartford, Connecticut.

6 MAY 1953

Die chinesische Nachtigall, ballet by Werner EGK, after Hans Christian Andersen's tale, is performed for the first time in Munich.

7 MAY 1953

Can-Can, musical comedy by Cole PORTER, recalling the highlights of the 1890's in Paris, when the can-can was regarded as the nadir of depravity, featuring such nostalgic tunes as *C'est Magnifique,* is produced in New York.

9 MAY 1953

Israeli Country Dances by the Latvian-born Israeli composer Marc LAVRY, a symphonic group of contrasting dance movements in an effective manner of Jewish musical folklore, is performed for the first time in Nazareth.

16 MAY 1953

Piano Concerto by the 43-year-old Rumanian composer Paul CONSTANTINESCU, in three movements—(1) *Allegro,* ingratiatingly utilizing authentic Rumanian melorhythms; (2) *Andante,* marked by a characteristic Balkan rhythmic asymmetry; (3) *Presto,* with thematic material derived from Transylvanian folk dances—is performed for the first time in Bucharest.

17 MAY 1953

Guernica, symphonic poem by the 27-year-old French-Canadian composer Clermont PEPIN, inspired by Picasso's *Guernica,* surrealistically conveying the sense of horror of the bombing of Guernica by the Nazi-Fascist planes during the Spanish Civil War with the angular atonal melodies expressing the animal cruelty of Picasso's distorted bull, and polytonal sequences reflecting the despair of massed humanity, is performed for the first time in Quebec, Wilfred Pelletier conducting. (The American première was given by the National Broadcasting Company Symphony Orchestra, on 23 August 1953.)

17 MAY 1953

Leon XANROF, French Composer who wrote the sentimental chansonette *Le Fiacre* launched by Yvette Guilbert in the 1890's which became a nostalgic souvenir of the pre-automotive era (his real name was Fournier, which he translated into Latin, Fornax, which, read backwards, makes Xanrof), dies in Paris at the age of 85.

22 MAY 1953

Der Tod zu Basel, oratorio by the 51-year-old Swiss composer Conrad BECK, tracing the history of disasters in Basel beginning with the polytonally dissonant unmelodious earthquake of 1356, is performed for the first time in Basel.

25 MAY 1953

A demonstration of electronic music is given for the first time in the world at the opening of the Music Festival of the Cologne Radio.

25 MAY 1953

The Harpies, one-act opera by Marc BLITZSTEIN, to his own libretto dealing with an oracular ancient Greek hounded by vengeful harpies, written in 1931, comes to a belated world première in New York.

25 MAY 1953

Second Symphony by the 31-year-old English composer Malcolm ARNOLD, in four movements: *Allegretto, Vivace, Lento* and *Allegro con brio,* written in the traditional symphonic idiom, is performed for the first time in Bournemouth, England.

26 MAY 1953

Kontra-Punkte for ten instruments by the 24-year-old German innovator Karlheinz STOCKHAUSEN, organized so that the interplay of the horizontal (melodic) and vertical (contrapuntal) lines results in a homogeneous dissonant florid counterpoint, with the instruments dropping out one by one until at the end the piano is left to fend for itself, is performed for the first time in the Electronic Studio of the West German Radio in Cologne.

26 MAY 1953

The Barber of New York, one-act opera by the Viennese composer Kurt MANSCHINGER, written under his pen name Ashley Vernon, dealing with a New York barber who refuses to shave the commander of a British ship, set to music in an ingratiatingly melodious and pleasingly harmonious manner, is performed for the first time in New York.

28 MAY 1953

Zoya Kosmodemyanskaya, symphony-legend by the 44-year-old Soviet composer Sergei RAZORYONOV, inspired by the heroic deed of a Soviet guerrilla girl hanged by the Nazis for arson in occupied Ukraine during World War II, with quotations from authentic guerrilla songs, is performed for the first time in MOSCOW.

28 MAY 1953

The 27th Festival of the International Society for Contemporary Music opens in Oslo, Norway, with the following program of orchestral music and instrumental concertos:

Passacaglia 1952 by Gian Francesco MALIPIERO; *Violin Concerto* by Arnold SCHOENBERG (first performed in Philadelphia on 6 December 1940); *Piano Concerto* in three movements by the Norwegian romantic composer Harald SAEVERUD; *Second Symphony* by the 32-year-old English composer Peter Racine FRICKER, in three movements which increase progressively in length, each presenting a different aspect of rondo form.

28 MAY 1953

Me and Juliet, musical comedy by Richard RODGERS, with book and lyrics by Oscar HAMMERSTEIN II, wherein a chorus girl enamored of the assistant manager of a theater has to resist the dastardly machinations of a desperate electrician who covets her, featuring the successful tango tune *No Other Love*, borrowed by Rodgers from his own score for the documentary film, *Victory at Sea*, is produced in New York.

30 MAY 1953

At the second concert of the 27th Festival of the International Society for Contemporary Music in Oslo the following program of chamber music is given:

Viola Sonata by the 26-year-old South African composer John JOUBERT, in five movements, in a neo-baroque style; *Partita* for unaccompanied flute by the 23-year-old Japanese composer Makoto MOROI, in six sections thematically derived from six dodecaphonic series; *Sextet* for wind instruments by the 41-year-old Chilean composer René AMENGUAL; *Piano Sonatina* in four movements by the 41-year-old Finnish composer Erik BERGMAN; *Du*, cycle of seven songs for voice and piano by the 37-year-old American mathematician Milton BABBITT with the vertical, horizontal and motivic organization subordinated to a unifying dodecaphonic series; *Piano Sonata* by the 37-year-old Argentinian composer Alberto GINASTERA, in four movements (first performed by Johana Harris in Pittsburgh on 29 November 1952) in which the structural elements reflect dodecaphonic procedures while the melorhythmic substance relates to ethnic Argentinian sources; and *Third String Quartet* in three movements by the 43-year-old Danish composer Vagn HOLMBOE.

30 MAY 1953

Dudaray (*The Curly One*), opera in four acts by the 47-year-old Soviet composer Evgeny BRUSILOVSKY, on the subject of interracial social comity among pre-revolutionary fishermen in a Khazakstan village, with a profusion of Russian and Khazak folk tunes, is produced in Alma-Ata.

31 MAY 1953

At the third concert of the 27th Festival of the International Society for Contemporary Music in Oslo, the following program of music for chamber orchestra is presented:

Le cimetière marin by the impressionistic Norwegian composer Fartein VALEN (1887–1952), inspired by the symbolist poem of Paul Valéry, and presenting an antinomy of the serenity of the dead in a seaside cemetery and the constant movement of the life-giving sea; *Octet* by the 46-year-old Java-born Dutch composer Henk BADINGS, in three movements of neo-classical provenance; *Concerto da camera* for piano and string orchestra by the 35-year-old Swiss composer Julien-François ZBINDEN, in three neo-Bachian movements; *Opus 3 aux son frappés et frottés* by the 29-year-old Belgian empiricist Karel GOEYVAERTS, for piano, violin, viola, cello, vibraphone, and percussion, written in the pointillistic technique of thematic dismemberment; and *Salutatio Angelis* for mezzo-soprano and 12 instruments by the English composer Anthony MILNER, to the Latin text of the 130th Psalm, in the form of a passacaglia.

2 JUNE 1953

At the fourth concert of the 27th Festival of the International Society for Contemporary Music in Oslo, the following program of symphonic music is presented:

Sixth Symphony in three movements, by the 60-year-old Swedish composer Hilding ROSENBERG; *Piano Concerto* by the 26-year-old German composer of dodecaphonic tendencies, Hans Werner HENZE; *Concertino* for trumpet and orchestra by the French avant-garde composer André JOLIVET; and *Le Zodiaque*, cantata by the 59-year-old Belgian composer of moderately modern music Jean ABSIL.

2 JUNE 1953

At the Coronation Services for Elizabeth II of England, a new *Te Deum* by Sir William WALTON, is performed, and his March, *Orb and Sceptre*, is played during the procession.

2 JUNE 1953

Variacionès Concertantes, suite for chamber orchestra by the 37-year-old Argentinian composer Alberto GINASTERA, containing eleven whimsical variations (one of them for doublebass solo), on an original theme of Argentinian flavor, is performed for the first time in Buenos Aires, with Igor Markevitch conducting.

2 JUNE 1953

Homage of the Queen, ballet by the 31-year-old British composer Malcolm ARNOLD, is performed for the first time at Covent Garden in London, in honor of the coronation of Queen Elizabeth II.

3 JUNE 1953

At the fifth concert of the 27th Festival of the International Society for Contemporary Music in Oslo, the following concert of chamber music is given:

Sonatina for clarinet and piano, in three movements by the 33-year-old Norwegian composer Hjort ALBERTSEN; *Piano Sonata 1952* by the 23-year-old Brazilian composer Roberto

SCHNORRENBERG, in three movements, set in a free dode-caphonic idiom; *String Quartet* by the almost 31-year-old Scottish composer Iain HAMILTON, in three contrasting movements; *Second Piano Sonata* in three movements by Busoni's disciple Phillipp JARNACH; *Sonata in G* for violin solo by the Israeli composer Paul BEN-HAIM, in three classically outlined movements; and *Das Nasobém*, a divertimento for chorus a cappella by the 32-year-old Swiss composer Franz TISCHHAUSER, to the macabre texts by Christian Morgenstern.

5 JUNE 1953

At the sixth and last concert of the 27th Festival of the International Society for Contemporary Music in Oslo, the following program of symphonic music is given:

Variazioni breve by the 33-year-old Danish composer Niels Viggo BENTZON, a theme with five baroque variations and a coda forming a synthesis of the whole work; *I speglarnas sal* (*In the Hall of Mirrors*), nine sonnets for solo singers, chorus and orchestra by the 36-year-old Swedish modernist Karl-Birger BLOMDAHL; *Flute Concerto* by the 72-year-old Dutch romanticist Sem DRESDEN, in three movements of a classical type; and *Concerto for Orchestra* by the grandmaster of Hungarian music Zoltan KODÁLY, written in the baroque manner, alternating motoric and lyric sections, with the principal theme of a pentatonic structure in an ancient Magyar mold.

8 JUNE 1953

Gloriana, opera in three acts by Benjamin BRITTEN on the subject of the unqueenly affair between Queen Elizabeth I and Essex to a libretto after Lytton Strachey's biographical study *Elizabeth and Essex*, written specially for the Coronation ceremony, glorying in Britannically shaped grandly confident triadic proclamations, is produced at a Gala Performance at Covent Garden in London, in the presence of Elizabeth II and the royal family, the first opera by a British composer so honored since King George II attended the performance of Handel's *Atalanta* in 1736.

9 JUNE 1953

Second Symphony by the 31-year-old Scottish composer Iain HAMILTON, in four movements of a classical formation and modernistic connotations, is performed for the first time at the Cheltenham Festival in England.

19 JUNE 1953

The Government of Czechoslovakia issues postage stamps honoring Leoš JANÁČEK (1.60 kronen) and Joseph SLAVÍK, renowned as the Paganini of Bohemia (75 hellers).

23 JUNE 1953

The Bolshoi Theater of Moscow presents the first complete performance of the grand opera *Decembrists* by the 63-year-old Soviet composer Yuri SHAPORIN, glorifying the five hanged conspirators in the abortive rebellion of 14 December 1825 (hence the historical nickname, Decembrists, Men of December) against the incumbent Tsar Nicholas I, set to music in a grand Russian style reaching a climax in the vocal quintet of the doomed Decembrists, to the rousing words of the poet Alexander Pushkin: "Have faith, comrade, our star will rise in happy rapture when Russia awakens from her slumber and will write our names on the ruins of autocracy."

26 JUNE 1953

Concerto for Oboe and Strings by the 31-year-old English composer Malcolm ARNOLD, in three neo-classical movements, is performed for the first time in London.

26 JUNE 1953

In the course of a series of concerts of modern music, *Die Woche für Neue Musik* at Frankfurt, two world premières are given:

Spiegelungen for orchestra by the 57-year-old Swiss-resident Moscow-born half-Russian half-German composer Vladimir VOGEL, in two movements, based on a dodecaphonic series consisting of two mutually inverted six-note groups (hence the title, mirrorings), with a tonifugal first movement *Lento espressivo*, and a firmly tonipetal second movement, *Allegro;* and *Cantata seculare* by the 48-year-old Hungarian composer resident in England Mátyás SEIBER, with its four movements titled after the four seasons, to a medieval Latin text, set to music in modernized ecclesiastical modes.

28 JUNE 1953

Abstrakte Oper No. 1 by the 50-year-old China-born Estonian-German Boris BLACHER, scored for three vocalists, two speakers, chorus and orchestra, to a libretto by Werner EGK set in a surrealistically unintelligible language projected in a stream of syllabic glossolalia with the component scenes identified only by their emotional content, e.g. Fear, Love No. 1, Pain, Panic, Love No. 2, to denote the abstraction from the concrete, is performed for the first time in the course of *Die Woche für Neue Musik* in Frankfurt.

9 JULY 1953

The French Government marks the 250th anniversary of the birth of Jean-Philippe RAMEAU by issuing a postage stamp for 15 francs bearing his likeness.

17 JULY 1953

On the occasion of the quadricentennial of the birth of the Russian patriot Ivan SUSANIN, glorified in Glinka's opera *A Life for the Czar,* a group of Russian opera singers stage a celebration in Susanin's native village of Domnino by performing several arias from Glinka's opera.

19 JULY 1953

Marie ASHTON, an Irish housewife, completes a 133-hour marathon of piano playing, claiming the world record for female pianofortitude, exceeding by one hour the previous record established by Syncopating Sandy of Bolton, England.

22 JULY 1953

Endymion, opera by the 49-year-old Australian composer John Henry ANTILL, is performed for the first time in Sydney.

26 JULY 1953

Concerto d'Orphée for violin and orchestra by the 52-year-old French composer Henri SAUGUET, in one protracted movement set in a curiously un-Orphean chromatic idiom, is performed for the first time at the Festival of Aix-en-Provence, in France.

26 JULY 1953

Concerto Grosso for Band by the 53-year-old American composer Joseph WAGNER, one of the earliest pieces in classical concerto grosso form written for band, is performed for the first time by the U.S. Marine Band in Washington.

31 JULY 1953

The Covent Garden Opera Company, on its South African tour, presents VERDI's *Aida* as the opening spectacle in Bulawayo, Southern Rhodesia, the first opera to be performed in the South African hinterland, a thousand miles from the coast, the singers and musicians having been transported by air.

15 AUGUST 1953

O.C. CASH, tax consultant for an oil company, founder of the Society for the Preservation and Encouragement of Barber Shop Quartet Singing in America (SPEBSQSA), dies in Tulsa, Oklahoma, at the age of 61.

15 AUGUST 1953

Larry Adler plays the mouth harmonica with the London Symphony Orchestra, Basil Cameron conducting, in the first performance of the *Concerto for Harmonica and Orchestra* by the Australian-born composer Arthur BENJAMIN.

17 AUGUST 1953

Der Prozess, opera in nine scenes by the 35-year-old austrian composer gottfried VON EINEM, to a libretto from the surrealist tale of Franz Kafka, in which a deracinated Central European adrift in the disoriented world of 1919 is awaiting a trial on unspecified charges by anonymous judges, set to music in an economically dissonant idiom animated by rhythmic propulsion, is produced in Salzburg.

18 AUGUST 1953

Captain Lovelock, one-act opera by the American composer John DUKE, is produced at Hudson Falls, New York. (The first New York performance took place on 20 February 1956.)

27 AUGUST 1953

Nicolai BEREZOWSKY, 53-year-old Russian-born American composer of ingratiatingly euphonious symphonies and chamber music breathing the simple joys of artistic self-expression, is found dead by his second wife in his New York apartment, a victim of intestinal congestion caused by a suicidal dose of powerful sedatives.

1 SEPTEMBER 1953

On his way to Indo-China to play for the embattled French Army there, the famous French violinist Jacques THIBAUD perishes in an airplane crash at Mount Cemet in the French Alps, carrying with him to fiery destruction two of his Stradivarius violins.

3 SEPTEMBER 1953

Viola Concerto by the 32-year-old English composer Peter Racine FRICKER is performed for the first time at the Edinburgh Festival by William Primrose, who commissioned the work, with the Philharmonia Orchestra conducted by Sir Adrian Boult.

8 SEPTEMBER 1953

La Partita a Pugni (*Prize Fight*), chamber opera by the 32-year-old Italian composer Vieri TOSATTI, dealing with a prize fight and a riot in the stadium ensuing in protest against the referee's decision, is performed for the first time at the Venice Festival.

15 SEPTEMBER 1953

Ornaments, for orchestra by Boris BLACHER, built on a series of metric progressions from 2 to 9 beats to a measure, then 2 to 8 beats, 2 to 7, 2 to 6, 2 to 5, etc., is performed for the first time at the Venice Festival.

17 SEPTEMBER 1953

Henry Holden HUSS, American composer and pianist, who once played his pieces at a reception for Tchaikovsky in New York in 1891, dies in New York at the age of 91.

1 OCTOBER 1953

Ein-Geb (*Ein-Gev*), symphonic fantasy by the 46-year-old Budapest-born Israeli composer Ödön PARTOS, composed during the bitter fight between Jews and Arabs in the valley of Ein-Gev, and based on the musical letters of Ein-Gev (E, G, B-flat), melodically developed in oriental scales, is performed for the first time by the Israel Philharmonic Orchestra in Ein-Gev, Leonard Bernstein conducting.

3 OCTOBER 1953

Sir Arnold BAX, English composer of loftily designed impressionistically flavored symphonies and symphonic poems, dies in Cork, Ireland (where he was on an educational mission) at the age of 69.

11 OCTOBER 1953

La Réveil des Oiseaux, ornithological symphony for piano and orchestra by Olivier MESSIAEN, with its melodic material drawn from an aviary of 37 song birds, exhibiting a remarkable similarity of atonal intervallic structures among such different species as a robin, a thrush, and a blackcap, with a universal preference for major sevenths and minor ninths, appearing also in such combinatory progressions as two perfect fourths separated by a tritone, is performed for the first time in the course of the Music Festival in Donaueschingen.

15 OCTOBER 1953

La porta verde, musical tragedy in four acts by the 70-year-old Italian composer Francesco SANTOLIQUIDO, is produced in Bergamo.

16 OCTOBER 1953

Darius MILHAUD conducts over the Italian Radio in Turin the world première of his *Fifth Symphony,* in four movements, *Vif et cinglant, Lent et tendre, Clair et leger, Alerte et rude.*

19 OCTOBER 1953

An aphoristic *Praeludium* by Igor STRAVINSKY, written in 1937 and scored for four saxophones, three trumpets, two trombones, strings, celesta, guitar and drums, is performed for the first time in the concert series of "Evenings on the Roof," in Los Angeles, conducted by Stravinsky's musical amanuensis Robert Craft, on the same program with Stravinsky's new orchestral setting of his piano piece *Tango*, written in 1940, his *Ragtime, Piano Rag Music, Ebony Concerto*, and three dances from *L'Histoire du Soldat.*

19 OCTOBER 1953

On the occasion of the centennial of the Steinway Piano Company, 35 pianists, in teams of four to ten for each number, give a polypianic rendition of CHOPIN's *Polonaise* in A major, SOUSA's march *Stars and Stripes Forever* and the first performance of Morton GOULD's *Inventions* for four pianos and orchestra.

20 OCTOBER 1953

Astutuli, "A Bavarian comedy" by Carl ORFF, in the form of a "Sprechstück," to his own text in a rustic Bavarian dialect, arranged for rhythmically inflected voices and 24 assorted percussion instruments, including musical glasses and a beer stein, with the timpani and the xylophone providing the dominant-tonic cadences, dealing with a cunning charlatan who inveigles local farmers to supply liquor and women for him, astutely addressing them in kitchen Latin "O Vos astutuli" (Oh you, little clever people), is performed for the first time in Munich.

21 OCTOBER 1953

The Inland Woman, one-act opera by the 49-year-old Scottish composer Erik CHISHOLM, is performed for the first time in Capetown, South Africa.

30 OCTOBER 1953

Emmerich KÁLMÁN, Hungarian composer of exhilarating operettas, among them the perennial favorite, *The Gypsy Princess*, dies in Paris at the age of 71.

4 NOVEMBER 1953

Elizabeth Sprague COOLIDGE, munificent American music patroness, herself a composeress, who despite her deafness (she could hear music only with a powerful hearing-aid apparatus) diverted a generous portion of her fortune as a Chicago canned-pork heiress to the promotion of modern music and performance of specially commissioned chamber music works at the Coolidge Festivals, dies in Cambridge, Massachusetts, in her 90th year.

6 NOVEMBER 1953

Atomic Bomb, symphonic fantasy on an extremely realistic subject by the 52-year-old Japanese composer Masao OKI is performed for the first time in Tokyo.

6 NOVEMBER 1953

Cello Concerto by the 50-year-old Russian-American composer Nicolas NABOKOV, subtitled *Les Hommages*, in three movements named *Serenata di Pietro* (for Peter Tchaikovsky), *Ballata d'Allessandro* (for Alexander Dargomyzhsky), and *Chorale di Michele* (for Michael Glinka), purporting to portray an impoverished Russian émigré driving a taxicab in Paris and humming tunes by Tchaikovsky, Dargomyzhsky and Glinka, is performed for the first time by the Philadelphia Orchestra, Eugene Ormandy conducting.

8 NOVEMBER 1953

The Magic Apple Tree, ballet by the 23-year-old Russian composer Andrei PETROV, is performed for the first time in Leningrad.

18 NOVEMBER 1953

The Government of Czechoslovakia issues a 30-heller stamp in honor of the famous Bohemian dramatic soprano Emmy DESTINN (1878–1930).

18 NOVEMBER 1953

Sixth Symphony by the 30-year-old American composer Peter MENNIN, animated by a neo-Baroque Italian spirit (Mennin's original name was Mennini), in three movements of functional music spiced with non-corrosive dissonances—(1) *Maestoso*, as a prelude to an *Allegro;* (2) *Grave*, marked by an economically applied emotive force; (3) *Allegro vivace*, set in an energetic aggressive manner and terminating in an abrupt cadential configuration—is performed for the first time as a commissioned work, by the Louisville Orchestra.

20 NOVEMBER 1953

The Taking of T'ung Khan, tone poem by the 34-year-old Chinese-born American composer Jacob AVSHALOMOV, with an orientally flavored orchestral score, is performed for the first time by the Detroit Symphony Orchestra, Leopold Stokowski conducting.

1 DECEMBER 1953

Carlos CHÁVEZ conducts the Chamber Orchestra of Los Angeles in the world première of his *Fifth Symphony* for string orchestra, in three linked movements, *Allegro molto moderato, Lento, Allegro con Brio*, marked by astutely drawn contrasts of thematic and dynamic factors, ranging in contents from loftily elegiac to powerfully elemental structures.

3 DECEMBER 1953

Kismet, musical extravaganza by Robert WRIGHT and George FORREST, derived from music by Alexander Borodin, disjoined, altered, dislocated and mutilated with the hit song *Stranger in Paradise* utilizing the lyrical portion of one of the *Polovetsian Dances* in *Prince Igor*, is produced in New York.

4 DECEMBER 1953

Daniel Gregory MASON, American composer of scrupulously academic symphonies and chamber music, one-time chairman of the Music Department of Columbia University, dies in Greenwich, Connecticut, at the age of 80.

4 DECEMBER 1953

Das Ende einer Welt, radiophonic opera in two acts by the 27-year-old German composer Hans Werner HENZE, representing a jazzy Doomsday to the accompaniment of a disoriented and disharmonious heterogeneous assemblage of instruments, is performed for the first time in Hamburg.

6 DECEMBER 1953

Rural Antiphonies by the American experimental composer Henry BRANT, scored for five conductors and five orchestras, each operating at its own autonomous tempo and meter, is performed for the first time in New York City.

6 DECEMBER 1953

Ivo CRUZ conducts in Lisbon the first performance of his *Sinfonia de Amadis*, in four romantically programmatic movements descriptive of the love of Amadis for Oriana, his retirement to a monastery at a crisis of their romance, and his return as a defrocked impenitent monk for a sensualized reunion at the Portuguese royal court festival.

6 DECEMBER 1953

First Symphony by the Swedish composer Gunnar BUCHT is performed for the first time in Stockholm.

7 DECEMBER 1953

First Symphony by the 25-year-old German-born American composer Samuel ADLER is performed for the first time in Dallas, Texas.

8 DECEMBER 1953

The Dress, one-act opera by Mark BUCCI, is produced in New York.

9 DECEMBER 1953

The Hungarian Government issues a series of postage stamps honoring LISZT, MOSONYI, ERKEL, BIHARI, GOLDMARK, BARTÓK and Zoltán KODÁLY, a rare distinction for the latter, still living and active.

11 DECEMBER 1953

Albert COATES, Russian-born English conductor, dies in Milnerton, near Capetown, South Africa, at the age of 71.

12 DECEMBER 1953

Une Cantate de Noël by Arthur HONEGGER, for baritone solo, children's voices, mixed chorus, organ and orchestra (sketched in 1941, but interrupted by the war, and not finished until 5 January 1953), with an instrumental intermezzo of popular Christmas songs containing special effects, e.g. singing *bouche fermée*, is performed for the

first time by the Chamber Orchestra of Basel, Paul Sacher conducting.

15 DECEMBER 1953

Fables by Ernst BACON for narrator and orchestra, partly to his own texts, is performed for the first time in New York.

16 DECEMBER 1953

The Rumanian Government issues a 55-lei postage stamp to commemorate the centennial of the birth of the Roumanian song composer Ciprian PORUMBESCU.

17 DECEMBER 1953

The first performance is given in Leningrad of the *Tenth Symphony* by Dmitri SHOSTAKOVICH (completed on 27 October 1953), thematically based on the musical letters of his name in German notation (D.SCH, in which S stands for Es, that is, E-flat, and H stands for B), in four movements:

(1) *Moderato* in E minor, wherein the monogram first appears in the form of initials (D, Es), is trilled over with the ascending semitone retaining its thematic connotations, reaching a climax in the recapitulation, supported by powerful drums; (2) *Allegro*, in B-flat minor, in constant motoric agitation in an almost constant fortissimo; (3) *Allegretto*, in C Minor, opening with a permutated monogram, then stating the four signature notes explicitly in the violins; (4) *Andante*, wherein the oboe, the flute, the bassoon and the clarinet echo each other with a broadly Russian theme, which subsequently grows into a fugato in the strings, leading to a kinetic *Allegro*, and accumulating momentum driving relentlessly towards the Finale in which the personal monogram is revealed in full power of declarative utterance, ending with an ostinato on four kettledrums, reiterating and pounding the four notes in mighty augmentation.

25 DECEMBER 1953

Sevil, opera in three acts by the 31-year-old Azerbaijan composer Fikret AMIROV, to a libretto centered on an emancipated Soviet woman of Baku named Sevil who renounces the traditional ways of Moslem life, abandons her obsolete polygamous husband, goes to Moscow for a scientific education, publishes a book and returns home in feminine glory, set to music with a profusion of native melorhythms encased in mellifluous Russian harmonies, is performed for the first time in Baku. (A revised version was produced in Baku, on 8 May 1955.)

27 DECEMBER 1953

The Capital of the World, ballet by George ANTHEIL, is produced in New York.

29 DECEMBER 1953

Wandering in Sorrow, opera in three acts by Antonio SPADAVECCHIA, 46-year-old Odessa-born Soviet composer of Italian descent, after the revolutionary trilogy by Alexei Tolstoy, is performed for the first time in Perm. (A new version, titled *The Flaming Years*, was produced in Perm on 8 April 1966.)

1954

2 JANUARY 1954

Notturno, an elegiac piece of nostalgic inspiration by Ernst TOCH is performed for the first time as a commissioned work by the Louisville Orchestra.

9 JANUARY 1954

Sinfonietta flamenca by Carlos SURINACH, 38-year-old Spanish composer, now resident in America, based on the flamenco rhythms of his Catalan birthplace, is performed for the first time in Louisville.

11 JANUARY 1954

Oskar STRAUS, Austrian composer of merry Viennese operettas including *The Chocolate Soldier*, freely modeled after the fantasmagorical Shavian comedy *Arms and the Man*, dies at Bad Ischl, at the age of 83.

15 JANUARY 1954

Fourth Symphony by the foremost Polish woman composer Grazyna BACEWICZ is performed for the first time in Cracow.

23 JANUARY 1954

Alvorado na Floresta Tropical (*Dawn in a Tropical Forest*), overture by the prime Brazilian composer Heitor VILLA-LOBOS, depicting in luscious instrumental colors the ornithological pandemonium in the Brazilian jungle at dawn, marked by a cornucopia of native melorhythms, is performed for the first time in Louisville, Kentucky.

23 JANUARY 1954

Septet by Igor STRAVINSKY for violin, viola, cello, clarinet, horn, bassoon and piano (or harpsichord), in three movements modeled after the baroque dance forms, *Allegro*, *Passacaglia* and *Gigue*, serving the functional purpose of a classical ensemble, couched in a frugal fugal polyphony and a parsimonious harmonic setting, is performed for the first time at the private estate of Dumbarton Oaks in Washington, with Stravinsky himself conducting.

28 JANUARY 1954

Kaspers Fettisdag, opera by the 61-year-old dean of Swedish composers, Hilding ROSENBERG, is performed for the first time in Stockholm.

1 FEBRUARY 1954

Eighth Symphony by the 78-year-old English composer Havergal BRIAN, in a single movement, in the key of B-flat minor, composed in 1949, and inspired by Goethe's ballad *Die Braut von Corinth*, set in constantly changing tempi, with the inclusion of two autocephalous passacaglias, is performed for the first time by the London Philharmonic Orchestra, Sir Adrian Boult conducting.

10 FEBRUARY 1954

Salvino de SILVA sets a world record for continuous guitar playing after 16 hours of supervised strumming in Lisbon.

12 FEBRUARY 1954

The Legend of a Stone Flower, ballet by Sergei PROKOFIEV, to a scenario from Ural fairy tales in which a piece of green malachite blossoms forth in melodious efflorescence, is produced posthumously at the Bolshoi Theater in Moscow.

13 FEBRUARY 1954

Variations for Piano and Orchestra by Wallingford RIEGGER, set in a vigorous vigesimosecular style, is performed for the first time as a commissioned work by the Louisville Orchestra.

21 FEBRUARY 1954

Ernst VON DOHNÁNYI, 76-year-old expatriate Hungarian composer, conducts in Athens, Ohio, the first performance of his first American orchestral piece, *American Rhapsody*.

23 FEBRUARY 1954

Atlantide, lyric and choreographic opera in four acts, by the 52-year-old French composer Henri TOMASI, after the novel of Pierre Benoit dealing with the polyandrogynous Queen of Atlantis (who has only a dancing, non-singing part), is produced in Mulhouse, Alsace.

27 FEBRUARY 1954

Triskelion, symphonic suite by the 45-year-old American composer Halsey STEVENS, symbolizing the relationship existing between the thematic ideas of the three movements of the suite, and their synthesis in a triskelion, a geometric figure of three branches radiating from the center, is performed for the first time in Louisville, Kentucky.

4 MARCH 1954

Cello Concerto by Ernst KRENEK is played for the first time in Los Angeles.

4 MARCH 1954

First Symphony by the Czech composer Karel HUSA is performed for the first time by the Belgian Radio Orchestra in Brussels.

8 MARCH 1954

Three Songs from William Shakespeare for mezzo-soprano, flute, clarinet and viola by Igor STRAVINSKY are performed for the first time in Los Angeles.

12 MARCH 1954

The Radio Hamburg broadcasts the first performance of the two completed acts of the posthumous opera *Moses und Aron* by Arnold SCHOENBERG, written in 1930–1932, scored for voices, bass, tenor, chorus and orchestra, with a profusion of percussion instruments, to his own biblical text dissecting the dialectical antinomy between Moses (inflected *Sprechstimme* in the bass register) as prophet of monotheistic Judaic philosophy and Aaron (tenor) as the pragmatic materialist, opening with the voice of God chanting the single vowel O, evolving in an intricate hermetic dodecaphonic polyphony of allegorical motives in a Schoenbergian relativistic musical space, where there is no absolute up or down, right or left, forward or backward, and culminating in the Dance Around the Golden Calf (Act II, scene 3) in which four naked virgins (two sopranos and two contraltos) are throttled and slaughtered by priests, while other girls, some clad, pass butcher knives and hold receptacles for the jets of blood from the coronary aortas of the victims, followed by a universal quaquaversal erotic orgy, with multifutuent youths shouting dodecaphonically, "Human procreativity is sanctified!"

(The original title of the work was *Moses und Aaron*, but Schoenberg, oppressed by triskaidekaphohia, aware that the number of letters in the title aggregates to 13, deleted the second A in Aaron, reducing the total to 12, an ideal dodecaphonic module. The *Dance Around the Golden Calf* was performed separately on 2 July 1951 in the course of the International Summer Course of New Music in Darmstadt. The first stage performance of the entire opera took place on 6 June 1954 in Zürich.)

13 MARCH 1954

Piano Concerto by the 23-year-old Spanish composer Cristóbal HALFFTER, nephew of Ernesto and Rodolfo Halffter, written in a neo-baroque manner with some atonal protuberances, is performed for the first time in Madrid.

13 MARCH 1954

Toccata Giocosa for orchestra by Gardner READ is performed for the first time as a commissioned work by the Louisville Orchestra.

14 MARCH 1954

Ludomir ROGOWSKI, Polish composer of colorful symphonic works scented with Slavonic suffusions further individualized by the use of a scale of alternating wholetones and semitones, which he believed to be of his invention, but which in chronological fact was used by Rimsky-Korsakov long before, dies at the age of 72, in Dubrovnik, Yugoslavia, where he spent most of his life.

15 MARCH 1954

The University Greys, opera in two acts and nine scenes by the 47-year-old American composer Arthur KREUTZ, to a libretto based on Maud Morrow Brown's novel of the same name in which a young man leaves his university studies to go to war, returning to die in the arms of his sweetheart whom he had married during his first leave, is produced for the first time by the University of Mississippi. (The work was commissioned by the University in 1953 and revived in 1961 to commemorate the centennial of the Eleventh Mississippi Regiment's departure to war. The Greys constituted a regiment drawn from men at the University, none of whom survived the war.)

17 MARCH 1954

Concerto for Two Pianos and Orchestra by Quincy PORTER, which won the Pulitzer Prize, is performed for the first time as a commissioned work by the Louisville Orchestra.

20 MARCH 1954

Rhapsodic Variations for orchestra and electronic tape by Otto LUENING and Vladimir USSACHEVSKY, the first score ever composed that combined electronic sounds with human musicians, is performed for the first time by the Louisville Orchestra in New York.

21 MARCH 1954

Piano Concerto by the 33-year-old English composer Peter Racine FRICKER is performed for the first time in London.

23 MARCH 1954

Slovo od Mladosti (*Message of Youth*), opera in three acts by the Yugoslav composer Danilo SVARA, is produced in Ljubljana.

24 MARCH 1954

Two one-act operas by Italian composers, *La Figlia del diavolo* by Virgilio MORTARI, and *La Gita in campagna* by Mario PERAGALLO, are performed for the first time at La Scala in Milan.

24 MARCH 1954

Willy FERRERO, American-born Italian conductor, who as a child prodigy before World War I astounded music lovers by actually conducting Mozart and Beethoven, dies in comparative obscurity in Rome at the age of 47, professionally reduced to the position of a provincial opera conductor.

26 MARCH 1954

La Voix de la mer, opera by the 60-year-old Belgian composer Jean ABSIL, to a libretto mystically identifying the sea as an abstract female figure which lures a mariner from his fleshly wife to the submarine realm of fluvial sensuality and oblivion in death, is performed for the first time at the Théâtre de la Monnaie in Brussels.

1 APRIL 1954

The Tender Land, opera in three acts by Aaron COPLAND, to a libretto by Horace Everett, with a locale in the American Midwest, dealing with a harvester who breaks his promise to elope with a farmer's daughter, and she decides to leave her family to wander in the tender land of the cornfields alone, set to music imbued with American melorhythms, including some quotations from actual folk tunes, and accoutred in economic but tonally resonant pandiatonic harmonies, is produced at the New York City Opera.

4 APRIL 1954

In his last public appearance, ten days after his 87th birthday, Arturo TOSCANINI conducts in Carnegie Hall, New York, a program of Wagner's music with the Symphony Orchestra of the National Broadcasting Company, and becomes pathetically confused in the *Tannhäuser* Overture, necessitating an interruption of the broadcast and the incongruous substitution of a recording of the *First Symphony* by Brahms.

4 APRIL 1954

The Transposed Heads, opera in six scenes by the 41-year-old Australian-born American composeress Peggy GLANVILLE-HICKS, after a story by Thomas Mann, dealing with two Brahmins who are beheaded in a thanatolatrous ritual, leading to a capital confusion of decapitated torsos when the widow of one magically restores the head of her minifutuent husband to the more attractively muscular torso of the other and then decides to immolate herself with both Brahmins in a spectacular suttee, set to music in a synthetic semi-Oriental demi-Occidental idiom, ornamented with a cincture of Hindu drumlets, is performed for the first time in Louisville, Kentucky.

5 APRIL 1954

Claude DELVINCOURT, 66-year-old French composer of operas, ballet and instrumental music in a hedonistic Gallic manner, dies in an automobile accident, at Bivio di Albinia, Orbetello, Italy.

14 APRIL 1954

Twenty-five Pages, an "open form" work for piano solo by the 27-year-old American composer Earle BROWN, a paradigm of a musical "mobile" in which some fragments, and indeed whole pages, can be freely permutated, is played for the first time in New York by the prime votary of the musical avant-garde, David Tudor.

18 APRIL 1954

Profile for Orchestra by the 30-year-old American composer Benjamin LEES is performed for the first time in New York.

1 MAY 1954

The Government of the Netherlands issues a postage stamp to commemorate the Dutch composer Willem PIJPER (1894–1947), the foremost impressionist of Holland.

6 MAY 1954

Ode an den Westwind for cello and orchestra by the 27-year-old German composer Hans Werner HENZE inspired by Shelley's poem, is performed for the first time in Bielefeld.

7 MAY 1954

Perfume Set to Music, for voices and orchestra, an olfactory pastiche by Harry REVEL, in six movements glorifying in wafting aural emanations six famous scents conjured up by the French perfumer Corday: *Jet, Toujours Moi, Posse-*

sion, L'Ardente Nuit, Zigane and *Fame,* is performed for the first time at the opening night of a special series of modernistic Pop Concerts in Carnegie Hall, in New York.

9 MAY 1954

Second Symphony in a single long movement by the turbulently melancholic Swedish composer Allan PETTERSSON, thematically set in a series of widely dispersed unstable intervals, ending in a deeply sunk moribund organ point on C, is performed for the first time on Swedish Radio in Stockholm.

13 MAY 1954

The Pajama Game, musical comedy by Richard ADLER and Jerry ROSS, based on Richard Bissell's novel 7 1/2¢ (with reference to a demand by the union for a raise of 7 1/2¢ per hour), retailing the high-jinks at the Sleep-Tite Pajama Factory, wherein the superintendent sings a duet with his own dictaphone-recorded voice (*Hey There*), the syncopated puffs of the steam heat pipes are transformed into a rhythmic dance, and both labor and management repair to Hernando's Hide-away to loll in tango rhythms in an intermittent illumination provided by lighted matches, is produced in New York.

14 MAY 1954

Concerto for Orchestra, by Tadeusz BAIRD, is first performed in Lodz.

15 MAY 1954

The Voice and *The Pumpkin*, two one-act operas by the Hungarian-American composer Leslie KONDOROSSY are performed for the first time by the American New Opera Theater Society in Cleveland, Ohio.

15 MAY 1954

Invocation and Dance for orchestra by the 47-year-old American composer Paul CRESTON is performed for the first time in Louisville.

16 MAY 1954

Clemens KRAUSS, Austrian conductor, scholarly interpreter of classical and romantic operas and symphonic works and a close associate of Richard Strauss, dies suddenly at the age of 61, in Mexico City.

19 MAY 1954

Charles IVES, solitary genius on the American musical scene who, shunning the crowds wrote the prophetic works limning the greatness, the humility and the daily joys of American life in an idiom presaging by many years the developments of modern techniques of composition, dies in New York at the age of 79.

20 MAY 1954

Il Contrabasso, one-act opera-grotesque after Chekhov's short story, by the Italian composer Valentino BUCCHI, is given for the first time in Florence.

22 MAY 1954

Le petit Faune, symphonic extracts from a ballet score by the 81-year-old French composer ROGER-DUCASSE, wherein the surviving Grecian divinities in the forest of Marly are dispersed by the intrusion of modern civilization, and the little faun is mortally stabbed by a polytechnical student who finds him innocently cuddled at his fiancée's flank in the grass, set to a delicately contrived impressionistic score with neo-Grecian modalities pierced by polyharmonies, is performed for the first time in the composer's home town of Bordeaux.

24 MAY 1954

The first National Macedonian opera, *Goce,* by the 29-year-old composer Kiril MAKEDONSKI to his own libretto depicting the uprising, under the leadership of Goce Delčev, of the people of Macedonia against Ottoman rule in 1903, is produced in Skopje.

27 MAY 1954

Hello, Out There, opera by the American composer Jack BEESON, is produced for the first time in New York.

29 MAY 1954

Eleventh Symphony by Henry COWELL subtitled *Seven Rituals of Music,* in seven stylistically disparate sections reflecting in a broad spectrum of instrumental colors the seven melosomatic phenomena—grief, work, love, dance, magic, war and death—is performed for the first time in Louisville.

30 MAY 1954

The 28th Festival of the International Society for Contemporary Music opens in Haifa, Israel, in the following program of orchestral music performed by the Israel Philharmonic Orchestra:

World première of *Odisseia de urea raça (The Odyssey of a Race),* symphonic poem by Heitor VILLA-LOBOS, expressive of his admiration for Israel: "When the Universe was formed, God created a heroic race which lived and suffered, and became victorious in Israel"; *Fourth Piano Concerto* by Darius MILHAUD, in three contrasting movements, written in a highly complex polytonal idiom demanding a maximum of pianofortitude, with Zadel Skolovsky as soloist; *Due Invenzioni* by the Italian neo-classicist Adone ZECCHI; and the first performance of *Symphony* in four movements by André JOLIVET.

31 MAY 1954

At the 28th Festival of the International Society for Contemporary Music in Israel, the following program of chamber music is given in Haifa:

Violin Sonata in three movements by the 54-year-old Italian composer Antonio VERETTI, dedicated "to an imaginary girl"; *5 Songs* by the 38-year-old South African composer Arnold VAN WYK; and *Second String Quartet* by Roger SESSIONS, in five movements based on three tetradecaphonic thematic groups consisting of 14 notes, of which 12 are different and two are duplicates, a dodecaphonic series of 12 non-repeated notes and a hendecaphonic series of eleven non-repeated notes, with numerous fugal developments in dissonant counterpoint.

1 JUNE 1954

Switzerland issues a commemorative postage stamp to mark the centenary of the death of the Swiss hymn composer Alberich ZWISSIG, with a musical quotation from his *Schweizer Psalm* which has attained the status of the Swiss National Anthem.

1 JUNE 1954

At the 28th Festival of the International Society for Contemporary Music in Israel, the world première of *David,* opera in five acts by Darius MILHAUD, is given in Jerusalem in oratorio form, to commemorate the three thousand years of the establishment of Jerusalem as the capital of Judea, with a chorus commenting on the event from the historical point of view.

2 JUNE 1954

At the 28th Festival of the International Society for Contemporary. Music in Israel, the following program of orchestral and choral music is given in Haifa:

Capriccio for string orchestra by the 39-year-old Dutch composer Marius FLOTHUIS, in three movements written in rococo manner; *3 Psalms* for chorus a cappella by the 27-year-old Danish composer Bernhard LEWKOWITCH; *Third String Quartet (Quartetto lirico)* by Mátyás SEIBER, Hungarian composer resident in London, imbued with the spirit of lyrical desolation and based on a pessimistically atonal hypododecaphonic series; and *La Resa di Calais,* ballad for soloists, chorus, strings and piano by the Italian composer Mario PANATERO.

3 JUNE 1954

At the 28th Festival of the International Society for Contemporary Music, the following program of orchestral and choral music is given in Haifa:

5 Variants of Dives and Lazarus by Ralph VAUGHAN WILLIAMS; *Violin Concerto* by Riccardo MALIPIERO, dodecaphonic nephew of Gian Francesco Malipiero; the world première of *Metamorphoses on Saibara* for voice and instruments by the 47-year-old Japanese composer Yoritsune MATSUDAIRA, based on dodecaphonically dislocated modalities of ancient pentatonic Japanese dance tunes; the world première of the *Viola Concerto* by the Posen-born 43-year-old Israeli composer Josef TAL (who abridged his name from the German Grünthal); and *Symphonie Concertante* by the dean of Swedish composers Hilding ROSENBERG.

4 JUNE 1954

At the 28th Festival of the International Society for Contemporary Music in Israel, the following program of chamber music is given in Haifa:

Variations on Bach Chorale by Michael GIELEN of Germany, resident in Buenos Aires; *First String Quartet* by the 63-year-old Israeli composer Erich-Walter STERNBERG; *Le Tombeau de Ravel* for harpsichord and five instruments by the 42-year-old Dutch composer Rudolf ESCHER; *Divertimento* for wind quintet by Saikkola LAURI of Finland; and *String Quartet* by the American composer Leon KIRCHNER.

6 JUNE 1954

At the 28th Festival of the International Society for Contemporary Music in Israel, the following program of orchestral music is given in Haifa:

Sinfonia Piccola by the Polish-Parisian composer Alexandre TANSMAN (performed for the first time in Paris on 27 November 1952); *Piano Concerto* by Arnold SCHOENBERG, played in a two-piano version; *Violin Concerto* by the 47-year-old Norwegian composer Klaus EGGE; and the world première of *4 Danzas* for orchestra by the Chilean composer Carlos RIESCO.

6 JUNE 1954

HAYDN's skull, which disappeared from his casket two days after his funeral in 1809, came into the possession of the Vienna Male Singing Society and eventually of the Society of Friends of Music in Vienna, where it was publicly exhibited in a glass case, is restored in solemn ceremony (after being sprinkled with holy water by Cardinal Innitzer of the Roman Catholic diocese of Vienna) to the rest of his skeleton in the marble sarcophagus at Eisenstadt, at the ancestral estate of Prince Esterhaz, where Haydn spent thirty years of his productive life. (The date 12 June 1938, assigned to the skeletal integration of Haydn in the Third Edition of *Music Since 1900*, is premature.)

7 JUNE 1954

At the concluding concert of the 28th Festival of the International Society for Contemporary Music in Israel, the following program is presented in Haifa:

Violin Sonata by Ahmed Adnan SAYGUN (Turkey); *Threnody* for piano by Jean COULTHARD (Canada); *Fourth Suite* for piano by Nikolas SKALKOTTAS (Greece); *Suite* of songs by Avraham DAUS (Israel); *Violin Sonata* by Hector TOSAR (Uruguay); *Variations on a Yugoslav Folk-Tune* for piano by Mirko CIPRA (Yugoslavia); *Second Piano Sonata* by Paul HINDEMITH (U.S.A.); *Leyenda del Ariel Criollo* for cello and piano by Aurelio DE LA VEGA (Cuba); and *Violin Sonata* by Don BANKS (Australia).

12 JUNE 1954

The First International Council of Composers opens in Rejkjavik, Iceland, presenting a program of Scandinavian and other music.

13 JUNE 1954

Nicolas OBOUHOV, the Russian expatriate who wrote ecstatic religious music and marked his scores with blood symbolic of that shed during the Russian Revolution and who signed his name "Nicolas l'illuminé" dies in Paris at the age of 62.

13 JUNE 1954

Concerto for tuba and orchestra by Ralph VAUGHAN WILLIAMS, in three classical movements, *Prelude, Romance, Rondo alla tedesca*, with two grand cadenzas of elephantine capers and borborygmic burps, is performed for the first time by the London Symphony Orchestra, with Philip Catelinet as tuba soloist, Sir John Barbirolli conducting.

17 JUNE 1954

Die Heimkehr, one-act opera by the Rumanian-Parisian composer Marcel MIHALOVICI, after Guy de Maupassant's novelette *Le Retour*, a tale of a soldier returning from the wars surrealistically greeted by a chorus of walls, doors, and windows of his own house, set to music with considerable dissonant angst and atonal disorientation, is performed for the first time in concert form on the Frankfurt Radio, to a German libretto. (The first stage performance took place in Düsseldorf on 9 November 1954; a revised version was produced in Hamburg on 23 January 1955.)

17 JUNE 1954

A Dinner Engagement, comic opera in one act by the 51-year-old English composer Lennox BERKELEY, to a libretto concerning an attempt of avaricious impoverished parents to marry their daughter to a certifiably authentic prince, unexpectedly succeeding through a fortuitous series of felicitous coincidences, written in an appropriately hedonistic modernistic manner, is performed for the first time at the Aldeburgh Festival.

17 JUNE 1954

Violin Concerto by the South African-born English composer John JOUBERT is performed for the first time at the York Festival in England.

19 JUNE 1954

The Italian Government issues a 25-lire postage stamp commemorating the centennial of the birth of the Italian opera composer Alfredo CATALANI.

6 JULY 1954

Murder in Three Keys, three compact one-act operas, *Black Roses, Dark Sonet*, and *Simoon*, each with a bizarre case of dubiously motivated homicide, by the 50-year-old Scottish composer Erik CHISHOLM, set in a modernistic idiom of high complexity, are performed for the first time in Greenwich Village, in New York.

8 JULY 1954

Circus, overture by Ernst TOCH, written in an artfully stylized mock-popular manner, with an ostentatiously vulgar march tune as a motto and an interlude of free improvisation in the brass, is performed for the first time at the summer season in Ravinia, Chicago, Isler Solomon conducting.

14 JULY 1954

Third Symphony by the 42-year-old English composer Stanley BATE, written in 1940, is performed for the first time at the Cheltenham Festival.

19 JULY 1954

Jean-Jules Aimable ROGER-DUCASSE, French composer of agreeable impressionistic music, dies in Le-Tallan-Médoc, near Bordeaux, at the age of 81.

20 JULY 1954

Les Caprices de Marianne, opera by the 53-year-old French composer Henri SAUGUET, is performed for the first time in Aix-en-Provence.

21 JULY 1954

Daelia, one-act opera by the American composer Hamilton FORREST, is produced in Interlochen, Michigan.

26 JULY 1954

The Soviet Government issues two commemorative postage stamps at 40 and 60 kopecks, bearing the likeness of the "father of Russian opera" Michael GLINKA on the occasion of the sesquicentennial of his birth.

27 JULY 1954

The Audition, one-act opera by the 34-year-old German-born American composer Alfred Grant GOODMAN, dealing with an aging actor who refuses to accept fatherly roles on the stage, but is finally persuaded by a kindly widow to reconcile himself to his age, written in a moderately modern idiom, is performed for the first time at the Ohio University Summer Opera Workshop, in Athens, Ohio.

28 JULY 1954

The Brothers, short opera by George ANTHEIL, is produced for the first time in Denver.

7 AUGUST 1954

Paris à nous deux, or *Le nouveau Rastignac,* opera-farce by Jean FRANÇAIX caricaturing the pretentiousness of modern Paris society, typified by Balzac's pompous *arriviste* Rastignac *redivivus* with a quartet of uncouth saxophones representing self-propelled geniuses among artists and musicians, is performed for the first time at the American Conservatory in Fontainebleau, an elegant Paris suburb.

14 AUGUST 1954

Concerto for mouth harmonica and orchestra by the English composer Malcolm ARNOLD is performed for the first time at the Promenade Concerts in London, with Larry Adler as soloist.

14 AUGUST 1954

The Lost Flute by the 55-year-old Russian-born composer Alexander TCHEREPNIN for narrator and orchestra, is presented for the first time at the Peninsula Music Festival at Fish Creek, Door County, Wisconsin, conducted by Thor Johnson, with the composer's wife Hsien Ming reciting the six Chinese poems of the text.

17 AUGUST 1954

Penelope, "opera semiseria" in two parts by the 43-year-old Swiss-born composer Rolf LIEBERMANN, taking place the 3,137th year after the end of the Trojan war, written in the style of modern antiquity, with baroque recitatives reflecting the Odyssean peripeties, contrasted with the dissonant counterpoint and stark bitonalities characterizing modern life, the score incorporating a recorded session of boogie-woogie, is performed for the first time in Salzburg.

25 AUGUST 1954

La Victoire de Guernica, oratorio for chorus and orchestra by the Italian modernist Luigi NONO, to the words by Paul Eluard descriptive of the inner meaning of the victory of man's spirit over evil, as illustrated by the spiritual victory of the victims of the Fascist air assault upon the Basque village of Guernica, written in an apocalyptically agonizing atonal idiom, is performed for the first time at the International Festival for New Music in Darmstadt.

26 AUGUST 1954

Pratical Cats, "an entertainment for children" for speaker and orchestra by the 49-year-old British composer Alan RAWSTHORNE, to the text by T. S. Eliot, is performed for the first time at the Music Festival at Edinburgh.

28 AUGUST 1954

Fifth Symphony (*Symphony for Strings*), in one movement, by the 39-year-old American composer Vincent PERSICHETTI, is performed for the first time by the Louisville Orchestra.

4 SEPTEMBER 1954

Study in Pianissimo, a dynamic symphonic essay by Boris BLACHER, is performed for the first time in Louisville.

7 SEPTEMBER 1954

Western Symphony by the 34-year-old Philadelphia-born composer Hershy KAY, in four movements based on authentic American tunes, ending with a symphonic barn dance subtitled *Saturday Night,* is performed for the first time as a ballet by the New York City Ballet Company, choreographed by George Balanchine, who commissioned the work.

8 SEPTEMBER 1954

Ralph VAUGHAN WILLIAMS conducts at the Three Choirs Festival in the Worcester Cathedral the first performance of his Christmas Cantata *Hodie,* for soprano, tenor, baritone, mixed chorus, boys' voices and orchestra, to texts from the Bible, Milton and other English poets.

11 SEPTEMBER 1954

Licinio REFICE, 71-year-old Italian composer of sacred music, collapses and dies on the podium while conducting his mystery play *Santa Cecilia* in Rio de Janeiro.

11 SEPTEMBER 1954

Four grandchildren of Robert SCHUMANN living in the United States bring a suit for libel in New York for nine million dollars against Loew's Inc., producers of the motion picture *Song of Life,* charging that it slanders the memory of their grandfather represented as insane and their grandmother Clara Schumann portrayed as having a non-platonic relationship with a clean-shaven Brahms, causing them "to suffer a loss of social standing, humiliation, mortification, chagrin and other mental anguish." (The suit was dismissed in view of the historical truth of Schumann's insanity.)

12 SEPTEMBER 1954

Leonard BERNSTEIN conducts at the International Festival of Contemporary Music in Venice the world première of his *Serenade* for violin solo, with Isaac Stern as soloist, string orchestra and percussion, inspired by Plato's *Symposium*, and set in five interrelated movements:

(1) *Phaedrus: Pausanias*, in which an initial fugato symbolizes the principle of erotic duality; (2) *Aristophanes*, expatiating satirically on human love; (3) *Erixymathes*, a rapid scherzo giving a physician's view on love as a scientific model of harmony of carnal components; (4) *Agathon*, chanting a melodious paeon to Eros in all aspects of amorous passion; (5) *Socrates: Alcibiades*, in which Socrates speaks of the daemon of love in measured didactic tones, while the mundane Alcibiades hurls at him a jazzified challenge.

14 SEPTEMBER 1954

Ivesiana, a ballet score put together from several short works by Charles IVES, *In the Inn, In the Night, Central Park in the Dark* and *The Unanswered Question*, is performed for the first time in this collage, choreographed by George Balanchine in New York.

14 SEPTEMBER 1954

The Turn of the Screw, chamber opera in two acts by Benjamin BRITTEN, after the somber novel of Henry James in which a Victorian governess battles manorial ghosts seemingly intent on subverting the souls of the children in her charge, scored for boy treble, girl treble, three sopranos, tenor and a 13-member orchestra in which the piano serves as harmonic backbone, the "screw" of the title being represented by a subject that "turns" through 15 variations, evolved during instrumental interludes between the 8 scenes of each act, the entire score encompassed within a vast modulatory scheme of alternating perfect fifths and thirds (or their inversions), forming a thematic dodecaphonic series, which is subjected to a whole lexicon of technical operations, transmutations and metamorphoses, creating a tense atmosphere of expressionistic Angst, is produced in Venice.

18 SEPTEMBER 1954

The Government of the Federal German Republic commemorates the fifth anniversary of the death of Richard STRAUSS by issuing a 40-pfennig stamp bearing his likeness.

18 SEPTEMBER 1954

Concerto for flute, strings, harp, celesta and percussion by Virgil THOMSON, "a portrait conceived as a concerto for nightingale and strings," in three movements, making use of mutually exclusive whole-tone scales as well as triadic harmonies according to an elaborate intervallic scheme, is performed for the first time at the Festival of Contemporary Music in Venice.

20 SEPTEMBER 1954

In Memoriam Dylan Thomas, Dirge, Canons and Song for tenor, string quartet and four trombones by Igor STRAVINSKY, set in reverberant tones evocativein their sonorous prosody of the lamented poet's Welsh voice, to the text of his celebrated poem "Do not go gentle into that good night," in which the apostrophe "Rage, rage against the dying of the light" recurs as an anguished refrain, evolving bio-melodically from a molecule of five thematic notes subjected to serialistic transmutations, is performed for the first time at the Monday Evening Concerts, Los Angeles, Robert Craft conducting.

22 SEPTEMBER 1954

Nelson, opera in three acts by the 51-year-old English composer Lennox BERKELEY, dealing with the great admiral's celebrated romantic affair with Lady Hamilton, is performed for the first time at Sadler's Wells in London. (A partial performance, with piano accompaniment, was given in London on 14 February 1953.)

28 SEPTEMBER 1954

Concerto des oracles for baritone, piano and orchestra by Germaine TAILLEFERRE, the sole female member of Les Six, is performed for the first time in Hilversum, Holland, with the 62-year-old composer playing the piano part.

2 OCTOBER 1954

Two operas by Gian Francesco MALIPIERO, *Il Festino* (originally broadcast over the Turin Radio on 6 November 1937) and *Donna Urraca*, are given their first stage performances in Bergamo.

3 OCTOBER 1954

Variazioni per orchestra by Luigi DALLAPICCOLA, with a subject built on a tone-row in which the first and last notes are related by a tritone, ranging in mood from a lyrical *Amoroso* to a raging *Con violenza*, is performed for the first time in Louisville.

17 OCTOBER 1954

Concerto for jazz band and symphony orchestra by the 44-year-old Swiss-born composer Rolf LIEBERMANN, written in the strict dodecaphonic idiom, in 8 movements (*Introduction, Jump, Scherzo I, Blues, Scherzo II, Boogie-Woogie, Interludium* and *Mambo*), in which the 12-note tone-row appears horizontally (melodically) in the piano, and vertically (harmonically) in the muted divisi strings, is performed for the first time at the Donaueschingen Music Festival.

17 OCTOBER 1954

In the course of the Donaueschingen Festival of Contemporary Music a program for prepared pianos is given including the world premières of two American works:

34'46.776" for two pianists by John CAGE, the title indicating duration of the music in minutes and seconds, the method of composition being derived from two sources, the Chinese book of oracles, *I Ching*, enabling one to tell fortune by six throws of coins, and observation of imperfections on a sheet of paper, so that a work is created which is completely free from the impedimenta of personal taste, knowledge of musical literature, and tradition; and *Intersection for Magnetic Tape* by Morton FELDMAN, the title referring to a street intersection at the moment when the green light is flashed, the score (in the form of a topographical diagram) indicating the approximate pitch (high, middle or low), the number of notes to be used, and determining the total duration of the work.

19 OCTOBER 1954

The era of Electronic Composition dawns with a broadcast from the Funkhaus of Cologne of seven works synthetically put together from fragments recorded on magnetic tape, mutated by the alteration of pitch, acceleration and deceleration of tempo, diffraction of tone color, denaturalization of the overtone series, dislocation of rhythmic symmetry and reversal of direction (forward to retrograde):

Glockenspiel and *Etüde über Tongemische* by Herbert EIMERT; *Studie I* and *Studie II* by Karlheinz STOCKHAUSEN; *Komposition No. 5* by Karel GOEYVAERTS; *Seismogramme* by Henri POUSSEUR; and *Formanten I and II* by Paul GREDINGER, all stemming from dodecaphonic esthetics, symbolized by the dodecahedron structure of the loudspeaker, suspended from the ceiling in the broadcasting studio.

19 OCTOBER 1954

Analfabeta, musical burlesque in one act by the 41-year-old Croatian composer Ivo LHOTKA-KALINSKI, to a libretto focused on an analphabetic municipal clerk who believes that analphabet is the name of a secret subversive political party and proceeds to take police action when he hears someone being called an analphabetic fellow, written in a satirically dissonant idiom in utilitarian modernistic harmonies marked by propulsive asymmetric rhythms, is produced in Belgrade.

20 OCTOBER 1954

Sisyphus, choreographic suite for orchestra by the 38-year-old Swedish composer Karl-Birger BLOMDAHL, depicting the atonal anguish of the frustrated Greek forced to roll a boulder uphill only to have it roll down again, is performed for the first time in Stockholm.

20 OCTOBER 1954

Pampeana No. 3, a symphonic pastorale by the 38-year-old Argentinian composer Alberto GINASTERA, making use of acrid polyharmonic complexities, a simulated *scordatura* on a guitar and a dodecaphonic series, while preserving the essential melorhythms of the pampas, is performed for the first time in Louisville.

23 OCTOBER 1954

Fifth Symphony by the 63-year-old Hungarian composer László LAJTHA, in two movements (*Très modéré* and *Vite et agité*), with their thematic consanguinity emphasized by the identical 16-bar endings of both movements, replete with lyrical and motoric Transylvanian melorhythms, is performed for the first time in Paris.

24 OCTOBER 1954

Bakhtior and Nisso, music drama in four acts by the Soviet composer Sergei BALASANIAN, dealing with the struggle of Tadzhik peasantry against the obsolescent feudal lords in Pamir supported by the decaying imperialist powers, with a didactic epilogue of the tragic Tadzhik situation, is performed for the first time in Stalinabad.

27 OCTOBER 1954

Franco ALFANO, Italian composer of effective melodramatic operas, dies in San Remo at the age of 78.

29 OCTOBER 1954

La Magicienne de la Mer, lyric legend in three scenes by the 73-year-old French composer Paul LE FLEM, wherein a modern siren, semi-undine demi-midinette lures fishermen of the city of Ys to her den of amphibious iniquity, eventually submerging the entire community, so that only the eternally resonant bells of the sunken cathedral give evidence of its former glories, is produced at the Opéra-Comique in Paris.

30 OCTOBER 1954

Claudio SANTORO, 34-year-old Brazilian composer, conducts in Rio de Janeiro the first performance of his Fourth Symphony, *Da Paz*, consecrated to the cause of international peace, set in optimistically consonant modalities, representing a distinct departure from his previous dodecaphonic proclivities and signalizing his adoption of the Soviet doctrine of Socialist Realism. (Santoro conducted *Da Paz* in Moscow on 21 March 1955.)

4 NOVEMBER 1954

A Tale of a Mask Maker, one-act opera by the 43-year-old Japanese composer Osamu SHIMIZU, dealing with a disfranchised samurai's love for the beauteous daughter of a lowly mask-maker in 1204, and ending in the death of both, set to music derived from ancient Nipponese melorhythms, is performed for the first time in Osaka.

10 NOVEMBER 1954

Juro Jánošík, opera in six scenes by the 43-year-old Czech composer Jan CIKKER, with action taking place in Slovakia during the turbulent years 1711–1713 and focused on a rebellious idealistic youth Juro Jánošík betrayed into the hands of the Austrian gendarmerie and sentenced to hang, written in an expansive folkloristic idiom with spacious melorhythms of Slavic content and invigorated by asymmetrical rhythms and admissible dissonances, is produced in Bratislava.

10 NOVEMBER 1954

Die stumme Serenade, comic opera by Erich Wolfgang KORNGOLD, composed in 1946, is performed for the first time in Dortmund, Germany.

17 NOVEMBER 1954

Sixth Symphony by the English composer Edmund RUBBRA, in four movements, with thematic substance derived from a tetraphonic motive, E-F-A-B, in various transmutations developed in tangentially tonal modalities spiced with non-toxic resolvable dissonances—(1) *Lento-Allegretto*, displaying a continuity of romantic development, in unobfuscated polyphony; (2) *Canto*, set in spacious harmonies with unimpeded melorhythmic current; (3) *Vivace impetuoso*, an unpretentious lyric scherzo; (4) *Poco Andante-Allegro moderato*, ending in a plagally approached unadulterated C major—is performed for the first time in London.

20 NOVEMBER 1954

The Cask of Amontillado, opera after Edgar Allan Poe by the 30-year-old black American composer Julia PERRY, is performed for the first time at Columbia University in New York.

21 NOVEMBER 1954

Karol RATHAUS, Polish-born German-bred composer and scholar whose modernistic music attracted brief attention in the period between the two wars, dies in New York, where he took refuge from European turmoil, at the age of 59.

23 NOVEMBER 1954

Sandhog, "ballad in three acts" based on the short story *St. Columbia and the River* by Theodore Dreiser, dealing with a true adventure of an Irishman, father of twins, employed as a "sandhog" in digging the tunnel under the North River in New York City in the 1880's, and who is blown up through the muck to the surface of the river, but escapes unscathed, featuring a *Work Song* and a *Sweat Song*, is produced in New York, with a folksy musical score by Earl ROBINSON.

26 NOVEMBER 1954

Concerto for Orchestra by the 41-year-old Polish composer Witold LUTOSLAWSKI, in three compactly functional movements—(1) *Intrada*, (2) *Capriccio, Notturno ed Ariosa*, (3) *Passacaglia, Toccata e Chorale*—couched in classical forms, with melorhythmic contents derived from Polish folk sources, is performed for the first time in Warsaw.

29 NOVEMBER 1954

Concerto for Orchestra by the 32-year-old Greek composer Yorgo SICILIANOS, written in a compact and resonant idiom of neo-Grecian baroque, is performed for the first time in Athens.

30 NOVEMBER 1954

Wilhelm FURTWÄNGLER, German conductor, cultured interpreter of the masterpieces of German music and a liberal champion of moderate modern music, dies in Baden-Baden at the age of 68.

30 NOVEMBER 1954

Concerto for bassoon, string orchestra, harp and piano by André JOLIVET in four varied movements, *Recitativo, Allegro giovale, Largo cantabile* and *Fugato*, is performed for the first time in Paris.

2 DECEMBER 1954

Déserts, symphonic poem by Edgar VARÈSE, scored for wind instruments, percussion and electronic sounds, the first work ever composed for orchestral instruments combined with a pre-recorded magnetic tape and conceived in anathematic idiom of agglutinated melorhythmic molecules, according to Varèse's doctrine of "organized sound," is performed for the first time in Paris.

(*Poem in Cycles and Bells* for tape recorder and orchestra by Otto Luening and Vladimir Ussachevsky was composed later than *Déserts*, but had its first performance two weeks earlier than Varèse's work. An even earlier work for live instruments combined with electronic sounds by Luening and Ussachevsky was their *Rhapsodic Variations*, first performed by the Louisville Orchestra in New York on 20 March 1954.)

2 DECEMBER 1954

Enrique SORO, Chilean composer of easily assimilable piano pieces tinted with local Andean color, dies in Santiago at the age of 70.

3 DECEMBER 1954

Troilus and Cressida, opera in three acts by William WALTON, to a libretto derived from Chaucer, wherein Prince Troilus of Troy perishes in his attempt to rescue the daughter of a treasonous high priest from Greek captivity, and she stabs herself to death, set to music in a dramatically impassioned neo-Handelian manner, intensified by an uninhibited use of modern dissonance, is produced at Covent Garden in London.

3 DECEMBER 1954

Prayers of Kierkegaard, oratorio by Samuel BARBER for soprano solo, chorus and orchestra, to the texts from the writings of the melancholy Danish philosopher whose fatalistic theology paradoxically influenced the deterministic trends of his preeminently mechanistic century, set to music with an authentic sentiment of Protestant hymnody and frequent flights into atonal and bitonal formations, is performed for the first time by the Boston Symphony Orchestra, Charles Munch conducting.

4 DECEMBER 1954

La Figlia di Iorio, "pastoral tragedy" in three acts by Ildebrando PIZZETTI (composed between 11 July 1953 and 18 April 1954), to a mystical libretto of Gabriele d'Annunzio, wherein the beautiful daughter of a self-styled magus is forced to flee from a massed assault of harvesters "intoxicated by the sun and wine" and finds refuge in the family of a young bridegroom who, inflamed by her, carries her to an oceanside grotto and kills his own father with an axe when the latter intrudes to ravish her, but is saved from the vengeance of the villagers when she assumes the guilt as a psychological incendiary, and goes to her death in the "purifying flames" of a sacred fire, set to music in rhapsodically pyromantic modalities, is performed for the first time in Naples.

4 DECEMBER 1954

Double Trouble, one-act opera by the 50-year-old expatriate German composer Richard MOHAUPT, in which a pair of identical twins named Hocus and Pocus are involved in a series of amatory imbroglios, set to music in the manner of an Italian opera buffa, is performed for the first time as a commissioned work by the Louisville Orchestra, vocal soloists and chorus.

10 DECEMBER 1954

Third Symphony by the 51-year-old Russian-born American composer Nikolai LOPATNIKOFF is performed for the first time in Pittsburgh.

11 DECEMBER 1954

Carlos CHÁVEZ conducts at the Music Festival in Caracas the world première of his *Third Symphony*, commissioned for this occasion by the playwright Clare Boothe Luce, in four movements, *Introduzione, Allegro, Scherzo,* and *Finale,* based on classical models without overt ethnical Mexican references. (The Fourth and Fifth symphonies of Chávez, though written later than the Third, were performed on earlier dates, the Fourth on 11 February 1953, the Fifth on 1 December 1953.)

14 DECEMBER 1954

Second Symphony by the 47-year-old French composer Tony AUBIN, is performed for the first time in Paris.

17 DECEMBER 1954

Fourth Symphony by Vincent PERSICHETTI, cast in the classical four movements—(1) *Adagio-Allegro,* (2) *Andante,* (3) *Allegretto,* (4) *Presto*—and conceived in a cyclically constructed form, judiciously equilibrated between lyric consonant episodes and dramatic dissonant interludes, is performed for the first time anywhere by the Philadelphia Orchestra, Eugene Ormandy conducting.

18 DECEMBER 1954

Die Brücke von San Luis Rey, radio opera by the 54-year-old German composer Hermann REUTTER, after Thornton Wilder's novel tracing back the lives of several people united in a catastrophe when a bridge collapses in Peru carrying them to their deaths, is given in its stage performance, in Essen. (First radio performance was given by the Frankfurt Radio on 20 June 1954.)

23 DECEMBER 1954

A Christmas Carol, musical television play by Bernard HERRMANN, is produced by the Columbia Broadcasting System in New York.

25 DECEMBER 1954

A commemorative stamp of 15 dinars to mark the centennial of the death of the Serbian composer Vatroslav LISINSKY (1819–1854) is issued in Yugoslavia.

27 DECEMBER 1954

The Saint of Bleeker Street, music drama in three acts by Gian Carlo MENOTTI, to his own libretto dealing with a mystically illuminated young woman in the Italian section of Greenwich Village in New York, whose religious frenzy causes psychosomatic stigmata to appear on her hands and feet on Good Friday at the conclusion of her aria in the first act, emulating the wounds of Christ, and whose brother strangles his fiancée when she taunts him regarding his quasi-incestuous brotherly love, and the "Saint of Bleecker Street" falls lifeless to the ground as she receives the nun's veil, set to music combining elements of religious chants with mundane balladry, and including a scene in a subway station in the best tradition of Italian Verismo, is produced in New York, with Menotti himself acting in the multiple capacities of coordinator and stage director.

1955

7 JANUARY 1955

Fantaisies symphoniques (Sixth Symphony) by Bohuslav MARTINU (completed on 23 April 1953), in three movements consisting of sections alternatively marked *Lento* and *Allegro,* with a germinal motive taken from Martinu's opera *Julietta,* and developed as a rhapsodic fantasy in a romantically impressionistic vein, is performed for the first time by the Boston Symphony Orchestra under the direction of Charles Munch, as a commissioned work for its 75th anniversary.

7 JANUARY 1955

Marian ANDERSON makes her debut at the Metropolitan Opera in New York, as Ulrica in Verdi's *Un Ballo in maschera,* the first Negro singer to be so distinguished.

14 JANUARY 1955

Heitor VILLA-LOBOS conducts the Philadelphia Orchestra in the world première of his *Eighth Symphony* in four movements, *Andante, Lento assai, Allegretto scherzando, Allegro giusto,* in which a spacious cantillation in the manner of Brazilian melorhythms is brought in contrast with stark dissonant harmonies, creating intermittent dramatic tension, and the world première of his *Concerto for Harp and Orchestra,* in four movements, *Allegro, Andante moderato, Scherzo, Allegro non troppo,* containing a long cadenza linking the third and fourth movements, with the eminent modernistic harpist Nicanor Zabaleta as soloist.

14 JANUARY 1955

Monaco issues a five-franc postage stamp to mark the 80th anniversary of the great humanist Albert SCHWEITZER.

15 JANUARY 1955

Third Symphony, in F sharp, by the 55-year-old Russian-born composer Alexander TCHEREPNIN, in four movements, *Lento, Allegro pessante, Adagio* and *Allegro*, written in a propellent rhythmic style, is performed for the first time by the Indianapolis Symphony Orchestra, Fabien Sevitzky conducting.

19 JANUARY 1955

Guillermo URIBE-HOLGUÍN, prime composer of Colombia, conducts in Bogotá the first performance of his *Third Symphony*.

23 JANUARY 1955

Symphonie de chambre, in E major, for 12 instruments, last work by Georges ENESCO (completed by him 28 May 1954), written in a rhapsodically elaborated rococo manner, is performed for the first time in Paris.

23 JANUARY 1955

Tudor Vladimirescu, opera-oratorio by the 40-year-old Rumanian composer Gheorghe DUMITRESCU dealing with the tragic hero of the Rumanian war for independence executed in 1821 by the Greek leader Ypsilanti on account of conflicting national aims, set in a sociologically realistic idiom, leaning strongly on folk music, is performed for the first time in Bucharest. (A partial performance of the work was given in Bucharest on 24 September 1951.)

25 JANUARY 1955

A Letter to Emily, chamber opera by the American composer Lockrem JOHNSON, is produced in Seattle.

27 JANUARY 1955

The Midsummer Marriage, opera in three acts by the 50-year-old English composer Michael TIPPETT, to his own libretto, dealing with two pairs of lovers mating symbolically with their own antinomic selves representing the masculine element in a woman and a feminine element in a man, set to music in a capaciously diatonic idiom diversified by opulently terraced dissonances, is produced at Covent Garden in London.

16 FEBRUARY 1955

La Conchiglia, short opera by the Italian composer Lino LIVIABELLA, after Robert Louis Stevenson's *The Bottle Imp*, is produced in Florence.

18 FEBRUARY 1955

Fifth Symphony, subtitled *Sinfonia Sacra*, by Howard HANSON (completed by him on 8 August 1954), inspired by the story of the first Easter in the Gospel according to St. John, and conceived as an architectonic triptych, consisting of a triune introduction, a trithematic middle section, and variants and mutations of these materials form-

ing a third division, founded on ecumenical ecclesiastical modalities and evolving with dramatic passion in powerfully resonant harmonies, is performed for the first time by the Philadelphia Orchestra under the direction of Eugene Ormandy.

21 FEBRUARY 1955

Four Russian Songs for soprano, flute, harp and guitar by Igor STRAVINSKY are performed for the first time at the Monday Evening Concerts in Los Angeles, Robert Craft conducting.

(Two of these songs are arrangements for voice and instruments of songs from *Four Russian Songs* for voice and piano completed on 23 October 1919; the other two are orchestrations of songs from *Three Tales for Children* for voice and piano completed on 21 June 1917.)

24 FEBRUARY 1955

Silk Stockings, musical comedy by Cole PORTER, inspired by the motion picture *Ninotchka*, urbanely satirizing the Soviet ways of Stalinist life (when a Soviet bureaucrat is informed that Prokofiev is dead, he observes: "I didn't even know he was arrested" and a commissar carries with him a copy of "Who's Still Who"), is produced in New York.

24 FEBRUARY 1955

Susannah, musical drama in two acts by the 28-year-old American composer Carlisle FLOYD, to his own libretto, fashioned after the biblical story of Susannah and the elders transferred to rural Tennessee, wherein a fire-breathing Baptist preacher defiles a virginal cornfed farm girl after watching her swim innocently in the nude, whereupon her brother slays him during a baptism exhibit, set to music in a simplicistically hymnal triadic idiom, with a modicum of modernistic bitonalities, is performed for the first time at Florida State University in Tallahassee. (The first New York performance of the opera was given at the New York City Center on 27 September 1956.)

27 FEBRUARY 1955

Mitologia, symphonic poem by the 62-year-old Portuguese composer Maurice SANDOZ, in two sections, *The Aeolian Harp* and *Sybil's Grotto*, is performed for the first time in Lisbon.

2 MARCH 1955

Le Serment, opera by the Parisianized Polish composer Alexandre TANSMAN, is produced in Brussels.

12 MARCH 1955

Charlie PARKER, nicknamed "Bird" (his real forenames were Charles Christopher), black American jazz saxophone player, a pioneer archpriest of bebop, dies at the unfulfilled age of thirty-four in a state of physical exhaustion caused by alcoholism and drug addiction, in the luxurious New York apartment of his ardent admirer Baroness Pannonica de Konigswarter.

12 MARCH 1955

First Symphony, in four movements, by the 34-year-old Soviet Armenian composer Karen KHACHATURIAN, nephew of Aram Khachaturian, is performed for the first time in Moscow.

13 MARCH 1955

First Symphony for strings by the 60-year-old Corsican-born French composer Henri MARTELLI, is performed for the first time in Paris.

14 MARCH 1955

Hand in Hand, opera by the Estonian composer Gustav ERNESAKS, dealing with the attempted sabotage of an Estonian electric power station by unliquidated Estonian counterrevolutionaries, with a jubilant finale as foes are foiled and the station begins to generate electricity, is produced in Tallin.

18 MARCH 1955

A Trip to Nahant, fantasy for orchestra by the American composer Randall THOMPSON, nostalgically depicting an excursion to the small town northeast of Boston, making use of euphoniously harmonized Americanistic tunes, is performed for the first time by the Philadelphia Orchestra, Eugene Ormandy conducting.

21 MARCH 1955

Olivier MESSIAEN, organist since 1932 at the Trinité in Paris, presents there the first integral performance of his *Livre d'Orgue,* in seven movements, *Reprise par interversion, Pièce en trio, Les Mains de l'Abîme, Chants d'oiseaux, Pièce en trio, Les Yeux dans les roues* and *64 durées,* written according to his theory of interrelated modalities, in which not only the notes, but durations and dynamic intensities are distributed according to a master plan of coordinated combinatorial parameters.

31 MARCH 1955

The first complete performance of Sergei PROKOFIEV's revised and abbreviated version of his opera *War and Peace,* after Tolstoy's epic novel, set to music with a natural fluency of modulating tonalities, rhythmically ebullient and rich equally in nostalgic lyrical quality and dramatic tension, is given posthumously in Leningrad.

2 APRIL 1955

The Wish, one-act opera by George ANTHEIL, to his own libretto about the death of a young couple in love in Greenwich Village in New York City, accentuating the fateful element in somber modalities, upon which the sounds of ubiquitous popular songs mundanely intrude, in a "synthesis of the mystic and the realistic," is performed for the first time in Louisville.

2 APRIL 1955

Il Giudizio Universale, opera in three acts by the 34-year-old Italian composer Vieri TOSATTI, in which members of the world bourgeoisie attend the Day of Judgment and confess their abominations perpetrated while maintaining a posture of social respectability, is produced at La Scala, Milan.

15 APRIL 1955

Numance, opera by the 54-year-old French composer Henry BARRAUD, based on a play by Cervantes dealing with the patriotic resistance of the Spanish town of Numantia to Roman invaders in 133 B.C., is performed for the first time at the Paris Opéra. (The symphonic predecessor of *Numance* was Barraud's *Symphonie de Numance,* performed at Baden-Baden on 3 December 1950.)

21 APRIL 1955

Il Cappello di paglia di Firenze (The Little Straw Hat of Florence), comic opera by Nino ROTA, is performed for the first time at the Teatro Massimo in Palermo.

24 APRIL 1955

Dance Overture by Paul CRESTON, a quadrinational musical tribute derived from the rhythms of the four powers that shaped the destiny of Florida: Spain (bolero), England (country dance), France (loure), and the United States (square dance), is performed for the first time at the convention of the National Federation of Music Clubs in Miami, Florida.

25 APRIL 1955

Die Füsse im Feuer, music drama by the 34-year-old Swiss composer Armin SCHIBLER, is produced in Zürich.

27 APRIL 1955

The Magic Mirror, opera in 3 acts by Wheeler BECKETT, is produced in Newark, New Jersey.

28 APRIL 1955

Fifth Symphony by the 45-year-old Rumanian composer Alfred MENDELSOHN is performed for the first time in Bucharest.

30 APRIL 1955

Dawn, operetta in three acts by the Albanian composer Kristo KONO, to a libretto depicting the successful discovery and condign lethal punishment of an unliquidated Albanian kulak scheming to murder a newly-wed socialistic couple, is produced in Tirana.

30 APRIL 1955

Kineska priča (Chinese Tale), ballet by the 60-year-old Croatian composer Krešimir BARANOVIĆ is performed for the first time in Belgrade.

1 MAY 1955

Heinz ARNTZ sets a world record for playing the piano without stopping, except for necessary physiological functions of ingestion, imbibation, elimination and brief dormition, for 423 hours (17 days and 15 hours).

486   4 May 1955

4 MAY 1955

Georges ENESCO, prime composer of modern Rumania, who began his career as an incredible child prodigy of fantastic natural gifts and became a virtuoso violinist and whose youthful *Rumanian Rhapsody* represents the most successful symphonic stylization of indigenous motives, dies in Paris at the age of 73.

5 MAY 1955

Damn Yankees, musical comedy by Richard ADLER and Jerry ROSS, based on Douglass Wallop's novel *The Year the Yankees Lost the Pennant,* a modern Faust story in which an elderly baseball fan sells his soul to the devil in exchange for the career of a rejuvenated pitcher, enabling his favorite team, the Washington Senators, to win the pennant from the New York Yankees with psychosomatic assistance from a reincarnated witch Lola, and then cheats the devil by refusing to play in the World Series, regains his soul and returns to his proper age, is produced in New York.

5 MAY 1955

Sixth Symphony by the 45-year-old Danish composer Vagn HOLMBOE, commemorating the tenth anniversary of the liberation of Denmark from Nazi occupation, is performed for the first time in Copenhagen.

9 MAY 1955

The Pot of Fat, chamber opera in six scenes by the American composer Theodore CHANLER, a fable of a cat and a mouse living in congenial matrimonial concubinage, who store a pot of fat away in the church as communal property, with the cat poaching on it surreptitiously, set to music in a gently satirical Gallic vein, with asymmetrical melorhythms supporting a tonal vocal line, is performed for the first time at the Longy School of Music in Cambridge, Massachusetts. (The first New York performance was given 22 February 1956.)

10 MAY 1955

A *Chilhood Miracle,* one-act opera by the American composer Ned ROREM, based on Hawthorne's story *The Snow Image,* set to music in a simple tonal idiom adorned with tolerable non-toxic dissonances, and *The Nightingale,* one-act opera by Bernard ROGERS, after Hans Christian Andersen's tale of the Chinese Emperor saved from a mortal illness by the singing of a forest nightingale, sustained in an impressionistic style, are performed for the first time by Punch Opera in New York.

11 MAY 1955

Violin Concerto by the dean of modern British composers Sir Arthur BLISS is performed for the first time in London.

12 MAY 1955

Two centuries have passed since the birth at Fontanetto da Po of Giovanni Battista VIOTTI, Italian virtuoso violinist and composer who dazzled the royal court of Marie Antoinette and fled from the French Revolution to London to die in penury and distress.

(Viotti had a brother, also named Giovanni Battista, who was born on 23 May 1753, and died in infancy on 10 July 1754. The surviving Viotti, who was given the same first names, was born on 12 May 1755. Through confusion, Viotti's bicentennial was widely celebrated on 23 May 1953, on the anniversary of the birth of the dead child.)

13 MAY 1955

The Ruby, a short opera by the American composer Norman DELLO JOIO, is performed for the first time in Bloomington, Indiana.

17 MAY 1955

Robert METZLER, 50-year-old Chicago church organist, obtains a court injunction against Miss Harriet Davis, 35, who, accompanied by her mother, systematically pursued him wherever he went after they met while walking their respective dogs, specifically charging her with blocking his car as he was leaving the church and creating a traffic jam. (Miss Davis claimed she was interested only in the inspiration received from his organ playing.)

18 MAY 1955

Francesco Balilla PRATELLA, futurist Italian composer who wrote the first opera about an aviator and whose futuristic idiom was anchored mainly on the whole-tone scale, dies in Ravenna, at the age of 75.

20 MAY 1955

What Men Live By, one-act opera-pastorale by Bohuslav MARTINU, adapted to an English libretto from Tolstoy's moralistic tale wherein a kindly cobbler tenders a helping hand to a pilgrim, a widow and a boy, and then learns in a veridical dream that he thereby received Christ, set to music with an equilibrated infusion of lofty modalities and mundane balladry, is performed for the first time on the stage at Hunter College in New York.

25 MAY 1955

The Commitee, comic opera in four scenes by the 33-year-old American composer Matt DORAN, detailing an examination for a Music Doctor's degree in a Western American university, with a multiplicity of academically inane questions, including one asking which symphony ends with a timpani beat on the dominant (the correct answer is the first symphony by the chairman of the committee), is produced for the first time at the Del Mar College of Music in Corpus Christi, Texas.

25 MAY 1955

The Fatal Oath, opera by the 54-year-old Russian-born American composer Boris KOUTZEN, to a libretto derived from Balzac's horror story *Le Grande Bretèche,* is performed for the first time anywhere in New York.

26 MAY 1955

Michel MAGNE conducts in Paris the first performance of his *Symphonie Humaine,* employing 150 players and making use of instruments producing inaudible sounds of slow low frequencies calculated to make a painful impact on the abdominal region of the listener.

30 MAY 1955

Incontri for 24 instruments by the Italian avant-garde composer Luigi NONO is performed for the first time in Darmstadt.

9 JUNE 1955

First Symphony by the Rumanian composer Sigismond TODUTA is performed for the first time in Bucharest.

11 JUNE 1955

Marcel SAMUEL-ROUSSEAU, French composer of operas, ballets and other works, son of Samuel-Alexandre Rousseau, whose first Christian name he added to his own last name to avoid confusion, dies in his native Paris at the age of 72.

11 JUNE 1955

Trumpet Concerto by the 25-year-old Russian composer Alexandra PAKHMUTOVA is performed for the first time in Moscow.

15 JUNE 1955

Feltámadt a tenger (The Sea is Rising), oratorio by the Communist Hungarian composer Ferenc SZABÓ, descriptive of the revolutionary upheaval of 1848 and dedicated to the "unforgettable memory of the Hungarian Soviet Republic of 1919," is performed for the first time in Budapest.

17 JUNE 1955

The 29th Festival of the International Society for Contemporary Music opens at Baden-Baden with the following program:

Seventh Symphony by the 45-year-old Danish composer Vagn HOLMBOE, in a neo-classical setting, in seven sections, *Allegro con fuoco, Intermezzo I, Adagio, Intermezzo II, Presto, Intermezzo III, Coda,* in which the intermezzi serve as intervallic mutations and rhythmic variants of the principal movements; *Variazioni per Orchestra* by the 51-year-old Italian expressionist Luigi DALLAPICCOLA (first performed as a commissioned work in Louisville on 3 October 1954); *Lied der Kentauren,* cantata for soprano and orchestra by the German composer Markus LEHMANN; *Musique pour cordes* by the Swiss composer Constantin REGAMEY, in three movements, *Andante, Marcia giocosa, Vivace assai,* in a conciliatorily tonal idiom in which the modulatory factor is replaced by dodecaphonic relativity, with the retention of a definitely sensed tonal barycenter in each movement: and *Third Symphony* by Carlos CHÁVEZ (first performed at the Festival of Caracas, on 11 December 1954)

17 JUNE 1955

At a meeting of the International Standards Organization in Stockholm, delegates of 37 nations agree to raise the pitch of the basic tuning note "A" from 435 (adopted at an international congress in Vienna in 1885) to 440 cycles.

18 JUNE 1955

At the 29th Festival of the International Society for Contemporary Music at Baden-Baden, the following works are presented:

Actus Tragicus for ten violins by the German-American composer Erich Itor KAHN, derived from a dodecaphonic subject but provided with a triadic epilogue as a tonal atonement of the atonal peripeties of the "tragic act" and constituting an Aristotelian catharsis; *Kammerkonzert* for piano, woodwinds and percussion by the Swedish avante-garde composer Karl-Birger BLOMDAHL, in four movements, *Lento, Allegro, Adagio, Presto; Arpiade* by the Moscow-born German-Russian composer Vladimir VOGEL of Switzerland, scored for soprano and a small ensemble, to dadaistic texts of eight poems, four in German and four in French, by the surrealist poet Hans Arp, athematically set to music, with syllabic values determining a corresponding instrumental color; the world première of *Le Marteau sans Maître* by the emergent leader of the avant-garde, 30-year-old Pierre BOULEZ, scored for contralto, alto flute, vibraphone, xylorimba (a heterozygotic product of xylophone and marimba), viola, guitar, and a covey of unloud drumlets, shakers and metallic percussion instruments, to the surrealistic texts of René Char, in nine sections containing three instrumental "commentaries" on the masterless martellation of the title.

19 JUNE 1955

At the 29th Festival of the International Society for Contemporary Music in Baden-Baden, two concerts of chamber music are given, one in the afternoon, one in the evening:

Afternoon concert: *String Quartet* in three movements by Herbert BRÜN of Israel, based on a dodecaphonic series; *Alpha and Beta,* a dodecaphonic piano piece by the Japanese composer Makoto MOROI, the title alluding to the most conspicuous stars in the Gemini constellation; *Piano Sonatina* by the Australian composer Peter SCULTHORPE; *5 Lieder* for voice, flute, clarinet and bassoon by the 54-year-old Austrian composer Hans Erich APOSTEL; *Trio* for oboe, clarinet and bassoon by the 29-year-old Danish composer Jan MAEGAARD; and *Third String Quartet,* subtitled *Quaretetto Lirico,* by the Hungarian-born naturalized British composer Mátyás SEIBER, in three contrasting movements, ending on a pessimistic note of cosmic desolation symbolized by an atonally disjunct melodic motto.

Evening concert: *Orchester-Ornament* by the 52-year-old China-born half-Estonian half-German composer Boris BLACHER, consisting of two fast and two slow movements, derived from an arithmetic series governing intervallic, metrical and rhythmic factors; *String Quartet* by the 28-year-old German composer Hans Werner HENZE, in three classically proportioned movements; *Chanson et Romance* for soprano and orchestra by the German composer Werner EGK, to the text of an old French love song; *The Creation* for baritone and orchestra by the German composer Wolfgang FORTNER, to the text by the American Negro poet Weldon Johnson, explaining the act of creation as the result of God's loneliness in a world without people; and *Variations for Orchestra,* op. 31, by Arnold SCHOENBERG.

20 JUNE 1955

At the 29th Festival of the International Society for Contemporary Music at Baden-Baden, the following program of chamber music is presented:

Sonata for two pianos by the Italian modernist Riccardo NIELSEN, in three parts thematically built on a 12-tone series; *Quartet* for flute, clarinet, bassoon and piano by the Norwegian composer Knut WIGGEN, in a paradodecaphonic idiom; *Sonata* for cello and piano by the 46-year-old American composer Elliott CARTER, in which he applies systematically the technique of "metric modulation" whereby an independent and usually incommensurate rhythm is superposed on the dominant meter and subsequently supersedes it as the main time signature; *Concertino* for flute, oboe, English horn and cello by the 34-year-old Swedish composer Ingvar LIDHOLM, in four movements, with the subject matter being derived from serialistic premises; and *Second String Quartet* in four movements by the English composer Francis BURT.

21 JUNE 1955

At the last concert of the 29th Festival of the International Society for Contemporary Music in Baden-Baden, the following program of symphonic music is presented:

Rhapsody for orchestra by the renowned pianist Arthur SCHNABEL, written in a neoclassical style with atonal excrescences in dissonant counterpoint; *Divertimento No. 1* for two violins and chamber orchestra by the Parisian Hungarian composer Tibor HARSÁNYI, in three movements of a classical countenance; *Suite* for string orchestra, piano and percussion by the Italian composer Gino CONTILLI, with a passacaglia based on a 12-tone series; and *Sinfonia* by the Spanish composer resident in England Roberto GERHARD, in three movements, derived from a basic 12-tone series with concomitant serial procedures in the intervallic and dynamic parameters.

22 JUNE 1955

Sixth Symphony by Johann Nepomuk DAVID is performed for the first time in Wiesbaden.

26 JUNE 1955

Musicwriter, a machine that can efficiently and speedily type in musical notation, invented by the American composer Cecil EFFINGER, is demonstrated for the first time at the exhibit of the National Office Machine Dealers Association, in Denver, Colorado.

26 JUNE 1955

The Hudson River Suite by Ferde GROFÉ, inspired by Washington Irving's story, the score of which includes a part for a trained dog's barking, a rescue squad siren, a police whistle and a set of bowling pins to represent the rumble of the ghostly group encountered by Rip Van Winkle in the Catskill Mountains, is performed for the first time in Washington, with Sally Herman as soloist, barking in lieu of a dog.

5 JULY 1955

To commemorate the centennial of the birth of the Russian composer Anatoly LIADOV, the Soviet government issues a postage stamp at 40 kopecks bearing his portrait and a few notes from a Russian song arranged by him.

5 JULY 1955

Zarya nad Dvinoi (*Dawn over the Dvina*), opera by the Ukrainian composer Yuli MEITUS, is performed for the first time in Kiev.

12 JULY 1955

The Hollow Men for chorus, clarinet, three trombones and piano by the 26-year-old American composer Donald KEATS, to words by T. S. Eliot, is performed for the first time in Hamburg, Germany.

8 AUGUST 1955

The Rope, opera by the American composer Louis MENNINI, brother of Peter Mennin (who cut off the last letter of his Italian name), commissioned by the Koussevitzky Music Foundation, is presented for the first time at the Berkshire Music Festival at Tanglewood, Massachusetts.

11 AUGUST 1955

A Lament for April 15, fiscal madrigal by the retired banker Avery CLAFLIN, who had some lessons with Erik Satie in Paris, to the text, verbatim, of the tax instruction sheet for filing statements of income on April 15 each year, set to music with gravity befitting the subject, in the polyphonic style of a secular oratorio, is performed for the first time at the Berkshire Center in Tanglewood, Massachusetts.

17 AUGUST 1955

Irische Legende, opera by the German composer Werner EGK, is performed for the first time in Salzburg.

22 AUGUST 1955

Olin DOWNES, for many years chief music critic of the New York *Times*, earnest defender of the ideal of good music marked by melodious godliness and harmonious cleanliness, of which Sibelius was a paradigm and Schoenberg its principal defiler, dies of cancer in New York at the age of 69.

7 SEPTEMBER 1955

After five years of residence in America, 78-year-old Hungarian composer Ernst VON DOHNÁNYI, sobbing with joy (as reported by his third wife), becomes a citizen of the United States.

13 SEPTEMBER 1955

Seventh Symphony, by Darius MILHAUD, in three contrasting movements, *Animé, Grave, Vif* completed by him in California on 15 May 1955, and written in a characteristically direct Gallic manner, without a key signature, but built around D, which is the first and the last note in the score, is performed for the first time in the course of the International Music Festival in Venice by the Orchestra of the Belgian Institute National de Radiodiffusion, as a commissioned work, conducted by Franz André.

15 SEPTEMBER 1955

The Flaming Angel, opera in five acts by Sergei PROKOFIEV, composed between 1919 and 1927, to a libretto from the medievalistic story by the Russian novelist Valery Bryusov, dealing with a young maiden tortured by the Inquisition for iniquitous communion with the Devil, comes to a belated posthumous stage production in the course of the Festival of Contemporary Music in Venice.

17 SEPTEMBER 1955

The German Federal Republic issues a 40-pfennig postage stamp commemorating the conductor Wilhelm FURTWÄNGLER.

18 SEPTEMBER 1955

Variazioni concertanti for piano and orchestra by the 35-year-old Rumanian-born Italian composer Roman VLAD, based on a succession of 12 different notes artfully extracted from a pseudo-dodecaphonic passage in Mozart's *Don Giovanni,* is performed for the first time in Venice.

24 SEPTEMBER 1955

Suite transocéane for orchestra by André JOLIVET is performed for the first time in Louisville, Kentucky, as a commissioned work, by the Louisville Orchestra.

7 OCTOBER 1955

Darius MILHAUD conducts the first performance, with the Boston Symphony Orchestra, of his *Sixth Symphony* in four movements, *Calme et tendre, Tumulteueux, Lent et doux,* and *Joyeux et robuste,* written in his characteristic cultured manner, vitalized by a constant influx of harmonious dissonances.

9 OCTOBER 1955

The Hungarian Government issues two stamps at 60 fellers and one forint honoring Béla BARTÓK, and bearing his portrait.

17 OCTOBER 1955

Pallas Athene Weint, opera in three acts with a prologue by Ernst KRENEK (completed in Los Angeles on 2 January 1955), to his own libretto, in which Pallas Athene sheds dodecaphonic tears over the subjugation of her city of Athens by the Spartans during the last phase of the Peloponnesian War in 404 B.C., with Socrates offering her diatonic consolation against a pentatonic accompaniment in gymnosophistical vigesimosecular counterpoint, is performed for the first time by the Hamburg State Opera.

23 OCTOBER 1955

Only a Dream, operetta by the Estonian composer Boris KYRVER, dealing with the love between an unemployed young architect and a salesgirl during the period between the two world wars, with local bourgeois color provided by interludes of obsolete jazz, is performed for the first time in Tallin.

28 OCTOBER 1955

Saeta, ballet by the 25-year-old Spanish composer Cristóbal HALFFTER, nephew of Ernesto and Rodolfo Halffter, is performed for the first time in Madrid.

29 OCTOBER 1955

Violin Concerto in A minor by Dmitri SHOSTAKOVICH, in four movements, a tranquil *Nocturne,* a limpid *Scherzo,* a stately *Passacaglia* leading by means of an extended cadenza into a whimsical *Burlesca,* is performed for the first time in Leningrad with David Oistrakh, to whom the *Concerto* is dedicated, as soloist.

4 NOVEMBER 1955

Credendum for orchestra by William SCHUMAN, in three movements, *Declaration, Chorale, Finale,* commissioned by the Department of State for UNESCO, couched in a grandly declarative oratorical manner and ending with a festive affirmation of faith in a lofty oriflamme of sonorous masses, is performed for the first time by the Cincinnati Symphony Orchestra, conducted by Thor Johnson.

5 NOVEMBER 1955

The new hall of the Vienna State Opera, rebuilt according to the plan of the old building destroyed in the Allied air raid, and equipped with a headlight suspended from the ceiling in lieu of the ornate chandelier of the romantic past, opens with a performance of BEETHOVEN's *Fidelio.*

6 NOVEMBER 1955

Griffelkin, fantasy opera in three acts by the 33-year-old American composer Lukas FOSS, to a German folk tale dealing with a mischievous adolescent devil who is given a day on earth as a reward for nasty behavior and decides to defect from Hell and embark on a life of humanistic endeavor, set to music in an inventively modernistic vein, including a skit of a discordant but basically diatonic Hell Conservatory, is produced as a commissioned work for television by the National Broadcasting Company in New York.

14 NOVEMBER 1955

Sixth Symphony by Henry COWELL is performed for the first time in Houston, Texas.

22 NOVEMBER 1955

Guy ROPARTZ, bearded patriarch of French music, composer of flamboyantly romantic operas and symphonic works, dies in his native mansion, Lanloup, not far from Guingamp, Côtes-du-Nord, Bretagne, at the age of 91.

24 NOVEMBER 1955

White Acacia, operetta in three acts by the Soviet composer Isaak DUNAYEVSKY (who died in Moscow on 25 July 1955), to a story of romantic love between a harpoonist and a girl radio operator on a Soviet whaling ship bound for the Antarctic, embellished by pseudo-tropical dance tunes characterizing the ship's passage through the equatorial zone, is produced posthumously in Moscow.

25 NOVEMBER 1955

Sixth Symphony by Walter PISTON, written in a distinct tonal idiom but devoid of an overt key signature, in four movements—(1) *Fluendo espressivo,* in sophisticated waltz time, opening with a permutated Bachian motto C-A-B-H and concluding with its conversion C-H-B-A; (2) *Leggerissimo vivace,* scherzo in 2/4 time, with muted trumpets contributing moments of jazzy syncopation; (3) *Adagio sereno,* with congested chromatic progressions alleviated by diatonic oxygenation, ending on an unadulterated B-A-C-H motto; (4) *Allegro energico,* a symphonic hallelujah in march time concluding on a focal A—is performed for the first time by the Boston Symphony Orchestra, as a commissioned work for its 75th anniversary, under the direction of Charles Munch.

26 NOVEMBER 1955

Grazina, symphonic ballad by the 60-year-old Ukrainian composer Boris LIATOSHINSKY, inspired by the poem by the great Polish writer Adam Mieckiewicz, descriptive of a 13th-century Polish girl who dons the armor of a friendly knight at night and perishes in a victorious combat against the invading crusaders, is performed for the first time simultaneously in Kiev and in Moscow.

27 NOVEMBER 1955

Arthur HONEGGER, French composer of noble gifts, who launched the first symphonic locomotive in his *Pacific 231*, and created a new type of the modern biblical and historical cantata in *Jeanne d'Arc au bûcher* and *Le Roi David*, whose musical language naturally absorbed dissonance as part of new euphony, dies in Paris at the age of 63.

30 NOVEMBER 1955

Josip SLAVENSKI, Yugoslav composer whose music presents native rhythms in modern dress, dies in Belgrade at the age of 59.

30 NOVEMBER 1955

Pipe Dream, musical play by Richard RODGERS, with book and lyrics by Oscar Hammerstein II, dealing with a vagrant girl who is saved from arrest by the madam of a fashionable bordello, and eventually finds happiness with a marine biologist, is produced in New York.

2 DECEMBER 1955

Third Symphony by Ernst TOCH, in three movements, *Molto Adagio*, *Andante tranquillo* and *Allegro impetuoso*, commissioned by the American Jewish Tercentenary Committee of Chicago, is performed for the first time by the Pittsburgh Symphony Orchestra. (It received the Pulitzer Prize in 1957.)

26 DECEMBER 1955

La Piccola Scala, a miniaturized adjunct of La Scala, is inaugurated in Milan with CIMAROSA's opera *Il Matrimonio segreto*.

26 DECEMBER 1955

Porgy and Bess, folk opera by George GERSHWIN, is performed for the first time in Russia, at the Leningrad Palace of Culture, by an all-Negro cast, the first American theatrical company to visit the Soviet Union.

31 DECEMBER 1955

Haru no Umi (*Sea at Springtime*), concerto for koto, flute and orchestra by the blind Japanese composer Michio MIYAGI, is performed for the first time by Shinichi Yuize, a member of the Kabuki Dance Group, as soloist on the koto, and the New York Philharmonic, André Kostelanetz conducting.

1956

3 JANUARY 1956

Alexandre GRETCHANINOFF, the last Mohican of the second generation of the Russian National School of composers, whose songs, imbued with the melodious melancholy of old Russia, have become perennial favorites, dies in New York, an expatriate for three decades, at the patriarchal age of 91.

5 JANUARY 1956

Violin Concerto by the 48-year-old Hungarian-born American composer Miklós RÓZSA, written in a brilliant Virtuoso style, replete with admissible modernities, and nontoxic polyharmonies, is performed for the first time by Jascha Heifetz with the Dallas Symphony Orchestra.

14 JANUARY 1956

Idyll of Theocritus for soprano and orchestra by the 59-year-old American composer Roger SESSIONS, to the text of an English translation of the second idyll by Theocritus, in which a Grecian damsel, deserted by her lover, manipulates, with the aid of Selene, a series of lunar invultuations to secure his return, set to music of impassioned austerity in a *sui generis* serial idiom, is performed for the first time in Louisville.

21 JANUARY 1956

On the occasion of the forthcoming bicentennial of MOZART's birth, Austria issues a commemorative stamp for 2 schillings 40 hellers with his image.

22 JANUARY 1956

Palamas Symphony for chorus and orchestra by the 72-year-old Greek composer Manolis KALOMIRIS, inspired by the poem of the modern Greek writer Kostis Palamas which pictures a decaying Balkan community revitalized by a masculine invasion of optimistic Gypsies, set to music with a profusion of exotic melorhythms accoutred in Italianate harmonies, is performed for the first time in Athens.

25 JANUARY 1956

Etruscan Concerto for orchestra, in three movements, by the Australian-born American composer Peggy GLANVILLE-HICKS, written in neo-archaic modalities purported to reflect the ethos of the ancient Etruscans, is performed for the first time in New York.

26 JANUARY 1956

Mtzyri, symphonic poem by the 31-year-old Georgian composer Otar TAKTAKISHVILI, inspired by a melodramatic tale of the Russian poet Mikhail Lermontov, descriptive of passionate mysteries in the forbidding chasms of the Caucasian mountains, is performed for the first time in Tbilisi.

27 JANUARY 1956

Erich KLEIBER, Austrian conductor, cultured interpreter of the classics and a valiant champion of modern music, who was the first to conduct Alban Berg's *Wozzeck*, dies in Zürich at the age of 65.

27 JANUARY 1956

On the bicentennial of MOZART's birth, West Germany and East Germany issue commemorative stamps bearing his likeness.

1 FEBRUARY 1956

Le Fou, opera in three acts by the 40-year-old French composer Marcel LANDOWSKI, dealing with the inventor of a powerful war weapon capable of destroying the besiegers of his city who refuses to divulge the secret of its manufacture to his concitoyens for fear that it would kill innocents as well as the guilty in the enemy camp, is produced in Nancy, France.

3 FEBRUARY 1956

Clarinet Concerto by Elie SIEGMEISTER, written in a vesuviatingly jazzy manner with nostalgic remissions in the blues tempo, is performed for the first time by the Oklahoma City Symphony, Guy Fraser Harrison conducting, with Earl Thomas as soloist.

13 FEBRUARY 1956

Peter Pan, symphonic fairy tale for orchestra by Ernst TOCH, inspired by J. M. Barrie's children's classic, in three sections reflecting in whimsical modalities and winged rhythms the adolescent antics of Peter Pan, is performed for the first time in Seattle.

14 FEBRUARY 1956

Zaria, opera in four acts by the 33-year-old Soviet composer Kirill MOLCHANOV, depicting in socialistically realistic modalities the revolutionary action on board the Russian cruiser Zaria (Dawn) in Petrograd harbor on the eve of the Soviet Revolution of October 1917, is produced in Perm.

15 FEBRUARY 1956

Symphony in E-Flat by Ernest BLOCH (completed on 8 March 1955), written in an energetically emotional style, in four movements—(1) *Tranquillo-Allegro deciso*, (2) *Allegro*, (3) *Andante*, (4) *Allegro deciso*—in cyclic construction, returning to the tonic base after a number of caracoles into distant keys, is performed for the first time in London.

15 FEBRUARY 1956

The Wife of Martin Guerre, opera by the 34-year-old American composer William BERGSMA, is produced in New York.

15 FEBRUARY 1956

Declamations for string orchestra and piano by Benjamin LEES is performed for the first time in Oklahoma City.

17 FEBRUARY 1956

Second Symphony by the 47-year-old Chilean composer Juan ORREGO-SALAS is performed for the first time in Minneapolis.

18 FEBRUARY 1956

Gustave CHARPENTIER, French composer whose "roman musical" *Louise* made history as the first French opera of the realistic school, dies in Paris at the patriarchal age of 95.

18 FEBRUARY 1956

Dr. Heidegger's Experiment, one-act opera by the American composer Sam RAPHLING, is produced in New York.

19 FEBRUARY 1956

Cello Concerto by the 32-year-old American composer Peter MENNIN is performed for the first time by Leonard Rose and the Juilliard School of Music Orchestra under the direction of Jean Morel, in New York.

23 FEBRUARY 1956

Leon KIRCHNER, 37-year-old American composer, plays with the New York Philharmonic Orchestra, Dmitri Mitropoulos conducting, the solo part in the first performance of his *Piano Concerto*, written in a functional neo-classical manner, in three movements, *Allegro*, *Adagio* and *Rondo*.

24 FEBRUARY 1956

The first performance is given in New York of the *Fifth Symphony* by Walter PISTON, commissioned by the Juilliard School of Music to commemorate the fiftieth anniversary of its foundation, written in a characteristic Pistonian Bostonian style and idiom, abstaining from using tonally explicit key signatures, but observing a sense of tonality, set in three symmetrically converging movements: (1) *Lento*, in rolling, barcarolling meter as an introduction to a propulsive, impulsive *Allegro con Spirito* soon initiating a deep, steep descent into an initial relented *Lento*; (2) *Adagio*, a dirge surging from the lower depths, embroidered with microrhythmic melismas, finally returning to the tenebrous caverns of the bass register; and (3) *Allegro lieto*, in prancing, dancing time in a mood of secular laetification in a clearly implied white key of perlucent C major. (Piston's *Sixth Symphony* received its first performance three months before, in Boston, on 25 November 1955.)

25 FEBRUARY 1956

Mario e il Mago, "choreographic action" in two acts by the 33-year-old Italian composer Franco MANNINO, to a scenario from a story of Thomas Mann taking place in an Italian spa in 1935, and dealing with the romantic competition between a balletmaster and a magician, is performed for the first time at La Scala in Milan.

25 FEBRUARY 1956

La Guerra, one-act opera by the 48-year-old Italian composer Renzo ROSSELLINI, to his own libretto portraying the horrible fate of a paralytic Italian mother with a Fascist-raped daughter and a Nazi-blinded son, is produced in Rome.

25 FEBRUARY 1956

Piano Concerto by the 30-year-old Vienna-born American composer Richard HOFFMANN, Schoenberg's last musical amanuensis in Los Angeles, thematically based on a dodecaphonic row and containing a rhythmic serialization, in international Morse code (.—..—.—.—.), of Mozart's scatological letter to his father dated 17 October 1777, and other verbal serialisms, is performed for the first time at the annual Contemporary Music Festival in Oberlin, Ohio.

2 MARCH 1956

Heitor VILLA-LOBOS conducts the Boston Symphony Orchestra in the world première of his *Eleventh Symphony*, in four movements, *Allegro moderato, Largo, Scherzo, Molto Allergo*.

9 MARCH 1956

Eugene GOOSSENS, English conductor of the Sydney Symphony Orchestra and director of the New South Wales State Conservatorium of Music is detained at Sydney Airport on the charge of importing 1,100 sexual photographs and other articles of an uninhibited nature into puritanical Australia, and in consequence is forced to resign both posts.

10 MARCH 1956

Séquence by the 28-year-old French composer Jean BARRAQUÉ, scored for soprano, piano, harp, violin, cello, celesta, glockenspiel, vibraphone, xylophone and percussion, to a French text translated from Nietzsche's philosophical works, in an atonal idiom in which the intervals of a tritone and a major seventh are the formative factors, is performed for the first time in Paris.

11 MARCH 1956

Sergei VASSILENKO, Russian composer of flamboyant symphonic and vocal music exuding the aura of oriental-ized Russianisms, dies in his native Moscow at the age of 83.

14 MARCH 1956

Symphonie 1953 by the 69-year-old Dutch modernist Daniel RUYNEMAN, in three movements, *Robusto e vivo, Largo, Allegro energico*, bearing a motto from François Villon, "Rien ne m'est sûr que la chose incertaine," with the opening theme built on consecutive perfect fourths, is performed for the first time in Utrecht.

14 MARCH 1956

Feria Magica for orchestra, by the 41-year-old Spanish-American composer Carlos SURINACH, is performed for the first time in Louisville.

15 MARCH 1956

My Fair Lady, musical play by Frederick LOEWE with lyrics by Alan Jay Lerner, adapted from George Bernard Shaw's play *Pygmalion*, in which a Cockney flower girl is transfigured into a modern Galatea by a fanatical phonetician and learns to enunciate the sentence "the rain in Spain stays mainly on the plain," with correct vowels, containing such ingratiating tunes as *I Could Have Danced All Night* and *I've Grown Accustomed to Her Face*, is produced in New York. (A preliminary performance of the play was given in New Haven on 4 February 1956.)

22 MARCH 1956

Porträttet, opera by the 63-year-old Swedish composer Hilding ROSENBERG, after Gogol's horror tale of a gold-laden portrait that comes to life to haunt its avaricious owner, is performed for the first time in concert form on the Stockholm Radio.

29 MARCH 1956

Don Juan de Mañara, radio opera by the 54-year-old French composer Henri TOMASI, is produced in Munich.

31 MARCH 1956

Comoedia de Christi Resurrectione, Easter passion play by Carl ORFF, scored for soloists, mixed chorus and children's voices, 3 pianos, 2 harps, 4 double basses and percussion, a surrealistic interlingual tale of the Resurrection, with historical planes translocated and parasynchronized, in which the Roman soldiers guarding the tomb are Bavarians, and the devil objurgates Christ in ecclesiastical Latin, is performed for the first time on the Munich Radio. (The first stage performance took place in Stuttgart on 21 April 1957.)

4 APRIL 1956

Symphony for Trombone and Orchestra by Ernest BLOCH, in three movements—(1) *Maestoso*, with the trombone solo making a series of eloquent declarations in quartal intervallic outcries; (2) *Agitato*, in which the trombone assumes the role of a prophet in exclamatory Hebraic incantations; (3) *Allegro deciso*, a rhetorical proclamation leading to a chromatic convergence to the cadential A major—is performed for the first time in Houston.

4 APRIL 1956

Fifth Symphony by the 49-year-old American composer Paul CRESTON, in three movements, *Con Moto*, flaunting the energy of monorhythmic challenge, *Largo*, expressive of passion, and *Maestoso-Allegro*, voicing poignant tenderness, the entire thematic material being derived from the initial subject by melorhythmic shifts, is performed for the first time in Washington.

7 APRIL 1956

Second Symphony by the 41-year-old American composer Gail KUBIK is performed for the first time in Louisville.

8 APRIL 1956

The Trial at Rouen, opera by the 43-year-old American composer Norman DELLO JOIO, a variant of his opera *Joan of Arc*, is performed for the first time on television by the National Broadcasting Company in New York.

12 APRIL 1956

First Symphony by the South African-born English composer John JOUBERT is performed for the first time in Hull, England.

13 APRIL 1956

Guillermo URIBE-HOLGUÍN, prime composer of Colombia, conducts in Bogotá the first performance of his *Fourth Symphony*.

16 APRIL 1956

Sixth Symphony (*Symphony for Winds*) by the 40-year-old American composer Vincent PERSICHETTI, in four classically arrayed movements, is performed for the first time by the Washington University Band in St. Louis.

21 APRIL 1956

Variations for Orchestra, a set by the 47-year-old American composer Elliott CARTER, based on the principle of topological congruity of thematic intervals, is performed for the first time in Louisville.

24 APRIL 1956

I Sette peccati, "musical mystery," with choreography and singing, by the 56-year-old Italian composer Antonio VERETTI, is produced at La Scala, in Milan.

26 APRIL 1956

First Piano Concerto by the 32-year-old Manchurian-born American composer of Russian parentage Benjamin LEES, couched in a civilized neo-classical manner vaccinated with immunologically prophylactic dissonances, is performed for the first time in Vienna.

2 MAY 1956

Eighth Symphony in D minor by Ralph VAUGHAN WILLIAMS, in four movements, of which the first, *Fantasia*, is a set of seven variations without a palpable theme, the second, *Scherzo alla marcia*, is an essay for wind instruments, the third, a *Cavatina*, a lyrical eclogue

for strings, and the finale, *Toccata*, a festival of saccadic sonorities enhanced by a proliferation of percussion, vibraphone, xylophone, gongs and bells, is performed for the first time in Manchester, England, under the direction of John Barbirolli.

3 MAY 1956

The Most Happy Fella, musical play by Frank LOESSER, to a story in which a senescent Californian wine grower, courting a restaurant waitress by mail, sends her a photograph of his handsome farmhand in lieu of that of his own unprepossessing self, and is distressed when she meets the proxy and becomes pregnant by him, set to music containing elements of grand opera and of Tin Pan Alley, and featuring the ingratiating love ballad *My Heart Is So Full of You*, is produced in New York.

6 MAY 1956

Sampiero Corso, lyric drama in three acts by the 54-year-old French composer Henri TOMASI, depicting in melodramatic colors the tempestuous career of the famous Corsican patriot who fought the encroachments of Genovese invaders in the 16th century, is produced in Bordeaux.

11 MAY 1956

Images of Youth, cantata in ten movements by the Polish-American composer Felix LABUNSKI, is performed for the first time in Cincinnati.

12 MAY 1956

On the occasion of the International Music Festival in Prague, Czechoslovakia issues postage stamps bearing portraits of MOZART (30 hellers), Joseph MYSLIVEČEK (45 hellers), and Jiří BENDA (60 hellers).

17 MAY 1956

Pantaloon, opera in three acts by the American composer Robert WARD, based on the play by Leonid Andreyev, *He Who Gets Slapped*, narrating the classically sad tale of a circus clown's infatuation for a bareback dancer, set to music in a sparse infra-modern triadically oriented idiom seasoned with euphonious dissonances, is performed for the first time by the Columbia University Opera Workshop in New York. (A revised version of the opera, under the title *He Who Gets Slapped*, was produced by the New York City Opera Company on 12 April 1959.)

19 MAY 1956

Seventh Symphony, the last work of the Czech composer Jaroslav ŘÍDKÝ, in four classically designed movements, conceived in a slightly modernized Dvořákian manner, devoid of key signatures, but opening and closing with a unison F sharp, is performed for the first time in Prague, a few weeks before Řídký's death on 14 August 1956.

20 MAY 1956

La Verité de Jeanne, oratorio by the 50-year-old French composer André JOLIVET, to the texts from the actual transcripts of the trial of *Joan of Arc*, is performed for the first time at the Festival of Domrémy, where she was born and where she first heard the acoustically implausible but subjectively convincing voices.

25 MAY 1956

Rona, opera in three acts by the 50-year-old German-born Croatian composer of Greek origin Boris PAPANDOPULO, dealing with the tragic love of a country girl for a non-peasant, is produced in Rijeka (Fiume).

27 MAY 1956

Igor STRAVINSKY's arrangement for chorus and orchestra of J. S. Bach's *Choral-Variationen über das Weihnachtslied* "Vom Himmel hoch da komm' ich her" is performed for the first time at the Ojai Festival, in Ojai, California.

30 MAY 1956

At a concert of electronic music presented at Cologne by the Westdeutscher Rundfunk the world premières of the following works are presented:

5 Stücke by the German theorist of modern musical trends Herbert EIMERT; *Doppelrohr* by the 28-year-old Swedish modernist Bengt HAMBRAEUS; *Klangfiguren II* by the geometrically inclined German composer Gottfried Michael KÖNIG; *Elektronische Komposition I* by the 58-year-old German composer of athematic, abstract and electronic music Hermann HEISS; *Interferenzen* by the 30-year-old German modernist Giselher KLEBE, portraying heterodynamic phenomena in wave mechanics; *Der Gesang der Jünglinge* by the German apostle of "total" music 27-year old Karlheinz STOCKHAUSEN, to the text from the Book of Daniel relating the miraculous survival of three monotheistic Hebrew youths in the midst of the Babylonian fiery turnace, in a polymetric and polydynamic setting with a voice singing topologically contorted and intervallically translocated infantiloquent rhymes antiphonally echoed by an undistorted children's choir subsequently translated by electronic manipulation to the infrasonic inaudible range; and *Spiritus Intelligentiae Sanctus* by Ernst KRENEK, containing an electronic interlude in a scale of 13 equal degrees, with canonic imitation obtained by rerecording the original materials at different speeds, thus raising or lowering the pitch, with the macrorhythm governing the general architectonic scheme of the work and auxiliary microrhythms determining the duration of thematic tones.

3 JUNE 1956

The 30th Festival of the International Society for Contemporary Music opens in Stockholm with the following program:

Concerto da camera for flute, English horn and string orchestra by Arthur HONEGGER, in three movements, written in 1948; *Suite* for brass instruments, percussion and string orchestra by the 24-year-old Swiss composer Rudolf KELTERBORN, in four neo-baroque movements; *Spisak (Inventory)*, 13 sketches for 13 performers, including two female voices, by the Yugoslav composer Dušan RADIĆ, surrealistically depicting animals, plants and pieces of furniture; *Sinfonia da camera* by the Swedish composer Sven Erik BÄCK, thematically built on a liberated dodecaphonic formula and developed in a neo-classical style; *El amor pasa* for soprano, flute and chamber orchestra by the Finnish composer Ahti SONNINEN, to texts from Spanish poems; and *Triple Concerto* for oboe, clarinet and bassoon in three movements by the Danish neo-baroque composer Niels Viggo BENTZON.

4 JUNE 1956

A Vision of Aeroplanes, motet for chorus and organ by Ralph VAUGHAN WILLIAMS, to a text from the Book of Ezekiel, describing the prophet's vision of manned flying machines propelled by a wheel in the middle of a wheel, is performed for the first time in London.

4 JUNE 1956

At the second concert of the 30th Festival of the International Society for Contemporary Music in Stockholm the following program of chamber music is presented:

Second String Quartet by the Corsican-born French composer Henri MARTELLI; *Kontra-Punkte* by Karlheinz STOCKHAUSEN, scored for 10 instruments, written in a pragmatic serialistic idiom calculated to correlate the factors of pitch, duration, dynamic strength and instrumental color in both horizontal (melodic) and vertical (contrapuntal) aspects; *Chorale-Motet* for chorus a cappella by the Austrian composer Anton HEILLER, written in a neo-ecclesiastic modal idiom; *Quintet* for wind instruments by the Norweigan composer Finn MORTENSEN, in three movements cast in a neo-classical form; *Violin Sonata* in three movements by the 21-year-old Icelandic composer Leifur THÓRARINSSON; and *Sixth String Quartet* in four movements by the dean of Swedish composers Hilding ROSENBERG.

5 JUNE 1956

At the third concert of the 30th Festival of the International Society for Contemporary Music in Stockholm the following program of orchestral music is presented:

Variations for Orchestra by the 26-year-old New Zealand composer Barry MOSS; *Ectoplasm* for electronic instruments, percussion and strings by the 27-year-old Japanese composer Toshiro MAYAZUMI, intended to effect a synthesis of preternatural psychic phenomena, Japanese Zen philosophy and Occidental ultra-modern techniques; *Idyll of Theocritus* for soprano and orchestra by Roger SESSIONS (first performed in Louisville on 14 January 1956); *Violin Concerto* in three movements by the 46-year-old Italian composer Mario PERAGALLO, written in 1953 and first performed at a contest in Rome in 1954, at which it carried the first prize; and *Fourth Symphony* by the 51-year-old Dutch composer Guillaume LANDRÉ, subtitled *Symphonie concertante*, in five movements, written in the dodecaphonic technique.

7 JUNE 1956

At the fourth concert of the 30th Festival of the International Society for Contemporary Music in Stockholm, the following program of Swedish music is given:

Ritornell for Orchestra by Ingvar LIDHOLM, in four movements, in which the term Ritornell indicates the return of the basic dodecaphonic theme in the form of an inversion or cancrizans; *Cantata* for soprano, flute, clarinet, cello and piano by Hilding HALLNÄS; *Missa Breves* for chorus a capella by Lars Erik LARSSON; and *Sinfonia espressiva*, in four movements by Gösta NYSTROEM.

8 JUNE 1956

At the fifth concert of the 30th Festival of the International Society for Contemporary Music in Stockholm, the following program of chamber music is presented:

Second String Quartet by the 44-year-old Canadian composeress Barbara PENTLAND; *Trio* for flute, oboe and bass clarinet by

Joaquín Homs OLLER of Spain; *Psalm VIII* for soprano, flute, cello and piano by the 56-year-old Italian composer Luigi CORTESE; *Elegia appassionata* for piano, violin, and cello by the 30-year-old German composer Giselher KLEBE; and *Second String Quartet* by Alan RAWSTHORNE of England.

9 JUNE 1956

The French Government issues a 15-franc postage stamp in honor of Maurice RAVEL, bearing his portrait.

9 JUNE 1956

Grozovan, opera in four acts by the 44-year-old Moldavian composer David GERSHFELD, to a libretto in the Moldavian language, dealing with the patriotic uprising of native guardsmen against the Turkish overlords of Moldavia in the middle of the 18th century, with a central dramatic episode touching on the fate of the heroic Grozovan and his young bride who is monstrously coveted by a lecherous janizary, set to music with a profusion of asymmetric Balkan melorhythms, is produced for the first time at the opening of the National Moldavian Theater in Kishinev, the capital city of the Soviet Socialist Republic of Moldavia.

10 JUNE 1956

At the sixth and last concert of the 30th Festival of the International Society for Contemporary Music in Stockholm, the following program of orchestral music is given:

Sinfonia concertante in five movements by the foremost Austrian theoretician and practitioner of dodecaphonic music Hanns JELINEK; *Violin Concerto* in four movements by the English composer Benjamin FRANKEL dedicated "to the memory of the six million" with the mournful motto of the falling minor second symbolizing the tragic fate of the Jews murdered by the Nazis; *Music for Orchestra* by the French composeress Marcelle DE MANZIARLY, in four movements set in the order of a classical suite; *Piano Concerto* by the Russian-born American composer Alexei HAIEFF, in three movements, centering on the key of C major with pandiatonic ramifications; and the coloristic *Pampeana No. 3* by the Argentine composer Alberto GINASTERA (first performed in Louisville on 20 October 1954), painting the pampas in palpitating melorhythms and modernistic polyharmonies.

10 JUNE 1956

Four hundred years have passed since the death in Magdeburg of the erudite German music theorist Martin AGRICOLA.

15 JUNE 1956

Passacaille for orchestra by Maurice JARRE, written in memory of Arthur Honegger, using the musical letters (H - - e g g e -) in Honegger's name in the principal subject, is performed for the first time at the Music Festival in Strasbourg.

17 JUNE 1956

Der Sturm, magic fairy tale in three acts, by Frank MARTIN, to a German libretto translated from the French version of Shakespeare's play *The Tempest,* written in an economically tonal idiom, with the application of polytri-

adic progressions, and ending in clear F-sharp major, is produced in Vienna.

21 JUNE 1956

Cain and Abel, electronic ballet by the Dutch composer Henk BADINGS, depicting the story of the first human murder with the aid of five acoustical layers and an optical siren which transforms an oscillating beam of light passed through a rotating disc to a photo-electric cell into melodies of varied timbres, with numerous other sonic effects produced by intermodulators of sinusoidal tones, is performed in The Hague for the first time.

23 JUNE 1956

Reinhold GLIÈRE, Russian composer of remote French extraction, who excelled in the melodious genre of harmoniously fashioned songs and whose grandiose symphony *Ilya Murometz* portrays the legendary giant of Russian folklore in grandisonant splendor, dies in Moscow at the age of 81.

25 JUNE 1956

Fifth Piano Concerto by Darius MILHAUD is performed for the first time at the Lewisohn Stadium, New York, with Stell Andersen as soloist and Pierre Monteux conducting the Stadium Symphony Orchestra.

26 JUNE 1956

Michio MIYAGI, 62-year-old blind Japanese virtuoso player on the koto, who composed a thousand pieces for it, dies in a railroad accident near Tokyo.

27 JUNE 1956

Pană Lesnea Rusalim, opera in three acts by the 47-year-old Rumanian composer Paul CONSTANTINESCU, dealing with an early 19th-century peasant girl participant in a Rumanian rebellion against the Turkish overlords, is performed for the first time in Bucharest.

7 JULY 1956

The Ballad of Baby Doe, folk opera in two parts by the 62-year-old American composer Douglas MOORE, to a libretto drawn from the real story of a historic personage named Elizabeth McCourt Doe, "the miner's sweetheart" of the American West, second wife of the "Silver Dollar King" Horace Tabor who built a fortune on silver but lost it when the U.S. went on the gold standard and died destitute in 1899, set to music in a melodious Americanistic idiom, imparting a flavor of authenticity by using actual tunes of the period, modernistically enlivened by shrewd rhythmic translocation and euphoniously dissonant counterpoint while maintaining a fine contrast of lyrical arias, dramatic duets, and individualized vocal ensembles, and further enhancing its realistic sense of history by introducing President Chester A. Arthur and silver-throated William Jennings Bryan singing of the economic glories of silver dollars, is performed for the first time at the Tabor Opera House in Central City, Colorado (elevation 8,500 feet) where the real Baby Doe luxuriated in the golden era of her silver prosperity, near Leadville (elevation 11,500 feet), where she spent 36 long years after her husband's death and was found frozen to death in a shack on 7 March 1935.

20 JULY 1956

The postal authorities of the German Democratic Republic (East Germany) issue two stamps, of the values of 10 and 20 pfennigs, commemorating the centennial of SCHUMANN's death, featuring a portrait of Schumann superimposed, through a fantastic dereliction of scholarship, on the reproduction of a few bars from Schubert's setting of Goethe's *Wanderers Nachtlied.* (The issue was withdrawn as soon as the misattribution was discovered, and a new set of stamps, with a musical example from a Schumann work, was issued on 8 October 1956.)

29 JULY 1956

The first demonstration of music produced by stalactites is given in the 65-acre Luray Caverns in Virginia on the Great Stalacpipe Organ by Leland W. SPRINKLE, its inventor, playing the Lutheran chorale *A Mighty Fortress Is Our God,* with five miles of wire electrically connecting the plungers that strike the stalactites tuned by careful grinding, and stereophonic effects achieved by staggered stalactites in natural cavernous air-conditioning maintaining the constant temperature of 54° Fahrenheit.

1 AUGUST 1956

Howard BRUBECK, 40-year-old Californian composer, conducts the San Diego Symphony in the first performance of his *Four Dialogues for Jazz Combo and Orchestra,* with the combo (combination of piano, alto saxophone, drums and doublebass) performing improvised patterns of notes and rhythms in jazzily logical coordination with the pre-composed orchestral parts, mostly adhering to metrical periods in powers of 2 (2^2, 2^3, 2^4, 2^5 bars each), and the last section, *Blues* in a 12-bar pattern.

5 AUGUST 1956

Second Symphony by the 32-year-old American composer Ned ROREM is performed for the first time at La Jolla, California.

9 AUGUST 1956

Bodas de Sangre, opera in three acts by the 61-year-old Argentinian composer Juan José CASTRO, to a libretto after the mystical play *Blood Wedding* of Federico García Lorca, is performed for the first time in Buenos Aires.

18 AUGUST 1956

On the Nature of Things, a spatial work by the 42-year-old American composer Henry BRANT, scored for string orchestra, wind instruments and glockenspiel, is performed for the first time in Bennington, Vermont.

20 AUGUST 1956

Edinburgh Overture by the 65-year-old English composer Sir Arthur BLISS, is performed for the first time as a festive introduction to the Edinburgh Festival of Music and Drama.

28 AUGUST 1956

Frescoes of Piero della Francesca, a symphonic suite in three movements by Bohuslav MARTINŮ, reflecting the deep veneration for the austere Italian Renaissance painter, is performed for the first time in Salzburg.

3 SEPTEMBER 1956

To commemorate the tenth anniversary of the death of the German operetta composer Paul LINCKE (1866–1946), the government of West Germany issues a 20-pfennig stamp reproducing his portrait against the background of a musical quotation from his famous march song *Das macht die Berliner Luft* from his operetta *Berliner Luft.*

5 SEPTEMBER 1956

Fourth Piano Concerto by Sergei PROKOFIEV for left hand alone, originally commissioned by the amputated Austrian pianist Paul Wittgenstein, but never played by him, in four movements—(1) *Vivace,* a virtuoso type of toccata artfully confined to the left-hand range of the solo part; (2) *Andante,* a tranquil essay making use of the entire keyboard; (3) *Moderato,* a vivacious scherzo marked by saltatory melodic exuberance; (4) *Finale,* cyclic metempsychosis of the initial *Vivace*—is performed for the first time in Berlin, 25 years after its composition, by the one-armed pianist Siegfried Rapp (who, like Paul Wittgenstein, lost his right arm from a shrapnel wound on the Russian front in World War I.)

6 SEPTEMBER 1956

An audience of 2,200 persons gathers in the concert hall of the Leningrad Conservatory to hear the Boston Symphony Orchestra, conducted by Charles Munch (the first American orchestra to play in the Soviet Union), in a program opening with the Soviet and American national anthems, and including BEETHOVEN's *Eroica,* Walter PISTON's *Sixth Symphony* and the Second Suite from RAVEL's *Daphnis and Chloe,* arousing spontaneous enthusiasm expressed in tumultuous applause, forcing the conductor to break his ingrained opposition to the playing of encores, and to oblige the audience with the rendition of *L'Apprenti Sorcier* by Paul DUKAS.

11 SEPTEMBER 1956

Concerto for harmonica and orchestra by the 57-year-old Russian-born composer Alexander TCHEREPNIN, is performed for the first time at the Venice Festival.

13 SEPTEMBER 1956

Igor STRAVINSKY conducts in the basilica of San Marco in Venice the first performance of his *Canticum Sacrum ad Honorem Sancti Nominis,* composed in the spirit of a devout offering on the bimillennium of St. Mark, patron saint of Venice, scored for tenor, baritone, chorus and orchestra, consisting of an introductory Dedicatio and five sections—(1) *Euntes in Mundum,* (2) *Surge aquilo,* (3) *Ad Tres Virtutes Hortationes,* (4) *Brevis Motus Cantilenae,* (5) *Illi autem profecti sunt*—set to Latin texts from the Vulgate, the three inner sections being the first works composed by Stravinsky entirely in a strict dodecaphonic technique, while the non-dodecaphonic sections 1 and 5 stand in palindromic relation to each other.

MURDER IN THE CATHEDRAL. (*Time* magazine headline for review of the concert)

23 SEPTEMBER 1956

König Hirsch, opera in three acts by the 30-year-old German composer Hans Werner HENZE, after Carlo Gozzi's play *Il Re Cervo*, in which a king dethroned by an impostor lives in the deep forest as a stag, but reassumes his human form, overthrows the usurper and returns to his people as their rightful king, scored for singers, speakers, chorus, and orchestra, is produced in Berlin.

25 SEPTEMBER 1956

Johannesburg Festival Overture by William WALTON, a jubilee piece written for the 70th anniversary of Johannesburg as a hedonistic rondo, devoid of an explicit key signature but eloquently oriented towards a focal D, making use of genuine South African tunes, is performed for the first time in Johannesburg, South Africa.

2 OCTOBER 1956

Ruth, one-act opera by Lennox BERKELEY, to a libretto after the Book of Ruth, is produced in London.

4 OCTOBER 1956

Fourth Piano Concerto, subtitled *Incantation*, by Bohuslav MARTINU, is performed for the first time at the Metropolitan Museum of Art, New York City, with Rudolf Firkušny as soloist and Leopold Stokowski conducting.

6 OCTOBER 1956

Piano Concerto by the 38-year-old Austrian composer Gottfried VON EINEM, in three cyclic movements, *Molto moderato*, *Adagio* and *Con spirito*, written in a neo-baroque idiom spiced by non-toxic dissonances, is performed for the first time in Hamburg.

10 OCTOBER 1956

The first "Warsaw Autumn" International Festival of Contemporary Music opens in Warsaw, inaugurating a series of concerts concluding on 21 October 1956, presenting works by STRAVINSKY, SCHOENBERG, Alban BERG, Béla BARTÓK, SZYMANOWSKI, RAVEL, HONEGGER, ENESCO, Benjamin BRITTEN, SHOSTAKOVICH, KHACHATURIAN, MIASKOVSKY, PROKOFIEV, Jacques IBERT, Darius MILHAUD, Georges AURIC, Henri DUTILLEUX, André JOLIVET, Jean MARTINON, Jean-Louis MARTINET, Olivier MESSIAEN, Henri BARRAUD, Leoš JANÁČEK, Bohuslav MARTINU, Lázló LAJTHA, and a number of contemporary Polish composers: Grazyna BACEWICZ, Tadeusz BAIRD, Andrzej DOBROWOLSKI, Wojciech KILAR, Stefan KISIELEWSKI, Witold LUTOSLAWSKI, Artur MALAWSKI, Zygmunt MYCIELSKI, Piotr PERKOWSKI, Theodor ROGALSKI, Kazimierz SEROCKI, Stanislaw SKROWACZEWSKI, Michal SPISAK, Boleslaw SZABELSKI, Antoni SZALOWSKI, Zbigniew TURSKI, Stanislaw WIECHOWICZ, Stanislaw WISLOCKI, and Boleslaw WOYTOWICZ.

10 OCTOBER 1956

The Belgian Congo and Ruanda-Urundi issue sets of stamps commemorating the bicentennial of the birth of MOZART.

12 OCTOBER 1956

Lorenzo PEROSI, elective composer of several pontiffs, whose professed goal was to recreate the reverential and scholarly spirit of Palestrina in his own oratorios, which he often performed at the Vatican, but whose recurrent mental aberrations interrupted his ecclesiastical and musical activities, dies in Rome at the age of 83.

14 OCTOBER 1956

Third Symphony by Alan HOVHANESS is performed for the first time by the Symphony of the Air in New York, Leopold Stokowski conducting.

17 OCTOBER 1956

Fourth Symphony by the 51-year-old Soviet composer Dmitri KABALEVSKY, in four traditional movements outlining a dramaturgic scenario of dialectic conflicts and an ultimate festive synthesis—(1) *Lento*, an evocatively bucolic introduction to the mainstream of a bithematically developed *Allegro molto;* (2) *Largo*, a solemn procession with the undertones of an undecided struggle; (3) *Allegretto capriccioso*, a humanistic scherzo in cyclic rondo form; (4) *Allegro*, a finale animated by the rhythms of a vigorous march reinforced by a masculine fugato—is performed for the first time in Moscow.

18 OCTOBER 1956

Potrait for violin and orchestra by the American composer Bernard ROGERS is performed for the first time in Cleveland.

18 OCTOBER 1956

The Sweet Psalmist of Isreal by the 59-year-old Israeli composer Paul BEN-HAIM (who Hebraized his original German name Frankenburger), in three sections—(1) *David Before Saul*, for harpischord and wind instruments, representing David's playing upon a lyre to pacify King Saul; (2) *Invocation*, for harp solo and strings, reflecting the spirit of the Lord speaking through David; (3) *Song of Degrees*, a set of variations for harpsichord, harp and orchestra—is performed for the first time in Tel Aviv.

19 OCTOBER 1956

Pokondirena tikva (Preening Pumpkin), comic opera in three acts by the 54-year-old Yugoslav composer Mihovil LOGAR, to a libretto recounting the absurd behavior of a self-inflated matron in a provincial central European town, set to music in the manner of a Viennese operetta, is performed for the first time in Belgrade.

21 OCTOBER 1956

Two one-act operas, *Unexpected Visitor* and *The Two Impostors*, by the 41-year-old Czech-born American composer Leslie KONDOROSSY, are produced in Cleveland.

21 OCTOBER 1956

The Unicorn, the Gorgon and the Manticore, a madrigal fable for chorus, 10 dancers and nine instruments by Gian Carlo MENOTTI, subtitled *The Three Sundays of a Poet*, to his own libretto descriptive of a magically endowed poet, who thrice emerges from his seclusion on Sundays, leading successively a promenade with a pet unicorn, a gorgon and a manticore, and creating such a demand among local women to obtain similar pets, that the populace is driven to distraction, set to music in a translucidly euphonious manner, making use of dramatic dissonances to point the surrealistic quality of the tale, is performed for the first time at the Library of Congress, in Washington, as a commissioned work by the Elizabeth Sprague Coolidge Foundation.

21 OCTOBER 1956

Second Symphony in D minor by the Rumanian composer Sigismond TODUŢA is performed for the first time in Cluj.

22 OCTOBER 1956

In the Drought, opera by the 29-year-old South African composer John JOUBERT, is performed for the first time in Johannesburg.

22 OCTOBER 1956

Déploration de Tonton, Chien Fidèle, solo cantata for voice and orchestra by Jean FRANÇAIX, deploring the death of a faithful dog named Tonton in somber neo-medieval modalities, is performed for the first time in Paris.

24 OCTOBER 1956

At the opening of the concert series Musik der Zeit at Cologne, the world première is given of *Il Canto Sospeso* (*Broken Song*) for three voices, chorus and orchestra by Luigi NONO, to the texts selected from letters written by members of European resistance groups in Nazi-occupied countries condemned to death, among them a 14-year-old Greek schoolboy and two young Russian girls, set to music in the manner of a modern litany, making use of the hoquet technique, in which words, broken into syllables, are given separately to different voices creating an anguished effect of human discontinuity, employing as serial determinants the row derived from the horizontalization of the GROSSMUTTERAKKORD consisting of all 12 different tones of the chromatic scale and all 11 different intervals and the Fibonacci series in which each number is the sum of the two preceding numbers.

26 OCTOBER 1956

Walter GIESEKING, eloquent master of the piano, born of German parents in Lyon, France, a superlative interpreter of German classics and French impressionists, dies in London at the age of 60.

30 OCTOBER 1956

Composition No. 6 aux objets sonores by the 33-year-old Belgian composer Karel GOEYVAERTS, an electronic montage based on a mode of 180 units of duration, resulting in such time signatures as 11/4 + 1/8 + 1/64, with this temporal-tonal continuum being subdivided into five sonorous agglomerations, is performed for the first time on the Brussels Radio.

30 OCTOBER 1956

Piano Concerto by the 51-year-old British composer Sir Michael TIPPETT is performed for the first time in Birmingham.

10 NOVEMBER 1956

Hécube, opera in two acts by the 46-year-old French composer Jean MARTINON, is performed for the first time in Strasbourg.

12 NOVEMBER 1956

Irma la Douce, comedy with music by Marguerite MONNOT, in which a Montmartre *poule* supports an indigent art student in his Paris studio out of her illicit earnings, with surrealistic developments ensuing when he grows a beard and masquerades as her maquereau and after a pogonotomy accuses the artist, i.e., himself, of killing the pimp, his alter ego, receives a life sentence for this pseudonymous ipsocidal crime, but escapes, returns to Sweet Irma and discloses his true artistic identity, is produced in Paris.

15 NOVEMBER 1956

Americana, a symphonic pastiche of American tunes, from old balladry to jazz, by the 72-year-old American composer Louis GRUENBERG, is performed for the first time in Cleveland.

16 NOVEMBER 1956

Two symphonic poems by the 70-year-old Belgian neo-romanticist Robert HERBERIGS, *Les Quatres Saisons* (after Breughel) and *La petite Sirène* (after Hans Christian Andersen) are performed for the first time in Brussels.

18 NOVEMBER 1956

The Men of Blackmoor, sociological opera in three acts by the 55-year-old English composer Alan BUSH, to a libretto by his wife Nancy Bush, dealing with a strike of English mine workers in the early period of industrial expansion, with a tragic romance developing between a downtrodden miner and the owner's liberal daughter, set to music in the spirit of socialist realism and harmonized in broad triadic modalities, is produced for the first time in Weimar, in the German version, under the title *Die Männer von Blackmoor.*

21 NOVEMBER 1956

Third Symphony by the Swedish composer Allan PETTERSSON is performed for the first time in Göteborg.

23 NOVEMBER 1956

Études pour orchestra à cordes, a symphonic suite for strings by Frank MARTIN, is performed for the first time in Basel.

24 NOVEMBER 1956

Guido CANTELLI, 36-year-old Italian conductor whose great talent earned for him the appellation "piccolo Toscanini," dies in an airplane crash at Orly, near Paris, en route to America to conduct a series of concerts with the New York Philharmonic.

29 NOVEMBER 1956

Bells Are Ringing, musical comedy by Jule STYNE, dealing with a sympathetic telephone switchboard operator who invades the apartment of a neurotic playwright and provides the feminine ministrations he physiologically and psychologically needs to finish his play, is produced in New York.

1 DECEMBER 1956

Candide, musical comedy by Leonard BERNSTEIN based on Voltaire's novella retailing the extraordinary adventures of an unregenerate idealist who retains his optimism through all the tortuous peripeteia during his forced peregrinations, set to music with a sense of hedonistic persiflage, and incorporating parodies on classical dance music, as well as the first detected 12-tone row in any musical comedy (in the introduction to the second act), is produced in New York. (A new redaction of Leonard Bernstein's *Candide,* as an "opera house version," with considerable changes in the libretto, was produced by the New York City Opera on 13 October 1982.)

4 DECEMBER 1956

The Intruder, one-act opera by the 32-year-old Vienna-born composer Robert STARER, is performed for the first time in New York.

14 DECEMBER 1956

Anabasis, cantata by the 40-year-old Swedish composer Karl-Birger BLOMDAHL, after Xenophon's classic battle epic, is performed for the first time in Stockholm.

14 DECEMBER 1956

The Open Window, opera by the 35-year-old British composer Malcolm ARNOLD, is produced in London.

26 DECEMBER 1956

1804, cantata by the Serbian composer Božidar TRUDIĆ, written to commemorate the sesquicentennial of the Serbian uprising against the Turkish janizaries, set in Slavic diatonic modalities and nutritiously triadic harmonies and containing recitatives to the accompaniment of the Balkan instrument gusli, is performed for the first time in Sarajevo.

26 DECEMBER 1956

Spartak, ballet by Aram KHACHATURIAN, to a scenario glorifying the Roman gladiator Spartacus who led the slaves in a temporarily successful uprising in 73–71 B.C., but was eventually defeated and killed, set to music in a series of dramatic numbers, abounding in marching rhythms and colorful harmonies rooted in firm pedal points, with spacious melodies and chromatic rivulets forming gratifying contrasts, is performed for the first time in Leningrad.

29 DECEMBER 1956

The Rumanian government issues two stamps of 55 bani and of 1.75 lei in honor of Georges ENESCO, the prime modern Rumanian composer who died in Paris on 4 May 1955.

30 DECEMBER 1956

Krakatuk, fantastic opera in three acts by the 60-year-old Polish composer Tadeusz SZELIGOWSKI, after E.T.A. Hoffmann's fairy tale *The Nutcracker* with the action transferred to old Warsaw and centered on the search, eventually successful after many an eerie peripeteia, of the magic nut Krakatuk, written in an ingratiatingly infantiloquent idiom, set in nutritious triadic harmonies, and spiced with non-toxic chromatic condiments, is produced in Gdańsk.

1957

1 JANUARY 1957

The Prince of the Pagodas, a ballet by Benjamin BRITTEN, is performed for the first time in London.

10 JANUARY 1957

Caino, one-act opera by the 74-year-old Italian composer Felice LATTUADA, after Byron's poem, is produced at La Scala, Milan.

11 JANUARY 1957

Eighth Symphony by the 49-year-old Java-born Dutch composer Henk BADINGS is performed for the first time in Hannover, Germany.

16 JANUARY 1957

Arturo TOSCANINI, "The Maestro," sublime Italian conductor whose fanatically meticulous interpretations of great musical masterworks and flaming devotion to his art set the loftiest standard of orchestral and operatic perfection, dies in his sleep at 8:40 A.M. in New York, a few weeks before his 90th birthday.

20 JANUARY 1957

Declaration, symphonic narrative by the 43-year-old American composer Morton GOULD, scored for two narrators, speaking chorus and orchestra, to the text of the

500   20 January 1957

Declaration of Independence, is performed for the first time by the National Symphony Orchestra, Howard Mitchell conducting, at the Inaugural Concert of the second Eisenhower administration held in Constitution Hall, Washington, D.C. (*A Declaration Suite* extracted from this work in five movements, *Liberty Bell, Midnight Ride, Concord Bridge, Summer '76,* and *Celebration,* was first performed by the Symphony of the Air, New York, on 14 February 1957.)

25 JANUARY 1957
Cello Concerto by William WALTON, in three movements, *Moderato, Allegro appassionato* and *Epilogue,* in which the interval of a major seventh governs melodic and harmonic parameters, is performed for the first time by Gregor Piatigorsky, by whom it was commissioned, and the Boston Symphony Orchestra, Charles Munch conducting.

26 JANUARY 1957
Dialogues des Carmélites, opera in three acts by Francis POULENC, dealing with the martyrdom of Carmelite nuns during the French Revolution, set to music in a reverential sentiment, with devout accents of Latin hymns and the turmoil of the revolutionary populace standing in dramatic contrast, culminating in the horrifying stroke of the guillotine, is produced at La Scala, Milan, with an Italian libretto translated from a French play adapted from an unproduced motion picture based on a German novel.

30 JANUARY 1957
Aculeo, symphonic suite by Alfonso LETELIER of Chile, is performed for the first time in Louisville.

1 FEBRUARY 1957
First Symphony by the 36-year-old American pianist and conductor Leo SMIT, in four neo-classical movements, is performed for the first time by the Boston Symphony Orchestra, conducted by Charles Munch.

2 FEBRUARY 1957
Jekyll and Hyde Variations for orchestra by Morton GOULD, portraying in an artfully atonal vein the mutation of a humane physician into a bestial murderer by way of a fugally agitated stretto and schizophrenically waltzing memories, is performed by the New York Philharmonic, Dimitri Mitropoulos conducting.

7 FEBRUARY 1957
TCHAIKOVSKY's *Symphony in E-Flat Major,* integrated and collated from uncoordinated sketches, is performed for the first time in Moscow. (The material from the symphony was used by Tchaikovsky in other works: the first movement in the *Third Piano Concerto;* two other movements in *Andante* and *Finale,* op. 79; another movement became *Scherzo-Fantasy,* op. 72)

9 FEBRUARY 1957
Mother Margarita, opera by the Yugoslav composer Krsto ODAK, is performed for the first time in Zagreb.

10 FEBRUARY 1957
La Grande Bretèche, television opera, after Balzac, by the 32-year-old American composer Stanley HOLLINGSWORTH, is performed for the first time by the National Broadcasting Company Television in New York.

11 FEBRUARY 1957
Great River (The Rio Grande), symphonic poem for orchestra and narrator by the 58-year-old American composer Ernst BACON, in twelve movements, to a text by the American novelist Paul Horgan, tracing the flow of the Rio Grande from its sources in New Mexico to the Gulf of Mexico, is performed for the first time in Dallas.

16 FEBRUARY 1957
Beg Bajazid, opera by the 45-year-old Slovak composer Ján CIKKER, dealing with a Turkish-reared Slovak boy who at the age of thirty becomes commander of an Ottoman punitive battalion in his native village and cruelly carries its entire population into slavery, discovering that his own old mother was among his victims, the realization of which enormity makes him abandon his promising military career and return to Slovakia to fight his former masters, set to music with a proliferation of Slavic melorhythms set in polytriadic harmonies, is produced in Bratislava.

16 FEBRUARY 1957
Josef HOFMANN, great romantic Polish-born pianist, who began his career as a child prodigy (when he toured America in 1887, the Boston Society for Prevention of Cruelty to Children succeeded in preventing pianistic cruelty to him, forcing a temporary suspension of his career), and an affable composer of unpretentious romantic trifles under the nom de plume Dvorsky, a Russian equivalent of the German word Hofmann, i.e. yardman, dies in Los Angeles at the age of 81.

19 FEBRUARY 1957
Maskal, symphonic suite by the Yugoslav composer Rudolf BRUČI (the title is derived from the Ethiopian folk festival of flowers), in three movements, is performed for the first time in Belgrade.

23 FEBRUARY 1957
La Donna è mobile, opera buffa by Riccardo MALIPIERO, dodecaphonic nephew of Gian Francesco Malipiero, the title alluding with ironic condescension to the famous aria from Verdi's *Rigoletto,* is performed for the first time in Milan.

23 FEBRUARY 1957
Ethel LEGINSKA, 70-year-old English-born pianist, composeress and conductoress (her real name was Liggins, but she adopted a Polish feminine surname, to improve her chances of success in a musical career), conducts in Los Angeles the world première of her opera *The Rose and the Ring* (after Thackeray's story).

24 FEBRUARY 1957

Lydian Ode, symphonic essay by Paul CRESTON, set in a mournful Lydian mode, is performed for the first time by the Wichita Symphony Orchestra as a commissioned work in memory of the donor's pianist sister.

26 FEBRUARY 1957

Sinfonia visionaria (*Ninth Symphony*), "in modo di rondo espansivo," by the Swedish composer Kurt ATTERBERG, scored for mezzo soprano, baritone, chorus and orchestra, is performed for the first time anywhere in Helsinki.

28 FEBRUARY 1957

Third Symphony by the 42-year-old American composer Gail KUBIK, with its thematic material extracted from his film music, in three movements—(1) *Slowly, broadly,* containing a long trumpet cadenza; (2) *Slowly, sadly;* (3) *Masquerade,* a vivacious polytonal charade—is performed for the first time by the New York Philharmonic, Dimitri Mitropoulos conducting.

28 FEBRUARY 1957

Sven-Erik BÄCK, 37-year-old Swedish composer, conducts at the Swedish Radio in Stockholm the first performance of his radio opera *Tranfjädrarna* (*Crane Feathers*), in one act and five tableaux, to a libretto after a Japanese Noh drama, in which a captive girlcrane sheltered by a farmer makes exquisite fabric for him from her own gossamer feathers, but flies away when he breaks his solemn promise never to look at her while she works when she assumes an aviohuman appearance, with her ornitho-antropoheterogenation represented by an optimistic dodecaphonic series, containing some triadic elements within a stark ambience of monodic ostinati and tintinnabulating dynamics. (The first stage performance was conducted by Bäck at the Swedish Royal Opera in Stockholm on 9 February 1958.)

28 FEBRUARY 1957

Ian PARROTT, 40-year-old British composer, conducts at the University College of Wales in Aberystwyth the concert version of his two-act opera *The Black Ram,* to a libretto in the Welsh language, dealing with an 18th-century baronet who drops his prize ram down the chimney of a stubborn Welshman when the latter refuses to sell his land, charges him with theft and gets him hanged in 1762, set to music with melorhythmic materials drawn from Welsh folk songs.

2 MARCH 1957

Wild Bara, opera in three acts by the 68-year-old Russian composer Anatoly ALEXANDROV, in which the proletarianized daughter of a disfranchised Carpathian peasant in the early 19th century starts a social upheaval, is performed for the first time in Moscow, in concert form.

2 MARCH 1957

A concert of Chinese music is given in Shanghai, presenting a *Mongolian Suite* for orchestra by U TSE-YUN,

New Year's Eve for strings by YAN-TSE and *Nostalgia for Fatherland* for chorus and orchestra by MASA-TZUNG.

8 MARCH 1957

Sixth Symphony by the 41-year-old American composer David DIAMOND, in three movements—(1) *Introduzione—Adagio interrotto—Allegro,* (2) *Adagio interrotto,* (3) *Deciso: Poco Allegro-Fuga*—with their thematic materials related to the initial opening theme of 12 non-different notes and the conjugate theme of 11 non-different notes, dynamically sustained as a succession of diastolic and systolic phrases and periods, and culminating in a magistral fugue, is performed for the first time by the Boston Symphony Orchestra, conducted by Charles Munch.

8 MARCH 1957

Bolaslav I, opera by the 69-year-old Bohemian composer Boleslav VOMÁČKA, dealing with the historical struggle between Duke Wenceslaus and his brother Boleslav, and ending with the murder of the former by the latter, is performed for the first time in Prague.

8 MARCH 1957

Othmar SCHOECK, Swiss composer of operas and symphonic works, a minor master of lyric Lieder in the purest romantic tradition, dies in Zürich at the age of 70.

Schoeck is a type rather like Beckett who gets up at 2:30 P.M. his wife says . . But he can write music all right. (James Joyce in a letter to his son George, 15 January 1935)

15 MARCH 1957

Second Symphony in E major by the 79-year-old Hungarian composer Ernst von DOHNÁNYI, is performed for the first time in its revised form by the Minneapolis Symphony Orchestra, Antal Dorati conducting. (The original version, written in 1944 was first performed in London on 23 November 1948.)

17 MARCH 1957

Fiesta, ballet by Morton GOULD, is produced in Cannes, France.

17 MARCH 1957

At the University of Illinois, in Urbana, two short operas are performed for the first time: Ernst KRENEK's *The Bell-Tower* after Melville, and Jan MEYEROWITZ's biblical music drama *Esther.*

19 MARCH 1957

The Second Festival of American Music opens in Caracas, Venezuela, and a prize of $10,000 for the best work submitted for performance is divided between Camargo GUARNIERI of Brazil for his orchestral *Chôro* and the Mexican composer Blas GALINDO for his *Sinfonía.*

21 MARCH 1957

1907, oratorio by the 47-year-old Rumanian composer Alfred MENDELSOHN, picturing in operatically dramatic tones the heroic rebellion of Rumanian peasantry against the oppressive landed gentry in 1907, is performed for the first time in Bucharest.

25 MARCH 1957

Camille ROBERT, French composer of the famous marching song of World War I, *Madelon*, which he wrote in 1911, dies at the age of 85 in Paris. (He was born inside the building of the Grand Opéra in Paris, where his father, the architect of the theater, made his residence.)

4 APRIL 1957

Tenth Symphony, by Heitor VILLA-LOBOS, written to celebrate the 400th anniversary of the founding of the Brazilian metropolis of São Paulo, scored for soloists, chorus and orchestra, to a text by a 16th-century Brazilian priest, is performed for the first time in Paris.

5 APRIL 1957

Guillermo URIBE-HOLGUÍN, 77-year-old Colombian composer, conducts in Bogotá the first performance of his *Sixth Symphony*, written in a spaciously harmonious and chromatically melodious manner of his venerated teacher Vincent d'Indy.

9 APRIL 1957

Howard HANSON conducts in Washington his choral *Song of Democracy*, to words by Walt Whitman, composed for the centennial celebration of the National Education Association of America in the spirit of assertion of democratic tonality, with polytriadic harmonies expressing the ideal of unity in American diversity, and concluding in an envoi in the patriotic key of E flat major.

12 APRIL 1957

Fourth Symphony by the American composer Wallingford RIEGGER, in three movements—(1) *Allegro moderato*, (2) *Allegretto con moto*, (3) *Sostenuto—Presto*—written in an advanced polytriadic idiom marked by stimulating dissonant counterpoint, is performed for the first time as a commissioned work at the Festival of Contemporary Arts, organized at the University of Illinois, in Urbana.

13 APRIL 1957

Second Symphony for orchestra and chorus by the 40-year-old American composer Ellis KOHS, and the cantata *To the God Who Is in the Fire* by the 46-year-old American composer of Armenian-Scottish extraction Alan HOVHANESS are performed for the first time at the Festival of Contemporary Arts, at the University of Illinois, in Urbana.

16 APRIL 1957

Nardone zagonetke (*Folk Riddles*), cantata by the 71-year-old Croatian composer Stevan HRISTIĆ, set to lively music in Balkanized asymmetrical meters, is performed for the first time in Belgrade, conducted by the composer.

19 APRIL 1957

Antal DORATI conducts the Minneapolis Symphony Orchestra (of which he is music director) in the first per-

formance of his dramatic cantata *The Way of the Cross*, to the English text after Paul Claudel, in 14 sections, descriptive of the successive stages of the Via Dolorosa.

1 MAY 1957

The Prodigal Son, ballet by the veteran Swedish composer Hugo ALFVÉN, on the scenario from the New Testament, with the inclusion in the score of some Swedish dances, is produced in Stockholm on his 85th birthday.

2 MAY 1957

Tadeusz KASSERN, 53-year-old Polish composer of numerous competent choral and instrumental pieces, commits suicide in New York under the double pressure of inoperable cancer and his inability to obtain a permit to remain in the United States after his defection from the Polish Consulate.

6 MAY 1957

The Boor, one-act opera by the 29-year-old American composer Dominick ARGENTO, to a libretto based on a play by Chekhov dealing with an ill-tempered young man who is about to propose to the lady of his heart but ruins his chances by starting a boorish argument about an inconsequential matter, set to music in a modernistically rambunctious vein, is performed for the first time in Rochester, New York.

6 MAY 1957

Michael GNESSIN, Russian-Jewish composer of expressive choral and instrumental music in a nostalgic Hebraic manner, dies in Moscow at the age of 74.

9 MAY 1957

Der Revisor, comic opera in five acts by the German composer Werner EGK, to a libretto drawn from Gogol's comedy deriding the corruption and incompetence of Tsarist bureaucracy, with municipal officers lavishing honors and money on an inconspicuous and impecunious stranger in the belief that he is a government inspector traveling incognito, culminating in the dramatic appearance of the real Revisor, arranged in the form of an Italian opera buffa, sprinkled with innocuous dissonances and introducing stylizations of Russian folksongs for couleur locale, is performed for the first time in Schwetzingen.

9 MAY 1957

Panfilo and Lauretta, opera in three acts by Carlos CHÁVEZ, dealing with a group of 14th-century aristocrats hiding in a Tuscan villa hoping to escape the raging pestilence, diverting themselves by impersonating their true natures in uninhibited play, during which a soldier gives a demonstration of carnal intercourse with a Florentine noblewoman, the sociosexual egalitarianism reaching the climax when a pestiferous monk invades their refuge with a theatrical troupe and infects guests and hosts alike with the bubonic plague, is produced at Columbia University in New York. (A revised Spanish version, under the title *El Amor propiciado*, was performed under the composer's direction in Mexico City on 28 October 1959.)

10 MAY 1957

Maxim SHOSTAKOVICH, son of Dmitri SHOSTAKO-VICH, plays the piano part in the first performance in Moscow of his father's *Second Piano Concerto,* dedicated to him, in three movements: (1) *Allegro,* in propulsive 4/4 time, with discursive lyric episodes; (2) *Andante,* in a ruminating Chopinesque manner in 3/4 time; and (3) *Allegro,* an energetic essay in optimistic major keys, with its predominant 2/4 time occasionally disequilibrated by asymmetric measures in compound 7/8 time.

11 MAY 1957

Two short operas, *Il Figliuol prodigo* and *Venere Prigioniera,* by Gian Francesco MALIPIERO, are produced at the Florence May Festival to honor the composer on the attainment (on 18 March) of the age of seventy-five. (A concert performance of *Il Figliuol prodigo* took place on the Italian Radio on 25 January 1953.)

12 MAY 1957

On the occasion of the annual Prague Spring Music Festival, the Government of Czechoslovakia issues a set of six postage stamps of the denominations of 60 hellers, bearing the portraits of eminent Bohemian composers and performers: Jan STAMIC (1717–1757) with a musical quotation from his *Frühlingssinfonie;* the virtuoso violinist Ferdinand LAUB (1832–1875); Joseph FOERSTER (1859–1951), with a musical quotation from the third act of his opera *Eva;* Vítězslav NOVÁK (1870–1949), with a musical quotation from his symphonic poem *In the Tatra Mountains,* and Otakar OSTRČIL (1879–1935) with a musical quotation from his opera *Poupe* in which the first note is erroneously printed as D-sharp instead of F-sharp.

15 MAY 1957

Dzhalil, opera in two acts by the 46-year-old Tatar Soviet composer Nazib ZHIGANOV, to a libretto by the Tatar composer Dzhaudat Faizy on the subject of the heroic life of the Tatar poet Musa Dzhalil, executed by the Nazis in 1944 after he was taken prisoner of war on charges of participation in underground activities, is performed for the first time in Kazan, with a Russian libretto. (A new revised version was produced in Kazan on 30 April 1964.)

17 MAY 1957

The definitive version of HAYDN's *Concerto in D major* for violoncello and orchestra, is performed for the first time in Vienna by Enrico Mainardi from the newly found authentic manuscript, signed in Haydn's own hand, "di me Giuseppe Haydn," thus settling beyond doubt Haydn's authorship of the work long attributed by doubting Haydnologists to Anton Kraft, Haydn's first cellist of Prince Esterházy's Orchestra.

20 MAY 1957

The Soviet Union issues a stamp of 40 kopecks in honor of Mili BALAKIREV, the enlightened mentor of the Russian National School.

22 MAY 1957

Una domanda di matrimonio, one-act opera buffa by the Italian composer Louis CHAILLY, after Anton Chekhov's playlet in which a youth about to propose to a girl becomes entangled in an abstract debate with her and only after making an angry departure recollects the object of his visit and mends matters by an immediate return and proposal in marriage, is produced at the Piccola Scala in Milan.

24 MAY 1957

Venus in Africa, fantasy-opera by George ANTHEIL, to a libretto about a virginal American youth traveling in Tunis who appeals to the statue of Venus for instruction in love, whereupon a native girl opportunely materializes to initiate him into advanced sexual techniques, with a musical score marked by saccadic rhythms and sophisticated balladry, fertilized by innocuous amorous dissonances, is performed for the first time by the opera group of the University of Denver.

24 MAY 1957

The Moon and Sixpence, opera in three acts by the 40-year-old English composer John GARDNER, based on Somerset Maugham's novel suggested by the life of Paul Gauguin, taking place in London, Paris and on a Pacific island, set to music in a colloquially simplicistic vein with some pseudo-exotic inflections, is performed as the first commissioned work of the Sadler's Wells Opera in London.

24 MAY 1957

Simonida, opera in three acts by the 46-year-old Yugoslav composer Stanojlo RAJIČIĆ, to a story of the 14th-century Byzantine damsel who is affianced to an aged Serbian king but falls in love with his son and, when the latter is blinded by the king's orders, dies from a psychosomatic inanition, is performed for the first time in Sarajevo. (A revised version was first performed in Belgrade on 17 April 1958.)

25 MAY 1957

A Feira, opera by the Portuguese composer Ruy COELHO, is produced in Lisbon.

25 MAY 1957

The Taming of the Shrew, comic opera in four acts, after Shakespeare, by the 54-year-old Soviet composer Vissarion SHEBALIN, written in a realistic idiom modeled after Mussorgsky, but containing a considerable admixture of modernistically enhanced tonal harmonies and polyharmonies, is produced in Kuibishev. (The first Moscow performance of the opera, in concert form, took place on 1 October 1955.)

31 MAY 1957

The 31st Festival of the International Society for Contemporary Music opens in Zürich, Switzerland, with a program of electronic music, comprising the following works:

Scambi by the 27-year-old Belgian composer Henri POUSSEUR; *Notturno* and *Syntaxis* by the 37-year-old Italian composer Bruno MADERNA; *8:37 Perspectives* and *Mutazioni* by the 31-year-old Italian composer Luciano BERIO.

1 JUNE 1957

The following orchestral works are presented at the 31st Festival of the International Society for Contemporary Music in Zürich, Switzerland:

Corales crillos by Juan José CASTRO of Argentina; *Scythian Suite* by PROKOFIEV; *Figures sonores* by Yoritsune MATSU-DAIRA of Japan; and *Sixth Symphony* by Karl Amadeus HARTMANN of Germany, in two large sections, a greatly protracted *Adagio*, Mahlerian in its proportions and philosophical concentration, and *Toccata*, generated by the motive of three notes, B-flat, B and A, with highly intricate variations and fugues.

2 JUNE 1957

The following works are presented at the third concert of the 31st Festival of the International Society for Contemporary Music in Zürich:

3 Volkstexte, op. 17, by Anton von WEBERN, for soprano, violin, clarinet and bass clarinet, written in 1924, in which the method of composition with 12 tones is employed by Webern for the first time after Schoenberg; *Concert Piece* for violin and piano by Mátyás SEIBER of Hungary and England; *Sonata* for trumpet, guitar and piano by the 32-year-old Italian composer Aldo CLEMENTI, employing the method of rhythmic serialism on repeated notes of natural harmonics, calculated to produce the effect of mechanized static immobility; *Contrasts* for clarinet, violin and piano by Béla BARTÓK; and *Frequencies* for piccolo, flute, guitar, doublebass, xylophone, vibraphone and percussion by the 20-year-old Swede Bo NILSSON, in which the dodecaphonic subject is presented in serial treatment in dynamics, tempi, coloration, duration, rhythms, and other aspects of musical composition, according to the formula:

$$\int (a + bx)^n dx = \frac{(a + bx)^{n+1}}{(n + 1)b} + C \ (n \neq -1)$$

3 JUNE 1957

During the course of the 31st Festival of the International Society for Contemporary Music in Zürich the following works are presented:

(1) *Concerto breve* for orchestra by Vittorio FELLEGARA of Italy, in a free non-classical, non-romantic, non-diatonic, non-chromatic, non-dodecaphonic but thematically coherent and sonorously integrated idiom; (2) *Eine Gotthard-Kantate* for baritone solo and string orchestra by the Russian-born Swiss resident composer Wladimir VOGEL, illustrating in expressively dodecaphonic melodies the vision of the poet Friedrich Hölderlin as he stood in contemplation at the St. Gotthard pass in the Alps; (3) *Recitativo ed Aria* for clavecin and orchestra by the 30-year-old Polish-born composer Roman HAUBENSTOCK-RAMATI, conceived as a neo-classical serial idea; (4) *5 Neapolitanische Lieder* for voice and chamber orchestra by the 30-year-old German expressionist composer Hans Werner HENZE, who took up residence on the island of Capri; (5) *Passacaglia* for small orchestra by the 32-year-old French composer Maurice JARRE, dedicated to the memory of Arthur Honegger; and (6) *Kammermusik No. 1* by Paul HIN-DEMITH, first performed in Donaueschingen on 31 July 1922.

3 JUNE 1957

Die Räuber, opera in four acts after Schiller by the 31-year-old German composer Giselher KLEBE, written in a heroic modern manner within a framework of unencumbered dissonances, is produced in Düsseldorf.

4 JUNE 1957

The 31st Festival of the International Society for Contemporary Music continues in Zürich with a concert presenting the following works:

3 Psalmen for soprano, tenor, chorus and orchestra by the Swiss composer Robert OBOUSSIER (who was fated to be assassinated five days later) composed in 1946–1947 under the impact of fresh memories of Nazi horrors and expressing in terms of simple tonal lyricism the successive sentiments of deep despair, nascent hope and liberating joy; *Concerto* for piano and orchestra by the 38-year-old American composer Leon KIRCHNER, of a sharply accentuated musical consistency within a classically clear formal design; *First Symphony* by the 31-year-old Chilean composer Gustavo BECERRA SCHMIDT, written in a volitionally synthetic idiom of tonal serialism; *Epitaph* for orchestra by the 33-year-old Austrian composer Karl-Heinz FÜSSL, dedicated to the memory of Anton von Webern, in 13 brief variations in the lapidary style of Webern himself with a maximum of dissipation in the distribution of orchestral registers and rhythmic units; and a *String Quartet* by the 32-year-old American composer Billy Jim LAYTON.

5 JUNE 1957

The 31st Festival of the International Society for Contemporary Music continues in Zürich with the following concert of Swiss music:

4 Etudes for string orchestra by Frank MARTIN; *Etudes* for voice and orchestra by Constantin RÉGAMEY; *Violin Concerto* by Willy BURKHARD; *Tre Mutazioni* for chamber orchestra by Jacques WILDBERGER; and *Amores* for tenor, trumpet, percussion and strings by Franz TISCHHAUSSER.

5 JUNE 1957

The Curious Fern, one-act opera by the American composer Meyer KUPFERMAN, is produced in New York.

6 JUNE 1957

The 31st Festival of the International Society for Contemporary Music in Zürich concludes with the first stage performance of Arnold SCHOENBERG's posthumous opera *Moses und Aron.*

8 JUNE 1957

Bluthochzeit, lyric tragedy in two acts by Wolfgang FORT-NER, after *Bodas de Sangre* by Federico García Lorca, written in an eclectic dodecaphonic technique with symbolic overtones (the mother's impassionate apostrophe to the knife suggests atonal schizophrenia, a dodecaphonic canon of two violins alludes to the mystery of the forest, etc.) is performed for the first time in Cologne. (The world première was originally scheduled for 25 May 1957 but was deferred on account of the illness of one of the performers; *Der Wald,* a section of the complete opera was first performed in its original version in Frankfurt on 25 June 1953.)

9 JUNE 1957

Robert OBOUSSIER, 56-year-old Swiss composer, is stabbed to death 17 times by his room companion at dawn, in their apartment in Zürich.

10 JUNE 1957

Putovanje (The Journey), the first television opera to be given in Yugoslavia, a satirical musical burlesque by the 43-year-old Croatian composer Ivo LHOTKA-KALINSKI, dealing with a petty functionary vegetating about 1900 who nourishes an unfeasible desire to travel to distant places, set to music in the tonally dissonant manner of utilitarian opera, is produced in Zagreb.

17 JUNE 1957

On the 75th birthday of Igor STRAVINSKY, his ballet *Agon* (completed on 27 April 1957, in Los Angeles, his dwelling place since World War II), an antiphonally designed realization of the ancient Greek *agon*, a prize contest, scored for 12 dancers, in 12 movements (the numbers symbolically signaling the incipient dodecaphony of Stravinsky's Third Style), is performed for the first time in Los Angeles in concert form, conducted by Stravinsky's loyal famulus, Robert Craft, and forming the following divisions:

(1) *Pas de Quatre* for 4 male dancers in diatonic ostentation; (2) *Double Pas de Quatre*, for 8 female participants, marked by petulant minor seconds in argumentative heterophony; (3) *Triple Pas de Quatre* for 8 female and 4 male dancers, with chromatic infoliation around the bisexual focal D; (4) *Prelude* in triadic disposition; (5) *First Pas de Trois*, containing a pandiatonic Saraband; (6) *Gaillarde*, a pantriadic neo-archaic divertissement; (7) *Coda* in fauxbourdon counterpoint; (8) *Interlude*, an aimbivalent equilibrium of C major and B flat minor triads; (9) *Second Pas de Trois*, in the form of a simple canonic bransle; (10) *Bransle Gay*, with the orchestra in vacillating meter against the steady triple rhythms of a single castagnette; (11) *Bransle de Poitou*, in the meter of a courante; (12) *Interlude;* (13) *Pas de Deux*, marked by wide intervallic saltation; (14) Four choreographic *Duos*, monophonically serialistic, in propulsive quarternote motion; (15) Four choreographic *Trios* in paraserialistic melos, leading to a coda as a reprise of the initial *Pas de Quatre* and concluding on a gymnosophistically quartal-quintal chord C-F-D-G-C. (The first stage performance of *Agon* took place in New York on 1 December 1957.)

22 JUNE 1957

First Symphony in five movements by Karl Amadeus HARTMANN, subtitled *Versuch eines Requiem*, for contralto solo and orchestra, composed in 1936 and revised several times, is performed in a final version in Vienna with words from Walt Whitman's *Leaves of Grass* in the solo voice.

26 JUNE 1957

Dos movimientos for a kettledrum and string orchestra by the 27-year-old Spanish composer Cristóbal HALFFTER, written in a constructivistically polyrhythmic manner, is performed for the first time in Madrid.

29 JUNE 1957

Ede POLDINI, Hungarian composer of pleasant piano pieces, of which *La Poupée valsante* became a semi-classical classic, dies in Vevey, Switzerland, at the age of 88.

3 JULY 1957

Richard MOHAUPT, German composer of various operatic and symphonic works in an enlightened modern manner, dies in Reichenau, Austria, at the age of 52.

6 JULY 1957

Henry FÉVRIER, French composer of romantic operas touched with Wagneromorphic drama, dies in Paris at the age of 81.

20 JULY 1957

Guillermo URIBE-HOLGUÍN, 77-year-old prime composer of Colombia, conducts in Bogotá the first performance of his *Seventh Symphony*.

23 JULY 1957

Two centuries have passed since Domenico SCARLATTI, originator of modern keyboard technique, died in Madrid, where he became a court composer, and where he successively married two Spanish ladies who bore him nine children, who in turn propagated in a geometric progression right into the 20th century, so that there are dozens of Scarlattis in the Madrid telephone book.

26 JULY 1957

Jacob and the Indians, opera in three acts by the 33-year-old American composer Ezra LADERMAN, is produced in Woodstock, New York.

30 JULY 1957

Sem DRESDEN, prime Dutch composer, author of romantic songs and instrumental pieces, dies at The Hague, at the age of 76.

2 AUGUST 1957

The Tower, one-act opera by the American composer Marvin David LEVY, is performed for the first time by the Santa Fe Opera Company on his 25th birthday.

3 AUGUST 1957

Pablo CASALS, 80-year-old grand maestro of the violoncello, takes in marriage as his third wife, his 20-year-old pupil, Martita Montañez, in a ceremony held in San Juan, Puerto Rico, an island which was to become his permanent residence and the site of the Casals Music Festivals.

11 AUGUST 1957

At the opening of the Munich Festival, Paul HINDEMITH conducts the world première of his opera *Die Harmonie der Welt*, in five acts, to his own text, dealing with the life and theories of planetary motion of the astronomer Johannes Kepler, reverting also to the astrological ideas of the Harmony of the Spheres. (A symphonic suite from the opera was performed in Basel on 24 January 1952.)

17 AUGUST 1957

Schule der Frauen, opera buffa in three acts by Rolf LIEBERMANN, after Molière's play *L'Escole des Femmes*, scored for six singers and chamber orchestra, in a German version, with Molière himself presiding over the action and expressing curiosity as to how his comedy would work out as an opera, is produced in Salzburg. (The original smaller concert version was first produced as a commissioned work in Louisville, Kentucky, on 3 December 1955; another version was presented in Zürich on 9 November 1957.)

17 AUGUST 1957

Gunther SCHULLER, 31-year-old American composer and jazzologist, spontaneously invents, during a lecture at Music Inn at the Berkshire Music Center in Tanglewood, near Lenox, Massachusetts, the term *Third Stream*, to define a type of composition in which elements of jazz are organized within a classical matrix, so that popular music becomes ennobled and respectable without losing its innate vitality and classical music acquires an indigenous vivacity of rhythmic progress. (The exact date and circumstances of the portentous epiphany communicated to the author, with proper certification, by Gunther Schuller himself.)

1 SEPTEMBER 1957

Dennis BRAIN, 36-year-old British virtuoso horn player, a scion of the family of horn players, is killed in an automobile accident after hitting a tree on a winding road in Hatfield, Hertfordshire, while driving at night at high speed from Edinburgh to London.

11 SEPTEMBER 1957

Concerto for two pianos and orchestra by Gian Francesco MALIPIERO, written in a fine pandiatonic manner, is performed for the first time at the music festival of Besançon, France, by the matrimonial duo pianists Janine Reding and Henri Piette.

20 SEPTEMBER 1957

Jean SIBELIUS, great Finnish composer whose tall physical stature and granitically noble countenance seemed to mirror the spiritual character of his music and the spacious melorhyrthms of Suomi folksongs, dies in his home at Järvenpää at the age of 91 as his poignant *Swan of Tuonela* is mournfully broadcast over the Finnish radio.

23 SEPTEMBER 1957

Two postage stamps in the denominations of 40 kopecks and one ruble, are issued by the Soviet Union in honor of the great proponent of national Russian music Vladimir STASOV (1824–1906).

24 SEPTEMBER 1957

Maratona di danza, ballet by Hans Werner HENZE, is performed for the first time in Berlin.

26 SEPTEMBER 1957

West Side Story, musical play by the protean 39-year-old Leonard BERNSTEIN, presenting an American counterpart of Romeo and Juliet, wherein two youthful gangs collide murderously in the tenements and playgrounds of West Side, Manhattan, between 80th and 90th Streets, engulfing the tragic romance across the fighting lines between an American boy and a Puerto Rican girl, the score containing the modern sentimental ballads *Maria* and *I Feel Pretty*, is produced in New York, marking a

musical event without precedent, a highly popular show with music written by the conductor of a major symphony orchestra, the Philharmonic of New York.

28 SEPTEMBER 1957

Third Symphony by the Rumanian composer Sigismond TODUŢA, subtitled *Ovid*, written in the commemoration of the second millennium of the birth of the Roman poet Ovid who was exiled by Emperor August to Rumania, is performed for the first time in Cluj, Rumania.

29 SEPTEMBER 1957

La Dame aux camélias, ballet by Henri SAUGUET, to a scenario after the famous melodrama of Alexandre Dumas, is produced at the Berlin Festival.

1 OCTOBER 1957

Fourteen Minutes Before the Start, a song by the Soviet composer Oscar FELTSMAN, depicting the expectant atmosphere before an aviator takes off on an important mission, destined to become the favorite air of the Soviet cosmonauts, is broadcast for the first time on Radio Moscow, three days before the launching of the first Sputnik. (Date and information obtained by the author from Oscar Feltsman.)

1 OCTOBER 1957

Thyl de Flandre, opera by the 47-year-old French composer and musicologist Jacques CHAILLEY, is produced in Brussels.

1 OCTOBER 1957

Seventh Symphony by the English composer Edmund RUBBRA, couched in polycentric modalities invested with polytriadic harmonies containing a generous injection of non-toxic dissonances, in three cyclic movements—(1) *Lento-Allegro moderato*, ending on "niente" in C major; (2) *Vivace e leggiero* a quasi-Vindobonic waltz-scherzo with a cadence on a thirdless C triad; (3) *Passacaglia and Fugue*, in circular construction, the last two bars being identical with the first two, and concluding in unpigmented C major—is performed for the first time in Birmingham, England, by the Birmingham Symphony Orchestra under the direction of the Polish composer-conductor resident in England, Andrzej Panufnik.

10 OCTOBER 1957

Three unnamed short pieces for chamber orchestra by Arnold SCHOENBERG, written in 1910, untitled and unpublished, but historically important since they demonstrate the transitional period from athematic atonality to organized panthematic dodecaphony, are performed for the first time by members of the Berlin Philharmonic Orchestra in West Berlin.

10 OCTOBER 1957

Seventh Symphony by the 61-year-old Austrian composer Johann Nepomuk DAVID is performed for the first time at Stuttgart.

11 OCTOBER 1957

Gauche, the Violoncellist, one-act opera buffa by the 45-year-old Japanese composer Osamu SHIMIZU, is produced in Osaka.

16 OCTOBER 1957

The centennial season of the Hallé Orchestra in Manchester, founded by Charles HALLÉ in 1858, opens with a *Flourish for Glorious John* written for the conductor John Barbirolli by Ralph VAUGHAN WILLIAMS.

17 OCTOBER 1957

Ralph BENATZKY, Czech-born composer of tuneful German operettas, of which *Im weissen Rössl* became a universal favorite, dies in Zürich at the age of 73.

18 OCTOBER 1957

Toccata for orchestra by Paul CRESTON is performed for the first time by the Cleveland Orchestra.

19 OCTOBER 1957

Gorski Vijernac (*Mountain Bouquet*), oratorio in three acts by the 46-year-old Herzegovinian composer Nikola HERCIGONIA, descriptive of the 1817 rebellion of Montenegro against its Ottoman overlords, in which the hero performs a personal sacrifice by subordinating his passion for a girl to his patriotism, containing 11-beat rhythms characteristic of the region, is produced in Belgrade.

24 OCTOBER 1957

Jean MARTINON conducts in Paris the first performance of his cantata *Le Lis de Saron* (*Rose of Sharon*), an impassionate Solomonian cantillation with a polytonal accompaniment.

25 OCTOBER 1957

Fantasy for piano by Aaron COPLAND, written for the 50th Anniversary of the Juilliard School of Music, receives its initial performances played twice (for better penetration and comprehension) in New York by William Masselos.

26 OCTOBER 1957

Mother, opera in four acts by the 44-year-old Soviet composer Tikhon KHRENNIKOV, after Maxim Gorky's novel, dealing with a protest strike by factory workers against a one-kopeck monthly tax, resulting in the strike leader's deportation to Siberia, where he is followed by his faithful beloved while his formerly apolitical mother takes over his work in distributing anti-Tsarist propaganda leaflets, set to music making ample use of the Marseillaise, the Warsaw Funeral March, the Prison Ballad, and other revolutionary songs popular during the period of the abortive Russian revolution of 1905, is produced at the Bolshoi Theater in Moscow.

26 OCTOBER 1957

Milana, opera in four acts by the Ukrainian composer Georgi MAIBORODA, dealing with a beautiful Soviet girl and her young Communist lover working in the resistance groups from 1939 to 1944 in the Fascist-governed part of Transcarpathia, until it was liberated by the Red Army and subsequently incorporated into the Ukrainian Soviet Socialist Republic, is performed for the first time in Kiev.

30 OCTOBER 1957

The world première is given in Moscow of the *Eleventh Symphony* by Dmitri SHOSTAKOVICH, subtitled *1905* (the year of the tragically abortive and yet romantically inspiring Russian revolution), set in four descriptive movements:

(1) *Palace Square,* postulating a static theme expressive of the inhumanity of the Tsarist regime interspersed with inchoate fragments of anguished church anthems, trumpet calls and ominous drum beats as background for the popular ballads *Listen!* and *The Prisoner;* (2) *January the Ninth,* the "Bloody Sunday" in St. Petersburg when the Cossack troops dispersed the crowd advancing on the Winter Palace to petition the Tsar for redress of grievances, musically portrayed by an eerie *scherzo-fugato,* interrupted by outcries of prayer and agony, with a militant workers' song *Boldly, Comrades, Step Forward!* marking the turn towards revolutionary decisions; (3) *Perpetual Remembrance,* opening with the melody of the revolutionary funeral march *You Fell a Victim to Fateful Struggle,* changing to the strains of *Welcome the Free Word of Liberty* and leading to the finale; (4) *The Alert,* using the melodies of *Warsaw March, Rage You Tyrants,* and *Let Us Uncover Our Heads,* with growing growls in the brass presaging the victorious revolution of 1917.

31 OCTOBER 1957

Baptism of Fire, opera in five scenes by the 48-year-old Estonian composer Gustav ERNESAKS, dealing with the abortive Russian Revolution of 1905, symbolized by the contrapuntal syncrasy of the old Tsarist anthem with the Marseillaise, popular among the revolutionary masses and sung to Russian words, is produced in Tallin.

2 NOVEMBER 1957

The Voice of Lenin, cantata for mixed chorus, children's chorus and orchestra by the Rumanian composer Alfred MENDELSOHN, is performed for the first time in Bucharest.

4 NOVEMBER 1957

Joseph CANTELOUBE, known as Canteloube de Malaret, after his family estate, French composer, whose tasteful quasi-impressionistic settings of songs from his native Auvergne have become favorites among singers, dies in Paris at the age of 78.

8 NOVEMBER 1957

The Gadfly, opera by Antonio SPADAVECCHIA, 50-year-old Odessa-born Soviet composer of Italian descent, to the novel of that name written in 1597 by the English novelist Ethel Voynich, dealing with an inspired British revolutionary who helped Garibaldi in the Italian struggle for independence, is produced in Perm.

16 NOVEMBER 1957

Medusa, ballet by the 39-year-old Austrian composer Gottfried von EINEM, is performed for the first time in Vienna.

18 NOVEMBER 1957

The Throne of God, cantata for mixed voices and orchestra by the 62-year-old American composer Leo SOWERBY, commissioned by the National Cathedral in Washington for its 50th anniversary, is performed for the first time in Washington.

22 NOVEMBER 1957

The government of the Democratic Republic of Germany issues two postage stamps in honor of two prominent Leipzig musicians, one for 10 pfennigs commemorating the organist Günther RAMIN who died on 27 February 1956, and for 25 pfennigs for the conductor Hermann ABENDROTH who died on 29 May 1956.

22 NOVEMBER 1957

The Sweet Bye and Bye, opera in three acts by the American composer Jack BEESON, to a discreetly fictionalized libretto suggested by the scandalous disappearance on 18 May 1926 of the famous female revivalist Aimée MacPherson, the builder of a personal temple in Southern California, is produced in New York.

22 NOVEMBER 1957

Fourth Symphony by Ernst TOCH in three movements, *Molto dolce, Molto tranquillo* and *Molto igualmente*, commissioned by the Women's Association of the Minneapolis Symphony Orchestra, and dedicated to the memory of Marion MacDowell (1857–1956) with a motto by the composer, addressing her as "indomitable, incandescent soul," and describing his symphony as a letter "written wholly upon your dictation," is performed for the first time by the Minneapolis Symphony Orchestra, Antal Dorati conducting.

25 NOVEMBER 1957

The Republic of Liberia issues a postage stamp bearing the musical notation of its National Anthem.

25 NOVEMBER 1957

Logaritmos No. 3 by the Italian composer Giorgio GASLINI, for string quartet concertante with string orchestra, xylophone and chimes, in two parts, in which the quartet is treated as a dodecaphonic logarithm to the duodecimal base of the ripieni, is performed for the first time in Rome.

28 NOVEMBER 1957

Othello, Shakespearean ballet by the foremost romantic composer of Soviet Georgia Alexei MACHAVARIANI, written in romantically melodramatic tones, is produced in Tbilisi.

29 NOVEMBER 1957

Erich Wolfgang KORNGOLD, once a *Wunderkind* who aroused enthusiasm by his precocious talent and was hailed by reputable musicians as a modern Mozart, dies in Hollywood, his refuge after the Nazi darkness descended on his native Vienna, as the result of debilitating apoplexy, at the age of 60.

2 DECEMBER 1957

Smrt Stefana Dečanskogo cantata by the Yugoslav composer Enriko JOSIF, in the form of a lamentation upon the death of the Serbian 14th-century king Stefan dethroned by his son, set to music in a neo-medieval style, is performed for the first time in Belgrade.

2 DECEMBER 1957

Third Symphony by the 36-year-old British composer Malcolm ARNOLD is performed for the first time in London.

3 DECEMBER 1957

Yugoslavia issues a postage stamp of 70 dinars in honor of the Serbian composer Stevan MOKRANJAĆ (1856–1914).

4 DECEMBER 1957

Pierre BOULEZ conducts the first performance in Cologne of his work *Le Visage nuptial* for soprano, contralto, chorus and orchestra.

6 DECEMBER 1957

Third Symphony by Roger SESSIONS, completed by him on 23 September 1957, in which a guiding dodecaphonic series is formed by a gradual accretion of thematic units, in four movements, *Allegro grazioso e con fuoco, Allegro un poco ruvido, Andante sostenuto e con affetto* and *Allegro con fuoco*, concluding on a seminal statement of the cumulative tone-row in decisive unisons, ending on a proleptic tonic B, is performed for the first time by the Boston Symphony Orchestra, under the direction of Charles Munch.

9 DECEMBER 1957

Konjanik (*The Horseman*), "cavalcade" for mixed chorus and chamber orchestra by the 39-year-old Triesteborn Yugoslav composer Emil COSSETTO, depicting a knight's night ride to a mysteriously receding battlefront, written in melodramatic march time, is performed for the first time in Zagreb.

19 DECEMBER 1957

The Music Man, musical play by the 55-year-old American composer Meredith WILLSON, to his own lyrics dealing with the satirical yet somehow patriotic subject of a traveling salesman of band uniforms and musical instruments who sold them to hicktown suckers, opens on Broadway in New York.

21 DECEMBER 1957

Eric COATES, English composer of descriptive symphonic pieces, of which the *Knightsbridge* march from his *London Suite* became widely popular, dies at the age of seventy-one in Chichester.

25 DECEMBER 1957

Labinska Vještica (*The Witch of Labin*), opera in two acts by the 43-year-old Croatian composer Natko DEVČIĆ, with the action centered on the religious strife between Protestants and Catholics in 16th-century Istria, is produced in Zagreb.

1958

10 JANUARY 1958

Alec ROWLEY, 65-year-old English composer of gracefully unpretentious music in smaller forms, collapses and dies during a tennis game in London.

15 JANUARY 1958

The Metropolitan Opera presents in New York the world première of *Vanessa*, opera in four acts by Samual BARBER, to the libretto by Gian Carlo Menotti, recounting the melodramatic tale of "a lady of great beauty" (Vanessa is a genus of butterflies to which an American variety, the "painted beauty," belongs) languishing "in a northern country about 1905," and the handsome young son of her dead lover who seduces her niece Erika, nearly causing her death as she tries to abort the fruit of their liaison, and who in the end marries Vanessa herself as a symbolic redemption of his father's defection long ago, set to music of colorful opulence freely applying chromatic, atonal, polytonal, and pandiatonic devices, with aerostatic melodies reposing on long-stemmed chords rooted in deep overtone-fertile basses, and with the vocal line varying from impassionate cantilena to ostentatiously prosaic spoken lines.

15 JANUARY 1958

Second Symphony by the 57-year-old American composer Colin MCPHEE, utilizing pentatonic scale forms and other melodic material collected by him during his sojourn in Bali, is performed for the first time by the Louisville Orchestra under the direction of Robert Whitney.

23 JANUARY 1958

Mosaics for orchestra by Howard HANSON, suggesting the interplay of colors, lights and shadows in a mosaic design by an astute polarization of instrumental timbres, is performed for the first time as a commissioned work by the Cleveland Orchestra in celebration of its 40th anniversary.

24 JANUARY 1958

Paul SACHER conducts the Chamber Orchestra of Basel in two world premières:

The Epic of Gilgamesh, cantata by Bohuslav MARTINU, in three parts, to the texts of newly deciphered Babylonian poems relating the story of a simple man of nature seduced by a dancer of the temple of Istar who dies to expiate his delinquency and posthumously warns King Gilgamesh of the lamentability of carnality and inexorability of perdition, with a musical score based on a brief archaically sounding theme artfully mutated into a series of variations; and *Kette, Kreis und Spiegel* a "symphonic drawing" by Ernst KRENEK, wherein the "chain" in the title refers to the interlocking arrangement of 48 forms of the basic dodecaphonic series, "circle" to the principle of rotation underlying it, and "mirror" to the ulti-

mate inverted form of the original configuration resulting from the preceding concatenations and rotations.

Whatever morphological kinship may be detected between adjacent sections is a result of similarities of intervallic shapes that may occur in neighboring forms of the tone-row, the vicinity of which, however, is a consequence of the premeditated serial arrangement and not dictated by requirements of a so-called musical nature. (Ernst Krenek, in *Extents and Limits of Serial Techniques* in *The Musical Quarterly*, April, 1960)

30 JANUARY 1958

Partita for Orchestra by William WALTON, in three movements—(1) *Toccata*, with thematic contents determined by the contraction of the octave to a major seventh and its subsequent fission into a tritone and a perfect fourth; (2) *Pastorale Siciliana*, in a luminescently Italian vein with a proliferation of trilled protuberances and; (3) *Giga burlesca*, a hedonistic rondo—is performed for the first time by the Cleveland Orchestra.

5 FEBRUARY 1958

Second Symphony by the 53-year-old English composer of Cornish stock Michael TIPPETT (completed after five years of work on 13 November 1957), in four movements—(1) *Allegro vigoroso*, opening with a round of impressive beats on low C's, immediately challenged by the gymnosophistical fifths in the horns a tritone away and proceeding thence along polytriadic lines; (2) a lyrically contemplative *Adagio molto e tranquillo;* (3) a scherzo, *Presto veloce*, built on additive rhythms in asymmetrical meters; and (4) *Allegro moderato*, a fantasia in four unrelated sections, ending on the pandiatonic conglomerate C-G-D-A-E—is performed for the first time by the British Broadcasting Corporation Symphony Orchestra, under the direction of Sir Adrian Boult (who had to restart the work after something went amiss in the exposition in the first movement, and apologized to the public for an incidence of unintentional polyrhythmic polyharmony resulting from a contrapuntal contretemps).

6 FEBRUARY 1958

The Dragon, one-act chamber opera by Deems TAYLOR, to a story of an Irish princess saved from a green Irish dragon by a prince masquerading as a cook, set to music in a flowingly melodious and ingratiatingly harmonious idiom, with occasional euphonious modernities injected for melodramatic effect, is performed for the first time by the New York University Opera Workshop, in a version accompanied by piano and organ in lieu of the original orchestral instrumentation.

8 FEBRUARY 1958

Il Vortice, opera in three acts by the 50-year-old Italian composer Renzo ROSSELLINI, is produced in Naples.

10 FEBRUARY 1958

Mythical Beasts by the American composer Henry BRANDT, scored for soprano and sixteen instruments, is performed for the first time in New York.

12 FEBRUARY 1958

The inaugural concert of *Structures Sonores*, an ensemble of sound-producing objects fashioned of glass and steel in modernistically asymmetrical shapes by François BASCHET, is given at the Schola Cantorum in Paris in a program of works specially written by Jacques Lasry, the co-builder of *Structures Sonores*, and including *Two Dances for the Crystal Coil-spring Dance, Metalic Prelidium, Cosmotony, Bolide* and *Mister Blues*.

12 FEBRUARY 1958

Second Symphony by the 29-year-old German-born American composer Samuel ADLER is performed for the first time in Dallas, Texas.

14 FEBRUARY 1958

Hungaria 1956, symphonic poem by the Polish composer Artur MALAWSKI, descriptive in somber tones of the sanguinary pacification by the Soviet Army of the Hungarian insurrection of 1956, is performed for the first time in Warsaw.

15 FEBRUARY 1958

The World of Paul Klee, symphonic suite by David DIAMOND, evoking by congenial melorhythmic configurations the impressions of four paintings by Klee—(1) *Grieving Child*, waltzing sadly in muted strings and muted brass; (2) *Black Prince*, strutting in dislocated march time; (3) *Pastorale*, in multiple triple meters, like a bark a-rolling in a barcarolle; (4) *Twittering Machine*, with disconnected gears set a-flutter by means of a large sheet of heavy paper shaken longitudinally to produce the sonic simulacrum of a miniaturized thunderclap—is performed for the first time by the Portland, Oregon, Junior Symphony Orchestra, Jacob Avshalomov conducting.

20 FEBRUARY 1958

Isidor PHILIPP, 94-year-old French pianist and famous pedagogue, dies in Paris of injuries sustained in a fall at the entrance of the Metro, which he continued to use despite his nonagenarian fragility.

25 FEBRUARY 1958

Aeneas-Silvius Symphonie by the 56-year-old Swiss composer Conrad BECK (his *Seventh Symphony*), written as an homage to the 15th-century humanist Aeneas-Silvius Piccolomini of Siena who became Pope Pius II and founded the University of Basel, set in a series of four variations, alternately rhetorical, hieratic, nostalgic and impetuous, is performed for the first time in Zürich.

27 FEBRUARY 1958

Miorița, oratorio by the 31-year-old Rumanian composer Anatol VIERU, to the words of a folk ballad about a stray sheep, based on two mutually exclusive tropes of six notes (C,D,F-sharp, G,B,C-sharp and E-flat, E,F,A-flat, A,B-flat), aggregating to a 12-tone series, set in effectively acerbic harmonies, is performed for the first time in Bucharest.

27 FEBRUARY 1958

Love in Transit, opera by the 40-year-old British composer Richard ARNELL, is performed for the first time in London.

1 MARCH 1958

Assassinio nella Cattedrale, opera-oratorio by the Italian grandmaster Ildebrando PIZZETTI, based on T.S. Eliot's play *Murder in the Cathedral*, and dealing with the assassination of Thomas à Beckett on the orders of Henry II of England in 1170, drawn in heroic modalities and resonant unencumbered harmonies, performed for the first time at La Scala, Milan.

1 MARCH 1958

First Symphony by the 35-year-old Greek composer Yorgo SICILIANOS, written in a neo-classical idiom revitalized by ambitonal, atonal and polytonal exfoliations, is performed for the first time by the New York Philharmonic Symphony Orchestra, Dimitri Mitropoulos conducting.

4 MARCH 1958

Pre-Classic Suite for orchestra by Paul CRESTON, in three movements (*Courante, Pavane* and *Galliard*) is performed for the first time in New Orleans.

5 MARCH 1958

Orchestral Variations by Aaron COPLAND, a symphonic transcription of his *Piano Variations* of 1930, derived, as was the original work, from an eleven-bar theme of a dramatically atonal nature, with an involute four-note figure, E, C, E-flat, C-sharp, constituting the thematic nucleus, is performed for the first time in Louisville.

7 MARCH 1958

Third Symphony by the 57-year-old French composer Henry BARRAUD, in four contracting movements freely conceived in a median modernistic manner, utilizing enriched tonality, polytonality, atonality, and occasionally nonthematic dodecaphony, is performed for the first time by the Boston Symphony Orchestra, Charles Munch conducting, on the same program with the première of Walter PISTON's *Viola Concerto*.

9 MARCH 1958

Second Symphony for strings and celesta by the 59-year-old French composer Marcel DELANNOY, in three well-balanced movements, is performed for the first time in Paris.

10 MARCH 1958

Pan by the 63-year-old Croatian composer Krešimir BARANOVIĆ, scored for narrator, voices and orchestra, is performed for the first time in Belgrade.

14 MARCH 1958

Third Concerto for String Orchestra by the innovative, but determinedly romantic Swedish composer Allan PETTERSSON is performed for the first time on the Swedish Radio in Stockholm.

16 MARCH 1958

Doubles, a set of symphonic variations by the apostle of ultramodern music Pierre BOULEZ, scored for a normal classical orchestra, in which the spatial positions of musical chairs are periodically shifted, with the application of novel dynamic effects such as simultaneous crescendo and diminuendo in the same chord, is performed for the first time in Paris.

19 MARCH 1958

Gallantry, one-act "soap opera" by Douglas MOORE, in which a hospital nurse is libidinously coveted by a lascivious surgeon about to perform an appendectomy on her fiancé, set to music in mock-melodramatic tones, is performed for the first time in New York.

22 MARCH 1958

Ninth Symphony by the 82-year-old English composer Havergal BRIAN, written in 1951, in three movements, *Allegro vivo* (prefaced by a slow introduction), *Adagio* and *Allegro moderato,* set in a modernistically individual experimental manner without overflowing the tonal boundaries of classical forms, scored for full orchestra and a substantial pod of drums, is performed for the first time by the London Symphony Orchestra, under the direction of Norman Del Mar.

24 MARCH 1958

Gruppen, spatial work by the 30-year-old German apostle of the avant-garde Karlheinz STOCKHAUSEN, for three chamber orchestras, each governed by individual serial parameters determining meter, rhythm, intervallic structure, dynamics, instrumentation and differentiated noises, with three synchronized conductors beating time in three different tempi ($M_1 = 70$, $M_2 = 113.5$, $M_3 = 94$), is performed for the first time at Cologne.

25 MARCH 1958

Emerson WHITHORNE, American composer, who in 1920 wrote the first piece of airplane music, dies in Lyme, Connecticut, at the age of 73.

26 MARCH 1958

Ongaku, a symphonic suite on Japanese themes by Henry COWELL, is performed for the first time in Louisville.

26 MARCH 1958

Musique Funèbre by the 45-year-old Polish composer Witold LUTOSLAWSKI, dedicated to the heroes and victims of Polish resistance groups against the Nazis, based on a symbolic tonal emblem of ascending tritones and descending semitones, is performed for the first time in Katowice, Poland.

27 MARCH 1958

The Heart of the Taiga, opera in four acts by the 59-year-old Soviet composer Lev KNIPPER, to a libretto dealing with the conflicts and achievements in the collective farms of Eastern Siberia, set to music in accordance with the doctrine of Socialist Realism, national in thematic materials and socialist in treatment, is performed for the first time, in concert form, in Moscow. (The first version of the opera, originally entitled *The Root of Life* written in 1949, was not produced.)

28 MARCH 1958

W. C. HANDY, "Father of the Blues," who learned to play the cornet by practicing on a cow's horn as a child, and whose *Memphis Blues,* which he published at his own expense ($32.50) in 1912, created a new genre of American music, dies in New York at the age of 84. (A commemorative stamp of 6 cents, showing W. C. Handy playing the trumpet, was issued in Memphis on 17 May 1969 on the occasion of the sesquicentennial of the city and to honor the birth place of Memphis Blues.)

28 MARCH 1958

First Symphony by the 39-year-old American composer George ROCHBERG, in three movements—(1) *Allegro risoluto,* written in an exclamatory triadic idiom with atonal implosions and onomatopeic ornithological episodes; (2) *Tema e variazioni,* a sepulchrally Calvinistic chorale drenched in lachrymal magma; (3) *Adagio-Allegro giocoso,* a marching procession in maximal dissonances ending in reiterative caudal chords—is performed for the first time in Philadelphia.

1 APRIL 1958

Alexander TCHEREPNIN, 59-year-old Russian composer, becomes an American citizen in Chicago.

2 APRIL 1958

Ninth Symphony in E minor by Ralph VAUGHAN WILLIAMS, his last, written at the age of 85, in four movements—(1) *Allegro moderato,* in a whimsically variegated sonata form with a rhapsodically wrought recapitulation; (2) *Andante sostenuto,* introduced by a romantic flügelhorn solo, with a meaningful stroke of the gong ushering in a clonic march tune; (3) *Allegro pesante,* a sophisticated scherzo in which three saxophones disport themselves with saltatory felinity, ending with a funereal side-drum tap; (4) *Andante tranquillo,* in two sections, exuding a species of tragic optimism, concluding with periodically inturgescent and detumescent E-major chords, vanishing into nothingness, marked *niente* in the score—is performed for the first time, a few months before the composer's death, by the London Philharmonic Orchestra, Malcolm Sargent conducting.

2 APRIL 1958

Nirvana-Symphony by the 29-year-old Japanese composer Toshiro MAYUZUMI, in six movements, comprising three Buddhist hymns and three "campanologies" (temple bell tones), symbolizing the ideal Buddhist state Nirvana, with a male chorus in 12 parts singing Zen chants, is performed for the first time in Tokyo.

3 APRIL 1958

A century has elapsed since the death in Paris at 79, of Sigismund Ritter von NEUKOMM, "fruitful composer, world famous conductor and organist, all-round musician and scholar" (as he is described on a plaque on the wall on the house in which he was born around the corner from Mozart's birthplace in Salzburg).

4 APRIL 1958

Ett Spel om Maria (*A Play on Mary*), scenic oratorio by the 38-year-old old Swedish composer Sven-Erik BÄCK, with dodecaphonically serialized Holy Family supported by the diatonic choral commentary, is performed for the first time in Stockholm.

5 APRIL 1958

Minotauros, choreographic suite for orchestra by the 41-year-old Swedish composer Karl-Birger BLOMDAHL, descriptive of the Cretan half-bull half-man devouring virgins in a dodecaphonic fury, is performed for the first time in Stockholm.

11 APRIL 1958

Second Symphony by the 43-year-old Siberian-born American composer Alexei HAIEFF, in three movements, transcribed from his piano sonata written in 1955, in a modernistically mannered neo-baroque style, is performed for the first time by the Boston Symphony Orchestra, Charles Munch conducting.

13 APRIL 1958

Van CLIBURN, 23-year-old Louisiana-born Texan pianist, spectacularly wins the first prize in the Tchaikovsky Contest in Moscow for his performance of Tchaikovsky's *First Piano Concerto* and Rachmaninoff's *Third Piano Concerto*, victoriously overtaking a number of young Russians, and arousing tremendous enthusiasm among music-loving Muscovites. (On 20 May 1958, a Van Cliburn Day was declared in New York, and he was given a ticker-tape parade, the first musician so honored.)

14 APRIL 1958

Titus Feuerfuchs, oder Liebe, Tücke und Perücke, burlesque opera by the Swiss composer Heinrich SUTERMEISTER, is produced in Basel.

14 APRIL 1958

Two one-act operas are performed for the first time by the opera workshop and orchestra of the Mannes College of Music in New York:

The Robbers by the 34-year-old American composer Ned ROREM, to his own libretto, involving multiple internecine slaughter among three murderers in a fight over their initial victim's money, set to music in a grimly dissonant idiom, with recurrent detonations of homicidal harmonies, and *The Pet Shop* by the 60-year-old Egyptian-born Italian composer Vittorio RIETI, wherein the daughter of a New York society woman marries a member of the canine jury influential in awarding first prize to her mother's dog, set to music in an appropriately hedonistic manner with a cornucopia of vivacious melorhythms.

15 APRIL 1958

The Second Quintet for piano and strings by Ernest BLOCH is performed for the first time at the opening concert of a music festival arranged by the Department of Music of the University of California, Berkeley.

17 APRIL 1958

The Rock, a symphonic prelude by Bohuslav MARTINU, is performed for the first time in Cleveland.

18 APRIL 1958

First Symphony by the 24-year-old American composer Easley BLACKWOOD (completed by him in December 1955, at the age of 22) conceived "along completely abstract lines," in four movements, *Andante maestoso, Andante comodo, Scherzo, Andante sostenuto,* written in a rhapsodically romantic vein, with a tropism towards triadic points of repose, sensitized by atonal divagations in a euphonious polyharmonic setting, is performed for the first time by the Boston Symphony Orchestra, Charles Munch conducting.

18 APRIL 1958

The First Inter-American Music Festival opens in Washington under the auspices of the Pan American Union, with a program including the first performance of *New England Episodes,* a symphonic suite by Quincy PORTER.

20 APRIL 1958

Two Brazilian works, *Twelfth Symphony* by Heitor VILLA-LOBOS, and *Chôro* for clarinet and orchestra by Camargo GUARNIERI, are performed for the first time at the First Inter-American Music Festival in Washington.

21 APRIL 1958

Dugme (*The Button*), musical grotesque in one act by the 44-year-old Croatian composer Ivo LHOTKA-KALINSKI, dealing with the desperate predicament of a petty functionary invited to an influential dinner, who cannot find the crucial collar button for his formal dress, set to music in an utilitarian modernistic idiom replete with non-corrosive polytriadic dissonances, is performed for the first time in Zagreb.

22 APRIL 1958

Eighth Symphony, by Darius MILHAUD, subtitled *Rhodanienne,* depicting in its four movements the progress of the river *Rhône,* from its source in the Swiss glacier through Lake Geneva to its emergence as a French river, and its division into several streams forming a conspicuous delta, is performed for the first time by the San Francisco Symphony, Enrique Jordá conducting, on the same program with the first performance of the *First Violin Concerto* by the 37-year-old American composer Andrew IMBRIE.

23 APRIL 1958

The Good Soldier Schweik, opera by the American composer of Czech origin Robert KURKA (who died of leukemia at the age of 35, on 12 December 1957), to a colloquial American libretto drawn from the Czech novel of Jaroslav Hasek, depicting the misadventures of a Czech soldier of the Austro-Hungarian Army in World War I, whose irrepressible habit of good-natured equivocation embroils him in fantastic troubles with the military, written in an unaffected folkloristic manner and scored for wind instruments and percussion only, is posthumously performed for the first time at the City Center in New York.

26 APRIL 1958

Seventh Symphony by the 66-year-old Hungarian composer László LAJTHA, in three movements devoid of key signatures but essentially tonal, scored for an orchestra with multiple percussion to be used in a genteel manner without "brutal noise," and couched in a modern style with a modicum of civilized dissonances, using a heraldic motto trumpeted in naked fifths, is performed for the first time anywhere in Paris, prior to the initial production on Lajtha's earlier *Sixth Symphony.*

29 APRIL 1958

Fifth Symphony, Jerusalem (with chorus), by the Russian-born American composer Lazare SAMINSKY, in two sections, (1) *The City of Solomon,* "of strife, tumult and pristine splendor," and (2) *The City of Christ,* "of a creed born in disillusion, transfigured into light," composed in 1929–1930, comes to a belated first performance in New York.

2 MAY 1958

The Lady of Shalott, ballet by Sir Arthur BLISS, dealing with the love-death of a maiden from the Arthurian legends, who dies of unrequited love for Sir Lancelot of the Lake, is produced at the University of California, Berkeley.

4 MAY 1958

Escurial, one-act opera by the 25-year-old American composer Marvin David LEVY, is produced in New York.

15 MAY 1958

Concert for Piano and Orchestra by the prime mover of the American avant-garde John CAGE, in which miniaturized precision is antinomially achieved through the application of the principle of indeterminacy of melorhythmic parameters, is performed for the first and (by definition) last time in its nonprecognitive unreproducible form by the pianist David Tudor with Merce Cunningham as choreographic conductor, in New York.

The Concert for Piano and Orchestra is without a master score, but each part is written in detail in a notation where space is relative to time determined by the performer and later altered by a conductor. Notes are of three sizes referring ambiguously to duration or amplitude. As many various uses of the instruments as could be discovered were subjected to the composing means which involved chance operations and the observation of imperfections in the paper upon which the music was written. The pianist's part is a "book" containing 84 different kinds of composition. The pianist is free to play any elements of his choice, wholly or in part, and in any sequence. (From John Cage's annotation in the catalogue of his works)

22 MAY 1958

The Music Festival at the University of California, Berkeley concludes with the first performance of *Requiem* by Randall THOMPSON, for double chorus *a cappella.*

28 MAY 1958

The Central Committee of the Communist Party of the Soviet Union issues a declaration amending its Resolution of 10 February 1948 which assailed the state of Soviet music and singled out PROKOFIEV, SHOSTAKOVICH, KHACHATURIAN and MIASKOVSKY for specific derogation as submissive followers of the decadent Western trends. (Complete text in the section Letters and Documents.)

30 MAY 1958

First Violin Concerto by Béla BARTÓK (composed between 1 July 1907 and 5 February 1908) in two contrasting movements, *Andante sostenuto* (later incorporated into the first section of *Two Portraits* for orchestra), representing an Ideal and based on a "personal" leitmotiv, D-F-sharp-A-C-sharp, of the Hungarian violinist Steffi Geyer for whom the Concerto was written, and who was in possession of the unpublished and unperformed manuscript until her death in 1956, and *Allegro giocoso,* a hedonistic rondo, is performed for the first time in Basel.

5 JUNE 1958

Sixth Symphony by the Rumanian composer Alfred MENDELSOHN is performed for the first time in Bucharest.

6 JUNE 1958

Geigy Festival Concerto for a "Basel Drum" and orchestra, by Rolf LIEBERMANN, commissioned by the chemical firm J. R. Geigy & Co., of Basel, Switzerland, on the occasion of its bicentennial, set in a hedonistically dodecaphonic idiom, is performed for the first time in Basel.

7 JUNE 1958

Zoologica, a symphonic suite by the 55-year-old German composer Günther RAPHAEL, is performed for the first time in Duisburg.

9 JUNE 1958

The Sun Over the Steppe, opera in three acts by the 55-year-old Soviet composer Vissarion SHEBALIN, dealing with the civil war in the Don River basin in 1919, depicting in strong contrasts the militant heroism of the Bolsheviks and the black treachery of the counter-revolutionary forces in a socialistically realistic melodic style making use of authentic Cossack folk tunes, is performed for the first time in Moscow, in concert form. (The first stage production took place in Moscow on 22 December 1959.)

9 JUNE 1958

The 32nd Festival of the International Society for Contemporary Music opens in Strasbourg with the following program:

Septour by Peter SCHAT of Holland; *Oratio Mechtildis* for chamber orchestra by Klaus HUBER (Switzerland); *Développements raréfiants*, suite for voice and small ensemble by Makoto MOROI (Japan); *Les Jeux* for baritone and string orchestra by Milko KELEMEN (Yugoslavia); and *Concerto* for clarinet, horn, violin, cello, piano and percussion, by Ralph SHAPEY (U.S.A.).

11 JUNE 1958

The following works are presented at the 32nd Festival of the International Society for Contemporary Music in Strasbourg:

Concertino for three trumpets and string orchestra by Egil HOVLAND (Norway); *Ritornell* for orchestra by Ingvar LIDHOLM (Sweden); *Sept poèmes de René Char* for vocal quartet and orchestra by Jean-Louis MARTINET (France); and *Concerto* for jazz band and orchestra by Rolf LIEBERMANN (Switzerland).

12 JUNE 1958

The following program is presented at the 32nd Festival of the International Society for Contemporary Music in Strasbourg:

Fantasia seria for string quartet by Fleming WEIS (Denmark); *No. 5 Zeitmasse* for wind quintet, by Karlheinz STOCKHAUSEN (Germany); *Variations* for violin, cello, and piano by Yori-Aki MATSUDAIRA (Japan); *Alma Redemptoris Mater* for six wind instruments by Peter Maxwell DAVIES (England); and *String Quartet* by Valentino BUCCHI (Italy).

13 JUNE 1958

The following works are presented at the 32nd Festival of the International Society for Contemporary Music in Strasbourg:

Overture in tre tempi, by Niccolò CASTIGLIONI (Italy); *Pre-variata* for orchestra, by Einojuhani RAUTAVAARA (Finland); *Concerto* for piano, sixteen wind instranents, and percussion, by Miches CIRY (France); *Fourth Symphony* in one movement, by Bernd Alois ZIMMERMANN (Germany); and *Variations symphoniques* by Miloš SOKOLA (Czechoslovakia).

14 JUNE 1958

The following works are presented at the 32nd Festival of the International Society for Contemporary Music in Strasbourg:

Third Symphony by Henry BARRAUD (France); *Jeux* by DEBUSSY; and *Sixth Symphony* by Darius MILHAUD (France).

14 JUNE 1958

The 32nd Festival of the International Society for Contemporary Music in Strasbourg continues with the following program:

Second String Quartet by Herbert BRÜN (Israel); *Piano Fantasy* by Aaron COPLAND (U.S.); *Second String Quartet* by Hans Erich APOSTEL (Austria); *Dialogues* for two violins by John EXTON (England); and *Trio* for piano, violin and cello, by Artur MALAWSKI (Poland).

15 JUNE 1958

At the 32nd Festival of the International Society for Contemporary Music in Strasbourg, Charles Munch conducts the world première of the *Second Symphony* by the 87-year-old French modernist Florent SCHMITT, op. 137 (the First Symphony being the *Symphonie Concertante* for orchestra and piano written in 1932), his last work (excepting a Mass for mixed chorus and organ performed after his death), in three movements (*Assez animé, Lent sans excès Animé*), set in a vigorously youthful style, full of rhythmic propulsion in the animated sections and harmoniously lyrical in the slow movement, without transcending, however, the admirably respectable modernity of his earlyworks, generously coloristic in the scoring and ostentatiously somber in the savagely rhythmed primitivistic episodes. (Other works on the program were BACH's *Violin Concerto* in A minor, Sergei PROKOFIEV's *Second Violin Concerto* and *Suite en fa* for orchestra by Albert ROUSSEL.)

15 JUNE 1958

The posthumous opera *François Villon* by the Dutch composer Sem DRESDEN opens the Holland Festival at Amsterdam.

18 JUNE 1958

Noye's Fludde, one-act opera by Benjamin BRITTEN after a 14th-century English miracle play dealing with Noah's Ark and the Flood, and scored for a pleasingly bruitous ensemble of recorders, bugles, handbells, drums, cups hit by wooden spoons, string instruments and piano, with singing parts for the principal characters, a spoken part for the Voice of God (accompanied by a wind machine), and children's voices for seven groups of seven pairs of animals—lions, oxen, swine, camels, asses, dogs, cats, polecats, etc. and birds—is performed for the first time in the church of the village of Orford, England, during the course of the annual Aldeburgh Music Festival.

20 JUNE 1958

The Scarf, one-act opera by the 32-year-old American composer Lee HOIBY, with a libretto drawn from Chekhov's short story *The Witch*, dealing with a frustrated wife cheered by a young mailman seeking shelter in their house during a blizzard, with a murderous ending (not in the original story) when she strangles her uninteresting husband with her long scarf, set in a moderately modern vein, is performed for the first time at the First Festival of Two Worlds, in Spoleto, Italy.

23 JUNE 1958

Armas JÄRNEFELT, Finnish composer of melodious and harmonious instrumental pieces tenderly interwoven with Suomian folksong patterns within a Germanic framework, dies in Stockholm, where he made his home for many years, at the age of 88.

27 JUNE 1958

Cuba issues a postage stamp of 4 centavos honoring the 19th-century musician and pedagogue Ignacio CERVANTES.

10 JULY 1958

Italy issues postage stamps commemorating the approximate centennial of the birth of PUCCINI and that of LEONCAVALLO, the two Italian composers who, with Mascagni, created *Verismo*, the modern type of operatic realism, with denominations of 25 lire each.

16 JULY 1958

Wuthering Heights, opera in three acts with a prologue by the 32-year-old American composer Carlisle FLOYD, after Charlotte Brontë's emotional story of dark passions in the inhibited atmosphere of the bleak heath in the moor-lands of Northern England, with a musical score of balladic design uncluttered by polyphonic complexity and limited to functional melodic elements, is performed for the first time as a commissioned work by the Santa Fe Opera Company, in Santa Fe, New Mexico. (A revised version, with the third act entirely rewritten, was produced by the New York City Opera on 9 April 1959.)

17 JULY 1958

Second Symphony for string orchestra by the 63-year-old Corsican-born French composer Henri MARTELLI, is performed for the first time in Paris.

18 JULY 1958

Homenaje a Bolívar for voices, chorus and orchestra by the prime composer of Colombia Guillermo URIBE-HOLGUÍN, is performed for the first time in Bogotá.

31 JULY 1958

Percy A. SCHOLES, enlightened English writer on music, whose *Oxford Companion to Music* is a unique example of imaginative lexicography and a treasure trove of wide-ranging information, dies a week after his 81st birthday in Vevey, Switzerland, his home for many long years.

5 AUGUST 1958

Josef HOLBROOKE, English composer of ambitious stage works, in which he tried to block the modernistic tide and adopted a simplified tonal idiom to please the great masses (who failed to respond), dies in London a month after his 80th birthday.

17 AUGUST 1958

Florent SCHMITT, "le sanglier des Ardennes," as he was once called to describe his emotional impetuosity and boar-like animal power associated with the inhabitants of his native Ardennes, composer of numerous symphonic and choral works in a bold modern style which enjoyed a certain succès d'estime and who continued to write until the end (his last work, a symphony, was performed in his presence at the Strasbourg Festival on 15 June 1958), dies in Neuilly near Paris at the patriarchal age of 87.

20 AUGUST 1958

Maria Golovin, opera in three acts by Gian Carlo MENOTTI, to his libretto, dealing with a blinded Italian veteran of World War II who falls in love with the beautiful wife of a Russian prisoner of war presumed dead, attempts to shoot her when her husband materializes, and departs in quest of a new life, set to music in a gorgeously Italianate idiom, burnished with modernistic atonalities and vitalized by incidental spurts of euphonious jazz, is performed for the first time at the International Exposition in Brussels, Belgium.

24 AUGUST 1958

Leo BLECH, German composer and conductor, dies in Berlin at the age of 87.

26 AUGUST 1958

Ralph VAUGHAN WILLIAMS, grand seigneur of English modern music, whose many symphonic and choral works combined enlightened nationalism with superlative mastery of technical resources, dies in London at the age of 85, shortly after the first performance of his *Ninth Symphony*.

1 SEPTEMBER 1958

Belgium issues a postage stamp of 30 centimes honoring the Belgian violinist Eugène Ysaÿe on the occasion of the centennial of his birth.

3 SEPTEMBER 1958

The Congregation of Rites of the Vatican issues an Instruction on Sacred Music, prohibiting the use in liturgical services of mechanical devices such as radio, phonograph, tape recorder or automatic organ players even in transmitting sermons or performances of sacred music.

12 SEPTEMBER 1958

Léonidas ou la cruauté mentale, opéra-bouffe by the Swiss composer Pierre WISSMER, is performed for the first time in Paris.

15 SEPTEMBER 1958

Egypt issues a postage stamp to honor the Arab musician Sayed DARWISH (1892–1923).

23 SEPTEMBER 1958

At the final concert of the International Festival of Contemporary Music in Venice, Igor STRAVINSKY conducts the first performance of his sacred work to the Latin text from the Lamentations of the Prophet Jeremiah, entitled *Threni*, scored for six soloists, chorus and orchestra, his first integrally serial composition, evolved from a unifying 12-tone subject.

3 OCTOBER 1958

The Diary of a Madman, opera in one act by Humphrey SEARLE, after Gogol's story descriptive of the inner state of a demented Russian government clerk, with the madman intoning his fantasies and delusions in insanely atonal intervallic leaps while the dissonant orchestra observes a schizophrenically logical dodecaphonic structure, and an eerie electronic tape accompanies the madder moments of the psychological bedlam, leading to a final outcry in an integral twelve-note blob, is performed for the first time at the Berlin Music Festival, Hermann Scherchen conducting.

3 OCTOBER 1958

Guillermo URIBE-HOLGUÍN, 78-year-old Colombian composer, conducts in Bogotá the first performance of his *Eigth Symphony*.

7 OCTOBER 1958

Fiesta, minuscule one-act opera by Darius MILHAUD, dealing with a shipwrecked sailor rescued by villagers who seduces the wife of one of them and is ignominiously thrown back into the sea, is performed for the first time in Berlin.

7 OCTOBER 1958

Genèse, electronic music for five oscillators by the prime composer of the Dutch avant-garde Henk BADINGS, tape-recorded in Eindhoven on four tracks of spatial sound, is performed in public for the first time in Brussels. (It was produced as a ballet under the title *Der Sechste Tag* in Innsbruck on 7 November 1959, and under the title *Mikrobiologisches* in Linz on 22 February 1960.)

13 OCTOBER 1958

A *Vision of Judgement*, oratorio by Peter Racine FRICKER, is performed for the first time at the Leeds Festival.

14 OCTOBER 1958

THE RCA ELECTRONIC MUSIC SYNTHESIZER, capable of producing any musical tone in any instrumental color, and of manipulating them by repetition, reverberation, dynamic intensification, rhythmic variegation, acceleration and deceleration, is patented by its inventors, H. F. OLSON and H. BELAR, of the Acoustical and Electromechanical Research Laboratory of the Radio Corporation of America. (The first public presentation of the RCA Electronic Music Synthesizer and music produced by the machine was made at the American Institute of Electrical Engineers Meeting in New York on 31 January 1956 by General David Sarnoff.)

16 OCTOBER 1958

Nocturne, a linked series of songs for voice and small orchestra, by Benjamin BRITTEN, to texts from poems by Shakespeare, Shelley, Keats, Tennyson, Coleridge, Middleton, Wilfred Owen and Wordsworth, with night being represented by the perennially incandescent key of C major and dawn by intrusive inflections of D-flat major, is performed for the first time at the Centennial Music Festival at Leeds.

18 OCTOBER 1958

Minnesota Symphony by the Norwegian composer Harald SAEVERUD, commissioned for the celebration of the centennial of the statehood of Minnesota, in four movements with subtitles suggesting the ethnic aspects of Scandinavian Minnesotans (*Once Upon a Time, Hope and Longing, Gay Day, Man and the Machine*) is performed for

the first time by the Minneapolis Symphony Orchestra, Antal Dorati conducting.

19 OCTOBER 1958

Poésie pour pouvoir by Pierre BOULEZ, scored for two orchestras conducted by two synchronized conductors (Hans Rosbaud and Boulez himself), with four large and four small loudspeakers placed on each wall and a rotating loudspeaker suspended from the ceiling (the rate of rotation is specified as a serial parameter), with a recorded narration of French poetry, electronically distorted so as to render it unintelligible, rising from a dehumanized sinusoidal sound to a limit of sonic variety, is presented for the first time at the Donaueschingen Festival.

21 OCTOBER 1958

Un Ballo in Maschera by VERDI, is brought out in Swedish at the Stockholm Opera, with the original libretto dealing with the assassination of Gustave II of Sweden in March 1792, instead of that of the absurd "governor" of Boston of the traditional version made under the pressure of the authorities in turbulent Italy fearing the dangers of the representation of regicide on the stage.

24 OCTOBER 1958

Lukas FOSS conducts the Pittsburgh Orchestra in the first complete presentation of his *Symphony of Chorales for Orchestra*, in four movements based respectively on Bach's chorales No. 90, No. 77, No. 139, No. 133 and containing in the second movement a fugue on the motive B-A-C-H, with consecutive entries at the interval of a tritone.

25 OCTOBER 1958

Osud, opera in three "romantic tableaux" by Leoš JANÁČEK, written in 1903–1904, and depicting symbolically and autobiographically the tragic frustrations of a composer Zivny (i.e. living) amid the inappreciative hordes of uncomprehending society, is performed on the stage for the first time in Brno, thirty years after the composer's death. (A concert performance of the work was given by the Brno Radio on 18 September 1934.)

27 OCTOBER 1958

Undine, a ballet by Hans Werner HENZE, is performed for the first time anywhere in London.

3 NOVEMBER 1958

Tenth Symphony by the 82-year-old English composer Havergal BRIAN, in a single compound movement entailing constant changes of tempi and set in a modernistic romantic idiom, scored for a large orchestra including a phalanx of drums requiring the services of ten players, is performed for the first time in London.

Completion of each of my symphonies is realized by Symmetry and Balance of Design. The Symphonies compose themselves. (From Havergal Brian's declaration of purpose made at the age of 94, on 7 May 1970, at the author's request)

7 NOVEMBER 1958

Variazioni Concertanti for orchestra by the 55-year-old Russian-born American composer Nikolai LOPAT-NIKOFF, consisting of the theme enunciated by strings pizzicato, four variations, and an energetic finale, is performed for the first time in Pittsburgh.

10 NOVEMBER 1958

Adventures of King Arthur, one-act opera buffa by the foremost woman composer of Poland Grazyna BACEWICZ, is performed for the first time on the Warsaw Radio.

27 NOVEMBER 1958

Artur RODZINSKI, fiery conductor of Dalmatian birth and Jewish-Polish origin, who acquired fame as a symphonic perfectionist and disciplinarian, and notoriety as a recalcitrant and intransigent artist, constantly at odds with the managerial world (he was discharged successively by the New York Philharmonic and the Chicago Symphony Orchestra in the middle of the season for violations of contractual agreements), dies of heart failure in Boston, while on a brief American engagement, at the age of 66.

28 NOVEMBER 1958

Fourth Symphony, subtitled *Crazy Horse Symphony* as a tribute to the legendary Sioux Indian Chief, by the 44-year-old American composer Charles MILLS, is performed for the first time in Cincinnati.

3 DECEMBER 1958

Mrika, first national Albanian opera, written by the Albanian composer Prenk JAKOVA, wherein a young Albanian girl named Mrika is sabotaged in her work involving the construction of a collective hydro-electric power plant by her treacherous temporary bride-groom acting at the behest of foreign imperialists, with the socialistically realistic ending vouchsafed when she overcomes all interventionist wiles and, as the plan is completed, marries a progressive coworker, set to music in a congenially optimistic idiom, based on proletarian Albanian tunes, is produced in Shkodra.

3 DECEMBER 1958

Second Symphony by the 34-year-old Harbin-born Russian-American composer Benjamin LEES, in three movements, *Andante mesto, Scherzo* and *Adagio,* in a contrastingly lyrical, hedonistic and meditative style, vitalized by propulsive rhythms, is performed for the first time in Louisville.

5 DECEMBER 1958

Fourth Symphony by the 59-year-old Russian-American composer Alexander TCHEREPNIN, in three movements, *Moderato, Allegro, Andante con moto,* melodically based on his favorite 9-note scale constructed by dividing the octave into three equal parts and interpolating two passing notes in each division with the polyphonic structure governed by the method described by him as *Interpoint (punctus inter punctum),* is performed for the first time by the Boston Symphony Orchestra, Charles Munch conducting.

11 DECEMBER 1958

Ikuma DAN, Japanese composer, conducts in Tokyo the world première of his grand opera *Yang Kwei-fei,* on an ancient Chinese tale dealing with a concubine of the Chinese Emperor who falls in love with the Emperor's eunuch, featuring a Mongolian wrestling dance as a choreographic interlude.

11 DECEMBER 1958

Sixth Symphony by Jean RIVER, in four contrasting movements, embanked within the bounds of traditional symphonic forms, is performed for the first time in Paris.

22 DECEMBER 1958

A century has passed since the birth in Lucca of Giacomo PUCCINI, who introduced into the world of Italian operatic melodrama a number of novel modernistic procedures, such as whole-tone scales, consecutive triads and ninth-chords, unresolved suspensions, sustained dissonances and even polytonality, without impairing the popular appeal and great commercial success of his productions.

1959

3 JANUARY 1959

Thirteenth Symphony by the 73-year-old prolific Rumanian composer Dimitrie CUCLIN is performed for the first time in Arad.

4 JANUARY 1959

O Vestido de Noiva, opera by the 67-year-old Portuguese composer Ruy COELHO, is produced in Lisbon.

24 JANUARY 1959

Moskva Tcheryomushki, the first operetta by Dmitri SHOSTAKOVICH, depicting the urban predicament of the newly wed Sasha and Masha, trying to obtain an apartment in the new housing development in the Moscow suburb of Tcheryomushki, with a score full of dulcet waltzes and hedonistic tunes, is produced in Moscow.

27 JANUARY 1959

The Volcano, opera in three acts by the Soviet composer Evgeny UTZEVICH, wherein a wily American capitalist named Octopus and his daughter who is employed by the Central Intelligence Agency are exposed by a native woman school teacher with the aid of the downtrodden Polynesian masses groaning under the yoke of the American military forces occupying, since 1945, a volcanic island in the South Pacific, is produced in Donetz.

30 JANUARY 1959

Paul HINDEMITH conducts the Pittsburgh Symphony Orchestra in the first performance of his *Pittsburgh Symphony*, composed for the bicentennial celebration of the city, in three movements, of which the first exploits quartal melodic patterns and their inversions, the second is a slow angular march ending with six instrumental variants of the Pennsylvania Dutch tune "*Hab lumbedruwwel mit me lumbeschatz*" and the last movement is based on an ostinato figure of six different notes, with a final somewhat jazzy subject to the words: "Pittsburgh is a great old town."

The Pennsylvania Dutch are very familiar to me; their German dialect is almost the same as that of my old home. I have always been acquainted with their way of life. And their Lieder are those which to this very day are sung in the countryside where they once originated. (Hindemith's statement in the program book)

31 JANUARY 1959

Fantasia Concertante for piano and orchestra by Bohuslav MARTINU in three movements, in a translucent neobaroque style, is performed for the first time in Berlin, with Margrit Weber, to whom the work is dedicated, as soloist.

5 FEBRUARY 1959

Curt SACHS, learned German musicologist, expert in Oriental musical cultures, dies in New York at the age of 77.

6 FEBRUARY 1959

La Vox humaine, one-act opera by Francis POULENC, a monologue for soprano, to a text by Jean Cocteau, in which a dejected girl vainly tries to regain the affection of her lover in a long responseless telephone monologue reaching its climax when she learns of his impending marriage, and still cries, "Je t'aime!" written in a monodically sensual simplified Debussyan idiom, with aerostatic harmonics supporting a fleshless and denuded vocal line (a Paris critic described the action as "Mélisande au telephone") is produced at the Opéra-Comique in Paris. (Date from the announcement of the work as "creation" in *Le Figaro* of 6 February 1959; the date given in the *Enciclopedia dello Spettacolo*, 17 February 1959, is tardy.)

7 FEBRUARY 1959

A Guide to the Life Expectancy of a Rose, one-act operafantasy by the 37-year-old American composeress Vivian FINE, to her own libretto, written in a sophisticated vigesimosecular idiom vitalized by prudential dissonances, is produced in concert form in New York.

8 FEBRUARY 1959

Third Symphony by Elie SIEGMEISTER is performed for the first time in Oklahoma City.

12 FEBRUARY 1959

George ANTHEIL, the whilom enfant terrible of American music whose *Ballet mécanique* depicts in expressive noises the ambience of the modern world amidst American-made machines, but whose later compositions reflect his disillusion in conventional modernity and a militant espousal of the eternal verities of tonal music, and whose lovelorn column "Boy Meets Girl" helped to patch up many a broken romance, dies in New York at the age of 58.

13 FEBRUARY 1959

Ivailo, opera in seven scenes by the 50-year-old Bulgarian composer Marin GOLEMINOV, to a libretto dealing with the Bulgarian uprising against their Mongolian overlords in 1280, led by the shepherd Ivailo, written in an expansive Italianate manner, with the inclusion of authentically Slavic popular chants of the period, is produced in Sofia.

13 FEBRUARY 1959

Parables by Bohuslav MARTINU, a symphonic suite in three sections, *Parable of a Sculpture* (after Saint-Exupéry, alluding to a mystical change in one who looks at a statue), *Parable of a Garden* (with reference to a psychic meaning of floral scent), and *Parable of a Labyrinth* (inspired by *Le Voyage de Thésée* by Georges Neveux, which postulates the mythological truth that without the aid of Ariadne and her guiding thread, Theseus would have never found his way out of the Cretan labyrinth), is performed for the first time by the Boston Symphony Orchestra, Charles Munch conducting.

17 FEBRUARY 1959

Percussion Concerto by André JOLIVET in four movements, *Robuste, Dolent, Rapidement* and *Allègrement,* is performed for the first time in Paris.

23 FEBRUARY 1959

Il Dottore di vetro, radiophonic opera by the 40-year-old Rumanian-born Italian composer Roman VLAD, dealing with a senescent Spanish doctor, dissuaded by a scheming barbering surgeon from marrying a nubile damsel who diagnoses the gout from which he suffers as a case of incipient vitrification resulting from unbridled sexual fantasies, is produced in Turin.

24 FEBRUARY 1959

Second Symphony by the English composer Lennox BERKELEY, in four movements of neo-classical content vitalized by an infusion of non-toxic dissonances, is performed for the first time in Birmingham.

25 FEBRUARY 1959

Gustave BECKER, American pianist and composer, who continued to give annual concerts even after he became a nonagenarian, dies at the age of 97 while visiting his daughter in Epsom, Surrey, England.

26 FEBRUARY 1959

Second Symphony by the 40-year-old American composer George ROCHBERG, in four sections, derived from a symmetrical 12-tone row of two groups of hexachords but free of dodecaphonic asceticism and admitting even explicit triadic formations, is performed for the first time by the Cleveland Orchestra, George Szell conducting.

28 FEBRUARY 1959

The Sons of Aaron, opera in two acts by the 37-year-old German-born American composer Siegfried LANDAU, to his own libretto from the Bible, is performed for the first time in Scarsdale, New York.

1 MARCH 1959

Capriccio for soprano, violin and orchestra by Rolf LIEBERMAN, in the form of a compact *Rondo* in which the main subject is taken from his opera *Leonore 40/45,* another theme is a dodecaphonic *Adagio* from a love song in his opera *Penelope,* and still another theme borrowed from his piano sonata, is performed for the first time in Paris.

1 MARCH 1959

Das Stundenlied, choral suite with orchestra by Gottfried VON EINEM, to nine poems by Bertolt Brecht on the nine hours of the Passion, in which Jesus appears as the Socialist victim of reactionary priests, is performed for the first time in Hamburg.

3 MARCH 1959

Thirteenth Symphony in five movements, subtitled *Madras Symphony,* by Henry COWELL, written during his sojourn in Madras, India, in the course of a world tour, in 1956, and completed in New York in 1958, inspired by the Indian talas (rhythmic patterns) and the ragas (scales or modes), is performed for the first time in Madras by the Little Orchestra of New York City under the direction of Thomas Scherman, during its Asian tour.

4 MARCH 1959

Third Symphony by the Norwegian composer Klaus EGGE, inspired by the spectacular display of aurora borealis during a transatlantic flight, in one movement opening and ending with an evocative *Adagio misterioso,* with an intermediate rapid section in asymmetrical rhythms, illustrative of the changing colors of the phenomenon, is performed for the first time in Louisville.

10 MARCH 1959

Summer Seascape, symphonic sketch by Howard HANSON, is performed for the first time by the New Orleans Symphony Orchestra.

15 MARCH 1959

Seventh Symphony by the 53-year-old German master of polyphonic dodecaphony, Karl Amadeus HARTMANN, in three movements, *Ricercare, Adagio Mesto* and *Virtuoses Scherzo,* is performed for the first time in Hamburg.

17 MARCH 1959

Rafaele d'ALESSANDRO, Swiss composer of pleasantly modern pieces, dies in Lausanne on his 48th birthday.

17 MARCH 1959

Quotations in Percussion by Arthur COHN, a quinquepartite suite for 103 percussion instruments, the largest phalanx of its type ever assembled for performance, among them a gigantic bass drum, a microsonic triangle, hydrophonic gong, the Brazilian concussion instrument reco-reco, cracked glass in a glass container, a doublebass placed on sawhorses and struck with drumsticks, a cat's meow and friction utensils such as a washboard, with a text from anonymous and non-anonymous authors, inter alia Walt Whitman and James Joyce, is performed for the first time in New York.

20 MARCH 1959

Symphonic Poem After Descartes by the 56-year-old American composer John VINCENT, in two parts of four sections each wherein the Cartesian principle of actuality is reflected by the thematic notes of the natural harmonic series, with the opening phrase by the solo timpani prosodically rhythmed in the basic words of Descartes, *Cognito ergo sum,* continuing through the musical representation of the Cartesian theory of planetary motions in *Vortex,* and of the geometric *Folium,* a Cartesian knot, and allusions to the philosopher's Catholic faith in quotations from medieval hymnody, concluding on a chord containing a series of overtones, is performed for the first time by the Philadelphia Orchestra, Eugene Ormandy conducting.

21 MARCH 1959

Monsieur Jabot, opera by the Swiss composer Roger VUATAZ, is performed for the first time in Geneva.

3 APRIL 1959

Fourth Symphony by the Swedish composer Gunnar BUCHT is performed for the first time in Stockholm.

5 APRIL 1959

Marie ASHTON, 238-pound housewife in Slough, England, completes 133 hours of uninterrupted (except for necessary physiological functions) piano pounding, establishing a world record of pianofortitude for the female of the species, although still falling far behind the accomplishment of Heinz Arntz of Germany who completed a piano marathon of 255 hours on 28 April 1953.

11 APRIL 1959

Eric BLOM, urbane, witty and caustic English writer on music, whose life of musical journalism culminated in the formidable accomplishment of editing the Fifth Edition of Grove's *Dictionary of Music and Musicians* in nine volumes, the largest music dictionary in the English language, dies in London at the age of 70.

13 APRIL 1959

Eduard VAN BEINUM, energetic and imaginative Dutch conductor, who commuted by plane via the North Pole between Los Angeles, where he was permanent conductor, and Amsterdam, where he was similarly engaged, dies suddenly at the age of fifty-seven while conducting a rehearsal of the Concert-gebouw Orchestra in Amsterdam.

16 APRIL 1959

Third Symphony by the 35-year-old American composer Ned ROREM, in five classically designed movements, opening with a *Passacaglia*, and couched in a euphonious idiom with an invigorating injection of non-toxic dissonances, is performed for the first time in New York. On the same program was *Second Symphony*, subtitled *Titans*, by the 30-year-old American composer William Joseph RUSSO.

23 APRIL 1959

On the Far Shores, opera in four acts by the Estonian composer Willem REJMAN, the action taking place in a country on the Indian Ocean "controlled by the military forces of a certain imperialist power" represented by a Mr. Lockhart and a Mr. Brown, whose sinister schemes of military and economic subjugation are foiled by a socialistic local teacher and an employee of the Soviet Embassy, is produced at Tallin.

25 APRIL 1959

Second Symphony by the 52-year-old Soviet Georgian composer Andrei BALANCHIVADZE is performed for the first time in Tbilisi.

26 APRIL 1959

Aurelia, opera in three acts by the 47-year-old Moldavian composer David GERSHFELD, to a Moldavian text, dealing with a local girl who dies a heroic death fighting the Nazis in Bessarabia, is produced in Kishinev.

26 APRIL 1959

Six Characters in Search of an Author, musical play by the 46-year-old Czech-born American-educated composer Hugo WEISGALL, after Pirandello's symbolic drama, with the dramatis personae being members of an opera company, so that the product represents a controlled and strictly circscribed opera rehearsal, set to music in a quasi-dodecaphonic idiom, is produced by the New York City Opera.

26 APRIL 1959

Kádár Kata, opera in two acts by the Hungarian composer Mihály HAJDU, after a grim Transylvanian tale in which the possessive mother of a youth in love with Kata drowns her in a pond, and as her body is incarnated in a flower, he follows her into the dark waters, is produced in Budapest.

27 APRIL 1959

The Hunted, opera by the 26-year-old American composer Martin MAILMAN, is performed for the first time in Rochester, New York.

12 MAY 1959

Fantaisie concertante for violin and piano by the 65-year-old Belgian composer Jean ABSIL is performed for the first time in Brussels.

15 MAY 1959

Mérope, opera in three acts by the Portuguese composer Joly Braga SANTOS, with the vocal line set in conformity with the natural prosody of the Portuguese language, is produced in Lisbon.

17 MAY 1959

Mirandolina opera by Bohuslav MARTINU, after Carlo Goldoni's comedy *La locandiera* (*The Mistress of the Inn*), is produced in Prague.

21 MAY 1959

Symphonic Epitaph, for narrator, chorus and orchestra by the 31-year-old Serbian composer Aleksander OBRADOVIĆ, extolling the heroism of mobilized workers who held off the Nazi assault during the invasion of Yugoslavia in 1941, is performed for the first time in Belgrade.

23 MAY 1959

Joshua, biblical oratorio by the 52-year-old Germanborn American composer and conductor Franz WAXMAN, is performed for the first time in Dallas, Texas.

31 MAY 1959

Aniara, "revue of mankind in space-time," by the 42-year-old Swedish composer Karl-Birger BLOMDAHL, wherein an animated female electronic brain Mima guides the space ship Aniara to Mars after the atomic disintegration of the earth, with the passengers delivering themselves nostalgically to the last terrestrial pleasures (a sex orgy in a hall of mirrors, a jazz session, etc.), the music running the entire gamut of expression from a Lesbian waltz to a jazz solo in 7/16, with some weird sounds on magnetic tape creating a suitable interplanetary mood, and recordings of the voices of Hitler, Khrushchev and Eisenhower remindful of the past forces of evil, half-evil and good, the nuclear musical motif being an involuted *Grossmutterakkord*, consisting of 12 different notes and 11 different intervals spiralling out of the central C, and ever returning to it, is performed for the first time at the Royal Opera in Stockholm.

3 JUNE 1959

Doña Beatriz, la Sinventura, opera by the Guatemalan composer Felipe SILIÉZAR, depicting the great inundation of 1541 in Guatemala during which a volcanic lake engulfed the palace of the Spanish colonial regents carrying Doña Beatriz, "the Luckless One," to her death, is produced in Guatemala City.

8 JUNE 1959

The PURCELL-HANDEL Festival opens in London (both composers were buried in Westminster Abbey) under the combined auspices of The Arts Council, the British Council, the British Broadcasting Corporation and the British Museum, continuing through 27 June, and featuring performances of operatic works, oratorios and solo compositions.

10 JUNE 1959

The 33rd Festival of the International Society for Contemporary Music opens in Rome with the following program of symphonic music:

Cheltenham Concerto for chamber orchestra by George ROCHBERG of the U.S.A.; *Skaldens Natt* for soprano, chorus and orchestra by the Swedish composer Ingvar LIDHOLM; *Omnia tempus habent*, cantata for soprano and 17 instruments by the German composer Bernard Alois ZIMMERMAN; and *Prolation* for orchestra by the 24-year-old English composer Peter Maxwell DAVIES.

10 JUNE 1959

Seraphine oder die stumme Apothekerin, opera by the Swiss composer Heinrich SUTERMEISTER, after Rabelais, is performed for the first time over the Zürich Radio.

11 JUNE 1959

At the 33rd Festival of the International Society for Contemporary Music in Rome, the following program of chamber music is given:

Eighth String Quartet by the dean of Swedish composers, Hilding ROSENBERG: *Serenata* for flute, viola, doublebass, harpsichord and percussion by Goffredo PETRASSI of Italy; *Nocturnos* for soprano and instruments by Hans Ulrich ENGELMANN of Germany; and *Three Blue Sketches* for nine instruments by Hanns JELINEK of Austria, written in a dodecaphonic jazz style with a serial sequence of meters and rhythms.

12 JUNE 1959

At the 33rd Festival of the International Society for Contemporary Music in Rome, the following chamber works are presented:

Mati (Mother) for voice and string quartet by the 28-year-old Yugoslav composer Alojz SREBOTNJAK; *Second String Quartet* by the Argentinian composer Alberto GINAS-TERA; *Three Studies* for cello and piano by the 35-year-old Australian composer Don BANKS; *Two Sonnets* for baritone, clarinet, viola and cello by the American composer Milton BABBITT; and *Ein irrender Sohn* for contralto and instruments by the 22-year-old Swedish composer Bo NILSSON.

13 JUNE 1959

At the 33rd Festival of the International Society for Contemporary Music in Rome, the following works by the winners of the International Competition of 1958 are presented, in an afternoon concert:

String Quartet by the 25-year-old American composer Ramiro CORTES; *Des Engels Anredung an die Seele* for tenor, accompanied by flute, horn, clarinet and harp, by the 34-year-old Swiss composer Klaus HUBER; *Six Poems of Dylan Thomas* for voice and instruments, by Riccardo MALIPIERO; and the cantata *Canticum Psalmi Resurrectionis* by the 28-year-old German composer Dieter SCHÖNBACH.

13 JUNE 1959

The 33rd Festival of the International Society for Contemporary Music in Rome presents an evening concert of the following symphonic works:

Sinfonia in Do, written by Manuel ROSENTHAL of France during his sojourn in America in 1949, and first performed in Paris on 12 June 1950; *Tartiniana Seconda* for violin and orchestra by Luigi DALLAPICCOLA (his first *Tartiniana* was written in 1951), on material from Tartini's unpublished works; *Quatre Essais* for orchestra by the 30-year-old Polish composer Tadeusz BAIRD (first performed in Katowice on 12 August 1958), wherein each of the four parts uses different instrumentation, in a protusion of emancipated dodecaphony; *Impromptus* for orchestra by Wolfgang FORTNER of Germany, built on a sequence of serial parameters; and STRAVINKSY's *Agon*, in which *sui generis* serial procedures and polyrhythmy form a synthesis of Stravinsky's earliest and latest methods.

14 JUNE 1959

Die tödlichen Wünsche, opera by the 33-year-old German composer Giselher KLEBE, after Balzac's novel *La Peau de Chagrin*, in which the owner of a magical piece of shagreen that fulfills his wishes is consumed by the inanition of success, is performed for the first time in Düsseldorf.

14 JUNE 1959

The 33rd Festival of the International Society for Contemporary Music in Rome continues with the following program of chamber works:

Suite de Kurpie for contralto and 9 instruments by the 32-year-old Polish composer Witold SZALONEK; *Trio* for clarinet, cello and piano by the 42-year-old Swedish composer Karl-Birger BLOMDAHL; and *Improvisations sur Mallarmé* for soprano and instruments by the French apostle of intransigent antideterminism in a calculated aleatory system of composition, Pierre BOULEZ.

15 JUNE 1959

At the 33rd Festival of the International Society for Contemporary Music in Rome the following works for chamber orchestra are presented:

Konstellationen, suite for strings by the 35-year-old Danish composer Per NØRGÅRD (first performed on the Danish Radio on 3 November 1958), spiritually and technically derived from the early period of Schoenberg, middle period of Alban Berg, and late period of Béla Bartók; *Concertino* for piano and chamber orchestra, by the 39-year-old French composer André CASANOVA; *Incontri* for 24 instruments by the 35-year-old Italian experimentalist Luigi NONO (first performed at the Darmstadt Festival on 30 May 1955); *Tre Studi* for chamber orchestra by the 34-year-old Italian composer Aldo CLEMENTI (first performed at the Festival for New Music in Darmstadt in 1957); *Oiseaux exotiques* for piano and orchestra by Olivier MESSIAEN, composed in 1955, conjuring up in sophisticated idealization the tweets, chirps, warbles, twitters and trills of polychromatic birds of Asia and America; and *Samai* for chamber orchestra by the Japanese composer Yoritsune MATSUDAIRA, a palimpsest of old Japanese court dance themes and serial parameters.

16 JUNE 1959

The 33rd Festival of the International Society for Contemporary Music in Rome concludes with a program of the following symphonic and choral works:

Permutazioni sinfoniche by the Dutch composer Guillaume LANDRÉ based on the medieval idea of hexachordal mutations, with centripetal tonal inflections; *Vier Gedichte von Stefan George* for mixed chorus with instrumental accompaniment, by the German composer Michael GIELEN, derived from a dodecaphonic radix, tonally solidified by recognizable repetitions of focal elements; *Trittico sinfonico* by the Finnish composer Nils-Eric FOUGSTEDT; and *Nachtstücke und Arien* for soprano and orchestra by the 32-year-old German modernist Hans Werner HENZE, depicting, with a modicum of modified dodecaphony, the passage from crepuscular to auroral hours.

17 JUNE 1959

A Hand of Bridge, for four solo voices and chamber orchestra by Samuel BARBER, to a libretto by Gian Carlo Menotti, revealing in audible asides the wishes, anxieties and fantasies of a bridge foursome: a florid businessman conjuring up an alabaster palace at Palm Beach with "twenty naked girls and twenty naked boys tending to my pleasures," a lawyer wondering where his unstabilized blond-tressed mistress was, and their vacuous wives engaged in inconsequential chatter, set to music in a tense polyrhythmic idiom, is performed for the first time at the Festival of Two Worlds in Spoleto, Italy.

17 JUNE 1959

The American popular pianist LIBERACE is awarded by a London tribunal the sum of 10,000 pounds in damages in his suit for defamation of character against the *Daily Mirror* of London and its columnist W. Connor (Cassandra) for suggesting in print that Liberace was a homosexual.

19 JUNE 1959

Salto Mortale, electronic opera by Henk BADINGS for five voices with electronic accompaniment, to the composer's libretto, in which a professor of biochemistry (lyric tenor) restores to life a recent suicide poet by using an elixir perfected by him and enabling him to vitalize dead bodies, if not too decayed, and who kills him again when the poet, whose voice suddenly changes from tenor to bass, forms a mutual attraction with the professor's favorite young laboratory assistant (a high soprano), is produced by the Dutch Television Network, as the first opera totally accompanied by an electronically recorded score.

21 JUNE 1959

On the occasion of the bicentennial of the foundation of the City of Pittsburgh, the Pittsburgh Symphony Orchestra presents the world premières of *Adagio and Scherzo* by Quincy PORTER, and *Paeans and Dances of Heathen Iberia* by Carlos SURINACH.

25 JUNE 1959

Clarinet Concerto by Guillaume LANDRÉ is performed for the first time in Amsterdam as part of the Holland Festival.

3 JULY 1959

Concerto for viola, strings and percussion in four movements by the 35-year-old Vienna-born Americanized Israeli composer Robert STARER, written in techniques suggested by similarly instrumented works by Béla Bartók and Frank Martin, is performed for the first time in Geneva.

5 JULY 1959

Concerto Grosso for orchestra by Heitor VILLA-LOBOS is performed for the first time in Pittsburgh.

7 JULY 1959

Ernest NEWMAN, nonagenarian English music critic who started out as a Liverpool bank clerk named William Roberts, adopted the symbolic pseudonym "earnest new man" and sailed forth on a brilliant career of musical journalism (he was columnist of *The Sunday Times* of London for 38 years until his retirement on his 90th birthday in 1958), author of a monumental Wagner biography and several books on opera, dies at Tadworth, Surrey.

9 JULY 1959

La Notte di un Nevrastenico, opera buffa by the 47-year-old Italian composer Nino ROTA, dealing with sexual frustrations of a neurasthenic youth bedeviled by the amorous groans made by a heterosexual couple occupying an adjacent room in his hotel, is performed for the first time in concert form in Turin.

14 JULY 1959

GROCK, Swiss-born musical clown whose real name was Adrian Wettach, who provided entertainment for half a century by playing on a tiny violin kept in a huge fiddle case, or trying to move the piano towards the bench before starting to play, dies at Imperia, Italy, at the age of 79.

15 JULY 1959

Ernest BLOCH, Swiss-born composer of impassioned Jewish-inspired music clad in sonorous modern harmonies, dies of cancer in Portland, Oregon, nine days before his 79th birthday.

In my works termed "Jewish" I have not approached the problem from without, by employing melodies more or less authentic or "Oriental" formulae, rhythms or intervals . . . No! I have but listened to an inner voice, deep, secret, insistent, ardent, an instinct much more than cold and dry reason, a voice which seemed to come from afar beyond myself, far beyond my parents. This entire Jewish heritage moved me deeply; it was reborn in my music. To what extent it is Jewish, to what extent it is just Ernest Bloch, of that I know nothing. The future alone will decide. (From Bloch's article in *Musica Hebraica* 1938)

17 JULY 1959

Janus by Paul CRESTON, a diptych consisting of a lyric prelude and a fast dance with a single theme for both sections, in unvarying triple time but greatly variegated as to rhythms and polyrhythms, is performed for the first time in Denver.

22 JULY 1959

Missa Breves for 3-part boys' voices and organ by Benjamin BRITTEN, according to the Catholic rite, to Latin words (*Credo* is omitted), is performed for the first time at Westminster Cathedral in London.

23 JULY 1959

The Bayreuth Festival opens with a performance of *Der Fliegende Holländer*, staged in an expressionistic and inherently un-Wagnerian manner by Wagner's grandson Wieland Wagner.

29 JULY 1959

The Union of Soviet Socialist Republics issues a postage stamp representing the statue of TCHAIKOVSKY.

9 AUGUST 1959

Emil František BURIAN, modern Czech composer who initiated voice bands performing in a prescribed rhythmic pattern but without definite pitch, dies in Prague at the age of 55.

9 AUGUST 1959

A *Faun in the Forest*, one-act opera by the English composer Gerald COCKSHOTT, is produced at the rustic White Barn Theater, in Westport, Connecticut.

15 AUGUST 1959

Alexandra, opera by the Israeli composer Menahem AVIDOM, dealing with the martyrdom of Alexandra, the last ruler of the Hasnonean dynasty, is produced in Tel Aviv.

16 AUGUST 1959

Wanda LANDOWSKA, grande dame of the clavecin, a noble instrument which she lovingly resuscitated from its Baroque quietus, and brought forth a bevy of pupils, dies at the age of 82 in her American retreat (where she lived since she was forced to abandon France as the German armies converged on Paris) at Lakeville, Connecticut.

16 AUGUST 1959

Pedro Humberto ALLENDE, Chilean composer who combined in his works the peculiar melorhythms of the Chilean countryside with impressionistic harmonies, dies in Santiago at the age of 74.

17 AUGUST 1959

Julietta, "opera semiseria" by the 35-year-old German composer Heimo ERBSE, based on the short story of Heinrich von Kleist, *The Marquise of O.*, relating the plight of a young Italian widow cast adrift during the Napoleonic wars and rescued from the rapacious soldiery by a noble German aristocrat, who, however, takes advantage of her fainting spell to incontinently ravish and impregnate her, redeeming himself by a proposal of honorable marriage, set to music in an appropriately hedonistic vein, is produced in Salzburg.

19 AUGUST 1959

Symphonic Prayer by Alexander TCHEREPNIN, thematically based on the 9-tone "Tcherepnin scale," a symmetrical progression of three groups, each containing a whole tone and two semitones, contrapuntally treated in his *sui generis* technique of *Interpunctus*, in which two-part complexes enter the interstices between wider two-part complexes, all immersed in euphonious dissonances, is performed for the first time as a commissioned work at the opening concert of the Pan American Festival in Chicago.

24 AUGUST 1959

The Eleventh International Edinburgh Festival opens with a presentation by the Royal Opera of Stockholm of Verdi's *Un Ballo in Maschera*, with the libretto restored to its original, in which King Gustav II of Sweden, and not the preposterous Riccardo, Governor of Boston, is assassinated by his secretary, in a Swedish translation and adaptation from the primary source, *Gustave III ou Le Bal masqué* by Eugène Scribe.

25 AUGUST 1959

On his 41st birthday, Leonard BERNSTEIN conducts in Moscow a concert of the New York Philharmonic Symphony Orchestra, on its grand tour of Europe, presenting the first Moscow performance of STRAVINSKY's *Le Sacre du Printemps* since the Soviet Revolution, and the first Soviet performance of *The Unanswered Question* by Charles IVES, encored in response to an ovation.

28 AUGUST 1959

Sinfonia for two orchestras by the British composer Iain HAMILTON is performed for the first time at the Edinburgh Festival.

28 AUGUST 1959

Bohuslav MARTINU, Czech composer of classically wrought symphonies animated by a deep emotional current and of many instrumental concertos and chamber music pieces, cast in a judiciously modernistic manner without ever relinquishing the basic sense of tonality, dies at the age of 68 in Liestal, Switzerland.

8 SEPTEMBER 1959

A souvenir sheet containing postage stamps for HANDEL (10 pfennigs), HAYDN (25 pfennigs), SPOHR (15 pfennigs), BEETHOVEN (20 pfennigs), and MENDELSSOHN (40 pfennigs) is issued in West Germany in conjunction with the opening of the Beethoven Hall in Bonn.

11 SEPTEMBER 1959

The 22nd International Festival of Contemporary Music opens in Venice, continuing through 26 September, and featuring opera, ballet, chamber music and electronic demonstrations, including three ultra-modern stage works by Italian composers: *Allez-hop*, mimed tale by Luciano BERIO; *Diagramma Circolare*, abstract melodrama by Alberto BRUNI; and *Il Circo Max*, a contemporary satire on café society by Gino NEGRI.

12 SEPTEMBER 1959

Prometheus, opera by Rudolf WAGNER-RÉGENY, is performed for the first time in Kassel.

12 SEPTEMBER 1959

The Third Festival of Contemporary Music opens in Warsaw with the world première of Tadeusz BAIRD's *Expression* for violin and orchestra, and works by SHOSTAKOVICH (*First Piano Concerto*), Anton VON WEBERN (*Six Pieces* for orchestra), SZYMANOWSKI (*Third Symphony*), and Boleslaw SZABELSKI (*Toccata* for orchestra).

14 SEPTEMBER 1959

At the Third Festival of Contemporary Music in Warsaw, the world premières of *Music for Strings, Horn and Percussion* by Grazyna BACEWICZ and *First Symphony* by Henryk GÓRECKI are given, as well as SZYMANOWSKI's *Fourth Symphony* and Luigi NONO's *Composizione per Orchestra*.

17 SEPTEMBER 1959

Strophes by the 25-year-old Polish avant-garde composer Krzysztof PENDERECKI, scored for soprano, speaker and ten instruments, to words from the Bible, Sophocles and other great sources, written in a highly complex athematic idiom, making use of serial and aleatory procedures, is performed for the first time at the "Warsaw Autumn" Festival.

20 SEPTEMBER 1959

Die Ermörderung Cäsars, one-act opera by the 34-year-old German composer Giselher KLEBE, is performed for the first time in Essen.

22 SEPTEMBER 1959

Josef Matthias HAUER, Viennese pioneer of 12-tone music based on symmetric six-note tropes (he had a rubber stamp made, which he used on his stationery, signed "the spiritual protagonist of 12-tone music and, despite many poor imitators, still the only one who knows and understands it"), dies in solitude and obscurity in a furnished room in Vienna, at the age of 76.

25 SEPTEMBER 1959

Gunther SCHULLER conducts in New York the first performance of his *Conversations* for string quintet and jazz quartet (piano, percussion, vibraphone and doublebass), containing aleatory interludes.

3 OCTOBER 1959

Plautus in Nonnenkloster, opera by the 70-year-old German composer Max BUTTING, is produced in Leipzig.

3 OCTOBER 1959

Second Symphony by André JOLIVET in three movements—(1) *Heurté*, marked by colliding sonorities (hence the subtitle); (2) *Fluide*, in a slow tempo with serially developed lyric motives; (3) *Vigoureux*, a hedonistic finale—is performed for the first time in Berlin.

4 OCTOBER 1959

A series of 18 autogenetic meetings is launched by the American writer, painter and musician Allan KAPROW at the Reuben Gallery in New York, with a cast of participants including visitors "who sit in various chairs," described as HAPPENINGS, thereby adding a winged word to the modern vocabulary.

The name "Happening" is unfortunate. It was not intended to stand for an art form, originally. It was merely a neutral word that was part of a title of one of my projected ideas. It was the word which I thought would get me out of the trouble of calling it a "theater piece," a "performance," a "game," a "total art," or whatever, that would evoke associations with known sports, theater, and so on. But then it was taken up by other artists and the press to the point where now all over the world it is used in conversation by people unaware of me, and who do not know what a "Happening" is. (From a recorded interview with Allan Kaprow, reproduced in *Happenings*, an anthology, published in New York, 1966)

4 OCTOBER 1959

Concerto for cello and orchestra, op. 107, by Dmitri SHOSTAKOVICH, in four sections, *Allegretto*, *Moderato*, *Cadenza*, and *Allegro con moto*, beginning and ending in E-flat major, characteristically Shostakovichian in its contrasts of relentless animation and ruminating lyricism, is performed for the first time in Leningrad by Mstislav Rostropovich, to whom the piece is dedicated.

4 OCTOBER 1959

Der arme Konrad, opera in five acts by the 50-year-old German composer Jean Kurt FOSTER, dealing with the peasant rebellion in Southern Germany in 1514, is produced in East Berlin.

12 OCTOBER 1959

Frigate Victory, opera by the Russian composer Boris ARA-POV, after Pushkin's novella *The Moor of Peter the Great*, is given its radio première in Leningrad.

17 OCTOBER 1959

Epitaphium für das Grabmal des Prinzen Max Egon zu Fürstenberg, a dodecaphonic offering by Igor STRAVIN-SKY on the tomb of the prince patron of the Donaueschingen Festival, scored for flute, clarinet and harp and consisting of eight statements of its unifying dodecaphonic theme, including inversion, retrograde and inverted retrograde, is performed for the first time at the opening of the annual Musiktage in Donaueschingen.

18 OCTOBER 1959

Vlast (*Authority*), third musical burlesque by the 46-year-old Croatian composer Ivo LHOTKA-KALINSKI, dealing with a pompous prime minister whose authority is deflated by ridicule, set to music in a utilitarian polytriadic manner making melodic use of a specialty devised heterotonal scale in the range of a minor ninth, is performed for the first time on the television network in Zagreb.

19 OCTOBER 1959

Stanley BATE, English composer of rhapsodic symphonies and neo-romantic chamber music, dies in London at the age of 47.

21 OCTOBER 1959

Concertino for doublebass and strings by the 35-year-old Croatian composer Milko KELEMEN is performed for the first time in Zagreb.

21 OCTOBER 1959

Violin Concerto by the 46-year-old Soviet composer Tikhon KHRENNIKOV, written in an optimistically vigorous manner, consonant with the ideals of Socialist Realism, is performed for the first time in Moscow.

22 OCTOBER 1959

A century has passed since the death in Kassel of Ludwig SPOHR, grand master of German music whose fame rivaled that of Beethoven and Mendelssohn, but whose obsolescent operas, oratorios, symphonies, concertos, chamber music, and songs rapidly decayed into archeological desuetude.

23 OCTOBER 1959

Beatrice, music drama in three acts by the 33-year-old American composer Lee HOIBY, based on Maeterlinck's play *Sœur Béatrice*, and dealing with a ravished nun driven to bordellos, who returns to the convent in her old age and meets a saintly prioress in whom she recognizes her other self as she might have been, and dies absolved of shame, is performed for the first time in Louisville.

23 OCTOBER 1959

Three New England Sketches, suite for orchestra by Walter PISTON, with romantic subtitles, *Seaside*, *Summer Evening* and *Mountains*, reflecting the "impressions, reminiscences, even dreams, that pervaded the otherwise musical thoughts of one New England composer," with coloristic sonorities permeating the essentially symphonic design, is performed for the first time at the 100th Worcester, Massachusetts Festival by the Detroit Symphony Orchestra, Paul Paray conducting.

23 OCTOBER 1959

Eagles, symphonic poem by Ned ROREM, is performed for the first time by the Philadelphia Orchestra, on his 36th birthday.

24 OCTOBER 1959

Seventh Symphony (*Liturgical*) by the 44-year-old American composer Vincent PERSICHETTI is performed for the first time by the St. Louis Symphony Orchestra.

28 OCTOBER 1959

Second Symphony by Roberto GERHARD, Catalan composer radicated in England since the Spanish Civil War, written in a serial polyphonic idiom, is performed for the first time in London.

28 OCTOBER 1959

La Vida de le Misión, posthumous Spanish-American opera by the German-born Texan composer Carl VENTH, is performed by the Symphony Society of San Antonio for the first and last time, a few months before his centennial, using the funds left by Venth's widow to satisfy the dead composer's lifelong desire to let the world hear it.

30 OCTOBER 1959

Kassiani, opera in four acts by the Greek composer George SKLAVOS, dealing with a Byzantine noblewoman who resolved to become a nun, is performed for the first time in Athens.

5 NOVEMBER 1959

The first performances of two symphonies by the 83-year-old English composer Havergal BRIAN are given in London: *Eleventh Symphony*, written in 1954, consisting of three contrasting movements and ending with a festive march; and *Twelfth Symphony*, written in 1957, in a single movement subdivided into three sections and concluding serenely after a fierce climax.

9 NOVEMBER 1959

Heeding the protest made by the Moslem population of Djakarta, the Indonesian Army Commander of the Fourth Military District of West Java issues a decree banning rock 'n' roll, cha-cha, and other American "social dances" as violating the Indonesian norm of decency. (Date and details communicated by the Embassy of Indonesia, Washington, D.C., in a communication to the author dated 21 June 1961.)

13 NOVEMBER 1959

Second Symphony by the 53-year-old American composer Ross Lee FINNEY is performed for the first time in Philadelphia.

16 NOVEMBER 1959

The Sound of Music, musical comedy by Richard RODGERS to the lyrics of Oscar HAMMERSTEIN II, suggested by the true story of Baroness Maria von Trapp, governess to the seven singing children of the widowed Austrian Baron Georg von Trapp (whom she subsequently married), who fled Austria en masse after the Nazi Anschluss in 1938 to find fame as the Trapp Family Singers, with a variety of eminently singable songs in the score, including the modernized solfage ditty, *Do-Re-Me*, is produced in New York.

17 NOVEMBER 1959

Heitor VILLA-LOBOS, great innovator of Brazilian music, inventive creator of the pan-Brazilian *Chôros* and of *Bachianas Brasileiras*, in which Bach-like polyphony forms the background for Brazilian melorhythms, and who believed that science, love of country and music form the triune entities expressing the idea of *Brasilidade*, dies in his native Rio de Janeiro at the age of 72.

26 NOVEMBER 1959

Albert KETÈLBEY, English composer of remote Danish origin, whose exotic pieces, such as *In a Persian Market*, *In a Monastery Garden*, *In a Chinese Temple Garden*, became fantastically popular among the musical bourgeoisie all over the world, and even penetrated via radio into the proletarian masses of the young Russian Soviet Socialist Republic, causing Soviet spokesmen for the arts to declare Ketèlbey's alluring exoticism a piece of cleverly masked imperialist propaganda, dies in Cowes, Isle of Wight, at the age of 84.

27 NOVEMBER 1959

Der Tod des Grigori Rasputin, opera in three acts by Nicolas NABOKOV (grown out of the one-act opera *The Holy Devil* first performed in Louisville on 18 April 1958), describing in naturalistic detail the astounding story of the painstaking murder in 1916 of the Russian "mad monk," by poison, bullets and drowning under ice, with quotations and stylizations of contemporary salon music (an old-fashioned phonograph is played on the stage), is produced at Cologne.

27 NOVEMBER 1959

Seven Studies on Themes of Paul Klee by the 34-year-old American composer Gunther SCHULLER, in seven movements depicting in various heterotonal colors seven paintings by Paul Klee, one of them, *The Twittering Machine*, lubricated with some quarter-tones, is performed for the first time by the Minneapolis Symphony Orchestra, Antal Dorati conducting.

6 DECEMBER 1959

Stanac, opera by the 64-year-old Croatian composer Jakov GOTOVAC, to a libretto from a 16th-century Croatian fable in which an aged shepherd named Stanac is induced by cunning swindlers to shave his beard and give his sheep away to nubile town girls in the expectation that these actions would rejuvenate him, but who

remains as phallically fallible as prior to his pogonotomy, is performed for the first time in Zagreb.

9 DECEMBER 1959

Legend, symphonic poem by the 38-year-old American composer Andrew IMBRIE, is performed for the first time by the San Francisco Symphony Orchestra.

11 DECEMBER 1959

Second Symphony by the 43-year-old French composer Henri DUTILLEUX, in three movements, *Animato, ma misterioso, Andantino sostenuto, Allegro fuocoso*, scored for 12 solo instruments and orchestra, with the two groups collectively independent of each other, resulting in a stereophonic antiphony and instrumental echolalia, is performed for the first time as a commissioned work by the Boston Symphony Orchestra, Charles Munch conducting.

11 DECEMBER 1959

Oedipus der Tyrann, "funeral play," after Sophocles, by Carl ORFF, is produced at Stuttgart.

11 DECEMBER 1959

Mela and Fair, orchestral essay by Henry COWELL, designed to effect a compatible blend of Hindu melorhythms (Mela is the Hindu word for country fair) with Americanistic fiddling tunes, is performed for the first time at the opening of the United States exhibit at the World Agricultural Fair in New Delhi, as a musical manifestation of the Fair's motto, "Food, Friendship, Freedom and Family."

13 DECEMBER 1959

The Sofa, a modern opera by the 52-year-old English composeress Elizabeth MACONCHY, is produced in London.

15 DECEMBER 1959

Blue Flame, opera in four scenes by the 48-year-old American composer Alan HOVHANESS, is performed for the first time in San Antonio, Texas.

18 DECEMBER 1959

Two days after his 77th birthday, Zoltán KODÁLY, veteran of Hungarian music, marries his 19-year-old pupil Sarolta Péczely. (His first wife, pianist and composer of salon music which she published in 1900–1905 under her first married name Emma Gruber, and whom Kodály married in 1910, died on 12 November 1958 at the age of 99.)

(Date of Kodály's second marriage and the age of the bride at the time was communicated to the author by Sarolta Kodály during a visit at the Kodály home in Budapest on 25 March 1963.)

18 DECEMBER 1959

Oratorio of Our Time for narrator, solo voices, chorus and orchestra by the Bulgarian composer Lubomir PIPKOV, to the words of six imaginary letters from a girl to a soldier, set to music in the effective manner of Socialist Realism and collective individualism, vitalized by a profusion of asymmetrical Balkan rhythms, is performed for the first time in Plovdiv.

24 DECEMBER 1959

La Mystère de la Nativité, oratorio by the prime composer of Switzerland Frank MARTIN, to a text from a 15th-century nativity play, picturing heaven (modally) and hell (atonally and dissonantly), and concluding with the presentation of Jesus in the temple, is performed for the first time in Geneva.

28 DECEMBER 1959

Three tenors, Ramon Vinay of Chile, Karl Liebl of Germany, and Albert Da Costa of the United States sing at the Metropolitan Opera House in New York the role of Tristan in the first, second and third acts of *Tristan und Isolde* respectively, all three being successively disabled by debilitating colds but making this valiant effort in order to prevent the cancellation of a sold-out performance, with the unaffected Swedish soprano Birgit Nilsson imperturbably singing the part of Isolde.

1960

2 JANUARY 1960

Fourth Symphony by Roger SESSIONS, written in celebration of the centennial of the State of Minnesota, in three movements—(1) *Burlesque,* a satirically atonal piece, punctuated by asymmetrical stresses; (2) *Elegy,* a somberly passionate invocation, receding into elegiac reverie; (3) *Pastorale,* a bucolic musical landscape in barcarolle-like rhythms—in a euphonious dissonant setting, is performed for the first time by the Minneapolis Symphony Orchestra, Antal Dorati conducting.

5 JANUARY 1960

Poems for Tables, Chairs and Benches by the 24-year-old Idaho-born experimentalist La Monte YOUNG, a visual and aural action in which furniture is moved, audibly by dragging or pushing on the floor, or inaudibly by lifting, with pre-programmed parameters indicating the timing of entrances and exits of the furniture movers and duration of each manipulation of a specific piece of furniture, is performed for the first time as part of the series of experimental music, at the University of California, Berkeley.

10 JANUARY 1960

Jabadao, choreographic tone-poem by the Corsican composer Henri TOMASI evoking the ancient Celtic action in Brittany, in which the devil (represented by five oboes in unison to emulate the obsolete instrument *bombarde*) captures the souls of incautious maidens who venture out on a midnight dance, is performed for the first time in Paris.

10 JANUARY 1960

Igor STRAVINSKY conducts in New York the world première of his *Movements for Piano and Orchestra,* in five divisions, written according to a personally furbished and punctiliously fashioned dodecaphonic method of composition, with the serial rows spaced horizontally while polyrhythmic patterns are designed for vertical perception.

Perhaps the most significant aspect of my new work is its "anti-tonality." I am amazed at this myself, in view of the fact that in *Threni,* triadic references occur in every bar. This new work is the most advanced, from the point of view of construction, of anything I have ever composed. Every aspect of the composition of the *Movements* was guided by the forms of the series—the sixes, the quadrilaterals, the triangles, etc. To me, the fact of the 12 tones is not as important as the fact of the serial function. The *Movements* have made me see that I am becoming not less but more of a serial composer. The rhythmic language of the *Movements* is also the most advanced I have so far used. I compose my polyrhythmic combinations to be heard vertically. . . . The five movements are related more by tempo than by "mood" or "character." . . . Construction replaces contrast. (From Stravinsky's program note)

15 JANUARY 1960

Spectra by the American composer Gunther SCHULLER, scored for a septuple orchestra, in seven parts, to convey the impression of the seven principal colors reflecting the heptatonic nature of the rainbow, is performed for the first time anywhere by the New York Philharmonic, Leonard Bernstein conducting.

22 JANUARY 1960

Tahmeela, symphonic poem by the Egyptian composer Halim EL-DABH, is performed for the first time by the Cairo Symphony Orchestra.

25 JANUARY 1960

La Coupole, symphonic poem by the 32-year-old French Composer Jacques BONDON, subtitled *Tableaux fantastiques d'un monde étrange* and presenting scenes of an extra-terrestrial world with scintillating metallic percussion, undulating tropes of woodwinds, oscillating divided strings, and vociferating brass, is performed for the first time in Paris.

1 FEBRUARY 1960

Arjuna, symphonic poem by Alan HOVHANESS, scored for small European-type orchestra with the Indian instrument *mridangam*, and couched in the Carnatic classical style, is performed for the first time at an all-Hovhaness concert in Madras, India, with the composer participating as pianist.

2 FEBRUARY 1960

Second Symphony by the Czech-born Canadian composer Oscar MORAWETZ is performed for the first time by the Toronto Symphony Orchestra.

5 FEBRUARY 1960

A Igreja do mar, opera by the Portuguese composer Frederico DE FREITAS, is performed for the first time in Lisbon.

9 FEBRUARY 1960

Ernst VON DOHNÁNYI, grand old man of Hungarian music, the last of the Mohicans of the Central European romantic school of music, whose first steps in composition received the blessings of Brahms, dies of a heart attack in New York City at 10:40 in the morning, at the age of 82.

12 FEBRUARY 1960

Attis, cantata by 38-year-old Wisconsin-born American composer Robert W. MOEVS, to the erotic latin verses from Catullus bemoaning the fate of a Phrygian youth who is compelled to sacrifice his virility to the Earth Goddess, is performed for the first time by the Boston Symphony Orchestra, Richard Burgin conducting.

22 FEBRUARY 1960

Concerto for Piano with wind instruments and percussion by the 30-year-old Welsh composer Alun HODDINOTT, in four movements set in a traditionally dissonant modern idiom, is performed for the first time in London.

25 FEBRUARY 1960

Music for Amplified Toy Pianos by John CAGE, the keyboard of each being limited to nine white keys with microphones attached to the instruments and wired loudspeakers distributed among the audience so that deafening decibels enter each human auricle, is performed for the first time by David Tudor, Cage's authorized pianist and faithful famulus, at Wesleyan University in Middletown, Connecticut.

29 FEBRUARY 1960

Bursać Nikoletina, symphonic poem by the Yugoslav composer Dragutin ČOLIĆ, named after a roguish character of northwestern Bosnian folklore, set to music permeated with asymmetrical Balkan dance rhythms, is performed for the first time in Belgrade.

1 MARCH 1960

Second Symphony by the 60-year-old American composer Joseph WAGNER, in four movements bearing self-explanatory titles—(1) *With dramatic intensity*, (2) *With continuous restless energy*, (3) *With dignified noble simplicity*, (4) *With strong drive*—is performed for the first time in Wilmington, Delaware. (A revised version was first performed in Providence on 12 February. 1963.)

1 MARCH 1960

Sinfonietta in E, in four movements, by Paul HINDEMITH, is performed for the first time, as a commissioned work, by the Louisville Orchestra, Robert Whitney conducting.

4 MARCH 1960

Hunchback-Horse, ballet by the 27-year-old Soviet composer Rodion SHCHEDRIN, after the famous Russian fairy tale dealing with an omnipotent pony, is produced in Moscow. (A revised version was produced in Leningrad on 21 December 1963.)

4 MARCH 1960

The American baritone Leonard Warren is fatally stricken on the stage of the Metropolitan Opera in New York at 9:55 P.M., after completing Don Carlo's aria *Urna fatale del mio destino* in the third act of Verdi's *La Forza del Destino*, and dies a few minutes later, at 10:03 P.M., of a massive cerebrovascular hemorrhage.

10 MARCH 1960

Svätopluk, historical opera by the 51-year-old Slovak composer Eugen SUCHOŇ, dealing with a Moravian prince who ordered the expulsion of followers of the Thessalonian brothers Cyril and Methodius, founders of the Slavic branch of the Greek Orthodox Church, and restored the Catholic liturgical service in Moravia, is performed for the first time in Bratislava.

18 MARCH 1960

Concertino for cello and orchestra, op. 132, by Sergei PROKOFIEV, left incomplete at his death, is performed for the first time in Moscow, in an idiomatically supplemented version by Mstislav Rostropovich.

18 MARCH 1960

Antal DORATI, 53-year-old Hungarian conductor, conducts the Minneapolis Symphony Orchestra, of which he is musical director, in the first performance of his *First Symphony*, in five movemements, designated by formal content: Sonata (*Vivace con brio*), Variazioni (*Andante*), Scherzo (*Presto*), Adagio (*Notturno*), and Rondo Finale (*Allegro robusto*), without key signatures but converging centripetally on a focal A, with thematic elements derived from chromatic permutation and containing spacious pentatonic melodies of millennial antiquity redolent of the primeval modes of the Szekels and Magyars in immemorial Pannonia, culminating in a terse and curt finale.

23 MARCH 1960

Magische Quadrate, symphonic fantasy by the 64-year-old Austrian composer Johann Nepomuk DAVID, intervallically derived from magic squares in which the sums of the horizontal, vertical and diagonal rows of numbers are constant, and depicting in its three movements the *Saturn Square* (constant sum 15), *Melancholia Square* (constant sum 34), and the *Witch Square* (constant sum 15), with the augends and the addends computed in semitones from an arbitrarily selected ground note designated by unity, is performed for the first time in Recklinghausen, Germany.

23 MARCH 1960

The Radio Station WEOK at Poughkeepsie, New York, issues a directive, replacing the term "Disk Jockey" for radio announcers who "ride" recordings of popular songs by "Musicaster" to avoid "unpleasant associations" resulting from revelations that disk jockeys accepted "payola" (payment by interested parties to promote particular songs on the air by broadcasting them at prime time with eloquent "plugs").

26 MARCH 1960

Concerto for Kazoo and Orchestra by the 36-year-old New York composer Mark BUCCI, originally titled *Concerto for a Singing Instrument* (so that any instrument with the range of a twelfth, including the human voice, can perform it), accompanied by strings, harp and celesta, and written in an uninhibitedly hedonistic manner, replete with unapologetically tonal melody dipped in a nontoxic dissonant sauce, is performed for the first time by the New York Philharmonic at a concert for young people, Leonard Bernstein conducting, with Anita Darian as Kazoo soloist.

28 MARCH 1960

Twelfth Symphony by Henry COWELL is performed for the first time by the Houston Symphony Orchestra, Leopold Stokowski conducting.

28 MARCH 1960

Fife and Drum Corps is organized in the U.S. Army to play on festive occasions on the fife and on the drums, colorfully attired in the costumes of Spirit of 1776.

28 MARCH 1960

Austrian Airlines inaugurates the flights of three Vickers Viscount planes carrying the name of Beethoven, Bruckner and Johann Strauss.

29 MARCH 1960

Ninth Symphony by Darius MILHAUD, commissioned by the Fort Lauderdale, Florida, Symphony Orchestra, in three movements, *Modérément animé*, *Lent et sombre* and *Alerte et vigoureux*, without key signatures but gravitating towards a barycentric F, is performed for the first time in Fort Lauderdale, under the direction of Mario di Bonaventura.

30 MARCH 1960

Joseph HAAS, whose liturgic works written in a grand Germanic manner (*Deutsche Singmesse*, *Deutsche Kindermesse*, *Deutsche Gloria*) with their emphasis on the hypostatic Germanism of God, seem to justify the appellation "Der Spielmann Gottes" bestowed on him by his admirers, dies in Munich 12 days after his 81st birthday.

5 APRIL 1960

Night Blooming Cereus, chamber opera in two scenes by the 33-year-old Canadian composer John BECKWITH, in which a gardening lady receives a visit by her daughter's daughter as an act of contrition to expiate her mother's elopement a generation before, with an emotional finale as the nocturnal cereus suddenly blossoms forth in the afternoon, set to music in a moderately modern idiom decussated with asymmetrical meters, and copulated in innocuous dissonant counterpoint, is produced in Toronto. (A concert performance took place on the Ontario Radio on 4 March 1959.)

14 APRIL 1960

The Woman of Andros, electronic ballet by Henk BADINGS, realized in the Philips Laboratory at Eindhoven on four tracks of spatial sound, is performed for the first time in Hannover, Germany.

23 APRIL 1960

Ferde GROFÉ leads the San Francisco Symphony Orchestra as guest conductor in the world première of his musicoramic *San Francisco Suite*, in four pictorial movements, *Gold Rush*, *Bohemian Nights*, *Mauve Decade* and *1906–1960*, the latter opening with a concentrated blast of ultra-seismological percussion to illustrate the famous San Francisco earthquake.

26 APRIL 1960

Boréal, an impressionistically Arctic symphonic poem by the 34-year-old Canadian composer François MOREL, is performed for the first time in Montreal.

27 APRIL 1960

Constellations for chamber orchestra by the 35-year-old Croatian avant-gardist Milko KELEMEN, in which melodic, rhythmic and dynamic groups continually return in varying combinations, is performed for the first time in Zagreb.

2 MAY 1960

Three centuries have passed since the birth in Palermo of Alessandro SCARLATTI, founder of the Neapolitan School of composition, composer of numerous effective oratorios and operas, and father of Domenico Scarlatti.

2 MAY 1960

Jugando al toro, ballet inspired by a bull fight, by the 30-year-old Spanish composer Cristóbal HALFFTER, is performed for the first time in Barcelona.

4 MAY 1960

Chvala Světla (*Praise of Light*), cantata in eleven sections by the 35-year-old Czech composer Svatopluk HAVELKA, marked by optimistically diatonic melodies and polytriadic harmonies, with a profusion of tritones in a section entitled "In Praise of Modern Fashion," is performed for the first time in Prague.

8 MAY 1960

Hugo ALFVÉN, Swedish composer of five symphonies and of a well-known Swedish orchestral rhapsody, *Midsommarvaka*, which he wrote in 1904, dies a week after his 88th birthday, at Faluns, Sweden.

9 MAY 1960

Botho von Steegan, 60-year-old refugee from East Prussia, sets fire to Beethoven's birthplace in Bonn, destroying the furniture and two early Beethoven autographs, a song *An Laura*, and the piano score of an early ballet, as a gesture of protest against the order by the West German authorities for his forcible deportation to East Germany.

10 MAY 1960

Goran, cantata by the Croatian composer Krešimir BARANOVIĆ, in five movements to the words by a Croatian poet who fell in the battle against the Nazis, is performed for the first time in Belgrade under the composer's direction.

10 MAY 1960

Stari mladić (The Old Bachelor), opera by the 58-year-old Yugoslav composer Tihomil VIDOŠIĆ, using folk melos of Istria for local color, is produced in Rijeka (Fiume).

11 MAY 1960

Una notte in Paradiso, opera by the 43-year-old Italian composer Valentino BUCCHI, is performed for the first time in Florence.

14 MAY 1960

Lucrezia BORI, famous Spanish-born soprano, whose real name, Borja, she changed to avoid any association with the murderous Lucrezia Borgia, dies in New York at the age of 72.

14 MAY 1960

Virgil THOMSON conducts at the State University College of Education in Potsdam, New York, the first performance of his *Missa pro Defunctis*, for chorus and orchestra, embodying elements ranging from earliest Christian chants to the jazzy inflections of modern America, harmonically dominated by the spirit of the major triad, moving in parallel formations and creating "evanescence and iridescence" in shifts of unstable tonality.

16 MAY 1960

Ludas Matyi, ballet by the 57-year-old Hungarian composer Ferenc SZABÓ, after a Hungarian fairy tale dealing with a proletarian youth who forces a dishonest merchant to pay him the price of his wild geese, set to suitably picaresque music, infused with melorhythms of Hungarian folksongs, is performed for the first time in Budapest.

19 MAY 1960

Tobias and the Angel, opera in two acts by Sir Arthur BLISS, on the biblical subject wherein the Archangel Raphael exorcises the demon who has been annoying the bride of Tobias, is produced in London.

20 MAY 1960

Les Amants captifs, opera by the 54-year-old French composer Pierre CAPDEVIELLE, in which Vulcan imprisons Venus and Mars in an invisible net on their adulterous bed, is performed for the first time in Bordeaux.

21 MAY 1960

Eighth Symphony by the 68-year-old Hungarian composer László LAJTHA, classically constructed in four movements, devoid of key signatures, with the basic tonal materials exfoliating in ostentatiously dissonant secundal concatenations, fertilized by an insemination of Transylvanian modalities, is performed for the first time in Budapest, anticipatorily to the first performance of his earlier *Sixth Symphony* which took place in Brussels on 12 December 1960.

22 MAY 1960

Der Prinz von Homburg, opera in three acts by the German composer Hans Werner HENZE, after an old melodrama by Heinrich von Kleist discoursing upon the peripeties of a German prince sentenced to die for neglecting his military duties in favor of love, reprieved at the last moment and given a victor's laurel, with a musical score of dynamic incandescence increasing in complexity from Italianate beginnings to a dodecaphonic climax, is produced in Hamburg.

24 MAY 1960

Primavera, symphonic suite in four vernal movements by the 44-year-old South African composer Arnold van WYK, thematically derived from songs by the 13th-century German minnesinger Neithart von Reuenthal, is performed for the first time in Bloemfontein, South Africa.

25 MAY 1960

Malcolm Frager, 25-year-old American pianist, plays at the Queen Elisabeth International Music Competition in Brussels the first performance of the *Piano Concerto* by the Belgian composer Marcel POOT specially written for the competition, and wins first prize, outdazzling a number of formidably equipped Russian pianists.

26 MAY 1960

Noc a Naděje (Night and Home), symphonic poem by the 38-year-old Czech composer Otmar MÁCHA, dedicated to the memory of the victims of the ghetto of Theresienstadt, the Nazi camp near Prague, with the anguished mood sustained by a monothematic progression of alternating semitones and sesquitones, is performed for the first time in the course of the International Music Festival in Prague, bearing the allusively vernal name Prague Spring (Prague was liberated from the Nazis in the spring).

27 MAY 1960

Fourth Symphony by the 56-year-old American composer Vittorio GIANNINI is performed for the first time at the Juilliard School of Music in New York.

27 MAY 1960

Violin Concerto by the 35-year-old ex-dodecaphonic French composer Serge NIGG, written in an eclectic idiom conforming to the doctrine of Socialist Realism adopted by him under the influence of the French Communist Party, is performed for the first time in Paris.

28 MAY 1960

Fifth Symphony by the Dutch composer Léon ORTHEL is performed for the first time in Rotterdam.

28 MAY 1960

Nazar Stodolya, opera in three acts by the Ukrainian composer Constantin DANKEVICH, to a libretto reciting the dramatic story of a valiant young Cossack in love with a glorious girl whose infamous father is bent on leading her to the connubial bed of an unspeakable colonel of the Tsarist Army, with true young love triumphant in the E-flat major finale, set to music in soaring modalities with melodramatic Slavic verve, is produced in Kharkov.

3 JUNE 1960

Der Zauberfisch, operatic ballad in two acts by the 68-year-old Bohemian-born Austro-German composer Fidelio FINKE, to a libretto drawn from a fairy tale by the Grimm brothers dealing with a shrewish fisherwoman who is endowed with worldly goods by a magic fish, but keeps demanding more until the fish deprives her of all her gains, set to music in a burlesque manner laden with sharp but tonal polyphonic dissonances, is performed for the first time in Dresden.

10 JUNE 1960

The 34th Festival of the International Society for Contemporary Music opens in Cologne with a program comprising two basic works by the founders of dodecaphonic and serial music, *Fünf Orchesterstücke* by Arnold SCHOENBERG and *Fünf Sätze* for string orchestra by Anton VON WEBERN.

11 JUNE 1960

A postage stamp of 30 centimes (with the overprint plus 10 francs) honoring BIZET, bearing his bewhiskered and bespectacled image and facsimiles of the title pages of *L'Arlésienne* and *Carmen*, with a Spanish fan and a tambourine shown in the foreground, is issued by the Administration des Postes et Télécommunications of France. (The date of issue of the stamp was to mark the 3000th performance of *Carmen* in Paris, but the jubilee performance was postponed.)

11 JUNE 1960

Benjamin BRITTEN conducts at the opening of the 13th Aldeburgh Festival the world première of his operatic setting in three acts of Shakespeare's *A Midsummer Night's Dream* to a libretto by Britten himself and his favorite tenor Peter Pears, with a heterogeneous musical score, containing atonal melodic devices to illustrate the surrealistic scene and animistic fantasy, while leaving the triadic foundations intact.

11 JUNE 1960

The 34th Festival of the International Society for Contemporary Music in Cologne presents the following program of chamber music:

Cori di Didone, for chorus and percussion, by the 36-year-old Venetian Luigi NONO, to the story of Dido's self-immolation, written in an expressive paradodecaphonic style; *Anagram* for four voices, speaking chorus and instruments, by the 28-year-old Argentinian-born avant-garde composer Mauricio KAGEL, conducted by him in world première, the anagram being represented in four surrealistic poems in German, in French, in Italian and in Spanish, in which only the consonants and vowels of the Latin palindrome from Dante's *Divina Commedia* "In girum imus nocte et consumimur igrni" are used (thus the sounds a, b, d, f, h, l, p, v and z are excluded); and *Kontake* for electronic sounds, piano and percussion, by the 31-year-old German innovator Karlheinz STOCKHAUSEN.

12 JUNE 1960

Spring, opera in two acts by the Albanian composer Tish DAIJA, taking place in Albania in the spring of 1944, and centered on a heroic partisan dying "with the name of the Communist Party on his lips" before the firing squad of the Nazi occupying forces, betrayed by an Albanian Fascist who failed in love rivalry for the hand of a beautiful mountain maiden, set to music in melodramatic colors of the traditional opera, with a stimulating injection of asymmetrical Albanian rhythms, is produced in Tirana.

12 JUNE 1960

The 34th Festival of the International Society for Contemporary Music in Cologne presents an orchestral concert in the following program:

Skolion by the Yugoslav Milko KELEMEN (Skolion being the Greek word for a table song or a round), with a considerable element of isorhythmic improvisation; *Mosaiken* by the 25-year-old Dutch-dodecaphonist Peter SCHAT; *Eighth Symphony* (*Rhôdanienne*) by Darius MILHAUD, (first performed at the Berkeley, California, Festival on 22 April 1958); *Poem* for viola and chamber orchestra by the 38-year-old American Czech Karel HUSA, based on a self-consistent tone-row; and *Spectra* by the American 34-year-old composer Gunther SCHULLER, in which the orchestra is subdivided into seven groups (as the spectrum is analyzed into seven principal colors), originally performed by the New York Philharmonic on 15 January 1960.

13 JUNE 1960

The 34th Festival of the International Society for Contemporary Music in Cologne presents a concert of orchestral music with three world premières:

Quaderni per Orchestrar by the 34-year-old Italian modernist Luciano BERIO, which reflects five pictorial images built to the principle of a freely gyrating mobile; *Motus Coleres* by the 39-year-old Swedish composer Ingvar LIDHOLM, based on a twofold serial and aleatory structure, rhythmic and timbric; and *Pli selon pli*, "portrait de Mallarmé" by Pierre BOULEZ, containing three improvisations derived from specific tonal data, but statistically indeterminate and multivalent.

14 JUNE 1960

The 34th Festival of the International Society for Contemporary Music in Cologne presents a concert of orchestral music in the following program:

Chorikon by the 36-year-old Greek composer Argyris KOUNADIS, based on three mutually invertible symmetric tone-rows; *Fourth Symphony* by the American composer Roger SESSIONS, originally written for the Minnesota Centennial in 1957, in three movements, *Burlesque, Elegy* and *Pastorale; Après-ludes,* "after-play" by the 27-year-old Italian composer Niccolò CASTIGLIONI, in which four interrelated fragments, built on a dichotomy of two different tempi (one metronomic, one motoric), are integrated into a functionally dialectic succession of discrete sonorous units, with dynamic elements maintaining a euphoniously aerostatic equilibrium; *Piano Concerto* by the 35-year-old Rumanian Parisian Marius CONSTANT, cast in a cyclic monothematic tripartite form; and *Musique en Relief* by the 34-year-old Pole Wlodzimierz KOTOŃSKI, in five short movements, written in a serial technique.

15 JUNE 1960

Martin Korda, D.P., opera in three acts by Henk BADINGS, to a symbolically realistic story of a displaced person (D.P.) impaled on the diagonal of a parallelogram of opposing political, social and economic forces after World War II, illustrated by irrational polyharmony, and culminating in a schizophrenic vision, scored for voices with electronic accompaniment, is produced at the opening of the Holland Festival in Amsterdam.

15 JUNE 1960

The 34th Festival of the International Society for Contemporary Music in Cologne continues with a chamber music concert comprising the following works:

Maqamat for flute and string quartet by the 52-year-old Hungarian-born Israeli composer Ödön PARTOS, Maqamat being an Arabic type of thematic melody serving as cantus firmus for improvisation; *Fantasy and Fugue* for piano by the 38-year-old Norwegian composer Finn MORTENSEN, written in a free dodecaphonic idiom; *String Quartet* by the American composer Arthur BERGER, conceived in a modified dodecaphonic idiom, with the serial row assembled cumulatively by discrete units; *Auf die ruhige Nachtzeit,* for soprano, flute, viola and cello by the 35-year-old Swiss composer Klaus HUBER, built in a mirror-like symmetric framework to a text of seven stanzas, each line of which contains seven syllables, while the nucleus of the thematic series is fissioned into mutually imitative halves; *Third String Quartet* by the 43-year-old Korean composer Isang YUN; and *Mobiles* for two pianos by the 30-year-old Belgian composer of serial music Henri POUSSEUR.

16 JUNE 1960

An orchestral concert is presented at the 34th Festival of the International Society for Contemporary Music in Cologne with the following program:

Omaggio by the 34-year-old German composer Giselher KLEBE, a neo-baroque homage to Italy; *Der Wein* for soprano and orchestra by Alban BERG, to the text of the German translation of Baudelaire's vinous poems, *L'âme du vin, Le vin des amants* and *Le vin du solitaire,* set in an impassionately expressionistic vein, composed in 1929, and first performed in Königsberg on 4 June 1930; *Aulodie* for oboe and orchestra by the 52-year-old German composer Wolfgang FORTNER, emulating the character and the sound of the ancient Greek wind instrument Aulos, written in an appropriately bland monodic idiom; and *Canti di Liberazione* for mixed chorus and orchestra by Luigi DALLAPICCOLA, written in an individualized dodecaphonic style.

17 JUNE 1960

The 34th Festival of the International Society for Contemporary Music in Cologne continues with a program of orchestral music, presenting the world première of *Fioriture* by the 43-year-old Swedish ultramodernist Karl-Birger BLOMDAHL; *Movements for Piano and Orchestra* by STRAVINSKY (first performed in New York on 10 January 1960); and *Requiem* for soprano and baritone solo, chorus and orchestra by the China-born Russian-Estonian composer acclimatized in Berlin, Boris BLACHER.

18 JUNE 1960

The 34th Festival of the International Society for Contemporary Music in Cologne presents the following program of miscellaneous music:

Ricercar and Doubles for 8 instruments by the 25-year-old English composer Peter Maxwell DAVIES, based on the old song *To Many a Well,* treated with the techniques of *Hoquetus, Isorythmics, Mensuration* and *Prolation* applied to a paradodecaphonic radix derived from the notes of the song, and scored for flute, oboe, clarinet, bassoon, horn, viola, cello and cembalo; *Introduzione-Sequenze-Coda* for 3 flutes, chimes and percussion by the 32-year-old Swedish composer Bengt HAMBRAEUS, based upon the acoustic concept of "Music in Space"; *Selektion I* for four groups of loudspeakers utilizing five basic sonorous units, by the pioneer atonalist and dodecaphonist Herbert EIMERT; *Cantata sacra* for tenor and six instruments by the 33-year-old Danish composer Bernhard LEWKOWITCH, a Latin hymn with a serial cyclic setting, with the number 12 playing the fundamental role in temporal division; *De la muerte a la mañana,* cantata by the 35-year-old German-born Chilean composeress Leni ALEXANDER, to words of Dylan Thomas, Thomas Wolfe and the Psalms, written in a paradodecaphonic idiom; and *Cantada* by the 29-year-old Catalan composer Xavier BENGUEREL, conceived in a neo-medieval manner.

19 JUNE 1960

The 34th Festival of the International Society for Contemporary Music concludes in Cologne with an orchestral concert comprising the following works:

Sixth Symphony by the veteran Dutch composer Matthijs VERMEULEN, subtitled *Les Minutes heureuses* (after a hemistichon from *Le Balcon* of Baudelaire, *Je sais l'art dévoquer les minutes heureuses*), in three continuous movements, with the thematic base derived from the syllables *La, do, ré,* phonetically spelling *L'Adoré,* for the Supreme Being, culminating in a canon for three trumpets on this theme; *Nobody Knows de Trouble I seen* for trumpet and orchestra by the German composer Bernd Alois ZIMMERMAN, molded after a Negro spiritual, with elements of pentatonicism inherent in the blues section; *Apparitions* by the 37-year-old Hungarian composer György LIGETI, wherein the title is taken in the French sense as a transitory manifestation or an ephemeral phenomenon, and connotes a reduction of the role of the height of pitch and the concomitant intervallic structure, melodic line and harmonic investiture, replaced by the sonic dimension of *Klangfarbe* in the taxonomic athematic distribution of discrete quanta within a given aural spectrum, in several acoustical layers of different densities ceaselessly colliding in their labyrinthine courses; and *Seventh Symphony* in three movements by the German master polyphonist Karl Amadeus HARTMANN.

21 JUNE 1960

In the course of the Music Festival in Strasbourg, the first complete performance is given of *Hieronymous Bosch* for orchestra by the 36-year-old French composer Serge NIGG, inspired by Bosch's famous triptych *The Garden of Terrestrial Delights* in the Prado Museum at Madrid, in three contrasting movements tonally limning the landscape of Hell, a man contemplating a rat through a glass tube, and the rosary of sin, written in Nigg's eclectic "third" manner (the first was dodecaphonic, the second, folklorically realistic, dictated by Nigg's Communist allegiance), reaching the point of dissonant paroxysm in the surrealistic portrayal of abomination of desolation and perversion of body and soul.

22 JUNE 1960

Tapshyrylmagan Hatlar (*Unposted Letters*), opera in four acts by the 50-year-old Tatar composer Dzhaudat FAIZY (real name Faizullin), to his own libretto in the Tatar language, is performed for the first time in Kazan.

23 JUNE 1960

The Ninth Annual Festival of Music and Dance in Granada, Spain, opens with the first performance of a posthumous work by Bohuslav MARTINU, *Suite on the Frescoes of Piero della Francesca,* in three movements, representing the varying moods portrayed by the painter, musically translated into the form of a free fantasia.

1 JULY 1960

On the occasion of the quincentenary of the University of Basel, *Cantata Academica* by Benjamin BRITTEN, to a Latin text taken from the university charter, and subdivided into 12 sections, each dominated by a different tonal center according to a premeditated 12-tone series (which appears discretely in direct and retrograde forms), written in an emphatically diatonic style dominated by major chords, and ending with a coda recapitulating the first section, is performed for the first time in Basel.

3 JULY 1960

The Newport Jazz Festival is ordered by the City Council of Newport, Rhode Island, to close down after a night of terror when thousands of young jazz lovers, failing to gain admission because Newport's Freebody Park was full to capacity, rioted, threw beer cans and bottles at the police, National Guardsmen, and Navy militia summoned to quell the disturbance with tear gas and strong firemen's hoses, leaving some fifty injured on both sides and necessitating the declaration of emergency and sealing off Newport County to all incoming vehicles, banning liquor sales, and cancelling the remaining concerts of the Festival at which several jazz luminaries were scheduled to appear.

7 JULY 1960

On the centennial of birth of Gustav MAHLER, Austria issues a postage stamp for one and a half schillings with his portrait.

9 JULY 1960

At a seminar on electronics in Darmstadt, the first public performance is given of the definitive version of *Etude concrète pour un seul coup de cymbale* lasting 2 minutes 35 seconds, by the 34-year-old Polish composer Wlodzimierz KOTOŃSKI, constructed in an integral serial technique by transposing the original sounds of the cymbal electronically to 11 different pitches of the chromatic scale and assigning to them different durations and dynamic intensities.

9 JULY 1960

Edward Burlingame HILL, American composer of impressionistic orchestral scores of subtle cerulean charm, an early follower of French modernism, teacher of many an American composer at Harvard University, whose father was a professor of chemistry there and whose grandfather was once its president, dies in his summer home in Francestown, New Hampshire, at the age of 87.

14 JULY 1960

The Lodger, opera in two acts by the English composeress Phyllis TATE, relating in nostalgically somber tones the predicament of an elderly couple who discover that their lodger is Jack the Ripper and who charitably let him leave and vanish into the London fog as a young detective on his trail takes time off to pay court to their daughter (thus protecting her from Jack's disembowelling propensities), is performed for the first time at the Royal Academy of Music, of which the composer was an alumna.

14 JULY 1960

On the last day of the 16th Festival of British Contemporary Music at Cheltenham, the world première is given of *Cosmos,* symphony in four movements by Reginald SMITH-BRINDLE, depicting the "everlasting infinities," "numberless firmaments," "confraternity of souls" and other cosmic and spiritual things, with the application of a variety of eclectic infra-modern technical devices.

14 JULY 1960

Sea Symphony for bass-baritone and orchestra by the 70-year-old American composer Philip JAMES, composed in 1928 and revised in 1945, is performed for the first time in Frankfurt, Germany.

15 JULY 1960

Hercules furens, music for the tragedy by Euripides by the Greek composer Yorgo SICILIANOS, is performed for the first time under the composer's direction in the ancient open arena in Epidaurus, in Greece.

23 JULY 1960

Ballet of Lights, with music by the Egyptian composer Halim EL-DABH, is presented in world première in front of the great Sphinx in Cairo.

27 JULY 1960

In commemoration of the 83rd anniversary of the birth of Ernst VON DOHNÁNY, the Governor of Florida proclaims it Dohnányi Day "in recognition of the pride felt by our citizens that he chose to live among them for the last twelve years of his life and chose Florida for his final resting place." (A similar proclamation was issued by the Governor of Florida on Dohnányi's 84th birthday in 1961.)

30 JULY 1960

The Fifth Annual Jazz Festival in Great Britain held on the green lawns of Lord Montagu of Beaulieu's estate, 68 miles south of London, is broken up at 11:15 P.M. when some ten thousand youths erupt in mass savagery under the influence of Americanized British jazz, and haul down the bandstand and the floodlights for the British Broadcasting Corporation filming the festival.

1 AUGUST 1960

Bolivia issues a series of 12 stamps (6 regular and 6 airmail) to honor the 19-year-old Bolivian violinist Jaime LAREDO (with the insignia of his name spelled in the musical notes, La, Re, Do), winner of the 1959 International Music Competition in Brussels, when he was selected as best among 37 contestants, playing a Stradivarius violin lent to him for the occasion on 31 May 1959, a week before his 18th birthday.

4 AUGUST 1960

Port Town, one-act opera by the 47-year-old German-born American composer Jan MEYEROWITZ, to a libretto by Langston Hughes, telling a symbolic tale of platonic love of a sailor in port for a dreamy schoolgirl quickly squelched by horrified townsfolk, with a musical score full of romantic vocalizing in lush harmonies, is performed for the first time at the Berkshire Music Center at Tanglewood, Massachusetts.

7 AUGUST 1960

André BLOCH, French composer of numerous operas and instrumental pieces, of which the *Suite palestinienne* for cello and orchestra, written by him at the age of seventy-five, gained considerable popularity, dies at Viry-Châtillon, near Paris, at the age of 87.

14 AUGUST 1960

The first musical broadcast via an artificial earth satellite is accomplished during the twenty-first pass of the American orbiting balloon Echo I between 2:44 and 2:55 A.M., when a taped recording of the patriotic hymn *America the Beautiful* is transmitted from the Bell Telephone laboratory at Holmdel, New Jersey, to the Jet Propulsion Laboratory at Goldstone, California,

20 AUGUST 1960

Rudolf MOSER, 68-year-old Swiss composer of classically organized and romantically inspired instrumental and vocal music, perishes in a 275-foot plunge during an Alpinist excursion near St. Moritz.

23 AUGUST 1960

Czechoslovakia issues a 40-heller postage stamp in honor of the Czech composer and conductor Oskar NEDBAL (1874–1930) and a 60-heller stamp in honor of the Czech opera composer Otakar Ostrčil (1879–1935).

2 SEPTEMBER 1960

At the 14th Edinburgh International Festival, the Royal Liverpool Orchestra conducted by John Pritchard gives the world première of the *Second Symphony*, by Sir William WALTON (completed on 22 July 1960), set in three well-balanced movements:

(1) *Allegro molto*, with propulsively masculine rhythms and resiliently leaping melody; (2) *Lento assai*, an elegiacally dulcet evocation; (3) *Passacaglia*, thematically proclaiming the three notes of the G minor triad plus nine more notes without duplication thus forming a 12-note series, and after ten variations, leading through an accelerated fugato to a Coda-Scherzando, and a grandiloquently unmitigated G major ending, with brass sonorities in triumphant fanfares.

3 SEPTEMBER 1960

Third Symphony by Humphrey SEARLE, psychologically tense in its darksomely upsurging calls (inspired by a visit to Mycenae and the sight of the ruins of the palace in which Agamemnon was supposed to be killed), is performed for the first time at the Edinburgh Festival.

8 SEPTEMBER 1960

Derby Day, a race-track overture by William ALWYN, is performed for the first time in London.

8 SEPTEMBER 1960

The Stockholm festival of modern Scandinavian music opens with a concert of orchestral works by the Swiss-born Gunnar BERG, 66-year-old Stockholm-born Maurice KARKOFF, 28-year-old Dane Per NØRGÅRD and the 40-year-old Finn, Nils-Eric FOUGSTEDT.

10 SEPTEMBER 1960

Puloined Happiness, opera in three acts by the Ukrainian composer Yuli MEITUS, wherein a rural damsel, believing her bridegroom to be dead, marries another and finds herself in a painful dilemma when he returns to reclaim his purloined happiness, is produced in Lvov.

14 SEPTEMBER 1960

Two centuries have passed since the birth in Florence of Luigi CHERUBINI, prolific composer of impeccable craftsmanship, who became a formidable disciplinarian as director of the Paris Conservatory.

18 SEPTEMBER 1960

First performances of two new works by two modern Polish composers are presented for the first time in the course of the Fourth International Festival of Contemporary Music, "The Warsaw Autumn," in Warsaw:

Wymiary czasu i ciszy (*Dimensions of Time and Silence*) for chorus and instruments by the 26-year-old leader of the Polish avant-garde Krzysztof PENDERECKI, intended as a musical counterpart of paintings by Paul Klee and other expressionist artists and creating a "space of sonic matter," with entrances of various instrumental bodies indicated in the score by red lines, the text vocalized on the decasyllabic Latin pentameter of the palindromic magic square

> SATOR
> AREPO
> TENET
> OPERA
> ROTAS

and in addition introducing permutations and rotations of consonants in the vocal line, converting the chorus into a percussion ensemble supplemented by sibilation and purified bruitism; *Tertium datur* by the 31-year-old ultra-modernist Boguslaw SCHAEFFER, subtitled "Treatise of composition for clavichord and instruments," following a method of facture neither classical nor modern (hence the title contradicting the rule of Aristotelian logic, *Tertium non dartur,* in syllogisms of mutually exclusive terms), making use of novel techniques with a free displacement of tonal centers and metrical stresses and written out in a pictorial notation in diagrams and geometric figures.

20 SEPTEMBER 1960

Ida Rubinstein, urbane and enterprising Russian-Jewish dancer and choreographer, who dazzled Paris for many years by her well-financed ballet presentations, for whom Debussy wrote *Le Martyre de Saint Sébastien,* Ravel wrote *Boléro* and Stravinsky *Le Baiser de la fée,* dies at an uncertain age (but old) in seclusive obscurity in the village of Vence on the French Riviera.

21 SEPTEMBER 1960

Rosamunde Floris, opera in three acts by Boris BLACHER, to a libretto wherein a promiscuous damsel premaritally impregnated by an unscrupulous gallant and abandoned by him, marries an aspiring librarian, after the latter defenestrates his previous fiancée, with a polymonotonous tension created by solitonal system of repetitious effects in variable meters, is produced at the Berlin Music Festival.

24 SEPTEMBER 1960

Mátyás SEIBER, 55-year-old Hungarian composer, resident in England from 1935, whose music astutely combines Magyar melos, baroque formality and dodecaphonic techniques, is killed in an automobile crash in Krueger National Park in Johannesburg, South Africa, during his stay there as visiting lecturer and composer.

25 SEPTEMBER 1960

Capriccio for piano and orchestra by the Israeli composer Paul BEN-HAIM, is performed for the first time in Tel Aviv.

27 SEPTEMBER 1960

At the 23rd Festival of Contemporary Music in Venice, Igor STRAVINSKY conducts the world premiere of his *Monumentum Pro Gesualdo di Venosa ad CD Annum,* an instrumental surrealization of three madrigals by Gesualdo, Prince of Venosa, composer, lutenist, and murderer by proxy (he is reputed to have hired assassins to overtake and kill his fleeing wife and her lover), on the occasion of the quadricentennial of his birth, the Stravinsky touch clearly pointed (*ex ungue leonem*) by the colloidal suspension of ornamental dissonances and forceful translocation of metric incipits, creating a distinctly vigesimosecular form of triune chirality.

27 SEPTEMBER 1960

At the opening concert of the Paris Festival (*Semaines Musicales de Paris*), the Philharmonic Orchestra of Leningrad presents a program of Russian music, under the auspices of the Comité National de la Musique and the patronage of the City of Paris, the Department of Seine, the Radiodiffusion française, and administered by the Chambre Syndicale des Organisateurs de Concerts. (Other foreign orchestras participating in Les Semaines Musicales de Paris were the Israel Philharmonic, the Orquesta Nacional of Madrid, and the Tokyo Radio Orchestra.)

30 SEPTEMBER 1960

Toccata Festiva, a dedicatory piece by Samuel BARBER, commissioned by Mrs. Mary Curtis Zimbalist on the occasion of the unveiling of a large cathedral organ, costing $175,000, at the inaugural concert of the 61st season of the Philadelphia Orchestra, is performed for the first time, with Eugene Ormandy, starting on his 25th season as music director, conducting.

30 SEPTEMBER 1960

Ernst KRENEK conducts in Hamburg the world première of his orchestral work *Quaestio Temporis* for chamber orchestra, based on a 12-tone series containing all eleven different intervals in symmetrically invertible positions so that two intervals equidistant from the center are complementary to an octave, and the central interval, a tritone, is complementary to itself, with the sum of these eleven intervals (66 semitones) taken as the basic temporal parameter determining six different speeds of the eleven principal sections of the work according to six terms of the Fibonacci series (in which each term equals the sum of the two preceding terms) from 2 to 21, decupled and metronomically applied to the duration of a quarter-note (20, 30, 50, 80, 130, and 210 to a minute) with further parameters of vertical density and horizontal spissitude reaching the ne plus ultra compression in the finale with 12 vertical layers and a sensory maximum of 14 successive notes per second, in the individual parts.

30 SEPTEMBER 1960

La Taillis ensorcelé, symphonic poem by the 32-year-old French composer Jacques BONDON, depicting a vegetable universe on another planet, possessing complex polyrhythmics of non-logarithmic growth rate, in a hyperserial melodic idiom, is performed for the first time in Paris.

1 OCTOBER 1960

Nigerian Folk Symphony by the prime Nigerian composer Fela SOWANDE, is performed for the first time in a broadcast by the British Broadcasting Corporation in London on the day of the proclamation of Nigeria's independence.

2 OCTOBER 1960

Free China, symphonic poem by the 55-year-old Soviet composer Boris ARAPOV, depicting in four connected movements the happy life, felicitous labor, festive jubilation, and earnest struggle for a still brighter Chinese future, making use of pentatonic Sinological materials, is performed for the first time in Leningrad.

7 OCTOBER 1960

Les Adieux, one-act opera by the 45-year-old French composer Marcel LANDOWSKI, in which a young woman refuses to open the door for her lover when he comes for his daily session, realizing that her infatuation with him is not sufficiently compelling, is produced in Paris.

8 OCTOBER 1960

The United States Post Office issues two stamps in the series Men of Liberty in honor of Ignace PADEREWSKI, great Polish composer and statesman, who went into exile after Hitler's attack on Poland, and died in America.

8 OCTOBER 1960

A Story of a Real Man, posthumous opera in four acts by Sergei PROKOFIEV, to a documentary libretto from the heroic life of a Soviet fighter pilot who returned to active service in combat in World War II, after having lost both legs, receives its first performance for the general public at the Bolshoi Theater in Moscow, with the actual hero of the opera, the flyer Maresyev, present in the audience. (A semi-private performance was given for selected public in Leningrad on 3 December 1948, but the score was summarily rejected by Soviet officials and music critics as inadequate to its theme and too dissonant in musical substance.)

In the modernistic antimelodic music of Prokofiev's opera *A Story of a Real Man,* the composer retains his old positions, condemned by the Party and by Soviet society. The spiritual world of the Soviet man who performs miracles of valor and heroism for the love of his fatherland holds no attraction for Prokofiev. He is still interested solely in the external effects of dramatic action and in naturalistic details. (Tikhon Khrennikov in *Pravda,* 4 January 1949)

Melodic generosity of this music, the bright songful arias, the especially powerful chracterization of the image of the hero made the production of *A Story of a Real Man* a great event in the cultural life of the capital. (*Pravda,* 9 October 1960)

"I am deeply moved" said the Hero of the Soviet Union Alexey Petrovich Maresyev. "Prokofiev's opera brought back to me the unforgettable events of the Great Patriotic War." He said this after attending the final rehearsal of Prokofiev's opera *A Story of A Real Man* on the stage of the Bolshoi Theater. After the end of the rehearsal, A. P. Maresyev warmly congratulated the artists, embraced and kissed the interpreter

of the part of Alexey. (Report of the impression received by the real pilot Maresyev whose story served as the foundation of the libretto, in *Izvestia,* 6 October 1960)

10 OCTOBER 1960

The Philharmonic Orchestra of Israel opens its international tour in Paris under the direction of Carlo-Maria GIULINI in a program containing a *Psalm* by the 25-year-old Israeli composer Noam SHERIFF.

14 OCTOBER 1960

Second Violin Concerto by Walter PISTON, distinguished by characteristically Pistonian directness of musical speech, translucency of contrapuntal fabric, and contrastfulness of the three ideally equilibrated movements, *Moderato, Adagio,* and *Allegro,* is performed for the first time by the Pittsburgh Symphony Orchestra, Joseph Fuchs soloist, William Steinberg conducting.

15 OCTOBER 1960

At the opening of the Musiktage für die zeitgenössische Tonkunst at Donaueschingen, a chamber music concert is presented with the following program of world premieres:

5 Bagatellen for wind quintet (flute, oboe, clarinet, bassoon, horn) by Wolfgang FORTNER, written in an unaffected vein of *Gebrauchsmusik;* first performance of the posthumous *Fourth String Quartet* by Bohuslav MARTINU, written in 1937 for a Paris friend, but never performed in public; *Szene I* for a chamber ensemble (2 flutes, 2 trumpets, harp, piano, percussion, and two empty wine bottles) by the precociously ultra-modernistic 23-year-old Bo NILSSON of Sweden whose serialistically conceived and surrealistically constructed music postulates the orderliness of systematic disorder; *Twelfth String Quartet* in quarter-tones by Alois HÁBA of Prague, in three movements designated by the traditional Italian terms, *Allegro energico, Andante cantabile, Allegro risoluto* but constructed athematically in melody, asymmetrically in periodicity and agglutinatively in successiveness, with the intervallic structure using the entire gamut of quarter-tones and their multiples, including "neutral" seconds (a quarter-tone larger than a minor second and a quarter-tone smaller than a major second), neutral thirds, sixths and sevenths, and pairs of neutral perfect intervals (fourths, fifths, octaves); *Tropi per complesso da camera* by the Milanese modernist Niccolò CASTIGLIONI, for flute, clarinet, violin, cello, piano and percussion, serially conceived as tropes of sonority, tempo, and even of bel canto; and *Kammermusik 1960* for 14 instruments by the 29-year-old Pomeranian composer Dieter SCHÖNBACH, in five movements with sonorously meaningless titles *Akuo, Siri I, Melog, Siri II, Khor,* selected to inspire constructivistically coloristic associations to help form an auditively subjective organization of the music.

16 OCTOBER 1960

On the second and last day of the Musiktage für die zeitgenössische Tonkunst at Donaueschingen, the world premières are given of the following works:

Suite of Dances by the 53-year-old Japanese modernist Yoritsune MATSUDAIRA, for three orchestras conducted by three conductors in non-coincidental tempi and meters, written in a serialistically procrusteanized style of ancient Japanese court music Bugaku (a genre of Gagaku); *Anaklasis* for strings and percussion by the 16-year-old Pole Krzysztof PENDERECKI, a serial interpretation of the anaclastic transposition of short and long syllables in the Ionic rhythms of Greek prosody, with associative tonal and metrical ideas (arithmetical progressions, rotation of tonerows, etc.), introducing quarter-tones as part of an intervallic series, making use of instrumental innovations such as the prepared piano, and resorting to diagrammatic notation for metric and rhythmic factors (the piece was hissed by the audience, but punitively encored by the conductor Hans Rosbaud); and *Chronochromie* for orchestra by Olivier MESSIAEN in 7 sections evolved from the considerations of time (*chronos*) and color (*chroma*), comprising 32 different note-values (durations) subjected to symmetrical permutation and melodic colors supplied by songbirds of France, Sweden, Japan, Mexico, and noise elements of waterfalls of the French Alps, the chronos and the chroma being mutually interactive, individual chroma being determined by corresponding chronos so that *Chronochromie* becomes the color of time.

19 OCTOBER 1960

Haiti issues a series of stamps (10 centimes, 20 centimes and 1 franc 50 centimes) in honor of the Haitian composer Occide JEANTY (1860–1936) with a musical quotation from his *1804 Marche Militaire*, commemorating the proclamation of independence of Haiti from France.

20 OCTOBER 1960

Time Cycle, by Lukas FOSS, a suite of four songs for soprano and orchestra to the texts by Auden, Housman, Kafka and Nietzsche, all of them concerned with clocks, bells and timepieces, and written in a highly rarefied pointillistically sharpened idiom beyond the borders of tonality, with interludes for a heterogeneous quartet (clarinet, cello, percussion and piano) improvising simultaneously but without collective precognition following individually subjective semi-aleatory ideas within the deterministic parameters of thematic matrices and serial instrumental rotation, is performed uniquely (for any other performance would inevitably be different in the improvised interludes) by the New York Philharmonic, Leonard Bernstein conducting, Adele Addison soprano, with Lukas Foss himself as piano aleatorist (the composed part of the piece without optional interludes was repeated at the end of the concert.)

21 OCTOBER 1960

Le Roi David, biblical music drama by Arthur HONEGGER, first performed in Mézières, near Lausanne, on 11 June 1921, and later revised as a symphonic psalm and oratorio, is presented for the first time as an opera at the Grand Opéra in Paris, arranged in 31 scenes interspersed by choral numbers and supplied with an additional dialogue, but without in any way altering the original musical score.

21 OCTOBER 1960

Seventh Symphony by William SCHUMAN, in four movements, *Largo assai*, *Vigoroso*, *Cantabile intensamente* and *Scherzando brioso*, conceived in a vigorous and intense 20th-century idiom replete with austere intervallic structures with a predilection for major sevenths and minor ninths, but ending unapologetically in sonorous E-flat major, is performed for the first time by the Boston Symphony Orchestra, Charles Munch conducting.

22 OCTOBER 1960

Time-Span, symphonic movement by George ROCHBERG, conceived in an abstractly constructivistic style in a serial technique of durations, with tonal elements in dodecaphonic distribution ascetically sampled in widely contrasting instrumental monosyllables in dynamic chiaroscuro, commissioned by the Junior Division of the Women's Association of the St. Louis Symphony Society on funds obtained through the sale of art by local modernist painters auctioned off on a Mississippi steamboat, is performed for the first time by the St. Louis Symphony Orchestra. (A revised version of the work was performed, under the title *Time-Span II*, on 19 January 1964 in Buffalo, the composer conducting.)

23 OCTOBER 1960

Preamble to Peace by Earl ROBINSON, oratorio based on the Preamble to the United Nations Charter, is performed for the first time by the Trenton Symphony Orchestra.

25 OCTOBER 1960

The Symphony Orchestra of Radio Tokyo presents, during its international tour, a program in Paris, featuring two Japanese works:

Euburi 2 tableaux by the 31-year-old Michio MAMIYA, composed in 1957, and representing a stylized impression of the dances and prayers at the Enburi festival during harvest time, with a profuse percussion section, including an enormously huge gong and an extraordinarily minuscule drum; and *Mandala*, symphonic poem by the 31-year-old Toshiro MAYUZUMI, attempting to translate Buddhist philosophy into musical terms, and based on a series of 10 notes derived from two sets of overtones of sacred bells of Japanese temples, each forming a pentatonic scale, with the tonics of the two sets distanced by a minor ninth, designed to acheive a scematic tonal representation of the sacred symbol of Oriental art, the mandala, with its concentrically arrayed geometric figures, and at the same time to suggest the concept of collective subconscious as promulgated by Carl Jung.

25 OCTOBER 1960

Thai, symphonic rhapsody by the 34-year-old Dutch composer Jurriaan ANDRIESSEN, based on four jazz tunes by King Phumiphol Aduldet of Thailand, is presented by the Royal Military Band of the Netherlands as a surprise for the musical monarch during a concert given by the municipality of The Hague at which he and Queen Juliana of Holland were guests of honor.

25 OCTOBER 1960

José PADILLA, Spanish composer of the popular tunes *Valencia* and *El Relicario*, ubiquitously played and sung in the 1920's, dies in Madrid at the age of 71.

28 OCTOBER 1960

The North German Radio Network presents the world première of *Carré* by Karlheinz STOCKHAUSEN, for four orchestras and four choruses placed on four podia and conducted by four conductors along the four walls of a square mess hall in Hamburg with the audience seated in a carré of rows of chairs at 90° to each other, the music based on a one-to-one correspondence of duration (macro-time) and height of pitch (micro-time).

30 OCTOBER 1960

Alfred HILL, Nestor of Australian composers, who wrote ballets, symphonic poems and chamber music utilizing melodic and rhythmic materials of the aboriginal Maoris, dies in Darlinghurst, near Sydney, a few weeks before his 90th birthday.

2 NOVEMBER 1960

Malcolm ARNOLD conducts the British Broadcasting Corporation Symphony Orchestra in London in the world première of his *Fourth Symphony,* in four movements, cast in his customary infra-modern but hedonistically vigorous style, with the inclusion of some Caribbean percussion used "non-exotically," and introducing in the *Scherzo* a 12-note palindrome "to express unpleasant emotion."

2 NOVEMBER 1960

Dimitri MITROPOULOS, 64-year-old Greek conductor of ecstatic genius, prodigious musician with a photographic memory and champion of ultra-modern music, dies suddenly of a heart attack, collapsing and falling on the podium of La Scala, Milan, after conducting 45 beats of the first movement of Mahler's *Third Symphony.* (According to his will, his body was cremated in Switzerland, since Italian law prohibits cremation, and flown by a Greek government plane to Athens for a non-religious ceremony, cremated bodies being unacceptable to the ritual of the Greek Orthodox Church, and placed in an urn in the Athens Conservatory of Music.)

6 NOVEMBER 1960

On the occasion of the sesquicentennial of the birth of the Hungarian pioneer of national opera, Ferenc ERKEL, the Hungarian government issues a 60-feller postage stamp.

6 NOVEMBER 1960

The Arsenal, opera by the Ukrainian composer Georgy MAIBORODA, is produced in Kiev.

7 NOVEMBER 1960

To commemorate the centennial of the birth of the Spanish national composer Isaac ALBÉNIZ, the Spanish government issues two postage stamps with his likeness, at 25 centavos and one peseta.

8 NOVEMBER 1960

Third Symphony by the 40-year-old English composer Peter Racine FRICKER is performed for the first time in London.

11 NOVEMBER 1960

The Brazilian Coffee Institute stages at the Music School of the University of Brazil in Rio de Janeiro the first Brazilian performance of Bach's *Coffee Cantata,* recounting the tribulations of a young German maiden whose father will not let her indulge in drinking such an aphrodisiac beverage which she herself finds "better tasting than a thousand kisses."

17 NOVEMBER 1960

Second Violin Concerto by Paul CRESTON is performed in a world première by Michael Rabin and the Los Angeles Philharmonic.

18 NOVEMBER 1960

A century has passed since the birth in the village of Kurylówka in Podolia (which was part of Poland until the Second Partition of 1793, when it was ceded to Russia) of Ignace Jan PADEREWSKI, the great piano virtuoso who thrilled multitudes in Europe and America during the Golden Age of romantic artistry at the turn of the century, composer of the perennially popular *Minuet* and also bigger things in various genres, Polish patriot and statesman who was briefly Prime Minister of Poland after World War I.

(Paderewski's date of birth is 6 November 1860 according to the old style Russian calendar, or 18 November new style. The Government of Poland issued a commemorative stamp of 2 zloty 50 groszy on the correct date 18 November 1960. Paderewski stamps for 4 and 8 cents were issued by the U.S. Post Office, in the Liberty Champions Series on 8 October 1960, not stated to be centennial, but several governors proclaimed the date of 6 November 1960 as Paderewski Day with specific reference to the centennial, among them Governor Nelson Rockefeller of New York. Governor Michael V. DiSalle of Ohio, issued a proclamation stating: "Whereas November 6, 1960 marks the one hundredth anniversary of the birth of Ignace Paderewski, noted Polish statesman and artist and Whereas, as a great piano virtuoso and composer Paderewski contributed countless hours of musical entertainment to the peoples of the world, Whereas, this great orator and patriotic leader fought a continuous never-faltering battle for Polish independence, and Whereas, in this centennial year of the birth of Paderewski, the Government of the United States is honoring him by issuing a stamp bearing his likeness in the Champion of Liberty series, Now, therefore, I, Michael V. DiSalle, Governor of the State of Ohio, do hereby proclaim November 6, 1960 as Paderewski Day." Similar statements, giving the centennial date as 6 November 1960 were issued by the governors of Illinois and Nebraska. Governor Price Daniel of Texas stated in his declaration that "October 1960 will mark the one hundredth anniversary of the birth of Ignace Paderewski." Maryland, Colorado, and Michigan held celebrations of Paderewski Day; the State of Minnesota proclaimed an American-Polish Friendship Day. The Proclamation of the governor of Michigan included the reminder that Podolia was "occupied" by Russia at the time of Paderewski's birth.)

25 NOVEMBER 1960

The era of soap operas, daily radio broadcasts telling stories of heartbreak, mental and physical illnesses, frustrated female amours, and teetering business enterprises (usually sponsored by manufacturers of soaps and detergents, hence also known as sudsy programs), formally comes to an end as the Columbia Broadcasting System removes from the ether the long enduring serials, *Ma Perkins,* veteran of 27 years of struggle to maintain her lumber mill (inaugurated 13 August 1933), *The Right to Happiness,* 20-year-old story of a nubile widow and perpetually adolescent son (inaugurated 22 January 1940),

Young Dr. Malone, wise and lovable, medically and socially (inaugurated 29 April 1940) and *The Second Mrs. Burton,* a widow infatuated with a young and unscrupulous artist (inaugurated 7 January 1946), the final episodes all provided with happy or at least morally gratifying endings, to the accompaniment of saturated diminished seventhchords on the organ, the instrument indissolubly linked to radio serials from time immemorial.

25 NOVEMBER 1960

Hachatur Abovian, opera in three acts by the Armenian composer Gebork ARMENIAN (changed from his real name Khachaturian in order to avoid confusion with his famous namesake), recounting in romantic tones the life and social activities of the bringer of enlightenment to Armenia in the first half of the 19th-century, is produced in Erevan, capital of the Armenian Soviet Socialist Republic.

3 DECEMBER 1960

Marko Polo, opera by the Yugoslav composer Ivo TIJARDOVIĆ, encompassing in three acts the epic travels of Marco Polo to China and back to Venice in the years 1271–1292, set to songful Italianate melodies with some pentatonic discursions in the scenes set in fabulous Cathay, is performed for the first time in Zagreb.

3 DECEMBER 1960

Camelot, musical revue by Frederick LOEWE, with book and lyrics by Alan Jay Lerner, drawn from the novel *The Once and Future King* by T. H. White, in which the fabled court of King Arthur at the legendary town of Camelot in West England is modernized and melodramatized in an ingratiatingly sentimental manner, with Guinevere familiarly called Jenny and Lancelot dubbed Lance, concluding with the nostalgic envoi, "Don't let it be forgot/That once there was a spot/For one brief shining moment/That was known as Camelot," is produced in New York.

5 DECEMBER 1960

Violin Concerto by the 38-year-old Czech composer Zdeněk LIŠKA, written in a modern virtuoso manner, is performed for the first time in Leningrad at a demonstration of the Czechoslovak theatrical spectacle *Laterna magica,* in which the violinist appears in a dual function as a performer in the flesh on the stage and as an actor in the film in close succession without losing the continuity of the action or of the music.

11 DECEMBER 1960

Carl ORFF conducts in Stuttgart the world première of his nativity play *Ludus de nato infante mirificus,* to his own libretto in the Upper Bavarian dialect intermingled with ecclesiastical Latin, employing toneless rhythmoloquy with a gymnosophistically monochromatic and an ascetically homophonic instrumental accompaniment.

12 DECEMBER 1960

Eleventh Symphony in C by Darius MILHAUD, pointedly subtitled *Romantique,* with its typically melodian Milhaudean three movements, *Intense, Meditatif, Emporté,* is performed for the first time by the Dallas Symphony Orchestra, as a specially commissioned work, Paul Kletzki conducting.

12 DECEMBER 1960

Sixth Symphony by the Hungarian composer László LAJTHA, in four romantically lyric movements, assertively tonal in spite of constant melismatic chromatization and conspicuous absence of key signatures, scored for a modern orchestra with an imposing battery of percussion instruments, which, the composer warns "messieurs les chefs d'orchestre" in a printed note are not to be allowed to produce "brutal noise," is performed for the first time in Brussels.

15 DECEMBER 1960

Lysistrata, comic opera with serious pacifist intent by the Rumanian composer Gherase DENDRINO, ending with a realistic release of actual white doves and cast in a Viennese manner with a lot of waltzing tunes, is performed for the first time in Bucharest under the composer's direction.

16 DECEMBER 1960

The Golden Child, television opera in three sections by Philip BEZANSON to a Christmas libretto by Paul Engle wherein a child's rag doll magically leads a California gold rusher of 1848, his pregnant wife, and a small daughter out of a snowy wilderness to a mining camp, with a subsequent birth of a male child in a manger, making use of some special effects such as an authentic moo of a cow, is produced in a 90-minute television broadcast from New York.

17 DECEMBER 1960

Ninth Symphony for string orchestra by Henk BADINGS is performed for the first time in Amsterdam.

17 DECEMBER 1960

Paul HINDEMITH conducts in Mannheim the world première of his opera *Das lange Weihnachtsmahl,* in one act, after Thornton Wilder's plotless play *The Long Christmas Dinner,* translated into German by Hindemith, recounting the tale of 90 Christmas dinners in a single American family through several generations between 1840 and 1930, the dead departing and the newly born arriving, with a musical score of formal self-sufficiency and tonal directness wherein resolvable dissonances are subordinated to the basically triadic harmony.

17 DECEMBER 1960

Eleven days before his 84th birthday, Pablo CASALS conducts in Acapulco, Mexico, the world première of his oratorio *El Pesebre* (*The Manger*), composed in the 1940's for a performance in celebration of the unconsummated downfall of General Franco, and conceived as a nativity play interwoven with Catalan folksong material.

19 DECEMBER 1960

A "realization" of MAHLER's unfinished *Tenth Symphony* in F-sharp major and minor, by the British musicologist

Deryck Cooke (of the five movements of the work, the first, *Adagio*, the second, a *Scherzo*, and 28 measures of the third, *Purgatorio*, exist in full score; the rest in "short score"), is performed for the first time by the Philharmonia Orchestra in London under the direction of Berthold Goldschmidt. (On 28 April 1963, Alma Mahler, his widow, wrote to Deryck Cooke, expressing her admiration for his intuitive but authentic completion, and rescinding her earlier prohibition of further performances of the work in this version.)

22 DECEMBER 1960

Die Natali, "chorale preludes for orchestra" by Samuel BARBER, glorifying Christmastide in its Latin title, which means "on the day of the Nativity," and including adroit variations of several Christmas songs, is performed for the first time in Boston by the Boston Symphony Orchestra under the direction of Charles Munch.

30 DECEMBER 1960

The Invitation, ballet by Mátyás SEIBER, Hungarian composer, long resident in London, to a libretto focused on two adolescents in love befriended by a perverse married couple, with the boy being seduced by the wife, and the

girl raped by the husband, set to music in an expressionistically concentrated, schematically sensual quasi-dodecaphonic idiom, is produced at Covent Garden in London, three months and six days after Seiber's tragic death.

30 DECEMBER 1960

Symphonic Engravings, a suite for orchestra by the Soviet composer of Azerbaijan, Kara KARAEV, drawn from his music to the film *Don Quixote*, and picturing the knight of the sorrowful countenance in funereal tones, grotesquely changing to an asymmetrically rhythmed gallop, with Sancho Panza represented by a rude, crude march, is performed for the first time in Baku.

30 DECEMBER 1960

Mariuta, opera in three acts by the Soviet composer Dmitri TOLSTOY, after the story *Forty-First* by Boris Lavrenev, dealing with a Soviet girl guerrilla fighter who is left to guard a White Russian officer taken prisoner during the civil war in Central Asia, falls in love with him, but despite their intimacy, kills him unhesitantly when he tries to join the crew of an anti-Bolshevik motor boat on the Aral Sea, as she did forty previous enemies, is performed for the first time in Perm.

1961

1 JANUARY 1961

Deseret, television opera by the 31-year-old American composer Leonard KASTLE, based on a romanticized episode in the life of Brigham Young, founder of the Mormon colony in the Utah desert called Deseret, dealing with his magnanimous surrender of his 25th bride-to-be to a young Union Army officer whom she loves, set to music in a liltingly melodious and meltingly harmonious manner with pleasing arias, vocal duets, trios, quartets, quintets and sextets, is produced by the National Broadcasting Company Television Opera in New York.

5 JANUARY 1961

Second Symphony, written by the 27-year-old American composer Easley BLACKWOOD, on a commission from the G. Schirmer music publishing firm to commemorate its centennial, set in a rhapsodically romantic vein with a cornucopia of exclamatory and proclamatory fanfares, mitigated by atonally chromaticized melodic lines and nervously agitated rhythms, in three movements, *Largo*, *Scherzo* and *Toccata*, well within the classical mold, each ending on a unisonal E, is performed for the first time by the Cleveland Orchestra, George Szell conducting.

8 JANUARY 1961

CLARINEN, accurate modern replicas of Bach trumpets, capable of performing baroque music with great agility, celerity and perfect articulation along the natural scale of the harmonic series, are sounded over the Cologne Radio.

9 JANUARY 1961

In a Vienna court, Heinrich SCHMID, vocal coach of the Vienna State Opera, is awarded 1000 schillings damages in his lawsuit against the critic Franz Endler for unfairness in his review of a song recital by Elisabeth Schwarzkopf given in Vienna on 19 May 1960 accompanied by Schmid, in which Endler said that Schmid "struggled sullenly with the notes and limped unsteadily" in Hugo Wolf's song *Das Köhlerweib ist trunken (The Collier's Wife Is Drunk)*, maliciously or ignorantly disregarding the fact that these supposed lapses were intentional for a vivid illustration of drunkenness in the syncopated piano part.

13 JANUARY 1961

An evening of electronic opera and other musical essays in time, space, and sound, is produced by David Johnson at the Cooper Union for the Advancement of Science and Art in New York in a program opening with *Cough Music* (a recorded montage of actual coughs nervously emitted by the audience during a New York ballet recital, electronically altered and rhythmically rearranged and magnified); *Two Sounds* (violin scrapings amplified to screeches); *Amazing Grace* (electronically scrambled Negro spirituals) and an opera, *The Peaceable Kingdom* by Dick HIGGINS, dedicated to the composer's brother Mark "murdered by Lumumba's racists" in the Congo, scored for speaking voices representing tropical animals, accompanied by electronically amplified sounds of three toy pianos.

15 JANUARY 1961

George BARATI, Hungarian-born American composer conducts the Honolulu Symphony Orchestra in the first performance of his symphonic poem *The Dragon and the Phoenix*, suggested by a Polynesian legend, with the Phoenix redivivus illustrated by ornithological echolalia in the woodwinds and the dragon evoked by pyrophoric eruptions in the brass accompanied by sonorific clangors of pythonic gongs.

20 JANUARY 1961

Gloria by Francis POULENC for soprano solo, chorus and orchestra, comprising six parts of the Catholic Mass, conceived in a perfervid religious spirit and set in exalted triadic modalities, is performed for the first time by the Boston Symphony Orchestra, Charles Munch conducting.

27 JANUARY 1961

Fourth Symphony by the Swedish composer Allan PETTERSSON is performed for the first time in Stockholm.

2 FEBRUARY 1961

Dance and Invocation for orchestra by the Israeli composer Paul BEN-HAIM is performed for the first time in Tel Aviv.

8 FEBRUARY 1961

Collages by the Catalan composer Roberto GERHARD, resident in England, a serial work for orchestra and tape-recorded noises, composed in emulation of the principles of abstract expressionism in modern art, with the organic music represented by humans while electronic sound generators take an independent course, except at nine specified points at which the two sonic streams cross each other, is performed for the first time in London by the Orchestra of the British Broadcasting Corporation.

The tape recording consisted entirely of noises; gusty escaping winds, the steam exhaust of a train, rattles, bangs, and moans, tappety-tapping, all without form, shape, rhythm or sequence, cropping up here and there. . . . To this hideous counterpoint the orchestra added its quota of unmelodic, unharmonious, unrhythmical music, notes snatched out of the blue, dissonances mercifully overwhelmed by the greater cacophony of noise issuing from the loudspeaker. Mr. Gerhard's composition was an attempt to imitate that form of painting known as collage, in which extraneous bits of material are stuck on to the painted canvas in the name of abstract art. The musical result was as meaningless as the graphic one. If ever the BBC has wasted public money on the rehearsal and performance of absolute rubbish, it was on this occasion.

One might as well have taken the orchestra to the Hungerford Bridge and allowed them to improvise to the chance noises of the railway and the river. Perhaps this is just what happened and Mr. Gerhard was just deceiving us. (*Musical Opinion*, London, March 1961, in a leading article entitled *Rubbish!*)

9 FEBRUARY 1961

Symphonic Dialogues for orchestra by the Polish-born American composer Felix LABUNSKI, inspired by Arthur Schnitzler's *Reigen*, an erotic farce of overlapping fornication, in which a member of one couple becomes heterosexually involved with a member of another, and the last of the series with the initial adulterer with whom the round originated, forming a pericyclically proleptic dichotomy, represented in the score by nine bithematic sections (a + b, b + c, c + d . . . h + a) flanked by mutually reversible prelude and postlude, is performed for the first time by the Cincinnati Symphony Orchestra, Max Rudolf conducting.

10 FEBRUARY 1961

As part of the ceremony marking the opening of the first part of the Niagara Power Project, Ferde GROFÉ conducts the Buffalo Philharmonic in Niagara Falls in the first performance of his symphonic *Niagara Falls Suite*, in four movements reflecting historical, social and political aspects of the mighty cataract: *The Thunderer of the Waters*, *Devil's Hole Massacre*, *The Honeymooners*, and *Power of Niagara 1961*.

10 FEBRUARY 1961

The Philadelphia Orchestra, conducted by Eugene Ormandy, gives the world première of the *Seventh Symphony* by Walter PISTON, written in a kinesthetic neo-baroque manner, with clear tonal epicenters but without explicit key signatures, in three movements:

(1) *Con moto*, in non-waltz 3/4 time, melodically perambulating the circumference of mutant tonalities, gravitating towards A; (2) *Adagio Pastorale*, in 6/8, an elegiac eclogue with exterior decorations in the woodwinds, agitated towards the middle but subsiding into a floatingly fluent fluvial flute solo in the envoi; (3) *Allegro festevole*, in 2/4, a vivacious essay in the manner of a symphonic toccata.

10 FEBRUARY 1961

1941, opera in three acts by the 58-year-old Croatian composer Mihovil LOGAR, to a libretto glorifying the patriotic resistance groups fighting the Nazis in occupied Belgrade, containing in the action a choreographic hallucination, is produced in Sarajevo.

17 FEBRUARY 1961

Purgatory, opera in one-act by the Bohemian-born American composer Hugo WEISGALL, to a libretto from a mystagogical play by William Butler Yeats, wherein a man slays his father to avenge his mother's death in childbirth, and many years later kills his own son to prevent him from victimizing the women of the future, set to music in parsimoniously dissonant counterpoint, and frugally arranged harmonies is performed for the first time in concert form at the Library of Congress in Washington.

20 FEBRUARY 1961

Percy GRAINGER, romantic Australian-born pianist and composer whose first steps in music were tenderly fostered by Grieg, and who wrote folksy pieces with homely English titles making ostentatious use of colloquial musical terms (such as "dished up for piano" instead of arranged, "louden lots" instead of crescendo, "middle fiddle" instead of viola, "room-music" for chamber music, "foursome" for quartet, and even "twenty-two-some" for an ensemble of twenty-two instruments), and whose own life as a wandering artist was full of heartache (his adored mother jumped to her death from the 18th floor of the Aeolian Hall Building on 42nd Street in New York in 1922), romance (he married the Swedish painter and poet Allea Viola Stroem in the Hollywood Bowl before an audience of 22,000 people and wrote a bridal song for her entitled *To a Nordic Princess*), virtue (he was utterly unmercenary, a vegetarian, teetotaler, and non-smoker, and never owned a hat), and eccentricity (he was once arrested as a suspicious character when he arrived for a concert in Wausau, Wisconsin, in 7° below zero weather wearing white ducks, a knapsack, but no hat or coat), dies in White Plains, New York, at the age of 78. Percy Grainger's Last Will and Testament directed in part:

. . . that my flesh be removed from my bones and the flesh destroyed. I give and bequeath my skeleton to the University of Melbourne, Australia, for preservation and possible display in the Grainger Museum.

22 FEBRUARY 1961

Nick LA ROCCA, jazz cornetist, founder in New Orleans of the Original Dixieland Band, the first white ensemble of this genre, who blazed his syncopated trail to Chicago, New York and the world, dies in his native New Orleans at the age of 71.

2 MARCH 1961

Ariadne, lyric opera in one act by Bohuslav MARTINU, in which Theseus appears as the Freudian *superego* that kills its own *id* personified by the Minotaur with the aid of Ariadne's psychoanalytic umbilical cord, set to music in an orderly succession of recitatives, ensembles, and instrumental interludes in a neo-Monteverdian monody, is produced posthumously in Gelsenkirchen, Germany.

2 MARCH 1961

Nonet for Strings by Aaron COPLAND, scored for three violins, three violas and three cellos, with a discrete distribution of contrapuntal entities in polyriadic harmonies gradually accelerating in canonic imitation, then subsiding into serene polyharmony, is performed for the first time at the Dumbarton Oaks Research Library as a commissioned work in honor of the 50th wedding anniversary, of Mr. and Mrs. Robert W. Bliss, owners of the Dumbarton Oaks estate in Georgetown, D.C.

2 MARCH 1961

An American music program of works by members of the Southeastern Composers' League is presented by the George Peabody College for Teachers in Nashville, Tennessee, comprising twelve innocuous pieces for various instrumental groups and a set of six *Fallopian-Tube Waltzes* by Peter FORD, a microsonic anatomical percussion piece, in which the process of ovulation is illustrated by a dozen raw eggs solo dropped from a stepladder into a metal basket on the floor.

3 MARCH 1961

Sabbatai Zevi, le faux Messie, "fresque lyrique" in four acts with a prologue, by Alexandre TANSMAN, to a libretto dealing with a seventeenth-century Jewish Kabbalist who inflames his Zionist followers with faith in him as a Messiah destined to assume the tiarone of Zion in the fatidic year 1666, but is arrested by the Sultan as he tries to enter the Holy Land, then part of the Ottoman Empire, and embraces the Islamic faith to save himself, is produced in Paris.

3 MARCH 1961

Paul WITTGENSTEIN, amputated Austrian pianist who, after losing his right arm in Russia during World War I, began a unique career as a left-hand virtuoso and who commissioned Ravel, Richard Strauss, Prokofiev and others to write left-hand piano concertos for him, dies at the age of 73 in Manhasset, Long Island.

4 MARCH 1961

A partial concert performance is given at Yankton College in South Dakota of *The American Volunteer*, an opera in four acts composed in 1889 by the Italian bandmaster Felice VINATIERI who served with the Union Army in the Civil War and joined General Custer, to leave him just before his last stand in the battle with Sitting Bull at Little Big Horn. (Vinatieri commemorated the famous battle in his band piece *General Custer's Last Indian Campaign*.)

8 MARCH 1961

Sir Thomas BEECHAM, autocratic British grandee of the conductorial baton whose revenue from hereditary wealth accumulated through the opulent sales of Becham's liver pills enabled him to organize and maintain a symphony orchestra and a Beecham Opera Company early in the century, and whose insouciant disdain for good manners (he remarked, after a horse defecated on the stage in *Aida* during a tenor aria, "the beast is rude, but a good music critic") was condoned in deference to his sovereign musicianship revealed in his impeccable interpretations of classical music and his championship of early modernists, dies in London of a cerebral hemorrhage at the age of 81.

10 MARCH 1961

Per un Don Chissiotta, opera by the 31-year-old French composer Jean-Pierre RIVIÈRE, is produced by the Piccola Scala in Milan as the winning work in the international opera competition held by the Ricordi publishing firm to mark the 150th anniversary of its existence.

11 MARCH 1961

Uno Sguardo dal Ponte, opera by Renzo ROSSELLINI, to a libretto after Arthur Miller's play *A View from the Bridge*, dealing with a tragedy of concupiscence among illicit Italian immigrants in New York, is produced in Rome.

19 MARCH 1961

The Unattainable Woman, opera in three acts by the 52-year-old Estonian composer Eugen KAPP, is produced in Tartu.

23 MARCH 1961

Il Calzare d' argento, sacred play in two acts by Ildebrando PIZZETTI, dealing with a medieval pauper who is accused of the theft of a sacred relic when a silver shoe falls into his hands from a crucifix in the Lucca Cathedral but is exonerated by Jesus descending from the cross to testify in his defense, is produced at La Scala in Milan.

31 MARCH 1961

L'Horloge de Flore, suite for solo oboe and small orchestra by Jean FRANÇAIX, in seven movements each named after a specimen in the Flower Clock of Linnaeus, classified according to the hour of expected bloom, from poisonberry (flowering at 3 A.M.) to Silene Noctiflore (flowering at 9 P.M.), and set in an appropriately floriated neoclassical manner, is performed in a world première by the Philadelphia Orchestra, Eugene Ormandy conductor, with John de Lancie, first oboist of the orchestra, who commissioned the work, as soloist.

2 APRIL 1961

Wallingford RIEGGER, American composer of extraordinary independence of spirit and broadness of outlook, whose creative catalogue ranged from pragmatic studies in the simplest possible forms and idioms (most of them published under a variety of common-sounding pseudonyms) to sharply dissonant atonal pieces of experimental but immediately effective works, dies in New York at the age of seventy-five, after an emergency operation for a clot on the brain as the result of head injuries sustained after he tripped on a leash of one of two quarrelsome dogs which he tried to separate and fell on the pavement near his home as he went out for a luncheon appointment with Otto Luening.

4 APRIL 1961

Tenth Symphony by Darius MILHAUD, in four movements, *Décidé, Expressif, Fantasque, Emporté*, conceived in Milhaud's characteristic style of sharp contrasts, formal cohesion, and harmonic bitonality, with resilient rhythms animating the fast episodes, is performed for the first time by the Portland, Oregon, Symphony Orchestra, as a commissioned work for the centennial of the State of Oregon.

5 APRIL 1961

Len LYE demonstrates at the Museum of Modern Art in New York his tangible motion sculptures creating their own musical compositions through incidental collisions of rods and rings and music-box flanges attached to them.

11 APRIL 1961

Revelation in the Courthouse Park, scenic extravaganza by Harry PARTCH, after *The Bacchae* of Euripides (in which a horde of nymphomaniacal Bacchantes kill and dismember the King of Thebes for trying to suppress their orgiastic cult), in a theatrical setting featuring folk singers, dancers, tumblers, drum girls, and an assortment of exotic instruments producing non-tempered scales and Greek modes and musique concrète on a tape recorder, is staged at the University of Illinois, Urbana, during its Festival of Contemporary Arts.

12 APRIL 1961

For the first time a song is sung in outer space, as Yuri GAGARIN, 27-year-old Soviet cosmonaut, sings the patriotic air by Shostakovich, "My homeland hears, my homeland knows where in the skies her son soars on," to voice his elation as gravity gradually returns to his weightless body and his spaceship Vostok, decelerated by retro-rockets, begins its parabolic descent over Central Africa a few minutes before landing in a fallow plowed field of the collective farm, Lenin's Way, near the city of Engels, some 400 miles southeast of Moscow, after the completion of the first circumterrestrial manned flight.

13 APRIL 1961

Intolleranza 1960, "scenic action" in two parts, political opera-oratorio by the 37-year-old Italian modernist Luigi NONO, to texts by Eluard, Mayakovsky, Brecht, and other revolutionary poets integrated into a realistically allegorical continuity of nightmarishly unconnected tableaux, in which a refugee is dodecaphonically tortured by four choruses electronically transmitted from the four points of the compass, and a magnificently irrelevant ballet in a mythical "Dummyland" culminates in the atomic explosion of a polydodecaphonic chord, is produced during the course of the XXIV International Festival of Contemporary Music in Venice, amid protests in the audience and shouted mutual insults, as a Neo-Fascist group "Ordine Nuovo" stages a demonstration, showering from a gallery typewritten copies of an anti-dodecaphonic manifesto, proclaiming that "the only thing that is missing in this season of festivals, is Music," refusing to believe that "this confusion of sound and disonances called dodecaphony represents even a minimal musical manifestation," declaring that "in it there is no concept of hierarchy, the fulcrum around which the principles are formed that have made traditional music an imperishable art" and concluding with the assertion that dodecaphony is "only a distribution of notes contrasting with one another and demonstrating what happens when democracy is carried into the field of music."

17 APRIL 1961

William Arundel ORCHARD, Nestor of Australian composers, couductors and pedagogues, dies six days short of his 94th birthday, at sea on board *Dominion Monarch*, at Latitude 23°49' South and Longitude 09°33' East, off Sydney, Australia.

20 APRIL 1961

Symphonic Prelude by Walter PISTON, designed in four musical "facets" contrasted by tempo, density of motion and mood, but united by a basic tonal center F, is performed for the first time by the Cleveland Orchestra, George Szell conducting.

22 APRIL 1961

Belgium issues a 6-franc postage stamp honoring the famous Belgian violinist Henri VIEUXTEMPS (1820–1881) and 2-franc postage stamp honoring the Belgian organist and song composer Willem de MOL (1846–1874).

24 APRIL 1961

Jeux Vénitiens, symphonic suite by the 48-year-old Polish composer Witold LUTOSLAWSKI, written in a complex polyphonic idiom subordinated to an interrelated system of thematic subjects according to a *sui generis* serial procedure, including aleatory episodes within a predetermined duration, is performed for the first time in Venice by the Cracow Symphony Orchestra.

27 APRIL 1961

In the course of the Second Inter-American Music Festival in Washington, Howard Hanson conducts the Eastman School Philharmonic in the first performances of two American works: *Fourteenth Symphony* in four movements by Henry COWELL and *Give Me the Splendid Silent Sun* for baritone and orchestra by Roy HARRIS, to the words of Walt Whitman.

30 APRIL 1961

Two world premières are given in the course of the Second Inter-American Music Festival in Washington, D.C.:

Symphony in Four Parts (Overture, Hymn, Ostinato, Toccata) by the Cuban-born Californian composer Aurelio de la VEGA and the grandiose *Cantata para América Mágica* for dramatic soprano and percussion orchestra of 53 instruments to ancient pre-Columbian texts by the Argentinian composer Alberto GINASTERA, in six divisions, invoking the magical powers of the dawn, love, warfare, phantasmagoria, agony and prophecy.

30 APRIL 1961

In the course of the Second Inter-American Music Festival in Washington, the Orquesta Sinfónica Nacional de Mexico gives the first performances of two symphonic works: *Lyric* by the Canadian vanguardist Harry SOMERS and *Third Symphony,* in four movements, by the Mexican composer Blas GALINDO.

30 APRIL 1961

Violin Concerto with Lights by the 47-year-old American composer Henry BRANT, wherein kaleidescopically activated beams of light are manipulated by five musicians manning/womanning five pushbuttons, is performed for the first time in New York.

1 MAY 1961

At a concert of works by Edgar VARÈSE in New York, his electronic scores *Déserts* and *Poème electronique* are performed, as well as a new version of *Ecuatorial* for men's chorus and orchestra, originally conceived in 1934.

1 MAY 1961

Forest Song, ballet by the Ukrainian composer Herman ZHUKOVSKY, on the subject of Soviet youth working on the virgin soil of intellect and emotion, abounding in mellifluous melodies and rich ginger-bread harmonies and quickened by stimulating dance rhythms, is produced in Moscow during a festival of Ukrainian music.

5 MAY 1961

Jean-Michel DAMASE, 33-year-old French composer conducts in Bordeaux the world première of his lyric comedy *Colombe,* to a libretto by Anouilh, dealing with an underflowered flower girl named Colombe who marries into a middleclass family, then becomes an actress and is successively seduced by the director, by an actor, by a poet, and finally by her husband's half-brother, but is forgiven when she agrees to renounce the theater and return to her florist's stand.

6 MAY 1961

The Scarlet Letter, first opera written in the United States by Walter KAUFMANN, in three acts to a libretto by the composer based on Hawthorne's novel of the same name set in Salem, Massachusetts, in the seventeenth century, is produced for the first time at Indiana University in Bloomington.

7 MAY 1961

Tkalci, opera in two acts by the Czech composer Vít NEJEDLÝ, after Gerhard Hauptmann's drama *Die Weber,* dealing with the desperate sabotage action of German weavers, who destroy not only the factory of their oppressive employer but also his private house, set to music in an expressive melodramatic vein, is posthumously performed for the first time in Plzén.

10 MAY 1961

Le Héros et son miroir, surrealist ballet by the 37-year-old avant-garde Croatian composer Milko KELEMEN, a dodecaphonic portrayal of a former hero who contemplates his own image in a retrospective mirror and suffers agonies at recalling his once glorious past, is produced in Paris.

15 MAY 1961

Krakatit, opera in two parts by the Czech composer Václav KASLÍK, after a novelette of Karel Čapek wherein the inventor of a powerful explosive Krakatit has a vivid hallucination that a group of anarchists forces him to use his invention to destroy society, and upon awakening becomes a militant pacifist, set to music in an explosively dynamic score including electronic sound, is produced in Ostrava.

18 MAY 1961

The Chopin Express, operating between Vienna and Warsaw, is inaugurated by the Austrian Federal Railways, leaving Vienna at 10 P.M. and arriving in Warsaw the next day at 11:09 A.M.

19 MAY 1961

Lancelot, two-act opera by the 25-year-old Czech composer Luboš FIŠER, to a libretto from the Arthurian legend dealing with a knight in love with a queen, is produced in Prague.

20 MAY 1961

Silas Marner, opera in three acts by the 34-year-old South African composer John JOUBERT after the novel of that name by George Eliot, dealing with an unjustly maligned village weaver who is vindicated through industry, prosperity, and love for a foundling, set to music in a triadic tonal idiom spiced with prudential non-corrosive dissonances, is produced at the South African College of Music in Capetown.

20 MAY 1961

Elegie für junge Liebende, opera in three acts by the 34-year-old German composer Hans Werner HENZE, to a libretto (originally in English) by W. H. Auden and Chester Kallman, dealing with an egocentric old poet who sends the younger of his two mistresses and her lover to their deaths in an expected snowstorm, in the Alps in 1910, calculated to provide the needed catalytic impulse for the completion of his literary masterpiece, an "elegy for young lovers," the score making use of a variety of expressive vocal resources, from whispers to screams, is performed for the first time in Schwetzingen. (The opera was first performed in English in Glyndebourne on 13 July 1961 under the original title *Elegy for Young Lovers*.)

25 MAY 1961

Rapsodie Cartésienne, orchestral rhapsody by the 61-year-old French composer Henry BARRAUD, written according to putative principles of Descartes, is performed for the first time in Paris.

25 MAY 1961

Il Mercante de Venezia, grand opera in three acts by Mario CASTELNUOVO-TEDESCO, the winning work in an international competition sponsored by the Italian manufacturer of the bitter-sweet apéritif Campari, greatly condensed from Shakespeare's play and equi-syllabically translated by the composer into Italian (so that the opera can be performed in English or Italian without rhythmic readjustments) and supplemented by Shakespeare's sonnet "O! Never say that I was false of heart" but with Shylock's forced conversion to Christianity omitted (being Jewish, Castelnuovo-Tedesco himself was compelled to leave Italy in 1939 when Mussolini espoused Hitler's antisemitic policy), the music soaring rhapsodically in the grandest Puccinian manner and the melodious vocal line immersed in luxuriant but never unduly dissonant harmonies, with but a single instance of explicit modernity when a dodecaphonic chord is erected to illustrate the wrong guesses of two pretenders to Portia's hand (the chord is resolved into the purest C major when the lucky Bassanio guesses right), is performed for the first time at the Maggio Musicale in Florence, where the composer's ancestors were bankers at the time when Shylock was a usurer in Venice.

29 MAY 1961

Ninth Symphony, subtitled *Aerosymfonien*, by the 41-year-old Danish composer Niels Viggo BENTZON, is performed for the first time in Odense.

31 MAY 1961

Radio Warsaw broadcasts the first performance of *Tren pamięçi ofiar Hiroszimy (Lament in Memory of the Victims of Hiroshima)* by the 27-year-old Polish composer Krzysztof PENDERECKI, scored for 24 violins, 10 violas, 10 cellos and 8 doublebasses, in graphic notation indicating special effects, such as the highest possible note, arpeggios on strings below the bridge, tapping, rapping, rasping, rattling, scraping and snapping at the body of the instruments, with the duration of individual measures marked by the actual time, from 4 to 30 seconds each, comprising sections of stochastic playing in a directed aleatory procedure, and calculated to give a distant impression of the atomic annihilation of the Japanese town of Hiroshima on 6 August 1945, with a simulacrum of human outcries of disembodied anguish and unsynchronized heartbeats in disarticulated infantiloquy in a tremor of microsonic formication in quarter-tones, concluding with a massive tonal cloud of gray matter, encompassing two octavefuls of icositetraphonic harmony.

3 JUNE 1961

The Right Hand of a Great Master, opera by the 57-year-old Georgian composer Shalva MSHELIDZE, to a libretto from the time of the internecine strife in the 11th century for the possession of Georgia, wherein the young Georgian king engages a captive architect to build a temple on the confluence of the Aragva and the Kura rivers, and upon finding out that he has seduced his favorite concubine, orders his right hand to be cut off, driving both him and her to suicide, is produced in Tbilisi.

5 JUNE 1961

Concerto for mouth harmonica and orchestra by Heitor VILLA-LOBOS, written in 1955, in three contrasting movements replete with humid Brazilian melo-rhythms and containing a tropically luxuriant cadenza, is performed posthumously for the first time during a Music Festival in Cartágena, Colombia, conducted by Guillermo Espinosa, with John Sebastian, the virtuoso harmonica player to whom the work is dedicated, as soloist.

5 JUNE 1961

In a deliberate hoax aimed at gullible listeners and uncritical music critics, the British Broadcasting Corporation presents a *Mobile for Tape and Percussion* by a non-existent 22-year-old Polish composer Piotr ZAK, consisting of a montage of random noises and other debris of musique concrète gathered around the studio.

The British Broadcasting Corporation policy of giving the musical avant-garde a hearing needs no justification, but there are bound to be occasional lapses: Piotr Zak's *Mobile* for electronic tape and two partially improvising percussion players, broadcast twice last night, sounded like one of them. The composer's refusal to publish a score suggests that he considers a consciously analytic approach a waste of the listener's time. It was certainly difficult to grasp more than the music's broad outlines, partly because of the high proportion of unpitched sounds and partly because of their extreme diversity. Without some idea of what could be relevant, it is not easy to say what is not. (*The Times*, London, 6 June 1961)

7 JUNE 1961

On his 50th birthday, Franz REIZENSTEIN, German-born English subject, plays in London the solo part in the first performance of his *Second Piano Concerto*, in three movements, written in a neo-romantic vein marked with diversified lyrico-dramatic episodes setting the tone of melancholy exhilaration.

9 JUNE 1961

The Greek Passion for voices and orchestra, last work by Bohuslav MARTINU, after the novel by the Greek writer Nikos Kazantzakis, *Christ Recrucified*, in which a bearded shepard, acting Christ in a passion play in a Greek village about 1900 A.D., identifies himself so completely with his role that he begins to preach unpopular sermons attacking capitalism and imperialism and is slain by a villager impersonating Judas, set to music embodying elements of Greek folksongs and Byzantine liturgical chants, is brought out posthumously at the Zürich Opera, under the direction of Paul Sacher on whose estate in Switerland Martinu completed the work on 15 January 1959, shortly before his death.

11 JUNE 1961

The 35th annual Festival of the International Society for Contemporary Music opens in Vienna with a program dedicated to the works of Anton von WEBERN:

Cantata, Das Augenlicht, op. 26, written in 1935, scored for mixed chorus and chamber orchestra, including a saxophone, xylophone, celesta, harp and mandolin, based on a 12-tone radix with predominantly small intervals, spelling the name B-A-C-H in its exposition, undodecaphonically harmonized in quartal formations superimposed on thematic major sevenths and their concomitant minor ninths; *First Cantata*, op. 29, for soprano solo, mixed chorus and orchestra, in three parts, written in 1939, based on a symmetrical 12-tone row composed of two-note tropes, of which the second constitutes a melodically inverted cancrizans, with the text of the third part referring to the transfiguration of the Three Graces represented by a fugue in the form of a Scherzo with variations; Webern's orchestral arrangement of Bach's *Ricercata* (the second fugue of the *Musikalisher Opfer* written for Frederick the Great); Bach's motet *Singer dem Herrn*, in four sections with a parallel instrumental accompaniment; and Webern's *Second Cantata*, op. 31, his last completed work, containing a complex four-part canon derived from a dodecaphonic radix.

12 JUNE 1961

The 35th Festival of the International Society for Contemporary Music in Vienna presents a special concert in a program comprising a *Rondino giocoso* for string orchestra by the Viennese composer Theodor BERGER, Mozart's *Violin Concerto* in G major, PROKOFIEV's *Second Violin Concerto* and MAHLER's *First Symphony*.

12 JUNE 1961

Hello, Kansas!, a musical play in observance of the hundredth anniversary of the statehood of Kansas by the American composer John POZDRO, is performed for the first time in Lawrence, Kansas.

13 JUNE 1961

At the third concert of the 35th Festival of the International Society for Contemporary Music in Vienna, the following program is given:

Musik for 22 solo string instruments by the Swiss composer Jacques WILDBERGER (a world première); *Sonata* for piano, five wind instruments, timpani and strings by the Czech composer Václav DOBIÁŠ, written in harmonious neo-baroque style; *Variationen* for 40 instruments by Michael GIELEN of Austria, with its theme represented by a tone row *in nuce*, followed by twelve variations governed by an arithmetical progression in a serial arrangement of instrumental groupings; and the eloquently sonorous *Arcana* by the grand maître of new music Edgar VARÈSE, consistently dissonant in its polyphonic fabric, with the exception of two bars of C major before the end inserted to create the sense of shattering discordance.

14 JUNE 1961

Forma Ferritonans, symphonic poem by the Swedish modernist Karl-Birger BLOMDAHL, written on commission from the Oxeloesund Steel Corporation in Sweden to celebrate the opening of its new manufacturing plant, illustrated by a progression beginning softly in the bass to symbolize the presence of unprobed iron ore in the bowels of the earth, and rising to a thundering "ferritonans" climax, picturing the rolling sheets of manufactured metal, is performed for the first time in Oxeloesund.

15 JUNE 1961

At the fourth concert of the 35th annual Festival of the International Society for Contemporary Music in Vienna, the following program of vocal and instrumental music is given:

Four *a cappella* choruses by the serialistic West German composer Winfried ZILLIG, derived from a dodecaphonic series, subjected to a rigorous canonic treatment; *Serenata* for chamber orchestra by Vittorio FELLEGARA of Italy, in one neo-baroque movement, set in unaltered 3/8 time; *Wymiary Czasu i Ciszy* by the 27-year-old Polish experimenter Krzysztof PENDERECKI, scored for a wordless and toneless 40-part chorus, singing, whispering, whistling (glissando), and flutter-tonguing on the voiceless gutturals, sibilants and labials (e.g., G B P K T) arranged in artfully contrived canonic configurations, wherein the "dimensions of time and silence" of the titles are measured in precisely indicated durations, the entire piece lasting exactly 8 minutes and 40 seconds; 3 *Lieder* by the 31-year-old Icelander Fjölnir STEFANSSON, with each song built on a symmetrically constructed dodecaphonic radix, and transpositions limited to the tritone; *Monody for Corpus Christi* by the 26-year-old British composer Harrison BIRTWISTLE, to the text from 16th-century English church songs, for soprano, flute, violin, and horn; *0,0,0,0, That Shakespeherian Rag* (the title being a line from T. S. Eliot's poem *The Waste Land*), scored for mixed chorus and a jazz combo, by the American composer Salvatore MARTIRANO, to four excerpts from Shakespeare, with words unnaturally syllabilized and abnormally articulated to cause the disjected members of the poetic line to form adventitious verbalities.

16 JUNE 1961

In the course of the 35th Festival of the International Society for Contemporary Music in Vienna, the world première is given of *Die Jakobsleiter*, unfinished oratorio by Arnold SCHOENBERG to his own theologically mystical text, derived from the biblical story of Jacob's dream of a celestial ladder, placing unclean souls of rationalists, skeptics and cynics at the bottom of the ladder, and geniuses at the top, with ascending and descending traffic maintained by the Archangel Gabriel busily reincarnating skeptics into believers and vice versa, the composition of which, begun in 1915, continued fragmentarily throughout 35 years almost until Schoenberg's death, the germinal musical idea already adumbrating the 12-tone method (the basic row being the sum of two hexachords: D, C-sharp, E, F, G, A-flat, plus C, E-flat, B, B-flat, F-sharp and A, the first group being used in different rhythms and registers), set in score according to Schoenberg's sketches and subsequent elucidations by Winfried Zillig, with the application of stereophonic "music in space," in accordance with the suggestion made by Schoenberg in a note written in English in 1944: "Today, October 1944, the problem of the *Fern-Orchester* and *Fern-Chöre* would best be resolved by being played behind the scene, by soundproof materials inaudible at the stage, but by microphones distributed so as to appear at different places of the hall," and a previous note written in German in 1921: "Chorus and soloists, at first chiefly on the platform, then gradually joined by the choruses stationed with the off-stage orchestras, so that in the end the music streams from all sides of the hall."

17 JUNE 1961

At the sixth concert of the 35th Festival of the International Society for Contemporary Music in Vienna, the following works are performed:

Felder for flute, vibraphone, tubular chimes, piano and a large assortment of percussion instruments by the Norwegian composer Björn Wilho HALLBERG, the "fields" of the title referring to units of the dimension of time during which each player is aleatorically independent, with the application of numerous special effects, such as the toneless clapping of the flute keys; *Calligraphy* for piano by the Japanese composer Keyiro SATO, calculated to express in a complex serialistic design the "pure vitality" of the music, comparable to the perfection of Zen-Buddhist calligraphy, attaining in the final stretto the intensity and internal concentration of the exalted state "kihakul"; *Haiku Settings* for voice and piano by the American composer Mel POWELL, to English tristychs from Japanese originals consisting of 5—7—5 syllables each, to be sung with head-tones changing to falsetto; *Canzone da sonare* for piano and percussion by the Japanese composer Shin-ichi MATSUSHITA, written with the application of aleatory concepts, in which each player is free to select any thematic fragments within a strict time limit, in a manner corresponding to the technique of Japanese brush painting; *Relazioni fragili* for cembalo and chamber orchestra by the Austrian composer Friedrich CERHA, in four parts, devised according to a complex serial concept, in which all elements of music are ordered and organized in their interdependent actions, with two women's voices treated as instruments and producing reverberations in the orchestra that change their secondary sexual characteristics to male sonorities; and *Composizione 3* for 12 instruments by the Italian composer Egisto MACCHI,

an essay in tone color, opening with an "extended zone of inconceivable pianissimo" and making use of quarter-tones.

18 JUNE 1961

The 35th Festival of the International Society for Contemporary Music in Vienna continues with the following program:

Three works by Anton von WEBERN: *Passacaglia*, op. 1, *Variationen* for orchestra, op. 30, and 6 *Stücke* for orchestra, op. 6; *Metamorphosen* for 23 solo string players by Richard STRAUSS, written by him during the last days of the fall of Germany, as a mournful testament of an 80-year-old German master of romantic music; *Second Piano Concerto* by the German-born Israeli composer Josef TAL, in one tripartite movement, based on a traditional modal cantillation of Jeremiah's lament, developed according to serial principles; and the world première of *Von der Liebe*, lyric fantasy for voice and orchestra by Gottfried von EINEM, consisting of four chromatically inflected songs about love with correspondingly romantic instrumental interludes.

19 JUNE 1961

At the 35th Festival of the International Society for Contemporary Music in Vienna, the following works are performed:

Tre Pezzi for cello and orchestra, *Fantasia*, *Capriccio* and *Epilogue* by the Hungarian-born British-naturalized composer of atonally inflected music, Mátyás SEIBER, who perished in an automobile accident in South Africa on 24 September 1960; *Monosonata* by the autodidact experimenter in the ultimate complexities of the musical language within humanly performable limits, 32-year-old Boguslaw SCHÄFFER of Poland, written for six string quartets subdivided into three uneven groups of one, two and three each, the whole work based on a single melodico-harmonic matrix, consisting of 8 different notes and 7 different intervals, with the contrapuntal and harmonic materials built from units from a single note to twice twelve notes, while other dimensions and parameters parallel these radices; *Strophes* by the 34-year-old Italian composer Franco DONATONI, empirically developed from an organic serial concept, with instrumental complexes built on the principle of the labyrinth the intersections of which constitute a matrix of unpredictable topographic events compounded of tone-clusters of various degrees of spissitude; *Sequences* for violin and four orchestral groups by the 42-year-old Polish composer living in Vienna, Roman HAUBENSTOCK-RAMATI, constructed according to the concept of a two-dimensional continuum of contrasting qualities—perpendicularity and linearity, staticism and mobility—in completely emancipated dissonant counterpoint; and *Chronochromie* for orchestra by Olivier MESSIAEN, making thematic use of song patterns of French, Swedish, Japanese and Mexican birds and of the rustling noises of waterfalls in the French Alps, with 32 different divisions of time (*chronos* of the title) and corresponding diversities of color (*chromos* of the title) forming a chronochromic hypostasy.

20 JUNE 1961

The 35th annual Festival of the International Society for Contemporary Music in Vienna concludes with the performance of three works by Béla BARTÓK: *Dance Suite*, *Violin Concerto* and *Concerto for Orchestra*.

22 JUNE 1961

At the Holland Festival in Amsterdam, Otto KLEMPERER, 76-year-old German conductor, leads the Concertgebouw Orchestra in the world première of his newly composed symphony in two movements, with an ending in which the *Marseillaise* is irrelevantly projected against a variation of an original theme, creating an element of surprise in polytonal counterpoint.

24 JUNE 1961

Gothic Symphony by the 85-year-old English composer Havergal BRIAN, in four movements, the last of which is an enormously protracted *Te Deum,* and the second movement a funeral march, written for a huge orchestra requiring a choir of 8 flutes (including a bass flute), 11 clarinets of various sizes (including a contrabass clarinet), 8 instruments of the oboe family (including the oboe d'amore and heckelphone), 16 kettledrums, a thunder machine and other noisemakers, 2 separate brass orchestras, 4 large choruses, a children's chorus and vocal soloists, is performed for the first time in Westminster, 42 years after the composition of the work.

30 JUNE 1961

Lee de FOREST, Iowa-born "Father of Radio" (as the title of his autobiography proclaimed), the Aladdin of the Audion, the magical lamp which he invented in 1906, which made radio possible by the addition of an essential third element, the grid, to the anode and the cathode of a vacuum tube; who courted a lady by closed-circuit radio (he married her, but the marriage was annulled shortly afterwards; his subsequent wives were a suffragist, a concert singer, and a motion picture actress), and who on 3 April 1909 engineered the first broadcast of a human voice when he installed two microphones along the footlights of the stage at the Metropolitan Opera House in New York and transmitted the singing of Enrico Caruso in *Cavalleria Rusticana* to a receiver in his home, dies in Hollywood whose flowering owed so much to his inventions in the field of the sound motion pictures and television, at the age of eighty-seven.

You have debased my child . . . You have made him a laughingstock of intelligence . . . a stench in the nostrils of the gods of the ionosphere. . . . (From Lee de Forest's letter to the National Association of Broadcasters on the 40th anniversary of the Audion tube, 1946)

12 JULY 1961

Irving CONN (real name Cohn), piano player who in 1922 set to music the fascinatingly self-contradictory verse, *Yes, We Have No Bananas,* which Frank Silver wrote down after talking to a Greek fruit-vendor at Lynnbrook, Long Island, and which became the great hit of the 1920's (the first four notes of the song are identical with Handel's *Halleluja* from the *Messiah,* but the similarity was in all probability coincidental), dies at Hudson, New York, at the age of 63.

20 JULY 1961

Lavinia, opéra-bouffe by Henry BARRAUD, to a modern story about a Neapolitan fruit-vendor who names his newly-born daughter Lavinia, and when a local journalist points out that Lavinia was the wife of Aeneas, ignorant neighbors decide that the child was the fruit of an illegitimate affair of the vendor's wife with Aeneas, leading to

all kinds of amusing contretemps, with an appropriately light but sophisticated musical score, is performed for the first time in the course of the summer festival at Aix-en-Provence.

23 JULY 1961

Grace BUMBRY, "die schwarze Venus," 24-year-old American Negro mezzosoprano, sings the role of Venus in *Tannhäuser* at the opening of the sacrosanct Wagner Festival in Bayreuth, the first black woman to appear in a Wagner opera, directed by Wagner's grandson Wieland Wagner and appearing not as an ample-bodied symbol of medievalistic sensuality, but as a magical presence clad in gold-black attire and standing immobile with outspread arms in the foreground of the stage.

3 AUGUST 1961

John CAGE conducts at the International Week of Today's Music in Montreal, Canada, the first performance of his *Atlas Eclipticalis* notated so that each part occupies space equal to a time at least twice as slow as clock time, with loudness being proportional to the size of notes on paper, the score being the product of chance operations by the placing of transparent templates on the pages of an astronomical atlas and inscribing the positions of stars.

7 AUGUST 1961

Early Dawn, opera in three acts by the 55-year-old American composer Norman LOCKWOOD to a libretto by Russell Porter dealing with the emotional unrest of two brothers torn between love and patriotism on the eve of the outbreak of the Civil War and making use of homespun folk materials cast in memorable melodies, is produced for the first time at the University of Denver, Thomas Scherman conducting.

16 AUGUST 1961

Szimfónia by Zoltán KODÁLY, his first symphony, completed in May 1961 at the age of 78, with a dedication to the memory of Arturo Toscanini in a line from a psalm ". . . is etenim saepenumero me adhortatus est . . ." (for indeed Toscanini often encouraged Kodály and voluntarily played his music), in three movements, *Allegro, Andante moderato* and *Vivo,* the outer movements in unobstructed C major in a virile binary march time, the inner movement a set of variations on an ancient quintuple-metered pentatonic Magyar chant melismatically situated in the proximity of G-sharp minor, is performed for the first time at the Lucerne Festival for which it was written, in the presence of the composer and his 20-year-old bride.

16 AUGUST 1961

Das Bergwerk zu Falun, opera by the 57-year-old German composer Rudolf WAGNER-RÉGENY, after a story by Hugo von Hofmannsthal painting in dark undertones the doom-laden progress of a death-obsessed collier, saturated with atonal forebodings, with occasional tonal relief brought about by rustic rhythms, is performed for the first time at the Salzburg Festival.

17 AUGUST 1961

C'est la guerre, opera in one act by the Hungarian composer Emil PETROVICS, to the verisimilitudinous story of a Hungarian deserter given refuge by a friend in Budapest in 1944, who is betrayed to the Nazis by her landlady avenging the loss of her two sons in battle, and is executed with his host whose wife, who has in the meantime fallen in love with him, defenestrates herself as the Nazi officer observes in French, "C'est la guerre," set to music in expressionistically dissonant harmonies replete with dramatic bitonalities, is performed for the first time in concert form on the Budapest Radio. (The first stage performance took place in Budapest on 11 March 1962.)

19 AUGUST 1961

Nausicaa, opera by the Australamerican composeress Peggy GLANVILLE-HICKS, to a libretto by Robert Graves from his book *Homer's Daughter,* advancing the frivolous notion that the epic *Odyssey* was created not by Homer but by his daughter, set to music in homophonic pseudo-Grecian modalities, ending in a sudden explosion of declarative C major, with soloists singing in English and the commentating chorus in Greek, receives its world première in Athens, in the Herodes Atticus amphitheater built in 161 A.D., situated on the southern slope of the Acropolis.

23 AUGUST 1961

Lembitu, opera in two acts by the 47-year-old Estonian composer Villem KAPP, relating the defeat administered to the crusading German Knights by the Estonians in the 12th century, is produced in Tallin.

5 SEPTEMBER 1961

The government of Rumania issues a 3-lei postage stamp to honor Georges ENESCO on the occasion of the Enesco Festival in Bucharest, and showing Enesco playing the violin and the initial bars of his *Third Violin Sonata.*

6 SEPTEMBER 1961

Double Concerto for harpsichord, piano and two chamber orchestras by Elliott CARTER, antiphonally constructed so that the two ensembles are mutually exclusive (except that each has a French horn), and are further musically separated by coopting different sets of preferred intervals, metronomic speeds and polyrhythmic schemes (the harpsichord group cultivates harsh dissonances and polyrhythmic combinations of 4 against 7 temporal units while the piano ensemble favors lighter dissonances and clearer consonances as well as less complex polyrhythms, viz. 5 against 3), the mutual exclusivity leading to complementality, synchronization, syncretism, synthesis and ultimately esthetic fusion, the whole continuous work subdivided into seven linked movements and forming in the process one of the most complex and yet most self-consistent works of modern music in a nondodecaphonic though mainly atonal matrix, is performed for the first time in the course of the 8th Congress at the International Society for Musicology in New York.

Craft: What composition by an American-born composer has most attracted you to date?

Stravinsky: Elliott Carter's *Double Concerto.* But analysis as little explains a masterpiece or calls it into being as an ontological proof explains or causes the existence of God. There, the word is out. A masterpiece, and by an American composer. (From a colloquy between Robert Craft and Igor Stravinsky in *Musical America,* New York, June 1962)

17 SEPTEMBER 1961

In the course of the First Music Festival of Israel (inaugurated on 26 August 1961), an open-air concert is presented in the amphitheater of Caesarea, built by Herod in 12 B.C., and dug up from the sands in 1959, in a program of instrumental music, with Pablo CASALS playing a Bach sonata for viola da gamba.

18 SEPTEMBER 1961

Blood Moon, opera by the 48-year-old American composer Norman DELLO JOIO, to a libretto dealing with the famed octoroon actress Adah Menken who prospered in New Orleans and New York at the time of the Civil War until her favorite lover discovered the 12 1/2% of denigrating Negro blood in her veins, set to music within the framework of Civil War tonality, varnished with a pandiatonic patina, is performed for the first time in San Francisco.

20 SEPTEMBER 1961

To mark the sesquicentennial year of the birth of Franz LISZT, the Hungarian Post Office issues a series of six perforate and six imperforate postage stamps in his honor.

(The German Democratic Republic issues a set of four Liszt stamps on 19 October 1961; Austria issued one Liszt stamp at 3 schillings on 20 October 1961, and Russia issued a 4-kopeck Liszt stamp on 31 October 1961.)

20 SEPTEMBER 1961

On the occasion of the centennial of the birth of the Australian-born prima donna Nellie MELBA, the Australian government issues a postage stamp in her honor.

24 SEPTEMBER 1961

An architectonically utilitarian and ostentatiously non-baroque building of the Deutsche Oper, constructed according to the modern findings of the science of acoustics, is officially opened on Bismarckstrasse in West Berlin to take the place of the renowned Städtische Oper, destroyed by aerial bombardment but restored in its original site on Unter den Linden in East Berlin.

25 SEPTEMBER 1961

Alkmene, opera by the 36-year-old German composer Giselher KLEBE, dodecaphonically dealing with Zeus who assumes the likeness of Amphitryon and materializes in his wife's bedroom to claim his marital right by Olympian proxy, is performed for the first time at the newly built Deutsche Oper in West Berlin.

28 SEPTEMBER 1961

Scherzo for piano and orchestra, an early work by BÉLA BARTÓK, written by him at the age of 23, and consisting of an introductory *Adagio* and a typically Hungarian *Allegro vivace,* with the influx of a considerable amount of rational dissonance, is performed for the first time in Budapest as part of the gradual process of Bartók's canonization in his native country.

30 SEPTEMBER 1961

A Man's Destiny, music drama by the 52-year-old Soviet composer Ivan DZERZHINSKY, dealing with a Soviet prisoner of war who escapes from Nazi captivity in 1943 and returns to his native village only to find that his wife and daughters were killed in an air raid but saves himself from suicidal despair by adopting an orphan boy, set to music in an illustratively realistic idiom (the Nazis are characterized by quotations from Kurt Weill's *Dreigroschenoper*), employing the Soviet accordion Bayan for realistic effect, is produced at the Bolshoi Theater in Moscow.

1 OCTOBER 1961

The world première is given in Leningrad of the *Twelfth Symphony* by Dmitri SHOSTAKOVICH, dedicated to the memory of Lenin, and subtitled *1917,* a triumphant sequel to his *Eleventh Symphony* (which commemorates the idealistically romantic and therefore unsuccessful revolution of 1905), encompassing in four movements the historic milestones of Lenin's life:

(1) *Revolutionary Petrograd (Allegro),* reflecting in opulent triadic harmonies the period from the abortive Russian revolution of 1905 to Lenin's arrival in Petrograd in April 1917; (2) *Razliv (Adagio),* descriptive of Lenin's hiding place in a Finnish retreat under an assumed name in the summer of 1917 when his arrest was ordered by the Russian Provisional Government; (3) *The Aurora (Allegro),* glorifying the cruiser *Aurora* which fired the first shots of the Soviet Revolution; (4) *Dawn of Humanity (Allegretto,)* portraying in eloquent sonorities and impassioned colors the Soviet victory of 7 November 1917.

7 OCTOBER 1961

Fifteenth Symphony by Henry COWELL, subtitled *Thesis,* is performed for the first time at Bowling Green, Kentucky.

12 OCTOBER 1961

The Wings of the Dove, opera in two acts by Douglas MOORE, after a psychological novel by Henry James wherein a British girl persuades her fiancé to ingratiate himself with a dying American heiress and induce her to bequeath her fortune to him, ending with an empty victory as the plan succeeds but their love is dead, set to a deliberately infra-modern, melodious and harmonious score, is performed for the first time in New York.

16 OCTOBER 1961

Do Russians Want War?, a song by Eduard KOLMANOVSKY, to the bitterly ironical words of the prime Soviet poet Evgeny Evtushenko, destined to become the most popular anti-war song, widely used at Soviet festivals and official celebrations, is broadcast for the first time on Radio Moscow. (Date obtained by the author from Kolmanovsky.)

17 OCTOBER 1961

Third Symphony by the 53-year-old Yugoslav composer Milan RISTIĆ, in four movements tracing chronologically the four stages of his life—youth, political struggle, Nazi occupation and liberation in a new socialist world—written in a neo-classical manner unified by a twelve-tone serial row without forsaking the essential tonality, is performed for the first time in Belgrade.

21 OCTOBER 1961

Peter RONNEFELD, a 26-year-old German composer, conducts at the Festival of the Music Theater of the 20th Century in Düsseldorf the world première of his four-act opera *Die Ameise,* wherein a voice teacher formicatingly enamored of his pupil Formica, strangles her in the middle of a coloratura aria, in his remorse cultivates a queen ant in his prison cell (hence the title *The Ant,* or in Latin, *Formica*) whom he teaches to sing, is released for good behavior and tries to get her into a ballet show dealing with the life in an anthill, collapses and dies when his incautious impresario steps on her, set to music in an eclectically dissonant style with such realistic episodes as a colloquy of convicts reminiscing about their sexual experiences and a male chorus lecturing in vulgar Latin on the mating modus operandi of ants.

21 OCTOBER 1961

The annual Donaueschingen Festival of Contemporary Music opens with the following program:

Monades III for chamber orchestra (world première) by Jacques GUYONNET (Switzerland); *Permutazioni* for wind quintet by Mátyás SEIBER (1905–1960) of Hungary and England; *Entelechie I* for 5 instrumental groups (world première) by Peter SCHAT (Holland); *Credentials or think, think lucky,* for voice and instruments (world première) by Roman HAUBENSTOCK-RAMATI (Poland); *Structures* for 2 pianos (vol. 2; world première) by Pierre BOULEZ (France).

22 OCTOBER 1961

The second concert of the two-day Donaueschingen Festival of Contemporary Music presents the following program:

Atmospheres for orchestra (world première) by Gyorgy LIGETI (Hungary); *Epifanie* for orchestra (world première) by Luciano BERIO (Italy); *Contrasts* for orchestra (world première) by Gunther SCHULLER; *Variations* for orchestra by SCHOENBERG.

23 OCTOBER 1961

Torquilla, oratorio by the Danish composer Niels Viggo BENTZON, to texts from Nevil Shute's tale of the atomic war between China and Russia ultimately engulfing the world in lethal cobalt radiation, is performed for the first time in Aarhus, Denmark.

26 OCTOBER 1961

Eighth Symphony by David DIAMOND (completed on 15 November 1960, on the day after the 60th birthday of Aaron Copland, to whom the work is dedicated), in two movements—(1) *Moderato-Adagio-Allegro vivo,* neurotically agitated and languidly anguished; (2) *Theme, Variations* and *Double Fugue,* derived from a 12-tone radix—is performed for the first time by the New York Philharmonic, Leonard Bernstein conducting.

26 OCTOBER 1961

The Crucible, opera by Robert WARD after Arthur Miller's play, dealing with the hysterical witch-hunt in Salem, Massachusetts, in 1692, set to music in a traditional operatic style, is produced in New York.

5 NOVEMBER 1961

The Flower of Remembrance, opera in three acts by the Albanian composer Kristo KONO, dealing with an Albanian youth fighting the oppressive Turkish rule in 1907, erroneously reported to have been torn apart by wild wolves, the news causing his faithful beloved to lose her reason thus saving her from a repuguant forced marriage, with a happy dénouement vouch-safed when she receives from him a symbolic flower of remembrance, instantly curing her amnesia, while her obtrusive suitor is frozen to death in the mountains, is produced in Tirana.

11 NOVEMBER 1961

Two short Flemish operas, *Jonker Lichthart* by Jef van HOOF, written in 1928 for a radio performance, and *St. Anthony's Great Temptation* by Louis de MEESTER, a modernistic interpretation of the horror-laden painting of Hieronymous Bosch, with electronic jazz symbolizing the agony of seduction, are performed in the Flemish language in Antwerp.

13 NOVEMBER 1961

At the invitation of President John F. Kennedy, Pablo CASALS takes part in a concert of chamber music in the White House, given in honor of Governor Luis Muñoz of Puerto Rico, the adoptive residence of Casals, his first appearance in the White House since he played for President Theodore Roosevelt in 1904.

14 NOVEMBER 1961

Concerto accelerato for violin and orchestra by the Serbian composer Dragutin GOSTUSKI in which the tempo is accelerated from *Largo* to *Allegretto* to *Presto* through its three atonally oriented movements, is performed for the first time in Belgrade.

20 NOVEMBER 1961

Gráficos for guitar and chamber orchestra by the 47-year-old Gibraltar-born Spanish composer Maurice OHANA, in three movements, based on melorhythms of the Andalusian *Cante hondo*, is performed for the first time in London.

25 NOVEMBER 1961

Vittorio GIANNINI conducts the Chicago Lyric Opera Company in the world première of his opera *The Harvest*, dealing with a somber tale of multilateral lust on an American farm circa 1900, wherein two brothers covet the third brother's young bride, who is ultimately stangled by their blind father when she rejects his groping advances.

2 DECEMBER 1961

Son of Science, cantata for the machine age for boys' voices, chorus, tenor, piano, percussion, and strings by the 31-year-old British composer Philip CANNON, is performed for the first time in Aylesbury.

6 DECEMBER 1961

The Padrone, two-act opera by George Whitefield CHADWICK, in which the figure of the padrone, in the period of Italian and Irish immigration in the late nineteenth century, symbolizes human corruption in the exploitation of poor immigrants, musically based "on the union of Wagner's symphonic recitative and Italian lyricism," with its four principal characters singing in Italian and all others in English, is produced in an abridged concert version in Carnegic Hall.

20 DECEMBER 1961

The Golden Bird, operatic fairy tale by the Bulgarian composer Marin GOLEMINOV, is produced in Sofia.

21 DECEMBER 1961

Covek je vidik bez kraja (A Man Is a Horizon Without End), cantata by the Yugoslav composer Rudolf BRUČI, to texts from letters written by doomed inmates of Nazi concentration camps, set to music in anguished chromatic convolutions, culminating in a heroic finale in optimistic major keys, proclaiming the ultimate faith in freedom, is performed for the first time in Belgrade.

25 DECEMBER 1961

Not Love Alone, opera in three acts by the 29-year-old Soviet composer Rodion SHCHEDRIN, is performed for the first time at the Bolshoi Theater in Moscow.

1962

9 JANUARY 1962

Seventh Symphony, subtitled *Les Contrastes*, by the French composer Jean RIVIER, written in a cultivated style of Gallic romanticism, is performed for the first time in Paris.

9 JANUARY 1962

Symphony for Strings by André JOLIVET, in three movements, *Farouche, Flottant*, and *Trépidant*, is performed for the first time in Paris.

10 JANUARY 1962

Orchestral Abstractions, symphonic suite by the 33-year-old American composer William SYDEMAN, in three movements written in a dramatically atonal idiom, is performed for the first time in New York.

11 JANUARY 1962

Princesse Pauline, opera-masque by the French composer Henri TOMASI, dealing with the amours of Napoleon's sister, is performed for the first time in concert form in Paris. (The first stage performance took place at the Opéra-Comique in Paris, on 21 June 1962.)

14 JANUARY 1962

Fifth Symphony by the Swedish composer Gunnar BUCHT is performed for the first time in Stockholm.

17 JANUARY 1962

Eighth Symphony by Roy HARRIS, commissioned by the San Francisco Symphony Orchestra on the occasion of its 50th anniversary, purporting to represent in stately modalities the five principal stages of the life of St. Francis, patron saint of San Francisco—Childhood and Youth, Renunciation of Mundane Joys, The Building of the Chapel with His Own Hands, Pantheistic Joy, Ecstasy after Premonition of Death—and concluding on a pandiatonically amplified C-major chord, is performed for the first time by the San Francisco Symphony Orchestra, Enrique Jordá conducting.

19 JANUARY 1962

Violin Concerto by the 76-year-old Austrian composer and music scholar Egon WELLESZ set in four classically designed movements, written in a post-romantic atonal idiom, is performed for the first time in Vienna.

20 JANUARY 1962

Fourth Symphony by Dmitri SHOSTAKOVICH, in three movements, *Allegretto poco moderato, Moderato con moto* and *Largo*, his most uncompromisingly dissonant work containing some remarkable canonic writing, which he composed in 1936 but withdrew after an unfavorable impression it produced on Soviet musicians during tentative rehearsals in Leningrad, is performed in public for the first time after an interval of 25 years in Moscow.

25 JANUARY 1962

Bold Island, symphonic suite by Howard HANSON, inspired by Bold Island off the coast of Maine, where Hanson spends his summers, is performed for the first time by the Cleveland Symphony Orchestra.

26 JANUARY 1962

Seventh Symphony by the 36-year-old American composer David DIAMOND, in three movements—(1) *Andante*, serving as a prelude to *Allegro ma non troppo*; (2) *Andante*; (3) *Allegro moderato*, accelerating through a succession of prodding indications of *Più mosso*, and reaching double quick time at the end—written in a tense dynamic idiom marked by anxious chromatic torques within a broadly diatonic framework, but invariably observing a classically designed cyclic thematic structure, is performed for the first time by the Philadelphia Orchestra, Eugene Ormandy conducting. (Diamond's *Eighth Symphony* was performed earlier, on 26 October 1961, by the New York Philharmonic.)

29 JANUARY 1962

Fritz KREISLER, one of the greatest violinists of the 20th century and composer of perennial favorites (*Liebesleid, Liebesfreud, Caprice Viennois*), as well as a number of original pieces which he ascribed to Vivaldi, Couperin, and several lesser classics, dies in New York City of a heart ailment four days before his 87th birthday.

5 FEBRUARY 1962

Jacques IBERT, French composer, consummate master of impressionistic tone painting, whose *Escales*, depicting in lavish instrumental colors the sundrenched ports of call in the Mediterranean basin, became a minor masterpiece of modern music, dies in his native Paris at the age of 71.

5 FEBRUARY 1962

Kragujevac, symphonic poem with chorus by the Serbian composer Dušan KOSTIĆ to the text of the poem *Bloody Fairy Tale* by a contemporary poetess dealing with the shooting by the Nazis of Serbian schoolboys in Kragujevac in occupied Yugoslavia in September 1941, with the application of modified dodecaphonic motives to express horror and anxiety, is performed for the first time in Belgrade.

14 FEBRUARY 1962

Chôro for violoncello and orchestra by Camargo GUARNIERI, written in the typical manner of Brazilian folksong rhapsody, with some astringent but always tonal harmonies, is performed for the first time in New York.

15 FEBRUARY 1962

Rehearsal Call, opera buffa in three acts by Vittorio GIANNINI, retailing the vicissitudes of three boys and three girls trying to find menial operatic jobs, such as ushers, in New York, with bits from Wagner and atonal arias illustrating their aspirations, is performed for the first time at the Juilliard School of Music in New York.

16 FEBRUARY 1962

Twelfth Symphony by Darius MILHAUD, subtitled *Rural*, is performed for the first time by the San Francisco Orchestra, Enrique Jordá conducting, on the Davis campus of the University of California, by which it was commissioned.

17 FEBRUARY 1962

A Song of Orpheus, written in a modernistically atonal manner, suggesting that Orpheus charmed men, animals and plants by the power of expressionistic angst, by William Schuman is first performed in Indianapolis, with Leonard Rose as soloist, Izler Solomon, conductor; the work was commissioned by the Ford Foundation.

17 FEBRUARY 1962

Bruno WALTER, German conductor who excelled in exemplary interpretations of the classics, devoted champion of the music of Mahler, dies at the age of 85 in Beverly Hills, California, where he settled after being forced to leave the darkness of Nazified Europe.

19 FEBRUARY 1962

Un amour électronique, opéra-bouffe by the 56-year-old Hungarian-born French composer Joseph KOSMA, in which a lady is enamored of a homuncular electronic robot who collapses when her husband asks him to square the circle, is produced in Paris.

22 FEBRUARY 1962

A month and six days after his 90th birthday, Henri BÜSSER, prolific French composer who remained faithful to the melodious and harmonious legacy of his teacher Gounod through all the vicissitudes of the ultramodern era in music, conducts the first performance of his *Concerto* for trumpet and string orchestra specially written for a nonagenarian concert in his honor at the Paris Conservatory.

23 FEBRUARY 1962

A Sermon, A Narrative and *A Prayer*, triptych by Igor STRAVINSKY to texts from St. Paul, The Acts of the Apostles, and a poem by Thomas Dekker, completed on 31 January 1962, scored for contralto, tenor, speaker, chorus and a medium-size orchestra including three gongs, piano and harp, written in a hermetic serial idiom, with a dodecaphonic radix germinating melodic, contrapuntal and harmonic integumenta, is performed for the first time by the Basel Chamber Orchestra, Paul Sacher (who commissioned the work) conducting.

26 FEBRUARY 1962

Eighteenth Symphony by the 86-year-old English composer Havergal BRIAN, in three movements, with two outer movements in marching time flanking a lyric middle movement, organically connected but thematically diversified, composed in 1961, receives its first performance at the opening concert of the St. Pancras Arts Festival in London, by the Polyphonia Symphony Orchestra, Bryan Fairfax conducting.

26 FEBRUARY 1962

Czechoslovakia issues two 10-heller postage stamps to mark the centennial of the birth of Czech composer and conductor Karel KOVAŘOVIC and the centennial of the death of Czech composer František SKROUP.

1 MARCH 1962

The Alcestiad, opera by the American composeress Louise TALMA to a libretto by Thornton Wilder, dealing with the ancient myth of a Greek woman whose devotion to Apollo won her release from Hades, is performed for the first time anywhere in Frankfurt, Germany.

6 MARCH 1962

Pervy Kosmichesky (The First Cosmic Ship), symphonic poem by the 57-year-old Ukrainian composer Gleb TARANOV, commemorating in optimistically triadic harmonies the first orbital flight of the Soviet Sputnik launched in 1957, and using the exact rhythmic formula of the Sputnik beep as a motto, is performed for the first time in Kiev.

9 MARCH 1962

Fantasy and Variations for piano and orchestra by Norman DELLO JOIO, with six variations on a thematic four-note cell, is performed for the first time by the Cincinnati Symphony Orchestra.

11 MARCH 1962

Symphony by 29-year-old Sergei SLONIMSKY, Soviet nephew of Nicolas Slonimsky, in three movements: *Lento, Vivace bruscamente, Largo-Allegro*, written in a melodically tense, rhythmically intense, and contrapuntally tensile idiom, ending with a magisterial triple fugue, is performed for the first time by the Leningrad Philharmonic, Arvid Jansons conducting.

15 MARCH 1962

The Singing Skeleton, one-act opera by the 50-year-old Japanese composer Osamu SHIMIZU, based on a harrowing horror tale of old Japan, is performed for the first time in Osaka.

16 MARCH 1962

Die Glücksfischer (Fishermen for Luck), opera in two acts by the 59-year-old German composer Mark LOTHAR, is produced in Nürnberg.

20 MARCH 1962

Violin Concerto by the Israeli composer Paul BEN-HAIM (who changed his real name Frankenburger to the Hebrew patronymic Ben-Haim which means Son of Life, when he fled to Palestine in 1933 from his native Munich darkened by the Hitlerian cloud) in three movements, *Allegro, Adante affettuoso, Cadenza e Finale,* set in the focal tonality of B major, but without an explicit key siguature, neo-classical in form, but embodying occasional scintillae of Judaic cantillation in the solo violin part, is performed for the first time in Tel Aviv by Zvi Zeitlin, for whom the work was written, accompanied by the Israel Philharmonic.

22 MARCH 1962

The Golem, opera in four acts by Abraham ELLSTEIN, to a libretto derived from the famous Jewish legend of a rabbi who by the magic of alchemy creates a destructive human creature, set to music in a Wagneromantic idiom seasoned with Judaic melismas, is produced by the New York City Opera, as a commission of the Ford Foundation.

23 MARCH 1962

Symphony (1962) by the 47-year-old American composer Irving FINE, in three movements, *Intrada,* suggestive of an ordered choreographic action, *Capriccio,* a hedonistic scherzo, and *Ode,* a dithyrambic fantasia with an epilogue, is performed for the first time by the Boston Symphony Orchestra, Charles Munch conducting.

26 MARCH 1962

A set of four airmail stamps is issued by Fidel Castro's government in Cuba to celebrate the opening of the Cuban international broadcasting service, containing the initial notes of the *Hymn of the 26th of July,* the Cuban national anthem commemorating the first act of Castro's victorious insurgence on 26 July 1953.

31 MARCH 1962

Meditationen über die Totenmaske von Amedeo Modigliani, cantata by the Moscow-born Swiss composer Wladimir VOGEL, aurally limning the visual art and the dramatic career of the Italian modernist painter Modigliani, from his humble beginnings to his death in Paris at the threshold of success and the suicide of his beloved model Jeanne, the musical scheme based on a 12-tone row and developed by a serial distribution of characteristic intervals (large atonal spans symbolizing the Greco-like elongation of Modigliani's portraits), is performed for the first time by the Radio Svizzera Italiana in Lugano.

31 MARCH 1962

Den gefundne Ofelia, electronic opera by the Danish composer Jorgen PLAETNER treating Ophelia and Hamlet in modern psychoanalytic terms, is performed for the first time in Copenhagen.

3 APRIL 1962

Manolis KALOMIRIS, Greek composer of Wagneromantic operas on ancient and modern Greek subjects, teacher of a generation of young Greek composers, dies in Athens at the age of 78.

5 APRIL 1962

The Communist Manifesto, oratorio by the Prague-born composer Erwin SCHULHOFF, written in 1932, to the classical text of Karl Marx, beginning with the celebrated sentence: "A ghost is walking across Europe, the ghost of Communism," set in declarative triadic harmonies, and ending with the appeal "Proletarians of all nations, unite!" in a virile Dorian mode, is performed posthumously in Prague, from a manuscript copy discovered in Russia.

5 APRIL 1962

Il buon soldato Svejk, opera in three acts by the 45-year-old Italian composer Guido TURCHI, to a libretto from the famous novel of Jaroslav Hašek, dealing with a marvelously passive Czech soldier Schweik whose demoralizing indifference exercises a salutary influence on the heterogeneous Austro-Hungarian Army in World War I of which he was a reluctant member, set to music in an aggressively atonal idiom and corrosively discordant harmonies and vitalized by pseudopopular rhythmic patterns, is produced at the Teatro alla Scala in Milan.

6 APRIL 1962

Cyrnos, opera in three acts by the 50-year-old French composer André AMELLER, dealing with the political struggle in 16th-century Corsica (Cyrnos is its Greek name) during which a Corsican soldier of fortune slays his wife who threatens to expose his scheme to deliver Corsica to the French, set to music in a melodramatically explosive style dulcified by a cerulean Mediterranean couleur locale, is produced in Nancy.

6 APRIL 1962

Transfigurations for piano and orchestra, a serial composition based on the principle of permutations, by the Yugoslav composer Milko KELEMEN, is performed for the first time by the Hamburg Radio.

9 APRIL 1962

Consort by John VINCENT, in three movements, scored for piano and strings in a neo-Elizabethan style in copulative antiphony with superimposed harmonic acridities and rhythmic asymmetries, is performed for the first time by the Seattle Symphony Orchestra, Milton Katims conducting.

12 APRIL 1962

Il Tamburo di panno, one-act opera by the Italian composer Orazio FIUME, modeled after the classical Japanese genre of *No,* is produced in Rome.

16 APRIL 1962

In the course of the Fifth International Festival of Music and Drama at Osaka, Japan, three Japanese composers conduct their own works:

Symphonic suite *The Silk Road* by the 38-year-old Ikuma DAN, in four movements, *Prelude, Pastorale, Dance* and *March,* a baroque treatment of old Japanese modes; *Nirvana Symphony* by the 33-year-old Toshiro MAYUZUMI, in six movements for orchestra, chorus with orchestrally imitated campanology, ending with a Zen hymn; and *Dark Mirror*, subtitled *Young Orpheus on a Theme of the Atomic Bomb*, by Yori-Aki MATSU-DAIRA, wherein a Japanese youth disfigured by radiation burns in Hiroshima meets a spiritual prostitute who gives him a magic mirror showing his face as it was before the atomic holocaust and who decides to have plastic surgery performed by a phantom surgeon from the land of the dead which may either cure or kill him.

16 APRIL 1962

Polymorphie by the 28-year-old Polish modernist Krzysztof PENDERECKI, scored for 48 string instruments in pluralistic counterpoint, in copulative synchronization and maximal harmonic combinatoriality, making use of diatonic, pandiatonic, pentatonic, chromatic and icositetraphonic progressions, is performed for the first time in Hamburg.

22 APRIL 1962

Majstori su prvi ljudi (Masters Are First Among Men), a musical comedy by the Serbian composer Dušan KOS-TIĆ, dealing with a modern Figaro manipulating the love affairs of his employers, is produced in Belgrade.

10 MAY 1962

In seinem Garten liebt Don Perlimplin Belison, comic opera by the 54-year-old German composer Wolfgang FORTNER, his third on the subject drawn from García Lorca's *Bodas de Sangre* (the first two were *Der Wald* and *Die Bluthochzeit*) wherein the minifutuent husband of an unusually mobile donna performs a self-induced schizophrenia, so that half the time he is a magnificently potent youth, his real self ultimately killing his fantasy ego in a semi-homicidal demisuicide, set to music in an appropriately divisive serial idiom, is performed for the first time at the opening of the Music Festival at Schwetzingen, Germany.

10 MAY 1962

Legend of Comrade Tito, cantata by the Yugoslav composer BORIS PAPANDOPULO, tracing in heroic verse and music the patriotic struggle against the Nazis of Yugoslav partisans under the command of President Tito of Yugoslavia, is performed for the first time in Zagreb.

15 MAY 1962

Sonority Canon for Four Solo Flutes Accompanied by 33 Flutes on Tape by Otto LUENING, the flutiest piece since Pan blew his syrinx, is performed for the first time at a concert of contemporary flute music at Columbia University in New York.

15 MAY 1962

Chorikon, symphonic tetraptych by the 38-year-old Greek composer Arghyris KOUNADIS, in four serially organized movements, artfully incorporating the modalities of popular Greek songs, is performed for the first time by the Berlin Philharmonic, with the composer's teacher, Wolfgang Fortner, conducting.

15 MAY 1962

Vision of Poets, a cantata for soloists, chorus and orchestra by the 38-year-old Manchurian-born American composer Benjamin LEES, in ten sections to words by Walt Whitman, is performed for the first time as a commissioned work at the dedication concert of the World's Fair Festival in Seattle, by the Seattle Symphony Orchestra, under the direction of Milton Katims.

17 MAY 1962

Concert for Eight, an octet for flute, clarinet, guitar, mandolin, double-bass, accordion, piano, and percussion, by the foremost Spanish avant-gardist making his home in London, Roberto GERHARD, is performed for the first time in London.

18 MAY 1962

Vzkriesenie (Resurrection), opera in three acts by the 50-year-old Slovak composer Jan CIKKER, after Tolstoy's moralistic novel centered on the sufferings of a debauched orphan girl in 1886, set to music in an expressionistically atonal idiom to reflect the psychic contradictions of her reformed seducer, is produced in Prague.

19 MAY 1962

Concerto for Violoncello and Orchestra in C major by Joseph HAYDN, in three cyclic movements, *Moderato, Adagio, Allegro di Molto*, long regarded as lost, is performed for the first time during the Spring Festival in Prague, from an 18th-century copy of the original, discovered in the archives of the National Museum of Prague.

21 MAY 1962

Momente, for soprano, singing, speaking and screaming choruses, instruments and percussion by the guru of the international avant-garde Karlheinz STOCKHAUSEN, is performed for the first time in Cologne.

24 MAY 1962

Srbija, cantata by the 45-year-old Serbian composer Rudolf BRUČI, patriotically extolling the valor of Serbia, set to music in a proclamatory triadic idiom, with occasional dodecaphonic arabesques in wordless solos and choral vocalises, is performed for the first time in Belgrade.

25 MAY 1962

The Coventry Cathedral Festival opens in the newly constructed church replacing the old historic shrine destroyed by the Nazi air attack of 1941, with the first performance of *The Beatitudes*, religious cantata by Sir Arthur BLISS to texts drawn from the Bible and from the writings of John Donne and other English poets.

25 MAY 1962

The first International Anton von Webern Festival opens at the University of Washington in Seattle with the first performance from the manuscript, recently discovered by Hans Moldenhauer, of the symphonic poem by Anton von WEBERN *Im Sommerwind*, written by him in 1904 at the age of 19.

29 MAY 1962

King Priam, opera in three acts by the 57-year-old English composer Michael TIPPETT, to his own libretto relating in colloquial prose the vicissitudes of the Trojan ruler whose son Paris abducted Helen, precipitating the Homeric wars, set to music in a frugal monodic idiom accompanied by a skeletonized instrumental group and percussion supporting the tonal spinal vertebrae while the guts of string instruments are often conspicuously absent, is performed for the first time in Coventry, England.

30 MAY 1962

At the consecration of the functionally modernized Cathedral of Coventry replacing the old Gothic edifice destroyed by the Germans from the air during World War II, Benjamin BRITTEN conducts the first performance of his *War Requiem* to the texts of the Latin *Missa pro defunctis* and nine poems by the young British poet Wilfred Owen killed a week before the Armistice of 1918, a musical setting anchored in the medieval diabolus in musica, the tritone, symbolizing the horror and the pity of war (Benjamin Britten himself was a conscientious objector during World War II), but remaining firmly within the framework of modulatory tonality.

30 MAY 1962

Journey into Jazz for narrator, jazz quartet and orchestra by the multi-faceted 36-year-old American composer and jazzologist Gunther SCHULLER is performed for the first time in Washington, D.C.

31 MAY 1962

The 36th Festival of the International Society for Contemporary Music opens in London with the following program:

World première of *Espejismos* (from *espejo*, mirror) by the nearly 38-year-old Argentine composer Carlos VEERHOFF, based on a dodecaphonic motto of two mutually exclusive whole-tone scales, one ascending, the other descending; STRAVINSKY's cantata *A Sermon, A Narrative* and *A Prayer* (first performed in Basel on 23 February 1962), to the texts from St. Paul's letter to the Romans (VIII, 24–25), his Letter to the Hebrews (XI, 1; XII, 29), Acts of the Apostles, VI–VII, and a prayer written by the playwright Thomas Dekker, culminating in a choral Alleluia, the thematic material being serially constructed with a dodecaphonic motto related to rhythmic values; *Antifone* for orchestra by Hans Werner HENZE, the antiphonal elements including not only thematic responses but the contrasts of tempi, dynamic tensions, articulation, and timbre, and even the seating arrangement, while the dodecaphonic series results from cumulation rather than exposition of melodic and harmonic elements; *Cujus Legibus Rotantur Poli* by the 37-year-old Swiss composer Klaus HUBER, to the Latin text from Aurelius Augustinus, wherein the central idea of the divine laws governing the terrestrial rotation around the polar axis is represented by spiral intervallic structures; and Arnold SCHOENBERG's *Variations for Orchestra*, op. 31.

2 JUNE 1962

To mark the centennial year of the birth of Gustave CHARPENTIER, whose *Louise* was a landmark of French operatic realism, the French Post Office issues a commemorative stamp of 30 centimes with an overprint of an additional 10 centimes.

2 JUNE 1962

In the course of the 36th Festival of the International Society for Contemporary Music in London, a concert of British music is given comprising the following works:

Partita for string quartet by John EXTON, 19-year-old disciple of Luigi Dallapiccola, written in 1957 in a free dodecaphonic idiom and consisting of seven movements in variation form; *The Queen's Epicedium* by PURCELL, written for the funeral of Queen Anne in 1694, multilaterally "realized" by Benjamin Britten; *The Deluge*, cantata for soprano, contralto and chamber ensemble by the Berlin-born 29-year-old naturalized English composer Alexander GOEHR to texts from the notes of Leonardo da Vinci dealing with the Flood; *Boyhood's End*, cantata with alternating sections of recitative and arioso, by Michael TIPPETT, composed in 1943 to texts from W. H. Hudson's autobiography reminiscing about adolescing in Argentina; *String Quartet* by Peter Maxwell DAVIES, 27-year-old member of the avant-garde, composed in 1961 according to a *sui generis* serial method, in one movement comprising four demarcatable sections; *Canticle No. 3* by Benjamin BRITTEN for voice and piano with interludes for French horn with piano, composed in 1954 to Edith Sitwell's *Canticle of the Rose* subtitled *The Raids, 1940, Night and Dawn*, wherein the inexorability of war, the ineluctability of night, and the indeterminacy of dawn are conjured up by spasmodic contractions of thematic intervals in variation forms.

3 JUNE 1962

Blackwood & Co., burlesque opera by the Swiss composer Armin SCHIBLER, in which a bed manufacturing company of New York City awards a free bed deluxe to a young honeymoon couple as part of a publicity campaign ("We stand behind every bed we sell"), with other companies advertising Sweetsex and Pepsi-Cola in neon signs next to Merry's Hotel, is produced in Zürich.

3 JUNE 1962

The following program for chamber orchestra is presented in London in the course of the 36th Festival of the International Society for Contemporary Music:

Lyric Variations by Reuben RADICA, 31-year-old Yugoslav composer, for string orchestra, in which the thematic notes and rhythmic values are subjected to integral organization; *Two Epigrams* for chorus a cappella by the 32-year-old Sicilian-born composer Girolamo ARRIGO, composed in 1957, to texts relating to Michelangelo's statue La Notte; *Suoni estremi* for speaker and string quartet by the 47-year-old Swiss composer Philipp EICHENWALD, to a text from the report of a landslide by an illiterate Sicilian woman illustrating the human reaction to catastrophic extremities (hence the title, Extreme Sounds); *Propos d'Alain*, for baritone and 12 instruments by Goffredo PETRASSI to words from the writings of the 12th-century French theologian Alain, the musical setting derived from postulated micro-structures as non-integral serial parts; and Darius MILHAUD's pioneer jazz ballet *La Création du Monde* of 1922 for 18 instruments. (*Constellation III* for organ and magnetic tape by the Swedish composer Bengt HAMBRAEUS listed in the printed program book of the Festival was not performed due to technical difficulties.)

4 JUNE 1962

In the course of the 36th Festival of the International Society for Contemporary Music in London the following program of orchestral music is presented:

Helian di Trakl, by the 39-year-old Italian composer Camillo TOGNI, a cycle of five songs for voice and chamber orchestra to poems of the German poet Georg Trakl, first performed in a version with piano in Darmstadt on 1 June 1955, and derived from a fundamental dodecaphonic series; *Mobiles* for violin and orchestra by the 37-year-old French composer Maurice JARRE, first performed at the Strasbourg Music Festival in 1961, consisting of six elements which the soloist is free to play in any order of ten prescribed permutations while the accompaniment remains an invariant, analogously with structural mobile arrangements of Alexander Calder; *Erotics*, a set of six songs for soprano and orchestra by the 33-year-old Polish composer Tadeusz BAIRD, first performed at the Warsaw Autumn Music Festival on 16 September 1961; *Double Concerto* for harpsichord, piano and two chamber orchestras by Elliott CARTER, written in 1961, according to an enormously complex and relentlessly logical scheme in which each of the two antiphonal instrumental groups is multilaterally organized in respect to intervals, rhythms, and tempi, without reference to a basic tone row or a common theme, in seven interconnected movements (first performed in New York on 6 September 1961); and Benjamin BRITTEN's *Violin Concerto*, composed in America in 1939.

6 JUNE 1962

The 36th Festival of the International Society for Contemporary Music in London concludes with a chamber music concert comprising the following works:

Moving Pulses for three voices and percussion by the 35-year-old Formosan composer Kejiro ESAKI, with three vocalists moving freely, on stage, under the stage and among the audience, written in the intonations of *No* in no known or unknown language; *Constructions* for two pianos by the 27-year-old Dutch composer Jan van VLIJMEN, totally serialized in pitch, meter and rhythm; *Haggadah* (*Legend*) for viola, percussion and piano by the Budapest-born Israeli composer Ödön PARTOS, in five short movements of oriental thematic provenance systematized in a dodecaphonic series; *Trio* for violin, cello and piano in three movements by Leopold SPINNER, 56-year-old Galician Pole resident in England since 1938; *Formantes* for two pianos by the Spanish composer Cristóbal HALFFTER, nephew of Rodolfo and Ernesto Halffter, in eight sections, of which the inner six are played in any order, in any form, and in any tempo, while the pitch, durations of notes and dynamics are fixed; and *Trio* for flute, guitar and percussion by the 36-year-old Polish composer Wlodzimierz KOTOŃSKI.

8 JUNE 1962

Alea for 8 loudspeakers, 8 tape recordings and 8 composers, compiled at random by the Danish composer Jorgen PLAETNER, is performed for the first time in Copenhagen.

8 JUNE 1962

The Outcasts of Poker Flat, one-act opera by the German-born American composer Samuel ADLER, after a story, by Bret Harte, is performed for the first time in Denton, Texas.

10 JUNE 1962

Cabeza de Vaca, cantata by George ANTHEIL, his last major work, completed in 1957, to the text by Allan Dowling, drawn largely from the reports of the Spanish explorer Alvar Nuñez Cabeza de Vaca to King Charles V

beginning with 17 June 1527 after his shipwreck in the Gulf of Mexico, his spiritual and medicinal help to Indians, adjudged by a papal encyclical to possess redeemable souls, set to music in a triadic harmony intensified at tense moments into tertian pyramids and dramatized by dissonant pandiatonicism, with topical and historical references made in sing-song see-sawing from the tonic to the dominant, pentatonic Indian chants, and ecclesiastical hymns (*Dies irae* is plainly alluded to), is presented in a posthumous world première in observance of Whitsuntide on the television network of the Columbia Broadcasting Company.

12 JUNE 1962

John IRELAND, English composer of instrumental and vocal pieces rooted in austere Celtic modalities accoutred in impressionistically colored harmonies, dies in Washington, England, at the age of 82.

13 JUNE 1962

Eugene GOOSSENS, English composer and conductor, whose expertly fashioned operas and symphonies set a mark of impressionistic modernism in England in the first third of the 20th century, for many years conductor of the Cincinnati Symphony Orchestra and later of the Sydney, Australia, Symphony Orchestra, dies in London at the age of 69.

14 JUNE 1962

Samsara, symphonic poem by Toshiro MAYUZUMI, is performed for the first time in Tokyo.

14 JUNE 1962

Noah and the Flood, biblical spectacle by Igor STRAVINSKY, narrated, mimed, sung, and danced, with literary material taken from the Book of Genesis and a collection of medieval miracle plays of Chester, England, is performed for the first time three days before Stravinksy's 80th birthday at a special television production by the Columbia Broadcasting Company, with Stravinsky himself presented visually as the conductor of the previously recorded and videotaped performance and a highly stylized choreography by George Balanchine, Stravinsky's associate in numerous ballets for many years, wherein Noah and his human companions in the Ark are introduced wearing neo-troglodytic two-dimensional expressionless masks and the paired animals are portrayed by artfully artless toys, the basically dodecaphonic musical score exhibiting utmost economy of design and maximalized individuality of instrumental parts, while hymnal choral numbers to Latin texts are set in heterophonically harmonious and diatonically melodious modalities.

Of hundreds of reviews of my New York work *Noah and the Flood*, most of them, like my every opus since 1905, were gratifyingly unfavorable, I found only yours entirely stupid and suppurating with gratuitous malice. The only blight on my 80th birthday is the realization that my age will probably keep me from celebrating the funeral of your senile music columnist. (A cable dispatched by Igor Stravinsky from Hamburg, Germany, and published in the New York *Herald Tribune* of 24 June 1962)

Stravinsky is a man trapped in his own narrowness and intolerance, so blinded by the praise of sycophants who want to vindicate his joining the twelve-tone camp that he leaps to an instantaneous attack upon everyone who dares to express an independent opinion about his work. . . . As to Noah . . . it was nothing but a slight pièce d'occasion of 20-minute duration embedded in a television medley both silly and artificial, and interrupted by repellant commercials. (Response to Stravinsky's cable by the music critic of the New York *Herald Tribune*, Paul Henry Lang, in the same issue)

17 JUNE 1962

On the occasion of Stravinsky's 80th birthday, Ernst KRENEK presents to him a musical offering, inscribed *Carissimo amico sapientissimo magistro*, a two-part vocal canon in Latin, containing 80 words, both words and music ending on C.

18 JUNE 1962

Atlántida, unfinished "scenic cantata" by Manuel DE FALLA (begun on 29 December 1928 and interrupted on 8 July 1946, four months and a week before his death), to the text from the Catalan poem by Mosé Jacinto Verdaguer describing the salvation of Spain by Hercules who tore it asunder from the continent of Africa to let the flood that submerged the island of Atlantis pass through the Pillars of Hercules into the Mediterranean, and culminating with the voyage of Columbus across the Ocean Sea, combining in the score the elements of a medieval miracle play, a mimodrama for the parts of Hercules and Columbus, and Spanish folklore (Queen Isabella dreams her prophetic dream of the New World to the strains of two folksongs, one Catalan, one from Granada), is performed for the first time, in a version completed by Falla's pupil Ernesto Halffter, at La Scala, Milan, Thomas Schippers conducting.

24 JUNE 1962

A fountain in honor of Richard STRAUSS is erected in Munich on the site of the house in which he was born and which was destroyed during air raids of 1943, with scenes from his opera *Salomé* sculptured on the central column.

25 JUNE 1962

Cuba's Daughter, opera by the 61-year-old Soviet composer Konstantin LISTOV, depicting in realistically romantic terms the heroic life of Angela Alonso, Cuban girl guerrilla, who fought in the ranks of Fidel Castro's insurrectionary forces in 1958, and who gave poison to her beloved to save him from torture after he was captured by the police, is performed for the first time in Voronezh.

A statuesque figure, black locks of hair falling on her shoulders; a handsome, courageous, and at the same time coquettish face; her hands naturally and decisively grasping an automatic rifle. . . . (From a description of Angela Alonso's appearance on a Soviet poster, 1961)

It is a great honor for me, a simple soldier of my country, that my life should be the subject of an opera. With the death of my beloved, all dreams of personal happiness were ended for me, but this news from Moscow made me happy once more. I am convinced that the opera will be a tremendous success because I am aware of the enormous talents of the Soviet people and of their sincere love for Cuba. (From Angela

Alonso's letter addressed to the Moscow correspondent of the Havana daily newspaper *Revolución*)

26 JUNE 1962

Psalmy Dawida (*Psalmus*), cantata by the 28-year-old Polish composer Krzysztof PENDERECKI, to texts from the Psalms of David, based on a neo-Gregorian cantus firmus diversifed by atonal protuberances and employing the dramatic effects of shouting and whispering in highly dissonant counterpoint, is performed for the first time in Cracow.

27 JUNE 1962

Ausgerechnet und verspielt, "Spiel-Oper" for television by Ernst KRENEK, to his own libretto in which a mathematician loses a lot of hard-earned-money using his highly scientific theory of probability at the roulette table, but breaks the bank by playing a series of consecutive numbers taken from the intervals in semitone units in a tone-row selected at random by a humanoid computer, is performed for the first time on television in Vienna.

28 JUNE 1962

Two Peruvian Preludes for orchestra by the 45-year-old American musician and scholar of formidable capacities in ubiquitous fields Robert STEVENSON, is performed for the first time in Philadelphia, Leopold Stokowski conducting. (A revised version, titled *Tres Preludios peruanos,* was premièred in Mexico City on 20 July 1963, Luis Herrera de la Fuente conducting.)

5 JULY 1962

Five Movements, suite for orchestra by the 39-year-old American composer Leslie BASSETT, derived from the concept of "pyramid sounds" in which the symmetrical portions in relation to the apex in each movement are thematically and dynamically related, is performed for the first time in Rome.

9 JULY 1962

Heterophonie, a compound of five successive and/or simultaneous heterophonic symphonic variations on a theme by the Argentinian-born German composer Mauricio KAGEL, optionally played or unplayed, with the tuning given by the oboe mischievously playing A-sharp instead of customary A, is performed for the first time in its third version at the International Summer Festival in Darmstadt. (The world première of the combined Versions I/II was given over the Cologne Radio on 22 May 1962.)

12 JULY 1962

A 20-pfennig postage stamp honoring Michael PRAETORIUS, German music theorist who died on his 50th birthday on 15 February 1621, with the reproduction of a tuning fork superimposed over three bars of a three-voice motet from his *Musae Sionae* (1614), is issued by West Germany.

21 JULY 1962

Robert STOLZ, 81-year-old Austrian composer, conducts at the open-air amphitheater in Bregenz, on Lake Constance, the world première of his 43rd operetta, *Trauminsel*, dealing with a Canadian archeologist infatuated with an Aztec belle, with the score incorporating the explosive sounds of actual fireworks.

23 JULY 1962

During the first intercontinental transatlantic telecast relayed by the American artificial satellite Telstar, the 312-Voice Mormon Tabernacle Choir transmits its performance of *The Battle Hymn of the Republic* from the foot of Mount Rushmore on which the heads of Washington, Jefferson, Lincoln and Theodore Roosevelt are imposingly hewn from the rock, at noon of local sidereal time (7:00 P.M. Greenwich time) during Telstar's 123rd orbit, and Ferruccio Tagliavini presents an aria from *Tosca* in the open theater of the Baths of Caracalla in Rome at 11:00, local sidereal time (6:00 P.M. Eastern daylight saving time) during Telstar's 124th orbit.

24 JULY 1962

The Wagner Festival in Bayreuth opens with a novel production, by Wagner's grandson Wieland WAGNER, of *Tristan und Isolde* wherein King Mark becomes Tristan's father, thus intensifying the incestuous element and introducing an Oedipus complex (justified by the archeological discovery of an inscription on the gravestone of a putative counterpart of Tristan as the son of a putative counterpart of King Mark), and Isolde languishes in her *Liebestod* but does not die, with an abstract stage set dominated by an enormous shaft as a phallic symbol.

6 AUGUST 1962

On the 17th anniversary of the atomization of Hiroshima, a grand cantata by the Japanese composer Masao OKI to a poem by Sankichi Toge in six movements: *August 6th* (with the atom bomb exploding on a dominant seventh-chord in triple forte), *At the First-Aid Stations, See My Eyes, For an Infant Soul, We Call to You, Take Back the Human* (ending on a C-major chord in triple forte), is performed for the first time in Tokyo.

Everybodies in the world should keep the verses from the bottom of Toge's heart in memory. This is, I believe, the straight-forward approach to make a restate for the continued existence and the well-being of the mankind, to take back the humanity being lost in our days. And this passage can be cut open only by the well-intentioned combination of the people, the honest and frank, innocent of flattering to power and wealth. This grand cantata is a today's art to be made out only by the Japanese. Through the creation and propagation of this work we, the today's Japanese, I believe, can fulfill one of our grave responsibilities for the peace of the mankind. And it is the desire of the Japanese heart in our time of the terror of atomic weapons. (From the introductory note in English in the printed score)

9 AUGUST 1962

Phonologie Symphonique by the Japanese composer Toshiro MAYUZUMI is performed for the first time in West Berlin.

12 AUGUST 1962

Constantin Palaeologus, last opera by the Greek composer Manolis KALOMIRIS, dealing with the Emperor of Byzantium whose defeat by the Turks in 1453 marked the end of the Eastern Empire, is produced in Athens, three months after the composer's death.

12 AUGUST 1962

Don Perlimplín, radio opera by the 42-year-old Italian conductor and composer Bruno MADERNA, after a text by Federico García Lorca, is broadcast for the first time over RAI Radio in Rome.

14 AUGUST 1962

The first vocal duet in outer space is heard around the world when Major Andrian Nikolayev and Lieutenant Colonel Pavel Popovich, the "heavenly twins" of the Soviet Cosmos orbiting the earth in tandem in their spaceships Vostok 3 and Vostok 4, establish radio contact and sing the *Astronaut Song* by the Soviet composer Oscar FELTSMAN: "I know, my friends that caravans of rockets/Will hurl us forward from star to star/And that on the dusty pathways of distant planets/Our footprints will leave their mark!"

Comrades Nikolayev and Popovich had more fun than their predecessors Gagarin and Titov. Not only did they maintain communication with Earth, but they could talk to each other and watch each other at work. And as you know, they even gave a sort of improvised concert for the Cosmos and sang a duet with a refrain which suits the occasion perfectly and corresponds to our future plans in the Cosmos. (From a speech by the Soviet Premier Minister Nikita Khrushchev in Moscow, delivered on 18 August 1962)

15 AUGUST 1962

The Second Israel Music Festival opens in Jerusalem with a grand spectacle called Folklore of a Nation, presenting the folkloric patterns of various communities of Israel in song and dance, with the participation of immigrants from Yemen, Kurdistan, North Africa, Arabia and India, culminating in an exhibition by the native-born Israelis, the Sabras.

19 AUGUST 1962

The Edinburgh Festival of Music and Drama opens with programs of varied fare and performers from all over Europe, featuring a grand presentation of works by Dmitri SHOSTAKOVICH, with the composer in attendance, including his ten symphonies, eight string quartets, cello concerto, violin concerto, cello sonata, piano quintet, songs and his orchestration of MUSSORGSKY's opera *Khovanshchina*, performed by the Belgrade Opera Company.

22 AUGUST 1962

The Edinburgh Festival of Music and Drama presents the world première of *Three Songs of Life and Love* by the Italian avant-garde composer Luigi NONO:

(1) *Sul Ponte di Hiroshima* for orchestra, picturing in angry dissonances the atomic annihilation of a man with a guitar standing on a bridge in Hiroshima on 6 August 1945 when the bomb fell; (2) an anguished solo for unaccompanied soprano vaulting atonal intervals in the narrative of an Algerian girl tortured by the French colons to secure information; (3) a protest against war, set in discordantly pacifistic heterophony.

23 AUGUST 1962

Irving FINE, American composer of fine instrumental music exquisitely equilibrated in a modernistic manner with occasional dodecaphonic explorations, dies in Boston of a massive heart attack at the age of 47.

31 AUGUST 1962

On the day of the Independence of Trinidad and Tobago, the government of the new nation within the British Commonwealth adopts as their national anthem a song by the Trinidad musician Patrick CASTAGNE, the winner in a competition among 1,150 entries, to his own words declaring the love of their "Islands of the blue Caribbean Sea" where "every race finds an equal place."

2 SEPTEMBER 1962

Igor STRAVINSKY conducts, sharing the podium with his constant assistant Robert Craft, in the course of the Second Israel Music Festival in Haifa, a concert of his orchestral music including the *Symphony in Three Movements* of 1945, the *Violin Concerto* of 1931, the *Ode* of 1943, and a symphonic suite from *The Firebird*, in the third revision made in 1945. (He conducted the same program in Jerusalem on 4 September 1962 and in Tel Aviv on 6 September 1962.)

6 SEPTEMBER 1962

Hanns EISLER, German composer of introspective atonal and dodecaphonic music according to the doctrine of his master Arnold Schoenberg and of optimistically triadic socialistic marches for the Soviet Army and proletarian choruses for East Germany, dies in East Berlin at the age of 64.

11 SEPTEMBER 1962

John LENNON, Paul MCCARTNEY, George HARRISON and Richard STARKEY ("Ringo Starr"), four young, brash and pert Liverpudlians destined to ascend the empyrean heights of fame, fortune and ubiquitous adulation under the inspired sobriquet THE BEATLES phonemically related to the rhythmic beat and the order of coleoptera, make their first recording together in a hallucinogenic rendering of two vocal quartets, *Love Me, Do!* and *P.S. I Love You*.

20 SEPTEMBER 1962

In the course of the Sixth Music Festival in Warsaw ("Warsaw Autumn") comprising a series of concerts of empiric, experimental, atonal, athematic, gymnosophistical, but invariably autocephalous and aggressively vigesimosecular music, three works by modernistic Polish composers are given for the first time:

Musica Ipsa by the 33-year-old composer Boguslaw SCHÄFFER, an instrumental concerto in three parts posing and resolving the problems of progressive variability of thematic material and a novel type of symphonic emotionalism, as opposed to formalized serialism; *Capriccio* for 24 instruments by the 36-year-old Jan KRENZ, subdivided into six groups of players and written in a polythematic succession of phrases and ideas governed by discrete dodecaphonic motives; and *Canon* by the 28-year-old Krzysztof PENDERECKI for orchestra and magnetic tape, scored for 52 string instruments and developed in three layers in canonic imitation among themselves, culminating in a stretto of 208 voices involving the recorded parts, making use of diatonic, pandiatonic, chromatic and icositetraphonic resources. (At other concerts of the Sixth Warsaw Festival the following works by Polish composers were presented: *Riff 62* by Wojciech KILAR, based on a constantly repeated jazzified refrain to characterize the spirit of the modern year 1962; *Variations Without a Theme* by Tadeusz BAIRD, presenting inconstant variants of an asomatous subject; *Concerto for Orchestra* by Grazyna BACEWICZ; and *Aphorisms* by Boleslaw SZABELSKI.)

23 SEPTEMBER 1962

At the inauguration of Lincoln Center for the Performing Arts in New York City, Leonard BERNSTEIN, conductor and music director of the New York Philharmonic, presents in the new Philharmonic Hall a concert televised by the Columbia Broadcasting System in the following program:

Gloria from BEETHOVEN's *Missa Solemnis;* the first performance of the specially commissioned work by Aaron COPLAND, *Connotations for Orchestra*, intended to express "the tension, aspirations, and drama inherent in the world today" set in a *sui generis* dodecaphonic technique, with the basic statement made by four spacious but highly dissonant chords of mutually exclusive groups of three notes, and an agitated rhythmic section in which the notes of the tone row are allowed free repetition; and the first movement of Mahler's *Eighth Symphony*, nicknamed *Symphony of a Thousand*, here performed by about 500 instrumentalists, soloists and choristers, including a children's choir.

24 SEPTEMBER 1962

At the second concert given in the Philharmonic Hall in Lincoln Center for the Performing Arts in New York City, the Boston Symphony Orchestra, under the direction of its newly appointed conductor Erich Leinsdorf of Vienna, presents the world première of *Piano Concerto* by Samuel BARBER, with John Browning as piano soloist, an exuberantly romantic, comprehensively pianistic work set in a centripetally tonal idiom in a peripheral tonal diaspora, with thematic phrases uncoiling in a diachromatic modality cadentially dissolving in triadic formations, in three movements:

(1) *Allegro appassionato*, opening with a somber germinal phrase for piano solo, evolving antiphonally with the orchestra in palpitatingly dramatic exchanges; (2) *Canzona*, a meditative adumbration of the old Italian contrapuntal form, with a prominent flute solo, accompanied by the piano playing guitar-like figurations; (3) *Allegro molto*, in unremitting 5/8 time, in the manner of a virtuoso toccata.

25 SEPTEMBER 1962

At the third concert given in the Philharmonic Hall at Lincoln Center for the Performing Arts in New York City, the first performance of Walter PISTON's *Lincoln Center Festival Overture* is presented by the Philadelphia Orchestra, Eugene Ormandy, conductor, on the same program with Aaron COPLAND's *Lincoln Portrait* with the United States Ambassador to the United Nations, Adlai Stevenson, acting as the narrator reciting Abraham Lincoln's words to the music, the program rounded off by both suites from *Daphnis et Chloé* by RAVEL, and Van Cliburn's playing of RACHMANINOFF's *Third Piano Concerto*.

26 SEPTEMBER 1962

After forty-eight years of absence from his native Russia, Igor STRAVINSKY appears in Moscow in a program of his music, conducting the Moscow State Symphony Orchestra in performances of his symphonic *Ode* of 1944, and his ballet suite *Orpheus* of 1947, with his assistant Robert Craft leading *Le Sacre du Printemps*, and Stravinsky concluding the concert with an encore, his arrangement of 1917 of the *Volga Boatmen's Song*.

28 SEPTEMBER 1962

At the Philharmonic Hall in Lincoln Center for the Performing Arts in New York the Juilliard School Orchestra presents the first performance of a commissioned work: *Toccata for the Sixth Day* by William BERGSMA, dean of the Juilliard School of Music.

30 SEPTEMBER 1962

Leonard Bernstein conducts at Philharmonic Hall in Lincoln Center for the Performing Arts in New York the first Young People's Concert of the season, including the first public performance of *Catacoustical Measures* by Daniel PINKHAM of Boston, originally composed as an acoustical test of the new Philharmonic Hall.

3 OCTOBER 1962

The Master of Boyana, opera in four acts by the 38-year-old Bulgarian composer Konstantin ILIEV, depicting the legendary story of an anonymous painter of 13th-century frescoes in the church at the village of Boyana near Sofia and his artistic victory over iconographic reactionaries who objected to the realistic interpretation of religious subjects and a concomitant consummation of his love for a chosen mate, set to music in an advanced idiom containing traits of Stravinsky's neo-Grecianism, Prokofiev's stylized Slavism and atonally oriented expressionism of Alban Berg, with unabashed Italian cantilena persisting in the vocal parts, is produced in Sofia.

4 OCTOBER 1962

Eighth Symphony by William SCHUMAN, President of Lincoln Center in New York, in three movements, the first and second in a slow tempo, and the finale a rapid rhapsodic rondo, written in a tensile polyharmonic idiom, is performed for the first time as a commissioned work by the New York Philharmonic Orchestra, Leonard Bernstein conducting on the same program with a memorial performance of the *Adagio* from *Notturno for Strings and Harp* by Irving FINE.

9 OCTOBER 1962

Fifth Symphony in C major by the Soviet composer Vissarion SHEBALIN, in the classical four movements, is performed for the first time in Moscow.

11 OCTOBER 1962

The Passion of Jonathan Wade, opera in three acts by Carlisle FLOYD, to his own libretto dealing with a noble-souled Yankee commander who marries a Southern belle in the post-bellum turmoil of 1866, undismayed by a rude raid of the Ku Klux Klan during their wedding, to a musical score bathed in lyrical melodiousness and set in the traditional sequences of arias, duets, and dramatic interludes in the orchestra, with some nice plantation ballads sung by a mamma named Nicey, is produced by the New York City Opera Company.

15 OCTOBER 1962

Leopold STOKOWSKI, 80 years old, but vigorous in his assertive musicianship, presents at Carnegie Hall in New York City the opening concert of his newly organized American Symphony Orchestra.

18 OCTOBER 1962

Concerto for Wind Quintet and Orchestra by the 49-year-old American composer Alvin ETLER, in three movements, in the style of a modern concerto grosso, is performed for the first time anywhere by the Tokyo Philharmonic with the New York Woodwind Quintet as quintuple soloists.

22 OCTOBER 1962

Bonjour Max Ernst, surrealistic cantata by the Danish composer Niels Viggo BENTZON is performed for the first time in Aarhus, Denmark, as a tribute to the modern master of abstract art.

24 OCTOBER 1962

0'00" (zero silence) "to be performed in any way by anyone," composed by John CAGE in Tokyo, as No. 2 after his longer silent work *4'33"*, receives its instantaneous first performance simultaneously with the writing of the first margination of the blank-page manuscript with the following instructions on the title page: "With any interruptions. Fulfilling in whole or part an obligation to others. No two performances to be of the same action, nor may that action be the performance of a 'musical' composition. No attention to be given the situation (electronic, musical, theatrical). In a situation provided with maximum amplification (no feedback), perform a disciplined action." (The title page is followed by three blank pages in the printed copy, retailing at 50 cents.)

25 OCTOBER 1962

Jacques PERROT, Parisian music hall artist known as "Tête de bois," gives an opening performance at the Olympia in Paris of his *Concerto pour une grande tête et orchestre*, for skull solo accompanied by doublebass, piano, xylophone and 20 violins, the cranial melodic range extending to three and a half octaves in dry weather and only one octave in case of rain, the dynamics gauged by tapping fingers for piano effect and a mallet for *mezzo forte*, a maximum of loudness, the finer nuances depending on the locality, the resonance areas including the parietal and occipital bones, maxilla, mandible, zygomatic arch, eye socket and mental process (bony promontory, forming the chin).

25 OCTOBER 1962

Opéra d' Aran by Gilbert BÉCAUD, a Parisian crooner nicknamed "Monsieur 100,000 volts" for his high electric potential with young audiences, to a libretto inspired by Robert Flaherty's film of the same name wherein two lovers on a bleak island outpost in the North Sea are forced to sail away in an unseaworthy boat into the ocean after they are charged with a local murder, with a musical score coagulating operatic ideas from Gounod to Puccini, is produced at the composer's own expense, accompanied by a gushing flood of crimson publicity, at the Théâtre des Champs-Elysées in Paris.

26 OCTOBER 1962

Piano Concerto by Gunther SCHULLER is performed for the first time by the Cincinnati Symphony Orchestra.

27 OCTOBER 1962

L'Opéra de Poussière, opera in two acts by the French composer Marcel LANDOWSKI, dealing with an ironic fate of an opera composer who kills himself when his fiancée leaves after a series of fruitless attempts to have his opera produced, with the attendant publicity arousing sudden interest in his opera which is produced posthumously with sensational success, is performed for the first time in Avignon, under the composer's direction.

2 NOVEMBER 1962

Albena, opera in five tableaux by the Bulgarian composer Parashkev KHADZHIEV, to a libretto from the village life in Dobrudja of the early 20th-century, based on a true story of an aberrant wife who becomes a passive accomplice in the murder of her husband by her lover, is performed for the first time in Varna. (In real life she was stoned by the villagers, but in the opera she is allowed to depart.)

3 NOVEMBER 1962

Concerto-Rhapsody for violin and orchestra by Aram KHACHATURIAN (originally named simply *Rhapsody*) is performed for the first time in Moscow, with Leonid Kogan as soloist.

A concerto is music with chandeliers burning bright; a rhapsody is music with chandeliers dimmed (a description Khachaturian used during his meeting with the author in Moscow on 7 December 1962)

4 NOVEMBER 1962

Second Symphony by the Soviet composer Andrei ESHPAY, conceived in a broadly Russian style with melodic inflections of his own ancestral pentatonicism of the Mongol Mari strain, and developed in an energetically lyrical vein, is performed for the first time in Moscow.

8 NOVEMBER 1962

Humphrey SEARLE conducts in Birmingham, England, the first performance of his *Fourth Symphony* in four movements on a monothematic idea of a dodecaphonic nature.

9 NOVEMBER 1962

Hamlet, Shakespearean opera in three acts by the 53-year-old Russian-born American composer Sergius KAGEN, is performed for the first time in Baltimore.

11 NOVEMBER 1962

The Legend of a Lake, ballet in three acts by the Bulgarian composer Pantcho VLADIGEROV, to a story of a patriotic Bulgarian damsel who opens the dikes to drown the foe attacking the village perishing herself in the flood, is produced at the Sofia National Opera, under the direction of the composer's son.

13 NOVEMBER 1962

Barcarolla fantastica, symphonic picture by the 48-year-old Dutch composer Hans HENKEMANS, written in a coloristically impressionistic manner influenced by the style of his teacher Willem Pijper, divisible into five episodes, all in the steady rhythms of 6/8 and 9/8, suggesting the Venetian gondola song, is performed for the first time by the Northern Philharmonic Orchestra in Groningen, Holland, on the occasion of its centennial.

20 NOVEMBER 1962

First Cello Concerto by André JOLIVET, in three expressive movements, *Méditatif*, *Hiératique* and *Cursif*, is performed for the first time in Paris.

26 NOVEMBER 1962

Synthesis for strings and percussion by the 40-year-old Greek composer Yorgo SICILIANOS, constructed according to a serial concept in which both melodic components and rhythmic units are coordinated in contrapuntal and harmonic complexes, is performed for the first time in Athens.

29 NOVEMBER 1962

Seventh Symphony by Jean RIVIER, in three movements, the inner a *Lento malinconico* the outer two, *Allegros*, economically constructed and centered on a single principal motive, is performed for the first time in Paris.

30 NOVEMBER 1962

Ouverture Philharmonique by Darius MILHAUD is performed for the first time by the New York Philharmonic at its new home in Lincoln Center for the Performing Arts in New York, as a specially commissioned work.

4 DECEMBER 1962

Concerto for two guitars and orchestra by Mario CASTELNUOVO-TEDESCO is performed for the first time in Toronto.

6 DECEMBER 1962

Gunther SCHULLER conducts in New York a concert of music entitled "American Iconoclasts" which includes works by Henry COWELL (*Polyphonica*) Stefan WOLPE, Edgar VARÈSE, John CAGE and Charles IVES, the latter represented by short pieces arranged by Gunther Schuller from undecipherable manuscripts in the Ives collection of the Yale University Library: *Chamber Orchestra Set No. 3* (*At Sea, Luck and Work, Premonitions*) and *Chromatimelodtune* written between 1913 and 1919 and prophetically containing motives of 12 different notes each.

8 DECEMBER 1962

Four centuries have passed since the death in Venice of Adrian WILLAERT, master of the secular madrigal, the instrumental ricercar, and the sacred motet, initiator of antiphonal writing for the two symmetrical choirs at San Marco, Venice, where he was *maestro di cappella* from 12 December 1527, teacher of Andrea Gabrielli Zarlino, and many foreign musicians of renown.

16 DECEMBER 1962

The Departure, opera in three acts by the 55-year-old English composer Elizabeth MACONCHY, is produced in London.

18 DECEMBER 1962

Thirteenth Symphony by Dmitri SHOSTAKOVICH, scored for bass soloist, male voices and orchestra, op. 113, to words by the 29-year-old Soviet poet Evgeny Evtushenko, in five movements—(1) *Adagio*, "*Babi Yar*," (2) *Allegretto*, "*Humor*," (3) *Adagio*, "*Women*," (4) *Largo*, "*Fears*," (5) *Allegretto*, "*Career*,"—of which the first includes an eloquent remembrance of the fate of thousands of Jews put to death by the Nazis at Babi Yar in Kiev in 1941 and a passionate appeal against anti-Semitism, is performed for the first time in Moscow. (Reacting to criticisms from high Communist quarters pointing out that not Jews alone were killed at Babi Yar, Evtushenko added a few words of the martyrdom of Russian and Ukrainian young men and women, along with the Jews.)

20 DECEMBER 1962

Katerina Ismailova, a new version of SHOSTAKOVICH's opera *Lady Macbeth of the District of Mzensk*, minus the naturalistic sexual intermezzo in the orchestra, is produced in Moscow.

30 DECEMBER 1962

Emil SIMON, Bessarabia-born 26-year-old Rumanian composer, conducts in Bucharest the world première of his cantata *Partidului* (*To the Party*) based on a musical anagram HBCA of Bach, and written in a realistically socialistic manner rich in optimistically opulent harmonies as an offering of thanks to the Communist Party "which has given a purpose to our lives and glory to our land."

1963

4 JANUARY 1963

Percussion Concerto by Henry COWELL is performed for the first time by the Pittsburgh Symphony Orchestra.

18 JANUARY 1963

Ninth Symphony by ROY HARRIS, "dedicated to the City of Philadelphia as the Cradle of American Democracy," in three movements bearing subtitles from the Constitution of the United States—(1) *Prelude*, "We the People," (2) *Chorale*, "To form a more perfect Union," (3) *Contrapuntal Structures*, "To promote the general welfare," in three sections, concluding on an optimistic bitonal chord of B major over G major— is performed for the first time by the Philadelphia Orchestra, Eugene Ormandy conducting.

18 JANUARY 1963

Riolama, Ten Places for Piano and Orchestra, by Ernst BACON is performed for the first time in Syracuse.

23 JANUARY 1963

Les Jumeaux, opera in three acts by the Rumanian-born Parisian composer Marcel MIHALOVICI, is performed for the first time in Brunswick, Germany.

24 JANUARY 1963

Fifth Symphony, subtitled *Sinfonia aforistica*, by the Swedish composer Hilding HALLNÄS, is performed for the first time in Göteborg.

25 JANUARY 1963

Mouvement Symphonique, subtitled *Bostoniana*, by Jacques IBERT, which constitutes the first movement of a larger work commissioned by the Boston Symphony Orchestra but left unfinished at Ibert's death, is performed for the first time by the Boston Symphony Orchestra, Charles Munch conducting.

25 JANUARY 1963

Eighth Symphony by the German master of symphonic modernism Karl Amadeus HARTMANN, in two principal parts, *Cantilena*, with a passionate, penetrating theme, derived from a structure of dispersed tritones, and *Dithyrambe*, motoric and frugally fugal, is performed for the first time in Cologne.

30 JANUARY 1963

Francis POULENC, second youngest of the French Six, "Musicien de la doulce France," as he was once poetically described, whose gift evolved from nihilistic beginnings to pure melodic poetry, and who knew how to combine mundane hedonism with religious contemplation, dies suddenly of a heart attack in Paris at the age of 64.

Like his name, he was both dapper and ungainly. His clothes came from Lanvin but were unpressed; his hands were scrubbed but the fingernails were bitten to the bone. . . . His social predilections were for duchesses and policemen. . . . He was deeply devout and uncontrollably sensual. (Ned Rorem in *Poulenc—A Memoir*, in *Tempo*, London, Spring 1963)

2 FEBRUARY 1963

Concerto for Orchestra by the 27-year-old Georgian Soviet composer Giya KANCHELI is performed for the first time in Tbilisi.

5 FEBRUARY 1963

Emancipation Symphony by the 46-year-old American composer Robert KELLY, written to celebrate the centennial of the Proclamation of Emancipation by Abraham Lincoln, written in an abstract 12-tone dodecaphonic idiom to demonstrate the democratic principles of tonal equality, is performed for the first time, in Washington.

6 FEBRUARY 1963

Piano Concerto in three movements by the 35-year-old French composer Jean-Michel DAMASE, written in the manner of Gallic baroque, is performed for the first time in Paris.

7 FEBRUARY 1963

Violin Concerto by the 66-year-old Slovenian composer Matija BRAVNIČAR, making use of the quasi-oriental Istrianic scale, is performed for the first time in Ljubljana.

8 FEBRUARY 1963

Violin Concerto by the 39-year-old American composer Benjamin LEES, born in Manchuria of Russian parents, in three movements of a classical nature, with the contrapuntal and harmonic elements forming a reticle of euphonious dissonance, is performed for the first time by the Boston Symphony Orchestra, Erich Leinsdorf conducting, Henryk Szeryng soloist.

9 FEBRUARY 1963

Requiem by Dmitri KABALEVSKY, commemorating the supreme sacrifice of the Soviet soldiers and citizens fallen victims to the Fascist aggression in eleven sections similar to the subdivisions of the Russian service for the dead, among them *Eternal Glory, I Shall Not Die, Remember,* and concluding with a prayerfully powerful appeal to the world to renounce war intoned by a children's chorus, is performed for the first time in Moscow.

15 FEBRUARY 1963

Spirit of the Avalanche, opera by the American composer Alan HOVHANESS, is performed for the first time anywhere in Tokyo.

16 FEBRUARY 1963

László LAJTHA, Hungarian composer of nine well-regulated symphonies, some of them revealing a deep melorhythmic sense of authentic Magyar music, dies suddenly of a heart attack in Budapest, at the age of 70.

17 FEBRUARY 1963

Violin Concerto by the Czech pioneer of microtonal music Alois HÁBA, composed in 1954 and based on athematic but homeorhythmic motives, exuberantly hendecaphonic and dodecaphonic in its melodic materials and paradoxically classical in form, is performed for the first time in Prague.

18 FEBRUARY 1963

Sinfonia montana, dodecaphonic symphony with programmatic content by the German composer Jürg BAUR, who was born on Armistice Day in 1918, is performed for the first time in Hagen.

22 FEBRUARY 1963

The Delta Chi Fraternity of Wayne State University in Detroit, Michigan, sets the world record for demolishing an upright piano and passing all its *disjecta membra* through a 9-inch hole in 4 minutes 51 seconds. (A group of British firemen in Christchurch, England, smashed 17 pianos on 12 July 1966 in a vain attempt to beat the world record of Wayne University, but their best time was 5 minutes 48 seconds.)

23 FEBRUARY 1963

The Darkened City, opera in three acts by the 52-year-old Americanized German-born composer Bernhard HEIDEN, dealing with the year of the plague, 1319, in East Anglia, during which a lethargic victim Lazarus rises from the mass of presumed cadavers frightening the populace and precipitating ecclesiastical hysteria, set to music in a measurably tonal, rhythmically propulsive manner, verisimilitudinarily illustrated by authentic passages of Gregorian chant, is produced by the Indiana University Opera Theater in Bloomington, Indiana.

28 FEBRUARY 1963

Il Diavolo in giardino, "historical pastoral comedy" in three acts by the 38-year-old Italian composer Franco MANNINO, centered on the famous swindle of a diamond necklace at the court of Marie Antoinette in Versailles, with the inclusion in the score of some popular airs of the time, written in a modernistically polyharmonic idiom, and ending on a dissonantly salinated chord of D major, is produced in Palermo.

3 MARCH 1963

Labyrinth, surrealist opera by Gian Carlo MENOTTI, to his own libretto in which a distraught bridegroom misplaces the key to his hotel room on his wedding night, gets lost in a maze of nightmarish corridors, meanders into a non-adjacent spatial continuum, is suspended weightless in an orbiting spaceship, and is measured for interment by an ultra-dimensional mortician while holding in his hand the crucial hotel room key, set to music with a somewhat atonal lilt, reverting to terrestrial tonality in non-cosmic scenes, is performed for the first time as a commissioned work by the National Broadcasting Company Television Opera Theater.

5 MARCH 1963

Tenebrae for orchestra by the 42-year-old American composer Louis MENNINI is performed for the first time in New Orleans.

8 MARCH 1963

On the 150th anniversary of the first concert of the Royal Philharmonic Society, William WALTON conducts the London Philharmonic in the first performance of his *Variations on a Theme by Hindemith*, derived from 36 bars of the opening section of the second movement of Hindemith's *Cello Concerto*, comprising nine variations and a fugal finale and concluding with the trumpet call from Hindemith's opera *Mathis der Maler*, astutely constructed as an amiable colloquy between the two composers, preserving under Walton's British patina Hindemith's characteristic tonal inflections.

8 MARCH 1963

Nikita KHRUSHCHEV, Premier of the Union of Soviet Socialist Republics, airs his views on music at a meeting of Communist Party leaders and representatives of Soviet literature and arts, in which he states his unalterable opposition to abstractionism, formalism and other petty bourgeois tendencies, and says that dodecaphony to him is plain cacophony, the pun being possible in Russian as well as in any other language. (Full text in Letters and Documents.)

13 MARCH 1963

Alceste, opera by the Dutch composer-engineer Ton de LEEUW, commissioned by the Netherlands Television Foundation, is performed for the first time on the Holland National Television network.

14 MARCH 1963

Frances MCCANN, 41-year-old American operatic soprano, is slain in a hotel room in Rome by her impresario Ernest Boxman who shoots himself too, dying a few days later.

16 MARCH 1963

Il Capitan Spavento, one-act opera by Gian Francesco MALIPIERO, is produced in Naples.

18 MARCH 1963

Concerto for Violin, Piano and Orchestra by the American composer Robert Russell BENNETT, is performed for the first time in Portland, Oregon.

19 MARCH 1963

Stereophony for Orchestra by the Canadian composer Harry SOMERS, based on a 12-tone series subdivided into three groups of four notes each, with orchestral instruments distributed in different places in the concert hall for stereophonic effect, is performed for the first time in Toronto.

21 MARCH 1963

Sixteenth Symphony in five movements by Henry COWELL, subtitled *Icelandic*, making thematic use of the open fifths characteristic of ancient runic chants projected on the tritone bases of the indigenous Lydian mode and integrated in a dodecaphonic series, is performed for the first time in Reykjavik.

27 MARCH 1963

Cello Concerto by the 36-year-old Rumanian composer Anatol VIERU, in one compact movement, written in an individually advanced idiom with the application of thematic tropes adumbrating dodecaphony, is performed for the first time in Geneva, as the prize-winning work for an international competition.

28 MARCH 1963

Fifteenth Symphony subtitled *Silver Pilgrimage*, by Alan HOVHANESS, is performed for the first time in New York.

1 APRIL 1963

To supplement the previously enforced prohibition of singing sad songs that undermine the nation's morale, the government of South Vietnam issues an order forbidding performances of American twist music.

2 APRIL 1963

Prophecy of Isaiah, last work by Bohuslav MARTINU, for chorus and orchestra is performed posthumously in Jerusalem, with the original Biblical text in English changed to corresponding verses in Hebrew.

4 APRIL 1963

Andromache's Farewell, scena for soprano and orchestra by Samuel BARBER, after an episode in *The Trojan Woman* by Euripides, relating to Andromache's tragic fate after she is carried to Greece by the victors as a war prize, set to music in a highly tense, euphoniously discordant idiom, is performed for the first time by the New York Philharmonic, Thomas Schippers conducting.

8 APRIL 1963

Concerto for Violin, Viola and Orchestra by the 42-year-old Slovenian composer Primož RAMOVŠ, in four connected movements for an orchestra without the violin and viola sections, and set in a free dodecaphonic technique, is performed for the first time in Ljubljana.

11 APRIL 1963

Sept Répons des Ténèbres, last work by Francis POULENC, commissioned by the New York Philharmonic in celebration of its opening season in Lincoln Center for the Performing Arts, scored for a boy soprano, boys' choir and orchestra, to Latin texts descriptive of the tenebrous days of Christ's Passion, with an atonally refracted medieval chant figure as a motto, is performed for the first time by the New York Philharmonic, under the direction of Thomas Schippers.

13 APRIL 1963

In the course of the 26th International Festival of Contemporary. Music in Venice, the world premières are given of *Quintet* for piano and strings by Alberto GINASTERA (Argentina), *Diagramma IV* for flute solo by Henryk GÓRECKI (Poland), *Polyphonie I* for alto flute and piano by Jacques GUYONNET (Switzerland), and *Recíproco* for flute, piano and percussion by Luis de PABLO (Spain).

14 APRIL 1963

In the course of the 26th International Festival of Contemporary Music in Venice, the Groupe de Recherches Musicales, led by the Paris electrical engineer Pierre SCHAEFFER, originator (in 1948) of musique concrète, presents a program of orchestral music with electronic montages in absolute world premières:

Collages by Philippe CARSON (France), *Alternances* by Bernard PARMEGIANI (France), *L' experience ambigue* by Jean-Etienne MARIE (France), *Tutti* by Ivo MALEC (Yugoslavia), *Synergies* by François-Bernard MÂCHE (France), *D'un bout à l' autre* by Edgardo CANTON (Argentina), *Éventail* by N'Guyen Van TUONG (Vietnam), *Pluriel* by François BAYLE (France), and *Compose-Composite* by Luc FERRARI (France).

16 APRIL 1963

In the course of the 26th International Festival of Contemporary Music in Venice, a chamber music concert presents the world premières of the following works:

Musica da camera for 9 instruments by Angelo PACCAGNINI; *Informel 2* for 15 instruments by Aldo CLEMENTI; *A Solemn Music* for voice and small ensemble to the words of Milton's poem by Niccolò CASTIGLIONI; *Elegie* for voice, violin, clarinet and guitar by Antonio VERETTI; and *Serenade No. 2* by the 30-year-old Californian avant-garde composer Morton SUBOTNICK.

23 APRIL 1963

In the course of the 26th International Festival of Contemporary Music in Venice, a concert of symphonic music is given comprising the following works:

World première of *Abracadabra* by the 81-year-old Italian grandmaster of music Gian Francesco MALIPIERO, for baritone and orchestra, in 8 episodes of neo-pastoral inspiration with the thematic material derived from the letters of the medieval magic word Abracadabra; Bruno MADERNA's *Concerto* for oboe and orchestra; and the world première of *Stratégie* by the Greek composer Iannis XENAKIS, a "musical competition" for two orchestras playing two different pieces comprising 19 musical divisions, the durations of which are determined by an IBM 7090 computer in Paris, each constituting a matrix of the game, with the conductor who carries out the stochastic data more efficiently being declared the winner (Maderna won on this occasion by *viva voce* acclamation against the Yugoslav conductor Konstantin Simonovic.)

23 APRIL 1963

Monsieur de Pourceaugnac, opera by Frank MARTIN, after Molière's farce, in which a pompous landlord to whom an ambitious bourgeois wants to give his daughter in marriage is beset by machinations organized by the unwilling bride, is declared debile by false doctors and bigamous by false lawyers until he is driven back to his country estate and the bride is free to marry her true lover, with a musical score written in a classical comic style and the orchestra supplemented by a xylophone, celesta, piano, harp, harpsichord and vibraphone, is produced at the newly rebuilt Grand-Théâtre in Geneva, Ansermet conducting. (The previously announced date for the première, 13 December 1962, was postponed.)

24 APRIL 1963

Novae de infinito laudes, cantata by the German composer resident in Italy, Hans Werner HENZE, to the texts of six essays of the martyr of science Giordano Bruno, discoursing learnedly upon celestial bodies, the basic four elements, the continuous mutation, the pleasure of motion, the sunrise and the Summum Bonum, set to music in a correspondingly catholic idiom, tonal, atonal, polytonal, serial, is performed for the first time in the course of the 26th International Festival of Contemporary Music in Venice.

25 APRIL 1963

Paul HINDEMITH conducts the New York Philharmonic in the world première of his *Concerto for Organ and Orchestra,* commissioned by the New York Philharmonic in celebration of its opening season in Lincoln Center and consisting of four movements: (1) *Crescendo—Moderato maestoso;* (2) *Allegro assai;* (3) *Canzonetta in Triads and Two Ritornelli,* with interludes for solo organ traversing 22 different major and minor triads in unrelated succession; (4) *Phantasy on Veni Creator Spiritus,* set to music in a resplendent neo-gothic Regeromorphic idiom (the score was completed on 1 February 1963 in the upper Palatinate, once the home ground of Max Reger).

26 APRIL 1963

Media in vita, symphonic oratorio by the Swiss composer Armin SCHIBLER, to the text of a patrological Latin poem reminding that middle life is half death and written in a neo-ecclesiastical style with two antiphonal choruses representing the dead and the living, is performed for the first time in Zürich.

30 APRIL 1963

Noah and the Flood, ballet with singing, by Igor STRAVINSKY, receives its first stage performance in Hamburg.

2 MAY 1963

Ninth Symphony, the last work by the Hungarian composer László LAJTHA, written in a structurally lucid, classically designed form, with melismatic melos suggesting the Magyar origins of its inspiration, is given a posthumous world première in Paris.

5 MAY 1963

On the 18th anniversary of the liberation of Holland from the Nazi occupation, Radio Hilversum presents the first performance of the oratorio entitled *5 mei: Zij (Fifth of May: They)* by Bertus VAN LIER.

10 MAY 1963

Still Are New Worlds for narrator, tape, choir and orchestra by the 56-year-old American composer Ross Lee FINNEY is performed for the first time in Ann Arbor, Michigan.

12 MAY 1963

The Bonn Council opens a Robert SCHUMANN Museum, housing his manuscripts and letters, in the private clinic in Endenich, now a suburb of Bonn, where Schumann was confined during the last three years of his life and where, during his intervals of lucidity, he wrote his last compositions.

13 MAY 1963

Highway No. 1, U.S.A., one-act opera by the American Negro composer William Grant STILL, glorifying in epic tones the main North-South automobile artery leading along the coast from Maine to Florida, is performed for the first time in Miami, Florida.

16 MAY 1963

Fifth Symphony by the 36-year-old German composer Hans Werner HENZE, in three movements: *Movimentado, Adagio, Moto perpetuo*, scored for orchestra sans clarinets and sans bassoons and couched in a searchingly atonal but tonipetal idiom keeping clear of totally organized dodecaphony which was Henze's preferred style before he settled on the island of Ischia in the Bay of Naples, is performed for the first time as a commissioned work by the New York Philharmonic, Leonard Bernstein conducting.

16 MAY 1963

One Hundred Devils and One Girl, operetta by Tikhon KHRENNIKOV, is produced in Moscow.

18 MAY 1963

Death of the Bishop of Brindisi, dramatic cantata by Gian Carlo MENOTTI, scored for orchestra, two soloists and a chorus of 525, including 325 children, dealing with the historic episode of the Children's Crusade of A.D. 1212, which was blessed by the Bishop of Brindisi who subsequently was tortured by conscience and responsibility for the tragic death of the adolescent crusaders when their ships foundered and sank, is performed for the first time in Cincinnati.

20 MAY 1963

Die Soldaten, opera in four acts by the German composer Bernd Alois ZIMMERMANN, is performed for the first time in Cologne.

22 MAY 1963

To commemorate the sesquicentennial of the birth of Richard WAGNER, the Soviet Union issues a 4-kopeck postage stamp with his portrait.

23 MAY 1963

Hymnody for wind instruments, percussion and two pianos by the dean of the Spanish musical avant-garde, Roberto GERHARD, who went to England after the Falangist victory in Spain, is performed for the first time in London.

27 MAY 1963

To mark the bicentennial of the birth of the French opera composer Etienne-Nicolas MÉHUL, France issues a 60-centime postage stamp in his honor.

28 MAY 1963

La Celestina, opera by Flavio TESTI, is produced in Florence during the Maggio Fiorentino Festival.

29 MAY 1963

Exactly 50 years after the world première of STRAVINSKY's *Le Sacre du Printemps* at the Théâtre des Champs-Elysées in Paris, Pierre Monteux, the original conductor, now 88, leads the London Symphony Orchestra in the Royal Albert Hall, London, in the presence of the composer.

It was a moving experience to watch these octogenarian partners in a 50-year-old crime receiving their ovation together. (*The Times*, London, 30 May 1963)

The short, bald composer sat forward eagerly, although in the shadows, as the orchestra presented a performance that the reviewers agreed came up to the occasion. Then it was all over and the audience exploded in applause. . . . Monteux turned to face the delirious audience and then immediately looked around the hall for his fellow octogenarian. Stravinsky, in a box, noticed the conductor's confusion, and whipped out a handkerchief to catch his attention. . . . As Monteux began the slow climb to the box through an admiring throng, Stravinsky continued to wave his handkerchief at the delighted audience. . . . After the two old friends embraced each other in the box, Monteux returned to the podium. (New York *Times*, 31 May 1963)

31 MAY 1963

Christopher Sly, comic opera by the 35-year-old American composer Dominick ARGENTO, based on a scene from Shakespeare's play *The Taming of the Shrew*, is produced in Minneapolis for the first time.

31 MAY 1963

Dualities, ballet by Humphrey SEARLE, is performed for the first time in Wiesbaden.

4 JUNE 1963

Byzantine Concerto for piano and orchestra by the 54-year-old Serbian composeress Ljubica MARIĆ, in three movements, thematically derived from elements of ancient Byzantine chants, set in baroque form and embellished by atonal and polytonal techniques, is performed for the first time in Belgrade.

7 JUNE 1963

Concerto for guitar and orchestra by Alfonso LETELIER is performed for the first time in Santiago, Chile.

8 JUNE 1963

The 37th Festival of the International Society for Contemporary Music opens in Amsterdam with the following program:

Ombres for orchestra by Ton DE LEEUW, 36-year-old Dutch composer of highly advanced music with philosophical undertones, in four movements utilizing some Indian ragas; *Les symphonies de timbres* by the 43-year-old Polish-born composer Roman HAUBENSTOCK-RAMATI, an essay in forms and sonorities and thematic metamorphoses in a peritonal idiom; *4 Songs*, op. 22 by Arnold SCHOENBERG; and *Eighth Symphony* by Karl Amadeus HARTMANN.

9 JUNE 1963

The second concert of the 37th Festival of the International Society for Contemporary Music in Amsterdam presents the following program:

Flökt (Fluctuations) for chamber orchestra by the 25-year-old Icelandic composer Thorkell SIGURBJÖRNSSON built on the scheme of expanding intervals and freely fluctuating instrumental sonorities; *Studio per 24,* an experimental sketch for 24 instruments by the 30-year-old Italian composer Giacomo MANZONI; *Um Mitternacht* for chorus by the Viennese composer Hans Erich APOSTEL, written in dynamically dimmed sonorities between pianissimo and mezzo forte, in a free chromatic idiom; *Aphorismes 9* by the 66-year-old Polish composer Boleslaw SZABELSKI, a succinct suite for 9 instruments in a somewhat impressionistic manner; *Improperia per voci,* by the 36-year-old Danish composer Bernhard LEWKOWITCH, to the Latin text of the Good Friday ritual containing the Lord's reproaches to his people, with an element of free improvisation in the inflected speech and requiring the audience to heave a deep sigh during the cadential fermata; *Constellations III* by the 35-year-old Swedish composer Bengt HAMBRAEUS, written for an electronically enriched organ with the application of the aleatory technique of calculated improvisation; and *Bugaku* by the 56-year-old Japanese composer Yoritsune MATSUDAIRA, in four movements for small orchestra based on melorhythms of ancient Japanese court dances with the application of the principle of indeterminacy as to the order of components and instrumentation.

10 JUNE 1963

The third concert of the 37th Festival of the International Society for Contemporary Music at Amsterdam presents the following program:

Elegia II by the 23-year-old Argentinian composer Armando KRIEGER for contralto, 2 flutes, piano and percussion, wherein the verticality of harmony is contrasted with the horizontality of the melorhythmic line and both are balanced by their common perpendicularity to instrumental timbre; *Sonata for flute and piano* by the 30-year-old Australian composer Richard MEALE opposing the static and dynamic aspects of symmetry and asymmetry and injecting elements of indeterminacy in contrapuntal combinations; *Erde und Himmel,* cantata by the 24-year-old Swiss composer Heinz HOLLIGER, in three movements, to words by a young Swiss suicide hovering between death and existence, the morbid oscillation portrayed by the devices of inversion and retrograde canon in an atonalized serialistic idiom; *Favola per clarinetto e batteria grande* by the 43-year-old Swedish composer Sven Erik BÄCK, in the narrative style of responsorial fabulation, with the clarinet speaking and assorted chimes and drums offering colorful comment; *Second String Quartet* by the Dutch composer Kees VAN BAAREN, written in a pre-classi-

cal form of a suite rich with improvised but pre-meditated cadenzas; and *Second Sonata* for piano by the prophet of French ultramodernism Pierre BOULEZ, written in 1948 when he was 22 and based on a cellular type of composition through cohesive agglutination and melorhythmic coagulation of component thematic ingredients.

12 JUNE 1963

The fourth concert of the 37th Festival of the International Society for Contemporary Music in Amsterdam presents the following program:

Variations on an Old Song by the great Dutch organist Sweelinck (1562–1621) orchestrated by Jan MUL; *Concerto* for two pianos and orchestra by the 49-year-old Belgian-born composer Luctor PONSE, in three movements, based each on a group of thematic intervals according to a serial technique; *Concerto for Orchestra No. 3* by the Indonesian-born 34-year-old Dutch composer Will EISMA, in three movements, with the thematic foundation of mutually exclusive symmetrically posited six-note tropes; *De Vogels,* overture by the Dutch composer Alphons DIEPENBROCK (1862–1921), after *The Birds* of Aristophanes; *Anagrams* for chamber orchestra by the 58-year-old Dutch composer Guillaume LANDRÉ, in four sections, in which the thematic materials are anagrammatically permutated; and *6 Symphonic Epigrams*, extremely brief, by the Dutch impressionist Willem PIJPER (1894–1947).

12 JUNE 1963

In the course of the 25th International Music Festival in Strasbourg, the world première is given of *Cantates pour une démente* by Maurice JARRE, scored for soprano, contralto, chorus and orchestra to texts from authentic letters by inmates of insane asylums, with the score notated both acoustically and pictorially, as a "partition-tableau," which can be read from left to right or from right to left, wherein the notes are represented by colors, dynamic intensity by the size of a color disc, 2 centimeters being the unit of time according to a chosen tempo so that 4,920 different versions could be produced in performance (hence the plural form of the title, *Cantates*).

13 JUNE 1963

The Fifth Concert of the 37th Festival of the International Society for Contemporary Music at Amsterdam presents the following program:

Serenade for flute, clarinet and bassoon by the 32-year-old Yugoslav composer Alojz SREBOTNJAK, written in the 12-tone technique, in six brief movements; *Quintet No. 2* for piano, clarinet, violin, viola and cello by the 30-year-old Czech composer Ilja ZELJENKA, written in a modified 12-tone idiom, with tonipetal tendencies; *Trio* for violin, clarinet and piano by the 32-year-old American composer Donald MARTINO, in 7 symmetric sections and derived from a series of consequential permutations of a predetermined set of 12 different notes; *Sonata* for cello solo by the 45-year-old German composer Bernd Alois ZIMMERMANN, in 5 sections, purporting to illustrate the passage from Ecclesiastes commenting upon planetary movements: ". . . et suis spatiis transeunt universa sub caelo"; *4 Studies* for wind quintet by the 44-year-old Swiss composer Robert SUTER, in 4 sections: *Couleurs, Mouvements, Improvisations* and *Polyphonie*, the content corresponding to the explicit intentions of the titles; and *String Quartet No. 6* by the 53-year-old Danish composer Vagn HOLMBOE, in four movements monothematic in ultimate derivation, but morphologically diversified in treatment.

14 JUNE 1963

The sixth and last concert of the 37th International Society for Contemporary Music Festival at Amsterdam presents the following program:

Canzone per orchestra by the 32-year-old Norwegian composer Arne NORDHEIM, in three movements in a terse contrapuntal idiom with the basic melorhythmic motto stated explicitly in the first six bars; *Three Movements for Orchestra* by the 48-year-old American composer George PERLE, set in a serial technique in which the rhythmic impulses are symmetrically distributed; *Arabescata* for orchestra by the 35-year-old Finnish composer Einojuhani RAUTAVAARA, in 3 graphic variations in which tones, durations, intervals, instrumental colors and dynamics are serially distributed; *Symphonie concertante* by Jacques IBERT for oboe and string orchestra couched in a neo-classical vein with coloristic effects; and *Threnody for the Victims of Hiroshima* by Krzysztof PENDERECKI for 52 string instruments.

15 JUNE 1963

Le Silence de la Mer, lyric drama in one act by the French composer Henri TOMASI, to a dramatic libretto from the time of Nazi occupation of France, in which a German officer of uncommon sensibilities who lodges in a French home tells the story of his life to an old man of the house and his niece, and then kills himself, is performed for the first time in Strasbourg.

18 JUNE 1963

The government of the People's Democratic Republic of Germany issues two postage stamps, at 20 and 25 pfennigs, marking the 75 years of the composition of the *Internationale*.

23 JUNE 1963

Die Errettung Thebens, opera in three acts by the Swiss composer Rudolf KELTERBORN, to his own libretto drawn freely from Aeschylus, in which seven princes from Argos assail the seven gates of Thebes, is produced in Zürich.

25 JUNE 1963

A Frenchman in New York, symphonic suite by the Gallic Novoeboracophile Darius MILHAUD, in six sight-seeing sections—(1) *New York with Fog on the Hudson* (impenetrably static in windless wind instruments); (2) *The Cloisters* (devotionally hymnal in neo-medieval polymodalities); (3) *Horse and Carriage in Central Park* (quadripedally nostalgic in equine saunter); (4) *Times Square* (cacophonously polychordal in quaquaversal commotion); (5) *Gardens on the Roof* (an urbanely aerated aerie); (6) *Baseball in Yankee Stadium* (fugally competitive, with pitcher and batter in vernacular antiphony)—is performed for the first time by the Boston Pops Orchestra, Arthur Fiedler conducting.

28 JUNE 1963

Figaro lässt sich scheiden, opera in two acts by the German composer Giselher KLEBE, a non-Mozartian projection, wherein characters of the famous Beaumarchais play are placed in the tourbillon of the French Revolution, with Figaro singing atonal arias in a dodecaphonic idiom, is produced by the Hamburg State Opera.

2 JULY 1963

Our Man in Havana, opera in three acts by the 31-year-old composer Malcolm WILLIAMSON of Australia, after the melodramatic novel by Graham Greene, with spies and counterspies matching wits in wry atonalities over ostentatious pseudo-Cuban rhythms, is produced in London.

4 JULY 1963

On the occasion of the Fourth Centennial of the founding of El Escorial, the Spanish Ministry of Information and Tourism inaugurates an international festival of music with the participation of groups of artists from Europe and America.

4 JULY 1963

The new Presidential Medal of Freedom, established by President John F. Kennedy's executive order to reward annually those "who contribute significantly to the quality of American life," is awarded among 31 recipients to the great Spanish violoncellist Pablo CASALS, outstanding Negro singer Marian ANDERSON and the Austrian pianist Rudolf SERKIN.

6 JULY 1963

Little Symphony by the 30-year-old German-born English composer Alexander GOEHR, written in memory of his father Walter Goehr and couched in a euphonious atonal idiom, is performed for the first time in York, England.

6 JULY 1963

Variations for Orchestra by the 40-year-old Californian composer Leslie BASSETT, each based on a quadripartite phrase, the segments of which possess an individual dynamic and color scheme, but are not related to a hypothetical theme conceivably implied in the variants, are performed for the first time in Rome. (Its first American performance was given by the Philadelphia Orchestra, Eugene Ormandy conducting, on 22 October 1965; in 1966 the work received the Pulitzer Prize in Music.)

25 JULY 1963

Wagner's grandson Wieland WAGNER is roundly booed by the Wagnerolatrous audience in Bayreuth after his modern production of *Die Meistersinger*, in which the fight scene in the second act becomes a donnybrook, and the polka and the samba are danced in the third act.

1 AUGUST 1963

Elemental by the American jazz pianist Dave BRUBECK, subtitled "Concerto for Anyone Who Can Afford an Orchestra," is performed for the first time by Brubeck's jazz quartet with the Arrangers Workshop Orchestra in Rochester.

20 AUGUST 1963

A six-concert series of avant-garde music opens in New York with the following program:

Dreams for piano by the American composer Frederic RZEWSKI; *Pour Clavier* by the Italian composer Silvano BUSSOTTI; *Klavierstück* by Karlheinz STOCKHAUSEN, inviting the pianist to dust the keyboard with talcum powder and perform glissandos with a pair of women's white gloves; and *Teatrino* by Giuseppe CHIARI, a multi-media presentation for five squeaking dolls, ping-pong balls, drums, electronic tape, an alarm clock and a lumber jack's saw with the piano obligato playing snatches from BEETHOVEN'S *Fifth Symphony*.

21 AUGUST 1963

The avant-garde concert series continues in New York presenting John CAGE'S *Variations II and III*, with electronically amplified sounds of various actions, such as drinking water, with a microphone pressed against his throat aggregating to the decibel count of the Niagara Falls, and a piece by Cage's Japanese disciple Toshi ICHIYANAGI activating the denuded piano wires and the wooden parts of two pianos manned by John Cage and his accommodating clairaudient famulus David Tudor.

26 AUGUST 1963

The third of the six concerts of avant-garde music is presented in New York, including *Water Music* and *Densities* by the 22-year-old American musician Joseph BYRD, for various instrumental ensembles; *High Contrasts* by Philip CORNER for an amplified harpsichord, with a profusion of silences between massive agglomerations of sonic materials; *Ludlow Blues* by Malcolm GOLDSTEIN, for a heterophonic group of wind instruments; and *Ergodos 1/2/3* by James TENNEY for electronic tape recording of animal noises.

27 AUGUST 1963

The fourth concert of the avant-garde series in New York presents the following program:

Two pieces for piano by the Swedish composer Bo NILSSON; *Schlagfiguren und Quantitäten* and *Zyklus* for percussion by Karlheinz STOCKHAUSEN; *Music for 3 pianos* by Toshi ICHIYANAGI, the Japanese composer; *Action Music* for piano by the American composer Alvin LUCIER, in which digital aleatorics are combined with bodily gestures; *Sonata* for 3 pianos by Christian WOLFF; *Two Piano Pieces* by Morton FELDMAN; *From Place to Place* for two pianos by David BEHRMAN; *Nursery Fable with Exegesis* for piano by Bertram BALDWIN; and *Corona for Pianists* by the Japanese composer Tru TAKEMITZU.

28 AUGUST 1963

In the course of the Edinburgh Festival of Music and Drama, the first performance is given of the *Concerto for Orchestra* by the British composer Michael TIPPETT, commissioned by the Edinburgh Festival Society, in three movements of neo-baroque consistency: (1) *Allegro*, without string instruments; (2) *Largo*, without wind instruments; (3) *Allegro*, for full orchestra.

1 SEPTEMBER 1963

Cantata Misericordium by Benjamin BRITTEN (completed on 25 May 1963), scored for piano, harp, timpani, solo string quartet, tenor, baritone, and chorus and string orchestra, written for the centenary of the International Red Cross, to a Latin dramatization of the parable of the Good Samaritan, in a tonal style with bitonal excrescences,

is performed for the first time in its spiritual birthplace, Geneva, at a Red Cross celebration, by the Orchestre de la Suisse Romande, Ernest Ansermet conducting.

2 SEPTEMBER 1963

Mary of Magdala, cantata for chorus and orchestra by Sir Arthur BLISS, is performed for the first time at the Three Choirs Festival, at the Worcester Cathedral.

3 SEPTEMBER 1963

Hungary issues a 40-forint postage stamp in honor of the Hungarian composer Leo WEINER, who died on 13 September 1962.

3 SEPTEMBER 1963

The avant-garde musical festival continues in New York City with the following program of young adventurous music:

Composition 1960, No. 13 by the 27-year-old Idaho-born composer La Monte YOUNG for cello solo letting the performer play anything at all to his taste (a Sammartini *Adagio* was actually played); *Projection 1* by Morton FELDMAN; *City Minds and Country Hearts* by Ornette COLEMAN; *Music for Cello and Piano* by Earle BROWN (partly aleatory); and 34' 46.776" for violin and piano by John CAGE, during which both players blow whistles, hurl cymbals, and perform other seemingly random actions, circumscribed by temporal parameters indicated in a sheet of instructions.

7 SEPTEMBER 1963

Second Symphony by Louis MENNINI, subtitled "da Festa," is performed for the first time by the Erie Philharmonic, as part of the sesquicentennial celebration of the founding of Erie, Pennsylvania.

9 SEPTEMBER 1963

The New York Festival of avant-garde Music concludes with a non-stop performance of Erik SATIE's piano piece *Vexations*, which according to Satie's instructions is to be played unremittingly 840 times, with the total duration of 18 hours 40 minutes at the estimated length of a single hearing of 80 seconds. (The event began at 6:00 P.M. on Monday 9 September and ended at 12:40 P.M. on Tuesday, 10 September with ten crepuscular, nocturnal, matutinal and diurnal pianists playing in relay.)

10 SEPTEMBER 1963

The Soviet Post Office issues commemorative postage stamps to honor Giuseppe VERDI and Alexander DARGOMYZHSKY on the sesquicentennial of their births, and the Ukrainian singer-composer Semyon GULAK-ARTEMOVSKY on the 100th anniversary of his birth.

21 SEPTEMBER 1963

The newly erected Place des Arts opens in Montreal, Canada, with a concert by the Montreal Symphony Orchestra, featuring the world première of *Miroir* by the Canadian composer Jean Papineau-COUTURE RAVEL's *La Valse* and MAHLER's *First Symphony*, led by the newly appointed music director of the Montreal Symphony, the youngest ever to head a major orchestra, 27-year-old

Indian conductor Zubin MEHTA, to the extrinsic accompaniment of protesting French-Canadian nationalists clamoring for entrance outside the hall and carrying placards saying "Étatisation de la Place des Arts," "Vive la nation Québecoise" and "e Québec se réveille."

22 SEPTEMBER 1963

Don Giovanni, one-act opera by Gian Francesco MALIPIERO, after Pushkin's drama *The Stone Guest*, is produced in Naples.

3 OCTOBER 1963

Violin Concerto by the prime Argentinian composer Alberto GINASTERA, is performed for the first time as a commissioned work by the New York Philharmonic, Leonard Bernstein conducting, Ruggiero Ricci soloist, set in three formalistically modernistic movements:

(1) *Cadenza e Studi*, opening with a prolonged cadenza, leading to six technical studies, unified by a common dodecaphonic series, the first exploiting multiple stops in the violin solo, the second in tertian formations, the third in changing intervals, the fourth in free figurations, the fifth employing high harmonics, and the sixth making use of tropes in quarter-tones, followed by a magistral coda summarizing the devices of all six studies; (2) *Adagio* for 22 soloists, a lyric interlude intended as an homage to the virtuosi of the New York Philharmonic; (3) *Scherzo pianissimo e Perpetuum mobile*, opening with a prologue for exotic drums and assorted chimes, played on the threshold of audibility at a very rapid tempo, with thematic fragments from Paganini's *Capriccios* passing fleetingly through the orchestra before the final precipitous flight of perpetual motion.

4 OCTOBER 1963

Sogno d'un tramonto d'autonno (*Dream of an Autumn Sunset*), one-act opera by Gian Francesco MALIPIERO originally written in 1913 as incidental music to a play by Gabriele d'Annunzio, dealing with a Venetian Dogaressa who schemes to destroy her love rival through ceraceous invultuation and acuminulate perforation of her waxen image, and induces an internecine carnage of carnally aroused men on the barges in the canals of Venice, is performed half a century after its composition on the Milan radio, in concert form.

6 OCTOBER 1963

Symphonie marine by Jacques IBERT, written in 1931 in a Gallically elegant, coloristic aquamarine manner but withheld by him from performance, is performed for the first time posthumously in Paris.

9 OCTOBER 1963

Hans Werner HENZE conducts in Berlin the first performance of his *Fourth Symphony*, with its material taken wholly from the discarded finale of the second act of his opera *König Hirsch*, in one movement which disperses its tonal energy in tangential atonalities, coming to rest on a soft multiple unison.

10 OCTOBER 1963

On the occasion of the sesquicentennial of VERDI's birth, a 30-lire stamp with his portrait is issued by Italy.

10 OCTOBER 1963

Gentlemen, Be Seated!, opera in two acts from the time of the American Civil War by the 50-year-old American composer Jerome MOROSS, which combines elements of a minstrel show, dance, and drama, with a "Mister Interlocutor" supplying commentary on the historic, social, and fictional characters and events, is produced in New York.

11 OCTOBER 1963

A concert of ultra-avant-garde American music is presented in New York City in a program comprising the world premières of the unpremeditated *Vertical Thoughts* in five perpendicular movements by Morton FELDMAN, abounding in non-aforethought canons, with players entering whenever they have a chance, and of his *Straits of Magellan*, a circumnavigatory "graph piece" with the compass pointing towards a tonal pole exercising great latitude of altitude of sound, as well as his threnody to the dead abstractional painter Franz Kline, *The Swallows of Salangan;* and four partially prepense pieces by Earle BROWN: *December 1952, Pentathis* (a demonstrative nonaseity derived from the pentathionate, a sulphur solution, with allusions to the five-event athletic contest Pentathlon), *Available Forms I*, in 27 accidental events, and *From Here*, the title referring to the common schizophrenic phrase, "You can't get there from here."

11 OCTOBER 1963

President John F. KENNEDY announces the formation of a new permanent national company of the Metropolitan Opera in association with the National Cultural Center in Washington.

11 OCTOBER 1963

Jean COCTEAU, Gallic inspirer of the arts, poet, dramatist, painter, stage designer, and newly elected member of the august French Academy (*Vu*, a Paris periodical, listed among the future impossibilities man's landing on the moon and Cocteau's election to the Academy), dies of a heart attack in his suburbanly Parisian country seat at Milly-la-Forêt at 1:30 P.M., at the age of 74, a few hours after the death caused by the hemorrhage of the spleen of Edith Piaf, 47-year-old, 90-lb., 4-ft., 10-in., French street singer, who was brought up in a brothel run by her grandmother and nicknamed Piaf (argot for a sparrow) by her souteneur, a cabaret owner shot to death in 1937.

13 OCTOBER 1963

Alexander TCHEREPNIN plays in Berlin the piano part in the world première of his *Fifth Piano Concerto*.

15 OCTOBER 1963

The new Philharmonic Hall, designed by the German architect Hans SCHAROUN, shaped as an asymmetrical polygon, with a seating capacity of 2,200, and acoustically accoutred with 136 pyramidal ceiling reflectors for sound (Helmholz resonators), festooned with neon light tubes, opens in West Berlin with a gala performance of Beethoven's *Ninth Symphony* by the Berlin Philharmonic Orchestra, under the direction of Herbert von Karajan.

16 OCTOBER 1963

Carmen Vitale, cantata by Alan RAWSTHORNE, to a medieval English text exhorting the hearers to practice carnal abstinence, with the hymn to St. John *Ut queant laxis,* used by Guido d'Arezzo as the foundation of the syllabic singing method, serving here as the cantus firmus, so that musical phrases enter a degree higher in each succeeding stanza, is performed for the first time in London.

20 OCTOBER 1963

The opening of the new Nisei Theater with a capacity of 1,350 seats and equipped with the most advanced electronic systems takes place in Tokyo, with the presentation of BEETHOVEN's *Fidelio* by the Deutsche Oper of West Berlin, comprising its entire personnel of 280 members.

20 OCTOBER 1963

Ut Unum Sint, symphonic piece by the Italian composer Renzo ROSSELLINI, inspired by the last words of Pope John XXIII uttered before his death, "That they may be one," from the Latin text of the Gospel according to St. John, Chapter 17, Verse 11, is performed for the first time by the Miami Symphony Orchestra, Fabien Sevitzky conducting.

21 OCTOBER 1963

The Last Savage, opera buffa by Gian-Carlo MENOTTI, to his own libretto dealing with a whimsical American heiress who undertakes a search for the abominable snowman in the high Himalayas, locates a putative specimen, imports him to her native Chicago and when he recoils in horror from abstract impressionist art, dodecaphonic music and beatnik poetry, takes him back to his mountain habitat and eventually marries him, set to music in urbane satirical tones, with illustrative persiflage of American avant-garde pursuits, is produced at the Opéra-Comique in Paris.

22 OCTOBER 1963

Synthesis for Orchestra and Electronic Sound by Otto LUENING is performed for the first time by the Erie, Pennsylvania, Philharmonic.

23 OCTOBER 1963

Symphony for Metal Orchestra (Seventeenth Symphony) by the American composer Alan HOVHANESS, is performed for the first time in Cleveland.

28 OCTOBER 1963

Juha, romantic opera by the Finnish composer Aarre MERIKANTO, composed in 1922, in which an elderly Finn named Juha kills himself after his chronologically and genetically more youthful bride lets herself be imprudently impregnated by a transient philanderer, set to music in somber tones vested in dramatically romantic Germanic harmonies in which the musical images of Sibelius and Richard Strauss coalesce, is performed for the first time on the stage in the small Finnish locality of Lahti, five years after Merikanto's death. (A radio pre-

mière of *Juha* was first performed in Helsinki on 3 December 1958, also posthumously, within nine weeks of the composer's death.)

28 OCTOBER 1963

Second Piano Concerto by Leon KIRCHNER, in two connected movements, written in a rhapsodically exhortatory style, gravid in its dissonant condensation, with a decoratively baroque piano part and minatory percussion, is performed for the first time by the Seattle Symphony Orchestra with the composer conducting, Leon Fleischer soloist.

1 NOVEMBER 1963

Two Negro music students are arrested in Jackson, Mississippi, by the city police and are held overnight on a charge of disturbing the peace in trying to attend, with two valid tickets, a concert given by the Royal Philharmonic Orchestra of London, under Sir Malcolm Sargent, at a segregated hall.

I understand that Sir Malcolm received a telephone call during the interval of his concert telling him of the arrest of the two students and asking him not to carry on with the concert. Unfortunately, the terms of our contract still applied, and no doubt he felt it his duty to play the advertised concert in full. (From a letter by the concertmaster of the Royal Philharmonic Orchestra, in the *Manchester Guardian Weekly,* 5 December 1963)

8 NOVEMBER 1963

Fifth Symphony in one long movement, by the individualistic, innovative, unfailingly romantic Swedish composer Allan PETTERSSON, is performed for the first time on the Swedish Radio.

11 NOVEMBER 1963

Echoi, suite of four movements by Lukas FOSS, scored for piano, clarinet, cello, assorted percussion and a garbage can, written according to a stochastic formula in which temporal freedom is given to the percussion player controlling the actions of his colleagues, is performed for the first time in New York, with Lukas Foss presiding at the piano.

12 NOVEMBER 1963

Anniversary Concerto: 75 by the 40-year-old American composer Robert EVETT, commissioned for the 75th anniversary of the Basic-Witz Furniture Industries of Wayneseboro, Virginia, in seven movements with instrumental solos expressive of individual pieces of mass-produced furniture, set in a fittingly automated rhythmic idiom, is performed for the first time in Washington.

12 NOVEMBER 1963

Paul HINDEMITH makes his last public appearance, conducting the Vienna Chamber Chorus in the first performance of his last work, a *Mass* for mixed choir *a cappella,* written in an austere neo-medieval polyphonic idiom, with transitional discords occasionally perturbing the reticent ambience of the music.

15 NOVEMBER 1963

Fritz REINER, Hungarian-born conductor, master technician of the baton, distinguished both in symphonic and operatic repertory, sympathetic interpreter of modern music, dies in New York at the age of 74.

17 NOVEMBER 1963

This Sacred Ground by David DIAMOND, a symphonic setting of Lincoln's Gettysburg Address, scored for orchestra, chorus and male voice is performed for the first time by the Buffalo Philharmonic Orchestra.

20 NOVEMBER 1963

Sixth Symphony by the Swedish composer Gunnar BUCHT is performed for the first time in Stockholm.

20 NOVEMBER 1963

The National Theater of Munich, housing the Staatsoper, opens its doors in a building reconstructed stone by stone, stucco by stucco, to produce an architectural facsimile of the original structure with its Corinthian columns and a 180-light chandelier destroyed in an Allied air attack on 18 October 1943, with a performance of *Die Frau ohne Schatten* by Richard STRAUSS, born in Munich 99 1/2 years before. (This was a preliminary opening for invited guests; the official opening for the general public took place on 23 November 1963 with a performance of Wagner's *Die Meistersinger* which had its première at the Munich National Theater in 1868.)

22 NOVEMBER 1963

At the Friday afternoon concert of the Boston Symphony Orchestra, having completed the first performance of the torturously atonal and minatory *Study for Orchestra No. 2* by the American composer William SYDEMAN, Erich Leinsdorf is apprised of the assassination of President Kennedy and announces the tragic news to the audience (there are cries: "No, no!"), then conducts the *Marcia funèbre* from Beethoven's *Eroica*.

23 NOVEMBER 1963

Twenty-five days before his unexpected death, Winfried ZILLIG conducts in Linz the world première of his seventh opera, in one act, *Das Verlöbnis*, depicting in an ironically solemn dodecaphonic idiom the joys and heartaches of rural love.

27 NOVEMBER 1963

Werner EGK conducts in the newly rebuilt National Opera Theater in Munich the world première of his opera in two acts, *Die Verlobung in San Domingo,* to his own libretto fashioned after a novella by Heinrich Kleist dealing with a miscegenational love affair in San Domingo during the native uprising against the French in the early 19th century, ending in tragedy with the innocent death at the hands of the white lover of the lovely mulatto girl unjustly suspected of spying, containing a half-hour interlude of tape recorded indigenous music.

29 NOVEMBER 1963

First Symphony by the 41-year-old American composer Irwin BAZELON is performed for the first time in Kansas City, Missouri.

2 DECEMBER 1963

The Knife, opera in two acts by the Welsh composer Daniel JONES, commissioned by the Welsh Committee of the Arts Council, to his own libretto, wherein a Negro accused of raping and murdering a white girl in a Southern mining town in 1866 is saved from lynching when a conscience-stricken white miner confesses the crime, is produced at Sadler's Wells in London.

2 DECEMBER 1963

The Sojourner and Mollie Sinclair, one-act opera by Carlisle FLOYD, to his own libretto delineating the conflict between an old-fashioned clan chieftain and a progressive-minded lass among the early Scottish settlers in the Carolinas, commissioned by the Carolina Charter Tercentenary Commission is produced in Raleigh, North Carolina.

2 DECEMBER 1963

Murder of a Great Chief of State, In Memory of John F. Kennedy, a brief symphonic piece by Darius MILHAUD composed in Paris on the day after the assassination, is performed for the first time in Oakland, California.

3 DECEMBER 1963

Aaron COPLAND conducts at the Munich National Opera Theater the world première of his ballet *Dance Panels in Seven Movements,* built in a translucidly intricate polyphonic reticle, with some jazzy interpolations.

5 DECEMBER 1963

Karl Amadeus HARTMANN, German master of modern polyphony, who adopted a viable individual style incorporating elements of pure classicism and prudential modernism, dies in his native town of Munich at the age of 58.

6 DECEMBER 1963

Genghis Khan, symphonic poem by the 56-year-old Berlin-born American composer Gene GÜTCHE (whose real name was Romeo Gutsche), expressionistically portraying the murderous character of the great Mongolian khan, is performed for the first time in Minneapolis.

7 DECEMBER 1963

A commemorative stamp honoring the centennial of Pietro MASCAGNI's birth, is issued in Italy.

9 DECEMBER 1963

Leonard BERNSTEIN conducts in Tel Aviv the world première of his choral *Third Symphony* subtitled *Kaddish,* inspired by the traditional Jewish prayer for the dead, originally commissioned by the Boston Symphony Orchestra, and re-dedicated to the memory of President John F. Kennedy.

10 DECEMBER 1963

Song of Human Rights, cantata by Howard HANSON commissioned by the United Nations Human Rights Organization, to texts from various sources including excerpts from the Inaugural Address of President John F.

Kennedy, is performed for the first time as part of the observance honoring the United Nations Human Rights day in Washington.

10 DECEMBER 1963

Ronald STEVENSON, 35-year-old English pianist and composer, plays at Capetown, South Africa, the first performance of his brobdingnagian *Passacaglia* for piano solo, lasting one hour and 20 minutes, and written as a tribute to Dmitri Shostakovich, based on the theme of Shostakovich's musical monogram, D.S.C.H. (D, Es, C, H in German notation), used by Shostakovich himself in his *Tenth Symphony*.

12 DECEMBER 1963

Symphony in One Movement by the 54-year-old Scottish composer Robin ORR, a dramatically introspective soundpiece marked by periodic outbursts of massive sonorities alternating with austerely pentatonic Caledonian progressions, and concluding with a series of immaculate open fifths, is performed for the first time in London.

20 DECEMBER 1963

The Lithuanian Soviet Socialist Republic issues a 4-kopeck stamp in honor of the prime modern composer of Lithuania, Mikas PETRAUSKAS (1873–1937).

20 DECEMBER 1963

Pacem in terris, choral symphony, op. 404, by Darius MILHAUD, to the Latin text from the 1963 encyclical of Pope John XXIII, in seven sections, proclaiming the imperative necessity of peace in a scientific age, rights of free movement, obedience to divine authority, spirit of justice, protection of political dissenters, disarmament and brotherhood of man, is performed for the first time at the inauguration of a new hall of the Paris Radio under the direction of Charles Munch. (It had its first church performance in the cathedral of Notre Dame in Paris on 1 June 1964, on the occasion of the 800th anniversary of the inception of its construction.)

21 DECEMBER 1963

Shlaúra, opera in three acts in the Bashkir language by the 46-year-old Bashkir Soviet composer Zagir ISMAILOV, is produced in Ufa.

28 DECEMBER 1963

Paul HINDEMITH, supreme musical craftsman of 20th-century Germany, whose ideals of immanent esthetics rooted in the mastery of tonal techniques has bridged the Bachian past with the logic of modern music, dies in Frankfurt, Germany, at the age of 68, following a series of four consecutive cerebrovascular strokes.

28 DECEMBER 1963

Triple Concerto for violin, piano, cello and orchestra, the last work by the Rumanian composer Paul CONSTANTINESCU, is performed for the first time in Bucharest eight days after his death.

31 DECEMBER 1963

The Government of South Africa bans the musical play *South Pacific* by Richard RODGERS on the ground that it encourages miscegenation.

1964

10 JANUARY 1964

Pierre BOULEZ conducts in Strasbourg the first performance of a fragment from his *Figures, Doubles, Prismes* for orchestra, conceived in blocks of double sonic prisms in *fortissimo* separated by cylindrical pillars of zero sonority in the "temps strié" (striated time), and representing the creative desire to "seize and organize the delirium."

13 JANUARY 1964

The House of Atreus, ballet by the Canadian composer Harry SOMERS, depicting the murder of Agamemnon and Electra's avenging wrath, written in an ironically philosophical manner with jazzy vignettes on a neo-Grecian canvas, is performed for the first time in Ottawa.

14 JANUARY 1964

Second Symphony by Quincy PORTER, in four classical movements+3, set in a dignified neo-baroque style with some atonal excrescences and polytonal protuberances, is performed for the first time in Louisville.

14 JANUARY 1964

Voyage Four, "spatial concert piece" by the American composer Henry BRANT, scored for 83 instrumentalists and a singer, is performed for the first time in New Haven, led by three conductors, with the players seated in different parts of the hall, on the balcony and on the stage, so as to create the impression of a stereophonic environment.

20 JANUARY 1964

Fourteenth Symphony by the prolific Swiss-American composer Ernst LÉVY is performed for the first time in Basel.

22 JANUARY 1964

Marc BLITZSTEIN, 58-year-old American composer of operas of social significance, dies in a hospital at Fort-de-France, Martinique, as a result of a savage beating arising out of a political altercation at the hands of three sailors the night before.

23 JANUARY 1964

Seventh Symphony, subtitled *Variation Symphony*, by the American composer Peter MENNIN, in five concise movements, charged with kinetic energy, is performed for the first time by the Cleveland Orchestra, George Szell conducting.

30 JANUARY 1964

Night Music I for soprano, piano and percussion by the 34-year-old American composer George CRUMB, to verses by Federico García Lorca, is performed for the first time in Paris.

7 FEBRUARY 1964

Fifth Symphony by Roger SESSIONS, a compact single-unit work written in a neo-classically formal serialistic idiom, and scored for a colorful orchestra, including xylophone, marimba, vibraphone, piano, harp and celesta, is performed for the first time by the Philadelphia Orchestra, Eugene Ormandy conducting.

9 FEBRUARY 1964

The Liverpudlian vocal quartet that assumed the name THE BEATLES (derived from the beat rather than the insect) is revealed to an expectant American public on the Ed Sullivan television show, instantly winning the hearts, eyes, ears, minds and viscera of millions of cisatlantic enthusiasts. (The Beatles presented a public concert in Washington, D.C., on 11 February 1964, as their first living contact with the subjugated American masses.)

14 FEBRUARY 1964

Concerto in C minor for cello and orchestra by the French composer Henri SAUGUET, is performed for the first time in Moscow by Mstislav Rostropovich, to whom the work is dedicated, under the direction of the composer.

17 FEBRUARY 1964

Athaliah, opera in two parts by the 51-year-old Czech-born American composer Hugo WEISGALL, based on Racine's play about Jezebel's murderous daughter, set in a lyrico-dramatic expressionistic idiom with dodecaphonic parameters, is performed for the first time by the Concert Opera Association in New York, conducted by its founder and director Thomas Scherman.

18 FEBRUARY 1964

Alexander bis, opera buffa in one act by Bohuslav MARTINU, is posthumously produced for the first time in Mannheim.

25 FEBRUARY 1964

Concerto-Monologue for cello and orchestra by the Soviet composer Lev KNIPPER, is performed for the first time in Moscow by Mstislav Rostropovich, to whom the concerto is dedicated.

6 MARCH 1964

Third Symphony by Ross Lee FINNEY, in three movements, each subdivided into three sections, each of the latter containing three themes of dodecaphonic connotations, is performed for the first time by the Philadelphia Orchestra, Eugene Ormandy conducting.

6 MARCH 1964

The Swedish pianist Karl-Erik Welin wounds himself in the knee with a power saw during the Stockholm performance of an enhanced piano piece by Knut WIGGEN requiring the explosion of a pyrotechnical device purporting to be a charge of dynamite and sawing off the legs of the piano preliminary to working over the keyboard with the intention of demolishing it, too. (Welin's knee injury was not grave, and the prognosis excellent. Because of his failure to operate the power saw properly, the Swedish music critic Sten Broman suggested the incorporation of classes in power saw handling at the Stockholm High School of Music.)

12 MARCH 1964

Benjamin BRITTEN conducts in Moscow the world première of his *Cello Symphony*, with Mstislav Rostropovich, to whom it is dedicated, as soloist.

13 MARCH 1964

Concerto in E major for cello and orchestra by the Soviet composer Boris TCHAIKOVSKY, unrelated to his great namesake, is performed for the first time in Moscow by Mstislav Rostropovich, to whom the work is dedicated.

13 MARCH 1964

Fifth Symphony, subtitled *Jephtha's Daughter*, by Ernst TOCH, in one movement (completed on 18 May 1963), coloristically scored for large orchestra that includes gong, chimes, xylophone, vibraphone, Chinese temple blocks and an anvil, depicting in melodramatic tones the tragic Biblical story of Jephtha's sacrifice of his daughter in obedience to the cruel command of the barbarous Jehovah, is performed for the first time by the Boston Symphony Orchestra, Erich Leinsdorf conducting.

15 MARCH 1964

Yolimba, oder Die Grenzen der Magie, opera "in one act and four love songs" by the 36-year-old German composer Wilhelm KILLMAYER, dealing with a televisonary robotesse scientifically furnished with supernumerary aphrodisiac organs, who shoots every man uttering or muttering the word love, but reaches the limits of her magic (hence the title) in her encounter with a sexless technician, and retreats to her native electronic world, is produced in Wiesbaden.

22 MARCH 1964

Royal Invitation, orchestral suite subtitled *Homage to the Queen of Tonga* by the 36-year-old American composer Dominick ARGENTO, is performed for the first time by the St. Paul Philharmonic in Minneapolis.

25 MARCH 1964

The octogenarian composer Robert STOLZ conducts at the Volksoper in Vienna the première of his 51st operetta, *Frühjahrs-Parade*, depicting the power of Viennese love in three different age groups, with 400 soldiers of the Austrian Army participating as non-singing marching uniformed auxiliary forces.

31 MARCH 1964

Umbrian Scene, tone poem by the 47-year-old American Negro composer Ulysses KAY, a tranquil symphonic work evoking the landscape of the Italian province of Umbria, is performed for the first time in New Orleans.

1 APRIL 1964

The Plague, oratorio by the Catalan composer Roberto GERHARD, resident in England since the Spanish Civil War, to a text from the novel of the same name by Albert Camus describing an imaginary outbreak of virulent pestilence in Oran, Algiers, in the 1940's, scored for singing, whispering, shouting, moaning and wailing voices, orchestra and air-raid sirens, is performed for the first time by the British Broadcasting Corporation in London, Antal Dorati conducting.

1 APRIL 1964

Božidar KUNC, 60-year-old Zagreb-born pianist and composer, who made his home in America from 1951, dies of a heart attack at 10:45 P.M., in a Detroit hospital, half an hour after completing a performance with the Detroit Symphony Orchestra of his *Piano Concerto* in B minor (of which he played the world première in Zagreb on 27 April 1934) at a special concert sponsored by the Croatian Board of Trade, in a program which also featured his sister, the singer Zinka Milanov.

4 APRIL 1964

Sir Gawain and the Green Knight, opera by the 33-year-old American composer Richard FELICIANO, is produced in San Francisco.

6 APRIL 1964

Elegy for J.F.K. by Igor STRAVINSKY, scored for baritone, two clarinets and corno di bassetto, to a poem by W. H. Auden, lamenting in the reverential tones of a liturgical threnody the death of an admired President fallen on 22 November 1963, based on a 12-tone series containing a proliferation of whole-tone progressions, symbolic of evil, and ending with a 3/8 bar of absolute silence, is per-

formed for the first time at one of the Monday Evening Concerts in Santa Monica, California.

15 APRIL 1964

La Venus d'Ille, lyric drama in two acts by the nonagenarian French composer Henri BÜSSER, to his own libretto relating the story of a statue of Venus found in the French provincial town of Ille who stuns a youth to death with a bracelet he playfully placed on her hand, is produced in Paris.

17 APRIL 1964

Notturno ungherese for orchestra by Miklós RÓZSA, Hungarian composer prospering in Hollywood, drawn from the remembered melorhythms of his Magyar adolescence, is performed for the first time by the Philadelphia Orchestra, Eugene Ormandy conducting.

19 APRIL 1964

Appassionata for orchestra by the German-born American composer Lothar KLEIN is performed for the first time in Dallas, Texas.

19 APRIL 1964

Montezuma, opera in three acts by Roger SESSIONS, dealing in atonally anguished colors with the fall of the last Aztec emperor, is performed for the first time anywhere in West Berlin.

20 APRIL 1964

Concerto-Symphony for cello and orchestra by the Bulgarian composer Lubomir PIPKOV, is performed for the first time in Moscow by Mstislav Rostropovich to whom the work is dedicated.

22 APRIL 1964

October, opera by Vano MURADELI, depicting in heroic Russian modalities the glorious Bolshevik Revolution of 25 October 1917, according to the Julian calendar of old Russia, corresponding to 7 November, Gregorian style, containing in the cast, for the first time on the stage, a singing part for Lenin, is performed for the first time in its complete stage version at the Palace of Congresses in the Kremlin in Moscow. (The concert version was first heard on the Moscow Radio on 5 December 1962.)

22 APRIL 1964

World's Fair Suite for orchestra by Ferde GROFÉ, in five movements epitomizing the main points of attraction of the New York World's Fair—*Unisphere, International, Fun at the Fair, Pavilions of Industry*, and *National*—performed as a specially commissioned work for the first time at the opening of the Fair, in rainy weather, for an audience of 63 people, and in the presence of the semi-paralyzed 72-year-old composer (he suffered a stroke in 1962).

24 APRIL 1964

The Swiss Exposition of Industry opens in Lausanne, architecturally reflecting the modern world in its wallless Pavilion Échange, with the world première of *Concert des Échanges* by Rolf LIEBERMANN, scored for 15 machines, including teletypes, cash registers, staplers and copying devices, timed by an electronic computer to last exactly 195 seconds.

2 MAY 1964

A memorial exhibition to mark the centennial of the death of Giacomo MEYERBEER, the sublime melodramatist of ultra-romantic operatic art, opens in his native Berlin.

7 MAY 1964

Sixth Symphony by the prime Mexican composer Carlos CHÁVEZ, in three movements, *Allegro risoluto, Adagio* and a *Passacaglia* with 43 variations, is performed for the first time as a commissioned work by the New York Philharmonic, Leonard Bernstein conducting.

8 MAY 1964

Under the auspices of the Elizabeth Sprague Coolidge Foundation, the Library of Congress presents the world premières of the piano quintets by Roberto CAAMAÑO of Argentina, Gustavo BECERRA SCHMIDT of Chile and *Structures* for piano and string quartet by the Cuban-born American composer Aurelio DE LA VEGA, in five movements, containing three structures with two intervening "mobiles."

10 MAY 1964

Epilogue to Profiles in Courage: J.F.K., a "symphonic dedication" by Roy HARRIS, lamenting in dark bitonalities punctuated by slow drum beats the loss to the world of a young American president, ending softly on the half-fulfilled promise of a G-major triad over a C-major chord, is performed for the first time in Los Angeles.

13 MAY 1964

Concerto for Cello and Orchestra by the Soviet composer Tikhon KHRENNIKOV is performed for the first time in Moscow by Mstislav Rostropovich, to whom the work is dedicated.

20 MAY 1964

At the opening concert of the Basel Festival of New Music from Germany and Switzerland, the first performance is given of *Épitaphe pour Évariste Galois,* "documented action" for soprano, baritone, narrators, speaking chorus, magnetic tape and orchestra by the 42-year-old Swiss composer Jacques WILDBERGER, depicting in six sections the tragically brief life of the French mathematician Evariste Galois, killed at the age of 20 in a duel in Paris, on 30 May 1832:

(1) *The Autopsy,* to the words of the official registry of death, detailing the exact nature of the mortal head wound; (2) *The Night before the Duel,* to the text of the last letter which Galois wrote, and concluding with the statement "Je meurs victime d'une infâme coquette," the word "coquette" being scanned to the rhythm of a mocking infernal dance; (3) *Mathematics,* depicting in a scientifically serial idiom the mathematical speculations of Galois as a schoolboy, punctuated by marginal remarks of his teachers; (4) *Politics,* presenting the facts of his republican agitation alter the mild Paris revolution of 1830, resulting in his arrest and imprisonment; (5) *The Death,* in which Galois voices

his hatred of all authoritarianism and sketches the ideas of his revolutionary mathematical theory of groups; (6) *Évariste Galois Illustre Mathématicien Français,* to the text of the inscription on the wall of the house in which Galois was born.

The mathematical achievement of Galois lies in the field of the theory of equations. He proved, with the aid of his newly developed theory of groups, that algebraic equations containing exponential powers higher than 4, cannot be solved in their general form. His discoveries formed the foundation of modern algebra. The group theory touches upon the problems of ornamentation, symmetries and permutations. Since these concepts, and particularly that of permutation, are integral parts of contemporary musical grammar, I became preoccupied with Galois. My work is an *hommage* to the unfortunate youth whose ideas are so important to us. These ideas are not "illustrated" in the music, but are present in its principle of organization. Thus, in the third section of my work, *Mathematics,* there are numerous interrelated permutation groups serving as a hidden steering system. (Elucidatory statement by Jacques Wildberger prepared at the author's request)

26 MAY 1964

A Vision of Therese, two-act opera by the 38-year-old Swedish composer Lars Johan WERLE, after Emile Zola's short story *Pour une nuit d'amour,* dealing with a provincial femme fatale who brings passion into the life of a flute-playing postal clerk, written in an idiom of anguished atonal tension, with realistic effects contributed by phonograph recordings, is performed for the first time during the Stockholm Festival of Music, Drama and Dance.

26 MAY 1964

Aaron COPLAND conducts the London Symphony Orchestra in the first performance of his *Music for a Great City* (commissioned by that orchestra on the occasion of its 60th anniversary), a symphonic cyclorama of sights and sounds of New York City, intensely realistic in its illustrative effects, in four tableaux, *Skyline, Night Thoughts, Subway Jam* and *Towards the Bridge.*

27 MAY 1964

The first International Seminar of Marxist Musicology opens in Prague, with delegates from the countries of the Socialist bloc, including the Soviet Union, East Germany, Hungary, Yugoslavia, Rumania and Bulgaria, assembled to discuss the dialectically correct interpretation of musical phenomena, in accordance with the Marxist doctrine of the identity of the real and epistemological worlds, and in the light of Lenin's theory of the sociological determinism of art.

28 MAY 1964

Taras Shevchenko, opera in four acts by the 50-year-old Ukrainian Soviet composer Georgi MAIBORODA, to his own Ukrainian libretto on the subject of the revolutionary life of the Ukrainian poet Shevchenko (1814–1861), is produced in Kiev.

28 MAY 1964

4 × 5, concerto for four quintets by the 57-year-old Russian-born Swiss composer Constantin REGAMEY, in five movements—*Perotinamente* (i. e., in the manner of Perotin), *Quasi una monodia, Condensazioni in moto, Mosaica e*

Corale, Concertando—is performed for the first time at the Basel Festival of New Music.

28 MAY 1964

The 38th Festival of the International Society for Contemporary Music opens in Copenhagen with the following program:

Konzertmusik für Blasorchester by Paul HINDEMITH, written in 1927, a defiant fanfaronade in blatant sonic outbursts of wind instruments, containing quotations from popular German music; *Muzyka epifaniczna* by Tadeusz BAIRD of Poland, first performed under the French title *Musique épiphanique* in Montreux, Switzerland, on 12 September 1963, a musical stream of consciousness, emulating the inspired glossolalia of the Apostles and the grammatic epiphany of James Joyce; *Ricercari* for orchestra by the 33-year-old Argentinian composer Antonio TAURIELLO; *Mutazioni*, four choreographic fragments for orchestra by the 37-year-old Italian composer Vittorio FELLEGARA, based on serial structures of tones and intervals; and *Fragment VI* for six orchestral groups by the 31-year-old Danish composer Per NØRGÅRD, realized in optical notation for microchronous divisions and metrical notation for macrochronous progressions.

29 MAY 1964

At the second concert of the 38th Festival of the International Society for Contemporary Music in Copenhagen, the following program of chamber music is presented:

Second Quintet for piano, clarinet, violin, viola and cello by the 31-year-old Czech composer Ilja ZELJENKA, set in a *sui generis* punctualistic idiom in which serialism is liberalized and dodecaphony mitigated by tonal centralism while rhythmic organization is governed by the contrast of symmetrical and asymmetrical figurations; *4 Pieces for String Trio* by the 34-year-old Polish modernist Boguslaw SCHAFFER, a suite of four short essays in virtuosity, demonstrating the execution of twisted sonorities, percussive effects on instrumental bodies, maximum velocity in glissandi, and diversification of pizzicati; *Being Beauteous* by the German expressionist Hans Werner HENZE, resident in Italy, for coloratura soprano, 4 cellos and harp to a poem of Rimbaud; *Pour violon et piano* by the 55-year-old Swiss-born Danish composer Gunnar BERG; *Sonant* for guitar, harp, doublebass and percussion by the Argentine-born German experimentalist Mauricio KAGEL, conceived *in statu nascenti* so that the complete execution of the work is immanently impossible, and the players are instructed to act, gesticulate and read aloud irrelevant texts borrowed from roulette (Faites votre jeu!) and from chess (Pièce touchée, Piece jouée), with instantaneous and simultaneous translation into their respective mother tongues; and *Bolos* for 4 trombones, written in collaboration by two Swedish composers, Jan BARK and Folke RABE.

30 MAY 1964

At the third concert of the 38th Festival of the International Society for Contemporary Music in Copenhagen, the following program of chamber music by Danish composers is given:

Passacaglie for flute, violin, cello and piano by the 41-year-old Poul Rovsing OLSEN, in five movements, each based on a different rhythmic mode; *Direction: inconnue* by 33-year-old Ib NORHOLM, inspired by a one-way street sign in which the direction of the arrow is ambiguous; *Cantata* for contralto and seven instruments by 40-year-old Axel BORUP-JORGENSEN; and *In Terra Pax* for clarinet, piano and percussion by 32-year-old Pelle GUDMUNDSEN-HOLMGREEN.

30 MAY 1964

In the course of the 18th Festival at Ojai, California, a program of international avant-garde and electronic music is given:

Samstirni by the Icelandic composer Magnus Blöndal JOHANNSSON; *Ensembles for Synthesizer* by Milton BABBITT, of the Columbia-Princeton Electronic Music Center; *Duo for Clarinet and Recorded Clarinet* by William O. SMITH, originally produced at the Studio di Fonologia Musicale in Milan; *Mikrostruktury* by the Polish composer Wlodzimierz KOTOŃSKI, recorded at the Experimental Studio of the Polish State Radio in Warsaw; *Rhythm Studies* on perforated piano tape by the American-born composer Conlon NANCARROW, living in Mexico and recorded in his home studio; *Events* by Mel Powell, prepared at the Electronic Music Studio at Yale University; *Tautalogos II* by Luc FERRARI, produced at the Centre de Recherche of the Radiodiffusion-Télévision Française in Paris; *La Sonate et les trois messieurs ou comment parler musique*, a surrealistic glossolalia by the French actor Jean TARDIEU, in which three people talk colloquially about the phenomenon of sonata form and its effect on the impressionable mind; *Selektion I* by Herbert EIMERT, produced at the Studio für Elektronische Musik in Cologne; and *Coordinates for Magnetic Tape* by the Cuban-Californian composer Aurelio DE LA VEGA, produced at the San Fernando Valley State College Electronic Laboratory in Northridge, California, in three movements: *Polynomial, Acoustical Measurements* and *Vectors*.

31 MAY 1964

The Mozart Express is launched by the Austrian Federal Railways, running between Vienna and Paris, leaving Vienna at 8:10 A.M., and after a stop at Salzburg, Mozart's birthplace, arriving in Paris at 11 P.M. (A train named Mozart Express was also run by the U.S. Occupation Forces between Munich and Vienna, during the period of 1946–1955.)

1 JUNE 1964

At the fourth concert of the 38th Festival of the International Society for Contemporary Music in Copenhagen, the following program is presented:

Diaglyphen for chamber orchestra by the 40-year-old German composer Günther BECKER, in which the sonorous materials are arranged in three categories, alpha, beta and gamma, corresponding to the horizontality, verticality and diagonality of spatial and temporal parameters; *Concerto rapsodico* for voice and orchestra by the 40-year-old Austrian composer Karl Heinz FÜSSL, esthetically conceived on the geodesic line connecting Mahler with Berg; *Hi-Kyo* for flute, piano, strings and percussion by the 34-year-old Japanese composer Kazuo FUKUSHIMA, the title meaning literally a flying mirror, the music combining traditional oriental elements with western serialism; *Tre occasioni* for soprano and orchestra by the 34-year-old Italian composer Girolamo ARRIGO, written to demonstrate that creative action may result from occasional opportunities; *Offrandes* for soprano and chamber orchestra by Edgar VARÈSE; and *Genesis II* for 15 performers by the 30-year-old Polish avant-garde composer Henryk GÓRECKI.

2 JUNE 1964

At the fifth concert of the 38th Festival of the International Society for Contemporary Music in Copenhagen, the following program is presented:

Movimento for harpsichord, piano and 9 wind instruments by the 36-year-old Italian composer Franco DONATONI, conceived as a serialized set of variations, in which the antagonism between the harpsichord and piano is neutralized by the intervention of the brass; *Lyric Songs* for mezzo soprano and 2 pianos by the 33-year-old German composer Dieter SCHÖNBACH in which the German verses are treated as sonic verbalities to he integrated into the musical fabric; *Alpha-Beth* for six wind instruments by the 27-year-old French composer Gilbert AMY, written as an exercise in modern sonorities; *String Quartet* by the 38-year-old Hungarian composer György KURTAG, in six movements with free thematic associations in non-dodecaphonic atonalities; *Impressions d'un Choral* for harpsichord by the 19-year-old Bulgarian-born Israeli composer Yitshak SADAI, in which the melodic materials of Bach's chorale *O Haupt voll Blut und Wunden* is organized hendecaphonically in two unequal tone-rows of six and five notes; and *The World Is Discovered*, instrumental motet in 6 movements by the 29-year-old English composer Harrison BIRTWISTLE.

3 JUNE 1964

The 38th Festival of the International Society for Contemporary Music in Copenhagen concludes with the following program of orchestral music:

Metamorphose II by the 32-year-old Catalan composer Enrique RAXACH, in 15 sections forming three main divisions, organized according to contrasts of rhythms and timbres: *Equivalences* by the 25-year-old French composer Jean Claude ÉLOY, striving to achieve a serene equilibration of contrasting dynamic, rhythmic and instrumental elements with Zen-like pauses of total immobility; *7 Hai-kai*, Japanese sketches by Olivier MESSIAEN, with the participation of the electronic keyboard instrument, Ondes Martenot; *Wisnania* (*Confessions*), three symphonic poems by the 37-year-old Polish composer Witold SZALONEK, for narrator, chorus and orchestra, in expressionist colors; *Faglarna* (*The Birds*) by the 52-year-old Finnish composer Erik BERGMAN, for baritone and a chamber ensemble in which coloristic instruments predominate, designed to picture the human desire to fly away into the light of outer space; and *Nausikaa ensam* for soprano, chorus and orchestra by the 43-year-old Swedish composer Ingvar LIDHOLM, written in a neo-romantic quasi-expressionistic style.

3 JUNE 1964

Martin's Lie, chamber opera by Gian Carlo MENOTTI, to his own libretto, in which a 12-year-old medieval orphan boy shelters a heretic and refuses unto death to reveal his hiding place to the inquisitors, is performed for the first time anywhere at the opening of the 17th consecutive Music Festival in Bath, England.

3 JUNE 1964

The Photo of the Colonel, opera in three acts by the English composer Humphrey SEARLE, to a play by the Rumanian-Parisian dramatist of the theater of the absurd Eugène Ionesco, dealing with a maniacal killer who terrorizes the townspeople by inquiries about "the photo of the colonel" and then murdering them, with the music based on three groups of four chromatically adjacent tones aggregating to a dodecaphonic series, is performed for the first time on the stage in Frankfurt. (The first concert performance was broadcast by the British Broadcasting Corporation on 8 March 1964, the composer conducting.)

4 JUNE 1964

Demeter, ballet by Boris BLACHER, is performed for the first time in Hannover.

6 JUNE 1964

Karl Marx, oratorio by the 31-year-old Estonian composer Jään RÄÄTS, to texts from Marx, employing spoken words as well as singing voices with an orchestral accompaniment, is performed for the first time in Tallin.

7 JUNE 1964

In the course of the centennial celebration of the birth of Richard STRAUSS, his unfinished mythological opera, *Des Esels Schatten*, focused on an ass's currier at the time of the "laughing philosopher" and father of the atomistic theory of matter Democritus, featuring a fauna of frogs, storks, tooth extractors and didactic scholars, arranged in six scenes from an incomplete manuscript by Karl Haussner, is presented for the first time in Ettal.

9 JUNE 1964

Louis GRUENBERG, Russian-born American-bred composer, whose opera *The Emperor Jones* momentarily gave the illusion of an American epic of the musical theater, and whose experiments in symphonic jazz earned him a footnote in modern music history, dies in Los Angeles in his 80th year.

11 JUNE 1964

A century has elapsed since the birth of the great German master of modern romantic music Richard STRAUSS.

11 JUNE 1964

English Eccentrics, "an entertainment in two acts" by the 32-year-old Australian composer Malcolm WILLIAMSON, a review in music of the history of British social non-conformists, is performed for the first time at the Aldeburgh Festival.

12 JUNE 1964

Paučina (The Weaving), opera by the 32-year-old Macedonian composer Toma PROŠEV, a sociopsychological drama portraying the lives of Slavic emigrants in America, is produced in Rijeka (Fiume).

12 JUNE 1964

First Symphony by the 20-year-old Polish composer Krzysztof MEYER is performed for the first time in Cracow.

13 JUNE 1964

Curlew River, "parable for church performance" by Benjamin BRITTEN, inspired by a medieval Japanese *No* play, with the action transferred to an ungeographic Curlew River in East Anglia, wherein a woman searching for her lost son learns that he has drowned in it, with an all-male cast, an orchestra of seven players, and singers voicing their parts in half-spoken sounds, while the contrapuntal fabric is decussated into sparse Spartan patterns, is performed for the first time in Orford Church as part of the Aldeburgh, England, Music Festival.

16 JUNE 1964

Ernst KRENEK conducts in Hamburg the first performance of his opera *Der goldene Bock* (*The Golden Ram*), to his own libretto in which the Argonaut Jason inadvertently breaks the time barrier, finds himself on Route 66 in the United States, marries the termagant Medea, divorces her after she serves him a dish of human soup made of the flesh of a Greek shipping magnate and flies back in time and space to ancient Greece in a jet plane called Chrysomallos (i.e., golden fleece), which is attacked by Medea transformed into a dinosaursized dragon (she is thrown off the liner and perishes), with an ironic finale when Greek customs officers seize the golden fleece as contraband, the music written in a complex but logically impeccable serial idiom embellished by pre-recorded electronic sounds.

21 JUNE 1964

Faust III, operatic trilogy by the Danish composer Nils Viggo BENTZON, to his own libretto, in which Goethe's *Faust*, James Joyce's Bloom in *Ulysses* and Kafka's Josef K. in *The Trial* are psychologically related through their fantasies of feminine projections and magical Mephistos, is produced for the first time in Kiel at the opening of a Scandinavian-German Music Festival.

25 JUNE 1964

Le Chant du dépossédé (The Song of the Dispossessed), after Mallarmé, for narrator, baritone and orchestra by the 40-year-old French composer Serge NIGG, is performed for the first time in Strasbourg.

27 JUNE 1964

Tongues of Fire, oratorio by the 38-year-old Greek composer Jani CHRISTOU, to a text from the liturgical ritual of Epiphany, composed in a *sui generis* serial technique of isotones and isochrones and culminating in a magisterial canonic glossolalia uttered by intrapuntally involved speaking chorus, is performed for the first time at the Bach Festival in Oxford, England.

1 JULY 1964

Pierre MONTEUX, grand old man of French music, whose unobtrusive command of the orchestra inspired respect of his musicians and admiration of his composers, dies in his American summer home at Hancock, Maine in his 90th year, a few months after the conclusion of his last tour as guest conductor of European orchestras.

3 JULY 1964

The Lady from Colorado, one-act opera by the American composer Robert WARD, his third opera and dealing with a real-life Irish immigrant girl whose spectacular marriage to a titled Englishman in a booming Colorado mining town in 1875 created a sensation in American society, is performed for the first time at the restored old opera house in Central City, Colorado.

4 JULY 1964

Concerto for Two Pianos and Orchestra by Walter PISTON is performed for the first time at the Second Congregation of the Arts at Dartmouth College, Hanover, New Hampshire.

15 JULY 1964

Morvoren, opera by the 34-year-old English composer Philip CANNON, to a libretto concerning an attractive Cornish mermaid who lures a susceptible altar boy to her aquatic realm, set to music in an expressionistically serialistic idiom, is performed for the first time in London.

24 JULY 1964

Don Rodrigo, opera by the prime composer of Argentina, Alberto GINASTERA, in nine scenes, each designated by a classical form (Rondo, Suite, Melodrama, Caccia and Scherzo, Nocturne and Duo, Aria Ternary Form, Canon and Aria, Arch Form), dealing with the semi-legendary 15th-century Spanish warrior Don Rodrigo who wages a patriotic war against the Moors, written in a dodecaphonic idiom enhanced by spatial serialism (12 dodecaphonic hunting horns are sounded from different points of compass in the hall to illustrate Don Rodrigo's desperate search for his beloved running in nude terror in the crepuscular forest; prophetic bells of liberty fill the hall ubiquitously in the scene of his death), is performed for the first time at the Teatro Colón in Buenos Aires as a specially commissioned work by the Argentine government.

2 AUGUST 1964

Piano Concerto by Vincent PERSICHETTI is performed for the first time at the Congregation of the Arts, Dartmouth College, Hanover, New Hampshire.

7 AUGUST 1964

André JOLIVET conducts in Mexico City the first performance of his *Third Symphony*, in four contrasting movements marked *Obstiné, Fulgural, Lyrique* and *Véhément*.

12 AUGUST 1964

Sinfonia Sacra, by Andrzej PANUFNIK, Polish composer resident in England, is performed for the first time at the Palace of Monaco as the prize-winning work in an international competition.

12 AUGUST 1964

I Hear an Army for soprano and string quartet by the 27-year-old American composer David DEL TREDICI, based on a poem by James Joyce, is performed for the first time in Tanglewood, Massachusetts.

12 AUGUST 1964

Sinfonia Sacra by Andrzej PANUFNIK, 50-year-old expatriate Polish composer, based on medieval plainchant of the Polish church, opening with three "visions" and concluding with a hymn based on *"Bogurodzica,"* a legendary Polish hymn of immense political and religious content, scored for four quadraphonically spaced trumpets, strings, percussion and orchestra, is performed for the first time in Monte Carlo, after receiving first prize in the Prix de Composition Musicale Prince Ranier III de Monaco.

23 AUGUST 1964

Abraham and Isaac, sacred ballad for baritone and chamber orchestra by Igor STRAVINSKY, written in an expressive dodecaphonic idiom, to the original Hebrew text from Genesis, is performed for the first time in Jerusalem in a concert hall situated in the immediate Vicinity of Mt. Moriah where an angel of the Lord stayed Abraham's hand as he was about to carry out the abominable act of filicide as originally ordered by the inhuman and treacherous Jehovah, with Stravinsky's Boswellian famulus Robert Craft conducting in the presence of the composer.

27 AUGUST 1964

Non-Stop for piano by the innovative master of Polish musical modernism Boguslaw SCHAEFFER is performed for the first time by a relay team of two pianists at the first Polish Happening in Cracow, with a total duration of eight hours.

30 AUGUST 1964

Concertino for piano, strings and percussion by the 29-year-old Greek composer Theodore ANTONIOU, written in a serial idiom in which the fundamental tone row grows cumulatively from an embryonic diatonic cellule, is performed for the first time in Athens.

3 SEPTEMBER 1964

Cello Concerto by the 61-year-old South African composeress Priaulx RAINIER is performed for the first time in London.

5 SEPTEMBER 1964

The entire company of La Scala of Milan opens its month-long guest season with a performance of PUCCINI's opera *Turandot*, at the Bolshoi Theater in Moscow, the first major European opera company to visit Soviet Russia.

5 SEPTEMBER 1964

A set of four stamps with portraits of the prime Rumanian composer of modern times, Georges ENESCO, is issued by Rumania on the occasion of the Third International Enesco Festival of Music and Drama in Bucharest.

6 SEPTEMBER 1964

The Water and the Fire, dramatic oratorio in four scenes by the English composer Anthony MILNER, on the theme of man's alienation from God, is performed for the first time in Herford, England, in the course of the Three Choirs Festival.

6 SEPTEMBER 1964

Hyperion, a "lyric spectacle" by the 44-year-old Italian conductor and composer Bruno MADERNA, is performed for the first time at the Venice Festival.

10 SEPTEMBER 1964

Vox Maris, symphonic poem by Georges ENESCO, his last work, completed by him a year before his death, symbolizing in romantic modalities the fate of a sailor lured by the "voice of the sea" to a watery grave, is performed for the first time in Bucharest.

17 SEPTEMBER 1964

Der Zerrissene, opera in two acts by Gottfried von EINEM, to a libretto arranged by Boris Blacher from a novel by Johann Nestroy, dealing with a disillusioned capitalist who finds that capital cannot buy happiness, set to music in an ostentatiously tonal manner immersed in a plasma of non-toxic dissonances and polytriadic parallelisms, is produced in Hamburg.

18 SEPTEMBER 1964

Carlos CHÁVEZ conducts in Mexico City the first performance of his orchestral *Resonancias*, commissioned by the Secretariat of Public Education in Mexico to celebrate the inauguration of the National Archeological Museum in Chapultepec, a polyphonic essay in ordered thematic resonances and rationally copulated dissonances, in a *sui generis* serial technique in which melorhythmic patterns are never duplicated, concluding with a serenely placed hendecaphonic chord.

20 SEPTEMBER 1964

Le nouveau locataire (The New Lodger), opera in one act by the 40-year-old avant-garde Croatian composer Milko KELEMEN, after a whimsical play by Ionesco, is produced in Münster, Germany.

22 SEPTEMBER 1964

Fiddler on the Roof, nostalgic musical depicting the life of intermittently pogromized Jews in Czarist Russia with music by Jerry BOCK and choreography by Jerome Robbins, opens in New York, destined to become one of the most durable popular musical spectacles in Broadway history.

1 OCTOBER 1964

The East Is Red, militant song of the Chinese Communist Party, is sung for the first time in Peking by a myriad of young Socialist voices. (Date obtained from Guozi Shudian, China Publications Center in Peking. A recording of the song was broadcast from space by the first Chinese satellite launched on 23 April 1970.)

1 OCTOBER 1964

Ernst TOCH, enlightened composer of symphonies, concertos, chamber operas, string quartets and other music, written in a cultured manner of modern romanticism, dies at the age of seventy-six in Los Angeles where he found his third home after his native Vienna and adoptive Berlin.

5 OCTOBER 1964

Meditation on Zeami, symphonic poem by the American composer Alan HOVHANESS, glorifying in pentatonic sonorities of massed trumpets accompanied by clangorous bells the legendary founder of the Japanese *No* drama, is performed for the first time by the American Symphony Orchestra in New York, Leopold Stokowski conducting.

7 OCTOBER 1964

Fifth Symphony by the English composer Humphrey SEARLE, written in a serial technique in the spirit of Anton von WEBERN to whose memory the score is dedicated, is performed for the first time by the Halle Orchestra in Manchester, England.

8 OCTOBER 1964

Natalia Petrovna, opera in two acts by the 38-year-old American composer Lee HOIBY, to a libretto from Turgenev's play *A Month in the Country,* characterizing in romantic modalities distilled in modernistic ambitonalities the emotional turmoils of 19th-century Russian women, is performed for the first time at the City Center in New York.

14 OCTOBER 1964

The First Festival of American and Spanish Music opens in Madrid in the following program of orchestral music:

Symphony No. 12 by Heitor VILLA-LOBOS (written in 1957 and first performed at the First Inter-American Music Festival in Washington on 20 April 1958); *Violin Concerto* by the Spanish-born Mexican composer Rodolfo HALFFTER, on his first visit of his native land; *Sinfonia* by the Cuban-American composer Aurelio DE LA VEGA (first performed at the Second Inter-American Music Festival in Washington On 30 April 1961), in four movements, *Obertura, Himno, Ostinato, Toccata,* based on four distinct dodecaphonic series fertilized by luxuriant rhythms; and *Lyric* for orchestra by the Canadian composer Harry SOMERS.

15 OCTOBER 1964

On the occasion of the 50th anniversary of the American Society of Composers, Authors and Publishers the United States Post Office issues a commemorative 5-cent stamp, depicting a lute, a clarion and an oblong music box.

15 OCTOBER 1964

Cole PORTER, American lyricist-composer, author of the nostalgic chromatic song *Night and Day,* the tropically pulsating, punningly sophisticated dance *Begin the Beguine,* and a number of other great melodies, dies of a kidney ailment in Santa Monica, California, at the age of 71.

15 OCTOBER 1964

At the second concert of the First Festival of Music of America and Spain in Madrid, the following program of chamber music is given:

Música para Muñecos de Trapo for clarinet and string quartet by the 64-year-old Spanish composer Victorino ECHEVARRIA, in five picturesque episodes depicting life among puppets; *String Quartet,* subtitled *Carlos III,* by the estimable Spanish composer of folkloristic Iberian music Conrado DEL CAMPO (1879–1953); *Quintet* for wind instruments by the prime composer of Chile Domingo SANTA CRUZ; and *Quintet* for piano and string quartet by the Mexican composer Blas GALINDO.

17 OCTOBER 1964

At the third concert of the First Festival of Music of America and Spain in Madrid, the following program of orchestral music is given:

Preludio Sinfónico by the Colombian composer Roberto PINE-DA-DUQUE; *Canticum in P. P. Johannem XXIII* by Ernesto HALFFTER of Spain; *Sinfonía* by Celso GARRIDO LECCA of Peru (first performed at the Second Inter-American Music Festival in Washington on 22 April 1960), in three contrasting movements based on a 12-tone series; and *10 Melodías Vascas* for orchestra by the Basque composer Jesús GURIDI (1886–1959) originally performed on 12 December 1941 by the Madrid Symphony Orchestra, based on authentic Basque tunes.

17 OCTOBER 1964

Couleurs de la Cité céleste, an apocalyptic suite by Olivier MESSIAEN, scored for a large orchestra with a resonant assortment of tinkling, banging and tintinnabulating percussion instruments, superadded upon ornithological chirping, twitting and crackling sounds of two birds from New Zealand and one from Brazil, is performed for the first time at the Donaueschingen Festival, under the direction of Pierre Boulez.

19 OCTOBER 1964

At the First Festival of American and Spanish Music in Madrid the following program is given:

Nonet for Solo Strings by Aaron COPLAND (first performed in Dumbarton Oaks on 2 March 1961), dedicated to Nadia Boulanger and performable by groups of 24, 36, or 48 instrumentalists; *Suite* for harp, strings and percussion by Virgil THOMSON, in three movements, in a world première, with Nicanor Zabaleta as soloist; *Capriccio* for harp and string orchestra by Walter PISTON, a world première, performed by Zabaleta; *Partita* for strings by Enrique SOLARES of Guatemala, in four movements of atonal connotation; and *Concerto Breve* of considerable duration by the Catalan composer Xavier MONTSALVATGE.

21 OCTOBER 1964

At the First Festival of American and Spanish Music in Madrid the following program of orchestral music is given:

Obertura Grotesca by the Spanish-born Argentinian composer Julian BAUTISTA (1901–1961), composed in 1932; *Concerto* for piano and orchestra by the Argentinian composer Roberto CAAMAÑO in three neo-classical movements; *Rutas* by the Dominican composer Manuel SIMO, in four movements in the neo-classical vein; *New England Episodes* by Quincy PORTER (first performed at the First Inter-American Music Festival at Washington on 18 April 1958); and *Concerto for Orchestra* by the Venezuelan composer Antonio ESTEVEZ.

22 OCTOBER 1964

At the First Festival of American and Spanish Music in Madrid the following program is given:

Cesuras by the Spanish composer Luis DE PABLO, for double trio of woodwind and string instruments consisting of freely serialized episodes separated by important pauses (hence the title); *Sincronismos No. 2* by the Argentinian composer Mario DAVIDOVSKY in which the basic instrumental quartet (flute, clarinet, violin and cello) is synchronized with a pre-recorded magnetic tape; *Lamentos* by the Peruvian composer Pozzi ESCOT, for voice and instruments, to the disembodied, dismembered and disfigured verbal elements taken from James Joyce and other authors, in five sections, each containing seventeen sound events; *Preludio* for magnetic tape by José Vicente ASUAR of Chile; *Composition for IBM Computer 7090* by Gerald STRANG of the U.S.; *Mixturas* by

Carmelo A. BERNAOLA of Spain, representing a painter's color mixtures; and *Constantes Rítmicas en el Modo Primero* by José SOLER of Spain.

24 OCTOBER 1964

The Virgin and the Faun, one-act opera by the Hungarian-born Californian composer Eugene ZÁDOR, wherein an impoverished family is compelled to sell their prized possession, a Renaissance painting of a shepherdess and a faun, with a happy ending secured when its young purchaser proposes to the daughter of the family, retaining the painting in their common home, written in a candidly harmonious and ostentatiously melodious manner, is performed for the first time anywhere by the Opera Workshop at the University of California, Los Angeles, with a piano accompaniment in the absence of an orchestra.

24 OCTOBER 1964

At the First Festival of American and Spanish Music in Madrid the following program is given:

Third Symphony in four movements, by the Chilean composer Juan ORREGO-SALAS; *Variaciones sobre un Tema Nordestino* for piano and orchestra by the Brazilian composer Camargo GUARNIERI; *Te Deum* by the Uruguayan composer Hector TOSAR; and *Sinfonia Sevillana* by the Spanish composer of the old nationalist school Joaquín TURINA.

26 OCTOBER 1964

At the First Festival of American and Spanish Music in Madrid the following program of chamber music is presented:

Second String Quartet by Roberto GERHARD, Catalan composer residing in England; *String Quartet* by Francisco ESCUDERO of Spain; *Soli II* for wind quintet by Carlos CHÁVEZ of Mexico; and *Quintet* for piano and string quartet by the Chilean composer Gustavo BECERRA SCHMIDT.

27 OCTOBER 1964

To reciprocate the visit of the La Scala troupe in Russia in September 1964, the Bolshoi Theater Opera Company of Moscow goes to Milan for a season of 23 performances, opening with a spectacularly colorful presentation of the unabridged version of Mussorgsky's *Boris Godunov*, the only alteration being the elimination from the cast of characters of the name Khrushchev (odious since Nikita Khrushchev's fall from Soviet power on 14 October 1964), which appears in Pushkin's drama and in Mussorgsky's opera, replacing it with an anonymous designation "nobleman."

28 OCTOBER 1964

At the First Festival of American and Spanish Music in Madrid the following program is given:

El Retablo de Maese Pedro, puppet play by Manuel DE FALLA; *Concierto de Estio* for violin and orchestra by the blind Spanish composer Joaquín RODRIGO; and *Improperios*, a sacred chorus by the Spanish composer Federico MOMPOU.

30 OCTOBER 1964

Vérnász, opera in three acts by the 33-year-old Hungarian composer Sándor SZOKOLAY, after the mystical play *Bodas de Sangre* by Federico García Lorca, dealing with a bloody feud between two village families, culminating in an elopement of a married man with his rival's lethal bride (she is a symbol of Death incarnate) on her wedding day, leading to the death of both contenders and the retribution in blood dealt to her as well, is produced in Budapest.

30 OCTOBER 1964

The 13th Festival of Chamber Music opens in the Coolidge Auditorium of the Library of Congress in Washington to commemorate the centennial of the birth of Elizabeth Sprague Coolidge, the founder of the festival, with a program including PURCELL's ode, *Celebrate This Festival*, and three world premières:

Parole di San Paolo by Luigi DALLAPICCOLA, for voice and instruments, set in a dramatic dodecaphonic style of Italian provenance, with the composer conducting; *In Time of Daffodils* by Riccardo MALIPIERO, dodecaphonic nephew of Gian Francesco Malipiero, a set of five songs to the texts by e. e. Cummings, scored for soprano, baritone and a chamber ensemble; and *Miserere Nobis*, a Mass for 18 wind instruments by the German modernist Giselher KLEBE, set in uncompromisingly dissonant Gothic counterpoint. (Aaron Copland's *Appalachian Spring*, originally commissioned by the Coolidge Foundation and performed for the first time at the 10th Coolidge Festival on 30 October 1944, was also included in the program.)

31 OCTOBER 1964

The First Festival of American and Spanish Music in Madrid concludes with the following program of orchestral music:

Second Symphony by the Panamanian composer Roque CORDERO; *Sinfonía de Don Rodrigo*, comprising three excerpts from the opera *Don Rodrigo* by Argentina's prime modernist Alberto GINASTERA; *Secuencias* by Cristóbal HALFFTER, ultra-modernistic nephew of Rodolfo and Ernesto Halffter, opening with an explosion of undifferentiated homogeneous noise as a manifestation of the primordial sonic universe, and progressing toward total organization and serialization of sonorous elements (first performed in Madrid on 16 June 1964); and the world première of *Sinfonia Aitana* (surnamed after a lofty mountain chain in the Levant), by the 78-year-old Spanish composer Oscar ESPLÁ, subtitled *A la música tonal, in memoriam*, as a gesture of resignation in the face of the decline of time-honored tonal concepts.

31 OCTOBER 1964

The second concert of the 13th Coolidge Festival in Washington continues with an afternoon program containing vocal pieces by MOZART and BEETHOVEN and the following pieces by modern composers:

Quartetto per Elisabetta, dedicatory piece by Gian Francesco MALIPIERO, in one movement, for string quartet; first performance of *Amaryllis*, variations for string trio by William SCHUMAN, based on an old English round and dedicated to the memory of Elizabeth Sprague Coolidge; *First String Quartet* by PROKOFIEV, originally composed for an early Coolidge festival in 1930; and the world première of *String Septet* by Darius MILHAUD, in four movements of which the second, subtitled *Étude de hasard dirigé*, represents a modernistic interplay of directed chance.

The evening program of 31 October 1964 contained a cantata by SCHUBERT; the first performance of *Sonata a quattro* by the Chilean Composer Juan ORREGO-SALAS, scored for flute, oboe, doublebass and harpsichord, in four movements; first performance of *Four Psalms* by Howard HANSON for baritone, two violins, two violas and two cellos; *Fifth String Quartet* by Béla BARTÓK, originally composed for a Coolidge Festival in 1934; and the first performance of *String Sextet* by Walter PISTON, in three movements of varied content in a neo-baroque manner.

31 OCTOBER 1964

Oblaci (The Clouds) by the 70-year-old Croatian composer Krešimir BARANOVIĆ, scored for mezzo-soprano and orchestra, is performed for the first time in Belgrade.

1 NOVEMBER 1964

At the afternoon concert of the 13th Coolidge Festival in Washington, the following program is given:

Come, Ye Sons of Art, cantata by Henry PURCELL; the world premiere of *Cantata* by the Cuban-Californian composer Aurelio DE LA VEGA, scored for two sopranos, contralto and chamber orchestra, in three movements, based on a dodecaphonic series: *Introduction, Contrapunctus primus, Contrapunctus secundus;* the world première of *The Feast of Love* by Virgil THOMSON for baritone and chamber orchestra, to the text from *Pervigilium Veneris*, written in an evocatively archaizing manner; *Herodiade*, orchestral recitation by Paul HINDEMITH; and the world première of *Bomarzo*, cantata for narrator, baritone and chamber orchestra by the prime composer of Argentina Alberto GINASTERA, in six sections, *The Horoscope, The Metaphysical Anxiety, The Portrait, In Search of Love, The Monsters of the Sacred Forest* and *Eternity of Bomarzo*, a dramatic hexalogy recounting the fateful career of the 16th-century hunch-hacked Prince Pier Francesco Orsini, Duke of Bomarzo, whose quest for immortality leads him to murder in the company of mystical alchemists and caballistic astrologers, eventuating in the transformation of the rocks in his garden into giant monsters in the gaping mouth of one of which he perishes, set to music employing a number of ultra-modern serial techniques, including the application of the involutes, evolutes and spirals of the *Grossmutterakkord* (invertible dodecaphonic all-interval chord invented by Nicolas Slonimsky on 13 February 1938).

4 NOVEMBER 1964

Napuštene (The Abandoned Ones, also known under the title *Las Apasionadas)*, ballet by the 40-year-old modernistic Croatian composer Milko KELEMEN, after a text by Federico García Lorca, is produced in Lübeck.

6 NOVEMBER 1964

Carnegie Hall is proclaimed a "Registered National Historic Landmark," and an appropriate plaque is unveiled in a special ceremony by Mayor Wagner of New York and representatives of the National Parks Service.

12 NOVEMBER 1964

One-Man Show, chamber opera by the 29-year-old British composer Nicholas MAW, dealing with an impecunious young art student whose back is discovered to be tattooed in a theoretically abstract pattern (actually it spells JOE upside down), and who therefore becomes the target of covetous art dealers, is performed for the first time in London.

13 NOVEMBER 1964

Gesangszene for baritone and orchestra, last work by the German master of symphonic counterpoint Karl Amadeus HARTMANN, to texts from the German translation of *Sodome et Gomorrhe* by Jean Giraudoux, is performed for the first time at Frankfurt, with an ending in speaking voice, following indications given by Hartmann himself at his deathbed on 15 December 1963.

15 NOVEMBER 1964

At the annual World Series of Roller Canaries in New York City, a quartet of canaries from Stony Creek, Ontario, is declared the winner for their excellence in schockels (a chuckling ha-ha-ha-ho-ho-ho), glucks (vocalized hen-like clucks), water rolls (gurgling trills) and flageolets (do-de-do-de), and for their scarcity of point-losing schwirrs (tearing sounds), locken (whistling), schnarrs (unvocal sibilation), aufzug (wheezing), schnatters and schnetters (a variety of schnarrs).

18 NOVEMBER 1964

Shunkan (The Banishment), one-act opera by the 53-year-old Japanese composer Osamu SHIMIZU, based on the folk tale of a rebellious priest exiled in 1177 to a desert island by the Japanese feudal lords, is produced in Tokyo.

21 NOVEMBER 1964

Willem van Saeftinge, opera by the 35-year-old Dutch composer Freddy DEVREESE, to a historical libretto, portraying the pragmatism of ecclesiastical authorities in medieval Flanders, is performed for the first time in Antwerp.

21 NOVEMBER 1964

Concerto for clarinet and orchestra by the American composer Easley BLACKWOOD is performed for the first time in Cincinnati.

26 NOVEMBER 1964

La nuit foudroyée, opera in four acts by the 36-year-old French composer Jacques BONDON, in which a diurnal man is held in thrall by a nocturnal woman who disintegrates in his arms with the dawn, is performed for the first time in concert form on the Paris Radio. (A stage production took place in Metz on 10 February 1968.)

30 NOVEMBER 1964

The Sun of the Incas, suite in six sections for soprano and 11 instruments by the 35-year-old Soviet modernist Edison DENISOV (he was named Edison because of his father's admiration for the inventive genius of Thomas Alva Edison), to the words of the Chilean Nobel-prize laureate Gabriela Mistral, and derived autonomously from a single series of 12 different notes, is performed for the first time in Leningrad.

30 NOVEMBER 1964

Tartuffe, fourth and last opera by the British composer Arthur BENJAMIN, completed shortly before his death in 1960 in vocal score, written in a relaxed opera-bouffe manner to suit Molière's comedy of hypocrisy, is performed for the first time in London under the direction of Alan Boustead who completed the orchestration of the opera.

3 DECEMBER 1964

Three Against Christmas, one-act opera by the American composer Andrew IMBRIE, dealing with the abolition of Christmas in a mythical town of Peebles, is performed for the first time at the workshop of the University of California in Berkeley.

6 DECEMBER 1964

The Pavilion of the Music Center for the Performing Arts in Los Angeles, one of the three structures erected at the cost of $33.5 million, opens its Dedication Week with a concert by the Los Angeles Philharmonic Orchestra, under the direction of its 28-year-old Indian conductor Zubin Mehta, officiating in his third season as musical director, in a program including *Fanfare* for massed brass and drums by Richard STRAUSS written by him for the Vienna Philharmonic in 1924, William SCHUMAN's *American Festival Overture,* Ottorino RESPIGHI's *Feste Romane* and BEETHOVEN's *Violin Concerto,* with Jascha Heifetz as soloist.

8 DECEMBER 1964

During the Dedication Week of the Pavilion of the Music Center for the Performing Arts in Los Angeles, the Los Angeles Philharmonic Orchestra, under the direction of Zubin Mehta, presents a program containing the First and the Ninth Symphonies of BEETHOVEN and the world première of *Elytres* (French for *elytra,* anterior pair of wings in the Coleoptera serving to protect the posterior pair) by Lukas FOSS, for twelve instruments playing only in the G clef and employing only the high half of the audible range to suggest the aleatorily aleate

motion of the insect wings, and based on the principle of controlled stochastic musical data, resulting in 12 times 24 probabilistic events during actual performance.

11 DECEMBER 1964

Alma Mahler Gropius Werfel, widow of Gustav Mahler, the divorced wife of the architect Walter Gropius (with whom she became amorously involved while still married to Mahler who was aware of this relationship and was moved to write "beautiful poems" about it), widow of the writer Franz Werfel, self-confessed inamorata of many another genius (in her memoirs, *And the Bridge is Love,* she names as her lovers Oskar Kokoschka, the painter, Paul Krammerer, the biologist, and Ossip Gabrilowitsch, the pianist), dies in New York in the fullness of her days, at the age of 85.

18 DECEMBER 1964

Concerto for koto and chamber orchestra by Henry COWELL, in three movements, the first using the characteristic descending Japanese mode (major third, minor second, major second, major third, minor second), the second set in a Western idiom, and the third combining the elements of both East and West, is performed for the first time in Philadelphia by the blind virtuoso koto player Kimio Eto, with Leopold Stokowski and the Philadelphia Orchestra.

28 DECEMBER 1964

The Execution of Stepan Razin, cantata for solo bass, chorus and orchestra by Dmitri SHOSTAKOVICH, to the text by the Soviet poet Evgeny Evtushenko, glorifying the career of the 17th-century rebel from Volga who rose against the power of the Tsar, is performed for the first time in Moscow.

1965

8 JANUARY 1965

Five Contrasts for Orchestra, a suite by the Hungarian-American composer Eugene ZÁDOR, presenting a quinquefoil of varied moods and culminating in a precipitous fugal avalanche, is performed for the first time by the Philadelphia Orchestra, Eugene Ormandy conducting.

14 JANUARY 1965

5 Métaboles, suite for orchestra by the 48-year-old French composer Henri DUTILLEUX, in five movements expressive of rhetorical metabolism in which the principal theme

of each *métabole* undergoes topological translocations suggested by the individual titles, *Incantatoire, Linéaire, Obsessionel, Torpide, Flamboyant,* written in the dissonant counterpoint of modern euphony, is performed for the first time by the Cleveland Orchestra, under the direction of George Szell.

19 JANUARY 1965

Concerto for String Quartet and Orchestra for string quartet and orchestra by Benjamin LEES, 41-year-old Manchurian-born American composer of Russian parentage, is performed for the first time in Kansas City.

20 JANUARY 1965

Alan FREED, American disc jockey who popularized the term Rock 'n' Roll to describe the stultifyingly monotonous type of syncopated music, originally known as rhythm-and-blues, whose ministrations at the turntable moved post-adolescent mobs to frenzy, and who was arrested, indicted and pleaded guilty to taking bribes, colloquially known as "payola" from publishers and recording companies to promote their inane ballads (he received a suspended sentence), dies at Palm Springs, California, at the age of 43.

20 JANUARY 1965

Requiem für Lumumba by Paul DESSAU, in 28 convulsive movements glorifying the martyred leader of Congo masses Patrice Lumumba, scored for two speakers, a speaking chorus and a wordless soprano voice, with a profusion of Central African percussion instruments, set in a dialectical dodecaphonic idiom but ending in triumphantly socialistic C-major, is performed for the first time in East Berlin.

24 JANUARY 1965

Cello Concerto by Jean MARTINON, French composer and conductor of the Chicago Symphony Orchestra, in three modernistic movements opening with a luxuriant cadenza and progressing through a passable labyrinth of asymmetrically rhythmed, polyharmonically integrated serial themes with conjugate tonal foci, is performed for the first time in Hamburg.

30 JANUARY 1965

Ukiyo (*Floating World*), ballad for orchestra by Alan HOVHANESS inspired by an old Japanese Buddhist concept of the unpredictability of fate, the music exfoliating from a single dramatic theme, and ending in a state of "controlled chaos," is performed for the first time in Salt Lake City.

2 FEBRUARY 1965

Antiphonies by the 28-year-old French composer Gilbert AMY, written for two orchestras in antiphonal competition, with a third orchestra entering the musical tournament to arbitrate polyphonic differences, is performed for the first time in Paris, with the composer and Bruno Maderna as synchronized conductors.

3 FEBRUARY 1965

Night Music II, four *Nocturnes* for violin and piano by the 35-year-old American composer George CRUMB, is performed for the first time in Buffalo, New York.

8 FEBRUARY 1965

First Symphony by the American composer Gunther SCHULLER, combining elements of formal classicism with the ingredients of the Third Stream (the term of his own invention denoting civilized jazz), is performed for the first time in Dallas.

15 FEBRUARY 1965

Die Soldaten, "pluralistic opera" by the 46-year-old German composer Bernd Alois ZIMMERMANN, based on an eighteenth-century play dealing with a naïve provincial girl whose unquenchable ambition to meet influential people leads her to yield to the psychological needs of every officer of the local garrison, is produced in Cologne. It is written in a highly original serial idiom, making use of multifarious techniques of the modern theater, from cinema to collage, incorporating in the score fragments of Bach's chorales and vesuviating epiphanies of polyrhythmic jazz, with dramatic pluralism emphasized by the subdivision of the stage into simultaneous but separate compartments.

24 FEBRUARY 1965

The Mines of Sulphur, opera by the 28-year-old English composer Richard Rodney BENNETT (the title is from one of Iago's speeches in Shakespeare's *Othello*), wherein a band of 18th-century English gypsies murder a rich old man but are driven to terrified confessions when a phantom theatrical troupe performs a play reenacting the murder, in addition contaminating them with plague, set to music in a suitably melodramatic modern idiom, permeated with non-infectious dissonances, is produced in London.

1 MARCH 1965

Clitennestra, music drama by Ildebrando PIZZETTI, depicting the classic tragedy of Clytemnestra, from her murder of Agamemnon to her death at the hands of her own children, Electra and Orestes, is produced at the Teatro alla Scala in Milan.

4 MARCH 1965

Narrative for Orchestra by the 41-year-old American composer William FLANAGAN is performed for the first time by the Detroit Symphony Orchestra.

4 MARCH 1965

In the course of the Buffalo Festival of the Arts Today a *Poème Symphonique* for 100 metronomes by the Hungarian composer György LIGETI is given its first American performance, with ten performers assigned the task of winding up the metronomes set at different speeds, the ending signalized by the expiration of the beats of the terminal metronome.

I composed my piece for 100 metronomes in 1962, partly as a sort of persiflage of chance music (believing that the little automatons can do this job better than human performers), partly as an experiment in "continuous form" resulting in a gradual "rhythmic diminuendo," the metronomes stopping one by one. Different polymetric patterns arise automatically; the slowest oscillating metronome remains alone at the end. The world première took place in September 1963 at the official party given by the burgomaster of Hilversum. All performers, with myself as conductor, wore full dress. The production was taped for television, but the film was never shown because the Senate of the City of Hilversum protested against the public showing and the burgomaster himself felt deeply offended. (From Ligeti's letter to the author, dated 21 May 1965)

5 MARCH 1965

Eighth Symphony by Walter PISTON, his first major work containing explicit dodecaphonic processes, scored for a full symphonic contingent and two nonarpeggiating harps, in three movements—(1) *Moderato mosso*, evolving from a somberly involuted 12-tone motive, with harmonic configurations anchored in tritones and perfect fourths; (2) *Lento assai*, a suite of variations marked by thematic imbrication in fugal progressions; (3) *Allegro marcato*, a propulsive rhythmic rondo, thematically purified by recurrent diatonic statements, and concluding on an ascetic thirdless C triad—is performed for the first time by the Boston Symphony Orchestra conducted by Charles Munch.

7 MARCH 1965

Third Symphony by the 31-year-old American composer Easley BLACKWOOD is performed for the first time in Chicago.

9 MARCH 1965

Gunther SCHULLER conducts the New Orleans Philharmonic Symphony Orchestra in the first performance of his orchestral *American Triptych: Three Studies in Texture*, in the following divisions:

(1) *Calder's Four Directions*, a musical realization of Alexander Calder's rotating mobiles representing a three-dimensional spatial counterpoint, with an intussusception of instrumental groups on the stage written in serial melodic formations; (2) *Pollock's Out of the Web*, illustrating Jackson Pollock's drip method of painting, applying an analogous aleatory dripping of notes and tone-colors; (3) *Davis's Swing Landscape*, written in an enriched jazz technique to convey the visual impression of paintings of Stuart Davis, with the musical course following three different tempo levels.

15 MARCH 1965

Inferno 1944, oratorio by Hellmuth Christian WOLFF, commemorating the massive Allied air assault on Dresden in 1944, is performed for the first time in Gera, East Germany.

19 MARCH 1965

The Emperor of Ice Cream, music drama by the 31-year-old American composer Roger REYNOLDS, derived from stochastically calculated probabilities of sonic incidence, is performed for the first time at the third 20th-Century Innovations Concerts in New York City, under the direction of Gunther Schuller.

25 MARCH 1965

Atomtod, opera by the 32-year-old Italian composer Giacomo MANZONI depicting in a surrealistically apocalyptic spirit the atom death of Planet Earth, with a handful of men surviving in ultra-scientific shelters but perishing in the end of mental inanition, is produced at the Piccolo Scala in Milan.

25 MARCH 1965

Lizzie Borden, opera by the 43-year-old American composer Jack BEESON, drawn from the famous parenticidal case of the 1890s in New England ("she gave her father forty whacks, and when she saw what she had done, she gave her mother forty-one"), written in a flippantly melodramatic vein, with topical allusions to hymnal chants, seasoned with expressionistic atonalities, is produced in New York.

26 MARCH 1965

On his 40th birthday Pierre BOULEZ conducts, at the Monday Evening Concerts in Los Angeles, the world première of his *Éclat* for divers instruments.

28 MARCH 1965

The Passion According to Saint Luke, oratorio by Randall THOMPSON, is performed for the first time in Boston.

2 APRIL 1965

The first stage performance of the opera *Deirdre* by the dean of Canadian composers, Healey WILLAN, to a libretto from the Irish legend of the Red Branch Knights of Ulster, set to music in a flamboyant Wagneromantic style, is presented in Toronto.

2 APRIL 1965

The Shape of Time for two antiphonal percussion and double-bass groups by the 38-year-old American composer Robert WYKES is performed for the first time in St. Louis, Missouri.

6 APRIL 1965

Das Lächeln am Füsse der Leiter, opera by the 43-year-old Italian composer Antonio BIBALO, after Henry Miller's story *The Smile at the Foot of the Ladder*, is produced at the Hamburg State Opera with a German libretto translated from the original Italian version, *Sorrisi ai piedi d'una scala*.

7 APRIL 1965

Der junge Lord, opera buffa in two acts by Hans Werner HENZE, dealing with a 19th-century Byronic English gentleman dallying in a provincial German town who manhandles a girl by mammary palpation, tears off his clothes and reveals himself as a circus ape, set to music in a mock-Verdian style, is performed for the first time in Berlin.

8 APRIL 1965

Calder Piece, by Earle BROWN for four percussion instruments silently accompanied by a mobile by Alexander Calder, is performed for the first time in Paris.

10 APRIL 1965

Philidor's Defense, symphonic poem by the 55-year-old Prague-born American composer Paul REIF, describing a famous chess game in 1858, is performed for the first time in New York.

11 APRIL 1965

The Final Ingredient, opera by the 34-year-old American composer David AMRAM, to the story of a Passover celebration by Jewish prisoners in a Nazi concentration camp, is performed for the first time as a commissioned work by the American Broadcasting Company, with the composer conducting.

11 APRIL 1965

Second Symphony by the 32-year-old Soviet composer Rodion SHCHEDRIN, in four movements, the third being a precisely notated process of tuning the orchestra, is performed for the first time in Moscow.

14 APRIL 1965

On the centennial day of Lincoln's assassination, *Abraham Lincoln Symphony* by Roy HARRIS, chronologically his tenth, for chorus, brass ensemble, two amplified pianos and percussion, in five movements, relating to five aspects of Lincoln's career, is performed for the first time at Long Beach, California.

17 APRIL 1965

A concert of Igor STRAVINSKY's music is given by the Chicago Symphony Orchestra, including two new pieces: *Variations*, based on a linear succession of twelve different thematic notes representing "musical mobiles" and *Introitus: T. S. Eliot in Memoriam*, scored for six male voices, harp, piano, viola, doublebass, four kettledrums and two gongs.

25 APRIL 1965

Concerto for Orchestra by the Catalan-born composer Roberto GERHARD, resident in England since 1936, is performed for the first time anywhere by the British Broadcasting Corporation Symphony Orchestra, in Boston during its American tour.

26 APRIL 1965

The American Symphony Orchestra, under the direction of Leopold Stokowski, gives the first integral performance of the grandiose *Fourth Symphony* by Charles IVES, composed between 1910 and 1916, in four movements:

(1) *Prelude: Maestoso adagio*, a solemnly intimate evocation of the American scene, with the hymn *Watchman, Tell Us of the Night*, as a central melodic idea; (2) *Allegretto*, derived from the music of the second movement of the *Concord Sonata*, depicting Hawthorne's transcendental ride in the "Celestial Railroad," and set in a fantastically complicated, polymetric, polyrhythmic, polyharmonic, and polycontrapuntal palimpsest, with particles of American songs, ballads and hymns strewn over the orchestral musicorama; (3) *Fugue, Andante con moto*, transcribed from Ives's *First String Quartet* written in 1896, subtitled *A Revival Meeting*, and fugally treated in a euphoniously dissonant vein; (4) *Largo maestoso*, derived from Ives's *Memorial Slow March* for organ composed in 1901 and based on the melody of the hymn *Nearer, My God, to Thee*, concluding on a philosophical concord, with drums marking time in the distance.

The esthetic program of the work is that of the searching questions of What? and Why? which the spirit of man asks of life. This is particularly the sense of the prelude. The three succeeding movements are the diverse answers in which existence replies. (From a program note written by Charles Ives for the performance of the second movement given in New York under the direction of Eugene Goossens on 29 January 1927)

30 APRIL 1965

The Torch of Prometheus, opera by the Czech composer Jan HANUŠ, wherein a modernized Prometheus steals atomic fire from heaven thus challenging the power of the monopoly of the dictatorial and imperialistic Olympus, is produced in Prague.

30 APRIL 1965

The Symphony Orchestra of the British Broadcasting Corporation presents the first of a series of six concerts of 20th-Century music at Carnegie Hall in New York with Antal Dorati, musical director, conducting. (The last concert of the series took place on 15 May 1965.)

2 MAY 1965

The Early Bird Satellite, launched by the American Telegraph and Telephone Company, transmits selections of hedonistically cosmopolitan band music from radio stations in Washington, Quebec and Portsmouth, England, and a chorus from Stockholm, in a synchronized rendition with Washington, of *Auld Lang Syne*, with 1/6 second's lag required for the radio signal to reach the satellite and bounce back to earth.

2 MAY 1965

The Seattle Symphony Orchestra, Milton Katims conductor, presents a Contemporary Festival Concert under a grant from the Rockefeller Foundation and under the auspices of the University of Washington School of Music, in the following program of first performances by American composers: *Oracles* by William BOLCOM; *Elegiac Symphony* by Donald KEATS; *Graffiti* by Roger REYNOLDS; and *Symphony of Overtures* by Donald ERB.

2 MAY 1965

Donald Erb's *Symphony of Overtures* was first performed on 11 February (not 2 May) 1965 at Indiana University in Bloomington (not the University of Washington).

4 MAY 1965

Intimation to the Living, cantata for narrator, chorus and orchestra by the Dutch composer Hans HENKEMANS, commissioned by the Artists Resistance Movement 1942–1945 of Holland, is performed for the first time in Amsterdam on the National Remembrance Day, marking the 20th anniversary of the liberation of Holland from the Nazis.

5 MAY 1965

Music for Solo Performer by the 34-year-old American composer Alvin LUCIER, in which encephalographic waves produced by a human brain activate percussion instruments, is performed for the first time in Waltham, Massachusetts.

7 MAY 1965

The Third Inter-American Music Festival opens in Washington with a program comprising the world premières of the following works:

Little Symphony by Luis Antonio ESCOBAR of Colombia; *Second Symphony,* subtitled *Billy Ascends,* by Robert EVETT of the United States, symbolizing the spiritual ascent of Billy Budd after his hanging in Herman Melville's classic story; *Concerto* for five timpani and orchestra by Jorge SARMIEN-TOS of Guatemala; *Concerto a tre* for violin, cello, piano and orchestra by Juan ORREGO-SALAS of Chile; and the first American performance of the *Sinfonia de Don Rodrigo* for dramatic soprano and orchestra by Alberto GINASTERA of Argentina.

7 MAY 1965

L'Hymne aux Morts, a suite in five movements to texts from the Vulgate, scored for a large orchestra with cow bells by Olivier MESSIAEN, chimes, gongs, and tamtams, is performed for the first time under the title *Et expecto resurrectionem mortuorum* at Sainte-Chapelle, Paris.

8 MAY 1965

In the course of the Third Inter-American Music Festival in Washington, five world premières of the following pieces of chamber music for strings are presented:

String Trio by Joaquin ORELLANA of Guatemala; *String Quartet* by Eduardo MATURANA of Chile; *Invention* for string trio by Carlos CHÁVEZ of Mexico; *Three Poems* for narrator and string quartet by Pozzi ESCOT of Peru; and *Second String Quartet* by Ezra LADERMAN of the United States.

9 MAY 1965

In the course of the Third Inter-American Music Festival in Washington, the following works are performed for the first time:

Rondo Rhapsody for orchestra by John VINCENT of the United States; *Duó Trágico* for piano and orchestra in memory of John F. Kennedy by Hector CAMPOS-PARSI of Puerto Rico; *Nueva York* by Leon SCHIDLOWSKY of Chile; *Third Symphony* by Domingo SANTA CRUZ of Chile; *Violin Concerto* by Roque CORDERO of Panama; *Symphonic Suite* by Pedro SANJUÁN of the United States.

11 MAY 1965

In the course of the Third Inter-American Music Festival in Washington, the following program of orchestral world premières is presented by the Buffalo Philharmonic Orchestra conducted by Lukas Foss:

Laudes by Celso GARRIDO-LECCA of Peru; *Concertino de cámara* by Alfonso MONTECINO of Chile; *Stray Birds,* triptych for baritone and eleven instruments by Hector TOSAR of Uruguay; *Vivencias I–IV* by Enrique ITURRIAGA of Peru; and *Violin Concerto* by Juan José CASTRO of Argentina.

12 MAY 1965

At the last concert of the Third Inter-American Music Festival in Washington the following program of first performances is given:

Sejatpar by Marina SAIZ of Panama; *Cello Concerto* by Claudio SANTORO of Brazil; *Transparencias* for six instrumental groups by Antonio TAURIELLO of Argentina; *Orchestra Variations* by Gerardo GANDINI of Argentina; and *Music for Piano and Orchestra* by Juan Carlos PAZ p of Argentina.

12 MAY 1965

The Spring Festival of Czechoslovakia opens in Prague, inaugurating a series of 71 concerts with the participation of Sadler's Wells Opera Company of London; Cleveland Orchestra, George Szell conducting; London Symphony Orchestra, George Solti conducting, Moscow Radio Symphony Orchestra, and the Czech Philharmonic (the Festival closed on 11 June 1965)

20 MAY 1965

The 39th Festival of the International Society for Contemporary Music opens in Madrid with the following program of symphonic music:

Stasimon B! by the Greek composer Yorgo SICILIANOS, for chorus and orchestra, to words from Euripides, constituting an attempt to revive ancient Greek modes with the aid of modern serial techniques; *Piano Concerto* by the 58-year-old Japanese composer Yoritsune MATSUDAIRA, in three movements, inspired by ancient Japanese court music, but constructed according to dodecaphonic procedures, lubricated by quartertones and diversified by aleatory devices; *Spiegel II* by the 39-year-old Austrian composer Friedrich CERHA, a cycle of six pieces for 55 string instruments, forming multiple reflecting surfaces of sonic chirality; and *Second Symphony,* in three movements, *Heurte, Fluide, Vigoureux,* by the 59-year-old French composer André JOLIVET, employing a free, eclectically atonal and adumbratively serial method of composition with an infusion of subtropical rhythms.

21 MAY 1965

At the 39th Festival of the International Society for Contemporary Music in Madrid, the following program of chamber music is performed:

3 Fantasias for clarinet and piano by the 32-year-old Berlin-born British composer Alexander GOEHR, combining the "fantastic" element in the Miltonian sense in a proliferation of fugal fancies with a modernistic profusion of unmitigated dissonances; *In Time of Daffodils* for soprano, baritone and a chamber group of instruments by the 50-year-old Italian composer Riccardo MALIPIERO, nephew of Gian Francesco Malipiero, to the texts, in English, of five surrealist poems by the American poet, e. e. Cummings; *Alpha-Beth* for six instruments by the 28-year-old French composer Gilbert AMY, in five movements illustrating various combinations of instruments and rhythms; *Polar* by the 35-year-old Spanish composer Luis de PABLO, in which heterogeneous groups of instruments are mutually polarized fence the title); *Concerto for String Instruments* by the 25-year-old Japanese composer Motohiko ADACHI, derived from a single agogic pattern; *Glühende Rätsel (Glowing Riddles)* by the 26-year-old Swiss composer Heinz HOLLIGER, for contralto and a small group of instruments, in five sections unified by a common melorhythmic pattern; and *Contrasts* for piano, violin and clarinet by Béla BARTÓK, in three dance movements.

21 MAY 1965

In C, an orchestral piece by the 33-year-old American composer Terry RILEY, obdurately sticking to the key of C, with an intrusive F sharp occasionally making its appearance as a fleeting *trompe l'oreille* effect, is performed for the first time in San Francisco.

22 MAY 1965

The Happy Prince, opera by the 33-year-old Australian composer Malcolm WILLIAMSON, after Oscar Wilde, scored for 8 soloists, chorus, semi-chorus, piano duet and percussion, is performed for the first time at the Farnham Festival in England.

22 MAY 1965

At the 39th Festival of the International Society for Contemporary Music in Madrid, the following program of symphonic music is performed:

Eufonia 64 by the 48-year-old Hungarian composer Rudolf MAROS for 24 wind instruments, two harps and percussion, in four symmetrical movements subordinated to the idea of an equilibrium of sound, form and notation; *In Nuce* by the 42-year-old Swedish composer Ake HERMANSON, consisting of a series of parallel variations in indeterminate notation, evoking an embryo's evolution into a foetus (hence the title, "in a nutshell"); *Hölderlin-Fragmente* by the 29-year-old German composer Aribert REIMANN, for soprano and instruments, to the mystical texts of Friedrich Hölderlin's poems, built on a free serial basis and developed in pointillistic images; *Music for Orchestra* by the 43-year-old Polish composer Andrzej DOBROWLSKI constructed in spatial matrices of instrumental groups; *Violin Concerto* by Alban BERG; and *Secuencias* by the 35-year-old Spanish composer Cristóbal HALFFTER, representing a succession of acoustical phenomena, beginning with white noise without rhythmic organization, and progressing towards increasingly complex integration of thematic sonorities.

24 MAY 1965

At the 39th Festival of the International Society for Contemporary Music in Madrid, the following program of chamber music is performed:

Music for Brass Quintet by the 39-year-old American composer Gunther SCHULLER, in three movements representing the integral calculus of differential melorhythmic fragments with a series of brief cadenzas improvised by the players in the jazz idiom; *Rondeaux per Dieci* by the 42-year-old Italian composer Camillo TOGNI, for soprano and nine instruments (aggregating to ten performers thus justifying the title), written in the manner of serialistic neo-classicism; *Sonata Canonica*, by the 28-year-old Czech composer Peter KOLMAN, an aphoristic composition for clarinet and bass clarinet thematically built on a permutating dodecaphonic series; *Divisions* by the 29-year-old Swiss composer Jürg WYTTENBACH for piano and strings in four movements, following the Baroque forms with improvised permutations of principal themes in free cadenzas; *Fresque sonore* for 7 instruments by the 43-year-old Japanese composer Shin-Ichi MATSUSHITA, evocative of oriental frescos with varied instrumental colors in an acoustical space; *Einst dem Grau* by the 28-year-old Dutch composer Ton DE KRUYF, inspired by a mystical poem of Paul Klee, and involving the application of dodecaphonic techniques; and *Destination 5* by the 30-year-old Israeli composer Noam SHERIFF, for two trumpets, two trombones, tuba and percussion, the duration of performance stipulated to be precisely five minutes, and the metric arrangements being derived from the geometric properties of the golden mean section.

25 MAY 1965

At the 39th Festival of the International Society for Contemporary Music in Madrid, the following program of Spanish music is performed:

Homenaje a Miguel Hernández for bass voice and orchestra to the words of Miguel Hernández, by the 32-year-old Spanish composer Antón García ABRIL; *Sonata del Sur* by the dean of Spanish composers Oscar ESPLÁ, for piano and orchestra, in three movements, permeated with melorhythms of Spanish secular and sacred music; *Ausencias de Dulcinea* by the blind Spanish composer Joaquín RODRIGO, a symphonic poem inspired by Cervantes and his vision of Dulcinea; *Canticum in P. P. Johannem XXIII* for soprano, bass and chorus, by the Spanish composer Ernesto HALFFTER; and *Desintegración morfológica de le Chacona de Bach* by the 53-year-old Spanish composer Xavier MONTSALVATGE, in which Bach's famous Chaconne for violin solo is morphologically fissioned, then reassembled in a new form.

26 MAY 1965

At the 39th Festival of the International Society for Contemporary Music in Madrid, the following program of symphonic music is presented:

Szene II by the 28-year-old Swedish composer Bo NILSSON, one of his three *Scenes for Orchestra* written in an abstractly theatrical manner; *Epitaffio* for orchestra and magnetic tape by the 34-year-old Norwegian composer Arne NORDHEIM, with only three words used in the text culled from the verses of the Italian poet Salvatore Quasimodo (Solo, Terra, Sera) interpreted as emotional signals for the music; *Freski symfoniczne* by the 43-year-old Polish composer Kazimierz SEROCKI, in four sections, each representing an imaginary fresco; *Symphony* by Anton VON WEBERN, in two movements, op. 21, his masterpiece of dodecaphonic chirality; *Abraham and Isaac* by Igor STRAVINSKY for baritone and orchestra; and *A Survivor from Warsaw*, for narrator, chorus and orchestra, by Arnold SCHOENBERG.

27 MAY 1965

The Judas Tree, "musical drama of Judas Iscariot," by the 30-year-old British composer Peter DICKINSON, for speakers, singers, chorus and chamber orchestra, wherein the tree on which Judas hanged himself is mystically identified with the tree of the true cross, utilizing in the score various forms of serial devices and electronic effects and simplicistically tonal harmonies, with the tritone (the medieval "diabolus in musica") representing Judas, progressing through a series of excruciating (*ex cruce*) discords to a theologically immaculate unison symbolizing the sacrificial identity of Jesus and Judas, is performed for the first time in the College of St. Mark and St. John in London.

28 MAY 1965

The 39th Festival of the International Society for Contemporary Music concludes in Madrid with the following program of music for chamber orchestra:

Iter inverso by the 40-year-old Italian composer Domenico GUACCERO, in two sections, *Da monodia a linee* and *Da linea a sfera*, illustrating a geometric expansion from linear melody to spherical harmony in a spatial distribution of instrumental sonorities; *Bomarzo*, cantata for narrator, baritone and instruments by the prime Argentinian composer, 49-year-old Alberto GINASTERA, revolving around a mad Florentine Duke and written in a serial idiom; *Combat T, N* by the 25-year-old French composer René KOERING, depicting in serially designed melodies and rhythms the composer's impression of the French Army maneuvers in which he participated; *Stabat Mater* for 3 unaccompanied choruses by the 31-year-old prime modernist of Poland, Krzysztof PENDERECKI, using liturgical chant patterns of the Catholic ritual surrounded by a raging stream of anguished dissonance; and *El Retablo de Maese Pedro* by Manuel DE FALLA, a "musical and scenic adaptation of the story of the ingenious Knight Don Quixote of La Mancha."

5 JUNE 1965

24 Hours, a festival of environmental anti-music is proffered in Wuppertal, Germany, featuring the following non-events:

String Quartet by George BRECHT (the four players shake hands mutually and depart); *Danger Music Number Six* by Dick HIGGINS (a silent piece); *Collective Composition* by György LIGETI, entitled *The Future of Music* (the composer appears with a stopwatch and scrutinizes the audience whose reaction constitutes the content of the composition); *Creep into the Vagina of a Living Whale* by the Korean composer Nam June PAIK (free improvisation with any animate object); *Count the Waves of the Rhine* by Nam June PAIK (a notated piece of music containing only rests and repeat signs); *Two Sounds* by La Monte YOUNG, a verbal piece containing the words "Two Sounds" but no actual sounds; *Music for the Ear* by Dick HIGGINS; *Composition 1960, No. 15* by La Monte YOUNG, a piece to be imagined only.

8 JUNE 1965

Erik CHISHOLM, Scottish composer of a number of sophisticated works in various genres, including expert stylizations of Oriental modes, dies in Rondebosch, South Africa, at the age of 61.

15 JUNE 1965

The 18th Holland Festival of Music and Drama opens in Amsterdam with a concert by the Concertgebouw Orchestra featuring the posthumous performance of *Salutation Joyeuse* by Anton van der HORST, Dutch composer who died in Amsterdam on 7 March 1965.

16 JUNE 1965

In the course of the Holland Music Festival two operas by Dutch composers are presented for the first time in Amsterdam:

De Droom (*The Dream*) by Ton de LEEUW, in which dreams are induced by a somnificent pillow, featuring a ballet based on 13 Haikai in English, set to music in an orientalistically modernistic vein, in a scientific notation so that the linear dimensions are proportional to the duration of each note; and *Jean Lévecq* by Guillaume LANDRÉ, to Guy de Maupassant's story *Le Retour,* wherein a vagabond returning to his abandoned and long remarried wife, agrees to disappear again so as not to disturb her new happiness, set in a euphoniously dissonant idiom.

20 JUNE 1965

L' Hymne aux Morts by Olivier MESSIAEN, commemorating the dead of the two world wars, is presented at the Cathedral of Chartres, on the occasion of the visit there of President Charles de Gaulle.

20 JUNE 1965

Traumspiel, first opera by the 28-year-old German composer Aribert REIMANN, after August Strindberg's symbolically realistic psychological drama *Ett Drömspel* (*The Dream Play*), couched in a lyrically expressionistic modern idiom asymptotically tending towards shifting tonal foci, is produced in Kiel.

24 JUNE 1965

Second Symphony by the French composer Marcel LANDOWSKI is performed for the first time in Strasbourg.

28 JUNE 1965

Moses und Aron, Arnold SCHOENBERG's unfinished expressionistic opera, is given its first London performance at the Royal Opera House in Covent Garden, eliciting shocked and prurient comments regarding the realistic mise-enscène of the climactic orgy depicting the sacrifice to the golden calf of three bare-bosomed virgins, who were, however, asked to turn their backs to the audience. (The fiery immolation of live animals was left out of the production owing to safety regulations forbidding the setting of fires on the stage.)

7 JULY 1965

Fibonacci-Mobile for string quartet, two pianos and a coordinator, by the modern magus of profoundly calculated yet humanly experienced music Ernst KRENEK, based on a Fibonacci series in which each successive number is the sum of the two preceding numbers, is performed for the first time at a festival of contemporary music in Hanover, New Hampshire.

14 JULY 1965

Leonard BERNSTEIN conducts the New York Philharmonic in the world première of his *Chichester Psalms,* for chorus and orchestra, commissioned by the Chichester Cathedral, to the Hebrew texts of Psalms 100, 23 and 131, set in a neo-ecclesiastical idiom of ascetic severity, marked by a proliferation of ominous harmonic collisions and asymmetrical rhythmic phrases. (The first performance in Chichester, England, took place at the Tri-Choir Festival, on 31 July 1965.)

21 JULY 1965

Le Rossignol de Boboli, one-act operatic "fable" by Alexandre TANSMAN, in which a nightingale, accidentally mutated into a human, is restored to his original avian identity thanks to the efforts of a devoted love bird, is produced in Nice.

4 AUGUST 1965

Cantos for orchestra by the 43-year-old Scottish composer Iain HAMILTON, designed according to the principles of instrumental serialism, in 5 sections: *Parade, Nocturne I, Sonata, Nocturne II, Declarations,* is performed for the first time in London.

10 AUGUST 1965

An estimated horde of 70,000 people gathers at the Sheep Meadow in Central Park, New York, to hear the first performance of a newly established series of outdoor concerts by the New York Philharmonic, in a program comprising the first performance of William SCHUMAN's

Philharmonic Fanfare, WAGNER's *Meistersinger Overture* and BEETHOVEN's *Ninth Symphony*, William Steinberg conducting. (Eleven more concerts were given by the New York Philharmonic in New York, Brooklyn and Queens attracting great crowds.)

10 AUGUST 1965

The government of Ecuador issues a memorial stamp for the composer of the Ecuadorian national anthem, the Corsican-born ethnically German musician Antonio NEUMANN (1818–1871).

21 AUGUST 1965

Nun's Priest's Tale, after Chaucer, scored for folk singer, electric guitar and small orchestra by the 58-year-old American composer Ross Lee FINNEY, is performed for the first time at Dartmouth College in Hanover, New Hampshire.

25 AUGUST 1965

The third annual Avant-Garde Festival opens in New York in a program of *Action Music* by the Korean composer Nam June PAIK, including an *Ommaggio a Cage* scored for a destructible upright piano, a dozen eggs, scissors for an instant haircut and tape-recorded noises, with the participation of the cellist Charlotte Moorman wearing a cellophane sheath and playing *Le Cygne* by SAINT-SAËNS in an oil drum filled with water. (The series concluded on 11 September 1965.)

2 SEPTEMBER 1965

Herr von Hancken, second opera in three acts by the Swedish composer Karl-Birger BLOMDAHL, dealing with a Swedish paterfamilias pursued by God for his blasphemous outrecuidance and saved from perdition by the devil whom he encounters in a European spa in 1806, set to music in a serialistic technique, in which the leading motives of God, man and devil are formed by permutated ingredients of the governing tonal series, is produced in Stockholm.

4 SEPTEMBER 1965

Albert SCHWEITZER, great Alsace-born humanitarian, who began his career as an organist and a Bach scholar, winner of the Nobel Peace Prize, who went to West Africa to serve the ailing natives as a physician, dies in the jungle hospital of Lambaréné in Gabon, founded by him, at the age of 90.

5 SEPTEMBER 1965

La Passion selon Sade, theatrical action for mixed media by the prime Italian avant-garde composer Sylvano BUSSOTTI evolving from a dodecaphonic motto and ramifying into varied atonal, polytonal, rhythmically dispersed, serialistically surrealistic musical motion purported to portray the sadistic bedroom philosophy of Marquis de Sade (1740–1814), is produced in the course of the Modern Music Festival in Palermo, Sicily.

The work is not all here; when the performers absorb the text they may recapitulate from memory all fragments that they remember, in order or in disorder, including errors of memory, without mutual communication, or any point of reference, gradually yielding and groping more and more during lapses of remembrance; Only when memory is completely extinct can the performance come to a FINE. (From Bussotti's postscript in the score of his *Tableaux vivants avant la Passion selon Sade*)

9 SEPTEMBER 1965

Julian CARRILLO, Mexican composer, pioneer in composition in quarter-tones, eighth-tones, sixteenth-tones and other fractional intervals, who promulgated the earliest theory of micro-intervals in his publication *Sonido 13* (i.e., sound beyond 12), dies in Mexico City at the age of 90.

14 SEPTEMBER 1965

Violin Concerto, composed in 1963, by the 83-year-old dean of Italian composers, Gian Francesco MALIPIERO, in three classically equilibrated movements, with a profusion of delicate violinistic filigree, is performed for the first time in Venice.

16 SEPTEMBER 1965

The Commonwealth Arts Festival opens in London with a concert by the Sydney, Australia, Symphony Orchestra featuring the first performance of *Violin Concerto* by the New Zealand composer Malcolm WILLIAMSON.

21 SEPTEMBER 1965

Piano Concerto by the Russian-born, quarter-French, quarter-Scottish, quarter-Russian, quarter-German, naturalized American composer Avenir de MONFRED, subtitled *Trois Aspects de la France*, in three movements, *France classique*, *France romantique* and *France populaire*, cast in an intensely melodious and harmonious idiom, redolent of the spirit of Liszt, Rachmaninoff and Debussy, diffused in a Gallic ambiance, is performed for the first time, 21 years after its composition, by the Bulgarian pianist Yury Boukoff and the Norddeutscher Rundfunk Orchestra in Hamburg.

23 SEPTEMBER 1965

Oba ko so (*The King Did Not Hang*), Nigerian folk opera for mixed media, including singing, dancing and acting, telling the story of the Nigerian god Shango, is performed at the Cardiff Commonwealth Arts Festival.

25 SEPTEMBER 1965

On the 20th anniversary of the death of Béla BARTÓK, the Budapest Radio presents a program of his music relayed by the American Communications Satellite Telstar to both hemispheres.

25 SEPTEMBER 1965

Der Traum des Liu-Tung, opera in four dream sequences by the 48-year-old Korean composer Isang YUN, after a medieval Taoist fable centered on a Zen-starred youth who lapses into catalepsy and awakens 16 years later, scored for a modern orchestra with a large array of oriental instruments, with singers oscillating between tempered intonation and oriental singsong, is produced for the first time in West Berlin.

29 SEPTEMBER 1965

Balkan Rhapsody for orchestra by the Bulgarian-born American composer Boris KREMENLIEV, written in a neo-romantic manner diversified by Balkan melorhflhmic asymmetries, is performed for the first time in Munich.

29 SEPTEMBER 1965

Petite Symphonie, subtitled *Scultura*, by the 36-year-old Polish composer Boguslaw SCHÄFFER, in five minuscule movements notated diagrammatically, in curvilinear, rectilinear and spiral geometric designs, conceived as a study in plastic forms (hence the association with sculpture in the subtitle) and exploring the entire sonic and dynamic spectrum, from fortississimo to pianissimo, ending in an ascending icositetraphonic glissando in the massed strings, is performed for the first time in the course of the 9th International Festival of Contemporary Music in Warsaw ("Warsaw Autumn").

30 SEPTEMBER 1965

In the course of the Commonwealth Arts Festival in London, the Sydney Symphony Orchestra presents the first performance of *Sun Music* by the 36-year-old Tasmanian composer Peter SCULTHORPE, climaxed by an integrated icositetraphonic sonic aggregate of 59 adjacent quarter-tones for string instruments.

2 OCTOBER 1965

A Bridge, Bulgarian opera by Alexander RAICHOV, depicting the Communist revolutionary and military action on the eve of the liberation of Sofia by the Soviet Army from the Nazis, is produced in Rusa, Bulgaria.

14 OCTOBER 1965

Sud, opera by the expatriate 34-year-old American composer Kenton COE to a libretto concerning homosexual practices in South Carolina on the eve of the Civil War, written in an incongruously eupeptic manner, is produced in Marseilles.

18 OCTOBER 1965

Die Ermittelung (*The Inquest*), oratorio by the Italian avant-garde composer Luigi NONO, to a text by Peter Weiss based entirely on the court transcript of trials of minor Nazi criminals, dramatized by electronic effects, consisting of eleven songs, each illustrating a bestial episode of murderous inhumanity, culminating with an account of the crematorium, is performed for the first time in Berlin.

18 OCTOBER 1965

Nineteenth Symphony by Henry COWELL, his last completed major work, in five movements cast in a grhythmically propulsive, melodically expansive and harmonically pellucid manner with occasional agglomerations of tone-clusters diversified by multifarious percussion including porcelain bowls, is performed for the first time by the Nashville, Tennessee, Symphony Orchestra, conducted by Willis Page.

24 OCTOBER 1965

On the 20th anniversary of the founding of the United Nations, *Voices for Today* for two choirs by Benjamin BRITTEN, specially written for the occasion, to a collage of anti-war texts ranging in period from Jesus and Socrates to Camus and Evtushenko, and concluding with a setting of Virgil's fourth eclogue which was believed by medieval theologians to be a prediction of the coming of Christ, used by Britten as a symbol of the coming of Peace, is performed for the first time in the General Assembly Hall in the United Nations Building in New York.

25 OCTOBER 1965

The Norwegian government issues a commemorative stamp in honor of the bicentennial of the Philharmonic Society of Bergen.

28 OCTOBER 1965

The Third International Festival of Visiting Orchestras opens in Carnegie Hall, New York, with a concert by the Detroit Symphony, conducted by Sixten Ehrling and featuring the first performance of *Lions*, symphonic poem by the 42-year-old American composer Ned ROREM, with a motto from Shakespeare, "The hind that would be mated by the lion must die for love," characterized by maundering blues played by a meandering jazz combo.

28 OCTOBER 1965

Requiem by Wilfred JOSEPH, a memorial choral symphony to the Jews slain by the Nazis, with the motto "Requiescant pro defunctis iudaeis," set to a Hebrew text of the Kaddish, is produced at La Scala, as the winner of the First International Composition Competition of the City of Milan.

2 NOVEMBER 1965

Jacobowsky und der Oberst, opera in four acts by Giselher KLEBE, after Franz Werfel's ironic play detailing the tragicomic adventures of a Jewish Pole who saves a snobbish Polish aristocrat after the military débacle in France in 1940, is produced at the Hamburg State Opera.

4 NOVEMBER 1965

Miss Julie, opera in two acts by Ned ROREM, after Strindberg's play dealing with a liaison between an aristocratic Scandinavian lady and her father's servant, set to music in a euphonious modernistic vein, with the application of rational dissonances, is produced in New York.

6 NOVEMBER 1965

Edgar VARÈSE, magisterial genius of new music, whose scientifically inspired works—*Intégrales, Hyperprism, Ionisation*—weave a magic carpet of "organized sound" and whose flamingly cryogenic symphonic pageants—*Amériques, Arcana, Déserts*—have established the principle of sonic illation and additive athematic development, the first modern composer to combine electronic elements with conventional instrumental timbres, dies in New York at the age of 81. (Varèse was born on 22 December 1883, not 1885, as he himself believed and as all biographical dictionaries indicate; from 1950 on he spelled his first name with a final d, Edgard, which was the original spelling in his birth certificate.)

15 NOVEMBER 1965

Musique for eleven wind instruments and timpani by the 36-year-old Soviet composer Edison DENISOV is performed for the first time in Leningrad.

16 NOVEMBER 1965

Pine Tree Fantasy for orchestra by the dean of American music, 71-year-old Walter PISTON, written as a tribute to his native state of Maine, in three cyclic sections, with an *Allegro deciso* flanked by two elegiac expositions, and modally converging on a focal C, is performed for the first time by the Portland, Maine, Symphony Orchestra.

19 NOVEMBER 1965

The National Polish Opera House, rebuilt and restored after its fiery destruction by the Nazi air force during the devastating onslaught on Poland in September 1939, is reopened in Warsaw.

21 NOVEMBER 1965

Eighth Symphony by the 69-year-old Austrian composer Johann Nepomuk DAVID, is performed for the first time in Stuttgart.

2 DECEMBER 1965

The New Music Workshop at the University of California, Los Angeles, presents a program of avant-garde music comprising the following manifestations:

Piano Piece No. 1 by George MACIUNAS, consisting of bringing an upright piano onto the stage; *Piano Piece No. 1* by La Monte YOUNG, composed at 2:10 A.M. on 8 November 1960 and containing the following instructions: "Push the piano up to a wall and put the flat side flush against it. Then continue pushing into the wall. If the piano goes through the wall, keep pushing in the same direction regardless of new obstacles"; and *Playable Music No. 4* by the Korean composer Nam June PAIK, performed by Joseph Byrd for the first time anywhere, fulfilling to the letter the directions "Cut your left arm very slowly with a razor (more than 10 centimeters)," shedding 7 cubic centimeters of blood in the process. (Someone in the audience shouted the exhortation "Encore! Use your throat!")

3 DECEMBER 1965

A second manifestation of the New Music Workshop of the University of California, Los Angeles, presents the world première of a patriotic octet for 8 or more instruments, *The Defense of the American Continent from the Viet-Cong Invasion* (subtitled *Communist Aggression Music No. 1*) by the 27-year-old American composer Joseph BYRD,

culminating with a polyphonic synchronization of *America the Beautiful* with *Deutschland, Deutschland über alles*.

5 DECEMBER 1965

The Cancelling Dark, radio opera by the British composer Christopher WHELEN, based on the true story of an aircraft crash-landing in the desert in which the doomed pilot and his sole passenger engage in a philosophical dialogue and self-induced hallucinations of women in their lives, is performed for the first time in London.

10 DECEMBER 1965

Henry COWELL, American composer, builder of novel sonic edifices, theorist of new musical resources, inventor of the tone-clusters played on the piano keyboard with elbows and forearms, animator and devoted champion of artistic innovations and modern techniques, dies in Shady, New York, at the age of 68.

11 DECEMBER 1965

La Princesse de Clèves, opera in five acts by Jean FRANÇAIX, reviving in a hedonistically modernistic neo-classical idiom the age of royal France, is performed for the first time in Rouen.

14 DECEMBER 1965

Mara, opera by the British composer John HASTIE, dealing with a sea nymph who induces a non-aqueous prince to marry her, set to music in an appropriately fanciful simplistic manner, modernized by atonal melismas in asymmetrical rhythms, is produced in Croydon, England.

17 DECEMBER 1965

Apocalypse for narrator, chorus and instruments by the 26-year-old Polish composer Edward BOGUSLAWSKI, written in an expansive grandiloquent manner, with allusions to ecclesiastical chants providing an eschatological ambience, is performed for the first time in Warsaw.

24 DECEMBER 1965

Ayikuli, Chinese opera composed collectively by a group of Communist musicians, adapted from a film entitled *Red Blossom on Tien Shan Mountains*, and dealing with a heroic Kazakh woman, a former slave, who becomes a revolutionary leader, is produced in Peking. —

30 DECEMBER 1965

Jean MARTINON conducts the Chicago Symphony Orchestra in the first performance of his *Altitudes*, symphony in three movements—*La Porte des Étoiles, Le Jardin Vertical and La Traversée des Dieux*—written for the Diamond Jubilee Season of the Orchestra, of which he is musical director.

1966

4 JANUARY 1966

Julius Caesar Jonesz, opera in two acts by the 34-year-old New Zealand-born English composer Malcolm WILLIAMSON, dealing with imaginative children who conjure up a surrealistic Polynesian fantasy, set to music in a deceptively unsophisticated manner, is produced at a children's theater in London.

19 JANUARY 1966

The 61-year-old British composer Michael TIPPETT conducts in London the first performance of his cantata in three parts, *The Vision of St. Augustine,* to Latin texts from St. Augustine's confessions, in which he comments on his instant realizations of the persistence of volition, evanescence of reified material objects and the relativity of time, making use of a variety of techniques, including vocal glossolalia, medieval hocket syncopation and thematic serialism, set in the classical forms of rondo and toccata, and concluding with a pious Alleluia.

31 JANUARY 1966

Twelfth Symphony, subtitled *Tunis,* by the Danish composer Niels Viggo BENTZON is performed for the first time in Aarhus.

4 FEBRUARY 1966

Zwischenfälle bei einer Notlandung, "reportage" for electronic devices, instruments and singers, in two phases and 14 situations, by Boris BLACHER, with an acoustically realistic aural report of incidents at a forced landing of an aircraft, introducing the contrasting characters of survivors, among them a cybernetics scientist, a journalist, a prima donna, a financier and a girl secretary, is produced in Hamburg.

5 FEBRUARY 1966

Sixth Concerto for piano and orchestra by the 83-year-old grand master of Italian music Gian Francesco MALIPIERO, in three cyclic movements, *Allegro, Lento, Allegro,* bearing the subtitle *delle macchine,* and ending with a stroke on the bass drum, is performed for the first time in Rome.

5 FEBRUARY 1966

Concerto for cello, seventeen woodwind instruments, percussion and harmonium by the 26-year-old Soviet composer Boris TISHCHENKO, in one monothematically conceived movement, written in an advanced modernistic dialectical style, is performed for the first time in Leningrad, Igor Blazhkov conducting, with Mstislav Rostropovich, to whom the Concerto is dedicated, as soloist.

6 FEBRUARY 1966

Piano Concerto by the Canadian composer Jean PAPINEAU-COUTURE, is performed for the first time in Toronto.

9 FEBRUARY 1966

Kardiogram I by the 23-year-old Swedish avant-garde composer Gunnar VALKARE, in the form of a coroner's report, to the French text, "Il meurt a Paris en 1867. . .," scored for four vocalists of different sexes, chorus and chamber orchestra, is performed for the first time in Stockholm.

10 FEBRUARY 1966

First Symphony by the 29-year-old English composer Richard Rodney BENNET, in three movements, *Allegro, Andante* and *Molto vivace,* scored for a large orchestra and employing a rich assortment of exotic percussion instruments, written in an expressionistic continental manner and a free serial idiom peculiar to the modern Albion while not renouncing tonality and hedonistically colorful means of musical expression within a distinctly vigesi-mosecular Weltanschauung, is performed for the first time in London.

11 FEBRUARY 1966

Mirror Twenty-five for chorus and orchestra by the 26-year-old Swedish composer Johnny GRANDERT in which the score includes a machine gun, and the chorus is invited to belch at some points, is performed for the first time in Stockholm.

11 FEBRUARY 1966

Psalm 140 for soprano and orchestra by Roger SESSIONS, in which David's prayer for deliverance from evil is expressed with eloquently dissonant and atonally explosive fervor, is performed for the first time by the Boston Symphony Orchestra, Erich Leinsdorf conducting.

12 FEBRUARY 1966

The Eternal Theme, symphonic poem by the 68-year-old Israeli composer Paul BEN-HAIM, in six movements—*Intrada, Fanfare, Prayer for the Innocent, Meditation, Rondo, Conclusion*—written in a neo-baroque formal manner, with six trumpets proclaiming the rabbinical belief in the eternal "song of all songs at the end of all time," is performed for the first time by the Israel Philharmonic Orchestra in Tel Aviv.

18 FEBRUARY 1966

Madrigals, Book I, for soprano, double-bass and the vibraphone by the 36-year-old American composer George CRUMB, to the text by Federico García Lorca, is performed for the first time in Philadelphia.

21 FEBRUARY 1966

The Phoenix, Fabulous Bird, tone poem by John VINCENT dedicated to the city of Phoenix, Arizona, and based on a soaring theme symbolizing the eternal rebirth of the fiery bird, is performed for the first time in Phoenix.

25 FEBRUARY 1966

Piece for Allison Knowles by the Korean composer Nam June PAIK, instructing the performer, a female, to take off 25 pairs of multicolored silk pieces of underwear and lift her remaining skirt to mark the coda, is demonstrated for the first time at an avant-garde happening in Los Angeles.

3 MARCH 1966

Relata I for symphony orchestra by the 49-year-old American composer-mathematician Milton BABBITT is performed for the first time, in Cleveland.

4 MARCH 1966

David DEL TREDICI conducts in San Francisco the first performance of his *Night Conjure-Verse*, scored for soprano, mezzo-soprano, woodwind septet and string quartet, to a text by James Joyce.

5 MARCH 1966

Excursion for orchestra by the 43-year-old American composer Irwin BAZELON is performed for the first time in Kansas City.

10 MARCH 1966

Concerto for four percussion soloists and orchestra by the 42-year-old American composer and percussion virtuoso William KRAFT is performed for the first time in Los Angeles.

11 MARCH 1966

Madrigals, Book II, for soprano, flute and percussion by the 36-year-old American composer George CRUMB, to text by Federico García Lorca, is performed for the first time in Washington, D.C.

18 MARCH 1966

The Judgment of St. Francis, one-act opera by the 38-year-old American composer Nicolas FLAGELLO, is produced in New York.

21 MARCH 1966

Mr. and Mrs. Discobbolos, minuscule opera by the 34-year-old American composer Peter WESTERGAARD, for two singers and six instrumentalists, to the whimsical poem by Edward Lear, with the aleatorically serial idiom of the music illustrating the rhymed glossolalia of the text, is performed for the first time at a concert of the Group for Contemporary Music at Columbia University in New York.

24 MARCH 1966

The First Inter-American Festival of the Arts opens in San Juan, Puerto Rico, with a program of choral music by Puerto Rican composers.

30 MARCH 1966

St. Luke Passion, oratorio by the 32-year-old Polish avant-garde composer Krzysztof PENDERECKI, to the Latin text of the Passion and Death of Jesus Christ according to St. Luke, composed in a fervidly devotional style, making use of the millennial devices of the Gregorian chant as well as of serial procedures of the mid-20th century, written in a special graphic notation, indicating the highest possible note by an isosceles triangle, and the lowest by an inverted one, with special symbols for various percussion effects, is performed for the first time at the Cathedral of Münster, Germany.

31 MARCH 1966

Markheim, opera in three acts by the 39-year-old American composer Carlisle FLOYD, after Robert Louis Stevenson's tale of a pawnbroker who is given a specious promise of a life of pleasure by a diabolical stranger, is produced in New Orleans.

2 APRIL 1966

The First Inter-American Festival of Arts in San Juan, Puerto Rico, concludes with a program of Latin American music, including the first performance of *Musica Festival* for chamber orchestra by the Puerto Rican composer Amaury VERAY.

3 APRIL 1966

Terrêtektorh for orchestra by Iannis XENAKIS, 43-year-old Rumanian-born Greek electronic engineer, active in Paris, foremost exponent of stochastic music, with the etymology of the title indicating earth (*terre*), tectonic (*tekt*) and action suffix *orh*, conceived as a sonotron, i.e. accelerator of sonic particles, disintegrator of acoustic masses and a synthesizer, covering the entire spectrum of sound, with an emphasis on noise elements, is performed for the first time at the Festival of Contemporary Music at Royan, France, conducted by Hermann Scherchen, with 88 musicians strewn among the audience, each equipped with a consortium of drumlets and policemen's whistles, "producing sounds similar to flames."

If desired, a rain of hail can surround each of the listeners, or perhaps a murmuration of a pine forest, or any other atmosphere or linear concept, static or in motion. The individual listeners will then find themselves as though sailing in a frail boat on a turbulent sea, or in a pointillistic universe of sonorous sparks moving in cumulous or isolated clouds. (Xenakis in a descriptive note, reproduced in the program book of the 1967 Warsaw Festival)

4 APRIL 1966

Luna 10, circumlunar unmanned orbiting "cosmic ship" launched by the Soviets, is activated to broadcast the *Internationale* to the earth for the opening of the sixth session of the 23rd Congress of the Communist Party of the USSR.

5 APRIL 1966

Cantata by Sergei PROKOFIEV, written in 1937 to glorify the 20th anniversary of the Soviet Revolution, scored for two choruses, military band, ensemble of accordions and percussion, to texts from Marx, Engels, Lenin and Stalin, judged ideologically and musically inadequate and therefore withheld from performance, is finally given a hearing at a public concert in Moscow, nearly thirty years after its composition, with the significant omission of the section of Stalin's texts in conformity with the process of de-Stalinization in Soviet politics and art.

6 APRIL 1966

Cello Concerto by the 60-year-old English composer Alan RAWSTHORNE, in three movements, *Allegro lirico, Mesto,* and *Allegro,* set a luminously bitonal harmonic idiom, gravitating towards a focal C, is performed for the first time in London.

14 APRIL 1966

The First Hellenic Week of Contemporary Music opens in Athens, Greece, in programs including the string quartets of SCHOENBERG, several works by Anton VON WEBERN and Olivier MESSIAEN and eleven world premières by modern Greek composers, among them *Trittys* for guitar, percussion and 2 doublebasses by the 37-year-old empiricist Nikos MAMANGAKIS (15 April) and *Praxis for 12* for strings, piano and percussion by the 40-year-old avant-gardist Jani CHRISTOU (18 April).

16 APRIL 1966

After 83 years of operatic splendor of the gilded age of America, the old baroque building of the Metropolitan Opera House of New York, inaugurated on 22 October 1883, where the golden voices of the past had resounded gloriously for the delectation of tax-free millionaires and aristocratic opera lovers, closes its antiquated doors with a final nostalgic performance of Puccini's opera *La Bohème,* before moving to a new home in the modernistically functional Lincoln Center for the Performing Arts.

28 APRIL 1966

In the series of "Symphonic Forms in the Twentieth Century," the New York Philharmonic under the direction of Leonard Bernstein presents the world premières of two works by the 50-year-old American composer David Diamond:

Fifth Symphony, composed intermittently between 1947 and 1964, and completed on the Island of Ponza, Italy, on 30 September 1964 (alter the completion and performances of his 6th, 7th and 8th Symphonies) in two large sections—(1) *Adagio-Allegro enegico,* opening with an unaccompanied English horn solo, achieving a dynamic climax in the second subject; (2) *Andante; Fuga; Allegretto; Adalgio,* with an intervallically angular but tonally centered fugue ending in a rhetorical solo cello summarizing thematic ideas from both movements—and *Concerto for Piano and Orchestra,* composed in 1949–1950, in three movements—(1) *Andante-Allegretto-Allegro,* set in an amalgamated form of sonata and rondo; (2) *Adagio, molto espressivo,* couched in a quasi-devotional mood; (3) *Allegramente,* a spirited rondo launched by a gay piccolo solo, in an unequivocal A major (conducted by David Diamond himself with Thomas Schumacher as soloist).

28 APRIL 1966

Concerto buffo for chamber orchestra by Sergei SLONIMSKY, written in an advanced technical style making use of serial and aleatory procedures in two movements, *Canonic Fugue* for 14 string instruments and trumpet and *Improvisation,* opening with a protracted flute solo and concluding with a tumultuous dance, is performed for the first time in Leningrad.

28 APRIL 1966

Carry Nation, opera in two acts by Douglas MOORE, nostalgically recreating the stormy career of Carry Nation, the redoubtable American lady who led a crusade against demon rum by smashing saloons and bars with her little hatchet, written in a fittingly grandiloquent idiom with a profusion of florid arias, is produced at the University of Kansas in Lawrence, Kansas.

28 APRIL 1966

Analigus, orchestral triptych by Cuban-born American composer Aurelio de la VEGA, in four movements, *Phases, Serenade, Pauses,* and *Partitus,* athematic in structure and designed as an exposition of contrasting sonorities (including the novel effect of the entire string section shuffling their feet to produce a rhythmic noise), but possessing nevertheless a logic of analogy (the title *Analigus* is a deliberate distortion of the word), is performed for the first time in Fullerton, California.

1 MAY 1966

Sinfonia by the 30-year-old English composer Nicholas MAW, in three movements, with an embryonic fourth movement fertilized in utero in the finale, conceived as a compressed cellular organism, expressionistically developed along atonal thematic lines, is performed for the first time at the Rutheford College of Technology in Newcastle-upon-Tyne, England.

6 MAY 1966

The Third Festival of Music opens in Caracas, Venezuela with a program of orchestral works by Latin American composers:

Partita 3 by Julian ORBÓN of Cuba; *New York* by Leon SCHIDLOWSKY of Chile; *Fantasia de Bolsillo* by José Luis MUÑOZ of Venezuela; *Sands* by Pozzi ESCOT of Peru; and *Abyssus* by Carlos TUXEN-BANG of Argentina.

8 MAY 1966

At the second concert of the Third Festival of Music in Caracas, the following works by Latin American composers are performed:

Homogramas I by Gustavo BECERRA SCHMIDT of Chile; *Música III* by Antonio TAURIELLO of Argentina; *12 Mobiles* by Jacqueline NOVA of Colombia; and *Sinfonia en Cuatro Partes* by Aurelio DE LA VEGA of Cuba and the United States.

11 MAY 1966

First Symphony by the 45-year-old American composer Andrew IMBRIE is performed for the first time in San Francisco.

11 MAY 1966

During the course of the Third Festival of Music in Caracas, the following works for various ensembles are performed for the first time anywhere:

Continuidades by Juan Carlos PAZ of Argentina; *Laudate Servum Domine*, cantata by Leopoldo BILLINGS of Venezuela; *Resonancias Tres* by Hilda DIANDA of Argentina; and *Discrepancia* by Lukas FOSS of the United States.

13 MAY 1966

During the course of the Third Festival of Music in Caracas, the Philadelphia Orchestra under the direction of Eugene Ormandy presents the world premières of *Concerto per corde* by Alberto GINASTERA of Argentina and *4 Piezas para orquesta* by Hector TOSAR of Uruguay.

14 MAY 1966

At the Third Festival of Music in Caracas, the Philadelphia Orchestra, under the direction of its guest conductor Stanislaw Skrowaczewski, presents the following program:

Variaciones concertantes by Alberto GINASTERA of Argentina; *Sensemayá* by Silvestre REVUELTAS of Mexico; the world première of *Ludus Symphonicus* by Edino KRIEGER of Brazil; *Medea's Dance of Vengeance* by Samuel BARBER of the United States; and *Canto for Orchestra* by Peter MENNIN of the United States.

14 MAY 1966

The Magic Chair, one-act opera by the Hungarian-born American composer Eugene ZÁDOR, in which a malingering bureaucrat is seated in a magic chair that forces him to tell scandalous truths about his management of municipal affairs, is performed for the first time (with piano instead of the orchestra) at Louisiana State University in Baton Rouge.

15 MAY 1966

At the Third Festival of Music in Caracas, two works by Venezuelan composers are given for the first time: *Sinfonietta Satirica* by Inocente CARREÑO and *Ballet Miniatura* by Blanca ESTRELLA.

15 MAY 1966

15 Prints After Dürer's Apocalypse, suite for orchestra by the 30-year-old Czech composer Luboš FIŠER, abstractly related to the apocalyptic visions embodied in the engravings of Albrecht Dürer, with melodic and harmonic materials serially derived from the basic mode of six notes, while the musical current is carried forward within precisely determined time units, is performed for the first time at the Prague Spring Music Festival.

16 MAY 1966

The Philadelphia Orchestra under the direction of Eugene Ormandy presents in the course of the Third Festival of Music in Caracas the world première of the posthumous *Ninth Symphony* by Heitor VILLA-LOBOS and the world première of *Sinfonia* by Roque CORDERO of Panama.

16 MAY 1966

Koshare, ballet by the American Indian composer Louis BALLARD, evoking the creation of the world as seen through the eyes of the Hopi Indians, is performed for the first time in Barcelona, Spain.

18 MAY 1966

Violin Concerto by William BERGSMA is performed for the first time under the composer's direction at Tacoma, Washington.

18 MAY 1966

The Third Festival of Music in Caracas closes with an orchestral program of music by Venezuelan composers, including *First Symphony* by Carlos FIGUEREDO; *Fantasia* for piano and orchestra by Nelly Mele LARA; *Giros Negroides* by Antonio LAURO; and *El Rio de las Siete Estrellas* by Evencio CASTELLANOS.

21 MAY 1966

Professor Mamlock, opera by the 52-year-old Slovak composer Ladislav HOLOUBEK to a libretto inspired by the European resistance movement against the Nazi occupation written in an angst-filled dodecaphonic idiom is performed for the first time in Bratislava, under the direction of the composer.

23 MAY 1966

Die schwarze Spinne, opera in three acts by Josef Matthias HAUER, after a mystical tale by the Swiss cleric Albert Bitzius (1797–1854), dealing with a peasant woman who attempts to outwit the devil incarnate by pretending to submit to his hideous proposal to surrender to him her unbaptized child for his iniquitous purposes, but who is transformed into a black spider and brings forth a proliferation of horrible arachnids instead, with thematic materials derived from a single tone-row, E, G sharp, D, F, A, C, D sharp, F sharp, B, C sharp, B flat and G, is performed posthumously for the first time in Vienna.

27 MAY 1966

Lake Ukereve, opera in five scenes by the 44-year-old Czech composer Otmar MÁCHA, to his own libretto dealing with the medical missionaries combating the effects of sleeping sickness in Central Africa in 1900, with eloquent arias and choruses supported onomatopoeically by stylized drums suggesting primitivistic rites, is produced in Prague.

29 MAY 1966

Der Tod des Empedokles, "scenic concerto" in one act by the German composer Hermann REUTTER, to the romantic poem by Friedrich Hölderlin, in which the ancient wise philosopher finds his private truth in a voluntary death in the crater of the volcano Aetna, is performed for the first time in Schwetzingen, on the same program with the revised version of Reutter's one-act opera buffa *Die Witwe von Ephesus* (first performed in Cologne on 23 June 1954).

31 MAY 1966

The Metropolitan Opera Company of New York opens its European season in Paris, its first visit since 1910.

2 JUNE 1966

17 Tage und 4 Minuten, opera buffa in three acts by Werner EGK, a fanciful version of Calderón's comedy *El mayor encanto amor*, with wandering Ulysses and nymphomaniacal Circe making love for exactly 17 days and 4 minutes surrounded by half-mythological, quarter-realistic and quarter-surrealistic creatures, is produced in Stuttgart.

4 JUNE 1966

Symphonie de marches by Henri SAUGUET is performed for the first time as a commissioned work at the International Congress of Railroads, in Paris, to stimulate the popular appreciation of train travel.

8 JUNE 1966

Der mysteriöse Herr X, opera in three acts by the Austrian composer Alfred UHL, is performed for the first time at the Vienna Festival of Music.

9 JUNE 1966

The Burning Fiery Furnace, a church parable by Benjamin BRITTEN, set for male voices, organ and instruments, to the biblical story of Shadrach, Meshach and Abednego and their miraculous survival in the Babylonian oven, written in an esthetically devotional, tensely modern musical idiom, is performed for the first time by the English Opera Group, without a conductor, in the course of the annual Aldeburgh Festival, founded by Britten.

10 JUNE 1966

Jeppe, opera by the Norwegian composer Geirr TVEITT, is performed for the first time in Bergen, Norway.

12 JUNE 1966

Herman SCHERCHEN, intellectual German conductor and an ardent champion of modern music, dies in Florence, whither he fled to escape the dark Nazi apocalypse, a day after his 75th birthday.

13 JUNE 1966

La Mère coupable, opera in three acts by Darius MILHAUD, to a libretto from a comedy by Beaumarchais, in which Figaro settles the amorous troubles of the daughter of the "culpable mother" Rosina, is performed for the first time in Geneva.

14 JUNE 1966

Doppio Concerto Grosso by the Japanese composer Michio MAMIYA, in three movements, scored for a violin and a percussion group as soloists with a large orchestra, opening in a neo-Nipponese manner with an explosive polycacophonous sound, but concluding with a pacifically Baroque perpetuum mobile, is performed for the first time by the Japan Philharmonic Symphony Orchestra in Tokyo.

18 JUNE 1966

Half a millennium has passed since the birth of Ottaviano PETRUCCI, the Venetian printer who was the first to publish a complete collection of part-songs from movable type.

23 JUNE 1966

In the course of the 18th International Music Festival in Strasbourg, three world premières are presented:

Expressions contrastées for orchestra, piano and percussion, by Charles CHAYNES, depicting the kaleidoscopic sensations induced by a psychic visit to an astral territory; *Le Marcheur Solitaire,* a monologue for orchestra by the 42-year-old American composer Eugene KURTZ, written in a "spatial idiom" derived from harmonic aggregates of 3, 6 and 8 serially arranged sounds; and *Chant après Chant*, a fragment from a projected but uncomposed epic *La Mort de Virgile* by the problematic French composer Jean BARRAQUÉ scored for 6 groups of percussion, piano and soprano and based on a series of varied rhythmic cells arranged in permutations and translocations.

23 JUNE 1966

In the course of the Holland Festival in Amsterdam the 31-year-old Dutch modernist Peter SCHAT conducts the first performance of his operatic triptych *Labyrinth* dealing with the three aspects of a woman (sexual, ideological, naturalistic) and intended as "a total theater" calculated to impose "disorientation by simultaneity of incongruities" through the use of mixed media, containing films, ballet, electronic sound, and chants in Latin, accompanied by an orchestra without violins, but with several double-bassoons, doublebasses and bass clarinets.

23 JUNE 1966

First Symphony by the Welsh composer William MATHIAS, in four movements with the overall tonal center of C and dedicated to his wife, is performed for the first time in Birmingham.

23 JUNE 1966

Sixth Symphony by the 80-year-old Austrian composer Egon WELLESZ, "an idea presented in three aspects," in three movements of cyclic facture, an introspective *Lento*, a light-hearted Viennese *Scherzo* and a philosophic *Adagio*, written in a Mahlerian style with dodecaphonic excrescences, is performed for the first time in Nuremberg.

28 JUNE 1966

Akrata by Iannis XENAKIS, 44-year-old Rumanian-born Greek engineer, architect and composer, scored for 15 wind instruments and a vibraphone, written according to his individual method of stochastic composition, in which the creative impulse delegates the process of composition to probabilistic events, and in which the melodic, rhythmic and dynamic parameters are of axiomatic subsumption and strict organization (the Greek title denotes total consistency), is performed for the first time during the English Bach Festival in Oxford.

3 JULY 1966

Deems TAYLOR, versatile American composer and writer whose operas *The King's Henchman* and *Peter Ibbetson* flashed with momentary, brilliance at the Metropolitan Opera, articulate master of ceremonies on radio programs and in whimsical movies (such as Walt Disney's *Fantasia*), literate music critic of an astute conservative persuasion, dies in New York at the age of 80.

3 JULY 1966

The White Gods, opera in three acts depicting the fearful Aztec view of the conquistadors by the 49-year-old American composer Robert KELLY, is performed for the first time in Urbana, Illinois.

7 JULY 1966

Purgatory, one-act opera by the 28-year-old British composer Gordon CROSSE, to a libretto after Yeats dealing with posthumous retribution, wherein a remorseful old man kills his son to end his family's crime-ridden history (he killed his father to avenge his brutal treatment of his mother, who died during his childbirth) and to secure the entrance to Purgatory for all of them, is produced at the Cheltenham Festival.

10 JULY 1966

The 17th Annual Music Festival opens in Dubrovnik, Yugoslavia, with the participation of the Zagreb Philharmonic, the Belgrade Philharmonic, the Cincinnati Symphony Orchestra and ensembles of Serbo-Croatian folk singers.

13 JULY 1966

Kinesis by the 31-year-old Greek composer Theodor ANTONIOU, for two groups of strings, is performed for the first time at the Athens Festival.

27 JULY 1966

The annual Israel Festival opens in Jerusalem with a specially commissioned work *A Festival Sinfonietta* by the Israeli composer Menahem AVIDOM, and the first performance in Israel of *Requiem* by BERLIOZ. (The Festival concluded on 23 August with a concert of chamber music.)

28 JULY 1966

Esculapio al Neon, musical fantasy by Ennio PORRINO, is performed posthumously in concert form, in Naples.

30 JULY 1966

Walter KAUFMANN conducts the Indiana University Opera Group in the world première of his opera *A Hoosier Tale*, to his own libretto, dealing with the marital miscegenation between a white trader and an Indian girl in old Indiana (Hoosier is a folksy epithet for inhabitants of Indiana), set in ostentatiously simplicistic harmonies, with quotations from American songs.

1 AUGUST 1966

Mesa, electronic musical event for cybersonic bandoneon devised by Gordon MUMMA and David TUDOR, is performed for the first time by its creators at an electronic laboratory in St. Paul de Vence, France.

5 AUGUST 1966

The Israel Philharmonic Orchestra embarks on a tour in the Far East, terminating on 19 September, presenting 16 concerts in Australia, 8 in New Zealand and 3 in Hong Kong, under the direction of Eliyahu Inbal, Zubin Mehta and Antal Dorati, and with the participation of the Israeli violinist Zvi Zeitlin.

6 AUGUST 1966

Die Bassariden, neo-Grecian opera by Hans Werner HENZE, to an English libretto by W. A. Auden and Chester Kallman, based on *The Bacchae* of Euripides, set to music in the form of a symphony in four movements within a single act, depicting the conflict between the Germanically tense dodecaphonic asceticism of a sexually repressed King of Thebes and the Italianate incandescent sensualism of the multifutuent, yet diatonically conditioned god of wine Dionysus, all this refracted through a prism of rococo mannerisms, is produced in Salzburg in the German version.

16 AUGUST 1966

Melorhythmic Dances by Carlos SURINACH, an orchestral suite of seven movements (*Fervid, Festive, Poignant, Tragic, Voluptuous, Vehement, Mournful*) is performed for the first time at the Meadow Brook Music Festival at Oakland University in Rochester, Michigan.

18 AUGUST 1966

Markings, symphonic essay by Ulysses KAY, dedicated to the memory of Dag Hammarskjöld, Secretary General of the United Nations until his death in a plane accident in the Congo in 1961, with the title taken from his own posthumous writings, in a single movement subdivided into four contrasting but interrelated sections, opening with an *Allegretto agitato* and progressing through a number of quietly turbulent moods, and ending on a pandiatonic question mark, is performed for the first time at the Meadow Brook Music Festival of Oakland University, in Rochester, Michigan, for which it was written.

21 AUGUST 1966

Pavane Variations for orchestra by Paul CRESTON, written in a dissonantly rhapsodic, sonorously explosive manner, ingratiatingly mitigated by lyrical moments of harmonic candor, is performed for the first time at the La Jolla Music Festival in California.

3 SEPTEMBER 1966

Belisa, opera after Federico García Lorca by the 43-year-old Danish composer and ethnomusicologist Poul Rovsing OLSEN, is performed for the first time in Copenhagen.

4 SEPTEMBER 1966

Le metamorfosi di Bonaventura, fantastic opera by the dean of Italian composers Gian Francesco MALIPIERO, in three acts tracing the madness of a Seville jester, written in a characteristic modern baroque style, is performed for the first time at the opening of the Festival of Modern Music in Venice.

6 SEPTEMBER 1966

Metamorphoses Ebrietatis, symphonic poem by the Swiss composer Armin SCHIBLER, is performed for the first time in Montreux, Switzerland.

9 SEPTEMBER 1966

The 40th Festival of the International Society for Contemporary Music opens in Stockholm with the following program of orchestral music played by the Stockholm Philharmonic Orchestra:

Improvisations symphoniques for piano and orchestra by the 55-year-old Hungarian composer Gabor DARVAS, in two movements, *Cadenza* and *Notturno*, in which the intervallic scheme is governed by the Fibonacci series, with improvised permutations; *Gesangsszene* by Karl Amadeus HARTMANN (1905–1963) of Germany, for baritone and orchestra, written in the manner of free recitative with euphonious dissonant accompaniment; *Transparencias* for 6 instrumental groups by the 35-year-old Argentinian composer Antonio TAURIELLO, based on a general serial principle; and *Syntagma* for orchestra by the 34-year-old Spanish modernist Enrique RAXACH, derived from a complex of parameters. (*Choros I* by Henryk GÓRECKI of Poland was listed in the program, but the performance was cancelled when it was discovered that the orchestral parts were contaminated by a plague of errors.)

10 SEPTEMBER 1966

The Royal Opera of Stockholm presents, in the framework of the annual Stockholm Festival, the world première of the two-act opera *Tronkrävarna (The Pretenders)* by the Swedish composer Gunnar BUCHT, after Ibsen's play *Kongsemnerne*.

10 SEPTEMBER 1966

Klimentu (To Kliment), oratorio by the 41-year-old Macedonian composer Vlastimir NIKOLOVSKI, an homage to an early Christian cleric set in Byzantine modalities, is performed for the first time in Skopje.

11 SEPTEMBER 1966

The second concert of the 40th Festival of the International Society for Contemporary Music in Stockholm presents the following program:

Octandre (the title means an 8-stamen plant) by Edgar VARÈSE (1883–1965), a florid instrumental octet in dissonant harmonies, composed in 1914; *Preludes* by the 69-year-old Polish composer Boleslaw SZABELSKI, in three movements unified by a 12-tone row; *Alveare vernat* for flute and instruments by the 41-year-old Swiss composer Klaus HUBER, written in a metamorphic serial idiom (the title means "spring appears in a beehive"); *Diaphonie* I for chorus and orchestra by the Argentine-born 34-year-old German-domiciled composer Mauricio KAGEL, set for chorus, orchestra and two film projectors casting the musical score derived from random photographic impressions on the screen; *Antistixis* by the 30-year-old Greek composer Yorgos APERGIS, written for three string quartets, in six consecutive events; *Improvvisazione* by the 34-year-old Italian composer Fausto RAZZI, for viola, 18 wind instruments and kettledrums, written as a free interplay of neo-baroque elements; and *Prologues* by the 27-year-old Polish composer Tomas SIKORSKI for a wordless female choir and a small ensemble.

12 SEPTEMBER 1966

The third concert of the 40th Festival of the International Society for Contemporary Music in Stockholm presents the following program of chamber music:

Second Wind Quintet by the 22-year-old Australian composer Ross EDWARDS, written in a freely atonal idiom, economically treated for an optimum effect; *De Profundis* by the 50-year-old Norwegian composer Knut NYSTEDT, for chorus a cappella; *Songs* by Charles IVES (U.S.A.); *Epitaphe* for two sopranos and flute, kettledrums, vibraphone, drums, piano and celesta, written in an expressionistically anguished atonal idiom by the 39-year-old Italian composer Vittorio FELLEGARA; *Music for Albion Moonlight* for soprano and instruments by the 28-year-old English composer David BEDFORD, based on thematic clusters of notes; and *Prisme* by the 33-year-old Danish composer Per NØRGÅRD, for mezzo-soprano, tenor, baritone, guitar and orchestra, in 8 movements.

13 SEPTEMBER 1966

At the fourth concert of the 40th Festival of the International Society for Contemporary Music in Stockholm the following program of chamber music is given:

Quattrodramma by the 71-year-old German composer Paul DESSAU, for four cellos, two pianos and a battery of percussion, written in a free serialistic idiom with aleatoric interludes; *The Tomb at Akr Caar* by the 52-year-old Finnish composer Bengt JOHANSSON, for voice and chamber chorus, to texts by Ezra Pound, set in a moderate polytonal idiom; *This Is Thy Glorification* by the 22-year-old Jerusalem-born Israeli composer Ron LEWY, for narrator, chorus and instruments; *Third String Quartet* by the 34-year-old Czech composer Marek KOPELENT, written as a study in altering tensions; *Elegie in friulano* by the 66-year-old Italian composer Antonio VERETTI, to words in the Frioulian dialect of North Italy, scored for voice, violin, clarinet and guitar, in 9 short movements; *Oro No. 2* by the 42-year-old Icelandic composer Leifur THORARINSSON, based on a free serial technique in aleatoric turbulence (hence the name, Oro, disturbance); *Torso* by the 42-year-old Danish composer Axel BORUP-JÖRGENSEN, written for two string quartets, one of which is tape recorded in advance; and *Kanon* by the 29-year-old Norwegian composer Alfred JANSON, written for a chamber orchestra and prerecorded tape.

14 SEPTEMBER 1966

At the fifth concert of the 40th Festival of the International Society for Contemporary Music in Stockholm, a program of Swedish music is given:

The first performance of *Il Cantico del sole* by the 47-year-old composer Siegfried NAUMANN, for soloists, chorus and orchestra, to the words of Francesco d'Assisi; *Coloratura IV* by the 26-year-old composer Jan W. MORTHENSON, representing a coloristic study of harmonic textures; and *Poesis* by the 45-year-old composer Ingvar LIDHOLM, a lyrico-dramatic study in contrasting sonorities of orchestral timbres.

15 SEPTEMBER 1966

The 40th Festival of the International Society for Contemporary Music in Stockholm presents its sixth and last concert in the following program:

Un día sobresale, by the 39-year-old German-born Argentinian composer Michael GIELEN, serialistically conceived as a pentaphony for five solo instruments, and five groups of five musicians each (of which one group is comprised of vocalists); *Les Sons* by the 39-year-old Polish composer Witold SZALONEK, scored for orchestra without violins and cellos, and conceived as a series of tonal tensions from pianississississimo to fortississississimo; *Etude III* by the 28-year-old French composer Jean-Claude ÉLOY, conceived as a concertino for 5 percussion players, piano, harp, celesta and a classical orchestra; *22 Pages* by the 32-year-old Dutch composer Joep STRAESSER, for wind instruments, 8 doublebasses, percussion and male voices, to a text by John Cage, for tenor, baritone, bass and an assorted ensemble of instruments; and *Transfiguration* by the 38-year-old Swedish composer Bengt HAMBRAEUS, a cycle of movements of instrumental and electronic music, in which any movement can be played individually or synchronously with any other.

16 SEPTEMBER 1966

The new Metropolitan Opera House, erected in Lincoln Center, New York, at the cost of $45,700,000, opens with a spectacular production of the specially commissioned opera *Antony and Cleopatra* by the American composer Samuel BARBER, in three acts and 16 scenes, conducted by Thomas Schippers and staged with flamboyant extravagance by Franco Zeffirelli (special prices were set at $250 for a single seat in rows A through M) requiring the participation, besides the soprano Leontyne Price (first Negro singer to take the part of Cleopatra in any opera), the bass Justino Diaz as Antony and tenor Jess Thomas as Octavian, of three horses, three goats and a camel, the scenery, including a sphinx, arrayed on multiple rotating platforms, making it possible to change the scene of action from Alexandria to Rome with cinematic celerity, and a musical score combining Italianate fervor of bel canto with a flair for intellectually modern melodic configurations, quartal intervallic progressions and acridly euphonious polyharmonies.

17 SEPTEMBER 1966

TIS-MW-2, a metamusical audio-visual spectacle by the 37-year-old Polish modernist Boguslaw SCHÄFFER, to a non-ontological alogical oneirological scenario for an illusory narrator reciting a series of discrete surrealistic fragments of irrationally oriented non-temporal events to the accompaniment of an indeterminate instrumental ensemble, with demoniac illuminations scintillating in sudden silences, anguished outcries, implosive borborigmuses and choreic singultations, is performed for the first time in the course of the 10th International Festival of Contemporary Music in Warsaw ("Warsaw Autumn").

18 SEPTEMBER 1966

Tomorrow, lyric drama in one act by the 38-year-old Polish composer Tadeusz BAIRD, to a libretto after Joseph Conrad's story of dark passions in a fishermen's village, ending with the murder of a seaman by his own father for an attempt to violate a girl who was the object of the father's senescent adoration, is produced in Warsaw in the course of the 10th International Festival of Contemporary Music ("Warsaw Autumn").

20 SEPTEMBER 1966

Muses of Sicily, cantata by the 40-year-old German composer Hans Werner HENZE is performed for the first time in Berlin as a commissioned work to mark the 175th anniversary of the Berlin Singakademie.

21 SEPTEMBER 1966

Ninth Symphony in three movements by the prime Italian symphonist Gian Francesco MALIPIERO, subtitled *Hélas*

because a presentiment of the death of his wife interrupted the composition of the finale and inspired an elegiac interlude, is performed for the first time in the course of the 10th Festival of Contemporary Music in Warsaw ("Warsaw Autumn").

21 SEPTEMBER 1966

Sixth Symphony, surnamed *Sinfonia Tragica*, by the 90-year-old English composer Havergal BRIAN, composed in 1948, consisting of three movements played without pause, receives its first performance, in London. (*Sinfonia Tragica* was originally an unnumbered work, but at the age of 92 the composer renumbered his earlier symphonies and discarded the *First Symphony* written in 1908; this ellipsis made *Sinfonia Tragica* his *Sixth Symphony*.)

23 SEPTEMBER 1966

George BARATI conducts the Honolulu Symphony Orchestra in the world première of his festival ode, *The Waters of Kane*, for chorus and orchestra, a symphonic invocation of the millennial legend of the magic waters struck from the rainbow of the Polynesian demiurge Kane, written in a primitivistic modernistic idiom, with thematic materials drawn from authentic Hawaiian chants, fertilized by hula rhythms tapped out on the native drum *puili* made of the split bamboo plant.

24 SEPTEMBER 1966

Altisonans, avian tone poem by Karl-Birger BLOMDAHL, produced by an electronic transmutation of elements of bird songs superimposed on the reduction to the audible spectrum of satellite signals and the impact of cosmic rays, is recorded in the Swedish Television Center in Stockholm.

25 SEPTEMBER 1966

On his 60th birthday Dmitri SHOSTAKOVICH is nominated Hero of Socialist Labor by the Soviet Government, and a concert of his music is given at the Moscow Conservatory, presenting the first performance of his *Second Violoncello Concerto* under the direction of his son Maxim Shostakovich, with Mstislav Rostropovich as soloist.

1 OCTOBER 1966

The 67-year-old German pianist Heinz ARNTZ plays, at the Long Island fair in Westbury, New York, his favorite march *Alte Kameraden*, establishing at 1 P.M. the world record of pianofortitude with 1054 hours of continuous piano playing (with two hours off each day for the physiological necessities of sleeping, eating and elimination), a pianistic marathon begun at 8:00 P.M. on 18 August 1966, in a Düsseldorf cafe, continued in a truck from Düsseldorf to Bremerhaven, in the salon of the liner United States and in another truck from the pier to the fair at Roosevelt Raceway in Westbury.

3 OCTOBER 1966

The new Jesse H. Jones Hall for the Performing Arts opens in Houston, Texas, with the Houston Symphony Orchestra, conducted by Sir John Barbirolli in a program including the first performance of a commissioned Amer-

ican work, *Ode to the Temple of Sound* by Alan HOV-
HANESS.

8 OCTOBER 1966

Amerika, opera by Roman HAUBENSTOCK-RAMATI,
after Kafka, written in an advanced serial idiom, with the
application of electronic techniques, is produced at the
Berlin Festival.

8 OCTOBER 1966

Requiem Canticles by Igor STRAVINSKY, for mixed chorus,
vocal soloists and orchestra, in 9 sections (6 vocal and 3
instrumental), set to abbreviated extracts from the
Requiem in the Latin ritual, and written in a reverential
neo-ecclesiastical Spirit but set in a specific serial idiom,
is performed for the first time at a semiprivate gathering
at Princeton University.

12 OCTOBER 1966

Esther, opera in two acts by the German composer Robert
HANELL, in which the non-Aryan animal warmth of a
young Jewish girl violinist is used by the Nazi doctors to
restore the life of an experimentally frozen Aryan youth,
with anti-fascist love blossoming forth between the two
enabling the girl to go to her death in a gas chamber with
a renewed hope in the inherent decency of at least one
German in a flood of Hitlerian diabolism, is produced at
the German State Opera in East Berlin.

12 OCTOBER 1966

Gunther SCHULLER conducts the Hamburg State
Opera in the world première of his three-act opera *The
Visitation,* inspired by the faceless terrors of Kafka's
novel *Der Prozess* and dedicated "to all men who,
through hate, injustice and oppression are denied freedom in their pursuit of happiness," with the action
transferred to the American South and focused on the
tragic fate of a black student suspected of harboring a
miscegenating sentiment towards a white girl, set to
music in a plenitude of modern techniques, ranging
from triadic serenity to integral serialism, and incorporating a jazz combo in the orchestral score, the action
subdivided into the following sections:

Act I. Scene 1. *A Warning* (jazzy portents and discordant
omens against the background of Negro chants). Scene 2.
Miss Hampton (atonal coloratura voicing anxiety and sympathy). Scene 3. *A Summoning* (brassy tumult in a drug store
where the intended victim is employed as a soda jerk).
Scene 4. *An Interrogation* (massive incursion of authoritarian
brass reinforced by traumatic drumbeats). Act II. Scene 1.
The Court House (ostentatiously egalitarian jurisprudential
disharmonies). Scene 2. *An Encounter* (police cars cruising
permissively past groups of racist men mobilizing in darkening streets). Scene 3. *The Lawyer* (tranquilizing legalities in
pseudo-humanitarian concordant counterpoint). Act III.
Scene 1. *The Nightclub Operator* (polytonal tides of inexorable
inhumanity). Scene 2. *The Preacher* (a specious paraclete
radiating phony euphony). Scene 3. *The Sacrifice* (polychordal onslaught by brutalized killers, with the recorded
voice of Bessie Smith, the Queen of the Blues, heard on a
distant phonograph providing sorrowful commentary). *Epilogue* (a funereal procession intoned by a toneless chorus
receding into timeless space).

16 OCTOBER 1966

Wieland WAGNER, grandson of Wagner and great-grandson of Liszt, who with his brother Wolfgang assumed the
directorship of the Bayreuth Festivals in 1951, and revo-
lutionized the production of Wagner's music dramas,
doing away with the stuffy Teutonic costumery which
was once *de rigueur* and introducing stark scenic symbolism (e.g., the erection of a phallic totem pole in *Tristan
und Isolde*), dies in Frankfurt at the age of 49.

25 OCTOBER 1966

Dr. Atom, surrealistic ballet by the 60-year-old Croatian
composer Boris PAPANDOPULO, is produced in Rijeka
(Fiume).

29 OCTOBER 1966

Music for Indiana, a symphonic sketch by Darius MIL-
HAUD, written for the sesquicentennial of the State of
Indiana, is performed for the first time in Indianapolis.

30 OCTOBER 1966

Sinfonia Tramontana, the last symphony by the Swedish
romantic composer Gösta NYSTROEM (1890–1966) is
performed posthumously in Stockholm.

31 OCTOBER 1966

Sinfonia II, subtitled *Susudil,* by the 43-year-old Danish
composer and ethnomusicologist Poul Rovsing OLSEN,
based on Arabic and Turkish modes, is performed for the
first time in Copenhagen.

4 NOVEMBER 1966

In Memoriam John F. Kennedy by the 38-year-old American
composer William SYDEMAN, for narrator and orchestra,
to a text including extracts from Kennedy's speeches and
comments by Kennedy's associates, containing allusions
to the funeral march from Beethoven's *Eroica* and to the
U.S. National Anthem, is performed for the first time by
the Boston Symphony Orchestra, Erich Leinsdorf conducting.

5 NOVEMBER 1966

Együtt és egyedül (Together and Alone), allegorical opera by
the 48-year-old Hungarian composer András MIHÁLY, in
which a perpetual wanderer seeking the location of
Dante's Inferno finds it in Hungary under the Nazi-dominated Fascistic regime, set to music in somberly discordant harmonies and ominously asymmetrical rhythms, is
produced in Budapest.

8 NOVEMBER 1966

Die Flucht, dramatic oratorio by the Russian-born, German-educated Swiss composer Wladimir VOGEL is performed for the first time in Zürich.

12 NOVEMBER 1966

Quincy PORTER, American composer of highly cultured
symphonic music set in a neo-classical style, dies in
Bethany, Connecticut, at the age of 69.

15 NOVEMBER 1966

Puntila, opera by Paul DESSAU, after a play by Bertolt Brecht, in 12 scenes with a prologue and an epilogue, dealing with four resolute women who expose the wickedness of an alcoholic landlord, written in a burlesque manner, including a series of ariosos and half-spoken dialogues, is produced in East Berlin.

17 NOVEMBER 1966

Fourth Symphony by the 64-year-old Swedish composer Sten BROMAN, in two sections *Fantasia* and *Finale,* unified by a permanent rhythmic pulse of 63 beats per minute, with all changes of tempo being multiples of this number and the melodic material drawn from a monoserial dodecaphonic matrix, the score containing a large complement of percussion instruments, including exotic drums, is performed for the first time by the Detroit Symphony Orchestra under the direction of its Swedish conductor Sixten Ehrling.

19 NOVEMBER 1966

Sixth Symphony by Roger SESSIONS, in three movements, written in a highly complex contrapuntal idiom, fertilized by the spermatic infusion of asymmetrically ejaculated rhythms, commissioned by the State of New Jersey for the celebration of its tercentenary, is performed for the first time in its entirety in Newark. (The first two movements were performed for the first time, before the third movement was completed, in Newark, on 19 January 1966.)

29 NOVEMBER 1966

The Violins of Saint-Jacques, opera in three acts by the 35-year-old Australian composer Malcolm WILLIAMSON, his fifth opera, in which phantom violins emerge from the sea on each anniversary of the cataclysmic eruption in 1902 of Mont Pelée on the Island of Martinique, with assorted zombies, among them a convertible Lesbian and an effeminate captain, arising from the foam in voodoo rituals, set to music in a sophisticatedly simplistic triadic idiom vivified by Caribbean rhythms, is produced by the Sadler's Wells Opera Company in London.

2 DECEMBER 1966

Double Concerto for oboe, harp and 18 string instruments by Hans Werner HENZE, written in a dissonant neobaroque idiom, is performed for the first time in Zürich.

11 DECEMBER 1966

Guayana Johnny (The Sugar Reapers), opera in two acts by the English socialist composer Alan BUSH, dealing with the downtrodden sugar plantation workers in British Guiana who successfully overwhelm the British colonial power in 1953, containing an episode of interracial passion of a handsome Negro for a diminutive Hindu maiden, set to music steeped in indigenous melorhythms, is performed for the first time in Leipzig.

11 DECEMBER 1966

Laura, comic opera by Béla TARDOS, Hungarian composer of meloromantic music, is produced posthumously in Debrecen, 23 days after the composer's death.

15 DECEMBER 1966

Triplum by Wolfgang FORTNER, a triptych in which the thematic condominium of component trinities is scored for a triune consortium of wind instruments, strings, percussion and three pianos, set in serially calculated triplicities of tripartite forms, is performed for the first time by the Basel Chamber Orchestra, Paul Sacher conducting.

18 DECEMBER 1966

Fourth Symphony by the English composer Benjamin FRANKEL is performed for the first time in London.

21 DECEMBER 1966

It Is Snowing, cantata by the Soviet composer Georgy SVIRIDOV, to words by Boris Pasternak, is performed for the first time in Moscow.

29 DECEMBER 1966

Concerto for Percussion and Orchestra in three movements by the 42-year-old American composer Donald ERB, is performed for the first time by the Detroit Symphony Orchestra.

1967

4 JANUARY 1967

Mary GARDEN, Scottish soprano singer who captured the imagination of the Paris public as Mélisande in Debussy's opera at its first performance in 1902 despite her burring accent, dies in her native town of Aberdeen in Scotland, a few weeks before her 93rd birthday. (She was born on 20 February 1874, not 1877, as she self-rejuvenatingly claimed.)

6 JANUARY 1967

André JOLIVET conducts in Moscow the first performance of his *Second Concerto* for cello and orchestra, with Mstislav Rostropovich as soloist.

6 JANUARY 1967

Piano Concerto by the 58-year-old American composer Elliott CARTER, in two movements, *Fantastico* and *Molto giusto,* conceived in the form of a double concerto grosso, in which a group of seven instruments acts as a polyphonic mediator between the piano and orchestra, with thematic materials organized in a serial totality of metrical, rhythmical, melodic, harmonic and contrapuntal parameters, is performed for the first time by Jacob Lateiner with the Boston Symphony Orchestra, Erich Leinsdorf conducting.

12 JANUARY 1967

Fourth Symphony by the 63-year-old Hungarian neoclassicist Paul KÁDOSA is performed for the first time in Budapest.

22 JANUARY 1967

Sixth Symphony by Ernst TOCH, in three movements, *Allegro comodo, Molto grazioso e leggiero* and *Allegro energico,* set in an endearing neoromantic mood, is performed posthumously for the first time by the Zürich Radio Orchestra.

24 JANUARY 1967

A symphony concert in a program of four specially commissioned works by American composers is presented at the University of Chicago to mark its 75th anniversary:

Music for the Magic Theater by George ROCHBERG, a musical collage of quotations from compositions by masters from Mozart to Varèse, interlinearly perlustrated by connective tissue of original motives; *Inflexions* for 14 players by the Argentine composer, resident in America, Mario DAVIDOVSKY, written in a modernistic idiom within the normal tempered scale; and *Un Voyage à Cythère* for soprano and ten instruments by Easley BLACKWOOD, depicting in impressionistic tones a journey to the island of Aphrodite.

27 JANUARY 1967

Concerto for Cello and Orchestra by Frank MARTIN in three movements—*Allegro moderato, Adagietto* and *Vivace*—writ-

ten in a pantonal style ranging from immaculate diatonicism to quasi-dodecaphonic chromaticism, is performed for the first time in Basel.

29 JANUARY 1967

Die Doppelgängerin, opera in three acts by the German-American composer Jan MEYEROWITZ, based on Gerhardt Hauptmann's play *Winterballad,* to a libretto of murderous violence and preternatural revenge by an alter ego of the victim (hence the title) in 16th-century Sweden, set to music in neo-medieval modalities, is performed for the first time in Hannover, Germany.

7 FEBRUARY 1967

Les Quasars (*Third Symphony*) for chorus and orchestra by the Canadian composer Clermont PEPIN, to his own poem extolling man's boldness in probing the mysterious quasi-stellar objects in remote space, in four movements—*Symphonie de lumières, Poésie de couleurs, Trajectories invisibles de présences* and *Lancinantes décorations de silence*—set in hyperimpressionistic harmonies, is performed for the first time in Montreal.

13 FEBRUARY 1967

Sinfonietta for string orchestra by Ernst TOCH, in three cyclic movements, is performed posthumously for the first time in Philadelphia.

14 FEBRUARY 1967

Fourth Symphony by the 46-year-old English composer Peter Racine FRICKER, in one continuous movement, subdivided into ten sections, written in a freely atonal idiom containing mutually independent dodecaphonic episodes, but gravitating towards a focal A as a key center, dedicated to the memory of his Hungarian teacher Mátyás Seiber (who died in an automobile catastrophe in South Africa on 24 September 1960) and embodying translucently veiled thematic allusions to several of Seiber's works, is performed for the first time in Wolverhampton, England.

15 FEBRUARY 1967

Nausikaa and *Die Bauerhochzeit,* scenic cantatas by Hermann REUTTER, newly arranged for the stage from his vocal cycle *Hochzeitslieder,* are performed for the first time on the stage in Mainz.

16 FEBRUARY 1967

Anis FULEIHAN, 66-year-old American composer, conducts the New York Philharmonic in the world première of his *Second Symphony* in five movements: *Moderato, Vivace, Andante con moto, Tempo di marcia* and *Allegro,* the latter based on a Greek song retained in Fuleihan's childhood memories of his native island of Cyprus.

24 FEBRUARY 1967

Kardiogram IV by the 23-year-old Swedish avant-garde composer Gunnar VALKARE, scored for four vocalists of different sexes, chorus and a chamber orchestra, is performed for the first time in Helsinki, Finland.

1 MARCH 1967

The inaugural concert is given in the newly built Queen Elizabeth Hall, London, in the presence of Queen Elizabeth II, presenting a program of music by English composers, from Henry PURCELL to Benjamin BRITTEN, including the first performance of Britten's *Hankin Booby* for chamber orchestra, based on English folksongs.

2 MARCH 1967

Variations for Cello and Orchestra, in one continuous movement, by Walter PISTON, written in his newly adopted dodecaphonic technique of composition, opening with a widely-spaced 12-tone chord, with the perfect fourth, tritones and their summational major sevenths being the principal "tendency intervals," the entire panchromatic panoply opened to include episodes in diatonic modalities and nutritious triadic harmonies, concluding on a starkly thirdless triad on D, is performed for the first time by the prime Soviet violoncellist Mstislav Rostropovich, with the London Symphony Orchestra on its American visit, conducted by Gennady Rozhdestvensky, in Carnegie Hall, New York.

4 MARCH 1967

Kaiser Jovian, opera in four acts by the 35-year-old Swiss composer Rudolf KELTERBORN, wherein Jupiter assumes the identity of the ephemeral Roman emperor Jovian (reigned 363–364 A.D.), marries his bride, and ultimately reveals himself and returns to Mt. Olympus, opening and ending with a vociferous dodecaphonic chord, is produced in Karlsruhe.

4 MARCH 1967

Arden muss sterben, a "political opera about ourselves" in two acts by the 34-year-old German-born English composer Alexander GOEHR, to a German libretto after an anonymous 16th-century English play *Arden of Feversham*, dealing with the murder of a faceless man by his wife and her lover, set to music as a series of interconnected variations immersed in an atonal magma, is performed for the first time by the Hamburg State Opera.

5 MARCH 1967

Eli, opera in 12 scenes by the German composer Walter STEFFENS, after a story by the Nobel laureate Nelly Sachs, dealing with a Jewish boy named Eli slain by an Ebreocidal Nazi as he plays a tune on his shepherd's pipe in the childish hope of summoning angels from heaven to his aid, set to music in "intervallically coherent atonal counterpoint" is produced in Dortmund.

5 MARCH 1967

Lukas FOSS conducts in New York, with the Soviet cellist Mstislav Rostropovich as soloist, the first performance of his *Concerto* for violoncello and orchestra, written in a highly advanced modern idiom and containing aleatory passages.

6 MARCH 1967

Zoltán KODÁLY, great master of modern Hungarian music who together with Béla Bartók early in the century traveled through the hills and dales of Southeastern Europe to collect thousands of authentic multinational folk melodies, composer of operas, symphonic, choral and instrumental music, dies in Budapest of a heart ailment at the age of 84.

9 MARCH 1967

The Servant of Two Masters, posthumous opera by Vittorio GIANNINI (who died in New York on 28 November 1966 at the age of 63), after the play by Carlo Goldoni, written in an effusively euphonious, harmonious and melodious idiom as a legacy of the composer's Italian ancestry, is brought out for the first time by the New York City Opera Company.

11 MARCH 1967

Geraldine FARRAR, American soprano, who rose to fame as a heart-rending Madama Butterfly, a role which she sang at the Metropolitan Opera with Caruso a hundred times, and colored her career by sensationally publicized affairs of the heart, dies at the age of 85 at her farmland retreat in Ridgefield, Connecticut, surviving by decades the purple era of her stardom.

17 MARCH 1967

Mourning Becomes Electra, opera in three acts by the 34-year-old American composer Marvin David LEVY, to a libretto condensed from Eugene O'Neill's trilogy, in which the scene of action is shifted from ancient Greece to a New England village in 1865, Agamemnon is phonetically anglicized into Ezra Mannon returning home from the Civil War, Clytemnestra becomes Christine, her lover Aegisthus is Adam Brant, Electra is Lavinia and her brother Orestes is Orin, set to music in an anguished atonal idiom embanked in compact dissonant counterpoint, is produced by the Metropolitan Opera Company as a commissioned work, at Lincoln Center, New York.

23 MARCH 1967

Stronger Than Death, opera in three acts by the Soviet composer Kyrill MOLCHANOV, focused on a Soviet hero of the defense of Brest-Litovsk against the Nazi assault in June 1941, is produced in Voronezh in the presence of the actual prototype of the story, Pyotr Gavrilov, Hero of the Soviet Union.

23 MARCH 1967

A memorial stamp is issued by the Malagasy Republic (Madagascar) in honor of the native composer Norbert RAHARISOA (1914–1963), a graduate of the Lyon Conservatory in France, who in 1959 wrote the national hymn of Madagascar.

24 MARCH 1967

Quintet for Groups by the 40-year-old American composer Benjamin Burwell JOHNSTON, in which the orchestra is divided into five contrasting sections of instruments, is performed for the first time by the St. Louis Symphony Orchestra.

25 MARCH 1967

To mark the centennial of the birth of Arturo TOSCANINI, the Italian government issues a 40-lire yellow and lavender commemorative stamp depicting the Maestro with a baton in his right hand.

31 MARCH 1967

The Bridge, "anti-opera" by the Czech composer Jaromil BURGHAUSER, to a symbolic libretto placed simultaneously at two points in time, in the revolutionary year of 1848 and in the socialist year of 1963, and located in space on a bridge which divides a town into two parts, set to music in modern serial techniques, is produced in Prague.

1 APRIL 1967

Polymorphie for 106 musicians by the French composer Michel DECOUST is performed for the first time in the course of the musical festival in Royan, France.

5 APRIL 1967

Mischa (a diminutive Slavic form for Michael) ELMAN, 76-year-old Russian-Jewish violinist whose playing was distinguished by an emotional richness of tone and romantic absorption in the music, dies suddenly of a heart attack in New York.

6 APRIL 1967

Los Caprichos, symphonic fantasy by the 40-year-old German composer Hans Werner HENZE, inspired by Goya's drawing of a witch riding a broom at the altitude of about 2,000 feet, is performed for the first time in Duisburg.

6 APRIL 1967

Concerto for Piano and Orchestra by Miklós RÓZSA, Hungarian-born composer domesticated in Hollywood, in three well-contrasted movements, vibrant with colorful Lisztian pianism, saturated with euphonious dissonances and vitalized by explosively asymmetrical rhythms, is performed for the first time by the Los Angeles Philharmonic Orchestra, with Zubin Mehta conducting and Leonard Pennario playing the solo part.

6 APRIL 1967

Chthonic Ode for orchestra by the American composer Paul CRESTON, a homage to the modern British sculptor Henry Moore, extolling in tersely dissonant harmonies the immanent chthonicism of his primitivistically transcendental sculptures, is performed for the first time in Detroit.

13 APRIL 1967

La Chanson de Roland, lyric opera in three acts by the 72-year-old French composer Henri MARTELLI, to the composer's own libretto after the medieval French epic, is performed for the first time in Paris.

14 APRIL 1967

Dies Irae, "Oratorium ob memoriam in perniciei castris in Oswiecim necatorum inexstingguibilem reddendam," for solo voices, chorus and orchestra, by the 33-year-old Polish modernist Krzysztof PENDERECKI, dedicated to the memory of men, women and children exterminated in Auschwitz (Oswiecim) by the Nazis, to Latin texts from Psalms and Apocalypse and Latin translations of poems by Louis Aragon, Paul Valery and others, as well as Greek texts of Aeschylus, is performed for the first time in Cracow. (Three days later it was performed at the inaugural of the Monument of Struggle and Martyrdom in Oswiecim.)

15 APRIL 1967

In honor of the 20th anniversary of UNESCO, the Republic of Togo issues a set of commemorative postage stamps of seven values (5, 10, 15, 20, 30, 45 and 90 francs) featuring portraits of Bach, Beethoven, Debussy and Duke Ellington.

16 APRIL 1967

Les Hauts de Hurlevent, opera in seven scenes after Emily Brontë's novel *Wuthering Heights,* by the French composer Thomas STUBBS, set to an appropriately romantic score in an ingratiatingly old-fashioned operatic idiom, is produced for the first time in Rouen, France.

17 APRIL 1967

The Crook, comic opera in two acts by the Israeli composer Menahem AVIDOM, the first musical satire on the government of Israel, wherein its fiscal troubles lead to the promulgation of a decree forbidding the population to breathe after the expiration of the deadline for payment of taxes, is produced in Tel Aviv.

18 APRIL 1967

Cosmic Mist, symphonic poem by the Texas-born composeress Radie BRITAIN, in three movements—(1) *In the Beginning,* (2) *Nebula,* (3) *Nuclear Fission*—illustrative of cosmogonic mysteries by means of chromatic implosions amidst tritone-laden harmonies, culminating in a subatomic fortississississimo, is performed for the first time at an unrehearsed orchestral symposium in Houston.

19 APRIL 1967

Cello Concerto by the Hungarian ultra-modernist György LIGETI, is performed for the first time in Berlin.

20 APRIL 1967

Carmen Suite, ballet arranged from Bizet's famous opera *Carmen* by Rodion SHCHEDRIN for strings and drums, with the music deromanticized by blunt percussive rhythms, is performed for the first time in Moscow, with Shchedrin's wife, Maya Plisetskaya, as prima ballerina.

27 APRIL 1967

La Duchesse de Langeais, opera in three acts by the French-Italian conductor Eugène BOZZA, written in a Puccinian lyrico-dramatic style, is performed for the first time in Lille, France.

27 APRIL 1967

Phorion for orchestra, electronic organ, and electric guitar by the 44-year-old ultra-modern American composer Lukas FOSS, a metamorphosis of Bach's violin *Partita in E* (*Phorion* means stolen goods in Greek, and the idea came to Foss in a dream when he heard, and observed on paper, "torrents of Baroque 16th-notes washed ashore by ocean waves and sucked in again"), with the thematic materials transmogrified by aleatory permutations, acrobatic inversions, congenial perversions and melorhythmic singultations, is performed for the first time by the New York Philharmonic, under the direction of Leonard Bernstein. *Phorion* was later incorporated into *Baroque Variations,* with thematic material derived not only from Bach's *Partita,* but also from Handel's suite in E major and Scarlatti's Sonata in E major.

29 APRIL 1967

Geschäftsbericht, minimal opera (duration 600 seconds) by the prime German Communist composer Paul DESSAU, a "business report" to the text of the indictment of the American aggression in Vietnam by the International Tribunal for War Crimes in Stockholm, with an epilogue in which dead American soldiers curse President Johnson for depriving them of their lives, is produced in Leipzig.

29 APRIL 1967

The Universal and International Exhibition EXPO 67 opens in Montreal to mark Canada's Centennial year with the presentation of specially composed oratorio *Terre des hommes,* to a French text, for orchestra, chorus and two narrators, by the Canadian composer Andre PREVOST, written in an inframodern idiom enlivened by rational dissonances, with the message exhorting mankind to regain the "perfumes of dawn."

30 APRIL 1967

At the World Festival of Music given in conjunction with Expo 67 in Montreal, the Stockholm Royal Opera makes its North American debut with Verdi's opera *Un Ballo in Maschera,* to the original libretto describing the assassination on 16 March 1792 of King Gustavus of Sweden, rather than that of the mythical "Governor of Boston" of the revised version.

1 MAY 1967

Diastasis, As in Beer (that is, a mixture of ingredients of malt from which beer is made), for two cybersonic guitars by Gordon MUMMA, is performed by its creator and Christian Wolff at Harvard University in Cambridge, Massachusetts.

2 MAY 1967

Venice, "an audiograph" for double orchestra and brass choirs by the American composer Morton GOULD, portraying, in seven "sonic postcards" the topography of Venice, its cafés, its canals and its pigeons, is performed for the first time by the Seattle Symphony Orchestra.

9 MAY 1967

A Criminal Court Judge in New York City gives a suspended jail sentence to Charlotte MOORMAN, 28-year-old American cellist for playing a recital in New York on 9 February 1967 in "topless" attire, with her rounded bosoms fully exposed to potentially innocent eyes.

13 MAY 1967

Concerto for flute and orchestra by Jean FRANÇAIX is performed for the first time in Schwetzingen, Germany.

14 MAY 1967

Galileo, oratorio by the American composer Ezra LADERMAN, depicting the prosecution by the Church of the great astronomer Galileo, is performed for the first time as a television drama with music by the Columbia Broadcasting Company in New York.

15 MAY 1967

Antiparallele, for piano and orchestra by the 46-year-old Slovenian composer Primoz RAMOVS, is performed for the first time at the Zagreb Festival.

16 MAY 1967

Voie for three choirs and orchestra by the 32-year-old avant-garde Slovenian-born composer and trombonist Vinko GLOBOKAR, to a text by Mayakovsky sung in Russian by a men's choir, in French by a women's choir, and in Slovenian by a mixed choir, is performed for the first time in Zagreb.

17 MAY 1967

Jonah, dramatic cantata by the American composer Daniel PINKHAM, is performed for the first time at the New England Conservatory of Music in Boston, as part of the celebration of its centennial.

19 MAY 1967

Bomarzo, opera in two acts by the 51-year-old Argentinian modernist Alberto GINASTERA, subdivided into 15 scenes saturated with effulgent sex, ecstatic violence and psychedelic hallucinations, dealing with the 16th-century Italian Duke of Bomarzo, to a libretto fashioned after a novel by the Argentine writer Manuel Mujica Lainez, featuring a seduction in a bordello, mass voyeurism, latent sodomy and ineffable perversions leading to Bomarzo's poisoning, set to music with the application of various serial techniques, a chord of 12 different notes and 11 different intervals being of germinal importance, is performed for the first time on the stage in Washington. (A cantata *Bomarzo* by Alberto Ginastera, with the same plot but a different score, was performed for the first time on 1 November 1964, also in Washington.)

22 MAY 1967

At the opening concert of the 11th Gulbenkian Music Festival in Lisbon, *Concerto for Violin, Piano and Orchestra* by the 69-year-old Brazilian composer Francisco MIGNONE is performed for the first time.

26 MAY 1967

Echoes of Time and the River: Processionals for Orchestra by the 37-year-old American composer George CRUMB is performed for the first time in Chicago, later receiving the 1968 Pulitzer Prize in Music.

26 MAY 1967

Madame Bovary, opera in two acts by the Swiss composer Heinrich SUTERMEISTER, after Flaubert's famous novel analyzing the adulterous life and pitiful death of a provincial Frenchwoman, is performed for the first time in Zürich.

1 JUNE 1967

Seventh Symphony by Ernst TOCH, his last, in four cyclic movements, *Molto lento, Allegro moderato, Allegro giocoso* and *Allegro risoluto*, is performed posthumously for the first time in Munich.

2 JUNE 1967

To Vishnu, tone poem by the 56-year-old American composer Alan HOVHANESS, depicting the solar god of the Hindus as the controlling deity of the galactic spheres, opening with a musical landscape of mildly dissonant chaos and culminating in a sonic pandemonium of bells and trumpets in a fiery orbit, is performed for the first time by the New York Philharmonic.

2 JUNE 1967

Sequencia, Coral e Ricercare, a neo-baroque symphonic suite by the 60-year-old Brazilian composer Camargo GUARNIERI is performed for the first time at the 11th annual Gulbenkian Music Festival in Lisbon.

2 JUNE 1967

Queen Elizabeth of England opens the 20th Music Festival of the Suffolk fishing village of Aldeburgh, with the Royal Artillery Band sounding fanfares from the opera *Gloriana* by Benjamin BRITTEN, founder of the Aldeburgh Festival, followed by a brief concert featuring Britten's choral overture *The Building of the House* written for the occasion.

3 JUNE 1967

Two chamber operas by British composers receive their first performances at the Aldeburgh Festival in England:

Castaway by Lennox BERKELEY, dealing with the dalliance of Odysseus with Nausicaa; and *The Bear* by William WALTON, after a comic play by Anton Chekhov in which an ill-mannered intellectual, about to propose to the lady of his heart, nearly ruins their future marital bliss by starting a polemical discussion with her.

12 JUNE 1967

Magic Prison for two narrators and orchestra by the 43-year-old American composer Ezra LADERMAN, based on the writings of Emily Dickinson, is performed for the first time by the New York Philharmonic, André Kostelanetz conducting.

17 JUNE 1967

Heroine, opera in two acts by the Albanian composer Vangjo NOVO, in which an Albanian girl guerrilla heroically refuses, despite inhuman torture, to disclose the names of the Communist-led partisans to the Nazi invaders in 1943, culminating in a total liberation of the land and the execution of local traitors, set to music according to the romantic formula of socialist opera, with tragedy and sacrifice in minor modes leading to a triumphant finale in marching major keys, is produced in Tirana.

18 JUNE 1967

Blumine, excised movement from Gustav MAHLER'S *First Symphony*, redolent of the flowery scent of the neologism of the title (taken by Mahler from a literary essay *Herbst-Blumine* of the romantic German writer Jean Paul), is performed for the first time in the 20th century, from a recently discovered manuscript, at the Aldeburgh Music Festival, in England, conducted by Benjamin Britten. (The first complete 20th-century performance of Mahler's First Symphony, in five movements, including *Blumine*, was given on 9 April 1968, in New Haven, Connecticut, by the New Haven Symphony Orchestra, Frank Brieff conducting.)

24 JUNE 1967

Die Blumen von Hiroshima, musical chamber play by the German composer Jean Kurt FOREST, dealing with a militant American pacifist who in 1955 marries a Japanese girl, survivor of the atom bombing of Hiroshima, despite the ominous possibility that the genes of their children might be affected by latent radiation, is produced in Weimar, conducted by the composer.

28 JUNE 1967

Triplum by Gunther SCHULLER, scored for orchestra in which the strings, the woodwinds and the brass constitute three self-sufficient entities (hence the title) functioning in the manner of a concertino, with a polyphonally effulgent climax, in conformity with the titular concept *e tribus unum*, is performed for the first time in Philharmonic Hall, Lincoln Center, New York.

2 JULY 1967

The Fifth Congregation of the Arts opens at Dartmouth College in Hanover, New Hampshire, under the direction of Mario di Bonaventura, with Aaron COPLAND, Hans Werner HENZE and Frank MARTIN participating as visiting composers, inaugurating a series of concerts comprising the following world premières:

Endecatode (eleven melodies) for chamber orchestra, in 11 visions, by the 85-year-old dean of Italian composers Gian Francesco MALIPIERO (5 July); *Estri* (improvisational fancies), a chamber symphony by Goffredo PETRASSI of Italy

(2 August); *Clarinet Concerto* by Walter PISTON (6 August); *Soli No. 4* for trumpet, horn and trombone by Carlos CHÁVEZ (9 August); and *Virtuose Musik* (Second Violin Concerto) by Boris BLACHER of West Germany (19 August).

3 JULY 1967

Fourth Symphony, subtitled *Das Siegeslied*, by the nonagenarian English polysymphonist Havergal BRIAN, to the text of Psalm 68 in the Lutheran German version and scored for soprano, double chorus and orchestra, comes to its belated first performance in London, thirty-four years after its composition.

7 JULY 1967

Toyon of Alaska (*The Lord of Alaska*) historical pageant-opera in three acts by Williard STRAIGHT, dealing with the Russian overlord of the Arctic Alexander Baranov who established the first settlement in Alaska in 1792, is produced in Anchorage during the centennial celebration of the purchase of Alaska by the United States from the Russian government in 1867 for the sum $7,500,000.

9 JULY 1967

A month after the glorious conclusion of Israel's six-day war against the overwhelmingly more populous adversaries of the surrounding Arab nations, the Israel Philharmonic Orchestra, under the direction of Leonard Bernstein and with Isaac Stern as the soloist, gives a concert on Mount Scopus on the Northeastern side of Jerusalem in a program including two works by converted Jewish composers, *Violin Concerto* by Felix MENDELSSOHN and *Second Symphony* by Gustav MAHLER, the latter with the final chorus sung in Hebrew.

17 JULY 1967

John COLTRANE, remarkable American jazz musician and a virtuoso on the tenor saxophone who initiated an enlightened type of composition and performing practice that led to the formation of sophisticated black primitivism, dies in Huntington, Long Island, New York, at the age of 40.

18 JULY 1967

Aequora Lunae, symphonic suite in seven movements by the 64-year-old South African composeress Priaulx RAINIER, symbolically portraying the astrological characteristics of the principal seven "seas" of the moon, is performed for the first time in Cheltenham, England.

20 JULY 1967

Concerto for trombone and orchestra by the Hungarian-American composer Eugene ZÁDOR, is performed for the first time in Meadow Brook, Michigan.

21 JULY 1967

The Bayreuth Festival opens its annual Wagner series, including three cycles of *The Ring of the Nibelung* in Wieland WAGNER's production as designed by him before his death in 1966.

23 JULY 1967

Doña Barbara, opera by the 43-year-old American woman composer Caroline LLOYD, resident in Venezuela for 15 years, is performed for the first time in Caracas.

29 JULY 1967

The Israel Philharmonic Orchestra commences a three-week tour of the United States and Canada, with an opening concert at Philharmonic Hall, Lincoln Center, in New York under the direction of William Steinberg, in a program of classical German music prefaced by an exultant *Fanfare to Israel* by the German-born Israeli composer Paul BEN-HAIM.

3 AUGUST 1967

The Rise and Fall of the Third Reich, cantata by the 35-year-old Argentinianborn American composer of Russian-Jewish parentage, Lalo (Boris) SCHIFRIN, adapted from his musical score to the moving picture of that name after the historical book by William Shirer, in which Satan sends his special envoy Adolf Hitler to Germany, and containing an actual recording of Hitler's rasping voice, couched in a musical style pervaded by atonal anxiety, is performed for the first time at the Hollywood Bowl by the Los Angeles Philharmonic Orchestra, chorus and soloists under the direction of Lawrence Foster.

6 AUGUST 1967

On the 22nd anniversary of the atomic obliteration of Hiroshima, a cantata entitled simply *Hiroshima* by the Italian composer Gaetano ZUFFRE, is performed for the first time as a dedicatory work by the Japanese Broadcasting Corporation in Tokyo.

8 AUGUST 1967

The production of the opera *Bomarzo* by the prime Argentinian composer Alberto GINASTERA, scheduled for performance at the Teatro Colón in Buenos Aires, is cancelled on orders of the military government of Argentina as "obsessed by sex and violence."

Bomarzo contains an excessive dose of scenes of violence and sex, which makes it unacceptable for the Argentine public. Perhaps the opera can be successful in Europe and in the United States, but it is our duty to protect our own people. I repeat that this measure was taken for strictly moral reasons, for we believe that the action of *Bomarzo* is not suitable for production in the Teatro Colón. (Statement of the Secretary of Culture of the Municipality of Buenos Aires)

8 AUGUST 1967

Jaromir WEINBERGER, 71-year-old Czech composer of one of the most durable comic operas of the twentieth century, *Schwanda*, driven to despondency because of his inability to produce further successful works, commits suicide by swallowing an overdose of barbiturates at his home in St. Petersburg, Florida, where he settled in 1939.

9 AUGUST 1967

Concert Piece for Syn-Ket and Orchestra by the 32-year-old American composer John EATON, the first of its genre, set for a portable electronic synthesizer invented by the Russian engineer Paul Ketoff (hence Syn-Ket), is performed for the first time at the Berkshire Music Festival at Tanglewood, Massachusetts.

10 AUGUST 1967

At the Expo 67 World Festival in Montreal, the Bolshoi Theater Opera Company of Moscow, in its first appearance in North America, presents MUSSORGSKY's great national opera *Boris Godunov.*

10 AUGUST 1967

Gita, electronic piece for chorus, brass ensemble and pre-recorded tape by the Canadian engineer-composer R. Murray SCHAEFER is performed for the first time at the Berkshire Festival, in Lenox, Massachusetts.

12 AUGUST 1967

War and Peace, monumental opera by Sergei PROKOFIEV is presented by the Bolshoi Opera as its second offering on its first tour in the Western Hemisphere, at Montreal, during the music festival of the Canadian Expo 67.

14 AUGUST 1967

At the Canadian Expo 67 World Festival in Montreal, the Bolshoi Theater Opera Company of Moscow presents the first Canadian performance of RIMSKY-KORSAKOV'S mystical opera *The Legend of the Invisible City of Kitezh,* popularly known as the Russian *Parsifal* (indeed, Wagnerian undertones are peculiarly discernible underneath the multicolored Russian harmonies).

25 AUGUST 1967

Die Sonnenfinsternis, cantata by the Swiss composer Conrad BECK, for contralto and chamber orchestra, philosophically reflecting upon the wonder of a solar eclipse, is performed for the first time at the International Musical Festival of Lucerne, Switzerland.

25 AUGUST 1967

Historien om en Moder (*Story of a Mother*), opera by the Danish composer Thomas KOPPEL, written by him when he was 17, to a sentimental story by Hans Christian Andersen, is produced in Copenhagen.

31 AUGUST 1967

Oxus, dramatic scene for voice and orchestra by Humphrey SEARLE, to the text from the final stanza of Matthew Arnold's poem *Sohrab and Rustum* relating the ancient Persian tale of Rustum fighting a tournament to the death against the young Tatar Sohrab on the river Oxus (Amu-Darya) in Central Asia, only to discover, after killing him, that he is his natural son by a Tatar concubine, set to music in a strict dodecaphonic idiom in disregard of the ethnomusicologically proper pentatonicism of Asian modalities, is performed for the first time in London.

2 SEPTEMBER 1967

Labyrinth, phantasmagoric opera in two acts by the 35-year-old Danish composer Per NØRGÅRD, in which the guide of a labyrinth in a sideshow at a country fair imagines himself in Dante's Inferno with a tape recorder blaring popular songs, is produced in Copenhagen.

3 SEPTEMBER 1967

The Death of Moses, cantata by the 56-year-old Israeli composer Josef TAL, written in the manner of a modern miracle play and combining mystic elements with allusions to historical reality, scored for voices, orchestra and electronic sound generators, is performed for the first time in Jerusalem.

4 SEPTEMBER 1967

Visage d' Axel, symphonic poem by the 43-year-old French composer Serge NIGG, in two sections, *Le monde visionnaire,* and *Le monde passionel,* after a poem by Villiers de l'Isle Adam, is performed for the first time in Paris.

13 SEPTEMBER 1967

Inscape, for orchestra by Aaron COPLAND (the title comes from a poem by Gerard Manley Hopkins), a "quasi-mystical illumination," with thematic materials derived from two basic 12-tone rows, is performed for the first time by the Orchestra of the University of Michigan in Ann Arbor. (The work, commissioned by the New York Philharmonic in observance of its 125th anniversary, came to its first New York performance by that orchestra on 20 October 1967.)

14 SEPTEMBER 1967

The Los Angeles Philharmonic Orchestra, under the direction of its 31-year-old Indian conductor Zubin Mehta, undertakes its first world tour with concerts in Belgium, Luxembourg, Rumania, Greece, France, Austria, Germany, Italy, Yugoslavia, Turkey, Cyprus, Iran and India. (The tour was completed on 6 November 1967, with a concert in Mehta's native city of Bombay.)

15 SEPTEMBER 1967

The Luck of Ginger Coffey, opera in three acts by the Canadian composer Raymond PANNELL, to a libretto retailing the vicissitudes of an Irishman in search of a newspaper job in Canada, set to music in an ingratiatingly eclectic idiom, containing rock 'n' roll, hymnology and French-Canadian folksongs, is produced in Toronto.

23 SEPTEMBER 1967

Louis Riel, music drama in three acts by the Canadian composer Harry SOMERS, centered on the dramatic career of the French-Canadian rebel who espoused the cause of the Metizo Indians in 1869 (he was 1/8 redskin and married a squaw), tried to overthrow the government and was hanged in 1886, to a bilingual libretto, set to music in a highly diversified idiom, containing serial devices, electronic effects and contemporary folksongs, is produced in Toronto.

30 SEPTEMBER 1967

Virineia, music drama by the 35-year-old Soviet composer Sergei SLONIMSKY, depicting the social and personal upheavals in the Russian countryside during the first year of the Russian Revolution, in seven ideologically and politically significant scenes—*The End of the Autocracy, The End of the Family, The End of Religious Faith, The Night, The Dawn, Political Meetings, Farewell*—centering on the fate of a simple Russian woman Virineia who breaks away from the chains of dull matrimony and obsolete religious faith, set to music deeply rooted in Russian melos, with the interpolation of purely illustrative orchestral tableau—a blizzard, a night's silence, a people's rumblings—is produced in Leningrad.

1 OCTOBER 1967

Seventh Symphony by Roger SESSIONS, written to observe the sesquicentennial of the University of Michigan, in three classically conceived movements, *Allegro con fuoco, Lento e dolce* and *Allegro misurato*, followed by a brief epilogue, set to music in dissonant polyphony with thematic strands formed by a serial pattern, is performed for the first time in Ann Arbor, the site of the University of Michigan, by the Chicago Symphony Orchestra, conducted by Jean Martinon.

4 OCTOBER 1967

The 41st Festival of the International Society for Contemporary Music opens in Prague with the following program of symphonic music:

Configurations by the Japanese composer Yori-Aki MATSU-DAIRA; *Perspectives* by the Greek neo-classicist Yorgo SICILIANOS; *Iniciativas* by the Spanish neo-classical abstractionist Luis de PABLO; and *Triplum* by the German modernist Wolfgang FORTNER.

5 OCTOBER 1967

At the second concert of the 41st Festival of the International Society for Contemporary Music in Prague the following orchestral works are given:

Shadows by the Italian modernist Girolamo ARRIGO; *Sigma* by the Yugoslav abstractionist Ivo MALEC; *Contra fidem* by the Polish neo-classicist Zbigniew RUDZINSKI, intended to exemplify "a struggle for a concise form in the non-traditional field of musical expression"; and *Symphony* for three instrumental groups by the Spanish modernist Cristóbal HALFFTER.

7 OCTOBER 1967

On Jazz Day in New York City, so designated by Mayor Lindsay, the orchestral *Jazzhattan Suite* by Oliver NELSON, specially composed for the occasion, has its first performance in Central Park, a natural location for Manhattanese jazzification, embanked between the protective towers of East Side and West Side and flanked by jazz-fecund maternal Harlem and an aggressively erectile paternalistic downtown genus.

7 OCTOBER 1967

At the 41st Festival of the International Society for Contemporary Music in Prague two fairy-tale operas by the Czech composer JIŘÍ PAUER, *The Talkative Snail* and *The Red Riding Hood*, are presented, on the same day with the following program of chamber music:

Dialogues for flute and harp by Jan KARP of Czechoslovakia; *Fragment IV from Shakespeare Sonnets* by Ton de KRUYF of Holland; *String Quartet* by Atilla BOZAY of Hungary; *String Quartet No. 15* by the 74-year-old Czech modernist Alois HÁBA, written in fifths of a tone; *Réseaux* by Francis MIROGLIO of France; and *Aria da capo* by Yitzhak SADAI of Israel.

8 OCTOBER 1967

At the 41st Festival of the International Society for Contemporary Music in Prague the following program of chamber music is presented:

For Two Violins by Robert du BOIS of Holland; *Trio* for oboe, viola and harp by Heinz HOLLIGER of Switzerland; *Presence* by Bernd Alois ZIMMERMANN of Germany; *Springtime* by Erik BERGMAN of Finland; and *Eufemias Mysterion* by Miloslav KABELÁČ of Czechoslovakia.

9 OCTOBER 1967

Concerto à ballo for orchestra by the 58-year-old Austrian composer Alfred UHL, in four movements set in a neo-baroque idiom diversified by modern harmonies, is performed for the first time by the Vienna Symphony Orchestra in New York, during its American tour.

9 OCTOBER 1967

At the 41st Festival of the Society for Contemporary Music in Prague, the following program of music by Czech composers is presented:

15 Prints After Dürer's Apocalypse by the 32-year-old composer Luboš FIŠER (first performed in Prague on 15 May 1966); *6 Etudes* for chamber orchestra by Miloslav ISTVAN; *Foam* for orchestra by Svatopluk HAVELKA; and *Transformations* by Roman BERGER.

10 OCTOBER 1967

At the last concert of the 41st Festival of the International Society for Contemporary Music in Prague the following program of symphonic music is presented:

Tsukishiro by the Japanese composer Kazuo FUKUSHIMA; *Métamorphose d' Écho* for voice and orchestra by the French composer Claude PREY, incorporating the natural inflections of conversation in French in the vocal part, echoed by the instruments; *Aura* by the Swedish composer Arne MELLNÄS, scored for a heterogeneous ensemble, including a clavier of beer bottles and exploding toy balloons, and set in a free aleatory idiom; *Studio No. 2* by the Italian composer Giacomo MANZONI; and *Sub rosa* by the Yugoslav composer Milko KELEMEN.

14 OCTOBER 1967

Meer der Stürme, symphonic poem by the foremost Communist composer of East Germany Paul DESSAU, an expansively optimistic fanfaronade, presaging in a proleptically realistic idiom the landing of Soviet cosmonauts in the Sea of Storms on the surface of the moon, is performed for the first time in East Berlin, on the occasion of the 50th anniversary of the Soviet Revolution. (In actual history, American astronauts made the first lunar landing, on 20 July 1969, in the Sea of Tranquility rather than in the Sea of Storms.)

15 OCTOBER 1967

Vertige d' Éros, symphonic poem by Gunther SCHUL-LER, written by him in 1945, at the age of twenty, in an erotically impressionistic idiom, achieves its belated first performance in Madison, Wisconsin.

17 OCTOBER 1967

Shulamith RAN, 20-year-old Israeli composeress, plays in Jerusalem the solo part in the first performance of her *Piano Concerto.*

17 OCTOBER 1967

Hair, a rollicking rock 'n' roll musical, with lyrics by several hands including William Shakespeare (in Hamlet's complaint about air pollution, smog and "a foul and pestilent congregation of vapors"), and music mostly by Galt MacDermot, a spontaneously designed far-out mass spectacle in which the audience is invited to get it on with the cast and vocally participate, featuring for the first time in the musical theater a scene of total nudity mitigated only by stroboscopically freaked-out lights, including such mind-blowing songs as *Let the Sunshine In,* the title song *Hair* and the psychedelically astrological chorus *Aquarius,* couched in the bemused plagal modalities of old English balladry with incredibly heavy raps laid on the audience by uninhibited proliferation of Anglo-Saxon profanity, opens in New York under the aegis of the Shakespeare Festival Public Theater. (It subsequently moved to the discotheque The Cheetah, and on 29 April 1968 inaugurated its highly auspicious Broadway run, proceeding thenceforward on a triumphant cephalotripsical tour of world capitals.)

19 OCTOBER 1967

On its first visit to the United States, the La Scala Company of Milan gives, in Carnegie Hall, New York, a performance of VERDI's *Requiem.*

21 OCTOBER 1967

Seven Counterpoints, orchestral suite by the English composer Peter Racine FRICKER, temporarily in residence at the University of California, Santa Barbara, is performed for the first time in Pasadena, California.

21 OCTOBER 1967

The first performance of the stage version of the scenic cantata *Nochebuena del Diablo* by the dean of Spanish composers Oscar ESPLÁ is given in Madrid.

22 OCTOBER 1967

Capriccio for violin and orchestra by the 33-year-old Polish modernist Krzysztof PENDERECKI is performed for the first time at the Donaueschingen Festival, with Wanda Wilkomirska as soloist.

22 OCTOBER 1967

Lontano for orchestra by the Hungarian ultra-modern composer György LIGETI, is performed for the first time at the Donaueschingen Music Festival.

24 OCTOBER 1967

Il Pozzo e il Pendolo (The Pit and the Pendulum), opera by the Italian composer Bruno BETRINELLI, after Edgar Allan Poe, is performed for the first time in Bergamo.

29 OCTOBER 1967

Eighth Symphony by the 52-year-old American composer Vincent PERSICHETTI, in four classically ordered movements vitalized by picaresque instrumental colors (including a lyric aria on the tuba) and an active percussion section, is performed for the first time at Baldwin-Wallace College in Berea, Ohio.

31 OCTOBER 1967

A Penny for a Song, comic opera by the 31-year-old English composer Richard Rodney BENNETT, to a story about a British eccentric who dresses up like Napoleon to issue the counter order cancelling the imagined invasion of Southern England by the French Army in 1804, precipitating a number of military alarms and absurdities, is produced in London.

2 NOVEMBER 1967

Concerto for doublebass and orchestra by Hans Werner HENZE, is performed for the first time as a commissioned work by the Chicago Symphony Orchestra, with Gary Karr soloist and Jean Martinon conducting.

3 NOVEMBER 1967

White Nights (the title refers to the subhorizontal sunlight during the summer nights in the sub-Arctic St. Petersburg), "musical chronicle" by Tikhon KHRENNIKOV, a pasquinade satirizing the last years of the Tsarist rule in Russia, with a cast of historical characters including the last Tsar Nicholas II, his Tsarina, and her coterie maneuvered by the sinister monk Gregory Rasputin (his last name derives from the Russian word for debauchery), set to music in the manner of Russian burlesque profusely interlarded with pseudo-Gypsy balladry, is performed for the first time in Moscow.

4 NOVEMBER 1967

The Gallant King, opera by the 61-year-old Slovak composer Alexander MOYZES, is produced in Bratislava.

6 NOVEMBER 1967

Tovarishch Andrei, opera-oratorio in ten scenes, with a prologue and an epilogue, by the 56-year-old Soviet composer Boris GIBALIN, a series of musical tableaux illustrating the revolutionary life of Jacob Sverdlov, known in the Tsarist underground as "Tovarishch Andrei," is performed for the first time in Sverdlovsk, the Ural city, formerly Ekaterinburg, renamed Sverdlovsk after Sverdlov who died in 1919.

7 NOVEMBER 1967

Der letzte Schuss, opera by the 33-year-old German composer Siegfried MATTHUS, to a libretto dealing with the romance between a Red Army girl guerrilla and a captured White Army officer during the civil war in Central Asia in

1919, whom she is assigned to guard and whom she shoots down (the "last shot" of the title) when he attempts to join the crew of an enemy motor boat in the Aral Sea, written in a modernistically decorative manner including electronic sounds, is produced in East Berlin as part of the celebration of the semicentennial of the Soviet Revolution.

7 NOVEMBER 1967

Sixth Symphony, subtitled *Musica Intima,* by the Swedish composer Hilding HALLNÄS, is performed for the first time in Malmo.

9 NOVEMBER 1967

La Fille de l'homme, lyric tragedy in three acts by the 61-year-old French composer Pierre CAPDEVIELLE, to a libretto dealing with an Italian railroad magnate who incites a woman employee to kill her lover, is performed for the first time in concert form on the Paris Radio. (A complete stage performance was given in Paris on 1 December 1967.)

9 NOVEMBER 1967

November Steps, symphonic sketch by the 37-year-old Japanese composer Toru TAKEMITSU, for solo biwa (lute) and shakuhachi (bamboo flute) and orchestra, creating in its static homophony the impression of autumnal immobility, with special effects in the percussion section, is performed for the first time by the New York Philharmonic under the direction of the Japanese conductor Seiji Ozawa.

13 NOVEMBER 1967

"Cross Talk No. 1," a concert of ultramodern music, is presented in Tokyo, featuring works by Charles IVES, and by three Japanese composers: *Chromamorphe 1* for seven instruments by Yuji TAKAHASHI; *Provisional Color* for piano by Shuko MIZUNO; and *Icon* for magnetic tape by Joji YUASA.

14 NOVEMBER 1967

The newly organized Orchestre de Paris makes its initial appearance in Paris under the direction of Charles Munch, in a program of works by Berlioz, Debussy and Stravinsky.

20 NOVEMBER 1967

Smell Piece for Mills College for frying pans and foods by the intransigently radical 30-year-old American avant-garde composer Robert MORAN, originally intended to produce a conflagration sufficiently thermal to burn down the college, is performed for the first time at Mills College in Oakland, California.

21 NOVEMBER 1967

Hodaya Min Hamidbar (*Thanksgiving from the Desert*), oratorio by the 70-year-old Israeli composer Paul BEN-HAIM, is performed for the first time at the Kibbutz Yagour in Israel.

25 NOVEMBER 1967

The Brothers Ulyanov, opera in three acts by the 64-year-old Ukrainian Soviet composer Yuli MEITUS, based on the life story of Vladimir Ulyanov (Lenin) and his brother who was hanged for the participation in the attempt to assassinate the Tsar Alexander III, is produced in Ufa.

30 NOVEMBER 1967

The first performance is given in the German Radio Studio in Cologne of *Hymnen,* electronic piece by the foremost proponent of new music Karlheinz STOCKHAUSEN, for a heterophonic ensemble, including an electronic accordion, recorded shrieks, wheezes and audible exhalations, a tacit viola played by moving the bow across the strings without touching them, a tamtam rubbed by paper rolls, subdivided into four parts with thematic materials derived from a number of national anthems, opening with dislocated versions of *Internationale* and the *Marseillaise* and concluding with a "hymunion in the harmondy of a Utopian Pluramon State," under the direction of Stockhausen himself, manipulating a circular rectangle of a rigorously indeterminate digital computer.

30 NOVEMBER 1967

The Decision, opera by the 39-year-old Scottish composeress Thea MUSGRAVE, to a libretto based on an actual case of a miner entombed for 23 days following a cave-in of rock in Scotland in 1835 (he died three days later), which so shocked the stolid British establishment that a government decision (hence the title) was made to ameliorate the conditions of mine workers and to prohibit the employment of women and children in the Scottish mines, is performed for the first time in London.

1 DECEMBER 1967

Neutron Star, by the 27-year-old Swedish composer Jan W. MORTHENSON, a sonic construction of the hypothetical neutron star created by an implosion of a decayed supernova, with its entire mass contracted to an electrically neutral body of about ten kilometers in diameter and a fantastic density of $10"$ g/cm^3 constituting the specific weight of the atomic nucleus denuded of electrons, in which the condensation of matter is symbolically represented by constantly increasing frequencies, beginning with the subsonic and ending in a heterodynamic echo, is constructed by means of multiple superpositions of electronic tapes at the Electronic Music Studio of the Swedish Broadcasting Station in Stockholm, with the aid of Computer SAAB D-21.

9 DECEMBER 1967

Die Witwe des Schmetterlings, opera in three scenes by the modernistically minded 50-year-old Korean composer Isang YUN, to an oneiric libretto in German based on an old lepidopteromorphic Chinese tale about a defunct functionary whose metempsychotic memory of having been a giant butterfly is reified when he emerges from his coffin as from a chrysalis and scares away his perfidious "butterfly widow" and her lover, set to music in an orientalized serial idiom, marked by angst-laden vocal atonalities and pierced by acute instrumental discords and horrendous asymmetric rhythms in an ample battery of percussion, is performed for the first time in Bonn in the absence of Isang Yun himself who was abducted with his wife from his West Berlin apartment on 17 June 1967 by South Korean agents, flown to Seoul to stand trial as a North Korean spy and sentenced to life imprisonment, but reprieved in March 1969 after the West German government threatened to cut its economic aid to South Korea in retaliation for illegal acts on German soil, with a contributory pressure exerted by the aroused intellectual community supported by a letter of protest signed by Igor Stravinsky and 23 other important composers.

12 DECEMBER 1967

On the 80th birthday of the Swedish composer Kurt ATTERBERG, his *Sinfonia visionaria* is performed for the first time in Malmö.

12 DECEMBER 1967

Mooga Pook, a tetraphallic action for dancers by the 22-year-old American composer Charles AMIRKHANIAN, notated on graph paper with anatomical precision, is performed for the first time in San Francisco.

14 DECEMBER 1967

Cello Concerto by the 70-year-old Israeli composer Paul BEN-HAIM is performed for the first time in Limburg, Holland.

14 DECEMBER 1967

Fourth Symphony, subtitled *New York*, by the 71-year-old Spanish-born naturalized English composer Roberto GERHARD, in one movement, written in an idiosyncratic serial idiom, cohesive in form, but free in the agglutination of its additive thematic elements, dedicated to the New York Philharmonic on the occasion of its 125th anniversary, is performed for the first time by that orchestra, William Steinberg conducting.

26 DECEMBER 1967

Two new operas by Yugoslav composers are presented for the first time in Zagreb:

Svjetleći Grad (*The Town of Light*), seventh opera by the 54-year-old Croatian composer Ivo LHOTKA-KALINSKI, probing the minds of mental patients in an asylum in a wide-ranging atonal idiom departing decisively from the Italianate musical language of his previous works; and *Adam i Eva* by the 51-year-old Slovenian composer Silvije BOMBARDELLI, dealing with man and wife meeting in the astral world after their respective terrestrial suicides, and settling their differences in an intentionally vulgarized monorhythmic manner with polytonal protuberances calculated to produce a surrealistic effect.

27 DECEMBER 1967

Landschaft aus Schreien, cantata by the 40-year-old Swedish composer Maurice KARKOFF, to the text of the Nobel-prize winning German Jewish poetess Nelly SACHS, recalling the horrors of the Nazi extermination camps, where "the landscape of screams tears the black bandage of the night," written for singing and spoken voice in an anguished atonal idiom, is performed for the first time by the Swedish Radio Station in Stockholm.

1968

4 JANUARY 1968

Third Symphony by the 64-year-old Russian-born American composer Nicolas NABOKOV, subtitled *A Prayer* and composed in memory of Pope John XXIII and J. Robert Oppenheimer, written in a solemn neo-medieval idiom distilled in impressionistic harmonies, is performed for the first time as a commissioned work by the New York Philharmonic, on its 125th anniversary, with Leonard Bernstein conducting.

8 JANUARY 1968

Babels Torn (*The Tower of Babel*), ballet by the Swedish composer Hilding ROSENBERG, is performed for the first time as a commissioned work at the Swedish Television Station.

8 JANUARY 1968

Rezsö SERESS, 68-year-old Hungarian composer of the song *Gloomy Sunday*, which precipitated a wave of Sunday suicides in the 1930s and was temporarily banned in Hungary and in the United States, jumps out of the window from the second floor of his apartment in Budapest (on a Monday), in a fit of despondency caused by a painful case of aortic stenosis in his head. (He died in a hospital on 12 January 1968. Information received from his widow.)

11 JANUARY 1968

The Equation ($x = o$), opera in one act by the 47-year-old English composer Geoffrey BUSH, scored for voices, cello solo, wind ensemble, organ and percussion, dealing polytonally with the incompatibility of war with morality or common sense, is performed for the first time in a London church.

11 JANUARY 1968

Chimes for orchestra by the 35-year-old Soviet composer Rodion SHCHEDRIN, in the form of a concerto for orchestra, written in a highly dissonant chromatic style with the orchestra in a state of constant furfuraceous commotion, punctuated by sounds of bells and culminating with a pistol shot, is performed for the first time as a commissioned work by the New York Philharmonic, Leonard Bernstein conducting.

18 JANUARY 1968

Anachronie I for orchestra by the 28-year-old Dutch composer Louis ANDRIESSEN, dedicated to the memory of Charles Ives, is performed for the first time in Rotterdam.

18 JANUARY 1968

Second Symphony by the 31-year-old English composer Richard Rodney BENNETT, in a single economically compact movement with a pluralistic network of thematic groups derived from a guiding dodecaphonic series and forming multifarious dissonant harmonies, is performed for the first time as a commissioned work by the New York Philharmonic, Leonard Bernstein conducting.

20 JANUARY 1968

Ode in Memory of Ché Guevara for clarinet, piano and percussion by the 38-year-old Soviet composer Edison DENISOV is performed for the first time in Moscow.

21 JANUARY 1968

Sixth Symphony, in a single very long movement, by the neo-romantic Swedish composer Allan PETTERSSON, culminating in a pessimistic conclusion in the melancholy key of B-flat minor, is performed for the first time on the Swedish Radio in Stockholm.

25 JANUARY 1968

Alpine Ballad, lyric opera in one act by the 84-year-old Soviet composer Andrei PASHCHENKO, to a libretto recounting the story of an affectionate international romance spontaneously exfoliating between a Russian soldier and an Italian girl during their flight from a Nazi concentration camp, is performed for the first time in Leningrad.

2 FEBRUARY 1968

On his 60th birthday, the Italian composer Renzo ROSSELLINI conducts in Monte Carlo the first performance of his seventh opera, *L'Avventuriere,* to a libretto dealing with a penitent retiring businessman who pays farewell visits to his estranged wife, his mistress and others whom he has wronged in his life, set to music in a peculiarly unadventurous Italianate idiom.

3 FEBRUARY 1968

Concert Piece for orchestra by the 38-year-old American composer Donald KEATS is performed for the first time in Columbus, Ohio.

4 FEBRUARY 1968

Stephen Crane, cantata for chorus and orchestra by the 51-year-old Negro American composer Ulysses KAY, to the texts of four poems by the short-lived American poet Stephen Crane (1871–1900), *Black Riders, Mystic Shadow, A Spirit* and *War Is Kind,* is performed for the first time in Chicago as a commissioned work in honor of the centennial of the Chicago Musical College.

5 FEBRUARY 1968

A Study in the Story of Human Stupidity, symphonic poem by the 24-year-old Swedish composer Gunnar VALKARE, is performed for the first time in Aarhus.

5 FEBRUARY 1968

Le Voyage, "musique électro-acoustique" by the pioneer of musique concrète Pierre HENRY, is produced in Grenoble as a ballet.

8 FEBRUARY 1968

Eleventh Symphony by Roy HARRIS, in a single cyclically constructed movement, commissioned by the New York Philharmonic on its 125th anniversary, and written as the expression of "emotional rather than intellectual ethos," is performed for the first time by the New York Philharmonic under the composer's own direction.

13 FEBRUARY 1968

Ildebrando PIZZETTI, Italian composer whose music combined the expansive melodiousness of his national heritage with modern chromatic harmonies, and whose operas revived the style of medieval mystery plays, dies in Rome at the age of 87.

20 FEBRUARY 1968

The Bride Comes to Yellow Sky, opera by the 46-year-old American composer Roger NIXON, from a story by Stephen Crane, written in a songful quasiatonal manner, descriptive of the purchase of a mail-order wife by an hombre in the Western frontier town called Yellow Sky, is produced at Eastern Illinois University. (The opera was revised and performed in San Francisco in a new version on 22 March 1969.)

20 FEBRUARY 1968

Fünf Geschichten vom Herrn Keuner for tenor and seven instruments by the 38-year-old Soviet composer Edison DENISOV, to original German texts by Bertolt Brecht, is performed for the first time in Berlin.

29 FEBRUARY 1968

Howard HANSON conducts the New York Philharmonic in the world première of his *Sixth Symphony,* in six compact movements, conceived in a broad neo-romantic style seasoned with euphonious dissonances and invigorated by stimulating asymmetrical rhythms.

29 FEBRUARY 1968

The Light in the Wilderness, oratorio by the American jazz pianist and composer Dave BRUBECK, in 12 sections, to segments of the New Testament, written in an ostentatiously elevated Handelian manner, vivified by jazzy inflections and incorporating neo-baroque cadenzas and free improvisations, is performed for the first time in Cincinnati.

5 MARCH 1968

Hamlet, opera by Humphrey SEARLE, to a libretto compressed from Shakespeare's play, with the thematic texture derived melodically and methodically from a 12-tone series, except for the scene of the tragedians, which is set in an ostentatiously tonal idiom in euphonious harmonies, is produced in Hamburg with a German libretto.

5 MARCH 1968

Reunion, a synthetic electronic work, formally determined by the movements of chessmen in a game between John CAGE and the famous Painter Marcel Duchamp on an electronic chess board built by Lowell Cross, takes place at a special session at the Polytechnical Institute in Toronto, Canada. (Duchamp gave Cage a handicap of a knight and still beat him handily.)

7 MARCH 1968

Ricercare, symphonic essay in a time-honored Baroque form by Walter PISTON, is performed for the first time as a commissioned work by the New York Philharmonic.

11 MARCH 1968

Schooltime Compositions by the English modernist Cornelius CARDEW, with "matrices arranged around vocal sounds, triangles, newspapers, balloons, noises, desire, keyboard, with many people working," in optative adaptation of a set of melodic, rhythmic and instrumental parameters, aiming by guessing, grasping, gasping, gaping, aping and ping, at creating dissipating pullulating "beautiful bodies in rags" in multidimensional media, are performed uniquely (first time is last time, each random a meander), by the Focus Opera Group at the International Students House in London, on the same bill with *Aventures* by the Hungarian ultra-avantgardist György LIGETI for three nonsensically syllabificating singers and seven instruments, and *Sur scene* by the Argentinian-born aleatorist Mauricio KAGEL for an omnivocal singer, three instruments and a mime.

12 MARCH 1968

Cantata for mixed choir, wind instruments and percussion by the 49-year-old Czech composer Zbynek VOSTRAK, to the words by Franz Kafka in Czech translation of the original German text, expressing the surrealistic anguish of quotidian reality in acute dissonant counterpoint is performed for the first time in Prague.

13 MARCH 1968

Seventh Symphony by the 92-year-old English composer Havergal BRIAN, written in 1948, in four elongated movements—(1) *Allegro moderato*, opening with an ebullient brass fanfare and proceeding with ponderous concentration; (2) *Allegro*, with discursive episodes; (3) *Allegro* alternating with *Adagio;* (4) *Moderato*, marked *Epilogue Once Upon a Time*, in an appropriately narrative romantic manner—is performed for the first time in London. (It was on this occasion announced as Brian's *Sixth Sympho-*

ny, owing to the variable numbering; in the final list of works made by Brian in 1968, the work was described as *Seventh Symphony*.)

14 MARCH 1968

Ordure dans l'air après la passion, instrumental nonet by the 24-year-old Swedish modernist Gunnar VALKARE, an atonally postcoital malefaction in malefaction, is performed for the first time in Stockholm.

15 MARCH 1968

Second Piano Concerto by the 44-year-old Manchurian-born American composer of Russian parentage Benjamin LEES, in three movements, *Allegro enfatico, Adagio vago* and *Allegro tempestoso*, set in an individually synthetic idiom incorporating heterogeneous elements redolent of the rhapsodic elegance of Rachmaninoff, the percussive volatility of Prokofiev and the primitivistic modernity of Béla Bartók, is performed for the first time by Gary Graffman and the Boston Symphony Orchestra, Erich Leinsdorf conducting.

16 MARCH 1968

Mario CASTELNUOVO-TEDESCO, Italian-born composer of harmonious operas, overtures, concertos, piano works and songs, whose spirit of cultured modernism transcended the bounds of tenacious traditions and inconstant fashions alike, dies at the age of 72 in Los Angeles, where he settled at the outbreak of the Second World War.

17 MARCH 1968

Votre Faust, opera by Henri POUSSEUR, treating the Faust legend in contemporary terms, with audience participation in the form of a vote in favor of one of the four proffered dénouements, is performed for the first time in concert form in Buffalo.

21 MARCH 1968

Fra Angelico, symphonic poem by the 57-year-old half-Armenian half-Scottish American composer Alan HOVHANESS, his opus 220, written as a tribute to the mystical medieval Italian master of the fresco and couched in a harmoniously translucent, orientalistically modal idiom, is performed for the first time by the Detroit Symphony Orchestra, Sixten Ehrling conducting.

24 MARCH 1968

Prometheus, opera by Carl ORFF, the third part of his trilogy of Greek tragedies, after *Prometheus Bound* of Aeschylus, set to the original ancient Greek text, in one continuous act, constituting a series of homophonic monologues, dialogues, trialogues, tetralogues and choruses in neo-Grecian diatonic modalities accoutred in rudimentary triadic harmonies and orchestrated for 4 pianos, 6 flutes, 6 oboes, 6 trumpets, 6 trombones, 4 banjos, 4 harps, 2 organs, 9 double-basses, 5 kettledrums and an ensemble of 70 percussion instruments, is performed for the first time in Stuttgart.

26 MARCH 1968

Blackboard Piece with Girls and Loops for two girls and two pitchproducing blackboards by the 31-year-old American avant-garde composer Jon HASSELL is performed for the first time in New York.

28 MARCH 1968

Fourth Symphony by the 61-year-old Norwegian composer Klaus EGGE, based on the initials of Bach and Egge himself, subtitled Sinfonica sopra B.A.C.H.—E.G.G.E., is performed for the first time in Detroit, Michigan.

28 MARCH 1968

Symphony by the 51-year-old American Negro composer Ulysses KAY, commissioned by the Illinois Sesquicentennial Committee, written in a classical manner, in the traditional four movements, with hypersensitive applications of dissonant counterpoint underlying the melodic flow, vivified by frequent detonations of jazzy syncopation, but shunning topical melodic references to the musical past of Illinois, is performed for the first time by the Chicago Symphony Orchestra, Jean Martinon conducting, in Macomb, Illinois.

29 MARCH 1968

Forte e Piano for two pianos and orchestra by the 46-year-old Polish composer Kazimierz SEROCKI is performed for the first time in Cologne.

31 MARCH 1968

La Symphonie pastorale, opera by the Dutch composer Guillaume LANDRÉ, after the autumnal novel by André Gide, dealing with the crepuscular passion of an aging Swiss minister for a blind orphan girl adopted by him, who recovers her sight and selects his son as her spiritual bridegroom, dying of mystical inanition just as the world of sight and love is uncovered for her, is performed for the first time in Rouen, France.

31 MARCH 1968

The Vancouver Symphony Orchestra, in British Columbia, with Meredith Davies conducting, gives the first performance of *Estudios Sinfónicos* by the prime Argentinian composer Alberto GINASTERA, titled in homage to Robert Schumann, and in emulation of his *Etudes symphoniques*, presented as a commissioned work on the occasion of the centennial of Canada, containing nine studies based on three chords, two of which are formed by six different notes, and one is pandodecaphonic, each serving as a biomusical nucleus.

4 APRIL 1968

Contextures: Riots—Decade '60 for orchestra by the 44-year-old American composer William KRAFT is performed for the first time in Los Angeles.

5 APRIL 1968

Piano Concerto by the American composer John CORIGLIANO is performed for the first time by the San Antonio Symphony, conducted by Victor Alessandro.

7 APRIL 1968

Oliver KNUSSEN, 15-year-old English schoolboy, conducts the London Symphony Orchestra in the first performance of his ambitious *First Symphony,* in four movements, *Allegro Brillante, Lento, Scherzo-Satira* and *Theme and Variations,* written in a thematically pluralistic hemidemisemiserial idiom redolent of Mahler, Shostakovich and Alban Berg, and culminating in a respectable fugato.

8 APRIL 1968

Concerto for Violoncello and Orchestra by Bernd Alois ZIMMERMANN, "en forme de pas de trois," in five movements, the "trois" being the three dramatic personae—the soloist, the orchestra and the ballet—employing, in addition to a regular orchestra, a cimbalom, a glass harp, a mandolin, a guitar and an electronic doublebass, is performed for the first time in Strasbourg, in concert form. (The first performance as ballet took place in Wuppertal on 12 May 1968.)

10 APRIL 1968

Full Circle, one-act opera by the 58-year-old Scottish composer Robin ORR, dealing with an inadvertent killer of a Scottish policeman in 1930 who is tracked down to his middle-class habitat, written in the form of a dramatic ballad, emphasizing the elegiac element in the killer's family life and his devotion to his loyal wife, is performed for the first time in Perth, Scotland.

12 APRIL 1968

Hétéromorphie for orchestra by the 40-year-old Rumanian composer Stefan NICULESCU is performed for the first time in Bucharest.

21 APRIL 1968

Rainforest, a musical event designed by David TUDOR and Gordon MUMMA with the Merce Cunningham Dance Company, is created for the first time by the Public Broadcast Laboratory Television Production in New York.

21 APRIL 1968

Concerto for Synket and Orchestra in three movements by Jerome ROSEN, with a portable electronic instrument, invented by the Russian acoustician in Rome named Paul Ketoff, is performed for the first time on the campus of the University of Washington in Seattle.

25 APRIL 1968

Rain, opera by the 61-year-old Russian composer Boris ARAPOV, based on Somerset Maugham's short story, is produced in Leningrad.

2 MAY 1968

Eighth Symphony by Roger SESSIONS, set in an austerely euphonious dissonant idiom, in one movement subdivided into contrasting sections, statically propulsive in its emotional tonus, thematically governed by a cybernetically functional dodecaphonic series, occasionally apocopated in hendecaphonic or decaphonic forms, is performed for the first time by the New York Philharmonic Orchestra as a commissioned work on the occasion of its 125th anniversary, William Steinberg conducting.

12 MAY 1968

First Symphony by the 32-year-old Georgian Soviet composer Giya KANCHELI, in two movements, *Allegro con fuoco* and *Largo,* is performed for the first time in Tbilisi.

18 MAY 1968

The Choir Invisible, choral symphony in three movements by the 41-year-old South African composer John JOUBERT, after a poem by George Eliot, wherein true immortals form an ethereal chorus in the ionosphere radiating spiritual goodness residual from the terrestrial virtues of its members before death, is performed for the first time in Halifax, England, with the composer conducting.

24 MAY 1968

Invocation-Concerto for violin and orchestra by the 47-year-old American composer Ralph SHAPEY, written in a pluralistic serial technique, with individual melodic ingredients limited to a few intervallic distances between two consecutive thematic notes, is performed for the first time in New York.

30 MAY 1968

The Marriage of Nyakato, one-act opera by the prime composer of Uganda Solomon MBABI-KATANA, to the story of a beautiful country girl Nyakato whose family witch doctor correctly interprets, in a psychedelic solo on an indigenous central African long horn, a Freudian dream of her father as a precognitive revelation of her becoming the bride of the tribal King, containing a number of African dances, with the music derived from original pentatonic and tetratonic African melodies, is performed for the first time in the City of Kampala in Uganda, with the composer himself presiding at the piano.

5 JUNE 1968

Two stage works by the 61-year-old British composer Elizabeth MACONCHY, *The Three Strangers,* opera after Thomas Hardy, and *The Birds,* operatic extravaganza after Aristophanes, are produced in London.

8 JUNE 1968

Punch and Judy, puppet show for sadistic children, in which Punch throws a baby into the fire, kills Judy, his doctor and his lawyer and escapes the hangman by a stratagem, with a deliberately oxymoronic score by the British composer Harrison BIRTWISTLE, in which murderous action is illustrated by elegiac music and human kindness by shattering discords, is produced at the Aldeburgh Festival in England.

10 JUNE 1968

The Prodigal Son, "parable for church performance," by Benjamin BRITTEN, to a Latin text, and based on a plainchant in the Phrygian mode, accompanied by a small orchestra including some exotic percussion instruments, is performed for the first time at the Aldeburgh Festival.

14 JUNE 1968

Karl-Birger BLOMDAHL, Swedish composer of original ideas and mastery of modern techniques, who made intelligent and effective use of electronic resources, and whose pessimistic views of the terrestrial destinies are reflected in his dodecaphonic interplanetary opera *Aniara,* dies of a heart ailment in Kungsängen, at 51 (his ashes were strewn over nearby Lake Mälaren).

19 JUNE 1968

The Fourth Inter-American Music Festival opens in Washington under the general direction of Guillermo Espinosa, Chief of the Music Division of the Pan American Union, with the following program of Latin American music:

Cantus Creationis for four instrumental groups by José Almeida PRADO of Brazil (a world première); *Xilofonías* for flute, oboe, bass clarinet, bassoon and percussion by Mario KURI-ALDANA of Mexico, in three movements, with the "wooden sound" of the xylophonic concept of the title provided by the drum section; *Contrasts* for two pianos and chamber orchestra by Gerardo GANDINI of Argentina (a world première); *Concertante* for timpani and chamber ensemble by Blas E. ATEHORTUA of Colombia (a world première); *Divertimento III (Density I)* by Cesar BOLANOS of Peru; and *Quodlibet III* for chamber ensemble, an aleatory composition within a given set of cybernetical temporal parameters, by Gabriel BRNCIC of Chile (a world première).

20 JUNE 1968

In the course of the Fourth Inter-American Music Festival in Washington, the following program of electronic music is given:

Animus I for trombone and tape by Jacob DRUCKMAN of the United States; *Dialogues I* by Francisco KROEPFL of Argentina, with a sonic material based on sinusoidal waves and filtered white sound; *Cross-Fire* for piano and taped piano by Carman MOORE of the United States, a "pièce de résistance for the entire family, rhythmically simple, based on Italian folksongs, complete with a home-cooked Chinese dinner" constituting a game of statement by the recorded tape and stochastic response by the human pianist; *Of Wood and Brass* by Vladimir USSACHEVSKY of the United States, in four distinct sections, electronically metamorphosed by topological translocations and soniferous dispersion of original sounds of trombones, xylophones and a Korean gong; musical score from the Polish documentary film, *The World in Which We Live* by Mesias MAIGUASHCA of Ecuador, beginning with sound of a giant rocket; *Juegos (Games)* for piano and magnetic tape by Gustavo BECERRA SCHMIDT of Chile, with the pianist superposing an unpremeditated solo on the recorded sound, including the applause and voices of an audience taped in 1966; and *Synchronisms No. 2* for four instruments and electronic sounds by Mario DAVIDOVSKY of Argentina, aiming at a consistent integration of volitional and mechanistic media.

21 JUNE 1968

On the 100th anniversary of the first production of Wagner's *Die Meistersinger,* West Germany issues a 30-pfennig stamp with a facsimile reproduction of the initial 12 bars of the Overture to the opera.

21 JUNE 1968

In the course of the Fourth Inter-American Music Festival in Washington, the following program of avant-garde music of Latin America is presented:

Elegy for Strings by Rafael APONTE-LEDÉE of Puerto Rico; *Canticum Instrumentalis* by Marlos NOBRE of Brazil, with the sonic materials subjected to multiserial treatment (a world première); *Eidesis II (1967-III)*, for 13 instruments by Alcides LANZA of Argentina, the title being derived from the Greek word "eidos" (idea) and from the oneiric phenomenon known in medicine as "eidetic dreams," wherein the kinetic energy of enormous charges of sensuality leads to a series of sonic orgasms, with some instruments tuned in quarter-tones resulting in orgiastic icositetraphonic implosions; *Fissions* by Edgar VALCÁRCEL of Peru, in four sections and three cadenzas, in which the sonic nuclei are fissioned with liberation of soniferous energy; and *Métamorphose d'après une lecture de Kafka*, for piano and 15 instruments, by Armando KRIEGER of Argentina (a world première), in which the super-imposition of various instrumental groups symbolize the anthropozoic metamorphoses in Kafka's tales.

23 JUNE 1968

Die Geschichte von einem Feuer, opera by the German composer Dieter SCHÖNBACH, a multi-media spectacle for chorus, orchestra and functional kinetic sculpture cybernetically directed by an electronic computer, to a libretto portraying three anonymous men engaged in quest of instances of nobility through eight periods of time, from ancient Greece to the present, is performed for the first time in Kiel.

23 JUNE 1968

In the course of the Fourth Inter-American Music Festival a program of orchestral and choral music is presented, in Columbia, Maryland, including the first performances of the *Piano Concerto* by Robert WARD of the United States, *Recitative and Variations for Orchestra* by Hector TOSAR of Uruguay, and *Hymn to the Americas* for soprano, chorus and orchestra by Rudolph SCHIRMER of Schirmer Inc., to a Spanish text, set in abecedarian triadic harmonies in the manner of rudimentary hymnody.

24 JUNE 1968

In the course of the Fourth Inter-American Music Festival in Washington, a program of string quartet music is presented, including the world premières of *Zinctum* by Sergio CERVETTI of Uruguay and *Quartet 1967* by Leon SCHIDLOWSKY of Chile.

25 JUNE 1968

In the course of the Fourth Inter-American Music Festival in Washington, the following world premières are given:

Myth of Dreams and Cosmogonies for wood-wind quintet by Alexis RAGO of Venezuela, in four movements, *Amavalica, Totemic Animals, The Venus of Seas and Constellations,* and *Petroglyphs,* suggested by ancient Indian legends; and *Divertimento on Themes by Paul Klee* by Roberto GARCÍA-MORILLO of Argentina for woodwind quintet, inspired by 21 sketches of the expressionistic Swiss painter Paul Klee, set to music in a synthetically codified style of sophisticated infantiphony.

27 JUNE 1968

In the course of the Fourth Inter-American Music Festival in Washington, a concert of avant-garde music of Spain is given, presenting the following program:

Objetos Sonoros by Ramón BARCE, in four divisions, derived from the concepts of plane geometry and spherical trigonometry, with centripetal filaments rotating around a central tonic G; *Geometrías* by Leonardo BALADA, derived from pointillistic tonal topology and linear homophony, introduced by a symbiotic exposition of both; *Three Pieces for Double Quintet and Percussion* by Antón GARCÍA-ABRIL, evolving from parameters of spontaneous cellular generation; *Antiphonismói* by Cristóbal HALFFTER, exploring the limits of compressibility of recurring improvisatory passages; *Caesuras* by Luis DE PABLO, for flute, oboe, clarinet, violin, viola and cello, the structure of which is determined by the aleatoric phenomena before and after thematic caesuras, or pauses; *Vertices* by Miguel Angel CORIA, derived from the serial principle of interchangeable vertical and horizontal parameters; *Car en effet* by Tomás MARCO, inspired by an inductive syllogism propounded by Pierre Boulez as a stochastic non sequitur after a lecture in Darmstadt in 1965, set to music emphasizing freedom of creative emission; and *Surface No. 1* for woodwind quartet, string quartet, piano and percussion by Carmelo A. BERNAOLA, illustrating a non-rigid codification of the formal elements of two-dimensional surfaces of three-dimensional solids.

27 JUNE 1968

Concerto for double-bass and orchestra by Gunther SCHULLER is performed for the first time in New York, conducted by the composer.

28 JUNE 1968

Malcolm ARNOLD conducts the BBC Northern Symphony in the first performance in Sheffield, England, of his *Sixth Symphony,* which draws its inspiration from the jazzy muse of the American saxophonist Charlie Parker, popularly known as the "Bird."

30 JUNE 1968

The Fourth Inter-American Music Festival concludes with a concert by the Washington National Symphony Orchestra, conducted by Walter Hendl, in the following program:

Sonic Landscape by Lester TRIMBLE of the United States, conceived as an abstract composition, which became concrete in the composer's mind when a jet airplane flew over his New York apartment with a deafening sonic boom (a world première); *Piano Concerto* by Antonio TAURIELLO of Argentina, subdivided into 11 structures with an optional synchronization between the soloist and the orchestra (a world première); *Poem of Itabira* for contralto and orchestra by Heitor VILLA-LOBOS (first performed in Rio de Janeiro on 30 December 1946); *Mount Gilboa* for tenor and orchestra, subtitled *Lamentations of David for the Death of Saul and Jonathan* by Julián ORBÓN of Cuba, dedicated to a Catholic nun of Jewish ancestry who perished in a Nazi concentration camp in Poland; and *Symphony with Theme and Five Variations* (*Third Symphony*) by Roque CORDERO of Panama, based on the concept of concentric specular reflections of the pluralistic structure inherent in the concept of variations (first performed in Caracas on 16 May 1966.)

6 JULY 1968

On the occasion of the 70th anniversary of the birth of Hanns EISLER, a disciple of Schoenberg who also wrote proletarian choruses and other socialist music, the government of the German Democratic Republic issues 8,000,000 postage stamps of 20 marks with his portrait, wearing glasses.

6 JULY 1968

Syzygy by the 31-year-old American composer David DEL TREDICI, scored for soprano, horn, bells, drums and chamber orchestra, to the text by James Joyce, symbolizing the precision of leptokurtic equilibration of two mutually related celestial bodies when they achieve straight-line alignment with a third body, is performed for the first time in New York.

9 JULY 1968

The Great Digest for chorus and organ, and *Missa Brevis,* to the Latin text, by Anthony GILBERT, with special effects, such as permanent tone-clusters produced by placing weights on the organ keyboard, and with the chorus clicking pebbles and whistling, are performed for the first time at the Cheltenham Festival.

16 JULY 1968

Naboth's Vineyard, a brief theatrical play with music by the 35-year-old Berlin-born English composer Alexander GOEHR, to a Latin text, with singers placed behind a partition while action is mimed on the stage, is performed for the first time in London.

28 JULY 1968

Concerto for Flute and String Orchestra by the 35-year-old American composer Easley BLACKWOOD is performed for the first time in the course of the 1968 Congregation of the Arts at Dartmouth College, Hanover, New Hampshire, with Robert Willoughby as soloist and Mario de Bonaventura conducting.

30 JULY 1968

The Festival of Israel is inaugurated in Jerusalem with the world première of the oratorio *Testimonium,* traversing the history of Jerusalem through the ages, with music by Zvi AVNI, Sergiu NATRA, Roman HAU-BENSTOCK-RAMATI, Yitzhak SADAI and Jehoshua LAKNER. (The Festival concluded on 31 August 1968 with a concert by the New York Philharmonic, Leonard Bernstein conducting.)

30 JULY 1968

Jon LEIFS, foremost composer of Iceland who succeeded in embodying the stark Arctic modalities of his native island in universal musical terms within the framework of romantic, largely Germanic harmonies, dies in Reykjavik at the age of 68.

1 AUGUST 1968

Ernst KRENEK conducts at the 1968 Congregation of the Arts at Dartmouth College, Hanover, New Hampshire, the first performance of his *Augenblick erinnert (Instant Remembered)* for soprano and orchestra. (At the same concert, the first public performance is given of the posthumous *Rondo* for string quartet by Anton VON WEBERN, written in 1906.)

2 AUGUST 1968

Sayings for Our Time for chorus and orchestra by the 37-year-old American composer Roger HANNAY, to a text from "current news media," is performed for the first time in Winston-Salem, North Carolina.

4 AUGUST 1968

Concerto for Violino Grande and Orchestra by the prime Polish modernist Krzysztof PENDERECKI, written for a 5-stringed violin, tuned c-g-d-a-e, composed in 1967 on a commission from the Swedish government for the Swedish lutier Hans Olof Hanson, the inventor of the Violino Grande, in a formally monistic but thematically pluralistic movement, is performed for the first time in its final version at the Congregation of the Arts at Dartmouth College, Hanover, New Hampshire, with Bronislaw Eichenholz as soloist.

4 AUGUST 1968

Second Symphony by the 35-year-old American composer Alan STOUT in, three movements, *Prologue, Processional* and *Recitative,* each subdivided into allusively baroque sections such as antiphons, trio ostinato, fanfares and apogaeum, filled with ostentatiously displayed polyphonic devices, is performed for the first time in Highland Park, Illinois, by the Chicago Symphony Orchestra, Seiji Ozawa conducting.

10 AUGUST 1968

Virginia City, Requiem for a Ghost Town, symphonic poem by Ferde GROFÉ, a tribute to the centennial celebration of St. Mary's of the Mountain Catholic Church, is performed for the first time in Virginia City, Nevada, where the famed Comstock City once throve on the Comstock lode of silver ore.

11 AUGUST 1968

Musique pour Nouvelle Orléans by Darius MILHAUD, in the characteristically melodious Milhandean three movements, *Large, Très lent et tendre* and *Vigoureux,* originally commissioned for the 250th anniversary of New Orleans in 1966 but rejected by the anniversary committee as spiritually, melodically, harmonically and orchestrally unfit, is performed for the first time, still under its original title, by the Aspen Festival Orchestra in Aspen, Colorado, conducted by the composer.

11 AUGUST 1968

Chamber Symphony by the American composer Andrew IMBRIE is performed for the first time at the Congregation of the Arts, at Dartmouth College, Hanover, New Hampshire.

13 AUGUST 1968

The Growing Castle, opera by the 36-year-old Australian composer Malcolm WILLIAMSON, his sixth, to his own libretto after Strindberg's mystical drama *A Dream Play*, dealing with a neurotic Scandinavian young woman who lives in an animated world of fantasy, set to music in a neo-Verdian manner of simplicistic sophistication, is performed for the first time in Dynevor Castle, Wales, as a commissioned work by Lord Dynevor, in concert form, with solo singers accompanied alternatively at the piano and at the harpsichord by the composer.

23 AUGUST 1968

Nomos for orchestra by the 34-year-old English composer Harrison BIRTWISTLE is performed for the first time in London.

24 AUGUST 1968

Rafael KUBELIK, Czech conductor and composer, launches an appeal to world musicians to boycott the nations which invaded Czechoslovakia with military force on the night of 20–21 August 1968—Russia, Poland, Hungary, Bulgaria and East Germany—and to refuse to maintain cultural relations with them until they evacuate the country. (The appeal was joined by Igor Stravinsky, Arthur Rubinstein, Yehudi Menuhin, Otto Klemperer, Bernard Haitink and Claudio Arrau.)

26 AUGUST 1968

Étude pour folklore II for orchestra by the 34-year-old French-born Slovenian composer Vinko GLOBOKAR, using such native instruments as gusle, tapan, double whistle and darabukka, in six sections subject to aleatory permutations, is performed for the first time in Frankfurt.

3 SEPTEMBER 1968

Juan José CASTRO, 73-year-old Argentinian composer of cultured symphonic and operatic works reflecting the melorhythmic resources of his country, dies in his native Buenos Aires after years of inanition caused by multiple apoplectic attacks.

5 SEPTEMBER 1968

La Femme et son Ombre, ballet by the 35-year-old French composer Jacques CHARPENTIER, after the mimodrama of Paul Claudel, is performed for the first time in Paris.

7 SEPTEMBER 1968

Traumdeutung (Meaning of Dreams), psychodrama for four choruses and four instruments (celesta, harp, vibraphone and guitar) by the 34-year-old French-born Slovenian composer Vinko GLOBOKAR, representing a Freudian psycho-analysis of four persons relating four dreams about an identical experience, is performed for the first time in Rotterdam.

21 SEPTEMBER 1968

The 42nd Festival of the International Society for Contemporary Music opens in Warsaw in conjunction with the 12th Festival of the "Warsaw Autumn," in the following program:

Symphonies for wind instruments by the 41-year-old Dutch composer Ton DE LEEUW; *Capriccio* for violin and orchestra by the 34-year-old Polish composer Krzysztof PENDEREC-KI (first performed at the Donaueschingen Festival on 22 October 1967); *Spiegel I* for orchestra by the 42-year-old Viennese composer Friedrich CERHA, the first of the seven works of that title suggesting a mirrorable musical structure; and *Requiem* for soloists, chorus and orchestra by the Translyvanian-born Hungarian composer György LIGETI (first performed in Stockholm on 14 March 1965).

22 SEPTEMBER 1968

At the 42nd Festival of the International Society for Contemporary Music in Warsaw, two concerts of instrumental and vocal music are given, one at noon and one in the evening in the following programs:

Noon: *Concerto for Six Musicians* by the 49-year-old Danish composer Niels Viggo BENTZON; *Rondo* by the 36-year-old Danish composer Per NØRGÅRD; *Quattro Monologhi* for oboe solo by the 41-year-old Polish composer Witold SZA-LONEK; *Song II* for mezzosoprano and percussion by the 25-year-old English composer Tim SOUSTER; *Amores* for "prepared piano" by the chief prophet of the American avant-garde John CAGE; *Espace et Rythme* for a percussion ensemble by the 40-year-old Rumanian composer Tiberiu OLAH; *Solo* for sliding trombone by John CAGE; *Sequenza V* for trombone solo by the 42-year-old Italian composer of the Italian avant-garde Luciano BERIO; and *Ricercare a 5* for trombone solo by the 51-year-old American composer Robert ERICKSON.

Evening: *Pantalan* for orchestra by the 38-year-old Spanish composer Agustin BERTOMEU; *Canti* for violin and orchestra by the 37-year-old Argentinian composer Antonio TAURIELLO; *Stabil-Instabil* for orchestra by the 44-year-old German composer Günther BECKER; and *Aïelet, fille de Iephte*, opera-mysterium by the Polish composer Augustin BLOCH.

23 SEPTEMBER 1968

At the 42nd Festival of the International Society for Contemporary Music in Warsaw, a concert of electronic music is given in the afternoon and two ballets by Polish composers in the evening with the following programs:

Afternoon: *Symphonie* by the 39-year-old Polish composer Boguslaw SCHÄFFER, an electronically constructed work represented in score by diagrammatic homologues suggesting alternative stochastic procedures, and employing generators of sinusoidal waves, saw-tooth oscillators, impulsions, filters, cyclic modulators, amplitude discriminators and white noise integrators comprising the entire spectrum of audible sounds; *Philomel* for mezzosoprano and a synthesized double-track magnetic tape by Milton BABBITT, 52-year-old American pioneer of integral musical serialization and advanced electronic techniques, in three sections, to the words of John Hollander after the classical myth of the metamorphosis of Philomel into a nightingale, in which the songs of other birds are represented by the vocal palimpsest on magnetic tape; *Telemusik* by the 40-year-old apostle of the German avant-garde Karlheinz STOCKHÄUSEN, an electronic work conceived during insomnia in Tokyo and realized as a dream of omniterrestrial music reflecting the human melorhythms of Asia, America, Africa and Europe; *Treni d'onda a modulazione di intensità* by the 42-year-old Italian ultramodernist Vittorio GELMETTI, consisting of 21 sonorous lines, each employing five different frequencies of sinusoidal, rectangular and irregular waves as well as filtered and white sounds, governed by statistical data; and *Hétérozygote* by the 39-year-old French composer Luc FERRARI, illustrating the growth of organisms of mixed chromasomal provenance, and comprising heterogeneous sound sources, such as speech, the barking of dogs, the bleating of sheep, the howling of winds, the splashing of water and other polyphonic ingredients of natural origin.

Evening: *Tytania i osiol* (*Titania and the Ass*), ballet by the 60-year-old Polish composer Zbigniew TURSKI; and *Pancernik Potiomkin* (*Dreadnaught Potemkin*), ballet for orchestra and magnetic tape by the 41-year-old Polish composer Juliusz LUCIUK, based on the historical episode of the mutiny on the Tsarist warship of that name.

23 SEPTEMBER 1968

The first "Styrian Autumn" festival of contemporary music opens in Graz with the following program:

Lux Aeterna for an a cappella chorus of sixteen voices by the 45-year-old Hungarian-born Austrian composer György LIGETI. The European première of *Aegrotavit Ezechias*, a motet for two female soloists and female chorus by Ernst KRENEK. The world première of *Mass* for chorus a capella by the 66-year-old Austrian composer Erich MARCHL. *Hiob (Job)*, a "sacra rappresentazione" for speaker, soloists, chorus and chamber ensemble by Luigi DALLAPICCOLA.

24 SEPTEMBER 1968

At the 42nd Festival of the International Society for Contemporary Music in Warsaw two concerts of orchestral music are given in the following programs:

Afternoon: *Crescendo e diminuendo* for harpsichord and 12 string instruments by the 39-year-old Siberian-born Soviet composer Edison DENISOV (he was named in honor of Thomas Alva Edison) designed as a bivalve palindrome, opening with a single B-flat of the first violin (*non vibrato*), growing in sonorous amplitude, and after reaching the peak, reverting in precise palindromic ending on the initial B-flat of the first violin (*non vibrato*), the total duration being six minutes, and all temporal parameters being divisible by six (the central orchestral tutti lasts 48 seconds, the number of instruments is 12, the harpsichord being a supernumerary free agent), first performance having been given in Zagreb on 14 May 1967, and first American performance on 18 May 1967 by the New York Philharmonic under the direction of Leonard Bernstein; *Mouvements* by the 34-year-old Bulgarian composer Ivan SPASOV, for 12 string instruments; *Divertimento d'Improvisation* for chamber orchestra by the 46-year-old Bulgarian composer Lazar NIKOLOV, giving aleatoric freedom to players within the determined parameters of the music; *Symphonie des timbres* by the 34-year-old Bulgarian composer Vasil KAZANDZHIEV, an essay in diversified instrumental timbres; *Requiem pour un jeune homme inconnu* for chamber orchestra by the 41 year-old Bulgarian composer Simeon PIRONKOV, a tribute to unknown men who died young; *Musica concertante* for chamber orchestra by the 44-year-old Bulgarian composer Georgi TUTEV, based on a dodecaphonic series, with applications of aleatory tone colors; *Divertimento for String Orchestra* by Béla BARTÓK.

Evening: *Iris* for orchestra by the 36-year-old Danish composer Per NØRGÅRD, an essay in instrumental iridescence (hence the title), in which the themes are the headlines of an "electric newspaper," employing collages of musical clichés; *Banka* for soprano and orchestra by the 34-year-old Korean-born Japanese composer Hiroaki MINAMI, to words by an ancient Japanese poet, meditating on the death of his wife, infant children and his own; *Tenebrae* for orchestra by the 43-year-old Swiss composer Klaus HUBER, in three parts without pause, suggesting three aspects of tenebrousness: solar eclipse, constant obscuration of life, and the Golgotha, making use of quartertones; and *Et exspecto resurrectionem mortuorum* for orchestra, by Olivier MESSIAEN of France, in five movements with biblical exergues for each, making use of Indian ragas, and including an imitation of a Brazilian jungle bird Uirapurú (Leucolepis modulator).

25 SEPTEMBER 1968

At the 42nd Festival of the International Society for Contemporary Music in Warsaw, two concerts of chamber music are given in the following programs:

Afternoon: *Training 68* for clarinet, trombone, cello and piano by the 36-year-old Polish composer Wojciech KILAR; *Pour quatre*, for clarinet, trombone, cello and piano by the 43-year-old Polish composer Wlodzimierz KOTOŃSKI; *Spirale I per uno* by the 38-year-old Polish composer Leoncjusz CIUCIURA, for voice and percussion, to the words of an existentialist monologue, written in the graphic notation of musical ideograms, with aleatoric latitude; *Polychromie* for clarinet, trombone, cello and piano by the 30-year-old Polish composer Zygmunt KRAUZE exploiting the polychromatic potentialities of different instrumental combinations; *Keyboard Studies* by the 33-year-old Californian composer Terry RILEY, a part of a vast work guided by intervallic and melodic parameters of indefinite duration (a record length achieved being eight hours in 1967); and *Plus-minus*, for clarinet, trombone, cello and three pianos by Karlheinz STOCKHÄUSEN, subtitled *2 × 7 Pages for Workout*, in which the diagrammatic instructions are deliberately latitudinous as though "transmitting the voice of deeply hidden anonymity undiscoverable even by the composer himself."

Evening: *Quick Are the Mouths of Earth* by the 34-year-old American composer Roger REYNOLDS, for chamber orchestra, in six parts, each subdivided into six sections, the instrumental ensemble comprising three mutually independent groups operating distinct types of spatial interludes, making allowance for aleatoric interpretation; *Cadencias II* by the 32-year-old Argentinian composer Gerardo GANDINI, written for 15 instruments as an essay of thematic mobility in indetermined expositions; *The Approach to the Hidden Man* by the 35-year-old Swiss composer Jacques GUYONNET, for mezzosoprano and chamber orchestra, written in graphically stochastic notation; *Canticum Zachariae* by the 31-year-old Czech composer Tadeáš SALVA, for soprano and chamber orchestra, to a biblical text, using various modern techniques but preserving a fixed tonal center; *Músicas de cámara* by the Spanish composer Carmelo Alonso BERNAOLA with a graphic notation indicating the stable parameters of the music; and *Tragoedia* by the 34-year-old English composer Harrison BIRTWISTLE, planned as a symbiotic form of absolute and theatrical music based on concentric layers.

Evening: *La passion selon Sade*, mimed oratorio by the 36-year-old Italian avant-garde composer Sylvano BUSSOTTI, in four suggestive tableaux vivants, *Mistico*, *Libertina*, *Demoniaco* and *Mortale*, with Marquis de Sade represented by a panerotic serial arrangement of the musical letters of Sade and Bach.

25 SEPTEMBER 1968

The first "Styrian Autumn" festival of contemporary music in Graz continues with the following program:

The world première of *Concerto* for guitar and string orchestra by the 42-year-old composer Thomas Christian DAVID. *Ode an die Musik* for alto and chamber orchestra by the England-domiciled master of ancient and new music Egon WELLESZ. *Concerto* for viola da gamba, string orchestra and percussion by the 41-year-old Austrian composer Paul ANGERER. *Nil admirari* by the 51-year-old composer Helmut EDER.

26 SEPTEMBER 1968

At the 42nd Festival of the International Society for Contemporary Music in Warsaw, two concerts are given, one in the afternoon and one in the evening, with the following program:

Afternoon: *Rondo* for string quartet by the 38-year-old Yugoslav composer Stanko HORVAT, in which the rondo form is treated serialistically with an ordered succession of instrumental rather than thematic entries; *Due Lamenti* for soprano and piano by the 35-year-old Hungarian composer Miklós KOCSÁR, in two movements, *Clamor* and *Malagueña*, to the texts of Federico García Lorca, using serialistic and aleatoric procedures; *Manzit* for clarinet, trombone, cello and piano by the 34-year-old Swedish composer Karl-Erik WELIN, a study in sonority in free serial techniques; *Crystals* for chamber orchestra by the 45-year-old Austrian composer Jacob GILBOA, who emigrated to Palestine in 1938, arranged in dodecagenic serial divisons, comprising 12 sections, each lasting 12 seconds, and each integrally mirrorable; *Cantata* by the 48-year-old Czech composer Zbyněk VOSTŘÁK, to the text by Kafka dealing with the frustration of an average man incapable of penetrating the mystery of reality (first performed under the composer's direction in Prague on 24 September 1966); *Improvvisazione III* for two sopranos, bass, percussion, flute, double-bass and harpsichord by the 36-year-old Italian composer Fausto RAZZI, the improvisatory element referring to the latitude given to the players to extend or reduce the duration of each note and raise or lower the pitch, but leaving other parameters stabilized; and *Continuum* by the 46-year-old Polish composer Kazimierz SEROCKI, scored for 123 percussion instruments, including xylorimbas, bottles, gourds, bells, gongs and drums, subdivided into 36 sections, the shortest lasting 4 seconds, and the longest 45 seconds (first performed at the Stockholm festival on 17 September 1967).

Evening: *Parades* for orchestra and two pianos by the 31-year-old Polish composer Zbigniew BARGIELSKI, in four movements, burlesquing the stolid stultification of salon music; *Piano Concerto* by the 61-year-old Dutch composer Kees van BAAREN, in one movement, written in a moderately modern idiom; *Paroles tissées* for tenor and orchestra by the 55-year-old Polish composer Witold LUTOSLAWSKI, in four contrasting divisions, to the text by the surrealist French poet Jean-François Chabrun, set in a lyrically expressionistic idiom (first performed at the Aldeburgh, England, Festival on 25 June 1965); and *Second Symphony* by Sergei PROKOFIEV.

26 SEPTEMBER 1968

The first "Styrian Autumn" festival of contemporary music in Graz continues with the following program featuring works by Yugoslav composers:

Tâches (Spots) for piano and chamber orchestra by the 38-year-old composer Stanko HORVAT. *Sequenzen* for chamber orchestra by the 30-year-old composer Igor KULJERIĆ. *Komposition* for Ondes Martenot and chamber orchestra by the 37-year-old composer Ruben RADICA. *Verklärungen (Transfigurations)* for baritone and chamber orchestra by the 38-year-old composer Krešimir ŠIPUŠ. *For-men und Flächen (Forms and Surfaces)* for chamber orchestra by the 31-year-old composer Dubravko DETONI.

26 SEPTEMBER 1968

Crystals by Jacob GILBOA, *Continuum* by Kazimierz SENOCKI and Cantata by Zbyněk VOSTŘÁK, originally scheduled for performance on this date at the Warsaw Autumn Festival, were not performed "for reasons of force majeure" (see full scheduled program in *Music Since 1900*). They were performed instead at the 1969 Festival in Hamburg: *Crystals* and *Cantata* on 22 June 1969, *Continuum* on 24 June 1969.

27 SEPTEMBER 1968

At the 42nd Festival of the International Society for Contemporary Music in Warsaw three concerts are given with the following programs:

Afternoon: *Spheroon* by the 36-year-old Yugoslav composer Vladan RADOVANOVIĆ, for chorus and tape, in palimpsest, glorifying the primordial dust of a chaotic tourbillion; and *Labiryntus II* by the prime Italian avant-gardist Luciano BERIO, for soprano, chamber orchestra, percussion and a vocal ensemble, superimposed on a tape recording.

Evening: *4 × 5*, concerto for four quintets by the 61-year-old Russian-born Swiss composer Constantin REGAMEY, scored for four contrasting groups of five instruments each, and based on a single series containing all different intervals, in five movements suggesting a millennial link with the Ars antiqua: *Perotinamente* (i.e., in the manner of Perotin), *Quasi una monodia, Condensazioni in moto, Musica e Corale,* and *Concertando; Epifanie* for mezzosoprano and orchestra by Luciano BERIO, a cycle of heterogeneous songs set to texts in French, English, Spanish and German, in an artful montage; *Serenata II* for flute and four instrumental groups by the 32-year-old Dutch composer Jan VAN VLIJMEN, in a single movement subdivided into five fragments of varied connotations; and *Figures, Doubles, Prismes* for orchestra by the French magus of modern music, Pierre BOULEZ, composed in 1958 and representing a deep probe into sonorous structures.

Late evening: Film music: *Altisonance* by the Swedish avant-garde composer Karl-Birger BLOMDAHL (1916–1968), in which the visual images from outer space are translated into altisonant frequencies, with the terrestrial ornithological sounds of the songs of the nightingale and the blackbird combined in an audio-visual montage with the static noise from the sun and the aurora borealis (first performed at the Festival of Art and Technology in Stockholm on 20 September 1966); and *Match* and *Solo* by the 36-year-old Argentinian-born German experimentalist Mauricio KAGEL obtained as a result of electronic synchronization, desynchronization and postsynchronization.

28 SEPTEMBER 1968

At the 42nd Festival of the International Society for Contemporary Music in Warsaw two concerts are given, one in the afternoon and one in the evening, in the following programs:

Afternoon: *14 Arten den Regen zu beschreiben* for flute, clarinet, violin, viola, cello and piano by the politically and musically radical composer Hanns EISLER (1898–1962), a cycle of 14 brief variations on a theme, written by Eisler in 1941; *Morsima-Amorsima* for piano, violin, cello and double-bass by the 46-year-old Rumanian-born Greek composer and engineer Iannis XENAKIS, prime theorist of the scientifically organized stochastic method of composition (*Morsima* means an event ordained by fate; *Amorsima*, by virtue of the privative *a*, means not ordained by fate) with parameters derived from the statistical findings of probabilities of tonal events calculated by a computer; *Triad III* for oboe, viola and cello by the 35-year-old English composer Justin CONNOLLY, the word triad here meaning simply a triunity of timbres; *Quartet* op. 22, for violin, clarinet, tenor saxophone and piano by Anton VON WEBERN, in two movements of color melody, canonic polyphony and serialistic pointillism; *Moments* for flute, clarinet, viola, cello and piano by the 27-year-old Polish composer Piotr WARZECHA, in a single movement written in a variety of modern techniques; and *Kammersymphonie*, op. 9, by Arnold SCHOENBERG.

Evening: *Tenth Symphony* by Dmitri SHOSTAKOVICH; *Second Piano Concerto* by the 35-year-old Soviet composer Rodion SHCHEDRIN (first performed by him with the Moscow Radio Orchestra on 5 January 1967), in three movements: (1) *Dialogues*, opening with an exergue in piano, echoed by the orchestra; (2) *Improvisation*, a toccata-scherzo, in which two dominant themes are freely copulated in versatile improvisatory manner; (3) *Contrasts*, wherein the piano plays single notes and chords as if tuning up the instrument, eliciting an antiphonal reaction from the orchestra; and *To the Memory of the Dead During the Years of the Siege of Leningrad*, symphonic poem by the 38-year-old Soviet composer Andrei PETROV, scored for strings, trumpets, two pianos and percussion, a musical dedication to the heroic human spirit to be recalled when "men will explore new planets and abolish war forever."

29 SEPTEMBER 1968

On the last day of the 42nd Festival of the International Society for Contemporary Music in Warsaw, two concerts are given, one at noon and one in the evening, with the following programs:

Noon: *Sonata per archi* by the 42-year-old German expressionist Hans Werner HENZE (first performed in Zürich on 21 March 1958), in two linked movements, *Allegro* and a theme with 32 variations, each having 8 bars; *Jubilus* by the 37-year-old French composer André LAPORTE, scored for brass and percussion, with the thematic material based entirely on the serial principle of 12 different notes and different dynamic and instrumental elements, incorporating organized aleatoric episodes; 5 *Chants* for mezzo-soprano and chamber orchestra by the 40-year-old Polish composer Tadeusz BAIRD, to the words of a Polish poetess who died young; *The Dorian Horizon* by the 37-year-old Japanese composer Toru TAKEMITSU, scored for two string ensembles; *Lineas y puntos* for 20 wind instruments and a double-track magnetic tape by the 38-year-old Spanish composer Cristóbal HALFFTER (first performed at the Donaueschingen Festival on 22 October 1967); and *Eufonia III*, for orchestra, by the 51-year-old Hungarian composer Rudolf MAROS, intended to create a euphonious modernistic impression, with a mirrorable section in the center of the piece.

Evening: *La Peau du Silence* for orchestra by the 33-year-old French composer François-Bernard MÂCHE, in five movements, *Plages*, *Manipulations*, *Poème*, *Migrations* and *Montage*, employing the imitation of the animal noises of marine life and nocturnal birds, in a montage of human sounds; *Canti* for soprano and orchestra by the 28-year-old Polish composer Edward BOGUSLAWSKI, for soprano and orchestra, based on a dodecaphonic series; *Second Concerto* for oboe and orchestra by the 48-year-old Italian composer Bruno MADERNA (first performed in Cologne on 10 November 1967); and *Fifth Symphony* by the 71-year-old Polish composer Boleslaw SZABELSKI, in a single movement, with a choral ending set to the text of abstract syllables.

29 SEPTEMBER 1968

Second Piano Concerto by Hans Werner HENZE, in one movement, subdivided into three sections, the first representing the auditory impressions of the Orient and evoking the clangs of the Japanese Gagaku orchestra in a pluralistic setting with specular intervallic reflections, the second, a scherzo with thematic elements intervallically refracted and prismatically dispersed, and the finale, a polyphonic fantasy inspired by the line from Shakespeare's sonnet, "the expense of spirit in a waste of shame," the whole intended to convey the existentialist philosophy derived from the optimistic realization of the inevitability of human decay, is performed for the first time in Bielefeld, Germany.

29 SEPTEMBER 1968

Ulisse, opera in two acts with a prologue by the 64-year-old Italian modernist Luigi DALLAPICCOLA, to his own Italian libretto after Homer's *Odyssey*, centered on Princess Nausicaa's insular interlude with Ulysses, and set in a *sui generis* dodecaphonic technique, with a fissile 12-tone-series forming two thematic hexachords, each subject to interior permutations, is performed for the first time at the Berlin Music Festival in a German version under the title *Odysseus*, conducted by Lorin Maazel.

2 OCTOBER 1968

Three Mysteries, opera-triptych by Niccolò CASTIGLIONI, based on three separate texts—*Silence*, inspired by a Japanese Noh play; *Chordination*, in a setting of a medieval English morality play; *The Fall of Lucifer and Aria*, developed from a scene in Shakespeare's *Romeo and Juliet*—written in an austere atonal manner with the utmost economy of sonic materials, is performed for the first time in Rome.

3 OCTOBER 1968

To Thee Old Cause, symphonic evocation by William SCHUMAN for oboe, brass, timpani, piano and strings, inspired by Walt Whitman's poem, and dedicated to the memory of the slain leaders of American society Martin Luther King and Robert F. Kennedy, is performed for the first time by the New York Philharmonic, Leonard Bernstein conducting.

3 OCTOBER 1968

Anna LOCKWOOD, 39-year-old New Zealand-born pioneer in aural, oral, visual, tactile, gustatory and olfactory techniques of composition, holds in London a musico-spiritualistic séance, at which a total combustion of an upright piano is achieved, crowned by the epiphany of the spirit of Beethoven who metapsychically records on magnetic tape some of his posthumous music in an astonishingly modern idiom. (Instructions for burning the piano read as follows: "Overtune the strings as high as possible so as to get maximum sound when they snap with the heat. Cover microphones with asbestos and fasten inside the piano. To start fire, splash small amount of kerosene at the back of the piano, in one corner, so that the fire spreads slowly.")

6 OCTOBER 1968

Quadri for jazz quartet and orchestra by the 42-year-old black American composer and jazz clarinetist William O. SMITH is performed for the first time in New York with the Modern Jazz Quartet as soloists.

7 OCTOBER 1968

I Have a Dream, solo cantata for voice and orchestra by Elie SIEGMEISTER, to the text based on the famous speech by Martin Luther King, is performed for the first time in Omaha.

9 OCTOBER 1968

Nine Rivers from Jordan, opera in three acts by the Czech-born American composer Hugo WEISGALL, to a libretto saturated with religious symbolism, in which a Christ-like British soldier in World War II lets a Judas-like German war prisoner escape, the first opera in history to employ four-letter words for sexual intercourse in dialogue, set to music in intransigently dissonant counterpoint, with some topical insertions, such as the singing of *Lili Marlene*, a song popular with both sides in the conflict, is produced by the New York City Opera.

10 OCTOBER 1968

Luciano BERIO, 42-year-old Italian avant-garde composer, conducts the New York Philharmonic and Swingle Singers in the first performance of his *Sinfonia*, surrealist musicorama in four parts: the first, making use of a text from an anthropological treatise on Brazilian mythology with dodecaphonic boulders crashing into the tidal waves of a totality of discordance; the second, in which the name of Martin Luther King is fissioned into its syllabic atoms; the third, a montage of thematic molecules in a disoriented version of Mahler's Resurrection Symphony, with disembodied motives from disemboweled Bach and Berlioz, Debussy and Stravinsky juxtaposed and superimposed in multidimensional counterpoint, while voices recite excerpts from the writings of Samuel Beckett and James Joyce subjoined to French graffiti from the walls of the Sorbonne during the student insurrection of May 1968; and the last, a sonic collage beginning with a whispering of atomized vocables and concluding with a panacoustical coagulation of aleatory matrices. In 1970 Luciano Berio remodeled the *Sinfonia* by rewriting the finale for greater tension and percussive punctuation; the revised score was first performed by the New York Philharmonic on 8 October 1970, Leonard Bernstein conducting.

10 OCTOBER 1968

Heracles, opera by the 33-year-old American composer John EATON, is performed for the first time in Turin, Italy.

13 OCTOBER 1968

Seventh Symphony by the remarkable Swedish composer Allan PETTERSSON, the most popular of all his symphonic works, and like most of his symphonies set in a single protracted movement diversified by clearly demarcated divisions in varying tempos, is performed for the first time by the Stockholm Philharmonic, conducted by Antal Dorati.

19 OCTOBER 1968

Hamlet, opera in three acts by the 37-year-old Hungarian composer Sándor SZOKOLAY, after Shakespeare, in a Hungarian translation adapted by the composer, is performed for the first time in Budapest.

26 OCTOBER 1968

The Scarlet Mill, opera in two acts by the 73-year-old Hungarian-born American composer Eugene ZÁDOR, after Ferenc Molnar's play *The Red Mill* having to do with an infernal red mill capable of corrupting the most virtuous man in Hell's epicenter, but failing when the only certifiably virtuous man found in the whole world proves to be absolutely incorruptible, set to music in a functionally modernistic manner saturated with tolerable discords, is performed for the first time by the Brooklyn College Opera Theater.

27 OCTOBER 1968

Fifth Symphony by the Austrian composer Karl WEIGL (1881–1945), surnamed *Apocalyptic*, in four movements— (1) *Evocation*, (2) *The Dance around the Golden Calf*, (3) *Paradise Lost*, (4) *The Four Horsemen*—conceived in a megasymphonious Bruckneromantic manner, polyphonically elaborated and harmonically inspissated, is performed for the first time, 23 years after its composition, by the American Symphony in New York under the direction of its sesquioctogenarian founder Leopold Stokowski.

27 OCTOBER 1968

Symphony '68, identified simply by year of composition (1968), by the 47-year-old Slovenian composer Primož RAMOVŠ in two movements set in a radically modernistic sonic language, is performed for the first time in Opatija, Yugoslavia.

27 OCTOBER 1968

Third Symphony, subtitled *Mikrosimfonija*, by the 41-year-old Serbian composer Aleksandar OBRADOVIĆ is performed for the first time in Opatija.

28 OCTOBER 1968

Bílá nemoc (The White Sickness), opera by the 51-year-old Czech composer Tibor ANDRAŠOVAN, is performed for the first time in Bratislava.

30 OCTOBER 1968

L'Apocalypse de Jean, electronic oratorio by the Parisian pioneer of concrete music Pierre HENRY, is performed for the first time in Paris.

5 NOVEMBER 1968

King Samuel, opera by the 43-year-old Macedonian composer Kiril MAKEDONSKI, to his own libretto depicting turbulent events in Macedonia in the tenth century, is produced in Skopje.

6 NOVEMBER 1968

Charles MUNCH, 77-year-old Alsatian-born conductor, known as "le beau Charles" for his patrician demeanor and sartorial elegance, who rose to the highest position in the music world after a late start (he made his conducting début at 42) and held the prestigious post of music director of the Boston Symphony Orchestra from 1949 to 1962, whose aristocratic insouciance in interpretations of the classics and idiosyncrasies of treatment (his irrepressible penchant for fast tempi gave rise in the orchestral milieu to the quip that the three degrees of musical celerity are *Presto, Prestissimo, Munchissimo*) aroused occasional perplexity, dies of a sudden heart attack in the early morning, in Richmond, Virginia, on the day he was to lead a concert there with the touring Orchestre de Paris, founded by him in 1967. (Date and hour of death from the official verdict by the Virginia State Medical Examiner. The obituary in The New York *Times* of 7 November 1968 erroneously datelined the Richmond dispatch about Munch's death as 5 November 1968.)

6 NOVEMBER 1968

Guillaume LANDRÉ, Dutch composer of nobly intentioned music in various genres, greatly esteemed within the confines of his native land, dies in Amsterdam at the age of 63.

8 NOVEMBER 1968

Changeant for cello and orchestra by the 44-year-old Croatian modernist Milko KELEMEN, suggesting the constant changes in musical continuity, is performed for the first time in Cologne.

8 NOVEMBER 1968

The Passion of Oedipus, opera in two acts by the American composer Roy TRAVIS, written in an advanced dissonant idiom, is performed for the first time by the Opera Workshop of the University of California, Los Angeles.

13 NOVEMBER 1968

Son of Heldenleben by the Canadian composer R. Murray SCHAFER, based on the themes of the quasi-autobiographical symphonic poem of Richard Strauss, is performed for the first time in Montreal.

17 NOVEMBER 1968

Katyń Epitaph, symphonic elegy by the 54-year-old Polish composer resident in England Andrzej PANUFNIK, dedicated to the memory of hundreds of Polish officers and soldiers slain in Katyń, Lithuania, in 1941, during the rapid advance of the Nazi armies into Russia, is performed for the first time in New York by the American Symphony, Leopold Stokowski conducting.

18 NOVEMBER 1968

Concerto for Two Pianos and Orchestra by Paul CRESTON is performed for the first time in Montevallo, Alabama, by the New Orleans Philharmonic Symphony, Werner Torkanowsky conducting.

24 NOVEMBER 1968

Kesa and Morito, opera in three acts by the Japanese composer Kan ISHII, to a horrendous tale of medieval Japanese passions, in which the reckless suitor of a friend's beauteous wife, scheming to murder the husband in the darkness of the night, severs with his sword the head of his beloved, and holding it aloft in faint moonlight realizes the enormity of his miscalculation, set to music in a cosmopolitan vigesimosecular idiom without ostentatious Nipponisms, is produced in Tokyo by an all-Japanese company of singers and instrumentalists.

27 NOVEMBER 1968

Second Symphony by the 48-year-old Soviet Armenian composer Karen KHACHATURIAN, in two movements, is performed for the first time in Moscow.

1 DECEMBER 1968

Second Concerto for string orchestra, composed in 1956 by the foremost Swedish composer Allan PETTERSSON, is performed for the first time on Swedish Radio, ten years after the performance of his *Third Concerto* for string orchestra.

3 DECEMBER 1968

Ars amatoria, cantata by the 45-year-old Austrian composer Gerhard WIMBERGER, in five parts to selected texts from Ovid's classical manual of sexual gymnastics written ca. 8 A.D., scored for soprano, baritone, chorus, jazz combo and chamber orchestra with the focal word *amor* intoned by the soprano in a long solo embracing a two-octave range, is performed for the first time in Berlin.

9 DECEMBER 1968

Musique pour l'homme by the Dutch composer Joep STRAESSER, for singing, speaking, shouting and whispering voices and a large orchestra, to the text in French of the Universal Declaration of the Rights of Man adopted by the United Nations in 1948, with quodlibets rendered deliberately unintelligible by heterosyllabification, is performed for the first time by the Concertgebouw Orchestra in Amsterdam.

9 DECEMBER 1968

A scheduled first performance in Hamburg of *Das Floss der Meduse (The Raft of the Medusa)*, "oratorio volgare e militare" by the German composer Hans Werner HENZE, dedicated to Ché Guevara, the fiery Cuban guerrilla fighter executed by the Bolivian soldiery during an abortive revolutionary operation, a setting of the story of the dramatic shipwreck of the French frigate Medusa in 1816 revealing a shocking lack of humanity among its superior officers who left 154 seamen and passengers to die on the raft made from the hulk of the wrecked ship, to a libretto in which the living sing in German while their dead comrades call to them in untranslated lines from Dante's *Divina Commedia*, is canceled when the chorus refuses to sing under a red banner installed on the stage. (Henze had said that world revolution was more important than world premières of new music.)

9 DECEMBER 1968

Stimmung (Tuning) by Karlheinz STOCKHAUSEN, scored for six shoeless singers sitting cross-legged in a circle with musical material selected from a matrix of fifty-one pitch patterns and occasionally intoning "magic names," is performed for the first time in Paris.

12 DECEMBER 1968

Yes Speak Out Yes, cantata by the 38-year-old Spanish composer Cristóbal HALFFTER, to the text by Norman Corwin, in honor of the twentieth anniversary of the United Nations Declaration of Human Rights, is performed for the first time in New York.

15 DECEMBER 1968

Epicycle, a continuum for mixed media by the 42-year-old Greek composer Jani CHRISTOU, designed to last any duration of time (millennia, decennia, lustra, years, months, weeks, days, hours, minutes, seconds, milliseconds, nanoseconds, picoseconds) "in a climate of total impassivity," with optional audience participation, is given its first finite presentation at a session of the Hellenic section of the International Society for Contemporary Music in Athens.

17 DECEMBER 1968

Spider-Song, a comic book and event by the 31-year-old American avant-gardist Stanley LUNETTA, in collaboration with Larry AUSTIN, is demonstrated for the first time in New York.

17 DECEMBER 1968

Les Pleurs, vocal cycle by the 39-year-old Russian composer Edison DENISOV, for a passionately tearful soprano accompanied by an anguished piano (with application of painful fingernail pizzicato and glissando on the grand piano strings) and three groups of exotic percussion instruments, to texts from age-long fitfully repetitious crying spells of Russian funeral folklore, portraying with soul-wrenching realism the nailing of the coffin's cover by strokes of claves, is performed for the first time in Brussels.

19 DECEMBER 1968

Help! Help! The Globolinks! a space opera by Gian Carlo MENOTTI, to his own libretto in English depicting the invasion of the earth by extraterrestrial globolinks (i.e., global links) who speak an electronic language of dodecaphonic provenance but who are vulnerable to the sounds of human music and are eventually routed by a school band playing a diatonic march, is produced at the Hamburg State Opera.

24 DECEMBER 1968

The Story of Ivan the Fool, cantata by Alexander TCHEREPNIN, for narrator, vocalists, chorus, orchestra and electronic devices, after Tolstoy's moralistic tale of a simpleton who outwits wiseacres, written in a folkloristic Russian style, is performed for the first time in a broadcast by the BBC in London, from a previously recorded tape conducted by the composer.

29 DECEMBER 1968

Sixty years after the devastating earthquake in Sicily on 28 December 1908, when some 75,000 people perished, a newly decorated Vittorio Emanuele Theater reopens in Messina, the epicenter of the tremor, with the production of Verdi's *Aida,* the opera which was last performed on the eve of the disaster, in the presence of several survivors, with the conductor using the same baton as the one wielded by the last maestro to conduct at the theater.

31 DECEMBER 1968

False Relationships and the Extended Ending for cello, violin, trombone, three pianos and chimes, by the 42-year-old American avant-garde composer Morton FELDMAN, is performed for the first time in the course of the Festival of New Music in Palermo, Sicily.

1969

7 JANUARY 1969

Six Studies of Francis Bacon for orchestra by the 44-year-old British composer Gerard SCHURMANN, comprised of *Figures in a Landscape, Popes, Isabel, Crucifixion, George and the Bicycle* and *Self-Portrait,* is performed for the first time in Dublin.

10 JANUARY 1969

Ninth Symphony by William SCHUMAN, subtitled *Le Fosse Ardeatine,* written under a deep impression of a visit at the Ardeatine Caves in Rome where the Germans shot, bombed and suffocated 335 Italians in 1944 in reprisal for the killing of 32 German soldiers by the Italian resistance groups, is performed for the first time by the Philadelphia Orchestra, Eugene Ormandy conducting.

14 JANUARY 1969

Asterism for piano and orchestra by the Japanese modernist Toru TAKEMITSU, written for a normal orchestra with a plethora of percussion, containing episodes of aleatoric sound and improvisation, is performed for the first time by the Toronto, Canada, Symphony orchestra, with Yuji Takahashi at the piano and Seiji Ozawa on the podium.

16 JANUARY 1969

Vladimir DUKELSKY, Russian composer who was born in a railroad station during his mother's journey to Pskov and became famous in America under an abbreviated cognomen Vernon Duke (which was suggested to him by George Gershwin), whose ballets and rarely played symphonies exhibit a cultured brand of listenable vigesimosecular modernism and whose popular songs, such as *April in Paris*, are poetic perennials of urban American music, dies in Santa Monica of a cardiac arrest during the second operation for a fulminant cancer of the lung, at an unfulfilled age of 65.

16 JANUARY 1969

Relata II for orchestra by the articulate enunciator of advanced musicomathematical techniques Milton BABBITT, a sequel to his *Relata I*, based on the idea of an intimate relationship between contrapuntal voices and concomitant rhythmic values in their mutual combinatoriality, is performed for the first time by the New York Philharmonic, Leonard Bernstein conducting.

17 JANUARY 1969

Third Symphony by the Manchuria-born 45-year-old American composer Benjamin LEES, is performed for the first time by the Detroit Symphony Orchestra, Sixten Ehrling conducting.

24 JANUARY 1969

Andrea del Sarto, opera in two acts by the 60-year-old French composer DANIEL-LESUR, inspired by the life of the famous Florentine painter, known as "Andrea senza errore," because of the impeccability of his fresco technique, is performed for the first time in Marseille.

31 JANUARY 1969

Music for Prague for band by the 47-yearold Prague-born Americanized composer Karel HUSA, in four diversified movements, with the third movement, *Interlude,* scored for percussion instruments only, and with the last section including a series of improvisations, the total effect being an integral representation of the historic, social, and cultural aspects of the great city, is performed for the first time in Washington, D.C. (A revised version of the score, for full orchestra, was performed for the first time in Munich on 31 January 1970.)

5 FEBRUARY 1969

Clarinet Concerto by the 40-year-old Scottish composer Thea MUSGRAVE, representing a set of variations on a diatonic tune, with the clarinet soloist instructed to ambulate among members of the audience, is performed for the first time in London.

13 FEBRUARY 1969

Hommage à Charles Ives for string orchestra by the 27-year-old Swedish composer Ulf GRAHN is performed for the first time in Trondheim, Norway.

14 FEBRUARY 1969

Hans Werner HENZE conducts in London the world première of his spoken cantata *Versuch über Schweine,* scored for speaker, chamber orchestra and jazz combo, the swine of the title being the contemptuous sobriquet for the rebellious West Berlin students in the restless days of 1968, accepted by them as an honorific title, to texts by the Chilean theorist of the doctrine of the Students for Democratic Society Gaston Salvatore, as a testimony of "the necessity of rebellion against the acceptance of the supposedly unalterable conditions of life."

15 FEBRUARY 1969

Second Symphony, subtitled *Epitaphium Stanislaw Wiechowicz in memoriam,* with mixed chorus by the 25-year-old Polish composer Krzysztof MEYER, is performed for the first time in Katowice.

18 FEBRUARY 1969

Enantiodromia (Opposed Pathways) for orchestra by the 43-year-old Greek composer Jani CHRISTOU is performed for the first time in Oakland, California.

19 FEBRUARY 1969

Photoptosis, symphonic movement by the 50-year-old German composer Bernd Alois ZIMMERMANN (the title denotes the drooping of the upper eyelid, due to the imperfect function of the levator palpebrae superioris under the influence of light), containing a montage of particles from Beethoven's *Ninth Symphony,* Scriabin's *Poem of Ecstasy,* Wagner's *Parsifal,* Bach's First Brandenburg Concerto and Tchaikovsky's *La danse de la fée dragée* from the *Nutcracker Suite,* is performed for the first time in Gelsenkirchen.

20 FEBRUARY 1969

Ernest ANSERMET, Swiss conductor of high cultural attainments whose interpretations of old and new masterpieces were marked by elegance and precision and who served as an apostle of early modern music but turned against the ultimate vigesimosecular trends and denounced dodecaphony in a dogmatic musicosophical tract, dies in Geneva at the age of 85.

26 FEBRUARY 1969

Love and Conception by the totally emancipated radical American composer Daniel LENTZ, scored for a heterogeneous assortment of incongruous events, bodily exertions and physiological sound emissions, and reaching an aleatory climax when the male piano soloist and his female page turner cuddle up under the open lid of a grand piano and proceed to simulate a concrete copulation while a coordinated radio program continues to blare away the solo piano part, is performed for the first time under the composer's direction at the assembly hall of the University of California in Santa Barbara. (The composer, a faculty member, was peremptorily discharged from his post after the event.)

28 FEBRUARY 1969

Luisella, opera in four acts by the 44-year-old Italian composer Franco MANNINO, expanded from his original one-act opera, to the libretto from a short story by Thomas Mann, in which a cuckolded husband dressed up as a woman at a beer party in a German provincial town in 1897 suffers a fatal cardiac arrest while singing the song "Luisella" composed by his wife's lover, with a lethally dissonant polychord serving as his epitaph, is performed for the first time in Palermo, conducted by the composer.

2 MARCH 1969

Die Reise, opera by the Swedish composer Lars Johan WERLE representing a dichotomy of reality and fantasy, written in an eclectic idom embracing tonality, serialism, electronic sound and sonic montage, and embellished by judiciously selected non-corrosive dissonances, is performed for the first time in Hamburg.

3 MARCH 1969

Ocean, opera by the 67-year-old Yugoslav composer Danilo ŠVARA after the drama by Leonid Andreyev, written in an expressionist manner including the use of dodecaphony, is produced in Ljubljana.

14 MARCH 1969

Muko Erabi (*The Marriage Contest*), comic opera in one act by Osamu SHIMIZU, to a libretto based on a folktale involving a contest of three suitors for the hand of the beauteous daughter of a prosperous landowner, won by a pauper who guesses rightly by choreographic palpation that his dance partner wearing a hideous demon's mask is his nuptial objective, is produced for the first time in Tokyo.

16 MARCH 1969

Hommage à Gauss for violin and orchestra by the 24-year-old French composer Alain LOUVIER, serially derived from the probability curve of the famous German mathematician Karl Friedrich Gauss, with a polyrhythmic percussion section portraying the differential calculus involved in the Gaussian equations, is performed for the first time in Paris.

16 MARCH 1969

The Plough and the Stars, opera in three acts by the American composer Elie SIEGMEISTER, based on the play of Sean O'Casey, depicting the agonies, the joys and human humor of the dramatic days during the Irish rebellion of 1915 and 1916 against the British domination, is performed for the first time at the 26th Festival of Contemporary Music of Louisiana State University in Baton Rouge, conducted by Peter Paul Fuchs.

23 MARCH 1969

Sixth Symphony by the 63-year-old English composer Benjamin FRANKEL, of Polish-Jewish parentage, in five movements unified by a common dodecaphonic series, in five movements, a spacious *Andante*, a waltzing *Allegro*, a ruminating *Adagio*, an elegiac *Intermezzo* and a rapid *Allegro* in quintuple time, immersed in resonant impressionistic carillons reflecting his philosophical "attitudes to things and people" and realistically directed towards progressive society, is performed for the first time by the Philharmonia Orchestra in London, Denis Vaughan conducting.

29 MARCH 1969

Songs, Drones and Refrains of Death by the 39-year-old American composer George CRUMB, scored for baritone, electric guitar, electric double-bass, amplified piano and two percussionists, to the text by Federico García Lorca, is performed for the first time in Iowa City, Iowa.

2 APRIL 1969

String Figures Disentangled by a Flute for flute and string orchestra by the 37-year-old American composer Joyce MEKEEL is performed for the first time in Boston.

3 APRIL 1969

Nomos gamma, for orchestra and percussion by Iannis XENAKIS, with performers strewn quaquaversally among unsuspecting members of the audience, sonically ranging from the gentlest coo to massive teratological borborygmuses, is performed twice in succession for maximum traumatic effect at the Music Festival in Royan, France.

5 APRIL 1969

The Seventh Trumpet for orchestra by the 42-year-old American composer Donald ERB is performed for the first time by the Dallas Symphony.

19 APRIL 1969

Let's Build a Nut House, opera in memory of Paul Hindemith by the 32-year-old American avant-gardist Robert MORAN, a wistfully perverse homage to the modern German creator of Gebrauchsmusik who wrote a children's opera, *Wir bauen eine Stadt* (*Let's Build a City*), is produced in San Jose, California.

22 APRIL 1969

Peter Maxwell DAVIES, 35-year-old English avant-garde composer, conducts in London the first performance of his *Eight Songs for a Mad King* for voice and instruments, including a large biscuit tin filled with glass fragments, illustrating the schizophrenic state of King George III and notated in the form of a cage with criss-crossed music staves.

24 APRIL 1969

Don Juan, ou l'Amour de la Géometrie, surrealist opera by the 51-year-old French composer Ivan SEMENOFF, is produced in Saint-Denis, near Paris.

29 APRIL 1969

The Lion, the Witch and the Wardrobe, opera in four acts, prologue and epilogue, by the English composer John MCCABE, to a libretto from a Christian parable of C. S. Lewis, with a cast of characters on three hypostatic levels, human (4 schoolboys), preternatural (a leonine Christ figure) and a bestiary (of superanimals), is performed for the first time at the Manchester, England, Cathedral Festival.

6 MAY 1969

Charles FUSSEL conducts the first performance of his *Second Symphony,* scored for soprano and orchestra, at the Eastman School of Music in Rochester, New York.

9 MAY 1969

Fifth Symphony by the 46-year-old American composer Irwin BAZELON is performed for the first time in Indianapolis.

9 MAY 1969

Igra riječi (Word Game) for two speakers, chorus, eight instruments and tape by the 54-year-old Croatian composer Natko DEVČIĆ, in which the sonic elements of the Serbo-Croatian language are represented in musical terms, is performed for the first time in Zagreb.

15 MAY 1969

Das Märchen von der schönen Lilie, opera in two acts after Goethe's gentle tale of pastoral love, by the 43-year-old German composer Giselher KLEBE, is performed for the first time in Düsseldorf.

16 MAY 1969

HPSCHD (Harpsichord, in vowelless computer language) by John CAGE, scored for seven amplified harpsichords, fifty-two film projectors, 340-foot circular screen, suspended sheets measuring 40×100 feet each and fifty-two channels of sound for magnetic tapes, is performed for the first time on the Urbana Campus of the University of Illinois.

16 MAY 1969

Musique romantique, unromantic piece for oboe, harp and string trio by the innovative Soviet composer Edison DENISOV, is performed for the first timein Zagreb.

17 MAY 1969

The United States Post Office issues a 6-cent stamp honoring W. C. HANDY, "Father of the Blues", and concomitantly celebrating the sesquicentennial of the City of Memphis, the scene of Handy's early triumphs, in which he is portrayed playing trumpet in deep blue against a purple background.

19 MAY 1969

Children's Crusade, cantata by the British composer Benjamin BRITTEN, evoking a historical event when many children perished at sea, is performed for the first time at St. Paul's Cathedral in London.

29 MAY 1969

Under Western Eyes, opera in three acts by the 42-year-old South African composer John JOUBERT, to a libretto fashioned from Joseph Conrad's tale of Russian revolutionary exiles in Geneva early in the 20th century, set to music in a sophisticated melodramatic manner salinated by the ingestion of Slavoromantic songs, is performed for the first time in the course of the Camden, England, Music Festival.

1 JUNE 1969

Rosemary BROWN, middle-aged British housewife and amateur pianist, gives the first performance, televised by the British Broadcasting Corporation Television Studio, of a *Moment Musical* for piano by Franz SCHUBERT, composed by him in 1969 and transmitted to her by posthumous telepathy. (A number of piano pieces by BACH, MOZART, BEETHOVEN, CHOPIN, LISZT, BRAHMS, DEBUSSY and RACHMANIOFF were similarly dictated to her at various times, proving that a prolonged state of death fatally affects the sense of elementary harmony even among musicians once known for their unerring skill in composition.)

2 JUNE 1969

The newly constructed auditorium of the Canadian National Arts Center, with a seating capacity of 2,373 persons, is inaugurated in Ottawa with a presentation of a specially commissioned ballet *Kraanerg* ("perfected energy") by the world's foremost cybernetic composer Iannis XENAKIS, to his own scenario depicting the domination of the earth by the youth in 2069 A.D. who decree the extermination of all humans over thirty years of age, with an apocalyptic accompaniment of a fantastically varied electronic score.

7 JUNE 1969

La Transfiguration de Notre Seigneur Jesus-Christ for chorhs and orchestra by the 61-year-old French composer Olivier MESSIAEN, in fourteen sections, covering all states of transfiguration, is performed for the first time in Lisbon.

20 JUNE 1969

The Hamburg State Opera presents, as part of the program of the 43rd Festival of the International Society for Contemporary Music, the world première of the demonological music drama in three acts *Die Teufel von Loudun* by the 35-year-old Polish magus of ultra-modern music Krzysztof PENDERECKI, to a libretto drawn from Aldous Huxley's novella dealing with the implosion of the *furor uterinus* among 17th-century Ursuline nuns in the southern French town of Loudun, whose latent sexuality was aroused to a feverish pitch by the virile presence of a macrophallic and multifutuent neighbor cleric whom they accused of invading their bodily orifices in the immund shape of a homuncular incubus, leading to a searching inquest by the Holy Inquisition and ultimately to his execution for communion with the devil on 18 August 1634, set to music with a maximal number of stylistic resources, from copulative heterophony of dissonant counterpoint in a plasma of pantechnical parameters to eschatological scatology in naturalistic onomatopoeia illustrated, e.g., by the sonic simulation of the expulsion of flatulent demons from the gastrointestinal tract of the prioress in an icositetraphonic series of brobdingnagian borborygmuses.

20 JUNE 1969

Violin Concerto in C by the 93-year-old English composer Havergal BRIAN, composed in 1934–1935, receives a belated first performance in London.

21 JUNE 1969

In the course of the 43rd Festival of the International Society for Contemporary Music in Hamburg, the following program of chamber music is given:

Redundanz II for string quarter by the 38-year-old Austrian composer Josef Maria HORVATH, based on the principle of statistical changes of melodic, rhythmic and esthetic parameters and involving thematic redundancies applicable in cybernetic calculus; *Trio* for flute, marimbaphone and guitar by the 37-year-old Hungarian composer László KALMÁR, written in linear counterpoint, in three linked movements; *Distributions* for strings by the 38-year-old Japanese composer Yori-Aki MATSUDAIRA, based on a gradual accumulation of discrete distributions of sonic materials, beginning with a simulacrum of tuning; *Paraphrase* for flute and piano by the 33-year-old Swiss composer Jürg WYTTENBACH, in six cyclical movements, with a motto of an invertible and reversible theme; and *Serenata* for a chamber ensemble by the 31-year-old Dutch composer Ton de KRUYF, in two movements representing a polythematic collage.

22 JUNE 1969

At the 43rd Festival of the International Society for Contemporary Music in Hamburg, two programs are given, one in the afternoon and one in the evening:

Afternoon program: *Mutatis Mutandis* for six players by the 32-year-old Rumanian-born Israeli composer Yehuda YANNAY, a study in intermutation of thematic parameters in horizontal and vertical dimensions, with an intussusception of independent elements at climactic points, eventually returning to the purified essences; *Übungen für Gydli*, for soprano, flute and harp, by the 55-year-old Czech composer Jan KAPR, to the words by his infant daughter nicknamed Gydli, with a congenially infantilo-quacious onomatopoeic instrumental accompaniment; *Still Life* for chamber ensemble by the 37-year-old Czech composer Marek KOPELENT, with a thematically serial, aerostatically ethereal suspension of single notes analogous with paintings of fruits, flowers and inanimate objects; *Crystals* for chamber ensemble by the 49-year-old Czech-born and Vienna-educated Israeli composer Jacob GILBOA, illustrating the symmetrical principles of crystallography in serial parameters; and *Cantata* for mixed choir, wind instruments and percussion by the 49-year-old Czech composer Zbynek VOSTRAK, to the words by Franz Kafka in Czech translation of the original German text, expressing the surrealistic anguish of quotidian reality in acute dissonant counterpoint.

Evening program: *Heterophonika idiomela* by the 45-year-old Constantinople-born Greek composer Arghyris KOUNADIS, exploring the combinatorial techniques of individual (*idio*) melos (*mela*) in heterophonic structures, in three individualized movements: (1) *The other Sebastian*, i.e., a non-Bach; (2) *La polonaise interrompue*, an essay, in an established form; (3) *The holy man of Arcueil*, a tribute to the musical grand seigneur of Arcueil, Erik Satie; *Siebengesang* by the 30-year-old Swiss composer Heinz HOLLIGER, a suite in seven sections for oboe, orchestra, voices and a loudspeaker, to amplify and alter the character of the oboe sound, with the composer him-

self playing the oboe; *Paraboles* for dramatic soprano and chamber orchestra by the 32-year-old French composer Paul MÉFANO; and *Septem Tubae* by the polished Polish composeress Bernadetta MATUSZCZAK, for chorus, orchestra, percussion and organ, to texts from the Apocalypse.

23 JUNE 1969

The 43rd Festival of the International Society for Contemporary Music in Hamburg presents a concert of choral and instrumental music with the following program:

Sonata for 5 woodwind instruments by the 33-year-old Danish composer Mogens Winkel HOLM, conceived as an instrumental drama in one act, with a considerable latitude in interpretation without actual improvisation; *Cantate pour elle* for soprano, harp and four magnetic tapes by the 44-year-old Zagreb-born French composer Ivo MALEC, in which the instruments are contrapuntally counterposed to their recorded images without identity of thematic substance; *Portrait* for two pianos and two percussion players by the 62-year-old Japanese composer Yoritsune MATSUDAIRA, an abstract portrait projected in five albums, with their order to be decided aleatorically by the players, but all must play the same number, involving free intussusception of themes and rhythms; and *Halleluja* for voices by the 37-year-old Argentine-born German composer Mauricio KAGEL, set to words in pseudo-Latin of liturgical type and verbalization until a freely chosen fermata, serving as a turning point to another section.

24 JUNE 1969

At the 43rd Festival of the International Society for Contemporary Music in Hamburg the following concert of choral and orchestral music is presented:

4 Novelettes for Chamber Orchestra by the 40-year-old Polish composer Tadeusz BAIRD, written in a cyclic form, in four movements, with the finale outlined in strictly controlled aleatoric distribution of sonic components; *Consolation II* for 16 voices by the 34-year-old German composer Helmut LACHENMANN, with the syllabification of the text obtaining thematic significance as tonal material; *Break* for piano by the 30-year-old German composer Hans-Joachim HESPOS, an essay in syncopated rhythms and polyharmony; *AMN* by the 39-year-old German composer Dieter SCHNEBEL, for 7 groups of speaking vocalists, to the text of a liturgy (AMB is the vowelless Hebrew spelling of Amen); and *Continuum* by the 47-year-old Polish composer Kazimierz SEROCKI, for 123 percussion instruments manned by six players, placed stereophonically as autonomous sonic transmitters, in 36 sections, the shortest of which lasts four seconds (first performed at the Stockholm Festival on 17 September 1967).

25 JUNE 1969

The 43rd Festival of the International Society for Contemporary Music in Hamburg presents the following program of symphonic music:

Symphony K by the 49-year-old Polish composer Roman HAUBENSTOCK-RAMATI, in which the letter *K* stands for Kafka's "everyman" oppressed by the incomprehension and incomprehensibility of the outside world and by the unanalizability of the subjective Angst, in three sections based on the instrumental portions of HAUBENSTOCK-RAMATI's opera *Amerika; Concerto* for violoncello and orchestra by the 51-year-old German composer Bernd Alois ZIMMERMANN, in five movements, *Introduzione, Allegro, Adagio, Tempo di marcia, Blues and Coda*, designed as a choreographic "pas de trois," with an optional ballet representation being the third performing entity; *Mutazioni* by the 42-year-old Polish composer Witold SZALONEK, for chamber orchestra, in three sections marked *Gajo, Espressivo, Molto agitato*, with "combined sonic effects" in the woodwind instruments, produced by an abnormal manipulation of keys; and *Imaginario II* by the 39-year-old Spanish composer Luis DE PABLO, an essay in timelessness, without a determinate beginning or ending, with the thematic material treated as an infinity of combinatoriality, so that the piece may last a mystical chiliad, a hebdomad of lustra, a quindecillion of picoseconds, a bissextile year, a sidereal day, or an imaginary number of non-zero moments.

27 JUNE 1969

The 43rd Festival of the International Society for Contemporary Music in Hamburg presents the following concerts of instrumental and vocal music:

La Musiquette II by the 35-year-old Polish composer Henryk Mikolaj GÓRECKI, a "musical crooked mirror of everyday life" scored for trumpets, trombones, two pianos and multiple percussion; *Reflection* by the 39-year-old Japanese composer Hifuni SHIMOYAMA, for 66 string instruments divided into three equal groups, reflecting one another in a sonic minor; *Echo* for soprano, boys' chorus, mixed chorus and orchestra by the 38-year-old Norwegian composer Arne NORDHEIM, to the texts in Italian by Salvatore Quasimodo, reflecting the oppression of Nazi occupation of Europe; *Le Roman de Kapitagolei* for orchestra by the 42-year-old Italian-born Swiss composer Giuseppe Giorgio ENGLERT, conceived in the form of a musical discourse, to a text of meaning-less vowel-rich phonemes suggesting a multiplicity of possible meanings; and *In alium* by the 25-year-old English composer John TAVENER, for soprano, string orchestra, organ, percussion and four tape recordings, to French, German, English and Latin texts sung by quadrilingual children simultaneously on four tapes (the title comes from the sentence, "Spem in alium nunquam habui," the first line of a choral motet by Thomas Tallis), first performed by the British Broadcasting Corporation Promenade Concert in London on 12 August 1968.

27 JUNE 1969

Richard MAXFIELD, American composer, realizer of the tussive symphonic piece entitled *Cough Music*, first performed in New York on 13 January 1961, commits suicide at the age of 42 by self-defenestration from a hotel room in Los Angeles.

29 JUNE 1969

Reconstruction, a brobdingnagian anti-imperialist pasquinade with a musical score by Louis ANDREISSEN, Reinbert DE LEEUW, Peter SCHAT, Misha MENGELBURG and Jan VAN VLIJMEN, denouncing Yankee incursions into bucolically vulnerable Latin American countries (Cuba is represented as a naked young bride exposed to the libidinous insults of an American Don Juan, who is eventually hurled all the way down to hell by a forty-foot statue of Ché Guevara), is produced at the Holland Festival in Amsterdam.

1 JULY 1969

Eryri for mixed chorus and orchestra by the 39-year-old Welsh composer Alun HODDINOTT is performed for the first time at the Investiture of the Prince of Wales in Cardiff.

3 JULY 1969

Bravo, Mozart, a playful homage by the 41-year-old American composer Dominick ARGENTO for chamber orchestra of Mozartean dimension, is performed for the first time in Minneapolis.

9 JULY 1969

Third Symphony by the British composer Lennox BERKELEY is performed for the first time at the Cheltenham Festival.

16 JULY 1969

A *Celtic Requiem*, dramatic cantata for soloists, children's chorus, chorus and orchestra by the 25-year-old British composer John TAVENER, is performed for the first time in London.

20 JULY 1969

The HARMONY OF THE SPHERES of the Pythagorean doctrine that interprets the position and movement of celestial bodies in terms of musical concordance is mystically manifested as the first men step on the silent surface of the moon.

21 JULY 1969

La Comédie, "anti-opera" by the 49-year-old Polish-born Austrian composer Roman HAUBENSTOCK-RAMATI, scored for one male and two female speechsingers and three percussionists, to a text by Samuel Beckett, is performed for the first time in St. Paul de Vence in Alpes-Maritimes, France.

25 JULY 1969

Douglas MOORE, American composer whose erudite symphonic and chamber music reflected the cultural trends of American cosmopolitanism, and who recreated in his "folk opera" *Ballad of Baby Doe* a historical moment of genuine Americana, dies in Greenport, Long Island, New York, at the age of 75.

30 JULY 1969

How Much Better if Plymouth Rock Had Landed on the Pilgrims, a historic wish-fulfillment for acoustic and electronic instruments, devised by the 21-year-old American composer David ROSENBLOOM, begins its continuous performance with a projected duration of about seventy-two hours at the Electric Ear Series of the Electric Circus in New York.

1 AUGUST 1969

Hra o láske a smrti (Play of Love and Death), opera by the 58-year-old Slovak composer Ján CIKKER, after a novella by Romain Rolland, is performed for the first time in Munich.

10 AUGUST 1969

Chuench'i, cycle of seven songs from the Chinese for voice and orchestra by the 45-year-old British composer Gerard SCHURMANN, is performed for the first time in Harrogate.

15, 16, 17 AUGUST 1969

The Woodstock Music and Arts Fair is held on the alfalfa field in Bethel, fifty miles south of Woodstock, New York, attended by nearly half a million celebrants and enthusiasts of rock 'n' roll, marijuana and angel dust, a three-day festival that crystallized the emotions of a generation of flower children and social rebels, evoking comparison with Mecca and Gettysburg as sites of historic events.

20 AUGUST 1969

Thirty-nine Minutes for Thirty-nine Autos by the 32-year-old American avant-garde composer Robert MORAN, "environmental work for thirty skyscrapers, thirty-nine auto horns, Moog synthesizer and human performers, employing 100,000 persons," directed from atop Twin Peaks in San Francisco and making use of autos, airplanes, searchlights and local radio and television stations, is revealed to the populace of San Francisco and the world for the first time.

24 AUGUST 1969

Aloys MOOSER, learned Swiss musicologist who sojourned early in the century in Russia and took lessons with Rimsky-Korsakov, author of exemplary volumes on Russian eighteenth-century music, dies in his native Geneva at the age of 92.

23 SEPTEMBER 1969

Sixth Symphony by the Swiss composer Robert BLUM is performed for the first time in Zürich.

24 SEPTEMBER 1969

Erasmi Monumentum for organ and orchestra by the distinguished Swiss composer Frank MARTIN, a musical homage to the great skeptical philosopher Erasmus who wrote *In Praise of Folly*, is performed for the first time in Rotterdam.

25 SEPTEMBER 1969

200,000 Taler, opera by the Manchurian-born composer Boris BLACHER after a tale by Sholom Aleichem, is performed for the first time in Berlin.

27 SEPTEMBER 1969

Fifth Symphony, subtitleed *Sinfonia dolce quasi passacaglia*, by the 63-year-old Norwegian composer Klaus EGGE, is performed for the first time in Oslo.

29 SEPTEMBER 1969

Fourteenth Symphony by Dmitri SHOSTAKOVICH, scored for soprano, bass and chamber orchestra, in eleven sections with texts by Federico García Lorca, Apollinaire, Rilke and the Russian poet Wilhelm Küchelbecker, a friend of Pushkin, each poem of a quasi-thanatological coloration, with the musical score revealing a tremendous inner tension within the threshold of tonality, is performed for the first time in Leningrad.

9 OCTOBER 1969

Fulgar (Lightning) for band, percussion, two harps, piano, celesta and tubular chimes by the 45-year-old French composer Serge NIGG is performed for the first time in Paris.

19 OCTOBER 1969

. . . pianissimo . . . for orchestra by the 34-year-old Soviet avant-gardist Alfred SCHNITTKE is performed for the first time at the Donaueschingen Festival of Contemporary Music.

22 OCTOBER 1969

Concerto for timpani and orchestra by the 63-year-old Croatian composer Boris PAPANDOPULO is performed for the first time in Zagreb.

23 OCTOBER 1969

Lovely Thing for piano by the American avant-garde composer Harold BUDD, with directions to the player: "Select a chord—if in doubt call me (in lieu of performance) at 213–662–7819 for spiritual advice," is performed for the first time in Memphis, Tennessee.

25 OCTOBER 1969

Continuum, subtitled *Trauerminuten für Dana Kosanova*, for chamber orchestra by the 34-year-old Bulgarian composer Bojidar DIMOV, commemorating a 15-year-old Czech girl student killed in the course of the Soviet invasion of Czechoslovakia in 1968, is performed for the first time in Graz.

25 OCTOBER 1969

The Strange Story of Arthur Rowe, opera by the 40-year-old Czech composer Ivan JIRKO, after Graham Greene's novel *Ministry of Fear*, is produced in Liberec.

29 OCTOBER 1969

Superball for four players with hand-held magnetic tape heads by the 32-year-old American avant-gardist Jon HASSELL is performed for the first time in Ithaca, New York.

11 NOVEMBER 1969

Jed z Elsinoru (Poison from Elsinore) by the Czech composer Karel HORKÝ, after the radio play *Urhamlet*, inspired by the conviction that the assassination of President Kennedy, like the murder of Hamlet's father in Shakespeare's tragedy, was the result of a struggle for power guided by a wily American Polonius who urges the reactionary government to conceal the truth, with a somber chorus voicing the conscience of America, is produced in Brno.

11 NOVEMBER 1969

Catharsis: Open Style for Two Improvisation Ensembles, Tapes and Conductors by the American composer Larry AUSTIN, exemplifying his concept of coordinated improvisation with optional beginnings and endings of individual sections, is performed for the first time in Oakland, California.

13 NOVEMBER 1969

Epimetheus USA, symphonic poem by the 62-year-old Berlin-born American composer Gene GUTCHË, conjuring up an American counterpart of the brother of the igniferous Prometheus and mundiferous Atlas and husband of the vitigerous Pandora, is performed for the first time in Detroit.

13 NOVEMBER 1969

Maria Triptychon for soprano, violin and orchestra by the 79-year-old Swiss composer Frank MARTIN, consisting of three separate works, *Ave Maria, Magnificat* and *Stabat Mater,* is performed for the first time in Rotterdam.

14 NOVEMBER 1969

The Lobster Quadrille by the 32-year-old American composer David DEL TREDICI, scored for soprano, folk group, mandolin, banjo, accordion and orchestra, inspired by the writings of Lewis Carroll, is performed for the first time in London, Aaron Copland conducting.

23 NOVEMBER 1969

La Voz del Silencio, one-act opera by the 33-year-old Argentine composer Mario PERUSSO, to a symbolistic libretto, with indeterminate characters described only by sex or age (a woman, a man, a youth, a visitor) colliding and rotating on the stage in aleatory motion, set to an appropriately atonal score, is produced for the first time at the Teatro Colón in Buenos Aires.

27 NOVEMBER 1969

Marriage of the Whale, symphonic chorus for three voices, chorus and orchestra by the 59-year-old Japanese composer Kozaburo HIRAI, is performed for the first time in Tokyo.

6 DECEMBER 1969

Lukas FOSS conducts in Hamburg the first performance of his *Geod,* a "musical action for orchestra, without development, without rhetoric," suggestive of the power of geodesic constructions, and scored for full orchestra.

9 DECEMBER 1969

Vesalii Icones by the 35-year-old English modernist Peter Maxwell DAVIES, scored for cello solo, small instrumental group and dancers, in fourteen sections, corresponding to fourteen anatomical drawings by the famous Renaissance anatomist Vesalius but audaciously paralleling successive postures of musculatures and skeletal figures with the stages of Christ's passions, the music varying eclectically from excruciating atonality expressing Christ's agony to ostentatious piano pounding in the manner of the Victorian music-hall to represent the Roman soldiery, is performed for the first time in London.

11 DECEMBER 1969

Fifth Symphony for baritone solo and orchestra, subtitled *Wine of Summer,* by the English polysymphonist Havergal BRIAN, comes to its belated first performance in London, thirty-two years after its completion.

1970

5 JANUARY 1970

Roberto GERHARD, Catalan-born composer who exchanged his Iberian legacy for a tense serialism, dies at the age of 73 in his English home at Cambridge, where he took political refuge after the lamentable defeat of the Spanish loyalists.

8 JANUARY 1970

Jani CHRISTOU, Greek composer of great inventive powers, creator of a style of composition striving to embrace a totality of humanistic and metaphysical expression, for which he designed a surrealistic graphic notation (indicating a psychological metamusical state by the Greek letter *psi,* aleatory usages by a pair of dice, etc.), and extending the form and duration of an individual work into an infinity of temporal units, dies tragically with his wife, while driving at excessive speed, near Athens, on the eve of his 44th birthday.

10 JANUARY 1970

Opsadno stanje (The State of Siege), opera by the 45-year-old Croatian composer Milko KELEMEN, after the surrealist tale *The Plague* by Camus, with the entire tonal fabric evolving out of a single motive and its derivatives, is produced in Hamburg under the German title *Der Belagerungszustand.*

14 JANUARY 1970

Improvisations on an Impromptu of Britten for orchestra by the 67-year-old British composer William WALTON is performed for the first time in San Francisco.

22 JANUARY 1970

Of Mice and Men, opera by the American composer Carlisle FLOYD, after Steinbeck's celebrated novel, is performed for the first time in Seattle.

28 JANUARY 1970

Intermission Piece by the 33-year-old American avant-garde composer Harold BUDD, designated to be played at random with the "amplitude spectrum barely audible" during intermission, with the audience "physically or conceptually absent," is realistically projected for the first time at Hartford, Connecticut, as the first of a long series of realizations all over the world wherever and whenever an intermission takes place, without the performers being aware of participating in a musical event.

30 JANUARY 1970

In Praise of Shahn, canticle for orchestra by the American composer William SCHUMAN, written in memory of the American Painter Ben Shahn, is performed for the first time in New York.

1 FEBRUARY 1970

Conspiracy Eight, an indeterminate composition by Gordon MUMMA for a digital computer and eight manipulators, is premiered at the Massachusetts Institute of Technology in Cambridge.

5 FEBRUARY 1970

Concerto for Orchestra by the 61-year-old American composer Elliott CARTER, written in a structural style in which notes, harmonies, rhythms and timbres become figures and parameters of a metageometric complex, is performed for the first time by the New York Philharmonic.

6 FEBRUARY 1970

La visita meravigliosa, opera after H. G. Wells by the brilliant 58-year-old Italian composer Nino ROTA, is performed for the first time in Palermo.

14 FEBRUARY 1970

Love 200 for rock band and orchestra by the 40-year-old Australian composer Peter SCULTHORPE is performed for the first time in Sydney.

17 FEBRUARY 1970

Alfred NEWMAN, native American film composer, one of the few successful writers of cinematic music who was not born in Vienna, author of nearly 300 motion picture scores which transmogrified the most marketable elements found in the symphonies of Tchaikovsky, in the piano works of Rachmaninoff, and in the operas of Wagner, dies in Hollywood at the age of 68.

22 FEBRUARY 1970

Von A bis Z, abecedarian opera by the 50-year-old Italian composer and conductor Bruno MADERNA, is produced in Darmstadt.

25 FEBRUARY 1970

Agape, "a celebration for priests, musicians, actors and poets," by the 39-year-old American avant-garde composer Larry AUSTIN, expressive of spiritual love as opposed to carnal lust, is performed for the first time in Buffalo, New York.

2 MARCH 1970

Metahudba (Metamusic) for orchestra by the 49-year-old Czech composer Zbyněk VOSTŘÁK is performed for the first time in Prague.

18 MARCH 1970

Rhapsody for Orchestra by the greatly esteemed American composer Roger SESSIONS is performed for the first time in Baltimore.

23 MARCH 1970

Carlos CHÁVEZ conducts in Houston, Texas, the first performance of his symphonic ode *Clio,* written in a firmly structured narrative technique symbolic of the Greek muse of history.

26 MARCH 1970

Count Down, an astronautical opera by the Italian composer Bruno BETIINELLI, is performed for the first time in Milan.

7 APRIL 1970

Polinteracões, a score of total music by the 33-year-old Brazilian pianist and composer Jocy DE OLIVEIRA, programmed as a synesthetic action involving sound, light and spatial effects such as inflatable floors and movable panels, comprising the impressions of the visual, aural, tactile, gustatory and olfactory senses, with an anatomic chart serving as a score for guidance of plural or singular participants, supplemented by a phonemic table indicating the proper verbalization of vocal parts, receives its first semiperformance on the occasion of the Catalytic Celebration of the Tenth Anniversary Festival of the New Music Circle in St. Louis. (It was interrupted in midcourse by the loud protest of the building superintendent as a noisy and noisome nuisance.)

8 APRIL 1970

The Martyred, opera by the American composer James WADE, longtime resident of Korea, to his own libretto dealing with the dramatic events of the Korean War in 1951, is produced in the Korean language in Seoul.

8 APRIL 1970

Grablegung Christi, Part I, of *Utrenja (Morning Prayer)* by the foremost Polish avant-garde composer Krzysztof PENDERECKI, scored for two choruses, five soloists and percussion, to a text of an old Slavonic church service, is performed for the first time at the Cathedral of Altenburg, East Germany.

13 APRIL 1970

Victory, opera by the 34-year-old British composer Richard Rodney BENNETT, after the novel by Joseph Conrad, is performed for the first time at the Royal Opera in Covent Garden, London.

13 APRIL 1970

Second Symphony by the 37-year-old Danish composer Per NØRGÅRD is performed for the first time in Aarhus.

14 APRIL 1970

Kingdom Come, a spatial work by the American composer Henry BRANT, based on a wordless text and calling for stage orchestra, balcony orchestra, sirens, slide whistles, bells and buzzers, is performed for the first time in Oakland, California.

26 APRIL 1970

The Mystic Trumpeter, after Walt Whitman, scored for narrator, chorus and orchestra by the 73-year-old American composer Howard HANSON, is performed for the first time in Kansas City, Missouri.

4 MAY 1970

Voyages, by the 36-year-old American composer Charles FUSSELL, scored for soprano, tenor, female chorus, piano and wind instruments, plus a recorded speaker, to texts by Hart Crane, is performed for the first time at the University of Massachusetts in Amherst.

7 MAY 1970

The Fisherman and His Wife, children's opera after a grim Grimm fairy tale by the versatile American composer Gunther SCHULLER, is performed for the first time in Boston, with the composer conducting.

9 MAY 1970

Symphony by the Berlin-born English composer Alexander GOEHR is performed for the first time in London.

9 MAY 1970

Il coccodrillo (The Crocodile), opera by the 53-year-old Italian composer Valentino BUCCHI, is produced in Florence.

10 MAY 1970

Fourteenth Symphony and *Twenty-first Symphony* by the macrosymphonic English composer Havergal BRIAN are presented in London as world premières.

22 MAY 1970

Zdravý nemocný (Le malade imaginaire), opera by the Czech composer Jiří PAUER to his own libretto based on the famous play of Molière, is produced in Prague.

24 MAY 1970

The Universal Prayer, for four soloists, chorus, three harps and organ by the Polish expatriate composer Andrzej PANUFNIK, to the poem by Alexander Pope, is performed twice in the same program to an audience of about 4,000 at its première at the Cathedral of St. John the Divine in New York, Leopold Stokowski conducting.

30 MAY 1970

Fibonacciana, concerto for flute and string orchestra by the 40-year-old Spanish composer Cristóbal HALFFTER, inspired by the cumulative accretion of numbers in the Fibonacci series (1, 2, 3, 5, 8, 13, 21, etc., each number being the sum of the preceding two), is performed for the first time in Lisbon.

31 MAY 1970

Violin Concerto by the 52-year-old Austrian composer Gottfried von EINIM is performed for the first time in Vienna.

4 JUNE 1970

Seventh Symphony by the British composer Benjamin FRANKEL, couched in an uncompromisingly dissonant vein, is performed for the first time in London.

8 JUNE 1970

Ombres, Hommage à Beethoven for string orchestra by the Bulgarian-born French music critic and composer André BOUCOURECHLIEV, is performed for the first time in Toulouse on the occasion of Beethoven's bicentennial.

12 JUNE 1970

Triple Concerto for piano, double-bass, drums and orchestra by the 31-year-old American composer William MCKINLEY is performed for the first time by the Chicago Symphony Orchestra.

19 JUNE 1970

The 44th Festival of the International Society for Contemporary Music opens in Basel with the stage performances of two short operas, *Der Traum des Liu-Tung* by the Korean composer Isang YUN (first produced in Berlin on 25 September 1965) and *Der magische Tänzer*, two scenes for two singers, two dancers, two actors, chorus, orchestra and tape by the 31-year-old Swiss composer and virtuoso oboist Heinz HOLLIGER.

20 JUNE 1970

At the second concert of the 44th Festival of the International Society for Contemporary Music in Basel, the following program of chamber orchestra music by Swiss composers is given:

Miroirs for winds, harp, piano, percussion and double-bass by Rudolf KELTERBORN; *Tempora* for violin and orchestra by Klaus HUBER; *Exécution ajourneé* for thirteen musicians by Jurg WYTTENBACH; *In my end is my beginning*, cantata after T. S. Eliot for soprano, tenor and chamber orchestra by Jacques WILDBERGER; and *Sonata per orchestra* by Robert SUTER.

21 JUNE 1970

At the third concert of the 44th Festival of the International Society for Contemporary Music in Basel, the following program for various instrumental and vocal groups is given in the morning:

Ikos by the Greek composer Dimitri TERZAKIS; *Ancora odono i colli* by the Italian composer Sylvano BUSSOTTI; *Hry* by Ilja ZELJENKA of Czechoslovakia; *Spectacles for Percussion and Tape* by Atli Heimir SVEINSSON of Iceland; and *Alternance pour percussion* by Makoto SHINOHARA of Japan.

21 JUNE 1970

At the fourth concert of the 44th Festival of the International Society for Contemporary Music in Basel, the following program is presented in the evening:

Requiem profanum for soprano, alto, baritone, strings and piano by Erkki SALMENHAARA of Finland; *Continuum II. Trauer-*

minuten für Dana Kosanova for chamber orchestra by Bojidar DIMOV of Bulgaria; *Nocturne,* after Nietzsche, for two choruses, two cellos, two percussion groups and harp by Alfred JANSON of Norway; *The Approach to the Midden Man II* after H. Michaux, for mezzo-soprano, chamber orchestra and tape by Jacques GUYONNET of Switzerland; and *XC,* after Ezra Pound, for soprano, chorus and chamber orchestra by Henrik-Otto DONNER of Finland.

23 JUNE 1970

At the fifth concert of the 44th Festival of the International Society for Contemporary Music in Basel, the following program of symphonic music is presented:

Altamira for chorus and orchestra by the Hungarian composer Zsolt DURKÓ. *Trajectoires pour violon et orchestre* by the French composer Gilbert AMY; *Étude pour Folklora II* by the Yugoslav composer Vinko GLOBOKAR; and *Variété* by the West German composer Peter Michael BRAUN.

24 JUNE 1970

Cello Concerto by the British composer Sir Arthur BLISS is performed for the first time at the Aldeburgh Festival with Mstislav Rostropovich as soloist.

24 JUNE 1970

At the sixth concert of the 44th Festival of the International Society for Contemporary Music in Basel, the following program of compositions for string quartet is given:

Steps of Silence by the Rumanian composer Anatol VIERU; *Aura* by the Spanish composer Tomás MARCO; *String Quartet* by the Australian composer Ross EDWARDS; and *String Quartet* by the Polish composer Witold LUTOSLAWSKI.

25 JUNE 1970

At the seventh concert of the 44th Festival of the International Society for Contemporary Music in Basel, the following program of chamber music is given:

...sentire... for flute, cello and piano by Sven-Erik BÄCK of Sweden; *Spell Respell* for electric bass clarinet and piano by Anthony GILBERT of England; *Wind Quintet* by Rudolf ESCHER of Holland; *Soliloquium No. 1* for solo flute by Zoltán JENEY of Hungary; and *La guerre* for soprano, piano, vibraphone, clarinet and two percussion groups by Ramon ZUPKO of the United States.

26 JUNE 1970

The 44th Festival of the International Society for Contemporary Music in Basel concludes with the following program of orchestral music:

Musik für Orchester by Andrzej DOBROWOLSKI of Poland; *Serenata II* by Antonio TAURELLO of Argentina; *Rondo,* after H. Heissenbüttel, for voice and orchestra by Hans Ulrich LEHMANN of Switzerland; *Tricolore IV* by Pelle GUDMUNNSEN-HOLMGREEN of Denmark; and *Plejaden II* by Günter KAHOWEZ of Austria.

27 JUNE 1970

Das kommt davon, oder Wenn Sardakai auf Reisen geht (That's What Happens, or When Sardakai Goes Traveling), opera by Ernst KRENEK, to his own libretto, is performed for the first time at the Hamburg State Opera.

5 JULY 1970

Thema for solo electrified oboe, four electric guitars, Hammond organ and eighteen wind instruments by the 35-year-old Dutch modernist Peter SCHAT is performed for the first time in Amsterdam.

14 JULY 1970

Waste Land Music, by the 26-year-old English avant-garde composer Tim SOUSTER, scored for saxophone, modulated piano, modulated organ and electronic synthesizer, is performed for the first time in London.

19 JULY 1970

The Rising of the Moon, opera by the 34-year-old British composer Nicholas MAW, is produced in Glyndebourne.

20 JULY 1970

Mme. Press Died Last Week at Ninety, an orchestral composition by the 44-year-old American ultramodernist Morton FELDMAN, commemorating his old Russian piano teacher, is performed for the first time in St. Paul de Vence, France.

25 JULY 1970

Tout un monde lointain for cello and orchestra by the 54-year-old French composer Henri DUTILLEUX is performed for the first time in Aix-en-Provence.

29 JULY 1970

John BARBIROLLI, British conductor of Italian and French parentage, whose impeccable taste won him numerous admirers, but whose lack of theatrical flamboyance became an obstacle to his success in the exteriorized musical societies of New York, and who was knighted in 1949 in appreciation for his devoted service to new and old English music, dies in London at the age of 70.

30 JULY 1970

George SZELL, Hungarian-born conductor of a tremendous organizing capacity, who commanded the Cleveland Orchestra with imperious discipline and geometrically balanced sonorities, dies in Cleveland, a victim of a conglomerate of disabling diseases, at the age of 73.

10 AUGUST 1970

Bernd Alois ZIMMERMANN, German composer of tense, expressionistic music, commits suicide in Königsdorf at the age of 52, leaving behind a post-humous *Requiem* in which the desperate motto "Worauf hoffen?" ("What can we hope for?") is answered by a suicidally pessimistic conclusion, "There is nothing that awaits us except death."

12 AUGUST 1970

Opera, a spectacle for mixed media by the Italian composer Luciano BERIO, in which calculated chaos is integrated into an oxymoronic theatrical action, is performed for the first time in Santa Fe, New Mexico.

26 AUGUST 1970

Notturni ed Alba (Nocturnes and Dawn) for soprano and orchestra by the 31-year-old English composer John MCCABE is performed for the first time in Birmingham, England.

27 AUGUST 1970

Septuria Lunaris, orchestral suite by the 28-year-old Swiss composer Matthias BAMERT, in seven movements, inspired by the seven "maria" on the face of the moon turned toward the earth, is performed for the first time at the Lucerne Festival.

27 AUGUST 1970

Marie Olénine D'DLHEIM, Russian soprano, who with her French husband Pierre d'Alheim perfervidly pursued the propaganda of Russian music in France, who joined the French Communist Party in 1949 and returned to Russia in 1959, dies in Moscow at the incredible, for sopranos, age of 100.

29 AUGUST 1970

Trobar clus for thirteen instruments by the 31-year-old American composer Barbara KOLB, wordlessly representing the ancient Provençal verse form of the rondeau, is performed for the first time in Tanglewood.

8 SEPTEMBER 1970

Essence of our Happiness, for tenor, chorus and orchestra by the British modernist composer Elisabeth LUTYENS, set in an atonally dodecaphonic idiom, is performed for the first time in London.

14 SEPTEMBER 1970

Hoe het is (What It's Like), for live electronic improvisers and fifty-two strings by the 31-year-old Dutch composer Louis ANDRIESSEN, is performed for the first time in Rotterdam.

18 SEPTEMBER 1970

Jimi HENDRIX, black American rock musician, dies in London at the age of 27, of asphyxiation induced by an overdose of barbiturates.

26 SEPTEMBER 1970

Dybuk, opera by the Czech-born Austrian composer Karl Heinz FÜSSL, is produced in Karlsruhe, West Germany.

29 SEPTEMBER 1970

Joe Hill, opera by the progressive British composer Alan BUSH, on the subject of the execution of the labor agitator Joe Hill in Salt Lake City on 19 November 1915, is performed for the first time in East Berlin.

1 OCTOBER 1970

Klangfarbenfunk I for orchestra, rock band and electronic sounds by the American composer Donald ERB is performed for the first time in Detroit.

1 OCTOBER 1970

Peter KONJOVIĆ, Serbian composer who succeeded in creating an indigenous type of national opera, making sensible use of the modalities of Serbian folk music couched safely within the tonal idiom of cosmopolitan romanticism, dies in Belgrade at the age of 88.

1 OCTOBER 1970

Catalogue des objets trouvés for chamber orchestra by the 44-year-old Austrian avant-gardist Friedrich CERHA is performed for the first time in West Berlin.

2 OCTOBER 1970

Daibutsu-Kaigen (The Great Image of Buddha), opera in three acts by the prime operatic composer of Japan, Osamu SHIMIZU, relating the dramatic events attendant upon the building of the great copper statue of Buddha in A.D. 747 in a Japanese village, is produced in Tokyo.

2 OCTOBER 1970

Norman DELLO JOIO conducts in Tampa, Florida, the first performance of his *Evocations* for chorus and orchestra.

6 OCTOBER 1970

Triplo Concerto a Tre in three movements by Gian Carlo MENOTTI is performed for the first time in New York.

10 OCTOBER 1970

Visions of Ishwara for orchestra by the 30-year-old black American composer Talib Rasul HAKIM, whose original name was Stephan A. Chambers before he converted to Sufism, is performed for the first time in New York.

14 OCTOBER 1970

Cello Concerto by the 57-year-old Polish composer of high intellectual attainments Witold LUTOSLAWSKI is performed for the first time in London, with Mstislav Rostropovich as soloist.

18 OCTOBER 1970

Five Fantasies of the Theater by Elie SIEGMEISTER, scored for multimedia participants, is performed for the first time at Hofstra University, Hempstead, New York.

18 OCTOBER 1970

Mantra für zwei Pianisten by Karlheinz STOCKHAUSEN, based on a triskaidecaphonic theme (with a perfunctory duplication of the central tone)—A, B, G-sharp, E, F, D, G, E-flat, D-flat, C, B-flat, G-flat, (A)—and *Heterogéneo* for two narrators, Hammond organ and orchestra by the 40-year-old Spanish composer Luis DE PABLO, are performed for the first time at Donaueschingen, West Germany, during the Days for Contemporary Music Festival.

20 OCTOBER 1970

At the third annual "Styrian Autumn" festival of contemporary music in Graz the following program is presented:

The world première of a partly aleatory *Formula (Edgar Varèse in memoriam)*, op. 261, for orchestra by the fantastically productive Danish composer Niels Viggo BENTZON; *Ionisation*, seminal work for percussion ensemble and two sirens by Edgar VARÈSE; *Luna* for orchestra by the 38-year-old Danish composer Per NØRGÅRD, dedicated to the moon, and commemorating the first lunar landing on 20 July 1969, in four phases (movements), using thirty-two notes employed in a horizontal serial arrangement in which certain notes fall in prescribed registers only; and the world première of an "open end" orchestral work appropriately titled *Floating*, by the 39-year-old Norwegian composer Arne NORDHEIM, which lacks a beginning and has no appointed ending. (At this point the audience was invited to vote which work they would like to have repeated; Varèse and Nørgaard were the winners.)

23 OCTOBER 1970

Black Angels (Thirteen Images from the Dark Land) for electric string quartet by the 41-year-old American composer George CRUMB is performed for the first time in Ann Arbor, Michigan.

23 OCTOBER 1970

The third annual "Styrian Autumn" festival of contemporary music in Graz continues with the following program of orchestral music:

Déserts, symphonic poem with electronic sound, by Edgar VAREAGSE; world première of *Irisation* by the 34-year-old Polish composer Marek STACHOWSKI, in three iridescent movements, each displaying an individual color effect; *Mouvement symphonique*, written in 1936, by the Serbian composer Slavko OSTERC (1895–1941); *Nasprotja (Contradictions)* for flute and orchestra by the 49-year-old Slovenian composer Primož RAMOVŠ, in three sections without pause, illustrating the motto *unus contra omnes;* and *Etude pour Folklora II* by the 36-year-old French-born, Yugoslav-educated composer Vinko GLOBOKAR, making use of microtones.

24 OCTOBER 1970

The third annual "Styrian Autumn" festival of contemporary music in Graz continues with the following program:

The world première of *Triga einer chroma tischen Leiter*, a collective, three-movement composition for eight players by Boris BLACHER and two of his pupils: the first movement, *West*, by Blacher, in five sections; the second movement, *Ost (East)*, by the 31-year-old Japanese composer Sesshu KAI, a sparsely conceived piece representing the infinite simplicity of Zen thought; and the third movement, *Südost (Southeast)*, by the 36-year-old Indonesian composer Paul Gutama SOEGIJO, representing a series of sonic oscillations; the world premiere of *Linien* for chamber ensemble by the 49-year-old Yugoslav-born composer living in Graz, Franz KORINGER, conceived as a progression of sonic "lines" that combine in sonic "surfaces"; the world première of *Musique pour Graz* for chamber orchestra by Darius MILHAUD; and *Octandre*, a modern classic for eight instruments by Edgar VARÈSE.

24 OCTOBER 1970

Kosmogonia, cosmopolitan work by Krzysztof PENDERECKI, is performed for the first time at the conference of the United Nations in New York. The work is scored for soprano, tenor, bass, chorus and orchestra, singing in Greek, Latin, Italian, Russian and English, in two parts—*Arche* (beginning), with a text from writings on the structure of the universe by Copernicus, Lucretius and the book of Genesis, and *Apeiron* (infinity), extolling the genius of man and exploration of the cosmos, drawing upon the poetic prognostications of Sophocles, Ovid, Leonardo da Vinci, and Giordano Bruno, and the pragmatic realization of the first Soviet cosmonaut Yuri Gagarin and the first American earth-orbiter John Glenn—all set in a fantastically diversified plasma of emancipated sounds.

26 OCTOBER 1970

The third annual "Styrian Autumn" festival of contemporary music in Graz continues with the following program:

Hyperprism, essay in sounding geometry, scored for wind instruments and percussion by Edgar VARÈSE; the world première of *Doppelt beflügeltes Band (Tape and Doubles)* for two pianos and tape by Ernst KRENEK, in five sections, the last of which uses elements of rock 'n' roll; the world première of *Zyklus* for cello, winds, harp and percussion by Wolfgang FORTNER, originally scored for cello and piano in 1964 and revised in the present amplified version in 1969; and the world première of KAMMERMUSIK 70 for wind quintet by the 30-year-old Vienna-born composer Martin BJELIK.

30 OCTOBER 1970

The third annual "Styrian Autumn" festival of contemporary music in Graz concludes with the following program:

Intégrales for wind instruments, double-bass and percussion by Edgar VARÈSE; *Chants et Prismes* for orchestra by the 51-year-old Polish-born, Austrian-domiciled composer Roman HAUBENSTOCK-RAMATI, written in 1957 and revised in 1967; the world première of PEINTURE for large orchestra by the 41-year-old Soviet composer Edison DENISOV, dedicated to the painter Boris Birger; *Pneuma* for thirty winds, organ, percussion and four transistor radios by the 31-year-old Swiss composer and master oboist, Heinz HOLLIGER (first performed at Donaueschingen on 18 October 1970); and *Heterogéneo* for two narrators, Hammond organ and orchestra by the 40-year-old avantgarde Spanish composer Luis DE PABLO.

30 OCTOBER 1970

Faisceaux-Diffractions for twenty-eight instruments by the 32-year-old French composer Jean-Claude ELOY is performed for the first time at the Library of Congress in Washington, D.C.

31 OCTOBER 1970

Second Symphony, subtitled *Chance*, by the 35-year-old Soviet Georgian composer Giya KANCHELI, in a single movement subdivided into three sections, is performed for the first time in Tbilisi.

31 OCTOBER 1970

Three modern American works are performed for the first time at the Coolidge Festival in Washington, D.C.:

1. *Ancient Voices of Children* for soprano and boy soprano by the 41-year-old American composer George CRUMB, to the text by Federico García Lorca, with two instrumental interludes, *Dances of the Ancient Earth* and *Ghost Dance*. Instrumentation and performance include a plethora of percussion, including Tibetan prayer stones, a musical saw, a paper-threaded harp, a glass rod, a toy piano, glissando produced by a small chisel with a smooth cutting edge on piano strings to obtain high overtones, and vocal production diversifier by expelling

breath violently like a sneeze, singing a glossolalia of vowels into the open piano, tongue clicking, shouting and whispering. 2. *Changes* for electronic tape and digital computer by the 28-year-old American composer Charles DODGE. 3. *Mass* for soprano, clarinet and the electronic synthesizers Syn-Mill (an electric generator based on a design of Robert Moog and built by Edward Miller) and Syn-Ket (a portable electronic generator built by the Roman sound engineer Paul Ketoff), by the 35-year-old American composer John EATON.

9 NOVEMBER 1970

Cocktail Party for any number of uninvited guests playing any number of undetermined instruments by the 30-year-old Uruguayan composer Sergio CERVETTI is performed for the first time in Malmö, Sweden.

9 NOVEMBER 1970

Fifth Symphony by William Grant STILL, subtitled *Western Hemisphere*, in four movements reflecting respectively the vigor, the beauty, the nervous energy and the humanity of the continent, composed in 1945 and based on thematic materials from an earlier symphony, is performed for the first time by the Oberlin College Orchestra at Oberlin, Ohio.

10 NOVEMBER 1970

Nattstycken (Nocturnes) for alto, speaker and chamber ensemble by the 37-year-old American composer Alan STOUT is performed for the first time in Chicago.

11 NOVEMBER 1970

A Record of Our Time, "protest piece" for chorus, narrator, soloist and orchestra by the 56-year-old American composer Gail KUBIK, is performed for the first time in Manhattan, Kansas.

12 NOVEMBER 1970

Ecology of the Skin by the 23-year-old American avantgarde composer David ROSENBLOOM, scored for tape machines, computers and brain ("an electroencephalographic experience for performer/leader and group-dynamic brain waves"), is performed for the first time as part of the Electric Ear Series of the Electric Circus in New York.

14 NOVEMBER 1970

Cassandra by the 35-year-old Greek-American avantgardist Theodore ANTONIOU, sound-action for dancers, actors, chorus, orchestra, tapes, lighting and projections, is performed for the first time in Barcelona.

17 NOVEMBER 1970

Sixth Symphony by the 48-year-old American composer Irwin BAZELON is performed for the first time in Kansas City, Missouri.

19 NOVEMBER 1970

Communication in a Noisy Environment, an event conceived by the 35-year-old American avant-gardist Gordon MUMMA, consisting of a number of artifacts (a racing Citroën car, with its horn blaring and neon-tubed windshield wipers swishing, a fire extinguisher emitting a foamlike spray, an amplified group of violins, clarinets, saxophones, police whistles and other music makers), takes place at the Automation House in New York.

24 NOVEMBER 1970

Third Symphony for soloists, double chorus, chamber chorus and orchestra by the 52-year-old American composer George ROCHBERG, containing quotations from Schütz, Bach, Mahler and Ives, is performed for the first time in New York.

29 NOVEMBER 1970

Frank ZAPPA'S rock group The Mothers of Invention performs at the Lyceum Ballroom in London a phallic song, *Penis Dimension*, in which the tenor soloist broods over the insufficient length of his male organ while a chorus of young girls contradicts his pessimistic assessment.

29 NOVEMBER 1970

Croisées des couleurs croisées (Crosses of the Crossed Colors) for female voice, an undetermined number of grand pianos, tape recorders and two radio receivers dialed aleatorily, to texts from Indian and Negro political speeches by the 41-year-old surrealist Belgian composer Henri POUSSEUR, is performed for the first time in New York.

2 DECEMBER 1970

The Knot Garden, opera in three acts by the 65-year-old British composer Sir Michael TIPPETT (he was knighted by Queen Elizabeth in 1966), to his own libretto with seven people raveled in a psychophysical knot—a white musician homosexually involved with a black poet, a physically mangled female revolutionary, an aging psychoanalyst and a fluttering nubile girl lusted after by a married man who renounces his nuptial vows with his possibly lesbian wife—all this immersed in a shimmering sea of iridescent instrumental colors, is produced at Covent Garden in London.

3 DECEMBER 1970

Piano Concerto in Six Movements by the 47-year-old American composer Ned ROREM, diversified by emphatically allusive titles (*Strands, Fives, Whispers, Sighs, Lava, Sparks*), is performed for the first time by the American pianist Jerome Lowenthal with the Pittsburgh Symphony Orchestra, William Steinberg conducting.

4 DECEMBER 1970

Tragedy of Man, opera by the 63-year-old Hungarian composer György RÁNKI, is produced in Budapest.

9 DECEMBER 1970

Quadrodram for clarinet, trombone, piano, percussion, dancer and film by the 44-year-old American composer and clarinetist William O. SMITH, is performed for the first time in Seattle.

31 DECEMBER 1970

Oedipe-Roi, electronic ballet by the 50-year-old Italian composer and conductor Bruno MADERNA, is performed for the first time in Monte Carlo.

31 DECEMBER 1970

Cyril SCOTT, british composer who domesticated the harmonies and timbres of french impressionism and created instrumental bagatelles of beguiling charm and exotic flavor, such as *Lotus Land,* pleasingly invoking the aura of Egypt, *Danse nègre* and *Jungle Book* after Kipling, but who strongly opposed any steps beyond his private Parnassus, and who described jazz as a work of the devil and embraced the astral beliefs of synthetic Hinduism, dies in Eastbourne, England, at the age of 91.

1971

5 JANUARY 1971

Eighth Symphony by the prolific 69-year-old British composer Edmund RUBBRA is performed for the first time in Liverpool.

10 JANUARY 1971

Triple Concerto for woodwinds, brass, jazz quintet and orchestra by the 40-year-old American composer David AMRAM is performed for the first time in New York.

21 JANUARY 1971

Pulsations for electronic keyboard, jazz band and orchestra by 38-year-old Argentinian-born American composer Lalo SCHIFRIN is performed for the first time in Los Angeles.

25 JANUARY 1971

Invitation à L'Utopie for narrator, two female voices, four-voice chorus and instrumental ensemble by the 41-year-old Belgian modernist Henri POUSSEUR is heard for the first time on a broadcast over Brussels Radio.

28 JANUARY 1971

Thirty-second Symphony by the English megasymphonist Havergal BRIAN achieves its first performance in London three years after its completion.

30 JANUARY 1971

The Mountaineers, the first national opera of the Dagestan in the Caucasus, by the 35-year-old native composer Shirvani CHALAYEV, depicting in dramatic colors and stark asymmetrical rhythms the socialist passions in a remote Caucasian village during the civil war of 1920, is produced in Derbent, Dagestan, U.S.S.R.

3 FEBRUARY 1971

Frieze, third chamber symphony by the polysymphonic Danish composer Vagn HOLMBOE, is performed for the first time on the state radio of Denmark in Copenhagen.

5 FEBRUARY 1971

The Contemporary, opera by the 56-year-old Bashkir composer Hussain AKHMETOV, is performed for the first time in Ufa, the capital of the Bashkir Soviet Socialist Republic.

5 FEBRUARY 1971

Cello Concerto, composed in 1964 by the macrosymphonic English nonagenarian composer Havergal BRIAN, is performed for the first time in London.

11 FEBRUARY 1971

Ein Gespenst geht um in der Welt (A Specter Roams About in the World), cantata for voice and orchestra by the foremost Communist composer of Italy, Luigi NONO, to the words of the portentous preamble of the Communist Manifesto by Marx and Engels, issued in 1848, scored for a seemingly innocuous soprano, a pointedly hoarse chorus representing the bourgeoisie and a cunningly mistuned orchestra, is performed for the first time in Cologne.

11 FEBRUARY 1971

Compases para preguntas ensimismadas (Bars for Self-querying Questions) by Hans Werner HENZE, for viola solo and twenty-two players (eleven strings, six winds, percussion, harp, harpsichord and celesta), written with an introspective reticence concerned with subtle nuances in a curiously impressionistic manner, is performed for the first time by the Chamber Orchestra of Basel under the direction of its founder and conductor Paul Sacher.

13 FEBRUARY 1971

Ostrov Afrodité (The Island of Aphrodite), opera in three acts by the 42-year-old Czech composer Jiří DVOŘÁČEK, to his own libretto after a play by Alexis Parnis, is performed for the first time in a German version in Dresden. Depicting the tense struggle in 1955 between the British colonial authorities and the rebellious nationalistic Greek populace on the island of Cyprus, the legendary birthplace of Aphrodite, the work is musically organized along the lines of Socialist Realism, with the national conflict characterized by tense trills and dramatic tremolos, ending in a triumphant C major as the mother of a Greek patriot perfidiously executed by the British magnanimously prevents the retaliatory execution of a kidnapped British officer.

13 FEBRUARY 1971

Leviathan for double bassoon and chamber orchestra by the 50-year-old English composer Ruth GIPPS is performed for the first time in London.

18 FEBRUARY 1971

Ninth Symphony by the extraordinary Swedish composer Allan PETTERSSON, set (as most of his symphonies) in a single gigantic movement, is performed for the first time in Göteborg, conducted by Sergiu Comissiona to whom the work is dedicated.

20 FEBRUARY 1971

Second Symphony by the 51-year-old French composer André CASANOVA is performed for the first time in Nice.

25 FEBRUARY 1971

Commemoration Symphony by Louis GESENSWAY is performed for the first time by the Philadelphia Orchestra.

27 FEBRUARY 1971

La Fontana, one-act opera by the Italian composer Mario BUGAMELLI, is performed for the first time in Trieste.

28 FEBRUARY 1971

Carmen, a collage from materials of Bizet's opera, by the 63-year-old German composer Wolfgang FORTNER, is performed for the first time in Stuttgart.

5 MARCH 1971

Ninth Symphony, subtitled *Sinfonia: Janiculum,* by the American composer Vincent PERSICHETTI, is performed for the first time by the Philadelphia Orchestra.

5 MARCH 1971

Tajemství elipsy (The Secret of Ellipsis) for orchestra by the 50-year-old Czech composer Zbynek VOSTŘÁK is performed for the first time in Prague.

12 MARCH 1971

Memory for electronic piano and electronic harpsichord by the Italian avant-garde composer Luciano BERIO is performed for the first time in New York, with the composer and Peter Serkin at the respective keyboards.

12 MARCH 1971

The Most Important Man, opera in three acts with music and libretto by Gian Carlo MENOTTI, in which a black man in an unnamed segregated nation invents an ultimate formula to attain total dominion of the world and himself achieves a liaison with an unpigmented woman, strangles his laboratory assistant and then destroys himself and the formula in a luminous death dance, set to music with a liberal application of Africanesque percussion, is performed for the first time at the New York City Opera.

12 MARCH 1971

The Capitoline Venus, opera by the American composer Ulysses KAY, is performed for the first time at the University of Illinois in Urbana.

19 MARCH 1971

Stille und Umkehr (Stillness and Return) for orchestra by the German composer Bernd Alois ZIMMERMANN, written in a thanatological spirit of ultimate quietude dissolving at the end into shimmering quarter tones, is performed for the first time in Nuremberg, seven months and nine days after his inexplicable suicide.

21 MARCH 1971

Octagon for piano and orchestra by the 45-year-old American composer William MAYER is performed for the first time by William Masselos as soloist with the American Symphony Orchestra under the direction of Leopold Stokowski in New York.

24 MARCH 1971

Second Symphony by the South African-born English composer John JOUBERT is performed for the first time in London.

4 APRIL 1971

The Scene-Machine, opera by the 36-year-old British composer Anthony GILBERT, is produced in Kassel, West Germany.

5 APRIL 1971

Prayer, a sound event with magnetic tape by the Italian avant-garde composer Luciano BERIO, is performed for the first time in New York.

6 APRIL 1971

Igor STRAVINSKY, musical demiurge of titanic powers, whose unique genius projected itself upon the world, transcending his Russian beginnings in achieving universality of technical means, and completing the cycle of creative expansion by adopting the serial method of composition during his last terrestrial years, dies in New York at the age of 88.

9 APRIL 1971

Écran for orchestra by the 44-year-old Rumanian composer Anatol VIERU is performed for the first time at the Royan Festival in France.

15 APRIL 1971

Fourth Symphony by the 38-year-old American composer Alan STOUT is performed for the first time by the Chicago Symphony Orchestra.

21 APRIL 1971

Andrey Kostenya, opera by the 80-year-old Byelorussian composer Nikolai ALADOV, is performed for the first time in Minsk.

23 APRIL 1971

First Symphony by the 43-year-old American composer Nicolas FLAGELLO is performed for the first time in New York.

23 APRIL 1971

Hallelujah, "a joyous phenomenon with fanfares" by the 34-year-old American avant-garde composer Robert MORAN, scored for marching bands, drum and bugle corps, church choirs, organs, carillons, rock 'n' roll bands, television stations, automobile horns and other sounding implements, is staged in Bethlehem, Pennsylvania, hopefully with the participation of its entire population of 72,320 inhabitants.

25 APRIL 1971

Staatstheater, "theatrical composition" for combined media by the Argentine-born German-domesticated avant-garde composer Mauricio KAGEL, is performed for the first time at the Hamburg State Opera.

26 APRIL 1971

A Moment of History, oratorio in five movements by the 50-year-old Soviet Armenian composer Karen KHACHA-TURIAN, to documented texts of the Soviet Revolution, is performed for the first time in Moscow.

29 APRIL 1971

Melusine, opera by the 35-year-old German composer Aribert REIMANN, to a libretto based on the medieval legend of a miscegenated Albanian princess who was doomed to change to a serpent from the waist down on Saturdays and who vanished forever after her husband surprised her during her weekly metamorphosis, is performed for the first time in Schwetzingen.

30 APRIL 1971

Fourth Symphony, subtitled *Das Testament,* for orchestra and two pianos tuned a quarter-tone apart, by the 50-year-old German composer Giselher KLEBE, is performed for the first time in Wiesbaden in the form of a ballet.

1 MAY 1971

The following program of modern pieces is performed for the first time at a special concert in Glasgow: *Bewegung* for orchestra by Luciano BERIO, *Horn Concerto* by Thea MUSGRAVE and *Alastor* by Iain HAMILTON.

2 MAY 1971

Forest Music for orchestra by the 32-year-old American-born Japanese composer Paul CHIHARA, forming a synthesis of his other instrumental pieces of sylvan inspiration (*Tree Music, Branches, Redwood, Willow, Rain Music, Driftwood, Logs*), and couched in a calligraphically impressionistic manner with pointillistic touches, is performed for the first time in Los Angeles.

4 MAY 1971

Busonism, an homage to the great romantic classicist Ferruccio Busoni for piano and orchestra by the Danish neoclassicist composer Niels Viggo BENTZON, is performed for the first time in Maimö, Sweden.

4 MAY 1971

Eppur si muove, orchestral piece by the 35-year-old Serbian composer Rajko MAKSIMOVIĆ, titled after Galileo's famous sotto voce asseveration, ". . . and yet it moves," after he was forced by the Inquisition in 1633 to recant his belief that the earth is an axially rotating and orbitally revolving celestial body, is performed for the first time in Belgrade.

5 MAY 1971

Opera Flies by the 50-year-old Egyptian composer Halim EL-LABH, to a libretto dealing with the tragic occurrence on the campus of Kent (Ohio) State University when four students were killed by National Guardsmen during an antiwar demonstration in 1970, the "flies" of the title referring to the victims, is performed for the first time in Washington, D.C.

9 MAY 1971

David VAN VACTOR conducts in Maryville, Tennessee, the first performance of his choral symphony *Walden,* to texts from Thoreau's celebrated individualistic work. (Billed as the *Third Symphony, Walden* was chronologically No. 4, his *Second Symphony* having actually been an orchestral suite and his *Third Symphony* recorded as *No. 2.* Van Vactor conducted a partial performance of *Walden* in Knoxville, Tennessee, on 1 March 1970.)

10 MAY 1971

Conflict for computerized sound by the 59-year-old Russian-born American composer Vladimir USSACHEVSKY, intended to represent the mystical struggle between two ancient deities, is performed for the first time in Salt Lake City.

16 MAY 1971

Owen Wingrave, television opera by Benjamin BRITTEN, based on a short story by Henry James dealing with a pacifist youth who suffers social reprehension for his convictions (as Britten himself had during World War II), is broadcast for the first time by the BBC in London.

16 MAY 1971

Chant d'Automne for soprano and orchestra by the 42-year-old Soviet composer Edison DENISOV (first-named in honor of Thomas A. Edison, and whose name is also an anagram, minus the *v,* of his family name), to poems by Charles Baudelaire, is performed for the first time in Zagreb.

17 MAY 1971

Der langwierige Weg in die Wohnung der Natascha Ungecheuer (The Tedious Journey to Natascha Monster's House), "show for seventeen" by Hans Werner HENZE, is performed for the first time in Rome in an Italian version.

18 MAY 1971

The Fifth Inter-American Music Festival opens in Washington, D.C., featuring the world premieres of *Reflections* for orchestra by the Uruguayan composer Antonio MAS-

TROGIOVANNI; *Piano Concerto* by Morris KNIGHT of the United States; *Checan III* for nineteen instruments by Edgar VALCARCEL of Peru; and *Plexus* for orchestra in varied degrees of sonorous density by the Uruguayan composer Sergio CERVETTI.

18 MAY 1971

Klič (The Key) by the 50-year-old Czech composer Ivo JIRÁSEK is performed for tbe first time in Prague.

19 MAY 1971

L'Opéra des Oiseaux, opera by Antoine DUHAMEL after *The Birds* of Aristophanes, is produced in Lyon.

20 MAY 1971

The second concert of the Fifth Inter-American Music Festival is presented in Washington, D.C., featuring the world premières of *Diagrams* for orchestra by Bias E. ATEHORTA of Colombia; *Concerto for Viola and Orchestra* by Robert PARRIS of the United States; *The Windhover*, for bassoon and orchestra by Robert EVETT of the United States; and *Colores Mágicos* for harp and chamber orchestra by the Uruguayan-born American composer José SÉREBRIER.

20 MAY 1971

Huckleberry Finn, opera after Mark Twain by the American composer Hall OVERTON, is performed for the first time at the Juilliard American Opera Center in New York.

21 MAY 1971

Sinfonia in Do for chorus and orchestra by the 38-year-old Italian composer Niccolò CASTIGLIONI, to texts from works of Ben Jonson, Dante, Shakespeare and Keats, is performed for the first time in Rome.

23 MAY 1971

Der Besuch der alten Dame, opera in three acts by Gottfried VON EINEM, to the surrealist libretto of Friedrich Dürrenmatt, is produced at the Vienna Festival. The old lady *(alten Dame)* of the title returns to her native locality in Switzerland where she had been seduced at a tender age and abandoned by her amoral lover, becomes rich in the world as Madame Clair Zachanassian (a contraction of millionaire names Zacharoff, Onassis and Gulbenkian) and promises the villagers untold riches on condition that they kill her erstwhile seducer, an offer which is ultimately accepted by the impoverished citizens—a tale set to music in a suitably melodramatic fashion in a brilliantly heterogeneous score.

28 MAY 1971

The Resurrection of Christ, the second part of the grand mass *Utrenja* by Krzysztof PENDERECKI, is performed for the first time at the Münster Cathedral.

29 MAY 1971

Icarus, ballet by the 38-year-old Soviet composer Sergei SLONIMSKY, to a scenario by his otherwise unrelated namesake Yuri Slonimsky, in seven tableaux, depicting in neo-Grecian modalities and propulsively asymmetrical rhythms the immortal dream of human flight by heroic Icarus, imprisoned on the island of Crete by the tyrannous archons who sabotage the sturdy wings of his craft and so precipitate him to his death, is performed for the first time in Moscow.

1 JUNE 1971

The 45th Festival of the International Society for Contemporary Music opens in London with an afternoon concert of modern chamber music featuring the following program:

Second String Quartet by the 40-year-old Dutch composer Carel BRONS, consisting of thirteen sections of which four are quasi-aleatory in respect to dynamics, duration, tempo and articulation; *Confluencia sobre do sostenido (Confluence upon C-sharp)* by the 41-year-old Spanish composer Agustín BERTOMEU, the title indicating that the thematic phrases and sections recurrently return to the focal C-sharp; *Projection* for string quartet by the 41-year-old Japanese composer Joji YUASA, in which a single sound is regarded as an acoustical compound of many potential sounds in the overtone series which acquire either melodically or contrapuntally their own thematic values; and *Abbreviaturen* by the 53-year-old German composer Jürg BAUER for thirteen solo string instruments, in four movements featuring microstructures, sound surfaces, tone clusters and aleatory passages.

1 JUNE 1971

At an evening concert of the opening day of the 45th Festival of the International Society for Contemporary Music in London, the following program of orchestral music is given:

J. D. E. by the 45-year-old Paris-born American composer Betsy JOLAS scored for fourteen instruments, the title suggesting an infinite meaninglessness; *Voyage into the Golden Screen* by the 38-year-old Danish composer Per NØRGÅRD, the texture of the music based on the constant acoustical interference between closely adjacent notes; *Praxis* for eleven strings and piano by the foremost representative of the Greek musical avant-garde Jani CHRISTOU, who perished on the eve of his 44th birthday on 8 January 1970 in an automobile accident near Athens; the titular word refers to purposeful action, contrasted to metapraxis, implying loss of emotional control, hysteric manifestations, such as six violinists striking the piano keyboard and the piano strings, at the same time furiously shouting the names of notes at random, the score being written out in associative notation with pictorial illustrations for metapractical actions; *Tetraeder* by the 43-year-old Austrian composer Irmfried RADAUER, with the musical events deriving from the number of apexes in a tetrahedron (hence the title), and scored for twelve instrumentalists seated in a manner suggesting the shape of an eponymous structure, the work concluding in an electronic coda generated by a computer; and *Chamber Concerto* by the 44-year-old apostle of ultramodernism, the Hungarian-born György LIGETI, scored for thirteen players and consisting of four movements of metarhythmic complexity resulting from parallel progressions of solo parts moving at different tempi. (This latter work was first performed at the Berlin Music Festival, 1 October 1970.)

2 JUNE 1971

On the second day of the 45th Festival of the International Society for Contemporary Music in London, an afternoon concert of instrumental and vocal music is given with the following program:

Turba by the 27-year-old Hungarian composer Miklós MAROS, for a chorus and a singing conductor, with the phonetic text of disjected syllables and improvisatory episodes in which the chorus represents the crowd of the Latin title; *Requiem* by the 40-year-old Chilean-born Israeli composer Leon SCHIDLOWSKY, to a Latin text, with twelve solo voices periodically rising to a screaming pitch; *False Relationship and the Extended Ending* by the 45-year-old American avant-garde composer Morton FELDMAN, written for two nonsynchronous instrumental groups occasionally coming to a fortuitous confluence . . .; and *Da un Divertimento* by the 24-year-old Sicilian avant-garde composer Salvatore SCIARRINO, for an instrumental ensemble, the title alluding to a planned divertimento which was never brought to completion.

2 JUNE 1971

The second day of the 45th Festival of the International Society for Contemporary Music in London continues in the evening with the following program:

An Imaginary Landscape for orchestra by the 37-year-old British avant-gardist Harrison BIRTWISTLE, with the musical design governed by a computer; *Second Piano Concerto* by Béla BARTOK; *Siebengesang* by the 32-year-old Swiss master oboist and composer Heinz HOLLIGER, the seven parts alluded to in the title representing various orchestral groupings, with the oboe as a focal solo instrument played by the composer; and *Variations for Orchestra*, op. 31, by Arnold SCHOENBERG.

3 JUNE 1971

On the third day of the 45th Festival of the International Society for Contemporary Music in London, the following program of orchestral music is presented:

Momentum, In Memoriam by the 54-year-old Hungarian composer Rudolf MAROS, father of Miklós Maros, whose work was played the day before, the memory evoked in the title being that of the fateful year 1945; *Enfiando per orchestra* by the 42-year-old Polish composer Augustyn BLOCH, composed for the Beethoven bicentennial and first performed in Beethoven's native city of Bonn on 12 October 1970 ("Enfiando" of the title meaning swelling out, for the music embodies a series of consecutive crescendos); *Haiku II* for voice and orchestra by the 44-year-old Dutch modernist Ton DE LEEIUW, modeled after the Japanese miniature verse form, fragmented and pitched together so that syllables from different poems form a series of synchronized multivocables; *Tartinia MCMLXX* for violin and orchestra by the 29-year-old Brazilian composer Jorge ANTUNES, employing microtonal structures derived from differential tones, the discovery of which is traditionally credited to Tartini (hence the title), in nine continuous sections; and *Per Bastiana Tai-Yang Cheng* by the 47-year-old Venetian avant-gardist Luigi NONO, the musical material derived from microtonal intervals contrapuntally surrounding the theme of the Communist Chinese anthem *Tai-Yang Cheng (The East Is Red)*.

4 JUNE 1971

In the course of the 45th Festival of the International Society for Contemporary Music in London the following program of chamber music is presented:

Zoom for clarinet and bongos by the 42-year-old Yugoslav composer Milan STIBILJT, the music marked by a prosodic rhythmic flow without a basic pulse; *Tételpár*, for oboe and piano by the 32-year-old Hungarian composer Attila BOZAY, in two movements (the title means a pair of movements) set in the cyclic form of Hungarian dances, in the dodecaphonic idiom; *Second String Quartet* by the 39-year-old English composer Hugh WOOD, constituting a continuous movement in thirty-nine sections, each shorter than the preceding one, except for a lyrical coda; and *Quartet* for two pianos and two percussion players by the 36-year-old Polish composer Zbigniew RUDINSKI, with the thematic material based on the principles of coexistence of opposition and a contrast between organized stable structures and nonorganized quasi-improvisatory materials.

4 JUNE 1971

A special concert of three stage works by the 39-year-old Berlin-born English composer Alexander GOEHR is presented in the evening at the Forty-fifth Festival of the International Society for Contemporary Music in London: *Naboth's Vineyard, Shadowplay-2* and *Sonata about Jerusalem*.

5 JUNE 1971

On the fifth day of the 45th Festival of the International Society for Contemporary Music in London the following program of chamber music is presented:

Variations for wind quintet, piano and recorded piano by the 36-year-old Australian composer Nigel BUTTERLEY, comprising fifteen variations on a dodecaphonic subject; *Tabuh Tabuhan* for wind quintet and two percussion players by the 42-year-old Australian composer Peter SCULTHORPE, making use of aboriginal rhythms; *Incredible Floridas* by the 39-year-old Australian composer Richard MEALE, in six movements inspired by poems of Arthur Rimbaud; and *Revelation and Fall* by the 36-year-old English avant-garde composer Peter Maxwell DAVIES, for sixteen instruments and a soprano part ranging in expression from Sprechgesang to screaming through a megaphone, containing a large battery of primitivistic percussion, a railway guard's whistle, an oil drum, a knife grinder, dulcimer and handbells, to texts by the Austrian suicide poet Georg Trakl.

6 JUNE 1971

Franz SCHUBERT'S *Unfinished Symphony,* completed by Gerald ABRAHAM, is performed for the first time in this heterogeneous form in Liverpool.

7 JUNE 1971

In the course of the 45th Festival of the International Society for Contemporary Music in London the following program of vocal and instrumental music by British composers is given:

Two Pomes for soprano, clarinet, trumpet, viola, and harp by the 28-year-old Bill HOPKINS, to words from *Pomes Penyeach* by James Joyce; *Second Piano Sonata* by 40-year-old Robert Sherlaw JOHNSON, in three movements making use of both the keyboard and the inside of the grand piano; *Poem of Wallace Stevens I* by 38-year-old Justin CONNOLLY, for soprano and seven instrumentalists; *Islands* for soprano, tenor, narrator and instruments by 65-year-old Elizabeth LUTYENS, evoking four islands described by Sophocles, Shelley, Stevenson and Rabelais; and *Leo* for chamber orchestra by the Catalan-born composer Roberto GERHARD (1897–1970), a work first performed at Dartmouth College in Hanover, New Hampshire, on 23 August 1969, the title bearing an astrological reference to the constellation of Leo.

8 JUNE 1971

On the concluding day of the 45th Festival of the International Society for Contemporary Music in London the following program is given in an afternoon concert:

Invariant for bass clarinet, piano and tape by the 42-year-old Czech composer Václav KUČERA, based on the principle of invariance of some elements in a cybernetic system and set in a free variation form; *Epitase* by the 35-year-old Swiss composer Eric GAUDIBERT, the title being derived from epitasis, the point in Greek dramaturgy at which the action approaches the climax, scored for harpsichord, string trio and magnetic tape; *Dialogue* for cello and seven instruments by the 36-year-old Soviet composer Alfred SCHNITTKE, set in somber colors, beginning and ending with a cello cadenza; and *Tetragon (Homage to Pablo Picasso)* by the 43-year-old Swedish modernist Bengt HAMBRAEUS, recorded on tape in four instrumental groupings with four separate loudspeakers placed in each of the four corners of the hall (whence the title, tetragon, a quadrangle), emulating Picasso's technique in multicolor painting visible on a big plate of glass.

8 JUNE 1971

The 45th Festival of the International Society for Contemporary Music in London concludes with the following program at an evening concert:

In eius memoriam by the 45-year-old American composer Seymour SHIFRIN, written in memory of a friend, in three lyric sections with long solos; *From the Tibetan Book of the Dead* for soprano, chorus and prerecorded tape of electronic and concrete sounds, by the 37-year-old Canadian composer R. Murray SCHAFER, to a text sung in the Tibetan language; *Versuch über Sprache,* by the 31-year-old German composer Nicolaus A. HUBER for quadrasonic tape, combining four unrelated linguistic fragments accompanied by instruments; *Chorali* by the 35-year-old Finnish composer Aulis SALLINEN, written for thirty-two wind instruments and percussion, in a hymn-like mode, with funereal allusions (the work is dedicated to the memory of the composer's dead parents); *Présence* for piano trio by the German composer Bernd Alois ZIMMERMANN (who committed suicide at the age of 52 on 10 August 1970), composed in 1961; *Atrées,* an homage to Blaise Pascal, pioneer in the theory of probability, by the foremost apostle of scientific electronic music, the Rumanian-born 49-year-old Greek composer Iannis XENAKIS, for ten players, the music being the result of a stochastic (probabilistic) calculation made on a computer, the title referring to the Cretan dynasty of the Atrides whose fates were determined both by fate and probability.

11 JUNE 1971

The Inspector General, opera by the Hungarian-American composer Eugene ZÁDOR after the famous Gogol comedy of mutual deception and misrepresentation in Czarist Russia, composed in 1928 and radically revised and orchestrated at a later date, with an English libretto by the composer, is given its first stage performance in Los Angeles.

15 JUNE 1971

In the course of the Holland Festival, the world première is given in Utrecht of *Spinoza,* opera in three acts by Ton DE KRUYF, dealing with the expulsion of Baruch Spinoza from the Jewish community of Amsterdam for his heterodoxal views of Hebrew patriarchs as fallible men,

with Spinoza's leitmotif derived from the first and the last letter-note of his name (S = Es = E-flat vs. A, forming the tritone, the "diabolus in musica" of medieval theorists), and symbolizing the rabbi's curse upon Spinoza, accompanied by an annihilating unison of C's, signifying the rigid rectitude of millennial tradition.

19 JUNE 1971

Summer and Smoke, opera in two acts by the 45-year-old American composer Lee HOIBY after a play by Tennessee Williams dealing with the unrequited love of a Mississippi girl who refuses to face reality and seeks refuge in a fantasy world, set to music in an emotional Mahlerian idiom with the application of expressionistic song-speech, is performed for the first time in St. Paul, Minnesota.

20 JUNE 1971

Geisterliebe, opera by the Korean composer domesticated in Germany, Isang YUN, is performed for the first time in Kiel.

25 JUNE 1971

Cornelius CARDEW, the British proponent of extreme modernism, presents in Newcastle-on-Tyne a performance of his Scratch Orchestra, featuring a piece by Greg BRIGHT instructing him to "behave as vulgarly as possible," while handing to children in the audience pieces of pink lavatory paper with copulative four-letter verbs written on them. (A second appearance by the orchestra was stopped by the municipal authorities.)

26 JUNE 1971

Guillermo URIBE-HOLGUÍN, prime composer of Colombia, author of symphonies written in the style of his teacher Vincent d'Indy, and of a remarkable set of piano pieces "en el sentimiento popular," reflecting the genuine modalities of Colombian songs and dances, dies in his native city of Bogotá at the age of 91.

27 JUNE 1971

Oh, Mr. Fogg, comic chamber opera by the 49-year-old Czech composer Jan FISCHER, satirizing the hero of Jules Verne's novel *Around the World in Eighty Days,* is produced in Saarbrücken, West Germany.

6 JULY 1971

Louis ARMSTRONG, the great "Satchmo" (satchelmouth) of American jazz, trumpeter extraordinary, dies in New York at the age of 71.

23 JULY 1971

Béatris, opera by the 38-year-old French composer Jacques CHARPENTIER, based on a true story of a fourteenth-century French matron brought to trial on a charge of consorting with demons and of having carnal relations with a priest, and whose eloquent defense saved her from execution, is performed for the first time at Aix-en-Provence.

12 AUGUST 1971

Yerma, posthumous opera by Heitor VILLA-LOBOS, to a symbolic drama by Federico García Lorca, depicting the inner torment of a woman remaining barren (*yerma*) because of her husband's inexplicable refusal to have marital relations with her, and her equally inexplicable refusal to find another man, culminating in her superhuman and successful effort to strangle her inactive mate to death, is produced with the original Spanish libretto in Santa Fe, New Mexico.

18 AUGUST 1971

The final version of *Second Symphony* for soprano and orchestra by the precocious 19-year-old English composer Oliver KNUSSEN, using texts from poems by Georg Trakl and Sylvia Plath, is performed for the first time by the Boston Symphony Orchestra under the direction of Gunther Schuller, in Tanglewood, Massachusetts.

28 AUGUST 1971

Two musical legends concerning the tragedy of Judas Iscariot by the 89-year-old Italian master Gian Francesco MALIPIERO, *L'iscariota* and *Uno dei dieci (One of the Twelve)*, both to his own libretti in which Judas is pictured as a true disciple of Christ, who by his betrayal intended to carry out the prophecy of resurrection, are produced in Siena.

8 SEPTEMBER 1971

Mass, a theater piece for singers, players and dancers, by the protean American composer, conductor, poet, conceptual actor, pianist and charismatically communicative lecturer Leonard BERNSTEIN, is performed for the first time at the opening of the John F. Kennedy Center for the Performing Arts in Washington, D.C. The work is set to texts from the Roman liturgy, in seventeen well-demarcated sections: (1) *Devotions Before Mass;* (2) *First Introit;* (3) *Second Introit;* (4) *Confession,* wherein the first subdivision, *Confiteor,* is based on mutually exclusive augmented, major, minor and diminished triads; (5) *Meditation #1;* (6) *Gloria;* (7) *Meditation #2;* (8) *Epistle: "The World of the Lord";* (9) *Gospel-Sermon: "God Said";* (10) *Credo;* (11) *Meditation #3: De Profundis, Part 1;* (12) *Offertory: De Profundis, Part 2;* (13) *The Lord's Prayer;* (14) *Sanctus;* (15) *Agnus Dei;* (16) *Fraction: "Things Get Broken";* and (17) *Pax: Communion.*

10 SEPTEMBER 1971

Fadograph from a Yestern Scene for orchestra by Samuel BARBER, after James Joyce's *Finnegans Wake*, is performed for the first time by the Pittsburgh Symphony Orchestra.

10 SEPTEMBER 1971

Beatrix Cenci, opera by Alberto GINASTERA dealing with a patricidal Italian matron who, in a complot with her mother and two brothers, exterminates her vicious Roman father, and who was beheaded on 11 September 1599 by papal order despite her defense in claiming that her father attempted incest upon her, is produced at the Kennedy Center in Washington, D.C.

18 SEPTEMBER 1971

The Stone Wall, a multimedia action for orchestra, chorus and a participant audience by the Australian avant-garde composer Malcolm WILLIAMSON, is performed for the first time by the BBC in London.

22 SEPTEMBER 1971

The Lovers for baritone, mixed chorus and orchestra by the American composer Samuel BARBER, to the text of the radical Chilean poet Pablo Neruda, is performed for the first time in Philadelphia.

7 OCTOBER 1971

Sixth Symphony by the 64-year-old Berlin-born American composer Gene GUTCHË is performed for the first time in Detroit.

9 OCTOBER 1971

Sonora for orchestra by the 39-year-old Serbian composer Vladan RADOVANOVIĆ, set in a surrealistically micropolyphonic technique of "sonoriferous sculpturing," is performed for the first time in Belgrade.

12 OCTOBER 1971

Jesus Christ Superstar, rock opera with music by the 23-year-old British composer Andrew LLOYD WEBBER and lyrics by the 26-year-old British writer Tim RICE, with Jesus appearing as a fanatically suicidal martyr and Judas as an earnest believer in Christ's immortality, originally presented as a record album, receives its first stage performance on Broadway in New York. (A choral version was produced in Kansas City, Kansas, on 15 May 1971.)

17 OCTOBER 1971

Planto por las victimas de la violencia (Plaint for the Victims of Violence) for chamber ensemble and tape by the 41-year-old Spanish composer Cristóbal HALFFTER is performed for the first time in Donaueschingen, West Germany.

23 OCTOBER 1971

Kâmakalâ, a "triangle of energies" for three orchestral groups and five choral ensembles by the 33-year-old French composer Jean-Claude ELOY, is performed for the first time in Paris, directed by three synchronized conductors.

24 OCTOBER 1971

Carl RUGGLES, grand old man of American music whose few instrumental works such as *The Sun Treader* and *Men and Mountains* are imbued with a sui generis American expressionism, dies at the age of 95 in Bennington, Vermont, where he had retired from the world to devote himself mainly to painting abstract canvases.

3 NOVEMBER 1971

The Sacrifice, ballet by the 40-year-old Hungarian composer Sándor SZOKOLAY, is performed for the first time in Budapest.

9 NOVEMBER 1971

Ashmedai, opera by the Israeli composer Josef TAL, is produced in Hamburg. The story deals with a minor devil known in Christian demonology as Asmodeus, who persuades an adventurous king to let him rule his domain for a year as a test of the people's loyalty to the throne, with an unexpected outcome when the population, enjoying the newly proclaimed freedom of sin, unanimously votes for Ashmedai's continuance in office for life (i.e., forever, demons being immortal). Thematic tritones (the "diabolus in musica" of the pietistic musicasters of the Dark Ages) are rampant in a score which is further diabolized by a variety of gliding licks, electronic clicks, percussive kicks and dodecaphonic ticks.

18 NOVEMBER 1971

Labyrinth for orchestra by Humphrey SEARLE is performed for the first time in Birmingham, England.

20 NOVEMBER 1971

Ninth Symphony, subtitled *Sinfonia semplice,* by the 66-year-old Estonian-born Swedish composer Eduard TUBIN, is performed for the first time in Stockholm.

26 NOVEMBER 1971

The British Prime Minister and amateur musician Edward Heath conducts the London Symphony Orchestra in a competent performance of Edward ELGAR'S *Cockaigne Overture.*

3 DECEMBER 1971

De Natura Sonoris No. 2 for strings, wind and percussion by the foremost Polish modernist Krzysztof PENDERECKI is performed for the first time at the Juilliard School of Music in New York.

3 DECEMBER 1971

Rhythmicana for rhythmicon and orchestra by Henry COWELL, written in 1931, with the solo instrument being an electrostatic tonal-rhythmic device constructed by Leon Theremin according to Cowell's specifications, receives a belated first performance at Stanford University, in Palo Alto, California, with an electronic apparatus replacing the original instrument.

7 DECEMBER 1971

Eighth Symphony by the prolific British composer Benjamin FRANKEL is performed for the first time in Liverpool.

8 DECEMBER 1971

Memories of Morning: Night, monodrama for soprano and orchestra by the 34-year-old British composer Gordon CROSSE, is performed for the first time in London.

12 DECEMBER 1971

Mantrajana, a Buddhist symphonic poem by the 29-year-old Swiss composer Matthias BAMERT, based on the belief in redemption through the repetition of sacred formulas (mantras) and scored for four Oriental gongs, to be struck at six different points each, and a non-Oriental orchestra, is performed for the first time by the American Sympbony Orchestra under the direction of the 89-year-old maestro Leopold Stokowski.

28 DECEMBER 1971

Max STEINER, Viennese-born master of cinematic melodramatic music that became a model of many emulators in the art, dies in Hollywood at the age of 83.

31 DECEMBER 1971

Colonel Jonathan the Saint, opera in four acts by Dominick ARGENTO, is produced in Denver, Colorado.

1972

1 JANUARY 1972

Maurice CHEVALIER, gallant French chansonnier whose beguilingly debonair delivery belied the torrid eroticism of his songs, dies in his native Paris at the age of 83.

8 JANUARY 1972

Fifteenth Symphony by Dmitri SHOSTAKOVICH, op. 141, in four classically designed movements in the benign key of C major, containing some innovations, such as a theme of twelve nonrepeated notes in a trumpet fanfare, an almost precise quotation from Rossini's *William Tell Overture* in the first movement, and the insertion of the Fate motive from Wagner's *Walküre* in the Finale, is performed for the first time by the Symphony Orchestra of the All-Union Radio and Television in Moscow, under the direction of Shostakovich's son, Maxim.

11 JANUARY 1972

From the Dead Sea Scrolls for chorus, children's chorus, two organs, tape and orchestra by the 51-year-old Czech-born Israeli composer Jacob GILBOA is performed for the first time in Hamburg.

16 JANUARY 1972

Lux Aeterna for Five Masked Players for soprano, bass flute (interchangeable with soprano recorder), sitar and two percussionists by the 42-year-old American composer George CRUMB is performed for the first time in Richmond, Virginia.

21 JANUARY 1972

Fourth Symphony by the 68-year-old Russian-born American, composer Nicolai LOPATNIKOFF is performed for the first time by the Pittsburgh Symphony.

25 JANUARY 1972

A Lincoln Address for narrator and orchestra by the American composer Vincent PERSICHETTI, to the text of Lincoln's second inaugural address of 4 March 1865, with the thematic materials adapted from his *Seventh Symphony* which was in turn derived from his work *Hymns and Responses*, receives its first performance by the St. Louis Symphony Orchestra conducted by Walter Susskind. The work was commissioned for the inaugural concert for President Richard Nixon's second term of office, but taken off the program on account of Lincoln's truculent invocation of the wrath of the Lord upon the rebellious South should they persist in their unrighteous struggle, a sentiment embarrassing to the Nixon Administration in the throes of liquidating the Vietnam War.

27 JANUARY 1972

Tenth Symphony by the 62-year-old Danish composer Vagn HOLMBOE is performed for the first time anywhere in Detroit, Sixten Ehrling conducting.

27 JANUARY 1972

The Labyrinth by the 55-year-old Italian composer Guido TURCHI is performed for the first time by the Chicago Symphony Orchestra.

28 JANUARY 1972

Treemonisha, opera by the black ragtime pianist Scott JOPLIN (who died of tertiary syphilis in an insane asylum in New York on 4 April 1917), to his own libretto portraying in a series of set pieces and arias permeated with the spirit of Afro-American songs and rhythms, the story of a black baby girl found under a tree near Texarkana by the compassionate woman Monisha (who, naturally, names her Treemonisha), involving Negro plantation scenes and weird voodoo rituals, enlivened by Joplin's infectious ragtime rhythms, receives its first full stage production three-score and two years after its composition, by an all-black cast as the final event of the Afro-American Musical Workshop Festival at Morehouse College in Atlanta, Georgia, orchestrated by T. J. Anderson, and conducted by Robert Shaw. (An early production in concert form was given by Joplin in New York in 1915.)

30 JANUARY 1972

Karel Boleslav JIRÁK, prolific Czech composer of six symphonies and many other works, dies at the age of 80 in Chicago, where, as an emigrant from Czechoslovakia, he spent the last 25 years of his life.

3 FEBRUARY 1972

The Natural Sound Workshop, founded by Kirk NUROCK and dedicated to the artistic exploration of bodily sounds, presents its first public performance in Greenwich Village in New York, with a group of naturally sounding men and women belching, burping, farting, hard breathing, regurgitating, sneezing, talking with mouths full, moaning, groaning, yowling, whistling, erupting in polyglot glossolalia, babbling, gabbling, blowing, singing while inhaling air, audibly stretching limbs and pandiculating, shaking, vibrating, lip-fluttering, tongue-clicking, snapping fingers, clapping hands, slapping exposed flesh, cracking bones, murmuring, mumbling, imitating animal sounds, rolling thighs, profusely salivating in chromatic tremolos, gargling, gurgling, gnashing teeth, making dental glissandos, sibilating, sighing, grunting, coughing, choking, gagging, cackling, giggling, cooing, tittering, yawning, cachinnating, whimpering, whining, shouting, screaming, chanting, bouncing, humping and somersaulting.

4 FEBRUARY 1972

Drumming by the American avant-gardist Steve REICH, in four long sections scored respectively for drums and a male voice, marimbas and female voices, glockenspiels, piccolos and whistles, suggesting in its intransigently concentrated drive the sound of the Indonesian gamelan accompanied by African drumming and rudimentary. American ragtime, Indian raga, Japanese gagaku, Australian boomerang and Afro-Cuban heterorhythmics, is performed in its entire length by the Steve Reich Ensemble in London.

4 FEBRUARY 1972

Splash, a space composition for double-bass and percussion by the 33-year-old German composer Hans-Joachim HESPOS, is performed for the first time on the German television network.

8 FEBRUARY 1972

Tikhon KHRENNIKOV, foremost proponent of Soviet Socialist Realism in music, plays the solo part in the first performance in Moscow of his *Second Piano Concerto* in C major, in three sections, *Introduction*, *Sonata* and *Rondo*.

11 FEBRUARY 1972

Partita for harpsichord, electric guitars, harp, double-bass and orchestra by Poland's prime musical modernist Krzysztof PENDERECKI is performed for the first time at the Eastman School of Music in Rochester, New York.

14 FEBRUARY 1972

The Trial of Mary Lincoln, opera by the 26-year-old American composer Thomas PASATIERI, based on the true story of the trial of Lincoln's widow, on the suspicion of Confederate sympathies, is performed for the first time on the National Educational Television network in the United States.

17 FEBRUARY 1972

Sixth Symphony by the Czech-American composer Kartel Boleslav JIRÁK is performed for the first time in Prague, eighteen days after his death in Chicago.

23 FEBRUARY 1972

Eighth Symphony by the individualistic Swedish composer Allan PETTERSSON, in two movements, set in an exalted empyrean idiom "to exorcise the fiendishness of existence and transfigure the repressed possibilities of happiness," alternating meditative episodes with contrasting martial passages, is performed for the first time by the Stockholm Philharmonic, Antal Dorati conducting.

25 FEBRUARY 1972

Den stora teatern (The Big Theater), opera by the 38-year-old Swedish composer Ulf BJÖRLIN, is produced in Göteborg.

1 MARCH 1972

Time Off? Not a Ghost of a Chance, "a charade in four acts and three interruptions" by the 65-year-old British composer Elisabeth LUTYENS, is produced in London.

2 MARCH 1972

Black Widow, opera by the American composer Thomas PASATIERI, is performed for the first time in Seattle, Washington.

3 MARCH 1972

Palast Hotel Thanatos by the 36-year-old German composer Dieter EINFELDT, a modernistic opera in one act dealing with the ghastly subject of multiple death, is performed for the first time in Hannover, Germany.

8 MARCH 1972

Cello Concerto by Krzysztof PENDERECKI is performed for the first time in Baltimore.

8 MARCH 1972

Seven Dodecaphonic Fragments for strings by the 71-year-old Slovenian composer Lucijan Marija ŠKERJANC, is performed for the first time in Ljubljana, not quite a year before his death.

16 MARCH 1972

The 1972 Pulitzer Prize-winning *Windows* for orchestra and large percussion section by the 43-year-old American composer Jacob DRUCKMAN, with the titular windows described as memories of memories and shadows of shadows, is performed for the first time by the Chicago Symphony Orchestra, Bruno Maderna conducting.

17 MARCH 1972

Vox Balaenae (Voice of the Whale) by George CRUMB, scored for three masked players performing on electric flute, electric cello and altered electric piano, with the musical material derived from the recordings made of the actual sounds produced by a humpback whale, is performed for the first time at the Library of Congress in Washington, D.C.

22 MARCH 1972

Non nova, orchestral piece by the 57-year-old Croatian composer Natko DEVČIĆ, set in an oscillating probabilistic technique within a controlled aleatory system, tantalizingly belying its negativistic title, and concluding with a cadenza for four percussion instruments, is performed for the first time in Zagreb.

23 MARCH 1972

Aura, symphonic poem by the Italian avant-garde composer and conductor Bruno MADERNA, is performed for the first time by the Chicago Symphony under the direction of the composer.

26 MARCH 1972

Spaces for orchestra by the 65-year-old American composer Ross Lee FINNEY is performed for the first time in Fargo, North Dakota.

28 MARCH 1972

Messe des voleurs, Les voleurs de Messe (Thieves' Mass, Mass Thieves) by the 35-year-old Basra-born French composer Paul MÉFANO, scored for electronics, organ, voices and instruments, is performed for the first time in Royan, France.

31 MARCH 1972

Symphony Between Piano and Orchestra by the 51-year-old Slovenian composer Primož RAMOVŠ, fashioned as a dialogue between the soloist and the orchestra, in three connected movements, is performed for the first time in Ljubljana.

3 APRIL 1972

Ferde GROFÉ, American composer whose picturesque orchestral *Grand Canyon Suite* became one of the most beguiling pieces in American semiclassical repertory and who served the cause of symphonic jazz by expertly orchestrating Gershwin's *Rhapsody in Blue*, dies in Santa Monica, California, at the age of 80.

3 APRIL 1972

Nigeria commemorates the seventy-fifth anniversary of the death of Johannes BRAHMS by issuing a 100-franc airmail stamp, adorned with his bearded portrait and a quotation from his *Lullaby*.

4 APRIL 1972

Stefan WOLPE, Berlin-born composer of Russian-Jewish extraction, who developed a highly personal—albeit unattractive to hoi polloi—style of writing, in which melodic angularity, intransigent atonality and intractable polytonality were combined with ancient Hebrew modalities and fertilized by polyrhythmic jazzicles, and who fled the Nazi monster to find peace in hospitable America where he became an admired teacher of an exclusive group of loyal local disciples, dies in New York a few months before reaching the biblical age of three-score and ten.

4 APRIL 1972

Seventh Symphony by the 59-year-old Welsh composer Daniel JONES is performed for the first time in London.

4 APRIL 1972

Fritz SPIEGEL, appearing at a "Tuesday Irritation Concert" at the Queen Elizabeth Hall in London, performs (not for the first time) his *Onanisms* for the solitary left hand on the phallomorphous piccolo and *Tactiles III* for two consenting male altos and prerecorded tape.

6 APRIL 1972

Lux, ballet by the 30-year-old Swedish composer Ulf GRAHN, is performed for the first time in Stockholm.

7 APRIL 1972

Towards Time's Receding by the American composer Robert WYKES, in three sections in a pyramidal profile, dynamically rising toward the middle and receding at the end, making use of attentuated impressionistic sonorities and asymmetrical rhythms, is performed for the first time in St. Louis.

8 APRIL 1972

Reflux, concerto for double-bass and wind ensemble by the 40-year-old American composer M. William KARLINS, is performed for the first time in Chicago.

14 APRIL 1972

Grass, concerto for double-bass and orchestra by the 33-year-old American composer Paul CHIHARA, is performed for the first time in Oberlin, Ohio.

14 APRIL 1972

Concertino for Chamber Orchestra by Roger SESSIONS, commissioned by the Fromm Music Foundation, in three movements with contrasting episodes spinning a fine web of astute variations, is performed for the first time (and immediately repeated) by the Contemporary Chamber Players of the University of Chicago, Ralph Shapey conducting.

14 APRIL 1972

Saint Louis, Roi de France, opera-oratorio in two parts by Darius MILHAUD to the poem by Paul Claudel, dramatically evolving as an operatic panorama of eleven scenes tracing the regal course of the canonized French King, is performed in a world première in Rio de Janeiro.

15 APRIL 1972

Julian by the 34-year-old American composer Charles FUSSELL, drama for orchestra and chorus after Gustave Flaubert's story of the apostate Roman emperor, is performed for the first time in Winston-Salem, North Carolina.

16 APRIL 1972

Anna Karenina, opera after Tolstoy by the Czech composer Emil HLOBIL, is produced in Ceské Budejovice.

20 APRIL 1972

Lord Byron, opera in three acts by Virgil THOMSON, to a libretto by Jack Larson, focused on the controversy regarding the erection of a monument to Lord Byron at Westminster Abbey, set to a characteristically Thomsonian, disarmingly bland melody, with candid allusions to such popular songs as *Auld Lang Syne*, *Ach du lieber Augustin* and *Three Blind Mice*, and ending in an apotheosis of disarmingly sharpless and alarmingly flatless C major, is performed for the first time at the Juilliard School of Music in New York.

24 APRIL 1972

Fourth Symphony by the 66-year-old English composer William ALWYN is performed for the first time in London.

27 APRIL 1972

Experimenta for a pianist and orchestra by the 42-year-old Polish modernist Boguslaw SCHAEFFER is performed for the first time in Poznań.

27 APRIL 1972

Second Symphony, subtitled *Isola Bella*, by the 41-year-old Danish composer Ib NØRHOLM is performed for the first time in Copenhagen.

3 MAY 1972

Allo, ici la terre (Hello, Earth Here), light and time show by the 43-year-old French composer Luc FERRARI with visual projections, of an indeterminate duration of a minimum of twenty minutes and a maximum of two hours, portraying the mortification of the beautiful Planet Earth, is presented for the first time in Bonn.

5 MAY 1972

Seventh Symphony by the 70-year-old Swedish composer Sten BROMAN, which includes electronic sound, is performed for the first time in Stockholm.

5 MAY 1972

Time Machine by the Dutch avant-garde composer Otto KETTING, inspired by the futuristic novel of H. G. Wells, scored for wind instruments and percussion in a highly dissonant counterpoint with major sevenths as anchor intervals and eruptive asymmetrical rhythms conveying the sense of acute temporal shifts into futurity, then reversing the time arrow toward the prehistoric past, with ecclesiastical chants coalescing into pandiatonic formations in a purifyingly white C major, is performed for the first time in Rotterdam.

11 MAY 1972

The Four-Note Opera by the 32-year-old American composer Tom JOHNSON, to his original libretto for five voices and piano in which the characters commit mass self-immolation at the end, the entire score based on four notes, A, B, D and E, in ostentatiously tetraphonic monotony fertilized by rhythmic diversification, is performed for the first time at the ultra-modern emporium the Cubiculo in New York, with a prelude for a rebellious tape recording which demands individualistic deprogramming.

12 MAY 1972

Intrata for orchestra by the Cuban-born American avant-garde composer Aurelio DE LA VEGA, written in an ingeniously impressionistic manner, with a concertino for string instruments in elaborately polyrhythmic patterns, is performed for the first time by the Los Angeles Philharmonic Orchestra, Zubin Mehta conducting.

13 MAY 1972

The Trumpet of the Swan for narrator and orchestra, to the text of E. B. White, with music by Benjamin LEES, is performed for the first time in Philadelphia.

14 MAY 1972

Piano Concerto by the Berlin-born British composer Alexander GOEHR is performed for the first time in Brighton, England, with Daniel Barenboim as piano soloist.

16 MAY 1972

Flower and Hawk, monodrama by the 45-year-old American composer Carlisle FLOYD, is performed for the first time in Jacksonville, Florida.

17 MAY 1972

Solstices (ou Les jours et las saisons tournent) for flute, clarinet, horn, double-bass and two percussionists by the 39-year-old Canadian composer Gilles TREMBLAY is performed for the first time in Montreal.

23 MAY 1972

Auto da fé, opera in eight episodes with prologue and epilogue by the 57-year-old Casablanca-born French composer Maurice OHANA, to his own libretto, scored for orchestra, triple chorus and electronics, "pour le plaisir de brûler les monstres," with a fiery crackling finale to portray the ritual burning of heretics, is performed for the first time in Lyon.

24 MAY 1972

Fourth Symphony by the inventive Yugoslav composer Aleksandar OBRADOVIĆ, in two movements, *Torches*, evolving from a generating dodecaphonic subject, and *Echoes*, dubbed "variations with a theme," the last variation being a canon for sixty voices, is performed for the first time in Belgrade.

26 MAY 1972

Eurydice, lyric drama by Jean-Michel DAMASE, to a play by Jean Anouilh, is produced in Bordeaux: A young man disenchanted with the unvirginal condition of a girl with whom he fell in love, lets her go after a quarrelsome night in a hotel; she is killed by an automobile and he spends the rest of his life in fantasies of her being a chaste nymph.

26 MAY 1972

Cantus arcticus, concerto for the voices of polar birds (on tape) and orchestra by the Finnish composer Einojuhani RAUTAVAARA, is performed for the first time in Oulu, Finland.

29 MAY 1972

Margaret Ruthven LANG, daughter of the Boston conductor and pianist Benjamin Johnson Lang, herself the composer of several symphonic overtures, piano pieces and songs, dies in her native Boston at the incredible age of 104.

1 JUNE 1972

The Triumph of Time for orchestra by the 37-year-old English composer Harrison BIRTWISTLE, based on an allegorical painting of Pieter Bruegel, embodying a huge funeral march of Mahlerian proportions, is performed for the first time by the Royal Philharmonic of London.

5 JUNE 1972

Wheel of the World, "entertainment" based on Chaucer's *Canterbury Tales* for actors, children's chorus, mixed chorus and orchestra by the 34-year-old British composer Gordon CROSSE, is performed for the first time at the Aldeburgh Festival.

7 JUNE 1972

Three Latin American Sketches, an orchestral set by Aaron COPLAND, astute stylizations of Mexican and Cuban melorhythms, is performed for the first time by the New York Philharmonic, André Kostelanetz conducting.

20 JUNE 1972

Cheap Imitation by John CAGE, a frankly titled orchestral piece, consisting of remembered fragments from Erik SATIE's *Parade*, is performed for the first time in Amsterdam.

20 JUNE 1972

Kitharaulos by Ernst KRENEK for harp (i.e., kithara), oboe (i.e., aulos), and string orchestra is performed for the first time in the course of the Holland Festival at The Hague.

20 JUNE 1972

To You for solo voice, six guitars, three bass guitars, four pianos, two Hammond organs, six humming tops and electronics by the 37-year-old Dutch composer Peter SCHAT is performed for the first time in Amsterdam.

22 JUNE 1972

Third Symphony by Sir Michael TIPPETT, in two movements, with a vocal part singing the blues, is performed for the first time by the London Symphony Orchestra, Colin Davis conducting.

22 JUNE 1972

The Wrestler, sacred opera by the 44-year-old German-born American composer Samuel ADLER, is produced for the first time in Dallas, Texas.

12 JULY 1972

Taverner, opera by the English modernist Peter Maxwell DAVIES, is performed for the first time at the Royal Opera House in Covent Garden, London. It is based on the life of John Taverner, English composer and organist who was incarcerated for a while for Protestant persuasions in the still Popish England in the early sixteenth century, but who subsequently became an energetic suppressor of Catholic monasteries, and is set to a modernistically polyphonic score applying hemidemisemidodecaphonic techniques, with a dramatic climax achieved when the soldiers of Henry VIII irrupt at the Mass service while the monks sing Taverner's own *Benedictus.*

17 JULY 1972

Den Fremmede (The Stranger), opera by the 49-year-old Danish composer Poul Rovsing OLSEN, is produced in Copenhagen.

18 JULY 1972

Goeran GENTELE, Swedish opera manager who was appointed general manager of the Metropolitan Opera House in New York as successor to Rudolf Bing, dies tragically in an automobile accident near Olbia, Sardinia, while on vacation with his family.

18 JULY 1972

Violin Concerto by Andrzej PANUFNIK, Polish-born composer of maternal English lineage, is performed for the first time by Yehudi Menuhin in London.

1 AUGUST 1972

Sim Tjong, opera by the 54-year-old Korean composer Isang YUN, is performed for the first time in Munich.

2 AUGUST 1972

Rudolph GANZ, Swiss-born musician who played the cello in his nonage, piano as an adolescent, began to compose romantically inspired music at an early maturity, went to America, became a highly respected piano teacher, and finally a competent symphonic conductor, who equally pleased untutored youth, skeptical professional players and financially endowed dowagers, dies in Chicago five years before reaching the centenary mark.

4 AUGUST 1972

Concerto for electronically amplified violin and orchestra by the uncompromising American avant-gardist Charles WUORINEN, written in an aggressively atonal style, is performed for the first time at Tanglewood, Massachusetts, by the avant-garde virtuoso Paul ZUKOFSKY and the Boston Symphony Orchestra under the direction of modern-minded Michael Tilson Thomas.

5 AUGUST 1972

David DEL TREDICI conducts in Saratoga, California, the first performance of his *Vintage Alice* for soprano, folk group and chamber orchestra, based on the text of the immortal tale by Lewis Carroll.

14 AUGUST 1972

Oscar LEVANT, American pianist whose neurasthenic self-deprecation made him a celebrity along the ephemeral pathways of Hollywood and New York, dies in Beverly Hills, California, at the age of 65.

14 AUGUST 1972

Tiger Balm, ballet by the fearless New Zealander Anna LOCKWOOD, scored for a montage of concrete music on tape, is presented by ICES (International Carnival of Experimental Sound) in London.

15 AUGUST 1972

Cornelia Faroli, opera by the 58-year-old Czech composer Rafael KUBELIK, is performed for the first time in Augsburg, West Germany, under the direction of the composer.

17 AUGUST 1972

Ronald STEVENSON, 44-year-old Brythonic composer, plays in London, with the New Philharmonia, Norman del Mar conducting, the piano part in the first performance of his *Second Piano Concerto,* subtitled *The Continents,* acoustically reflecting the primal elements of native music in each of the five continents: Africa, hypnotically percussive; Australia and Asia, in pentatonic drone; Europe, West and East, concluding with a sonorific Russian march; North America, in an ebullient exposition of ragtime; and South America, an exotic apotheosis of the spirit of dance, with an epilogue in which the piano hammers out a reiterated chord "to assert human rights of many nations but only one race—the human race."

24 AUGUST 1972

Great Learning, Paragraph One, by the uncompromising British avantgardist Cornelius CARDEW, wherein violence exercised by the revolutionary masses against the ruling class is justified by dialectical materialism of history, set for screechingly agonizing voices, deafening organ, loudly tapped stones, whistling solos and delirious drumming, and illustrated visually by sixteen ideograms of the Chinese text of the revolutionary slogan "Apply Marxism-Leninism-Mao Tse-tung thought in a living way to the problems of the present," is performed for the first time at the radio broadcast of the Promenade Concerts Series in London, by the Scratch Orchestra, with the composer conducting.

27 AUGUST 1972

Prometheus Bound for chorus, solo voices and orchestra, by the foremost Mexican composer Carlos CHÁVEZ, is performed for the first time at the Cabrillo Festival in Aptos, California, under the direction of the composer.

27 AUGUST 1972

Four centuries have passed since Claude GOUDIMEL, the French Huguenot who published the earliest editions of French Protestant chorales and composed music anticipatory of the homophonic style of Palestrina, died in the flames of the murderous St. Bartholomew Night in Lyon.

28 AUGUST 1972

René LEIBOWITZ, Polish-born composer and theorist, an astute explicator of dodecaphonic techniques, dies at his home in Paris at the age of 59.

2 SEPTEMBER 1972

Ich wandte mich und sah an alles unrecht, dass geschah unter der Sonne (I turned about and observed all the unjustices that occured under the sun), ecclesiastical action for two speakers, solo bass and orchestra, commissioned by the town of Kiel in connection with the Olympic Games of 1972, the last work of the suicidal pessimist Bernd Alois ZIMMERMANN, is performed for the first time in Kiel, West Germany.

5 SEPTEMBER 1972

Sixth Piano Concerto by Alexander TCHEREPNIN is performed for the first time in Lucerne.

7 SEPTEMBER 1972

A postage stamp of the denomination of 1.30 francs is issued by the Republic of Liechtenstein in honor of the American piano manufacturer Theodore STEINWAY (1883–1957), who was himself an impassioned philatelist.

7 SEPTEMBER 1972

Lorenzaccio, opera by the 41-year-old Florentine composer Sylvano BUSSOTTI, is performed at the opening of the Thirty-fifth International Festival of Contemporary Music in Venice.

16 SEPTEMBER 1972

Concerto for flute, oboe and orchestra by the foremost Hungarian modernist György LIGETI is performed for the first time in Berlin.

21 SEPTEMBER 1972

Flute Concerto by Walter PISTON, in a single movement comprised of three sections—*Aliquanto lento, Lento espressivo, Allegro assai*—with the thematic material pullulating in major sevenths and minor seconds in compact dissonant harmonies, is performed for the first time by the Boston Symphony Orchestra, with its first flutist Doriot Anthony Dwyer as soloist and Michael Tilson Thomas conducting.

28 SEPTEMBER 1972

Eighth Concerto for orchestra by the 74-year-old Italian composer Goffredo PETRASSI is performed for the first time in Chicago.

3 OCTOBER 1972

Audiospectrum for orchestra by the 39-year-old Slovenian composer Darjan BOŽIĆ, purporting to draw a parallel between optic and sonic waves and colors, with the entire spectrum extending from stillness (white) to deafening sonorous masses (black), is performed for the first time in Ljubljana.

5 OCTOBER 1972

A Ring of Time by the 44-year-old American composer Dominick ARGENTO, a cyclic orchestral suite of preludes and interludes, each being a variation on a fundamental tone row, revealed in its manifest form in a postlude entitled *Homage to Gustav Mahler,* the music traversing the seasonal—vernal, estival, autumnal and hibernal—moods, is performed for the first time by the Minnesota Orchestra to celebrate its seventieth anniversary, under the direction of Stanislaw Skrowaczewski.

7 OCTOBER 1972

Mother Svea, radio opera by the Swedish composer Hans EKLUND, is performed for the first time in Stockholm.

9 OCTOBER 1972

The 46th Festival of the International Society for Contemporary Music opens in Graz, Austria, with the first performance of the complete cycle of the theater work, *Spiegel I-VII*, by the 46-year-old bellwether of the Austrian avant-garde Friedrich CERHA, under his own direction, the title denoting seven mutually reflecting musical mirrors.

10 OCTOBER 1972

Wilderness Journal, symphony for bass-baritone, contralto, organ, orchestra, rubber-razzer, vibra-slap, mechanical cricket and sounds of nature (on tape) by John LA MONTAINE, based on texts from the *Essays and Journals* of Henry David Thoreau, in fifteen movements, based on a twelve-tone theme and its retrograde to portray the simplicity of Thoreau's contemplation, is performed for the first time in Washington, D.C., by the National Symphony Orchestra, Antal Dorati conducting.

10 OCTOBER 1972

On the second day of the 46th Festival of the International Society for Contemporary Music in Graz, the following program of instrumental music is presented:

Mouvements circulatoires for two chamber orchestras by the 65-year-old Japanese composer Yoritsuné MATSUDAIRA, modeled after the gagaku type of old Japanese court music, with the constituent orchestral groups intertwined in a circulatory movement; *To Earle,* by the 45-year-old Italian composer Franco DONATONI, for chamber orchestra, dedicated to the American ultramodernist Earle BROWN; *Theme* for oboe solo, two guitars, organ and wind ensemble by the 37-year-old Dutch member of the extreme avantgarde Peter SCHAT; and *Chemins II B* for orchestra by the intransigent Italian innovator, 47-year-old Luciano BERIO, representing a radical metamorphosis of an earlier *Chemins II.*

10 OCTOBER 1972

Addio Garibaldi by Girolamo ARRIGO, "épopée musicale" in which the heroic Italian irredentist is betrayed by his patriotic followers to the accompaniment of a miscegenated orchestra, is produced at the Opéra-Comique in Paris.

11 OCTOBER 1972

On the third day of the 46th Festival of the International Society for Contemporary Music in Graz the following program is presented at an afternoon concert:

Lamentatio Jeremiae Prophetae, composed in 1941 by the astute Austrian modernist Ernst KRENEK, long domiciled in America, with thematic material derived from the fundamental tetrachord of the lamentation of the prophet Jeremiah according to the Catholic ritual and expanded into a dodecaphonic series by a process of melodic multiplication, modulation, rotation and permutation, scored for chorus a cappella; *Cromofonética* by the 30-year-old Brazilian composer Jorge ANTUNES, for vocal quartet, each voice being given three determined pitches, aggregating to the sonorous matrix of twelve different tones; *Nuits* by the Rumanian-born Greek apostle of stochastically calculated musical gospel Iannis XENAKIS, for twelve voices, dedicated to four political prisoners in Greece, making use of a variety of vocal techniques, including Japanese nasal sounds and neomedieval onomatopoeia; and *Landschaften* by the 38-year-old Indonesian composer Paul Gutama SOEGIJO for chorus, lamenting the barbarity of the American war in Southeast Asia, making use of indeterminate melodic and rhythmic structures.

11 OCTOBER 1972

The third day of the 46th Festival of the International Society for Contemporary Music in Graz continues at an evening concert with the following program of theatrical music:

Glossolalie by the 42-year-old German composer Dieter SCHNEBEL, in which Pentecostal Babel becomes music; *Repertoire* by the 42-year-old Argentine-born apostle of the cosmopolitan avant-garde, now radicated in Germany, Mauricio KAGEL, conceived as a piece of "instrumental theater," in which actors who are also musicians perform according to a strict metronomical sequence but are free as to the use of materials of their musicodramatic action; and *Ping* by the 38-year-old American avant-garde composer Roger REYNOLDS, scored for a variety of electronically amplified instruments, with the participation of visual elements.

12 OCTOBER 1972

On the fourth day of the 46th Festival of the International Society for Contemporary Music in Graz, the following program is given at an afternoon concert:

Musica per ventiquattro (24) by the 36-year-old Italian avant-garde composer Umberto ROTONDI, starting with monophonic synchrony of the 24 instruments and eventually achieving a totally independent instrumental confabulation leading to a creative disintegration; *Musica polymetrica* by the 40-year-old Slovak composer Ilja ZELJENKA, based on the principle of metric modulation with asymmetrical displacements of structural fragments in multi-temporal instrumental combinations; *Al naar gelang* by the 49-year-old Belgian modernist Karel GOEYVAERTS, in five instrumental groups, programmed by players and audience by mutual consent; *Preludes and Fugue* by the 59-year-old Polish master composer Witold LUTOSLAWSKI, with the application of aleatory techniques in the sixth subject of the fugue.

12 OCTOBER 1972

On the fourth day of the 46th Festival of the International Society for Contemporary Music in Graz the following program is performed at an evening concert:

What's Next by the 41-year-old Japanese modernist Yori-Aki MATSUDAIRA, an aleatory quodlibet for toy instruments, motorcycles, bottles and a soprano; *Six Likes for Solo Tuba*, by the 37-year-old Greek modernist Theodore ANTONIOU, consisting of six comparatives (like a march, like a song, etc.),

with the tuba used in extreme high and low ranges; and *Karma-Dharma Drama* by the 51-year-old Rumanian-born Greek composer Anestis LOGOTHETIS, an audio-visual piece combining the spiritual elements of Indian karma, Buddhistic dharma and Greek drama.

13 OCTOBER 1972

Third Symphony by the English composer Ian PARRON is performed for the first time at Aberystwyth.

13 OCTOBER 1972

On the fifth day of the 46th Festival of the International Society for Contemporary Music in Graz, the following program is given:

Cummings Is the Poet, an instrumental composition by the formidable apostle of the French avant-garde Pierre BOULEZ, inspired by the poetry of the American surrealist e.e. cummings; *Costellazioni* by the 27-year-old Austrian modernist Robert WITTINGER, in four connected instrumental movements designed to create coordinated constellations of sonorities; *Melancolia* for violin and orchestra by the 41-year-old Hungarian modernist Josef Maria HORVATH, inspired by an etching of Dürer, wherein a magic square of coordinate numbers serves as the matrix . . .; and *inwendig voller Figur . . .* by the 48-year-old Swiss composer Klaus HUBER, scored for several choruses and various instruments to texts in Greek, Latin, German and English from the Apocalypse.

14 OCTOBER 1972

On the sixth day of the 46th Festival of the International Society for Contemporary Music in Graz, the following program is presented:

Stop by the German apostle of scientific modern music Karlheinz STOCKHAUSEN, scored for six instrumental groups enriched by aleatory noises, to be stopped as soon as any sensible degree of coordination is accidentally attained; *Disturbances* by the 30-year-old Swedish composer Sven-David SANDSTRÖM, for six brass instruments, three of which are tuned a quarter tone lower than the rest; *Stanza* for harp and magnetic tape by the 42-year-old Japanese modernist Toru TAKEMITSU; *Omnipotence* by the 31-year-old Argentine composer Carlos Roqué ALSINA, for two soloists and chamber orchestra, the title connoting desire to communicate omnipotentially with art, people, nature and time; *Circle for Twelve Players* by the 33-year-old Swiss oboe virtuoso and composer Heinz HOLLIGER, in which the players are assigned instruments at random whether they can play them or not; *Die Glocken sind auf falscher Spur* by the 46-year-old German-born composer Michael GIELEN, constructed according to an intricate system of basic intervals and inspired by surrealist poetry; *Linaia* by the master of electronic and stochastic construction Iannis XENAKIS; and *Concerto Grosso* by the 38-year-old French-born composer of Yugoslav extraction Vinko GLOBOKAR, in five sections in which the instrumentalists are instructed to vacillate in their behavior toward each other and their colleagues in the orchestra with a chorus offering encouraging advice.

14 OCTOBER 1972

The mortal remains of Alexander GLAZUNOV, who died in Paris on 21 March 1936, are transferred from their burial site in the cemetery at Neuilly and interred at the laura of Alexander Nevsky in Leningrad, in proximity to the graves of Glinka, Tchaikovsky and Rimsky-Korsakov.

15 OCTOBER 1972

Polytope, audiovisual spectacle by the panjandrum of scientific music Iannis XENAKIS, is performed for the first time in its completely automatized stochastic version, accompanied by laser projections, in Cluny, France.

15 OCTOBER 1972

On the seventh day of the 46th Festival of the International Society for Contemporary Music in Graz, the following program is presented at an afternoon concert:

Galaxias for organ by the 75-year-old Argentine modernist Juan Carlos PAZ, written in the manner of an aleatory passacaglia; *Traces de . . .* for organ by the 35-year-old German composer Hans Joachim HESPOS, inspired by the great Baroque master of instrumental polyphony Girolamo Frescobaldi; *Non pulsando* for organ by the 46-year-old Italian composer Giuseppe ENGLERT; *Mein blaues Klavier* by the 45-year-old Chilean composer Juan ALLENDEBLIN, for organ, barrel organ and Jew's harp, inspired by a melancholic entry in Kafka's diary; and *Variations III*, a specimen of indeterminate music by the intransigent American innovator John CAGE.

15 OCTOBER 1972

On the seventh day of the 46th Festival of the International Society for Contemporary Music in Graz, the following program is given at an evening concert:

Signals, a constructivist piece for voices by the Argentine modernist Eduardo BERTOLA; *Commiato* by the 68-year-old Italian modernist Luigi DALLAPICCOLA, for instruments and voices, being a dirge and farewell for a departed friend; *Erinnerung an eine Winterabenddämmerung* by the 46-year-old Rumanian-born Hungarian György KURTÁG, an instrumental impression of a winter evening; *Musiken* by the 29-year-old Silesian-born American composer Rolf GEHLHAAR, written with the application of concrete sounds, including scratching, scraping and grinding; *Engramas* for nine musicians and thirteen instruments by the 38-year-old Argentine composer Rufo HERRERA, purporting to represent a subconscious excursion into the engrams of the embryonic and fetal past; and *Contraction*, computer music for thirteen instruments, by the 45-year-old Austrian composer Irmfried RADAUER.

16 OCTOBER 1972

On the eighth day of the 46th Festival of the International Society for Contemporary Music in Graz, the following program is presented:

Seak by the 35-year-old Korean composer Junsang BAHK, for chamber ensemble (*seak* means delicate music), dedicated to the memory of the Austrian modernist Hanns Jelinek based on an alternation of momentarily homogeneous groups of sounds; the *Straits of Magellan*, a geographical fantasy by the 47-year-old American modernist Morton FELDMAN, for seven instruments treated as purveyors of either extremely attenuated or imposingly massive sounds; *Melodies* by the 49-year-old Hungarian apostle of ultramodern impressionism György LIGETI, a condominium of melodic figures which grow gradually into rhythmically pulsating polyphonic conglomerates; *Opus Ghimel* by the 27-year-old Venetian conductor and composer Giuseppe SINOPOLI, the melodic, rhythmic and contrapuntal texture being determined by digital computers; and three pieces named for Danish girls, *Nina Larker, Tina Norlov, Susanne Rudkjobing,* by the 31-year-old American composer active in Denmark, Maurice WEDDINGTON.

17 OCTOBER 1972

The 46th Festival of the International Society for Contemporary Music in Graz concludes with the following program:

Unisonos by the 45-year-old Rumanian composer Stefan NICULESCU, in which the thematic unisons expand into a temporary polyphony only to be retracted into the original monophony; *Chant d' automne* by the 44-year-old mathematically trained Russian composer Edison DENISOV, for instrumental ensemble, inspired by a poem of Charles Baudelaire; *Concerto* for cello and orchestra by the masterly Polish modernist Witold LUTOSLAWSKI; and *Nicina* for orchestra by the 38-year-old Slovenian composer Lojze LEBIĆ, a piece connoting the fear of a mysterious menace, written in an idiom marked by polyphonic mobility.

20 OCTOBER 1972

Eighth Symphony by the Welsh composer Daniel JONES is performed for the first time at the Swansea Festival in Wales.

21 OCTOBER 1972

Décollage for two speaking choruses, electric guitar, electrically amplified cello, electric organ and magnetic tape by York HÖLLER, descriptive of the disintegration of palimpsestic collage, is performed for the first time at the Donaueschingen Festival.

22 OCTOBER 1972

Arbor, cantata to texts of Goethe, Dante, Shakespeare, Hitler, Mussolini, Martin Luther King and Ché Guevara by the 41-year-old Catalonian composer Xavier BENGUEREL, scored for soloists, four speakers, chorus and orchestra, is performed for the first time in Barcelona.

23 OCTOBER 1972

Elisabeth Tudor, operatic scenes by the 65-year-old German composer Wolfgang FORTNER, dealing with the lives of Queen Elizabeth I of England and Mary Stuart, "Queen of Scotland, former Queen of France, pretender to the English throne, murderess of her husband the King, and perjurer, executed in 1587," is produced in Berlin.

27 OCTOBER 1972

Soundings for eleven instruments and electronic tape by the 33-year-old American composer Barbara KOLB is performed for the first time at Lincoln Center in New York. (A revised version for full orchestra was premiered by the New York Philharmonic, Pierre Boulez conducting, on 11 December 1975.)

2 NOVEMBER 1972

Second Violin Concerto by the German composer Hans Werner HENZE, concluding with a prerecorded vocal homage by Hans Magnus ENZENSBERGER to the German mathematical logician Kurt Gödel who, enunciated his mind-boggling "Gödel's theorem," according to which in any sufficiently rich axiomatic system there is always an undecidable theorem, is performed for the first time in Basel.

8 NOVEMBER 1972

Seventh Symphony, subtitled *Israel*, by the French pianist-composer Robert CASADESUS, written in 1970 "in admiration for the people of Israel," but not specifically derived from Jewish motives, scored for a large orchestra with a textless chorus of men, women and children intoning the vowel "A," in three movements—*Maestoso, Andante dolce* and *Presto con fuoco*—is performed in a posthumous world premiere (Casadesus died in Paris on 19 September 1972 at the age of 73) by the Musica Aeterna Orchestra and Chorus in New York, Frederic Waldman conducting.

9 NOVEMBER 1972

Prayer of the Emperor of China on the Altar of Heaven on 21 December 1539 by the American composer Ron NELSON, scored for a variety of Sinoid percussion, a Chinese bell-tree, electric piano, piccolo playing in quarter tones, organ and chorus, and containing some aleatory passages, with the Emperor's prayer gradually submerged in the flood of tinkling and jangling sounds, is performed for the first time at Lawrence University in Appleton, Wisconsin, as a work commissioned for its 125th anniversary.

12 NOVEMBER 1972

Rudolf FRIML, Prague-born American composer of successful operettas, among them *The Firefly, Rose Marie* and *The Vagabond King*, as well as songs such as *Donkey Serenade* and *Indian Love Call*, dies in Hollywood twenty days before his 93rd birthday.

15 NOVEMBER 1972

Chronoplastic for orchestra by the 43-year-old Japanese composer Joji YUASA is performed for the first time in Tokyo.

16 NOVEMBER 1972

Heliogabalus Imperator, a musical allegory by Hans Werner HENZE, is performed for the first time by the Chicago Symphony Orchestra as a commissioned work on the occasion of the orchestra's 80th anniversary. A highly dissonant and flamboyantly sonorous orchestration quite realistically represents the advent to the Roman Empire of the adolescent Syrian Varius Avitus, who elevated the Assyrian god Baal to the pantheon of the Roman deities and who reigned under the name Heliogabalus to render homage to Helios, the sun, to which Baal was sacred, who erected a statue of Baal with a giant phallus of black stone imported from Syria, who ostentatiously deflowered a vestal virgin in front of a Christian church, and who was finally murdered with his equally paganized mother by outraged Roman soldiers in A.D. 220.

22 NOVEMBER 1972

Ninth Symphony by the scholarly Viennese octogenarian Egon WELLESZ, composed in seventeen days in 1971, set in three cyclic movements of a Baroque triptych in an expressionistic quasi-dodecaphonic idiom bristling with acoustically acute thematic major sevenths and minor ninths, maintained in somber tones and concluding in a hymnal mood, is performed for the first time in Vienna.

24 NOVEMBER 1972

Anti-Concerto for clarinet and orchestra by Paul Walter FÜRST is performed for the first time in Vienna, by the Austrian Radio Orchestra, with the soloist playing abnormal music on a normal clarinet.

27 NOVEMBER 1972

Symphony in F-sharp by the erstwhile wunderkind Erich Wolfgang KORNGOLD, cast in luscious modalities of late German romanticism, reaches a belated first performance, many years after the composer's death, by the Munich Philharmonic.

28 NOVEMBER 1972

Havergal BRIAN, Nestor of British music, who through the long years of nonrecognition obdurately persisted in composing large orchestral works until he exceeded Miaskovsky's record of symphonic proliferation by writing 32 symphonies, dies at last in his rural home at Shoreham-by-the-Sea, Sussex, England, at the age of 96.

10 DECEMBER 1972

Leo SMIT conducts the Buffalo Philharmonic in the first performance of his symphonic poem *Caedmon*.

16 DECEMBER 1972

Winter Solstice for soprano, baritone, chorus and instruments by the 58-year-old Polish composer Andrzej PANUFNIK is performed for the first time in London.

27 DECEMBER 1972

Anna LOCKWOOD, the eccentric composer from New Zealand, sinks an upright piano in Little Matthew Lake on the Toad Hall Ranch in Amarillo, Texas, to a depth of three feet, leaving it there to continue sinking in the muddy bottom, while her husband, Harvey Matusow, brandishes a bottle of gin and blows a cadenza on his clarinet.

27 DECEMBER 1972

Fourth Symphony by the 49-year-old Serbian composer Vasilije MOKRANJAC, set in a single movement in which all ideas are derived from the opening twelve-tone row, is performed for the first time in Belgrade.

1973

5 JANUARY 1973

Pierre BOULEZ conducts in New York the first performance of his innovative score . . . *explosante/fixé* . . . for vibraphone, harp, violin, viola, cello, flute, clarinet, trumpet and Halaphone—a computerized electronic instrument named after its inventor Peter Haller and capable of projecting individual sounds metamorphosed as to pitch and timbre according to programmed instructions, thus acting as a superior stochastic transponder—projecting the modified sounds vectorially around the hall via flexibly positioned loudspeakers in fixed explosions (hence the title, derived from an essay by the grand prophet of Surrealism André Breton).

12 JANUARY 1973

Moira, "music in C for large orchestra," a tribute to the Greek goddess of Fate, by Werner EGK is performed for the first time in Nuremberg.

12 JANUARY 1973

Steel Symphony by the 39-year-old Spanish-born composer Leonardo BALADA is performed for the first time by the Pittsburgh Symphony Orchestra.

14 JANUARY 1973

Speculum Speculi (Mirror of a Mirror) for flute, oboe, bass clarinet, double-bass, piano, vibraphone, four drums and three gongs by the 34-year-old American composer Charles WUORINEN, representing "a sectional set of variations," with a dodecaphonic matrix serialized to correspond proportionally to the duration of each thematic note, so that intervallic leaps are from a shorter note to a longer one, is performed for the first time in Grand Forks, North Dakota, by an ensemble called Speculum Musicae.

18 JANUARY 1973

Tintomara, opera by the romantically conservative 46-year-old Swedish composer Lars Johan WERLE, dealing with a mystical creature named Tintomara and bearing reference to the regicide in Sweden in 1792 (which was also the subject of Verdi's opera *Un ballo in maschera*), is produced in Stockholm.

18 JANUARY 1973

Raumzeit Y (Space-time Y) by the German modernist Dieter SCHNEBEL is performed for the first time in Düsseldorf.

23 JANUARY 1973

Third String Quartet by Elliott CARTER, conceived as an interplay and a contest of two duos, one of a violin plus cello and one of a violin and viola, in the characteristical-ly Carterian system of metrical modulation here megametrically expanded to a simultaneity of noncoincident sections (one dual group plays four sections against the other's six), and tempo marks as divergent as Maestoso pitched against a simultaneous Furioso, all these tremendous complexities somehow resulting in the creation of a serene concordance of uncompromising dissonances, is performed for the first time by the Juilliard String Quartet in New York.

6 FEBRUARY 1973

As a demonstration of the perishability of music, an upright piano is dropped to its utter destruction from a chartered helicopter from an altitude of 300 feet near the Detroit airport under the auspices of radio station WDET.

7 FEBRUARY 1973

Chamber Concerto for double-bass by the 31-year-old Swedish composer Ulf GRAHN is performed for the first time in Santa Barbara, California.

7 FEBRUARY 1973

Love's Labour's Lost, opera by the 69-year-old Russian-born American composer Nicolas NABOKOV, in three acts, to a libretto by W. H. Auden and Chester Kallman after Shakespeare, is performed for the first time in its original English version by the West-Berlin Deutsche Oper at its visiting appearance in Brussels.

8 FEBRUARY 1973

Makrokosmos, Volume I (*Twelve Fantasy-Pieces after the Zodiac for Amplified Piano*) by the American composer George CRUMB is performed for the first time in Colorado Springs. (Volume II is first performed in New York on 12 November 1974.)

9 FEBRUARY 1973

Kyldex I (abbreviation of Kybernetischluminodynamische Experimente) by the prime apostle of concrete music Pierre HENRY, set for five electronically activated erotic sculptures, human dancers, fifteen programmed audiovisual sequences of variable durations determined by audience reaction, nine light-effect complexes, stroboscopic projections and a striptease (da capo ad lib.), extracurricularly accompanied by recorded dog barks and various assorted animal and human eructations, is produced in Hamburg.

19 FEBRUARY 1973

Roger SMALLEY conducts in London his *Strata* for strings, a macédoine of traduced quotations from works of Beethoven, Wagner, Mahler, Debussy, Schoenberg,

Stravinsky, Anton von Webern, Ligeti, Stockhausen and Boulez.

28 FEBRUARY 1973

Violin Concerto by the 67-year-old French composer André JOLIVET is performed for the first time in Paris.

28 FEBRUARY 1973

The United States Postal Service puts out an eight-cent commemorative stamp for George GERSHWIN on the 35th anniversary of his death, in Beverly Hills, California, portraying a profile of Gershwin and a montage of characters from his opera *Porgy and Bess.*

3 MARCH 1973

Yaroslav the Wise, opera by the 70-year-old Ukrainian composer Yuli MEITUS, glorifying an early Russian prince, is produced in Donetsk.

9 MARCH 1973

Karlheinz STOCKHAUSEN conducts in London the first production of his multimedia pantomime *Ylem,* purporting to represent the formation of the primordial first substance (Hyle in Greek) which expands to a full size universe and contracts to its initial atom every 80 billion years, with players instructed to wander and roam probabilistically with eyes closed carrying their instruments around and playing on them at will, finally congregating around the center of the contracted universe represented by a grand piano, electronium, three synthesizers and a closed television circuit.

16 MARCH 1973

Satyrikon, opera after Petronius by the 53-year-old Italian composer and conductor Bruno MADERNA, is produced in Scheveningen, Holland. (The first American performance was in Tanglewood, Massachusetts, on 6 August 1973.)

16 MARCH 1973

Universe, symphonic poem by the 37-year-old Soviet composer Alexander NEMTIN, reconstructed, recreated and synthesized from SCRIABIN's fragmentary sketches of his *Acte Préalable,* a preliminary to his projected cosmic *Mysterium,* and drawing more or less literally on Scriabin's piano pieces, the eighth sonata, *Guirlandes* and preludes from opus 74, and including a "color keyboard" paralleling Scriabin's own associations (C = red, G = orange, D = yellow, F-sharp = violet, etc.), with wordless chorus entering toward the end as it did in Scriabin's "Poem of Fire," *Prométhée,* is performed for the first time in Moscow under the direction of Kirill Kondrashin.

22 MARCH 1973

Second Piano Concerto by the foremost Argentine modernistic composer Alberto GINASTERA, completed by him only the day before, is performed for the first time by the prestidigital pianist Hilde Somer to whom it is dedicated, with the Indianapolis Symphony Orchestra under the direction of Izler Solomon. The work is in four movements, the first being a set of 32 variations on the seven notes D, F, A, C-sharp, E, G, B-flat of the abrasively dissonant initial chord of the second choral exposition of the Finale of Beethoven's *Ninth Symphony,* dodecaphonically developed by the complementary five notes; the second, a progressively polymetric *Scherzo* for the left hand alone; the third, a pensively homophonic *Quasi una fantasia;* and the last, *Cadenza e Finale,* a display of maximal pianofortitude with 1,860 eighth notes at ten per second and containing passages of sonic pandemonium with the application of tone clusters and aleatory interludes.

27 MARCH 1973

Levins Mühle (Levin's Mill), opera by the 29-year-old German composer Udo ZIMMERMANN, is produced in Dresden.

31 MARCH 1973

Fourth Symphony by the 66-year-old American composer Ross Lee FINNEY is performed for the first time in Baltimore.

7 APRIL 1973

Pantagleize, opera in three acts by the Viennese-born American composer Robert STARER, to an ironic political drama by the Belgian playwright Michel de Ghelderode in which a bumbling colonial general precipitates a revolution in an unnamed Belgian colony in West Africa by unwittingly uttering a secret signal "Oh, what a lovely day!" and scored in a highly dynamic atonal expressionistic idiom, with some mandatory injection of tetraphonic African motives, is produced at Brooklyn College.

14 APRIL 1973

Espace dernier, aleatory music for chorus, six instrumental groups and tape, completed by the 30-year-old Rumanian composer Costin MIEREANU in 1965, is performed for the first time in Royan, France.

16 APRIL 1973

Milena, cantata for soprano and orchestra by the brilliant Argentine composer Alberto GINASTERA, to texts from Kafka's letters, is performed for the first time in Denver, Colorado.

17 APRIL 1973

Infidelio, chamber opera by the 66-year-old British composer Elisabeth LUTYENS, completed in 1956, is given a belated first performance in London.

19 APRIL 1973

Violin Concerto, subtitled *Les Mécanismes de la mémoire,* by the 30-year-old Spanish composer Tomás MARCO, is performed for the first time at the Royan Festival in France.

20 APRIL 1973

The Picture of Dorian Gray, ballet after Oscar Wilde by the 67-year-old Russian composer Boris ARAPOV, is performed for the first time in Leningrad.

21 APRIL 1973

Metamorphic Variations for orchestra by the 81-year-old British composer Sir Arthur BLISS is performed for the first time in London under the direction of Leopold Stokowski.

23 APRIL 1973

Myshkin, opera by the 38-year-old American composer John EATON, after *The Idiot* by Dostoyevsky, is produced in Bloomington, Indiana.

23 APRIL 1973

Trumpet Concerto by the American composer Fisher TULL is performed for the first time in Houston with James Austin as soloist and Lawrence Foster conducting the Houston Symphony Orchestra.

23 APRIL 1973

Genesis, opera by the 41-year-old Australian composer Malcolm WILLIAMSON, is performed for the first time in London.

28 APRIL 1973

Musica Sacra for string orchestra by Alexander TCHEREP-NIN is performed for the first time during the Easter Festival in Lourdes, as lame and halt worshippers gather from all parts of the world in hope of a supernatural cure.

4 MAY 1973

Requiem by the prolific Swiss composer Frank MARTIN is performed for the first time in Lausanne.

4 MAY 1973

Gilgamesh, opera by the 40-year-old Danish composer Per NØRGÅRD, is produced in Aarhus.

5 MAY 1973

Transformations, opera by the 38-year-old American composer Conrad SUSA, inspired by a poem by Anne Sexton, with symbolic themes illustrating the characters and events of children's fairy tales transmuted into surrealistic images, is performed for the first time by the Minnesota Opera in Minneapolis.

8 MAY 1973

Collage for string quartet, woodwind quintet and percussion by the 49-year-old Manchurian-born Russian-reared American composer Benjamin LEES (his natal family name was Lysniansky), the title referring to the collating of two independent musical groups and to thematic contents of their parts while wood blocks and snare drums punctuate the rhythms, is performed for the first time as a commissioned work at the University of Wisconsin in Milwaukee.

10 MAY 1973

Unter dem Milchwald, opera by the 38-year-old German composer Walter STEFFENS, to a libretto fashioned from the poem *Under Milkwood* by Dylan Thomas, is produced in Hamburg.

15 MAY 1973

Notturno by the 42-year-old American composer Donald MARTINO, scored for a chamber ensemble and resonant percussion, set in three distinguishable movements and nineteen perceivable subsections making use of preliminary noises, key-clicks of the flute and clarinet, blossoming into tones of definite pitch, is performed for the first time in New York, and later awarded the Pulitzer Prize.

19 MAY 1973

Second Symphony by the English composer Havergal BRIAN, completed in 1931, is performed posthumously for the first time in Brighton.

25 MAY 1973

Piano Concerto by the Hungarian-American composer George BARATI is performed for the first time under the composer's direction in Santa Cruz, California.

31 MAY 1973

The trilogy *Lustro* by the 39-year-old Canadian composer R. Murray SCHAFER, consisting of three separately composed works—*Divan i Shams i Tabriz* for seven singers, tape and orchestra; *Music for the Morning of the World* for voice and tape; and *Beyond the Great Gate of Light* for seven singers, tape and orchestra—is performed for the first time in its entirety in Toronto.

5 JUNE 1973

Canticum Canticorum Salomonis (Solomon's Song of Songs) for chorus and orchestra by Krzysztof PENDERECKI is performed for the first time in Lisbon, under the composer's direction.

14 JUNE 1973

Seventh Symphony by the 64-year-old Serbian composer Milan RISTIĆ is performed for the first time in Belgrade.

16 JUNE 1973

Death in Venice, opera by Benjamin BRITTEN, after the novella of that name by Thomas Mann, is produced at the Aldeburgh Festival in England. It centers upon the fateful trip to Venice of an aging famous German writer Gustav Aschenbach (the name means a brook of ashes), where he platonically observes an Apollonian Polish adolescent boy disporting himself with Grecian grace on the beach, leading to his dismaying realization of forbidden love, and ultimately succumbing to the raging cholera epidemic, and is written in an austere, yet dramatic manner: Aschenbach's part is almost entirely in recitative; the Polish youth is represented choreographically, without words. (Thomas Mann himself visited Venice in 1911 and saw there the prototype of the Polish boy portrayed in his novella. As an old man, living in Sweden, the hero of *Death in Venice* recalled seeing Thomas Mann in Venice sixty years earlier. A motion picture based on *Death in Venice* changed Gustav Aschenbach to a composer, strongly suggesting Gustav MAHLER, and making use of Mahler's music on the soundtrack. This act of artistic travesty was denounced by Mahler's family and surviving friends. Mann had incurred the anger of Arnold SCHOENBERG for appropriating his musical genius in the novel *Doctor Faustus;* see Part Two, 13 November 1948, below.)

17 JUNE 1973

Masada 967, opera in fifteen scenes by the 62-year-old Polish-born Israeli composer Josef TAL, is performed for the first time in Jerusalem.

18 JUNE 1973

The 47th Festival of the International Society for Contemporary Music opens in Reykjavik with the following program of works by Icelandic composers:

Quartet for flute, clarinet, bass clarinet and horn by 27-year-old Jónas TÓMASSON; *Five Pieces* for piano in a neoromantic vein by 32-year-old Halflidi HALLGRÍMSSON; and *Requiem* by the prime composer of Iceland, Jón LEIFS (1899–1968).

19 JUNE 1973

On the second day of the 47th Festival of the International Society for Contemporary Music in Reykjavik, the following program of chamber music by Scandinavian composers is presented at an afternoon concert:

Ohm by the 42-year-old Norwegian Arne NORDHEIM. *Pieces* for solo flute by the 51-year-old Norwegian composer Finn MORTENSEN; *Sonatina* for woodwind quintet by the 51-year-old Trieste-born Norwegian resident composer Antonio BIBALO; *Yan Guan* by the 44-year-old Norwegian composer Sigurd BERGE; *Quintet* for woodwinds by the 32-year-old Finnish composer Erkki SALMENHAARA; and *Etwas für . . . for* woodwind quintet by the 39-year-old Swedish composer Karl-Erik WELIN.

19 JUNE 1973

On the second day of the 47th Festival of the International Society for Contemporary Music in Reykjavik, the following program is given at an evening concert:

The Girl with an Umbrella for actor, guitar and tuba by the 37-year-old Greek composer Vasilis TENIDIS; *Musique piquante* for violin and piano by the 41-year-old Czech composer Marek KOPELENT, written in a candidly hedonistic manner; *Fourteen Epigrams for Oscar Wilde* by the 53-year-old Czech-born Israeli composer Jacob GILBOA, for speaker, piano and prerecorded piano played at double speed; *Suggestion* for clarinet solo by the 26-year-old Dutch composer Bart SCHURINK; *Meta-Phrases* by the 29-year-old American composer Homer LAMBRECHT, for saxophone and bass clarinet; *Lo tirtsakh* by the 37-year-old French composer Maurice BENHAMOU, for soprano, representing a vocal panorama of world terror from Hiroshima to the assassination of Martin Luther King (*Lo tirtsakh* means "Thou shalt not kill" in Hebrew); *Three Flutes and Percussion* by the 39-year-old Korean composer Chung Gil KIM, synchronizing Oriental and Occidental traits, with liberal application of dodecaphony; *Eidos* by the 47-year-old Japanese composer Hidenori TOKUNAGA, scored for saxophone and magnetic tape and representing the Socratic "idea" (eidos) of the universality of the human mind; and *Chamber Concerto* for twelve performers by the 26-year-old Norwegian composer Olav Anton THOMMESSEN.

20 JUNE 1973

On the third day of the 47th Festival of the International Society for Contemporary Music in Reykjavik, the following program is presented:

An Old Song of the Sun and the Moon and the Fear of Loneliness for soprano, flute, piano and electronic sounds by Paul PEDERSEN of Canada; *Toccata* for soprano and flute by Harry FREEDMAN of Canada; *Synchronisms VI* for piano and magnetic tape by the Argentine-born American composer Mario DAVIDOVSKY; *Récit de Deux pour Trois Exécutants* for soprano, flute and piano by Bengt HAMBRAEUS of Sweden; *Trialogue* for soprano, flute and piano by the Canadian composer John WEINZWEIG; *Madrigal IV* for soprano, flute, piano and magnetic tape by Bruce MATHER of Canada; *Goathemala* for soprano and flute by the Belgian composer Karel GOEYVAERTS; *Voice* for flute and electronics by the Japanese composer Toru TAKEMITSU; and *Bizzarreries* for soprano, flute, piano and magnetic tape by Atli Heimir SVEINSSON of Iceland.

21 JUNE 1973

On the fourth day of the 47th Festival of the International Society for Contemporary Music in Reykjavik, *A Tea Symphony or The Perils of Clara,* "a kitsch opera in nine drinks" for soprano, flute and piano by Gabriel CHARPENTIER, with a libretto by the composer, is presented at a noon concert.

21 JUNE 1973

On the fourth day of the 47th Festival of the International Society for Contemporary Music in Reykjavik, the following program is presented at an afternoon concert:

Tautologos, a flexible piece for instruments by Luc FERRARI of France; *Thanks to St. George* for cello solo by the Swedish composer Olov FRANZÉN; *Mimicry,* an onomatopoeic piece imitating sounds of nature by Bengt-Emil JOHNSON of Sweden; *Albumblätter* for piano by Luca LOMBARDI of Italy; *Stamp Music* by Ingvar LIDHOLM of Sweden; *Extrasensory Conception IV* by Sten HANSON of Sweden; and *Quo vadis?* by Anders ELIASSON of Sweden.

21 JUNE 1973

On the fourth day of the 47th Festival of the International Society for Contemporary Music in Reykjavik, the following program is presented at an evening concert:

Dream About a House, a pantomime with orchestral accompaniment by the 39-year-old Icelandic composer Leifur THÓRARINSSON; *Quasi niente,* a piece for relaxation, a soft chair, a dark room, closed eyes and open ears by the 40-year-old Swedish composer Arne MELLNÄS; *Etymon* for voice and instruments by the 43-year-old English composer James STEVENS. *Bagatelles* for instruments by the 40-year-old Austrian composer Franz ENDRES; *Three Bagatelles* for instruments by the 34-year-old Italian composer Armando GENTILUCCI; *Notturno* for orchestra by the 38-year-old German composer Helmut LACHENMANN; and *Folk Music* for non-synchronized orchestral groups by the 35-year-old Polish composer Zygmunt KRAEUZ.

22 JUNE 1973

Second Symphony, subtitled *Copernican Symphony,* for soprano, baritone, chorus and orchestra by the 39-year-old Polish composer Henryk Mikolaj GÓRECKI, is performed for the first time in Warsaw.

22 JUNE 1973

On the fifth day of the 47th Festival of the International Society for Contemporary Music in Reykjavik, the following program of chamber music, mostly by German composers, is presented:

Music for piano and four speakers by Paul-Heinz DITTRICH; *La-Sen No. 2* for solo cello by Maki ISHI of Japan; *Sotto voce* for flute, violoncello and piano by Friedhelm DOHL; *Trifolum* for flute, violoncello and piano by Hans ZENDER; *Four Short Studies* for solo cello by Bernd Alois ZIMMERMANN; *Mit/gegen sick selbst I* for flute and magnetic tape by Erhard KARKOSCHKA; *Multiple Five* for flute and cello by Roman HAUBENSTOCK-RAMATI of Austria; and *Rondo* for piano by Niels Frederic HOFFMAN.

23 JUNE 1973

The 47th Festival of the International Society for Contemporary Music in Reykjavik concludes with a program of string quartets by the Dutch composers Ton DE LEEUW and Enrique RAXACH, and by the Polish master of modern music Witold LUTOSLAWSKI.

6 JULY 1973

Third Oboe Concerto by the 53-year-old Italian composer and conductor Bruno MADERNA is performed for the first time in Amsterdam.

6 JULY 1973

Otto KLEMPERER, grand master of the German art of imperious orchestral playing whose renditions of symphonies of Beethoven and Mahler bore the stamp of authentic greatness, but who as a non-Aryan was exiled by the racially besotted National Socialist clique that had held Germany in obscurantist thrall, dies in Zurich at the age of 88.

7 JULY 1973

La reine morte (The Dead Queen), lyric drama by the 65-year-old Italian composer Renzo ROSSELLINI, with a libretto after Henri de Montherlant dealing with political and emotional upheavals at a Renaissance court, is performed for the first time in Monte Carlo.

18 JULY 1973

Krzysztof PENDERECKI conducts the London Symphony Orchestra in Peterborough Cathedral in the first performance of his First Symphony.

19 JULY 1973

Faciebat Anno 1973 for twenty-four violins and orchestra by the 48-year-old Rumanian-born French composer Marius CONSTANT is performed for the first time in Paris.

27 JULY 1973

Cacega Ayuwipi, written for thirty-five percussion instruments (the title means "The Decorative Drums") by the American Indian composer Louis BALLARD, is performed for the first time in Washington, D.C.

1 AUGUST 1973

Gian Francesco MALIPIERO, grand master of Italian music, fertile composer of operas, symphonies, concertos and chamber works, dies in Treviso, at the venerable age of 91.

7 AUGUST 1973

The Hidden Landscape for orchestra by the 26-year-old British composer Nicola LEFANU is performed for the first time in London.

13 AUGUST 1973

Thea MUSGRAVE, 45-year-old Scottish composer, conducts at a Promenade concert in London the first performance of her *Viola Concerto,* worked out on finely textured neo-Baroque lines, with her husband Peter Mark as soloist.

20 AUGUST 1973

De Temporum Fine Comoedia (A Play of the End of Time) by Carl ORFF, in three scenes—*The Sybils, The Anchorites* and *Dies Ill*—is produced in Salzburg.

22 AUGUST 1973

Lennox BERKELEY conducts in Birmingham, England, the first performance of his orchestral work *Voices of the Night.*

5 SEPTEMBER 1973

Tamu-Tamu (meaning "guests" in Indonesian), chamber opera in two acts by the most successful opera composer in the United States, Gian Carlo MENOTTI, commissioned by the Ninth International Congress of Anthropological and Ethnological Sciences, with the libretto by Menotti himself, sung and partly spoken in English and Indonesian, the plot dealing with victims of American air attacks in Southeast Asia, is produced in Chicago.

9 SEPTEMBER 1973

Polyptyque, six images of the Passion of Christ, for violin and two string orchestras by the 83-year-old Swiss composer Frank MARTIN, is performed for the first time in Lausanne.

14 SEPTEMBER 1973

The Philadelphia Orchestra under the direction of Eugene Ormandy, the first American orchestra ever to visit China, presents a concert in Peking with a program including the *Third Symphony* by Roy HARRIS, MOZART's *Haffner Symphony* and the *First Symphony* of BRAHMS.

15 SEPTEMBER 1973

Yvonne, Prinzessin von Burgund, opera by Boris BLACHER, in which a sadomasochistic prince weds the ugliest bride he can find, with a score designed to express "the agony of suffering in the language of Euclid," and written in a characteristically Blacherian dissonantly rhythmic idiom, is produced in Wuppertal, West Germany.

22 SEPTEMBER 1973

Stone Litany—Runes from a House of the Dead by the British composer Peter Maxwell DAVIES, scored for mezzo-soprano and orchestra, is performed for the first time in Glasgow.

25 SEPTEMBER 1973

Cello Concerto by the Soviet composer Edison DENISOV is performed for the first time in Leipzig.

27 SEPTEMBER 1973

Jot, oder Wann kommt der Herr zurück?, a mock-mystical opera by the 50-year-old Swiss composer Klaus HUBER, in three parts entitled *Sandstone Figures, How to Heal Wounds* and *Concrete Theater,* with the action of theologically metaphysical content (the mysterious word Jot in the title may be the Berlin dialect for Gott, God), is produced in Berlin.

9 OCTOBER 1973

Initium, an orchestral work by Carlos CHÁVEZ, is performed for the first time by the Akron Symphony Orchestra.

9 OCTOBER 1973

Third Symphony, subtitled *Day's Nightmare,* by the 42-year-old Danish composer Ib NØRHOLM, is performed for the first time in Copenhagen.

11 OCTOBER 1973

Third Symphony by the 38-year-old Soviet Georgian composer Giya KANCHELI is performed for the first time in Tbilisi.

14 OCTOBER 1973

The Truth About Windmills, chamber opera by the 66-year-old American composer Alec WILDER, is produced in Rochester, New York.

19 OCTOBER 1973

The City, suite for orchestra and narrator in five movements by the 40-year-old American troubadour Rod MCKUEN, professionally arranged from his semi-improvised tunes and rhythms by Paul RUHLAND, in five sections, with the untutored "poet-composer" himself narrating his own lines, depicting in pseudo-Whitmanesque verbal images the various aspects of an American city, is performed for the first time by the Louisville Orchestra under the direction of Jorge Mester.

20 OCTOBER 1973

Autumnmusic for orchestra and electronic sound by the 46-year-old American composer Donald ERB is performed for the first time in New Haven, Connecticut.

20 OCTOBER 1973

Queen Elizabeth II of England officially opens the giant opera house of Sydney, Australia, designed in the form of a ship under full sail by the Danish architect Jørn Utzon at a cost of about $150 million and fourteen years in construction, the ceremony being followed by a performance of Beethoven's *Ninth Symphony* by the Sydney Symphony Orchestra conducted by Willem Van Otterloo. (Actually,

the initial public performance at one of the four different auditoriums of the Sydney Opera House was given on 28 September 1973, when Prokofiev's opera *War and Peace* was performed.)

22 OCTOBER 1973

Pablo CASALS, the greatest master of the cello of the twentieth century and a noble spokesman for universal peace, who left his native Spain after it was captured by the fascistic General Franco, and who eventually settled in Puerto Rico, the native island of his mother, dies at the patriarchal age of 96 in San Juan.

25 OCTOBER 1973

First Violin Concerto by Bohuslav MARTINU, composed in 1932, in three movements, which lay dormant for 40 years, is brought to a belated performance by the Chicago Symphony Orchestra, fourteen years after Martinu's death, with soloist Josef Suk, grandson of the composer Josef Suk and great-grandson of Dvořák, Georg Solti conducting.

26 OCTOBER 1973

Mutazioni for orchestra by the 30-year-old East German composer Udo ZIMMERMANN is performed for the first time in Dresden.

28 OCTOBER 1973

Soundscapes I for flute, bass clarinet, English horn and percussion by the 31-year-old Swedish composer Ulf GRAHN is performed for the first time in Washington, D.C.

30 OCTOBER 1973

Masada, oratorio by the 41-year-old American composer Marvin David LEVY, depicting in dramatic diction the heroic defense of a group of Jewish patriots who chose death rather than surrender in the last struggle of Judea against Roman soldiery at the ancient Jewish fortification of Masada, composed as a montage of tonal blocks superimposed on a collage of melodic patterns including synagogal cantillation, is performed for the first time in Washington, D.C.

3 NOVEMBER 1973

Matrix Symphony (Sinfonia da requiem) for three narrators and orchestra by the 55-year-old Croatian composer Branimir SAKAČ, in three movements—*Ylem, Caspar Casparius* and *Gentle Fire*—constructed upon a matrix with serial submatrices, is performed for the first titne in Opatija, Yugoslavia.

3 NOVEMBER 1973

Noon I! Kwak, a neo-Mayan exclamation by a San Franciscan teen-ager, Jim NOLLMAN, for seventeen performers consisting of thirty-three respirations accompanied by a continuous "duration, chorus" reciting in equal time pulses "kwak, kwak, kwak . . .," is performed for the first time in a tunnel in Golden Gate Park in San Francisco.

4 NOVEMBER 1973

Concerto for violin, cello and string orchestra by Halsey STEVENS, written in an alternately lyric and compactly modern style, is performed for the first time by the University of Southern California Symphony Orchestra, with soloists Eudice Shapiro and Gabor Rejto, Daniel Lewis conducting.

11 NOVEMBER 1973

First Symphony by the prolific Canadian composer Violet ARCHER is performed for the first time in Vancouver.

13 NOVEMBER 1973

Ani Maamir, oratorio by Darius MILHAUD, (the title means "I believe" in Hebrew), composed in the manner of a Biblical confabulation of the three patriarchs Abraham, Isaac and Jacob, demanding justice for the Jewish people from God, who eventually comes down and weeps with them, is performed for the first time in New York.

13 NOVEMBER 1973

Bruno MADERNA, modernistic Italian conductor and composer, a man of tremendous hulk (estimated avoirdupois, 100 kilos), the result of unrestrained bulimia, a bon vivant having an insatiable appetite for young female flesh (he acquired a 15-year-old girlfriend when he was 31), dies of inoperable cancer in Darmstadt, West Germany, where he lived, conducted and taught, at the age of 53.

14 NOVEMBER 1973

Enivrez-vous (Get Drunk!), "new electroacoustical experiment," by the pioneer of musique concrète Pierre HENRY, an agglomeration of sonorous structures generated by six tape recorders, two triple systems of perpetual aleatory music and a complex modulator of impulses and beats, plus Tibetan trumpets, ornithological trills, Hindu prayers, quotations from Monteverdi, and a waltz by Johann Strauss, is produced in Bordeaux, under the composer's direction.

18 NOVEMBER 1973

Alois HÁBA, Czech pioneer of music in quarter tones, third tones and sixth tones, who codified microtones and developed a special notation for them, dies in Prague at the age of eighty. (His younger brother, Karel Hába, also a valiant investigator of mini-intervals, predeceased Alois almost exactly by one year, dying in Prague on 21 November 1972.)

20 NOVEMBER 1973

Interval, a scoreless aleatory piece by Karlheinz STOCKHAUSEN for piano four hands, to be performed by two blindfolded pianists, who had to be friends, is realized in New York by two female pianists, one of whom had to be brought from Washington, D.C., because the first pianist did not have a close piano-playing friend in New York.

21 NOVEMBER 1973

Piano Concerto by William KRAFT, timpanist of the Los Angeles Philharmonic, written in a modernistically romantic genre with a plethora of percussion, is performed for the first time by the Los Angeles Philharmonic, Zubin Mehta conducting, Mona Golabek soloist.

21 NOVEMBER 1973

Piano Concerto by the 49-year-old British composer Gerard SCHURMANN is performed for the first time in Portsmouth with John Ogdon as soloist.

4 DECEMBER 1973

Centering, explicitly "closed-form" notated work for violin and ten instruments by the American musical innovator Earle BROWN, containing a mobile inner structure as the only reference to the "open-form" method of composition proselytized by him in most of his works wherein constituent sections and fragments can be freely reordered, is performed for the first time in Manchester, England.

5 DECEMBER 1973

Gli Spaziali (The Space People), opera by Wladimir VOGEL, in three interlingual parts—*Leonardo da Vinci* (in Italian and German), *Roman de la Lune,* after Jules Verne (in French and German), and *Present Exploration of the Universe* (in German, English and Russian)—set in a dodecaphonized neo-Renaissance polyphonic manner, is produced in Zürich.

6 DECEMBER 1973

Fourth Symphony by Elie SIEGMEISTER, in four classically symmetric movements, scored for a very large orchestra, including a whole arsenal of Western and exotic percussion instruments, and written in a sharply aggressive dissonant idiom relieved by unapologetically melodious passages, is performed for the first time by the Cleveland Orchestra under the direction of Lorin Maazel.

9 DECEMBER 1973

Candomblé, song cycle for soprano, piano and percussion by the 64-year-old Croatian composer Bruno BJELINSKI, based on sacred texts of Afro-Brazilians and incorporating stylistic elements of Latin American folklore, is performed for the first time in Zagreb.

14 DECEMBER 1973

Variations and Epilogue for cello and orchestra, an orchestrated version of a 1946 work for cello and piano by the 70-year-old Russian-born American composer Nicolai LOPATNIKOFF is performed for the first time by the Pittsburgh Symphony Orchestra, William Steinberg conducting.

30 DECEMBER 1973

Henri Paul BUSSER, French composer and conductor, author of numerous operas, ballets, concert overtures and organ pieces, who served as conductor at the Paris Opéra for nearly half a century, dies in Paris in the fullness of his years at the patriarchal age of 101.

30 DECEMBER 1973

Istrianic Frescoes, cantata by the 67-year-old Croatian composer Boris PAPANDOPULO, inspired by frescoes found in the churches in Beram, Istria, in three movements—*The Three Kings, Dance of Death* and *The Angels Sing*—is performed for the first time in Zagreb.

1974

4 JANUARY 1974

Hans Werner HENZE conducts in London the first performance of his *Stimmen (Voices)*, an album of twenty-two songs for mezzo-soprano, tenor and fifteen players manipulating some eighty different instruments, to texts of Italian, German, Cuban and American ballads, reflecting Henze's radical politics.

4 JANUARY 1974

Two musical stamps are issued in Czechoslovakia by the Federal Ministry of Post and Communications: one commemorating the centennial of the birth of the Bohemian composer Josef SUK, and one for the sesquicentennial of the birth of Bedřich SMETANA, each in the denomination of sixty hellers.

14 JANUARY 1974

Tenth Symphony by the turbulently romantic Swedish composer Allan PETTERSSON, set (as most of his symphonies) in one throbbing movement, and the only one to end in fortissimo, receives its first public performance in Stockholm (a recorded performance was broadcast over Swedish Television on 16 December 1973). The composer himself was in absentia, confined to a hospital bed tormented by chronic rheumatoid arthritis.

15 JANUARY 1974

Piano Personnage for piano and chamber ensemble by the 48-year-old Rumanian-born French composer Marius CONSTANT is performed for the first time in Paris.

23 JANUARY 1974

Colori ed improvvisazioni for orchestra by the 62-year-old Finnish composer Erik BERGMAN is performed for the first time anywhere in Zeeland, Holland.

24 JANUARY 1974

Introduction and Masque by the erstwhile prodigy of British music, 23-year-old Oliver KNUSSEN, is performed for the first time by the Boston Symphony Orchestra.

28 JANUARY 1974

Valiant Deed, symphonic poem by the 94-year-old Galician-Ukrainian composer Stanislaus LUDKEWYCZ, glorifying the brave exploit of a revolutionary fighter, is performed for the first time in Kiev.

1 FEBRUARY 1974

Through and Through for orchestra by the 31-year-old Swedish composer Sven-David SANDSTRÖM is performed for the first time in Stockholm.

2 FEBRUARY 1974

Jean ABSIL, prolific Belgian composer whose variegated piano pieces and other works represent the golden mean of performable and listenable modernistic music, dies in Brussels at the age of 80.

3 FEBRUARY 1974

On the occasion of the centennial of Gertrude Stein, a piece by Charles AMIRKHANIAN, entitled *she she and she,* for three male voices, is broadcast from Berkeley, California.

5 FEBRUARY 1974

Sganarelle, one-act comic opera by the Canadian composer Violet ARCHER, to her own libretto based on the first of the several plays of Molière wherein Sganarelle appears as an old duped fool, is produced in Edmonton, Canada.

5 FEBRUARY 1974

Five separate works by the 31-year-old Rumanian composer Costin MIEREANU—*Amnar, Rod, Amurg, Zbor* and *Apo*—collectively described as "reécriture spatio-temporelle," scored for chamber groups, film and tape, are performed for the first time in Paris.

9 FEBRUARY 1974

Concerto for orchestra, three electric guitars, piano, saxophone and percussion by the 41-year-old Soviet composer Sergei SLONIMSKY, in three sections, dramatic, lyric and festive, concluding with a simulacrum of a jam session, is performed for the first time in Leningrad.

15 FEBRUARY 1974

Kurt ATTERBERG, dean of Swedish music, composer of a number of sonorous symphonies and several impressively dramatic operas regularly performed by the Royal Opera of Sweden, guardian of eternal musical values solidly rooted in four-part harmony, dies in Stockholm at the age of 86.

16 FEBRUARY 1974

Einstein, opera by the 79-year-old German composer Paul DESSAU, in which Einstein laments dodecaphonically that his discoveries resulted in the atomic murder of Hiroshima and Nagasaki and who is actually manhandled by an American military policeman when he resists the attempt by authorities to force him to cooperate in further atomic research, and whose two colleagues reflect the Manichean polarity of good (Communist) and bad (Imperialist) states of soul, is produced in East Berlin.

19 FEBRUARY 1974

Elevamini (First Symphony) by the 42-year-old Australian composer Malcolm WILLIAMSON, in three movements, written in 1957 in a style of sustained triads, rhythmic exertion and serial melos, is performed for the first time in Liverpool.

22 FEBRUARY 1974

Kosmochromie I for four loudspeakers and orchestra by the 63-year-old Dutch composer Berend GILTAY is performed for the first time in Utrecht.

23 FEBRUARY 1974

Breakfast Rhythms for clarinet and five instruments by the 35-year-old American composer Joan TOWER is performed for the first time in New York.

25 FEBRUARY 1974

Concerto for Orchestra by the British composer Richard Rodney BENNETT is performed for the first time in Denver.

1 MARCH 1974

Das Orchester by the 39-year-old cosmopolitan Slovenian composer Vinko GLOBOKAR, in five suggestive sections (*Independence, Dependence, Promenade, Machine* and *Metamorphosis*) representing a free "happening" analyzing the historically important instrumental ensemble, is performed for the first time in Bonn, sans a baton-wielding, constricting conductor.

4 MARCH 1974

The first performance of *La cubana, oder ein Leben für die Kunst,* vaudeville by Hans Werner HENZE, is broadcast by NET Opera Theater in New York. (The stage première took place the following year, in Munich on 28 May 1975.)

5 MARCH 1974

The Seagull, opera by Thomas PASATIERI with a libretto based on a play by Chekhov, centered on the character of a young woman who is unloved and has to feed herself emotionally on psychological debris like a seagull in the wake of a brilliantly lighted ship, is produced for the first time in Houston, Texas.

10 MARCH 1974

Antoine et Cléopâtre, opera by Emmanuel DE BONDEVILLE, after Shakespeare's play, thematically based on two leading motives, one for Anthony and one for Cleopatra, immersed in fluid impressionistic harmonies, is produced in Rouen, France.

13 MARCH 1974

The Story of Vasco, opera by the 35-year-old British composer Gordon CROSSE, dealing with an Italian barber caught in a European war in the middle of the nineteenth century who, unwittingly recruited as a spy for the losing side, is unexpectedly proclaimed as a hero and dies in dodecaphonic glory, is produced by the Sadler's Wells Company in London.

15 MARCH 1974

L'Héritière, opera by Jean-Michel DAMASE, in which a rich father who cannot forget that in childbirth his daughter was the unwitting cause of death of her mother and who breaks her engagement to the man she loves by cutting off her inheritance, set to music in a mildly modernistic idiom, is produced in Nancy, France.

16 MARCH 1974

The Catiline Conspiracy, opera by the Scottish composer Iain HAMILTON, to a libretto by the composer based on Ben Jonson's play and centered on Cicero's famous apostrophe (Quousque tandem Catilina abutere patientia nostra?—How long then, Catilina, will you abuse our patience?) is performed for the first time in Stirling, Scotland.

17 MARCH 1974

Mockery, a scherzo for piano and dance orchestra written in 1933 by the American composer John J. BECKER, is given its belated première in a posthumous performance in New York.

21 MARCH 1974

Second Symphony by the 47-year-old Rumanian composer Anatol VIERU is performed for the first time in West Berlin.

26 MARCH 1974

The Beach of Falesá, first opera by the Welsh composer Alun HODDINOTT, based on a short story by Robert Louis Stevenson, is produced by the Welsh National Opera Company in Cardiff, Wales.

30 MARCH 1974

Dorian Gray, opera by the Dutch composer Hans KOX, after the novel by Oscar Wilde in which the portrait of the beauteous English lad painted by one of his admiring friends grows old, while Dorian himself engages in "love that dares not speak its name," is produced in The Hague.

30 MARCH 1974

Music for a Summer Evening by George CRUMB for two amplified pianos and two percussionists busily blowing penny whistles and shaking thunder sheets, subtitled *Makrokosmos III,* in five romantically inspired movements suggesting a Kantian categorical imperative in a system of practical reason—*Nocturnal Sounds, Wanderer-Fantasy, The Advent, Myth* and *Music of the Starry Night*—with epigraphs from Quasimodo, Pascal and Rilke, is performed for the first time in Swarthmore, Pennsylvania.

16 APRIL 1974

Incident at Wounded Knee by the American Indian composer Louis BALLARD, scored for chamber orchestra and evoking the tragic massacre of the Oglala Sioux Indians in the Dakotas in the nineteenth century, in four sections—*Procession, Prayer, Blood and War* and *Ritual*—is performed for the first time in St. Paul, Minnesota.

17 APRIL 1974

Aum (Om) for harp and orchestra by the 40-year-old English-born American composer Bernard RANDS, the title being a mantric word of three sounds representing the hypostatic union of Brahma, Vishnu and Siva, is performed for the first time in London.

27 APRIL 1974

Two works by the 30-year-old Finnish composer Leif SEGERSTAM, *Patria* for orchestra and *Six Songs of Experience*, after Blake and Auden, for soprano and stereophonically placed conductorless orchestra, are performed for the first time in Stockholm.

1 MAY 1974

The Image of Man for chorus and orchestra by the 42-year-old American composer Michael COLGRASS is performed in Spokane, Washington, in a world première.

3 MAY 1974

This Music Seems Very Familiar, comic skit based on materials from Mozart's operas by the 39-year-old Danish composer Bent LORENTZEN, scored for four singers and tape, is performed for the first time in Kiel, West Germany.

5 MAY 1974

Seventh Symphony by the 52-year-old British composer Malcolm ARNOLD is performed for the first time in London.

5 MAY 1974

The Winter of the World for cello and chamber ensemble by the 67-year-old British composer Elisabeth LUTYENS is performed for the first time in London.

8 MAY 1974

The Gates of the Dream for soloists, chorus and orchestra by the 60-year-old British musicologist and composer Wilfrid MELLERS is performed for the first time in York, England.

16 MAY 1974

Dybbuk by Leonard BERNSTEIN, a ballet based on the Yiddish mystical play by Shlomo Ansky in which the errant spirit of a dead young man enters the body of his bereaved bride who then has to be torturously exorcised by knowledgeable rabbis to save her body and soul, is choreographed for the first time in New York by Jerome Robbins for New York City Ballet.

17 MAY 1974

New England's Prospect for choruses, narrator and orchestra by the 47-year-old American composer Donald ERB, commissioned for the one hundredth anniversary of the Cincinnati May Festival, is performed there for the first time.

20 MAY 1974

Sinfonia Concertante for flute, harp and strings in two movements by the Polish composer Andrzej PANUFNIK, now dwelling in England, numerically his *Fourth Symphony*, gravitating to the tonal center of C, expressing his devotion to his wife whose name was Camilla, but avoiding the use of explicit major or minor C triads, is performed for the first time in London.

23 MAY 1974

Dali for large orchestra by the 22-year-old American avant-garde composer Richard HAYMAN, composed at the command of Salvador Dali and microscopically notated on a toothpick with instructions to "ascend chromatically in slow pulse," is performed for the first time in New York.

24 MAY 1974

Edward Kennedy ELLINGTON, known to the world of popular music as Duke Ellington, who created a Harlem "jungle style" of big band playing characterized by piercing trumpets and intensely syncopated jazz rhythms, and who himself composed orchestral and choral music in the elevated concert manner of the blues, dies in New York at the age of 75.

28 MAY 1974

Eighth Symphony by the 65-year-old Serbian composer Milan RISTIĆ, in three movements, the elegiac middle one being a eulogy for Ristic's teacher, Alois Hába, is performed for the first time in Belgrade.

2 JUNE 1974

Wolkenloses Christfest: Requiem for baritone, cello, and orchestra by the 37-year-old German composer Aribert REIMANN is given its first ever performance in Landau, celebrating the 700th anniversary of the city.

5 JUNE 1974

Arnold SCHOENBERG's mortal remains are brought back from Los Angeles, where he died on 13 July 1951, to his native Vienna during the centennial year of his birth.

8 JUNE 1974

An American Requiem by the 60-year-old avant-garde American composer Henry BRANT, a memorial observance of the Watergate scandal, to a text from the Old Testament, with seventeen instrumentalists sitting on the stage and five others spatially scattered in the concert hall, is performed for the first time in Mt. Lebanon, Pennsylvania.

11 JUNE 1974

Thea MUSGRAVE conducts the first performance, in Aldeburgh, England, of her opera *The Voice of Ariadne*, after a novella by Henry James, *The Last of the Valerii*, with the action, taking place in Rome in 1870, concerned with Marco Valeri, who digs up an ancient statue of the goddess Juno in his Roman estate and becomes so infatuated with his find that his American wife decides to rebury it, the "voice of Ariadne" symbolizing Valeri's neglected wife.

14 JUNE 1974

It Is Not Here, light-and-sound piece by the 22-year-old American avantgardist Richard HAYMAN, is realized in Morse code at the Museum of Modern Art in New York.

18 JUNE 1974

Cendrées for chorus and orchestra by Iannis XENAKIS, creator of a mathematically logical stochastic style of composition, is performed for the first time in Lisbon.

22 JUNE 1974

Darius MILHAUD, noble French composer who began his career as a member of the modernistic group Les Six and who by the strength of his inventive talent organized the modern techniques of polytonality and polyrhythmics into a distinctive universal style of composition, whose catalogue embraces works of every genre, and who continued to compose music despite his long, crippling illness, dies in Geneva at the age of 81.

23 JUNE 1974

The Strumpet, opera by the 47-year-old Czech composer Ivan JIRKO, is produced in Olomouć.

30 JUNE 1974

Chlopi (Townspeople), opera by the 61-year-old Polish composer Witold RUDZINSKI, depicting in passionate Polonian tones the heroic futility of the national Polish insurrection of 1863 against the Russians, is performed for the first time in Warsaw.

11 JULY 1974

Libertas, cantata in three movements for brass, chorus and orchestra by the 68-year-old Croatian composer Boris PAPANDOPULO, an homage to the free and artistic city of Dubrovnik during the fifteenth through eighteenth centuries of its existence, with the motto, "Non bene pro toto libertas venditur auro" (Liberty cannot be sold for gold), is performed for the first time in Dubrovnik.

25 JULY 1974

Symparanekromenoi for orchestra by the 30-year-old Hungarian-born Canadian composer John FODI, the title being a Greek polynome translatable as *Those who are living lives that are spiritually entombed*, is performed for the first time in Toronto.

8 AUGUST 1974

The original version of *Chords* for orchestra by the 31-year-old American composer Fred LERDAHL, designed as a mosaic of alternatively consonant and dissonant chords, is performed for the first time at the Berkshire Music Center in Tanglewood. (A revised version was performed for the first time by the New York Philharmonic under the direction of Arthur Weisberg on 3 June 1983.)

17 AUGUST 1974

This Worlde's Joie, oratorio to words from early English texts by the Welsh composer William MATHIAS, in four sections designed to reflect the seasons of the year and the span of human life, is performed for the first time at the Fishguard Music Festival, Wales.

3 SEPTEMBER 1974

Harry PARTCH, American "transcontinental hobo," as he liked to style himself, who during his wanderings fashioned a whole band of homemade instruments to which he attached folksy names, such as blow-boys (a hybrid of bellows and an automobile horn), dies in San Diego, California, at the age of 73.

3 SEPTEMBER 1974

Shenandoah, ingratiatingly tuneful musical play by Gary GELD, a nostalgic recollection of the terrible battle in the Shenandoah Valley in 1862 during the American Civil War, is produced in East Haddam, Connecticut, preliminary to its New York opening 13 December 1974.

6 SEPTEMBER 1974

Le Jeu de Sainte Agnes, "ecclesiastical action" to texts from a fourteenth-century manuscript by the 49-year-old Rumanian-born French composer Marius CONSTANT, scored for six singers, five actors, one dancer, Hammond organ, electric gnitar, trombone and percussion, is performed for the first time in Besançon.

19 SEPTEMBER 1974

Ghost and Dream Dancing for orchestra by the 40-year-old British composer Anthony GILBERT is performed for the first time in Birmingham.

6 OCTOBER 1974

Mack and Mabel, a musical comedy by Jerry HERMAN relating in sentimental semifictional tones the unmarried amours of the American silent movie producer Mack Sennett and his beloved Mabel Normand, is produced in New York.

11 OCTOBER 1974

Violin Concerto by the Ukrainian-born Canadian composer George FIALA is performed for the first time in Winnipeg.

12 OCTOBER 1974

Fête galante et pastorale, space music for a castle by the 36-year-old Polish composer and pianist Zygmunt KRAUZE, utilizing thirteen tapes and six instrumental groups, is performed for the first time in Graz, Austria.

18 OCTOBER 1974

Third Symphony by the English composer Havergal BRIAN, completed in 1932, is given its first performance posthumously, broadcast by the BBC in London.

20 OCTOBER 1974

Tristan, richly allusive score by Hans Werner HENZE for piano, orchestra and recorded tapes, in six movements, containing quotations from a medieval troubadour song, *Lamento di Tristan*, as well as references to Wagner's *Tristan und Isolde*, with a climatic discordant uproar epitomizing the social turmoil of the modern world, is performed for the first time in London by the London Symphony Orchestra, Colin Davis conducting.

20 OCTOBER 1974

Brass Quintet by the 65-year-old American composer Elliott CARTER, arranged in a neo-Baroque manner with instrumental groups forming transitory concertinos, and with each instrument specializing in an individually apportioned interval, is performed for the first time in London, broadcast by the BBC.

20 OCTOBER 1974

O-ke-wa by the fearlessly dissident American composer Daniel LENTZ, a ritual chant to onomatopeic words of the Seneca Indian tribe, scored for twelve voices, two drummers and four bone raspers shuffling around the audience from dusk to dawn shaking small bells with piercing sounds, is performed for the first time, under the direction of the indomitable composer himself, in Rotterdam, Holland, by the group called San Andreas Fault, so named after the major fracture of the earth's crust running northwestward through southern California.

22 OCTOBER 1974

The 48th Festival of the International Society for Contemporaiy Music, held in Holland, opens in Rotterdam with the following program:

Gieter (Watering Can) for orchestra by the 23-year-old Dutch composer Guus JANSSEN, in five movements arranged in a steadily decelerating progression, with one instrument after another committing a musical hara-kiri, figuratively disemboweling itself until only a whiff of rarefied air remains at the end; *Parodia ad Perotinum* by the 40-year-old German composer Georg KRÖLL, based on an organum of the great master of the Ars Antiqua (*parodia* here means emulation, not parody); *Heaventree* by the 26-year-old British composer Nigel OSBORNE, a poem of poems, represented by the polymorphic world of European verse, with the matrix assembled from Latin, French, German, Italian, Russian and Polish vocables, in four movements, based on fricative, vocal, plosive and nasal sounds; and *Chronoplastic* for orchestra by the 45-year-old Japanese composer Joji YUASA, a member of the transsonic group of Tokyo, the work being a combination of static and kinetic fields with transitional mutations of both the temporal (chrono) and spatial (plastic) elements fused in the cosmic environment and leading to terrestrial catharsis.

23 OCTOBER 1974

Karlheinz STOCKHAUSEN conducts the South West German Radio Symphony in London in the first performance of his work *Inori*, employing a mime as a tacit soloist with an electronic ensemble.

23 OCTOBER 1974

On the second day of the 48th Festival of the International Society for Contemporary Music the following program of electronic music is presented at an afternoon concert in Utrecht:

Les ailes by the 49-year-old Polish composer Wlodzimierz KOTOŃSKI, in which the wings in the title indicate the eternal desire of humankind to fly into cosmic spaces; *Basic Barrier*, a computerization by the Hungarian composer Támás UNGVARY, representing an inexorable separation of finite human entities; *Keiserens nye slips (The King's New Necktie)*, generated by a computer and ending in a sonic vacuum symbolic of the nonexistent cravat by the 38-year-old Norwegian composer Kåre KOLBERG; and *Alphas und andere Rhythmen* by the 31-year-old German physicist Ulricke TRÜSTEDT and her husband, 35-year-old Dieter TRÜSTEDT, a synthetic piece generated by statistic impulses, various sequencers and square wave beats.

23 OCTOBER 1974

On the second day of the 48th Festival of the International Society for Contemporary Music, the following program of orchestral music is given in an evening concert in Utrecht:

A Song of Degrees by the 33-year-old American composer Curtis SMITH, in which piano strings are bowed under the lid; *Innervation II* by the 28-year-old Japanese composer Masaru TANAKA, in which the floating rhythms are supposed to affect the nervous system; *Parodie* by the 36-year-old Korean composer Junsang BAHK, scored for flute, cello, percussion and electroacoustic equipment; *Bien* by Tona SCHERCHEN, modernist daughter of the conductor Hermann Scherchen, representing constant mutations of sonic ingredients without altering the indivisible entity of the goodness implied in the title; *Rotation* by the 27-year-old Persian composer Doriansch DOWLATSHAHI, derived from classical Iranian modes; and *Aerophonie* by the 35-year-old German composer Wilfried MICHEL, structured along sonorific lines.

24 OCTOBER 1974

Eleventh Symphony by the prolific Swedish composer Allan PETTERSSON is performed for the first time in Bergen, Norway.

24 OCTOBER 1974

On the third day of the 48th Festival of the International Society for Contemporary Music in Holland, the following program of chamber music is presented in Rotterdam:

Limine for string trio by the 36-year-old Italian composer Davide ANZAGHI, based on an interplay of long sustained notes and florid atonal counterpoint; *Tre Studi per Quattro* for four recorders by the 56-year-old German composer Jürg BAUR, a compendious work of rotating thematic fragments, overblown harmonic tones and aleatory episodes; *Annäherung* for brass by the 23-year-old German composer Christian DETHLEFFSEN, expressing erotic approximations; *Trio* for harp, viola and oboe by the 31-year-old German composer Hans DARMSTADT; and *String Quartet* by the 27-year-old Japanese composer Katsuhiro TSUBONOH.

25 OCTOBER 1974

On the fourth day of the 48th Festival of the International Society for Contemporary Music the following program is presented in Rotterdam:

Arabeschi by the 42-year-old Italian composer Niccolò CASTIGLIONI; *Cello and Orchestra* by the 48-year-old American original Morton FELDMAN; and *Abschied*, symphonic poem by the 36-year-old Dutch composer Reinbert DE LEEUW, reflecting the paroxysm and expiration of nineteenth-century romanticism.

26 OCTOBER 1974

On the fifth day of the 48th Festival of the International Society for Contemporary Music the following afternoon program of orchestral music is presented in Rotterdam:

Tre Pezzi by Rob DU BOIS; *The Magic of Music* for chorus by Ton DE LEEUW; *Sound of Silence* for brass band by Tera de Marez

OYENS; *Sound Poem in Shikara Tala* for chorus by David PORCELIJN; *Sage de Vénise* for percussion by John HELSDINGEN; and *Milaraspa* for two choruses, eight instrumental groups and narrator by Bernard VAN BEURDEN.

26 OCTOBER 1974

On the fifth day of the 48th Festival of the International Society for Contemporary Music in Holland, the following program is presented at an evening concert in The Hague:

Lied per tredici (13) strumenti by the 47-year-old Italian composer Franco DONATONI, based on thirteen sounds subordinated to fifteen variants in thirty-two beats; *Wind Quintet* by the 29-year-old English composer Stephan Peter LAWSON; *Fond Youth Is a Bubble* by the 21-year-old English composer Benedict MASON; *A Pair of Wings* for three sopranos by the 24-year-old English composer Nicholas SACKMANN to text by the fifteenth-century English poet Stephen Hawes; *Quanta* for violin and wind ensemble by the 33-year-old Brazilian composer Fernando CERQUEIRA; and *Elements of Logic* by Jan VRIEND, 36-year-old Dutch composer, and Jos KUNST, 38-year-old Dutch composer, working in collaboration, scored for an impressive ensemble of five flutes, seven clarinets, six bassoons, nine saxophones and brass, the logic in the title being the syllogism leading from given premises to the total reorganization of the world and the philosophy of humankind.

27 OCTOBER 1974

On the sixth day of the 48th Festival of the International Society for Contemporary Music in Holland the following program of orchestral music is presented at an afternoon concert in Amsterdam:

Time Machine by the 39-year-old Dutch composer Otto KETTING, based on a single ten-tone chord, with the anachronistic C major scale intruding into the orderly progression of thematic elements; *Aura* by the generally admired and deeply mourned Italian composer and conductor Bruno MADERNA (1920–1973), inspired by the contrapuntal art of the Italian masters of the Renaissance; *Through and Through* by the 32-year-old Swedish composer Sven-David SANDSTRÖM, the title alluding to the lengthy melodic line symbolic of the indestructibility and interminability of true art; and *Prelude, Interlude et Aprèslude* by the 67-year-old Japanese composer Yoritsuné MATSUDAIRA, written in a free form of old Japanese dances in which the tempi of participating instruments are not compatible.

27 OCTOBER 1974

On the sixth day of the 48th Festival of the International Society for Contemporary Music in Holland the following program of orchestral music is presented at an evening concert in Amsterdam:

Fan It by the 29-year-old Dutch composer Jacques BANK, suggesting that the music is an ever-expanding and contracting fan; *Querimonia* for cello and orchestra by the 29-year-old French composer Jacques LENOT, based on a twelve-tone series that gradually annexes alien twelve-tone themes until it expands to sixty tones, with the cello querimoniously sticking to the primordial dodecaphonic series; and *Sette Canzoni alla tristezza* by the 26-year-old Italian modernist Claudio BILUCAGLIA, the seven songs of sadness of the title referring to the 8-seven recent deaths of Stravinsky, G.M. Gatti, Casals, Picasso, Neruda, Malipiero and Maderna.

28 OCTOBER 1974

The 48th Festival of the International Society for Contemporary Music in Holland concludes in Hilversum with the following afternoon program:

Opus 6 by the 21-year-old German composer Wolfgang VON SCHWEINITZ, with several flutes playing in monodic conjunction against heterophonic strings; *Lunar Possession Manual 1973* for soprano and various instruments by the 29-year-old American-born composer of Dutch extraction Burr VAN NORSTRAND, with subliminal selenological allusions to calendarical lunacy of Endymionlike youths; *Rondo* by the 27-year-old Italian composer Salvatore SCIARRINO for flute solo accompanied by a shimmering ensemble of violins; *Aus aller Welt stammende* by the 36-year-old Polish composer Zygmunt KRAUZE, based on a folk melody of central Poland; and *Second Concerto* for piano and nineteen instruments by the 36-year-old German composer Aribert REIMANN.

1 NOVEMBER 1974

Double-bass Concerto by the 62-year-old French composer Jean FRANÇAIX is performed for the first time in Frankfurt.

9 NOVEMBER 1974

Egon WELLESZ, greatly cultured composer of the Viennese school, an early associate of Schoenberg, who was also an eminent music historian and lucid analyst and codifier of the modalities of Byzantine music, dies in his ninetieth year, in Oxford, England, where he held a professorship at the University after being forced by the Nazis to leave his native Vienna.

10 NOVEMBER 1974

Six Grand Pianos Bash Plus Friends by the 61-year-old American composer Henry BRANT, scored for six grand pianos, three piccolos, trumpet, trombone and percussion, is performed for the first time in Riverdale, New York City.

12 NOVEMBER 1974

Makrokosmos, Volume II (*Twelve Fantasy-Pieces after the Zodiac for Amplified Piano*) by the American composer George CRUMB is performed for the first time in New York. (Volume I was first performed in Colorado Springs on 8 February 1973.)

15 NOVEMBER 1974

A Bayou Legend, opera by the dean of American black composers William Grant STILL, to a libretto by his wife, Verna Arvey, reflecting an old legend of the region of Biloxi within a stone's throw of Still's own birthplace in Woodville, Mississippi, in which a young Cajun falls in love with an astral creature, is hanged for consorting with spirits, but unites with her in the beyond, written in a melodious operatic style fertilized by sensitively authentic Southern melorhythms, is produced for the first time, thirty-three years after its composition, by the all-black troupe of Opera/South in Jackson, Mississippi.

17 NOVEMBER 1974

Fifth Symphony by the Yugoslav composer Aleksandar OBRADOVIĆ, in a symmetrically subdivided single movement, is performed for the first time in Opatija.

20 NOVEMBER 1974

Des Canyons aux étoiles, grandiose musicorama for piano and orchestra by the 65-year-old French composer Olivier MESSIAEN, inspired mainly by the topography and ornithology of Bryce Canyon in Utah, replete with Messiaenic songbird calls against an instrumental accompaniment including the specially designed Eolophone (wind machine) and Geophone (earth machine, a tray of sand shaken harmoniously), in twelve tableaux depicting the ascent from the deep canyons to stars in the sky, is performed for the first time in New York by Musica Aeterna, which commissioned the work, with Messiaen's wife Yvonne Loriod, wearing a star-studded gown, as piano soloist and Frederic Waldman conducting.

21 NOVEMBER 1974

Frank MARTIN, eminently cultured Swiss composer, whose operas, symphonic, choral and chamber music are marked with spiritual distinction and technical fluency embracing the entire spectrum of modern devices including modified dodecaphony, dies in his adoptive home in Naarden, Holland (he was married to a Dutch woman), at the age of 84.

21 NOVEMBER 1974

Eighth Symphony by Peter MENNIN, cast in four movements, each with Biblical overtones—*In the Beginning, Day of Wrath, Out of the Depths* and *Praise Ye the Lord*—written in a straightforward neoclassical style with the tonal foundation clearly in evidence through a complex and often dissonant network of well-placed notes, is performed for the first time by the New York Philharmonic, Daniel Barenboim conducting.

1 DECEMBER 1974

The Ministry of Post and Communications of Czechoslovakia issues a postage stamp in honor of the Czech violinist František ONDŘÍČEK (1857–1922), with an impressive photographic image of him holding a violin under his right arm.

6 DECEMBER 1974

Charles WUORINEN, the intransigent American composer, plays with the New York Philharmonic, Erich Leinsdorf conducting, the solo part in tbe world première of his one-movement *Second Piano Concerto,* for an electronically amplified piano exercising a sonic hegemony, with the orchestra functioning as a duplicator, fragmentor and integrator of the discordant musical materials.

9 DECEMBER 1974

Holly from the Bongs, opera by the 37-year-old British composer Gordon CROSSE, is produced in Manchester.

11 DECEMBER 1974

Sixth Symphony in four neoclassically ordained movements by the 76-year-old Italian-American composer Vittorio RIETI is performed for the first time in New York.

13 DECEMBER 1974

Hod po mukah Ambroza Matije Gupca zvanog Beg (The Torturous Journey of Ambrose Matija Gubec, Named Beg), scenic oratorio by the 67-year-old Croatian composer Ivan BRKANOVIĆ, an epic portrayal of the bloody peasant uprising in Croatia of 1573, led by Gubec, is produced in Zagreb.

20 DECEMBER 1974

André JOLIVET, brilliant composer of instrumental and vocal music in a modernistic vein, with elements of classicism, romanticism and impressionism, integrated into a distinct personal idiom which included occasional dodecaphony and electronic sound, who traveled far and wide to conduct concerts of his works, organized in Paris a progressive performing group Spirale and in his leisure moments wrote poetry, dies in Paris at the age of 69.

26 DECEMBER 1974

Knudåge RIISAGER, prolific symphonic composer of modern Denmark, author of numerous pragmatically effective instrumental works and imaginatively constructed ballets, dies in Copenhagen at the age of 77.

1975

8 JANUARY 1975

San Francisco Polyphony by György LIGETI, spiraling forth from a melorhythmic pulse in the eye of the sonorific hurricane to extreme turbulence as a transcendental image of the grand city of St. Francis with its heterogeneous topography and eclectic Occidental-Oriental population, its imposing modern edifices, and its ancient Spanish missions over the bay, is performed for the first time by the San Francisco Symphony under the direction of Seiji Ozawa.

8 JANUARY 1975

Richard TUCKER, the son of Jewish immigrant parents in New York, whose real name was Reuben Ticker, who reached the summit of singing artistry as a leading tenor at the Metropolitan Opera House, dies suddenly of a heart attack in Kalamazoo, Michigan, on the day of an announced concert there, at the still vigorous age of 61.

9 JANUARY 1975

The Chagall Windows for orchestra by the 35-year-old English composer John MCCABE, inspired by the phantasmagorically colorful stained-glass windows by the Russian-Jewish-French-American painter Marc Chagall, is performed for the first time by the Hallé Orchestra in Manchester England.

13 JANUARY 1975

Fourth Symphony by the 39-year-old Soviet Georgian composer Giya KANCHELI, commemorating the semimillennium of the death of Michelangelo, in a single movement, is performed for the first time in Tbilisi. (The U.S. première was given by the Philadelphia Orchestra on 13 January 1978.)

18 JANUARY 1975

Ein wahrer Held (A Real Hero), opera by the 49-year-old German composer Giselher KLEBE, after Synge's play *The Playboy of the Western World,* is performed for the first time in Zürich.

6 FEBRUARY 1975

A new version of Samuel BARBER's opera *Anthony and Cleopatra,* radically rewritten and reorchestrated, with the libretto restructured by Gian Carlo MENOTTI, and the musical fustian and tinsel removed from the original score of the abortive production at the Metropolitan Opera House in New York on 16 September 1966, is performed anew under the direction of Menotti at the Juilliard School of Music in New York.

13 FEBRUARY 1975

Prismen for flute, oboe, clarinet, harp, percussion and orchestra by the 67-year-old German composer Wolfgang FORTNER is performed for the first time in Basel.

14 FEBRUARY 1975

Das Geheimnis des entwendeten Briefes, opera by the German composer Boris BLACHER, after *The Purloined Letter* by Edgar Allan Poe, is produced in Berlin.

19 FEBRUARY 1975

Luigi DALLAPICCOLA, the Italian composer whose cosmopolitan ideals and modern expertise in dodecaphonic techniques did not affect the profoundly Italian essence of his music, dies in Florence at the age of 71.

21 FEBRUARY 1975

Still and Moving Lines of Silence in Families and Hyperbolas, a fantastical aleatory divertissement by the fearlessly nonconformist 43-year-old radical American composer Alvin LUCIER, is performed for the first time in New York.

14 MARCH 1975

Quintet Concerto for two trumpets, French horn, trombone, tuba, and orchestra by the 58-year-old American composer Ulysses KAY is performed for the first time in New York.

15 MARCH 1975

Galileo Galilei for vocal soloists, chorus and orchestra by the 49-year-old American composer Lee HOIBY, glorifying the Italian astronomer who set the earth in motion in defiance of the clerical edict legislating that it should stand still, is performed for the first time in Huntsville, Texas.

20 MARCH 1975

Turbae ad passionem Gregorianam, sacred work in a Gregorian manner by the 58-year-old Argentine composer Alberto GINASTERA, scored for three singers, choir of treble voices, mixed chorus and orchestra, is performed for the first time as a commissioned work by the Mendelssohn Club of Philadelphia on the occasion of its centennial.

27 MARCH 1975

Sir Arthur BLISS, the English composer who began his career as a radical modernist early in the century, moderated his musical language to a point of total tonal respectability, was knighted in 1950 and appointed Master of the Queen's Musick in 1953, dies in London at the age of 83.

2 APRIL 1975

Pierre BOULEZ conducts the first performance of his orchestral work *Rituel in memoriam Bruno Maderna* in London.

4 APRIL 1975

Violin Concerto by the 56-year-old American composer George ROCHBERG, in five movements, titled *Introduction, Intermezzo, Fantasia, Intermezzo, Epilogue,* wherein the odd-numbered sections are related in thematic and structural materials, whereas the two Intermezzi differ in mood, the first scherzoid, the second, lulling, the total being cast in an outspoken historical sequence of thematic and stylistic structures, ranging from the classically Mozartian to the post-Romantic modernistic techniques, illustrating Rochberg's return to the musical traditions, is performed for the first time by Isaac Stern and the Pittsburgh Symphony Orchestra conducted by Donald Johanos.

4 APRIL 1975

Al Gran Sole Carico d'amore (the title, "In the great sun laden with love," is a line from a poem by Rimbaud), a panoramic socialistic orera by Luigi NONO, in several historic tableaux portraying the French Commune of 1871, Czarist Russia shaken by bloody revolt, social upheavals in Cuba and Chile, and culminating in the American debacle in Vietnam, with a female quartet commenting on the passing events as stages in class struggle, making use of dodecaphonic progressions as promulgated by Nono's father-in-law, Arnold Schoenberg, is produced in Milan.

11 APRIL 1975

Ensembles for Seventeen by the 25-year-old Israeli pianist and composer Shulamit RAN, set for high female voice and sixteen instrumentalists, to a text from the concluding lines of *Othello,* is performed for the first time, and immediately repeated, by the Contemporary Chamber Players of the University of Chicago, Ralph Shapey conducting.

11 APRIL 1975

The Dawns Are Quiet Here, opera by the 52-year-old Soviet composer Kirill MOLCHANOV, describing in a series of lachrymogenic scenes the horrors of the Nazi invasion of Russia, contrasted with the heroic patriotic repulse, replete with folklike tunes and rousing military marches in the finest tradition of Socialist Realism, is produced at the Bolshoi Theater in Moscow.

16 APRIL 1975

Noise and Silence for harpsichord, celesta and percussion by the 43-year-old Soviet composer Sofia GUBAI-DULI-NA is performed for the first time in Moscow.

19 APRIL 1975

Abaris ou Les Borédes, last opera by Jean-Philippe RAMEAU, completed by him shortly before his death in 1764, the plot dealing with a priest of Apollo in love with the Queen of Bactria, who cannot marry her because she is a Boréade, a descendant of the wind god Boréas, and must marry a windy relative, with a happy dénouement secured as Abaris opportunely discovers that he, too, is a boreal through his nymph mother, is performed 211 years after its composition for the first time anywhere by the Monteverdi Choir and Orchestra in London.

29 APRIL 1975

Two; onwards: inwards, outwards, (upwards, downwards) .. . aroundwards . . . towards . . . for two pianos and orchestra by the 31-year-old Finnish composer and conductor Leif SEGERSTAM is performed for the first time in Helsinki.

1 MAY 1975

The government of Nicaragua issues a set of fifteen stamps depicting the world's greatest opera singers in their most famous roles alongside a musical excerpt from each particular opera, starting with the denomination of one centavo and featuring not only dead persons, according to philatelic convention (among them Melba, Chaliapin and Caruso), but also living singers (among them Callas, Nilsson and Gobbi).

2 MAY 1975

A Concord Cantata by the 76-year-old American composer Randall THOMPSON, written for the bicentennial of Concord, Massachusetts, is performed there for the first time.

8 MAY 1975

Roqué CORDERO conducts in Normal, Illinois, the first performance of his *Six Mobiles for Orchestra.*

10 MAY 1975

Karel HUSA conducts in Boulder, Colorado, the first performance of his piece for narrator and orchestra, *The Steadfast Tin Soldier.*

13 MAY 1975

Der lange Weg zur grossen Mauer (The Long Road to the Great Wall), opera by the Austrian composer Kurt SCHWERT-SIK, is produced in Ulm.

14 MAY 1975

Fourth Symphony by the 31-year-old Polish composer Krzysztof MEYER is performed for the first time in Zagreb.

19 MAY 1975

Celebration for tape and orchestra by the 44-year-old American composer Roger HANNAY is performed for the first time in New York.

20 MAY 1975

i.330, opera by the 47-year-old French composer Jacques BONDON, to a libretto after the socio-futural novel *We* by the Russian expatriate author Eugene Zamiatin written in 1920, wherein humans of a remote future are forbidden to make love or to think, and are identified only by number and code letter under the rule of a "benefactor," set to music in an appropriately mechanistic idiom, is produced at Nantes.

27 MAY 1975

Ave Maris Stella by the 40-year-old British composer Peter Maxwell DAVIES, scored for flute, clarinet, marimba, piano, viola and cello, derived from medieval plainchant and consisting of nine contrasting sections forming a self-generative sonata principle, is performed for the first time at the Bath Festival by the music-theater group called The Fires of London.

3 JUNE 1975

Heaven Music by the 44-year-old avant-garde composer Larry AUSTIN, scored for a congregation of exulting flutes, is performed for the first time in Tampa, Florida.

18 JUNE 1975

Partizanka Ana (Freedom Fighter Anna), opera in one act by the 61-year-old Yugoslav composer Rado SIMONITI, depicting the Yugoslav people's fight against the Nazi forces, is produced in Ljubljana.

20 JUNE 1975

Simfonija Faronika for chorus and orchestra by the 78-year-old Slovenian composer Matija BRAVNIČAR is performed for the first time in Ljubljana.

24 JUNE 1975

Cello Concerto by the 45-year-old Spanish composer Cristóbal HALFFTER is performed for the first time in Granada, Spain.

24 JUNE 1975

Eighth Symphony, with chorus, subtitled *In candidum*, by the 82-year-old Swedish composer Hilding ROSENBERG is performed for the first time in Malmö. (N.B. This work underwent extensive revision. The subtitle and chorus were dropped, and by 1980, when the revision was completed, it was for orchestra only. The finalized version was premiered in Malmö on 3 November 1981.)

8 JULY 1975

The Philosopher in the Kitchen, "gastronomic meditation" for contralto and orchestra by the 43-year-old German-born Canadian composer Lothar KLEIN, is performed for the first time in Toronto.

13 JULY 1975

Still Life, with Moonbeams for orchestra by the 30-year-old South African composer Peter KLATZOW is performed for the first time in Johannesburg.

17 JULY 1975

Ratsumies (The Horseman), opera by the 40-year-old Finnish composer Aulis SALLINEN, is produced at the Savonlinna Opera Festival.

9 AUGUST 1975

Dmitri SHOSTAKOVICH, supreme Soviet composer whose symphonies, concertos and chamber music created a powerfully dramatic and poignantly lyrical style that combined classically melodious and romantically harmonious manners of composition with a proclamatory modern idiom, dies of lung cancer in Moscow, at the age of 68.

2 SEPTEMBER 1975

Viimeiset Kiusaukset (The Last Temptations), opera by the 53-year-old Finnish composer Joonas KOKKONEN, to a libretto dealing with the Finnish evangelist Paavo Ruotsalainen, who revived the purity of the Finnish Lutheran churcla in the first half of the nineteenth century, set to music in a passionate hymnal style in sonorous Mussorgskian harmonies, is performed for the first time in Helsinki. (The first American performance took place at the Metropolitan Opera in New York on 26 April 1983.)

20 SEPTEMBER 1975

Captain Jinks of the Horse Marines, musical comedy by the 54-year-old American composer Jack BEESON, is performed for the first time in Kansas City, Missouri.

21 SEPTEMBER 1975

The Young Penis Symphony (a.k.a. First Symphonie) by the Korean composer Nam June PAIK is performed for the first time in San Francisco by a cast of ten young (and not so young) penises protruded through a Japanese rice paper curtain, followed by a female sequel, *La Mamelle (The Young Breast Symphony)*, composed by Ken FRIEDMAN, and featuring a pair of protruding mammary glands.

24 SEPTEMBER 1975

Lowell CROSS presents in Iowa City the total realization of SCRIABIN's symphonic poem *Prometheus*, including the mystic part for color organ (*luce*) on a specially designed electronic keyboard which coordinates color projections to accompany changes of pitch in the score, with James Dixon conducting the University of Iowa Symphony Orchestra.

11 OCTOBER 1975

Assembly and Fall, symphonic poem by Ned ROREM, is performed for the first time by the North Carolina Symphony Orchestra conducted by John Gosling.

20 OCTOBER 1975

Unseen Leaves for soprano, oboe, tapes, slides and lights by the 47-year-old American composer Lawrence MOSS is performed for the first time in Washington, D.C.

21 OCTOBER 1975

Symphony 1972, Phoenix for orchestra by the 30-year-old South African composer Peter KLATZOW is performed for the first time in Cape Town (Kaapstad).

22 OCTOBER 1975

Third Symphony by the celebrated British novelist Anthony BURGESS (who began his career as a composer), in four movements, classically formal, romantically expansive and typically English in its tonal impact, with a literary coda for tenor and baritone from Shakespeare's *Love's Labour's Lost*, to the lines of the pedant Holofernes who sings a snatch of a Venetian ballad, accompanied by a mandolin, with ornithological allusions to the hooting of an owl, the spring song of the cuckoo and the trilling of the nightingale, ending in a formidable explosion of C major, is performed as a commissioned work by the University of Iowa Symphony Orchestra, conducted by James Dixon.

24 OCTOBER 1975

Twenty-sixth Symphony by the fantastically fertile American composer of Armenian stock Alan HOHANESS, is performed for the first time iu San Jose, California.

24 OCTOBER 1975

An die Nachgeborenen (To Posterity) for soloists, chorus and orchestra by the 57-year-old Austrian composer Gottfried VON EINEM is performed for the first time in New York.

25 OCTOBER 1975

The 49th Festival of the International Society for Contemporary Music opens in Paris with an orchestral concert in the following program:

Sillages by the 33-year-old Swiss composer Michel TABACH-NIK; *Stratus* by the 37-year-old Japanese composer Yoshihisa TAÏRA; *Phases* by the 41-year-old Dutch composer Ton BRUYNÈL; and *Aum*, thematically representing the mystical triad of sounds symbolizing Brahma, Vishnu, and Siva by the English-born American composer Bernard RANDS (first performed in London on 17 April 1974).

25 OCTOBER 1975

The 49th Festival of the International Society for Contemporary Music continues in Paris with the following concert of electronic works:

Pace for tape by the 44-year-old Norwegian composer Arne NORDHEIM; *Le Départ pour la lune* for electroacoustical tape by the 31-year-old French composer Georges BOEUF; *Música para sintetizador* for electroacoustical tape by the 44-year-old Argentine composer Francisco KRÖPFL; and *Thunders of Spring Over Distant Mountains* for tape by the 32-year-old American composer Robert MORRIS.

26 OCTOBER 1975

On the second day of the 49th Festival of the International Society for Contemporary Music in Paris the following works are presented:

Naissances for oboe and string trio by the 44-year-old French composer Claude LEFEBVRE; *Ensaio* for mezzo-soprano, double-bass and cymbals by the 38-year-old Brazilian composer Mario FICARELLI; *Simulation* for tuba solo by the 44-year-old Japanese composer Yori-Aki MATSUDAIRA; two conjunct pieces by the 30-year-old Italian composer Fernando GRILLO: *Paperoles* for double-bass solo and *Étoile* for cello solo; *Point/Lines* for clarinet, tape and projections by the 28-year-old Polish composer Krzysztof KNITTEL; *Disappearances* for piano and tape by the 38-year-old Swedish composer Bengt-Emil JOHNSON; *Wild Flowers* for two pianos by the 29-year-old British composer Michael FINNISSY; *Segni* for piano by the 38-year-old Italian composer Davide ANZA-GHI; *Frieze* for four pianos by the 33-year-old American composer John MCGUIRE; *In memoriam Johannes Ockeghem* for electronic tape by the 39-year-old Slovenian composer Ivan PARIK; *Waga Kokora, Imada . . .* for electronic tape by the 25-year-old Japanese composer Kazutaka TAZAKI; and *Mobile* by the 44-year-old Polish composer Eugeniusz RUDNICK.

27 OCTOBER 1975

On the third day of the 49th Festival of the International Society for Contemporary Music in Paris the following program is presented:

Soria Moria for string orchestra by the 43-year-old Argentine composer Gerardo GANDINI; *Ka* for saxophone, double-bass and orchestra by the 37-year-old German composer Hans Joachim HESPOS; *D* for orchestra by the 28-year-old British composer Barry GUY; *Duel*, a ludibund piece for two orchestras and two conductors, by the mathematical Greek composer Iannis XENAKIS; and the world première of *Prelude, Interlude and Postlude* for orchestra by the 68-year-old Japanese composer Yoritsuné MATSUDAIRA.

27 OCTOBER 1975

The third day of the 49th Festival of the International Society for Contemporary Music in Paris continues at a night concert featuring the following program of electronic-acoustic works:

Epicentrum by the 25-year-old American composer Carter THOMAS; *La Panaderia* by the 36-year-old Argentine composer Eduardo KUSNIR; *Titre perdu* by the 24-year-old French composer Michel REDOLFI; *Slopes* by the 29-year-old British composer Denis SMALLEY; and *Tokyo 1969* by the 42-year-old Japanese composer Toshi ICHIYANAGI.

28 OCTOBER 1975

On the fourth day of the 49th Festival of the International Society for Contemporary Music in Paris the following symphonic works are presented:

Me-Ti by the 27-year-old Italian composer Sandro GORLI; *Passage* by the 47-year-old Japanese composer Ryo ENDO; and *Vagues, Chemins, le Soufflé* by the 29-year-old French composer Gérard GRIEY.

At a later concert on the same day, the following electronic works are presented:

Midnight by the 33-year-old Finnish composer Antero HONKANEN; *Bestiary* by the 30-year-old American composer Barry SCHRADER; *Panoramic sonore* by the 38-year-old Japanese composer Akimichi TAKEDA; and *Aion* by the 36-year-old German composer Nicolaus HUBER.

30 OCTOBER 1975

The 49th Festival of the International Society for Contemporary Music in Paris concludes with the following program of symphonic works:

Befragung by the 27-year-old German composer Peter RUZI-KA; *Portraitspiel* by the 35-year-old German composer Wilfried MICHEL; and *Fumon 2* by the 45-year-old Japanese composer Hifumi SHIMOYAMA.

10 NOVEMBER 1975

Fifth Symphony, subtitled *We Are the Echoes*, by the German-born American composer Samuel ADLER, scored for mezzo-soprano and orchestra, is performed for the first time in Fort Worth, Texas.

10 NOVEMBER 1975

Utmost for wind quintet, trumpet, trombone, tuba and percussion by the 33-year-old Swedish composer Sven-

David SANDSTRÖM is performed for the first time in London, Pierre Boulez conducting.

20 NOVEMBER 1975

Regnbueslangen (The Rainbow Snake) for orchestra by the 39-year-old Danish composer Erik NORBY, after an American Indian fable, is performed for the first time in Copenhagen.

21 NOVEMBER 1975

Aurora for orchestra by the 53-year-old Scottish composer Iain HAMILTON is performed for the first time in New York.

22 NOVEMBER 1975

Piano and Orchestra for piano and orchestra by the innovative American avant-gardist Morton FELDMAN is performed for the first time in Metz, France.

22 NOVEMBER 1975

Friedrich BLUME, grand master of German musicology, founder of the voluminous historical and biographical encyclopedia *Die Musik in Geschichte und Gegenwart*, dies in his native town of Schlüchtern, West Germany, at the age of 82.

5 DECEMBER 1975

Air Music, ten variations for orchestra by the 52-year-old American composer Ned ROREM, which was to win the 1976 Pulitzer Prize, marked by gay urbanity with a harmonious whiff of Parisian *je ne sais quoi*, is performed for the first time by the Cincinnati Symphony Orchestra, Thomas Schippers conducting.

8 DECEMBER 1975

Mass in Honor of the Blessed Virgin Mary by the 62-year-old American composer Norman DELLO JOIO is performed for the first time in Washington, D.C.

16 DECEMBER 1975

Der Kaiser von Atlantis, opera by the Austrian composer Viktor ULLMANN, written in 1944 at the Theresienstadt concentration camp in Czechoslovakia shortly before his transfer to Auschwitz where he was put to death, the score turning up in 1972 in the hands of the British conductor Kerry Woodward who restored the barely legible manuscript, is produced for the first time in Amsterdam.

1976

4 JANUARY 1976

A Wisconsin Symphony by the American composer Otto LUENING, reflecting the multifarious ethnic origins of the people of Wisconsin in some recognizable strains of regional folksongs and some unrecognizable modifications thereof (such as a retrograde version of the state song, "Oh, Wisconsin"), in four movements, scored for a lush orchestra magnified by electronic sonorities, is performed for the first time in Milwaukee, the composer's birthplace, Kenneth Schermerhorn conducting the Milwaukee Symphony Orchestra.

5 JANUARY 1976

Georges MIGOT, significant French composer whose music, though rarely played outside of France, has the appealing virtue of modern euphonism, dies in Levallois near Paris at the age of 84.

6 JANUARY 1976

Oscar ESPLÁ, Spanish composer of fine Iberian-flavored instrumental and vocal pieces, dies in Madrid at the age of 89.

8 JANUARY 1976

Bi-Centurion for orchestra by the 68-year-old German-born American composer Gene GUTCHË, commemorating the United States bicentennial, is performed for the first time in Rochester, New York.

11 JANUARY 1976

Music for a Festive Occasion by the American composer Donald ERB, scored for orchestra, electronic sounds and forty water goblets, is performed for the first time by the Cleveland Orchestra, Lorin Maazel conducting.

13 JANUARY 1976

Concertino Pastorale, subtitled *A Forest Rhapsodie*, for two flutes and orchestra, by the American composer John BECKER (1886–1961), completed in 1933, containing a "Rustic Dance" that imitates the song of the meadowlark, written in a highly dissonant idiom, with the flutes tuned a quarter tone apart, is performed posthumously for the first time at the Cincinnati Conservatory of Music.

16 JANUARY 1976

Concerto for Piano Trio and Orchestra by the 61-year-old Italian composer Riccardo MALIPIERO, nephew of Gian

Francesco Malipiero, is performed for the first time in Milan.

23 JANUARY 1976

Paul ROBESON, great black American bass whose performing genius extended to Shakespearean plays and whose singing was of extraordinary sonorous and yet profoundly lyric quality, but whose radical political beliefs aroused barbarian wrath among reactionary groups of the American populace, dies in Philadelphia at the age of 77.

24 JANUARY 1976

The Beth Alpha Mosaic for female voice, chamber ensemble and tape by the 55-year-old Czech-born Israeli composer Jacob GILBOA is performed for the first time in Chicago.

28 JANUARY 1976

Phlegra for eleven instruments by the 53-year-old Greek composer Iannis XENAKIS is performed for the first time in London.

29 JANUARY 1976

Concertmasters, a concerto for three violins and orchestra by the American composer Michael COLGRASS, a vividly Vivaldian triple concerto with proleptic leaps into dodecaphony and other modern devices, is performed for the first time by the violinists Gordon Staples, Bogos Mortchikian and Joseph Goldman with the Detroit Symphony Orchestra, Aldo Ceccato conducting.

4 FEBRUARY 1976

Portugalin nainen (*The Woman of Portugal*), opera by the 35-year-old Finnish composer Erkki SALMENHAARA, is produced in Helsinki.

5 FEBRUARY 1976

The Adequate Earth for two male narrators, baritone, three choruses and orchestra by the 49-year-old American composer Robert WYKES, set to Donald Finkel's poems about Antarctica, is performed for the first time in St. Louis.

10 FEBRUARY 1976

Bicentennial Symphony, 1976 (Symphony No. 14) for chorus and orchestra by the prime American symphonist Roy HARRIS is performed for the first time by the National Symphony Orchestra in Washington, D.C., Antal Dorati conducting. (N.B. Although billed as Harris's "fourteenth symphony," in actuality this was Harris's "thirteenth" and last symphony.)

10 FEBRUARY 1976

Southern Harmony for orchestra by the 59-year-old American composer Ulysses KAY is performed for the first time in Raleigh, North Carolina.

13 FEBRUARY 1976

Lily PONS, glamorous French coloratura soprano whose slender beauty and thrush-like trills fascinated audiences in opera and solo recitals all over the world and whose fame reached such universality that a locality in Maryland was named Lilypons in her honor dies in Dallas, Texas, at the age of 77.

20 FEBRUARY 1976

Colloquy for orchestra, tape and various chairs by the Russian-born American composer Vladimir USSACHEVSKY is performed for the first time in Salt Lake City by the Utah Symphony Orchestra, Maurice Abravanel conducting.

20 FEBRUARY 1976

Dreamsound by the 24-year-old American avant-gardist Richard HAYMAN, a sleep event in which the composer makes various sounds for the benefit of slumbering participants, is snored for the first time in Berkeley, California.

24 FEBRUARY 1976

A Mirror on Which to Dwell for soprano and nine players by the 67-year-old American composer Elliott CARTER, to a cycle of six poems by Elizabeth Bishop, is performed for the first time in New York.

27 FEBRUARY 1976

Echoes from an Invisible World by Leslie BASSETT, a romantically inmpressionistic orchestral piece, with the title taken from a phrase by the Italian patriot Giuseppe Mazzini and suggesting reality reflected in the world of fantasy, is performed for the first time, as part of the American bicentennial celebration, by the Philadelphia Orchestra, conducted by Eugene Ormandy.

29 FEBRUARY 1976

Bilby's Doll, opera composed for the United States bicentennial by the 49-year-old American composer Carlisle FLOYD, wherein Doll, a young French girl brought to America by a sea captain named Bilby, is accused of witchcraft by Bilby's wife (who contends that Doll had caused to wither the fetus in her womb), eventually becomes herself convinced that she is a witch and prays for Satan to come to her rescue, is produced in Houston.

1 MARCH 1976

Jean MARTINON, French composer of modernistically programmatic symphonies and other works, who also had a fine career as a conductor in France and America, dies in Paris at the age of sixty-six.

3 MARCH 1976

Mary, Queen of Scots, ballet by the 36-year-old British pianist and composer John MCCABE, is produced in Glasgow.

8 MARCH 1976

Piano Concerto by the American pianist and composer William BOLCOM is performed for the first time by Bolcom as soloist with the Seattle Symphony Orchestra, Milton Katims conducting.

11 MARCH 1976

Trombone Concerto by Donald ERB is performed for the first time by Stuart Dempster on the trombone with the St. Louis Symphony Orchestra under the direction of Leonard Slatkin.

11 MARCH 1976

Fifth Symphony by the 69-year-old American composer David VAN VACTOR is performed for the first time in Knoxville, Tennessee.

19 MARCH 1976

Second Piano Concerto for four soloists, chorus, and strings, subtitled *Landscapes of the Mind I,* by the 49-year-old American composer Marga RICHTER, is performed for the first time in Tucson, Arizona, with William Masselos as soloist.

19 MARCH 1976

Vox Humana, song cycle by the melancholically existential Swedish composer Allan PETTERSSON, scored for organ, strings and voices, in three parts to words by Latin American proletarian poets and American Indian songsters, concluding with the poem *The Great Joy* by the communist Chilean Nobel Laureate Pablo Neruda, is performed for the first time on the Swedish Radio.

25 MARCH 1976

Cello Concerto by the Korean-born German-resident composer Isang YUN is performed for the first time in Royan, France.

30 MARCH 1976

Zodiac for orchestra by the English composer Richard Rodney BENNETT, a United States bicentennial commission, is performed for the first time by the National Symphony Orchestra under the direction of Antal Dorati in Washington, D.C.

30 MARCH 1976

Ines de Castro, opera by the 30-year-old American composer Thomas PASATIERI, based on an apparently true historical episode involving the mistress of Pedro I of Portugal who was assassinated by a court clique in 1355, whose corpse was exhumed by her imperial lover who forced her assassins to kiss her skeletal remains during her postmortem coronation, is produced in Baltimore.

31 MARCH 1976

Second Violin Concerto by the American composer Ross Lee FINNEY is performed for the first time by Robert Gerle on the violin with the Dallas Symphony Orchestra conducted by Louis Lane, to celebrate the one hundredth convention of the Music Teachers National Association.

1 APRIL 1976

Symphony of Spirituals by the American composer Morton GOULD is performed for the first time by the Detroit Symphony Orchestra under the direction of Aldo Ceccato.

1 APRIL 1976

Third Violin Concerto by David DIAMOND is performed for the first time by Piotr Janowski on the violin with the New York Philharmonic conducted by Leonard Bernstein.

2 APRIL 1976

Nicolaus Copernicus, oratorio by the 79-year-old Polish organist and composer Boleslaw SZABELSKI, composed to glorify the semimillennium of the birth of the great Polish astronomer who put the earth in axial and circumsolar motion, is performed for the first time in Poznań (actually with a calendarical delay of three years: Copernicus was born in 1473).

6 APRIL 1976

Tenth Symphony by William SCHUMANN, subtitled *American Muse,* in three symmetric movements—a slow movement flanked by two fast ones—is performed for the first time by the National Symphony Orchestra of Washington, D.C., Antal Dorati conducting, on the same program with two other world premières of works by Schuman: *The Dead Young Soldiers,* for soprano, French horn, woodwinds and strings, a lamentation to words by Archibald MacLeish, and a new concert version of Schuman's baseball cantata, *Casey at the Bat,* for baritone-reciter, soprano, chorus and orchestra.

13 APRIL 1976

Sinfonia di Sfere (Symphony of the Spheres), the fifth symphony by the 62-year-old Polish-born British composer Andrzej PANUFNIK, in three palindromic movements, each of which evolves from a focal monomelodic cell, with the central section of the middle movement mirroring itself in an orgiastic dance, is performed for the first time in London.

14 APRIL 1976

Vaque-T'ao for orchestra by the 38-year-old Swiss-born French composer Tona SCHERCHEN-HSIAO, daughter of the famous conductor Hermann Scherchen, is performed for the first time in Paris.

15 APRIL 1976

Passion for solo voices, chorus and orchestra by the 43-year-old American composer Alan *STOUT,* with Christ portrayed by a male trio symbolizing the Trinity, employing occasional serial devices, aleatory passages and microtonal harmonies, is performed for the first time as a commissioned work by the Chicago Symphony Orchestra, Margaret Hillis is conducting.

23 APRIL 1976

Meeting for Equal Rights: 1866, cantata by the 62-year-old American composer Vivian FINE, is performed for the first time in New York.

24 APRIL 1976

Music for Eighteen Musicians for violin, cello, two clarinets, four pianos, four female voices, three marimbas, two xylophones and a metallaphone by the 39-year-old American composer Steve REICH, who unintentionally became the guru of modern minimalism by extracting a maximum effect from a minimum of musical material, is performed for the first time in New York.

24 APRIL 1976

Morton GOULD conducts the first performance of his *American Ballads* for orchestra, in Queens, New York.

24 APRIL 1976

The Voyage of Edgar Allan Poe, opera by the fertile American composer Dominick ARGENTO, depicting a hallucinatory voyage into Poe's past shortly before his death, recalling his marriage to a child bride, her early death, his recovery of her from the region of death, and her second final death, with copious quotations from Poe's poem *Annabel Lee*, is performed for the first time in St. Paul, Minnesota.

25 APRIL 1976

Magic, Magic, Magic for chorus and chamber orchestra by the 61-year-old American composer Gail KUBIK is performed for the first time in San Antonio, Texas.

25 APRIL 1976

Statement 1976 for soprano, chorus brass, strings and percussion by the 72-year-old American composer Irwin FISCHER, commemorating the United States bicentennial, is performed for the first time in New Haven, Connecticut.

28 APRIL 1976

Animus-Anima for orchestra by the 27-year-old Canadian composer Steven GELLMAN is performed for the first time in Paris.

2 MAY 1976

New Land, New Covenant for soloists, children's chorus, mixed chorus and orchestra by the 79-year-old American composer Howard HANSON, to words by Isaac Watts, T. S. Eliot, John Newton, the Bible and the Declaration of Independence, is performed for the first time in Bryn Mawr, Pennsylvania.

4 MAY 1976

Varii Capricci, a symphonic suite by the prime British composer Sir William WALTON, is performed for the first time in London. (A choreographed version was produced by the Royal Ballet in London on 19 April 1983.)

6 MAY 1976

America, 1976, choral symphony written for the American bicentennial by the 62-year-old Polish-American composer Jacques BERLINSKI, is performed for the first time in San Diego.

6 MAY 1976

Concerto for Bassoon and Low Strings in five movements by the remarkable 44-year-old Soviet composer Sofia GUBAIDULINA, of ethnic tatar origin, in which the bassoon indulges in audacious acrobatic feats of atonal saltation with tricky trills, transcendental tremolos, labial glissandos and shrieks and laughter through the tube, accompanied by four cellos and three double-basses in a visuviation of euphonious discords deployed over their entire diapason, is presented for the first time in the Hall of the Union of Soviet Composers in Moscow, with Valery Popov as soloist in a prescribed series of salto mortale virtuosity.

11 MAY 1976

Second Symphony for solo voices, chorus, and orchestra by the 55-year-old American composer William BERGSMA, subtitled *Voyages*, is performed for the first time in Great Falls, Montana.

14 MAY 1976

Landscapes and Remembrances for soloists, chorus and orchestra by Gian Carlo MENOTTI is performed for the first time in Milwaukee.

20 MAY 1976

Third Symphony, subtitled *Rustica*, by the 51-year-old Macedonian composer Vlastimir NIKOLOVSKI, incorporating folk instruments such as the zurla, tapan and kaval, is performed for the first time in Skopje.

22 MAY 1976

Flute Concerto by the 47-year-old Soviet composer Edison DENISOV is performed for the first time in Dresden.

27 MAY 1976

Colonial Variants for orchestra by the American composer Norman DELLO JOIO is performed for the first time by the Philadelphia Orchestra under the direction of Eugene Ormandy.

12 JUNE 1976

The Last of the Mohicans, opera by the 36-year-old American composer Alva HENDERSON, is produced in Wilmington, Delaware.

19 JUNE 1976

Das Mädchen aus Domremy, opera by the 51-year-old German composer Giselher KLEBE, based on Schiller's play dealing with Joan of Arc, is performed for the first time in Stuttgart.

23 JUNE 1976

Kinkakuja (The Temple of the Golden Pavilion), opera by the 41-year-old Japanese composer Toshirō MAYUZUMI, is performed for the first time in Berlin.

3 JULY 1976

Ode to Freedom, violin concerto by the fruitful American composer Alan HOVHANESS is performed for the first time by the National Symphony Orchestra in Wolf Trap Farm Park near Washington, D.C., with Yehudi Menuhin as soloist and André Kostelanetz conducting.

12 JULY 1976

We Come to the River, "action for music," by the radical German composer Hans Werner HENZE, centered on a murderous army general, attacked by demented pacifists who gouge his eyeballs, set to a score ranging from insanely inappropriate bel canto to planned pandemonium as the musicians invade the stage to the deafening sounds of a marching band, with celestial diaphony superimposed on an infernal cacophony, is produced for the first time at Covent Garden in London.

13 JULY 1976

Max BUTTING, prolific German composer who adopted varied techniques from academic euphony to sophisticated dodecaphony, dies in Berlin at the age of 88.

19 JULY 1976

Visions of Terror and Wonder for mezzo-soprano and orchestra by the 42-year-old American composer Richard WERNICK, to texts from the Bible and the Koran in Hebrew, Arabic and Greek, is performed for the first time at the Aspen Music Festival in Colorado, later winning the 1977 Pulitzer Prize in music.

25 JULY 1976

Einstein on the Beach, phantasmagorical spectacle by the surrealistically minimalistic American composer Philip GLASS, to the scenario of a dadaistically propended dramatist Robert Wilson, in which hypnopompic events are oxymoronically juxtaposed in a deliberately antisyllogistical sequence, is produced at the Festival of Avignon, France. (The first American performance was given at the Metropolitan Opera in New York on 21 November 1976.)

26 JULY 1976

Die Versuchung (The Temptation), opera in two acts by the 65-year-old Polish-born Israeli composer Josef TAL, is produced at the Munich Festival.

4 AUGUST 1976

First Symphony, subtitled *The Halcyon*, by Gian Carlo MENOTTI, is performed for the first time in Saratoga Springs, New York, by the Philadelphia Orchestra conducted by Eugene Ormandy.

6 AUGUST 1976

Gregor PIATIGORSKY, famed Russian violoncellist whose romantic talent was served by a total virtuosity and who was the favorite soloist of Richard Strauss (he called him "mein Don Quixote," for Piatigorsky played the cello solo in that work many, many times under the composer's direction), and who eventually settled in America, dies in Los Angeles of lung cancer at the age of 73.

8 AUGUST 1976

David DEL TREDICI conducts in San Francisco the first performance of his orchestral work *An Alice Symphony*, subtitled *Illustrated Alice*, inspired by the works of Lewis Carroll. (An operatic *Alice* by Del Tredici was performed on 7 October 1976.)

28 AUGUST 1976

My Kinsman, Major Molineux, one-act opera, after Nathaniel Hawthorne, by the 30-year-old American composer Bruce SAYLOR, is produced in Pittsburgh.

2 SEPTEMBER 1976

Third Symphony for chorus, organ and orchestra by the 44-year-old Danish composer Per NØRGÅRD is performed for the first time in Copenhagen.

5 SEPTEMBER 1976

Something to Do, cantata-musical by the 62-year-old American composer Morton GOULD, is performed for the first time in Washington, D.C.

24 SEPTEMBER 1976

Missa elettronica by the foremost Polish master of experimental modern music Boguslaw SCHAEFFER, consisting of five liturgical choral sections (*Kyrie, Gloria, Credo, Sanctus* and *Agnus Dei*) separated by electronic interludes, the tonal armamentarium including heterophony and polytonality, is performed for the first time at the Evangelical Church of Warsaw as part of the Warsaw Autumn Festival.

29 SEPTEMBER 1976

Two synchronized scores by John CAGE, *Renga* (a Japanese poetic structure, in graphic notation comprising 361 drawings by Thoreau), and *Apartment House 1776* for four vocal soloists, representing four ethnic groups of America in 1776, featuring a pseudo-Indian chief rhythmically slapping his belly, are performed as a pluralistic bicentennial tribute by the Boston Symphony Orchestra, conducted by Seiji Ozawa.

7 OCTOBER 1976

Final Alice, "an opera, written in concert form" by the 39-year-old American composer David DEL TREDICI, spoken and sung by an amplified soprano to a text from Lewis Carroll's *Alice's Adventures in Wonderland* and *Through the Looking Glass*, scored for a large orchestra that includes a theremin, a banjo, an accordion and a mandolin, set in a beguilingly euphonious, harmonious and melodious idiom, and ending with the soloists signing off by counting to thirteen in Italian, in sly allusion to the composer's name (tredici = 13), is performed for the first time by the Chicago Symphony Orchestra, with Barbara Hendricks as narrator-soloist and Sir Georg Solti conducting.

8 OCTOBER 1976

Slovenica for orchestra by the 45-year-old Slovenian composer Alojz Srebotnjak, in three movements (*Antiphone, Dance* and *Mourning Chant*), based on modernistically treated archaic Slovenian folk modalities, is performed for the first time in Ljubljana.

13 OCTOBER 1976

Charles WUORINEN conducts in Cleveland the first performance of his *Tashi Concerto* for four instruments and orchestra, with the Tashi Chamber Music Ensemble as soloists.

22 OCTOBER 1976

Mi-parti for orchestra by the masterly Polish composer Witold LUTOSLAWSKI is performed for the first time in Rotterdam.

24 OCTOBER 1976

The 50th Festival of the International Society for Contemporary Music opens in Boston with the following program of music by Canadian composers, presented at an afternoon concert:

Offrandes III by the 47-year-old Quebec composer Serge GARANT, scored for three cellos, two harps, piano and percussion, the third of a series of his works inspired by Bach's *Musical Offering; Madrigal III* by the 37-year-old Toronto-born composer Bruce MATHER, scored for contralto, marimba, harp and piano; *Lalita: Shadows II* by the 37-year-old Nova Scotian composer Robert AITKEN, derived from a matutinal Hindu imploration and scored for flute solo and ensemble; . . . *le sifflement des vents porteurs de l'amour* . . . (a quotation from a Renaissance canticle), by the 46-year-old Quebec composer Gilles TREMBLAY, scored for flute and percussion, evoking the whistling of winds bringing streams of love; and *Arcana* by the Ontario-born 43-year-old avant-garde composer and theorist R. Murray SCHAFER, the title referring to a mysterious text in Egyptian hieroglyphs discovered in the ninth century, scored for several singers intoning symbolic phonemes with the accompaniment of an instrumental ensemble.

24 OCTOBER 1976

The second concert of the 50th Festival of the International Society for Contemporary Music in Boston is given in the evening with the following program:

Chanson for soprano and instruments by the 48-year-old Italian composer Vittoria FELLEGARA, written in an antifunctional harmonic system to a text from *Matines* by Paul Eluard; *Second Symphony* by the 24-year-old Glasgow-born composer Oliver KNUSSEN, scored for soprano and chamber orchestra, illustrating the hypnopompic state of a dreamy sleeper; *Origo* for orchestra by the 45-year-old Hungarian-born Austrian composer Josef Maria HORVATH, purporting to represent the origin of a species as part of a genus, in which the various aspects of the music trace the evolutionary lines of all art; and *Meridian* by the 42-year-old British composer Harrison BIRTWISTLE for voices and instruments in convoluted interplay.

25 OCTOBER 1976

On the second day of the 50th Festival of the International Society for Contemporary Music in Boston the following afternoon program is given:

Strömung for orchestra by the 54-year-old Japanese composer Yoshirō IRINO (first performed in Teheran on 17 September 1973), the title suggesting a saying of Confucius that all things pass away as in a stream, scored for a shimmering continuum of subdued harmonies; *Études for Two Pianos* by the 32-year-

old Montreal-born, composer John HAWKINS, in three movements of which the finale is polymetric; *Nightflies* by the 33-year-old Swedish composer Daniel BORTZ, scored for voice, clarinet, trombone, percussion, piano, electric organ and cello, set to a symbolistic Swedish text; *Argia Ezta Ikusten* by the 47-year-old Basque composer Carmelo A. BERNAOLA, scored for clarinet, vibraphone, assorted percussion and piano, to text by the Basque poet Gabriel Aresti; *Solentiname* for instrumental group by the 38-year-old Venezuelan composer Alfredo DEL MONACO, the title being a solemn homage to the commune of Solentiname in Nicaragua; *Music for Winds, Percussion, Cello and Voices* by the 50-year-old American composer Rolv YTTREHUS, in a serial system of composition.

25 OCTOBER 1976

On the second day of the 50th Festival of the International Society of Contemporary Music in Boston, the following program of chamber music is given in an evening concert:

Portrait of Lili Boulanger by the 33-year-old Brazilian composer Almeida PRADO, scored for string quartet, flute and piano, written as an homage to the early blooming and untimely withered French composer Lili Boulanger, using fragments of her melodies; *Meditación en Fa* for oboe solo by the 39-year-old Uruguayan composer Juan José ITURRIBERRY, structured on the persistent note F, with occasional microtonal oscillations around it; *Mosaico* by the 37-year-old Dutch composer Ton DE KRUYF, for oboe and string trio, and consisting of seven short movements separated by graded pauses; *Sonata* for flute and piano by the 46-year-old Hungarian composer Jozsef SOPRONI, written in a free sonata form; and *Chamber Music No. 2* by the 52-year-old American composer Leonard ROSENMAN, scored for chamber orchestra, singer and electronic tape to the text of the martyred Spanish poet Federico García Lorca.

26 OCTOBER 1976

On the third day of the 50th Festival of the International Society for Contemporary Music in Boston, the following program is presented in an afternoon concert:

Drei Bilder von Li Tai-bo by the 53-year-old Korean composer In-Chan CHOI, scored for singer, flute, harp, cello and percussion to the text of three poems by the ancient Chinese poet Li Tai-bo; *Indian Summer* for chamber ensemble by the 47-year-old Slovenian composer Milan STIBILJ, glorifying the colorful forests of early autumn in America; *Disegno per Sestetto d'Ottoni* for brass sextet, by the 29-year-old Swedish composer Anders ELIASSON; *Else (Hommage)* by the 66-year-old Israeli composer Josef TAL, intended to describe a colloquy with people of Jerusalem, scored for vocalist, narrator and chamber group, and inspired by the poems of Else Lasker-Schüler; *Two Pieces for Four Clarinets* by the 49-year-old Israeli composer Tzvi AVNI; *Pequeño Triptico* for two pianos and percussion by the 36-year-old Argentine composer José MARANZANO; and *Piece for Trumpet and Seven Instruments* by the Berlin-born, American composer Stefan WOLPE (1902–1972).

26 OCTOBER 1976

On the third day of the 50th Festival of the International Society for Contemporary Music in Boston, an evening concert is given with the following program of orchestral music performed by the University of Iowa Symphony Orchestra conducted by James Dixon:

The Rainbow Snake by the 40-year-old Danish composer Erik NORBY, inspired by the Indian legend of the serpentine origin of the rainbow (first performed in Copenhagen on 20 November 1975); *Entropies* by the 38-year-old Swiss composer Jim GRIMM, descriptive of the dialectical contradiction beween order and disorder; *Concerto for Orchestra* by the 40-year-old British composer Anthony PAYNE, built on a process of gradual intervallic convolution; *Catena* by the 42-year-old Korean composer Sukhi KANG, representing a concatenation of sixty fragments.

26 OCTOBER 1976

Concerto for string quartet, winds, brass and percussion by Walter PISTON is performed for the first time in Portland, Oregon.

27 OCTOBER 1976

On the fourth day of the 50th Festival of the International Society for Contemporary Music in Boston, the following program of chamber music is given in an afternoon concert:

String Quartet III/b by the 39-year-old Czech composer Tadeáš SALVA; *Piano Sonata* by the 36-year-old French composer René KOERING; *Geometrics* for string quartet by the 30-year-old American composer Robert POLLOCK, based on the geometric progressions of rhythms, intervals and tempi; *Piano Control* by the 39-year-old Swiss composer Thomas KESSLER, in which the solo piano part is regulated by a synthesizer generating different pitches, timbres, rhythms and dynamics; and *String Quartet* by the 44-year-old Australian composer Richard MEALE, based on a chaconne forming variations in a complex chordal progression.

27 OCTOBER 1976

On the fourth day of the 50th Festival of the International Society for Contemporary Music in Boston, the following program is presented in an evening concert by the Boston Symphony Orchestra under the direction of Seiji Ozawa:

Renga with *Apartment House 1776* by the formidable 64-year-old American iconoclast John CAGE, originally performed by the Boston Symphony Orchestra on 29 September 1976, embodying two collated scores played with aleatory freedom under the supervision of the conductor and making use of any instruments to form a desired balance; *Anarchia* for percussion and orchestra by the 47-year-old Cretan composer Nikos MAMANGAKIS in which the serial principle is evolved to the point of total anarchy; and *Chronicles* by the 50-year-old American composer Seymour SHIFRIN, to Hebrew texts from the Old Testament.

28 OCTOBER 1976

Con tutta forza for 41 wind instruments and six percussionists by the 34-year-old Swedish composer Sven-David SANDSTRÖM is performed for the first time in Stockholm.

28 OCTOBER 1976

On the fifth day of the 50th Festival of the International Society for Contemporary Music in Boston, a concert of chamber Music is given with the following program:

Alborada for viola and piano by the 23-year-old Venezuelan composer Emilio MENDOZA; *String Quartet No. 6* by the 43-year-old British-born Australian composer John EXTON; *Fourth Piano Sonata* by the 46-year-old Finnish composer

Usko MERILÄINEN; *Air* for soprano, percussion and piano by the 33-year-old Norwegian composer Magne HEGDAL; and *Concerto a Quattro* for string quartet by the 32-year-old Canadian composer John FODI.

29 OCTOBER 1976

On the sixth day of the 50th Festival of the International Society for Contemporary Music in Boston, the following program of works by American composers is given in an afternoon concert:

Crossworks for chamber ensemble by the 32-year-old composer Paul LANSKY; *Six Études* for piano by the 61-year-old learned composer/theorist George PERLE; *Bittere Nüsse*, songs romanticizing acrid nuts by the 48-year-old John HUGGLER; *Songs of Nature* by the 38-year-old New York composer John HEISS; *Block Songs* for soprano and children's toys by the 46-year-old T. I. ANDERSON; *Six Dumbshows* by the 38-year-old John HARBISON, scored for flute, clarinet, violin, cello and electric piano, with material taken from his opera, *Winter's Tale*, after Shakespeare.

29 OCTOBER 1976

On the sixth day of the 50th Festival of the International Society for Contemporary Music an evening concert of electronic music is presented at the Massachusetts Institute of Technology in Cambridge, featuring the following works:

Resa for computer by the 49-year-old Norwegian-born, German-educated Swedish composer Knut WIGGEN (*resa* is the Swedish word for travel); *Chimaera* for bass clarinet and tape by the 46-year-old Spanish-born Dutch composer Enrique RAXACH; *Ars recte computandi (Art of Correct Calculation)* by the group BBK, organized in 1973 and consisting of Pierre BARBAUD, Frank BROWN and Genevieve KLEIN; *Electra* for tape by the 44-year-old Yugoslav composer Vladan RADOVANOVIĆ; *Harry's Wonderland* for bass clarinet and tape by the 45-year-old Belgian composer André LAPORTE; and *Group Variations II* by the 42-year-old American composer Benjamin BORETZ.

30 OCTOBER 1976

On the seventh day of the 50th Festival of the International Society for Contemporary Music in Boston, the following program is presented in an afternoon concert:

Catena, a chain of episodes for chamber ensemble by the 41-year-old Hawaiian composer Donald SUR; *Cantus Contra Cantum II* for violin and cello by the 49-year-old French composer Jacques-Louis MONOD; *Valentine* for solo double-bass by the 48-year-old American composer Jacob DRUCKMAN, with the player sadistically assaulting the instrument with bow and timpani stick while singing sustained tones with loudly punctuating accents; *String Quartet* by the 37-year-old Florida-born composer Ellen Taaffe ZWILICH, in four movements involving some clever contrapuntal convolutions while keeping the melody in a pleasingly fluid state; *Echoes and Anticipation* by the 53-year-old American composer Ezra LADERMAN, scored for oboe and seven instruments in three movements, *Nuances*, *Strata* and *Changing Textures*.

30 OCTOBER 1976

The 50th Festival of the International Society for Contemporary Music in Boston concludes with an evening concert with the New England Conservatory Symphony

Orchestra, under the direction of Gunther Schuller, performing the following program:

Fassade by the 40-year-old German composer Helmut LACHENMANN, projecting a rectilinear marching meter in contrapuntal internal articulations; *Inner Space* by the 37-year-old American composer David STOCK, gravid with clusters of sonic matter mutually interacting in several different tempi; *Voix* by the 36-year-old Portuguese composer Jorge PEIXINHO, scored for mezzo-soprano and chamber orchestra, leading to a gradual disintegration of the material into autonomous elements, with all participants, including the audience, becoming distraught but still attempting to follow the guiding thread of the music; *Sinfonia* by the 30-year-old Dutch composer Tristan KEURIS, in four parts connected by a fragmentary tissue; and *Jazz Concerto* by the 47-year-old master of Polish modern music Boguslaw SCHAEFFER, in which jazz elements are organized in an arresting classical form.

31 OCTOBER 1976

Jonah, opera after the tragedy by Marin Sorescu, by the 50-year-old Rumanian composer Anatol VIERU is produced in Bucharest.

4 NOVEMBER 1976

Cello Concerto by the American composer Donald ERB is performed for the first time by Lynn Harrell and the Rochester (New York) Philharmonic Orchestra, conducted by David Zinman.

5 NOVEMBER 1976

In Wildness is the Preservation of the World, orchestral fantasy after Thoreau by the 39-year-old American composer Brian FENNELLY, is performed for the first time in Davenport, Iowa.

9 NOVEMBER 1976

Rosina LHÉVINNE, grande dame of Russian piano pedagogy who taught a plethora of wunderkinder of all ages in Europe and America and who gave brilliant duo-piano recitals with her virtuoso pianist husband Josef LHÉVINNE whom she survived by 31 years, dies at the matriarchal age of 96 in Glendale, California.

12 NOVEMBER 1976

Walter PISTON, enlightened master of music whose works embody the best cultural achievement of American music and who as a Harvard University professor educated a number of talented composers, dies in his home at Belmont, Massachusetts, at the age of 82.

14 NOVEMBER 1976

Night of the Moonspell, three-act opera by Elie SIEGMEISTER, based on Shakespeare's *Midsummer Night's Dream,* with the action transferred to a festive mardi gras in Louisiana circa 1900, set to music full of euphonious dissonance and rhythmic asymmetries in depicting Cajun voodoo rites, is produced in Shreveport, Louisiana, as a commissioned United States bicentennial piece.

14 NOVEMBER 1976

The Secret History of the Birth of the Nation for narrator, chorus and orchestra by the 64-year-old American composer

Don GILLIS is performed for the first time in York, Pennsylvania.

15 NOVEMBER 1976

Fourth Symphony by the American composer George ROCHBERG is performed for the first time by the Seattle Youth Symphony.

20 NOVEMBER 1976

Jubilee, opera by Ulysses KAY, with the action taking place on an antebellum plantation in Georgia, in which both the slave owner and his slaves unite in an optimistic jubilee when all men are really equal, is performed for the first time in Jackson, Mississippi.

26 NOVEMBER 1976

Isis and Osiris, lyric drama by the enlightened British composer Elisabeth LUTYENS, is performed for the first time at Morley College in London.

1 DECEMBER 1976

Letter from Mozart by Michael COLGRASS, a pseudo-epistolary musical collage of Mozartomorphic tunes culled from genuine bits of Mozartiana, and mulcified in a plasma of polyrhythmic, polymetric, polytonal and sometimes aleatory ingredients, requiring two conductors to beat non-coincident meters, is performed for the first time in New York.

4 DECEMBER 1976

Benjamin BRITTEN, greatly endowed British composer whose many operas and church parables established a harmonious link with the Elizabethan era of English music and who succeeded in creating a modern idiom along national lines, as exemplified in his operas *Peter Grimes, The Turn of the Screw* and *Gloriana,* composed for the coronation of Queen Elizabeth II, as well as in his educational music for the young, such as *Let's Make an Opera,* and who was elevated to the peerage of Great Britain in 1976 and became a Lord, dies in Aldeburgh at the age of 63.

10 DECEMBER 1976

Triptih dalmatinskih gradova (Triptych of Dalmatian Cities) for orchestra by the 70-year-old Croatian composer Milo CIPRA is performed for the first time in Zagreb.

17 DECEMBER 1976

Kabale und Liebe, opera by the 58-year-old Austrian composer Gottfried VON EINEM, after Schiller's play, is produced in Vienna.

20 DECEMBER 1976

Windungen for twelve cellos by the 54-year-old Greek mathematician-musician-philosopher Iannis XENAKIS is performed for the first time in Bonn.

24 DECEMBER 1976

Symphonic Movement by the reclusive, hermetically individualistic Swedish composer Allan PETTERSSON is performed for the first time on Swedish Radio.

29 DECEMBER 1976

On the occasion of the centennial of the birth of Pablo CASALS, three years, nine weeks and five days after his death in exile from fascistic Spain, the royal government of new democratic Spain issues a postage stamp in his honor, and the municipal assembly of Barcelona attaches the name of Calle Casals to a city street.

1977

1 JANUARY 1977

Roland HAYES, inspired black singer whose parents were former slaves, dies in Boston at the age of 89.

5 JANUARY 1977

Der Schuhu und die fliegende Prinzessin, opera by the 33-year-old German composer Udo ZIMMERMANN, the Schuhu being a wise birdman who captured the flying princess of Tripoli in midair, set to music with electroacoustical ornithomorphic effects, is produced in Dresden.

17 JANUARY 1977

Chamber Concerto for viola d'amore and eleven instruments by the 35-year-old Swedish composer Ulf GRAHN is performed for the first time in Washington, D.C.

19 JANUARY 1977

Ninth Symphony by the 68-year-old Serbian composer Milan RISTIĆ, written in a neoclassical manner, is performed for the first time in Belgrade.

2 FEBRUARY 1977

The Royal Hunt of the Sun, opera by Iain HAMILTON, composed in 1966–1968 to a libretto arranged from Peter Shaffer's play dealing with the fall of the Inca Empire and the death of the Inca sun king Atahualpa, with a score full of ominous pentatonic invocations, is produced for the first time by the English National Opera in London.

6 FEBRUARY 1977

Malooley and the Fear Monster, a "family opera" in one act by the American composer John POZDRO, is performed for the first time in Lawrence, Kansas.

7 FEBRUARY 1977

Palinode for orchestra and computer synthesis by the 34-year-old American composer Charles DODGE is performed for the first time in New York.

17 FEBRUARY 1977

Symphony of Three Orchestras by the foremost modern American composer Elliott CARTER, derived from the concept of the Baroque concerto grosso, with each of the component orchestras representing a concertino of soloists set against the entire ensemble, in twelve movements preceded by a spacious exordium and concluded by a grandiloquent peroration, is performed for the first time by the New York Philharmonic Orchestra, Pierre Boulez conducting.

22 FEBRUARY 1977

Culminations for orchestra by the 34-year-old Swedish composer Sven-David SANDSTRÖM is performed for the first time on Swedish Radio.

23 FEBRUARY 1977

The Prophet, oratorio by the American composer Gardner READ, based on text by the Lebanese mystic Kahlil Gibran, is performed for the first time by the Boston University Orchestra and Chorus.

14 MARCH 1977

Tamburlaine, lyric drama for radio, in twenty-four scenes, lasting about eighty-five minutes without a break, by the Scottish composer Iain HAMILTON, based on Marlowe's play dealing with the legendary Mongol warrior, is performed for the first time in London.

22 MARCH 1977

ČSV for orchestra by the 35-year-old Norwegian composer John PERSEN, the ambiguous acronym of the title meaning "dare to admit you are a Lapp," is performed for the first time in Oslo.

26 MARCH 1977

The 150th anniversary of BEETHOVEN's death is marked in Peking by a televised performance of his *Fifth Symphony,* revoking the ban on Beethoven, heretofore denounced by the cultural Chinese authorities as an imperialistic revisionist bourgeois composer.

1 APRIL 1977

Symphony in D Major, in the style of Mozart by the 33-year-old Polish composer Krzysztof MEYER, written in such an authentic Mozartean idiom as to confuse and seduce even the most suspicious of the Mozartologists, is performed for the first time in Poznan, on April Fool's Day.

4 APRIL 1977

Eugene ZÁDOR, Hungarian-American composer of operas and symphonic works, many of them steeped in Magyar folklore, dies of cancer of the prostate gland in Hollywood at the age of 82.

14 APRIL 1977

Lily, opera by the 58-year-old, hemidemisemimodernistic American composer Leon KIRCHNER, based on the novel *Henderson the Rain King* by Saul Bellow (Lily is Henderson's lissom wife), scored with a variety of quaquaversal expressionistic techniques, including a chorus singing in a made-up African language, is performed for the first time by the New York City Opera.

21 APRIL 1977

Symphony in nine movements for large orchestra and six solo instruments by the innovative Polish modernist Boguslaw SCHAEFFER is performed for the first time in Wroclaw, with the composer at the piano as one of the soloists.

24 APRIL 1977

Damals, by the 69-year-old German composer Wolfgang FORTNER, after text by Samuel Beckett, scored for mime, narrator, mezzo-soprano, baritone, harpsichord, guitar, piano and live electronics, is performed for the first time in Baden-Baden.

27 APRIL 1977

Violin Concerto by the 43-year-old Polish modernist Krzysztof PENDERECKI is performed for the first time in Basel.

29 APRIL 1977

Quartet Plus for narrator and double string quartet by the 54-year-old American composer Lukas FOSS is performed for the first time in New York.

2 MAY 1977

Fifth Symphony, subtitled *Visions of Time,* by the American composer Elie SIEGMEISTER is performed for the first time by the Baltimore Symphony Orchestra conducted by Sergiu Comissiona.

3 MAY 1977

Fleuves (Rivers) for orchestra by the 44-year-old Canadian composer Gilles TREMBLAY is performed for the first time in Montreal.

4 MAY 1977

Forty Piano Études in Modus Lascivus by the 75-year-old Hungarian-American violist and composer Tibor SERLY is performed for the first time in its entirety by the composer's wife, Miriam Molin, in New York.

5 MAY 1977

Star-Child by George CRUMB, subtitled *A Parable for Soprano, Antiphonal Children's Voices, Male Speaking Chorus and Large Orchestra,* supplemented by a peal of 20 handbells and carillons of bell ringers, with the text in Latin from the Vulgate, is performed for the first time by the New York Philharmonic led by Pierre Boulez, aided and abetted by three simultaneous conductors.

5 MAY 1977

Fluctuante-Immuable for large orchestra by the 38-year-old French composer Jean-Claude ELOY, suggesting in its title the immutability of fluctuation, is performed for the first time in Paris under the direction of Jean-Claude Casadesus.

13 MAY 1977

Neither by the American modernist Morton FELDMAN, a monodrama after an original text by Samuel Beckett, scored for soprano and orchestra, is performed for the first time in Rome. (The American première took place in New York on 21 November 1978.)

14 MAY 1977

On the opening day of the 51st Festival of the International Society for Contemporary Music in Bonn, the following program is presented at an afternoon concert:

Quemadmodum for string quartet by the 34-year-old Hungarian composer Zoltán JENEY, the relative pronoun of the title indicating a reference to traditional structures; *Seul opus 38* for bass clarinet solo by the 36-year-old Chicago-born Danish-resident composer Maurice WEDDINGTON; and *A Wind/Tornado Piece/Cyclone* by the 29-year-old American composer Joan LA BARBARA, with the audience placed in the static eye of the hurricane.

14 MAY 1977

At an evening concert on the first day of the 51st Festival of the International Society for Contemporary Music in Bonn, the following program of choral music under the slogan "Spaces with Voices—Voices of the Innerspace" is presented:

Integrale Musik with tape by the 30-year-old German composer Peter Michael HAMEL; *Ritual for the Thirsty Earth* for seven voices and instruments by the 46-year-old Rumanian composer Myriam MARBE, derived from Rumanian folk tunes; *Sanctus* for ten solo voices, ten metronomes, bells and chorus by the 33-year-old Brazilian composer Jamary OLIVEIRA; *The Gentleness of Rain Was in the Wind* for three female and three males voices by the 47-year-old Austrian composer Gerhard RÜHM; *Les Sources Transfigurées* for vibraphone, tam-tam and vocal ensemble by the 34-year-old Belgian composer Andre VAN BELLE; and *Requiem Hashshirim* for choir by the 31-year-old Venetian conductor-composer Giuseppe SINOPOLI.

15 MAY 1977

On the second day of the 51st Festival of the International Society for Contemporary Music in Bonn the following program of "Music of a Special Sound" is presented at an afternoon concert:

Genklang for five pianists by the 30-year-old Danish composer Karl Aage RASMUSSEN; *Jackson* for bass-baritone by the Australian composer Helen STANDRING, to a text of letters by the black inmate of Soledad Prison George Jackson; *Influx* for string quartet by the 44-year-old Japanese composer Hidenao ITO; *Cluster* for an optional number of pianists, and *Piano Trio*, by the 34-year-old Mexican composer Mario LAVISTA; and *Appels* for seven wind instruments, two percussionists, piano and double-bass by the 38-year-old French composer Michael LEVINAS.

15 MAY 1977

At an evening concert on the second day of the 51st Festival of the International Society for Contemporary Music in Bonn, the following program announced as "Music for Children with Children: I" is given:

Kommunikationsspiele, a demonstration with a youth group by the 40-year-old Swiss composer Hans WÜTHRICH; *Pieces* for instruments constructed by school children, program supervised by the British instructor Hugh DAVIES; and *Jeux avec le Scriptoson* (games with a scientifically scripted phonograph disc) by the 30-year-old French composer Jean Ives BOSSEUR.

15 MAY 1977

Moses, opera by the 43-year-old Hungarian composer Zsolt DURKÓ, is performed for the first time in Budapest.

16 MAY 1977

On the third day of the 51st Festival of the International Society for Contemporary Music in Bonn, the following program of "Music with Exotic Sounds" is presented:

Cabotaje IIIc for flute and tape by the 37-year-old Uruguayan composer Ariel MARTINEZ; *Chanson* for wind instruments by the 45-year-old Italian composer Mario BERTONCINI; *Kontrasignatur* for double-bass and tape by the 37-year-old German composer Wilfried MICHEL; *Transpositio ad infinitum* for solo cello by the 53-year-old Swiss composer Klaus HUBER; and *Ach Golgatha!* for harp, organ and percussion by the 54-year-old Belgian composer Karel GOEYVAERTS, based on a passage from Bach's *St. Matthew Passion*.

18 MAY 1977

On the fourth day of the 51st Festival of the International Society for Contemporary Music in Bonn an orchestral concert is given with the following program:

Morphogenesis by the 24-year-old German composer Hans-Jürgen VON BOSE; *Gespenster (Ghosts)* for singer/narrator, tape and orchestra, to a text by Bertolt Brecht, by the 38-year-old German composer Nicolaus A. HUBER; and *Houdini Symphony* by the 42-year-old avant-garde Dutch composer Peter SCHAT, scored for four soloists, chorus and orchestra, in four movements drawn from his circus opera on the life of the famous magician Houdini. (The entire opera was produced in Amsterdam on 29 September 1977.)

19 MAY 1977

A Water Bird Talk, a protracted monologue to the music of Dominick ARGENTO, adapted from Chekhov's parodistic lecture on the harm on tobacco smoking, is performed for the first time at the Brooklyn Academy of Music in New York.

19 MAY 1977

On the fifth day of the 51st Festival of the International Society for Contemporary Music in Bonn, two programs featuring "Music for Children with Children" are presented, including *Fountains of My Sky* by the 35-year-old Rumanian composer Horatio RADULESCU; *Yobikake (The Call)* by the 26-year-old Japanese composer and educator Chisako SHIMIZU; and *Polyagogie* by the Greek master of pedagogical stochastics Iannis XENAKIS.

19 MAY 1977

The fifth day of the 51st Festival of the International Society for Contemporary Music in Bonn continues at an evening concert of "All Sound-Space Music" with the following program:

Orange Air, collaborative work by the American composers Richard FEIT and Richard SCHAER; *Peripathetisches zur Lage* by the 42-year-old Austrian composer Otto M. ZYKLAN; *Dentist Music* by the 39-year-old Polish-born composer Piotr LACHERT, conceived as a kind of orthodontic laboratory of the musical future; and *The Sinking of the Titanic* for instruments and projections by the 34-year-old British composer Gavin BRYARS, based on hymns played by the ship band before the unsinkable *Titanic* went down at 2:20 A.M. on 15 April 1912.

20 MAY 1977

On the sixth day of the 51st Festival of the International Society for Contemporary Music in Bonn, an afternoon concert featuring the following program of "Narrative Music" is presented:

Piano Concerto by the 43-year-old Italian composer Danilo LORENZINI; *Kouklokosmos (Puppet World)*, an electronic fairy tale by the 44-year-old Greek composer Stephanos WASSILIADIS; *Solo* for piano and live electronics by the 29-year-old Finnish composer Jukka TIENSUU; and *Hörfilm (Audio Film)*, audio-visual environment for tape, multivision and headphones by the 29-year-old Chilean-born Hungarian composer János DARVAS.

20 MAY 1977

The sixth day of the 51st Festival of the International Society for Contemporary Music in Bonn continues with the following program at an evening concert of orchestral music, presented under the general rubric "Reflections":

Variations on a Theme by Mozart by the 24-year-old German composer Wolfgang VON SCHWEINITZ; *Reflections of Narciss and Goldmund* for two chamber orchestras, harp, piano and celesta by the 24-year-old British composer Robert SAXTON, inspired by the novel by Hermann Hesse; *Ding (Thing)* by the 34-year-old Swiss composer Roland MOSER; and *Accanto* for clarinet and orchestra by the 42-year-old German composer Helmut LACHENMANN.

21 MAY 1977

The 51st Festival of the International Society for Contemporary Music in Bonn concludes with a program of orchestral works by four international grand masters of modern music: *Punkte* by Karlheinz STOCKHAUSEN; *Don* by Pierre BOULEZ; *Piano Concerto* by John CAGE; and *Il Canto sospeso* by the innovative Italian composer Luigi NONO.

6 JUNE 1977

A *Gentle Spirit*, chamber opera after a story by Dostoyevsky by the 34-year-old British composer John TAVENER, is produced in London at the Bath Festival.

18 JUNE 1977

The Martyrdom of Saint Magnus, chamber opera in one act and nine scenes by the British composer Peter Maxwell DAVIES, is performed for the first time at the twelfth-century Orkney Cathedral, in Kirkwell, where Saint Magnus was buried, recounting the saga of the unnatural murder of the pious Earl Magnus by his own cousin in 1117, to the composer's libretto drawn from George Mackay Brown's novel *Magnus*, the thematic material derived from medieval plainchant.

22 JUNE 1977

Napoli milionaria, comic opera by the 65-year-old Italian composer Nino ROTA, making sport of the American occupation of Naples in 1945 that produced black-market Neapolitan millionaires, is produced in Spoleto.

26 JUNE 1977

Karadjordje (Black George) or *Seme zla (The Seed of the Wicked)*, television opera by the 66-year-old Serbian composer Stanojlo RAJIČIĆ to the text by Ivan Studen, depicting the psychological aspect of the conflicts between Karadjordje and Miloš Obrenović, the leaders of the first and second Serbian revolts against Ottoman rule in the early nineteenth century, ending in Karadjordje's defeat, is produced on Belgrade Television.

6 JULY 1977

The Ice Break, opera by Sir Michael TIPPETT dealing with the reunion of a political prisoner with his family after a great many years, involving the estrangement of his son who questions his father's courage and his daughter who offers herself to a black athlete in a gesture of atonement for racial guilt, all this heavily embroiled in a network of semiotics, symbols and psychedelic signals implanted in a complex contrapuntal web, is produced at the Royal Opera House, Covent Garden, in London.

29 JULY 1977

Fourth Symphony by the 71-year-old Russian composer Boris ARAPOV, scored for mezzo-soprano, baritone, narrator, two choirs and orchestra, is performed for the first time in Leningrad.

7 AUGUST 1977

Seventh Symphony, subtitled *A Sea Symphony*, for orchestra and chorus by the 80-year-old American composer Howard HANSON, to text from Walt Whitman, is performed for the first time for the fiftieth anniversary of the National Music Camp at Interlochen, Michigan.

16 AUGUST 1977

Elvis PRESLEY, superduper star of American rock 'n' roll, popularly described as "Elvis the Pelvis" because of his habit of rotating the lower part of his torso, whose fantastically successful career ended in a bottomless pit of erotic perversity and conspicuous drug consumption, expires at his lavishly accoutered home at Memphis, Tennessee, at the age of 44.

17 AUGUST 1977

Petro PETRIDIS, Greek composer of great cultural attainments (he could recite Homer in extenso from memory), dies in Athens at the age of 85.

20 AUGUST 1977

Voyager I, American spacecraft, is shot off on a mission to reconnoiter Jupiter, Saturn and Uranus, containing a two-hour recorded message for any extraterrestrial beings owning a phonograph who may intercept it, including musical bits by the three B's and a rock piece by a fourth B, Chuck Berry.

6 SEPTEMBER 1977

Mary, Queen of Scots, opera by the 49-year-old Scottish composer Thea MUSGRAVE, is produced at the Edinburgh Festival.

13 SEPTEMBER 1977

Leopold STOKOWSKI, symphonic conductor of unequaled histrionic gifts whose patrician appearance suggested his paternal Polish origin, and who as music director of the Philadelphia Orchestra for many years created a unique Stokowski sound, dies still in full possession of his artistic powers at Nether Wallop, Hampshire, England, at the fulfilled age of 95.

16 SEPTEMBER 1977

Maria CALLAS, prima donna assoluta, born in New York of Greek parents, whose career was in itself a series of operatically melodramatic peripeteias and whose temperamental antics on and off stage were the favorite pabulum of sensational newspaper stories, dies suddenly of a heart seizure in her Paris apartment at the age of 53.

22 SEPTEMBER 1977

Dawnpath, chamber opera by the 30-year-old British composer Nicola LEFANU, is produced in London.

29 SEPTEMBER 1977

Houdini, a circus opera by the Dutch composer Peter SCHAT, scored for seven soloists, chorus, orchestra, dancers, escapologists and acrobats, is produced in Amsterdam. (An orchestral version, titled *Houdini Symphony*, was first performed in Bonn on 18 May 1977.)

29 SEPTEMBER 1977

Alexander TCHEREPNIN, prolific Russian composer, son of the romantically nationalist composer Nicolas Tcherepnin, who departed from ancestral legacy, lived in China and Paris, eventually becoming an American citizen, joined the modern movement by among other things adopting a scale of nine degrees and practicing a rhythmic polyphony which he called interpunctus, dies suddenly at the age of 78 while returning from a walk with his Chinese wife, Lee Hsien-ming, at the entrance of his Paris apartment.

29 SEPTEMBER 1977

On the occasion of the semimillennial anniversary of Uppsala University, *Twelfth Symphony* by the romantic Swedish composer Allan PETTERSSON, entitled *De Döda på Torget (The Dead in the Marketplace)* for chorus and orchestra, inspired by the poetry of the Chilan Nobel Laureate Pablo Neruda and throbbing with irreconcilable discords in a turbulent polyphonic setting voicing a heart-rending protest against the unspeakable cruelty of the military Chilean regime, is performed for the first time by the Stockholm Philharmonic.

6 OCTOBER 1977

Fourth Symphony in one movement by Sir Michael TIPPETT, set in a dissonant idiom, restrained by a disciplined classical form, completed on 18 April 1977, is performed for the first time as a commissioned work by the Chicago Symphony Orchestra, Sir Georg Solti conducting.

8 OCTOBER 1977

Requiem for chorus, organ, piano, electric bass, electric guitar, brass, percussion and celesta by the 42-year-old Soviet modernist Alfred SCHNITTKE is performed for the first time in Budapest.

11 OCTOBER 1977

Songfest, a suite of twelve pieces for six singers and orchestra by Leonard BERNSTEIN, is performed for the first time in Washington, D.C.

14 OCTOBER 1977

Bing CROSBY, immensely popular American crooner and a talented cinematic comedian, dies suddenly during a game of golf at La Moraleja Golf Course outside of Madrid, at the age of 74.

15 OCTOBER 1977

Westerlings, "four songs and a prayer with seascapes" for unaccompanied chorus by the 43-year-old British composer Peter Maxwell DAVIES, to a text by George Mackay Brown utilizing traditional Orkney Norn (a language native to the residents of the Island of Orkney, out of common use for over two hundred years), receives its first performance by the BBC Singers at the Concert Hall, Broadcasting House in London, John Aldis conducting. (The American première by the Berkeley Contemporary Chamber Players, Christopher Fulkerson conducting, took place on 26 March 1984.)

5 NOVEMBER 1977

Guy LOMBARDO, Canadian-born American bandleader, wizard of the golden sound, publicized as the purveyor of "the sweetest music this side of Heaven," whose New Year's radio and television broadcasts became the quintessence of American life, dies in Houston, Texas, at the age of 75.

13 NOVEMBER 1977

Strange Tenderness of Naked Leaping for orchestra by the 46-year-old American composer of Polish descent Lucia DLUGOSZEWSKI is performed for the first time in Santa Fe, New Mexico.

17 NOVEMBER 1977

English Horn Concerto by the 61-year-old American composer Vincent PERSICHETTI is performed for the first time in New York.

30 NOVEMBER 1977

A Flock Descends Upon the Pentagonal Garden for orchestra by the 47-year-old Japanese composer Toru TAKEMITSU is performed for the first time in San Francisco.

1 DECEMBER 1977

American Cantata for tenor, soprano, two speakers, chorus and orchestra by the 55-year-old American composer Lukas FOSS is performed for the first time in New York.

6 DECEMBER 1977

Clarinet Concerto by the 39-year-old American composer John CORIGLIANO is performed for the first time in New York.

21 DECEMBER 1977

Johann Nepomuk DAVID, Austrian composer of a number of compactly wrought symphonies and pieces of chamber music, dies in Stuttgart at the age of 82.

1978

10 JANUARY 1978

Timbres, Espace, Mouvement for orchestra by the French composer Henri DUTILLEUX is performed for the first time by the National Symphony Orchestra, conducted by Mstislav Rostropovich, in Washington, D.C.

16 JANUARY 1978

Aeneas on the Saxophone for voices, clarinet, French horn, trombone, viola and double-bass by the American composer Ezra SIMS, based on a sui generis eighteen-tone scale, is performed for the first time on the composer's fiftieth birthday at the Dinosaur Annex in Boston.

17 JANUARY 1978

Sixth Symphony, subtitled *Sinfonia Mistica*, by the eminent Polish-born (naturalized British) composer Andrzej PANUFNIK, based heavily on hexalogical numerology (six sections, six recurring melodic patterns, six triads at the root of the harmonies, six rhythmic units in every bar), is performed for the first time by the Northern Sinfonia under the direction of Christopher Seaman, in Middlesborough, England.

18 JANUARY 1978

Ivan DZERZHINSKY, Soviet composer who wrote music fitting to perfection into the scheme of Socialist Realism and who received an exceptional verbal accolade from Stalin himself after the production of his dialectically patriotic opera *And Quiet Flows the Don* to a libretto fashioned from the Bolshevistically orthodox eponymous novel by Sholokhov, dies in Leningrad, largely unsung and unhailed, at the age of 68.

19 JANUARY 1978

L'invitation au voyage for chamber orchestra and speaker by the 39-year-old Swiss-born French composer Tona SCHERCHEN-HSIAO, daughter of the famous conductor Hermann Scherchen, is performed for the first time in Paris, under the direction of Pierre Boulez.

2 FEBRUARY 1978

First Symphony by the English composer Peter Maxwell DAVIES is performed for the first time in London.

12 FEBRUARY 1978

The Women in the Garden, chamber opera for five singers and nine instruments by the 64-year-old American composer Vivian FINE, to her own feminist libretto portraying Emily Dickinson, Isadora Duncan, Gertrude Stein and Virginia Woolf, is produced in San Francisco.

13 FEBRUARY 1978

Fiery Wind for orchestra by the radical 43-year-old American modernist Roger REYNOLDS is performed for the first time in New York.

20 FEBRUARY 1978

Arietten for piano and orchestra by the 60-year-old Austrian composer Gottfried VON EINEM, is performed for the first time in Berlin.

22 FEBRUARY 1978

Introitus for piano and chamber orchestra by the 46-year-old Soviet composer Sofia GUBAIDULINA, of Tatar paternity and Russian maternity, is performed for the first time in Moscow.

27 FEBRUARY 1978

Fifth Symphony by the 42-year-old Soviet Georgian composer Giya KANCHELI, dedicated to the memory of his parents, is performed for the first time in Tbilisi.

2 MARCH 1978

Janus for trombone and jazz orchestra by the 51-year-old American composer and jazz clarinetist William O. SMITH is performed for the first time in Seattle.

12 MARCH 1978

Witold LUTROSLAWSKI conducts the Berlin Philharmonic in the first performance of his *Les Espaces du sommeil* for baritone and orchestra, with Dietrich Fischer-Dieskau as soloist.

14 MARCH 1978

Adieu Robert Schumann for contralto and orchestra by the Canadian composer R. Murray SCHAFER, to text from Clara Schumann's diaries chronicling Schumann's madness, is performed for the first time in Ottawa.

17 MARCH 1978

Deaï for three orchestras by the 50-year-old American composer, conductor and educator Gunther SCHULLER is performed for the first time in Tokyo. (The first American performance was in Tanglewood, Massachusetts, on 4 August 1979.)

6 APRIL 1978

Nicolas NABOKOV, Russian composer, first cousin of the novelist Vladimir Nabokov, who lived in Paris and in America and wrote a number of fine ballets and symphonic music in a modernistic but quite pleasurable vein, dies in New York at the age of 74.

6 APRIL 1978

Triptychon by the 70-year-old German composer Wolf-gang FORTNER, in three parts—*Hymnus I* for six brasses, *Improvisation* for large orchestra and *Hymnus II* for eighteen-voice string orchestra—is performed for the first time in Düsseldorf.

12 APRIL 1978

Le Grand Macabre, eschatological anti-opera by the musical thaumaturgist Györgi LIGETI, dealing with the apocalyptic ultima hora and written in a gloriously antimusical idiom of beguiling allure, with singers shouting and whispering inarticulate vocables, to the altered text adapted from dramas by the Belgian surrealist Michel de Ghelderode, the action being set in a chimeric town of Breugelland, and centered on the thanatopherous necroczar who sexually mutilates a local hausfrau before ordering the world's end, but shrinks himself into a death mask when the forces of life refuse to stop functioning, is produced for the first time in Stockholm.

14 APRIL 1978

Claudia L'egare, fourth opera by the 60-year-old American composer Robert WARD, to a libretto dealing with an American counterpart of Ibsen's independent woman Hedda Gabler, with the action taking place in Charleston, South Carolina, shortly after the Civil War, is produced by the Minnesota Opera in St. Paul.

18 APRIL 1978

Stark såsom Döden (Strong Like Death), church opera by the 35-year-old Swedish composer Sven-David SAND-STRÖM, is produced in Stockholm.

20 APRIL 1978

Fireballs for orchestra by the 34-year-old Polish composer Krzysztof MEYER is performed for the first time in Warsaw.

21 APRIL 1978

Danton and Robespierre, opera by the 43-year-old American composer John EATON, is performed for the first time in Bloomington, Indiana.

1 MAY 1978

Aram KHACHATURIAN, brilliant Soviet composer born in Tiflis, Georgia, of Armenian parents, whose quasi-Oriental ballet music throbs with animal energy and whose harmonies richly resonate with euphonious bitonalities, dies in Moscow of lung cancer at the age of 74.

6 MAY 1978

The 52nd Festival of the International Society for Contemporary Music opens in Stockholm with a city event of Fireworks and Water Music, coordinated by Lars-Gunnar Bodin, Sten Hanson, Bengt Emil Johnson, Ame Mellnäs, Jan W. Morthenson and Leo Nilson.

7 MAY 1978

On the second day of the 52nd Festival of the International Society for Contemporary Music, the following

program of chamber music is presented at an afternoon concert in Stockholm:

Miroirs for harpsichord and tape by the 40-year-old Canadian composer Micheline Coulombe SAINT-MARCOUX, consisting of six "moments" representing six "jeux de miroirs" (plain mirror, magic mirror, concavec mirror, parabolic mirror, extension mirror and superimposed mirror), all polyphonically mirrored; *Discantus III* for solo saxophone by the 40-year-old Finnish composer Paavo HEININEN, treating the saxophone as a lyric instrument as well as a playful jazz medium; *Inundations: Willow* for soprano, piano and tape by the British composer Stephen MONTAGUE, to a text limited to four words of various amorous implications; *The Lost Jugglery* for mezzo-soprano, cello, piano and percussion by the 28-year-old Swedish composer Mikael EDLUND, portraying the territorial struggle of several players seeking dominance; and *Toujours plus . . .* for harpsichord and organ by the 33-year-old French composer Graciane FINZI, a study in cumulative dodecaphony.

7 MAY 1978

The second day of the 52nd Festival of the International Society for Contemporary Music in Stockholm continues at an evening concert with the following program of orchestral works:

Partiels by the 32-year-old French composer Girard GRISEY, an analytic essay on the overtone series; *Consort Music* by the 31-year-old Austrian-born Finnish composer Herman RECH-BERGER, constructed of a series of ten subsidiary consorts, each formed by a Morse code rhythm; *Love-Charm Songs* for voice and orchestra by the 39-year-old Finnish composer Jarmo SERMILÄ, to texts from South American Tupi-Indian magic incantations; and *Inner Light III* by the 39-year-old British composer Jonathan HARVEY, being an invocation of the solipsistic notions of the philosopher Rudolf Steiner.

8 MAY 1978

On the third day of the 52nd Festival of the International Society for Contemporary Music, the following program of chamber music and multimedia works is presented at an afternoon concert in Stockholm:

Row Music for solo piano by the 39-yearold American composer William HELLERMANN, reflecting an Oriental mantra in a twelve-tone row derived from Alban Berg's *Mutterakkord; Il y a mille et mille soleils* for flute, harp and percussion by the French composer Nicole LACHARTRE, inspired by the notion of thousands of dying and resurrecting suns; *The Poem*, a video composition by the American composers Barbara SYKES, Tom DEFANTI, Drew BROWNING and Bob SNYDER; *Mobile* for solo cello by the Polish composer Anna MACIEJASZKAMINSKA, containing eighteen segments of which six are subdivided into sixty structural articulations; and *Inharmonique* for computer sounds and voice by the French composer Jean-Claude RISSET.

9 MAY 1978

Twelve weeks before his death, Carlos CHÁVEZ conducts at the InterAmerican Music Festival in Washington, D.C., the first performance of his *Trombone Concerto*.

9 MAY 1978

On the fourth day of the 52nd Festival of the International Society for Contemporary Music, an afternoon concert of chamber music with the following program is given in Helsinki:

Hirmos for soprano, alto, tenor, bass and chamber orchestra by the 49-year-old Greek composer Michael ADAMIS, to texts from medieval Byzantine hymnology; *Breath* for soprano, tape and chamber ensemble by the 48-year-old Japanese composer Hifumi SHIMOYAMA, to words from the Japanese traditional Noh drama; *Images* for electric piano, electric bass and two percussionists by the 33-year-old Canadian composer Donald STEVEN, consisting of seven miniatures designed to explore the musical dimensions of time and space; *Three Pieces for Piano* by the 55-year-old Uruguayan composer Hector TOSAR, based on thematic groups of three, four and twelve notes; *Bedu* for baritone and chamber ensemble by the 58-year-old Israeli composer Jacob GILBOA, in eight sections of metamorphoses of a Bedouin call; *Elixir*, a miniconcerto for flute and chamber ensemble by the 35-year-old American composer Joseph SCHWANTNER; and *Routine Investigations* by the 52-year-old American composer Morton FELDMAN, an esoteric inquiry into the nature of sound.

9 MAY 1978

On the fourth day of the 52nd Festival of the International Society for Contemporary Music taking place in Helsinki, the following program of orchestral music is given at an evening concert:

Topo Ostinato by the 42-year-old Iranian-born Austrian composer Iraj SCHIMI, a musical essay on the correlation of the composer's proclivities and a listener's propensities; *Concerto Seven*, "for Daniel in the lion's den," for violin and orchestra by the 37-year-old Austrian composer Dieter KAUFMANN, being fragments from *Concertomobil*, a symbol of constant inner struggle between the composer and performer; *Atembogen* by the 39-year-old Swiss oboe virtuoso and composer Heinz HOLLIGER, an idyll reigning between silence and sound; *Tide* by the 43-year-old Danish composer Bent LORENTZEN, progressing from a single tenuous tone to a sonoriferous finale; *Piano Concerto* in one movement by the 40-year-old Polish composer Zygmunt KRAUZE; and *The Turning Point* by the 34-year-old Finnish composer Pehr Henrik NORDGREN, inspired by a sojourn in a small Japanese village.

10 MAY 1978

On the fifth day of the 52nd Festival of the International Society for Contemporary Music, the following program of chamber music is presented at an afternoon concert in Helsinki:

Music for Upright Piano and Amplified Cello by the 51-year-old Finnish composer Einojuhani RAUTAVAARA; *Triptych* for three French horns by the 34-year-old Greek composer Agapitos AGAPITOS, a serially organized piece freely extending into an entire domain of available tones; *Solfatára* for saxophone and percussion by the 67-year-old Finnish composer Erik BERGMAN, inspired by the sulfuric fumes of an extinct volcano near Naples; *Divertimento* for violin and chamber orchestra by the 30-year-old Italian composer Umberto ROTONDI, based on a psychic automatism along surrealist lines; *Sinistro* for guitar and accordion by the 30-year-old Finnish composer Jukka TIENSUU, being a darksome synthesis of intuitive and stochastic formations; and *Nosotros (We)* for violin, clarinet, vibraphone and piano by the 38-year-old Spanish composer Jesús VILLA-ROJO, an individualistically collective invocation of experimental laboratory work.

10 MAY 1978

On the fifth day of the 52nd Festival of the International Society for Contemporary Music, the following program of chamber music is given at an evening concert in Helsinki:

Octet by the 43-yearold French composer François-Bernard MÂCHE, set in the traditional classical form with novel excrescences; *Sirato (Lament)* by the 61-year-old Hungarian composer Rudolf MAROS, derived from a Hungarian folk song expressing sorrow; *Akāša* for six trombones by the 30-year-old Finnish composer Mikko HEINIÖ, the title meaning the sound-carrying medium, with aleatory rhythms; *Relations* for flute and piano by the 47-year-old Japanese composer Makoto SHINOHARA, symbolizing a relationship between two persons in alternating cordiality and discord; *Music for Chambers* by the 37-year-old Italian-born American composer Marc-Antonio CONSOLI, an amalgam of three separate compositions; and *Six Turkish Folk Poems* by the 48-year-old Dutch composer Theo LOEVENDIE.

11 MAY 1978

On the sixth day of the 52nd Festival of the International Society for Contemporary Music, the following program of electroacoustic music is presented at an afternoon concert in Helsinki:

Traum des Einsamen (Dream of the Lonely One) by the 42-year-old Swedish composer Támás UNGVARY; *Music for the Morning of the World* for soprano with four-channel tape by the 45-year-old Canadian composer R. Murray SCHAFER, inspired by medieval Persian poetry, both erotic and religious; *Microhabitat* by the 39-year-old English-born Yugoslav composer Paul PIGNON, a musical reverberation of artificial intelligence; *. . . From Behind the Unreasoning Mask* for trombone, percussion and four-channel tape by the 44-year-old American composer Roger REYNOLDS, framed by six simultaneous transient events with some improvisatory intercalations; and *Rothko* by the 28-year-old Belgian composer Peter BEYLS, a musical reflection of the abstract expressionistic work of the suicidal painter Mark Rothko.

11 MAY 1978

The sixth day of the 52nd Festival of the international Society for Contemporary Music continues with the following program of orchestral music given at an evening concert at Helsinki:

In Memoriam by the 39-year-old Brazilian composer Marlos NOBRE, dedicated to the composer's father who was an amateur guitar player; *Spur* for accordion and orchestra by the 47-year-old Norwegian composer Arne NORDHEIM, the title suggesting an impulse generated in the subconscious; *Cantata Y* by the 43-year-old Hungarian composer Sandor BALASSA, composed for the 700th anniversary of the town of Györ; and *Time of Orchestral Time* by the 49-year-old Japanese composer Joji YUASA, in three parts, each designated to represent a single macrocosm lasting twenty minutes.

12 MAY 1978

On the seventh day of the 52nd Festival of the International Society for Contemporary Music, the following program of intermedia and music theater is presented in Helsinki:

Penetrations VI by the 49-year-old Argentine-Canadian composer Alcides LANZ; *Oedipe Sphinz/Crimes sans initiales* by the French composer Gherasim Luca-Gilles EHRMANN; and *Synchrone Klänge aus dem Rauschen* by the 35-year-old German composer Ulrike TRÜSTEDT, comprising elements of environmental noises and semiotics.

12 MAY 1978

Sixth Symphony by the Yugoslav composer Aleksandar OBRADOVIĆ, subtitled *Explicatio duplex, expressio triplex,* in three movements—*Allegro* for wind instruments, *Largo* for strings and *Finale* for full orchestra, repeating the musical contents of both previous movements (hence the Latin subtitle)—is performed for the first time in Belgrade.

13 MAY 1978

On the eighth day of the 52nd Festival of the International Society for Contemporary Music, the following program of chamber music is presented in Helsinki:

Voice of the Shades for soprano, violin and clarinet by the 39-year-old Australian composer Jennifer FOWLER; *Music for Violin Solo* by the 32-year-old American composer Daria SEMEGEN, in which the violin makes use of tone clusters and other unviolinistic sonorities; *Q for Five* for soprano saxophone and chamber ensemble by the 26-year-old British composer Jonty HARRISON, with Q assigned five different functions, including a cue and a queue; *Ritos* for harp by the 39-year-old Brazilian composer Ricardo TACUCHIAN, in which primitive Indian rituals are organized in a sophisticated modern technique; *I Am Goya*, to the text of Andrey Voznesensky, for bass baritone and chamber ensemble by the 30-year-old British composer Nigel OSBORNE, reminiscing of the hideous Russian war winter of 1941; and *Biálogo* for French horn, guitar and tape by the 28-year-old Portuguese composer Paulo BRANDÃO, a dialectic interchange between the guitar and the French horn resulting in a biological synthesis.

14 MAY 1978

On the ninth day of the 52nd Festival of the International Society for Contemporary Music, the following program of chamber music is presented at an afternoon concert ill Helsinki:

Metaboles IV for string quartet by the 32-year-old Austrian composer Klaus AGER, illustrating the musical metabolism through a seventy-two-tone system, including overtones and combination tones; *String Quartet No. 2* by the 37-year-old Finnish composer Erkki JOKINEN; *Cordes Plus* for viola and tape by the 42-year-old French composer Maurice BEN-HAMOU, in which the viola is given four extra strings (which explains the title); *Vĕdomí souvislosti (Imaginable Connections)* for string quartet by the 49-year-old Czech composer Václav KUČERA, in which a stream of dissonance leads to a final fugue; and *Mutationen XII* for string quintet and tape by the 59-year-old Brazilian composer Claudio SANTORO, representing the process of democratization of electronic music by giving the performers equal rights to decide what to play.

14 MAY 1978

The 52nd Festival of the International Society for Contemporary Music concludes in Helsinki with the following program of percussion music presented at an evening concert:

Redskap by the 27-year-old Swedish composer Klas TOR-STENSSON, the title meaning a tool for solving the problems of musical structure; *Campanella* by the 43-year-old Polish composer Zbigniew RUDZIŃSKI, in which a variety of bells and other metal percussion instruments results in a sonoriferous tintinnabulation (hence the title); *Sound First!* by the 51-year-old Japanese composer Michiharu MAT-SUNAGA, being an exclamatory celebration of sound as a primary element of all music; *A-Hun* by the 50-year-old Japanese composer Minoru KOBASHI, the title being a Sanskrit word beginning with the opening of the mouth and ending with the closing of it; and *Siderals*, an audiovisual composition by the 35-year-old Polish composer Marta PTASZYŃSKA, the title suggesting constellations that are in constant motion, requiring 117 percussion instruments to account for it.

22 MAY 1978

The National Afro-American Philharmonic Orchestra, with an all-black personnel, presents its first concert at the Academy of Music in Philadelphia under the direction of James Frazier.

30 MAY 1978

Fourth Symphony by the 75-year-old English composer Sir Lennox BERKELEY is performed for the first time by the Royal Philharmonic Orchestra under the direction of Sir Charles Groves in London.

2 JUNE 1978

A World Within, tape composition for ballet consisting of multitrack recordings of a horn by the 31-year-old British composer Giles SWAYNE, based on the life of the Brontë sisters, is performed for the first time in Stoke-on-Trent.

7 JUNE 1978

Thirteenth Symphony by the solipsistic Swedish composer Allan PETTERSSON is performed for the first time in Bergen, Norway.

9 JUNE 1978

Thirty-fifth Symphony by the interminably fruitful 67-year-old American composer Alan HOVHANESS, scored for Korean instruments and orchestra, is performed for the first time in Seoul, Korea.

16 JUNE 1978

The Two Fiddlers, opera for young people by the 43-year-old British composer Peter Maxwell DAVIES, is performed for the first time in Orkney.

21 JUNE 1978

Evita, a show by the 30-year-old British wonderboy of the musical theater, Andrew LLOYD WEBBER, based on the fantastic career of the cabaret singer who married the Argentine populist dictator Juan Perón, and who became an object of well-nigh goddesslike worship among the Argentine populace after her untimely death of cancer ("Don't cry for me, Argentina," she sings), is produced in London.

11 JULY 1978

Third Symphony, subtitled *Hommages* and paying tribute to both Haydn and Carl Nielsen, by the 39-year-old English composer John MCCABE is performed for the first time by the Royal Philharmonic Orchestra of London under the direction of Charles Dutoit.

13 JULY 1978

Second Symphony for vocal soloists, chorus and orchestra by the 53-year-old English composer Anthony MILNER is performed for the first time in Liverpool.

17 JULY 1978

Seven Pollock Paintings for eight wind and string players by the 25-year-old American composer Roger BOUR-LAND, in seven movements including *Eyes in the Heat, Peacocks Afraid of the Color, The Saint,* and *Lavender Mist,* with occasional use of literal musico-pictorial equivalences, receives its first ever performance at Tanglewood by members of the Berkshire Music Festival Orchestra, Patricia Handy conducting.

18 JULY 1978

Violin Concerto by the 49-year-old Soviet composer Edison DENISOV is performed for the first time in Milan.

2 AUGUST 1978

Carlos CHÁVEZ, thaumaturgical Mexican composer, conductor and educator whose works conveyed the essence of Latin American lore within the contrapuntal set of cosmopolitan musical science and who for years guided the destinies of new music of his land, dies in Mexico City at the age of 79.

5 AUGUST 1978

At a meeting of citizens of Parowan, Utah, it is resolved to name a local mountain Mt. Messiaen, in honor of the French composer Olivier MESSIAEN, who spent a month in Utah in 1973 and wrote a symphonic work, *Des Canyon aux etoiles,* to glorify the natural beauty of the state.

18 AUGUST 1978

The Duchess of Malfi, opera by the 35-year-old American composer Stephen Douglas BURTON, is produced at Wolf Trap Farm Park near Washington, D.C.

25 AUGUST 1978

Sunday Morning, eight-part symphonic suite by the American composer Ned ROREM, inspired by the eponymous poem by Wallace Stevens, is performed for the first time by the Philadelphia Orchestra in Saratoga Springs, New York, conducted by Eugene Ormandy.

5 SEPTEMBER 1978

Piano Concerto by the Soviet composer Edison DENISOV is performed for the first time in Leipzig.

8 SEPTEMBER 1978

Pantcho VLADIGEROV, prime Bulgarian composer whose ballets, symphonic music and chamber music are permeated with asymmetrical native melorhythms, dies in Sofia at the age of 79.

14 SEPTEMBER 1978

Essay No. 3 for orchestra by Samuel BARBER is performed for the first time by the New York Philharmonic, conducted by Zubin Mehta on his debut as the orchestra's newly appointed musical director.

26 OCTOBER 1978

First Symphony by the intransigent Dutch modern composer Peter SCHAT, commissioned by the city of Amsterdam to commemorate the 90th anniversary of the Concertgebouw Orchestra, is performed for the first time by that orchestra in Amsterdam, Colin Davis conducting.

2 NOVEMBER 1978

Viola Concerto by the 50-year-old American composer Jacob DRUCKMAN is performed for the first time by Sol Greitzer as soloist with the New York Philharmonic conducted by James Levine.

3 NOVEMBER 1978

Exotic Suite for two violins, two electric guitars, saxophone and percussion by the 46-year-old Soviet composer Sergei SLONIMSKY, in three parts—*Configurations, Love's Tears* and *Dance with a Tambourin*—is performed for the first time in Leningrad.

16 NOVEMBER 1978

Spatial Concerto, subtitled *Questions from "Genesis,"* for piano, sixteen women's voices and orchestra by the adventurous American composer Henry BRANT, in one continuous movement consisting of ten nonrecurring sections, with the pianist instructed to play on the strings under the lid, is performed for the first time by the Tucson Symphony, conducted by George Trautwein, with Hilde Somer as a courageous piano soloist.

17 NOVEMBER 1978

Dr. Heidegger's Fountain of Youth, opera by the 57-year-old American composer Jack BEESON, based on the story by Nathaniel Hawthorne, is produced for the first time in New York.

22 NOVEMBER 1978

Fourth Symphony by the American composer Easley BLACKWOOD is performed for the first time by the Chicago Symphony Orchestra conducted by Sir Georg Solti.

25 NOVEMBER 1978

Frankenstein!!, a "pandemonium" by the 35-year-old Austrian composer Heinz Karl GRUBER, for a baritone chansonnier who recites children's verses in a mockscary manner, and orchestra, is performed for the first time in London. (A version for a vocalist and a twelve-member ensemble was performed for the first time at the Berlin Festival of New Music on 30 September 1979.)

29 NOVEMBER 1978

Paradise Lost, "sacra rappresentazione" by the prime Polish modernist composer Krzysztof PENDERECKI, originally planned for a production during the 1976 American bicentennial, comes to a belated performance by the Lyric Opera of Chicago.

30 NOVEMBER 1978

Punainen viiva (The Red Line), opera by the 43-year-old Finnish composer Aulis SALLINEN, to the composer's own libretto based on a Finnish novel by Ilmari Kianto (1874–1970) dealing with an unexpected victory of women's suffrage in Finland in 1907 (the red line of the title was the mark of support on the new social order to be put on the ballot), set to music in a highly dramatic manner with a strong injection of Finnish folk modalities and an ample infusion of unambiguous dissonance, is performed for the first time in Helsinki. (The first American performance took place at the Metropolitan Opera in New York on 27 April 1983.)

2 DECEMBER 1978

Jazavac pred sudom (The Badger Before the Jury), the first nationalist opera of Bosnia by the 77-year-old composer Vlado MILOSEVIĆ, inspired by a folk legend wherein Austro-Hungarian rule in Bosnia is wittily satirized, is produced in Sarajevo (the historic locality where a Bosnian youth assassinated the heir to the Austrian throne in the summer of 1914, precipitating the First World War).

3 DECEMBER 1978

William Grant STILL, whose popularity earned for him the appellation "Dean of Afro-American Composers," and whose many works were profoundly infused with the pride of his race as expressed in his use of folklike thematic sources, dies in Los Angeles at the age of 83.

10 DECEMBER 1978

Syringa, cantata by the American composer Elliott CARTER, scored for soprano and chamber ensemble, is performed for the first time in New York.

18 DECEMBER 1978

Triple Concerto for clarinet, bass clarinet, contrabass clarinet and chamber orchestra by the 47-year-old American composer Donald MARTINO is performed for the first time by the Group for Contemporary Music, at the Manhattan School of Music in New York.

1979

9 JANUARY 1979

Un enfant appelle for soprano, cello and orchestra by the 63-year-old French composer Marcel LANDOWSKI, to poems of Marie-Noël, is performed for the first time in Washington, D.C., with Galina Vishnevskaya and Mstislav Rostropovich as spousal soloists.

11 JANUARY 1979

Gaku-no-Michi (Voices of Music) by the 40-year-old French composer Jean-Claude ELOY set for four tapes, originally recorded at the Nippon Studio of electronic music in Tokyo in 1978 with an admixture of concrete music, is performed publicly for the first time in its totality lasting four hours at the Autumn Festival in Paris.

16 JANUARY 1979

Thirty-sixth Symphony for solo flute and orchestra by the indefatigable Alan HOVHANESS is performed for the first time by Jean-Pierre Rampal and the National Symphony Orchestra in Washington, D.C., under the direction of Mstislav Rostropovich. On the same concert the *Contrabassoon Concerto*, the first concerto ever written for this instrument, plying the depths of the sound spectrum, by the learned American composer Gunther SCHULLER, receives its première with Lewis Lipnick as soloist.

18 JANUARY 1979

Reflections of Emily for treble voice, piano, harp and percussion by the 55-year-old American composer Peter

MENNIN, to texts from poems of Emily Dickinson, is performed for the first time in New York.

25 JANUARY 1979

The intransigent Italian avant-gardist Luciano BERIO conducts in Los Angeles the first performance of his *Ritorno degli Snovidenia (Return of Dreams; snovidenia* is a Russian word for dream visions) for cello and thirty instruments.

29 JANUARY 1979

Affertones of Infinity, symphonic poem by the American composer Joseph SCHWANTNER, which won the 1979 Pulitzer Prize, is performed for the first time by the New York Philharmonic, Lukas Foss conducting.

29 JANUARY 1979

Third Violin Concerto by the 44-year-old Soviet composer Alfred SCHNITTKE is performed for the first time in Moscow.

3 FEBRUARY 1979

Galileo Galilei, opera by the American composer Ezra LADERMAN, originally written as an oratorio for television, to the libretto by Joe Darion, is performed for the first time in Binghamton, New York.

3 FEBRUARY 1979

Musique pour un Vernissage by the 40-year-old American composer Barbara KOLB, scored for flute, violin, viola and guitar, originally intended to be played as "furniture music" or "music to walk by" à la Satie, is premièred as a concert piece at the Kennedy Center in Washington, D.C., Leon Fleischer conducting.

10 FEBRUARY 1979

A *Solo Requiem* for soprano and two pianos by the 62-year-old American composer of mathematical bent Milton BABBITT is performed for the first time in New York.

24 FEBRUARY 1979

Lulu, opera by Alban BERG with the unfinished third act completed by Friedrich CERHA, is performed for the first time in its enhanced version in Paris with Pierre Boulez conducting.

1 MARCH 1979

Palintropos for piano and orchestra by the 35-year-old British composer John TAVENER is performed for the first time in Birmingham, England.

7 MARCH 1979

Klaus EGGE, romantically inclined, intellectually inventive Norwegian composer, who signed his scores with the autobiographical notes E-g-g-e, dies in Oslo at the age of 72.

17 MARCH 1979

Orpheus, a story in six scenes by the 52-year-old German composer Hans Werner HENZE, is given its world première by the Württemberg State Opera in Stuttgart.

24 MARCH 1979

Concerto for flute, oboe and orchestra by the 49-year-old Soviet composer Edison DENISOV is performed for the first time by Aurele Nicolet and Heniz Holligev as soloists with the orchestra of the West German Republic in Cologne.

10 APRIL 1979

Nino ROTA, Italian composer of operas, oratorios, and symphonic works in a pleasingly modernized settecento manner, dies in Rome at the age of 67.

11 APRIL 1979

Teuta, ballet in three acts by the 73-year-old Croatian composer Boris PAPANDOPULO, glorifying in martial sonorities the imperious Queen Teuta of the once powerful ancient kingdom of Illyria on the eastern shores of the Adriatic, who daringly defied Rome until she was finally subdued by the Roman navy in 228 B.C., is produced in Novi Sad, Yugoslavia.

12 APRIL 1979

Fifteenth Symphony, with chorus, subtitled "*I have faith in this earth,*" by the 59-year-old Soviet composer Moisei VAINBERG, is performed for the first time in Moscow.

20 APRIL 1979

Sial for Baroque instruments and chamber ensemble by the 60-year-old Croatian composer Branimir SAKAČ, representing in musical terms the two principal elements of the earth's crust, silicon (Si) and aluminum (Al), is performed for the first time in Zagreb.

22 APRIL 1979

Miracles for boys' choir and orchestra by Gian Carlo MENOTTI, to words from verses written by children, is performed for the first time in Fort Worth, Texas.

28 APRIL 1979

Concerto piccolo for a saxophone player performing alternatively on four saxophones (bass, tenor, alto, soprano) and for six percussionists by the 50-year-old Soviet composer Edison DENISOV is performed for the first time in Bordeaux.

28 APRIL 1979

Mangrove for orchestra by the Australian composer Peter SCULTHORPE is performed for the first time in Sydney, on the eve of his 50th birthday.

30 APRIL 1979

Full Moon in March, opera by the 40-year-old American composer John HARBISON, to a text by Yeats, is performed for the first time in Cambridge, Massachusetts.

1 MAY 1979

Cheers for orchestra by the brilliant American composer Morton GOULD is performed for the first time in Boston.

2 MAY 1979

Quintets for orchestra by the 57-year-old American composer Lukas FOSS is performed for the first time in Cleveland.

3 MAY 1979

Medea, opera by the 52-year-old American composer Ray LUKE, is produced in Boston.

4 MAY 1979

Eighth Symphony by the 57-year-old English composer Malcolm ARNOLD is performed for the first time by the Albany (New York) Symphony.

18 MAY 1979

As of a Dream by the 66-year-old American composer Norman DELLO JOIO, scored for narrator, chorus and orchestra to a text by Walt Whitman, is performed for the first time in Midland, Michigan.

19 MAY 1979

Animalen (The Animals), opera by the 53-year-old Swedish composer Lars Johan WERLE, to a libretto treating the fateful antagonism between America and Russia in which representatives of both nations hurl their slogans at each other, but whose enmity is unexpectedly challenged by the animals of the world who force both sides to reconcile their differences, is produced in Göteborg.

3 JUNE 1979

La Loca, opera by the 67-year-old Italian-born composer Gian Carlo MENOTTI, commissioned by the San Diego Opera to honor the quinquegenarian opera mistress Beverly Sills, based on the trne story of fifteenth-century Juana of Castile who goes mad after her husband, father and son try to usurp her throne and contrive to have her incarcerated for nearly fifty years, is produced in San Diego, with Sills herself in the leading role.

5 JUNE 1979

Kentervilski duh (The Ghost of Canterville), comic opera by the 73-year-old Croatian composer Boris PAPANDOPU-LO, after the satirically fantastic tale by Oscar Wilde, is produced in Osijek.

9 JUNE 1979

Aureole for orchestra by the American composer Jacob DRUCKMAN, commissioned by and dedicated to Leonard Bernstein, is performed for the first time by the New York Philharmonic Orchestra, Bernstein conducting.

17 JUNE 1979

Concerto Festivo by the 64-year-old Polish composer Andrzej PANUFNIK, in three movements, *Pomposo* for brass only, *Lirico* for strings and wood-winds and *Giocoso* for full orchestra, is performed for the first time by the London Symphonic Orchestra, without a conductor.

21 JUNE 1979

Octet by the 42-year-old American composer Steve REICH, scored for string quartet, two pianos and two clarinets (doubling on flute and piccolo), is performed for the first time by members of the Netherlands Wind Ensemble under the direction of Reinbert de Leeuw, at Radio Frankfurt.

23 JUNE 1979

Symphonie en l'honneur du Soleil by the 82-year-old French composer Jean RIVIER is performed for the first time on the "Day of the Sun" in Paris, as a commission of the French Ministry of Culture.

27 JUNE 1979

Paul DESSAU, German composer, one of the most fervent and intelligent practitioners of socialist music in a fitting amalgam with *Gebrauchsmusik,* who however refused to abandon his endemic experimentalism, dies in East Berlin at the age of 84.

10 JULY 1979

Arthur FIEDLER, Boston-born and -bred scion of a German-Jewish family of musicians, who from a humble beginning as a viola player in the Boston Symphony rose to the heights of pop fame as conductor of the celebrated Boston Pops Orchestra, ministered to a relaxed summer audience undisturbed by the clinking of beer mugs and clanking of salad dishes, dies in Brookline, Massachusetts, of a recurrent heart attack at the age of 84, just short of completing half a century of presiding over the Pops, and deeply mourned by the people of Boston.

12 JULY 1979

Hymn for chorus and orchestra by the 40-year-old British composer Jonathan HARVEY, written for the 900th anniversary of the Winchester Cathedral, is performed there for the first time.

23 JULY 1979

"Music is no different from opium. . . . Opium produces one kind of sensitivity and lack of energy, music another. . . . Music is a treason to our country, . . . and we should cut it out and replace it with something instructive" (Ayatollah Khomeini, Ramadan exhortation to revolutionary masses in Teheran).

9 AUGUST 1979

Nymph and Satyr, ballet by the 82-year-old American composer Howard HANSON, is performed for the first time in Chautauqua, Tennessee.

20 AUGUST 1979

The Winter's Tale, opera after Shakespeare by the 40-year-old American composer John HARBISON, is performed for the first time in San Francisco.

6 SEPTEMBER 1979

Third Symphony by the 27-year-old British composer Oliver KNUSSEN is performed for the first time by the BBC Symphony Orchestra in London.

10 SEPTEMBER 1979

Stanislaus LUDKEWYCZ, Polish composer and educator, who composed romantic tone poems and piano works inspired by Ukrainian lore, and who as a soldier in the Austrian army was taken prisoner by the Russians in the First World War, dies in Lwów (after 1945 spelled Lvov as part of the Ukrainian Socialist Republic) at the all but incredible age of one hundred, honored by the Soviet government with the Order of the Red Banner.

11 SEPTEMBER 1979

The 53rd Festival of the International Society for Contemporary Music opens in Athens with the following program:

Das Glashaus, operetta for seven musicalizing actors by the 42-year-old Swiss composer Hans WÜTHRICH-MATHEZ, conducted by the composer; *Minimal* for bass clarinet, electronic manipulations and automatic percussion by the 28-year-old German-born Dutch composer Michael FAHRES; *The Horn of Plenty,* a musical cornucopia for amplified horn, percussion and tape by the 43-year-old Belgian composer Claude A. COPPENS, with the rhythmic organization derived from all prime numbers up to 1,453 (the year when Constantinople fell to the Turks), in five acts symbolizing the senses of the eye, the ear, the brain, the tongue and the nose; and *Kijo,* theater piece for baritone and five percussionists by the 51-year-old Japanese composer Minoru KOBASHI.

12 SEPTEMBER 1979

On the second day of the 53rd Festival of the International Society for Contemporary Music in Athens, the following program of Swiss music is presented at an afternoon concert:

Zeitraum for violin, alto flute, cello and bass clarinet by 36-year-old Urs Peter SCHNEIDER; *Von Magischem Nr. 7* by 35-year-old Peter STREIFF, scored for two horns, organ, two strings and piano, based on an automatic script in graphic notation; and *Schattenküsse* for solo piano by 36-year-old Rolland MOSER, written in an ostentatiously comprehensible idiom.

12 SEPTEMBER 1979

On the second day of the 53rd Festival of the International Society for Contemporary Music in Athens, the following program is given at an early evening concert:

Piano Duo by the 33-year-old Italian composer Luca LOMBARDI; *Blick der Natur* for soprano, mezzo-soprano, clarinet, horn and percussion by the 51-year-old Slovenian composer Jakob JEŽ with a text of pure acoustic quality without imposition of a specific means; *Intervals* for chamber choir, flute, cello and harp by the 45-year-old Dutch composer Joep STRAESSER; *Refractions* for two amplified pianos by the 36-year-old Swedish composer Mats PERSSON, symbolizing an acoustic refraction of several different sounds; *Stabat Mater* for a cappella choir by the 33-year-old Norwegian composer Olav Anton THOMMESSEN; and *Beta* by the 43-year-old Austrian composer Klaus AGER, originally intended for the duration of twenty-four hours and requiring forty-eight vocalists, forty-eight percussion players, and twelve tam-tams, ballet and lights, with performers executing bilabial and dental vocables, striving to achieve an unending flow of sound.

12 SEPTEMBER 1979

The second day of the 53rd Festival of the International Society for Contemporary Music continues in Athens, with a late night concert featuring the following program of electronic works:

Cellule 75 for piano, percussion and tape by the 33-year-old French composer Luc FERRARI; *Homenaje a la flecha clavada en el pecho de Don Juan Deaz de Solis (Homage to the arrow plunged into the breast of Don Juan Deaz de Solis)* for tape by the 39-year-old Uraguayan composer Coriún AHARONIAN; and *En Pyri (In Fire)* by the 46-year-old Macedonian composer Stephanos VASSILIADIAS, scored for amplified double-bass, tape and projections, in memory of the great Greek composer Jani Christou who perished in an automobile accident.

13 SEPTEMBER 1979

On the third day of the 53rd Festival of the International Society for Contemporary Music in Athens the following program is given in an afternoon concert:

Sol-Jay by the Australian composer Helen STANDRING, scored for two trombones and concerned with the psychology of freedom; *Stichomythia II* for solo guitar by the 44-year-old Greek composer Theodore ANTONIOU; *Colori* for solo piano by the 44-year-old Danish composer Bent LORENTZEN, in five movements symbolized by five perceived colors, red, white, gold, azure and black, with the last movement reflecting the Latin American music of black composers; *Inter-mezzo* for six flutes by the 39-year-old Slovak composer Juraj BENES; ac, the metrical foundation being represented by a minim divided into six to eleven semiquavers; *Piano Piece I* by the 45-year-old Berlin-born composer Erhard

GROSSKOPF, conceived as a quasi sonata; CELLO EINSATZ for solo cello by the 48-year-old East German composer Paul-Heinz DITTRICH; and *Syneirmoni (Associations)* for chamber ensemble by the 69-year-old Hellenist Yannis PAPAIOANNOU.

13 SEPTEMBER 1979

On the third day of the 53rd Festival of the International Society for Contemporary Music in Athens, the following program of modern Hungarian music is given at an evening concert:

Capricorn Concerto for chamber orchestra by the 46-year-old Miklós KOCSÁR; *Monologo*, for violin by the 48-year-old László KALMÁR; *Quartet* by the 49-year-old László SÁRY, based on a serial set of tones, rhythms and dynamics; *Improvisation* for cimbalom by the 46-year-old István LÁNG; *Improvisations I* for zither solo by the 40-year-old Attila BOZAY; *Eight Duos* for violin and cimbalom and *In Memory of a Winter Sunset* for soprano, violin and cimbalom by the 53-year-old György KURTA; aag; and *Pro Somno Igoris Stravinsky Quieto*, a memorial piece for chamber ensemble by the 58-year-old András SZÖLLÖZY.

14 SEPTEMBER 1979

On the fourth day of the 53rd Festival of the International Society for Contemporary Music in Athens a special presentation is given at Delphi of *The Midnight Sun* by the 50-year-old Japanese composer Joji YUASA, a double homage to Apollo, Greek god of the Sun, and Amaterasu, the Japanese sun god.

15 SEPTEMBER 1979

On the fifth day of the 53rd Festival of the International Society for Contemporary Music in Athens, an afternoon concert is given with the following program:

Tromboffolón for horn, trumpet, trombone (interchangeable with tuba) and tape by the 49-year-old Uruguayan composer Ariel MARTÍNEZ; *Tayutai* for koto and baritone by the 47-year-old Japanese composer Makoto SHINOHARA, analyzing psychological dilemmas between hope and despair; *Korpus et Antikorpus* by the 36-year-old Brazilian composer Agnaldo RIBEIRO, scored for thirteen instruments and representing the sonic battle between life-asserting generators (corpus) and life-denying sound generators (anticorpus); *Encomium to Skalkottas* for solo clarinet by the 50-year-old Greek composer Nikos MAMANGAKIS, being an homage to the late Greek composer Nikos Skalkottas; *Arsis* for flute, two pianos, two percussionists and double-bass by the 26-year-old Venezuelan composer Emilio MENDOZA; *Il Fa-To-Re* for solo recorder by the 32-year-old Austrian-born Finnish composer Herman RECHBERGER, the tonal materials being derived from the three notes F, B-flat and G; and *Stationen* for wind ensemble by the 30-year-old German composer Raimund JÜLICH.

15 SEPTEMBER 1979

The fifth day of the 53rd Festival of the International Society for Contemporary Music in Athens continues with an evening concert presenting the following program of Polish music:

Quartet for four actors consisting of twenty-five musical and nonmusical scenes by the 50-year-old foremost empiricist Boguslaw SCHAEFFER; *Spirale II* by 49-year-old Loencjusz SIUCIURA, scored for flute, cello, harpsichord, celesta and piano; *Dichromia* for flute and piano by 51-year-old Adam

WALACIŃSKI, a study in contrasts of two colors; *Lamentation* by 54-year-old Andrzej NIKODEMOWICZ, scored for soprano, flute, cello and two pianos; *C'est-à-dire* by 33-year-old Józef RYCHLIK, scored for flute, cello, harpsichord, two pianos and tape, the title being an explicative French expression meaning "that is to say"; *Bel canto* for soprano, cello, celesta and percussion by Krystyna MOSZUMARŃSKA-NAZAR; and *Heraklitiana* by Boguslaw SCHAEFFER, a spectacle for four actors (speaking four different European languages), piano and tape, inspired by the maxim of Heraclitus that all life is motion.

16 SEPTEMBER 1979

The sixth day of the 53rd Festival of the International Society for Contemporary Music in Athens continues with an evening concert presenting the following program of Austrian music:

Scenes from the opera *Daidalia oder das Leben einer Theorie* by the 58-year-old Bulgarian-born ethnically Greek composer, resident of Austria, Anestis LOGOTHETIS; *Curriculum* for thirteen wind instruments by the 53-year-old Austrian modernist and scholar Friedrich CERHA; *Gegenstimme* for voice, cello and tape by 38-year-old Wilhelm ZOBL; *Cacophony-Euphony* for actress, tape and live electronics by 38-year-old Dieter KAUFMANN, representing the dichotomous imbalance of dissonances and consonances; *Sonata* for solo cello by the 60-year-old Polish-born cosmopolitan composer Roman HAUBENSTOCK-RAMATI; and *Frankenstein Suite*, a "pandemonium" for baritone, quintet and toy instruments by 36-year-old Karl Heinz GRUBER.

17 SEPTEMBER 1979

Fifth Symphony for string Orchestra by the 36-year-old Polish composer Krzysztof MEYER is performed for the first time in Bialystok.

17 SEPTEMBER 1979

On the seventh day of the 53rd Festival of the International Society for Contemporary Music in Athens, an afternoon concert is given featuring the following works:

Piano by the 53-year-old American ultramodernist Morton FELDMAN; *Quartet* for flute and strings by the 50-year-old Greek composer Michael ADAMIS; *Quilisma* for piano and string quartet by the 47-year-old Italian composer Niccolo CASTIGLIONI; *Strangeness, Charm, and Color* for piano, two trumpets and trombone by the 36-year-old German composer Rolf GELHAAR, portraying the subatomic particles (quarks, whose characteristics arc denoted by the titular terms), in their constant collisions, consisting of twenty-seven exponentially related structures; and *Liturgia Profana* by the Greek composer Dimitris TERZAKIS, scored for choir, soloists, cellos and percussion.

17 SEPTEMBER 1979

The seventh day of the 53rd Festival of the International Society for Contemporary Music in Athens continues with a late-afternoon concert of modern British chamber music, in the following program:

Solo/Ensemble by the 27-year-old Dominic MULDOWNEY, scored for percussion soloist and ensemble of piano, flute, clarinet, viola, and cello, and requiring the percussionist to move among his three groups of instruments as part of a "ritualized game"; *Cantata* for oboe and string trio by the 27-year-old Oliver KNUSSEN; and *Ave Maris Stella* by the 45-year-old Peter Maxwell DAVIES, scored for flute, clarinet, violin, cello, piano, and percussion and based on the familiar plainsong of the same title.

17 SEPTEMBER 1979

The seventh day of the 53rd Festival of the International Society for Contemporary Music in Athens continues with a late evening concert of the following program of electronic music:

Terrortorium for tape by the 30-year-old Greek composer Vanghelis KATSOULIS, portraying the apocalyptic horrors of life and death; *Androgyny* for quadraphonic tape by the 32-year-old Canadian composer Barry TRUAX, inspired by the *I Ching,* implying the simultaneous presence of the male/female elements; *Antiphony I* for tape by the 50-year-old Greek composer Nikiphoros ROTAS; and *Myr* for computer-controlled tape, electronic transformations and slide projections by the 28-year-old Swedish composer Roll ENSTRÖM, representing the chaotic state of the world and the necessity of mankind to prove its right to exist.

18 SEPTEMBER 1979

On the eighth day of the 53rd Festival of the International Society for Contemporary Music in Athens, the following program of American music is presented at an afternoon concert:

Synchronisms No. 6 for piano and electronic sounds by the 45-year-old Argentine-born American composer Mario DAVIDOVSKY; *Granites* for piano by the 84-year-old composer/astrologer Dane RUDHYAR, written in 1929, representing a continuity of sonorities in its five connected sections; *Philomel* for soprano and tape by the 63-year-old musical mathematician Milton BABBITT, inspired by the myth of Philomel who acquired the voice of a nightingale after she was raped by the King of Thrace, with the various mutations arranged in serial tropes; *Two Stevens Songs* for soprano and tape by 38-year-old John MELBY to the text of two poems by Wallace Stevens; and *Five Pieces for Piano* by the 82-year-old master of American music Roger SESSIONS, written in the modified twelve-tone system.

18 SEPTEMBER 1979

The eighth day of the 53rd Festival of the International Society for Contemporary Music continues in Athens with the Danish Radio Symphony Orchestra presenting the following program at an evening concert:

The Statue of III by the 33-year-old Japanese composer Katsuhiro TSUBONOH; *Music in Twilight* for piano and orchestra by the 40-year-old Polish composer Tomasz SIKORSKI, in a single movement; *Flute Concerto* by the 47-year-old Icelandic composer Atli Heimir SVEINSSON; and *Twilight* by the 47-year-old Danish composer Per NØRGÅRD.

18 SEPTEMBER 1979

At a special archaeological event at the Philopappos Hill facing the Acropolis in Athens in the context of the Fifty-third Festival of the International Society for Contemporary Music, a multimedia spectacle is presented at night with music by the 28-year-old French composer Patrick FLEURY under the title *Espace IX.*

19 SEPTEMBER 1979

On the ninth day of the 53rd Festival of the International Society for Contemporary Music in Athens two concerts of music by the greatly esteemed and deeply mourned Greek composer Nikos SKALKOTTAS (1904–1949) are presented, including thirty-six piano pieces, an overture, violin concerto and *Symphony* in one movement, subtitled *The Return of Ulysses*.

20 SEPTEMBER 1979

On the tenth day of the 53rd Festival of the International Society for Contemporary Music in Athens the following program of chamber music is presented at an afternoon concert:

Carols for solo trombone and percussion by the 25-year-old Rumanian composer Serban NICHIFOR; *Fast Dances, Slow Dances* for piano by the 33-year-old British composer Michael FINNISSY, performed by the composer; *La espiral eterna* for solo guitar by the 40-year-old Cuban composer Leo BROUWER; *Mono-status* for three clarinets by the 26-year-old British composer Avril ANDERSON; and *Tremor* for violin and tape by the 39-year-old Swedish composer Jan W. MORTHENSON.

20 SEPTEMBER 1979

The 53rd Festival of the International Society for Contemporary Music in Athens concludes with the following program of chamber music at an evening concert:

Carmen Criaturalis for solo horn, strings, and percussion by the Argentine composer Alicia TERZIAN; *Ach, trauriger Mond (Oh, Sad Moon)* for percussion and chamber orchestra by the 31-year-old German composer Theo BRANDMÜLLER, a lament for Federico García Lorca, murdered by the Falangists during the Spanish Civil War; *God's Duet* from *Les Enfants du Sable* for baritone, soprano and chamber ensemble by the 37-year-old Greek composer Georg COUPOUROS; *Dasselbe ist nicht dasselbe (The Same Is Not the Same)* for solo side drum by the 40-year-old German composer Nikolaus A. HUBER, expressing the self-contradiction of all music; *Sternengesang* for chamber orchestra by the 32-year-old Lithuanian-born Israeli composer Michael BAROLSKY, reflecting the tenets of Kabbalistic mysticism; and *Canción desesperada* for soprano, two basses and chamber orchestra by the 38-year-old Spanish composer Francisco OTERO.

29 SEPTEMBER 1979

Ivan WYSCHNEGRADSKY, Russian composer who for years lived in France and wrote music in quarter tones and other microtonal intervals, and who enjoyed recognition within a circumscribed group of admirers of his fine character and of his distinguished talent, dies in Paris at the age of 86.

30 SEPTEMBER 1979

Te Deum for soloists, chorus, and orchestra by the foremost Polish composer Krzysztof PENDERECKI, who combines ultramodernism with fervent Catholicism, is performed for the first time in Assisi, Italy.

1 OCTOBER 1979

Thérèse, opera by the 35-year-old British composer John TAVENER, is produced at Covent Garden in London.

1 OCTOBER 1979

Roy HARRIS, extraordinary American composer whose symphonies and chamber music reflect in their rough-

hewed harmonies and modally inflected melodies the stark sound of essential America, who found symbolic significance in the circumstance of his birth in Lincoln County, Oklahoma, on Lincoln's birthday, dies in Santa Monica, California, at the age of 81.

10 OCTOBER 1979

Apocalyptica, "scenic vision" by the 55-year-old Croatian composer Milko KELEMEN, a multimedia spectacle wherein biblical associations serve as allegorical symbols for the alienation of people of the totalitarian and atomic era, is produced in Graz, Austria.

20 OCTOBER 1979

Opus Cygne for flute and orchestra by the 48-year-old Italian composer Sylvano BUSSOTTI is performed for the first time in Baden-Baden, West Germany.

22 OCTOBER 1979

Nadia BOULANGER, the legendary nourrice of several generations of American composers, including Aaron Copland, Roy Harris, Walter Piston, Virgil Thomson, Elliott Carter and David Diamond, as well as of such moderns as Igor Markevich, Jean Françaix, Lennox Berkeley and Dinu Lipati, whose own artistic credo was encompassed within the neoclassical traditions of Stravinsky and Ravel, dies in Paris, blind and nearly deaf, at the age of 92.

25 OCTOBER 1979

Violin Concerto by the 59-year-old American composer Earl KIM is performed for the first time by Itzhak Perlman and the New York Philharmonic Orchestra under the direction of Zubin Mehta.

2 NOVEMBER 1979

Arctica for orchestra by the Finnish composer Erik BERGMAN is performed for the first time in Utrecht, Holland.

16 NOVEMBER 1979

The Donner Party, "dramatic opera in three acts" by the American composer Ronald MCFARLAND, to the story of stranded travelers in the Rockies in the winter of 1846 who resorted to cannibalism of dead comrades to survive, is produced for the first time at Chico State University in California. (The second performance took place on 31 July 1982, at the Squaw Valley Theater in the historic town of Squaw Valley, near Donner Pass in Nevada.)

16 NOVEMBER 1979

Amorgos by the 44-year-old French composer François-Bernard MÂCHE, scored for twelve instruments and sea waves recorded at Amorgos Island of the Cyclades group of the Greek Aegean Islands, is performed for the first time in concert form at a festival in Metz, France.

18 NOVEMBER 1979

Celestial Mechanics, subtitled *Makrokosmos IV*, cosmic dances for amplified piano, four hands, by the 50-year-old American composer George CRUMB, is performed for the first time in New York.

24 NOVEMBER 1979

Second Symphony by the 47-year-old Soviet composer Sergei SLONIMSKY, in three movements: *Andante,* in which three basic themes intertwine creating a shimmering succession of alternatingly lyric, dramatic and elegiac moods; *Vivace ben ritmato,* permeated with urban refrains and plunging into the syncopated rhythms of Soviet jazz; and *Lento cantabile,* leading to the fugal finale in an ornamental *ricercar,* is performed for the first time in Leningrad, Gennady Rozhdestvensky conducting.

29 NOVEMBER 1979

Flores musicales for violin, oboe, cello and psaltery electronically manipulated by the 36-year-old composer Ivan TCHEREPNIN, son of Alexander Tcherepnin, grandson of Nicholas Tcherepnin, is performed for the first time in Boston.

3 DECEMBER 1979

Eleven young rock fans die of asphyxiation, crushed by multitudes at the doors outside Riverfront Coliseum in Cincinnati trying to get seats to hear a concert by the pronominally named British group, THE WHO.

7 DECEMBER 1979

A *Christmas Carol,* opera by the remarkable Scottish composer Thea MUSGRAVE, is performed for the first time by the Virginia Opera Association in Norfolk.

9 DECEMBER 1979

Concerto for piano and string orchestra by the 45-year-old Soviet composer Alfred SCHNITTKE is performed for the first time in Leningrad.

16 DECEMBER 1979

Not by Might, oratorio based on the Books of the Maccabees by the 41-year-old American organist and composer Simon SARGON, is performed for the first time in Dallas, Texas.

30 DECEMBER 1979

Richard RODGERS, greatly endowed American composer of popular music whose *South Pacific* became a Broadway classic, dies in New York at the age of 77.

1980

17 JANUARY 1980

Ninth Symphony by the highly significant, independently thinking American composer Roger SESSIONS, in three movements, incorporating for the first time in his music a full-fledged twelve-tone row, is given its world première by the Syracuse (New York) Symphony Orchestra, Christopher Keene conducting.

17 JANUARY 1980

Gradations for orchestra by the Soviet composer Vladimir ZAGORTSEV is performed for the first time, 14 years after its completion, by the New York Philharmonic, Zubin Mehta conducting.

24 JANUARY 1980

Three Colloquies for French horn and orchestra by the 69-year-old American composer William SCHUMAN is performed for the first time by Philip Myers as virtuoso soloist with the New York Philharmonic Orchestra directed by Zubin Mehta.

25 JANUARY 1980

Second Violin Concerto by the recondite Swedish composer Allan PETTERSSON, employing some of his own ballad tunes, is performed for the first time on the Swedish Radio in Stockholm.

8 FEBRUARY 1980

Erschöpfung der Welt (Exhaustion of the World), opera by the Argentine-born German-radicated noumenally cosmopolitan composer Mauricio KAGEL, is produced in Stuttgart.

19 FEBRUARY 1980

Variations for winds, strings and keyboards by the 43-year-old soi-disant minimalist American composer Steve REICH is performed for the first time in New York. (A revised version for full orchestra was first performed by the San Francisco Symphony on 14 May 1980.)

23 FEBRUARY 1980

In Memory of a Summer Day for soprano and orchestra by the American composer David DEL TREDICI, Part I of his serial tone poems *Child Alice,* inspired by Lewis Carroll's children's classic, and which won for him the 1980 Pulitzer Prize, is performed for the first time with Phyllis Bryn-Julson, soprano, and the St. Louis Symphony Orchestra, Leonard Slatkin conducting. (Part II was first performed 13 September 1980, Part III 8 May 1981, Part IV 19 November 1981.)

1 MARCH 1980

The Cry of Clytaemnestra, opera by the 45-year-old American composer John EATON, is performed for the first time in Bloomington, Indiana.

5 MARCH 1980

Ringed by the Flat Horizon for orchestra by the 20-year-old British composer George BENJAMIN is performed for the first time in Cambridge.

23 MARCH 1980

Joan TOWER plays in New York for the first time her piano work *Petroushskates*, having a dual allegiance to Stravinsky's ballet and Olympic Games ice skaters.

28 MARCH 1980

Farne for orchestra by the 32-year-old British composer Nicola LEFANU is performed for the first time in Bradford.

29 MARCH 1980

Annunzio Paolo MANTOVANI, Italian conductor and composer of popular music, who became a British subject and achieved fame as the harmonious creator of the melodious "Mantovani sound" conducive to listening pleasure among worldwide multitudes, dies in Tunbridge Wells at the age of 74.

1 APRIL 1980

The Trumpet Major, opera after Thomas Hardy by the 50-year-old Welsh composer Alun HODDINOTT, is produced in Manchester.

5 APRIL 1980

Max BRAND, Austrian composer, a pioneer of modern "machine music" of which his opera *Maschinist Hopkins*, to his own libretto, was an examplar, dies in undeserved oblivion at Langenzersdorf, near Vienna, at the age of 83.

7 APRIL 1980

Sixth Symphony by the 44-year-old Soviet Georgian composer Giya KANCHELI is performed for the first time in Tbilisi. (A revised version was given in Leipzig on 22 October 1981, conducted by Kurt Masur.)

12 APRIL 1980

Iubilum for orchestra by the remarkable Argentine composer Alberto GINASTERA, commissioned for the 400th anniversary of the city of Buenos Aires, is performed for the first time there in the Teatro Colón.

23 APRIL 1980

Cello Concerto by the 52-year-old Serbian composer Aleksandar OBRADOVIĆ is performed for the first time in Belgrade.

23 APRIL 1980

Second Symphony, subtitled *St. Florian*, for chorus and orchestra by the 45-year-old Soviet avant-garde composer Alfred SCHNITTKE, is performed for the first time anywhere by the BBC Symphony Orchestra in London, Gennadi Rozhdestvensky conducting.

1 MAY 1980

Second Symphony, subtitled *Christmas Symphony*, by the 46-year-old Polish composer Krzysztof PENDERECKI, containing a musicial quotation from the hymn *Silent Night*, is performed for the first time by the New York Philharmonic at Avery Fisher Hall in New York, under the direction of Zubin Mehta, to whom the score is dedicated.

8 MAY 1980

Copernicus (Rituel de mort), chamber opera for soloists, instrumentalists and tape by the 32-year-old Canadian composer Claude VIVIER, is produced in Montreal.

10 MAY 1980

A Lyric Symphony by the 53-year-old American composer Robert WYKES is performed for the first time in St. Louis, Missouri.

12 MAY 1980

Piano Concerto by the 41-year-old American composer John HARBISON, written in an effective manner deliberately using the lyrical, dramatic and prestidigital techniques of yore, while retaining the thematic anchors of free atonality and euphonious dissonances, is performed for the first time by the American Composers Orchestra in New York, Gunther Schuller conducting, with Robert Miller as soloist. (It subsequently received the Kennedy Center Award for playable American instrumental music.)

14 MAY 1980

Folk Sinfonia by the 62-year-old Yugoslav composer Boris ULRICH, a collage of medieval and Renaissance elements combined with folkloric motives, culminating with a metamorphosed quotation from Monteverdi's *Incoronazione di Poppea*, is performed for the first time in Zagreb. (It was also produced as a ballet in Zagreb on 9 May 1981.)

18 MAY 1980

Jesu Hochzeit, opera by the 62-year-old Austrian composer Gottfried VON EINEM, in which Christ takes a wife, scandalizing the whole of Christendom, is produced in Vienna.

21 MAY 1980

Prism for orchestra by the American composer Jacob DRUCKMAN is performed for the first time by the Baltimore Symphony Orchestra under the direction of Sergiu Comissiona.

24 MAY 1980

Far calls, Coming far! for violin and orchestra by the 49-year-old Japanese modernist Torui TAKEMITSU, the title being taken from the final paragraph of James Joyce's *Finnegans Wake*, and based on a motive of six notes (E-flat, E, A, C-sharp, F and A-flat), is performed for the first time in Tokyo by Ida Kavafian with the Tokyo Metropolitan Orchestra.

2 JUNE 1980

The world première is presented at Bath, England, of Elliott CARTER's *Night Fantasies* for piano, commissioned by and dedicated to four pianists, Paul Jacobs, Gilbert Kalish, Ursula Oppens and Charles Rosen, each of whom subsequently played the work during the 1983 Elliott Carter Festival at the University of Southern California in Los Angeles. (The Bath première was given by Oppens.)

18 JUNE 1980

Notations for orchestra by the cerebrally celebrated French composer Pierre BOULEZ is performed for the first time by the Orchestra de Paris, Daniel Barenboim conducting.

20 JUNE 1980

Allan PETTERSSON, remarkable Swedish composer of symphonic and other music permeated with the spirit of radical melancholy, who said about himself, "I am not a composer, I am a voice crying out in the noise of the times," dies in Stockholm crippled by a plethora of degenerative diseases, at the age of 79.

21 JUNE 1980

Hermetic British composer Peter Maxwell DAVIES conducts in Kirkwall, Orkney, the first performance of his work *The Yellow Cake Revue* for singers and piano, to a text by the composer which inveighs against the ominous threat of covertly radioactive uranium mining in the Orkney Islands.

28 JUNE 1980

José ITURBI, brilliant Spanish pianist acclaimed for his genuine Iberian virtuosity, dies in Hollywood at the age of 84.

28 JUNE 1980

Yoshiro IRINO, Japanese composer who was born in Vladivostok, Siberia, who wrote music in highly advanced techniques permeated with genuine Nipponese melorhythms, dies in Tokyo at the age of 58.

29 JUNE 1980

The 54th Festival of the International Society for Contemporary Music in Israel opens with a concert of chamber music in Jerusalem presenting the following program:

Dialogo 3 for two pianos by the 37-year-old Swedish composer Daniel BÖRTZ; *Renascence* for clarinet solo and tape by the 38-year-old American composer Jonathan D. KRAMER; *The Sunflower* for string quartet by the 26-year-old Danish composer Erik HÖJSGAARD; *Aspro* for clarinet, trombone, cello and piano by the 32-year-old Finnish composer Jukka TIENSUU, the title suggesting singularly rough, austerely barren, acridly pungent and hermetically morose substances; *Arnold Schoenberg in Memoriam* for string quartet by the 39-year-old Polish composer Bronislaw PRZYBYLSKI, based on a tone row composed on the musical letters in Schoenberg's name; *Epigano* for guitar solo by the 43-year-old Portuguese composer José António LOPES E SILVA, the title signifying the living endurance of the immediate past; *Strides* for piano solo by the 51-year-old Dutch composer Theo LOEVENDIE, based on Harlem "stride paino" jazz technique; and *About an Old Tune* for piano quartet by the 51-year-old Russian-born Israeli composer Mark KOPYTMAN, the music being an echo of Jewish tunes in a heterophonic setting.

30 JUNE 1980

On the second day of the 54th Festival of the International Society for Contemporary Music in Israel, a choral concert is presented in Jerusalem with the following program:

Yogi by the 36-year-old japanese composer Mayako KUBO; *Requiem* for twelve solo voices by the 49-year-old Chilean-born Israeli composer Leon SCHIDLOWSKY; *Jarchas de dolor de ausencia (Solace in the Sadness of Absence)* by the 50-year-old Spanish composer Cristóbal HALFFTER; *Motetus paraburi* for mezzo-soprano, tenor and baritone by the 43-year-old Swiss composer Hans Ulrich LEHMANN; and *Chorbuch* for choir, piano and harmonium by the 49-year-old Argentine-born German empiricist Mauricio KAGEL.

1 JULY 1980

On the third day of the 54th Festival of the International Society for Contemporary Music in Israel, the following program of orchestral music is presented at an afternoon concert in Jerusalem:

Scintilla Prisca for cello and piano by the 43-year-old American composer Brian FENNELLY, an homage to his late wife Priscilla (the title means pristine spark); *2 + 2 + 2 + 2* for two flutes, two clarinets, two violas and two cellos by the 33-year-old French composer Gérard GARCIN; *String Quartet* by the 30-year-old Belgian composer Franklin GYSELYNCK; *Zalmen*, subtitled *Madness of God*, for violin by the 43-year-old American composer Norman DINERSTEIN, evoking the Yom Kippur celebration in Russia; and *Koss* for brass quintet by the 42-year-old German composer Hans-Joachim HESPOS.

1 JULY 1980

On the third day of the 54th Festival of the International Society for Contemporary Music in Israel, the following program of chamber music is presented by the Jerusalem Symphony Orchestra at an evening concert:

Concerto by the 24-year-old Austrian composer Thomas PERNES, based on a harmonic progression of 38 chords burgeoning into a series of 132 chords in 38 rhythmic patterns; *Cello Concerto* by the Hungarian master of ingeniously interwoven musical patterns, György LIGETI, using a sui generis technique of micropolyphony; *Portrait* for harpsichord and orchestra by the 53-year-old Italian composer Franco DONATONI; and *Program Music 1980* by the 53-year-old German-born Israeli composer Tzvi AVNI, in four pictorial movements: *The Machine Game, The Dream of the Broken Mirror, Magritte—A Dilemma?*, a surrealistic superposition of incongruous visual and tonal elements producing a new reality, and *It's a Busy Day in the Beehive*, picturing the death of a male hornet after mating with the queen bee.

2 JULY 1980

On the fourth day of the 54th Festival of the International Society for Contemporary Music in Israel, an afternoon concert of electroacoustic music is presented with the following program in Tel Aviv:

Clouds by the 45-year-old Swedish composer Lars-Gunnar BODIN; *Echoes* by the 43-year-old Argentine composer Beatriz FERREYRA; *Return to Clarity* by the 31-year-old Israeli composer Mike SHADOWSKY; *The Pulses of Time* by the 34-year-old New Zealand-born English composer Denis SMALLEY; *Half-Synthetic Boxtrot* by the Finnish composer Marja VESTERINEN, the piece being a parody of a pop concert; and *Mr. Frankenstein's Babies* by the 32-year-old German composer Klaus RÖDER, the title representing the microtonal divisions of the composer's own voice.

2 JULY 1980

On the fourth day of the 54th Festival of the International Society for Contemporary Music in Israel, an early evening concert of chamber music is given in Tel Aviv with the following program:

Solstice for clarinet, violin, cello and electronics by the 34-year-old Rumanian-born Israeli composer Gabriel IRANYI; *Territoires de l'oubli (Territories of Oblivion)* for piano by the 33-year-old French composer Tristan MURAILL; *Metamorphoses* for flute and string quartet by the 46-year-old Korean composer Sukhi KANG; *Four Songs to Icelandic Poems* for contralto, piano, cello and flute by the 28-year-old Icelandic composer Hjalmar RAGNARSSON; *Iambe* for chamber ensemble by the 44-year-old French composer Michel DECOUST, written in iambic prosody, alternating short and long pulses; *String Quartet No. 2* by the 41-year-old Hungarian composer Attila BOZAY; *Homenaje a Marcel Duchamp* for guitar and flute, a tribute to the famous painter and masterful chess player, by the 35-year-old Spanish composer Francisco ESTÉVAZ; and *Mesmerized* for mezzo-soprano, piano, three trumpets and three percussionists by the 37-year-old Dutch composer Jacques BANK, to text from the diary of the English poet Gerard Manley Hopkins.

2 JULY 1980

On the fourth day of the 54th Festival of the International Society for Contemporary Music in Israel, a late evening concert, announced as "New Dimensions in Music," is given in Tel Aviv with the following program:

Minos' for harpsichord by the 29-year-old Finnish composer Anneli ARHO; *Fall* for cello, trombone and piano by the 25-year-old Swedish composer Lars SANDBERG; *Wind Drumming* for woodwind quintet and four percussionists by the 31-year-old Danish composer Pool RUDERS; *Psalm 117* for double-bass by the 30-year-old Rumanian-born Israeli composer Dan LUSTGARTEN; and *Oralleluiants* for soprano and chamber ensemble by the 48-year-old Canadian composer Gilles TREMBLAY, the title being a biverbal compact of "orants" (people praying) and "alleluia."

3 JULY 1980

On the fifth day of the 54th Festival of the International Society for Contemporary Music in Israel, the following program of chamber music is presented in Beersheba:

Hael for violin, string orchestra and percussion by the 44-year-old Jewish-French composer Maurice BENHAMOU, a musical interpretation of the eighteenth Benediction of the Jewish liturgical calendar glorifying the Lord; *On a Delphic Reed* for oboe solo by the 32-year-old Italian composer Sandro GORLI, scored for oboe solo; *Cars et cordes* for basset horn, two English horns, two French horns, strings and harpsichord by the 37-year-old Dutch composer Geert VAN KEUTLEN; . . . *With Neither Boundary Nor Rim . . .* by the 56-year-old Swiss composer Klaus HUBER, scored for viola solo (the title is

taken from the poem by Hui-k'o, founder of Chinese Zen Buddhism); and *Violet Elegy for Monseigneur Rainero* by the 38-year-old Brazilian composer Jorge ANTUNES, scored for children's chorus and piano, dedicated to the memory of the progressive Archbishop Oscar Arnulfo Romero of El Salvador, slain in the cathedral by right-wing death squads, with the violet color of the title represented by the thematic note E.

5 JULY 1980

The 54th Festival of the International Society for Contemporary Music in Israel concludes with a concert of chamber music at the Kibbutz Shefayim with the following program:

Mensurale by the 41-year-old Italian composer Armando GENTILUCCI, scored for strings and set in the polyphonic idiom of the Flemish "canone mensurale;" *Sextet* by the 27-year-old Venezuelan composer Emilio MENDOZA; *Expressions* for strings by the 52-year-old Hungarian composer Kamillo LENDVAY; *Heu de cordes*, an educational "game of strings" with some optional electroacoustical devices echoing the music, by the 34-year-old French composer Fernand VANDENBOGAERDE; *What Name Shall I Call*, a song cycle for soprano and chamber ensemble by the Polish-born 71-year-old composer Shlomo YOFFE, to texts by a member of the Kibbutz who fell in the Yom Kippur War; and *Ison I* by the 53-year-old Rumanian composer Stefan NICULESCU, for 14 wind instruments (the word *ison* is taken from a term of Byzantine monody, wherein a melody is accompanied by a specially assigned long-held tone).

5 JULY 1980

Branchings for orchestra by the 51-year-old American composer Donald KEATS is performed for the first time at the Colorado Music Festival in Boulder.

12 JULY 1980

Sopiana for flute, piano and magnetic tape by the 45-year-old French composer François-Bernard MÂCHE is performed for the first time in Pecs, Hungary.

20 JULY 1980

The Last Twilight, theater piece for chorus, brass and percussion, setting D.H. Lawrence's 1923 poem *Men in New Mexico* by the 52-year-old Scottish composer Thea MUSGRAVE is performed for the first time in the open-air Paolo Soleri theater in Santa Fe, New Mexico, complete with a processional, torches, and campfires.

23 JULY 1980

Cry for 28 amplified solo voices, depicting the creation of the world, by the 34-year-old British composer Giles SWAYNE, is performed for the first time in London.

2 AUGUST 1980

Pollicino, or *The New Adventures of Tom Thumb*, "community opera" by the 54-year-old German modernist Hans Werner HENZE, is performed for the first time in Montepulciano, Italy.

15 AUGUST 1980

Summer Solstice, symphonic poem by Ezra LADER-MAN, is performed for the first time by the Philadelphia Orchestra under the direction of Michael Tilson Thomas in Saratoga Springs, New York.

20 AUGUST 1980

Eleventh Symphony by the 79-year-old English composer Edmund RUBBRA is performed for the first time by the BBC Northern Symphony Orchestra in London.

22 AUGUST 1980

Triple Concerto for violin, viola, cello and orchestra by the 75-year-old British composer Sir Michael TIPPETT, in three integrated sections, with the concertino of three participating soloists figuratively curtseying before the ripieni, is performed for the first time in London, Sir Colin Davis conducting the London Symphony Orchestra.

22 AUGUST 1980

Piers Plowman, opera-cantata in two acts to the poem of William Langland by the 56-year-old British composer of Dutch and Hungarian descent Gerard SCHURMANN, is performed for the first time at the Three Choirs Festival held in the Gloucester Cathedral.

24 AUGUST 1980

Double Concerto for oboe, harp and chamber orchestra by Witold LUTOSLAWSKI is performed for the first time by the virtuoso oboist Heinz Holliger with his wife Ursula as harpist at the Ursula Collegium Musicum in Lucerne under the direction of Paul Sacher.

1 SEPTEMBER 1980

The Post Office of Great Britain issues a set of commemorative postage stamps glorifying four English conductors: 12 pence for Sir Henry WOOD; 13 1/2 pence for Sir Thomas BEECHAM; 15 pence for Sir John BARBIROLLI; and 17 1/2 pence for Sir Malcolm SARGENT.

5 SEPTEMBER 1980

Satyagraha, opera by the 43-year-old American composer Philip GLASS, dedicated to the political theory of *Satya* and *agraha* (truth and resolution in the original Sanskrit) and adapted from the Indian epic Bhagavad-Gita, the libretto dealing with the life of Mahatma Gandhi in South Africa before his ascent to glory as a prophet of nonviolence, in six ritualistic tableaux with timeless, motionless, changeless music (at one point Gandhi walks at night singing a scale E to E 30 times; at another point a progression of second inversions of a triad is repeated 143 times), is produced in Rotterdam, Holland.

13 SEPTEMBER 1980

Happy Voices by the 43-year-old American composer David DEL TREDICI, Part II of his symphonic series *Child Alice,* based on *Alice in Wonderland* and *Through the Looking Glass* by Lewis Carroll, is performed for the first time by the San Francisco Symphony Orchestra, Edo De Waart conducting. (Part I was first performed 23 February 1980, Part III 8 May 1981, and Part IV 19 November 1981.)

15 SEPTEMBER 1980

The Servants, opera by the 46-year-old Welsh composer William MATHIAS, to a libretto by Iris Murdoch, is produced by the Welsh National Opera in Cardiff.

24 SEPTEMBER 1980

Orchestra for orchestra by the 49-year-old American composer Richard FELICIANO is performed for the first time in San Francisco.

1 OCTOBER 1980

Entrata for orchestra by Luciano BERIO is performed for the first time by the San Francisco Symphony.

8 OCTOBER 1980

Symphony No. 2, True and Eternal Bliss, for six flutes, six oboes, six trumpets, trombone, tuba, percussion, piano, and solo voice, by the unique 61-year-old Soviet composer Galina USTVOLSKAYA, based on a text by Hermannus Contractus (1013–1054) found in *Monuments of Mediaeval Latin Literature from the 10th to 12th Centuries,* is premiered in Leningrad.

10 OCTOBER 1980

Maurice MARTENOT, French inventor of the Ondes Martenot for electronic keyboard, dies as a result of a vélocipede accident in Paris four days before his 82nd birthday.

11 OCTOBER 1980

A Musical Toast, subtitled *A Fanfare in Memory of André Kostelanetz,* by Leonard BERNSTEIN is performed for the first time by the New York Philharmonic, Zubin Mehta conducting.

12 OCTOBER 1980

Ludi Leopoldini (Leopoldian Games), variations on a theme of Leopold I, Holy Roman emperor 1640–1705, for orchestra by the 62-year-old Austrian composer Gottfried VON EINEM, is performed for the first time in Berlin.

30 OCTOBER 1980

Requiem by the 51-year-old Soviet composer Edison DENISOV, set for soprano, tenor, chorus and orchestra to the trilingual (German, French, English) text by the modern German poet Francisco Tanzer, in five sections (*Anflug des Lächelns, Fundamental Variation, Danse permanente, Automatic Variation, La Croix*) and containing a quotation from Mozart's *Requiem,* is performed for the first time in Hamburg.

28 NOVEMBER 1980

Two Minor Desperations for chamber orchestra by the 56-year-old German-born American conductor Gerhard SAMUEL is performed for the first time by the San Francisco Symphony Orchestra, the composer conducting.

28 NOVEMBER 1980

Where the Wild Things Are, fantasy opera by the 28-year-old Scottish composer Oliver KNUSSEN, the central character being a small boy confronted with monsters singing in "pidgin Yiddish," and the whole score a mosaic of some 25 interdependent microforms, is performed for the first time, in its first version, in Brussels. (The eventual definitive version was first performed on 9 January 1984 in London.)

28 NOVEMBER 1980

Apocalypsis for soloist, chorus and orchestra by the 47-year-old Canadian composer R. Murray SCHAFER, an allegorical spectacle about the destruction of the world according to St. John the Divine, is performed for the first time in London, Ontario.

29 NOVEMBER 1980

Violin Concerto by the 50-year-old Spanish composer Cristóbal HALFFTER is performed for the first time in Madrid.

4 DECEMBER 1980

Orpheus in Pecan Springs, ballad opera by the 63-year-old American composer William LATHAM, to a libretto by Thomas Holliday, is performed for the first time in Denton, Texas.

8 DECEMBER 1980

John LENNON, 40-year-old British singer and song writer, the social philosopher of the glorious Liverpudlian band The Beatles, is gunned down in front of his New York apartment by an assailant besotted by his adulation of Lennon to the point of identifying himself with him.

24 DECEMBER 1980

Alec WILDER, American composer of versatile talents equally amusing in operas, operettas, musical comedies and finely structured chamber music, who was also capable of writing popular songs in a hedonistic and ingratiating style, dies in Gainesville, Florida, at the age of 73.

1981

18 JANUARY 1981

All Done from Memory for violin solo by the 53-year-old American composer Ezra SIMS, based on an eighteen-tone scale of his own device, is performed for the first time by Janet Packer at a Dinosaur Annex Concert in Boston.

23 JANUARY 1981

Samuel BARBER, American composer whose patrician style in composition was etched along fine romantic lines and yet stamped with an unmistakably modernistic imprint and whose poignant *Adagio for Strings* became one of the most affecting and most frequently played American instrumental works, dies of cancer in New York at the still creative age of 70.

25 JANUARY 1981

Third Symphony, subtitled *Sevastopol,* by the 65-year-old Soviet composer Boris TCHAIKOVSKY, unrelated to the great Tchaikovsky, is performed for the first time in Moscow.

31 JANUARY 1981

Mary Stuart, opera-ballad by the 49-year-old Soviet composer Sergei SLONIMSKY, in three tableaux to a historically accurate libretto by Yakov Gordin, wherein the march of events related by folk narrators traces the fate of the tragic Queen of Scotland, with the sinister Protestant minister John Knox leading the resistance to the Catholic ruler, set to music with all astute application of genuine Scottish melorhythms, invested ill darksome dissonant harmonies, is produced in Kuibishev, U.S.S.R. (A Leningrad performance followed on 18 April 1981, and on 26 May 1984 the opera was produced, in a German translation, in Leipzig.)

13 FEBRUARY 1981

Aïs for solo percussionists, amplified baritone and orchestra by the 58-year-old Greek composer and musical mathematician Iannis XENAKIS is performed for the first time in Munich.

19 FEBRUARY 1981

Abélard and Héloïse, fifth opera by the 63-year-old American composer Robert WARD, based on the tragic story of the medieval theologian Abélard who was brutally castrated by the uncle of his secret bride Héloïse, is performed for the first time in Charlotte, North Carolina.

26 FEBRUARY 1981

Second Symphony by the 46-year-old British composer Peter Maxwell DAVIES, in four classically designed movements, thematically derived from a variety of sources including the plainsong melody *Nativitas Tua, Dei Genetrix*, sacred to the birthday of the Virgin Mary (which happens also to be the composer's own birthday, about 1954 years later), is performed for the first time by the Boston Symphony Orchestra, Seiji Ozawa conducting.

26 FEBRUARY 1981

Howard HANSON, grand American composer and educator who proclaimed his faith in the eternal values of musical romanticism, whose symphonies expressed his deeply felt affinity to his Scandinavian ancestry, dies in Rochester at the age of 84.

1 MARCH 1981

Canti Lunatici for soprano and nine instruments by the 47-year-old British-born American composer Bernard RANDS, based on lunar poems in English, French, German, Italian and Spanish, is performed for the first time at the Contemporary Music Festival at California Institute of the Arts in Valencia.

10 MARCH 1981

Ninth Symphony, subtitled *Sinfonia Capricciosa*, by the 57-year-old American composer Peter MENNIN, is performed for the first time by the National Symphony Orchestra under the direction of Mstislav Rostropovich in Washington, D.C.

10 MARCH 1981

The Czechoslovak Federal Ministry of Telecommunications issues a set of postage stamps which includes three honoring the composers Mikulas SCHNEIDER-TRNAVSKY, MOZART and SHOSTAKOVICH.

20 MARCH 1981

Million d' Oiseaux d'or for orchestra by the 56-year-old French composer Serge NIGG is performed for the first time in Boston by the Toulouse Orchestra on its United States tour.

23 MARCH 1981

Partita for violin and orchestra by the 51-year-old Soviet composer Edison DENISOV is performed for the first time in Moscow by Leonid Kogan, soloist, with his son Pavel Kogan conducting the orchestra.

28 MARCH 1981

The Trojan Women, ballet for orchestra by the 59-year-old Czech-born American composer Karel HUSA, is performed for the first time by the Louisville Symphony Orchestra under the direction of the composer.

2 APRIL 1981

Orphikon, a symphony in three movements by the Czech conductor and composer Rafael KUBELIK, is performed for the first time by the New York Philharmonic Orchestra under the direction of the composer.

4 APRIL 1981

Dnevnik jednog ludaka (Diary of a Madman), television opera by the 70-year-old Serbian composer Stanojlo RAJIČIĆ, to the composer's own libretto after Gogol's tale, is produced on Belgrade Television.

8 APRIL 1981

Sixth Symphony by the British composer Robert SIMPSON is performed for the first time by the London Philharmonic Orchestra conducted by Sir Charles Groves.

10 APRIL 1981

Concerto for orchestra by the 49-year-old Swedish composer Ulf GRAHN is performed for the first time in Cincinnati.

12 APRIL 1981

La mujer y su sombra, opera by the 38-year-old Mexican composer Miguel ALCAZAR, to a libretto of Paul Claudel dealing with an Oriental woman who cannot move without her shadow, which possesses a different personality and a different voice, set to music in a sonorously somber atonal idiom, with an ample assortment of drums and cymbals, is performed for the first time in Mexico City.

15 APRIL 1981

Clarinet Concerto by the Polish-born American composer Stanislaw SKROWACZEWSKI, is performed for the first time by Joseph Longo as soloist with the Minnesota Orchestra, Skrowaczewski conducting.

15 APRIL 1981

Harmonium by the 34-year-old American composer John ADAMS, scored for chorus and orchestra, containing three sections—*Negative Love* to words by John Donne, *Because I Could Not Stop for Death* and *Wild Nights*, both to words by Emily Dickinson—is performed for the first time in San Francisco, Edo de Waart conducting.

18 APRIL 1981

Skorogovorka (Russian for "tongue twister") for wind orchestra and percussion by the 31-year-old Swedish composer Johnny GRANDERT is performed for the first time on Swedish Radio in Stockholm.

20 APRIL 1981

The Composers in Red Sneakers, a Boston-based consortium of composers comprised of Roger BOURLAND, Robert ALDRIDGE, Thomas Oboe LEE, Christopher STOWENS, Gary PHILO, and Amy REICH, presents its first ever concert at Old Cambridge Baptist Church in Cambridge, Massachusetts, spawning a growth of "composer groups" throughout Boston in the 1980s.

23 APRIL 1981

Ravi SHANKAR, North Indian sitar virtuoso, performs his *Rāga-Mālā (Garland of Ragas)* with the New York Philharmonic Orchestra conducted by his Parsi compatriot Zubin Mehta.

708   23 April 1981

23 APRIL 1981

Concerto for violin, cello and chamber orchestra by the 45-year-old Estonian composer Arvo PÄRT is performed for the first time in London.

24 APRIL 1981

Violin Concerto by the American composer Ellis B. KOHS is performed for the first time by Eudice Shapiro, with Daniel Lewis conducting the University of Southern California Orchestra in Los Angeles.

24 APRIL 1981

Willie Stark, opera by Carlisle FLOYD, modeled after the career of Huey Long, with a marginal participation of other American demagogues such as Bilbo, Talmadge, Wallace and McCarthy, set with illustrative realism but occasionally drifting into a sentimental music, is produced for the first time in Houston, Texas.

29 APRIL 1981

Trumpet Concerto by the 54-year-old American composer Donald ERB is performed for the first time by Don Tison as soloist with the Baltimore Symphony Orchestra, Sergiu Comissiona conducting.

30 APRIL 1981

Descencio by the remarkably innovative Soviet composer of Tatar origin Sofia GUBAIDULINA, depicting the glossolalia descended upon the Apostles of Pentecost that enabled them to "speak in tongues" (the scoring, in three groups of threes—three trombones, three percussionists and three stringed instruments, harp, piano and celesta—is symbolic of three Trinities), is performed for the first time at the Centre Pompidou in Paris.

2 MAY 1981

Alan HOVHANESS, prodigiously prolific 70-year-old American composer of Armenian antecedents, conducts the first performance by the Vermont Symphony of his *Forty-sixth Symphony*, subtitled *To the Green Mountains*.

6 MAY 1981

Angel of Dusk, concerto for double-bass and orchestra by the 53-year-old Finnish composer Einojuhani RAUTAVAARA, dedicated to the memory of Olga Koussevitzky, the last widow of the fabled double-bass virtuoso and illustrious conductor Serge Koussevitzky, is performed for the first time on the Finnish Radio in Helsinki.

7 MAY 1981

Anna Karenina, opera by the Scottish composer Iain HAMILTON after Tolstoy's novel of adulterous passion, the penalty for which was death (the epigraph on the novel was from the Bible, "The Vengeance is Mine, I shall repay"), is performed for the first time by the English National Opera in London.

8 MAY 1981

All in the Golden Afternoon by the greatly gifted 44-year-old American composer David DEL TREDICI, Part III of the symphonic series *Child Alice*, based on *Alice in Wonderland* by Lewis Carroll, commissioned by ARCO Petroleum Products Co. in honor of Eugene Ormandy's 80th birthday, is performed for the first time by Benita Valente, soprano, and the Philadelphia Orchestra, Ormandy conducting. (Parts I and II were respectively premiered on 23 February and 13 September 1980, Part IV on 19 November 1981.)

9 MAY 1981

The Infernal Machine for orchestra by the 32-year-old American composer Christopher ROUSE, after a play by Jean Cocteau retelling the Oedipus myth, the infernality of the music being represented by an instrumental *perpetuum mobile* setting, is performed for the first time by the University of Michigan Symphony Orchestra at the Evian Festival in France. (This work later became the middle movement of Rouse's *Phantasmata*.)

11 MAY 1981

Cats, an ailurolatrous musical by the unfailingly successful 33-year-old British tunesmith Andrew LLOYD WEBBER, inspired by *Old Possum's Book of Practical Cats* by the felinamorous poet T. S. Eliot, is produced in London. (The first Broadway production took place on 7 October 1982.)

17 MAY 1981

The world première is given at Castle Herrenchiemsee, near Munich, of *Symphony in F Major* for two oboes, two horns, strings, and harpsichord, in three movements, apparently composed by MOZART at the age of 9.

18 MAY 1981

Sequoia for orchestra including 54 percussion players by the 42-year-old American composer Joan TOWER is performed for the first time by the American Composers Orchestra in New York.

20 MAY 1981

Das Opfer der Kerze (The Sacrifice of the Candle) for instrumental and electronic ensemble by the 60-year-old Czech composer Zbyněk VOSTŘÁK is performed for the first time in Baden-Baden, West Germany.

1 JUNE 1981

De Tijd (Time) for winds, pianos, harps, guitars, percussion and women's voices by the 41-year-old Dutch composer Louis ANDRIESSEN, portraying the passage of time and its synthesis when, as Dante said, "tutti i tempi son presenti," is performed for the first time in Amsterdam.

10 JUNE 1981

Rupturas for chamber ensemble by the 40-year-old Brazilian composer Fernando Barbosa de CERQUEIRA is performed for the first time by Musica Nova at the Reitoria of the Federal University of Bahía in Salvador, Bahía, P. Bastianelli conducting.

18 JUNE 1981

The Gay Men's Chorus presents its first open air concert on Capitol Hill in Washington, D.C., in a program of works by BRUCKNER, SCHUBERT, SIBELIUS, IVES, COPLAND, RIEGGER, Randall THOMPSON, Irving BERLIN and George GERSHWIN, singing from memory, marking perhaps the greatest exhibit of technical expertise and purity of intonation since the sublime castratosphere of the Italian Baroque.

6 JULY 1981

Aurora Natola, wife of Alberto GINASTERA, plays the solo part in his *Second Cello Concerto,* dedicated to her, at its first performance in Buenos Aires.

30 JULY 1981

Vociano, a theater work for soprano and piano by the 60-year-old American composer Pia GILBERT, based on imaginary languages suggesting Slavic, Central European, and Oriental phonemes, receives its first performance at the Aspen Music Festival.

10 AUGUST 1981

Akhmatova: Requiem for soprano, baritone and ensemble by the 37-year-old British composer John TAVENER to poems by Anna Akhmatova (1889–1966), the Russian poetess intermittently ostracized by the Soviet authorities for the suffused eroticism of her verse, is performed for the first time in Edinburgh.

17 AUGUST 1981

Robert Russell BENNETT, American composer and arranger of extraordinary dexterity whose own works were respectable presentations of American and cosmopolitan themes, dies in New York at the age of 87.

26 SEPTEMBER 1981

The 55th Festival of the International Society for Contemporary Music in Belgium opens with the following program of electronic music and mixed media in an afternoon concert in Brussels:

Uitgebreid parametrisch nr. 3B for trombone and electronics, and *Parametrische modellen* for solo computer/synthesizer by the 34-year-old Belgian composer Joris DE LAET; *Animus* for trombone and tape by the 53-year-old American composer Jacob DRUCKMAN; *From a Pitch to a Voltage* for trombone and electronics by the Belgian composer Leo VERNHEYEN; and Four experimental pieces for various ensembles by the 43-year-old Polish composer Piotr LACHERT.

26 SEPTEMBER 1981

At the first evening concert of the 55th Festival of the International Society for Contemporary Music in Brussels, the following program of choral and organ music is presented:

Veni Sancte Spiritus—Veni Creator by the 42-year-old Australian composer Jennifer FOWLER; *Les Anges de l' Apocalypse* by the 49-year-old Belgian composer Paul UY (pseudonym for Uyttebroeck); *Lapponia* by the 70-year-old Finnish composer Erik BERGMAN, picturing sunless winter, midnight summer sun and polar storm in Lapland; *Ricercar* by the 53-year-old

Swedish composer Bengt HAMBRAEUS; *Doe* by the 45-year-old Belgian composer Frans GEYSEN; *Musique de Jour* by the 55-year-old French composer Betsy JOLAS; *Choral Concerto No. 1* by the 39-year-old Spanish composer Tomás MARCO; and *Organum III* by the 47-year-old French composer Xavier DARASSE.

27 SEPTEMBER 1981

On the second day of the 55th Festival of the International Society for Contemporary Music in Belgium, the following program is presented in Brussels:

Swinging Music by the Polish composer Kazimierz SEROCKI (1922–1981); *Empirical Rag* by the 44-year-old American composer Brian FENNELLY; *Humpty Dumpty Sat on a Waltz* by the American-born Israeli composer Joan Franks WILLIAMS; *Danse des ministres chez M. Pompidou* by the 52-year-old French composer Luc FERRARI; *Fantastic Rondos* by the 43-year-old Icelandic composer Atli Heimir SVEINSSON; *A Flemish Round* by the 50-year-old Belgian composer André LAPORTE; *Warsaw Workshop Waltz* by the 41-year-old Portuguese composer Jorge Rosado PEIXINHO; *Dal-a* by the 47-year-old South Korean composer Sukhi KANG; *Dance Vision* by the 51-year-old Greek composer Iannis IOANNIDIS; and *Sweet Sixteenths, a Cakewalk* by the 37-year-old American composer William ALBRIGHT.

28 SEPTEMBER 1981

On the third day of the 55th Festival of the International Society for Contemporary Music in Belgium, the following program of chamber music is presented at an afternoon concert in Brussels:

Double for two prepared pianos by the 37-year-old Hungarian composer László VIDOWSZKY; *Episodes* for trombone solo by the 34-year-old Israeli composer Dan YUHAS; *Voix intérieure* for two cellos by the 51-year-old East German composer Paul-Heinz DITTRICH; *Dianima* for two cellos by the 27-year-old Norwegian composer Ole LÜTZOW-HOLM; *Time and Motion* for bass clarinet by the 38-year-old British composer Brian FERNEYHOUGH; and *Regime II, Type A* for two pianos by the 42-year-old Canadian composer Bruce MATHER.

28 SEPTEMBER 1981

On the third day of the 55th Festival of the International Society for Contemporary Music in Belgium, the following program is presented at an evening concert in Brussels:

Concerto for Percussion and Wind Ensemble by the 60-year-old Prague-born naturalized American composer Karel HUSA; *Frises* for wind orchestra by the Belgian composer Jacqueline FONTYN; *Essay* for horn and wind ensemble by the 52-year-old Belgian composer Jan SEGERS; and *Rhapsodie* for wind orchestra by the 67-year-old Belgian composer Jean LOUEL.

29 SEPTEMBER 1981

On the fourth day of the 55th Festival of the International Society for Contemporary Music in Belgium, an afternoon concert of electronic music and mixed media is presented in Ghent with the following program:

Yantra 8 for piano and tape by the 35-year-old Cuban-born Canadian composer Sergio BARROSO, based on an old Tibetan cosmogram generating intermitable melorhythms; *Kompositie 1979* for tape by the 59-year-old Dutch composer Jan BOERMAN; *Sonata* for double-bass and tape by the 50-

year-old Belgian composer Lucien GOETHALS; *Das Unrecht in meinem Bad (Injustice in My Bath)* for tape and slides by the 26-year-old Austrian composer Martin SCHWARZENLÄNDER; *Estallido breve* for bass clarinet and tape by the 31-year-old Argentine composer Ricardo MANDOLINI; *Hanging* for tape by the 35-year-old Swedish composer Tommy ZWEDBERG; and *Monologo II* for clarinet, piano and tape by the Chinese composer Man-Yee LAM.

29 SEPTEMBER 1981

On the fourth day of the 55th Festival of the International Society for Contemporary Music in Belgium, the following program is presented at an evening concert of chamber music in Ghent:

Octet for flute, oboe, bass clarinet, tuba, violin, viola, double-bass and piano by the 33-year-old American composer David OLAN; *Rainbow Studies* for piano and wind quartet by the 35-year-old British composer Colin MATTHEWS; *Voci Siciliani (Sicilian Voices)* for mezzo-soprano, flute, clarinet, guitar and string quartet by the 40-year-old, Italian-born American composer Marc-Antonio CONSOLI; and *Sonata* for cello, piano solo and chamber ensemble by the 38-year-old British composer Tim SOUSTER.

30 SEPTEMBER 1981

On the fifth day of the 55th Festival of the International Society for Contemporary Music in Belgium, the following program is presented at an afternoon concert of theater music and mixed media in Brussels:

124 E. 107th St. for percussion, narrator-actor and tape by the 34-year-old Puerto Rican composer William ORTIZ-ALVARADO, depicting the Puerto Rican urban experience in the United States and deploying Afro-American rhythms; *Roundabouts* for four marimbas by the 47-year-old Dutch composer Joep STRAESSER; *Bouffe* for a person alone on stage by the 35-year-old British composer Michael FINNISSY; *Cardini*, spoken solfeggio for solo voice by the 51-year-old Italian composer Paolo CASTALDI, the text consisting exclusively of note names; *Music* for tape and bass clarinet by the 60-year-old Polish composer Andrzej DOBROWOLSKI; and *The Temporary and Tentative Extended Piano*, sound-theater by the 32-year-old American composer Carson KIEVMAN.

30 SEPTEMBER 1981

On the fifth day of the 55th Festival of the International Society for Contemporary Music in Belgium, an early evening concert of electronic music is given in Brussels with the following program:

. . . la taupe by the 36-year-old French composer Christian CLOZIER; *Orchestrations I* by the American composer Joe DAVIDOW; *Ascents* by the 27-year-old American composer Michael William GILBERT; *Llanto* by the 27-year-old Uruguayan composer Leo MASLIAH; *Chanta Khat* by the 39-year-old American composer Michael RANTA; and *Cantico* by the 54-year-old Portuguese composer Affonso SOUZA.

30 SEPTEMBER 1981

On the fifth day of the 55th Festival of the International Society for Contemporary Music in Belgium, the following program of chamber music is given at an evening concert in Brussels:

Such a Nice Lady for clarinet, violin, viola, cello and piano by the 41-year-old American composer Alvin SINGLETON;

Linia for chamber ensemble by the 28-year-old Australian composer Gerard BROPHY; *Mythologies* for flute, clarinet, trumpet, violin, cello and harp by the 33-year-old British composer Nigel OSBORNE; and *La Vita Nuova* for soprano and chamber ensemble by the 46-year-old British composer Nicholas MAW.

1 OCTOBER 1981

Sadhana for cello and chamber orchestra by the American composer Paul CRESTON, inspired by the philosophy of the Indian poet Rabindranath Tagore, cast in the form of theme and variations, is performed for the first time, in honor of Creston's imminent 75th birthday, by the Los Angeles Chamber Orchestra under the direction of Gerard Schwarz, in El Cajon, California.

1 OCTOBER 1981

On the sixth day of the 55th Festival of the International Society for Contemporary Music in Belgium, the following program of chamber music is presented at an afternoon concert in Brussels:

Pasargada T.50 for recorder quartet by the 50-year-old Brazilian composer Brenno BLAUTH; *Capriccio* for trumpet solo by the 49-year-old Czech composer Marek KOPELENT; *Eleven Echoes of Autumn* for violin, alto flute, clarinet and prepared piano by the 52-year-old American composer George CRUMB; *The Eighth Ancestor* for baroque flute, alto recorder, cello and harpsichord by the 29-year-old American composer Beth ANDERSON, to a Zen text in which an eighth ancestor discusses the idea that logical argument is not the way to truth; *Signes en blanc* for piano by the 52-year-old Soviet composer Edison DENISOV; and *Landschappen III* for brass quintet by the 36-year-old Belgian composer Wilfried WESTERLINCK.

1 OCTOBER 1981

On the sixth day of the 55th Festival of the International Society for Contemporary Music, an early evening concert for wind orchestra is given in Brussels with the following program:

Eroptosis by the 22-year-old Belgian composer Luc BREWAEVYS; a fantastically dissonant but clearly identifiable *Variations on America*, based on *My Country 'tis of Thee*, by Charles IVES; *Meditation* by the 56-year-old American composer Gunther SCHULLER; *Tuten und Blasen* by the 40-year-old Austrian composer Dieter KAUFMANN; and *La Tromba è mobile* by the French-born composer of Slovenian descent Vinko GLOBOKAR.

1 OCTOBER 1981

On the sixth day of the 55th Festival of the International Society for Contemporary Music in Brussels, a special chamber music concert is presented in the evening in connection with the exhibit "Musicians, Painters, Poets, and Their Scores," featuring the following program:

Le Jardin des secrets by the 38-year-old Rumanian-born French composer Costin MIEREANU; *Glimpses* by the 40-year-old French composer André MOURET; *Autre Temps-Autres Moeurs* by the 39-year-old French composer François NOWAK; *Portrait de John Cage* by the Belgian composer Françoise VAN KESSEL; *Satie's Dream* by the 34-year-old French composer Jean-Yves BOSSEUR; *Erratum musical* by Marcel DUCHAMP; and *Les Noces d'Icare et Mnémosyne* by the 52-year-old Belgian composer Henri POUSSEUR.

2 OCTOBER 1981

On the seventh day of the 55th Festival of the International Society for Contemporary Music in Brussels, the following program of chamber music is presented at an afternoon concert:

Hymnos for piano by the 42-year-old Polish composer Tomasz SIKORSKI; *Un grand sommeil noir* for soprano, flute and harp to words by Paul Verlaine by the 38-year-old Polish composer Marta PTASZYŃSKA; *Rege (Tale)* for two identical and a third different kind of instrument by the 27-year-old Hungarian composer Zsolt SEREI; *Tetramegrate* for harp, celesta, harpsichord and piano by the 33-year-old Italian composer Adriano GUARNIERI; *Riverberi* for two pianos by the 51-year-old Belgian composer Raymond BAERVOETS; and *Modèle réduit* for bass clarinet and piano by the 52-year-old Belgian composer Henri POUSSEUR.

2 OCTOBER 1981

On the seventh day of the 55th Festival of the International Society for Contemporary Music in Brussels, the following program of orchestral music is given at an evening concert:

And the mountains rising nowhere . . . for wind orchestra, piano and percussion by the 38-year-old American composer Joseph SCHWANTNER; *Violin Concerto* by the 45-year-old Belgian composer Philippe BOESMANS; *Innanzi* for double-bass and orchestra by the 40-year-old Swiss composer Gérard ZINSSTAG; and *Aquatilis* by the 33-year-old Belgian composer Jean-Louis ROBERT.

2 OCTOBER 1981

On the seventh day of the 55th Festival of the International Society for Contemporary Music in Brussels, a solo clarinet recital is given by Florian Popa in a program of the following works:

Sonata by the 53-year-old Rumanian composer Tiberiu OLAH; *Amour* by the 53-year-old German master of scientific music Karlheinz STOCKHAUSEN; *Consonance IV* for clarinet and tape by the Rumanian composer Liana ALEXANDRA; *Claribior* by Eugen WENDEL; and *Chalumeau* by the 47-year-old Yugoslav composer Lojze LEBIĆ.

3 OCTOBER 1981

On the eighth day of the 55th Festival of the International Society for Contemporary Music in Brussels a theater piece by the American film composer Richard LERMAN, *Incident at Three Mile Island*, subtitled *Perhaps an Elegy for Karen Silkwood*, dealing with the accident that befell the worker Karen Silkwood at a possibly radioactive laboratory, is performed at an afternoon concert.

3 OCTOBER 1981

On the eighth day of the 55th Festival of the International Society for Contemporary Music in Brussels, the following program is presented at a late afternoon concert:

Symphony for Open Strings by the 42-year-old Dutch composer Louis ANDRIESSEN; *Concerto* for piano, twenty-four instruments and carillons by the 56-year-old Italian composer Aldo CLEMENTI; *Double* for winds and double-basses by the 56-year-old Italian composer Guido BAGGIANI; and *LO* for trombone and twelve strings by the Swiss-born French composer Tona SCHERCHEN-HSIAO.

3 OCTOBER 1981

On the eighth day of the 55th Festival of the International Society for Contemporary Music in Brussels, the following program of orchestral music is given at an evening concert:

Hé, très doulz Roussignol joly, variations on old French ballads and virelais, by the 44-year-old German composer Rolf RIEHM; *Égalisation* for twenty-five musicians by the 50-year-old Japanese composer Makoto SHINOHARA; *Sori* by the 36-year-old South Korean composer Younghi PAGH-PAAN; and *Variations* by the 29-year-old German composer Reinhard FEBEL.

4 OCTOBER 1981

On the ninth day of the 55th Festival of the International Society for Contemporary Music in Brussels, the following program of chamber music is presented at a morning concert:

Winternacht for flute, clarinet, cornet, horn, violin, cello and piano by the 29-year-old Danish composer Hans ABRAHAMSEN; *Lokale Musik T2: Leichte Tänze* by the 32-year-old German composer Walter ZIMMERMANN; and *Chlebnicov* for chamber orchestra by the 30-year-old German composer Robert PLATZ, an homage to the Russian dadaistic poet of the title.

4 OCTOBER 1981

The 55th Festival of the International Society for Contemporary Music in Brussels concludes with an evening concert of the following program of orchestral music:

Liederen for wind instruments, two pianos and double-bass by the 35-year-old Dutch composer Diderik WAGENAAR; *Transit* for forty-eight strings by the 50-year-old Belgian composer André LAPORTE; *Litanie III* for orchestra by the 58-year-old Belgian composer Karel GOEYVAERTS; *Scenes from Basho* for orchestra by the 52-year-old Japanese composer Joji YUASA; and *Morendo* for orchestra, mixed choir and tape by the 41-year-old Swedish composer Jan MORTHENSON.

15 OCTOBER 1981

Violin Concerto by the American composer Robert STARER is performed for the first time by Itzhak Perlman and the Boston Symphony Orchestra, Seiji Ozawa conducting.

18 OCTOBER 1981

Répons by Pierre BOULEZ, written for an ensemble of twenty-four instruments placed in the middle of the hall and six other players stationed against the walls, all these connected to a musical computer system capable of reacting to human gestures, is performed for the first time at the Donaueschingen Festival of Contemporary Music in West Germany.

22 OCTOBER 1981

Fourth Symphony for brass and orchestra by the 57-year-old American composer Ezra LADERMAN is performed for the first time by the Los Angeles Philharmonic under the direction of Carlo Maria Giulini, as a musical salutation on the occasion of the 80th birthday of Dorothy Chandler, the munificent founder of the Los Angeles Music Center.

23 OCTOBER 1981

Concerto for orchestra by the supremely intellectual American composer Roger SESSIONS, in three connected sections, *Allegro, Largo* and *Allegro maestoso*, couched in a characteristically Sessionesque manner, successively lyrical, earnestly calm and festive, united by a latent polyphony of tremendous acoustical force, is performed for the first time by the Boston Symphony Orchestra as a commissioned work for its centennial.

30 OCTOBER 1981

Fourth Symphony, subtitled *Indian Rose Garden and Chinese Witch Lake*, inspired by the works of the Swiss "mental deviant" Adolf Wo;älfi (1864–1930), by the 49-year-old romantically intellectual Danish composer Per NØR-GÅRD is performed for the first time in Hamburg.

2 NOVEMBER 1981

Thea MUSGRAVE conducts the Royal Philharmonic Orchestra in London in the first performance of her orchestral work *Peripeteia*, written to celebrate the bicentenary of the birth of the London music publisher Vincent Novello.

5 NOVEMBER 1981

Third Symphony by the 45-year-old Soviet composer of German origin Alfred SCHNITTKE is performed for the first time in Leipzig.

5 NOVEMBER 1981

La Tragédie de Carmen, opera by the 66-year-old Rumanian-born French composer Marius CONSTANT, is produced in Paris.

13 NOVEMBER 1981

Double Concerto for piano, cello, and orchestra by the American composer Ned ROREM is performed for the first time in Cincinnati. (Soon after the première, Rorem changed the title to *Remembering Tommy* [in memory of Thomas Schippers, the conductor], which is also the title of the third of the work's ten movements.)

19 NOVEMBER 1981

Quaint Events, fourth and last part of an orchestral series by the 44-year-old American composer David DEL TREDICI, inspired by Lewis Carroll's children's classic *Alice in Wonderland*, is performed for the first time by the Buffalo Philharmonic under the direction of Julius Rudel. (The previous three parts of Del Tredici's orchestral pieces descriptive of Alice's adventures were, respectively, the Pulitzer Prize-winning *In Memory of a Summer Day* for soprano and orchestra, first performed in St. Louis, 23 February 1980; *Happy Voices* for soprano and orchestra, first performed in San Francisco on 16 September 1980; *Child Alice* for soprano and orchestra, first performed in Philadelphia, 8 May 1981; other pieces by Del Tredici pertaining to Alice are *Vintage Alice, Adventures Underground* and *An Alice Symphony*.)

19 NOVEMBER 1981

Sixth Symphony by the 75-year-old American composer David VAN VACTOR is performed for the first time in Knoxville, Tennessee. (A version for band was premièred at Ball State University in Kentucky on 13 April 1983.)

21 NOVEMBER 1981

Tehillim (*Psalms* in Hebrew) for four sopranos, percussion, woodwinds, electric organs and string quartet by the 45-year-old American composer Steve REICH, who, turning away from his primitivistically minimalistic and pervasively repetitive musical patterns, came to pursue the recessive traits of his ancestral Judaism, is performed for the first time in Houston, Texas. (A full orchestral version was performed on 16 September 1982 by the New York Philharmonic, Zubin Mehta couducting.)

24 NOVEMBER 1981

Forty-seventh Symphony, subtitled *Walla Walla, Land of Many Waters*, for soprano and orchestra by the interminably productive American composer Alan HOVHANESS is performed for the first time in Walla Walla, Washington.

26 NOVEMBER 1981

Fourteenth Symphony, completed by the passionately romantic Swedish composer Allan PETTERSSON in 1978, is performed posthumously, for the first time, in Stockholm.

13 DECEMBER 1981

Cornelius CARDEW, intransigent British avant-gardist who conducted a group called Scratch Orchestra and composed such works as *Three Winter Potatoes* scored for piano, triangles, balloons but no potatoes, and who toward the end of his career became a prophet of militant latitudinarianism and disestablishmentarianism, embraced the doctrine of Mao Dzedung, vehemently denounced his erstwhile idols Stockhausen and Cage and penitently renounced his own former ultramodernistic notions of art, dies at the age of 45 in a preposterous street accident in London, run over by a truant automobile.

20 DECEMBER 1981

An Occurrence at Owl Creek Bridge, radio opera for baritone, three speakers, tape and orchestra by the 53-year-old Scottish composer Thea MUSGRAVE, is performed for the first time in London.

23 DECEMBER 1981

Magnifico, festive overture by the 65-year-old Serbian composer Vitomir TRIFUNOVCÍ, glorifying the patriotic Serbian resistance to the Nazi invaders during the Second World War, is performed for the first time in Belgrade.

27 DECEMBER 1981

Hoagy CARMICHAEL, American jazz pianist and composer of popular songs among which *Stardust* became a sentimental American classic, dies at his retreat at Rancho Mirage, California, at the age of 81.

1982

14 JANUARY 1982

Cello Concerto by the 59-year-old American composer George WALKER is performed for the first time by Lorne Munroe as soloist with the New York Philharmonic, Zubin Mehta conducting.

22 JANUARY 1982

Three Hallucinations for orchestra by the 43-year-old American composer John CORIGLIANO, derived from his score to the film *Altered States,* is performed for the first time in Syracuse, New York.

25 JANUARY 1982

Undici colori (Eleven Colors) for solo bassoon, stamping right foot and slide projections by the 56-year-old Cuban-born American composer Aurelio DE LA VEGA is performed for the first time in Los Angeles.

28 JANUARY 1982

Eighth Symphony, subtitled *Sinfonia Votiva,* by the Polish composer Andrzej PANUFNIK, is performed for the first time by the Boston Symphony Orchestra under the direction of Seiji Ozawa.

2 FEBRUARY 1982

Cinque (5) sonetti del Michelangelo Buonarroti for voice and chamber orchestra by the fantastically individualistic British Parsi composer Kaikhosru Shapurji SORABI is performed for the first time in Toronto, nearly 60 years after its composition.

9 FEBRUARY 1982

Der gelbe Klang, experimental stage composition by the Expressionist Russian painter Vasily KANDINSKY, published in a literary form in the compendium of modern aesthetics *Der Blaue Reiter* in 1912, a theater spectacle consisting of five intensely yellow images with a musical score chanted by a basso profondo, tenor and chorus, fashioned by the Russian composer Thomas VAN HARTMANN, comes to a belated realization at the Guggenheim Museum in New York.

13 FEBRUARY 1982

Symphony No. 10, F.D.R., by the 55-year-old American composer Meyer KUPFERMAN, composed as a "portrait" of Franklin Delano Roosevelt for the 100th anniversary of his birth, is premiered by the Hudson Valley Philharmonic in Kingston, New York.

18 FEBRUARY 1982

Phantasmagoria, a Fantasy, compacted from sketches of the projected *Universe Symphony* by Charles IVES, arranged by Larry AUSTIN for orchestra, narrator, tape

and digital synthesizer, is performed for the first time at North Texas State University in Denton.

19 FEBRUARY 1982

Requiem: De ur alla minnen fallna (Requiem: Mutely the Bereaved Memories Speak) for four soloists, mixed chorus, children's chorus and tape by the 39-year-old Swedish composer Sven-David SANDSTRÖM is performed for the first time in Stockholm.

20 FEBRUARY 1982

John ADAMS, 35-year-old modernistic pluralistic minimalist American composer, conducts the San Francisco Symphony in the first performance of his *Grand Pianola Music,* scored for two winds, two brass, three percussionists, three female singers and two pianos.

20 FEBRUARY 1982

Prologo e Fantasia for orchestra by the 79-year-old British composer Sir William WALTON is performed for the first time in London.

21 FEBRUARY 1982

Margot la Rouge, opera by Frederick DELIUS written in 1902 but laid aside for 80 years before it was unearthed from the dusty heap of forgotten manuscripts, to a story dealing with an originally virtuous girl becoming a *fille de joie et de détresse* on Paris boulevards, and her pimp, killed by her fiancé, is performed for the first time by the BBC orchestra and chorus in London. (The first stage performance was given in St. Louis on 9 June 1983, conducted by the faithful Deliusian Eric Fenby.)

26 FEBRUARY 1982

Wonder's Edge by the 45-year-old American composer Harold Budd, scored for piano, electric guitar and electronics, is performed for the first time in San Francisco.

3 MARCH 1982

Symphonic Study, composed in 1928 by the Finnish composer Aarre MERIKANTO (1893–1958), its manuscript mutilated by the composer in 1956 and inscribed "Unplayable; may it remain so," is premiered in Helsinki in a 1981 reconstruction by his former pupil Paavo HEININEN.

5 MARCH 1982

Concerto de la fidélité for soprano and orchestra, written in 1981 by the still creatively functioning 89-year-old French composer Germaine TAILLEFERRE, is performed for the first time in Paris.

6 MARCH 1982

Food, a stylistically eclectic theater piece for soprano, baritone, trumpet, piano, and snare-drum by the 60-year-old American composer Pia GILBERT, to a culinary text taken from John Cage's "Where Are We Eating? And What Are We Eating?" incorporating a recipe for sweet nut rolls, receives its first performance at the Contemporary Music Festival at the California Institute of the Arts in Valencia.

6 MARCH 1982

Meteor Farm by the 68-year-old American composer Henry BRANT, scored for orchestra, jazz band, two percussion ensembles, two sopranos, Javanese gamelan orchestra, West African drummers and South Indian musicians, is performed for the first time at Wesleyan University in Middletown, Connecticut, directed by the composer.

7 MARCH 1982

Quiet Music for orchestra by the 49-year-old Soviet composer Sergei SLONIMSKY is performed for the first time in Leningrad.

9 MARCH 1982

La Vera Storia, veristic opera by the Italian avant-gardist Luciano BERIO, employing singers, actors, dancers and acrobats and featuring the Swingle Singers offstage and a wordless soprano, is performed for the first time at La Scala, in Milan, under the direction of the composer.

12 MARCH 1982

The Telltale Heart, chamber opera by the 35-year-old American composer Daniel KESSNER, after a scary tale by Edgar Allan Poe, is performed for the first time in Utrecht, Holland.

12 MARCH 1982

Eighth Symphony by the 76-year-old Austrian composer Marcel RUBIN is performed for the first time in Vienna.

18 MARCH 1982

Sonneries for orchestra by the 55-year-old American composer Donald ERB is performed for the first time in Rochester, New York.

20 MARCH 1982

Second Symphony, subtitled *Birds of Sorrow*, by the 43-year-old American composer Paul CHIHARA is performed for the first time in Los Angeles.

29 MARCH 1982

Carl ORFF, German composer and theorist whose scenic oratorio *Carmina Burana* to texts assembled from medieval student songs became a classic of modern music despite the general unfamiliarity of the idioms employed (Latin, old French, Catalan, etc.), and who initiated an attractive method of musical training by constructing a whole ensemble of sonoriferous instruments, dies in Munich at the age of 86.

31 MARCH 1982

The Orchestral Noises of October Nights for orchestra by the 31-year-old American composer James UNDERWOOD is performed for the first time in Bloomington, Indiana.

3 APRIL 1982

The Shivaree, opera by the Canadian composer John BECKWITH, dealing with a successful if maddening shivaree (i.e., charivari, a wedding-night mock serenade) staged by the young lover of the third wife of a middleaged merchant in rural Ontario ca. 1900, is produced in Toronto.

6 APRIL 1982

Southern Voices by the 40-year-old American avant-garde composer Doris HAYS, incorporating seven solos for soprano and piano with the orchestra imitating southern speech patterns, is performed for the first time in Chattanooga, Tennessee.

14 APRIL 1982

A Bride from Pluto, opera by Gian Carlo MENOTTI, is produced at the Kennedy Center in Washington, D.C.

15 APRIL 1982

Offertorium for violin and orchestra by the 50-year-old half-Tatar, half-Russian Soviet composer Sofia GUBAIDULINA, the title referring to the mercurially appearing, disappearing and reappearing "Royal Theme" given to Bach on his visit to Potsdam on 7 May 1747 by King Frederic the Great, herein surrounded by a flowering abundance of original thematic material forming atonal asymptotes to shifting central tones, and magniloquently fructified by sonorific orchestration, is performed for the first time by the Soviet violinist Oleg Kogan with the Culture Symphony Orchestra in Moscow, conducted by Gennadi Rozhdestvensky.

20 APRIL 1982

Les Hommages by the 56-year-old American composer Ronald MCFARLAND, a smorgasbord of twentieth-century pianistic styles in "twenty-four preludes in twenty-four keys," two each in the manner of Poulenc, Satie, Prokofiev, Stravinsky, Chopin, Berg, Joplin, Fauré, Bartók, Gershwin, Liszt and Ravel, is performed for the first time by Caesar Cancino in San Anselmo, California.

2 MAY 1982

Il tessuto d'Arabeschi for flute and string quartet by the 89-year-old British Parsi composer Kaikhosru Shapurji SORABJI is performed for the first time in Philadelphia.

5 MAY 1982

First Symphony, subtitled *Three Movements for Orchestra*, by the American composer Ellen Taaffe ZWILICH is performed for the first time by the American Composers Orchestra in New York under the direction of Gunther Schuller, later winning the 1983 Pulitzer Prize in Music (the first such award to a female composer).

9 MAY 1982

Concerto for Piano and Orchestra by the El Salvador composer Germán CÁCERES receives its first ever performance at the 13th Inter-American Music Festival in Washington, D.C.

11 MAY 1982

Black Pentecost, cantata by the English composer Peter Maxwell DAVIES, decrying industrial air pollution, is performed for the first time in London by the varivocal soprano Jan DeGaetani and tenor Michael Rippon with the Philharmonia Orchestra under the direction of Simon Rattle.

15 MAY 1982

Brachot Para Golda Meir, op. 109, for orchestra by the Colombian composer Bas Emilio ATEHORTUA, dedicated to the late Prime Minister of Israel, receives its first ever performance at the 13th Inter-American Music Festival in Washington, D.C.

23 MAY 1982

Count-Down for sixteen-part choir and two percussionists by the 35-year-old British composer Giles SWAYNE is performed for the first time at the Bath Festival.

30 MAY 1982

Tod ist ein langer Schlaf (Death Is a Long Sleep), variations on a theme by Haydn for cello and orchestra by the 53-year-old Soviet composer Edison DENISOV, is performed for the first time in Moscow.

4 JUNE 1982

Minutes Till Midnight, opera in two acts by the 64-year-old American composer Robert WARD, centered on an idealist atomic scientist who inadvertantly invents an annihilating doomsday bomb, opens the three-week New World Festival of the Arts in Miami, Florida.

6 JUNE 1982

The Silken Drum, chamber opera by the 43-year-old Icelandic composer Atli Heimir SVEINSSON, is produced in Reykjavik.

7 JUNE 1982

Solo Observed for piano, cello, vibraphone, and electric organ by the 43-year-old American composer Lukas FOSS is performed for the first time at the New World Festival of the Arts in Miami, Florida.

19 JUNE 1982

The Postman Always Rings Twice, opera by Stephen PAULUS after the novel by James M. Cain, is produced in St. Louis.

21 JUNE 1982

Forty-eighth Symphony, subtitled *Vision of Andromeda,* by Alan HOVHANESS is performed for the first time by the Minnesota Orchestra at the New World Festival of the Arts in Miami, Florida.

25 JUNE 1982

Memento, concerto for two pianos and orchestra by the 50-year-old American composer Michael COLGRASS, is performed for the first time by the Minnesota Orchestra at the New World Festival of the Arts in Miami, Florida.

28 JUNE 1982

Sixth Symphony for organ and orchestra by the 75-year-old American composer Paul CRESTON is performed for the first time in Washington, D.C.

4 JULY 1982

Sinfonietta della Notte for orchestra by the American composer Gloria COATES is performed for the first time in Lund, Sweden.

5 JULY 1982

Crossings for pure wave oscillator and small orchestra by the 51-year-old American composer Alvin LUCIER, inspired by "observing the flow of water around obstacles in Colorado trout streams and the recurring images of migrating animals and people crossing the rivers of vast continents," receives its first ever performance by members of the Chicago Symphony Orchestra and Wallace McMillan, soloist, as part of the 4th annual New Music America Festival in Chicago.

10 JULY 1982

Maria JERITZA, prima donna assoluta, of Czech parentage (her real name was Jedlitzka), whose career took her to the heights of fame in Europe and America, and to whom Richard Strauss dedicated in 1948 his last song *Malven* ["Der geliebten Maria diese letzte Rose," he inscribed on the manuscript—(For) Beloved Maria, this last rose], dies in Orange, New Jersey, at the age of 94. (The song was first publicly performed on 10 January 1985.)

18 JULY 1982

Stern Grove Grand Ceremonial Overtures by the American composer Henry BRANT, scored for two chamber orchestras, jazz drummer and three martial karate artists, one of them being Brant's son Joaquin Ives Brant, is performed for the first time in San Francisco. (The title was subsequently changed to *Horizontals Extending.*)

31 JULY 1982

The Confidence Man, first opera by the American composer George ROCHBERG, based on Herman Melville's novel, is produced for the first time at the Santa Fe Opera in New Mexico.

22 AUGUST 1982

Image, Reflection, Shadow for instrumental sextet by the British composer Peter Maxwell DAVIES is performed for the first time at the Lucerne Festival.

16 SEPTEMBER 1982

Housewarming for orchestra by the multifariously gifted American composer Morton GOULD is performed for the first time in Baltimore.

17 SEPTEMBER 1982

Three Sisters Who Are Not Sisters, opera by the 55-year-old American composer David AHLSTROM to the words of Gertrude Stein, is performed for the first time in San Francisco.

21 SEPTEMBER 1982

Concerto for two violins and orchestra by the 41-year-old Finnish composer Erkki SALMENHAARA is performed for the first time in Helsinki.

22 SEPTEMBER 1982

Beyond Neon: Post-Commercial Sound Sculptures for French horn and orchestra by the imaginative 36-year-old Norwegian composer Olav Anton THOMMESSEN is performed for the first time in Minneapolis.

1 OCTOBER 1982

Vermont Counterpoint for eleven flutes, ten of them recorded on tape, by the 46-year-old American composer Steve REICH, who inadvertently became the prophet of musical minimalism by virtue of primitivistic maximalism of repeated patterns in his works, is performed for the first time in New York.

2 OCTOBER 1982

Avanti! (Forward!) for orchestra by the 50-year-old Latvian-American composer Gundaris PONÉ is performed for the first time in Washington, D.C.

4 OCTOBER 1982

Glenn GOULD, Canadian-born pianist of extraordinary gifts who devoted endless hours to etch the technical ingredients to the point of crystal-clear lucidity in the works of Bach, and who became virtually an anchorite in self-imposed seclusion, dies suddenly in Toronto at the age of 50.

4 OCTOBER 1982

Koyaanisqatsi (a Hopi Indian word meaning "life out of balance"), film without words using the techniques of acceleration and lentification, with musical accompaniment featuring the deep voices of native American Indians, by the extraordinary American composer Philip GLASS—whose motto seems to be *e minimis multum,* or *festina lente* (oxymoronic maxim meaning "hurry slowly") is premièred at Radio City Music Hall Film Festival in New York.

14 OCTOBER 1982

Kinetic Poem for piano and orchestra by the 52-year-old Finnish composer Usko MERILÄINEN is performed for the first time in Helsinki.

15 OCTOBER 1982

Third Symphony in one movement by the 62-year-old Soviet Armenian composer Karen KHACHATURIAN is performed for the first time in Moscow.

16 OCTOBER 1982

Violin Concerto by the 33-year-old Danish composer Poul RUDERS is performed for the first time in Copenhagen.

19 OCTOBER 1982

Sixteenth Symphony by the 62-year-old Soviet composer Moisei VAINBERG is performed for the first time in Moscow.

23 OCTOBER 1982

Soldier Boy, Soldier, opera by the 54-year-old black American composer T. J. ANDERSON, to a libretto by Leon Forrest dealing with a black Vietnam veteran's return home, is performed for the first time at Indiana University in Bloomington.

29 OCTOBER 1982

Doctor Faustus Lights the Lights, opera by the 55-year-old American composer David AHLSTROM to words of Gertrude Stein, is performed for the first time in San Francisco.

30 OCTOBER 1982

The 56th Festival of the International Society for Contemporary Music, in conjunction with the Styrian Autumn Festival, opens in Graz, Austria, with the following program of brass band music presented at a morning concert:

Entmilitarisierte Zonen (Demilitarized Zones), march paraphrases by the 39-year-old Austrian composer Heinz Karl GRUBER; *Ständchen für einen Potentaten (Serenade for a Potentate)* for cello and brass band by the 41-year-old Austrian composer Dieter KAUFMANN; *Altiplano* by the 47-year-old Swedish composer Folke RABE, depicting the life among the Inca descendants in the high plateau of the Andes; *Prinz Johannes Wanderung* by the 52-year-old Austrian composer Franz SCHÖGGL; and *Ragtime and Habaneras* by the 56-year-old German composer Hans Werner HENZE, consisting of eleven miniatures.

30 OCTOBER 1982

The first day of the 56th Festival of the International Society for Contemporary Music continues in Graz with the following works presented throughout the evening:

Fireworks for orchestra by Igor STRAVINSKY; *Fürst Igor, Stravinsky* for bass and chamber ensemble by the 51-year-old Argentine-born German ultramodernist Mauricio KAGEL, with material drawn from Borodin's opera *Prince Igor* and his namesake Igor Stravinsky; *Atmospheres* for orchestra by the 59-year-old Hungarian master modernist György LIGETI, first performed at the Donaueschingen Festival on 22 October 1961; *Avant d' Être (Before Being)* for violin, cello and six wind players by the 28-year-old Greek composer Nicos CORNILIOS, depicting in macrorhythmic structures the fetal anticipation of imminent parturition; *Credo in US* for chamber ensemble by the prime American innovator John CAGE; *Improvisation sur Mallarmé* for soprano and orchestra by the greatly influential French composer of dialectically structured musical edifices Pierre BOULEZ; *Tem* for orchestra by the 44-year-old German composer Volker HEYN, in which a tone cluster stretched across the entire diapason of acoustical sounds is eventually compressed into a single tone, the *Tem;* and *Tea for Two* for orchestra, the famous tune of Vincent YOUMANS variegated and orchestrated by Dmitri SHOSTAKOVICH and used in one of his early ballets.

31 OCTOBER 1982

On the second day of the 56th Festival of the International Society for Contemporary Music in Graz, the following works are presented:

Kreuzspiel for orchestra by the 54-year-old legislator of elusive aleatory molecules of tonal monads Karlheinz STOCK-HAUSEN; *Tristes* for chamber orchestra by the 36-year-old French composer Jean-Claude WOLFF, in which the wistful essence of the music, expressed in sequences of atonal Angst, is cast in aquatic green colors; *Configurations* for orchestra by the 25-year-old Austrian composer Gerhard PRÄSENT, depicting the inexorable machinery of modern life; *Quintette à la Memoire d' Anton Webern* for chamber orchestra by the 54-year-old Belgian composer Henri POUSSEUR, written in a strict canonic style typical of the Webernian web; *Sonata* for two pianos by the 59-year-old Belgian composer Karel GOUYVAERTS, forming an oxymoronic synthesis of Webern's dodecaphony with Messiaen's neo-Gregorianism; *Piano-Piano* for solo piano by the 32-year-old Uruguayan composer Carlos DE SILVEIRA, in which musical cellular motives alternate with pregnant silences; *Nocturnes* for piano and tape by the remarkable 47-year-old French linguist, philosopher and composer François-B. MÂCHE; *Piano Variations* by the inventive German modernist Hans Werner HENZE; *We Think for the Future* for piano by Cornelius CARDEW, the uncompromising English concocter of inexorably incongruous and overwhelmingly illogical repetitive sonic structures who lost his life when he was run over on 13 December 1981 by a mindless automobilist; *Necessity is a Mother . . .* for three actresses and amplified double-bass by the 42-year-old American composer Alvin SINGLETON, a wordless theater piece glorifying motherhood; and *Piece for Small Orchestra String Quartet*, and ten *Studies for Player Piano* by the 70-year-old American composer, living in Mexico, Conlon NANCARROW, the initiator of piano music composed directly on perforated player-piano rolls in hyperpianistic counterpoint.

1 NOVEMBER 1982

On the third day of the 56th Festival of the International Society for Contemporary Music in Graz, the following electronic works are presented:

Gioco di Velocità by the 29-year-old Italian composer Roberto DOATI; *La Folia* by the 28-year-old Polish composer Pawel SZYMANSKI; *Ode for Elestase* by the 29-year-old Japanese composer Akira NISHIMURA; *Opus 1* by the 24-year-old Austrian composer Martin SIEREK; *Pourquoi astu jeté ta pantoufle? (Why Did You Throw Your Slipper?)* by the 23-year-old French composer Xavier GRACIA; *Wellenmusik II* by the 33-year-old Japanese composer Takehito SHIMAZU; and *The Stones of Jerusalem* by the 42-year-old Israeli composer Joseph DORFMAN.

Continuing throughout the afternoon and evening, the Festival presents the following works:

Die sechs Vermessenen (The Six Surveyors) for piano by the supremely intellectual 82-year-old Austrian-born master composer Ernst KRENEK; *Two Pianos and Violin* by the 30-year-old American composer Bunita MARCUS, a modernistically contrapuntal *ménage à trois*; *Four North American Ballads* for piano by the 44-year-old American composer Frederic RZEWSKI, in which simple folk tunes are magnified through tonal augmentation and compressed through melodic diminution, incorporating improvisatory sections; *Gamelan Corn* by

Philip CORNER; and a set of violin solo works including *Soundings* by Malcolm GOLDSTEIN.

2 NOVEMBER 1982

On the fourth day of the 56th Festival of the International Society for Contemporary Music in Graz, a morning concert of electronic music by Latin American composers presents the following program:

Creación de la tierra by the Belgian-born Colombian composer Jacqueline NOVA (1936–1975); *Suiana-Wanka* by the 27-year-old Uruguayan composer Fernando CONDON; *Imposible a la Equis* by the 45-year-old Guatemalan composer Joaquín ORELLANA; *Gran Tiempo* by the 42-year-old Uruguayan composer Coriún AHARONIAN; *Tramos (Stretches)* by the 43-year-old Argentine composer Eduardo BÉRTOLA; *. . . después el silencio. . . (. . .After the Silence. . .)* by the 42-year-old Argentine composer Hilda DIANDA; and *Huauqui* by the 42-year-old Argentine composer Graciela PARASKEVAIDIS.

2 NOVEMBER 1982

The fourth day of the 56th Festival of the International Society for Contemporary Music in Graz continues throughout the evening, presenting the following works:

Somos nueve (We Are Nine) for nine instrumentalists by the 33-year-old American composer Alfredo RUGELES, written in the manner of a modernized concerto grosso; *Interiors* for chamber ensemble by the 28-year-old Australian composer Trevor PEARCE, in twelve sections with subterranean juxtapositions and subliminal interpolations rich in deliberately meaningless tonal dislocations and psychosomatic coagulations; *Missa Viva 1978* for orchestra by the 39-year-old Israeli composer Arie SHAPIRA, with a verbal allusion to Tel Aviv (which means the Hill of Spring in Hebrew) and to an anonymous girl's name Aviva so that Missa viva when coalesced into Missaviva pays court to Aviva and Tel Aviv, with the sonic climax serving as an anticlimatic peroration; *The River* for orchestra by the 27-year-old French composer Pascal DUSAPIN, in which the aquatic flux is figuratively split into microhydrographical monads; *Thanatos Eros*, symphonic improvisations for orchestra by the 52-year-old German composer Dieter SCHNEBEL, wherein love and death merge into an oxymoronic liebestod; *Katabiosis* for ensemble by the 27-year-old Scottish composer Stephen FERGUSON, descriptive of the breakdown of living cells in an atonal progeria; *Tres impressoẽs cancioneirigenas* for chamber ensemble by the Brazilian composer Jorge ANTUNES, the third word in the title being a combination of two Portuguese words, cancioneiro (chanson) and cancerigenas (carcinogenic), the "three impressions" pronouncing damnation on the dictatorial period of former Brazilian politics; and *Die Atmer der Lydia* for orchestra by the 32-year-old Swiss composer Christoph DELZ, a "transcomposition" of pulmonary functions of an unidentified female named Lydia.

3 NOVEMBER 1982

On the fifth day of the 56th Festival of the International Society for Contemporary Music in Graz, a concert of electronic music from Austria presents the following program:

Excerpts from "Faust" after Nikolaus Lenau by Werner RUTTINGER; *Suite on E* by 34-year-old Werner RADITSCHNIG; *ORC 17* by 36-year-old Klaus AGER; *Fantasmata* by the 61-year-old Bulgarian-born composer Anestis LOGOTHETIS; *Memento* by the 45-year-old Polish-born composer Ryszard KLISOWSKI; *Mugl entsteigt (Mugl Descends)* by 29-

year-old Günther RABL; *Bach* by the Japanese composer resident in Germany Mayako KUBO; *Uraufführung (First Performance)* by 22-year-old Klaus KARLBAUER; *Spital* by the 30-year-old French-born composer Flora ST. LOUP; and *Requiem* by 29-year-old Bruno LIBERDA.

3 NOVEMBER 1982

The fifth day of the 56th Festival of the International Society for Contemporary Music in Graz continues throughout the evening with the following program:

Pezzo grazioso for wind quintet by the 46-year-old Polish composer Marek STACHOWSKI; *Once Upon a Time* for wind quintet by the 31-year-old Finnish composer Anneli ARHO, a musical remembrance of a pleasant day; *Second Brass Quintet* by the 42-year-old Austrian composer Günther KAHOWEZ, based on folk songs and medieval sequences; *The Tyger* by the 40-year-old Swedish composer Sven-David SANDSTRÖM, inspired by the macroailurophiliac poetry of William Blake; *Palinode No. 4* and *Four Lovesongs by Oswald von Wolkenstein*, two choral works by the 38-year-old composer Hubert STUPPNER; *Cantos del Capitán* for soprano and piano, towords of the great Chilean poet Pablo Neruda, by the 44-year-old Chilean composer Sergio ORTEGA; *The Seasons* for chorus by the 43-year-old Swiss composer and oboe virtuoso Heinz HOLLIGER, after poems by Friedrich Hölderlin; and *Ritornella, the Cosmic Wheel* for chorus by the 34-year-old Canadian composer Michel-Georges BRÉGENT, an homage to an ancient selenologist who flourished ca. 2300 B.C.

4 NOVEMBER 1982

On the sixth day of the 56th Festival of the International Society for Contemporary Music in Graz, the following electronic works are presented:

Sinfonie Konkret by the 24-year-old Austrian composer Martin SIEREK; *Chaceol-Music for the Early Evening* by the 27-year-old Austrian composer Martin SCHWARZENLANDER; *Minimal Splitting Movements* by the 29-year-old Austrian composer Werner JAUK; *Current Loops* by the 38-year-old German-born composer Helmut DENKER; *Orquideas Primaverales (Spring Orchids)* by the 43-year-old Argentine composer Eduardo KUSNIR; *Austera* by the 46-year-old Argentine composer Oscar BAZÁN; *Natal del Rei (The King's Birthday)* by the 42-year-old Uruguayan composer Conrado SILVA; *La Cuidad (Caution)* by the 27-year-old Bolivian composer Cergio PRUDENCIO; and *Ceremonias* by the 39-year-old Argentine composer Lionel FILIPPI.

4 NOVEMBER 1982

The sixth day of the 56th Festival of the International Society for Contemporary Music in Graz continues with the following program presented in the evening:

Samba for chamber ensemble by the 47-year-old Danish composer Bent LORENTZEN, a modernistic transfiguration of the Brazilian folk dance; *Polifonica, Monodia, Ritmica* for chamber orchestra by the 58-year-old Italian composer Luigi NONO, the most prominent practitioner of dodecaphonic realizations of classical forms; *Music for Orchestra No. 6* by the 61-year-old Polish composer Andrzej DOBROWOLSKI, symbolizing the embryonic and fetal formation of unicellular motives; *Alabaster* for three orchestras by the 31-year-old Japanese composer Isao MATSUSHITA, in which the constituent groups represent the three a's in the word alabaster, all bathed in the milky color of the substance in question; *Homenaje a Federico García Lorca* for chamber orchestra by the revolutionary Mexican composer Silvestre REVUELTAS (1899–1940), an homage to the great Spanish poet slain by

Franco's fascists; *Nocturnes II* for orchestra by the 63-year-old Polish composer Roman HAUBENSTOCK-RAMATI, a wistful invocation of the fading of the light; *Saudades do Parque Balneario Hotel* for alto saxophone and piano by the 60-year-old Brazilian composer Gilberto MENDES, being a nostalgic tribute to a hotel in a Brazilian spa; *À Varsovie* for orchestra by the 41-year-old Polish composer Bronislaw K. PRZYBYLSKI, a dedication to the long-suffering city of Warsaw; and *Concerto* for alto saxophone and twelve players by the 46-year-old Austrian composer Erich URBANNER.

5 NOVEMBER 1982

The 56th Festival of the International Society for Contemporary Music in Graz concludes with the following program:

Mutatio Perpetua for chamber ensemble and tape by the 48-year-old Korean composer Sukhi KANG, an experiment in tonalities, dynamics, rhythm and articulation, consisting of seventy-three musical units combining and separating in perpetual mutations; *Giardino religioso (Religious Garden)* for chamber ensemble by the cosmopolitan conductor and composer Bruno MADERNA (1920–1973); *Cantata for Makronissos* by the 35-year-old Greek composer Thanos MAKROUTSIKOS, composed in the concentration camp of Makronissos where the composer was confined by the reactionary military authorities; *Fasce* for orchestra by the 56-year-old Austrian composer Friedrich CERHA; *Entrata/Encore* by the 57-year-old Italian modernist Luciano BERIO; and *A Handsome-Smooth-Sweet-Smart-Clear Stroke; or else play not at all* for orchestra by the 38-year-old British composer Michael NYMAN, the title being taken from *Musick's Monument* by Thomas Mace, published in London in 1676.

7 NOVEMBER 1982

Double Concerto for piano, cello and orchestra by the 58-year-old American composer Benjamin LEES is performed for the first time in New York.

9 NOVEMBER 1982

Bumberboom: Scherzo diabolique for orchestra by the 48-year-old Canadian composer Sydney HODKINSON is performed for the first time in Montreal.

11 NOVEMBER 1982

Igor STRAVINSKY'S draft of *Le Sacre du Printemps* breaks all auction records when it sells for 330,000 pounds sterling at Sotheby's of London to the Paul Sacher Collection in Basel.

19 NOVEMBER 1982

The posthumous première of the *Fifteenth Symphony* by the romantic Swedish composer Allan PETTERSSON, completed in 1978, is given in Stockholm.

23 NOVEMBER 1982

Tenebrae, concerto for cello and orchestra by the 51-year-old Norwegian composer Arne NORDHEIM, is performed for the first time in Washington, D.C.

28 NOVEMBER 1982

Passio Domini nostri Jesu Christi secundum Joannum for chorus and ensemble by the 47-year-old Estonian composer Arvo PÄRT is performed for the first time in Munich.

15 DECEMBER 1982

Third Symphony by the 50-year-old Soviet composer Sergei SLONIMSKY, in four conjointed movements, *Andante, Allegro, Presto* and *Adagio*, making use of dodecaphonic progressions and microtones, is performed for the first time in Leningrad.

20 DECEMBER 1982

Artur RUBINSTEIN, Polish-born Jewish pianist of titanic powers, an inspired performer of profoundly human music, unexcelled interpreter of Chopin and Schumann, and self-acknowledged lover of many women, dies at the extreme age of 95 in his apartment in Geneva, which he shared with his last object of admiration, who helped him to write his candid autobiography.

1983

11 JANUARY 1983

Krzysztof PENDERECKI conducts the Berlin Philharmonic Orchestra in the first performance of his *Second Cello Concerto* with Mstislav Rostropovich as soloist.

18 JANUARY 1983

Concerto for kettledrum, trumpet and orchestra by the 48-year-old German composer Siegfried MATTHUS is performed for the first time in East Berlin.

18 JANUARY 1983

Concerto for Violin and Orchestra (1948) by the experimental American composer John J. BECKER (1886–1961), compatriot of Ives, Cowell, Ruggles, and Riegger with whom he comprised "the American Five," set in a single movement of vivid, dissonant counterpoint, polytonal rhythms, and rich chordal structures, all cast in an overtly coloristic orchestration, receives its first ever performance by the Chattanooga Symphony Orchestra.

30 JANUARY 1983

Sinfonia Ricercata for organ and violinless and percussionless orchestra by the 52-year-old Spanish composer Cristóbal HALFFTER is performed for the first time in Vienna.

3 FEBRUARY 1983

The two-evening spectacle *United States* by the 35-year-old avant-garde performance artist Laurie ANDERSON, a multimedia epic on the themes of politics, money and love, opens for its first complete performance at the Brooklyn Academy of Music in New York.

9 FEBRUARY 1983

Frank ZAPPA, radical rock musician and enthusiastic admirer of ultramodern classical music, presides over a concert in San Francisco commemorating the approxi-

mate centennials of the birth of Edgar VARÈSE and Anton von WEBERN, conducting Varèse's *Ionisation* and *Intégrales*. The balance of the program included Varése's *Poème electronique* and *Offrandes* and *Variations for Piano, op. 27*, and vocal works by Anton von Webern, conducted by Jean-Louis LeRoux.

10 FEBRUARY 1983

Concerto for Orchestra by the 43-year-old British composer and pianist John MCCABE is performed for the first time in London.

12 FEBRUARY 1983

Eubie BLAKE, black American musician, master of piano ragtime who proudly demonstrated unfailing digital fluency on television well into his 99th year, dies in Brooklyn five days after reaching the glorious mark of 100 years of age.

17 FEBRUARY 1983

Eleventh Symphony by the industrious Danish composer Vagn HOLMBOE is performed for the first time in Copenhagen.

22 FEBRUARY 1983

Sir Adrian BOULT, English conductor of impeccable classical bent who presented a number of congenial performances of works by modern British composers, dies in Tunbridge Wells at the age of 93.

24 FEBRUARY 1983

Sixteenth Symphony by the Swedish composer Allan PETTERSSON (1911–1980), originally designated *Alto Saxophone Concerto*, written for the American saxophonist Fred Hemke, is performed for the first time, posthumously, with Hemke as soloist, in Stockholm.

7 MARCH 1983

Igor MARKEVITCH, greatly talented Russian composer and conductor who rose to sudden fame in Paris where he became known as "second Igor," (the first being, of course, Stravinsky) and who later devoted himself mainly to conducting, dies in Antibes, France, at the age of 70.

7 MARCH 1983

Claude VIVIER, 34-year-old Canadian composer, is murdered in his Paris apartment where he was installed on a Canadian government subsidy, stabbed 24 times by a chance acquaintance and strangled with pads of paper stuffed in his mouth to stifle his cries for help. (His body was discovered on 12 March 1983.)

8 MARCH 1983

Sir William WALTON, illustrious British composer who began his career as an *enfant terrible* of modern music and who in his maturity created operatic and symphonic masterpieces in the aristocratic British tradition, dies at the island of Ischia in Italy where he lived for many years, three weeks before his 81st birthday.

11 MARCH 1983

A Death in the Family, opera by the 57-year-old American composer William MAYER, based on the emotionally moving semiautobiographical 1958 Pulitzer Prize-winning novel by James Agee, is performed for the first time in Minneapolis.

12 MARCH 1983

To the Edge of Dream for guitar and orchestra by the 52-year-old Japanese composer Toru TAKEMITSU is performed for the first time in Liège, France.

18 MARCH 1983

Siddharta, opera by the 50-year-old prime Danish composer Per NØRGÅRD, is produced in Stockholm.

19 MARCH 1983

Salambo, opera by the eminent Austrian composer Josef Matthias HAUER (1883–1959), receives its posthumous première performance over Austrian Radio in Vienna.

3 APRIL 1983

Counterbomb Renga, a spectacle by about one hundred poets and musicians protesting against the proliferation of nuclear weapons, conceived and coordinated by the 63-year-old Estonian-born Canadian composer Udo KASEMETS, is relayed by the Canadian Broadcasting Corporation.

5 APRIL 1983

Dialogues for violin, cello, and orchestra by the 65-year-old American composer Robert WARD is performed for the first time in Chattanooga, Tennessee.

10 APRIL 1983

Third Piano Concerto by the Soviet composer Tikhon KHRENNIKOV is first performed in Moscow, with the composer as soloist.

14 APRIL 1983

Elisabeth LUTYENS, English composer who wrote music in different genres marked by an effective use of modern techniques while preserving the melodic essence of English folk music, dies in Hampstead at the age of 76.

21 APRIL 1983

Piano Concerto by the 36-year-old American composer Peter LIEBERSON, gifted son of a talented father, Goddard Lieberson, commissioned by the Boston Symphony Orchestra for its centennial, is performed for the first time by Peter Serkin as soloist, Seiji Ozawa conducting the Boston Symphony.

23 APRIL 1983

Triple Duo by Elliott CARTER, scored for flute and clarinet, violin and cello, and piano and percussion, is performed for the first time in Symphony Space in London, by a group called Fires of London.

24 APRIL 1983

The Australian-born pianist Geoffrey Douglas Madge courageously plays the American première of Kaikhosru Shapurji SORABJI'S formidable four-hour piano work, *Opus Clavicembalisticum*, at the University of Chicago.

27 APRIL 1983

Poem for piano and orchestra by the 59-year-old Serbian composer Vasilije MOKRANJAC, his last large work, set in a lyrical meditative manner, is performed for the first time in Belgrade.

29 APRIL 1983

Padre Libertador for chorus and orchestra by the 74-year-old Argentine-born Venezuelan folklorist and composer Isabel ARETZ, in three movements (*La palabra mágica, Tiempo difícil*, and *Despierta con el pueblo*), receives its first performance at a 25th anniversary concert of the Inter-American Music Festival in Washington, D.C.

30 APRIL 1983

George BALANCHINE, Russian choreographer extraordinaire (his real name was Balanchivadze, and his country of origin was Georgia, in the Caucasus), who transplanted himself and his art to New York, dies at the age of 79, crippled by a dreadful neurological illness that reduced his once lithe body to the state of a mindless mass of flesh.

6 MAY 1983

Ra, multimedia work with audience participation by the 49-year-old Canadian composer R. Murray SCHAFER, based on the myth of the Egyptian sun god, is presented in a continuous performance from dawn to dusk in Toronto.

12 MAY 1983

Sounder Rounds for orchestra by the innovative American composer Earle BROWN is performed for the first time in Saarbrücken, Germany.

14 MAY 1983

Second Symphony, subtitled *Summer Music,* by the 48-year-old Welsh composer William MATHIAS is performed for the first time by the Royal Liverpool Philharmonic Society.

17 MAY 1983

Organ Concerto by the masterly 82-year-old Austrian-born American composer Ernst KRENEK is performed for the first time by Martin Haselböck as soloist with the Melbourne Symphony Orchestra under the direction of John Hopkins.

18 MAY 1983

Guitar Concerto by the 40-year-old Swedish composer Sven-David SANDSTRÖM is performed for the first time in Malmö.

19 MAY 1983

Fratres I for string orchestra and percussion by the 47-year-old Estonian composer Arvo PÄRT is performed for the first time in Göteborg, Sweden.

20 MAY 1983

Seventh Symphony, subtitled *Ecliptical Instincts,* by the 52-year-old Danish composer Ib NØRHOLM is performed for the first time in Copenhagen.

31 MAY 1983

Second Sinfonia by the 34-year-old English composer Nigel OSBORNE is performed for the first time by the Leicestershire Schools Symphony Orchestra, Peter Fletcher conducting.

2 JUNE 1983

The English Cat, comic opera by Hans Werner HENZE, is performed for the first time in Schwetzingen, West Germany.

2 JUNE 1983

Afterimages for orchestra by the 42-year-old Italian-born American composer Marc-Antonio CONSOLI, in three movements, *October Lights Refrains, Elegiac Lullaby* and *The Dream at the End of Joy Tract Road* (the name of a country street in the Adirondack mountains, where Consoli spent time during his American sojourn), is performed for the first time by the New York Philharmonic, conducted by Raymond Leppard.

3 JUNE 1983

Raleigh's Dream, opera by the Scottish composer Iain HAMILTON, is performed for the first time in Durham, North Carolina.

3 JUNE 1983

Foci I for orchestra by the 58-year-old American composer Leonard ROSENMAN, the entire work being derived from the opening chord in the woodwinds forming its first focus, is performed for the first time in its revised version by the New York Philharmonic, Arthur Weisberg conducting. (The original version, for chamber ensemble, was first performed in New York by the Los Angeles Chamber Orchestra, conducted by Gerard Schwarz, on 11 April 1981.)

8 JUNE 1983

Canti del Sole for tenor and orchestra by the English-born American composer Bernard RANDS, winner of the 1984 Pulitzer Prize, which presents a day's progression from dawn to dusk through a continuous setting of poems in several languages about the sun, is performed for the first time by Paul Sperry as soloist with the New York Philharmonic, Zubin Mehta conducting.

17 JUNE 1983

A Quiet Place by Leonard BERNSTEIN, constituting a sequel to his one-act opera *Trouble in Tahiti* produced in 1952, is staged for the first time in Houston, Texas.

17 JUNE 1983

Peter MENNIN, American composer of symphonies in a faultless neoclassical manner touched with Mediterranean songfulness (he was of an Italian family and his real name was Mennini), dies in New York at the age of 60, a victim of incurable lung cancer.

19 JUNE 1983

Seid nüchtern und wachet . . . (Be wakeful and Watchful . . .), cantata by the 48-year-old Soviet composer of German origin Alfred SCHNITTKE, based on a version of the Faust legend published in 1587 under the title *Historia von Doktor Johann Fausten,* and commissioned by the Vienna Choral Academy for its 125th anniversary, is performed for the first time in Vienna. (Its Moscow première took place on 23 October 1983.)

24 JUNE 1983

Second Symphony by the 48-year-old Dutch composer Peter SCHAT is performed for the first time by the Rotterdam Philharmonic Orchestra.

25 JUNE 1983

Alberto GINASTERA, immensely talented Argentine composer who began his career as a fashioner of pulsating Latin American rhythms in song and symphony, but who developed a stern code of advanced atonal, polytonal and dodecaphonic techniques in his later works, dies in his home in Geneva, Switzerland, racked by lung cancer, at the age of 67.

10 JULY 1983

Werner EGK, significant German composer who allegedly changed his original and undistinguished name Mayer to a seemingly self-complimentary acronym for "ein grosser (or even, ein genialer) Komponist," but who claimed that he did so as a tribute to his wife, Elizabeth Karl (with the middle guttural letter added "for euphony"), whose music was marked by pleasingly acrid harmonies and dense contrapuntal involvement, dies in Inning, near Munich, at the age of 82.

16 JULY 1983

Second Symphony, subtitled *Reflections*, by the 61-year-old Czech-born American composer Karel HUSA is performed for the first time in Greensboro, North Carolina.

17 JULY 1983

Cello Concerto by the 80-year-old English composer Sir Lennox BERKELEY is performed for the first time in Manchester.

23 JULY 1983

Georges AURIC, French composer, member of the legendary group Les Six (the others were Milhaud, Honegger, Poulenc, Durey and Germaine Tailleferre), dies in Paris at the age of 84.

27 JULY 1983

Piano Concerto by the 31-year-old British composer Dominic MULDOWNEY is performed for the first time in London.

17 AUGUST 1983

Ira GERSHWIN, supreme American lyricist who wrote the great libretti for his brother George's musicals in gloriously rhymed verse, dies at his home in Beverly Hills, California, at the age of 86.

23 SEPTEMBER 1983

Akhenaten by the 76-year-old German-born American composer Gene GUTCHË, in a version for tenor, chorus, and orchestra, is performed for the first time in St. Louis.

29 SEPTEMBER 1983

Third Symphony by the highly distinguished Polish composer Witold LUTOSLAWSKI, who worked on it for nearly ten years, is finally performed after its successful completion, in Chicago.

30 SEPTEMBER 1983

À l'approche du Feu méditant by the 45-year-old French composer Jean-Claude ELOY, set for the traditional Japanese Gagaku ensemble, with two choirs of Buddist monks and five Bugaku dances, is performed for the first time in Tokyo.

1 OCTOBER 1983

Fourth Symphony by the 51-year-old Soviet composer Sergei SLONIMSKY, dedicated to the memory of his father, the novelist Mikhail Slonimsky, in four movements, *Allegro scherzando*, *Andante*, *Allegro maziale* and *Marcheofunèbre*, is performed for the first time in Kuibishev on the Volga River. (Its first Leningrad performance took place on 23 March 1984.)

4 OCTOBER 1983

The Photographer, theater piece by the ingeniously simplistic American composer Philip GLASS, in three acts of drama, concert music and dance, portraying in vivid colors the extraordinary life of the pioneer motion-analyzing photographer Eadweard Muybridge, who was the first to prove that, like a galloping horse, a trotting horse had at moments all four hooves off the ground, who killed the lover of his wife but won an acquittal in a sensational trial, is performed in a new version, with the subtitle *Far From the Truth*, at the Brooklyn Academy of Music. (The world première of the original version took place at the Holland Festival in June 1982.)

7 OCTOBER 1983

Wenn Bach Bienen gezüchtet hätte (If Bach Had Raised Bees), concertino for harpsichord, electric bass guitar, electric tape and ensemble by the 48-year-old Estonian composer Arvo PÄRT, based on the theme B-A-C-H, is performed for the first time in Graz, Austria.

7 OCTOBER 1983

Double Concerto for flute, bassoon and orchestra by the 57-year-old Austrian avant-garde composer Friedrich CERHA is performed for the first time in Graz.

8 OCTOBER 1983

Concerto primaverile (Spring Concerto) for violin and string orchestra by the 51-year-old Soviet composer Sergei SLONIMSKY, in three movements, *Allegro capriccioso*, *Romanze* and *Vivace ben ritmato*, is performed for the first time in Vilnius, by Sergei Stadler, soloist, and the Lithuanian Chamber Orchestra under the direction of Saulus Sondetskis. (A Leningrad performance was given on 17 October 1983.)

9 OCTOBER 1983

Monodrama for cello and orchestra by the 31-year-old German composer Wolfgang RIHM is performed for the first time in Graz.

19 OCTOBER 1983

Otadžbina (The Fatherland), oratorio by the Serbian prime romantic composer Petar KONJOVIĆ (1883–1970), in three "singing actions" inspired by the epic folksong about the Serbian defeat in the Battle of Kosovo in 1389, is produced in Belgrade.

20 OCTOBER 1983

Double-bass Concerto by Gian Carlo MENOTTI is performed for the first time by James VanDemark as soloist with the New York Philharmonic, Zubin Mehta conducting.

29 OCTOBER 1983

The 57th Festival of the International Society for Contemporary Music opens in Aarhus, Denmark, with a performance of *I Ching* for percussion solo by the 51-year-old Danish composer Per NØRGÅRD, after the ancient Chinese book of oracles based on 64 different states of all living things, in four movements: *Thunder Repeated, the Image of Shock*; *The Taming Power of the Small*; *The Gentle, the Penetrating;* and *Towards Completion: Fire Over Water*.

At an afternoon concert, the following program of chamber music by Danish composers is presented:

Aquarelles by 38-year-old Ole BUCK; *Pianissimo Furioso* by 36-year-old Karl Aage RASMUSSEN, an oxymoronic etude in which inner fury is expressed in soft sounds; *Haven med stier der deleg sig (The Garden with Separating Paths)*, to text of Jorge Luis Borges, by 52-year-old Ib NØRHOLM, with its seven instruments all following separate metronome beats; *Perceptive Constructions* by 51-year-old Henning CHRISTIANSEN, in four sections, being an essay in aggressive simplicity without falling into psychedelic abecedarianism; and *Seadrift* by 51-year-old Per NØRGÅRD, in two movements, *Being Together* and *Torn Apart*, inspired by the poetry of Walt Whitman.

29 OCTOBER 1983

The first day of the 57th Festival of the International Society for Contemporary Music continues in Aarhus with the following program of symphonic works at an evening concert:

Tre Concerti Piccoli by the 57-year-old German composer Hans Werner HENZE, a set of interludes from his ninth opera, *The English Cat*, which deals with an innocent victim of ailurophobia; *Third Symphony* by the 70-year-old Polish composer Witold LUTOSLAWSKI; and *Fifth Symphony* by the Danish classical romanticist Carl NIELSEN (1865–1931).

29 OCTOBER 1983

On the first day of the 57th Festival of the International Society for Contemporary Music in Aarhus, a nocturnal concert of chamber music is presented with the following program:

Night Fantasies for solo piano by the 75-year-old American composer Elliott CARTER, suggested by a hypnopompic interlude of nocturnal wakefulness; *Pyonkyong* for piano and percussion by the 38-year-old Korean composer trained in Germany Younghi PAGH-PAAN; *String Quartet* by the 28-year-old French composer Pascal DUSAPIN; and *Fourth String Quartet* by the 78-year-old Italian composer Giacinto SCELSI.

30 OCTOBER 1983

On the second day of the 57th Festival of the International Society for Contemporary Music in Aarhus, *Mantra* by Karlheinz STOCKHAUSEN for two pianists, tape, ring modulator, woodblocks and antique cymbals, subdivided into thirteen cycles integrated into a mystical invocation of Hindu ritual, is presented at an afternoon concert. At a later concert, the following program entitled "Is Darmstadt Alive?" is presented:

/L for amplified piano, four hands, by the 35-year-old Finnish composer Jukka TIENSUU, an essay in modulated sonorities; *String Quartet* by the 34-year-old British composer Jonathan HARVEY, in one movement based on gradual expansion of melodic ornaments; *Second String Quartet* by the 40-year-old British composer Brian FERNEY-HOUGH, a labyrinthine exercise in serialistic melodies and pauses; *Salut für Caudwell* for two guitars by the 48-year-old German composer Helmut LACHENMANN, dedicatory essay to a modern esthetician; and *Tetras* for string quartet by the 61-year-old commanding master of teleological structures Iannis XENAKIS, set in a tetradic ensemble.

30 OCTOBER 1983

The second day of the 57th Festival of the International Society for Contemporary Music continues in Aarhus, at an evening concert with the following program:

Treppenmusik (Staircase Music) for saxophone quartet, clarinet quartet, string quintet and electronics by the 39-year-old Canadian composer John REA, a musical counterpart of Dutch artist M. C. Escher's heterodimensional ladders; *Epigrams*, to a text by Takis Antoniou, for soprano and chamber orchestra by the 48-year-old Greek composer Theodore ANTONIOU, influenced by Byzantine hymnology; Two Parts from *Four Compositions*, "Plain Song" and "Variations" for flute, clarinet, horn, piano and string quintet by the 34-year-old Danish composer Poul RUDERS; *Two Shôgas (Two Solfeges)* for soprano, flute, oboe, percussion, harp, piano and violins by the 76-year-old Japanese composer Yoritsuné MATSUDAIRA, sonorous exercises in onomatopeia; and *Incenters* for trumpet, horn, trombone and chamber group by the 55-year-old American composer Jacob DRUCKMAN, corresponding in geometry to a triangle inscribed in a circle or a pyramid within a sphere, with blocks of brassy sounds set against the equilibrium in the rest of the ensemble.

31 OCTOBER 1983

On the third day of the 57th Festival of the International Society for Contemporary Music in Aarhus, a morning concert of electronic mixed media from Scandinavia presents the following program:

Openings by the composer and visual artist team Par and Jörgen LINDGREN, an attempt at a musical utopia in a conflict with electronic and concrete sounds; *In Dagbrott (Daybreak)* by the 32-year-old Swedish composer Rolf ENGSTRÖM, corresponding to the palimpsest or pentimento in painting; *Organ Music 1980* by the 44-year-old Hungarian-born composer Akos RÓZMANN; and *À propos Marcel* by the 47-year-old poet/composer/sonologist Sten HANSON and 47-year-old photographer/artist Nino MONASTRA, an artistic commentary on the famous modern painter and chessmaster Marcel Duchamp.

31 OCTOBER 1983

On the third day of the 57th Festival of the International Society for Contemporary Music in Aarhus, an afternoon concert of minimal music presents the following program:

Music for Mallet Instruments, Voices and Organ by the 47-year-old American composer Steve REICH, based on the technique of the gradual phase displacement and stratification of the parameters of thematic content; *Litanie I* for piano by the 60-year-old Belgian composer Karel GOEYVAERTS, an elaboration of Balinese and African techniques of drumming; *Impho 102/6* for six crotales (miniature cymbal clapper-pairs) by the 40-year-old Hungarian composer Zoltán JENEY, the title being the Telex number of a hotel in Tokyo; *The Knight of Richerenches* for two pianos by the 35-year-old Ukrainian-born Canadian composer Lubomyr MELNYK, invoking the legend of the medieval Knights of the Temple; and *Music for Horns, Piano and Cymbals* by the 41-year-old American, composer John MCGUIRE, consisting of a chain of thirty-six sections of responsorial exchange.

31 OCTOBER 1983

The third day of the 57th Festival of the International Society for Contemporary Music continues with the following program at an evening concert in Aarhus:

Bells of Light for four choirs by the 24-year-old Canadian composer James HARLEY, to a text of syllabic phonemes gradually shifting phases to construct a sound sculpture; *Carrousel-Constellations* for two pianos, flute, cello and percussion by the 36-year-old Canadian composer Walter BOUDREAU, a cycle of nine pieces reflecting the topographical aspects of the nine planets of the solar system; *Three Pieces for Two Pianos, Eight Hands* by the 28-year-old Dutch composer Robert NAS-VELD, based on octotonic and enneatonic scales; *Linea* for two pianos and percussion by the 58-year-old Italian composer Luciano BERIO, involving a constant reshaping of a simple basic melody; and *Trio for Violin, Horn and Piano* by the 60-year-old cosmopolitan modernist György LIGETI, in three movements based on heterometric variations on asymmetrical melodies.

31 OCTOBER 1983

On the third day of the 57th Festival of the International Society for Contemporary Music in Aarhus, the following program, entitled "From Composition to Improvisation," is presented at a late night concert:

Recitatons for voice without accompaniment by the 38-year-old Greek-born French composer Georges APERGHIS, consisting of fourteen fragments of aleatory music, each marked by an expressive command, such as "secretive," "contemptuous," etc.; *Japan*, one of the works from *For Times to Come*, which consists of seventeen texts of Intuitive Music by the 55-year-old German master of modernity Karlheinz STOCK-HAUSEN; *n* for four uncoordinated instrumental parts by the 37-year-old British composer Michael FINNISSY; *Turba* for double-bass solo by the 29-year-old British composer Oliver KNUSSEN; *Echo III* for trumpet solo and tape by the 40-year-old British composer Roger SMALLEY; and *Organic Music* for any number of instruments by the New Zealand-born British composer Lyell CRESSWELL, giving improvisatory freedom to the performers.

1 NOVEMBER 1983

On the fourth day of the 57th Festival of the International Society for Contemporary Music at Aarhus, the following program is presented at an afternoon concert, under the general heading "Neotonality":

Heavy Metal Two-step for brass quintet by the British composer David SUTTON-ANDERSON, with the imperious tuba entry establishing a commanding Gestalt; *Fratres* for violin and piano by the 48-year-old Estonian composer Arvo PÄRT, in which the meandering violinistic figures and solemn hymnodic harmonies are united in an appeal for the brotherhood of men; *For Renée* for flute, cello, piano and percussion by the 45-year-old Icelandic composer Thorkell SIGURB-JÖRNSSON, a birthday salutation in five moments; *C'est la mer melée au soleil (It is the Sea Mixed with the Sun)* for guitar solo by the 29-year-old Danish composer Erik HØJSGAARD, to a poem by Arthur Rimbaud; and *In Dark Times*, eight songs to texts by Bertolt Brecht by the 31-year-old British composer Dominic MULDOWNEY, scored for soprano, tenor, bass, flute, clarinet, viola, cello and piano.

1 NOVEMBER 1983

The fourth day of the 57th Festival of the International Society for Contemporary Music in Aarhus continues with an evening concert of "Theatrical Expressions," featuring the following program:

De profundis for piano four hands by the 34-year-old Belgian composer Paul BEELAERTS, a hymnal lament; *Heiligenle-*

gende for recorder, eight-part vocal ensemble, speaker and tape by the 42-year-old Austrian composer Dieter KAUF-MANN, based on Psalm 129 by Ernesto Cardenal, the Nicaraguan priest imprisoned under dictator Somoza; *Tuba mirum* for tuba player by the 37-year-old British composer Trevor WISHART, representing a prisoner in a mental hospital; and *Questions* for thirty-two voices by the 54-year-old Japanese composer Joji YUASA, in six movements depicting both physical and metaphysical inquiries.

At a late night concert wind instrumentalists Morten Carlsen and Jesper Zeuthen present a program of improvisational fusion music, combining folk and art music from the Third World with Western avant-garde jazz.

2 NOVEMBER 1983

On the fifth day of the 57th Festival of the International Society for Contemporary Music, *Sinfonie querrière et amoureuse* for organ by the 51-year-old Italian composer Niccolò CASTIGLIONI is performed at a morning concert in the Aarhus Cathedral. At an afternoon concert, the following program, under the general heading "The Social Commitment," is presented by the Dutch orchestra De Volharding (The Perseverance):

Tango for Jet by 37-year-old Diderik WAGENAAR; *Balada do amor militante* to the text of Manuel Alegre by 38-year-old Portuguese-born Dutch composer Amilcar Vásques DIAS; *Blues voor de Volharding* by 29-year-old Huub DE VRIEND; *Workers Union* by 44-year-old Louis ANDRIESSEN; *Järn (Iron)* by Klas TORSTENSSON; *Moeilijkheden (Difficulties)* by 39-year-old Klaas DE VRIES; *On Jimmy Yancey* by Louis ANDRIESSEN; and *Dressoir* by 48-year-old Russian-born Dutch composer Misha MENGELBERG.

2 NOVEMBER 1983

The fifth day of the 57th Festival of the International Society for Contemporary Music continues with the Aarhus Symphony Orchestra presenting the following program at an evening concert:

Arc of Life by the 83-year-old great composer Ernst KRENEK, a philosopher of modern music who successfully combines profound truths of life with dodecaphonic artistry; *Gondwana* by the 36-year-old French composer Tristan MURAIL, the title referring to the mythical sunken continent; *Beati pauperes II (Blessed Be the Poor)* with vocal soloists by the 59-year-old Swiss composer Klaus HUBER, a "Kontrafaktur" of two motets by Orlando Lassus; and *Symphony, Antiphony* by the 51-year-old Danish composer Pelle GUNDMUNDSEN-HOLMGREEN, a pair of homogeneous and heterogeneous works.

At a night concert the Australian pianist Geoffrey Douglas Madge performs *Opus Clavecembalisticum*, the brobdingnagian masterpiece by the supreme British Parsi individualist Kaikhosru Shapurji SORABJI.

3 NOVEMBER 1983

On the sixth day of the 57th Festival of the International Society for Contemporary Music in Aarhus, the following audiovisual works are presented at an early afternoon concert:

Claustraphonie by the 48-year-old Swiss composer Jürg WYT-TENBACH, a salad bowl of musical quotations from Schubert to Schoenberg to the Beatles; *Patches of Life*, an opera-oratorio for television by the 40-year-old Swedish composer Daniel BÖRTZ, extolling nature's struggle against man's lust for destruction; and *Kasaanin Synty (The Genesis of Kazan)* by the 37-year-old Finnish composer Pekka SIRÉN, based on an old Mordvinian poem telling the story of self-immolation among the pagan population of Kazan on the Volga river.

3 NOVEMBER 1983

The sixth day of the 57th Festival of the International Society for Contemporary Music continues in Aarhus with an afternoon concert featuring the following electronic works:

Bouwstenen for bass clarinet and multiple tape delay by the 39-year-old Dutch composer Harry SPARNAAY; *Berceuse* for tape by the 50-year-old Polish composer Eugeniusz RUDNIK; *Violin Control* for violin and synthesizer by the 46-year-old Swiss composer Thomas KESSLER; *Voyage au Centre de la Tête* for tape by the 51-year-old French composer François BAYLE; and *Invention V* for percussion and electronics by the 31-year-old Norwegian composer Kjell SAMKOPF.

3 NOVEMBER 1983

On the sixth day of the 57th Festival of the International Society for Contemporary Music in Aarhus, the following program of chamber music is presented at an evening concert:

String Quartet by the 29-year-old Hungarian composer Miklós CSEMICZKY; *Sei danze* for violin solo by the 34-year-old Italian composer Fernando MENCHERINI; *Brains and Dancin'* for string quartet by the 33-year-old Swedish composer Mikael EDLUND, purported to reflect the cerebral and choreographic elements in music; *Oriens III* for three flutes by the 35-year-old Brazilian composer Ronaldo COUTINO DE MIRANDA, in three movements of diversified content; *Looking at Silence* for cello solo by the 43-year-old Israeli composer Joseph DORFMAN, with the cello tuned in scordatura, which determines its atonal character; and *Tashi Quartet* for clarinet, violin, cello and piano by the 37-year-old American composer Peter LIEBERSON, son of the renowned recording executive Goddard Lieberson.

4 NOVEMBER 1983

On the seventh day of the 57th Festival of the International Society for Contemporary Music in Aarhus, the following program featuring Danish music is presented at an afternoon concert:

Second String Quartet by 31-year-old Hans ABRAHAMSEN; *Fresques*, Part III, for guitar solo by 74-year-old Swiss-born Gunnar BERG; *Mambo* for clarinet, cello and piano by 48-year-old Bent LORENTZEN, inspired by the rhythms of Afro-Cuban music; *A Dream in Violet* for string trio by Poul Rovsing OLSEN (1922–1982), based on an eight-note theme converging on the central middle A in the coda; *String Quartet* by 27-year-old Steen PADE; and *Piano Quintet* by 59-year-old Axel BORUP-JØRGENSEN.

4 NOVEMBER 1983

The seventh day of the 57th Festival of the International Society for Contemporary Music continues in Aarhus at an evening concert with the Danish Radio Symphony Orchestra performing the following program:

Le Pinceau (The Paint Brush) by the 39-year-old Japanese composer Yoshiyuki DOI, a shimmering palette of super-imposed and interwoven timbres; *The Magic Mountain* for piano and orchestra by the 34-year-old British composer John HOP-

KINS, after the novel by Thomas Mann describing the tragic monotony of a tubercular retreat; *Otto poesie da un soldo (Eight Poems for a Penny)* for tenor and orchestra, inspired by the writings of James Joyce, by the 37-year-old Italian composer Claudio BILUCAGLIA; and *Space* for four orchestral groups by the 30-year-old Rumanian-born German resident composer Adriana HÖLSZKY, depicting the vivacious cosmogony of the Maori people of New Zealand.

4 NOVEMBER 1983

The 57th Festival of the International Society for Contemporary Music in Aarhus concludes with the following program at a late night concert:

Dressur for trio of wooden percussion instruments by the audacious experimenter who was born in Argentina and took residence in Germany, Mauricio KAGEL, herein purporting to advocate the training of musicians similar to the *dressage* of performing horses; *Invention* for tape by the 45-year-old Venezuelan composer Alfredo DEL MONACO, an electronic study focusing on the relationship between duration and tone color; *Tango* for clarinet, cello, piano and trombone by the 29-year-old Polish composer Tadeusz WIELECKI, in which the participating instruments dance a tango with one another; *Six Songs* for voice and piano by the 40-year-old British composer Mick WILSON, to his own words; and *On Shooting Stars*, an homage to the Chilean folksinger/poet/playwright Victor Jara who fell victim of the military clique in Chile, for chamber ensemble by the 33-year-old Australian composer Vincent PLUSH.

7 NOVEMBER 1983

Morephonemena, highly serialized work for twelve unaccompanied voices to a text created from phonemes by the 57-year-old American composer Milton BABBITT, in which every musical feature of the work relates to the number 12 (twenty-four consonants and twelve vowels in the text, twelve minutes in length, written in twelve-tone style, etc.), is given its first performance at the San Francisco Museum of Modern Art by the vocal ensemble Ariel, Christopher Fulkerson conducting.

7 NOVEMBER 1983

Germaine TAILLEFERRE, the last surviving member of Les Six, the French group of early modernists, dies in Paris at the age of 91.

7 NOVEMBER 1983

Gallery 83 for chamber ensemble by the 60-year-old American composer and timpanist William KRAFT, based on paintings by the composer, Claude Monet and Jackson Pollock, receives its first performance at the San Francisco Museum of Modern Art, the composer conducting.

13 NOVEMBER 1983

Viola Concerto by the 31-year-old German composer Wolfgang RIHM is performed for the first time in West Berlin.

19 NOVEMBER 1983

Perfect Lives (Private Parts), video opera by Robert ASHLEY, in seven acts each lasting exactly 25 minutes and 50 seconds, with the composer narrating his song in quasi-singing vocal inflections, is televised from New York.

28 NOVEMBER 1983

Saint François d'Assise, first opera by the 74-year-old French composer of devotional and ornithological music Olivier MESSIAEN, to his own libretto suffused with deep religious thought and depicting the immanent aspects of Grace in the soul of Saint Francis, who was himself a devout birdman, its melodious score replete with trills and refrains characteristic of flying creatures, in five sections culminating with an angelic choir vibrant with the sounds of an Ondes Martenot and a wordless women's chorus, is performed for the first time at the Paris Opéra.

4 DECEMBER 1983

Claudio SANTORO, Brazilian composer of progressive tendencies in music as well as in politics, conducts in Rio de Janeiro the first performance of his *Tenth Symphony.*

1984

11 JANUARY 1984

De Snelheid (Velocity), orchestral poem by the modern flying Dutchman Louis ANDRIESSEN, a study in reciprocally counteractive forces reflected in relative velocity of instrumental parts, is performed for the first time as a commissioned work by the San Francisco Symphony Orchestra under the direction of its Dutch conductor Edo de Waart.

14 JANUARY 1984

Paul BEN-HAIM, accomplished Israeli composer who fled his native Germany and established himself in Israel, changing his real name Frankenburger to the Hebrew appellation Ben-Haim (meaning "son of bliss"), who wrote a number of orchestral and vocal works inspired by Biblical themes, dies in Tel Aviv at the age of 84.

24 JANUARY 1984

Ralph SHAPEY conducts the first performance of his *Double Concerto* for violin, cello and Orchestra at the Juilliard School of Music in New York.

28 JANUARY 1984

Prismatic Variations by the 57-year-old American composer Donald ERB, scored for orchestra with the participation of three harmonicas, slide whistle, piano, electric piano, electric organ and about eighty young people in the audience, is performed for the first time as a commissioned work by the St. Louis Symphony Orchestra, Leonard Slatkin conducting.

2 FEBRUARY 1984

Bells, an anti-war work by the 62-year-old American composer Pin GILBERT, to texts taken from Bertrand Russell, John Cage, Gertrude Stein, and others, opening with the Sanskrit apostrophe, "We want more cows!" accompanied by a whole campanology of popular demands, is performed for the first time at El Camino College in Torrance, California.

10 FEBRUARY 1984

Dances from the Sacred Harp, four-movement work based on hymn tunes from borrowed from *The Original Sacred Harp,* by the 31-year-old American composer Roger BOURLAND, is given its first ever performance by the Boston Musica Viva at Jordan Hall in Boston.

11 FEBRUARY 1984

Howl for three dogs and twenty human voices organized by Kirk NUROCK, founder of the Natural Sound Center, is performed for the first time in New York.

18 FEBRUARY 1984

Western Springs by the American composer Henry BRANT, a spatial assembly for two orchestras, two choruses and two jazz combos, in five sections descriptive of hot springs in five Western states, is performed for the first time by the La Jolla Civic/ University Orchestra at the University of California in San Diego.

21 FEBRUARY 1984

Dhammapada for soprano, harp and percussion, after the classic Buddhist epic poem, by the 51-year-old Soviet composer Sergei SLONIMSKY, is performed for the first time in Leningrad.

26 FEBRUARY 1984

Konstantin DANKEVICH, nationalistic Ukrainian composer who achieved a dictatorial position by establishing a proper socialistic type of composition but who nonetheless failed to satisfy the extreme demands of proper Communist ideology in his operatic treatment of Russian history, dies at the age of 78 in the Ukrainian capital of Kiev.

9 MARCH 1984

Concerto for timpani and orchestra by the 60-year-old American composer and percussion virtuoso William KRAFT is performed for the first time by Thomas Akins as soloist with the Indianapolis Symphony Orchestra, John Nelson conducting.

10 MARCH 1984

The Black Theatre of Hermes Trismegistos to text and music by the 50-year-old Canadian composer R. Murray SCHAFER, for actors, singers and instrumentalists, depicting marriage according to the rites of medieval alchemists, is performed for the first time at the Contemporary Music Festival at the California Institute of the Arts in Valencia, California.

14 MARCH 1984

Scritti di Leonardo, the first musical setting of words by Leonardo da Vinci, by the 29-year-old American composer Christopher FULKERSON, for tenor solo, vocal quartet and instrumental ensemble of viola, guitar, harp, flute and bass clarinet and set in a "simultaneous form" arising from the sometimes overlapping, sometimes sequential and sometimes simultaneous placement of its numerous arias, quartets and instrumental pieces, receives its first performance by Patrick Neve as tenor soloist and the vocal ensemble Ariel at the San Francisco Museum of Modern Art, the composer conducting.

17 MARCH 1984

Sendings by Kirk NUROCK, hopefully scored for winds, three guinea pigs and a Siberian husky, with the application of microtonal pulses and circular breathing, is performed for the first time at the Natural Sound Center in New York.

17 MARCH 1984

The Desert Music for 27 amplified voices and orchestra by the 47-year-old American composer Steve REICH, from the book of poems, *The Desert Music,* by William Carlos Williams, is heard for the first time over West German Radio, Cologne, in a performance by the Cologne Chorus and Symphony Orchestra of West German Radio conducted by Peter Eötvös.

21 MARCH 1984

Violin Concerto by Roy HARRIS, his 1949 second attempt at a violin concerto (a 1938 violin concerto was never completely orchestrated and was incorporated into his Third Symphony) and scheduled for performance in 1950 but rejected by the imperious conductor George Szell after the orchestral parts turned out to be in disarray, is retrieved and performed for the first time in Wilmington, North Carolina, by the North Carolina Symphony Orchestra, Greg Fulkerson as soloist, Gerhardt Zimmermann conducting.

22 MARCH 1984

First Symphony by the 45-year-old American composer John HARBISON is performed for the first time in Boston.

24 MARCH 1984

Akhenaton, opera by the 48-year-old American composer Philip GLASS, based on the story of the Eighteenth-Dynasty pharaoh who introduced monotheism to Egypt, is performed for the first time at the Württemberg State Theater, Dennis Russell Davies conducting.

27 MARCH 1984

Starlight Express, a musical by the 36-year-old topnotch British melorhythmicist Andrew LLOYD WEBBER, the central characters being steam locomotives performed by singing actors on roller skates, is produced in London.

2 APRIL 1984

Contextures II: The Final Beast by William KRAFT, scored for soprano, tenor and two ensembles, one of modern instruments, the second of historical instruments, to texts from a 3,000-year period, including Homer, Psalms, Longfellow, etc., commissioned by the Los Angeles Philharmonic, is performed for the first time by the Los Angeles Philharmonic New Music Group, the composer conducting.

5 APRIL 1984

The Mask of Time for four soloists, large chorus and orchestra by the grand and royally ennobled 79-year-old British composer Sir Michael TIPPETT is performed for the first time by the Boston Symphony Orchestra, Colin Davis conducting.

12 APRIL 1984

Fourth Symphony by the 49-year-old Soviet modernist Alfred SCHNITTKE is performed for the first time in Moscow.

20 APRIL 1984

Cantata No. 6, Flower Songs for mixed chorus and string orchestra by the 68-year-old American composer Vincent PERSICHETTI is performed for the first time in Philadelphia.

23 APRIL 1984

Sunday in the Park with George, musical by the versatile American composer and lyricist Stephen SONDHEIM, inspired by the painting by Georges Seurat entitled "A Sunday Afternoon on the Island of La Grande Jatte," astutely transmuting Seurat's pointilistic techniques into a colorful panneau of a merry Paris of yore populated by moustachioed, sideburned boulevardiers and visited by stolid American tourists, is produced in New York.

24 APRIL 1984

The Abduction of Figaro, an innocuous mockery in the form of a Mozartean pasticcio in which Don Giovanni is Donald Giovanni and Papageno is Papa Geno, by P.D.Q. BACH, a.k.a. Peter SCHICKELE, the amiable American mountebank of performing arts, is produced in Minneapolis.

26 APRIL 1984

Count BASIE, black American bandleader who led his groups from the piano keyboard using grunts and eyelid movements to give specific cues for dynamics, tempo and timbre, and who received the honorific sobriquet Count in appreciation of the nobility of his interpretations (his real name was William), dies in Hollywood, Florida, at the age of 79.

14 MAY 1984

Fourth Symphonic Fantasy by the 83-year-old American composer Otto LUENING is performed for the first time in New York.

15 MAY 1984

The Moscow Contemporary Music Festival opens with a concert of symphonic music in the following program:

Overture to the opera *Colas Breugnon* by the 79-year-old doyen of Soviet music Dmitri KABALEVSKY; *Double Concerto* for violin, cello and orchestra by the 57-year-old Rumanian composer Anatol VIERU; *Querela pacis (The Dispute of Peace)* for two choirs and orchestra by the 57-year-old Norwegian composer Oddvar S. KVAM, to words after Erasmus; *Self-Portrait*, a set of orchestral variations by the 51-year-old Soviet composer Rodion SHCHEDRIN; *Eighth Concerto for Orchestra* by the 79-year-old Italian composer Goffredo PETRASSI; and *Second Rhapsody* by the Soviet conductor Evgeny SVETLANOV.

Our Spring Music Festival is intended to popularize the music of composers promoting the ideals of humanism and democracy in their compositions, strengthening peace and friendship among peoples. The progressive mission of the Moscow Festival has found its reflection in the motto: "Music for Humanism, for Peace and Friendship among Nations." This motto is especially topical these days— days of concern for the fates of humanity, days when imperialist forces threaten the existence of world civilization. We, however, believe in the power of Reason and Good, in the power of Art uniting people in the name of Life and Beauty. (From the introductory address by Tikhon Khrennikov, Secretary-General of the Union of Soviet Composers.)

16 MAY 1984

On the second day of the Moscow Festival the following program is presented at a noon concert:

The Song of Peace for mixed choir a cappella by the 63-year-old Greek composer Iakovos HALIASSAS; *Song of 3 June 1983*, a cantata on the opening of the Library of Stockholm University by the 46-year-old Swedish composer Eskil HEMBERG; *Podhozarje (In the Hills of Khozara)* for chorus by the 51-year-old Yugoslav composer Vojin KOMADINA; *El Jicaro* for chorus by the 67-year-old Nicaraguan composer Juan MORENO; *Second String Quartet* by the 54-year-old Japanese composer Michio MAMIYA; *Piano Pictures* by the 31-year-old composer from Cyprus Nicolas ECONOMU, performed by the composer; and *Sixth String Quartet* by the 55-year-old Australian composer Peter SCULTHORPE.

16 MAY 1984

The second day of the Moscow Festival continues with an evening concert featuring the following program of symphonic works:

Western Suite by the 75-year-old American composer Elie SIEGMEISTER; *Cello Concerto* by the 56-year-old Japanese composer Nobuo TERHARA; *Symphonic Prologue* by the 45-year-old Bulgarian composer Georgi MINCHEV; *Flute Concerto* by the 50-year-old East German composer Siegfried MATTHUS; and *Piano Concerto*, subtitled *Let Korea Be United,* by the North Korean composer Jun Chun NAM.

17 MAY 1984

On the third day of the Moscow Festival, the following program of chamber music is presented:

Three Pieces for string quartet by the Argentine composer Alicia TERZIAN; *Five Pieces* for piano by the 60-year-old Egyptian composer Gamal ABDEL-RAHIM; *Trio Concertante* for violin, viola and cello by the 38-year-old Czech composer Ladislav KUBIK; *Brass Quintet* by the 54-year-old Hungarian composer Emil PETROVICS; *Synthesen* for string quartet by the 57-year-old East German composer Siegfried KÖHLER; *Sonatina* for flute and piano by the Ecuadoran composer Claudio AIZAGA; and three pieces from *Six humeurs* for cello and piano by the 54-year-old Belgian composer Jacqueline FONTIJN.

17 MAY 1984

The third day of the Moscow Festival continues at an evening concert with the following program of symphonic works:

Simon Bolivar, overture for orchestra by the 54-year-old Mexican composer Enrique SANTOS; *Viola Concerto* by the 78-year-old East German composer Ernst Hermann MEYER; *Festive Prologue* by the 59-year-old Austrian composer Thomas Christian DAVID; *Le Bal des Pendus*, to poems from Rimbaud, by the 85-year-old French composer Emmanuel BONDEVILLE; *Piano Concerto* by the 30-year-old Luxembourg composer Walter CIVITA-REALE; and *Clarinet Concerto* by the Bulgarian composer Lubomir PIPKOV (1904–1974).

18 MAY 1984

On the fourth day of the Moscow Festival the following program of chamber music is presented at an afternoon concert:

Prelude and Fugue, subtitled *Epitaph to Béla Bartók*, for cello and piano by the 55-year-old Finnish composer Einojuhani RAUTAVAARA; *Movement* for cello and piano by the 66-year-old Hungarian composer András MIHÁLY; *Piece* for cello and piano by the Nigerian composer Akin EUBA; *Serenade* for cello by the 57-year-old German composer Hans Werner HENZE; *Six Japanese Folksongs* for cello and piano by the 54-year-old Japanese composer Michio MAMIYA; *Rítmicas* for wind quintet and piano by the Cuban composer Amadeo ROLDÁN (1900–1939); *Pieces* for guitar by the 42-year-old Mexican composer Miguel ALCAZAR; *Kuema (Wave)* for string quartet by the 54-year-old Finnish composer Usko MERILÄINEN; and *Pieces* for piano by the 52-year-old Norwegian composer Arne NORDHEIM.

18 MAY 1984

The fourth day of the Moscow Festival continues with the following program of choral music:

The Will for soloist and mixed choir by the 59-year-old Yugoslav composer Vlastimir NIKOLOVSKI; *Bells Clanging* for reciter, soloists, mixed choir, oboe and percussion, in sixteen movements, by the 44-year-old Soviet composer Valery GAVRILIN; *Three Estonian Songs* for mixed choir, entitled *Windmill, Tying up the Finger* and *Ship*, by the 54-year-old Estonian composer Veljo TORMIS; and *The Pushkin Wreath*, concerto for choir by the 68-year-old Soviet composer Georgy SVIRIDOV.

18 MAY 1984

On the fourth day of the Moscow Festival the following program of symphonic works is presented at an evening concert:

Unfinished March by the 59-year-old Tunisian composer Salah EL-MAHDI; *Double-bass Concerto* by the 81-year-old Italian composer Virgilio MORTARI; *Third Symphony* by the 77-year-old Soviet composer Andrei BALANCHI-VADZE; *Invincible Revolution*, hymn of Soviet-Afghan Friendship by the 54-year-old Afghani composer Salim SARMAST; *Cello Concerto* by the 63-year-old Soviet composer Karen KHACHATURIAN; and *Metamorphosen über ein Fragment von Mozart* for flute, oboe, string quartet and orchestra by the 67-year-old Austrian composer Helmut EDER.

19 MAY 1984

On the fifth day of the Moscow Festival the following program of chamber music is presented at a noon concert:

First String Quartet by the 50-year-old Hungarian composer Zsolt DURKÓ; *Legend of the Raven* for piano by the Canadian composer Alex PAUK; *Musica Viva* for percussion by the 43-year-old Cuban composer José LOYOLA; *Duets for Two Violins* by the 51-year-old Slovak composer Ilja ZELJENKA; and *Third String Quartet* by the 68-year-old Norwegian composer Knut NYSTEDT.

19 MAY 1984

The fifth day of the Moscow Festival continues with the following program of chamber music at an afternoon concert:

Nocturne for tenor, seven obbligato instruments and strings by the British composer Benjamin BRITTEN (1913–1976); *Guitar Concerto* by the Brazilian composer Heitor VILLA-LOBOS (1887–1959); *Frescoes of Saint Sophia in Kiev,* symphony-concerto for harp and chamber orchestra by the 43-year-old Soviet composer Valery KIKTA; *Concierto Barroco* for piano, violin and chamber orchestra by the 58-year-old Colombian composer Luis Antonio ESCOBAR; and *Eighth Symphony* for chamber orchestra by the 40-year-old Soviet composer Mirsadyk TADJIEV.

19 MAY 1984

On the fifth day of the Moscow Festival the following program of symphonic works is presented at an evening concert:

Orpheus in Hiroshima, concert version of the opera for soloists, mixed choir and orchestra by the 58-year-old Japanese composer Yasushi AKUTAGAWA; *Concerto for Orchestra* by the 62-year-old Bulgarian composer Alexander RAICHEV; *Violin Concerto* by the 82-year-old Spanish composer Joaquín RODRIGO; and *Memory* by the 71-year-old Slovak composer Ján CIKKER.

20 MAY 1984

On the sixth day of the Moscow Festival the following program of chamber and choral music is presented at an afternoon concert:

Funeral Music, dedicated to the memory of Ché Guevara, for chamber orchestra by the 56-year-old Spanish composer Ramón BARCE; *Sonata* for piano, wind quintet, strings and timpani by the Czech composer Václav DOBIÁŠ (1909–1978); *Divertimento* for flute, strings and celesta by the 81-year-old Soviet composer Andrei SHTOGARENKO; and *Romancero of Love and Death* to the text by Federico García Lorca for mixed choir, two electric guitars, piano and percussion by the 54-year-old Soviet composer Nicolai SIDELNIKOV.

20 MAY 1984

On the sixth day of the Moscow Festival the following program of symphonic works is presented at an early afternoon concert:

Fragments from the ballet *Yerma* by the 43-year-old Filipino composer Francisco FELICIANO; *Violin Concerto* by the 66-year-old Filipina composer Lucrecia KASILAG; Suite from the ballet *Kni* by the 56-year-old Vietnamese composer Van KY; Suite from the comic opera *King Pomádé's New Clothes* by the 76-year-old Hungarian composer György RÁNKI; *Piano Concerto* by the 69-year-old Turkish composer Bülent TARÇAN; and *Chorali* for 32 winds, percussion, harp and celesta by the 49-year-old Finnish composer Aulis SALLI-NEN.

20 MAY 1984

On the sixth day of the Moscow Festival the following program of symphonic works is presented at an evening concert:

Intrada by the 59-year-old Austrian composer Fritz LEITER-MEYER; *Second Symphony,* subtitled *The Age of Anxiety,* for piano and orchestra by the 65-year-old American composer Leonard BERNSTEIN; *Festivity* by the 38-year-old Soviet composer Tolib-khon SHAKHIDI; and *Second Piano Concerto* by the 79-year-old Soviet composer Dmitri KABALEVSKY.

21 MAY 1984

The American première of *The Trials of Peter the Hebrew,* chamber opera by the 54-year-old French composer Henri POUSSEUR, drawing from an incident in the life of Arnold Schoenberg when at the age of 70 he was denied a grant from the Guggenheim Foundation, in three acts divided into 21 sections, each of which represents a conflict between an individual (Schoenberg, Moses, Abraham, Noah) and a social group (population, generation, class), is produced in Los Angeles. (The original version was premièred in Berlin in 1974 under the title *Die Erprobung des Petrus Hebraicus.*)

21 MAY 1984

On the seventh day of the Moscow Festival the following program of chamber music is presented at a noon concert:

Concerto for Strings by the Argentine composer Alberto GINASTERA (1916–1983); *Concerto for String Orchestra* by the 70-year-old Rumanian composer Ion DUMITRESCU; *Clarinet Concerto* by the 83-year-old American composer Aaron COPLAND; *Music for String Orchestra* by the 62-year-old Finnish composer Joonas KOKKONEN; *Four Love Sonnets* to the words of Shakespeare for baritone, strings and harpsichord by the Polish composer Tadeusz BAIRD (1928–1981); and *Adagio* for strings and vibraphone by the 33-year-old Mongolian composer Tsogzolyn NATSAGDORDG.

21 MAY 1984

The seventh day of the Moscow Festival continues at an afternoon concert with the following program of works for wind orchestra:

March on Russian Folk Themes by the Soviet composer Nicolai IVANOV-RADKEVIGH (1904–1962); *Heroic Prelude* by the 60-year-old East German composer Heinz ARENZ; *Concertino* for piano, wind instruments, percussion and harp by the

55-year-old Hungarian composer Kamilló LENDVAY; *English Rhapsody* for brass band by the 53-year-old Norwegian composer Trevor FORD; *Spanish Metamorphoses* for two wind orchestras by the 45-year-old Czech composer Eugene ZÁMEČNIK; Finale from *Sakarska Suite* by the Bulgarian composer Filip KUTEV (1903–1982); *Poème du Feu* by the 51-year-old French composer Ida GOTKOVSKY; *Concerto* for saxophone and wind orchestra by the Soviet composer Mikhael GOTLIB (1907–1978); *Variations on a Japanese Folk Song Theme* by the 56-year-old Dutch composer Henk VAN LIJNSCHOOTEN; *Olympic Overture* by the 43-year-old Czech composer Ivana LOUDOVÁ; *Circus Suite* by the Swedish composer Julius JACOBSON; *Overture Ritmica* by the 52-year-old East German composer Klaus-Peter BRUCH-MANN; and *March for Spartakiad* by Sergei PROKOFIEV (1891–1953).

21 MAY 1984

On the seventh day of the Moscow Festival the following program of symphonic works is presented at an evening concert:

Women—Heroines of the Native South by the Vietnamese composer Nguyen Thi NHUNG; *Tout un monde lointain . . .* to the text by Baudelaire for cello and orchestra by the 68-year-old French composer Henri DUTILLEUX; *A Heavy Harvest in the Fields of Chkhonsan* by the North Korean composer Kim Ok SON; *Memory* by the Moroccan composer Mustapba BEN-NIS; *Oboe Concerto* by the 59-year-old Soviet composer Andrei ESHPAI; and *Sixth Symphony* by the 62-year-old Italian composer Mario ZAFRED.

22 MAY 1984

On the eighth day of the Moscow Festival the following program of chamber music is presented at a noon concert:

Ancient Voices of Children for soprano, child's voice and instrumental ensemble by the 54-year-old American composer George CRUMB; *Folk Songs* for soprano and seven instruments by the 58-year-old Italian composer Luciano BERIO; *Three Madrigals* for soprano and five instruments by the 49-year-old Soviet composer Alfred SCHNITTKE; and *About Love and Nostalgia* for chamber orchestra by the 50-year-old Argentine composer Bruno D'ASTOLI.

22 MAY 1984

On the eighth day of the Moscow Festival the following program of symphonic works is presented at an evening concert:

Violin Concerto by the 53-year-old Soviet composer Andrei PETROV; *Fifth Symphony* by the 57-year-old German composer Hans Werner HENZE; and *Requiem* for five soloists, mixed chorus and orchestra by the 77-year-old Portuguese composer Fernando LOPES-GRAÇA.

23 MAY 1984

On the ninth day of the Moscow Festival the following program of chamber music is presented at an afternoon concert:

Adagio for Strings by the American composer Samuel BAR-BER (1910–1981); *Variations on a Theme of Haydn* for cello and orchestra by the 55-year-old Soviet composer Edison DENISOV; *Concerto Funebre* for violin and string orchestra by the German composer Karl Amadeus HARTMANN (1905–1963); and *Concerto* for two string orchestras by the 79-year-old British composer Sir Michael TIPPETT.

23 MAY 1984

On the ninth day of the Moscow Festival the following program of symphonic works is presented at an evening concert:

Music in Memory of Leonid Kogan, subtitled *Missa pro defunctis*, for soloists, mixed chorus and orchestra by the 60-year-old Italian composer Franco MANNINO; *Theme and Eight Variations* by the 58-year-old Soviet composer Boris TCHAIKOVSKY; *Second Cello Concerto* by the 50-year-old Polish composer Krzysztof PENDERECKI; and *Symphonic Metamorphoses on Gesualdo* by the 65-year-old German composer Jürg BAUR.

24 MAY 1984

The Moscow Festival of Contemporary Music concludes with the following program of symphonic works:

Seventh Symphony, subtitled *Spring*, for soloists, chorus and orchestra by the 58-year-old Greek composer Mikis THEO-DORAKIS and *Third Piano Concerto* by the 70-year-old Soviet composer Tikhon KHRENNIKOV, with himself as soloist.

4 JUNE 1984

Bamboula Squared for orchestra by the 46-year-old American composer Charles WUORINEN is performed for the first time in New York.

7 JUNE 1984

A Haunted Landscape by the 54-year-old American composer George CRUMB, scored for orchestra, amplified piano and a set of exotic instruments including Caribbean steel drums, Cambodian angklungs, Japanese Kabuki blocks, the Brazilian cuica and the Appalachian hammered dulcimer, the title reflecting the mystery of certain places on the planet Earth, with a unifying factor provided by a low B-flat, is performed for the first time in New York, Arthur Weisberg conducting.

16 JUNE 1984

Bran(d)t aan de Amstel by Henry BRANT, the nonpareil American artificer of unearthly sounds in a terrestial environment, scored for ten dozen flutes, choirs and bands, carilloneur, four Dutch hand organs and sundry sonorifers, is presented for the first time in Amsterdam, Holland, in a procession on boats and barges plying the canals of Amsterdam.

20 JUNE 1984

The Double Life of Amphibians, electronic tone poem by the 51-year-old American composer Morton SUBOT-NICK, featuring fourteen performers interacting with a computer, in three parts, *Ascent into Air* (written especially for IRCAM's computer system in Paris and premièred there on 18 January 1982), *The Burghers of Calais* and *The Fluttering of Wings* for string quartet and computer, is performed for the first time in its entirety at the Los Angeles Olympic Arts Festival.

1 JULY 1984

The King Goes Forth to France, opera by the 49-year-old Finnish composer Aulis SALLINEN, is produced in Helsinki.

4 JULY 1984

Concertorama for synthesizer/amplified piano and amplified orchestra by the American composer James SELLARS, in a festive art-rock/disco style, receives its first ever performance by the Hartford Symphony, Yvar Mikhashoff, soloist, as part of the 6th annual New Music America Festival in Hartford, Connecticut.

9 JULY 1984

Randall THOMPSON, American composer who took pride in writing music in a euphonious traditional manner without being seduced by modern innovations, whose choral work *The Testament of Freedom* to words by Thomas Jefferson became a national classic, and who for many years taught composition at Harvard University, dies in Boston at the age of 85.

14 JULY 1984

Sweeney, opera by the Broadway composer Stephen SONDHEIM, ingeniously arranged from his successful musical *Sweeney Todd* (which was originally produced in New York on 1 March 1979 and which ran for 557 performances) after a grisly tale, *The String of Pearls, or the Fiend of Fleet Street*, published serially in a London newspaper in 1846, dealing with a mad barber who cuts the throats of his unsuspecting customers for his even madder landlady who uses the throats and other meaty parts for her culinary concoctions ("Man eats man," Sweeney sings), is produced in Houston, Texas. (The first New York performance was given by the New York City Opera on 11 October 1984.)

17 JULY 1984

La Prison, cantata for soprano, cello and orchestra by Marcel LANDOWSKI, with cellist Mstislav Rostropovitch, his wife, Galina Vishnevskaya, as soprano soloist, Jean-Claude Casadesus conducting the Orchestre National de Lille, is performed for the first time anywhere at Aix-en-Provence.

20 JULY 1984

Gail KUBIK, inventive American composer who wrote symphonies and other works of merit but made a popular hit with his idiomatic setting of the animated cartoon *Gerald McBoing-Boing*, dies in Covina, California, at the age of 69, a victim of a deadly tropical disease, kala-azar, which he contracted during one of his trips to Africa.

29 JULY 1984

American Sing for orchestra by the 70-year-old American composer Morton GOULD, commissioned for the opening concert of the Los Angeles Olympic Games, is performed for the first time at the Hollywood Bowl.

31 JULY 1984

Paul LE FLEM, doyen of French music criticism, who was also a composer (he continued to write music until the age of 95 when he lost his sight almost totally), dies at the incredible age of 103 years, four months, and thirteen days at his summer retreat in Trégastel (Côtes-du-Nord), France.

2 AUGUST 1984

Love of Don Perlimplín, one-act opera by the American composer Conrad SUSA, after the eponymous play by Federico García Lorca, who described it as an "erotic lace-paper valentine," is produced at State University of New York at Purchase.

12 AUGUST 1984

Un Re in ascolto (A King Listening), "musical action" in two parts by Luciano BERIO, is performed for the first time in Salzburg, Lorin Maazel conducting.

14 AUGUST 1984

John COUSINS, 40-year-old member of the faculty at Canterbury University in Christchurch, New Zealand, presents the first British demonstration of his Urinal Technique of Composition, inspired by the sound of dripping water in a New Zealand canyon, by urinating on a set of glass tubes covered with rubber membranes and producing an untempered scale of melodious tones.

11 SEPTEMBER 1984

Fourth Violin Concerto by the 49-year-old Soviet composer Alfred SCHNITTKE is performed for the first time in West Berlin.

12 SEPTEMBER 1984

Organ Concerto by the 49-year-old English composer William MATHIAS is performed for the first time by Gillian Weir as soloist with the BBC Welsh Symphony Orchestra under the direction of Erich Bergel in London.

23 SEPTEMBER 1984

The 58th Festival of the International Society for Contemporary Music opens in Toronto, Canada, with an afternoon concert of mostly choral music, in the following program:

Two pieces by the 51-year-old experimental Canadian composer R. Murray SCHAFER, *Sun* to plural words for sun in multiple tongues, and *Epitaph for Moonlight*, being an ear-training exercise for school children; *Carnatus* by the enterprising Norwegian composer Cecile ORE to texts of Latin names for butterflies and moths; *Choralis* by 36-year-old Nigel OSBORNE of Great Britain in a pluralistic hemidemisemioriental manner (only the first and third sections of the work were performed); *L'Infinito* by 51-year-old Arno MELLNÄS of Sweden, to words by Giacomo Leopardi; *Monodie* by the 45-year-old Canadian composer Robert AITKEN for flute and voices with the composer himself piping up; and *Car nos vignes sont en fleur* by the 58-year-old Dutch composer Ton DE LEEUW, to words from the biblical *Song of Songs*.

24 SEPTEMBER 1984

Concerto for bassoon, cello and orchestra by the 55-year-old Soviet composer Edison DENISOV is performed for the first time in Venice.

24 SEPTEMBER 1984

On the second day of the 58th Festival of the International Society for Contemporary Music in Toronto, an afternoon concert of works for solo piano and solo flute is presented with the following program:

Pieces of Piano by the 26-year-old American composer Scott LINDROTH, which require adjustments of piano strings to make them sound like an Oriental gamelan; *Distancias* for piano by the 41-year-old Argentine composer Mariano ETKIN, the distances of the title referring to the antagonistic employment of distant registers of the keyboard; *En ré* for piano by the 61-year-old Uruguayan composer Hector TOSAR, centered on the thematic tone of D, modified harmonically, rhythmically, dynamically and timbrally, with application of direct action on the strings; *Rivers* for piano by the 47-year-Old Canadian composer Ann SOUTHAM, a Chopinesque piece in which fundamental and incidental motives appear in polytonal superimposition; *Flute Sonata* by the 56-year-old Rumanian composer Tiberiu OLAH, set in three sections separated by deep silences and interspersed with slap-tonguing doubled by the performer's natural voice lapsing into the non-tempered zones of sound; *Yta I* for flute solo by the 26-year-old Finnish composer Esa-Pekka SALONEN, set in a fast, "sempre nervoso" tempo; *Traits suspendus* for amplified double-bass flute by the 47-year-old Iraqi-born French composer Paul MÉFANO, using antiflutational sounds like the tongue-ram, slap-tones and circular respiration, producing sounds by inhaling as well as exhaling; *Man-Pa (Huge Stream)* for solo flute accompanied by a triskaidecaphiliac coven of multifarious flutes in all sonic registers by the 50-year-old Korean composer Sukhi KANG, purporting to represent stormy winds blowing through a bamboo thicket; *Conspiracies* for solo flute accompanied by a whole sanhedrin of flutes by the 37-year-old American composer Martin BRESNICK, the title meaning breathing together, rather than plotting; and *Ryoanji II* by the fearless American disestablishmentarian guru John CAGE, with some flute glissandi the notation of which was inspired by the pattern of stones bounding the famous rock-and-sand garden at the Zen Buddhist temple in Kyoto.

24 SEPTEMBER 1984

On the second day of the 58th Festival of the International Society for Contemporary Music in Toronto, an evening concert is presented in a program of the following symphonic works:

Canti del Sole for tenor and orchestra by the 50-year-old spiritually modernistic British-born American composer Bernard RANDS, to texts by a number of romantic European poets all glorifying the circadian and seasonal cycles of the sun; *Miroirs célestes* by the 41-year-old Rumanian-born French composer Costin MIEREANU, conceived as a narrative reflection of celestial mirrors with multiple images in a sort of musical palimpsest; *Exú* for violin and orchestra by the 31-year-old Australian composer Gerard BROPHY, the title being one of the many ingenious names of the devil, with a reference to the demonic nature of Paganini, whose virtuosity was attributed to Satan; and *Divertmento No. 7* for French horn and string orchestra by the 71-year-old Canadian composer John WEINZWEIG, in nine interconnected sections linked by horn solos.

25 SEPTEMBER 1984

On the third day of the 58th Festival of the International Society for Contemporary Music in Toronto, an afternoon piano recital is given by Ivar Mikhashoff, featuring the following program:

For Cornelius by the American composer Alvin CURRAN, a memorial to the British creator of Scratch Music, Cornelius Cardew, who was killed by an errant automobile in 1981; a selection of piano waltzes by Philip GLASS, Lou HARRISON, Milton BABBITT, Robert MORAN, John CAGE and Virgil THOMSON; *Mort de Phèdre* by the 52-year-old Italian composer Sylvano BUSSOTTI; *Tangos* from the *International Tango Collection* by John CAGE, Marlos NOBRE, Betsy JOLAS, Zoltan JENEY, William DUCKWORTH, Conlon NANCARROW, Anthony GENGE and others; *Achilles and the Tortoise* by the 52-year-old Danish composer Per NØRGÅRD, illustrating the famous paradox of the Greek philosopher Zeno on the infinite divisibility of a given distance; and *Piano Piece No. 4* by the 46-year-old American composer Frederic RZEWSKI, based on a Chilean folksong.

25 SEPTEMBER 1984

The third day of the 58th Festival of the International Society for Contemporary Music in Toronto continues with an evening concert of chamber music featuring the following program:

Tesserae III for solo viola by the 47-year-old American composer Brian FENNELLY, the title referring to the mosaic construction of the music, with each motive representing a four-cornered unit; *Trio op. 21* for clarinet, cello and piano by the 28-year-old Finnish composer Jouni KAIPAINEN; *Walk the Line* for solo percussion and string ensemble by the 31-year-old Canadian composer Henry KUCHARZYK; *For Marimba and Tape* by the 39-year-old Australian composer Martin WESLEY-SMITH; and *Dzei (Voices of Fire)* for chamber ensemble by the 52-year-old Canadian composer Gilles TREMBLAY, ostensibly depicting the transmutation of elements by the spirit of fire as conceived by the Greek philosopher Heraclitus.

25 SEPTEMBER 1984

Gespenstersonate, opera by the 48-year-old German composer Aribert REIMANN, after Strindberg's play *The Ghost Sonata*, is produced in Berlin.

26 SEPTEMBER 1984

On the fourth day of the 58th Festival of the International Society for Contemporary Music in Toronto, an afternoon concert of chamber music presents the following program:

Six Melodies for Violin and Keyboard by the 72-year-old guru of new American music John CAGE, composed in 1950, reflecting his penetrating study of Oriental homophony; *Breakfast Rhythms I & II* for clarinet, piano, percussion, cello, violin and flute by the 45-year-old American composer Joan TOWER, a domestic celebration of matutinal prandium set in enjoyable visceral modalities; *Synchronisms No. 6* for piano and electronic tape by the 50-year-old Argentine composer Mario DAVIDOVSKY; *Three for Six* in three movements for six instruments by the 63-year-old American composer Ralph SHAPEY, written in the technique of massive collage; *First String Quartet* by James DILLON; and *Ancora* for string quartet by the 44-year-old Swedish composer Jan MORTHENSON.

26 SEPTEMBER 1984

On the fourth day of the 58th Festival of the International Society for Contemporary Music in Toronto, the following program of orchestral works is presented at an evening concert:

Vanishing Points by the 40-year-old Canadian composer John REA, the title alluding to the half-tints in art creating a vanishing point in infinite perspective; *Ritratto (Portrait)* for 18 players by the 26-year-old Finnish composer Magnus LINDBERG, in four sections: diagonals, polarities, linearities and verticals; *Into the Distant Stillness* . . . by the 42-year-old Canadian composer Brian CHERNEY, written as part of a triptych of stillnesses for various instrumental combinations; *Alchemies* by the 33-year-old Canadian composer John BURKE, in which a central chord is transmuted into heterogeneous elements in varying tonal colors; and *Mirage* by the 51-year-old Canadian composer Alex PAUK, purporting to reflect the phantasmagoria of aural intangibilities, optical refractions, topographical distortions and retinal illusions.

27 SEPTEMBER 1984

In the course of the 58th Festival of the International Society for Contemporary Music in Toronto, *Chaconne* for viola and orchestra by the 52-year-old American composer Michael COLGRASS, inspired by the famous *Chaconne* of Bach, is performed for the first time.

27 SEPTEMBER 1984

On the fifth day of the 58th Festival of the International Society for Contemporary Music in Toronto, an afternoon concert of chamber music is presented with the following program:

Musica for five instruments by the Argentine composer Marcello KOC; *Ambivalencia* by the Mexican composer Manuel ENRIQUEZ; *Feedback* by the Chilean composer Juan Amenabar RUIZ; *Tableaux* by the Italian-born Australian composer Riccardo FORMOSA; *Three Monograms* by the Argentine composer Salvador RANIERI; *Estrias* by the Brazilian composer Raul DO VALLE; and *Rhapsody on a Gagaku Theme* by the 77-year-old Japanese composer Yoritsuné MATSUDAIRA.

27 SEPTEMBER 1984

On the fifth day of the 58th Festival of the International Society for Contemporary Music in Toronto, the following program of electronic works is presented at an evening concert:

Rubrics for bassoon and electronics by the 36-year-old American composer David GRIMES; *Love in the Asylum* by the 32-year-old American composer Michael MCNABBY, a computerized tribute to modified insanity; *Sticherarion* by the 41-year-old American composer Larry LAKE, an electronic version of a Byzantine collection of stylized psalm melodies making a joyful noise unto God; *Clim of the Clough* by the 37-year-old American composer David JAEGER, a submissive celebation of the famed Canadian bandit; *Klang* by the 32-year-old British composer Jony HARRISON, a sonorific clang of exuberant onomatopoeic motives; and *Wildfire* by the 41-year-old American composer James MONTGOMERY, a sequentially structured work in which the traditional string trio textures are transfigured into electronic equivalents.

28 SEPTEMBER 1984

On the sixth day of the 58th Festival of the International Society for Contemporary Music, the following program is presented in Montreal:

Sonata for orchestra by the 30-year-old Polish composer Pawel SZYMANSKI; *Concertante in moto perpetuo* for oboe solo and chamber ensemble by the 32-year-old British composer Simon BAINBRIDGE; *Turns* for violin and koto by the 53-year-old Japanese composer Makoto SHINO-HARA; *East* for orchestra by the 51-year-old Canadian composer R. Murray SCHAFER, a musical meditation of an Oriental nature; *Lonely Child* for soprano and chamber orchestra by the Canadian composer Claude VIVIER (1948–1983); and *Plages* by the 55-year-old Canadian composer Serge GARANT, an orchestral suite of entities of time and of color with the basic material formed of five notes.

29 SEPTEMBER 1984

On the seventh day of the 58th Festival of the International Society for Contemporary Music in Montreal, an afternoon concert of chamber music is presented with the following program:

Pearls by the 34-year-old Canadian composer Alexina LOUIE, a group of pieces of diminutive structures suggesting a string of pearls; *Arpeggio* by the 37-year-old American composer John CELONA, based on a heptatonic series of notes worked in a combinatorial process generated by a digital synthesizer; *Tellus* by the 72-year-old Canadian composer Barbara PENTLAND, the title meaning earth, herein regarded as a living planet, the music being worked out by aleatory processes involving the vision of a roll of surf on a sandy beach; *Escalator* by the 30-year-old Canadian composer Owen UNDERHILL, a series of successive escalations rich in hidden transmutations of an elementary design; *Hesitation* by the 33-year-old American composer Stephen CHATMAN, a vanishing dialogue between the violin and celesta, dissolving into a sonic nirvana; and *Elegy* by the 45-year-old Canadian composer Bruce MATHER, a lyrical memorial to an artistic friend.

30 SEPTEMBER 1984

On the eighth day of the 58th Festival of the International Society for Contemporary Music in Montreal, the following program for chamber ensemble is presented at an evening concert:

Gestalten (Forms) by the 23-year-old South Korean composer Unsuk CHIN, a musical evocation of three paintings by Paul Klee; *Five Epigrams* by the 45-year-old Cuban guitarist and composer Leo BROWER; *Cantos del amor y la eternidad* by the 58-year-old Argentine composer Rodolfo ARIZAGA; *Shantiniketan* by the Argentine composer Alicia TERZIAN; *Tres impresoes cançoneirigenas* by the Brazilian composer Jorge ANTUNES; and *Quintet* by the Argentine composer Guillermo GRAETZER.

1 OCTOBER 1984

On the ninth day of the 58th Festival of the International Society for Contemporary Music in Montreal, an afternoon concert of percussion music is presented with the following program:

Circuit I for six percussionists by the 55-year-old Canadian composer Serge GARANT; *Kétiak* for six percussionists by the 31-year-old Japanese composer Akira NISHIMURA, based on Balinese dance motives; *Etats* for violin and six percussionists by the 58-year-old American-born Parisian composer Betsy JOLAS; *Vertiges* by the 31-year-old Canadian composer Pierre TROCHU, the vertiginous elements in the work being symbolized by the prestidigitation of the marimba player; and *Pulau Dewata* by the Canadian composer Claude VIVIER, for any combination of percussion instruments, thematically based on Balinese modalities.

An evening concert by the Montreal Symphony is conducted by Charles Dutoit in a program that includes *Exemplum in memoriam Kwangju* by the 67-year-old politically active South Korean composer Isang YUN, dedicated to the victims of the massacre in Kwangju, perpetrated by the brutal Korean police on 28 May 1980.

1 OCTOBER 1984

On the ninth day of the 58th Festival of the International Society for Contemporary Music in Montreal, a late evening concert by the Arditti String Quartet presents the following chamber works:

Quartet op. 1 by the 58-year-old Hungarian composer György KURTÁG; *Adagissimo* by the 41-year-old British composer Brian FERNEYHOUGH; *Ricercate* by the 31-year-old American composer Susan BLAUSTEIN; *Fifth Quartet* by the 32-year-old German composer Wolfgang RIHM; *Solos and Shadows* by the 36-year-old Danish composer Karl RASMUSSEN; and *String Quartet* by the 41-year-old British composer Roger SMALLEY.

1 OCTOBER 1984

Fifth Symphony by the 52-year-old Soviet composer Sergei SLONIMSKY (incidentally a nephew of the American musicologist Nicolas Slonimsky), in three movements: *Presto* unified by a dominant rhythmic pulse; *Andante* related in its melodic content to the freely flowing folk tunes of the "mother river" of eternal Russia, the Volga; *Vivace*, an energetic apotheosis of motoric gaiety in bell-like sonorities, is performed for the first time in the Volga town of Kuibishev and dedicated to the quadricentennial of the city, originally named Samara.

2 OCTOBER 1984

On the tenth day of the 58th Festival of the International Society for Contemporary Music in Montreal, an afternoon concert of electronic works is presented with the following program:

Points de fuite (Vanishing Points) by the 58-year-old French-born Canadian composer Francis DHOMONT; *Chronaxie ou Ce désert acharnement de couleurs* for percussion and tape by the 30-year-old Canadian composer Serge ARCURI; *Conte-à-Nino* by the 38-year-old French composer Philippe MÉNARD, an electronic fairy tale realized on the digital synthesizer; *Petite musique sentimentale* for piano and tape by the 38-year-old Canadian composer Yves DOAUST; *Manu Militari* for tuba and tape by the 29-year-old Canadian composer André Luc DESJARDINS; *Étude à la quatre-vingt-dix-neuvième nuit* by the 29-year-old Canadian composer Claude FRENETTE; *Vortex* by the 38-year-old New Zealand composer Denis SMALLEY; and *Rite of Passage* by the 30-year-old Swedish composer Anders HILLBORG.

2 OCTOBER 1984

On the tenth day of the 58th Festival of the International Society for Contemporary Music in Montreal, the Society of Contemporary Music of Quebec Ensemble performs the following program at an evening concert:

Planetary Folklore II by the 29-year-old Japanese composer Mamoru FUJIEDA, making use of canonic processes from Bach's *Musical Offering; Tangente* by the 31-year-old Canadian composer Pierre TROCHU, wherein disjointed events seek their tangential focus; *Écrits sur toiles (Written on Canvases)* by the 48-year-old French composer Gilbert AMY, an essay in form of variations based on letters by R. M. Rilke; and *Pohjatuuli* by the 38-year-old Canadian composer Michel

LONGTIN, the title being the Finnish word for North Wind, drawing inspiration from Sibelius.

3 OCTOBER 1984

The 58th Festival of the International Society for Contemporary Music concludes in Montreal with a performance by the group Les Événements du Neuf, featuring the following program at an afternoon concert:

Oleada for bass soloist and instrumental ensemble by the 56-year-old Spanish composer Ramon BARCE, to a text inspired by Apollonius of Rhodes, in four scenes depicting the legends of the Argonauts, Orpheus, Theseus and the conquest of the Golden Fleece, with the voice in Sprechgesang; *Plastiques Faber* for four recorder players by the 31-year-old French composer Daniel TOSI, written for the Faber Quartet (faber meaning artisan in Latin), the specification "plastique" referring to a graphic notation employed herein; *Observatons on Weather Forecast* by the 55-year-old Japanese composer Joli YUASA, a meteorological fantasy for a vocal duo; and *Voix intimes* for two sopranos, clarinet quartet and percussion by the 33-year-old Canadian composer Denis GOUGEON.

In the evening, the musical theater piece *Transit* by the 46-year-old Canadian composer Micheline Coulombe SAINT-MARCOUX, depicting the anxiety of a woman waiting in an airport, is produced.

3 OCTOBER 1984

Creations, two scenes from *Genesis*, for narrator and chamber orchestra by the 46-year-old American composer John CORIGLIANO, is performed for the first time in Milwaukee, Wisconsin.

3 OCTOBER 1984

Cosmic Cycle for orchestra by the 89-year-old American composer, painter and mystical philosopher Dane RUDHYAR is performed for the first time in Milwaukee, Lukas Foss conducting.

12 OCTOBER 1984

Sinfonia by the 47-year-old American composer Olly WILSON is performed for the first time by the Boston Symphony Orchestra, Seiji Ozawa conducting.

12 OCTOBER 1984

Celebration for Orchestra, festive piece by the 45-year-old American composer Ellen Taaffe ZWILICH, is performed for the first time in Indianapolis, John Nelson conducting.

22 OCTOBER 1984

Spleen, opera in two acts by the 53-year-old Catalonian composer Xavier BENGUEREL, is premiered in Barcelona.

24 OCTOBER 1984

Minette Fontaine, opera by the black American composer William Grant STILL (1895–1978), completed in 1958, depicting the life of the French opera diva in New Orleans in the 1880's, is given its posthumous world première in Baton Rouge, Louisiana.

25 OCTOBER 1984

The American première of *Desert Music* for orchestra by Steve REICH, to a text of poems by William Carlos Williams, is performed by Steve Reich and Musicians, with chorus and members of the Brooklyn Philharmonic Orchestra, Michael Tilson Thomas conducting, in New York. (The absolute first performance took place in Cologne, Germany, in March 1984.)

29 OCTOBER 1984

Forgiving and forgetting the émigré status of the great Russian basso Fyodor CHALIAPIN, the Soviet authorities arrange to transfer his remains from Paris, where he died in 1938, to the Novodevichy Cemetery in Moscow, alongside the graves of Scriabin, Prokofiev and Shostakovich.

Without Russia Chaliapin found life tedious and abhorrent. Now he is returned to his motherland, and we bow deeply to him for all he did for the culture of his country and his people. Let the native earth be light on him. (From a graveside eulogy by the Russian bass singer Evgenyi Nesterenko.)

31 OCTOBER 1984

Hora eius, eight motets for three sopranos by the 53-year-old Hungarian composer László KALMAR, to a Latin text depicting Christ's disciples on the night of the crucifixion calling to one another on the Mount of Olives, receives its first complete performance in San Francisco by the vocal ensemble Ariel, conducted by Christopher Fulkerson.

3 NOVEMBER 1984

Sixth Symphony by the 75-year-old American composer Elie SIEGMEISTER, characterized by him as a "search for intensity of expression" and using a vast armamentarium of melodic, harmonic, rhythmic and timbral means, in three movements reflecting the dialectically dramatic, hedonistically exuberant and solipsistically meditative moods, all this enlivened by diversified percussion battery, is performed for the first time by the Sacramento Symphony Orchestra, Carter Nice conducting.

21 NOVEMBER 1984

Concerto Quaternio for violin, flute, oboe, trumpet and orchestra with tape-recorded human voice by the 59-year-old American composer Gunter SCHULLER is performed for the first time by the New York Philharmonic, Zubin Mehta conducting.

1 DECEMBER 1984

The Bride Stripped Bare by Her Bachelors, Even for solo singers, orchestra and chorus by the 49-year-old American composer and critic Charles SHERE, to a surrealistic text based on Marcel Duchamp's painting *The Large Glass* as well as his numerous verbal and literary utterances, is produced for the first time at Mills College in Oakland, California.

1 DECEMBER 1984

Seventh Symphony by the 58-year-old German modernist Hans Werner HENZE is performed for the first time in Berlin. (The United States première took place on 18 April 1985, the composer conducting the Cleveland Orchestra.)

13 DECEMBER 1984

Oboe Concerto by the 66-year-old American composer George ROCHBERG, in four distinct sections, set in an enhanced tonal style without any attempts at surreal virtuosity, is performed for the first time by the New York Philharmonic as a commissioned work, with Joseph Robinson as oboe soloist and Zubin Mehta conducting.

14 DECEMBER 1984

Bernard RANDS conducts the San Diego Symphony Orchestra in the first performance of his orchestral suite *Le Tambourin*.

15 DECEMBER 1984

Wayang V for piano and orchestra by the 33-year-old American jazz pianist and composer Anthony DAVIS, conceived in four attaca movements entitled *Opening Dance*, *Wet Dreams*, *March*, and *Keçak* ("Wayang" is the Indonesian shadow puppet theater, while "Keçak" is a Balinese monkey chant), is premiered by the San Francisco Symphony, with the composer as soloist, John Adams conducting.

22 DECEMBER 1984

Les Fourberies de Scapin, opéra-bouffe in three acts by the 48-year-old Soviet composer Yuri FALIK, after Molière's comedy dealing with an audacious valet, modeled after the rascal servant Scapino in the Italian commedia dell'arte, is performed for the first time in Tartu, Estonia.

1985

1 JANUARY 1985

Montségur, opera by the 69-year-old French composer Marcel LANDOWSKI, is produced in Toulouse.

9 JANUARY 1985

Sir Robert MAYER, German-born British philanthropist and erstwhile piano wunderkind, who with his first wife, a concert singer, started in London a series of youth concerts, dies in London at the incredible age of one hundred and five, five years after marrying, as a nuptially hopeful centenarian, a lady of an uncertain but definitely postnubile age named Jacqueline Noble.

10 JANUARY 1985

The last known song written by Richard STRAUSS, dated 23 November 1948, consisting of 72 bars in the key of E-flat major, set for soprano and piano, entitled *Malven* (mallow flowers) dedicated to his favorite singer, Maria Jeritza (it is inscribed "my last rose"), and depicting an "odorless flower resembling a tear-stained and pallid face, washed by the golden, heavenly light," is performed for the first time anywhere in New York as an encore to the New York Philharmonic program by Kiri Te Kanawa, with piano accompaniment. (The original manuscript was purchased in 1984 by a New York philanthropist from the estate of Maria Jeritza, for an incredible sum of $60,500.00.)

10 JANUARY 1985

riverrun for piano and orchestra by the 54-year-old avant-garde composer Toru TAKEMITSU, inspired by the famous first word of Joyce's *Finnegans Wake,* which begins in the middle of a sentence and ends in the middle of the same sentence, the river being Dublin's Liffey, is performed for the first time by the American proponent of modern music Peter Serkin, son of the romantic pianist Rudolf Serkin, and the Los Angeles Philharmonic.

11 JANUARY 1985

Jacob's Room, monodrama in two parts based on Virginia Woolf's novel of that name and *Eleni* by Nicholas Gage, by the 51-year-old American composer Morton SUBOTNICK, scored for string quartet and voice and set in an agonizingly permuted quasitonal idiom, is performed for the first time in San Francisco by the Kronos String Quartet and Subotnick's Wife, soprano Joan La Barbara. (Later, a third part was added, to the text of Elie Weisel, portraying the horrors of Nazi transportation of Jews to their final destination, death.)

16 JANUARY 1985

Rhapsody for violin and orchestra by the 46-year-old American composer Charles WUORINEN (completed on 5 December 1983), thematically based on one of Stravin-sky's unfinished sketches (G, E, F, D-flat, C, A) with the total time span of 19 minutes and 31 seconds, is performed for the first time by Daniel Kobialka and the San Francisco Symphony, Edo de Waart conducting.

18 JANUARY 1985

Partita for violin and piano by the 71-year-old Polish composer Witold LUTOSLAWSKI (who, in 1988, orchestrated the piece) is premiered in St. Paul, Minnesota, by Pinchas Zukerman and Marc Neikrug.

23 JANUARY 1985

A Jerome KERN postage stamp, at the new price of 22 cents, designed by James Sharpe of Westport, Connecticut, and overseen by Jack Williams, program manager for philatelic design, goes on sale by the U.S. Postal Service to mark (four days early) the centennial of his birth. (Kern himself was a noted philatelist.) The dedication ceremony, attended by Hal David, president of ASCAP, and Kern's daughter, Betty Kern Miller, from Danville, Kentucky, took place in the main gallery of the Library of Performing Arts at Lincoln Center.

24 JANUARY 1985

Requiem for soloists, chorus and orchestra by the scholarly 63-year-old American composer Andrew IMBRIE, written in mournful memory of his intellectually endowed young son, who died suddenly, to texts from the traditional Latin Requiem, Kyrie, Dies Irae, Offertorium and Benedictus, interspersed with devotional poems by Willim Blake, George Herbert and John Donne, suffused with darksomely lucent tense, dense, contrapuntally saturated sonic masses in mutually conciliated dissonances, is performed for the first time by the San Francisco Symphony Orchestra and Chorus, conducted by Edo de Waart.

28 JANUARY 1985

Symphony No. 59 by the extraordinarily prolific 73-year-old American composer of Armenian-Scottish descent Alan HOVHANESS is premiered in Bellevue, Washington.

13 FEBRUARY 1985

Forty years after an apocalyptic assault by vengeful British and American air fleets upon the defenseless, porcelainlike, lovely town of Dresden, setting its fragile habitations on hellish fire, incinerating 35,000 living people, Dresden's legendary Opera House, where Weber and Wagner once led their works, is restored to its former glory with punctilious attention to artistic detail, and opens its first postwar season with a performance of Weber's opera *Der Freischütz,* symbolically proclaiming unceasing struggle against brutality, oppression and autocracy.

14 FEBRUARY 1985

Winds of Nagual—Musical Fable for Wind Ensemble on the Writings of Carlos Castaneda by the 52-year-old American composer Michael COLGRASS is performed for the first time at the New England Conservatory of Music in Boston.

17 FEBRUARY 1985

Music for Twelve for chamber ensemble by the 66-year-old American composer Leon KIRCHNER is performed for the first time by the Chamber Players of the Boston Symphony Orchestra at the New England Conservatory of Music, the composer conducting.

19 FEBRUARY 1985

Third Symphony by the British composer Peter Maxwell DAVIES is performed for the first time in Manchester, England.

22 FEBRUARY 1985

Efrem ZIMBALIST, SR., eminent Russian-born American violinist and teacher, dies in Reno, Nevada, at the age of 96.

23 FEBRUARY 1985

Three centuries have elapsed since the birth in the Saxon town of Halle of Georg Friedrich HÄNDEL, creator of operas, oratorios and instrumental music of incomparable magnificence, who emigrated to England where he changed the spelling of his name to George Frideric Handel, a close contemporary of Bach who was born not far from him on the plains of Saxony but whom he never met. (The tombstone of Handel in Westminster Abbey bears the date of his birth as 23 February 1684, a discrepancy owing to the calendar of the time in which the years began in March.)

1 MARCH 1985

Harriet, the Woman Called Moses, opera by Thea MUS-GRAVE, Scottish composer dwelling in America, to the story of the valiant abolitionist Harriet Tubman who smuggled Negro slaves to freedom in Canada before the Civil War, is performed for the first time by the Virginia Opera in Norfolk, conducted by the composer's husband, Peter Mark.

1 MARCH 1985

Harriet, the Woman Called Moses, opera by the 56-year-old Scottish composer Thea MUSGRAVE, is staged in Norfolk, Virginia.

6 MARCH 1985

The Black Spider, opera by the 30-year-old Scottish composer Judith WEIR, based on the 1842 novel *Die schwarze Spinne* by Jeremias Gotthelf and a contemporary news report from Krakow, is staged in the Crypt of Canterbury Cathedral.

7 MARCH 1985

Symphony in one movement, with solo commentary from electric piano, by the 28-year-old Finnish composer Jouni KAIPAINEN is performed for the first time in Helsinki.

12 MARCH 1985

Eugene ORMANDY, the ultra-professional Hungarian conductor who as successor to the aureole-laureled Leopold Stokowski perfected the "Philadelphia sound" of the great Philadelphia Orchestra and who held the podium for a record 44 years before yielding it to his Italian successor, Riccardo Muti, in 1980, dies of a prosaic pulmonary ailment in Philadelphia, at the age of 85.

15 MARCH 1985

Contrabassoon Concerto by the 58-year-old American composer Donald ERB, a rare opus for this unwieldy instrument, is performed for the first time by Gregg Henegar as soloist with the Houston Symphony Orchestra, Sergiu Comissiona conducting.

15 MARCH 1985

Ritual for orchestra by the 50-year-old Russian composer Alfred SCHNITTKE is premiered in Novosibirsk.

16 MARCH 1985

Roger SESSIONS, great American composer of densely contrapuntal, harmonically complex and yet poetic and lyrical eight symphonies, two operas, technically demanding concertos, tersely crafted chamber pieces, intransigently unyielding to the public tastes ("my music was born difficult," he once explained), who earned the devotion of his many students and colleagues, and whose intellectual equipment included profound knowledge of philosophy, philology and history (he spoke four languages besides English), dies as a result of a cerebral hemorrhage in Princeton, at the age of 88.

21 MARCH 1985

Three hundred years have passed since the birth in the Saxon town of Eisenach of Johann Sebastian BACH, the great lawgiver of music whose importance is comparable to that of Aristotle in philosophy and Leonardo da Vinci in art, and whose scientific precision of technique in counterpoint, fugue, harmony, and sonorous structures of instrumentation became an instructive model for untold generations of composers.

21 MARCH 1985

Harmonielehre for orchestra by the 38-year-old American composer John ADAMS, in three tonally tried but ultimately true movements culminating in the sunlit "Meister Eckhardt and Quackie," its title drawn from Schoenberg's exhaustive 1911 treatise but alluding no less to harmony in the sense of spirit and psychology, is premiered by the San Francisco Symphony Orchestra, Edo de Waart conducting.

12 APRIL 1985

Casanova's Homecoming, lyrical opera buffa in three acts by the 57-year-old American composer Dominick ARGENTO, to an original libretto based on "'histoire de ma vie" by Jacques Casanova, set in the first week of Carnival season, 1774 Venice, is staged in St. Paul, Minnesota.

18 APRIL 1985

Flute Concerto by the multifaceted American composer Morton GOULD is performed for the first time by the Chicago Symphony Orchestra, Georg Solti conducting.

19 APRIL 1985

Behold the Sun, an opera by the 52-year-old English composer Alexander GOEHR, is produced in Duisberg in a German version as *Die Wiedertäufer.*

19 APRIL 1985

Eating Living Monkeys for orchestra by the 28-year-old American composer David LANG, the source of the title being a story told among eighteenth-century colonial powers that the Chinese Imperial family ate the brains of living monkeys and which the composer considers "one example of the many rumors, lies, and insults which preceded armed conflict between the East and West," is premiered in Cleveland.

6 JUNE 1985

Der Wald, concerto for kettledrums and orchestra by the 51-year-old German composer Siegfried MATTHUS, is premiered in Dresden.

13 JUNE 1985

March to Tonality for orchestra by the 48-year-old American composer David DEL TREDICI is performed for the first time by the Chicago Symphony Orchestra under the direction of Michael Tilson Thomas, for whom the work was written.

6 JULY 1985

Sinfonia Sacra for organ and orchestra, composed in 1908 by the French organist-composer Charles-Marie WIDOR (1844–1937), is performed for the first time in Haarlem, Holland, Albert de Klerk, soloist.

13 JULY 1985

"Live Aid," the first global rock concert, a telethon to raise money for famine victims in Africa, opens simultaneously in Philadelphia and London, televized to about 150 countries and watched by something like 1,500,000,000 people, expected to raise something like $70,000,000, with the Philadelphia portion utilizing about 90,000 nails driven into the 23,744 square-foot plywood stage and 75 miles of cable connecting 16 tons of lighting equipment with 2 million watts of power, and involving 37 acts and 30 equipment changes, with hundreds of spectacular celebrities gracing the stage with their uninhibited crooning and howling presence, and hundreds of humble roadies donating their essential labor.

26 JULY 1985

Penthode by the eminent 76-year-old American composer Elliott CARTER, quintuple quartet for five groups comprised of varying balances of brass, string, wind, and percussion instruments, referentially signifying "experiences of connectedness and isolation," with each group possessing its own "repertory of expressive characters embodied in its own special field of speeds and musical intervals," receives its first ever performance at London's Royal Albert Hall by the Ensemble InterContemporain and the Ensemble Orchestral de Paris conducted by Pierre Boulez.

26 JULY 1985

Genrik LITINSKY, scholarly and versatile Soviet composer and teacher who achieved mastery in modern techniques of counterpoint, but who was also capable of adapting the cultural elements of Mongolian and other folk elements in popular music (he wrote operas based on native rhythms and natural harmonies of Yakut tribes), but who was unfairly discriminated against as not following the empty letter of National Socialism, dies in Moscow at the age of 84.

27 JULY 1985

Tuning for orchestra by the 46-year-old English composer John McCABE is premiered in s'Hertogenbosch.

18 AUGUST 1985

Il ritorno d' Ulisse in patria, realization of Monteverdi's opera by the socially tempered 59-year-old German composer Hans Werner HENZE, is staged in Salzburg.

24 AUGUST 1985

Paul CRESTON, American composer whose real name was Giuseppe Guttoveggio, a variant of his nickname "Crespino" (given by his schoolmates after a role he acted in a play), and who in his major musical works introduced such alien time signatures as 6/12 and 3/9, dies in San Diego at the age of 78.

24 AUGUST 1985

Lancelot, opera by the 63-year-old Scottish composer Iain HAMILTON, is staged in Arundel, England.

24 AUGUST 1985

Symphony No. 3, Symphony of Lamentations, for chamber orchestra by the 31-year-old Russian composer Sergei PAVLENKO, in one movement and commemorating the 100th anniversary of Igor Stravinsky's birth, receives its first ever performance at the Cabrillo Music Festival in Aptos, California, by the Cabrillo Festival Orchestra, Dennis Russell Davies conducting.

4 SEPTEMBER 1985

Kraft (*Power*) in two large movements for solo ensemble of six players and orchestra (with a percussion section requiring electric drum) by the volcanic 27-year-old Finnish composer Magnus LINDBERG is performed for the first time in Helsinki.

13 SEPTEMBER 1985

Dane RUDHYAR, French-born composer of mystical persuasion whose real name, Daniel Chennevière, he changed to the old Sanskrit surname, astrologically related to the red planet Mars and the month of his birth, who wrote a limited amount of works mostly for piano and also painted pictures of supernatural significance, dies in San Francisco at the age of 90. (When asked by his fourth wife whom he expected to meet beyond, he answered, "Myself.")

15 SEPTEMBER 1985

Alax for three identical instrumental ensembles by the 63-year-old Greek-born French composer Iannis XENAKIS is premiered in Cologne.

19 SEPTEMBER 1985

Seeded 44-year-old American rock artist Frank ZAPPA, self-proclaimed opponent of the Parents Music Resource Center (PMRC), an organization which, opposing the glorification of sex, violence, and drugs in song lyrics, made such demands upon the Recording Industry Association of America (RIAA) as the labeling of record albums as to lyric content and the rating of record albums in a system akin to that in effect for film, appears in the first of a series of highly publicized hearings involving the Senate Commerce, Technology, and Transportation Committee, the PMRC, and the RIAA, in which he described the PMRC proposal as ". . . an ill-conceived piece of nonsense which fails to deliver any real benefits to children and promises to keep the courts busy for years, dealing with the interpretational and enforcemental problems inherent in the proposal's design." (See complete text in Letters and Documents.)

26 SEPTEMBER 1985

Symphony No. 3 by the 68-year-old Korean-born German composer Isang YUN is premiered in Berlin by the Saarbrücken Radio Symphony.

27 SEPTEMBER 1985

Symphony No. 3 by the 42-year-old English composer David MATTHEWS is premiered in Sheffield.

28 SEPTEMBER 1985

Judith, opera by the 51-year-old German composer Siegfried MATTHUS, is staged in Berlin.

4 OCTOBER 1985

On the first day of the 59th Festival of the International Society for Contemporary Music in Amsterdam, an opening concert by the Radio Chamber Orchestra conducted by Ernest Bour is presented with the following program:

Concertino for Chamber Orchestra by the American composer Ross BAUER; *Tya* by the Australian composer Michael WHITICKER, its title the aboriginal word for "earth" or "flowering time"; *Chamber Symphony* in one movement by the American composer Jon CHENETTE; and *Corpus cum Figuris* by the 36-year-old Danish composer Poul RUDERS, in one movement, vaguely inspired by Adrian Leverkühn's fictional musical composition "Apocalipsis Cum Figuris" from Thomas Mann's monumental novel *Dr. Faustus*.

5 OCTOBER 1985

On the second day of the 59th Festival of the International Society for Contemporary Music in Amsterdam, two concerts are given in the following sequence:

An afternoon concert in two segments: (1) a performance by the Silesian Quartet of string quartets by the Polish composers Eugeniusz KNAPIK and Aleksander LASOŃ; (2) "National programme of traditional music of Venezuela," performed by the Orquesta de Instrumentos Latinoamericanos (ODILA), including traditional works as well as contemporary compositions by Venezuelan composers, in the following program: *Proyecto Odila* for Latin American instruments by Javier ALDANA; *Magia*, "love dialogue" for two mbiras and chamber ensemble by Randy ARRIECHI; and *Etnocidio* by Emilio MENDOZA.

An evening concert of chamber works performed by the Hague Philharmonic conducted by Friedemann Layer, in the following program: *Madi (Knot)* for twelve instruments by the Korean composer Younghi PAGH-PAAN, in four parts, with the conductor marking time in his dual role of percussionist; *Prisma* by the Greek composer Michael TRAVLOS, with a melodic fragment built on a minor second serving as the formal connecting element; *Dérive* for flute, clarinet, violin, cello, vibraphone, and piano by the 60-year-old French composer Pierre BOULEZ; and *Flexio* by the 55-year-old Netherlands composer Theo LOEVENDIE, in two atonal movements, commissioned by the Dutch Ministry of Culture for the 90th anniversary of the Concertgebouw Orchestra.

6 OCTOBER 1985

On the third day of the 59th Festival of the International Society for Contemporary Music in Amsterdam, three concerts are given in the following sequence:

An afternoon concert of vocal works performed by the Radio Chamber Choir conducted by Robin Gritton, in the following program: ". . . *Nudo que ansi juntáis* . . ." by the 60-year-old Swiss composer Klaus HUBER, based on the confrontation of two Spanish texts (Teresa de Ahumada y Cepeda [de Avila] [1515–1582] and Pablo Neruda); *Ngano* for mezzo-soprano, tenor, eight-part chorus, flute, and two percussionists by the 39-year-old English composer Michael FINNISSY, with each of its four sections characterized by different vocal and/or instrumental combinations, its text derived from rhymes and folksongs of the Venda Africans; and three works by Irish composers: a selection from *Verona Preludes* by Gerard VICTORY, *Au Milieu* by Gerald BARRY, and *Oileain* by John BUCKLEY.

A late afternoon concert of organ works performed by Willem Tanke, in the following program: *Sweelinck-Variations* by the 58-year-old Netherlands composer Ton de LEEUW, based on the beginning of Sweelinck's variations on "Mein junges Leben hat ein End"; *Fa-Si* by the 59-year-old Italian composer Luciano BERIO, the composer's only work for organ and based thematically on the interval of a major third indicated in its title; *Splendid Isolation*, passacaglia by the 51-year-old Netherlands composer Joep STRAESSER, in five sections (Toccata, Fantasia 1, Passacaglia, Toccata 2, and Fantasia 2); and *Fanfare II*, designed for an organ with three manuals and pedal board and based on the four verses of the Kyrie of Machaut's Notre-Dame Mass by the 49-year-old Belgian composer Philippe BOESMANS.

An evening concert of orchestral works performed by the Radio Symphony Orchestra conducted by Lucas Vis, in the following program: *Verblendungen (Dazzlings)* for small orchestra and four-channel digital tape by the Finnish composer Kaija SAARIAHO, dedicated to Esa-Pekka Salonen; *Musik-*

Geschichte for piano and orchestra by the 55-year-old German composer Werner HEIDER; *Piece for orchestra No. 3,* in one monothematic movement by the 47-year-old Polish composer Zygmunt KRAUZE; and *De Snelheid (Velocity)* by the 46-year-old Netherlands composer Louis ANDRIESSEN.

7 OCTOBER 1985

On the fourth day of the 59th Festival of the International Society for Contemporary Music in Amsterdam, three concerts are given in the following sequence:

An early afternoon concert of prize-winning works from the 13th International Competition for Electroacoustic Music Bourges in cooperation with Gaudeamus, in the following program: *Im-mobile* by the Norwegian composer Cecilie ORE, utilizing synthesized and concrete sounds; *Transparency* for harp and tape by the Japanese composer Takayuki RAI, realized on the two PDP-15 computers at Utrecht's Institute of Sonology; *Nebula Prospect* by the Finnish composer Patrick KOSK, a "simple play" with structures and colors; and *Kristallwelt,* the first of three parts of a cycle of electronic pieces mixing sounds of early Asian instruments (Chinese woodblock, rîn, Japanese temple gong, et al.) by the German composer Michael OBST.

A mid afternoon concert of solo and ensemble pieces, in the following program: *Concert Etude* for piano by the American composer Todd BRIEF; *Trama* for violin by the Italian composer Mauro CARDI, winner of the 1984 Gaudeamus prize; *Ferma E'l'Antica Voce . . .* for soprano and piano on a poem by Salvatore Quasimodo ("Erato e Appolion") by the Italian composer Marco LASAGNA; *Spirali: quand'i caldi raggi fuggon (Spirals: When the warm rays flee)* for clarinet by the Italian composer Giuseppe SOCCIO; *Spektra* for three celli by the Korean composer Unsuk CHIN, in five small sections representing various light effects; and *Apax* for eight wind instruments by the Italian composer Luigi ABBATE.

An evening "National Programme of Austria" performed by Nouvelle Cuisine-Electric Big Band conducted by Wolfgang R. Kubizek, in the following program: *Oblesse n'oblige,* antiwar piece in two parts by Christian MÜHLBACHER; *Oktett* for jazz ensemble by Wolfgang R. KUBIZEK; and *Fast Steps for Giants,* incorporating Latin American, Cuban, disco, and funk rhythms by Christoph CECH; and, after intermission, "National Programme of the Netherlands," in the following program: *Strides* and *Walk* for piano, both by Theo LOEVENDIE; *Brake* and *Woeha* for piano, both by Guus JANSSEN; *Trajekten* by Willem VAN MANEN, melding traditional French music with 1960s jazz; and *Carrara,* in three phrases, by Paul TERMOS.

8 OCTOBER 1985

On the fifth day of the 59th Festival of the International Society for Contemporary Music in Amsterdam, three concerts are given in the following sequence:

An early afternoon concert of prize-winning works from the 13th International Competition for Electroacoustic Music Bourges in cooperation with Gaudeamus, in the following program: *A quiet disturbance* for tape mixing FM radio materials from Toronto and sounds from the composer's private studio by the Belgian composer Peter BEYLS; *Musica en la noche* by the Spanish composer José Manuel BERENGUER, named after Aldous Huxley's "Night Music" and realized on the Alpha Syntauri and Mountain Computer synthesizer systems; and *Naturel-Culturel* by the 45-year-old Rumanian composer Octavian NEMESCU, based on the "egg or seed" note of g, with an optimal length of 21'.

A mid afternoon "National Programme of Iceland," performed by the Icelandic Trio (cello, clarinet, and piano), in the following program: *Dans* for solo cello by Snorri Sigfús BIRGISSON; *Burned Bright Lights of Both Eyes,* trio in one movement/four sections by Gudmundur HAFSTEINSSON; and *Trio* by Hjalmar H. RAGNARSSON; and, after intermission, "National Programme of Sweden," in the following program: *Fractal,* "multimedia show" for tape and slide projections by Rolf ENSTRÔM; *Den förstenade (The petrified one)* for mezzo-soprano and tape by Pär LINDGREN, reflecting upon mankind's awkward relationship with nature; and *Yáin* for tape by Åke PARMERUD.

An evening "National Programme of Belgium," performed by the Nieuwe Muziekgroep conducted by Mark De Smet, in the following program: *Squib* by Frank NUYTS, one in a series of works based on the number 7 ("squib" in old English denoting fireworks that explode "7" times); *Pampa* by Lucien GOETHALS, the monotony of the title (itself suggested by a poem by the Argentine poet Ricardo Guiraldes) reflected in an ostinato motive; *Icarus' Flight (Ascension II)* for self-actualized piano by André LAPORTE; and *Chances* (Version II) for 17 performers in three double systems by Jacques CALONNE; and, after intermission, "National Programme of the German Federal Republic," performed by the Ensemble Modern conducted by Lothar Zagrosek, in the following program: *Saitenspiel (Flechtwerk 5)* for 18 instruments by Walter ZIMMERMANN, commissioned by Ensemble Modern; and *Mouvement—vor der Erstarrung* by Helmut LACHENMANN, comprised of various "noise-like" events.

9 OCTOBER 1985

On the sixth day of the 59th Festival of the International Society for Contemporary Music in Amsterdam, three concerts are given in the following sequence:

An early afternoon concert of electroacoustic music, in the following program of works by Netherlands composers: *Denk mal das Denkmal* by Ton BRUYNÈL, "something to play during a lunch-break concert at a disarmament conference"; *Clair-Obscur* by Ton de LEEUW, commissioned by the Groupe de Recherches Musicales de Paris, its title referring to paintings of Rembrandt and comprised of blocks of materials which surface and unfold "in their own way"; and *Ontketening II* for percussion, live electronics, and tapes by Jan BOERMAN.

A midafternoon "National Programme of Japan," performed by the Hato Ensemble, in the following program: *Requiem Saecularem* by Yori-Aki MATSUDAIRA, to a text drawn from the World War II diary of the Japanese poet Eiji Usami, based on materials derived from 964 chords; *Dan-So (Dislocation, Bend)* for an ensemble of spatially dislocated violin, cello, and piano by Toshio HOSOKAWA; *Inter-posi-play-tion No. 2* by Joji YUASA; and *Nétri et Rôëï, dans le style de Gagaku* by Yoritsuné MATSUDAIRA, inspired by Gagaku singing and attempting to "modernize the atmosphere of the Japanese musical tradition."

An evening concert of chamber works, in the following program: *Pour les vingt doigts* for piano by the Italian composer Riccardo FORMOSA, composed via "Gestalt-logic" and loosely based on the letters contained in the names of the work's dedicatees (Katherine Ryder and Richard Toop); and *Sonancias III* for two pianos and two percussionists by the 46-year-old Brazilian composer Marlos NOBRE, dedicated to Pierre Metral, conductor of the Bartók Ensemble of Geneva; and, after intermission, "National Programme of Portugal," performed by Grupo de Música Contemporânea de Lisboa and presented in a vishual/scenic conception by choreographer/dancer Wanda Ribeiro da Silva, director of the Escola

Superior de Danca, in the following program: *Momento* (occasionally aleatoric) by Constança CAPDEVILLE; *Recondita Armonia* by Clotilde ROSA, inspired by both Puccini and the composer's father, the *Tosca*-loving tenor José Rosa; *Nocturnal* for guitar, percussion, and dance by J. A. LOPES E SILVA; and *Meta-formoses* for bass clarinet and ensemble by Jorge PEIXINHO.

9 OCTOBER 1985

X: The Life and Times of Malcolm X, opera in three acts with a libretto derived from the black leader's autobiography, by the 34-year-old black American composer and jazz pianist Anthony DAVIS, is given its first full-scale production in Philadelphia. (The "official" world première is claimed for the New York City Opera production of 28 September 1986.)

10 OCTOBER 1985

On the seventh day of the 59th Festival of the International Society for Contemporary Music in Amsterdam, two concerts are given in the following sequence:

An afternoon concert of electroacoustic works, in the following program: *Octuor* by the Argentine composer Horacio VAGGIONE, realized at Paris' IRCAM using a PDP-10 computer and the Music-10 language; *Stirae (Icicles)* by the English composer Alistair N. MACDONALD, its sound sources including rubbed and struck wine glasses; *Kinesis* by the English composer Ian DEARDEN, utilizing four sound sources (stone attack, metal attack, glass tone, and tam-tam resonance) heard in both "raw" and "developed" states; and *Forty-three* by the American composer and Associate Director of the Columbia-Princeton Electronic Music Center Pril SMILEY.

An evening "National Programme of Hong Kong" featuring traditional and contemporary music for Chinese instruments, in its first half consisting of works for Gu zheng, gu qin, pipa, and erhu, and in its second half consisting of compositions by contemporary composers from Hong Kong, in the following program: *Almond Flower Reflection* for ensemble by Kuan NAICHUNG, inspired by the travels of the Sung Dynasty lyric poet Jian Bai-she; *Cantilena* for pipa by Law WING-FAI, in three sections, each beginning with a passage imitating drums; *Longing for the native land* for gu zheng by Shi KUMPOR, based on intervals of a fourth and a fifth; *Silk Music* for er-hu, dong-xioa, and gu-zheng by Richard TSANG; and *Twilight Swallows* for ensemble by the American-born but China-assimilated composer Tim WILSON (a.k.a. Wai TINGSUN), inspired by the "silk and bamboo" chamber music of Southeast China.

10 OCTOBER 1985

Symphony No. 4, Memorial Candles, by the 61-year-old American composer Benjamin LEES, commemorating the 40th anniversary of the end of the Nazi Holocaust in its setting of poems by the Nobel Prize-winning poet Nelly Sachs (a Holocaust survivor), set in three massive movements with a large obbligato part for violin, is given its first ever performance in Dallas, Pinchas Zukerman soloist.

11 OCTOBER 1985

On the eighth day of the 59th Festival of the International Society for Contemporary Music in Amsterdam, two concerts of note are given in the following sequence:

A mid afternoon "National Programme of Israel," in the following program: *Beyond the Curtain* for violin, viola, cello, and piano by Tzvi AVNI, in one uncharacteristically Romantic movement; *Deux Impromptus pour piano (nr. 2)* by Ami MA'AYANI; *Realm* for amplified cello by Gabriel IRANYI; and *Piano Quartet* by Josef TAL; and, after intermission, "National Programme of Norway," performed by the NY Musikks Ensemble conducted by Christian Eggen, in the following program: *The Savage,* "4 impressions for 6 players" ("Awakening," "Sub Stellarum," "Games," and "In the Jungle") by Antonio BIBALO; *Echo of an Echo* by Olav Anton THOMMESSEN, an acoustic version of the composer's music for a TV-ballet, "Echo"; and *Make Believe Rag for (Dancing) Soprano* by Magne HEGDAL, with both music and text composed via chance operations applied to Scott Joplin's popular "Maple Leaf" rag.

An evening concert of chamber works, in the following program: *Vanada* for keyboards (including two synthesizers), brass, and percussion by the American composer Michael TORKE, its title the composite of the two principle characters of Nabokov's novel, Ada, or Ardor, and its musical materials the conjoining of "serial time point composition, American minimalism, and black disco music"; *Solidity* for oboe, clarinet, bass clarinet, bassoon, string quartet, piano, and harp by the Japanese composer Talayuki RAI; *Carceri d'Invenzione I* for 13 instruments lasting some thirteen minutes by the 42-year-old English composer Brian FERNEYHOUGH, commissioned by the London Sinfonietta; *Ritos Ancestrales de Una Cultura Olvidada* by the Argentine composer Alejandro Iglesias ROSSI, to ancient Quechua hymns and ritual *jaillis* (poems sung while working), in nine parts; *Vórtice* for six bass clarinets and three contrabass clarinets by the 53-year-old Netherlands composer Enrique RAXACII, in one "continuous concentric movement"; and *Lamentoros, Badinerie vocale et instrumental en forme d'un Grand Double Carillon* by the 49-year-old Swiss composer Jürg WYTTENBACH.

12 OCTOBER 1985

On the ninth day of the 59th Festival of the International Society for Contemporary Music in Amsterdam, two concerts of note are given in the following sequence:

A midafternoon concert of mostly piano works, in the following program: *Klavierstück XII* by the 57-year-old German composer Karlheinz STOCKHAUSEN; *Campagne in Campi Aperti* by the Swedish composer Jan SANDSTRÖM; *Slow Lament* for soprano and piano, a 16-minute, one-movement elegy on the poem "Lamento Lent" by Pablo Neruda by the American composer Todd BRIEF; and *Music for Piano Nr. 5* by the American composer Jonathan D. KRAMER, based on six notes of the chromatic scale.

An evening "National Programme of Australia," performed by Ensemble Flederman, in the following program: *Miniature III* for flute, trombone, percussion, and piano by Carl VINE, in three rhythmically distinct sections; *Ways-Byways* by Keith HUMBLE, in five virtuosic parts; *Ganymede/Prometheus* by Graham HAIR, with its *Ganymede* being an "inverse double" of its *Prometheus;* and *Snark-Hunting* for flute, percussion, keyboards, cello, and tape by Martin WESLEY-SMITH, a "nonsense piece" loosely based on Lewis Carroll's whimsical "The Hunting of the Snark."

13 OCTOBER 1985

On the tenth and final day of the 59th Festival of the International Society for Contemporary Music in Amsterdam, two concerts are given in the following sequence:

A midafternoon concert of vocal works performed by Het Nieuw Ensemble conducted by Otto Ketting, in the following program: *12 Songs* for female voice and piano by the 42-

year-old Hungarian composer Zoltán JENEY, to texts by e.e. cummings, Tandori Dezsö, William Blake, and Friedrich Hölderlin; *Tour pour violon and piano*, an "exercise in restriction" by the Netherlands composer Joël BONS; *Alba (Tre poesie di Vincenzo Cardarelli)* for soprano and four instruments by the 54-year-old Belgian composer Jacqueline FONTYN; and *Clos de Vie (In memoriam Claude Vivier)* by the Canadian composer José EVANGELISTA, its four sections cast in a monodic texture of unisons, based on a cyclical melody and closing with a quotation from Vivier's *Lonely Child*.

An evening concert, "Gaudeamus Music Week," with the following program: *Försvinna (To Disappear)* for bass clarinet, and contrabass clarinet, and string orchestra by the English composer James CLARKE, inspired in part by the electric storms of the west coast of Finland; *O Dormiente, che cosa e' sonno?* by the Italian composer Paolo RICCI, based on two texts dealing with death; *Track* by the Australian composer Michael SMETANIN; and *Bewegingen* for fifteen instruments grouped into wind, string, and percussion quintets by the Netherlands composer Klaas DE VRIES.

14 OCTOBER 1985

Emil GILELS, Russian pianist who reached the rank of world virtuoso, dies in Moscow just five days before his 70th birthday.

20 OCTOBER 1985

Piano Concerto by the inventive 68-year-old American composer Lou HARRISON is premiered in New York, Keith Jarrett, soloist.

20 OCTOBER 1985

Challenger for orchestra by the 59-year-old American composer Meyer KUPFERMAN, conceived in 1983 as a tribute to the *Challenger* space shuttle, is first heard in New York, less than four months prior to the craft's tragic explosion after liftoff on January 28, 1986, on a mission that included the schoolteacher Christa McAuliffe.

31 OCTOBER 1985

The Los Angeles Philharmonic conducted by Leonard Slatkin gives an opening orchestral concert of the 7th annual New Music America Festival in Los Angeles in a program including *Auroras* by the 68-year-old American composer Robert ERICKSON, and the first ever performance of *Encounter* (1977), dramatic sequence in five scenes for piano and orchestra, by the French-born American composer and writer on psychospiritual and astrological matters Dane RUDHYAR (1895–1985).

2 NOVEMBER 1985

Piano and String Quartet by the 59-year-old American composer Morton FELDMAN receives its first performance by the Kronos Quartet and Aki Takahashi as part of the 7th annual New Music America Festival in Los Angeles.

4 NOVEMBER 1985

The Los Angeles Philharmonic New Music Group conducted by Lucky Mosko presents a concert as part of the 7th annual New Music America Festival in Los Angeles in a program including *Fog Tropes* (1982) for brass sextet (pairs of trumpets, trombones, and horns) and tape of collected sea sounds, including the plaintive keening of seagulls, by the 43-year-old American composer Ingram MARSHALL, and the first ever performance of *Fanfare erafnaF*, played sequentially both forward and backward by a stereophonically subdivided orchestra, by the 28-year-old American composer Rand STEIGER.

5 NOVEMBER 1985

Symphony No. 2, Espacio cerrado, by the 43-year-old Spanish composer Tomás MARCO, a "study of circular time," is performed for the first time ever by the Berlin Symphony Orchestra in Ravenna, Italy.

5 NOVEMBER 1985

The Key to Songs, music for an imaginary ballet by the 52-year-old American composer Morton SUBOTNICK, based on Max Ernst's collage-novel *A Week of Kindness or the Seven Deadly Elements*, in two rollicking parts and scored for two pianos, xylophone, marimba, vibraphone, viola, cello, and live electronics, receives its second ever performance at the 7th annual New Music America Festival in Los Angeles.

7 NOVEMBER 1985

Ceremonial for Orchestra by the 50-year-old English-born American composer Bernard RANDS is premiered in San Diego by the San Diego Symphony, David Atherton conducting.

10 NOVEMBER 1985

Symphony No. 58, Symphony Sacra, for soprano, baritone, chorus, and orchestra by the prolific 74-year-old American composer of Armenian-Scottish descent Alan HOVHANESS, is premiered in Valparaiso, Indiana.

13 NOVEMBER 1985

Symphony No. 2, Cello Symphony, by the 46-year-old American composer Ellen Taaffe ZWILICH is premiered in San Francisco.

14 NOVEMBER 1985

Proclamation (1982) by the veteran American composer Aaron COPLAND, in an authorized orchestration by Philip Ramey, is premiered in New York on the occasion of the composer's 85th birthday.

17 NOVEMBER 1985

Symphony No. 9 for baritone and orchestra by the 70-year-old American composer David DIAMOND, in two hyper-Romantic movements enhanced by the setting of four sonnets of Michelangelo reflecting upon man's mortality and lasting some forty-five minutes, inspired by Dimitri Mitropoulos for whom it was intended as a memorial, is premiered in New York, Leonard Bernstein conducting.

23 NOVEMBER 1985

Bright Blue Music for orchestra by the 24-year-old American composer Michael TORKE is premiered in New York.

12 DECEMBER 1985

Quartet No. 5, In Memoriam Henri Michaux (1984), by the remarkable and mysterious 80-year-old Italian composer Giacinto SCELSI is premiered by the Arditti String Quartet in Rome.

13 DECEMBER 1985

Violin Concerto by the 62-year-old Polish-born American composer and conductor Stanislaw SKROWACZEWSKI, a lyric and transparent three-movement work for orchestra without violins and trumpets but with fortified winds, brass, and percussion suggesting new relationships between the soloist and orchestra, receives its first performance in Philadelphia.

1986

4 JANUARY 1986

Hell's Angels, opera by the 37-year-old English composer Nigel OSBORNE, dealing with secular protectors of the human species, is staged in London.

6 JANUARY 1986

Viola Concerto by the 51-year-old Soviet composer of German descent Alfred SCHNITTKE, who developed a *sui generis* modern Baroque style, is performed for the first time in Amsterdam.

10 JANUARY 1986

Archetypon for orchestra by the 61-year-old modernistic Croatian composer Milko KELEMEN is heard for the first time in Hannover.

17 JANUARY 1986

Concerto for Violin and Orchestra by the American composer Richard WERNICK, recipient of the prestigious 1986 Kennedy Center Friedheim Award, is performed for the first time in Philadelphia, one day after the composer's 52nd birthday.

19 JANUARY 1986

Piano Concerto by the 69-year-old American composer Milton BABBITT, cast in a multiserial but inwardly compelling organized setting, receives its premiere performance in New York.

24 JANUARY 1986

Piano Concerto, composed in 1931 by the American composer Marc BLITZSTEIN (1905–1964) and heard previously only in a two-piano reduction, is premiered posthumously with orchestra at New York's Cooper Union, Robert Black soloist.

13 FEBRUARY 1986

Starckdeutsche Lieder und Tänze for baritone and orchestra by the 50-year-old Austrian composer of the avant-garde Kurt SCHWERTSIK, set to humorous texts of Matthias Koeppel and bearing an intentional misspelling of *Starkdeutsche,* is premiered in Vienna.

13 FEBRUARY 1986

Edmund RUBBRA, English composer of contrapuntally involved, and for that reason highly respectable, symphonic and chamber works that enjoyed minimal hearings in Great Britain but virtually none elsewhere, dies at the accomplished but insufficiently fulfilled age of 85 in Gerrards Cross.

21 FEBRUARY 1986

Myung-Whun CHUNG, extraordinary Korean-born American conductor, makes his Metropolitan Opera debut in New York with a performance of Verdi's seldom performed *Simone Boccanegra.*

12 MARCH 1986

Symphony No. 6, Aphorisms, for choir and orchestra by the 69-year-old Finnish composer Einar ENGLUND, to words by Heraclitus, receives its premiere performance in Helsinki.

13 MARCH 1986

Three Sisters, opera after Chekhov's sad play dealing with a family's tragic triple indecision by the 40-year-old American composer Thomas PASATIERI, is staged in Columbus, Ohio.

13 MARCH 1986

Symphony No. 5 by the 67-year-old American composer George ROCHBERG, an uncharacteristically chromatic work in seven sections framed by an *Episode* and a closing *Finale,* all performed without pause, commissioned for the 150th anniversary of the founding of the city of Chicago, is heard for the first time in a performance by the Chicago Symphony Orchestra, Sir Georg Solti conducting.

20 MARCH 1986

On the first day of the 60th Festival of the International Society for Contemporary Music in Budapest, significantly curtailed in proportion by the successive illness of its participants, an opening gala recital by the pianist Adám Fellegi is given with the following program:

Nuages gris (1881), *Etude de Concert*, No. 3 (1848), *Aux Cypres de la Villa D'Este 1.* (1867–77), *Sunt lacrymae rerum, en mode hongrois* and *Sursum corda* from the third series of *Années de Pèlerinage*, and *Csardas macabre* (1882), all by the revered Hungarian composer Franz LISZT; *Cloud-Variations* by the Hungarian composer Miklós SUGÁR, on a theme from Liszt's *Nuages gris; Fantasy* by the Chinese composer Cong SU; and *Fantasy* by the Italian composer Gulin CORRADO.

21 MARCH 1986

On the second day of the 60th Festival of the International Society for Contemporary Music in Budapest, two concerts are given in the following sequence:

A late afternoon performance by the Kodály Quartet of *String Quartets* by the German composer Paul-Heinz DITTRICH (in eight segments corresponding to the segments of Hölderlin's "Das Nächste Beste") and by the Swiss composer André RICHARD.

An evening concert of orchestral works performed by the Savaria Symphony Orchestra conducted by János Petró, in the following program: *Prismes pour Orchestre* by the Japanese composer Karen TANAKA, a "tone picture" evoking light through a prism; *Dedica* for amplified oboe and orchestra by the Italian composer Riccardo FORMOSA, in two sections exploiting the expected potentials of the soloist's abilities and resources; *Tashi Gomang* by the 53-year-old American composer Pauline OLIVEROS, its title translating from Tibetan as "good flying" and its musical materials metaphorically equating to earthly elements; *Concerto for Viola and Orchestra* by the Argentine composer Marcelo KOC, in three movements; and *A Carlo Scarpa Architetto al suoi Infinitie Possibili* by the 62-year-old Italian composer Luigi NONO, a one-movement work with extraordinarily slow metronome indications, commissioned by Hans Zender for the Hamburg Philharmonic Orchestra.

22 MARCH 1986

On the third day of the 60th Festival of the International Society for Contemporary Music in Budapest, a program entitled "Contemporary Jazz Concert" is heard at the Academy of Music Concert Hall featuring progressive, avant-garde works by the leading Hungarian jazz composers János GONDA and György SZABADOS.

23 MARCH 1986

On the fourth day of the 60th Festival of the International Society for Contemporary Music in Budapest, three concerts are given in the following sequence:

A morning concert of pedagogical pieces by Hungarian composers, presented under the auspices of the Composers' and Music Education Sections of the Association of Hungarian Musicians and performed by the Ensemble of the Budapest Mókus-street Music School, conducted by Oszkár Balázs, students of the preparatory class and resident Ensemble of the Ferenc Liszt Academy of Music, and the Orchestra of the Vác Music School, conducted by László Fazekas, in the following program: *Fives* for five tuned percussion instruments played by three performers, composed by Gábor KÓSA; *Chamber Music for*

Six Cow-Bells, based on a scale of six notes performed at intervals of one second in arch form, by László ZEMPLÉNI; *Hexagramm* for six percussionists by László SÁRY; *Games* (excerpts) for piano by György KURTÁG; *Quintetto* (two of four movements only) for brass ensemble by Sándor BALASSA; *Musica Agile* by Miklós SUGÁR, in four movements, composed for the Budapest Brass Quintet; and *Ludus Stellaris*, a quasi-improvisational piano piece by Zsolt DURKÓ.

A late afternoon concert of chamber works, in the following program: *Yuunoqui'iye* for cello by the Mexican composer Julio ESTRADA, emerging from the "primordial needs of the imagination," the third of four so-named pieces for solo instruments (*Yuunoqui'iye* translating as: in Zaptec, "yuu" = earth, "noqui" = fresh, without stones, and, in Nahuatl, "iye" = the number 3); *Yours Sincerely* for clarinet by the Yugoslav composer Marko RUZDJAK; *Sur Les Points* for piano by the Irish composer Gerald BARRY; *Per Limina* for piano by the Italian composer Fernando MENCHERINI; and *Pentagram* for prepared piano surrounded by five groups of different, untuned percussion instruments (metal, glass, pottery, wood, stone) by the 46-year-old Hungarian composer László SÁRY.

An evening concert of chamber works performed by the Youth Chamber Studio Ensemble conducted by Zsolt Serei, in the following program: *Secret Theatre* by the 51-year-old English modernist composer Harrison BIRTWISTLE, with the orchestra divided into two groups ("Cantus" and "Continuum"), its title referring both to a poem by Robert Graves and to the secret rites of Greek drama, commissioned by the London Sinfonietta and premiered at a concert celebrating the composer's 50th birthday in London in 1984; *Ergo Sum* by Suzanne GIRAUD; *Trajet* for piano, slight ring modulation, and eleven players by the Belgian composer Luc BREWAEYS, in three sections moving from rhythmic stasis to complexity, bridged by two cadenzas and based on a five-note chord; *Comme un Silène Entr-ouvert* by the Canadian composer Denys BOULIANE, commissioned by Ensemble Köln and subsidized by the Canada Council of the Arts; and *At First Light* for fifteen players by the English composer George BENJAMIN, inspired by a late Turner oil painting, "Norham Castle, Sunrise," in which ". . . solid objects—fields, cows and the castle itself—virtually appear to have melted under the intense sunlight."

24 MARCH 1986

On the fifth day of the 60th Festival of the International Society for Contemporary Music in Budapest, two concerts are given in the following sequence:

A late afternoon concert of chamber works, in the following program: *Cantus II* for violin, viola, and cello by the 56-year-old Ukrainian-born Israeli composer Mark KOPYTMAN, based on micro-intonations of Jewish tunes; *Insight* for two violins and viola by the Italian composer Ada GENTILE; *Six Pieces* for violin, horn, and piano— "Serenade," "Arabesque," "Blues," "Marcia funèbre," "Scherzo Misterioso," and "For the Children"—by the 33-year-old Danish composer Hans ABRAHAMSEN; *Sestina d'Autunno* for viola, cello, double bass, guitar, mandolin, and percussion by the 81-year-old Italian composer Goffredo PETRASSI, subtitled "Veni, creator, Igor" and dedicated to Stravinsky on the 1982 centenary of his birth; and *Tres Piezas para Cuartet de Cuerdas* by the Argentine composer Gabriel VALVERDE.

An evening concert of musical theater works, in the following program: *Spheres and Cubes*, with music by Lazsló DUBROVAY and Miklós MAROS and directed by Róbert Bánky as part of a series of six experimental pantomime performances by the Hungarian State Puppet Theatre entitled *Puppets and*

Clowns; The Nose, with music by János DECSÉNYI, directed by Géza Bologh, who adapted Gogol's original story; *Acte Sans Paroles I and II* by the intransigent French playwright and novelist Samuel Beckett, directed by Kató Szönyi and Géza Balogh; and *Aventures* for chamber ensemble and three voices by György LIGETI, its script created and adapted by Dezsö Szilégyi involving various stage props in place of characters and playing upon a general theme of amorous intrigue, ably directed by Kató Szönyi.

25 MARCH 1986

On the sixth day of the 60th Festival of the International Society for Contemporary Music in Budapest, two concerts are given in the following sequence:

A late afternoon concert of chamber pieces, in the following program: a taped realization of *Touch* for piano by Lars SANDBERG; *DLJA . . .* for B-flat clarinet, alto saxophone, flügelhorn, flugabone, and bass trombone by the German composer Hans Joachim HESPOS, commissioned by the West German TV station ZDF for the 1982 centenary celebration of Igor Stravinsky's birth; *Images* for clarinet and percussion by the Brazilian composer Ronaldo MIRANDA, in four movements evocatively titled *Omens, Games, Transparencies,* and *Searches;* and a taped realization of *Extension* for violin and piano by the German composer Mathias SPAHLINGER.

An evening concert of chamber works, in the following program: *Orfeo* for string orchestra, in three brief movements, by the Australian composer Gerard BROPHY; *Isomérie* for string orchestra by the 47-year-old French composer Roger TESSIER; *Eisler Ensemble Pieces,* "1. For Cornelius" and "2. Dig a Hole in the Meadow," for clarinet, violin, cello, and piano by the 52-year-old American composer Christian WOLFF; *Scenes from a Novel,* "15 Songs to Poems by Rimma Dalos," its title referring to Ingmar Bergman's famous film *Scenes from a Marriage,* for soprano, cimbalom, violin, and double bass by the 60-year-old Rumanian-born Hungarian composer György KURTÁG; and *Rite of the Black Sun* for pop-infused percussion quartet and seven optional dancers by the American composer Anne LEBARON, in nine sections corresponding to nine sections of text from Antonin Artaud's "The Dance of Tutuguri: Rite of the Black Sun," extracted from his 1947 radio play, "To Have Done with the Judgement of God."

26 MARCH 1986

On the seventh and final day of the 60th Festival of the International Society for Contemporary Music in Budapest, two concerts are given in the following sequence:

An afternoon concert of chamber works, in the following program: *Septet* for chamber ensemble by the German composer Bruno STROBL, in four segments symbolizing the elements (earth, fire, air, and water); *Parabola* for guitar by the 47-year-old Cuban composer and virtuoso guitarist Leo BROUWER; *Estigma* for guitar by the Portuguese composer Paulo BRANDÃO, ". . . a structure of spatial attractions and repulsions between the elements of sound and silence," in two parts with a variable, reflected second section, dedicated to the guitarist and composer Lopes e Silva; and *Theme with Variations* for violin and piano by the 58-year-old Bulgarian composer Simeon PIRONKOFF.

An evening concert of orchestral works, in the following program: *Calyx* for harp and 26 wind and string instruments, with all but harp divided into three opposing groups, by the Hungarian composer Zsolt SEREI; *Gemma* for chamber ensemble of six woodwinds, six brass, and six-part strings by the Hungarian composer Rudolf MAROS, in three movements, the outer two being slow laments; and Béla BARTÓK's *Concerto for Orchestra.*

3 APRIL 1986

Sir Peter PEARS, remarkable English tenor who created most of Benjamin Britten's operatic roles and who was Britten's constant companion and inspiration in life and on the stage, dies in Aldeburgh at the age of 75.

14 APRIL 1986

Coming Forth Into Day, choral symphony with narration by the 35-year-old American composer Libby LARSEN, incorporating speeches by Jehan Sadat, widow of the slain leader of Egypt, is staged in St. Paul, Minnesota, Jehan Sadat, narrator.

20 APRIL 1986

Vladimir HOROWITZ, on his return to Russia after years of absence, at the age of 81, gives an internationally televised recital at the Moscow Conservatory.

20 APRIL 1986

Byung-ki HWANG, foremost Korean kayagum player and composer, makes his New York recital debut at Carnegie Hall in a program with San Won Park on the changgu (an hourglass drum) of Sanjo (formal, traditional kayagum music) and his own translucent works, including *Chimhyangmu, The Forest,* and *The Silk Road.*

23 APRIL 1986

Harold ARLEN (whose real Jewish name was Hyman Arluck), American composer of highly popular songs, among them *Stormy Weather,* dies in New York City at the age of 81.

24 APRIL 1986

Symphony No. 60, To the Appalachian Mountains, by the prolific 75-year-old American composer of Armenian-Scottish descent Alan HOVHANESS is heard for the first time in Knoxville, Tennessee.

4 MAY 1986

Symphony No. 6 for soprano, bass, and orchestra by the 35-year-old American composer Brian ISRAEL, to texts from the Bible and Langston Hughes, is premiered in Syracuse, four days before the composer's untimely death of leukemia.

7 MAY 1986

Abertura Halley for orchestra by the 32-year-old Brazilian composer Paulo Costa LIMA receives its first ever performance by the Orquestra Sinfônica da Bahía in Salvador, Bahía, Ernst Widmer conducting.

14 MAY 1986

Symphony No. 5 in one movement by the 57-year-old Finnish composer Einojuhani RAUTAVAARA is performed for the first time in Helsinki.

16 MAY 1986

Capriccio for Clarinet and Orchestra, *"Rossini in Paris,"* by the 58-year-old American composer Dominick ARGEN-TO receives its premiere performance in St. Louis.

21 MAY 1986

The Mask of Orpheus, opera by the 51-year-old English composer Harrison BIRTWISTLE, is staged at the English National Opera in London.

11 JUNE 1986

Music for Men, Women, and Reflecting Walls for pure wave oscillator by the 55-year-old American composer Alvin LUCIER is performed for the first time in New York.

13 JUNE 1986

Benny GOODMAN, proverbial jazz clarinetist and bandleader who was popularly crowned King of Swing, dies in New York at the age of 77.

15 JUNE 1986

Stephen Climax, enormously successful opera by the 49-year-old German composer and conductor Hans ZENDER, is staged in Frankfurt.

19 JULY 1986

The 58-year-old English conductor Sir Colin DAVIS, leading an ill-received, modernist version of Beethoven's *Fidelio*, brings an end to fifteen years of service as music director of the Royal Opera House, Covent Garden.

15 AUGUST 1986

Die schwarze Maske, opera by the 52-year-old Polish composer krzysztof PENDERECKI, is staged in Salzburg.

15 AUGUST 1986

Ritorna Vivaldi . . . E Tutti for string orchestra by the 32-year-old Brazilian composer Paulo Costa LIMA receives its first-ever performance by the Orquestra Sinfônica of the Federal University of Bahía in Salvador, Bahía, Ernst Widmer conducting.

22 AUGUST 1986

Mary Stuart, opera on the life and death of the Catholic Queen of Scotland by the 54-year-old Russian composer Sergei SLONIMSKY, is premiered (in the Russian language) at the Edinburgh Festival in Scotland.

4 SEPTEMBER 1986

". . . but this is a landscape, monsieur Dali!" for orchestra by the 56-year-old Finnish composer Usko MERILAINEN, characterized by an extensive use of silence, is first heard in Helsinki.

11 SEPTEMBER 1986

Classical Variations on Colonial Themes for orchestra by the 72-year-old American composer Morton GOULD is given its premiere performance in Pittsburgh.

11 SEPTEMBER 1986

Remembering Gatsby for orchestra by the 47-year-old American composer John HARBISON is heard for the first time in Atlanta.

12 SEPTEMBER 1986

Viola Concerto, Remembering Child, by the 54-year-old Danish composer Per NØRGÅRD, dedicated to the memory of Samantha Smith, a 13-year-old American schoolgirl who wrote to Soviet premier Yuri Andropov in 1983 expressing fear about the possibility of nuclear war and who died two years later in an air crash while returning from filming a television series in London, is premiered in St. Paul, Minnesota, with Pinchas Zuckerman as soloist and conductor.

13 SEPTEMBER 1986

Jubilee Games, concerto for orchestra and electronic playback by the 68-year-old American composer and conductor Leonard BERNSTEIN, is performed for the first time by the Israel Philharmonic in New York. (A three-movement revised version, with an added movement, "Benediction," originally premiered as a separate piece with baritone voice titled *Opening Prayer*, was completed in 1988.)

19 SEPTEMBER 1986

Captain Eo, three-dimensional, synaesthetic video space odyssey by the international superstar performer Michael JACKSON, opens at the Disneyland Theme Park in Anaheim, California.

20 SEPTEMBER 1986

Queenie Pie, musical composed by Duke ELLINGTON, left unfinished and later completed by others, is staged in Philadelphia.

23 SEPTEMBER 1986

Amsterdam opens an 85 million pound (sterling) Muziek-theater to protests from environmental and anti-nuclear groups.

25 SEPTEMBER 1986

Concerto for Orchestra by the 65-year-old, Czech-born American composer Karel HUSA is premiered by the New York Philharmonic, Zubin Mehta conducting.

26 SEPTEMBER 1986

Symphony No. 3, The Tricentennial, by the 66-year-old American composer Lester TRIMBLE, composed for the 300th anniversary of the city of Albany, New York, is premiered in Troy, New York, shortly before the composer's untimely death and one day before its first hearing in Albany.

3 OCTOBER 1986

Symphony No. 6 by the 62-year-old Bulgarian composer Konstantin ILIEV, intended to "hold the wisdom of the happy and ill-fated years of my life," is premiered in Russe, Bulgaria.

4 OCTOBER 1986

Symphony No. 61 by the 75-year-old American composer of Armenian-Scottish descent Alan HOVHANESS receives its première performance in Boise, Idaho.

9 OCTOBER 1986

Drala for orchestra by the 39-year-old American composer Peter LIEBERSON, son of recording executive and occasional composer Goddard Lieberson, its title combining Tibetan words for "enemy" and "above," is performed for the first time in Boston.

9 OCTOBER 1986

Phantom of the Opera, musical of operatic proportions by the 38-year-old English composer Andrew LLOYD WEBBER, is staged at Her Majesty's Theatre in London.

20 OCTOBER 1986

Himlens Hemlighet (*Secret of Heavens*), television ballet by the 51-year-old Finnish composer Aulis SALLINEN, based on his *Symphonies Nos. 1, 3,* and *4,* is mounted for the first time over Swedish Television.

25 OCTOBER 1986

Phantasmata for orchestra by the 37-year-old American composer Christopher ROUSE, a triptych of "dream images" comprising the separate pieces *The Evestrum of Juan de la Cruz in the Sagrada Famiglia at 3 A.M., The Infernal Machine,* and *Bump,* is given its première integral performance in St. Louis.

28 OCTOBER 1986

On Freedom's Ground: An American Cantata for baritone, chorus, and orchestra by the 76-year-old American composer William SCHUMAN, composed for the rededication of the Statue of Liberty, is performed for the first time in New York.

29 OCTOBER 1986

The Man Who Mistook His Wife for a Hat, opera by the 42-year-old English composer Michael NYMAN, based on one of several neurological case histories documented in Oliver Sacks's best-selling book of the same name, opens in London, with the composer conducting from the keyboard.

29 OCTOBER 1986

Symphony in A by the 62-year-old American composer Ben JOHNSTON, in three microtonal movements (*Martial with bite, Leisurely, relaxed,* and *Like a hoedown*), scored for an orchestra with limited wind instruments but a full complement of strings, is given its first ever performance at the acoustically well-suited First United Methodist Church of Rocky Mount, North Carolina.

30 OCTOBER 1986

Oedipus Memnetai (*Oedipus Remembers*) for bass-baritone narrator/soloist, six-part mixed chorus, and chamber ensemble by the 74-year-old veteran American film composer David RAKSIN, commissioned by the Elizabeth Sprague Coolidge Foundation, is premiered at a Special Founder's Day Concert at the Library of Congress in Washington, D.C.

10 NOVEMBER 1986

A Crack in the Bell for vocal soloist, three keyboardists, and optional chamber orchestra by the 45-year-old American composer Daniel LENTZ receives its premiere performance in Los Angeles by members of the Lentz Ensemble and the Los Angeles Philharmonic New Music Group.

13 NOVEMBER 1986

Keqrops for piano and orchestra by the 64-year-old Greek-born French composer Iannis XENAKIS, the title teasingly identified by the composer as coming either from a fusion of the Greek words *krekoo* ("to play an instrument by tapping the strings with the bow") and *opsis* ("looking"), or from a reference to the legendary Egyptian-born Greek ruler Keqrops I, who was said to have the double personality of a dragon and a man, receives its first ever performance in New York.

15 NOVEMBER 1986

Goya, opera by the 75-year-old, Italian-born American composer Gian Carlo MENOTTI, is mounted in Washington, D.C., with Placido Domingo, who commissioned the work, in the title role.

15 NOVEMBER 1986

Alexandre TANSMAN, cultured Polish-born, French composer of lucid modernistic music in a cosmopolitan style (one of his most popular piano pieces was titled *Sonatine Transatlantique*), dies in Paris at the age of 89.

16 NOVEMBER 1986

An Idyll for the Misbegotten for amplified flute and three percussionists by the 57-year-old American composer George CRUMB is premiered in Toronto.

21 NOVEMBER 1986

The Flight Into Egypt for voices, chorus, and small orchestra to biblical texts by the 47-year-old American composer John HARBISON is performed for the first time in Boston, later winning the 1987 Pulitzer Prize in Music.

13 DECEMBER 1986

12 Kleine Elegien for Renaissance instruments by the 60-year-old German composer Hans Werner HENZE is performed for the first time ever in Cologne.

19 DECEMBER 1986

Symphony No. 2, Visions, for soprano, tenor, and orchestra by the 30-year-old American composer Richard DANIELPOUR, with a text from Dylan Thomas's "Vision and Prayer," is first performed in San Francisco.

1987

3 JANUARY 1987

Symphony No. 4, Hayovel (*Jubilee*), by the 76-year-old Polish-born Israeli composer Josef TAL is performed for the first time in Tel Aviv by the Israeli Philharmonic in a concert celebrating its 50th anniversary.

15 JANUARY 1987

Formazioni for orchestra by the 61-year-old Italian composer Luciano BERIO is premiered in Amsterdam.

4 FEBRUARY 1987

Walter LIBERACE, uniquely popular American pianist of partly Polish and partly Italian descent whose pianistic virtuosity earned him commercial success in nightclubs under the name Busterkeys, and who satisfied mass audiences with easily digestible musical pap and built to his specification a swimming pool in the form of a grand piano, dies in his richly appointed California estate near Palm Springs, of physical and mental desuetude at the pitiful age of 67.

6 FEBRUARY 1987

Symphony No. 1 by the 39-year-old Swedish composer Anders ELIASSON is premiered over Swedish Radio in Stockholm.

14 FEBRUARY 1987

Dmitri KABALEVSKY, prime Soviet composer who wrote works for the theater, the orchestra, and for solo instruments that symbolize the essence of national music of new Russia and possess a peculiar socialist realism that combines Russian classicism with revolutionary dependence of harmony and the songful quality of new melos, dies in Moscow at the accomplished age of 82.

12 MARCH 1987

Determined Swiss tenor Hugues CUÉNOD makes his belated operatic debut as the Emperor in *Turandot* with the Metropolitan Opera in New York just three months before his 85th birthday.

13 MARCH 1987

Gerald MOORE, preeminent English piano accompanist who also wrote amusing books on his experiences with singers at the keyboard, dies in Penn, Buckinghamshire, at the age of 88.

21 MARCH 1987

Piano Concerto, In Memoriam Gideon Klein, by the 36-year-old Czech composer Vojtech SAUDEK, a "symbolic picture" of the Czech pianist and composer Gideon Klein (1919–1945) who perished at Auschwitz, and incorporat-

ing a theme from Klein's *String Trio* of 1944, is premiered in Prague.

25 MARCH 1987

Die Hamletmaschine, musical theater piece in five parts by the 35-year-old German composer Wolfgang RIHM, to his own libretto adapted from a text by Heiner Müiller calling for three Hamlets, is staged for the first time in Mannheim.

26 MARCH 1987

Eugen JOCHUM, eminent German conductor, dies in Munich at the age of 85.

2 APRIL 1987

Buddy RICH, colorful American jazz drummer and bandleader, dies in Los Angeles at the unfulfilled age of 69.

3 APRIL 1987

I Hear the Water Dreaming for flute and orchestra by the 56-year-old Japanese composer Toru TAKEMITSU is performed for the first time in Indianapolis.

13 APRIL 1987

Erwin NYIREGYHÁZI, Hungarian pianist who achieved fame as a prodigious *Wunderkind* of the keyboard, and who composed playable rhapsodies that impressed some simple-minded critics as equal to Liszt in brilliance and inspiration, and whose personal life with nine successive wives led to lengthy absences from public view, dies in solitude in a poor people's home in Los Angeles at the age of 84.

16 APRIL 1987

Concerto for Brass and Orchestra by the 60-year-old American composer Donald ERB, in three short movements, the second of which using quotations from the seventh-century Lutheran hymn "Alle Menschen müssen Sterben," with intermittent improvization and a percussion section enhanced by mounted wine glasses, harmonicas, and an array of mallet instruments, is premiered in Chicago.

21 APRIL 1987

Vladimir FELTSMAN, prominent Russian pianist, gives his first Moscow recital in nearly a decade, having been barred from public performance after making unsuccessful application for emigration to Israel in 1979.

28 APRIL 1987

Geometry of Sound for eighteen soloists by the 54-year-old Russian composer Rodion SHCHEDRIN is performed for the first time in Cologne.

2 MAY 1987

Symphony No. 8, Sinfonia breve, by the 89-year-old Italian-born American composer Vittorio RIETI is performed for the first time in Lafayette, Indiana.

6 MAY 1987

Symphony No. 9, Sinfonia d'estate, by the 67-year-old Swedish composer Sven-Eric JOHANSON is premiered in Malmö.

8 MAY 1987

Concerto for Viola and Orchestra by the 53-year-old American composer Richard WERNICK is performed for the first time in Annandale-on-Hudson, New York.

13 MAY 1987

Symphony No. 2 by the 48-year-old American composer John HARBISON is premiered in San Francisco.

16 MAY 1987

Tycho, chamber opera by the 38-year-old Danish composer Poul RUDERS, inspired by the last days of Danish astronomer Tuco di Braga, is mounted for the first time in Aarhus.

26 MAY 1987

Symphony No. 1 by the 41-year-old English composer Robert WALKER is heard for the first time in Exeter.

2 JUNE 1987

Andrés SEGOVIA, renowned Spanish virtuoso of the guitar which he handled as a contrapuntal instrument of many colors, dies in Madrid at the accomplished age of 94.

21 JUNE 1987

Abram CHASINS, greatly gifted American virtuoso pianist and composer of highly successful semiclassical piano pieces, one of which, *Flirtation in a Chinese Garden*, in an orchestral arrangement, was the first American composition to be conducted by Arturo Toscanini, dies in New York of a multiple consort of ailments, beginning with retinitis pigmentosa and ending with cancer, at the age of 83.

8 JULY 1987

A Night at the Chinese Opera by the 33-year-old Scottish composer Judith WEIR is mounted for the first time in Cheltenham.

24 JULY 1987

Carnival of Wales for orchestra by the 52-year-old Welsh composer William MATHIAS is performed for the first time in Cardiff.

10 AUGUST 1987

Billy JOEL kicks off a six-night tour of the Soviet Union with a performance at Moscow's 20,000-seat Olympic stadium, at which he dedicates the song "Honesty" to the late Soviet folk hero Vladimir Bysotsky.

14 AUGUST 1987

Vincent PERSICHETTI, remarkable American musician who played the organ, double bass, and tuba, and who worked up a formidable contrapuntal skill that he applied in his symphonies and in his numerous piano sonatas and other instrumental and choral pieces, dies in Philadelphia at the age of 72, but not before specifying that his body be given over to medicine for experimentation.

3 SEPTEMBER 1987

Morton FELDMAN, much beloved American composer of the experimental school, dies in Buffalo at the age of 61 after a mercifully brief but hopeless battle with pancreatic cancer. (In less than two years after his passing, Feldman's once sparse discography has mushroomed and performances of his works have become commonplace; some two dozen works have been composed in his memory, including those by Ingram Marshall, Charles Amirkhanian, Charlemagne Palestine, John Adams, Charles Dodge, and Lucky Mosko.)

11 SEPTEMBER 1987

RUR, passacaglia for orchestra by the 37-year-old Czech composer Otomar KVECH, based on a theme of Karel Čapek's play *R.U.R. (Rossum's Universal Robots)*, is premiered in Plzen, Czechoslovakia.

17 SEPTEMBER 1987

Symphony No. 5 for baritone and orchestra by the Korean-born German composer Isang YUN, to words by Nelly Sachs, is heard for the first time in Berlin, on the occasion of the composer's 70th birthday.

19 SEPTEMBER 1987

Der Turm, opera by the Polish-born Israeli composer Josef TAL, is mounted for the first time in Berlin, one day after the composer's 77th birthday.

1 OCTOBER 1987

Symphony No. 3, Jesus Messiah, Save Us!, for five oboes, five trumpets, trombone, three tubas, three double basses, percussion, piano, and solo voice, by the 68-year-old individualistic Soviet composer Galina USTVOLSKAYA, based on the same Contractus text used in her *Second Symphony* (8 October 1980), is premiered in Leningrad.

4 OCTOBER 1987

Oedipus, music theater piece by the 35-year-old German composer Wolfgang RIHM, after Hölderlin's translation of the drama by Sophocles, is mounted in Berlin.

5 OCTOBER 1987

The Electrification of the Soviet Union, optimistically modernistic opera by the 39-year-old English composer Nigel OSBORNE, after Pasternak's *The Last Summer*, is staged in Glyndebourne.

7 OCTOBER 1987

The Four Sections for orchestra by the 51-year-old American composer Steve REICH is heard for the first time in San Francisco.

9 OCTOBER 1987

Campagne di Ravello for orchestra by the 49-year-old American composer John CORIGLIANO, composed for Sir Georg Solti's 75th Birthday Gala Concert, is premiered in Chicago.

15 OCTOBER 1987

Masada, oratorio for narrator, tenor, chorus, and orchestra by the 55-year-old American composer Marvin David LEVY, composed in 1973, is performed for the first time in Chicago.

16 OCTOBER 1987

Symphony No. 6 by the 69-year-old American composer George ROCHBERG is heard for the first time in Pittsburgh.

22 OCTOBER 1987

Nixon in China, opera by the 40-year-old American composer John ADAMS, to a historically accurate story of President Richard Nixon's sensational five-day trip to China in 1972 with Kissinger, which opened the theretofore closed Communist country, is staged for the first time as part of the eighth annual New Music America Festival in Houston.

23 OCTOBER 1987

On the first day of the 61st Festival of the International Society for Contemporary Music held in the consecutive host cities of Cologne, Bonn, and Frankfurt, two concerts of note are given in Cologne in the following sequence:

A late afternoon concert performed by the Cologne Radio Symphony Orchestra conducted by Hans Zender and the Cologne Radio Chorus conducted by Herbert Schernus of works by the 82-year-old Italian composer Giacinto SCELSI, in the following program: *Phlat: "Ein Blitzstahl . . . und der Himmel öffnete sich"* for chorus, organ, and orchestra; *Hurqualia: Ein anderes Königreich* for five percussionists and orchestra; *Hymnos* for orchestra; and *Uaxuctum: Die Legende der Maya-Stadt, die sich selbst aus religiösen Gründen zerstörte* for seven percussionists, chorus, and orchestra.

An evening concert of electronic works: *Embryo* for violin, piano/synthesizer, string trio, tape, and live electronics by the Danish composer Ivar FROUNBERG; and *Chansons*, to a text by Erich Fried for mezzo-soprano, bass clarinet, synthesizer, two percussionists, and tape by the German composer Michael OBST.

24 OCTOBER 1987

On the second day of the 61st Festival of the International Society for Contemporary Music, three concerts of note are given in Cologne in the following sequence:

A late afternoon concert of mixed-media works, in the following program: *Derviche/Le Robert*, twenty-six "Klanggedichte" by the German composer Bernard HEIDSIECK; *Compléments de noms* by the German composer Michèle MÉTAIL, setting nouns from an endless poem of some 15,000 verses begun in 1973; three works by the American composer Peter ROSE: *The Pleasures of the Text*, a live audiovisual presentation integrating "direct address, invented languages, ideographic subtitles, sign language, and simultaneous translation"; *Secondary Currents*, an "imageless" film, and *Babel*; and *That Dada-*

Strain for amplified voice and bass, conceived and with texts by the American poet Jerome ROTHENBERG and with music by the American bassist Bertram TURETSKY, integrating in duet fashion poetic addresses to four Dada fathers (Tzara, Ball, Schwitters, and Picabia).

An evening concert of mixed-media works, in the following program: *Die faule Vernunt*, "Hörspiel" for contrabass, two horns, four percussion, and two voices by the German composer Carola BAUCKHOLT; and *Angelus*, a 45-minute "biographical litany" by the Austrian composer Gerhard RÜHM.

An evening concert of vocal works, in the following program: *Si ch'io vorrei morire, Quel augellin che canta*, and *Zefiro torna e'l bel tempo rimena* by Claudio MONTEVERDI; *Linie, Zirkel, Kreis* after politically and theologically controversial texts by Kurt Marti for five solo singers by the German composer Günther BECKER; *Resta di darmi noia, Al mio gioir il ciel si fa sereno*, and *Moro lasso al mio duolo* by Carlo GESUALDO; *La justa* for four singers by Mateo FLECHA; *Caccia barbara* for five vocal soloists by the Yugoslav composer Jakob JEŽ, inspired by Bartók's *Allegro barbaro;* and *Martin, Fyez vous y si vous voulez*, and *Les cris de Paris*, three songs for four and five voices by Clément JANNEQUIN.

25 OCTOBER 1987

On the third day of the 61st Festival of the International Society for Contemporary Music, four concerts of note are given in Cologne in the following sequence:

An afternoon concert of solo and ensemble pieces, in the following program: Réunion for two circling violinists tuned a quarter tone apart by the 56-year-old Japanese composer Yori-Aki MATSUDAIRA; *Sonatina* for two violins by the 70-year-old Korean composer Isang YUN, in one movement/four sections, symbolizing the balance of Taoist yin and yang; *Jūshichingen-No-Umare (The Birth of the Bass Koto)* for 17-string koto by the 56-year-old Japanese composer Makota SHINOHARA; *Cheminement* for soprano and ensemble by the 56-year-old Belgian composer Jacqueline FONTYN; and *Kreta-Grosser Traum*, cantata for speaker, soprano, tenor, and instrumental ensemble by the 52-year-old Greek composer Theodore ANTONIOU, utilizing both Oriental and Occidental sound structures in its setting of a text by Demetris Kakavelakes describing the turbulent history of the island of Crete.

An afternoon concert of works for string quartet performed by the Leonardo Quartet, in the following program: *Acoso y muerte de un hombre* by the Chilean composer Sergio ORTEGA, based on a portion of the composer's in-progress opera, *Pedro Paramo; Hölderlin Lesen*, with speaker, by the 40-year-old German composer Hans ZENDER, integrating musical "languages" of the present with those of Höderlin's time and closing with a fugue based on a theme of Beethoven; and *Fragmente-Stille, an Diotima* by the prominent and political 63-year-old Italian composer Luigi NONO, based on passing fragments of text drawn from poems by Höderlin.

An evening concert of orchestral works performed by the German Chamber Philharmonic of Frankfurt, in the following program: *Tre pezzi per due pianoforti con accompagnamento d'orchestra* by the Italian composer Luca LOMBARDI, an orchestral version of his earlier *Piano Duo* (1977–79); *Konzert für Violoncello und Orchester* by the 64-year-old Hungarian composer György LIGETI, in two complementary movements; *Orchesterbuch*, eight "ceremonies" to a text by Robert Walser by the Swiss composer Urs Peter SCHNEIDER; and *Suite (im alten Stil)* for string orchestra by the revered Austrian composer Arnold SCHOENBERG.

An evening program of electronic works, "Elektronische Nacht: Lateinamerika—Europa," in the following program:

FMelodies for cello, percussion, and computer sounds by the Ecuadorian-born German composer Mesias MAIGUASHCA; *Una Música, un Rumor, un Símbolo* by the Argentine composer Gabriel VALVERDE, its title drawn from the last verse of a poem by Jorge Luis Borges and intermingling concrète and electronic sounds; *Flute Control* for flute and computer by the 50-year-old Swiss composer Thomas KESSLER; *Encuentros para un Fin de Siglo* for tape by the Chilean composer Eduardo CÁCERES, in tripartite form with coda; *Impulso y Medida* for percussion and tape by the Argentine composer Alberto SCUNIO; *Annäherung an Francesco Petrarca: Francisci Petrarche laureati poete rerum vulgarium fragmenta et alia*, "Hörspiel" of "speech" and "public" sounds by the German composer Hans Ulrich HUMPERT; *The Transistor Radio of St. Narcissus* for flügelhorn, tape, and live electronics by the 44-year-old English composer of the extreme avant-garde Tim SOUSTER, its title referring to a passage from Thomas Pynchon's novel "The Crying of Lot 49," and moving musically from sonic chaos to order; and *Ejercicio de Aire: 2|c + c|2 × 2*, one of 18 tape pieces collectively entitled *Civilization or Barbarism* by the Argentine composer Bernardo KUCZER.

26 OCTOBER 1987

On the fourth day of the 61st Festival of the International Society for Contemporary Music, three concerts of note are given in Cologne in the following sequence:

An afternoon program of solo and chamber works, in the following program: *Steps* for piano by the Italian composer Marcella MANDANICI, based on pitches (A, B-flat, D-flat, C, and B) from a theme of Bartók; *Dream-Landscapes, Book II*, from "Portrait of Apollinaire" for piano by the 40-year-old English composer Douglas YOUNG, with each of its three movements (*River, Journey,* and *Distances*) revolving symmetrically around a central, designated pitch; *One-Man-Cha-Cha* for voice and piano by the American composer and vocalist Meredith MONK, merging materials from *The Games* (1983) and *Turtle Dreams* (1982); and *Frenetico il longing di amara*, "intimate ritual" involving "echoing orbits" and "spectrum pulses" with microtimbre changes for bass flute, bass voice, and "sound icon" (bowed vertical piano with spectral scordatura) by the Rumanian composer Horatiu RADULESCU.

A late afternoon concert of solo and ensemble works, in the following program: *Die Taube des fernen Pinienhaines* (Psalm 56) for bass flute by the Rumanian-born German composer Eugen-Mihai MÁRTON; *Lichtbogen* for nine instruments and live electronics by the Finnish composer Kaija SAARIAHO; *Poem* for voice and instrumental ensemble to words by the German-born Israeli poet Pinhas Yasar by the Israeli composer Ella LAZAR; and *Maro und Stille* for violin, soprano, piano, five wind instruments, timpani, and chorus by the German composer Robert H. P. PLATZ.

A late afternoon performance of chamber and orchestral works, performed by Frankfurt's Ensemble Modern conducted by Ernest Bour, in the following program: *Wandlungen*, five passacaglia for 25 instruments and live electronics by the Portuguese-born French composer Emmanuel NUNES; and *Violin Concerto*, op. 61, by Ludwig van BEETHOVEN.

27 OCTOBER 1987

On the fifth day of the 61st Festival of the International Society for Contemporary Music, three concerts of note are given in Bonn, in the following sequence:

A morning performance of *Die Mannequins*, one-act chamber opera in three scenes by the 52-year-old Polish composer Zbigniew RUDZIŃSKI, to a libretto adapting the prose of the Polish-Jewish author Bruno Schulz.

A late afternoon concert of solo and ensemble works, in the following program: *Flux* for cembalo by the Irish composer Jerome DE BROMHEAD, commissioned by the Dublin Festival of 20th-Century Music; *Canzonetta*, in three parts (A-B[= P-Q-Q']-A), and *Spright the Diner*, both for piano trio by Klarenz BARLOW; *Portraits of Marilyn, Ursula, Deborah,* and *Marianne*, and *Gathering Together* for piano eight-hands (each player responsible for 22 keys) by the 55-year-old American composer and active suffragette Pauline OLIVEROS; *Stichworte—Stichnoten* by the prime German experimental composer Dieter SCHNEBEL; and *White Man Sleeps* for viola da gamba, percussion, and two cembali by the South African composer Kevin VOLANS, one of 14 "African Paraphrases," its title referring to a dance step in Nyanga panpipe music in which the pipes are replaced by soft rattles, allowing the white landowner a respite for sleep.

An evening performance of a new mixed-media musical theater work, *Les Emigrés*, by the 53-year-old French composer Vinko GLOBOKAR, in three parts: *Misere* for five speakers, orchestra (on tape), and jazz trio, *Realités / Augenblicke* for film, slides, and tape, and *Sternbild der Grenze* for orchestra, puppet show, and seven singers.

28 OCTOBER 1987

On the sixth day of the 61st Festival of the International Society for Contemporary Music, three concerts of note are given in Frankfurt in the following sequence:

An early afternoon concert of ensemble pieces, in the following program: *Zona* for cello and seven instruments by the Finnish composer Magnus LINDBERG; *Long Peace March*, a militant musical patchwork for chamber ensemble by the 53-year-old internationally minded and musically Minimalist American composer Christian WOLFF; and *Coming Together* for voice and instruments by the 49-year-old American composer Frederic RZEWSKI, based on a letter written by the political prisoner Sam Melville, long known for his leadership in the Columbia University protests and one of 43 people to lose their lives in the 1971 Attica uprising.

A late afternoon concert of ensemble pieces, performed by Ensemble Contrechamps conducted by Philippe Albèra, in the following program: *Momento II* for clarinet, cello, and piano by the Uruguayan composer Diego LEGRAND, in two contrasting movements; *Arpège* for flute, clarinet, violin, cello, piano, and vibraphone by the 60-year-old Italian composer Franco DONATONI; *Vox Faucibus Haesit* for flute, clarinet, violin, cello, and piano by the Argentine composer José Luis CAMPANA; and *Musique de Rue* for flute, clarinet, violin, cello, piano, percussion, and tape by the Swiss composer André RICHARD, intermingling incidental street noise with musically structured materials, inspired by the Italian street musicians of Abruzzi.

An evening performance of chamber works performed by the Ensemble InterContemporain, conducted by Arturo Tamayo, in the following program: *Jalons* for 15 instruments by the 65-year-old Greek-born French composer Iannis XENAKIS; *Erinnere dich an G . . .* for double bass solo and eighteen instrumentalists by the 62-year-old Swiss composer Klaus HUBER, in four parts with introduction; *Symmolpa III* for five instrumental groups by the Greek composer Georges KOUMENDAKIS; and *Niobé (ou le rocher de Sipyle)* for twelve mixed voices, soprano, and eight instrumentalists by the French composer Pascal DUSAPIN.

29 OCTOBER 1987

On the seventh day of the 61st Festival of the International Society for Contemporary Music, three concerts of note are given in Frankfurt in the following sequence:

A late afternoon concert of mostly percussion pieces, in the following program: *Antiphony 8 (Revolution)* for percussion and four-channel tape by the 61-year-old American composer Kenneth GABURO, the second act of his gargantuan theater piece, *The Scratch Project: Acts*, with the percussionist in the role of actor, acrobat, and dancer, played from memory and representing some 40 percussion instruments; *I Can Fly* for percussion and tape by the German composer Klaus Hinrich STAHMER; *An Idyll for the Misbegotten* for amplified flute and drums by the 58-year-old American composer George CRUMB, an apocalyptic environmental vision incorporating quotations from Debussy's *Syrinx* and two lines ("The moon goes down. There are shivering birds and withering grasses") from the eighth-century Chinese poet Ssu-K'ung Shu; and *A Doll's House Story*, an allegorical tale of toys running amok in a department store for four percussionists by the Hungarian composer István MÁRTA.

An evening performance of solo and ensemble pieces performed by the London Sinfonietta conducted by Lionel Friend, in the following program: *Syrinx* for flute by Claude DEBUSSY; *Introduction et Allegro* for harp, string quartet, flute, and clarinet by Maurice RAVEL; *Sun's Dance*, a work of continuous energetic variation for ten players by the English composer Colin MATTHEWS; *Erinnerung* for chamber ensemble by the South Korean composer Man-Bang YI, in three movements (*Window, Column-Cathedral*, and *Roof-Courtyard*) collectively representing the outward characteristics of traditional Korean architecture; and *Suite from "'Histoire du Soldat"* for clarinet, flute, trumpet, trombone, violin, contrabass, and percussion by Igor STRAVINSKY.

An evening installation and performance by the 56-year-old American composer Alvin LUCIER, in a program of his *Bird and Person Dyning* (1975), *Music for Pure Waves, Bass Drums, and Acoustic Pendulums* (1980), and *Music for a Solo Performer (1965)*.

29 OCTOBER 1987

Woody HERMAN, versatile American clarinetist and bandleader for whom Stravinsky wrote his popular *Ebony Concerto*, which he premiered at New York's Carnegie Hall on March 25, 1946, dies in Los Angeles at the age of 74.

30 OCTOBER 1987

On the eighth day of the 61st Festival of the International Society for Contemporary, Music, three concerts of note are given in Frankfurt in the following sequence:

A late afternoon concert of solo and ensemble works, in the following program: *D'(H)ommage oder Freu(n)de, nicht . . .* for trombone by the Swiss composer Jürg WYTTENBACH, an homage to Beethoven's "Ode to Joy" and "Conversation Books," composed for the Pro Musica (IGNM), Zürich, in honor of its 50th anniversary; *Scène du va et vient* for cello, contrabass, bass clarinet, and actor by the French composer Luc FERRARI; and—*ihre Geschichte*—for vocal soloists and ensemble by the German composer Mia SCHMIDT, to texts by the composer and Christa Reinig about woman and child abuse.

An evening concert of ensemble works, "'Itineraire (Paris)," in the following program: *Désintégrations* for tape and 17 instruments by the French composer Tristan MURAIL; *La montée des oiseaux* for contrabass and *Concerto pour piano espace No. II* for piano, flute, trumpet, cello, percussion, and 4-channel tape, both by the French composer Michaël LEVINAS; *Artifices* for ensemble and live electronics by the Swiss composer Gérard ZINSSTAG; and a programatically untitled new work by the Belgian composer Luc BREWAEYS.

An evening performance of a new music theater work, *Missa nigra*, "Kammerspiel II" for seven instrumental players, actor, conductor, and tape by the German composer Friedrich SCHENKER, to texts adapted by the composer from the Latin requiem, performed within a scene consisting of pedestals occupied by seven masked and costumed musicians, conductor, and actor, with one additional player, seated to the side, operating live electronics, synthesizer, and tapes.

31 OCTOBER 1987

On the ninth day of the 61st Festival of the International Society for Contemporary Music, two concerts of note are given in Frankfurt in the following sequence:

A concert of instrumental and vocal works, in the following program: *Lyrische Szenen* for chamber ensemble by the 62-year-old Polish composer Włodzimierz KOTOŃSKI; *Right After* for chamber ensemble by the Norwegian composer Åse HEDSTRØM, its title derived from a work by the painter Eva Hesse (1936–70); *Commission* for baritone and chamber ensemble by the 57-year-old German composer Werner HEIDER, to texts by the unmasked Fascistic American poet Ezra Pound; *Abeer: Guernica—Hommage à Pablo Picasso* for sixteen-voice a cappella choir by the Polish composer Elzbieta SIKORA; and *Kanons, Motetten und Hymnen aus "Polyptychon,"* three cycles on religious texts for a capella vocal ensemble by the Swiss composer Balz TRÜMPY.

An evening concert of symphonic works, in the following program: *Ein Tag tritt hervor (Un dia sobresale)* for piano, five instrumental soloists (vibraphone, marimba, harmonium, Ondes Martenot, and electric guitar), and five groups of like instruments (metal percussion, wood and hide percussion, clarinets, voices, and strings), to texts by Pablo Neruda, by the 60-year-old Austrian composer and conductor Michael GIELEN; *A la fenêtre recelant* for orchestra by the Italian composer Mario GARUTI; *Ein Brief*, "concert scene" for mezzo-soprano and orchestra by the 55-year-old German composer Mauricio KAGEL, the "brief" of the title comprised of only two words, "My love"; and *Landscape with Martyrdom* for orchestra by the American composer George LOPEZ, the title taken from Peter Brueghel's "Landscape with Martyrdom of St. Catherine," with its images of fire, smoke, army, mountains, seas, and torture wheel given musical substantiation in its setting of words representing ". . . the three poles of inanimate nature, society, and the individual in intense conflict with society."

1 NOVEMBER 1987

On the tenth and final day of the 61st Festival of the International Society for Contemporary Music, four concerts of note are given in Frankfurt in the following sequence:

A morning performance and reading by the 75-year-old American composer John CAGE in a program that includes two versions of his *Music for 13*, one in a series of unconducted works (*Music for . . .*) for various instrumental combinations.

An afternoon concert of chamber works, performed by Karlsruhe's Ensemble 13 conducted by Manfred Reichert, in the following program: *Canto XVII (Divina Commedia)* for instrumental ensemble by the Netherlands composer David COPPOOLSE, set in a nonfunctionally tonal setting and inspired by Dante Alighieri; *Nocturne I* for two opposing instrumental groups by the German composer Reinhard FEBEL; *La flamme lumineuse* for flute, cello, and piano by the English composer Stephen REEVE, the last in a trilogy of pieces based on Belgian composer Henri Pousseur's *Icare Obstiné* (1972); and *Chiffre VII* for piano and chamber ensemble in seven cyclic parts by the 35-year-old German composer Wolfgang RIHM.

An afternoon retrospective concert of chamber works, "IGNM 1923/1987," with the following program: *String Quartet No. 3* by the 87-year-old Austrian-born American composer Ernst KRENEK, dedicated to Paul Hindemith; *AA-GAI* for cello by the South Korean composer Younghi PAGH-PAAN, its title comprised of two Chinese ideograms loosely translated as "Appreciation in Song"; *Scène 3* for cello and tape by the 48-year-old French composer Roger TESSIER; *Iter* for cello by the Italian-born Australian composer Riccardo FORMOSA, its title referring, in Latin, to "voyage, journey, or path"; and *Quintett für Streichquintett und Klarinette*, op. 30, by the German composer Paul HINDEMITH.

An evening presentation of works by the 59-year-old German composer Karlheinz STOCKHAUSEN, in the following program: *Xi* for flute, the title signifying, in Greek, an unknown quantity, playable on any wind instrument bearing keys or valves or on any synthesizer capable of producing microscales; *Drachenkampf und Argument* for trumpet, trombone, synthesizer, tenor, bass, percussion, and two dancers, comprising two scenes from Act 3 of his *Thursday* from *Light*, conceived as independent versions in 1986–87 for the "Nuits de la Fondation Maeght"; *Vision* for tenor, trumpet, dancer, electric organ, and magnetic tape, the final scene of his *Thursday* from *Light* in which the character of Michael appears as tenor, trumpet, and dancer; and *Donnerstags Abschied (Michaels Abschied)* for trumpet on 5-track recording.

15 NOVEMBER 1987

Violin Concerto No. 1 by the 56-year-old American composer Nancy VAN DE VATE is heard for the first time in Pittsburg, Kansas.

2 DECEMBER 1987

Valis, video opera for actors, vocal soloists, piano/electronic keyboards, percussion/electronic percussion, computer-generated tape, and video projections, all synthesized and transformed via computer by the technologically inspired 34-year-old composer and director of M.I.T.'s Experimental Media Laboratory Tod MACHOVER, with an original libretto adapted from the science fiction novel by Phillip K. Dick of the same name, is mounted in Paris.

6 DECEMBER 1987

In Memoriam Vincent Persichetti for winds, brass, and percussion by the 59-year-old American composer Jacob DRUCKMAN is premiered in New York.

10 DECEMBER 1987

Jascha HEIFETZ, the most celebrated violinist of the 20th century, who began his career as an incredibly accomplished wunderkind in Russia and ended his spectacular violinist life in self-imposed retreat in Los Angeles, dies at the age of 86.

11 DECEMBER 1987

Symphony No. 2, War with the Newts, by the 52-year-old Czech composer Jirí TEML, inspired by the novel of the same title by the Czech writer Karel Čapek, is premiered in Brno.

12 DECEMBER 1987

Europeras 1 & 2, chance-determined, musicodramatic stage collage by the 75-year-old American veteran composer John CAGE, receives its premiere performance, unconducted, by the Frankfurt Opera, roughly one month after its scheduled première was postponed due to a mysteriously set fire.

1988

1 JANUARY 1988

From the Eye of the World for orchestra by the 67-year-old Canadian composer Norman SYMONDS is performed for the first time in Toronto.

11 JANUARY 1988

Trumpet Concerto by the 51-year-old South African-born Canadian composer Malcolm FORSYTH is premiered in Montreal.

19 JANUARY 1988

Eugene MRAVINSKY, autocratic chief conductor of the Leningrad Philharmonic for nearly half a century, dies in Leningrad at the fullness of his days at the age of 85.

21 JANUARY 1988

Symphony No. 1 by the 38-year-old American composer Christopher ROUSE is performed for the first time in Baltimore.

29 JANUARY 1988

Sinfonietta I for orchestra by the 72-year-old American composer George PERLE is heard for the first time in St. Paul, Minnesota.

4 FEBRUARY 1988

Enharmonic Variations for piano and chamber ensemble by the Italian-born American composer Vittorio RIETI is performed for the first time in New York, Bennett Lerner soloist, in a program celebrating the composer's 90th birthday, one week after the fact.

11 FEBRUARY 1988

Concerto for Trumpet and Orchestra by the prolific 66-year-old Czech-born American composer Karel HUSA, in the standard three-movement form (*Maestoso-Allegro, Molto moderato,* and *Allegro*) for an orchestra including two trumpets but no low brass, is premiered in Chicago, Adolph Herseth, soloist.

13 FEBRUARY 1988

Leon GOOSSENS, extraordinary English oboist whose brother was equally prominent as a composer and conductor, dies in Tunbridge Wells at the accomplished age of 90.

14 FEBRUARY 1988

Frederick LOEWE, Viennese-born, American composer of popular Broadway shows, among them the great hit *My Fair Lady,* using George Bernard Shaw's socialized comedy *Pygmalion,* dies in Palm Springs at the age of 84.

27 FEBRUARY 1988

Music for 4 for string quartet, one in a series of computer-generated compositions (*Music for . . .*) with unspecified instrumentation by the 75-year-old American composer John CAGE is premiered by the Arditti Quartet in Middletown, Connecticut.

29 FEBRUARY 1988

Piano Concerto by the 64-year-old Hungarian-born Austrian composer György LIGETI is premiered in its final five-movement version in the Mozart Room of the Konzerthaus Society in Vienna, with the brothers Mario and Anthony di Bonaventura as conductor and soloist, respectively. (The original three-movement version was first heard in Graz, Austria, on 23 October 1986.)

4 MARCH 1988

Vast, ballet by the 43-year-old Australian composer Barry CONYNGHAM, is mounted for the first time in Melbourne.

18 MARCH 1988

Symphony No. 14, Moments of Peace, for high baritone and orchestra by the 44-year-old Finnish composer and conductor Leif SEGERSTAM, to texts by John Gracen Brown, is premiered in Stockholm.

24 MARCH 1988

Cello Concerto by the 47-year-old Finnish composer Erkki SALMENHAARA is performed for the first time in Lahti.

29 MARCH 1988

Symphony No. 5, Kalmar Nyckel, by the 64-year-old American composer Benjamin LEES, named for the ship that brought the Finns and Swedes who founded the city of Wilmington, Delaware (some 350 years earlier), is premiered in Wilmington.

8 APRIL 1988

Symphony No. 6 by the 82-year-old Austrian-born Swedish composer Hans HOLEWA is premiered in Stockholm.

8 APRIL 1988

Malin: Pictures of History, opera for chorus, brass, and archeological instruments by the 68-year-old Swedish composer Torsten NILSSON, is mounted for the first time ever in the Belmont Heights Baptist Church in Nashville, Tennessee.

16 APRIL 1988

H'un (Lacerations): In Memoriam 1966–76 for orchestra by the 33-year-old Chinese composer Bright SHENG, dissonant music reflecting the composer's emotions about the period of China's Cultural Revolution, is performed for the first time in New York.

29 APRIL 1988

Strathclyde Concerto No. 1 for oboe and orchestra by the 53-year-old English composer Peter Maxwell DAVIES, the first of ten *Strathclyde Concertos* commissioned by the Regional Council of Strathclyde, the political section of Scotland that includes Glasgow, and the Scottish Chamber Orchestra, is premiered in Glasgow.

7 MAY 1988

Montag aus Licht, third in a projected cycle of seven operas, one for each day of the week, by the 59-year-old German composer Karlheinz STOCKHAUSEN, is heard for the first time in Milan.

17 MAY 1988

Hwan Myung for traditional Korean instruments by the 42-year-old Korean composer Byung-Dong PAIK is performed for the first time in Seoul.

18 MAY 1988

The Fall of the House of Usher, opera after Poe by the 51-year-old American composer Philip GLASS, is staged in Cambridge, Massachusetts.

20 MAY 1988

Nymphea: Jardin Secret III for string quartet and live electronics by the imaginative 34-year-old Finnish composer Kaija SAARIAHO is performed for the first time in New York.

29 MAY 1988

Der Garten, chamber opera by the 77-year-old Polishborn Israeli composer Josef TAL, is mounted for the first time ever in Hamburg.

1 JUNE 1988

Symbolon for orchestra by the 49-year-old American composer Ellen Taaffe ZWILICH is performed by the New York Philharmonic under the baton of ZUBIN Mehta for the first time in Leningrad, symbolically, on one of Russia's "white nights."

13 JUNE 1988

La Célestine, opera by the 74-year-old French composer Maurice OHANA, is mounted for the first time ever in Paris.

17 JUNE 1988

Orait for dancers and vocal ensemble by the 53-year-old American composer Gordon MUMMA is performed for the first time in Santa Cruz, California.

17 JUNE 1988

Greek, opera by the 28-year-old English composer Mark Anthony TURNAGE, is mounted for the first time in Munich.

24 JUNE 1988

Symphony No. 4, Prayer, by the 69-year-old iconoclastic Soviet composer Galina USTVOLSKAYA, scored for soprano, trumpet, tamtam, and piano and based on the same Contractus text used in her *Second* (8 October 1980) and *Third* (1 October 1987) *Symphonies*, is heard for the first time in Heidelberg, Germany.

1 JULY 1988

Lex VAN DELDEN, remarkable Dutch composer whose works embraced a number of original techniques and who derived his inspiration from such diversified subjects as a railway timetable and the Nazi invasion of Holland, dies in his native city of Amsterdam at the age of 68.

5 JULY 1988

Concerto for Kettledrums and Orchestra by the 53-year-old Austrian composer Kurt SCHWERTSIK is performed for the first time in Vienna.

7 JULY 1988

Nearly 43 years after his death, Béla BARTÓK's remains are removed from the Ferncliff Cemetery in Hartsdale, New York, and taken to Budapest for a regal state funeral.

8 JULY 1988

The Making of the Representative for Planet 8, musical theater work by the 51-year-old American composer Philip GLASS, to a libretto adapted from Doris Lessing's book of the same name, is staged in Houston.

10 JULY 1988

Pacifica for orchestra by the 38-year-old Australian composer Vincent PLUSH is performed for the first time in Aspen, Colorado.

11 JULY 1988

Sound Round for orchestra and electronics, composed in 1973 by the 45-year-old American composer Stephen MONTAGUE, is heard for the first time in Manchester, England.

22 JULY 1988

Cataclismas, choreographed scenic cantata for soloists, chorus, and orchestra by the 46-year-old Brazilian composer Fernando Barbosa de CERQUEIRA, to poems by J. C. de Melo Neto, Antônio Brasileiro, and Nei B. Lopes, receives its first ever performance at the 20th Annual Festival of Inverno.

26 JULY 1988

Symphony No. 4 by the 40-year-old English composer Jonathan LLOYD is performed for the first time in London.

2 AUGUST 1988

Sea and Sky for orchestra by the 42-year-old English composer Michael FINNISSY is premiered in London.

9 AUGUST 1988

Giacinto SCELSI, Italian composer who wrote music of determinately novel technique reaching into determined serialism while somehow retaining his native Italian strain, dies in Rome at the age of 83.

15 AUGUST 1988

Chevaux-de-frise and *Diner*, two orchestral works by the 36-year-old Irish composer Gerald BARRY, are premiered on a double-bill program in London.

15 AUGUST 1988

Hans STUCKENSCHMIDT, greatly knowledgeable German music historian and critic who was born in Strasbourg when it was part of Germany, dies in Berlin at the age of 86.

19 AUGUST 1988

Piano Concerto by the 75-year-old Polish composer Witold LUTOSLAWSKI, in four tightly knit movements with rhythmic intricacies enriched by intermittent aleatoric passages, all performed without pause, receives its premiere performance at the Salzburg Festival.

19 AUGUST 1988

Composer-to-Composer, an international gathering of composers founded by Charles Amirkhanian and John Lifton and presented by the Telluride Institute, with resident composers Brian ENO, Virko BALEY, Paul DE MARINIS, Kyle GANN, Lou HARRISON, Terry RILEY, Stephen SCOTT, Laurie SPIEGEL, Sarah HOPKINS, Vincent

PLUSH, Peter SCULTHORPE, Denys BOULIANE, and Lepo SUMERA, culminates a week of private sessions with its first three-day festival of public concerts, panel discussions, and a film/video presentation in the historic Sheridan Opera House in Telluride, Colorado.

15 SEPTEMBER 1988

Prometheus Kommt, Olympic Torch Music of the Seoul Olympiad by the 53-year-old Korean composer Sukhi KANG, is performed for the first time in Seoul.

23 SEPTEMBER 1988

At a concert of the 31st Warsaw Autumn Festival, two works are given their first public performances: *Masks*, three pieces for piano composed in 1916 by the eminent Polish composer Karol SZYMANOWSKI (1882–1937) and orchestrated and reordered in 1984 by the 62-year-old Polish conductor and composer Jan KRENZ; and *Symphony No. 5* by the 80-year-old Paris-domiciled Polish composer Roman PALESTER.

24 SEPTEMBER 1988

Viola Concerto, apparently the last work by the remarkable Swedish composer Allan PETTERSSON (1911–1980), is posthumously premiered in West Berlin from an undated, late manuscript discovered among the composer's effects in the mid-1980s.

29 SEPTEMBER 1988

Violin Concerto in one short movement, subtitled *Putování-dusicky* (*Pilgrimage of a Little Soul*), by the revered Czech composer Leoš JANÁČEK (1854–1928), composed in 1926 in London and laid aside after some of its materials were transferred to other works, discovered and reconstructed by the Janáček Collected Works editors Leoš Faltus and Miloš Štedron (who, in 1985, also reconstructed Janáček's late four-movement symphony *The Danube*), receives its belated premiere performance in Brno.

7 OCTOBER 1988

A *Quaker Reader* for chamber orchestra by the 64-year-old American composer Ned ROREM, an orchestration of eight of the eleven pieces of his solo organ suite of 1975, is performed for the first time ever in New York.

9 OCTOBER 1988

Symphony No. 3 by the 38-year-old Estonian composer Lepo SUMERA is heard for the first time in Tallinn.

13 OCTOBER 1988

Concerto for Flute by the 62-year-old American composer Gunther SCHULLER is premiered in Chicago.

14 OCTOBER 1988

Kaikhosru SORABJI, uniquely endowed, English-born composer who claimed the dubious ancestral origin of Parsi, worshippers of fire (his real name was Leon Dudley), but who was undoubtedly a genuine, demented genius whose keyboard works of enormous length and supernatural complexity demanded fantastic technique and total devotion to the composer himself, who signalized separation from the common folk by a sign in front of his lodgement, "Visitors Unwelcome," dies at his English estate in Wareham, Dorchester, at the Methuselian age of 96.

15 OCTOBER 1988

Symphony No. 4 by the 73-year-old French composer Marcel LANDOWSKI is performed for the first time ever in Paris.

15 OCTOBER 1988

String Quartet No. 3, Canon 3/4/5/6, by the 75-year-old American-born Mexican composer Conlon NANCARROW receives its premiere performance by the Arditti Quartet in Cologne.

19 OCTOBER 1988

Katadrone: Contrecri for orchestra by the 56-year-old Canadian composer Gilles TREMBLAY receives its premiere performance in Montreal.

22 OCTOBER 1988

The 62nd Festival of the International Society for Contemporary Music, presented in conjunction with the Asian Composers League, opens in Hong Kong with an evening concert by the Hong Kong Philharmonic Orchestra conducted by Kenneth Schermerhorn, in the following program: *Transit* for orchestra by the Chinese composer CHANG Wing-Wah, "inspired by the various ways of communication and exchange of human thoughts, feelings and ideas"; *Projetto traki*, two pieces for orchestra by the Italian composer Dario MAGGI; *Toki-no-ito II* for piano and orchestra in five parts by the Japanese composer Isao MATSUSHITA; *Kafka-Fragments and Pavanne*, poetry in seven "songs" by the German composer Detlev MÜLLER-SIEMENS; Oboe Concerto by the 45-year-old Swedish composer Daniel BÖRTZ; and *Mudang* for orchestra by the Korean composer Manbang YI, intermingling the sacred and profane.

23 OCTOBER 1988

On the second day of the 62nd Festival of the International Society for Contemporary Music in Hong Kong, three concerts of note are given in the following sequence:

A midafternoon performance of *El Cimarrón* (1970), music theatre work for baritone, flute, guitar, and percussion by the 62-year-old German composer Hans Werner HENZE, recounting in free-form notation the heroic life of a Cuban slave, adapted from *The Biography of a Runaway Slave* by Esteban Montejo.

A late afternoon of chamber works, in the following program: *Scattered Shadows* for guqin (7-string zither) utilizing a Chinese pentatonic scale enhanced by natural harmonics by the American-born Chinese composer Tim WILSON; *Reflections* for two pianists and two percussionists in three symmetrical parts by the Korean composer Nahm-hee CHUNG; *Tempus Ex Machina* by the German composer Jens-Peter OSTENDORF; *Yün* ("reverberations") by the Chinese-born American composer CHOU Wen-chung; *Spiral* for cello, piano, and percussion by the Cambodian-born American composer Chinary UNG; and *After Spring* for two pianos by the Chinese composer LAM Bun-ching.

An evening concert of orchestral works performed by the Hong Kong Chinese Orchestra conducted by Kuan Nai-chung, in the following program: *Flowing Water*, symphonic picture based on a guqin piece of the same name by the Chinese composer CHAN Pui-fang; *Autumn Execution* in five "chapters" by the Chinese composer Doming LAM; *Concerto for Wind Instruments, Song of Deities*, by the Chinese composer Qu XIAOSONG, in three movements (*Heavenly King: River Spirit, Mountain Monster and Ghost*, and *Worshipping*) based on the "Nine Odes" by Qu Yuan; *Three Meditations* (*Endless Sky, Mother Earth*, and *Unity of Heaven and Man*) by the Chinese composer Richard TSANG; *Journey to Lhasa* by the Chinese composer KUAN Nai-chung, in four parts variously depicting the Tibetan Highlands; and *Tien Yuan (The Root of Heaven)* by the Taiwanese composer HSU Po-yun.

24 OCTOBER 1988

On the third day of the 62nd Festival of the International Society for Contemporary Music in Hong Kong, two concerts of note are given in the following sequence:

A midafternoon piano recital by pianist Yvar Mikhashoff, in the following program: *Opening* by the 51-year-old American composer Philip GLASS; *Study in Five Parts* by the Netherlands composer Richard RIJNVOS; *Achilles and the Tortoise* by the 56-year-old Danish composer Per NØRGÅRD; *Ballade* by the Chinese composer Ye XIA-OGANG; plus tangos by Jo KONDO, Ralph SHAPEY, and Conlon NANCARROW.

An evening concert of vocal works performed by EXVOCO (Expanded Voice Company), in a program including *Tout en roulant les RR* by Michel SEUPHOR; *Jet te veux, Chansons d'amour*, and *La Diva de l'Empire* by Erik SATIE; *Corinthian 1, 13* by Thomas LAUCK; *Verfluchung* by Mathias SPAHLINGER; and *Song Books I–II* by John CAGE.

25 OCTOBER 1988

On the fourth day of the 62nd Festival of the International Society for Contemporary Music in Hong Kong, three concerts of note are given in the following sequence:

An afternoon concert of contemporary music from the People's Republic of China, jointly presented by the ISCM and the Hong Kong Institute for the Promotion of Chinese Culture, in the following program: *Warring Drums* by ZHANG Da-long; *Autumn Wilderness* by GAO Wei-jie; *Reminiscing the Moon* by WU Shao-xiong; Quartet *"Yun"* by CUI Wen Yu; *Nuwa;* by CAO Guang-ping; *Taiji* by ZHAO Xiao-sheng; *Sketches of an Amusement Park* by ZU Jiangiang; *Morning Glory, Dusk, Goddess of the Moon* by LUO Zhong-rong; and *In Distance* by TAN Dun.

A late afternoon piano recital performed by pianist Yvar Mikhashoff, in the following program: *Solo* by the 66-year-old American composer Lukas FOSS; *The Tide* by the Chinese composer YOUNG Shui-ting; *Topologies* by the English composer Chris DENCH; *Palais de Marai* by the American composer Morton FELDMAN; and *Piano Piece No. 4* by the 50-year-old American composer Frederic RZEWSKI.

An evening concert of chamber works performed by the Hong Kong Ensemble, in the following program: *Tango del Desamparo*, an autobiographical contemplation of death by the Argentine composer Luis NAON; *Trio II* for flute, bass clarinet, and harp by the Italian composer Giulio CASTAGNOLI; *Icons* for clarinet, piano, and tape by the American composer James PRIMOSCH, its title suggested by Madeleine L'Engel's "Walking on Water," in which artists are called upon to form "icons of the true"; *BXR 6* by the Spanish composer Albert Llanas RICH; *Introduction and Capriccio* by the Hungarian composer Pál RÓZSA, in two movements; *Moments of Rising Mist* for chamber ensemble by the American composer Jay Alan YIM, loosely inspired by a Chinese scroll painting of a landscape; and *A Place of Fire* by the Israeli composer Yinam LEEF, to a text by the late Israeli poet Zelda.

25 OCTOBER 1988

A 25-Year Retrospective Concert of the music of the 48-year-old iconoclastic American composer Dary John MIZELLE is given by Essential Music at New York's Symphony Space, in the following program: *Through a Glass . . .* for tarogato (1987); *Sonata No. 2—Polyvalence* for piano (1985); *Six Pieces for Violin and French Horn* (1963); *Violin Fantasy* (1975–88); *Polyphonies I* for shakuhachi with quadraphonic tape and tape delay (1976); *Interplay* for clarinet and violin (1979); and *Lake Mountain Thunder* for percussion and tarogato (1981).

26 OCTOBER 1988

Symphony No. 7, Hyönteissinfonia (Insect Symphony), by the 39-year-old Finnish composer Kalevi AHO, a continuation of the satirical pose adopted in his opera *Insect Life* composed the year before and based on a play by Josef and Karel Čapek in which a drunken and narcissistic vagrant is the only human character and ultimately discovers that human life is but a form of insect life, composed in an intentionally postmodern and polystylistic idiom of six episodic movements titled *The Tramp and the Parasitic Hymenopteran and Its Larva, The Butterflies, The Dungbeetles, The Grasshoppers, The Ants*, and *Dayflies*, with "the symphony's overall form . . . a negation of the conventional striving forwards (as) each new movement questions the preceding one, acting as its antithesis," is premiered in Helsinki.

26 OCTOBER 1988

On the fifth day of the 62nd Festival of the International Society for Contemporary Music in Hong Kong, three concerts of note are given in the following sequence:

An early afternoon "music performance event" involving students from all over Hong Kong of *Suling* for ten flutes, ten bamboo percussion instruments, and ten Chinese gongs by the Filipino composer Jose MACEDA.

An afternoon concert, "Asian Composer's League Young Composers Concert," comprised of entries submitted for the Asian Composer's League "Young Composers Awards," in the following program: *Reminiscence* by the Chinese composer LAM Shun; *In Memory of Ben Pangosban* by the Filipino composer Jonathan B. HAYAG; *The Unsent Letter* by the Taiwanese composer YEUNG Kam-fung; *Music from a High Altitude* by the New Zealand composer Gareth FARR; *Distraction* by the Japanese composer Masataka MATSUO; *Sacrificial Rite* by the Chinese composer MO Wu-ping; and *Of Minds and Men* by the Australian composer Peter MYERS.

An evening cello and piano recital by Siegfried Palm and Zygmunt Krauze, in the following program: *Two Pieces* (1899), *Sonata* (1914), and *Three Small Pieces*, op. 11, by Anton WEBERN; *Maya* by Tomás MARCO; *Sonata (Dialogo e Capriccio)* by György LIGETI; *Five Nocturnes*, op. 10b, by

Kurt SCHWERTSIK; *To the Master* by Giacinto SCELSI; and *Unguis incarnatus est* by Mauricio KAGEL.

27 OCTOBER 1988

On the sixth day of the 62nd Festival of the International Society for Contemporary Music in Hong Kong, three concerts of note are given in the following sequence:

An afternoon concert of compositions by members of the Asian Composers League performed by the Hong Kong Ensemble, in the following program: *Writing on the Sand*, seven settings of haiku by Raydia d'Elsa by the 50-year-old New Zealand composer David FARQUHAR; *Sous-Entendu* by the Korean composer KIM Dong-su, in two sections; *Passage for Stereo Amplified Bass Flute* by the 56-year-old Japanese composer Makota SHINOHARA, based on seventeen independent fragments; *Trivalence II* by the 45-year-old Japanese composer Shin-Ichiro IKEBE; *Sun Soundic* for flute, clarinet, violin, cello, piano, percussion, and tape by the Chinese composer LAW Wing-fai; *Death Be Not Proud* for flute, mezzo-soprano, and two-channel electronic sound by the Chinese composer Clarence MAK, inspired by a poem of the same name by the English poet John Donne (1572–1631); *Sketches* for oboe and piano in three continuous sections by the foremost Singaporean composer LEONG Yoon-pin; and *Territory II* by the Japanese composer Takehito SHIMAZU, a process piece involving seventeen tone groups in ABC form.

A late afternoon organ recital performed by Paul Griffiths, in the following program: *Zum Lied der Weisheit* by the Swiss composer Ulrich GASSER; *Strahlen* by the Canadian composer David EAGLE, requiring assistance during performance to control registration; *Pusat* by the German composer Dieter MACK, the second of three formulaic pieces comprising his *Organcycle; Reincarnation* by the Taiwanese composer TSENG Shing-kwei, making use of three themes ("Yin," "Yang," and "Transmigration"); *Elevation III* by the Japanese composer Harue KUNIEDA; *Recitative, Aria and Chorale* by the American-born Chinese composer David GWILT, based on a well-known hymn tune; *Prelude/Postlude on "Wer Nur Den Lieben Gott"* by the Chinese composer Daniel LAW, based on a choral tune by Georg Neumark (1657); and *Toccata and Fugue* by the Taiwanese composer MA Shui-lung.

An evening performance by the Arditti String Quartet of *String Quartets* by the Finnish composer Kimmo HAKOLA, the English composer Gavin BRYARS (*No. 1, Between the National and the Bristol*), the English composer Brian FERNEYHOUGH (*No. 3*), and the Hungarian-born Austrian composer György LIGETI (*No. 2*).

27 OCTOBER 1988

Concerto for Orchestra by the 38-year-old American composer Steven STUCKY is performed for the first time in Philadelphia.

28 OCTOBER 1988

On the seventh day of the 62nd Festival of the International Society for Contemporary Music in Hong Kong, two concerts of note are given in the following sequence:

A late afternoon performance by the Arditti String Quartet of *String Quartets* by the Australian composer Liza LIM (*Pompes Funebres*), the Japanese composer Akira NISHIMURA (*Heterophony*), the Taiwanese composer PAN Hwang-long (*No. 3*), and the 66-year-old Greek-born French composer Iannis XENAKIS (*Tetras*).

An evening concert by the Messiaen Quartet and others, in the following program: *Talea (The Machine and the Weeds)*, quintet by the French composer Gérard GRISEY; *Music for Six Performers*, in three parts adapted from an unfinished opera based on a story of Edgar Allan Poe by the Japanese composer Tatsuhiko NISHIOKA; *Red Sun—Chill Wind* for flute and piano by the 42-year-old Australian composer Anne BOYD, a "meditation" upon words by the great Japanese haiku poet Basho; and *Quartet for the End of Time* in eight movements for violin, clarinet, cello, and piano by the 79-year-old French composer Olivier MESSIAEN.

29 OCTOBER 1988

On the eighth day of the 62nd Festival of the International Society for Contemporary Music in Hong Kong, three concerts of note are given in the following sequence:

A midafternoon concert performed by the Hong Kong Ensemble, in the following program: *Symmolpa 4* by the Greek composer George KOUMENDAKIS, for four different sound groups (wind, percussion, piano, and strings); *Music for a Thousand Autumns* by the Canadian composer Alexina LOUIE, in three movements reflecting three periods of the composer's life, its first movement a "call" to the late Canadian composer Claude Vivier; *Carnyx* by the Rumanian composer Serban NICHIFOR; *Beast from Air*, a protest against the continuing worldwide detonation of nuclear devices, by the Australian composer Brenton BROADSTOCK; *Fables, that Time Invents* by the Italian composer Alessandro MELCHIORRE, its title taken from a line of poetic text by the American poet John Ashbery; and *". . .though what made it has gone"* for mezzo-soprano and piano by the Norwegian composer Rolf WALLIN, its text comprised of fragments from "Whoever finds a horseshoe" (1923) by the Jewish-Russian author Osip E. Mandelstam.

A late afternoon concert by the Messiaen Quartet, in the following program: *Tristess* by the Japanese composer Karen TANAKA, in a spiral design inspired by Edgar Allan Poe's "The Raven"; *Nocturnes*, seven short pieces cast in two movements by the French composer Gérard PESSON; *Romanza* by the Icelandic composer Hjalmar RAGNARSSON; *Tongen* by the Yugoslavian composer Uros ROKJO; plus works by Arnold SCHOENBERG, Harrison BIRTWISTLE, and Gilbert AMY.

An evening concert of orchestral works performed by the Tokyo Philharmonic Orchestra conducted by Tadaaki Otaka, in the following program: *Staub* by the 52-year-old German composer Helmut LACHENMANN, a "prologue" to Beethoven's *9th Symphony; Syrensong* by the English composer Simon HOLT, dedicated to the English writer-critic William Mann; *Threnody (for the victims of Hiroshima)* for fifty-two instruments by the 54-year-old Polish composer Krysztof PENDERECKI; and *Orion and the Pleiades* for cello and orchestra in two sections linked with an interlude by the 58-year-old leading Japanese composer Toru TAKEMITSU.

29 OCTOBER 1988

Fearful Symmetries for orchestra by the 41-year-old American composer John ADAMS is premiered in New York, the composer conducting.

29 OCTOBER 1988

Songs of the Aztecs for soloist and orchestra by the 56-year-old Argentine-American composer Lalo SCHIFRIN is performed for the first time in Teotihuacan, Mexico.

10 NOVEMBER 1988

The 100th anniversary of the birth of the American composer Johanna Magdalena BEYER (1888–1944) is celebrated with the first of two commemorative concerts by Essential Music in New York in a program which includes the first known performances of her *Three Songs: Timber Moon, Stars, Songs, Faces, and Summer Grass* (1933) and *March for 30 Percussion Instruments* (1939).

10 NOVEMBER 1988

Concerto Grosso No. 4/Symphony No. 5 (a single work) by the 53-year-old German-born Russian composer Alfred SCHNITTKE is heard for the first time in Amsterdam.

12 NOVEMBER 1988

Missa: Cahlemer Messe for four solo voices, two choruses, orchestra, and organ by the 58-year-old German composer Dieter SCHNEBEL is performed for the first time in Berlin.

12 NOVEMBER 1988

The 100th anniversary of the birth of the American composer Johanna Magdalena BEYER (1888–1944) is celebrated with the second and last commemorative concert by Essential Music in New York in a program of first ever performances of her *Percussion Suite* (1933), *Dissonant Counterpoint* for piano, in eight movements (193?), *Gebrauchs-Musik* for piano (1934), and *String Quartet No. 2* (1936), as well as her *Music of the Spheres* in its first realization with strings.

13 NOVEMBER 1988

Antal DORATI, Hungarian-born, naturalized American musician who made a signal career as both a conductor and composer, dies in Gerzensee, Switzerland, at the age of 82.

16 NOVEMBER 1988

Quasi una fantasia for piano and chamber orchestra by the 62-year-old Rumanian-born Hungarian composer György KURTÁG is heard for the first time in Berlin.

19 NOVEMBER 1988

A *Kennedy Portrait* for narrator and orchestra by the 65-year-old American composer William KRAFT commemorating the 25th anniversary of the assassination of President John F. Kennedy, is performed for the first time ever in Boston.

21 NOVEMBER 1988

Akathist of Thanksgiving: Glory to God for Everything for soloists, chorus, and orchestra by the 44-year-old English composer John TAVENER is heard for the first time in Westminster Abbey, London.

4 DECEMBER 1988

Concerto Grosso by the 74-year-old American composer Morton GOULD is premiered in New York.

4 DECEMBER 1988

The Seasons for orchestra by the 60-year-old Scottish composer Thea MUSGRAVE is performed for the first time ever in London.

11 DECEMBER 1988

Whispers Out of Time for string ensemble by the 55-year-old American composer Roger REYNOLDS receives its first performance in Amherst, Massachusetts, later winning the 1989 Pulitzer Prize in Music.

13 DECEMBER 1988

Forty-year-old American vocalist/composer Bonnie BARNETT organizes the first *Global Hum*, a live video satellite broadcast sponsored by the World Philharmonic Orchestra as part of the Music and Peace Event, extending the curative community principles at work in her earlier *Tunnel Hums* (1983, 1984, 1986), *Auto Hum* (1985), and *America Hum* (1986), with singers in Moscow, Geneva, Montreal, Santa Fe, New Mexico, and Irvine, California, invited to sing along with the generating *Hum*mers in San Francisco.

1989

12 JANUARY 1989

The Struggle Between the Realistic and Formalist Trends in Music, subtitled "Anonymous Words and Music," a pedagogical cantata for four basses, small chorus, and piano, composed c. 1948 by the revered Soviet composer Dmitri SHOSTAKOVICH (1906–1975), receives its posthumous première performance in Washington, D.C.

19 JANUARY 1989

Symphony No. 1 by the 40-year-old English composer Jonathan LLOYD is heard for the first time in Birmingham.

20 JANUARY 1989

The W. of Babylon, opera by the 50-year-old American composer Charles WUORINEN, receives its first complete performance in San Francisco.

26 JANUARY 1989

At the White Edge of Phrygia for orchestra by the 45-year-old American composer Stephen MONTAGUE is heard for the first time in London.

1 FEBRUARY 1989

Strathclyde Concerto No. 2 for cello and orchestra by the 54-year-old English composer Peter Maxwell DAVIES, the second of ten *Strathclyde Concertos* commissioned by the Regional Council of Strathclyde, the political section of Scotland that includes Glasgow, and the Scottish Chamber Orchestra, is performed for the first time in Glasgow.

2 FEBRUARY 1989

Trombone Concerto by the 49-year-old American composer Ellen Taaffe ZWILICH is performed for the first time in Chicago, Sir Georg Solti conducting.

3 FEBRUARY 1989

Ash for orchestra by the 28-year-old American composer Michael TORKE is performed for the first time in St. Paul, Minnesota.

17 FEBRUARY 1989

Cortège for orchestra by the 43-year-old English composer Colin MATTHEWS is premiered in London.

18 FEBRUARY 1989

Symphony No. 9 by the 56-year-old Soviet composer Sergei SLONIMSKY is performed for the first time in Leningrad.

22 FEBRUARY 1989

. . . Body and Shadow . . . for orchestra by the 53-year-old English-born American composer Bernard RANDS is performed for the first time in Boston.

24 FEBRUARY 1989

The Last Unicorn for orchestra by the 47-year-old Italian-born American composer Marc-Antonio CONSOLI, recounting the animal's adventures and death at the hands of hunters, is performed for the first time ever in New York.

24 FEBRUARY 1989

The Wound-Dresser for baritone and orchestra by the 42-year-old American composer John ADAMS, to a libretto adapted from Walt Whitman's poem of the same title, is heard for the first time in St. Paul, Minnesota, the composer conducting.

2 MARCH 1989

Cello Concerto by the 67-year-old Czech-born American composer Karel HUSA is premiered in Los Angeles.

5 MARCH 1989

Talking to the Sun, song cycle/theater piece by the 60-year-old American composer William RUSSO, is performed for the first time in Chicago.

6 MARCH 1989

O-kawa no Uta (Song of the River) for mezzo-soprano, baritone, and orchestra by the 73-year-old Japanese composer Kunio TODA is performed for the first time in Tokyo.

13 MARCH 1989

Kinetics for orchestra by the 31-year-old Finnish composer Magnus LINDBERG is performed for the first time in Helsinki.

23 MARCH 1989

Brangle for orchestra by the 60-year-old American composer Jacob DRUCKMAN, in three kinetic movements (*Macho, Languorous,* and *Driven*), its title derived from the fifteenth-century French branle (Brangle), one of the steps of the courtly basse dance (brangle [brangill] or brawl was the popularized sixteenth-century English form, mentioned in passing in Act III, Scene i of Shakespeare's *Love's Labour's Lost*), receives its first ever performance in Chicago.

30 MARCH 1989

An American in L.A. for rhythmically infused orchestra and synthesizer by the 48-year-old American composer

Daniel LENTZ, in three movements (*Freeway Estampie, Beach Pavan,* and *Smog Vamp*), is performed for the first time in Los Angeles.

2 APRIL 1989

Controversial 55-year-old English conductor Roger NOR-RINGTON makes his auspicious New York debut at Carnegie Hall conducting the *8th* and *9th Symphonies* of Beethoven.

6 APRIL 1989

101 by the 76-year-old veteran experimental American composer John CAGE is premiered by 101 prepared but unconducted players of the Boston Symphony Orchestra.

7 APRIL 1989

Popol Vuh for orchestra by the Argentine composer Alberto GINASTERA (1916–1983), commissioned by Eugene Ormandy in 1975 and left with only seven of its projected eight movements completed at the time of the composer's death, its title the name of the sacred Mayan book of creation, is premiered in St. Louis.

8 APRIL 1989

Odyssey for orchestra by the 53-year-old English composer Nicholas MAW receives its first complete performance in London. Begun in 1972 and, after several interruptions, completed in 1985, the score, titled to reflect the composer's quest for reconnections to musical traditions, comprises an *Introduction, 4 Parts,* and an *Epilogue* that together total more than 90 minutes, making *Odyssey* possibly the longest orchestra-only stretch of music ever composed.

17 APRIL 1989

Aspects of Love, musical by the phenomenally successful 41-year-old English composer Andrew LLOYD WEBBER, opens in London.

28 APRIL 1989

Symphony in Three Movements by the 53-year-old American composer Charles SHERE is performed for the first time in Berkeley, California.

28 APRIL 1989

Chasing the Sunset for orchestra by the 37-year-old American composer Lawrence RAPCHAK is performed for the first time in New York.

19 MAY 1989

What Where, chamber opera after Beckett by the 49-year-old Swiss oboist and composer Heinz HOLLIGER, is given its first ever staging in Frankfurt.

25 MAY 1989

Raumklang X for orchestra and four instrumental groups by the 59-year-old German composer Dieter SCHNEBEL is heard for the first time in Cologne.

29 MAY 1989

The Plumber's Gift, opera by the 52-year-old English composer David BLAKE, is staged in London.

3 JUNE 1989

Epitaph, a collection of 18 titled and untitled pieces for 30 jazz musicians by the revered American jazz bassist and composer Charles MINGUS (1922–1979), composed sporadically over a 20-year period beginning around 1940 and discovered on blurred and torn manuscript pages without instrumental parts during a cataloging project of Mingus's works, receives its posthumous premiere in a reconstructed arrangement by Gunther SCHULLER in New York by a large jazz orchestra including Wynton Marsalis and John Handy, Schuller conducting.

17 JUNE 1989

Miserere for soloists, chorus, ensemble, and organ by the 53-year-old Estonian composer Arvo PÄRT is heard for the first time in Rouen, France.

24 JUNE 1989

A Question of Taste, opera by the 63-year-old American composer Gunther SCHULLER, is mounted for the first time in Cooperstown, New York.

3 JULY 1989

Veitsi (The Knife), opera by the 51-year-old Finnish composer Paavo HEININEN, is staged in Savonlinna, Finland.

16 JULY 1989

Herbert VON KARAJAN, great Austrian conductor who was able to personify in his stature and in his eloquent gesture the national greatness of the music of Wagner, the stormy spirit of Beethoven, and the melodious genius of Mozart, dies in his estate near Salzburg at the fulfilled age of 81.

18 AUGUST 1989

Composer-to-Composer, an international gathering of composers founded by Charles Amirkhanian and John Lifton and presented by the Telluride Institute, with the resident composers Joan LA BARBARA, John CAGE, Anthony DAVIS, Julio ESTRADA, Ricardo DAL FARRA, Tom JOHNSON, Jin Hi KIM, Tania LÉON, Annea LOCKWOOD, Conlon NANCARROW, Morton SUBOTNICK, TRIMPIN, and Walter ZIMMERMANN, culminates a week of private sessions with its second three-day festival of public concerts, panel discussions, and a film/video presentation in the historic Sheridan Opera House in Telluride, Colorado.

4 SEPTEMBER 1989

The 63rd Festival of the International Society for Contemporary Music opens in Amsterdam with an evening concert of works for symphonic band in the following program:

Lof der Duisternis for wind orchestra by the 41-year-old Dutch composer Gilius VAN BERGEIJK, in six "gloomy reflections" (*Reflection, Nocturne, The Conjurer, Ritual Dance, Chorale,* and *Shadows*) built on a somber and repetitive minor tone series; *Concert* for alto saxophone and symphonic wind band by the Dutch composer Simon BURGERS, based on a "giant-tone scale" exploring a range of seven octaves governing melodies, harmonies, and instrumentation; and *Preparatori 22'* for wind orchestra by the 57-year-old Spanish-born Dutch composer Enrique RAXACH, in two parts, symbolizing "rising, appearing, and starting" and "temporary, transition, and bypass," composed during the millennial advent of Catalonia and bringing together modal and atonal elements in a structure based on two pitch-controlling triads.

5 SEPTEMBER 1989

On the second day of the 63rd Festival of the International Society for Contemporary Music in Amsterdam, an evening concert of chamber works is presented with the following program:

Aqueous Fire for clarinet and percussion by the Portuguese composer Paolo BRANDÃO, consisting of four fragments (2 + 2) and coda; *Sound Carvings from Rano Rareku* for flute, percussion, piano, and double bass by the 33-year-old Irish composer Piers HELLAWELL, named after the quarry in which the carving of Easter Island statues took place and consisting of 23 micro-movements arranged symmetrically around the central twelfth movement, all based on a single Balinese Gamelan melody; and *Recitatives & Ariosos, "erchenmusik,"* for piano, cello, and clarinet, in three movements, by the seasoned 55-year-old Polish composer Henryk Mikolaj GÓRECKI.

6 SEPTEMBER 1989

Det Tempererede Klaver VIII, op. 532, the eighth hour-and-a-quarter long complete cycle of 24 preludes and fugues for piano by the colossally prolific 70-year-old Danish composer Niels Viggo BENTZON is premiered in Humlebaek, Denmark.

6 SEPTEMBER 1989

On the third day of the 63rd Festival of the International Society for Contemporary Music in Amsterdam, three concerts of note are given in the following sequence:

An afternoon concert of chamber and solo works, in the following program: *Breakthrough 1* for cello and flute by the Chinese composer Doming LAM, transitionally favoring avant garde principles, inspired by the bodily gestures and percussion effects of Beijing opera; *Music for Bass Clarinet and Tape* by the American composer Cort LIPPE, in five parts, its tape aspect created at Paris's CEMAMU using the graphics-oriented computer-music system UPIC designed by Iannis Xenakis; *Stråkkvartett* for tape by the 36-year-old Swedish composer Åke PARMERUD; *Children's Games,* subtitled *Pieter Brueghel Inspirationen für Flöte, Basklarinette, und Klavier,* by the 60-year-old Czech composer Václav KUČERA, in four movements, played without pause; and *Canparus* for bassoon by the Brazilian composer Aylton ESCOBAR.

An afternoon concert entitled "Contemporary Music in Korea" and devoted to the music of the respected 54-year-old Korean composer Sukhi KANG, in the following program: *Nong* for piano and flute, in five parts, its title alluding to the vibrational phenomenon characteristic of traditional Korean music; *Odyssee* for tape, concrète music comprised of manipulated bicycle sounds collected at a crossroad; *Lung,* synaesthetic film work dedicated to the great Buddhist priest, Gu San, and based on Korean motives; and *Feng Hwang,* cinematic "Zen meditation" based on a transformation process applied to groups of shapes, its pictorial aspect being various forms of religious dance and its sounds transformed into repetitive and incremental layers via computer.

An evening concert of chamber and solo works by Korean composers, in the following program: *Canzone II* for piano by Unsuk CHIN; *Guitariana* for two guitars by Byungdong PAIK with contrasting, often improvisatory materials provided to each of eleven parts, linear and assertive in the second guitar and chordal and passive in the first, converging solidly in the closing coda; *Micrology I* for 2 pianos by Kangyul Ih LEE, a chordal setting based on minute timbral changes comprised of small interval classes, with repetition of tones indicating "breathing" silences and changes of tones indicating movement; *Nong* for piano and flute by Sukhi KANG; and *Myeng II* for clarinet, bassoon, flute, and piano by Cheng-Ick CHANG, a 12-tone work tinged with modal elements with the basic tone of A-flat serving both central and linearly generative functions.

7 SEPTEMBER 1989

On the fourth day of the 63rd Festival of the International Society for Contemporary Music in Amsterdam, three concerts of note are given in the following sequence:

An afternoon concert of solo and ensemble pieces, in the following program: *Duo staccato* for violin and piano by the 46-year-old Spanish-born Canadian composer José EVANGELISTA, featuring a pervasive, cyclical cantus firmus outlined in a heterophonic manner, with an abundance of staccato attacks heard against legato lines; *Polysono* for bassoon by the 51-year-old Swiss composer Thomas KESSLER, "a trio for soloist" comprised of traditional etudes: one extended and melodic with near-silent legato bowings of very high pitches, one an energetic "perpetuum mobile," and one fortissimo throughout with overriding staccato rhythms of very low-pitched materials; *Salamanca* for violin, viola, and cello by the 29-year-old Argentine composer Alejandro IGLESIAS-ROSSI, named after places where, according to Argentine mythology, the devil meets his witches; and *Strophen* for 8-part chorus by the Greek composer Nikos DRELAS, inspired by polyphonic music of Ipiro.

An afternoon concert of ensemble pieces, in the following program: *Ecarts* for piano and marimba by the Belgian composer Benoît MERNIER, part of a cycle-in-progress of pieces for piano and percussion combining homogenous and heterogenous elements, exploiting here the similarities of tone colors of the marimba and piano through different registers, with an impression of stability provided by near-static harmonic development; *Me Recurdas Tanto Y Nada (Música Nocturna)* for soprano and chamber ensemble by the spanish composer eduardo perez MASEDA, based on two original texts, both extolling the memory of night and one of bitter cold, with the words, heard only in the second and fourth parts, serving both musico-semantic and poetic-representational functions, its five parts-played without pause; *Strano* for oboe, horn, bassoon, and bass clarinet by the 49-year-old Swedish composer Jan W. MORTHENSON; *Psychomachia* for soprano and cello by the 41-year-old Icelandic composer Thorsteinn HAUKSSON, based on a portion of *Psychomachia* or *The Fight for Man's Soul* by Aurelius Prudentius Clemens (348–c. 410), with both text and music portraying virulent battles between "Virtues" and "Vices"; *Vannspiel (Water Mirror)* for violin, cello, and piano by the 29-year-old Norwegian composer Nils Henrik ASHEIM, a contrast of line and points, with the note A representing the horizontal line ("water mirror") and the vertical points, appearing in short or long sequences, comprised of rapid staccato accents, slowly evolving repetitive series, and melodic fragments; and *Camino de Camino* for soprano, flute, bass clarinet, viola, and piano by the 46-year-old Argentine composer Mariano ETKIN, named for a musician-shepherd of the area, Gregorio Caminos, and for the area itself, Caminos, without specific programmatic references but exploring the general phenomena of borders and fusions.

An evening concert of chamber works, in the following program: *Zahgurim, whose number is twenty-three and who kills in an unnatural fashion . . .* for minimally amplified bass recorder and four percussionists by the Dutch composer Richard RUJNVOS, the title drawn from William Burroughs's *Cities of the Red Night* and the musical content exploiting the multiphonic capabilities of the Aulos bass recorder, which is uncharacteristically pitted against the battery of percussion; *Del sogno di Icaro* for flute and percussion by the Italian composer Giovanni BONATO, consisting of determinate (recorder) and indeterminate (percussion) materials related through the lyric, prepared vibraphone—first antagonistically, then symbiotically—inspired by the image of a gentle fall and painless absorption at the bottom; *Recursion* for piano, celesta, vibraphone, glockenspiel, and percussion by the 25-year-old American composer Nicholas HOPKINS, consisting of the interaction of six discrete and highly individualistic structures, the recursive principle of its title extending into all levels of the musical parameters, with a shimmering treble tessitura and performance gestures emanating from characteristics unique to the playing of each instrument; *Pianotrio (for violin, cello and piano, 1984)* by the 42-year-old Dutch composer Tristan KEURIS, "a work which bewitched the listener like a heap of evaporated passion" at its 1985 première in Amsterdam by the Mendelssohn Trio; *4 Fragments* for piano by the leading 57-year-old Danish composer Per NØRGÅRD, with its third and fourth fragments comprised of material based on the infinity series and its first and second fragments marked by amorphous rhythms and "unison polyphony"; and *Lethe* for two pianos, eight hands by the innovative 54-year-old French classicist and composer François-Bernard MÂCHE, a subjective homage to Poland, one in a series of works named for the rivers of the Greek underworld (Lethe is the river of oblivion).

8 SEPTEMBER 1989

On the fifth day of the 63rd Festival of the International Society for Contemporary Music in Amsterdam, three concerts of note are given in the following sequence:

An afternoon concert of electroacoustic works, in the following program: *Etapper* by the 35-year-old Norwegian composer Cecilie ORE on a text from Ole Robert Sunde's novel *Kontrapunktist*, with spoken and whispered sounds from the author's reading transmuted and transfigured through analogue and digital filtering and echoing techniques; *Le voyage au paradis*, five images derived from fragments taken from Robert Muris' posthumous sketches of "Die Reise ins Paradies" from *Der Mann ohne Eigenschaften* by the 48-year-old Austrian composer Dieter KAUFMANN, depicting the ill-fated love between a boy and girl twin, Ulrich and Agathe, and laying bare the ". . . secret lusts of the hermaphrodite, separated into two beings, whose secret nobody who touches him can guess;" and *Kristallwelt*, first in a cycle of three electronic pieces by the 34-year-old German composer Michael OBST, based on sound materials comprised of the overtones and spectra created by the electronic manipulation of sound materials drawn from ancient Asian instruments (Chinese woodblock, Japanese temple gong, small Chinese tamtam, et al.), the overture setting the sonic stage for an evocation of nature's self-transformation.

An afternoon concert of prize-winning works at the International Competition for Electroacoustic Music Bourges 1989, in the following program: a taped rendition of *Four Inventions* for piano and live computer electronics by the Japanese composer Takayuki RAI, with each invention divided into three parts, each governed by one of ten separate microcode programs which include real-time frequency modulations with a continuous input signal, amplitude modulation, and feedback techniques; *Salto mortal* for computer-sequenced synthesizer and sampler by the Venezuelan composer Julio de ESCRIVAN, its title deriving from the Spanish phrase equating to "somersault," oscillating between sonance and color and making extensive use of FM-programmed and a few sampled sounds, originally intended for dance, explaining its numerous rhythmic cues; *Shrinking Times* by the 35-year-old Hungarian composer Gyula PINTÉR, in tripartite structure; *Konstruktie IV, Part 1* by the 23-year-old Dutch composer Ronald PHILIPPI; and *Jeu* by the 34-year-old Canadian composer Robert NORMANDEAU, incorporating the sounds of Paris subway musicians as well as excerpts from Karlheinz Stockhausen's *Hymnen* and Perotin's *Siderunt Omnes*.

An evening concert performed by the Radio Philharmonic Orchestra conducted by Gunther Schuller, in the following program: *Timepieces for Orchestra* by the 50-year-old English composer Jonathan HARVEY, in three movements, the orchestral players choosing, in performance, which of two conductors (usually beating different tempi) to follow; *Three Sonnets* for alto saxophone and orchestra by the 42-year-old Dutch composer Tristan KEURIS; and *Between* for cello and orchestra by the 57-year-old Danish composer Per NØRGÅRD, addressing in three movements three possible relationships between soloist and orchestra.

9 SEPTEMBER 1989

On the sixth day of the 63rd Festival of the International Society for Contemporary Music in Amsterdam, three concerts of note are given in the following sequence:

A morning concert of solo organ pieces performed by Gottfried Sembdner, in the following program: *Organum V* by the 55-year-old French composer Xavier DARASSE; *Etude Nr. 1, "Harmonies"* by the 67-year-old Hungarian-born Austrian composer György LIGETI, beginning with a cluster of ten notes, each finger depressing one key, the color changing only in response to the fingers slightly shifting on the keys, and ending with a chord of only three notes; *Three Strange Visions of Hieronymus Bosch* for organ by the 69-year-old Czech-born Israeli composer Jacob GILBOA, in three movements (*The Haywain*, *Paradise*, and *The Ship of Fools*); *Pari Intervallo*, constructive piece by the 53-year-old Estonian composer Arvo PÄRT; and *Jets d'Orgue* by the 50-year-old Dutch composer Jan VRIEND, first in a projected three-part work, with the role of the organist's two assistants being as prominent as that of the organist himself.

An afternoon concert of chamber works, in the following program: *Holzwege* for nine instruments by the Italian composer Pietro BORRADORI; *Chorus* by the Italian composer Giovanni BONATO, comprised of two interwoven processes equating broadly to "sound events" and counterpoint, set in an atmosphere of rhythmic unfolding, with constant decelerations and accelerations creating an over-all sense of temporal elasticity; *Jeu de . . .* by the Italian composer Paolo RIMOLDI, in nine sections (4 + 1 + 4), with the first four decelerating and diminishing in volume at the proportion of 8:7 and the second four accelerating and increasing in volume at a corresponding, reverse proportion, returning the work, at its close, to the opening speed, the central section in a contrasting slow tempo; *Assonance III* for cello, bass clarinet, and piano by the 30-year-old Swiss composer Michael JARRELL; *Un recitativo* by the Italian composer Stefano GERVASONI, to a text by Franco Fortini, "Come mai le fogli," with *Sprechstimme* handling of the vocal part; and *Take Off*, "mechanical ballet" for seven players by the 27-year-old English composer David SAWER, programmatically inspired by photographs depicting the successive failures and ultimate success of the Wright brothers in their first flight on 17 December 1903 at the Kill Devil Hills, Kitty Hawk, North Carolina.

An evening concert of orchestral and choral works, in the following program: *Alentour* by the French composer Henri KERGOMARD, the title referring to the preponderance of low tones, suggesting "impressions from far away" and set in an overall texture of musical repetitions and dynamic extremes; *On Taoism* by the iconoclastic Chinese composer Tan DUN, its textless vocal aspect and purely instrumental elements inspired by both Taoism and Chinese calligraphy, and with its Western instruments made to sound like those of China; *Kassandra* by the innovative 54-year-old French classicist and composer François-Bernard MÂCHE, an unprogrammatic impression of the mythical character of the title as the "sensual source of all lucidity," in ten sections moving from shadow to light, evoking the ambient street sounds of the legendary city of Cassandra; and *Pangäa—Symphony Fragment* by the West German composer Karl-Wieland KURZ, a symphonic potpourri glorifying historically unessential music.

10 SEPTEMBER 1989

Symphony No. 4 by the 55-year-old English composer Peter Maxwell DAVIES is premiered in London.

10 SEPTEMBER 1989

On the seventh and final day of the 63rd Festival of the International Society for Contemporary, Music in Amsterdam, two concerts of note are given in the following sequence:

A morning concert of mostly chamber pieces, in the following program: *Play* for clarinet and piano by the 42-year-old Dutch composer Tristan KEURIS, set in metrically free form; *Aliunde* for clarinet, soprano, percussion (including Indian tabla), and Akai S900 synthesizer with MIDI keyboard by the innovative 54-year-old French composer François-Bernard MÂCHE, the title alluding to the introduction and incorporation, in performance, of "foreign" sampled sounds that occur in unspecified time intervals; *Anatomic Safari* for accordion by the preeminent 57-year-old Danish composer Per NØRGÅRD in 9 movements—*Respiration, Movement, Clusters, Fluctuations, Reaction, Percussion, Vertigo, Toccata,* and *Fantasy*—collectively exploring the trodden and untrodden potentials of the instrument; and *. . . kaum einen Hauch* for clarinet, piano, and cello by the German composer Jörg BIRKENÖTTER, an interpretation of Goethe's poem "Ein Gleiches," its repetitious musical materials articulating the overall structure.

An afternoon concert of chamber music, in the following program: *Have your trip* for harp, guitar, and mandolin by the Italian composer Fausto ROMITELLI, in twelve pictographic images collectively depicting twelve angles of the same object; *Monade* for oboe by the German composer Claus Steffen MAHNKOPF, dedicated to the oboist Peter Vealethe, its title alluding to the philosophical aesthetics of Leibnitz, Benjamin, and Adorno, throughout exploring the technical capabilities of the instrument in a virtually unplayable matrix of instructions in its score, the player having to find his way through the labyrinth to a place of fundamental expression; *For the Republic* for alto trombone, marimba, and 22-channel digital tape by the English composer Ian WILLCOCK, a musical manifesto owing its inception to two inspired quotations, one from Cornelius Cardew and one from Plato (*The Republic*), each concerned with the conscience of the experimental; *Sacrificial Rite in Village* for string quartet by the Chinese composer Mo WUPING, an emotional setting refusing

to merge East and West but seeking to present the composer's ideas about distinctions without edification; *I Open and Close* for string quartet by the English geneticist-turned-composer Richard BARRETT, sixth in an eleven-part series of works entitled *Fictions*, commissioned by the BBC and first performed by the Arditti Quartet, for whom it was composed, in London on 15 December 1988; and *Nymphea: Jardin Secret III*, an evocative piece for string quartet and live electronics by the 36-year-old Finnish composer Kaija SAARIAHO.

13 SEPTEMBER 1989

Sonance-Resonance: Welche Töne? for orchestra by the eminent 70-year-old Hungarian-born Canadian composer István ANHALT is premiered in Toronto.

14 SEPTEMBER 1989

Festum for orchestra by the 63-year-old Italian composer Luciano BERIO is premiered in Dallas.

22 SEPTEMBER 1989

Arias & Barcarolles, first conceived as six songs with prelude and postlude for soprano, baritone, and two pianos by the 71-year-old veteran American composer Leonard BERNSTEIN, the title derived from a 1960 comment to the composer by President Eisenhower about his liking music with a theme and "not all them arias and barcarolles," in an authorized orchestration for strings and percussion by the prolific 33-year-old Chinese composer Bright SHENG, receives its first ever performance in Brookville, New York.

22 SEPTEMBER 1989

Peace Talks for ethnic percussion instruments, based on the concept of global union of socially and politically troubled nations by the 32-year-old American composer and percussionist Michael PUGLIESE, is heard for the first time in Berkeley, California.

22 SEPTEMBER 1989

Irving BERLIN, supremely effective composer of genuinely fashioned American popular songs, among them such classics as *God Bless America*, which nearly became an American national anthem, disregarding the fact that he was born in Russia and that his real Jewish name was Israel Balin, and who made millions of dollars for himself and his American family, dies at the incredible age of 101 in New York.

30 SEPTEMBER 1989

Virgil THOMSON, American composer of great originality, seen particularly in his opera *Four Saints in Three Acts* (actually more than four saints and more than three acts) setting the nonsense verse of Gertrude Stein as well as in his numerous and elegant songs, and whose music criticisms chronicled the many-forked road of American music since before World War II, dies in New York at the ripened age of 92.

2 OCTOBER 1989

Symphony No. 12 by the 79-year-old Danish composer Vagn HOLMBOE, commissioned by the BBC Wales, is given its first hearing in Cardiff.

5 OCTOBER 1989

Ritual for orchestra, *Cello Concerto No. 1*, and *Symphony No. 3*, all by the 54-year-old Russian composer Alfred SCHNITTKE, form the first concert of an unprecedented ten-day, twelve-concert retrospective of the works of the Soviet composer, held in Stockholm with the participation of Gennady Rozhdestvensky, Eri Klas, Okku Kamu, Eric Ericson, the Stockholm Philharmonic, Gidon Kremer, Ivan Monighetti, and Viktoria Posmikova.

12 OCTOBER 1989

L'Okanga La Ndju Pene Luambo Makiadi, socially conscious African singer, songwriter, and guitarist and founding leader of O.K. (later T.P.O.K.) Jazz, known as FRANCO to his literally millions of fans, dies in Zaire at the age of 51, just months after a critically acclaimed U.S. tour.

14 OCTOBER 1989

The ten-day, twelve-concert retrospective of the works of the 54-year-old Russian composer Alfred SCHNITTKE closes with a concert comprised of his *Requiem* and *Symphony No. 4*. (In all, 41 works from six genres were presented.)

17 OCTOBER 1989

Symphony No. 7 for organ and orchestra by the 60-year-old Welsh composer Alun HODDINOTT is heard for the first time at the Swansea Festival.

18 OCTOBER 1989

Symphony by the Czech composer Viktor ULLMANN (1898–1944), completed in a short score on 22 August 1944 as his five-movement *Piano Sonata No. 7*, three movements bearing notes for orchestration and the rest realized by the 41-year-old Freiburg music professor Bernard Wulff, is premiered in Stuttgart by an orchestra comprised of the five Baden-Württemberg music academies on the 45th anniversary of the composer's death. (Ullman was imprisoned at the Terezín [Theresienstadt] concentration camp in Czechoslovakia [8 September 1942–15 October 1944, then transferred to Auschwitz on 16 October 1944, where he died. Wulff described the final "Variations and Fugue on a Hebrew Folksong" as a ". . . final reckoning with European culture, which allowed things like Terezín to happen." James Reid Baxter, writing for *Tempo* [No. 171, December 1989], described it as ". . . simply the most disturbing music I have ever heard.")

27 OCTOBER 1989

New Year, opera by the esteemed 84-year-old English composer Sir Michael TIPPETT, is mounted for the first time in Houston.

28 OCTOBER 1989

Three Chinhai Folk Songs for chorus and orchestra by the precocious 35-year-old Chinese composer Bright SHENG is performed for the first time in Boston.

2 NOVEMBER 1989

Pro et Contra for orchestra by the leading 57-year-old Russian composer Sofia GUBAIDULINA, in three slow movements of opposing textures and dynamics with parts for prepared harpsichord and extended percussion as well as numerous solos for tuba, double bass, and contrabassoon, all of which moves gradually to a subtle thematic synthesis of the Russian hymn "Alleluia," is premiered in Louisville, Kentucky.

3 NOVEMBER 1989

The 64-year-old Greek composer and political activist Mikis THEODORAKIS signs his name to a manifesto condemning the divisive policies of the former Socialist government of Andreas Papandreou and ends four years of musical silence by appearing on an Athens stage before a crowd of 70,000 admirers, singing songs of protest and love in the name of national unity.

5 NOVEMBER 1989

Vladimir HOROWITZ, fantastically, fabulously gifted prestidigital pianist who spread his luminous stardom from darkest Russia to sunlit America, and who fascinated the greatest masters of the instrument such as Rachmaninoff by his inborn technique and romantic inspiration but whose life in music was made turbulent by torturous interruptions owing to his strange self-doubt, dies unexpectedly in New York at the peak of his great career, two years after his triumphant return to Russia after a half century of absence, at the age of 86.

7 NOVEMBER 1989

Indigenous Instruments for a microtonally-detuned "Pierrot" ensemble by the 33-year-old American composer Steven MACKEY, the first in a series of works conceived as "vernacular music from a culture that doesn't really exist," is performed for the first time in San Francisco by the San Francisco Contemporary Music Players, Stephen Mosko conducting.

10 NOVEMBER 1989

Industrial Symphony No. 1, a dark and disturbing theatrical evocation of love's ending and survival by the *enfant terrible* of film and television direction David LYNCH (whose television series "Twin Peaks" attained national cult status), combining sound and movement in a "bed" of quirky, blues-based music by Angelo BADALAMENTI, is mounted for the first time at the Brooklyn Academy of Music's Opera House in New York.

10 NOVEMBER 1989

23 Facts in 2 Acts, "brass fantasy" for musicians, dancers, chorus, and actors by the 48-year-old American jazz trumpeter and composer Lester BOWIE receives its first ever performance at the Brooklyn Academy of Music's Majestic Theater in New York.

11 NOVEMBER 1989

A collaborative, sold-out concert of works by the 77-year-old American-born Mexican composer Conlon NANCAR-

ROW and the 37-year-old German-born American composer TRIMPIN (who, to date, has transferred the 75 player piano rolls of Nancarrow to computer database), including pieces for four computer-controlled pianos and interactive sound sculpture, is given at the Baldwin Showroom in New York as part of the 11th annual New Music America Festival.

12 NOVEMBER 1989

Symphony No. 3 by the 59-year-old Estonian composer Eino TAMBERG is performed for the first time in Tallinn.

16 NOVEMBER 1989

Music in Abstract Lines for orchestra by the 51-year-old American composer Gloria COATES is premiered in New York.

16 NOVEMBER 1989

A melodious medley of occasionally delectable orchestral trifles including *Paris, Good for Goodie, Bird's Lament,* and *Stamping Ground* by the personally eccentric and musically eclectic American composer Louis HARDIN, a.k.a. MOONDOG to those privvy to his impromptu performances on the corner of 53rd and 6th in New York throughout the 1960s, receives its first performance by the Brooklyn Philharmonic Symphony Orchestra conducted by Lukas Foss at the Brooklyn Academy of Music's Majestic Theater in New York.

28 NOVEMBER 1989

Krakow Concerto for percussion and orchestra and *Katyń* for chorus and orchestra (dedicated to the victims of the Katyń Forest massacre) by the 58-year-old American composer Nancy VAN DE VATE are performed for the first time in Krakow.

1 DECEMBER 1989

The Master and Margarita, significant opera after Bulgakov by the eminent 57-year-old Soviet composer Sergei SLONIMSKY, is given its first Russian performance in Leningrad.

23 DECEMBER 1989

Preeminent 71-year-old American conductor and composer Leonard BERNSTEIN conducts the first of two celebratory performances of Beethoven's *9th Symphony* scheduled for either side of the Berlin Wall at the Kaiser Wilhelm Memorial Church, a World War II memorial in West Berlin. The second performance is heard on December 24, at the Schauspielhaus in East Berlin. On Christmas Day, both performances were telecast to the world. (The multinational orchestra for both performances was comprised of members from the Bavarian Radio Symphony Orchestra in Munich, augmented by players from New York, London, Paris, Dresden, and Leningrad.)

26 DECEMBER 1989

Lennox BERKELEY, significant British composer of expertly fashioned music in an impressive modern Baroque manner that he described as "modern English," dies in London at the fulfilled age of 86.

1990

4 JANUARY 1990

Vladimir USSACHEVSKY, innovative Russian-born American composer and founder of the Columbia-Princeton Electronic Music Center, dies in New York at the age of 78.

8 JANUARY 1990

Tableaux (after Kandinsky) for piano and orchestra by the 57-year-old Bulgarian-born American composer Henri LAZAROF, with each of its nine sections intending to evoke one of the nine letters in the Russian painter's name, is premiered in Seattle, Garrick Ohlsson soloist.

11 JANUARY 1990

Symphony No. 5 by the 51-year-old American composer William BOLCOM, cast in four eclectic movements, the second of which, *Scherzo Mortale,* combining "Abide With Me" on contrabass with the wedding march from Wagner's *Lohengrin* on contrabassoon, and the third of which, *Hymne à l' Amour,* incorporating an excerpt from Wagner's *Tristan und Isolde,* receives its first ever performance in Philadelphia.

19 JANUARY 1990

Concerto for Piano Three Hands for two pianos and chamber orchestra by the 64-year-old American composer Gunther SCHULLER is performed for the first time in Springfield, Illinois, with Lorin Hollander and Leon Fleisher as soloists.

26 JANUARY 1990

Duplicates, "perpetual cadenza" in three movements for two pianos and orchestra, by the 66-year-old American composer Mel POWELL, commissioned by new music patroness Betty Freeman, receives its first-ever performance in Los Angeles, later winning the 1990 Pulitzer Prize in Music.

1 FEBRUARY 1990

Symphony No. 10 by the 75-year-old English-domiciled Polish composer Andrzej PANUFNIK receives its first ever performance in Chicago.

13 FEBRUARY 1990

Music for Prague 1968 by the Czech-born American composer Karel HUSA, fraught with symbolism and conceived as a tribute to Czech resolve in the wake of the Soviet invasion of Czechoslovakia in August of 1968 and banned from performance in the composer's homeland while it received over 7,000 performances worldwide in both concert-band and orchestral versions, is finally performed in Czechoslovakia, in Smetana Hall in Prague, by the Bohuslav Martinů Philharmonic of Zlín, conducted by the composer.

15 FEBRUARY 1990

The Enchanted Loom for orchestra by the 51-year-old American composer Barbara KOLB is premiered in Atlanta, Georgia.

22 FEBRUARY 1990

Cello Concerto by the 75-year-old American composer Ezra LADERMAN, in one long movement in A-B-A' form, is heard for the first time in Chicago, Yo-Yo Ma, soloist.

24 FEBRUARY 1990

A retrospective concert of the entire *oeuvre* of eight works by the 84-year-old American jazz violinist and composer William RUSSELL is given in New York with a program including his first composition in more than 50 years, *Tango* for percussion, composed to accompany his earlier *3 Dance Movements*, as well as première performances of his *Concerto for Trumpet and Percussion* (1937) and *Ogou Badagri* (1933) for percussion, based on Voodoo rites.

24 FEBRUARY 1990

Symphony No. 3, Journey Without Distance, for soprano, chamber chorus, and orchestra by the 34-year-old American composer Richard DANIELPOUR, commissioned by the Foundation for Inner Peace and based on the psychological text *A Course in Miracles*, is premiered in Akron, Ohio.

10 MARCH 1990

Machaut à ma Manière for orchestra by the 55-year-old English composer Sir Harrison BIRTWISTLE is premiered in Hamburg.

15 MARCH 1990

Symphony No. 1 by the 52-year-old American composer John CORIGLIANO, in three highly referential movements, the third, *Epilogue*, inspired in its mosaic-like interweaving of motifs by "The Quilt," itself woven out of literally thousands of fabric panels designed and con-

structed by family and friends of those who have died of AIDS, is premiered in Chicago.

16 MARCH 1990

Ernst BACON, American composer of great intellectual power who devised a unique individual technique of mutual imitation of the visual relationship of the white and black keys in triadic chords of the right and left hand, and who also wrote romantic songs of great impressive power, dies in Orinda, California, at the age of 91.

22 MARCH 1990

Der Kuhnhandel, operetta composed in 1934 by the German-born American composer Kurt WEILL (1900–1950), receives its posthumous première performance in Düsseldorf.

22 MARCH 1990

Sasima for orchestra by the 36-year-old Puerto Rican composer Roberto SIERRA is performed for the first time in San Antonio, Texas.

3 APRIL 1990

Sarah VAUGHAN, beloved black American jazz singer known for her soulful renditions of such songs as *Broken-Hearted Melody* and *Whatever Lola Wants* and through her numerous appearances with bona fide symphony orchestras, including the Los Angeles Philharmonic conducted by Michael Tilson Thomas in 1982, dies in Los Angeles at the age of 66.

12 APRIL 1990

Prisons of the Mind for orchestra by the 76-year-old American composer Henry BRANT, "spatial symphony" designed to the acoustic dimensions of the Dallas Symphony's new Morton H. Meyerson Symphony Center, inspired by drawings by the eighteenth-century Venetian architect Giovanni Battista Piranesi and calling on some 314 musicians (the Dallas Symphony Orchestra divided, two high school concert bands, and two Caribbean steel-drum ensembles) and eight conductors, all strategically placed throughout the hall, receives its first-ever, rather well-tolerated performance in Dallas.

21 APRIL 1990

The Lifework of Juan Diaz for orchestra by the 38-year-old American composer Lawrence RAPCHAK, loosely based on a story by Ray Bradbury, is performed for the first time in Chicago.

25 APRIL 1990

Portrait of Raoul Wallenberg: Symphony for three narrators, chorus, children's chorus, and orchestra by the 56-year-old Swedish composer and conductor Ulf BJÖRLIN, to a text commemorating Swedish diplomat Raoul Wallenberg (1912–c. 1947), whose daring exploits in Nazi-held Hungary in 1944 are credited with saving the lives of tens of thousands of Jews, and who was awarded honorary U.S. citizenship posthumously in 1981, is premiered in Palm Beach, Florida, with the veteran actors Cliff Robertson,

Ruth Warrick, and Fritz Weaver as narrators and the Greater Palm Beach Symphony, Choral Society, and Public School Chorus, all conducted by the composer.

25 APRIL 1990

Dexter GORDON, legendary jazz tenor saxophonist and bebop innovator who played with such luminaries as Lionel Hampton, Fletcher Henderson, Dizzy Gillespie, Fats Navarro, and Louis Armstrong, and whose sterling performance in the 1986 film 'Round Midnight secured him an Oscar nomination for Best Actor, dies in Philadelphia, of kidney failure, at the age of 67.

26 APRIL 1990

Marea (Tides) for large chamber orchestra by the 32-year-old Finnish composer Magnus LINDBERG, opening with six "waves," is performed for the first time in London.

28 APRIL 1990

Patmos, "Azione musicale" in seven acts by the 37-year-old German composer Wolfgang von SCHWEINITZ, to a libretto adapted from the Book of Revelations by D. E. Salter, is performed for the first time at the Munich Biennale.

29 APRIL 1990

Sesubun—Day of Change for two live performers, sound engineer, piano, and tape by the American composer-poet Alison KNOWLES, with sounds collected in and around a Japanese shrine and cities that, since Basho (1644–1694), have practiced the bean-throwing ceremony each February 3 or 4 alluded to in the title, driving out the devil and welcoming spring in one fell swoop, commissioned by Klaus Schöning and the WDR, is performed for the first time in New York as part of the second Acustica International Festival.

2 MAY 1990

Floof, subtitled Songs of a Homeostaic Homer, for soprano, clarinet, piano, cello, synthesizer, and percussion by the 31-year-old Finnish composer and conductor Esa-Pekka SALONEN, based on a science fiction novel by Stanislau Lem in which attempts to create a poetry machine fail miserably, is first heard in a revised version in London. (The original version was premiered at the Sibelius Academy in Helsinki on 27 August 1988.)

2 MAY 1990

Violin Concerto by the seasoned 81-year-old American composer Elliott CARTER, in four sections/three movements—an opening Impulsive, a middle conjoined Tranquillo and Angosciato, and a final Scherzando—with devilishly difficult solo passages handled with aplomb by the Norwegian violinist Ole Böhm (who co-commissioned the work), is given its first performance in San Francisco.

3 MAY 1990

Piano Concerto No. 3 in E-flat Major, composed c. 1839 by the venerable Hungarian composer Franz LISZT (1811–1886), receives its posthumous premiere perfor-

mance by the Chicago Symphony Orchestra with Janina Fialkowska, soloist, Kenneth Jean conducting.

8 MAY 1990

Luigi NONO, great modern composer, one of the most adventurous creators of stage and other musical works based on intransigent equalization of dissonance in harmony and polyrhythms in counterpoint, with the application of a battery of percussive instruments, whose adherence to political extremism included membership in the Italian Communist Party beginning when Italy was still controlled by the terrorist fascist regime, and who eventually married Arnold Schoenberg's daughter, dies in his native Venice at the age of 66.

8 MAY 1990

Opus sine nomine, oratorio by the 89-year-old Austrian-born American composer Ernst KRENEK, is performed for the first time in Vienna as part of a celebratory concert in anticipation of his 90th birthday.

17 MAY 1990

Vincent, opera by the 61-year-old Finnish composer Einojuhani RAUTAVAARA, based on letters written by Vincent van Gogh to his brother Theo, is staged for the first time in Helsinki.

18 MAY 1990

Concord/Eendracht for orchestra by the 40-year-old Australian composer Vincent PLUSH is performed for the first time in Utrecht.

25 MAY 1990

Frankenstein: The Modern Prometheus, opera by the 39-year-old American composer Libby LARSEN, is performed for the first time in St. Paul, Minnesota.

26 MAY 1990

Pioneers, mixed-media musical theater work by the 39-year-old American composer Paul DRESHER, is staged for the first time at the Spoleto Festival in Charleston, South Carolina.

31 MAY 1990

Cello Concerto by the 49-year-old American composer Stephen ALBERT, in four stark, Romantic movements lasting some thirty minutes, is heard for the first time in Baltimore, Yo-Yo Ma soloist.

11 JUNE 1990

Rap group 2 LIVE CREW'S double album As Nasty As They Wanna Be, featuring such songs as "Me So Horny" and "If You Believe in Having Sex," is ruled obscene by a federal judge in Fort Lauderdale, Florida, the first musical recording ever to be banned by a court. A nationwide antiobscenity campaign followed: a Fort Lauderdale record store owner was arrested for selling the album; San Antonio police ordered record store workers to remove Nasty from their shelves or face arrest; the city council in Huntsville, Alabama, extended its antiobscenity ordinance to include live performances in order to block an impending appearance by the group. In a concert in Duluth, Georgia, 2 LIVE CREW performed under the watchful eyes of officials, singing only cleaned-up versions of their songs while the audience irreverently filled in the expurgated language. Prior to the ban, the album had sold some 1.7 million copies; after the ban it quickly hit the 2 million mark.

14 JUNE 1990

Marie Galante, "Suite Panaméenne" with vocal numbers in their original instrumentation by the German composer Kurt WEILL (1900–1950), is given its first ever performance by the Matrix Ensemble as part of the 10th Almeida Festival of Contemporary Music and Performance, marking the 90th anniversary year of his birth.

15 JUNE 1990

It's All the Same to Me for bass and orchestra by the 62-year-old American composer John DOWNEY is first heard during an all-Downey concert of three of his works in Lvov in the western Ukraine, the composer conducting.

16 JUNE 1990

A concert by the pianist Yvar Mikhashoff of ten world premieres for piano is given at the 10th Almeida Festival of Contemporary Music and Performance with the following program: *Prelude* by the Japanese composer Mamoru FUJIEDA, *Signs and Pictures* by the Norwegian composer Åse HEDSTRØM, *When Alysander Our King was Dede* by the Scottish composer James CLAPPERTON, *Le Strade dell'Aurora* by the Italian composer Alessandro SBORDONI, *There Be Dragons* by the American composer Michael MCCANDLESS, *Prelude* by the Canadian composer Rodney SHARMAN, *The Masque of the Red Death* by the Danish composer Bent SØRENSEN, *For Flying Away Birds* by the Russian composer Alexander GUGEL, *Soledades* by the Spanish composer Carlos GALÁN, *Satie's Sixth Nocturne* by the American composer Nils VIGELAND, *L'Isola di Euthanasio* by the Rumanian composer Serban NICHIFOR, and *Five Spirals* by the Brazilian composer Augusto VALENTE.

17 JUNE 1990

Europeras 3 & 4 for eight singers, two pianos, and six gramophone operators by the iconoclastic 77-year-old American composer John CAGE, making use of 150 years of plundered European opera remixed and renewed in a new, peculiarly American whole, receives its première staging at the 10th Almeida Festival of Contemporary Music and Performance.

25 JUNE 1990

Peggy GLANVILLE-HICKS, Australian composer of a number of diversified works for the stage, gathering her inspiration from ancient Greek modalities and Hindu mythology as well as from contemporary subjects, dies in Sydney at the age of 77.

13 JULY 1990

Composer-to-Composer, an international gathering of composers founded by Charles Amirkhanian and John Lifton

and presented by the Telluride Institute, with resident composers Geri ALLEN, Laurie ANDERSON, Henry BRANT, Hugh DAVIES, Ge GANG-RU, Robert MORRIS, Pauline OLIVEROS, Larry POLANSKY, Roger REYNOLDS, I Wayan SADRA, Leo SMIT, and Gerhard STÄBLER, culminates a week of private sessions with its third three-day festival of public concerts, panel discussions, and a film/video presentation in the historic Sheridan Opera House in Telluride, Colorado.

16 AUGUST 1990

Mein Tod. Requiem in Memoriam Jane S. for soprano and orchestra by the 38-year-old German composer Wolfgang RIHM, to a text by Wolf Wondratschek, is heard for the first time at the Salzburg Festival.

1 SEPTEMBER 1990

Carpe diem!, concerto for clarinet and small orchestra by the 33-year-old Finnish composer Jouni KAIPAINEN, is performed for the first time in Helsinki.

3 SEPTEMBER 1990

First Symphony, subtitled *Himmelhoch jauchzend—zum Tode betrübt* by the 41-year-old Danish composer Poul RUDERS is premiered by the BBC Orchestra in London, later winning the 1990 Royal Philharmonic Society/ Charles Heidsieck Champagne Award for "outstanding accomplishments in British musical life" by virtue of its "adventurous sense of scale and design, and the mastery of large orchestral forces."

8 SEPTEMBER 1990

La cancion de las Antillas for orchestra by the 32-year-old Puerto-Rican born American composer Raymond TORRES-SANTOS is performed for the first time in San Juan.

22 SEPTEMBER 1990

The 64th Festival of the International Society for Contemporary Music opens in Oslo with an evening concert, performed by the Bergen Philharmonic Orchestra and Bergen Opera Choir, in the following program:

Der Atem der verletzten Zeit for orchestra by the Yugoslavian composer Uros ROJKO, based on manipulations of the overtone series; *Troerinnen*, operatic cantata on a Greek text adapted from Euripides' "The Trojan Women," for three female singers, women's choir, and orchestra by the Korean composer Unsuk CHIN; an orgiastic *Bacchanal* for organ solo and orchestra by the 45-year-old American composer William ALBRIGHT; and *The Howl of the Thousand Throats* for soprano, recitant bass, chorus, and orchestra by the Argentine composer Alejandro IGLESIAS-ROSSI, in seven parts based on ancient texts of the Qwechuas, the Peruvian and Bolivian Indian tribe that ruled the Inca Empire at the time of the Spanish Conquistadors.

23 SEPTEMBER 1990

On the second day of the 64th Festival of the International Society for Contemporary Music in Oslo, four concerts of note are given in the following sequence:

An afternoon concert of "Harmonic Chant" by the American composer-vocalist David HYKES, self-accompanied on tanpura, svarpeti, zither, 12-string fretless guitar, and Casio SK5 sampler, in a program including his *Behind All This Going, Going Toward Oneself, Harmonic Mass,* and *Windhorse Riders.*

An afternoon concert of chamber works, performed by Cikada led by the foremost Norwegian conductor of contemporary music, Christian Eggen, in the following program: *. . . and No Birds Sing* for flutes, clarinets, violin, piano, and percussion by the Australian composer Brenton BROADSTOCK, the third of three works protesting environmental devastation, its title borrowed from John Keats's dreary poem "La Belle Dame sans Merci" (1819); the quasi-improvisational *Ouçam a Somados Sons que Soam* for flute, clarinet, piano, percussion, and strings by the 50-year-old avant-garde Portuguese composer Jorge PEIXINHO; the Rousseau-inspired *Locus Solus (Solitary Place)* for two percussionists by the Argentine composer Mariano ETKIN; and *Et Cetera* for flute, clarinet, violin, cello, piano, and percussion by the 48-year-old Norwegian-Lapp composer John PERSEN.

An evening concert of vocal works performed by Singcircle, in the following program: *Rosaces 4* for four amplified voices and 4-channel prerecorded tape by the English composer Jonty HARRISON, inspired by the rose windows of Chartres Cathedral; *Son Entero* for four voices and computer by the Argentine composer Alejandro VIÑAO, its text drawn from "El Son Entero" by the Cuban poet Nicolas Guillén; *Vox II* for four amplified voices, stereo tape, harmonizer, and delay-system incorporating Japanese Bunraku puppet-theatre recitation, vocal music of Mali, and songs of frogs, monkeys, and birds, all fused with contemporary extended vocal techniques and accompanied by a tape backdrop of environmental sounds, by the English composer Trevor WISHART; *Tre Canti Popolari* for four (or more) mixed voices, in a textually ambiguous setting of alternating unison and microtonal passages by the Italian composer Giacinto SCELSI; and *Tigida Pipa* for four amplified voices, percussion, and tape by the American composer Stephen MONTAGUE, described by *The Financial Times* as a ". . . brilliantly sustained tongue-twisting, tempo-twisting vocal toccata."

An evening concert of solo and ensemble works, in the following program: *Novelette* for violin and piano by the Netherlands composer Willem JETHS; *Crystalline* for piano in seven short parts by the Japanese composer Karen TANAKA; *Variations* for piano by the Icelandic composer Hrodmar Ingi SIGURB-JÖRNSSON; *RAPS IV* for violin by the Italian composer Giampaolo CORAL; *Ciclos* for cello and piano, the second of its three cyclic parts nested within the first and the third nested within the first and second, by the Brazilian composer Roseanne YAMPOL-SCHI; and *Petals* for cello and electronics by the Finnish composer Kaija SAARIAHO, derived from her earlier *Nymphea: Jardin Secret III* for string quartet and live electronics and dedicated to the cellist Anssi Karttunen.

24 SEPTEMBER 1990

On the third day of the 64th Festival of the International Society for Contemporary Music in Oslo, three concerts of note are given in the following sequence:

An afternoon concert of electronically enhanced chamber and solo works, in the following program: the award-winning *Voix Blanche* for Ondes Martenot and tape by the Canadian composer Gilles GOBEIL; *Météores* for tape by the Canadian composer Francis DHOMONT, third of a four-movement work entitled *Chroniques de la Lumière*, impressionistically akin to a visual "happening"; *Chordis Canam* for harpsichord and tape by the Netherlands composer Roderik DE MAN; and *Qudrat* for three percussion (octoban drums, kettle drums, glass chimes, Chinese cymbals, et al.) and three Yamaha DX7 synthesizers by the Norwegian composer Lasse THORESEN,

its title translating, in Arabic, as "strength, power, force, potency, ability."

An evening concert of microtonal music is performed by Newband, in the following program: *Rain Spell* for flute, clarinet, harp, piano, and vibraphone by the 59-year-old leading Japanese composer Toru TAKEMITSU; *Haikai* for flute and zoomoozophone by the revered and iconoclastic 78-year-old American composer John CAGE, one in a series of modular works modeled after Japanese haiku; *Thus* for flute, clarinet, Yamaha DX7 synthesizer, zoomoozophone, percussion, and stroke rods by the Norwegian composer Lasse THORESEN, thematically based on a Norwegian cattle call; *Continental Drift* for clarinet, amplified harp, Yamaha DX7 synthesizer, zoomoozophone, and percussion by the American composer Mathew ROSENBLUM, juxtaposing materials drawn from both 19-note and 12-note (tempered) octaves; and *Incredible Time (to Live and Die)* for flute, Yamaha DX7 synthesizer, Korg digital drums, zoomoozophone, and percussion by the American composer (and Newband member) Dean DRUMMOND.

An evening orchestral concert performed by the Norwegian Chamber Orchestra, in the following program: *Ariel* for oboe, tape, and string orchestra by the Swedish composer Anders NILSSON; *Winter's Tale (La Novella d' Inverno)* for string orchestra by the 47-year-old Polish composer and percussionist Marta PTASZYŃSKA, inspired by the surrealist paintings of Ernst, Tanguy, and de Chirico, with conscripted juxtapositions of transmutated and synthesized motives and rhythms from Vivaldi's *Four Seasons; Pitangus Sulphuratus* for flute and string orchestra by the Venezuelan composer Adina IZARRA, based on the call of the Great Kiskadee (whose Latin name is reflected in the title); *Apocaliptica II* for piano and string orchestra by the Chilean composer Santiago VERA-RIVERA; and *Shaker Loops* for seven solo strings by the 43-year-old American composer John ADAMS.

25 SEPTEMBER 1990

On the fourth day of the 64th Festival of the International Society for Contemporary Music in Oslo, two concerts of note are given in the following sequence:

An afternoon concert of chamber works, in the following program: *Zampugn* for twenty-nine bells by the Swiss composer Daniel OTT; *Angel's Music* for string quartet by the Danish composer Bent SØRENSEN, inspired by paintings of angels playing music (i.e., Fra Angelico's "The Linauoli Triptych," begun in 1433), with constant use of glissandi and cast in a three-part structure in a ratio relationship of 5:6:4; *Music for Re-tuned Instruments* for variously prepared flute, violas, cello, and piano by the Czech composer Martin SMOLKA; *Third Quiet Music* for eight contrabasses by the American composer Leonard PAYTON; and *Gesta* for saxophone ensemble by the Italian composer Tonino TESEI.

An evening concert of orchestral works performed by the Norwegian Radio Orchestra, in the following program: *Saisir* for chamber orchestra by the Norwegian composer Åse HED-STRØM; inspired by words and images of Henri Michaux; *Nasjonalsang (National Anthem)* for trumpet, trombone, orchestra, and tape by the 53-year-old Norwegian composer Alfred JANSON, dedicated to the Norwegian State Railways; and *Music für Tasteninstrumente und Orchester* (two pianos, two electric organs, and orchestra) by the 58-year-old German composer Mauricio KAGEL.

26 SEPTEMBER 1990

On the fifth day of the 64th Festival of the International Society for Contemporary Music, four concerts of note are given in the following sequence:

An early afternoon concert of works by Norwegian composers, in the following program: The first ever performance of three motets for men's choir, *O Salutaris Hostia*, *Quia vidisti me*, and *Ostore Konge Davids Søn*, by Fartein VALEN (1887–1952); *Suite* for microinterval guitar by Bjørn FONGAARD (1919–1980), performed on a fretless electric guitar designed by the composer to realize works composed in his "n-tonal" system allowing for any division of the octave; *Intermezzo* for soprano, violin, and tape by Gunnar SØNSTEVOLD, dating from 1958, the first Norwegian work to utilize electronic effects; a Neoclassical Sonata for solo flute by Finn MORTENSEN (1922–1983); and *My Ancestors* for violin and piano by Harald SAEVERUD.

A midafternoon concert of ensemble works, in the following program: *The Thundering Scream of the Seraphim's Delight* for double bass, color video, and electronic sound by the American composer Reynold WEIDENAAR; *Encore!*, "ticks and tricks for an actress and a cello player" by the 54-year-old Swiss composer Jürg WYTTENBACH, its text a tale from "Rose et Vert-Pomme" (1894) by Alphonse Allais; *Evidence of Things Unseen* for slide projections and electroacoustic music, joint work by the Swedish composer Robert DOUKKALI and the American composer William BRUNSON, inspired by arts of Tantric tradition; and *Electronic Purgatory*, live multimedia work for keyboard and interactive electronics by the Canadian composers Kristi ALLIK and Robert MULDER, loosely inspired by Dante's *Divine Comedy* in a tripartite structure of *Purgatory*, *Inferno*, and *Paradise*.

A late afternoon concert of chamber works, in the following program: *Chio no tsukkage* for 17-string koto, cello, and piano by the 60-year-old Japanese composer Hifumi SHIMOYAMA, its title derived from the famous medieval Japanese literary text recited by the koto player in the latter half of the piece; *Labyrinth* for cello and accordion by the 53-year-old Polish composer Zbigniew BARGIELSKI, originally *Labyrinth of the Forgotten Glance* for cello and piano (1984); *Piece for Accordion with Screen* by the Australian composer Caroline WILKINS; *La Voce* for cello by the 51-year-old Netherlands composer Louis ANDRIESSEN, named for the poem by Cesare Pavese recited during performance; *Ygghur: Old Age-Memories-Catharsis-Liberation*, third part of a *Trilogia* subtitled "The Three Stages of Man" by the Italian composer Giacinto SCELSI (1905–1988); *Ligatura: Message to Frances-Maria: The Unanswered Question* for cello, two violins, and celesta by the 64-year-old Hungarian composer György KURTAG; and *Epicycles* for solo cello and twelve instruments by the 68-year-old Greek-born French composer Iannis XENAKIS.

An evening concert of works for string quartet by the Cuarteto Latinoamericano, in the following program: *Danger of the Disappearance of Things* by the English composer Simon HOLT; *Kinesis-2* by the Spanish composer Zulema DE LA CRUZ; *String Quartet* No. 2 by the Polish composer Aleksander LASON; *Visas* by the Italian composer Stefano SCODANIBBIO, named after the only book by the Genoese poet Vittorio, its title denoting a central theme of travel; and *Praesens Subitus* by the Norwegian composer Cecilie ORE.

27 SEPTEMBER 1990

On the sixth day of the 64th Festival of the International Society for Contemporary Music in Oslo, four concerts of note are given in the following sequence:

An early afternoon concert of electronic pieces, in the following program: *Music for Oboe and Tape* by the Russian composer Sergei BELCHUKOV, "filled with love to Byelorussian land, alarm for its future, for the state of nature which asks for help"; *Oppbrudd* for tape by the Norwegian composer Tor HALMRAST, based on only one sound sample and com-

posed with only one nonlinear algorhythm; *El Reposo del Fuego* for synthesizers and digital tape by the Canadian composer John OLIVER, its title taken from poems by the Mexican writer Jos-Emilio Pacheco, portions of which are recited on tape; and *Triple Concerto* for flute, cello, piano, and computer by the Argentine composer Alejandro VIÑAO, demanding extraordinary synchronicity between the players and computer.

A late afternoon concert of vocal works performed by the Swedish Radio Choir, in the following program: *Sounds, Shadows. . . .* for eight a cappella voices by the Israeli composer Yinam LEEF setting Esperanto texts by L. L. Zamenho; *Four Late Poems and an Epigram of Rainer Maria Rilke* for soprano by the 38-year-old English composer Oliver KNUSSEN; *Breathing Room: July* for a cappella choir by the Swedish composer Anders ELIASSON, setting the epic poem of Tomas Tranströmer, the last recipient of the Nordic Council Prize of Literature, in three movements with text scattered freely throughout; and *Kolo* for mixed choir, trombone, and electronics variously grouped and distributed throughout the performance space by the 56-year-old French composer Vinko GLOBOKAR.

An evening world première performance of *Yuki-Yuki-Te* (*Gone on-and-on*), conceived and performed by Japanese dancer/choreographers Rika TATEOKA and Minoru HIDESHIMA, a mixed media dialogue between ". . . Age and Youth, body and soul, new music and ancient tradition, contemporary dance and classical theatre, between the Noh and Butoh performing arts," in seven acts, with music (scored for computer and 17-string koto), text, and computer programming by Takehito Shimazu, Noh choreography by Tetsuo Shiozu, butoh choreography by Hideshima, scenography and costumes by Michel Boulang, and light design by Lysverket.

An evening concert of orchestral works performed by the Chamber Orchestra of Georgia, in the following program: *Concerto Grosso I* for two violins, harpsichord, prepared piano, and string orchestra by the 56-year-old German-born Russian composer Alfred SCHNITTKE, in six movements performed without pause, with reworked excerpts from famous film-scores (Khrazhanovsky's *The Butterfly*, Shepitko's *The Ascent*, Klimov's *Agony*, et al.); *Cronicas* for twenty-two strings by the Argentine composer Osvaldo GOLIJOV, intentionally reminiscent of Middle Eastern religious music; and *Morning Prayers* for chamber orchestra and tape, first in a series entitled *Life Without Christmas* by the 55-year-old Georgian composer Giya KANCHELI.

28 SEPTEMBER 1990

On the seventh day of the 64th Festival of the International Society for Contemporary Music in Oslo, three concerts of note are given in the following sequence:

An early afternoon concert of ensemble works performed by the Oslo Sinfonietta and Cikada, both conducted by Christian Eggen, in the following program: *Io* for chamber orchestra, tape, and live electronics by the Finnish composer Kaija SAARIAHO, named after one of the moons of Jupiter, the nonharmonic sounds produced by the double bass and bass flute providing the model for both overall chord structure and tape aspect; *Allegories* for flute, clarinet, horn, violin, cello, percussion and synthesizer by the French composer Tristan MURAIL; *UR* for five players and electronics by the Finnish composer Magnus LINDBERG, with the acoustic instruments amplified and integrated in four channels to effect a smooth merger with the many synthetically generated sounds; and *Partiels* for 18 musicians by the French composer Gérard GRISEY.

A late afternoon concert of orchestral works performed by the Oslo Philharmonic Orchestra, in the following program: *Echanges* for orchestra and electronics by the Swiss composer André RICHARD; *Helle Nacht,* concerto for violin and orchestra by the 58-year-old Danish composer Per NØRGÅRD, a four-movement work so rich in influences it was described as ". . . a kaleidoscopic, pluralistic, expressive world of romantic Danish song, rhapsodic, dramatic virtuosity, Brahms, Mahler, Bartók, Ligeti, and much, much more"; *Heterophony of Two Pianos and Orchestra* by the Japanese composer Akira NISHIMURA, winner of the 36th (1988) Otaka Prize; and *Kinetics* for orchestra by the Finnish composer Magnus LINDBERG, an extraordinarily popular work in the Nordic orchestral literature and dedicated to the conductor Esa-Pekka Salonen.

An evening concert of chamber works performed by Borealis, in the following program: *Listening to Fishermen's Songs,* "musical drawing" of a poem by Ye Weilian for flute, clarinet, horn, violin, cello, and piano by the Chinese composer David MAK CHI PIU; *Wantilan* for alto flute and percussion by the German composer Dieter MACK, named for the Balinese term for a village performance hall and based on a fixed gong cycle repeated eight times with a cantus firmus that forms the melodic base; *Litanie IV* for soprano, flute, clarinet, violin, cello, and piano by the 67-year-old Belgian composer Karel GOEYVAERTS, reminiscent of Balinese and African ritual musics; *Nadir* for flute, viola, and tape by the Greek composer Christos HATZIS; and *O Bali* for piano, vibraphone, flutes, violins, cello, and contrabass by the Canadian composer José EVANGELISTA.

29 SEPTEMBER 1990

On the eighth day of the 64th Festival of the International Society for Contemporary Music, two concerts of note are given in the following sequence:

A late afternoon concert of ensemble works performed by the Oslo Sinfonietta, in the following program: *L'ECRAN parfum* for six violins and three percussion, second in the *Nine Rivers* cycle by the English composer James DILLON; *Musical Graffiti,* "virtuoso drawings" for amplified piano, large ensemble, and tape with cosmic sounds (recorded via satellite) by the Norwegian composer Asbjørn SCHAATHUN; *Essete 1mar* for soprano, baryton, wind quartet, string quartet, and basso continuo by the Greek composer Giorgos KOUMENDAKIS; and *Märchenbilder,* "Six fairytale pictures" of "Mendelssohn-like lightness" for chamber orchestra by the 37-year-old Danish composer Hans ABRAHAMSEN.

An evening world premiere performance of *Macbeth,* opera by the 68-year-old Italian-born Norwegian composer Antonio BIBALO, based on the play by Shakespeare.

30 SEPTEMBER 1990

On the ninth and final day of the 64th Festival of the International Society for Contemporary Music in Oslo, an afternoon concert is given by the Youth Brass Band of Nanset and trumpet soloist Ole Edvard Antonsen, conducted by Karel Husa, in the following program: *Opus Partus* for symphonic band by the Norwegian composer Bjørn Korsan HOEMSNES; *Perpetuus,* "11-minute exploration" for chamber orchestra by the Polish composer Hanna KULENTY; *Concerto for Trumpet and Wind Orchestra* and *Concerto for Wind Ensemble,* two virtuosic, three-movement works by the 69-year-old Czech-born American composer Karel HUSA; and *Magma VII* for fourteen wind instruments by the Uruguayan composer Graciela PARASKEVAIDIS.

8 OCTOBER 1990

Rainbow for orchestra by the 62-year-old Scottish composer Thea MUSGRAVE is performed for the first time in Glasgow.

11 OCTOBER 1990

Sotheby's of New York hosts an auction of the "Property from the Estate of Virgil THOMSON" at which the contents of the composer's ninth-floor apartment at the historic Chelsea Hotel (where he lived for more than half a century) are sold for the benefit of the Virgil Thomson Foundation, Ltd. Among the most coveted items were a fine black silk brocade vest belonging to Gertrude Stein ($18,000) and an art deco ebonized wood and chrome dining table, reputedly "Shanghai-ed" from the basement of the apartment of *Modern Music* magazine pioneer Minna Ledermann and her husband Mell Daniel, which hosted legendary meals for some of the twentieth-century's most illustrious cultural figures ($6,500). Also included in the sale were Thomson's American Rococo Revival walnut bedstead ($1,100), in which much of his post-World War II music was composed, a collection of 43 (many first) edition works by Gertrude Stein ($14,000), some bearing personal inscriptions by the poet, and numerous paintings by the composer's lifetime companion, Maurice Grosser.

14 OCTOBER 1990

A contingent of 14 South Korean experts in traditional Korean music cross into Communist North Korea through the truce village of Panmunjom, 35 miles north of Seoul, on an unprecedented eleven-day visit to attend a "unification music festival" sponsored by the Seoul government, the first visit of its kind since Korea divided at the end of World War II.

14 OCTOBER 1990

Leonard BERNSTEIN, true American genius who became the first native musician to head the New York Philharmonic as a brilliant conductor and whose other talents included the composition of Broadway hits such as *West Side Story,* but who also showed remarkable gifts as a writer and even a poet (his sonnets were comparable to those of Edna St. Vincent Millay), not to mention his ability to fascinate audiences as a lecturer and a television instructor in music, dies in New York at an unfulfilled age of 72, broken down by a pitiless combination of progressive emphysema and lung inflammation, culminating in heart failure.

19 OCTOBER 1990

From Me Flows What You Call Time for percussion quintet and orchestra by the 60-year-old Japanese composer Toru TAKEMITSU is heard for the first time in New York.

19 OCTOBER 1990

Symphony by the 40-year-old Israeli-born American composer Shulamit RAN, later to win the 1991 Pulitzer Prize in Music, is heard for the first time in Philadelphia.

21 OCTOBER 1990

MIDORI (real name Goto Mi Dori), fantastically gifted 19-year-old Japanese *Wunderkind* of the violin, makes her New York recital debut at Carnegie Hall.

27 OCTOBER 1990

Xavier CUGAT, versatile Spanish-born American bandleader who achieved popularity in his fanciful arrangements of Latin American dances and who was variously married to jazz singers, dies in his native Barcelona at the advanced age of 90.

29 OCTOBER 1990

An Angel Moves Too Fast to See for bass, percussion, and ensemble of 101 guitars by the American Minimalist composer and founder of the alternative performance space The Kitchen in New York Rhys CHATHAM, is performed in an opening concert of the 12th annual New Music America Festival in Montreal.

2 NOVEMBER 1990

Symphony No. 4, Last Symphony, for baritone and orchestra by the 73-year-old American composer Lou HARRISON, utilizing texts derived from coyote stories of native Americans (including those of Daniel Harry Steward), receives its first ever performance by the Brooklyn Philharmonic conducted by Dennis Russell Davies at the Brooklyn Academy of Music's Opera House in New York.

2 DECEMBER 1990

Aaron COPLAND, the first American composer to generate a truly native form of composition that combined the American jazz idiom with highly developed modernistic techniques, dies of multiple disabling ailments 18 days after reaching the age of 90 in North Tarrytown, New York.

6 DECEMBER 1990

Fifth Symphony by the 58-year-old Danish composer Per NØRGARD is premiered by the Danish Radio Symphony in Copenhagen as a commissioned work celebrating the twin 125th anniversaries of the births of Jean Sibelius and Carl Nielsen and forming part of a concert that also includes the *Fifth Symphonies* of each of the Scandinavian masters.

7 DECEMBER 1990

Concierto a cuatro for saxophone quartet and orchestra by the 60-year-old Spanish composer Cristóbal HALFFTER is premiered by the Sigurd Rascher Saxophone Quartet and the Southwest German Radio Orchestra in Baden-Baden.

8 DECEMBER 1990

Suite for violin and string orchestra, op. 117, by the great Finnish composer Jean SIBELIUS (1865–1957), long considered unfinished but discovered to have been completed by the composer c. 1930, is heard for the first time at a concert celebrating the 125th anniversary of his birth in Lahti in a performance by the Lahti Symphony Orchestra conducted by Osmo Vanska.

9 DECEMBER 1990

"orchester in stereo mit 5 sinustönen for two orchestras" by the 32-year-old Korean composer Kunsu SHIN, with identical, limited materials (F and B-flat) distributed to all instruments, independent of tone ranges or tuning systems (so "neither captain, nor slaves"), and without connection to either Korean or Western European musical tradition but suggesting both, is premiered in Kamen, Germany.

18 DECEMBER 1990

Paul TORTELIER, French cellist who also devoted his life to the cause of improving human life and government and who spent some time at an Israel kibbutz to test the work of a new communal life, dies in Villarceaux at the age of 76.

1991

6 JANUARY 1991

Bronze, piano concerto by the 29-year-old American composer Michael TORKE, is performed for the first time in New York.

17 JANUARY 1991

Concerto for Double Orchestra: A Play Within a Play by the 66-year-old American composer Ezra LADERMAN, the outer two movements of which, for full orchestra, frame three inner movements for chamber orchestra, is premiered by the New Jersey Symphony Orchestra in New Brunswick.

19 JANUARY 1991

Fifth Symphony, Amen, a setting of the "Lord's Prayer" for baritone, oboe, trumpet, tuba, violin, and a precisely measured, thick plywood cube struck with wooden mallets by the 71-year-old Soviet composer

Galina USTVOLSKAYA is premiered at Alice Tully Hall in New York, Joel Sachs conducting.

24 JANUARY 1991

Piano Concerto by the 75-year-old American composer George PERLE is premiered in San Francisco by the San Francisco Symphony, David Zinman conducting, Richard Goode soloist.

9 FEBRUARY 1991

World's Turning for orchestra by the 44-year-old American composer Peter LIEBERSON, an evocation of the seasons of the year, is premiered in San Francisco by the San Francisco Symphony, Herbert Blomstedt conducting.

10 FEBRUARY 1991

The Widening Gyre for orchestra by the 63-year-old American composer Wayne PETERSON is performed for the first time in New York.

16 FEBRUARY 1991

Ljodasinfonia (Sound Symphony) for soloists, chorus, and orchestra by the 32-year-old Icelandic composer Hródmar Ingi SIGURBJÖRNSSON is first heard in Reykjavik as part of the final orchestral concert of the week-long Myrkir Musikdagar (Dark Music Days) Festival.

22 FEBRUARY 1991

Atlas, opera by the 48-year-old American composer and vocalist Meredith MONK, in three sections ("Personal Climate," "Night Travel," and "Invisible Night") depicting the misadventures of the fictional explorer Alexandra Daniels (including encounters with spirits from other realms and struggles with personal and societal demons), with textless vocal lines defining situations and reflecting emotions, directed by Monk and Pablo Vela and with orchestration by Wayne Hankins, opens at the Houston Grand Opera.

22 FEBRUARY 1991

On the Verge/Troubadour Songs for string quartet and scordatura electric guitar by the 35-year-old American composer Steven MACKEY, avoiding the obvious rock/classical/electric-acoustic oppositions by placing five equal string instruments into a musical landscape equally foreign to all, is premiered by the Kronos Quartet and the composer as soloist at Stanford University in Stanford, California.

23 FEBRUARY 1991

As Saddam Hussein's forces fired a Scud missile at Israel, just moments before the U.S. deadline for his leaving Kuwait, Zubin Mehta was conducting a performance of the Israeli Philharmonic with the violinist Isaac STERN at the Jerusalem theater. The audience duly donned their gas masks, and the orchestra quickly left the stage. Stern, however, undaunted by the warning of the sirens, returned to the stage and played a saraband for solo violin by Bach. On 25 February 1991 *The New York Times* noted Stern's courage as follows: "An old Jewish custom holds that if a guest at a wedding is stricken or even dies, the service should continue nonetheless to affirm the primacy of life. In the same spirit, Mr. Stern nobly and dramatically affirmed the primacy of art and civilization, even as distant cannons thundered and missiles cut a frightening path through the sky."

28 FEBRUARY 1991

Symphony No. 3 by the 52-year-old American composer John HARBISON is performed for the first time in Baltimore.

10 MARCH 1991

Elie SIEGMEISTER, American composer who wrote music glorifying the mass movement of the people and who became a musical spokesman for a new America, dies of a brain tumor in Manhasset, Long Island, at the age of 82.

18 MARCH 1991

A special 90th birthday tribute to the Viennese-born American composer Ernst KRENEK entitled "Entarte Musik" is given in Los Angeles in conjunction with exhibits at the Los Angeles County Museum of Art and the Los Angeles Philharmonic's Dorothy Chandler Pavilion with the following program: *Arc of Life* (1981), *Durch die Nacht* (1931), *The Dissembler* (1979), and *Kleine Symphonie* (1928).

19 MARCH 1991

The Death of Klinghoffer, opera by the 44-year-old American composer John ADAMS, in collaboration with librettist Alice Goodman, stage director Peter Sellars, and choreographer Mark Morris, and cocommissioned by Brussels, Lyons, Brooklyn, Los Angeles, San Francisco, and Glyndebourne, in two dramatically uneven, 80-minute acts relating the October 1985 seizure of the Italian cruise ship *Achille Lauro* by four Palestinian terrorists and the scandalously senseless murder of the pathetic, wheelchairbound American Jew of the title, all sonically bathed in Adams's inimitable neo-Romantic, post-Minimalist music, electrically infused with electronic instruments and amplification throughout, is staged for the first time in Brussels.

20 MARCH 1991

The USSR Radio-Television Concert Orchestra gives the first concert in its history of works devoted entirely to a living American composer, the 65-year-old Kirke MECHEM, in a program that includes his overture *The Jayhawk* and *Symphonies Nos. 1* and *2,* conducted by the American conductor Corrick Brown and performed in the historic Hall of Columns, simultaneously broadcast throughout the USSR.

27 MARCH 1991

Pega esta nêga . . . a chêra (Hold this blackie . . . and smell her) for flute and piano by the 37-year-old Brazilian composer Paulo Costa LIMA, based on a folksong from the San Francisco River, is heard for the first time at the Reitoria of the Federal University of Bahía in Salvador, Bahía.

6 APRIL 1991

Symphony No. 3 by the 62-year-old American composer James DREW is performed for the first time in Providence, Rhode Island, Andrew Massey conducting.

11 APRIL 1991

Byzantium for vocal soloist and orchestra by the 86-year-old English composer Sir Michael TIPPETT, its text drawn from Yeats, is performed for the first time in Chicago.

14 APRIL 1991

Frederick Douglass, three-act opera completed in 1983 by the 74-year-old American composer Ulysses KAY, to a fictionalized libretto concerning the post-Civil War activities of the former slave-turned-abolitionist/ activity and lecturer, incorporating music from the period as well as Haitian folk songs, is staged for the first time by the New Jersey State Opera in Newark.

23 APRIL 1991

Julia, chamber opera for 11 voices and 14 instruments by the 59-year-old Swiss composer Rudolf KELTERBORN, in which the setting of Shakespeare's *Romeo and Juliet* is changed to the West Jordan region and its essential conflict made an Israeli-Palestinian dispute, is staged for the first time in Zürich.

28 APRIL 1991

Haiku for violin, cello, and chamber orchestra by the 26-year-old American composer Augusta Read THOMAS, a five-movement concerto based on Haiku by Basho, each movement corresponding to a different Haiku but sharing certain core musical materials exposed in the first movement, *Skylark on Moor*, is performed for the first time in New York.

28 APRIL 1991

Slobberin' Goblins for chamber ensemble by the 43-year-old American composer Donald GRANTHAM, a "malevolent little scherzo based on a dream about three small children who refused to chew with their mouths closed," receives its first ever performance in New York.

5 MAY 1991

A Centennial Day Gala performance celebrating the 100th anniversary of Carnegie Hall, New York's famed concert stage that steered the course of literally countless musical careers, among them Benny Goodman, the Beatles, Isaac Stern, Frank Sinatra, Van Cliburn, Edith Piaf, Billie Holiday, and Judy Garland, as well as numerous orators, suffragettes, and political and religious activists, is given in New York by the New York Philharmonic jointly conducted by Zubin Mehta and James Levine, in two consecutive programs:

An afternoon performance, featuring solo artists Placido Domingo, the Empire Brass, Marilyn Horne, Midori, Jessye Norman, Samuel Ramey, Mstislav Rostropovich, and Pinchas Zukerman, in the following program: *Third Fanfare for the Uncommon Woman* by Joan TOWER; *Egmont Overture*, op. 84, by Ludwig van BEETHOVEN; "The Trumpet Shall Sound"

from *Messiah* by George Frideric HANDEL; "Simple Gifts," "Long Time Ago," and "At the River" from *Old American Songs*, arranged by Aaron COPLAND; "Quando le sere al placido" from *Luisa Miller* by Giuseppe VERDI; "Dich, teure Halle" from *Tannhäuser* by Richard WAGNER; "Allegro maestoso" from *Sinfonia Concertante in E-flat Major*, K. 364, by Wolfgang Amadeus MOZART; and *Till Eulenspiegel's Merry Pranks*, op. 28, by Richard STRAUSS.

An evening concert featuring solo artists Alfred Brendel, Yo-Yo Ma, Leontyne Price, Isaac Stern, and the New York Choral Artists, Joseph Flummerfelt, director, in the following program: *Fanfare for the Common Man* by Aaron COPLAND; *Fantasia in C minor for Piano, Chorus, and Orchestra*, op. 80, by Ludwig van BEETHOVEN; "Allegro" from *Concerto in A minor for Violin, Cello, and Orchestra*, op. 102, by Johannes BRAHMS; "Zweite Brautnacht" from *Die ägyptische Helena* by Richard STRAUSS; and "Langsam, Ruhevoll, Empfunden" from *Symphony No. 3* by Gustav MAHLER, this performance dedicated to the memory of Leonard Bernstein.

8 MAY 1991

Rudolf SERKIN, Austrian-born American pianist, performer, and eminent teacher, dies in his American residence in Guilford, Vermont, at the age of 88.

15 MAY 1991

Requiem für Rilke for tenor and orchestra by the 65-year-old Austrian composer Friedrich CERHA, drawn from his 1986 opera *Der Rattenfänger*, is premiered in Vienna.

16 MAY 1991

Concerto for orchestra by the 52-year-old American composer Joan TOWER is premiered by the St. Louis Symphony, Leonard Slatkin conducting.

17 MAY 1991

The Wayward Barstow: Eight Hitchhiker Inscriptions from a Highway Railing at Barstow, California (1941; rev. 1954), stage work depicting the Depression years of a hobo by the iconoclastic American composer Harry PARTCH (1901–1974), directed by Tom O'Horgan and performed by Dean Drummond and Newband, is realized in its first fully staged production on Partch's original instruments in New York.

20 MAY 1991

Capriccio for two horns and strings by the 48-year-old English composer David MATTHEWS, composed for the 70th anniversary of the birth of the *sui generis* English horn player Dennis Brain, whose life was cut tragically short at the age of 36 in an automobile accident in 1957, is premiered in London.

23 MAY 1991

Wilhelm KEMPFF, masterful representative of the gradually waning German school of piano playing, after suffering hopelessly and helplessly of the debilitating Parkinson's disease that made it impossible for him to play the piano, terminating his grand career, which included a remarkably late American concert tour that he undertook nearing his septuagenerian turn of life, dies in Positano, Italy, at the age of 95.

28 MAY 1991

Van Gogh Video Opera by the American composer Michael GORDON, in which the painter is schizophrenically portrayed by three singers against a backdrop of twenty-four video monitors, accompanied by a chamber ensemble and raucous rock band, is performed for the first time in New York.

30 MAY 1991

Gawain, opera in two acts by the 56-year-old English composer Sir Harrison BIRTWISTLE, to a "poetic libretto" by David Harsent based on an anonymous 14th-century poem about the supernatural encounter of Gawain and the Green Knight, symbolic of the opposition of Christianity and pagan sorcery, is heard for the first time in London.

1 JUNE 1991

Ojai Festival Overture by the 56-year-old English modernist composer Peter Maxwell DAVIES is premiered by the Scottish Chamber Orchestra in Ojai, California.

9 JUNE 1991

Claudio ARRAU, Chilean-born but German-trained master pianist who gave his first public concert at the age of five and who was trained by Martin Krause, a pupil of Franz Liszt, and whose authentic renditions of Beethoven's music were legendary and who spent decades in the U.S. before becoming a citizen in 1979, dies in the Austrian city of Mürzzuschlag, past the supremely artistic age of 88.

21 JUNE 1991

Symphony No. 4 by the 58-year-old Irish composer Seóirse BODLEY is performed for the first time in Parma, Italy.

28 JUNE 1991

Joy for orchestra, the third work in an orchestral trilogy that also includes *Kinetics* and *Marea*, by the Finnish composer Magnus LINDBERG is heard for the first time in Porvoo, Finland, one day after his 33rd birthday, Jukka-Pekka Saraste conducting.

28 JUNE 1991

Liverpool Oratorio for soprano, tenor, chorus, cathedral boys' chorus, and orchestra by the 49-year-old ex-Beatle Paul MCCARTNEY, composed in collaboration with the 55-year-old American-born English conductor and film composer Carl DAVIS, receives its first ever performance in Liverpool.

7 JULY 1991

Ubu Rex, opera by the eminent 58-year-old Polish composer Krzysztof PENDERECKI, its libretto an adapted version of Alfred Jarry's 1896 proto-Surrealist play *Ubu Roi*, in two one-hour-long acts incorporating quotations from the composer's earlier sacred works, receives its first mounting by the Bavarian State Opera at the Munich Opera Festival, Michael Boder conducting.

7 JULY 1991

Riket är ditt (*Thine Is the Kingdom*), comic chamber opera by the 33-year-old Swedish composer Jonas FORSSELL, after the stage play by Kim Procopé about a Chilean refugee family hidden from Swedish police by nuns in a convent, in three acts and twelve scenes each dedicated to one of the apostles, a mélange of tragedy and farce and the sacred and the profane, is premiered in Vadstena, Sweden.

11 JULY 1991

Composer-to-Composer, an international gathering of composers founded by Charles Amirkhanian and John Lifton and presented by the Telluride Institute, with resident composers Aleanor ALBERGA, Louis ANDRIESSEN, Paul DRESHER, Janice GITECK, Fred HO, Alan HOVHANESS, Zakir HUSSAIN, Alicia TERZIAN, G. S. SACHDEV, Pamela Z, and Tom ZÉ, culminates a week of private sessions with its fourth four-day festival of public concerts, panel discussions, and a film/video presentation in the historic Sheridan Opera House in Telluride, Colorado.

19 JULY 1991

Summer Lightning for orchestra by the 63-year-old American composer Jacob DRUCKMAN is heard for the first time at the Tanglewood Music Festival in Lenox, Massachusetts.

3 AUGUST 1991

Music, Untangled in Distant Woods for orchestra, commissioned for the 50th anniversary of the Tanglewood Music Center, by the 37-year-old Scottish composer Judith WEIR, is first heard in Tanglewood, Massachusetts.

7 AUGUST 1991

Violin Concerto, composed in 1978 by the 68-year-old English-born American composer Raymond WILD-ING-WHITE, comprised of a series of cadenzas, each accompanied by a different instrumental choir, one including a toy piano and one (for violin and percussion) requiring the concertmaster to roll a pair of dice across the stage à la John Cage, is premiered by the Grant Park Symphony in Chicago, Eugene Gratovich soloist.

7 AUGUST 1991

An Alice Symphony by the 54-year-old American composer David DEL TREDICI—incorporating his *Speak Gently/Speak Roughly*, *The Lobster Quadrille*, *'Tis the Voice of the Sluggard*, *Who Stole the Tarts?*, and *Dream Conclusion*—is given its first complete performance at the Tanglewood Music Festival in Lenox, Massachusetts.

15 AUGUST 1991

O Vôo do Colibrî (*The Flight of the Colibrî*) for instrumental ensemble by the eminent Brazilian composer Lindembergue CARDOSO (1939–1989), dedicated to Felipe Silvestre, receives its second ever performance at the Reitoria of the Federal University of Bahía in Salvador, Bahía.

27 AUGUST 1991

Concerto for Cello and Orchestra by the 59-year-old Russian composer Sofia GUBAIDULINA is premiered at the Helsinki Festival.

30 AUGUST 1991

Malin, subtitled *The Doors of History Open Wide,* opera by the 70-year-old Swedish composer Torsten NILSSON, to an archeologist's libretto recounting a museum tour that entices a young girl's imagination to recreate historical Swedish environments from the bronze age to the medieval period as she moves from site to site, with the orchestra augmented by ancient percussion instruments, is staged in its entirety for the first time at the Historical Museum on Narvavägen in Stockholm.

4 SEPTEMBER 1991

Concerto for Piano and Orchestra by the 33-year-old Finnish composer Magnus LINDBERG is premiered at the Helsinki Festival, Paul Crossley soloist.

8 SEPTEMBER 1991

Alex NORTH, American composer of remarkably effective musical scores for dramatic movie and television productions, who developed a technique of composition far beyond the common Hollywood manner, dies in Pacific Palisades, California, at the age of 80.

8 SEPTEMBER 1991

The 65th Festival of the International Society for Contemporary Music in Zürich opens with a performance at the Zürich Opera of *3 × 1 ÷ CH + X* for mezzo-soprano, choir, and twelve percussionists by the 80-year-old Swiss composer Rolf LIEBERMANN. (The work, a commission of the Expert Commission of Music for the "Festival of Four Cultures," was premiered at the Théâtre du Jorat in Mézières [Lausanne] on 26 June 1991.)

11 SEPTEMBER 1991

Berliner Momente II for Orchestra by the 43-year-old Canadian composer Walter BOUDREAU, inspired by the destruction of the Berlin Wall and reunification of Germany, a follow-up to the composer's 1988 *Berliner Momente,* receives its first ever performance by the Toronto Symphony, Günther Herbig conducting.

13 SEPTEMBER 1991

On the second day of the 65th Festival of the International Society for Contemporary Music in Zürich, an opening concert, "Orchestra 1," by the Basler Madrigalisten, Freiburger Vokalensemble, Basel Sinfonietta, and Elektronisches Studio der Musik-Akademie Basel, conducted by Arturo Tamayo, is given in a program of *Erniedrigt - geknechtet - verlassen - verachtet . . .* for solo voices, choir, orchestra, and tapes by the 66-year-old Swiss composer Klaus HUBER, in seven "polytempic" parts in which the simultaneous use of different languages, setting texts by Ernesto Cardenal, Florian Knobloch, Carolina Maria de Jesus, and George Jackson, as well as the spatial disposition of the performers, suggests cultural and social identity, all set in a complex score in which extreme collisions of dynamics indicates the direction of the music as a "Passion of the exploited, oppressed people of our time."

14 SEPTEMBER 1991

On the third day of the 65th Festival of the International Society for Contemporary Music in Zürich, three concerts are given in the following sequence:

An early evening concert of chamber works, "Chamber Music I," in the following program: *Trois airs de Genji Monogatari* for soprano, sho, flute, and koto, inspired by and composed for Yumi Nara, with each of its airs preceded by an atmosphere-provoking instrumental prologue and each air itself divided into four structurally complex parts, by the 84-year-old Japanese composer Yoritsuné MATSUDAIRA; *In Freundschaft* for bassoon, one of several movements of a larger work with the same title, each composed for a different solo instrument, conceived in three layers (horizontal polyphony), by the 63-year-old German composer Karlheinz STOCKHAUSEN; *Warkocz Bereniki (Tress of Berenice)* for capricious solo piano by the 31-year-old Polish composer Jerzy KORNOWICZ; and *Involtura sonora* for bassoon and cello, conceived as a confrontation between and among three characterized musical structures connected by pedal points, by the 42-year-old Argentine composer José Luis CAMPANA.

An evening orchestral concert, "Orchestra 2," performed by the Radio Orchestra Cracow, with Stefan Kamasa, solo violist, conducted by Räto Tschupp and James Wood, in the following program: *Einklang,* op. 1 (second version 1988/89; rev. 1990/91) by the 28-year-old German composer Tobias P. M. SCHNEID; *Concerto per viola ed orchestra,* in one movement distinguished by four large cadenzas, by the 57-year-old Polish composer Krzysztof PENDERECKI; *Oreion* by the 38-year-old English composer James WOOD; and *Queensland Music* by the 57-year-old Slovenian composer Lojze LEBIĆ, in four parts, composed ". . . as a result of the noble cooperation between Sound Australian and the Union of Yugoslav Composers."

A late-night concert, "Nocturne I," with the following program: *Two Choral Songs to Enzensberger* ("Prozession" and "Mund") by the 56-year-old Danish composer Bent LORENTZEN; *Les Adieux* for piano, rigorously structured as a pitch-time cycle, by the 64-year-old Dutch composer Ton de LEEUW; *Advent* for choir with soprano and alto solos (1959), with texts drawn from the Old and New Testaments and the Apocrypha, by the 52-year-old Swiss composer and oboist Heinz HOLLIGER; and *Reclaimed Prefu II* for two pianos and choir, based on J. S. Bach's "1st Prelude and Fugue" from *The Well-Tempered Clavier* enhanced by traditional ornamentation techniques of Chinese folk music, its fugal section distinguished by a superimposed text by the classical Chinese poet Su-Shi, by the Chinese-born Australian composer Julian J. YU.

15 SEPTEMBER 1991

On the fourth day of the 65th Festival of the International Society for Contemporary Music in Boswil, Switzerland, three concerts are given in the following sequence:

A morning chamber concert, "Concert"* with the following program: *Petra,* variations for two pianos, by the 48-year-old American composer Maryanne AMACHER; *String Quartet,* "travelogue" in five continuous parts, by the 37-year-old English composer Benedict MASON; *Projection* for cello and piano, composed in 1967 as part of a series of pieces with the same title, by the 62-year-old Japanese composer Joji YUASA; and *Grand Duet* for cello and piano by the 72-year-old Russian composer Galina USTVOLSKAYA. (*Although this concert followed the design and general content of the preceding and succeeding programs of chamber music, its title was not the sequentially proper "Chamber Music II," but simply "Concert," by request of one of its featured composers, Galina USTVOLSKAYA, who claims her music is "never chamber music.")

An afternoon concert of chamber works, "Chamber Music III," with the following program: *Huítzitl* for soprano Ganassi recorder by the 27-year-old Mexican composer Gabriela ORTIZ-TORRES, written for Horacio Franco, its title the Aztec word for "hummingbird"; *Celliphonia* for cello and tape, in which ". . . the laws of acoustics, psychoacoustics, and electroacoustics . . . govern both micro and macro-form," by the 42-year-old Rumanian composer Calin IOACHIMESCU; *Time and the Bell* for percussion and live electronics by the 41-year-old Danish composer Ivar FROUNBERG, originally commissioned by the Lerchenborg Music Days 1990 and premiered at Lerchenborg Castle by percussionist Gert Sorenson, to whom it was dedicated, on 5 August 1990; *Szenen (Jelentek)* for two flutes in five movements by the 36-year-old Hungarian composer József SÁRI; and *Amitayus Buddha: String Quartet No. 2*, in five movements extolling the virtues of Korean burial rites, by the 46-year-old South Korean composer Manbang YI.

An early concert of chamber works, "Chamber Music IV," with the following program: *Prognostication* for flute, two violins, double-bass, and piano by the 28-year-old Japanese composer Noriko HISADA; *GEHEN, fragment* (1989) for clarinet, violin, and cello, one in a series of instrumental pieces that refer programmatically to a text of the same name by Thomas Bernhard, by the 38-year-old Swiss composer Thomas MÜLLER; *Voodoo Child* for soprano and seven instruments, setting two stanzas from Sappho's "To a Young Girl," by the 25-year-old Australian composer Liza LIM; *A même les échos I* for "furiously virtuosic" solo violin by the 33-year-old Finnish composer Kimmo HAKOLA; *Dämmerung, Musica per Sette* (flute, alto saxophone, trumpet, trombone, violin, cello, and percussion) by the 30-year-old Argentine composer Pedro PALACIO; and *And So Becomes the Water* for flute, clarinet, violin, cello, piano, and percussion by the 46-year-old Japanese composer Masao ENDO.

16 SEPTEMBER 1991

On the fifth day of the 65th Festival of the International Society for Contemporary Music in Zürich, three concerts are given in the following sequence:

An early evening concert of chamber works, "Chamber Music V," with the following program: *Das Narrenschiff* for soprano, two clarinets, and percussion, setting ten short comments from "Das Narrenschiff" ("The Nave of the Lunatics") by the 15th-century Strasbourg humanist Sebastian Brant, by the 37-year-old French composer Thierry LANCINO; *Le modelle di Delacroix* for cello, overlaying semitones and quarter-tones with micro-intervals through the use of a double bow (a technique developed by Frances-Marie Uitti, to whom the work is dedicated) by the 41-year-old Italian composer Arduino GOTTARDO; *Space* for flute, clarinet, and piano by the 22-year-old Korean composer Shinwoo LEE; *Io* for cello by the 30-year-old Spanish composer Jesús RUEDA, utilizing microtones and glissandi on all four strings, its title that of one of Jupiter's moons discovered by Galileo Galilei; *Estranging* for flute and clarinet by the 44-year-old Italian composer Fernando SILEONI; and *Verstörung* for bass clarinet, cello, and piano by the 34-year-old English composer James CLARKE, its title taken from the 1974 novel by Thomas Bernhard.

An evening orchestral concert, "Orchestra 3," with the following program: *Signos para cuerdas* by the 48-year-old Swiss composer Fritz VOEGELIN; *Cooperation* for eight Japanese and eight Western instrumentalists, each of whom, initially paired across cultures, appears once as a soloist, by the 59-year-old Japanese composer Makota SHINOHARA; and *Jahreszeiten*, op. 12, for piano and small orchestra in four seasonal movements by the 41-year-old Swiss composer Christoph DELZ.

A late-night performance, "Nocturne II," of *Antiphony X (Winded)* for solo organist and eight-channel tape, the latest in a series of ten completed works of the same name, each exploring the interactive potentials between electroacoustic sounds and live performers, by the 65-year-old American composer Kenneth GABURO.

16 SEPTEMBER 1991

Oboe Concerto by the 73-year-old Korean-born German-resident composer Isang YUN is premiered in Berlin, Heinz Holliger soloist and Dennis Russell Davies conducting.

17 SEPTEMBER 1991

On the sixth day of the 65th Festival of the International Society for Contemporary Music in Zürich, two concerts are given in the following sequence:

An early evening concert of chamber works, "Chamber Music VI," with the following program: *Shiver* for mezzosoprano and eight instrumentalists, a setting of one of Pietro Aretino's texts from "Sonetti lussuriosi" (1524), by the 38-year-old Australian composer Gerard BROPHY; *Wirbeltanz* for 11 musicians by the Korean composer Sueyoun HONG; and *Kryptogramm for Nine Musicians* (first movement only) by the 35-year-old German composer Klaus K. HÜBLER. (As the I.S.C.M. catalog notes: "Since Klaus K. Hübler became seriously ill in 1989, the first movement of *Kryptogramm for Nine Musicians* is for the present the end of his activity as a composer.")

An evening concert of chamber works, "Chamber Music VII," with the following program: *2nd String Quartet* by the 65-year-old Austrian composer Friedrich CERHA; *Allegro Sostenuto* for clarinet, cello, and piano, commissioned by clarinetist Eduard Brunner who, with Walter Grimmer and Gerhard Oppitz, performed its Cologne première, by the 55-year-old German composer Helmut LACHENMANN; *Onda di ghiaccio* for 16 instruments, embodying fractal mathematics, by the 34-year-old Norwegian composer Rolf WALLIN; *String Quartet* by the 41-year-old Azerbaijanian composer Frangis ALI-SADE; and *. . . ancora viva tra le sue rovine* for mezzo-soprano, seven instruments, and live electronics, with a text by the Italian poet Mario Luzi and loosely inspired by informal conversations with the semiologist Gino Stefani, by the 30-year-old Italian composer Paolo RIMOLDI.

18 SEPTEMBER 1991

On the seventh day of the 65th Festival of the International Society for Contemporary Music in Winterthur, Switzerland, two concerts are given, in the following sequence:

An afternoon concert of chamber works, "Chamber Music VIII," with the following program: *Noun*, "fretwork cycle" for guitar solo by the 37-year-old Finnish composer Harri SUILAMO; *Herzuhr* for speaker, female voice, and percussion, with a text derived from Heiner Müller's "Hamletmaschine" and its music the sounds ("noises") of children's mechanical toys, by the 36-year-old South Korean composer Song-On CHO; *Sonant* for guitar, harp, double-bass, and membranophones in ten formally malleable movements, played without pause, by the 59-year-old Argentinian-born German composer Mauricio KAGEL; DER SCHLAF, "montage of heterogenous acoustical sketches" for tape and dancer by the 56-year-old German composer Georg KATZER; *Sicher sein . . .* for speaker and tape, its title derived from the advertising slogan of the morally questionable Swiss Bank Corporation, "Sicher sein, Bankverein," by the 44-year-old Swiss composer Max E. KELLER; and *Lost and Found,* "a performance" in which a percussionist plays only his own body while reciting a letter written to his parents by an American soldier eventually killed during the Vietnam War, by the 53-year-old American composer Frederic RZEWSKI.

An evening orchestral concert, "Orchestra 4," by the Stadtorchester Winterthur with Veit Scholz, solo bassoonist, conducted by Mark-Andreas Schlingensiepen, with the following program: *Maharal Dreaming,* free orchestral fantasy based on the composer's opera *Golem,* by the 42-year-old English composer John CASKEN; *Le isole* for orchestra in five stereophonically arranged groups, three with percussion, one of violins, and one of strings by the 36-year-old Japanese composer Tomoyuki HISATOME; and *Concerto for Bassoon and Orchestra,* op. 49, in three sections exploring acoustic and architectural phenomena, by the 37-year-old Rumanian composer Liviu DANCEANU.

19 SEPTEMBER 1991

On the eighth day of the 65th Festival of the International Society for Contemporary Music in Zürich, four concerts are given, in the following sequence:

An early afternoon concert of chamber works, "Chamber Music IX," featuring two works for string quartet by Spanish composers: *El silencio va más deprisa al revés* by 29-year-old César CAMARERO, a selection of the 1990 Gaudeamus Young Composers' Competition and revised for this concert, and *Extracto* (new version), in twelve continuous sections, by 33-year-old Enrique X. MACÍAS.

An early evening concert of chamber works, "Chamber Music X," with the following program: *Arsenic and Old Lace* for harpsichord and string quartet by the 43-year-old Finnish composer Jukka TIENSUU; *Novars,* electro-acoustic or acousmatic music, "dedicated to 'Musique Concrète' and to Pierre Schaeffer, its *unfortunate inventor*," by the 65-year-old French-born Canadian composer Francis DHOMONT; and *Ring Shades* for percussionist and taped stereo electronic music by the Chinese composer Kwok-Ping John CHEN.

An evening concert of chamber works, "Chamber Music XI," with the following program: *The Snake Pit* for clarinet, viola, cello, and piano/harpsichord, making unprogrammatic reference to the 1948 film of the same name, by the 31-year-old Australian composer Stephen CRONIN; *Ombra* for English horn by the 57-year-old Swiss composer Heinz MARTI; *Nada superflue/floue,* opera fragment for displaced female voice and piano by the 53-year-old Swiss composer Rainer BOESCH; *AA-GA I* for cello, the Chinese ideograms of its title loosely equating to "veneration in song," by the 46-year-old South Korean composer Younghi PAGH-PAAN; *Klavierstück II* for two pianos, minimalistically concerned with the playing of a single tone after its opening, afterthought prelude, by the 34-year-old Swiss composer Martin WEHRLI; and *Madam He* for soprano, oboe, cello, and piano by the 29-year-old Australian composer Mary FINSTERER, the title being a fusion of "She" and "He" from the two-character radio play "Radio I" by Samuel Beckett.

A late-night concert, "Nocturne III," with the following program: *Troïte* for clarinet, percussion, and piano, its musical "discourse . . . developed with a slow and permanent variation of motives reminiscent of archaic Rumanian folklore," by

the 40-year-old Rumanian composer Doïna ROTARU; *Trakl-Fragmente* for mezzo-soprano and piano by the 41-year-old German composer Manfred TROJAHN; *Hölderlin-Fragmente,* "unborn song cycle" for mezzo-soprano and piano by the 39-year-old German composer Wolfgang RIHM; and *Trakl-Fragmente* for mezzo-soprano, bass, and two pianists by the 39-year-old Swiss composer Alfons Karl ZWICKER.

20 SEPTEMBER 1991

On the ninth day of the 65th Festival of the International Society for Contemporary Music in Zürich, two concerts are given, in the following sequence:

An evening concert of orchestral works, "Orchestra 5," with the following program: *Neumas: como un concierto de cámara* for chamber orchestra by the 34-year-old Mexican composer Ignacio BACA-LOBERA; *Polyphony* for string quartet and string quintet by the 25-year-old South Korean composer Young Sug CHANG; *Sinfonia concertante: A Mozartean Episode* for chamber orchestra and computer-music narrative, its text derived from ten letters written by Mozart to his father during the period 22 November 1777–9 July 1778 by the 61-year-old American composer Larry AUSTIN; *Scroscio* for ten instruments by the 27-year-old Finnish composer Veli-Matti PUUMALA; and *Second Symphony* for 13 string instruments (1984), commissioned by Elzbeta and Krzysztof Penderecki, by the prematurely deceased Polish composer Andrzej KRZANOWSKI (1951–1990).

A late-night performance, "Tage für Neue Musik Zürich I" (an independent but integrated and complementary part of the World Music Days 91), by the 60-year-old American composer Alvin LUCIER, in which the composer as performer makes "the inaudible audible" through electronic projection of his brain waves.

21 SEPTEMBER 1991

On the tenth day of the 65th Festival of the International Society for Contemporary Music in Zürich, two concerts are given, in the following sequence:

A six-hour marathon of Swiss folk music presented by curator Brigitte Bachmann-Geiser at the Kornhaus Burgdorf, located twenty kilometers north of the Swiss capital Berne, inhabited by some 1,600 people and being distinguished by its new center for folk music and national/traditional costumes of Switzerland.

An evening concert of theater music, "Tage für Neue Musik Zürich II," with the following program: *schlag-ZEITschlag* for four players and *Nouvelles chansons violées pour une violiniste chantante* by the 55-year-old Swiss composer Jürg WYTTENBACH; *Le rire physiologique* for baritone and piano (1982), a "kagelesc parable about the drama of the oppressed musician," with a text adapted from Raymond Devos, and *Fidélité* for harp (1982), dedicated to Brigitte Sylvestre, by the 45-year-old Greek-born French composer Georges APERGHIS; and *Présentation fürzwei* from *Quatre degrés* "scenic work" for speaker/baritone and pianist in which the piano "plays the part of a defective 'music box' as a source of incessant sound" and the speaker that of a street hawker or cabaret announcer, by the 59-year-old Argentinian-born German composer Mauricio KAGEL.

21 SEPTEMBER 1991

Awakenings for chamber ensemble by the 44-year-old American composer-vocalist Joan LA BARBARA is performed for the first time as part of the 25th anniversary celebration of the Center for New Music at the University of Iowa.

22 SEPTEMBER 1991

On the eleventh day of the 65th Festival of the International Society for Contemporary Music in Zürich, three concerts are given, in the following sequence:

A morning concert of chamber works, "Chamber Music XII," with the following two-part program: I: a series of works for two quarter-tone pianos: *Intégrations,* op. 67 (1967) and *Prélude No. 5* from *24 Préludes dans tous les tons de l'échelle chromatique diatonisée à 13 sons,* op. 22 (1934; rev. 1960s) by the Russian master composer of microtonal music Ivan WYSCHNEGRADSKY (1893–1979); *4 Arabesques* by the 33-year-old Swiss composer Dieter JORDI; eight "sketches and curiosities" from *Kabinett mit Vierteltönen* by the 48-year-old Swiss composer Roland MOSER; *Klavierstück III* by the 34-year-old Swiss composer Martin WEHRLI; and *Romanze* by the 59-year-old Czech composer Marek KOPELENT; and, II: a series of chamber works: *Momenti unici* for tenor saxophone, cimbalom, and percussion by the 67-year-old Swiss composer Franz FURRER-MÜNCH; *Redes Cristalinas* for harpsichord, harp, guitar, vibraphone, and marimbaphone, emphasizing sonorous combinations, by the Spanish composer José Manuel LÓPEZ LÓPEZ; and *G.P.P. for 7* by the 42-year-old Polish composer Zbigniew BAGIŃSKI.

An afternoon concert, "Tage füt Neue Musik Zürich III," with the following program: *Mikrophonie I* (1964) for tamtam, two microphones, two filters, and volume faders by the 63-year-old German composer Karlheinz STOCKHAUSEN; *Nemos Orgel* for organ and tape, answering the question as to how Captain Nemo's organ would have sounded onboard the *Nautillus* in Jules Verne's *20,000 Leagues Under the Sea,* by the 52-year-old Ecuadorian composer Mesías MAIGUASHCA; and *Tumbler* for violin, marimbaphone, and computer, based on a short rhythmic phrase that introduces the work and is later extensively developed, by the 40-year-old Argentine composer Alejandro VIÑAO.

An evening orchestral concert, "Orchestra 6," by the Orchestra della Svizzera Italiana and Singkreis der Engadiner Kantorei, conducted by Francis Travis and Ueli Haesler, with the following program: *Recollection* for piano and chamber orchestra utilizing five kinds of figurations and quoting pieces by the Polish composers Serocki, Chopin, and Szymanowski, by the 60-year-old Japanese composer Yori-Aki MATSUDAIRA; *Diafonia—La Creación* for two sopranos and ensemble, loosely inspired in its acrid but ultimately resolving dissonances by a duet for two voices and continuum by Claudio Monteverdi, by the 47-year-old Dutch composer Klaas de VRIES; *Trois Poèmes de Samuel Beckett* for a cappella choir by the 58-year-old Danish composer Pelle GUDMUNDSEN-HOLMGREEN; and *Wirklicher Wald* (1983) for soprano, cello, mixed choir, and orchestra, utilizing texts by Rilke and fragments from the Book of Job (14) in Hebrew, by the 60-year-old Norwegian composer Arne NORDHEIM.

23 SEPTEMBER 1991

On the twelfth day of the 65th Festival of the International Society for Contemporary Music in Zürich, an orchestral concert, "Orchestra 7," is given by Ensemble Modern and London Voices with Aurèle Nicolet, solo flutist, in a performance of *Scardanelli-Zyklus* for flute, mixed choir, orchestra, and tape, to texts by Hölderlin, by the 57-year-old Swiss composer-conductor-oboist Heinz HOLLIGER.

24 SEPTEMBER 1991

Concerto for Piano and Small Orchestra by the 80-year-old Polish composer Stefan KISIELEWSKI, conceived for nonstop pianist providing "figurative background" for soloists from the orchestra, is premiered during the 34th Warsaw Autumn Festival. (Kisielewski spoke of this work as "the greatest agony of my life . . . a kind of sea monster for me, or a nightmare capable of enslaving a man for years." Begun in the spring of 1980, its composition was interrupted by Poland's period of martial law and the composer's general health problems, including surgery. Finally, in early 1990, after learning that he was going blind, Kisielewski took a magnifying glass to a rest home and one year later finished the work. He died in Warsaw just three days after its premiere.)

26 SEPTEMBER 1991

Genesis, cantata in five movements for chorus and orchestra by the 53-year-old American composer Charles WUORINEN, extolling God the creator with traditional chants woven into modern contrapuntal ecstasy, its middle movement a Vulgate setting of the first Biblical chapter and opening verses of the second followed by an orchestral-only, big-bang fourth movement, is premiered in San Francisco as a joint commission with the Honolulu Symphony and Minnesota Orchestra, Herbert Blomstedt conducting.

27 SEPTEMBER 1991

A Little Travelin Music (The Can Opener) for Orchestra by the 57-year-old Canadian-American composer Sidney HODKINSON, is first heard in Rochester.

2 OCTOBER 1991

Leviathan, lyric-fantastic chamber opera by the 31-year-old German composer Detlev GLANERT after Thornton Wilder's "eviathan," published as one of sixteen plays in his 1928 collection *The Angel That Troubled the Waters,* chronicling a young shipwrecked prince who encounters a mermaid who asks for his soul in return for whatever he wishes and who is devoured by a sea monster when he refuses to trade, is staged for the first time in Hamburg.

4 OCTOBER 1991

KPFA radio in Berkeley, California, dedicates its newly constructed, two-story broadcast facility at 1929 Martin Luther King Jr. Way with a live national satellite broadcast of *Homage to Pacifica* by the 74-year-old American composer Lou HARRISON, a 40-minute work for five soloists, gamelan orchestra, and mixed chorus, with texts on the subject of war by Chief Seattle, Mark Twain, and the composer, commissioned by the Gerbode Foundation of San Francisco. Written in protest of the U.S. invasion of Iraq, the piece is highlighted by a concerto movement for harp solo with gamelan in the style of Handel and two duets for bassoon and "Ptolemy duple," a metallophone built by William Colvig for the occasion. Other works on the inaugural program, produced and narrated by KPFA Music Director Charles Amirkhanian, included a piano performance recorded in 1949, the first year of the station's existence, by the late Henry COWELL,

Grande Rag Brilliant by Gary NOLAND, a 15-minute rag introducing KPFA's new Yamaha Disklavier grand piano, featuring fugues, frozen grace-notes to produce tone clusters, and a lengthy passage in which the music modulates up and down a half-tone each measure ("the turntable change of speed effect"), and *Raga Jai Jai Vanti* (*In Praise of Beauty*), performed by two of the greatest living practitioners of North Indian classical music, G. S. Sachdev (bansuri) and Zakir Hussain (tabla).

5 OCTOBER 1991

The Tiger's Tail for orchestra by the 45-year-old American composer Joelle WALLACH, its title taken from the expression "Catch a tiger by the tail," with music reflecting both the animal's plush, seductive beauty and its dangerous excitement through contrasting soft and loud sonorities, is given its first public performance by the Bay Area Women's Philharmonic in San Francisco, JoAnn Falleta conducting.

6 OCTOBER 1991

Symphony No. 65, op. 428, subtitled *Artstakh*, by the Armenian-American composer Alan HOVHANESS, is premiered as part of an all-Hovhaness concert celebrating the composer's 80th birthday at Carnegie Hall in New York City, the composer conducting.

13 OCTOBER 1991

On the thirteenth and final day of the 65th Festival of the International Society for Contemporary Music in Zürich, an orchestral concert is given by the Tonhalle Orchestra, Christiane Edinger, violinist, Alicja Mounk, conductor, with the following program: *Chronogram* by the 32-year-old Austrian composer Gerhard E. WINKLER, utilizing seven types of sounds from a traditional orchestra (string outbursts, tutti repetitions, brass calls, etc.); *Violin Concerto* in two conciliatory movements by the 44-year-old German composer Peter Michael HAMEL; *Babel* in one movement by the 64-year-old Swiss composer Giuseppe G. ENGLERT; and *Musique pour les soupers du Roi Ubu*, "ballet noir en sept parties et une entrée" for actress and orchestra, a 20-minute work freely adapting the activities of the central character of Alfred Jarry's pre-Surrealistic theater piece, in a musical framework rife with quotations and collage, by the important German composer Bernd Alois ZIMMERMANN (1918–1970).

13 OCTOBER 1991

Black Light for orchestra by the 38-year-old American composer Daniel ASIA and *Piano Concerto No. 2* by the 67-year-old American composer Ezra LADERMAN are premiered by the American Composers Orchestra in New York City.

17 OCTOBER 1991

The Face of the Night, The Heart of the Dark by the 64-year-old American composer Wayne PETERSON, subsequent winner of the 1992 Pulitzer Prize in Music, receives its first ever performance by the San Francisco Symphony, David Zinman conducting.

17 OCTOBER 1991

Wind Canticle, one-movement concerto for clarinet and orchestra by the 50-year-old American composer Stephen ALBERT, is premiered in Philadelphia.

20 OCTOBER 1991

Co—wie Kobalt for double-bass and orchestra by the 42-year-old German composer Gerhard STÄBLER, inspired by the element of its title and by the poem "Agglutinati all'oggi" by the Italian poet Giuseppe Ungaretti (1888–1970), the text of which is transformed over a rhythmic foundation into Morse codes of various durations, the featured double-bass performing unusually high pitches produced by natural and artificial harmonics, is premiered at the Donaueschinger Musiktage Festival, Stefano Scodanibbio soloist, Michael Gielen conducting.

25 OCTOBER 1991

National Park Suite for Orchestra by the 44-year-old American-born Canadian composer Michael HORWOOD, commissioned jointly by six Canadian orchestras and commemorating both U.S. and Canadian national parks as a sequel to his 1986 *Amusement Park Suite*, is first heard in Peterborough, Ontario.

26 OCTOBER 1991

Native Dancers for orchestra by the 61-year-old American composer Eric STOKES is first heard in Anchorage, Alaska.

27 OCTOBER 1991

Sir Andrzej PANUFNIK, greatly esteemed Polish-born composer who left his country in protest against its stubborn Communistic policies and settled in London, where he was in due time honored by the rarely bestowed title of "Sir," dies in London at the age of 77.

2 NOVEMBER 1991

Bacchanterna, opera after Euripides' play *The Bacchae* by the 48-year-old Swedish composer Daniel BÖRTZ, who claims that "all the madness of fundamentalism is contained in the play about the failure of the last great matriarchate," is directed by the Swedish film director Ingmar Bergman in its première performance by the Stockholm Opera.

7 NOVEMBER 1991

Karolju for chorus and orchestra by the 42-year-old American composer Christopher ROUSE is given its first performance in Baltimore.

9 NOVEMBER 1991

Symphony in Waves by the 31-year-old American composer Aaron Jay KERNIS, in five movements, each inspired by a different variety of ocean waves, is heard in its first complete performance in New York, Gerard Schwarz conducting.

10 NOVEMBER 1991

Torquemada (The Great Inquisitor) for baritone, chorus, and instrumental ensemble by the 58-year-old Spanish-born

American composer Leonardo BALADA is premiered in Pittsburgh.

11 NOVEMBER 1991

Mexico City Blues for orchestra by the 56-year-old American Minimalist composer Terry RILEY, commissioned by the Brooklyn Philharmonic Orchestra and the Serge Koussevitzky Music Foundation, receives its first ever performance at the Brooklyn Academy of Music's Opera House in New York, conducted by Dennis Russell Davies.

13 NOVEMBER 1991

El Dorada, symphonic work in two movements (*A Dream of Gold* and *Soledades*), the first a gradual crescendo depicting the destructive probing of the continent brought about by nearly 500 years of gold fever, by the 44-year-old American composer John ADAMS, is premiered in San Francisco, the composer conducting.

14 NOVEMBER 1991

Swords and Plowshares, oratorio for four voices and orchestra, drawn from fourteen texts by ten authors grouped as seven reflecting the horrors of war and seven extolling peace, by the 68-year-old American composer Ned ROREM, is heard for the first time in Boston.

14 NOVEMBER 1991

Tropicalia for orchestra by the 38-year-old Puerto Rican composer Roberto SIERRA is played for the first time by the Milwaukee Symphony for which he is composer-in-residence.

21 NOVEMBER 1991

Concerto Fantastique for orchestra by the 70-year-old American composer Ralph SHAPEY is first performed by the Chicago Symphony Orchestra, the composer conducting in place of an ailing Daniel Barenboim. (This work was later nominated by a jury of musicians for the 1992 Pulitzer Prize in Music. However, in a controversial reversal by the Pulizer Prize board, the award ultimately went to Wayne PETERSON for his symphonic work *The Face of the Night, The Heart of the Dark*.)

1 DECEMBER 1991

Canciones for solo clarinet and small orchestra by the 63-year-old German composer Frank Michael BEYER is given its first ever performance in Berlin.

4 DECEMBER 1991

Double Concerto for Violin, Cello, and Orchestra by the 52-year-old American composer Ellen Taaffe ZWILICH is premiered in Louisville.

7 DECEMBER 1991

Concerto for Clarinet and Orchestra by the 69-year-old German-born American composer Lukas FOSS is premiered in Los Angeles. (Technically speaking, this is Foss's second clarinet concerto. The first, composed in 1941, was later [1944] revised into his *Piano Concerto No. 1*.)

11 DECEMBER 1991

Strathclyde Concerto No. 5 for violin, viola, and orchestra by the 57-year-old English composer Peter Maxwell DAVIES, the fifth of ten proposed *Strathclyde Concertos*, is performed for the first time in Glasgow.

19 DECEMBER 1991

The Ghosts of Versailles, "grand opera buffa" in two acts by the 53-year-old American composer John CORIGLIANO, to a libretto by William Hoffman based on Beaumarchais' play *La Mère coupable* written as a sequel to his *Le barbier de Séville* and *Le mariage de Figaro*, for which Hoffman was called upon by Corigliano "to create a libretto that did not set me in 1792 but in a world of smoke and haze from which I could leap in and out of the past," bringing Beaumarchais himself, Marie Antoinette, Louis XVI, and other French aristocrats of the Revolutionary era back as ghosts to the palace of Versailles where Beaumarchais stages a Figaro opera-within-an-opera meant to court the queen he has phantomly loved for 200 years and which eventually turns into an attempt by Beaumarchais and Figaro to spare her historic fate (the orchestra plays "La Marseillaise" when her head ultimately rolls again), with the music at times teasingly quoting Rossini's and Mozart's famous Figaro treatments, is premiered with Teresa Strata, Marilyn Horne, and Håkan Hagegård at New York's Metropolitan Opera (its first premiere in twenty-five years), James Levine conducting.

23 DECEMBER 1991

Ernst KRENEK, Austrian-born composer of many works of surprising originality who began his kaleidoscopic career with the production of a sensationally successful modernistic opera, *Jonny spielt auf,* and who eventually went to the United States to settle in the subtropical Californian community of Palm Springs, dies there of a respiratory infection at the age of 91.

1992

1 JANUARY 1992

There for guitar and strings (1991) by the 43-year-old English composer Jonathan LLOYD receives its first performance in Aldeburgh.

5 JANUARY 1992

Honey and Rue, song cycle which would become the most widely-performed score by the brilliant 62-year-old German-born American pianist, conductor, and composer André PREVIN (real name Andreas Ludwig Priwin), is heard for the first time in New York, Kathleen Battle soloist, composer conducting.

9 JANUARY 1992

Concerto for the New World for wind quintet, strings, and percussion (1991) by the 53-year-old American composer, pianist, and teacher William Thomas MCKINLEY is heard for the first time in New York.

13 JANUARY 1992

Sueños en España, cantata for mezzo-soprano, tenor, children's chorus, mixed chorus, and orchestra (1991), by the 59-year-old Hungarian-born Israeli composer and teacher André HAJDU is given its first ever performance in Jerusalem.

15 JANUARY 1992

On the occasion of his 32nd birthday, *Second Symphony* by the American composer Aaron Jay KERNIS is performed for the first time in New York.

16 JANUARY 1992

Stèle à la mémoire d'une jeune fille for flute and strings (1991) by the prominent French composer Jean Yves DANIEL-LESUR (real name, Daniel Jean Yves Lesur) is given its first ever performance in Fresnes.

19 JANUARY 1992

Five² for English horn, two clarinets, bass clarinet, and timpani (1991) by the singularly inventive and much beloved 79-year-old American composer, writer, philosopher, and visual artist of ultramodern tendencies John (Milton) CAGE (Jr.) is performed for the first time in Cologne.

20 JANUARY 1992

Nocturnal for flute quartet, piano, double bass, and percussion (1991) by the 58-year-old English composer Justin (Riveagh) CONNOLLY is given its first ever performance in London.

21 JANUARY 1992

The Duenna, or The Double Elopement, opera in three acts to an original libretto by the composer after Sheridan's *The Duenna* (1775), comprised of various intersected amours, mistaken identities, and other embroilments of 18th-century Seville also at work in both Thomas Linley Sr.'s comic opera of the same name (1775) and in Sergei's Prokofiev's *Betrothal in a Convent* (1946), by the eminent Spanish-born English composer Roberto GERHARD (1896–1970) receives its posthumous premiere in Madrid.

22 JANUARY 1992

The American soprano Patricia BROOKS, whose best roles were Gilda, Lucia, Violetta, Massenet's Manon, Sophie, and Mélisande, dies in Mount Kisko, New York, at the tender age of 54.

23 JANUARY 1992

The prodigious 20-year-old American violinist Gil SHAHAM makes his Carnegie Hall recital debut in New York.

27 JANUARY 1992

The eminent Russian composer and pedagogue Boris (Alexandrovich) ARAPOV, whose compositions represented to perfection the evolutionary character of Soviet music, taking their source from the Russian traditions of the previous centuries and making ample use of ethnic materials of the constituent regions of the immense territory of the U.S.S.R., dies in his native St. Petersburg at the seasoned age of 86.

28 JANUARY 1992

Second Piano Concerto (1991) by the eminent 76-year-old American composer, music theorist, and pedagogue George PERLE receives its first ever performance in Columbus, Ohio.

29 JANUARY 1992

Delight of the Muses for orchestra and first performed in Stony Brook, New York (Nov. 9, 1991), by the prominent 53-year-old American composer, pedagogue, pianist, and conductor Charles (Peter) WUORINEN receives is first ever performance as a ballet in New York.

31 JANUARY 1992

The Hungarian writer on music Péter P(ál) VÁRNAI, who, in addition to his writings on contemporary Hungarian music and musicians, wrote authoritatively on Verdi, including *Verdi Magyarországon* (Verdi in Hungary; 1975) and *Verdi-operakalauz* (Verdi's Operas; 1978), dies in his native Budapest at the age of 69.

1 FEBRUARY 1992

The 29-year-old Argentine tenor, conductor, and composer José CURA makes his operatic debut as the Father in a performance of Hans Werner Henze's *Pollicino*, fairy tale for music (1979–80), in Verona.

2 FEBRUARY 1992

Walking Again for piano by the accomplished 44-year-old American nun-turned-composer, pianist, administrator, presenter, and teacher Bernadette (Marie) SPEACH receives in first ever performance in New York.

3 FEBRUARY 1992

Song of Penance for Hyperviola, computer voice, and large chamber ensemble by the noteworthy 38-year-old American cellist, conductor, and composer Tod MACHOVER receives its first performance in Los Angeles.

4 FEBRUARY 1992

The eminent 60-year-old Russian conductor Gennadi (Nikolaievich) ROZHDESTVENSKY, son of the Russian conductor and pedagogue Nikolai Anosov and husband of the Russian pianist Viktoria Postnikova, and who, in 1982, founded and became chief conductor of the State Symphonic Orchestra of the Soviet Ministry of Culture in Moscow, conducts the ensemble at its United States debut in New York.

5 FEBRUARY 1992

Corrente I for chamber orchestra (1991–92) by the 33-year-old Finnish composer Magnus (Gustaf Adolf) LINDBERG is heard for the first time in the composer's native Helsinki.

6 FEBRUARY 1992

Funeral Music for Queen Mary, a transcription and elaboration of music by the great English composer Henry Purcell for wind orchestra, by the 43-year-old American composer, teacher, conductor, and writer on music Steven (Edward) STUCKY is heard for the first time in Los Angeles.

9 FEBRUARY 1992

The admired Hungarian-born American pianist Andor FOLDES (actually, Földes), esteemed for his performances of the Classical and early Romantic masters but who also displayed a special affinity for the music of Bartók, dies in Herrliberg, Switzerland, at the reasonable age of 79.

12 FEBRUARY 1992

The Romanian-American soprano Stella (real name, Florica Vierica Alma Stela Blasu) ROMAN, who was active with the Metropolitan Opera from 1941 to 1950, becoming best known for such roles as Gioconda, Amelia, Leonora in *Il Trovatore*, Desdemona, and Tosca, dies in New York at the well-seasoned age of 87.

14 FEBRUARY 1992

Avoaha for chorus, percussion, and two pianos (1991) by the 77-year-old French composer and pianist Maurice OHANA is performed for the first time in Aix-les-Bains.

15 FEBRUARY 1992

The eminent American composer, music educator, and administrator William (Howard) SCHUMAN, whose music was characterized by great emotional tension, maintained by powerful asymmetric rhythms, his contrapuntal structures works reaching a great degree of complexity and being saturated with dissonance without, however, losing their essential, signature tonal references, dies in his native New York at the ripened age of 81.

16 FEBRUARY 1992

Harbour with Ships (Five Impressions) for brass quintet (1991) by the esteemed 53-year-old English pianist, music educator, and composer John MCCABE is given its first performance in Salford.

18 FEBRUARY 1992

On Buying a Horse for medium voice and piano (1991) by the 37-year-old English composer Judith WEIR receives its first ever performance in Edinburgh.

19 FEBRUARY 1992

Third Symphony, subtitled *Symphony of Sorrows* (1991), by the brilliant 69-year-old German-born American pianist, conductor, and composer Lukas FOSS (real name, Fuchs) is given its premiere performance in Chicago.

20 FEBRUARY 1992

The noted French conductor and teacher Pierre DERVAUX, who, during his tenure as music director of the Orchestre Symphonique de Québec (1968–71), the Orchestre Philharmonique des Pays de la Loire (1971–78), and in Nice (1979–82), became especially admired for his brilliant and colorful interpretations of the French repertoire, dies in Marseilles at the reasonable age of 75.

22 FEBRUARY 1992

The eminent American musicologist Gilbert CHASE, who from 1951 to 1953 was cultural attaché at the American Embassy in Lima, from 1953 to 1955 in Buenos Aires, and from 1958 to 1960 in Belgium, and who, in 1963, organized the first Inter-American Conference on Musicology in Washington, D.C., dies in Chapel Hill, North Carolina, at the ripe age of 85.

24 FEBRUARY 1992

Sur la nappe d'un étang glacé for nine instruments and tape (1991) by the notable 62-year-old Russian composer and teacher Edison DENISOV receives its premiere performance in Paris.

25 FEBRUARY 1992

Kullervo, opera, by the prominent 56-year-old Finnish composer Aulis SALLINEN, receives its first mounting in Los Angeles, with the distinguished Finnish baritone and opera administrator Jorma Hynninen in the title role, conducted by the Finnish conductor Ulf Söderblom.

26 FEBRUARY 1992

Flute Concerto (1991) by the 53-year-old Canadian composer and teacher Jacques (Joseph Robert) HÉTU is heard for the first time in Ottawa.

27 FEBRUARY 1992

Eighth Symphony, subtitled *Indian Sounds,* for tenor or soprano solo vocalise or soprano and alto duet and orchestra (1991), *Cette Blanche Agonie* for soprano and chamber orchestra, after Mallarmé (1988–91), and *Wir tönen allein* for soprano and chamber orchestra, after Celan (1989–91), three works by the compelling 53-year-old American composer Gloria COATES, are heard for the first time in a concert in Dresden.

28 FEBRUARY 1992

Fourteen Variations by Piotr Bikont and Krzysztof Knittel on Fourteen Variations by Edwin Moran on Fourteen Words by John Cage for voices and computers (1986–92) by the 44-year-old Polish composer Krzysztof KNITTEL is performed for the first time in Wrocław.

1 MARCH 1992

Concert Piece for microtonally-tuned viola, flute, clarinet, cello, and small orchestra (1990) by the innovative 64-year-old American composer Ezra SIMS is given its first ever performance in Cambridge, Massachusetts.

2 MARCH 1992

ShamanSong for voice, percussion, and tape by the 44-year-old American composer and experimental vocalist Joan LA BARBARA (Linda, née Lotz), wife of the respected American composer Morton Subotnick, is heard for the first time in Athens.

3 MARCH 1992

Sharp Thorne for four solo voices (1991–92) by the 42-year-old English composer John (Arthur) CASKEN is given its first ever performance in Durham.

6 MARCH 1992

The eminent Hungarian-born Swiss composer and pedagogue Sándor VERESS, who, from 1958 to 1977, taught musicology at the University of Bern, becoming a naturalized Swiss citizen in 1975, dies there at the respectable age of 85.

8 MARCH 1992

Plus II for clarinet and cello by the prominent 43-year-old Finnish harpsichordist, pianist, conductor, teacher, and composer Jukka TIENSUU is given its first performance in the composer's native Helsinki.

9 MARCH 1992

Athanor for ten instruments (1991) by the versatile 56-year-old French composer, musicologist, and philologist François-Bernard MÂCHE is heard for the first time in Brussels.

10 MARCH 1992

The Italian composer and teacher Franco MARGOLA, who, in addition to serving as director of the Messina Conservatory (1938–40), taught at the conservatories in Cagliari, Bologna, Milan, Rome, and Parma, dies in Brescia, not far from his home town of Orzinuovi, at the age of 83.

11 MARCH 1992

Medeamaterial, opera (1991), by the productive 36-year-old French composer Pascal DUSAPIN is first mounted in Brussels.

12 MARCH 1992

Fábula for guitar (1991–92) by the eminent 62-year-old Spanish composer and teacher Luís (Alfonso) de PABLO (Costales) is given its premiere performance in Madrid.

13 MARCH 1992

Adolfo ODNOPOSOFF, Argentine cellist and teacher and brother of the Argentine violinist Ricardo Odnoposoff, and for whom several Latin American composers, including Roque Cordero, Rodolfo Halffter, Eduardo Mata, Floro Ugarte, and Antonio Tauriello, wrote special works, dies in Denton, Texas, at the age of 75.

14 MARCH 1992

Night Prayers, in a version for string quartet and tape, by the notable 56-year-old Georgian composer Giya (Alexandrovich) KANCHELI is performed for the first time in Vienna.

19 MARCH 1992

The Russian mezzo-soprano Nina (Nikolaievna) TERENTIEVA makes her Metropolitan Opera debut in New York singing Eboli, a role she'd previously sung in Los Angeles (1990) and which she later in the year would reprise at the San Francisco Opera.

20 MARCH 1992

Bird Gong Game for improvising soloist and chamber ensemble by the doubly-talented 44-year-old English double bass player and composer Barry (John) GUY is first heard in Glasgow.

21 MARCH 1992

Woodwind Quintet (1965) by the 45-year-old American composer and teacher Bruce (Stuart) SAYLOR is given its first ever performance in Sunnyside, New York.

23 MARCH 1992

Summer 1990, trio for violin, cello, and piano (1990) by the significant, award-winning 73-year-old American composer and teacher George ROCHBERG is first heard in Philadelphia.

24 MARCH 1992

Roái for orchestra (1991) by the eminent 69-year-old Greek-born French composer Iannis XENAKIS is given its first ever performance in Berlin.

26 MARCH 1992

Pocta životu (Homage to Life) for orchestra (1988–89) by the prominent 63-year-old Czech composer, pedagogue, music theorist, and administrator Ctirad KOHOUTEK, brother of the astronomer Luboš Kohoutek, is given its premiere performance in Brno.

27 MARCH 1992

Harald SAEVERUD, prominent Norwegian composer and father of the talented Norwegian composer known as Ketil Hvoslef (real name, Saeverud), and whose music was permeated with characteristically lyrical Scandinavian Romanticism, with Norwegian folk melos as its foundation, dies in Siljustl at the remarkable age of 94.

28 MARCH 1992

The Czech composer Josef MATĚJ , whose early works were characterized by folk-song inflections of the Lachian region of his birth, but after 1960 were inflected with coloristic oriental elements, as well as a discreet use of dodecaphonic techniques, dies in his native Brušperk at the age of 70.

29 MARCH 1992

The Austrian baritone and opera administrator Eberhard WAECHTER, who ended his too-brief career as director of the Vienna Volksoper (from 1987) and as co-director of the Vienna State Opera (from 1991), dies in his native Vienna at the lamentable age of 62.

31 MARCH 1992

Johannes Stein, oder Der Rock des Kaisers, monodrama (1990–91), by the 56-year-old Austrian composer, teacher, and conductor Erich URBANNER is first heard in Vienna.

8 APRIL 1992

Vor dem singenden Odem (alla memoria di Luigi Nono) for flute, clarinet, violin, cello, and piano (1990) by the 35-year-old Italian composer, conductor, teacher, and writer on music Alberto CAPRIOLI is performed for the first time in a newly-revised version in Bologna.

9 APRIL 1992

The Song of Majnun, opera, by the remarkable 36-year-old Chinese composer Bright SHENG, to a libretto by the erudite *New Yorker* magazine music critic Andrew Porter based on an Islamic legend, is first mounted at the Chicago Lyric Opera, where the composer serves as composer-in-residence.

12 APRIL 1992

The Mouse Metamorphosed Into a Maid for voice (1991) by the prominent 59-year-old German-born English composer and teacher (Peter) Alexander GOEHR, son of the German-born English conductor and composer Walter Goehr, is first performed in Columbia, South Carolina.

13 APRIL 1992

Zhizn's idiotom (Life With an Idiot), opera (1990–91), by the respected 57-year-old Russian composer of German descent Alfred (Garrievich) SCHNITTKE is first mounted in Amsterdam.

16 APRIL 1992

The English contralto Alfreda (Rose) HODGSON, whose concert repertoire ranged from Bach to Britten, dies in her native Morecombe at the tender age of 51.

21 APRIL 1992

Hope Chest for chamber quartet (1991) and *Copperhead* for electric quartet of woodwinds, electronics, keyboard, bass, and percussion, two works by the extremely promising 35-year-old American composer Mikel (actually, Michael Joseph) ROUSE, are performed for the first time in New York.

22 APRIL 1992

Tre canzone senza parole for orchestra by the remarkable 58-year-old American composer Bernard RANDS, husband of the talented American composer Augusta Read Thomas, is first performed in Philadelphia.

23 APRIL 1992

Finale e aria for soprano, string quartet, and orchestra (1991) by the 59-year-old Italian composer, teacher, and writer on music Giacomo MANZONI is heard for the first time over Milan's RAI.

24 APRIL 1992

Violin Concerto by the seasoned 53-year-old American composer, pianist, and teacher Joan (Peabody) TOWER is performed for the first time in Salt Lake City.

25 APRIL 1992

Seraphic Games for orchestra by the outstanding 67-year-old American composer Jacob (Raphael) DRUCKMAN is given its premiere performance in Costa Mesa, California.

26 APRIL 1992

Songs Without Voices for eight instruments by the lovable 39-year-old English composer and conductor (Stuart) Oliver KNUSSEN is heard for the first time in New York.

27 APRIL 1992

Olivier (Eugène Prosper Charles) MESSIAEN, outstanding French composer and pedagogue, one of the most original of modern composers, whose music made use of a wide range of resources, from Gregorian chant to oriental rhythms, and who strove to find a relationship between progressions of musical sounds and religious concepts (he was a mystic by nature and a Catholic by religion), dies in Clichy, Hauts-de-Seine, at the age of 83.

29 APRIL 1992

The English composer Stephen (Michael Harding) OLIVER, who early on revealed a special talent for composing dramatic scores, including among his mature works for the stage *La Bella e la bestia* (Batignano, July 26, 1984), *Exposition of a Picture* (London, June 24, 1986),

Mario ed il mago (Batignano, Aug. 5, 1988), and *L'Oca del Cairo* (Batignano, July 30, 1991), dies in London at the lamentable age of 41.

30 APRIL 1992

Double Cello Concerto by the 45-year-old Dutch composer and teacher Tristan KEURIS is heard for the first time in Manchester.

1 MAY 1992

Eye on Genesis II for orchestra by the respected 62-year-old Japanese composer and teacher Jōji YUASA is given its first ever performance in Tokyo.

3 MAY 1992

The Sands, concerto for string quartet and orchestra (1991), by the significant 56-year-old American composer and performer Terry (Mitchell) RILEY is performed in Salzburg as the first-ever new music commission from the Salzburg Festival.

5 MAY 1992

Bartók Variations for string quartet (1989) by the 60-year-old English composer, pianist, and teacher Malcolm (Leyland) LIPKIN is heard for the first time in Newbury.

7 MAY 1992

P'tit Pierre et la Sorcière du placard à balais, children's opera (1991), by the eminent 77-year-old French composer and administrator Marcel (François Paul) LANDOWSKI, great-grandson of celebrated Belgian violinist and composer Henri Vieuxtemps and son of the sculptor Paul Landowski, is mounted for the first time ever in Colmar.

8 MAY 1992

Since Armstrong, piano concerto (1989), by the spirited 41-year-old American composer Libby LARSEN (actually, Elizabeth Brown) is performed for the first time in Minneapolis.

9 MAY 1992

The Canadian composer, music educator, and conductor Keith (Warren) BISSELL, adept at the Orff Schulwerk method who, in addition to his works for professional performance, wrote much music for the young, dies in Newmarket, near Toronto, at the respectable age of 80.

12 MAY 1992

The distinguished English pianist, harpsichordist, and musicologist (Macario) Santiago KASTNER, an authority on Hispanic keyboard music who, in addition to writing several important books, edited works by Portuguese and Spanish composers, dies in Lisbon at the age of 73.

14 MAY 1992

Gitanjali for soprano and small orchestra (1990) by the 58-year-old Canadian composer, writer, and educator R(aymond) Murray SCHAFER is first performed in Ottawa.

15 MAY 1992

The distinguished American music educator and ethnomusicologist Willard RHODES, founding member (1953) and first president (1956–58) of the Society for Ethnomusicology, in which connection he accumulated a most valuable collection of Amerindian folk music, both notated and recorded (many pressings of which were released by the Library of Congress), dies in Sun City, Arizona, just three days after his 91st birthday.

15 MAY 1992

The 66th Festival of the International Society for Contemporary Music in Warsaw opens with two concerts, in the following sequence:

A late afternoon concert at the Royal Castle Ball Room of *5 Songs to Words by Kazimiera IŁłakowiczówna*, for woman's voice and piano (1956–58), by the eminent 79-year-old Polish composer and pedagogue Witold LUTOSŁAWSKI.

An evening orchestral concert performed by the Warsaw National Philharmonic Orchestra and Choir, conducted by Stanisław Skrowaczewski, with special guest artists Ewa Pobłocka, piano, and Elżbieta Towarnicka, soprano, in the following program: *Lumen* for chorus, symphonic orchestra, and Yamaha DX7 synthesizer (1987) by the Polish composer Jacek GRUDZIEŃ; *Für Klara* (1983), piano concerto dedicated to both Clara Schumann and Cara Kaufmann, in three movements: *1. On perishing—and how to fight against it, 2. Stifling in the salon*, and *3. Survival*, by the Austrian composer Dieter KAUFMANN; *Symphony No. 2* for soprano and orchestra (1990/91), in one continuous movement, inspired by the heat and beauty of the Sahara desert, the folk music of Tunisia, and the invasion of Kuwait by Iraq, to texts drawn from John Milton's *Paradise Lost*, by the Icelandic composer John A. SPEIGHT; *Iconography* (1983), a commission from the Southern African Rights Organization in three movements (*Skadubeeld/Silhouette, Ilusie/Illusion*, and *Kinetika/Kinetics*), concluding with an iconoclastic quotation from J.S. Bach's *St. Matthew Passion*, by the South African composer Hans ROOSENSCHOON.

16 MAY 1992

Sunde. Fall. Beil., opera after Dumas' *Catherine Howard* (1990–91), by the prolific German organist, teacher, and composer Gerhard STÄBLER, is mounted for the first time ever in Munich.

16 MAY 1992

On the second day of the 66th Festival of the International Society for Contemporary Music in Warsaw, four concerts are given in the following sequence:

A late morning concert of "mini-operas" for children at the Teatr Wielki (Opera House), Chamber Hall, performed by the Ensemble of the Łódź Opera House, conducted by Aleksander Tracz, in the following program: *Sir Elephant* (1991), to a libretto by Wanda Chotomska, in prologue and five scenes, by the Polish composer Jan OLESZKOWICZ; *The Piano Teacher* (1991), to a libretto by Fer Bank extolling the importance of both piano practice and playing with dolls, by the Dutch composer Jacques BANK; *The Little Match-Girl* (1991), to a libretto after Hans Christian Andersen, the music following in the tradition of the operatic writing of Britten, Orff, and Janáček, by the Russian composers Sergei BANEVICH and Dmitri SMIRNOV; *Kocia wojna* (A Cat Fight) (1991) by the Italian composer Gino MICHELAZZI; and *The Promise* (1991) by the German composer Joschi KRÜGER.

A late afternoon concert at the Centre of Contemporary Art, performed by Vienna's Ensemble 20. Jahrhundert, conducted by Peter Burwik, with special guest artist Jutta Geister, mezzo-soprano, in the following program: *Jappaments à la Lune* for mezzo-soprano and chamber ensemble (1991), setting to music eight poems by the Quebec poet and playwright Claude Gauvreau, by the Canadian composer Christopher BUTTERFIELD; *Fax* for chamber ensemble (1990) by the Spanish composer Jep NUIX; *Panische Walzer 8 & 9* for chamber ensemble (1990) by the German composer Volker HEYN; *Creatoria II* for indeterminate instrumentation (1964 et seq.) by the Polish composer Leoncjusz CIUCIURA; and *Vierzehn mal eins* for chamber ensemble of 14 virtuoso soloists (1991/92) by the Austrian composer Gerd KÜHR, freely based on the horn theme of his earlier composition, *Für Bläserquintett*.

An evening performance at the Teatr Wielki (Opera House), Main Stage, by the Choir and Orchestra of the Łódź Opera House, conducted by Andrzej Straszyński, of *The Devils of Loudun* (1969), opera in three acts by the eminent 58-year-old Polish composer, pedagogue, and conductor Krzysztof PENDERECKI, after the drama by J. Whiting, based on the book of the same name by Aldous Huxley, itself a documentary report on the famous and quite sordid trial of Loudun in central France in the first half of the 17th century.

A late-night performance at the Academy of Music by the pianists Andrzej Dutkiewicz, Szabolcs Esztényi, Eugeniusz Knapik, and Jerzy Witkowski of *Canto Ostinato* (1979) by the Dutch composer Simeon ten HOLT.

17 MAY 1992

On the third day of the 66th Festival of the International Society for Contemporary Music in Warsaw, seven concerts are given in the following sequence:

A mid-day performance at Rynek (Market Square) by the Warsaw Chamber Opera Choir, conducted by Rszard Zimak, of *6 Kurpie Songs* for a cappella mixed chorus (1928–29), one of the most original works of the eminent Polish composer Karol SZYMANOWSKI (1882–1937).

A second mid-day concert, this one at the Royal Castle, Concert Hall, performed the Silesian String Quartet, in the following program: *Second String Quartet* (1990) by the German composer Matthias PINTSCHER and *String Quartet* (1990), in three movements, performed attaca, each based on song fragments— in the first two movements, settings of medieval Spanish romances, and, in the third, a ballad from Banfshire, Scotland— by the 37-year-old English composer Judith WEIR.

A third mid-day concert, this one given in the Meadows around the Royal Castle, of a mixed media celebration of the Kurpie region, including an installation, "The Sounds of Earth," an exhibition of old cinema posters, and a musical folklore film, *The Wedding in the Kurpie Region*, by Mieczysław Adamek, in two parts, *I. Nuptials* (1982/83) and *II. Caping* (1985).

A late afternoon performance at the Old School Church by Adrianna Biedrzyńska, actress, and Edward Kulka, sound engineer, of *Alice...ou la boîte à image* (1988), a story about Alice's world, "full of surprises, madness, humor, and sometimes anxiety," by the French composer Bernard FORT.

A second late-afternoon concert, this one given at the Amphitheatre, performed by the Kraków Percussion Group, with guest artists Issy Rudnik, trombone, Jan Pilch and Sławomir Berny, percussion, and Theodore Anzelotti, accordion, in the following program: *Earth Will Have Her Say...or...*

Say What? for trombone, percussion, and tape (1990) by the American composer Diego MINCIACCHI; *Molto Semplicemente* for accordion (1988/89) by the Swiss composer Daniel OTT; and *Stoneware: Ritual for the exorcism of evil spirits* for six percussionists (1990) by the Norwegian composer Rolf WALLIN.

An early evening concert at the Collegiate Basilica, performed by Andrzej Chrosiński, organ, Aleksander Szebeszczyk, horn, Robert Duda, horn, Krzysztof Specjał, horn, Tadeusz Boniecki, horn, Zbigniew Koźlik, accordion, and Tadeusz Wielecki, double-bass, in the following program: *In nomine lucis V* for organ (1974) by the remarkable Italian composer Giacinto SCELSI (1905–1988), dedicated to Franco Evangelistic, a close friend to the composer and co-founder of the Nuova Consonanza group for contemporary music; *Hörner-Stimmen aus einem unbekannten Requiem* for four horns (1990) by the Romanian composer Dan DEDIU; seven pieces in either canon (strict form) or continuous variation (open form): *Requiem, Dies irae, Tuba mirum, Rex tremendae, Recordare, Confutatis,* and *Lacrimosa, Duo* for accordion and double bass (1987) by the Polish composer Wojciech NOWAK; and *Pari Intervallo* for organ (1976) by the outstanding 56-year-old Estonian-born Austrian composer Arvo PÄRT, comprised of two lines moving in parallel, hence the title.

An evening performance at the Rynek (Market Square), by The Third Year Students of the State High Drama School at Warsaw and the Concert Orchestra of the Polish Army, conducted by Edward Miller and Grzegorz Mielimąka, with special guest artist Mariusz Pędziałek, oboe, directed by Piotr Cieślak, with stage setting by Agnieszka Zawadowska, choreography by Emil Wesołowski, and sound engineering by Edward Kulka and Krzysztof Suchodolski, of *Kanal* (1990), a spatially-arranged, multi-media environment event for solo oboe or clarinet or trumpet, singers, actors, dancer, brass, percussion, and electronic tapes, by the English composer Margaret Lucy WILKINS.

18 MAY 1992

On the fourth day of the 66th Festival of the International Society for Contemporary Music in Warsaw, two concerts are given in the following sequence:

A late afternoon concert at the Academy of Music, performed by the Silesian String Quartet, with special guest artists Louise Bessette, Szabolcx Esztényi, and Jerzy Witkowski, piano, and Piotr Wawreniuk, trombone, in the following program: *Monodías Españolas* for piano (1988) by the Canadian composer José EVANGELISTA, in 18 movements of unequal duration ranging from 20 seconds to three minutes, with melodies (worksongs, ballads, entertainment songs, dances, religious songs, etc.) drawn from different parts of Spain, *Annäherungen an Gegenwart* for string quartet (1986/87) by the Swiss composer Hans WÜTHRICH-MATHEZ; *Labyrinth Promenade II* for trombone (1989) by the Taiwanese composer Hwang-Long PAN, in open form notation wherein its 26 segments are arranged in alphabetical order; *Dwa utwory na kwartet smyczkowy* by the Polish composer Paweł SZYMAŃSKI; and *Prime* for two pianos (1987), a set of six variations, by the Irish composer Ian WILSON.

An evening concert at St. Hyacinth's Church, performed by the Polish Radio Choir and the Silesian Philharmonic Orchestra and Choir, conducted by Wojciech Michniewski, with special guest artists Krzysztof Szmyt, tenor, Jerzy Artysz, baritone, and Beatriz Blanco, mezzo-soprano, in the following program: *Prajña-naya Symphony* for chorus and orchestra (1983) by the Japanese composer Yutaka TAKAHASHI; *Holzwege* for strings (1972) by the Polish composer Tomasz SIKOWSKI, based on an idea expressed in an essay by Martin Heidegger of the same name wherein *Holzwege* is expressed as a symbol of life; *El Patio y la Lluvia, Trio de Pedro Páramo* for child soprano, tenor, baritone, mezzo-soprano, alto, and orchestra, by the Chilean composer Sergio ORTEGA, to texts from *Pedro Páramo*, the first and last novel of the Mexican writer Juan Rulfo; and *Beatus Vir* for baritone, chorus, and orchestra (1979) by the celebrated 58-year-old Polish composer Henryk Mikołaj GÓRECKI, the title referring to both the Saint and the Pope, the text a compilation of different biblical psalms.

19 MAY 1992

On the fifth day of the 66th Festival of the International Society for Contemporary Music in Warsaw, two concerts are given in the following sequence:

A late afternoon concert at the SARP (Association of Polish Architects), Warsaw Department, by Jane's Minstrels Ensemble of Lodon, with Jane Manning, soprano, and special guest artists Krzysztof Wojtyniak, trombone, and Dorota Imiełowska, cello, in the following program: *Muertango* (1989) by the Argentine composer Luis NAÓN; *Poem for the Nations Demise I* for soprano and four instruments (1991), to a text by Tu Mu (803–852) entitled *Bo Chin - Huai (Moorning he Chin-huai River)*, by the Chinese composer Tzzy Sheng LEE; *De Profundis* (1990), cycle of four songs inspired by the poetry of Michelangelo, by the Slovak composer Iris SZEGHY; *Ombre* for bass recorder, bass flute, soprano, and harp (1988), to a text by Rainer Rilke, by the American composer Matthew KIROFF; *Relève d'esquisse* (excerpts) (1964; rev. 1982) by the French composer Michel DECOUST; *Relève d'esquisse* (excerpts) (1964; rev. 1982), and *Sounds* for five vocalists (1983) by the Israeli composer Hagar KADIMA.

An evening performance at the Teatr Wilki (Opera House), Main Stage, by Władysław Wigura, stage setting, David Earle, Ewa Wycichowska, and Barbara Goławka, choreography, and the Polish Dance Theatre (Poznań), in the following program: *Karma* (1991), dramatic stage work scored for a string instrument (i.e. the rebab, scored in graphic notation), wind instruments, oboe, flute, piccolo, percussion, i.e. the tabla, set to syllabic time-cycles named *Karma-talas*), and a gamelan selection, by the English composer Valerie ROSS; *Mournes* (1990), a series of staged litanies based on a five-note figure, by the Argentine composer Osvaldo GOLIJOV; and *Hell Screen* (1989), dance work, by the Chinese composer Man-Yee LAM, inspired by the Japanese writer Ryunosuke Akutagawa and the tragic events in Beijing, June 1989, in two parts, the first filled with tranquility and serenity, and the second with indignation and horror.

20 MAY 1992

On the sixth day of the 66th Festival of the International Society for Contemporary Music in Warsaw, two concerts are given in the following sequence:

A late afternoon concert at the Academy of Music, given by the Camerata Vistula, conducted by Piotr Borkowski, with special guest artists Szabolcs Esztényi, piano, Lucy Wakeford, harp, and Krzysztof Bąkowski, violin, with sound engineering by Krzysztof Suchodolski and Javier Alvarez, in the following program: *Strophes*, partita for piano (1990) by the Russian composer Mikołaj STOMA; *Acuerdos por Diferencia* for harp and computer by the Mexican composer Javier ALVAREZ; *Partita* for piano (1988) by the American composer Diego LUZURIAGA, in four parts: *Toccata 1, Aureum, Fantasia*, and *Toccata 2; Drones* for violin and piano (1991) by the Dutch composer Theo LOEVENDIE, the piano section initially exposing eight pedal tones (drones), which increasingly

overlap, producing bell-like resonances; *Pas Au Delà* for piano (1989) by the English composer Roger REDGATE, its title taken from the book *Octobiography* by Jacques Derrida, a careful reexamination of Nietzsche's autobiography; and *Zalouh* for clarinet, trombone, tuba, piano, and four actors (1971) by the Greek composer Dimitrios DRAGATAKIS, the title a conjoining of two syllables, *Za* and *louh*, united to express screaming, an interjection, agony, etc., taken from the poem of the same title (*Zalouh*) by Toula Tolia.

An evening concert at the Polish Radio Concert Studio S-1, performed by the Łódź Philharmonic Orchestra, conducted by Jorge Antunes and Daniel Gazon, with special guest artist Barbara Górzyńska, violin, with sound engineering by Barbara Okoń-Makowska, in the following program: *Successions* for orchestra by the 57-year-old Korean composer Sukhi KANG, with an often present B-A-C-H sequence; *Attributumok* for orchestra (1990) by the Hungarian composer József SÁRI, paying hidden tribute to those composers from the 15th, 16th, and 20th centuries for whom the construction principle played a significant role; *Skrin*, violin concerto (1990), by the Swedish composers Sven AHLBÄCK and Karin REHNQVIST, in three parts: *1. skrin* (double meaning of *shriek* and *box*), *2. koral* (*Chorale*), and *3. grovt och grant* (*rough/coarse and fine* or simply *low and high*); *Pequeñas* (1990), eight pieces for varying instrumental ensembles, by the Uruguay composer Alvaro CARLEVARO; *Idiosynchronie* for orchestra (1991) by the Brazilian composer Jorge ANTUNES; and *July '90* for orchestra (1990) by the Dutch composer Margriet HOENDERDOS.

20 MAY 1992

King Gesar for narrator and eight instrumentalists (1991–92) by the respected 45-year-old American composer Peter LIEBERSON, son of the well-known English-American recording executive and composer Goddard Lieberson, is given its first ever performance in Munich.

21 MAY 1992

On the seventh day of the 66th Festival of the International Society for Contemporary Music in Warsaw, two concerts are given in the following sequence:

A late afternoon concert at the Academy of Music, performed by Frankfurt am Main's Ensemble Modern, conducted by Friedrich Suchodolski, with special guest artists Ruben Seroussi, guitar, Sharon Cooper, mezzo-soprano, and Ralf Popken, countertenor, with sound engineering by Krzysztof Suchodolski, in the following program: *Differencias II* for guitar and orchestra (1990) by the Israeli composer Ruben SEROUSSI; *Phantastische Figuren* for six instruments (1991) by the Japanese composer Tetsuya OMURA; *Black Light* for chamber ensemble (1991) by the English composer Andrew TOOVEY, inspired by descriptions of both light and sun found in the early pages of *L'Etranger* by Albert Camus, mixed with mortuary and funeral images; and *La Terre des Hommes* for chamber ensemble by the Swiss composer Klaus HUBER, its title drawn from a text by Simone Weil.

An evening concert given at the National Philharmonic, Chamber Music Hall, by Sinfonia Varsovia, conducted by Reinbert de Leeuw, with special guest artists Barbara Skoczyńska, percussion, and Joanna Kozielska, harp, in the following program: *Canto a Mi Misma* for chamber orchestra (1986/87) by the Argentine composer Alicia TERZIAN, with the instrumentalists divided into two string quartets, the remaining instruments forming a semicircle around the conductor, who performs on a tam-tam at certain points in the score, with all performers intoning poetry by Nerdu, Prevert, Whitman, Alonso, Beckett, and others, the purely musical aspects often drawing directly upon the composer's earlier works; *Viola* for strings (1989) by the Italian composer Giorgio TEDDE, *Yarrageh,* nocturne for percussion and orchestra (1989), by the Australian composer Ross EDWARDS, the title an aboriginal word meaning "the spirit of Spring"; and *King, Queen and Ace* for harp and small ensemble (1989) by the prominent 67-year-old Danish composer and pedagogue Per NØRGÅRD, in three movements, each preceded by a prelude.

22 MAY 1992

On the eighth day of the 66th Festival of the International Society for Contemporary Music in Warsaw, four concerts are given in the following sequence:

A late afternoon performance at the National Philharmonic, Chamber Music Hall, by the Amadeus Chamber Orchestra (Poznań), conducted by Agnieszka Duczmal, with special guest artist Louise Bessette, piano, in the following program: *Memories of a Landscape II* for string ensemble (1988) by the Canadian composer James HARLEY, inspired by memories of the Okanagan Valley, particularly the Kalamalka Lake area, where the composer grew up, in five continuous "scenes" which are developed through thirteen section of varying lengths; *Hirai IV* for piano and chamber orchestra (1990) by the Japanese composer Masataka MATSUO; *La Gioia,* suite for string instruments (1991), by the Polish composer Włodzimier KOTOŃSKI; and *Intermezzo* for chamber orchestra (1989/90), a commission from the Swedish Radio for the Stockholm Sinfonietta, by the Swedish composer Daniel BÖRTZ.

An evening marathon concert of chamber music, given at the Centre of Contemporary Art, performed by the Choir of the Music Academy, conducted by Ryszard, with guest soloists Shelley Hirsch, performer, Jerry Young, tuba, Krzysztof Bąkowski, violin, Szabolcs Esztényi, piano, Egidius Streich, violin, Sylwia Żytyńska, percussion, Bayazet Akhundov, violin, and Javanashir Kulijev, saz, in the following program: *Travelogue,* suite for voice and tape (1990/91), by the American composer Joshua FRIED, scored for two synchronized prepared tapes and one live performer, with Tape I, consisting of the accompaniment, heard only by the audience and Tape II, consisting of various vocal sounds, heard only by the performer (via headphones); *The Dancing King* for tuba and tape (1988) by the American composer Jesse AYERS, the title referring to King David of ancient Israel, who, upon the recapture of the Ark of the Covenant from Israel's enemies, *danced before the Lord with all his might* (II Samuel, 6:14); *The Cognition of Music...* for violin, piano, and tape (1990) by the Polish composer Jarosław SIWIŃSKI; *Tumblers* for violin, marimba, and computer (1989/90) by the Portuguese composer Alejandro VIÑAO, *Sonate* for violin and saz (1980) by the Azerbaijan composer Javanashir KULIYEV; and *Survol* for mixed chorus (1991) by the Finnish composer Herman RECHBERGER, with a score written on eight graphic pages (timetables), with two additional pages providing information regarding entrances and exits, which are additionally projected on a large screen.

A late-night jazz concert given at the Centre of Contemporary Art featuring the Bill Frisell Band, comprised of William Frisell, guitar, bass guitar, and clarinet, Kermit Driscoll, bass guitar, and Joey Baron, percussion.

An all-night Marathon Concert, "Musical Hyde Park," given at the Centre of Contemporary Art,

wherein anyone may present his or her own (or a collective) piece, solo or band improvisation, etc., performed either by themselves or with others at their own expense, the time limit for each performance being fifteen minutes, with the participants providing their own instruments and equipment.

22 MAY 1992

The noted Hungarian composer György RÁNKI, who won distinction as a composer of both serious and popular works, dies in his native Budapest at the seasoned age of 74.

23 MAY 1992

Tropic for six players by the eminent 63-year-old Australian composer and teacher Peter (Joshua) SCULTHORPE is given its first ever performance in Brighton.

23 MAY 1992

On the ninth and last day of the 66th Festival of the International Society for Contemporary Music in Warsaw, two concerts are given in the following sequence:

A late afternoon concert at the Church of the Visitation of Our Lady, given jointly by the Bornus Consort and Warsaw's Camerata Vistula, conducted by Piotr Borkowski, with special guest artist Rober Lawaty, baritone/countertenor, in the following program: *Poème Lyrique II* for baryton and eleven musicians (1991) by the Chinese composer Qigang CHEN, relating the poetry of Su Shu (1037–1101) from the Song dynasty period; *Voices* for three singers and two percussionists (1986) by the Japanese composer Hifumi SHIMOYAMA, the intoned text taken from *Kojiki* (Japan's oldest written history) and *Man'yôshû* (the ancient anthology of Japanese poetry); *Cadman Requiem* for four voices, two violas, and cello (1989) by the significant 49-year-old English composer and teacher Gavin BRYARS, in memory of the composer's friend, Bill Cadman, who was killed in the Pan Am Flight 103 Lockerbie air disaster, in five sections, setting two traditional Requiem texts (*Requiem* and *Agnus dei*), as well as *In Paradisum,* Bede's paraphrase of Caedmon's *Creation Hymn* (in Latin), and the original Caedmon poem (in 7th century Northumbrian); and *Choralvorspiel* for chamber ensemble (1987) by the Russian composer Vladimir TARNOPOLSKY.

An evening orchestral concert at the National Philharmonic, Concert Hall by the National Philharmonic Orchestra, conducted by Ives Prin, with special guest artists Andrew Ball and Jarosław Siwiński, piano, in the following program: *Symphony No. 2* (1979) by the 54-year-old Lithuanian composer and teacher Osvaldas BALAKAUSKAS; *Musica pro Musica* for symphonic orchestra (1987) by the 49-year-old American composer, music theorist, teacher, and writer on music American composer Jonathan D. KRAMER, contrasting sonorities and juxtaposing elements of music from both East and West; *5 Misterios Eleusicos* for orchestra (1979) by the 54-year-old Mexican composer Federico IBARRA; and *Piano Concerto No. 2* (1991), in three movements, played attaca, by the 31-year-old Polish composer Hanna KULENTY.

25 MAY 1992

Piano Quartet (1990–91) by the remarkable 48-year-old Polish composer and teacher Krzysztof MEYER is given its first performance in Cologne.

27 MAY 1992

Visions for string quartet by the seasoned American composer and teacher Roger (Lee) REYNOLDS is heard for the first time in Tokyo.

29 MAY 1992

The Ukrainian-born Canadian violinist, violist, conductor, and composer Leon ZUCKERT, husband of the poet

Ella Bobrow, who collaborated with him on many of his songs, all composed in the tonal tradition, dies in Toronto at the reasonable age of 88.

30 MAY 1992

Scherzo for percussion ensemble (1956) by the outstanding German composer Karl Amadeus HARTMANN (1905–1963) is given its belated premiere performance in Munich.

31 MAY 1992

Hölderlin lesen III, *"denn wiederkommen,"* for string quartet and speaking voice (1991) by the distinguished 55-year-old German conductor, composer, and pedagogue (Johannes Wolfgang) Hans ZENDER is heard for the first time in Hombroich.

1 JUNE 1992

Grand Spiral ("Desert Flowers Bloom") for orchestra (1990) by the strikingly original 49-year-old Cambodian-born American composer Chinary UNG is performed for the first time in Sendai, Japan.

5 JUNE 1992

Concerto grosso for orchestra and electronics by the noted 64-year-old Italian composer and pedagogue Franco DONATONI is performed for the first time in Bologna.

6 JUNE 1992

A *Christmas Round* (1990) and *O, Do Not Move* (1990), two works for chorus by the remarkable 48-year-old English composer John (Kenneth) TAVENER, are given their first performance at a concert in London.

7 JUNE 1992

Mozart on Mortality for soprano and six instruments by the notable 48-year-old English composer, conductor, and writer on music Michael (Laurence) NYMAN is performed for the first time in London.

8 JUNE 1992

The Austrian composer and pedagogue Alfred UHL, whose music was patterned after Classical forms, with emphasis on contrapuntal clarity, dies in his native Vienna just three days after his 83rd birthday.

11 JUNE 1992

Second Piano Concerto by the 30-year-old American composer, pianist, and conductor Lowell LIEBERMAN, *Second Piano Concerto*, subtitled *Concerto of the Americas*, by the 59-year-old Argentine-American pianist, conductor, and composer Lalo (Boris) SCHIFRIN, and *Fourth Piano Concerto*, subtitled *Sharp Keys* (1991) by the 59-year-old Russian composer Rodion (Konstantinovich) SHCHEDRIN, are all heard for the first time in Washington, D.C.

12 JUNE 1992

Easter Dawning for carillon (1991) by the highly innovative 62-year-old American composer George (Henry, Jr.) CRUMB is heard for the first time in Dayton, Ohio.

13 JUNE 1992

The outstanding 28-year-old German violinist Anne-Sophie MUTTER gives the first ever performance of Wolfgang Rihm's *Gesungene Zeit* in Zürich with the Collegium Musicum Orchestra, Paul Sacher conducting.

14 JUNE 1992

Tania, opera, inspired by the Patty Hearst-Symbionese Liberation Army exploits by the gifted 41-year-old black American composer and pianist Anthony DAVIS is performed for the first time in Philadelphia.

16 JUNE 1992

A *Hidden Music* for orchestra by the 55-year-old English composer and music critic Anthony (Edward) PAYNE, husband of the English soprano Jane Manning, is given its premiere performance in London.

17 JUNE 1992

An adaptation and translation of a French music-theater piece, *Jumelles*, by James Giroudon, Pierre Alain Jaffrennou, and Michel Rostain, as *The Silent Twins*, is made by the versatile 58-year-old American composer, writer on music, teacher, and pioneer of new music theater Eric SALZMAN and performed for the first time at the London Opera Festival.

18 JUNE 1992

Serendib for orchestra (1991–92) by the remarkable 45-year-old French composer Tristan MURAIL is given its premiere performance in Paris.

19 JUNE 1992

Sixth Symphony (1991) by the prominent 81-year-old German-born Israeli composer, pianist, conductor, and pedagogue Josef TAL (real name, Joseph Gruenthal) is performed for the first time in Eschede.

20 JUNE 1992

The distinguished English conductor Sir Charles (Barnard) GROVES, who acquitted himself equally and admirably in the orchestral, operatic, and choral repertory, dies in London at the age of 67.

22 JUNE 1992

The singularly inventive and much beloved American composer John (Milton) CAGE (Jr.) gives a stellar performance of one of last compositions in his "number series," *One^{12}* for solo voice, in Perugia.

24 JUNE 1992

Cello Concerto (1991) by the eminent 77-year-old Polish-born English conductor and composer Sir Andrzej PANUFNIK is performed for the first time in his native London.

25 JUNE 1992

Seasons Fantastic for chorus and harp (1991–92) by the seasoned 55-year-old American composer, teacher, and pianist David WARD-STEINMAN receives its first ever performance in San Diego.

28 JUNE 1992

Vitya VRONSKY, prominent Russian-born American pianist and widow of the Russian-born American pianist and composer Victor Babin (1908–1972), with whom she often appeared in duo-recital concerts in a repertoire extending from Bach to Babin, dies in Cleveland at the ripened age of 82.

29 JUNE 1992

The eminent Italian conductor Mario ROSSI, long-time chief conductor of the RAI Orchestra in Turin (1946–69) who became especially well known for his performances of contemporary music, dies in his native Rome at the remarkable age of 90.

30 JUNE 1992

Bariolage for harp (Geneva, March 23, 1992), *Immer Neu* for oboe and harp (Sermoneta, Italy, June 30, 1992), and *Immer Song* for oboe (Witten, April 25, 1992), three independent works combined to form *Trilogy* for oboe and harp by the outstanding 83-year-old American composer and teacher Elliott (Cook) CARTER (Jr.), is performed for first time in Sermoneta.

1 JULY 1992

Voyage, fantasy for organ (1991), by the 42-year-old American composer, organist, and teacher Dan (Steven) LOCKLAIR, receives its first ever performance in Atlanta.

3 JULY 1992

Of Discoveries for two guitars and orchestra by the 38-year-old Puerto Rican composer Roberto SIERRA is heard for the first time in Chautauqua, New York.

5 JULY 1992

The body of Ignacy (Jan) PADEREWSKI, celebrated Polish pianist and composer, having been removed from Arlington National Cemetery and returned to Free Poland, is accorded a Mass and state burial at the St. John the Baptist Cathedral in Warsaw, with President Bush of the United States and President Walesa of Poland in attendance.

5 JULY 1992

The fiery Argentine bandoneón player, bandleader, composer, and arranger Astor PIAZZOLLA, much beloved the world over, especially for his iconoclastic reworkings of the traditional tango, dies in Buenos Aires at the age of 71.

9 JULY 1992

Und der Engel sprach..., ballet (1991), by the 71-year-old Austrian composer and teacher Paul KONT is mounted for the first time in Vienna.

12 JULY 1992

Violin Concerto (1991) by the prominent 43-year-old American composer and teacher Christopher (Chapman) ROUSE is given its first ever performance in Aspen.

15 JULY 1992

The German-born Israeli musicologist (Esther) Edith GERSON-KIWI, a prolific and versatile writer whose subjects included Renaissance, Classical, Romantic, and contemporary music, and the ethnic music of the Middle East, on which she became an outstanding authority, dies in Jerusalem at the reasonable age of 84.

16 JULY 1992

Il re Teodoro in Venezia, a new version of Paisiello's opera (1991–92), by the outstanding 66-year-old German composer Hans Werner HENZE is staged for the first time in Montepulciano.

23 JULY 1992

Interludi: Musica per il Mito di Eco e Narciso, opera, by the prominent 67-year-old Italian composer and pedagogue Aldo CLEMENTI is mounted for the first time in Gibellina.

29 JULY 1992

The prominent Welsh composer and teacher William (James) MATHIAS, whose music followed a basically tonal path notable for its craftsmanship, adept handling of instrumental and vocal forces, and euphonious appeal, dies in Menai Bridge at the lamentable age of 57.

2 AUGUST 1992

Hikari no Toride, Kaze no Shiro for chorus by the notable 59-year-old Japanese composer Toshi ICHIYANAGI is heard for the first time in Nakaniida.

7 AUGUST 1992

First Symphony, subtitled *Da Pacem Domine* (1991), by the 48-year-old Australian composer Ross EDWARDS is given its premiere performance in Perth.

8 AUGUST 1992

Terrestial Music, double concerto for violin, piano, and strings, by the 64-year-old American composer, pianist, and teacher Mary Jeanne VAN APPLEDORN is heard for the first time in Nagano, Japan.

9 AUGUST 1992

The significant and iconoclastic American composer William RUSSELL (real name, Russell William Wagner), who broke his more than 40-year compositional silence on Feb. 24, 1990, for a retrospective concert of his works in New York by writing a percussion *Tango* to accompany his *3 Dance Movements* (1933), in a program which also included the belated premieres of his *Concerto for Trumpet and Percussion* (1937) and *Ogou Badagri* (1933), dies in New Orleans at the seasoned age of 77.

10 AUGUST 1992

Veni, Veni, Emmanuel, percussion concerto, by the precocious 33-year-old Scottish composer, conductor, and teacher James MACMILLAN is heard for the first time in London.

11 AUGUST 1992

New World: An Opera About What Columbus Did to the "Indians" (1991) by the 42-year-old American composer, pianist, and conductor Leonard J(ordan) LEHRMAN is mounted for the first time in Huntington, New York.

12 AUGUST 1992

John (Milton) CAGE (Jr.), the singularly inventive and much beloved American composer, writer, philosophy, and visual artist of ultramodern tendencies, whose mature life's work centered on the development and implementation of sophisticated chance procedures applied to music, literature, and art, dies of a stroke in New York just weeks shy of his 80th birthday.

14 AUGUST 1992

Fifth Symphony, subtitled *Koreańska* (Korean; 1991–92), by the eminent 58-year-old Polish composer, pedagogue, and conductor Krzysztof PENDERECKI is heard for the first time in Seoul.

16 AUGUST 1992

Fourth Symphony for tenor and orchestra by the 42-year-old German composer and teacher Manfred TROJAHN is given its premiere performance in Hamburg.

17 AUGUST 1992

Three works for soprano and ensemble by the significant 57-year-old Austrian composer, horn player, and teacher Kurt SCHWERTSIK—*Human Existence, Singt meine Schwäne,* and *Der Herr weis was der Wil*—are performed for the first time in Dartington.

19 AUGUST 1992

A Vocalise for Einstein, computer piece (1991), by the 53-year-old New Zealand composer, teacher, and horn player John (Francis) RIMMER is heard for the first time in Auckland.

23 AUGUST 1992

The American composer David AHLSTROM, best known for the operas *3 Sisters Who Are Not Sisters*, after Gertrude Stein (San Francisco, Sept. 17, 1982), *Doctor Faustus Lights the Lights*, after Gertrude Stein (San Francisco, Oct. 29, 1982), and *America, I Love You*, after e.e. cummings (San Francisco, June 25, 1983), dies in San Francisco at the age of 65.

24 AUGUST 1992

Funeral Music for brass quintet by the 60-year-old English composer and teacher Hugh (Bradshaw) WOOD is given its premiere performance at the Three Choirs Festival.

30 AUGUST 1992

Low Symphony, effectively incorporating music by musical compatriots David Bowie and Brian Eno, by the phenomenally popular 55-year-old American composer Philip GLASS is performed for the first time in Munich.

2 SEPTEMBER 1992

Das Schloss, opera (1989–91), by the innovative 56-year-old German composer, pianist, and teacher Aribert REIMANN is mounted for the first time in Berlin.

4 SEPTEMBER 1992

The Austrian composer, musicologist, publisher, and music critic Karl Heinz FÜSSL, who, during his tenure as head of production for Universal Edition oversaw its Urtext Editions and who was closely associated with the publication of the works of Haydn, Mozart, Johann Strauss, and Mahler, dies in Eisenstadt at the modest age of 68.

5 SEPTEMBER 1992

The eminent Persian-born American musicologist of Armenian descent Armen CARAPETYAN, who, in 1945, became founder-director of the American Institute of Musicology, with headquarters in Rome and Cambridge, Massachusetts, where he diligently pursued his labors until 1980 dies, in Francestown, New Hampshire, at the seasoned age of 83.

8 SEPTEMBER 1992

Sygnaly I (Signals) for orchestra by the 57-year-old Polish composer Zbigniew PENHERSKI is heard for the first time in his native Warsaw.

10 SEPTEMBER 1992

Air and Angels for orchestra by the promising 28-year-old American composer Augusta Read THOMAS, wife of the respected American composer Bernard Rands, is heard for the first time in Washington, D.C.

11 SEPTEMBER 1992

Die Sonnevanger for orchestra (1990) by the confident Dutch-born South African composer Hans ROOSEN-SCHOON is given its premiere performance in Cape Town.

12 SEPTEMBER 1992

The Gardens of Adonis, opera (1959), in a revised version (1977–81), by the distinguished 79-year-old Moravian-born American composer and pedagogue Hugo (David) WEISGALL is heard for the first time in Omaha.

14 SEPTEMBER 1992

Alice TULLY, American mezzo-soprano, soprano, and music patroness, generous scion of a family of wealth, celebrates her ninetieth birthday at a New York gala held in her honor at Lincoln Center.

15 SEPTEMBER 1992

Her Anxiety for soprano and ensemble (1991) by the youthful 32-year-old English composer Mark-Anthony TURNAGE is performed for the first time in London.

16 SEPTEMBER 1992

The Ukrainian composer and pedagogue Andrei (Yakovlevich) SHTOGARENKO, long-time director of the Kiev Conservatory (1954–68), where he also was a professor (from 1960), dies in Kiev just weeks shy of his 90th birthday.

17 SEPTEMBER 1992

Roger (Francis) WAGNER, seasoned French-born American choral conductor, founding director of the celebrated Roger Wagner Chorale, with which he toured extensively in the United States, Canada, and Latin America, dies in Dijon at the age of 78.

18 SEPTEMBER 1992

Oboe Concerto (1991–92) by the veteran 49-year-old English composer and writer on music David (John) MATTHEWS, brother of the equally talented English composer, writer on music, and broadcaster Colin Matthews, is given its first ever performance in his native London.

19 SEPTEMBER 1992

103 for orchestra and the abstract film *One*¹¹, two works by the remarkable American composer John (Milton) CAGE (Jr.) (1912–1992), receive their posthumous and simultaneous premieres in Cologne.

20 SEPTEMBER 1992

Gloria for orchestra (1991–92) by the 57-year-old German composer Georg KATZER is heard for the first time in Berlin.

21 SEPTEMBER 1992

Gathering Together for two keyboards and two mallet percussion by the lovable American composer, pianist, teacher, and writer on music William (Ervin) DUCKWORTH is given its first ever performance in Rome.

22 SEPTEMBER 1992

Landscapes, song cycle for soprano and piano trio, by the distinguished 65-year-old South African-born English composer and teacher John (Pierre Herman) JOUBERT is heard for the first time in Cheltenham.

23 SEPTEMBER 1992

Settings for small orchestra by the remarkable 59-year-old American composer and teacher Mel POWELL (real name, Melvin Epstein) is given its premiere performance in Los Angeles.

24 SEPTEMBER 1992

Bang! for piano and orchestra by the promising 38-year-old American composer Tobias PICKER is performed for the first time for the opening of the 150th anniversary season of the New York Philharmonic.

25 SEPTEMBER 1992

Musik zu Kafka II for percussionist by the productive 66-year-old German composer, pedagogue, organist, and harpsichordist Ruth ZECHLIN is heard for the first time in Heidelberg.

26 SEPTEMBER 1992

The Commission, "operatic episode" (1954), by the remarkable and innovative American composer Henry (Dixon) COWELL (1897–1965) receives its posthumous premiere in Woodstock, New York.

27 SEPTEMBER 1992

Las Indias Olvidades, concerto for harpsichord and eleven instruments (1990), by the 51-year-old Uruguayan-born American composer and teacher Sergio CERVETTI is given its first ever performance in Alicante.

28 SEPTEMBER 1992

Concerto for violin and strings (1991) by the multi-talented 65-year-old Yugoslav composer, pedagogue, writer on music, painter, and poet Aleksandar OBRADOVIĆ is heard for the first time in Belgrade.

29 SEPTEMBER 1992

Let the Earth Bring Forth for chamber ensemble 45-year-old Russian composer, conductor, and teacher Nikolai KORNDORF is given its first ever performance in Amsterdam.

30 SEPTEMBER 1992

Univers de lumière, symphonic poem for reciter and orchestra (1990–91), by the energetic 47-year-old French composer and teacher Graciane FINZI is heard for the first time in Seville.

1 OCTOBER 1992

Prophet Bird for chamber orchestra, after Robert Schumann, by the 62-year-old American composer and teacher Eric (Norman) STOKES receives its first ever performance in St. Paul, Minnesota.

3 OCTOBER 1992

The prominent Czech-born American conductor Zdenek (originally Zdeněk Mácal) MACAL becomes a naturalized American citizen at a special ceremony held during a concert he conducts with the Milwaukee Symphony Orchestra.

4 OCTOBER 1992

The German tenor Peter KLEIN, whose operatic roles included Valzacchi in *Der Rosenkavalier,* Basilio, Mime in the *Ring* cycle, the Captain in *Wozzeck,* and Monsieur Taupe in *Capriccio,* dies in Vienna at the age of 85.

4 OCTOBER 1992

Hadra, installation for 20 independent tape sources by the innovative 39-year-old American composer Ron FEIN, an enveloping surround-sound composition for stationary or mobile audience and incorporating ritual music from the around the world, is heard for the first time in Seattle.

5 OCTOBER 1992

The accomplished 39-year-old American soprano Erie MILLS sings Orazio in the United States premiere of Georg Friedrich Handel's *Muzio* in New York.

8 OCTOBER 1992

Violin Concerto (1990), in a second, revised version, by the eminent 69-year-old Hungarian-born Austrian composer and pedagogue György (Sándor) LIGETI, great-nephew of the celebrated Hungarian violinist and pedagogue Leopold Auer, is performed for the first time in Cologne.

9 OCTOBER 1992

"...Zwei Gefühle...", Musik mit Leonardo for orchestra by the respected 56-year-old German composer and pedagogue Helmut (Friedrich) LACHENMANN is given its first ever performance in Stuttgart.

11 OCTOBER 1992

Monticello Trio for violin, cello, and piano by the talented 53-year-old American composer Barbara KOLB is heard for the first time in Charlottesville, Virginia.

12 OCTOBER 1992

The Voyage, allegorical opera commissioned by the Metropolitan Opera in New York to commemorate the 500th anniversary of the discovery of America, by the successful 55-year-old American minimalist composer Philip GLASS is first mounted in New York.

16 OCTOBER 1992

Music for cello and orchestra by the distinguished 73-year-old American composer, pedagogue, conductor, and pianist Leon KIRCHNER is given its first performance in Philadelphia.

17 OCTOBER 1992

Violin Concerto by the 45-year-old American composer David OTT is heard for the first time in Reading, Pennsylvania.

18 OCTOBER 1992

Fraktale, "Concerto Philharmonico," composed for the 150th anniversary of the Vienna Philharmonic by the outstanding 74-year-old Austrian composer Gottfried von EINEM, is heard for the first time in the orchestra's home city.

19 OCTOBER 1992

The French conductor, composer, and writer on music Maurice LE ROUX, who utilized serial procedures in his compositions, which included the ballets *Le Petit Prince* (1949) and *Sables* (1956), and who published a number of books in Paris, including *Introduction à la musique contemporaine* (1947), *Monteverdi* (1947), *La Musique* (1979), and *Boris Godounov* (1980), dies in Avignon at the age of 69.

20 OCTOBER 1992

The German-born American conductor, violinist, and composer Werner TORKANOWSKY, long-time (1963–77) music director of the New Orleans Philharmonic, and then of the Bangor Symphony Orchestra (from 1981), dies in Bar Harbor, Maine, at the moderate age of 66.

21 OCTOBER 1992

In honor of his 80th birthday, the eminent Hungarian-born English conductor Sir George SOLTI (real name, György Stern) is awarded the first Hans Richter Medal from the Vienna Philharmonic.

23 OCTOBER 1992

William MASSELOS, American pianist and teacher who acquired a fine reputation as an exponent of modern music, who gave the belated premiere of Charles Ives's *First Piano Sonata* (1949) as well as the premieres of Aaron Copland's *Piano Fantasy* (1957) and Ben Weber's Piano Concerto (1961), dies in New York at the age of 72.

24 OCTOBER 1992

Rain Tree Sketch II: In memoriam Olivier Messiaen for piano by the preeminent 62-year-old Japanese composer Tōru TAKEMITSU is performed for the first time in Orléans.

25 OCTOBER 1992

The Goat That Couldn't Sneeze, musical comedy, by the distinguished 73-year-old Chilean composer and musicologist Juan (Antonio) ORREGO-SALAS is staged for the first time in Bloomington, Indiana.

26 OCTOBER 1992

Symfonie dzwonów (Bell Symphonies) *I-III* for piano (1988–91) by the 62-year-old Polish composer and teacher Romuald TWARDOWSKI is performed for the first time in Warsaw.

28 OCTOBER 1992

Group of 7 for reciter, viola, and orchestra (1991) by the 72-year-old Canadian composer and teacher Robert (Comri) TURNER is given its premiere performance in Ottawa.

29 OCTOBER 1992

Overture Concertante for orchestra by the esteemed 69-year-old American composer, organist, choral conductor, and teacher Daniel (Rogers) PINKHAM (Jr.) is performed for the first time ever in Boston.

31 OCTOBER 1992

McTeague, opera, by the 54-year-old American pianist and composer William (Elden) BOLCOM, husband of the American mezzo-soprano Joan (Clair) Morris, is staged for the first time in Chicago.

2 NOVEMBER 1992

Nocturnes I for flute, violin, viola, cello, and percussion by the 68-year-old American composer, pianist, and teacher Robert PARRIS is performed for the first time in Washington, D.C.

4 NOVEMBER 1992

The Swiss-born French composer and pedagogue Pierre WISSMER, the 1983 recipient of the Grand Prix Musical of Geneva for his creative efforts, which revealed an adept handling of both traditional and contemporary styles, dies in Valcros, France, at the age of 77.

5 NOVEMBER 1992

Éclairs sur l'Au-Delà for orchestra (1987–91) by the outstanding French composer and pedagogue Olivier (Eugène Prosper Charles) MESSIAEN (1908–1992) receives its posthumous premiere in New York.

6 NOVEMBER 1992

Café of the Ghosts: Fantasy-Trio on a Moroccan Beggar's Song for violin, cello, and piano by the 53-year-old American writer on music and composer Phillip RAMEY is given its first ever performance in Sacramento, California.

7 NOVEMBER 1992

The distinguished Polish-born violinist, conductor, and pedagogue Henri TEMIANKA, who was was equally esteemed as a violin soloist and chamber player, conductor, and teacher, dies in Los Angeles just days before his 86th birthday.

8 NOVEMBER 1992

Seventy-Four for orchestra by the outstanding senior composer, writer, philosopher, and visual artist John (Milton) CAGE (Jr.) (1912–1992) receives its posthumous premiere performance in New York.

13 NOVEMBER 1992

Kneeling Dance, in an arrangement for six pianos, by the gifted 43-year-old South African-born Irish composer Kevin VOLANS is given its first ever performance in Southhampton.

14 NOVEMBER 1992

Over Eternal Peace, chamber concerto for bassoon and fourteen players, by the 37-year-old Armenian composer Yuri KASPAROV is performed for the first time in Zürich.

16 NOVEMBER 1992

Im Namen der Liebe, song cycle for man's voice and piano, by the 69-year-old Austrian composer, conductor, and pedagogue Gerhard WIMBERGER receives its first performance in Salzburg.

17 NOVEMBER 1992

Bitter Fruit, chamber opera, by the promising 33-year-old Irish composer Fergus JOHNSTON is staged for the first time in Dublin.

18 NOVEMBER 1992

The noted American soprano Dorothy KIRSTEN, whose finest roles included Manon Lescaut, Cio-Cio-San, Marguerite, Louise (coached by the composer), and Nedda in *Pagliacci*, and who also sang in several films, including *The Great Caruso*, dies in Los Angeles at the respectable age of 82.

21 NOVEMBER 1992

The outstanding Italian flutist and teacher Severino GAZZELLONI, who pursued an international career as a soloist and recitalist of the first magnitude, excelling in an expansive repertoire ranging from the Baroque masters to the most demanding exponents of the contemporary avant-garde, dies in Cassino, near Rome, at the age of 73.

22 NOVEMBER 1992

Ballade au vibraphone for vibraphone and small orchestra by the 67-year-old French composer Antoine DUHAMEL, son of the writer Georges Duhamel and the comedienne Blanche Albane, is premiered in Chambéry.

23 NOVEMBER 1992

Roy ACUFF, popular American country music singer, guitarist, and songwriter who was a featured artist with his Smoky Mountain Boys on the "Grand Ole Opry" radio program in Nashville, and whose best known songs included *Night Train to Memphis* and *Wabash Cannonball*, dies in Nashville at the well-seasoned age of 89.

24 NOVEMBER 1992

The French organist, pianist, teacher, and composer Henriette PUIG-ROGET, "chef de chant" at the Paris Opéra (1937–40; 1946–57) and then professor of piano accompaniment and score reading at the Paris Conservatory (1957–79), dies in Paris at the accomplished age of 82.

25 NOVEMBER 1992

Strathclyde Concerto No. 7 for double bass and orchestra by the eminent 58-year-old English composer and conductor Sir Peter Maxwell DAVIES is given its first ever performance in Glasgow.

26 NOVEMBER 1992

Wind Pictures for chorus and orchestra (1991) by the 44-year-old Finnish composer and musicologist Mikko HEINIÖ is performed for the first time in Turku.

27 NOVEMBER 1992

...das Gesegnete, das Verfluchte, four sketches for orchestra (1991), by the 44-year-old German composer and Intendant Peter RUZICKA receives its premiere performance in Munich.

29 NOVEMBER 1992

The Italian stage designer and opera director Filippo SANJUST, whose most distinguished productions included *Ariadne auf Naxos* (1976) and *Falstaff* (1980) in Vienna, *L'incoronazione di Poppea* (1979) in Brussels, and *Simon Boccanega* (1980) at Covent Garden, and who was chosen by Hans Werner Henze as designer for the premieres of his *Der junge Lord* in Berlin in 1965 and for his *The Bassarids* at the Salzburg Festival in 1966, dies in his native Rome at the modest age of 67.

3 DECEMBER 1992

Eleventh Symphony by the eminent 77-year-old American composer David (Leo) DIAMOND is given its premiere performance in New York.   •

4 DECEMBER 1992

The eminent 57-year-old Japanese conductor Seiji OZAWA, son of a Buddhist father and a Christian mother, makes his Metropolitan Opera debut in New York conducting *Eugene Onegin*.

5 DECEMBER 1992

Gold Are My Flowers, cantata/melodrama for soprano, baritone, and chamber group, by the 51-year-old American composer, pianist, and teacher Curtis O(tto) B(ismarck) CURTIS-SMITH is performed for the first time in Houston.

6 DECEMBER 1993

Concerto-Cantata for flute and orchestra (1991–92) by the celebrated 58-year-old Polish composer Henryk (Mikołaj) GÓRECKI is performed for the first time in Amsterdam.

7 DECEMBER 1992

The 150th anniversary of the New York Philharmonic is celebrated with a concert featuring three celebrated conductors: the formidable 67-year-old Frenchman Pierre BOULEZ, conducting Debussy's *La Mer;* the eminent 65-year-old German Kurt MASUR, conducting Dvořák's *New World Symphony;* and the impassioned 56-year-old Indian Zubin MEHTA, conducting Strauss's *Till Eulenspiegels lustige Streich,* all stellar performances which are televised live to the nation via PBS.

8 DECEMBER 1992

Monday and Tuesday for chamber ensemble by the energetic 31-year-old American composer and pianist Michael TORKE receives its first ever performance in London.

9 DECEMBER 1992

Études aperçues for vibraphone and five bells and *Musique pour Delphine* for violin and cello, two works by the distinguished 66-year-old French-American composer and teacher Betsy JOLAS, daughter of the poet and journalist Eugène Jolas, known in his own right as the founder and editor of the literary journal *transition*, are performed for the first time in Paris.

13 DECEMBER 1992

O Magnum Mysterium for chorus (1991) in an expanded setting (1992) by the esteemed 54-year-old American composer, conductor, and teacher John (Harris) HARBISON receives its first ever performance in Boston.

14 DECEMBER 1992

Mimo II for oboe and orchestra by the spirited 36-year-old Finnish conductor and composer Esa-Pekka SALONEN is performed for the first time in his native Helsinki.

15 DECEMBER 1992

Cello Sonata by the distinguished 66-year-old Romanian composer and musicologist Anatol VIERU is heard for the first time over Radio classique in Paris.

17 DECEMBER 1992

The American composer, pianist, and teacher Edwin GERSCHEFSKI, who attracted particular notice for his settings of exact texts from newspapers, magazines, and business letters in several of his vocal scores, dies in Athens, Georgia, at the ripened age of 83.

18 DECEMBER 1992

The promising 32-year-old Mexican tenor Ramón (Arturo) VARGAS makes his Metropolitan Opera debut in New York as Edgardo.

21 DECEMBER 1992

The celebrated Russian-born American violinist Nathan (Mironovich) MILSTEIN, renowned for his technical virtuosity and musical integrity, and who also composed a number of violin pieces, including *Paganiniana* (1954), and also prepared cadenzas for the violin concertos of Beethoven and Brahms, and whose autobiography appeared as *From Russia to the West* (N.Y., 1990), dies in London, ten days shy of his 89th birthday.

26 DECEMBER 1992

The distinguished Russian-born Swiss pianist and teacher Nikita MAGALOFF, son-in-law of the eminent Hungarian-born American violinist and teacher Joseph Szigeti (1892–1973), and who was renowned for his lyrico-dramatic interpretations of Chopin, with lapidary attention to detail, dies in Vevey at the age of 80.

29 DECEMBER 1992

The Swiss organist, teacher, and composer Torsten SÖRENSON, whose many fine works ranged from large forces to lieder, dies in Uddevalla at the mature age of 84.

31 DECEMBER 1992

The legendary 67-year-old German baritone (Albert) Dietrich FISCHER-DIESKAU makes his farewell public appearance as a singer at the Bavarian State Opera.

1993

1 JANUARY 1993

The 49-year-old American baritone William PARKER makes his last public concert in Minneapolis.

6 JANUARY 1993

The famous black American jazz trumpeter and bandleader "Dizzy" (John Birks) GILLESPIE, without question one of the greatest trumpeters in jazz history and practice, a true virtuoso on his instrument, extending its upper ranges and improvising long passages at breakneck speed, dies in Englewood, New Jersey, at the seasoned age of 75.

8 JANUARY 1993

Violin Sonata, subtitled *Invisible Lilacs* (1992), by the 38-year-old American composer Tobias PICKER is performed for the first time in his native New York.

10 JANUARY 1993

Cello Concerto by the remarkable 69-year-old Chinese-born American composer Chou WEN-CHUNG is given its first ever performance in New York.

11 JANUARY 1993

Concerto for flute and chamber orchestra (1992) by the eminent 59-year-old Polish composer, pedagogue, and conductor Krzysztof PENDERECKI is heard for the first time in Lausanne.

13 JANUARY 1993

The esteemed Brazilian composer, conductor, and teacher (Mozart) Camargo GUARNIERI, whose extensive catalogue of music, skillfully crafted in a tonal style, was basically reflective of Brazilian national elements, dies in São Paulo just weeks shy of his 86th birthday.

15 JANUARY 1993

The great American lyricist Sammy CAHN (real name, Samuel Cohen), who composed countless songs, often in collaboration with others, including *Call Me Irresponsible* (for *Papa's Delicate Condition,* 1963, Academy Award), *My Kind of Town* (for *Robin and the Seven Hoods,* 1964), *I Should Care* (for *Thrill of a Romance,* 1945), and, especially, an English-language rendition of *Bei mir bist du schön,* made popular by the Andrews Sisters, dies in Los Angeles at the age of 79.

17 JANUARY 1993

Woefully Arranged for soprano, baritone, chorus, boy's chorus, and orchestra by the 66-year-old pianist, organist, conductor, writer on music, and composer Francis (John) ROUTH is heard for the first time in London.

18 JANUARY 1993

Gomorra, musical spectacle, originally composed in 1970–72, then withdrawn, by the 50-year-old Austrian composer, conductor, chansonnier, and double bass player, H(einz) K(arl) "Nali" GRUBER, great-great-grandson of the Austrian composer Franx Xaver Gruber, is performed for the first time in a new version (1984–91) in his native Vienna.

19 JANUARY 1993

The Belgian composer Renier VAN DER VELDEN, who in 1970 was made a member of the Royal Flemish Academy of Arts, Letters, and Sciences, dies in his native Antwerp just days after his 83rd birthday.

20 JANUARY 1993

The outstanding 59-year-old American mezzo-soprano Marilyn (Bernice) HORNE sings at the inauguration of President Clinton in Washington, D.C.

21 JANUARY 1993

The significant Slovak composer and pianist Ján ZIMMER, whose music was marked by a mastery of form, technique, and expression, sometimes utilizing 12-tone and other modern techniques, and who generally forged his own course as a worthy representative of the Slovak tradition, dies in Bratislava at the age of 66.

22 JANUARY 1993

The eminent Finnish musicologist Erik (Werner) TAWASTJERNA, who after a brief career as a concert pianist devoted himself to musicology, serving for over two decades (1960–83) as a professor at the University of Helsinki, dies in Helsinki at the age of 76.

23 JANUARY 1993

Episodes for viola, cello, and piano (1992) by the esteemed 59-year-old Austrian-born American composer and pedagogue Robert STARER is heard for the first time in Hartford, Connecticut.

25 JANUARY 1993

Sonata-Aria for cello and piano (1992) by the significant 74-year-old American composer and teacher George ROCHBERG is given its first ever performance in Houston.

26 JANUARY 1993

The intriguing American composer and teacher Kenneth (Louis) GABURO, whose numerous teaching posts included Kent State University (1950), McNeese State University (1950–54), the University of Illinois (1955–67), the University of California at San Diego (1967–75), where he was founder-director of the Studio for Cognitive Studies in San Diego (1975–83), and the University of Iowa (from 1983), dies in Iowa City at the age of 66.

28 JANUARY 1993

Elégie balkanique for flute, guitar, and percussion (1992) by the innovative 58-year-old French composer, trombonist, conductor, and teacher Vinko GLOBOKAR is performed for the first time in Hamburg.

31 JANUARY 1993

The Hungarian musicologist Ernő LENDVAI, who became best known as a distinguished writer on the life and works of Béla Bartók, dies in Budapest at the lamentable age of 67.

2 FEBRUARY 1993

The notable Italian baritone Gino BECHI, who became best known for his Verdi roles, among them Falstaff, Amonasro, Hamlet, Iago, and Nabucco, and who in later years was active as a teacher and opera producer, dies in his native Florence at the age of 79.

3 FEBRUARY 1993

The significant Belgian composer Karel (August) GOEYVAERTS, a pioneer in his country of serialism, spatial music, and electronic techniques, dies in his native Antwerp at the age of 69.

4 FEBRUARY 1993

Concerto for piano, left-hand, and orchestra (1991) by the brilliant 69-year-old American composer, pianist, and writer Ned ROREM, son of a medical economist and a civil right activist, is performed for the first time by the Curtis Institute of Music Symphony Orchestra, Gary Graffman soloist, conducted by André Previn.

5 FEBRUARY 1993

Fourth Symphony by the veteran 81-year-old Polish composer and conductor Witold LUTOSŁAWSKI is heard for the first time in Los Angeles.

6 FEBRUARY 1993

The Romanian composer and teacher Dan CONSTANTINESCU, long-time faculty member at the Bucharest Conservatory (1950–55; 1956–92), dies in his native Bucharest at the age of 61.

9 FEBRUARY 1993

Głowa Meduzy I (Medusa's Head I) for one to three recorders (1992) by the 65-year-old Polish composer and pedagogue Witold (Józef) SZALONEK is given its first ever performance in Berlin.

11 FEBRUARY 1993

Second Symphony, subtitled *quasi una fantasia* (1989–92), by the 66-year-old Polish conductor and composer Jan KRENZ is heard for the first time in Bonn.

12 FEBRUARY 1993

Labour for orchestra (1992) by the adventurous 58-year-old French composer, trombonist, conductor, and teacher Vinko GLOBOKAR is given its first performance in Cologne.

13 FEBRUARY 1993

A Poet to His Beloved for tenor, flute, string quartet, and piano by the precocious 31-year-old American composer, pianist, and conductor Lowell LIEBERMANN is heard for the first time in his native New York.

14 FEBRUARY 1993

First Symphony (1992) by the 65-year-old American composer and teacher John (Wilham) DOWNEY is given its first ever performance in Palatine, Illinois.

17 FEBRUARY 1993

Thirteen for flute, oboe, clarinet, bassoon, trumpet, trombone, tuba, two xylophones, and string quartet (1992) by the eminent American composer, writer, philosopher, and visual artist John (Milton) CAGE (Jr.) (1912–1992) is given its posthumous premiere in Gütersloh.

18 FEBRUARY 1993

Viola Concerto by the 46-year-old American composer Peter LIEBERSON, son of the English recording executive and composer Goddard Lieberson, is performed for the first time in Toronto.

19 FEBRUARY 1993

Trio des trois I for violin, piano, and percussion (1991) by the accomplished 45-year-old American composer, pianist, administrator, presenter, and teacher Bernadette (Marie) SPEACH is performed for the first time in New York.

20 FEBRUARY 1993

Polyhedra for woodwind quintet (1992) by the 70-year-old American composer and pedagogue Allen Dwight SAPP, Jr., receives its first performance in Dodge City, Kansas.

22 FEBRUARY 1992

Third Concerto for viola and orchestra by the innovative 44-year-old American composer, pianist, and teacher William Thomas MCKINLEY is performed for the first time in New York.

24 FEBRUARY 1993

Rainforest Images, collaborative audio piece, by the 54-year-old American composer Barton (Keith) MCLEAN and his wife, the 50-year-old American composer Priscilla MCLEAN, is performed for the first time in Cincinnati.

25 FEBRUARY 1993

Third Symphony (1992) by the remarkable 53-year-old American composer Ellen Taaffe ZWILICH is heard for the first time in New York, conducted by the Indonesian conductor and pianist of Chinese descent Jahja Ling.

27 FEBRUARY 1993

The Italian violinist Pina (actually, Giuseppina) CARMIRELLI, founder of both the Boccherini Quintet (1949) and the Carmirelli Quartet (1954), dies in Carpena at the age of 79.

2 MARCH 1993

El Simurgh, Book I, The Conference of the Birds for piano and tape (1991) by the promising 32-year-old Argentine composer Ezequiel VIÑAO is given its premiere performance in London.

4 MARCH 1993

Midnight for chorus (1992) by the remarkable 64-year-old Scottish composer Thea MUSGRAVE receives its first ever performance in San Antonio.

5 MARCH 1993

Zyklus for organ (1992) by the 56-year-old Austrian composer, teacher, and conductor Erich URBANNER is performed for the first time in Vienna.

8 MARCH 1993

The black American singer and bandleader Billy ECKS-TINE (real name, William Clarence Eckstein), nicknamed "Mister B," whose prominent recordings included *Billy Eckstine's Imagination* (1958), *Billy Eckstine and Quincy Jones at Basin Street East* (1961), and *My Way* (1966), dies in his native Pittsburgh at the age of 78.

11 MARCH 1993

Gewandhaus-Sinfonie for soprano, children's chorus, organ, and orchestra (1992–93) by the esteemed 58-year-old German composer Siegfried MATTHUS is heard for the first time in Leipzig.

12 MARCH 1993

Violin Concerto (1992) by the 40-year-old American composer and teacher Stephen (Paul) HARTKE is performed for the first time ever in Troy, New York.

13 MARCH 1993

Blackmail (1992–93), music for Alfred Hitchcock's silent film of the same name, by the 44-year-old English composer Jonathan LLOYD is heard for the first time in Paris.

16 MARCH 1993

The distinguished German musicologist Erich VALENTIN, whose mature writings included *Die schönsten Beethoven-Briefe* (Munich, 1973), *Lübbes Mozart-Lexikon* (Bergisch-Gladbach, 1983), and *Don-Juan-Reflexionen: Eine Auswahl literarischer Zeugnisse* (Augsburg, 1988), dies in Bad Aibling at the respectable age of 86.

18 MARCH 1993

Organ Concerto by the 46-year-old Dutch composer and teacher Tristan KEURIS is performed for the first time in Amsterdam.

19 MARCH 1993

Sinfonia (1988) by the outstanding, multi-talented 63-year-old Polish composer, pianist, pedagogue, writer on music, stage manager, and playwright Bogusław (Julien) SCHAEFFER is heard for the first time in Opole.

24 MARCH 1993

Between the Wings of the Earth for chamber orchestra by the accomplished 42-year-old Canadian composer Michael (Bass) MATTHEWS receives its premiere performance in Winnipeg.

25 MARCH 1993

Revolution for two pianos and four percussion, amplified (1992–93), by the versatile 50-year-old American composer, pianist, teacher, and writer on music William (Ervin) DUCKWORTH is performed for the first time in New York.

26 MARCH 1993

Trookh for trombone and orchestra (1991) by the eminent 70-year-old Greek-born French composer, music theorist, and teacher Iannis XENAKIS is given its first ever performance in Stockholm.

27 MARCH 1993

Death and Fire: Dialogue with Paul Klee for orchestra (1991–92) by the significant 35-year-old Chinese composer Tan DUN is heard for the first time in Glasgow.

29 MARCH 1993

The American baritone William PARKER, who, after contracting AIDS, commissioned a number of composers to contribute selections to *The AIDS Quilt Songbook*, and who, with the baritones Kurt Ollman, William Sharp, and Sanford Sylvan, gave the premiere of the cycle at New York's Alice Tully Hall in 1992, dies in New York at the lamentable age of 49.

30 MARCH 1993

Requiem de Jean Cocteau for baritone, dancers, reciters, and orchestra by the interesting 67-year-old French composer Antoine DUHAMEL, son of the writer Georges Duhamel and the comedienne Blanche Albane, is given its first ever performance in Fresnes.

31 MARCH 1993

The eminent Spanish harpist Nicanor ZABALETA (Zala), who did much to further the cause of contemporary harp music by commissioning works from many notable composers, among them Villa-Lobos, Rodrigo, Montsalvatge, Milhaud, Krenek, Piston, Hovhaness, and Farkas, dies in San Juan, Puerto Rico, at the ripened age of 86.

1 APRIL 1993

Comoedia for Soprano and 6 Players by the 38-year-old French composer Pascal DUSAPIN is heard for the first time in Toulouse.

2 APRIL 1993

Frauenleben, nine lieder for viola and orchestra (1992), by the distinguished 66-year-old French-American composer and teacher Betsy JOLAS, daughter of the poet and journalist Eugène Jolas, best known as the founder and editor of the literary journal *transition*, is first heard in Paris.

3 APRIL 1993

The celebrated 69-year-old German mezzo-soprano Christa LUDWIG makes her farewell appearance at the Metropolitan Opera singing the role of Fricka in Richard Wagner's *Die Walküre*.

4 APRIL 1993

The Jogger and the Dinosaur for rapper and orchestra by the extraordinarily talented 79-year-old American composer and conductor Morton GOULD is performed for the first time in Pittsburgh.

8 APRIL 1993

The celebrated black American contralto Marian ANDERSON, aunt of the greatly talented black American James (Anderson) DePreist, one of America's outstanding musicians who, on Jan. 7, 1955, became the first black singer to appear at the Metropolitan Opera in New York when she made her debut as Ulrica, who would later receive such honors from governments and institutions of higher learning as the U.S. Medal of Freedom (1963), a gold medal from the U.S. Congress (1977), and the National Medal of Arts (1986), dies in Portland, Oregon, at the extraordinary age of 96.

9 APRIL 1993

Sound of the Independent Speaker for sampler, electric guitar, and percussion by the 32-year-old American composer, instrumentalist, improviser, and sampling specialist Annie (actually, Anne) GOSFIELD is heard for the first time in New York.

13 APRIL 1993

Adagio for orchestra by the eminent 77-year-old American composer, music theorist, and pedagogue, George PERLE is performed for the first time in New York.

15 APRIL 1993

Colossos or Panic: Symphonic Fragment after Goya for orchestra (1991–92) by the prominent 60-year-old German-born English composer and teacher (Peter) Alexander GOEHR, son of the German-born English conductor and composer Walter Goehr, is heard for the first time in Boston.

16 APRIL 1993

Violin Concerto by the significant 66-year-old American composer and teacher Donald (James) ERB receives its premiere performance in Grand Rapids, Michigan.

19 APRIL 1993

The noted Mexican composer and pedagogue Blas GALINDO (Dimas), whose extensive output displayed a genuine respect for traditional forms, the folkloric element of his early works giving way to a sophisticated use of dissonance without abandoning accessibility, dies in Mexico City at the seasoned age of 83.

20 APRIL 1993

Jacob's Room, opera, by the respected 60-year-old American composer and teacher Morton SUBOTNICK, husband of the American vocalist and composer Joan LaBarbara, is first performed in Philadelphia.

21 APRIL 1993

Third Piano Concerto (1992) by the distinguished 72-year-old American composer and pedagogue Andrew (Welsh) IMBRIE is heard for the first time in his native New York.

22 APRIL 1993

The 37-year-old German tenor Wolfgang SCHMIDT makes his Metropolitan Opera debut in New York as Wagner's Siegfried.

23 APRIL 1993

The outstanding 26-year-old Italian mezzo-soprano Cecilia BARTOLI makes a sensational U.S. operatic stage debut with the Houston Grand Opera as Rosina.

26 APRIL 1993

4 Preludes for piano (1992) by the promising 22-year-old Polish composer and clarinetist Paweł MYKIETYN is first performed in Warsaw.

29 APRIL 1993

Run for orchestra (1992) by the rising 31-year-old American composer and pianist Michael TORKE is given its first ever performance in New York.

1 MAY 1993

Awed Behavior, music theater piece (1992–93), by the extraordinarily talented 42-year-old American composer and performer Paul (Joseph) DRESHER is staged for the first time in Los Angeles.

2 MAY 1993

A Tangled Web for chamber orchestra by the 55-year-old American-born Canadian composer and teacher Thomas (Michael) SCHUDEL is heard for the first time in Regina.

4 MAY 1993

C.A.G. for flute, violin, vibraphone, and guitar by the respected 68-year-old Italian composer and pedagogue Aldo CLEMENTI is first performed in Bologna.

7 MAY 1993

Il Suono di Enormi Distanze for mezzo-soprano and large ensemble (1992–93) by the 48-year-old New Zealand composer Lyell (Richard) CRESSWELL is heard for the first time in Glasgow.

8 MAY 1993

The revered American choreographer, stage director, and occasional composer Alwin (Theodore) NIKOLAIS, who composed the music for many of his dance productions, including works in the electronic medium, his principal choreographic innovation being the technique of body extension by tubular projections and disks attached to the head and upper and nether limbs, so that his biped dancers became stereogeometrical figures, dies in New York at the age of 80.

10 MAY 1993

From Saibai for violin and piano by the eminent 64-year-old Australian composer and teacher Peter (Joshua) SCULTHORPE is given its premiere performance in New York.

11 MAY 1993

The Hungarian composer Iván PATACHICH, who in 1971 established the electronic music studio EXASTUD (Experimentum Auditorii Studii) in his native Budapest, dies there at the age of 70.

14 MAY 1993

Rodrigue et Chimène, opera (1890–92) left in piano score by the great French composer (Achille-) Claude DEBUSSY (1862–1918), whose music created new poetry of mutating tonalities and became a perfect counterpart of new painting in France, is reconstructed by Richard Smith, orchestrated by Edison Denisov, and given its posthumous premiere in Lyons.

15 MAY 1993

She Sleeps Perhaps for mezzo-soprano and chamber orchestra by the 57-year-old Serbian composer and teacher Rajko MAKSIMOVIĆ is performed for the first time in Novi Sad.

16 MAY 1993

The Cave, documentary video opera (1990–93), by the outstanding 56-year-old American composer Steve (actually, Stephen Michael) REICH is given its first public screening in Vienna.

19 MAY 1993

Fourth String Quartet by the 60-year-old English composer and teacher Hugh (Bradshaw) WOOD is first heard over the BBC in Birmingham.

20 MAY 1993

Visitatio Sepulchri, music theater piece (1992–93), by the 33-year-old Scottish composer, conductor, and teacher James MACMILLAN receives its first ever staging in Glasgow.

21 MAY 1993

Discours IX for two pianos by the 58-year-old French composer, trombonist, and teacher Vinko GLOBOKAR is heard for the first time in Saarbrücken.

22 MAY 1993

The remarkable Polish-born American pianist and pedagogue Mieczyslaw HORSZOWSKI, who, on Oct. 31, 1991,

at the astounding age of 99, gave his last recital in Philadelphia, thus bringing to a close one of the most outstanding performing and teaching careers of the 20th century, dies in Philadelphia at the remarkable age of 100.

23 MAY 1993

Fourth Symphony by the accomplished 38-year-old Australian composer and pianist Carl VINE is given its first hearing in Sydney.

25 MAY 1993

Álmodj Bachot (Dream Bach), musical play (1991), by the Hungarian composer Frigyes HIDAS is mounted for the first time in Budapest on the occasion of the composer's 65th birthday.

26 MAY 1993

The Dutch pianist, teacher, and composer Cor de GROOT, winner of the Vienna piano competition in 1936, and later active as a piano teacher in The Hague and as a librarian and archivist in Hilversum, dies in his native Amsterdam at the age of 78.

27 MAY 1993

Violin Concerto by the distinguished 71-year-old Czech-born American composer, conductor, and pedagogue Karel HUSA is given its first ever performance in New York.

28 MAY 1993

Madrigales de Entonces for chorus (1991) by the colorful 67-year-old Cuban-born American composer, teacher, and writer on music Aurelio de la VEGA is heard for the first time in Mexico City.

30 MAY 1993

The innovative black American jazz pianist, electric keyboardist, bandleader, and composer Sun RA (real name, Herman Blount), who as a composer developed an abrasive and complex style in which avant-garde techniques were combined with electronic resources, dies in his native Birmingham, Alabama, at the age of 79.

31 MAY 1993

Singing Child, children's opera, by the preeminent 81-year-old Italian composer Gian Carlo MENOTTI is staged for the first time in Charleston, South Carolina.

2 JUNE 1993

Hvörf for strings (1992) by the 39-year-old Icelandic composer Áskell MÁSSON is heard for the first time in his native Reykjavík.

4 JUNE 1993

Gra for clarinet by the outstanding 84-year-old American composer and teacher Elliott (Cook) CARTER (Jr.) receives its first ever performance in Sermoneta.

5 JUNE 1993

Samuel Beckett: What is the Word, in its original version for voice and piano (1990), by the eminent 67-year-old Hungarian composer and teacher György KURTÁG is heard for the first time in Vienna.

8 JUNE 1993

The Argentine composer, pedagogue, and pianist Roberto CAAMAÑO, author of the valuable compendium *Historia del Teatro Colón* (3 vols., Buenos Aires, 1969) and *Apuntes para la formación del pianista profesional* (Buenos Aires, 1979), dies in his native Buenos Aires at the age of 69.

10 JUNE 1993

The esteemed American soprano Arleen (Joyce) AUGER, who in 1986 was chosen to sing at the royal wedding of Prince Andrew and Sarah Ferguson in London, dies in Amsterdam of a fatal brain tumor at the pitiable age of 53.

11 JUNE 1993

Second Piano Concerto, subtitled *Pensées*, with live electronics (1992–93), and *Pensées*, Requiem for piano, orchestra, and electronics (1990–91), two works by the respected 49-year-old German composer York (Georg) HÖLLER, are performed for the first time in Cologne.

12 JUNE 1993

Jetzt Immer Schnee for chamber chorus and chamber ensemble by the remarkable 61-year-old Russian composer Sofia (Asgatovna) GUBAIDULINA is given its premiere performance in Amsterdam.

13 JUNE 1993

Third String Quartet (1992–93) by the rising 41-year-old Polish composer, conductor, and teacher Aleksander LASOŃ is performed for the first time in Ontario.

14 JUNE 1993

Doppio coro for organ by the 68-year-old Croatian-born French composer, conductor, and teacher Ivo MALEC is given its first performance in Paris.

17 JUNE 1993

Odyssey for soprano, bass-baritone, sixteen instruments, computer-processed sound, and lighting (1989–93) by the veteran 58-year-old American composer and teacher Roger (Lee) REYNOLDS is performed for the first time in Paris.

18 JUNE 1993

Archipelago S. for orchestra by the outstanding 63-year-old Japanese composer Tōru TAKEMITSU is performed for the first time in Aldeburgh.

19 JUNE 1993

Rathenau, opera (1991–92), by the 64-year-old German-born Australian bassoonist, conductor, and composer George (actually, Georg) DREYFUS is given its first ever staging in Kassel.

20 JUNE 1993

Eblana: A Symphonic Portrait of Dublin (1990–91) by the respected 71-year-old Irish composer, conductor, and broadcasting administrator Gerard (real name, Alan Loraine) VICTORY is heard for the first time in Belfast.

22 JUNE 1993

Fourth Piano Sonata (1987–88), formerly numbered the *Sixth*, by the 54-year-old American writer on music and composer Phillip RAMEY is performed for the first time in Tangier, Morocco.

23 JUNE 1993

Initium for orchestra (1992) by the rising 32-year-old Japanese composer Karen TANAKA is given its first ever performance in her native Tokyo.

25 JUNE 1993

Pipa Rhyme for Pipa and 14 players by the energetic 40-year-old Chinese composer and teacher Chen YI is heard for the first time in New York.

28 JUNE 1993

The celebrated Bulgarian bass Boris (Kirilov) CHRISTOFF, brother-in-law of the famous Italian baritone Tito Gobbi (1913–1984), and most renowned for his dramatic portrayal of Boris Godunov, which recalled the interpretation of Chaliapin, dies in Rome at the age of 79.

2 JULY 1993

Memento mori for orchestra (1992–93) by the respected 64-year-old Australian composer and teacher Peter (Joshua) SCULTHORPE is heard for the first time in Perth.

3 JULY 1993

...beside the still waters: Variations and Interludes, concerto for piano, violin, cello, and orchestra (1992), by the 66-year-old American composer Marga RICHTER is given its first ever performance in Greensboro, North Carolina.

4 JULY 1993

Fanfare for Sagamore Hill for brass quintet by the 75-year-old American composer, pianist, and teacher J(oseph) Willard ROOSEVELT, grandson of President Theodore Roosevelt, is performed for the first time in Oyster Bay, New York.

7 JULY 1993

Baa-Baa Black Sheep, opera, by the talented 45-year-old English composer Michael (Fitzhardinge) BERKELEY, son of the significant English composer Sir Lennox (Randall Francis) Berkeley, is performed for the first time in Cheltenham.

8 JULY 1993

Die Zufriedenheit for tenor and piano, after Hölderlin, by the 65-year-old German composer and teacher Wilhelm KILLMAYER is heard for the first time in Munich.

12 JULY 1993

Sunset Boulevard, musical setting of the striking 1950 Billy Wilder film by the tremendously successful 45-year-old composer Sir Andrew LLOYD WEBBER, brother of the talented English cellist Julian Lloyd Webber, is first staged in London.

13 JULY 1993

Darting the Skiff for strings (1992–93) by the 43-year-old English composer and teacher John (Arthur) CASKEN is first performed in Cheltenham, the composer conducting.

15 JULY 1993

The Romanian composer and teacher Ovidiu VARGA, composer of much vocal music, including the oratorio *Scînteia Eliberăii* for soloists, chorus, and orchestra (1954) and the *Cantata bucuriei* for soloists, chorus, and orchestra (1960), dies in Bucharest at the age of 79.

19 JULY 1993

The eminent Polish-born American violinist and conductor Szymon GOLDBERG, who taught at Yale University (1978–82), the Juilliard School in New York (from 1978), the Curtis Institute of Music in Philadelphia (from 1980), and the Manhattan School of Music in New York (from 1981), and who from 1990 until his death conducted the New Japan Philharmonic in Tokyo, dies in Ôyama-machi, Japan, at the well-seasoned age of 84.

21 JULY 1993

The esteemed Swiss conductor and composer Paul MÜLLER-ZÜRICH (real name, Müller), whose music evolved from early Romantic influences to reflect neo-Baroque practices in a contemporary, tonal style, dies in Lucerne at the respectable age of 95.

22 JULY 1993

Mrs. Dalloway, chamber opera (1992), by the energetic 42-year-old American composer Libby (actually, Elizabeth Brown) LARSEN is mounted for the first time in Cleveland.

23 JULY 1993

The Gates, music theater piece, by the greatly talented 42-year-old American composer and performer Paul (Joseph) DRESHER in collaboration with the choreographer Margaret Jenkins is staged for the first time in Lee, Massachusetts.

25 JULY 1993

The Lord's Prayer for chorus by the remarkable 49-year-old English composer John (Kenneth) TAVENER is heard for the first time in Bury St. Edmunds.

26 JULY 1993

The greatly renowned 57-year-old Italian tenor Luciano PAVAROTTI gives a concert before some 500,000 people in New York's Central Part, a concert also viewed by countless others via a live telecast over PBS.

2 AUGUST 1993

Refren (Refrain) for piano by the 54-year-old Polish composer and pianist Zygmunt KRAUZE is performed for the first time in Schleswig-Holstein.

5 AUGUST 1993

The significant Slovak composer and pedagogue Eugen SUCHOŇ, one of the creators of the modern Slovak style of composition, based on authentic folk motifs and couched in appropriately congenial harmonies, dies in Bratislava at the respectable age of 84.

6 AUGUST 1993

Still Life with a Cello (for cello) by the aspiring 32-year-old Polish composer Hanna KULENTY is performed for the first time in Schleswig-Holstein.

6 AUGUST 1993

Amber Waves, installation for 20 independent tape sources by the innovative 39-year-old American composer Ron FEIN, an enveloping surround-sound composition for stationary or mobile audience and incorporating American music of various styles, is heard for the first time in Seattle.

8 AUGUST 1993

The Maid of the Mist and the Thunderbeings, dance piece first performed in Buffalo on Oct. 18, 1991, by the pre-eminent 62-year-old native American composer and music educator Louis (Wayne) BALLARD is heard for the first time as a symphonic suite in Aptos, California.

11 AUGUST 1993

Honor, Honor, spiritual for soprano and chorus first performed in New York on May 3, 1993, by the 47-year-old American composer and teacher Bruce (Stuart) SAYLOR is first heard in an arrangement for voice in piano in Chicago.

16 AUGUST 1993

Holocaust Memorial Cantata by the 50-year-old Polish composer, percussionist, and teacher Marta PTASZYŃSKA is performed for the first time in Schleswig-Holstein.

17 AUGUST 1993

Concerto for flute, vibraphone, harpsichord, and strings by the notable 64-year-old Russian composer and teacher Edison DENISOV is given its first ever performance in Lucerne.

21 AUGUST 1993

The brilliant American mezzo-soprano Tatiana TROYANOS, a leading member of the Metropolitan Opera in New York, excelling there in such roles as Amneris, Brangäne, Eboli, the Composer, Kundry, Didon, Santuzza, Orlovsky, Adalgisa, and Geschwitz, and where, in 1992, she created the role of Queen Isabella in Philip Glass's *The Voyage,* dies of cancer in her native New York at the pitiable age of 54.

22 AUGUST 1993

Ritornello for eight cellos (1992–93) by the eminent 63-year-old Spanish composer and teacher Luís (Alfonso) de PABLO (Costales) is performed for the first time in Santander.

26 AUGUST 1993

Serenade for strings (1990) by the productive 49-year-old English composer, teacher, and writer on music Robin (Greville) HOLLOWAY is first heard in Worcester.

27 AUGUST 1993

The Everlasting Voices, cantata for chorus and organ, by the respected 71-year-old Irish composer, conductor, and broadcasting administrator Gerard (real name, Alan Loraine) VICTORY is given its premiere performance in Belfast.

28 AUGUST 1993

Hommage a quelque'un for guitar and strings by the 66-year-old Polish composer Juliusz (Mieczyslaw) ŁUCIUK is performed for the first time in Hannover.

29 AUGUST 1993

Swing Dance for orchestra (1992) by the 53-year-old Czech-American composer Tomáš SVOBODA, son of the renowned mathematician Antonin Svoboda, is first heard in Billings, Montana.

2 SEPTEMBER 1993

The Hungarian conductor Miklós ERDÉLYI, long associated as a répétiteur and conductor with the Hungarian State Opera in his native Budapest, and author of *Schubert* (Budapest, 1963; 2nd ed., 1979), dies in Budapest at the moderate age of 65.

6 SEPTEMBER 1993

The Italian composer and pedagogue Virgilio MORTARI, who numbered among his accomplishments the completion of Mozart's unfinished score *L'Oca del Cairo* (Salzburg, Aug. 22, 1936), dies in Rome at the respectable age of 90.

9 SEPTEMBER 1993

The American singer of popular music Helen O'CONNELL, whose most popular recordings included *Tangerine, I Remember You*, and *When the Sun Comes Out*, and who became widely known as a television personality via NBC-TV's "Today Show" (1956–58) and her own "Helen O'Connell Show" (1957), dies in San Diego at the age of 73.

11 SEPTEMBER 1993

The eminent Austrian-born American conductor Erich LEINSDORF (real name, Landauer), who, from 1962 to 1969, held the prestigious appointment of music director of the Boston Symphony Orchestra, and who published a semi-autobiographical and rather candid book of sharp comments, *Cadenza: A Musical Career* (Boston, 1976), as well as *The Composer's Advocate: A Radical Orthodoxy for Musicians* (New Haven, 1981), followed by the posthumous volume *Erich Leinsdorf on Music* (Portland, Oreg., 1997), dies in Zürich at the reasonable age of 81.

12 SEPTEMBER 1993

Lieder und Tanze for mezzo-soprano and chamber ensemble, after the television opera *La Cubana oder Ein Leben für die Kunst* (1992–93), by the outstanding 67-year-old German composer Hans Werner HENZE is performed for the first time in Zürich.

13 SEPTEMBER 1993

Madre Juana, opera (1986), by the 47-year-old Mexican composer Federico IBARRA (Groth) is first staged in his native Mexico City.

14 SEPTEMBER 1993

Viola Concerto (1990) by the respected 62-year-old American composer and record producer Nancy VAN DE VATE is performed for the first time in Kraków.

15 SEPTEMBER 1993

The Dutch musicologist Frits (Rudolf) NOSKE, long-time professor of musicology at the University of Amsterdam whose mature writings included *The Signifier and the Signified: Studies in the Operas of Mozart and Verdi* (The Hague, 1977), *Sweelinck* (Oxford, 1988), and *Saints and Sinners: The Latin Musical Dialogue in the Seventeenth Century* (Oxford, 1992), dies in Ariolo, Switzerland, at the age of 72.

16 SEPTEMBER 1993

The Czech conductor František JÍLEK, who acquired a fine reputation through his championship of the music of his homeland, most notably works by Smetana and Janáček, dies in Brno at the age of 80.

17 SEPTEMBER 1993

L'estuaire du temps for orchestra by the innovative 58-year-old French composer, musicologist, and philologist François-Bernard MÂCHE is first performed in Strasbourg.

18 SEPTEMBER 1993

3 Pieces for three recorders and metronome by the 39-year-old Polish composer Paweł SZYMÁNSKI is performed for the first time in Basel.

19 SEPTEMBER 1993

The Hungarian composer, conductor, administrator, and teacher András MIHÁLY, three-time recipient (1952, 1954, and 1964) of the Erkel Prize, and in 1955 of the Kossuth Prize, and who was made a Merited Artist (1969) and an Outstanding Artist (1974) by the Hungarian government, dies in his native Budapest at the age of 75.

21 SEPTEMBER 1993

Winterreise, "composed interpretation" of Schubert's song cycle for tenor and small orchestra, by the distinguished 56-year-old German conductor, composer, and pedagogue (Johannes Wolfgang) Hans ZENDER is performed for the first time in Frankfurt am Main.

22 SEPTEMBER 1993

The distinguished Greek-born American conductor of Spanish-Portuguese Sephardic descent Maurice ABRA-VANEL, on whose 90th birthday (Jan. 6, 1993), the Utah Symphony Orchestra's concert hall was renamed in his honor, dies in Salt Lake City at the respectable age of 90.

24 SEPTEMBER 1993

The gifted 45-year-old Turkish-born American violinist of Armenian descent Ani KAVAFIAN, sister of the equally gifted violinist Ida Kavafian, performs as soloist in the premiere performance of Tod Machover's *Forever and Ever*, concerto for Hyperviolin and chamber orchestra, with Hugh Wolff and the St. Paul (Minneapolis) Chamber Orchestra.

25 SEPTEMBER 1993

William and the Bomb for narrator and orchestra by the esteemed 66-year-old English composer Wilfred JOSEPHS is performed for the first time in Cardiff.

26 SEPTEMBER 1993

MGV (Musique à Grande Vitesse) for orchestra and *The Piano Concerto*, two works by the notable 49-year-old English composer, conductor, and writer on music Michael (Laurence) NYMAN, are performed for the first time in Lille.

27 SEPTEMBER 1993

The revered 52-year-old Spanish tenor and conductor Plácido DOMINGO and the greatly renowned 57-year-old Italian tenor Luciano PAVAROTTI appear at the 25th anniversary of the Metropolitan Opera, Domingo singing Siegmund in Act 1 of *Die Walküre* and Pavarotti singing Otello in the first act of Verdi's opera, in a live radio broadcast heard around the world.

29 SEPTEMBER 1993

Violin Concerto by the distinguished 57-year-old English composer and teacher Nicholas (John) MAW is premiered in New York.

30 SEPTEMBER 1993

Orloj for orchestra by the 42-year-old American conductor and composer Lawrence RAPCHAK is given its first ever performance in Omaha.

1 OCTOBER 1993

Eighth Symphony (1992–93) by the outstanding 67-year-old German composer Hans Werner HENZE is heard for the first time in Boston.

2 OCTOBER 1993

3 Fantasy Movements for cello and orchestra, based on the earlier *3 Fantasy Pieces* for cello and piano (1971), by the accomplished 43-year-old Israeli pianist and composer Shulamit RAN is performed for the first time in Berkeley, California.

3 OCTOBER 1993

Don Quijote de la Mancha, theatrical adventure after Cervantes (1989–91), by the distinguished 46-year-old German conductor, composer, and pedagogue (Johannes Wolfgang) Hans ZENDER is given its first ever performance in Stuttgart.

6 OCTOBER 1993

Santika Ekatala (Sanskrit for "Harmony to Ward Off Evil Consequences") for orchestra by the promising 32-year-old Korean composer Unsuk CHIN is performed for the first time in Tokyo.

8 OCTOBER 1993

Troubadours: Variations for guitar and chamber orchestra by the notable 55-year-old American composer John (Paul) CORIGLIANO, son of the notable American composer John Corigliano, is performed for the first time in St. Paul, Minnesota.

9 OCTOBER 1993

Languido for bass flute and live electronics (1992–93) by the iconoclastic 63-year-old German composer Dieter SCHNEBEL is given its first performance in Graz.

10 OCTOBER 1993

Symphonic Melismas by the 78-year-old Spanish-born American composer and conductor Carlos SURINACH is given its first performance in Miami.

11 OCTOBER 1993

The much admired American pianist and composer Yvar (real name, Ronald Mackay) MIKHASHOFF, a champion of American music of the 19th and 20th centuries who, in 1982, organized the Holland Festival's two-week-long celebration of 200 years of Dutch-American friendship through a series of nine thematic concerts covering 250 years of American music, dies in Buffalo, New York, at the lamentable age of 52.

12 OCTOBER 1993

The German-born American publishing executive and writer on music Hans (Walter) HEINSHEIMER, a brilliant stylist in both German and English who contributed numerous informative articles to *Melos, Musical Quarterly, Holiday, Reader's Digest*, etc., and who published the entertaining books *Menagerie in F-sharp* (N.Y., 1947), *Fanfare for Two Pigeons* (1952), and *Best Regards to Aida* (published in German as *Schönste Grüsse an Aida*; Munich, 1968), dies in New York at the fulfilled age of 93.

14 OCTOBER 1993

The Golem, opera (1980), by the prominent 59-year-old Australian composer, pianist, teacher, and writer on Larry SITSKY is given a belated premiere in Sydney.

15 OCTOBER 1993

Tribute to Portinari for orchestra by the 79-year-old Brazilian composer, violinist, and conductor César GUERRA-PEIXE is heard for the first time in Rio de Janeiro.

16 OCTOBER 1993

Dream Steps, dance suite for flute, viola, and harp, in a choreographed version, by the 44-year-old American composer, organist, and teacher Dan (Steven) LOCK-LAIR is performed for the first time in Raleigh, North Carolina. (A concert version premiere followed in Washington, D.C., on 24 October 1993.)

20 OCTOBER 1993

Fresh Dances for the Late Tchaikovsky, ballet, by the respected 57-year-old English composer and music critic Anthony (Edward) PAYNE, husband of the English soprano Jane Manning, is mounted for the first time in London.

21 OCTOBER 1993

The 42-year-old American soprano Sharon SWEET sings Lina in the first staging of Giuseppe Verdi's *Stiffelio* by the Metropolitan Opera in New York.

24 OCTOBER 1993

Grendel's Mother for orchestra by the 42-year-old American composer James UNDERWOOD receives its first ever performance in Bloomington, Indiana.

25 OCTOBER 1993

Plejady (Pleiades) for violin and piano by the 63-year-old Polish composer and teacher Romuald TWARDOWSKI is given its first performance in Warsaw.

26 OCTOBER 1993

Solar for chamber ensemble by the significant 40-year-old Finnish composer Kaija (Anneli) SAARIAHO is performed for the first time in Antwerp.

29 OCTOBER 1993

The 33-year-old Italian conductor Carlo RIZZI makes his Metropolitan Opera debut in New York conducting a performance of *La Bohème*.

31 OCTOBER 1993

A Deviant Fantasy for four clarinets by the prolific 33-year-old English composer Mark-Anthony TURNAGE is first performed in London.

1 NOVEMBER 1993

The Twittering Machine for chamber orchestra, after the Klee painting, by the 40-year-old American composer and teacher Cindy MCTEE is given its first ever performance in Pittsburgh.

3 NOVEMBER 1993

Leon THEREMIN (real name, Termen), Russian inventor of the space-controlled electronic instrument that bears his name, dies in Moscow at the respectable age of 97.

4 NOVEMBER 1993

The first-ever "Other Minds" Festival, under the artistic direction of Charles Amirkhanian, opens at the Center for the Arts at Yerba Buena Gardens in San Francisco with a concert in the following program: the first-ever performances of *Contraption No. 1* and *Study No. 47* for extended woodwinds and prepared piano by the remarkable 81-year-old American-born Mexican composer and innovator in the technique of recording notes on a player-piano roll Conlon NANCARROW; the world premiere of *Music* for extended woodwinds by the 41-year-old German-born inventor, practitioner, and builder of sound sculpture and computerized acoustic instruments TRIMPIN; a work-in-progress commissioned by New Langton Arts with sponsorship from the National Endowment for the Arts, *Early that summer* by the American composer and co-founder of New York's internationally-acclaimed festival, Bank on a Can, Julia WOLFE; and *Improvisations* by the American composer and Kora virtuoso Foday Musa SUSO.

5 NOVEMBER 1993

On the second day of the first-ever "Other Minds" Festival at the Center for the Arts at Yerba Buena Gardens in San Francisco, a concert is given in the following program: *Lily, Woman Shaman of Ali Mountain*, and *Sorrow Song of Meng Jiangnu*, three works by Chinese-born American composer and pianist Jon JANG; *Mad Rush* for piano (1979) by the outstanding 56-year-old American composer Philip GLASS; *Duo for Piano and Percussion* by the Canadian composer (and former pupil and wife to the outstanding American composer Morton FELDMAN) Barbara Monk FELD-MAN; and *Nocturne* for violin and piano (1947), *Music for 3* (1984), and *In a Landscape* (1948), three works by the singularly inventive and much beloved American composer, writer, philosopher, and visual artist of ultramodern tendencies John CAGE (1912–1992).

6 NOVEMBER 1993

On the third day of the first-ever "Other Minds" Festival at the Center for the Arts at Yerba Buena Gardens in San Francisco, a concert in the following program: *Full Spectrum Voice* by the leading 52-year-old American baritone, composer, and producer Thomas BUCKNER; *Light Songs* for voice and piano (1988) by the 50-year-old American composer, singer, and filmmaker Meredith MONK; *A Berkelium Canon* by the American composers the distinguished 48-year-old avant-garde composer, influential radio producer, and arts administrator of Armenian descent Charles AMIRKHANIAN and the innovative 40-year-old improvisational guitarist and keyboardist Henry KAISER; and *Selected Studies* for player piano by the remarkable 81-year-old American-born Mexican composer, innovator in the technique of recording notes on a player-piano roll Conlon NANCARROW.

7 NOVEMBER 1993

On the fourth and final day of the first-ever "Other Minds" Festival at the Center for the Arts at Yerba Buena Gardens in San Francisco, two events of note are given, in the following sequence:

An afternoon program of film and video presentations by and about guest composers, featuring *Ellis Island* by the 50-year old American composer, singer, and filmmaker Meredith (Jane) MONK; *Atalanta Strategy*, television opera (1984), by the pioneering 63-year-old American composer, performer, director, and writer Robert (Reynolds) ASHLEY; and "Philip Glass" and "John Cage," two works from the *Four American Composers* series by the 51-year-old Welsh film director, writer, painter, and librettist Peter GREENAWAY.

An evening concert featuring *Empire* for voices and tape and *The Producer Speaks*, two works by the pioneering 63-year-old American composer, performer, director, and writer Robert (Reynolds) ASHLEY, as well as recent works by the versatile American vocalist and instrumentalist Jai UTTAL.

11 NOVEMBER 1993

The Finnish composer and teacher Olavi PESONEN, whose works followed along traditional lines, dies in his native Helsinki at the reasonable age of 84.

12 NOVEMBER 1993

Alternativer Baukasten for chamber ensemble by the 67-year-old German composer, pedagogue, organist, and harpsichordist Ruth ZECHLIN is heard for the first time in Nuremberg.

14 NOVEMBER 1993

Schoenberg's Space for violin, cello, and piano by the 38-year-old Armenian composer Yuri KASPAROV is given its premiere performance in Hamburg.

16 NOVEMBER 1993

The esteemed Czech-born Austrian soprano Lucia POPP, who won accolades for her roles in operas by Mozart and Strauss, especially Pamina, Despina, Zerlina, Susanna, Zdenka, Sophie, and the Countess, as well as the Queen of the Night, dies in Munich, just days after her 54th birthday.

18 NOVEMBER 1993

The remarkable 81-year-old American composer of film music David RAKSIN is guest of honor at the Ecrans Sonores Festival in Biarritz, France, where the day is declared "David Raksin Day."

20 NOVEMBER 1993

The 67th Festival of the International Society for Contemporary Music in Mexico opens at the Pirámides de Teotihuacán with a program entitled "Percusiones y Electroacústica en Teotihuacán," performed by Los Ejecutores, percussion ensemble, conducted by Aldo Brizzi; and Adrian Peacock, bass, Stefano Scodanibbio, Luis Antonio Rojas, and Valeria Theirry, double bass, and Benjamín Alarcón, Félix Méndez, Clemente Sanabria, Hernando Castro, and David Abrego, trombones, conducted by Diego Minciacchi, in the following program: *Awithlaknannai...dal gioco degli dei* (1992) for four percussionists arranged to form a circle, in an amplified setting by the Italian composer Nicola CISTERNINO; *Políptico* (1983), a virtuosic piece for percussionists, with Latin American musical sources set in a free structure, by the Mexican composer and violinist Manuel ENRÍQUEZ; and *Westbau aus "Der Dom"* for bass, double bass, trombones, and electronic sounds (1992) by the American composer Diego MINCIACCHI, the third in a series of works composed

with mixed techniques of audiodigital production, performable in both indoor and outdoor spaces.

21 NOVEMBER 1993

On the second day of the 67th Festival of the International Society for Contemporary Music in Mexico, two concerts are given in the following sequence:

A mid-day concert, "Texturas Sonoras para Cuerdas," given at the Museu Nacional de Arte (MUNAL) by Gonzalo Salazar and Magnus Andersson, guitar, Bozena Slawinska, cello, Armando Merino, piano, and Stefano Scodanibbio, double bass, in the following program: *Sonata* for solo guitar (1992) by the Uruguay-born Mexican composer Hebert VAZQUEZ, in two contrasting movements, with coda; *Changes* for solo guitar (1983) by the well-seasoned 84-year-old American composer Elliott CARTER, first performed by David Starobin, for whom it was written, on the occasion of the composer's 75th birthday, Dec. 11, 1983; *Antagonia* for solo cello (1990) by the Portuguese composer Alexandre DELGADO, with scordato tuning, wherein the first and second strings are tuned half a tone lower than normal, dividing the instrument into two "antagonic" fields, i.e. two perfect fifths separated by an augmented fourth; *Colloid* for ten-string guitar (1988–91), dedicated to Magnus Andersson, by the Welsh-born English composer Richard BARRET; *Esplorazione del bianco* for solo double bass by the Italian composer Salvatore SCIARRINO; *In deepening light* for piano and double bass (1989) by the Canadian composer Rodney SHARMAN, first performed at the 1989 Huddersfield Festival by Robert Black and Anthony de Mare, to whom the work is dedicated; and *Valentine* for solo double bass (1969) by the respected 65-year-old American composer Jacob DRUCKMAN.

An early evening concert at the Sala Nezahualcóyotl del Centro Cultural Universitario, "La Expresion Nórdica," performed by Ensemble CIKADA, conducted by Christian Eggen, in the following program: *Solve e Coagula* (1992) by the Norwegian composer Rolf WALLIN; *Our whisper woke no clocks* for piano and chamber ensemble, inspired by lines from a poem by W.H. Auden, by the Norwegian composer Asbjørn SCHAATHUN; *Ex* (1993) by the Norwegian composer John PERSEN and *AbUno* (1992) by the Norwegian composer and teacher Lasse THORESEN, both composed especially for CIKADA; and *UR* for five instruments and live electronics by the 35-year-old Finnish composer Magnus LINDBERG.

22 NOVEMBER 1993

The celebrated English novelist, critic, and occasional composer Anthony BURGESS (real name John Anthony Burgess Wilson Burgess), author of the disturbing *A Clockwork Orange* (1962), followed by such novels as the *Napoleon Symphony* (1974) and his major literary achievement, *Earthly Powers* (1980), and who, as a composer, produced a respectable body of works notable for being refreshingly rhythmical and tonal, but not without quirky quartal harmonies and atonal diversions, dies in London at the age of 76.

22 NOVEMBER 1993

On the third day of the 67th Festival of the International Society for Contemporary Music in Mexico, four events are given, in the following sequence:

An early morning series of lectures and presentations at the Sala Manuel M. Ponce del Palacio de Bellas Artes, entitled "Alrededor del Concepto Oriental del Tiempo" and moderated by Daniel Catán (Mexico), featuring Hilda Parades (Mexico), "The concept of time in the music of India," Valerie Ross (Malaysia), "Juxtaposition of Eastern and Western Time Concepts," Arturo Salinas (Mexico), "Time and space in the ritual drums of Tarahumara Indians and in an electroacoustic composition composed by computer," Max Stern (Israel), "The concept of time in aleatory composition," and Joji Yuasa (Japan), "Monochronic time, polychronic time; countable time and uncountable time."

A mid-day concert entitled "Música Mínima para Piano," "In Memoriam Walter Maas" (founder of the Gaudeamus Foundation), performed by Michael Finnissy, piano, at the Sala Manuel M. Ponce del Palacio de Bellas Artes, in the following program: *L'Alouette des champs (Petites Esquisses d'Oiseaux)* by the French composer Olivier MESSIAEN, *Tres miniaturas del siglo XX* by the Mexican composer Graciela AGUDELO, *Air III* by the Norwegian composer Yngve SLETTHOLM, *Rauda* (Lament) by the Lithuanian composer F.R. BAJORAS, *México (Intexterior No. 4)* by the Japanese composer Tetsuji EMURA, *Prelude No. 2 (La naissance de la saison nouvelle)* by the Brazilian composer Celso MOJOLA, *after-image* by the English composer Howard SKEMPTON, *...desde que naçe...* by the English composer Michael FINNISSY, *Tras la ventana* by the Mexican composer Ana LARA, *Mazurek (1926)* by the Polish composer Karol SZYMANOWSKI, *Winterday* by the Italian composer Vittorio FELLEGARA, *Brief Exaltation* by the Belgian composer André LAPORTE, *Aphorismus (aus katalog I)* by the Austrian composer Christian OFENBAUER, *Níu* (Nine) by the Icelandic composer Snorri Sigfús BIRGISSON, *Haze* by the Chinese composer Jin-Fong YANG, *Spectacle pour un instant* by the Romanian composer Octavian NEMESCU, *Ostinato* by the Romanian composer Nicolae BRINDUS, *Prelude I* by the Serbian composer Milan MIHAJLOVIC, *Attax (Sonate met 394 Aanslagen per minuut)* by the Dutch composer Daan MANNEKE, *Waving* by the Uruguayan composer Clotilde ROSA, *Preludio* by the Argentine composer Martin PAVLOVSKY, *Mikro-Toccata* by the Israeli composer Jacob GILBOA, *Opera transcriptions: La Rondine* by the Canadian composer Rodney SHARMAN, *Afterpiece* by the Irish composer Raymond DEANE, *Dream* by the American composer John CAGE, *Images of bells* by the Chinese composer Richard TSANG, *Sin título* by the Uruguayan composer Hector TOSAR, *Alla burla* by the Hungarian composer József SÁRI, *View-lines* by the Swedish composer Erik FORARE, *From "Das Leonara notenbuch"* by the Irish composer Piers HELLAWELL, and *Night* by the Australian composer Peter SCULTHORPE.

A late afternoon concert at the Anfiteatro Simón Bolívar entitled "Contra La Muerte," performed by the Latin American String Quartet, in the following program: *Yiddishbbuk* (1992) by the Argentine composer Osvaldo GOLIJOV, in three movements, the first commemorating three children interned by the Nazis at Terezin, the second bearing the initials of the writer Isaac Bashevis Singer, and the last the initials of Leonard Bernstein; *Toki-no-ito I* (Threads of time; 1985), in four movements, each in of four parts, by the Japanese composer Isao MATSUSHITA; *String quartet, in memoriam Barry Anderson & Tomasz Sikorski* (1989–93), by the 50-year-old American composer and pianist Stephen MONTAGUE, the final version of which was completed and performed by the Smith Quartet for the composer's 50th Birthday Concert in London's Purcell Room on March 23, 1993; and *Cuartet número 2* (1992–93), an "African-Caribbean aesthetic experience" in two movements, *Nocturne* and *Homage to Nanny (Dance)*, by the Costa Rican composer and guitarist Alejandro CARDONA.

An evening concert at the Anfiteatro Simón Bolívar entitled "Figuras Momentáneas con Instrumentos Solistas," performed by the Divertimento Ensemble, directed by Sandro Gorli, with special guest artists Louise Bessette, piano, Garth Knox, viola, and Cayetano Castaño, oboe, in the following program: *Piano concertant* (1987), in four movements, "Deciso," "Fugace," "Canto," and "Furioso," by the Canadian composer José EVANGELISTA, *De l'instant où* (1987) by the Italian composer Alessandro MELCHIORRE, the title referring to an impressive text by Andre Breton, *Arpège* for six instruments (1986) by the noted 66-year-old Italian composer and pedagogue Franco DONATONI, *La del alba sería...* by the Mexican composer Manuel MORA, the title drawn from the first words of chapter IV in Cervantes's *Quixote* and referring to the first hour of dawn, and *Journey of the Virgin Spirit* for solo oboe and chamber ensemble by the 27-year-old English composer Julian Anthony BUTCHER.

23 NOVEMBER 1993

On the fourth day of the 67th Festival of the International Society for Contemporary Music in Mexico, three events are given, in the following sequence:

A mid-day concert at the Sala Manuel M. Ponce del Palacio de Bellas Artes entitled "Homenaje a Nancarrow: El Tiempo: Último Confín de la Música," performed by the Arditti String Quartet, enhanced by Trimpin's *Vorsetzer*, in a program of works by the remarkable 71-year-old American-born Mexican composer, innovator in the technique of recording notes on a player-piano roll, Conlon NANCARROW, including *Studies for Player Piano # 21 (Canon X)*, *#3a* (from the *Boogie-Woogie Suite*), *#36, #12, #29,* and *#43, String Quartet #1, Studies for Player Piano #37* and *#41c* (for two player pianos, a simultaneous playing of #s 42a and 41b), in a version for player piano and Trimpin's Vorsetzer, *Toccata for violin and player piano*, and *String Quartet #3*.

A late afternoon concert at the Sala Manuel M. Ponce del Palacio de Bellas Artes entitled "Desafíos para Alientos," performed by Horacio Franco, recorders, Salvador Torre, flute, Abel Pérez Pitón, clarinet, Federico Mobdelci, bass saxophone, and Barry Hall, MIDI violin, in the following program: *2 Caprichos* for virtuoso solo recorder by the Mexican composer Armando LUNA; *Encantamiento* (1990) for two recorders (one player) by the Mexican composer Daniel CATÁN; *Pythikos nomos* for solo flute by the Cyprus composer Faidros KAVALLARIS, first performed on April 4, 1990, in Nicosia, Cyprus, by Pierre Yves Artaud, to whom it is dedicated; *Deade (n) Turn left* for solo clarinet by the Belgian composer Baudouin de JAER; *From the abyss* for solo bass saxophone by the Italian composer and teacher Tonino TESEI; and *Concerto in D* for violin and DMIX computer by the Israeli composer Daniel OPPENHEIM.

An evening concert at the Alcázar del Castillo de Chapultepec entitled "Evocación de Rituales," performed by the Orquesta Filarmónica de la Ciudad de México, conducted by Jorge Sarmientos, in the following program: *Oxkintok*, fantasy for orchestra, by the Mexican composer Hilda PAREDES, the title drawn from both the Mayan word with three different meanings: *Ox* (three), *kin* (sun), and *tok* (flint), as well as referring to the ruins being discovered near Maxcanú in Yucatán; *Durch die Erde geht ein riss gegen das vergessen* (1990) by the 44-year-old German composer Ernst H. FLAMMER; *Orchestral Theatre I: Xun* (1990) by the significant 36-year-old Chinese composer Tan DUN, part one of a significant three-part commission from the BBC; *Tzilini* (Tolling bells; 1992) by the Mexican composer Carlos Sanchez GUTIERREZ, based on the composer's earlier *Calacas y Palomas* for two pianos (1991), its title referring to "the percussive and eternally resonant character of both works: a dialogue between continuous and incisive waves and the murmuration of crystal"; and *Trinkets of little value* for mezzo-soprano and orchestra (1986–91) by the Canadian composer and recorder and MIDI instruments player Peter HANNAN, to texts taken from a "dictionary" of about 200 native words found at the end of Jacques Cartier's account of his second voyage to Canada in 1535.

23 NOVEMBER 1993

The Brazilian composer, violinist, and conductor César GUERRA-PEIXE, who, as a composer plunged headlong into the torrent of dodecaphony, but about 1949 changed his orientation and reclaimed his Brazilian roots, nurtured by melorhythmic folksong resources, dies in Rio de Janeiro at the age of 79.

24 NOVEMBER 1993

On the fifth day of the 67th Festival of the International Society for Contemporary Music in Mexico, three events are given, in the following sequence:

A mid-day series of lectures and presentations entitled "El Tiempo en la Música de Algunos Compositores Americanos Contemporáneos," given at the Casa Borda, Taxco., Gro., and moderated by Ricardo Miranda (Mexico), featuring Monika Fürst-Heidtmann (Germany), "Tempo as an essential element in the composition of Conlon Nancarrow's *Studies* for player piano," Carole Gubernikoff (Brazil), "Time in John Cage's *Sonatas and Interludes* and *Music of Changes*," David Vayo (U.S.A.), "The concept of time in the music of the USA," and Ricardo Zohn-Muldoon (Mexico), "The tepidness of time."

An early afternoon concert at the Iglesias de Santa Prisca, Taxco, entitled "Sonido y Unidad," performed by Ensemble Aventure, conducted by Bernhard Wulff, in the following program: *Monolith* (1991) by the German composer Thomas BRUTTGER, commissioned by Ensemble Aventure, with the choice of instruments corresponding to the instrumentation of Edgar Varèse's *Octandre; Chants* by the Venezuelan composer Alfredo del MONACO; *Ohne Hölderlin* by the German composer Nicolaus A. HUBER; *Zerblasen: Wind brakings* for seven wind instruments and double bass (1992–93) by the Swiss composer Max E. KELLER; *Music for Het trio* by the Romanian composer Liana ALEXANDRA; and *Sendas* (1992) by the Uruguayan composer Graciela PARASKEVAIDIS, in four movements" "cortante," "cantante," "agresivo," and "de baile," loosely corresponding to lines of text by Juan Gelman: *I. but we look fearfully the passing roa, II. we ask to which other inferno will it lead, III. an inferno in the hand is worth two in the bush,* and *IV. and freedom becaomes a pain of the body.*

An early evening concert at the Iglesia de Santa Prisca, Taxco, entitled "Tejidos y Fluídos Sonoros," performed by the Arditti String Quartet, in the following program: *String Quartet No. 2,* entitled *Reigen seliger Geister* (1989) by the 47-year-old German composer and pedagogue Helmut LACHENMANN; *ishini' ioni* (1984–90) by the 50-year-old Mexican composer, theoretician, historian, and pedagogue Julio ESTRADA; and *String Quartet No. 2* (1968) by the eminent 70-year-old Hungarian-born Austrian composer and pedagogue György LIGETI.

24 NOVEMBER 1993

Strathclyde Concerto No. 8 for bassoon and orchestra and *A Spell for Green Corn: The MacDonald Dances* for orchestra, two works by the eminent 59-year-old English composer and conductor Sir Peter Maxwell DAVIES, are heard for the first time in Glasgow.

25 NOVEMBER 1993

On the sixth day of the 67th Festival of the International Society for Contemporary Music in Mexico, three concerts are given, in the following sequence:

A mid-day concert at the Ex-Escuela de Medicina (Antiguo Palacio de la Inquisición)/Patio entitled "Mitos, Raices y Culturas Ancestrales," performed by Los Ejecutores, percussion ensemble, Armando Merino, piano, Ricardo Gallardo, percussion, Ruth Ramírez, mezzo-soprano, Horacio Franco, recorder, and Cuauhtémoc Rivera, violin, conducted by Ricardo Gallardo, in the following program: *Border Crossing* for percussion quartet (1991) by the American composer David VAYO, its partly autobiographical title reflecting the composer's interest and involvement as a North American in the culture of the lands south of "la frontera"; *Scintillation II* for percussion by the Chinese-born Australian composer Julian Jing-JunYU; *Critical Point* for piano and percussion by the 44-year-old Japanese composer and teacher Takehito SHIMAZU; *Rogosanti* (1986) by the English composer James WOOD, the title the Sanskrit word for healing or quieting of disease, reflecting the work's essential elements wherein evil is represented by a rhythmic cell from North India called "Ata Trisra" and performed by drums and wood instruments, and the good spirit by a rhythmic cell from South India called "Dhamar-tala" and performed by metal instruments; and *Flores del viento II* for mezzo-soprano, recorder, violin, and percussion by the Mexican composer Ricardo ZOHN-MULDOON, utilizing texts primarily written by his sister, Laura (with the exception of one, *El río pasa,* an old Otomi poem translated into Spanish by Angel M. Garibay).

A late afternoon concert at the Sala Manuel M. Ponce del Palacio de Bellas Artes entitled "El Mensaje de los Dioses," performed by the Arditti String Quartet, with special guest artists Brenda Mitchell, soprano, and Stefano Scodanibbio, double bass, in the following program: *Invención No. 2* for solo cello (1987–90) by the 36-year-old Mexican composer Ignacio BACALOBERA; *Desiderantur* for violin and viola (1992) by the Italian composer and virtuoso double bassist Stefano SCODANIBBIO, fourth in a series of six duets (all inspired by writers) composed for possible combinations of bowed instruments, its title based on the first poem of *Laborinthus,* an anthology by Eduardo Sanguineti, to whom the work is dedicated; *Fourth String Quartet,* with soprano (1989–90), by the 50-year-old English composer and teacher Brian FERNEYHOUGH; *Vom Grund bis zum Scheitel* for solo double bass (1991–92) by the 44-year-old German organist, teacher, and composer Gerhard STÄBLER, based on the composer's earlier *Co-wie Kobalt* for double bass and orchestra (1989/90), both inspired by Giuseppe Ungaretti's poem; *Agglutinati all'oggi, Ikhoor* for string trio (1978), in seven sections, by the eminent 71-year-old Greek-born French composer, music theorist, and teacher Iannis XENAKIS; and *String Quartet No. 3* (1963) by the remarkable Italian composer Giacinto SCELSI (1905–1988), in five uniquely programmatic movements: *I. With great tenderness (dolcissimo), II. The spirit calls: dualism, ambivalence, conflict (drammatico), III. The soul awakens..." (con transparenza), IV. ...and falls once more into pathos, but now with a sense of imminent release (con tristezza),* and *V. Liberation, Catharsis.*

An evening concert at the Ex-Escuela de Medicina (Antiguo Palacio de la Inquisición)/Auditorio entitled "Ecos, laments, shadows," performed by the Divertimento Ensemble, conducted by Sandro Gorli, with special guest artists Marianne Lund, Ana Valdez, Amelia Sierra, Teresa Guillermo, and Rosaura Gorra, sopranos, in the following program: *Trois études* by the French composer Michaël LEVINAS; *The harp of fire,* song cycle based on five musical poems by the Indian poet Rabindranath Tagore, by the 33-year-old Dutch composer Jan Rokus van ROOSENDAEL; *Syster, min syster* for soprano and chamber ensemble by the Danish composer Mogens Winkel

HOLM, to three texts by the Swedish-Finnish poet Edith Södergran (1892–1923) drawn from her anthology *Rosenaltaret* (The altar of the rose, 1919); *Elegía* (1991) for four sopranos and chamber ensemble by the Mexican composer Gabriela ORTIZ, to texts comprised of brief phrases from the liturgy of the Requiem; and *Shadowland* by the Danish composer Bent SØRENSEN, in four movements, "Fluente," "Luminoso," "Lontano, quasi un funerale," "Maniaco don delicatezza," and "Sostenuto, molto calmo," in the proportions 4-7-4-3.

25 NOVEMBER 1993

The distinguished 46-year-old Yugoslav mezzo-soprano Marjana LIPOVŠEK makes her North American debut as Fricka in Richard Wagner's *Die Walküre* at the Lyric Opera of Chicago.

26 NOVEMBER 1993

On the seventh day of the 67th Festival of the International Society for Contemporary Music in Mexico, four events are given, in the following sequence:

A morning-long series of lectures and presentations at the Sala Manuel M. Ponce del Palacio de Bellas Artes, featuring Jonathan Kramer (U.S.A.), "The perception of musical time," Alessandro Melchiorre (Italy), "Between musical amnesia and memory," Celso Mojola (Brazil), "Structural possibilities in imminent time for the organization of a musical work," and Thomas Reiner (Australia), "A chameleon named musical time."

An early afternoon concert at the Sala Manuel M. Ponce del Palacio de Bellas Artes entitled "Modelos, Paisajes, Descripciones y Juegos Ciberneticos," performed by Louise Bessette, piano, and Trío Neos, in the following program: *Model XV (Sahihi)* for solo piano (1988) by the outstanding 64-year-old Polish composer, pianist, pedagogue, writer on music, stage manager, and playwright Boguslaw SCHAEFFER, utilizing throughout its eleven minute duration intervals derived of B-Es-C-H (Boguslaw Schaeffer), thus *Sahihi*, which means, in Suaheli, signature, in eleven sections (A to K); *Ivoren Landschap* for two pianos (1992) by the 52-year-old Indonesia-born Dutch composer Roderick De MAN, utilizing specially-made "chord laths" which allow the player to play and sustain extremely large chords; *Domino I* for solo piano (1986) by the French composer Philippe BOIVIN; *Descrizione Umoristica* for high soprano and piano (1990) by the German composer Andre WERNER, to texts built of extracts form a theater piece by Pier Paolo Pasolini, *Pilade*, especially the fifth episode, wherein Atena gives a prophecy to Oreste, in five scenes, each with special registers and articulations for both singer and pianist; *Divertimento No. 2,* op.84, for clarinet, bassoon, and piano (1990), subtitled "cybernetic," by the Chilean composer and physician Hernán Ramírez AVILA, in four movements, the last a set of theme and variations; and *Para tres* by the 40-year-old Puerto Rican composer Roberto SIERRA.

A late afternoon concert at the Sala Jaime Torres Bodet del Museu Nacional de Antropología entitled "Latidos, Ritmos y Colores," performed by La Camerata, conducted by Harry Sparnaay, in the following program: *Expulsie* (1988; rev. 1990) by the 34-year-old Dutch composer Theo VERBEY, in four parts, forming a triptych with the composer's earlier *Inversie* for ten instruments (1987) and *Contractie* for flute, bass clarinet, and piano (1988); *Concertino Colorum* for flute and eleven instruments by the Ecuadorian composer Diego LUZURIAGA, utilizing frequency modulation as a method for generating harmonic support; *Sable, In memoriam Edmond Jabès* by the 33-year-old French composer Gualtiero DAZZI; and *Clock of the past II* (1988), a commission from Paris's Le chant du monde by the Lithuanian composer Bronius KUTAVICIUS.

An evening concert at the Teatro del Palacio de Bellas Artes entitled "Espacios, Aguas, Luces, Eternidades," performed by the Orquesta Sinfónica Nacional, conducted by Aldo Brizzi, with special guest artist Gerardo Gandini, piano, in the following program: *Intexterior No. 5* by the 33-year-old Japanese composer Tetsuji EMURA, the words *interior* and *exterior* conjoined in the title to suggest interplay between the private and the public; *Paisaje imaginario* for piano and orchestra (1988) by the Argentine composer and pianist Gerardo GANDINI, in three movements: "Descripción de las aguas," "Descripción de la noche," and "Descripción del fuego," commissioned by the BBC Welsh Symphony Orchestra and first performed in 1989 in Cardiff, conducted by Odaline de la Martinez, with the composer as soloist; *Tamara: Profile of Lights* by the Mexican composer Francisco NÚÑEZ; and *Symphonic Karma* (1991), winner of The Akutagawa Award for Music Composition, by the 40-year-old Japanese composer Yutaka TAKAHASHI.

27 NOVEMBER 1993

On the eighth and last day of the 67th Festival of the International Society for Contemporary Music in Mexico, two concerts are given, in the following sequence:

A mid-day concert at the Palacio de Bellas Artes entitled "Electronic nostalgias," performed by Ensemble CIKADA, conducted by Christian Eggen, with special guest artist Adriana Díaz de Léon, vocalist, in the following program: the award-winning *River of January* for diverse ensemble and live electronics (1991) by the 39-year-old American composer Rick BAITZ; *Divertimento* (1991) by the Swedish composer Anders NILSSON; *Qawan Escoipe* for vocalist and chamber ensemble by the Argentine composer Octavio LÓPEZ; and *String Quartet* (1956) by the outstanding Italian-born German conductor, composer, and teacher Bruno MADERNA (1920–1973), regarded by many as his most original work with respect to instrumental invention.

An evening concert at the Cholula, Puebla, entitled "Cholula, Un Vaniloquio Campanero," arranged by Spanish composer, performer, and musicologist Llorenç BARBER, the role of the tañedores (bell ringers) performed by students and teachers from Conservatorio Estatal de Puebla, Escuela de Música de la Universidad de Puebla, and Escuela Nacional de Música de la UNAM, coordinated by Rubén López Cano, conducted by Llorenç Barber.

27 NOVEMBER 1993

The American pianist and composer Jerry (Edward) HUNT, who, as a pianist, championed the cause of contemporary music, and who, as a composer, produced a number of multimedia works in which he utilized the most varied elements, ranging from live performers and performance spaces to video and microwave detection systems, dies in Canton, Texas, just three days shy of his 50th birthday.

1 DECEMBER 1993

Alto Saxophone Concerto (1989) by the 48-year-old American composer and teacher Eugene O'BRIEN is given its first ever performance in Bloomington, Indiana.

2 DECEMBER 1993

Of Reminiscences and Reflections for orchestra by the senior American composer, conductor, and music educator Gunther (Alexander) SCHULLER is premiered in Louisville.

4 DECEMBER 1993

The seeded, outspoken American rock artist Frank (actually, Francis Vincent) ZAPPA, who, in addition to his ground-breaking work with his forward-thinking rock band The Mothers of Invention, produced a number of truly astonishing full orchestral scores reveling in artful dissonant counterpoint, including *Bob in Dacron and Sad Jane* and *Mo' 'n Herb's Vacation,* and the cataclysmic *Penis Dimension* for chorus, soloists, and orch., the latter with an anatomically precise text, dies of inoperable prostate cancer in Los Angeles at the pitiable age of 52.

5 DECEMBER 1993

Concerto for Strings (1947–50) and *Triptychon* for flute, oboe, clarinet, horn, and strings (1948–51), two works by the notable 57-year-old Austrian composer, conductor, and pedagogue Friedrich CEHRA, are given their first ever performance in Vienna, the composer conducting.

8 DECEMBER 1993

Let's Get This Show on the Road: An Alternative View of Genesis, opera, by the 58-year-old American composer and teacher John (Charles) EATON is premiered in Chicago.

9 DECEMBER 1993

Walker, chamber opera (1992), by the respected 65-year-old black American composer and teacher T(homas) J(efferson) ANDERSON (Jr.) is staged for the first time in Boston.

10 DECEMBER 1993

The American mezzo-soprano, soprano, and music patroness Alice TULLY, a scion of a family of wealth whose legacy includes Alice Tully Hall at New York's Lincoln Center, dies in New York at the seasoned age of 91.

12 DECEMBER 1993

The eminent 64-year-old German conductor of Hungarian descent Christoph von DOHNÁNYI, grandson of the eminent Hungarian pianist, composer, conductor, and pedagogue Ernst (Ernő) von Dohnányi and husband of the remarkable German soprano Anja Silja, conducts Beethoven's *Ninth Symphony* in a gala concert at Cleveland's Public Auditorium, marking the 75th anniversary of the founding of the Cleveland Orchestra.

14 DECEMBER 1993

The Czech musicologist Milan POŠTOLKA, who authored respected books on Czech music of the 18th century (Prague, 1961) and on the young Franz Joseph Haydn (Prague, 1988), dies in his native Prague at the moderate age of 61.

21 DECEMBER 1993

The Russian tenor Ivan (Semyonovich) KOZLOVSKY, an artist of imaginative power who, in addition to giving operatic performances and recitals in programs of the classical repertoire as well as Russian and Ukrainian songs, expanded his activities into stage direction, striving to synthesize dramatic action with its musical realization, dies in Moscow at the accomplished age of 93.

24 DECEMBER 1993

The English organist, organ designer, and teacher Ralph (William) DOWNES, who designed many notable organs, including the instrument for London's Royal Festival Hall, dies in London at the ripened age of 89.

1994

6 JANUARY 1994

The Bulgarian-born Austrian composer of Greek parentage Anestis LOGOTHETIS, who employed a highly personalized "integrating" musical notation, making use of symbols, signs, and suggestive images, playing on a performer's psychological associations, dies in Lainz at the age of 72.

9 JANUARY 1994

The noted 54-year-old German mezzo-soprano, opera producer, and Intendant Brigitte FASSBÄNDER, daughter of the German baritone Willi Domgraf-Fassbänder, makes her New York recital debut at Alice Tully Hall.

10 JANUARY 1994

The significant Swedish composer Sven-Erik BÄCK, who experimented with serialism and, later, electronic sound, producing particularly notable liturgical works, dies in his native Stockholm at the age of 74.

12 JANUARY 1994

Ervallagh for alto saxophone (1993) by the 46-year-old English composer and teacher Nicola (Frances) LEFANU, daughter of the medical historian William LeFanu and the composer Elizabeth Maconchy, is given its first ever performance in London.

13 JANUARY 1994

56 Blows (Quis Custodiet Custodies?) for orchestra, based on the Rodney King beating by the Los Angeles police (1992), by the 53-year-old black American composer Alvin (Elliot) SINGLETON, receives its premiere performance in the city of brotherly love, Philadelphia.

14 JANUARY 1994

Fantasy for orchestra (1993) by the remarkable 54-year-old American composer Ellen Taaffe ZWILICH is heard for the first time in Long Beach, California.

15 JANUARY 1994

The Dream of Valentino, opera (1993), by the greatly talented 66-year-old American composer Dominick ARGENTO is staged for the first time in Washington, D.C.

17 JANUARY 1994

Tre intermezzi for string trio (1993–93) by the 57-year-old Polish composer and pedagogue Marek STACHOWSKI is given its first ever performance in Kraków.

20 JANUARY 1994

Mysteries of the Macabre for trumpet and orchestra (1974–77; rev. 1992) by the eminent 70-year-old Hungarian-born Austrian composer and pedagogue György (Sándor) LIGETI, great-nephew of the celebrated Hungarian violinist and pedagogue Leopold Auer, is heard for the first time in Paris.

23 JANUARY 1994

Cello Concerto by the prominent 44-year-old American composer and teacher Christopher (Chapman) ROUSE is premiered in Los Angeles.

26 JANUARY 1994

The American composer, teacher, and computer music pioneer Lejaren (Arthur) HILLER (Jr.), whose scientific bent led him to explore the application of electronics and computers to composition, and who, with Leonard Isaacson, produced the *Illiac Suite,* his fourth string quartet (1955–56), the first composition composed with the aid of a computer, dies in Buffalo at the age of 69.

27 JANUARY 1994

English Horn Concerto (1992) by the brilliant 70-year-old American composer, pianist, and writer Ned ROREM, son of C. Rufus Rorem, a medical economist, and Gladys Miller Rorem, a civil rights activist, is performed for the first time in New York, Thomas Stacy soloist.

28 JANUARY 1994

Symphony No. 5, dubbed *Universe Symphony,* a reworking of the incomplete *Universe Symphony* (1911–28; 1951) by Charles Ives by the 63-year-old American composer and teacher Larry (Don) AUSTIN, in which Ives's "universe of tones" ranges from fully scored to fragmentary measures on 36 manuscript pages, and which Austin "completed" over a period ranging from 1974 to 1993 with a scoring that includes tape and digital synthesizer in three sections requiring seven orchestras of varying sizes to be led by five conductors, is performed for the first time at the University of Cincinnati College-Conservatory of Music.

30 JANUARY 1994

The noted Austrian musicologist Walter KOLNEDER, whose significant writings included *Anton Webern: Einführung in Werk und Stil* (Rodenkirchen, 1961; Eng. tr., 1968, as *Anton Webern: An Introduction to His Works*), *Geschichte der Musik: Ein Studien- und Prüfungshelfer* (Heidelberg, 1961; 5th ed., 1973), *Musikinstrumentenkunde: Ein Studien- und Prüfungshelfer* (Heidelberg, 1963; 3rd ed., 1972), and *Anton Webern: Genesis und Metamorphosen eines Stils* (Vienna, 1973), dies in Karlsruhe at the age of 83.

31 JANUARY 1994

Und: Das Feste ist in vollem Gange, cello concerto (1993), by the remarkable 62-year-old Russian composer Sofia (Asgatovna) GUBAIDULINA is heard for the first time in La Palmas, Canary Islands.

1 FEBRUARY 1994

Draumkvedet for nine voices, chorus, and electroacoustic sounds by the significant 62-year-old Norwegian composer Arne NORDHEIM is given its first ever performance in Oslo.

2 FEBRUARY 1994

La Princesse Blanche, opera (1993), by the accomplished 54-year-old Canadian composer, pianist, and teacher (James) Bruce MATHER is mounted for the first time in Montreal.

3 FEBRUARY 1994

Szatan w Goraju (Satan in Goray), ballet for flute, piano, violin, cello, and tape (1993), by the productive 46-year-old Polish composer Krzysztof KNITTEL is heard for the first time in Philadelphia.

5 FEBRUARY 1994

The remarkable German soprano Tiana (Luise) LEMNITZ, whose most celebrated portrayals included Pamina, Sieglinde, Desdemona, Micaëla, Octavian, and the Marschallin, dies in Berlin at the remarkable age of 96.

6 FEBRUARY 1994

The noted English conductor, teacher, and writer on music Norman (René) DEL MAR, father of the English conductor and musicologist Jonathan (Rene) Del Mar, whose distinguished career culminated with posts as principal guest conductor of the Bournemouth Sinfonietta (1982–85) and as artistic director of the Århus Symphony Orchestra (1985–88), dies in Bushey at the seasoned age of 74.

7 FEBRUARY 1994

During a rehearsal for her starring role in the revival of *La Fille du Régiment,* the outstanding 45-year-old black American soprano Kathleen (Deanna) BATTLE is summarily dismissed from New York's Metropolitan Opera roster by its general manager Joseph Volpe for "objectionable behavior."

9 FEBRUARY 1994

The distinguished American violinist Louis KAUFMAN, who gave numerous first performances of works by contemporary composers, among them a violin concerto by Dag Wiren (Stockholm, Oct. 25, 1953), as well as first American performances of violin works by Milhaud, Knipper, Martinů, and others, dies in Los Angeles at the respectable age of 88.

10 FEBRUARY 1994

Sinfonia Concertante for saxophone quartet and wind ensemble by the 56-year-old American-born Canadian composer and teacher Thomas (Michael) SCHUDEL is given its first performance in Winnipeg.

13 FEBRUARY 1994

Voices from the Gallery for soprano, tenor, baritone, and piano (1990) by the 57-year-old American composer, teacher, and pianist David WARD-STEINMAN is heard for the first time in San Diego.

17 FEBRUARY 1994

Partita for orchestra (1993) by the outstanding 85-year-old American composer and teacher Elliott (Cook) CARTER (Jr.) is heard for the first time in Chicago.

19 FEBRUARY 1994

The accomplished Italian-born American composer and teacher Vittorio RIETI, who, after becoming a naturalized American citizen on June 1, 1944, taught at the Peabody Conservatory of Music in Baltimore (1948–49), the Chicago Musical College (1950–53), Queens College in New York (1958–60), and New York College of Music (1960–64), and whose style of composition represented an ingratiating synthesis of cosmopolitan modern tendencies, dies in New York at the remarkable age of 96.

20 FEBRUARY 1994

Medea, ballet, by the promising 40-year-old German composer Hans-Jürgen von BOSE is given its first ever performance in Zürich.

22 FEBRUARY 1994

String Quartet (1988) by the prominent 79-year-old Italian composer, pedagogue, administrator, and writer on music Riccardo MALIPIERO, nephew of the eminent Italian composer Gian Francesco Malipiero, is heard for the first time in Milan.

23 FEBRUARY 1994

Your Rockaby for soprano saxophone and orchestra (1992–93) by the precocious 33-year-old English composer Mark-Anthony TURNAGE is premiered in London.

24 FEBRUARY 1994

The successful American singer of popular music Dinah (originally, Frances Rose) SHORE, known for such hit songs as *Blues in the Night* (1942), *I'll Walk Alone* (1944), *Buttons and Bows* (1948), and *Dear Hearts and Gentle People* (1949), and as a television personality via her own "Dinah Shore Show" in the early 1950s and later on via the television variety program, "Dinah Shore Chevy Show" (1956–63), dies in Beverly Hills at the age of 76.

25 FEBRUARY 1994

The outstanding 53-year-old Belgian bass-baritone José (real name, Joseph Van Damme) VAN DAM makes his Carnegie Hall recital debut in New York.

26 FEBRUARY 1994

The American pioneer in audio equipment who was also a munificent music patron Avery (Robert) FISHER, who, in 1973, gave the New York Philharmonic $10 million to renovate the interior of Philharmonic Hall, which, in 1976, was inaugurated at a gala concert in which it was officially renamed Avery Fisher Hall in his honor, and who also created the Avery Fisher Prize, a significant award given to outstanding musicians of the day, dies in New Milford, Connecticut, at the seasoned age of 88.

1 MARCH 1994

The understated Russian-American composer Alexei (Vasilievich) HAIEFF, whose music followed Igor Stravinsky's neo-Classicism, observing an austere economy of means, but achieving modernistic effects by a display of rhythmic agitation, often with jazzy undertones, dies in Rome at the age of 79.

2 MARCH 1994

Song in Winter, originally scored for harpsichord, di, and zheng (1993) but rewritten in a version of flute, zheng, piano, and percussion by the effective 40-year-old Chinese composer and teacher Chen YI is heard for the first time in Boston.

3 MARCH 1994

The promising Italian conductor Roberto ABBADO, nephew of the outstanding Italian conductor Claudio Abbado and the accomplished pianist and composer Marcello Abbado, makes his Metropolitan Opera debut in New York conducting *Adriana Lecouvreur*.

4 MARCH 1994

Fanfare for Los Angeles for orchestra (1993) by the lively 44-year-old American composer, teacher, conductor, and writer on music Steven (Edward) STUCKY is heard for the first time in Los Angeles.

7 MARCH 1994

The career of the famous 70-year-old famous Spanish soprano Victoria de LOS ANGELES (real name, Gómez Cima) continues unabated as she enters her eighth decade, highlighted by a well-received recital appearance at New York's Alice Tully Hall.

10 MARCH 1994

String Music for orchestra by the extraordinarily talented 80-year-old American composer and conductor Morton GOULD is heard for the first time in Washington, D.C.

11 MARCH 1994

The eminent Italian music scholar and bibliographer Claudio SARTORI, founding director of the Ufficio Ricerche Musicali in 1965, its aim to conduct a thorough codification of Italian musical sources, providing information on all manuscripts and published music in Italy before 1900, on all published librettos in Italy down to 1800, and on all literature on music in Italy, and who additionally served as editor-in-chief of *Dizionario Ricordi della musica e dei musicisti* (Milan, 1959), dies in Milan at the reasonable age of 80.

12 MARCH 1994

Mario and the Magician, opera (1991–93), by the respected American composer and music patron Francis THORNE, grandson of the American writer on music Gustav Kobbé, is performed for the first time in New York.

15 MARCH 1994

A Hoy Calendar for chorus (1994) and *Chat Moss* for orchestra (1993), two works by the eminent 59-year-old English composer and conductor Sir Peter Maxwell DAVIES, are performed for the first time in Liverpool.

16 MARCH 1994

The American composer, pianist, and organist (Charles) Russell WOOLLEN, who, although considered a minor composer, with the bulk of his manuscripts remaining unpublished at the time of his death, with Robert Evett and Robert Parris contributed to the development of the so-called "Washington School of Composers" that flourished in the 1960s and 1970s, dies in Charlottesville at the age of 61.

18 MARCH 1994

The notable American composer and pedagogue William (Laurence) BERGSMA, whose style of composition was that of classical Romanticism, having a strong formal structure without lapsing into modernistic formalism, the Romantic side of his music reflected in his melodious lyricism, dies in Seattle at the age of 72.

20 MARCH 1994

The Four Reasons, concerto for chamber orchestra (1993), by the 71-year-old American composer and pedagogue Allen Dwight SAPP, Jr. is performed for the first time in Cincinnati.

21 MARCH 1994

The notable 40-year-old Russian conductor Valery (Abissalovich) GERGIEV makes his Metropolitan Opera debut in New York conducting *Otello.*

23 MARCH 1994

Idyll No. 3 for small orchestra (1993) by the 50-year-old English composer, teacher, and writer on music Robin (Greville) HOLLOWAY is premiered in Poole.

24 MARCH 1994

The American flutist, conductor, teacher, and composer David VAN VACTOR, who, as a composer, adhered mainly to basic tonalities, enhanced with ingeniously contrived melodic gargoyles, creating a simulation of atonality, with the rhythmic vivacity of his inventive writing creating a cheerful, hedonistic atmosphere, dies in Los Angeles at the age of 87.

25 MARCH 1994

The outstanding 27-year-old Italian mezzo-soprano Cecilia BARTOLI makes her first appearance at the John F. Kennedy Center for the Performing Arts in Washington, D.C.

26 MARCH 1994

Dialog über Wasser for acoustic guitar and electric guitar by the 59-year-old French composer, trombonist, conductor, and teacher Vinko GLOBOKAR is heard for the first time over the WDR in Cologne.

28 MARCH 1994

The Riot for three players (1993) by the significant 54-year-old English composer Jonathan (Dean) HARVEY is premiered in Bristol.

30 MARCH 1994

New York Rock, musical, by the visible 61-year-old Japanese-born American vocalist, songwriter, and performance artist Yoko ONO, widow of the beloved member of The Beatles John Lennon, is performed for the first time in New York.

31 MARCH 1994

With Bells On, fanfare for symphonic winds and percussion, by the outstanding 65-year-old American composer and teacher Jacob (Raphael) DRUCKMAN is heard for the first time in Los Angeles.

1 APRIL 1994

Römer VIII, 26 for soprano, alto, organ, and live electronics ad libitum by the distinguished 57-year-old German conductor, composer, and pedagogue (Johannes Wolfgang) Hans ZENDER is premiered in Kassel.

4 APRIL 1994

Amazonia (Desafio XVIII) for voice and guitar (1993) by the notable 55-year-old Brazilian composer, pianist, and conductor Marlos NOBRE is given its first ever performance in New York.

5 APRIL 1994

Fantazia for string quartet (1993) by the 40-year-old English composer and teacher Robert (Louis Alfred) SAXTON is heard for the first time in his native London.

6 APRIL 1994

Anthony PARATORE, 49, and Joseph PARATORE, 46, outstanding American duo-pianist brothers, give the premiere of William Bolcom's *Sonata* for two pianos in Lafayette, Indiana.

7 APRIL 1994

The noteworthy 46-year-old American conductor Gilbert LEVINE conducts the Royal Philharmonic of London and the choir of St. Peter's Basilica in a concert of reconciliation for the victims of the Holocaust in the presence of Pope John Paul II in Rome.

8 APRIL 1994

Plus V for accordion and strings by the prominent 45-year-old Finnish harpsichordist, pianist, conductor, teacher, and composer Jukka TIENSUU is heard for the first time in Tampere.

9 APRIL 1994

Baobab 4, dance piece for flute, clarinet, alto saxophone, trombone, acoustic and electric guitar, bass, two pianos, balafon, reciter, three women's voices, and dancer, by the accomplished 46-year-old American composer, pianist, administrator, presenter, and teacher Bernadette (Marie) SPEACH, is performed for the first time in New York.

10 APRIL 1994

Aria Hebraique for oboe and strings (1984) by the respected 83-year-old American composer, teacher, and conductor Leon STEIN is given its first ever performance in Los Angeles.

11 APRIL 1994

Vents capricieux ser le clavier for flute, oboe, clarinet, bassoon, and piano (1993) by the prominent 77-year-old Canadian composer, teacher, and administrator Jean PAPINEAU-COUTURE, grandson of the Canadian musician Guillaume Couture, is heard for the first time in his native Montreal.

12 APRIL 1994

Concert Études for violin and computer synthesis by the accomplished 51-year-old American composer and teacher Charles (Malcolm) DODGE is given its first performance in New York.

14 APRIL 1994

Gawain, opera in two acts, by the noted 49-year-old English composer Sir Harrison (Paul) BIRTWISTLE, to a "poetic libretto" by David Harsent after the anonymous 14th-century English poem *Sir Gawain and the Green Knight* about the supernatural encounter of Gawain and the Green Knight, symbolic of the opposition of Christianity and pagan sorcery, which was first produced in London on May 30, 1991, is revised and given a second premiere in London.

15 APRIL 1994

Concertpiece for marimba and orchestra by the 44-year-old American composer and teacher Maurice WRIGHT is performed for the first time in Boston.

17 APRIL 1994

The eminent 69-year-old Italian tenor Carlo BERGONZI gives his farewell New York concert at Carnegie Hall.

20 APRIL 1994

Clarinet Concerto by the 48-year-old English composer, teacher, and conductor Edward GREGSON is given its premiere performance in Manchester.

21 APRIL 1994

English Horn Concerto by the visible 34-year-old American composer Aaron Jay KERNIS is heard for the first time in San Francisco.

22 APRIL 1994

Rise for orchestra (1993) by the promising 29-year-old Irish composer Ian WILSON is premiered in Ulster.

23 APRIL 1994

Magnum ignotum for flute/alto flute, two oboes, two clarinets, two bassoons, two horns, double bass, and tape by the notable 58-year-old Georgian composer Giya (Alexandrovich) KANCHELI is heard for the first time in Witten.

25 APRIL 1994

Cicada for two pianos by the gifted 44-year-old South African-born Irish composer Kevin VOLANS is heard for the first time in Los Angeles.

26 APRIL 1994

The significant Mexican composer, violinist, and teacher Manuel ENRÍQUEZ, a leading composer of the post-Chávez generation in Mexico, whose early works show the influences of Hindemith, Bartók, and jazz, later progressing into the vanguard of severe constructivism, employing dodecaphony, serialism, sonorism, indeterminacy, and graphic notation, dies in Mexico City at the modest age of 67.

29 APRIL 1994

Prologue and Narrative, incidental music for cello and orchestra, by the 64-year-old Canadian-born American composer, pianist, conductor, and teacher Yehudi WYNER, son of the Russian-American pianist, conductor and composer Lazar Weiner and husband of the American soprano Susan Davenny Wyner, is given its premiere performance over the BBC in Manchester.

30 APRIL 1994

Third String Quartet (1993) by the esteemed 55-year-old American composer, conductor, and teacher John (Harris) HARBISON receives its first ever performance in Waltham, Massachusetts.

1 MAY 1994

Violin Concerto (1993) by the 67-year-old Romanian composer Theodor GRIGORIU is performed for the first time in Indianapolis.

4 MAY 1994

The admired 38-year-old American soprano Cheryl STUDER makes her Carnegie Hall recital debut in New York.

5 MAY 1994

Evensong for orchestra (1993) by the significant 67-year-old American composer and teacher Donald (James) ERB is heard for the first time in Cleveland.

6 MAY 1994

Cello Concerto (1993) by the respected 43-year-old American composer, conductor, and teacher Donald CROCKETT is premiered in Chatham, New Jersey.

7 MAY 1994

String Quartet (1917) by the remarkable Czech-born American composer Bohuslav (Jan) MARTINŮ (1890–1959) is given its posthumous premiere in Zürich.

8 MAY 1994

Amalia's Secret for piano, drum set, guitar, bass, and cello by the innovative 35-year-old American composer, performer, and programmer Nick (actually, Nicholas Russel) DIDKOVSKY is heard for the first time in New York.

9 MAY 1994

Songs of Desperation and Comfort for mezzo-soprano and chamber orchestra (1993) by the 59-year-old American composer and teacher John (Charles) EATON receives its first ever performance in Cleveland.

11 MAY 1994

Sonata for solo violin by the multi-talented 67-year-old English pianist, organist, conductor, writer on music, and composer Francis (John) ROUTH receives its first performance in London.

13 MAY 1994

Apollonia's Circus, opera, by the 63-year-old American composer and teacher Eric (Norman) STOKES is mounted for the first time in Minneapolis.

14 MAY 1994

9 Pieces for orchestra (1993) by the striking 58-year-old German composer, pianist, and teacher Aribert REIMANN is heard for the first time in Houston.

15 MAY 1994

Divertimento for flute and strings by the 74-year-old American composer and teacher Paul FETLER is given its first performance in New York.

16 MAY 1994

Terra incognita for ten strings and piano by the accomplished 55-year-old Polish composer and pianist Zygmunt KRAUZE is heard for the first time in Bonn.

17 MAY 1994

Ocean, the final collaboration between the remarkable American composer John CAGE and his preeminent American choreographer partner Merce CUNNINGHAM, with two overlaid scores, one for orchestra, *1-95* (1993) by the inventive 40-year-old American-Canadian composer,

instrument maker, and performer Andrew (David) CULVER (after an idea by Cage), and one for live electronics, *Soundings: Ocean Diary* (1994), by the significant 68-year-old American pianist and composer David (Eugene) TUDOR, with costumes and lighting by Marsha Skinner, in 128 movement phrases, with omnidirectional placement of 114 musicians, and performed in the round (in a circular space), receives its first ever staging in Brussels.

18 MAY 1994

G.F.F.... for five instruments by the prominent 68-year-old Italian composer and pedagogue Aldo CLEMENTI is heard for the first time in Rome.

19 MAY 1994

Ligeia, chamber opera (1991-94), by the promising 30-year-old American composer Augusta Read THOMAS, wife of the respected American composer Bernard Rands, is premiered in Evian.

20 MAY 1994

MR (Marina and Rainer), chamber opera (1989), by the 47-year-old Russian composer, conductor, and teacher Nikolai KORNDORF is heard for the first time in Munich.

22 MAY 1994

Paschale for organ (1993) by the accomplished 67-year-old Polish composer Juliusz (Mieczyslaw) ŁUCIUK is given its premiere performance in Kraków.

23 MAY 1994

The admired American composer and teacher Radie BRITAIN, whose compositions followed along traditional lines, inspired by various American subjects, and whose autobiography appeared posthumously as *Ridin' Herd to Writing Symphonies* (Lanham, Md., 1996), dies in Palm Springs, California, at the respectable age of 95.

25 MAY 1994

Journeys & Secrets for chorus and chamber orchestra by the 52-year-old American composer, teacher, and pianist Paul Alan LEVI is heard for the first time in his native New York.

28 MAY 1994

The gifted 35-year-old American soprano Renée FLEMING appears as Mozart's Countess at the opening of the new opera theater at the Glyndebourne Festival.

30 MAY 1994

Elegia for wind quintet and string quintet (1993) by the 73-year-old Hungarian composer and musicologist András SZŐLLŐSY is given its first performance in Berlin.

1 JUNE 1994

Piano Concerto, after Brahms's *Piano Quartet*, op.25 (1992), by the esteemed 60-year-old German composer Siegfried MATTHUS is performed for the first time in Berlin.

818   2 June 1994

2 JUNE 1994

The English musicologist Jerome (Lawrence Alexander) ROCHE, who brought out the books *Palestrina* (London, 1972) and *The Madrigal* (London, 1972; 2nd ed., 1990), and, with his wife, Elizabeth Roche, the useful reference source, *A Dictionary of Early Music from the Troubadours to Monteverdi* (London, 1981), dies in Durham at the pitiable age of 52.

3 JUNE 1994

Die Schönheit des Morgens for viola and piano by the 66-year-old German composer and teacher Wilhelm KILL-MAYER is performed for the first time in Dresden.

5 JUNE 1994

First String Quartet by the respected 47-year-old American composer Peter LIEBERSON, son of the English-American recording executive and composer Goddard Lieberson, is heard for the first time in Halifax.

6 JUNE 1994

Violin Concerto: Hommage à György Kurtág (1990) by the admired 67-year-old German composer, pedagogue, organist, and harpsichordist Ruth ZECHLIN is given its premiere performance in Chemnitz.

8 JUNE 1994

Yad Vashem: An Impression for chamber orchestra by the 66-year-old American composer and teacher John (Wilham) DOWNEY is heard for the first time in Milwaukee.

10 JUNE 1994

Orpheus Descending, opera, by the 48-year-old American composer and teacher Bruce (Stuart) SAYLOR is staged for the first time at the Lyric Opera of Chicago, where from 1992 to 1994 he serves as composer-in-residence.

11 JUNE 1994

Piano Concerto, subtitled *Shiva's Drum* (1993-94), by the 46-year-old American composer, conductor, and teacher Dan WELCHER is heard for the first time at Texas's Round Top Festival.

12 JUNE 1994

Songs of the Slave for bass-baritone, chorus, and orchestra (1993) by the gifted 68-year-old American composer, conductor, and lecturer on music Kirke (Lewis) MECHEM is performed for the first time in Los Angeles.

13 JUNE 1994

No Longer Very Clear, aria for soprano, string quartet, and harpsichord, by the 53-year-old Uruguayan-born American composer and teacher Sergio CERVETTI is heard for the first time over New York's WNYC.

15 JUNE 1994

Echoes of Normandy for tenor, tape, organ, and orchestra by the distinguished 70-year-old Manchuria-born American composer and teacher Benjamin LEES is premiered in Dallas.

17 JUNE 1994

The German composer Kurt HESSENBERG, who possessed great facility in composition, evolving an effective idiom, fundamentally Classical, but containing Wagnerian elements in dramatic passages, with occasional infusion of prudential modernistic devices, and whose most successful work was *Struwwelpeter* (1933), a suite for small orchestra based on a well-known German children's tale, dies in his native Frankfurt am Main at the age of 85.

18 JUNE 1994

Les Rois Mages, cantata for voices, flute, and trumpet, by the eminent 79-year-old French composer and administrator Marcel (François Paul) LANDOWSKI, son of the sculptor Paul Landowski and great-grandson of the celebrated Belgian violinist and composer Henri Vieux-temps, is performed for the first time in Bayoux.

19 JUNE 1994

Amen for chorus by the notable 56-year-old American composer and teacher John (Paul) CORIGLIANO, son of the respected American composer John Corigliano, is given its first ever performance in Montreat, North Carolina.

21 JUNE 1994

La Belle et la bête, opera, by the outstanding 57-year-old American composer Philip GLASS, after the deeply moralistic fable of *Beauty and the Beast*, is staged for the first time in Gibellina.

24 JUNE 1994

The Canadian composer, music critic, teacher, and administrator Jean (d'Auray) VALLERAND, who published the books *Introduction a la musique* (Montreal, 1949) and *La Musique et les tout-petits* (Montreal, 1950), and whose compositions followed along neo-Romantic lines, later tinged with serial techniques, dies in his native Montreal at the age of 78.

30 JUNE 1994

Nocturne for piano by the significant 81-year-old French composer Jean FRANÇAIX is heard for the first time in Paris.

3 JULY 1994

The Kingdom of God for chorus, after Francis Thompson, by the admired English composer and teacher Hugh (Bradshaw) WOOD is premiered in London.

4 JULY 1994

The Piano Dreams of Empire (for piano) by the 41-year-old American composer and teacher Stephen (Paul) HARTKE is performed for the first time in Los Angeles.

7 JULY 1994

Cello Concerto by the enormously successful 62-year-old American composer and conductor John (Towner) WILLIAMS, best known for his voluminous work in television and motion pictures, is performed for the first time in Tanglewood.

8 JULY 1994

The Tempest, opera (1988–90), by the 63-year-old American composer, music theorist, and teacher Peter (Talbot) WESTERGAARD is mounted for the first time in Lawrenceville, New Jersey.

10 JULY 1994

Bisbigliando for harpsichord (1993) by the 49-year-old New Zealand composer Lyell (Richard) CRESSWELL is heard for the first time in Viitasaari.

13 JULY 1994

Second Chamber Symphony by the notable 64-year-old Russian composer and teacher Edison DENISOV is premiered in Tokyo.

14 JULY 1994

Journey Through a Japanese Landscape, concerto for marimba and wind orchestra (1993–94), by the remarkable 66-year-old Scottish composer Thea MUSGRAVE is heard for the first time in Cheltenham.

15 JULY 1994

Three Quartets for saxophone quartet, string quartet, and brass quartet by the noteworthy 50-year-old English composer, conductor, and writer on music Michael (Laurence) NYMAN is given its first ever performance in Tokyo.

18 JULY 1994

The Fox and the Magpie for tenor, baritone, soprano saxophone, horn, bassoon, and piano by the 59-year-old Austrian composer, horn player, and teacher Kurt SCHWERTSIK is performed for the first time in Sydney.

19 JULY 1994

The eminent Czech-born American pianist and pedagogue Rudolf FIRKUŠNÝ, who became known as a champion of the music of Leoš Janáček and who also gave first performances of Frank Martin's *Third* (Dallas, Nov. 20, 1949) and *Fourth* (N.Y., Oct. 4, 1956) *Piano Concertos* as well as first performances of piano concertos of Gian Carlo Menotti (No. 1; Boston, Nov. 2, 1945) and Howard Hanson (Boston, Dec. 31, 1948), dies in Staatsburg, New York, at the reasonable age of 82.

20 JULY 1994

Piano Quartet (1993) by the respected 46-year-old Finnish composer and musicologist Mikko HEINIÖ is heard for the first time in Kuhmo.

23 JULY 1994

On the occasion of his 66th birthday, the distinguished American pianist, conductor, and teacher Leon FLEISHER is soloist in the premiere performance of *Piano Concerto* for left-hand and orchestra by the brilliant 71-year-old German-born American pianist, conductor, and composer Lukas FOSS (real name, Fuchs), with the Boston Symphony Orchestra at Tanglewood, Seiji Ozawa conducting.

25 JULY 1994

Adagio and Rondo for violin and strings by the respected 63-year-old American composer and record producer Nancy VAN DE VATE is heard for the first time in Lancut, Poland.

4 AUGUST 1994

The German conductor and teacher Jürgen JÜRGENS, who cultivated works of the Baroque period, while not neglecting modern music of a polyphonic nature, and also edited works of Claudio Monteverdi and Alessandro Scarlatti, dies in Hamburg at the moderate age of 68.

5 AUGUST 1994

Passacaglia and Fugue for organ by the seasoned 78-year-old Japanese composer and teacher Kunio (actually, Morikuni) TODA receives its premiere performance in his native Tokyo.

6 AUGUST 1994

Music for Here for bassoon, viola, and cello by the distinguished 68-year-old French-American composer and teacher Betsy JOLAS, daughter of the poet and journalist Eugène Jolas, known in his own right as the founder and editor of the literary journal *transition*, is heard for the first time in Norfolk, Virginia.

10 AUGUST 1994

Mass for the 21st Century for soloists, chorus, and orchestra by the versatile 57-year-old black American composer, conductor, teacher, and writer on music Carman (Leroy) MOORE is given its first ever performance in New York.

11 AUGUST 1994

Tenebrae for piano (1992–93) by the esteemed 55-year-old English pianist, music educator, and composer John MCCABE is performed for the first time in Harrogate.

13 AUGUST 1994

The French violinist, music educator, and composer Raymond GALLOIS-MONTBRUN, long-time director of the Paris Conservatory (1962–83) and whose cantata *Louise de la miséricorde* won the 1944 Prix de Rome, dies in Paris at the age of 75.

14 AUGUST 1994

Puhetta (Talk) for chorus (1993) by the 54-year-old Finnish trumpeter and composer Jarmo (Kalevi) SERMILÄ is premiered in Hämeenlinna.

18 AUGUST 1994

The German bass Gottlob FRICK, best known as a fine Wagnerian, who excelled particularly as Gurnemanz and Hagen, but who was also admired for his portrayal of Rocco in *Fidelio*, dies in Mühlacker, near Pforzheim, at the age of 88.

19 AUGUST 1994

The French conductor Louis (Georges François) de FROMENT, who from 1958 to 1980 served as chief conductor of the Luxembourg Radio Symphony Orchestra, dies in Cannes at the age of 72.

21 AUGUST 1994

Incantation for harp by the 47-year-old French composer Jean-Claude WOLFF is first performed in Rheims.

22 AUGUST 1994

Intarsi, chamber concerto for piano and ensemble (1993–94), by the 69-year-old Swiss composer and pedagogue Klaus HUBER is premiered in Lucerne.

23 AUGUST 1994

Wave Mechanics I for orchestra by the youthful 33-year-old Japanese composer Karen TANAKA is performed for the first time in Tokyo.

24 AUGUST 1994

Sallie Chisum Remembers Billy the Kid for soprano and piano by the brilliant 65-year-old German-born American pianist, conductor, and composer André (George) (real name, Andreas Ludwig Priwin) PREVIN is given its first ever performance in Lenox, Massachusetts.

28 AUGUST 1994

The Chilean composer and teacher Alfonso LETERLIER (-LLONA), who would be honored in 1996 when the faculty of arts of the University of Chile renames the Alfonso Letelier Llona Branch in his memory, dies in his native Santiago at the age of 81.

2 SEPTEMBER 1994

3 Preludes for orchestra by the 49-year-old Dutch composer and teacher Tristan KEURIS is heard for the first time in Amsterdam.

3 SEPTEMBER 1994

inter for small orchestra by the eminent 64-year-old German composer Dieter SCHNEBEL is performed for the first time in Frankfurt am Main.

8 SEPTEMBER 1994

Javelin for orchestra by the spirited 32-year-old American composer and pianist Michael TORKE is given its first ever performance in Atlanta.

10 SEPTEMBER 1994

Dangerous Liaisons, opera, by the respected 59-year-old American composer Conrad SUSA is mounted for the first time in San Francisco, with Renée Fleming in the role of Mme. de Tourvel.

11 SEPTEMBER 1994

The Italian harpsichordist Luciano SGRIZZI, who championed the vast collection of harpsichord sonatas by Domenico Scarlatti, and who edited many performing editions, ranging from Monteverdi to Pergolesi, dies in Monaco at the age of 83.

13 SEPTEMBER 1994

Excelsior K-2 for piano and chamber orchestra by the 77-year-old American composer and educator William P(eter) LATHAM is heard for the first time in Fort Worth, Texas.

14 SEPTEMBER 1994

Cello Concerto by the successful 38-year-old American composer Richard DANIELPOUR is given its first ever performance in San Francisco.

15 SEPTEMBER 1994

A Study of Shade for orchestra (1989), in a version for small orchestra (1992), by the 40-year-old Polish composer Paweł SZYMÁNSKI is performed for the first time in Warsaw.

16 SEPTEMBER 1994

Subito for violin and piano (1992) by the prime Polish composer and conductor Witold LUTOSŁAWSKI (1913–1994) is given its posthumous premiere over Indianapolis's WFYI.

19 SEPTEMBER 1994

The distinguished American musicologist Carleton Sprague SMITH, who was an instructor in history at Columbia University (1931–35) and at New York University (1939–67) and who also served twice as chief of the Music Division at the New York Public Library (1931–43; 1946–59), dies in Washington, Connecticut, at the seasoned age of 89.

21 SEPTEMBER 1994

Mnamas Xapin Witoldwi Lutoslavskiemu (In Memory of Witold Lutosławski) for two horns and two trumpets by the eminent 71-year-old Greek-born French composer, music theorist, and teacher Iannis XENAKIS is given its first performance in Warsaw.

22 SEPTEMBER 1994

The respected English-born American jazz pianist, clarinetist, writer on music, and composer Leonard (Geoffrey) FEATHER, author of such valuable reference works on jazz as *The Encyclopedia of Jazz in the '60s* (1966), *The Encyclopedia of Jazz in the '70s* (1976), *The Passion for Jazz* (1980), and *The Jazz Years: Earwitness to an Era* (1987), dies in Encino, California, at the age of 80.

23 SEPTEMBER 1994

Titus Magnificus, fanfare for orchestra, by the 61-year-old American composer and teacher Vincent MCDERMOTT is heard for the first time in Cincinnati.

24 SEPTEMBER 1994

Głowa Meduzy II for one to three flutes (1993) by the 67-year-old Polish composer and pedagogue Witold (Jósef) SZALONEK is given its first ever performance in Berlin.

25 SEPTEMBER 1994

Trois Rivières for percussion quartet and electronics by the significant 41-year-old Finnish composer Kaija (Anneli) SAARIAHO is heard for the first time in Strasbourg.

29 SEPTEMBER 1994

The outstanding 38-year-old Italian mezzo-soprano Cecilia BARTOLI regales audiences at the opening of the 1994-95 season of New York's Carnegie Hall when she appears as soloist with the equally outstanding 70-year-old English conductor Sir Marriner NEVILLE in a program with the Academy of St. Martin-in-the-Fields that was subsequently telecast throughout the United States by PBS.

30 SEPTEMBER 1994

Concerto for electric guitar and instrumental ensemble (1993) by the 69-year-old Polish composer and pedagogue Włodzimierz KOTOŃSKI is heard for the first time in Apeldoorn.

1 OCTOBER 1994

The 68th Festival of the International Society for Contemporary Music in Stockholm opens with two concerts, in the following sequence:

An early evening performance aboard the Regalskeppet Vasa with "welcome" pieces by French composer André CHINI, Israeli composer Dror FEILER, and Swedish composers Sten HANSON, Anders HILLBORG, Arne MELLNÄS, Ivo NILSSON, Kent OLOFSSON, and Karin REHNQVIST, with sound and light design by Åke Parmerud, performers including the Stockholm Chamber Brass, Stockholm Percussion Trio, and Stockholm Saxophone Quartet, with special guest artists Susanne Rosenberg, vocals, Helén Jahren, oboe, Ivor Nilsson, trombone, and Jörggen Pettersson, saxophone.

A late night event at the Fylkingen, featuring three sound and video installations open, which continue throughout the festival week: *Variations on gravity*, video/audio installation by Dinka PIGNON, with sound design by Erik Mikael KARLSSON; *"Stockholm 1957,"* installation for video, banderol, and CD by Josef DOUKKALI; and *"This is a revelation,"* sound-installation by Kent TANKRED.

1 OCTOBER 1994

Narcissus, opera (1992–94), by the promising 39-year-old Swiss-born Austrian composer, conductor, and teacher Beat FURRER is staged for the first time in Graz.

2 OCTOBER 1994

On the second day of the 68th Festival of the International Society for Contemporary Music in Stockholm, two concerts are given, in the following sequence:

An early evening program of works at The Concert House, main auditorium, performed by the Malmö Symphony Orchestra, conducted by Arvo Volmer, with special guest artist Pierre-Yves Artaud, flute, in the following program: *Six poems from Neruda's "Alturas.."*(1993) by the American composer David FELDER; *Spyralis II* (1991) for flute(s) and orchestra by the Romanian composer Doina Marilena ROTARU; the world premiere of *Espacios Inasibles* by the Brazilian composer Gabriel VALVERDE, comprised of two individual works, *Fragmentaciones* and *Luminar;* and *Appari-*

tions (1958-59) by the eminent 71-year-old Hungarian-born Austrian composer and pedagogue György LIGETI.

An evening concert at St. Jacob's Church performed by Jeff Pressing, vocals and keyboards, Susanne Rosenberg, Lena Willemark, Margaretha Ljunggren, and Cecilia Wessman, sopranos, Helena Gabrielsson and Roberto Pellegrini, percussion, Maurizio Saiu, baritone, Helena Ströberg and Annika Sjunnesson, mezzo-sopranos, and Boel Adler and Helena Bjarnle, altos, with sound design by Giorgio Tedde, in the following program: *His Master's Voice* for solo performer (live voice and vocal samples triggered by MIDI keyboard) by the Australian composer Jeff PRESSING; *Puksånger-lockrop* for solo voices and percussion by the Swedish composer Karin REHNQVIST, exploring vocal techniques used in early Swedish folk music, especially "kulning," the solo technique once used out of doors for herding cattle and communicating over long distances; *Vox (seconda parte),* for solo voices and percussion, by the Italian composer Giorgio TEDDE, part of a larger composition exploring largely unused expressions of the human voice; and *g pdegi-n n gara* (Down with the shell; 1992) by the Korean composer Nahm-Hee CHUNG, based on the critical Korean poem of the same name by Dong-Yeop Shin.

2 OCTOBER 1994

Dialog über Erde for percussion by the radical 60-year-old French composer, trombonist, conductor, and teacher Vinko GLOBOKAR is heard for the first time at Australia's Barossa Festival.

3 OCTOBER 1994

On the third day of the 68th Festival of the International Society for Contemporary Music in Stockholm, three concerts are given, in the following sequence:

A mid-day concert at the Stockholm Cultural Centre, the auditorium performed by The Futurum Ensemble, conducted by Kjell-Inge Stevensson, with special guest artist Amelie Fleetwood, soprano, and the Örebro Chamber Orchestra, conducted by B Tommy Andersson, with special guest artist Mats Widlung, piano, in the following program: *Tre Laudi* (1936–37) by the remarkable Italian composer Luigi DAL-LAPICCOLA (1904–1975); a setting of a medieval hymn to the Virgin, a study for the opera *Volo di Notte*, after Saint-Exupéry's novel *Vol de nuit, Under a Rest* for piano and tape/live electronics (1992–93) by the Swedish composer Anders BLOMQVIST; *Hommage en cristal* by the 33-year-old Japanese composer Karen TANAKA, an hommage to Luciano Berio, who provided a series of 23 notes that serve as the work's harmonic field; and *Sinfonietta*, op.10 (1932), composed in an "objective, Hidemith-inspired" style, by the important Swedish composer and pedagogue, Lars-Erik LARSSON (1908–1986).

An evening concert at The Concert Hall, main auditorium, performed by The Budapest Tomkins Vocal Ensemble and the Stockholm Symphonic Wind Orchestra, conducted by Olivier Cuendet, with special guest artists Terje Lerstad, bass clarinet, Roger Carlsson, cimbalom, Ildikó Monyók, recitation, and Casba Király, pianino, in the following program: *Bihuà* (Fresco) (1990) by the Chinese composer Yiu-Kwong CHUNG, inventor of the I-Ching Composition System (ICCS) which integrates fundamental Chinese yin-yang philosophy with Western contemporary compositional and analytical theories (set and prolongation); *Symphonies for Winds* (1920), in memory of Claude Debussy, by the great Russian-born French, later American, composer, one of the supreme masters of 20th-century music, whose works exercised the most profound influence on the evolution of music through the emancipation of rhythm, melody, and harmony Igor STRAVINSKY (1882–1971); *Actions, Interpolations and Analyses*, symphonies for bass clarinet and large ensemble, in five parts, by the Norwegian composer Asbjørn SCHAATHUN; and *Samuel Beckett: What is the word?* for voice and piano (1990) by the eminent 68-year-old Hungarian composer and teacher György KURTÁG.

A late night concert at the Stockholm Cultural Centre performed by Kristine Scholz and Mats Persson, piano, Nanae Yoshimura, soh, and Kifu Mitsuhashi, shakuhachi in the following program: *...für Zwei Klaviere (Studie II)* by the German composer Clemens GADENSTÄTTER; *Soh-Oh-Ka* (1990) by the Japanese composer Tetsuya OMURA; and *Fantasia Contrappuntistica* for two pianos (1921), "choral variations over 'Ehre sei Gott in der Höhe,' followed by a quadruple fugue over a fragment from Bach," by the greatly admired Italian-German pianist, pedagogue, and composer Ferruccio BUSONI (1866–1924).

3 OCTOBER 1994

Tenth String Quartet (1993–94) by the remarkable 51-year-old Polish composer and teacher Krzysztof MEYER is given its first ever performance in Poznań.

4 OCTOBER 1994

On the fourth day of the 68th Festival of the International Society for Contemporary Music in Stockholm, four events are given, in the following sequence:

A mid-day concert at the Stockholm Cultural Centre performed by the Stockholm Broken Consort, conducted by Pascal Rophé, with special guest artists Irvine Arditti, violin, and Tommie Lundberg, bass clarinet, in the following program: *5 Orchestral Pieces*, op.10 (1911–13) by the remarkable Austrian composer Anton WEBERN (1883–1945); *Riti neurali* by the Italian composer Luca FRANCESCONI; *Presentiment* for chamber ensemble and tape (1992) by the Russian composer Dmitry YANOV-YANOSVKY, and *Essaims-Cribles* for bass clarinet and instrumental ensemble (1986–88) by the Swiss composer Michaël JARRELL, a commission from Pro Helvetia and dedicated to Jürg Wyttenbach and Ernesto Molinari.

A mid-afternoon Seminar on Interpretation No. 1 at the Royal Swedish Academy of Music, featuring the French flutist Pierre-Yves ARTAUD, who concludes his course of master classes at the Stockholm College of Music with a public seminar on interpretation.

An evening concert at The Berwald Hall performed by the Gävleborg Symphony Orchestra, conducted by Hanna Koivula, and The Swedish Radio Choir, conducted by Tönu Kaliuste, in the following program: *Cristal au soleil couchant* for orchestra with three instrumental groups (1992) by the Chinese composer Shuya XU, *Petrarch Suite*, to four sonnets by Francesco Petrarca (1991), for baritone, chorus, and orchestra, by the eminent 82-year-old Finnish composer, conductor, music critic, and pedagogue Erik BERGMAN; *The Rain on Thin Glass Legs* for chamber choir or eight voices (1987) by the Lithuanian composer Nomeda VALENČIŪTĖ, setting three lines from H. Radusaka's poem, *The Rain, Sonetto di Michelangelo*, op.17, No.1 (1932), by the noted Norwegian composer Fartein VALEN (1887–1952); *Forms of Emptiness* by the significant 55-year-old English composer Jonathan HARVEY, ceremonial work for mixed chorus to texts from the Buddhist Heart Sutra, in the original Sanskrit; and four poems by e.e. cummings, and *Time and Again* (1987) by the 50-year-old Canadian composer, teacher, and concert producer John REA.

A late-night concert at the Fasching Jazz Club featuring Anders Jormin, bass, Per Jørgensen, trumpet, Harald Svensson, keyboards, Severi Pyysaalo, vibraphone, and Lisbeth Diers, percussion, in the following program: *Roman* for saxophone quartet (1988), in four chapters, divided by interludes and built as a dramatic narration, by the Norwegian composer Lasse THORESEN; the world premiere *Acordeón de roto Corazón* by the Mexican composer Javier ALVAREZ; the first installment of a long-term composition project with the Stockholm Saxophone Quartet, *Link/Sequence* (1990) for five saxophones, small percussion instruments, synthesizer, and tape by the Swedish composer Bo RYDBERG; and the world premiere of *Jord,* a suite of self-contained movements, by the well-known Swedish jazz performer and composer Anders JORMIN.

5 OCTOBER 1994

On the fifth day of the 68th Festival of the International Society for Contemporary Music in Stockholm, three concerts are given, in the following sequence:

A mid-day concert at the Stockholm Cultural Centre performed by Ars Nova, conducted by Michael Bartosch, with special guest artist Kerstin Pettersson, soprano, in the following program: *Noctal 1, 2, and 3* (1992) for flute, clarinet, violin, cello, and piano by the Argentine composer José Luis CAMPANA; *Lost Voice* (1992), in three continuous parts, by the Azerbaijan composer Zaur FAKHRADOV; *23 lines from Emily Dickinson* (1989), in three parts, by the Bulgarian composer Ivan SPASSOV; and *U-mul* (The Well; 1991/92) by the Korean composer Younghi PAGH-PAAN.

An evening concert at The Concert Hall, the Grünewald auditorium, performed by Kammarensemble (The Chamber Ensemble), conducted by Jonathan Nott, with special guest artists Magnus Andersson, guitar, Sylvie Altenburger, viola, and Irvine Arditti, violin, in the following program: *Eco errante* by the Uruguayan composer Alvaro CARLEVARO; *Surfing* (1990) by the Belgian composer Philippe BOESMANS; *Octandre* for flute, oboe, clarinet, bassoon, horn, trombone, and double bass (1923) by the remarkable French-born American composer, who introduced a totally original principle of organizing the materials and forms of sound, profoundly influencing the direction of new music Edgar VARÈSE (1883–1965); and *Terrain* for violin and eight instruments (1991–92) by the significant 51-year-old English composer Brian FERNEYHOUGH, its title drawn from the homonymous poem by A.R. Ammons.

A late-night concert at the Stockholm Cultural Centre performed by The Zetterqvist String Quartet (Mats Zetterqvist, violin, June Gustafson Lyng, violin, Håkan Olsson, viola, and Ewa Rydström, cello) and The Tale String Quartet (Tale Olsson, violin, Patrik Swedrup, violin, Ingegerd Kierkegaard, viola, and Helena Nilsson, cello), with Anders Blomqvist, diffusion, in the following program: *Salto Mortal* (1989), winner of the 2nd Prize in the International Electro-acoustic Music Competitions at Brouges, by the Venezuela composer Julio D'ESCRIVAN; *String Quartet No. 1* (1923–24) by the greatly significant Czech composer Leoš JANÁČEK (1854–1928); *Klagovisor* (Laments; 1982–88) by the Hungarian composer Ákos RÓZMANN, in 13 movements comprised of short musical fragments performed on a Hungarian peasant zither using a double bass bow; and *String Quartet No. 2* by the English composer Valerie Ross, with Eastern influences inspired by a spectacular performance by the Semarah Ratih Gamelan of Ubud on May 21, 1993.

6 OCTOBER 1994

Saboreando el Gusto Cubano for violin, piano, and percussion by the 51-year-old American composer, teacher, pianist, and writer on music Peter (Kenton) WINKLER is performed for the first time in Havana.

6 OCTOBER 1994

On the sixth day of the 68th Festival of the International Society for Contemporary Music in Stockholm, four events are given, in the following sequence:

A mid-day concert at the Stockholm Cultural Centre performed by Ma, an ensemble comprised of violin (Staffan Larson), clarinet (Bo Petterson), saxophone (Christer Jonsson), and piano (Love Derwinger), conducted by its founder, violinist Staffan Larson, in the following program: *Prudent views of my love passing by the seasons* (1991) by the Croatian composer Marko RUŽDJAK, originally conceived as three separate movements but later intertwined; *Occasus* (1991) by the Portuguese composer Joǎo RAFAEL, a commission from Lisbon's Gulbenkian Foundation; *Durchscheinende Etüden, Simultankonzept IV* (1993–94) by the German composer Caspar Johannes WALTER, the last and most complicated in a series of short pieces derived from graphic originals (sheets of paper with dots); and *La Sabbia del Tempo* for flute, clarinet, synthesizer, violin, viola, and cello (1991–92) by the Italian composer Fausto ROMITELLI.

A mid-afternoon Seminar on Interpretation No. 2 at the Royal Swedish Academy of Music, moderated by Davis Osmond Smith, featuring two interpreters — Trio des Lyres member Anna Lindal and founding violinist of the acclaimed Arditti String Quartet Irvine Arditti — who perform, compare, and comment on their interpretations of the famous piece *Sequenza VIII* for violin (1976) by Luciano Berio.

An evening concert at The Music Museum performed by members of Omnibus Wind Chamber Orchestra, the Linné Quartet, and Uppsala Chamber Soloists, conducted by Petter Sundkvist, with special guest artists Per Lundberg, piano, Hugo Noth Trio (Hugo Noth, accordion, Hector Guedes, baritone, and Mario de Secondi, cello), HOT 3 (Terje Thiwång, flute, Torbjörn Helander, viola, and Stefan Östersjö, guitar), and Trio des Lyres (Anna Lindal, violin, Nils-Erik Sparf, viola, and Chrichan Larson, cello), in the following program: *O versa*, an orchestration of an earlier work for solo piano, by the Icelandic composer Atli INGÓLFSSON; *Et puis plus rien le rève* by the Slovenian composer Uros ROJKO, to texts by Ingeborg Bachman, William Carlos Williams, and Guillaume Apollinaire, *Trio II* for flute, viola, and guitar by the Spanish composer and founder of Multifonia in France and Spain (a society for the promotion of contemporary music) José Manuel López LÓPEZ; *Des Dichters Pflug* (1986) by the 69-year-old Swiss composer and pedagogue Klaus HUBER; and *Minnewater* (1988), subtitled *Thousands of Canons*, by the Danish composer Bent SØRENSEN, with direct references to the compositional technique by which all layers and elements in the music are constantly imitated.

A late-night concert at the Stockholm Cultural Centre performed by Paula Hoffman and Malin Gjörup, sopranos, Anders Kilström and Ann-Sofie Klingberg, piano, Niklas Andersson and Mats Wallin, clarinet, Åsa Åkerberg and Torbjörn Nilsson, cello, and Anders Blonqvist, diffusion, in the following program: *I am wind on sea* (1987) for woman's voice, two crotales, and two woodblocks, both played by the singer, written expressly for the American mezzo-soprano Aylish Kerrigan, by the Irish composer John BUCKLEY; *Numerous branches of ramified plaits* by the Polish composer Tadeusz WIELECKI; *Le vertige inconnu* (1993) for tape by the Canadian composer Gilles GOBEIL, realized at France's Groupe de musique expérimentale de Bourges (GMEB); *Je brûle, dit-elle un jour à un camarade* (1991) by the French composer Philippe LEROUX, an homage to the poet Edmond Jabès, who died on January 1, 1991; and *Lerchen-Trio* (In Memoriam

of Olivier Messiaen, 1992) for clarinet (or alto clarinet), cello, and piano by the Dutch composer Theo LOEVENDIE.

7 OCTOBER 1994

Through Interior Worlds, ballet, by the accomplished 51-year-old American composer and teacher Joseph SCHWANTNER is staged for the first time in a concert version in Nashville, Tennessee.

7 OCTOBER 1994

On the seventh day of the 68th Festival of the International Society for Contemporary Music in Stockholm, four events are given, in the following sequence:

A mid-day concert at the Stockholm Cultural Centre performed by The Nordia Ensemble and members of Stockholm Symphonic Wind Orchestra, conducted by Niklas Willén, in the following program: *Echo-Mime* for solo clarinet with clarinet sextet (1992) by the Chinese composer Richard TSANG, a sound sculpture using the homogeneous tone color of the clarinet as its only sonic resource; *Jacob's Ladder* (1990) by the 43-year-old Russian composer Dmitri SMIRNOV, a commission by the London Sinfonietta by the Michael Wyner Trust and one of several imaginary ballets by the composer inspired by the drawings of William Blake; *inné* by the Swedish composer Madeleine ISAKSSON; and *En pares* for chamber ensemble (1993) by the Mexican composer Gabriela ORTIZ, in which pairs of instruments are located opposite each other to create a stereo effect.

A mid-afternoon Seminar on Interpretation No. 3 at the Royal Swedish Academy of Music in which composers, musicians, and musicologists, including Philippe Boesmans, Brian Ferneyhough, Chrichan Larson, Asbjørn Schaathun, and David Osmond-Smith, discuss a number of questions concerning the problems of interpretation in the music of our time.

An evening orchestral concert at The Berwald Hall performed by The Swedish Radio Symphony Orchestra, conducted by Leif Segerstam, in the following program: *ignis noster* for large orchestra (1991–92), a commission from the BBC Proms for the BBC Symphony Orchestra, by the Scottish composer James DILLON, and *Passage/Paysage* (1989/90) for large orchestra, the concluding portion of a three-part cycle (*Extension*, 1979/80 and *Inter-Mezzo, concertato non concertabile tra pianoforte e orchestra*, 1986), by the German composer Mathias SPAHLINGER.

A late-night concert at the Stockholm Cultural Centre performed by Peter Rydström, flute, Mats Wallin, clarinet, Julia Whybrow, alto recorder, Magnus Andersson, guitar, and Anders Blomqvist, diffusion, in the following program: *Specimens* (1991) for flute, clarinet, AKAI 1000 HD, and Apple Macintosh Computer (1991) by the Serbian composer Srdan HOFMAN, realized at Belgrade's Sound Studio, *Scambi* (1957) by the radical 65-year-old Belgian composer and pedagogue Henri POUSSEUR, *Weeds in Ophelia's Hair* (1992) by the German composer Rolf RIEHM, first performed on May 29, 1992, at the 4th Insel Festival, Hombroich, by Julia Whybrow, treble recorder, *Perspectives* for electronic sounds (1957) by the eminent 68-year-old Italian composer, conductor, and pedagogue Luciano BERIO, and *Downstream* for guitar and computer-processed guitar sounds (1991–92) by the American composer Josh LEVINE.

8 OCTOBER 1994

On the eighth and final day of the 68th Festival of the International Society for Contemporary Music in Stockholm, two concerts are given, in the following sequence:

A mid-day concert at the Stockholm Cultural Centre performed by The Futurum Ensemble, conducted by Kjell-Inge, with special guest artist Michael Weinius, baritone, in the following program: *Angels* for six muted trumpets (1920–21) by the remarkable American composer Carl RUGGLES (1876–1971); *Keep the Change* for eight bells (1989) by the Swedish composer Sten MELIN; and *Cantata Bomarzo*, op.32 (1964) by the greatly talented Argentine composer Alberto GINASTERA (1916–1983), a commission from the Elizabeth Sprague Coolidge Foundation in Washington, D.C., making use of the same libretto by Manuel Mujica Láinez that served his opera *Bomarzo* (1966/67), which created a sensation at its production in Washington, D.C., on May 19, 1967, by its unrestrained spectacle of sexual violence.

A mid-afternoon program at The Concert Hall performed by Royal Stockholm Philharmonic Orchestra, conducted by Markus Stenz, in the following program: *Mémoire vive* for orchestra (1988–89) by the French composer Philippe HUREL, dedicated to Catie, Raphaële, Thibault, and Pierre; *Tenout* (1990) by the Israeli composer Betty OLIVERO, a commission from the Cologne Radio Symphony Orchestra who gave the first performance of the work as part of a Festival of Israeli and Jewish Music; *Timeline*, subtitled *Concerto No. 2 for Orchestra* (1989), with extensive use of percussion, by the Finnish composer Usko MERILÄINEN; and *Eye on Genesis II* for orchestra (1992) by the respected 65-year-old Japanese composer and teacher Joji YUASA, commissioned and premiered by the NHK Symphony Orchestra.

9 OCTOBER 1994

The Myrrh-Bearer for viola, chorus, and percussion (1993) by the remarkable 50-year-old English composer John (Kenneth) TAVENER is performed for the first time in his native London.

10 OCTOBER 1994

The Russian composer Nikolai KARETNIKOV, whose advanced scores were not welcomed in official circles, and whose opera *Til Ulenshpigel* (Till Eulenspiegel; 1985) had to be recorded in secret, which prompted Gerard McBurney on BBC Radio 3 to dub it the first *samizdat* opera, dies in his native Moscow at the age of 64.

13 OCTOBER 1994

The remarkable 29-year-old French soprano Natalie DESSAY makes her Metropolitan Opera debut in New York as Fiakermilli in Richard Strauss's *Arabella*.

14 OCTOBER 1994

For Your Eyes Only for orchestra (1989) by the innovative 41-year-old American composer and instrumentalist John ZORN is given its first ever performance in a revised version in New York.

16 OCTOBER 1994

Dans la marche: Hommage à Witold Lutosawski for orchestra by the noted 51-year-old German composer, conductor, pedagogue, and Intendant Udo ZIMMERMANN is given its first ever performance in L'Aquila.

19 OCTOBER 1994

The outstanding 28-year-old Welsh bass-baritone Bryn (in full, Bryn Terfel Jones) TERFEL gives his highly acclaimed Metropolitan Opera debut in New York as Mozart's Figaro.

21 OCTOBER 1994

The Second Mrs. Kong, opera (1993–94), by the prime 60-year-old English composer Sir Harrison (Paul) BIRTWISTLE is staged for the first time in Glyndebourne.

22 OCTOBER 1994

Tangenten for voice and instrumental ensemble by the 43-year-old Austrian conductor, teacher, and composer Günther ZECHBERGER is heard for the first time over Istanbul's Turkish Radio.

23 OCTOBER 1994

The masterful Greek-born American composer and teacher Nicolas ROUSSAKIS, whose works, including *Concertino* for percussion and woodwinds (1973), *Ode and Cataclysm* for orchestra (1975), *Ephemeris* for string quartet (1979), *Fire and Earth and Water and Air* for orchestra (1980–83), *The God Abandons Antony*, cantata for narrator, chorus, and orchestra (1987), and *To Demeter* for orchestra (1994; N.Y., Oct. 29, 1995), although marked by an aggressive modernity of idiom are nonetheless satisfyingly playable and surprisingly pleasurable even to untutored ears, dies in New York at the lamentable age of 60.

26 OCTOBER 1994

5 Bagatelles for oboe and piano (1993) by the respected 62-year-old English composer, pianist, and teacher Malcolm (Leyland) LIPKIN is heard for the first time in London.

27 OCTOBER 1994

Hues for orchestra (1993) by the 45-year-old American composer, organist, and teacher Dan (Steven) LOCK-LAIR is performed for the first time in Fayetteville, North Carolina.

28 OCTOBER 1994

Percussion Concerto (1993–94) by the 68-year-old Argentine-German composer Carlos VEERHOFF is given its first ever performance in Munich.

31 OCTOBER 1994

Quest for guitar, soprano saxophone, two percussion, harp, and contrabass (1990) by the distinguished and highly innovative 65-year-old American composer George (Henry) CRUMB (Jr.) receives its first performance in a newly-revised version in Vienna.

2 NOVEMBER 1994

Rosa, "horse drama" in two acts and twelve scenes, by the inspired 55-year-old Dutch composer Louis ANDRIESSEN, who hails from a remarkably musical family which includes his father, the eminent Dutch organist and composer Hendrik Andriessen, his uncle, the Dutch pianist, teacher, and composer Willem (Christian Nicolaas) Andriessen, and his brother, the talented Dutch composer Jurriaan Andriessen, to a libretto by the remarkable 52-year-old Welsh film director, writer, painter, and librettist Peter GREENAWAY, set in the 1950s and concerning a fictitious Brazilian pianist who lives in a former slaughterhouse, is devoted to his favorite horse, and writes only music for Wild West films, is first mounted in Amsterdam

4 NOVEMBER 1994

Entrata for four horns, three trumpets, three trombones, tuba, and timpani by the celebrated 60-year-old Polish composer, pedagogue, and conductor Krzysztof PENDERECKI is heard for the first time in Cincinnati.

5 NOVEMBER 1994

The black American bass-baritone McHenry BOATWRIGHT, who created the central role in Gunther Schuller's opera *The Visitation* (Hamburg, Oct. 12, 1966), dies in New York at the age of 66.

6 NOVEMBER 1994

Fourth Symphony, subtitled *Symphonie fleuve*, by the distinguished 42-year-old German composer and teacher Wolfgang (Michael) RIHM is heard for the first time in Hamburg.

9 NOVEMBER 1994

Carmel Eulogies, symphonic poem for the 75th anniversary of the Oslo Philharmonic, by the ascending 45-year-old Norwegian composer and teacher Lasse THORESEN is heard for the first time in Oslo.

10 NOVEMBER 1994

The esteemed black American jazz singer, pianist, and songwriter Carmen MCRAE, a fine exponent of the bop style with exceptional scat ability who gave remarkable renditions of both jazz and pop ballads, dies in Beverly Hills at the age of 74.

11 NOVEMBER 1994

The significant English composer of Irish descent Dame Elizabeth MACONCHY, mother of the talented English composer Nicola LeFanu, who developed a style peculiarly her own, tonally tense, contrapuntally dissonant, and coloristically sharp in instrumentation, dies in Norwich at the respectable age of 87.

15 NOVEMBER 1994

Dittico baciato for chorus and orchestra by the promising 38-year-old Italian composer, conductor, teacher, and writer on music Albert CAPRIOLI is given its first ever performance in Bologna.

17 NOVEMBER 1994

last things, I think, to think about for bass-baritone, piano, and computer-processed sound by the veteran 60-year-old American composer and teacher Roger (Lee) REYNOLDS is heard for the first time in New York.

18 NOVEMBER 1994

Fanfare for Peace for orchestra by the 51-year-old Polish composer, percussionist, and teacher Marta PTASZYŃSKA is performed for the first time in Cincinnati.

19 NOVEMBER 1994

7 Movements for saxophone, harp, percussion, and fourteen strings by the 54-year-old Hungarian composer László SÁRY is given its first ever performance in Budapest.

21 NOVEMBER 1994

Kristallene Gusli for orchestra by the brilliant 61-year-old Russian composer Rodion (Konstantinovich) SHCHEDRIN is performed for the first time in Moscow.

22 NOVEMBER 1994

The Seeds Long Hidden..., orchestral variations, by the 58-year-old English composer and music critic Anthony (Edward) PAYNE, husband of the English soprano Jane Manning, is premiered in his native London.

24 NOVEMBER 1994

Fresk (Fresco) *III* for orchestra (1993) by the 70-year-old Polish composer and pedagogue Krystyna MOSZUMAŃSKA-NAZAR is heard for the first time in Kraków.

26 NOVEMBER 1994

Espace for orchestra by the versatile 44-year-old English composer, conductor, writer on music, and teacher Roger (Michael) MARSH is performed for the first time in Huddersfield.

27 NOVEMBER 1994

The highly talented 38-year-old American soprano Sylvia MCNAIR makes her recital debut at New York's Alice Tully Hall.

28 NOVEMBER 1994

The Russian-American pianist, teacher, and composer (Sviatoslav) Soulima STRAVINSKY, son of the great Russian-born French, later American, composer Igor Stravinsky, who early on became known as a fine interpreter of his father's piano works and whose own compositions included several chamber pieces, including three string quartets and a *Cello Sonata*, dies in Sarasota, Florida, at the age of 84.

1 DECEMBER 1994

The 33-year-old Italian conductor Daniele GATTI makes his first appearance at the Metropolitan Opera in New York conducting *Madama Butterfly*.

2 DECEMBER 1994

Moires for quartet and tape by the multi-talented 59-year-old French composer, musicologist, and philologist François-Bernard MÂCHE is heard for the first time over Paris's Radio France.

4 DECEMBER 1994

Cantate pour le temps de Noël for soloists, mixed chorus, women's chorus, boy's chorus, strings, harpsichord, and organ (1929) by the greatly renowned Swiss composer and pedagogue Frank (Théodore) MARTIN, left unfinished at his death in 1974 but later completed by the composer's widow, Maria Martin, and the conductor Alois Koch, is given its posthumous premiere in Lucerne.

5 DECEMBER 1994

The German-born American pianist, conductor, teacher, and composer Carl FUERSTNER, long-time (1963–82) principal opera coach at the Indiana University School of Music in Bloomington, Indiana, where he also conducted operas, and music director of the Bloomington Symphony Orchestra (1981–89), dies in Bloomington, Indiana, at the age of 82.

8 DECEMBER 1994

Sixth Symphony by the outstanding 68-year-old German composer Hans Werner HENZE is performed for the first time in a new version in Munich.

9 DECEMBER 1994

Scrooge, concert scene from "A Christmas Carol" for bass-baritone, chorus, and orchestra, by the 48-year-old American composer Robert Xavier RODRIGUEZ is given its first ever performance in El Paso, Texas.

10 DECEMBER 1994

The Swiss composer and teacher Robert (Karl Moritz) BLUM, in whose extensive output he utilized various contemporary means of expression, from polytonal to 12-tone writing, dies in his native Zürich at the fulfilled age of 94.

11 DECEMBER 1994

The Azerbaijani composer and teacher Avet TERT-ERYAN, whose music was made forceful with ancient

sonorities, employing a dramatic character that verged on barely-controlled chaos, with the backbone of his relatively small output exploring paths that were daring in the Soviet Union of the 1970s, often giving solo roles to folk instruments such as the duduk, zurna, and kemancha, dies in Yekaterinburg at the modest age of 65.

17 DECEMBER 1994

The neo-conservative American pianist, teacher, and music critic Samuel LIPMAN, whose numerous teaching posts included Marymount College in Tarrytown, New York (1963–72; chairman of the music dept., 1968–71), the Curtis Institute of Music (from 1969), the Manhattan School of Music (1972–87), the New England Conservatory of Music in Boston (1984–86), and the Juilliard School in New York (from 1986), dies in New York at the lamentable age of 60.

19 DECEMBER 1994

The 46-year-old American conductor Gilbert LEVINE becomes only the fourth Jew in history to receive the papal Equestrian Order of St. Gregory the Great.

21 DECEMBER 1994

Nagoya Marimbas for two marimbas by the outstanding 58-year-old American composer Steve (actually, Stephen Michael) REICH is heard for the first time in Nagoya City.

24 DECEMBER 1994

The Angels for chorus by the significant 55-year-old English composer Jonathan (Dean) HARVEY is given its first performance in Cambridge.

1995

3 JANUARY 1995

The Slovak composer Tadeáš SALVA, whose music embraced sonorism with occasional excursions into aleatory procedures, dies in Bratislava at the pitiable age of 56.

4 JANUARY 1995

The compelling 32-year-old Russian soprano Galina GORCHAKOVA makes her Metropolitan Opera debut in New York as Cio-Cio-San.

5 JANUARY 1995

The French composer Francis(co) LOPEZ, whose career centered on the composition of light works for the French

musical theater in Paris, mostly in collaboration with the adept librettist and lyricist Raymond Vincy, including their first outing, the operetta *Le Belle de Cadix* (Dec. 24, 1945), as well as *Andlousie* (Oct. 25, 1947), *Quatre Jours à Paris* (Feb. 28, 1948), *Pour Don Carlos* (Dec. 17, 1950), *Le Chanteur de Mexico* (Dec. 15, 1951), *La Route fleurie* (Dec. 19, 1952), *À la Jamique* (Jan. 24, 1954), and *Méditerranée* (Dec. 17, 1956), many of which became classics and were made into films, dies in Paris at the age of 78.

6 JANUARY 1995

Percussion Concerto (1991) by the 51-year-old American composer and teacher Joseph SCHWANTNER is premiered in New York.

7 JANUARY 1995

Der Sturz des Antichrist, opera (1935), by the Austrian composer, pianist, conductor, and music critic Viktor ULLMANN, who ended his tragic last days in the concentration camp in Auschwitz on or about Oct. 15, 1944, is given its posthumous premiere in Bielefeld.

8 JANUARY 1995

Troika for eleven instruments (1994) by the 43-year-old American conductor and composer Lawrence RAPCHAK is given its first ever performance in Chicago.

10 JANUARY 1995

A Winter's Tale, originally scored for soprano and piano, by the prominent 56-year-old American composer, pedagogue, pianist, and conductor Charles (Peter) WUORINEN is given its first performance in a version for soprano, clarinet, horn, string trio, and piano in Houston.

11 JANUARY 1995

The distinguished Russian-born American violinist and pedagogue Josef GINGOLD, a guiding force in establishing the International Violin Competition of Indianapolis, which he served as first honorary chairman and president of the jury in 1982, positions he held again in 1986 and 1990, dies in Bloomington, Indiana, at the respectable age of 85.

14 JANUARY 1995

The distinguished Scottish conductor Sir Alexander (Drummond) GIBSON, founder (1962) of Glasgow's Scottish Opera, which he served as artistic director (until 1987), and who as a conductor became equally admired as an interpreter of the orchestral and operatic repertoire, dies in London at the age of 68.

15 JANUARY 1995

Rough Road for flute and guitar (1994) by the 67-year-old American composer and teacher John (William) DOWNEY is heard for the first time over Chicago's WFMT.

16 JANUARY 1995

Third Symphony, entitled *Inner Communications* (1994), by the notable 61-year-old Japanese composer Toshi ICHIYANAGI is performed for the first time in Yokohama.

18 JANUARY 1995

Third Symphony, entitled *Jesus, Messiah, Save Us!* (1983), by the significant 75-year-old Russian composer and pedagogue Galina (Ivaovna) USTVOLSKAYA is heard for the first time in Amsterdam.

19 JANUARY 1995

Second Symphony for soprano and orchestra (1993) by the 61-year-old American composer, teacher, and conductor Richard WERNICK is performed for the first time in Philadelphia.

20 JANUARY 1995

Simón Bolívar, opera (1989-92), by the remarkable 64-year-old Scottish composer Thea MUSGRAVE is mounted for the first time in Norfolk, Virginia.

21 JANUARY 1995

Harvey Milk, highly successful operatic treatment in three acts by the prominent 34-year-old American composer Stewart (Farrell) WALLACE, to a libretto by Michael Korie based on the tragic murders of San Francisco mayor George Moscone and city supervisor Harvey Milk by disgruntled ex-city supervisor Dan White, is first mounted at the Houston Grand Opera, earning Wallace encomiums both in the United States and abroad.

23 JANUARY 1995

They Come Dancing for orchestra (1994) by the 42-year-old American composer Tina DAVIDSON receives its first performance in Roanoke, Virginia.

26 JANUARY 1995

The notable Australian piano accompanist and teacher Geoffrey (Penwill) PARSONS, who pursued an international career as a piano accompanist to many leading artists of his day, dies in London at the age of 65.

28 JANUARY 1995

The prominent Italian tenor Ferruccio TAGLIAVINI, long-time husband of the Italian soprano and mezzo-soprano Pia Tassinari, dies in his native Reggio Emilia at the age of 81.

29 JANUARY 1995

Pygmalion for baritone and string quartet (1989) by the 69-year-old Austrian-Canadian composer and teacher Gerhard (Joseph) WUENSCH is heard for the first time in London, Ontario.

2 FEBRUARY 1995

Failing Kansas, first in what would be a trilogy of operas (framed by *Dennis Cleveland*, 1996, and *The End of Cinematics*, 1999), by the formidably original 38-year-old American composer Mikel (actually, Michael Joseph) ROUSE, after Truman Capote's *In Cold Blood*, is staged for the first time in New York.

5 FEBRUARY 1995

Third Symphony for strings (1994) by the outstanding 58-year-old American composer Philip GLASS is given its first ever performance in Künzelsau.

6 FEBRUARY 1995

The highly-regarded 36-year-old American mezzo-soprano Jennifer LARMORE makes her Metropolitan Opera debut in New York as Rosina.

8 FEBRUARY 1995

Trio for oboe, bassoon, and piano (1978) by the 48-year-old black American composer and teacher Joyce

Solomon MOORMAN is heard for the first time in a revised version in New York.

9 FEBRUARY 1995

Ring, Time for symphonic wind ensemble (1994) by the productive 41-year-old English composer and teacher Robert (Louis Alfred) SAXTON is premiered in his native London.

10 FEBRUARY 1995

5 Poems for woodwind quintet (1994) by the distinguished 73-year-old Czech-born American composer, conductor, and pedagogue Karel HUSA is performed for the first time in New York.

11 FEBRUARY 1995

Polarization for two percussionists (1994) by the promising 33-year-old Japanese composer Karen TANAKA is heard for the first time over Paris's Radio France.

12 FEBRUARY 1995

Braises for amplified harpsichord and orchestra (1994) by the versatile 59-year-old French composer, musicologist, and philologist François-Bernard MÂCHE is heard for the first time over Paris's Radio France.

13 FEBRUARY 1995

Magnificat for voice, flute, and guitar by the 48-year-old American composer and teacher Bruce (Stuart) SAYLOR is premiered in Chicago.

15 FEBRUARY 1995

Invocation for horn, timpani, and chimes (1994) by the award-winning 45-year-old Israeli pianist and composer Shulamit RAN is heard for the first time in Los Angeles.

16 FEBRUARY 1995

Quatuor V for string quartet (1994) by the distinguished 68-year-old French-American composer and teacher Betsy JOLAS, daughter of the poet and journalist Eugène Jolas, well known as the founder and editor of the literary journal *transition*, is performed for the first time in her native Paris.

18 FEBRUARY 1995

Four Marian Antiphons: III, Regina Coeli Laetare for organ by the productive 68-year-old English pianist, organist, conductor, writer on music, and composer Francis (John) ROUTH is heard for the first time in London.

21 FEBRUARY 1995

Automobile Graveyard, opera after Fernando Arrabal, by the 65-year-old American composer and teacher Robert (Paige) CEELY is staged for the first time in Boston.

22 FEBRUARY 1995

Fanfares and Arias for wind ensemble (1994) by the respected 45-year-old American composer, teacher, conductor, and writer on music Steven (Edward) STUCKY is heard for the first time in Boulder, Colorado.

23 FEBRUARY 1994

Organ Concerto (1994) by the multifaceted 53-year-old American organist, harpsichordist, fortepianist, conductor, and composer Anthony NEWMAN is given its first ever performance in Englewood, New Jersey.

24 FEBRUARY 1995

Zion for wind ensemble (1994) by the 46-year-old American composer, conductor, and teacher Dan WELCHER is performed for the first time in Boulder, Colorado.

28 FEBRUARY 1995

The respected American pianist and teacher Leonard SHURE, who numbered among his pupils David del Tredici, Gilbert Kalisch, Gary Karr, Ursula Oppens, and Pinchas Zukerman, and who as a pianist became particularly admired for his performances of Beethoven, Schubert, and Brahms, dies in Nantucket, Massachusetts, at the age of 84.

2 MARCH 1995

Second Symphony (1994) by the prominent 46-year-old American composer and teacher Christopher (Chapman) ROUSE is performed for the first time in Houston.

3 MARCH 1995

Soleil Noir/Chitra for nine players, one technician, and live electronics (1993–94) by the significant 55-year-old English composer Jonathan (Dean) HARVEY is given its first performance in Brussels.

5 MARCH 1995

Brief Mass for chorus (1993) by the 45-year-old American composer, organist, and teacher Dan (Steven) LOCKLAIR is heard for the first time in Portland, Maine.

7 MARCH 1995

City Life for ensemble by the extraordinarily gifted 58-year-old American composer Steve (actually, Stephen Michael) REICH is performed for the first time in Metz.

10 MARCH 1995

The German-born American organist, conductor, and composer Herbert FROMM, author of the books *The Key of See: Travel Journey of a Composer, Seven Pockets*, and *On Jewish Music: A Composer's View*, and able composer of an extensive body of music for the synagogue, dies in Brookline, Massachusetts, at the accomplished age of 90.

11 MARCH 1995

Concertino for piano and strings (1989) by the 67-year-old French composer and pianist Jean-Michael DAMASE is heard for the first time in Rueil-Malmaison.

12 MARCH 1995

Orpheus for chamber orchestra (1994) by the esteemed 72-year-old black American composer, pianist, and teacher George (Theophilus) WALKER is performed for the first time in Cleveland.

14 MARCH 1995

The admired Irish composer, conductor, and broadcasting administrator Gerard (real name, Alan Loraine) VICTORY, long-time associated as a deputy director and then director of music at Radio Telefis Eireann and creator of an extensive body of music in various genres and styles, all handsomely crafted and couched in a generally accessible idiom, dies in his native Dublin at the age of 73.

15 MARCH 1995

Herma for cello and strings (1994–95) by the 53-year-old Icelandic cellist and composer Haflidi (Magnus) HALLGRÍMSSON is heard for the first time in Glasgow.

16 MARCH 1995

The distinguished Swiss composer Heinrich SUTERMEISTER, who in his works placed prime importance upon the composer's responsibility to communicate directly with his listeners, dies in Vaux-sur-Morges at the age of 84.

17 MARCH 1995

Percussion Symphony (1994), fifth symphony of the 40-year-old Australian composer and pianist Carl VINE is heard for the first time in Sydney.

21 MARCH 1995

blueS No. 5 for piano and orchestra (1992) and *Double Concerto* for two violins and orchestra (1988), two works by the outstanding 65-year-old Polish composer, pianist, pedagogue, writer on music, stage manager, and playwright Bogusław (Julien) SCHAEFFER are heard for the first time in Warsaw.

23 MARCH 1995

Music for percussion and orchestra (1994) by the outstanding 64-year-old Estonian composer and pedagogue Eino TAMBERG is premiered in his native Tallinn.

25 MARCH 1995

Appassionatamente (1995), fantasy for orchestra, after the music drama *Das verratene Meer* (1993–94), by the masterful 68-year-old German composer Hans Werner HENZE is performed for the first time in Vienna.

26 MARCH 1995

Marimba Concerto (1994) by the 55-year-old Czech-American composer Tomáš SVOBODA, son of the renowned mathematician Antonin Svoboda, is heard for the first time in Portland, Oregon.

28 MARCH 1995

Theme and Variations for piano (1948) by the 77-year-old American composer, pianist, and teacher J(oseph) Willard ROOSEVELT, grandson of President Theodore Roosevelt, is heard for the first time in a revised version in Long Island, New York.

29 MARCH 1995

Woman Without Adornment for reciter and piano (1994) by the accomplished 57-year-old American composer, pianist, administrator, presenter, and teacher Bernadette (Marie) SPEACH in collaboration with Thulani Davis is performed for the first time in a version scored for reciter and chamber ensemble in New York.

30 MARCH 1995

The second "Other Minds" Festival, under the artistic direction of Charles Amirkhanian, opens in San Francisco at the Center for the Arts at Yerba Buena Gardens with a concert in the following program: *String Quartet No. 2*, entitled *Secret Desire to Be Black* (1988), by the respected 54-year-old black American composer Alvin SINGLETON; *Ascension* for guitar (1993) by the significant 59-year-old American composer and performer Terry (Mitchell) RILEY; the world premiere of *Gemini* for solo violin, Zeta MIDI violin, and interactive computer (1994) by Mari KIMURA; *Varied Trio* for violin, piano, and percussion (1987) by the inventive 78-year-old American composer and performer Lou (Silver) HARRISON; and the world premiere of *The Prism I* and *2* for piano, trumpet, and trombone by Muhal Richard ABRAMS.

31 MARCH 1995

On the second day of the second "Other Minds" Festival at the Center for the Arts at Yerba Buena Gardens in San Francisco, a concert in the following program: *Narcisse* (1993) by Ashot ZOGRABYAN; "The Gift" from *Salome Dances for Peace* (1985–86) by the significant 59-year-old American composer and performer Terry (Mitchell) RILEY; *There Goes the Neighborhood* (1994) by Don BYRON; *Fog Tropes II* (1993) by the remarkable 52-year-old American composer Ingram MARSHALL; and *Ghost Opera* (1994) by the significant 38-year-old Chinese composer TAN DUN, featuring the pipa virtuoso, Wu Man.

1 APRIL 1995

December for strings by the gifted 33-year-old American composer and pianist Michael TORKE is premiered in Des Moines.

1 APRIL 1995

On the third and final day of the second "Other Minds" Festival at the Center for the Arts at Yerba Buena Gardens in San Francisco, a concert is given in the following program: *Five Short Pieces* for guitar and percussion (1952–78) by the inventive 78-year-old American composer and performer Lou (Silver) HARRISON; *Compulsive Caress* for guitar (1993) by the 31-year-old Greek pianist and composer Calliope TSOUPAKI; *Trees* (1992) for two violins and viola by the 34-year-old American composer Frances WHITE; *Toccata* for violin and pianola (1935) by the remarkable 82-year-old American-born Mexican composer and innovator in the technique of recording notes on a player-piano roll Conlon NANCARROW; *Etude for Pianola* (1930; rev. 1952) by the great Russian-born French, later American composer, one of the supreme masters of 20th-century music, Igor STRAVINSKY (1882–1971); and *Sierran Songs* for baritone, piano, and percussion (1994) by the remarkable 52-year-old American composer Ingram MARSHALL.

2 APRIL 1995

The notable 59-year-old Austrian composer, conductor, and pedagogue Friedrich CERHA conducts the first performance of his *Viola Concerto* (1993) in his native Vienna.

3 APRIL 1995

Clarinet Concerto by the outstanding 65-year-old Polish composer, pianist, pedagogue, writer on music, stage manager, and playwright Bogusław (Julien) SCHAEFFER is performed for the first time in Kraków.

6 APRIL 1995

Weisen von Liebe, Leben und Tod for middle voice and orchestra by the esteemed 60-year-old German composer Siegfried MATTHUS is given its first ever performance in Berlin.

8 APRIL 1995

"The Narrow Road into the Deep North: Bashô" for orchestra by the 65-year-old Japanese composer Jōji YUASA receives its first performance in his native Koriyama.

11 APRIL 1995

Komungo Permutations No. 3 for Korean mabrain bamboo flute and western flutes by the talented 37-year-old South Korean composer and komungo player Jin Hi KIM is heard for the first time in Los Angeles.

12 APRIL 1995

The 5 Sacred Trees, concerto for bassoon and strings (1992–94), by the enormously successful 63-year-old American composer and conductor John (Towner) WILLIAMS is first heard in his native New York.

14 APRIL 1995

The loveable American folksinger Burl (Icle Ivanhoe) IVES, popular as a singer and dramatic actor as well as author of an autobiography, *Wayfaring Stranger* (N.Y., 1948), and the anthologies *The Burl Ives Songbook* (1953) and *The Burl Ives Book of Irish Songs* (1958), dies in Anacortes, Washington, at the age of 85.

16 APRIL 1995

Chamber Concerto for accordion and ensemble by the 48-year-old Dutch composer and teacher Tristan KEURIS is heard for the first time in his native Amsterdam.

17 APRIL 1995

Dwa dialogi (Two Dialogues), originally scored for instrumental ensemble, by the 70-year-old Polish composer and pedagogue Krystyna MOSZUMAŃSKA-NAZAR is performed for the first time in an orchestral version in Szczecin.

18 APRIL 1995

New York Moonglow for chamber ensemble by the talented 56-year-old American composer Barbara KOLB is heard for the first time in New York.

20 APRIL 1995

Family Tree for narrator and orchestra (1992) by the outstanding 64-year-old Japanese composer Tōru TAKEMITSU is premiered in New York.

21 APRIL 1995

Mata Hari, chamber opera (1994), by the 61-year-old American composer and teacher Vincent MCDERMOTT is staged for the first time in Dallas.

23 APRIL 1995

Seventh Symphony, entitled *Angel of Light* (1994), by the eminent 66-year-old Finnish composer and pedagogue Einojuhani (actually, Eino Juhani) RAUTAVAARA is performed for the first time in Bloomington, Indiana.

26 APRIL 1995

Madrugada for soprano, actors, and musicians (1992–95) by the accomplished 44-year-old Canadian composer Michael (Bass) MATTHEWS is premiered in Winnipeg.

28 APRIL 1995

The Czech soprano Hana JANKŮ, best known for her work in the Czech repertory but also for such roles as Gioconda, Elsa, Kundry, Desdemona, and Ariadne, dies in Vienna at the lamentable age of 54.

29 APRIL 1995

Carrington for orchestra and *Concerto* for harpsichord and strings, two works by the notable 51-year-old English composer, conductor, and writer on music Michael (Laurence) NYMAN is heard for the first time in his native London.

1 MAY 1995

Black Water, opera after Joyce Carol Oates, by the noted 68-year-old American music administrator and composer John DUFFY is staged for the first time in Philadelphia.

4 MAY 1995

The Russian-born American violinist Louis KRASNER, who commissioned and gave the first performances of Alban Berg's *Violin Concerto* (Barcelona, April 19, 1936) and Arnold Schoenberg's *Violin Concerto* (Philadelphia, Dec. 6, 1940), dies in Brookline, Massachusetts, at the age of 91.

5 MAY 1995

Memory for orchestra, written for the 50th anniversary of the liberation of Denmark by the 86-year-old Danish pianist, teacher, and composer of Polish parentage Herman D(avid) KOPPEL, father of the Danish composer Thomas Herman Koppel, is performed for the first time in Århus.

6 MAY 1995

Odysseus' Women for orchestra by the masterful 55-year-old Dutch composer and teacher Louis ANDRIESSEN, son of Hendrik (Franciscus), nephew of Willem (Christiaan Nicolaas), and brother of Jurriaan Andriessen, is heard for the first time in Rotterdam.

7 MAY 1995

Oboe Concerto (1994) by the esteemed 56-year-old English pianist, music educator, and composer John MCCABE is performed for the first time in Isle of Wight.

8 MAY 1995

Dorian Gray, opera (1993–94), by the versatile 44-year-old American composer, pianist, and conductor Lowell LIEBERMANN is first staged in Monte Carlo.

10 MAY 1995

Libertas Vincit for reciter, chorus, and chamber orchestra to celebrate the 50th anniversary of the liberation of Norway from Nazi occupation (1994) by the esteemed 79-year-old Norwegian choral conductor, organist, pedagogue, and composer Knut NYSTEDT is performed for the first time in Oslo.

11 MAY 1995

I Was Looking at the Ceiling and Then I Saw the Sky, song play by the award-winning 48-year-old American composer John (Coolidge) ADAMS is performed for the first time in Berkeley, California.

16 MAY 1995

The Austrian soprano Gertrud GROB-PRANDL, best known for her Wagnerian roles, most notably Ortrud, Brünnhilde, and Isolde, dies in her native Vienna at the age of 77.

19 MAY 1995

Corridors of Light for baritone, oboe, strings, and percussion (1994) by the 58-year-old American composer, choral conductor, and organist William (Edward) FERRIS is performed for the first time in his native Chicago.

20 MAY 1995

The eminent black American composer and teacher Ulysses Simpson KAY, long-time faculty member at the Herbert H. Lehman College in New York (1968–1988), whose music followed a distinctly American idiom, particularly in its rhythmic intensity, while avoiding ostentatious ethnic elements, dies in Englewood, New Jersey, at the age of 78.

24 MAY 1995

The gifted 15-year-old American violinist Sarah CHANG is soloist in the Mendelssohn *Violin Concerto* with the New York Philharmonic conducted by Kurt Masur, a performance telecast live to the nation by PBS.

27 MAY 1995

Die Weise von Liebe und Tod des Cornets Christoph Rilke for speaker and orchestra (1944) by the Austrian composer, pianist, conductor, and music critic Viktor ULLMANN, who ended his days in the concentration camp in Auschwitz on or about Oct. 15, 1944, receives its posthumous premiere in a partial reconstruction by H. Brauel in Prague.

29 MAY 1995

Albumblatt for flute, guitar, and vibraphone by the prominent 70-year-old Italian composer and pedagogue Aldo CLEMENTI is performed for the first time in Rome.

1 JUNE 1995

Watt for trombone and orchestra (1994) by the 40-year-old French composer Pascal DUSAPIN is premiered in Las Vegas.

3 JUNE 1995

Double Concerto for violin, cello, and orchestra, winner of the Grawemeyer Award of the University of Louisville, by the 55-year-old French-born American composer of Russian descent Ivan (Alexandrovich) TCHEREPNIN, son of Alexander (Nikolaievich) and brother of Serge (Alexandrovich) Tcherepnin, both noteworthy composers in their own right, is performed for the first time in Cambridge, Massachusetts.

4 JUNE 1995

Kristnikvede for chorus and orchestra, written to celebrate the 1,000th anniverary of Christianity in Norway by the esteemed 79-year-old Norwegian choral conductor, organist, pedagogue, and composer Knut NYSTEDT is heard for the first time in Moster.

5 JUNE 1995

The highly-regarded American pianist and teacher Johana HARRIS (née Beula Duffey), widow of the masterful American symphonist Roy Harris and for a time wife of the talented American composer Jake Heggie, dies in Los Angeles at the age of 82.

8 JUNE 1995

On the occasion of her 48th birthday, *Calligraphy II/Shadows* for voice and Chinese instruments by the gifted American composer and experimental vocalist Joan (Linda née Lotz) LA BARBARA, wife of the prominent American composer Morton Subotnick, is performed for the first time in New York.

9 JUNE 1995

The Wildman, opera, by the 48-year-old English composer and teacher Nicola (Frances) LEFANU, daughter of the medical historian William LeFanu and the composer Elizabeth Maconchy, and wife of the Australian composer David Lumsdaine, is staged for the first time in Aldeburgh.

11 JUNE 1995

Akashic Prelude on a Theme of Paul Bowles for piano by the respected 55-year-old American writer on music and composer Phillip RAMEY is heard for the first time in Santa Cruz, California.

12 JUNE 1995

The celebrated Italian pianist and pedagogue Arturo Benedetti MICHELANGELI , whose technical mastery made him one of the great keyboard exponents of the Romantic repertoire, his sympathies ranging from early music to the 20th century, dies in Lugano at the age of 75.

14 JUNE 1995

The Estonian composer and teacher Els AARNE, longtime faculty member of the Tallinn Conservatory (1944–1974), dies in Tallinn at the age of 78.

17 JUNE 1995

Helios, oboe concerto (1994), by the remarkable 67-year-old Scottish composer Thea MUSGRAVE is given its first ever performance in Orkney.

19 JUNE 1995

The Polish pianist and teacher Maria WIŁKOMIRSKA, who hailed from a distinguished family of Polish musicians which included her father, the violinist and teacher Alfred Wiłkomirski, dies in Warsaw at the seasoned age of 91.

21 JUNE 1995

Songs of Despondency and Grief for chorus and instruments (1980–94) by the eminent 69-year-old Hungarian composer and teacher György KURTÁG is heard for the first time in Amsterdam.

22 JUNE 1995

Historia von D. Johann Fausten, opera (1989–93), by the prominent 60-year-old Russian composer of German descent Alfred (Garrievich) SCHNITTKE is premiered in Hamburg.

23 JUNE 1995

The 69th Festival of the International Society for Contemporary Music opens in Germany with a concert at Essen's Aalto-Theater performed by the Essen Philharmonic, conducted by Wolf-Dieter Hauschild, with special guest artist Anthony de Mare, piano, in the following program: *Klavierkonzert* (1931) by the remarkable and innovative American composer Henry COWELL (1897–1965), in three movements: *1. Polyharmony, 2. Tone cluster,* and *3. Counter rhythm; In den Stunden des Neumonds*, symphonic poem (1910), by the Ukrainian composer Nicolai ROSLAWEZ (1881–1944); *Piano Mechanics* for solo piano (1981–87) by the innovative Canadian composer Gordan MONAHAN; *Arcana* for large orchestra (1925–27; rev. 1960) by the remarkable French-born American composer who introduced a totally original principle of organizing the materials and forms of sound, profoundly influencing the direction of new music, Edgar VARÈSE (1883–1965), inspired by the cosmology of Paracelsus,

and a 1937 arrangement of Johannes Brahms' *Piano Quartet No 1* in G major, op. 25, for large orchestra by the great Austrian-born American composer whose new method of musical organization in 12 different tones related only to one another profoundly influenced the entire development of modern techniques of composition, Arnold SCHOENBERG (1874–1951), in four movements, *1. Allegro, 2. Intermezzo. Allegro ma non troppo, 3. Andante con moto,* and *4. Rondo alla zingarese. Presto.*

24 OCTOBER 1995

On the second day of the 69th Festival of the International Society for Contemporary Music in Germany, three concerts are given, in the following sequence:

A mid-day concert at Essen's Kunstschacht Katernberg performed by the Schlagquartett Köln, Michael Lentz, live and recorded voice, Lesley Olson, flute, Rosiya Suzuki, bass recorder, and the Essener Flute Ensemble, conducted by Christoph Erkens, in the following program: *Taltal* for four percussionists (1993) by the Argentine composer Mariano ETKIN; *S'Geypo* for 16 flutes (1989/1993) by Ramon Pagayon SANTOS; *Slippery When Wet* for 18 musicians (1995) by Amnon WOLMAN; *Drawing* for solo bass recorder (1992) by the Japanese composer Hitoshi NAKAMURA; *hass------- flüstern*, variations for two speakers, clapping and stamping (1994) by the German composer Josef Anton RIEDL; *El en gris* for two percussionists (1992) by the Argentine composer Maria Cecilia VILLANUEVA; *hacia la noche* for flute (1985) by Ana LARA; and *Tribadabum extensif sur rythme fantome* for an unspecified number of percussion (1981) by the 60-year-old French composer, trombonist, conductor, and teacher of Slovenian descent, Vinko GLOBOKAR.

A late afternoon concert at Essen's Zeche Zollverein-Wipperhalle performed by the Trio Recherche, Freiburg, comprised of Melise Mellinger, violin, Barbara Maurer, viola, and Lucas Fels, cello, with special guest artist Stefano Scodanibbio, double bass, in the following program: *String Trio* (1968) by the Swiss composer Thomas KESSLER; *String Trio*, op.20 (1926–27) by the remarkable Austrian composer Anton WEBERN (1883–1945), in two movements: *1. Sehr langsam* and *2. Sehr getragen und ausdrucksvoll; Trittico for Gertrude Stein* for double bass (1989) by the 52-year-old English composer and teacher Brian FERNEYHOUGH; *PLC-Abstract* for double bass (1968/1972) by the 64-year-old American composer and long-time music director for the Los Angeles County Museum of Art Dorrance STALVEY; *Mar del Olvido* for violin, cello, and double bass (1994–95) by the Italian composer and virtuosic double bassist Stefano SCODANIBBIO; *String Trio No. 2* (1955) by the English composer of extreme avant-garde tendencies, one of the founding members of the Scratch Orchestra, a heterogeneous group for performances of new music, militantly latitudinarian and disestablishmentarian, Cornelius CARDEW (1936–1981); and *String Trio* (1995) by Frank COX.

An evening concert at Essen's Grugahalle performed by numerous forces, including the Niederländischer Rundfunkchor, Hilversum, Solistenchor Freiburg, Ensemble Modern, Orchester des Polnischen, etc., conducted by Eberhard Kloke, and featuring guest soloists Monika Meier-Schmid, soprano, Susanne Otto, alto, and Dietmar Wiesner, flute, in the following program: *Ave Maria* from *Four Sacred Pieces* for four soloists and a cappella chorus (1889) by the great Italian opera composer whose genius for dramatic, lyric, and tragic stage music has made him the perennial favorite of a multitude of opera enthusiasts Giuseppe VERDI (1813–1901), his last composition, in which he made use of the so-called *scala enigmatica* (C, D , E, F , G , A , B, and C); *Diastema* for two orchestras with one conductor (1991–92) and *Diastasis* for two orchestras without conductor (1991–92), two works by the 46-year-old German composer Walter ZIMMERMANN; *Leonora Overture No. 3*, op.72a (1806) by the great German composer whose unsurpassed genius, expressed with supreme mastery in his symphonies, chamber music, concertos, and piano sonatas, revealing an extraordinary power of invention, marked a historic turn in the art of composition Ludwig van BEETHOVEN (1770–1827); *Super Flumina Babylonis* for soprano, alto, chamber orchestra, and strings ad libitum (1995) by the Japanese composer Toshio HOSOKAWA; *Second Orchestral Set* (1909–15) by Charles IVES (1874–1954), one of the most remarkable American composers, whose individual genius created music so original, so universal, and yet so deeply national in its sources of inspiration that it profoundly changed the direction of American music, in three movements: *1. An Elegy to Our Forefathers, 2. The Rockstrewn Hill Join in the People's Outdoor Meeting,* and *3. From Hanover Square North, at the End of a Tragic Day, the Voice of the People Again Rose; Piano Mechanics* for solo piano (1981–87) by the innovative Canadian composer and performance artist Gordan MONAHAN; *Ecuatorial* for bass, four trumpets, four trombones, piano, organ, percussion, and Thereminovox (1932–34) by the remarkable French-born American composer, who introduced a totally original principle of organizing the materials and forms of sound, profoundly influencing the direction of new music, Edgar VARÈSE (1883–1965); and *Caminantes...Ayacucho* for orchestra, chorus, soloists, flute, and live electronics (1987) by the remarkable Italian composer who earned a unique place in the history of modern music through his consistent devotion to social problems Luigi NONO (1924–1990).

24 JUNE 1995

The outstanding 31-year-old German violinist Anne-Sophie MUTTER appears as soloist in the premiere performance of Krzysztof Penderecki's *Second Violin Concerto* with the MDR Symphony Orchestra in Leipzig under Mariss Jansons's direction.

25 JUNE 1995

On the third day of the 69th Festival of the International Society for Contemporary Music in Germany, two concerts are given, in the following sequence:

A late afternoon concert at Essen's Zeche Zollverein-Lesebandhalle performed by the Klangforum Wien, conducted by Peter Rundel, with guest artist Isabella Cholette, oboe, in the following program: *Bidan-Sil* for oboe and nine instruments (1993–94) by the Korean composer Youngi PAGH-PAAN, *Trojtza* for 15 players (1990) by Carmen Maria CÂRNECI, *Parabel 8* (1993) by the Bulgarian composer Bojidar SPASSOV, and *Lonicera caprifollum* for ensemble and tape (1993) by the 27-year-old Austrian composer Olga NEUWIRTH.

An evening concert at Essen's Zeche Zollverein-Lesebandhalle performed by the Experimentalstudio des SWF, Klangforum Wien, conducted by Peter Rundel, with guest artists Eugen Procter and Hannes Hellmann, speakers, and Annette Bik, violin, in the following program: *Nacht-Schaten* for ensemble (1991) by the 42-year-old Swiss composer Georg Friedrich HAAS, *Narcissus-Fragment* for two speakers and ensemble (1993–94) by the 40-year-old Swiss-born Austrian composer, conductor, and teacher Beat FURRER; *Aussenhäute* for clarinet, saxophone, violin, and cello (1989) by the Austrian composer Gerhard WINKLER; *La Battaglia* for ensemble (1994) by the Italian composer Antonio PILEGGI, *Glidif-a sonar e cantar* for bass- and double bass clarinet, two double basses, and live electronics (1989/1991) by the Swiss compos-

er André RICHARD; and *Anahit. Poème lyrique dédié à Vènus* for solo violin and 18 instruments (1965) by the remarkable Italian composer Giacinto SCELSI (1905–1988).

26 JUNE 1995

On the fourth day of the 69th Festival of the International Society for Contemporary Music in Germany, three concerts are given, in the following sequence:

A mid-day concert at Essen's Folkwang-Hochschule-Neue Aula, the first of several matinee concerts of electronic works presented by the Institut für Computertechnik und Electronische Medien (ICEM) der Folkwang-Hochschule Essen, in the following program: *Unknown Journey* (1992) by Joshua K.B. CHAN, *Rebus I* (1990) by Srdjan HOFMAN, *Image: The Pop Can* (1993) by Ronald ALFORD, *Là où vont les nuages pour Ondes Martenotsysteme* (1991) by Giles GOBEIL, and *Pyrotechnika* (1993) by Steve ADAMS.

A late afternoon concert at Essen's Alte Synagoge performed by Mitglieder der Musikfabrik NRW, in the following program: *Lenzmusik I* for violin, clarinet, and piano (1992) by the German composer Erhard GROSSKOPF, *Myoung-Sang* (Meditation) for soprano or tenor and percussion (1984) by the Korean composer Kyu Yung CHIN, and *Wiederholt Annäherung* for clarinet, trombone, cello, and piano (1992–93) by the German composer Jörg BIRKENKÖTTER.

An evening concert at Essen's Alte Synagoge performed by MusikFabrik NRW, conducted by Johannes Kalitzke, in the following program: *from fear and thunder, dreams...* for chamber ensemble (1987–88) by the German composer Robert HP PLATZ; *Chu Ky VII* for harp and ensemble (1986) by the Vietnamese composer Ton-Chat TIÊT; *Music for 12*, op. 34, for ensemble (1989) by the Russian composer Jelena FIRSSOWA; and *Come and Go* for ensemble (1994) by the English composer Andrew TOOVEY.

27 JUNE 1995

Josef, opera (1993–95), by the prominent 84-year-old German-born Israeli composer, pianist, conductor, and pedagogue Josef (real name, Joseph Gruenthal) TAL is staged for the first time in Tel Aviv.

27 JUNE 1995

On the fifth day of the 69th Festival of the International Society for Contemporary Music in Germany, four concerts are given, in the following sequence:

A mid-day concert at Essen's Folkwang-Hochschule-Neue Aula, the second matinee concert of electronic works presented by the Institut für Computertechnik und Electronische Medien (ICEM) der Folkwang-Hochschule Essen, in the following program: *sud* (1985) by Jean Claude RISSET, *Klangkörper* (1994) by Thomas GERWIN, *Point Virgule* (1990) by Jean François DENIS, *Breathing Room* (1990) by Hildegard WESTERKAMP, *MiniSérie* (1990) by Roxanne TURCOTTE, and *Yun Mu 3* (1993) by Jung-hae LEE.

A late afternoon concert at Duisburg's Karmel-Kirche performed by The Barton Workshop (Amsterdam) featuring an untitled work for flute and string quartet (1994) by the innovative 37-year-old Korean composer Kunsu SHIM.

An evening concert at Duisburg's Mercatorhalle performed by the Sinfonieorchester des Saarländischen Rundfunks, conducted by Marcello Viotti, with featured guest artists Thomas Zehetmair, violin, and Thomas Larcher, piano, in the following program: *Kammerkonzert* for piano, violin, and 13 wind instruments (1923–25) by the greatly significant Austrian

A late-night concert at Essen's Folkwang-Hochschule-Innenhof, an open-air concert of electronic works presented by the Institut für Computertechnik und Electronische Medien (ICEM) der Folkwang-Hochschule Essen, in the following program: *The Bell Drama* (1993-94) by Friedhelm Hans HARTMANN, *Pyrócua* (1994) by Ralf R. OLLERTZ, *Turenas* (1972) by the American composer John CHOWNING, *Dinosaur Music* (1986) by William SCHOTTSTAEDT, and *Valdrada* (1988) by the 34-year-old American composer Frances WHITE.

30 JUNE 1995

On the eighth day of the 69th Festival of the International Society for Contemporary Music in Germany, two concerts are given, in the following sequence:

A mid-day concert at Essen's Folkwang-Hochschule-Neue Aula, the fifth and last matinee concert of electronic works presented by the Institut für Computertechnik und Electronische Medien (ICEM) der Folkwang-Hochschule Essen, in the following program: *just-more-idle chatter* (1987) by the 51-year-old American composer and teacher Paul LANSKY; *Étude pathétique* (1948) by the 84-year-old French acoustician, composer, and novelist Pierre SCHAEFFER; *Skweeit-Chupp* (1990) by Zack SETTEL; *Funktion blau* (1969) by Gottfried Michael KOENIG; *cut* (1988) by Lutz GLANDIEN; *Mortous Plango, Vivos, Voco* (1980) by the significant 56-year-old English composer Jonathan HARVEY; and *Mambo á la Braque* (1990) by Javier ALVAREZ.

An evening concert at Bochum's Jahrhunderthalle performed by the Hilliard-Ensemble, Philharmonisches Orchester der Stadt Nürnberg, and Philharmonia Hungarica, conducted by Eberhard Kloke, in the following program: *Viderunt omnes V. Notum fecit* (gradual for Christmas and Circumcision), *Veni creator,* and *Alleluja,* three works by PEROTIN (also called Perotinus Magnus and Magister Perotinus), the celebrated composer who flourished in the 12th century; *Diastema* for two orchestras with one conductor (1991–92) and *Diastasis* for two orchestras without conductor (1991–92), two works by the 46-year-old German composer Walter ZIMMERMANN; *Ficciones* for orchestra (1980) by the Mexican composer Mario LAVISTA; Lieder for baritone and orchestra by the great Austrian composer and conductor Gustav MAHLER (1860–1911): 1. "Revelge" from *14 Lieder aus des Knaben Wunderhorn* (1892–1901), 2. "Ich bin der Welt abhanden gekommen" from *Rückert-Lieder* (1901–03), 3. "Um Mitternacht" from *Rückert-Lieder* (1901–03), 4. "Der Tambourgesell" from *14 Lieder aus des Knaben Wunderhorn* (1892–1901), and 5. "Wo die schönen Trompeten blasen" from *14 Lieder aus des Knaben Wunderhorn* (1892–1901); *Polyèdre* for orchestra (1987) by the Japanese composer Yoshihisa TAÏRA; *The Unanswered Question* for chamber orchestra (1906) by Charles IVES (1874–1954), one of the most remarkable American composers, whose individual genius created music so original, so universal, and yet so deeply national in its sources of inspiration that it profoundly changed the direction of American music; *Overture* to *Lohengrin* (1847–48) by the great German composer whose operas, written to his own librettos, radically transformed the concept of stage music, postulating the inherent equality of dramatic and symphonic writing, and establishing the uninterrupted continuity of the action, Richard WAGNER (1813–1883); and *Yuan* for orchestra (1988) by the Chinese composer Qigang CHEN.

1 JULY 1995

Powder Her Face, chamber opera in eight scenes by the gifted 24-year-old English composer Thomas (Joseph Edmund) ADÈS, to a libretto by the maverick novelist Philip Henscher based on the scandalous life of Margaret, Duchess of Argyll (1912–1993), the beautiful and alluring English socialist whose marriage to the Duke of Argyll ended in a sensational trial in which she was charged with slander, forgery, and various adulteries, is given its premiere staging at the Cheltenham Festival.

1 JULY 1995

On the ninth day of the 69th Festival of the International Society for Contemporary Music in Germany, four concerts are given, in the following sequence:

An early afternoon concert at Essen's Grillo Theater performed by CIKADA (Oslo), conducted by Christian Eggen, in the following program: *Solentiname* for flute, clarinet, piano, violin, and percussion (1972–73) by the Venezuelan composer Alfredo del MONACO; *Dark Glasses* for ensemble (1988) by the Canadian composer Rodney SHARMAN; *Ning* for clarinet and string trio (1989) by the Norwegian composer Rolf WALLIN; *Pièce pour violon et piano* (1975) by the short-lived Canadian composer Claude VIVIER (1948–1983); *Funeral Procession* for ensemble (1989) by the 36-year-old Danish composer Bent SØRENSEN, and *Neue Komposition* for ensemble (1995) by the Swedish composer Henrik STRINDBERG.

A late afternoon concert at Essen's Kreuzeskirche performed by Cappella Artis Novae, Essen, conducted by Chrisoph Erkens, with special guest artists Stephan Rath, lute, and Andreas Fröhling and Gary Verkade, organists, in the following program: *Improvisation ajoutée,* music for organ (1962/68) by the notable 63-year-old Argentine composer and pedagogue Mauricio KAGEL; "Qui risi Tirsi" from *Il sesto libro di madrigali* for five voices, "con uno dialogo," and seven voices, with basso continuo (1614), "Lamento della Ninva" from *Concerto: Settimo libro de madrigali, con altri generi de canti* for one to four and six voices, with basso continuo (1619), and "Ballo e Glori" from *Madrigali guerrieri et amorosi con alcuni opuscoli in genere rappresentativo, che saranno per brevi episodii frà i canti senza gesto: Libro ottavo* for one to eight voices and instruments, with basso continuo (1638), three pieces by the great Italian composer Claudio MONTEVERDI (1567–1643); *Icarus* for four solo speakers and tape (1993) by the English composer Katharine NORMAN; *Vox 5* for tape (1986) by Trevor WISHART; *sns* for organ (1975) by Hans-Joachim HESPOS; and *Wiegenlied, Brentano* for sixteen speakers and tape (1993) by the German composer Achim Christian BORNHÖFT.

An evening concert at Essen's Saalbau performed by NDR-Sinfonieorchester, conducted by Hans Zender, with guest artist Pierre-Laurent Aimard, piano, in the following program: *Piano and Orchestra* (1975) by the significant American composer and pedagogue Morton FELDMAN (1926–1987); *The Unanswered Question* for chamber orchestra (1906) by Charles IVES (1874–1954), one of the most remarkable American composers, whose individual genius created music so original, so universal, and yet so deeply national in its sources of inspiration that it profoundly changed the direction of American music; *A Shape of Time* for piano and orchestra (1980) by the Japanese composer Jo KONDO; *Manfred Overture,* op.115 (1848–49), by the great German composer of surpassing imaginative power whose music expressed the deepest spirit of the Romantic era Robert SCHUMANN (1810–1856); and *Hymnos* for orchestra (1963), in three parts, by the remarkable Italian composer Giacinto SCELSI (1905–1988).

A late-night concert at Oberhausen's Gasometer performed by the Institut für Computermusik und elektronische Medien (ICEM) der Folkwang-Hochschule and Accroche Note, Strasbourg, in the following program: *Klangraum Interaktiv II* (1995) by the German composers Thomas NEUHAUS and Gerald ECKERT; *Improvisation und Werke,* performed by

Accroche Note of Strasbourg, including compositions by Marc MONNET (*Chansons imprévues* for solo voice), Sylvano BUSSOTTI (*Voliera. Concerto a l'acquila* for ensemble), James CLARKE (*Afterglow* for soprano and ensemble), Iannis XENAKIS (*Kren* for trombone), and John CAGE (*Fontana Mix*); *Aux mains de l'espace* (1993) by the German composer Gerald ECKERT; and *La cloche sans vallées* (1993) by the German composer Ludger BRÜMMER.

2 JULY 1995

On the tenth and final day of the 69th Festival of the International Society for Contemporary Music in Germany, a concert is given at Essen's Aalto Theater performed by the BBC Symphony Orchestra, London, conducted by Péter Eötvös, with guest artist Márta Fábián, cimbalom, in the following program: *Jeux. Poème dansé* (1912) by the great French composer whose music created new poetry of mutating tonalities and became a perfect counterpart of new painting in France Claude DEBUSSY (1862–1918), in two movements, *Très lent - Scherzando (Tempo initial), Psychokosmos* for cimbalom and orchestra (1993) by the 41-year-old Hungarian conductor, composer, and pedagogue Péter EÖTVÖS; and *Symphony No. 7* (1983–84) by the outstanding 49-year-old German composer Hans Werner HENZE, in four movements: *1. Tanz, 2. Ruhig bewegt, 3. Unablässig in Bewegung,* and *4. Ruhig, verhalten.*

3 JULY 1995

Barries Deviant Fantasy for string quartet and referee's whistles by the 35-year-old English composer Mark-Anthony TURNAGE is premiered in London.

5 JULY 1995

Daedalus Remembers for cello and orchestra by the 37-year-old English composer Simon HOLT is performed for the first time in Cheltenham.

7 JULY 1995

The German contralto Marga HÖFFGEN, who in 1953, shortly after her operatic debut, made a highly successful appearance in Vienna as a soloist in Johann Sebastian Bach's *St. Matthew Passion* conducted by Herbert von Karajan, dies in Müllheim at the age of 74.

8 JULY 1995

Concerto for guitar and strings by the 51-year-old Australian composer Ross EDWARDS is given its first ever performance in Darwin.

9 JULY 1995

Alicia, opera, after Lewis Carroll (1989–90), by the 48-year-old Mexican composer Federico IBARRA (Groth) is staged for the first time in his native Mexico City.

12 JULY 1995

The talented American pianist Alan MARKS, whose innate virtuoso technique allowed him to interpret with perfect stylistic fidelity piano works by classical as well as modern composers, dies in Berlin at the pitiable age of 46.

15 JULY 1995

The Woman is a Devil, opera (1993), by the 59-year-old Russian-born American composer and teacher David FINKO is staged for the first time in Philadelphia.

16 JULY 1995

Fünf Lieder der Sappho for soprano and piano (1993–95) by the 67-year-old German composer and teacher Wilhelm KILLMAYER is given its premiere performance in his native Munich.

17 JULY 1995

The German composer Rainer KUNAD, who was principally influenced by Lutosawski, with some indirect inspiration from Penderecki and Henze, and who found his métier as a composer for the theater, dies in Tübingen at the lamentable age of 58.

20 JULY 1995

The Russian composer Alexander PIRUMOV, whose *Prelude and Toccata* (1962) and *Scherzo* (1974) became required pieces for the Tchaikovsky Piano Competition, dies in Moscow at the age of 65.

22 JULY 1995

Singin' in the Dark (Songs of the American Frontier) for chorus and orchestra by the energetic 42-year-old Chinese composer and teacher Chen YI is performed for the first time in San Francisco.

23 JULY 1995

The Children for mezzo-soprano or baritone and piano by the 36-year-old Scottish composer, conductor, and teacher James MACMILLAN is heard for the first time over London's BBC Radio 3.

26 JULY 1995

Palatsi (The Palace), opera (1991–93), by the prominent 60-year-old Finnish composer Aulis SALLINEN is mounted for the first time in Savonlinna.

27 JULY 1995

The brilliant Hungarian-American composer Miklós RÓZSA, who won Academy Awards for his grandiloquent film scores to *Spellbound* (1945), *A Double Life* (1947), and *Ben-Hur* (1959), dies in Los Angeles at the age of 88.

31 JULY 1995

A Spring Cadenza for cello (1994) by the 46-year-old English composer and teacher John (Arthur) CASKEN is given its first ever performance in Sydney.

5 AUGUST 1995

The prominent Polish-born Israeli composer and administrator Menahem AVIDOM (real name, Kalkstein), whose extensive output, of wide stylistic variety, utilized folk modalities of the Middle East as well as dodecaphony, dies in Herzliya at the accomplished age of 87.

6 AUGUST 1995

The French organist, pedagogue, and composer André (Edouard Antoine Marie) FLEURY, long-time organist at the Cathedral and as a professor at the Conservatory in Dijon (1949–71) who also composed two organ symphonies (1947, 1949) and many other organ works, dies in Le Vésinet at the remarkable age of 92.

11 AUGUST 1995

Moon and Star for chorus and orchestra by the 41-year-old English composer Judith WEIR is given its first ever performance in London.

12 AUGUST 1995

In Paradisum for men's chorus by the 41-year-old Polish composer Paweł SZYMAŃSKI is performed for the first time in Sendai.

16 AUGUST 1995

Requiem of Reconciliation for soprano, alto, tenor, baritone, chorus, and orchestra, a collaborative endeavor with independent movements by the eminent 62-year-old Polish composer, pedagogue, and conductor Krzysztof PENDERECKI (*Agnus Dei aus "Requiem der Versöhnung"*), the significant 64-year-old Norwegian composer Arne NORDHEIM (*Lacrimosa*), and the noteworthy 66-year-old Japanese composer Jōji YUASA (*Responsorium*), is first performed in Stuttgart.

19 AUGUST 1995

The ground-breaking French acoustician, composer, and novelist Pierre SCHAEFFER dies in Aix-en-Provence at the age of 85.

21 AUGUST 1995

The Russian-born English conductor Anatole FISTOULARI, for a time (1942–1956) married to Gustav Mahler's daughter Anna, dies in London, just one day after his 88th birthday.

23 AUGUST 1995

The remarkable 83-year-old American composer of film music David RAKSIN conducts the United States Marine Band in transcriptions of three of his film works.

29 AUGUST 1995

Trio for oboe, bassoon, and piano (1994) by the significant 83-year-old French composer Jean FRANÇAIX is first heard in Rotterdam.

31 AUGUST 1995

Bassoon Concerto (1994–95) by the 63-year-old Czech-born Canadian composer, bassoonist, and teacher Rudolf KOMOROUS is given its premiere performance in Rotterdam.

1 SEPTEMBER 1995

Second Organ Concerto by the esteemed 72-year-old American composer, organist, choral conductor, and teacher

Daniel (Rogers) PINKHAM (Jr.) is performed for the first time in Rheinland-Pfalz.

2 SEPTEMBER 1995

Don Quixote tanzt Fandango, overture (1944), by the Austrian composer, pianist, conductor, and music critic Viktor ULLMANN, who ended his life in the concentration camp in Auschwitz on or about Oct. 15, 1944, is given its posthumous premiere in a partial reconstruction by B. Wulff in Lucerne.

3 SEPTEMBER 1995

Det sjungande trädet (The Singing Tree), opera, by the eminent 82-year-old Finnish composer, conductor, music critic, and pedagogue Erik (Valdemar) BERGMAN, for which he was awarded the Nordic Council Music Prize, is staged for the first time in Helsinki.

5 SEPTEMBER 1995

Part II of the 3-part *...wir aber singen*, symphonic cycle for cello and orchestra, by the 42-year-old German composer Wolfgang von SCHWEINITZ is performed for the first time in Hagen.

6 SEPTEMBER 1995

A Parade for M.T.T. for orchestra by the beloved 78-year-old American composer and performer Lou (Silver) HARRISON, honoring his close friend, the equally beloved American conductor Michael Tilson Thomas, is performed for the first time in San Francisco.

8 SEPTEMBER 1995

The Austrian bass-baritone Erich KUNZ, greatly esteemed in buffo roles, as an operetta singer, and as an interpreter of popular Viennese songs, whose most successful operatic roles were Papageno, Leporello, Figaro, and Beckmesser, dies in his native Vienna at the age of 86.

13 SEPTEMBER 1995

Adagio Tenebroso for orchestra (1994) by the outstanding 86-year-old American composer and teacher Elliott (Cook) CARTER (Jr.) is performed for the first time in London.

15 SEPTEMBER 1995

The 47-year-old Brazilian pianist Arnaldo COHEN makes his U.S. debut as a soloist with the Lexington (Kentucky) Philharmonic.

17 SEPTEMBER 1995

Eine kleine Herbstmusik for eleven instruments by the precocious 24-year-old Polish composer Paweł MYKIETYN is premiered in Warsaw.

18 SEPTEMBER 1995

First Symphony by the 70-year-old Polish composer and pedagogue Włodzimierz KOTOŃSKI is heard for the first time in his native Warsaw.

19 SEPTEMBER 1995

Going Up 2 for chamber orchestra by the 34-year-old Polish composer Hanna KULENTY is premiered in Warsaw.

20 SEPTEMBER 1995

The exceptionally gifted 50-year-old black American soprano Jessye NORMAN is the featured soloist with the New York Philharmonic under Kurt Masur's direction in a gala concert telecast live to the nation by PBS marking the opening of the orchestra's 53rd season.

21 SEPTEMBER 1995

S., opera, by the 53-year-old American composer and teacher Ronald (Christopher) PERERA is mounted for the first time in Northampton, Massachusetts.

22 SEPTEMBER 1995

The American experimental filmmaker, computer-graphics artist, and Pythagorean-inspired speculative theorist of the analogies between music and the visual arts John WHITNEY dies in Santa Monica, California, at the age of 78.

24 SEPTEMBER 1995

The well-known American string and conducting pedagogue Elizabeth A(dine) H(erkimer) GREEN, author of the widely consulted textbook *The Modern Conductor* (1961; 6th ed., 1997), dies in Ann Arbor at the age of 89.

28 SEPTEMBER 1995

Night Prayers, originally scored for string quartet and tape (Vienna, March 14, 1992), by the notable 60-year-old Georgian composer Giya (Alexandrovich) KANCHELI is performed for the first time in a version for soprano saxophone, strings, and tape (1994) in Stuttgart.

29 SEPTEMBER 1995

The Padrone, opera (1912–13), by the eminent American composer and teacher George Whitefield CHADWICK (1854–1931), has its belated posthumous premiere in a concert performance in Thomaston, Connecticut.

30 SEPTEMBER 1995

Blueskonzert for piano and orchestra by the 54-year-old black American composer Alvin (Elliot) SINGLETON is heard for the first time in Houston.

1 OCTOBER 1995

Pastorale for flute, oboe, clarinet, bassoon, and horn by the 57-year-old Polish composer and pianist Zygmunt KRAUZE is given its first ever performance in Budapest.

2 OCTOBER 1995

The German composer and teacher Helmut DEGEN, whose music was couched in a well-defined, neo-Classical idiom, with strong points of reference to Baroque forms, dies in Trossingen at the age of 84.

3 OCTOBER 1995

The 38-year-old Russian soprano Nina RAUTIO makes her debut at the Metropolitan Opera in New York as Aida.

6 OCTOBER 1995

The 39-year-old Czech composer Ivo MEDEK collaborates with the 70-year-old Czech composer and teacher Alois Simandl PIŇOS and the 53-year-old Czech composer and musicologist Miloš ŠTĚDROŇ on the opera *Věc Cage aneb Anály avantgardy dokořań* (The Cage Affair, or the Avant-Garde Chronicles Flung Open), which has its premiere performance in Brno.

6 OCTOBER 1995

The Vienna Art Orchestra, led by the extraordinary 42-year-old Swiss-born Austrian musician Mathias RÜEGG and joined by special guest artists Anna Lauvergnac and Monika Trotz, gives the first ever performance of *nine immortal evergreens for eric dolphy*, comprised of Dolphy's *Prologue, Out There, Hat & Beard, 245, Miss Ann, Gazzelloni, Something Sweet, Something Tender, Straight Up & Down,* and *Jitterbug Waltz* in able arrangements by Rüegg, at the Stadtheater in Bruck/Leitha.

7 OCTOBER 1995

Let's Begin Again for chorus and orchestra by the remarkable 51-year-old English composer John (Kenneth) TAVENER is heard for the first time in Norwich.

8 OCTOBER 1995

Tenth Symphony, entitled *Drones of Druids on Celtic Ruins* (1993–94), by the compelling 56-year-old American composer Gloria COATES is given its premiere performance in Erding.

8 OCTOBER 1995

The prominent American conductor and music administrator Christopher KEENE, who ended his career as artistic supervisor (1982–83), music director (1983–86), and general director (1989–95) of the New York City Opera, becoming well known for his championship of rarely-heard operas, dies in New York of AIDS-induced lymphoma at the age of lamentable age of 48.

10 OCTOBER 1995

Innocence for soprano, tenor, chorus, cello, and organ (1994) by the remarkable 51-year-old English composer John (Kenneth) TAVENER is heard for the first time in his native London.

12 OCTOBER 1995

Aura for orchestra (1991–92) by the 51-year-old German composer York (Georg) HÖLLER is premiered in Chicago.

13 OCTOBER 1995

Momo, opera, by the notable 62-year-old Japanese composer Toshi ICHIYINAGI is staged for the first time in Tokyo.

15 OCTOBER 1995

4 Last Songs for mezzo-soprano, violin, and piano by the accomplished 75-year-old Canadian composer and teacher Robert (Comrie) TURNER is heard for the first time in Winnipeg.

17 OCTOBER 1995

Glint for clarinet, violin, and piano by the outstanding 67-year-old American composer and teacher Jacob (Raphael) DRUCKMAN is performed for the first time in New York.

18 OCTOBER 1995

Concerto for piano and winds by the gifted 46-year-old South African-born Irish composer Kevin VOLANS is given its first ever performance in Rotterdam.

20 OCTOBER 1995

Masse, Macht und Individuum for orchestra and four instrumental soloists by the active 64-year-old French composer, trombonist, conductor, and teacher Vinko GLOBOKAR is heard for the first time in Donaueschingen.

26 OCTOBER 1995

The prominent 33-year-old Russian baritone Dmitri HVOROSTOVSKY makes his Metropolitan Opera debut in New York as Yeletsky in Tchaikovsky's *The Queen of Spades*.

27 OCTOBER 1995

Pamietam for mezzo-soprano and orchestra by the 54-year-old American composer, pianist, and teacher Richard (Edward) WILSON is heard for the first time in Annandale-on-Hudson, New York.

28 OCTOBER 1995

Evaernesto, duo concertante for flute, clarinet, and chamber ensemble, by the versatile 38-year-old Italian composer, conductor, teacher, and writer on music Alberto CAPRIOLI is premiered in Vienna.

29 OCTOBER 1995

The legendary American editor and writer on music Minna DANIEL (née Lederman), whose internationally-renowned journal *Modern Music* (1924–46) served as a literary forum for contemporary composers by publishing essays and reviews by such musical activists as Virgil Thomson, John Cage, Elliott Carter, Marc Blitzstein, and Paul Bowles, dies in New York at the remarkable age of 99.

30 OCTOBER 1995

The Austrian-born American violinist Erica MORINI (real name, Siracusano), who, after the Anschluss in 1938, emigrated to the United States and in 1943 became a naturalized American citizen, dies in New York at the accomplished age of 91.

31 OCTOBER 1995

The English composer and teacher Alan (Dudley) BUSH, who from 1925 to 1978 served as professor of composition at the Royal Academy of Music, and who, in 1935, joined the Communist Party, to which he remained deeply committed, and who, in 1936, founded the Workers' Music Association, which he served as president from 1941 to 1976, dies in Watford at the seasoned age of 94.

1 NOVEMBER 1995

The eminent Irish music critic Desmond (Christopher) SHAWE-TAYLOR, who from 1958 to 1983 served as music critic of the *Sunday Times,* and whose writings, including *Covent Garden for the World of Music Series* (London, 1948), were notable for their unostentatious display of wide learning, dies in Long Crichel, Dorset, at the age of 88.

2 NOVEMBER 1995

The Ascent of the Equestrian in a Balloon for orchestra by the 43-year-old American composer and teacher Stephen (Paul) HARTKE is heard for the first time in Washington, D.C.

3 NOVEMBER 1995

The important Korean-born German composer and teacher Isang YUN, whose career was dramatically interrupted on June 17, 1967, when he and his wife were brutally abducted from West Berlin by secret police agents of South Korea, and forced to board a plane for Seoul, where they were brought to trial for sedition (Yun was sentenced to life imprisonment, his wife given three years in jail), which act of lawlessness perpetrated on the territory of another country prompted an indignant protest by the government of West Germany, which threatened to cut off its substantial economic aid to South Korea, and also prompted some 23 celebrated musicians, Igor Stravinsky among them, to issue a vigorous letter of protest, resulting in their eventual release after nearly two years of detention, dies in Berlin at the respectable age of 78.

7 NOVEMBER 1995

Venezianisches, concerto for harpsichord and strings (1994) by the productive 69-year-old German composer, pedagogue, organist, and harpsichordist Ruth ZECHLIN is given its first performance in Flensburg.

10 NOVEMBER 1995

The admired 36-year-old Norwegian soprano Elizabeth NORBERG-SCHULZ makes her Metropolitan Opera debut in New York as Verdi's Oscar.

12 NOVEMBER 1995

Kaï for nine players by the eminent 73-year-old Greek-born French composer, music theorist, and teacher Iannis XENAKIS is premiered in Oldenburg.

15 NOVEMBER 1995

Bagatelle für A. W. for violin, clarinet, tenor saxophone, and piano by the 41-year-old Polish composer Paweł SZYMÁNSKI is heard for the first time in Bratislava.

16 NOVEMBER 1995

Violin Concerto (1993–95) by the outstanding 56-year-old Swiss oboist, conductor, pedagogue, and composer Heinz HOLLIGER is premiered in Lausanne.

17 NOVEMBER 1995

The American composer and teacher Salvatore MARTIRANO, who composed works in a progressive avant-garde idiom, applying the quaquaversal techniques of unmitigated radical modernism, free from any inhibitions, dies in Urbana, Illinois, at the age of 68.

19 NOVEMBER 1995

Turning To for two flutists by the accomplished 57-year-old American composer Gloria COATES is heard for the first time in Munich.

24 NOVEMBER 1995

Fanfare of Rings for orchestra, for the 100th anniversary of the Cincinnati Symphony Orchestra (1994), by the prominent 65-year-old American composer and teacher Eric (Norman) STOKES is heard for the first time in Cincinnati.

25 NOVEMBER 1995

The respected American soprano Sheri (Kay) GREENAWALD makes her Metropolitan Opera debut in New York as Kurt Weill's Jenny.

28 NOVEMBER 1995

Mosaïques for flute, viola, and guitar (1991) and *Trois solitudes* for cello and piano (1993), two works by the 49-year-old French composer Jean-Claude WOLFF are premiered in Echirolles.

30 NOVEMBER 1995

Violin Concerto by the eminent 80-year-old French composer and administrator Marcel (François Paul) LANDOWSKI, son of the sculptor Paul Landowski and great-grandson of the celebrated Belgian violinist and composer Henri Vieuxtemps, is heard for the first time in Paris.

1 DECEMBER 1995

The Austrian-born American conductor and teacher Frederic WALDMAN, long-time teacher at the Juilliard School of Music in New York (1947–67), where, as music director of its Opera Theater, he conducted the American premieres of Richard Strauss' *Capriccio* (1954) and Zoltan Kodály's *Háry János* (1960), and who, in 1961, founded the Musica Aeterna Orchestra and Chorus, which he conducted in enterprising programs of rarely-heard music of the past and present eras, ranging from Monteverdi to Rieti, dies in New York at the respectable age of 92.

3 DECEMBER 1995

String Trio (1995) and *Fahlstimmig* for soprano, three women's voices, and chamber ensemble (1995), two works by the 64-year-old German composer and teacher Paul-Heinz DITTRICH, are heard for the first time in Berlin.

5 DECEMBER 1995

The German composer Reiner BREDEMEYER, who was an astute experimenter while at the same time adhering to the tenets of classical forms and avoiding the extremes of modernism, dies in Berlin at the modest age of 66.

6 DECEMBER 1995

Tanzende Faune for orchestra (1914) and *Des Turmes Auferstehung* for two basses and orchestra, after Werfel (1921), two works by the eminent German composer and music educator Carl ORFF (1895–1982), are given their posthumous premieres in the composer's native Munich.

7 DECEMBER 1995

A Sobbing Pillow of Man, opera, by the 70-year-old American composer William (Robert) MAYER is staged for the first time in his native New York.

8 DECEMBER 1995

Concerto festivo for violin and orchestra (1993–95) by the 44-year-old Polish composer, conductor, and teacher Aleksander LASOŃ is heard for the first time in Kraków.

10 DECEMBER 1995

Silver Echoes of Distant Bells for mezzo-soprano and string quartet by the admired 52-year-old Polish composer, percussionist, and teacher Marta PTASZYŃSKA is premiered in New York.

13 DECEMBER 1995

Elegy V for strings by the 54-year-old Finnish composer and musicologist Erkki (Olavi) SALMENHAARA is given its first ever performance in Paris.

14 DECEMBER 1995

Ottava alta, violin concerto, by the 70-year-old Croatian-born French composer, conductor, and teacher Ivo MALEC is premiered in Luxembourg.

15 DECEMBER 1995

Concertino for chamber orchestra and tape by the promising 42-year-old Puerto Rican composer Roberto SIERRA is performed for the first time in New York.

19 DECEMBER 1995

Burning Meditation for baritone, harp, tubular bells, and string quartet by the innovative 48-year-old Japanese composer Sômei SATOH is given its first performance in a revised version in New York.

25 DECEMBER 1995

The legendary Russian-born American musicologist, composer, and conductor of manifold endeavors Nicolas (actually, Nikolai Leonidovich) SLONIMSKY, uncle of the respected Russian composer Sergei (Mikhailovich) Slonimsky and nephew of the equally legendary piano teacher Isabella Vengerova, and revered author/editor of such respected tomes as the *Thesaurus of Scales and Melodic Patterns* (1947), successive editions of *Baker's Biographical Dictionary of Musicians* (N.Y., 1958, 1978, 1984, 1992), and two editions of the present and now-classic *Music Since 1900* (N.Y., 1937; 5th ed., rev., 1994), dies in Los Angeles at the remarkable age of 101.

28 DECEMBER 1995

The promising 30-year-old American soprano Patricia RACETTE makes her Metropolitan Opera debut in New York as Musetta.

31 DECEMBER 1995

The American musicologist Robert U(riel) NELSON, long-time faculty member at the University of California at Los Angeles (1938–70), and author of the valuable study *The Technique of Variation* (Berkeley and Los Angeles, 1948), dies in Los Angeles at the respectable age of 93.

1996

2 JANUARY 1996

The distinguished 69-year-old Austrian soprano Leonie RYSANEK makes her farewell appearance at the Metropolitan Opera in New York singing the role of the Countess in Tchaikovsky's *The Queen of Spades*.

4 JANUARY 1996

The distinguished German musicologist Anna Amalie ABERT, daughter of the eminent German musicologist Hermann Abert, dies in Kiel at the seasoned age of 89.

8 JANUARY 1996

The American music and drama critic Howard TAUBMAN, long-time music and drama critic (1929–1972) of the *New York Times*, dies in Sarasota, Florida, at the age of 88.

9 JANUARY 1996

Danse Africaine for soprano and piano (1991) by the 49-year-old black American composer and teacher Joyce Solomon MOORMAN is performed for the first time in New York.

11 JANUARY 1996

Merlin-Liederbuch for four voices and chamber ensemble (1981–96) by the 68-year-old German composer and teacher Wilhelm KILLMAYER is premiered in his native Munich.

12 JANUARY 1996

For the Musicians of the Queen: Fanfare and Fugues for orchestra (1994) by the 52-year-old American composer Dennis EBERHARD is heard for the first time in his native Cleveland.

18 JANUARY 1996

The remarkable 35-year-old English soprano Jane EAGLEN makes her Metropolitan Opera debut in New York as Donna Anna.

19 JANUARY 1996

Cristalline II for piano (1995–96) by the 34-year-old Japanese composer Karen TANAKA is given its first ever performance in Yokohama.

20 JANUARY 1996

A string orchestra version of Schubert's String Quartet No. 14, D.810, *Der Tod und das Mädchen*, by the esteemed 61-year-old German composer Siegfried MATTHUS is given its premiere performance in Berlin.

25 JANUARY 1996

The German opera director Ruth BERGHAUS, who, in her productions pursued a radical course laden with symbolism and satire, and who, from 1980 to 1987, was an opera director at the Frankfurt am Main Opera, where she oversaw outstanding productions of Waner's *Parsifal* (1982) and the *Ring* cycle (1985–87), dies in Zeuthen at the age of 68.

26 JANUARY 1996

The black American conductor Henry LEWIS, who from 1960 to 1976 was married to the outstanding American mezzo-soprano Marilyn Horne, dies in New York at the lamentable age of 63.

28 JANUARY 1996

Air for flute (1995) by the outstanding 65-year-old Japanese composer Tōru TAKEMITSU is performed for the first time in Oberwil.

31 JANUARY 1996

Trio for piano, oboe, and bassoon (1994) by the brilliant 66-year-old German-born American pianist, conductor, and composer André (George) (real name, Andreas Ludwig Priwin) PREVIN is heard for the first time in New York.

1 FEBRUARY 1996

The imaginative American composer, pianist, and performance artist Randy (actually, James Randolph) HOST-

ETLER dies suddenly at the pitiable age of 32 of undiagnosed Addison's Disease.

2 FEBRUARY 1996

The beloved American singer, dancer, actor, choreographer, and film director Gene (real name, Eugene Curran) KELLY, star of a number of acclaimed Hollywood films, including *An American in Paris* (1951), *Singin' in the Rain* (1952), *On the Town* (1949), and *Invitation to the Dance* (1956), and winner, in 1994, of the National Medal of Arts, dies in Beverly Hills at the age of 83.

5 FEBRUARY 1996

The Italian conductor, writer on music, and composer Gianandrea GAVAZZENI, who, in addition to being known especially for his interpretations of the Italian operatic repertory was also a prolific writer, numbering among his publications *Donizetti* (Milan, 1937), *Le feste musicali* (Milan, 1944), *Musicisti d'Europa* (Milan, 1954), *La musica e il teatro* (Pisa, 1954), *La morte dell'opera* (Milan, 1954), and *Diario di Edimburgo e d'America* (Milan, 1960), and who also composed the opera *Paolo e Virginia* (1932; Bergamo, 1935) and the ballet *Il furioso all'isola di S. Domingo* (1940), dies in his native Bergamo at the ripened age of 86.

6 FEBRUARY 1996

Group Sax for five saxophonists by the 66-year-old American composer and teacher Robert (Paige) CEELY is heard for the first time in Boston.

7 FEBRUARY 1996

Triple Concerto for piano, violin, cello, and orchestra (1995) by the remarkable 56-year-old American composer Ellen Taaffe ZWILICH is performed for the first time in Minneapolis.

8 FEBRUARY 1996

Hidden Voice 1 for chamber orchestra (1995) by the significant 56-year-old English composer Jonathan (Dean) HARVEY is given its first ever performance in London.

9 FEBRUARY 1996

The outstanding 29-year-old Italian mezzo-soprano Cecilia BARTOLI makes her Metropolitan Opera debut in New York as Despina.

10 FEBRUARY 1996

Music for Ten for ten instruments by the productive 66-year-old American composer and teacher Robert (Paige) CEELY is heard for the first time in Cambridge, Massachusetts.

11 FEBRUARY 1996

Exultet Coelum laudibus for organ by the versatile 69-year-old English pianist, organist, conductor, writer on music, and composer Francis (John) ROUTH is premiered in London.

14 FEBRUARY 1996

Seasons in Hell: A Life of Rimbaud, opera (1992–94), by the 72-year-old American composer Harold BLUMENFELD is mounted for the first time in Cincinnati.

19 FEBRUARY 1996

The noted black American soprano and music educator Dorothy (Leigh) MAYNOR, founder of the Harlem School of the Arts in 1963, which she served as its executive director until her retirement in 1979, dies in West Chester, Pennsylvania, at the seasoned age of 85.

20 FEBRUARY 1996

The outstanding Japanese composer Tōru TAKEMITSU, whose award-winning scores demonstrated his mastery in combining the refined craftsmanship of oriental music with the innovative usages of Western avant-garde music, dies in his native Tokyo at the modest age of 65.

21 FEBRUARY 1996

The esteemed 72-year-old German-born American pianist and pedagogue Menahem PRESSLER makes his belated Carnegie Hall recital debut in New York.

22 FEBRUARY 1996

The ascending 34-year-old Italian conductor Daniele GATTI makes an auspicious United States debut with the New York Philharmonic conducting Gustav Mahler's *Sixth Symphony*.

23 FEBRUARY 1996

Trzy fragmenty do słów Stanisława Wyspiańskiego (3 Fragments to Words by Stanisław Wyspiański) for voice and piano by the celebrated 62-year-old Polish composer Henryk (Mikoaj) GÓRECKI is heard for the first time in Zakopane.

24 FEBRUARY 1996

La Terre for soprano, piano, and orchestra (1995) by the respected 57-year-old Polish composer and pianist Zygmunt KRAUZE is performed for the first time in Paris.

26 FEBRUARY 1996

Double Concerto for violin, cello, and orchestra (1995) by the 48-year-old American composer David OTT is given its first ever performance in Indianapolis.

28 FEBRUARY 1996

Ecstatic Songs for high voice and piano (1989–1996), in three parts, after Whitman, by the 45-year-old American composer, conductor, and teacher Donald CROCKETT, is given its first complete performance in Los Angeles.

29 FEBRUARY 1996

Trio for piano, violin, and cello (1995) by the 35-year-old Argentine composer Ezequiel VIÑAO is heard for the first time in New York.

1 MARCH 1996

Koïranoï for orchestra (1994) by the eminent 73-year-old Greek-born French composer, music theorist, and teacher Iannis XENAKIS is given its premiere performance in Hamburg.

4 MARCH 1996

The American country-music comedienne, country-music singer, and pianist Minnie PEARL (real name, Sarah Ophelia née Colley Cannon), whose introduction to her audiences with a shrill "Howdyyyyyyyyyyy! I'm just so proud to be here!," and her out-of-tune vocalisms and her ubiquitous hat (complete with dangling price tag) making her a popular favorite, and who was a member for many decades of the "Grand Ole Opry" and later a regular on the television show "Hee Haw," dies in Nashville, Tennessee, at the age of 83.

5 MARCH 1996

Fantasy Pieces for piano (1995) by the admired 65-year-old American composer and recorder producer Nancy VAN DE VATE is heard for the first time in Utrecht.

7 MARCH 1996

Concerto for flute and chamber orchestra (1992) by the eminent 62-year-old Polish composer, pedagogue, and conductor Krzysztof PENDERECKI is heard for the first time as a *Clarinet Concerto* (1995) in Prague.

11 MARCH 1996

Concerto for violin, accordion, and chamber orchestra (1994) by the notable 70-year-old Austrian composer, conductor, and pedagogue Friedrich CERHA is premiered in his native Vienna, the composer conducting.

17 MARCH 1996

Galina, opera (1995), by the eminent 81-year-old French composer and administrator Marcel (François Paul) LANDOWSKI, son of the sculptor Paul Landowski and great-grandson of the celebrated Belgian violinist and composer Henri Vieuxtemps, is performed for the first time in Lyons.

18 MARCH 1996

...à la Duduki for orchestra (1995) by the notable 60-year-old Georgian composer Giya (Alexandrovich) KANCHE-LI is performed for the first time in Mannheim.

19 MARCH 1996

Oratio brevis for organ (1995) by the productive 71-year-old Polish composer and pedagogue Krystyna MOSZU-MAŃSKA-NAZAR is given its premiere performance in Kraków.

20 MARCH 1996

Sinfonietta (1994–95) by the 69-year-old Polish conductor and composer Jan KRENZ is given its first ever performance in Zürich.

21 MARCH 1996

Sallie Chisum Remembers Billy the Kid for soprano and piano (1994) and *Vocalise* for soprano, cello, and orchestra (1995), two works by the brilliant 66-year-old German-born American pianist, conductor, and composer André (George) (real name, Andreas Ludwig Priwin) PREVIN are performed for the first time in Boston.

22 MARCH 1996

The American composer and teacher Robert Hall LEWIS, who taught for many years at both the Peabody Conservatory of Music in Baltimore (from 1958) and at Johns Hopkins University (1969–80), dies in Baltimore at the age of 69.

26 MARCH 1996

Der Idiot, scenic mimodrama (1952), by the outstanding 69-year-old German composer Hans Werner HENZE is given its first ever performance in a newly-revised version (1990) in Basel.

28 MARCH 1996

Pinturas de Tamayo for orchestra (1995) by the versatile 46-year-old American composer, teacher, conductor, and writer on music Steven (Edward) STUCKY is performed for the first time in Chicago.

29 MARCH 1996

Tallbrem Variations for five percussion and orchestra by the 56-year-old Canadian composer, pianist, and teacher (James) Bruce MATHER is premiered in his native Toronto.

31 MARCH 1996

Lamento mémoire for viola and chamber orchestra by the admired 70-year-old French composer Antoine DU-HAMEL, son of the writer Georges Duhamel and the comedienne Blanche Albane, is performed for the first time in Fresnes.

4 APRIL 1996

The American composer and teacher Paul COOPER, whose diverse compositions followed an eclectic course in which he utilized various styles in a distinct and original manner, dies in Houston at the age of 69.

5 APRIL 1996

Waiting for Charlie for 15 players by the successful 46-year-old English composer, conductor, writer on music, and teacher Roger (Michael) MARSH is performed for the first time in Apeldoorn.

9 APRIL 1996

Ôgenraku for Gagaku ensemble and shomyo (1980) by the notable 63-year-old Japanese composer Toshi ICHIYANAGI is performed for the first time in a version for Gagaku ensemble in Tokyo.

10 APRIL 1996

The prominent 32-year-old Italian tenor Roberto ALAGNA makes his Metropolitan Opera debut in New York as Rodolfo.

13 APRIL 1996

The eminent 67-year-old American pianist and music educator Gary GRAFFMAN and the distinguished 67-year-old American pianist, conductor, and teacher Leon FLEISHER join forces as duo-soloists in the premiere of William Bolcom's *Gaea* for piano, two left-hands, and orchestra, with the Baltimore Symphony Orchestra, David Zinman conducting.

14 APRIL 1996

Jubilation for orchestra by the remarkable 56-year-old American composer Ellen Taaffe ZWILICH is performed for the first time in Athens, Georgia.

16 APRIL 1996

Third Concerto for Orchestra (1981–94) by the 52-year-old English composer, teacher, and writer on music Robin (Greville) HOLLOWAY is premiered in London.

20 APRIL 1996

The Marx Sisters, opera (1994–95), by the multi-talented 67-year-old German-born Australian bassoonist, conductor, and composer George (actually, Georg) DREYFUS is heard for the first time in Bielefeld.

21 APRIL 1996

Shadows for two alto saxophones by the 65-year-old American composer and teacher Eric (Norman) STOKES is given its first ever performance in Minneapolis.

24 APRIL 1996

The Spanish pianist Rafael OROZCO, winner in 1966 of the 1st prize in the Leeds Competition and thereafter best known for his interpretations of the Romantic repertoire, dies in Rome at the lamentable age of 50.

25 APRIL 1996

Still Life for orchestra (1995) by the 54-year-old Icelandic cellist and composer Haflidi (Magnus) HALLGRÍMSSON is premiered in Glasgow.

26 APRIL 1996

Vortex Temporum I, II, and *III* for piano and five instruments (1994–96) by the respected 49-year-old French composer and teacher Gérard GRISEY is given its first complete performance in Witten.

2 MAY 1996

Uninterrupted Movement for solo cello, four cellos, and others (1995) by the prominent 63-year-old German-born English composer and teacher (Peter) Alexander GOEHR, son of the German-born English conductor and composer Walter Goehr, is performed for the first time in Manchester.

4 MAY 1996

Blow Out for organ and orchestra (1995) by the esteemed 62-year-old German composer Siegfried MATTHUS is premiered in Dresden.

5 MAY 1996

Blue Serge and *Marble Hunt*, two works for sampler by the 35-year-old American composer, instrumentalist, improviser, and sampling specialist Annie (actually, Anne) GOSFIELD are performed for the first time in Lucerne.

7 MAY 1996

Duetti, dance piece (1995), by the gifted 46-year-old South African-born Irish composer Kevin VOLANS in collaboration with Matteo Fargion is premiered in Ghent.

8 MAY 1996

Musik for three percussionists (1995) by the 69-year-old German composer, pedagogue, organist, and harpsichordist Ruth ZECHLIN is given its first performance in Saarbrücken.

9 MAY 1996

Sonata for eight cellos (1994) by the 49-year-old French composer Jean-Claude WOLFF is performed for the first time in Rencontres.

12 MAY 1996

The German soprano Margit SCHRAMM, whose vast and impressive repertoire included German and Austrian operettas, dies in Munich at the age of 60.

15 MAY 1996

The admired Italian soprano and mezzo-soprano Pia TASSINARI, widow of the prominent Italian tenor Ferrucio Tagliavini, and whose repertoire included such diverse roles as Mimi, Tosca, Manon, and Marguerite, as well as Amneris and Carmen, dies in Faenza at the respectable age of 92.

17 MAY 1996

Neljä Mustapään laulua (Four Songs to Words by Mustapää) for soprano and piano (1995) by the 55-year-old Finnish composer and musicologist Erkki (Olavi) SALMENHAARA is heard for the first time over Finnish Radio.

18 MAY 1996

Les Enfants terrible, dance-opera, by the phenomenally-successful 59-year-old American composer Philip GLASS is staged for the first time in Zug.

19 MAY 1996

The Greek conductor Spiros ARGIRIS, who from 1986 until a dispute with the festival's founder, Gian Carlo Menotti in 1992, was music director of the Festival of Two Worlds in Charleston, South Carolina, and Spoleto, Italy, who rejoined his association with the Charleston organization in 1993, dies in Nice at the pitiable age of 47.

20 MAY 1996

Combustion Chamber for Sampler, Electric Guitar, and Percussion, a collaborative work of the 35-year-old American composer, instrumentalist, improviser, and sampling specialist Annie (actually, Anne) GOSFIELD and the 37-year-old adventurous American guitarist, composer, and improviser Roger (Wayne) KLEIER, is performed for the first time in Ulm, Germany.

21 MAY 1996

Sigrancia-Ballade for baritone and orchestra (1995) by the distinguished 69-year-old French-American composer and teacher Betsy JOLAS, daughter of the poet and journalist Eugène Jolas, best known as the founder and editor of the literary journal *transition*, receives its first ever performance in London.

24 MAY 1996

The outstanding American composer and teacher Jacob (Raphael) DRUCKMAN, whose distinguished body of works demonstrated an assured handling of various contemporary means of expression, ranging from 12-tone procedures and electronics to traditional and new Romantic elements, and whose mastery of orchestration was particularly notable, dies in New Haven, Connecticut, at the age of 67.

28 MAY 1996

The Russian composer and musicologist Julian (Grigorievich) KREIN, son of the Russian composer Grigori (Abramovich) Krein, and whose music was inspired by both Russian and French models, resulting in works of notable lyricism and harmonic inventiveness, and who published several monographs (all in Moscow), including ones on Falla (1960), Debussy (1962), Ravel (1962), and his uncle Alexander (Abramovich) Krein (with N. Rogozhina; 1964), dies in his native Moscow at the age of 83.

30 MAY 1996

Quodlibet for wind trio (1995) by the 60-year-old Polish composer and pedagogue Marek STACHOWSKI is performed for the first time in Kraków.

1 JUNE 1996

Songs for a Winter's Evening for Soprano and Orch. (1995) by the remarkable 68-year-old Scottish composer Thea MUSGRAVE is given its first ever performance in Dumfries.

2 JUNE 1996

The prominent Spanish soprano Pilar (real name, Pilar Lorenza García) LORENGAR, recipient of the Medallo d'Oro de Zaragoza of Saragossa and the Order of Isabella de Catolica (1965) as well the San Francisco Opera Medal (1989), and whose finest roles included Donna Anna, Fiordiligi, Countess Almaviva, Alice Ford, Eva, and Mélisande, dies in Berlin at the age of 68.

4 JUNE 1996

A realization of the unfinished *Universe Symphony* (1911–16) by the foremost American composer Charles IVES (1874–1954) by the 40-year-old American microtonalist composer Johnny REINHARD, distinguished from a similar effort by the American composer Larry Austin in its exclusive use of music composed by Ives, is performed by 71 musicians at the American Festival of Microtonal Music at New York's Lincoln Center.

5 JUNE 1996

A.E.T. for chamber ensemble by the notable 52-year-old English composer, conductor, and writer on music Michael (Laurence) NYMAN receives its premiere performance at the Salisbury Festival.

10 JUNE 1996

Kuïlenn for nine winds (1995) by the eminent 74-year-old Greek-born French composer, music theorist, and teacher Iannis XENAKIS is heard for the first time in Amsterdam.

12 JUNE 1996

Time Rocker, opera in a prologue and 30 (some subdivided) scenes by the musically-astute 54-year-old American singer, guitarist, and composer Lou REED, to a futuristic libretto by the composer with text by Darryl Pinckney, directed and designed by the notable 54-year-old American theater director, stage designer, and dramatist Robert WILSON, is first staged at Hamburg's Thalia Theater.

14 JUNE 1996

Chinese Myths, cantata for men's chorus and orchestra, by the versatile 43-year-old Chinese composer and teacher Chen YI is given its first performance in San Francisco.

17 JUNE 1996

Preludium & Fughetta for piano (1986) by the outstanding Finnish composer (Sven) Einar ENGLUND is performed for the first time in Helsinki on the occasion of the composer's 80th birthday.

20 JUNE 1996

Little Requiem for koto and strings by the eminent 67-year-old Australian composer and teacher Peter (Joshua) SCULTHORPE is given its first ever performance in Sydney.

21 JUNE 1996

Mysterious Numbers for flute, clarinet, violin, cello, piano, and percussion by the versatile 53-year-old American composer, pianist, teacher, and writer on music William (Ervin) DUCKWORTH is performed for the first time in Orlando, Florida.

22 JUNE 1996

The Hungarian-born American cellist, conductor, and composer George (real name, György Baráti) BARATI, whose last significant posts included executive director of the Montalvo Center for the Arts and conductor of the Montalvo Chamber Orchestra in Saratoga, California (1968–1978) and music director of the Santa Cruz County Symphony Orchestra in Aptos, California (1971–1980), where, in 1991, the George Barati Archive was opened at the University of California at Santa Cruz Library, dies in San Jose, California, at the age of 83.

24 JUNE 1996

Horse d'oeuvres for mezzo-soprano and orchestra by the 42-year-old English composer Judith WEIR is performed for the first time in London.

26 JUNE 1996

Tears of the Angels for violin and strings (1995) by the remarkable 52-year-old English composer John (Kenneth) TAVENER is premiered in his native London.

27 JUNE 1996

Suite from Nemo for orchestra by the 65-year-old American composer and record producer Nancy VAN DE VATE is heard for the first time in Ruse, Bulgaria.

30 JUNE 1996

Invisible Curve for flute, violin, viola, cello, and piano by the 35-year-old Japanese composer Karen TANAKA is premiered in Yokohama.

1 JULY 1996

Schlachthof 5, dramatic work after Vonnegut's *Slaughterhouse 5*, by the 42-year-old German composer Hans-Jürgen von BOSE is mounted for the first time in his native Munich.

2 JULY 1996

"Are You Ready, Brother?" for piano trio by the 49-year-old Russian composer, conductor, and teacher Nikolai KORNDORF is premiered in Amsterdam.

4 JULY 1996

A Child's Prayer for two treble soloists and chorus by the 36-year-old Scottish composer, conductor, and teacher James MACMILLAN is given its first ever performance in London.

5 JULY 1996

The Doctor of Myddfai, opera (1993–96), by the eminent 61-year-old English composer and conductor Sir Peter Maxwell DAVIES is staged for the first time in Cardiff.

7 JULY 1996

Celebration Fanfare for orchestra by the distinguished 74-year-old Czech-born American composer, conductor, and pedagogue Karel HUSA is performed for the first time in Oneonta, New York.

9 JULY 1996

Ere long we shall see...", concerto brevis for organ and orchestra (1995–96), by the 46-year-old American composer, organist, and teacher Dan (Steven) LOCKLAIR is premiered in New York.

10 JULY 1996

Duos for horn and string quartet (1995) by the eminent 81-year-old American composer, music theorist, and pedagogue George PERLE is performed for the first time in Kalamazoo, Michigan.

11 JULY 1996

The World's Ransoming for orchestra and English horn obbligato (1995–96), part I of *Triduum*, a triptych additionally comprising the *Cello Concerto* (1996) and the *Symphony, Vigil* (1997), by the 36-year-old Scottish composer, conductor, and teacher James MACMILLAN is performed for the first time in London.

14 JULY 1996

Violin Sonata, entitled *Vineyard* (1994), by the brilliant 67-year-old German-born American pianist, conductor, and composer André (George) (real name, Andreas Ludwig Priwin) PREVIN is heard for the first time in Katonah, New York.

23 JULY 1996

Brain Opera by the innovative 42-year-old American cellist, conductor, and composer Tod MACHOVER is premiered in New York.

24 JULY 1996

Recalling a Serenade for clarinet, two violins, viola, and cello by the 42-year-old Polish composer Paweł SZYMÁNSKI is given its first performance in Kuhmo.

25 JULY 1996

Hyperstring Trilogy for Hypercello, Hyperviola, Hyperviolin, and chamber orchestra (1991–93) by the productive 42-year-old American cellist, conductor, and composer Tod MACHOVER is given its first performance in a revised version in New York.

27 JULY 1996

The 31-year-old American soprano Patricia RACETTE creates the title role of Emmeline Mosher in *Emmeline*, opera by the 42-year-old American composer Tobias PICKER, at the Santa Fe Opera.

6 AUGUST 1996

Symfonietta Concertante for flute, cello, and chamber orchestra (1995) by the 85-year-old German-born American composer and pedagogue Bernhard HEIDEN is performed for the first time in Ernen, Switzerland.

7 AUGUST 1996

The Italian conductor Francesco MOLINARI-PRADELLI, best known as an able interpreter of the Italian operatic repertoire, dies in Marano di Castenaso at the age of 85.

8 AUGUST 1996

The Swedish composer Åke (Oscar Werner) HERMANSON, who pursued a style of concentrated brevity marked by an alternation of short contrasting motifs, a usage he defined as "pendulum dynamics," dies in Stockholm at the age of 73.

9 AUGUST 1996

Château de l'âme for soprano and orchestra by the significant 43-year-old Finnish composer Kaija (Anneli) SAARIAHO is performed for the first time in Salzburg.

10 AUGUST 1996

Vlepondas for soprano, baritone, and cello by the remarkable 52-year-old English composer John (Kenneth) TAVENER is premiered in Delphi.

11 AUGUST 1996

The Orchestra of St. Luke's of New York, conducted by Yehudi MENUHIN, and the New York Choral Society, directed by John Daly Goodwin, join forces to present "A Benefit Tribute to Yehudi Menuhin" at Lincoln Center's Avery Fisher Hall, featuring the world premiere performances of *Lullaby* for kora, dousongoni, and string sextet by Foday Musa Suso, *Romance of Hsiao and Ch'in* for two violins and string orchestra (1995) by Chen Yi, *Hunem-Iduhey* for violin and cello by Iannis Xenakis, *Innocence* for soprano, violin, and shō by Somei Satoh, *Credo* for clarinet, two violins, and string orchestra by Poul Ruders, and *Cabbages and Kings* for soprano, chorus, four solo violins, clarinet, and orchestra by David Del Tredici, as well as numerous works by other notable composers in their United States premieres.

13 AUGUST 1996

The significant American pianist and composer David (Eugene) TUDOR, best known for his innovative work with the Merce Cunningham Dance Company in the medium of live electronic performance, dies in Tomkins Cove, New York, at the age of 70.

15 AUGUST 1996

Tantamounts for four flutes and string quartet by the 66-year-old American composer and teacher Eric (Norman) STOKES is given its first ever performance in New York.

16 AUGUST 1996

Nuun for two pianos and orchestra by the 41-year-old Swiss-born Austrian composer, conductor, and teacher Beat FURRER is heard for the first time in Salzburg.

17 AUGUST 1996

Gesang am Brunnen, oratorio for soprano, tenor, baritone, chorus, and chamber orchestra, by the 69-year-old Polish composer Juliusz (Mieczyslaw) ŁUCIUK is premiered in Hannover.

23 AUGUST 1996

The Dutch composer Jurriaan ANDRIESSEN, nephew of the Dutch pianist, teacher, and composer Willem (Christiaan Nicolaas) Andriessen (1887–1964) and brother of the 57-year-old Dutch composer Louis (Joseph) Andriessen, and whose television opera *Kalchas* (Dutch TV, June 28, 1959) was the first such score to be produced in the Netherlands, dies in Haarlem at the age of 70.

6 SEPTEMBER 1996

The Romanian composer and pedagogue Ion DUMITRESCU, brother of the Romanian composer Gheorghe Dumitrescu (1914–1996), dies in Bucharest at the age of 83.

7 SEPTEMBER 1996

Séraphim, music theater work, by the distinguished 42-year-old German composer and teacher Wolfgang (Michael) RIHM is staged for the first time in Stuttgart.

7 SEPTEMBER 1996

The 70th Festival of the International Society for Contemporary Music opens in Copenhagen with two programs, in the following sequence:

Two installations open at The Museum of Modern Art, to run for the duration of the Festival week: Japanese composer Kazue MIZUSHIMA's "String Telephone" and a sound installation by the German ensemble Klangfach 6.

An early evening concert at The Royal Riding School, in the following program: *Lulu*, opera (1928–35), by the greatly significant Austrian composer whose music combined classical clarity of design and highly original melodic and harmonic techniques that became historically associated with the Second Viennese School Alban BERG (1885–1935), his second, to a libretto derived from two plays by Wedekind, left unfinished at the time of his death.

8 SEPTEMBER 1996

On the second day of the 70th Festival of the International Society for Contemporary Music in Copenhagen, three concerts are given, in the following sequence:

A mid-afternoon concert at The Royal Stock Exchange performed by the Athelas Ensemble, in the following program: *City of Threads* by the Dutch composer Anders NORDENTOFT, *J.S.B. Meditations* for chamber ensemble (1992) by the Bulgarian conductor and composer Georgi TUTEV (1924–1994), and *Un Train pour l'Enfer* (1993) by the Canadian composer Denis GOUGEON.

A late afternoon concert at The Court Theatre performed by The Danish Trombone Quartet, the World Music Days Percussion Ensemble, and The Danish Cello Ensemble, conducted by Henrik Vagn Christensen, in the following program: *Percussion Studies I & II* for guitar (1990–93) by the Brazilian composer Arthur KAMPELA, *Sept Collones* for four trombones (1993) by the Dutch composer Jesper HENDZE, *Rain Forest/Jungla* for five percussion (1992) by the Venezuelan composer Emilio MENDOZA, and *Su-Itzalak* for eight cellos (1991) by the Spanish Ramon LAZKANO.

An evening performance at The Other Opera of *The Last Virtuoso*, music theater piece. by the Danish composer Lars KLIT.

9 SEPTEMBER 1996

On the third day of the 70th Festival of the International Society for Contemporary Music, three concerts are given, in the following sequence:

A mid-afternoon concert at the Museum of Modern Art, Arken performed by the LINensemble, in the following program: *AK-47* for piano and live electronics (1994) by the Australian composer Matthew HINDSON; *Capriole* for bass clarinet and viola (1991) by the Finnish composer Kimmo HAKOLA; *Bla Tradgard* for violin, cello, and piano by the Swedish composer Mikael EDLUND; and *In the Silence of Time* for clarinet, percussion, piano, and violin (1994) by the Japanese composer Michiharu MATSUNAGA.

A late afternoon concert at the Museum of Modern Art, performed by the Esbjerg Ensemble, in the following program: *Liofa* for eight instruments (1994) by the 37-year-old Irish composer Fergus JOHNSTON, *Wunderblumen* for chamber ensemble by the 51-year-old Norwegian composer Bent LORENTZEN, *Elja* for chamber ensemble by the Icelandic composer Askel MASSON, and *Akrostichon-Wortspiel* for soprano and chamber ensemble by the 35-year-old Korean composer Unsuk CHIN.

An evening performance at The Museum of Modern Art of *In gewohnter Umgebung II*, music theater piece, by the German composer Carola BAUCKHOLT.

10 SEPTEMBER 1996

On the fourth day of the 70th Festival of the International Society for Contemporary Music in Copenhagen, three concerts are given, in the following sequence:

A mid-afternoon concert at The Tycho Brahe Planetarium, "Electroacoustic Concert I," in the following program: *Jurel* for two-channel tape (1990–93) by the Spanish composer Adolfo NUÑEZ; *Advaya* for cello, keyboard, and live electronics (1994) by the 57-year-old English composer Jonathan HARVEY; and *Asylen* for tape and slides (1992) by the Swedish composer Rolf ENSTROM.

A late afternoon concert at the Copenhagen City Museum performed by the Bernardel String Quartet, with special guest artist, Eydis Fransdottir, oboe, in the following program: *String Quartet No. 2* (1994) by the Venezuelan composer Victor VARELA, *Oboe Quintet* by the Irish composer James CLARKE, and *String Quartet*, entitled *Fluchtig wie Wind und Welle...* by the Luxembourg composer Rene HEMMER.

An evening concert at the Tivoli Concert Hall performed by The Tivoli Symphony Orchestra, with special guest ensemble, the Mandelring Quartet, conducted by Tamas Veto, in the following program: *TOI-tu...* (1994) by the Argentine composer Jose Luis CAMPANA, *Interview avec D.* (1993–94) by the notable 64-year-old Argentine composer and pedagogue Mauricio KAGEL, and *Concerto Grosso* (1990) by the noted 63-year-old Danish composer Pelle GUDMUNDSEN-HOLMGREEN.

11 SEPTEMBER 1996

On the fifth day of the 70th Festival of the International Society for Contemporary Music in Copenhagen, three concerts are given, in the following sequence:

A mid-afternoon concert at The Church of the Holy Ghost performed by The Zapolski Quartet and Musica Ficta, in a performance of *Lung Ta* for string quartet (1992) by the Canadian composer Linda BOUCHARD and *Word* for four vocal soloists (SATB) by the American composer Michael PISARO.

A late afternoon concert at The Round Tower performed by The Prison Players, conducted by Frans Rasmussen, in the following program: *Les Murs* for two mezzo-sopranos and two trumpets by the Dutch composer Robert ZUIDAM; *Prison Music I, II*, and *IV* for three sopranos, three oboes, and harp by the Danish composer Mogens Winkel HOLM; and *Horizon Caree* for soprano, flute, guitar, and harp by the Chilean composer Fernando GARCIA.

An evening performance The Ferry, Kronborg, of *Ophelia/Ophelia*, music theater piece (1994), by the English composer Andrew POPPY.

12 SEPTEMBER 1996

On the sixth day of the 70th Festival of the International Society for Contemporary Music in Copenhagen, four concerts are given, in the following sequence:

A mid-afternoon concert at The Tycho Brahe Plantarium, "Electroacoustic Concert II," in the following program: *Espace/Escape* for two-channel tape (1989) by the Canadian composer Francis DHOMONT, *Yo* for controller suit and live electronics (1994) by the Norwegian composer Rolf WALLIN, and *Sorgsang II* by the Danish composer Birgitte ALSTED.

A late afternoon concert at The National Museum performed by The Danish Chamber Players, in the following program: *Litanie con Epitaffio* for flute, bass clarinet, vibrafone, piano, violin, viola, and cello by the Belgian composer André LAPORTE; *Vispera de mi* for flute, clarinet, percussion, piano, violin, and cello by the Spanish composer Jesus TORRES; *The Buddhist Verse* for flute, guitar, percussion, and cello by the Taiwanese composer Jeanny Sun YING-CHIEH; and *Landscape #3* for nine instruments by the 51-year-old Danish composer Ole BUCK.

An evening concert at the Tivoli Concert Hall performed by The Danish National Radio Symphony Orchestra, with special guest artist Max Artved, oboe, conducted by Thomas Dausgaard, in the following program: *H'un (Lacerations): In Memoriam 1966–1976* (1987) by the remarkable 40-year-old Chinese composer Bright SHENG, first runner-up for the 1989 Pulitzer Prize in Music; *Oboe Concerto*, op.46 (1994) by the 39-year-old Finnish composer Jouni KAIPAINEN; *Durchscheinende Etüde* (1991/92) by the German composer Caspar Johannes WALTER; and *Symphony No. 4* (1988–92) by the eminent Polish composer Witold Lutosławski (1913–1994).

An evening performance at the Albertslund Music Theatre of *Nuit des Hommes*, music theater piece (1994–95), by the prominent 64-year-old Danish composer Per NØRGÅRD.

13 SEPTEMBER 1996

On the seventh day of the 70th Festival of the International Society for Contemporary Music in Copenhagen, two concerts are given, in the following sequence:

A mid-afternoon concert at The Tycho Brahe Planetarium, "Electroacoustic Concert III," in the following program: *Four Seasons* for two-channel tape (1994) by the Slovenian composer Bor TUREL, *Unes, voix de basse* for double bass and live electronics (1995) by the French composer James GIROUDON, a new work by the French composer Jean-François ESTAGER, *Ode to the South-facing Form* for two-channel tape (1992) by the American composer Mark WINGATE, and *James Kamotho Kimani* for two-channel tape (1994) by the Welsh-born Canadian composer John WYNNE.

A late afternoon concert at The Royal Stock Exchange performed by the Athelas Ensemble, in the following program: *Mundo Perdido* for chamber ensemble (1992) by the Austrian composer Gerd KÜHR, *Rent a Ricercar* for eight musicians (1992) by Martin SMOLKA, and *Red George Square* for chamber ensemble (1994) by the English composer Ross CAMPBELL.

14 SEPTEMBER 1996

On the eighth and final day of the 70th Festival of the International Society for Contemporary Music in Copenhagen, a mid-day concert is given at The Other Opera, performed by Christian Martinez and Lars Graugaard, in the following program: *Le Cru et Le Cuit* for percussion (1990–93) by the Brazilian composer Jorge ANTUNES, *Election of the Beauty Queen* for piano by the Slovak composer Miro Bazlik, and *Manic Psychosis* for flute (1992) by the Japanese composer Motoharu KAWASHIMA.

15 SEPTEMBER 1996

The Brazilian conductor and composer Eleazar de CARVALHO, husband of the Brazilian composer and pianist of French and Portuguese descent Jocy de Oliveira, who ended his days as artistic director of the São Paulo State Symphony Orchestra, dies in São Paulo at the respectable age of 84.

24 SEPTEMBER 1996

Epifora for piano and tape by the ascending 25-year-old Polish composer and clarinetist Paweł MYKIETYN is heard for the first time in Warsaw.

27 SEPTEMBER 1996

Ein Landarzt, radio opera, after Kafka (1951), and *Das Ende einer Welt*, radio opera (1953), two works by the outstanding 59-year-old German composer Hans Werner HENZE, are given first performances in revised versions over Cologne's WDR.

28 SEPTEMBER 1996

Since Dawn, tone poem for narrator, chorus, and orchestra (1995), by the 47-year-old American composer, organist, and teacher Dan (Steven) LOCKLAIR is given its first performance in Winston-Salem, North Carolina.

30 SEPTEMBER 1996

Tinguely-Fanfare for brass ensemble by the prominent 66-year-old Spanish composer and conductor Cristóbal HALFFTER (Jiménez-Encina), nephew of Ernesto (1905–1989) and Rodolfo (1900–1987) Halffter (Esriche), is given its first ever performance in Basel.

2 OCTOBER 1996

Outis, opera, by the eminent 70-year-old Italian composer, conductor, and pedagogue Luciano BERIO is staged for the first time in Milan, with the 51-year-old English baritone Alan (John) OPIE in the title role.

3 OCTOBER 1996

Cello Concerto (1996), part II of *Triduum*, triptych additionally comprising *The World's Ransoming* for orchestra and English horn obbligato (1995–96) and *Symphony, Vigil* (1997), by the 37-year-old Scottish composer, conductor, and teacher James MACMILLAN is performed for the first time in London.

4 OCTOBER 1996

Ittidra for string sextet by the eminent 74-year-old Greek-born composer, music theorist, and teacher Iannis XENAKIS is premiered in Frankfurt am Main.

5 OCTOBER 1996

Tristes Tropiques, opera, by the innovative 50-year-old Greek composer Georges APERGHIS is mounted for the first time in Strasbourg.

13 OCTOBER 1996

Concerto for Orchestra, Fallingwater, by the 49-year-old English double bass player and composer Barry (John) GUY is performed for the first time in his native London.

15 OCTOBER 1996

In the Woods for guitar (1995) by the outstanding Japanese composer Tōru TAKEMITSU (1930–1996) is given its posthumous premiere in the composer's native Tokyo.

17 OCTOBER 1996

Piano Concerto by the outstanding American composer and teacher Jacob (Raphael) DRUCKMAN (1928–1996) receives its posthumous premiere in the composer's native New Haven.

18 OCTOBER 1996

Holy Canticles for chorus by the 47-year-old American composer, organist, and teacher Dan (Steven) LOCKLAIR is heard for the first time in Winston-Salem, North Carolina.

20 OCTOBER 1996

Lonh for soprano and electronics, the winning work of the Nordic Council's Music Prize of 2000 by the significant 44-year-old Finnish composer Kaija (Anneli) SAARIAHO, is performed for the first time in Vienna.

25 OCTOBER 1996

Heathcote's Inferno for symphonic wind ensemble by the 46-year-old English composer, conductor, writer on music, and teacher Roger (Michael) MARSH is premiered in Manchester.

26 OCTOBER 1996

Lichte Spiele for violin, viola, cello, and piano by the esteemed 62-year-old German composer Siegfried MATTHUS is performed for the first time in Berlin.

26 OCTOBER 1996

Gnarly Buttons, concerto for clarinet and small ensemble, by the marvelous 49-year-old American composer and conductor John (Coolidge) ADAMS, a commission by the London Sinfonietta and Present Music in three movements, each based on a "forgery" of an "imagined musical model" — "The Perilous Shore," "Howdown (Mad Cow)", and "Put Your Loving Arms Around me" — is given its first ever performance by the London Sinfonietta.

27 OCTOBER 1996

Psalm 150 for treble voices and optional voices and/or instruments by the eminent 67-year-old Australian composer and teacher Peter (Joshua) SCULTHORPE is premiered in Launceston.

28 OCTOBER 1996

Violin Concerto, In Memory of Toru Takemitsu, by the innovative 67-year-old Japanese composer and teacher Jōji YUASA is heard for the first time in Tokyo.

29 OCTOBER 1996

Dennis Cleveland, the first-ever "talk show" opera by the formidably original 39-year-old American composer and performer Mikel ROUSE, second in a trilogy framed by

Failing Kansas (1994) and (ultimately) *The End of Cine-matics* (1999), inspired by the John Ralston Saul's brilliant 1992 study of the tyranny of reason in the 20th century, *Voltaire's Bastards*, and capturing the essence of that most banal and bizarre of American pastimes—the TV talk show—while marrying the absolute best of both pop and classical music worlds, is mounted for the first time at The Kitchen in New York.

30 OCTOBER 1996

Second Piano Concerto by the 58-year-old Polish composer and pianist Zygmunt KRAUZE is performed for the first time in Tokyo.

31 OCTOBER 1996

Coexistence for shakuhachi and strings (1994) by the notable 63-year-old Japanese composer Toshi ICHIYANAGI is performed for the first time in a version for Ondes Martenot and orchestra in Osaka.

3 NOVEMBER 1996

Die Glasmenagerie, opera, by the 74-year-old Italian-born Norwegian composer of Slovak descent Antonio (Gino) BIBALO is staged for the first time in Trier.

7 NOVEMBER 1996

Second Sonata for strings (1995) by the outstanding 70-year-old German composer Hans Werner HENZE is performed for the first time in Leipzig.

8 NOVEMBER 1996

Transfigured Goat for soprano, baritone, clarinet, and piano by the 55-year-old American composer, pianist, and teacher Richard (Edward) WILSON is given its first ever performance in Poughkeepsie, New York.

10 NOVEMBER 1996

In Rides the Dust for flute, tenor saxophone, trumpet, trombone, two percussion, two pianists (at one piano), and strings by the 36-year-old American composer, instrumentalist, improviser, and sampling specialist Annie (actually, Anne) GOSFIELD is performed for the first time in Prague.

11 NOVEMBER 1996

The important Estonian composer and pedagogue Eugen (Arturovich) KAPP, son of the equally significant Estonian composer Artur Kapp, and whose operas *Tasuleegid* and *Vabaduse laulik* won Stalin Prizes in 1946 and 1950, respectively, as did his ballet *Kalevipoeg*, in 1952, dies in Tallinn at the age of 88.

13 NOVEMBER 1996

Pol.Kolchis.Nucleus for chamber ensemble by the distinguished 44-year-old German composer and teacher Wolfgang (Michael) RIHM is premiered in Badenweiler.

15 NOVEMBER 1996

Carmen Natale for strings by the 43-year-old English composer and teacher Robert (Louis Alfred) SAXTON is performed for the first time in Bristol.

16 NOVEMBER 1996

Throstle's Nest Junction for orchestra by the prime 62-year-old English composer and conductor Sir Peter Maxwell DAVIES is performed for the first time in his native Manchester.

17 NOVEMBER 1996

Maximum est unum for mezzo-soprano, two choruses, and orchestra by the distinguished 44-year-old German composer and teacher Wolfgang (Michael) RIHM is performed for the first time in Freiburg im Breisgau.

18 NOVEMBER 1996

The 36-year-old German baritone Andreas SCHMIDT makes his New York recital debut.

19 NOVEMBER 1996

Koan for orchestra by the distinguished 59-year-old German conductor, composer, and pedagogue (Johannes Wolfgang) Hans ZENDER is performed for the first time in Freiburg im Breisgau.

20 NOVEMBER 1996

Minidoka for viola, clarinet, harp, percussion, and tape by the 58-year-old American composer, arranger, and teacher Paul (Seiko) CHIHARA is premiered in New York.

21 NOVEMBER 1996

Transcendental Modulations for orchestra (1993) by the eminent 91-year-old American composer, music theorist, and pedagogue George PERLE is heard for the first time in New York.

22 NOVEMBER 1996

Étude de technique et de sonorité for violin and piano by the eminent 91-year-old French composer and administrator Marcel (François Paul) LANDOWSKI, son of the sculptor Paul Landowski and great-grandson of the celebrated Belgian violinist and composer Henri Vieuxtemps, is performed for the first time in Paris.

23 NOVEMBER 1996

The notable Russian composer and teacher Edison DENISOV, whose extensive output demonstrated his remarkable command of a wide variety of contemporary techniques and procedures in creating scores of a pronounced individuality, dies in Paris at the age of 67.

24 NOVEMBER 1996

The third "Other Minds" Festival, under the artistic direction of Charles Amirkhanian, opens in the San Francisco Bay Area with two concerts at the University of California at Berkeley's Hertz Hall, in the following sequence:

An afternoon concert, in the following program: *The Blue Melody* for chamber ensemble (1993) by the Chinese composer Kui DONG; the world premiere performance of *Trio for Violin, Piano, and Percussion* by the 61-year-old American writer on music and composer Charles SHERE; *Endless Shout* for piano (1994) by the respected black American composer, performer, and computer/installation artist George LEWIS; *Two Waltzes* for piano (1986/90) by the American composer, ethnomusicologist, and writer on music Mitchell CLARK, in two movements, *I. Same Old Waltz* and *II. Fairly New Waltz;* and *No More* for chamber ensemble (1985) by the 59-year-old black American composer, conductor, and teacher Olly (Woodrow) WILSON, in five movements, *I. ..., II. We Have No Heroes, III. No More, IV. I Can Sit,* and *V. Return To Us.*

An evening performance by the Kronos Quartet, with technical direction by Larry Neff and lighting environment by Marian Zazeela, of Chronos Kristalla (Time Crystals) from The Magic Chord x 4 (1990) by the 61-year-old American composer of the extreme avant-garde La Monte YOUNG.

25 NOVEMBER 1996

Song Cycle for soprano and double bass by the remarkable 65-year-old Russian composer Sofia (Asgatovna) GUBAIDULINA is performed for the first time in Huddersfield.

26 NOVEMBER 1996

The prominent New Zealand soprano Dame Joan (Hood) HAMMOND, who was made an Officer (1953), a Commander (1963), and a Dame Commander (1974) of the Order of the British Empire, and whose finest operatic roles included Beethoven's Leonore, Violetta, Marguerite, Tatiana, Rusalka, Salome, and Tosca, dies in Bowral, Australia, at the age of 84.

27 NOVEMBER 1996

Seventh Symphony, entitled *The Dreams of Gandalf,* by the prominent 61-year-old Finnish composer Aulis SALLINEN is premiered in Göteborg.

28 NOVEMBER 1996

Lumor, seven lieder spirituels for saxophone and orchestra, by the distinguished 70-year-old French-American composer and teacher Betsy JOLAS, daughter of the poet and journalist Eugène Jolas, best known as the founder and editor of the literary journal *transition,* is performed for the first time in Paris.

29 NOVEMBER 1996

L'inquiétude for mezzo-soprano and instrumental ensemble (1995) by the 50-year-old French composer Jean-Claude WOLFF is heard for the first time in Meylan.

2 DECEMBER 1996

The extraordinary 30-year-old American countertenor David DANIELS makes his New York recital debut at Lincoln Center.

3 DECEMBER 1996

Thirteenth String Quartet, entitled *Island Dreaming,* with mezzo-soprano, by the eminent 67-year-old Australian composer and teacher Peter (Joshua) SCULTHORPE is premiered in Paris.

6 DECEMBER 1996

Roscobeck for cello and double bass by the eminent 74-year-old Greek-born French composer, music theorist,

and teacher Iannis XENAKIS is given its first performance in Cologne.

7 DECEMBER 1996

Perso per Perso, opera, by the 64-year-old Italian composer Guido BAGGIANI is mounted for the first time in his native Naples.

9 DECEMBER 1996

The Mother of Black-Winged Dreams, opera (1995), by the 35-year-old Polish composer Hanna KULENTY is staged for the first time in Munich.

11 DECEMBER 1996

Fantazia on the Notes E, Eb, C, B, and A for piano by the 43-year-old English composer and teacher Robert (Louis Alfred) SAXTON is heard for the first time in his native London.

12 DECEMBER 1996

Words of the Sea for orchestra (1995–96) by the 32-year-old American composer Augusta Read THOMAS, wife of the celebrated 62-year-old American composer Bernard Rands, is premiered in Chicago.

13 DECEMBER 1996

The Hungarian-born American bass Lorenzo ALVARY, who, after emigrating to the United States in 1938 appeared regularly at both the San Francisco Opera (1939–1977) and the Metropolitan Opera in New York (1942–1978), dies in New York at the age of 87.

15 DECEMBER 1996

The Dutch composer and teacher Tristan KEURIS, whose music evolved along postserial lines to embrace athematic writing with an assured command of technique, form, and structure, dies in Amsterdam at the pitiable age of 50.

17 DECEMBER 1996

Midwest Celebration for orchestra by the distinguished 75-year-old Czech-born American composer, conductor, and pedagogue Karel HUSA is performed for the first time in Chicago.

20 DECEMBER 1996

Valse Boston for piano and strings by the notable 61-year-old Georgian composer Giya (Alexandrovich) KANCHELI is given its first ever performance in Stuttgart.

23 DECEMBER 1996

Tietäjien lahja (The Gift of the Maji), chamber opera (1993–94), by the eminent 68-year-old Finnish composer and pedagogue Einojuhani (actually, Eino Juhani) RAUTAVAARA is seen for the first time over Finnish TV.

28 DECEMBER 1996

The 39-year-old English baritone Anthony MICHAELS-MOORE makes his Metropolitan Opera debut in New York as Marcello.

1997

3 JANUARY 1997

The distinguished Dutch organist, pedagogue, and composer Cornelis KEE, father of the noted 69-year-old Dutch organist, teach, and composer Piet(er Willem) Kee, dies in his native Zaandam at the respectable age of 96.

9 JANUARY 1997

Seventh Symphony, entitled *Siedem Bram Jerozolimy* (Seven Gates of Jerusalem) for solo voices, chorus, and orchestra (1996), by the eminent 63-year-old Polish composer, pedagogue, and conductor Krzysztof PENDERECKI is heard for the first time in Jerusalem.

11 JANUARY 1997

Venus und Adonis, opera (1993–95), by the outstanding 70-year-old German composer Hans Werner HENZE is mounted for the first time in Munich.

13 JANUARY 1997

The 37-year-old Italian-born American conductor Antonio PAPPANO makes his Metropolitan Opera debut in New York conducting *Eugene Onegin*.

16 JANUARY 1997

L.A. Variations for orchestra (1996) by the spirited 38-year-old Finnish conductor and composer Esa-Pekka SALONEN is premiered in Los Angeles.

17 JANUARY 1997

Flute Concerto (1996) by the 37-year-old Irish composer Fergus JOHNSTON is given its first performance in a revised version in his native Dublin.

18 JANUARY 1997

The distinguished American opera administrator Ardis (Joan) KRAINIK, who, during her tenure as artistic administrator (1975–1981) and general director (from 1981) of the Chicago Lyric Opera, molded it into one of the most prestigious opera companies in the world, renovating its Civic Opera House, commissioning new scores, and establishing a composer-in-residence program, dies in Chicago at the age of 67.

26 JANUARY 1997

Concerto Grosso for two violins and chamber orchestra (1996) by the 53-year-old Polish composer, percussionist, and teacher Marta PTASZYŃSKA is premiered in her native Warsaw.

28 JANUARY 1997

The Swiss conductor Edmond de STOUTZ, founder in 1954 of the Zürich Chamber Orchestra (1954) and the Zürich Concert Choir (1962), in whose programs he invariably included works by contemporary composers, dies in his native Zürich at the age of 76.

30 JANUARY 1997

Rough Magic for orchestra (1996–97) by the 38-year-old American composer and teacher Jay Alan YIM is performed for the first time in Chicago.

31 JANUARY 1997

Erlkönig, fantasy for orchestra after Schubert (1996), by the outstanding 70-year-old German composer Hans Werner HENZE is given its first performance in Paris.

2 FEBRUARY 1997

Die Welt der Mongolen, opera (1996), by the avant-garde 61-year-old Austrian composer, horn player, and teacher Kurt SCHWERTSIK is mounted for the first time in Linz.

5 FEBRUARY 1997

String Quartet Concerto (1996) by the 52-year-old New Zealand composer Lyell (Richard) CRESSWELL is heard for the first time in Aberdeen.

6 FEBRUARY 1997

Quintet, subtitled *Five Objects Darkly*, for bass clarinet, horn, violin, viola, and piano (1996) by the prominent 64-year-old German-born English composer and teacher (Peter) Alexander GOEHR, son of the German-born English conductor and composer Walter Goehr, is premiered in Los Angeles.

8 FEBRUARY 1997

The important German musicologist Walter WIORA, whose principal achievement was his advocacy of a system of "essential research" in musicology that utilized both traditional and contemporary principles, dies in Tutzing at the seasoned age of 89.

9 FEBRUARY 1997

The 48-year-old Brazilian pianist Arnaldo COHEN makes his New York recital debut at the Frick Collection.

13 FEBRUARY 1997

Saetas for orchestra (1996) by the 45-year-old American conductor and composer Lawrence RAPCHAK is heard for the first time in Chicago.

18 FEBRUARY 1997

The French conductor of Portuguese-American descent Antonio (Jacques) de ALMEIDA, who, in addition to appearing with many of the world's major orchestras and opera houses during his career was active in researching and editing the works of Offenbach, dies in Pittsburgh at the age of 68.

19 FEBRUARY 1997

The distinguished Czech composer, conductor, and musicologist Jarmil (real name, Jarmil Michael Mokrý) BURGHAUSER, who became a leading figure in the restoration of the musical life of his country by serving as chairman of the Guild of Composers and as a member of the rehabilitation committee of the Ministry of Culture, dies in Prague at the age of 75.

20 FEBRUARY 1997

The Belly of the Whale for chorus (1996) by the 52-year-old New Zealand composer Lyell (Richard) CRESSWELL is performed for the first time in Glasgow.

21 FEBRUARY 1997

Seventh Symphony (1990–91) by the compelling 58-year-old American composer Gloria COATES is given its first ever performance in Munich.

26 FEBRUARY 1997

Aubade for orchestra (1996) by the 46-year-old American composer, conductor, and teacher Donald CROCKETT is performed for the first time in Los Angeles, the composer conducting.

1 MARCH 1997

The Conquistador, opera, by the 64-year-old American composer Myron S(amuel) FINK is mounted for the first time in San Diego.

3 MARCH 1997

"2 plus 2" dla Witolda ("2 plus 2" for Witold) for violin, cello, and two pianos by the 45-year-old Polish composer, conductor, and teacher Aleksander LASOŃ is premiered in Katowice.

4 MARCH 1997

Concerto for clarinets and orchestra (1996–97) by the 74-year-old American composer and pedagogue Allen Dwight SAPP, Jr., receives its first performance in Cincinnati.

8 MARCH 1997

Double Concerto for saxophone, cello, and orchestra (1996–97) by the notable 52-year-old English composer, conductor, and writer on music Michael (Laurence) NYMAN is given its first ever performance in his native London.

10 MARCH 1997

60e Parallèle, opera, by the 44-year-old French composer Philippe MANOURY is mounted for the first time in Paris.

11 MARCH 1997

Symphony 1997: Heaven Earth Mankind for orchestra, two treble choruses, solo cello, and the recently unearthed bronze bells (the so-called "Bianzhong" bells) from the Hubei province of China dating from nearly 500 years B.C. (performed by the Imperial Bells Ensemble of China) by the significant 39-year-old Chinese composer Tan DUN after a commission for Hong Kong's 1995 reunification ceremonies is given its first United States performance at Lincoln Center's Avery Fisher Hall in New York, Yo-Yo Ma cello soloist.

12 MARCH 1997

"Henry Cowell's Musical Worlds: A Centennial Festival," 13 ambitious days and nights of panels and concerts celebrating the life's work and continuing influence of the remarkable and innovative American composer Henry (Dixon) COWELL (1897–1965), jointly sponsored by the Institute for Studies in American Music, The New School, World Music Institute, 92nd Street Y, and The New York Public Library for the Performing Arts, opens with the ISAM Symposium "Modernity and Tradition I: The Many Worlds of Henry Cowell," at Levenson Recital Hall, Brooklyn College, the seasoned American musicologist H. Wiley Hitchcock the keynote speaker.

12 MARCH 1997

Quad—In memoriam Gilles Deluze, concerto for violin and small orchestra (1996), by the 41-year-old French composer Pascal DUSAPIN is performed for the first time in Paris.

13 MARCH 1997

Odradek: Hommage à Franz Kafka for orchestra by the prominent 66-year-old Spanish composer and conductor Cristóbal HALFFTER (Jiménez-Encina), nephew of the important Spanish composer and conductor Ernesto (1905–1989) and the eminent Spanish-born Mexican composer Rodolfo (1900–1987) Halffter (Escriche), is given its premiere performance in Prague.

16 MARCH 1997

Contrepoint barbare for violin, cello, accordion, and tape (1996) by the innovative 62-year-old French composer, trombonist, conductor, and teacher Vinko GLOBOKAR is heard for the first time in Lyons.

17 MARCH 1997

Qi for flute, cello, piano, and percussion (1996–97) by the energetic 43-year-old Chinese composer and teacher Chen YI is performed for the first time in San Francisco.

18 MARCH 1997

Celo, cello concerto (1996), by the 41-year-old French composer Pascal DUSAPIN is premiered in Caen.

20 MARCH 1997

As part of its 135th anniversary season, the Brooklyn Academy of Music hosts "BAM Salutes Sondheim," an evening celebration of song, dance, and concert work devised and directed by Hugh Woodridge in honor of the brilliant 66-year-old American composer and lyricist Stephen (Joshua) SONDHEIM, featuring the Brooklyn Philharmonic Orchestra, the New York City Gay Men's

Chorus, and such solo luminaries of the musical theater as Angela Lansbury, Liz Callaway, Len Cariou, Davis Gaines, Kitty Carlisle Hart, Judy Kaye, Julia Migenes, and Elaine Stritch. (In addition to innumerable songs from Sondheim's most popular musicals, also heard were premiere performances of *A Very Short Violin Sonata* [1951], performed by Christina Sunnerstam Prince, and *Variations on a Theme—Katie Malone* for piano [1949], performed by Peter Cincotti.)

20 MARCH 1997

Nuits, adieux for four voices and live electronics (1991) by the significant 44-year-old Finnish composer Kaija (Anneli) SAARIAHO is given its first performance in a version for chorus in Paris.

22 MARCH 1997

Peanuts Gallery for piano and orchestra (1996) by the remarkable 57-year-old American composer Ellen Taaffe ZWILICH is premiered in New York.

23 MARCH 1997

Ipso for clarinet (1994) by the 41-year-old French composer Pascal DUSAPIN is given its first performance in Caen.

24 MARCH 1997

Oral Poetry of the Native American for chorus and flute by the notable 64-year-old Japanese composer Toshi ICHIYANAGI is heard for the first time in Tokyo.

25 MARCH 1997

The Galloway Mass for unison voices, chorus or cantor, and organ (1996) by the 37-year-old Scottish composer, conductor, and teacher James MACMILLAN is premiered in Ayr.

27 MARCH 1997

Petite Symphonie Concertante for violin and orchestra by the distinguished 70-year-old French-American composer and teacher Betsy JOLAS, daughter of the poet and journalist Eugène Jolas, best known as the founder and editor of the literary journal *transition*, is first performed in Besançon.

29 MARCH 1997

The Danish composer and pedagogue (Niels) Finn HØFFDING, long-time teacher (1931–1969) and director (1954–1969) at the Royal Danish Conservatory of Music in Copenhagen and whose large compositional output followed along post-Nielsen lines, dies in Frederiksberg at the remarkable age of 98.

31 MARCH 1997

Sozu Baba for voice (1996) by the 47-year-old English composer, conductor, writer on music, and teacher Roger (Michael) MARSH is performed for the first time in Utrecht.

2 APRIL 1997

The Ukrainian composer Yuli (Sergeievich) MEITUS, who for the most part adhered to the tenets of Soviet realism in his extensive output, which included numerous operas, dies in Korovograd at the seasoned age of 94.

3 APRIL 1997

Wieman's treibt, so geht's for bass clarinet and tape by the 67-year-old American composer and teacher Robert (Paige) CEELY is performed for the first time in Boston.

4 APRIL 1997

"Celestes Schubertiades" for two flutes, two oboes, two clarinets, two bassoon, and two horns, after Schubert (1996), by the significant 84-year-old French composer Jean FRANÇAIX is given its first ever performance in Meran.

6 APRIL 1997

He's Our Dad for soprano, keyboard, and computer-generated sound by the innovative 43-year-old American cellist, conductor, and composer Tod MACHOVER is performed for the first time in Boston.

7 APRIL 1997

Time...and Again for violin and piano by the notable 61-year-old Georgian composer Giya (Alexandrovich) KANCHELI is heard for the first time in London.

9 APRIL 1997

Memory and Hope: Essays for orchestra by the 70-year-old Austrian-born American pianist, conductor, teacher, and composer Karl (Georg) KOHN is performed for the first time in Stockton, California.

10 APRIL 1997

The Padrone, opera in two acts by the eminent American composer George W(hitefield) CHADWICK (1854–1931), to a libretto in which the figure of the padrone, in the period of Italian and Irish immigration in the late 19th century, symbolizes human corruption in the exploitation of poor immigrants, musically based "on the union of Wagner's symphonic recitative and Italian lyricism," with its four principal characters singing in Italian and all others in English, is seen in its first complete stage production in Boston.

11 APRIL 1997

Land Mystery for shakuhachi and koto by the notable 64-year-old Japanese composer Toshi ICHIYANAGI is performed for the first time in Tokyo.

12 APRIL 1997

Trio for flute, guitar, and drum set (1991) by the 50-year-old black American composer and teacher Joyce Solomon MOORMAN is heard for the first time in Teaneck, New Jersey.

14 APRIL 1997

Caught By The Sky With Wire for cello and percussion by the 38-year-old American composer, performer, and programmer Nick (actually, Nicholas Russel) DIDKOVSKY is given its first ever performance in New York.

14 APRIL 1997

Mysterious Numbers for flute, clarinet, violin, cello, piano, and percussion (1996) by the versatile 44-year-old American composer, pianist, teacher, and writer on music William (Ervin) DUCKWORTH is given its first ever performance in a version for orchestra in Cleveland.

15 APRIL 1997

Mancala for two violins by the 43-year-old Polish composer, percussionist, and teacher Marta PTASZYŃSKA is performed for the first time in New York.

16 APRIL 1997

The Density of Memory for clarinet trio and orchestra by the 60-year-old American composer and teacher George (William) FLYNN is heard for the first time in Chicago.

17 APRIL 1997

The Magic Number for soprano and orchestra (1995) by the brilliant 68-year-old German-born American pianist, conductor, and composer André (George) (real name, Andreas Ludwig Priwin) PREVIN is given its first ever performance in New York.

19 APRIL 1997

Night Journey for piano (1996) by the 66-year-old American composer and record producer Nancy VAN DE VATE is premiered in Eisenstadt.

20 APRIL 1997

5 Studien and 1 Collage for chamber ensemble (1996) by the productive 70-year-old German composer, pedagogue, organist, and harpsichordist Ruth ZECHLIN is heard for the first time in Potsdam.

23 APRIL 1997

Piccolo Concerto (1996) by the eminent 62-year-old English composer and conductor Sir Peter Maxwell DAVIES is premiered in Nottingham.

24 APRIL 1997

The remarkable American composer and teacher Robert ERICKSON, who, in addition to teaching for 20 years (1967–1987) at the University of California at San Diego published the interesting volumes *The Structure of Music: A Listener's Guide to Melody and Counterpoint* (1955) and *Sound Structure in Music* (1975), dies in Encinitas, California, at the age of 80.

24 APRIL 1997

The remarkable American-based string quartet the KRONOS QUARTET gives the first of three programs of world premieres at San Francisco's Theater Artaud, featuring *Altar de Muerto* by Gabriela Ortiz, *Raising Shadow* by P.Q. Phan, *Going Going Gone* by Anne LeBaron, and *Collected Songs Where Every Verse is Filled with Grief* by Alfred Schnittke.

25 APRIL 1997

3 Faces of Love, chamber cantata for soprano, tenor, baritone, chamber organ or harpsichord, and lute, after John Wilmot, Earl of Rochester, by the distinguished 70-year-old South African-born English composer and teacher John (Pierre Herman) JOUBERT is given its first ever performance in Oxford.

27 APRIL 1997

On the Annunciation of the Blessed Virgin for chorus and organ (1996) and *The Halie Speerit's Dancers* for children's chorus and piano (1996), two works by the 37-year-old Scottish composer, conductor, and teacher James MACMILLAN are heard for the first time in Cambridge.

1 MAY 1997

Sanctus Adalbertus Flos Purpureus for mezzo-soprano, tenor, baritone, chorus, and orchestra by the 70-year-old Polish composer Juliusz (Mieczyslaw) ŁUCIUK is heard for the first time in Częstochowa.

2 MAY 1997

Swell for piano, guitar, sampler, violin, and cello (or any combination of instruments) by the productive 36-year-old American composer, instrumentalist, improviser, and sampling specialist Annie (actually, Anne) GOSFIELD is performed for the first time in New York.

4 MAY 1997

Short Stories for flute, viola, and harp (1995) by the 46-year-old American composer, conductor, and teacher Donald CROCKETT is given its first ever performance in Eugene, Oregon.

5 MAY 1997

The Russian-born French composer, ethnomusicologist, and broadcasting administrator Tolia NIKIPROWETZKY, who pursued important ethnomusicological missions to Mauritania (1960), Senegal (1962), Niger (1963), and Cameroun (1965) and who (from 1969) was active with the French Radio, dies in Paris at the age of 80.

9 MAY 1997

The noted Swiss musicologist Willy HESS dies in his native Winterthur at the age of 90.

10 MAY 1997

The Marriages Between Zones Three, Four, and Five, opera, by the outstanding 60-year-old American composer Philip GLASS is staged for the first time in Heidelberg.

11 MAY 1997

Job, oratorio for soprano, alto, tenor, bass, chorus, and orchestra, by the eminent 62-year-old English composer and conductor Sir Peter Maxwell DAVIES is heard for the first time in Vancouver, British Columbia.

13 MAY 1997

Arcanum for soprano, oboe/horn, trombone, string quintet, and percussion (1996) by the 36-year-old Argentine composer Ezequiel VIÑAO is given its first performance in New York.

14 MAY 1997

Jahr lang ins Ugewisse hinab for orchestra (1995–96) by the notable 71-year-old Austrian composer, conductor, and pedagogue Friedrich CERHA is performed for the first time in his native Vienna, the composer conducting.

15 MAY 1997

Capriccio for piano and strings (1994) by the 48-year-old Polish composer Piotr MOSS is heard for the first time in Warsaw.

16 MAY 1997

Balseros, subtitled *A Sage of Exile—The Cuban Rafters' Journey To The Promised Land*, opera utilizing a dense, multi-layered collage of voices, an Afro-Cuban drum (bata) ensemble, an orchestra ensemble of timpani and trumpets, and electronic processing, by the pioneering 67-year-old American composer, performer, director, and writer Robert (Reynolds) ASHLEY, to a bilingual (Spanish and English) libretto by Maria Irene Fornes, featuring core members of Ashley's opera ensemble, including Sam Ashley, Tom Buckner, Tom Hamilton, Jacqueline Humbert, and Joan La Barbara, as well as singers from the Florida Grand Opera's Young Artists program, is mounted for the first time by the Florida Grand Opera in Miami.

17 MAY 1997

Hymn of the Unwaning Light for chorus (1996) by the remarkable 53-year-old English composer John (Kenneth) TAVENER is performed for the fist time in Sherbourne Abbey.

18 MAY 1997

Kwiaty (Flowers) for flute, piccolo flute, oboe, clarinet, and piano (1996–97) by the 72-year-old Polish composer and pedagogue Krystyna MOSZUMAŃSKA-NAZAR is given its first ever performance in Kraków.

19 MAY 1997

Ereia for string quartet, guitar, bass, drum set, piano, soprano saxophone, flute, trumpet, and bass clarinet by the 38-year-old American composer, performer, and programmer Nick (actually, Nicholas Russel) DIDKOVSKY is performed for the first time in Victoriaville, Quebec.

21 MAY 1997

Invocazioni intorno for horn and percussion by the 51-year-old Polish composer and teacher Józef RYCHLIK is heard for the first time in Kraków.

22 MAY 1997

The remarkable 37-year-old English soprano Jane EAGLEN makes her first appearance with the New York Philharmonic in New York, singing the "Liebestod" from *Tristan und Isolde* under Kurt Masur's direction.

23 MAY 1997

Réponse a "letters" après "second thoughts" for soprano, flute, accordion, and percussion by the innovative 62-year-old French composer, trombonist, conductor, and teacher Vinko GLOBOKAR is performed for the first time in Hannover.

25 MAY 1997

Le fils de l'air/Der Sohn der Luft or *L'enfant changé en jeune homme*, ballet (1995–96), by the outstanding 70-year-old German composer Hans Werner HENZE is staged for the first time in Schwetzingen.

31 MAY 1997

Pensée écartelée for percussionist by the innovative 62-year-old French composer, trombonist, conductor, and teacher Vinko GLOBOKAR is heard for the first time in Whitehaven.

4 JUNE 1997

Dragon Bond Rite, cross-cultural mask dance drama by the talented 39-year-old South Korean composer and komungo player Jin Hi KIM, in five scenes (*I: Dawn*, *II: Place Mute of Light*, *III: What Pleasure*, *IV: Air Here*, and *V: Endstart*) based on Japanese noh theatre and featuring Korean, Japanese, Indian, Indonesian, and Mongolian artists, is staged for the first time at New York's Japan Society, who commissioned the work.

6 JUNE 1997

Piano Concerto (1996) by the 35-year-old Korean composer Unsuk CHIN is performed for the first time in Cardiff.

7 JUNE 1997

The Finnish organist, teacher, and composer Sakari (Tuomo) MONONEN, active mainly as an organist and teacher in his native country, dies in Espoo at the moderate age of 68.

10 JUNE 1997

Cathedral, a five-year work created especially for the Internet by the adventurous 54-year-old American composer, pianist, teacher, and writer on music William (Ervin) DUCKWORTH, incorporating acoustic and computer music, live webcasts, and newly-created virtual instruments, goes online for the first time, its planned completion to take place in 2001 in a live and online 48-hour concert with sounds incorporated into the piece from sites around the globe.

12 JUNE 1997

Piano Concerto (1996–97) by the respected 43-year-old English composer Judith WEIR is heard for the first time in London.

13 JUNE 1997

The Country of the Blind, chamber opera (1996–97), and *Twice Through the Heart* for mezzo-soprano and 16 players (1994–96), two works by the admired 37-year-old English composer Mark-Anthony TURNAGE, are premiered in Aldeburgh.

14 JUNE 1997

Hopper's Wife, opera, by the prominent 36-year-old American composer Stewart (Farrell) WALLACE, its libretto a sexually-charged treatment of the life of the American painter Edward Hopper, is staged for the first time in Long Beach, California.

15 JUNE 1997

Miatsoom (in the Armenian language, Reunion; 1994–97), a 26-minute tape piece, by the multi-talented 52-year-old American avant-garde composer, influential radio producer, and arts administrator of Armenian descent Charles (Benjamin) AMIRKHANIAN is given its world premiere via the California radio stations KPFA in Berkeley and KFCF in Fresno, based on recordings made during a 1994 two-week visit by the composer and his father, Benjamin Vresh ("Revenge") Amirkhanian, two months after the genocidal massacre of over 1,000,000 Armenians by the Ottoman Turkish government, and including recordings of the ambience of a 4th century cave church at Gehrart and another more modern one in the religious capital of Etchmiadzin, a tour guide speaking broken English in the national historic museum, Amirkhanian's last remaining relatives in the Republic of Armenia singing traditional Armenian love songs and laments.

18 JUNE 1997

The AMERICAN SYMPHONY ORCHESTRA LEAGUE opens a four-day national conference, "America's Orchestras: A National Priority," featuring a keynote address on leadership in the arts by William J. Perry, former Secretary of Defense, as well as briefings on current legislation by two members of the Congressional Arts Caucus, Senator Robert F. Bennett, a Republican from Utah, and Representative Louise Slaughter, a Democrat from New York.

20 JUNE 1997

Between Two Worlds: The Dybbuk, opera (1994–95), by the 47-year-old Israeli pianist and composer Shulamit RAN is heard for the first time in Chicago.

21 JUNE 1997

The admired German bass Karl RIDDERBUSCH, known especially for his Wagnerian roles, which included King Marke, Fafner, Hagen, and Daland, dies in Wels, near Linz, at the modest age of 65.

23 JUNE 1997

Sea-Change for orchestra by the eminent 75-year-old Greek-born French composer, music theorist, and teacher Iannis XENAKIS is premiered in London.

24 JUNE 1997

Homage to Novalis for flute, harp, two cellos or cello, and viola (1996) and *Fairytale Suite* for flute (1997), two works by the compelling 58-year-old American composer Gloria COATES, are premiered in Passau.

29 JUNE 1997

Giro for orchestra (1982) by the spirited 38-year-old Finnish conductor and composer Esa-Pekka SALONEN is first heard in its newly-revised version in Porvoo.

1 JULY 1997

Third String Quartet, entitled *Diódia* (1995), by the remarkable 53-year-old English composer John (Kenneth) TAVENER is heard for the first time in West Cork.

5 JULY 1997

Four-Horned Fandango for four horns and orchestra (1995–96) by the productive 37-year-old English composer Mark-Anthony TURNAGE is performed for the first time in Birmingham.

6 JULY 1997

Die Aussicht for soprano, flute, guitar, violin, and cello (1996) by the significant 44-year-old Finnish composer Kaija (Anneli) SAARIAHO is given its first ever performance in Manta, Italy.

7 JULY 1997

Gebild for piccolo trumpet, two percussionists, and 20 strings by the distinguished 45-year-old German composer and teacher Wolfgang (Michael) RIHM is given its first performance in a newly-revised version in Lucerne.

8 JULY 1997

Aleksis kivi, opera (1995–96), by the eminent 68-year-old Finnish composer and pedagogue Einojuhani (actually, Eino Juhani) RAUTAVAARA is staged for the first time in Savonlinna, with the distinguished 56-year-old Finnish baritone and opera administrator Jorma HYNNINEN in the title role.

10 JULY 1997

First Clarinet Concerto (1986) by the 69-year-old American musicologist, inventor, and composer James (Myron) COHN is given its first ever performance in Lubbock, Texas.

11 JULY 1997

Melodies for piano by the 67-year-old Japanese composer and teacher Jōji YUASA is heard for the first time in Tokyo.

11 JULY 1997

The first of three concerts under the title "Ten Years of Essential Music" ("essential" here referring both to the essential New York-based new music ensemble Essential Music, co-directed by two American composer-musicians John KENNEDY and Charles WOOD, and to the essential music they perform) is given at The Kitchen in New York, featuring *Music of the Spheres* (1938) for two violins, cello, triangle, and lion's roar by Johanna M. Beyer; *Between Categories* (1969) for two violins, two cellos, two pianos, and chimes by Morton Feldman; *Percussion Piece* (1968) by David Jackman; *Two²* for two pianos by John Cage; and *Another Sunrise* for two pianos, marimbula, and percussion by Peter Garland. (Subsequent evenings, on 12 July and 13 July 1997, feature works, in addition to Wood and Kennedy, by Dary John Mizelle, Kurt Schwitters, William Russell, Cornelius Cardew, James Tenney, Mitchell Clark, William Duckworth, Robert Ashley, and Kyle Gann.)

12 JULY 1997

Love-Song for guitar and strings by the prime 68-year-old Australian composer and teacher Peter (Joshua) SCULT-HORPE is given its first ever performance in Darwin.

16 JULY 1997

Intimate Immensity, interactive multimedia work by the 64-year old American composer Morton SUBOTNICK, incorporating laser disc imagery, nature images, stage sets (pianos and computers), and lighting design, featuring the characters She (performed by Subnotnick's wife, Joan La Barbara), He (Thomas Buchner), Cyber-Angel (I Nyoman Wenten), and The Hand (Nanik Wenten, on laser disc), and relating in ten scenes, without intermission, an apocalyptic tale of the composer's late-20th century love affair with technology, with text freely inspired by the writings of Gaston Bachelard, David Rothenberg, Kafka, Lewis Mumford, and Marshall McLuhan, is performed for the first time at LaGuardia Theater as part of the 1997 Lincoln Center Festival in N.Y.

18 JULY 1997

Hoch soll er Leben for horn, two trumpets, trombone, and tuba by the brilliant 68-year-old German-born American pianist, conductor, and composer André (George) (real name, Andreas Ludwig Priwin) PREVIN is performed for the first time in New York.

20 JULY 1997

À Sainte Dévote for orchestra by the eminent 82-year-old French composer and administrator Marcel (François Paul) LANDOWSKI, son of the sculptor Paul Landowski and great-grandson of the celebrated Belgian violinist and composer Henri Vieuxtemps, is performed for the first time in Monte Carlo.

26 JULY 1997

Percussion Concerto by the significant 58-year-old English composer Jonathan (Dean) HARVEY is given its first ever performance in London.

28 JULY 1997

Le grand macabre, opera in two acts by the eminent 73-year-old Hungarian-born Austrian composer and pedagogue György (Sándor) LIGETI, to a libretto by Michael Meschke and the composer after Michel de Ghelderode in which the action is set in a chimeric town of Breugelland and the story centered on the thanatopherous necro-czar who sexually mutilates local hausfrau before ordering the world's end, but who shrinks himself into a death mask when the forces of life refuse to stop functioning, is mounted for the first time in a newly-revised version in Salzburg.

1 AUGUST 1997

The legendary Russian pianist Sviatoslav (Teofilovich) RICHTER, a foremost interpreter of the Russian repertoire and also rightly acclaimed the world over as a supreme master of the great Romantic repertoire, dies in Moscow at the age of 82.

7 AUGUST 1997

The admired 41-year-old American soprano Barbara BONNEY, wife of the outstanding Swedish baritone Håkan Hagegård, makes her New York recital debut at Alice Tully Hall.

8 AUGUST 1997

The English lutenist, guitarist, singer, and teacher Robert SPENCER, lutenist with the Julian Bream Consort (from 1960) and the Deller Consort (from 1974) whose repertoire embraced works from the Renaissance to the contemporary era, dies in Woodford Green, Essex, at the age of 67.

10 AUGUST 1997

The remarkable American-born Mexican composer Conlon NANCARROW, innovator in the technique of recording notes on a player-piano roll, which he put to use in an astonishingly innovative body of original works, dies in Mexico City at the age of 84.

11 AUGUST 1997

Feria for orchestra by the 39-year-old Finnish composer Magnus (Gustaf Adolf) LINDBERG is heard for the first time in London.

15 AUGUST 1997

Flute Sonata (1996) by the significant 85-year-old French composer Jean FRANÇAIX is premiered in Chicago.

17 AUGUST 1997

Fifth Symphony, entitled *Time Perspective* and *Existence* for clarinet and piano, two works by the notable 64-year-old Japanese composer Toshi ICHIYANAGI, are given their first performances, the first over Tokyo's NHK, and the second in Yokohama.

19 AUGUST 1997

Rochester Triptych for chorus and organ, after John Wilmot, Earl of Rochester (1991–92), by the distinguished 70-year-old South African-born English composer and teacher John (Pierre Herman) JOUBERT is heard for the first time in a version for chorus and orchestra in Hereford.

22 AUGUST 1997

A Welcome Ode for chorus and optional piano duet/percussion or optional organ/percussion by the 52-year-old English composer, teacher, and conductor Edward GREGSON is given its first ever performance in Sunderland.

23 AUGUST 1997

De Coloribus for chamber ensemble by the distinguished 45-year-old German composer and teacher Wolfgang (Michael) RIHM is heard for the first time in Lucerne.

2 SEPTEMBER 1997

The prominent Austrian-born English opera manager Sir Rudolf (Franz Joseph) BING, whose tenure as general manager of the Metropolitan Opera in New York (1950–1972) was distinguished, if at times controversial, and whose other accomplishments included the colorful books *5,000 Nights at the Opera* (N.Y., 1972) and *A Knight at the Opera* (N.Y., 1981), dies in New York at the seasoned age of 95.

5 SEPTEMBER 1997

The eminent Hungarian-born English conductor Sir Georg (real name, György Stern) SOLTI, long-time conductor of the Chicago Symphony Orchestra, in which capacity he achieved a triumph as an interpreter and orchestra builder, so that the "Chicago sound" became a synonym for excellence, and with which he showed himself an enlightened disciplinarian and a master of orchestra psychology, so that he could gain and hold the confidence of the players while demanding from them the utmost in professional performance, dies in Antibes at the respectable age of 84.

5 SEPTEMBER 1997

The tenure of the 68-year-old Iranian-born American opera director and administrator Lotfi (actually, Lotfollah) MANSOURI is marked with the major renovation of the San Francisco Opera House and its gala reopening concert conducted by Donald Runnicles.

8 SEPTEMBER 1997

Mini Stories for narrator, soprano, and small ensemble by the 55-year-old Icelandic cellist and composer Haflidi (Magnus) HALLGRÍMSSON is heard for the first time in Thurso, Scotland.

11 SEPTEMBER 1997

Diary Fragments 3 for two violins, viola, and cello (1996) by the 58-year-old Finnish trumpeter and composer Jarmo (Kalevi) SERMILÄ is given its first ever performance in St. Gallen.

12 SEPTEMBER 1997

Staden, opera (1996), by the 54-year-old Swedish composer and teacher Sven-David SANDSTRÖM is mounted for the first time in Stockholm.

14 SEPTEMBER 1997

Graal Théâtre for violin and orchestra (1994) by the significant 44-year-old Finnish compoer Kaija (Anneli) SAARIAHO is heard for the first time in a version for violin and chamer orchestra in her native Helsinki.

15 SEPTEMBER 1997

First Trio for piano, violin, and cello by the 42-year-old French composer Pascal DUSAPIN is given its first ever performance in St. Jean-de-Luz.

16 SEPTEMBER 1997

The American soprano Helen JEPSON, whose roles of note included Eva in *Die Meistersinger von Nürnberg*, Marguerite in *Faust*, Desdemona in *Otello*, and Nedda in *Pagliacci*, dies in Bradenton, Florida, at the accomplished age of 92.

17 SEPTEMBER 1997

Reigaku for alto flute by the 68-year-old Japanese composer and teacher Jōji YUASA is heard for the first time in Berlin.

19 SEPTEMBER 1997

Cram Jin Quotient for electronically-altered string quartet by the innovative 37-year-old American composer, instrumentalist, improviser, and sampling specialist Annie (actually, Anne) GOSFIELD is given its first performance in New York.

20 SEPTEMBER 1997

Credo for orchestra by the 45-year-old Polish composer, conductor, and teacher Aleksander LASOŃ is premiered in Poznań.

22 SEPTEMBER 1997

Extant for bassoon and eight instruments by the 46-year-old American composer, conductor, and teacher Donald CROCKETT is performed for the first time in Pittsburgh.

24 SEPTEMBER 1997

3 Faces of Love, chamber cantata for soprano, tenor, baritone, chamber organ or harpsichord, and lute, after John Wilmot, Earl of Rochester (1997) by the distinguished 70-year-old South African-born English composer and teacher John (Pierre Herman) JOUBERT is given its first performance in a reduced version for soprano, tenor, baritone, and piano in Windsor.

25 SEPTEMBER 1997

The significant French composer Jean FRANÇAIX, whose large output demonstrated his Gallic refinement and wit, dies in Paris at the age of 85.

26 SEPTEMBER 1997

Of Things Exactly As They Are for soprano, baritone, chorus, and orchestra by the distinguished 78-year-old American composer, pedagogue, conductor, and pianist Leon KIRCHNER is given its first ever performance in Boston.

26 SEPTEMBER 1997

The 71st Festival of the International Society for Contemporary Music opens in Seoul with two concerts, in the following sequence:

A late afternoon concert at the Seoul Arts Center, Garden performed by Austria's Klangmobil, with special guest artist Emil Rider, clarinet and soprano saxophone, in the following program: *Moving Bells* and *Reflexionen 3* by Herbert GLASSL, *Endless Variation* and *CLB512* by Klaus AGER, and *Klangquadrat* by Bruno Strobl.

An evening concert at the Seoul Arts Center, Concert Hall performed by the KBS Symphony Orchestra, with special guest artists Lotta Tejle and Nina Lugn, monologists, Lena Willemark and Kang Tong-suk, violin, and Per Salo, piano, conducted by Yves Prin, in the following program: *Solsangen* by the Swedish composer Karin REHNQVIST, *Violin Concerto No. 3* (1992) by the important Korean-born German composer and teacher Isang YUN (1917–1995), and *Piano Concerto*, subtitled *Concerto in due Tempi* (1994–95) by the prominent 65-year-old Danish composer and pedagogue Per NØRGÅRD, a commission from the Léonie Sonning Music Foundation.

27 SEPTEMBER 1997

The eminent German-American violist and pedagogue Walter TRAMPLER, a master of his instrument who did much to create an audience for the viola and who showcased many contemporary scores, including newly-commissioned works by Luciano Berio and Simon Bainbridge, dies in Port Joli, Nova Scotia, at the age of 82.

27 SEPTEMBER 1997

On the second day of the 71st Festival of the International Society for Contemporary Music continues in Seoul, three concerts are given, in the following sequence:

A late afternoon concert at the Seoul Goethe-Institute performed by the The Tokyo Symphony and S-Color Quartet, in the following program: *Adamento* op.64, by the Romanian composer Liviu DANCEANU, a new work by the Korean composer Su Yuon HONG, *Music for Two* by the Bulgarian composer Russi TARMAKOV, *Loquela* by the English composer Caroline WILKINS, and *Reconciliation* by the Japanese composer Ayaka MURKUMO.

An evening concert at the National Theater, central hall, performed by Germany's Ensemble Avantgarde, with special guest artist Ksenija Lukic, soprano, in the following program: *Tre Voci* for soprano and chamber ensemble (1988) by the significant 56-year-old Norwegian composer Norwegian composer Arne NORDHEIM; *klavier & Klavier* by the German composer and pianist Steffen SCHLEIERMACHER; *Music for Five* by the singularly inventive and much beloved American composer, writer, philosopher, and visual artist of ultra-modern tendencies American composer John CAGE (1912–1992), realized from the composer's *Music for* ____ series, for any solo from or combination of voice, flute, oboe, clarinet, horn, trumpet, trombone, four percussionists, two pianos, two violins, viola, and cello (1984; rev. 1987); *Fêtes de la Faim & Plainte* by the Canadian composer James ROLFE; and *Teibstoff* by the German composer Carola BAUCKHOLT.

An evening concert at the National Theater, small hall, "Electronic Music 1," presented by the Korean Electronic Music Association, with special guest artist Yi Chi-yong, kayagum, in the following program: *Scratches* by the Finnish composer Jukka RUOHOMOKI, *Mannam* by the Mexican composer Javier ALVAREZ, *Tuduri* by the Korean composer Seong-joon MOON, *VOXII* by the Argentine composer Jorge SAD, and *Respiro* by the Norwegian composer Ragnhild BERSTAD.

28 SEPTEMBER 1997

Symphony, entitled *Vigil*, by the 38-year-old Scottish composer, conductor, and teacher James MACMILLAN, Part III of *Triduum*, a triptych additionally comprising *The World's Ransoming* for orchestra and English horn obbligato (1995–96) and *Cello Concerto* (1996), is heard for the first time in London.

28 SEPTEMBER 1997

On the third day of the 71st Festival of the International Society for Contemporary Music continues in Seoul, four concerts are given, in the following sequence:

A morning performance, entitled "Traditional Korean Music 1," given at Seoul's Sungkyunkwan of Munmyojereak, Confucian ritual music performed by members of the Traditional Korean Music Society.

An early afternoon concert at the National Theater, outdoor stage, performed by the Korean Festival Ensemble, with special guest artist Graziela Bortz, horn, in the following program: *Layers for a Transparent Orgasm* by the Brazilian composer Arthur KAMPELA, *Homothetie et Quantité Sonores* by the Albanian composer Alexander PECI, *Fantasie Mecanique* by the Korean composer Yun-suk JIN, and new works by the Yugoslav composer Tatjana Tanya MILOSEVIC and the Dutch composer Jacques BANK.

An evening concert at the National Theater, main hall, performed by the Seoul High School of Art Symphony, with special guest artist Chae Hui-chul, cello, conducted by Yoo Bong-Hun, in the following program: *Amphora* for piano and orchestra (1993) by the Russian composer Olga RAYEVA; *Green Pig, Broken Twigs* for young people's chorus and youth orchestra (1996) by the Chinese composer Joyce Bee Tuan KOH, a musical collection of limericks written and illustrated by Edward Lear in his book entitled *The Book of Nonsense;* and *Urack* by the Korean composer Yong-shi PAKI.

An evening concert at the Yeongang Hall performed by Sylvia Nopper, soprano, Matthias Wursch, percussion, Thomas Kessler, vocals, and Wolfgang Heiniger, electronics, in the following program: *Drum 1 for Percussion* by the Korean composer Chong-hae YI, *Morite* by Giorgio TADDE, *Wassermusik* by Wolfgang HEINIGER, *Corps a Corps* by the innovative 51-year-old Greek composer Georges APERGHIS, *Bleu* by Jacques DEMIERRE, and *Voice Control* by the American composer Thomas KESSLER.

29 SEPTEMBER 1997

Overnight Mail for chamber ensemble by the energetic 36-year-old American composer and pianist Michael TORKE is given its first performance in Amsterdam.

29 SEPTEMBER 1997

On the fourth day of the 71st Festival of the International Society for Contemporary Music continues in Seoul, three concerts are given, in the following sequence:

A late afternoon concert at the National Theater, small hall, performed by America's Ensemble Continuum, conducted by co-founder and ensemble pianist Joel Sachs, in the following program: *Sky and the Song of the Deep Blue* by the Korean composer Ki-pom KIM; *Elliott Ness* by the Argentine composer Sebastian ZUBIETA; *Quartet for Piano and Strings* by the Israeli composer Betty OLIVERO; *Four on the Floor* by the spirited 46-year-old American composer Libby LARSEN; *Trio Tropical* for violin, cello, and piano (1992) by the 43-year-old Puerto Rican composer Roberto SIERRA; and *Lady Chatterly's Dream* by the American composer Jon DEAK.

An evening concert at the National Theater, main hall, performed by The Netherlands' ASKO Ensemble and the Het Trio, with special guest artist Toon van Ulsen, trombone, conducted by Stefan Asbury, in the following program: *Gramvousa* by the Dutch composer Roderik de MAN, *Westen* by the notable 65-year-old Argentine composer and pedagogue Mauricio KAGEL, *Birds and Bells* by the Danish composer Bent SØRENTSEN, and *Pot'ae-p'yung in 1997* by the Korean composer Shin-u YI.

An evening concert at the National Theater, small hall, performed by the Taegu Municipal Chorus, in the following program: *Elegie pour les villes detruites* by the prominent 70-year-old Dutch composer and teacher Ton de LEEUW; *Te Deum* for soloists, chorus, and orchestra (1978–80) by the eminent 63-year-old Polish composer, pedagogue, and conductor Polish composer Krystof PENDERECKI; *Alpabeto Apocalittico* by the Italian composer Tonino TESEI; and *Viriditas* by the English composer James DILLON.

30 SEPTEMBER 1997

Ox Mountain Was Covered by Trees for soprano, countertenor, baritone, and orchestra (1990) by the 43-year-old English composer Judith WEIR is performed for the first time in a reduced version for soprano, countertenor, and piano in London.

30 SEPTEMBER 1997

On the fifth day of the 71st Festival of the International Society for Contemporary Music in Seoul, three concerts are given, in the following sequence:

A late afternoon concert at the National Theater, small hall, performed by the Contemporary String Quartet, with special guest artist Jane Manning, soprano, in the following program: *Three Poems in French* for soprano and string quartet (1989) by the 77-year-old American composer and pedagogue of Korean descent Earl Kim, *Akroate Hadal* by Olga NEUWIRTH, and new works by both the Korean composer Choi MYUNG-HUN and the 54-year-old Spanish composer Tomás MARCO.

An evening concert at the National Theater, main hall, performed by Laughing Stone, with Maria Berquet, in a program comprised of *Landscapes of the Soul* by the German composer and performance artist Maria BERQUET and *Sori* by the Korean composer Shin-cha HONG.

An evening concert at the National Theater, small hall, performed by the Echo Ensemble, with special guest artist King Kyung-su, percussion, in the following program: *The Seafarer* by the English composer Joby TALBOT, *Zao Shin* by the Taiwanese composer Pei-Yu SHIN, *A Song Taken from a Poem by the Venerable Yongsan* by the Korean composer Chae-uk KIM, and *Neumes* for six percussionists (1996) by the 65-year-old Spanish-born Dutch composer Enrique RAXACH.

1 OCTOBER 1997

On the sixth day of the 71st Festival of the International Society for Contemporary Music in Seoul, three concerts are given, in the following sequence:

A late afternoon concert at the Arirang TV Studio, entitled "Electronic Music 2," presented by the Electronic Music Studio of the Basel Music Academy, with special guest artist Lori J. Fredrics, soprano, in the following program: *Notarimbalo* by the Polish composer Jaroslaw SIWINSKI, *Vagvisa For Mitt Ofedda Barn* by the American composer Howard FREDRICS, IZARRA, *VOJM* by the Venezuelan composer Adina, and new works by both the Uruguayan composer Cariun AHARONIAN and Ake PARMERUD.

An evening concert at the Seoul Arts Center, recital hall, performed by the Seoul Motet Chorus and S-Voclissimo, conducted by Pak Chi-yong, in the following program: *Noche oscura* by the Canadian composer Jose EVANGELISTA, *On the eve of the 2nd year anniversary of Morton's death* by the Cuban-born American composer Orlando J. GARCIA, *Go

Skin! by the Korean composer Nahn-hee CHUNG, and *Les Chants de l'Amour* for chorus and synthesizer (1982–84) by the 51-year-old French composer and teacher Gérard GRISEY.

An evening concert at the Arirang TV Studio performed by Mircea Ardeneanu, percussion, and Kurt Widmer, baritone, in the following program: *New York* by Christoph NEID-HOFER; *Assonance VII* by the French composer Michael JARREL; *Hölderlin Lieder (Hölderlin: An...)* for tenor and piano (1988–89) by the eminent 71-year-old Hungarian composer and teacher György KURTÁG; *Kassandra* for amplified baritone and percussion (1987) by the eminent 74-year-old Greek-born French composer, music theorist, and teacher Iannis XENAKIS; and *The End* by Jacques BANK.

2 OCTOBER 1997

On the seventh day of the 71st Festival of the International Society for Contemporary Music, two concerts are given, in the following sequence:

An evening performance at the Namyangju Duomul Workshop performed by Australia's Elision Ensemble, with special guest artist Deborah Kayser, soprano, conducted by Sandro Gorli, in the following program: *Voodoo Child* by the Australian composer Lisa LIM; *Time and Motion Study No. 1* for bass clarinet (1971–77) and *On Stellar Magnitudes*, two works by the 53-year-old English composer and teacher Brian FERNEYHOUGH; *Algor* by David YOUNG; *Sacred Song I* by the Korean composer Man-bang YI; and a work by the German composer Helmut LACHENMANN.

An evening concert performed by the Russian String Trio, with special guest artists Nelly Lee, soprano, and Sergei Maltcev, piano, in a program of (unspecified) works by the Armenian composer Tigran MANSURIAN, the Russian composer Alfred SCHNITTKE, the Abchazian composer Nodar CHANBA, the Israeli composer Mark KOPYTMAN, the Korean composer KIM Sunnam, and the Russian composer Edison DENISOV.

3 OCTOBER 1997

Visions for two sopranos and chamber ensemble (1993) by the 55-year-old American composer and teacher Ronald (Christopher) PERERA is given its first performance in Cambridge, Massachusetts.

3 OCTOBER 1997

On the eighth and final day of the 71st Festival of the International Society for Contemporary Music in Seoul, two concerts are given, in the following sequence:

A late afternoon performance at the Seoul Arts Center, Towol Hall, given jointly by the Salm gwa Kkum Singers, Tokyo Chamber Singers, and Chamber Ensemble (Japan), of a new chamber opera by the respected 62-year-old Korean composer Sukhi KANG.

An evening concert at the Seoul Arts Center, concert hall, performed by the Korea Chamber Music Ensemble, with special guest artists Cho Young-hae and Yoo Mi-suk, sopranos, conducted by Kim Duck-ki, in the following program: *Kon* by the Korean composer Song-on CHO, *Concerto for Cello and Chamber Orchestra* by the Croatian composer Srdan DEDIC, *I'm nobody, who are you?* by the Belgian composer Marc de HERTOGH, and *Su Ziaoziao's Tomb* by the Chinese composer Yang YONG.

4 OCTOBER 1997

The Austrian-born American conductor and opera administrator Henry HOLT, who from 1966 to 1984 was general director of the Seattle Opera, where he conducted its acclaimed Wagner Festivals, dies in Charlottesville, Virginia, at the age of 63.

5 OCTOBER 1997

Nostradamus, computer-generated piece for the Internet, by the versatile 54-year-old American composer, pianist, teacher, and writer on music William (Ervin) DUCKWORTH is heard online for the first time.

7 OCTOBER 1997

Oberon Concerto for flute and instrumental ensemble by the 46-year-old Serbian composer and teacher Zoran ERIČ is performed for the first time in his native Belgrade.

9 OCTOBER 1997

The Shadows of Time for orchestra by the distinguished 81-year-old French composer and teacher Henri DUTILLEUX is given its first ever performance in Boston.

10 OCTOBER 1997

Concerto IV for ensemble by the versatile 70-year-old English pianist, organist, conductor, writer on music, and composer Francis (John) ROUTH is performed for the first time in London.

11 OCTOBER 1997

The Prophecy for children's chorus and instruments by the 38-year-old Scottish composer, conductor, and teacher James MACMILLAN is premiered in London.

12 OCTOBER 1997

A Solemn Overture for orchestra by the prominent 52-year-old Finnish composer Aulis SALLINEN is performed for the first time in Monte Carlo.

15 OCTOBER 1997

Scree for cello, piano, and percussion by the productive 46-year-old American composer, conductor, and teacher Donald CROCKETT is heard for the first time in Bowling Green, Ohio.

17 OCTOBER 1997

D'après un eri for piano by the 58-year-old Canadian composer, pianist, and teacher (James) Bruce MATHER is premiered in Ottawa.

18 OCTOBER 1997

Hymn do świętego Wojciecha (Hymn to the Holy Adalbert) for chorus and winds by the eminent 63-year-old Polish composer, pedagogue, and conductor Krzysztof PENDERECKI is performed for the first time in Gdańsk.

19 OCTOBER 1997

Melusine, opera, by the strikingly original 61-year-old German composer, pianist, and teacher Aribert REIMANN is staged for the first time in Munich.

19 OCTOBER 1997

Concierto Clasico for piano and orchestra by the 61-year-old Mexican composer, conductor, and music educator Héctor QUINTANAR is performed for the first time in Guanajuato City.

20 OCTOBER 1997

Passacaglia for orchestra by the notable 58-year-old Brazilian composer, pianist, and conductor Marlos NOBRE receives its first ever performance in his native Recife.

22 OCTOBER 1997

The 41-year-old American tenor Bruce (Edwin) FORD makes his Metropolitan Opera debut in New York as Count Almaviva.

24 OCTOBER 1997

The prominent 53-year-old American conductor Leonard (Edward) SLATKIN, son of the American violinist and conductor Felix Slatkin, leads the National Symphony Orchestra in the opening of its refurbished concert hall at the Kennedy Center in Washington, D.C.

26 OCTOBER 1997

Third Symphony, entitled *1999*, for chorus and orchestra (1996–97) by the 45-year-old Polish composer, conductor, and teacher Aleksander LASOŃ is heard for the first time in Kraków.

29 OCTOBER 1997

The Judgement of Calliope/Das Urteil der Kalliope, satyr play, after Auden and Kallman (1964), by the outstanding 71-year-old German composer Hans Werner HENZE is mounted for the first time in Giessen.

31 OCTOBER 1997

Cosmos Haptic IV for cello and piano by the respected 68-year-old Japanese composer and teacher Jōji YUASA is performed for the first time in Tokyo.

2 NOVEMBER 1997

Salute for flute, clarinet, horn, trombone, piano, percussion, violin, and cello by the admired 47-year-old American composer, teacher, conductor, and writer on music Steven (Edward) STUCKY is given its first ever performance in Ithaca, New York.

3 NOVEMBER 1997

The spirited American percussionist and composer Michael (Gabriel) PUGLIESE, who performed extensively with the Merce Cunningham Dance Company and who also appeared as a rock drummer and made numerous rock arrangements, including one of Henry Mancini's *Peter Gunn*, for percussion quartet, dies mysteriously in New York at the pitiable age of 41.

5 NOVEMBER 1997

Songs, Dances, and Ellipses for string quartet by the 44-year-old English composer and teacher Robert (Louis

Alfred) SAXTON is heard for the first time in his native London.

7 NOVEMBER 1997

The outstanding American mezzo-soprano, later soprano, Margaret HARSHAW, who was particularly successful in Wagnerian roles, including Isolde, Sieglinde, Kundry, Elisabeth, and all three parts of Brünnhilde, dies in Libertyville, Illinois, at the respectable age of 88.

8 NOVEMBER 1997

Golden Flute for flute and orchestra by the admired 44-year-old Chinese-born American composer and teacher Chen YI is given its first performance in Duluth.

9 NOVEMBER 1997

Sufi Dance for guitar by the significant 58-year-old English composer Jonathan (Dean) HARVEY is heard for the first time in Nottingham.

11 NOVEMBER 1997

Apolytikion of St. Martin for chorus by the remarkable and prolific 53-year-old English composer John (Kenneth) TAVENER is performed for the first time in his native London.

12 NOVEMBER 1997

The fourth "Other Minds" Festival, under the artistic direction of Charles Amirkhanian, takes place at the Cowell Theater in the Fort Mason Center in San Francisco, in the following program: *Chorale Times Two* for violin and electro-acoustic band (1996–97); the second movement from the *Concerto for Violin & Electro-Acoustic Band*, and *RetroDisrespective* for electric guitar with digital delays and digital signal processing (1997), two works by the 46-year-old American composer and performer Paul (Joseph) DRESHER; *Patterns of Plants—The Seventh Collection* (1997) and *Patterns of Plants—The Fifth Collection* (1996), two works by the innovative Japanese composer Mamoru FUJIEDA; and *Ruen Pair* (1993) by the innovative 44-year-old American composer and performer Carl STONE, a computer-generated score based on a short piece of 18th-century music.

13 NOVEMBER 1997

Pensieri Sospesi for flute, clarinet, violin, viola, cello, and piano by the 56-year-old Italian-born American composer and teacher Marc-Antonio CONSOLI is given its first performance in Mexico City.

15 NOVEMBER 1997

Spring Dreams for chorus by the productive 44-year-old Chinese composer Chen YI is performed for the first time in Ithaca, New York.

18 NOVEMBER 1997

The Story Behind the Song is Forgotten for flute, oboe, clarinet, piano, cello, and percussion by the prolific 43-year-old English composer Judith WEIR is performed for the first time in London.

20 NOVEMBER 1997

Crépuscules for piano (1996) by the 51-year-old French composer Jean-Claude WOLFF is premiered in his native Paris.

21 NOVEMBER 1997

The English composer and writer on music Robert (Wilfred Levick) SIMPSON, long-time music producer of the BBC (1951–80), and winner of the Carl Nielsen Gold Medal of Denmark (1956) and the Bruckner Medal (1962), dies in Tralee, Ireland, at the age of 76.

22 NOVEMBER 1997

Quatuor VI: Avec clarinette for clarinet and string trio by the distinguished 71-year-old French-American composer and teacher Betsy JOLAS, daughter of the poet and journalist Eugène Jolas, best known as the founder and editor of the literary journal *transition*, is heard for the first time over Paris's Radio France.

23 NOVEMBER 1997

Wolf Lieder: In der Frühe, Um Mitternacht, Das verlassene Mägdlein, and *Nun wandre, Maria*, orchestrated by the innovative 51-year-old French composer and teacher Gérard GRISEY for mezzo-soprano and instrumental ensemble, are heard for the first time over Paris's Radio France.

26 NOVEMBER 1997

The admired 32-year-old Austrian mezzo-soprano Angelika KIRCHSCHLAGER makes her Metropolitan Opera debut in New York as Annio.

27 NOVEMBER 1997

Reflections on a Martyrdom for orchestra by the distinguished 70-year-old South African-born English composer and teacher John (Pierre Herman) JOUBERT is performed for the first time in Birmingham.

28 NOVEMBER 1997

Slow Right Arm for double bass and Baroque violin by the 47-year-old English composer, conductor, writer on music, and teacher Roger (Michael) MARSH is heard for the first time in Huddersfield.

3 DECEMBER 1997

Iphis, opera, by the 40-year-old Uzbekistan-born Australian composer Elena KATS-CHERNIN is mounted for the first time in Sydney.

4 DECEMBER 1997

The Selfish Giant, choreographic tone poem, by the 47-year-old American composer and teacher Jay REISE is heard for the first time in London.

6 DECEMBER 1997

Dopo la vittoria for chorus by the outstanding 62-year-old Estonian-born Austrian composer Arvo PÄRT is given its first ever performance in Milan.

7 DECEMBER 1997

When Famous Last Words Fail You for baritone, chorus, and orchestra, the first installment of the monumental series of *Immortality Songs* by the pioneering 67-year-old American composer, performer, director, and writer Robert ASHLEY is performed for the first time by the American Composers Orchestra at New York's Carnegie Hall, Thomas Buchner, baritone, Sam Ashley, Jacqueline Humbert, and Joan LaBarbara comprising the chorus, with Tom Hamilton, electronics, and conducted by Dennis Russel Davies. (Also on the program is the world premiere of *Microsymph* by the lesser-known American composer Sebastian Currier, a five-movement symphony squeezed into ten minutes and including a 60-billion nanosecond scherzo.)

8 DECEMBER 1997

Chansons cachées for piano by the eminent 82-year-old American composer, music theorist, and pedagogue George PERLE is heard for the first time in Boston.

9 DECEMBER 1997

Certus for orchestra by the 36-year-old Polish composer Hanna KULENTY is performed for the first time in Amsterdam.

11 DECEMBER 1997

The Raft for voices, dancers, and string quartet by the accomplished 47-year-old Canadian composer Michael (Bass) MATTHEWS is given its first performance in Winnipeg.

12 DECEMBER 1997

Cello Concerto by the gifted 48-year-old South African-born Irish composer Kevin VOLANS is performed for the first time in Munich.

13 DECEMBER 1997

Brooklyn, October 5, 1941 for piano, baseballs, and catcher's mitt by the experimental 37-year-old American composer, instrumentalist, improviser, and sampling specialist Annie (actually, Anne) GOSFIELD is given its first performance in New York.

18 DECEMBER 1997

The Argentine conductor Michelangelo VELTRI, who ended his varied career as artistic director of the Teatro Colón in Buenos Aires, and who as a guest conductor appeared in Vienna, Berlin, Salzburg, Amsterdam, Paris, Marseilles, Monte Carlo, Turin, Philadelphia, and Washington, D.C., dies in his native Buenos Aires at the lamentable age of 57.

19 DECEMBER 1997

Ka Himeni Hehena (in the Hawaiian language, The Raving Mad Hymn) for four speaking voices and tape by the multi-talented 52-year-old American avant-garde composer, influential radio producer, and arts administrator of Armenian descent Charles (Benjamin) AMIRKHANIAN is performed for the first time in Paris at the Cité de la Musique, Salle des Concerts, the second of three concerts in a series called "Amérique: Made in the USA," the composer performing with conductor David Robertson, utilizing a tape of prerecorded sounds drawn from a concert of the Ensemble Intercontemporain.

19 DECEMBER 1997

The notable 44-year-old Russian conductor Valery (Abissalovich) GERGIEV, from 1997 principal guest conductor of the Metropolitan Opera in New York, conducts the orchestra there in the first performance of Buketoff's edition of *Boris Godunov.*

23 DECEMBER 1997

My Guardian Angel for chorus and audience by the respected 43-year-old English composer Judith WEIR is heard for the first time in London.

25 DECEMBER 1997

The Italian opera director Giorgio STREHLER, who was closely associated with the Théâtre de l'Europe at the Odéon in Paris and whose background as an actor was instrumental in forging his vision of the serious and comic elements of theatrical scores, particularly in his productions of works by Mozart and Verdi, dies in Lugano at the age of 76.

1998

3 JANUARY 1998

The American musicologist Louise (Elvira) CUYLER, long-time faculty member at the University of Michigan (1929–42; 1945–75), later (1975) becoming the Neilson Distinguished Professor at Smith College, and whose publications included *The Emperor Maximilian I and Music* (London, 1973) and *The Symphony* (N.Y., 1973; 2nd ed., 1995), dies in beautiful Carmel-by-the-Sea, California, at the age of 92.

6 JANUARY 1998

The Russian composer and pianist Georgi (Vasilevich) SVIRIDOV, whose *Oratorio pathétique* (1959) was one of the most successful works by a Soviet composer as per the tenets of socialist realism, dies in Moscow at the age of 82.

11 JANUARY 1998

The Czech composer Miroslav RAICHL, whose career was largely devoted to teaching and administrative work in the Union of Czechoslovak Composers, dies in Pardubice at the age of 67.

13 JANUARY 1998

Miranda's Lament for soprano, clarinet, harp, violin, and contrabass (1997) by the significant 45-year-old Finnish composer Kaija (Anneli) SAARIAHO is heard for the first time in Järvenpää.

14 JANUARY 1998

The German composer, conductor, and pedagogue Peter Jona KORN, whose compositional style was a pragmatic Romanticism marked by polycentric tonality in the framework of strong rhythmic counterpoint, dies in Munich at the age of 75.

15 JANUARY 1998

The eminent Italian musicologist Nico (actually, Antonino) PIRROTTA, an erudite scholar of wide interests who greatly distinguished himself in the study of Renaissance polyphony and Baroque opera, and whose important books included *Music and Culture in Italy from the Middle Ages to the Baroque: A Collection of Essays* (Cambridge, Mass., and London, 1984) and *Don Giovanni's Progress: A Rake Goes to the Opera* (N.Y., 1994), dies in his native Palermo at the age of 89.

16 JANUARY 1998

Pulcinellas Erzählungen for chamber orchestra, after the ballet *Le disperazioni del Signor Pulcinella* (1996), *Zigeunerweisen und Sarabanden* for orchestra, after the ballet *Le fils de l'air* (1996), and *Minotauros Blues* for six percussionists (1996), three works by the outstanding 71-year-old German composer Hans Werner HENZE, are premiered in Cologne.

17 JANUARY 1998

Fourth String Quartet (1997) by the 56-year-old American composer, pianist, and teacher Richard (Edward) WILSON is performed for the first time in New York.

24 JANUARY 1998

Marie Antoinette, opera (1996–97), by the 54-year-old Swedish composer Daniel BÖRTZ is staged for the first time in Stockholm.

26 JANUARY 1998

The outstanding 34-year-old German violinist Anne-Sophie MUTTER and the distinguished 51-year-old American pianist, fortepianist, and teacher Lambert (Thomas) ORKIS open their marathon tour in Hannover, which will continue on to such cities as Berlin, Zürich, Madrid, Amsterdam, Rome, N.Y., Chicago, Philadelphia, Boston, Los Angeles, Dresden, Milan, Paris, London, Shanghai, Seoul, Buenos Aires, and Vienna before concluding with a benefit concert at the Beethovenhaus in Bonn on Dec. 17, 1998.

29 JANUARY 1998

The Capeman, the first-ever musical by the popular 48-year-old American singer, guitarist, and songwriter Paul SIMON, based on the troubled and troublesome life of the teenage Puerto Rican gang leader Salvador "The Capeman" Agron who, convicted in 1959 of the merciless killing of two rival gang members, was sentenced to death at the age of 16 (but was subsequently pardoned, in 1979, by then-governor Nelson Rockefeller, only to die seven years later), co-written with Nobel laureate Derek Walcott, with sets and costumes by Bob Crowley, and with directors in succession too numerous to mention, merging doo-wop, gospel, salsa, and rock 'n' roll, opens at the Marquis Theatre in New York. (The work, financially unsuccessful in the extreme, closed on March 28, 1998, after 59 previews and 68 performances.)

30 JANUARY 1998

The American tenor Richard CASSILLY, who from his debut as Radames on January 20, 1973, enjoyed a lengthy association with the Metropolitan Opera, appearing from 1978 in such roles as Tannhäuser, Don José, Tristan, Samson, Otello, Jimmy Mahoney in *Mahagonny*, and Captain Vere in *Billy Budd*, dies in Boston on the age of 70.

31 JANUARY 1998

The 42-year-old American soprano Barbara BONNEY, wife of the outstanding Swedish baritone Håkan Hagegård, makes her Carnegie Hall recital debut in New York.

4 FEBRUARY 1998

The esteemed American conductor and teacher Margaret (Eleanor) HILLIS, from 1957 until her retirement in 1994 the able conductor of the chorus of the Chicago Symphony Orchestra (under Fritz Reiner), dies in Evanston, Illinois, at the age of 76.

7 FEBRUARY 1998

Sechs Gesänge nach Fragmenten von Nietzsche for mezzo-soprano and orchestra (1997) by the 49-year-old German composer and Intendant Peter RUZICKA is given its first ever performance in Stuttgart.

8 FEBRUARY 1998

Sonoris causa for orchestra (1997) by the 72-year-old Croatian-born French composer, conductor, and teacher Ivo MALEC is performed for the first time in Paris.

11 FEBRUARY 1998

Lorca Sketches for strings by the accomplished 47-year-old Canadian composer Michael (Bass) MATTHEWS is heard for the first time in Winnipeg.

14 FEBRUARY 1998

The French composer Antoine TISNÉ, who from 1967 to 1992 served as an inspector of music for the French Ministry of Culture, dies in Paris at the age of 65.

15 FEBRUARY 1998

The versatile American composer, conductor, lexicographer, and publishing executive Arthur COHN, long-time Director of Serious Music at Carl Fischer and author of such useful books as *The Collector's Twentieth-Century Music in the Western Hemisphere* (N.Y., 1961), *Twentieth-Century Music in Western Europe* (N.Y., 1965), *Recorded Classical Music: A Critical Guide to Compositions and Performances* (N.Y., 1981), *The Encyclopedia of Chamber Music* (N.Y., 1990), and *The Literature of Chamber Music* (4 vols., Chapel Hill, 1997), dies in New York at the age of 87.

17 FEBRUARY 1998

The Swiss-born Dutch pianist, teacher, and composer Luctor PONSE, long-time member (from 1964) of the Institute for Sonology at the University of Utrecht and also founder of the electronic music studio at the Groningen Conservatory, dies in Amsterdam at the age of 83.

18 FEBRUARY 1998

Phoenix Rising for orchestra (1997) by the remarkable 69-year-old Scottish composer Thea MUSGRAVE is performed for the first time in London.

19 FEBRUARY 1998

The American country-music singer, guitarist, and banjo player Grandpa (actually, Louis Marshall) JONES, whose recording of *Mountain Dew* (1947) was a popular favorite in the comedic country genre, dies in Nashville, Tennessee, at the age of 84.

20 FEBRUARY 1998

Farewell Music for orchestra (1997) by the remarkable 54-year-old Polish composer and teacher Krzysztof MEYER is performed for the first time in Warsaw.

25 FEBRUARY 1998

Elegia per Carlo Michelstaedter for oboe and instruments by the 41-year-old Italian composer, conductor, teacher, and writer on music Alberto CAPRIOLI is heard for the first time in Bologna.

28 FEBRUARY 1998

The black American baritone (Robert) Todd DUNCAN, creator of the role of Porgy in Gershwin's *Porgy and Bess* in New York (Oct. 10, 1935) and subsequently the first black American to become a member of a major opera company when he made his first appearance at the New York Opera City on Sept. 28, 1945, as Tonio, dies in Washington, D.C. at the seasoned age of 95.

1 MARCH 1998

The Greek conductor Miltiades CARIDIS, successively chief conductor of the Philharmonia Hungarica in Marl kreis Recklinghausen (1960–67), chief conductor of the Oslo Philharmonia (1969–75), Generalmusikdirektor of the Duisburg Symphony Orchestra (1975–81), and chief conductor of the Niederösterreichisches Tonkünstler Orchestra in Vienna (1981–85), dies in Athens at the age of 74.

7 MARCH 1998

The distinguished Austrian soprano Leonie RYSANEK, much loved for her performances in such roles as Kostelnička in *Jenůfa* in San Francisco (1986) and Kabanicha in *Kat'á Kabanová* in Los Angeles (1988), and whose lesser-known younger sister Lotte Rysanek (b. Vienna, March 18, 1928) attained a fine reputation in Vienna as a lyric soprano, dies in her native Vienna at the age of 71.

8 MARCH 1998

The 50-year-old American composer and teacher Neil (Burton) ROLNICK and the 59-year-old American composer Joel CHADABE, having joined forces in 1995 on 2 Places @ Once, an ongoing project exploiting the possibilities of teleconferenced musical and video performance, give their first ever public performance simultaneously at The Kitchen in New York and the Electronic Cafe International in Santa Monica, California.

10 MARCH 1998

Burnham Wick for orchestra (1997) by the 55-year-old English composer and writer on music David (John) MATTHEWS, brother of the 52-year-old English composer, writer on music, and broadcaster Colin Matthews, is heard for the first time in Birmingham.

12 MARCH 1998

Fresco for orchestra (1997) by the 39-year-old Finnish composer Magnus (Gustaf Adolf) LINDBERG is performed for the first time in Los Angeles.

14 MARCH 1998

Little Concerto for Strings (1961) by the significant 58-year-old English composer Jonathan (Dean) HARVEY is heard for the first time in its 1997 revised version in London.

17 MARCH 1998

Kanon pokajanen for chorus by the outstanding 62-year-old Estonian-born Austrian composer Arvo PÄRT is given its premiere performance in Cologne.

19 MARCH 1998

Virgin Mother Creatrix for chorus by the talented 59-year-old American composer Barbara KOLB is heard for the first time in Indiana, Pennsylvania.

22 MARCH 1998

Regina, opera (1848), by the celebrated German composer (Gustav) Albert LORTZING (1801–1851), with a libretto by the composer revised by Adolf L'Arronge and first performed in Berlin on March 21, 1899 as *Regina, oder Die Marodeure,* is staged for the first time in its original version in a new critical edition in Gelsenkirchen.

26 MARCH 1998

Violin Concerto (1997) by the remarkable 58-year-old American composer Ellen Taaffe ZWILICH is performed for the first time in New York.

29 MARCH 1998

Canto VIII: Shir Hashirim-Lied der Lieder for soloists, chorus, live electronics, and orchestra (1992–96) by the distinguished 61-year-old German conductor, composer, and pedagogue (Johannes Wolfgang) Hans ZENDER receives its first complete performance in Saarbrücken.

31 MARCH 1998

The American musician Donald KNAACK (aka The Junkman) unveils the first of six musical playstations, *The Rasping Rack,* effectively recycling found scrap wood, metal, plastic, and other materials into imaginative "instruments" upon which he performs, at Stratton Mountain, Vermont, who commissioned the work, before a rapt (if slightly mystified) audience of skiers and snowboarders.

3 APRIL 1998

The Canadian choral conductor, teacher, and editor Elmer (Walter) ISELER, especially known for his interpretations of masterworks from the Tudor and 20th century eras and an ardent champion of the music of Healey Willan, dies in Toronto at the age of 70.

6 APRIL 1998

Quintet for clarinet and strings (1995) by the 58-year-old Canadian composer, pianist, and teacher (James) Bruce MATHER is first performed in Montreal.

10 APRIL 1998

Manuel de Résurrection for mezzo-soprano and two samplers by the multi-talented 63-year-old French composer, musicologist, and philologist François-Bernard MÂCHE is heard for the first time over Paris's Radio France.

11 APRIL 1998

The loveable French-born American composer of Russian descent Ivan (Alexandrovich) TCHEREPNIN, who hailed from a remarkably musical family that included his father, Alexander (Nikolaievich) Tcherepnin, and his brother of Serge (Alexandrovich) Tcherepnin, dies in Boston at the pitiable age of 55.

13 APRIL 1998

The San Francisco Contemporary Music Players is joined by virtuoso guitarist David Tanenbaum and virtuoso percussionist William Winant for a program which includes the premiere performances of *Peque ño Concierto* by the significant 44-year-old Puerto Rican composer Roberto SIERRA, *Dias de los Muertos* for guitar and percussion by the seminal 62-year-old American composer and performer Terry (Mitchell) RILEY, and *Transcription* for strings and percussion, based on Buddhist chant from the native country of the ascending Korean composer Hyo-shin NA, at San Francisco's Yerba Buena Center for the Arts.

14 APRIL 1998

Strong on Oaks, Strong on the Causes of Oaks for orchestra (1997) by the noteworthy 54-year-old English composer, conductor, and writer on music Michael (Laurence) NYMAN is heard for the first time in his native London.

15 APRIL 1998

Concerto for harpsichord, oboe, and strings, a reconstruction of J.S. Bach's BWV 1059, by the multifaceted 56-year-old American organist, harpsichordist, fortepianist, conductor, and composer Anthony NEWMAN is performed for the first time in Seattle.

17 APRIL 1998

Sea Dreams by the innovative 54-year-old American composer David MASLANKA is premiered simultaneously in a unique "netcast" over the Internet on seven university campuses from Oregon to New York.

17 APRIL 1998

The 72nd Festival of the International Society for Contemporary Music opens in Manchester with three events, in the following sequence:

A late-afternoon performance outside of The Bridgewater Hall, during rush hour, by Urban Strawberry Lunch, the world's finest ensemble of scrap instrumentalists, of *A Good Hoot,* wherein the instruments of the ensemble are joined by "...the instrument too often pressed in anger and frustration: the car horn."

An evening concert at The Bridgewater Hall performed by the BBC Philharmonic Orchestra, with special guest artist Peter Donohoe, piano, conducted by Peter Maxwell Davies, in the following program: *Angels* (1920–21) by the American composer Carl RUGGLES (1876–1971), *Windows* (1996) by the Dutch composer Jan Rokus van ROOSENDAEL, *Piano Concerto in D* for the left hand alone (written for Paul Wittgenstein, 1929–30) by the great French composer Maurice RAVEL (1875–1937), in three movements, *Lento, allegro,* and *tempo primo,* and *Worldes Blis,* "motet" for orchestra by the eminent 63-year-old English composer and conductor Peter Maxwell DAVIES.

A late night concert at The Bridgewater Hall, "Duos for Classical Accordions," performed by James Crabb and Geir Draugsvoll, accordionists, in the following program: *A Conversation with a Shadow* by the 61-year-old Polish composer Zbegniew BARGIELSKI; *De Profundis* for solo accordion by the remarkable 66-year-old Russian composer Sofia GUBAIDULINA, in one movement, dedicated to Friedrich Lips, who premiered the work in Moscow in 1980, its title referring to the Latin version of Psalm 130, "Out of the depths I cry to thee, O Lord," with the psalm verses symbolically presented in the music; *Jeux d'anches* for solo accordion (1990) by the 39-year-old Finnish composer Magnus LINDBERG; *On the Banks of the Eternal Second* (1995) by the 46-year-old Norwegian composer Magnar ÅM; *Kommos* (1995) by Klaus Ib JORGENSEN; *Music for Duo* by Valdis ZILVERIS; and Three Tangoes: *Escualo, Oblivion,* and *Fear* by the fiery Argentine bandoneón player, bandleader, composer, and arranger Astor PIAZZOLLA (1921–1992).

18 APRIL 1998

On the second day of the 72nd Festival of the International Society for Contemporary Music in Manchester, eleven events are given, in the following sequence:

A noon-time performance in front of Manchester's Town Hall of *Horn Concerto* (for an Orchestra of Automobiles) by the 55-year-old American composer Stephen MONTAGUE, displaying in a brief ten minutes "...the automobile's inherent musical talents and its natural flair for gesture, polish and rapt attention."

A noon-time performance at the Castlefield Viaducts of *Resonating Arch* by the English electronic artist Joseph HYDE, "...reflecting the history of the Castlefields area as a vital rail and waterways transport and communications hub for the city, from former glories such as Central Station (now the GMEX Centre) to the newly-built Bridgewater Canal."

A noon-time installation opening at Manchester's Town Hall of two works: *Corridors of Power,* a collaborative, interactive installation by Alexandra JULYAN, visual artist/sculptor, and Cameron SINCLAIR, composer, comprising a guided tour around Manchester's Town Hall, suggesting just a few of the things that can happen behind closed doors; and *Standing Waves* by the English composer Joseph L. ANDERSON, a site specific installation of automated acousmatic music, revealing the "...implicit harmonies and tunes our ears to the strange music and grand measure of Manchester Town Hall."

An early afternoon installation opening at The Green Room *Bird Organ* by Isobel BOWLER and Michael WOLTERS, situated around a bush set in the middle of the Green Room, the initial bird songs eventually completely replaced by the sounds of the various activities of New Music '98. (Note: A bird organ is a miniature forerunner of the barrel organ invented in the 17th century, originally used to teach songbirds to sing tunes.)

An early afternoon event at The Bridgewater Hall by Urban Strawberry Lunch performing *Ambient Blx,* a forerunner to the performance to follow of *Song of the Building,* an installation culminating in performances inside and outside the Bridgewater Hall, using the architectural forms expressed in the building and applying them to music, with weird and wonderful sonic devices which react to human, urban, and environmental stimulation.

An early afternoon concert at the RNCM Lord Rhodes Room entitled "ICCC (Inter-Conservatoire Composers' Consortium) Festival (I)," performed by the RNCM New Ensemble, in the following program: *Hypermusic* (1997) by the English composer Tim BENJAMIN, for 12 players arranged in three widely spaced groups of four, a musical equivalent to hypertext, a literary technique in which the reader chooses a path through the text by following linked words, in six movements; *Heat Death* by the largely self-taught English composer Colin SUTTON, in four movements wherein the woodwinds (hot) and strings (cold) come into contact with each other; *November night-gathering of seven lonely yoru-no-tsuru* by the Uruguayan composer Reynaldo YOUNG (Note: the composer explains: "*tsuru* - amazing bird-like creature of the origami family, thus living in appropriately folded paper popular for preventing illness as for being carrier of good fortune [curiously without being aware of these properties themselves], and *yoro-no-tsuru* - that specimen which stubbornly insists on wandering single and by night, strangely enough considering that they are not gifted with good night-vision and that they really would enjoy each other's company, if they had any chance"); and *A mirror on which to dwell* by the outstanding 89-year-old American composer and teacher Elliott CARTER, cycle of six songs for soprano and chamber ensemble to poems by Elizabeth Bishop: *Anaphora, Argument, Sandpiper, Insomnia, View of the Capitol from the Library of Congress,* and *A Breath.*

An early afternoon launch of the Green Room as the Festival Music Technology Centre with an installation of Sound Intermedia's *Festival Jukebox,* a cutting-edge, 8-channel surround sound loudspeaker system, giving demonstrations, workshops, and hands-on remixing sessions.

A mid-afternoon performance aboard the Walk The Plank Theatre Ship, Salford Quays, performed by COMA (Contemporary Music Making for Amateurs), conducted by Michael Finnissy, with sound projection by Stephen Montague, of *The Sinking of the Titanic* for orchestra and tape (1995) by the significant 55-year-old English composer Gavin BRYARS, a multimedia, meditative collage work composed of excerpts from pieces the drowning orchestra might have been playing as it sank into the sea.

A late afternoon concert at the RCNM Sema Group Concerto Hall performed by PSAPPHA, conducted by Paul MacAlindin, in the following program: *Canto de ascensión y recuerdo* for flute, B-flat clarinet, violin, and cello (1992–93) by the Argentine composer Arturo GERVASONI, in two parts, based on common elements found in music of all styles throughout history (tension and release, continuity and discontinuity, etc.); *Horn Trio* by the eminent 64-year-old Hungarian-born Austrian composer and pedagogue György LIGETI, in four movements: *Andantino con tenerezza, Vivacissimo molti ritmico, Alla marcia,* and *Lamento: Adagio,* an "homage" to Johannes Brahms; *Profits d'outremer* for wind, brass, and strings (1997) by the Taiwanese composer Sue-Ya WANG; *Echo Canyon* for chamber ensemble (1995) by the 37-year-old Japanese composer Karen TANAKA, inspired by Utah's Bryce Canyon; and *Khorovod* (Round Dance) for fifteen players (1994) by the English composer Julian ANDERSON, drawing on Russian, Turkish, Romanian, and Lithuanian melodies.

An evening performance at the RNCM Siemens Opera Theatre performed by the Arditti String Quartet and Nash Ensemble, with special guest artist, Claron McFadden, soprano soloist, conducted by Andrea Quinn, with a pre-concert conversation featuring Sir Harrison Birtwistle and Sir John Drummond, of *Pulse Shadows* for soprano, string quartet and ensemble of two clarinets, viola, cello, and double bass by the eminent 63-year-old English composer Harrison BIRTWISTLE, a flexible conjoining of *Nine Movements for String*

Quartet (five Fantazias and four Friezes) (1991–96) and *Nine Settings of* [Paul] *Celan* for soprano, two clarinets, viola, cello, and double bass (1989–96).

An evening performance at The Green Room by the Base Chorus & Unity Theatre of *The Golden Boy,* a darkly comic music theatre drama by the English composer Patrick DINEEN.

An evening installation opening on the 12th floor, Sunlight House, Quay St., of *Look Out,* for voice, instruments, and sampler within a large-scale video installation presented high over the city by the English composers Keith JOHNSON and Alex BRADLEY.

19 APRIL 1998

Fiddle Suite for huqin and strings (1997) by the 45-year-old Chinese composer and teacher Chen YI is heard for the first time in Tokyo.

19 APRIL 1998

On the third day of the 72nd Festival of the International Society for Contemporary Music in Manchester, seven concerts are given, in the following sequence:

A late morning concert at the RNCM Sema Group Concert Hall entitled "ICCC Festival (II)," performed by The Pentagon Ensemble (from the RSAMD), conducted by Joel Thomas, in the following program: *Five Pieces* by the Australian composer Christine MCCOMBE; *To Each Other Strangers* by the English composer Sonja GROSSNER, in three movements; *Wind Quintet* by the youthful English composer Jayson MACKIE, in two movements; and *6 Bagatelles* (1953) by the eminent 64-year-old Hungarian-born Austrian composer and pedagogue György LIGETI : I, *Allegro con spirito,* II, *Rubato, Lamentoso,* III, *Allegro grazioso,* IV, *Presto ruvido,* and V, *Adagio, Mesto (Béla Bartók in memoriam).*

A mid-day concert at the City Art Gallery Pre-Raphaelite Room performed by London's Arditti String Quartet, in a program comprised of a solo, a duo, a trio, and a quartet, exploring the full range of the ensemble: *Glosse,* for string quartet, by the eminent 72-year-old Italian composer, conductor, and pedagogue Luciano BERIO; an obligatory finalists' piece to the Borciani Competition, *Envoûtements I* (1996) for solo violin by the French composer Suzanne GIRAUD; *Traumwerk,* 12 duos for two violins (1995), by the Scottish-born English composer James DILLON, its title derived from Albrecht Durer's descrption of his enigmatic and inventively playful "marginalia," designed for the prayer book commissioned by the Emperor Maximillian in 1515; and *String Trio* (1995) by the respected 55-year-old English composer and teacher Brian FERNEYHOUGH, "a series of inter-locking, large-scale units and a series of shorter 'interventions'," making something which "more closely resembles a cassation or baroque trio sonata than any of the sonata-form derivatives typical of the quartet."

An early afternoon performance at the Palace Hotel Ballroom by the Manchester Camerata, with special guest vocalists, Eleanor Bron and Sam West, conducted by Gregory Rose supported by the William Walton Foundation, of *Façade* (1921) by the eminent English composer Sir William WALTON (1902–1983), an "entertainment" for small chamber ensemble to poems by Edith Sitwell declaimed by speakers in notated rhythms.

A mid-afternoon concert at the RNCM Sema Group Concert Hall performed by COMA, conducted by Simon Foxley, in the following program: *The Forest of Clocks,* for voices, orchestra, and assorted small percussion, including metronomes and ping pong balls by the English composer Philip CASHIAN; to texts by Neruda, Lorca, and Kathleen Raine; *Dark Sun* by the 55-year-old American composer Stephen MONTAGUE, an orchestral threnody incorporating period radio broadcast recordings, first performed in 1995 during the 50th anniversary week of the bombing of Hiroshima and Nagasaki; and *Aspects of Leaving* by the prominent 65-year-old Danish composer and pedagogue Per NØRGÅRD.

A late afternoon concert at the RNCM Sema Group Concert Hall entitled "ICCC Festival III," performed by the Guildhall New Music Ensemble, conducted by Pablo Gonzalez, in the following program: *South of the City* (1997) by the English composer William ATTWOOD; *Kantak* for piccolo and instrumental ensemble by the Spanish-born English composer Gabriel ERKOREKA, influenced by Basque folklore in its melodic elements and its varied, irregular rhythms; *Requiescat* by the English composer Luke BEDFORD, inspired by Oscar Wilde's poetic lament of the same name; and *Nonet* for violin, viola, cello, double bass, flute, clarinet, oboe, bassoon, and horn (1959) by the remarkable Czech-born American composer Bohuslav MARTINŮ (1890–1959).

An evening concert at The Bridgewater Hall performed by Joanna MacGregor, piano, with special guest Iain Ballamy, saxophone, and Andrew Stones, digital projections,* in the following program: Hughe Ashton's *Ground,* for solo piano, by the great English composer William BYRD (c.1540–1623), found in the first volume of the Fitzwilliam Virginal Book; *Traced Overhead,* for piano, by the remarkable 28-year-old English composer and pianist Thomas ADÈS, in three movements, *I: Sursum: Velocissimo quasi senza peso, II: Aetheria: Giusto e chiarissimo,* and *III: Chori; Forlorn Hope Fancy* by the great English composer and famous lutenist John DOWLAND (1563–1626), one of his most solitary lute pieces; *Harrison's Clocks* by the eminent 63-year-old English composer Harrison BIRTWISTLE, in four movements, *Clock I, II, III,* and *IV* (although only *I, II,* and *IV* were performed here); *Contrapunctus No. 2* from the unfinished *The Art of the Fugue* by the most revered member of the illustrious Bach family, Johann Sebastian BACH (1685–1750); *Player Piano Studies Nos. 3c, 6,* and *11* by the remarkable American-born Mexican composer Conlon NANCARROW (1912–1997), innovator in the technique of recording notes on a player-piano roll; *Tango* and *Piano Rag Music* by the great Russian-born French, later American composer, one of the supreme masters of 20th-century music, whose works exercised the most profound influence on the evolution of music through the emancipation of rhythm, melody, and harmony, Igor STRAVINSKY (1882–1971); *Nashville Nightingale,* in an arrangement by Michael Finnissy, by the immensely gifted American composer George GERSHWIN (1898–1937); *42nd St.,* in an arrangement by Alasdair Nicolson, by Harry WARREN; *Piano Variations* (1930) by the greatly distinguished and exceptionally gifted American composer Aaron COPLAND (1900–1990); and *Walpurgis Night* by Iain BALLAMY.

A late-night performance at The Bridgewater Hall by Django Bates' Human Chain, comprised of Bates (keyboard/horn), Iain Ballamy (alto sax), Michael Mondesir (bass guitar), and Martin France (drums), joined by Joanna MacGregor (piano) for the first half of the performance.

Some Charts to Go By: Digital Projections for Joanna MacGregor. Macintosh-based sequences related to both the artist's moving-image work and various manipulations of archive drawings and photographs he has typically presented as image/text works, light-boxes, or large-scale transparency projections within installations.

20 APRIL 1998

On the fourth day of the 72nd Festival of the International Society for Contemporary Music in Manchester, four concerts are given, in the following sequence:

An early afternoon concert at the RNCM Lord Rhodes Room performed by the RNCM Chamber Ensemble, with special guests artists Zygmunt Krause, piano, and Jonathan Scott, harpsichord conducted by Garry Walker, in the following program: *Piano Quintet* (1993) by the 59-year-old Polish pianist and composer Zygmunt KRAUZE, comprised of five independent instrumental songs linked by interludes to form a lyrical suite cosisting of images and promenades, first composed for the opening of an exhibition of Wladyslaw Strzeminski's art works; *Mystic Play of Shadows* (1995), string quartet movement, by the American-born Irish composer Jane O'LEARY; and *Concerto* for harpsichord, flute, oboe, clarinet, violin, and cello (1926) by the great Spanish composer Manuel (Maria) de FALLA (y Matheu) (1876-1946).

A late afternoon program at The Green Room of electro-acoustic music performed by Sound Intermedia's surround-sound Festival Jukebox, in the following program: *Nuit Cendre* (1996) by the Canadian composer Gilles GOBEIL, a free adaptation of the underground worlds described in Jules Verne's *Journey to the Centre of the Earth; Jeux Imaginaires* (1993) by the Swedish photographer-turned-composer and artist Åke PARMERUD, a fantasy on time and strategies found in a famous game of chess (Karpov v. Kasparov, 22nd round, World Championship, 1992); and *Figuras Flamencas* (1995) by the Brazilian composer Mario VERANDI, with source materials including samples from Spanish flamenco music and spoken texts from Lorca's *Blood Wedding*.

An evening concert at the RNCM Sema Group Concert Hall performed by the RNCM Symphony Orchestra & New Ensemble, with the UK Conservatories Ensemble, conducted by Elgar Howarth, Baldur Brönniman, and Clark Rundell, and joined by special guest artist Tomoko Mukalyama, piano, voice, and koto, in the following program: *Koexistenz für Zwei Gruppen* (1996–97) by the Korean composer Jontae HA, in five parts, each with a melody called *Sorigeul*, treated in different ways and expressing a theme in the Bible; *Tao* for solo piano, four women's voices, and orchestra (1996) by the significant 48-year-old Dutch composer and teacher Louis ANDRIESSEN, the second part of a larger work in three movements; *Trilogy of the Last Day, Tiroirs* (1997) by the English composer David SAWER, in one continuous movement made up of interlocking episodes; *Concerto* for nine instruments, op.24 (1934) by the remarkable Austrian composer Anton WEBERN (1883–1945); and *Memorial* for large orchestra (1992–93) by the 52-year-old English composer, writer on music, record producer, and broadcaster Colin MATTHEWS.

A late-night program of electro-acoustic music at The Green Room performed by Sound Intermedia's surround-sound Festival Jukebox, in the following program: *Cympergon* (1995) by the Chinese composer and visual artist Joyce Wai-chung TANG, exploring the timbral potential of originally recorded sound samples of cymbal, paper, and gong; *Nemietoia* (1994) by the Brazilian composer Rodolfo CAESAR, its title an anagram of *meia-noite* (midnight); and *Crystal Music* (1993) by the Canadian composer Stéfane ROY.

20 APRIL 1998

The Austrian musicologist Othmar WESSELY, long-time president of the Publishing Society for Monuments of Music in Austria (1974–1991) and author of such noteworthy books as *Musik in Oberösterreich* (Linz, 1951), *Die Musikinstrumentsammlung des Oberösterreichischen Lan-*

desmuseums (Linz, 1952), *Johann Joseph Fux und Johann Mattheson* (Graz, 1966), *Johann Joseph Fux und Francesco Antonio Vallotti* (Graz, 1967), *Pietro Pariatis Libretto zu Johann Joseph Fuxens "Costanza e fortezza"* (Graz, 1969), and *Johann Joseph Fux: Persönlichkeit, Umwelt, Nachwelt* (Graz, 1979), dies in Vienna at the age of 75.

21 APRIL 1998

On the fifth day of the 72nd Festival of the International Society for Contemporary Music in Manchester, five concerts are given, in the following sequence:

A late afternoon program of electro-acoustic music at The Green Room performed by Sound Intermedia's surround-sound Festival Jukebox, in the following program: *Del cuadro a la postergación* (1994) by the Brazilian composer Patricia MARTÍNEZ, based on the painting *The nail in the picture* by Gunter Eucker; *Phrenos* (1997) by the German composer Ludger BRUEMMER; and *Klang, Kar und Melodie* (1996) by the American composer Mark WINGATE, a tape piece inspired by the ultra-organized, super-rational, post-12-tone academic serialism of the late 20th century.

A late afternoon concert at the RNCM Sema Group Concert Hall performed by the RNCM Wind Orchestra, with special guest artists Stephen Wibley, marimba, Ben Palmer, xylophone, and Sophie Hastings, percussion, conducted by Clark Rundell, in the following program: *Marimba Spiritual* (1984) by the Japanese composer Minoru MIKI, dedicated to Keiko Abe, the virtuoso solo part accompanied by three percussionists who, free to choose within their groups of instruments, play in turn on metallic and wooden instruments and drums; *Concertino for Xylophone* (1962; rev. 1967) by the Hungarian composer Istvan LANG; and *Zildjian concerto* for percussion and symphonic wind band (1995) by the Croatian composer Mladen TARBUK, in two movements, *In colore di blu* and *Per popola popolare*, inspired by the brilliant percussionist Igor Lesnik.

An evening performance at the Nynex Arena performed by Belgium's acclaimed Rosas Dance Company, with the Ictus Ensemble, of *Just before*, with choreography and direction by Anne Teresa De Keersmaeker, and featuring music by John CAGE, Steve RECIH, Iannis XENAKIS, Magnus LINDBERG, Pierre BARTHOLOMÉE, Thierry De MEY, and Claude DEBUSSY.

An evening concert at the RNCM Lord Rhodes Room performed by the North West Composers' Association Concert, with special guest artists Deborah Jacob, soprano, Richard Casey, piano, Stephen Wibley, percussion, and Joanna Patton, clarinet, in the following program: *Deformierte Texte* by the English composer James CLARKE; *Three Songs*, "Winter Evening Landscape: Dunham Park, "From Alderley," and "I've Got a Penny," by the English composer Paul CRUNDEN-WHITE, who, nearly blind from birth, composes with the assistance of modern telescopic low vision aids; *The Guardian Angel* by the English composer Geoffrey KIMPTON; *I Know a Bank* and *A Faery Song* by the English composer and teacher Margaret WEGENER; two pieces composed in the 1950s for a school production of *A Midsummer Night's Dream*, *Del Fuego* for solo marimba (1993) by the Spanish composer, cellist, and conductor Tomás GARRIDO; *Dewpoint* by the English composer David ELLIS, a cycle of four songs to words by Douglas Rawlinson, originally conceived in 1955 for soprano, clarinet, harp, and string orchestra; *Requiem* (1996) by the English composer Kevin George BROWN, inspired by a collection of three poems by the Australian-born Russian poet Irina Kizminskaya; *Nigredo* by the English composer Simon HOLT; *Financial Targets* by the English composer Jeremy PIKE, in two movements, *1. Competition Entry*, and *2. Lost for Words*, both settings of satirical poems by Christopher Cunningham; and *The Radio Song* by the English composer Kevin MALONE, a techno-love song consisting of tightly woven web of pop music clichés nested within Baroque-inflected concert music.

A late-night program of electro-acoustic music at The Green Room performed by Sound Intermedia's surround-sound Festival Jukebox, with special guest artist Dimiris Marinos, mandolin, in the following program: *The Voter Registration Act* by the American composer Michael PISARO, a collage comprised of short excerpts of rock music, mainly British punk from 1977 to 1979; *Relief* for electronics (1996) by the Swedish composer Jens HEDMAN, the second piece in a trilogy with the collective title *RE-cycle; Artifices* (1989) by the French-born Canadian composer Francis DHOMONT, the second movement of *Chroniques de la lumière*, an impressionistic sonic version of visual elements based on a concept by the Montreal artist Luc Courchenes and realized in the composer's studio, Studio 123 and INA-GRM in Paris; and *Tantrum* for amplified mandolin and tape (1992) by the American composer C.P. FIRST.

22 APRIL 1998

On the sixth day of the 72nd Festival of the International Society for Contemporary Music in Manchester, four concerts are given, in the following sequence:

An early afternoon concert at the RNCM Sema Group Concert Hall performed by The Goldberg Ensemble, directed by Malcolm Layfield, in the following program: *Esquisses I* (1988) by the 49-year-old English composer and teacher Nigel OSBORNE, a work for eleven solo strings which began life as sketches for the opera *The Electrification of the Soviet Union; Das Lied der Unfruchtbaren* for flute and thirteen strings (1995/96) by the Korean composer Uzong CHOE, inspired by a text found in Chapter 54 of the Old Testament Book of Isaiah; *Time Out* for flute, harp, four violins, two violas, and two cellos (1995) by the 43-year-old Swiss-born Austrian composer, conductor, and teacher Beat FURRER; and [10] *Variations on a Theme of Frank Bridge* for strings (1937) by the outstanding English composer Benjamin BRITTEN (1913–1976).

A late afternoon recital by Peter Lawson, piano, at Chetham's School of Music, in the following program: *Tombeau de Messiaen* for piano and tape (1994) by the significant 48-year-old English composer Jonathan HARVEY; six pieces from a total of 38 by Portuguese and Spanish composers comprising the "Album de Colien," commissioned by Cecilia Colien Honegger, each lasting around 1 1/2 minutes: Ernest Martinez IZGUIERDO, *Altermança*, Augustin Charles SOLER, *Joc*, David del PUERTO, *Intrata*, Alexandre DELGADO, *Pequena Obsessão Compulsiva*, Alvaro SALAZAR, *Apuntes para un Meccano*, and Joan GUINJOAN, *Recordant Albéniz; The King of France* (1993) by the 43-year-old English composer Judith WEIR, a set of variations for solo piano on the Spanish/Arabic folk song *El Rey de Francia*, as sung by Seraphic Jews at the time of their exile; *Somewhere Submarine* by the English composer David PRIOR, an "underwater voyage" for piano and tape; and *The Faraday Wheel* by the English composer Paul ROBINSON, in three movements, *1. Mr. Maltbys' Machine, 2. On a curious class of optical deception*, and *3. Mr. Maltbys' Machine (reprise)*.

An evening concert at the RNCM Sema Group Concert Hall* performed by the BBC Philharmonic Orchestra, with special guest artists Ernst Kovacic and Lydia Mordkovich, violins, conducted by Martyn Brabbins, in the following program: *Nextwave Fanfare* for orchestra (1992) by the Australian composer Mary FINSTERER, written to celebrate the Brooklyn Academy of Music's Next Wave Festival, *Violin Concerto* (1995) by the 49-

year-old English composer Jonathan LLOYD, in three movements, *Reality, Fantasy*, and *Limbo*, dedicated to Ernst Kovacic; *On Beholding a Rainbow* (1997), by the 63-year-old English composer and teacher Anthony GILBERT, in three movements, *Passacaglia nascondita, Cantilena-slow and still;* and *Variazioni in moto perpetuo-flowing, legato, a little rubato*, commissioned by the BBC Philharmonic, and *Psalm 20* for orchestra (1994/96) by the Korean composer Shinuh LEE, based on biblical Psalms and ancient Hebrew music.

A late-night concert at the RNCM Sema Group Concert Hall performed by the Apollo Saxophone Quartet and RNCM Wind Orchestra, conducted by Timothy Reynish and Clark Rundell, in the following program: *Dream Carousels*, triptych for wind orchestra (1989), by the 63-year-old English composer and teacher Anthony GILBERT, its movements being *...and shadow theatre begins..., ...cyclone breeze in the house of infinity...*, and *...moths batter the dark...orbit the skull...; Distant Variations* (1996/97) by the 48-year-old English composer and teacher John (Arthur) CASKEN, a one-movement concerto grosso for saxophone quartet and wind orchestra; *Alembic* (1992) by the Irish composer Raymond DEANE, for symphonic wind band and composed for student players; and *Versuch über einen Marsch* by Marcel WENGLER.

* Prior to this performance, at 6:15 p.m., four soloists from the BBC Philharmonic and Fast Forward (featuring 100 students and teachers from Knowsley Teachers' Centre) present *Symposium* by Ivor Hodgson and *On Meeting at Knowsley Lane*, conducted by Bill Connor.

23 APRIL 1998

On the seventh day of the 72nd Festival of the International Society for Contemporary Music in Manchester, five concerts are given, in the following sequence:

An early afternoon concert at the Whitworth Art Gallery performed by the Apollo Saxophone Quartet, with special guest artist Simone Rebello, percussion, in the following program: *July* (1995) by the spirited 36-year-old American composer Michael TORKE, fusing funk, pop, and classical styles; *Saxophone Quartet* (1993) by the German composer Eckardt BEINKE; *Music for Saxophones* (1987) by the short-lived Dutch composer and teacher Tristan KEURIS (1946–1996), originally conceived as *Concerto for Saxophone Quartet and Orchestra*, a commission from the Rascher Saxophone Quartet; *Bulchenska Ratchenitsa* by Youri YOUNAKOV, Papasov's saxophonist, and Radi KAZAKOV, bassist, taken from the repertoire of Ivo Papasov's Bulgarian wedding band, high energy dance music arranged for the Apollo Saxophone Quartet by Mike Hammett; and *Kaval Sviri* (1990) by Peter LYONDEV, originally performed by the Bulgarian choir Le Mystère des Voix Bulgares, arranged for saxophone quartet by Rob Buckland.

A late afternoon concert at Chetham's School of Music performed by Chetham's Contemporary Music Ensemble, conducted by Jeremy Pike, in the following program: *Carillon* for six digital grand pianos (1996) by the Swiss composer Peter BENGSTON; *Concerto for Bassoon and Chamber Ensemble* by the English composer Jeremy PIKE, in three movements, *Andante con moto, Presto*, and *Lento ma non troppo-Presto; Still Sleeping* by the 37-year-old English composer Mark-Anthony TURNAGE, originally written for piano as a lullaby for the composer's elder son, William, when he was three months old; and *Verstelwerk* (Mending) for tenor saxophone, percussion, and chamber orchestra (1996) by the Dutch composer Guus JANSSEN, based on a series of 12 triads.

An evening concert at The Bridgewater Hall performed by the Hallé Orchestra, with special guest artists Christian Tetzlaff, violin, Penelope Walmsley-Clark, soprano, and soloists from the Royal Northern College of Music, conducted by Kent Nagano, in the following program: *Apparitions* (1956; rev. 1958–59) by the eminent 64-year-old Hungarian-born Austrian composer and pedagogue György LIGETI, in two movements, *Lento* and *Agitato*, *Château de l'âme* by the significant 45-year-old Finnish composer Kaija SAARIAHO; five songs for solo soprano, women's chorus, and orchestra: *1. La liane, 2. A la terre, 3. La liane, 4. Pour repousser l'esprit*, and *5. Les formules*, to texts drawn from ancient Hindu and Egyptian sources; *Violin Concerto* (1935) by the greatly significant Austrian composer whose music combined classical clarity of design and highly original melodic and harmonic techniques that became historically associated with the Second Viennese School Alban BERG (1885–1935), in two movements, *Andante-allegretto* and *Allegretto-adagio;* and *Ekphrasis (continuo II)* (1990) by the eminent 72-year-old Italian composer, conductor, and pedagogue Luciano BERIO.

An evening performance at The Dancehouse by the Shobana Jeyasingh Dance Company of *Intertense,* with choreography by Wayne McGregor and music by Andy COWTON and *Intimacies for a Third Order,* with choreography by Shobana Jeyasingh and music by Michael GORDON.

A late-night concert at The Bridgewater Hall, Barbirolli Room, performed by the South Bank Gamelan Players, in the following program: *Gendhing Bonang Tukung* (traditional); *My Mother's House* by Robert CAMPION, on a poem by Androula Pistolas for soprano, mezzo-soprano, and gamelan; *Philemon and Baukis* for violin and gamelan by the inventive 80-year-old American composer Lou HARRISON; *The Dissolving Tree* for mezzo-soprano and gamelan by Symon CLARKE, a suite of songs on poems by Miroslav Holub; *Ketawang Puspåwarnå* (traditional); *Waiting for the Wind* by the Italian composer Salvatore SCIARRINO; and *Short Ride in a Fast Machine* for orchestra (1986) by the prominent 51-year-old American composer John ADAMS, in a gamelan arrangement by Symon Clarke.

23 APRIL 1998

Why is this night different? for string quartet (1997) by the 38-year-old Scottish composer, conductor, and teacher James MACMILLAN is performed for the first time in London.

24 APRIL 1998

The Icelandic composer Leifur THÓRARINSSON, who was equally active as a music critic, dies in his native Reykjavík at the modest age of 63.

24 APRIL 1998

On the eighth day of the 72nd Festival of the International Society for Contemporary Music in Manchester, five concerts are given, in the following sequence:

An early afternoon performance at the RNCM Sema Group Concert Hall by PSAPPHA, with special guest artist Sally Bruce-Payne, mezzo-soprano, conducted by John Carewe, of *Le Marteau sans maître* for alto, alto flute, guitar, vibraphone, xylorimba, percussion, and viola (1953–55; rev. 1957) by the greatly significant 73-year-old French composer and conductor Pierre BOULEZ.

A late afternoon concert at the RNCM Sema Group Concerto Hall performed by the Royal Northern College of Music Brass Band and Brass Ensembles, with special guest artists Peter Mainwaring, trumpet, and Jeremy Holland Smith, organ, conducted by James Gourlay, in the following program: *Hymns at Heaven's Gate* by the 62-year-old English composer and conductor Elgar HOWARTH; *Erasmus* for trumpet, trom-

bone, and tape (1996) by the 60-year-old Lithuanian composer and teacher Osvaldas BALAKAUSKAS, a "polytextural narration," wherein the "texts" are 1. signals, 2. minimalistic refrains (prerecorded), 3. pointillistic episodes, 4. jazzy monologues and dialogues, and 5. organum-like choruses, played live; *Okna* (Stained Glass Windows), *After Marc Chagall* (1977), by the 69-year-old Czech composer, teacher, organist, and pianist Petr EBEN, a cycle in four movements, first performed in Prague in 1997, the year of Chagall's 90th birthday; and *Dances and Arias* by the 52-year-old English composer, teacher, and conductor Edward GREGSON, in one continuous movement alternating fast and slow sections (Dance-Aria I-Dance [scherzo]-Aria II-Dance).

An evening concert at The Bridgewater Hall performed by the London Sinfonietta, conducted by James Wood (preceded at 6:30 p.m. by a pre-concert talk and performance given by composers David Sawyer and Fraser Trainer who introduce Kagel's *Orchestrion-Straat* and an education project involving members of the London Sinfonietta and pupils from Winstanley College, Wigan, and The King's School, Macclesfield), in the following program: *Warp* for orchestra (1994) by the Chinese composer Xiaoyong CHEN; *Idées fixes,* subtitled *Sonata for 13* by the prominent 65-year-old German-born English composer and teacher Alexander GOEHR, in one continuous movement; *The Parliament of Angels* for mixed ensemble (1993) by James WOOD, inspired by a series of 15th-century frescos in the crypt of Bayeux Cathedral depicting "Musical Angels," each seen playing a different musical instrument; and *Orchestrion-Straat* for chamber ensemble (1995–96) by the notable 66-year-old Argentine composer and pedagogue Mauricio KAGEL.

A late-night recital by Jens Christensen, organ, at The Bridgewater Hall, in the following program: *Spring from Four Seasons* (1996) by the outstanding 68-year-old Polish composer, pianist, pedagogue, writer on music, stage manager, and playwright Bogusław SCHAEFFER, in four large movements, named for the seasons, each movement divided into three parts, according to the number of months contained in each (performed here were "March, April and May"); and five movements from the originally seven-movement *The Planets* (1982–96) by the 63-year-old Danish composer Bent LORENTZEN (*1. Mars, 2. Mercurius, 3. Jupiter, 4. Venus*, and *5. Saturnus*).

A music theatre double bill at The Green Room performed by the Royal Northern College of Music, comprised of *Exposition of a Picture* (1986), opera in one act, by the English composer Stephen (Michael Harding) OLIVER (1950–1992), and *The Bridge* (1996), opera in one act, by the English composer Tim BENJAMIN, winner of the £10,000 first prize in the 1996 Stephen Oliver Prize for Contemporary Opera.

25 APRIL 1998

Przebudzenia (Awakenings), ballet, by the 50-year-old Polish composer Krzysztof KNITTEL is performed for the first time in Poznań.

25 APRIL 1998

On the ninth and final day of the 72nd Festival of the International Society for Contemporary Music in Manchester, five concerts are given, in the following sequence:

A late morning concert at the RNCM Lord Rhodes Room performed by the Nossek String Quartet, in the following program: *String Quartet No. 3*, entitled *Super Hoqueti David* [Machaut], by the 53-year-old English composer and teacher Anthony GILBERT; *String Quartet No. 1* by the English composer David ELLIS, in four movements, *Allegro inquieto, Quasi presto, Lento,* and *Allegretto; String Quartet,* op.69, by the English composer Stuart SCOTT, in three movements, *1. Allegro ma non troppo, 2. Lento,* and *3. Allegro energico; Fast Forward* by the English composer Kevin MALONE; and *String Quartet No. 3,* op. 19 (1924), by the important Austrian composer and conductor of partly Jewish descent Alexander ZEMLINSKY (1871–1942), in four movements, *Allegretto, Thema mit Variationen: Geheimnisvoll bewegt, Romanze: Sehr mässige Achtel,* and *Burleske: Sehr lebhaft.*

An early afternoon performance at the RNCM Sema Group Concert Hall by PSAPPHA of *Kontakte* for electronic sounds, piano, and percussion (1960) by the outstanding 69-year-old German composer Karlheinz STOCKHAUSEN.

"The Four Seasons" at The Green Room, a family concert combining the skills of contemporary music ensemble Apollo Saxophone Quartet with the words of the popular Manchester performance poet Lemn Sissay, featuring a new collaborative piece, mixing poetry and music, created especially for the Festival.

A late afternoon concert at the RNCM Sema Group Concert Hall performed by the BBC Singers, with special guest artists Simon Limbrick and Julian Warburton, percussion, Nancy Ruffler, flute, Kim Porter, alto, and Neil MacKenzie, tenor, conducted by Simon Joly, in the following program: *Cinq Réchants* for chamber chorus (1949) by the outstanding French composer and pedagogue Olivier MESSIAEN (1908–1992); *Nuits* for twelve voices (1967) by the remarkable 75-year-old Greek-born French composer, music theorist, and teacher Iannis XENAKIS; *Six Kurpian Songs* by the outstanding Polish composer Karol SZYMANOWSKI (1882–1937); *Il Rozzo Martello* for chorus (1997) by the eminent 63-year-old English composer and conductor Peter Maxwell DAVIES, based upon a Michaelangelo sonnet, written for and dedicated to the BBC Singers; and *Ngano* (Evening Songs) for mezzo-soprano, tenor, chorus, flute, and two percussion (1983–84) by the 52-year-old English composer Michael FINNISSY, a model of community music-making from the people of the Northern Transvaal in Africa but using original pitches and rhythms (derived from European aesthetic sources rather than African ones).

An evening concert at The Bridgewater Hall (preceded by a pre-concert talk, Elliott Carter in conversation with Sir John Drummond) performed by the BBC Symphony Orchestra, with guest artists Susan Bickley, mezzo-soprano, and Kim Walker, bassoon, conducted by Oliver Knussen, in the following program: *Praeludium* for brass, bells, and percussion (1962) by the greatly renowned 93-year-old English composer Sir Michael (Kemp) TIPPETT, written to celebrate the 40th anniversary of the BBC; *Lullaby* for 29 solo strings and two harps (1947) by the eminent Polish-born English conductor and composer Sir Andrzej PANUFNIK (1914–1991); *Ad Ora Incerta* by the 45-year-old English composer Simon BAIN-BRIDGE; four orchestral songs for mezzo-soprano, bassoon, and orchestra (1994), to texts from Primo Levi, *1. Il canto del corvo, 2. Il tramonto di Fossoli, 3. Lunedi,* and *4. Buna,* winner of the 1997 Grawemeyer Award of the University of Louisville; and *Symphonia* by the outstanding 89-year-old American composer and teacher Elliott CARTER, an orchestral trilogy in three movements, *1. Partita, 2. Adagio tenebroso,* and *3. Allegro scorravole.*

26 APRIL 1998

Lives and Times of Angels, oratorio, by the multifaceted 56-year-old American organist, harpsichordist, fortepianist, conductor, and composer Anthony NEWMAN is premiered in Mt. Kisco, New York.

29 APRIL 1998

Cello Dreaming for cello, strings, and percussion by the eminent Australian composer and teacher Peter (Joshua) SCULTHORPE is performed for the first time in Manchester, England, in celebration of his 69th. birthday.

30 APRIL 1998

Triodion for chorus by the outstanding 62-year-old Estonian-born Austrian composer Arvo PÄRT is heard for the first time in London.

2 MAY 1998

Bimini Place for piano and electric guitar (or any combination of instruments), *Chivas* for sampler and electric guitar (in collaboration with R. Kleier), and *Djerassi Suite* for sampler and electric guitar (in collaboration with R. Kleier), three works by the innovative 37-year-old American composer, instrumentalist, improviser, and sampling specialist Annie (actually, Anne) GOSFIELD are performed for the first time ever in Alburquerque.

5 MAY 1998

Wake Up...And Die for solo cello and orchestral cello section (1996) by the remarkable 54-year-old English composer John (Kenneth) TAVENER is performed for the first time at the Beauvais Festival.

6 MAY 1998

The outstanding 42-year-old Swedish mezzo-soprano Anne Sofie von OTTER makes her Carnegie Hall recital debut in New York.

8 MAY 1998

The American trombonist, conductor, teacher, and composer Raymond (Eugene) PREMRU, who gave masterclasses in trombone virtuosity throughout the world and also taught at various institutions, including the Oberlin College Conservatory of Music (from 1988), dies in Cleveland at the modest age of 63.

11 MAY 1998

Elegia No. 2 for cello and strings (1987) by the 48-year-old Polish composer Piotr MOSS is given its first ever performance in Warsaw.

12 MAY 1998

A Fiddler's Tale for narrator, clarinet, bassoon, trumpet, trombone, violin, bass, and percussion by the outstanding 36-year-old black American trumpeter Wynton MARSALIS, to a text by Stanley Crouch, conceived as a companion piece to Igor Stravinsky's *Histoire du soldat* (1918), with which it is often paired in concert, is given its first complete performance in New York as part of the Jazz at Lincoln Center series.

16 MAY 1998

Gymel for two oboes by the 68-year-old American composer and teacher Robert (Paige) CEELY is heard for the first time in Cambridge, Massachusetts.

18 MAY 1998

Deutsches Stück mit Hamlet for two soloists and orchestra by the distinguished 46-year-old German composer and teacher Wolfgang (Michael) RIHM is performed for the first time in Frankfurt am Main.

21 MAY 1998

Concertino for Orchestra (1997–98) by the 34-year-old American composer Augusta Read THOMAS, wife of the remarkable 64-year-old American composer Bernard Rands, is heard for the first time in Rochester.

22 MAY 1998

Frozen Horizon for orchestra by the 37-year-old Japanese composer Karen TANAKA is premiered in Bergen.

23 MAY 1998

Zoom and Zip for strings (1997) by the 40-year-old Uzbekistan-born Australian composer Elena KATS-CHERNIN is given its first ever performance in Canberra.

25 MAY 1998

Thrène for flute, clarinet, violin, cello, and piano (1997) by the 51-year-old French composer Jean-Claude WOLFF is heard for the first time in l'Avray.

28 MAY 1998

Salammbô, opera, after Flaubert (1992–93), by the 45-year-old French composer Philippe FÉNELON is staged for the first time in Paris.

29 MAY 1998

Ghost Dance for orchestra by the versatile 55-year-old American composer, pianist, teacher, and writer on music William (Ervin) DUCKWORTH is performed for the first time in Charleston, South Carolina.

31 MAY 1998

The Polish conductor, pianist, pedagogue, and composer Stanisław WISŁOCKI, who from 1955 was a professor at the State Higher School of Music in Warsaw, where he held its conducting chair from 1958, and who from 1961 to 1968 conducted the National Philharmonic in Warsaw, dies in Warsaw at the age of 76.

1 JUNE 1998

Jeu parti for violin and piano (1997) by the 62-year-old Polish composer and pedagogue Marek STACHOWSKI is heard for the first time in Kraków.

5 JUNE 1998

Angels, miracle play (1998), and *The Diva*, opera (1979), two works by the 61-year-old American composer, choral conductor, and organist William (Edward) FERRIS, are staged for the first time, the latter in a newly-revised version, in Evanston, Illinois.

7 JUNE 1998

The pioneering American discographer William (Joseph) SCHWANN, best known for his *Schwann Record Catalog*, founded in 1949, the first monthly compilation of available recordings in the world, dies in Burlington, Vermont, at the age of 85.

9 JUNE 1998

Certum ex Incertis for orchestra by the 44-year-old English composer Judith WEIR is heard for the first time in Birmingham.

10 JUNE 1998

The outstanding Italian organist and teacher Fernando GERMANI, who, blessed with a brilliant technique and an amazing memory, became best known for his championship of the music of Bach, dies in his native Rome at the seasoned age of 92.

11 JUNE 1998

The Italian mezzo-soprano Lucia VALENTINI-TERRANI, known particularly for her roles in operas by Rossini and Verdi, dies in Seattle at the lamentably young age of 49.

12 JUNE 1998

Asanga for percussion (1997) by the gifted 48-year-old South African-born Irish composer Kevin VOLANS is premiered in Berlin.

14 JUNE 1998

String Theory for amplified string quartet by the gifted 42-year-old American composer Steven MACKEY is given its first ever performance by the Kronos Quartet, for whom the work was written, at an afternoon concert of the San Francisco Symphony's "American Mavericks" series at Davies Symphony Hall.

15 JUNE 1998

Doctor Ox's Experiment, opera (1988–95), by the significant 55-year-old English composer and teacher (Richard) Gavin BRYARS is mounted for the first time in London.

19 JUNE 1998

Agate Slice for cello, violin, and percussion by the talented 42-year-old South Korean composer and komungo player Jin Hi KIM is performed for the first time by Frances Marie Uitti, Mifune Tsuji, and Titiana Koleva at Festival Nieuwe Muziek 1998's "Women in the Avant Garde" in Middleburg, The Netherlands.

21 JUNE 1998

Harp Concerto (1996) and *Western Front* for orchestra (1997), two works by the 67-year-old American composer and record producer Nancy VAN DE VATE, are premiered in Olomouc.

23 JUNE 1998

The American composer Herbert HAUFRECHT, active as a collector of folk music and author of such volumes as *Folk Sing* (1960), *'Round the World Folk Sing* (1964), *Travelin' on with the Weavers* (1966), *The Judy Collins Songbook*

(1969), and *Folk Songs in Settings by Master Composers* (1970), dies in Albany, New York, at the age of 88.

25 JUNE 1998

The American conductor and composer Richard (Henry Horner) BALES, who in 1942 became the first music director of the National Gallery of Art in Washington, D.C., and who in 1943 founded the National Gallery Orch., which he conducted until his retirement in 1985, dies in Lake Ridge, Virginia, at the age of 83.

27 JUNE 1998

Shining Forth, concerto for cello and small orchestra, by the promising 33-year-old Irish composer Ian WILSON is given its first ever performance in London.

28 JUNE 1998

A Tone Poem for Victims of Racism and Hatred for orchestra by the 52-year-old black American composer and teacher Joyce Solomon MOORMAN is heard for the first time in Olomouc.

30 JUNE 1998

The Italian baritone Renato CAPECCHI, who was particularly successful as a buffo artist, winning special praise for his portrayals of Rossini's Figaro, Dr. Bartolo, Dulcamara, Don Pasquale, and Gianni Schicchi, dies in Milan at the age of 74.

3 JULY 1998

The English composer and conductor George (Walter Selwyn) LLOYD, whose compositions included the operas *Iernin* (1933–34; Penzance, Nov. 6, 1934), *The Serf* (1936–38; London, Oct. 20, 1938), and *John Socman* (1949–51; Bristol, May 15, 1951), in which he embraced an unabashedly Romantic style of pleasurable accessibility, dies in London at the age of 85.

7 JULY 1998

The 5th String, opera (1980), by the 48-year-old American composer and teacher Maurice WRIGHT is mounted for the first time in Des Moines.

8 JULY 1998

The Slovak composer and teacher Miloslav KOŘÍNEK, long-time theory and composition teacher (1949–1985) and assistant director (from 1962) at the State Conservatory in Bratislava, dies there at the age of 73.

9 JULY 1998

Effi Briest, ballet, by the 44-year-old Romanian-born German composer, teacher, and writer on music Violeta DINESCU is staged for the first time in Magdeburg.

11 JULY 1998

Credo for soloists, chorus, and orchestra (1996–98) by the preeminent 64-year-old Polish composer, pedagogue, and conductor Krzysztof PENDERECKI is heard for the first time in Eugene, Oregon.

13 JULY 1998

Harpsichord Sonata by the 58-year-old American writer on music and composer Phillip RAMEY is performed for the first time in Yorkshire, England.

14 JULY 1998

The Dutch pianist, teacher, and composer of Polish heritage Herman D(avid) KOPPEL, father of the 54-year-old Danish composer Thomas Herman Koppel, dies in his native Copenhagen at the respectable age of 89.

17 JULY 1998

The distinguished Italian conductor and composer Lamberto GARDELLI, a notable interpreter of the Italian operatic repertory and composer of four original operas, dies in Munich at the age of 82.

22 JULY 1998

The outstanding German baritone Hermann PREY, who numbered among his finest operatic roles Count Almaviva, Papageno, Guglielmo, and Rossini's Figaro, dies in Munich at the age of 69.

23 JULY 1998

The Hungarian-born Belgian violinist and pedagogue André GERTLER, best known as an advocate of contemporary scores but who also played standard repertoire works and wrote cadenzas for Mozart's G major *Violin Concerto*, K.216, and Beethoven's *Violin Concerto*, dies in Brussels at the age of 90.

31 JULY 1998

Second Clarinet Concerto (1996) by the 70-year-old American musicologist, inventor, and composer James (Myron) COHN is performed for the first time in Cali, Colombia.

1 AUGUST 1998

The remarkable 38-year-old English soprano Jane EAGLEN returns to the Seattle Opera to sing Isolde, which proved a triumph.

3 AUGUST 1998

The prominent Russian composer of German descent Alfred (Garrievich) SCHNITTKE, one of the boldest experimenters in modernistic composition in Soviet Russia, dies in Hamburg at the lamentable age of 63.

4 AUGUST 1998

Prometheus Wept (August 6, August 9, 1945) for strings by the 54-year-old American composer Dennis EBERHARD is performed for the first time ever in Shaker Heights, Ohio.

8 AUGUST 1998

3 Lieder nach Texten der Hildegard von Bingen for mezzo-soprano and flute (1996) by the gifted 72-year-old German composer, pedagogue, organist, and harpsichordist Ruth ZECHLIN is given its premiere performance in Weimar.

9 AUGUST 1998

5 Lightnings for orchestra (1997) by the significant 60-year-old Finnish composer and teacher Paavo (Johannes) HEININEN is heard for the first time in Turku.

21 AUGUST 1998

The Canadian clarinetist, saxophonist, and composer Norman SYMONDS, one of Canada's early champions of the "3rd stream" idiom who also composed works in an Expressionist vein, dies in Toronto at the age of 77.

24 AUGUST 1998

Un Grand Sommeil noir for voice and piano (1906) and *Tuning Up* for orchestra (1947), two works by Edgard (Victor Achille Charles) VARÈSE (1883–1965), the remarkable French-born American composer who introduced a totally original principle of organizing the materials and forms of sound, the first in an orchestration by Antony Beaumont and the second as developed by the remarkable 75-year-old Chinese-born American composer Chou WEN-CHUNG from fragments "suggesting the sound of an orchestra tuning up" for a score to the film *Carnegie Hall*, are heard for the first time in Amsterdam.

1 SEPTEMBER 1998

Schumann-Fantasie for orchestra (1997) by the distinguished 61-year-old German conductor, composer, and pedagogue (Johannes Wolfgang) Hans ZENDER is premiered in Cologne.

8 SEPTEMBER 1998

Ears Stretch a Sensitive Sail for percussionist and string quartet by the 56-year-old Icelandic cellist and composer Haflidi (Magnus) HALLGRÍMSSON is performed for the first time ever in Thurso, Scotland.

10 SEPTEMBER 1998

Double Concerto for two guitars and orchestra (1995) by the notable 59-year-old Brazilian composer, pianist, and conductor Marlos NOBRE is given its first ever performance in São Paulo.

11 SEPTEMBER 1998

Phantasiestück in C.'s Manier for cello and orchestra by the notable 72-year-old Austrian composer, conductor, and pedagogue Friedrich CERHA, originally premiered in Vienna on Nov. 24, 1989, with the composer conducting, is expanded to a *Cello Concerto* (1996) and given its first ever performance in Berlin.

17 SEPTEMBER 1998

The respected American composer, pianist, organist, and teacher William (Hugh) ALBRIGHT, who pursued an active career as a pianist and organist, excelling in ragtime, jazz, and contemporary works, and in whose compositions he pursued quaquaversal methods of experimental music, using varied techniques according to need, dies in Ann Arbor, Michigan, at the pitiable age of 53.

18 SEPTEMBER 1998

Galileo, chamber opera, by the noteworthy 59-year-old New Zealand composer, teacher, and horn player John (Francis) RIMMER is staged for the first time in his native Auckland.

19 SEPTEMBER 1998

A Streetcar Named Desire, opera in three acts by the brilliant 59-year-old German-born American pianist, conductor, and composer André (George) (real name, Andreas Ludwig Priwin) PREVIN, to a libretto by Philip Littell after the play by Tennessee Williams, is mounted for the first time under the composer's direction in San Francisco, with the gifted 39-year-old American soprano Renée Fleming in the role of Blanche.

21 SEPTEMBER 1998

Stretto for flute, clarinet, cello, and guitar by the 37-year-old Polish composer Hanna KULENTY is given its premiere performance in Warsaw.

26 SEPTEMBER 1998

White Raven, opera (1991), by the outstanding 61-year-old American composer Philip GLASS is mounted for the first time in Lisbon.

1 OCTOBER 1998

The Ives editor and scholar David PORT takes Charles Ives's uncompleted sketches for an "overture-concerto" meant as an Emerson portrait, of which some of the material found its way into Ives's *Concord Sonata*, and produces a "practical" reconstruction he dubs the *Emerson Concerto* for piano and orchestra (1996–98), which is premiered by the Cleveland Orchestra, Alan Feinstein soloist.

2 OCTOBER 1998

Pierre de Coeur for chamber ensemble (1997) by the 67-year-old German composer and teacher Paul-Heinz DITTRICH is performed for the first time in Dresden.

6 OCTOBER 1998

Fourth String Quartet by the brilliant 76-year-old German-born American pianist, conductor, and composer Lukas FOSS (real name, Fuchs) is given its first ever performance in Buffalo, New York.

7 OCTOBER 1998

Chaos, opera by the innovative American composer Michael GORDON, to a futuristic libretto by Matthew Macguire dealing with the moral dilemma of two rogue scientists whose discoveries into the realm of chaos threaten their jobs and their lives, with Marie and Pierre Curie making appearances as helpful navigators in the Chaos Zone, is first staged at The Kitchen in New York.

8 OCTOBER 1998

The distinguished Romanian composer and musicologist Anatol VIERU, founder-director of the Musiques parallèles concerts (1970–84), at which he presented the first Romanian performances of works by such modern masters as Schoenberg, Varèse, and Ives, and who, as a composer, developed a highly personal compositional style in which microstructures served as the foundation upon which to build scores notable for their inventive handling of modal, tonal, and serial elements, dies in Bucharest at the age of 72.

10 OCTOBER 1998

Sessionals for brass quintet by the 67-year-old American composer and writer on music Jack GOTTLIEB is performed for the first time ever in Dobbs Ferry, New York.

13 OCTOBER 1998

Great Sandy Island for orchestra by the eminent 69-year-old Australian composer and teacher Peter (Joshua) SCULTHORPE is premiered in Tokyo.

15 OCTOBER 1998

Double Concerto for violin, cello, and orchestra by the brilliant 74-year-old American composer, pianist, and writer Ned ROREM, son C. Rufus Rorem, a medical economist, and Gladys Miller Rorem, a civil rights activist, is performed for the first time in Indianapolis.

17 OCTOBER 1998

The respected Latvian-born American writer on music and pedagogue Joseph MACHLIS, author of the immensely popular book, *The Enjoyment of Music* (N.Y., 1955; 8th ed., 1999), dies in New York at the respectable age of 92.

24 OCTOBER 1998

The Other Voice, chamber opera, by the esteemed 74-year-old Austrian-born American composer and pedagogue Robert STARER is staged for the first time in Kingston, New York.

26 OCTOBER 1998

The iconoclastic English-born American composer, performer, music publisher, and writer Dick (actually, Richard Carter) HIGGINS, long-time partner of the innovative poet Allison Knowles, and a proponent of the intermedia group of composers who advocated the union of music with other allied arts and was active in the first "happenings," dies in Quebec City, Canada, at the age of 60.

27 OCTOBER 1998

String Quartet by the ascending 27-year-old Polish composer and clarinetist Paweł MYKIETYN is given its first ever performance in London .

27 OCTOBER 1998

Chana's Story, song cycle, the internationally-acclaimed 61-year-old American composer and teacher David DEL TREDICI is given its first ever performance in San Francisco, the composer accompanying the mezzo-soprano Miriam Abramowitsch.

30 OCTOBER 1998

Für Celia affettuoso for chorus by the distinguished 72-year-old French-American composer and teacher Betsy

JOLAS, daughter of the poet and journalist Eugène Jolas, well known as the founder and editor of the literary journal *transition,* is performed for the first time ever in Paris.

5 NOVEMBER 1998

Epitaphium tempori pereunti for chorus and orchestra by the 66-year-old Lithuanian composer Bronislovas KUTAVIČIUS is performed for the first time in Odense, Denmark.

6 NOVEMBER 1998

The German conductor and orchestral Intendant Wolfgang STRESEMANN, son of Gustav Stresemann, who was the distinguished chancellor and foreign minister of the Weimar Republic, dies in Berlin at the seasoned age of 94.

7 NOVEMBER 1998

American City for piano and wind ensemble by the 61-year-old American composer and teacher George (William) FLYNN is heard for the first time in Chicago.

8 NOVEMBER 1998

From Across La Manche for strings by the 66-year-old English composer, pianist, and teacher Malcolm (Leyland) LIPKIN is performed for the first time in Canterbury.

9 NOVEMBER 1998

Four Marian Antiphons: II, Ave Regina Coelorum for organ by the multi-talented 71-year-old English pianist, organist, conductor, writer on music, and composer Francis (John) ROUTH is given its first ever performance in London.

11 NOVEMBER 1998

Sonata for solo guitar by the prominent 68-year-old Spanish composer and conductor Cristóbal HALFFTER (Jiménez-Encina), nephew of the important Spanish musicians Ernesto and Rodolfo Halffter (Escriche), is performed for the first time in Vienna.

13 NOVEMBER 1998

Percussion Concerto by the 74-year-old Polish composer and pedagogue Krystyna MOSZUMAŃSKA-NAZAR is given its first ever performance in Kraków.

14 NOVEMBER 1998

Five Simic Songs for soprano and string quartet by the 43-year-old American composer and teacher Eric (David) CHASALOW is performed for the first time ever in Waltham, Massachusetts.

17 NOVEMBER 1998

The Swiss composer and teacher Norbert MORET, who turned to full-time composition late in life but whose music gained almost immediate international attention (his *Violin Concerto* and *Cello Concerto* being commissioned and premiered by, respectively, Anne-Sophie Mutter and Mstislav Rostropovich), dies in Fribourg, just three days shy of his 77th birthday.

19 NOVEMBER 1998

The Nightingale's to Blame, opera (1996–98), by the promising 40-year-old English composer Simon HOLT is staged for the first time in Huddersfield.

20 NOVEMBER 1998

Fifth Symphony, entitled *Les lumières de la nuit*, by the eminent 84-year-old French composer and administrator Marcel (François Paul) LANDOWSKI, son of the sculptor Paul Landowski and great-grandson of the celebrated Belgian violinist Henri Vieuxtemps, is premiered in Paris.

21 NOVEMBER 1998

The Polish composer, teacher, and organist Tadeus PACIORKIEWICZ, long associated (from 1954) as faculty member, dean of its composition, theory, and conducting department, and rector of the Warsaw State College of Music, dies in Warsaw at the seasoned age of 82.

22 NOVEMBER 1998

The greatly renowned 63-year-old Italian tenor Luciano PAVAROTTI celebrates his 30th anniversary with the Metropolitan Opera with a gala performance with the company.

1 DECEMBER 1998

The Dutch organist, choral conductor, pedagogue, and composer Albert de KLERK, who, as an organist, became particularly admired for his improvisational skills, and whose extensive repertoire included the complete organ works of César Franck and Hendrik Andriessen, dies in his native Haarlem at the age of 81.

11 DECEMBER 1998

Billy and Zelda, opera, by the 45-year-old American composer Tina DAVIDSON is staged for the first time in Wilmington, Delaware.

13 DECEMBER 1998

"20 dia 4" ("20 for 4") for string quartet by the 47-year-old Polish composer, conductor, and teacher Aleksander LASOŃ is given its premiere performance in Rybna.

18 DECEMBER 1998

Double Concerto for flute, harp, and orchestra by the esteemed 64-year-old German composer Siegfried MATTHUS is heard for the first time in Dresden.

19 DECEMBER 1998

Il mondo assurdo del Signor B. for viola and tape (1997) by the 59-year-old Finnish trumpeter and composer Jarmo (Kalevi) SERMILÄ receives its first ever performance in Florence.

22 DECEMBER 1998

Piece for Strings by the notable 63-year-old Georgian composer Giya (Alexandrovich) KANCHELI is heard for the first time in Dresden.

24 DECEMBER 1998

The 35-year-old American conductor and musicologist Patrick SUMMERS makes his auspicious Metropolitan Opera debut in New York conducting *Die Fledermaus*.

31 DECEMBER 1998

The outstanding 38-year-old American soprano Deborah VOIGT and the greatly admired 33-year-old Austrian mezzo-soprano Angelika KIRCHSCHLAGER are the featured soloists with the New York Philharmonic, conducted by the esteemed 71-year-old German conductor Kurt MASUR, in a New Year's Eve Gala Concert televised live to the nation by PBS.

1999

1 JANUARY 1999

The American violinist and musicologist W(illiam) Thomas MARROCCO, long-time professor of music at the University of California at Los Angeles (1950–77) as well as author of *Fourteenth Century Italian Cacce* (Cambridge, Mass., 1942; 2nd ed., rev. and aug., 1961), *Music in America: An Anthology* (with H. Gleason; N.Y., 1964), *Medieval Music* (with N. Sandon; London, 1977), *Inventory of Fifteenth Century Bassedanze, Balli and Balletti in Italian Dance Manuals* (N.Y., 1981), and *Memoirs of a Stradivarius* (N.Y., 1988), dies in Eugene, Oregon, at the age of 89.

2 JANUARY 1999

The esteemed Swiss opera administrator and composer Rolf LIEBERMANN, whose works for the stage were composed mostly in an experimental idiom, sharing the influence of hedonistic eclecticism, French neo-Classicism, and Viennese dodecaphony, dies in Paris at the age of 88.

4 JANUARY 1999

The American composer and pedagogue Allen Dwight SAPP, Jr., long-time dean (1978–80) and professor of composition (1978–93) at the University of Cincinnati College-Conservatory of Music, dies in Cincinnati at the age of 76.

8 JANUARY 1999

Kabir Padavali for soprano and orchestra (1997) by the prominent 39-year-old American composer and teacher Christopher (Chapman) ROUSE is heard for the first time in Minneapolis.

14 JANUARY 1999

Natural History for soprano and orchestra (1998) by the productive 44-year-old English composer of Scottish heritage Judith WEIR is premiered in Boston.

21 JANUARY 1999

The eminent French musicologist and composer Jacques CHAILLEY, authoritative writer on many subjects, including medieval music, the music of ancient Greece, music history, and the music of Bach, Mozart, Wagner, and others, whose books included *Les Passions de J.S. Bach* (1963; 2nd ed., rev., 1984), *Tristan et Isolde de Wagner* (1963; 2nd ed., 1972), *Le "Carnaval" de Schumann* (1971), *Le Voyage d'hiver de Schubert* (1975), *Parsifal de R. Wagner, opéra initiatique* (1979), *La Musique grecque antique* (1979) and *La musique et son langage* (1996), dies in Montpellier at the seasoned age of 88.

23 JANUARY 1999

Voices from the Ancient World for flute trio and percussion (1998) by the remarkable 70-year-old Scottish composer Thea MUSGRAVE is heard for the first time in Glasgow.

24 JANUARY 1999

Concerto for viola and strings (1998) by the 62-year-old Polish composer and pedagogue Marek STACHOWSKI is premiered in Warsaw.

25 JANUARY 1999

The renowned American conductor Robert (Lawson) SHAW, a master of the choral repertoire and for more than half a century America's preeminent choral conductor (his 13 Grammy Awards and numerous honorary doctorates attest to the unbounded esteem and admiration he was accorded during his remarkable career), dies in New Haven, Connecticut, at the respected age of 82.

26 JANUARY 1999

The Swedish conductor, pianist, and composer Rune WAHLBERG, who, after serving as music director of the Göteborg City Theater (1943–51), was music director in Kramfors (1953–57), Hofors (1957–64), Härnösand (1964–69), and Hudiksvall (1969–75), dies in his native Gävle at the ripened age of 88.

27 JANUARY 1999

The German opera director and administrator August EVERDING, who, in addition to staging operas during his tenures with the Hamburg State Opera (1973–1977) and at the Bavarian State Opera in Munich (1977–1982), where he subsequently was Generalintendant of the Bavarian State Theater (1982–93) and then founder-president of the Bavarian Theater Academy (from 1993), worked as a guest opera director at the Bayreuth Festival, the Savonlinna Festival, London's Covent Garden, New York's Metropolitan Opera, and other music centers, dies in Munich at the age of 70.

30 JANUARY 1999

The outstanding 43-year-old Canadian tenor Ben HEPPNER makes his New York recital debut at Carnegie Hall.

3 FEBRUARY 1999

Como anhela la cierva for soprano and orchestra (1998) by the outstanding 63-year-old Estonian-born Austrian composer Arvo PÄRT is heard for the first time in Santa Cruz.

5 FEBRUARY 1999

Viviane of Avalon for dramatic coloratura soprano and orchestra by the 38-year-old Argentine composer Ezequiel VIÑAO, arranged from the opera *Merlin*, after Caleb Carr (1998), is heard for the first time ever in Paris.

6 FEBRUARY 1999

Piece for oboe and strings (1998) by the notable 63-year-old Georgian composer Giya (Alexandrovich) KANCHELI is premiered in Amsterdam.

7 FEBRUARY 1999

Rockpool Dreaming for soprano saxophone and strings by the eminent 69-year-old Australian composer and teacher Peter (Joshua) SCULTHORPE is performed for the first time in Newcastle, New South Wales.

8 FEBRUARY 1999

The distinguished 52-year-old English bass John (Rowland) TOMLINSON portrays Arnold Schoenberg's Moses at his Metropolitan Opera debut in New York in a remarkable production staged by the ascending 45-year-old English opera producer Graham VICK.

12 FEBRUARY 1999

It Almost Passed in a Dream for flute, bass marimba, harmonic canon, adapted guitar, and cello, an ensemble enhanced by the inclusion of Harry Partch/Newband Instruments, by the innovative 38-year-old American composer, instrumentalist, improviser, and sampling specialist Annie (actually, Anne) GOSFIELD is performed for the first time in New York.

14 FEBRUARY 1999

Ninth Symphony (1997–98) by the prominent Russian composer of German descent Alfred (Garrievich) SCHNITTKE (1934–1998), in a revised version completed by the eminent 67-year-old Russian conductor, Gennadi (Nikolaievich) ROZHDESTVENSKY, son of the Russian conductor and pedagogue Nikolai Anosov, following the composer's instruction (1998), is given its first ever performance in Hamburg.

15 FEBRUARY 1999

The Dutch composer Jan MASSÉUS dies in Bilthoven at the respected age of 86.

16 FEBRUARY 1999

The distinguished Norwegian composer and organist (David) Johan KVANDAL (real name, Johansen), son of the Norwegian pianist, music critic, and composer David Monrad Johansen (1888–1974), dies in Oslo at the age of 79.

17 FEBRUARY 1999

The German soprano Sabine HASS, best known for her Wagner and Strauss roles, dies in Klagenfurt at the lamentable age of 49.

23 FEBRUARY 1999

The English conductor and composer Ruth (Dorothy Louisa) GIPPS, founder-conductor of the London Repertoire Orchestra (1955–86), founder-conductor of the London Chanticleer Orchestra (from 1961), and music director of the Rondel Ensemble, a wind group, dies in Eastbourne, East Sussex, just three days after her 78th birthday.

24 FEBRUARY 1999

Xi (Nucleus) for ensemble and tape (1998) by the respected 37-year-old Korean composer Unsuk CHIN is premiered in Paris.

6 MARCH 1999

Maria Paradis, opera, by the 50-year-old Danish conductor and composer Bo HOLTEN is staged for the first time in Odense.

8 MARCH 1999

The respected 51-year-old German baritone Franz GRUNDHEBER makes his Metropolitan Opera debut in New York as Rigoletto.

9 MARCH 1999

The outstanding Canadian composer and pianist Harry (Stewart) SOMERS, whose musical idiom was quaquaversal, absorbing without prejudice ancient, national, and exotic resources, from Gregorian chant to oriental scales, from simple folkways to electronic sound, all handled with fine expertise, brought to bear on his historical opera, *Louis Riel*, which was performed at the Kennedy Center in Washington, D.C., on Oct. 23, 1975, as part of America's Bicentennial celebration, dies in his native Toronto at the age of 73.

11 MARCH 1999

Vulcan, orchestral fanfare, by the 60-year-old New Zealand composer, teacher, and horn player John (Francis) RIMMER is given its first ever performance in his native Auckland.

12 MARCH 1999

The celebrated American-born English violinist, conductor, and humanitarian of Russian-Jewish descent Yehudi, Lord Menuhin of Stoke d'Abernon MENUHIN, brother of the American pianist Hephzibah Menuhin (1920–1981), dies in Berlin at the age of 82.

16 MARCH 1999

The American composer and teacher Eric (Norman) STOKES, whose early interest in collage and mixed media scores prompted him to pursue an eclectic experimental course, producing works leavened with imagination, lyricism, and wit, dies in a fatal automobile accident in Minneapolis at the age of 68.

17 MARCH 1999

Triple Concerto for horn, bass clarinet, marimba, and orchestra by the 57-year-old American composer, pianist, and teacher Richard (Edward) WILSON is performed for the first time in New York.

21 MARCH 1999

The admired 52-year-old Irish mezzo-soprano (later soprano) Elizabeth CONNELL and the esteemed 56-year-old Austrian baritone Bernd WEIKL appear as Senta and Wagner's Dutchman, respectively, at the opening of the new Macau Cultural Centre.

23 MARCH 1999

The Italian composer, writer, and teacher Vieri TOSATTI, long-time teacher at the Pontificio Istituto di Musica Sacra (1966–86) and the Conservatorio di Santa Cecilia (1973–80) in Rome, and whose compositions followed along conservative lines in an eclectic style, dies in his native Rome at the age of 78.

24 MARCH 1999

Après un silence for violin and chamber orchestra (1998) by the 49-year-old English composer and teacher John (Arthur) CASKEN is heard for the first time in Newcastle.

25 MARCH 1999

The fifth "Other Minds" Festival, under the artistic direction of Charles Amirkhanian, opens in San Francisco at the Cowell Theater at the Fort Mason Center, featuring special guest artist Margaret Leng Tan, pianist, in the following program: "Fanfare" from *The Winged Energy of Delight* for toy piano and toy percussion (1997) by the 39-year-old American composer, timpanist, and conductor John KENNEDY; *Dinky Toys* (1979), arranged for toy pianos, by the 47-year-old Portuguese composer and pianist António Pinho VARGAS; *Louis' Loops, Songs,* and various solo piano pieces by the versatile 30-year-old English composer and formidable pianist Errollyn WALLEN; *East Broadway* for toy piano and toy boombox (1996) by the American composer and co-founder of the internationally-acclaimed New York new music festival, Bang on a Can, Julia WOLFE; *Ductwork* for chamber ensemble (1997) by the French-Canadian composer Linda BOUCHARD; *Islands* for soprano saxophone, clarinet, English horn, trumpet, and trombone (1998) by the respected 67-year-old American composer Alvin LUCIER; and the world premiere of *Les Émois d'Aphrodite* for synthesizers, piano, percussion, and clarinet (1998) by the multi-faceted French composer Luc FERRARI.

26 MARCH 1999

On the second day of the fifth "Other Minds" Festival in San Francisco, a concert is given at the Cowell Theater at the Fort Mason Center, featuring special guest artist Margaret Leng Tan, pianist, in the following program: *Mirabella (A Tarantella)* for toy piano (1995) by the 56-year-old American composer and pianist Stephen (Rowley) MONTAGUE; *Eleanor Rigby* by John LENNON/ Paul MCCARTNEY (1966), arranged by Toby TWINING for toy piano; *Nothing Is Real (Strawberry Fields Forever)* for piano and teapot with miniature sound system (1990) by the respected 67-year-old American composer Alvin LUCIER; *Three 2-Part Studies* for player piano (1942) by the remarkable American-born Mexican composer and innovator in the technique of recording notes on a player-piano roll Conlon NANCARROW (1912–1997), arranged for two toy pianos by Margaret Leng TAN; *Rapture* for viola and piano (1998) by the versatile 30-year-old English composer and formidable pianist Errollyn WALLEN; *Mirrors* for piano (1989) by the 47-year-old Portuguese composer and pianist António Pinho VARGAS; and selections by American trombone legend Julian PRIESTER and brilliant jazz improviser on tenor and soprano saxophones, flute, and piano Sam RIVERS for trombone, saxophone, and electronics.

27 MARCH 1999

Horn Concerto (1995–96) by the prominent 71-year-old Swedish composer, organist, musicologist, and pedagogue Bengt HAMBRAEUS is heard for the first time over Swedish TV.

27 MARCH 1999

On the third and final day of the fifth "Other Minds" Festival in San Francisco, a concert is given at the Fort Mason Center, featuring special guest artist Margaret Leng Tan, pianist, in the following program: *Presque Rien No. 4, "La remontée du village"* (1998), tape piece by the multi-faceted French composer Luc FERRARI; *Suite for Toy Piano* (1948) by the singularly inventive and much beloved American composer, writer, philosopher, and visual artist of ultramodern tendencies John CAGE (1912–1992); *General Complex* for two toy pianos (1995) by the 47-year-old Portuguese composer and pianist António Pinho VARGAS; *Sweet Chinoiserie* (1995) by the 51-year-old American composer and accordionist Guy KLUCEVSEK, in three movements—*Not With My Chopsticks You Don't!*, *Silent as Swans*, and *The Mark of a Hero*—arranged by the composer for toy pianos, toy accordion, melodica, toy drums and rattles, glasses, soya sauce dishes, and cat food cans; *Satie Blues* (1989) and *Nightmare Rag* (1989), two works for piano and toy piano, by Toby TWINING; and *Sight of Hand* (1999), *Shiva* (1994), *Drum Roll* (1998), *Click* (1989), and *Talking Stick* (1998), five works by the successful American composer Mary Ellen CHILDS.

28 MARCH 1999

Trio supra "et sola facta" for clarinet, violin, and piano (1998) by the distinguished 72-year-old French-American composer and teacher Betsy JOLAS, daughter of the poet and journalist Eugène Jolas, best known as the founder and editor of the literary journal *transition*, is performed for the first time in Washington, D.C.

1 APRIL 1999

Piece for orchestra (1998–99) by the 40-year-old Finnish composer Magnus (Gustaf Adolf) LINDBERG is given its first ever performance in Cleveland.

3 APRIL 1999

The English composer and lyricist Lionel BART (real name, Begleiter), creator of the enormously popular *Oliver!* (London, June 30, 1960), after Dickens's *Oliver Twist*, as well as a number of other stage successes, dies in his native London at the moderate age of 68.

10 APRIL 1999

The extraordinary 33-year-old American countertenor David DANIELS makes his Metropolitan Opera debut in New York as Arsamene.

14 APRIL 1999

Dust, multi-media television opera, by the pioneering 69-year-old American composer, performer, director, and writer Robert (Reynolds) ASHLEY, in collaboration with Y. Yoshihara, is given its first ever stage performance in New York.

17 APRIL 1999

Girlanda (Garland) for eight flutes by the 70-year-old Polish composer and teacher Adam WALACIŃSKI is heard for the first time in his native Kraków.

22 APRIL 1999

Saturnalia for double bass (1996) by the 74-year-old Croatian-born French composer, conductor, and teacher Ivo MALEC is performed for the first time in his native Zagreb.

24 APRIL 1999

What We Can See of the Sky Has Fallen for orchestra (1998–99) by the productive 34-year-old Irish composer Ian WILSON is given its first ever performance in his native Belfast.

25 APRIL 1999

Bassoon Sonata (1997) by the brilliant 70-year-old German-born American pianist, conductor, and composer André (George) (real name, Andreas Ludwig Priwin) PREVIN is performed for the first time in New York.

27 APRIL 1999

The Hungarian-born Swiss soprano Maria STADER (originally, Molnár), especially admired for her interpretations of Bach and Mozart, but was esteemed for her performances of works by A. Scarlatti, Gluck, Bruckner, and Mahler, dies in Zürich at the respectable age of 87.

28 APRIL 1999

Des Saisons en enfer, opera, by the 74-year-old Romanian-born French conductor, composer, and teacher Marius CONSTANT, whose credits include the composition of the signature theme for the popular TV program, *The Zwilight Zone* (1959), is mounted for the first time in Monte Carlo.

29 APRIL 1999

Two Paths for two violas and orchestra (1998) by the remarkable 67-year-old Russian composer Sofia (Asgatovna) GUBAIDULINA is given its first ever performance in New York.

30 APRIL 1999

Who's Afraid of Red, Yellow, and Blue?, saxophone concerto (1998), by the ascending 34-year-old Irish composer Ian WILSON is performed for the first time in Ulster.

1 MAY 1999

Ernst Toller: Requiem for an Idea for actor and cello by the accomplished 48-year-old Canadian composer Michael (Bass) MATTHEWS is given its first performance in Winnipeg.

2 MAY 1999

Antikrist, biblical opera (1921–39), by the distinguished Danish composer and organist Rued (Immanuel) LANGGAARD, first heard over Danish Radio on June 28, 1980, is given its belated stage premiere in Innsbruck.

4 MAY 1999

Double Violin Concerto by the gifted 49-year-old South African-born Irish composer Kevin VOLANS is performed for the first time in Belfast.

8 MAY 1999

Concerto breve for strings (1998) by the 68-year-old Polish composer and teacher Romuald TWARDOWSKI is premiered in Warsaw.

9 MAY 1999

The English violinist and conductor Harry BLECH, founder of a variety of ensembles, including the Blech String Quartet (1933), which he served as first violinist until it disbanded in 1950, the London Wind Players (1942), the London Symphonic Players (1946), the London Mozart Players (1949), which he served as conductor until 1984 when he was made its conductor laureate, and the London Mozart Choir (1952), dies in his native London at the respectable age of 89.

10 MAY 1999

Triple Double for oboe, English horn, bassoon, and tape by the productive 69-year-old American composer and teacher Robert (Paige) CEELY is performed for the first time in Brookline, Massachusetts.

12 MAY 1999

Whistling in the Dark for chamber ensemble by the innovative 48-year-old American composer, conductor, and teacher Donald CROCKETT is heard for the first time in Los Angeles.

14 MAY 1999

Scenes for Piano IV, Bretagne by the multi-talented 72-year-old English pianist, organist, conductor, writer on music, and composer Francis (John) ROUTH is given its premiere performance in London.

15 MAY 1999

Hidden Voice 2 for chamber ensemble and compact disc by the significant 60-year-old English composer Jonathan (Dean) HARVEY is performed for the first time in London.

17 MAY 1999

Temenos, with Mermaids and Angels for orchestra (1998) by the eminent 64-year-old English composer and conductor Sir Peter Maxwell DAVIES is heard for the first time ever in Dublin.

18 MAY 1999

The Canadian conductor and composer William (Alexander) MCCAULEY, successively music director of York University (1960–69), the O'Keefe Centre (1960–87), Christopher Chapman Films (1969-70), Seneca College (1970–78), and the North York Symphony Orchestra (1972–88), dies in Alliston, Ontario, at the seasoned age of 82.

19 MAY 1999

Continuum for organ and tape (1991) and *String Quartet* (1992), two works by the 52-year-old Russian composer, conductor, and teacher Nikolai KORNDORF, are premiered in his native Moscow.

21 MAY 1999

Eleanor's Gift, cello concerto, by the productive 46-year-old Chinese composer and teacher Chen YI, originally premiered in San Francisco on Dec. 10, 1998, is given its first ever performance in a revised version in New York.

22 MAY 1999

A program of works for guitar and drum set by the imaginative 40-year-old American composer, performer, and programmer Nick (actually, Nicholas Russel) DIDKOVSKY, comprised of first ever performances of his *One Wooden Leg, Stuffed, The Corpse Was Born Half As Long As Life, The Round Nose of Some 20 Years*, and *Two Languages Take Twice As Long*, is given in Vandoeuvre, France.

23 MAY 1999

Pater noster for men's chorus and organ (1997) by the 74-year-old Polish composer and pedagogue Krystyna MOSZUMAŃSKA-NAZAR is heard for the first time in Kraków.

26 MAY 1999

The respected Swiss conductor and philanthropist Paul SACHER, husband to Maja Stehlin, widow of Emmanuel Hoffmann, whose father founded the Hoffmann-La Roche pharmaceutical firm, makers of the drugs Valium and Librium, through whose fortune was able to pursue his goal of commissioning works from the leading composers of the 20th century (in all, over 200, including scores by Stravinsky, Bartók, Strauss, Honegger, Hindemith, Martin, Britten, Henze, and Boulez, many of which received their premieres under his direction), and who in 1986 established the Paul Sacher Foundation in Basel, which would ultimately house the archives of Stravinsky (purchased for $5,250,000), Webern, Martin, and Maderna, among others, dies near his native Basel at the respectable age of 93.

30 MAY 1999

Litany to the Virgin Mary of Supraśl for alto, chorus, and chamber orchestra by the 72-year-old Polish composer Juliusz (Mieczyslaw) ŁUCIUK is given its premiere performance in Kraków.

3 JUNE 1999

Chaconne for violin and orchestra (1997), used in the film score *The Red Violin* (1998) by the noteworthy 61-year-old American composer and teacher John (Paul) CORIGLIANO, son of the American violinist John Corigliano (1901-1975), is given its first performance as a suite for violin and orchestra in New York.

4 JUNE 1999

Sinfonietta for orchestra (1998) and *Une lecture de Marie Noël* for two flutes, two clarinets, trombone, percussion, piano, and cello (1999), two works by the notable 52-year-old French composer Jean-Claude WOLFF, are heard for the first time in Le Blanc-Mcsnil.

6 JUNE 1999

A *Toy Symphony* for six soloists and chamber orchestra by the 56-year-old American composer and pianist Stephen (Rowley) MONTAGUE is given its premiere performance in Bath.

8 JUNE 1999

The Golden Door for chorus and chamber ensemble by the 57-year-old American composer and teacher Ronald (Christopher) PERERA is heard for the first time in New York.

13 JUNE 1999

Prairie Dawn for clarinet and orchestra (1998) by the 49-year-old American composer and teacher Stephen (George) CHATMAN is premiered in Vancouver.

16 JUNE 1999

The American organist, teacher, and composer Rayner BROWN, long-time organist at Wilshire Presbyterian Church (1941–77) and professor of music at Biola University in La Mirada, California (1950–77), dies in Los Angeles at the age of 87.

18 JUNE 1999

An Aphrodite for oboe (1998) and *Aphorismen zu Goethes Urworte Orphisch* for oboe and harpsichord (1998), two works by the prolific 72-year-old German composer, pedagogue, organist, and harpsichordist Ruth ZECHLIN, is performed for the first time in Passau.

25 JUNE 1999

The American composer and musicologist Everett (Burton) HELM, an accomplished linguist who contributed articles to various music magazines in several languages and made a specialty of the music of Yugoslavia, dies in Berlin at the age of 85.

27 JUNE 1999

The outstanding Finnish composer (Sven) Einar ENGLUND, whose works, while continuing along the path of neo-Classicism, revealed a mastery of concentrated power, invention, and lyricism which placed him among the foremost composers of Finland, and whose *Second Symphony*, entitled *The Blackbird Symphony*, first performed in Helsinki on Oct. 8, 1948, became one of his most celebrated works, dies in Helsinki at the age of 83.

28 JUNE 1999

The Czech composer Luboš FIŠER, whose music is often associated with paintings, archeology, and human history, his style of composition employing effective technical devices without adhering to any particular doctrine, with his *15 Prints after Dürer's Apocalypse* for orchestra (1964–65), his most successful work, receiving the UNESCO prize in Paris in 1967, dies in his native Prague at the premature age of 63.

29 JUNE 1999

Sonata da chiesa for flute and organ (1998) by the 49-year-old American composer, organist, and teacher Dan (Steven) LOCKLAIR is performed for the first time in Knoxville, Tennessee.

30 JUNE 1999

The respected American pianist and teacher Beveridge WEBSTER, son of Beveridge Webster, the founder-director of the Pittsburgh Conservatory, and who acquired a notable reputation for his insightful performances of the music of Debussy and Ravel, dies in Hanover, New Hampshire, at the well seasoned age of 91.

6 JULY 1999

The eminent Spanish composer and teacher Joaquín RODRIGO, whose music, expertly crafted, was reflective of the colors and melorhythms of Spain, and whose most celebrated score is the *Concierto de Aranjuez* for guitar and orchestra (1939; Barcelona, Nov. 9, 1940) became a classic during his own lifetime, dies in Madrid at the remarkable age of 97.

7 JULY 1999

The Days Before Death Destruction & Detroit III, musico-dramatic stage work by the remarkable 57-year-old American theater director, stage designer, and dramatist Robert WILSON, to a libretto after Umberto Eco's *The Island of the Day Before*, with music by Ryuichi Sakamoto (founder of the techno-pop group Yellow Magic Orchestra [YMO] and winner of an Academy Award for his film score for *The Last Emperor*), is mounted for the first time in New York.

9 JULY 1999

The American pianist and teacher Samuel SANDERS, an influential figure from 1963 at the Juilliard School of Music, where he was instrumental in establishing its master's degree program in accompaniment, and whose later career was hampered with recurrent heart problems, which led to open heart surgery, followed by heart transplants in both 1990 and 1998, dies in his native New York at the modest age of 62.

10 JULY 1999

La fille joue aux oiseaux de nuit for recorder(s) and tape (1998) by the 59-year-old Finnish trumpeter and composer Jarmo (Kalevi) SERMILÄ is given its first ever performance in Viitasaari.

15 JULY 1999

Forever Escher for double quartet (string quartet and saxophone quartet) (1995) by the respected 51-year-old American composer, arranger, and teacher Paul (Seiko) CHIHARA is heard for the first time ever in Chautauqua.

16 JULY 1999

Ritual Incantations for cello and chamber orchestra (1998) by the admired 35-year-old American composer Augusta Read THOMAS, wife of the remarkable American composer Bernard Rands, is given its first ever performance in Aspen.

20 JULY 1999

Řecké pašije (Greek Passion), musical drama after Kazantzakis (1955–59), by the remarkable Czech-born American composer Bohuslav (Jan) MARTINŮ (1890–1959), is given its first ever performance in Bregenz in its original version as reconstructed by Ales Brezina.

24 JULY 1999

Central Park, opera, by the notable 37-year-old American composer and pianist Michael TORKE, in collaboration with R. Beaser and D. Drattell, is mounted for the first time in Glimmerglass, New York.

26 JULY 1999

Autumn Gardens for orchestra by the eminent 70-year-old Finnish composer and pedagogue Einojuhani (actually, Eino Juhani) RAUTAVAARA is performed for the first time in London.

29 JULY 1999

Aerial, trumpet concerto (1998–99), by the 56-year-old Austrian composer, conductor, chansonnier, and double bass player H(einz) K(arl) "Nali" GRUBER, great-great-grandson of the Austrian composer Franz Xaver Gruber (1787–1863), is given its premiere performance in London.

30 JULY 1999

Second Symphony (1998–99) by the 53-year-old Latvian composer and teacher Pēteris VASKS is heard for the first time in Bournemouth.

31 JULY 1999

Trio for clarinet, cello, and piano (1997–98) by the remarkable 55-year-old Polish composer and teacher Krzysztof MEYER is performed for the first time in Hitzaker.

11 AUGUST 1999

Quarries for piano, four-hands, by the esteemed 76-year-old American composer, organist, choral conductor, and teacher Daniel (Rogers) PINKHAM, Jr., is premiered in Rocca di Cambio.

18 AUGUST 1999

Third Piano Concerto, entitled *Gift of Dreams* (1998), by the eminent 70-year-old Finnish composer and pedagogue Einojuhani (actually, Eino, Juhani) RAUTAVARA is heard for the first time in Tampere.

21 AUGUST 1999

Fifth Symphony by the respected 56-year-old English composer and writer on music David (John) MATTHEWS, brother of the 53-year-old English composer, writer on music, and broadcaster Colin Matthews, is performed for the first time in their native London.

24 AUGUST 1999

The Egyptian-born French guitarist and teacher of Greek and Italian descent Alexandre LAGOYA, long time husband and partner of the respected French guitarist Ida Presti (1924–1967), dies in Paris at the age of the 70.

28 AUGUST 1999

Summer, opera, after Edith Wharton (1997–99), by the imaginative 50-year-old American composer Stephen (Harrison) PAULUS, is mounted for the first time in Pittsfield, Massachusetts, with the 51-year-old American bass-baritone John (Taylor) CHEEK creating the role of Lawyer Royall.

7 SEPTEMBER 1999

Dixit Farouche for soloists, chorus, and chamber orchestra by the 74-year-old French composer Antoine DUHAMEL, son of the writer Georges Duhamel and the comedienne Blanche Albane, is performed for the first time ever in d'Ambronay.

8 SEPTEMBER 1999

The Czech composer Klement SLAVICKÝ, whose career was hampered for more than 40 years due to the reign of the Communist regime in his native country, but who emerged, with the collapse of Communism in Czechoslovakia in 1989, as a respected elder statesman of Czech musical life, and whose *Fourth Sinfonietta*, entitled *Pax hominibus in universo orbi*, dedicated to the United Nations in honor of its 40th anniversary in 1985, was awarded the U.N. Gold Commemorative Medal, dies in Prague at the respectable age of 88.

9 SEPTEMBER 1999

The Carbon Copy Building, comic-book opera, by the imaginative 42-year-old American composer David LANG is mounted for the first time in Turin.

10 SEPTEMBER 1999

The distinguished Spanish tenor of Austrian descent Alfredo KRAUS (Trujillo), a consummate artist with a voice of remarkable beauty, particularly noted for his portrayals of Rossini's Count Almaviva, Don Ottavio, Ernesto in *Don Pasquale*, Des Grieux, Nadir in *Les Pêcheurs de perles*, and Massenet's Werther, dies in Madrid at the age of 71.

13 SEPTEMBER 1999

Canto a García Lorca for voice and cello octet (1998) and *Beiramar* for voice and cello octet (1999), two works by the notable 60-year-old Brazilian composer, pianist, and conductor Marlos NOBRE, are performed for the first time in Amsterdam.

14 SEPTEMBER 1999

The renowned Hungarian-born American cellist and pedagogue János STARKER celebrates his 75 birthday by performing as soloist in a gala performance of the Brahms *Double Concerto* with the Indiana University Phiharmonic in Bloomington, Indiana, conducted by Rostropovich.

16 SEPTEMBER 1999

What Next?, the first opera by the outstanding 90-year-old American composer and teacher Elliott (Cook) CARTER, Jr., is staged for the first time in Berlin.

17 SEPTEMBER 1999

Fifth Symphony by the spirited 48-year-old American composer Libby (actually, Elizabeth Brown) LARSEN is performed for the first time in Denver.

18 SEPTEMBER 1999

Commencement de siècle for chamber ensemble and live electronics by the ascending 28-year-old Polish composer and clarinetist Paweł MYKIETYN is premiered in Warsaw.

22 SEPTEMBER 1999

The Heart Piece, opera, by the 52-year-old Polish composer Krzysztof KNITTEL, in collaboration with John King, is staged for the first time ever in his native Warsaw.

24 SEPTEMBER 1999

The Swedish organist, choirmaster, teacher, and composer Torsten NILSSON, who excelled as a composer of liturgical works, and who introduced many innovations in his organ music, such as static tone-clusters and specified periods of thematic improvisation, dies in Stockholm at the age of 79.

25 SEPTEMBER 1999

Brûlis for clarinet, cello, and piano by the versatile 64-year-old French composer, musicologist, and philologist François-Bernard MÂCHE is heard for the first time in Venice.

25 SEPTEMBER 1999

The 73rd Festival of the International Society for Contemporary Music opens in Romania and Moldavia with a concert at Bucharest's Romanian Atheneum performed by the Philharmonic Orchestra "George Enescu," with special guest artists Zygmunt Krauze, pianist, and The Rascher Saxophone Quartet, conducted by Christian Mandeal, in the following program: *Acalanto* by the Norwegian composer Peter TORNQUIST, *Cantico I* by the Slovenian composer Lojze LEBIC, *Piano Concerto No. 2* by the 60-year-old Polish composer and pianist Zygmunt KRAUZE, and *Chimères* by the German composer Theo BRANDMÜLLER.

26 SEPTEMBER 1999

The 36-year-old Argentine tenor, conductor, and composer José CURA makes his Metropolitan Opera debut in New York as Turiddu.

26 SEPTEMBER 1999

On the second day of the 73rd Festival of the International Society for Contemporary Music in Romania and Moldavia, three concerts are given, in the following sequence:

A late afternoon concert at Bucharest's Auditorium Hall performed by Pro Contemporania, conducted by Iuri Florea, in the following program: *Illusion of time* by the Belgian composer Walter SCHRAEYEN, *Intimacy* by the Israeli composer Vladimir SCOLNIC, *Aksak* by the Dutch composer Theo LOEVENDIE, *À la recherche* by the Swiss composer Jean-Luc DARBELLAY, *L'arrivée à Cythère* by the German composer Thomas BEIMEL, and *Terra incognita* by the Argentine composer Gabriel VALVERDE.

An evening concert at Bucharest's Radio Symphony Orchestra Hall performed by the Chamber Orchestra "Virtuosi," with special guest artist Anca Varolomei, cellist, conducted by Horia Andreescu, in the following program: *Ululation* by the Finnish composer Jukka KOSKINEN, *Cello Concerto* by the Taiwanese composer Hwang-Long PAN, *Sinfonia* by the Venezuelan composer Alfredo RUGELES, and *Undecimum* by the Romanian composer Stefan NICULESCU.

A late evening concert at Bucharest's Arcub Hall, "Multimedia I," performed by Daniel Kientzy, saxophones, and Reina Portuondo, electronics, in the following program: *Saxatile* by the French composer Jean Claude RISSET, *Pulsions* by the distinguished Romanian composer and musicologist Anatol VIERU (1926–1998), *Lisboa, tramway 28* by the Polish composer Elzbieta SIKORA, *Violet ritual p.a.a.* by the 57-year-old

Brazilian composer and teacher Jorge ANTUNES, *Noir, trois neiges d'un paysage* by the French composers James GIROUDON and Jan François ESTAGER, and *Itee* by the French composer Gilles RACOT.

27 SEPTEMBER 1999

On the third day of the 73rd Festival of the International Society for Contemporary Music in Romania and Moldavia, four concerts are given, in the following sequence:

A late afternoon concert at Bucharest's Auditorium Hall, with the following program: *UL* by the Russian composer Alexander LITVINOVSKY, *Ciclos para cuarteto de cuerdos* by the Chilean composer Aliocha Solovera ROJE, *Spiritus tuus in nobis* by the Slovak composer Egon KRAK, *About Time* by the Czech composer Michal MACOUREK, and *The Realing-Up* by the Czech composer Edvard SCHIFFAUER.

A late afternoon concert by Game, conducted by Alexandru Matei, in the following program: *Morning Hill* by the Chinese composer Clarence MAK, *No tocar* by the Mexican composer Eduardo Soto MILAN, *Digital signals* by the Dutch composer David Clair LITTLE, and *Time and Space* by the Romanian composer Tiberiu OLAH.

An evening concert at Bucharest's Radio Symphony Orchestra Hall performed by the Chamber Orchestra Radio, with special guest artist Andrei Kivu, cello, conducted by Christian Brancusi, in the following program: *Canticello* for cello and orchestra by the Albanian composer Thoma SIMAKU, *Intervall 19* by the German composer Ernstalbrecht STIEBLER, and *Parallels* by the Ukrainian composer Karmella TSEPKOLENKO.

An evening performance by the Children's Choir of the Arts' School, O. Bancila', Iaşi, and La Camerata' Ensemble, Iaşi, conducted by Jorge Antunes and Doru Morariu, of *Rimbaudiannisia MCMXCV* by the 57-year-old Brazilian composer and teacher Jorge ANTUNES.

28 SEPTEMBER 1999

On the fourth day of the 73rd Festival of the International Society for Contemporary Music in Romania and Moldavia, four concerts are given, in the following sequence:

A late afternoon at Bucharest's Auditorium Hall performed by the Archaeus Ensemble, conducted by Liviu Danceanu, in the following program: *The Legend of Dreams* by the Romanian composer Ulpiu VLAD, *Retratos de Macondo* by the Venezuelan composer Adina IZARRA, *Sounds Etudes* by the Moldova composer Ghenadi CIOBANU, *Bird in the Tangled Sky* by the Canadian composer Jocelyn MORLOCK, and *Dancing to my Spirit* by the Japanese composer Takuo KOCHI.

A late afternoon concert by Repertorium, with Inna Oncescu, piano, Adina Radu, percussion, Christiana Budescu, percussion, and Mihai Vartosu, piano, in the following program: *Hora* by the Israeli composer Ari Ben SHABETAI, *In the Memories* by the Japanese composer Stoshi OHMAE, *Masques* by the Spanish composer Jesús TORRES, and *Echoes' white* by the American composer Jason ECKARDT.

An evening concert at Bucharest's Radio Symphony Orchestra Hall performed by the Symphonic National Radio Orchestra and Choir, with special guest artists Pierre Yves Artaud, flute, and Fredrik Burstedt, violin, conducted by Ludovic Bacs and Aurel Grioras, in the following program: *Symphony* by the Danish composer Bent SØRENTSEN, *Vocalizes of the Sea* by the Romanian composer Theodor GRIGORIU, *Concerto* for flute and string orchestra by the Azerbaijan composer Ismail GAJIBEKOV, and *Violin Concerto* by the Swedish composer Per MARTENSSON.

A late night concert at Bucharest's Aula UCMR, with the following program: *Paganihilismo* by the Austrian composer Dieter KAUFMANN, *Thrausmata* by the Australian composer Ros BANDT, *Synthyphonye* by the Bulgarian composer Lubomir MITZEV, *When Timbre Comes Apart* by the Norwegian composer Joran RUDI, and *Lopa Varg* by the Swedish composer Anders BLOMQVIST.

29 SEPTEMBER 1999

On the fifth day of the 73rd Festival of the International Society for Contemporary Music in Romania and Moldavia, three concerts are given, in the following sequence:

A late afternoon concert at Cluj-Napoca's Music Academy Hall performed by Trio Contraste, with special guest artist Andrei Deleanu, piano, in the following program: *Duel* by the Yugoslav composer Srdan HOFMAN, *Sax* by the Chilean composer Mario MORA, *Wing of Prayer* by the American composer Melinda WAGNER, and *Introversion III* by the German composer Eckart BEINKE.

A late afternoon concert by the Percussion Ensemble of Cluj-Napoca, conducted by Grigore Pop, in the following program: *A la Sombra de la Higuera* by the Bolivian composer Cergio PRUDENCIO, *Letah* by the Brazilian composer Roberto VICTORIO, *Triplum* by Gabriel IRANY, *Fase II* by the Mexican composer Ignacio Baca LOBERA, *As ?* by the Taiwanese composer Jer-Huei CHEN, and *Puls* by the Finnish composer Tapio TOUMELA.

An evening concert at Cluj-Napoca's Music Academy Hall performed by Christina Muresan, piano, and Florin Ghic, electronics, in the following program: *Do You Remember the Chirping of Crickets?* by the Hungarian composer János DECSÉNYI, *Morfe Technes* by the Swedish composer Joakim SANDGREN, *Trail of Tears* by the Japanese composer Yasuhiro TAKENAKA, *Earth Haze* by the Norwegian composer Natasha BARRETT, and *Dinergy 2* by the Japanese composer Tamami TONO.

29 SEPTEMBER 1999

In doppelter Tiefe for mezzo-soprano, alto, and orchestra by the distinguished 47-year-old German composer and teacher Wolfgang (Michael) RIHM is given its premiere performance in Berlin.

30 SEPTEMBER 1999

On the sixth day of the 73rd Festival of the International Society for Contemporary Music in Romania and Moldavia, two concerts are given, in the following sequence:

A late afternoon concert at Cluj-Napoca's Music Academy Hall performed by the Antifonia Choir, conducted by Constantin Rapa, in the following program: *Madrigale* by the Italian composer Marcella MANDANICI; *Gesualdo* by the Argentine composer Miguel BELLUSCI; *Non Stop* by the Finnish composer Mikko HEINIO; *Little Chamber Music* by the Chinese composer Richard TSANG; *Coro primo* by the Italian composer Pippo MOLINO; *Callings* by the Romanian composer Nicolae TEODOREANU; *Auroram Lucifer* by the German composer Caroline WILKINS; *Miserere* by the esteemed 84-year-old Norwegian choral conductor, organist, pedagogue, and composer Knut NYSTEDT; *7 Haiku* by the Mexican composer Jorge CORDOBA; *Versuri de dor* by the Romanian composer Vasile HERMAN; and *Uvedenrode* by the Romanian composer Constantin RAPA.

An evening concert at Cluj-Napoca's Music Academy Hall performed by the Chamber Orchestra 'Ars Nova, with special guest soloists Gh. Rosu, Marius Budoiu, and Flavius Trif, conducted by Cornel Taran, with the following program: *Oreste-Odeipe 1* by the Romanian composer Cornel TARANU, *Nonet* by the Icelandic composer Kjartan OLAFSSON, *Quatuor à trios 1* by the French composer Fernand VANDER-BOGAERDE, *Into the blue* by the English composer Rebecca SAUNDERS, *Cvintet* by the Moldova composer Vladimir BELEAEV, *De Tierra* by the American composer Ricardo Zohn MULDOON, and *Fern and E. Green: 'A' miniature* by the Canadian composer Michelle BOUDREAU.

1 OCTOBER 1999

On the seventh day of the 73rd Festival of the International Society for Contemporary Music in Romania and Moldova, three concerts are given, in the following sequence:

A late afternoon concert at Cluj-Napoca's Music Academy Hall performed by Traject, chamber ensemble, conducted by Sorin Lerescu, in the following program: *Libres en el sonido pressos, en el sonido* by the Uruguayan composer Graciela PARASKEVAIDIS, *Ariel* by the Australian composer Eve DUNCAN, *Discussions* by the Israeli composer Menachem ZUR, *Segles* by the Lithuanian composer Jurgis JUOZA-PAITIS, and *Spectacle for an instant* by the 59-year-old Romanian composer Octavian NEMESCU.

A late afternoon recital by Andrei Tanasescu and Scott Tinney, pianists, with special guest pianist Camelia Goila, in the following program: *Prosegisi 11* by the Greek composer Anastasios VASILIADIS, *For Two Pianos* by the Dutch composer Robert ZUIDAM, *Epiphora* by the Polish composer Pawel MYKIETYN, *Sonata para piano nr. 4* by the Mexican composer Leonardo CORAL, *Le Temple du Silence* by the Bulgarian composer Gheorghi ARNAOUDOV, *Undulation A* for piano (1996) by the 67-year-old Japanese composer Makoto SHINOHARA, *For piano 1* by the English composer Richard EMSLEY, and *Let's play* by the Uruguayan composer Juan Felipe SILVEIRA.

An evening concert at Cluj-Napoca's Philarmony Orchestra Cluj Hall performed by The Philharmonic Transilvania, with special guest artists Dorina Mangra, violin, Kiraly Csaba, piano, Emil Sein, saxophone, and Pierre Yves Artaud, flute, conducted by Remus Georgescu, in the following program: *Violin Concerto* by the Luxembourg composer Marcel WENGLER; *Piano Concerto* by the Croatian composer Dubravko DETONI; *Saxophone Concerto* by the Irish composer John BUCKLEY; *Concerto No. 3*, subtitled *Magics Cercles*, for flute and orchestra, by the Romanian composer Doina ROTARU; and *Altaic Ritual* by the Korean composer June-Hee LIM.

2 OCTOBER 1999

The Austrian-born New Zealand conductor Georg (Bernard) TINTNER, who in 1937 became an assistant conductor at the Vienna Volksoper but in 1938 was compelled by the Anschluss to flee the Nazis, after which he settled in New Zealand, where he served in various directorial capacities, dies by his own hand in Halifax at the age of 82.

3 OCTOBER 1999

On the eighth day of the 73rd Festival of the International Society for Contemporary Music in Romania and Moldova, a concert is given at Chisinau's Philharmonic Orchestra Hall, performed by the Symphonic Orchestra of Chisinau, with guest soloists Virgil Francu, flute, and Sergiu Helioglu, piano, conducted by Valentin Doni, in

the following program: *Simfonia* by the Moldova composer Dmitri KITSENKO, *Modalis 11*, flute concerto, by the Romanian composer Sorin LERESCU, *Stanze* by the Moldova composer Vasile ZAGORSCHI, *Echo* by the Korean composer Jie-Sun LIM, and *Moment bacovian* by the Moldova composer Ghenadie CIOBANU.

4 OCTOBER 1999

Nipson for countertenor and viol consort (1998) by the remarkable 55-year-old English composer John (Kenneth) TAVENER is heard for the first time in Norwich.

4 OCTOBER 1999

On the ninth day of the 73rd Festival of the International Society for Contemporary Music in Romania and Moldova, two concerts are given, in the following sequence:

A late afternoon concert at Chisinau's Organ Hall, with the following program: *The Persistence of Memory* by the English composer Richard CAUSTON, *Reality* by the significant 61-year-old Finnish composer and teacher Paavo HEININEN, *Dialects* by the Azerbaijan composer Zaur FAHRADOV, *Toccata Longa* by the Brazilian composer Calimerio SOARES, *Evening* by the Taiwanese composer Wang Sue YA, and *Par-ci, par-la* by the Canadian composer Chan Ka NIN.

An early evening concert at Bacau's Philarmony Hall performed by the Game Ensemble, in the following program: *Danza del dahina* by the Spanish composer Carmen VERDU, *Relief I, II* by the 58-year-old German composer and pedagogue Dieter ACKER, *A Silver Thread* by the Irish composer Jean O'LEARY, *Concerto* for piano and percussion by the Romanian composer Dan DEDIU, *L'abime de Pascal* by the Romanian composer Liviu DANCEANU, and *Necronomicon* by the Spanish composer Tomás MARCO.

5 OCTOBER 1999

The distinguished French organist and teacher Marie-Madeleine (née Chevalier) DURUFLÉ, an authoritative interpreter of the works of her husband, the eminent French composer Maurice Duruflé, and who also excelled as an interpreter of Widor, Vierne, Dupré, and Langlais, dies in Paris at the age of 78.

5 OCTOBER 1999

On the tenth day of the 73rd Festival of the International Society for Contemporary Music in Romania and Moldova, two concerts are given, in the following sequence:

An early evening concert at Bacau's Philarmony Hall performed by the Archaeus Ensemble, Quartet Florilegium, Game Ensemble, and Duo Valentina Sandu and Dan Dediu, in the following program: *Micro-pseudo-requiem* by the Romanian composer Liviu DANCEANU, *Double I* by the French composer James GIROUDON, *Idile and Guerrille* by the Romanian composer Dan DEDIU, *Trio* by the 58-year-old German composer and pedagogue Dieter ACKER, *Quartet No. 4* by the Spanish composer Tomás MARCO, *String Quartet* by the Finnish composer Daping QIN, and *Sombra de Alilanto* by the Spanish composer Carmen VERDU.

An evening concert at Chisinau's Organ Hall performed by Traject, chamber ensemble, conducted by Sorin Lerescu, in the following program: *Delirium* by the English composer James CLARKE, *Skyin* by the Icelandic composer Karólína EIRÍKS-DÓTTIR, *Reflection of the Sun in the Water* by the Russian composer Dmitry LYBIN, *Catalan Tales* by the Irish composer Ian WILSON, *Wavelets* by the Greek composer Leontios HADJILEONTIADIS, and *Spectacle for an Instant* by the 59-year-old Romanian composer Octavian NEMESCU.

6 OCTOBER 1999

On the eleventh day of the 73rd Festival of the International Society for Contemporary Music in Romania and Moldova, two concerts are given, in the following sequence:

An early evening concert at Bacau's Philarmony Hall performed by Archaeus' Ensemble, with special guest artist Adriana Cioaba, soprano, in the following program: *Gothic Concerto* by the Romanian composer Dan DEDIU, *Winter Music* by the 71-year-old Italian composer and teacher Italian composer Vittorio FELLEGARA, *Lorna* by the Romanian composer Carmen VERDU, *Light and shade—setting off* by the Russian composer Yuri KASPAROV, *Traces* by the French composer James GIROUDON, *Duo* by the Irish composer Jane O'LEARY, and *Septett* by the 58-year-old German composer and pedagogue Dieter ACKER.

An evening concert at Iaşi's Philarmony Hall performed by Chisinau's Ars Poetica Ensemble, in the following program: *Music to an Unshot Motion Picture* by the Finnish composer Jarmo SERMILA, *Expectation* by the Moldova composer Iulian GOGU, *Deviation* by the Austrian composer Karlheitz ESSL, *Sonata* by the Moldova composer Pavel RIVILIS, *Las Mariposas bailan...en la nada* by the Italian composer Luca BELCASTRO, and *Concerto No. 2* by the Moldova composer Oleg PALYMSKI.

7 OCTOBER 1999

The outstanding 56-year-old Hungarian soprano Eva MARTON portrays Turandot at the reopening of the restored Gran Teatre del Liceu in Barcelona.

7 OCTOBER 1999

On the twelfth day of the 73rd Festival of the International Society for Contemporary Music in Romania and Moldova, seven concerts are given, in the following sequence:

An early evening concert at Bacau's Philarmony Hall performed by the Philarmonic Orchestra "Mihail Jora," with special guest artists Tiziana Moneta, piano, Adriana Cioaba, soprano, and Serban Novac, bassoon, conduced by Ovidiu Balan, in the following program: *Primo vere* by the 71-year-old Italian composer and teacher Vittorio FELLEGARA, *Animal Farm* by the Finnish composer Daping QIN, *Bassoon Concerto* by the Russian composer Yuri KASPAROV, *Sinfonietta No. 1* by the Spanish composer Tomás MARCO, and *Islands of Discovery* by the Irish composer Jane O'LEARY.

An evening concert at Iaşi's Philarmony Hall performed by Musica Viva Ensemble, conducted by Florin Simion, in the following program: *Secret Message* by the Slovenian composer Uros ROJKO, *A Cinque* by the Yugoslav composer Dejan DESPIC, *Crystals* by the Slovak composer Alexander MIHALIC, *Reminiscences* by the Hungarian composer Miklos SUGAR, *In modo rustico* by the Croatian composer Stanko HORVAT, *Colours and Cents of the Night* by Petr POKORNY, *Entre le ciel et l'enfer* by the Romanian composer Irinel ANGHEL, *Ekagrata* by the Ukrainian composer Ludmila YURINA, and *Quintetto* by the Bulgarian composer Velislav ZAIMOV.

An evening concert at Timişoara's Music School Hall performed by the Timişoara Ensemble, in the following program:

Je est un autre by the French composer Jose Luis CAMPANA; *Soprano Only* for six sopranos and ensemble by the 59-year-old American composer and writer on music Tom JOHNSON, with stage direction by Alexander Bayer; *Lavrea* for piano by the Italian composer Luigi MORLEO; *Flying in New York at Summer Night* for flute, clarinet, cello, and marimba by the Korean composer Chan Ji KIM; *Reticoli di diffrazioni* for piano by the Italian composer Riccardo SANTOBONI; *Curses* for solo vocalist, vocalists, and tape by the American composer Sever TIPEI; *Supercalifragillisticexpialidoceus* for tape by the Japanese composer Yusuke IWASAKI; and *New York* for cello and marimba by the Korean composer Jiyoung JUNG.

An evening concert by Duo Manoleanu, in the following program: *Letters to Walt Whitman* by the American composer Dinu GHEZZO, *Three Songs From Love* by the American composer Christopher SCINTO, and *Extravaganze* by the German composer Helge HUNG.

An evening concert by Trio Contraste, with guest pianist Andrei Deleanu, in the following program: *Duel* by the Yugoslav composer Srdan HOFMAN, *Sax para sax* by the Chilean composer Mario MORA, *Wing and Prayer* by the American composer Melinda WAGNER, and *Introversion III* by the German composer Erkart BEINKE.

An evening concert by Trio Contraste and musicians from New York University, in the following program: *Dances of the Spirit* by the American composer Ron MAZVREK, *Shan* by the Taiwanese composer Chianan YEN, *Six Bagatelles* by the 77-year-old American composer Leo KRAFT, *Voices* by the Korean-born American composer Young-mi HA, *Trio* by the American composer Paul LEE, *Elegy for Cassandra* by the English composer John GILBERT, *Trez* by the Korean composer Joug Suh LEE, and *Imaginary Voyages* by the American composer Dinu GHEZZO.

An evening recital by Christel Nies, soprano, in the following program: *Die Landschaft in meine Stimme* by the German composer Klaus Hindrich STAGMER; *Wie entzweit durch das Seil* by the German composer Violeta DINESCU; *Aria* (1958) by the singularly inventive and much beloved American composer, writer, philosopher, and visual artist of ultramodern tendencies American composer John CAGE (1912–1992); *Flammenzeichen* by the Korean composer Younghi Pagh PAAN; and *Sequenza III* (1965) by the eminent 73-year-old Italian composer, conductor, and pedagogue Luciano BERIO.

8 OCTOBER 1999

Piano Concerto "No. 3" by the greatly renowned Polish composer Frédéric (-François) (actually, Fryderyk Franciszek) CHOPIN, in a reconstruction by Alan Kogosowski based on the composer's *Allegro de Concert*, which Chopin had indicated was the first movement of a *Third Piano Concerto*, is performed for the first time in Detroit.

8 OCTOBER 1999

On the thirteenth and final day of the 73rd Festival of the International Society for Contemporary Music in Romania and Moldova, three concerts are given, in the following sequence:

An early evening concert at Bacau's Philarmony Hall performed by Archaeus' Ensemble, in the following program: *Les murs, ciels et silence* by the French composer James GIROUDON, *Bassoon Sonata* by the 58-year-old German composer and pedagogue Dieter ACKER, *Segundo Albor* by the Spanish composer Tomás MARCO, *Shadja* by the Spanish composer Carmen VERDU, *Landscape fading into infinity* by the Russian composer Yuri KASPAROV, *Red anthem* by the

Finnish composer Daping QIN, *Wiegendlied (Lullaby)* by the 71-year-old Italian composer and teacher Italian composer Vittorio FELLEGARA, and *Domestic Music* by the Romanian composer Liviu DANCEANU.

An evening concert at Iaşi's Philarmony Hall performed by the Philarmonic Orchestra 'Moldova, with guest soloist Daniel Kientzy, saxophone, conducted by Gheorghe Costin, in the following program: *"Under Pressure,"* saxophone concerto, by the Swiss composer Dieter AMMAN; *Chapter Three/Stage 1* by the 67-year-old Spanish-born Dutch composer Enrique RAXACH; *Egovision* by the Romanian composer Mihaela VOSGANIAN; and *Saxophone Concerto* by the Romanian composer Calin IOACHIMESCU.

An evening concert at Timişoara's Philarmony Hall performed by the Philharmonic Orchestra 'Banatul', with special guest soloists Florian Croitoru, violin, Voichita, oboe, and Ionut Bogdan Stefanescu, flute, conducted by Remus Georgescu, in the following program: *Violin Concerto* by the significant 68-year-old Norwegian composer Arne NORDHEIM; *Symphonia* by the Polish composer Maciej ZIELINSKI; *Helios*, oboe concerto (1994), by the remarkable 71-year-old English composer Thea MUSGRAVE; *Oberon*, flute concerto, by the 47-year-old Serbian composer and teacher Zoran ERIČ; and *Obertura de Concierto* by the Chilean composer Juan LEMANN.

9 OCTOBER 1999

Passacaglia for cello (1997) by the 52-year-old Russian composer, conductor, and teacher Nikolai KORNDORF is heard for the first time in Amsterdam.

11 OCTOBER 1999

The Polish composer and teacher Zbigniew WISZNIEW-SKI, whose awards included the RAI Award in the International Prix Italia Competition in Sorrento (1959), 1st prize in the Premiere Semaine Chrétienne Internationale de TV competition in Monaco (1969), and the Prime Minister's Award of Poland (1972), dies in Warsaw at the age of 77.

13 OCTOBER 1999

Josef Süss, opera (1998–99), by the 39-year-old German composer Detlev GLANERT is mounted for the first time in Bremen.

14 OCTOBER 1999

Second Piano Concerto, entitled *Red Garuda* (1998–99), by the 52-year-old American composer Peter LIEBERSON, son of the English-American recording executive and composer Goddard Lieberson (1911–1977), is premiered in Boston.

16 OCTOBER 1999

The 49-year-old American baritone David PITTMAN-JENNINGS makes his New York debut in Luigi Dallapiccola's opera *Il Prigioniero* in a concert performance with the Montreal Symphony Orchestra under the direction of Charles (Edouard) Dutoit.

21 OCTOBER 1999

Fifth Piano Concerto by the brilliant 66-year-old Russian composer Rodion (Konstantinovich) SHCHEDRIN is performed for the first time in Los Angeles.

22 OCTOBER 1999

Gondwana-Land for orchestra by the eminent 70-year-old Australian composer and teacher Peter (Joshua) SCULTHORPE is premiered in Malvern, England.

23 OCTOBER 1999

Tower, opera, by the prominent 70-year-old Welsh composer and teacher Alun HODDINOTT is mounted for the first time in Swansea.

28 OCTOBER 1999

The American composer Robert LINN, long-time faculty member (from 1958) and chairman of the theory and composition department (from 1973) at the University of Southern California in Los Angeles, dies there at the age of 74.

29 OCTOBER 1999

American Muse for baritone and orchestra by the 49-year-old American composer, teacher, conductor, and writer on music Steven (Edward) STUCKY is given its first ever performance in Los Angeles.

30 OCTOBER 1999

Heroikon for mezzo-soprano, baritone, reciter, chorus, and orchestra (1974) by the 70-year-old Polish composer Jan FOTEK is premiered in Warsaw.

1 NOVEMBER 1999

The Irish pianist, musicologist, and composer Howard FERGUSON, whose neo-Classical scores frequently incorporated English, Scottish, and Irish folk songs, dies in Cambridge at the respectable age of 91.

10 NOVEMBER 1999

The Austrian-born American violinist and pedagogue Felix GALIMIR, who taught successively at the Juilliard School of Music in New York (from 1962), the Curtis Institute of Music in Philadelphia (from 1972), and the Mannes College of Music in New York (from 1977), where his quartet, the Galimir String Quartet, which subsequently acquired a fine reputation for its performances of contemporary music, was in residence, dies in New York at the age of 89.

11 NOVEMBER 1999

Oltra mar for chorus and orchestra, after Amin Maalouf and Abou Saîd (1998–99), by the significant 47-year-old Finnish composer Kaija (Anneli) SAARIAHO is premiered in New York.

12 NOVEMBER 1999

The French pianist and teacher Gaby (née Gabrielle L'Hôte) CASADESUS, wife of the eminent French pianist and composer Robert Casadesus, with whom she organized the Robert Casadesus International Piano Competition in Cleveland in 1975, which became the Cleveland International Piano Competition in 1994, dies in Paris at the remarkable age of 98.

14 NOVEMBER 1999

The Hungarian-born American pianist and pedagogue György SEBÖK, a long-time professor at the Indiana University School of Music in Bloomington, where he was made a Distinguished Professor in 1985, and whose engagements took him all over the world as a soloist with orchestras, dies in Bloomington, Indiana, at the age of 77.

17 NOVEMBER 1999

Espacios for cello and piano (1998) by the distinguished 80-year-old Chilean composer and musicologist Juan (Antonio) ORREGO-SALAS is premiered in Washington, D.C.

19 NOVEMBER 1999

Cantiques des degrés for chorus and orchestra by the outstanding 64-year-old Estonian-born Austrian composer Arvo PÄRT is given its first ever performance in Monte Carlo.

21 NOVEMBER 1999

Of Whirlwind Underground for E-flat clarinet, bass clarinet, bass trombone, cello, and double bass by the 55-year-old New Zealand composer Lyell (Richard) CRESSWELL is performed for the first time in Auckland.

23 NOVEMBER 1999

6 Gesänge aus der Arabischen for tenor and piano (1997–98) by the outstanding 73-year-old German composer Hans Werner HENZE is heard for the first time in Cologne.

24 NOVEMBER 1999

Canto I for string ensemble by the respected 49-year-old English composer, conductor, writer on music, and teacher Roger (Michael) MARSH is premiered in Huddersfield.

1 DECEMBER 1999

Writing to Vemeer (1997–99), opera, by the inspired 60-year-old Dutch composer Louis (Joseph) ANDRIESSEN, son of Hendrik (Franciscus) Andriessen and brother of Jurriaan Andriessen, to a libretto by the brilliant 57-year-old Welsh film director, writer, painter, and librettist Peter GREENAWAY, is given its lavish first-ever staging in Amsterdam.

5 DECEMBER 1999

The American composer, pianist, and teacher Robert PARRIS, whose early compositions pursued a tonal path but whose later works adopted atonal procedures, dies in Washington, D.C., at the age of 75.

6 DECEMBER 1999

Musical Offerings for piano, left-hand (1998), by the eminent 84-year-old American composer, music theorist, and pedagogue George PERLE is given its first ever performance in New York.

8 DECEMBER 1999

Diverti-memento for orchestra (1997) by the veteran 79-year-old Canadian composer and teacher Robert (Comrie) TURNER is heard for the first time in Winnipeg.

12 DECEMBER 1999

The American pianist, teacher, and composer Leo SMIT, whose neo-Classical style of composition was marked by a strong contrapuntal fabric belying the influence of Stravinsky, with whom he had personal contact, dies in Encinitas, California, at the age of 78.

16 DECEMBER 1999

The American soprano Ruth WELTING who also appeared frequently as a noteworthy lieder artist dies in Ashville, North Carolina, at the age pitiable age of 51.

19 DECEMBER 1999

The American musicologist Martin BERNSTEIN, author of the successful textbook *An Introduction to Music* (N.Y., 1937; 4th ed., rev., 1972 with M. Picker), and brother of Artie (actually, Arthur) Bernstein (b. N.Y., Feb. 3, 1909; d. Los Angeles, Jan. 4, 1964), a classically trained cellist who became a leading jazz bassist in the 1930s and '40s, playing with many big bands, including Jimmy Dorsey's, dies in his native New York just days after his 95th birthday.

20 DECEMBER 1999

The Great Gatsby, opera after F. Scott Fitzgerald, by the esteemed American composer, conductor, and teacher John (Harris) HARBISON is mounted for the first time in New York on the occasion of the composer's 61st birthday.

22 DECEMBER 1999

The eminent French composer and administrator Marcel (François Paul) LANDOWSKI, son of the sculptor Paul Landowski and great-grandson of the celebrated Belgian violinist Henri Vieuxtemps, dies in Paris at the age of 84.

30 DECEMBER 1999

Crown Prince Friedrich, opera, by the esteemed 65-year-old German composer Siegfried MATTHUS is mounted for the first time ever in Rheinsberg.

31 DECEMBER 1999

Schrumpf-Symphonie by the innovative 64-year-old Austrian composer, horn player, and teacher Kurt SCHWERTSIK receives its premiere performance in Salzburg.

2000

1 JANUARY 2000

Jubilee and Psalm for chorus (1999) by the esteemed 76-year-old American composer, organist, choral conductor, and teacher Daniel (Rogers) PINKHAM (Jr.) is performed for the first time in Boston.

2 JANUARY 2000

Concert de Gaudi for guitar and orchestra (1999) by the prominent 50-year-old American composer and teacher Christopher (Chapman) ROUSE is given its first ever performance in Hamburg.

4 JANUARY 2000

The American music critic and writer on music Henry PLEASANTS, whose numerous, sometimes controversial books on music included *The Agony of Modern Music* (1955), *Death of a Music? The Decline of the European Tradition and the Rise of Jazz* (1961), and *Opera in Crisis: Tradition, Present, Future* (1989), dies in London at the seasoned age of 89.

6 JANUARY 2000

Sixth Symphony (1999) by the prominent 67-year-old Danish composer and pedagogue Per NØRGÅRD is premiered over the Danish Radio.

7 JANUARY 2000

Tara's Dream for orchestra (1999) and *Fanfare for the Millennium* for orchestra (1999), two works by 49-year-old American composer and teacher Stephen (George) CHATMAN, are given their first performance in Vancouver.

8 JANUARY 2000

The eminent 70-year-old German conductor of Hungarian descent Christoph von DOHNÁNYI, grandson of the equally eminent Hungarian pianist, composer, conductor, and pedagogue Ernst (Ernő) von Dohnányi (1877–1960) and husband of the remarkable 64-year-old German soprano Anja Silja, conducts the Cleveland Orchestra in the Gala Celebration Concert opening the refurbished Severance Hall, the ensemble's home.

11 JANUARY 2000

The American composer Barney (Sanford) CHILDS, best known as a composer for his cultivation of indeterminate structures and, as a writer, for his collaborative publication with Elliott Schwarz, *Contemporary Composers on Contemporary Music* (N.Y., 1967; rev. 1998), dies in Redlands, California, at the age of 73.

12 JANUARY 2000

First Violin Concerto, entitled *Messenger* (1998–99), by the 35-year-old Irish composer Ian WILSON receives its first ever performance in Dublin.

21 JANUARY 2000

Fanfary "50" (Fanfares "50") for chamber ensemble (1999–2000) by the 48-year-old Polish composer, conductor, and teacher Aleksander LASOŃ is heard for the first time in Warsaw.

22 JANUARY 2000

The Italian tenor Carlo COSSUTTA, who made his first appearance appearance at the Teatro Colón in Buenos Aires as Cassio in 1958 and returned there a decade later to create the title role in Alberto Ginastera's *Don Rodrigo* in 1968, dies in Udine at the age of 67.

25 JANUARY 2000

Arthur, Part 1: Arthur Pendragon, ballet (1999), by the esteemed 60-year-old English pianist, music educator, and composer John MCCABE is heard for the first time in Birmingham.

26 JANUARY 2000

The famous 49-year-old Spanish tenor and conductor Plácido DOMINGO makes his belated U.S. recital debut in Chicago.

27 JANUARY 2000

The remarkable Austrian pianist Friedrich GULDA, who while praised for his intellectual penetration of the music of Bach, Beethoven, and Mozart also became intensely fascinated by jazz, particularly in its improvisatory aspect, which he construed as corresponding to the freedom of melodic ornamentation in Baroque music, and who, in 1956, made an acclaimed appearance at New York's Birdland, dies in Weissenbach at the modest age of 69.

30 JANUARY 2000

The famous 49-year-old Spanish tenor and conductor Plácido DOMINGO makes his New York Carnegie Hall recital debut, just four days after his belated United States recital debut in Chicago.

2 FEBRUARY 2000

7 Boleros for orchestra (1998) by the outstanding 73-year-old German composer Hans Werner HENZE is given its premiere performance in Las Palmas.

5 FEBRUARY 2000

Fourth Symphony, entitled *The Gardens*, for chorus, children's chorus, handbells, and orchestra (1999) by the remarkable 60-year-old American composer Ellen Taaffe ZWILICH is heard for the first time in East Lansing, Michigan.

6 FEBRUARY 2000

The Canadian composer and teacher Barbara (Lally) PENTLAND, who adopted a pragmatic method of cosmopolitan modernism, employing dissonant linear counterpoint and dodecaphonic melodic structures within the framework of Classical forms, dies in Vancouver at the ripened age of 88.

8 FEBRUARY 2000

Pastorales Vorspiel by the talented Austrian composer Hans (actually, Johann Carl Maria) ROTT (1858–1884), whose scant works, housed in Vienna's Österreichische Nationalbibliothek, were admired by such revered compatriot composers as Gustav Mahler and Anton Bruckner, receives its posthumous premiere in Vienna.

11 FEBRUARY 2000

Intimations for piano and orchestra by the 58-year-old American composer, pianist, and teacher Richard (Edward) WILSON is performed for the first time in Annandale-on-Hudson, New York.

12 FEBRUARY 2000

Nell'ombra, nella luce for string quartet (1999–2000) by the spirited 50-year-old American composer, teacher, conductor, and writer on music Steven (Edward) STUCKY is given its first ever performance in Pittsburgh.

15 FEBRUARY 2000

Ring Out Wild Bells to the Wild Sky for soprano, chorus, and orchestra (1999–2000) by the talented 35-year-old American composer August Read THOMAS, wife of the esteemed American composer Bernard Rands, is given its premiere performance in Washington, D.C.

16 FEBRUARY 2000

The Silver Tassie, opera (1999), by the productive 39-year-old English composer Mark-Anthony TURNAGE is mounted for the first time in London.

17 FEBRUARY 2000

Timepiece for orchestra (1999) by the 46-year-old American composer and teacher Cindy MCTEE is premiered in Dallas.

21 FEBRUARY 2000

The Canadian composer and teacher Violet ARCHER (originally, Balestreri), whose works, influenced by Hindemith, were strong, polyphonically disciplined, and generally kept within organized tonality, with occasional dodecaphonic episodes, dies in Ottawa at the respectable age of 86.

23 FEBRUARY 2000

Don Quijote, opera, by the prominent 69-year-old Spanish composer and conductor Cristóbal HALFFTER (Jiménez-Encina), nephew of the esteemed Spanish musicians Ernesto (1905–1989) and Rodolfo (1900–1987) Halffter (Escriche), is staged for the first time ever in Madrid.

24 FEBRUARY 2000

Last Dance for orchestra (1999) by the respected 61-year-old American composer, pianist, and teacher Joan (Peabody) TOWER is given its premiere performance in New York.

26 FEBRUARY 2000

What Sheet Herd for erh hu (Chinese fiddle), voice, and computer by the innovative 41-year-old American composer, performer, and programmer Nick (actually, Nicholas Russel) DIDKOVSKY receives its first performance in Warwick, New York.

2 MARCH 2000

The remarkable American instrument maker and performer William COLVIG, long time partner and colleague of the celebrated American composer Lou (Silver) Harrison, and whose original gamelan instruments include those housed at the University of California at Berkeley and at Mills College in Oakland, dies in Capitola, California, just two weeks short of his 83rd birthday.

4 MARCH 2000

Water and Stone for eight players (1999) by the productive 38-year-old Japanese composer Karen TANAKA is performed for the first time in Paris.

5 MARCH 2000

The English tenor (Basil) Alexander YOUNG (real name, Youngs), who was particularly admired for his performances of Handel's music, dies in Macclesfield at the age of 79.

6 MARCH 2000

Tjenerindens Fortaelling (The Handmaid's Tale), opera, after Margaret Atwood (1997–98), by the 50-year-old Danish composer Poul RUDERS is mounted for the first time in Copenhagen.

9 MARCH 2000

The Canadian composer Jean COULTHARD, long-time faculty member in composition at the University of British Columbia (1947–1973) and who, in 1978, was named an Officer of the Order of Canada, dies in her native Vancouver at the seasoned age of 92.

16 MARCH 2000

The Scottish baritone, conductor, and pedagogue Roy (Galbraith) HENDERSON, who was especially esteemed as a concert singer, becoming well known for his championship of music by English composers, dies in London at the remarkable age of 100.

16 MARCH 2000

The sixth "Other Minds" Festival, under the (guest) artistic direction of Carl Stone, opens in San Francisco with a concert at Theater Artaud, in the follow program: *The Three Strange Angels* for bass drum, bullroarer, and piano (1972–73) by the 46-year-old American composer, publisher, and writer on music Peter GARLAND; *Greet-*

ings: Escalay (Water Wheel) for oud and vocals by Hamza el DIN, to Arabic lyrics by Ismail Hasan; *Memory Pieces* for piano (1992–97) by the 41-year-old American composer David LANG, comprised of *cage* (in memory John Cage), *spartan arcs* (in memory Yvar Mikhashoff), *wed* (in memory Kate Ericson), *grind* (in memory Jacob Druckman), *diet coke* (in memory Bette Snapp), and *cello* (in memory Anna Cholakian); *Solo Improvisations* for violin and viola composed (and performed) by the 66-year-old black American jazz violinist, bandleader, and composer Leroy JENKINS; and *Flying Sparks and Heavy Machinery*, octet for strings and percussion inspired by industrial sounds, by the 37-year-old American composer, instrumentalist, improviser, and sampling specialist Annie (actually, Anne) GOSFIELD.

17 MARCH 2000

On the second day of the sixth "Other Minds" Festival in San Francisco, a concert is given at Theater Artaud, in the follow program: *String Quartet No. 3* (1994), subtitled "There must be some way out of here," by the successful Dutch composer Jacob ter VELHUIS, in two movements; *Rain Study* for piano and *Blue Yellow River* for kayageum, cello, and double bass, two works by the respected African composer Hyo-shin NA; *Bright Angel—Hermetic Bird* for piano (1996) by the 46-year-old American composer, publisher, and writer on music Peter GARLAND; and *Melody* for melodica (1998) and *Burdocks* (1970–71) for guitar, cello, koto, electronics, french horn, sampler, percussion, and melodica, two works by the seasoned 64-year-old French-born American composer and teacher Christian WOLFF.

18 MARCH 2000

On the third and final day of the sixth "Other Minds" Festival in San Francisco, a performance is given, in cooperation with electromechanik, a project of Blasthaus Gallery, at the Justice League of *Electro Pollution* by the American "scanner" Robin RIMBAUD (aka scanner) and *Synchronia* by the popular American artist, writer, and musician Paul MILLER (aka Dj Spooky that Subliminal Kid).

20 MARCH 2000

The respected American composer, teacher, and pianist Vivian FINE, who was particularly adept at writing vocal and instrumental works in a dissonant but acceptable style, dies in Bennington, Vermont, at the age of 86.

21 MARCH 2000

The Man Who Hated Pets for guitar and drum set by the innovative 41-year-old American composer, performer, and computer programmer Nick (actually, Nicholas Russel) DIDKOVSKY is performed for the first time ever in Grenoble, France.

25 MARCH 2000

Piano Sonata by the eminent 74-year-old Italian composer, conductor, and pedagogue Luciano BERIO is performed for the first time in London, Rolf Hind pianist.

4 APRIL 2000

Concerto for percussion and wind ensemble (1998) by the accomplished 49-year-old Canadian composer Michael (Bass) MATTHEWS is heard for the first time in Winnipeg.

11 APRIL 2000

The innovative American composer, performer, teacher, and inventor Lucia DLUGOSZEWSKI, whose most noteworthy creation was the so-called timbre piano (c.1951), a revamped conventional piano activated by striking the strings with mallets, or having the strings bowed and picked, and who became especially successful as a composer for the dance, and as such was closely associated with the Erick Hawkins Dance Company, dies in New York at the unfulfilled age of 68.

13 APRIL 2000

The English composer Inglis GUNDRY, whose writings on music included *Opera in a Nutshell* (1945), *The Nature of Opera as a Composite Art* (1947), and *Composers by the Grace of God: A Study of Music and Religion* (1989), dies in his native London just weeks shy of his 95th birthday.

14 APRIL 2000

The 34-year-old American soprano Patricia RACETTE creates the role of Love Simpson in Carlisle (Sessions) FLOYD (Jr.)'s *Cold Sassy Tree* at the Houston Grand Opera.

18 APRIL 2000

The American composer, conductor, and teacher Martin MAILMAN, who, late in life, was greatly celebrated for his works for concert band, receiving the American Bandmasters Association/NABIM Award for his *Exaltations* (1983) and both the National Band Association/Band Mans Award and the American Bandmasters Association/Ostwald Award for his *For Precious Friends Hid in Death's Dateless Night* (1989), dies in Denton, Texas, at the modest age of 67.

25 APRIL 2000

The prominent Danish pianist, pedagogue, and composer Niels Viggo BENTZON, known well as a prolific composer of avant-garde scores encompassing happenings, audio-visual scores, and graphic notation, but who also found time to write music criticism, publish poetry, and paint, whose cousin was the Danish composer Jørgen Bentzon (1897–1951), dies in his native Copenhagen at the age of 80.

27 APRIL 2000

Eighth Symphony, subtitled *The Journey* (1999), by the eminent 71-year-old Finnish composer and pedagogue Einojuhani (actually, Eino Juhani) RAUTAVAARA is performed for the first time in Philadelphia.

28 APRIL 2000

Piece for triple string quartet by the 47-year-old American composer Tina DAVIDSON is given its first ever performance in Philadelphia.

29 APRIL 2000

CassandraComplex, music theater piece, after Christa Wolf (1993–94), by the iconoclastic 50-year-old German organist, teacher, and composer Gerhard STÄBLER is staged for the first time in Wiesbaden.

1 MAY 2000

The German-born American composer and pedagogue Bernhard HEIDEN, long-time (1946–81) and highly respected faculty member of the Indiana University School of Music in Bloomington whose compositions followed along neo-Classical lines, dies in Bloomington, Indiana, at the ripened age of 89.

5 MAY 2000

Rapture for orchestra (1999) by the prominent 51-year-old American composer and teacher Christopher (Chapman) ROUSE is heard for the first time in Pittsburgh.

13 MAY 2000

The notable Italian tenor Cesare VALLETTI, whose admired vocal gifts placed him in the forefront of the bel canto revival of his day, dies in Genoa at the respectable age of 87.

16 MAY 2000

The American composer, choral conductor, and organist William (Edward) FERRIS dies in his native Chicago of a heart attack at the age of 73 while rehearsing Verdi's *Requiem.*

17 MAY 2000

The noted American composer and teacher Ellis (Bonoff) KOHS, who authored such useful manuals as *Music Theory, a Syllabus for Teacher and Student* (2 vols., N.Y., 1961), *Musical Form: Studies in Analysis and Synthesis* (Boston, 1976), and *Musical Composition: Projects in Ways and Means* (Metuchen, N.J., 1980), dies in Los Angeles just days after his 84th birthday.

19 MAY 2000

The American music educator, conductor, and composer Gideon W(illiam) WALDROP, long-time dean of the Juilliard School in New York (1963–1985), dies in New York at the age of 80.

20 MAY 2000

The celebrated French flutist, conductor, and teacher Jean-Pierre (Louis) RAMPAL, whose vast repertoire ranged from the Baroque masters to jazz, from the music of Japan to that of India, and from arrangements to specially commissioned works (Poulenc and Jolivet wrote pieces for him), and whose countless concerts and recordings did more than those of any other flutist of his time to bring his instrument into the mainstream of musical life, dies in Paris at the age of 78.

24 MAY 2000

An "Otto Luening Centennial Concert" in honor of the noted 99-year-old American composer, music educator, flutist, and conductor Otto (Clarence) LUENING is given in New York.

30 MAY 2000

The American jazz singer, tenor saxophonist, and bandleader Tex (real name, Gordon) BENEKE dies in Santa Ana, California, at the age of 86.

4 JUNE 2000

The esteemed Estonian composer and pedagogue Lepo SUMERA, whose profound influence in his native country emanated not only from his astounding compositions but also from his involvement with the Estonian Radio (1973-78), the Estonian Music Academy (1976–99), and the Estonian Composers Union (1993–2000), and who served from 1990 to 1992 as minister of culture of the Republic of Estonia, dies in his native Tallinn at the lamentable age of 50.

15 JUNE 2000

The Tale of the Genji, opera, by the 70-year-old Japanese composer Minoru MIKI is staged for the first time in St. Louis.

16 JUNE 2000

"An Antheil Centennial Concert," presented by the San Francisco Symphony and San Francisco's "Other Minds" Festival, featuring such works of the remarkable American composer George (Georg Johann Carl) ANTHEIL (1900–1959) as his *Ballet Mécanique, A Jazz Symphony* (in its original version), and his *Second Sonata* for violin accompanied by piano and drums, in a program featuring the Abel-Steinberg-Winant Trio (William Winant, Julie Steinberg, and David Abel), and conducted by Michael Tilson Thomas, is given in San Francisco as part of the 2000 American Mavericks Festival. (The concert was preceded on June 11, 2000, by a full-day Antheil event which included a panel discussion, slide lecture, and German film director Michael Meert's public premiere screening of *Bad Boy of Music,* originally produced for German television).

17 JUNE 2000

Musikalische Antworten auf Johann Sebastian Bach for flute and organ (1999) by the 73-year-old German composer, pedagogue, organist, and harpsichordist Ruth ZECHLIN is heard for the first time in Rheinsberg.

21 JUNE 2000

The prolific American composer of Armenian-Scottish descent Alan (Vaness Scott) HOVHANESS (real name, Chakmakjian), whose more than 370 opus numbers included a symphonic score *And God Created Great Whales,* in which the voices of humpback whales recorded on tape were used as a solo with the orchestra and which was performed to great effect in the campaign to save the whale from destruction by human (and inhuman) predators, dies in Seattle at the respectable age of 89.

1 JULY 2000

...Song in Sorrow... for orchestra by the respected 36-year-old American composer August Read THOMAS, wife of the esteemed American composer Bernard Rands, written in memory of the students killed by the National Guard at Kent State University, is performed for the first time by the Cleveland Orchestra at the Blossom Music Festival, Jahja Ling conducting.

21 JULY 2000

The remarkable Scottish composer Iain (Ellis) HAMILTON, who, despite coming late to music, after graduating as a scholarship student from the Royal Academy of Music garnered such prestigious awards as the Dove Prize (1950), the Royal Philharmonic Society Prize (1951), the Koussevitzky Foundation Award (1951), the Edwin Evans Prize (1951), the Arnold Bax Gold Medal (1957), and the Vaughan Williams Award (1974), dies in London at the age of 78.

24 JULY 2000

The esteemed American violinist, conductor, and pedagogue Oscar SHUMSKY, father of the respected violist Eric Shumsky (b. Port Chester, N.Y., Dec. 7, 1953), with whom he frequently appeared in chamber music concerts, dies in Rye, New York, at the age of 83.

28 JULY 2000

Triptychon 2000 for orchestra by the respected 74-year-old German composer, pedagogue, organist, and harpsichordist Ruth ZECHLIN is given its first ever performance in Passau.

15 AUGUST 2000

Clémence, opera after Amin Maalouf (1999–2000), by the significant 47-year-old Finnish composer Kaija (Anneli) SAARIAHO is staged for the first time in Salzburg.

26 AUGUST 2000

...which was the son of... for chorus by the outstanding 64-year-old Estonian-born Austrian composer Arvo PÄRT is given its first ever performance in Reykjavík, Thorgerdur Ingólfsdóttir conducting.

5 SEPTEMBER 2000

At the initiative of German music critic Heinz-Klaus Metzger, German composer/scholar Rainer Riehn, and German composer/organist Jakob Ullman, all inspired by a passage from Harry Partch's *Genesis of a Music* (wherein that "fateful day at Halberstadt" is chronicled as introducing the tyranny of the 12-part division of the octave), The John CAGE *Organ Project* begins in the town of Halberstadt in Eastern Germany with the construction of an organ and is to continue for some 639 years with a performance of John Cage's *Organ2/ASLSP* (As Slow As Possible), originally intended to last 20 minutes. While the performance begins officially on this date, the 88th anniversary of Cage's birth, the first chord will not be sounded for another year and a half. (The extension of the work to over half a millennium is to commemorate the completion of the town's first famous organ, built 639

years previous. The head of the John Cage Organ Foundation stated further that the tempo is being drawn out to that extreme to stand in marked contrast to the breathless pace of modern life.)

14 SEPTEMBER 2000

Concerto for flute and harp by Anders KOPPEL is performed for the first time in Aabenraa, Denmark, by the Sønderjyllands Symphony, with special guest artists Thomas Jensen, flute, and Benedikte Johansen, harp.

15 SEPTEMBER 2000

ENGINE 27, a technologically-advanced performance space founded by Jack Weisberg, with unique variable acoustic possibilities and surround-sound technology located at 173 Franklin Street in New York City, opens its doors for the first time with a festival of electronic music entitled "EMF @ Engine 27," masterminded by the 61-year-old Joel CHADABE, American composer and director of the Electronic Music Foundation, beginning with an artful, spatialized installation of *Bird Cage* (1972) by the veteran American composer of experimental music John CAGE (1912–1992). (The remainder of the premiere Fall 2000 season was to feature elaborate new works by such notable electronic composer/musicians as Larry Austin, Earle Brown, Darren Copeland, Annea Lockwood, Warren Burt, Hildegard Westerkamp, Stevie Wishart, Jim Denley, Rik Rue, Amanda Stewart, Tom Buckner, and Tom Hamilton.)

21 SEPTEMBER 2000

Perturbed Spirit for orchestra by the English composer Giles SWAYNE is performed for the first time at the Royal Northern College of Music in Manchester.

22 SEPTEMBER 2000

Millennium Fantasy for piano and orchestra by the remarkable 61-year-old American composer Ellen Taaffe ZWILICH is performed for the first time by the Cincinnati Symphony Orchestra, Jeffrey Biegel pianist, Jesús López-Cobos conducting.

22 SEPTEMBER 2000

Tirol Concerto for piano and orchestra by the extraordinarily successful 63-year-old American composer Philip GLASS is heard for the first time ever at the Festival Klangspuren in Tyrol, Austria, performed by the Stuttgart Chamber Orchestra.

29 SEPTEMBER 2000

The 74th Festival of the International Society for Contemporary Music opens in Luxembourg with an early evening concert at the Cercle Municipal Luxembourg performed by the Schweizer Kammerorchester, with special guest artists Marius Ungureanu, alto, and Carlo Jans, flute, conducted by Klaus Arp, in the following program: *Overture* to the popular operetta *Mumm Séis* by the Luxembourg composer Edmond de la FONTAINE (1823-1891), known for much of his life as simply DICKS; *Viola Concerto No. 2*, subtitled *Lichtung des Schreiseins* (1998), by the Romanian composer Dan DEDIU; *Unto These Yellow*

Sands, concerto for two oboes, two horns, and strings, by the Danish composer and director of the electro-acoustic department at the Carl Nielsen Academy of Music in Denmark Lars GRAUGAARD; and *Flute Concerto* (1999) by the Luxembourg composer and conductor Marcel WENGLER, commissioned by the National Orchestra of Portugal and premiered that same year with Luxembourg flutist Carlos Jans as soloist, the composer conducting.

29 SEPTEMBER 2000

Crouching Tiger Concerto by the significant 43-year-old Chinese composer Tan DUN is heard for the first time at the Barbican Festival in London, performed by the London Sinfonietta.

30 SEPTEMBER 2000

On the second day of the 74th Festival of the International Society for Contemporary Music in Luxembourg, six concerts are given, in the following sequence:

A late morning concert at the Cercle Municipal Luxembourg performed by the Ensemble Antipodes, in the following program: the world premiere of *Albedor III* for octet by the German composer Helmut ZAPF; *Labyrinth, Promenade IX* by the Taiwanese composer Hwang-Long PAN; *Evolution* by the Japanese composer Makoto SHINOHARA, comprised of 45 short fragments classified into three characters: revolting, introverted, and positive-active; *Ein Garten für Orpheus* (1996) by the Swiss composer Jean-Luc DARBELLAY, a commission from the Leipzig Radio (MDR) to celebrate the 70th anniversary of the Bauhaus of Dessau; *String Trio* by the Taiwanese composer Tsung-Hsien YANG; *Tempus* by the Venezuelan composer, teacher, and ethnomusicologist Emilio MENDOZA; and *Anaktoria* for clarinet, bassoon, horn, string quintet, and double bass (1969) by the eminent 78-year-old Greek-born French composer, music theorist, and teacher Iannis XENAKIS, exploiting micro-intervals of quarter- and third-tones, precisely notated, but also less precise bending pitches and glissandi.

An early afternoon concert at the Cercle Municipal Luxembourg performed by the Quatour de Saxophones de Luxembourg, in the following program: *Tangled Loops* for saxophone and piano by the American composer Jason Eckardt; *Rituals for Forgotten Faces* by the South African composer Bongani NDODANA, one in a series of pieces for various instruments and ensembles in which musical language is based on African and hexatonic modes, drawing from many influences to create a "neo-African" sound; *Monotaurus* by the Luxembourg composer and teacher Claude LENNERS, a study in velocity and virtuosity; *Saxophone Quartet* (1996) by the Irish composer John BUCKLEY, the second of three successful works by this composer exploring the expressive capabilities of the saxophone (the others being *Arabesque,* 1990, for solo alto saxophone, and *Concerto for Alto Saxophone and Strings,* 1997); *To the edge of the corridors* by the Chinese composer, arranger, writer, and broadcaster So Ting CHEONG; *Coupe de Dés* by the Luxembourg composer and founding conductor of the largely-amateur Orchestre de Chambre de Luxembourg René HEMMER; *Opcit* by the French composer and musicologist Philippe HUREL, the title taken from the Latin phrase "opus citatum" and alluding to the composer's earlier *Eolia* for solo flute (1982), both pieces made up of characteristic studies which follow each other in an increasing order of complexity; and *Passamezzo,* quartet for saxophones, by the Dutch composer and teacher Theo VERBEY, based on a four-note theme, similar to such early Baroque forms as the Passacaglia and the Chaconne.

An early afternoon performance at the Cercle Municipal Luxembourg by Hannover's Das Neue Ensemble of *For Philip Guston* for flute, alto flute, percussion, piano, and celesta (1984) by the significant American composer and pedagogue Morton FELDMAN (1926–1987).

A late afternoon concert at the Conservatoire de Musique Esch/Alzette performed by The Peärls Before Swïne Experience, in the following program: the world premiere of *Hermione's Dream* by the 64-year-old Belgian composer Philippe BOESMANS; *Goyoh* (Stillness) for two instruments by the Korean composer and teacher Hae-Sung LEE; the world premiere of *Short Fall* by the 43-year-old American composer and co-founder of the internationally-acclaimed New York festival Bang on a Can, David LANG; *Eclat du soir* by the Japanese composer and teacher Yuriko Hase KOJIMA, with aleatoric passages, inspired by the play of light around the Château de Fontainebleau in France, where the piece was conceived during the Fontainebleau Summer Music Festival; *Zi Yun Xiao Sa* for two instruments by the Chinese composer Ming Chi CHANG; the world premiere of *A presto* by the Swedish composer Mats LARSSON, dedicated to The Peärls Before Swïne Experience, "a convincing drama with simple means," lasting some four minutes in length, and divided into ten parts, in a very fast tempo; and *Feuilles à travers les cloches* for flute, violin, cello, and piano (1998) by the remarkable 53-year-old French composer Tristan MURAIL.

An evening program at the Théâtre Municipal Esch/Altzette entitled "Der Gelbe Raum," comprised of works attempting "...to evaluate, from the new viewpoint of the aesthetics of performance and within the spatial constraints of the Esch theatre, the artistic parameters of music, light and image, bringing them together into synaesthesia and giving them a new definition in terms of their inter-relations through this specific link." Performed by Hannover's Das Neue Ensemble, with special guest artists Annette Robbert, soprano, Anina Papazian, mezzo-soprano, and Thomas Holzapfel, baritone, conducted by Eberhard Kloke, with lighting by Thilo Reuther, and set design by Klaus Merkel.

Part I: *3 Little Pieces* for chamber orchestra (1911) by the great Austrian-born American composer whose new method of musical organization in 12 different tones related only to one another profoundly influenced the entire development of modern techniques of composition Arnold SCHOENBERG (1874–1951); *The Unanswered Question* (1906), in a version for two flutes, oboe, clarinet, two trumpets, string quintet, and two singers, by the American composer Charles IVES (1874–1954), one of the country's most remarkable, whose individual genius created music so original, so universal, and yet so deeply national in its sources of inspiration that it profoundly changed the direction of American music; and *Der Andere,* melodrama for mezzo-soprano and instruments by the German composer Moritz EGGERT, after the novel *The Outsider* by H.P. Lovecraft (1890–1937).

Part II: *Thousands of bundled straw II* for two voices, bass recorder, violin, and percussion by the Australian composer Davis YOUNG, the second movement of a larger cycle with a total of seven movements, the title derived from a myth surrounding the Ichibata-Yakushi Buddhist Temple, situated on a hill overlooking Lake Shinji-ko, in Hirata-City, Shimane Prefecture, Japan; *Todesmusik,* D.758, for soprano, mezzo-soprano, baritone, and piano (1822), to texts by Schober, by the great Austrian composer, a supreme melodist and an inspired master of lieder Franz SCHUBERT (1797–1828); *Ich plante zu sprechen* for two soprano voices, baritone, two violins, viola, cello, and double bass, to texts by Monika Köhn, by the Luxembourg composer Jeannot HEINEN; and *Tientos del dia infinito* for soprano, flute, guitar, cello, and percussion (1998) by the Spanish composer and teacher Augustín Charles SOLER, based on texts by Frederico García Lorca chosen to symbolize the infinite circle of the day.

Part III: *Spatial Ayres* for soprano, chamber orchestra, and tape by the 51-year-old German composer, teacher, and organist Gerhard STÄBLER; *The Unanswered Question* (1906), in a version for speakers, instruments, and tape, by the great American composer Charles IVES (1874–1954); and Wassily Kandinsky's *Der Gelbe Klang* (1912), in a new version by the prominent Russian composer of German descent Alfred SCHNITTKE (1934–1998) entitled *Zhyoltïy zvuk* (Yellow Sound), ballet (1973/74/83), first performed in Saint Bomme, France.

A late-night concert at the Kulturfabrik Esch/Alzette performed by the Tanztheater Basel, with choreography by Jean-Guillaume Weis, music realizations by Electronisches Studio der Musikhochschule Basel, directed by Josh Jürgen Martin, lighting by Lutz Deppe, and featuring dancers Sophie Faudot, Randi De Vlieghe, and Jean-Guillaume Weis, in the following program: *Histoires de Sons* by the Spanish composer and performer Eduardo POLONIO; *Currents* by the Swedish composers Jens HEDMAN and Pauline SUNDIN, a musical tribute to Stockholm, each of its four sections portraying the city from different sound perspectives through materials recorded during the period 1996 to 1998; and *Derrière la porte la plus éloignée...* by the Canadian composer Gilles GOBEIL.

1 OCTOBER 2000

On the third day of the 74th Festival of the International Society for Contemporary Music in Luxembourg, four concerts are given, in the following sequence:

A late morning concert of live electronic works at the Théâtre des Capucins Luxembourg, performed by The B.E.A.M. (Basel Electric Art Messengers) and guests, comprised of Sylvia Nopper, soprano, Matthias Würsch, percussion and piano, Wolfgang Heiniger, percussion and live electronics, Thomas Kessler, live electronics, Marcus Weiss, saxophone, Anton Kernjak, piano, Lanet Floers Otero, clarinet, Julia Schröder, violin, Karin Löffler, violin, Natalja Alexandrowa, viola, and Michael Keller, cello, in the following program: *Implantate* by the German composer Kilian SCHWOON, *Four constellations before dawn* by the Italian composer Manuel CECCHINATO, *Wassermusik* by Swiss composer Wolfgang HEINIGER, *Tangata Vocale* by the Argentine-born French composer José Luis CAMPANA, and *Erinnerungen an Shakespeare* by the prominent 69-year-old Swiss composer and pedagogue Rudolf KELTERBORN.

A late afternoon concert at the Château de Vianden performed by America's Ensemble Continuum, conducted by Joel Sachs, in the following program: *Piano Trio No. 1* by the Korean composer Jong Woo KIM, in one movement, in three sections, the first made up of long and short melodic lines with a staccato character, the second imitating a passage taken from a previous chromatic melody, and the third and last a postlude to wind up the whole; *Tema y variaciones* for clarinet and piano (1999) by the 46-year-old Puerto Rican composer Roberto SIERRA, its theme a "note collection" forming the basis for the succeeding variations, which, while continuous, were composed in twelve distinct sections; *Interrupted Song* by the Azerbaijan composer Oleg FELZER (1939–1998); *Proverbs of Hell* for soprano and chamber ensemble by the Italian composer Alberto COLLA, to texts extracted from *The marriage of heaven and hell* by William Blake; *Aşk Havasi* for solo cellist by the Azerbaijan composer Franghiz ALI-ZADEH, throughout which the performer sings, both upon the instrument and with the voice, the world premiere of *Nguurraa* by the Luxembourg composer Georges LENTZ; and *Daimon II* by the American composer Francis SCHWARTZ.

A late afternoon concert at the Eglise St-Michael Luxembourg performed by the Ensemble Antipodes, with special guest artists Alain Wirth, organ, and Charles Consbruck, trumpet, in the following program: *Camera aeolia* by the English composer Caroline WILKINS, the title referring to the wind-producing mechanism of a mechanical organ, as described by Athanasius Kirchner in 1650; *Appel interstellaire* by the outstanding French composer and pedagogue Olivier MESSIAEN (1908–1992); *...and the Sun?*, for five instrumental parts, all moving from melody to stasis, by the Hungarian composer László SÁRY; the world premiere of *Les Lunes de Jupiter* by the Luxembourg composer Roland WILTGEN; *Tres Noches sin Luna* by the Venezuela composer Diana ARISMENDI, in three movements utilizing texts by e.e. cummings, as well as gestures, physical expression, and spatial movements from the players; and *Seven Visions from the Apocalypse of Saint John* by the Belgian composer André LAPORTE, comprised of an introduction for organ and seven trumpet-calls, each followed by a more or less extensive organ piece.

An evening concert at the Eglise Sts-Pierre-et-Paul Echternach performed by London's Arditti String Quartet, in the following program: *Nunatak* by the Swedish composer Jonas BOHLIN, first heard as accompaniment to a dance performance in New York and as soundtrack to the documentary film, *Wintership*, its title translated as "mountains buried in ice"; *String Quartet No. 2* (1997) by the Finnish composer Kimmo HAKOLA, in five movements, materially consistent with the composer's *String Quartet No. 1*, composed some eleven years earlier; *Uy u t'an* by the Mexican composer Hilda PAREDES, in four sections, its title an expression in the Mayan language of Mexico's Yucatan translating to "listen how they talk"; *String Quartet No. 4* by the Tatarstan composer Rashid KALIMOULLIN, in one movement with through-composed dramatic development and much improvisation, with the initial intonation of "Sakura," a Japanese folk song, a peculiar leitmotiv; and *String Quartet No. 3* by the English composer James DILLON.

2 OCTOBER 2000

In One Single Movement by the 56-year-old remarkable English composer John TAVENER is heard at the South Bank Centre as part of the "Tavener Festival," performed by the Pentonville Prison Chorus and the Tibetan Temple Bowls Ensemble.

2 OCTOBER 2000

On the fourth day of the 74th Festival of the International Society for Contemporary Music an evening concert is given at the Conservatoire de Musique Luxembourg performed by Paris's Ensemble Intercontemporain-IRCAM, with special guest soloists Emmannuelle Ophèle, MIDI flute, Sophie Cherrier and Marine Perez, flute, and Jean-Jacques Gaudon, trumpet, conducted by Jonathan Nott, in the following program: *Aura (par-delà les résonances)* by the Argentine composer Carlos GRÄTZER; *Trojtza* by the German composer Carmen Maria CÂRNECI, in four modernistic movements, each following an uneven path, full of "crossings, overlaps, sudden or subtle changes in direction"; *Agregados* for small orchestra by the Spanish composer Carlos Satué ROS, in three basic structures which combine to create a larger and more complex architecture; *...explosante-fixe...* (1972) by the greatly significant 75-year-old French composer and conductor Pierre BOULEZ, founder of IRCAM's Ensemble Intercontemporain, the title borrowed from a quotation by André Breton, heard here in its most current version, completely rewritten, both instrumentally and electronically, now scored for three flutes (one connected to a computer), woodwind ensemble, brass, and strings.

3 OCTOBER 2000

On the fifth day of the 74th Festival of the International Society for Contemporary Music in Luxembourg, three concerts are given, in the following sequence:

An early afternoon concert at the Cercle Municipal Luxembourg performed by the Luxembourg Sinfonietta, with special guest artists Ruth-Maria Nicolay, soprano, Assaf Levitin, baritone, and Nicholas Isherwood, bass, conducted by Marcel Wengler, in the following program: *"Löwe, leih' mir Deine Stimme"* by the German composer Theo BRANDMÜLLER, *in den hohen trompeten der bäume* by the French composer Claude LEFEBVRE, and *Der unbekannte Engel* by the Luxembourg composer Marcel WENGLER.

A late afternoon concert at the Conservatoire de Musique Luxembourg performed by the Orchestre de Flûtes Français, with special guest flutist Pierre-Yves Artaud, conducted by Pierre-Alain Biget, in the following program: the world premiere of *Shaman's Songs*, a concerto-like work for solo flute, flute orchestra, and percussion, by the Bulgarian composer Yassen VODENITCHAROV, in four parts, a tribute to Igor Stravinsky; the world premiere of *Wings of Light* by the Romanian composer Doina ROTARU, a ritual in five sections, composed for Pierre-Yves Artaud and the ensemble OFF; *Le chant des aires* by the French composer Alain LOUVIER; and the world premiere of *Seven Ways to Djebel Chambi* by the Luxembourg composer Luc ROLLINGER.

An evening concert at the Deutsche Bank Luxembourg performed by the Prague Chamber Orchestra, with special guest soloists Ladislav Kozderka, trumpet, and David Svec, piano, conducted by Ondrej Kukal, in the following program: *Burnout* for chamber ensemble (1996) by the Dutch composer and teacher Toek NUMAN; *Delusions on Mozart's Ave Verum Corpus* by the Israeli composer Ari BEN-SHABETAI, in five movements "a la concertante," played without pause, the fifth encompassing a slow, distorted rendition ("like an unreal reflection through a cracked mirror") of Mozart's motet *Ave Verum Corpus;* the world premiere of *Trumpet Concerto* by the 68-year-old Czech composer Marek KOPELENT; *Hymn and Ara* for chamber orchestra by the 48-year-old Polish composer, conductor, and teacher Aleksander LASOŃ; *A Winged Creature* by the Czech composer Miroslav PUDLÁK, in six sections: *1. Apparition, 2. Flight, 3. Legend, 4. Dance, 5. Meditation,* and *6. Procession*, a commission from the Academy of St. Martin in the Fields Orchestra; *Sonata for Strings No. 2* (1995) by the outstanding 74-year-old German composer Hans Werner HENZE; and *At the End of the Road* by the Yugoslav composer Dejan DESPIĆ, an autobiographical work comprised of snippets of music previously composed by Despić, as well as a theme comprising some of the letters of his name, translated into tones D-E(j)-A-(n) D-Es(Eflat)-(pi)-C.

4 OCTOBER 2000

On the sixth day of the 74th Festival of the International Society for Contemporary Music in Luxembourg, four concerts are given, in the following sequence:

A late morning concert at the Château de Clervaux performed by the Ensemble Saxas (Accordéon, Percussion), in the following program: *Meeting* by the Luxembourg composer and founding member of the "Quatuor de Saxophones de Luxembourg" Marco PÜTZ, *Vue sur les jardins interdits* for saxophone quartet (1974) by the radical 71-year-old Belgian

composer and pedagogue Henri POUSSEUR, *...Whose Sun constructs perpetual Noon...* by the Luxembourg composer Marcel REUTER, and *No way out* by the Luxembourg composer Camille KERGER.

An afternoon concert at the Eglise de Marnach performed by Carlo Jans, flute, and Vania Lecuit, violin, in the following program: *Agra* by the Australian composer Mark ZADRO, *Puntas* (1995) by the Uruguayan composer and systems engineer Silvia SUÁREZ, composed via a computer program created especially by the composer as a means of "parametric generation of musical materials, that are afterwards modified during composition"; the world premiere of *Soliloquy* by the Albanian composer and humanities research fellow Thoma SIMAKU; and *Meditations sobre Abya-Yala* by the Mexican composer Graciela AGUDELO, the title alluding to one of the few pre-Hispanic names of America (consigned in its unknown history), or *Abya-Yala*, "land of bursting maturity," given to the country by the Cuna Indians of Panama.

A late afternoon concert at the Vieille église St-Laurent, Diekirch performed by the Arta Woodwind Quintet and Flute Trio, in the following program: *Quinteto de Vientos* by the Chilean composer Carlos ZAMORA, built upon rhythmic elements of Latin-American dances, in two movements, *Chacarera* and *Trote*, with cadenza; *Deformation* for 3 flutes by the Korean composer Seung-woo PAIK; *5 Egemere Moments* by the Romanian composer Dora COJOCARU, short musical fragments with contrasting character (*Animato/Scorrevo/Concitato/Addolorato/Ardente*); and *Four Brazilian Songs* by the Brazilian composer Liduino PITOMBEIRA, utilizing a 12-tone row (8-10-3-5-0-2-9-11-6-4-7-1) that quickly evolves into a Brazilian northeastern modal music.

An evening concert at the Centre des Arts Pluriels Edouard Juncker, Ettelbruck performed by Frankfurt am Main's Ensemble Modern, conducted by Dominique My, in the following program: *Entre Belacqua et Nell* by the Canadian composer and founder/director of Musiques Itinérantes Michelle BOUDREAU, *Maze* by the Australian composer Raffaele MARCELLINO, and *Jagden und Formen* for chamber ensemble (1999) by the distinguished 48-year-old German composer and teacher Wolfgang RIHM, first performed at Paris's Festival d'Automne .

5 OCTOBER 2000

On the seventh day of the 74th Festival of the International Society for Contemporary Music in Luxembourg, two concerts are given, in the following sequence:

An early afternoon concert at the Cercle Municipal Luxembourg performed by the Grand Orchestre d'Harmonie des Guides, conducted by Capitaine-Commandant Chef de Musique Norbert Nozy, in the following program: *Masada* by the Russian-born Israeli composer Boris PIGOVAT, named for the ancient mountaintop fortress in southeast Israel near the Dead Sea, the site of the Jews' last stand against the Romans after the fall of Jerusalem in 70 A.D., now a symbol of Israeli national heroism; *Concert Piece for Symphonic Band & Percussion* by the Norwegian composer and flutist Guttorm KITTELSEN; *Minimo* for wind orchestra (1997) by the Croatian composer Krešimir SELETKOVIĆ, composed for and first performed by the Croatian Army Symphony Wind Orchestra; *Phantasmagoria* for celesta and wind orchestra (1998) by the French composer Régis CAMPO, commissioned and first performed by the Orchestre national d'île-de-France, under the baton of Scott Sandmeier; *Danse funambulesque* (1925) by the Belgian composer and violinist Jules STRENS (1893–1971); and *Marche du Premier régiment des guides* by the Belgian composer Valentin BENDER (1801–1873).

An evening concert at the Arsenal Metz performed by the Orchestre Philharmonique du Luxembourg, with special guest soloists Béatrice Rauchs, piano, Celina Lindsley, soprano, and Roland Hermann, baryton, conducted by Fabrice Bollon, in the following program: *Konzertstück No. 2* for orchestra (1994–96) by the Lithuanian composer Vytautas BARKAUSKAS, a typical, well-constructed concertante, commissioned by the Lithuanian National Philharmonic; *Canticum Tremulum* by the Japanese composer Hiroyuki YAMAMOTO, with all sounds articulated in an ambiguous manner, reflecting the composer's belief that performers are fundamentally unable to realize a truly clear or straight tone; *Rondo* for piano and orchestra by the Swedish composer Lars EKSTRÖM, in a single movement; *WU-YU* by the Chinese-born Australian composer Julian YU, the title referring (in ancient Chinese) to "rain-making ceremonies performed in times of drought," in two essential sections; and *Duodramen* by the notable 68-year-old Argentine-born German composer and pedagogue Mauricio Kagel.

6 OCTOBER 2000

Cranks and Cactus Needles for flute, piano, violin, and cello by the productive 40-year-old American composer, instrumentalist, improviser, and sampling specialist Annie (actually, Anne) GOSFIELD is performed for the first time ever in Luxembourg.

6 OCTOBER 2000

Triptych for orchestra by the Norwegian composer Asbjørn SCHAATHUN is performed for the first time in Oslo by the Oslo Philharmonic.

6 OCTOBER 2000

On the eighth day of the 74th Festival of the International Society for Contemporary Music in Luxembourg, three concerts are given, in the following sequence:

A noontime concert at the Villa Louvigny Luxembourg performed by MusikFabrik, conducted by James Avery, in the following program: *Codename Orpheus* by the Finnish composer John TALLGREN, soundtrack for the film of the same name by film director Gösten Kraken, the title the same as that of the conversational character appearing in the novel *The Medusa Frequency* by Russell Hoban; *Annäherugen* by the German composer Günter STEINKE, a homophonic work for ensemble whose instruments are made to form a single large instrument through the composer's use of "event-fields"; *Apoteosi del blu* (1998) by the Italian composer Valerio SANNICANDRO, modeled after a painting of Vassili Kandinsky (*Im Blau*), wherein the composer "gives to all of its elements a music parameter and to each geometrical figure a different musical character"; and the world premiere of *Grave* by the English composer Ian WILLCOCK, who calls this a most "dark, contemplative, and pessimistic piece."

A late afternoon concert at the Stadtgalerie Saarbrücken performed by the Miso Ensemble Portugal, in the following program: *De l'Étant Qui Le Nie* by the Portuguese composer and instrumentalist Paula AZGUIME; *Salamander II* by the Japanese composer Hiroyuki ITOH, the title referring to the perpetually cold mythological reptile that was said to live in fire; *Réitérations* by the Portuguese composer João RAFAEL; *The Trap for Two* by the Ukrainian composer Julia GOMELSKAYA; and *Pulse Code Modulation* by the Portuguese composer, poet, and percussionist as well as founding director of Miso Ensemble Portugal Miguel AZGUIME.

An evening concert at the Funkhaus Halberg, Grosser Sendesaal, Saarbrücken, performed by the Sinfonieorchester des Saarländischen Rundfunks, with soloists Ksenija Lukic, soprano, Christoph Späth, tenor, Yaron Windmüller, baritone, and the Mitglieder des Kammerchores Saarbrücken, conducted by Oswald Sallaberger, in the following program: *Aurora Australis* by the Australian composer Bozidar KOS, "reminiscent" of the atmospheric phenomenon of the "southern lights"; the world premiere of *Orchesterstück* 7 by the Austrian composer Herbert GRASSL; and *Die Erde ist eine Schale von Dunkelm Gold* by the German composer Rolf RIEHM, concert scene for soprano, tenor, baritone, and orchestra in two movements: *1. Garten. Nacht und Mondschein* (in its world premiere performance), and *2. Leonce und und....*

7 OCTOBER 2000

Dead Man Walking, first full-scale opera (some three hours) by the promising 39-year-old American pianist and composer Jake (actually, John Stephen) HEGGIE, to a fluid libretto by Terrence McNally based on the Oscar-winning film after the novel of the same name by Sister Helen Prejean, in a mostly tonal idiom incorporating jazz, rockabilly, and gospel, is staged for the first time by the San Francisco Opera, Patrick Summers conducting.

7 OCTOBER 2000

On the ninth and final day of the 74th Festival of the International Society for Contemporary Music in Luxembourg, four concerts are given, in the following sequence:

A mid-day recital at the Orangerie, Domaine Thermal Mondorf-les-Bains performed by Béatrice Rauchs, piano, and Vania Lecuit, violin, in the following program: *Three Monothematic Pieces* by the Slovenian composer Ljubo RANCIGAJ; *Prélude et fugue* by the Slovak composer and teacher Vladimir BOKES; *Portrett Nr. 6* (1997–98) by the Icelandic composer Snorri Sigfús BIRGISSON, one of seven such musical "portraits" of an individual, the whole dedicated to Jón Nordal; *Ciulionis's Sketches* by the Lithuanian composer Anatolijus SENDEROVAS; *Enigma*, mysterious, emotive, and appropriately named music by the Mexican composer Lucia ALVAREZ; and *Where two become one* by the Israeli composer Nurit JUGEND.

A "Lunch-Concert-Spectacle" at the Remich-Grevenmacher, Bâteau du plaisance Marie Astrid, Mosel-Fahrgastschiff, featuring Sophie Proost, soprano, Yannchen, Hoffmann, mezzo-soprano, Fernando Presley Jr., tenor, Carlo Hartmann, baritone, and Marco Bettendorf, piano, in a performance of *De Scholdschäin* (1855) by the Luxembourg composer Edmond de la FONTAINE (1823–1891), known for much of his life as simply DICKS, the first musical comedy in the Luxembourg language.

An early afternoon concert at the Eglise Ehnen performed by Mariette Lentz, soprano, Aude Rocca-Serra, harp, Dimitris Marino, mandolin, and Isabelle Kayser, flute, in the following program: the world premiere of *Trois chansons d'amour* by the Luxembourg composer and teacher Johny FRITZ; *Contrapuntal Variations* for solo mandolin (1999) by the American composer Craig FIRST, in three movements which may be performed alone or in any sequential or simultaneous fashion, a commission by Dimitris Marinos as part of the national series of works sponsored by Meet the Composer Arts Endowment Commissioning Music/USA with support form the Helen F. Whitaker Fund; *Sequenza III* for solo voice (1965) by the eminent 74-year-old Italian composer, conductor, and pedagogue Luciano BERIO; and *Serenade* for soprano and harp by the Japanese composer and teacher Harue KUNIEDA.

An evening concert at the Conservatoire de Musique Luxembourg performed by London's BBC Symphony Orchestra, with special guest artists Shi Min, Peking opera actress, Nancy Lundy, soprano, and Zehuai Zhang, puppeteer, conducted by Pascal Rophé and Tan Dun, in the following program: *Giro* (1982; rev. 1997) by the spirited 42-year-old Finnish conductor and composer Esa-Pekka SALONEN; *Variations* (1994–97) by the 68-year-old English composer and teacher Hugh WOOD, a commission from the BBC, in ten variations, mainly fast and short and mostly performed attacca; *The Stations of the Sun* (1997–98) by the English composer Julian ANDERSON, with both seasonal and religious connotations, the superficial form being four linked sections, with coda; and *Orchestral Theatre IV: The Gate* (1999) by the respected 43-year-old Chinese composer Tan DUN, part of a decade-long concern, to date four works, concerned "with the reconciliation of apparent contrasts between 'primitive' ritual and the modern concert hall experience, performer and audience, and Eastern and Western culture."

8 OCTOBER 2000

An afternoon marathon concert featuring chamber and electronic works by the 72-year-old Israeli composer Herbert BRÜN takes place at Krueger Hall at Barnard College, directed by Keith Moore and Taimur Sullivan, and featuring an international roster of performers.

12 OCTOBER 2000

Harp Concerto by the eminent 72-year-old Finnish composer and pedagogue Einojuhani (actually, Eino Juhani) RAUTAVAARA is performed for the first time by the Minnesota Orchestra, Kathy Kienzle harpist, with Osmo Vänskä conducting.

15 OCTOBER 2000

Piano Concerto by the Danish composer Hans ABRAHAMSEN is performed for the first time in Oslo by the BIT 20 Ensemble, with special guest soloist Annemarie Fjord Abildskov, piano.

18 OCTOBER 2000

Solo Transformed for piano and orchestra by the brilliant 78-year-old German-born American pianist, conductor, and composer Lukas FOSS (real name, Fuchs) is performed for the first time by the Minnesota Orchestra, Peter Serkin soloist, and Eiji Oue conducting.

22 OCTOBER 2000

The 50-year-old black American pianist Leon BATES makes his Carnegie Hall recital debut in New York in a program including works by Edward MacDowell, Aaron Coland, Samuel Barber, and Tōru Takemitsu.

22 OCTOBER 2000

"The Ernst Krenek Centennial," hosted by the Austrian Cultural Institute New York, opens with the first of six concerts devoted to the works of the remarkable Austrian-born American composer Ernst KRENEK (originally, Křenek) (1900–1991), whose intellect responded equally to his musical philosophy and his imaginative technique of composition, with performing ensembles including the Austrian Chamber Symphony, soloists of the Camerata Academica Salzburg, soloists of the American Symphony Orchestra, and the Queens College Orchestra, soloists including Wolfgang Holzmaier, and Russel Ryan, and featuring such works as *Double Concerto*, op.124 (1950), *Symphonic Music* for nine instruments, op.11 (1922), *First String Quartet*, op.6 (1921), *Second Symphony*, op.12 (1922), and *Suite* for flute and piano, op.147 (1954).

25 OCTOBER 2000

And Every Sparke Shivering for piano quintet by the 56-year-old New Zealand composer Lyell (Richard) CRESSWELL is given its premiere performance in Auckland.

27 OCTOBER 2000

Vølvens Spådom for soprano, boys' chorus, and orchestra by the American-born Danish composer Andy PAPE is given its first ever performance in Copenhagen by the Copenhagen Philharmonic, with special guest artists Hane Fischer, soprano, and the Copenhagen Boys Choir.

28 OCTOBER 2000

Håndslag for orchestra by the prominent 68-year-old Danish composer and pedagogue Per NØRGÅRD is first performed by the Danish Radio Symphony in Copenhagen.

29 OCTOBER 2000

The EOS Orchestra, conducted by Jonathan Sheffer and featuring the American baritone Kurt Olllmann, presents "A Tribute to PAUL BOWLES" at the 92nd Street Y in New York, including footage from the documentary film *Let It Come Down: The Life of Paul Bowles*, as well as the first ever performances of *Romantic Suite* and *Secret Words: A Suite of Six Songs*, and excerpts from his incidental music to the Tennessee Williams's play *The Glass Menagerie*.

10 NOVEMBER 2000

Ländler Land for three cellos and two pianos by the 54-year-old American composer Daniel GOODE is performed for the first time by the DownTown Ensemble (Sarah Cahill and Joseph Kubera, pianists, and Michael Finckel, Pitnarry Shin, and Alex MacKenzie, cellists) in a program entitled "Waltzing With Pianos and Cellos," which also features Robert Ashley's *Viva's Boy*, Morton Feldman's *Intermission 6*, Michael Finckel's *Sinister Plaining*, Matthias Hauer's *Labyrinthischer Tanz*, and Blue Gene Tyranny's *The Decertified Highway of Dreams*, at the Renee Weiler Concert Hall at New York's Greenwich House Music School.

11 NOVEMBER 2000

The New York Chamber Symphony, conducted by Gerard Schwarz and featuring violin soloist Elmar Oliveira, gives the first ever performance of *Sinfonia Concertanto* by the respected 68-year-old Bulgarian-born American composer and pedagogue Henri LAZAROF, in New York at Lincoln Center's Alice Tully Hall.

12 NOVEMBER 2000

Three Balladen for bass-baritone and piano by Georg SCHÖNBERG, eldest son of the great Austrian-born American composer Arnold (Franz Walter) Schoenberg (originally, Schönberg) (1874–1951) and nephew of the important Austrian composer and conductor Alexander von Zemlinsky (1871–1942), is performed for the first time at the German Evangelical Lutheran Church of St. Paul in New York, Peter Ludwig, bass-baritone, Peter Vinograde, pianist.

15 NOVEMBER 2000

The American Symphony Orchestra presents the world premiere performances of *Cello Concerto* by the significant 71-year-old American conductor and composer Harold FARBERMAN, Eugene Moye, soloist, and *Timpani Concerto* by the outstanding 63-year-old American composer Philip GLASS, Jonathan Haas and Benjamin Herman, soloists, at Lincoln Center's Avery Fisher Hall in New York.

16 NOVEMBER 2000

Tequila Sunrise for orchestra by the 54-year-old American composer Robert X. RODRÍGUEZ is given its first ever performance by the Knoxville Symphony in Knoxville, Tennessee.

16 NOVEMBER 2000

Dorian Gray: A Symphonic Portrait, suite after the opera by the 39-year-old American composer, pianist, and conductor Lowell LIEBERMAN is first performed by the Dallas Symphony Orchestra, Andrew Litton conducting.

26 NOVEMBER 2000

And Furthermore, They Bite for orchestra by the American conductor, composer, and pianist Robert KAPILOW is given its first ever performance by the National Symphony in Washington, D.C.

30 NOVEMBER 2000

Second Symphony by the notable 62-year-old American composer and teacher John CORIGLIANO is given its first ever performance by the Boston Symphony Orchestra, Seiji Osawa conducting.

3 DECEMBER 2000

Birds of Minnesota for orchestra by the innovative 43-year-old American composer David LANG is performed for the first time by the Minnesota Orchestra in Minneapolis.

5 DECEMBER 2000

"Days of Bohuslav Martinů," a series of events devoted to the life and work of the eminent Czech composer Bohuslav MARTINŮ, begins at the Czech Center New York with the U.S. premiere screening of *Bohuslav Martinů and America*, a documentary about the 12 years he spent in the United States, directed by Jiri Mekvasil and written by Nekvasil and Ales Brezina. Featured in the film are such of Martinů's colleagues as Charles Rosen, Michael Steinberg, David Diamond, Ned Rorem, and Peater Stearns, among others. (Other, subsequent, events of the series, which continues to 29 January 2001, include "Exhibition: The Life and Work of Bohuslav Martinů," a significant collection of reproductions of photographs and facsimiles of letters, drawings, and original scores from the holdings of the Bohuslav Martinů Institute in Prague; a piano recital featuring Martinů's works by Erik Entwistle; and a video screening of *Return From Exile*, a 1998 documentary also by Brezina and Nekvasil, and centering on Martinů's life in Europe.)

6 DECEMBER 2000

The House of the Seven Gables, opera, by the inventive American composer Scott EYERLY to an original libretto based on Hawthorne's classic novel, is mounted for the first time at the Manhattan School of Music in New York.

7 DECEMBER 2000

Commotio by the 52-year-old Danish composer, conductor, and teacher Hans Aage RASMUSSEN is heard for the first time in Copenhagen, in an orchestral version, performed by the Danish Radio Symphony.

11 DECEMBER 2000

New Dance Alliance of New York, in cooperation with Dixon Place, presents "Performance Mix," a program of dance, music, and multi-discipline works including two short world premieres of *The Origin of Things: A Sung Prayer* and *Inauguration: A Nightmare Memory*, the first an excerpt from *WARNING!: eXplicit Material*, a large-cast musical spectacle, and the second an excerpt from a new solo piece called *MONKS & SLUTS (& STATESMEN, Oh My!)*, both live action, cutting-edge, movement-driven music theater pieces by the talented 30-year-old American composer and performer David RODWIN.

14 DECEMBER 2000

A mini-, three-day festival celebrating the work of the outstanding French composer and pedagogue Olivier MESSIAEN (1908–1992) begins at New York's Cooper Union with a recital concert by Elizabeth Farnum, soprano, and Phillip Bush, pianist, of *Poèmes pour Mi* for soprano and piano (1936) and *Chants de terre et de ciel*, song cycle for soprano and piano (1938), the latter after texts by the composer.

LETTERS
AND DOCUMENTS

Motu Proprio of Pope Pius X on Sacred Music

Instruction on Sacred Music

I *General Principles*

§ 1. Sacred music, being a complementary part of the solemn liturgy, participates in the general scope of the liturgy, which is the glory of God and the sanctification and edification of the faithful. It contributes to the decorum and the splendor of the ecclesiastical ceremonies, and since its principal office is to clothe with suitable melody the liturgical text proposed for the understanding of the faithful, its proper aim is to add greater efficacy to the text, in order that through it the faithful may be the more easily moved to devotion and better disposed for the reception of the fruits of grace belonging to the celebration of the most holy mysteries.

§ 2. Sacred music should consequently possess, in the highest degree, the qualities proper to the liturgy, and in particular *sanctity* and *goodness of form*, which will spontaneously produce the final quality of universality.

It must be *holy*, and must, therefore, exclude all profanity not only in itself, but in the manner in which it is presented by those who execute it.

It must be *true art*, for otherwise it will be impossible for it to exercise on the minds of those who listen to it that efficacy which the Church aims at obtaining in admitting into her liturgy the art of musical sounds.

But it must, at the same time, be *universal* in the sense that while every nation is permitted to admit into its ecclesiastical compositions those special forms which may be said to constitute its native music, still these forms must be subordinated in such a manner to the general characteristics of sacred music that nobody of any nation may receive an impression other than good on hearing them.

II *The Different Kinds of Sacred Music*

§ 3. These qualities are to be found, in the highest degree, in Gregorian Chant, which is, consequently, the Chant proper to the Roman Church, the only chant she has inherited from the ancient fathers, which she has jealously guarded for centuries in her liturgical codices, which she directly proposes to the faithful as her own, which she prescribes exclusively for some parts of the liturgy, and which the most recent studies have so happily restored to their integrity and purity.

On these grounds Gregorian Chant has always been regarded as the supreme model for sacred music, so that it is fully legitimate to lay down the following rule: *the more closely a composition for Church approaches in its movement, inspiration and savor the Gregorian form, the more sacred and liturgical it becomes; and the more out of harmony it is with that supreme model, the less worthy it is of the temple.*

The ancient traditional Gregorian Chant must, therefore, in a large measure be restored to the functions of public worship, and the fact must be accepted by all that an ecclesiastical function loses none of its solemnity when accompanied by this music alone.

Special efforts are to be made to restore the use of the Gregorian Chant by the people, so that the faithful may again take a more active part in the ecclesiastical offices, as was the case in ancient times.

§ 4. The above-mentioned qualities are also possessed in an excellent degree by Classic Polyphony, especially of the Roman School, which reached its greatest perfection in the sixteenth century, owing to the works of Pierluigi da Palestrina, and continued subsequently to produce compositions of excellent quality from a liturgical and musical standpoint.

Classic Polyphony agrees admirably with Gregorian Chant, the supreme model of all sacred music, and hence it has been found worthy of a place side by side with Gregorian Chant, in the more solemn functions of the Church, such as those of the Pontifical Chapel. This, too, must therefore be restored largely in ecclesiastical functions, especially in the more important basilicas, in cathedrals, and in the churches and chapels of seminaries and other ecclesiastical institutions in which the necessary means are usually not lacking.

§ 5. The Church has always recognized and favored the progress of the arts, admitting to the service of religion everything good and beautiful discovered by genius in the course of ages—always, however, with due regard to the liturgical laws. Consequently modern music is also admitted to the Church, since it, too, furnishes compositions of such excellence, sobriety, and gravity, that they are in no way unworthy of the liturgical functions. Still, since modern music has risen mainly to serve profane uses, greater care must be taken with regard to it, in order that the musical compositions of modern style which are admitted in the Church may contain nothing profane, be free from reminiscences of motifs adopted in the theatres, and be not fashioned even in their external forms after the manner of profane pieces.

§ 6. Among the different kinds of modern music, that which appears less suitable for accompanying the functions of public worship is the theatrical style, which was in the greatest vogue, especially in Italy, during the last century. This of its very nature is diametrically opposed to Gregorian Chant and classic polyphony, and therefore to the most important law of all good sacred music. Besides the intrinsic structure, the rhythm and what is known as the *conventionalism* of this style adapt themselves but badly to the requirements of true liturgical music.

III *The Liturgical Text*

§ 7. The language proper to the Roman Church is Latin. Hence it is forbidden to sing anything whatever in the vernacular in solemn liturgical functions—much more to sing in the vernacular the variable or common parts of the Mass and Office.

§ 8. As the texts that may be rendered in music, and the order in which they are to be rendered, are determined for every liturgical function, it is not lawful to confuse this order or to change the prescribed texts for others selected at will, or to omit them either entirely or even in part, unless when the rubrics allow that some versicles of the text be supplied with the organ, while these versicles are simply recited in the choir. However, it is permissible, according to the custom of the Roman Church, to sing a motet to the Blessed Sacrament after the *Benedictis* in a Solemn Mass. It is also permitted, after the Offertory prescribed for the Mass has been sung, to execute during the time that remains a brief motet to words approved by the Church.

§ 9. The liturgical text must be sung as it is in the books, without alteration or inversion of the words, without undue repetition, without breaking syllables, and always in a manner intelligible to the faithful who listen.

IV *External Form of the Sacred Compositions*

§ 10. The different parts of the Mass and the Office must retain, even musically, that particular concept and form which ecclesiastical tradition has assigned to them, and which is admirably brought out by Gregorian Chant. The method of composing an *introit*, a *gradual*, an *antiphon*, a *psalm*, a *hymn*, a *Gloria in excelsis*, etc., must therefore be distinct from one another.

§ 11. In particular the following rules are to be observed:

(a) The *Kyrie*, *Gloria*, *Credo*, etc., of the mass must preserve the unity of composition proper to their text. It is not lawful, therefore, to compose them in separate movements, in such a way that each of these movements form a complete composition in itself, and be capable of being detached from the rest and substituted by another.

(b) In the office of Vespers it should be the rule to follow the *Cæremoniale Episcoporum*, which prescribes Gregorian Chant for the psalmody and permits figured music for the versicles of the *Gloria Patri* and the hymn.

It will nevertheless be lawful on greater solemnities to alternate the Gregorian Chant of the choir with the so-called *falsi-bordoni* or with verses similarly composed in a proper manner.

It is also permissible occasionally to render single psalms in their entirety in music, provided the form proper to psalmody be preserved in such compositions; that is to say, provided the singers seem to be psalmodising among themselves, either with new motifs or with those taken from Gregorian Chant or based upon it.

The psalms known as *di concerto* are therefore forever excluded and prohibited.

(c) In the hymns of the Church the traditional form of the hymn is preserved. It is not lawful, therefore, to compose, for instance, a *Tantum ergo* in such wise that the first strophe presents a romanza, a cavatina, an adagio and the *Genitori* an allegro.

(d) The antiphons of the Vespers must be as a rule rendered with the Gregorian melody proper to each. Should they, however, in some special case be sung in figured music, they must never have either the form of a concert melody or the fullness of a motet or a cantata.

V *The Singers*

§ 12. With the exception of the melodies proper to the celebrant at the altar and to the ministers, which must be always sung in Gregorian Chant, and without accompaniment of the organ, all the rest of the liturgical chant belongs to the choir of levites, and, therefore, singers in church, even when they are laymen, are really taking the place of the ecclesiastical choir. Hence the music rendered by them must, at least for the greater part, retain the character of choral music.

By this it is not to be understood that solos are entirely excluded. But solo singing should never predominate to such an extent as to have the greater part of the liturgical chant executed in that manner; the solo phrase should have the character or hint of a melodic projection (*spunto*), and be strictly bound up with the rest of the choral composition.

§ 13. On the same principle it follows that singers in church have a real liturgical office, and that therefore women, being incapable of exercising such office, cannot be admitted to form part of the choir. Whenever, then, it is desired to employ the acute voices of sopranos and contraltos, these parts must be taken by boys, according to the most ancient usage of the Church.

§ 14. Finally, only men of known piety and probity of life are to be admitted to form part of the choir of a church, and these men should by their modest and devout bearing during the liturgical functions show that they are worthy of the holy office they exercise. It will also be fitting that singers while singing in church wear the ecclesiastical habit and surplice, and that they be hidden behind gratings when the choir is excessively open to the public gaze.

VI *Organ and Instruments*

§ 15. Although the music proper to the Church is purely vocal music, music with the accompaniment of the organ is also permitted. In some special cases, within due limits and with proper safeguards, other instruments may be allowed, but never without the special permission of the Ordinary; according to prescriptions of the *Cæremoniale Episcoporum*.

§ 16. As the singing should always have the principal place, the organ or other instrument should merely sustain and never oppress it.

§ 17. It is not permitted to have the chant preceded by long preludes or to interrupt it with intermezzo pieces.

§ 18. The sound of the organ as an accompaniment to the chant in preludes, interludes, and the like must be not only governed by the special nature of the instrument, but must participate in all the qualities proper to sacred music as above enumerated.

§ 19. The employment of the piano is forbidden in church, as is also that of noisy or frivolous instruments such as drums, cymbals, bells and the like.

§ 20. It is strictly forbidden to have bands play in church, and only in special cases with the consent of the Ordinary will it be permissible to admit wind instruments, limited in number, judiciously used, and proportioned to the size of the place—provided the composition and accompaniment be written in grave and suitable style, and conform in all respects to that proper to the organ.

§ 21. In processions outside the church the Ordinary may give permission for a band, provided no profane pieces be executed. It would be desirable in such cases that the band confine itself to accompanying some spiritual canticle sung in Latin or in the vernacular by the singers and the pious associations which take part in the procession.

VII *The Length of the Liturgical Chant*

§ 22. It is not lawful to keep the priest at the altar waiting on account of the chant or the music for a length of time not allowed by the liturgy. According to the ecclesiastical prescriptions the *Sanctus* of the Mass should be over before the elevation, and therefore the priest must here have regard for the singers. The *Gloria* and the *Credo* ought, according to the Gregorian tradition, to be relatively short.

§ 23. In general it must be considered a very grave abuse when the liturgy in ecclesiastical functions is made to appear secondary to and in a manner at the service of the music, for the music is merely a part of the liturgy and its humble handmaid.

VIII *Principal Means*

§ 24. For the exact execution of what has been herein laid down, the Bishops, if they have not already done so, are to institute in their dioceses a special Commission composed of persons really competent in sacred music, and to this Commission let them entrust in the manner they find most suitable the task of watching over the music executed in their churches. Nor are they to see merely that the music is good in itself, but also that it is adapted to the powers of the singers and be always well executed.

§ 25. In seminaries of clerics and in ecclesiastical institutions let the above-mentioned traditional Gregorian Chant be cultivated by all with diligence and love, according to the Tridentine prescriptions, and let the superiors be liberal of encouragement and praise toward their young subjects. In like manner let a Schola Cantorum be established, whenever possible, among the clerics for the execution of sacred polyphony and of good liturgical music.

§ 26. In the ordinary lessons of Liturgy, Morals, Canon Law given to the students of theology, let care be taken to touch on those points which regard more directly the principles and laws of sacred music, and let an attempt be made to complete the doctrine with some particular instruction in the aesthetic side of sacred art, so that the clerics may not leave the seminary ignorant of all those subjects so necessary to a full ecclesiastical education.

§ 27. Let care be taken to restore, at least in the principal churches, the ancient *Scholæ Cantorum,* as has been done with excellent fruit in a great many places. It is not difficult for a zealous clergy to institute such *Scholæ* even in smaller churches and country parishes—nay, in these last the pastors will find a very easy means of gathering around them both children and adults, to their own profit and the edification of the people.

§ 28. Let efforts be made to support and promote, in the best way possible, the higher schools of sacred music where these already exist, and to help in founding them where they do not. It is of the utmost importance that the Church herself provide for the instruction of her choirmasters, organists, and singers, according to the true principles of sacred art.

IX Conclusion

§ 29. Finally, it is recommended to choirmasters, singers, members of the clergy, superiors of seminaries, ecclesiastical institutions, and religious communities, parish priests and rectors of churches, canons of collegiate churches and cathedrals, and, above all, to the diocesan ordinaries to favor with all zeal these prudent reforms, long desired and demanded with united voice by all; so that the authority of the Church, which herself has repeatedly proposed them, and now inculcates them, may not fall into contempt.

Given from Our Apostolic Palace at the Vatican, on day of the Virgin and Martyr, St. Cecilia, November 22, 1903, in the first year of Our Pontificate.

PIUS X, POPE

Mediator Dei of Pope Pius XII on the Sacred Liturgy

The Adornment of Churches and Altars

§ 191. As regards music, let the clear and guiding norms of the Apostolic See be scrupulously observed. Gregorian chant, which the Roman Church considers her own as handed down from antiquity and kept under her close tutelage, is proposed to the faithful as belonging to them also. In certain parts of the liturgy the Church definitely prescribes it; it makes the celebration of the sacred mysteries not only more dignified and solemn but helps very much to increase the faith and devotion of the congregation. For this reason, Our predecessors of immortal memory, Pius X and Pius XI, decreed—and We are happy to confirm with Our authority the norms laid down by them—that in seminaries and religious institutes, Gregorian chant be diligently and zealously promoted, and moreover that the old *Scholæ Cantorum* be restored, at least in the principal churches. This has already been done with happy results in not a few places.

Gregorian Chant and Congregational Singing

§ 192. Besides, "so that the faithful take a more active part in divine worship, let Gregorian chant be restored to popular use in the parts proper to the people. Indeed it is very necessary that the faithful attend the sacred ceremonies not as if they were outsiders or mute onlookers, but let them fully appreciate the beauty of the liturgy and take part in the sacred ceremonies, alternating their voices with the priest and the choir, according to the prescribed norms. If, please God, this is done, it will not happen that the congregation

hardly ever or only in a low murmur answer the prayers in Latin or in the vernacular." A congregation that is devoutly present at the sacrifice, in which our Saviour together with His children redeemed with His sacred blood sings the nuptial hymn of His immense love, cannot keep silent, for "song befits the lover" and, as the ancient saying has it, "he who sings well prays twice." Thus, the Church militant, faithful as well as clergy, joins in the hymns of the Church triumphant and with the choirs of angels, and, all together, sing a wondrous and eternal hymn of praise to the most Holy Trinity in keeping with words of the preface, "with whom our voices, too, thou wouldst bid to be admitted."

§ 193. It cannot be said that modern music and singing should be entirely excluded from Catholic worship. For, if they are not profane nor unbecoming to the sacredness of the place and function, and do not spring from a desire of achieving extraordinary and unusual effects, then our churches must admit them since they can contribute in no small way to the splendor of the sacred ceremonies, can lift the mind to higher things and foster true devotion of soul.

§ 194. We also exhort you, Venerable Brethren, to promote with care congregational singing, and to see to its accurate execution with all due dignity, since it easily stirs up and arouses the faith and piety of large gatherings of the faithful. Let the full harmonious singing of our people rise to heaven like the bursting of a thunderous sea and let them testify by the melody of their song to the unity of their hearts and minds, as become brothers and the children of the same Father.

§ 211. Given at Castel Gandolfo, near Rome, on the 20th day of November in the year 1947, the 9th of Our Pontificate.

PIUS XII

The Black List of Disapproved Music

At the Convention of the Society of St. Gregory of America, held in Rochester, New York, May 4–6, 1922, the publication of a list of music not in accordance with the MOTU PROPRIO was authorized. The works of the following composers and the particular compositions listed below are clearly antagonistic to the principles enunciated in the document issued by Pope Pius X.

In preparing this section it was considered sufficient to mention the titles of only a few of the "most popular" of the objectionable Hymnals, Choir-Books, etc., still to be found in so many choir lofts.

It would be manifestly impossible to print a complete list of all the works which fall under this head. The purpose of the Society is to draw attention to the type of composition which is clearly opposed to the principles of the MOTU PROPRIO.

All the Masses by the following composers:

ASHMALL	LAMBILLOTTE
BATTMANN	LEJEAL
BORDESE	LEONARD
BROWN (WILL. M.S.)	LEPREVOST
CONCONE	LOESCH
CORINI	MARZO
DURAND	MERCADANTE
FARMER	MERLIER
GANSS	MILLARD
GENERALI	PONIATOWSKI
GIORZA	SILAS
KALLIWODA	STEARNS
LA HACHE	TURNER
	WIEGAND

Of CHARLES GOUNOD's, the following Masses:

St. Cecilia	De Paques (No. 3)
Sacred Heart	

The musical value of the religious compositions of MOZART, JOSEPH HAYDN, SCHUBERT, G. ROSSINI,* C. M. VON WEBER does not enter into the question. The exception taken is their purely liturgical unfitness according to the principles declared in the MOTU PROPRIO. All the Vespers and Psalms, by

ALDEGA	MARZO
BRIZZI	McCABE
CAPOCCI	MERCADANTE
CERRUTI	MILLARD
CORINI	MODERATI
GENERALI	STEARNS
GIORZA	WIEGAND
LEJEAL	ZINGARELLI

* Not to be confused with Rev. Carlo Rossini, whose compositions stand approved.

The Requiem Masses by

CHERUBINI
MADONNA
GIORZA
OHNEWALD

Hymn- and Choir-Books

ST. BASIL'S HYMNAL
BERGE HYMNALS
CANTICA PUERORUM, EDUARDO MARZO
LAUS ET PRECES, EDUARDO MARZO
COLLECTION FOR SODALISTS, A. H. ROSEWIG
CONCENTUS SACRI, A. H. ROSEWIG
CATHOLIC CHOIR BOOK, P. GIORZA
CATHOLIC CHOIR MANUAL, G. M. WYNNE
SALVE, VOLUME I, P. GIORZA
GLORIA, VOLUME II, P. GIORZA
LAUS DEO, VOLUME III, P. GIORZA
THE CHAPEL HYMN BOOK
CATHOLIC YOUTH'S HYMN BOOK, CHRISTIAN
  BROTHERS
MAY CHIMES, SRS. NOTRE DAME
PETER'S CLASS BOOK
PETER'S CATHOLIC HARMONIST
PETER'S CATHOLIC HARP
PETER'S SODALITY HYMN BOOK
SUNDAY SCHOOL HYMN BOOK
VADE MECUM, KELLY
WERNER'S COLLECTION OF SEVEN PIECES
WREATH OF MARY

Miscellaneous Disapproved Music

STABAT MATER—G. ROSSINI

All of Rossini's compositions should be excluded from the Catholic choir. These works are unchurchly, to say the least. The "Stabat Mater" is most objectionable from a liturgical standpoint.

REGINA COELI—P. GIORZA

All compositions by P. Giorza should be eliminated from the repertoire of the Catholic choirs. The composer wrote any number of "Ballets." He did not change his style one iota when he put sacred words to these utterly secular melodies. The worst example of this "Ballet" style in church is the setting of the "Regina Coeli," which, sad to relate, is still sung in many of our churches.

JESU DEI VIVA—G. VERDI

Taken from the opera "Attila." This number is another favorite among Catholic choirs. Verdi did not write this for use in the Church, but for one of his operas. He would have been the first to object to its use in its present form, since it is neither fitting nor appropriate.

THE AVE MARIAS by

LUZZI, MILLARD, VERDI, BACH-GOUNOD, MASCAGNI, LAMBILLOTTE, KAHN, ETC.

All arrangements and adaptations of Operatic Melodies, such as Sextet from "Lucia di Lammermoor," Quartet from "Rigoletto," arias from "Tannhäuser," "Lohengrin," "Othello," etc.

SALVE REGINA, C. Henshaw-Dana
BORDESE'S COMPOSITIONS . . . ALL

Songs in English, such as

The End of a Perfect Day
Face to Face
Beautiful Isle of Somewhere
O Promise Me
I Love You Truly
There's a Beautiful Land on High
Good Night, Sweet Jesus
Wedding Marches
  From "Lohengrin"—R. Wagner
  From "Midsummer Night's Dream"—F. Mendelssohn

NOTE: The Society of St. Gregory, at its convention held in Rochester, New York, May 4–6, 1922, registered an emphatic protest against the efforts made by certain publishers of Catholic Church Music to create an impression that "revised editions" of Masses by Mozart, Haydn, Schubert, Weber, Gounod, Millard, Giorza, Farmer, Kalliwoda and other composers of the operatic school were edited to conform to the requirements of the MOTU PROPRIO.

Because a certain number of repetitions have been eliminated from these unacceptable works it does not follow that they are metamorphosed, through this process, into liturgical compositions. No amount of revision, editing or truncating can create a devotional composition out of a work that is intrinsically secular in character. Pope Pius X, in his MOTU PROPRIO, made clear the distinction between the secular and the sacred style.

The attempt of certain publishers to "hoodwink" a gullible public by using in an indiscriminate manner the caption "In accordance with the MOTU PROPRIO" deserves the condemnation of every friend of liturgical art. A flagrant example of this attempt to pull wool over the eyes of the innocent is found in the publication of the popular song "Silver Threads Among the Gold" as an "Ave Maria Stella" under the caption "In accordance with the MOTU PROPRIO."

What the Society of St. Gregory has condemned in the way of unliturgical music applies to those so-called Revised Hymnals which have merited the disapproval of the authorities simply because the compilers and editors have chosen to disregard the very plain recommendations contained in the MOTU PROPRIO.

Three Anti-Modernist Poems: 1884, 1909, 1924

I

Directions for Composing a Wagner Overture

[From an American newspaper, *ca.* 1884]

A sharp, where you'd expect a natural.
A natural, where you'd expect a sharp.
No rule observe but the exceptional
And then (first happy thought) bring in a Harp!

No bar a sequence to the bar behind,
No bar a prelude to the next that comes.
Which follows which, you really needn't mind:—
But (second happy thought!) bring in your Drums!

For harmonies, let wild discords pass;
Let key be blent with key in hideous hash;
Then (for last happy thought!) bring in your Brass!
And clang, clash, clatter—clatter, clang and clash.

A Sufferer

II
[From the New York *World,* inspired by some music of
Richard Strauss, *ca.* January 1909]

Hark! from the pit a fearsome sound
That makes your blood run cold.
Symphonic cyclones rush around—
And the worst is yet untold.

No—they unchain those dogs of war,
The wild sarrusophones,
A double-bass E-flat to roar
Whilst crunching dead men's bones.

The muted tuba's dismal groan
Uprising from the gloom
And answered by the heckelphone,
Suggest the crack of doom.

Oh, mama! is this the earthquake zone?
What ho, there! stand from under!
Or is that the tonitruone
Just imitating thunder?

Nay, fear not, little one, because
Of this sublime rough-house;
'Tis modern opera by the laws
Of Master Richard Strauss.

Singers? they're scarcely heard nor seen—
In yon back seat they sit,
The day of Song is past, I ween;
The orchestra is it.

III
[From the Boston *Herald,* February 1924,
inspired by Stravinsky's *Sacre du Printemps*]

Who wrote this fiendish "Rite of Spring,"
What right had he to write the thing,
Against our helpless ears to fling
Its crash, clash, cling, clang, bing, bang, bing?

And then to call it "Rite of Spring."
The season when on joyous wing
The birds melodious carols sing
And harmony's in everything!

He who could write the "Rite of Spring"
If I be right, by right should swing!

Manifesto of Futurist Musicians

I address myself to the young, for only the young will listen to me and understand me. But there are those who are born old,

coming into the world like a somber spectre of the past, a tumid cryptogram of venom. Neither words nor ideas have any meaning for them. Their destiny is imposed on them. It is death.

I address myself to the young, because they become naturally excited about new things, Present and living. They must follow me, faithfully, ardent, through the pathways of the future, where our intrepid brothers, Futurist poets and painters, precede us in glory, beautiful in their rage, violent in their rebellion and luminous in their animating genius.

A year ago a committee composed of Pietro Mascagni, Giacomo Orefice, Guglielmo Mattioli, Rodolfo Ferrari and the critic Gian Battista Nappi, selected my Futurist opera *La Sina d'Vargoun,* written to my own libretto in free verse, as the winner of the prize of 10,000 lire in a contest, the money to be used to defray the expenses of the production of my work recognized as superior to other entries. The first performance, given in December, 1909, at the Teatro Communale in Bologna, was received with great enthusiasm, some insipid and stupid criticisms, generous support of friends, and the high honor of vituperation by numerous enemies.

Having triumphantly entered the Italian musical scene, and established contact with audiences, publishers and critics, I could judge with a maximum of self-possession the intellectual mediocrity and mercantile ignorance which have reduced Italian music to a uniform genre of vulgar melodrama, placing it in absolute inferiority in comparison with the Futurist developments in other countries.

In Germany, after the glorious revolutionary era dominated by the sublime genius of Wagner, Richard Strauss elevated the most bizarre type of instrumentation to the level of a vital artistic achievement. Yet even Strauss is unable to disguise the aridity, the mercantilism and the banality of his soul under harmonic mannerisms and clever acoustical effects. He attempts, however, to redeem his past by ingenious innovations.

In France, Claude Debussy, a profound artist, is a man of literature rather than a musician, swimming in a serene lake of tenuous, delicate, azure harmonies, immersed in an instrumental symbolism of monotonous polyphony by means of a whole-tone scale. It is a novel system, but still a device implying a voluntary limitation, and Debussy does not always succeed in covering up the indifferent quality of his thematic and rhythmic invention and his almost total lack of ideological development. In his music, this development becomes a primitive and infantile periodic repetition of a short and poverty-stricken theme, or of a monotonous and vague rhythmic pattern. He resorts in his operatic formulas to the obsolete concepts of the Florentine Camerata, which in 1600 gave birth to melodrama, but has not achieved a complete reform of the art of music drama even in its own country. Nonetheless, more than any one else, Debussy valiantly fights against the past and often emerges victorious. Charpentier may be ideologically stronger than Debussy, but musically he is inferior.

In England, Edward Elgar, who presides over the destruction of the past with considerable élan by amplifying the classical symphonic forms, attempting a thematic development in multiform variations on the same subject, and seeking equilibrated effects to satisfy our complex sensibilities in a variety of instrumental combinations, if not in their exuberance.

In Russia, Modest Mussorgsky, innovating the spirit of Rimsky-Korsakov, repudiates the tradition by instilling the national primitive element in formulas inherited from others and by seeking dramatic truth and harmonic freedom. In Finland, a new art is being nurtured against the background of national poetry. The music of Sibelius testifies to its strength.

And in Italy? Music schools, conservatories and academies of music are vegetating miserably. In these sanctuaries of impotence, teachers and professors, illustrious defectives, are perpetuating the old traditions and are fighting every attempt to extend the musical ambience. The result is a cautious repression, elimination of all liberal and bold tendencies, unceasing mortification of impetuous intelligence; unconditional support of mediocrity which knows how to copy and criticise; prostitution of great musical glories of the past. It is an arsenal of deadly weapons against the growing genius; the reduction of study to futile acrobatics, practiced in the perpetual agony of a retarded and already dead culture.

Young musical talents, stagnating in the Italian conservatories, set their sights on the alluring mirage of opera under the auspices of important publishing firms. The majority reduces this art to a very low level through lack of basic ideas and poor technique; very few new operas reach the stage and of these many have to be financed by the composers for the sake of an ephemeral success and polite tolerance.

Pure instrumental composition is the final refuge of these frustrated opera composers, and, to exonerate themselves, they predict the end of music drama as an obsolete and antimusical form. At the same time they confirm the universal belief that Italians are not born to write orchestral music, and demonstrate their ineptness in this noble and vital genre of composition.

The fortunate few who overcome all obstacles and obtain the favors of large publishing houses to whom they become bound by illusory and humiliating contracts, are slaves who sell their art. The merchant publishers issue orders, assign commercial limits to forms of music drama and set up as models the low, sickly and vulgar operas of Giacomo Puccini and Umberto Giordano. They are willing to pay the librettists, particularly those who manufacture their scripts according to the manner of a pasticcio baked by such writers as Luigi Illica, fetid cakes called operatic librettos. These publishers reject all works that transcend mediocrity; with their vested monopoly they make profit from their merchandise and forestall even a timid attempt at rebellion. They assume the tutelage and the privilege over popular tastes, and in complicity with the critics maintain the monopoly of bel canto in Italian opera, strangling and suffocating the throat of the nation.

Only Pietro Mascagni, himself the creation of a publisher, has enough courage to rebel against traditional art, against publishers and the deceived and spoiled public. By his personal example, first and the only one in Italy, Mascagni has torn the veil off the shame of publishing monopolies and the venality of the press and has hastened the day of our liberation from the mercantile Tsarism of the dilettantes. With a force of genius Pietro Mascagni has made real attempts at innovation in the music and librettos of his theatrical works, even though he has not as yet succeeded in freeing himself from traditional forms.

Futurism is a rebellion of life, of intuition and of sentiment, a thundering and impetuous spring. It wages implacable war on musicians who repeat, prolong and exalt the past to the detriment of the future. It proclaims the conquest of artistic action, amoral, free and imaginative.

I raise the red banner of Futurism to the sun in open air, sounding a clarion call under this flaming symbol to those among young composers who have a heart with which to love and to fight, a mind to conceive ideas, and boldness immune to cowardice. I rejoice in setting myself free from the chains of tradition, of doubt, of opportunism and of vanity.

I repudiate the title of Maestro, which is a stigma of mediocrity and ignorance, and hereby confirm my enthusiastic adherence to Futurism. For the young, for the ardent, for the courageous, I issue these irrevocable instructions:

1. We must convince young composers to desert music schools, conservatories and academies, and to adopt free study as the only means of regeneration.

2. We must combat with assiduous energy the fatally venal and ignorant critics, to free the public from the maleficent influence of their writings and to found for this purpose an independent musical journal, resolutely opposing the criteria of conservatory professors and of those who have been degraded by them.

3. We must abstain from the participation in any contest with the usual sealed envelopes and compulsory fees of admission, denouncing publicly the mystifications involved in them and exposing the incompetence of juries, generally composed of cretins and imbeciles.

4. We must keep aloof from commercial or academic circles, treating them with contempt, and preferring a modest life to the affluence of those through whom art is being sold.

5. We must liberate the individual musical consciousness from all imitation of the past, we must feel and sing with one's soul directed towards the future, receiving inspiration from nature in all its manifestations, human and extrahuman, and exalt man as a symbol of perennial regeneration in intimate relationship with nature.

6. We must destroy the pretense of well-made music, that rhetoric of impotence, and proclaim the unique ideal of Futurist Music, absolutely different from any written before. We must create in Italy a Futurist musical taste. We must destroy pedantic, academic and soporific values, and to regard the phrase, "Let us turn to the past" as odious, stupid and vile.

7. We must proclaim the reign of the singer as finished and demand that the vocal part in a work of art should correspond to that of an orchestral instrument.

8. We must change the term "opera libretto" to "dramatic and tragic poem set to music," substituting free verse for metrical prosody. Every opera composer must be the author of his own literary text.

9. We must combat categorically the historical reconstructions and the traditional mise en scène, and condemn the opposition to the use of contemporary dress in opera as stupid.

10. We must deprecate ballads in the manner of Tosti and the loathsome Neapolitan songs, as well as sacred music which has no reason to exist now that the decline of religious faith is complete, and which has become a monopoly of impotent conservatory directors and incompetent priests.

11. We must generate in the audiences a constantly increasing hostility against the exhumations of old operas, which hamper the chances of modern composers; we must exalt in music all that is revolutionary and original, treat the insults and the ridicule of the moribund opportunists as an honor.

And now let the defenders of the past turn against me with all the fury they are capable of, while I stand serenely smiling, not caring a whit. I climb over the past and in a loud voice I issue a summons to young musicians to gather under the banner of Futurism, launched by the poet Marinetti in Paris last year, which has since conquered the greatest intellectual centers of the world.

BALILLA PRATELLA, MUSICIAN
Milan, 11 October 1910

[Translated from the Italian by Nicolas Slonimsky]

Technical Manifesto of Futurist Music

All innovators are futurists in relation to their own times. Palestrina would have thought that Bach was mad. Bach would have rendered a similar judgment about Beethoven, and Beethoven would have described Wagner as crazy. Rossini claimed that he finally understood Wagner's music by playing it upside down. Verdi, after he heard the overture to *Tannhäuser,* said in a letter to a friend that only an insane person could have written it.

Today we find ourselves at the threshold of a glorious madhouse, for we declare without hesitation that counterpoint and fugue, still considered the most important branch of the musical curriculum, represent nothing more than the ruins of the history of polyphony of the period between the Flemish School and Bach.

We hear laments that young musicians are no longer capable of inventing melodies, doubtless alluding to the type of melodies cultivated by Rossini, Bellini, Verdi or Ponchielli. But melody is now conceived harmonically; harmony is felt through complex combinations and successions of sounds, thus creating new melodic resources. This development marks the end, once and for all, of paltry imitators of the past, who have no longer any reason to exist, and of various venal purveyors to the low tastes of the public.

We, the Futurists, proclaim that the traditional modes derived from major, minor, augmented, and diminished intervals, and even the novel scales of whole tones, are merely special cases of the harmonic and atonal chromatic scale. We also declare as invalid the concepts of consonance and dissonance. From the innumerable combinations and varied relations derived from the chromatic scale there will blossom forth a Futurist Melody. Such a melody will be a synthesis of harmony, similar to an ideal line formed by the incessant flowering of thousands of ocean waves with unequal crests.

We, the Futurists, predict progress and eventual victory over the chromatic atonal mode, after a search and the realization of an enharmonic mode. While chromaticism makes use of all sounds contained in a scale made up of semitones, the enharmonic mode, by incorporating small subdivisions of tones, offers to our renewed sensibilities a maximum of determinable combinatorial sounds and novel relations of chords and timbres. Above all, the enharmonic mode makes it possible to use natural instinctive intonations and modulations of enharmonic intervals, unavailable to us because of the artificial structure of our tempered scale, a condition we intend to change. We, Futurists, have for a long time cherished these enharmonic intervals found only in the natural dissonances of orchestral instruments which are differently tuned and in the spontaneous songs of the people sung without preoccupation with art.

The rhythms of modern dances, monotonous, limited and decrepit, must yield to a free polyrhythmic art. The alternation and succession of all possible meters and rhythms will achieve an equilibrium only in the genius and esthetic sense of the creative artist. Technical mastery of instrumentation must be acquired experimentally.

All this will be possible when conservatories, music schools and academies of music are deserted and are forced to close down, so that musical studies can be pursued in absolute freedom. Teachers of today will become experts of tomorrow, objective guides and collaborators of students; they will cease the unconscionable corruption of nascent geniuses by forcing them to drag themselves behind their personality and by imposing on them their own errors and their own criteria. We conclude:

1. Melody is a synthesis of harmony, in which major, minor, augmented and diminished triads are special cases of a generic chromatic atonal mode.

2. Enharmonic relationships are magnificent victories of Futurism.

3. The monopoly of the modern dance must be broken, since its rhythms are special cases of flee rhythm, in the sense that the rhythm of a hendecasyllable is a special case of a strophe in free verse.

4. By effecting a fusion of harmony and counterpoint, we must create polyphony in the absolute sense, such as has never been attempted before.

5. We must master all expressive technical and dynamic elements of instrumentation and regard the orchestra as a sonorous universe in a state of constant mobility, integrated by an effective fusion of all its constituent parts.

6. All musical forms are created by generative emotional motives.

7. A revival of traditional forms, dead and buried, of a classical symphony must be prevented.

8. All stage works must be regarded as symphonic forms.

9. It is imperative that opera composers should write their own librettos, their own dramatic theatrical poems. The symbolic action of such a poem must spring from the composer's own creative imagination, reinforced by the determination to develop emotional motives. Librettos written by others would force the composer to accept from others the rhythms of his own music as well.

10. Free verse is the only means of obtaining polyrhythmic freedom.

11. All forces of nature, tamed by man through his continued scientific discoveries, must find their reflection in composition—the musical soul of the crowds, of great industrial plants, of trains, of transatlantic liners, of armored warships, of automobiles, of airplanes. This will unite the great central motives of a musical poem with the power of the machine and the victorious reign of electricity.

BALILLA PRATELLA, MUSICIAN
Milan, 11 March 1911

[Translated from the Italian by Nicolas Slonimsky]

The Art of Noises

Futurist Manifesto

MY DEAR BALILLA PRATELLA, GREAT FUTURISTIC COMPOSER:

In the crowded Costanzi Theater, in Rome, while I was listening with my futurist friends Marinetti, Boccioni, and Balla to the orchestral performance of your overwhelming MUSICA FUTURISTA, there came to my mind the idea of a new art: the ART OF NOISES, a logical consequence of your marvelous innovations.

Life in ancient times was silent. In the nineteenth century, with the invention of machines, Noise was born. Today Noise is triumphant, and reigns supreme over the senses of men. For many centuries life evolved in silence, or, at the most, with but a muted sound. The loudest noises that interrupted this silence were neither violent nor prolonged nor varied, since—if we overlook such exceptional phenomena as hurricanes, tempests, avalanches, waterfalls—nature is silent.

Noises being so scarce, the first *musical sounds* which man succeeded in drawing from a hollow reed or from a stretched string were a new, astonishing, miraculous discovery. By primitive peoples musical sound was ascribed to the gods, regarded as holy, and entrusted to the sole care of the priests, who made use of it to enrich their rites with mystery. Thus was born the conception of musical sound as a thing having an independent existence, a thing different from life and unconnected with it. From this conception resulted an idea of music as a world of fantasy superimposed upon reality, a world inviolate and sacred. It will be readily understood how this idea of music must inevitably have impeded its progress, as compared with that of the other arts. The Greeks themselves—with their theory of music (systematized mathematically by Pythagoras) which permitted the use of a few consonant intervals only—greatly limited music's scope and excluded all possibility of harmony, of which they knew nothing.

The Middle Ages, with their modifications of the Greek tetrachord system, with their Gregorian chants and their folk songs, enriched the art of music. Yet they continued to regard music from the point of view of *linear development in time*—a narrow view of the art which lasted several centuries and which persists in the more complicated polyphony of the Flemish contrapuntists. The *chord* did not exist: the flow of the individual parts was never subordinated to the agreeable effect produced at any given moment by the ensemble of those parts. In a word, the medieval conception of music was horizontal, not vertical. An interest in the simultaneous union of different sounds, that is, in the chord as a complex sound, developed gradually, passing from the perfect consonance, with a few incidental dissonances, to the complex and persistent dissonances which characterize the music of today.

The art of music at first sought and achieved purity and sweetness of sound; later, it blended diverse sounds, but always with intent to caress the ear with suave harmonies. Today, growing ever more complicated, it seeks those combinations of sounds that fall most dissonantly, strangely, and harshly upon the ear. We thus approach nearer and nearer to the MUSIC OF NOISE.

This musical evolution parallels the growing multiplicity of machines, which everywhere are assisting mankind. Not only amid the clamor of great cities but even in the countryside, which until yesterday was ordinarily quiet, the machine today has created so many varieties and combinations of noise that pure musical sound—with its poverty and its monotony—no longer awakens any emotion in the hearer.

To excite and exalt our senses, music continued to develop toward the most complex polyphony and the greatest variety of orchestral timbres, or colors, devising the most complicated successions of dissonant chords and preparing in a general way for the creation of MUSICAL NOISE. This evolution toward noise was hitherto impossible. An eighteenth-century ear could not have endured the dissonant intensity of certain chords produced by our modern orchestras—triple the size of the orchestras of that day. But our own ears—trained as they are by the modern world, so rich in variegated noises—not only enjoy these dissonances but demand more and more violent acoustic emotions.

Moreover, musical sound is too limited in qualitative variety of timbre. The most complicated of orchestras reduce themselves to four or five classes of instruments differing in timbre: instruments played with the bow, plucked instruments, brass winds, wood winds, and percussion instruments. So that modern music, in its attempts to produce new kinds of timbre, struggles vainly within this little circle.

We must break out of this narrow circle of pure musical sounds, and conquer the infinite variety of noise-sounds.

Everyone will recognize that every musical sound carries with it an incrustation of familiar and stale sense associations, which predispose the bearer to boredom, despite all the efforts of innovating musicians. We futurists have all deeply loved the music of the great composers. Beethoven and Wagner for many years wrung our hearts. But now we are satiated with them and derive much greater pleasure from ideally combining the noises of street-cars, internal-combustion engines, automobiles, and busy crowds than from rehearing, for example, the "Eroica" or the "Pastorale."

We cannot see the immense apparatus of the modern orchestra without being profoundly disappointed by its feeble acoustic achievements. Is there anything more absurd than to see twenty men breaking their necks to multiply the meowling of a violin? All this will naturally infuriate the musicomaniacs and perhaps disturb the somnolent atmosphere of our concert halls. Let us enter, as futurists, into one of these institutions for musical anemia. The first measure assails your ear with the boredom of the already-heard and causes you to anticipate the boredom of the measure to come. Thus we sip, from measure to measure, two or three different sorts of boredom, while we await an unusual emotion that never arrives. Meanwhile we are revolted by the monotony of the sensations experienced, combined with the idiotic religious excitement of the listeners, Buddhistically intoxicated by the thousandth repetition of their hypocritical and artificial ecstasy. Away! Let us be gone, since we shall not much longer succeed in restraining a desire to create a new musical realism by a generous distribution of sonorous blows and slaps, leaping nimbly over violins, pianofortes, contrabasses, and groaning organs. Away!

The objection cannot be raised that all noise is loud and disagreeable. I need scarcely enumerate all the small and delicate noises which are pleasing to the ear. To be convinced of their surprising variety one need only think of the rumbling of thunder, the howling of the wind, the roar of a waterfall, the gurgling of a brook, the rustling of leaves, the receding clatter of a horse's hoofs, the bumping of a wagon over cobblestones, and the deep, solemn breathing of a city at night, all the noises made by wild and domesticated animals, and all those that the human mouth can produce, apart from speaking or singing.

Let us wander through a great modern city with our ears more attentive than our eyes, and distinguish the sounds of water, air, or gas in metal pipes, the purring of motors (which breathe and pulsate with an indubitable animalism), the throbbing of valves, the pounding of pistons, the screeching of gears, the clatter of streetcars on their rails, the cracking of whips, the flapping of awnings and flags. We shall amuse ourselves by orchestrating in our minds the noise of the metal shutters of store windows, the slamming of doors, the bustle and shuffle of crowds, the multitudinous uproar of railroad stations, forges, mills, printing presses, power stations, and underground railways.

Nor should the new noises of modern warfare be forgotten. Recently the poet Marinetti, in a letter from the trenches of Adrianopolis, described to me in admirably unfettered language the orchestra of a great battle: *"every 5 seconds siege guns splitting the belly of space with a* TZANG-TUMB-TUUUMB *chord revolt of 500 echos to tear it to shreds and scatter it to infinity In the center of these* TZANG-TUMB-TUUUMB *spied out breadth 50 square kilometers leap reports knife-thrusts rapid-fire batteries Violence ferocity regularity this deep bass ascending the strange agitated insane high-pitched notes of battle Fury, panting breath eyes ears nostrils open! watching! straining! what joy to see hear smell everything everything taratatata of the machine guns frantically screaming amid bites blows traak-traak whipcracks pic-pac pum-tumb strange goings-on leaps height 200 meters of the infantry Down down at the bottom of the orchestra stirring up pools oxen buffaloes goats wagons pluff plaff rearing of horses flic flac tzing tzing shaak hilarious neighing iiiiii stamping clanking 3 Bulgarian battalions on the march croooc-craaac* (lento) *Shumi Maritza or Karvavena* TZANG-TUMB-TUUUMB *toctoctoctoc*

1	2	3	4	5	6
Booms Thunderclaps Explosions Crashes Splashes Roars	Whistles Hisses Snorts	Whispers Murmers Mutterings Bustling noises Gurgles	Screams Screeches Rustlings Buzzes Cracklings Sounds obtained by friction	Noises obtained by percussion on metals, wood, stone, terracotta	Voices of animals and men: Shouts Shrieks Groans Howls Laughs Wheezes Sobs

(rapidissimo) *crooc-craac* (lento) *officers' yells resounding like sheets of brass bang here crack there* BOOM *ching chak* (presto) *chachacha-cha-chak up down back forth all around above look out for your head chak good shot! Flames flames flames flames flames collapse of the forts over behind the smoke Shukri Pasha talks to 27 forts over the telephone in Turkish, in German Hallo! Ibrahim!! Rudolf! Hallo! Hallo, actors playlists echos prompters scenarios of smoke forests applause smell of hay mud dung my feet are frozen numb smell of saltpeter smell of putrefaction Timpani flutes clarinets everywhere low high birds chirping beatitudes shade cheep-cheep-cheep breezes verdure herds dong-dang-dong-ding-baaaa the lunatics are assaulting the musicians of the orchestra the latter soundly thrashed play on Great uproar don't cancel the concert more precision dividing into smaller more minute sounds fragments of echos in the theater area 300 square kilometers Rivers Maritza Tundja stretch out Rudopi Mountains standing up erect boxes balconies 2000 shrapnel spraying exploding snow-white handkerchiefs full of gold* srrrrrrr-TUMB-TUMB *2000 hand-grenades hurled shearing off black-haired heads with their splinters* TZANG-srrrrrr-TUMB-TZANG-TUMB-TUUUMB *the orchestra of the noises of war swells, beneath a long-held note of silence in high heaven gilded spherical balloon which surveys the shooting. . ."*

We must fix the pitch and regulate the harmonies and rhythms of these extraordinarily varied sounds. To fix the pitch of noises does not mean to take away from them all the irregularity of tempo and intensity that characterizes their vibrations, but rather to give definite gradation or pitch to the stronger and more predominant of these vibrations. Indeed, noise is differentiated from musical sound merely in that the vibrations that produce it are confused and irregular, both in tempo and in intensity. Every noise has a note—sometimes even a chord—that predominates in the ensemble of its irregular vibrations. Because of this characteristic note it becomes possible to fix the pitch of a given noise, that is, to give it not a single pitch but a variety of pitches, without losing its characteristic quality—its distinguishing timbre. Thus certain noises produced by rotary motion may offer a complete ascending or descending chromatic scale by merely increasing or decreasing the speed of the motion.

Every manifestation of life is accompanied by noise. Noise is therefore familiar to our ears and has the power to remind us immediately of life itself. Musical sound, a thing extraneous to life and independent of it, an occasional and unnecessary adjunct, has become for our ears what a too familiar face is to our eyes. Noise, on the other hand, which comes to us confused and irregular as life itself, never reveals itself wholly but reserves for us innumerable surprises. We are convinced, therefore, that by selecting, co-ordinating, and controlling noises we shall enrich mankind with a new and unsuspected source of pleasure. Despite the fact that it is characteristic of sound to remind us brutally of life, the ART OF NOISES must not limit itself to reproductive imitation. It will reach its greatest emotional power through the purely acoustic enjoyment which the inspiration of the artist will contrive to evoke from combinations of noises.

See table above for the futurist orchestra's six families of noises, which we shall soon produce mechanically.

In this list we have included the most characteristic fundamental noises; the others are but combinations of these.

The rhythmic movements within a single noise are of infinite variety. There is always, as in a musical note, a predominant rhythm, but around this may be perceived numerous secondary rhythms.

CONCLUSIONS

1. Futurist musicians must constantly broaden and enrich the field of sound. This is a need of our senses. Indeed, we note in present-day composers of genius a tendency toward the most complex dissonances. Moving further and further away from pure musical sound, they have almost reached the *noise-sound*. This need and this tendency can only be satisfied *by the supplementary use of noise and its substitution for musical sounds*.

2. Futurist musicians must substitute for the limited variety of timbres of the orchestral instruments of the day the infinite variety of the timbres of noises, reproduced by suitable mechanisms.

3. The musician's sensibility, liberating itself from facile, traditional rhythm, must find in noises the way to amplify and renew itself, since each noise offers a union of the most diverse rhythms, in addition to the predominant rhythm.

4. Since every noise has in its irregular vibrations a general, predominating tone, it will be easy to obtain, in constructing the instruments which imitate it, a sufficiently wide variety of tones, semitones, and quarter tones. This variety of tones will not deprive any single noise of its characteristic timbre but will merely increase its tessitura, or extension.

5. The practical difficulties in the construction of these instruments are not serious. Once the mechanical principle producing a given noise is found, one may vary its pitch by applying the general laws of acoustics. For example, in instruments employing rotary motion the speed of rotation will be increased or diminished; in others, the size or tension of the sounding parts will be varied.

6. Not by means of a succession of noises imitating those of real life, but through a fanciful blending of these varied timbres and rhythms, will the new orchestra obtain the most complex and novel sound effects. Hence every instrument must be capable of varying its pitch and must have a fairly extensive range.

7. There is an infinite variety of noises. If, today, with perhaps a thousand different kinds of machines, we can distinguish a thousand different noises, tomorrow, as the number of new machines is multiplied, we shall be able to distinguish ten, twenty, or thirty thousand different noises, not merely to be imitated but to be combined as our fancy dictates.

8. Let us therefore invite young musicians of genius and audacity to listen attentively to all noises, so that they may understand the varied rhythms of which they are composed, their principal tone, and their secondary tones. Then, comparing the varied timbres of noises with those of musical tones, they will be convinced how much more numerous are the former than the latter. Out of this will come not merely an understanding of noises, but even a taste and an enthusiasm for them. Our increased perceptivity, which has already acquired futurist eyes, will then have futurist ears. Thus the motors and machines of our industrial cities may some day be intelligently pitched, so as to make of every factory an intoxicating orchestra of noises.

I submit these statements, my dear Pratella, to your futuristic genius, and invite you to discuss them with me. I am not a professional musician; I have therefore no acoustic prejudices and no works to defend. I am a futurist painter projecting into an art he loves and has studied his desire to renovate all things. Being therefore more audacious than a professional musician could be, caring nought for my seeming incompetence, and convinced that audacity makes all things lawful and all things possible, I have imagined a great renovation of music through the Art of Noises.

LUIGI RUSSOLO
Milan, 11 March 1913
[Translated from the Italian by Stephen Somervell]

Down With the Tango and *Parsifal!*

Futurist Circular Letter to Certain Cosmopolitan Friends who Arrange Tango Tea Parties and Parsifalize.

A year ago, responding to a questionnaire, I denounced the debilitating poison of the tango. This epidemic swinging gradually invades the whole world. It threatens to corrupt all races by gelatinizing them. We must therefore inveigh with full force against the imbecility of this fad and turn back the sheepish current of snobbism.

The ponderous English and German tangos are mechanized lusts and spasms of people wearing formal attire who are unable to exteriorize their sensibilities, and plagiarize Parisian and Italian tangos. They are copulated mollusks, who stupidly alter, morphinize and pulverize the felinity and savagery of Argentina.

To possess a woman one does not rub against her but penetrates her! A knee between the buttocks? It should be mutual! You will say, this is barbarism! All right then, let us be barbarians! Down with the tango and its languid thrills! Do you believe that it is exciting to look into each other's mouth and ecstatically relish each other's teeth like a couple of hallucinating dentists? Do you find it amusing to uncork one another to get a spasm out of your partner without ever achieving it yourself, or maneuver the pointed toes of your shoes like a hypnotized cobbler? It is like Tristan and Isolde who delay their *frissons* to excite King Mark. It is a medicinal dropper of passion, a miniature of sexual anguish, a sugared pastry of desire, lust in open air, delirium tremens, hands and feet of alcoholics, coitus mimed for the cinema, a masturbation waltz! Fie on this skin diplomacy! Hail the savagery of brusque possession and the fury of muscular, exalting and fortifying dance! Tangos are slow and patient funeral processions of sex that is dead! In the name of health, force, will power and virility we spit on the tango and its superannuated enervations!

If the tango is bad, *Parsifal* is worse, because it inoculates an incurable neurasthenia with its floods and inundations of mystical lachrimosity. *Parsifal* is a systematic depreciation of life, a cooperative factory of gloom and desperation, an unmelodious discharge of squeamish stomachs, indigestion and heavy breath of virgins at forty, complaints of queasy and constipated old priests, sales in bulk and retail of remorse and elegant ennui for snobs. It is an insufficiency of blood, kidney weakness, hysteria, anemia and chlorosis! It is a brutalization of man in ludicrous progressions of vanquished and wounded notes, snorting of drunken organs, wallowing in the vomit of bitter leitmotives, tears and false pearls of Mary Magdalene sitting in décolletage at Maxim's, polyphonic purulence of the wound of Amfortas, lachrymose somnolence of the Knights of the Holy Grail and preposterous satanism of Kundry. Away with all that obsolete offal!

Mesdames et Messieurs, Queens and Kings of Snobbism, you owe absolute obedience to us, the Futurists, the living innovators. Surrender to the enthusiastic putrefaction of the crowds the corpse of Wagner, this innovator of fifty years ago, whose music, surpassed today, by Debussy, by Strauss, and by our own great Futurist Pratella, no longer means anything. We will teach you to love the living, oh dear slaves and sheep of snobbism! And here is the most persuasive argument: It is no longer fashionable to love Wagner and *Parsifal,* played everywhere, even in the provinces, or to give tango tea parties like all the good petits bourgeois. So quit the mollifying dances and rumbling organ sounds. We have something more elegant to offer you! Tango and *Parsifal* are no longer chic!

F.T. MARINETTI
Milan, 11 January 1914
[Translated from the French by Nicolas Slonimsky]

Futurist Manifesto of Aeromusic

Synthetic, Geometric, Curative

Our futurist temperament, accelerated by the dynamic quality of mechanical civilization, has attained a hypersensitivity thirsting after essence, speed, and trenchant decision.

Long declamations, hesitating analyses and endless trains of words-lamentations-and-bells die in boredom for the ears of those who are swiftly rising in the air.

The futurist movement, created by a synthesis of Italian innovators inspired with originality and speed, has taught and continues to teach the religion of speed, that is, the attempt to synthesize the world from above.

For, beyond all prosody, beyond free verse and outside the bonds of syntax, we have been able to obtain the synthesis and the synoptic simultaneity of unconstrained tables of words of a new poetry. Furthermore, we shall create a new futurist aeromusic whose law is synthesis—brevity beyond all music.

Music, by its very nature sensuous, enveloping, penetrating and persisting in the nerves after the fashion of a vapor or a perfume, tends towards analysis, while showing itself apt at summing up all the infinity of sensations in a stirring moment—thanks to its harmonic densities.

As futurist poets and musicians

a) We condemn music for music's sake which borders fatally on the fetishism of a set form, on virtuosity or technicism. Virtuosity and technicism have alienated Bach, Beethoven and Chopin from synthesis, and they have confined their genius in a maniacal pursuit of musical architecture and of music for music's sake, scattering and chilling the stirring ardor, the themes and the "finds" in the midst of tiresome development and depressing repetitions.

b) We condemn the custom of setting to music obsolete poems and subjects, the kind that composers, with their usual incompetence, are fatally bound to choose.

Only synthesis of free words can enable music to fuse with poetry.

c) We condemn imitation of classical music. In art, every return is a defeat, or disguised impotence. We must invent, that is to say, extract a personal musical emotion from life.

d) We condemn the use of popular songs, which has led spirits as perspicacious and cultivated as Stravinsky and most inspired talents, as Pratella and Malipiero, away from synthesis in an artificial and monotonous primitivism.

e) We condemn imitations of jazz and negro music, killed by rhythmic uniformity and the absence of inspired composers, long Pucciniesque lamentation asthmatically interrupted by slaps and by the syncopated tom-tom of railway trains.

Futurist music, a synthetic expression of great economic, erotic, heroic, aviational, mechanical dynamism, will be a curative music.

We shall have the following types of syntheses, which will enable us to live sanely in speed, to fly, and to win in the greatest war of tomorrow.

Sonorous block of feelings. Decisive crash. Spatial harmony. Howling interrogation. Decision framed by notes. The regularity of the air motor. The caprice of the air motor. Interpenetration of joyful notes. Triangle of songs suspended at a thousand metres. Musical ascension. Fresh fan of notes over the sea. Aerial simultaneity of harmonies. Anti-human and anti-impressionist expression of the forces of nature. Coupling of echoes.

Italian musicians, be futurists, rejuvenate the souls of your listeners by swift musical syntheses (not exceeding a minute), thunderously arousing the optimistic and active pride of living in the great Italy of Mussolini, which will henceforth be at the head of the Machine Age!

F.T. MARINETTI
MAESTRO GIUNTINI

[From the Italian monthly magazine,
Stile futurista, August 1934]

History of the
Dalcroze Method of Eurhythmics

1ST PERIOD—GENEVA, 1903–1910

It was as a professor of solfège at the Conservatory of Geneva that Jaques-Dalcroze became interested in the difficulty his students had in singing accurately. In an attempt to correct this fault, he began to make them walk in rhythm. This formed the basis of the exercise known as "stepping the time-values" ("faire des pas") which has slowly developed into eurythmics.

It was in 1903 that the first "steps" were taken. In 1904 Dalcroze continued to improve and elaborate his exercises, although the refusal of the Conservatory to accept his ideas had forced him to give private lessons. In 1905 the Conservatory allowed him to give his first demonstration (15 April), and on the first of July he expounded the principles of his method before a Conference held at Soleure (VI Tagung der Schweizerischen Tonkünstler). In spite of this, official institutions still

denied him their support, and he continued to give private courses, constantly attracting more and more pupils.

After frequent conferences and demonstrations, the study of eurythmics was introduced into the conservatories at Zurich and Basel (autumn of 1905 and spring of 1906).

The first summer class took place between 23 August and 8 September 1906, at Geneva, with enrollments. It was followed by three more, also in Geneva: from 1 to 15 August 1907 (115 students); 1–15 August 1908 (130 students); and 2–16 August 1909 (140 students).

Meanwhile Dalcroze and several of his pupils were giving demonstrations outside Switzerland, and in 1907 a course of eurythmics was opened at Paris and at Brussels. The year 1907 also witnessed the first meeting of the Society of Eurythmics (Société de Gymnastique Rythmique) at Geneva.

In 1908 conferences and demonstrations took place in Berlin, Dresden, Munich, and Husum. In 1909 other courses were started and the demonstrations increased, including Paris, Heidelberg, and Vienna.

The method was launched. In 1910, at the beginning of the year, Dalcroze gave other demonstrations at Paris and Brussels, then in Berlin, Leipzig, and Dresden. As a result of this last visit he was offered the Institut de Dresde-Hellerau, so that he might have a place in which to put his theory into practice, and on 3 October Dalcroze and fifteen of his pupils left Geneva for Hellerau.

2ND PERIOD—HELLERAU, 1910–1914

Jaques-Dalcroze arrived in Dresden in October 1910, and it was in this city, at Ständehaus, that the first lessons were given. The cornerstone of the buildings of Hellerau was laid on 26 April 1911, and in November of the same year began a course in eurythmics. But it was in 1912 that Hellerau, garden city of Europe built by Germany's greatest architects, was fittingly dedicated. In June and July of that year the great Festival of Jaques-Dalcroze took place, with a musical program composed of Gluck's *Orpheus* and *Echo et Narcisse* by Dalcroze himself. It was a landmark in the history of the art: 4141 people came from Germany and other countries to take part in the celebration. The second Festival was held a year later. *Orpheus* was performed in its entirety, and more than 5000 people attended. It is difficult to convey an impression of the brilliance of this period in the history of Hellerau. All the artists of Europe were there at one time or another, including such outstanding figures as Paul Claudel, Karl Storck. Bernard Shaw, Prince Wolkonsky (Director of the Imperial Theatres of Russia), Adolphe Appia, Nijinsky, as well as all the stars of Diaghilev's Ballet Russe, Max Reinhardt, and many others.

The history of eurythmics was not concentrated, however, at Hellerau. In 1913 alone, Dalcroze gave demonstrations in six cities of Germany and seventeen cities outside, while other professors were introducing his method in 36 other cities. Foreign governments sent commissions to Hellerau to study this new educational system. Dalcroze was invited to present his innovation at the International Congress of Physical Education at Paris; before the royal family of Belgium; and at the International Congress of Music Professors at Berlin.

In Europe and elsewhere the study of eurythmics was growing; 23 cities (9 countries) introduced it into their public schools, and 19 cities (7 countries) into their Conservatories of Music. There are Dalcroze schools in Berlin, Breslau, Budapest, Dresden, Frankfort, Kiev, London, Moscow, Nürnberg, St. Petersburg, Prague, Warsaw, and Vienna; and eurythmics is taught in 127 cities of the following countries: Germany, America, England, Austria, Belgium, Spain, Finland,

France, Holland, Hungary, Italy, Poland, Russia, Sweden, and Switzerland.

The year 1914 marks the end of the splendid activity of Hellerau. On 4 February, Wolf Dohrn, the great organizer of the Institute, died as the result of a mountain-climbing accident. At the beginning of the year Jaques-Dalcroze had come to Geneva to direct the preparations for the great "Fête de Juin." The war came, and he never returned to Hellerau.

3RD PERIOD—GENEVA, 1915–1935

After several months of confusion, when all hope had been lost of reorganizing a center for eurythmics, the Institute of Geneva was finally opened (12 October 1915). In spite of the war, its enrollment for the first year included 397 pupils, representing 16 nationalities.

Everywhere there was a similar effort to keep the new movement alive. In Switzerland eurythmics was taught in fourteen cities, and included in the curricula of the conservatories at Berne, Basel, and Zurich.

In England there were 1392 pupils in March 1916; and all during the war Dalcroze continued, in spite of the danger of crossing the Channel, to visit the English schools.

Although there was no large school in France at this time, there was a Club de Gymnastique Rythmique at 52 rue de Vaugirard, Paris.

In the United States instruction was now given in seven cities, beginning in 1915 with the first Jaques-Dalcroze Institute.

Sweden, Holland, and Russia continued the work and sent reports to Geneva. Each year one or the other of these countries distinguished itself by an increase in the number of students or by expansion into more and more of the cities.

In 1919 Geneva held its first postwar summer course, which has been followed by many others, and relations were renewed with Germany.

In 1926 the first Congrès du Rythme was held in Geneva, a huge demonstration which held out great hope for the future of eurythmics. In August of the same year was founded the International Union of Professors of the Jaques-Dalcroze Method. On this occasion the approximate number of pupils throughout the world was estimated at 22,700.

In 1927, Dalcroze was invited to Frankfort to give conferences and demonstrations at the International Exposition of Music. It marked his triumphal return to Germany, and the press welcomed him with great enthusiasm.

The United States announced in 1927 that 22 cities had courses in eurythmics; and in 1929 England counted 5574 pupils divided among 144 schools.

From 1915 to 1935 more than 125 demonstrations were given in Switzerland; from 1920 to 1935 Dalcroze gave more than sixty demonstrations in nine other countries.

Eurythmics can be said to exist in more than thirty countries, among which are South Africa, Germany, England, Australia, Austria, Belgium, Canada, Chile, Denmark, Egypt, Spain, United States, Finland, France, Greece, Holland, Italy, Ireland, Japan, Lithuania, Morocco, the Natale, Norway, New Zealand, Palestine, Poland, Portugal, Russia, Sweden, Switzerland, Czechoslovakia, and Yugoslavia.

From 1915 to 1934 the Institute at Geneva had 7253 pupils, representing forty-six nationalities.

[From the *Association Jaques-Dalcroze* at Geneva]

Society for Private Musical Performances in Vienna

(A Statement of Aims, Written by Alban Berg)

The Society was founded in November, 1918, for the purpose of enabling Arnold Schoenberg to carry out his plan to give artists and music-lovers a real and exact knowledge of modern music.

The attitude of the public toward modern music is affected to an immense degree by the circumstance that the impression it receives from that music is inevitably one of obscurity. Aim, tendency, intention, scope and manner of expression, value, essence, and goal, all are obscure; most performances of it lack clarity; and specially lacking in lucidity is the public's consciousness of its own needs and wishes. All works are therefore valued, considered, judged, and lauded, or else misjudged, attacked, and rejected, exclusively upon the basis of one effect which all convey equally—that of obscurity.

This situation can in the long run satisfy no one whose opinion is worthy of consideration, neither the serious composer nor the thoughtful member of an audience. To bring light into this darkness and thus fulfill a justifiable need and desire was one of the motives that led Arnold Schoenberg to found this society.

To attain this goal three things are necessary:

1. Clear, well-rehearsed performances.

2. Frequent repetitions.

3. The performances must be removed from the corrupting influence of publicity; that is, they must not be directed toward the winning of competitions and must be unaccompanied by applause, or demonstrations of disapproval.

Herein lies the essential difference revealed by a comparison of the Society's aims with those of the everyday concert world, from which it is quite distinct in principle. Although it may be possible, in preparing a work for performance, to get along with the strictly limited and always insufficient number of rehearsals hitherto available, for better or worse (usually the latter), yet for the Society the number of rehearsals allotted to works to be performed will be limited only by the attainment of the greatest possible clarity and by the fulfillment of all the composer's intentions as revealed in his work. And if the attainment of these minimum requirements for good performance should necessitate a number of rehearsals that cannot be afforded (as was the case, for example, with a symphony of Mahler, which received its first performance after twelve four-hour rehearsals and was repeated after two more), then the work concerned should not, and will not, be performed by the Society.

In the rehearsal of new works, the performers will be chosen preferably from among the younger and less well-known artists, who place themselves at the Society's disposal out of interest in the cause; artists of high-priced reputation will be used only so far as the music demands and permits; and moreover that kind of virtuosity will be shunned which makes of the work to be performed not the end in itself but merely a means to an end which is not the Society's, namely, the display of irrelevant virtuosity and individuality, and the attainment of a purely personal success. Such things will be rendered automatically impossible by the exclusion (already mentioned) of all demonstrations of applause, disapproval, and thanks. The only success that an artist can have here is that (which should be most important to him) of having made the work, and therewith its composer, intelligible.

While such thoroughly rehearsed performances are a guarantee that each work will be enabled to make itself rightly understood, an even more effective means to this end is given to the Society through the innovation of weekly meetings* and by frequent repetitions of every work. Moreover, to ensure equal attendance at each meeting, the program will not be made known beforehand.

Only through the fulfillment of these two requirements—thorough preparation and frequent repetition—can clarity take the place of the obscurity which used to be the only impression remaining after a solitary performance; only thus can an audience establish an attitude towards a modern work that bears any relation to its composer's intention, completely absorb its style and idiom, and achieve that intimacy that is to be gained only through direct study—an intimacy with which the concert-going public can be credited only with respect to the most frequently performed classics.

The third condition for the attainment of the aims of the Society is that the performances shall be in all respects private; that guests (foreign visitors excepted) shall not be admitted, and that members shall be obligated to abstain from giving any public report of the performances and other activities of the Society, and especially to write or inspire no criticisms, notices, or discussions of them in periodicals.

This rule, that the sessions shall not be publicized, is made necessary by the semi-pedagogic activities of the Society and is in harmony with its tendency to benefit musical works solely through good performance and thus simply through the good effect made by the music itself. Propaganda for works and their composers is not the aim of the Society.

For this reason no school shall receive preference and only the worthless shall be excluded; for the rest, all modern music—from that of Mahler and Strauss to the newest, which practically never, or, at most, rarely, is to be heard—will be performed.

In general the Society strives to choose for performance such works as show their composers' most characteristic and, if possible, most pleasing sides. In addition to song, pianoforte pieces, chamber music, and short choral pieces, even orchestral works will be considered, although the latter—since the Society has not yet the means to perform them in their original form—can be given only in good and well-rehearsed 4-hand and 8-hand arrangements. But the necessity becomes a virtue. In this manner it is possible to hear and judge a modern orchestral work divested of all the sound-effects and other sensuous aids that only an orchestra can furnish. Thus the old reproach is robbed of its force—that this music owes its power to its more or less opulent and effective instrumentation and lacks the qualities that were hitherto considered characteristic of good music—melody, richness of harmony, polyphony, perfection of form, architecture, etc.

A second advantage of this manner of music-making lies in the concert style of the performance of these arrangements. Since there is no question of a substitute for the orchestra but of so rearranging the orchestral work for the piano that it may be regarded, and should in fact be listened to, as an independent work and as a pianoforte composition, all the characteristic qualities and individualities of the piano are used, all the pianistic possibilities exploited. And it happens that in this reproduction—with different tone quality—of orchestral music, almost nothing is lost. Indeed, these very works, through the sureness of their instrumentation, the aptness of their instinctively chosen tone-colors, are best able to elicit from the piano tonal effects that far exceed its usual expressive possibilities.

* At that time, every Sunday morning from 10 to 12, in the Society's small concert hall.

At the first nine meetings, the following works were performed;

Béla Bartók, 14 Bagatelles, Op. 6 (twice)
Alban Berg, Piano Sonata, Op. 1
Claude Debussy, Two Song Cycles: Proses Lyriques (twice) and Fêtes galantes (twice); Trois Nocturnes pour orchestre, arr. for 2 pianos 4 hands by Maurice Ravel (twice)
Josef Hauer, Nomos in seven parts, Op. 1, and Nomos in five parts, Op. 2
Gustav Mahler, 7th Symphony, arr. for piano 4 hands (twice); Five songs from "Des Knaben Wunderhorn" (twice)
Hans Pfitzner, Five Songs, Op. 26
Max Reger, Introduction, Passacaglia, and Fugue for 2 pianos 4 hands, Op. 96 (twice); Sonata for piano and 'cello in A minor, Op. 118 (twice)
Franz Schreker, Vorspiel zu einem Drama, arr. for piano 4 hands (twice)
Alexander Scriabin, Sonata for piano No. 4 (twice); Sonata for piano No. 7 (twice)
Richard Strauss, Don Quixote, Op. 35, arr. for 2 pianos 4 hands (twice)
Igor Stravinsky, Trois pièces faciles and Cinq pièces faciles pour piano à 4 mains (twice)
Anton von Webern, Passacaglia for orchestra, Op. 1, arr. for 2 pianos 6 hands
Alexander von Zemlinsky, Four Songs, Op. 8

The following works are in rehearsal and are (among others) planned for performance:

Alban Berg, Vier Lieder, Op. 2
Julius Bittner, Sonata for piano and 'cello
Ferruccio Busoni, Six Elegies for piano
Gustave Charpentier, Poèmes Chantés, for solo voice and chorus
Claude Debussy, La Mer, 3 esquisses symphoniques, arr. for 2 pianos 4 hands
Fidelio Finke, Piano pieces
Egon Kornauth, Violin sonata
E.W. Korngold, Violin sonata, Op. 6
Gustave Mahler, 6th Symphony, arr. for piano 4 hands by A. von Zemlinsky
Viteslav Novak, Erotikon, piano pieces
Hans Pfitzner, Piano quintet in F minor, Op. 23
Maurice Ravel, Two Hebrew Songs
Max Reger, Suite for 'cello, Op. 131c; Sonata for violin and piano, Op. 139, Sonata for clarinet and piano, in B minor, Op. 107
Franz Schreker, Kammersymphonie, arr. for 2 pianos 4 hands
Cyril Scott, Sonata for violin and piano, Op. 57
Richard Strauss, Symphonia domestica, Op. 53, arr. for 2 pianos 4 hands
Igor Stravinsky, Berceuses du chat, Chansons avec ensemble, Pribaoutki, Chansons plaisantes
Josef Suk, "Erlebtes und Erträumtes," piano pieces; "Ein Sommermärchen," symphonic poem arr. for piano 4 hands
Anton von Webern, "Entflieht auf leichten Kähnen," mixed chorus a capella, Op. 2
Karl Weigl, String quartet in E major
Alexander von Zemlinsky, Six Songs (Maeterlinck), Op. 13; 2nd String Quartet, Op. 15

Finally it should be mentioned that, in addition to the performances listed, there were lectures and other meetings serving the purposes of the Society.

The financial means for accomplishing these ends were obtained in the following ways:

1. Through the regular membership dues.
2. Through voluntary contributions over and above these dues.
3. Through occasional voluntary gifts from non-members.

Following are the official membership rates:

The weekly evening meetings of the Society count as concerts to which members subscribe for a season. The subscription rates for the selected category of seats may be paid in advance for the whole season, or in quarterly, monthly, or even weekly installments, although the member obligates himself to pay all the installments for a complete season. In addition, upon joining the Society and at the beginning of each season, introductory fees must be paid, their amount varying with the location of the seats.

There are four categories of seats. The least expensive (IV) cost 1 Krone a week; the next (III) 2 Kronen; the next (II) 3 Kronen: the first category is reserved for those who voluntarily pay more.

In accordance with these rates, see table below for membership dues.

This grading of dues was devised in order to share the considerable expenses of the Society equitably and in proportion to the ability of members to pay. It is naturally expected that those who are in a position to make greater sacrifices will avail themselves of the first two categories.

Upon joining this Society, members must fill in and mail the appended form, declaring knowledge of and willingness to abide by the statutes.

PRESIDENT: ARNOLD SCHOENBERG
16 February 1919

EXTRACT FROM THE STATUTES

4. Any person of honorable and unblemished character and willing to accept the regulations may become a member.

6. The members of the Society are obligated

   a. to further the aims of the Society and to avoid acts prejudicial to them.
   b. to pay membership dues for the current year, even in case of premature cessation of membership.
   c. not to injure the cause served by the Society.

8. The direction of the Society consists of

   a. the President, Arnold Schoenberg, the duration of whose tenure is not limited;
   b. a committee of from ten to twenty (chairman, secretary, etc.) chosen by the General Assembly in agreement with the President.

9. The President has a completely free hand in the direction of the Society. He decides upon the kind and amount of the expenditures necessary to the work of the Society: fees paid to participants and the committee members specified in section 10, rental of halls, payment for lectures, administrative expenses, etc. He has also the right to remit wholly or in part the dues of worthy and needy members.

12. All decisions of the General Assembly, including elections, changes in statutes, dissolution of the Society, etc., require for their validity the consent of the President.

[Translated from the German by Stephen Somervell]

What Is Atonality?

(A radio talk given by Alban Berg on the Vienna *Rundfunk*, 23 April 1930, and printed under the title *"Was ist atonal?"* in 23, the music magazine edited by Willi Reich, No. 26/27, Vienna, 8 June 1936)

Interlocutor: Well, my dear Herr Berg, let's begin!

Alban Berg: You begin, then. I'd rather have the last word.

Int.: Are you so sure of your ground?

Berg: As sure as anyone can be who for a quarter-century has taken part in the development of a new art—sure, that is, not only through understanding and experience, but—what is more through faith.

Int.: Fine! It will be simplest, then, to start at once with the title of our dialogue: What is atonality?

Berg: It is not so easy to answer that question with a formula that would also serve as a definition. When this expression was used for the first time—probably in some newspaper criticism—it could naturally only have been, as the word plainly says, to describe a kind of music the harmonic course of which did not correspond to the laws of tonality previously recognized.

Int.: Which means: In the beginning was the Word, or rather, a word, which should compensate for the helplessness with which people faced a new phenomenon.

Berg: Yes, that, but more too: This designation of "atonal" was doubtless intended to disparage, as were words like arhythmic, amelodic, asymmetric, which came up at the same time. But while these words were merely convenient designations for specific cases, the word "atonal"—I must add, unfortunately—came to stand collectively for music of which it was assumed not only that it had no harmonic center (to use tonality in Rameau's sense), but was also devoid of all other musical attributes such as melos, rhythm, form in part and whole; so that today the designation as good as signifies a music that is no music, and is used to imply the exact opposite of what has heretofore been considered music.

Int.: Aha, a reproach! And a fair one, I confess. But now tell me yourself, Herr Berg, does not such a distinction indeed exist, and does not the negation of relationship to a given

annually		a) 52 Weekly Rates		b) 12 Monthly Rates		c) Quarterly Rates	
		Introductory	Weekly	Introductory	Monthly	Introductory	Quarterly
		Kr.	Kr.	Kr.	Kr.	Kr.	Kr.
4th Category	60.	8.	1.	6.	4.50	6.	13.50
3rd category	120.	16.	2.	12.	9.	12.	27.
2nd category	180.	24.	3.	18.	13.50	18.	40.50
1st category	300.	34.	5.	30.	22.50	30.	67.50
or	400.	36.	7.	40.	30.	40.	90.
or	500.	40.	9.	80.	35.	80.	105.
etc.							

tonic lead in fact to the collapse of the whole edifice of music?

Berg: Before I answer that, I would like to say this: Even if this so-called atonal music cannot, harmonically speaking, be brought into relation with a major-minor harmonic system—still, surely, there was music even before that system in its turn came into existence . . . .

Int.: . . . and what a beautiful and imaginative music!

Berg: . . . so it doesn't follow that there may not, at least considering the chromatic scale and the new chord-forms arising out of it, be discovered in the "atonal" compositions of the last quarter-century a harmonic center which would naturally not be identical with the old tonic . . . . We already have today in the "composition in twelve tones related only to each other" which Schoenberg has been the first to practice, a system that yields nothing in organization and control of material to the old harmonic order.

Int.: You mean the so-called twelve-tone rows? Won't you tell us something more about them in this connection?

Berg: Not now; it would lead too far afield. Let us confine ourselves to this notion of "atonality."

Int.: Agreed. But you have not yet answered my question whether there does not indeed exist a distinction such as that implied in the word between earlier music and that of today, and so whether the giving up of relationship to a keynote, a tonic, has not indeed unsettled the whole structure of music?

Berg: Now that we have agreed that the negation of major and minor tonality does not necessarily bring about harmonic anarchy, I can answer that question much more easily. Even if certain harmonic possibilities are lost through abandonment of major and minor, all the other qualities we demand of a true and genuine music still remain.

Int.: Which, for instance?

Berg: They are not to be so quickly listed, and I would like to go into that more closely—indeed, I must do so, because the point in question is to show that this idea of atonality, which originally related quite exclusively to the harmonic aspect, has now become, as aforesaid, a collective expression for music that is no music.

Int.: No music? I find that expression too strong; nor have I heard it before. I believe that what the opponents of atonal music are most concerned with is to emphasize the implied antithesis to so-called "beautiful" music.

Berg: That view you take from me. Anyhow, this collective term "atonality" is intended to repudiate everything that has heretofore made up the content of music. I have already mentioned such words as arhythmic, amelodic, asymmetric, and could name a dozen more expressions derogatory of modern music: like cacophony and manufactured music, which are already half forgotten, or the more recent ones like linear music, constructivism, the new factuality, polytonality, machine music, etc. These terms, which may perhaps properly apply in individual special instances, have all been brought under one hat to give today the illusory concept of an "atonal" music, to which those who admit no justification for this music cling with great persistence, purposing in this single word to deny to the new music everything that, as we said, has heretofore constituted music, and hence its right to exist at all.

Int.: You take too black a view, Herr Berg! You might have been entirely justified in that statement of the case of a while ago. But today people know that atonal music for its own sake can be fascinating, inevitably in some cases—where there is true art! Our problem is only to show whether atonal music may really be called musical in the same sense as all earlier music. That is, to show, as you have said, whether if only the harmonic foundation has changed, all the other elements of former music are still present in the new.

Berg: That I declare they are, and I could prove it to you in every measure of a modern score. Prove above all—to begin with the most important—that in this music, as in any other, the melody, the principal voice, the theme, is fundamental, that the course of the music is in a sense determined by it.

Int.: But is melody in the traditional sense at all possible in atonal music?

Berg: Yes, of course, even vocal melody.

Int.: Well, so far as song is concerned, Herr Berg, atonal music surely does follow a new path. There is certainly something in it that has never been heard before, I would almost like to say, something temporarily shocking.

Berg: Only as concerns harmony: on that we agree. But it is quite wrong to regard this new melodic line as taking a path entirely new, as you declare, in comparison with the usual characteristics of melodic procedure, or even as never before heard and shocking. Nor is this true of a vocal line, even if it is marked with what someone recently described as intervals of an instrumental chromaticism, distorted, jagged, wide-spaced; nor that it thereby totally disregards the requirements of the human voice.

Int.: I never said that, but I cannot help feeling that vocal melody and melody in general does seem never to have been treated like that before.

Berg: That is just what I am objecting to. I maintain on the contrary that vocal melody, even as described, yes, caricatured, in these terms, *has always existed*, especially in German music; and I further maintain that this so-called atonal music, at least in so far as it has emanated from Vienna, has also in this respect naturally adhered to the masterworks of German music and not—with all due respect—to Italian bel-canto opera. Melody that is linked with harmony rich in progressions, which is almost the same thing as being bold, may naturally, so long as one doesn't understand the harmonic implications, seem "distorted"—which is no less the case with a thorough chromatic style of writing, and for which there are hundreds of examples in Wagner. But take rather a melody of Schubert, from the famous song "Letzte Hoffnung." Is that distorted enough for you? [Berg here gives further examples—from Schubert: "Wasserfluth," bars 11–12, "Der stürmische Morgen," bars 4–8, 15–18; and from Mozart, *Don Juan* in particular to show that even in the classics vocal melody may be constantly on the move, expressive in all registers, animated and yet capable of declamation—indeed, an ideal instrument.] But you will also see by these examples from the classics that it has nothing to do with atonality if a melody, even in opera-music, departs from the voluptuous tenderness of Italian cantilena—an element you will furthermore seek in vain in Bach, whose melodic potency nobody will deny.

Int.: Granted. But there seems to be another point in which the melody of this so-called atonal music differs from that of earlier music. I mean the asymmetrical structure of melodic periods.

Berg: You probably miss in our music the two- and four-bar periodicity as we know it in Viennese classicists and all the romantics, including Wagner. Your observation is correct, but you perhaps overlook the fact that such metrical symmetry is peculiar to this epoch, whereas in Bach, for example, it is only to be found in his more homophonic works and the suites that derive from dance-music. But even in the Viennese classics, and especially in Mozart and Schubert, we observe again and again—and quite particularly in their most masterly works—efforts to break away from the restraints of this square symmetry. [Here Berg cites examples from *Figaro*.]

This art of asymmetric melodic construction developed still further in the course of the nineteenth century (just

think of Brahms . . . "Vergebliches Ständchen," "Am Son-
ntagmorgen," or "Immer leiser wird mein Schlummer"),
and while the four-bar period preponderates in Wagner
and his followers (they clung to this earlier style-factor in
favor of other innovations, notably in the harmonic field),
even at this time there is a very clear tendency to give up
the two- and four-bar form. A direct line runs here from
Mozart through Schubert and Brahms to Reger and
Schoenberg. And it is perhaps not without interest to
point out that both Reger and Schoenberg, when they discussed the asymmetry of their melodic periods, pointed
out that these follow the prose of the spoken word, while
strictly square-rhythmed melody follows, rather, metrical
speech, verse-form. Yet, as with prose itself, unsymmetri-
cal melodies may be no less logically constructed than
symmetrical melodies. They too have their half and full
cadences, rest and high points, caesuras and bridges, introductory and concluding moments which, because of their
directional character, may be compared with modulations
and cadences, To recognize all this is to feel in them
melody in the truest sense of the word.

Int.: . . . and perhaps even find them beautiful.

Berg: Quite right! But let us go on: This freedom of melodic
construction is naturally accompanied by freedom of
rhythmic organization. Because the rhythm of this music
has undergone a loosening process—let us say through
contraction, extension, overlapping of note-values, shifting of strong beats, as we see it quite particularly in
Brahms—does not mean that the laws of rhythm are dispensed with; and the term "arhythmic" for this treatment,
which after all represents just another refinement of the
artist's means, is just as silly as "amelodic." This rhythmic
treatment is particularly conditioned too by the multilin-
earity of the new music; we seem, indeed, to be finding
ourselves in a time which very much resembles Bach's.
For as that period, through Bach himself, wrought a
change from pure polyphony and the imitative style (and
the concept of the church modes), to a style of writing
built on major-minor harmony, so now we are passing out
of the harmonic era, which really dominated the whole
Viennese classic period and the nineteenth century, slowly
but incessantly into an era of preponderantly polyphonic
character. This tendency to polyphony in so-called atonal
music is a further mark of all true music and is not to be
dismissed just because it has been nicknamed "linear
structure."

Int.: Now I think we have arrived at a most important point.

Berg: Yes, at counterpoint!

Int.: Right! The essence of polyphony of course consists in
the interordination and subordination of voices, voices,
that is, which have a life of their own. Here again we are
dealing with the harmonic aspect; I mean, the individual
lives of all the voices give rise to a second, a new life, that
of the collective sound . . . .

Berg: . . . which is of course not accidental, but consciously
built and heard.

Int.: Now that is just what surprises me. Then is that elemental interplay of atonal voices, which seem to me to lack
any such essential contrast as would give rise to a strong
internal life, also achieved by conscious construction, or is
it the play of some admittedly highly inspired chance?

Berg: That question—to be brief and not too theoretical—I
can answer with a truth won from experience, an experience that springs not only from my own creative work but
from that of other artists to whom their art is as sacred as it
is to me (so anachronistic are we of the "atonal" Viennese
school!). Not a measure in this music of ours—no matter
how complicated its harmonic, rhythmic, and contrapuntal
texture—but has been subjected to the sharpest control of
the outer and the inner ear, and for the meaning of which,

in itself and in its place in the whole, we do not take the
artistic responsibility quite as much as in the case of some
very simple form—as a simple motive or a simple harmonic progression—the logic of which is at once clear to the
layman.

Int.: That explanation seems to me to make sense. But if so, it
almost seems as though the word "atonal" must be a mis-
nomer for this whole tendency in music.

Berg: Why, that's what I've been saying the whole time, trying
to make it clear to you.

Int.: But then you, that is, your music, must somehow have
some relation to the *formal* elements of earlier music too?
If my guess is correct, this very music—the word "atonal"
doesn't sound right after what we've said—strives to keep
in close touch with order forms?

Berg: With form itself; and is it any wonder then that we
should turn back to the older forms as well? Is this not a
further proof of how conscious contemporary practice is of
the entire wealth of music's resources? We have just seen
that this is the case in all serious music. And since this
wealth of resources is apparent in every branch of our
music simultaneously—I mean, in its harmonic development, in its free melodic construction, in its rhythmic variety, in its preference for polyphony and the contrapuntal
style, and finally in its use of all the formal possibilities
established through centuries of musical development—
. . . no one can reproach us with our art and tag it as "atonal," a name that has become almost a byword of abuse.

Int.: Now you have made an important declaration, Herr
Berg. I am somewhat relieved, for even I thought that the
word "atonal," whencesoever it came, had given rise to a
passing theory foreign to the natural course of musical
development.

Berg: That would suit the opponents of this new music of
ours, for then they would be right about the implications
which really lie in the word "atonal," which is equivalent
to anti-musical, ugly, uninspired, ill-sounding and destructive; and they would furthermore be justified in bemoaning such anarchy in tones, such ruination of music's heritage, our helpless state of deracination. I tell you, this
whole hue and cry for tonality comes not so much from a
yearning for a keynote relationship as from a yearning for
familiar concords—let us say it frankly, for the common
triads. And I believe it is fair to state that no music, provided only it contains enough of these triads, will ever
arouse opposition even if it breaks all the holy commandments of tonality.

Int.: So it is still sacred to you, after all, good old tonality?

Berg: Were it not, how could such as we—despite the skepti-
cism of our generation—maintain faith in a new art for
which Antichrist himself could not have thought up a
more diabolical appellation than that word "atonal"!

[Translated from the German by M. D. Herter Norton]

Letter from Arnold Schoenberg on the Origin of the Twelve-Tone Method of Composition

DEAR MR. SLONIMSKY: The "Method of composing with
twelve tones" had many "first steps" (*Vorversuche*). The first
step happened about December 1914 or at the beginning of
1915 when I sketched a symphony, the last part of which
became later the "Jakobsleiter," but which never has been
continued. The Scherzo of this symphony was based on a
theme consisting of the twelve tones. But this was only one of
the themes. I was still far away from the idea to use such a
basic theme as a unifying means for a whole work.

After that I was always occupied with the aim to base the structure of my music consciously on a unifying idea, which produced not only all the other ideas but regulated also their accompaniment and the chords, the "harmonies." There were many attempts to achieve that. But very little of it was finished or published.

As an example of such attempts I may mention the piano pieces op. 23. Here I arrived at a technique which I called (for myself) "composing with tones," a very vague term, but it meant something to me. Namely: In contrast to the ordinary way of using a motive, I used it already almost in the manner of a "basic set of twelve tones." I built other motives and themes from it, and also accompaniments and other chords—but the theme did not consist of twelve tones. Another example of this kind of aim for unity is my "Serenade." In this work you can find many examples of this kind. But the best one is the "Variationen," the third movement. The theme consists of a succession of fourteen tones, but only eleven different ones, and these fourteen tones are permanently used in the whole movement. With lesser strictness still I use the tones of the first two measures in "Tanzszene."

The fourth movement, "Sonett," is a real "composition with twelve tones." The technique is here relatively primitive, because it was one of the first works written strictly in harmony with this method, though it was not the very first—there were some movements of the "Suite for Piano" which I composed in the fall of 1921. Here I became suddenly conscious of the real meaning of my aim: unity and regularity, which unconsciously had led me this way.

As you see, it was neither a straight way nor was it caused by mannerism, as it often happens with revolutions in art. I personally hate to be called a revolutionist, which I am not. What I did was neither revolution nor anarchy. I possessed from my very first start a thoroughly developed sense of form and a strong aversion for exaggeration. There is no falling into order, because there was never disorder. There is no falling at all, but on the contrary, there is an ascending to higher and better order.

ARNOLD SCHOENBERG
Hollywood, California
3 June 1937

Letter from Anton Von Webern

ANTON VON WEBERN
MARIA ENZERSDORF
BEI WIEN, IM AUHOLZ 8
AUSTRIA

14 January 1937

MUCH ESTEEMED MR. SLONIMSKY:

Your friendly letter with enclosures brought me very special joy. To realize that you have taken the trouble of making my music accessible to children and that you have actually *succeeded* in doing so gives me uncommon satisfaction and real consolation. That you used my own score to arrange it for children is a friendly thought on your part, and it makes me happy that the notes that I have written appear on the Children's Page, dedicated specially to children.* Yes, it is true that if the so-called adults, the grown-ups, had as few prejudices as children, then everything would be quite different.

I am glad to give you the dates of composition of my *5 Orchesterstüke* Op. 10, which you want. I wrote, in the years between 1911 and 1913, with long interruptions, about twenty pieces, as expressions of musical lyricism, and selected five of them to include in opus 10. The dates of composition of

these five pieces are 28 June 1911, 13 September 1913, 8 September 1913, 19 July 1911 and 6 October 1913. The first performance of these pieces took place at the Festival of the International Society for Contemporary Music in Zurich on 22 June 1926, under my direction. I am very much interested in the book on modern music that you are writing.** Do you need more dates about my works? I hope to hear from you again soon, and I salute you most cordially.

Yours,
ANTON VON WEBERN

* In 1936, Slonimsky reproduced in its entirety No. 4 of Op 10 containing only six bars, with an upbeat, in 3/4 time, on the Children's Page of the *Christian Science Monitor,* and arranged it graphically, with the pictures of the instruments used in the score—clarinet, trumpet, trombone, mandoline, celesta, harp, snare drum, violin and viola—drawn next to the clef.

** This book was the first edition of *Music Since 1900,* published in 1938.

Gebrauchsmusik and *Gemeinschaftsmusik*

(From a letter to the author from B. Schott's Sons,
dated Mainz, 16 June 1936)

The word *Gebrauchsmusik* seems to have come into use in the postwar period. It is hard to define its meaning exactly. With the mechanization of music through radio and gramophone, with the increasingly organized musical life in Germany, and also owing to political circumstances, many composers, some on their own initiative, some because they were commissioned, began writing music for special purposes. The most obvious examples were compositions for the radio and musical illustrations for films; in brief, all compositions which called for no independent value in themselves but served only a special use (*Gebrauch*). When the expression *Gebrauchsmusik* was first used it is not possible to establish. It is not an official description, such as might head a section of a catalogue; its opposite would be art music, concert music, absolute music.

With *Gemeinschaftsmusik* the case is somewhat different. The postwar trend towards a polyphonic style gave rise to a new type of musicmaking, cultivated especially by the youth and distinguished from the customary orchestral style in that every voice has an importance of its own, i.e., all voices are equal, forming a new *Gemeinschaft* (community) in which new joy is found. This was true not only of instrumental music but also of all sorts of vocal music or the combination of both. In this connection we speak of "activating" the listener; as distinguished from the old "middle-class concert life," the main emphasis in the new youth is put less on listening to compositions written for the concert hall than on making music themselves. Correspondingly, it is no longer the virtuoso who plays the leading role, but the group, the community. This group arose, as we said above, out of the spirit of the new music itself and would not have been possible had not the composers of the day been turning always further from the romantic style, back to the *Spielmusik* of the middle ages and of the eighteenth century.

As a leader of modern music Hindemith was probably the first important composer to write for these purposes. He published such compositions under the title of *Das Neue Werk* in 1927 [Schott], so that it is justifiable to regard this time as approximately the birth-hour of the concept of *Gemeinschaftsmusik*. The expression must have been first used in Schott's catalogue about this time.

We understand that in the United States *Gemeinschaftsmusik* is translated by "sociable music." We no longer use this expression in our catalogues but speak instead of *Singund Spielmusik* (music to be sung and played), which seems to correspond better to the spirit of the music than the former term. We believe that the word *Gemeinschaftsmusik* went out of fashion with the political turn in Germany in 1933, perhaps because it came into being in the era just preceding.

Letter from George Bernard Shaw

4, WHITEHALL COURT (130) LONDON, S.W.1.
PHONE: WHITEHALL 3160.
TELEGRAMS: SOCIALIST, PARL-LONDON.

2nd September 1936

DEAR SIR, Within my lifetime there has been a complete liberation of modulation from its old rules. All the composers, great and small, have now availed themselves fully of this. New modes have been tried, like the whole-tone (or organ tuner's) scale of Debussy; and the obsolete modes have been played with a little. But all this music was in terms of some tonality or other, however sudden and frequent its modulations and transitions might be. And the harmonic practice was so free that the scale became a 12 note scale with nothing of the old tonality left but a keynote. Still, as long as there was a keynote there was no fundamental difference between Bach and Richard Strauss.

Schönberg tried to get loose from the keynote by writing pieces in listening to which you could not guess which was to be the final chord, because there was no tonal cadence. The revolutionary young composers rushed in at this new game and dropped key signatures; so that their scores were a mass of accidentals; but Schönberg exhausted the fun of this and relapsed more and more into tonality. This drift is apparent in all the big composers now. It is hard to say that the symphonies of Sibelius are in this key or that; but when we come to know his symphonies by heart as we know those of Mozart and Beethoven they will appear as tonal to us as Elgar's.

In short the post-Wagnerian anarchy is falling into order as all anarchies do pretty soon; and I expect soon to hear the Wagnerian flood of endless melody getting embanked in the melodic *design* of Bach and Handel.

Faithfully,
G. BERNARD SHAW

Nicolas Slonimsky Esq.
238 Hemenway Street
Boston
Massachusetts
U.S. America.

Letters from Charles E. Ives

West Redding
Connecticut
14 July 1929

Dear Mr. Slonimsky: Last Spring Henry Cowell told me that you had been kind enough to ask for a score of mine which your orchestra* might play. I should have written before but have been laid up for some months back and haven't been able to attend to things—even correspondence; and also was not sure I could get anything ready by next fall, as all of my scores are for larger orchestras. But I have one** which I got out the other

day and played for Henry Cowell who liked it and thought it should be played, and could be, with some revisions reducing it to the chamber group. The 1st and last movement lend themselves quite readily, but the 2nd which has some old "brass-band and town-tune" things in it, has a considerable brass part. But, I remember, this (in part) was first played by a theater orchestra as a kind of topical march. They made it go quite well with only a cornet and trombone,—a piano taking off the rest of the brass. So, I think, it can be brought down with the help of a piano part. At any rate I'm going ahead with it on this basis and should have it ready to send you in September. I am glad to do this anyway and you must not feel at all obligated to play it. You may not like it, and even if you do, you may not think it advisable or practicable to present—that will be quite alright. This score was written quite some years ago and won't loosen up much of a modern "sword-swallower"— but the subject matter I feel justifies its existence. It has some colloquial spots which the older generations of New Englanders (including mine) will get. But please feel perfectly free to do whatever you think best with it.

I have heard with pleasure that you and your organization are making a valuable contribution to music and to Boston. I wish I could hear it and also am very anxious to hear some of your music. I'm glad *New Music* will publish some of it soon.***

Henry Cowell left last week for California, after spending a few days with us. You will like to hear his experiences abroad, especially in Russia. He is a courageous "advance guard" all in himself. I tell him he is a better ambassador than some of our more famous ones.

Hoping to have the pleasure of meeting you before long, I am with best wishes,

Sincerely yours,
CHAS. E. IVES

* The Chamber Orchestra of Boston.

** *Three Places in New England.*

*** *Studies in Black and White* for piano published by *New Music Quarterly* in its October 1929 issue.

---

164 East 74 Street
New York
29 December 1929

Dear Mr. Slonimsky: The copy of the score* is being photographed and will be sent you this week. I hope you may like it. It adapted itself more readily than I supposed to the smaller orchestra. There are some places where the woodwind may be too heavy for the number of strings—for instance, at the end of the 3rd movement there is a rather mean, off-rhythm, inner part for the oboe, which may be omitted, letting the oboe play along with the trumpet on the main tune—there were originally 3 trumpets here. However, do anything you think best.

There will be a pianist and in the middle movement an extra drum player to be engaged, if you decide to play it; and I shall want to take care of this and any other extra expense that you may be put to in playing it. I would also appreciate it if you will have the parts copied in Boston and get some careful person to correct them and send me the bill. I hope you have been well and that your work is going along successfully.

I am, with best wishes for the New Year,

Sincerely yours,
CHAS. E. IVES

* *Three Places in New England.*

164 East 74th Street
New York
16 January 1930

Dear Mr. Slonimsky: Thank you much for your letter. I greatly appreciate what you say and that you feel the music* is worth playing. It doesn't seem right that you should be placed in so much uncertainty about carrying on the concerts**—it is work that should not be circumscribed. The Boston symphony Directors ought to lend more of a hand, if only from their sense of duty to music in Boston (we won't say from their sense of music). However, anything that's any good, works out slowly—usually, I suppose.

I was very sorry not to go to your concert Sunday, but I have not been able to get out at all recently. Was glad to see that the critics were favorably impressed—and I hope you felt the same way.

Your comment in the *Boston Evening Transcript* is very interesting and so well put. It seems to me that Paul Rosenfeld's interest in words is keener than his judgment of music. Probably I ought not to say that as I know very little of the music he talks about. Something I read of his some years ago rather gave me that impression. When you come to New York again I hope to have the pleasure of seeing you.

I am, with kind regards,

Sincerely,
CHAS. E. IVES

* *Three Places in New England.*

** With the Chamber Orchestra of Boston, founded by Slonimsky in 1927.

164 East 74th Street
New York
8 February 1930

Dear Mr. Slonimsky: Henry Cowell telephoned us this morning, that you will come down for the rehearsals on the 16th. It is good of you to do so. Mrs. Ives and I would like very much to have you stay with us while you are here and we hope you can and will come as soon as you can before Sunday and stay over the weekend at least.

Looking forward to your visit I am, with best wishes.

Sincerely,
CHARLES E. IVES

164 East 74 Street
New York
February 1930

Biography of Charles E. Ives: Born In Danbury, Conn. U.S.A., Oct. 20, 1874. Studied with his father, who was a music teacher and bandmaster. Played, as a boy, in the town bands and churches. Graduated from Yale College in the Class of 1898; while in college took the courses in music under Prof. Horatio W. Parker; Organ master, Centre Church, New Haven, Conn., 1892–98; Organ master and Director of Music, Central Presbyterian Church, New York to 1902. Entered business in 1898. Member of the firm of Ives & Myrick, 46 Cedar St., New York.

(See over for "nice" music)

For smaller orchestra or chamber music:

1. Theater or Chamber Orchestra Set
2. 2nd movement for *Holiday* set (strings, 1 horn, 1 flute, bells)
3. 1st Violin Sonata
4. 3 Pieces for Trumpet and Piano
5. Movements from 1st and 2nd Piano Sonatas
6. Book of 114 Songs

For larger orchestra:

7. 4th Symphony; 2nd movement published by New Music Edition, San Francisco
8. 1st Orchestra Set, *Three Places in New England*
9. 2nd Orchestra Set (no name)
10. *Decoration Day* (from *Holiday* set)
11. *Fourth of July* (from *Holiday* set)
12. Orchestra & Chorus: *Lincoln, the Great Commoner*

164 East 74th Street
New York
17 February 1930

Dear Mr. Slonimsky: I must write just a line to tell you what a fine time I had yesterday—it was quite a memorable occasion, for us, at least. It was good of you to come. Mrs. Ives and I will expect you in 2 weeks; we would like to have you stay with us while you are here—but you must do whatever is most convenient for you. You must be here part of the time, at least—and all the time if you can. We want you to feel free to come and go as you would in your own home.

I can't write as I would like to, the lame hands make it hard.—So good-bye for a short while.

Sincerely,
CHAS. E. IVES

You left your baton here. It feels rather ethereal so I won't mail it for it may be broken—unless you want me to.

164 East 74 Street
New York
26 February 1930

Dear Mr. Slonimsky: We are very glad you will be with us. Don't trouble to telephone, but come right up—we are not going out.

I think Henry Cowell told you that both his and my things were accepted by the committee*—you did it as far as my music was concerned.

Sincerely,
CHAS. E. IVES

* The Pan American Association of Composers, which sponsored Slonimsky's concerts in New York and in Europe.

164 East 74 Street
New York
28 April 1930

Dear Mr. Slonimsky: I was sorry to miss you last week—found your letter here upon getting back Saturday. We got out to hear Henry's concerto with the Conductorless Orchestra. It was strongly stimulating and carried us high in many places—will tell you more about it when I see you which I hope will be soon. Was glad to hear that the date for the concert next year has been arranged.* Please let me know whenever I can do anything in the matter. Will send along the suggested songs as soon as I can get to it.

Yours sincerely,
CHARLES E. IVES

* 10 January 1931, in New York.

West Redding
Connecticut
27 May 1930

Dear Mr. Slonimsky: We are up here now for the summer—and so I'm afraid we missed you again in New York—but Mrs. Ives and I hope you may find it convenient to come down here and see us some time this summer. I suppose it's too early to know just what your plans will be, but we expect to be here right along. It's too bad you won't be in France this summer—you see how the virtuous sins of committees and men (assuming committees are men) throw their "long shadows o'er innocent humanity."* But we won't be cast down by this particular Inter-Rational Committee—and they may see Casey driving his own hearse some day! Personally I put it up to the Republican Party of ours—it's just one of the many hard-boiled, old lady, soft-stuff things they are responsible for. They kept us out of Geneva—and you can't blame Europe much for wanting to keep us out of everything—except their hotels.

I wrote to Dr. Goldberg** saying I was mailing the book of songs to him—but as I looked for one to wrap up, I found there were no complete copies here—only those that I'd cut single copies from—so some of the pages are missing—but not many. I will send him one of these now and a complete copy later soon as I can get hold of one. I think next fall I'll get some more printed perhaps adding some others.

Sincerely yours,
CHAS. E. IVES

* Slonimsky had some difficulties in traveling with his Russian passport before he became a citizen of the United States in 1931.

** Isaac Goldberg (1887–1938), American writer who planned to do an article on Ives.

West Redding
Connecticut
30 May 1930

Dear Mr. Slonimsky: Our letters crossed—I guess. I'm glad the ring is cleared for the first bout. I don't know that I'm much qualified to give suggestions, but will do the best I can. The original plan that you and Henry Cowell had of giving 3 things and repeating them is by far the best. From what I hear from all sides—especially from the ears that have been most of their lives fed on the consonant heritage—is that a long program of modern pieces leaves them confused and tired—which is a bad thing for them (and the music) and all concerned. A short program they get better—sometimes!

When you come to New York in June perhaps you can run up here, but if you haven't the time I can come to New York for a day and meet you—I have to go down every so often. Do whatever you find most convenient. With best wishes, I am

Sincerely,
CHAS. E. IVES

West Redding
Connecticut
8 June 1930

Dear Mr. Slonimsky: We're very glad you will make us a visit—it will be fine to have you here. It won't do you any harm to get away from the routine, Boylston Street and city noise. This is a good place to rest if you feel like it or to work if you feel like it or to meditate or all three at once. Bring some old clothes and your bathing suit—on a hot day you may like to dive into "My Little Pool" (but it has nothing on yours).*

We're a little uncertain about the last part of June—we may have to be away for a few days—but how about the first week in July—or if more convenient for you the second week. Suit yourself—only be sure to come.

There used to be a way of getting down via Boston, Albany and Pittsfield and down the Housatonic River—but probably the best way to come down is the main line to South Norwalk, and we will meet you there. If you are to go to New York first, there are several good trains up here—we're about 60 miles from New York.

I didn't have in mind so much scaring away the "gentler part" of the audience, by the quality of the program (they will have to stand for that) as by the "quantity." If they get too much they go home groggy.

Have just gone through the book of songs and will mail it today. Some of the pages are gone. I can't seem to find any more whole copies.

Sincerely,
CHAS. E. IVES

* References to Slonimsky song *My Little Pool*.

West Redding
Connecticut
6 September 1930

Dear Mr. Slonimsky: Thank you for sending the magazines. Your "conductorless conductor" philippic is fine*—and a swinging comment on the history and evolution of this species—his rise and fall—rather his ups and downs. Though I doubt if he is any more to blame than most of the lady patrons! When you say "some conductors have mastered the art of beginning and stopping with the orchestra"—you made "some hit off"—Mark Twain could do no better.

It was fine to have you here with us—we enjoyed your visit exceedingly—both the old and young generation—you project yourself generously into each. We hope to see you here again before long—come anytime, only let us know 2 or 3 days before, so we can be sure to be here. We are thinking of making a few days family visit up the state. Don't let the arranging of the songs take up any time you need for other work—do it entirely at your convenience— there's no hurry.**

Sincerely yours,
CHAS. E. IVES

* Slonimsky's article on conductors and conducting in the magazine *Plain Talk*, published in the fall issue of 1930.
** Ives asked Slonimsky to orchestrate the accompaniment of some of his songs.

Quebec, Canada
October 1930

Dear. Mr. Slonimsky: Your letter came when we were leaving. We didn't intend as much of a trip as this but Mrs. Ives seemed pretty much tired out with the long job of housekeeper, chauffeur, nurse and general caretaker—and needed a rest. We will probably stay around here until the latter part of the month, depending on how we feel and will probably stop over for a little family visit at Williamstown, Mass. on the way back. I'm sorry not to be more certain as we want to see you in Redding again. But if that isn't possible will hope to see you in New York the first part of November. Will write when our plans are more certain.

This city is the cliff, the country about and the waters in the river all seem beautiful to us. Looking at the inscriptions on the monuments and all the children only 2 years old and speaking French—make us feel in a foreign land—and we are. We went to the old English church this morning. The "Plain Chant" and canticles, sung by everybody in unison, each one making a little music of his own to Mr. Tallis—may stand as a point of departure into collective composing—and the universal "Lyre." I'll now stop this and say good night.

Sincerely yours,
CHAS. E. IVES

West Redding
Connecticut
14 November 1930

Dear Mr. Slonimsky: We're back from the North Pole.* I was about to write that we were to stay on here longer when a water shortage came along and it looked as if we would have left to New York before this—and may have to any day now. If you are down there next week or so, please call up the house (Butterfield 5449)—if we're not there, perhaps you can run up here—if you don't mind drinking skimmed milk and washing in the dew. Telephone here is 43-5 Redding. At any rate I'll let you know as soon as we get to New York.

I want to thank Dr. Goldberg for his article in the Mercury.** Mrs. Ives and I appreciated it greatly. He has a way of putting things that is not common to most writers of music criticism, or to writers in general for that matter. We hope that we may have the pleasure of meeting him before long.

How are you and how are things going? If I can do anything about the concert,*** please let me know.

Sincerely,
CHAS. E. IVES

* Ives had just returned from a trip to Quebec.

** *The American Mercury,* edited by H. L. Mencken, of which Isaac Goldberg was a regular contributor.

*** The concert of the Chamber Orchestra of Boston in New York, scheduled for 10 January 1931.

West Redding
Connecticut
23 November 1930

Dear Mr. Slonimsky: Our letters crossed, I think—and probably you didn't get mine before leaving for Washington. We fully expected to have had to leave for New York last week, but just after writing, a three days' rain came, and the spring is up and we're going to stay here until after Thanksgiving. Will be at 164 West 74 on December 1st, and shall hope to see you there soon after. Mrs. Ives and I want you to stay with us when in the city and we hope you can.

As I remember you thought to start rehearsals about December and so think it just as well to send the enclosed now.*

Thank you much for sending the Phonograph Monthly article—you hit things off—and make that which may be somewhat uninteresting to the general reader, interesting to him. We will have to work out some plan this winter to have your orchestra make some records—through a company, if they'll undertake it—if not, we'll go it alone.

We've had an exciting day—a new grandniece, a fight with a polite skunk, and in between—Sir Jim Jeans which Mrs. Ives has been reading to me.

Sincerely yours,
CHAS. E. IVES

* A substantial check toward expenses connected with the New York concert of the Chamber Orchestra of Boston, scheduled for 10 January 1931.

---

164 East 74 Street
New York
20 December 1930

Dear Mr. Slonimsky: If it isn't too late, this might be put in the first paragraph* after "in 1914": "it was arranged, by the writer's request a while ago for chamber orchestra." It won't do any harm to have people know, if only by a slight inference, that you aren't afraid to ferret out a nonentity and do the unpopular thing etc. You're the only conductor that ever asked me to do anything. This score would never have gotten off the shelf, if it hadn't been for you.—Come down soon.

Sincerely,
CHAS. E. IVES

* In Nicolas Slonimsky's program notes on *Three Places in New England*, performed for the first time by Slonimsky and his Chamber Orchestra of Boston in New York on 10 January 1931.

---

164 East 74 Street
New York
26 December 1930

Dear Mr. Slonimsky: Thank you for your card and letter and enclosures. It seems to me there is no particular hurry in having the notice of the "repetitions" printed. Henry will be here Sunday and I'll find out how he feels about it. Personally, I should just say that these will be separated and let it go at that—with possibly a paragraph to the effect that as these 3 things happen to be made to a great part of new materials etc., in general structure, rhythm, harmony etc., which may not be easy to get on the first hearing, they are repeated. Also, I don't know that we ought to assume if a listener stays to hear something repeated it is a sign of his approval—it may be just the opposite—or at least a willingness to give it another chance. Radio: Art and business all hitched up together. $91\frac{3}{8}\%$ (I like to be precise) of all radio and phonograph records— are "sebaceous cysts," and soft ones at that—and they sell—though if a 3-year-old is always fed candy for breakfast he will always be a 3-year-old—and the oatmeal market will die. The letter from the Victor Co.—"all commitments are made by themselves"—unnecessary statement!—just look at them, g— d— soft-headed lists!—$94\frac{5}{8}\%$ "ta ta" stuff. However, in a day or so, I'm going to see how we can get in touch and at least take a crack at both the ether and Victor. Please don't worry about the concert—either the business part or wrong-note part. Hope to see you soon.

Hastily,
CHAS. E. IVES

164 East 74 Street
New York
30 December 1930

Dear Mr. Slonimsky: Yours just at hand. Take out the oboe, by all means, in 1st-2 measures, p. 27 before letter H; these notes were originally for a 2nd flute (ad lib.).*

At letter O, p. 39, do as you think best. Perhaps if the violins and piano could pound the waltz out somewhat it might do—I used to find if 2 countertunes in about same register were played by 2 brass instruments the contrast was sometimes lost. However, the quality of the trumpets seems different today than when I played one. But do anything in this or other places you think advisable. Will see you tomorrow—come right up—if convenient—but come up anyway. Will let you know about the repetition notice** as soon as I see Henry. He has not come yet.

Sincerely,
CHAS. E. IVES

* Slonimsky conducted the first performance of *Three Places in New England* in New York on 10 January 1931, with his Chamber Orchestra of Boston, composed of Boston Symphony Orchestra players with one of each of the wind instruments.

** Slonimsky proposed a program of three pieces by American composers to be played twice, at the beginning and at the end of the concert, so as to give the audience a second chance to become acquainted with the unfamiliar American idiom, but eventually it was decided not to do so.

---

164 East 74 Street
New York
5 January 1931

Dear Mr. Slonimsky: Henry is back, looking strong for action, after a very successful turn in Havana.

We are looking forward to seeing you here. The radio plan looks more possible. Will tell you all about it on Wednesday.

Am sending the enclosed* right on so you can deposit in your account before you leave. The records will be made alright—Victor** or Vanquished notwithstanding.

Hastily,
CHAS. E. IVES

* A personal check towards expenses for Slonimsky's European trip.

** The Victor Recording Company.

---

164 East 74 Street
New York
26 February 1931

Dear Mr. Slonimsky: I'm glad you have a pain in the throat and not in the heart—but if you had it would be quite alright. I'll learn you how to give a cuss word a good "vita propria."

We are glad you'll be down next week and will expect you. Remember you have the right key, not a strange key in your pocket.

Now here is an important job for you. Mrs. Ives wrote today to Mrs. Prof. Kingsley Porter about the Paris concerts, asking her and his help, saying that you would call her up to try to see her—we hear they are going abroad shortly. They live at Elmwood, Cambridge, in the old James Russell Lowell house. Prof. Porter is connected now with Harvard.

Sincerely,
CHAS. E. IVES

West Redding
Connecticut
8 May 1931

Mons! Mon Dieu!—Mon' Lisa—Bon Ami (not the mild sapolio)—Bon Soir—Cher—Chez—French is a too violent language for me—no *good* cuss words—I understand it perfectly (when it's translated).

I hope attending to so many difficulties etc. at one time won't tire you all out, and that the managers will do their part. A friend of mine who is gradually getting interested in American music (seeing that article of Henry's started it*) and may be of substantial help later—suggests that programs, notices etc. be put in "steamers" sailing from New York to France between now and June.** Your manager, he says, can get in touch with the "pursers" etc. sailing for Cherbourg—and also that notices be distributed to the hotels etc. However this is not advice—do anything you think best. Don't worry too much about the situation (that's good advice which I hate to have anyone give me— g—d—)

If not too much trouble please have a dozen or so programs and notices sent to me as soon as possible—as we have heard of a few friends who are going abroad this month.

Now that you are a regular Yankee,*** you will spit through your teeth, talk through your nose, cuss between syllables and let 'em "learn you" in Paris how to compose real American stuff. Our best wishes to you.

Sincerely,
CHAS. E. IVES

* A reference to an article by Henry Cowell, entitled (amazingly enough), *Four Little Known Modern Composers: Chávez, Ives, Slonimsky, Weiss*, published in the ephemeral magazine *Aesthete*, New York, August 1928.

** Slonimsky's Paris concerts took place on 6 and 11 June 1931.

*** Slonimsky received his American citizenship papers in April 1931.

West Redding
Connecticut
28 May 1931

Dear Monsieur—Beaucoup! We were glad to get your letters. Both came this A.M. It's 'most mail time—and just a line, so it will catch tomorrow's boat.

That's quite alright about Varèse. I don't blame him for wanting something new played. Have arranged with the Chase National Bank to cable their Branch Office in Paris a credit of $250 to you, which you can draw on by your personal check whenever you need any. Do whatever is necessary to be done, please, and don't worry. Nobody can read by Roman Candles. I agree with Henry that now you are over there, there's no need to hurry back if there are things that can be done—for instance, the English concert. And if there isn't enough left to carry out the work, let me know. The concert will go alright. Just kick into the music as you did in the Town Hall—never mind the exact notes or the right notes, they're always a nuisance. Just let the spirit of the stuff sail up to the Eiffel Tower and on to Heaven. Never mind the ladybirds, male and female, in the audience—they're dear and nice—or the cuffs—they never should be worn.* But you are a good boy.

I hope you can get in enough rehearsals, and if you can't, do it anyway and we will fix it up somehow. Don't bother with mine too much because it is harder—the others won't get any too much rehearsing.

I think probably it is advisable to put at least one notice in the leading papers; they do a lot for music and a lot against it.

Hastily,
CHAS. E. IVES

* Slonimsky complained that the cuffs of his shirt in full dress kept sticking out during the concert.

————

West Redding
Connecticut
12 June 1931

*Dear "Very Good Eddie":** We much appreciated your thought in sending the cables.** I sent the long one on to Henry. All I can say is that you are a good boy—with or without cuffs.*** Mrs. Ives is rejoicing to know and so am I that your courage, genius and character are receiving recognition and appreciation. You had a hard job—music-wise, other-wise and business-wise— and rather heavy responsibility. I hope all the composers will realize what you have done for them. To the public, a composer can say, no matter how it goes "my music *is* what it is"—regardless of what Geo. says—but a conductor has to break it into the existence of others—some of whom are "nice-pussy-boys"—ta-ta—some job! We wouldn't have been much surprised if the "Françoises" had hung a "blot" on the "Amerricaine." I wouldn't have blamed them much if they had—to my way of thinking "these U.S." during the last 10 years or so politically, and otherwise have been backward in coming forward. If Wilson had been running things—"bigger" things would have gone on. Your cables indicate that the French have been quite open and fairminded—thanks to you to a great extent. The "old gals" over here (I mean music critics—I often get them mixed up) are pretty soft under the "ears"—some, at least, are.

I hope now you can "let down" a little and get in some vacation days. It will be fine to see you again, but I hope you feel justified in staying as long as you want. How about the English and other concerts?

Please give my thanks to Varèse for all he has done. I hope his music went well and was appreciated. The enclosed**** is but a mark of respect between one citizen and another. When I see that so many get too much for doing so little (Josie Hoff-"frau",***** for instance) and you nothing for doing so much, then I like to have a hand in the opposition. I hope you had enough to get by on. If convenient, will you save me a dozen or so program notes.

What do you think of trying to make a few records?

Kindest greetings to your mother and you from all of us.

Sincerely,
CHAS. E. IVES

* A colloquialism current in the 1920s meaning "a good guy." popularized by Jerome Kern's 1915 musical of that name.

** Reporting his Paris concerts of American music.

*** Slonimsky had trouble with the cuffs of his full-dress suit which kept sticking out in the sleeves when he conducted an agitated passage.

**** A substantial personal check.

***** Josef Hofmann.

————

West Redding
Connecticut
10 July 1931

*Dear Columbus Et Vespuccius:** We understand you continue your Voyage of Discovery and take sail again soon. But Uncle Deac, your "rustic" friend says that there are some things that should not be discovered in America—so don't bother—-discover only a new move in chess—and, we hope, Redding. Will you stop here on your way to Boston or come down later? We expect to be away late in August till perhaps around the second week in September. Do whatever is convenient—but we all want to see you.

The papers, notes, etc., just at hand.** Your accomplishment has been remarkable. It is fine to have those estimates of your work and the rest. The French writers seem to listen and think more carefully than many do over here—we have too much snap judgment—without the "snap."

Philip Hale has it in for the American moderns—says they are just trying to pull same stuff as European moderns are, etc., etc. The thing seems to me not only unfair but it is not by any means all the truth—and half-truths are more insidious than an "honest lie." He says your program should have been much finer: E. B. Hill, Loeffler, Deems Taylor, and Arthur Foote. He forgets all about Vick Herbert and Carrie Bond, also Richard Wagner and Puccini. Well—your trunk will contain evidence enough to smother that "nice old lady."***

Henry is much pleased with your success and says he hopes to have you conduct some concerts in California this fall. If there is anything I can do, let me know. The enclosed is just to be on the safe side (not towards the sofa).****

There is much to talk with you about, but I will have to stop here—my hands and arms have been bothering again*****—it's hard to handle a pen but the meanest part is not to be able to play the piano when I want. However—am better now than I was last week.

With cordial greetings and congratulations,
Yours sincerely,
CHAS. E. IVES

* Reference to the opening paragraph of an article in the Paris publication *Le Canard enchaîné* by André Coeuroy, entitled *Découverte de l' Amérique:* "Nous venons, sans blague, de découvrir l'Amérique, grâce à un Christophe Colomb qui, parti de Russie, est allé à Boston recueillir pour nous des témoignages authentiques de la creation musicale américaine. Ce Christophe Colomb s'apelle Nicolas Slonimsky."

** Reports and reviews of Slonimsky's Paris concerts of American music given on 6 and 11 June 1931.

*** Philip Hale, music and drama editor of *The Boston Herald*, published on 7 July 1931 an editorial article entitled *Mr. Slonimsky in Paris*, in which he wrote: "Nicolas Slonimsky of Boston, indefatigable in furthering the cause of the extreme radical composers, has brought out in Paris orchestral compositions by Americans who are looked on by our conservatives as wild-eyed anarchists. Are these Parisians to be blamed if they say that the American composers thus made known to them are restless experimenters or followers of Europeans whose position in the musical world is not yet determined?"

**** A substantial check.

***** Ives suffered from a severe diabetic condition and a muscular tremor.

————

West Redding
Connecticut
18 August 1931

Dear Mr. Slonimsky: Thank you very much for the program note. Mrs. Ives and I think it is excellent—and one of the best things you've done. You "get in 'em good." The enclosed is just about as you had it, with a few corrections in details—one about Prof. Parker—whom I don't want to be unfair to. Parker seldom got horrified or mad, usually he'd just "smile" and not say much, sometimes he'd get a little bothered or puzzled.*

Well, we think of you and Miss Adlow** (who "was" and "is") with a very great and deep satisfaction. It's really a source of happiness to us, to think of you both— and of your new life.

In the "Barn dance" let 'em git it going—no pretty tones and long bowing. I think one violin (off stage) *pppp* plays in "off part" with the song, will be best. Hope you can make out my unclear writing. I'm quite ashamed of it.

Greetings, to you both,
CHAS. E. IVES

* Slonimsky wrote in his program note that Horatio Parker, with whom Ives studied at Yale University, was "horrified" by unresolved dissonances in the music Ives submitted to him.

** Slonimsky married Dorothy Adlow, art critic of *The Christian Science Monitor*, in Paris, on 30 July 1931, with Varèse as best man.

West Redding
Connecticut
17 September 1931

Dear Columerica: You're back, I guess, about now from shooting the buffalo—with robes and scalps.* And if not— it's quite alright, too. I hope you had a satisfactory time and found Henry well and sitting on the end of his summer symphony, loafing.

We came up here for a boat ride. It seems great to us to get back to this wilderness, a log cabin and living with the moose again. And we're staying longer than we expected.

Am sending the enclosed according to your instructions. Some Tombstone inscriptions** and pieces, to be or not to be played, and a "face." And when I look at it, I apologize. When is a man, not a man? Answer: When he has his picture taken. However, this is the last picture I'll ever have taken. So I'll stop talking.

We all send best wishes to you both, and shall hope to see you both soon. Will probably go back sometime next week.

As ever, Sincerely,
CHAS. E. IVES

* Slonimsky was conducting in the West in the fall of 1931.
** Biographical data requested by Slonimsky.

West Redding
Connecticut
20 October 1931

*Dear Mr. Ambassador,** As I learn that this is my birthday, I will celebrate by sitting down in a moderately comfortable chair and writing you. As you know, birthdays should be either forgotten or celebrated—I always do both—it's far better—for what.

We are wondering how you both are. We greatly appreciated the letter from your wife—and her art articles. They are extremely interesting, so clearly thought and beautifully written. It is a comment on the ways of the layman—and human nature (in her "Art and Publicity")—the congenital habit of man, "thinking for himself," after the "nice" teacher has told him *what* to think for himself—and his art of enjoying something he never can enjoy. I hope your plans for the work abroad are coming on as you want, and as soon as there is anything I can do, you will let me know. Last week Ich hatte, morgen früh ein froelich blatt (one of the best words in the

English language) vom liebe Heinrich er sagt**—that (and you probably have already heard) the Berlin Philharmonic Orchestra to give two concerts of American music, and you are to conduct one of them and the regular German conductor the other—why don't you do both! Henry was here on the day before he sailed. He seemed quite in sympathy with your foreign plans—and also said that, thanks to you the San Francisco concert was more of a success than usual and I hope you felt the same. We will be in New York before long—depending on how far the thermometer and water goes down—probably around the first part of November and we hope to see you there and to have the pleasure of a visit from you both— all of my family want to be most kindly remembered to all of your family.

Sincerely,
CHARLES E. IVES

* A Paris reviewer referred to Slonimsky as the American ambassador of music.

** Ives' own brand of German. "Heinrich" is Henry Cowell.

West Redding
Connecticut
17 November 1931

Dear Americain: As you see we're still here, the weather holding up and some warm days staying around, kept us longer than we expected. But we expect to go to New York next week—probably not later than the 20th and we hope you and Mrs. Slonimsky can come down to see us soon.

We have lots of things to talk over—and cuss about. No, I remember I've turned over a new leaf (page 7), and have locked all the best cuss words in the cellar closet and thrown the key down the well.

The new circulars are good ones. I'd like a few more, to send to some philistines, though it will probably make some bellow. My arms have been bothering again, and I can't write or play much and I'm sour. So good-bye.

Hoping to see you both soon,

Sincerely,
CHAS. E. IVES

I had a letter from Robert Schmitz, who is going to be in Paris after the first of the year, and who says he will be glad to play the piano at the Paris concerts. He knows that set of mine which I gave to you (a semi-piano concerto). Schmitz is well known in Paris—he's a friend of Monteux and has played with him. He's also the discoverer of Milhaud. How's that soft-seat Koussevitzky, the lily? Is he still bothering you and hornswoggling the puritans?

---

164 East 74 Street
New York
January 1932

*Dear N.S.A.**:* this doesn't mean "no swearing allowed" nor "no silence aloud,"

I had a long talk with Henry the day after you left. I told him what I told you about the "hythmicon" situation as I had got to thinking about it after our meeting—and we went into it from all angles. It relieved my mind to know especially that the new one would really be nearer to an instrument, than a machine. There will be a "lever" that can readily change the "tempo" with pedals and also the "tones" etc. It wasn't so much the question of having another made—as I think it ought to—it will be improved, transported, and studied on— but the main question is whether it is yet time to present it at Paris—and if so how is the best way to do it. Henry feels as I do about that—and after the demonstration at the New School for Social Research next Tuesday we can know better how to do it. I sent the remitted check to Mr. Theremin yesterday— and he's started the building. It will be yours and Henry's—I just want to help—and sit under its "shadow" on a nice day.**

I was glad to hear that you feel better about the 3 other pieces of mine at the Paris concert. Good, clear parts are made. It can be put like this: Three Pieces for (Large) Orchestra: I. *The Cage*, II. *The 4th of July*, III. *An Elegy*. Hoping to see you soon.

> Sincerely,
> CHAS. E. IVES

* The initials stand for Nicolas Slonimsky Adlow (Dorothy Adlow-Slonimsky).

** The "hythmicon" was constructed by Leon Theremin in New York, at Henry Cowell's specifications. Cowell wrote a special piece *Rhythmicana* for it, but it was too late to be used at Slonimsky's second series of concerts in Paris, given on 21 and 25 February 1932.

> London
> July 1932

Dear N.S. Am. Ambas! I felt very, *very* badly in not seeing you again that time in New York. I was just about in the end of one of those g— d— low sloughs, when a man can't be anything and doesn't know it—couldn't eat, sleep, think, or even cuss moderately!

We have been in Westmoreland living "slow with the sheep." The lakes and mountains and country are beautiful. We admire the English ways. When they get run over, they smile and say sorry (C♯→B♭) to the taxi driver!

Our plans are indefinite—but are going to Germany (and will see Henry) and probably to France. I will write a long and a nice letter to you soon—when I can lose the vibrato.*

I appreciate deeply all that you have done, your interest, help and above all your friendship—which will last through Eternity even to the day after the "4th of July."** I am glad to report that I am much better than I've been for sometime. You see, I have a remarkable doctor in New York (he's no good when you're sick)—but when I told him on leaving that I was going to take a pint of ale every night he said—"Don't do that—remember, three pints a day keep the doctor away— and drink good ale when you can." He was quite right. Eat, drink and be merry, for tomorrow we live on Main Street.

> Sincerely,
> CHAS. E. IVES

* Ives had increasing difficulties handling the pen, but insisted on writing in longhand to friends.

** Title of Ives' symphonic piece, from the *Holidays* set.

> Interlaken, Switzerland
> October 1932

Dear Mr. Slonimsky: To play the "Washington B.D."* in New York as you propose seems to me much the best! I hope the players don't give too much trouble—flat tires. Have you ever been in "Zwitzerland?" Well—I have!— for a month! And we think seriously of staying on till 1974.** We are in a little place just out of the village— nobody around but 2 goats and this

"young frau."*** Traveling doesn't seem to agree with us, and we may stay here for some while—perhaps go to Italy later.

> Sincerely,
> CHAS. E. IVES

* *Washington's Birthday*, from Ives' *Holidays* set, which Slonimsky conducted and recorded for the New Music Records.

** Ives was born in 1874.

*** Mt. Jungfrau.

> Taormina, Sicily
> Christmas, 1932

Remembrance to you both from this family. Best wishes for the New Year and many of them—but of course, not too many! We are in this country of great beauty—living in a little stone hut, on a side hill overlooking the Ionian toward the boot of Italia. We hope to stay here till Spring. We hear you did heroic work at the last concert against the opposition of the Union and "Premature Comment" girls.*

It is much appreciated. You see I'm getting so I can write (almost nice) and will send you a nice long letter soon, writin' regular.

> CHAS. E. IVES

* Slonimsky was to conduct a concert in New York sponsored by the Pan American Association of Composers on 1 November 1932, but there were difficulties with the Musicians' Union, and the concert had to be postponed until 4 November. However, the New York Evening *Sun* published a disparaging account of the event in its issue of 2 November 1932, two days before it took place.

> Taormina, Sicily
> 5 February 1933

Io Te Saluto Signore! "Buona Bonaparte di Batone"—and you are a good boy, even if you shoot old ladies in the elbow. You have been doing great work—and the Los Angeles battle was an extraordinary feat—a literal triumph for you. I'm glad they speak of your courage as well as your genius—Questo mi piace—and all the family who read with enthusiasm the tributes to your Napoleonic Forelock,* your rostrumic authority, your imagination, to say nothing of your "Riding master" ability. That article "An Old Lady Gets 3 Shots" etc. is one of the best of its kind we have ever seen.** José Rodriguez writes as though he were writing to get something off his chest and not to fill up a newspaper column. In spite of its ploy of comedy, it is convincing and dignified: of a man who thinks, and thinks for himself, and a literary "something" besides. Everybody in Boston aged over 38 years 6 months ought to read it***—but "Parlo troppo presto!"

It can't be long now before you get a permanent job with some big orchestra, I hope in the East—you've done so much for practically nothing—it makes me mad—and Mrs. Ives too. "Mi dia una hatto!"**** Though many a true word lodges in the teeth and though it's a long road that has no saloon, thou'll be there, with Aurora!—Non posso aspetto tanto!!****

It was good to know that the Pan American concert has been arranged for the 1934 Italian Festival—"Guggenheim" or not, you will have to be there—even if we have to train a nice eagle to fly you over. "Vogliamo anche un salotto"— when you're there— "Swatta di woppo, non troppo!"

We are here on a side hill of lemons and oranges—have you been in Sicily?—that is, early in the morning?—The sun comes out of Greece over the Ionian sea—which is quite alright and then a nice breeze over Calabria, brings it to your eye—but with it lemons, and madamigelle on the other eye! "Mi mandi un barbiere alle otto!" But this is a place of great beauty—and we can lead a quiet, "peasant" kind of life, which agrees with us. When the sun shines it is as our June— when not, it is like "Election Day" and Republicans! It is the color "buono mollo"—in everything and everywhere that makes up scenery here. There are many artists here—no musicians. "Lo voglio molto forte." Will probably stay here until the first part of March or so, and then go to some of the Italian cities for a while and may sail back from Naples—or possibly, a boat to England and back that way—"desidero un sigaro forte." When you write again it would be best to mail to our London address, the Guaranty Trust Co., 50 Pall Mall.

Ex Libris—Scriptor Romanus
401 B.C.

"Signore, io te saluto—ancora e ancora!"

* A woman reporter in California said that Slonimsky had a "Napoleonic forelock."

** José Rodriguez published in a local magazine a review of Slonimsky's Los Angeles concerts of December, 1932 under the title "Old Lady Gets Three Shots in the Arm." the old lady being the Los Angeles Philharmonic and the three shots being Ives, Cowell and Slonimsky.

*** Slonimsky was 38 1/2 years old when he conducted his Los Angeles concerts.

**** Samples of Ives' own brand of Italian.

London, England
May 1933

Dear "Nap"—Con Forelock:* Thank you very much for your letters—which we all enjoyed. We wanted to see more of Italy— but traveling around, hotels, etc. don't seem to agree with me somehow. So we came more directly on to England. Will stay here, "quiet and slow" until we sail—probably in July.

I hope things are going forte with you. When do you get back from Russia and are you going there? Is Russia a musical nation—like Italy—I mean is Russia a musical nation?—or do they like nice voices? I hear from Henry occasionally—he is now in California and says that America *is* a musical nation (out there). I didn't intend to get this old subject in this letter—but an article in an English paper this morning—"Are we a musical nation?" brought it—I am sorry. There is nothing in a musical nation—not even music! for a nation is only a nation—but a good cigar is et al!

It seems a long time since we've seen you—and it is. I hope next year things will work out better for all of us. Just now it seems a bad time for "carrying on" the work— all armies are apparently out of breath and supplies—but another year we must resume.

Yours as ever,
CHAS. E. IVES

P.S. Am not sure, but think before leaving I told you that in cleaning house preparatory to being away so long, I found several of the old scores, etc.—from which some of the songs were taken—I had forgotten some of them or thought they were not kept—so before arranging any songs it would be better to wait until we can get together again and look over these manuscripts. I also found some other things—or parts of them—that might do for short, chamber pieces, some of only 4 or 5 instruments—among them was a set of half-dozen pieces called "Cartoons," "A 3 minute Yale-Princeton Football Game," "Gyp the Blood & Hearst!" (which is worst?), "The Gen. Slocum Disaster," "Mike Donlin at the Bat," "Central Park in the Dark," etc. Some of them are topics of "those days," but why not!—"D.K.E. & ΦU," "Yale Campus," "Cal-

cium Light Night." When we get back will have Hanke** copy what he can—they were mostly in lead pencil, some rather indistinct—I think you will like some of them. One thing, they won't take much rehearsal and only a very few players. I'm looking these over. I was impressed with this— that I now have good advice for young composers—"If you write anything you think is good, copy it out in ink" and "If you write anything you think is no good, copy it out in ink!"

Auf wiedersehn—but not yet "good-bye"—and if you go to Russia come back before sunset—for it's long since we've seen you around the table.

* A reference in a Los Angeles newspaper review which said that Slonimsky's forelock was Napoleonic.

** Ives' regular copyist.

West Redding
Connecticut
18 August 1933

Dear Pater-Familias! The new message this morning was received by all the Ives family with enthusiasm—we send warmest congratulations to her father and mother—and also to Electra!*—may good health (even in the 1st tooth) be hers—may she live in happiness and not behold tragedy— except over the footlights! We were just about to write—in fact, Mrs. Ives had pen in hand—to see if Mrs. Dorothy Adlow and Mr. Nicolas Slonimsky could not come and see us over the Labor Day Holidays—but Electra steps in—as "Generations and Destiny" have done before—but wont it be possible for you to run down sometime before long? It has been far too long since we've seen you. Just let us know 2 or 3 days ahead—and we can meet you either in Bridgeport (Bridgeport is better for most trains) or South Norwalk if you come from Boston.

We have been settled in America for a few weeks, gradually getting our bearings on household Penates back into place. Have seen no one yet but the family etc., though have heard from Henry Cowell and Carl Ruggles—they're both well—one seething, and one cussing. Well—as soon as the family situation warrants your departure, please come down and see us in Redding—there's a new Eddington book—a new hammock and some mice—(not nice) moth-eaten scores, old and sore, for you to look at. Give our love to the baby and the mother—and keep some for the "Ole man-Papa!"

Ever yours,
CHAS. E. IVES

* Electra Slonimsky was born in Boston on 16 August 1933.

West Redding
Connecticut
1 November 1933

Padre Bon Appetito Di Electra!* We were glad to get your letter and know that the family keeps well—that Electra thrives under you as "Dispenser of Rations" speaks well for her "toleration!"

To be in Mr. Birchard's catalogue is more of an honor to *me* than to him—that is, I consider myself the honored one—as he is the only American publisher, as far as I know, who has published music he believed should be published, yet knowing it would bring him certain loss and the ridicule, or at best a "nice smile" from the trade. Please, tell him how much I appreciate his interest. You told him, I presume, that we wanted parts engraved and he should include this in the amount.**

We expect Henry up for a day soon—next to N.S. he is the busiest man in New York.

A letter from Mr. Aaron Copland says he is writing an article about my songs for "Modern Music" and I am sending him some of those old manuscripts (photos) to help him get the facts straight, etc.

CHAS. E. IVES

* Infant daughter of Slonimsky, who occasionally took care of her feeding.

** Slonimsky arranged with the C. C. Birchard Co. of Boston to publish *Three Places in New England*, with Ives paying for the engraving and other expenses in full.

———

West Redding
Connecticut
4 November 1933

Dear Padre: I am answering your 3 letters "to once"—2 came yesterday and one this morning. I don't know exactly what to say about the score. The estimate is somewhat more than I had thought of "laying out" just at the present time.* The score, of course, will have to be engraved—but would this other process in making the parts, come out just as clearly as the engraved parts?** Also, another point that I've heard about through Henry's troubles and others, is the question of "performance fees." It apparently often means a law suit and prevents performance. Henry says Stokowski returned a score recently saying that the Philadelphia Orchestra would not pay fees, etc. I would be willing to make any business arrangement that Mr. Birchard would suggest, so that "performance fee" could be cut out. If this can be done, I think I might as well go ahead and have the score made, on the estimate in letter. Also please ask them to let me know a few days in advance when payments are to be made.

I greatly appreciate your willingness to help me correct the proofs. I can't see that green-white proof paper. Can't find a score here but have one in New York. Our best to family,

Ever yours,
CHAS. E. IVES

Have extra pencil—I revert to it—can steer it with less vibrato than pen.

* The arrangement with the Birchard Co. was that Ives would pay for the engraving and printing of the score and parts of *Three Places in New England*.

** Slonimsky had suggested photographing parts individually from the score.

———

West Redding
Connecticut
5 December 1933

Dear Padre: I would have written before but have been somewhat out of shape for the last few weeks, and am still kept on "my back" most of the time—to much "ritin', talkin', playin', and cussin'," they say.

Thank you much for what you have done, and also Mr. Birchard. Am sending the enclosed check for $200 on account.

Am not sure I'd make any changes in the score—the drum part at beginning of the second movement, I wrote that way, so the "down beat" bass drum, would go along as they play it on main beats, not after beats. On Page 27 think it might be easier for drum and piano to play as it is written, or both ways might be printed—would also keep 2nd viola here. There are 2 or 3 places (short phrases only), when it might be better for

horn than trumpet. But I will look it through again in a few days and write more. Generally speaking, I don't like to change anything after once finished. But you may be right.* We can tell better when we see the proofs.

It was fine to hear that Mrs. Slonimsky had such a success in Pittsburgh. We do hope to see you both—wrong— you 3, soon after we get to New York. But we may stay here till after Christmas. Our love to Electra and you all. As ever,

Sincerely,
CHAS. E. IVES

Please excuse paper, pencil and ritin'. As you see there is no "tremolo" with nice pencil. The enclosed was sent me by an unmusical friend and you may like to see it. Needn't send back.

* Slonimsky had made several suggestions for uniform notation in various parts of the score of *Three Places in New England*.

———

West Redding
Connecticut
12 December 1933

Dear Padre: You are a good boy to take so much trouble over the score.* Most of the ways you suggest are advisable I think. The work looks well done—I will start today to go over the proofs, etc. and will get them back in a week or so.

I meant to have written you before, but forgot to say that Mrs. Ives says she will get you a copy of the Kodak picture for the "Transcript"**—if you can't get it from "Modern Music"—and that is none of my business to remark upon!

Ever yours,
CHAS. E. IVES

**Three Places in New England.*

** Slonimsky was writing an article on Ives for the Boston *Evening Transcript*.

———

West Redding
Connecticut
16 December 1933

Dear N.S.P. I've started in on going over the proofs—and I ran right into a "mess" that I thought was straightened out when Hanke made the parts. In all the strings mostly I, II and Viola, there should be some consistent way of showing when they play together and in parts. I asked Hanke to both "down and up" stems on all strings (except Bass) unless there were long passages of a page or more where there is only one part, then just one stem would do, if "unis." or "a due" or "non div." or some indication to that effect, was put. I will do the best I can to straighten these out, but it will take a little time. You will probably know the best way to make it clearest to the players. There are also mistakes I didn't correct, for instance on p. 2—note tied to another, but a dot over 1st note which of course is impossible. I am sorry to give you and the engraver so much trouble—but it's better to get it right now—even if it takes longer—and there is no hurry anyway.

Another point: As there is no staff for tuba at beginning of movements, there should be some note to indicate to conductor that tuba plays only when separate staff occurs. I haven't a tuba part here. The old score that had this was cut up and pasted when the photo-copy was made. I think you have the tuba copy I made from that. Haven't had time to cover all the points in your "questionnaire" but will in a few days and will then send.

Your conductor's note is "well put"—for some conductors it will be a help and others it will (according to what I hear of some conductors)—it will mix them up so they will "side-step" the whole job—it will make others "sour."—If used, I think it better than sent out when parts are asked for—or sent only to conductors whom you know are "bright" enough to "get it." There are some conductors that I'd send it to just as it stands, but there are others who I wouldn't like to have think (as it came ostensibly from me) that I underrate their intelligence— for instance Goossens. The last paragraph, as it stands, would seem to doubt one's ability to learn something new ("unable" could be the word). However, we can decide about that later. There are very few, if any, conductors with your "gifts"—I think most of them could not learn to beat 2 ups, and if they try to, would make things worse. I sent your copy of conductor's note to my brother's office to have a copy made, and will send it back with one or 2 suggestive changes.

Ought to get the proofs here corrected and back to you in a week or so. I hope my corrections etc., can be made out, I have used lead pencil, as my pen wobbles so. With our best to all the family,

Yours as ever,
CHAS. E. IVES

West Redding
Connecticut
19 December 1933

Dear Padre: Mrs. Ives has been expecting to go down and do some Christmas shopping, but hasn't for one reason or another. She wanted to get something for Electra's first Christmas— something that she (Electra) would be willing to have in her wardrobe—or has she already started her library? So we are sending the enclosed—and it may be just as well—as Mater (not Padre) will know better what will be the things for her.

Haven't been able to do much on the proofs yet*—have had a few off days—but will get the first movement back to you soon—also questionnaire etc.

But we send our kindest remembrances, with care and affection to you "three."

Ever yours,
CHAS. E. IVES

* Of *Three Places In New England*, in the process of publication by the C. C. Birchard Co. in Boston.

West Redding
Connecticut
24 December 1933

Dear N.S.P.: Electra's Christmas letter is a poem—and so is her signature. May her first New Year's be a happy one and may she have many nice ones, but not too nice!

The newspaper clipping with a list of composers, etc.— didn't mention Henry Cowell and made us sore, and we were about to burn it up when a fine and illuminating article came to our eye—by a Boston lady—Dorothy Adlow* (you will remember seeing her in Paris, I think)—so it went into our archive and not the fire.

Am about to send you the proofs of the first movement— all corrected—sometime. There are many minor things as stems, bows, etc. which I should have fixed before sending to engraver. They may kick about the extra work, I'm making

them and I wouldn't blame them. Am sending a check for Bir-chard Co.—please ask them to let me know what the balance is, after January 1st and I'll settle the 2nd week in January and will hope to see you. Will let you know definitely later. We then can go over everything, notes etc. before final printing.

Sincerely,
CHAS. E. IVES

* Mrs. Nicolas Slonimsky, art critic of *The Christian Science Monitor*.

West Redding
Connecticut
26 December 1933

More—Proofs, etc.

1) Stems, bow marks, etc. for div. strings—(my fault— thought this had been done when parts were made)—as there are already so many double stems (up and down)—might be better to do this all through instead of "unis."

2) Last measure p. 19—have put 2nd Cello part in 1st Bass (this is better I think—sometimes a Cello sounds too loud and scratchy down there).

3) Would have title and name only on cover and title page and not in very large print.

4) On page 15—would put metronome at 80 as 72 seems too big a jump from preceding.

5) p. 17—metronome marks changed a little.

6) p. 19—bottom corner—date in very small print (1911). Henry thinks all dates should go in.

7) p. 14—memo over RH piano in small print suggesting—2 players ad lib.

8) Opposite p. 19—(last music page of I)—would put verse (program) in small print—would have these programs at end and not at beginning of movements. Rather not feature the programs etc. before the music.

9) Think that whatever conductor's instructions should go in a note printed on separate sheet and be sent out when parts are sent and not in score. I think your "note" about beating the 2 rhythms is excellent and well put, even as it stands, if it got before men of your genius, brains and courage—but where are they? Most conductors, if they should be told to beat 2 together would fall over in a nice-looking swoon and give up the whole job—and it gives them another excuse for not playing anything. The 2 slight revisions I've made, would make it more optional and not sound quite so much as if I were laying the law down. And from some experience, asking most men to do a new way, only makes them do it worse.

There are 2 or 3 other points that might go into conduc-tor's note—for instance, about playing the piano at places— optional 2 players and when also, way of playing end of the third movement, holding ff chord till *sordini* are put on, etc. Also organ part. But we can decide about these things when we get together again.

Will send answers to your questionnaire soon—after going over the second movement about which it refers to most.

My corrections, etc.—are not any too clear—and if you or the engraver can't make some out, let me know— there's no great hurry about the job exactly—is there? We might take our time and do it as well as possible.

C.E.I.

West Redding
Connecticut
3 January 1934

*Dear "Nap"** I take my pen in hand to write you a long tiresome letter about why A is quite natural & 2/4 nice but wrong—but Happy new Year, first, to you all!

The engraver, when he sees my marks on the proofs of the II movement, which I'm mailing you today, may get quite sore—I wouldn't blame him. I should have gone through them, specially the strings before it was sent to him. I've done the best I could to straighten it out—& I hope you & he can make out the corrections, etc., for instance:

1) If div. bow marks up & down are in one measure & then only the "up" in the next, the "down" players might not know what to do always—keep on—or stop— All these things I've tried to fix with the least trouble to the engraver. But he may have a better way.

2) If parts are to be made from the score, as you suggested, all the marks will have to go in each staff—a great many are in—but not all—for instance the "roller" . . . just before letter A.

3) In II movement, a piccolo often plays with a flute, sometimes in unison, sometimes, octave higher. I tried to show this by a "note" over flute part. But a separation in II in percussion part should be made for the player.

4) In some places, an extra player for the piano is better— so have put at beginning (Piano for 2 players ad lib)—the passages etc. can be suggested in the conductor's note, to go with parts—I do not like too many observations in score.

5) Horn parts were all left out on pages 53–54 (didn't try to copy them in)—engraver can take it from photo score.

6) 2 measures before—would put in the regular parts—not the *ossia*—or both.

7) At H. p. 35—when the 2 bands play. Your plan of the separate time for each is good and a great improvement. But I think it's important to show in the score, where each fits into the other—so have kept Piano as it was with dotted lines up to show how it stands with the II and have put back II Viola part as it was to show how II Viola stands with I.

8) Have kept the first 5 measures of II as it was. So the drum parts keep the bass drum on main beat—the rest of the orchestra miss the beats.

There are other things but can't think of them now. When they send the corrected proofs back, I wish they could be with the black notes on white paper—these white notes blur my eye—and I can't work as steadily as on black on white, which is not very steadily at that. Am not starting over the III proofs for a little while—to give the eye a let-up.

What concert is to be in March, which Varèse spoke to you about? It's very good of him to have you play something of mine. I might suggest 2 short but active songs— and the quiet "In the Night" for orchestra: 1) "The New River" (p. 42, New Music edition, about 40 seconds), 2) "December," p. 40 (about 30 seconds), 3) "In the Night" (3rd movement, Theater Orchestra Set, New Music edition, about 2 minutes). This gives a contrasting group—short (about 4 minutes), not many players, not many rehearsals, & not very expensive!

The "December" ought to be sung by 3 to 10 fat basses (raucous voiced) and the "New River" by 1 or 2 men or 1 man and a lady (to A-sharp). "In the Night" without a voice.

But the "New River" and "December" will have to have the old scores copied and parts made (you have I think photos of these which you might look over). When you get back will have this done. As I remember there are some measures in the old scores that are rather indistinct, but not many—and it won't take

long to have copies made. Also I think the "New River" takes 2 Saxophones, but one and a trombone would do it. Good night.

C.E.I.

* Again a reference to the "Napoleonic forelock" that a California reporter found in Slonimsky's physical appearance.

164 East 74 Street
New York
11 January 1934

Dear Interpreter (of tongues and Sounding Brass—not the Psalmist's kind—but all nice music)—

Do you beat 2 rhythms when interpreting a lecture? We would have liked to have seen its setting. We're back in this gas-grained city. If we didn't have this house on our hands, we wouldn't come at all. When are you coming down? We hope soon—only we're sorry that just now, as our nephew is living with us, and in the only spare room— but we're having a room fixed for him in the attic (my floor), which Mrs. Ives thinks will be ready about the first of next month—as they have to run heating pipes, etc. up—but the next time you must stay with us.

Am returning the 2 pages—This (*ossia* place) way is good, I think & would go ahead with it. Haven't started going over the III yet. Haven't been quite in shape for a week or so and getting back to this "onus" doesn't help. Will you please ask them to send me another proof of the III in black & white (& charge it to me). After I look at those white notes on green, for about 10 minutes they all start to move around—like rice in green soup to my eyes—but you are a good boy to take so much trouble and we hope to see you soon.

Our love to all the family and Electra and Matre and Padre.

C.E.I.

I haven't seen anybody yet—and won't until I can get up to an 84 = ♩—except you.

164 East 74 Street
New York
5 February 1934

Dear Padre! Since writing you we have had some low days—Uncle Deac died—quite suddenly after a stroke. You remember him living with us in Redding—the oldest of our generation—and one of the last of the old type, now quite vanishing—and the world loses something undefinable.

Weiss & Riegger came in—and also Varèse—they are all full of plans—which I hope will work out. They told me first that Reiner was to conduct the Town Hall concert—that made me *sore*—but Varèse telephoned the other day that *you* were to conduct it—which is *quite* right—very much quite alright!

Have been rather slow correcting the last movement,* but have now got it cleared up and am mailing it to you today. On last page, the quotation from the poem should be printed in small print, in the way the other movements were done—have put in last page of photo to show. Please tell the engraver that I want to see the last proofs of the whole thing, including verses, programs, etc. before it goes to press. And also please ask them to send the balance of the bill as soon as they know what it is. I put in a few things about playing the piano, etc. that ought to go with "conductor's note." Will show these to you later.

When are you coming down, and how much does Electra weigh today?

CHAS. E. IVES

N.S.P.! Atoms are indivisible—so are 32nd-notes. From p. 74 each 2 measures are put down as such, through p. 80. In other words these "backwater waves" are put in a prescriptive formula which exists only on paper—so when played exactly right—it's wrong—like Arthur Evans' cow. Don't read the above again but just tell the engraver I've tried to make as little trouble as I could—and the attached sheet makes the lower staff piano, from p. 74 to 80, clear, uniform and nice. The real music is all put in the footnote to p. 74.

C.E.I.

* *Three Places In New England.*

---

164 East 74 Street
New York
6 February 1934

Dear N.S.P. We thank you—Mr. Parker*—and the Transcript—for your effort, interest and space. Do you handle the pen, the baton or the nursing bottle the best? Electra may have her special vote—but we vote for all three! Will you please ask them to save a dozen (or 25 better, because old copies are hard to get) copies and have them sent here whenever convenient—and we will send you a London Spectator** someday. I turned in the corrected proofs of the third movement*** yesterday to the proper department (= N.S.P.) We can talk about pagination and other matters when you come down—as you say that will be soon. Don't bother about the score, am having clean copies made from the manuscript of the 2 chorus songs "New River" and "December," which Varèse says are on the program together with the "In the Night" set.**** Good night to you all.

CHAS. E. IVES

Please ask Birchard Co. to let me see final proofs before sending to press.

* H. T. Parker, drama and music editor of the Boston Evening *Transcript.*
** The only periodical that Ives and Mrs. Ives ever read; they did not subscribe to any American newspaper or magazine.
*** Of *Three Places in New England.*
**** New York concert under the auspices of the Pan American Association of Composers scheduled for 15 April 1934 in Town Hall, New York.

---

15 February 1934
New York
164 East 74 Street

Dear Padre: It was fine to have you with us around the family—and we hope it won't be in the distant future before Madre and the Papina, may join around it too—Electra will be quite old enough to travel soon—having a birthday every 6 months.

The final proofs to the second movement* came today. Have only as yet looked at the first page—and the *ossia* drum part there probably will be of help, and would let it stay. It shouldn't take me long to check it all over and will send it back next week. I suppose they haven't forgotten that I haven't seen the final proofs of the first movement yet and will send it—also proofs of the written pages, i.e. verses, programs etc.

The notes you ask about on page 60 last measure are right now, the oboe and viola are OK. As I see it, here it is more a matter of where the voices lead to than their relation vertically to others. In the R.H. piano the upper A's are all flat and the lower A's natural. If the upper staff piano is taken by one player 2 hands it's quite easy to play. In fact 2 players (except in a very few places) are better than one. This week there have been several more instances of need of some "résumé"—but comprehen-

sive and under one cover, & convenient to mail—a teacher and lecturer in Philadelphia writes for something like that, a pianist and lecturer etc. in a college in Louisville, in a letter which came this A.M. asks for data, etc. for his lectures and yesterday a letter from Homeyer & Co., 458 Boylston St., Boston saying they have requests for my music and ask where it is published and for description pamphlets, etc. etc. I have had many requests etc. like this, and nothing to send—except odds and ends, scraps, and now the Musical Quarterly are all out, 1 copy left**—no more copies—so to have what is wanted under one cover and convenient to mail is quite necessary. Also the booklet should help sell both the new score*** and the songs etc.

The enclosed photo MSS of the original organ piece, later the "In the Night" will show in the upper manual the general idea of the 2 upper string parts which were left out—and which should get in. I will copy out these 2 measures later and send. I'm sorry to bother you with this long badly written letter. If you can't read it—it will be quite alright! It reminds me of a "Raphaelic Sky"—it's so different.

Our love to the family,
Sincerely,
CHAS. E. IVES

* Of *Three Places in New England.*
** *The Musical Quarterly* of January 1933 with an article on Ives by Henry Bellamann.
*** *Three Places in New England*, published by C. C. Birchard Co. of Boston.

---

164 East 74 Street
New York
21 February 1934

*Dear N.S.P.** The final corrected proofs were mailed to you this A.M.—so the job is done—most—only the prose and conductor's note, which is short and only to be copied. Will send it soon. I want to thank you for your help, interest and eyes—you were a good boy—and how is Electra!

We rather looked for you last week, but hope to see you soon. The parts are being made for the 2 choruses and a photo of "New River" score in your own handwriting is to be sent you. There was one measure (when they sing "Taraboomdeay") that I thought the strings better play with piano. You have, I think the score to the other song—"December." If not, will have one sent or give you one when you come down, which I hope will be soon.**

Another letter came in this A.M. from a music school asking for data, biography, then half lost—so that a booklet will save me a lot of trouble and cussing—it is digest of criticism, notes, etc. It takes me a whole day to get things together, and really needed.

How does Electra like it here in America? Our love to her and her mother and Padre.

Sincerely,
CHAS. E. IVES

* Nicolas Slonimsky Padre.
** Slonimsky arranged some songs of Ives for voice and orchestra to be performed at his concert in April 1934 in New York.

---

164 East 74 Street
New York
22 February 1934

*Dear N.S.P.** In writing you yesterday I meant to have sent the enclosed which Henry sent me. It might help in the booklet. It's from the "Music Lovers Guide" of February 3rd. And I also meant to have asked you to look at the last 15 pages to the end of the 2nd movement of my 4th Symphony which Henry published some years ago. Playing only the percussion group and a piano, or both pianos, would do for a piece or study in rhythms and percussion:

10 players, besides piano player (1, 2 or 3):

1 Gong	1 Indian drum
1 Light Gong or Cymbal	1 Timpani
hung up	1 Low Bell
1 Cymbal	1 High Bell
1 Bass Drum	1 Triangle
1 Snare Drum	

And to get the wood percussion, a xylophone would go well playing the piccolo part.

If you have a copy you might look it over and see what you think about it. It seems to me it makes a coherent musical sense, this way, even without the orchestra. In fact, this and other parts of this symphony I remember playing when I was working on it, with a few drums, kitchen tables, bells, etc. and the rhythmic lines seemed to hold up by its own. However, it may not do, but look it over. Will send a copy I have here to you marked as suggested when I mail back the proofs of the second movement** within a few days. The final proof to the first movement will be ready for any time. When you have the song scores copied, let me know what it will be and I'll send the check.

CHAS. E. IVES
Good night to all,

* Nicolas Slonimsky Padre.

** Of the score of *Three Places in New England.*

---

way except Sat. P.M.)—am quite sure, in sending the copy back with these 2 measures, I explained to the engraver to go by these—if he had he would have saved himself and us trouble. When they send the I and III final proofs, if the former proofs, with corrections in, could be sent also it would save time in checking up. The other engravers (New Music) always did that.

I don't care about the cover page—as long as the letters aren't = (are not) big, especially my name. Would just have *Three Places in New England* (an orchestral set) and the separate titles of each movement inside.

You are a good copyist—but I had no intention of having you take so much trouble and time to copy those scores. All I thought was that you would go over them with the copyist and perhaps go over a measure or passages that seemed indistinct, etc.

I've gone over the "December" as best I could. There are a few places, I can't quite make out in the old copy but its near enough and have had a photostat made, which will save time making parts etc. This and your copy will be sent back to you in a day or so.

A letter from Henry says some 70 people subscribed last month to the New Music Quarterly Records at $5 a person— it is surprising! In these Pan American concerts some good recordings ought to result. I hope so. Apparently the time, according to Henry's expression, is a problem—4 1/2 minutes or less to each side.

Good night to all,

Yours,
CHAS. E. IVES

* Third movement of *Three Places in New England.*

---

164 East 74 Street
New York
24 February 1934

Dear N.S.P.S.—2nd S = "Scriba"— You were a good boy to make copies—but am sorry for the misunderstanding about "Duty"—that isn't to be sung, and besides it's for a large orchestra. I'd no idea of having it copied, as I remember it was on the desk and just gave it to you for future reference. I hope it didn't take much time. The "December" looks well done and plain but I can't correct the last part until you send me the ink copy I made for the last photo page. I can't see that old copy now—happen to be going through one of those "bad eye" periods when everything blurs, unless very clear.

Am sending tomorrow the second movement* finished, There were a few mistakes but unimportant—have put a snare drum in that 11/8 measure that always bothered so— a drum was there once to make it clear to players.

Does Electra like New England winter? Love to all the family,

Ever yours,
CHAS. E. IVES

* Of *Three Places in New England.*

---

164 East 74 Street
New York
5 March 1934

Dear N.S.P. Am sending back the 6 pages you sent of the III* proofs. You are right—let them take p. 77 from correct copy (correct on paper, though you can't make me play it that nice

---

164 East 74 Street
New York
7 March 1934

Dear N.S.P. The scores and the voice parts of the songs came today.* Didn't mean to have you do all that work— I thought you'd just look or lean over the "scribe's" shoulder and point to a bad note. They are all plain and I'll have the parts copied here and your voice pages photostated. Now don't do anymore copying, you have more to do than that. They will probably send the proofs to the first movement of *Three Places* soon and then the worst of the job will be done. Please excuse this very bad letter.

Will hope to see you soon.

CHAS. E. IVES

* Orchestral arrangements made by Nicolas Slonimsky for his New York concert 15 April 1934.

---

164 East 74 Street
New York
24 April 1934

Dear N.S.P. Are you there—with both arms! et al. Please be sure to come in and see us if you're down Sunday, the 29th. Thanks for the notices from the Boston paper. The printed proof copy for Birchard Co. came yesterday, mostly O.K. Am mailing back today.

Ever yours,
CHAS. E. IVES

Is it nice to like music?

———

164 East 74 Street
New York
1 May 1934

Dear N.S.P. Mrs. Ives was disturbed that you have to come way down here to do those recordings, perhaps several times and instead of getting paid for it you even have to pay your own traveling expenses. She doesn't think it fair—nor do I, and I'm enclosing something to make us feel better.*

Your plan for the recording seems the best. One side *Lilacs*** 4 minutes, other side *Barn Dance,**** In the Night***** about the right time—and better to have time and space than otherwise.

Ever yours,
CHAS. E. IVES

* A characteristic Ivesian way of blaming Harmony Ives for his own noble impulses.
** By Carl Ruggles.
*** From *Washington's Birthday* of Ives.
**** By Ives.

———

West Redding
Connecticut
5 June 1934

Dear N.S.P. Riegger writes that the records went well, and that you did "nice work, old boy!" and the players were *serious and enthusiastic*—also that a few days ago Salzedo told him that *In the Night* was one of the best records he had ever heard—Riegger adds: "Salzedo is *very* critical." I hope Henry will like them and that they will help in this work.*

We are all glad to be back on the hill again and for me more sleep—less cuss. We hope you can get down before the summer is over.

We all send our best to you both,

Sincerely,
CHAS. E. IVES

* The recordings of *Washington's Birthday* and *In the Night* were made by Slonimsky for the New Music Edition, founded and edited by Henry Cowell.

———

West Redding
Connecticut
7 August 1934

Dear Padre! I've been on the point of writing you for many days back—but I'll have to admit for sometime I didn't seem to be able to keep in decent shape—and had to give up doing about everything. It's humiliating and makes me mad. Mrs. Ives has decided, backed up by all the family plus the M.D., that the best thing to do now is to sail over to England and stay there for 2 or 3 months—anyhow for good or otherwise, we're going to sail on August 10. Our address (as before) is c/o Guaranty Trust Co., 50 Pall Mall, London.

Everybody seems to like the records*—you did a good job—a hard one. I appreciate all you have done deeply and "I take off my hat." I've been wondering if I owe Birchard and Co. anything. The data, etc. for the little brochure (is that spelled OK? My Irish is bad!) will be sent in a few days to you from the office typewriter. It has (1) a short biography (including name and date of birth) (2) a list of compositions, etc. (3) Digest of Comment. Besides these, the verses and program for the "3 Places in New England" which are printed

in the score might go in, and I suppose whatever (but short) forenote the publisher thinks ought to be made—but *Please NO Picture* of me or any nice man anywhere!

The digest of comment has been arranged in preferential order by one who thinks he knows—but I suppose—[Here Ives had to stop. His handwriting was so shaky that the words were hardly intelligible, and his adopted daughter Edith took over: "Dear Mr. Slonimsky: I am now writing for daddy. Here is a hug, etc."]

* Slonimsky recorded *Washington's Birthday* for New Music Records.

———

164 East 74 Street
New York
12 December 1934

Dear N.S.P. Was just about to write you when your letter came. We were glad to know you all are well and that Electra is learning how to talk, or not how to talk, I can't quite make out—but both are best. We've been back for a while—as yet haven't been able to do anything I wanted to, but am getting better now and expect to be a human being soon—whatever that is! I appreciate the trouble you have taken about the printing etc. I don't know how many copies of the score should be printed. I remember that you said both you and Mr. Birchard thought a certain number should be sent to conductors, libraries, schools etc. Perhaps 300 would be enough to start with. But do whatever seems advisable and please let me know about a week ahead and I'll send the check for it. I will be glad to look over the proofs for the brochure any time. A few later things have been sent me that might go in or perhaps you may have something too. I feel the need of this, as I'm getting an increasing number of inquiries, etc. from papers, teachers, students, et al.—asking for data this book will give and which I'm never able to put my hands on when wanted—and some of the letters, I'm ashamed to say, I haven't even answered.

Mrs. Ives and Edie join me in kindest remembrances to you and yours.

Ever yours,
CHAS. E. IVES

———

164 East 74 Street
New York
January 1935

Dear N.S.P. Here is the printed matter corrected as well as I can, and with some suggestions. Would vote for the outside page not to be in gaudy, loud-mouthed colors that all nice* magazines and books have, but rather in plain letters and color. Mrs. Ives says a light grey—and if I were you I would take her advice. Ask Electra's mother to tell her husband that wives know more about color than men. And how do you like it in America and when are you coming to New York?

C.E.I.

* It should be remembered that Ives used the word "nice" with a strong feeling of revulsion.

———

164 East 74 Street
New York
April 1935

Dear N.S.P.! Thanks for your letter and for sending the proofs of the conductor's note. There are some references to pages, etc. I can't quite make out—so think I'll wait for a copy of the printed score to check up with. And there's no hurry I think, about this proof, as it is only to be sent out with the parts.

I'm very glad you are to conduct the concert in Denver. Robert Schmitz was here about a month ago but was not certain about the concert. Schmitz is a fine man—brains and courage. Milhaud told me that Debussy said that Schmitz had more music sagacity than most young men he knew. Please ask Birchard Co. to send me the bill for the printing, etc. as soon as it is done.

Hoping to see you again before long—and with kindest wishes from us all to Electra, her mother and you.

I am yours ever,
CHAS. E. IVES

West Redding
Connecticut
11 May 1935

*Dear N.S.P.!!** You are a good boy to send me the article and translation***—They were well written. I can see how you can write good English—but how did you learn Russian?

Am glad our parts*** came out so well. There is just one place I noticed that might help. It's the drum part in the 2nd movement, when playing the "off rhythm"—it might help the drummer if his part was cued in as the piano part in the score is. However, this can be easily done later.

Everybody at church except the one who ought to be— "arreta prodita"—bad Latin for Electra to correct!**** I expected to send back a score from New York. Will do so soon. There's one item in it, that makes no sense. "Don't play first measure unless there are 3 trombones"—now if it had said—"don't play first measure unless there is a good conductor" that would be the most sensible note ever written—the only conductor's note ever needed!

Please ask Birchard and Co. to send a copy of score to the 2 names enclosed. And if they also will send a half dozen (or more) copies to me, I'll appreciate it. Will also pay for the postage if I should. We all send best wishes to you and yours,

Ever yours,
CHAS. E. IVES

* N.S. Padre.

** An article on American music published in the Moscow monthly *Sovietskaya Musica*.

*** Makeshift photocopies of individual parts from the published score of *Three Places in New England*.

**** Electra's first language was Latin.

West Redding
Connecticut
October 1935

Dear N.S.P. This is just a line of welcome home. Will write in more detail as soon as I get in better pen-handling (not pan-handling) shape. We all send out best remembrances to Electra, her mother and dad.

Ever yours,
C.E.I.

164 East 74 Street
New York
November, 1935

Dear N.S.P. I'm sorry to report that I haven't been able to attend to those various things you wrote me about last sum-

mer— For some time past haven't been in shape to do anything I want to— As for music, sometimes for days at a time—can't see it, hear it or play it—not even a nice wrong note! But am getting somewhat out of this spell and hope soon to be more like a human being. May things go well with all of you. Best wishes again.

Ever yours,
CHAS. E. IVES

West Redding
Connecticut
23 November 1937

Dear N.S.P. You are a good boy! A gigantic and difficult job! The book* came. Many thanks. Anybody can write a good symphony—yet it takes a better man to conduct it. But only you and Sam Johnson can write a good Encyclopedia. Now give your mind and body a good rest—take it easy—just conduct the Boston Symphony for the old ladies for 10 seasons—then you will be able to do your big work again. A memorable day! Ahoy!

Ever yours,
CHAS. E. IVES

*First edition of *Music Since 1900*.

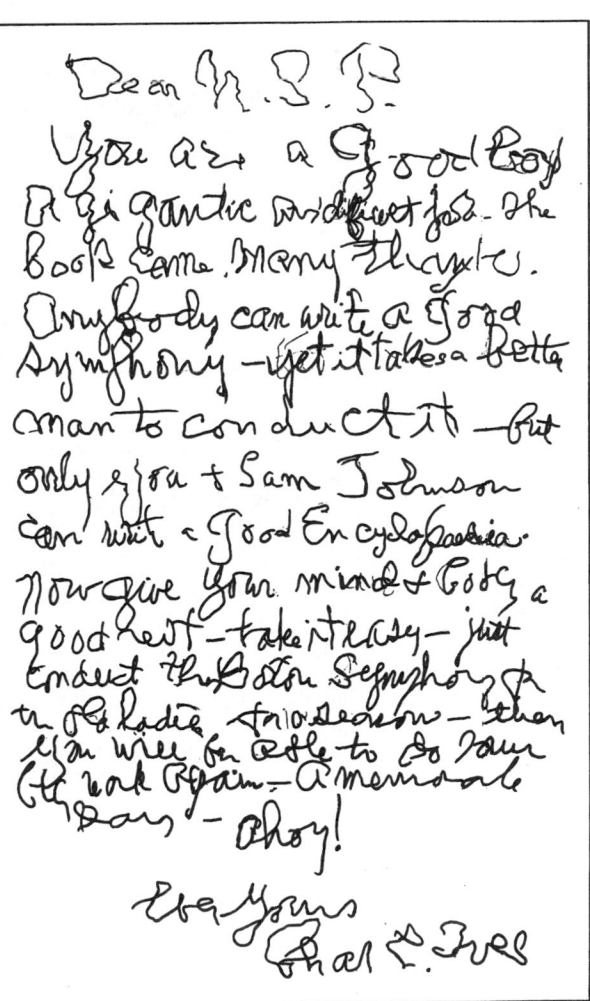

Letters from Edgar Varèse

Paris
26 April 1931

Dear Mr. Slonimsky, I have just received the program of your New York concert with the Pan-American Association of Composers, and it is very gratifying for me to know from your program notes how you feel about my music. I hope that when you have your own orchestra you will conduct my big works.

Cowell writes me of a prospective concert in Paris. May I suggest—may I even insist—that you play *Intégrales* instead of *Octandre*. I have already written Cowell and Salzedo my reasons for it. *Intégrales* was played here only once two years ago—not under favorable conditions—and yet provided a sensation. There is a demand for a repeat performance, and I think that the announcement of *Intégrales* on your program would help fill your hall.

I am looking forward to seeing you soon here in Paris—and having at last the pleasure of hearing you conduct.

With kindest regards.

Yours sincerely,
EDGAR VARÈSE

Paris
12 October 1931

Cher Ami, Merci pour votre lettre. Cowell wrote me from Hamburg immediately after his landing. If I can, I will go to Berlin to see him, but it is rather problematical on account of the depletion of my "gold mines." He told me about your success in California, which does not surprise me but does not prevent me from congratulating you most sincerely.

Orchestre Symphonique de Paris. The February concerts* must be made an immense success, and they must be given with all possible assurance of artistic results—with all the necessary rehearsals, etc. I will occupy myself with the task of molding the orchestra—a labor of slow penetration which is of absolutely prime importance. Good will on earth is secure, but as for the stars, it is up to us to reach them. Such a success will be the trampoline which will enable us to jump. Without it we cannot start. It is therefore imperative that you should take steps to obtain the necessary resources to realize this project.

Arcana. There is a great deal of talk about it, and an atmosphere of great and sympathetic expectation is created around this score. It will be published within a fortnight and I will send you a copy at once.

Everything moves along, and it is only the question of time—and perseverance in the imposed discipline, but—and I have the bad taste of Cato in insisting on it— Paris in February and the repercussions of this event is the condition *sine qua non* of the future successes. The road is open—but we must not start in the spirit of adventure—everything must be calculated in the preparation of this effort.

Cowell writes me—and it makes me happy—about the interest that certain important women in Southern California show for your appearances there.

To recapitulate, and to make use of your own words: it is imperative to organize a series of concerts of great musical importance in Europe. True—but the launching start must be in Paris. We have two immediate goals: intense concentration on the two February concerts—and their triumph. Am content with the projected concerts culminating in the performance of my *Amériques.* Do not forget to bring your own set of Chinese blocks for *Arcana.* If you find a good tamtam—deep—sonorous—warm—gargantuan—bring it along too. I work a great deal. Full of ideas fight and energy.

VARÈSE

* Slonimsky was engaged to conduct two concerts with the Orchestre Symphonique de Paris, on February 21 and 25, 1932, featuring Varèse's *Arcana.*

Paris
21 November 1931

Cher Ami, Thank you for your kind letter, article, translation and photograph.

Havana. If you will have, as Caturla* told Alejo Carpentier,** an orchestra large enough for *Le Sacre du Printemps,* I would like very much that my *Amériques* should be included in the program. See what you can do about it, and allow me to remind you of what I insist upon in regard to *Intégrales* for Paris. This is a psychological strategy. I know where I am going and what will follow. But, after all, we have a common cause, and I am happy that it is so. Have faith in my "hard-boiled" experience and don't mind this renewed insistence. My plan is clearly drawn—its development is logical—its results assured. You, Cowell, Salzedo, Ruggles, Riegger, Ives, Weiss—we must group together in a bloc. So you can see that there is no question of personal vanity. You know me well enough to realize that prima donna posturing is the least of my preoccupations. So try to do everything possible, and also the impossible.

Berlin. Let us decide on *Arcana.* You will have full knowledge of the score after the concert of the Orchestre Symphonique de Paris. The score has been sent to you. Despite all my care I am sure that your lynx eye will still find some errors. Let me know. People already talk about this concert—there are great expectations, and we must make it a resounding success—not only for our own satisfaction but also as a point of departure for further activities.

Russia. I saw the Soviet attaché who is doing all he can. He said that great interest in my works is developing there. I told him that I was very happy to hear about that, but that they should be played in such a way as to render them justice. I told him that you were the "mechanic" of my choice*** and that I wanted to have my works revealed in Russia by you. Some friends who just came from Russia brought some very flattering reports concerning me. But they also anticipate a great deal of red tape which is rampant in the U.S.S.R. This proves that the countries of old Europe and the U.S. have no reason to envy the Russians. But I am doing my best. Naturally, there is no question about defraying the expenses for the Russian concerts.

I am glad that you are seeing Salzedo—he is a dear and an old friend of mine. I am happy that my modest opinion about your person and your talents has moved you. I had a long conversation about you with Florent Schmitt, and you have his complete sympathy. He also is a wonderful comrade. Needless to say, you are free to quote all that is of interest to you in my letter to Salzedo. My opinions are not divided according to categories, and my admiration for you is expressed in public as well as in private.

Votre
VARÈSE

* Cuban composer.

** Cuban novelist and writer on music.

*** Varèse used to call Slonimsky "mon mécanicien," voicing his belief that performers should be regarded as mechanics carrying out the composer's engineering plans.

Paris
24 December 1931

Cher Ami, O.K. for *Intégrales* in Berlin and Budapest. The only thing on which I insist is that only the players should be on the stage, as you did in Paris, and that the rest of the orchestra should remain back stage and return to their seats after the performance of this work. Please get a string drum from Carl Fischer in New York—it costs only a dollar or two—and take it with you, because it is impossible to find one in Europe. They call it Lion's Roar, a stupid name, more suitable to describe the rumblings of a Methodist minister. O.K. also for Cuba to do *Amériques* after the fusion of the two orchestras in Havana. Merci. You and the score look like Siamese Twins on the photograph.

Arcana. We will correct the mistakes in the score together in Paris. I am glad that you are beginning to study it and I will be happy to hear this première of the new version under your intelligent and precise direction. Your progress does not surprise me. I have opened an unlimited credit for your future.

Do you think that there might be persons in New York interested in our group who could lend us support? Speak about it to Salzedo—he could give you good advice concerning the matter. Here, in Paris, unfortunately nothing. Crisis . . . Crisis < *ff* Crisis. But you will have a full house for your concerts in February. Not only myself but my friends will make sure of it. Amical souvenir.

VARÈSE

Letter from the Japanese League of Composers

Tokyo
22 March 1936

Dear Sir! I am a master of Hacsoh-ha composer's Society. I have read your letter with great rejoice. Hacsoh-ha is a group of my students, so all members are yet young about 20 years old, because I am yet 30 years. They have no interesting national compositions in their past. I have also no works in pure Japanese style. We Japanese composers, now and past, are studying European Harmony and Theory.

Of course, we have a earnest desire to complete our pure national music in future. We have many mystic melodies and wonderful scales in past, but we have no theories now and past. So we must at first, anyhow, study the perfect theories by West. We young Japanese composer is trying every test to using our old scales on our work. But non of them succes about it.

It is necessary to Japan, or it is a duty of Japanese composers, to complete a work and theories about it. We must compose or find new Japanese pure music in Western high style, in its instrumentation, systems and theorical elements.

Every group of Japanese composers or privatly earnestly trying this new work, but non of them complete it.

For instance, I send my score "Thema and Variations" for string trio to you. You will find easily from it only a European music, not a Japanese colour you needed. I know you will disappointed after reading my score. There will exist only a imitation of Western music.

I am very sorry, that you must wait a complete Japanese works in future; four or five years after. I believe that we will complete it recently.

Mr. Yokota, Nakano, Hirai are all my student and they are yet poor as young, so this time I will not send their works to you. But, I have many students about 150 members, and I will heartily send you when they will complete it.

Many thanks to your kind letter to our Japanese composer in far East. We feel so many happies that we are musician, such a international artist. Please remember me and teach us as long as possible. I have a riliance on my hard will to complete our new National music.

My honourable conductor! please encourage me hereafter. Good by!

from your
TAIJIRO GOH

The Ideological Platform of the Russian Association of Proletarian Musicians

Music and the Classes

(This is the third and last formulation of the platform of the RAPM, adopted in 1929. The first formulation was published in the magazine *Musikalnaya Nov*, No. 12, 1924; the second in No. 1 of the magazine *Music and October* for 1926. The RAPM was dissolved by government decree 23 April 1932.)

Reflecting the general evolution of class society, the music of the past evolved along two main paths: on the one hand the music of the toilers, the exploited, and the oppressed classes (the so-called folk music), on the other hand the feudal bourgeois music, which comprises virtually the entire bulk of written "cultured" music.

The position of this or that class at a given historical moment determines the development of these two musical cultures.

The brilliant spread of the musical culture of the ruling classes was determined by its possession of the tools of material, technical culture in the domain of everyday life as in that of the special musical field (complicated musical instruments, special technique of their manufacture, special educational institutes, music printing, etc.).

On the contrary, the music of the oppressed and exploited classes, despite its deep musical significance, remains at a primitive stage as far as cultural, technical and material means are concerned.

The above conditions give the ruling classes the possibility of utilizing the creative forces of the exploited masses. At certain moments of history musicians of the ruling classes address themselves to the art of the oppressed classes and, taking their most valuable possession, nourish their own music entirely with the vitalizing juice of folk music.

The bourgeoisie of the period of well-developed capitalism exerts, as a ruling class, profound moral influence on all strata and classes of the population, systematically poisoning the worker's mind. This influence is shown in the ideology of a certain fraction of the working masses and in their everyday life, as a result of which we find tendencies of degeneration and disintegration in the artistic tastes of some of its members. In the field of music this degeneration follows on the one hand the line of urban romance, on the other that of religious petty bourgeois estheticism, and very recently, the erotic dance of the contemporary capitalist city (fox-trot, Charleston, jazz music, etc.).

Since the emergence of social differentiation and stratification in the country, similar tendencies may be noted in folk music; having undergone the influence mentioned above, it becomes contaminated with songs alien to its nature (all sorts of "patriotic," "religious" songs and also those mentioned above), and, inasmuch as it reflects the psychology of different social strata in the country (on the one hand that of toilers, workers, on the other hand that of the exploiting parasitical elements), it ceases to be uniform.

While defining the class nature of one or another musical composition, it is imperative to consider its ideological emotional content expressed by corresponding sonorous material.

Musical Culture of the Past

During the bourgeois revolution and its struggle with remnants of feudal society, the bourgeoisie appeared as the bearer of economic and cultural progress, and its ideologists, among them composers, expressed the aspirations of a great majority of the population. At that time the bounds of cultural intercourse among men were comparatively wide and the bourgeois artists reflected the views of this wide community. This could not but affect in a beneficial way the artistic output of the bourgeois artists, inasmuch as inspiration, enthusiasm, and creative power increase in the direct ratio to the number of recipients among the popular masses.

The creative production of composers reflecting active and heroic sentiments of the revolutionary bourgeoisie, compared to the rest of the musical legacy, appears nearest to the psychology and world outlook of the contemporary proletariat, inasmuch as it possesses a more realistic, a more objective attitude.

This musical legacy, representing the best in musical culture of the past, has also evolved the highest type of musical form. The creative production of Beethoven and Mussorgsky may be cited as specimens of this highly-developed culture.

Bourgeois music in its latest period (that of the entrance of capitalism into its highest stage, financial capitalism) has reflected the process of general decay and disintegration of bourgeois culture. During this period music begins to cultivate decadent moods, and engages in the following pursuits:

a. Cultivation of sensual and pathologically erotic moods emerging as a result of narrowing interests of a bourgeoisie degenerating morally and physically; cultivation of musical materials reflecting primitive psychology of the nations whose cultural evolution has stopped at early stages ("barbarism," specific "colonial" exotic music, etc.).

b. Mysticism, feeling of oppressiveness as a premonition on the part of the bourgeoisie of the impending social catastrophe and the end of bourgeois rule.

c. Reproduction in a musical work of the movement of the contemporary capitalist city with its milling humanity and industry. This naturalistic streak in contemporary music is a symptom of its decay and of the inner devastation of the bourgeoisie, the inadequacy of its ideological-emotional world to serve as a "means of communication among men" and inspiration for composers. Hence, the so-called "emotionalist" trends in music and, specifically, urbanist music that reduces itself to a more or less successful reproduction of noises.

d. Cultivation of primitive coarse subjects as a means, on the part of the bourgeoisie, to slow up the process of degeneration and to fight the proletariat that threatens "anarchy" for the bourgeoisie after the Revolution.

The decadent subject-matter of bourgeois music determines its form. Under the influence of decadent moods the inner meaning of music becomes diluted; technical elements gain ascendancy and music splits into factions according to its formal elements. In contemporary decadent bourgeois music the most characteristic elements are:

a. Hypertrophy of harmonic, vertical concepts, resulting in utter monotony and poverty of metrical, rhythmical design, which leads towards distortion of the musical phrase and loss of dynamic power, and disappearance of melos that causes the vocal crisis of bourgeois opera.

b. Hypertrophy of the polyphonic principle, accompanied by complete negation of the modal groundwork of music (so-called linear music).

c. The pursuance of alogical spasmodic rhythms.

d. The striving towards so-called absolute self-dependent "constructivistic" music, mechanistically built, and claiming to produce an emotional response of a predetermined nature. The school of composition inculcating this attitude (the so-called theory of "manufacture" of musical compositions) contributes to the complete disappearance of creative urge, replaced by dead mechanical schematicism.

During this last period the bourgeoisie, disguising its class interests under convenient slogans, makes claim to "objective," formal, technical "attainments," rejects the legacy of the classical past, and promotes "novelty," "contemporaneity" and "progress" in a narrow, formal, technical sense. These trends in contemporary bourgeois music, symptomatic of the psychological distress of the bourgeoisie, are a direct result of its decay and degeneration.

The Proletarian Revolution and the Contemporary Situation on the Musico-Ideological Front

A long chain of circumstances prevents the proletariat from mastering the fine arts, music and literature, and from producing their own protagonists in the arts, and specifically in music. These circumstances are:

First, the proletariat has begun the social revolution not waiting for the complete development of its culture within the framework of capitalistic society (despite the fact that the process of cultural development has started long before the acquisition of power by the proletariat, and that in certain fields proletarian culture has attained great heights).

Second, the social revolution of the proletariat has started in a land whose working class was at a very low cultural level.

Third, a great deal of creative power has been spent during a long civil war, and an industrial upbuilding accompanied by the greatest difficulties.

In view of this and many other circumstances the proletariat which exercises hegemony in social policy and general economy, does not exercise this hegemony in cultural pursuits, and, in particular, in the arts.

The absence, at this moment of the hegemony of the proletariat in the arts gives the opportunity to ideologists of intermediate and even openly inimical social strata to pursue their artistic aims along bourgeois lines and even influence the policies of proletarian institutions by foisting their ideology on them. The NEP 'New Economical Policy' and the numerous bureaucratic distortions of the Soviet State apparatus contribute to the process of this insidious penetration. Besides, a great majority of proletarian artistic groups, in contrast with the proletariat which openly proclaims the class character of its artistic organizations, strives to conceal this affiliation under the guise of societies "scientific," "interpretative," "creative" and such, while actually serving enemy ideology. In music, for instance, the reactionary character of the right wing of musical society and its connection with the bureaucratic circles of the old regime force this group to maintain secret solidarity without forming any open organizations.

Social organizations and trends existing in music reflect on the one hand the general class differentiation and the existence of social stratification among these classes, on the other hand the various peripeteia of class struggle, uniting and disuniting, as they do, the heterogeneous social formations.

At the present time there exist among musicians the following trends reflecting the ideology of fundamental social groups:

a. A group of musicians that has been formed under the influence of the bureaucratic circles of the old regime, sponsors of art and music. At the present time this group, in view of absence of all connection with living art in all fields, has completely degenerated into a dead and retrograde epigonism incapable of contributing anything vital to music. Members of this group have managed, however, to entrench themselves in several important educational institutions.

b. A comparatively significant force, represented by a so-called group of "contemporaries" that reflects the ideology of the one-time "vanguard" young Russian bourgeoisie and bourgeois intelligentsia and that defends the tenets of modern decadent bourgeois art. The vitality and significance of this group stand in undeniable connection with the presence in the economy of our land, along with a socialistic section, of a comparatively strong capitalist current productive of bourgeois ideology. In some measure the ideology of this group is sustained by the penetration into the U.S.S.R. of bourgeois influences from the capitalist countries.

c. In the course of the next few years there must be expected a rise of the intermediate strata and classes, the village and city intelligentsia. Being a motley conglomeration of heterogeneous phenomena, this grouping requires that we discriminate in passing judgment on them. Along with sincere and honest companion-of-the-road citizenry striving to understand the proletariat and reflect its world outlook in its creative production and musical activity, there exist here certain grossly adaptationist trends that do not go beyond outward exhibitionistic "revolutionariness," and are essentially alien or even inimical to the proletariat.

d. In the course of the last five years there has been considerable progress of proletarian art contributing to penetration of proletarian influence among the artistic intelligentsia. This proletarian group of musicians is potentially strong, thanks to its connection with a class now in the vanguard of history.

RAPM

The non-enforcement of hegemony of the proletariat in the divers ideological fields and specifically in the domain of art cannot, of course, continue for any considerable time. After the very first successes in the task of economic recuperation, the proletariat will assemble and solidify its cultural powers to repel the petty-bourgeois influences and heighten the cultural level of the masses, in which there is observable a huge growth of independent activity, not solely in the political and economical fields but also in general culture. Voluntary proletarian organizations have contributed to this growth in no small measure and are at the same time a determining factor in this growth. Such are, in the domain of the arts, the Associations of Proletarian Artists, organizations historically given to the proletariat as conscious expressions of the historical process.

The fundamental task of the Proletarian Artistic Associations is to establish the hegemony of the proletariat in various fields of the arts.

In the domain of music, such an organization is embodied in the Russian Association of Proletarian Musicians (RAPM) which unites musicians active in the proletarian advance-guards on the various sections of the front of class war, among them on the musico-ideological section.

The ultimate aim of the RAPM is extension of the hegemony of the proletariat to the music field. At present it sets the following concrete tasks:

a. Extension of the proletarian Communist influence to the musical masses, re-education and reorganization of these masses in order to direct their work and creative talents towards Socialist upbuilding.

b. Creation of Marxist musicology and Marxist musical criticism, critical absorption of the musical culture of the past and of contemporary musical literature from the viewpoint of the proletariat.

c. Demonstration of proletarian musical creative productions and creation of necessary conditions for complete development and growth of proletarian music.

Toward the accomplishment of these tasks the RAPM

a. poses at its open meetings the most urgent problems in the domain of creative work, Marxist musicology, mass action and pedagogical musical work;

b. expounds, through the medium of the Soviet professional and party press, and also the organs of the RAPM, its fundamental ideas, heightens the social, scientific-musical and artistic level of the musical masses, analyzes and gives a musico-sociological evaluation of musical literature, pointing out the path of new musical work in city and country;

c. while helping the working and peasant masses to create their own music, organizes musical education of these masses for which purpose it encourages proletarianization of music schools and formation of music-teaching cadres in the conservatories, and also discusses in special conferences, problems of method in musical work among the masses and the individual circles in workers' clubs;

d. poses and discusses the problems of formation of new interpretative ways and begins the work of sanitation of our concert masses, organizing its own exemplary choral and orchestral collectives, and also groups of individual performers.

In its interrelations with various groupings of musicians, the RAPM is guided by the general policy of the proletariat and the party in relation toward various social categories. Neither the circumstance that the working class has already acquired power, nor the special character of musical problems deters the proletariat from fighting against ideological influences opposed to the proletariat on the musical front. As to the intermediate, the so-called companion-of-the-road groupings, the RAPM deems it necessary and useful to attract these groups unquestioningly into creative, scientific and educational work in the domain of music and to utilize them in practical work.

"While weeding out the antiproletarian and the counter-revolutionary elements and fighting the ideology of the new bourgeoisie among some of the companions-of-the-road, it is imperative to exercise tolerance towards the intermediate ideological forms, patiently helping them to form comradely relationship with the cultural powers of Communism." (From the resolution of the Central Committee of the All-Russian Communist party on the party policy in literature.)

In their creative work, composers, members of the Association of Proletarian Musicians, strive above all to reflect the rich, full-blooded psychology of the proletariat, as historically the most advanced, and dialectically the most sensitive and understanding class.

Following the dialectical and not the mechanistic laws of evolution, composers, members of the RAPM, strive to create gradually new musical forms and a new style born of its artistic subject matter.

The interrelation of content and form is regarded by the RAPM as a dialectical unity.

Thus, while not accepting any form of contemporary bourgeois music that in its content is opposed to the proletariat, the RAPM proclaims the slogan of learning the craft first of all from those among composers of the past who reflected in their creative output the subject matter close to the revolutionary ideas of the proletariat.

New musical forms are created and will be created by the proletariat. Proletarian music must "penetrate into the innermost masses of workmen and peasants, unite the thought and the will of these masses and raise them" for further struggle and construction, organizing their class consciousness in the direction of the ultimate victory of the proletariat as builder of Communist society.

(Translated from the Russian by Nicolas Slonimsky)

Resolution of the Union of Soviet Composers Condemning Anti-Soviet Activities

The composers of Moscow, musical activists and members of the Union of Soviet Composers, assembled at a session on the occasion of the trial of the anti-Soviet Trotskyist Center, express their profound indignation at the criminal activity of the Trotskyists, the vilest column of the world Fascist counter-revolution. Inveterate sworn enemies of socialism, dastardly enemies of the working class and its great Party of Lenin and Stalin, attempted to take away from us the achievements of the proletarian revolution, restore capitalism, and impose upon the country the Fascist yoke.

The enemies miscalculated again. In the land of victorious socialism, they failed to find support for their heinous designs, and, having sunk to the lowest level of degradation, became a direct agency of German and Japanese Fascism.

The murder of the best sons of the working class, espionage and diversion, sabotage of the defensive power of the Soviet Union, auctioning off piecemeal the great Soviet fatherland—there is no infamy of which these monstrous Trotskyist outcasts are not capable of perpetrating. There is no room on earth for this vile band!

Soviet composers join their voices to the unanimous demand of the Soviet people—to shoot down every one of these traitors who attempted to destroy our happy life. We are convinced that Soviet justice will expose all the criminal nests of the Trotskyists and their accomplices from the Bukharinovite camp, and will cleanse our Fatherland of this scum of Fascism.

Resolution

United by the great idea of socialism, its ranks closed around the Communist Party and our beloved leader and friend, Comrade Stalin, the Soviet people, having crushed the Fascist beast, strengthening and fortifying revolutionary vigilance, will continue its heroic struggle for the happy future of human kind.

(Published in *Sovietskaya Musica*, Moscow, January 1937)

Soviet Musical Policy, 1948

Resolution of the Central Committee of the All-Union Communist Party (Bolsheviks) of 10 February 1948

The Central Committee of the All-Union Communist Party (Bolsheviks) considers that the opera *Great Friendship* (music by Muradeli, libretto by Mdivani), produced by the Bolshoi Theater of the Union of Soviet Socialist Republics on the Thirtieth Anniversary of the October Revolution, is a defective anti-artistic work, in its music and its libretto.

The basic defects of the opera are rooted, first of all, in the music. The music of the opera is inexpressive and weak. It has not a single memorable melody or aria. It is confused and discordant; it is built on continuous dissonances, and ear-splitting combinations of sounds. Occasional lines and scenes, making a pretense of melodiousness, are suddenly interrupted by discordant noises, alien to a normal human ear, which produce a depressing effect on the listener. There is no organic connection between the music and the stage action. The vocal part of the opera, choruses, solos, and ensembles, make a distressing impression. As a result, the resources of the orchestra and the singers remain unused.

The composer did not take advantage of the richness of folk melodies, songs, refrains and dance airs, so abundant in the art of the nations of the USSR, and especially in the art of the nations of North Caucasus, where the action represented in the opera takes place.

In the pursuit of false "originality" in his music, the composer Muradeli ignored the best traditions of classical opera in general, and particularly of Russian classical opera distinguished by inner substantiality, melodic richness, breadth of range, national spirit, and elegant, attractive and clear musical form, the qualities which made Russian operas the best in the world, an art beloved by and accessible to broad strata of the people.

The libretto of the opera is historically false and artificial; it pretends to represent the struggle for the establishment of Soviet power and amity of nations in North Caucasus in 1918–1920. In this opera the wrong impression is created that such Caucasian nations as the Georgians and Osetins were at that time inimical to the Russian people, which is historically false inasmuch as the obstacle blocking the establishment of the friendship of nations during that period in North Caucasus were the Ingushs and Chechens.

The Central Committee of the All-Union Communist Party (Bolsheviks) considers that the fiasco of Muradeli's opera is the result of the fallacious, and, for the art of a Soviet composer, fatal formalistic path taken by Comrade Muradeli.

As was demonstrated at the conference of Soviet musicians, held in the Central Committee of the All-Union Communist Party (Bolsheviks), the fiasco of Muradeli's opera is not an isolated case, but is closely connected with a precarious condition of contemporary Soviet music and with the spread among Soviet musicians of formalistic tendencies.

As far back as 1936, in connection with the appearance of the opera by D. Shostakovich, *Lady Macbeth of the District of Mzensk*, *Pravda*, the organ of the Central Committee of the All-Union Communist Party (Bolsheviks), subjected to sharp criticism the anti-national formalistic distortions in the music of Shostakovich, and exposed the harm and danger of this trend for the destinies of the development of Soviet music. *Pravda*, acting upon the instructions of the Central Committee of the All-Union Communist Party (Bolsheviks), clearly formulated the demands presented by the Soviet people to their composers.

Despite these warnings, and despite the directives given by the Central Committee of the All-Union Communist Party (Bolsheviks) in its resolutions regarding the magazines *Zvezda* and *Leningrad,* the cinema film *Great Life,* and measures for improvement of the repertoire of dramatic theaters, no reorientation of any kind was made in Soviet music. Occasional successes of some Soviet composers in the field of song writing that received recognition and attained wide popularity in our country, in film music, etc., do not alter the general picture of the situation. Particularly bad are the conditions in symphonic and operatic production, with reference to composers who adhere to the formalistic anti-national movement. This movement has found its fullest expression in the works of composers such as Comrades Shostakovich, Prokofiev, Khachaturian, Shebalin, Popov, Miaskovsky, and others, in whose music formalistic distortions, and anti-democratic tendencies which are alien to the Soviet people and its artistic tastes, are represented with particular obviousness. The characteristic features of this music are the negation of basic principles of classical music; the preachment of atonality, dissonances and disharmony, supposedly representative of "progress" and "modernism" in the development of musical forms; the rejection of such all-important concepts of musical composition as melody, and the infatuation with the confused, neuropathological combinations which transform music into cacophony, into a chaotic agglomeration of sounds. This music is strongly reminiscent of the spirit of contemporary modernistic bourgeois music of Europe and America, reflecting the dissolution of bourgeois culture, a complete negation of musical art, its impasse.

An essential trait of the formalistic movement is also the rejection of polyphonic music and polyphonic singing, based on simultaneous combination and development of a series of independent melodic lines, and the cultivation of a monotonous type of unison music and song, often without words, in violation of the system of many-voiced singing harmony peculiar to our people, all of which leads to impoverishment and decline of music.

Trampling upon the best traditions of Russian and western classical music, rejecting these traditions as supposedly "obsolete," "old-fashioned," and "conservative"; haughtily snubbing those composers who are conscientiously trying to absorb and develop the concepts of classical music as adherents of "primitive traditionalism" and "epigonism," many Soviet composers, in their pursuit after a false conception of novelty, have in their music torn themselves away from the ideals and artistic tastes of the Soviet people, have cloistered themselves in a narrow circle of specialists and musical epicures, have debased the lofty social role of music and narrowed its significance, limiting it to the gratification of the perverted tastes of esthetizing egocentrics.

The formalistic movement in Soviet music has engendered among some Soviet composers a one-sided cultivation of complex forms of instrumental wordless symphonic music, and a supercilious attitude towards such musical genres as opera, choral music, popular music for small orchestras, national instruments, vocal ensembles, etc.

All this inevitably leads to a loss of fundamentals of vocal culture and dramatic mastery, so that the composers forget how to write for the people, as evidenced by the fact that no Soviet operas comparable to Russian classical operas have been produced in recent years.

The break between some Soviet musicians and the people has led to the formulation of the corrupt "theory" that the people fail to understand the music of many contemporary Soviet composers because they have not "grown up" enough to appreciate their intricate compositions; that they will understand it a few centuries hence, and that one should not be embarrassed if some musical works do not find an audience. This thoroughly individualistic and radically anti-national theory has contributed even more to the segregation of some composers and musicologists from the people, from the criticism of Soviet society, and has driven them into their shells.

The cultivation of all these and similar views causes the greatest harm to Soviet musical art. A tolerant attitude towards these views means the spread among those active in Soviet musical culture of tendencies alien to it, leading to an impasse in musical development, to the liquidation of musical art.

The fallacious, anti-national, formalistic tendency in Soviet music exerts a pernicious influence on the preparatory study and education of young composers in our conservatories, especially in the Moscow Conservatory (Director Comrade Shebalin) where the formalistic tendency is predominant. Students are not inculcated in respect for the best traditions of Russian and western classical music; they are not brought up to love national art and democratic musical forms. The creative output of many students of our conservatories consists in blind imitation of the music of Shostakovich, Prokofiev, and others.

The Central Committee of the All-Union Communist Party (Bolsheviks) finds an altogether intolerable situation in Soviet music criticism. The leading posts among critics are occupied by opponents of Russian realistic music and adherents of decadent formalistic music. Every new work by Prokofiev, Shostakovich, Miaskovsky, Shebalin, is acclaimed by these critics as "a new victory of Soviet music" and they glorify in this music its subjectivism, constructivism, extreme individualism, and technical complications of the idiom, i.e., exactly that which should be subjected to criticism. Instead of combating the harmful views and theories alien to the principles of socialist realism, music critics promote them, hailing the composers who share these false artistic concepts as the advance guard in art.

Musical criticism has ceased to express the opinion of Soviet society, the opinion of the nation, and has become a mouthpiece of individual composers. Some music critics, instead of writing objective criticisms, have begun, because of personal friendship, to fawn upon this or that musical leader, glorifying their works in every conceivable way.

All this means that a section of Soviet composers has not yet outlived the vestiges of bourgeois ideology, nourished by the influence of contemporary decadent western European and American music.

The Central Committee of the All-Union Communist Party (Bolsheviks) considers that this unfavorable situation on the front of Soviet music has resulted from the incorrect line in Soviet music, pursued by the Committee of the Fine Arts attached to the Council of Ministers of the USSR, and the Organizational Committee of the Union of Soviet Composers.

The Committee of the Fine Arts of the Council of Ministers of the USSR (Comrade Khrapchenko) and the Organizational Committee of the Union of Soviet Composers (Comrade Khachaturian) have failed to propagandize realistic concepts in Soviet music, the basis of which is the recognition of the tremendous progressive role of classical heritage, and especially of traditions of the Russian musical school, the utilization of this heritage and promotion of its further development, combining high ideational values with the artistic perfection of musical form, the genuineness and realism of music, its profound organic connection with the people, and with the people's musical and vocal art; a high professional mastery, and at the same time simplicity and accessibility of musical works—instead of all this, they have actually encouraged the formalistic movement alien to the Soviet people.

The Organizational Committee of the Union of Soviet Composers has become the tool of a group of composer-formalists, the hotbed of formalistic distortions. The Organizational Committee has created a suffocating atmosphere in which creative discussions are absent. The leaders of the Organizational Committee, and the musicologists grouped around them, heap praise upon anti-realistic, modernistic products undeserving of support, whereas works distinguished by their realistic character and by an effort to continue and to develop the classical heritage, are declared of secondary importance, remain unnoticed and are ignored. Composers who flaunt their "advanced" and "arch-revolutionary" ideas in music act in the Organizational Committee as proponents of the most backward and provincial conservatism, revealing a supercilious intolerance towards the slightest manifestations of criticism.

The Central Committee of the All-Union Communist Party (Bolsheviks) considers that the atmosphere, and the attitude towards the problems of Soviet music, created in the Committee of the Fine Arts at the Council of Ministers of the USSR and in the Organizational Committee of the Union of Soviet Composers, cannot be tolerated any longer, for they inflict the greatest harm upon the development of Soviet music. In recent years the cultural demands and the standard of artistic taste of the Soviet people have grown to an extraordinary degree. The Soviet people expect from their composers products of high quality in all forms, in opera, in symphonic music, in vocal art, in choral and dance music. In our country, composers are given unlimited opportunities, and all necessary conditions have been created for a genuine flowering of musical culture. Soviet composers have a listening audience such as no composer ever knew in the past. It would be unforgivable not to take advantage of all these richest potentialities, and not to direct one's creative efforts along the correct realistic path.

The Central Committee of the All-Union Communist Party (Bolsheviks) resolves:

(1) To condemn the formalistic movement in Soviet music as anti-national and leading to liquidation of music.

(2) To urge the Department of Propaganda and Agitation of the Central Committee and the Committee of the Fine Arts to correct the situation in Soviet music, to liquidate the defects pointed out in the present Resolution of the Central Committee, and to secure the development of Soviet music in the realistic direction.

(3) To call upon Soviet composers to realize fully the lofty requirements of the Soviet people upon musical art; to sweep from their path all that weakens our music and hinders its development, and assure an upsurge of creative work that will advance Soviet musical culture so as to lead to the creation in all fields of music of high-quality works worthy of the Soviet people.

(4) To approve organizational measures of the corresponding Party and Soviet organs, designed to improve the state of musical affairs.

Discussion at a General Assembly of Soviet Composers, Moscow, 17–26 February 1948

Speech of A. A. Zhdanov

Comrades, the Central Committee of the All-Union Communist Party (Bolsheviks) has decided to assemble a conference of Soviet musicians for the following reasons.

Recently the Central Committee took part in the social preview of the new opera by Comrade Muradeli, *Great Friendship*. You can well imagine with what attention and interest the Central Committee anticipated the very fact of the appearance of a new Soviet opera. Unfortunately, the hopes of the Central Committee were not justified. The opera *Great Friendship* turned out to be a failure.

What were, in the opinion of the Central Committee, the reasons, and what were the circumstances which led to the bankruptcy of this opera? What are the basic defects of this opera?

Speaking of the basic defects of the opera, one must first of all mention its music. In the music of this opera there is not a single memorable melody. The music does not reach the listener. It is not by accident that a rather considerable and sufficiently qualified audience, consisting of no fewer than five hundred people, did not respond during the performance to any part of the opera.

The music of the opera turned out to be very poor. The substitution of inharmonious and at the same time noisy improvisations for melody transformed the opera into a chaotic assortment of screeching sounds. The resources of the orchestra in the opera are utilized to a very limited extent. Throughout a major portion of the opera, the musical accompaniment consists of but a few instruments, and only once in a while, sometimes in the most unexpected places, the whole orchestral ensemble enters in stormy, discordant, and often cacophonic interventions, getting on the nerves of the listener and violently perturbing his mood. This disharmony, this lack of correspondence between the music and the actions, moods, and events, represented on the stage in the course of the opera, produces a depressing effect. A drum intrudes on the most lyrical moments of intimate sentiments; on the other hand, in the scenes of fighting and excitement, when the action on the stage portrays heroic events, the music for some reason becomes soft and lyrical. This creates a break between the musical accompaniment and the moods which the artists are supposed to reflect on the stage.

Despite the fact that the opera treats a very interesting period, the epoch of the establishment of Soviet power in North Caucasus, with all the complexity of its multinational society, and the diversity of forms of class struggle, demanding an adequate picture of the eventful life of the nations of North Caucasus, the music of the opera is alien to the national art of the peoples of North Caucasus.

When Cossacks are on the stage (and they play an important role in the opera), their appearance is not signalized in the music or in the singing by anything characteristic of the Cossacks, of their songs and their music. The same is true in regard to the people of the mountains. If the action includes the dancing of a Lezghinka, its melody does not remind us of any popular rhythms of the Lezghinka. In his pursuit of originality, the composer introduces his own music for the Lezghinka, an unimpressive, tedious music, which is much poorer, much less attractive than the traditional popular music of the Lezghinka.

The pretense of originality permeates the entire score of the opera. The music produces, I should say, a stultifying impression on the listener. Some stanzas and scenes of a lyrical or semi-melodious nature, or those that pretend to be melodious, are suddenly interrupted by noise and shrieking in fortissimo, reminding us of the noise on a building lot, at the moment when excavators, stone crushers and cement mixers go into action. These noises, alien to the normal human ear, demoralize the listener.

A few words regarding the vocal part of the opera: choral, solo, and ensemble singing. Here, too, one must mention the poverty of the entire vocal line of the opera. They say that this opera has complex singing melodies. We do not find it so. The vocal part of the opera is poor, and cannot stand a critical comparison with that wealth of melody and breadth of range to which we are accustomed in the classical operas. In this opera the largest orchestral capacities of the Bolshoi Theater and the magnificent vocal abilities of its singers are left unused. This is a great error. It isn't right to bury the talents of the singers of the Bolshoi Theater, giving them the range of half an octave, or two thirds of an octave, when they can sing two octaves. One should not impoverish art, and this opera represents the impoverishment, the drying-up of art, musical as well as vocal art.

The Committee of the Fine Arts, and particularly its chairman Comrade Khrapchenko, holds the chief responsibility for this affair. He widely publicized the opera *Great Friendship*. More than that, even before the opera was reviewed and approved by listeners, it was announced for production in a number of cities, in Sverdlovsk, Riga, and Leningrad. In the Moscow Bolshoi Theater alone, according to the Committee's statement, six hundred thousand rubles were spent on its production.

This means that the Committee of the Fine Arts, having passed a bad opera for a good one, not only proved itself incompetent in the task of leadership in art, but demonstrated its irresponsibility in having induced the state to expend large sums of money without justification.

If the Central Committee of the All-Union Communist Party (Bolsheviks) is not correct in defending the realistic direction and classical heritage in music, let it be said openly. It may be that the old musical norms have outlived their time; perhaps they should be rejected and be replaced by a new, more progressive direction. One must declare it openly, without hiding in the corner, and without smuggling anti-democratic formalism in music as contraband under the slogan of supposed devotion to the classics, and loyalty to the ideals of socialist realism. It is bad, it is not quite honest. One must be frank and declare outright whatever Soviet musicians have to say on this question. It would be dangerous, and downright fatal for the interest of the development of Soviet art, if the repudiation of the cultural heritage of the past, and the adoption of degraded music, were cloaked in a toga of supposedly genuine Soviet music. Here we must call things by their true names.

Declaration of Tikhon Khrennikov

The Central Committee of our Party in its Resolution of 10 February 1948 severely branded the anti-democratic formalistic tendencies in Soviet music. The immediate reason for the intervention of the supreme Party organs into musical affairs was the new opera *Great Friendship* by Muradeli, staged by the Bolshoi Theater of the USSR in the days of the thirtieth anniversary of the October Revolution.

It was established that repeated directives of the Party on the problems of art were not carried out by the majority of Soviet composers. All the conversations about "reconstruction," about switching of composers to folkways, to realism, remained empty declarations. Almost all composers who worked in the field of large forms kept aloof from the people, and did not enjoy popularity with the broad audiences. The people knew only songs, marches and film music, but remained indifferent towards most symphonic and chamber music. Concerts in which Soviet symphonic novelties were performed were attended very poorly, whereas classical programs almost invariably filled the hall. Soviet people, in their letters to concert organizations and to the Radio Committee, often voiced their perplexity and at times their protests against the incomprehensible and complicated music of a number of Soviet composers.

The leading figures of our Party and the Central Committee of the All-Union Communist Party (Bolsheviks) have frequently expressed themselves on the subject of Soviet art, directing its development along the path of Socialist realism, and cleansing it of harmful influences and alien ideology. Let us recall the words of V. I. Lenin on the tasks of Soviet art, his appeals in favor of a folk direction in art, his defense of Russian classical heritage against the assaults of the Association of Proletarian Culture; let us further recall the conferences of the Committee for Agitation and Propaganda at the Central Committee of the All-Union Communist Party (Bolsheviks) on the problem of music, held in 1925 and 1929 at the peak of the activity of the Association for Contemporary Music; the Resolution of the Central Committee of the All-Union Communist Party (Bolsheviks) of 23 April 1932 regarding the reorientation of literary and artistic organizations; the articles in the newspaper *Pravda*, "Confusion Instead of Music," and "Ballet Falsification" in 1936; the resolutions of the Central Committee of the All-Union Communist Party in 1946 concerning the periodicals *Zvezda* and *Leningrad*, the film *Great Life*, and the repertory of the drama theaters. We cannot fail to mention the utterances of Comrade Zhdanov at the philosophical discussions of June 1947, and particularly the principal thesis of his declaration: the thesis of the intransigent struggle for the purity of Soviet ideology as the most advanced and the most progressive in the world.

Among the directives of the Central Committee of the All-Union Communist Party (Bolsheviks) dealing with art, the Resolution on Muradeli's opera *Great Friendship* is particularly important for the destinies of Soviet music. This Resolution deals a decisive blow to the anti-democratic formalist movement which has spread in Soviet music. It administers a crushing blow to modernist art as a whole. At the same time this Resolution directs Soviet music onto the Path of realism leading to the development and integration of the best traditions of musical classicism and musical art of the nations of the USSR, the path of truly democratic art, the creation of which the Soviet people expects from its composers.

The Central Committee of the All-Union Communist Party (Bolsheviks) points out in its Resolution that formalistic distortions and anti-democratic tendencies have found their fullest expression in the works of such composers as Shostakovich, Prokofiev, Khachaturian, Popov, Miaskovsky, Shebalin, and others. In the music of these composers we witness a revival of anti-realistic decadent influences calculated to destroy the principles of classical music. These tendencies are peculiar to the bourgeois movement of the era of imperialism: the rejection of melodiousness in music, neglect of vocal forms, infatuation with rhythmic and orchestral effects, the piling-up of noisy ear-splitting harmonies, intentional illogicality and unemotionality of music. All these tendencies lead in actual fact to the liquidation of music as one of the strongest expressions of human feelings and thoughts.

In Soviet music, particularly during the last three or four years, there has been increasingly noticeable a break between the listener and musical art. Indicative in this respect is the fiasco with the public of the majority of works written by Soviet composers in recent years: Muradeli's opera *Great Friendship*; Prokofiev's *Festive Poem*, his cantata *Blossom Forth the Mighty Land* and the *Sixth Symphony*; Miaskovsky's *Pathetic Overture* and the cantata *Kremlin at Night*; Shostakovich's *Poem of Fatherland*; Khachaturian's *Symphonie-Poème*, and others.

In the music of the majority of Soviet composers there is noted an over-emphasis on purely abstract instrumental forms, not characteristic of the classical Russian movement in music, and a lack of interest in program music on concrete subjects of Soviet life. Exaggerated attention is given to chamber music written for a handful of connoisseurs, while ignoring such mass consumption forms as the opera.

The composers became engrossed in formalistic experimentation with artificially inflated and impracticable orchestral combinations (such as the inclusion of twenty-four trumpets in Khachaturian's *Symphonie-Poème*, or the incredible scoring for sixteen double-basses, eight harps, four pianos, to the exclusion of the rest of the string instruments, in Prokofiev's *Ode on the End of War*). Such music could not be performed by any of the provincial orchestras; and the gala performances in the Moscow Philharmonic evoked nothing but bewilderment among the listeners by the irrational use of orchestral sonorities, at times actually causing physical suffering. Musical instruments were not used in their natural medium. Thus, the piano was converted into a percussion instrument (as in the fist blows on the keyboard in Prokofiev's *Sixth Sonata*); the violin was transformed from a songful, tender instrument into a grunting, percussive one. The clarity and logic of harmonic progressions were sacrified in favor of intentional complexity of acoustical combinations; natural chords were turned into "timbre-sounds," into blots and inkspots of sound.

A peculiar writing in code, abstractness of the musical language, often reflected images and emotions alien to Soviet realistic art—expressionistic tenseness, neuroticism, escape into a region of abnormal, repulsive, and pathological phenomena. This defect is noticeable in many pages of Shostakovich's *Eighth* and *Ninth Symphonies,* and the *Piano Sonatas* of Prokofiev. One of the means of escape from reality was also the "neo-classical" tendency in the music of Shostakovich and his imitators, the resurrection of melodic turns and mannerisms of Bach, Handel, Haydn, and other composers, which were reproduced in a decadently distorted manner.

The musical art of the people and, above all, Russian folk songs were not favored by the aforementioned composers. When occasionally they turned toward folk melodies they arranged them in an overcomplex decadent manner alien to folk art (as in Popov's *Third Symphony on Spanish Themes*, and in some arrangements of Russian folk songs by Prokofiev).

All these creative faults are typical expressions of formalism.

Formalism is a revelation of emptiness and lack of ideas in art. The rejection of ideas in art leads to the preachment of "art for art's sake," to a cult of "pure" form, a cult of technical devices as a goal in itself, a hypertrophy of certain elements of the musical speech at the price of a loss of integrity and harmoniousness of art.

The Resolution of the Central Committee of the All-Union Communist Party (Bolsheviks) indicates that one of the traits of formalist music is the rejection of singing polyphony and a retreat towards a cerebral, dry, artificial counterpoint in the so-called linear style, or else the adoption of primitive unison writing.

The cultivation of form as a goal in art leads in the end to the disintegration of form itself and to the loss of high-quality professional mastery.

As Comrade Zhdanov has profoundly pointed out, the philosophical background of these views is subjective idealism. The artist imagines himself to be the appraiser and final judge of his art. He cares little about the listening human society. Personal caprice, a random whim, an extreme inconsiderateness, and the subjectivism of the isolated author are sharply contrasted with the requirements and expectations of his environment: "This is the way I feel, and I don't care what my listeners think about it."

Comrade Zhdanov has said in this connection that if an artist does not expect to be understood by his contemporaries, it leads to desolation, to an impasse. If a true artist,

says Comrade Zhdanov, finds that his work is not understood by the listeners, he must figure out first of all why he failed to please the people, why the people cannot understand him.

The theory and practice of formalism is a complete negation of democratic aspirations of the Russian classical composers and of the progressive representatives of music criticism. Great musicians of the past addressed their art to a contemporary audience, to their people, and not to their remote descendants.

Soviet composers of the formalistic persuasion ignored these progressive traditions of Russian classicism. It is not by accident that Comrade Zhdanov said to the composers-formalists present at the conference in the Central Committee: "One must admit that the landlord Glinka, the government clerk Serov and the member of nobility Stasov were more democratic than you are."

The anti-democratic formalistic direction of Soviet music is closely connected with the bourgeois decadent music of the contemporary West and the modernistic music of pre-revolutionary Russia.

The present musical art of western Europe and America reflects the universal dissolution and spiritual impoverishment of bourgeois culture. One cannot name a single composer of the West who is not infected with formalistic diseases, subjectivism and mysticism, and lack of ideological principles. The apostle of reactionary forces in bourgeois music, Igor Stravinsky, with equal impartiality writes a Catholic Mass in a stylized decadent style, or jazz pieces for the circus. The latest musical "genius" of contemporary France, Olivier Messiaen, writes mystical music on subjects from the Bible and medieval Catholic works. Contemporary operas of the German composers Hindemith, Krenek, Alban Berg, the Englishman Britten, the American Menotti, are a conglomeration of wild harmonies, far removed from natural human song. In this music there is frankly proclaimed a reversion to the primitive savage cultures of prehistoric society; eroticism is glorified along with psychopathology, sexual perversion, amorality and the shamelessness of the contemporary bourgeois heroes of the twentieth century.

In the well-known opera by Krenek, *Sprung über den Schatten,* nearly all the characters are absolutely amoral individuals. In that opera there is even a special chorus of sexual psychopaths-masochists. In the opera by the German composer Max Brand, *Machinist Hopkins,* the principal characters are murderers and erotomaniacs. Machinist Hopkins himself is a vile fascist caricature of a leader in a workers' movement, and is represented as a lustful beast, a base exploiter of women.

In Hindemith's *Sancta Susanna* religious erotomania is portrayed with repulsive naturalism. Similar pathology characterizes the neurotic operas of Alban Berg, and, among recent operas, *The Medium* by Gian-Carlo Menotti which enjoys tremendous success with the bourgeois public in America. The central character of this opera is a professional swindler, a woman spiritualist who suffers from alcoholism, and in addition is a murderess.

In Russian music formalistic ideas flourished particularly during the reaction after the Revolution of 1905. Among characteristic examples of decadent art in music are Stravinsky's *Le Sacre du Printemps,* Prokofiev's *Buffoon,* and a number of other works by these composers. The man who inspired and commissioned the majority of these works was Serge Diaghilev, one of the most prominent ideologists of Russian modernism.

Diaghilev was the organizer of a modernistic group of artists, known as "The World of Art." He urged artists and musicians to sever connections with the great realistic traditions of Russian art: "Down with the traditions of the Mighty

Five, of Tchaikovsky. They are obsolete and limited national phenomena; it is time to merge Russian art in a common European culture"—such was the frank and cynical slogan of Diaghilev and other representatives of the modernistic camp.

The modernist element in Russian music is the revelation of frank sycophancy before the Western music market, a desire to gain favor with the foreign audience, to titillate the nerves of the surfeited bourgeois listener-snob with exotic Russian "Asianism."

For Diaghilev's ballet in Paris, Stravinsky wrote *Petrouchka*, *Le Sacre du Printemps*, *Les Noces*, the opera *Le Rossignol*, and Prokofiev wrote his ballet *The Buffoon*, and other works.

The principal goal of the composers of these works is to escape from the contemporary world of humanity into the world of abstraction. Stravinsky himself, in his article, "What I Wished to Express in *Le Sacre du Printemps*" (*Music*, monthly magazine, 1913), writes: "I evoke neither human joy nor human sadness; I move towards a greater abstraction." His reversion to the images of "primordial earth" he explains by a desire to reflect "that fear which lives in every sensitive soul in contact with mysterious forces." This reversion to antediluvian barbaric images, the depiction of savagery and bestial instincts of a prehistoric man, of a Scythian, is found in some poems of the Russian writers of the bourgeois-modernistic type. In these poems, there is sounded an alarm before the "coming Ham," the plebeian who must come and destroy the beauty and the well-being of the bourgeois regime. In *Le Sacre du Printemps* Stravinsky expressed these moods in boisterous, chaotic, intentionally coarse, screaming sonorities. "Rhythm and motion, not the element of feeling, are the foundations of musical art," asserted Stravinsky. With Diaghilev's blessings Stravinsky uses, in *Petrouchka* and *Les Noces*, some elements of Russian life to mock at Russian customs and to please the European spectator by the express emphasis on Russian "Asianism," crudity, animal instincts, sexual motives. Ancient folk strains are here grotesquely distorted, twisted, and are served as if reflected in a crooked mirror. These so-called "irony and grotesque" are in evidence also in Prokofiev's ballet *The Buffoon*, in which the "exoticism" of old Russian folkways is relished in a decadent manner. The musical language of this work is related to the above-named ballets of Stravinsky. The continuation of the same line of "Russian grotesque" is seen in Stravinsky's comic opera "after Pushkin," *Mavra*, written in 1922. From this opera there is a direct line to the two defective operas by Shostakovich, *The Nose* and *Lady Macbeth*.

Paralleling this line Stravinsky and other new composers of the West, such as Hindemith in Germany, launched in the 1920s a "new" slogan (actually it is closely connected with the first line): "Back to Bach!" This meant that in a number of works there were revived polyphonic devices mechanically transplanted from Bach. They were ornamented by "new" harmonies, transforming the whole thing into cacophony. This reversion to Bach led to the composition by Stravinsky of the so-called *Symphony of Psalms*, in which there are stridently combined the old Bachian devices of polyphonic writing with the ear-splitting "contemporary" harmonies. The meaning of this mixture is well expressed in the composer's dedication of this Symphony: "Dedicated to the Almighty Lord and to the American Philharmonic Society."*

The music of Soviet composers of the 1920s and 1930s offers numerous instances of formalistic tendencies in Soviet music: Shostakovich: the opera *The Nose*, *Second Symphony*,

Third Symphony; Prokofiev: the ballet *The Prodigal Son*, *On the Boristhenes*, *Pas d'acier*, the opera *The Flaming Angel*, *Third Symphony*, *Fourth Symphony*, *Fifth Piano Concerto*, *Fifth Piano Sonata*; Mossolov: *Iron Foundry*, *Newspaper Advertisements*; Knipper: the opera *North Wind*, *Tales of a Porcelain Buddha*; Deshevov: the opera *Ice and Steel*; Miaskovsky: *Tenth Symphony*, *Thirteenth Symphony*, *Third Piano Sonata*, *Fourth Piano Sonata*; Feinberg: *Piano Sonatas*, *First Piano Concerto*; Shebalin: *Lenin Symphony*, *Second Symphony*; Popov: *First Symphony*; Liatoshinsky: *Second Symphony*; Boelza: *First Symphony*, *Second Symphony*, songs; Polovinkin: *Telescopes* for orchestra, *Accidents* for piano; Litinsky: Quartets and Sonatas; Shcherbachev: *Third Symphony*, etc.

The formalistic element in music is particularly strong in the *Eighth Symphony*, the *Ninth Symphony*, and the *Second Piano Sonata* by Shostakovich; in the *Sixth Symphony*, the opera *War and Peace*, and a number of piano works by Prokofiev; in *Symphonie-Poème* by Khachaturian; in the Quartet and String Trio by Shebalin; and in the *Third Symphony* by Popov. In Miaskovsky's music we find a one-sided preoccupation with instrumental music and a lack of interest for vocal and operatic music, which had a detrimental effect on the melodic idiom of his instrumental compositions, particularly the *Third Piano Sonata* and the *Fourth Piano Sonata*, written in the 1920s, but newly revised by the composer in recent years.

The influence of formalism is strongly felt in the creative work of young composers. The imitation of negative traits of the music by Shostakovich and Prokofiev, the infatuation with decadent thematics, exoticism and mysticism became almost a routine phenomenon in the creative output of the young generation of Soviet composers.

Formalistic distortions are also strongly reflected in the education of young composers in conservatories, particularly in the Moscow Conservatory. This is obviously connected with the fact that some composers mentioned in the Resolution of the Central Committee of the All-Union Communist Party (Bolsheviks) as representative of the formalistic movement (Shostakovich, Shebalin and Miaskovsky) are professors of the Moscow Conservatory, and Shebalin is its director.

The almost total contamination of young composers with the harmful influence of western music, the imitation of negative qualities of Soviet composers belonging to the formalist school, neglect of the traditions of musical classicism, particularly Russian classicism, and of the art of the nations of the USSR, testifies to the fact that the formalist movement plays a decisive role in the education of the young cadres of composers.

The Central Committee of the All-Union Communist Party (Bolsheviks) notes an altogether intolerable condition of Soviet music criticism. Our critics have lost the most important quality of Russian progressive criticism. They have ceased to fight for the high aspirations of art, for the ideals of realistic and democratic art.

The orientation towards Stravinsky as the most progressive phenomenon in contemporary music is found in the treatise of A. Ogolevetz, *Introduction to Contemporary Musical Thought*. In essence the entire "theory" of A. Ogolevetz is, objectively speaking, a theoretical support of formalism, and is an anti-Leninist and anti-Marxist work.

The musical departments of the periodical, *Soviet Art*, and other newspapers, and the monthly *Sovietskaya Musica* did not fight for the ideals of democratic art but lent their pages to apologists for the formalist movement. The Committee of Fine Arts has often shown the inclination to stifle even the most timid attempts to criticize the formalist movement. Thus, at the personal directive of Comrade Khrapchenko, chairman of the Committee of Fine Arts, critical articles about the *Ninth Symphony* of Shostakovich (among them an

---

* The inscription in the score of Stravinsky's *Symphony of Psalms* reads: "Composed for the glory of God and dedicated to the Boston Symphony on the occasion of the fiftieth anniversary of its existence."

article by Keldysh strongly condemning this symphony) were not allowed for publication in *Sovietskaya Musica*.

The policy of the Committee of Fine Arts, the Organizational Committee, and the Musical Fund, in the Section for Promotion and Propaganda of Soviet music, reflected above all the interests of the formalist school. Thus, the Musical Fund published the obviously fallacious formalistic compositions of the type of the *Second Symphony* of Boelza and the *Fourth Symphony* of Shostakovich, not to mention numerous editions of different versions of works by a narrow group of composers of the formalist school.

The Committee on Fine Arts did not take suitable measures toward the development of Soviet music in the realistic direction; it failed to promote the composition of operas, choral music, popular music for small orchestras, music for national instruments, vocal ensembles, etc. Commissions given to composers by the Committee of Fine Arts did not direct Soviet music along the correct path. The system of commissions was basically a form of material security for the leading group of composers of the formalist school. The major part of State commissions for the year 1947 was taken up by abstract, textless, instrumental forms. Prokofiev alone received eight commissions, among them one for the preparation of a "new" version of his *Fourth Symphony* derived from his ballet *The Prodigal Son*, which was condemned by Soviet society.

The decisive role in the Music Section of the Committee for Stalin Prizes was played by the same composers, representatives of the formalist movement. Some products of decadent art, which failed to find recognition with the general public, were nominated for a prize on the basis of a hearing by the narrow circle of specialists. Almost every new work by "leading" composers was automatically promoted as a prize work, year after year.

Soviet composers must reject as useless and harmful garbage all the relics of bourgeois formalism in musical art. They must understand that the creation of high-quality works in the domain of the opera, symphonic music, songwriting, choral and dance music, is possible only by following the principles of socialist realism.

Our duty is to mobilize all our creative strength and to give a worthy response, in the shortest possible time, to this appeal of our Party, to the appeal of our great leader Comrade STALIN.

Statement by Vano Muradeli

The Central Committee of our Party in its historic Resolution has subjected my opera *Great Friendship* to a just and severe criticism.

The Resolution establishes the fact that my opera is an anti-artistic composition, corrupt both from the musical and political standpoint. I fully agree with this absolutely correct evaluation of my opera.

A. A. Zhdanov, in his historic report to the General Assembly of Soviet Composers, exposed in clear terms the false formalistic tendencies in my opera *Great Friendship*.

The speech of Zhdanov will remain forever in my memory as an impassioned appeal to Soviet composers to serve our people with honesty and devotion, and to fight determinedly and unswervingly for the great ideals of building up Communist society in our country.

Addressing the Union of Soviet Composers, I wish to state the causes of my major creative errors. There are several reasons for my failure. I shall attempt to analyze them in full.

(1) Although I have been a convinced exponent of composition inspired by folk songs, I was unable to pursue this realistic path. Instead, attracted by false innovations, I have accepted the formalistic techniques of musical modernism.

(2) My isolation from other composers, which was a result of my "aristocratic" position in the Organizational Committee, deprived me of the opportunity of heeding their Bolshevik criticism, and receiving their professional advice.

(3) I have not made adequate study, and have not acquired sufficient professional knowledge of the operatic heritage of the great Russian and Western classics.

(4) Having been completely engrossed in the composition of my opera, I neglected to work on the improvement of my ideological political education.

(5) My over-confidence and self-complacency, my exaggerated preoccupation with professional activities, carelessness and haste, resulted in retarding the progress of my work.

(6) I failed to pay attention to the voice of the people and to their ideological and spiritual requirements. I lost the sense of true actuality and its vital imperatives. My opera *Great Friendship* failed to portray the life of the people, or its art, in any of its native phases. This shows that I have lost contact with the life of our people.

I grew up in the atmosphere of folk music. My first compositions hardly differed from simple songs of the people. In my later works—*Four Georgian Songs, Symphonic Dance,* and *Ten Heroic Songs*—I again turned for inspiration to these sources of people's music.

How could it have happened that I failed to introduce a single folk song in the score of my opera? It seems strange and almost incredible to me, and can be explained only as a manifestation of my inherent snobbishness. Apart from that, I did not possess sufficient mastery and craftsmanship for writing a large operatic work and building a music drama. In a number of places in my opera I indulged in technical tricks to obtain novel effects. Thus my opera was deprived of natural feeling and logical development.

There is no justification for these techniques in my opera, for the absence of folk songs, for the over-elaborateness, and at times crudity of my musical language. All this deprives my opera of the sense of reality, leading me towards a false formalistic path.

I have before me a definite task, to realize fully and unequivocally the seriousness of my creative errors, and to correct these errors with ideological honesty in my future works. The Resolution of the Central Committee of the All-Union Communist Party (Bolsheviks) is a new and vivid manifestation of interest and solicitude shown by our Party for the destinies of Soviet socialist culture. This historic Resolution constitutes for Soviet composers a clear creative program presaging a mighty uplift of Soviet musical culture. I will try with all my heart to earn the right to continue my devoted service to our Soviet music.

Statement of Dmitri Shostakovich

As we look back on the road traversed by our art, it becomes quite clear to us that every time that the Party corrects errors of a creative artist and points out the deviations in his work, or else severely condemns a certain tendency in Soviet art, it invariably brings beneficial results for Soviet art and for individual artists.

The directives of the Central Committee of the All-Union Communist Party (Bolsheviks) are inspired by the desire to raise the standard and the significance of art in the development of our Soviet Society.

When in 1936 the central organ of our Party, *Pravda*, severely condemned my opera *Lady Macbeth of the District of*

Mzensk and pointed out my serious aberrations, my formalism, this creative failure affected me profoundly. I gave it a great deal of thought, trying hard to derive from it all the necessary lessons. It seemed to me that in the years following, my art began to develop in a new direction, I strove to provide an answer in my work to the great and stirring problems that faced the whole Soviet land, the whole Soviet people. It seemed to me that to a certain extent I managed to eradicate the pernicious elements pointed out in *Pravda:* the over-complication of the musical language, the elaboration of musical thought, etc.

This severe but just criticism by the Party made me study more intensely the works of the Russian classics and Russian national art. In that light I regarded my work on Mussorgsky's opera *Boris Godunov* when I worked on its orchestration and on its editing.

As I look back mentally at all I have written after *Lady Macbeth,* it seems to me that in my symphonic works and chamber music there appeared elements new to my art, which when developed should have given me the opportunity of finding a path to the heart of the Soviet people. However, this did not materialize. I now can clearly see that I overestimated the thoroughness of my artistic reconstruction; certain negative characteristics peculiar to my musical thought prevented me from making the turn that seemed to be indicated in a number of my works of recent years. I again deviated in the direction of formalism, and began to speak a language incomprehensible to the people.

Now, when the Party and our entire nation, speaking through the Resolution of the Central Committee of the All-Union Communist Party (Bolsheviks), condemn this tendency in my music, I know that the Party is right; I know that the Party shows solicitude for Soviet art and for me as a Soviet composer.

All the resolutions of the Central Committee of the All-Union Communist Party (Bolsheviks) regarding the art of recent years, and particularly the Resolution of 10 February 1948 in regard to the opera *Great Friendship*, point out to Soviet artists that a tremendous national uplift is now taking place in our country, our great Soviet nation.

Some Soviet artists, and among them myself, attempted to give expression in their works to this great national uplift. But between my subjective intentions and objective results there was an appalling gap.

The absence, in my works, of the interpretation of folk art, that great spirit by which our people lives, has been with utmost clarity and definiteness pointed out by the Central Committee of the All-Union Communist Party (Bolsheviks).

I am deeply grateful for it and for all the criticism contained in the Resolution. All the directives of the Central Committee of the All-Union Communist Party (Bolsheviks), and in particular those that concern me personally, I accept as a stern but paternal solicitude for us, Soviet artists.

Work—arduous, creative, joyous work on new compositions which will find their path to the heart of the Soviet people, which will be understandable to the people, loved by them, and which will be organically connected with the people's art, developed and enriched by the great traditions of Russian classicism—this will be a fitting response to the Resolution of the Central Committee of the All-Union Communist Party (Bolsheviks).

In my *Poem of Fatherland* I attempted to create a symphonic work infused with songfulness and melodiousness. It proved to be unsuccessful.

On the basis of the principles clearly given in the Resolution of the Central Committee of the All-Union Communist Party (Bolsheviks), I shall try again and again to create symphonic works close to the spirit of the people from the standpoint of ideological subject matter, musical language and form.

I shall still more determinedly work on the musical depiction of the images of the heroic Soviet people.

I am now at work on the music for a cinema film, *Young Guard,* and I have begun an opera of the same title. I hope that in these compositions I shall partially achieve the aims of which I spoke here.

Some of my songs have attained a certain popularity among the people. Now, equipped with the directives of the Central Committee of the All-Union Communist Party (Bolsheviks), I shall again and again try to create Soviet mass songs.

I have no doubt whatsoever that Soviet music is on the eve of a tremendous creative uplift. This uplift will develop on the basis of the realization in the art of Soviet composers of the wise and just directives of the Central Committee of the All-Union Communist Party (Bolsheviks).

I appeal to all composers to bend their efforts to the task of the realization of this remarkable Resolution.

Statement of Aram Khachaturian

The Resolution of the Central Committee of the All-Union Communist Party (Bolsheviks) is the expression of the will of our people and fully reflects the opinion of the Soviet people regarding our music.

The Resolution of the Central Committee of the All-Union Communist Party (Bolsheviks) brings liberation to us, Soviet musicians. Indeed one feels as if we have thrown off the chains that have held us for many years. Despite my depressed moral state (for understandable reasons), I have a feeling of joy and satisfaction.

We feel easier, more free; there is before us a clear path, a road for Soviet music to pursue its swift progress. I see this path clearly, and I have only one desire, to correct by creative work all my previous errors.

How could it happen that I have come to formalism in my art? I made use of many folk songs, particularly my native Armenian songs. I have also used other national songs, Russian, Ukrainian, Georgian, Uzbekian, Turkmenian, and Tartar songs. I wrote a number of compositions based on these songs.

I have always declared that I do not recognize nonmelodic music; I have always maintained that melody is the foundation of musical composition. But despite the fact that I stood on these seemingly correct creative positions, I have committed formalistic errors.

I see two reasons for these errors. The first is my preoccupation with technique. I have often been reproached for my insufficient technical equipment. This was reflected in my consciousness. My desire to achieve a complete technical mastery imperceptibly resulted in an over-emphasis on technique, which is particularly evident in my *Symphonie-Poème.*

I have reached formalism because of my cultivation of abstract technique.

When music critics and musicologists were telling me that it was about time for me to go beyond the national confines, to renounce the supposedly narrow stylistic direction of my music, I listened attentively to these ideas. I failed to repudiate these harmful creative positions in time. In recent years I have moved farther and farther away from my native Armenian element; I wanted to be cosmopolitan.

Andrey Adreyevitch Zhdanov in his statement at the meeting in the Central Committee of the Party said that internationalism in music can develop only on the basis of enrichment and flowering of national music, and not by erasing the national elements.

Creative errors and formalistic leanings in our music could not but influence my work in the Organizational Committee, which became a hotbed of formalism. It could not fight formalism with members who either fully or partly stood on formalistic positions, or else were sympathizers. As the principal leader of the Organizational Committee, I had every opportunity to inaugurate and lead the struggle with this phenomenon in music. But I failed to do so.

I turned out to be a poor leader, and my methods of work in the Organizational Committee were undemocratic. In recent years I stood aloof from our composers' life. Members of the Organizational Committee became "grands seigneurs" proud of their "creative achievements," and as a result found themselves generals without an army. Criticism and self-criticism in the Organizational Committee were stifled.

The Resolution of the Central Committee declares that the Organizational Committee maintained a suffocating atmosphere, devoid of all creative discussion. One of the chief reasons interfering with the work of the Organizational Committee was a lack of unity among its members. We were preoccupied with petty quarrels and our personal interrelations. We forgot that we were appointed to guide the Union of Soviet Composers, that we were expected to lead all other composers. Hypocritically, paying compliments to one another, we, the members of the Organizational Committee, actually were highly antagonistic to each other.

I accept full responsibility for the unfavorable situation on the front of Soviet music, which was created as a result of the incorrect line in the domain of Soviet music, established by the Organizational Committee.

I wish to point out another very serious danger. I want to warn those comrades who, like myself, hoped that their music, which is not understood by the people today, will be understood by the future generations tomorrow. It is a fatal theory. In our country, millions of people, the entire Soviet nation, are now arbiters of music. What can be higher and nobler than writing music understandable to our people and to give joy by our creative art to millions?

I urge all Soviet composers, and above all, Shostakovich, Prokofiev, Shebalin, Popov, Miaskovsky, and Muradeli, to answer the stern but just Resolution of the Central Committee of the All-Union Communist Party (Bolsheviks) by a decisive reorientation of their musical views, and to prove by their artistic production the thoroughness and the sincerity of their reorientation.

Our principal task is now to unite on the basis of the Resolution of the Central Committee, to work as much as possible, and as well as possible, and to prove by deeds that Soviet composers are marching in the vanguard of victorious Soviet culture.

Letter from Prokofiev

The state of my health prevents me from attending the General Assembly of Soviet Composers. I therefore wish to express my ideas in regard to the Resolution of the Central Committee of the All-Union Communist Party (Bolsheviks) of 10 February 1948, in the present letter. I request that you read it at the Assembly if you find it expedient.

The Resolution of the Central Committee of the All-Union Communist Party of 10 February 1948 has separated decayed tissue in the composers' creative production from the healthy part. No matter how painful it may be for many composers, myself included, I welcome the Resolution of the

Central Committee of the All-Union Communist Party (Bolsheviks), which establishes the necessary conditions for the return to health of the whole organism of Soviet music. The Resolution is particularly important because it demonstrates that the formalist movement is alien to the Soviet people, that it leads to impoverishment and decline of music. It points out with ultimate clarity the aims that Soviet composers must attain to be of the greatest service to the Soviet people.

As far as I am concerned, elements of formalism were peculiar to my music as long as fifteen or twenty years ago. Apparently the infection caught from contact with some western ideas. When formalistic errors in Shostakovich's opera *Lady Macbeth of the District of Mzensk* were exposed by *Pravda*, I gave a great deal of thought to creative devices in my own music, and came to the conclusion that such a method of composition is faulty.

As a result, I began a search for a clearer and more meaningful language. In several of my subsequent works—*Alexander Nevsky, A Toast to Stalin, Romeo and Juliet, Fifth Symphony*—I strove to free myself from elements of formalism and, it seems to me, succeeded to a certain degree. The existence of formalism in some of my works is probably explained by a certain self-complacency, an insufficient realization of the fact that it is completely unwanted by our people. The Resolution has shaken to the core the social consciousness of our composers, and it has become clear what type of music is needed by our people, and the ways of the eradication of the formalist disease have also become clear.

I have never questioned the importance of melody. I love melody, and I regard it as the most important element in music. I have worked on the improvement of its quality in my compositions for many years. To find a melody instantly understandable even to the uninitiated listener, and at the same time an original one, is the most difficult task for a composer. Here he is beset by a great multitude of dangers: he may fall into the trivial or the banal, or into the rehashing of something already written by him. In this respect, composition of complex melodies is much easier. It may also happen that a composer, fussing over his melody for a long time, and revising it, unwittingly makes it over-refined and complicated, and departs from simplicity. Undoubtedly, I fell into this trap, too, in the process of my work. One must be particularly vigilant to make sure that the melody retains its simplicity without becoming cheap, saccharine, or imitative. it is easy to say, but not so easy to accomplish. All my efforts will be henceforth concentrated to make these words not only a recipe, but to carry them out in my subsequent works.

I must admit that I, too, have indulged in atonality, but I also must say that I have felt an attraction towards tonal music for a considerable time, after I clearly realized that the construction of a musical work tonally is like erecting a building on a solid foundation, while a construction without tonality is like building on sand. Besides, tonal and diatonic music lends many more possibilities than atonal and chromatic music, which is evident from the impasse reached by Schoenberg and his disciples. In some of my works in recent years there are sporadic atonal moments. Without much sympathy, I nevertheless made use of this device, mainly for the sake of contrast, in order to bring tonal passages to the fore. In the future I hope to get rid of this mannerism.

In my operatic production I have been often criticized for the predominance of recitative over cantilena. I like the theater as such, and I believe that a person who attends the opera has a right to expect not only auditory, but also visual impressions; or else he would go to a concert and not to the opera. But every action on the stage is closely associated with recitative; on the other hand, cantilena induces a certain immobility on the stage. I recall the painful experience of watching the action in some of Wagner's operas, when during a whole act, lasting nearly an hour, not a single person moved on the stage. This fear of immobility prevented me from dwelling on cantilena too long. In connection with the Resolution, I thought over this problem with great care, and came to the conclusion that every operatic libretto has elements demanding the use of the recitative, while other elements imperatively require a treatment in the arioso style. But there are also sections (and these sections take up considerable space, adding up perhaps to one-half of the entire opera) which the composer may treat as he wishes, either as a recitative or as an arioso. Let us consider, for example, the scene of Tatiana's letter from *Eugene Onegin*. It would have been quite simple to write most of it in the form of a recitative, but Tchaikovsky preferred cantilena, and so made the letter scene into a sort of aria, which has this additional advantage that it is accompanied by stage action, giving satisfaction not only to the ear but also to the eye. This is the direction which I intend to take in my new opera on a contemporary Soviet subject, *A Tale of a Real Man* by Polevoy.

I am highly gratified that the Resolution has pointed out the desirability of polyphony, particularly in choral and ensemble singing. This is indeed an interesting task for a composer, promising a great pleasure to the listener. In my above-mentioned opera, I intend to introduce trios, duets, and contrapuntally developed choruses, for which I will make use of some interesting northern Russian folk songs. Lucid melody, and as far as possible, a simple harmonic language, are elements which I intend to use in my opera.

In conclusion, I should like to express my gratitude to our Party for the precise directives of the Resolution, which will help me in my search of a musical language, accessible and natural to our people, worthy of our people and of our great country.

Letter to Stalin

Dear Iosif Vissarionovich: The composers and musicologists of the Soviet capital, assembled for the discussion of the historic Resolution of the Central Committee of the All-Union Communist Party (Bolsheviks) of 10 February 1948 regarding the opera by Muradeli, *Great Friendship*, send to you, our beloved leader and teacher, a warm salute and wishes for good health.

We are tremendously grateful to the Central Committee of the All-Union Communist Party (Bolsheviks) and personally to you, dear Comrade Stalin, for the severe but profoundly just criticism of the present state of Soviet music, and for the interest which you and the Central Committee of our Party have shown for the progress of Soviet music, and for us, Soviet musicians.

The conference of Soviet musicians with the Central Committee of the All-Union Communist Party (Bolsheviks), and particularly the speech of Comrade Zhdanov, and the Resolution of the Central Committee of the All-Union Communist Party (Bolsheviks) of 10 February 1948, are events of historical significance; the extraordinarily powerful, profound and precise analysis of the contemporary state of Soviet music, the clear directives for the elimination of defects in Soviet music give us inestimable help, a testimony of the great power and prophetic vision of the Communist Party.

We, composers and musicologists of the city of Moscow, recognize the complete justice of the Party's criticism of Soviet music, which is now freeing itself from the deadening impact of bourgeois-formalist routine, from the influence of decadence.

It is obvious to us that, having entered the path of formalistic pseudo-modernism, the representatives of the movement condemned in the Resolution of the Central Committee of the All-Union Communist Party (Bolsheviks) have disassociated themselves from folk music and song, have forgotten the musical language of their native land, have debased themselves to the point of subjecting their talents to models and dogmas of western European and American modernism. Confronted with the Soviet people, whose voice sounds in every line of the Resolution of the Central Committee of the All-Union Communist Party (Bolsheviks), we admit that many of us have forgotten the great traditions of Russian musical realism. The words of the great genius, Glinka, who declared "Music is created by the people, and we, artists, only arrange it," have not found their adequate expression in the art of Soviet composers. As a result, the national element has been ignored in our operatic and symphonic production, and the fallacious "theory," subjectively idealistic in its essence, has been circulated to prove that broad masses of listeners are supposedly not "grown up" enough to understand contemporary music.

For us, Soviet musicians, it is all the more painful to realize that we have failed to draw correct and logical conclusions from the warnings that have been repeatedly sounded by our Party whenever Soviet music has deviated from its true realistic path. The articles, *Confusion Instead of Music* and *Ballet Falsification*, published in *Pravda* twelve years ago, the Resolutions of the Central Committee of the All-Union Communist Party (Bolsheviks) concerning the magazines *Zvezda* and *Leningrad*, and the motion picture *Great Love*, and the article, *Regarding the Repertory of Dramatic Theatres and Measures for Its Improvement*, were not followed, as it was with profound justice pointed out in the Resolution of the Central Committee of the All-Union Communist Party (Bolsheviks), by any reorientation in Soviet music. Soviet composers and critics have failed to appreciate duly the timely and precise directives of the Central Committee of the All-Union Communist Party (Bolsheviks), and so have caused the heaviest detriment to Soviet musical culture. Only their lack of contact with the life of the nation can account for the fact that our composers were unable to evaluate in full the colossal and unprecedented growth of artistic tastes and requirements of the broad popular masses, and for that reason were unable to satisfy these tastes and requirements of the great Soviet people.

Your personal suggestions, dear Iosif Vissarionovich, regarding the task of building the Soviet classical opera, given by you in your talk with the composer Dzerzhinsky in connection with his opera, *Quiet Flows the Don*, remain a fighting program of our creative effort. We shall bend every effort to apply our knowledge and our artistic mastery and to produce vivid realistic music reflecting the life and struggles of the Soviet people.

The creative isolationism of composers must be ended once and for all. There is no place for bourgeois individualism in the musical art of a country where the artist is given every opportunity for a full development of his creative individuality, where he is surrounded with solicitude and care, of which the artists of bourgeois countries dare not even dream. In no country has a composer such an audience as in our land.

The Soviet artist is the servant of the people. This is the first conclusion that all Soviet composers and musicologists ought to make, and the creative art of every Soviet musician must be subordinated entirely to this lofty democratic principle. Not for the snobs should sound our music, but for our whole great people.

We assure you, our beloved leader and teacher, that the appeals of the Central Committee of the All-Union Communist Party (Bolsheviks) addressed to us, Soviet musicians, will become a fighting program of our creative art. We shall give all our strength to the new and unparalleledly great flowering of Soviet musical art.

We give to you and to the whole Soviet people a sworn pledge that we shall direct our work along the path of socialist realism, tirelessly laboring to create, in all musical forms, models worthy of our great epoch, striving to make our music beloved by the whole great Soviet people, so that the great ideas that inspire our nation in its universally historic deeds of valor shall find living and vivid expression in our art.

Long live the Lenin-Stalin people, the nation-worker, nation-victor that has earned the right for the most progressive socialist art in the world!

Long live the Lenin-Stalin Central Committee of the All-Union Communist Party (Bolsheviks)!

Long live our leader and teacher, father of the nation, great STALIN!

Letter of Protest from Four Soviet Composers

To the Editor of Izvestia: American newspapers have reported the release of the film *The Iron Curtain*. We know that this film pursues the aim of slandering our homeland, of fanning enmity and hatred for the Soviet people, in order to please the enemies of world peace and security.

With deep indignation we have learned from a report of the *New York Times* that excerpts from our musical works are being used in this film.

Needless to say, none of us ever gave, or could have given, his consent for the use of our music in any form whatsoever in the picture *The Iron Curtain*.

Knowing beforehand that Soviet composers would indignantly reject any such offer, the agents of the American Twentieth Century-Fox Corporation resorted to a swindling trick in order to steal our music for their outrageous picture. American reactionaries decided to supplement, by the theft of our works, the anti-Soviet forgeries on which their film is based.

The fact that these gentlemen enjoy full opportunity for political blackmail, that they ignore elementary rights of composers in making unwarranted use of their creative work, proves once more that manners and morals exist in the United States under which the rights of the individual, freedom of art, and democratic principles, to which allegiance is solemnly vowed, are in reality most unceremoniously trampled underfoot.

While expressing categorical protest against such methods, against this cynical infringement on the freedom of art, we resolutely insist that our music be removed from the film *The Iron Curtain*.

D. SHOSTAKOVICH, S. PROKOFIEV
A. KHACHATURIAN, N. MIASKOVSKY
April 1948

Declaration of the Central Committee of the Communist Party of the Soviet Union Amending and Canceling the Resolution of 10 February 1948 and Restoring the Dignity and Integrity of Soviet Composers Attacked in That Resolution

The Central Committee of the Communist Party of the Soviet Union notes that the Resolution of the Central Committee

dated 10 February 1948, and dealing with the opera by V. Muradeli, *Great Friendship,* has on the whole played a positive role in the development of Soviet music. In this Resolution the aims in the development of Soviet musical art were defined on the basis of the principles of Socialist Realism, with emphasis placed on the significance of the relationship between art and the life of the Soviet people, as on the importance of the best democratic traditions of musical classicism and folk art. The Resolution justly condemned the formalistic tendencies in music and ostensible innovations which took it away from the people into a circle of estheticizing gourmands. The development of Soviet music during the subsequent years confirmed the correctness and the timeliness of the Party's judgment.

However, the evaluation of the creative work of individual composers contained in this Resolution was in a number of instances unfair and unjustified. The opera by Vano Muradeli, *Great Friendship,* had faults that merited specific criticism, but these faults did not justify the description of this opera as formalistic. Talented composers, Comrades Prokofiev, Shostakovich, Khachaturian, Shebalin, Popov, Miaskovsky and others who showed faulty tendencies in some of their works, were peremptorily described as representatives of the formalist trends inimical to the people.

In this Resolution, specifically in the criticism of Muradeli's opera, there was made, contrary to historical facts, an artificial discrimination against some of the peoples of the northern Caucasus. Some incorrect evaluations in the Resolution reflected the subjective approach towards certain works of art on the part of J. V. Stalin. It was further demonstrated in the one-sided judgment of individual works of art and in the biased criticism of the operas *Bogdan Khmelnitsky* by Konstantin Dankevich and *From the Bottom of My Heart* by Herman Zhukovsky in the editorial articles of the newspaper *Pravda* published at J.V. Stalin's behest in 1951. As is well known, in his judgments regarding these problems, Stalin was under the negative influence of Molotov, Malenkov and Beria. Despite the fact that the libretto and the music of the opera *Bogdan Khmelnitsky* had faults, there was no justification in describing them as "gross ideological errors." The unwarranted reproaches contained in this article in *Pravda* were repeated later on in a number of other articles and statements. The editorial article of *Pravda* regarding the opera *From the Bottom of My Heart,* which included some correct critical judgments of its music and of its libretto, also included obvious exaggerations and bias.

The Central Committee of the Communist Party of the Soviet Union resolves: (1) to note that the Resolution of the Central Committee of 10 February 1948 with regard to the opera by Vano Muradeli *Great Friendship,* while correctly tracing the direction of the development of Soviet art along the lines of folk forms and realism, and containing just criticism of erroneous formalistic tendencies in Soviet music, passed unjust and unjustifiably harsh judgment on works by many Soviet composers, disclosing the negative traits that marked the period of the cult of personality; (2) to rule that the evaluation of the operas *Bogdan Khmelnitsky* and *From the Bottom of My Heart,* given in the editorial articles of the newspaper *Pravda,* is incorrect and one-sided and to recommend to the editorial board of the newspaper *Pravda,* on the basis of the present decision, to prepare an editorial article containing a many-sided and profound analysis of the fundamental problems of the development of Soviet musical art; (3) to suggest to the regional and local committees and to the Central Committees of the Communist Parties of the Republics of the Union, and to the Ministry of Culture of the Union of Soviet Socialist Republics, to initiate in the professional unions of creative art workers and in the institutes of the arts the requisite explanatory work in connection with the present Resolution, with the view of raising the ideological and artistic level of Soviet musical art, and the further solidarization of the creative intelligentsia on the basis of Communist ideology and the strengthening of the links connecting Soviet arts with the life of the people. (Dated 28 May 1958)

Declaration of the Second International Congress of Composers and Musicologists in Prague, 29 May 1948

We, composers and musicologists of different countries, gathered at the Second International Congress of Composers and Musicologists in Prague from 20 May to 29 May 1948, organized by the Union of Czech Composers, have, after discussions and conferences lasting for ten days, unanimously agreed on the following declaration.

Music and musical life of our epoch are undergoing a profound crisis. This crisis is characterized by the sharp conflict between so-called serious music and so-called light music.

So-called serious music is becoming increasingly individualistic and subjective in its content, and increasingly complex and constructivistic in its form.

So-called light music is becoming increasingly banal, impersonal, and standardized; in many countries it is made the object of a monopolized commercial industry, and becomes a piece of merchandise.

So-called serious music has lost the proper balance of its individual musical elements. In some cases, rhythmic and harmonic elements are over-emphasized, and the melodic elements rejected; in others, formally constructivistic elements are the determinants; or else, the logical development of the musical thought is replaced by a formless melodization and esthetizing imitation of old contrapuntal writing. But no formal ingenuities can conceal the ideational vacuity of the majority of these works.

On the other hand, so-called light music confines itself exclusively to primitive melodies, entirely ignoring all other elements. It is usually based on the most vulgar, most commonplace melodic formulas, exemplified particularly by American popular music.

These tendencies, supposedly opposite, are in reality two sides of the same nefarious phenomenon, and are conditioned by the same social process.

The more evident these defects are in contemporary serious music, the more complex its form and subjective contents, the smaller is its audience, while vulgar popular music penetrates deeper and deeper the musical life of different countries and peoples, contributing to the debasement and banality of perception of its many millions of listeners and perverting their musical tastes.

We, the delegates gathered at the Second International Congress of Composers and Musicologists in Prague, note that this situation is particularly inadmissible in our time when new social forms are being created, and when human culture enters a new era, posing before the creative artist new and urgent tasks.

The International Congress does not intend to give any concrete recipes or instructions for writing music; it is understood that each nation must find its own ways and methods. However, the reasons and the essence of the contemporary crisis in music ought to be understood by all, and we must apply a united effort to solve it.

A successful solution of the crisis in contemporary music seems to be possible under the following conditions:

(1) If composers renounce in their art the tendencies of extreme subjectivism; then their music would express great, new, and progressive ideas and aspirations of the popular masses and progressive ideals of contemporary life.

(2) If creative artists turn decisively towards national culture of their lands and become its true defenders against the cosmopolitan tendencies of contemporary life, for true internationalism in music is attained only on the basis of the strengthening of national culture.

(3) If the attention of composers is directed first of all towards musical forms that are most concrete in their contents, particularly operas, oratorios, cantatas, songs, mass choruses, etc.

(4) If composers and music critics become active and practical workers in the musical education of their peoples.

The Congress urges composers of the whole world to write music in which high artistic qualities combine with creative individuality and deep and genuine folk art.

The Congress considers that exchange of experience and ideas among progressive composers and musicologists of all nations is now an acute and urgent necessity. To achieve this, progressive musicians must unite their forces, first of all in their own countries, which ought to lead in the nearest future to the formation of a union of progressive composers and musicologists of all countries.

The Congress states its conviction that such an association of progressive composers and musicologists of all countries, by arduous and determined work will solve the protracted contemporary musical crisis, and will restore to music its lofty and noble role in society. Only under such conditions will music become a mighty factor in the solution of the great historic tasks facing all progressive mankind.

For the Praesidium of the Second International Congress of Composers and Musicologists in Prague:

A. Estrella (Brazil); V. Stojanov (Bulgaria); St. Lucky, A. Kypta, A. Sychra, Jar. Tomásek (Czechoslovakia); Roland de Candé (France); M. Flothuis, M. Rebling (Holland); O. Danon, N. Devcic (Yugoslavia); Denés Bartha (Hungary); Zofia Lissa (Poland); Hanns Eisler (Austria); A. Mendelsohn (Rumania); Tikhon Khrennikov, Boris Yarustovsky, Yuri Shaporin (USSR); Georges Bernard (Switzerland); Alan Bush, Bernard Stevens (Great Britain).

Declaration Made by Nikita Khrushchev on 8 March 1963 Stating His Views on Music in Soviet Society

In music, as in other arts, there are many genres, styles and forms. No one proposes to declare a ban on any of these styles and genres. But we want to stipulate our own attitude towards music, its tasks and its creative direction. To put it briefly, we are for melodic music, rich in content, which stirs the souls of men, generating strong feelings. We are against cacophonic music. . . . When I hear the music of Glinka, tears of joy appear in my eyes. Perhaps it is no longer fashionable, and I am not a young man, but I like to listen to David Oistrakh when he plays the violin, and I like to hear the massed collective of violins in the orchestra of the Bolshoi Theater. I do not know what this violin collective is called in professional terms. I have heard it many times, and always had great pleasure. Of course, I have no pretensions to claim that my feeling for music should become a general norm for everyone. But we refuse to encourage people who pass off cacophony for real melody and who regard music universally loved by the people as obsolete. Every nation has its musical traditions and loves its popular songs. I was born in a Russian village and was brought up in an atmosphere of Russian and Ukrainian music, of its folk songs. I derive great pleasure from listening to songs by Solovyov-Sedoy, or to Kolmanovsky's song to the words of the poet Evtushenko, "Do Russians Want War?" I like many Ukrainian songs, for instance *Rushnitchok* by Maiboroda. I listen and want to listen more and more. We have many good composers who have written many fine songs, but as you understand I cannot enumerate them all. In musical composition there are serious defects. One cannot consider the current infatuation with jazz music as a normal phenomenon. We are not against all jazz music; there are all kinds of jazz music. Dunayevsky knew how to write good music for jazz orchestra. I like some songs performed by the jazz orchestra conducted by Leonid Utyosov. But there is also music which makes one feel like vomiting, and causes colic in one's stomach.—After the recent plenum of the Union of Composers of the Russian Socialist Federal Soviet Republic, Comrade Shostakovich invited us to a concert at the Kremlin Convention Hall. Although we are all very busy we went to hear it, because we were told that it was going to be an interesting concert. And indeed there were some interesting numbers on the program. But then they put on a jazz band, then another, then another, and then all three together. Even good jazz is hard to take in quantity, but this kind of jazz bombardment was beyond endurance. And there was no place to hide. Music in which there is no melody produces nothing but irritation. They tell us that such opinions as mine reveal a lack of understanding. It is true that it is impossible to understand some jazz music which is repugnant to the ear. We must object also to so-called modern dance seeping through from the west into our land. I traveled through the country a great deal. I watched Russian, Ukrainian, Kazakh, Uzbek, Armenian and Georgian dances. They are beautiful dances and pleasant to watch. But what they call modern fashionable dance is simply indecent, an orgy and the devil knows what. They say that such obscenities one can witness only among the shakers. I cannot vouch for it because I never attended shakers' meetings. But it seems that among our creative workers there are young people who are eager to prove that melody in music has lost its right to exist and that it ought to be replaced by some new kind of music, dodecaphonic music, music of noises. A normal person finds it difficult to understand what is hidden behind the word dodecaphonic, but in all probability it is the same as cacophonic. Well, this cacophonic music we totally reject. Our people cannot include such trash in our ideological armament. (Shouts in the audience: "Right!") We need music that inspires, that calls for heroic deeds and for constructive labor. When a soldier goes to war, he takes all that he needs with him, and the regiment band never leaves him. It inspires him during the army march. Music for such bands can be written only by composers who adhere to positions of socialist realism, who remain close to everyday life and to the problems of national struggle, those who are supported by the people. Our political stand in art is that of intransigent opposition to abstractionism, formalism and other bourgeois perversions of this type. It is Lenin's line, which we have unswervingly followed, and which we will continue to follow. (APPLAUSE)

Charter of the Union of Soviet Composers

Confirmed by the Second All-Union Congress of Soviet Composers, 1957

I *General Statement*

The Union of Soviet Composers is a voluntary social organization which unites composers and musicologists actively par-

ticipating in the development of Soviet musical art. Having creatively mastered the Marxist-Leninist theory which equips an artist with the capacity of observing the authentic truth of life in all its complexity and totality, Soviet composers are guided by the method of Socialist Realism. This method demands from composers a faithful reflection of reality in its revolutionary development and high mastery in the artistic representation of life's images. In opening many-sided opportunities for the revelation of individual peculiarities of one's talent, Socialist Realism predicates a wealth and variety of artistic styles and a broad creative initiative in the struggle for ideals of Communism and for the national essence of the multi-national Soviet art of music.

II *Tasks of the Union of Composers of the USSR*

The Union of Composers of the USSR sets the following tasks for itself:

1. Cooperation and unionization of Soviet composers and musicologists with the purpose of creating ideologically valid musical works of high artistic content which would contribute to the building of Communism in our country.

2. Creative development of the best traditions of Russian and other musical cultures of the Soviet Union as well as those of foreign classical music and intensive promotion of Soviet musical culture, socialist in content and national in form.

3. Development of Soviet musicology, analysis of foremost problems of musical aesthetics on the basis of Marxism-Leninism, as well as of important questions of musical history and theory.

4. Establishing Soviet music as a progressive force of world music culture and irreconcilable struggle against the influences of bourgeois ideology.

5. Ideological and political education of Soviet composers and musicologists, aiding them in their creative growth and the evolution of their professional mastery, and an intensive spread of creative discussion, as a fundamental method of the Union's activities.

6. Establishment of creative and organizational contacts with Soviet performers.

7. Establishment of creative contacts with the representatives of literature, cinema, the theater and fine arts.

8. Establishment of creative contacts with composers and musicologists of the nations of people's democracies and with progressive musical organizations and representatives of other foreign countries; promotion of the best works of Soviet music abroad and the best works of foreign music in the USSR.

9. Socio-creative advice to musical institutions and organizations which are connected with music, such as orchestras, radio, television, music publishing firms, musical educational institutions, clubs, palaces of culture, professional musical press and musical sections of the general press.

10. Aid to the members of the Union of Soviet Composers in a deep and many-sided study of the life and culture of the peoples of the USSR and of foreign countries.

11. Aid to the members of the Union of Soviet Composers in the improvement of the cultural and material conditions of their life and work and in the safeguarding of their authors' rights.

To carry out these aims the Union of Soviet Composers takes the following course of action:

1. Organizes discussions about important creative and scientific problems, musical compositions and musicological works.

2. Promotes the progress of young composers and musicologists, aiding their ideo-political growth and perfecting their artistic mastery.

3. Organizes expeditions for study and recording of the creative music of the nations of the USSR.

4. Promotes intensively the development of musical creativity of nonprofessional groups.

5. Organizes creative visits of the Union's members at plants and factories, at construction sites, at collective farms and state farms, at service branches of the Soviet Army and Soviet Navy; and arranges creative meetings with listeners.

6. Organizes exchanges of creative experiences among composers and musicologists of the fraternal republics of the USSR.

7. Organizes exchanges of creative experiences among composers and musicologists of the Soviet Union and musical representatives of foreign countries.

8. Organizes competitions for the best works in different types of musical composition and musicology and for the best performance of works by Soviet composers.

9. Propagandizes the achievements of Soviet music by means of publishing musical works and musicological books, organizing concerts, discussions, lectures, etc.

III *Contingent of the Union of Composers of the USSR*

1. The following are qualified for membership of the Union of Soviet Composers:

   a. Composers of works of a high professional caliber possessing individual socio-artistic significance.
   b. Music critics and musicologists whose scientific works, critical essays and activity as lecturers and propagandists have actively contributed to the development of creative practical work and to the theory of Soviet musical art.

2. Members of the Union of Soviet composers enjoy the right of a decisive vote at general assemblies; of electing and of being elected as delegates to congresses, plenary, meetings and conferences; of electing and being elected to the guiding and controlling organs of the Union.

3. Members of the Union of Soviet Composers must take active part in the work of the Union, must contribute to the attainment of its goals, must observe discipline established by the Union and must fulfill all requirements of the present Charter.

4. Application for membership must be submitted to local branches of the Union of Composers of the USSR, enclosing works and other materials relating to the creative musical, musicological and social activity of the applicant.

   The Directorate of a regional or local union numbering fewer than twenty members has a right to accept for membership composers and musicologists having special musical and educational qualifications. An applicant is accepted by a majority of no less than two-thirds of the total membership.
   Composers' unions of fraternal republics of the USSR numbering fewer than twenty members each, must submit the candidacy of applicants accepted for membership in the Union of Soviet Composers to the Secretariat of the Union of Composers of the USSR for confirmation.

Admission to the membership of composers and musicologists not having special musical and educational qualifications must be confirmed by the Secretariat of the Union of Composers of the USSR. Rejection of candidacy is subject to appeal to the Directorate of the Union of Composers of the USSR.

5. Persons admitted to membership in the Composers' Union are assessed annual dues of 36 rubles and receive a membership card of the Union of Composers of the USSR.

6. Expulsion from membership of the Composers' Union is effected by a majority of no less than two-thirds of the membership of the Directorate of the corresponding local branch of the regional Union of Composers in the following cases:

   a. Deprivation of rights to vote by court action.
   b. Incompatibility of a member's activities with the aims and policies of the Union of Composers of the USSR.
   c. Perpetration of anti-social actions.
   d. Creative inactivity over a period of three years when not induced by illness or other justifiable cause, and also unconscientious attitude towards professional work.
   e. Systematic avoidance of participation in the socio-creative work of the Union.
   f. Failure to pay membership dues for a year.
   g. A member's own desire to leave the Union.

7. The decisions of the Directorate of the Union of Composers regarding expulsion from membership can be appealed to a superior organization, including the Congress of Soviet Composers.

IV *Guiding Organs of the Union of Composers of the USSR*

1. The highest guiding organ of the Union of Composers of the USSR is the Congress of Composers which convenes every four years.

2. Election of delegates to the All-Union Congress of Composers is conducted according to the rules established by the Directorate of the Union of Composers of the USSR. These delegates are elected by secret ballot in national assemblies. When a Soviet republic includes regional branches, delegates are elected at regional meetings or general assemblies.

3. The Congress of Soviet Composers performs the following functions:

   a. Passes on the questions of ideologically creative policy of Soviet music and Soviet musicology.
   b. Discusses and rules on the reports of the Directorate and the Control Committee of the Union of Composers of the USSR.
   c. Discusses and rules on the acceptance of the Charters of the Union of Composers and of the Musical Fund of the USSR.
   d. Elects central guiding and control organs of the Union of Soviet Composers.

4. Besides the periodical congresses of the Union of Soviet Composers, extraordinary congresses may be called to consider questions of an urgent nature. Such extraordinary congresses are summoned by the Directorate of the Union of Soviet Composers of the USSR for the following considerations:

   a. For its own reasons.
   b. At the request of not less than one-half of the membership of the Union of Soviet Composers.
   c. At the request of the Control Committee.
   d. At the request of Directorates of no fewer than five branches in Soviet republics or regional bodies, each of which numbers no fewer than fifty members of the Union of Soviet Composers.

When such requests are made, the Directorate of the Union of Composers of the USSR is obliged to summon an extraordinary congress within sixty days.

5. In the interval between congresses, the Directorate of the Union of Soviet Composers elected by secret ballot at the Congress, performs the functions of the executive organ.

6. In the interval between congresses, the Directorate of the Union of Soviet Composers performs the following functions:

   a. Provides guidance for the entire creative activity of the Union of Soviet Composers.
   b. Rules on fundamental problems touching on the creative, organizational and financial activities of institutions and enterprises of the Union of Composers.
   c. Guides the activity of all composers' unions in the fraternal republics of the USSR.
   d. Considers and confirms the accounts of the activities of the Directorate of the Musical Fund of the USSR.

   Congresses of composers' unions of the republics of the USSR are summoned by the Directorate of the corresponding local branches of the Union of Soviet Composers.

7. Plenary sessions of the Union of composers of the USSR are assembled at least twice a year.

8. The Directorate of the Union of Composers of the USSR elects a Secretariat from among its members, composed of a First Secretary and subordinate secretaries the number of which is determined by the Directorate.

9. The Directorate of the Union of Soviet Composers performs the following functions during the period between plenary sessions:

   a. Organizes and provides constant guidance for the ideological creative activities of the Union of Soviet Composers on the entire territory of the USSR.
   b. Provides guidance for the current activities of the Union of Composers of the USSR.
   c. Provides representation in behalf of the Directorate of the Union of Composers of the USSR at all state and social institutions.
   d. Considers creative accounts of organizations of composers of fraternal Soviet republics.
   e. Provides guidance for the activity of the Directorate of the Musical Fund of the USSR.

10. The Secretariat of the Union of Soviet Composers must present an accounting of its activities to the Directorate of the Union of Soviet Composers at least twice a year.

11. In the autonomous Soviet republics, as well as in regional districts, local unions of composers may be organized when a minimum of five members of the Union of Soviet Composers are available there.

    In the autonomous Soviet republics and regional districts in which there are available fewer than five members of the Union of Soviet Composers, a general assembly of the latter elects a plenipotentiary of the Union of Composers in that particular Soviet republic or regional district. The candidacy of such a plenipotentiary is confirmed by the Directorate of the corresponding local union of composers.

12. The Charter of the Union of Composers of the USSR is binding for all republican and regional branches. The quantitative contingent and the constitution of guiding organs of local unions of composers as well as the schedules of congresses and regional meetings are determined by the resolutions of such congresses and of regional

meetings, taking into account the peculiarities of each particular organization.

13. The Directorate of each of the regional branches of the Union of Soviet Composers provides guidance for the activities of the Union of Composers on the territories of the corresponding Soviet republics or regions.

    The resolutions of the All-Union congresses and of the Directorate of the Union of Composers of the USSR are binding for all branches of the Composers' Union.

14. For the purpose of checking on the management of the property and finances of the Union of Soviet Composers and its subsidiary institutions, a Control Committee is elected at each congress by secret ballot. Members of the Control Committee cannot concurrently be members of the Directorate of the Union of Soviet Composers.

    The Control Committee must submit reports of its activities to the Congress of Soviet Composers.

15. Republican and regional controlling organs are elected at corresponding congresses and general assemblies. In organizations of composers numbering fewer than twenty members, control organs are not elected.

V *Property Rights and Other Privileges of the Union of Composers of the USSR*

1. The Union of Composers of the USSR and those of individual republics and regions assume the rights of juridical persons, with all corollaries thereof, in pursuance of established laws, including possession, acquisition of property, signing of contracts, legal claims and liabilities, arbitration, etc.

2. The Directorate of the Union of Soviet Composers assumes the duty of safeguarding of authors' rights of the members of the Composers' Union in the territory of the USSR and, through corresponding Soviet organs abroad, takes necessary measures to protect other rights of members of the Union of Soviet Composers.

3. The Union of Soviet Composers maintains, with joint responsibility before the Directorate and the Secretariat of the Union of Soviet Composers, a financially autonomous organization possessing the rights of a juridical person, the Musical Fund of the USSR, whose principal task is to render aid for the creative activities of composers and musicologists, and which concentrates the entire administrative and financial services for the improvement of the material and cultural needs of members of the Union of Soviet Composers.

4. The Directorate of the Musical Fund of the USSR is appointed by the Directorate of the Union of Soviet Composers.

5. The Union of Soviet Composers maintains the following organizations:

   a. A publishing press, *The Soviet Composer*, whose task is the publication and wide distribution of Soviet musical literature of all types, as well as of scientific and popularizing works by Soviet musicologists.
   b. All-Union Bureau for Propaganda.

   Both organizations are financially independent and have the rights of juridical persons.

6. The Secretariat of the Union of Composers of the USSR takes charge of the activity of the Central House of Composers which constitutes an independent organization possessing the rights of juristic persons.

7. The financial funds of the Union of Soviet Composers are provided from the following sources:

   a. Budgetary appropriations from State organs.

b. Membership dues.

c. Income from the Property of the Union of Soviet Composers.

8. The Union of Soviet Composers and its subsidiary organizations are exempt from State or local taxes, dues or custom fees.

9. The Union of Soviet Composers extends its activity throughout the territory of the USSR.

10. The Directorate of the Union of Soviet Composers is domiciled in Moscow.

11. The Union of Soviet Composers has its seal inscribed THE UNION OF COMPOSERS OF THE USSR.

12. Unions of composers in other Soviet republics and regions have corresponding seals.

Appeal for Peace Addressed to Musicians of the World at the International Manifestation Held in East Berlin on 2 November 1961

On the 2nd November, 1961, leading composers and musicologists from the Soviet Union, the People's Republic of Poland, the Czechoslovak Socialist Republic, the People's Republic of Bulgaria, the People's Republic of Rumania, and the People's Republic of Hungary, met in the Apollo Hall of the German State Opera in Berlin to give their names, together with their colleagues from the German Democratic Republic, to a Manifestation for the Conclusion of a German Peace Treaty, for the securing of peace in the world. In an Appeal, the musicians from seven Socialist countries call on composers, musicians and musicologists of the whole world to help them realize this aim, which is for the wellbeing of mankind.

Nathan Notowicz, Secretary of the Union of German Composers and Musicologists, welcomed the foreign guests, as well as leading representatives of public and cultural life in the German Democratic Republic. The delegates of the various countries then made the following statements.

Dmitri Shostakovich, Soviet Union

Dear Friends, The question of the conclusion of a Peace Treaty with Germany and the final removal of the remnants of the Second World War is a question which today deeply moves all simple people in the world—moves the whole of mankind.

We Soviet people follow with great attention events in the heart of Europe, where the forces of progress, freedom, and peaceful creation fight against the forces of reaction, revanchism and militarism. It is well known that the West German revanchists do not want peace for Germany. They want to plunge the German people again into the terrible hellfire of a war. Can we, who are dedicated to peaceful and humanistic creative work, accept that the gigantic riches which are created by the working people, be transformed into a death-dealing weapon of horror and destructiveness never before known? No! No! and once again No! Every one of us to whom the joys of peaceful work are so dear has the duty today to raise his voice in defense of peace and justice. There must not be a single painter, actor or musician in the world who does not passionately protest against the preparations for an atomic battle.

Of great importance for the maintenance and consolidation of peace is the problem of the removal of the remnants of the Second World War, the peaceful solution of the German question, and on this basis, the normalisation of the situation in West Berlin.

The fact that there is no German Peace Treaty creates an uncertain situation and is a help to the aggressive forces.

We are of the opinion that a Peace Treaty is the only correct solution of the German question and we stand firm for the conclusion of this Peace Treaty based on mutually acceptable terms. We are convinced that the Peace Treaty will contribute towards normalising the mutual relations of States, will prevent a new world war and will relax international tension.

Our country is an enormous industrial power but we do not threaten anyone and we are of the opinion that all differences can be solved peacefully.

We musicians have the fate of the German people particularly at heart—the people of outstanding workers, great scholars, thinkers and eminent composers. We have only to remember that Germany presented the world with the genius Beethoven, who passionately called on the peoples of the earth to unite.

We long for the time when the whole of Germany will be united under the banner of peace and progress and will be forever a peace-loving happy country.

I shall never forget the tragedy of my birthplace, Leningrad, which suffered barbarous bombing and a cruel hunger blockade. Hundreds of thousands of the people of Leningrad, including women, children and old people, died of hunger or through the bombs. Can we allow mankind to suffer an even more terrible fate?

My dear friends—musicians from various countries, we stand passionately for the defence of peace and the happiness of the peoples, for the peaceful solution of the German question. Let us defend the right of the peoples for a peaceful happy life. Let beautiful and inspiring music sound all over the world rather than the hateful wailing of the sirens.

I call upon my colleagues in all countries of the earth to follow our appeal and raise your voices to defend peaceful creative work for the happiness and freedom of the people.

Stefan Sledzinski, People's Republic of Poland

Dear Colleagues, Sixteen years have already passed since the ending of the Second World War, but the whole world still feels the terrible results of this war.

The frightful irreplaceable losses in people and in goods which Polish culture and the whole of mankind suffered during the last war, during the fascist occupation, are for us—the representatives of Polish culture and Polish musical life—not only a past burdening us like a nightmare, but also a painful lesson showing us what fascism and imperialism lead to.

We shall never forget this lesson, just as many other peoples, including the German people, have not forgotten. For that reason we shall always be found in the forefront with those who stand for the right of mankind to peace and who work for that peace, no matter which country and in what form the hydra of fascism and imperialism raises its head.

Sixteen years ago when the whole world made the firm decision "Never again War," it looked as though the shadow of war had been banished for ever. It looked as though not only all the peoples, but also those who had been responsible for their fate, had drawn the correct lessons of history.

Time has shown however that for certain states and imperialist circles the terrible destruction was not enough. They place the world in danger of a new war, incalculable in its consequences and which threatens the existence of life on the earth altogether. We composers and musicians of all countries cannot wait indifferently for such a destructive war which would mean the destruction of all life and the highest achievements of the creative human spirit. We believe that works of art and not destructive tools are the expression of the endeavours of a true man.

Therefore we have the duty to defend peace which is so necessary for the development of art. And therefore we have the right to raise our voices for its defense.

Despite the frightful destruction of the last war—and may it be the last—we have developed art and science to a high degree in our country, thanks to our work and thanks to the care of the party and government. We Polish artists and musicians understand that we are also defending all achievements in the sphere of music when we call for a fight for peace. We do not want the destruction of our Philharmonic and Symphonic Orchestras, opera houses and music schools, reconstructed with such effort and more beautiful than before. We do not want that our rich musical creations be destroyed so that in Poland music is silenced as it was during the dark years of the war and the occupation.

We want every citizen of our country to be able to hear music in peace, to be receptive to its beauty and obtain joy from it. And we believe that musicians of all countries have the same aim.

We think that the more people in the world correctly understand music and its message the less will brutal actions be able to provoke conflicts and wars.

Allow me, on behalf of the Union of Polish composers and all representatives of musical life in Poland to express our complete agreement with the initiative of the Composers Union of the GDR for the signing of an Appeal for the Conclusion of a Peace Treaty with Germany and the peaceful settlement of the German problem. We believe that in this way the source, from which the unleashing of a new war threatening the existence of mankind stems, will be removed.

At the same time I take this opportunity of conveying warmest greetings to our colleagues in the German Democratic Republic on behalf of the Polish cultural workers, and wish you victory in your noble fight for a just cause, which is also ours.

Antonin Sychra, Socialist Republic of Czechoslovakia

Ladies and Gentlemen, This is my 18th visit to Berlin and today I want to speak about my experiences and memories.

I first visited the German Democratic Republic in 1950. At that time the situation was very complicated and, in many respects unfavourable. The food shops, and others were pretty empty. Everywhere there were ruins. And when you spoke to someone about the political situation, and particularly with the young people, you had the impression that you heard the correct opinion but that actually you were hearing meaningless phrases which had no clear and live content. Of course it only looked like this from the outside. For instance at the musicological congresses on the life and work of Johann Sebastian Bach it was quite different. There you felt the clear, ideological, purposeful position. Together we created a new picture of J. S. Bach and in so doing, unexpectedly found that we were seeing a reflection of the new forceful life in the GDR, a reflection of the new political path which the German Democratic Republic was taking.

During the World Festival I saw the GDR, and particularly Berlin, in another light. Berlin was international, full of life, joy and movement. Some other festivals, especially in Moscow, were perhaps more colourful and also bigger, but none of them could be compared with the Berlin Festival in the matter of fighting spirit. When you spoke there with someone on topical questions, you felt—and this was bound up with the whole atmosphere—that you were no longer hearing phrases but real experiences which formed the basis of a firm world outlook.

Then there were other meetings, the Beethoven Congress, the Schubert celebrations, lectures at the Humboldt University, discussions and meeting of the Composers Union. We made many valuable new friendships and gathered many deep impressions and fought many fights together.

One thing I find particularly important. In the German Democratic Republic you see how every question of science and art is bound up with life and the political struggle. Sometimes it happens that we cultural workers are too liberal. We are not always vigilant enough when we judge new western trends in art, new experiments or opinions. In the GDR the situation is different. Here all conflicts and contradictions seem to be sharper and more immediate. When you get to know the present situation here well, you have to agree with our German colleagues that it is necessary to have all these things out—thoroughly and from the party point of view.

When we speak today of the help of the socialist states for the German Democratic Republic we must bear in mind that this is a mutual help. It is help for those who are holding the outpost of our whole socialist camp. Through this help we shall all be stronger and firmer. With this in mind I welcome this meeting, which is bound up with an important turning point in world history, on behalf of the Union of Czechoslovak Composers and of the whole Czechoslovak people.

Petko Stainoff, People's Republic of Bulgaria

Ladies and Gentlemen, The whole of mankind is experiencing exciting and fateful days. At this critical moment all peace-loving and honest people are looking to the leading statesmen of the big powers. We know that war destroys all the prerequisites for the development of science and culture, together with the well-being and progress of mankind. We, the Bulgarian musicians, follow with deep sympathy all events in connection with the maintenance of the dearest possession of mankind—peace. If we undertake all efforts and do all in our power—however little that is—to contribute towards the maintenance of peace, we fulfill the most urgent duty of all responsible musicians. The Bulgarian composers and musicologists are united in assuring their German colleagues, and the whole world, that they fight side by side with them for the solution of this serious problem—the security and well-being of the German people.

Our peace-loving and industrious Bulgarian folk works for our beloved homeland and leads it along the road to Socialism with an enthusiasm and energy it never before possessed. The Bulgarian people, who took this road to the bright future of Communism out of conviction and at the price of its own blood, will guard this precious thing. This does not merely concern the Bulgarian people. It is a question of the maintenance of peace in the whole world, for the road of one people to Socialism and Communism is reached only through firm and fraternal friendship with other nations who work for peace.

In the present critical period the Berlin question appears to be one of the most dangerous problems out of which a world of conflict can arise. We are of the opinion that this problem must be solved as quickly as possible and that the danger of conflagration for a new world war be removed. Every possibility that Berlin would be used as the starting point of any conflict must, from the start, be prevented. The German people long for peace and quiet in order that they can still better use their strength and capabilities, which they have proved over the centuries, for the building up of their material and spiritual life. More than ever before the German people need peace in order to be able to work.

We, the Bulgarian musicians, stand firmly behind the decision of the German and Soviet peoples to sign the Peace Treaty with Germany, because we are convinced that this will be beneficial not only to the German people but to the whole of mankind.

My dear German colleagues, the Bulgarian composers, who respect and esteem your creative work, greet, through you, the whole German people, and promise to you and to the whole world not to desert you at this time, no matter what the difficulties which may arise in the solution of such an important question for you and the whole of mankind. We are prepared to declare our solidarity with the delegates of all countries at this congress and to sign the Appeal in which artists all over the world are called upon to stand for a speedy successful solution of the German question, and for the settlement of all problems in connection with the maintenance of world peace. With all our hearts we wish our esteemed German colleagues strength and confidence in their creative social-political work and determination in the defense of our mutual cause.

Ferenc Szabó, People's Republic of Hungary

Dear Colleagues, Dear Friends, In the course of its thousand years of history our people had to fight for hundreds of years against the German aggressors, who under the slogan "Drang nach Osten" continuously attacked our fatherland in order to destroy its national state and to plunder and subject our people so that our country could become part of the German Reich.

At the turn of the 17th century the superior force was victorious and our national state was destroyed. Our vanquished and plundered fatherland became an Austrian colony for almost three centuries.

All this reached a pinnacle in the frightful flood of death and destruction of the Second World War. The reactionary rulers of Hungary of that time drove the suppressed Hungarian workers and peasants by the hundreds of thousands into the battlefield, forcing them to die for the interests of German imperialism. German imperialism and fascism devastated our country, sent hundreds of thousands of our sons to their deaths and supported, with its whole power, the reactionary rulers of our country.

We do not nourish resentment against the German working people. Humanist German thought, which is rooted in the people, German literature and music, decisively influence the development of Hungarian culture. The great classics of German music—Bach, Handel, Beethoven, Mendelssohn, Schumann, Wagner—are continuously performed in our concerts and opera houses. We Hungarian composers learned the laws of beauty of the classical music from Bach's chorale. Through intensive study of the Bach Fugues and of his two- and three-part inventions we completed our knowledge of counterpoint. The wealth of forms and the perfection of Beethoven's works was, and is, the highest ideal for every Hungarian composer.

We esteem and love all that is valuable which the German people in the fields of science, thought, art and literature have created. We are bound by ties of friendship to the working people of the German Democratic Republic. We gladly visit them because we know and see that militarism and fascism have been torn out by the roots in the German Democratic Republic. With trust and sympathy we observe the impressive development of their country and are prepared to fully support all efforts and the fight of the working people in the interest of their sovereignty and their socialist achievements.

We must not forget however that on the other side of the borders of the German Democratic Republic there exists another Germany, where aggressive German militarism and fascism lives on and prepares a new world war. We have no right to forget that the rulers of the present West Germany again dream of the conquest and plundering of other countries. An official organ of the government of the German Federal Republic issued a map—and it is still being distributed—on which one-half of the Hungarian People's Republic, which was never German soil and which has belonged to Hungary for a thousand years, appears as "stolen" German territory.

It becomes ever more clear that the imperialist powers have given West Germany the role of ignition button to press, which is to unleash a new world war. It can explode tomorrow setting the world in flames and bringing the danger of death to mankind. The aggressive revanchists, who were once Hitler's generals, can take over the ignition button tomorrow and there is only one possibility of saving mankind from a third devastating and bloody world war—the settlement of the German question through the conclusion of a Peace Treaty.

We, Hungarian composers, musicologists and artists want to live and work with all artists in the world in peace and security. We have many plans and we wish to finish the works we have begun. We want to further develop the art and musical culture of our people who are building Socialism. We want to give our people and the whole world still more beauty, confidence, faith and strength. That is what we are living and working for. And for that we need peace and security. That is why we demand that the German Peace Treaty be concluded.

On behalf of the Hungarian composers, musicologists and musicians I declare that we are in agreement with the aims, and with the content and text of the Appeal. We are prepared to sign this Appeal and to support it with all our strength in Hungary and in the whole world.

Hanns Eisler, German Democratic Republic

With grief and care I turn, above all, to my colleagues in West Germany. Their situation is difficult. First because of the peculiarities of the profession. Music—in contra-distinction to the other arts—has still retained archaic traits of the unconscious, bluntness. To a certain extent the ear is more backward than the quick eye. This has contributed to form the musician type, who seeks to remain outside the quarrels of the world, who does not recognise his social situation and does not want to be involved in the great discussions of our time. He does not want to have anything to do with politics but he forgets that politics have to do with him—that the general interests are also his interests and that you can't live outside society but only vegetate. Such an attitude also harms his art. But to take part in the fight for the noblest task of our century—the defence and maintenance of peace—means also to look after his own private interest.

The pressure which is put on him, the pressure of the state apparatus of the Federal Republic, the newspapers, radio and television stations, which make anyone who shows only sympathy for Socialism, or who in the most modest way stands for recognition of the German Democratic Republic and for the Peace Treaty, into a suspected, dangerous person, who, if nothing worse happens to him, will be forced down to earth through economic boycott. Add to this that young composers are driven into a style of music, through the music critics, through the radio and by the juries of musical festivals, which separates them from their listeners and leads to sectarianism. So it happens that often young talented people, appear like old men in their works and experienced composers behave like experimental beginners, in order to appear on the music markets. Such an attitude changes into a social attitude and the isolated composer isolates himself from social life.

So as not to be misunderstood—I was and I am for what is new in music. But experiments must have a meaning and not be pseudo experiments such as were discarded long ago—artistically and therefore also socially meaningless. The danger is that those who do not play the game do not get performed and are thrown overboard as useless, or they remain silent. If they play the game they deform or squander their talent in sectarian circles.

I do not say this in order to begin a debate on esthetics, but only to describe the difficulties of the West German composers. Because however they compose and whatever differences we have, everything gives way today to the decisive question of peace. Music is made by people for people and if the people are destroyed then music is destroyed also.

In the western world they speak of the great crisis and the danger of a new terrible war which threatens to wipe out the world. We do not believe that there is real ground for a world crisis. What are the grounds?

I find it difficult to repeat what is said daily. The words are bitter in my mouth and I repeat them, only they should be said here and by me: the Government of the Soviet Union proposes that both German States should be recognised, that a Peace Treaty be signed with both German States and that the situation in West Berlin be normalised. It is prepared to give the Treaties into the custody of the United Nations and to guarantee adherence to them in every possible way.

The answer of a number of western governments—above all the Federal Republic—was a threat of war, hate propaganda against the people of the socialist camp and particularly against the German Democratic Republic—threats of which Goebbels need not have been ashamed. That gangsters spit out their hate against the Soviet Union is not new but the heat and the vulgarity of this propaganda is no accident. A former SS general said "The post-war period is at an end and we are now in the prewar period." In West Germany you can write, print and distribute such criminal sayings. West German politicians speak of the highest risks which must now be taken. Fascists and revanchists sit in high and the highest government posts. Judges once again stretch out their blood-stained shoes under High Court benches and the fascist scum once again greedily looks toward the East. The big bankers, the monopolists and the big landowners again speak of freedom. What do they mean? The basic folly of our epoch—anti-Communism—as Thomas Mann said, has been made the leading idea of the State. Why? Because the Soviet Union wants to conclude a Peace Treaty with both German States. This propaganda of hate has increased since the 13th August when our government took measures which were absolutely necessary.*

In their own interests the West German colleagues must tear down the veil which hangs over the truth. They must resist. They must immunise themselves against the hatred of big business—hatred against the most noble idea of mankind—Socialism and Communism. Just imagine what possibilities will exist for us all when there is such a Peace Treaty and normalisation of the situation in West Berlin—no worry about the future, an atmosphere freed of poison, peaceful competition between the nations.

So, we musicians are also called upon to take our part in the fight for peace with our works, and—wherever we are—through our personal stand.

May we not be lacking in strength and courage.

* Reference to the Berlin Wall, built on 13 August 1961.

Appeal Adopted by All Who Attended the Manifestation:

To Composers, Musicologists and Musicians All Over the World, Mankind is threatened by the danger of a new war—the most terrible and perhaps the last in history. Yet the possibility exists of turning aside the danger and of banning war and weapons for ever.

In this situation we address ourselves to our colleagues all over the world. When, 25 years ago, the anti-fascists stated that Hitler meant war, many did not believe it. Today, we who have experienced the horrors of war and the fiends in the shape of man who unleashed it, we affirm that the West German revanchists and generals, made more cunning but no wiser as a result of the last war, are preparing a new one. They do not even attempt to hide the fact. The identical mad plans of 25 years ago, and for the most part the same men, are used. In barely disguised terms they speak of a new order in Europe and of a military attack on the German Democratic Republic and other socialist countries, which they call "liberation," just as Hitler did in similar cases. Openly and shamelessly they demand an army of 400,000 armed with atomic weapons. They have, already, leading positions in NATO.

However, not only has the relation of forces in the world changed in favour of peace—in Germany also the situation has changed. There were always millions who wanted peace and they are also there today in West Germany. Up to now they have not had the strength to thwart the German militarists' war policy. The measures taken by the government of the German Democratic Republic on 13th August saved world peace and were a mighty blow by the German people, on German soil, against German militarism. With this action, against which German militarism curses and groans, the fight against war has entered a new phase in the whole world. The next thing will be the conclusion of a German Peace Treaty. Through the existence of the German Democratic Republic the forces of peace inside Germany are, for the first time in history, so strong, so confident, and so organised that they are in a position to prevent a war—together with the peace-loving people of the whole world.

In the western countries various factors combine to show the people what happens in the socialist countries in a completely false light. We, the citizens of the socialist countries, assure you that war will never be started by a socialist country. No-one here can profit from the making of atom bombs or other war material. The production of weapons is a necessity for our countries, and one which we would gladly renounce. Our countries, especially the Soviet Union, have made gigantic plans during the course of which the face of the earth and the fate of the people will be thoroughly changed in the next few years. In order to realise those plans we need peace and nothing but peace.

In the countries of western Europe and the United States the argument that a new war would be so terrible that no-one can want it or begin it, is often heard. It is true that this argument has validity if it depended on reason and clear consideration. But the militarists have plans which, it is true, envisage millions of dead in their own country (the "specialists" call it "Megadead"), but which principally reckon with the complete destruction of the socialist countries. It is of course a false speculation as sensible people in all leading countries understand. But those who expect that the West German militarists and the militarists of other capitalist countries think clearly and soberly, are themselves guilty of false speculation. War cannot be avoided by relying on the good sense of those whose object in life it is to make war.

The idea still prevails that nothing can be done against a threatening war or, that at the best, only professional politicians know what ought to be done. Protected by such arguments war is prepared. However, recently, and particularly since the 13th August the recognition that peace can be saved when millions of people make it their business, has grown in many countries. The comprehension that there are two German States and that this reality must be recognised, is coming to be accepted in the neutral countries of Asia and Africa, but also in England, the United States and other countries.

The neutralisation of the West Berlin conflagration centre, the confirmation by Treaty of the existing Oder-Neisse-frontier, an atomic-weapon-free zone in Central Europe and the acceptance of both German States in UNO, can be achieved by peaceful negotiations. They are reasonable demands which serve peace and are therefore in the best interests of us all.

Dear colleagues your voices carry weight. Appeal to your people, to the public and to the government of your countries. It is high time that the remains of the Second World War be removed and the preparations for a third war be smashed.

We none of us can imagine a life without music! Do not let us forget that without life there is no music!

[Official English text]

Musical Ideology of the Nationalist Socialist (Nazi) Party

I propose to show to German musicians what used to be and then to call for their help to establish what ought to be.

A great heritage ran the peril of being undone. A whole generation grew up which had to a large degree lost the zeal for the strength and purity of German art as it was created by the masters, a generation which all too often as in everyday life confused freedom with license, which placed the brain above the heart, which preferred to cultivate all that is alien and international rather than native. No longer did their hearts beat faster—the German true beat—they called this concept reactionary.

Then, as National Socialism captured more and more hearts, the firmament of art began to be streaked with lightning flashes. Those among us who had always identified themselves with German art, felt that the power which emanated from this movement had to do not only with the realities of life but also possessed a deeper spiritual world concept, a nucleus from which a new hope was blossoming also for German art. Thus we, too, became comrades-in-arms, and so there arose the *Kampfbund für deutsche Kultur*, indissolubly connected with the names of Alfred Rosenberg and Hans Hinkel, their founders and first leaders, and WE BEGAN TO MARCH. From one place to another, everywhere there were things to be cleaned up—there was enough dirt! Meanwhile, there the great work of the Reichsskulturkammer was slowly unfolding, which embraced all artistic professions, and which reached its peak in the unforgettable speech of its founder, Minister Goebbels, at its inauguration in November 1933. Thus was painstakingly created an instrument which in its great idea of steady progress could put art and artists to service as well. This betokens not alone an organizational reform but also the watch over the spiritual and artistic life of the nation under the guidance of the Reichskulturkammer, and especially, the Reichsmusikkammer, a watch not to impose restrictions to art but to protect it from influences that degrade and alienate it from the German soul.

And this must be the wish and the hope of all of us, involving the unforgettable words of Adolf Hitler: "Had the artists known what I will some day do for them, they would all be on my side."

[From a chapter in *Rückblick und Ausblick*, by Paul Graener, German composer, published in *Deutsche Kultur im Neuen Reich*, Berlin, 1934]

Hearings Regarding Hanns Eisler: Committee on Un-American Activities House of Representatives, Washington, D.C. 24, 25, and 26 September 1947

J. Parnell Thomas, New Jersey, Chairman*

Karl E. Mundt, South Dakota	John W. Wood, Georgia
John McDowell, Pennsylvania	John E. Rankin, Mississippi
Richard M. Nixon, California**	J. Hardin Peterson, Florida
Richard B. Vail, Illinois	Herbert C. Bonner, North Carolina

Robert E. Stripling, Chief Investigator

Donald T. Appell, Special Investigator

Stripling: When and where were you born?
Eisler: 6 July 1898, in Leipzig, Germany.
Stripling: What is your occupation?
Eisler: I am a composer.
Stripling: Musical composer?
Eisler: Musical composer—may I add, of international reputation.
Stripling: Of international reputation?
Eisler: Yes.
Stripling: In what institutions did you receive your musical education?
Eisler: In Vienna, at the Academy. I am the pupil of the famous composer Arnold Schoenberg, one of the greatest living masters of modern music.

Stripling: Mr. Chairman, the loudspeaker equipment doesn't seem to be working, and I am sure everyone is having a good bit of difficulty in hearing. Could I ask for a slight recess to see if it is possible to get the equipment working?
The Chairman: All right.

Stripling: Mr. Eisler, on August 5, 1938, the Acting Secretary of Labor issued an order permitting you and your wife to remain until January 21, 1939, before departing from the United States. On January 9, 1939, you filed an application to extend the time of your temporary stay for six months. In March 2, 1939, the Assistant Secretary of Labor ordered your deportation from the United States.
Eisler: Yes, I remember this quite well.
Stripling: And you were given an extension until April 7, 1939.
Eisler: Yes, Hitler was already in Austria, and being deported to Germany would have meant my execution.
Stripling: During 1940 you were employed in various capacities. Will you outline these for the committee?
Eisler: I was employed as professor of music at the New School for Social Research. And I got a grant from the Rockefeller Foundation.

* On 3 December 1949, J. Parnell Thomas was sentenced to 6–18 months imprisonment, after pleading no contest and throwing himself on the mercy of the court on charges of misappropriation of government funds, putting on the Congressional payroll a number of his relatives who never did any work, including a bed-ridden 71-year-old aunt of his wife, and extorting kickbacks from employees. He was released on 9 September 1950 on parole, and subsequently obtained full pardon from President Truman.

** In 1968 Richard M. Nixon was elected President of the United States.

Stripling: Now, Mr. Eisler, are you now, or have you ever been a Communist?

Eisler: I am not now a Communist. I remember I made, when I was a young man, in 1926, an application for the German Communist party, but I found out very quickly that I couldn't combine my artistic activities with the demands of any political party, so I dropped out.

Stripling: Mr. Eisler, you have been the foremost figure in the revolutionary movement of the Soviet Union in the musical field, have you not?

Eisler: No, sir. The Soviet Union has wonderful composers and I never was in the foreground of the movement of the Soviet Union at all.

Stripling: Mr. Chairman, I have here a copy of *The Daily Worker* of January 15, 1935. I should like to introduce this into the record. It states: "Hanns Eisler will arrive here January 27. The famous revolutionary composer, who has been living in exile in Paris and London since the advent of Hitler, is well known in Europe and America for his brilliant compositions, which include K-u-h-l-e W-a-m-p-e." Would you pronounce it for us?

Eisler: Kuhle Wampe. This is a motion picture which I did in 1932 in Berlin.

Stripling: Hell on Earth, Comintern, M-a-s-s-n-a-h-m-e.

Eisler: What is that last one, please?

Stripling: M-a-s . . .

Eisler: M-a-s . . . Would you be so kind, please?

Stripling: M-a-s . . . (exhibits printed paper).

Eisler: Massnahme, which is a German word meaning Expedient.

Stripling: And the next one?

Eisler: Tempo der Zeit, which means The Tempo of our Times.

Stripling: And the next one?

Eisler: Rot Front, which means Red Front.

Stripling: Red Front?

Eisler: Yes.

Stripling: Did you compose all of them?

Eisler: Yes.

Stripling: Mr. Chairman, I have here *The Daily Worker* of February 18, 1935, which contains an article entitled "Noted Composer of Comintern Arrives for U.S. Concert Tour—Hanns Eisler Exiled from Germany and His Music Banned."—The Communist Party in Germany had to fight the old beer garden atmosphere and nationalistic ditties of the middle class which had gone their way to the masses. In this cultural and musical development, the German workers were led by Hanns Eisler. The class struggle in Germany, strikes, barricades, May First celebrations, and other demonstrations are bound up with his name. Eisler, however, was not happy in the surroundings of the musical bourgeoisie. To be one of a great number of decadent musicians meant a futility stagnating to his talents. Only when Eisler came into the struggle of the working class did he find his medium and with it grew his power of composing music which expressed not only the life and battles of the German workers but of the working class of the entire world.

The Chairman: What is it you are reading from now?

Stripling: From *The Daily Worker*, Mr. Chairman, concerning Mr. Eisler's arrival in the United States in 1935.

The Chairman: Is that the Communist *Daily Worker*, the organ of the Communist Party in the United States?

Stripling: It is the official organ of the Communist Party.

The Chairman: That is what I wanted the record to show.

Stripling: Mr. Eisler, have you on a number of occasions said, in effect, that music is one of the most powerful weapons for the bringing about of the revolution?

Eisler: Napoleon said . . .

The Chairman: Never mind Napoleon. You tell what you said.

Eisler: I consider myself, in this matter, a pupil of Napoleon. I think in music I can enlighten and help people in distress, in their fight for their rights . . .

Stripling: You have written a lot of songs, Mr. Eisler, have you not?

Eisler: I have written not only songs. Here is a book printed by a subversive organization, the Oxford University Press, but I cannot say that I am a member of the Oxford University Press.

Stripling: Mr. Chairman, I should like to introduce a translation of an article which appeared in *Sovietskaya Musica*, in March and April of 1933 issue, "For a Solid Front of all Proletarian and Revolutionary Musicians." (Reads)

Eisler: May I object to the reading of articles of this kind, old articles from a different time, because it can only create a kind of hysteria against me.

The Chairman: Mr. Stripling, what is the purpose of your reading these excerpts?

Stripling: The purpose is to show that Mr. Eisler is the Karl Marx of Communism in the musical field and he is well aware of it.

Eisler: I would be flattered.

Stripling: Mr. Chairman, I intend to show that the International Music Bureau, as a section of the Communist International, was a major program of the Soviet Union in their effort to bring about a world revolution and establish a proletarian dictatorship. This International Music Bureau, which Mr. Eisler conceived and reorganized in 1935, after he had been in the United States, carried on extensive activities, which I shall be glad to introduce into the record. Now, I would like to question Mr. Eisler about the origin of it.

Eisler: It was my idea and the idea of my friends.

Stripling: Mr. Eisler, who composed the Internationale?

Eisler: A man called Pierre Degeyter. It was written around 1888.

Stripling: Did you ever belong to an organization known as the Pierre Degeyter Music Club?

Eisler: I gave a lecture there once.

Stripling: In the United States?

Eisler: In the Pierre Degeyter Club.

Stripling: Do you consider it to be a Communist organization?

Eisler: Mr. Stripling, I don't ask anybody if he is a Communist or not when I go to a club and speak.

Stripling: I have here a song book, entitled *Red Song Book*. This was published, prepared by the Workers Music League, with the hammer and sickle on the front, and they feature on the back the song Comintern by Hanns Eisler. Would you like to read the words?

Eisler: You have a better pronunciation than I.

Stripling: (reading):

> Oh, you who are missing,
> Oh, comrades in dungeons,
> You're with us, you're with us,
> This day of our vengeance.
> No Fascists can daunt us,
> No terror can halt;
> All lands will take flame
> With the fire of revolt,
> All lands.
>
> The Comintern calls you,
> Raise high Soviet banner
> In steeled ranks to battle.
> Raise sickle and hammer
> Our answer: Red Legions
> We raise in our might;
> Our answer: Red Storm Troops

We lunge to the fight.
Our answer Red Storm Troops.

From Russia victorious
The workers' October
Comes storming reactions
Regime the world over
We're coming with Lenin
For Bolshevik work
From London, Havana,
Berlin and New York,
From London.

Rise up, fields and workshops!
Come out workers, farmers!
To battle march onward,
March on world stormers!
Eyes sharp on your guns,
Red banners unfurled,
Advance Proletarians
To conquer the world.
Advance Proletarians.

Is this one of your little ditties that someone adopted?

Eisler: This song was written in 1926. This is a translation. When was the song printed here?

Stripling: Beg pardon?

Eisler: When was it printed here?

Stripling: This was published in 1932 in New York.

Eisler: In 1932 I was in Berlin. I am not responsible for literary translations. My song was written in Germany for a theater performance on the anniversary of the German revolution in 1918.

McDowell: Who wrote the words, Mr. Stripling?

Stripling: By Victor Jerome.

Eisler: In 1932.

Stripling: Other songs which appear in this issue are the Internationale, The Barricades, The Builders, Comrades, The Bugles Are Sounding, Solidarity, The Workers Funeral March, and others.

Eisler: Very beautiful melody there.

Stripling: I have another one here, Mr. Eisler, entitled "America Sings."

Eisler: Yes.

Stripling: That was published by the Workers Book Shop, in New York, which is the official publishing house of the Communist Party. Among the songs which are contained in *America Sings* are *Comintern, Comrades, The Bugles Are Sounding, Internationale, Red Air Fleet, Red Flag, Rounds, Salute to Life, Scottsboro Boys, Solidarity Forever,* and for some unknown reason, *The Star Spangled Banner.* I have here, Mr. Chairman, an article entitled *The Revolutionary Musical Front,* by Gregory Schneerson, which appeared in the magazine *Sovietskaya Musica* of May 1933. It says: "The Workers League has published songs by Hanns Eisler and by Soviet composers which have been translated into the English language. The American comrades have succeeded in getting into the movement a number of outstanding musicians and theorists. Great assistance in theoretical courses has been given by the Pierre Degeyter Music Club in New York, organized by the League. The work in the club is being conducted by such great musicians as Henry Cowell, Charles Seeger, and others. The League has over 6,000 active members. A number of large choruses and orchestras make the league one of the strongest and outstanding factors in the International Musical Revolutionary front." Mr. Eisler, when you were in Moscow in 1935, did you give out some interviews or write some articles?

Eisler: I think I gave interviews, as usual. Mostly ideas about Germany.

Stripling: I have an article here written by you, which appeared in *Sovietskoe Iskusstvo,* July 29, 1935, and it has your picture, and is printed in Russian. The title is *The Destruction of Art.* You state: "Still, I am an optimist with regard to the future because I believe in the inexhaustible strength of the organized masses. The dark epoch of Fascism makes it clear to every honest artist that close cooperation with the working masses is the only way of dealing with creative art. Only in a revolutionary struggle will an artist find his own individuality. Similar developments can be observed in America where the well-known composer Aaron Copland has written a mass song *The First of May.* An active role is also played in the workers' musical movement by Henry Cowell, of San Francisco. These events, which only three years ago could hardly have been imagined, proved that for a real artist there is only one way, the road toward revolution. It would not be long before there would not be left a single great artist on the other side of the barricades. Revolutionary music is now more powerful than ever. Its political and artistic importance is growing daily." Mr. Eisler, what do you mean by "on the other side of the barricades"?

Eisler: Will you repeat the title of this article?

Stripling: The title of it was *The Destruction of Art.*

Eisler: By whom?

Stripling: By Hanns Eisler.

Eisler: No, I didn't destroy art. I spoke on how Fascism has destroyed art.

The Chairman: I don't think that is responsive to the question. What was your question, Mr. Stripling?

Stripling: I asked him what he meant when he referred to "the other side of the barricades."

Eisler: I meant, in Germany, to fight against Hitler. That was my real belief.

Stripling: The next matter, Mr. Chairman, I would like to introduce, is a translation of an interview with Hanns Eisler, which appeared in the *Evening Moscow* of June 27, 1935. This is quoting you, Mr. Eisler "I left Germany after the Reichstag fire. Therefore, I have only second-hand information about the latest events in the musical life of Germany. It is natural and logical that all efforts to promote the workers' musical movement are radically suppressed by the Fascist regime. Not only are the workers' unions persecuted by the Fascists but also the leftist elements among the bourgeois composers. Even Paul Hindemith who, in view of the tragic shortage of people on the musical front, was hurriedly reinstated by the Hitlerites, has now lost their confidence. Considerable time must pass before a young generation of second-class musicians will grow up who will satisfy the political and artistic expectations of Adolf Hitler. For the time being the leadership in the musical world of Germany is divided between Hans Pfitzner and the very old Richard Strauss. Actually, Pfitzner's popularity was never significant. But Strauss was once great. The scores which he is composing now do not add any glorious pages to the history of his creative art. Recently the first performance of his new opera based on a libretto by Stefan Zweig took place at Dresden. The permission to produce a play by Zweig, who is a Jew, in present-day Germany reveals the pressing desire to compensate Strauss for his obedience. Alas, this seems to have been the only compensation for all his efforts. His opera had a dubious success. In London, where I went directly from Germany, I wrote a symphony in which I tried to solve a number of purely technical musical problems. There, an outstanding conductor, Ernest Ansermet, conducted the first performance of my symphony. I intend to follow up this musical work by a new symphony dedicated to the victims of the Fascist terror. From England I proceeded to America. I have the most pleasant recollections about this trip. First of all, I succeeded in giving there a great number of concerts for the benefit of political prisoners. Secondly, I gave a whole series of popular lectures on German Fascism. These lectures were always attended by very large audiences. For instance, in New York about 5,000 people listened to the lectures. In Hollywood and Los Angeles the audience consisted not only of workers but of numerous representatives of the progressive intelligentsia. I am extremely pleased to report a considerable shift to the left among American artists. I do not believe it would be an exaggeration to say that the best people in the musical world of America (with very few exceptions) share at present extremely progressive ideas. Their names? They are Aaron Copland, Henry Cowell, Wallingford Riegger, the outstanding musical theoretician Charles Seeger, the greatest specialist on modern music Nicolas Slonimsky, and finally the brightest star on the American musical horizon, the great conductor, Leopold Stokowski. Recently he even dared to play the Internationale at a concert. This nearly caused a riot." Mr. Eisler, did you write a song entitled *In Praise of Learning?*

Eisler: Yes.

Stripling: I will read the words to this one verse. It says:

> Learn now the simple truth,
> You, for whom the time has come at last.
> It is not too late.
> Learn now the A, B, C,
> It is not enough, but learn it still.
> Fear not, be not downhearted,
> Begin, you must learn the lesson,
> You must be ready to take over,
> You must be ready to take over.

What do you mean, "You must be ready to take over"?

Eisler: This song appeared in a play which I wrote the music for. It was written in 1929 in Berlin. The play was based on the famous novel by Maxim Gorki. This theater piece was sung by workers on the stage.

The Chairman: You didn't mean that you must be ready to take over now, did you?

Eisler: I can't understand your question.

The Chairman: You said as it applied to Germany.

Eisler: Not only to Germany. It was a song in a show. It applied to the situation on the stage.

Stripling: It was shown in the United States. He wrote the music for it in the United States.

Eisler: No, I wrote the music in 1929 or 1930 in Berlin. It was produced in Copenhagen, in New York and in Paris. It was a theater play.

The Chairman: It doesn't apply only to Germany but applies to France and Italy and the United States?

Eisler: This song applies to the historical structure of the Russian people from 1905 until 1917.

The Chairman: Would you write the same song here in the United States now, about "You must take over" here in the United States?

Eisler: No.

The Chairman: You have changed your opinion, then?

Eisler: No, but I am a guest, a stranger here, and the labor movement can handle their affairs themselves. That is what I mean.

Stripling: Mr. Eisler, did you ever send greetings to the Soviet Union?

Eisler: Sure.

Stripling: You don't hate Stalin, Mr. Eisler?

Eisler: Pardon?

Stripling: Do you hate Stalin?

Eisler: No.

Stripling: Why did you tell the immigration authorities that you hated Stalin?

Eisler: I cannot remember the fact. If I really made such a stupid remark I was an idiot.

Stripling: You said, "I hate Stalin just as I hate Hitler" when you were before the immigration authorities.

Eisler: I am surprised. There must be a misunderstanding, or it is a completely idiotic, hysteric remark.

The Chairman: Do you remember?

Eisler: I don't remember the remark. I think that Stalin is one of the greatest historical personalities of our time.

Stripling: This message, Mr. Chairman, refers to Stalin's Constitution, by Hanns Eisler, and reads: "Hearty greetings to the Constitution of the great socialistic state, based on the great principle, From Each According to his Abilities, to Each According to his Work. It is almost impossible to encompass the tremendous consequences which your Constitution will have for future instruction of the new socialist culture. Each success for the Soviet Union is success for the international proletariat. It gives us courage in struggle and binds us to give all our strength in the defense of the Soviet Union."

Eisler: Did I write this?

Stripling: It says "By Hanns Eisler, hearty greetings."

Eisler: I cannot remember. It is quite possible that I did.

Stripling: The Great Soviet Encyclopedia, Mr. Eisler, published in Moscow, in 1933, prints your picture and says: "Hanns Eisler, born 1898, composer, Communist, is at the head of the proletarian movement in German music." Is that an error on the part of this Great Soviet Encyclopedia to refer to you as a Communist?

Eisler: It is an error. They call everybody a Communist who is active like me. I would be a swindler if I called myself a Communist. The Communist underground workers in every country have proved that they are heroes. I am not an hero. I am a composer.

Stripling: Did you write the music for a play *Die Massnahme?*

Eisler: Sure.

Stripling: Would you describe it to the committee.

Eisler: It goes back to an old Japanese play. I wrote the music for it.

Stripling: It dealt with party strategy?

Eisler: Yes.

Stripling: It had to do with four young Communists, did it not?

Eisler: Yes, sir.

Stripling: And three of the Communists murdered the fourth one because they felt he would be a menace to the cause, is that correct?

Eisler: Yes.

Stripling: That is the theme of it?

Eisler: Yes.

Stripling: The real title of the play is *Disciplinary Measure*, isn't that right?

Eisler: Yes, it is a poetical philosophical play.

Stripling: Mr. Chairman, I don't think we can finish with Mr. Eisler before lunch. We will have to call him back to the stand.

The Chairman: All right, we will recess.

Stripling: Mr. Eisler, you stated that you have a sister in the United States.

Eisler: Yes.

Stripling: By the name of Ruth Fischer.

Eisler: Yes.

Stripling: Do you recall receiving a letter from her on April 27, 1944, addressed to you and your wife?

Eisler: I don't recall it. What kind of letter was it, please?

Stripling: In this letter she accused you and her brother Gerhard of being agents of the GPU. She stated as follows (reading): "If the local branches of the GPU can succeed in making clever arrangements for a natural death it will not succeed this time. Not for you nor for Gerhard Eisler, Chief of the

German GPU division in the United States. . . . This time it will not be made so easy for you. You always play with terror and are always afraid to take your responsibility for your acts. I have made the following preparations: Three physicians have given me a thorough examination. I am now in good health. There is no cause for natural death. I am constantly under a physician's care and am taking care of myself in a sensible manner. The doctors are informed and in case of any trouble they will testify accordingly. A number of reputable journalists and politicians have been informed and possess a copy of this letter. A number of German emigrants have also been apprised." Do you recall receiving this letter?

Eisler: Really not. I don't recall getting such a letter. I think the letter is absolutely idiotic.

The Chairman: If I had received a letter like that, or anyone in this room, particularly if it was from our sister, they would remember.

Eisler: Maybe my wife put it away. But let us say, for the sake of the record, that I received this letter.

McDowell: Mr. Eisler, did you write the *Ballad to Paragraph 218?*

Eisler: I write only music.

McDowell: You remember the words?

Eisler: Sure.

McDowell: Did you write the *Ballad of the Maimed?*

Eisler: Of what, please?

McDowell: Ballad of the Maimed, the hurt, the injured.

Eisler: I wrote music to it.

McDowell: Have you read the words?

Eisler: Yes.

McDowell: Did you write *Ballad of Nigger Jim?*

Eisler: I wrote the music.

McDowell: You didn't write the words.

Eisler: No.

McDowell: Did you read the words?

Eisler: I read the words.

McDowell: Did you write *Song of the Dry Bread?*

Eisler: Yes, it was in a play.

McDowell: Did you write the words?

Eisler: No. I never write the words.

McDowell: Did you read the words?

Eisler: Sure.

McDowell: Did you write *Song of Demand and Supply?*

Eisler: It is one of the songs of the . . .

McDowell: Did you write the words?

Eisler: No.

McDowell: Did you read the words?

Eisler: Yes.

McDowell: I would like to say, Mr. Chairman, that I think all members of the committee should examine these exhibits that I have here, and that I have just named to Mr. Eisler, who maintains he is a composer of the music. This is matter that couldn't be sent through the mails in the United States. It deals with affairs that are entirely out of political matters, entirely out of anything except perhaps that of medicine. Obscenity is a poor word for it. I don't know what the custom is in Germany or in Austria, but such words as are in those sheets have no place in any sort of a civilization.

Eisler: They are considered as great poetry.

McDowell: They are considered as what?

Eisler: Great poetry.

McDowell: Great poetry?

Eisler: Yes.

McDowell: Well, great poetry as we are taught in America has nothing to do with that kind of truck. Among other things there is a song in there apparently dedicated or written because of the laws prohibiting abortion.

Eisler: Yes.

McDowell: In Germany.

Eisler: Yes.

McDowell: This song ridicules the law . . .

Eisler: Yes.

McDowell: Opposing the prohibition of abortions.

Eisler: Yes.

McDowell: In other words, this song would, I presume, in your Communist fashion of thinking, urge that the law opposing abortion be disregarded.

The Chairman: I would suggest that we don't get very deep into the question of abortion.

Rankin: I understand that you have complained that this committee has smeared you.

Eisler: Yes, Mr. Rankin.

Rankin: When you make that charge you are making that charge against a Committee of the Congress of the United States. You realize that, do you?

Eisler: Yes.

McDowell: This Committee is governed by the rules of the House of Representatives. Nothing that this Committee has done is in violation of the rules of the House, or in conflict with the laws of common decency. Now, where do you get any authority for saying that this committee has smeared you?

Eisler: I haven't any authority at all, but if you had made such a hearing without giving, every week the last 12 months, things about me which are not even sometimes the truth, it would be different. But when you have distortions or inventions of somebody which told it to one of the members of the committee, when you go into this fantastic press campaign against an artist, I am sure every red-blooded artist will be, after one year, after you nearly ruined him, very angry about this.

Rankin: I am conscious, when I look at this filth here, to which Mr. McDowell has referred . . .

Eisler: Pardon me, Mr. Rankin. It is not filth.

Rankin: I am conscious that anybody that would write that stuff would certainly not have much respect for the Congress of the United States. But this Committee has given you more than a fair deal, more than a fair trial, more than you would have gotten in any other country in the world. In any other country in the world you would have fared worse than you have in the United States, if you had carried on the same class of conduct that has been brought out by the testimony here.

Eisler: I don't know, Mr. Rankin, how you are familiar with American poetry.

Rankin: American what?

Eisler: Poetry.

Rankin: Poetry.

Eisler: An American writing. This is not American poetry or American writing. This was written in German. It is not translated. It was written in Berlin in 1927 or 1928 or 1929. I say, again, it is great poetry. We can have different tastes in art, but I cannot permit, Mr. Rankin, that you call my work by such names. I protest against that.

Rankin: I suppose that I am as familiar with American poetry and with English poetry generally as any Member of either House. And anybody that tries to tell me that this filth is poetry certainly reads himself out of the class of any American poet that has ever been recognized by the American people.

Eisler: I am sorry . . .

Rankin: I don't believe I have anything further, Mr. Chairman.

McDowell: Mr. Eisler, you wrote the poem *About Killing?*

Eisler: No. I put it together from poetry. I cannot write words, you know.

McDowell: Mr. Chairman, I would like permission to read these nine lines, which is the entire poem, that Mr. Eisler put together.

Rankin: I reserve the right to object. But we will hear him read it.

McDowell: (reading):

> Terrible it is to shed blood,
> Hard it is to learn to kill
> Bad it is to see people die before their time,
> But we must learn to kill,
> We must see people die before their time,
> We must shed blood,
>
> So that no more blood may be shed.

Eisler: This is a correct anti-Fascist statement. When Heydrich was killed by the Czech people, I agreed with this. He was a gangster, and he killed innumerable good people. This is poetry and not reality. The difference between art and real life has to be reconsidered. Take Hollywood—at every street corner you can see the most cruel pieces of art, and you can read stories in mystery magazines that you can buy in every drug store, which are horrible. I don't like such stuff. This is a little philosophical poem directed against gangsters.

Rankin: Mr. Chairman, the American people, of course, have just whipped Hitler, but the thing that shocks me is that while our boys were dying by the thousands over there to get Hitler's heel off their necks, some of these people come here and attempt to foment revolution in the United States. It is about time the American people woke up and put a stop to it.

The Chairman: Mr. Eisler, the Chair wishes to direct you to remain in the United States.

Stripling: Mr. Appell, were you directed by the Committee to make an investigation as to Mr. Eisler's status as a visiting lecturer and professor with the New School for Social Research in New York?

Appell: I was, sir.

Stripling: I may say, Mr. Chairman, the purpose of Mr. Appell's testimony is to show that Mr. Eisler's position with the New School for Social Research was used merely as a subterfuge in order for him to remain here.

Appell: On May 2, 1935, Dr. Alvin Johnson, the director of the school, wrote Eisler that he was appointed visiting professor of music for the academic year 1935–36. On March 29, 1938, Dr. Johnson, with the apparent purpose of qualifying Eisler as a non-quota visa applicant, changed Eisler's status from lecturer in music to professor in music. In this letter, Dr. Johnson stated that the New School and its students were so enthusiastic over his work as a visiting lecturer that they wanted him to remain permanently. Mr. Chairman, with respect to this appointment which was prompted by the overwhelming enthusiasm of the New School and its students, I should like to refer to the pay record and attendance cards of the New School for Social Research in substantiation of the overwhelming enthusiasm. In the two courses conducted by Eisler from October 5, 1935 to January 18, 1936, no more than eight students attended the course of Musical Composition, and only three attended the course on the Crisis of Modern Music.... When Dr. Johnson wrote the letter prompted by the overwhelming enthusiasm, Eisler had seven students attending the lecture on Musical Composition, one student attending the lecture on Counterpoint, with the third course having been cancelled after the first lecture.

Stripling: Mr. Chairman, a number of the songs which Mr. Eisler composed the music for, the words were provided by Bertolt Brecht, who will be one of the witnesses in the Hollywood investigation, who is a Communist. Did your investigation disclose that Bertolt Brecht has also been brought to this country in a similar manner by the New School?

Appell: Apparently, he was.

Rankin: Mr. Appell, would you say this was a Communist school of instruction?

Appell: No sir, I do not say that it is a Communist school.

Rankin: It was spreading Communist propaganda?

Appell: I have no evidence that the school itself has put out any Communist propaganda, but I know that the members of the faculty of the New School for Social Research are very prominently displayed in our files.

Rankin: Do you know whether or not Mrs. Eleanor Roosevelt was familiar with this situation when she urged the admission of Hanns Eisler into the United States?

Appell: I do not, Sir.

Rankin: Did you read her recent article in the *Ladies Home Journal?*

Appell: No sir, I haven't.

Rankin: It is the most insulting communistic piece of propaganda that was ever thrown in the faces of the women of America. I am just wondering if she was familiar with all of this Communist infiltration when she was trying to get Hanns Eisler into the United States.

Appell: I do not know that, Sir.

Rankin: I want to point out that her action was not official. She did not represent the party in power in trying to get these Communists returned or readmitted to the United States. And she certainly doesn't represent the better element of the American people in this Communist propaganda that she has written in the *Ladies Home Journal.*

The Birth of Jazz

Come on there, Professor, string up the big harp and give us all a tune! The Seals are down from Boyes Springs for tomorrow's first engagement with the Sox and now we'll get a round of real baseball. The squad numbers fifteen men and reached the city shortly after 10 o'clock, having departed from the Spa before the camp was awake. Everybody has come back to the old town full of the old "jazz" and they promise to knock the fans off their feet with their playing.

What is the "jazz"? Why, it's a little of that "old life," the "gin-i-ker," the "pep," otherwise known as the enthusiasalum. A grain of "jazz" and you feel like going out and eating your way through Twin Peaks. It's that spirit which makes ordinary ball players step around like Lajoies and Cobbs. The Seals have it and we venture to say that everybody in the big town who has ever stopped to "pan" the San Francisco club in the past several months will be inoculated with it by the time the coming string of games is over.

"Hap" Hogan gave his men a couple of shots of "near-jazz" last season and look at what resulted—the Tigers became the most ferocious set of tossers in the league. Now the Seals have happened upon great quantities of it in the quiet valley of Sonoma and they're setting the countryside on fire. The team which speeded into town this morning comes pretty close to representing the pick of the army. Its members have trained on ragtime and "jazz" and Manager Del Howard says there's no stopping them. Class will not be denied, and whether they are ball players or not the members of the first squad will not be wanting in spirit and determination.

For the fans' information it is sufficient to state that Del Howard while he is manager of that San Francisco club will give them a first-class run for their money. He's a real ball player, excelling in several branches of the sport—the most important of all of which is—baseball sense.

Meanwhile, keep your eye on the Seal outfit. The players are just brimming over with that old "Texas Tommy" stuff and there is a bit of the "jazz" in everything they do.

["Scoop" Gleeson, *The Bulletin*, San Francisco, 6 March 1913]

Spring in a baseball training camp is all too often a season of sore arms, "charley horses" and crushed hopes. But that of 1913, when the San Francisco Seals took up a temporary abode at Boyes Springs, in Sonoma County, was different. For one thing Del Howard was installed as manager and the change ushered in a new spirit of enthusiasm and anticipation. For another, Art Hickman had arrived on the scene in the guise of a camp follower. He came up ostensibly to take a rest, but really to do a little fraternizing with his friends the newspaper correspondents.

It was this happy set of circumstances that launched Hickman on his career as a popular orchestra leader and marked the birth of a new syncopation in dance tunes, which soon won its way under the name of "jazz."

Hickman, whose home originally was in Oakland, had spent some time in his youth, dancing with his sister, Pearl, in professional engagements. He had played trap drums and picked at a piano in one of the city's places of amusement. Then had been named entertainment manager at the Chutes Theater. During his stay at the springs he went on several outings with the newspaper crowd. Up to Jack London's ranch at Glenn Ellen, where Jack was working away on "John Barleycorn." Over to the winery and the early California landmarks at Sonoma. But mostly he turned up to sit in the sun in the bleachers when the Regulars and Yannigans, selected from the baseball squads, put in their afternoons playing practice games. It was a pleasant and indolent way to enjoy a vacation. Perhaps Hickman had the idea all the time and was only awaiting such an opportunity to try it out. But it was his suggestion that it might be a good plan to put on a couple of dances and relieve the tedium of the evenings. He said it wouldn't cost much and that if the management at the springs would cooperate, with room and board, he thought he could induce several musicians out of work, to come up for a vacation. That was how his first group of players was assembled. As a feature Hickman included a banjo player in his orchestra—some one said he got the notion from watching one of the Negro orchestras at Purcell's on the Barbary Coast.

Similarly the very word "jazz" itself came into general usage at the same time. We were all seated around the dinner table at Boyes one evening and William ("Spike") Slattery, then sports editor of *The Call*, spoke about something being the "Jazz," or the old "gin-i-ker fizz."

"Spike" had picked up the expression in a crap game. Whenever one of the players rolled the dice he would shout, "Come on, the old jazz."

For the next week we gave "jazz" a great play in all our stories. And when Hickman's orchestra swung into action for the evening's dances, it was natural to find it included as "the jazziest tune rooters in all the Valley of the Moon." On one of the evenings James Woods, then manager of the Hotel St. Francis, and former Police Judge Jack Sullivan, visitors to the camp, attended the dance. Woods was at once struck by the melody of the band. "How long has this been going on?" he asked. He was introduced to Hickman and forthwith the latter was engaged to assemble an orchestra for the St. Francis. Soon all San Francisco was dancing to the "Rose Room Fox Trot" by Art Hickman.

("Scoop" Gleeson, *The Call Bulletin*, San Francisco, 3 September 1938)

Unclassified Document, Department of the Army: Communist Vulnerabilities to the Use of Music in Psychological Warfare

In my search of documentary evidence connecting musical practices with political events, I came upon the mention of a "laboratory" within the United States Department of the Army that investigated the ways and means of influencing the policies of the Soviet Union by broadcasting Western music of a humanistic nature. The purely musical purpose of such broadcasts was to counteract the prevalence of marching tunes and patriotic songs typical of Soviet music. I wrote the Department of the Army for a copy of the declaration of aims of this musical laboratory. To my surprise, the Department of the Army replied that no such laboratory existed. Yet references to its work appeared in reputable sources. I wrote to my friend William Lichtenwanger, then head of the Reference Department of the Music Division of the Library of Congress, asking him to make further inquiries on the subject. Accordingly, he addressed an inquiry to the Department of the Army, but received a reply that such documents were classified information. He then repeated his request under the recently promulgated Freedom of Information Act. This time he received a copy of the document, marked "Unclassified." The present text represents the most important parts of this remarkable document.—Ed.

Objectives

1. The original research requirement for this study came from the Operations and Training Branch, Propaganda Division, Office of the Chief of Psychological Warfare. This requirement called for lists of musical selections appropriate for use in propaganda broadcasts by Army operational units to certain specified target audiences. For this reason, initial attention in the research was concentrated upon problems of an operational nature. As the project progressed, however, it acquired the broader aspect of vulnerability research—the vulnerabilities of the Soviet Union and selected European Communist countries to the use of music in psychological warfare. Inquiry was directed toward:

   (a) Finding the major areas of vulnerability to the use of music in psychological warfare, through a study of the recent music practices of target countries.
   (b) Selecting compositions judged most appropriate for exploiting these vulnerabilities.

2. The operational objectives of the research were:

   (a) To facilitate procurement of music recordings by the Department of the Army for use in psychological warfare programs.
   (b) To guide Army psychological warfare operators in exploiting the propaganda possibilities in music broadcasts to audiences in the Soviet Union, Czechoslovakia, Hungary, Poland, Rumania, Yugoslavia, Bulgaria, and Albania.

3. It was considered appropriate to these objectives to present the research findings in three parts:

   (a) A textual report which analyzes the music situation in the target countries, estimates the vulnerabilities resulting from that situation and from the nature of music as a medium of communication, and suggests ways in which those vulnerabilities may be exploited through psychological warfare. This report may be found on pages 3–18 of this volume. A brief discussion of the ways in which music performers recently escaped from Communist countries may be used as additional sources of information for psychological warfare units and as a reservoir of talent for broadcasts employing music is presented in Appendix A, pages 21–25 of this volume.

(b) A brief handbook-type summary for each target country studied, containing a calendar of its national holidays and festivals, an analysis of its recent musical diet, a list of its important music performers and ensembles, and a selected list of sources where further music information pertinent to the target country can be obtained. These summaries are attached as Appendices B through I of the textual report, and may be found on pages 27–84 of this volume.

(c) A catalogue which provides an individual listing for music recordings judged most suitable for use by psychological warfare operators, together with facts about the recordings which may be useful for procurement and propaganda purposes. This catalogue is separate from the present volume. Its contents are briefly described in Appendix J, pages 85–86 of this volume.

Summary of Findings

1. Music is currently regulated in the Soviet Union, Czechoslovakia, Hungary, Poland, Rumania, Bulgaria, and Albania in accordance with a policy formulated in the Soviet Union by the late Andrei A. Zhdanov in 1948.

2. In certain aspects, the policy reflects the musical tastes of the people, tending to approve music which the majority of the people likes and to disapprove that which the majority does not like. Current policy demands simple, melodic music, using traditional harmonies and rhythms, prefers songs over instrumental music, favors the more popular pre-Communist composers over contemporary composers (both Western and indigenous), and prohibits the playing of modern Western jazz and art music. Folk music is in the highest favor, and music showing contemporary Western influences is disapproved.

3. In other aspects, current policy is designed to further the political and propaganda goals of the Communist regimes. It provides an opportunity to control "subversive" cliques of musical artists, enlists popular support for the regime in terms of the emotional responses induced by officially approved music, provides an opportunity for propaganda through the music, serves to "popularize" the intellectual accomplishments of the music world, and provides an additional opportunity to condemn Western culture.

4. The chief vulnerabilities in the countries studied (with the exception of Yugoslavia) to the use of music in psychological warfare would seem to be these:

(a) The official policies on music illustrate the regimes' distrust of all free and individual expression, and reveal how the desire of the regimes to preserve their own power conflicts with the desires of the people.

(b) The failure of the Communist approved musical diet wholly to satisfy certain target groups disposes them favorably toward United States programs offering music they like but cannot hear over their own Communist-controlled media of communication.

COMMUNIST VULNERABILITIES TO THE USE OF MUSIC
IN PSYCHOLOGICAL WARFARE

by

James S. Young

Approved:

Carleton F. Scofield
CARLETON F. SCOFIELD
Director of Research
Psychological Warfare Division

Meredith P. Crawford
MEREDITH P. CRAWFORD
Director
Human Resources Research Office

The George Washington University
HUMAN RESOURCES RESEARCH OFFICE
operating under contract with
THE DEPARTMENT OF THE ARMY

Technical Report 4
March 1954

Copy_____of 250
Log No.   A-2848

REGRADED UNCLASSIFIED ORDER
SEC ARMY BY TAG PER
7 5 0 2 4 4

(c) The nature of music itself makes it valuable for inducing desired moods, creating a certain emotional atmosphere for broadcasts, and suggesting certain ideas.

Cautions

1. The findings of this research cannot supplant area knowledge. They may serve to guide the psychological warfare operator who is not acquainted with the music practices of the target countries and to provide a convenient reference for area specialists.

2. The findings of this research are not based on firsthand testing or interviewing of escaped target nationals to ascertain actual music preferences in the target countries. Sources used include publications, interviews with music and area specialists, and monitoring reports of music broadcast by selected radio stations in the target countries.

3. Alienation of target audiences may result from (a) broadcasting music unattractive to the audience, (b) overemphasizing a single type of music, a single technique of presentation, or musical as against verbal programs.

4. The psychological warfare operator who uses music for propaganda purposes will be competing with the Communists' well-formulated and systematic programs of indoctrination through music. Failure to display equal skill may not only reduce the effectiveness of music as a United States propaganda weapon, but may even generate negative attitudes toward United States propaganda efforts employing other techniques.

Operational Suggestions

Note: Inasmuch as the Army research requirement which necessitated this study presented problems of an operational nature, certain suggestions for the guidance of personnel conducting psychological warfare operations have been made on the basis of the research accomplished. These suggestions, listed below, are offered with the understanding that broader policy objectives and the immediate operational situation may limit their usefulness.

1. The diverse content of musical expression and the various emotional responses elicited by music listening suggest that music can be adapted for the following purposes in psychological warfare:

    a. To express certain United Nations and United States values
    b. To popularize the expression of antagonism toward the Communist regime
    c. To popularize the expression of favorable attitudes toward the United States
    d. To increase nationalistic sentiments
    e. To illustrate propaganda themes
    f. To promote themes of internationalism
    g. To increase the audience appeal of fables or legends which have political overtones
    h. To attract attention, to induce certain moods, and to impute connotations to verbal matter
    i. To induce the defection of target artists

2. The use of contemporary indigenous music having pro-Communist connotations as well as compositions frequently broadcast by the Communist radio should for the most part be avoided in United States broadcasts.

3. Modern Western music of the dissonant or "radical" type—among both jazz and art music repertories—should not be used in United States broadcasts.

4. Both the Communist music policies and the music preferences of target groups (with respect to performers as well as compositions) can change rapidly and unpredictably. Psychological warfare operators intending to use music for propaganda purposes should, therefore, supplement the information contained in this report with intelligence on the current musical diet and references of the audience to be reached. Current intelligence, for instance, might void both suggestions 2. and 3. in the case of certain target audiences.

Foreword

The following text begins with an analysis of the official Soviet music policy promulgated in 1948 by the late Andrei Zhdanov. Although many factors contributed to this policy, the specific directives laid down in the policy represent what, at that time, seemed to Communist officials the most expedient way of making musical expression serve the propaganda and political objectives of their regime. As indicated in the text, it is likely that the Zhdanov policy will be changed or even supplanted altogether, and, since the writing of this report, there have been indications that the Malenkov regime is attempting to erase Zhdanov's influence. Even if the directives of the Zhdanov policy change, however, it is unlikely that the basic aims of this policy will be abandoned. For these aims are rooted in a fundamental tenet of Communism: that all artistic expression must embody, portray, and teach Communist values, and perform a function useful to Communist society. Thus, because music is regarded under Communism as a political and propaganda resource, the desire of the Communist propaganda machine to make use of it will not easily be thwarted. The techniques of employing this resource (the Zhdanov policy, for example) may vary from time to time, but any policy changes will be limited by those basic Communist values which require the subordination of cultural activity to the interests of the regime.

In order to reserve the strategic and tactical value of this report against revisions of the Zhdanov policy, the discussion has not been limited to a description of that policy. Instead, the Zhdanov policy is used as a starting point for discussing the more enduring goals which the policy was designed to serve. This approach, it is hoped, will enable propaganda specialists to make a meaningful appraisal not only of the Zhdanov policy, but also of the policies which may succeed it. It is hoped particularly that the information provided will enable the reader to recognize, where it exists, the underlying continuity and consistency in what may appear to be drastic changes in the Zhdanov policy.

It should be emphasized that this report discusses vulnerabilities other than those stemming from Communist political control over music. The text, together with the appendices, is designed as background material to guide propaganda specialists in using the catalogue of music recordings supplied by this research.

Origins of Communist Music Policy

In commemoration of the thirtieth anniversary of the Russian Revolution, in December 1947, a new opera entitled *The Great Fellowship*, by the Georgian composer Vano Muradeli, was performed at the Bolshoi Theater in Moscow. It was a "closed" performance, given for about 500 high-ranking Soviet officials, one of whom presumably was Stalin himself. At the end of the performance, such an intense dispute developed about the music that the director of the theater suffered a heart attack and died on the spot.

Immediately thereafter, music compositions by modern Soviet composers were expurgated from concert repertories in the Soviet Union. Rumors personally critical of certain outstanding Russian composers began to circulate, as did speculation about the possibility of a "purge" in the music world.

All doubt vanished in the middle of January, 1948. Russian composers, music teachers, and critics were summoned to a meeting by the Central Committee of the Communist Party to hear a blistering attack on contemporary Soviet music and musicians delivered by the late Andrei A. Zhdanov, Party Chief of Leningrad during the German siege, and cultural spokesman for the Party.

Following the musicians' meeting, the Party published a decree denouncing by name the six idols of Soviet music—Shostakovich, Prokofiev, Khachaturian, Shebalin, Popov, and Miaskovsky. They were accused of disregarding the "social role of music," of catering to the "degenerate tastes of a handful of estheticising individualists," of indulging in "decadent bourgeois formalism," and of manifesting "anti-People" tendencies.

Immediately after publication of the decree, Shostakovich and Miaskovsky were expelled from their teaching posts at the Moscow Conservatory, and Shebalin was dismissed as its director. Khachaturian was removed from his position as Secretary General of the Union of Soviet Composers and from the chairmanship of its Organizing Committee, which, in conjunction with the Committee on Arts of the Ministry of Education, decides what music works will be published and recommends those to be performed. Other familiar figures in the music world were arrested. Several months later a Party member suggested that composers infected with bourgeois tendencies "could very profitably move out of Moscow to the periphery of the vast Soviet land and get their inspiration from a close contact with the life of the people in the provinces, in collective farms and factories."

The new music policy begun in the Soviet Union in 1948 was later exported to the satellite countries. Eight months after the January meeting in Moscow, the first Working Congress of Czechoslovak Composers and Musical Scholars published directions for musicians that were strictly in accordance with the Soviet decree. In 1949, Polish composers were summoned to a meeting at Logow which turned out to be strikingly similar to the Moscow convention presided over by Zhdanov. The outcome of the Logow meeting was a demand for "breaking down the formalistic influence of the West" and "applying the methods of socialist realism . . . either by creating new musical forms . . . or by an increasingly stronger accentuation of the essentially ideological content in music." Soon thereafter, official attention was directed to the schooling of singers' collective groups. Rumanian musicians suffered a purge in 1952. As in the Soviet Union, the theme of the purge was formalism, and its result the development of a militant, combative, and partisan music, reflecting the "realities" of working class life, according to Party orders. After the purge, courses in Marxism and Leninism were conducted for musicians by the Rumanian Federation of Composers. Thus far, Hungary, Bulgaria, and Albania seem to have escaped purges, although in all of these countries, the radio music diet is generally restricted to compositions which currently enjoy the approval of the Soviet Communist Party.

Since 1948, many of the composers attacked in the Soviet decree have produced works designed to restore them to the Party's graces, but their acceptance by the Party has been only partial. A considerable amount of their music is still banned in the Communist world, and the Party has officially reported that "some formalist elements" still persist in their works and their "transformation [is] proceeding rather slowly."

The purpose and effect of the new policy has been to cramp musical expression into a role utilitarian to the Communist state. This "utility" music is fostered by the use of two techniques: prescribing musical standards for composers, and educating musicians in Communist doctrine. Traditionally accepted music likewise is manipulated to make it politically useful by such techniques as symbolizing its content in political terms or associating the music with political, economic, or military events. The same end is served by lending the prestige of the official media of communication to favored works, denying a hearing for works with adverse connotations, slanting with pro-Communist language the texts of familiar songs, and "capturing" the names of great composers of the past and imputing Communist ideas to their works.

The cultural offensive inside the Soviet Union has by no means been limited to music; music was merely the last victim. Similar attacks against literature and philosophy (also launched by Zhdanov), the graphic arts, drama, and cinema preceded the attack on music. But of these victims, music suffered the most radical and violent assault. That this should be the case is surprising, especially since the composers singled out for denunciation by the 1948 decree had long been the ones most highly revered in Soviet music. With the music-loving public, theirs were household names; they were idolized by the government and showered with numerous Stalin prizes for their compositions. Only once previously, in 1936, had any of the musicians named in the 1949 decree been criticized by the Party. This offender was Shostakovich, who was reprimanded by *Pravda* for "formalistic tendencies" in his opera *Lady Macbeth of Mtzensk*. Shostakovich had returned to Party grace by 1948, however. Less than a year before the 1948 attack, the leading Russian music historian and critic Asafiev wrote of Shostakovich that he could not have created subsequent to the reprimand in 1936 "those immense human symphonies which are the admiration of the whole world" had it not been the prior "fatherly directness and care" shown by the Party in 1936.

The 1948 policy was a reversal of the official attitude not only toward the leading composers themselves, but also on the merit of various music forms developed under Soviet rule. Before 1948, the symphonic form was in highest favor; according to Asafiev, "The great revolutionary struggle of our people, the building of Socialism in our country, the gigantic upsurge in all fields of human activity, the mighty growth of artistic and scientific thought in our country . . . is reflected in our music; and all that was best and most important in this respect we find in the music of our *symphonists*" (emphasis added). However, less than a year after Asafiev had made this statement, symphonic music was singled out by Zhandov for particularly strong criticism. The principal complaints were that composers had devoted more attention to symphonic than to operatic music and that—what the Party now views as one of the cardinal musical sins—"as a result of the underestimation of folk music by our symphonic composers," they had allowed symphonic music to become divorced from native folk music expression.

Why, then, did the Party take such a sweeping interest in music? Part of the answer lies in the fact that a political unit of totalitarian pretensions, by the logic of its own assumptions, is committed to an extension of its authority into even those areas of behavior which are least critical for the maintenance of political control and ideological solidarity. Specific applications of political authority to such areas of behavior are further encouraged when, as in the case of Russian Communism, the totalitarian ideology calls for reforming the very substance of culture itself. Likewise, extremist measures are resorted to when the regime becomes insecure, and tends to fear every uncontrolled or truly spontaneous activity as a potential source of disaffection.

Another significant factor in the 1948 attack is the fact that new music, like other art forms embodying novel and original concepts, is almost never readily accepted by the larger public, and in fact frequently provokes strongly hostile reactions. Thus it becomes possible for a dictatorial policy, under the guise of expressing the affirmative desires of a majority of the people, to condemn vast segments of contemporary repertories and approve the more familiar and traditional styles without risking protest from the listening public.

Another partial explanation for the Party's sudden and disruptive attack on music may have been that a musical clique professionally jealous of the denounced musicians was trying to gain favor. Competition within the Party, in which Zhdanov and Georgi Malenkov were then rivals, may also have been a factor; Zhdanov, having been entrusted with responsibility for cultural matters in the Party, may have used this opportunity to gain the favor of Stalin, whose artistic tastes, like Zhdanov's, were plebeian.

In this general context, however, other factors contributed more directly to the Soviet music policy. These factors, and the vulnerabilities they indicate, can best be understood by evaluating, first, the content of that policy and, second, the ways in which the Communist state benefits by it. Such an analysis may also provide a basis for evaluating future changes in Soviet music policy.

Music Approved by the Party

What is currently regarded by the Communist Party as the music most suitable for the ears of the populations it controls?

(1) *Music that is not "formalistic."* "Formalism" in musical expression may be described as overemphasis on external form as against content. It implies an elaborate structure of motifs or themes not unified by an underlying principle, a concern with craftsmanship rather than thought content, and, in its extreme form, reliance on established forms at the expense of originality. As described by one of Zhdanov's followers, it occurs "whenever the composer shows an insufficient creative will to follow [the] road of life's fundamentals to the utmost limit of his consciousness. If he is creatively lazy, he will stop at the beginning of the road, and the thread that leads him to the final goal snaps. His musical images, as a result, become vague, incomplete, and distorted."

This question of form and content is one of the central problems of the artist, a problem inherent in artistic endeavor itself. How to be original in thought and at the same time to express it musically in a form that is understandable in comparison with existing, familiar forms cannot be settled for the artist by political guidance. Nevertheless, because the problem is ever present for the practicing artist, it renders him extremely vulnerable to criticism for failure to solve it.

The simple fact that extreme formalism tends to produce inferior music imparts a certain validity to the use of formalism as a standard for music criticism. However, when applied with political reference, it ceases to have a definable meaning. For example, the Communist Party characterizes most Western music as formalistic, while Russian music, with the exception of the genre criticized in the 1948 decree, is called nonformalistic. Although it is generally true that Russian composers have demonstrated less skill in the matter of musical organization, they nevertheless have relied largely upon the music forms developed in the West, and not a few of them would be classified as formalists. One such musician is the pre-Communist Russian composer, Scriabin. Yet he is currently favored by Communist music policy makers. When, for example, in the midst of the 1948 controversy, he was charac-

terized by a writer in the Communist magazine *Soviet Literature* as a degenerate formalist of the worst sort, the music policy makers behind the Iron Curtain rose to his defense and denounced the writer of the article. Ironically enough, however, the best examples of formalism—defined by the Party as resulting from a failure of creative energy—are to be found in contemporary Soviet compositions which were written in conformity with the very policy which denounces it. For the policy set forth in 1948 has had the effect of inducing composers to imitate the music forms approved by the Party (especially folk music) and to avoid expressing original ideas for fear of not conforming to the officially approved stereotypes.

The concept of formalism that is applied by the Party in criticism of contemporary Soviet and Western music is derived only superficially, therefore, from musical principles. This concept is dictated chiefly by political considerations and expediency, for the formalistic music which Party usage considers unworthy of Communist-controlled audiences turns out to be compositions that either are associated with the West or are not of the type that engenders widespread interest among the masses of the population. That the basis of the whole policy is political in nature becomes apparent from the aspects of the policy which are discussed in the following sections.

(2) *Simple and melodic music.* It follows from the Party's desire to have composers put more "content" into musical expression that its interest goes further in specifying what content is acceptable.

With respect to musical material itself, atonal or strongly dissonant music, as well as music which is overly "naturalistic" (that is, involves excessive use of drums, cymbals, and the like), is regarded as "false, vulgar, and pathological . . . filled with idealistic emotion, alien to the broad masses of the people, and addressed to the few . . . to the elite." In contrast, "singable" melodies are desired.

With respect to musical ideas, "program music" is preferred to "absolute music." The reason is transparent: because program music conveys an impression of a definite series of images, scenes, or events, it is easier to understand and is better adapted as a vehicle of propaganda than absolute music, which is nonrepresentational in nature.

This attitude is in line with the broader outlines of the policy stated by Zhdanov to the effect that the "intrinsic function" of music is to "give pleasure." Hence, any music which the people "cannot understand" is bad. It is under this criterion of "understandability" that the present policy favors long-established music over modern music. For the longer an art work survives in history, the more familiar, and in this sense the more understandable, it becomes. The radical, "disharmonious" type of modern music is considered particularly undesirable, even though its content is apparently pro-Communist; not only is it unpopular and not "useful to society," but it also "affects the correct psycho-physiological functioning of man." If a composer produces disharmonious or atonal works for the sake of sheer novelty, the musical worth of his compositions is certain to be inferior. But a mere reading of Zhdanov's language shows that his criticism reflects more a suspicion of novel and unfamiliar expression than refined musical judgment. The official attitude may be summed up in the phrase: "It's what we don't understand that's dangerous." Or, as the Russian satirist Saltykov said, during the Czarist regime: "What I don't understand is undoubtedly dangerous to the security of the state." In this aspect, too, Communist music policy reflects the necessity of the totalitarian state to suspect everything which, due to lack of knowledge or other reasons, it cannot fully control.

(3) *Music using subjects from Communist doctrine and Soviet life.* Of all the standards demanded of new music, this is the most obviously political in nature. Examples of music fitting

this requirement are Beli's "In Defense of Peace," and Prokofiev's "Story of a Real Man" which deals with the heroism of a Soviet fighter pilot who learned how to fly again after having lost both legs.

It is in this connection that the recurrent conflict arises between the internationalist orientation of Communism and the nationalist orientation of Russian politics. Zhdanov dismissed this problem by pronouncing that "one cannot be an internationalist in music, or in any other realm, without being at the same time a genuine patriot of one's own country . . . internationalism arises from the very flowering of national art." To indulge in the "contraband" music forms imported from the West is, for the Russian musician, to become a "homeless cosmopolitan."

(4) *Vocal and operatic music.* The Communist Party favors songs over purely instrumental music, particularly songs that call for large choruses. For this requirement, too, the motivation is obviously political, for vocal music has certain propagandistic values above instrumental music—namely, that it allows for mass participation, is better adapted to convey specific political ideas, and is usually simpler and more understandable than instrumental music, not only because it must have words, but also because its melodies must conform to the limitations in range of the human voice.

(5) *Folk music.* The epitome of the Communist Party's musical standards is folk music. It is constantly eulogized by Party spokesmen: "Just as the lily, in its glorious and chaste beauty, eclipses the brilliance of brocades and precious stones, so folk music, thanks to its very childlike simplicity, is a thousand times richer and stronger than all the artifices of the learning taught by pedants in the conservatories and musical academies." This fulsome comparison is probably indicative of the real Communist attitude toward art music, an antagonism that is tantamount to denying the validity of this form of music altogether, except as it incorporates folk themes. In contrast, folk music enjoys such high favor because it is a communal, rather than an individualistic art; it is naturally adapted for group participation and more often than not is sung; it uses native subjects; and, simple in melody, harmony, and form, it is readily understood by proletarian and peasant alike.

What the policy amounts to, then, is an espousal by the Communist Party of certain esthetic values, none of them novel in themselves: "realism," comprehensibility, simplicity and tunefulness, beauty, and a preference for popular and folk ideas and for music that is sung. While these values may have an integrity of their own, they cannot be judged solely on their merits because they have been adapted to serve not esthetic, but political ends. So aptly do these values serve the regimes' conquest of power as to suggest that they have been expropriated by the Party chiefly for that reason. An examination of the ways in which Communist music policy benefits the state makes this conclusion even more convincing.

Political Advantages in Controlling Musical Expression

(1) One of the most important benefits to the Communist state is the opportunity that control provides for maintaining surveillance over composers, music theorists, and critics. Traditionally—in Russia, at least—criticism of the prevailing regime, having been denied an effective political outlet, was expressed through the medium of art, particularly literary art. Thus, with some justification in Russian history, artistic groups are regarded as traditional sources of disaffection and political criticism.

But there is a deeper reason for official control over artists in a totalitarian society. One of the historic attributes of artistic activity is the high value placed upon individuality. The

artist insists on the privilege of thinking "freely" and of perceiving without being restricted to the usual patterns. Russian artists in the past have particularly stressed the need for individuality and freedom in order to be truly creative. Illustrative of their thinking on this matter are the statements of the late Nicolas Berdyaev, an exiled member of the Russian intelligentsia: "It is only in the creative act that man prevails over the oppression and enslavement of extraneous influences . . . [creative activity] is individual and indeed rebellious in nature, involving conflict between man and his environment . . . the basic characteristic of a creative act consists in not being wholly determined by its medium, and [in] that it comprises something new, something which cannot be derived from the external world in which it is embodied, or indeed from some fixed repository of ideal forms which press upon the creator's imagination."

Zhdanov himself did not overlook the possible anarchistic implications in this type of thinking; one of the criticisms he made most vehemently was of music that was "rampantly individualistic." It does not appear at all surprising, then, that not one of the arts has escaped state control in the Soviet Union.

Thus, artists in general, and musicians in particular, should be especially susceptible targets for psychological warfare which plays upon this theme and encourages them to defect. The defection of an important artist from the Soviet Union would have an extremely high propaganda value.

(2) By allying itself with longer-established, more familiar, and better-liked music, the regime cultivates the support of the larger public and can receive credit for recognizing "good music." Furthermore, the pleasurable and inspirational emotions that are a part of the musical experience can be associated with, and turned to the advantage of, the regime.

(3) The Communist state also benefits from the way in which control permits the manipulation of music for purposes of conveying verbal propaganda. In this connection, it should be remembered that current policy favors songs, which are particularly adapted for this purpose. Propaganda that is put into musical form is less overt and, because it is cloaked in a pleasing melody, is less likely to evoke the defenses that an individual may put up against spoken propaganda.

(4) Control over music also serves to further the Communist goal of "popularizing" intellectual accomplishment and activity. One of the concerns of the pre-Communist Russian intelligentsia was justifying the divorce from the life of the people that intellectual activity entails. In the past, various segments in the Russian intelligentsia have resolved this problem by foregoing specialized intellectual life altogether and "returning to the soil"—to the people. While elements of this solution are apparent in the Communist answer, the current solution is more nearly that of bringing culture—used here in the lay sense—to the people, rather than the people to culture. This, to justify intellectual accomplishments, such as art music compositions, they must be simplified in order that they may be comprehensible to the masses. This fact is abundantly clear in Zhdanov's requirement that music be "understandable."

(5) Controlling the music diet of the people also provides an additional opportunity to condemn Western culture, to forestall any Western influence that may penetrate the Iron Curtain through music, and to impress the people with the superiority of Russian or native culture.

In summation, the current Communist music policy is based upon considerations of politics and expediency, and is guided by two frequently conflicting goals: first, and more important, to further the propaganda and political goals of the Party; second, to avoid violating the music tastes of the majority. Consequently, sudden and unpredictable shifts may be made in the specific directives laid down in the policy without altering the basic political goals which the policy was designed to serve. Evidence of strong public approval or disapproval of certain composers or compositions, personal jealousies within the music profession, the personal conduct of a musician or his expression of an unpopular viewpoint—all these things, and not solely the music principles stated in the official pronouncements, affect the Party's stand on individual cases. The psychological warfare operator should always attempt, therefore, to ascertain the current music situation prior to choosing his propaganda themes.

Major Areas of Communist Vulnerability to Music

The nature and implications of Communist music policy have been discussed here at length because it is the fact of control—the existence of a music policy as such—which gives rise to the major vulnerabilities of Communist countries to the use of music in psychological warfare.

(1) Control over musicians is one example of Communist tyranny. It is an especially revealing example because it illustrates specifically the higher value placed by Communism upon the interest of the "community" or "collective life" than upon the dignity of individual men, and because it shows how this "community interest" is being used by the Party as a disguise for its own self-interest. This situation provides a valuable opportunity for exploitation in psychological warfare, and the example of Communist music policy is all the more effective for this purpose because music is so obviously a field virtually unrelated to political interests, and thus least justifiably subject to political control. For this reason, it should be possible, by emphasizing the controls placed on music artists, to convey to target audiences the idea not only that the Party is dedicated chiefly to its own interest, but that, in serving itself, the Party threatens in a concrete way the freedom of activity and expression of those who still enjoy it. It is true, of course, that religious-like devotion to the task of unifying a community can excuse, in the eyes of the faithful, even the most extreme customs of human liberty. Certainly, unless attention is called to the fact, the devotees of such a cause can overlook the deprivations of a small group such as musicians. Their zeal should not be underestimated.

However, even with no exploitation whatever by the West, the music policy initiated by the Soviet Union has been itself sufficient to become a source of major embarrassment to Communists outside Russia. The Communist policy toward music in particular, and art in general, "has caused Russia more harm abroad, among Left-wing, and predominantly pro-Soviet intelligentsia, than anything else . . . The most powerful Communist Party in the West, that in France, has the strongest mental reservations about Soviet art policy . . . In Poland and Czechoslovakia, the whole Communist and Left-wing intelligentsia are perturbed and embarrassed by what has happened in Russia in the field of culture." This embarrassment has not been limited to intellectuals abroad; many of the Soviet musicians themselves have become in varying degrees disillusioned as a result of the policy. It is this group that should be particularly susceptible targets for psychological warfare. However, just as music is only one of many forms of expression which have been suppressed in Communist regimes, likewise the potential target in the exploitation of current Communist music policy is by no means limited to musicians. The policy can be used to illustrate the regime's attitude toward free expression in general.

Whether or not it exists in a situation of "thought control," music stands as a symbol of freedom and individuality of expression. It lends itself, therefore, to a psychological warfare theme developed along the following lines:

By dictating musical standards to composers and by banning all compositions that are individualistic or imaginative, or in some other way do not conform to these standards, the regime has denied the freedom of the artist to create and of the listener to hear music of his own choosing. Why won't the regime let people hear certain music? Why is it afraid of music? By playing its own, and not the people's music, it has betrayed the true values of the (Russian) people.

This vulnerability can be exploited not only verbally but also through music. One of the simpler techniques is to broadcast familiar and well-liked music composed by target nationals which has been officially or unofficially banned. In this way, target audiences may be reminded of the deprivations caused by the regime. It is important to recognize, however, that banning is seldom done overtly. The fact that Party organs condemn a certain composer or composition does not necessarily mean that he or his work will be formally banned. The more usual technique is simply the silent removal of the offender from radio and concert repertories: thus he or his work is consigned to oblivion.

(2) A second vulnerability lies in the fact that the Communist policy of reforming music is bound to encounter ingrained popular preferences for music which the Party does not approve, or popular resistance to compositions which the Party does approve. This puts our own psychological warfare operators in the advantageous position of being able to give Communist-controlled audiences a music fare more to their liking than the one they now receive.

The present policy shows that Communist policymakers have realized that the music tastes of the people cannot be changed overnight, and they have in most instances selected for approval those compositions which are most popular and disapproved those which are not well-liked. There are situations in which popular preferences seem not to have been satisfied, however. In Hungary, for example, there is evidence of resistance to the disproportionate amount of Russian music performed, as compared with Hungarian selections. Hungarian Communist officials feel that they cannot safely foster any substantial amount of Hungarian music because it is for the most part nationalistic in character. Before the Communist coup, Czechoslovakia had developed a distinct liking for Western swing, and to a lesser extent for jazz. In 1949, the charge of "decadence" hurled at Bing Crosby by one of the Party's cultural spokesmen precipitated a riot in Prague. In Russia itself, it appears that Western swing (not "hot" jazz), which is now totally banned, would have a considerable audience. Rumanian urban and upper-class audiences now hear very little of the French music for which they had, during the 1930's, developed a considerable liking—particularly songs of the Charles Trenet and Maurice Chevalier type. In the satellite countries generally, the well-liked, easygoing music in the coffee house and cabaret style of the 1930's is no longer heard. With only a few exceptions, too, religious music is not heard on radios in the Communist world; yet it is improbable that all Communist-controlled peoples have exchanged completely the orthodoxy of the Roman, Greek, or Russian Church for the orthodoxy of Communism.

Furthermore, there is a distinct monotony to the music issuing from the Communist radio. Much of it is pure propaganda, only thinly disguised in music. The "swing" music imitates the Western type, but it would not be considered of even mediocre quality in this country. Folk music is broadcast in great quantity, accompanied by the usual themes of proletarianism. Since the 1948 decree, the "non-art" music of Communist-ruled peoples has tended to become stereotyped, in harmony, melody, and rhythm. After years of this sort of music diet the audiences, especially in the satellites, might welcome a change.

(3) There are other vulnerabilities less directly related to current Communist policy and more directly stemming from

the nature of music itself. At first appearance the propaganda value in music alone may seem slight, but in the various target countries considered in this research music is important in the cultural life of the people as a common form of group participation. Because of its unique tonal, rhythmic, and harmonic combinations, music constitutes a means of ready access to people's minds. For this reason, when propaganda content is injected, music still has the advantage of seeming less weighted with the political overtones which so often stigmatize speech as "mere propaganda." Thus, although music is less effective than speech in communicating specific ideas (unless used in conjunction with verbal matter), it frequently becomes more effective than speech as a means of suggestion or connotation. This is especially true where direct expression is likely to be inaccurate, suspect, repetitious, or too naive or sophisticated to engender respect. Certainly the Communist Party itself recognizes such possibilities in music, as is evidenced by the attention it has devoted to manipulating the musical idiom and to influencing the output of composers.

With skillful presentation of music compositions in psychological warfare operations, it should not be difficult to establish in the minds of the listeners an association between the American sources and the pleasurable, inspirational, or nostalgic feelings that are a part of the musical experience provided by the American radio.

Exploitation of Vulnerabilities Through Music

Some examples of the uses to which music can lend itself for psychological warfare to the Communist countries considered in this research are as follows:

(1) *To express United Nations and United States values.* A great deal of music can be used, with a minimum of verbal explanation, to reveal our more admired national characteristics, our cultural diversity, our freedom, and our knowledge of and respect for the characteristics of target populations and United Nations peoples. Folk music such as our Western melodies may be of great value for this type of presentation, because it may serve to generate interest and curiosity in our broadcasts and, through them, in other aspects of democratic life as well; folk music from other United Nations countries will serve the same purpose. Since the music of nonbelligerent nations (especially South America) has a minimum of political overtones, it can be used in the more subtle type of propaganda designed to suggest the values in nonpartisanship, apathy toward war, and preoccupation with private or domestic concerns.

(2) *To popularize the expression of antagonism, toward the regime or of favorable attitudes toward the United States.* In song, music acts as a medium for verbal communication. Although the words of songs may empress subversive thoughts, songs may nevertheless achieve wide circulation due to their melodic appeal. This has often been the case with revolutionary songs. It may be profitable to broadcast versions of songs widely known in the target countries, therefore, in which the familiar words have been subtly twisted or replaced with ridiculous or pro-Western verse. In this way, the familiar songs of target peoples may be rendered useless for Communist purposes, and may also provide a way of venting antagonism toward the regime that is less risky than conversation or publication. Just as the German song "Lili Marlene" was adapted by the Allies in World War II, a catchy American tune may be adopted by the target people and serve to attract attention to our broadcasts. In using native songs, operators should be cautioned that Communists frequently change the words of familiar songs to include pro-Communist matter. An attempt to ascertain whether this has occurred should be made before using such songs.

(3) *To increase nationalistic sentiments.* One of the techniques Russia uses to control satellite countries is the neutralization of any nationalistic sentiments which may obstruct the ultimate "Russification" of the satellite's culture. The broadcasting of music that is peculiar to the target satellite—especially banned anthems and other music having nationalistic connotations—can aid in impeding "Russification" by keeping nationalistic sentiments alive: it can also reveal United States sympathy with the principle of national self-determination for target peoples.

(4) *To illustrate propaganda themes.* The plots of some music compositions, especially operas, and the experiences of some composers may provide vivid illustrations for propaganda themes. For example, a dramatization of Shostakovich's life, with appropriate musical illustrations, to show the inconsistency of his treatment by the Party, may focus public attention on the composer and may make target audiences more aware of certain oppressive aspects of Communist rule. Similarly, propaganda use can be made of the tragic opera "Boris Gudunov," by the 19th century Russian composer Moussorgsky. This story of a usurper who betrayed the people and became czar provides an opportunity for drawing parallels with the present Communist leadership.

(5) *To promote themes of internationalism.* There exists a substantial repertory of selections based upon musical themes or legends from countries other than the native country of the composer, which may be used as a medium for propaganda seeking to emphasize the community of interest between the peoples of target countries and the free world. Compositions of this type by target nationals which have been banned because of their "cosmopolitanism" or because they were written in a Western country may be especially useful. They can serve to promote an understanding that the ideas of brotherhood and internationalism originally espoused by the Communist movement have since been betrayed by the regime for the sake of its own entrenchment in power. This may be a particularly potent theme in view of the fact that current Communist music policy probibits the use of Western ideas by native composers. The late Sergei Prokofiev's "Overture on Hebrew Themes" is an example of banned music valuable for the purpose of pointing up this betrayal of ideals. The banning of such a work illustrates the consequences in Communist controlled countries of attempting to utilize freely the cultural heritage of all lands.

(6) *To heighten the audience appeal of fables or legends which have political overtones.* Because of their allegorical content and the simplicity of their form, fables and legends may assume effective political overtones when used in a propaganda context. They are particularly suited, too, for audiences with many diverse interests and capabilities, and should stimulate the interest of larger audiences than can be reached through the broadcasting of absolute, or nonrepresentational, music. Some fables and legends have already been adapted to music. Two examples are Prokofiev's "Peter and the Wolf" and "A Walk in the Forest" by the American composer, Herbert Haufrecht. The audience appeal of other fables and legends which have not been adapted to music may be greatly increased if musical illustrations are used in conjunction with their narration. Fables and legends lending themselves to musical illustration can undoubtedly be found in the folklore of target peoples.

(7) *To attract attention, to induce certain moods, and to impute connotations to verbal matter.* Some musical compositions, phrases, and instruments have highly distinctive and easily identifiable rhythmic, tonal, or "mood" qualities which lend themselves readily to symbolic interpretation. Others may have been associated with historical events and former ways of living. These compositions, phrases, or instruments may be used to identify particular persons, broadcasts, transmitters, or

situations, or may be interpolated in verbal programs to connote such things as humor, ridicule, disgust, sarcasm, strength, defiance, impending doom, sadness, and nostalgia. Thus the opening three short and one long notes of Beethoven's Fifth Symphony were commonly used as a victory symbol in World War II. At the present time, Radio Free Europe is featuring in its Hungarian broadcasts an old and rare Hungarian instrument called the tarogato, which has been banned by the Communist government because of its nationalistic associations.

The selection of music compositions which will exploit the possibilities listed above is not an easy task. Guidance could be offered more confidently if opportunity were provided for conducting tests upon and interviewing escaped target nationals in order to ascertain actual music preferences in the target countries, especially for music which has not recently been heard by their populations, jazz in particular.

As a general principle, indigenous contemporary music having pro-Commmist connotations and other music broadcast frequently by the Communist radio should not be used in United States broadcasts. The repetition in United States broadcasts of music with Communist connotations might reinforce these connotations, and the repetition of music frequently heard over the Communist radio would not be likely to stimulate audience interest in United States broadcasts. The latter is especially true in those Communist countries where individuals are punished for listening to United States broadcasts.

Modern Western music of the dissonant or radical type—among both jazz and art music repertories—is liable to evoke a confused or adverse response. Unless current intelligence indicates a preference for such music on the part of the target audience, therefore, this type of music also should not be used in United States psychological warfare.

In selecting music that is attractive to the target audience, the operator should be guided primarily by current intelligence on the music preferences in the target countries. In many cases, the Communist Party, for purposes of expediency, has adopted the music most popular with the populations it controls and has stamped it with pro-Communist connotations. Of this music, only those compositions having a definite value for United States psychological warfare broadcasts should be used, and special care should be taken to dissociate these compositions from Communist values. In some instances, the Communist-sponsored music diet has failed to fully satisfy the music preferences of the people. Advantage should be taken of all such situations, and use made of those compositions which the target audiences like but cannot hear over their own officially controlled media of communication.

One final warning is in order. Failure to employ a high degree of skill in using music for psychological warfare purposes may produce an effect that is not merely negative, but severely detrimental to psychological warfare objectives—detrimental because what the Party has told the target audience about Western music and music appreciation may be confirmed, and because the adverse responses induced by an unintelligent use of music may be transferred to non-musical programs. It is highly desirable, therefore, for the psychological warfare operator conducting music broadcasts to have the benefit of some knowledge, either his own or that of advisers, of the music history of the target area. Most important, however, is that the operator supplement the findings and suggestions of this report with current intelligence on the music diet and preferences of the *particular* audience he is attempting to reach.

Utilization of Escaped Music Performers

Musicians who have escaped from Communist countries can be valuable sources of information for psychological warfare units and can provide an effective reservoir of talent for broadcasts using music. A discussion of their potential usefulness is presented in this separate appendix because of its special importance for psychological warfare operations.

Recently escaped musicians have an intimate and fresh knowledge about many aspects of music in target countries, especially the style and types of music which are currently popular and recent changes in the officially controlled music diet of the people. This kind of information was largely inaccessible to research, and hence is dealt with only briefly in the foregoing report. Musicians coming through the Iron Curtain would be the best possible sources of information for checking and supplementing the findings presented in this report. In addition, they would have information which could suggest new psychological warfare themes involving the use of music. Psychological warfare operators without current information of the kind known to such musicians run the risk of broadcasting music which is no longer popular with the audiences they are attempting to reach or music which has recently been sponsored by the Commnunist Party or in other ways converted to Communist use.

Escaped music performers can be used in several ways to improve the effectiveness of music broadcasts. They can supply operators with compositions valuable for psychological warfare which are not available on records, or, if available, are of inferior broadcast quality. Many compositions of value for psychological warfare (especially folk music and music by native composers of the target country) have never been put on discs. Such hindrances as these could be overcome by having escaped performers tape-record or live-broadcast some of these compositions. Live broadcasts are considerably better than canned programs, being more dramatic and having more of an aura of immediacy and reality than the usual recorded presentation.

Singers can be used to translate the words and change the style of certain American songs in a way that would be understandable and attractive to target audiences. During World War II, the Office of Strategic Services commissioned Marlene Dietrich to record certain American songs in the German style and language in order to attract listeners to U.S. propaganda broadcasts to Germany. This technique may greatly increase the effectiveness of native American songs. In addition, such singers would be able to substitute pro-U.S. verse for the words of Communists songs, or subtly to twist the words of Communist songs to make them appear ridiculous or anti-regime.

Performances by escaped musicians—especially singers—would help to attract listeners to U.S. broadcasts. Such musicians know the style and type of music preferred by their fellow citizens and can "speak" to them in their own language. Many recordings of native music which are commercially available in the United States are performed by Americans who have little knowledge of, or feeling for, the style familiar to target audiences. Others, performed by native artists but recorded in the United States, have been Americanized in some way—as in style, words, or instrumentation. Both types are less useful for psychological warfare purposes than performances by artists who have the immediate feel of their native land. Broadcast performances by escaped performers could be supplemented with their comments about the compositions (adding a personal quality to the broadcast) and also, perhaps, accounts of their escape from behind the Iron Curtain.

The fact that creative artists flee Communist countries is in itself a potent propaganda weapon. Many musicians have emigrated from these countries because of the difficulty of carrying on their professional activities under surveillance by the Communist Party. However, one of the chief hindrances to the emigration of target musicians is their fear of being unable to attain some degree of recognition and to have an opportunity for exercising their skills. To induce defection, therefore, it might be appropriate to offer them an opportunity to perform over the radio and to make a few tape record-ings. These recordings could, in turn, be a valuable contribu-tion to the U.S. psychological warfare effort. For the more important musicians of the target countries, it may be fruitful to suggest the professional rewards and satsfactions they would receive should they come to the United States, with-out exaggerating the hospitality that would be extended to them by music circles in this country.

Although escaped musicians have occasionally in the past been used in various U.S. wartime broadcasting opera-tions, no systematic effort to contact such people and utilize their talents appears to have been made. Undertaking an effort of this kind would add to the usefulness of the research reported in the foregoing text. It would provide a continuing and useful flow of intelligence for operators in the field. It might vastly improve the effectiveness of psy-chological warfare programs using music. For these reasons, the potential usefulness of such persons has been briefly outlined here to provide a basis for further exploration by psychological warfare planning and operations personnel. A partial list of musicians known to have emigrated recently from Communist countries, and a sample radio script illus-trating the use of escaped musicians in broadcasts are given below as an aid to future planning.

Partial List of Escaped Musicians

Andre, Lydia
  Estonian singer (last heard of in Hamburg, Germany, where she recorded Estonian folk songs for the International Refugee Organization)
Andrejew, Galina
  Russian singer (last heard of in Munich, Germany, working as waitress in a cafe)
Black Sea Cossacks
  Russian choir (last heard of in Nurnberg, Germany)
Christova, Liliana
  Bulgarian pianist (last known address: 220 Katernbergerstrasse, Wuppertal-Elberfeld, Germany)
Darzins, G.
  Latvian organist and music teacher (last known address: Spokane Conservatory, Spokane, Washington, where he was teaching music)
Ese-Seps, Ludmila
  Latvian singer (last heard of in Hamburg, Germany, where she recorded Latvian songs for the United Nations Relief and Rehabilitation Administration)
Estonian Men's Choir
  (last heard at Geislingen IRO camp near Stuttgart, Germany)
Joachim (sthal), Walter
  German cellist (last heard of in Hamburg, Germany, working as entertainer at the Cafe Faum Betrieb)
Kalnins, A.
  Latvian composer (recently emigrated to Canada)
Karolyi, Julian
  Hungarian pianist (last known address: Hollywood, Calif.)
Lesta-Miller, Lydia
  Estonian pianist (last heard of in Hamburg, Germany, where she recorded Estonian keyboard music for UNRRA)
Medins, J.
  Latvian composer (last heard of in Sweden)
Nahruns, Ingus
  Latvian cellist (recently emigrated to New York City)
Nemerov, Boris
  Russian singer (last heard of in Munich, Germany, working in a night club)
Russian Men's Choir
  (last heard of in a Displaced Persons camp near Stuttgart, Germany)
Toi, Roman
  Estonian composer and choral director (last heard of in Toron-to, Canada, where he was directing an Estonian men's choir)
Tubin, Eduard
  Estonian composer (last heard of in Hamburg, Germany)

Zsigmondy, Denes
  Hungarian violinist (last known address: 13b Ammerland, Stronbergersee, Bavaria, Germany)

Sample Radio Script

(NOTE: The radio script reproduced below was prepared by the Mutual Network for broadcast on Good Friday, 1951. The broad-cast was designed for consumption by U.S. audiences, and illus-trates the kind of recognition which has been given to escaped music performers. However, the script should be read with a consideration of the propaganda possibilities in beaming similar programs to Communist audiences.)

MUSIC: *Theme. Establish, then under*

PRYOR: In cooperation with the United Nation's Internation-al Refugee Organization, the Mutual Network brings you a special half hour program of music for Good Friday, as sung by refugees in the IRO's Displaced Persons camps in Western Germany. We begin with an old Russian version of the Lord's Prayer, sung by a Russian men's choir, and recorded by Rein Narma and Ralph Scott in a refugee camp near Munich. This is Don Pryor at IRO headquar-ters in Geneva, Switzerland.

MUSIC: *Theme up to close*

PRYOR: Like all DPs under the care of the International Refugee Organization, these Russian singers are still wait-ing for a chance to emigrate to some new, free country. Meanwhile, they sing and pray for a new life. Now, a choir of Black Sea Cossacks in Nurnberg, Germany, sings a musi-cal prayer in the ancient Slaviansky language of the Ortho-dox church. Slaviansky is to the Russian language approxi-mately what Latin is to our Western languages, and is said to have originated around the time of Ghengis Khan.

MUSIC: *Cossack Liturgical*

PRYOR: The feeling of desolation and despair is expressed by Roman Toi, a former Estonian refugee, in this original com-position, sung for the first time by an Estonian Men's Choir of Geislingen, near Stuttgart. The composer has since been transported by IRO to Canada, where he is now making a new life. His song—"My Life is a Deserted Heath."

MUSIC: *"My Life is a Deserted Heath"*

PRYOR: Next, a Polish Men's Choir of refugees in DP camp at Wildflecken—a former SS training center—singing "Kyrie Eleison" in Latin.

MUSIC: *Kyrie Eleison*

PRYOR: In the next number, you may notice that the melody is strangely similar to the Pilgrim's song, from "Tannhaüs-er." Actually, it's another version of "The Lord's Prayer," sung by a mixed choir of Latvian refugees, during a church service in Nurnberg, Germany.

MUSIC: *Latvian Lord's Prayer*

PRYOR: Now, an old Cossack folk song of the season, sung by the Black Sea Cossacks in a DP camp near Nurnberg.

MUSIC: *Cossack folk song*

PRYOR: Next, another seasonal folk song, this time from Estonia—sung by an Estonian choir of 27 voices in one of the IRO's Displaced Persons camps at Geislingen, Ger-many.

MUSIC: *Estonian Nocturne*

PRYOR: Let's return now to the Black Sea Cossacks at Nurn-berg, singing another liturgical number from the Orthodox service.

MUSIC: *Cossack Liturgical. Pause 3 seconds, then up theme for 12 seconds and under*

PRYOR: Now, with our Russian Men's Choir singing "The Lord's Prayer" we bring to an end this special Good Fri-day program of music by the Displaced, recorded in DP camps operated by the International Refugee Organiza-tion, and transcribed at the Organization's headquarters in Geneva, Switzerland.

Resolution of the Fire and Police Research Association of Los Angeles on the Subversive Perils of American Folk Music

Officers	Board of Directors
Russell B. Weck, President	Edward Bakula
Irving L. J. Kasper, Vice-president	Charles Blank
Edward Bakula, Secretary-treasurer	Gordon M. Browning
	John C. Coleman
	Frank Cutter
	Kenneth Gustafson
	Irving L. J. Kasper
	Norman H. Moore
	Karl G. Thor
	Russell B. Weck

October 4, 1963

Mr. Nicolas Slonimsky:
295 Beacon Street
Boston, Massachusetts

Dear Mr. Slonimsky: Thank you for your letter of September 28, 1963 requesting a copy of our resolution which we sent to the House Committee on Un-American Activities regarding communist infiltration into the field of folk singing. We are enclosing a copy of this resolution and we have no objection to your reproducing it, provided it is reproduced in toto and without any alterations.

Very truly yours,
PAUL R. JACKSON, Member
Board of Directors

Resolution

WHEREAS, there is increasing and cumulative evidence indicating a deep interest in, and much activity by the Communist Party, USA, in the field of Folk Music, and

WHEREAS, Folk Music has been successfully used in the past by great political movements in history, particularly in the USSR, and

WHEREAS, the dialectics of the Communist movement have successfully used, and are now using all modes and media of communication with young people, including the subtleties and the verbal subterfuges of applied dialectics in both poems and songs, and

WHEREAS, it is becoming more and more evident that certain of the "Hootenannies" and other similar youth gatherings and festivals, both in this country and in Europe have been used to brainwash and subvert, in a seemingly innocuous but actually covert and deceptive manner, vast segments of young people's groups, and

WHEREAS, the youth of our nation is acknowledged to be a major target of the Communist Conspiracy, and

WHEREAS, there is much evidence indicating an accelerated drive in the Folk Music field is being made on or near the campuses of a number of high schools and colleges by certain individuals of questionable motivation, including members of the Communist Conspiracy,

THEREFORE, be it resolved that the Fire and Police Research Association of Los Angeles in its regular monthly meeting of August, 1963, hereby formally requests the Congress of the United States, through its House Committee on Un-American Activities, to investigate Communist subversive involvement in the Folk Music field, that the continued, effective misuse of this media may not be made, and that it may not be further used as an unidentified tool of Communist Psychological or Cybernetic Warfare to ensnare and capture youthful minds in the United States as it has so successfully and effectively captivated them abroad.

Adopted by the Board of Directors, August 7, 1963.

Debate on Folk Music at the United States Senate

Remarks of Senator Kenneth B. Keating and Others on Folkmusik (From Congressional Record, Thursday September 26, 1963, Volume 109, No. 154)

October 7, 1963

Mr. Nicolas Slonimsky
295 Beacon Street
Boston, Massachusetts

Dear Mr. Slonimsky: Thank you for requesting a copy of my recent speech on hootenannies.

I am very pleased to enclose a copy of the complete text for your information.

Very sincerely yours,
KENNETH B. KEATING

Mine Enemy—The Folk Singer

Mr. Keating: Mr. President, it will come as a shock to many Senators, but according to a resolution of a certain Los Angeles civic organization the Communists have developed a new secret weapon to ensnare and capture youthful minds in America—folk music.

No one who serves in Congress could reasonably entertain any illusions, no matter what might be the thrust of Soviet policy at any given time, about any possible letup in the intensity and earnestness of the Soviet pursuit toward its ultimate goal of world domination. Nor, based on our experiences with and knowledge of Soviet tactics, can one ever safely underestimate the capacity of communism for devising and employing whatever techniques are necessary to accomplish its long-range ends, from outright military takeover and occupation and the violent coup d'etat, to espionage, sabotage, subversion, propaganda, economic warfare, and perversion of the political and social processes of free societies to its own evil purposes. Nevertheless, I am stunned by the revelation that folk music is part of the Communist arsenal of weapons.

The resolution adopted by this organization, called the Fire and Police Research Association of Los Angeles, Inc., describes folk music as—and I quote from the resolution—"an unidentified tool of Communist psychological or cybernetic warfare."

For the benefit of any Senators who may not be fully familiar with the term "Cybernetics," I looked it up in the dictionary, and it means "a comparative study of the control system formed by the nervous system and brain and mechano-electrical communication systems, such as computing machines."

I ask unanimous consent that the text of the resolution be printed in the RECORD following my remarks.

The *Presiding Officer* (Mr. *Kennedy* in the chair). Without objection, it is so ordered.

Mr. Keating: Mr. President, this amazing document maintains that "the dialectics of the Communist movement have successfully used, and are now using all modes and media of communication with young people, including the subtleties and the verbal subterfuges of applied dialectics in both poems and songs" and that "it is becoming more and more evident that certain of the 'Hootenannies' in this country and in Europe have been used to brainwash and subvert"—and now, listen to this—"in a seemingly innocuous but actually covert and deceptive manner, vast segments of young people's groups." It closes with a fervent plea for a congressional investigation of this "unidentified tool of Communist psychological and cybernetic warfare" which is being used "to ensnare and capture youthful minds in the United States as it has so successfully and effectively captivated them abroad."

I had always had the impression that if anything was thoroughly American in spirit, it was American folk music. To be sure, I was perfectly aware of certain un-American influences in it, like Elizabethan balladry, English Protestant hymns and spirituals, and, with respect to jazz and in some cases the Negro spiritual, native African rhythms. But in my naivete I had never considered these un-American influences to be of a sinister nature and simply passed them off as part and parcel of the melting-pot tradition which has contributed so much in the way of variety and interest to the American cultural heritage.

In the light of this resolution, however, I have given this subject renewed attention. Have we ever considered, for example, that the music of our national anthem, the Star-Spangled Banner, is based upon an English folk melody—a drinking song, no less—"To Anacreon in Heaven"?

Of course, I realize that folk music tradition is grounded in movements of political, economic, and social unrest and I did not expect to find in music which originated among sharecroppers, miners, union organizers, factory workers, cowboys, hill folk, wanderers, and oppressed Negroes—a pattern of tribute and praise to such symbols of orthodoxy as the gold standard, the oil depletion allowance, and the standing rules of the U.S. Senate.

I knew that in reviewing the evidence I would be in for a share of lyrical protest against war, depression, economic exploitation, the plight of the Negro, the farmer, the worker, the railroaded convict, and, generally, the poor and down-trodden. I knew I would also come across music, as I actually did, dedicated to Robin Hood folk heroes like Jesse James, Pretty Boy Floyd, and Billy the Kid. And so I made allowances for the basic cultural factors operative in the folk music field. No one could possibly imagine the members of the board of directors of General Motors sitting around a conference table composing ditties in honor of defense contracts, while it is not surprising that coal miners should have come up with a protest song, "Sixteen Tons," crying "Saint Peter, don't call me, 'cause I can't go; I owe my soul to the company store."

I might interject at this point that the reason I recite rather than sing these words is that I know I would be breaking the Senate's rules if I did anything to provoke a Senate "hootenanny."

Mr Humphrey: Mr. President, will the Senator yield?

Mr. Keating: I yield.

Mr. Humphrey: I have examined the rules of the senate, knowing of the Senator's speech. I do not recall seeing anything in the rules which would prohibit the Senator from singing, except his own good judgment.

Mr. Aiken: Are there any other reasons?

Mr: Keating: My voice is not of the best. Some of the citations bearing out this thesis are better sung than said. There is in the gallery an old friend and associate of my office who could sing them. But I think it best that I do not sing them.

Mr. Humphrey: Particularly without musical accompaniment.

Mr. Keating: I would not be able to do that, anyway. If I used a guitar, I would have to use a left-handed guitar.

Mr. Humphrey: Let us not do anything "left" here.

Mr. Keating: No; let us do everything right.

But when I began to look into the folk music business, I began to find that where there is smoke, there is fire—which perhaps explains how the Fire and Police Research Association gets into the act, too.

The first significant discovery I made was that from this Nation's very beginnings folk music had indeed been used, "in a seemingly innocuous but actually covert and deceptive manner, to incite violations of the laws of the United States." Why, even "Yankee Doodle" has fallen victim to misuse in this fashion, as it did during President Jefferson's embargo of 1808 imposed to prevent our embroilment in the Napoleonic wars. Just listen to this plea to run the embargo:

> Attention pay ye bonny lads
> And listen to my Fargo
> About a nation deuced thing
> Which people call Embargo
>
> Yankee doodle, keep it up
> Yankee doodle, dandy
> We'll soak our hide in home-made rum
> If we can't get French brandy
>
> I've got a vessel at the wharf
> Well loaded with a cargo
> And want a few more hands to help
> And clear the cursed Embargo
>
> Yankee doodle, keep it up
> Yankee doodle, dandy
> We'll soak our hide in home-made rum
> If we can't get French brandy

Now it seems perfectly obvious to me that if people went around singing this today, we would be in a pretty fix with our shipping ban against Castro. Before we knew it, we would have rum-running out of Cuba in American bottoms.

While we are on the subject of the whisky trade, this is another area for grave concern. Apparently, some of our folk music takes a pretty cavalier attitude toward the enforcement of our Internal Revenue laws and could easily brainwash our young people into total disrespect for all law and order. The song, "Darlin' Cory," is a prime example of this:

> Wake up, wake up, darlin' Cory
> What makes you sleep so sound?
> The revenue officers a-comin'
> Gonna tear your still house down

Or, for another example, the now very popular, "Copper Kettle," which contains the lines:

> My daddy he made whisky
> My granddaddy did, too
> We ain't paid no whisky tax
> Since 1792

If enough people went around singing this at hootenannies, Americans might soon get the idea that they don't have to pay their taxes. After all, the family in the song got away without paying them for 171 years. And if the Government loses its ability to collect taxes to pay for our defense effort, we would be wide open for a Communist takeover, would we not?

This sinister folk music plot for disarmament takes more direct form than merely inciting Americans not to pay their taxes. Consider, for example, this pacifist Negro spiritual:

> Gonna lay down my sword and shield
> Down by the river-side
> Down by the river-side
> Down by the river-side
> Gonna lay down my sword and shield
> Down by the river-side
> And study war no more.

It should be especially noted that this song tells us not only to lay down our arms, but also—in the words of the Fire and Police Research Association—it uses "the subtleties and the verbal subterfuges of applied dialectics" by implying, by the words "And study war no more," that we should close down West Point, Annapolis, the Air Force Academy, and the War College, get rid of our ROTC program in our Nation's colleges and universities, and thus cut off our supply of trained military officers to lead us in our defense against communism. If we do not realize that this "seemingly innocuous" Negro spiritual is "actually covert and deceptive," we have obviously been duped.

Now the Communists have also been known to sow the seeds of dissension in capitalist countries by turning people against their own political leaders. There's an Ozark folk song—and perhaps one of the Senators from Arkansas can enlighten me as to its origin—that goes like this:

Yes, the candidate's a dodger, yes, a well-known dodger
Yes, the candidate's a dodger, and I'm a dodger, too
He'll meet you and greet you and ask you for your vote
But look out, boys, he's dodging for a note.

To be quite honest, I am not sure I understand all the "subtleties and verbal subterfuges" of these "applied dialectics." For example, what does the fellow mean when he sings, "And I'm a dodger, too"? Is he saying he is a draft-dodger and advocating resistance to the enforcement of the selective service laws? And then, what is meant by the words that the candidate is "dodging for a note"? Is he trying to undermine American faith and confidence in America's political leaders by implying that all they are interested in are "notes," that is to say, campaign contributions? I hope Senators will read the RECORD carefully tomorrow and fill me in on what may be an example of subtle regional dialectics.

These examples must give pause to every patriotic American who may have taken folk music for granted in the past. But there is one concern I still have about a congressional investigation of folk music proposed by the Fire and Police Research Association of Los Angeles. What I fear is that such an investigation would stimulate the writing of new folk music making fun of congressional investigations. This shows how devious the Communists really are. First they subtly use the verbal subterfuges of applied dialectics in folk music, knowing full well that organizations like the Fire and Police Research Association of Los Angeles are always on guard against them and sooner or later will demand a congressional investigation. Then, once a congressional investigation of folk music is held, the Communists set about composing new folk music impugning the integrity of Congressional investigations, like this folk song of a few years ago:

> Who's gonna investigate the man who investigates me?
> I don't doubt my loyalty
> But how about what his may be?
> Who'll check the record of the man who checks
>   the record of me?
> Seems to me there's gonna be an awfully long line.
>
> One more problem puzzles me
> Pardon my strange whim

> But who's gonna investigate the man who investigates
>   the man who investigates him?

This shows that there may be no logical stopping place once an investigation of folk music goes forward. Any such investigation would ultimately have to be extended ad infinitum, to take in a study of the folk songs composed in response to the investigation itself, which can go on indefinitely. But perhaps all this simply shows how devious the Communists are, perpetually tying up the valuable time of our elected officials and diverting their attention from other subversive activities which they engage in.

It all boils down to a gigantic plot, one that has been brought to our attention before, most notably, by the assistant minority leader, the senior Senator from California [Mr. Kuchel], based on letters he has received from constituents whose keen alertness to matters involving our national security is fully equal to that of the Fire and Police Association of Los Angeles, Inc. And so, now, to the list of subversive individuals, institutions, and ideas, which presently includes the United Nations, the income tax, the Chief Justice of the United States, the Girl Scouts of America, fluoridation of the water supply, the last four Presidents of the United States, beatniks, Harvard University, civil rights demonstrations, expenditures for mental health, the Arms Control and Disarmament Agency, coffee houses, every Secretary of State since William Jennings Bryan, professors of anthropology, back-door spending, metro government, Jews, *Time* magazine, the Council on Foreign Relations, firearms registration, the Protestant clergy, the two United States Senators from New York plus between 77 and 83 of their colleagues and proposals for Federal aid to mass transportation—to this list of Communist-inspired persons and ideas we must now add, merciful heavens, American folk music. And who knows what lies ahead?

Already there are signs that the Communists are going beyond folk music in their plot to subvert America, but I shall not dwell on that. Consider for a moment the inroads which have been made into the popular music field by such songs as "The Moon Belongs to Everyone. The Best Things in Life Are Free."

Mr. President, we ought to be grateful that we have a Constitution—that it protects the right of everyone to sing out as well as speak out whenever the spirit moves him. There is a fire of freedom in this document called the Constitution which no amount of researching by organizations such as the Fire and Police Research Association of Los Angeles will ever succeed in putting out.

This resolution is but another demonstration of the absurd lengths to which the amateur ferrets of the radical right will go in their quixotic sallies against the Communist menace. As the great FBI Director J. Edgar Hoover has often warned, vigilante charges such as these can breed the atmosphere of suspicion and confusion which tends not only to undermine free institutions but, of equal concern, to divert our energies from tackling the real threats posed by international communism to our liberty and security. With devotion to our freedoms, with trust in the American ideal of cultural diversity, with, above all, a sense of proportion and discernment in meeting the challenges of our times, I for one have every faith that—in the words of that inspiring song—we shall overcome.

Mr. Russell: Mr. President, will the Senator from New York yield?

Mr. Keating: I yield to the Senator from Georgia.

Mr. Russell: The remarks just made by the Senator from New York are a valuable contribution to the permanent record of the Senate. They bring to the attention of the American people the deep tolerance of these days and also show that the sense of humor has not been entirely extinguished by the complexities of the age in which we live.

But having paid tribute to the Senator's tolerance, I must express regret that he did not include in his magnificent defense of some of the things we have known in years gone by the song "Dixie." I did not hear him include that song in the list of things he defended. I am sure he would not desire to conclude his remarks without extending the mantle of Keating tolerance to overlap "Dixie" because it was written by a constituent of one of his predecessors in the Senate.

Mr. Keating: That is my understanding. "Dixie" was written by a New Yorker and is, of course, one of the great songs of the folk tradition. I am happy to include it in the engulfing embrace of these remarks. I am sure the Fire and Police Research Association of Los Angeles would find something subversive in it, but I fail to see how "Dixie" could undermine our security in any way.

Mr. Pell: Mr. President, I wish to congratulate the Senator from New York [Mr. Keating] on his spoof of the charges that folk music is a subversive wing of the Communist conspiracy.

The past summer we had the most successful music festival in the form of a folk festival that we have ever had in Newport. More people came to it, they were better shaved, and more enjoyment was received by our local citizens than had ever before been the case in any form of public entertainment.

When it is suggested, because of political reasons, that we should clamp down on forms of art expression, I think we are treading dangerously close to totalitarianism. This approach is very akin to that of the Kremlin with regard to impressionist artists and jazz musicians. Certainly it is not an approach that we should emulate.

Accordingly, I am very glad indeed that the Senator from New York has spoken as he has.

Letter from Ralph Nader Sounding Alarm at the Noise Pollution of the Aural Environment by the Rock-'n'-Roll Bands

May 31, 1969

Hon. Warren G. Magnuson
Chairman, Senate Labor-HEW Appropriations Subcommittee
U.S. Senate

Hon. Philip Hart
Chairman, Subcommittee on the Environment
Senate Commerce Committee
U.S. Senate

Dear Senators Magnuson and Hart: Noise trauma is being viewed as an increasingly serious environmental hazard by scientists as the noise level of our working and public surroundings continues rising. Acoustic trauma from rock and roll music is emerging as a very real threat to the hearing quality of young people who expose themselves to substantial durations of this music by live rock groups with high amplification. The nature of this hazard and its avoidance merit our attention if only to foresee and forestall even more aggravated risks and focus public concern on noise traumas of all kinds in our occupational and public environments. This country may be producing a new generation of young Americans with impaired

hearing before they reach the age of 21. It is in this context that the following information may be helpful:

The American Medical Association, the Workmen's Compensation Board of New York State and other similar groups consider exposure to noise levels over time between 85–90 db (decibels) to be hazardous to an individual's hearing. Some individuals are more susceptible to ear damage than others. The degree of hearing loss depends on a variety of important noise characteristics—most prominently the noise intensity, the frequency composition of the noise and the distribution and length of exposure to the noise. These are crucially important relationships. For example, given equivalent intensities, high frequencies are more harmful than lower frequencies. If high frequencies are prominent, as they are in rock and roll music, the risk of damage to the hearing is 100 times greater at 120 decibels than at 90 decibels. Other factors which have greater or different effects upon the hearing mechanism include rhythm, resonance and reflection. For rock-and-roll music bands, reflection is high because of the customary bare, hard walls, floors and ceilings that permit such reflection back to the microphones of the individual instruments and of the hall amplification systems. There are few absorptive surfaces. The worst sound pressure levels come from the playing of "hard rock" as distinguished from "folk rock" and "soul music."

The typical rock band's instruments are provided with high gain amplifiers and large speaker systems whose output is usually reamplified by two or more powerful sound reinforcement systems. Decibel level measurements in several Washington, D.C. establishments ranged between 100 to 116 decibels. With headphones, 125 decibels were attained. Readings in other areas of the country have shown similar levels but also higher levels, reaching on occasion in some discotheques levels of 125 to 138 decibels. The pain threshold level is 140 decibels for most people.

A number of recent studies by specialists have comprised a basis for urging further studies. Highly amplified rock music in relatively small, high reflection rooms has been around for several years. Studies are just beginning to catch up with this electronically facilitated acoustic assault, however.

In 1967, a study by Charles P. Lebo, M.D., Kenward S. Oliphant, E.E., and John Garrett, M.D., based on measurements obtained in two rock-and-roll music establishments in San Francisco, concluded that noise levels and frequency distributions therein "can produce temporary auditory threshold shifts and is of an order that has been recognized as entailing risk of permanent ear damage." These sound measurements exceeded the State of California ear damage risk criteria for industrial establishments. Dr. Lebo et al. noted that "noise greater than 92 decibels in sound pressure composed of frequencies primarily between 500 and 8,000 Hz (cycles per second) and sustained for a period of one hour will produce as much as 40 decibels threshold shift in the area of 4,000 Hz in approximately 10 percent of the ears exposed, no measurable shift in another 10 percent, and between 5 and 30 db shift in the remaining 80 percent of ears. Their data showed sound pressures with these frequencies to prevail in the musical establishments they studied. Their final conclusion is noteworthy:

> "We believe that we have demonstrated that the noise levels produced by some live rock-and-roll bands with the aid of high amplification unmistakably exceed those considered safe for prolonged exposure. Attenuation of the amplification to safe levels would substantially reduce the risk of ear injury in the audience and performers and, in the opinion of the authors, would still permit enjoyment of the musical material."

A later study (1968) by Dr. Lebo and K. P. Oliphant declared that "the sound pressure levels produced by a typical symphony orchestra in a typical concert hall during fortissimo passages for full orchestra are well below the acoustic trauma hazard strata." "The noise output of the rock groups is likely to be particularly ototraumatic because of factors other than sound pressure peaks alone. These factors include compressed dynamic range, narrow band amplification, and continuity from the addition of amplified and reamplified reverberation to the early arrival sound." Indicating a path of further inquiry, the authors suggest that the "use of certain drugs by some rock and roll listeners may further reduce the effectiveness of the protection afforded by the stapedius and the tonsor tympani."

Another study by Dr. David M. Lipscomb, director of audiology clinical services at the University of Tennessee, showed damage and destruction to the cells in an unprotected ear of a guinea pig exposed to 90 hours of go-go music spread over a three month period at intervals similar to the habits of the average teen-ager. The cells in the unprotected right ear were either displaced, collapsed or totally missing, while the left ear, protected by a plug, showed no signs of damage. (The guinea pig was chosen because its ear's biochemical process was very similar to that of man.) In the tests, go-go music was recorded and played back to the guinea pig at the identical sound level measured at a Knoxville discotheque. Dr. Lipscomb said that he "used 120 decibels as the sound level for these tests," but sound in various discotheques were measured at a peak of 138 decibels, "only two decibels below the pain threshold."

Quite significantly, what prompted Dr. Lipscomb's experiment was the routine screening of entering freshmen at the University of Tennessee which discovered a large number with measurable hearing loss. "We were shocked to find that the hearing of many of these students had already deteriorated to a level of the average 65-year-old person," said Dr. Lipscomb. Tests were then conducted involving 3,000 Knoxville public school students and showing a marked increase in the prevalency of high frequency hearing loss as the student moves from the sixth grade to high school senior—a period during which his exposure to recreational noises increases, according to Professor Lipscomb. Five percent of the 1,000 students tested at the sixth grade level suffered measurable hearing loss. This prevalence rose to 14 percent of the 1,000 students at the ninth grade level and approximately 20 percent of the 1,000 high school seniors. Professor Lipscomb believes that we have reached the point that "the young people are losing sufficient hearing to jeopardize their occupational potential." He urged entering into "a program or the consequences are going to be pretty dire."

A University of Florida audiologist, Dr. George T. Singleton, tested the hearing of ten 14-year-olds before a rock-and-roll dance. During the dance he measured the sound intensity of the room and found the sound level to be 106–108 db in the middle of the floor and 120 decibels next to the bandstand. It did not fall below the established safety limit of 90 db until he was forty feet outside the building. All ten teenagers showed some temporary loss of hearing with the greatest hearing loss occurring in the high-frequency range involving consonantal sounds.

An exceptional hazard for rock fans comes through the headphone. Damage, both temporary and permanent, can be extraordinary with headphones. Serious symptoms during usage of high volume headphones are: buzzing or tickling of the ear, tinnitus or ringing in the ear or temporary loss of hearing.

The hazard to the musicians is of course the greatest because of their longer exposure time. A recently published study (February 1969) observed five members of a rock-and-roll musical combo in Michigan before, during and after a rehearsal. Peak sound levels generated in the practice room ranged from 120 to 130 decibels (compared to the 120 deci-

bels from a Saturn moon rocket measured at the press site). All the players reported ringing in the ears after the rehearsal with the head noises persisting for two of the players from one to two days. The authors warned that such exposure may produce progressive, accumulative and permanent inner ear damage. They recommend that such musicians wear customized ear defenders to reduce by 20 to 30 db the intensity of noise reaching the ears. (Rupp, R. R., & Koch, L. J., Univ. of Michigan.) Similar findings come from Dr. James Jenger of the Houston Speech and Hearing Center who tested a five man combo, all under 23 years of age and three of whom suffered slight permanent damage. Although discussion with discotheque performers and workers produce regular admissions of hearing loss, surprisingly little attention has been given this problem by occupational safety specialists and labor unions.

Why is rock music played so loudly? This question also has received little study. Some light was shed in a Michigan State study by Dr. William F. Rintelmann, who showed less alarm than other researchers. He asked 66 college students last year why such music was played so loudly. Here is his report:

"The most commonly given response was that the high intensity makes up for the mediocre quality, that mistakes are not as readily noticed when the volume is so high and that musicians 'drown out their own mistakes.' The second most often given response was that the very loud music commands the attention of the listeners, 'takes control of their minds' by blocking out any environmental sounds such as talking, glasses rattling, etc. and almost forces them to dance in a manner that they feel releases tension. Following are some quotes from the responses gathered which may express this concept more clearly: 'It surrounds the people totally in the rock and roll atmosphere; it turns them on,' 'It makes you get worked up into a frenzy that serves to release a lot of tension and energy,' 'The type of dancing that is popular today would look a little strange with soft music.' A third frequently given response concerned the physical effect of the music on the body, the actual vibration of the body to the beat of the music. As one student said, 'It is supposed to captivate the body physically.' A fourth frequently given response was that the musicians feel that the louder they play, the better they are. Since the more powerful amplifiers are more expensive, louder music also implies a successful group. The authors also received this impression from the musicians themselves. . . . As a final point, perhaps the classic comment of all, given by one of the students who felt that the music was played at about the right intensity level, was 'It provides people of this age with the opportunity to congregate without having to communicate.'"

Rock band music impairing hearing involves both occupational and consumer issues. It typifies the growing pervasiveness of a trauma too charitably called noise pollution. The federal government should be concerned about it, but is doing little. Congress has done almost nothing. I believe it would be most salutary for you, in your respective official positions noted above, to conduct brief hearings that will bring together the relevant knowledge, etch the major problems, educate the public and the states and municipalities which have the immediate legal responsibility. Whether these jurisdictions wish to classify such musical performances, above a certain sound pressure and frequency level, as public nuisances, or whether they wish to require ear protectors for musicians and band hall workers, or whether they may require certain absorptive surfaces in the halls or rooms, will depend on sound public information and awareness. Your Subcommittees can provide this important service as well as prod the Executive Branch into greater activity in this area of acoustic abuse and other areas as well.

Thank you for your consideration and your continuing interest in the well-being of the consumer.

Sincerely yours,
RALPH NADER

Statement on the Mobilization of the Masses to Use Mao Tsetung's Thought to Transform the Literary, Musical, Art and Theater Front in China

Following Chairman Mao's great teaching that "there is no construction without destruction," the workers' Mao Tsetung Thought propaganda team stationed at the China Opera and Dance-Drama Theatre has mobilized the masses there to carry out protracted and deep-going revolutionary mass criticism. This was to help the literary and art workers to raise their consciousness of class struggle and the struggle between the two lines and change their old ideology, so that they would gradually shift their stand over to the side of the workers, peasants and soldiers.

In the past year, the mental outlook of the literary and art workers in this theatre has undergone a profound change.

The China Opera and Dance-Drama Theatre was one of the literary and artistic organizations under the direct control of the arch renegade Liu Shao-chi and the counter-revolutionary revisionist Chou Yang and their gang. In the decade and more before the cultural revolution, the handful of capitalist roaders there made use of this theatre in their frantic opposition to Chairman Mao's revolutionary line in literature and art. They actively pushed Liu Shao-chi's counter-revolutionary revisionist line and energetically peddle feudal, bourgeois and revisionist trash in literature and art. As a result, emperors, kings, generals and ministers, scholars and beauties and foreign mummies overran the stage. The theatre thus became one of the places used for restoring capitalism and creating counter-revolutionary public opinion.

After the propaganda team entered this theatre, it followed Chairman Mao's instruction to "thoroughly criticize and repudiate reactionary bourgeois ideas in the sphere of academic work, education, journalism, literature and art and publishing, and seize the leadership in these cultural spheres" and his other great teachings and analysed the specific conditions there. Members of the team were of the opinion that, to ensure that the proletariat firmly occupies and transforms this position, it is essential to take a firm grasp of the class struggle in the ideological and political spheres, use the powerful weapon of revolutionary mass criticism to eliminate the pernicious influence of Liu Shao-chi's counter-revolutionary revisionist line in literature and art, get rid of the bourgeois individualist ideology, and use Mao Tsetung Thought to thoroughly remould the world outlook of the literary and art workers.

The propaganda team successively ran several Mao Tsetung Thought study classes which made the proletarian revolutionaries and other revolutionary masses in the theatre even more determined to carry out deep-going revolutionary mass criticism. In these classes, they studied Chairman Mao's great theory of continuing the revolution under the dictatorship of the proletariat and came to a clearer understanding of the fact that, since the great cultural revolution, although organizationally the proletariat has already seized back that portion of power usurped by the bourgeoisie, its struggle against the bourgeoisie in the ideological and political spheres has not ended. Only by waging protracted and deep-going revolutionary mass criticism

to thoroughly criticize the counter-revolutionary revisionist line in literature and art and eliminate its pernicious influence, and by letting Mao Tsetung Thought occupy all positions can the dictatorship of the proletariat be effectively consolidated and strengthened and the restoration of capitalism prevented. Only thus can we ensure that our literature and art will always advance triumphantly along Chairman Mao's revolutionary line.

On the basis of such an understanding, the revolutionary masses of the whole theatre were filled with enthusiasm and the tide of their revolutionary mass criticism surged higher and higher.

Having repeatedly studied Chairman Mao's great teaching "This question of 'for whom?' is fundamental; it is a question of principle," the propaganda team deeply realized that the focus of the struggle between the two lines in literature and art is the question of whom literature and art should serve. In order to transform the literary and art ranks with Mao Tsetung Thought, the fundamental thing to do is to unfold criticism of the sinister counter-revolutionary revisionist line in literature and art so that the literary and art workers can gradually shift their stand over to the side of the workers, peasants and soldiers, to the side of the proletariat.

Through revolutionary mass criticism, the revolutionary masses of the theatre ascertained more fully the perfidious ambition of the arch renegade Liu Shao-chi in frenziedly pushing a sinister counter-revolutionary revisionist line in literature and art in a vain attempt to subvert the dictatorship of the proletariat and restore capitalism. They further heightened their consciousness of class struggle and the struggle between the two lines.

Accusation of the sinister revisionist line in literature and art which had poisoned them was a profound education for the revolutionary literary and art workers on the question of whom to serve.

One opera singer had worked as a cowherd for a landlord in the old society when he was only 13. In 1946, he jumped out of this pit of misery and joined the revolution. He became an actor in an army cultural troupe. In the difficult years of the War of Liberation, his heart was wholly dedicated to the revolution and the cause of saving China, and he portrayed only the workers, peasants and soldiers. After the liberation of the whole country, he came to the cities. Poisoned by the sinister counter-revolutionary revisionist line in literature and art, his thoughts and feelings changed. For many years before the cultural revolution, he was preoccupied with making a reputation for himself and took the revisionist road of desiring only to improve his art while remaining aloof from politics. His roles were confined to those of young nobles and feudal talents. Once, the theatre put on the big poisonous weed *The Peddler and the Lady*. He played the title role and was acclaimed by the capitalist roaders. He later became a member of the national stage artists' association. In this way, his thoughts and feelings became further divorced from the working people, and he sank even deeper in the mire of revisionism.

The revolutionary mass criticism woke him up with a start. Recalling how his thoughts and feelings had changed from the time he was a poor cowherd to his rise as the actor in the role of the peddler in the play, he said indignantly: "It was Liu Shao-chi's counter-revolutionary revisionist line which influenced me to divorce myself from the working people, forget the revolution and, through 'peaceful evolution,' embark on the revisionist road. It is the Great Proletarian Cultural Revolution personally initiated and led by Chairman Mao that saved me. I am determined to study Mao Tsetung Thought well, thoroughly rid myself of the poison of Liu Shao-chi's sinister literary and art line, and serve the workers, peasants and soldiers with all my heart."

Deliberately "honoring" some of the literary and art workers with the titles of "well-known actor," "well-known director" or "well-known script writer," the handful of capitalist roaders in the theatre gave them high pay and provided them with lucrative means of livelihood. This lured those literary art workers whose bourgeois world outlook had not been remoulded well into chasing after personal fame and gain and taking the revisionist road of concentrating on raising their level of artistic skill and of keeping aloof from proletarian politics. As the days went by, they became more and more divorced from the labouring people, from productive labour and revolutionary practice and slid farther and farther down the revisionist road.

One young dance-drama actress was a typical representative of the "three well-knowns and three highs." After enjoying her performance in the sinister dance-drama *Mermaid*, Liu Shao-chi lavished praises on her and personally instructed the theatre's capitalist roaders to increase her salary by three grades and gave her membership in the national dance association. Indeed, they spared no effort to corrupt her.

During the revolutionary mass criticism, the masses deeply realized from this young woman's vivid example that "the 'three well-knowns and three highs' were truly arsenic used by Liu Shao-chi to poison the literary and art workers. It was a soft sword which drew no blood but killed people." From her own painful experience, the dancer who was deeply poisoned by the revisionist line came to understand that the criminal aim of Liu Shao-chi and his agents in promoting this vile policy was to use fame and gain as bait to drag the literary and art workers into the mire of revisionism and turn them into tools for restoring capitalism. She said: "To be revolutionary literary and art workers, it is imperative first of all to solve the question of whom to serve. If this fundamental question is not solved, we will lose our bearings, go astray and run counter to Chairman Mao's revolutionary line in literature and art. And the result will be that the harder we work, the greater the harm we do to the revolution."

Revolutionary mass criticism has enabled the theatre's revolutionary masses to bring about a tremendous change in their mental outlook. Led by the workers' propaganda team, they often go to factories, mines and rural people's communes to take part in manual labour and receive re-education by the proletariat. They have gradually raised their level of class consciousness and consciousness of the struggle between the two lines, and their thinking and feelings are merging more and more with those of the workers, peasants and soldiers. Recently, while helping the rural communes with the summer harvest, sowing and field management, they joined the poor and lower-middle peasants in farm work and lived, studied and carried on the cultural revolution together with them. During work breaks, they gave performances for the poor and lower-middle peasants, enthusiastically propagating Mao Tsetung Thought, extolling the poor and lower-middle peasants' profound proletarian feelings of cherishing ardent love for the great leader Chairman Mao and their advanced deeds displaying love of the socialist collective economy. In addition to carrying water and sweeping courtyards for the poor and lower-middle peasants, they helped them mend and sew clothes and wash quilts and beddings. Full of praise, the commune members said: "We poor and lower-middle peasants welcome such literary and art workers."

[*Peking Review*, 1 August 1969]

Has Absolute Music No Class Character?

By Chao Hua of the Arts Department of the Central Institute for Nationalities

[*Peking Review*, No. 9, 1 March 1974]

The following excerpts from official Chinese publications represent the period of the extreme anti-Western and isolationist trend in the People's Republic of China, usually associated with the so-called Cultural Revolution. They are here reproduced as documentary evidence of irrationality that strikes otherwise intelligent people and forces them to embrace the most fantastic notions of history and civilization.—Ed.

With the deepening of the movement to criticize Lin Piao and rectify the style of work and new victories being continually won in the struggle-criticism-transformation in the realm of the superstructure, an excellent situation prevails in the country. But the class struggle and the two-line struggle on the art and literary front remain very sharp and complex. The recent weird contention that so-called absolute music has no social content but simply expresses contrasting and changing moods is a sign of a return to the revisionist line in art and literature.

Should the reactionary nature of this erroneous view be exposed or not? This is a cardinal issue of right and wrong and we cannot treat it casually. It involves the question of whether or not the Marxist-Leninist theory of class struggle should be recognized as a universally applicable truth, whether or not the proletarian dictatorship should be exercised in the ideological realm, and whether the Marxist critical attitude should be adopted towards the bourgeois arts or whether they should be "taken over wholesale" as the revisionist fallacies of Chou Yang and his like advocated; it involves the question of whether the proletarian revolution in art and literature can be carried through to the end.

Absolute music in general refers to instrumental music without a descriptive title as to theme or content and it usually is designated by its musical form or tempo. For example, "Symphony in F Major," "Concerto in C Minor," "Largo," "Allegro" and so on.

Bourgeois theorists have long spouted that absolute music is a form of "pure music," devoid of social content and class nature. They fallaciously contend that music is "simply fantasy, not reality" and that "music is music, and nothing else." The modern revisionists, while paying lip-service to music's ties with social life, actually blur the class distinction between proletarian and bourgeois music by describing absolute music as "of the people," "realistic" and so forth. Why should both the bourgeoisie and the revisionists concoct all sorts of arguments to obscure the class character of art? It is because bourgeois ideology, including bourgeois art and literature, serves to prop up the capitalist system. They dare not openly acknowledge the exploiting class character of their art and literature. Instead, to disguise the essential substance of capitalist exploitation, they pose as representatives of the whole people in order to deceive the labouring masses.

Marxist-Leninists hold that all works of music, both absolute and programme music, as a form of ideology "are products of the reflection in the human brain of the life of a given society." Music without titles descriptive of their theme or content is by no means merely "a form of the flow of sounds." Not giving their works a descriptive title is only a means by which composers cover up the class content of their works. In fact, a composer clearly has in mind what he wants to praise or oppose and what content and mood he means to convey, when he is composing absolute music.

When the German bourgeois composer Beethoven (1770–1827) was asked the meaning of his *Sonata No. 17*, a composition without a descriptive title, he replied: "Please read Shakespeare's *The Tempest*." That play, we know, preaches the bourgeois theory of human nature. Of course, the means of expression of music are different from those of literature. Music uses melody, rhythm and harmony to evoke scenes, tell a story or convey emotion, thereby expressing quite plainly or relatively subtly and deviously the composer's world outlook, ideas and feelings. But in any case, the social and class content, thoughts and feelings so expressed can never be abstract, unintelligible "fantasy," for they can be grasped by applying the Marxist theory of knowledge and method of class analysis.

Take for instance the representative work *Symphony in B Minor* (the *Unfinished Symphony*) by Schubert (1797–1828), an Austrian bourgeois composer of the romantic school. The class feelings and social content it expresses are quite clear, although it has no descriptive title. This symphony was composed in 1822, when Austria was a reactionary feudal bastion within the German Confederation and the reactionary Austrian authorities not only ruthlessly exploited and oppressed the workers and peasants, but also persecuted and put under surveillance intellectuals with any bourgeois democratic ideals. Petty-bourgeois intellectuals like Schubert saw no way out of the political and economic impasse, and lacking the courage to resist they gave way to melancholy, vacillation, pessimism and despair, evading reality and dreaming of freedom. This work of Schubert's expressed these class feelings and social content. The opening phrase is sombre and gloomy. The whole symphony continues and expands on this emotion, filling it with petty-bourgeois despair, pessimism and solitary distress. At times the dreaming of freedom does come through but this, too, is escapist and negative.

Absolute music composed in Europe in the 18th and 19th centuries are products of the European capitalist society, upholding the interests of the bourgeoisie and serving the capitalist system. The content and the ideas and feelings with which they are saturated have an unmistakably bourgeois class nature. Marx pointed out: "Capital comes 'into the world' dripping from head to foot, from every pore, with blood and dirt." And it is this blood and dirt that bourgeois music extolls. Although certain compositions to some extent progressive in the sense of being antifeudal, they failed to mirror proletarian thoughts and feelings of their time; and they are, of course, still more incompatible with our socialist system today under the dictatorship of the proletariat. Then why dismiss their class content and extol them? Yet even today there are some who would feed our young people on these musical works uncritically and intact. Where would this lead our young people?

Some devotees of bourgeois absolute music often try to cover up its class nature by holding forth in empty terms on the contrasting, changing moods it presents. This is a reactionary viewpoint of the bourgeois theory of a common human nature transcending classes. For these moods are none other than those of delight and anger, joy and sorrow which vary, as do all men's ideas and feelings, according to the times and society people live in and the class they belong to. Lu Hsun mercilessly repudiated this bourgeois trash that all men, share common emotions and feelings. He said: "of course, it is human nature to know delight and anger, joy and sorrow but the poor are never worried about losing money on the stock exchange, an oil magnate cannot know the trials of an old woman collecting cinders in Peking, and victims of famine will hardly grow orchids like rich old gentlemen . . . ." Are there any feelings that are not stamped with the brand of a class?

"Joy" can be presented in sharply contrasted ways. Thus the music for the despotic landlord's birthday celebrations in the third scene of the modern revolutionary dance-drama *Red Detachment of Women* uses frivolous melody and erratic rhythm to expose the landlord's wanton extravagance and profligacy built on the suffering of the working people. In contrast, the magnificent stirring music of the dance by soldiers and civlians in the next scene presents the brilliant sunshine and jubilation in the revolutionary base. Did these two musical passages project the same emotions?

Again, take the subject of "sorrow." The grief of a feudal monarch after his overthrow is expressed in the verses written by Li Yu, the last king of the Southern Tang kingdom in the 10th century, as he hankered in captivity after his former decadent life in the palace.

> Carved balustrades, jade flagstones still remain,
> But those rosy cheeks are gone.
> How great my lord's grief?
> Endless as the spring river flowing to the east!

But the proletarian fighter Lu Hsun portrayed sorrow of a very different nature when he wrote:

> A host of dark, gaunt faces in the brambles,
> Yet who dare shake the earth with lamentation?
> I brood over our whole far-stretching land
> And in this silence hear the peal of thunder.

This indignant denunciation of the savage oppression of the people by the Japanese invaders and Kuomintang reactionaries conveys the class hatred and national enmity of millions of working people. This militant lamentation has nothing at all in common with the grief of a feudal monarch over the loss of his kingdom. To claim that one melody could be used to express these two diametrically opposed feelings would be sheer charlatanry.

As for empty talk about "bright," "healthy" melodies, devoid of class content, this is the metaphysical approach which the revisionists usually resort to when peddling their bourgeois wares. Chou Yang once brayed that the American bourgeoisie whom Walt Whitman extolled was "the new man," "healthy, broad of mind, with high ideals, a pair of working hands, and eternally optimistic" and that that "shiny example" was "worthy of emulating and copying." But we are aware if the proletariat really were to "emulate" and "copy" the bourgeoisie, then what awaits us is not "bright skies" but the darkness of the dungeon.

The bourgeoisie may well believe that the works of the 18th-century Austrian bourgeois composer Mozart embody "bright" and "healthy" sentiments. But we working people know clearly that these sentiments cannot compare with the exuberant and impassioned feelings expressed by the chorus *The Sun Rises* in the seventh scene of *The White-Haired Girl*. Brimming over with jubilation, this chorus extols Chairman Mao, the red sun in the hearts of the Chinese people, as well as the Communist Party, and evokes the soul-stirring scene "of the land of hibiscus glowing in the morning sun" and the emancipation of the downtrodden peasants. No bourgeois music can even remotely compare with this unrestrained healthy burst of joy evoked by this chorus.

Chou Yang and company also raved that "music is a universal language," in order to concoct a theoretical basis for their attempt to peddle the wholesale Westernization of music. In fact, every class speaks its own language and there is no such thing as a so-called universal language transcending classes. *The Internationale* which rings throughout the world is the common language of the proletariat only. The bourgeoisie tremble at the sound of this melody. Lenin aptly said: "In whatever country a class-conscious worker finds himself, wherever fate may cast him, however much he may feel himself a stranger, without language, without friends, far from his native country—he can find himself comrades and friends by the familiar refrain of *the Internationale*."

For over eighty years this stirring song has inspired workers of all countries to unite to smash the old world and fight for the realization of communism. All reactionaries, however, regard this battle-song of the proletariat as a fearful menace and do all in their power to prevent *The Internationale* from circulating among the people. Hence, do the reactionaries share a common language with the Proletariat?

Liu Shao-chi, Lin Piao, Chou Yang and their gang, however, shared a common language with the bourgeoisie and all reactionaries at home and abroad, for these renegades, like all imperialists, revisionists and reactionaries, opposed proletarian revolution and proletarian dictatorship and vainly tried to restore capitalism in China. This was like the futile efforts of Confucius, the mouthpiece and defender of ancient China's slave-owning class, who, grieving that "the rites were lost and music was ruined," tried desperately to propagate reactionary music aimed at benumbing and enslaving the people while frantically attacking the new rising folk music in order to preserve the collapsing slave system.

Like the other forms of art, music has always been an instrument of class struggle, and on the art and literary front the class struggle and the two-line struggle have always been extremely acute. In the course of the Great Proletarian Cultural Revolution and the movement to criticize Lin Piao and rectify the style of work, great victories have been won on this front and intellectuals have made much progress, but the pernicious influence of revisionist wares peddled by Liu Shao-chi, Lin Piao, Chou Yang and company for a long time, such as "art and literature of the whole people" and "art and literature to nourish people," is deep-seated and still far from being eliminated. Some people talk about bourgeois classical music with great relish, are mesmerized by it and prostrate themselves before it, showing their slavish mentality for all things foreign. They are nihilists with regard to national art. Their reverence for foreign things is actually reverence for the bourgeoisie. If this erroneous thinking of extolling foreign things and belittling Chinese things is not criticized and repudiated, then proletarian art and literature will not be able to develop and Chairman Mao's revolutionary line in art and literature cannot be implemented.

We do not exclude foreign things indiscriminately. We should conscientiously study the revolutionary theory developed by Marx, Engels, Lenin and Stalin. We should learn from the revolutionary experience of the working class and revolutionary people of all countries and learn from and acquire advanced sciences and technology. We should critically assimilate certain techniques from classical bourgeois music, but we must not uncritically swallow anything and everything. And we must never throw ourselves at the feet of bourgeois artists. As Engels said: "The characterization of the ancients no longer suffices today." We must adhere to the principle of "making the past serve the present and foreign things serve China," learn from the experience in creating the model revolutionary theatrical works and turn out proletarian music and art worthy of our time.

Comrade Chou En-lai pointed out in the political report of the Tenth National Congress of the Communist Party of China that "we should attach importance to the class struggle in the superstructure, including all spheres of culture" and that "we should continue to carry out well the revolution in literature and art." The historical experience of the class struggle on the art and literary front shows that the ideology of the bourgeoisie and all other exploiting classes cannot be buried and done away with by a criticism or two. We must conscientiously study the documents of the Tenth Party Congress, implement the spirit of the Tenth Party Congress, take the Party's basic line as the key link, further deepen the movement to criticize Lin Piao and rectify the style of work and link them to reality in criticizing revisionism and bourgeois world outlook; we must continue to advance along the revolutionary path pointed out by Chairman Mao, and we must never go backwards. We must be on guard and resist a return of the revisionist line in art and literature. We must resolutely defend and develop the fruits of the Great Proletarian Cultural Revolution and carry the Proletarian revolution in art and literature through to the end!

[*Translation of an article published in "Renmin Ribao,"*
January 14, 1974]

Criticize the Revisionist Viewpoint in Music

By Chu Lan

[*Peking Review*, No. 9, 1 March 1974]

Following is the translation of a commentary entitled "Grasp the Essence, Deepen the Criticism" by Chu Lan which appeared in "Renmin Ribao" recently.—Ed.

The mass struggle to criticize Lin Piao and Confucius is now developing in depth. The discussion on programme and absolute music and the criticism of the revisionist viewpoint which professes that bourgeois classical music has "no profound social content" are also being carried out in a more and more deep-going way. This is a sharp struggle in the field of art and literature between the proletariat and the bourgeoisie and between Marxism and revisionism. The practice of struggle proves that it is most necessary to criticize this erroneous view. We must make this criticism a part of the struggle to criticize Lin Piao and Confucius and carry it through to the end.

In order to carry out criticisms more profoundly, we must take class struggle and the two-line struggle as the key link and see through superficial appearances to grasp the essence of the revisionist viewpoint. Only in this way can we completely demolish the revisionist viewpoint and make it abhorrent.

Marxism teaches us that in examining a problem we should look at its essence. The essence of our problem is not whether musical works have titles or not. The main thing is the political content of the class they express and the political line of the class they serve. All bourgeois music, programme and absolute, are weapons to shape opinion to serve the bourgeoisie for seizing and consolidating political power. Numerous facts in the history of music show that absolute music, or music without titles, is merely a means by which bourgeois composers conceal the class content of their works. For certain political aims and to meet the needs of struggle, composers sometimes give descriptive titles to their works and sometimes not. But even if given a descriptive title, this can be disregarded and the work played in manner far from what the title implies.

Are not impressionist and modernist musical work often designated with such titles as "pines," "fountains" and "moonlight"? But analysis of them from class viewpoint can clearly reveal the decadent, chaotic life and depraved sentiments of the bourgeoisie the weird cacophony represents. The music of the modern revisionists in particular, frequently under the guise of "revolutionary" titles, slanders and distorts in an unbridled way the revolutionary struggles of the people and heroic images of the working people, and vilely attacks the dictatorship of the proletariat and the socialist system. It can thus be seen that whether a musical work has a descriptive title or not does not in the least change the political content and class essence it expresses, nor the objective social function it performs. Hence, the basic problem lies in the stand, viewpoint and method we adopt towards bourgeois works of music, including programme and absolute music. The crux of the contention is whether one takes the stand of the proletariat, upholds the Marxist class viewpoint and method of class analysis and, taking into account the historical development of class struggle of a specific period, critically analyses the class content of bourgeois music, or whether one takes the stand of the bourgeoisie and replaces concrete class analysis with empty talk about abstract concepts such as "contrasting and changing moods," "healthy" and "bright," which actually is publicizing the bourgeois "theory of human nature" and covering up the class essence of musical works to hoodwink and beguile the broad masses.

We must never abandon class analysis and engage in empty talk as to whether a piece of music has or has not any "profound social content." In class society, all works of art have their concrete social content of a specific class. There is absolutely no such thing as social content that is abstract or above classes and neither is there such a thing as abstract "profundity." The real aim in publicizing bourgeois musical works as having "no profound social content" is to cover up the class content reflected in the music of the bourgeoisie. This can lead only to the revolutionary people lowering their vigilance against corruption by bourgeois ideology and facilitate bourgeois cultural penetration and provide a cover for the bourgeoisie to seize positions from the proletariat in the field of art and literature.

The appearance of the revisionist viewpoint denying the class character of musical works is no isolated, individual, accidental phenomenon. It is the concentrated expression of a tendency in society and in music circles today to make a fetish of foreign things and restore the old order of things. This tendency is reflected in the question of whether or not there is any social content in bourgeois music, both absolute and programme; it is also reflected in composing music, performing music and teaching music. And not only in music, but also in other fields of art. They differ in form only.

A reflection in music of the theory of "the dying out of class struggle" is the publicizing of the bourgeois theory of human nature, denying that music has a class character. We must thoroughly expose this and carry out serious criticisms against it.

The essence of the revisionist viewpoint in this question of absolute and programme music is the landlord-bourgeois theory of human nature. This theory of human nature which denies the class character of music is brought over from the European bourgeoisie and can also be traced back to the doctrine of Confucius, the ideological representative of the decadent slave-owning class of China. We must further criticize this revisionist viewpoint in the course of the struggle to criticize Lin Piao and Confucius.

Chairman Mao has pointed out: "The class struggle between the proletariat and the bourgeoise, the class struggle between the different political forces, and the class struggle in the ideological field between the proletariat and the bourgeoisie will continue to be long and tortuous and at times will even become very acute." We must fully understand the protractedness of the struggle in this field. In our struggle to criticize Lin Piao and Confucius, we must combine it with the actual class struggle in the realm of ideology, particularly in art and literature (including music), carry out sustained revolutionary criticism of all revisionist views and ideological trends which are unfavourable to the development of socialist art and literature and, in the course of tempestuous struggles, further consolidate and develop the socialist positions in the field of art and literature.

Record Labeling

Hearing Before the Committee on Commerce, Science, and Transportation United States Senate

NINETY-NINTH CONGRESS
FIRST SESSION ON CONTENTS
OF MUSIC AND THE LYRICS OF RECORDS

SEPTEMBER 19, 1985

Printed for the use of the Committee on Commerce, Science, and Transportation

Committee on Commerce, Science, and Transportation
  JOHN C. DANFORTH, Missouri, *Chairman*
  BOB PACKWOOD, Oregon
  BARRY GOLDWATER, Arizona
  NANCY LANDON KASSEBAUM, Kansas
  LARRY PRESSLER, South Dakota
  SLADE GORTON, Washington
  TED STEVENS, Alaska
  BOB KASTEN, Wisconsin
  PAUL S. TRIBLE, JR., Virginia
  ERNEST F. HOLLINGS, South Carolina
  RUSSELL B. LONG, Louisiana
  DANIEL K. INOUYE, Hawaii
  WENDELL H. FORD, Kentucky
  DONALD W. RIEGLE, JR., Michigan
  J. JAMES EXON, Nebraska
  ALBERT GORE, JR., Tennessee
  JOHN D. ROCKEFELLER IV, West Virginia
  W. ALLEN MOORE, *Chief Counsel and Staff Director*
  RALPH B. EVERETT, *Minority Chief Counsel and Staff Director*

Contents

Opening statement by the Chairman
Opening statement by Senator Hollings
Opening statement by Senator Trible
Opening statement by Senator Gore

LIST OF WITNESSES

Baker, Susan, Parents Music Resource Center; accompanied by Pamela Howar, president; Sally Nevius, treasurer; Tipper Gore; and Jeff Ling
Denver, John
Fritts, Edward O., president, National Association of Broadcasters; William J. Steding, executive vice president, Central Broadcast Division, Bonneville International Corp.: Robert J. Sabatini, Jr., WRKC-FM, King College, Wilkes-Barre, PA; and Cerphe Colwell, Reston, VA
  Prepared statements:
    Mr. Fritts
    Mr. Steding
Gortikov, Stanley M., president, Recording Industry Association of America, Inc.
Hawkins, Hon. Paula, U.S. Senator from Florida
Snider, Dee, of Twisted Sister
Stuessy, Dr. Joe, University of Texas at San Antonio, and Dr. Paul King, Memphis, TN
  Prepared statement
Waterman, Millie, National PTA vice president for legislative activity, Mentor, OH; accompanied by Arnold Fege, director, governmental relations
Zappa, Frank, accompanied by Larry Stein, counsel
  Prepared statement

ADDITIONAL ARTICLES, LETTERS, AND STATEMENTS

Bonk, James E., executive vice president, Camelot Enterprises, Inc., statement
Bonniwell, Rev., R. Edgar, Faith Christian Fellowship Church, letter
Bradley, Hon. Tom, Mayor, city of Los Angeles, CA., statement
Citizens Against Music Censorship, statement
Gross, Martha Winter, Ph.D., statment
Lynn, Barry W., legislative counsel, American Civil Liberties Union, letter

Record Labeling

THURSDAY, SEPTEMBER 19, 1985

U.S. Senate, Committee on Commerce, Science, and Transportation, *Washington, DC*

The committee met, pursuant to notice, at 9:40 a.m., in room SR-253, Russell Senate Office Building, Hon. John Danforth (chairman of the committee) presiding.

Staff members assigned to this hearing: Kathy Meier, staff counsel; Dale Brown, professional staff member; and Cheryl Wallace, minority staff counsel.

OPENING STATEMENT BY THE CHAIRMAN

The CHAIRMAN. Ladies and gentlemen, this hearing is on the subject of the content of some, and I want to underscore the word "some," not all rock music, which it has been pointed out by a number of people as having really broken new ground as to the content of music and the lyrics that are used in music.

There have, I suppose, always been cases of songs that are suggestive in one way or another. However, certain rock music that is now being sold deals very explicitly with sexual subjects. Some music glorifies violence in various forms, sexual violence. Some music advocates the use of drugs, drug abuse, and so on.

And so, the reason for this hearing is not to promote any legislation. Indeed, I do not know of any suggestion that any legislation be passed. But to simply provide a forum for airing the issue itself, for ventilating the issue, for bringing it out in the public domain.

The concern is that the public at large should be aware of the existence of this kind of music, and the fact that it is now available to kids, and that kids of all ages are able to buy it.

It is my understanding that various private groups have been holding discussions with people who are in the music publishing and music industry to try to achieve some sort of understanding with respect to the labeling of records so that at least the whole family knows what is in them, and not just the child who buys the record.

That seems to me to be a reasonable suggestion, but the point of this hearing is not for me to make any particular suggestions, but to simply provide forum so that the whole issue can be brought to the attention of the American people.

I want to say a word about this hearing. We have a number of witnesses. They have all been given specific time limits for their testimony, as is always the case in Commerce Committee hearings. It is going to be necessary for me to enforce those time limits strictly, and therefore I would ask the witnesses to do so voluntarily.

Your prepared text of your statements will be included in the record automatically. You don't even have to ask for permission for them to be in the record. They will be included in the record automatically, so you don't have to take some of your time asking permission. It will be done.

With respect to the content of the statements, to describe what is in the music that is in question, will, I am sure, require some witnesses to use words and describe things that will shock the sensitivities of many of us in this room, and many who are watching these proceedings on television, and I just wanted to warn you of that in advance so that if children have the TV on, their parents can know what is in store for them.

I want witnesses to be able to inform the Senate of their points of view and the facts as they know them. But I would also hasten to say to witnesses that when you go beyond description and needlessly use expressions that may be in bad taste, this is a hearing of a Senate committee, and this is the Government of the people of this country. It is really theirs, and I would hope that standards would be used to the extent possible in your discussions and in your testimony which bears that in mind.

Senator Hollings.

OPENING STATEMENT BY SENATOR HOLLINGS

Senator HOLLINGS. Mr. Chairman, I first want to commend the Parents Music Resource Center for bringing this to the Nation's attention. I have had the opportunity to attend a showing, you might say, or presentation of this porn rock, as they call it. In the test of pornography, one of the things to look at is whether or not it has any redeeming social value. There could be an exception here, because having attended that presentation, the redeeming social value that I find is inaudible.

I have a hard time understanding it. Paul, since I traveled the country for 3 years, they said they could not understand me. Maybe I could make a good rock star. I do not know.

But in all candor, I would tell you it is outrageous filth, and we have got to do something about it. I take the tempered approach, of our distinguished chairman, and commend it. Yet, I would make the statement that if I could find some way constitutionally to do away with it, I would.

I noticed on the media yesterday morning something about a tax bill. I have looked into that. That does not pertain to this particular hearing, but we do know that the broadcast airwaves give more or less, the most limited of protected speech, because the airwaves do belong to the American public. They invade the privacy of the homes. We do know under the law of pornography that children are given a special protection.

I want everyone to know I am keeping that foremost in mind, and I am asking the best of constitutional minds, if there is some way in the world to try to limit it as we go along with the voluntary labeling. I commend those who are now beginning to label. That is what we would like to have, truth in labeling. I do not think we can outlaw pornography. I do not have that in mind at all. But take 6 to 7 hours daily—the average listening time, Senator, as I understand, by the youngsters of this particular porn rock and rock music and everything else of that kind. Well, let us say rock music and intersperse it with pornography. This is a matter of national concern, and it is something that we have got to give some kind of attention to within the constrictions of free speech.

So, I will be looking from the Senator's standpoint, not just to bring pressures to try to see if there is some constitutional provisions to tax, but an approach that can be used by the Congress to limit this outrageous filth, suggestive violence, suicide, and everything else in the Lord's world that you would not think of. Certainly the writers and framers of our first amendment never perhaps heard this music in their time, never considered the broadcast airwaves and certainly that being piped into people's homes willy nilly over the air. I will be listening closely.

I am sorry—we also have another Defense Appropriations markup—that I must leave here shortly, but I will be in and out. It is not because I am not interested. I am very interested in trying our level best to limit and control as best we can, for the tender young ears of America, the porn rock that will be presented here. I have heard some of it, and I am sure you have.

The CHAIRMAN. Senator Trible.

OPENING STATEMENT BY SENATOR TRIBLE

Senator TRIBLE. Mr. Chairman, a brief statement if I may. More than 2,300 years ago Plato recognized that music is a powerful force in our lives, that music forms character and therefore plays an important part in determining social and political issues. In Plato's words, "When modes of music change, the fundamental laws of the state change with them."

Perhaps Daniel O'Connell, the 18th-century Irish nationalist, expressed it best when he said, "Let me write the songs of a nation, and I care not who makes its laws."

Our culture powerfully affects individual character. When we are constantly confronted by that which is coarse, we become coarsened. Repeated exposure to song lyrics describing rape, incest, sexual violence, and perversion is like sandpaper to the soul. It rubs raw one's sensibilities, resulting in a state of emotional numbness, in the words of George Will. One becomes literally demoralized.

Now, the subject of suggestive lyrics on a child may not be cataclysmic. Rather, the emotional damage is more subtle. The effect on a troubled child, however, can be disastrous, pushing that child over the emotional precipice, and to the extent that individual attitudes are influenced, this becomes a very real social problem.

The linkage between experience, thought, and action necessarily leads to concern about the consequences for society, and it demands a response from each of us, not the self-appointed guardians of the national morality, as someone suggested, but as concerned citizens and leaders of a great and lasting republic.

To paraphrase John Donne, any man's death or harm diminishes me because I am involved in mankind. Likewise, we are all involved in the American social and political experiment, and what damages our children and diminishes their future harms us all.

The mere announcement of this hearing led to cries of censorship. The Issue before us, however, is not censorship. Censorship, according to the classic legal definition, is the review of publications for the purpose of prohibiting publication, distribution, or production of material deemed objectionable as obscene, indecent, or immoral. The key word in that definition is prohibition.

The issue before us is not prohibition, but rather the exercise of moral suasion, the labeling of offensive lyrics, and other efforts aimed at encouraging restraint regarding the time, place, and manner of certain speech in question. That does not constitute censorship.

The first amendment is not under attack here. The Constitution is many things to many people, but they do not serve it well, those who thoughtlessly invoke its words to defend their every word and action.

Mr. Chairman, I am a Senator, and I am also a father. Being a parent of two small children is the most important task I will ever have. If I were to serve in Congress for decades, and be acclaimed a great statesman, I will have failed in my life if I fail to serve my children's best interests, to protect them during their youth, and provide for their needs, to encourage their education.

These are all important, but I will be measured, indeed, we will all be measured by how we teach our children right from wrong, by whether we impart respect for self and for others, by whether we pass on to the future generations the sense of moral and ethical principle.

That is what this hearing is all about. I believe this may well be the most important hearing conducted by the Commerce Committee this year. I look forward to working with you and my colleagues on this committee, the Parents Music Resource Center, the recording and broadcast industries, and responsible citizens everywhere to respond to this very real problem.

Thank you, Mr. Chairman.

The CHAIRMAN. Thank you, Senator Trible.

Senator Gore.

OPENING STATEMENT BY SENATOR GORE

Senator GORE. Thank you very much, Mr. Chairman. I would like to thank you and commend you for calling this hearing. Because my wife has been heavily involved in the evolution of this issue, I have gained quite a bit of familiarity with it, and I have really gained an education in what is involved.

The two most important things I have learned which have changed my initial attitude to this whole concern are, No.1, the proposals made by those concerned about this problem do not involve a Government role of any kind whatsoever. They are not asking for any form of censorship or regulation of speech in any manner, shape, or form.

What they are asking for is whether or not the music industry can show some self-restraint and working together in a manner similar to that used by the movie industry, whether or not they can come up with a voluntary guide system for parents who wish to exercise what they believe to be their responsibilities to their children, to try to prevent their children from being exposed to material that is not appropriate for them.

The second thing I have learned over the past several months is that the kind of material in question is really very different from the kind of material which has caused similar controversies in past generations. It really is very different, and I think those who have not become familiar with this material will realize that fact when they see some of the examples that involve extremely popular groups that get an awful lot of play, some of the most popular groups around now.

I was interested when the hearing was first announced to have the opportunity to ask the heads of the record companies whether or not they felt some responsibility. I am told by staff that every single one of the chief executive officers invited to participate chose to decline that invitation.

I fully understand that, but I wanted to note that fact for the record, and I think that they should take a look at what their companies are doing and just ask themselves as human beings whether or not this is the way they want to spend their lives, if this is the way they want to earn a living, if this is the kind of contribution they want to make to the society in which we live.

No one is proposing or contemplating the government answering that question for them, but as citizens of this country it seems to me we have the right to ask them whether or not they wish to answer the question, and I hope that they will. Thank you, Mr. Chairman.

The CHAIRMAN. Senator Gore, thank you very much.

I want to point out that I have received a letter from Mr. Robert McConnell, vice president of CBS, stating that CBS received the invitation to appear here too late to prepare his testimony, that he is very interested in the hearings, and would be willing to appear at some later time.

Senator Rockefeller.

Senator ROCKEFELLER. No statement, Mr. Chairman.

The CHAIRMAN. Senator Gorton.

Senator GORTON. Thank you, Mr. Chairman.

I am here to hear the witnesses, and I do not need to hold us off any further by any opening statement.

The CHAIRMAN. The first witness is Senator Paula Hawkins, who has joined us here at the committee dais. Senator Hawkins, we are delighted to have you here.

STATEMENT OF HON. PAULA HAWKINS, U.S. SENATOR FROM FLORIDA

Senator HAWKINS. I commend you, Mr. Chairman and the committee, for holding this all important hearing. As chairman of the Children, Family, Drugs, and Alcoholism Subcommittee, this is a subject that I am very familiar with.

The wealth of a nation is measured by its children. We decided as a committee in the last 18 months to hold hearings discussing the role of the media in drug abuse and prevention and education. There we learned that by the fourth grade children have already decided whether or not to take drugs. We asked the question, does the media behave responsibly in portraying values to our children.

In the second hearing, on the issue of alcohol advertising in the broadcast media, we weighed heavily the first amendment considerations involved when the media portrayed behavior which many Americans find objectionable. Today we are raising the question how far should society go to keep young children from being exposed to images and words which may run counter to parents' values and beliefs and values.

It is the parent we blame if the child gets on drugs. It is the parent we blame if the child commits suicide. It is the parent we blame if the child burns down a building. Just how much guilt can we place on these parents without giving them some assistance?

As Senator Gore has so eloquently stated, it has been 30 years since Elvis first shook his hips on the Ed Sullivan Show, and here we are talking about the content of rock music and its presentation in records, on album covers, and advertising concerts, and in rock video.

Much has changed since Elvis' seemingly innocent times. Subtleties, suggestions, and innuendo have given way to overt expressions and descriptions of often violent sexual acts, drug taking, and flirtations with the occult. The record album covers to me are self-explanatory.

I would like to show a sampling of record covers.

[The record covers follow:]

There is no question about the message. I still hear art is art, and in America artists are supposed to be free to express themselves, but who has the responsibility to regulate? Parents? The music industry? The Government?

I speak as a legislator. I speak as a parent, a veteran who has brought three children through adolescence. I know the temptations dangled in front of teenagers and I know the frustrations parents experience all through this process. The sense of hopelessness when you get the feeling your child will not listen to you.

There is in these times often a need to look to a force outside yourself for help. The question we must ask is, should the force be the Government, and that is what this hearing is designed to determine.

I believe it will be helpful before we proceed any further to get an idea of what it is we are talking about.

One criticism of the rock industry is the way it portrays values in rock videos which are viewed by the kids. There are suggestions that the move to label rock albums be extended to videos as well. I do not watch much television. I am not sure how many of my colleagues get much opportunity to watch any of the music video shows now available on cable and free TV.

I brought along two videos from which to choose which I believe are representative of the kind of presentations which cause the problem. The first is by the group Van Halen.

[The rock video "Hot for Teacher" by Van Halen was shown.]

The CHAIRMAN. Senator Hawkins, just a minute.

Now, this is a very large crowd today. We have allowed people in beyond the capacity of this room. We are not going to have any demonstrations. No applause, no demonstrations of any kind.

Senator HAWKINS. I thank the chairman. The title of that tape was "Hot for Teacher."

The next video is by the group Twisted Sister, and we will show you a brief portion of that. This is a very popular video.

[The video "We're Not Going to Take It" by Twisted Sister was shown.]

Senator HAWKINS. Mr. Chairman, I think a picture is worth a thousand words. This issue is too hot not to cool down. Parents are asking for assistance, and I hope we always remember that no success in life would compensate for failure in the home.

The CHAIRMAN. Senator Hawkins, thank you very much.

The next witness is Susan Baker, Mrs. James Baker, from the Parents Music Resource Center.

Mrs. Baker, thank you very much for being with us. Please proceed.

STATEMENT OF SUSAN BAKER, PARENTS MUSIC RESOURCE CENTER, ACCOMPANIED BY PAMELA HOWAR, PRESIDENT; SALLY NEVIUS, TREASURER; TIPPER GORE; AND JEFF LING

Mrs. BAKER. Thank you very much, Mr. Chairman. We would like to thank you and the committee for the opportunity to testify before you.

The CHAIRMAN. Could you please speak directly into the microphone, thank you.

Mrs. BAKER. Before I begin, I would like to introduce the president of the PMRC, Pam Howar, and our treasurer, Sally Nevius.

The Parents Music Resource Center was organized in May of this year by mothers of young children who are very concerned by the growing trend in music toward lyrics that are sexually explicit, excessively violent, or glorify the use of drugs and alcohol.

Our primary purpose is to educate and inform parents about this alarming trend as well as to ask the industry to exercise self-restraint.

It is no secret that today's rock music is a very important part of adolescence and teenagers' lives. It always has been, and we don't question their right to have their own music. We think that is important. They use it to identify and give expression to their feelings, their problems, their joys, sorrows, loves, and values. It wakes them up in the morning and it is in the background as they get dressed for school. It is played on the bus. It is listened to in the cafeteria during lunch. It is played as they do their homework. They even watch it on MTV now. It is danced to at parties, and puts them to sleep at night.

Because anything that we are exposed to that much has some influence on us, we believe that the music industry has a special responsibility as the message of songs goes from the suggestive to the blatantly explicit.

As Ellen Goodman stated in a recent column, rock ratings:

The outrageous edge of rock and roll has shifted its focus from Elvis's pelvis to the saw protruding from Blackie Lawless's codpiece on a WASP album. Rock lyrics have turned from "I can't get no satisfaction" to "I am going to force you at gunpoint to eat me alive."

The material we are concerned about cannot be compared with Louie Louie, Cole Porter, Billie Holliday, et cetera. Cole Porter's "the birds do it, the bees do it," can hardly be compared with WASP, "I, f-u-c-k like a beast." There is a new element of vulgarity and violence toward women that is unprecedented.

While a few outrageous recordings have always existed in the past, the proliferation of songs glorifying rape, sadomasochism, incest, the occult, and suicide by a growing number of bands illustrates this escalating trend that is alarming.

Some have suggested that the records in question are only a minute element in this music. However, these records are not few, and have sold millions of copies, like Prince's "Darling Nikki," about masturbation, sold over 10 million copies. Judas Priest, the one about forced oral sex at gunpoint, has sold over 2 million copies. Quiet Riot, "Metal Health," has songs about explicit sex, over 5 million copies. Mötley Crüe, "Shout at the Devil," which contains violence and brutality to women, over 2 million copies.

Some say there is no cause for concern. We believe there is. Teen pregnancies and teenage suicide rates are at epidemic proportions today. The Noedecker Report states that in the United States of America we have the highest teen pregnancy rate of any developed country: 96 out of 1,000 teenage girls become pregnant.

Rape is up 7 percent in the latest statistics, and the suicide rates of youth between 16 and 24 has gone up 300 percent in the last three decades while the adult level has remained the same.

There certainly are many causes for these ills in our society, but it is our contention that the pervasive messages aimed at children which promote and glorify suicide, rape, sadomasochism, and so on, have to be numbered among the contributing factors.

Some rock artists actually seem to encourage teen suicide. Ozzie Osbourne sings "Suicide Solution." Blue Öyster Cult sings "Don't Fear the Reaper." AC/DC sings "Shoot to Thrill." Just last week in Centerpoint, a small Texas town, a young man took his life while listening to the music of AC/DC. He was not the first.

Now that more and more elementary school children are becoming consumers of rock music, we think it is imperative to discuss this question. What can be done to help parents who want to protect their children from these messages if they want to?

Today parents have no way of knowing the content of music products that their children are buying. While some album covers are sexually explicit or depict violence, many others give no clue as to the content. One of the top 10 today is Morris Day and the Time, "Jungle Love." If you go to buy the album "Ice Cream Castles" to get "Jungle Love," you also get, "If the Kid Can't Make You Come, Nobody Can," a sexually explicit song.

The pleasant cover picture of the members of the band gives no hint that it contains material that is not appropriate for young consumers.

Our children are faced with so many choices today. What is available to them through the media is historically unique.

The Robert Johnson study on teen environment states that young people themselves often feel that they have: One, too many choices to make: two, too few structured means for arriving at decisions: and three, too little help to get there.

We believe something can be done, and Tipper Gore will discuss the possible solution. Thank you.

Mrs. GORE. Thank you, Mr. Chairman.

We are asking the recording industry to voluntarily assist parents who are concerned by placing a warning label on music products inappropriate for younger children due to explicit sexual or violent lyrics.

The Parents Music Resource Center originally proposed a categorical rating system of explicit material. After many discussions with the record industry, we recognize some of the logistical and economic problems, and have adjusted our original suggestions accordingly. We now propose one generic warning label to inform consumers in the marketplace about lyric content. The labels would apply to all music.

We have asked the record companies to voluntarily label their own products and assume responsibility for making those judgments. We ask the record industry to appoint a one-time panel to recommend a uniform set of criteria which could serve as a policy guide for the individual companies. Those individual recording companies would then in good faith agree to adhere to this standard, and make decisions internally about which records should be labeled according to the industry criteria.

We have also asked that lyrics for labeled music products be available to the consumer before purchase in the marketplace. Now, it is important to clearly state what our proposal is not.

A voluntary labeling is not censorship. Censorship implies restricting access or suppressing content. This proposal does neither. Moreover, it involves no Government action. Voluntary labeling in no way infringes upon first amendment rights. Labeling is little more than truth in packaging, by now, a time honored principle in our free enterprise system, and without labeling, parental guidance is virtually impossible.

Most importantly, the committee should understand the Parents Music Resource Center is not advocating any Federal intervention or legislation whatsoever. The excesses that we are discussing were allowed to develop in the marketplace, and we believe the solutions to these excesses should come from the industry who has allowed them to develop and not from the Government.

The issue here is larger than violent and sexually explicit lyrics. It is one of ideas and ideal freedoms and responsibility in our society. Clearly, there is a tension here, and in a free society there always will be. We are simply asking that these corporate and artistic rights be exercised with responsibility, with sensitivity, and some measure of self-restraint, especially since young minds are at stake. We are talking about preteenagers and young teenagers having access to this material. That is our point of departure and our concern.

Now, Mr. Chairman, one point we have already made, that the material that has caused the concern is new and different. It is not just a continuation of controversies of past generations. To illustrate this point, we would like to show a slide presentation, and to this end I turn the microphone over to Jeff Ling, who is a consultant to our group, and he will show you some of the material that we are talking about.

Thank you.

Mr. LING. Mr. Chairman, if we could have the lights turned down.

[Slides were then shown.]

Mr. LING. Mr. Chairman and distinguished members of the committee, thank you for allowing me to speak to you today. The purpose of this presentation is to acquaint you with the type of material that is in question.

I will be covering the themes of violence and sexuality. Bear in mind that what you are about to see and hear is a small sample of the abundant material available today. Today the element of violent, brutal erotica has exploded in rock music in an unprecedented way. Many albums today include songs that encourage suicide, violent revenge, sexual violence, and violence just for violence's sake.

This is Steve Boucher. Steve died while listening to AC/DC's "Shoot to Thrill." Steve fired his father's gun into his mouth.

A few days ago I was speaking in San Antonio. The day before I arrived, they buried a young high school student. This young man had taken his tape deck to the football field.

He hung himself while listening to AC/DC's "Shoot to Thrill." Suicide has become epidemic in our country among teenagers.

Some 6,000 will take their lives this year. Many of these young people find encouragement from some rock stars who present death as a positive, almost attractive alternative.

The album I am holding up in front of you is by the band Metallica. It is on Electra Asylum records. A song on this album is called "Faith in Black." It says the following. "I have lost the will to live. Simply nothing more to give. There is nothing more for me. I need the end to set me free."

"Death greets me warm. I will just say good-bye."

Consider the self-destructive violence that is encouraged in their song "Whiplash." "Bang your head against the stage like you never have before. Make it rain, make it bleed, make it really sore. In a frenzied madness, now is the time to let it rip, to let it fucking loose. We are gathered here to maim and kill, for this is what we choose."

Ozzie Osbourne on his first solo album, shown here, sings a song called "Suicide Solution." Ozzie insists that he in no way encourages suicidal behavior in young people, and yet he appears in photographs such as these in periodicals that are geared toward the young teenage audience.

For those of you who cannot make that out because of the lights, it is a picture of Ozzie with a gun barrel stuck into his mouth.

This is the cover of Twisted Sister's high selling LP for Atlantic Records called "Stay Hungry." An example of Twisted Sister's appeal to young people is evident in the back to school contest being run by MTV. First prize is a get together with Twisted Sister. The first prize is a meeting with Twisted Sister.

The hit song from the album, "We're Not Going to Take It," was released as a video, which you saw just a moment ago, a video in which the band members proceed to beat up daddy, who will not let them rock. Their first album, which has been rereleased by Atlantic Records, is called "Under the Blade."

The title song includes words like "Your hands are tied, your legs are strapped, you are going under the blade." In lyrics from the song "Shoot them Down," the band sings, "They think we are fools who want to make their own rules. It only gets us madder. They think they are hot. Well, I say they're not. They shoot us down for fun. If they don't want to play, then let's make them pay. Shoot them down with a fucking gun."

This is the cover of AC/DC's brandnew album for Atlantic Records, "Fly on the Wall."

One of the songs from the album "Back in Business" was released as a single for airplay and included the words, "Don't you struggle or try to bite. You want some trouble. I am the king of vice. I am a wrecking ball. I am a stinging knife. Steal your money. Going to take your life."

Of course, AC/DC is no stranger to violent material. Their song "Squealer" contained the following. "She said she had never been balled before, and I don't think she'll ball no more. Fixed her good."

One of their fans I know you are aware of is the accused Night Stalker.

Judas Priest sings of violent rape in their song "Eat Me Alive" from their Columbia Records released "Defenders of the Faith." "Squealing in passion as the rod of steel injects. Gut wrenching frenzy that deranges every joint. I am going to force you at gunpoint to eat me alive."

The band Great White in their album "On Their Knees" sings these words "Knocking down your door, going to pull you to the floor, taking what I choose, never going to lose, going to drive my love inside you, going to nail your ass to the floor."

This is Mötley Crüe. Their albums for Electra Asylum sell millions, and they are one of the top 10 grossing concert bands this year. Their albums include songs like "Bastard." "Out goes the light. In goes my knife. Pull out his life. Consider that bastard dead."

"Live Wire." "I will either break her face or take down her legs. Get my ways at will. Go for the throat and never let loose. Going in for the kill."

And "Too Young to Fall in Love." "Not a woman, but a whore. I can taste the hate. Well, now I am killing you. Watch your face turning blue."

This is the cover of the new album by the band Abattoir.

The title song is about a homocidal maniac, and notice on the cover the arms of the man wrapped around the woman. In one hand is a long knife. The other hand holds a hook being pressed against the woman's breast.

This is the cover of an album entitled "Rise of the Mutants" by the band Impaler.

Notice the man with the bloody meat in his mouth and hand. He is kneeling over the bloody arm of a woman.

The back cover shows a woman with a bloody face at the feet of the drummer.

While both of these albums were released on independent labels as opposed to major labels, they are reviewed and featured in teen rock magazines and are available in local record stores.

This band, WASP, recently signed a $1.5 million contract with Capitol Records. This is their first release. The capital item is entitled "The Torture Never Stops." Violence permeates the album as well as their stage show, which has included chopping up and throwing raw meat into the audience.

Drinking blood from a skull.

And until recently the simulated rape and murder of a half-nude woman.

This single is available in record stores across the country. The cover features the cod piece that lead singer Blackie Lawless wears on stage. In this picture, there is blood dripping down his stomach, hands, and off of the blade between his legs. The song that accompanies this photo is "Fuck Like a Beast."

This band, Piledriver, fuses together the elements of sexual violence and occult in the song "Lust." I forgot. It is right here in front of me. The song is called "Lust." The lyrics say, "Hell on fire. Lust, desire. The devil wants to stick you. The devil wants to lick you. He wants your body. He wants your spirit. Naked twisting bodies, sweating. Prince of darkness. Prince of evil. Spread your legs and scream. This is no dream. Degradation. Humiliation. Thrusting, shoving. Animals humping. He is like a dog in heat. You are just another piece of meat. Craving demons fill you with pain. Now you are bloodied and stained, hurt and beaten. He will possess you. He will molest you. Sex with Satan. Sex with Satan."

While we will not consider the subject in depth at this time, it should be noted that occultic themes, primarily Satanism, is prevalent among such bands as Slayer, Venom, and Merciful Fate, one of whose albums is shown in this picture.

Let us move on to sexuality, a theme which has been part of rock music since its beginning. Today's rock artists are describing sexual activity and practice in terms more graphic than ever before. Many of you are aware of Purple Rain, the multimillion seller by Prince. Much has been said about the song "Darling Nikki" from the album. "I met a girl named Nikki. I guess you could say she was a sex fiend. I met her in a hotel lobby masturbating with magazines."

Another album by Prince called "Dirty Mind" presents a positive attitude toward the subject of incest.

These lyrics are from the song called "Sister." "I was only 16, but I guess that is no excuse. My sister was 32, and kind of alone. My sister never made love to anyone but me. Incest is everything it' said to be."

This is the cover of the album "Stakk Attakk" by the band Wrath Child. The back cover of this album, which is available to young children in record stores, included this photo of a nude woman on the back of the album. Songs include "Sweet Surrender." "I lick my lips and make advances. You lay on down and let me in. But you can't fight. You've got no choice. I will take you down and rub my cream in."

Another song on an earlier album called "Cock Rock Shock" said the words "We are going to fuck you" and "Oh, you fucking little bitch."

This is Mötley Crüe's album, "Shout at the Devil," double platinum. The song on the album we are concerned with here is "Ten Seconds to Love." "Touch my gun, but don't pull my trigger. Shine my pistol some more. Here I come. Reach down real low. Slide it in real slow. You feel so good. Do you want some more? I have got one more shot. My gun is still warm."

The band KISS, popular with young people, "At All Times," their brandnew album, was released just yesterday, includes songs such as "Fits Like a Glove." "Ain't a cardinal sin, baby. Let me in. Girl, I am going to treat you right. Well, goodness sakes, my snake's alive, and it is ready to bite. Baby, let me in. It fits like a glove. I think I am going to burst. When I go through her it is like a hot knife through butter."

And the song, "Give Me More." "Hot blood, need your love. Hard as rock, can't get enough. Want to feel you deep inside, pumping through my veins. Fill you to the core, like a dog to the bone. Make you sweat, make you moan. Come on, lick my candy cane."

This is Betsy. She is the lead singer of a band called Bitch. The album is called "Be My Slave." It is available in record stores. One of the songs is called "Give Me a Kiss." "The way you grab me makes my knees shake. The way you pull my arms makes my body quake. The way you yank my hair, it just makes me want to kill you. I will take off my clothes. Kick me in the shins. Come on and slap me in the face, and I will get down on my knees and move you like this."

And the song "Leatherbound." "The whip is my toy. Handcuffs are your joy. You hold me down, and I am screaming for more. When you tie me up and gag me, the way you give me pain, come on, give me lashes."

The Rolling Stones on their album "Under Cover" also sang of sadomasochistic activities in the song "Tie You Up." "The pain of love, you dream of it, passion it. You even get a rise from it. Feel the hot come dripping on your thigh from it. Why so divine, the pain of love."

Even the Jacksons' mainstream pop music today, their song, "Torture," was released as a video, and was shown on national TV. That video included pictures of women dressed in leather bondage, masks, with whips in their hands, in chains, and wrapped up in handcuffs.

Some artists take their pornograph rock to the stage. This is a picture of Wendy O'Williams in concert. Concerts that young adolescents can attend.

[End of slide presentation.]

Mr. LING. How bad can it get? The list is endless. This album was released just recently by a band called the Mentors. It was released in an album with the label Enigma Records, which also launched Mötley Crüe's career. The album includes songs like "Four-F Club," "Find Her, Feel Her, Fuck Her, and Forget Her," "Free Fix for a Fuck," "Clap Queen," "My Erection is Over," and the song "Golden Showers," which says these words, "Listen, you little slut, do as you are told, come with daddy for me to pour the gold. Golden showers. All through my excrement you shall roam. Bend up and smell my anal vapor. Your face is my toilet paper. On your face I leave a shit tower. Golden showers."

Mr. Chairman, that concludes my remarks. I thank you.

[The materials referred to follow:]

The CHAIRMAN. I am sorry. Your time has expired.

Mrs. Gore, let me begin by asking you, you have children, I understand.

Mrs. GORE. Yes, I do, four children, 12, 8, 6, and 2.

The CHAIRMAN. Does the 12-year-old buy records?

Mrs. GORE. Yes, she does, and she has been buying them since she was 7 or 8. Not a lot, but occasionally.

The CHAIRMAN. Do you have any way of knowing what is on the records that she buys?

Mrs. GORE. No, I do not have any way of knowing that.

The CHAIRMAN. There is nothing on the face of the album which would notify you if the record has pornographic material or material glorifying violence?

Mrs. GORE. No, there is nothing that would suggest that to me at this time.

The CHAIRMAN. And it would be unrealistic, wouldn't it, for a parent to go into the record store and play the record in its entirety to find out what the words are?

Mrs. GORE. Well, it is. Normally you are not allowed to open a record and play it until after you have purchased it.

The CHAIRMAN. Now, Mr. Ling, you pointed out at the beginning of your presentation that you do know of a couple of cases where kids have committed suicide while listening to rock music that advocates suicide.

Do you believe that those are rare cases of rock music influencing behavior, or do you think that it is more commonplace? In other words, do you think that this music is tasteless, but that it really does not have very much effect, or do you think that the music has some negative consequences?

Mr. LING. I think it has great effect. As one who has worked with teenagers and college students on a professional level for the last 10 years, I have watched the things that they have watched, and listened to what they have listened to. I have seen their behavior influenced and encouraged by this music.

More importantly, sir, the problem is that the music might reflect the behavior, attitudes, values of those in the 18 or older bracket. However, when that music is listened to by 12-year-olds, 11-year-olds, and 10-year-olds, it moves from the area of being a reinforcer and an encourager into the role of educator, and many of these young children are being educated in these things before they have any kind of frame of reference to properly put it in.

The CHAIRMAN. Senator Gore.

Senator GORE. Well, Mr. Chairman, a statement was submitted for the record from Dr. Thomas Ridecki which bears upon the question about whether or not behavior is influenced by music. If it is appropriate, I would like that to be included in the record.

The CHAIRMAN. Without objection.

Senator GORE. I would just like to reinforce a couple of statements that were made in prepared testimony. I believe, Ms. Baker, you began by saying that what you're proposing and what the group is proposing does not involve any request for Government action, is that correct?

Mrs. BAKER. That's right.

Senator GORE. When you responded to the Chairman a minute ago, you said there is no way you can tell if the record has pornographic material or material glorifying violence. In fact, some of the material has an album cover design which will indicate it, but some does not, is that correct?

Mrs. GORE. That is correct. Some of the album covers are very explicit. In fact, they look like they should be in Playboy or Penthouse, some of them, and they are in the record bins available to young children. But others, you can not tell.

I bought the "Purple Rain" album for our 11-year-old and I did not know that "Darling Nikki" was on it, and I felt that it was inappropriate for her and her 8- and 6-year-old sisters to hear a song describing a girl masturbating in a hotel lobby with a magazine.

I had no warning. In fact, all I know was that Prince was the new creative teen idol on the scene and had just received a Grammy Award. So I would have appreciated it if I had known that before purchase.

Senator GORE. Well, I appreciate that. Thank you, Mr. Chairman.

The CHAIRMAN. Senator Rockefeller.

Senator ROCKEFELLER. It does not matter to me who answers this question, but there is a difference between the material that Mr. Ling presented and the videotapes that we viewed earlier. For example, I thought that the presentation that your particular panel made was much more to the point than the previous presentation. It was not only graphic and shocking, but there was not any question as to where to draw the line.

If something is graphic, does that cross the line? Does it have to be explicit? I understand, that 80 record companies have agreed to conform to the labeling principle.

Where should the line be drawn as to what is fantasy, which is disturbing to a parent and yet is not as dangerous as something which is graphic, explicit, and clearly dangerous to teens and pre-teens with vulnerable, unformed values?

One cannot stop everything. The companies, you are saying, are going to have to make the judgment. In your conversations with them, how do they define the line that should not be crossed?

Mrs. GORE. In our conversations with Mr. Gortikov, he has made it clear that this is a difficult area. We suggested that the industry appoint an industry-wide panel of some consumer representatives one time to discuss the set of criteria that would be used.

It would not be a list of words. It would be simply a policy statement, such as, we will be sensitive to lyrics that talk about graphic brutality toward women, violence, rape, explicit sexuality. We believe that the record companies and those individuals within those companies are best left to make those subjective decisions. There will always be areas of gray, but what we want from them is an affirmation that they will be sensitive to this concern as they individually apply a warning label within their individual companies.

We need for them to be able to get together and say, we will do this in good faith, we will go back to our individual companies, we will make those subjective decisions and judgments ourselves. That is what we are asking them to do.

Senator ROCKEFELLER. Do you think the record companies had been planning on doing this before you all approached them? I mean, this business has been going on, MTV and all the rest of it for some time now.

I do not know how long you have been in existence, but the problem is bad and apparently getting worse. It brings to the fore the terror that exists on the part of all parents, and goes to the whole question of what it is that our children are learning and seeing that confronts us every day.

Was this simply the result of your conversations with them, that they suddenly agreed to decide to do some labeling?

Mrs. BAKER. Senator, over a year and a half ago the National PTA passed a resolution and wrote to the music industry, direct recording industry, asking them to label sexually explicit, violent, profane, or material that encouraged the use of drugs and alcohol. And that, as far as I know, got no response from the industry.

But there have been calls for this sort of thing. Some, very few but some, albums have been labeled as objectionable to some people. So there has been a little bit of this done in the industry in the past, but it has been very small. And our hope is that there would be a uniform application across the board in the recording industry to give parents and consumers warning when explicit, blatant, violent material is in the album or any music product.

Senator ROCKEFELLER. Those companies which are declining to go along with labeling, which I take it to be about 20 percent of the volume, what are they giving as reasons for not going along?

Mrs. BAKER. We have not had direct conversations with them. We have been speaking with Stanley Gortikov, who is head of the Recording Industry Association of America, and he represents the majority of companies that produce the majority of records. And so I could not speak to that.

Senator ROCKEFELLER. Is there any serious doubt with serious people to whom you have talked that there is a direct relationship between violence and disturbing tendencies and occurrences among young people and the proliferation of this type of material that we have seen this morning. Is there any serious doubt that there is not a direct relationship between those two?

Or are there some who would argue that you are simply trying to suppress first amendment rights?

Mrs. BAKER. Well, some make the point—and it is certainly true—that sex and violence pervade every level of our society today. So we would just say that music, which is a very important part of young people, young people who are forming their characters and developing their value systems, learning how to relate to the opposite sex—even what they think about sex is not defined in their minds yet.

We think that it does have an influence on these young minds. But we are certainly do not blame music for the ills, all the ills that exist in the teenage population, the younger children.

Senator ROCKEFELLER. Is the relationship between the escalation of the so-called MTV phenomenon and the things that we have seen this morning, and the problems that exist in the teenage population is incontrovertible in your mind?

Mrs. BAKER. Absolutely.

Senator ROCKEFELLER. Thank you, Mr. Chairman.

The CHAIRMAN. Senator Gorton?

Senator GORTON. No questions, Mr. Chairman.

The CHAIRMAN. Senator Exon?

Senator EXON. Mr. Chairman, thank you very much.

I have been around here a while and I have been through many hearings in many committees, including Armed Services on the MX missile, the strategic defense initiative, Commerce Committee on a whole wide range of deregulation, Budget Committee with regard to the national debt and what we are going to do about cutting down expenditures of the Federal Government. This is the largest media event, both in this room and the people waiting outside, that I have ever seen.

I want to first congratulate you ladies for coming here and testifying on the concerns which you have. It seems to me that this should be voluntarily worked out without Federal legislation and without regulations.

Rock music does not appeal to me at all, but it does to my kids and it does to my grandchildren. Therefore, I agree generally with the thesis that has been brought forth here this morning, that in the arts, even though that term might be used loosely the way I view it—one of the things that I find it most difficult to do is to impose upon others what my particular beliefs are, whether those beliefs be to my children or to my grandchildren.

I do happen to believe, though, that you were correct in the thrust, I believe, of what we saw this morning, some of which was personally offensive to me and other things that were not. We all have our own individual goals, I guess, and how we view those.

I guess a key question that I would like to ask you is, if there is one thing that has come through loud and clear to me at least, it is that you do not want Federal legislation and you do not want Federal regulation, at least at this time. Is that correct?

Mrs. GORE. Yes, that is correct. We do not want legislation to remedy this problem. The problem is one that developed in the marketplace. The music industry has allowed the excesses that you saw and we believe the music industry is the entity to address those excesses. We would like them to do this voluntarily. We propose no legislative solution whatsoever.

Senator EXON. When you say legislation, do you also include the term that I use, regulation?

Mrs. GORE. Yes.

Senator EXON. Well, given that and given what I think I tried to put forth as my feelings on this, Mr. Chairman, I suppose it is nice to have these hearings and discuss these things, because I think it is a concern. But I wonder, Mr. Chairman, if we are not talking about Federal regulation and we are not talking about Federal legislation, what is the reason for these hearings in front of the Commerce Committee?

Can anyone answer that? I did not schedule these hearings. I am glad to be here to take part in them. But sometimes I wonder why these media events are scheduled and for what possible reason, if we are not being asked to do anything about it.

The CHAIRMAN. I think that the point is that there are problems that exist in the country that are not necessarily solved by legislation or by regulation. Fortunately, the be-all and end-all of the United States is not legislation that is enacted by Congress.

I think the point of the hearings is to provide a forum for airing what a lot of people perceive of as a real problem.

Senator EXON. Well, Mr. Chairman, that may well be and that may well be an intention of what the Congress should or should not do. As one member of the Congress, I think that we indulge in too many publicity events that are far beyond the scope of regulation and legislation, which I think is our primary purpose.

The CHAIRMAN. Senator Kasten.

Senator KASTEN. Mr. Chairman, thank you. I have no questions at this time.

The CHAIRMAN. Senator Hawkins?

Senator HAWKINS. Mrs. Baker, this is one Senator who feels that there is no absolute right to free speech. It has been my experience no one has the absolute right to yell "Fire" in a theater which is not on fire.

I believe no one has the right to poison our children with the kinds of lyrics that you have shown this committee so graphically today.

And to get back to my original tenet, I would like to know, in your experiences as mothers, where did your children first hear of the record that they asked for the money to purchase? Did they hear that on MTV? Did they see the videotape preview on MTV? Or was it on a radio station?

Mrs. BAKER. Well, my 8 year old hears music on her clock-radio. I mean, she does not have tapes and records at this stage in her life, but she does listen to the radio.

Senator HAWKINS. And then from that she decides she would like the entire album?

Mrs. BAKER. Yes, that is right.

Senator HAWKINS. So the original exposure to this kind of—I cannot think of a good word for it, but pornography rock—would be through the public airwaves, whether it be MTV or a radio station?

Mrs. BAKER. Well, Senator, I will say this, that basically most broadcasters are very responsible. There are a few hard rock stations that play things that are pornographic, but basically your main stations do not play the worst offenders.

They will play a song on an album that will get into the top 40 and maybe have some violence or sexually explicit lyrics on the album. They will not play, generally, a song that is sexually explicit.

Times are changing, though, because recently Sheena Easton's "Sugar Walls," which is really a fairly graphic song about female genital arousal, has been on the charts and it is played 10 to 12 times a day. That is one of our concerns, that this is becoming more and more mainstream, and we feel this is the time to talk about it.

Senator HAWKINS. And if the labeling took place as you have requested, do you envision that prior to the disc jockey playing that on the radio that he would read the label?

Mrs. BAKER. Well, I will tell you. All program directors know exactly what they are playing on their records. They do not need a label to know that. That is part of their business and that is part of their job, and they know exactly what they are playing.

So I would say that it is not going to be a help for the program directors and DJ's. It is going to be a help for parents. We are the ones that need the information. Those in the business know.

Senator HAWKINS. And do you have certain stations that you do not allow your child to listen to in the home?

Mrs. BAKER. Well, it has not come to that in my house, with just an 8 year old. The big ones, you know, that is another matter. But most of them are grown and they can make their own decisions about that.

This is for the young. She is not—the heavy metals is not something. It is others that she likes to listen to.

Senator HAWKINS. Well, it is my understanding it is no longer possible to have a successful rock album without a video; that MTV is widely viewed by children, whether their parents are home or not.

Has your group met with representatives of the TV industry?

Mrs. BAKER. Yes, we have, and MTV was originally begun to promote records. I mean, that is the whole purpose of it. And there have been some really fun things done with MTV and some really awful things done. So we have talked with them, but we will meet with them again.

Senator HAWKINS. What was their response?

Mrs. BAKER. Well, their response was that they already had standards in place. We had thought that their standards should be a little tighter for younger viewing audience. But we will be asking them to label videos that have violent or sexually explicit material in them, so that parents will know, and also to consider clustering very safe—"safe" is not a good word, but I mean harmless—videos at a time when the young audience would be viewing. So that would be our suggestion to them.

Senator HAWKINS. And when are you meeting with them again?

Mrs. BAKER. In the near future.

Senator HAWKINS. Thank you.

The CHAIRMAN. Thank you very much for being here. I know that for all of you it was not the most pleasant of experiences to read some of the lyrics in public. But it was very helpful and we appreciate your attendance.

John Denver is on the witness list. He has had to leave the hearing room for another engagement. He plans to be back. So the next witness will be Mr. Frank Zappa.

Mr. Zappa, thank you very much for being with us. Please proceed.

STATEMENT OF FRANK ZAPPA, ACCOMPANIED BY LARRY STEIN, COUNSEL

Mr. ZAPPA. My name is Frank Zappa. This is my attorney Larry Stein from Los Angeles.

Can you hear me?

The CHAIRMAN. If you could speak very directly and clearly into the microphone, I would appreciate it.

Mr. ZAPPA. My name is Frank Zappa. This is my attorney Larry Stein.

The statement that I prepared, that I sent you 100 copies of, is five pages long, so I have shortened it down and am going to read a condensed version of it.

Certain things have happened. I have been listening to the event in the other room and have heard some conflicting report as to whether or not people in this committee want

legislation. I understand that Mr. Hollings does from his comments. Is that correct?

The CHAIRMAN. I think you had better concentrate on your testimony, rather than asking questions.

Mr. ZAPPA. The reason I need to ask it, because I have to change something in my testimony if there is not a clearcut version of whether or not legislation is what is being discussed here.

The CHAIRMAN. Do the best you can, because I do not think anybody here can characterize Senator Hollings' position.

Mr. ZAPPA. I will carry on with the issue, then.

Senator EXON. Mr. Chairman, I might help him out just a little bit. I might make a statement. This is one Senator that might be interested in legislation and/or regulation to some extent, recognizing the problems with the right of free expression.

I have previously expressed views that I do not believe I should be telling other people what they have to listen to. I really believe that the suggestion made by the original panel was some kind of an arrangement for voluntarily policing this in the music industry as the correct way to go.

If it will help you out in your testimony, I might join Senator Hollings or others in some kind of legislation and/or regulation, unless the free enterprise system, both the producers and you as the performers, see fit to clean up your act.

Mr. ZAPPA. OK, thank you.

The first thing I would like to do, because I know there is some foreign press involved here and they might not understand what the issue is about, one of the things the issue is about is the First Amendment to the Constitution, and it is short and I would like to read it so they will understand. It says:

Congress shall make no law respecting an establishment of religion or prohibiting the free exercise thereof, or abridging the freedom of speech or of the press, or the right of the people peaceably to assemble and to petition the government for a redress of grievances.

That is for reference.

These are my personal observations and opinions. I speak on behalf of no group or professional organization.

The PMRC proposal is an ill-conceived piece of nonsense which fails to deliver any real benefits to children, infringes the civil liberties of people who are not children, and promises to keep the courts busy for years dealing with the interpretational and enforcement problems inherent in the proposal's design.

It is my understanding that in law First Amendment issues are decided with a preference for the least restrictive alternative. In this context, the PMRC demands are the equivalent of treating dandruff by decapitation.

No one has forced Mrs. Baker or Mrs. Gore to bring Prince or Sheene Easton into their homes. Thanks to the Constitution, they are free to buy other forms of music for their children. Apparently, they insist in purchasing the works of contemporary recording artists in order to support a personal illusion of aerobic sophistication. Ladies, please be advised: The $8.98 purchase price does not entitle you to a kiss on the foot from the composer or performer in exchange for a spin on the family Victrola.

Taken as a whole, the complete list of PMRC demands reads like an instruction manual for some sinister kind of toilet training program to house-break all composers and performers because of the lyrics of a few. Ladies, how dare you?

The ladies' shame must be shared by the bosses at the major labels who, through the RIAA, chose to bargain away the rights of composers, performers, and retailers in order to pass H.R. 2911, The Blank Tape Tax, a private tax levied by an industry on consumers for the benefit of a select group within that industry.

Is this a consumer issue? You bet it is. The major record labels need to have H.R. 2911 whiz through a few committees before anybody smells a rat. One of them is chaired by Senator Thurmond. Is it a coincidence that Mrs. Thurmond is affiliated with the PMRC?

I cannot say she is a member, because the PMRC has no members. Their secretary told me on the phone last Friday that the PMRC has no members, only founders. I asked how many other District of Columbia wives are nonmembers of an organization that raises money by mail, has a tax-exempt status, and seems intent on running the Constitution of the United States through the family paper-shredder. I asked her if it was a cult. Finally, she said she could not give me an answer and that she had to call their lawyer.

While the wife of the Secretary of the Treasury recites "Gonna drive my love inside you" and Senator Gore's wife talks about "bondage" and "oral sex at gunpoint" on the CBS Evening News, people in high places work on a tax bill that is so ridiculous, the only way to sneak it through is to keep the public's mind on something else: Porn rock.

Is the basic issue morality? Is it mental health? Is it an issue at all? The PMRC has created a lot of confusion with improper comparisons between song lyrics, videos, record packaging, radio broadcasting, and live performances. These are all different mediums and the people who work in them have the right to conduct their business without trade-restraining legislation, whipped up like an instant pudding by "The wives of Big Brother."

Is it proper that the husband of a PMRC nonmember/ founder/ person sits on any committee considering business pertaining to the blank tape tax or his wife's lobbying organization? Can any committee thus constituted find facts in a fair and unbiased manner? This committee has three that we know about: Senator Danforth, Senator Packwood, and Senator Gore. For some reason, they seem to feel there is no conflict of interest involved.

Children in the vulnerable age bracket have a natural love for music. If as a parent you believe they should be exposed to something more uplifting than "Sugar Walls," support music appreciation programs in schools. Why have you not considered your child's need for consumer information? Music appreciation costs very little compared to sports expenditures. Your children have a right to know that something besides pop music exists.

It is unfortunate that the PMRC would rather dispense governmentally sanitized heavy metal music than something more uplifting. Is this an indication of PMRC's personal taste or just another manifestation of the low priority this administration has placed on education for the arts in America?

The answer, of course, is neither. You cannot distract people from thinking about an unfair tax by talking about music appreciation. For that you need sex, and lots of it.

The establishment of a rating system, voluntary or otherwise, opens the door to an endless parade of moral quality control programs based on things certain Christians do not like. What if the next bunch of Washington wives demands a large yellow "J" on all material written or performed by Jews, in order to save helpless children from exposure to concealed Zionist doctrine?

Record ratings are frequently compared to film ratings. Apart from the quantitative difference, there is another that is more important: People who act in films are hired to pretend. No matter how the film is rated, it will not hurt them personally.

Since many musicians write and perform their own material and stand by it as their art, whether you like it or not, an imposed rating will stigmatize them as individuals. How long before composers and performers are told to wear a festive little PMRC arm band with their scarlet letter on it?

Bad facts make bad law, and people who write bad laws are in my opinion more dangerous than songwriters who celebrate sexuality. Freedom of speech, freedom of religious thought, and the right to due process for composers, performers and retailers are imperiled if the PMRC and the major labels consummate this nasty bargain.

Are we expected to give up article 1 so the big guys can collect an extra dollar on every blank tape and 10 to 25 percent on tape recorders? What is going on here? Do we get to vote on this tax?

I think that this whole matter has gotten completely blown out of proportion, and I agree with Senator Exon that there is a very dubious reason for having this event. I also agree with Senator Exon that you should not be wasting time on stuff like this, because from the beginning I have sensed that it is somebody's hobby project.

Now, I have done a number of interviews on television. People keep saying, can you not take a few steps in their direction, can you not sympathize, can you not empathize? I do more than that at this point. I have got an idea for a way to stop all this stuff and a way to give parents what they really want, which is information, accurate information as to what is inside the album, without providing a stigma for the musicians who have played on the album or the people who sing it or the people who wrote it. And I think that if you listen carefully to this idea that it might just get by all of the constitutional problems and everything else.

As far as I am concerned, I have no objection to having all of the lyrics placed on the album routinely, all the time. But there is a little problem. Record companies do not own the right automatically to take these lyrics, because they are owned by a publishing company.

So, just as all the rest of the PMRC proposals would cost money, this would cost money too, because the record companies would need—they should not be forced to bear the cost, the extra expenditure to the publisher, to print those lyrics.

If you consider that the public needs to be warned about the contents of the records, what better way than to let them see exactly what the songs say? That way you do not have to put any kind of subjective rating on the record. You do not have to call it R, X, D/ A, anything. You can read it for yourself.

But in order for it to work properly, the lyrics should be on a uniform kind of a sheet. Maybe even the Government could print those sheets. Maybe it should even be paid for by the Government, if the Government is interested in making sure that people have consumer information in this regard.

And you also have to realize that if a person buys the record and takes it out of the store, once it is out of the store you can't return it if you read the lyrics at home and decide that little Johnny is not supposed to have it.

I think that that should at least be considered, and the idea of imposing these ratings on live concerts, on the albums, asking record companies to reevaluate or drop or violate contracts that they already have with artists should be thrown out.

That is all I have to say.

The CHAIRMAN. Thank you very much, Mr. Zappa. You understand that the previous witnesses were not asking for legislation. And I do not know, I cannot speak for Senator Hollings, but I think the prevailing view here is that nobody is asking for legislation.

The question is just focusing on what a lot of people perceive to be a problem, and you have indicated that you at least understand that there is another point of view. But there are people that think that parents should have some knowledge of what goes into their home.

Mr. ZAPPA. All along my objection has been with the tactics used by these people in order to achieve the goal. I just think the tactics have been really bad, and the whole premise of their proposal— they were badly advised in terms of record business law, they were badly advised in terms of practicality, or they would have known that certain things do not work mechanically with what they suggest.

The CHAIRMAN. Senator Gore.

Senator GORE. Thank you very much, Mr. Chairman.

I found your statement very interesting and, although I disagree with some of the statements that you make and have made on other occasions, I have been a fan of your music, believe it or not. I respect you as a true original and a tremendously talented musician.

Your suggestion of printing the lyrics on the album is a very interesting one. The PMRC at one point said they would propose either a rating or warning, or printing all the lyrics on the album. The record companies came back and said they did not want to do that.

I think a lot of people agree with your suggestion that one easy way to solve this problem for parents would be to put the actual words there, so that parents could see them. In fact, the National Association of Broadcasters made exactly the same request of the record companies.

I think your suggestion is an intriguing one and might really be a solution for the problem.

Mr. ZAPPA. You have to understand that it does cost money, because you cannot expect publishers to automatically give up that right, which is a right for them. Somebody is going to have to reimburse the publishers, the record industry.

Without trying to mess up the album jacket art, it should be a sheet of paper that is slipped inside the shrink-wrap, so that when you take it out you can still have a complete album package. So there is going to be some extra cost for printing it.

But as long as people realize that for this kind of consumer safety you are going to spend some money and as long as you can find a way to pay for it, I think that would be the best way to let people know.

Senator GORE. I do not disagree with that at all. And the separate sheet would also solve the problem with cassettes as well, because you do not have the space for words on the cassette packs.

Mr. ZAPPA. There would have to be a little accordion-fold.

Senator GORE. I have listened to you a number of times on this issue, and I guess the statement that I want to get from you is whether or not you feel this concern is legitimate.

You feel very strongly about your position, and I understand that. You are very articulate and forceful.

But occasionally you give the impression that you think parents are just silly to be concerned at all.

Mr. ZAPPA. No; that is not an accurate impression.

Senator GORE. Well, please clarify it, then.

Mr. ZAPPA. First of all, I think it is the parents' concern; it is not the Government's concern.

Senator GORE. The PMRC agrees with you on that.

Mr. ZAPPA. Well, that does not come across in the way they have been speaking. The whole drift that I have gotten, based upon the media blitz that has attended the PMRC and its rise to infamy, is that they have a special plan, and it has smelled like legislation up until now.

There are too many things that look like hidden agendas involved with this. And I am a parent. I have got four children. Two of them are here. I want them to grow up in a country where they can think what they want to think, be what they want to be, and not what somebody's wife or somebody in Government makes them be.

I do not want to have that and I do not think you do either.

Senator GORE. OK. But now you are back on the issue of Government involvement. Let me say briefly on this point that the PMRC says repeatedly no legislation, no regulation, no Government action. It certainly sounded clear to me.

And as far as a hidden agenda, I do not see one, hear one, or know of one.

Mr. ZAPPA. OK, let me tell you why I have drawn these conclusions. First of all, they may say, we are not interested in legislation. But there are others who do, and because of their project bad things have happened in this country in the industry.

I believe there is actually some liability. Look at this. You have a situation where, even if you go for the lyric printed thing in the record, because of the tendency among Americans to be copycats— one guy commits a murder, you get a copycat murder—now you've got copycat censors.

You get a very bad situation in San Antonio, TX, right now where they are trying to pass PMRC-type individual ratings and attach them to live concerts, with the mayor down there trying to make a national reputation by putting San Antonio on the map as the first city in the United States to have these regulations, against the suggestion of the city attorney, who says, I do not think this is constitutional.

But you know, there is this fervor to get in and do even more and even more.

And the other thing, the PMRC starts off talking about lyrics, but when they take it over into other realms they start talking about the videos. In fact, you misspoke yourself at the beginning in your introduction when you were talking about the music does this, the music does that. There is a distinct difference between those notes and chords and the baseline and the rhythm that support the words and the lyrics.

I do not know whether you really are talking about controlling the type of music.

The CHAIRMAN. The lyrics.

Mr. ZAPPA. So specifically, we are talking about lyrics. It began with lyrics. But even looking at the PMRC fundraising letter, in the last paragraph at the bottom of the page it starts looking like it is branching into other areas, when it says: "We realize that this material has pervaded other aspects of society. 'And it is like what, you are going to fix it all for me?"

Senator GORE. No. I think the PMRC's acknowledging some of the statements by some of their critics who say: Well, why single out the music industry.

Do I understand that you do believe that there is a legitimate concern here?

Mr. ZAPPA. But the legitimate concern is a matter of taste for the individual parent and how much sexual information that parent wants to give their child, at what age, at what time, in what quantity, OK. And I think that, because there is a tendency in the United States to hide sex, which I think is an unhealthy thing to do, and many parents do not give their children good sexual education, in spite of the fact that little books for kids are available, and other parents demand that sexual education be taken out of school, it makes the child vulnerable because if you do not have something rational to compare it to when you see or hear about something that is aberrated you do not perceive it as an aberration.

Senator GORE. OK, I have run out of time.

Thank you, Mr. Chairman.

The CHAIRMAN. Senator Rockefeller.

Senator ROCKEFELLER. No questions, Mr. Chairman.

The CHAIRMAN. Senator Gorton.

Senator GORTON. Mr. Zappa, I am astounded at the courtesy and soft-voiced nature of the comments of my friend, the Senator from Tennessee. I can only say that I found your statement to be boorish, incredibly and insensitively insulting to the people that were here previously; that you could manage to give the first amendment of the Constitution of the United States a bad name, if I felt that you had the slightest understanding of it, which I do not.

You do not have the slightest understanding of the difference between Government action and private action, and you have certainly destroyed any case you might otherwise have had with this Senator.

Thank you, Mr. Chairman.

Mr. ZAPPA. Is this private action?

The CHAIRMAN. Senator Exon.

Senator EXON. Mr. Chairman, thank you very much.

Mr. Zappa, let me say that I was surprised that Senator Gore knew and liked your music. I must confess that I have never heard any of your music, to my knowledge.

Mr. ZAPPA. I would be more than happy to recite my lyrics to you.

Senator EXON. Can we forgo that?

Senator GORE. You have probably never heard of the Mothers of Invention.

Senator EXON. I have heard of Glen Miller and Mitch Miller. Did you ever perform with them?

Mr. ZAPPA. As a matter of fact, I took music lessons in grade school from Mitch Miller's brother.

Senator EXON. That is the first sign of hope we have had in this hearing.

Let us try and get down to a fundamental question here that I would like to ask you, Mr. Zappa. Do you believe that parents have the right and the obligation to mold the psychological development of their children?

Mr. ZAPPA. Yes, I think they have that right, and I also think they have that obligation.

Senator EXON. Do you see any extreme difficulty in carrying out those obligations for a parent by material falling into the hands of their children over which they have little or no control?

Mr. ZAPPA. Well, one of the things that has been brought up before is talking about every young children getting access to the material that they have been showing here today. And what I have said to that in the past is a teenager may go into a record store unescorted with $8.98 in his pocket, but very young children do not.

If they go into a record store, the $8.98 is in mom or dad's pocket, and they can always say, Johnny, buy a book. They can say, Johnny, buy instrumental music; there is some nice classical music for you here; why do you not listen to that.

The parent can ask or guide the child in another direction, away from Sheena Easton, Prince, or whoever else you have been complaining about. There is always that possibility.

Senator EXON. As I understand it from your testimony—and once again, I want to emphasize that I see nothing wrong whatsoever; in fact, I salute the ladies for bringing this to the attention of the public as best they see fit. I think you could tell from my testimony that I tend to agree with them.

I want to be very careful that we do not overstep our bounds and try and—and I emphasize once again—tell somebody else what they should see. I am primarily worried about children.

It seems to me from your statement that you have no obligation—or no objection whatsoever to printing lyrics, if that would be legally possible, or from a standpoint of having the room to do that, on records or tapes. Is that not what you said?

Mr. ZAPPA. I think it would be advisable for two reasons. One, it gives people one of the things that they have been asking for. It gives them that type of consumer protection because, if you can read the English language and you can see the lyrics on the back, you have no excuse for complaining if you take the record out of the store.

And also, I think that the record industry has been damaged and it has been given a very bad rap by this whole situation because it has been indicated, or people have attempted to indicate, that there is so much of this kind of material that people object to in the industry, that that is what the industry is.

It is not bad at all. Some of the albums that have been selected for abuse here are obscure. Some of them are already several years old. And I think that a lot of deep digging was done in order to come up with the song about anal vapors or whatever it was that they were talking about before.

Senator EXON. If I understand you, you would be in support of printing the lyrics, but you are adamantly opposed to any kind of a rating system?

Mr. ZAPPA. I am opposed to the rating system because, as I said, if you put a rating on the record it goes directly to the character of the person who made the record, whereas if you rate a film, a guy who is in the film has been hired as an actor. He is pretending. You rate the film, whatever it is, it does not hurt him.

But whether you like what is on the record or not, the guy who made it, that is his art and to stigmatize him is unfair.

Senator EXON. Well, likewise, if you are primarily concerned about the artists, is it not true that for many many years, we have had ratings of movies with indicators as to the sexual content of movies and that has been, as near as I can tell, a voluntary action on the part of the actors in the movies and the producers of the movies and the distributors?

That seems to have worked reasonably well. What is wrong with that?

Mr. ZAPPA. Well, first of all, it replaced something that was far more restrictive, which was the Hayes office. And as far as that being voluntary, there are people who wish they did not have to rate their films. They still object to rating their films, but the reason the ratings go on is because if they are not rated they will not get distributed or shown in theaters. So there is a little bit of pressure involved but still there is no stigma.

Senator EXON. The Government does not require that. The point I am trying to make is—and while I think these hearings should not have been held if we are not considering legislation or regulations at this time, I emphasized earlier that they might follow.

I simply want to say to you that I suspect that, unless the industry "cleans up their act"—and I use that in quotes again—there is likely to be legislation. And it seems to me that it would not be too far removed from reality or too offensive to anyone if you could follow the general guidelines, right, wrong, or indifferent, that are now in place with regard to the movie industry.

Mr. ZAPPA. Well, I would object to that. I think, first of all, I believe it was you who asked the question of Mrs. Gore whether there was any other indication on the album as to the contents. And I would say that a buzzsaw blade between a guy's legs on the album cover is a good indication that it is not for little Johnny.

Senator EXON. I do not believe I asked her that question, but the point you made is a good one, because if that should not go to little minds I think there should be at least some minimal activity or attempt on the part of the producers and distributors, and indeed possibly the performers, to see that that does not get to that little mind.

Mr. Chairman, thank you very much.

The CHAIRMAN. Senator Hollings.

Senator HOLLINGS. Mr. Zappa, I apologize for coming back in late, but I am just hearing the later part of it. I hear that you say that perhaps we could print the words, and I think that is a good suggestion, but it is unfair to have albums rated.

Now, it is not considered unfair in the movie industry, and I want you to elaborate. I do not want to belabor you, but why is it unfair? I mean, it is accurate, is it not?

Mr. ZAPPA. Well, I do not know whether it is accurate, because sometimes they have trouble deciding how a film gets to be an X or an R or whatever. And you have two problems. One is the quantity of material, 325 films per year versus 25,000 4-minute songs per year, OK.

You also have a problem that an album is a compilation of different types of cuts. If one song on the album is sexually explicit and all the rest of it sounds like Pat Boone, what do you get on the album? How are you going to rate it?

There are little technical difficulties here, and also you have the problem of having somebody in the position of deciding what's good, what's bad, what's talking about the devil, what is too violent, and the rest of that stuff.

But the point I made before is that when you rate the album you are rating the individual, because he takes personal responsibility for the music; and in the movies, the actors who are performing in the movie, it does not hurt them.

Senator HOLLINGS. Well, very good. I think the actual printing of the content itself is perhaps even better than the rating. Let everyone else decide.

Mr. ZAPPA. I think you should leave it up to the parents, because not all parents want to keep their children totally ignorant.

Senator HOLLINGS. Well, you and I would differ on what is ignorance and education, I can see that. But if it was there, they could see what they were buying and I think that is a step in the right direction.

As Senator Exon has pointed out, the primary movers in this particular regard are not looking for legislation or regulations, which is our function. To be perfectly candid with you, I would look for relations or some kind of legislation, if it could be constitutionally accomplished, unless of course we have these initiatives from the industry itself.

I think your suggestion is a good one. If you print those words, that would go a long way toward satisfying everyone's objections.

Mr. ZAPPA. All we have to do is find out how it is going to be paid for.

Senator HOLLINGS. Thank you, Mr. Chairman.

The CHAIRMAN. Senator Hawkins.

Senator HAWKINS. Mr. Zappa, you say you have four children?

Mr. ZAPPA. Yes, four children.

Senator HAWKINS. Have you ever purchased toys for those children?

Mr. ZAPPA. No; my wife does.

Senator HAWKINS. Well, I might tell you that if you were to go in a toy store—which is very educational for fathers, by the way; it is not a maternal responsibility to buy toys for children—that you may look on the box and the box says, this is suitable for 5 to 7 years of age, or 8 to 15, or 15 and above, to give you some guidance for a toy for a child.

Do you object to that?

Mr. ZAPPA. In a way I do, because that means that somebody in an office someplace is making a decision about how smart my child is.

Senator HAWKINS. I would be interested to see what toys your kids ever had.

Mr. ZAPPA. Why would you be interested?

Senator HAWKINS. Just as a point of interest.

Mr. ZAPPA. Well, come on over to the house. I will show them to you.

Senator HAWKINS. I might do that.

Do you make a profit from sales of rock records?

Mr. ZAPPA. Yes.

Senator HAWKINS. So you do make a profit from the sales of rock records?

Mr. ZAPPA. Yes.

Senator HAWKINS. Thank you. I think that statement tells the story to this committee. Thank you.

The CHAIRMAN. Mr. Zappa, thank you very much for your testimony.

Mr. ZAPPA. Thank you.

'The statement follows:'

Statement of Frank Zappa

These are my personal observations and opinions. They are addressed to the PMRC as well as this committee. I speak on behalf of no group or professional organization.

The PMRC proposal is an ill-conceived piece of nonsense which fails to delivery any real benefits to children, infringes the civil liberties of people who are not children, and promises to keep the courts busy for years, dealing with the interpretational and enforcemental problems inherent in the proposal's design.

It is my understanding that, in law, First Amendment Issues are decided with a preference for the least restrictive alternative. In this context, the PMRC's demands are the equivalent of treating dandruff by decapitation.

No one has forced Mrs. Baker or Mrs. Gore to bring Prince or Sheena Easton into their homes. Thanks to the Constitution, they are free to buy other forms of music for their children. Apparently they insist on purchasing the works of contemporary recording artists in order to support a personal illusion of aerobic sophistication. Ladies, please be advised: the $8.98 purchase price does not entitle you to a kiss on the foot from the composer or performer in exchange for a spin on the family Victrola. Taken as a whole, the complete list of PMRC demands reads like an instruction manual for some sinister kind of "toilet training program" to house-break all composers and performers because of the lyrics of a few. Ladies, how dare you?

The ladies' shame must be shared by the bosses at the major labels who, through the RIAA, chose to bargain away the rights of composers, performers, and retailers in order to pass H.R. 2911, The Blank Tape Tax: A private tax, levied by an industry on consumers, for the benefit of a select group within that industry. Is this a "consumer issue"? You bet it is. PMRC spokesperson, Kandy Stroud, announced to millions of fascinated viewers on last Friday's ABC Nightline debate that Senator Gore, a man she described as "A friend of the music industry," is co-sponsor of something she referred to as "anti-piracy legislation". Is this the same tax bill with a nicer name?

The major record labels need to have H.R. 2911 whiz through a few committees before anybody smells a rat. One of them is chaired by Senator Thurmond. Is it a coincidence that Mrs. Thurmond is affiliated with the PMRC? I can't say she's a member, because the PMRC has no members. Their secretary told me on the phone last Friday that the PMRC has no members . . . only founders. I asked how many other D.C. wives are non-members of an organization that raises money by mail, has a tax-exempt status, and seems intent on running the Constitution of the United States through the family paper-shredder. I asked her if it was a cult. Finally, she said she couldn't give me an answer and that she had to call their lawyer.

While the wife of the Secretary of the Treasury recites "Gonna drive my love inside you . . .", and Senator Gore's wife talks about "Bondage!" and "oral sex at gunpoint," on the CBS Evening News, people in high places work on a tax bill that is so ridiculous, the only way to sneak it through is to keep the public's mind on something else: "Porn Rock".

The PMRC practices a curious double standard with these fervent recitations. Thanks to them, helpless young children all over America get to hear about oral sex at gunpoint on network TV several nights a week. Is there a secret FCC dispensation here? What sort of end justifies THESE means? PTA parents should keep an eye on these ladies if that's their idea of 'good taste'.

Is the basic issue morality? Is it mental health? Is it an issue at all? The PMRC has created a lot of confusion with improper comparisons between song lyrics, videos, record packaging, radio broadcasting, and live performances. These are all different mediums, and the people who work in them have a right conduct their business without trade-restraining legislation, whipped up like an instant pudding by The Wives of Big Brother.

Is it proper that the husband of PMRC non-member/founder/person sits on any committee considering business pertaining to the Blank Tape Tax or his wife's lobbying organization? Can any committee thus constituted 'find facts' in a fair and umbiased manner? This committee has three. A minor conflict of interest?

The PMRC promotes their program as a harmless type of consumer information service providing 'guidelines' which will assist baffled parents in the determination of the 'suitability' of records listened by 'very young children'. The methods they propose have several unfortunately side effects, not the least of which is the reduction of all American Music, recorded and live, to the intellectual level of a Saturday morning cartoon show.

Teen-agers with $8.98 in their pocket might go into a record store alone, but 'very young children' do not. Usually there is a parent in attendance. The $8.98 is in the parents pocket. The parent can always suggest that the $8.98 be spent on a book.

If the parent is afraid to let the child read a book, perhaps the $8.98 can be spent on recordings of instrumental music. Why not bring jazz or classical music into your home instead of Blackie Lawless or Madonna? Great music with no words at all is available to anyone with sense enough to look beyond this week's platinum-selling fashion plate.

Children in the 'vulnerable' age bracket have a natural love for music. If, as a parent, you believe they should be exposed to something more uplifting than sugar walls, support Music Appreciation programs in schools. Why haven't you considered your child's need for consumer information? Music Appreciation costs very little compared to sports expenditures. Your children have a right to know that something besides pop music exists.

It is unfortunate that the PMRC would rather dispense governmentally sanitized Heavy Metal Music, than something more 'uplifting'. Is this an indication of PMRC's personal taste, or just another manifestation of the low priority this administration has placed on education for The Arts in America? The answer, of course, is neither. You can't distract people from thinking about an unfair tax by talking about Music Appreciation. For that you need sex . . . and lots of it.

Because of the subjective nature of the PMRC ratings, it is impossible to guarantee that some sort of 'despised concept' won't sneak through, tucked away in new slang or the overstressed pronunciation

of an otherwise innocent word. If the goal here is total verbal/moral safety, there is only one way to achieve it: watch no TV, read no books, see no movies, listen to only instrumental music, or buy no music at all.

The establishment of a rating system, voluntary or otherwise, opens the door to an endless parade of Moral Quality Control Programs based on "Things Certain Christians Don't Like". What if the next bunch of Washington Wives demands a large yellow "J" on all material written or performed by Jews, in order to save helpless children from exposure to 'concealed Zionist doctrine'?

Record ratings are frequently compared to film ratings. Apart from the quantitative difference, there is another that is more important: People who act in films are hired to 'pretend'. No matter how the film is rated, it won't hurt them personally. Since many musicians write and perform their own material and stand by it as their art (whether you like it or not), an imposed rating will stigmatize them as individuals. How long before composers and performers are told to wear a festive little PMRC arm band with their Scarlet Letter on it?

The PMRC rating system restrains trade in one specific musical field: Rock. No ratings have been requested for Comedy records or Country Music. Is there anyone in the PMRC who can differentiate infallibly between Rock and Country Music? Artists in both fields cross stylistic lines. Some artists include comedy material. If an album is part Rock, part Country, part Comedy, what sort of label would it get? Shouldn't the ladies be warning everyone that inside those Country albums with the American Flags, the big trucks, and the atomic pompadours there lurks a fascinating variety, of songs about sex, violence, alcohol, and the devil, recorded in a way that lets you hear every word, sung for you by people who have been to prison and are proud of it.

If enacted, the PMRC program would have the effect of protectionist legislation for the Country Music Industry, providing more security for cowboys than it does for children. One major retail outlet has already informed the Capitol Records sales staff that it would not purchase or display an album with any kind of sticker on it.

Another chain with outlets in shopping malls has been told by the landlord that if it racked "hard-rated albums" they would lose their lease. That opens up an awful lot of shelf space for somebody. Could it be that a certain Senatorial husband and wife team from Tennessee sees this as an 'affirmative action program' to benefit the suffering multitudes in Nashville?

Is the PMRC attempting to save future generations from SEX ITSELF? The type, the amount, and the timing of sexual information given to a child should be determined by the parents, not by people who are involved in a tax scheme cover-up.

The PMRC has concocted a Mythical Beast, and compounds the chicanery by demanding 'consumer guidelines' to keep it from inviting your children inside its sugar walls. Is the next step the adoption of a "PMRC National Legal Age For Comprehension of Vaginal Arousal". Many people in this room would gladly support such legislation, but, before they start drafting their bill, I urge them to consider these facts:

(1) There is no conclusive scientific evidence to support the claim that exposure to any form of music will cause the listener to commit a crime or damn his soul to hell.

(2) Masturbation is not illegal. If it is not illegal to do it, why should it be illegal to sing about it?

(3) No medical evidence of hairy palms, warts, or blindness has been linked to masturbation or vaginal arousal, nor has it been proven that hearing references to either topic automatically turns the listener into a social liability.

(4) Enforcement of anti-masturbatory legislation could prove costly and time consuming.

(5) There is not enough prison space to hold all the children who do it.

The PMRC's proposal is most offensive in its "moral tone". It seeks to enforce a set of implied religious values on its victims. Iran has a religious government. Good for them. I like having the capitol of the United States in Washington, DC, in spite of recent efforts to move it to Lynchburg, VA.

Fundamentalism is not a state religion. The PMRC's request for labels regarding sexually explicit lyrics, violence, drugs, alcohol, and especially occult content reads like a catalog of phenomena abhorrent to practitioners of that faith. How a person worships is a private matter, and should not be inflicted upon or exploited by others. Understanding the Fundamentalist leanings of this organization, I think it is fair to wonder if their rating system will eventually be extended to inform parents as to whether a musical group has homosexuals in it. Will the PMRC permit musical groups to exist, but only if gay members don't sing, and are not depicted on the album cover?

The PMRC has demanded that record companies "re-evaluate" the contracts of those groups who do things on stage that THEY find offensive. I remind the PMRC that groups are comprised of individuals. If one guy wiggles too much, does the whole band get an "X"? If the group gets dropped from the label as a result of this 're-evaluation' process, do the other guys in the group who weren't wiggling get to sue the guy who wiggled because he ruined their careers? Do the founders of this tax exempt organization with no members plan to indemnify record companies for any losses incurred from unfavorably decided breach of contract suits, or is there a PMRC secret agent in the Justice Department?

Should individual musicians be rated? If so, who is qualified to determine if the guitar player is an "X", the vocalist is a "D/A" or the drummer is a "V". If the bass player (or his Senator) belongs to a religious group that dances around with poisonous snakes, does he get an "O"? What if he has an earring in one ear, wears an Italian Horn around his neck, sings about his astrological sign, practices yoga, reads the Quaballah, or owns a rosary? Will his "occult content" rating go into an old CoIntelPro computer, emerging later as a "fact," to determine if he qualifies for a home-owner loan? Will they tell you this is necessary to protect the folks next door from the possibility of 'devil-worship' lyrics creeping through the wall?

What hazards await the unfortunate retailer who accidently sells an "O" rated record to somebody's little Johnny? Nobody in Washington seemed to care when Christian Terrorists bombed abortion clinics in the name of Jesus. Will you care when the "friends of the wives of big brother" blow up the shopping mall?

The PMRC wants ratings to start as of the date of their enactment. That leaves the current crop of 'objectionable material' untouched. What will be the status of recordings from that Golden Era to censorship? Do they become collector's items . . . or will another "fair and unbiased committee" order them destroyed in a public ceremony?

Bad facts make bad law, and people who write bad laws are, in my opinion, more dangerous than songwriters who celebrate sexuality. Freedom of Speech, Freedom of Religious Thought, and the Right to Due Process for composers, performers and retailers are imperiled if the PMRC and the major labels consummate this nasty bargain. Are we expected to give up Article One so the big guys can collect an extra dollar on every blank tape and 10 to 25% on tape recorders? What's going on here? Do WE get to vote on this tax? There's an awful lot of smoke pouring out of the legislative machinery used by the PMRC to inflate this issue. Try not to inhale it. Those responsible for the vandalism should pay for the damage by voluntarily rating themselves. If they refuse, perhaps the voters could assist in awarding the Congressional "X", the Congressional "D/A", the Congressional "V", and the Congressional "O". Just like the ladies say: these ratings are necessary to protect our children. I hope it's not too late to put them where they really belong.

The CHAIRMAN. The next witness is John Denver.

John, thank you very much for being with us.

STATEMENT OF JOHN DENVER

Mr. DENVER. Good morning, Mr. Chairman. It is a great pleasure to be with you, and I apologize for running in and out. I seem to be testifying and briefing many people here on Capitol Hill today, and it causes the ingoing and outgoing.

Honorable Chairman, members of the committee, ladies and gentlemen: It is a great honor and a privilege to appear before you this morning and to take advantage of the opportunity given me in our free society to speak my mind, to give voice to my opinions in a public forum in front of not only the leadership of our great country, but the press, the media, and through them all who might be listening around our country and around the world.

I am here to address the issue of a possible rating system in the recording industry, labeling records where excesses of explicit sex and graphic violence have occurred and, furthermore, references to drugs and alcohol or the occult are included in the lyrics.

These hearings have been called to determine whether or not the Government should intervene to enforce this practice. Mr. Chairman, this would approach censorship. May I be very clear that I am strongly opposed to censorship of any kind in our society or anywhere else in the world.

I have had in my experience two encounters with this sort of censorship. My song "Rocky Mountain High" was banned from many radio stations as a drug-related song. This was obviously done by people who had never seen or been to the Rocky Mountains and also had never experienced the elation, celebration of life, or the joy in living that one feels when he observes something as wondrous as the Perseides meteor shower on a moonless, cloudless night, when there are so many stars that you have a shadow from the starlight, and you are out camping with your friends, your best friends, and introducing them to one of nature's most spectacular light shows for the very first time.

Obviously, a clear case of misinterpretation. Mr. Chairman, what assurance have I that any national panel to review my music would make any better judgment?

To my knowledge, my movie "Oh God" was not banned in any theaters. However, some newspapers refused to print our advertisements, and some theaters refused to put the name of the film on the marquee.

I do not believe that we were using the name of our Lord in vain. Quite the opposite, we were making a small effort to spread his message that we are here for each other and not against each other.

Discipline and self-restraint when practiced by an individual, a family, or a company is an effective way to deal with this issue. The same thing when forced on a people by their government or, worse, by a self-appointed watchdog of public morals, is suppression and will not be tolerated in a democratic society.

Mr. Chairman, the suppression of the people of a society begins in my mind with the censorship of the written or spoken word. It was so in Nazi Germany. It is so in many places today where those in power are afraid of the consequences of an informed and educated people.

In a mature, incredibly diverse society such as ours, the access to all perspectives of an issue becomes more and more important. Those things which in our experience are undesirable generally prove to be unfurthering and sooner or later become boring. That process cannot and should not be stifled.

On the other hand, that which is denied becomes that which is most interesting. That which is hidden—excuse me. That which is denied becomes that which is most desired, and that which is hidden becomes that is most interesting. Consequently, a great deal of time and energy is spent trying to get at what is being kept from you. Our children, our people, our society and the world cannot afford this waste.

It was my pleasure to meet with radio programmers and broadcasters from all over the country this past week in Dallas. They expressed their concern about this issue and the direction in which it seemed to be going. They also expressed their willingness to practice the discipline and self-restraint that I mentioned earlier, especially when they were given direction by their listeners. I believe this to be true, because they are in business to please their listening audience.

I would like to acknowledge the PMRC for bringing this issue to the attention of not only our industry, but our Government and our people. It is obvious that we are dealing with a real problem which warrants our concern. I would like to point out, however, that we address ourselves not to the problem, but to the symptoms.

I suggest that explicit lyrics and graphic videos are not so far removed from what is seen on television every day and night, whether it be in the soap operas or on the news, and that we should point our finger at the recording industry while watching the general public at a nationally televised baseball game chant in unison "The Blue Jays suck" is ludicrous.

The problem, Mr. Chairman, in my opinion has to do with our willingness as parents to take responsibility for the upbringing of our children, to pay attention to their interests, to respond to their needs, and to recognize that we as parents and as individuals have a greater influence on our children and on each other than anything else could possibly have.

To quote a wise old man from ancient China: "If there be righteousness—" not self-righteousness; that is not part of the quote. "If there be righteousness in the heart, there will be beauty in the character. If there be beauty in the character, there will be harmony in the home. If there be harmony in the home, there will be order in the Nation. And if there be order in the Nation, there will be peace in the world."

I thank you very much. Mr. Chairman, if I may add a couple of personal words. I am a father of two children, both adopted, and I have a lot of friends in the music business, other rock performers who have children also, and all of them, including myself, we have a great concern for our children. That is why I am here today.

In my experience, sir, all over the world one of the most interesting things about the music that young people are listening to is it gives us as adults a very clear insight as to what is going on in their minds. We can know what they are thinking by listening to the music that they surround themselves with.

The people that I have had the opportunity to talk with, the troubled children, the teenagers who are considering suicide, what they expressed to me is a real frustration in their lives, an inability to communicate with their parents, an inability to understand or to envision any kind of a possible future because of the nuclear threat that we live under.

They do not see things getting better economically. They do not see things getting better for the small businessman, for the small farmer. They do not see a future for themselves.

It is my opinion that it is out of this that some young people put a gun into their mouths and pull the trigger. We can turn this around, sir. We can address the reality of a problem and not deal with just the symptoms, and create not only a better world for our children but for ourselves and all of humanity.

We can end hunger. We can rid the world of nuclear weapons. We can learn to live together as human beings on a planet that travels through the universe, living the example of peace and harmony among all people.

The CHAIRMAN. John, thank you very much for your excellent statement.

You talked about the importance of, in your words, an informed and educated people, and about the importance of communication between parents and their children. And as I understand it, that is exactly the point that was made by the Parents Music Resource Center group that was here earlier. That is, they are not asking for censorship, they are not asking for Government action.

Nobody has proposed that to my knowledge. There is no legislation that is pending that in any way suggests any censorship. The point is not less information. Nobody is trying to prevent rock stars from singing whatever they want or music

companies from publishing whatever they want. The question is one of communication and openness.

Senator Exon said earlier, if we are not legislating why have a hearing? Frequently we have oversight hearings in the Congress, and one of the reasons for it is to just air what is going on, to bring it out in the open, to increase information, not to reduce information.

What the mothers are saying is that they do not have sufficient information. They want to know more, they want to be more informed. They do not want less information. They do not want censorship. They want more information. They want to know.

They do not want what goes on in their homes simply to be a matter between the music artist, the rock star, and their 11- or 12-year-old, 13-year-old child. They want to be in on the act, too, and all they want is more information as to what is going on.

And it would seem to me that that is a reasonable request for them to make, that it is reasonable for all of us to be in on the act, rather than just to have almost a private relationship between our kids and somebody outside the home.

Mr. DENVER. I understand, Senator, and I applaud what is taking place here today. My concern is that it sort of feels like, if we are bringing this issue to the Congress through the Senate, there is a very real possibility that legislation is going to be acted upon. I understand that.

The CHAIRMAN. Zero.

Mr. DENVER. But several gentlemen have said that if it looks like it is possible to make legislation, some of you today have said, if it is possible to make legislation that you would go further with this if there is a constitutional way to do that.

The CHAIRMAN. Just believe me, zero chance of legislation. I do not think anybody has introduced a bill, and I do not really think that is a possibility at all.

The only question is is there a possibility of, first, bringing the issue before the country.

Mr. DENVER. And you have done that and I applaud that.

The CHAIRMAN. Just talk about it and ventilate our concerns.

And secondly, is there a possibility of increasing the information that is available to parents of kids, who have the real responsibility for raising those children and for establishing whatever values those children are going to have?

Mr. DENVER. I understand.

The CHAIRMAN. Senator Hollings.

Senator HOLLINGS. Welcome. I am glad to see you working, in addition to the hunger field, the hunger of the body, and the hunger of the mind, John. I am delighted to work with you on this.

There are some differences. For one thing, as an old trial lawyer, we know well that Clarence Darrow made a 9-hour summation in the *Scopes* trial. A trial lawyer today is competing with television and television performers. If he makes more than a 9-minute summation, he has lost the jury, his case, and everything else. The parent is in competition with that 6 hours of rock coming over radio and TV.

Now, it is pleasant to talk about parents and their duties and responsibilities, but they are in one heck of a competition out there. We do know that perhaps with television in many, many instances, parents are trying to do their best—in the *Hinckley* case and what have you—they tried and tried, but did not realize. You say that the parents have a greater influence. Not necessarily so.

An additional point we have to keep in mind is the proposition of the limited use of protected speech in the broadcast media. You mentioned just coming back from the radio and TV broadcasters convention last week and their tendering self-rule or regulation. Will that discipline develop? It has not. The only censorship movement now is that of our recent group that has gotten any kind of offer or recognition of the problem itself.

We know, talking about free speech, that the broadcast airwaves belong to the people. We will take a radio station in my own backyard using four-letter-words. The FCC fined them. That was not unconstitutional. We do have some authorities, we do have some responsibilities there.

They are not all clean-cut John Denvers. On the contrary, I have not listened to too much. It seems like the majority is otherwise.

I think that the aura or atmosphere developing in this particular hearing is developing to make sure that we do not do nothing, or to transmit, rather, back to the original problem, pornography, suicide, all of this other stuff coming out of these records.

Now, the other gentleman said print the words. I, rather like that, since I would not have to read it. He would read it one way, obviously, and I would read it differently, and there is that human error involved.

Do you have any recommendation for the committee other than just do nothing? I mean, you have talked in beautiful terms—you are the best I have seen—on peace—and I am not speaking facetiously—the family and responsibility and the wonderful human nature. I am with you on the stars, we are both supporters of Cousteau, and I have authored in this particular committee, the oceanography programs.

Barring all of that, are you saying do nothing?

Mr. DENVER. No, sir, I am not saying do nothing. And that is exactly why I am here and why I applaud this hearing and applaud what these ladies, what the PMRC has presented to us.

Senator HOLLINGS. Well, I think we have got to be sensible about it. But like you say—particularly with at least the radio and TV, I cannot read the words coming there. I can see that difference between Mr. Zappa and myself. A person of free volition can go in and read the language and see the words there. I would not have to read it.

Then, to not have some inhibition, some kind of discipline, as you describe it, within the broadcast media, we flunk the course, because there are 6 hours of that thing steaming and beaming into the home.

Mr. DENVER. Well, you know, Senator—excuse me if I am interrupting.

Senator HOLLINGS. No, sir.

Mr. DENVER. When I was raised, television was just coming out and, golly, it was an attractive medium. And I could sit there in front of that TV set and watch it all day. My parents set some restrictions on how much time I could watch television during the week, especially when I was going to school, and I could choose the programs that I wanted to watch.

And I think this is kind of an influence that we can exercise as parents on our children. Just because it is on 7 hours does not mean our kids are going to sit there and watch it that whole time, and we can give them a certain amount of time.

And over here, for me one of the things that I am fortunate with is my children and I live in beautiful country and we have a lot of activities which really call us outdoors, call us together and away from the boob tube. I do not watch very much television.

And I think we can exercise this kind of influence on our children even in a city environment.

Senator HOLLINGS. You and I are different—I mean, you and I are the same. We do not watch much TV. I do not watch that much television, obviously.

But the record is otherwise. They are watching television as much as the instructions in the classrooms of the public schools and more. All surveys show that, so it is being watched. That is the fact, and living in the real world, where you and I would like to restrict our children and my grandchildren now, it is a real problem. It is real problem.

And I guess you know from being a master at the art that, where you start off selling that record is to get it accepted at some good programming, some good broadcasting, and then the sales follow. You cannot print those words ahead of time so I will know to cut the television off quick.

Whatever it is, unless that discipline develops, in other words, with the broadcast media, we are going to be forced, somewhere with regulations, through the FCC or otherwise I do not think the American public is going to go along just with a nice hearing up in Washington. I think there is going to have to be something more developed and some kind of discipline, as you indicate.

I am trying to find out from you, how you develop that discipline a little bit better than what has been developed?

Mr. DENVER. Well, I think that a good beginning to addressing this real problem is this hearing that is taking place. What most concerns me, aside from potential legislation which might be enacted, which we have heard today is not going to be the case, is that the whole presentation made by the PMRC comes from in my experience a foundation of fear.

The only thing we have to fear, as President Roosevelt said, is fear itself. I am not afraid of anything. I am not afraid of what my children might see. I am not afraid of anything that might be shown them or done in their presence that would lessen my influence on them or their opportunity to grow, to be fine upstanding adults, and perhaps some day serve in this very august body.

Senator HOLLINGS. Well, most respectfully, President Roosevelt never heard these records.

The CHAIRMAN. Senator Gore.

Mr. DENVER. I think the things that he heard were far worse, sir.

The CHAIRMAN. Senator Gore.

Senator GORE. Thank you very much, Mr. Chairman.

It is an honor to be able to ask some questions. I have been a fan for a long time, Mr. Denver, not only of your music but also of your contributions to efforts such as Farm Aid at the present time, world peace, and your trips to the Soviet Union and elsewhere.

Do you see the trend of increased sexual explicitness and violence in some rock music that is outlined by this presentation? Have you ever been to a Mötley Crüe concert, for example?

Mr. DENVER. No, sir.

Senator GORE. Do you agree that there does seem to be a growing trend, at least in the heavy metal area, that emphasizes explicit violence and sex and sado-masochism and the rest? You are aware of that music, are you not?

Mr. DENVER. Yes.

Senator GORE. Why do you think that has been growing in popularity?

Mr. DENVER. Again, sir, my experience, not only in this country but all over the world, is that music today is the medium which most specifically tells us what is going on in young people's minds, not what is being put into them but what reflects what they are interested in.

I think that this addresses itself to a much graver problem in fact, the source of the symptom that we are discussing here today.

Senator GORE. Well, if a 10-year-old listens to a song glorifying rape, that is not reflecting what is in that 10-year-old's mind, is it?

Mr. DENVER. I do not think so. I do not think there are many 10-year-olds who know what rape is.

Senator GORE. I am not sure I would agree with that.

If you have an explicit description of a suicide, in a song that seems to glorify and promote suicide, young people are aware of that.

Mr. DENVER. Senator Gore, excuse me for interrupting. If I could count the number of times that a mother or father has come up to me or a child has come up to me and said, if I do not get your autograph my mother is going to kill me, if I do not get your autograph my daughter is going to kill me—you know, just this is a part of our language. And there might be a slight difference, but I do not think it is as big as you point out.

In a way, this video that we watched here today I think is probably a fantasy that every kid has about his father at some point in time. It may not be exactly those particular graphics. It may be out on the farm and being able to take your dad out and put a board to his fanny. But this goes on. This is a part of growing up.

And our society has gotten increasingly complex. There are many more images to reach from. They all have an impact on the child's mind.

And I am saying that the small percentage of records that we are discussing here today compared to the 125,000 songs that are released every year is miniscule and it is not going to affect our children to a degree that we need to be fearful of.

We need to be conscious of it. We need to concern ourselves and we need to communicate with our children and have them feel comfortable with communicating with us.

Senator GORE. Let me come back to the question about suicide. Let us say you have a popular rock star who has a lot of fans, who sings a song that says suicide is the solution, and appears in fan magazines with a gun barrel pointed in his mouth and promotes material that seems to glorify suicide.

The United States has one of the highest rates of teen suicide of any country in the world. The rate has gone up 300 percent in the last decade among young people, while it has remained constant among adults.

Do you think it is a responsible act for a record company to put out a song glorifying suicide and for the artist to promote the album by putting a gun in his mouth in a simulation of suicide?

MR. DENVER. I would not like to be the one to tell a record company or an artist what to do. I certainly think the picture you have described is deplorable, and if I found that in my home I would talk to my kids about it and get rid of it.

The CHAIRMAN. Could I interrupt? It is my understanding that you have to leave. Is that correct?

Mr. DENVER. Senator, I appreciate that. Yes, I have an appointment with NASA at noon and if it is possible I would like to go to that. But I also really appreciate being able to discuss this with you all and I am happy to stay.

The CHAIRMAN. Let me ask, are there any more questions?

Senator GORE. Mr. Chairman, I will stop my questions at this time and wish Mr. Denver good luck in getting on the Space Shuttle.

Mr. DENVER. Thanks very much. I appreciate that.

The CHAIRMAN. Senator Exon has a question and I think Senator Pressler has.

Senator EXON. Mr. Denver, thank you very much for being here. I appreciated your testimony. I do not know you, but, although it may lead to the beginning of the end of your career, I like your music.

Senator EXON. In fact, I think I know you. I think a friend of yours, Rainbow Terrain, has talked about you. She is an art instructor and a friend of my wife's, and I kind of think I know you through her.

Just one basic question. Please clarify for us, what is your opinion to the key question that has been asked time and time again here, and you have alluded to it: Are you for the printing of material on records? Are you for or against, or are you for or against any kind of a rating as long as it is done voluntarily between the records companies and the producers?

That is my key question. And I would simply say one more time, which I have said every time I have had this microphone this morning, I think it is wrong to imply that, although no bills have been introduced, that bills might not be introduced. And I want to hold that threat, for what it is worth, over the head of trying to accomplish some free enterprise volunteerism that most people have agreed to.

What do you think about a free enterprise volunteerism, getting together and either printing or coming up with a rating program of some kind that would be properly displayed in the records?

Mr. DENVER. I am opposed. As an artist, I am opposed to any kind of a rating system, voluntarily or otherwise. I think putting lyrics on the sleeve of an album or a jacket of an album is no problem for me.

Again, I think it goes beyond reading the words, and I bring up again the song "Rocky Mountain High." You know, some people, high is high, and high is getting stoned and high is a feeling of elation, celebration of life.

As I told the people in the Soviet Union when I had the privilege of singing for them there, I sang "Rocky Mountain High" and then I described what "high" meant to me. And I said to them, that is how I feel having the privilege of singing for you.

That is how I feel having the opportunity to participate in my Government here today.

Senator EXON. Thank you, Mr. Denver.

Thank you, Mr. Chairman.

The CHAIRMAN. Senator Pressler.

Senator PRESSLER. I guess that ties in with my question. Your basic line is that you are against any type of Government action in this area, or indeed any voluntary labeling?

Mr. DENVER. I would be, yes.

Senator PRESSLER. Thank you very much.

The CHAIRMAN. John; thank you very much. Thank you for your patience, for waiting so long.

Mr. DENVER. Thank you, Senator. It is a great privilege to be with you all.

The CHAIRMAN. Thank you.

Next we have Mr. Dee Snider of Twisted Sister, Freefall Talent Group.

Mr. Snider, thank you for being here.

STATEMENT OF DEE SNIDER, OF TWISTED SISTER

Mr. SNIDER. Thank you for having me here.

I do not know if it is morning or afternoon. I will say both. Good morning and good afternoon.

My name is Dee Snider. That is S-n-i-d-e-r. I have been asked to come here to present my views on "the subject of the content of certain sound recordings and suggestions that recording packages be labeled to provide a warning to prospective purchasers of sexually explicit or other potentially offensive content."

Before I get into that, I would like to tell the committee a little bit about myself. I am 30 years old, I am married, I have a 3-year-old son. I was born and raised a Christian and I still adhere to those principles. Believe it or not, I do not smoke, I do not drink, and I do not do drugs.

I do play in and write the songs for a rock and roll band named Twisted Sister that is classified as heavy metal, and I pride myself on writing songs that are consistent with my above-mentioned beliefs.

There are many facets to this complex issue and time does not permit me to address all of them. However, my feelings are expressed for the most part by the August 5, 1985, letter to the Parents Music Resource Center from Mr. Stanley Gortikov, president of the Recording Industry Association of America.

This letter was a formal response to the PMRC petition of the RIAA. The only part of this document I do not support is Mr. Gortikov's unnecessary and unfortunate decision to agree to a so-called generic label on some selected records. In my opinion this should be retracted.

Since I seem to be the only person addressing this committee today who has been a direct target of accusations from the presumably responsible PMRC, I would like to use this occasion to speak on a more personal note and show just how unfair the whole concept of lyrical interpretation and judgment can be and how many times this can amount to little more than character assassination.

I have taken the liberty of distributing to you material and lyrics pertaining to these accusations. There were three attacks in particular which I would like to address.

Accusation No. 1. This attack was contained in an article written by Tipper Gore, which was given the forum of a full page in my hometown newspaper on Long Island. In this article Ms. Gore claimed that one of my songs, "Under the Blade," had lyrics encouraging sadomasochism, bondage, and rape.

The lyrics she quoted have absolutely nothing to do with these topics. On the contrary, the words in question are about surgery and the fear that it instills in people. Furthermore, the reader of this article is led to believe that the three lines she quotes go together in the song when, as you can see from reading the lyrics, the first two lines she cites are an edited phrase from the second verse and the third line is a misquote of a line from the chorus.

That the writer could misquote me is curious, since we make it a point to print all our lyrics on the inner sleeve of every album. As the creator of "Under the Blade," I can say categorically that the only sadomasochism, bondage, and rape in this song is in the mind of Ms. Gore.

Accusation No. 2. The PMRC has made public a list of 15 of what they feel are some of the most blatant songs lyrically. On this list is our song "We're Not Gonna Take It," upon which has been bestowed a "V" rating, indicating violent lyrical content.

You will note from the lyrics before you that there is absolutely no violence of any type either sung about or implied anywhere in the song. Now, it strikes me that the PMRC may have confused our video presentation for this song with the song with the lyrics, with the meaning of the lyrics.

It is no secret that the videos often depict story lines completely unrelated to the lyrics of the song they accompany. The video "Were Not Gonna Take It" was simply meant to be a cartoon with human actors playing variations on the Roadrunner/Wile E. Coyote theme. Each stunt was selected from my extensive personal collection of cartoons.

You will note when you watch the entire video that after each catastrophe our villain suffers through, in the next sequence he reappears unharmed by any previous attack, no worse for the wear.

By the way, I am very pleased to note that the United Way of America has been granted a request to use portions of our "We're Not Gonna Take It" video in a program they are producing on the subject of the changing American family. They asked for it because of its "light-hearted way of talking about communicating with teenagers."

It is gratifying that an organization as respected as the United Way of America appreciates where we are coming from. I have included a copy of the United Way's request as part of my written testimony. Thank you, United Way.

Accusation No. 3. Last Tuesday a public forum regarding the lyric controversy was held in New York. Among the panelists was Ms. Gore. Trying to stem the virtual tidal wave of antiratings sentiment coming from the audience, Ms. Gore made the following statement:

I agree this is a small percentage of all music, thank goodness. But it is becoming more mainstream. You look at even the t-shirts that kids wear and you see Twisted Sister and a woman in handcuffs sort of spread-eagled.

This is an outright lie. Not only have we never sold a shirt of this type; we have always taken great pains to steer clear of sexism in our merchandise, records, stage show, and personal lives. Furthermore, we have always promoted the belief that rock and roll should not be sexist, but should cater to males and females equally.

I feel that an accusation of this type is irresponsible, damaging to our reputation, and slanderous. I defy Ms. Gore to produce such a shirt to back up her claim. I am tired of running into kids on the street who tell me that they cannot play our records any more because of the misinformation their parents are being fed by the PMRC on TV and in the newspapers.

These are the only three accusations I have come across. All three are totally unfounded. Who knows what other false and irresponsible things may have been said about me or my band.

There happens to be one area where I am in complete agreement with the PMRC, as well as the National PTA and probably most of the parents on this committee. That is, it is my job as a parent to monitor what my children see, hear, and read during their preteen years. The full responsibility for this falls on the shoulders of my wife and I, because there is no one else capable of making these judgments for us.

Parents can thank the PMRC for reminding them that there is no substitute for parental guidance. But that is where the PMRC's job ends.

The beauty of literature, poetry, and music is that they leave room for the audience to put its own imagination, experiences, and dreams into the words. The examples I cited earlier showed clear evidence of Twisted Sister's music being completely misinterpreted and unfairly judged by supposedly well-informed adults.

We cannot allow this to continue. There is no authority who has the right or the necessary insight to make these judgments, not myself, not the Federal Government, not some recording industry committee, not the PTA, not the RIAA, and certainly not the PMRC.

I would like to thank the committee for this time, and I hope my testimony will aid you in clearing up this issue.

The CHAIRMAN. Thank you, Mr. Snider.

Mr. Snider, let us suppose that there is music which, say, glorifies incest; not yours, but suppose that there is some music that glorifies incest. Do you think parents should know about it, or do you think that it is just a matter between whoever is selling the record and whoever is buying it?

Mr. SNIDER. As I said in my testimony, I think it is very important that parents be aware that these lyrics exist.

The CHAIRMAN. How could they find out about it?

Mr. SNIDER. Well, quite simply, as a parent myself and as a rock fan, I know that when I see an album cover with a severed goat's head in the middle of a pentagram between a woman's legs, that is not the kind of album I want my son to be listening to.

If I read a title on the back of, say, Somebody's Ice Cream Castle, a title called "If the Kid Can't Make You Come," whatever it is, I realized that is a sexually explicit song. By just looking at the cover, looking at the lyrics, looking at, I should say, the titles, that should cover just about all bases.

The few albums that do not express their intentions on the cover or in the song titles. I think a parent could take it home, listen to it. And I do not think there are too many retail stores that would deny them the ability to return the album for something different.

The CHAIRMAN. Do you think that most parents, or even kids for that matter, know everything that is on an album when they buy it, when the child buys the album?

Mr. SNIDER. I do not know half the things that are on half the albums I own. Some of the bands I listen to, I listen for musical reasons. Other bands I listen to for lyrical reasons.

I know that AC/DC, one of my favorite bands, sings a lot of songs glorifying hell and damnation. I am a Christian. I do not believe—I do not want to go to hell and I do not want to be damned for all time. But I do like the feel of the songs. The lyrics have no effect on me.

Other bands who have more to say, I listen to their words and I learn from their words.

The CHAIRMAN. Do you think that now there is adequate basis for parents to know what is on the records that their kids are buying?

Mr. SNIDER. I think if they really are concerned, there is. But quite honestly, I do not think that the majority of parents are in reality as concerned as the PMRC or myself. I do not think they really want to spend the time to listen to what they might consider to be a bunch of noise. They put it on and they cannot understand a thing that is being said anyway.

And so I think most of them do not spend enough time with it.

The CHAIRMAN. Senator Hollings.

Senator HOLLINGS. Yes. Mr. Snider, I think I would just take the opportunity to make an observation. You and I would differ as to what is obscene or what is shocking or what is vulgar, and persons of goodwill will differ on that particular score.

I think that somewhere in this hearing record, we should not be on the defensive and we should not create the atmos-

phere that we are powerless. The absolute nature of your statement that we do not have any authority—I only want to refer everyone to the Pacifica Foundation case, where the Federal Communications Commission was questioned as to its power to regulate public radio and TV broadcasts that was indecent but not obscene.

You see, they differed between what was indecent, what was obscene, and what was shocking. They had the seven dirty words. I think everyone remembers that case on the west coast, and the Supreme Court of the United States found that the FCC positively had the authority, and the responsibility.

I am quoting from the language of the Supreme Court:

Patently offensive, indecent material presented over the airwaves confronts the citizen not only in public, but also in the privacy of the home. The individual's right to be left alone, plainly outweighs the first amendment rights of an intruder.

This is not just a forum to rally one way or the other and hope something happens. This is a forum with a definite responsibility with respect to Congress in enunciating the duties of the Federal Communications Commission, which have been constitutionally followed.

I understand your opinion. That is why we invited you up here, to hear your words and not mine. I think that the general nature of all of this testimony of noting censorship, and first amendment absolutism, does not pertain with respect to the broadcast media. That is, of course, the main media that I guess you would agree to actually sell the records, would it not be?

Mr. SNIDER. Yes. Except I would like to clarify something. I said no authority has the right or necessary insight. I did not say you were not able to. I said you do not have the right or I do not have the right or the RIAA.

Also, we are talking about the airwaves as opposed to a person going with their money to purchase an album to play in their room, in their home, on their own time. The airwaves are something different.

I think that the FCC and even MTV have done a fair job in keeping profanity and obscenity and things like that off the public airwaves. But as far as what you listen to in your own home, that is something totally different, I feel in my opinion.

Senator HOLLINGS. I think that the record ought to be elaborated to show just that.

Previously, about 5 or 6 years ago, we had the TV networks before this committee, and pursuant to that particular hearing they then came back. I remember CBS specifically. They demonstrated how they had this film, and then got together with the producer and removed certain scenes of violence and certain four-letter words, and did not offend the producer's sense of art in the production itself.

We have made some progress. The bottom line with respect to these particular records, the Supreme Court has found, is that there is that right and that responsibility.

Thank you, Mr. Chairman.

The CHAIRMAN. Senator Gore.

Senator GORE. Thank you very much, Mr. Chairman.

Mr. SNIDER. Excuse me. Are you going to tell me you are a big fan of my music as well?

Senator GORE. No, I am not a fan of your music. I am aware that Frank Zappa and John Denver cover quite a spectrum, and I do enjoy them both. I am not, however, a fan of Twisted Sister and I will readily say that.

Mr. Snider, what is the name of your fan club?

Mr. SNIDER. The fan club is called the SMF Fans of Twisted Sister.

Senator GORE. And what does "SMF" stand for when it is spelled out?

Mr. SNIDER. It stands for the Sick Mother Fucking Fans of Twisted Sister.

Senator GORE. Is this also a Christian group?

Mr. SNIDER. I do not believe profanity has anything to do with Christianity, thank you.

Senator GORE. It is just an interesting choice. I was getting the impression from your presentation that you were a very wholesome kind of performer, and that is an interesting title for your fan club.

You say your song "Under the Blade" is about surgery. Have you ever had surgery with your hands tied and your legs strapped?

Mr. SNIDER. The song was written about my guitar player, Eddie Ojeda. He was having polyps removed from his throat and he was very fearful of this operation. And I said: Eddie, while you are in the hospital I am going to write a song for you.

I said it was about the fear of operations. I think people imagine being helpless on a table, the bright light in their face, the blade coming down on them, and being totally afraid that they may wake up who knows, dead, handicapped. There is a certain fear of hospitals. That is what, in my imagination, what I see the hospitals like.

Senator GORE. Is there a reference to the hospital in the song?

Mr. SNIDER. No, there is not. But there is not a reference to a woman, sado-masochism, or—well, bondage, yes.

Senator GORE. There is just a reference to someone whose hands are tied down and whose legs are strapped down, and he is going under the blade to be cut.

Mr. SNIDER. Yes, there is.

Senator GORE. So it is not really a wild leap of the imagination to jump to the conclusion that the song is about something other than surgery or hospitals, neither of which are mentioned in the song?

Mr. SNIDER. No, it is not a wild jump. And I think what I said at one part was that songs allow a person to put their own imaginations, experiences, and dreams into the lyrics. People can interpret it in many ways.

Ms. Gore was looking for sado-masochism and bondage and she found it. Someone looking for surgical references would have found that as well.

Senator GORE. Why do you think there is so much sado-masochism and bondage in some of these new songs?

Mr. SNIDER. I cannot speak for the other artists. I am really only here to defend myself, and hopefully by speaking for myself as one person, songwriter in a band that I feel has been unjustly dumped on, that will just warn us of the dangers of what we are trying to do here. I really cannot speak for the other bands.

Senator GORE. Now, you made reference to a comment about T-shirts. I would simply note for the record that the word "T-shirts" was in plural, and one of them referred to Twisted Sister and the other referred to a woman in handcuffs. And it was not intended, as I understand it, to say that you appear with a woman in handcuffs.

There are a lot of different T-shirts and advertisements around today. I have noticed from some of the fan magazines particularly featuring heavy metal music that little sado-masochistic outfits are advertised, with the fingerless gloves

and spikes and studs on them, and that these little S&M outfits are marketed to teens and preteens. Is that correct?

Mr. SNIDER. Well, they are marketed. Who buys them I am not sure.

I would just like to say, in reference to the comment about T-shirts, I have with me a taped cassette of the exact——

Senator GORE. No, I am reading from your transcript of it in your statement.

Mr. SNIDER. I will have to check the transcript, but when it was said there was no question she was referring to a Twisted Sister T-shirt. There was no question If I played the tape for anybody.

Senator GORE. Well, in your own transcripts it is in plural, "T-shirts," and two examples are cited. But I do not want to belabor that point.

Now, you said that you can look at the titles of albums and look at the covers and tell what kind of material is inside. Does the title "Purple Rain" give you an indication that the material is about masturbation?

Mr. SNIDER. You mean the album title, "Purple Rain"? No, it does not. I did not say in all cases. I believe I covered that there are occasional albums that are a bit misleading. I said I do not think a store would refuse a parent who came in and said, "I do not like what is on this record. I would like my money back."

Senator GORE. So the choice the parent has, then, is to sit down and listen to every song on the album; right?

Mr. SNIDER. Or read the lyrics if they are on the record.

Senator GORE. I think that is pretty general agreement that if the lyrics are printed that is one possible solution for this.

Let us suppose the lyrics are not printed. Then what choice does a parent have? To sit down and listen to every song on the album?

Mr. SNIDER. Well, if they are really concerned about it I think that they have to.

Senator GORE. Do you think it is reasonable to expect parents to do that?

Mr. SNIDER. Being a parent is not a reasonable thing. It is a very hard thing. I am a parent and I know. OK. I am a new parent. I only have one child, maybe. But I am learning that there is a lot to being a parent that you did not expect. It is not just always a cute baby. There is a lot of labor, a lot of time, and a lot of effort that goes into it. It is not totally pleasurable.

Senator GORE. And you will find when they get a little bit older that when they are exposed to the kinds of themes that we were presented with earlier, if you love your child you are going to be concerned about that. And if you want to protect that child from unnecessary exposure to inappropriate material, you sometimes need a little help, the kind of guidance that is presented in the movie industry.

It is totally unreasonable in my view to expect parents to sit down and listen to every single song in the albums that their children buy in order to fulfill their responsibilities as parents.

Now, the only thing in your statement that I felt at all comfortable about was when you said you shared some of the concerns of the PMRC. I would simply conclude by expressing the hope that artists and the record companies will find a way to manifest that mutual concern in some self-restraint, and show a responsibility and give parents a break.

You are right: It is tough being a parent. It is even tougher being a kid. And if both are going to be able to deal with the kind of material that is coming out in popular music, it seems to me the industry has a responsibility to give them a little help.

Thank you, Mr. Chairman.

The CHAIRMAN. Senator Rockefeller.

Senator ROCKEFELLER. Mr. Snider, do you feel that you have a responsibility as an artist to those who would hear those words that you write?

Mr. SNIDER. I feel a tremendous responsibility. And as I said, I do not put anything down on a record that I cannot stand behind 100 percent. I do not sing about drugs, sex, alcohol. I do not advocate sexism, the use of drugs and drinking, and so I do not write about those things. I only write about things I believe in.

Senator ROCKEFELLER. And that is the way you define what your responsibility is—that is, not to write about things that you do not believe in?

Mr. SNIDER. Yes; I would say to write about things that you can stand behind. I feel myself to be a moral person and I think that I have a lot of positive things to tell people about. And like I said, everything on my records I will stand behind and say, "Yes, I wrote those words and this is what it meant and this is what I was trying to say—Yes."

Senator ROCKEFELLER. Do you think that parents, not only those who are in PMRC but other parents who are concerned here and across the country about the development of new trends in music and the lyrics that go along with that music, are naive or somehow missing the point?

Do you think that they are unduly worried about some of these writings about sado-masochism, suicide, rape, and other things? Do you think that this is not really a serious problem for this country and our young people?

Mr. SNIDER. That is sort of a multiple question. I do not think they are naive and I do not think that at times they are unduly worried. But I do think sometimes they take it overly serious.

I mean, there are monster movies on all the time, they have been going on for ages, and people watch a monster movie and they get scared, and they walk away and it was just a movie. Rock and roll many times is the same thing, to try to get an effect of either laughter, sadness. A lot of the heavy metal bands are trying to scare people and just make them scared like a horror movie.

Vincent Price is not having problems because he has done all of these monster pictures. He is just an actor. I am not going to say I am just an actor, but I am entertaining people and a lot of these bands are entertaining people.

And when they were reading some of these lyrics before, I could not help but laugh. I mean, I had not heard some of them, but some of the lyrics were ridiculously ridiculous. I mean, a kid, even a kid reading that I think would go, oh my God, what is going on? It is ridiculous is the only word I can think of, some of the lyrics.

Senator ROCKEFELLER. In the vehemence with which you attacked Senator Gore's wife, I detected a defensiveness somehow on your part, a lack of assuredness on where you stand on this. Why did you feel it necessary to attribute some of the qualities to her that you did? Why was that important to your testimony?

Mr. SNIDER. First of all, I was not attacking Senator Gore's wife. I was attacking a member of the PMRC.

Senator ROCKEFELLER. You were attacking Senator Gore's wife by name.

Mr. SNIDER. Her name is Tipper Gore, is it not? I did not say the Senator's wife. I said Tipper Gore.

Second, defensive. I have been working very hard. I believe in the music that I play. I believe we have a very bad reputation and I have been doing a lot on my part to try and say, hey, this is not a bad thing, this is fun, this is fantasy.

Kids are coming out, they are screaming, they are yelling, they are letting out their emotions, and they are going home, they are feeling better because they let out a lot of their frustrations.

As I said, I pride myself on writing lyrics that are not offensive and that are saying something positive. Most of our songs are about personal freedom. And when somebody tells me, after all I have done to fight against sexism, that I have a shirt with a spread-eagled woman——

Senator ROCKEFELLER. All you have done to what?

Mr. SNIDER. All I have done to fight sexism. The whole Twisted Sister thing is very ambiguous: guys wearing make-up. We do not act like women; we act like men. We do not cater to the males or females in the audience. It is just one audience.

So when someone says there is a song about sado-masochism and bondage, or someone says "We're Not Gonna Take It" is violent lyrical content, which is what it has been rated for, yes, I am defensive. Yes, that gets me angry. I am trying to get adults to see that heavy metal is not totally a bad thing.

Senator ROCKEFELLER. How many months in the course of a year do you spend on the road away from home?

MR. SNIDER. In the course of a year, it would be tough to say. Over a 2-year period, I would spend about 11 months on the road and 13 months at home recording albums, things like that, doing videos.

Senator ROCKEFELLER. Eleven months on the road in a 2-year period?

Mr. SNIDER. Yes, because you do a tour and then you go and record albums. I have been off the road now for 10 months.

Senator ROCKEFELLER. Do you take your child with you?

Mr. SNIDER. He comes sometimes.

Senator ROCKEFELLER. Nine years from now when your child is 12 and in school, will you take your child with you?

Mr. SNIDER. Absolutely.

Senator ROCKEFELLER. When your child is in school?

Mr. SNIDER. Oh, no. Thank you for clarifying. No, I would not take him out of school.

Senator ROCKEFELLER. Then how would it be possible for you to, as a responsible parent, to spend the time that you suggest listening to these records and finding out what it is that you want your son to listen to and what you do not want him to listen to?

Mr. SNIDER. To be perfectly honest, 9 years from now I am going to be well retired and I will be spending more time with my son than any other parent probably ever spends. And that is one of the beautiful things about rock and roll, is that I can retire hopefully at a very early age.

But even now, I am very lucky that I have a wife who I have been going with for 10 years now, we have been married for 4, who is the most incredible mother. And while I am gone, she fills the role, and has a very difficult job, too, of mother and father.

Senator ROCKEFELLER. Do you expect later on, then, that she will be going through these records?

Mr. SNIDER. I think both of us will be doing that.

Senator ROCKEFELLER. Do you expect me to believe that?

Mr. SNIDER. You can. I am terminally teenage. I will be listening to my son's records.

Senator ROCKEFELLER. What about families where both parents have to work, which is an increasing phenomenon in this country now, because they have to survive? And the whole notion of parents sitting down and listening to record after record, tape after tape—that is what you suggested—does that not strike you as just a little bit naive and unrealistic?

Mr. SNIDER. No, it does not, because I know the reality of the record-buying market as a record buyer. With my allowance, I was able to, if I was lucky, afford maybe one album a week at the most. Usually it was one a month. Albums cost anywhere from $6 to $10, and that is a lot of money to a teenager, or to a pre-teenager it is a ridiculous sum.

And to a teenage kid that is a considerable amount of money. And so to listen to one record a week, I do not consider that a hardship.

Senator ROCKEFELLER. Might I ask just one final question, Mr. Chairman?

The CHAIRMAN. Bearing in mind that it is 12:30 and we have a lot of witnesses left, yes.

Senator ROCKEFELLER. I will bear that in mind and will not ask the question.

The CHAIRMAN. Senator Pressler.

Senator PRESSLER. Basically, I want to get down to your recommendations in terms of governmental action, either by this committee or by any Government body. You would recommend no governmental action in this area?

Mr. SNIDER. Absolutely.

Senator PRESSLER. What about industry actions? Would you recommend any type of voluntary labeling?

Mr. SNIDER. I do not feel that the industry—it has been expressed by many other people that each artist has an individual agreement. One of the big things is artistic freedom in your contract. I do not think the industry can pass a ruling on that.

Senator PRESSLER. And so your legislative recommendations, would that apply just to—not to broadcast? You would put broadcast and things that are over the airwaves in a different category than things people buy and show in their homes?

Mr. SNIDER. Well, I think we are talking about the purchase of albums and the lyrical content on the albums. That is what I am directing it to at this time.

Senator PRESSLER. So you would disagree with any action on those albums, be they by private industry or Government, any type of labeling?

Mr. SNIDER. If somebody would ask me what my opinion was, I had said earlier that I did not think there would be a problem for a parent to return an album they had taken home and and found it dissatisfactory. I would like to believe that, but some retail stores will give you a hassle if you try to return an open album.

If you want a solution, maybe they could bring back—in the fifties, you could listen to an album in the store before you purchased the album. Most record stores play the albums in the store, and there is usually a stack of those albums opened already that, if you want to go over and take a glance at the cover, which I have done many times myself, you could go over and do that.

So if you want to take some sort of industry action, I would think it would be to force the retail stores to allow people to return product that they are not satisfied with: satisfaction guaranteed.

Senator PRESSLER. Thank you very much.

The CHAIRMAN. Mr. Snider, thank you very much.

Mr. SNIDER. Thank you for your time.

[The material referred to follows:]

The CHAIRMAN. The next witness is Mrs. Millie Waterman, the National PTA vice president for legislative activity.

Ms. Waterman, thank you very much for being here.

Please proceed.

STATEMENT OF MILLIE WATERMAN, NATIONAL PTA VICE PRESIDENT FOR LEGISLATIVE ACTIVITY, MENTOR, OH, ACCOMPANIED BY ARNOLD FEGE, DIRECTOR, GOVERNMENTAL RELATIONS

Mrs. WATERMAN. Thank you, Senator.

I have accompanying me Mr. Arnold Fege, director of governmental relations for the National PTA. I ask that he sit up here with me.

Mr. Chairman, members of the Subcommittee on Communications, I thank you for this opportunity to address the issue of record and cassette lyric labeling. I am Millie Waterman, vice president for legislative activity for the National PTA, the Nation's largest volunteer child advocacy association comprising 5.6 million members in over 25,000 local units in 50 State congresses, the District of Columbia and Europe. The National PTA is a nonprofit organization interested in the protection of health, education, and welfare of children and youth.

Throughout the history of recorded music there have been complaints about the contents of some songs. The outcry over music lyrics began to rise with the introduction of rock and roll more than 30 years ago.

Senator GORE. Mr. Chairman, I am having trouble hearing the witness.

The CHAIRMAN. If you would withhold, Ms. Waterman, I want to apologize for the noise. If the officer could keep the door closed, I would very much appreciate it.

Please continue.

Mrs. WATERMAN. Thank you, Mr. Chairman.

Throughout the history of recorded music, there have been complaints about the contents of some songs. The outcry over music lyrics began to rise with the introduction of rock and roll. While parents and others interested in the well being of children have continued to voice their concern, the recording industry took no action to address this current concern until August of 1985.

Briefly, the problem is that there are many songs which include lyrics that may not be appropriate for young children or that send messages that may be dangerous to individuals or society. Some examples of songs that might be inappropriate for children are those that contain profane language, sexual references, vulgarity or violence. Those that could be dangerous to individuals or society include songs that promote suicide, practice of the occult, rape, incest, murder or bondage, among others.

Until now, no one has suggested a reasonable solution to the problem. By reasonable, we mean a solution that would not involve any form of censorship but would protect consumers from exposure to materials they feel may be harmful to themselves or children. Until 1984, no specific proposals were made or acted upon by either the public or the industry, at least none that we know of, that did not involve censorship.

In June of 1984, the National PTA's convention body, representing the 5.6 million members of the PTA, adopted a resolution which points out that an unsuspecting public may buy records, tapes and cassettes which contain explicit language, sexual references and inferences to situations not commonly recommended for all age groups. Further, it addressed the fact that there is currently no rating system in use for evaluating the content of recordings, nor any markings on jackets or covers to indicate the content. The resolution calls on the PTA to encourage recording companies to consider the explicit contents of some songs and their responsibility to an unsuspecting public. It also calls for recording companies to label record, tape and cassette covers and indicate the nature of the questionable content.

In October of 1984 the president of the National PTA sent a letter to 30 record companies and the Recording Industry Association of America explaining the resolution and suggesting that the industry convene a panel of consumer, industry and recording artist representatives to establish standards that all record companies could apply to determine which recordings need to bear a warning label.

Because our proposal to establish standards has been met with misunderstanding and confusion in the music industry, I would like to clarify it for this committee. We are not suggesting that the panel review every new song and rate it accordingly. We are suggesting that the panel produce written guidelines that each record company can follow to evaluate its own products.

The need for such standards was made clear in a response sent to the National PTA by the Recording Industry president, Stanley Gortikov on November 16, 1984, which said, "There are wide variations, company to company, within our industry in respect to artists, contractual relationships, marketing considerations and product services." With such different practices among companies, different standards might be applied to labeling records which would only confuse the consumers and therefore provide minimal benefit.

In May of 1985 the president of the National PTA invited the presidents or representatives of 62 record companies and the Recording Industry to meet with PTA representatives at a luncheon in New York City which was scheduled for May 30. Only seven companies replied, and all declined to attend. However, three companies did offer to meet with the PTA privately to discuss the issues involved. Due to scheduling conflicts, those meetings have not yet been arranged.

In August of 1985 the Recording Industry announced that it had received agreement from 19 record companies to label recordings they deemed appropriate with a warning of some kind. The suggested wording offered was "Parental Guidance: Explicit Lyrics."

We view this as a very positive step by the music industry. It demonstrates that the industry finally recognizes there is a serious problem that affects millions of music consumers and that this problem must be addressed.

Our concern is that the industry's proposal does not define what explicit lyrics are. What is explicit to one company may be acceptable to another. In addition, it does not address the use of dangerous lyrical themes, such as the promotion of drug and alcohol use or the committing of crimes.

While a "Parental Guidance" warning would provide some relief, it does not adequately solve the entire problem, which is that music consumers have no way of knowing exactly what they are getting until they take a recording home and play it.

Together with the Parents' Music Resource Center, the National PTA is proposing that the entire music industry agree upon an appropriate symbol that would be used to designate recordings containing explicit sexual language, violence, profanity, the occult and glorification of drugs and alcohol. We are suggesting that the letter "R" be used because it is familiar to consumers as a warning that material may be inappropriate for young people or sensitive adults as part of the movie rating system. "R" would not suggest restriction. It would be used only as an alert to consumers.

Such a label would need to be either adhered to or printed on the actual recording cover, not the cellophane wrapper. For this system to work as a means for parents to monitor the music their children are bringing into their homes, they need to see the warning, which could be removed along with a cellophane wrapping.

In addition, we recommend that the lyrics on all music recordings labeled "R" be provided in some way outside the packaging. If the lyrics could not be printed on the outside of music packages, then it might be made available in some other form at record stores for consumer review. Providing lyrics will let each individual determine for himself, or herself whether an "R" recording would be appropriate for personal use. We believe that the music industry should determine the best means for providing lyrics to consumers.

In conclusion, I would like to make it clear to this committee that the National PTA would in no way encourage nor support censorship of the music industry.

Second, we are asking that the use of a warning labeling system be a voluntary one undertaken by the music industry as part of its responsibility to its customers.

And, finally, the National PTA believes it is the responsibility of parents to control the types of musical materials their children listen to in their homes. Without a warning system, parents have no way to know what they are buying for their children or what their children are buying, unless then listen to every single recording.

We hope to continue our dialog with the industry as a whole, and individual record companies, until an agreement is reached that will satisfy all parties involved.

I thank this committee for the opportunity to testify.

The CHAIRMAN. You do not believe that under the present state of affairs sufficient information is available to parents to allow them to participate in the decision as to what is in their homes?

Mrs. WATERMAN. No, sir, there is nothing that as you buy a record or tape or cassette in most records that allows you to know what is in that, and we believe that there should be a label so that they know what they purchase.

The CHAIRMAN. Do you think it is realistic to expect parents to actually sit down and play the rock music that is going into the home?

Mrs. WATERMAN. Do I believe they should play every record?

The CHAIRMAN. Do you think it is realistic to expect that they will?

Mrs. WATERMAN. I think that when they themselves buy it, if they know what it is——

The CHAIRMAN. If a child brings a record into the home, do you think that as a practical matter the parents are going to be sitting down and listening to the record?

Mrs. WATERMAN. I think that parents to be good parents. Right now they are blindfolded, Mr. Chairman, by when they purchase a record or a tape or a cassette they do not know what is in it, and I say take the blindfold off of those parents and let them know what they buy, and then it is their responsibility of what they play in that home.

The CHAIRMAN. Senator Hollings.

Senator HOLLINGS. I thank Ms. Waterman, Mr. Chairman, and yield my time.

The CHAIRMAN. Senator Gore.

Senator GORE. Thank you, Mr. Chairman.

I would like to note for the record that the National PTA was the first organization to make this issue a major concern. In October of 1984 you passed a resolution at your national convention requesting assistance from the record industry. Is that correct?

Mrs. WATERMAN. That is correct, Senator.

Senator GORE. As a result of that resolution, you then contacted the major record companies asking for a response to your request that they voluntarily put ratings on albums, is that right?

Mrs. WATERMAN. That is correct.

Senator GORE. How many of the major record companies responded to that letter from the National PTA?

Mrs. WATERMAN. I think I told you in my testimony, seven. Very few of them. And the meetings, of course, never came off. Seven companies replied, sir.

Senator GORE. Seven companies?

Mrs. WATERMAN. Yes.

Senator GORE. Did any of them respond favorably?

Mrs. WATERMAN. No.

Senator GORE. None of them did?

Mrs. WATERMAN. No.

Senator GORE. You asked for a meeting with the record companies, is that right?

Mrs. WATERMAN. That is right.

Senator GORE. But that meeting has not yet occurred, is that right?

Mrs. WATERMAN. That meeting has never taken place, sir.

Senator GORE. Did you get the feeling that you were being stonewalled by the industry, or that they were resisting any effort to engage in a dialog with you?

Mrs. WATERMAN. You would have that feeling. However, 19 companies have agreed that there would be some kind of labeling. "Parental Guidance: Explicit Lyrics." So there is a movement of concern certainly if those 19 have agreed.

Senator GORE. Do you share the concern of the PMRC that if these record companies are going to voluntarily label albums and cassettes, the set of criteria governing when a label is appropriate and when it is not, should be industry-wide and not just according to the different criteria of each individual company?

Mrs. WATERMAN. Senator Gore, we feel that a panel of the music industry should sit down and do the guidelines and standards so that all of them are the same. Otherwise it would not—one company would be one way, one would be the other. It needs to be uniform.

Senator GORE. Now, although there are some differences between the remedies you have suggested and those suggested by the PMRC, if I am correct, the two organizations have met and worked out a common approach that meets the concerns of both groups, is that correct?

Mrs. WATERMAN. The president of the National PTA has had a meeting with the PMRC, and we agree on three things. I felt that the agreement was on the need for labeling, the need for lyrics to be placed so that a parent or a buyer could see what they were, and also the panel needed to be convened of the music industry, that it be voluntarily done.

Senator GORE. Well, I congratulate you for the leadership offered by the PTA in this matter. I hope you will keep it up, and will carry this message to your local chapters throughout the country.

Thank you very much for appearing.

Mrs. WATERMAN. Thank you, Senator Gore.

Senator GORE. Thank you, Mr. Chairman.

The CHAIRMAN. Senator Riegle?

Senator RIEGLE. Thank you, Mr. Chairman.

We have been involved this morning in the Banking Committee, as you may know, with the nominee for the position of head of the FDIC. We have also had the Social Security issue on the Senate floor, at least prospectively, and that has occupied myself and others of us.

I would like to ask you, Mr. Chairman—on the basis of the response, I may want to pose another question to the witness. Has an argument been advanced as to why rating systems have been and seem to be effectively used in rating motion pictures and therefore cannot as readily be adapted to records?

I mean, has there been any convincing reason presented as to why it can be done apparently with some effectiveness in that area of creative material and not as readily done in the record area?

The CHAIRMAN. There has been very little discussion of the relationship between ratings of motion pictures and ratings of records. There has been some reference to it, but very little discussion.

Senator RIEGLE. I take it that the position that has been advanced by the record spokesmen that have appeared is to the effect that full disclosure, any kind of a presenting and writing of the lyrics, when we have material that would be in this area, that would be offensive to many people, that the full disclosure is somehow seen as an invasion of rights? Is that the thrust of the argument that has been advanced?

The CHAIRMAN. I am hesitant to characterize other people's arguments. Mr. Zappa took the position that the printing of lyrics would be something that would be satisfactory to him. He thought that a rating system would be arbitrary and would falsely impugn the integrity of people in the music business.

Senator RIEGLE. Well, it seems to me that that bridge has been crossed in the motion picture business, in effect. Now, the two are not exactly the same, but I think the proposition is essentially the same.

Would it be the view of the National PTA that having taken that step with respect to motion pictures and now having a system there which seems to have met with the general acceptance by both artists and moviemakers as well as the public, that that would be an example of something that would work just as readily in the record business?

Would that be your view?

Mrs. WATERMAN. I think what we are asking for, Senator, is a rating system. You know the National PTA has been on record over the years on their concern on television violence, on their concern on movies, and we did ask for a rating system in movies. We are not asking for a rating system or label on the records restricting age. What we are asking is that that label does provide the consumer who wishes to buy or chooses not to, that he knows what is within that record. So we would not be putting age on it. But the National PTA has been on record in their protection of children and youth over nearly 90 years now in their concern on media, and we have in no way ever encouraged censorship, but we have always asked that the private industry limit themselves to knowing what is good and have a responsibility to society and children.

And the National PTA in the 1984 convention took this step because they were very concerned on what their children were hearing on records and what they as a parent, when they went to buy, had no way to knowing.

Senator RIEGLE. How do you envision, or how does the National PTA envision the best way if standards are going to be established. How would you see that done?

Mrs. WATERMAN. Well, the industry is going to have to clean their own house, just to be very frank. We have asked for a voluntary panel of the music industry that they can choose their own people to set up their guidelines and their standards, and we would certainly work with them in any way that we could, and we hope that this is done.

I think there has been some concern voiced here today. I listened very intently to the artists and to the PMRC and to everyone else that has testified, and there are obviously, and on this panel also, and there has been obvious concern as to what this hearing is all about.

I think that we will come to a responsible solution to this.

Senator RIEGLE. So the PTA is not suggesting any kind of a system as to how these ratings would be done, or what they would be or what would be included or left out, but rather, that you would like to see the recording industry and the artists sit down together and develop their own methodology? Is that the idea?

You are not trying to put yourself in that standard-setting business?

Mrs. WATERMAN. Senator, I think to answer your question completely, the resolution spoke very clearly to the rating, the label that should be violence or profanity or sex or occult or drugs. The knowing what is in the package was very important to the people of that convention of which there were thousands.

Now, when you are saying adding, that we believe voluntarily, we are hoping that the music industry will set up this panel, will set up their guidelines and their standards, and that it will be pleasing to all of us who are concerned.

Senator RIEGLE. My time has expired at this point, Mr. Chairman.

The CHAIRMAN. Thank you very much, Mrs. Waterman, for your testimony and for your patience in waiting so long.

Mrs. WATERMAN. Thank you for the forum.

The CHAIRMAN. The next witness is Mr. Stanley Gortikov, president, Recording Industry Association of America.

Mr. Gortikov, thank you for your patience.

Please proceed.

STATEMENT OF STANLEY M. GORTIKOV, PRESIDENT, RECORDING INDUSTRY ASSOCIATION OF AMERICA, INC.

Mr. GORTIKOV. Thank you, Mr. Chairman and members of the committee.

Your staff has advised me that I have 10 minutes for my statement.

I am Stanley Gortikov, president of the Recording Industry Association of America, and our member companies which I represent today create and market about 85 percent of the recordings sold in the United States.

We understand, of course, that this hearing was called to respond to the expressed protests of the Parents' Music Resource Center relating to the content of rock music recordings. And to confront that challenge, of course, each record company may exercise its own discretion. However, 24 of our member companies have reached consensus to foster a fair balance between the concerns of the PMRC and those of recording companies, performers, creators, and music buyers and listeners.

Briefly summarized, the PMRC desires recording companies to be sensitive to younger children in regard to the explicit content of certain recordings and to provide the means by which parents may exercise reasonable discretion over such recordings.

In response to that basic quest of the PMRC, let me tell you what recording companies are able and willing to do, what they cannot or will not do, and why.

First what we can and will do. To begin, we respect those parental concerns. Our constructive response is this: On future releases containing explicit lyrics, recording companies individually will include a packaging inscription that will state "Parental Guidance— Explicit Lyrics." This will highlight such content for any concerned parent to exercise discretion. And that move by the recording companies directly addresses the core concern of the PMRC.

For the record companies this is a significant step which we do approach, although with trepidation. It is as far as we can and should go.

The described parental guidance inscription is not a universally popular solution. Many feel that the inscription goes too far and represents "caving in" to the PMRC. Creative people are saying so, and you heard that. So are thoughtful journalists in media responses, some of which accompany our written statement as appendixes A to D.

But there are some PMRC recommendations that we just cannot accommodate. The first relates to ratings. We will not rate the 25,000 new recorded songs we release each year as originally requested by the PMRC. We would not even know how, let alone trust annointed experts to do so. By whose standards would such ratings be determined? For what audience ages? For what religious, geographic, or societal backgrounds? For what degree of permissiveness or stricture?

Nor will we by separate ratings differentiate between violent, sexual, substance abuse, or occult content. I doubt if any really concerned parent needs to favor or deplore any one of those categories over the others. However, if the PMRC or any other organization really wants ratings, it is free to set up its own private systems, just as the Catholic Church has done for movies.

Second, in respect to lyrics, we cannot consistently imprint on the outside of recordings the lyrics of the songs within or reproduce them for broadcasters. Music publishers usually own those rights, not record companies. Further, we cannot commit 50 percent of the space available on an LP jacket to lyrics alone; and cassettes are just too small to permit lyric display.

Third, in respect to in-store, the PMRC has asked that retailers be required to place explicit recordings behind counters or in special wrappers and to keep a master set of all lyrics on hand in stores. Recording companies do not have such rights or control. Retailers run their own businesses. Many are self-service with inadequate staffs to implement such actions. They also must serve the needs of the 95 percent of their music purchasers who are not younger children.

Fourth, concerts, according to the PMRC, record companies should "reassess contracting artists who engage in violence, substance abuse, or explicit sexual behavior in concerts attended by minors, and encourage ratings for such concerts." Again, record companies are devoid of control over concert performances or artist deportment. The best control, of course, is parental supervision of the concert attendance of their children.

Fifth, radio, at PMRC urging, President Eddie Fritts of the NAB requested that record companies provide complete lyrics of all recordings supplied to radio stations. That, too, is not uniformly possible. Companies just do not consistently have the right to reproduce lyrics for such purposes. Further, the staff of those radio stations which program music already include music experts. They program and play what they choose to, mindful of their own standards, regulations, audiences, demographics, advertisers, and creative preferences.

What I have just presented, then, summarizes what recording companies can and cannot do. Nevertheless, to our planned parental guidance inscription, the PMRC has said it is not enough. PMRC instead wants an industry panel to prepare common qualifications for such an inscription. Again, what superior wisdom would any such panel possess to proclaim a national standard for our diverse populace?

The PMRC itself has not needed guidelines to identify lyrics they have exposed to you here today. No star panel can make endless laundry lists of no-no's that can handily apply to every future lyric written. Lyrics just do not come only in the convenient form of four-letter words. They deal with interpretations, imagery, allusions. And a master bank of right/wrong or good/bad characterizations is likely to become a first step toward censorship, a concept which is abhorrent and fundamentally inconsistent with creative freedom and American values.

In this hearing today you have heard some understandable protests by the PMRC. We plan to act upon these concerns seriously. However, I also must spotlight five equally important truths that are essentially ignored by the PMRC in its media pronouncements, but hopefully which will be recognized by this committee.

The first relates to unfairness. The sheer number of offensive recordings is minute compared with the total mass of recordings released by the industry. Yet the narrow targeting of the PMRC unfairly characterizes all artists and all companies as universal practitioners of evil.

Second, positives. Whereas some lyrics may be objectionable the mass of lyrics reflects either pure entertainment or socially positive attitudes and practices. If recordings do in fact affect young minds, as maintained by the PMRC, then the heavy thrust of our industry's input is positive, not negative.

Other forces. The PMRC, and therefore this committee is focusing solely on rock music. But why is only rock music unfairly singled out for the scrutiny of the PMRC and the U.S. Senate while all other explicit negative influences on younger children go untargeted? What about movies and magazine ads, prime time television, soap operas, books, cable programs? If there is to be a negative review of negative forces in the environment of younger children, let it be a review of all such forces, not one which focuses on rock music alone. If the PMRC somehow were to be able to purify all music according to its own standards, who is going to purify the remainder of their children's world?

Fourth, behavior. The PMRC concentrates on modes of human behavior that it finds objectionable, but those realities are not invented by record companies, songwriters or performers. Adults in the society, some of them parents, are the real initiators of those extremes. Recorded music reflects rather than introduces society's values and the realities of human conduct, both good and bad.

And last, in respect to rights, although in this forum we address the rights of parents and younger children, we cannot submerge the rights of others. We are on delicate ground here in respect to censorship and the first amendment. We must not trample the rights of parents and other adults whose standards do not coincide with those of the PMRC or any other group. Further, recording artists and songwriters have their own rights and freedoms of expressions and even have contractual protections that legally must be respected. We must assure that the noble intentions of the PMRC do not somehow get translated into a dilution of the rights and freedoms of others.

Those five realities which I have just articulated merit the consideration of this committee, too. And as to the PMRC, I am getting a little apprehensive about its motives and fervor. Recording companies have offered to meet the core concern of the PMRC. Yet, without waiting to see even how the program operates, they tell us that is not good enough. The PMRC has said clearly it does not want censorship, but I fear that the only acceptable translation of the wishes of the PMRC will somehow constitute a de facto first stage form of censorship.

The PMRC now seems committed to impose its will on an entire creative community and on broadcasters, on record retailers, and thus on all who buy and hear recorded music. The PMRC seeks to revamp the structural patterns of an industry, to hold our feet to the fire. As the PMRC expands its actions and themes, its medium is becoming more vital than its message.

I appeal to the PMRC by saying "enough, already." I hope it takes a pride in what it has spotlighted and achieved, and in the response it definitely has triggered. I hope it does not allow a thirst for press, public and Government attention to gain priority over the olive branch we offer.

The members of the PMRC are parents. I and many of my colleagues are parents, too. The PMRC has no monopoly on love and concern for kids. Child supervision is my personal parental responsibility, and the degrees of control versus freedom are mine alone to set. I certainly would not be content to assign any part of my responsibility to some outside surrogate, like a record company, a radio station, a censorship panel, a government body, or a parent organization.

"Censorship" can take subtle forms and need not not be confined to a deliberate surgical excising of dirty words. Censorship, in one of its manifestations, can be the stifling of the creative act—an insidious filtering out of creative energy—a homogenizing of creative output.

Some musical content may be considered offensive. We offend some people some of the time. Down through the ages, there always has been shocks in popular music—even from prime shockers like Cole Porter, Elvis Presly, and the Beatles. I cannot recall, however, definitive damage to children from any one of them. We here today, in fact, are ourselves some of those "victimized" children.

Some of our music, then, may cause one to wince. That wincing, the fleeting moments of discomfort, are the occasional prices one pays to get access to basic creative energy, to the talent pool, to the resources of excitement from which music and all art forms flow. One risks strangling those precious energies by rules and criteria and panels and coalitions and inquiries and even inscriptions.

Sure, maybe the PMRC can sanitize our music for their kids if they are strident enough. They can clean up their kids' world and find even greater examples of explicitness if they choose to go to the walls of our Nation's museums and art galleries and to the book shelves of our libraries. Sanitize, then paralyze—purify, then stultify. We cannot be a party to such stifling. We trust that neither will the U.S. Senate.

Thank you.

[The attachments referred to follow:]

The CHAIRMAN. I have a couple of comments for you, Mr. Gortikov, and then a couple of questions.

You say that the PMRC is holding your feet to the fire, and the record companies' feet to the fire. They are doing that by publicizing the problem, right?

Mr. GORTIKOV. By publicizing the problem?

The CHAIRMAN. Yes. I mean, you do not object to anybody publicizing their concerns, do you?

Mr. GORTIKOV. No, but it is the degree, the narrowness of the focus, the ignoring of the——

The CHAIRMAN. Why should anybody not publicize any problem that occurs to them? If people are concerned about values in a society, if they are concerned about what is available to their kids, why should they not publicize it? The whole music industry lives on publicity, thrives on publicity. Why should concerned parents not be able to publicize their problems and their concerns as well?

Mr. GORTIKOV. I am not saying they should not, but by the same token, I want to publicize to you these other aspects that put this thing in proper perspective.

The CHAIRMAN. Well, I am glad you are here, but it seems to me that it is perfectly reasonable and even commendable for concerned parents to say wait a second, we are concerned about what is going on in this country, and we are going to call attention to it. We are not going to sweep it under the rug. We are not going to leave this just a matter between record companies and teenaged kids. We are going to talk about it and bring it out in the open. That is how we are going to try to hold people's feet to the fire, just by publicizing it.

That is reasonable I think.

Mr. GORTIKOV. It is reasonable providing the perspective is accurate. The perspective has not been.

The CHAIRMAN. Well, do you deny the testimony of the PMRC and the lyrics that they read to us this morning?

Mr. GORTIKOV. No.

The CHAIRMAN. It just seems to me that as matter of objective fact, the lyrics are there, and those lyrics are being sold to whoever wants to walk into a store and buy them.

Mr. GORTIKOV. You are absolutely right, and they focus on the negative impact of those lyrics, as they see it, on their children. What they do not say, for example, is take the "We Are the World" record. I promise you that their children learned more from the USA for Africa "We Are the World" record in respect to generosity, giving, caring, brotherhood, sacrifice. Those positive messages are just as important as the negative ones, and I only ask perspective and balance.

The CHAIRMAN. I think that was absolutely commendable, that record, and I have said so many times. But I also think that it is reasonable for parents to express concern and to do so very openly if records, in fact, suggest or even glorify incest or violence or suicide.

Mr. GORTIKOV. Well, what we are espousing, we have taken action in response to that. We are not sitting here ignoring what has been said, what has been publicized. We are taking action. We ask that that action be given a chance in the marketplace to work.

The CHAIRMAN. Now, if a PG rating, or some sort of rating were given records, there would have to be some basis for giving it, would there not? You would not just draw names out of a hat. There would be some basis for determining what got the label and what did not, right?

Mr. GORTIKOV. Yes.

The CHAIRMAN. Who would decide that?

Mr. GORTIKOV. The individual companies would make the determination that a given record with explicit content in these various areas that have been mentioned would warrant the inscription.

The CHAIRMAN. What if the company's whole business is to try to make as much money as possible by selling smut?

Mr. GORTIKOV. You may even find that the application of this inscription will enhance, not deter, sales.

The CHAIRMAN. It might, but what if it were to determine that it was deleterious to record sales and that it was not going to apply the label to the record at all? Then what would you do? What would your suggestion be?

Mr. GORTIKOV. Well, if a company chooses to ignore and not apply this or do it unfairly, I have a hunch that PMRC would rise again and approach you and approach the public for redress. But give it a chance to work. Let's not decide in front that the intentions or the motivations or effects of the program will not work. That is unfair.

It is a judgmental and it is an imperfect system, just like——

The CHAIRMAN. Well, I cannot blame them for being a little bit wary about the motives of record companies that are right now making their profits by peddling lyrics that glorify rape and incest and drugs and suicide and violence to children. Why should they feel that that is any great custodian of the values of their kids?

Mr. GORTIKOV. Yes, but on the other hand they are not saying that the content of records should be changed; they are only asking that they be identified. We are making a step to identify them.

The CHAIRMAN. But they are asking that somebody assume responsibility for identifying them, and I do not think that there is much basis for feeling that the record companies are terribly responsible.

Why would somebody who is making a profit selling records glorifying incest be a responsible body to disclose anything?

Mr. GORTIKOV. Why is the motion picture industry, which rates itself, responsible?

The CHAIRMAN. Does each company rate itself?

Mr. GORTIKOV. The Motion Picture Association itself rates its own.

The CHAIRMAN. Well, you do not want your association to rate anybody; you want each company to do it individually.

Mr. GORTIKOV. Because I do not think there are standards that can be developed for lyrics. Lyrics are not like motion pictures. Standards, precise standards, cannot be developed for language.

The CHAIRMAN. Well, nothing is precise, but I think, it is just clear to me that what we heard today is so clearly pornographic and obscene, that it does not take too much guessing in that case, does it?

Mr. GORTIKOV. No, it is not, and that is why I say there would be no problem in attaching the inscription. For example, every lyric that was exposed here today would certainly qualify. And I have even suggested to the PMRC that if it has a preferred set of standards or guidelines, give them to me. Let me communicate those to the record companies.

I have not had a response from them.

The CHAIRMAN. Well, I think you have come some distance, but it seems to me that looking at it from the standpoint of what we heard earlier today, it really is not adequate to just say every record company does whatever it wants by way of labeling.

Mr. GORTIKOV. No, every record company would apply an inscription when the content of lyrics is explicit. I do not think it is very difficult to determine when lyric content is explicit, any more than the PMRC has had any problem in determining the explicitness of the items that were aired here today.

The CHAIRMAN. Senator Gore?

Senator GORE. Thank you very much, Mr. Chairman.

There are some spokesmen for the industry who because of the length of this witness list understandably could not be included. One of them is George David Weiss, president of the Songwriters Guild of America, and he prepared a very short, 2½ page statement which, with your permission and with unanimous consent, I would like to put into the record.

The CHAIRMAN. Without objection.

Senator GORE. Mr. Gortikov, your exchanges with the chairman have illuminated the degree to which your industry has been willing to respond to the concerns expressed about explicit lyric content. I would like to follow along with the train of questioning begun by the chairman.

You have recognized that there are legitimate concerns on the part of parents, correct?

Mr. GORTIKOV. Right.

Senator GORE. You have recognized that the industry has some responsibility to help parents in fulfilling their own responsibility as parents, correct?

Mr. GORTIKOV. Correct.

Senator GORE. Where you begin to part ways with the PMRC the PTA and others is in your refusal to acknowledge that the industry as a whole has such a responsibility. Your position is that 24 companies should apply 24 different sets of criteria in determining what material warrants a label and what material does not, correct?

Mr. GORTIKOV. No. I do not think there will be 24 different sets of criteria. I think it will be a simple problem to identify the type of material that was exposed to you today, just as the PMRC has exposed that to you. I see no problem in doing that.

If it does not work, then some corrective action might be appropriate, but give it a chance.

Senator GORE. It seems that either the industry feels a sense of responsibility or it does not. If it does, then the key question is why can't the industry get together and develop an industry-wide set of criteria the same way the movie industry does, the same way dozens of industries around this country meet what they conceive to be their responsibilities to the public in a collective way?

If you just leave it up to each individual company, then those who have been least responsible in the past are going to be the least responsible in the future. If, on the other hand, there is an industry-wide recognition that there is some responsibility to the public, then the industry ought to be willing to convey that sense of responsibility to its individual members.

Mr. GORTIKOV. I go back to my testimony. You are dealing with lyrics. You are not dealing with motion pictures which have a precise image. We are dealing with lyrics here, and I think that there is no problem in a record company identifying what is or is not explicit sexuality or explicit violence. I do not see a problem here.

And other than a set of guidelines that is going to say we will identify explicit sexuality, we will identify explicit violence, when you get into words, how are you going to convert that to a precise set of guidelines? I just think it is impossible to do.

Senator GORE. Some would say that it is even more difficult to engage in such a task with visual images in the movies than it is with the lyric content.

Mr. GORTIKOV. Well, I have been told by an executive of the rating entity of the Motion Picture Association that it has no written guidelines, that what it does is subjective and judgmental, to the best of its capability. But they do not have any guidelines.

Senator GORE. Do they have an industrywide standard?

Mr. GORTIKOV. They do not have any guidelines that develop what those ratings are.

Senator GORE. But now, the individual movie companies do not rate their own movies, do they?

Mr. GORTIKOV. No; their association does.

Senator GORE. According to an industrywide sense of what is appropriate, right?

Mr. GORTIKOV. That is what I am saying. They state they have no such guidelines, that it is judgment on the part of the six or seven raters as to whether a motion picture qualifies for certain age exposure, or R or X.

Senator GORE. Well, I cannot believe that it is a totally ad hoc approach.

Mr. GORTIKOV. Well, this is what I was told by a senior executive as recently as yesterday.

Senator GORE. The movie industry has specific categories, and there have been debates and appeals about the appropriateness of a movie falling into one category or another. There is a dialog about where a movie fits, but when that dialog takes place, it is the industry as a whole which is making the decision.

With the recording industry you are suggesting that each individual company make the judgment on its own. I am saying in response that the companies that have been really irresponsible in promoting suicide and all the other things that we have heard here, are going to be the least likely to exhibit a sense of responsibility on their own.

Do you not agree with that?

Mr. GORTIKOV. Not necessarily. I do not, because of the records that you have exposed here today. Although I do not know the company that originates each one of them, they do represent a spectrum, a wide range of industry companies. Those same companies produce a wide array of records that would not so qualify for exposure here today.

Senator GORE. To a small degree, it seems to me that your industry has been forthcoming, and no one should minimize the fact that you have said these companies will be willing on their own to have labels. But there are two problems that I see and hate. I am not referring to the suggestion from Mr. Zappa and others that the lyrics be printed—I agree with that suggestion. But there are two problems that I see with your specific proposal.

Number one, there is no industrywide acceptance of responsibility.

Mr. GORTIKOV. That is not true.

Senator GORE. It appears to be true because you are saying that the individual companies are going to determine the labeling criterion on their own, individually.

Mr. GORTIKOV. That in aggregate constitutes——

Senator GORE. And only some of them.

Mr. GORTIKOV. That in aggregate constitutes an acceptance. I have not had any turn me down, and these companies, these 24 companies, represent somewhere between 80 and 85 percent of the totality of the industry. All companies in the industry are not our members. I cannot speak for them.

Senator GORE. Second, the wording of the label you have suggested translates into PG, basically, Parental Guidance, which has become associated over the years in the minds of the public with material in the movie industry which is generally considered suitable for young children. There has been kind of an erosion of the meaning of PG. But you know, 5, 6-year-olds will routinely watch PG movies, and their parents have come to feel in many cases that PG means maybe one or two bad words, and that it is not really a bad thing.

But the material we saw this morning, if translated into the sphere of the movie industry, would be X or certainly R. If you are going to only have one label, should it not be one that does not engender confusion in the minds of parents who might equate that parental guidance with the same meaning that it has acquired through the long experience of the movie industry?

Mr. GORTIKOV. We were not proposing to use PG. We were using the full language, "Parental Guidance—Explicit Lyrics." The words "parental guidance" we lifted right out of communications I received from the PMRC, and on that the choice of words was predicated. So it was not intended to relate or not to relate to the motion picture industry.

Senator GORE. But I take it that this is a matter that you are still engaged in some dialog about, is that correct?

Mr. GORTIKOV. Well, we felt that it was adequate. If it is not, then we have to go back to the drawing board.

Senator GORE. All right, thank you.

Thank you, Mr. Chairman.

The CHAIRMAN. Senator Riegle?

Senator RIEGLE. Thank you, Mr. Chairman.

I think as this discussion goes along, most people would agree that we do not want to end up with some legislated standard or framework here and I think the industry association should properly take the lead.

I would like to make a couple of suggestions to you because I do not think what you have said today is as adequate as it needs to be.

I have listened very carefully to what you have said, and you have said in effect that you think each of the companies can figure this out for themselves—what explicit material is—and make that judgment. If that is so, then I think the association as a whole can just as readily do it. You can decide as a body what in fact meets that test of explicit material or lyrics, and establish that as a standard on your own. You can keep other people out of it, but I think you do have a responsibility to do it within the industry. I think it ought to apply industrywide.

I do not think you should have a situation where different companies can go a different way and in a sense do something that, if they decide not to honor that or the feeling that meets the general sense within the industry, then the whole industry in a sense falls under the shadow of that kind of an extreme judgment.

I think if your association has any meaning and power, you ought to step up to that and you ought to do it before somebody else tries to do it for you.

Second, I think where there are explicit lyrics, I think there ought to be a written text. I think you ought to provide it, and I do not think there is any excuse for not doing it other than cost. These records, whether they are singles or albums, carry a high enough price tag that if it costs an extra 5 cents or 3 cents or whatever it does on the margin to print out what the text is when you have explicit material, I think it ought to be there. I think that still leaves it with the public to make a judgment, and decide what they want to buy or not want to buy. To simply say there are explicit lyrics and not have a way for somebody to see what that means and whether or not in the sense of a particular family or parent, who would decide that that is something they would not encourage their chil-

dren to have. If in fact you are saying there are explicit lyrics here but we are not going to tell you what it is, and you have got to actually take and listen to the record, I do not think that is sufficient.

I think in that case—and I gather Frank Zappa took that position earlier, that he had no problem when lyrics are printed, and if it costs you 2 or 3 or 4 or 5 cents more to put that on the inside of the record cover. I just think you ought to do it.

That falls, in my view, in the area of full disclosure. Again, it does not tell people how they should make the judgment, but it at least puts people in a position to be able to make an informed judgment.

I want to make an additional point with respect to the movies because you were talking about the fact that there is a difference here.

Well obviously, there is normally a verbal side to the movie, or there is a sound side to the movie as well as what one sees on the screen. Of course, if we are just talking about a record, it would be the lyrics, and you would not, of course, have the video part of it.

It seems to me that if they are able to set, in a sense, an industrywide standard, albeit with, I gather, 400 movies a year versus maybe 25,000 songs, so we are talking about a much bigger task within the record industry. They have found a way within the movie industry association to set up a working rating system far more complex than you are talking about. They have a variety of grades, and as was said, it is not just PG, but they have X rated and they have various ratings along the way. They have found a way to take and do that job in an area that I think is even more difficult because you are not only just rating the actual word content of a movie, you are also making some kind of a qualitative judgment about what is actually seen on the screen.

I think your job is easier. I think in fact, and in a sense, you are saying that because you have already admitted that point when you said here that you are going to draw the line in terms of disclosure at the point at which explicit lyrics are used, your choice of words. So it seems to me that in light of that, it is really quite easy to establish for yourself an industrywide standard and expect that others in the industry will adhere to that standard.

I would be frank to say to you, if you do that, I think that would be a helpful step. If somebody did not want to—somebody in the industry basically did not want to adhere to that, then I think the industry, the remaining companies have some obligation to differentiate themselves from whoever that might be.

Again, I think that to the extent that you can do this among yourselves that is a far better way to try to have this done. Frankly, the examples we have heard today, are the most extreme examples. Obviously the ones that were cited earlier in terms of violence or incest or suicide or what have you, the most extreme examples that are out there today are the ones that are used to illustrate the problem. But I think almost everybody is troubled by those extreme examples, and I think at the very least we ought to have a way of being fully informed about them so that parents are in a stronger position, and for that matter, young people for themselves, in their own behalf, are in a better position to try to make some kind of a qualitative judgment.

I think you have taken a step here, but I think you can go somewhat further on your own, and I think it would be constructive to have you to do so.

Mr. GORTIKOV. May I respond?

Senator RIEGLE. Please.

Mr. GORTIKOV. Please understand several things about the application of lyrics on the outside, say, of an album jacket. I repeat that these lyrics are owned by music publishers, not record companies. The right to reproduce has to come from them. In some cases it would be easy. In a given album there could be as many as 10 different music publishers represented. Rights, therefore, may come from eight of them or nine of them, but not from the one that is the key one.

If such lyrics were exposed on the outside, and those lyrics tend to be—

Senator RIEGLE. I do not necessarily say that they ought to be on the outside, but they ought to be such that if somebody is going to buy the album, maybe it is a fold-open album, they can open it and take a look at it.

Mr. GORTIKOV. But all albums are shrink-wrapped with plastic, and they would have to be on the outside or would not be visible. This raises another question: If questionable lyrics such as those protested here today were printed on the outside of an album, would we be again castigated by parents for daring to expose such explicit language to the younger children, and maybe be called before a committee to have to explain ourselves for daring to reveal such objectionable material.

Senator RIEGLE. Look, let me tell you something. I think there is a way to solve that problem, and there are probably a lot of different ways to solve it. Just in terms of what comes to mind, I realize the way records come now. You could certainly have two sides—you could have a paneled container with the records on one side, and I have seen them like that. I own some myself.

It is a matter of cost. It is not a matter of the fact that you cannot do it. I guess what I would like to establish with you, is that you are a lot better off once you have decided that explicit lyrics are there, to make the full disclosure. I think you should do that. I do not think you should fight it. I think you should find the most efficient way to do it so that people have the information to make a competent judgment. I think you are on a lot sounder ground if you do that than if you are reluctant about it for basically reasons of cost or inconvenience.

The CHAIRMAN. Mr. Gortikov, I just wanted to correct one statement that you made. You referred to being hauled before a committee. You were not hauled before this committee.

Mr. GORTIKOV. I did not say that I was.

The CHAIRMAN. You were not subpoenaed to come here.

Mr. GORTIKOV. No, sir, I am sorry, I did not say that word.

The CHAIRMAN. You are here voluntarily, right?

Mr. GORTIKOV. I was talking in the future.

The CHAIRMAN. Well, we do not haul people before committees, at least this committee.

Thank you, sir.

Mr. GORTIKOV. Thank you.

The CHAIRMAN. Next we have a panel, Dr. Joe Stuessy, University of Texas at San Antonio, and Dr. Paul King, Memphis, TN.

Dr. Stuessy, will you proceed, please?

STATEMENTS OF DR. JOE STUESSY, UNIVERSITY OF TEXAS AT SAN ANTONIO, AND DR. PAUL KING, MEMPHIS, TN

Mr. STUESSY. Yes, sir.

Mr. Chairman. Senators and guests, thank you for allowing me to make a few remarks.

I have submitted a substantial written testimony. I hope you will take the chance to read it because my 5-minute speech will be rather brief and just try to hit the main topics. Substantiation is in the written documentation.

Let me see if I can convey to you what we know from the field of music psychology about music and its interrelationship with people. I should say that I am on the music faculty of the University of Texas at San Antonio. I hold a Ph.D. in music, and have taught a course in the history of rock music for 12 years at two universities.

The first thing we know is that music affects behavior. Many children will say I listen to that stuff, but it does not affect me. In fact, Mr. Snider said exactly those words earlier today. He said, it does not affect me. We have known intuitively for centuries, and it has been proven conclusively by scientific studies in recent decades that music does affect behavior.

Music affects our moods, emotions, attitudes, and our resultant behavior. Music affects us psychologically and physiologically. This fact explains why we have choirs and organs at church, why we have bands at football games, Muzak in stores, business offices, and doctors' offices. It explains why there are military marches, discoteques, music behind movies and TV, Jazzercise, and most importantly, commercial jingles.

We know some other things about the way music interacts with people. We know that music is an aid to verbal retention. Any verbal message that you receive, you are more likely to remember if it is in a musical context.

We also know that repetition increases our preference for that which is repeated. The more we hear things, the more likely we are to internalize it and like it.

We also know that coordinated multisensory input reinforces music's message. The more senses that can be involved in receiving a coordinated message, the more likely that message is to impact upon our conscious and subconscious.

Although this next point may seem contradictory to the previous one, it is really not, and that is that there is such a thing as exclusionary input, that is to say, input which blocks out all other inputs, thus removing distractions. We also know that exclusionary input increase the impact on the mind of the messages being received.

Today's heavy metal music is categorically different from previous forms of popular music. It contains the element of hatred, a meanness of spirit. Its principal themes are, as you have already heard, extreme violence, extreme rebellion, substance abuse, sexual promiscuity and perversion and Satanism. I know personally of no form of popular music before which has had as one of its central elements the element of hatred.

The message may be either overt or covert. In the case of the overt message, we are talking of course about a message which is being reinforced by music, something we have said increases the verbal message's impact. It is being reinforced by repetition, primary and secondary repetition; primary meaning that within the same song a given hook line is repeated as many times as 30 or 40 times in a 3 or 4 minute span; secondary repetition comes about because frequently the words are very difficult to understand. Typically, the teenager therefore will listen repetitively, over and over and over, to understand the words and frequently be able to transcribe them.

The message is reinforced by multisensory input such as the album covers, which have been discussed, the looks of the performers, their theatrics on stage, the visual representations such as MTV, volume levels, etc. And the message is reinforced in individual headphone listening, which is a type of exclusionary listening that I referred to earlier.

The message may also be covert or subliminal. Sometimes subaudible tracks are mixed in underneath other, louder tracks. These are heard by the subconscious but not the conscious mind. Sometimes the messages are audible but are backwards, called backmasking. There is disagreement among experts regarding the effectiveness of subliminals. We need more research on that.

We hear frequently about the first amendment problem. In closing, I would say that while we must protect our first amendment freedoms, we must also protect minors from the abuse of those freedoms. The first amendment, as I understand it, is not a blank check. There are legal, constitutional limitations when we feel that the abuse or the use of a freedom negatively impacts the health of another segment of society. Use of the airwaves for pornography and immoral purposes, especially when aimed at minors, must be controlled somehow. Given the American philosophy, I think we have given the so-called creative artists a wide berth. We have given them more than the proverbial inch, and I believe they have taken more than the proverbial mile.

Somehow we must send a message to the recording and radio industry, enough is enough; you have gone too far. Parents are fighting this scourge all over the country. We plead for help from city councils, radio stations, advertisers and the record industry itself.

I hope that this committee will find a way to send a message to the industry: clean up your act or we will do it for you.

In the words of the heavy metal band, Twisted Sister, "we're not going to take it anymore."

Thank you.

[The statement follows:]

Statement of Dr. Joe Stuessy

I

A Few Brief Remarks About My Background
(Or, "Who is this guy?")

I like rock and roll. I am a former professional rock musician (at the local level); about half of my rather extensive record collection is rock music. I hold a Ph.D. in music from the Eastman School of Music and am currently a Professor of Music at The University of Texas at San Antonio. I was among the first in the nation to teach a university course in the history of rock music (that was in 1973; in 1985 there are many such courses). I have taught this course at two universities (Southern Methodist University and The University of Texas at San Antonio). I have had over 3,000 students in that course over the intervening twelve years.

A full résumé is appended to this testimony if further information is desired.

II

Some Things We Know About Music and Human Behavior
(Or, "I listen to that stuff, but it doesn't affect me!")

A. Music affects behavior. This simple fact has been known intuitively for centuries. For example, Plato's mentor, Damon, said that music can "not only arouse or allay different emotions, but also inculcate all the virtues—courage, self-restraint, and even justice."[1] Many centuries later, Martin Luther said, "Music is one of the greatest gifts that God has given us; it is divine and therefore Satan is its enemy. For with its aid, many dire temptations are overcome; the devil does not stay where music is."[2] We can probably assume that Martin Luther was not familiar with Heavy Metal!

In the twentieth century, especially in the last four decades, tons of research has been done on the interrelationship of music and human behavior. Although each study addresses slightly different aspects of this general premise, the aggregate conclusion is clear; music affects human behavior. It affects our moods, our attitudes, our emotions, and our behavior. It affects us psychologically and physiologically.

Anthropologist A. P. Merriam in his book *The Anthropology of Music* says, "The importance of music, as judged by the sheer ubiquity of its presence, is enormous.... There is probably no other human cultural activity which is so all-pervasive and which reaches into, shapes, and often controls so much of human behavior."[3] In his study of George Orwell's *1984*, Dr. Paul Haack summarized the numerous references to music as follows: "The most striking feature of these references is the constant, blatant propagandizing and mind controlling function that the music serves."[4]

Music can make us feel relaxed, scared, patriotic, ambitious, mad, sad, happy, romantic, reverent, etc. The fact that music affects behavior is the foundation of the entire science of music therapy, a field in which music is applied as a therapeutic tool to modify aberrant behavior.

Think for a moment of just a few of the ways that the presence of music affects our average daily lives:

1. Music in business offices, if properly structured, can have a positive (or negative) affect on worker efficiency. Companies such as Muzak, Inc. have done many studies which document this fact.
2. Similarly, music in doctors' and dentists' offices is used to relax patients and calm anxieties. In some cases, music has been used as an aid in pain reduction.
3. Music in retail establishments is used to partially sedate the shopper, making him/her more receptive to marketing stratagems.
4. Music at sporting events is used to inspire enthusiasm for the home team (fight songs, Alma Maters, etc.).
5. "The Star-spangled Banner" and other patriotic tunes are played on July Fourth celebrations (and other times) to inspire a feeling of pride and patriotism.
6. Music accompanies movies and television shows and is used to affect the viewers emotions and expectations. For example, when the camera slowly proceeds up a dark path with woods on either side, the presence of "spooky" music heightens our expectation that someone is going to jump out from behind a tree, brandishing a knife. We become nervous and apprehensive; we tighten up and hold onto our seats; our pulse and heartbeat quicken. These effects would be less likely if the music at that moment were the theme song from "I Love Lucy!"
7. When you think about it, dancing is a rather silly-looking activity. Next time you see a dance floor filled with people, imagine the same exact scene, but *without music*. Kinda stupid, isn't it? Either people would be jumping spastically around for no apparent reason (fast tune), or they would be draped over each other in a near-motionless embrace (slow tune). What makes this silly behavior OK? MUSIC!
8. Bugle calls and marches have historically been used to intensify courage on the part of men in battle. The right music prepares us to charge over that next hill, bayonets poised, ready to meet the enemy (or our own death).
9. When we are entering church on Sunday mornings, we are greeted with the reverent sounds of an organ. Choirs sing songs of praise. The congregation sings hymns of faith. All of this is done for a reason. It reinforces and enhances our reverence, our faith, our love of God, and our determination to live better lives.
10. An entire industry today is based on the idea that people will put on skimpy outfits and travel miles away several times per week for the purpose of exercising and sweating. And they'll pay for the privilege! Without music, this activity is just plain hard work. *With music*, it's fun! Jazzercise and similar exercise-to-music activities are flourishing all over the nation.
11. Perhaps the best example of music affecting behavior is the commercial jingle. The Sears, Penneys, Toyotas, Dr. Peppers, and Budweisers of the world spend millions annually on catchy advertising slogans set to music. I'll have more to say about that later. For now, let's assume that the companies which spend hundred of thousands of dollars to get their musical jingle on a Super Bowl broadcast for a few seconds are really not stupid! They know exactly what they are doing. They know that such a message will increase the likelihood of the listeners buying their services or products. It works.

B. Music is an aid in verbal retention. Studies (Lathom, 1970; Mann, 1979; Wintle, 1978) have shown that we can memorize and retain verbal information better if that information is presented in a short, catchy musical setting. The makers of *Sesame Street* certainly knew that and used it most effectively in teaching letters and numbers via their "commercials" for the letter K or the number 8. Currently a hotel chain is running a national advertising campaign in which they sing their telephone number. They are correct in thinking that it is more likely to be remembered because of the catchy rhythmic/melodic context. Once implanted, such verbal information stays with us a long time. For example, if I say, "Oh what a feeling, —," I'll bet you can fill in the blank with a car manufacturer's name. You can probably even sing the tune—in rhythm! How many other jingles can you still remember from *years* ago? Try "Baseball, hot dogs, apple pie, and —," or "Wouldn't you like to be a — too," or "See the USA in your —." That last one is thirty years old!

C. Repetition increases our preference for that which is repeated. Again, studies (Verveer, 1933; Mull, 1940; Meyer, 1960; Bartlett, 1969; Pantle, 1977) have shown that even if we are not favorably impressed with a piece of music the first time we hear it, most often such pieces tend to grow on us. As we become more familiar with it, begin to understand it, and as it becomes more "internalized," we not only find ourselves liking it more, but actually catch ourselves whistling it or singing it *subconsciously*— (that's important, by the way!). Think of one of your personal favorites (whether it's Beethoven or the Beatles). Can you remember the very first time you heard it? Were you as wild about it then as you are now? Probably not. There are always a few exceptions—the piece we love on first hearing. But all of Top 40 radio is based on the premise that repetitive listening increases preference for that which is repeated.

D. Coordinated multi-sensory input reinforces any message. Salesmen know this. If a salesman can coordinate a major presentation so that his client hears his message verbally, reads his message in printed form, sees some slides and a few graphs, etc., the impact of his message will be greater. Teachers know this. Some of the finest teaching I have seen involved a coordinated presentation with verbal, written, and visual factors all focused to teach a given concept.

E. "Exclusionary" input also enhances the impact of a message. (This seems to conflict with item D above, but notice that important word "coordinated" in item D.) By exclusionary input, I mean single-source input which blocks out all other conflicting or distracting inputs. Would you want to give an important political speech in the middle of Grand Central Station at the 5:00 p.m. rush hour? Probably not. You simply would not have people's undivided attention. There would be too many distractions. We know that we are bombarded with aural input every minute. Even in a relatively quiet room, there may be the sound of air-conditioning systems, flourescent lights buzzing, shoes squeaking, papers rustling, chairs scooting, not to mention the internal sounds of our own heartbeat, pulse, and respiration—*plus* anyone who is speaking and any music that is playing. Imagine how much more effectively our mind could concentrate on a message if most of these competing sounds were blocked out.

F. Stimulative music, while stimulating some bodily processes, may actually sedate others. This fact is suspected, but not yet proven conclusively to my knowledge. But we do know that some things stimulate some aspects of our activities while depressing others. For example, three or four stiff alcoholic drinks may make you the life of the party (stimulated), but at the same time you may slur your words or trip over the carpet (these and other faculties have been numbed or depressed). It is an interesting contradictory effect of some so-called "stimulants."

III

Is Heavy Metal Really Different?

(Or, "Isn't this just the same old fuddy-duddies against the same old rock and roll?")

A. New musical styles have typically elicited negative reactions. The waltz was considered a deprived and licentious phenomenon which should never replace the more proper minuet.

Stravinsky's *Rite of Spring* was soundly booed at its premiere and described as primitive and animalistic. Jazz was berated as decadent and immoral music. And, of course, rock and roll was declared to be noisy and sexually provocative music from the beginning.

So here we are in 1985; again, a group of people is decrying the negative and potentially harmful effects of an abrasive musical style. Is this current debate just more of the same, or is it really something different? Is it just a matter of degree or is it a difference in kind?

Both! We all know that differences in degree can be so extreme that they become differences in kind. Zero and 120 are differences in degree on the Fahrenheit scale; but the difference in degree is so great that we perceive them as opposites ("cold" and "hot" respectively). When we drive a car a 90 mph, that is just a difference in degrees from 10 mph; but we call one speed "slow" and the other one "fast." As we move along any continuum, we reach a point where the characteristics of one end are categorically different (opposite) from the characteristics of the other end.

Rock and roll has always been a rebellious music. It has often had sexual overtones. In fact the terms "rocking" and "rolling" were euphemisms for sexual intercourse in rhythm and blues music (the style from which rock emerged).

So, is heavy metal just a difference in degree from Elvis, Little Richard, Jerry Lee Lewis, etc.? Or is it categorically different? Greg Stevens (former Program Director for San Antonio heavy metal station KISS-FM) says, "It's the typical rebellion of rock. It's just the modern day version of that same rebel in black leather that Elvis Presley expressed in the '50s."[5]

But why, then, do so many reasonable, fairly "hip" people (even staunch rock and roll fans) sense that there is something really *different* about heavy metal—that it is more than a simple extension of good old rock and roll? Dwight Silverman, a writer for the *San Antonio Light*, may have put his finger on it best when he wrote, "Heavy Metal rock 'n' roll is a different beast from the music that ruled the late '60s and early '70s, the music that was supposed to bring a generation together. Heavy metal is a mean-spirited music. In it, women are abused, parents are objects of derision and scorn and violence, education is a foolish waste of time. Rock 'n' roll always has been a music of rebellion and frustration, but never of hatred."[6]

Hatred. A mean-spirited music. To my knowledge, their has never been a popular style of music which had as a central characteristic the element of *hate*. This is something new and different. Its seeds may be found back in the mid-1960s. It was nourished and developed in the late '60s and throughout the '70s. It has burst upon the 1980s as a full-grown force.

To understand the difference between earlier rock and current heavy metal, it is useful to make direct comparisons of songs from each period which address similar topics. For example, compare two songs about school and the educational experience. In the late 1950s, Chuck Berry released a song called "School Days." In it, he describes a typical school day ("the teacher is teaching the Golden Rule," and "Your studyin' hard and hopin' to pass"). Note particularly the reference to school dismissal: "Soon as 3 o'clock rolls around, you finally lay your burden down."[7] He goes on to say that our typical teenager leaves school, goes to a "juke joint," listens to some rock and roll and dances. Now compare that to "School Daze" by WASP. They refer to school as "a textbook madhouse," "a juvenile jail," "a blackboard jungle," and "a homework hellhouse." And what do they say about school dismissal? "Tick, tock, 3 o'clock, I'm sitting' here counting off the days; a fire bell ringing hell and I'd sure love to see it blaze—Burn it down! (screamed)."[8]

To consider two songs, one from the early '60s and one from the early '80s, which are almost like teen anthems. Bob Dylan's "Blowin' in the Wind" advised the younger generation of their goals in creating a better world. "... how many times must the cannon balls fly before they're forever banned" and "... how many years can some people exist before they're allowed to be free?"[9] The song speaks of love of fellow man, peace, and racial equality. Again, contrast that with Ozzy Osbourne's "Rock 'n' Roll Rebel." After many lines of deprecation of "them" (parents and other authority figures), Ozzy threatens, "Do what you will to try and make me conform, but I'll make you wish that you had never been born; cause I'm a rock 'n' roll rebel and I'll do as I please."[10]

Finally, compare two songs which refer to the age-old parent-child conflict within the family. The Coasters ('50s) sang a song called "Yakety-yak." Each verse recites typical parental commands (e.g., "you just put on your coat and hat, and walk yourself to the laundry mat; and when you finish doin' that, bring in the dog and put out the cat.")[11] The hook line is "Yakety-yak—don't talk back." The message seems to say to the teenager, "yeh, I understand your problem." But it never suggests violence or open rebellion, and certainly not hatred. But the song's 1980s counterpart might be a song by Twisted Sister called "We're Not Gonna Take It." They have a different message for parents:

"Oh you're so condescending; your gall is never-ending;
We don't want nothin', not a thing from you.
Your life is trite and jaded, boring and confiscated;
If that's your best, your best won't do.

Oh, Oh, we're right, we're free, we'll fight, you'll see!

We're not gonna take it; no, we're not gonna take it;
We're not gonna take it anymore
[screamed: Just you try and make us!]"[12]

The accompanying video shows a teenager who is transformed into Twisted Sister lead singer D. Snider, who proceeds to attack the teen's father.

We could continue, but perhaps the message is clear. The current heavy metal is categorically different from the earlier rock 'n' roll. Even if we could agree that the difference is merely one of degree, we must conclude that the degree of difference is so great as to be a difference in kind.

IV

Is There, Then, Reason To Think That Heavy Metal
Can Affect Human Behavior? (Or, "So what!")

A. Most of the successful heavy metal music projects one or more of the following basic themes:

a. extreme rebellion
b. extreme violence
c. substance abuse
d. sexual promiscuity/perversion (including homosexuality, bisexuality, sado-masochism, necrophilla, etc.)
e. Satanism

Testimony by Mr. Jeff Ling will provide more than ample evidence of heavy metal's projection of these themes.

B. These five basic themes are projected by overt messages. Let us now see how the music works to affect behavior, as based upon the principals discussed in section II above.

1. Remember that music reinforces verbal retention. The messages of commercial advertisers are more easily retained in our memory because they are set into a musical content. If you can still recall "See the USA in your Chevrolet," (assuring you are old enough to remember it from 30 years ago!), we can conclude that the message was firmly stored in your subconscious for later retrieval. Similarly, heavy metal lyrics, especially "hook lines" like "We're not gonna take it anymore," or "Lick it up," or "Eat me alive" are going to be stored in the current teenager's subconscious. The teen may or may not act upon this information, but we can be relatively certain that the mind has stored it away for future reference.

2. We said that repetition reinforces the message. With heavy metal, there are two kinds of repetition. I refer to them as primary and secondary repetition. Primary repetition is integral to a given song per se. Catchy hook lines are repeated over and over within a song. For example, in "Lick It Up" by KISS, the hook line (the title) is repeated thirty times in this four-minute piece. That's an average of one line every eight seconds. If I were to repeat a short message to you thirty times in the next four minutes, I'll bet you would remember it for quite a while! And remember that as an additional retention aid, the hook line is set to music. The hook line (and title) "Eat Me Alive" by Judas Priest is repeated eighteen times in 3 minutes. Twisted Sister's line "We're Not Gonna Take It" is repeated 24 times in three minutes and forty seconds. Let's face it: you never heard "See the USA in your Chevrolet" that often, yet your subconscious can still retrieve it.

Secondary repetition is more elusive. Adults often have difficulty understanding the words to heavy metal rock songs. And guess what! So do the kids. But they are determined to grasp every profound nugget of wisdom their heavy metal mentors spew forth! So they put on headphones and play the songs over and over, for hours if necessary, in order to decipher the words. Often they write them down in notebooks. In the process, more repetitive listening reinforces the message even further.

3. Recall that coordinated multi-sensory input also reinforces messages. The message of heavy metal music bombards our senses from every direction. The album covers display Satanic symbols, portrayals of violence, open and free sex, and angry defiance. The names of the groups, the song titles, the names of the performers (e.g., Blackie Lawless), the words of the songs, and the liner notes reinforce one or more of the basic themes. The facial expressions, the hair, the clothes all contribute to the same messages. The videos and the histrionic antics of the live stage performance add a strong visual impact. The light shows, the smoke devices, and the sheer volume add impact. One can literally *feel* the music at a live concert, as the rib cage vibrates with every beat. Heavy metal is a media expert's dream-come-true. If the youngsters at the live concert happen to be smoking marijuana (as a great many do), please add the senses of smell and taste. That about rounds out all five senses: you hear it, you see it, you feel it, you taste it, and you smell it!

4. As mentioned earlier, "exclusionary" input enhances the impact of a message. The phenomenon usually results from the parents' yelling for the teenager to "turn it down," or "turn it off," or "go to your room to listen to that stuff!" Often, they do just that. They go to their rooms, and put on the headphones (volume up, of course). When that happens, exclusionary input takes over. Now all distracting or competing input is blocked out. The heavy metal becomes the sole point of concentration. Now the teenager's mind need not be distracted by dishes rattling in the kitchen, little brother watching sitcoms in the next room, the dog barking, or even the telephone ringing (now *that's* a problem!). Literally, they can't hear it thunder! But heavy metal now has a direct, unfettered freeway straight into the mind.

5. Finally, we *suspect* that stimulative music (heavy metal surely qualifies) may stimulate certain bodily functions while actually sedating others (much like alcohol). The simplicity, the repetitive beat, and the uniformity of timbre and dynamics may contribute to a lowered level of consciousness. This may be why parents report that when their youngsters sit in apparent headphoned reverence while listening to music, they seem almost trancelike. If this is true (and we must admit that this phenomenon has yet to be scientifically substantiated to my knowledge), it would imply that while in such a state, the listener has a greater susceptibility to suggestions. When our conscious mind "dozes off," our subconscious is left with its guard down and rather indiscriminately accepts all input. Further study of this possible phenomenon is needed.

C. There has been much speculation about the use of covert messages (subliminals) in heavy metal music. It is said that two kinds of subliminals exist.

1. *Subaudibles (forward messages)*. Most contemporary rock recordings consist of multiple tracks (at least 10) which are mixed together at various dynamic levels. It is possible that one such track could contain a verbal message (Satanic, sexual, or anything). This track could be mixed in at such a low level that the other tracks easily cover it. If heard by itself, it would be audible; but mixed underneath fifteen or more other tracks, it is inaudible to the conscious mind. But, as the theory goes, the *subconscious* mind soaks up (and stores) all input. This type of message to the subconscious is one type of "subliminal" message. (A variant on this technique is to record the message normally, and then mix it in at high speed. Again, the conscious mind misses it; but does the subconscious?)

2. *Backmasking (backwards messages)*. Some messages are presented to the listener backwards. While listening to a normal forward message (often somewhat nonsensical), one is simultaneously being treated to a backwards message (in other words, the lyric sounds like one set of words going forward, and a different set of words going backwards). Some experts

believe that while the conscious mind is absorbing the forward lyric, the subconscious is working overtime to decipher the backwards message. Of course by spinning the record backwards (or by tape manipulation), the conscious mind gets a chance to hear the message too!

There has been much controversy about subliminals (both forward subaudibles and backmasking). Several countries (e.g. Belgium, Great Britain) have banned the used of subliminals. The National Association of Broadcasters issued a rule forbidding its members' use of subliminals.[13] The FCC says that the use of subliminals in advertising is "inconsistent with the obligations of the license. . . [and] contrary to the public interest." They continued, "whether effective or not, such broadcasts are clearly intended to be deceptive."[14] A United Nations study concluded that "the cultural implications of subliminal indoctrination is a major threat to human rights throughout the world."[15] Aryeh Neier (formerly executive director of the ACLU) said, "People have a right to go about their business without being subjected to manipulation they don't even know about."[16] Olivia Goodkin, an attorney, said in testimony before the U.S. House Committee on Transportation, Aviation, and Materials (hearing on subliminal communication technology) that "undisclosed subliminal communication poses an unusual kind of captivity . . . since the audience cannot avert its eyes or shut its ears or retreat to private places if it does not even know that the communication is taking place."[17] Subliminals are, at the very least, an invasion of privacy.

Again, more research is needed to determine the actual extent to which subliminals are used and the extent to which they influence the listener.

V

Summary

A. We know that music affects behavior. Anyone who says, "I listen to heavy metal, but it doesn't affect me" is simply *wrong*. Granted, it affects different people to different degrees, and in different ways. The healthy, stable, mature personality will, in fact, be minimally affected by heavy metal. But many, especially teenagers and pre-teens, are still shaping their self-identities. They are malleable, beset by internal and external conflicts about authority (especially parents), drugs, sex, theology, education, etc. They are in the process of defining who and what they are. At such a time, heavy metal's influence can be significant.

What should we as a society do to protect minors from the negative, often outright pornographic influences of heavy metal? What *can* we do? Parental awareness (and hopefully resultant counter-influences) is a desirable first step. But this can be ineffective. By his very nature, the teenager often does exactly the opposite of what the parent suggests. Anything stronger than suggestion (such as outright control) often leads to full-scale rebellion (especially if heavy metal music has already pounded its message in).

Can society in general (through its elected officials) help? Maybe. But what about the first amendment to the Constitution? *While we must protect our first amendment freedoms, we must also protect minors from the abuse of those freedoms.* The first amendment is *not* a blank check! There are legal, constitutional limitations. Any freedom carries responsibilities. Use of the public airwaves for pornographic and immoral purposes, especially when aimed at minors, must be controlled somehow. Open retail availability of pornographic records should be treated just as any other retail of pornography (books, "adult" movies, etc.).

Given the American philosophy, we have awarded the so-called creative artist a wide berth. We have given them *more* than the proverbial inch; and they have taken more than the proverbial mile. Indeed, our prior liberality may go a long way toward explaining how we have arrived at this unhappy point today.

Somehow we must send a strong message to the recording and radio industries. "Enough is enough! You have gone too far." Parents, teachers, ministers, and civic leaders are fighting this scourge all over the country. We plead for help from city councils, radio stations, advertisers, retailers, and the record industry itself!

I hope that this committee will find a way to send a message to the industry: "Clean up your act or we will do it for you!" In the words of Twisted Sister, "We're not gonna take it anymore!"

NOTES

[1] Donald A. Hodges, *The Significance of Music*, an unpublished manuscript, p. 9).

[2] *Ibid.*

[3] A. P. Merriam, *The Anthropology of Music* (Chicago: Northwestern University Press, 1964)

[4] Hodges, *op. cit.*, p. 94.

[5] (unsigned article), "A loud mix of rebellion, energy make heavy metal," *San Antonio Light*, Sunday, March 10, 1985, page A16.

[6] Dwight Silverman, "Drugs, violence steal the show," *San Antonio Light*. Sunday, March 10, 1985, page A16.

[7] "School Days" by Chuck Berry, Inc.: published by ARC Music Corporation (BMI).

[8] "School Daze" by Blackie Lawless: published by Zomba Enterprises, Inc.

[9] "Blowin' in the Wind" by Bob Dylan, *Writings and Drawings*, © 1973 Bob Dylan: published by Alfred A. Knopf, Inc., New York, page 33.

[10] "Rock 'n' Roll Rebel" by Ozzy Osbourne, © Nymph Music, Inc. (BMI).

[11] "Yakety-yak" by Jerry Leiber and Mike Stoller: published by Tiger (BMI).

[12] "We're Not Gonna Take It" by D. Snider, © 1984 Snidest Music Co. (ASCAP).

[13] Dan and Steve Peters, *Rock's Hidden Persuader: The Truth About Backmasking* (Minneapolis: Bethany House Publishers, 1985), page 17.

[14] *Ibid.*, page 19.

[15] *Ibid.*

[16] *Ibid.*, page 73.

[17] *Ibid.*, page 111.

The CHAIRMAN. Thank you, sir.

Dr. King.

Dr. KING. My name is Paul King, and I am a child and adolescent psychiatrist. I treat kids with serious drug problems. I have been treating adolescents for 9 years.

Senator RIEGLE. Excuse me. Could you pull the mike a little closer?

Dr. KING. I have been treating adolescents for over 9 years, and have formerly also been a New York City high school teacher. So I have been working with teenagers for over 14 years now.

The kids that I treat, some are delinquent, some are suicidal, others are violent, even homicidal. Many are sexually promiscuous. Nearly all of my patients worship heavy metal music.

My comments are not really my own but reflect what I have learned from the kids that I see each and every day in my practice. I would like to talk about two points. One is to answer the question about whether music influences young people or not, and the other is the issue about parents and the type of guidance, and what is the nature of sufficient guidance for parents in this issue.

With the aid of sophisticated marketing techniques, entertainers are elevated to the role of deities, to be worshipped by youth as if they are gods. Long hours are spent listening to heavy metal rock music, with some performers portraying themselves as charismatic leaders. The young person may then identify with the words of the song, "You've given me a new belief." "Belief" has religious connotations, "And soon the world will love you sweet leaf." Sweet Leaf, by Black Sabbath, Warner Brothers Records. Adolescents tell me sweet leaf refers to marijuana.

Rebellion and hate are common themes. "Children of the Grave," by Black Sabbath: "Revolution on their minds/The children march/Against the world they have to live in/Oh the hate that's in their hearts." The group leader is a preacher, and the young person who becomes involved with the lyrics develops a belief system, internalizes a belief system based on those lyrics.

Heavy metal refers to a type of music that was first developed in England. The music is loud and powerful, with most of the strength coming from electric guitars. The makeup or facial expressions are either hateful or demonic or have symbols and costumes representing power, which is the basic core issue. Examples, facial painting in what Kiss used to wear, tatoos of snarling animals, black leather, chains, motorcycles. We have seen examples. Members of the group Mötley Crüe wear pentagrams.

Verbal overtures are extremely philosophical. Let me give you a few examples. "The Number of the Beast" by Iron Maiden, which is Zomba Enterprises, and it goes "Woe to you, oh earth and sea./ For the Devil sends the beast with wrath,/because he knows the time is short./Let him who has understanding reckon/the number of the beast,/for it is a human number./His number is 666." The 666 refers to the Beast from Revelations.

Young people "Shout at the Devil." It has a prologue. It is not even the music, it is a prologue with a very clear message, the idea so that that could be clearly listened to. "In the beginning/the court of good always overpowered/the evils of all man's sins./But in time, the nations grew weak,/and our cities fell to slums/while evil stood strong.../In the dusts of hell/lurked the blackest of hates./For he whom you fear/awaits you."

"But now, many many lifetimes later/lay destroyed, beaten down/only the corpses of rebels/ashes of dreams and blood stained streets./It has been written/that those who have the youth have the future./So come now children of the beast./Be strong and shout at the devil."

The heavy metal groups themselves state that this is all in fun and that they are not into Satan worship. Whether this is true or not is not important. Young people feeling inadequate can have an instant sense of power from the music and identification closely with the lyrics. Heavy metal portrays the power and glory of evil. Adolescents with emotional and/or drug problems, which I treat every day, become further involved in delinquent behavior, violence, acts of cruelty and Satan worship. The glamorization of violence, sex, and drugs leads to further problems with directing young people's attitudes. Obviously, as a child psychiatrist, that is what I do, is try to help direct young people's attitudes and direct parents.

As Nikki Sixx of Mötley Crüe said in Hit Parader, "We like to live life to the fullest, and if that means driving your car into a wall at 70 miles per hour or doing three chicks at once, that's OK with us." In describing their form of music, "Yeah, apple pie, Chevrolet, tight jeans, Mötley Crüe, pizza, drugs and sex."

What is missing in today's teenagers identifying so strongly with heavy metal music? The music represents power, and the lyrics give purpose and meaning to those who have not been able to identify with the values they were raised with. Drugs and alcohol are often used while listening to heavy metal in order to feel the power more acutely and escape into the fantasies that are vividly portrayed on MTV. Escape alone may be harmless, but drug induced altered states of consciousness combined with the message of hatred and violence in heavy metal is dangerous. There are problems in attitude, changes in thinking and new values develop. Eighty-three percent of my patients have been listening to heavy metal for several hours per day, and over 50 percent know the words and write them down. And in fact, they do that in school, write down the words to the lyrics.

The drugs make the youngster suggestible to the message of the song. This is especially true with psychedelic mood-altering drugs, LSD, PCP and marijuana.

Heavy metal is presented to kids as a religion. The adolescents are vulnerable because their sense of identity has not been formed. Their sense of meaning and purpose in life is missing. They sense in themselves a need to rebel. The topics are sex, violence, and the power of evil. The emotional hunger in these young people is met in the form of music, chemical use, and promiscuous sexual behavior, the crazier, the better. The term "partying" refers to being under the influence of drugs and listening to the heavy metal music and lyrics. Drug dependent teenagers often party alone, soaking in the lyrics and allowing it to influence their attitudes.

In heavy metal evil acts are glorified to new heights in concerts. Gunpowder is lit, people are hung and placed in coffins, demonic figures are produced, and property is destroyed. There are many stories about portrayal of evil acts on the stage, and the crowd goes wild.

One of the most pathological forms of evil is in the form of the cult killer or deranged person who believes it is OK to hurt others or to kill. The Son of Sam who killed eight people in New York was allegedly into Black Sabbath's music. Ricky Kasso, the teenager in Long Island who stabbed his friend, took out his eyes, and then hung himself, followed Black Sabbath and Judas Priest. That is in Rolling Stone in November where they interviewed the kids that were at the funeral.

Most recently, the individual identified by the newspapers as the Night Stalker has been said to be into hard drugs and the music of the heavy metal band AC/DC.

This is not to say that the music made them into killers, but that in their insane, drug-crazed thinking, identification strongly with the lyrics of the songs. I see the same process in my work with chemically dependent and hateful teenagers.

Every teenager who listens to heavy metal certainly does not become a killer. Young people who are seeking power over others through identification with the power of evil find a close identification. The lyrics become a philosophy of life. It becomes a religion. Young people in our treatment program recovering from drug problems, do, we ask them to give up heavy metal for at least a year so that they are not again overtaken by feelings of resentment, hate, and the urge to party. Partying, which teens identify as a combination of drug use and hard rock music, is a strong stimulus to go back to that "Highway to Hell," which is an AC/DC song.

Young teens who already think too much with their hormones and too little with their heads, succumb to heavy metal bombardment.

Thank you, Mr. Chairman.

The CHAIRMAN. Gentlemen, thank you very much.

One 16-year-old music listener said to me—in fact, she is my daughter—you know, I really do not pay very much attention to the words. And my concern, said she, with labeling is that a label would simply underscore the fact that there are words here that really should be listened to, and that therefore, said she, labeling can make the situation worse, not better.

Do you think she has a good point or not?

Mr. STUESSY. I think she has a point there. Frequently that can in fact be the case. I think it is a matter of communicating to the record industry and related industries, whether it is through labeling, whether it is through ordinances such as are being considered today in San Antonio and other places, that we are not going to take this anymore. Do something. Clean up your act. Many of the problems Mr. Gortikov related just a few moments ago—that we cannot do this or that and if we print lyrics, then we might be guilty of pornography—there is a very simple answer. Get off that stuff, move on to something else. The industry itself creates the market for this.

The CHAIRMAN. Well, the industry could obviously stop making records that advocated this sort of behavior, but we are not talking about that today. All we are talking about is making information available to parents. The information that is available to parents is also available to children, and the question that was raised by my daughter was, well, does labeling not simply underscore the problem and call attention to it so that the kids are more likely to be paying attention to the words and, therefore, be influenced by the words more than otherwise?

Dr. KING. I do not feel that would happen. The young people who have serious drug problems are into the words. They specifically listen through the music for the lyrics because the lyrics give them the kinds of messages that they are looking for, rebellion, hate, violence, sex, the types of testimony that we have heard earlier. Those young people that do not listen for the lyrics pretty much are into just the beat of the music, and they know that some of the lyrics may be offensive, but they are not into it, so they do not listen for it. They just stay with the beat of the music.

The CHAIRMAN. You are saying the negative effect would not apply universally to everyone who heard the music, but it would apply to those people particularly on drugs who were susceptible to it.

Dr. KING. Yes, sir.

Mr. STUESSY. Nevertheless, even though an individual is not consciously absorbing the words, subconsciously they are being heard and registered.

The CHAIRMAN. Senator Gore.

Senator GORE. Thank you very much, Mr. Chairman.

I would like to first say it is nice to have a fellow Tennesseean on the panel here. Dr. King practices in Memphis, and I am delighted to hear your testimony, and yours, Dr. Stuessy.

In view of the lateness of the hour and the fact that we still have a panel to go, please forgive me if I just have a brief interchange with you.

If I could summarize the two presentations I would say both of you agree, based upon your experience, that there is a connection between messages received through this kind of material and behavior on the part of those who listen to it a lot or become really wrapped up in it.

Is that a fair summary?

Dr. KING. Yes, that is a fair summary. That is what the patients tell me.

Mr. STUESSY. That is exactly right. We could fill the room with research studies to prove that.

Senator GORE. So there is not much disagreement about that fact?

Mr. STUESSY. Not really.

Senator GORE. Well, I may submit some additional questions in writing. It would not be onerous for you to respond in writing, if you would be willing to do so. We may just do it that way and save some time.

Thank you very much for your testimony.

Thank you, Mr. Chairman.

The CHAIRMAN. Thank you both very much.

Finally, we have a panel consisting of Mr. Eddie Fritts, president, National Association of Broadcasters; Mr. William Steding, executive vice president, Central Broadcasting Division, Bonneville International Corp.; Mr. Robert Sabatini, WRKC-FM, Wilkes-Barre, PA; and Mr. Cerphe Colwell, Reston, VA.

Mr. Fritts, your name is first on the list. Why do you not proceed first.

STATEMENTS OF EDWARD O. FRITTS, PRESIDENT, NATIONAL ASSOCIATION OF BROADCASTERS; WILLIAM J. STEDING, EXECUTIVE VICE PRESIDENT, CENTRAL BROADCAST DIVISION, BONNEVILLE INTERNATIONAL CORP.; ROBERT J. SABATINI, JR., WRKC-FM, KING COLLEGE, WILKES-BARRE, PA; AND CERPHE COLWELL, RESTON, VA

Mr. FRITTS. Thank you, Mr. Chairman.

As you have mentioned, I represent the National Association of Broadcasters whose membership includes more than 4,500 radio stations and over 850 commercial television stations.

Of the 25,000 or so individual songs which are released each year, only a small number have lyrics which genuinely raise parental concern. As the principal trade association of the broadcasting industry, the main avenue of action for NAB when a problem such as the porn rock phenomenon arises is to generate industry awareness and sensitivity, and particularly the awareness of those at the top of our industry.

Thus, on May 13, 1985, I wrote executives of the more than 800 radio and television station group owners in the United States to alert them to the public concern that was developing over the issue of porn rock. Several articles have also been written on the subject for our weekly newsletter, which is sent to every NAB member.

The broadcasting industry response to my letter has been generally very favorable. In a number of cases senior executives wrote or told me in person that they had not been aware of the explicit nature of some of the music being played on their stations until they received my letter.

Some songs they found inappropriate for their audiences were removed from the play lists, and new songs are now being monitored more carefully. Additionally I believe the industry as a whole now has a higher level of sensitivity to this problem and to the general desirability of maintaining certain levels of good taste in programming.

A few weeks after I sent out my letter to the group owners, we discussed the porn rock problem at a meeting of the executive committee of the NAB board of directors. The conclusion which emerged was that we might be able to help our members respond by asking the record companies to supply copies of the lyrics when they make new records available to broadcasters. Thus, on May 31, 1985, I wrote to the chief executives of 45 record companies that together account for in sales for about 85 percent of the Nation's recorded music, and I asked that all recordings made available to broadcasters in the future be accompanied by copies of the songs' lyrics.

Although there was a good deal of support for this proposal among broadcasters, the recording industry was not overwhelmed by the idea and subsequently rejected it.

Since we became involved in this issue, I and other members of the NAB staff have been in regular contact with Mrs. Tipper Gore and Mrs. Susan Baker and other leaders of the Parents Music Resource Center. Last week at the Radio Management and Programming Conference in Dallas, NAB sponsored a major session on this issue which I chaired. It featured presentations by Mrs. Gore and others from the PMRC, and by Stanley Gortikov, president of the RIAA, who graciously agreed to participate on the panel.

I view this panel as another step in our effort to make broadcasters understand the nature of the public concern about the issue so that they can formulate an appropriate response.

The FCC expects each licensee to determine what the words or lyrics on a record are before the record is broadcast, and the FCC holds each broadcast licensee responsible for what it puts on the air. But even more importantly, broadcasters are held responsible in their local communities. If our listeners and our advertisers are not pleased with us, they will turn us off, the ultimate censor.

Each station must choose for itself how best to serve its own respective community, and not all listeners will like what every station in the marketplace has to offer. NAB will never attempt to intrude into any station's programming judgments. What we have endeavored to do is to balance the need for voluntary industry restraint with a strong sensitivity to first amendment concerns.

I think this effort has been successful. All in our industry now know that there is a problem which needs to be addressed and that they must make a conscious decision about how to respond to the concerns about porn rock as they go about serving their audiences in their respective communities.

Thank you, Mr. Chairman

[The statement follows:]

Statement of Edward O. Fritts, President, National Association of Broadcasters

Mr. Chairman, members of the Subcommittee, my name is Edward O. Fritts. I am president of the National Association of Broadcasters ("NAB"), an organization which represents more than 4500 radio stations, 850 television stations, and the major commercial broadcast networks. I appreciate the opportunity to join with you today to discuss the problem of what has come to be called "porn rock."

Before talking about what NAB has done to respond to this phenomenon, I think it is important to focus on the scope of the problem itself. More than 25,000 individual songs are released on record in the United States every year. Not all of these, of course, are rock music, and many recordings—much to the disapointment of the artists and their record companies—rapidly go from release to obscurity. Nonetheless, it is important to remember that literally thousands of songs are competing for public attention in the rock music marketplace each year.

Of this number, a small group have lyrics which are so sexually explicit or violent or deal with the use of drugs and alcohol or with the occult in such a way as to raise some parental concern. Those parents who are concerned fear that the music at issue may have a detrimental impact on their children. Of this limited number of songs, only a very few ever receive any meaningful airplay.

I bring this information to the subcommittee's attention, Mr. Chairman, not to minimize the importance of the subject we are discussing today, but because—especially in several of the press reports in recent months—there has been some tendency to confuse the exceptions with the rule.

Now, what has NAB done to respond to this problem? As a trade association the main avenue of action open to us when a problem such as this arises is to generate industry awareness and sensitivity, and, particularly, the awareness of those at the top. Therefore, on May 13, 1985, I wrote executives of the more than 800 radio and television station group owners in the United States to alert them to the public concern that was developing over "porn rock." I included in that mailing the letter that the founders of what is now the Parents Music Resource Center had sent me on the subject, as well as a column from one of the major news magazines. That same week, I followed up on the mailing with a story in Highlights, our weekly newsletter for all NAB members, including a reprint of the text of the letter sent to the group owners.

The broadcasting industry response to my letter was generally very favorable. Although a few broadcasts viewed even this informational mailing as a veiled attempt at censorship, many felt that it raised an issue deserving of immediate attention. Top management, even in rel-

atively small station groups, must delegate most day-to-day decisions about what's on the air to program staff. In a number of cases, senior executives wrote or told me in person that they had not been aware of the explicit nature of some of the music being played on their stations until they received my letter. Some songs they found inappropriate for their audiences were removed from their playlists, and new releases are being monitored more carefully. Through the letter itself, and through numerous articles about the letter and the reaction to it which appeared in the trade press, I believe the industry now has a higher level of sensitivity to this problem, and to the general desirability of maintaining certain levels of good taste in programming. In many cases programming changes have been made, and that will continue.

Several weeks after I sent out the letter to the group owners, we discussed the "porn rock" problem at a meeting of NAB's Executive Committee. That is the group of broadcasters elected by our Board of Directors to oversee the organization's day-to-day operations. The conclusion which emerged from the Executive Committee discussion was that one way in which we might be able to help our members respond to the "porn rock" problem would be to ask the record companies to supply copies of the lyrics when they make new records available to broadcasters.

Thus, on May 31, 1985, I wrote to the chief executives of 45 record companies that together account for the sales of over 90 percent of the nation's records, and asked that "all recordings made available to broadcasters in the future be accompanied by copies of the songs' lyrics." I explained that we were asking for this assistance not only to help the station program directors, but also to aid station owners and managers in going through the dozens of new releases, many of them recorded in a way that makes understanding the lyrics quite difficult.

Although there was a good deal of support for this proposal among broadcasters, our friends in the recording industry were not overwhelmed by the idea. Only a handful of responses were received, and they were generally negative in tone, although one very small company did send a copy of the lyrics it had supplied with a new singles release. Most recently, the Recording Industry Association of America has formally rejected the proposal on behalf of its members, arguing both that the record companies don't always have the right to reproduce lyrics for such purposes, and that it's the responsibility of every station to know what it broadcasts.

Since NAB got involved in this issue, I and other members of our staff have been in regular contact with Tipper Gore, Susan Baker and the other leaders of the Parents Music Resource Center. We have striven to understand their concerns, and to assist them in familiarizing themselves with the workings of our industry. Last week, at the Radio '85 Management and Programming Convention in Dallas, I chaired a panel session on "porn rock" which featured a lengthy presentation by Mrs. Gore. I am pleased that Stan Gortikov, the president of RIAA, also graciously agreed to participate on that panel. I view this panel as another step in our effort to make broadcasters aware of the public concern about this issue, so that they can formulate their own response.

The FCC expects each licensee to determine what the words or lyrics on a record are before the record is broadcast, and the FCC holds each broadcast licensee responsible for what it puts on the air. But even more importantly, broadcasters are held responsible by their local communities. We are there every day. Indeed, every hour our communities vote on how well we are doing. If our listeners and our advertisers are not pleased with us, they will turn away, in the ultimate censure of our activity.

Each station must choose for itself how best to serve its community, and not all listeners will like what every station in the marketplace has to offer. That is part of the extraordinary diversity of our industry, and that is as it should be. NAB will never attempt to intrude into any station's programming judgments. That would be improper both legally and as a matter of policy. What we have endeavored to do is to balance the need for voluntary industry restraint with a strong sensitivity to First Amendment concerns. I think this effort has been successful. Everyone in our industry now knows that there is a problem to be addressed, and that they must make a conscious decision about how to respond to the concerns about "porn rock" as they go about serving their audiences.

I appreciate the consideration of the Subcommittee in permitting me to let you know of the action NAB has taken.

Thank you very much.

FRITTS LETTER TO BROADCAST STATION GROUPS

National Association of Broadcasters,
Washington, DC, May 13, 1985.

DEAR : The lyrics of some recent rock records and the tone of the related music videos are fast becoming a matter of public debate. The subject has drawn national attention through articles in publications like Newsweek and USA Today and feature reports on TV programs like "Good Morning, America."

Many state that they are extremely troubled by the sexually explicit and violent language of some of today's songs. An example that has been cited is the song with words which say in part:

"I knew a girl named Nikki
I guess you could say she was a sex fiend
I met her in a hotel lobby
masturbating with a magazine."

The pre-teen and teen audiences are heavy listeners, viewers and buyers of rock music. In some communities, like Washington, D.C., parents and other interested citizens are organizing to see what they can do about the music in question, which at least one writer has dubbed "porn rock."

I wanted you, as one of the leaders in the broadcasting industry, to be aware of this situation. For your information, I am enclosing the recent Newsweek column as well as a letter I received from a group of influential Washington area residents.

It is, of course, up to each broadcast licensee to make its own decisions as to the manner in which it carries out its programming responsibilities under the Communications Act.

Sincerely.

FRITTS LETTER TO RECORD COMPANIES

National Association of Broadcasters,
Washington, DC, May 31, 1985.

DEAR : I am writing you, as a leader in the recording industry, to ask your assistance in a matter of concern to many of us in broadcasting.

The sexually explicit and violent nature of some of today's songs raises difficult issues of selectivity for those broadcasters who program rock and other contemporary music. The sheer volume of new records (and videos) made available to broadcasters, as well as the recording techniques sometimes used, make it extremely difficult for broadcast owners, managers, and program directors to be fully aware of the lyrics of all of the music their stations are being asked to air.

NAB has neither the ability nor the desire to place itself in any way in the role of censor of the music that broadcasters are presenting to the public. We do believe, however, that with your help we can play a constructive role by assisting broadcasters in making reasoned programming choices.

At its May meeting, NAB's Executive Committee asked that I write you to request that all recordings made available to broadcasters in the future be accompanied by copies of the songs' lyrics. It appears that providing this material to broadcasters would place very little burden on the recording industry, while greatly assisting the decision-making of broadcast management and programming staffs.

I look forward to hearing from you on this proposal and learning your thoughts on the problem of selectivity that the broadcasting and recording industries confront.

Sincerely.

The CHAIRMAN. Thank you, Mr. Fritts.

Mr. Steding.

Mr. STEDING. First of all, I would like to take the opportunity to thank the Senate Commerce Committee for bringing together a panel of witnesses today for the purpose of analyzing carefully the issue of pornographic rock and its impact on American youth today. It is my hope that a consensus can be reached toward resolving the issue in a self-regulatory manner.

Bonneville International has consistently advocated the limiting of Federal regulatory involvement to those areas of significant public concern not susceptible to voluntary self-regulation. However, because of the importance of this issue, if all voluntary efforts fail and the problems inherent in the airing of pornographic lyrics continue unabated, it is my personal opinion that some form of legislation may be appropriate.

I think it is very important that we understand what the issue is that is before us today. What this issue is about is the influence of today's popular artists on American youth and the abusive behaviors which some artists desire to popularize through their lyrics and music videos. What this issue is about is about consumer information, not censorship. It is about freedom of information, freedom of choice.

We can, however, have little hope of resolving this issue without the compliance and cooperation of every contributor to the marketing chain of contemporary music. While the recording artists cry for freedom of expression and cloak themselves in the Nation's highest principle, the first amendment, they, through popularizing abusive behaviors, deplore the common principle of responsibility to their fellow man.

All we are asking for is that these artists and these record companies come clean with America regarding the disclosure of their lyrics and the content of their music prior to funneling it through the powerful chain of distribution that includes not only record retailers but radio stations. We are not asking for the editing of music or the exclusion of lyrics from public consumption. What we are asking for is responsible disclosure of product information to the public so that the radio stations and the consumer can make a more informed decision regarding these records' exposure on their airwaves or their consumption in the home.

Over the last few years I have been highly involved with this issue from the standpoint of promoting its resolution in the broadcasting industry. One of the primary objections that people throw out to the idea of not playing music which is offensive in nature is that a radio station cannot compete in a marketplace if they do not play all these songs. I come before you today as evidence of one station in one market, KAFM in Dallas-Fort Worth, TX that has risen to great success over the last 3 years since entering the contemporary hit radio format and adopting policies of eliminating offensive music. Since August 1982, the time we went into the format and adopted these policies, the station has risen in success from 24th out of 27 to a high ranking of third. The stations remain competitive in the marketplace today as advertising revenues have increased more than six times those of 1982, and profits have increased by similar amounts.

Our financial success is due not only to increases in ratings but also due to the fact that several of our advertising clients will advertise with our station and not with our competitors simply because they know that their commercial will not air in an offensive environment.

Our success on the air in radio has also been duplicated on television in Dallas-Fort Worth. Through cooperation with Gaylord Broadcasting Co.'s KTVT Channel 11, KAFM simulcasts a music video program called Texas Hit Review. The program, I am proud to say, is No. 1 in its time period and beats, in fact, the network of the same nature produced by NBC called Friday Night Videos.

We have a similar policy in place for the selection of music videos for the production of Texas Hit Review as we do for selecting songs for air play.

The point is this: Be it on radio or television, we have succeeded at KAFM in presenting positive music to our marketplace.

As this committee is well aware, the Communications Act places the responsibility of all programming decisions directly on the licensee of each station. Even so, if I had to cite any negative about the process KAFM goes through to exercise that licensee responsibility as it relates to its music programming, it would be the lack of information available to the station. The station manager has no regular access to the opinion or input from the recording artist or the songwriter.

This lack of broad representation for information and input led KAFM in the spring of 1983 to propose a National Music Review Council to the industry for the purposes of creating a national awareness of this destructive impact of objectionable lyrics and to achieve self-regulation on the issue of offensive or pornographic lyrics.

Our proposal provides for the establishment of four councils located in New York, Detroit, Nashville and Los Angeles, where 90 plus percent of all contemporary music is produced. These councils would represent every segment of the marketing chain of music. In other words, each council would constitute itself by having membership representing the recording artists and songwriters, the record companies, record distributors, the broadcasters, the record retailers and the consumers. These councils would review the contemporary music produced in their respective markets, and if acceptable, based on the policy developed therein, the record would receive the seal of approval much like a Good Housekeeping Seal, on the album cover before it went to the radio stations for consideration for air play or before it went to record retail outlets for consideration of purchase by the consumer.

We have to say in 1983 the response to our proposal was mixed at best. To quote Stanley Gortikov in his response written to us in August 19, 1983, "I just deplore in principle any single review body sitting in judgment as to what is right for all Americans to hear."

I find it ironical that now Mr. Gortikov is proposing that the record companies sit as a single review body in judgment and label records which may or may not be offensive based on their own judgments. I guess what he meant in 1983 was that he deplored any single review body, that is not his own.

This brings us up to the current efforts and current proposals before this committee. In concept, the National Music Review Council proposal differs from other proposals brought before this committee in a couple of very key areas. First of all, it advocates the representation of every element of the marketing chain of music. Second, it advocates positive labeling of music which is acceptable. Third, it seeks the voluntary cooperation of broadcasters and retailers in using their discretion as to what is played or what is sold through their retail outlets.

Ladies and gentlemen, what we have today is to consider what is practical, what is reasonable, what creates the highest benefit for the real world and society as a whole. What we need on the issue of pornographic rock is a consumer information thrust which gives the National Music Review Council the opportunity to review every piece of contemporary music before it enters the American marketplace, and label that music as acceptable or not.

Whether this is in the form of ratings or positive labeling or whatever, the important thing is to make those judgments and seek the compliance of the radio station and the record retailer when it comes to the distribution of these products. All we are asking for is that a parent has a better chance of rearing their young adults, or that the teenager has a better chance of avoiding these types of popularized abusive behaviors being promoted by some recording artists.

[The statement follows:]

STATEMENT OF WILLIAM J. STEDING, EXECUTIVE VICE PRESIDENT, CENTRAL BROADCAST DIVISION, BONNEVILLE INTERNATIONAL CORP.

THE ISSUE:

First of all, I'd like to take the opportunity to thank the Senate Commerce Committee for bringing together a panel of witnesses this morning for the purpose of analyzing carefully the issue of porno-

graphic rock and its impact on American youth today. It is any hope that a consensus can be reached toward resolving this issue in a self-regulatory manner. Bonneville has consistently advocated the limiting of federal regulatory involvement to those areas of significant public concern not susceptible to voluntary self-regulation. However, because of the importance of this issue, if all voluntary efforts fail, and the problems inherent in the airing of pornographic lyrics continue unabated, it is my personal opinion that some form of legislation may be appropriate.

I think it's very important that we understand the issue that is before us today. What this issue is about, is about the influence of today's popular artists on American youth and the abusive behaviors which some artists desire to popularize through their lyrics and music videos.

What this issue is about, is about the thousands of young Americans who spend six hours a day with their favorite rock radio station and who adopt practices of deviant and destructive behavior because a popular recording artist has expressed his or her endorsement of such behavior to the point that young Americans feel this may be a means by which to gain popularity among their peers.

What this issue is about, is about young Americans who indulge in abusive behavior involving drugs, alcohol, sex and violence, to the sometimes permanent detriment of themselves and others.

What this issue is about, is about a North Dallas teenager committing suicide by carbon monoxide asphyxiation while listening to a Pink Floyd album which glorifies suicide as a logical way out.

What this issue is about, is about Richard Rameriz, suspected Los Angeles night stalker, who killed and terrorized fourteen people while being obsessed with the rock group AC/DC, and their 1979 album, "Highway to Hell".

What this issue is about, is about the negligence of recording artists, record companies, record distributors, radio stations and record retailers, in not informing the public about the potentially dangerous impact of some of these products on our highly impressionable young American public.

What this issue is about, is about freedom of information and freedom of choice.

We can, however, have little hope of resolving this issue without the compliance and cooperation of every contributor to the marketing chain of contemporary music. While the recording artists cry for freedom of expression, and cloak themselves in the nation's highest principle, the First Amendment, they deplore with great regularity the common laws of this land and the common principles of responsibility to their fellow man. All we're asking for is that these artists, and these record companies, come clean with America regarding the disclosure of their lyrics and the content of their music prior to funneling it through the powerful chain of distribution that includes not only record retailers, but radio stations. We are not asking for the editing of music or the exclusion of lyrics from public consumption. What we are asking for is responsible disclosure of product information to the public, so that the radio station and the consumer can make a more informed decision regarding these records' exposure on the airwaves or their consumption in the home.

KAFM RADIO:

Over the last three years, I have been highly involved with this issue from the standpoint of promoting resolution of this issue in broadcasting. One of the primary objections that people throw out to the idea of not playing music which is offensive in nature, is that a radio station cannot compete in a marketplace if they do not play all these songs. I come before you today as evidence of one station in one market, KAFM in Dallas/Fort Worth, Texas, that has risen to great success over the last three years since entering the Contemporary Hit Radio format and adopting policies of eliminating offensive music.

In July of 1982, I was National Sales Manager of Bonneville International Corporation's radio properties in Seattle, Washington. At that time, Ken Hatch, Senior Vice President of Bonneville, asked me to move to Dallas to take over KAAM and KAFM radio, also owned by Bonneville International Corporation. KAAM and KAFM were ranked 24th out of 27 stations in the market, and were losing millions of dollars each year. In July of '82, we made the decision to go into the brand new version of Top 40 Radio, called by the industry Contemporary Hit Radio. It was apparent at that time that the playing of top hits, or singles as the industry calls them, would be a format opportunity for several years to come, following the decline of the album-oriented rock stations who played the harder rock and longer album cuts of music.

In August of 1982, our stations' management team settled on a Statement of Purpose to guide our management process. Our Statement of Purpose was and is today:

"We will be the dominant voice in the community while upholding high standards and values for youth. We will operate a highly profitable organization, recognized as innovators of business systems, dedicated to the continuous development of employees as industry leaders, founded in a strong sense of business ethics."

Subsequent to this Statement of Purpose, we composed a music policy to support specifically our intention of 'upholding high standards and values for youth'. Our music policy, stated specifically:

"A title or lyric is objectionable if specific reference is made to sex or the sex act, the use of drugs, or when a specific expletive, used normally as a swearword is contained therein. The song would either be deleted from playlist consideration or the objectionable lyric edited entirely from that particular song. Innuendo or double entendre in the lyric or lyrics may or may not be construed as objectionable. The decision to delete or edit is left up to the management of each individual radio station."

At KAFM, we decided to take a position against offensive lyrics. Every week, we review the songs brought to us by the record company promoters in the hope of finding the four or five songs that we believe will be big hits. While this process is highly complex, it does involve one final decision regarding offensive lyrics. After all the music has been considered, the Vice President of Programming and the General Manager, sit down and review each piece of music again for lyrical content. If the song is acceptable, it is added to the playlist. If it is unacceptable, it is either edited for airplay or eliminated from consideration. If the General Manager and the Vice President of Programming cannot make a clear decision, the piece of music is played for the Youth Advisory Board, which is made up of 12 youth members of the community and youth leaders of the community. These 12 people review music on a regular basis, as well as advise the station on promotional policies and community service projects. After the piece of music has passed all these tests, it is added to the playlist.

Since August of 1982, the stations have risen in success from 24th out of 27 to a high ranking of third. The stations remain competitive in the marketplace today as advertising revenues have increased more than six times those of 1982, and profits have increased by a similar amount. Our financial success is due not only to increases in ratings, but also due to the fact that several of our advertising clients will advertise with our station and not with our competitors simply because they know that their commercial will not air in an offensive environment.

Our success on the air in radio has also been duplicated on television in Dallas/Fort Worth. Through cooperation with Gaylord Broadcasting Company's KTVT Channel 11 in Dallas/Fort Worth, KAFM simulcasts a music video program called the "Texas Hit Review" on Friday and Saturday nights, from 12 midnight to 2 AM. The program, I'm proud to say, is #1 in its time period, and beats, in fact, the network program of the same nature produced by NBC called "Friday Night Videos." Quite an accomplishment, considering that the program is on an independent TV station, up against a slick, highly financed network program. We have a similar policy for the music program, "Texas Hit Review," that we follow when selecting videos. Our policy on music videos is that

"A music video is objectionable when the graphic exploitation of sex, drugs or violence exists. In other words, when specific visual reference is made to sex, or the sex act, particularly featuring exposed body parts to refer to this action, or if there is a specific visual reference to the use of drugs as a positive effect on a human being, or violence in the form of excessive aggression leading to murder, rape, or similar acts. All decisions regarding the deletion or editing of objectionable materials is left up to the individual management of the radio and television station."

The point is this, be it on radio or television, we have succeeded at KAFM in presenting positive music to our marketplace. If that isn't proof enough for you about the attitudes and opinions of these listeners and viewers of Contemporary Hit Radio, let me refer you to some research recently conducted in Dallas/Fort Worth which reflects the same appetite for positive music rather than offensive music.

In July, 1985, KAFM commissioned Coleman Research Group to answer several questions regarding the radio station and the musical tastes of the Dallas/Fort Worth Contemporary Hit Radio listener. Sampling 400 people through telephone research, ages 15 to 29, we asked questions to measure the extent to which references to drugs, sex, violence and alcohol in hit songs today offend listeners. It's astonishing to learn that not only was a high percentage of the audience bothered by references to drugs, sex, alcohol or violence, but the sub-group that was most offended in that 15 to 29 age population, were the 15 to 18 year olds. 48% of the people in that age group said that they were either very or somewhat bothered by the above mentioned references. More importantly, the 19 to 29 year old age group trailed the 15 to 18 year old age group by 9 percentage points in their preference for a radio station that does not play lyrics that make overt references to drugs, sex, alcohol or violence. That 15 to 18 year old age group said that 43% preferred radio stations that did not play that type of music. Of the 15 to 18 year olds, when asked, "What should radio stations do about songs that include overt references to drugs, sex, alcohol or violence", 65% said "Don't play them", "Edit them", or "limit their exposure." Now remember, these are 15 to 18 year olds. Only 12% of that population said "Do nothing"; 18% said, "Play them as is." Finally, we asked the question, "Would you listen to a radio station that removes potentially offensive lyrics?" 60% of the 15 to 18 year olds said "Yes."

While some of these figures do not indicate a vast majority in all cases, you have to remember that in radio, the #1 station in the market may only have a 10% market share of listeners. Consequently, a 60% preference level for any given type of programming is a very large opportunity for a radio station. To quote Coleman Research's summary on this issue, they said, "The research suggests that the majority of listeners are willing to listen to a station that edits lyrics. In fact, some listeners like that KAFM edits lyrics."

As this committee is well aware, the Communications Act places the responsibility of all programming decisions directly on the licensee of each station. Even so, if I had to cite any negative about the process KAFM goes through to exercise that licensee responsibility, as it relates to its music programming, it would be the lack of information available to the station. The station manager has no regular access to the opinions or input from the recording artist, the music publisher, the recording company, or, except in limited circumstances, the consumer. This lack of broad representation for information and input led KAFM, in the Spring of 1983, to propose a National Music Review Council to the industry for the purposes of creating a national awareness of the destructive impact of objectionable lyrics, and to achieve self-regulation on the issue of offensive or pornographic lyrics.

NATIONAL MUSIC REVIEW COUNCIL PROPOSAL:

Our proposal provides for the establishment of four councils, located in New York, Detroit, Nashville and Los Angeles, where 90% of all contemporary music is produced. These councils would represent every segment of the marketing chain of music. In other words, each council would constitute itself by having membership representing the recording artists and songwriters, the record companies, the record distributors, the broadcasters, the record retailers and the consumers. These councils would review the contemporary music produced in their respective markets and, if acceptable, based on the policy developed therein, the record would receive the seal of approval, much like the Good Housekeeping seal, on the album cover before it went to the radio station for consideration for airplay, or before it went to the record retail outlets for consideration of purchase by the consumer.

We have to say, in 1983 the response to our proposal was mixed, at best. To quote Stanley Gortikov, in his response written to us on August 19, 1983, "I cannot support any nationalization of such a procedure, no matter how feasible it is for any one station such as your own. I just deplore in principle any single review body sitting in judgment as to what is right for all Americans to hear." I find it ironical that now, Mr. Gortikov is proposing that the record companies sit as a single review body, in judgment, and label records which may or may not be offensive, based on their own judgments. I guess what he meant in '83 was that he deplored any single review body that's not his own. We also flew to New York and had meetings with heads of Columbia Records and Warner Record Labels. In both cases, while executives of these companies thought the idea was an excellent idea and right for their children, they knew that it was too cumbersome an issue for them to deal with, with respect to the big money contracts they had with their artists. To quote one radio executive, he said,

"Can you imagine paying Mick Jagger of Rolling Stones five million dollars just to walk in the studio, and then tell him he can't sing certain lyrics?" Recording artists and record companies aside, industry response to our proposal at that time, from the record distributors and retailers, was positive. Bromo Distributors, the largest distributor in the area of Texas, was very supportive of our efforts, as were Leiberman Brothers, Minneapolis. This brings us up to the current efforts and the current proposals before this Committee.

In concept, the National Music Review Council proposal differs from other proposals brought before this Committee in a couple of very key areas. First of all, it advocates the representation of every element in the marketing chain of music, such that every one has a voice in the decision or judgment made on a particular piece of music. Second, it advocates the positive labeling of music which is acceptable, rather than drawing attention to that which is unacceptable. Third, it seeks the voluntary cooperation of broadcasters and the record retailers in using their discretion as to what is played or sold through their retail outlets regarding that music which is not accepted or approved by the Council. We feel that the benefits to the industry and to the consumer of this type of proposal far exceed the cost of implementing such a process. If we can save one young life from suicide, or several thousand lives from abusive behaviors popularized by some of today's recording artists, we have created a social benefit which far outweighs these negligible costs of administration.

For those who would seek to work against this effort by giving it the false label of censorship, we cite the opinion of Jeremiah S. Gutman, President of the New York Chapter of the American Civil Liberties Union and a member of the A.C.L.U. National Board of Directors. Mr. Gutman, while not endorsing the purposes of the N.M.R.C., said that "Individually owned media of communication have an absolute right to broadcast or not to broadcast whatever they please. The people that come together with the National Music Review Council have a First Amendment right to associate peaceably together and to attempt to persuade others to associate with them and to follow their recommendation on musical taste."

SUMMARY:

The issue we're faced with today is a social/consumer issue . . . not an issue of freedom of speech. We are not advocating the censorship of lyrics, or of music, to the American public. What we are advocating is a higher degree of information disseminated to those people who directly distribute that music to the American consumer, the radio station and the record retailer. It's simply irresponsible and negligent not to provide this information, considering the profound effect that this music has on American youth. Contemporary Hit Radio is one of the most dynamic influences on the emotions and the behavior of people in their pre-teen years. This population spends an average of six hours a day with rock radio stations in America. That's more time typically than they spend at school and with their parents combined. The impact of the lyrical content of songs is intensified by the charismatic appeal and fame of the recording artists, and the natural tendency to achieve a sense of identification with the artist is as powerful today as at any time in the 20th century. Broadcast and recording technology, and the ability to bring music into virtually every aspect of daily life has made Contemporary Hit music an integral part of the consciousness of today's youth. For many, it is more than entertainment, it is an accompaniment to day to day existence. Young artists have always dictated styles of personal appearance and dress. Today, however, that influence on the thoughts, emotions and behavior of their audiences has created a new responsibility for artists, the production companies which record their music, and the broadcasters who air Contemporary Hit music on radio and television. That responsibility is to establish ethical boundaries for the content of their communication, be it a lyric, and in the case of music videos, the visual content of their performances.

Unfortunately, a few artists have decided to abuse their power by popularizing abusive behavior along the lines of sex, drugs and violence. This issue is, therefore, one of social benefit vs. social cost. We are not asking for undue government interference. All we're asking for is that we decide to live by necessary rules for civilized society. For the same reasons we have laws about 21-year-old drinking ages, and laws mandating seat belt use, we need to seek measures which protect us against the influences of ill-intentioned popular artists. When it comes to regulatory intervention, some people think that it's a black and white situation . . . you either have to be completely for it, or completely against it. But, to quote Lee Iaccoca on the issue of mandatory seat belts, he says, "As with anything else, you have to look at the circumstances. There are areas of life where the government has to act to protect society. Only in America do we allow the idealogues to prevail over the demands of safety." He goes on to say, "What these purists seem to forget is that the damage done by not using seat belts raises our taxes. Increases car insurance rates, and harms us and our loved ones, and if that's not an intrusion on my freedom. I don't know what is." I feel Mr. Iaccoca's arguments for mandatory seat belt laws apply to pornographic lyrics as well.

Ladies and gentlemen, what we have to do today is to consider what is practical, what is reasonable, what creates the highest benefit for the real world and society as a whole. What we need on the issue of pornographic rock is a consumer information thrust which gives a National Music Review Council the opportunity to review every piece of Contemporary music before it enters the American marketplace, and label that music as acceptable or not. Whether this is in the form of ratings, or positive labeling, or whatever, the important thing is to make these judgments and seek the compliance of the radio station and the record retailer when it comes to the distribution of these products. Some people have said to me, "Well, isn't this the job of the parents?" I say to them, that the job of being a parent in today's society is more complex and time-consuming than it has been in recent years. With so many dual family incomes, the mother and father are highly preoccupied with the business of providing for a family. All we're asking for is that the parent has a better chance of rearing their young adult, or that the teenager has a better chance of avoiding the types of popularized abusive behaviors being promoted by some recording artists today. As long as we agree with the practicality of 21 year old drinking ages, and 55-mile an hour speed limits, we should have the fortitude to step up and handle this very delicate situation as it pertains to music and its relationship to young adults.

I ask today for your commitment in seeking some type of review process, complied with by all members of the music industry, including everyone from the artist to the consumer, in an effort to keep in check the potential harm to America's #1 resource, American youth.

Thank you very much for your time and for your consideration.

The CHAIRMAN. Mr. Sabatani.

Mr. SABATANI. Thank you very much.

My name is Robert Sabatani, Jr. I am speaking on behalf of WRKC-FM, and that is at King College in Wilkes-Barre, PA, not in New York or Kentucky or Camp Springs, MD.

We are very concerned about record labeling and its impact on college radio programming. College radio is generally alternative programming, playing music which has not been discovered by our commercial brothers yet. WRKC prides itself on playing these songs, giving listeners in the Wyoming Valley a musical alternative.

Some of this music could fall under the categories of sexually explicit, promoting drug use or violent, as we are discussing today. But what do these titles mean? Everyone here can find songs that truly offend our tastes. Some of this music could be played by radio stations; in fact, many are. But at WRKC we restrict their air play to late night hours. We exercise discretion over what and when music is played.

There is a great range between Disney and Deep Throat in lyrical content. That music makes up a sizable share of our alternative programming. This music talks about the human conditions, love, hate, sex, violence, and the need to escape. These artists are making a statement about society, and they should remain unhindered in expressing themselves. Groups that support record labeling say they do not want to censor records, but they ignore the effect that an X label has on a radio station, a retailer and a record company.

A chilling effect would encourage record companies to sign artists that do not cause controversy, like requiring a warning label. Less music would be available, and that would be something that offends no one. This chilling effect would cut back on available programming for alternative music stations and deprive all of us of significant music.

Smaller labels without the large roster of artists to fall back on would be the hardest hit. These labels which we are very dependent on are vulnerable because they do not have the financial resources to fight labeling restrictions or the muscle to convince retailers and radio stations to stock and play their music.

Radio stations do not exist in a vacuum. We are dependent on record companies and retail outlets, just as they are dependent upon us. If a record store declines to carry records with a warning label, maybe record sales of a group of artists fall in that area, even though a radio station is playing their music. So a record promotion executive says to himself, wow, no record sales in this area; I guess the radio stations are not very effective. Let's take their name off the mailing list.

College radio does not have the financial resources that our larger brothers have, so we are very dependent upon record companies for programming material.

Maybe a radio station does not want to play labeled records. Listeners then lose the opportunity to judge for themselves what is obscene or violent and what is not. We are also concerned about what announcers would be required to do before playing a labeled song. Should we say, this record contains sexually explicit material; listener discretion is advised? Actually, that would not be too bad of an idea. Forbidden fruit usually has its followers, and we can certainly use the boost in our ratings.

We question what constitutes violence, sexually explicit or promotion of drug use. We could spend a year throwing examples back and forth, but in my written testimony I have left you with a few examples to mull over.

Will record companies be required to label all types of music, rock, jazz, classical, soul, country, patriotic? Will older as well as newer material be covered?

We look forward to the day when we see a violence or sex label on a Frank Sinatra record because it contains "Mack the Knife" or "Strangers in the Night." Then we will believe that this is not an attempt to put down currently popular music.

Underlying this discussion about record labeling is the unstated assumption that records cause changes in their children's behavior, especially among those who have already got problems. Does rock music negatively affect children? We have all heard about studies when a researcher puts ten 7-year-olds in a room with baseball bats and then plays "aggressive music." Inevitably, the boys use the baseball bats, leading the researcher to partially concluded that music contributes to aggressive behavior.

But has there ever been any research conducted in the real world? It is naive of us to believe that labeling records so parents can know what their children are listening to will alter their behavioral patterns. Let's look at our children's environment before we go gung-ho into labeling. Rape, murder and everything else imaginable abounds on daytime and prime time television. Domestic violence scars thousands more than any record ever could.

Maybe we should ask ourselves why is there violent or sexually explicit lyrics out there? People are focusing on some ill-defined specifics of society's breakdowns and are not looking for the cause. Some people here said music reflects our society. In Barron's last week there was a chart showing different music trends, and basically what it said was that when music becomes downbeat, aggressive, that something is wrong with society. Maybe we should take a look at that.

We hope that the general public becomes more aware of what their children are listening to and respond if they believe that unacceptable values are influencing their children. This could be accomplished better by writing one article for a popular magazine, like Ladies' Home Journal, then a year's worth of warning labels, and would not be censorship, which record labeling is.

We have heard a couple of comments about the Night Stalker. It is inferred that this music by AC/DC contributed to this guy's committing murders. I put that in the same category as the Twinkie defense used in San Francisco and the television defense where the kid said he saw the murder on Kojak and felt compelled to commit the same thing in Florida. Let's look at how many people have been killed in the name of God. Do you want to ban God?

We thank the committee for allowing us, and me, the opportunity to testify on behalf of WRKC in Wilkes-Barre, PA.

Thank you.

The CHAIRMAN. Mr. Colwell.

Mr. COLWELL. Good afternoon.

I would like to thank you for the invitation to speak this afternoon on the subject of what some would call the explicit nature of lyrics in today's popular music. My name is Cerphe Colwell, and I am a radio announcer on WWDC, DC-101, FM, here in Washington DC, and also a co-host of a segment of panorama on Channel 5 television, also here in Washington, DC.

I have been employed in radio for 16 years in this market. Although others today have made the strong argument on the legitimate concerns raised by the subject, that is not my primary purpose for this appearance today. I believe that neither I nor any other individual is fully qualified to render judgments regarding the moral implication of any form of artistic expression, including contemporary music. However, for those who choose to make such judgments, there are some very real dangers that any proposed action to control or to limit the availability of certain records will amplify the problem that they seek to solve.

Many people have argued here today that today's popular music is merely a reflection of today's more explicit society. And certainly it cannot be disputed that from movies to print to television we are almost constantly exposed in every form of media to both explicit and graphic depictions of our modern world. However, to point an accusing finger solely at contemporary music demonstrates a fundamental misapprehension of the problems and concerns at hand and any attempted "solutions."

First, as our society has become more sophisticated, young people in general have become more sophisticated. Thus, any of the perceived harms that many feel will result from today's songs must be viewed weekly in the proper social context. Ralph Cramden promised his wife weekly trips to the moon back in the 1950s. We were not patently outraged when this happened, words and actions which today would be offensive, per se. Nevertheless, now as then, we as a society are sophisticated to place such scenes in the proper context. And I think certainly few of us would elevate The Honeymooners as a TV show that advocated spouse abuse.

Similarly, today's young people viewing musicians that to all outward appearances would offend their parents, are intelligent and sophisticated enough to place such performers in their proper context and to make their own judgments. In fact, many of these musicians are viewed as little more than glorified comic book characters. To underestimate the ability of young people today to make these perceptions just begins to expose the problems that antiregulatory steps would create.

Second, it must be recognized that any attempt to impose a standardized rating system similar to that for motion pictures is an overreaction to the perceived problem and could in fact produce results contrary to those intended. Mr. Chairman, your daughter had a good point on listening to lyrics, that it may indeed raise the attention to these lyrics that is not happening right now.

The effect of a backlash against such a rating system is a point surely that been raised by a few, and will not be repeated here now.

In that regard, however, it must be noted that the songs complained of today represent a very small fraction of all popular music currently being produced, and by highlighting just a small percentage of that music as "explicit" or needing of "parental guidance" is only going to serve to unduly focus attention on these subjects. This result is more probable due to the traditional perceptions of young people that popular music is an exclusive voice of their peer group.

As a radio personality for over 16 years, I have seen radical and fundamental changes in this business. Be assured that the nature of radio has significantly changed from the free-form days of the 1960's, and further be assured that no song is played on contemporary music stations that has not been previously reviewed by station personnel. These people are aware of FCC guidelines as well as community standards of our listening audiences, and quite simply, the economic marketplace defines what is broadcast. An FCC license is far too valuable to be jeopardized by the playing of songs that would offend their audiences.

Similar considerations apply to other segments of the industry such as the record companies and distributors. Again, it comes down to the fact that a particular song or record will not be made or distributed unless there is an acceptable market willing to receive it.

The inherent problem of determining standards to categorize lyrical content on a broad national level is the fact that parental ability to set guidelines for their children will be directly undermined. It cannot be disputed that every community in this country is different, just as every young person is different. A national rating system will deprive all parents everywhere of responding to what they believe is in the best interest of their child.

Finally, a proposed rating system for lyrics offers no assurance that these problems complained of here today will simply vanish or diminish, even if certain songs are targeted as offensive and effectively kept from young listeners. The explicitness of all of today's media would surely continue.

Nevertheless, should it be determined that some action is necessary, it is important that such a step be taken with extreme caution so as to overreach and effectively ban all popular forms of musical expression or to chill the creative talents of contemporary musicians and artists. Any such effort must be carefully designed to ensure that fairness is applied by those whose judgements and interpretations will control dissemination of popular music. All segments of the music industry, as well as society at large must be allowed adequate input into this.

Further hearings should be conducted, fully exploring all sides of these issues, and many of the people appearing before this committee today I think would be a natural starting place, for while the symptoms of our modern society are being examined here today, precipitous action will be a false cure, at best, and just another disease at worst.

Thank you.

The CHAIRMAN. Thank you, Mr. Colwell.

You know, when I looked at this witness list yesterday, I wondered what today's hearing would hold in store for the Commerce Committee, and I must say I looked at it with some trepidation. I was concerned about the problem of maintaining some degree of decorum in the committee room, what sorts of statements would be rendered by the various witnesses. I did not expect that we would wait for our last panel to testify to hear the most cynical statement that I have heard yet, and that is Mr. Sabatani's testimony.

You are the director of programming for a college radio station?

Mr. SABATINI. No, sir. I am testifying on behalf of the radio station.

The CHAIRMAN. Oh, you are testifying on behalf of a college station?

Mr. SABATINI. Yes, sir.

The CHAIRMAN. Does your testimony reflect their views?

Mr. SABATINI. Yes, it does, sir.

The CHAIRMAN. I'll tell you, the cynicism of whoever is running your college station blows my mind. I thought that there was some degree of idealism left. Your testimony is, as I understand it, the problem with this all is that it interferes with people's ability to make a buck.

Mr. SABATINI. No, sir. What it interferes with is our ability— well, we are not making any money off of it.

The CHAIRMAN. Yes, but the whole thrust is that people will not send you records to play, business will go down, dollars will not come in, people will not be spending money. That was what I got out of your testimony, that the great value is the pursuit of the dollar.

Mr. SABATINI. Or the great value might be that we are allowed to listen to music.

Now, we have to pay for music, at least on the disk, by buying disks. Now, music coming into a radio station, that comes to us generally free. We play that. Now, for us for people to hear it, we have to play it, and if retailers do not stock it or if retailers will not stock it and it gets back to the record companies that this music is not selling, then another type of music is affected, too, that is not necessarily what you would call porn rock.

The CHAIRMAN. I will just say that I have not advocated legislation, and do not. My whole thought in holding this hearing is that there are concerns and there are values out there in the country beyond the value of the dollar. And that whatever value system we have in the country is brought into play by letting that system work and speak to what is happening in the country. And therefore, to me, the idea of bringing out into the open what is in these lyrics and then allowing some system for labeling so that families can know what is in the lyrics is simply a matter of openness and disclosure and permitting the values of this country to be exercised for better or worse.

Maybe we as a people will decide that incest and rape are perfectly fine. I do not think that that is the attitude of the American people if they know the facts. I think the attitude of the American people if they know the facts is that this is not what we want to stand for as a people, and this is not what we want to stand for as a country.

I think that the attitude of mothers and fathers is this is not the kind of thing that we really want in our home. That is the use of a value system.

I understand the approach that if you have any labeling or any disclosure maybe it will interfere with people's dollars. But it just seems to me that there are things other than the pursuit of the dollar which should be considered in this country. To say that if you tell people that this record deals with suicide, then our radio station is not going to have as many dollars is no argument against disclosure.

Mr. SABATINI. I think a lot of broadcasters believe that we should have a lyric sheet, and I think that we should have a lyric sheet. It gives us the opportunity and it gives the parents the opportunity to judge what is on the music. But who is to say? I mean, we are all very tied into this, and the economic forces that say, OK, this stuff, this music is bad, that is how bad music fades out into oblivion, because the economic forces push it out.

The CHAIRMAN. You say who is to say, and everybody here has said that today. Who is to say? Who is to say? Parents are to say. Families are to say. Communities are to say.

That is what makes values in this country. It is not Congress. We hopefully reflect the values of the country. We do not make the values of the country.

Hopefully parents, families, and communities will say what is tolerable and what is not according to our value system. That is all the parents group is asking for. All they are asking is, just put it out in the open, and let the parents say.

Mr. SABATINI. A lyric sheet would be acceptable to them.

The CHAIRMAN. Maybe so. I am not part of this negotiation. Senator Gore has indicated that he thinks it is a good idea. Senator Gore.

Senator GORE. Yes; I do think that lyric sheets might be a solution to this problem. If the industry could work out the remaining problems associated with getting the publishing companies to cooperate with the record manufacturers to have lyric sheets available to the DJ's and to parents, I think it could be a very good way to solve this problem.

I want to elaborate on one point for the record, Mr. Chairman, and that is to underscore the fact that the National Association of Broadcasters was the first group that responded to these concerns as they were being initially raised. The NAB immediately wrote letters to broadcasters around the country and said, look, this is a real problem, we have a responsibility as an industry, and formally requested lyric sheets from the record companies.

I want to say for the record that I think these actions reflect very well on the sense of responsibility on the part of the NAB and on the leadership of Eddie Fritts in that respect. It was a very good step, and considering the reaction received from some other elements of the entertainment industry, a courageous step. You got a lot of criticism for your actions, I am told.

I want you to know that there are a whole lot of people who appreciate your leadership and believe that you did the right thing.

Mr. Steding, I think your heart is obviously in the right place, and you have made a commercial success out of imposing some standards on the material that you play, and I wish you the best.

I would like to say I have some concerns about the National Music Review Council idea. I understand that your radio station or stations sometimes change the words of songs in order to have them comply with airplay criterion. Is that right?

Mr. STEDING. The process at the stations includes a review of every piece of music that comes into the organization on a weekly basis, which sometimes can be as many as 100 records form record companies, and we go through a very complex process in terms of determining the four or five songs that we may potentially wish to add to our play list.

The very last step before we put it on the air is to review the song between myself and between the vice president of programming of lyrical content, and we do have a policy that we follow that states basically that if we find it offensive along the lines of popularizing abusive behaviors that involve sex, violence, or drugs or alcohol, that we will do one of two things.

We will either not play the song in its entirety. We will just abandon it from consideration. Or we will edit the music with

the compliance of the record company before we put it on the air.

Now, of course, we have two reasons why we do that. One is that we have a very high responsibility granted us by the FCC to represent the public interest, and along the lines of that responsibility review the music that we play on the radio station.

But also I think it really puts the issue flat back on the recording industry, and that when faced with the option of not having their song played, they very readily wish to have it edited, as long as we will play it and add it to our play list.

Senator GORE. I certainly applaud your willingness to refrain from playing songs which you consider offensive and inappropriate for your audience. However, I have some real concerns about editing or actively changing the words. You say you make these changes with the compliance of the record companies?

Mr. STEDING. Well, the record promoters who come and bring the music to our station each week are well aware and in fact have made suggestions at times of which lyrics to edit before air play, because they understand our position.

Senator GORE. It is obviously a complex legal question. I think it is noble to not play songs which you think are offensive. But I have some concern about going ahead and playing the songs and taking out the individual words you think are offensive. I would think the artist and the record companies may have something to say about that.

Again, however, it is obvious that your heart is in the right place, and you would like to give support to the effort to increase sensitivity within the recording industry, encouraging some self-restraint.

Mr. Sabatini, you belittled the connection between AC/DC and the alleged Nightstalker. I do not think it is fair to blame the record company or the artists for what this accused, evidently psychotic murderer did.

But at the same time, there have been a number of violent acts associated with that same rock group. In this particular case the accused had a hat with the name of the group on his forehead and wrote the words of the songs on the walls of his victims as they lay dying in their beds. According to his acquaintances, he was a big, big fan of the band and in fact, one of their songs spells out what a nightstalker does.

These facts, when combined with the incidences of young kids committing suicide while listening to other songs from the same group glorifying suicide, suggest to me that the company that is making a lot of money from the sales of these records ought to be willing to ask—are we doing something wrong here? Do we not have some responsibility to this country in which we live, to the people of whom we are a part? Does it not trouble you, that there have been several instances associated with these explicit lyrics from just this one group?

Mr. SABATINI. Yes; it does. I cannot comment for a record company or for a group saying that we should not have these songs on. That would be outside of my bounds. But yes, it is troubling. But can you say that definitely the song is going to make this person, this individual person, whether they have drug problems or whatever, commit crimes? Is there that direct correlation?

Senator GORE. Well, I do not think it is fair to draw a direct correlation.

Mr. SABATINI. It is troubling, yes.

The CHAIRMAN. Senator Trible.

Senator TRIBLE. Mr. Chairman, very briefly, first I want to thank you for your leadership and for giving this committee the opportunity to hear from many witnesses today, and to talk about a very important issue.

I want to commend you, Mr. Fritts, and the National Association of Broadcasters for your very constructive response, and I simply want to observe that probably the most important word in a democracy is "no," that in a free society not everything goes, that unbridled freedom leads to chaos and to loss of freedom.

The Supreme Court has said that freedom of speech is not without limitation, and I would hope that within this industry there would be a measure of self-restraint, and I would encourage the leaders of the industry to respond responsibly to this very real national concern to exercise a measure of restraint, and I think everyone's interest would be better served.

Absent that I would predict there would be a response from the elected officials of the people of this country who are very concerned about these kinds of activities, and who have judged them destructive, destructive of lives, destructive of our society.

Thank you, Mr. Chairman.

The CHAIRMAN. I want to thank the members of the committee for their diligence today. And I want to thank all witnesses, and especially the members of the last panel, for staying with us for such a long period of time. That concludes a 5-hour hearing.

[Whereupon, at 2:30 p.m., the committee was adjourned, to reconvene upon the call of the Chair.]

Additional Articles, Letters, and Statements

STATEMENT OF HON. TOM BRADLEY, MAYOR, CITY OF LOS ANGELES, CA

Attempts by narrow and isolated segments of our society to censor the lyrics of American popular music are not new. In the 1930's, pressure from censors forced Variety not to list the work of music legends Gene Autry and Jimmy Rodgers. The 1950's and 1960's saw zealous efforts to inhibit the lyrics and the performing styles of entertainment superstars such as Elvis Presley and Little Richard. In 1963, the Federal Communications Commission conducted a farcical month-long investigation of the Kingsmen's classic song "Louie, Louie."

Fortunately, the would be censors have lost nearly every round against American popular music, and generations of Americans have grown up with the legacy of free thought and unfettered expression guaranteed by the First Amendment.

Today, the acrid smell of censorship is in the air once again. Even though this Committee is not yet considering any specific legislation, the unmistakable threat of censorship now hangs over the American recording industry. The fact that these hearings are being held at all sends a clear message to the American music community. Meet the artistic demands of a few influential individuals, or face Congressional hostility on many different fronts.

The time has come to strip the veneer of respectability from the proposals offered by the would-be censors; we must recognize those proposals for what they really are. The censors want nothing less than a national system of ratings to categorize each of the tens of thousands of recordings released every year by the American music industry. The censors want to take away from parents the responsibility of deciding what kind of music their children should hear. Instead, the censor would have some annointed or appointed undemocratic committee decide questions that have always been properly left to the family.

There is no logical end to the arguments made by the would-be censors. If tens of thousands of recordings should be rated every year, why not impose the similar rating standards on books? Why not require authors to publish potentially objectionable passages in a special section of their books so that parents can easily review them?

Indeed, the proposals set forth before this Committee raise the frightening specter of government intrusion into American arts and culture. A few song lyrics—no matter how objectionable to some—do not deserve the attention of the United States Congress. Nor do these lyrics justify opening the Pandora's box of censorship—a box that is firmly and securely shut by the First Amendment.

The censorship proposals also open the door for the extreme kinds of narrow-mindedness and provincialism. For example, the would-be censors appearing before your Committee have focused entirely on rock and roll lyrics, while completely ignoring country music. This selectivity has more than a little to do with personal preferences and political constituencies than with concern for America's youth. Can we expect the same sort of arbitrary considerations to influence a national ratings system? Or can we expect the next wave of censors to shift their attack to lyrics they describe as "unpatriotic" or "un-American?" The dragon of censorship, once loosed, will not be easy to recapture.

The censorship proposals are also doomed to failure. Placing warning labels on record albums will do nothing but attract children to the "forbidden fruit," to precisely those songs the censors have decided are objectionable.

The American music industry does not deserve to be made the scapegoat for the problems that some see in our society. America's performing artists represent a multi-billion dollar industry that has always been quick to aid those in need. Surely we have not forgotten the scourge of the McCarthy era, when the ravings of a single prominent senator wreaked economic havoc on an entire industry and ruined many lives. We must not permit similar economic and personal devastation to be inflected on the music industry.

If there is concern about the lyrics to a few songs, the solution lies with the American family—not with the government, not with a small group of self-annointed censors. Parents must become involved in their children's lives; they must be concerned to find what albums their children are listening to. The censorship plans of a small fragment of our society can never substitute for the advice and supervision of caring, concerned parents.

The lure of headlines cannot justify the forum that this Committee has given to those who would restrict free speech. America's highest legislative body must stand squarely behind the First Amendment. The United States Congress should not sanction—in even the slightest way—the effects of those who regard the first amendment as an inconvenience rather than as the cornerstone of our democracy.

STATEMENT OF THOMAS E. RADECKI, M.D., CHAIRPERSON, NATIONAL COALITION ON TELEVISION VIOLENCE

Violent and Degrading Imagery in Rock Music Videos

The National Coalition on Television Violence (NCTV) has been monitoring rock music videos on national television channels since October, 1983. We have also completed a study comparing rock music lyrics from 1963, 1973, and 1983. We have gathered reports from other researchers from U.S. universities on violence in rock music videos and its impact on normal college students. What we have found is a major increase in the quantity and intensity of violence in rock music itself and even more so in rock music videos. We have also found a virtual absence of any non-violent rock music video viewing hours available to the public on any national cable or broadcast television channel. We have found research that documents the harmful effects of violent music video entertainment even on normal college students.

NCTV's own study of rock music lyrics found a major 115 percent increase in the use of violent lyrics since 1963 in rock music's top 40 lists. The character of this violence has also changed, becoming much more intense. Songs of rape and sadism were virtually non-existent in 1963, but have become fairly common in the 1980's. Rock music has even developed a subculture known as heavy metal which glamourizes violence and anti-social attitudes. However, songs of violence and sexual violence have become increasingly common in other rock music entertainment as well.

To date, NCTV has monitored over 1300 rock music videos from MTV, WTBS's Nighttracks, and the USA Network: 35 percent of these contain explicit physical violence, 9 percent contain anger or threats of violence, 2 percent contain violence which is used in an educational manner, 50 percent non-violent, and 4 percent pro-social. Violence on MTV and WTBS have been very similar in amount, averaging 17.9 acts of violence per hour. This level of violence showed little change from October 1983 and November 1984, while there has been a small decrease in violence in 1985.

In all, 44 percent of all music videos contained violence or suggestions of violence. Almost half of these violent videos contained violence between men and women. Women were as violent against men as men were against women. A major theme was a portrayal of hatred and intense violence between the sexes as being common-place and acceptable. Although women were as violent as men, they were more often portrayed in a negative light: 13 percent of violent videos contained sadistic violence, where the attacker actually took pleasure out of committing the violence.

Violence in music videos is considerably more common than violence in rock music lyrics, themselves. The visuals in music videos have been found to contain three times as many acts of violence as the lyrics. A fair number of videos with violence in the visual track have absolutely no violence in the lyrics themselves. In addition to violence, sexist and sexually degrading images, cigarette and alcohol abuse, and other anti-social behaviors are frequently portrayed in rock music videos with cigarette abuse being considerably more often portrayed than on prime-time television.

The impact of rock music videos can be seen in the powerful effect they have had on record sales as reported by the industry itself. A survey in Newsweek magazine reported that 50 percent of music video viewers replay the video in their minds when they later hear the record played on radio.

Other researchers have found the same high levels of violence as found by NCTV. Dr. Richard Caplan of the University of Akron in Ohio completed a study of 200 MTV videos and found the violence averaged 17 acts per hour. Women were more negatively portrayed and were shown as having lower morals and other undesirable traits. Dr. Caplan also did a monitoring of Nick Rocks, the Nickelodeon music video program owned by Warner Communication. He found the same high level of violence on Nick Rocks as he found on MTV.

Sherman and Dominick of the University of Georgia in a second study and Jerome and Dorothy Singer of Yale University in a third study report finding up to 60 percent of MTV videos to contain violence.

Research on the effects of music video violence amounts to three studies, all done on college students. These studies warn of harmful effects from the large amounts of violence found by the above researchers. Virtually no government funding has been available for this research despite well over $20,000,000 of funding by U.S. federal and state governments to the film industry in the past year alone.

(The film industry and the music video industry have a tremendous overlap with Warner and CBS being the first and second largest producer of rock music records and videos.)

One research study, done by a University of Massachusett's student for her Ph.D. dissertation, found that college students who watched MTV were more depressed than other students. Since this was a correlational study, a cause-effect relationship cannot be concluded with certainty. However, its findings are similar to research by Monroe Lefkowitz finding that 10-year-old girls and 20-year-old women also become more depressed when consuming heavier diets of TV violence. Jennings Bryant found a similar increase in anxiety and depression in a controlled study of college students consuming a diet heavy in TV violence.

Two studies have been done with violent music videos which have reported harmful effects in controlled studies. Dr. Susan O'Reilly and Dr. Sharas Rehman of the University of Miami in Oxford, Ohio reported that students became somewhat more desensitized to violence after viewing only five violent videos. Dr. Rehman has completed a second study at Pennsylvania State University and found similar effects in a larger study of over 100 college students. Although these studies did not look to see if there were long term effects, millions of young American children are never more than 24 hours away from rock music and music video entertainement.

Although music video violence is not necessarily more violent than primetime television, there are several key factors that must be remembered. 1) Research has found overwhelming evidence that violence on prime-time television has important harmful effects on normal children and adult viewers. This was the conclusion of the U.S. Surgeon General, the National Institute of Mental Health's expert panel, the U.S. Department of Justice, and the U.S. Attorney General's Task Force on Family Violence. 2) Music videos appeal to a young age group that has less ability to find out about the harmful effects of violent entertainment. 3) Music videos contain a higher level of violence between the sexes and of sadistic violence than is found on prime-time TV. 4) The viewer has absolutely no choice on music video programs. There are no viewing periods in which the viewer can be assured of non-violent and non-degrading programming. At least on prime-time television, a viewer knows that certain viewing hours, e.g. the Cosby Show, Family Ties, Webster, etc. will be non-violent and the A-Team and Mike Hammer will be violent. Thus, there is no way for a parent, child or adult to feel confortable at the present time that he or she will be able to enjoy an hour of rock music videos without sudden, unexpected images of violence, sadism and callous sexual protrayals. 5) MTV music video entertainment is a monopoly. By virtue of exclusivity contracts, essentially restraint of trade, MTV has guaranteed that it alone will have access to the newest videos from the major record companies. Until recently, MTV has been owned by Warner Communications, the number one owner of rock music companies.

Despite overwhelming evidence of harm, there are no warnings of harm, and no non-violent, non-degrading alternatives in rock music video entertainment. Because MTV has a monopoly as the nation's only rock music video networks, having bought out its competitors, and because there is limited access to any new such networks, due to the monopolistic nature of cable television, it is virtually certain that no national alternative will arise.

NCTV considers it the responsibility of the U.S. government to assure that America's young viewers are informed on a regular basis. Consumers have the right to be informed when a harmful product is being sold. Consumers, especially in monopolistic situations, also have a right to non-harmful alternatives. To expect the industry to police itself against its own financial self-interest is unreasonable and a renunciation by government of its function of assuring an open and honest marketplace.

The U.S. government, by its total inaction to date on this issue, has been irresponsible in its duty to the American people. It has allowed a monopolistic industry to program American young people for its own financial self-interest. Numerous people within the industry itself think that there is too much violence in current rock music entertainment. However, it is not the responsibility of the industry nor the ability of the industry to police itself. U.S. court decisions have spoken quite clearly in the case of the National Association of Broadcasters that it is the responsibility of the federal government to set standards for the marketplace. No public group that I know of has suggested censorship. Indeed what we are seeing at the present time is censorship by the industry. MTV, for example, has consistently refused to allow debate on its own channel about this important issue and has turned down several dozen invitations to debate this issue on national television and radio programs.

NCTV is asking today's Senate committee to take specific action. There have now been some 14 U.S. government hearings on violence and pornography entertainment since 1954. Not once in all of this time has either the U.S. House or the U.S. Senate ever taken one single action to correct this problem. Not once has any House or Senate committee recommended that America's young people be given the honest information on a regular basis on television or guarantee that they be provided with alternatives.

NCTV would like to see this committee recommend the following legislative steps to the U.S. Senate: 1) Require that all music video programs set aside at least 33% of viewing time, in one hour segments, for non-violent and non-degrading entertainment and that these program hours be announced ahead of time so that they can be published in TV guides. 2) Require a 30 second informational warning, designed by the Surgeon General, the FCC, or concerned public interest groups, be shown once for every three hours of music video programming. These warnings would inform the viewer on scientific findings about the effects of violent and degrading entertainment on viewers. This would allow viewers to be informed and make up their own minds, the opposite of censorship. 3) Require that an independent panel be constructed to rate all music video programming and that these ratings be displayed in the upper left hand corner of the screen for 10 seconds at the beginning of each video.

Reports in Billboard magazine make it quite clear that the only reason that MTV and the rock music industry is even talking to the Parent Music Resource Center is that there is a threat of legislation. It is virtually certain that such a threat cannot and should not be continued forever. Any recent small improvement on music video entertainment is sure to be transient if no action is taken by this committee. Sensible public action, compatible with the First Amendment can and should be taken. It would have a major beneficial effect on the rock music industry and young people in the U.S. and around the world.

I fear that this committee will do nothing and thus become the 15th U.S. governmental hearings resulting in no action. I fear that this committee will be afraid to exercise its responsibility to the American people and assure that America has an open and honest marketplace for music entertainment. Only by breaking down restraints of trade and guaranteeing consumers regular and honest information will this problem be resolved. From NCTV's monitoring of rock music and other forms of entertainment covering the past 20 years,

it is very likely that violence and sexual degradation will only get worse if the U.S. government refuses to correct this situation. I hope and pray that this committee will consider this issue serious and take action to require proper information and alternatives be made available to America's children and young people.

STATEMENT OF THE CITIZENS AGAINST MUSIC CENSORSHIP [CAMC]

From the outset, Citizens Against Music Censhorship (CAMC) would like to apologize for not being here with you today at this hearing, but want to assure you that on behalf of music's millions of fans, we are following the issue quite closely.

I present this testimony to you today as a California resident whose home state includes the huge music industry; as a music consumer and as Legislative Advocate for CAMC. In a nut shell, CAMC is opposed to the inroads that are being made in an effort to censor music and thus the activities of organizations that try to censor or restrict the individual rights of choice provided to us as artists and consumers by the United States Constitution, before they are ever utilized.

With this in mind, I will take but a few minutes of your time to quickly highlight many of the problems we find with this movement; even with the establishment of just a simple rating system, one using V for violent, D for drugs and so on.

To start with, CAMC finds that any proposal designed to censor music, immediately restricts the freedom of thought and artistic creativity process; by either making it tougher for an artist to pen, release or sell a new poem, song or phrase or simply by deciding what can and can not be purchased by selected consumers before that product is on the shelves.

Second, if you start censoring with Rock and Roll (everyone's first choice since Elvis Presley and the Beatles), where do you stop? Is it with Soul? Country and Western? Opera? Dance? Art? And who knows what else—laser light shows? Yet out of all of this, one point does stand clear: once started, the program will have to be carried over into every specific music field, definitely costing time, money and possibly valuable works of art; if not simply through increased avenues of red tape.

Third, and falling directly in line with #2, is that no one knows were this movement will start. Will we start by censorship only today's music, or are we going to go back into the past and put clothes on the Venus De Milo, rewrite Edgar Allan Poe, the 1812 Overture or the 1930's edition of Minnie the Moocher.

Fourth, the establishment of any rating system will cause problems for radio stations, because these rules will force the creation and establishment of special time zones designed for the air play of special songs and of course groups. Is this what we want from a free thinking and artistically inclined society?

Fifth, CAMC firmly believes that the establishment of any rating system will increase the costs of records and tapes to consumers, because there is more red tape for an artist and company to go through before they can release their music. And who do you think is going to pay for that? No doubt about it, the music fan.

Sixth, CAMC feels that the establishment of any rating system will only make the artist(s) that these rules are designed to affect, even more popular, because people will become curious about their works, in the same way they did with Playboy and Penthouse in the 50's and 60's.

Seventh, who will constantly be in charge of deciding what will be censored, and then what its rating will be? Will it be Congress, the President or better yet, a regulatory body or school teachers?

As you can see from this simple overview, the issue of censorship in music not only opens up the proverbial can of worms, but none the less, will cause a dramatic restructuring of the entertainment community in California and America, thus affecting millions of lives and dollars.

Next, I would like to directly refute a couple of misconceptions that have been brought to the forefront of this issue by the media.

First, do people know what is contained in the albums before they purchase them? The answer to this is definitely yes, and can be answered simply by pointing to marketing strategies that make sure that the album or song to be released is in the hands of the Radio Stations, sometimes weeks or months in advance so that their listeners may review the record and in turn, create excitement about its impending release.

Second, the articles have clearly brought into focus the question of parental responsibility and their role in raising the children of the 80's. I mean is it fair for a parent to complain about the material their children listens to, when they do not control or pay attention to the shows their children watch, the clothes they wear, the magazines they read or the friends they keep?

In conclusion, in this era of import competition and stagnant imaginations, we as community leaders should be looking at ways to both protect and promote one of the nation's largest and most important social, artistic and economic industries (not to mention ways upon which to expand our artistic community), rather than ways upon which to bring them down—something that music censorship does. Please, as we end this hearing today, let us promise to ourselves and the nation, that we will not move one step closer to music and artistic censorship in any way shape or form.

STATEMENT OF JOHN H. MARMADUKE, PRESIDENT, WESTERN MERCHANDISERS, HASTINGS BOOKS AND RECORDS

I am John H. Marmaduke, President of Western Merchandisers and Hastings Books & Records, a wholesaler and a retailer of music, books and video in 15 states in the Southwest.

I have a mixture of experiences that lends me to support the voluntary labeling of recorded material such as Polygram Records has initiated and the RIAA has promoted.

First, I am a parent of three children under the age of 10 so I and my wife have found some lyrics unsuitable for our children. In some cases, after the fact. Secondly, as a book retailer, I know that censorship doesn't work. Third, as a retailer, I am concerned that due to the expanding universe many artists are taking with lyrics that our problem is going to become more acute.

My experience leads me to believe it is time our industry regulated itself. Allowing parents to be determinate of what lyrics are appropriate for their children by labeling our product is the only workable solution.

As a retailer, I'm concerned that current parental concern over lyrics will end up painting all music retailers with a broad brush. Even though any form of labeling may halo the product of some such as "Banned in Boston" did for books and movies. I'm willing to take that risk because it's a much more reasonable approach to a real problem. Most of our business is done in malls where families frequent. Our image is one of a family music store. We encourage this through our decor, customer service, selection, and in-store airplay. We want to do nothing to jeopardize our appeal to the entire family. This is why we feel an industry wide cooperative to label explicit lyrics is a family oriented approach.

From my years of experience in the book industry with it's many travails of censorship, I am most certain any form of attempt to label product such as X, D, or O will prove unworkable due to the very nature of censorship. It is an impossible task to appoint someone whose personal criteria will have to fill in the wide gaps between censorship definition.

In fact, finding someone who could understand all the lyrics, much less interpret them to someone's definition of what constitutes an X, O, or D would be difficult enough. It has to be one of the most impossible job descriptions ever given.

Instead, I think the stickering of explicit lyrics puts the responsibility directly where it belongs: on the parents of the children. It is a family problem and can only be solved in that environment.

I appreciate the opportunity to submit this statement to the Committee.

STATEMENT OF JAMES E. BONK, EXECUTIVE VICE PRESIDENT, CAMELOT ENTERPRISES, INC.

The issue of lyrical content in popular music has received much attention of late from the Parents Music Resource Center, the Parent Teachers Association, the Recording Institute Association of America, the National Association of Recording Merchandisers and the recently-formed Musical Majority, along with other segments of the record industry: songwriters, performers, broadcaster, record labels, and the like. As the parent company of Camelot Music, one of the nation's leading mall-oriented retail chains of pre-recorded music with locations in 26 states, we at Camelot Enterprises, Inc., share many of the concerns that have been expressed regarding this issue.

As is true of any other large corporation, our ranks include a great number of parents—therefore, we understand the perspective of the PMRC and the PTA. Beyond the concern that we have for our own children, we have a natural interest in this topic, because it is obvious that the youth of America play a significant role in determining our industry's fortune. Since so much of our product is targeted for a young market, it would be irresponsible for us to ignore the impact that music has on a youth's emotional and social development. Our company has expressed deep concern, to our suppliers and within trade associations, regarding this topic and the need to examine its ramifications. We are committed to do so until a reasonable solution can be reached.

However, at the same time, we also share the concerns that have been expressed from many quarters of the music business. While we believe that Ben Franklin and John Adams may not have had some of today's controversial songwriters in mind when they framed the Bill of Rights, we realize that song lyrics are a First Amendment issue. On that note, we foresee the possibility of a "Witch Hunt" atmosphere, which some of the proposed solutions seem to encourage.

Furthermore, we fear that many of the discussions surrounding this issue unfairly cast a negative light on the music industry. As is true of any business, we do have problems that must be addressed—but overall, we at Camelot feel that the music community make a positive contribution to our society. Music offers a constructive diversion to the pressures of everyday life, and on occasion, the craft has been a healthy forum to express relevant issues that affect our society—both from conservative and liberal viewpoints. And this year alone, we have seen literally hundreds of individual performers devote their time and talents to help shape a better world.

In a year that will be remembered for such worthwhile efforts as U.S.A. For Africa, Live Aid, and Farm Aid, to mention just a few of our industry's worthy charitable ventures, the reputation of the entire music business is suffering as a result of the bickering that surrounds the issue of lyrics and label coding. It is a classic case where the actions of a few seem to outweigh the actions of the majority, because the song lyrics that are now under scrutiny do not represent the masses.

For the most part, industry leaders are sympathetic to the issues that have been raised in these discussions, and are aware of their responsibility to today's impressionable youth. Many recording artists are also aware of that responsibility. However, we are finding that our industry is being subjected to a dark image because we are being judged by the exception, rather than the rule.

The music retailer has a unique perspective in this discussion. Unlike the songwriter, the artist or the label executive, unlike the PMRC or the PTA, we are the conduit through which the public receives its music. As such, we have a vested interest in this topic. The music retailer is the most accessible target for the complaints and objections that questionable lyrics may inspire, a fact that sets us apart from the rest of our industry. What sets us apart from the PMRC and the PTA is the fact that we have a sharper perspective for the day-to-day realities of the retail world, and therefore, we have a keener awareness for the impracticalities of solutions that have been proposed to address this situation.

Our company has been in the music business for 29 years and I personally for 18 years, so we feel confident in making two key observations. First, this is by no means a new problem. Many of the same attitudes that are surfacing today led to a network executive's decision to only show Elvis Presley from the waist up during his first appearance on "The Ed Sullivan Show." And as RIAA president Stanley Gortikov has pointed out, controversy surrounding music dates back to the days of Plato and Socrates. That historic perspective leads to my second observation, namely, that there is no easy solution to this problem. Most of the remedies that have been laid on the table are "quick fixes," when in fact, there is no quick fix for this situation.

It has been proposed that record labels voluntarily place "Parental Guidance" warning stickers on releases that may contain objectionable lyric content. One need only look at the movie industry and its rating system to realize the shortcomings of this solution. In many cases, the "R" rating entices, rather than discourages, teens to attend films which portray excessive sexual and/or violent acts. In fact, there have been several instances when some studios have elected to add such footage to a movie to ensure an "R" rating, thereby increasing the chances for a box office success.

It is a simple fact that with many teens, if you tell them they cannot do something, they are more likely to seek out that forbidden fruit. Teenagers are known for their independence, a simple manifestation of their maturing process. When you tell the average teen that he or she cannot see a given movie, you stir their curiosity to the point where they want to see it all the more. I fear that the same would be true with stickered "Parental Guidance" albums and cassettes. Then, what happens if artists are record companies find that "stickered" product entice extra sales? Rather than discourage the artist or performer from engaging in content of questionable taste, you may actually promote the practice.

Finally, there's another reason that the "PG" sticker looks impractical from a retailer's perspective. Camelot's store managers and salespeople can tell you that it is a very rare occa-

sion when the average teen brings Mom and Dad along to the record store. Therefore, this so-called solution offers no means for enforcement.

It has also been proposed that a coalition of record executives and concerned parents form a review board, which would be charged with the task of combing in excess of 25,000 new songs annually for excessive references regarding sexual or violent acts, drug and alcohol abuse, and messages that promote the occult. My first fear with this "quick fix" is that it seems to condone the dark spector of censorship.

It must be acknowledged that some songs cross a fine line in these areas of concern, but who is in a position to judge when that line has been crossed? While it's easy to point out blatant sexual references in some of the songs that led to PMRC's stated concerns, I wonder what sort of verdict would be passed on such mainstream hits from the past, like Charlie Rich's "Behind Closed Doors," or Starland Vocal Band's "Afternoon Delight," which made more subtle references to a similar subject matter. Obviously, while some people may have objected to those songs, those songs were palatable to enough people that they became best sellers. We run the risk not only of stifling a songwriter's creativity and freedom of expression. We could actually deprive the general public of hearing songs that relate to common experiences, emotions, and thoughts.

Along that same line, I wonder how a song like the recent hit "I Want A New Drug" by Huey Lewis and the News would fare before a review board. On the surface, it would appear that the song title refers to the very intent of this discussion. However, upon study of the lyrics, you find that the song actually condemns drug use, and in fact the "new drug" referred to in the title is the singer's love for a lady friend.

Rather than clearing up the situation, this proposal instead opens up a Pandora's Box of First Amendment objections. We must remember that in music, as is true of any creative venture, it is extremely difficult to establish a reasonable set of standards for taste that would be acceptable to all people. It is said that beauty is in the eye of the beholder; that same philosophy applies to lyrics that may or may not be objectionable.

My second fear regarding a review board and the suggested "R" rating leans in another direction. Instead of encouraging songwriters and performers who cross the lines of acceptable tastes to look for more constructive subject matter, the review process may offer them a place to hide. Rather than taking the responsibility to elevate their songs' content, they could point to the review board as a convenient out with the attitude of "Go ahead and rate my record. I'll write what I damn well please." Again, if it appears that records that have been unfavorably rated find increased sales with youngsters and teenagers, you will further aggravate and call attention to the situation rather than solve it.

Finally, I wonder how feasible it would be for a review board to deal with the enormous task of rating all new songs that are released in a year. At least 4,000 new albums are released each year, accounting for in excess of 25,000 new songs. While some have raised the moral question of "who has the right" to determine lyrics which may or may not be offensive, a more practical question may well be who has the time for such a task?

Camelot Enterprises, Inc., is sympathetic to the legitimate concerns that have been illuminated by PMRC. Where we differ is the manner in which we would solve the problem. After all, the creative process cannot be legislated, just as you cannot legislate a person's thoughts.

A recent development seems to indicate a healthier solution to this dilemma. Former Prince cohort Morris Day, whose previous performances with the group The Time were frequently punctuated with overt sexual references, apparently has paid attention to the issues raised by PMRC. It has been reported that he voluntarily took an eraser to his own lyrics for an upcoming solo release in an effort to broaden his acceptance in the mainstream audience. We haven't heard the record yet, so we can't really say how successful his editing efforts have been, but Day has stated, "I don't want kids quoting me and not sounding kosher." This is the direction that our industry must instill within artists and songwriters to address this delicate situation. The best cure for this problem lies not in legislation, but in a sense of accountability on the part of the creative community.

As an industry, the music business must make a vigorous effort to ensure that the content of all released product falls within acceptable public standards. We must face up to that obligation. In fact, our company president, Paul David, and his counterparts from other national retailers and wholesalers, are working through the National Association of Recording Merchandisers to stress the importance of this topic throughout our entire industry. However, it is my firm belief that such action must be an internal effort. Otherwise, we must be careful not to infringe on musical artists' legal and creative rights. If these concerns are addressed in a positive nature, it is entirely possible that influential recording artists could be enticed to speak out against the negative topics that brought this controversy to a head. Such cooperation is not likely if they feel their hand has been forced through legislation.

In terms of protecting the value structures of today's youth, the primary responsibility has always been, and will always be, in the home. Stickers on records and decisions by review boards will not teach America's youth the difference between right and wrong. That valued task remains in the hands of parents. Through example, through open communication, and through caring direction, America's parents can exert far more influence over their children's values and behavior than any song with questionable lyrics will ever impact.

STATEMENT OF MARTHA WINTER GROSS, PH.D., WASHINGTON, DC

As a mother of two pre-adolescent children and as a licensed, practicing psychologist, sex therapist and sex educator in the nation's capital, I feel I can no longer afford to remain silent and powerless, as many of us have, over the type of entertainment our children are being exposed to by a multi-billion-dollar industry which exploits and manipulates them at a crucial time in their sexual development.

Like many of you on this committee, I belong to a generation that was steeped in and guided by tradition. There were rules when we were growing up. We were taught the rights and the wrongs, the shoulds and the shouldn'ts, the dos and the don'ts.

But as we grew older we were caught up in the sexual and cultural revolution of the 1960s when those rules were scrutinized, questioned—and, by some of us—abandoned—in pursuit of "freedom" to find our own sexuality, our own sexual values, our own morality. From those times we have emerged—the concerned, anxious and not-to-be-so-envied parents of today—confused and ambivalent about sexuality in general. Our conflict extends itself into the ways in which we communicate or can't—our verbal and nonverbal messages about sex which we give to our children.

We want to protect our children but not repress them; we want them to be free but provided with standards and guidelines that will help them become sexually healthy adults. Because of our own uneasiness and conflicts over the changing sexual mores and roles, many of us have done what we

were most comfortable with, what was easiest—and that is to say very little to our children about sex. Some of us have opposed sex education being taught in the schools, saying that was the role of the parents. But how many of us have assumed that responsibility? By our abdication, we leave the sexual education of our children in the hands of the purveyors of pornography in the music, print, television, film, and video industries.

We have no one to blame but ourselves. The entertainment industry is only responding as any good capitalist would—producing whatever is profitable in response to supply and demand. Dick Clark, who fathered rock and roll to the world on "American Bandstand," recently said in a television interview, "'We give them what they buy.'"

Our childrens' heroes, more than likely, are rock stars. And some of those rock stars—in their lyrics and in their videos—extol violence, sadism and masochism, sexism, the subordination of women, devil worship, and drug abuse.

Fortunately, the real trash, the most destructive and harmful rock videos, represents only a small percentage of the market and has a limited exposure. Music videos can be fun and entertaining and their potential for creating positive messages is unlimited and exciting.

The telecommunications explosion has robbed our children of their innocence. Television has introduced them to adult problems and emotional issues they sometimes are unprepared to handle. Frequently, they learn about sex and violence before they learn about sex and love.

Some might ask what is the difference between this form of entertainment and what we were exposed to in our teenage years. The difference, definitely, is in the explicitness of the message and in its presentation.

It is true that Elvis shocked our parents with his suggestive, pelvic gyrations, but he wasn't subjugating anybody—he wasn't expressing violence. CBS-TV even censored our view of those swival hips on "The Ed Sullivan Show," making them that much more tempting. But many of the messages in the songs and performances of the "King of Rock and Roll" were about love, romance and heartbreak. While some of his words had sexual overtones and were suggestive, they were explicit and they were not violent.

The messages of some of today's heavy metal rock—in lyrics and music video productions—convey explicit violence and abuse. Sexual messages, traditionally conveyed in music, are no longer communicated in suggestive terms or words. Masochism and sadism are conveyed as acceptable and normal standards of behavior. Some performers have admitted they feel compelled to add risque lyrics and music video scenes to entice the buying market. War scenes and scenes of nuclear devastation are presented in a flip, light-hearted manner, making them that much more pernicious. There is no connotation of pain. Most of the objects of violence and pain are women who are shown as liking it. The viewer becomes numbed—desensitized—to the hurt, the pain, the criminality of violent acts. The message communicated is that aggressiveness is an accepted—valued—way of life.

The fusion of violence and sexual explicitness in some of the rock music lyrics and music videos our pre-adolescents and adolescents are being exposed to is antithetical to the values of respectful treatment of one another that we as sex educators and sexologists are trying to create and to communicate.

While I'm not prepared to say that the violence and sexual explicitness communicated in some of today's rock music causes antisocial behavior, I certainly think it sets the stage. What I have seen and heard recently being produced by some in the rock music industry creates a damaging climate—a subculture—for teen-agers who are not old enough to make wise decisions about what they can emotionally handle and what they can not. It is a pervasive influence during a critical period of their development when attitudes, identity and values are being molded.

The time of sexual development for adolescents is a tumultuous, intense period as they experience a complicated mix of strong emotions and physical longings. I'm sure each of you remembers that period in your lives. This is a time they experience the pleasure and pain never before experienced and they are confronted with a variety of pressures arising from their new sexual consciousness. This is when they are learning about themselves, their bodies, their own sexuality and how to treat one another.

Two of the main developmental issues faced in adolescence are the struggles with identity and heterosexual relationships. Exposure to the cynical, violent, demeaning, sex and drug-laden messages conveyed by some of today's rock performers can be extremely damaging to pre-adolescents and adolescents during their formative years.

The subliminal messages in some of this rock music doesn't bolster optimism in teen-agers at a time when they most need it. And those of us in the mental health profession see the damage that results when people are unprepared to handle violent and sexually explicit messages they receive.

Statistics make commentaries about our times; but, sadly, and too often, we do not pay attention until the figures knock us into awareness. Are you comfortable learning from researchers that every 90 minutes someone in this country between the ages of 15 and 24 commits suicide? We're talking about 5,800 lives being wasted each year!

By the time the average youngster reaches the age of 18, he's seen 17,000 hours of violent deaths via television. He is absorbed in a rock music culture that advocates drugs or death as an escape from his adolescent pain. And statistics tells us that 80 percent of all people who try to take their own lives have been drinking heavily.

We are all alarmed by the dramatic surge of teen-age suicides in the last three decades. Adolescents' feelings are so intense, their emotions so volatile. Their impulsiveness and vulnerability make them high suicide risks. They become confused over their sexuality, drugs, violence, expectations and demands from peers, parents and society. Their psychological defenses break down, leaving them in despair. They haven't had enough life experience to understand that their pain will not last and that they have internal resources available to survive the disappointments.

Teen-age pregnancies are at an all-time high and our children are bombarded daily on the airwaves with free-love proclamations. Children, like many adults, are turning to alcohol and drugs to deal with anxiety and stress. And rock music lyrics encourage—rather than discourage—their use. Abused or neglected youngsters are running away from home in greater numbers, ending up making their living on the streets as prostitutes or criminals. Child pornography is increasing, and where there is child pornography there are child abusers. An alarming number of children are being reported missing—many of them never to be found or found dead at the hands of a molester.

Drs. Ed Donnerstein of the University of Wisconsin, Dolf Zillmann of Indiana University and Neil Malamuth of UCLA have shown through their much-cited sexual violent studies that pornography, violent and nonviolent, affects normal men and normal women. Their research has shown that pornography desensitizes viewers, increases male acceptance of aggression toward women, trivializes rape, and distorts our perception of rape and forced sex—promoting the age-old myths that women are sex objects who enjoy rape and torture.

Since the current research of the effects of violent pornography measures only attitudes, we cannot predict which men will act out aggressive tendencies stimulated by pornography. A lot of variables come into play when a man commits rape or child abuse—such as his background, his value system, his psychological make-up, his perception of sex, violence and women. Those are the very factors being shaped in the developing young person exposed to the violence and sexual explicitness in some of today's rock music and rock music videos.

MTV—the pioneering 24-hour all-music cable channel aimed at 12 to 34-year-olds—constantly exposes an estimated 20 million people daily to rock video. MTV programming chief Bob Pittman has publically acknowledged the influence he knows his product has on people's lives.

He candidly told a Ms. magazine reporter, "when you're dealing with a music culture . . . music serves as something beyond entertainment. It's really a peg they use to identify themselves."

It would be impossible to shelter our children from being exposed to the sex and violence of the media today. Censorship or labeling violent and sexually explicit records and music videos will only make them more attractive. Censorhip has always produced negative results and violates the principles of free speech that are precious to all of us.

Even a rating system similar to that used by the film industry would be effective only if parents monitored their children's purchases of records and music videos. But most teenagers make their own purchases, unsupervised. Once the purchases are opened, they cannot be returned. The kids share or copy each other's records, tapes and videos and then lose themselves in the music from their stereo headsets. Many parents are so relieved not to be disturbed by the blaring music, they don't take the time to find out what is absorbing the interest of their children under those headsets.

What can be done to clean up the entertainment our children are exposed to?

I feel the power of the almighty dollar which fuels the industry can be applied by parents to force reform in the lyrics and images being produced by the record companies. I believe it is the parents who hold the ultimate power as consumers to force the rock music industry to clean up its act.

It is the broadcaster's—the radio and television stations—who introduces the new records and videos to the buying public. Unless the stations play them, they are doomed in the ratings and thus assigned to dusty corners in warehouses.

Because many broadcasters have been caught off guard by playing new releases that record companies have sent to them without accompanying lyrics, the National Association of Broadcasters has requested record companies to include song lyrics with all promotional releases sent to radio stations. I strongly support the NAB request. If the companies agree to this request and the station still chooses to play music containing violent and sexually explicit messages, then parents can put pressure on station managers and businesses who advertise on the station. Station owners and advertisers respond when their profits are threatened.

Parental consumer pressure on broadcasters not to play the objectionable records and videos will force the record and video producers and the performers to tone down the violence and sexual explicitness of their products.

I feel this is the most sensible and effective way we can attack the pornographic rock music problem. It's a consumer issue—and I believe consumer pressure—not censorship, labeling, or new legislation—will generate the necessary reform.

STATEMENT OF THE NATIONAL RADIO BROADCASTERS ASSOCIATION

The National Radio Broadcasters Association ("NRBA") is a non-profit trade association representing approximately 2,000 AM and FM radio stations located throughout the United States. We appreciate the opportunity to present our views on the issues surrounding the lyrics of current songs which are sexually explicit or promote offensive conduct ("offensive lyrics"), especially as any remedial action would impact on the operation of radio broadcast stations.

Various suggestions have been made involving the regulation of offensive lyrics, including legislation requiring warning labels on records containing sexually explicit lyrics or the adoption of a federal rating system. While the NRBA is sympathetic to the concerns which have been raised about such lyrics, we believe that the adoption of legislation would be an inappropriate approach.

First, as an overall matter, philosophically it is difficult to believe that the imposition of warning labels on records is going to spark the interest of heretofore unconcerned parents. It is also difficult to believe that the posting of "X" ratings on records is going to discourage the sale of offensive music. To the contrary, an "X" rating will likely attract attention to such recordings and lead directly to an increase in sales.

From the perspective of radio broadcasters, any regulation of the record industry with respect to lyrics would necessarily impact on the radio broadcast industry, as one of the staples of most radio programming is the playing of records. Thus, the imposition of regulations would necessitate increased review by the Federal Communications Commission ("FCC") of the programming judgments of licensees. The FCC would be required to determine whether particular lyrics in a recording were in violation of regulations (which in this very complicated First Amendment area of the law would be difficult to draft and be amorphous at best), whether any part or all of the recording could be broadcast or whether it could only be broadcast at certain times of the day, when younger children are unlikely to be listening. And, in the event that the FCC were to find a licensee's decisions in a particular factual situation to be unreasonable, sanctions would necessarily be imposed upon the licensee. Such an approach, even if it could be tailored to meet constitutional requirements, would thus not only be burdensome, but would also be redundant in that Sections 1461 et seq of Title 18 of the United States Criminal Code already deal with the mailing, importation, transportation and broadcast of obscene, profane and/or indecent material and provide for criminal sanctions for violations. These sections of the Code, of course, are equally applicable to record producers and distributors.

Certainly, broadcasters are concerned about the problem of offensive lyrics, a problem which centers around the recording industry and not the broadcast industry. As good citizens and businessmen who are responsible to the communities they serve, broadcasters can be relied upon to monitor music and lyrics before broadcast. It has already been well established that broadcasters are policing themselves and screening out offensive recordings. Furthermore, insofar as any legislation would necessarily impact on the radio broadcast industry, the marketplace is the best guarantor of operation in the "public interest." The listening public will not tolerate for long a station which does not serve its needs and interests. The tune-out factor is a tough master. Who can better determine the interests of the people residing in a local community and how best to serve those needs and interests than the people residing in the community itself?

Therefore, while we are sympathetic with those who are offended by sexually explicit and other offensive recordings, the NRBA strongly believes that another law is not the answer. Legislation which of necessity intrudes upon, and interferes with, the free play of commercial marketplace forces and the operation of broadcast licensees should be kept to a minimum, especially when there are already laws in place and social forces in existence which are available to deal with the problem.

FAITH CHRISTIAN FELLOWSHIP CHURCH,
Blue Ash, OH, September 13, 1985.

Senator BARRY GOLDWATER.
Senate Commerce Committee.
Washington, DC.

DEAR SENATOR GOLDWATER AND MEMBERS OF THE COMMERCE COMMITTEE: I respectfully request that the sermon entitled Don't Let Them Do It, Daddy, containing important statistical data regarding pornography and audio pornography, as well as the attached petition, be added into the hearing record on behalf of the Faith Christian Fellowship Church. In addition, as a member of the Citizens Concerned For Community Values and as participants in the National Coalition Against Pornography, we ask that you stand against the dissemination of this material to the youth of our nation.

Audio pornography has easy availability and we desire that restraints be applied, so that the moral eyesight of our youth will not be gouged out. The corrupting influence of pornography in all of its forms degrades human life and results in deviant behavior. Responsible leadership cannot neglect this important area of our national life.

Love, the highest form of sanity, demands that we protect our most important natural resource—the young people of this great country, who will represent our nation in future years. Therefore, it is our sincerer prayer that you will repond and stop this hideous seduction.

Sincerely,
Rev. R. Edgar Bonniwell, M.Div., Th.M.

AMERICAN CIVIL LIBERTIES UNION,
Washington, DC, September 16, 1985.

Hon. JOHN C. DANFORTH

Chairman, Senate Commerce, Science, and Transportation Committee, Washington, DC

DEAR SENATOR DANFORTH: I am writing to express the concern of the American Civil Liberties Union regarding your upcoming September 19 hearing on proposals to label sound recording with some form of rating system or disclaimers to indicate their contents.

In our view, it is inappropriate for a committee of the United States Congress to serve as a set of official music critics or to evaluate the content of lawfully produced and distributed material. Virtually every newspaper, magazine, and network talk show has chronicled the efforts of the Parents Music Resource Center and other groups to "warn" parents of lyrics which they claim present offensive ideas about sex, violence, rejection of parental authority, substance abuse, or the occult. Although it is certainly permissible for such private groups of parents, religious leaders, or others to critique lyrics which they find offensive for any reason, the effect of giving official recognition to these positions through a Congressional inquiry can cast a substantial chill over free expression.

The decision to hold hearings about song lyrics sends the unmistakable signal to writers, producers, distributors, and broadcasters of this form of music that their actions are under scrutiny and that official intervention, in the form of federal legislation, could descend on them from the wings. These hearings seem designed not to warn parents about content so much as to warn persons in the recording industry that they must either "voluntarily" alter their product or face new statutory or regulatory initiatives. The threat of forthcoming censorship is palpable. This is particularly true where the product is often marketed through the regulated broadcasting industry. Any "label warning" means that broadcasters will need to decide whether to play "labelled" material and those who ignore the labels will undoubtedly face pressure at the time of license renewal.

Recent witness lists indicate that a few songwriters will be present to address charges leveled at rock music. It is certain that specific lyrics will be discussed as examples of what is "wrong" with rock music. The writers of all these lyrics will not be present to respond, even if that was their desire. Moreover, creative artists should not even be expected to explain or justify their work in an official forum such as a Congressional hearing.

The ACLU knows that many persons in the recording business feel great distress over Congressional activity in this arena. Although I realize that you are determined to hold these hearings, I wanted to voice out objections and ask that this letter be included in the record of the proceedings.

Sincerely.

Barry W. Lynn,
Legislative Counsel

STATEMENT OF MTV NETWORKS INC.

MTV: Music Television and Video Hits One/VH-1

MTV Networks Inc. is committed to presenting its viewing public with programming of the highest quality and standards. The Program Standards department has responsibility for a specific area of that commitment, ensuring that programming presented meets standards of good taste and community acceptability. To understand the process involved in applying program standards to video music, it is also important to understand the concepts and elements which led to the popularity of this imaginative and exciting art form.

In 1981 MTV Networks Inc. created an environment which gave life to the video music medium—MTV: Music Television. The phenomenal success of MTV: Music Television gave rise in 1985 to the creation of the company's second successful video music service, VH-1/Video Hits One. Video music is created and produced by recording companies and artists who supply clips to MTV Networks Inc. Video music encompasses a wide spectrum of popular tastes, ranging from straight forward concert footage to elaborately choreographed conceptual vignettes. MTV Networks Inc. has fostered and encouraged an experimental approach to developing this new art form, and the company continues to be a catalyst bringing together innovative, imaginative, and creative forces representing all that is new and exploratory in music, style, fashion and culture.

MTV and VH-1 have a charter to present and promote video music in a manner designed to entertain viewers and to satisfy their programming preferences while fulfilling the company's social responsibility to present programming of the highest quality. In short, the company recognizes alike the legitimate scope of artistic freedom of expression and the legitimate expectations of viewers for programming meeting accepted community standards. Accordingly, MTV Networks Inc. has voluntarily adopted the following program content guidelines:

Videos which endorse or condone illegal drug abuse or alcohol abuse will not be aired by MTV. Depictions of narcotic addiction and alcohol abuse, if presented, will be shown only as self-destructive, anti-social behavior. Videos aired will not promote, glamorize, or show as socially acceptable the use of illegal drugs or the abuse of legal drugs.

MTV will not air videos containing explicit, graphic or excessive depictions of sexual activities. When sexual themes are key to a video's concept or plot, they must be depicted with intelligent regard for commonly accepted standards of taste and propriety and not in a manner that would appeal to prurient interests.

Speech shall be consistent with the standards that prevail throughout a substantial portion of the viewing audience. Obscenity is unacceptable.

Pornographic material is prohibited.

Derogatory characterizations of any ethnic, racial or religious group will be avoided.

Videos containing gratuitous violence are unacceptable. Depictions of violence, if used, must be essential to the development of a video's theme, plot or concept. Violence may not be used to stimulate the audience or to invite imitation nor may it be shown or offered as an acceptable solution to human problems. Exceptional care must be taken in instances where women and children are victims of, or are threatened by, acts of violence.

Each video submitted to MTV for consideration is reviewed to determine whether it conforms to our guidelines. To understand the review process, it is important to recognize video music as an expressive art form, which may sometimes be controversial and thought provoking—and which is subject to highly personalized areas of taste and interpretation. As in any art gallery, MTV presents exploratory and imaginative art forms, the interpretation of which may occasionally generate honest disagreements among individuals who respond differently to their messages. The review process demands difficult, subjective judgments which reflect sensitivity and concern. Yet, clearly it will be impossible for everything to appeal to all people at all times.

Our guidelines are designed to provide an appropriate balance between our responsibility to our viewers and their preferences and the needs of creative artists to express and explore new ideas—to experiment, lead and innovate. To help achieve the balance, Program Standards maintains a liaison with, but independence from other company departments. It is supervised by a Vice President of Program Standards and Public Responsibility who reports directly to the President and Chief Executive Officer. The application of the principles which our guidelines express is sophisticated and complex. The result is the preservation of their spirit and intent in tandem with the artistic integrity of our high quality programming.

MTV Networks Inc. was built on creativity, the creativity of people. Unlike businesses delivering some material piece of hardware, ours delivers an extension of human expression. Artists, writers, directors, producers, programming management and viewers with specialized talents, tastes, opinions, attitudes and ideas help MTV Networks Inc. create its unique programming environment. Our sensitivity to viewers' desires for innovative programming is blended with our close working relationships in the creative community. The result is that MTV Networks Inc. offers its audience the best programming available—that which embodies sensitivity to creative and community standards.

STATEMENT OF GEORGE DAVID WEISS, PRESIDENT, SONGWRITERS GUILD OF AMERICA

I'm grateful for this opportunity to testify.

I find myself on the triple horns of a dilemma. First of all, I'm here to speak not officially as the president of the Songwriters Guild of America but personally, as a parent. I want to state in as strong a manner as I possibly can that I deplore the violent and sexually explicit themes that are creeping into our pop music literature.

There are those who say that today's teenagers are too sophisticated to be negatively affected by these lyrics. Well, if they want to take the risk of throwing those youngsters to the moral wolves and hope they'll come out all right, good luck; let it be on their conscience. But I would caution them to remember this: don't underestimate the power of ideas. They have historically been deadlier than bullets. And it becomes far more serious, and I become much more deeply concerned, when our pre-teenagers are so freely exposed to these songs and their suggestions.

Children of that age are hardly mature enough to deal with such lyrics and make judgments about them. Yet, through the airwaves, and the records their siblings purchase and bring into their home, kids hear this material day after day after day. Artists have become such idols, such role models, that youngsters sport a Michael Jackson white glove, frills a la Madonna, etc. If kids imitate their heroes to this degree, can absorption and acting out of a lyrical idea be far behind? Personally, I would not like to risk guessing wrong on that one.

Horn number two: Speaking now as a songwriter, I consider it much more artistic, and a far richer creative challenge, to employ innuendo and subtlety in lyric writing rather than blatancy.

Oh sure, it's a lot simpler going for the obvious, spouting the gutter language, reaching for the common titillating denominator, but who ever said writing was going to be easy?

I agree with others who say that almost all segments of society today are bombarding us with salacious, prurient and explicit material; but why is that an excuse for the music industry to join them? Why lower our standards to their level? Society has to start somewhere to stop this headlong dash into moral oblivion.

Those of us in the public eye must accept responsibility, particularly in regard to youngsters.

What an opportunity for songwriters! Bob Dylan and writers of his talent and caliber, with songs like "Blowin' in the Wind" appealed to the best in people, not the basest. And who will deny that those fine writers raised the perceptions of a generation and helped! What a contribution we can make by resisting the tide that seems to be swelling, and by sticking to our good taste guns and writing as cleverly, as beautifully as we can.

Aye, but there's the rub! Which brings me to the third horn of my dilemma.

When I say "good taste", the obvious riposte would be "in whose opinion?" In this particular presentation, of course, I advocate "my opinion." Yet, at the same time, I would shun like the plague a position, for instance, that would make me "administrator" of good taste. And I would fight with every ounce of my strength allowing Washington to decide officially and with the sanctions of law, what is or isn't acceptable, what a creator may or may not write.

Once the Pandora's Box of censorship is opened, no one will escape its spreading poison. Not writer or artist, not record company or broadcaster, no one. And I don't believe anyone down through the ages has yet devised a method of stuffing suffocation back into the Box.

Once out, forever out.

So, what to do?

Some months ago, I called for an industry-wide dialogue relating to this problem and the advisability of voluntary self-restraint. There have been some steps taken, perhaps not enough. The shock and wrath of parents are still gathering as they become more aware of what many of these songs are saying. And so everyone knows, when the public is aroused, Congress is too. After all, our legislators take their lumps often enough on issue after issue; isn't it nice (they're probably thinking) to be on the side of the angels for a change?

Here's the opportunity to make up for a multitude of omissions and co-missions. How can we blame them for wanting to rush pell-mell into the melee, and champion what is declared, by many, a righteous cause?

But, if ever it is true that haste makes waste, it would in this case make devastation.

Ladies and gentlemen of Congress and those who are close to you, I urge you to think long and hard before you even consider loosing censorship upon this land.

There was one other thing I called for some months ago. I'll be the first to admit that it might be an unrealistic, super idealistic suggestion, but here goes. All of us at various stages of our lives are subjected to and vulnerable to peer pressure. Well, perhaps if some of our great artists, like the Lionel Richies, who showed their power and influence with "We Are The World," were to use personal persuasion by calling up those who deal in porn lyrics and saying "Hey c'mon, don't do that. It ain't no good for the kids, for our industry. Straighten up and fly right guys." Then I truly believe that the embarrassment of peer pressure would get more response from many of these porn writers and artists than a hundred guns to their heads.

In closing, I want to say that ultimately it may all come down to economics.

If we put Xs on records, they'll probably sell millions. It's the old Boston ban the book syndrome. On the other hand, if parents, and kids, stopped buying these records, record executives wouldn't be too happy. Of necessity, they'd have to discuss this with their producers, their artists, and so on down the line.

Possible results; no profits? Exit porn.

There they are, the triple horns of my dilemma. No solutions, lots of hope. Plus my thanks to you for affording all of us the opportunity to talk, which after all may itself be the solution.

DICTIONARY
OF TERMS

Abecedarianism. As the etymology of the word indicates, ABECEDARIANISM (A-B-C-D-arianism) is alphabetarian in its nature. But ABECEDARIANISM is not necessarily a pejorative term. It takes a highly trained intellect and technical skill to create a truly Abecedarian masterpiece, as demonstrated, for instance in the self-inverted redundant prose of Gertrude Stein. Musical ABECEDARIANISM is far from tonal INFANTILOQUY. Stravinsky's *Piano Pieces for 5 Fingers*, Bartók's *Mikrokosmos* and Casella's *Valse diatonique* from his *Pezzi infantili* are illustrations of sophisticated ABECEDARIANISM. Abecedarian effects are naturally produced by small children banging at random on the white keys of the piano keyboard at the level of their heads, often resulting in the unintentional formation of interesting pandiatonic patterns vivified by asymmetrical rhythms. The walk across the keys by Domenico Scarlatti's cat provided the inspiration for a fugue; the critics who described the music they did not like as puerile or cat music had an imperfect understanding of the constructivist potentialities of random tonal juxtaposition.

Ablation. Extreme luxuriance of decorative and ornamental elaborations in the post-Romantic period of modern music resulted, through surfeit, in a profound repugnance to such practices. An inevitable consequence was a drastic ABLATION of all non-essential thematic excrescences and protuberances from a finished composition. A process of subjective ABLATION impelled some modern composers to revise their early works and reduce their instrumental luxuriance to an economic functional organization. The most striking instance of such ABLATION is Stravinsky's reorchestration of the score of his ballet *The Firebird*, removing some supernumerary instruments, excising florid cadenzas and in effect plucking the fiery bird of its iridescent plumage. Most audiences prefer the original luxuriant version to this later parsimonious arrangement.

Absolute Music. The term ABSOLUTE MUSIC is applied to music that is free from programmatic designs, psychological affiliations or illustrative associations; its Latin etymology connotes independence. In its function ABSOLUTE MUSIC is parasynonymous with ABSTRACT MUSIC, but the two terms are differentiated in their temporal points of reference. ABSOLUTE MUSIC is of ancient heritage, while ABSTRACT MUSIC is a relatively recent phenomenon, marked by structural athematism in an atonal context.

Abstract Music. Abstraction in music implies a separation of sonic structures from representational images, whether pictorial or psychological. ABSTRACT MUSIC is the antonym of all musical styles that are concrete or naturalistic; abstract works are usually short, athematic and rhythmically asymmetric. Intellectual fantasy, rather than sensual excitation, is the generating impulse of ABSTRACT MUSIC; its titles are derived from constructivistic and scientific concepts: Structures, Projections, Extensions, Frequencies, Sound. The German composer Boris Blacher has developed a successful form of ABSTRACT OPERA in which concrete action takes place in a swarm of discrete sonic particles, disjected words in several languages and isolated melodic fragments.

ABSTRACT EXPRESSIONISM, a term applied to nonobjective painting, is sometimes used to describe musical works of abstract quality with expressionistic connotations. A subsidiary genre of ABSTRACT MUSIC is ALEATORY MUSIC, in which the process of musical cerebration is replaced by a random interplay of sounds and rhythms.

Absurd Music. The vocable *surd,* cognate with *sourdine,* implies a muted sound; *Absurd* suggests a becalmed truth, but not necessarily nonsense. There are mathematical equations that seem to contradict common sense; in fact, square roots that cannot be resolved precisely, are called irrational numbers, or by the now obsolete term surd, a cousin of ABSURD. The inner validity of absurd logic was enunciated by Tertullian when he said: "Credo quia absurdum est." Oxymoronic pairs, such as "passionate indifference," or "glacial fire," are intrinsically absurd, and yet eloquent in their self-contradiction. ABSURD MUSIC cultivates analogous incompatibilities. It is particularly effective in modern opera, where a scene of horror may be illustrated by a frivolous waltz, or a festive celebration by the somber strains of a funereal march. The modern techniques of POLYTONALITY and ATONALITY represent MUSIC OF THE ABSURD to the withered sensitivity of an old-fashioned ear.

Accompaniment. In modern music, ACCOMPANIMENT transcends its traditional ancillary function and becomes an integral part of the entire composition. The simplest form of modern ACCOMPANIMENT is that of POLYTONALITY, in which the melody is set in one key and the harmony in another. Rhythmically, the modern ACCOMPANIMENT rarely follows the inflections of the melody; deliberate oxymoronic usages are enhanced by translocated accents.

Acousma. An auricular disturbance induced in hostile audiences by ULTRA-MODERN MUSIC, is known as ACOUSMA. Music critics, even those not suffering from professional indigestion, are chronically prone to ACOUSMA, and their discomfort is often reflected in their reviews.

Acoustics. By definition, acoustical phenomena are fundamental to all music. The overtone series, which is the generator of the basic major triad, is also the source of nominal dissonances. The tritone, deprecated as "diabolus in musica" by medieval scholiasts, is the foundation stone of ATONALITY, POLYTONALITY and other modern techniques. Acoustically, it is the 45th overtone at the distance of 6 1/2 octaves from the fundamental note, with which it forms a concord. Scriabin, theorizing ex post facto, regarded his MYSTIC CHORD as a consonance, because its constituents approximate the high overtones. An interesting practical application of the acoustical properties of the overtone series is found in Ravel's *Boléro*, where at one point the melody is accompanied by a group of flutes and piccolos constituting the 6th, 8th, 10th and 12th overtones progressing in parallel formations. In the score Ravel marks the gradually decreasing dynamics of these high notes, corresponding to a natural tapering of the strength of overtones in higher elevations. This calculated enhancement of natural overtones affects the timbre of the solo instrument. If performed correctly with

1045

the dynamics scrupulously observed, the solo player will find to his dismay that his instrument has undergone a curious change in its tone color. With the aid of electronic means of tone production, this effect can be produced artificially, generating hybrid sonorities such as a half-bassoon and a half-trombone, or a timbre which is a third-oboe, a third-clarinet and a third-violin.

Rhythms can be combined in special proportions with the overtone series. In 1932 Henry Cowell, in collaboration with Leon Theremin, constructed the *Rhythmicon*, an instrument which generates a series of rhythmic beats in an overtone series, the number of beats being proportional to the position of each overtone, so that the octave has two beats per time unit, the interval of the 12th, three beats, the major third over two octaves, five beats, etc. This arrangement makes it possible to devise polyrhythmic counterpoint of great variety and unique sonority. Acoustical innovations and improvements in the purity of intonation are not without musical perils, however. Perfect tuning in orchestral performance would generate differential tones and make a sonic jungle out of a classical symphony. The desire of modern architects to attain acoustical perfection often leads to orchestral pollution in the concert hall. Old-fashioned rococo architecture, with its ornate brocades and heavy curtains, contributed the necessary dampening of sounds and echoes that secured harmonious euphony. Modern acousticians eliminated the decorations, removed the tasselled seat covers and cushioned surfaces, replacing them by plywood and plastic, and added an array of mobiles suspended from the ceiling to eliminate microsonic impurities. But these elaborations resulted in some unwelcome side-effects. Parasitical noises were neutralized, but a variety of unsuspected musical micro-organisms, overtones and differential tones, rose from the instruments themselves, flooding the hall in a harmonious plasma that all but destroyed the natural equilibrium of tonal imperfections and mutual reverberations that were responsible for the rich resonance intuitively achieved by the musical architects of the past. The consequences of such modernization were painfully evident in the scientifically designed Philharmonic Hall at Lincoln Center in New York. The resulting acoustical anarchy was fortunately corrected by an ingenious rearrangement of the physical properties of the auditorium and the stage, so that the natural heterogeneity of sonic euphony was restored.

Action Music.
The term ACTION MUSIC is applied to compositions resulting from an impulsive melosomatic urge. Like IMPRESSIONISM, the term itself arose by analogy with painting. ACTION ART implies a free wielding of the brush in which the unpremeditated splash of color becomes a creative enzyme for the next projection. In ACTION MUSIC there is no calculated design; the initial reflex generates a successive series of secondary reflexes in a network of musico-neural synapses, resulting in the formation of dynamically propelled sounds.

ACTION MUSIC is primarily a manifestation in MIXED MEDIA, or HAPPENINGS with audience participation, in which the spontaneous psychological and physiological excitations determine the course of events. Composers of ACTION MUSIC usually provide a set of instructions, leaving specific decisions to the performers.

ACTION MUSIC is a mass phenomenon, which transcends national boundaries and energies in similar forms in many lands, like self-flagellation of medieval penitents and tergiversations of the whirling dervishes. This ubiquity of incidence is paralleled by the SYNCRETISM of cultures in ACTION MUSIC. Western practitioners of the genre tend to annex the contemplative philosophies of the East, while Oriental composers of ACTION MUSIC adopt serialistic methods and mathematical parameters. In mass manifestations, ACTION MUSIC often finds its audible expression in the ululations of pullulating populations.

Additive Composition.
As the term implies, ADDITIVE COMPOSITION is effectuated by a series of successive additions to an initial thematic statement. The connection is mechanistic by definition, but if by chance, or subliminal design, a dominant melorhythmic figure emerges, a paradoxical rondo is the result.

Adjunction.
Melodic, rhythmic or harmonic ADJUNCTION is produced by a juxtaposition of compatible thematic particles. Such a method suggests a less mechanistic connection than in ADDITIVE COMPOSITION, and a possibility of a thematic unity is not excluded. The Belgian composer Désiré Pâque used the term *Adjonctian constante* to describe an episodic use of recurrent or nonrecurrent motives.

Aerostatic Suspension.
In Impressionistic scores, the shimmering interference of euphonious dissonances generates a sonic inversion which forces the lighter elements to ascend into the upper harmonic regions. At some point an equilibrium of overtones and differential tones is established. This euphony, with ethereal sonorities wafted by the winds of flutes, oboes, clarinets and flageolet-like upper strings, suggests a physical convection which may be described as AEROSTATIC SUSPENSION.

Agglutination.
When successive melorhythmic particles are not unified by common tonality or melorhythmic similarity, the resulting type of composition may be described as AGGLUTINATION, a gluing together. The method differs from ADDITIVE COMPOSITION in possessing a greater malleability in the process of coalescence. On the other hand, it lacks the inherent compatibility that is present in the method of ADJUNCTION.

Aleatory Music.
The word ALEATORY is derived from the Latin "alea," that is, a die. (Julius Caesar exclaimed after crossing the Rubicon, "Alea jacta est.") ALEATORY MUSIC in the literal sense is not a new invention. "Dice music" was a popular parlor game in the 18th century. A celebrated example is *Musikalisches Würfelspiel*, attributed to Mozart. In the second half of the 20th century, composers of the AVANT-GARDE introduced true ALEATORY methods. A pioneer work was *Music of Changes* by John Cage, derived from chance operations found in the ancient Chinese book of oracles *I-Ching* in which random numbers are obtained by throwing sticks. By drawing an arbitrary table of correspondences between numbers and musical parameters (pitch, note-value, rests) it is possible to derive a number of desirable melorhythmic curves. Human or animal phenomena may also serve as primary data. Configurations of fly specks on

paper, pigeon droppings on a park bench, the design of crushed mosquitoes on wallpaper, the parabolic curve of an expectoration directed towards a spittoon, dissection of birds as practiced in ancient Rome, etc. are all excellent materials for ALEATORY MUSIC. At a HAPPENING in an American mid-western university, the anal discharge of a pig, which was administered a clyster, was used as an Aleatory datum. Mauricio Kagel has made use of partially exposed photographic film for ALEATORY composition. The composer-engineer Iannis Xenakis organizes ALEATORY Music in STOCHASTIC terms, which possess the teleological quality absent in pure ALEATORY pursuits. Among affiliated subjects of ALEATORY MUSIC are PROBABILITY, INFORMATION THEORY, STOCHASTIC COMPOSITION, CYBERNETICS, EXPERIMENTAL MUSIC, COMPUTER MUSIC, EMPIRICAL MUSIC and INDETERMINACY.

Algorithm.

In mathematical usage, an ALGORITHM is an operator devised for the solution of problems arising in the theory of numbers. Directions given in puzzle canons to indicate the time and the interval of entry are ALGORITHMS. The most ubiquitous ALGORITHM in modern music is the TRITONE. It compasses a chord containing 11 different intervals, for the sum of the first 11 numbers equals 66, which corresponds in semitone units to 5 1/2 octaves, the tritone being half an octave. The TRITONE is also the operating ALGORITHM in the problem of distributing 12 different notes of the chromatic scale into four mutually exclusive triads. Here the modus operandi is to build two major triads separated by a tritone, and two minor triads a whole tone higher whose tonics are also at a distance of a tritone (e.g., C major, F-sharp major, D minor, G-sharp minor). Magical properties emerge from such operations. It is remarkable, for instance, that four mutually exclusive triads can be arranged only by using a pair of major triads and a pair of minor triads, and that no other distribution is possible. But it is also possible to split the chromatic scale into a group of diminished, minor, major and augmented triads, one of each, a symmetric and elegant solution, suggesting similarly elegant formulas in mathematics. Algorithmic composition is a virgin field for experimentation in modern techniques.

Allusive Quotation.

Folk songs, contrapuntal elaborations on a given cantus firmus, quotations from the doom-laden chant *Dies irae*, have been for centuries a favorite resource of ALLUSIVE QUOTATIONS. Richard Strauss inserted the theme of the funeral march from Beethoven's *Eroica* in the score of his *Metamorphosen*, a dirge on the death of Germany, written during the last weeks of World War II. Alban Berg quoted Bach's chorale *Es ist genug* at the conclusion of his *Violin Concerto* as a memorial for Manon Gropius, daughter of Mahler's widow by a second marriage, who died young. Quotations from a composer's own scores are not rare; a notorious modern example is the egocentric series of quotations used by Strauss in the score of his tone poem *Ein Heldenleben*. But perhaps the most extraordinary assembly of assorted thematic memos, memories and mementos is found in *Sinfonia* by Luciano Berio, in which he quotes metamorphosed fragments from works of Mahler, Debussy, Ravel and others.

Alphabetical Monograms.

The origin of musical notation is alphabetical or syllabic. The names of the notes of the initial hexachord of the major scale were taken by Guido d'Arezzo from the first syllables of a Latin hymn, and this syllabic nomenclature is still in use in the Latin countries and in Russia. In German, the musical notes are designated by letters from A to H; thanks to this alphabetic denomination, it is possible to contrive musical themes out of words and names comprising these letters, the most illustrious example being the theme B-A-C-H. That such an artificial method of thematic invention does not hamper a composer of genius, is proved by Schumann's *Carnaval*, which is based on the spelling of the name of the town of ASCH (in German nomenclature either A-flat, C, B or A, E-flat, C, B). Dmitri Shostakovich based the main themes of his *Tenth Symphony* and the *Eighth String Quartet* on his ALPHABETICAL MONOGRAM, in German nomenclature, D.SCH. Mario Castelnuovo-Tedesco extended his system of ALPHABETICAL MONOGRAMS to 25 letters of the Italian alphabet, arranging the notes chromatically and filling two full octaves from A to Z.

Ambulation.

AMBULATORY activities by performers during a concert in the process of playing is a particular case of SPATIAL DISTRIBUTION, in which the position of the players in physical space is treated as an independent parameter. AMBULATION is also related to VECTORIALISM; in both the direction of the source of sound depends on the placement, stationary or kinetic, of the performers. In an AMBULATORY composition, the players are usually instructed to make their entrances on the stage while playing the initial bars upon their instruments which they carry with them. Some avant-garde composers even demanded the pushing of a grand piano on the stage while performing a one-arm composition on the keyboard. Rational AMBULATION is practiced in *Antiphones* for string quartet by the Soviet composer Sergei Slonimsky. In the opening of the work the cello player, originally seated in the middle of the last row of the concert hall, is instructed to walk with his instrument to the stage, while playing passages in a non-tempered scale; the other players are engaged in walking movements one after another, in a manner of an ambulatory fugato.

Anagrams.

By analogy with literal ANAGRAMS, in which words and sentences are derived from a given matrix (e.g., "Flit on, cheering angel" from Florence Nightingale), notes of a musical subject can be rearranged in order to generate plausible thematic variations. The 12 notes of the chromatic scale yield 479,001,600 possible permutations suitable for dodecaphonic usages. Polyanagrams, formed by linear (melodic), vertical (harmonic) and oblique (fugal) parameters, are comprised in the generic term COMBINATORIALITY, introduced by Milton Babbitt. Perhaps the most intricate Polyanagram is *Anagrama* by the Argentine-born avant-garde composer Mauricio Kagel, scored for speaking chorus, 4 vocalists and instruments, to the text derived from Dante's *Divina Commedia*, subject to a number of permutations forming plausible sentences in different languages.

Analphabetism.

There is a marked difference between musical ANALPHABETISM and ABECEDARIANISM.

While ABECEDARIANISM is the art of using artless formulas, ANALPHABETISM is the inability to use even a limited tonal vocabulary owing to a faulty technique of composition. The most obnoxious type of ANALPHABETISM is FRAUDULENT MODERNISM, mimicking advanced idioms and putting wrong notes in elementary harmonies. In its most innocent and disarming form, ANALPHABETISM approaches INFANTILOQUY. It is only when it raises its turgid tentacles above the level of harmless romantic indulgence that ANALPHABETISM becomes its literal self, i.e. illiteracy.

Anamnesis. A vivid memory of a psychologically important event that passes the mind simultaneously with another seemingly identical experience is popularly attributed to METEMPSYCHOSIS, a remembrance of a previous incarnation. ANAMNESIS is a similar explosion of memory, but it is devoid of any mystical notions. In music, an unexpected appearance of a thematic motive amid irrelevant melorhythmic events is ANAMNESTIC.

Anarchy and Autarchy. Innovating composers since the time of Wagner have been accused of promoting musical ANARCHY. An educated French music critic wrote after attending the first performance of Debussy's *Pelléas et Mélisande*, "No, I will never have anything to do with these anarchists of music!" But when Schoenberg enunciated his method of composition with 12 tones related only to one another, the outcries against atonal ANARCHY changed to charges of esthetic AUTARCHY. To refute such accusations, Schoenberg wrote, in a letter from Hollywood dated 3 June 1937, and addressed to Nicolas Slonimsky: "What I did was neither revolution nor anarchy. I possessed from my very first start a thoroughly developed sense of form and a strong aversion for exaggeration. There is no falling into order, because there was never disorder. There is no falling at all, but on the contrary, there is an ascending to a higher and better order."

Animal and Human Noises. The introduction of parts for animals into musical composition is an old and cherished fantasy. Imitations of bird songs have been part of music since the Middle Ages; but an actual sound of a bird occurs for the first time in Ottorino Respighi's *Pines of Rome* which includes a phonograph recording of a Roman nightingale. When a dog incidentally barked during a recording of Walte Piston's ballet suite *The Incredible Flutist,* the conductor decided to keep it in the final recording. A part for cat's meow appears in the score of Nicolas Slonimsky's piece *Anatomy of Melancholy,* to be enacted by a real cat whose tail is pulled during the performance. Electronic transcriptions provide an opportunity to supply recorded or synthetic animal noises. The tape recording of the cetacean song of a humpback whale has been incorporated into the symphonic poem *And God Created Great Whales* by the American composer Alan Hovhaness. Human noises—whistling, shrieking, grunting—were cultivated by the Italian Futurists and further propagated by the cosmopolitan AVANT-GARDE.

Anti-Music. ANTI-MUSIC is a concept formulated by analogy with the hypothetical phenomenon of Anti-Matter, in which the electrical charges of subatomic particles are reversed, so that the physical encounter between matter and Anti-Matter would result in mutual annihilation. ANTI-MUSIC reverses the acoustical charges of consonances and dissonances. The valences in the series of overtones are similarly reversed, so that the diminishing intervals in the upper part of the harmonic series are regarded as increasingly euphonious concords, and those close to the fundamental tone as discords, requiring a resolution. A manual of ANTI-MUSIC is yet to be written. Triadic formations, tonal sequences, symmetric periods and harmonious cadences would be ruled out in such a textbook. ANTI-MUSIC of this nature would then be taught in elementary schools along with the physical principles of anti-matter. But old music would not be entirely excluded. In special seminars, courses will be given in ANTI-ANTI-MUSIC, in which consonances will regain their respected status, while dissonances will once more be relegated to a dependency. It is even possible that in the fantastic world of ANTI-MUSIC, tolerance will be granted to such teratological practices as those of Bach, Beethoven, Brahms, Debussy and Schoenberg.

Anti-Opera. While ANTI-MUSIC is still in its embryonic stage, ANTI-OPERA flourishes on the contemporary scene. Its modest beginnings consisted in the reversal of the Aristotelian unity of place and action. In the world of ANTI-OPERA, it is not enough to use librettos that make no sense; this has long been achieved in classical Italian opera. What is required is deliberate violence wrought on logic, drama and comedy. Withal, ANTI-OPERA must be utterly solemn. The vocal parts must be written in an anti-larynx idiom. After the completion of an ANTI-OPERA, the score must be fractured, splintered, fragmented and then reassembled in a random montage, making sure that no inadvertent euphony or any non-Anti-Musical matter would result. ANTI-OPERA may include elements of the opera of the absurd, but there are differences. In the opera of the absurd, there is drama in the very absurdity of the libretto, while in ANTI-OPERA the dialogue is an *actus interruptus*, without any continuity. ANTI-OPERA belongs to the category of MIXED MEDIA, approaching in its total absence of cohesion the improvisatory qualities of a HAPPENING.

Aposiopesis. In oratorical practice, APOSIOPESIS is a sudden interruption of a speech as if in a state of overwhelming emotion. A locus classicus is Neptune's exhortation to his disobedient winds, "Quos ego. . . ." in Virgil's *Aeneid*. In music, APOSIOPESIS is used to best effect in opera. In Neo-Classical works, a dramatic break in a cadence or a rhythmic elision of a beat is a counterpart of APOSIOPESIS.

Asomatous Variations. Etymologically, the adjective ASOMATOUS signifies incorporeality, the lack of a soma, a material body. In composition, ASOMATOUS VARIATIONS are metamorphoses of an absent theme. Often a theme is cumulative, building up part by part, a practice as frequent among classical composers as in ultra-modern music. In DODECAPHONIC MUSIC, the principal series is sometimes evolved by such a cumulative thematic accretion. ASOMATOUS VARIATIONS serve a descriptive purpose in Vincent d'Indy's *Istar Variations*. In this work, portraying the passage of the goddess Istar through seven gates, at each of which she deposits a part of her garments, the theme does not appear in its totality until the final gate is reached. Elgar's *Enigma Variations* are based on a clearly outlined subject, but Elgar repeatedly hinted that this visible theme is but a counterpoint to a prime motive, which remains ASOMATOUS. Composers of the AVANT-GARDE cultivate the art of ASOMATOUS VARIATIONS with such determination that, in some ultra-modern works, an accidental repetition of a motive automatically marks the end of performance.

Asymmetry. Classical music is based on an orderly succession of symmetric periods and phrases; modern composers relish asymmetrical patterns. Often a simple, quasi-abecedarian tune is deliberately thrown out of symmetry by the addition or elision of a rhythmic unit, while the accompanying figure continues its preordained course. Compound meters are intrinsically asymmetric, as are the subdivisions of binary and ternary meters into unequal groups. Such subdivisions are typical of Serbian, Croatian, Bulgarian, Macedonian and Rumanian folk music. Béla Bartók makes artistic use of such meters derived from the multi-ethnic folkways of his native Transylvania.

Athematic Composition. ATHEMATIC COMPOSITION is the product of a deliberate effort to separate the melodic line into segregated groups of phrases and motives bearing no relation to one another. ATHEMATIC MUSIC does not adhere to any formal organization; a work without connected themes can therefore start and end at any point. Karlheinz Stockhausen arranges some of his works in segments which can be played in any order whatsoever, with this stipulation that when a performer, accidentally or intentionally, arrives at the same segment, it marks the ending. ATHEMATIC COMPOSITION tends towards atonal designs, in which the principle of non-repetition of melodic material is paramount. An athematic work need not be incoherent or inchoate; successive melodic statements may be related by a preferential use of a certain interval or a certain rhythmic configuration. In this sense, it may be said that an ATHEMATIC COMPOSITION has either zero or an indefinitely large number of themes.

Atonality. Etymologically, ATONALITY is a negative concept which connotes the absence of tonality. The term was first applied by hostile critics as a derisive description of a type of modern composition in which tonality was almost entirely disfranchised and integral chromaticism served as the guiding principle of melodic writing. Atonal composers avoid the repetition of a particular tone in order to preclude the appearance of an adventitious tonic. By natural predisposition such melodies invited a dissonant harmonization. Under such circumstances the key signature becomes superfluous. The desire to obviate the tonic-dominant relationship in atonal writing has led to the replacement of the perfect fifth by the tritone and of the octave by a major seventh. One of the most frequently occurring chordal formations in ATONAL MUSIC is a contraction of the four-part major triad, with the octave reduced to a major seventh, the fifth to a tritone and the major third to a sesquitone: C-E-G-C→C-D-sharp-F-sharp-B. The same chord can be obtained by raising the lowest note a semitone leaving the upper three notes unaltered: C-E-G-C→C-sharp-E-G-C. This chord may also be analyzed as a diminished-seventh chord with an unresolved appoggiatura. Consecutive blocks of such chords at a distance of a minor third are favorite devices of IMPRESSIONIST composers.

The gradual atrophy of tonality has resulted in the non-repetition of essential melodic notes, culminating in the organization of melodic writing making use of all 12 different tones. Tertian melodies and harmonies, affiliated with triadic structures, gave way to quartal and quintal progressions. Ascending or descending melodic fourths became the hallmark of atonal writing, gradually approaching the asymptote of integral dodecaphony in a cumulative PAN-DIATESSARON, an edifice of perfect fourths comprising all 12 tonics of the cycle of scales in the counterclockwise direction. Atonal structures guided by the principle of non-repetition are found in many works by 20th-century composers. An interesting example is an ornamental passage in Stravinsky's opera *Le Rossignol*, introducing the song of the Chinese nightingale. It traverses two ascending perfect fifths, a descending minor sixth, an ascending major seventh, an ascending minor third, a descending major third and an ascending major seventh. Not a single note is repeated, and the characteristic atonal interval of a major seventh occurs twice.

Tonal scales and modes derive their individuality from asymmetry of the pattern of tones and semitones. Atonal progressions are formed by the division of the octave into equal parts: two tritones, or three major thirds, four minor thirds, six major seconds, or 12 semitones. An augmented triad consisting of two major thirds is regarded as a dissonance in traditional harmony. When in 1903 the Russian composer Vladimir Rebikov used an augmented triad as the concluding chord of his opera *The Christmas Tree*, his daring was decried by academic critics. The diminished-seventh chord, consisting of minor thirds, is also an atonal dissonance, requiring a resolution into a triad. An atonal scale of 8 notes, obtained by the interpolation of symmetrically placed major or minor seconds in the sesquitone scale, is a frequently used coloristic device. It is described in Russian music dictionaries as Rimsky-Korsakov's scale. The WHOLE-TONE SCALE, representing the division of the octave into six equal parts, is a progression of a distinctly atonal nature, for it lacks the tonic-dominant complex and the leading tone.

The musical notation of ATONAL MUSIC, which in the larval phase of chromatic harmony bristled with double-sharps and double-flats, has been functionally simplified. When the fiction of a phantom tonality could no longer be maintained, double-sharps, double-flats and such vestigial tonal symbols as E-sharp and B-sharp, F-flat and C-flat were replaced by their enharmonic equivalents.

The cradle of ATONALITY is Central Europe, the birthplace of Freud's psychoanalysis, Kafka's existential Angst, the asymmetrical imagery of Kandinsky and the relativistic universe of Einstein. It seems fitting that these artistic and scientific developments occurred at about the same time. The controlled hesitancy, directed anxiety and Hesychastic omphaloskepsis of the period could be musically expressed with congenial intimacy only by atonal constructions. The circumstance that the TRITONE, the "diabolus in musica" of the medieval theorists, became the cornerstone of ATONALITY is a most significant reversal of musicosophical concepts of good and evil. It is also interesting to note that the tritone, being half an octave, is a neutral interval. On the psychological level this neuter quality suggests sexlessness. In his *Harmonielehre* Schoenberg remarks that "angels, our higher nature, are also sexless." In this assertion Schoenberg contradicts St. Thomas Aquinas who argued that angels must be of the masculine gender because Jacob wrestled with one and he would not have wrestled either with a woman or with a neuter hermaphrodite.

ATONAL melodies cultivate wide intervallic leaps, in order to avoid the monotony of consecutive small intervals. Although individual phrases in ATONAL MUSIC are usually short, the cumulative melodic curve appears long and sustained. Moreover, there is a singular sense of equilibrium inherent in a good atonal melody, in which the incidence of high notes is balanced by a countervailing group of low notes, with the solid central range representing a majority of essential notes. The computation of the relative frequency of individual notes in an ATONAL MELODY reveals the characteristics of the bell-shaped probability curve of Gauss. Since the duration of an individual note affects the general equilibrium of a melody, the sum of the products of duration in arbitrary units multiplied by the distance in semitones from the center of the melodic range must be zero, if the intervals below the central line are to be counted with a minus sign.

Several systems of atonal notation have been proposed in which accidentals are replaced by special symbols. Joseph Matthias Hauer suggested a multilineal staff. Jefim Golyscheff, a Russian who was active in Germany after World War I as composer and painter, and who eventually settled in Brazil, notated sharps with a cross inside a white circle and designated note values by stems. A similar notation was adopted by the Russian composer Nicolas Obouhov. He gave a demonstration of it at a concert of his works in Petrograd on 3 February 1916; he called his system "Absolute Harmony."

Herbert Eimert gives the following description of the essence of ATONALITY in his *Atonale Musiklehre* (1924): "Atonality, as the word itself implies, lacks modes, major and minor keys, and eliminates the entire harmonic apparatus of tonal music—cadences, leading tones, anticipations, resolutions, enharmonism, altered tones, etc.— as well as the concept of consonance and dissonance in their technical harmonic, but not psychological, aspects. The 12 mutually unrelated and independent tones of the tempered scale form the material of ATONAL MUSIC. The foundation of atonal material is therefore not a scale, or a progression of tones, but a group of tones, a complex, and specifically the only possible number of different tones, namely 12 tones." Hauer has this to say about ATONALITY: "In atonal music there are no tonic, dominant, subdominant, degrees, resolutions, consonances, dissonances, but only the 12 intervals of equal temperament; its scales consist therefore of 12 tempered semitones. In an ATONAL MELODY all purely physical, sensual, as well as trivial and sentimental elements, are eliminated, and its law, its *nomos*, is only that the 12 tones of the tempered scale must be played again and again."

Schoenberg and Alban Berg deprecated the use of the term ATONALITY. Berg concluded his talk on the subject, broadcast over the Vienna Radio on 8 June 1936, with these words: "Antichrist himself could not have thought up a more diabolical appellation than ATONAL!"

Aud Music. Optical art has given rise to a concentrated type of visual craft known as Op Art. By analogy, auditory art in its intense modern organization may be termed Aud Music. Op Art makes its impact felt by a direct assault on the visual nerve. Aud Music directs its onslaught against the auditory nerve. If *trompe l'oeil* in Op Art deceives the eye by rotating spirals, three-dimensional palimpsests, etc., the technique of *trompe l'oreille* in Aud Music confuses the ear by an unnerving succession of explosive musical fragments and sudden silences. Op Art and Aud Music freely combine in Audio-Visual syndromes. Fascinated by the optically concentric grooves of a phonograph disc, the painter Picabia called it Optophone.

To paraphrase Apollinaire, AUD MUSIC explores "a rational use of non-similitudinarianism." It makes music out of elements that are non-musical. Op Art tends to become music; modern artists often depict musical objects, such as a realistic metronome with an eye on the pendulum by Man Ray, which he entitled *Object of Destruction*, or a burning tuba by René Magritte. AUD MUSIC makes use of sound producing objects that are not musical instruments, as exemplified by the symphonic poem for 100 metronomes of György Ligeti. Other examples of Aud and Op Art acting in concert are Sculptures Sonores, sound-producing sculptures. Engineering applications of Aud Music are illustrated by the *Rhythmicon*, constructed by Theremin and Henry Cowell and the *Sonotron*, an acoustical accelerator built by Iannis Xenakis on the model of the Cyclotron and designed to synthesize sonic particles into a sound mass.

Jean Cocteau spoke of "oreilles myopes," referring to those suffering from auditory astigmatism. White light, analyzed by the spectroscope into primary colors, has inspired Op Art; by analogy, a linear evolution of a sonic complex generates AUD MUSIC.

Augenmusik. Music for the Eye is a term of opprobrium often applied to works that look orderly and plausible on paper but are unimpressive to the ear. Yet visual symmetry usually corresponds to a fine musical organization. Composers of the AVANT-GARDE have adopted the patterns of AUGENMUSIK as points of departure for their musical inspiration. Anestis Logothetis, a Bulgarian-born Greek composer, exhibited his scores of AUGENMUSIK in Vienna, bearing characteristic geometric titles, such as Cycloid, Culmination, Interpolation, Parallax, Concatenation. Villa-Lobos experimented with MILLIMETRIZATION by transferring a chart, a curve, or a silhouette onto a piece of graph paper, with the ordinate corresponding to intervals in semitones and the abscissa to the duration of a note.

Auricular Stimuli. Some musical ears are so sensitive that they perceive sonic stimuli at the threshold of audibility; they are also capable of generating such impulses from within, while reading a musical score, providing a realistic illusion of audible sounds. The secret of the process of composition, particularly of IMPRESSIONIS-TIC music, may lie in this type of inner stimulation. Such AURICULAR STIMULI perhaps explain the enigmatic title of a piece by Ravel, *Sites auriculaires*. The phenomenon of inner AURICULAR STIMULI may well be measurable and ought to be investigated by otologists.

Autogenetic Composition. AUTOGENETIC COMPOSITION, especially in modern music, is the function of melodic invention that makes the development of the basic idea seem inevitable. Bach anticipated the process in his riddle canons; modern composers, proceeding from premises entirely different from those of Bach, apply the method in advanced techniques. AUTOGENETIC COMPOSITION is an intelligent evaluation of the potentialities of an original invention.

Automatic Composition. True AUTOMATIC COMPOSITION can become a reality only with a considerable advance of electronic music. A photoelectric cell may be used to trigger selected groups of notes and to imprint them on a rotating roll of paper. A coordinating device can be constructed to dictate rhythms. An automatic musical typewriter can recapitulate whole sections of a composition. AUTOMATIC MUSIC should not be confused with automatic writing as employed by spiritualists. A British housewife appeared on television in the summer of 1969 and claimed that her diluted imitations of works by Schubert and Liszt were dictated to her by them, and that she wrote them down automatically. Her claims were never subjected to controlled examination, but if substantiated they would prove that a prolonged state of death fatally affects the ability to compose even among celebrated musicians.

Avant-Garde. The term AVANT-GARDE is the heir to a long series of terms descriptive of progressive art—Modern, Ultra-Modern, New, Modernistic, Experimental, Empiric. The unfortunate derivation from the military vocabulary does not seem to dismay progressive composers who accept the term as an honorable profession of artistic faith. The paradox is complicated by the fact that many AVANT-GARDE composers move in the direction of nullification of music as a complex art, with absolute zero as prospective Doomsday, as music diminishes in bulk and mass. There is an advantage to this minimusification, since the diminution in sonic mass, motion and duration, leads to a corresponding increase in the sensitivity of perception. When a composer writes a work consisting of a sustained note continuing indefinitely, the listener learns to appreciate the slightest variations in dynamics and pitch. After this, even a simple succession of two different tones would appear diversified and attractive.

Bebop. BEBOP, Rebop, or simply BOP, is one of the many onomatopoeic vocables descriptive of jazz techniques. The most striking characteristic of BEBOP is its maximal velocity, sometimes reaching 20 notes a second in clear articulation, with a strong off-beat stress. The invention of the term and the technique is generally attributed to the African-American jazz player Dizzy Gillespie. BEBOP is marked by irregular syncopation, a widely ranging melody of quasi-atonal configurations and, most impor-

tantly, by an accompaniment in rapidly changing modernistic harmonies, making use of unresolved dissonances and polytonal combinations. The verbalization of BEBOP can be traced to a counting jingle *Four or Five Times*, a disc issued by the Victor Company in 1928, in which the following line occurs, "BEBOP one, BEBOP two, BEBOP three." BOP as a verb was used in the comic strips in the 1920s, meaning to hit or to clobber. An erudite discussion of BOP is found in an article by Peter Tamony in the Spring, 1959, issue of the San Francisco periodical *Jazz*.

Bitonality. As the term indicates, BITONALITY is the simultaneous use of two different keys. The most effective type of BITONALITY is the combination of two polarized major triads whose tonics lie on the diametrically opposite points in the cycle of scales, and form the interval of a tritone. The sum of the absolute values of sharps or flats in the key signatures of such triads is always six (e.g., C major and F-sharp major, with zero sharps and six sharps respectively, or A-flat major and D major with key signatures of 4 flats and 2 sharps). The most frequently employed type of BITONALITY is the complex of C major and F-sharp major triads, which forms the harmonic foundation of Stravinsky's *Pétrouchka*, and is often called "Pétrouchka Chord." It is also known as "Parisian Chord," on account of the vogue that it subsequently acquired among Paris composers. The chord is of a clearly pianistic origin, with the white keys of C major contrasted with the black keys of F-sharp major; indeed, Stravinsky had originally planned to use these bitonal materials in a *Konzertstück* for piano and orchestra, and this accounts for the important piano part in the score of *Pétrouchka*. Acoustically, the most advantageous position of these two chords is the spacing of one in open harmony, in root position in the low register, and of the other in close harmony in the first inversion of the triad (e.g., C, G, E, A-sharp, C-sharp, F-sharp). In this disposition, the outer voices, the middle voices and the inner voices are all in the relationship of a tritone. It is of importance to note that the major hexachords based on such polarized scales aggregate to 12 different notes. BITONALITY of minor triads is encountered more seldom owing to poor acoustical balance of such combinations. In NEO-CLASSICAL music, a modal type of BITONALITY has come into existence, as exemplified by such complexes as C major and D major, in the Lydian mode. Such cases of BITONALITY are also part of PANDIATONICISM. Another type of BITONALITY is a combination of two major or minor triads with a tone in common, for instance C major combined with E major or E-flat major, favored particularly by composers of ethnic associations, among them Vaughan Williams and Roy Harris. It is interesting that a decreasing progression of intervals, beginning with 9 semitones and ending with 3 semitones, will form a bitonal major chord consisting of triads in second inversions (e.g., G, E, C, G, C-sharp, F-sharp, A-sharp, C-sharp) and that an increasing progression from 3 semitones to 9 semitones will form a bitonal combination of two minor triads in root positions (e.g., D, F, A, D, G-sharp, D-sharp, B, G-sharp). All these types of BITONALITY pursue the aims of euphony, either by polarization or by Pandiatonic approximation. A very important non-euphonious type of BITONALITY is homonymous BITONALITY of major and minor triads in close harmony (e.g., C, E, G, C, E-flat, G), with a friction point at a semitone between the major and the minor third of the same triad. It was cultivated assiduously by Stravinsky from his earliest period. In its linear devolution, it offers a stimulating quasi-atonal melodic design.

In his variations on the tune of *America,* written in 1891, Charles Ives combines F major with A-flat major. In order to bring out the bitonal resonance, he marks one of the tonalities *pianississimo* and the other *fortissimo.*

Blues. The word Blue is an old American colloquialism expressing melancholy. The BLUES, in plural, is an American ballad form, marked by leisurely syncopation, 4/4 time, in slow tempo. In its melancholy lilt, the BLUES forms the counterpart of the Elegy, the Bohemian Dumka or the Brazilian Modinha. Its distinctive characteristic is the "blue note" of the flatted seventh in major keys; the third is often flatted too. The sentiment of the BLUES reflects the long history of the suffering of the Negro people in the South; some elements in the Negro Spirituals and in Stephen Foster's songs are direct progenitors of the BLUES. The first composer of the BLUES in the modern sense was W. C. Handy; his songs, *The Memphis Blues* (1911) and *The St. Louis Blues* (1914), established the genre. On 17 May 1969 the United States Post Office issued a commemorative 6-cent stamp showing W. C. Handy playing the trumpet, with the legend "Father of the Blues." Ravel has a BLUES movement in his VIOLIN SONATA. The most famous concert piece in the BLUES idiom is Gershwin's *Rhapsody in Blue.* In its classic form, BLUES consists of a series of 12-bar strophes, with the following harmonic progression: 4 bars of tonic, 2 bars of subdominant, 2 bars of tonic, 1 bar of dominant, 1 bar of subdominant and 2 bars of tonic; the plagal cadence is *de rigueur.* As in all jazz, there are infinite variations on this harmonic succession, with atonal protuberances in the melody and pandiatonic excrescences in the accompaniment.

Boogie-Woogie. Like most terms of JAZZ music, BOOGIE-WOOGIE is an onomatopoeic alliterative word suggesting a certain type of rhythmic beat. BOOGIE-WOOGIE invaded the public arena at a concert of popular American music given in Carnegie Hall in New York on 23 December 1938. It is the only JAZZ form that has adopted an explicit classical model, of the type of passacaglia and chaconne, with the principal theme given in the bass and thus determining the harmonic scheme. The pattern of BOOGIE-WOOGIE is remarkably regular. It consists of a 12-bar period: 4 bars of tonic harmony, 2 bars of subdominant harmony, 2 bars of tonic harmony, 2 bars of dominant harmony and again 2 bars of tonic harmony. As in all JAZZ forms, the meter is in 4/4 time, but the rhythmic pattern is set in rapid motion, most often with dotted-eighth notes followed by sixteenth-notes. The bass is usually written in even eighth-notes, in broken octaves, and is sometimes described as "walking bass." The persistent eighth-notes rhythm is suggested by the title of an early BOOGIE-WOOGIE song, *Beat Me Daddy, Eight to the Bar.*

Bop. BOP is an apocope of BEBOP; possibly it preceded BEBOP, for the exclamatory flagellant expletive BOP appears in American comic strips in the 1920s, invariably followed by an exclamation point.

Boustrophedon. is an ancient system of writing and reading in alternate directions, one line from left to right, and the next from right to left. The Greek etymology of the word derives from oxen turning around as in plowing a field. Ophthalmologists find the BOUSTROPHEDONIC alignment beneficial in relieving the strain of shifting of the eye from right to left at the end of a line. In modern times, books have been published in a BOUSTROPHEDONIC arrangement, but no attempt has been made to publish music according to similar principles. The retrograde form of a thematic series is, to all effects and purposes, BOUSTROPHEDONIC.

Bruitism. BRUITISM is a genre of musical composition consisting of noises. The pioneer work of BRUITISM was *Arte dei Rumori* by the Italian Futurist Luigi Russolo, in which he codified the noises of friction, attrition, sibilation, percussion and concussion. Edgar Varèse elevated the inchoate BRUITISTIC scheme to a purely musical form in his epoch-making work *Ionization.*

Chirality. The etymology of CHIRALITY (from the Greek *cheir,* hand) connotes the symmetry of human hands. Lord Kelvin, who coined the term, proposed the following definition: "I call any geometrical figure, or a group of points, CHIRAL, and say it has CHIRALITY if its image in a plane mirror, ideally realized, cannot be brought to coincide with itself." Since music evolves in time and not in space, a composition that possesses CHIRALITY must consist of two symmetrical halves, the first note or chord being identical with the last, the second with the penultimate, the third with the antepenultimate, etc. In other words, musical CHIRALITY is achieved by the technique of specular reflection, or retrograde imitation. In spatial terms of musical performance, CHIRALITY exists between the first violin and second violin sections in an orchestra, if they are placed traditionally to the left and to the right of the conductor.

Chromatic Torsion. Chromatic melodies are most effective when they are involuted towards a central tone in a spiral. The effect of constant vectorial changes during which such a central tone is approached alternately from above and from below, may be described as CHROMATIC TORSION. An interesting example is the theme of the Queen of Shemaha in Rimsky-Korsakov's opera *Le Coq d'or,* in which CHROMATIC TORSION (and contortion) is effectively applied along the stems of diminished-seventh chord harmonies.

Circatonalitarianism. The employment, whether successive or quaquaversal, of all 12 minor and major modalities in a single composition may be called CIRCATONALITARIAN, by analogy with the biological term Circadian. CIRCATONALITARIAN structures are present literally in POLYTETRACHORDS, which traverse 12 major or minor tetrachords.

Circuitry. Modern scores for MIXED MEDIA performances often have the appearance of blueprints for the electric circuits in scientific instruments and digital computers. An early example of musical CIRCUITRY is the part marked *Luce* in Scriabin's *Prometheus,* intended to fill the concert hall with changing colors corresponding to fluctuations in instrumental timbre. The detailed directions as to lighting given by Schoenberg in his monodrama *Erwartung* are in the same category. The Russian composer Nicolas Obouhov, who called himself "Nicolas l'Illuminé," designed an electronic instrument in the form of a cross, called *Croix Sonore*. In the CIRCUITRY of some ultramodern scores the SPATIAL DISTRIBUTION of instruments becomes a musical parameter. Elliott Carter, Lukas Foss, Krzysztof Penderecki, Jani Christou, Sylvano Bussoti, Iannis Xenakis, John Cage and others, wrote works stipulating the position of each instrument in relation to the rest of the ensemble.

Collective Nouns. The following are suggestions for COLLECTIVE NOUNS to designate groups of musical instruments: a fluviality of flutes, an exhalation of piccolos, a conviviality of clarinets, a scabrosity of bassoons, a promiscuity of saxophones, an oriflamme of French horns, a plangency of oboes, an ambrosia of harps, a flourish of trumpets, a pomposity of trombones, a phlogiston of tubas, a circumspection of pianos, an enfilade of violins, a reticence of violas, an elegance of cellos, a teratology of doublebasses, a titillation of triangles, and the Brobdingnagian borborygmuses of bass drums.

Combinatoriality. In general topology the concept of COMBINATORIALITY applies to the functional congruence of geometrical figures of the same order of continuity. Thus a square can be brought into topological congruence with a circle because all the points of the former are in an enumerable correspondence of the other. On the other hand, the geometry of figure 8 cannot be made congruent with a square or a circle without cutting. The American composer and theorist Milton Babbitt extended the term COMBINATORIALITY to serial techniques. The parameter of continuity in dodecaphonic writing is the order of succession of the 12 thematic notes in their four forms, basic, retrograde, inversion and inverted retrograde, all of which are combinatorially congruent. Furthermore, the tone-row can be functionally divided into two potentially congruent groups of six notes each, or three groups of four notes each, or four groups of three notes each, with each such group becoming a generating serial nucleus possessing a degree of subsidiary COMBINATORIALITY. Extending the concept of COMBINATORIALITY to other parameters of serial music, a state of total SERIALISM is attained, in which not only the actual notes of a series, but also meter, rhythm, intervallic configurations, dynamics and instrumental timbres are organized in sets and subsets. The subsets in turn are organized as combinatorial derivations, possessing their own order of continuity and congruence. Of these, the most fruitful is the principle of rotation, in which each successive set is obtained by the transposition of the first note of the series to the end of a derived set. Thus the first set, 1,2,3, . . . 12, appears after rotation as subset 2, 3, 4, 5, . . . 12, 1, or as 3, 4, 5, 6, . . . 12, 1, 2, etc. Inversion, retrograde and inverted retrograde can be subjected to a similar type of rotation. The additive Fibonacci series, in which each number equals the sum of the two preceding numbers, as in 1, 1, 2, 3, 5, 8, 13, 21, is another fertile resource for the formation of sets, subsets and other derivations. The Fibonacci numbers can be used for building non-dodecaphonic tone-rows, in which case the

numbers will indicate the distance from the central tone in semitones, modulo 12, so that 13 becomes functionally identical with 1, 21 with 9, etc. The numerical field of COMBINATORIALITY is circumscribed by 12 different notes. But experiments have been conducted, notably by Ernst Krenek, with artificial scales of 13 equal degrees, obtained with the aid of electronic instruments. Potential uses of COMBINATORIALITY operating with sets of more than 12 notes in an octave are limitless.

Commodious Nomenclature. The musical avant-garde does not oppose euphony on general principle. Harmonious progressions are tolerated in modern music. The compromise between the prospective music of the future and the modality of the past is often achieved by resorting to COMMODIOUS NOMENCLATURE, as exemplified by the neologisms NEO-CLASSICAL, NEO-BAROQUE, NEO-ROMANTIC, and beyond that by the exotic terms VECTORIALISM, LIPOGRAMMATICISM or SPATIAL SERIALISM. New Music, Modern Music, Contemporary Music, etc., once progressive slogans, have long been overgrown with a fungus of obsolescence. Futurism itself, a rebellious cry of the dawn of the century, is now an academic object of historical study.

Computer Music. Digital computers are ideal purveyors of random numbers, which in turn can be converted into musical parameters. Such data furnish the natural sources for ALEATORY MUSIC. Care should be taken, however, not to program COMPUTER MUSIC excessively, for such input would amount to the dictation of the programmer's own musical ideas, which are often lamentable.

Conjugated Counterpoint. By definition, counterpoint is a conjugation of two or several melodic parts, but too often in common practice contrapuntal techniques follow harmonic formulas, to the detriment of the interdependence of component voices. It is therefore useful to introduce the term CONJUGATED COUNTERPOINT in its etymological sense of "opposite notes yoked together." The locus classicus of CONJUGATED COUNTERPOINT is the second movement of Béla Bartók's *Concerto for Orchestra*, in which conjugated pairs of wind instruments are arrayed in succession and intussusception.

Contrapuntal Intussusception. In many modern scores contrapuntal groups are arranged in pairs, and each pair becomes an individual entity which is subsequently combined with another prefabricated pair, and yet another. When two such pairs are widely separated in their ranges, an opportunity is presented for an intussusception of a new pair, forming a structure of six contrapuntal voices in three subdivisions. Alexander Tcherepnin made systematic use of this technique in his method of INTERPOINT (Contrapunctus inter punctum).

Controlled Improvisation. An arrangement of available thematic elements, following a definite formal design and confined within a specified period of time, has been described as CONTROLLED IMPROVISATION. Accordingly, the performer selects attractive or significant motives and phrases of an otherwise non-integrated work, as though drawing pre-set lines from a printer's tray, resetting them at will, duplicated, fragmented, or upside-down. Karlheinz Stockhausen, Lukas Foss, Earle Brown, and others have availed themselves of this manner of composition.

Counterpoetry. An apt term coined by the American composer Mikel Rouse to describe the use of multiple unpitched voices in strict metric counterpoint, which enable the exploration of complex, overlapping harmonies of meaning and emotion as these correspond to the equally complex and overlapping harmonies of the music "bed" on which they lie. In his one-man opera *Failing Kansas*, based on the events surrounding the murder of the Clutter family in Holcomb, Kansas (treated in quasi-documentary fashion in Truman Capote's novel *In Cold Blood*), Rouse employed COUNTERPOETRY as a highly-effective means of evoking the internal, interpersonal conflicts and emotions that precipitated this tragedy.

Country Music. As it is practiced in the American South, COUNTRY MUSIC is deeply imbued with sentimental balladry, with curiously oblique cadences that impart an archaic flavor to the melody. The syncopated beat, characteristic of RAGTIME and JAZZ, is practically absent in these bland songs. Through the medium of radio and television, COUNTRY MUSIC spread far and wide in the United States, eventually coalescing with ROCK 'N' ROLL.

Cubism. The musical counterpart of CUBISM in art is the erection of massive sonorous complexes moving *en bloc* at different speeds and angular motion. Such harmonic boulders produce the best effect in POLYTRIADIC STRUCTURES, CUBISTIC music must be static, with a low potential. There should be no intermediate melodic or harmonic shifts between CUBISTIC complexes, but tremolo effects within each unit may contribute to resonant power congruent with massive sonic structures.

Cybernetics. The word CYBERNETICS is derived from the Greek root for governing. As defined by its originator Norbert Wiener, CYBERNETICS is the exercise of human control over mechanical and electrical apparatus, especially in the field of communication. In music, CYBERNETICAL data are collected by various ALEATORY, intuitive or other means; the resulting materials are translated into a system of musical parameters, and a viable outline is drawn. It is in the selection and the programming of CYBERNETICAL elements that a composer can assert his personality. In music, CYBERNETICAL SERENDIPITY plays a beneficial part. Novel ideas often suggest themselves during the process of mutation and permutation of thematic elements, contributing to the all-important problem of musical communication.

Cyrenaic Hedonism. Hedonistic traits in modern music developed as a natural psychological reaction to the cataclysm of World War I. Composers and the public sought relaxation in hedonistic dalliance, Cyrenaic in its complete orgiastic abandon and Sybaritic in its quest for mindless comforts. The center of this cult of music for pleasure was France; it enjoyed a particular vogue between 1920 and 1935, when the slogan of NEW SIMPLICITY was launched as an antidote to post-Romantic solipsism. In form and content this new music cultivated the elegant conceits of the French rococo period, with an emphasis on Epicurean qualities designed to please the palate. Historically, it was the long-delayed fruition of the musical cuisine of Rossini, with occasional polyharmonies and asymmetric rhythms used for modern seasoning.

Dadaism. The word DADAISM was invented by Tristan Tzara of 8 February 1916 at a congenial gathering of friends in a Zürich café. According to one of the many versions, the word *Dada* owes its origin to French infantiloquy as a sort of dental lallation. Esthetically, *Dadaism* was the product of the frustrations endured during the First World War. Its philosophy was entirely negative. Derived from the vociferously proclaimed detestation of all art, music and poetry, DADAISM stood close to FUTURISM in its furious onslaught on all established values, but failed to offer a new art to replace the old. Despite its violently negative code, DADAISM prepared a well-manured ground for the flowering of such fertile stylistic vegetation as SURREALISM. DADAISM also cast its proleptic shadow on the AVANT-GARDE of the 1960s and the improvisatory art of the HAPPENINGS.

Decomposition and Reassembly. The technique of DECOMPOSITION AND REASSEMBLY is suggested by the title of a painting by the Futurist artist Umberto Boccioni, "Scomposizione," in which the normal head of a woman is fragmented and reassembled in a topologically non-congruent shape. The idea is applicable to modern music. A melody can be fractured and its elements redistributed in a different configuration. Variations, tonal and atonal, can be experimentally rearranged, melodically, harmonically and rhythmically. DECOMPOSITION AND REASSEMBLY may provide interesting and novel combinations of thematic materials and stimulate a disadvantaged composer to explore the laws of musical congruence far beyond his ordinary capabilities.

Demolition. Public DEMOLITION of musical instruments as part of new techniques of the American and British AVANT-GARDE came into vogue shortly after the conclusion of World War II, possibly as a sado-masochistic exercise of aggressive tendencies, frustrated by the unconditional surrender of the ex-enemies. Contests in the swiftness of destroying upright pianos have been held in clubs and colleges. According to the established rules of the game, a piano had to be reduced to comminuted fragments that could be passed through an aperture of specified dimensions (usually a circle 6 inches in diameter). In Stockholm, Sweden, a young pianist concluded his recital by igniting a dynamite charge previously secreted inside the piano, blowing it up. An exploding splinter wounded him in the leg. The American AVANT-GARDE composer La Monte Young set a violin on fire at one of his exhibits.

Bakunin, the scientific anarchist, said, "Die Lust der Zerstörung ist eine schaffende Lust." This "creative impulse of destruction" has received its full vindication in the anti-piano activities of the modern times.

Demotic Music. DEMOTIC MUSIC is a generic category that comprises all genres of popular music—rural, urban, pop, country, folk, western, jazz, tin-pan alley, commercial jingles. Modern applications of the sources of DEMOTIC MUSIC are obtained by diatonic translocation, atonal dismemberment and rhythmic compression. Hexachordal diatonic melodies may be metamorphosed into complex melorhythmic progressions without losing their DEMOTIC morphology. ABECEDARIAN MUSIC for children is a fruitful source of such topological transformation. Not all simple music is necessarily DEMOTIC, unless the folk quality is expressed in a composed work with utmost fidelity. Some obscure composers have succeeded in producing tunes that seem to be authentically DEMOTIC. The universally popular tune, *Dark Eyes*, regarded by many as an autochthonous Russian Gypsy song, is actually a violin piece, entitled *Valse-hommage* composed by a German band leader active in Russia in the 1880s. The Neapolitan ballad *Funiculi-Funicula*, mistaken by many for a genuine folk tune, was written by an Italian vocal teacher resident in London.

Dialectics.

Etymologically, DIALECTICS is a discourse. Musical DIALECTICS may be a useful term to describe a kind of meaningful antiphony, an orderly exchange of melodic statements, sufficiently divergent to imply the sense of a debate and yet unified by a general melodic, rhythmic or harmonic idea. Music in a dialectical form ought to be by definition a succession of free associations, not too strict in grammar and syntax, replete with asymmetrical rhythms and unresolved dissonances. The term is large enough to cover many idioms and techniques, from NEO-CLASSICAL structures to SERIAL COMPOSITION.

Dilapidation of Tonality.

The disappearance of explicit key signatures from the notation of modern composition was the first symptom of the DILAPIDATION OF TONALITY and deterioration of traditional harmony. The key signature has a reason for existence in NEO-CLASSICAL works in which the tonic-dominant relationship is still extant and triadic modulations strong. But the dormant chromaticism erupts all the more viciously against tonal restraints, and the key signature, if it is set down at all, exists only to be denied. The chromaticization of the modern idiom during the last decades of the 19th-century resulted in an enormous proliferation of double-sharps and double-flats. As enharmonic modulation reared its multicolored head, the antinomy between the tonality symbolized by the key signature and the florid panchromatic display reached the point of arithmetical incompatibility. Seven notes of the diatonic scale represented by seven positions on the music staff and seven letters of the alphabet were to provide notation for the 12 different notes of the chromatic scale. Academic musicians, eager to reserve the fiction of eminent tonality, and being unable to find a common denominator between 7 and 12, erected a fantastic network of accidentals; triple sharps and triple flats pullulate in the *Canons and Fugues* of Wilhelm Middelschulte. A whole section, acoustically equivalent to C major, masquerades in intervallic enharmonies as B-sharp and D-double-flat major in the piano part of Ravel's *Trio*. Debussy was similarly involved in exotic structures of double-flats and double-sharps in a triadic passage of his *Feuilles mortes*.

Even in the 19th century, tonality was often nominal and the key signature an armature without a function.

Intermezzo No. 4, op. 76, by Brahms is ostensibly in B-flat major, but the tonic triad is not reached until the final two bars. This type of tonal convention may be described as teleological tonality in which the tonic is the goal rather than the point of departure. The language of ATONALITY arose from the products of the decay of tonal relationships. Genuinely atonal melodies lack the homing instinct; they meander and maunder without the beacon of a tonic in sight. The attraction of the tonic does not exist in atonal writing; the members of an atonal melody are weightless. This atonal assembly deprived of tonal gravity came to be organized by Arnold Schoenberg in a mutually gravitating dodecaphonic complex. Key signatures are obviously superfluous in atonal and dodecaphonic music, but not in POLYTONALITY where different key signatures are used simultaneously.

The supremacy of tonality demanded that each composition should end in the same key, or in a related key, in which it began. How strong the prerequisite of this tonal uniformity was felt by composers of the 19th century is illustrated by a whimsical annotation of Richard Strauss in his song entitled *Wenn*, published in 1897. In the original version, the principal key is D-flat major, but the final seven bars and the concluding chord are in D major. Strauss supplied an alternative coda in which the transition was made to the original key, with the following footnote: "Vocalists who may perform this song before the end of the 19th century are advised by the composer to transpose the last seven bars a semitone lower so as to arrive at the end of the song in the same key in which it began."

Dislocation of Melodic Lines.

A special case of modern variation is a linear DISLOCATION OF A MELODIC LINE. A high note may be pulled upwards and a low note may be pulled downwards without disrupting the intervallic balance of the melody itself. Virtually any tonal melodic line can be topologically transformed into a dodecaphonic series, with ascending intervals retaining their upward direction and descending intervals conserving their downward motion. Stationary notes in the melody may be pulled upwards or downwards at will. Examples of intervallic and modulatory translocation can be found in NEO-CLASSICAL compositions. Translocation is also an excellent resource of modern burlesque.

Displaced Tonality.

A modernistic resource in tonal techniques, which has been successfully applied by composers who are reluctant to abandon tonality altogether, is a DISPLACEMENT of the tonic by an instant modulation a semitone higher or a semitone lower. Translocation by larger intervals is not effective. Major scales are more suitable for such translocation because of the greater intervallic strength within a major tetrachord, while minor tetrachords are often ambiguous. Transposition of the initial three notes of a major scale a semitone higher or lower forms a group of six different notes; a similar translocation in a minor key will entail a duplication of one member of the series. Examples of melodic translocations are found in many works of Prokofiev and Shostakovich.

Dissonant Counterpoint.

The term DISSONANT COUNTERPOINT came into usage in the 1920s as a sort of apologetic declaration by proponents of ATONAL

MUSIC. It emphasized the functional equality of dissonance and consonance in all types of contrapuntal techniques. In fugal writing, in particular, a strong tendency was evinced to use the tritone as the interval of entry, instead of the traditional perfect fifth of the tonic-dominant complex. DISSONANT COUNTERPOINT does not exclude consonances but puts them on probation. However, the perfect octave, as a cadential interval, is generally shunned by the theoreticians of DISSONANT COUNTERPOINT, and is usually replaced by a major seventh.

Dodecaphonic Music.

In historical perspective, DODECAPHONIC MUSIC is the product of a luxuriant development of chromatic melody and harmony. A conscious avoidance of all tonal centers led to the abolition of key signature and a decline of triadic harmony. The type of composition in which all tonal points of reference have been eliminated became known as ATONALITY. It was from this paludous atmosphere of inchoate ATONALITY that the positive and important technical idiom of dodecaphonic composition was gradually evolved and eventually formulated by Arnold Schoenberg as the "method of composing with 12 tones related only to one another." Schoenberg's first explicit use of his method occurs in his *Serenade*, op. 24, written in 1924. Five fundamental ideas underlie Schoenberg's method: (1) Dodecaphonic monothematism in which the entire work is derived from a 12-tone row (*Tonreihe*) which comprises 12 different notes of the chromatic scale. (2) The tone-row is utilized in four conjugate forms: the original, retrograde, inversion, and retrograde inversion. (3) Although the order of the notes in the tone-row is rigidly observed, the individual members of the series can be placed in any octave position, a peculiar feature of dodecaphonic music which results in the wide distribution of the thematic ingredients over the entire vocal or instrumental range of a single part or over sections of different parts. (4) Since each of the 4 forms of the basic 12-tone series can be transposed to any starting point of the chromatic scale, the total of all available forms is 48. (5) Melody, harmony and counterpoint are functions of the tone-row, which may appear in all its avatars, horizontally as melody, vertically as harmony and diagonally as canonic counterpoint. It may also be distributed partly in melodic progressions, partly in harmonic or contrapuntal structures, creating DODECAPHONIC MELOHARMONY or MELOCOUNTERPOINT. Because of the providential divisibility of number 12, the 12-tone row can be arranged in 6 groups in 2-part counterpoint, 4 groups in 3-part counterpoint (or harmony), 3 groups in 4-part harmony or 2 groups in 6-part harmony.

In a communication sent to Nicolas Slonimsky in 1939, Ernst Krenek describes the relationship between ATONALITY and the method of composing with 12 tones as follows: "ATONALITY is a state of the musical material brought about through a general historical development. The 12-tone technique is a method of writing music within the realm of ATONALITY. The sense of key has been destroyed by ATONALITY. The method of composing with 12 tones was worked out in order to replace the old organization of the material by certain new devices."

Schoenberg was not alone in his dodecaphonic illumination. Several musicians, mostly in Austria and Germany, evolved similar systems of organizing the resources of the chromatic scale in a logical and self-contained system of composition. Jef Golyscheff, Russian composer and painter who lived in Germany and eventually settled in Brazil, worked on the problem as early as 1914, and in 1924 published a collection which he called *12 Tondauer Musik*, making use of 12 different tones in thematic structures. At about the same time Nicolas Obouhov invented a system which he called "Absolute Harmony" and which involved the use of all 12 chromatic tones without doubling; he played his piano pieces written in this system at a concert in Petrograd on 3 February 1916.

Passages containing 12 different notes in succession, apart from the simple chromatic scale, are found even in classical works. There is a highly chromaticized passage in Mozart's *G Minor Symphony* derived from three mutually exclusive diminished-seventh chords, aggregating to 12 different notes. The main subject in the section "Of Science" in the score of *Also sprach Zarathustra* by Richard Strauss contains all 12 different notes of the chromatic scale, but they remain uninverted, untergiversated and otherwise unmetamorphosed, and thus cannot be regarded as a sampler of dodecaphonic writing.

Liszt's *Faust Symphony* opens with a theme consisting of four successive augmented triads descending by semitones comprising all 12 different tones, but it cannot be meaningfully described as an anticipation of the dodecaphonic method. Charles Ives has a 12-tone series of different chromatic notes in his instrumental piece *Tone Road No. 3*, which he wrote in 1915. This intuitive invention is important not only as an illustration of his prophetic genius, but also as another indication that dodecaphonic ideas appeared in the minds of musicians working in different parts of the world, completely independent of each other.

Among scattered examples of 12-tone composition of the pre-dodecaphonic years is *L'adieu à la vie* for piano by Alfredo Casella, which ends on a chord of 12 different notes. An amusing example of dodecaphonic prevision is the *Hymn to Futurism* by César Cui, written in 1917, when the last surviving member of the Russian Mighty Five was 82 years old. Intended as a spoof, the piece contains a passage of three mutually exclusive diminished-seventh chords in arpeggio adding up to 12 different notes, and another passage comprising two mutually exclusive augmented triads with a complementary scale of whole tones passing through the unoccupied six spaces, forming another series of 12 different notes. The fact that Cui had two dodecaphonic series in his short composition demonstrates that even in a musical satire the thematic use of 12 different notes was a logical outcome of the process of tonal decay, serving as a fertilizer for the germination of dodecaphonic organisms.

Schoenberg was intensely conscious of the imperative need of asserting his priority in the invention of the method of composition with 12 tones. Among contenders for the honor was Fritz Klein, the author of an extremely ingenious composition for orchestra, *Die Maschine*, subtitled "eine extonale Selbstsatire," published in 1921 under the characteristic pseudonym "Heautontimorumenos" (i.e., Self-Tormentor). This pseudonym Klein took from the title of a play by Terence, which contains the famous aphorism: "Homo sum; humani nil a me alienum puto." Klein's score contains a remarkable array of inventions: a "Mutterakkord" containing 12 different notes and 11 different intervals, a "Pyramidakkord," patterns of rhythmically repeated 12 notes, etc., all presaging the future developments of integral serialism. When queried by Nicolas Slonimsky regarding Klein's role in the history of dodecaphonic composition, Schoenberg replied (in English): "Although I saw Klein's 12-tone compositions abut 1919, 1920 or 1921, I am not an imitator of him. I wrote the melody for *Scherzo* composed of 12 tones in 1915. In the first edition of my *Harmonielehre* (1911), there is a description of the new harmonies and their application which has probably influenced all these men who now want to become my models."

A much more formidable challenge to Schoenberg's dodecaphonic priority was made by Joseph Matthias Hauer of Vienna, who had experimented with 12-tone composition independently from Schoenberg. But his method differed from Schoenberg's in essential aspects. He built 12-tone subjects from 6-tone "tropes," and allowed free permutation of each trope, a concept that was entirely alien to Schoenberg's fundamental doctrine of thematic ordering of the tone-row. Still, Schoenberg regarded Hauer's theories as sufficiently close to his own method to take notice of them. Schoenberg described the dodecaphonic situation in Vienna in a retrospective note published in the program book of a concert of his chamber music given in New York in 1950: "In 1921 I showed my former pupil Erwin Stein the means I had invented to provide profoundly for a musical organization granting logic, coherence and unity. I then asked him to keep this a secret and to consider it as my private method with which to do the best for my artistic purposes." (The arcane character of this report calls to mind a Latin cryptogram in which the astronomer Huygens encoded his discovery of the rings of Saturn to insure the priority of his observations.) "If I were to escape the danger of being his imitator," Schoenberg continued, "I had to unveil my secret. I called a meeting of friends and pupils, to which I also invited Hauer, and gave a lecture on my new method, illustrating it by examples of some finished compositions of mine. Everybody recognized that method was quite different from that of others." Hauer refused to surrender his own claims as the spiritual protagonist of 12-tone music. A man of an irrepressible polemical temper, he even had a rubber stamp made, which he used in his private correspondence, and which carried the following legend: "Josef Matthias Hauer, der geistiger Urhaber und trotz vielen schlechten Nachahmern immer noch der einziger Kenner und Könner der Zwölftonmusik."

Although Schoenberg's title to the formulation and practical application of the method of composing with 12 tones was finally recognized, in 1948 he came into an unexpected collision with a fictional claimant, Adrian Leverkühn, the hero of Thomas Mann's novel *Doktor Faustus*, described as the inventor of the 12-tone method of composition. In an indignant letter to the editors of the *Saturday Review of Literature* Schoenberg protested against this misappropriation of his invention. The idea that Leverkühn might be considered as a fictional portrait of Schoenberg himself infuriated him. "Leverkühn is depicted," Schoenberg wrote, "from beginning to end,

as a lunatic. I am seventy-four and I am not yet insane, and I have never acquired the disease from which this insanity stems. I consider this an insult."

John Stuart Mill once expressed fears that musical invention might soon exhaust its resources, considering the limited number of melodies that could be derived from the eight degrees of the major or the minor scale. He reckoned without the eventual proliferation of chromatic melodies. There are 479,001,600 permutations of 12 units, and as many possible melodies consisting of 12 different notes each. In the dodecaphonic firmament, the melodic horizon is practically unlimited.

The properties of 12-tone composition are truly magical. A priori, it would seem impossible that the 12 notes of the chromatic scale could be arranged in four mutually exclusive triads, considering that its organization was the product of negation of tonality. Yet it has been found empirically that there are two basic solutions of this problem, each capable of three transpositions. But there is a limiting condition: two of these triads must be major and two minor. On the basis of C, these solutions are: (1) C major, D minor, F-sharp major, G-sharp minor; (2) C major, B-flat major, G-sharp minor and F-sharp minor. The ever-present tritone is the interval between the tonics of each pair in the first solution, and between the tonics of the first and last triad in the second solution. It is also possible to distribute the 12 chromatic tones in a group containing a diminished triad, a minor triad, a major triad and an augmented triad. Furthermore it is possible to arrange four mutually exclusive triads in a continuous chain of major and minor thirds, forming a chord of the minor 23rd, e.g., F-sharp major, E major, D minor, C minor in an ascending series. This is the unique solution of this particular problem. The symmetry of these arrangements is extraordinary. These findings were first published in 1947 in Nicolas Slonimsky's *Thesaurus of Scales and Melodic Patterns*, and have been since verified by a digital computer without adding any new solutions.

Far from being sterile excogitations, the theory of mutually exclusive triads has had its practical application long before it was explicitly formulated. A passage including four mutually exclusive triads occurs in the concluding section of Debussy's *Prélude à l'Après-midi d'un Faune* (E major, C minor, D major, B-flat minor, with the melody descending chromatically from G-sharp down to F).

The method of composing with 12 tones related only to one another did not remain a rigid dogma. Its greatest protagonists, besides Schoenberg himself, were his disciples Alban Berg and Anton von Webern. Somewhat frivolously, they have been described as the Vienna Trinity, with Schoenberg the Father, Berg the Son, and Webern the Holy Ghost. Both Berg and Webern introduced considerable innovations into the Schoenbergian practice. While Schoenberg studiously avoided triadic constructions, Alban Berg used the conjunct series of alternating minor and major triads capped by three whole tones as the principal subject of his last work, the *Violin Concerto* (1935). Schoenberg practically excluded symmetric intervallic constructions and sequences, but Alban Berg inserted, in his opera *Lulu*, a dodecaphonic episode built on two mutually exclusive whole-tone scales. Anton von

Webern dissected the 12-tone series into autonomous sections of 6, 4 or 3 units in a group, and related them individually to one another by inversion, retrograde and inverted retrograde. This fragmentation enabled him to make use of canonic imitation much more freely than would have been possible according to the strict Schoenbergian doctrine.

The commonly used term for DODECAPHONIC MUSIC in German is Zwölftonmusik. In American usage it was translated literally as 12-tone music, but English music theorists strenuously object to this terminology, pointing out that a tone is an acoustical phenomenon and that DODECAPHONY deals with the arrangement of written notes, and that it should be consequently called 12-note music. In Italy the method became known as *Dodecafonia* or *Musica dodecafonica*. Incidentally, the term *Dodecafonia* was first used by the Italian music scholar Domenico Alaleona in his article *L'armonia modernissima* published in *Rivista Musicale* in 1911 but it was applied there in the sense of total chromaticism as an extension of Wagnerian harmony.

The proliferation of dodecaphony in Italy was as potent as it was unexpected, considering the differences between Germanic and Latin cultures, the one introspective and speculative, the other humanistic and practical. Luigi Dallapiccola was one of the earliest adepts, but he liberalized Schoenberg's method and admitted tonal elements. In his opera *Il Prigioniero*, written in 1944, he made use of four mutually exclusive triads.

The greatest conquest of Schoenberg's method was the totally unexpected conversion of Igor Stravinsky whose entire esthetic code had seemed to stand in opposition to any predetermined scheme of composition; yet he adopted it when he was already in his seventies. Many other composers of world renown turned to dodecaphonic devices as a thematic expedient without full utilization of the four basic forms of the tone-row. Béla Bartók made use of a 12-tone melody in his *Second Violin Concerto*, but he modified its structure by inner permutations within the second statement of the tone-row. Ernest Bloch, a composer for whom the constrictions of modern techniques had little attraction, made use of 12-tone subjects in his *Sinfonia Breve* and in his last string quartets. English composers who have adopted the technique of 12-tone composition with various degrees of consistency are Michael Tippett, Lennox Berkeley, Benjamin Frankel, Humphrey Searle and Richard Rodney Bennett. William Walton makes use of a 12-tone subject in the fugal finale of his *Second Symphony*. Benjamin Britten joined the dodecaphonic community by way of tonality. In his expressionist opera *The Turn of the Screw*, he adopts a motto of alternating perfect fifths and minor thirds (or their respective inversions), aggregating to a series of 12 different notes. The Spanish composer Roberto Gerhard, who settled in England, wrote in a fairly strict dodecaphonic idiom. In France the leader of the dodecaphonic school is René Leibowitz, who also wrote several books on the theory of 12-tone composition. Wladimir Vogel, a Russian-born composer of German parentage, making his home in Switzerland, has adopted Schoenberg's method in almost all of his works. The Swiss composer Frank Martin has extended the principles of dodecaphonic writing to include a number of tonal and modal ramifications.

In America Schoenberg's method has found a fertile ground, not only among his students but also among composers who had pursued different roads. Roger Sessions, Virgil Thomson and David Diamond followed Schoenberg's method with varying degrees of fidelity. Aaron Copland used the dodecaphonic technique in some of his chamber music works; in the orchestral compositions entitled *Connotations* commissioned for the opening concert of Lincoln Center, New York, in 1962, he applied the totality of DODECAPHONY to characterize the modern era of music. Walter Piston interpolated a transitional 12-tone passage in his ballet suite *The Incredible Flutist*. He resisted integral dodecaphony until his septuagenarian calendae, when in his *Eighth Symphony* he adopted Schoenberg's method in all its orthodoxy. Leonard Bernstein inserted a 12-tone series in the score of his *Age of Anxiety* to express inner agitation and anguished expectancy of the music. Samuel Barber made an excursion into the dodecaphonic field in a movement of his *Piano Sonata*. Gian Carlo Menotti turned dodecaphony into parody in his opera *The Last Savage* to illustrate the decadence of modern civilization into which the hero was unexpectedly catapulted from his primitivistic habitat.

In Soviet Russia dodecaphony still remains officially unacceptable as a "formalistic" device. (In a speech delivered in Moscow on 8 March 1963, Nikita Khrushchev, then Prime Minister of the Soviet Union, observed: "They call it dodecaphony, but we call it cacophony.") Nevertheless, some blithe spirits of the young Soviet generation, among them Andrei Volkonsky, Valentin Silvestrov and Sergei Slonimsky, have written and published works in the 12-tone idiom.

The following is a summation of theoretical postulates, subsidiary lemmata and practical usages of dodecaphonic techniques.

(1) The generating dodecaphonic series must be constructed in such a way as to establish a strong mutual valence of the component members, relating them only to one another in accordance with Schoenberg's prescription, and avoiding any suggestion of chordal derivation, particularly that of a triad nature.

(2) Intervals most suitable for the construction of a viable series are those that carry no tonal affiliation, with particular reference for the major seventh, the minor ninth, and the tritone. Since the intervallic difference between the major seventh and the tritone is a perfect fourth and the difference between the minor ninth and the tritone is a perfect fifth, these differential intervals have acquired a peculiar structural importance in DODECAPHONIC MUSIC, provided they do not appear poised strategically in the potential relationship of the tonic and dominant, or tonic and subdominant. Melodic successions of perfect fourths or perfect fifths are favored since they tend towards atonal asymptotes. Historically, such quartal and quintal progressions led to the distinctive evolution of atonal patterns preceding the formation of strictly dodecaphonic conformations.

(3) Identical intervals between successive pairs of thematic tones are to be used with circumspection so as not to impair the individuality of members of the tone-row

and prevent their degeneration and entropic coalescence into chromatic or diatonic scales or into easily decipherable chordal combinations.

(4) Although the original tone-row must be stated in full in the exposition, immediate repetition of a single tone in the series is not to be regarded as a disruptive factor, for such repetition may be simply a synonym for a rhythmic prolongation.

(5) Since the concept of tonality is irrelevant to DODECAPHONIC, MUSIC, the key signature is automatically eliminated. For the same reason chromatic alterations pertinent to tonal usages and modulation are reduced to their simplest enharmonic equivalents; double-sharps and double-flats are completely eliminated. Some dodecaphonic composers insist on prefixing every note with a sharp, flat or natural, but this type of notation is visually distracting and wasteful.

(6) Functional and operative equivalence of melody, harmony and counterpoint is of fundamental importance to the dodecaphonic techniques and constitutes its most innovative feature; thus the 12 tones of the series may be distributed either horizontally in melodic lines, vertically in harmonic columns, or diagonally in contrapuntal formations becoming different dimensions of a unified dodecaphonic space.

(7) Triadic chordal formations are unacceptable in vertical constructions as well as in horizontal melodies. Major triads, particularly in root positions, are inadmissible; their inversions are to be avoided in conspicuous positions. Only slightly less objectionable are minor triads in root positions, but inversions of minor triads in an atonal context are often tolerated. Explicit dominant-seventh chords, implying as they do the presence of the leading tone, are incompatible with the atonal essence of dodecaphony. Similarly obnoxious are diminished-seventh chords because of their connotations as leading-tone harmonies and also because of their uniform intervallic structure.

(8) PANDIATONICISM and POLYTONALITY have no place in the dodecaphonic vocabulary on account of their tonal derivation. Generally speaking, acoustical euphony, inflated sonorities and facile fluidity of harmonic progressions are contrary to dodecaphonic esthetics; any external effects of a melodious or harmonious nature are in conflict with the austere spirit and philosophical severity of the serial designs.

(9) Although the fundamental series and its derivations are available in 12 transpositions, such exhaustive utilization of serial materials is rarely found in actual works. Paradoxically, the most favored transpositions, particularly in sections corresponding to recapitulation in classical forms, stand in a quartal-quintal relationship, demonstrating once more the strength of the classical legacy in dodecaphonic composition. One would expect frequent transpositions at a tritone, but such is not the case, because the tritone is apt to be of strategic use in the original series, and would duplicate itself in such a transposition.

(10) The formal structure of works written in the 12-tone idiom is remarkably conservative, following the classical models of variations, passacaglia, prelude, suite, or serenade. The most striking instance of this classical consciousness is the organization of Alban Berg's expressionistic opera *Lulu*, a definitely serial work, which nevertheless contains individual sections bearing titles of Baroque forms. Variations are especially congenial to dodecaphonic organization, with the 12-tone row representing the theme and the retrograde, inversion and inverted retrograde being the three basic variations.

(11) Large forms, such as sonatas and symphonies, are not suited to dodecaphonic treatment owing to the essentially tonal thematic relationship between the exposition, the development and the recapitulation. For similar reasons, dodecaphonic treatment cannot be applied to fugal forms. Canonic imitation is possible when the 12-tone row is fragmented into subdivisions of 3, 4, or 6 notes each, as in some works by Anton von Webern, where such infradodecaphonic segments stand in a structural symmetric relationship of inverted and retrograde correspondence to one another.

(12) Polymetric and polyrhythmic developments are but rarely encountered in DODECAPHONIC compositions. Binary and ternary time signatures of the classical type are prevalent, while compound meters are rare. Triplets, quintuplets and other groups of prime divisions of note values are virtually absent because of the difficulty of fitting such groups into the serial melodic-harmonic scheme. Certain rhythmic predilections may be noted, especially the "Schoenberg Sigh," consisting of a short note on the strong beat immediately followed by an unstressed long note.

(13) In orchestration, traditional scoring prevails. There is no inclination to introduce exotic or unusual instruments; the flexaton in the score of Schoenberg's *Variations for Orchestra* is an exception. Special percussion effects are alien to the spirit of DODECAPHONIC MUSIC. On the other hand, there is a great variety of sound-color (*Klangfarbe*), with a fine gradation of dynamic elements.

(14) Historically, esthetically and structurally, 12-tone music is an evolutionary product of the ultra-chromatic modalities of the post-Wagnerian school of composition. The algorithms of chromatic convergence and divergence in DODECAPHONIC harmony are common. An experimental proof of this evolutionary origin of DODECAPHONIC melody and harmony may be provided by a calculated cancellation of a minimal number of sharps or flats, never exceeding a shift of a semitone, with the resulting product being an essentially diatonic composition with functional chromatic passing notes. Conversely, a simple diatonic melody may be metamorphosed into a DODECAPHONIC series provided that invariance of the vectorial factor is observed, so that the directional intervallic design remains unaltered. Repeated notes in the original diatonic melody can be replaced by their immediate neighbors. Operating according to these procedures, the Viennese melody *Ach du lieber Augustin*, the initial refrain of which happens to contain 12 notes if the last repeated note is omitted, can be transmuted dodecaphonically according to the following formula, in which the capital letters represent the notes of the original tune, ascending intervals are designated by the plus sign, descending intervals by the minus sign, and the numbers

are semitone units: G, A, G + 1, F + 1, E + 1, C + 2, C + 1, D + 2, G + 4, G + 3, E − 1, C. It is to be observed that in this case a conscious effort has been made to retain the first and last notes of the original melody, thus preserving an explicit dominant-tonic relationship.

(15) The hereditary characteristics of the DODECA-PHONIC techniques strongly point to their ultimate classical origins. The very foundation of the thematic arrangements in inversions and retrograde forms is an old classical and even pre-classical method of varying a thematic subject. Furthermore, there seems to be a tendency in the works of Schoenberg, Berg and Anton von Webern to extend the field of classical devices, particularly in the use of ostinati composed of a segment of the 12-tone row. Thus the tolerance of an immediate repetition of a thematic tone is extended to the repetition of a thematic fragment.

In view of the possibility of such DODECAPHONIC self-pollination, there is no reason to fear that DODECAPHONIC COMPOSITION would degenerate into an endless permutation of the available 479,001,600 combinations resulting from the factorial algorithm (12!). The second and the third generations of composers of 12-tone music have devised other methods of serial construction, the most interesting of them being a sort of DODECAPHONIC amputation, which reduces the 12-tone row to a hendecaphonic or decaphonic group of thematic notes. An attractive resource is to leave the amputated member of the series completely out of the account until the very end of a composition, when it would suddenly appear like a *tonus ex machina* and, suspended in a protracted fermata, would assert itself as a triumphantly recessive prodigal tonic.

Duodrama. DUODRAMA is a modern type of dramatic presentation, in which only two actors conduct a dialogue, usually reciting their reciprocal experiences retrospectively without coming to a dramatic clash. It lends itself naturally to chamber opera.

Electronic Music. ELECTRONIC MUSIC was revealed to the world on 5 August 1920 when the Russian engineer and cello player Leon Theremin gave a demonstration of his *Thereminovox* at the Moscow Technological Institute. The apparatus consisted of a set of cathode tubes, a vertical antenna and a metal arc; the sound was produced heterodynamically by the movement of the right hand which changed the electric potential in the area, creating a differential tone which determined the height of pitch. The left hand manipulated the field in the vicinity of the metal arc, regulating the power and the timbre of the sound. In constructing this instrument Theremin seemed to carry out Lenin's dictum that "socialism is proletarian dictatorship plus electrification." Theremin's invention was followed by a number of electronic instruments, among which the most successful was *Les Ondes Martenot*, a keyboard instrument for which a number of modern French composers wrote special works. In Germany, Joerg Mager constructed an electronic instrument which he called *Sphärophon*, and later developed other models, *Partiturophon* and *Kaleidophon*. A more practical and a more successful electronic instrument was *Trautonium* manufactured by Friedrich Trautwein; Hindemith wrote some

music for it. Oscar Sala introduced some innovations into the *Trautonium* in an electronic organ which he called *Mixtur-Trautonium*.

Unlimited musical horizons opened to ELECTRONIC MUSIC with the introduction of the so-called *Synthesizers*, capable of producing any frequency with the utmost precision and distributing the relative strength of the overtones so as to create any desired instrumental timbre. With the aid of *Synthesizers* it becomes possible to construct scales of any number of equal degrees. Ernst Krenek wrote a piece of music containing 13 equal parts of the octave. Among the capacities of the modern *Synthesizer* is the reproduction of a recorded composition at any speed without altering the pitch. No problem of articulation arises, for the generation of the sound is electronic, completely independent of all mechanical elements. In 1969 the American engineer, providentially named Moog, perfected a portable synthesizer which advanced the techniques of ELECTRONIC MUSIC further.

ELECTRONIC MUSIC requires special notation. One of the earliest attempts at a practical system was made in 1937 by Percy Grainger in his *Free Music* for 4 electronic instruments constructed by Theremin, indicating pitch and dynamic intensities in a four-part score on graph paper.

Elegant Variation. In his *Modern English Usage,* Fowler describes frivolous verbal substitutions as ELEGANT VARIATIONS. The phrase is suitable, with the application of similar gentle scorn, to some musical procedures. Variations that vary for the sake of variance, with an objective of sophisticated elegance of expression, are as offensive in their tautological and often teratological variety as their counterparts in literary diction. Reger's *Variations on a Theme by Mozart* are typical examples of ELEGANT VARIATION, turgid in reference, redundant in treatment. On the other hand, Rachmaninoff's 18th variation in his *Rhapsody on a Theme of Paganini* is both elegant and varied, for it represents an exact inversion of the minor triadic theme, resulting in a completely transformed, yet morphologically congruent melody, in which the ascending minor triadic figure of the theme becomes a descending major triadic figure.

Empirical Music. In application to modern techniques of composition, EMPIRICAL MUSIC suggests a pragmatic rather than an inspirational approach. It is, however, less cerebral, less laboratorian than EXPERIMENTAL MUSIC.

Enharmonic Ambivalence. The Janus-like nature of an enharmonic tone, performing two different functions at a modulatory junction, opens the portals of chromatic modulation and establishes a democratic omnivalence of the 12 different tones in dodecaphonic melody and harmony. In this view, chromatic harmony is a functional derivative of ENHARMONIC AMBIVALENCE.

Entropy. The luxuriant development of chromatic harmony and the concomitant equalization of enharmonic pairs may be described as musical ENTROPY, in which the component thematic particles become evenly distributed in melody and harmony. In physics, ENTROPY signalizes the dissipation of KINETIC ENERGY, the neutralization of electric potentials and an ultimate thermodynamic stability of inertial matter. The pessimistic cosmology that postulates the eventual end in a total passivity of the universe does not, however, constitute a categorical imperative for composers. Nothing prevents them from reversing the process of ENTROPY and reinstating the primacy of selected modalities. Verdi said: "Torniamo all 'antico: sarà un progresso."

Environment. The concept of musical ENVIRONMENT embraces the totality of technical resources. Ideally, the function of a composer is to establish a favorable ENVIRONMENT for these techniques, and apply powerful detergents to remove the accumulated tonal impurities. Particularly toxic is chromatic supererogation; conversely, a fine atonal work may suffer from excessive triadic infusion. The ENVIRONMENT also includes the parameters of VECTORIALISM; spatial arrangement of instruments on the stage is clearly environmental in its function. In this larger sense, the function of ENVIRONMENT comprises not only every technical aspect of musical composition but also the conditions of the performance itself.

Ethnic Resources. National musical cultures have developed from two distinct resources: the ethnic legacy and universally adopted techniques of composition. When Villa-Lobos was asked "What is folklore?" he replied, "I am folklore!" By this declaration he meant to say that in his original melodic inventions he gave expression to the artistic consciousness of the Brazilian people. In his *Bachianas brasileiras*, Bachian counterpoint gives ancillary service to ethnic Brazilianism. Charles Ives created single-handedly a modern American idiom that employs ETHNIC RESOURCES in a perfect SYNCRETISM of substance and technique. In Russia, the primacy of ETHNIC RESOURCES is maintained partly by the national spirit of the people and partly by the ideological principles of SOCIALIST REALISM which prescribes the realistic style of music within the framework of national modalities.

Ethnic musical materials are not necessarily incompatible with modern techniques. It is possible to arrange a popular tune dodecaphonically by applying various intervallic extensions and compressions, while retaining the vectorial parameters of the original melody. Perhaps the most congenial modern technique in making use of ETHNIC RESOURCES is PANDIATONICISM, in which the tonal functions are preserved and enhanced.

Etiology. The study of causation, or ETIOLOGY, is of importance not only in medicine and physics, but also in the fine arts. Particularly informing is the ETIOLOGY of ultra-modern music which is often likened by hostile observers to a symptom of mass dyscrasia. But to its adepts new music is the revelation of a superior psyche. Dostoyevsky, who suffered from epilepsy, advances the daring notion that during an epileptic *grand mal* the mind penetrates the ultimate mysteries of life and death. Similarly, the manifestations of the musical AVANT-GARDE, whether in the popular or technically complex field, are to their participants the proleptic vistas of the new universal art. Schoenberg, more than any other composer, endured endless abuse on the part of uncomprehending critics, but he never doubted the correctness of his chosen path. Edgar Varèse, who was similarly abused, wrote in a personal letter in 1931: "I know where I am going, and what will follow. My plan is clearly drawn, its development logical, its result assured." In the perspective of history both Schoenberg and Varèse proved right. The ETIOLOGY of their genius is a lesson for the future.

Euphony. Etymologically, EUPHONY implies a happy sound, but it is not necessarily synonymous with consonant harmony. A succession of dissonances, if they follow a natural tonal sequence, may sound entirely euphonious to the ear, while a progression of disembodied open fifths or disemboweled multiple octaves could register as uneuphonious and unsettling. Psychological apperception is the determining factor in this aural impression. Generally speaking, soft dissonances are tolerated better than loud consonances. Even more decisive is the factor of linear EUPHONY. A single line of an atonal melody impresses an untutored ear as an unacceptable dissonance, even though no simultaneous complex of sounds is involved. If an atonal melody were to be performed at a very slow tempo with long silences between the individual notes, no linear disharmony could then result. But the faster the tempo, the more disruptive to the peace of mind does an atonal melody become. It should be remembered that the word *harmonia* meant a melody in ancient Greek music. A rapid succession of tones unconnected by a uniform tonality will appear as a meaningless jumble of notes to an inexperienced listener. On the other hand, a musician trained in the art of listening to serial music will accept atonal melodies as legitimate expressions of a musical sentiment. The linearity of melody depends exclusively on the instant dampening of a sound in the cochlea without a tinnitus, but the memory of the previous sound persists, much in the manner that the retina of the eye retains the static images of a cinematographic film. It would be interesting to speculate on the possible course of music as an art if the cochlea, too, possessed the ability to retain sounds for a fraction of a second. Suffice it to say that all music, vocal, instrumental or percussive, would then become polyphonic.

Evolution and Devolution. In a famous definition, Herbert Spencer describes the process of EVOLUTION as an integration of matter and concomitant dissipation of motion, during which matter passes from an indefinite, incoherent homogeneity to a definite, coherent heterogeneity. He specifically included music in this process, with reference to the increasing complexity resulting from rhythmic changes and modulatory progressions, its specialization and its gradual differentiation from poetry, drama and dance. In recent times, however, the evolutionary process has been reversed. Once more, as in antiquity, music has entered into an intimate association with the theater and dance in the modern genre of MIXED MEDIA. ALEATORY procedures have accentuated the DEVOLUTION of music by increasing the element of homogeneity and the degree of randomness of distribution of constructive elements.

It may be argued that DEVOLUTION was unavoidable since the integration of music in the Spencerian sense has achieved its maximum of coherence in such techniques as the dodecaphonic method, and that a recoil from the stone wall of determinism reversed the evolutionary process, resulting in an esthetic passivity, in which kinetic energy is reduced to zero. In the practice of the AVANT-GARDE, the demobilization of technical resources has reached the point of melo-rhythmic asceticism, with only a few different notes being used in an entire work, as though emulating the legendary philosopher Cratylus who spent his declining years by moving the index finger of his right hand to and fro in front of his nose in the firm belief that this motion was the only demonstrable truth.

Experimental Music.

All music is EXPERIMENTAL; tradition is merely a congealed experiment. Chromatic harmony was EXPERIMENTAL in Wagner's time, and its ultimate dodecaphonic development became the most important type of EXPERIMENTAL MUSIC of the 20th century. Perhaps the most literally correct application of EXPERIMENTAL MUSIC is represented by aleatory operations, in which the manipulator merely sets the scene of action and nature supplies an EXPERIMENTAL answer. With every turn of the esthetic wheel, EXPERIMENTAL MUSIC was decried and deprecated by the adepts of the preceding prevalent style as repugnant to normal senses. In the second half of the 20th century, EXPERIMENTAL MUSIC finally moved into its proper enclave, that of the laboratory, where composers and experimenters conducted their research with electronic instruments and computers. There is a danger, however, that an imaginative computer may be hampered in its inventive productions by the limitations of the musical engineer who would program the data so as to adapt them to a preordained order, and in so doing would convert the machine into a mere servant. In one of such man-made pseudo-computerized compositions, the ending consists of a protracted C major coda which no computer in its right mental circuit could possibly turn out. The only valid programming of musical composition is that generated by a collection of random numbers ejaculated like so many embryonic sea-horses out of their male parent's pouch, to be translated into notes and rhythms according to a predetermined code. In all such experiments caution should be taken to prevent a disgorgement of data from becoming a personal regurgitation of the programmer.

Expressionism.

EXPRESSIONISM stands in a reciprocal relationship to IMPRESSIONISM, as its functional and psychological counterpart. IMPRESSIONISM derives its source of inspiration from external sources, whereas EXPRESSIONISM conjures up its images in the inner world of the human psyche and exteriorizes its states as an intimate subjective report. IMPRESSIONISM tends to be pictorial and exotic; EXPRESSIONISM is introspective and metaphysical. Impressionistic literature, art and music are easily projected outside; EXPRESSIONISM is an arcane medium, born in the deepest recesses of the psychic complex and cannot easily be translated into the common language of the arts. The receiver of colorful images of Impressionist art or music has the means of comparing the precise reality with the artist's impressions of it. No such scale of comparison is available to an outside recipient of Expressionist art, for it is a product of the artist's dream in which the dreamer experiences shock and surprise despite the fact that he is both the author and the victim of his own dreams. Because of this duality of the Expressionistic process, the art of EXPRESSIONISM itself suffers from the trauma of illogic; it is characterized by the breakdown of illation and by the disruption of the consequential processes of psychic transmission. The unreality of EXPRESSIONIST drama, poetry, painting and music, is the greatest obstacle for general comprehension. But once the curtain is removed and the secret images of a dreamer reach the observer in the form of poetry, art or music, EXPRESSIONISM becomes a universal medium of mass communication and the greatest multiplier of artistic emotion.

It is natural that because of the basic antinomy between the sources of IMPRESSIONISM and EXPRESSIONISM, each should generate a distinctive musical language. IMPRESSIONISM thrives on equilibrated euphony of harmonious dissonances, while EXPRESSIONISM prefers the harsh syntax of ATONALITY. The coloristic opulence of Impressionist music is obtained through the expansion of tonal materials into the spacious structures of resonant harmonies and exotic scales. EXPRESSIONISM, on the other hand, communicates its deep-seated anxieties through chromatic congestion and atonal dispersion. IMPRESSIONISM builds its thematic contents on fluctuating modality, block harmonies and parallel progressions of triadic formations. EXPRESSIONISM rejects modality, tonality and all diatonic textures. Its melodies are constructed parabolically, away from a putative tonic. In its evocation of the classical past, IMPRESSIONISM integrates the diatonic materials into the enhanced edifices of PANDIATONICISM. The harmonic idiom of EXPRESSIONISM is formed by the superposition of fourths and fifths. Progressions of consecutive perfect fourths or fifths result in the formation of 12 different notes in a panchromatic complex, preparing the foundation of the method of composing with 12 tones related only to one another, as formulated by Schoenberg.

There are profound differences in the historic, cultural and geographic factors in the development of IMPRESSIONISM and EXPRESSIONISM. IMPRESSIONISM is Gallic, EXPRESSIONISM Germanic. The French syllabification of IMPRESSIONISTIC poetry is a paradigm of euphonious instrumentation, with the vowels acquiring specific weights and distinctive colors. The German texts of EXPRESSIONIST songs offer no sonorous gratification of resonant vocables, but in their guttural strength they seem to deepen the penetration of the philosophical and often mystical notions underlying the words.

Though IMPRESSIONISM in music is a close counterpart of pictorial art, no Impressionist composer of any stature has ever tried his hand at painting pictures. EXPRESSIONISM is basically a psychic development with no esthetic contact with painting, and yet composers of the Expressionist school, notably Schoenberg and Berg, possessed a striking talent for painting in the EXPRESSIONIST style. Jef Golyscheff, the composer of early atonal music, emigrated to Brazil and became an Expressionist painter. Carl Ruggles, an American composer who developed a sui generis EXPRESSIONIST style in an atonal idiom, abandoned composition entirely and devoted himself to abstract painting.

Fasciculation. In view of the vagueness of such terms as section, part, division, subdivision, period, phrase, etc., it might be useful to introduce into musical nomenclature the term FASCICLE to designate a self-sufficient fragment of a musical work. Particularly, it is useful in application to serial music. In dodecaphonic exposition, FASCICLE I, FASCICLE II, FASCICLE III and FASCICLE IV would indicate the four forms of the basic tone-row. In NEO-CLASSICAL compositions FASCICULATION may easily replace the conventional Baroque designations of sequences, modulatory digressions and the like. This type of nomenclature may also contribute to the analytical clarity of theoretical discussion.

Fetishes and Taboos. In the inexorable course of history and of the arts, FETISHES of yesterday become TABOOS of tomorrow. The following modernistic FETISHES of the recent musical past have become TABOOS: (1) The diminished-seventh chord, once favored by Italian opera composers, the *Accorde di Stupefazione*, used to melodramatize the high points in operatic action. Verdi, who was responsible for some of the most effective applications of this "Chord of Stupefaction," often in parallel chromatic progressions, in his own operas, issued a stern warning to young composers not to abuse it. No self-respecting composer of today would resort to such unsophisticated practices, except for musical persiflage. (2) Tonal sequences, particularly those rising or descending by degrees, known as *Rosalias*, after an old popular Italian ballad, "Rosalia, mia cara." Indeed, sequences of any kind have virtually disappeared from 20th-century music. (3) The WHOLE-TONE SCALE, once a FETISH of IMPRESSIONISM, has now sunk into noxious desuetude as a cinematic effect used to portray strutting Nazis, mad scientists or schizoid females on the sound track. (4) Parallel progressions of major-ninth chords and consecutive formations of second inversions of major triads at intervals of minor thirds, one of the most prized formulas of IMPRESSIONISM. (5) The *Pétrouchka Chord*, known also as *Parisian Chord*, consisting of two major triads at the distance of a tritone. This early instance of BITONALITY, which became a FETISH of modern French music in the second quarter of the 20th century has been disfranchised and relegated to the category of FRAUDULENT MODERNISM. There are even signs and tokens on the firmament that the sacrosanct FETISH of the 20th century, the DODECAPHONIC method of composition, is on the point of deciduous decay, losing its dodecuple integrity and degenerating into the lipogrammatic hendecaphonic or decaphonic series.

Formalism. The term FORMALISM has acquired a specific pejorative meaning in Soviet esthetics, as a method inimical to the essence of desirable art. The *Encyclopedic Music Dictionary*, published in Moscow in 1966, defines FORMALISM as follows: "FORMALISM represents an artificial separation of form from content, and the attribution to formal elements of self-sufficient primary values to the detriment of musical content. . . . In contemporary esthetics, FORMALISM becomes a method of art hostile to realism and cultivated especially by the adepts of MODERNISM. FORMALISM is based on the theory of art for art's sake, counterposing the artist to society and art itself to life, seeking to create an artistic form detached from objective reality. The governing precepts of FORMALISM are the negation of ideological and realistic content of a work of art, a construction of arbitrary new forms, combined with the denial of national cultural heritage. In the final analysis, FORMALISM results in the abolition of artistic imagery and disintegration of formal coherence. In musical practice, FORMALISM rejects the ideational and emotional musical values and denies the capacity of a musical work to reflect reality. Proponents of FORMALISM attempt to justify their fallacious doctrine by pointing out the specific nature of music as an art lacking the external connection with the world of real objects, such as is present in painting or sculpture, and intrinsically incapable of conveying a concrete narrative characteristic of literature. The esthetic teaching of Marxism refutes FORMALISM by a scientific approach to music as a special form of social ideology. The reactionary theories of FORMALISM are assiduously cultivated in books and articles by the apologists of musical MODERNISM. The struggle for the correct formulation of SOCIALIST REALISM leads to the removal of FORMALISM from its pedestal. One should not confuse FORMALISM, however, with genuine individual originality or with true innovation in the field of musical forms and in the inner substance of a composition, which constitute an unalienable part of authentic realistic art."

Formant. FORMANT is an acoustical term, indicating the relative strength of partial overtones that determines the timbre of a musical instrument. In ultra-modern nomenclature, a FORMANT is the catalytic element that forms, deforms and transforms a given timbre into another by means of electronic manipulation.

Fraudulent Modernism. Commercially successful composers of marketable semi-classical music, eager to gain esthetic equality with sophisticated musicians, like to inject dissonant notes into their ABECEDARIAN and often ANALPHABETIC productions; proudly, they exhibit pieces using 12 different notes in a more or less chromatic order to earn membership in socially distinguished DODECAPHONIC circles. A combination of emaciated melodies in a spurious atonal manner and dietetic harmonies heavily spiced with discordant irrelevancies, is the essence of FRAUDULENT MODERNISM. Its adepts often parade in panel discussions, glibly bandying about mispronounced names of the latest celebrities of the AVANT-GARDE. FRAUDULENT MODERNISM fails because of the technical inadequacy of its practitioners and of their naive belief that wrong notes are the credentials of advanced sophistication.

Frugal Ankyloglossia. Art thrives on economy of means, but modernistic frugality must not be allowed to reach the point of tonal ANKYLOGLOSSIA. The criterion is a freedom of expression without cacuminal retroflection.

Furniture Music. In his sustained effort to degrade music and to reduce it to a menial level, Erik Satie was prompted to inaugurate a demonstration of *Musique d'ameublement*, which he defined as "new music played during intermission at theatrical events or at a concert, designed to create a certain ambience." At an actual performance at the Paris Art Gallery, Satie placed his musicians in separate groups, and urged the public to treat them as functional objects, to speak loudly and not to listen with professional attention. The performers were free to play anything they wished regardless of the repertoire selected by their confrères.

Futurism. FUTURISM is a modern movement in the arts that emerged in Italy early in the 20th century, under the aegis of the Italian poet Marinetti. Its musical credo was formulated by Balilla Pratella in his *Manifesto of Futurist Musicians* issued in Milan on 11 October 1910 and supplemented by a *Technical Manifesto of Futurist Music* of 11 March 1911. On 11 March 1913 Luigi Russolo published his own *Futurist Manifesto*. In these declarations the Italian FUTURISTS proclaimed their complete disassociation from classical, romantic and IMPRESSIONIST music and announced their aim to build an entirely new music inspired by the reality of life in the new century, with the machine as the source of inspiration. And since modern machines were most conspicuous by the noise they made, Pratella and Russolo created a new art of noises, *Arte dei Rumori*. Russolo designed special noise instruments and subdivided them into six categories. His instruments were rudimentary and crude, with amplification obtained by megaphones, but there is no denying that the Futurists provided a prophetic vision of the electronic future of fifty years later. It is interesting to note that most Futurist musicians and poets were also painters. Their pictures, notably those of Luigi Russolo, emphasized color rather than machine-like abstractions, and generally approximated the manner of Abstract EXPRESSIONISM. In the music by Pratella and others we find a profusion of modern devices of their Futurist day, with a foremost place given to the WHOLE-TONE SCALE. The Futurists gave monody preference over polyphony, and steady rhythm to asymmetry. The future of the Futurists appears passé, but they opened the gates to the experimenters of the actual chronological future, which none of them lived to witness.

Game Music. Games of musical compositions, in which cards, each containing a musical phrase, are put together according to special rules, are of considerable antiquity. One such game, *Musikalisches Würfelspiel* was put on the market in London in 1806 and was announced as "Mozart's musical game, enclosed in an elegant box instructing in a system of easy composition by mechanical means of an unlimited number of waltzes, rondos, horn pipes, reels and minuets." The attribution to Mozart is spurious, but the game itself has a certain ingenuity. The players were to throw a pair of dice, and the number indicated the particular card containing a musical phrase. Since the sequence was arranged so that each card was interchangeable with other cards containing melodies in approximately the same range set in similar harmonies, there was obviously no danger of running into difficulties. A much more modern conceit was suggested by an English musician William Hayes in his book entitled *The Art of Composing Music by a Method Entirely New, Suited to the Meanest Capacity*, published in 1751, in which the author, with a rather crude satirical intent, explained the principle of the game: "Take a

brush with stiff bristles (like a toothbrush), dip it into an inkwell, and, by scraping the bristles with the finger, spatter with one sweep a whole composition onto the staff paper. You have only to add stems, bar lines, slurs, etc., to make the opus ready for immediate performance. Whole and half-notes are entirely absent, but who cares for sustained tones anyway!" This is indeed a proleptic anticipation of methods of composition used by the AVANT-GARDE 200 years after the publication of this lively manual.

An interesting modern game can be devised using several sets of dodecaphonic cards, each set containing all 12 notes of the chromatic scale. The deck is shuffled and distributed among players. One after another, the players put down duplicates in their hands and collect a missing note of the next dodecaphonic series from the cards put down by other players. The winner is the player who first assembles all 12 different notes.

The most ambitious musical game of the modern era is *Stratégie* by Iannis Xenakis, first performed at the Venice Festival on 23 April 1963. In it, two conductors lead two different orchestras in two uncoordinated works. The audience declares the winner, taking into consideration the excellence of each orchestral group, marking points on the scoreboard for most striking rhythms, best color effects and finest instrumental solos.

Modern scores descriptive of games are numerous. Arthur Honegger wrote a symphonic movement *Rugby*, Arthur Bliss composed a ballet entitled *Checkmate*, Paul Reif selected *Philidor's Defense* as the title of a work for a chamber orchestra, inspired by a chess game played in 1858. Stravinsky portrayed a poker game in his *Jeu de Cartes*, a ballet in three deals in which the joker is defeated by a royal flush in hearts. A more abstract score by Stravinsky, entitled *Agon*, also portrays a game. Debussy's ballet score *Jeux* depicts an allegorical game of tennis.

Gauche Dexterity. Satire and burlesque depend for their effect on a deliberate violation of traditional rules of melodic structure, rhythmic symmetry and harmonic euphony. A sophisticated imitation of such semi-literate gaucherie often becomes an art in itself. Examples are many: Stravinsky reproduces the heterogeneous harmony of the barrel organ in *Pétrouchka;* Darius Milhaud tonalizes the natural cacophony of a barroom in the score of *Le Bœuf sur le toit*. Erik Satie elevated the dexterity of his gaucherie into a high art of musical persiflage; he was helped in it by his lack of an academic technique of composition; it was easier for him than for real masters to imitate ineptitude.

Gebrauchsmusik. The term GEBRAUCHSMUSIK, or Utilitarian Music, came into vogue shortly after the end of World War I; its earliest mention is found in the German magazine *Signale für die Musikalische Welt* of December 1918. GEBRAUCHSMUSIK promoted the utilization of new mechanical instruments, the radio, the phonograph and music for the films. A variety of GEBRAUCHSMUSIK was GEMEINSCHAFTSMUSIK, Community music, which cultivated choral singing. The term GEMEINSCHAFTSMUSIK was later changed to Sing- und Spielmusik, in the generic category of HAUSMUSIK. Probably the first work written specially for such groups by a modern composer was *Das neue Werk* by Paul Hindemith. Stylistically, GEBRAUCHSMUSIK has developed a type of modern melody, rhythm, harmony and orchestration making free use of utilitarian dissonance, polytonal combinations and polymetric arrangements. An innovation in GEBRAUCHSMUSIK is spoken rhythmic song, a variant of SPRECHSTIMME. In opera, the librettos were usually satirical and political, with a radical bent, especially PROLETARIAN MUSIC. From Germany, operatic GEBRAUCHSMUSIK was transplanted to America, where economic impoverishment contributed to its popularity. GEBRAUCHSMUSIK had little success in Russia, France or Italy, countries with a rich operatic culture, in which there was no necessity of reducing operatic productions to miniature dimensions. HAUSMUSIK, and GEBRAUCHSMUSIK in general, relied on the participation of the audience. Children's music is a natural product of GEBRAUCHSMUSIK. Hindemith wrote the first piece of GEBRAUCHSMUSIK designed specially for singing and acting by children, *Wir bauen eine Stadt.*

Gemeinschaftsmusik.
GEMEINSCHAFTSMUSIK is a term used by German composers to designate communal singing or playing; although of ancient origin, the practice was popularized as part of the program of HAUSMUSIK, in the generic category of GEBRAUCHSMUSIK.

Gestalt.
GESTALT is a fashionable psychological term which, in an attractively misapprehended scientific German nomenclature, connotes an ensemble of apperceptions produced by a series of sensory stimuli. The word, which can be literally translated as form, figure or appearance, indicates a psychological interaction between the physical nature of a given phenomenon and the inner interpretation of it by a receptive mind. The shape of a white vase against a uniformly black background may be perceived as two human figures facing each other if the symmetric sides of the vase are drawn to resemble silhouettes. In music, GESTALT is capable of many interpretations, of which the most literal is enharmonic ambivalence, as for instance the perception of a triad as a dissonance in the context of alien harmonies. Thus, if a C major triad is sounded immediately after an unrelated dominant-seventh chord based on E-flat, the ear would demand its resolution into the dissonant syndrome of the preceding dominant-seventh chord. Generally speaking, GESTALT is apprehended as an entire ensemble of musical parameters, comprising form, proportional distribution of consonances and dissonances, diatonic or chromatic tropism, symmetry or asymmetry of melorhythmic figurations, etc.

Graphic Notation.
Ever since 1000 A.D. when Guido d'Arezzo drew a line to mark the arbitrary height of pitch, musical notation has been geometric in its symbolism. The horizontal coordinate of the music staff still represents the temporal succession of melodic notes, and the vertical axis indicates the simultaneous use of two or more notes in a chord. Duration values have, through the centuries of evolution, been indicated by the color and shape of notes and stems to which they were attached. The composers of the AVANT-GARDE, eager to reestablish the mathematical correlation between the coordinates of the musical axes have written scores in which the duration was indicated by proportional distance between the notes. Undoubtedly such geometrical precision contributes to the audio-visual clarity of notation, but it is impractical in actual usage. A passage in whole-notes or half-notes followed by a section in rapid rhythms would be more difficult to read than the imprecise notation inherited from the past. In orchestral scores, there is an increasing tendency to cut off the inactive instrumental parts in the middle of the page rather than to strew such vacuums with a rash of rests. A graphic system of tablature notation was launched in Holland under the name *Klavarskribo*, an Esperanto word meaning keyboard writing. It has been adopted in many schools in Holland.

New sounds demanded new notational symbols. Henry Cowell, who invented tone-clusters, notated them by drawing thick vertical lines attached to a stem. Similar notation was used for similar effects by the Russian composer Vladimir Rebikov. In his book, *New Musical Resources*, Cowell tackled the problem of non-binary rhythmic division and outlined a plausible system that would satisfy this need by using square, triangular and rhomboid shapes of notes. Alois Hába of Czechoslovakia, a pioneer in microtonal music, devised special notation for quarter-tones, third-tones and sixth-tones.

As long as the elements of pitch, duration, intervallic extension and polyphonic simultaneity remain in force, the musical staff can accommodate these elements more or less adequately. Then noises were introduced by the Italian Futurists into their works. In his compositions, the Futurist Luigi Russolo drew a network of curves, thick lines and zigzags to represent each particular noise. But still the measure and the proportional lengths of duration retained their validity. The situation changed dramatically with the introduction of ALEATORY processes and the notion of indeterminacy of musical elements. The visual appearance of aleatory scores assumes the aspect of ideograms. John Cage, in particular, remodeled the old musical notation so as to give improvisatory latitude to the performer. The score of his *Variations I* suggests the track of cosmic rays in a cloud chamber. His *Cartridge Music* looks like an exploding supernova, and his *Fontana Mix* is a projection of irregular curves upon a strip of graph paper. The Polish Avant-Garde composer Krzyztof Penderecki uses various graphic symbols to designate such effects as the highest possible sound on a given instrument, free improvisation within a certain limited range of chromatic notes, or icositetraphonic tone-clusters.

In music for MIXED MEDIA, notation ceases to function per se, giving way to pictorial representation of the actions or psychological factors involved. Indeed, the modern Greek composer Jani Christou introduces the Greek letter *psi* to indicate the psychology of the musical action, with geometric ideograms and masks symbolizing changing mental states ranging from complete passivity to panic. The score of *Passion According to Marquis de Sade* by Sylvano Bussotti looks like a surrealistic painting with musical notes strewn across its path. The British Avant-Garde composer Cornelius Cardew draws black and white circles, triangles and rectangles to indicate musical action. Iannis Xenakis prefers to use numbers and letters indicating the specific tape recordings to be used in his musical

structures. Some composers abandon the problem of notation entirely, recording their inspirations on tape.

The attractiveness of a visual pattern is a decisive factor. The American Avant-Garde composer Earle Brown
draws linear abstractions of singular geometric excellence. Karlheinz Stockhausen often supplements his
analytical charts by elucidatory (or tantalizingly obscura-
tive) annotations.

The chess grandmaster Tarrasch said of a problematical chess move: "If it is ugly, it is bad." *Mutatis mutandis,*
the same criterion applies to a composer's musical graph.

Gymnosophistical Homophony. The description
Gymnosophist is applied to an Indian sect that flourished about 1,000 A.D. who preached abstinence from
carnal delights, refused to wear clothes and limited
themselves to the simplest modes of communication.
Etymologically, the word is derived from the Greek roots
for "naked" and "wisdom." Archaizing usages and affectation of utmost simplicity in musical composition may
well be called GYMNOSOPHISTICAL; naked fifths, in
particular, when applied ostentatiously in modern works,
creating the impression of luxurious abstemiousness, are
GYMNOSOPHISTICAL. Erik Satie, in his sophisticated
practice of GYMNOSOPHISTICAL harmonies in such
works as *Gymnopédies*, provides a perfect example of the
style, deliberately bleak in its renunciation of harmonious carnality and yet thoroughly modern in its invocation of secret rites and suggested aberrations. For different reasons, Stravinsky adopted GYMNOSOPHISTICAL
modalities in his neo-Grecian works, as a reaction against
the proliferation of colorful sonorities in instrumental
music, including his own. GYMNOSOPHISTICAL
HOMOPHONY is a natural medium also for neo-ecclesiastical composition in quintal or quartal gemination.

Happenings. A HAPPENING is a colloquial gerund
that has assumed a substantive value as a result of collective activities among American theater workers, painters,
poets and musicians in the 1950s. The word itself was
first used in this sense in the 1959 issue of the *Anthologist,*
a review published by Rutgers University. It featured an
article by Allan Kaprow, teacher of Art History at Rutgers, entitled *The Demiurge,* in which he announced his
aim of creating an entirely new art. As an illustration he
appended the outline of a script, with a caption, "Something to Take Place: a HAPPENING." Kaprow and others
staged in October 1956 in a New York art gallery, a production under the name 18 HAPPENINGS in 6 parts.
The audience was distributed in 14 groups seated in
chairs at random, and its participation in the action was
earnestly solicited. The spectacle was synaesthetic, with
sound, multicolored lights, and peripheral tactile and
olfactory impressions. There were also "visual poems,"
of the graffiti type randomly lettered in crayon on walls
and placards, with such communications as "My Toilet is
Shared by the Man Next Door who is Italian." The
musical part consisted of aleatory superfetations of loud-
speaking musical and anti-musical sounds. Activities
included various commonplace HAPPENINGS performed with the meaningful air of an artistic act. Allan
Kaprow made an ex post facto statement bemoaning his
choice of the word HAPPENING as unfortunate, but con-

ceded that it helped him to achieve an all-embracing
inclusivity in describing the uninhibited exhibits of the
AVANT-GARDE. In the meantime, HAPPENING entered
the language, penetrating the common speech so deeply
that everyday events are often described as HAPPEN-
INGS simply because they have taken place at all. The
term became popular in Europe as Le Happening, El
Happening, Il Happening or Das Happening.

Hausmusik. After a long period of alienation from the
masses, modern composers in Germany came to the conviction that music should cease to be a hermetic art for
select audiences and should be returned to its source, the
home. HAUSMUSIK, as such "home music" became
known, was a development parallel to GEBRAUCHS-
MUSIK. Dissonant harmony and asymmetric rhythms
were not excluded, as long as the performance did not
present technical difficulties. Usually HAUSMUSIK was
written for voices or SPRECHSTIMME, with piano
accompaniment and obbligato parts for instruments easy
to play, such as recorders, clarinets and violins.

Hebetude and Lubricity. A recipe for a musical work
providing sensory and intellectual gratification is a judicious mixture of dissonant HEBETUDE and euphonious
LUBRICITY. As a product of intellectual elucubration,
hebetudinous abstruseness results from indiscriminate
use of Dodecaphonic, Hendecaphonic, Pandiatonic or
Polymodal Combinatorialities. Modernistic LUBRICITY,
on the other hand, flows from an incontinent evacuation of
artificially flavored euphonious fluids sublimated in a
feculent plasma. Hebetudinous excogitations by Hesy-
chastically minded introverts occasionally reveal serendip-
itous technicalities of interest, as demonstrated by tonal
inventions in *Die Maschine* by Fritz Klein, while lubricious-
ly scabrous effluvia of an ABECEDARIAN composer are
usually productive of homogeneous sonic matter of gluti-
nous consistency, fetid, infertile and degenerative.

Hendecaphonic Serialism. With the gradual relaxation of dodecaphonic strictures in the orthodox Schoenbergian doctrine, serial composers have begun to resort
to a lipogrammatic device of omitting a member of a 12-
tone subject, reducing the series to a HENDECAPHON-
IC form, containing only 11 tones. The missing tone,
conspicuous by its absence, may be introduced in the
coda with a panache suggesting the apparition of an actual tonic.

Hirsute Chromaticism. A judicious mixture of chromatic and diatonic modes in a serial work is entirely valid
as a mode, idiom or a style. What cannot be tolerated in a
modern composition of any pretensions to self-consisten-
cy is the hairy growth of chromatics upon a diatonic or
pandiatonic melodic and harmonic surface, with mem-
branous pellicles obscuring the melorhythmic lines without protecting them. When instances of such HIRSUTE
CHROMATICISM occur inadvertently, a depilatory agent
should be applied in order to restore the basic musical
design. At the same time, care should be taken not to fall
into the extremes of unesthetic alopecia.

Homeological Variations. Modern variations are
often derived from a subject by topological extensions and

compressions of the constituent intervals and rhythms, a process known as HOMEOLOGICAL. This term denotes the compatibility of geometric figures which can be topologically altered without disrupting the continuity of their perimeters. Thus, a triangle can be stretched or crumpled like rubber and brought into congruity with a square or a circle, but not with a torus which is morphologically non-congruent with triangles, squares or circles. In modern music, a diatonic melody may be analogously compressed and extended by intervallic changes, but it cannot be converted into a pointillistic configuration or a hocketus, without violating topological laws.

Homonymity. In music, as in verbal communication, identical sounds often acquire different connotations according to the context. For example, *mental process* in anatomy refers not to the state of mind but to the bony promontory that forms the chin, the key word being derived from *mentum*, chin, not from *mens*, mind, while the word *process* comes from proceed in the sense of outgrowth. A C-major chord, if written with an F-flat instead of E, loses its white immaculacy and becomes a dissonant suspension over the A-flat major triad. HOMONYMITY plays a particularly significant role in DODECAPHONIC MUSIC. A segment of a 12-tone series may prove to be homonymous with another form of the same series. This fragmentary replication is of great structural importance in the theory and practice of COMBINATORIALITY.

Hörspiel. In search of a term that would apply to a great variety of musical works, the practitioners of GEBRAUCHSMUSIK in Germany selected the generic appellation HÖRSPIEL. Literally, HÖRSPIEL means a play for hearing: usually it is a short composition for a solo instrument, a small instrumental ensemble, or a choral group. In its idiom, a HÖRSPIEL should not appear strange to untutored ears, but non-toxic dissonances should not be shunned. A HÖRSPIEL is related to the practice of HAUSMUSIK.

Icositetraphony. As the etymology of the term indicates, ICOSITETRAPHONY deals with music using 24 equal intervals in an octave (icosi = 20; tetra = 4; phone = sound), i.e., in quarter-tones. A tone-row composed of 24 different notes in quarter-tones is an icositetraphonic series. In modern works ICOSITETRAPHONY usually occurs in conglomerates, as in the coda of Krzysztof Penderecki's *Threnody for the Victims of Hiroshima* and in Sergei Slonimsky's *Concerto Buffo*.

Illation. In logic and rhetoric, ILLATION is a conclusion drawn from given premises. In music, ILLATION represents a consistent development of thematic ideas, a logical progression from one idea to the next. ILLATION is particularly important in DODECAPHONIC structures, in which the basic series serves as a postulate from which all subsequent patterns are derived.

Imbricated Counterpoint. Canonic imitation in stretto formation may be described as IMBRICATED COUNTERPOINT, because it follows the pattern of roof shingles or tiles, all of the same size and all partly covered by adjacent shingles.

Immaculacy. The irresistible attraction that C major exercises on many modern composers is a curious phenomenon. Scriabin ends his *Poème de l' Extase* with a protracted coda of IMMACULATE C major in a veritable sunburst of white-hot flame on the waves of the luminiferous ether. C major was also the favorite key of Prokofiev, a composer whose esthetic precepts were diametrically opposed to Scriabin's; to him C major was simply a pianistic convenience lying naturally under the fingers. Pianistically, C major is associated with whiteness, but on many old keyboard instruments the keys of diatonic C major were black. Also pianistic in origin is PANDIATONICISM; a great many pandiatonic constructions in piano works are examples of C-major IMMACULACY. Even Schoenberg, for all of his anti-triadic teachings, succumbed to the temptation: his *Piano Concerto* ends on an enhanced C-major chord.

Impressionism. The term IMPRESSIONISM was first used in an article by Louis Leroy published in the Paris journal *Charivari* in its issue of 25 April 1874, to characterize the type of painting cultivated by French artists who exhibited at the Paris Salon des Refusés, with specific reference to *Sunrise* by Claude Monet, subtitled "an impression." This painting was Impressionistic in the sense that it brought out the subjective impact of the landscape on the artist, as it registered in his inner eye. Far from being offended by the irony implied in the word IMPRESSIONISM, the French modernists of the time accepted it as an honorable title. It was not the first time in cultural and political history that a sobriquet intended as a pejorative appellation was elevated to the dignity of a dictionary definition. When the French aristocrats dismissed the Paris revolutionaries as sansculottes, because they did not wear the culottes, the knee breeches, the expression was adopted triumphantly by the populace. When the German Kaiser described the British expeditionary force in World War I as "a contemptible little army," the English gleefully accepted this depreciative nomination, turning its sharp point against the Germans themselves as their vaunted superiority began to crumble. A group of American realistic painters, active in the first decade of the 20th century was described as Ashcan School by reactionary critics, and it was under that name that the group had proudly entered the annals of American art. The term Baroque originally meant uncouth, ungainly or bizarre, but it has risen in its semantical evolution to represent the noblest period in the history of fine arts.

Only slightly less derisive than IMPRESSIONISM was the term Symbolism, applied to modern French poets whose imagery dealt with symbols rather than with realities. The word Symbolism appeared for the first time in print in the Paris daily *Le Figaro* of 18 September 1886. As IMPRESSIONISM in art, Symbolism was the product of a reaction against the hegemony of academic realism. The painter Courbet said, "Le réalisme c'est la négation de l'idéal." To poets and to painters alike, music was the supreme medium of artistic expression. Paul Verlaine formulated this belief in the famous line, "De la musique avant toute chose." He insisted that words themselves should be selected for the quality of their sound: "Les mots seront choisis en tant que sonores."

Gauguin declared that he sought to achieve a musical expression in his exotic paintings: "Je cherche plus la suggestion que la description, comme le fait la musique." Conversely, the spectrum of light appears as a determining factor of musical expression to composers of the Impressionist school. Debussy spoke of "lumière sonore," such as is produced by an analytical diffraction of tones. The constant interchange of auditory and visual aspects in music and in art is illustrated by the titles both of Impressionist paintings and musical compositions. Whistler gave musical captions to his painting—symphonies, Nocturnes—while titles of Debussy's works are often taken from painting—Esquisses, Images. Poets were apt to speak of music that can be seen and of paintings that can be heard. After hearing Debussy's *Prélude à l'Après-midi d'un Faune*, Stéphane Mallarmé, whose poem inspired the work, inscribed the book to Debussy, with a quatrain, which equates word, light and sound in one sensation: "Sylvain d'haleine première/Si ta flûte a réussi/Ouïs toute la lumiére/ Qu'y soufflera Debussy!" In a modern tale of fantasy a scientist transplants the optical nerve to the ear and the auditory nerve to the eye, so that the human subjects on whom he performed this experiment heard colors and saw tones.

In *Les Fleurs du Mal,* Baudelaire said: "J'aime avec fureur les choses où le son se mèle à la lumière."

The interpenetrability of all senses, including the olfactory and the gustatory, was the dream of poets, artists and musicians. Baudelaire wrote: "Les parfums, les couleurs et les sons se répondent." In his essays *À rebours,* Huysmans conjures up an organ of liqueurs. As the organist pulls out the stops, each discharges a drop of wine accompanied by the sound of corresponding instrumental color. The clarinet gives the taste of curaçao sec; the oboe serves kummel; for the flute there is anisette; for the trombone gin and whiskey, while the tuba filters strong vodka.

The flight from nominalism among poets, painters and musicians of France a hundred years ago had a touch of mystical taboo which forbade the naming of the deity in primitive religions. Mallarmé wrote: "To name an object is to suppress three quarters of the enjoyment of a poem; to divine gradually, to suggest that is to dream." In order to be effective, art had to be a matrix of uncertainties. The French poet Charles Brugnot wrote the lines which Ravel selected as an epigraph for his piano suite *Gaspard de la nuit:* "Je croyais entendre/une vague harmonie enchanter mon sommeil/et près de moi s'épandre un murmure pareil/ aux chants entrecoupés d'une voix triste et tendre."

Above all, IMPRESSIONISM should not serve a utilitarian purpose or perform a function. Henri de Regnier spoke of "le plaisir délicieux et toujours nouveau d'une occupation inutile." Ravel put these words in the score of his *Valses nobles et sentimentales.*

If the aim of IMPRESSIONISM is to suggest uncertain images, then such images must be clothed in uncertain sounds; in music such sounds are dissonances. The yearning desire for dissonant harmonies can be traced back to Horace's pithy oxymoron, "Concordia discors," and to Keats, who said that "discords make the sweetest airs." Verlaine was explicit when he spoke poetically of

"accords harmonieusement dissonants." Dissonances are indeed harmonious in Impressionist music as discordant tones are suspended in airy equilibrium above the sustained basses that support columns of natural overtones.

Walter Pater said: "Impressionism is a vivid personal reflection of a fugitive effect." Spectral evanescence lies in the nature of Impressionist art and music. Sounds that suggest perfumes are ephemeral; they shimmer, they waver, and they vanish. Impressionist melodies are transparencies of a magic lantern; the images succeed each other without organic cohesion. There is no thematic development; the progress of the music depends on contrasts of contiguous thematic statements and colorful juxtapositions of sound. IMPRESSIONISM shuns the grandiosity of epic arts and the emotionalism of romance. No human passions invest the scores of Impressionist music, and the sonorities are never overwhelming. It is characteristic of Impressionist composers that in the selection of their subjects they favor the moon over the sun. Verlaine's poem *Clair de Lune* inspired Debussy's famous piano piece. Schoenberg, in his *Pierrot lunaire,* a work that possesses distinct Impressionistic qualities, selected a group of poems focused on a moonstruck lover with the pale disk of the moon projected on the back of his garment.

A suggestion of sensuality is often more forceful than a realistic description of carnality. Whispered words are more enervating than raucous outcries. Distant rhythms of throbbing drums, brief effervescences of quickly extinguished melodic phrases, muted instrumental colors, all this suggests faint mementos of passionate events. Debussy's most dyspeptic critic Camille Bellaigue (who was Debussy's classmate at the Paris Conservatoire) grudgingly admitted that Debussy's music "fait peu de bruit," but, he added malevolently, it makes "un vilain petit bruit." John Ruskin exploded in righteous indignation against modern French music: "Musicians, like painters, are almost virulently determined in their efforts to abolish the laws of sincerity and purity, and to invent, each for his own glory, new modes of dissolute and lascivious sound." When Debussy's *Prélude à l'après-midi d'un Faune* was first performed in Paris in 1894, a cautionary notice was inserted in the program: "The poem of Mallarmé, which inspired Debussy, is so sadistic that the management decided not to print it in the program book, because young girls attend these concerts." The great romanticist of French music Gounod, addressing students at the Paris Académie des Beaux Arts on 20 October 1883, warned them: "Do not be seduced by those hollow words, Realism, Idealism, Impressionism. They belong to the nihilist vocabulary, which now constitutes modern art."

Paul Verlaine described IMPRESSIONISM in a line of singular intimacy as "la chanson grise où l'Indécis au Précis se joint." And he summarized the esthetic code of Symbolist poetry and Impressionist art in a challenging invitation, "Pas la Couleur, rien que la Nuance!" The formula fits the music of French IMPRESSIONISM to perfection: in it the indecisiveness of the design is mitigated by the precision of execution. Bright colors are relinquished in favor of infinitesimally subtle nuances. Just as the eye is trained to differentiate between light and shadow in Impressionist art, so the ear is disciplined to discriminate between the measured quanta of sonic impulses in Impressionist music.

IMPRESSIONISM is the differential calculus of music, in which the infinitesimal particles of coloristic sound are integrated into a potent musical factor. Debussy himself insisted that he was a realistic composer and he deprecated the term IMPRESSIONISM. He wrote to his publisher Durand, in March 1908: "I am trying to create musical reality, the kind that some imbeciles call IMPRESSION-ISM, a term which I consider most unfitting."

IMPRESSIONISM has created its own tonal vocabulary and harmonic syntax. Its inspiration came from remote antiquity in time and far distances in space. When the Paris Exposition of 1889 presented Oriental dancers from Indochina with their strange bell-like musical instruments, Debussy and his friends found new resources in the polychromatic monody of the exotic modes from the East, free from contrapuntal and harmonic artificiality of western music. At the same time manufactured products from Japan began to arrive at the Paris markets, wrapped in Japanese rice paper with the symbolic prints by unknown masters. It was this wrapping paper, rather than the goods it enveloped, that provided pictorial resources to many French painters. Debussy selected a Japanese drawing of a typhoon wave for the cover of his score of *La Mer*. James Gibbons Huneker was not far wrong in his horrified contemplation of Debussy as a revenant from the East. "If the western world ever adopted eastern tonalities," he wrote, "Claude Debussy would be the one composer who would manage its system. I see his curious asymmetrical face, the pointed fawn ears, the projecting cheekbones. The man is a wraith from the East. His music was heard long ago in the hill temples of Borneo; was made as a symphony to welcome the head-hunters with their ghastly spoils of war!"

The innovations introduced by Impressionist techniques are as significant in the negation of old formulas as in the affirmation of the novelties. They may be summarized in the following categories:

MELODY: (1) Extreme brevity of substantive thematic statements. (2) Cultivation of monothematism and the elimination of all auxiliary notes, ornaments, melodic excrescences and rhythmic protuberances. (3) Introduction of simulacra of old Grecian and ecclesiastical modes calculated to evoke the spirit of serene antiquity in stately motion of rhythmic units. (4) Thematic employment of pentatonic scales to conjure up imitative sonorities and tintinnisonant Orientalistic effects. (5) Coloristic use of the scale of whole tones for exotic ambience. (6) Rapid iteration of single notes to simulate the rhythms of primitive drums.

HARMONY: (1) Extension of tertian chord formations into chords of the eleventh, or raised eleventh, and chords of the thirteenth. (2) Modulatory schemes in root progressions of intervals derived from the equal division of the octave into 2,3,4,6 and 12 parts in preference to the traditional modulations following the order of the cycle of fourths and fifths. (3) Motion by block harmonies without transitions. (4) Preferential use of plagal cadences either in triadic harmonies or extended chordal formations. (5) Quartal harmonies used as harmonic entities which move in parallel formations. (6) Modal harmonization in root

positions of perfect triads within a given mode, with the intervallic relationships between the melody notes and the bass following the formula 8, 3, 5, 8, etc. when harmonizing an ascending scale or mode, and the reverse numerical progression 8, 5, 3, 8, etc. in harmonizing a descending scale or mode, excluding the incidence of the diminished fifth between the melody and the bass; the reverse numerical progression, 8, 5, 3, 8, 5, etc. for an ascending scale results in a common harmonization in tonic, dominant and subdominant triads in root position; the same common harmonization results when the formula 8, 3, 5, 8, 3, etc. is applied to the harmonization of a descending scale; this reciprocal relationship between a modal and a tonal harmonization is indeed magical in its precise numerical formula. (7) Intertonal harmonization in major triads, in which no more than two successive chords belong to any given tonality, with the melody moving in contrary motion to the bass; since only root positions of major triads are used, the intervals between the melody and the bass can be only a major third, a perfect fifth and an octave. In harmonizing an ascending scale, whether diatonic, chromatic or partly chromatic, the formula is limited to the numerical intervallic progression 3, 5, 8, 3, 5, etc., and the reverse in harmonizing a descending scale, i.e., 8, 5, 3, 8, 5, 3, etc. Cadential formulas of pre-Baroque music are often intertonal in their exclusive application of major triads in root positions. A remarkable instance of the literal application of the formula of intertonal harmonization is found in the scene of Gregory's prophetic vision in Mussorgsky's opera *Boris Godunov*, in which the ascending melodic progression, itself intertonal in its peculiar modality, B, C-sharp, E, F-sharp, G, is harmonized successively in the major triads in root positions, E major, C-sharp major, A major, F-sharp major, E-flat major. Another instance of intertonal harmonization occurs in the second act of Puccini's opera *Tosca*, in which the motto of the chief of police, a descending whole-tone scale in the bass, is harmonized in ascending major triads in root positions, in contrary motion; the intervallic relationship between the melody and the bass follows the formula 8, 3, 5, 8, 3, 5, 8,. (8) Parallel progressions of inversions of triads, particularly second inversions of major triads, with the root progression ascending or descending in minor thirds, so that the basses outline a diminished-seventh chord. (9) Parallel progressions of major ninth-chords, also with a bass moving by minor thirds. (10) Parallel progressions of inverted dominant-seventh chords, particularly 6/5/3 chords. (11) Free use of unattached and unresolved dissonant chords, particularly suspensions of major sevenths over diminished-seventh chords. (12) Cadential formulas with the added major sixth over major triads in close harmony.

COUNTERPOINT: (1) A virtual abandonment of Baroque procedures; abolition of tonal sequences and of strict canonic imitation. (2) Reduction of fugal processes to adumbrative thematic echoes, memos and mementos. (3) Cultivation of parallel motion of voices, particularly consecutive fourths and organum-like perfect fifths.

FORM: (1) Desuetude of sectional symphonies of the classical or romantic type, and their replacement by coloristic tone poems of a rhapsodic genre. (2) Virtual disappearance of thematic development with its function being taken over by dynamic elements. (3) Cessation in the practice of traditional variations, discontinuance of auxiliary embellishments, melodic and harmonic figurations whether above, below or around the thematic notes and the concomitant cultivation of instrumental variations in which the alteration of tone color becomes the means of variegation. A theme may be subjected to augmentation or diminution and in some cases to topological dislocations of the intervallic parameters. Thus the tonal theme of Debussy's *La Mer* is extended in the climax into a series of whole tones. (4) Homeological imitation of melorhythmic formulas of old dance forms, often with pandiatonic amplification of the harmony. (5) A general tendency towards miniaturization of nominally classical forms, such as sonata or prelude.

INSTRUMENTATION: (1) Coloristic employment of unusual instrumental combinations. (2) Predilection for attenuated sonorities, with muted strings and muted brass, and considerable expansion of the role of woodwind instruments and of the decorative sonorities of the harp and the celesta. (3) Projection of evocative but brief solos, often in unusual registers. (4) The planting of deep pedal points over which the strings and the woodwinds are suspended in aerostatic equilibrium, often with a muted horn, trumpet or trombone, penetrating the euphonious mist. (5) Careful cultivation of multiple divided strings. (6) Periodic sonic expansions and compressions, massive heavings and sudden recessions. (7) Fluctuation of dynamic rhythms and constant oscillation of thematic particles. (8) Fragmentation of melodic patterns and pulverization of ingredients in tremolos. (9) Heterogeneous instrumental combinations tending to alter the natural tone color of an individual instrument. (10) Frequent application of dynamic antiphony of homogeneous or heterogeneous instrumental groupings.

Inaudible Music. Since electronic instruments are capable of generating any frequency, it is possible to reproduce sounds below and above the audible range. The first work for infrasonic and ultrasonic wavelengths was the INAUDIBLE symphony entitled *Symphonie Humaine* by the French composer Michel Magne, conducted by him in Paris on 26 May 1955. Its movements were entitled *Epileptic Dance, Thanatological Berceuse* and *Interior View of an Assassin*. The INAUDIBLE version was unheard first, followed by a hearing of an audible transcription. The mystical Russian composer Nicolas Obouhov devised in 1918 an INAUDIBLE instrument which he named Ether, theoretically capable of producing infrasonic and ultrasonic sounds ranging from five octaves below the lowest audible tone to five octaves above the highest audible tone. But Obouhov's instrument was never constructed. Avant-garde composers working in mixed media often compose visual music, which can be seen but not heard. A poetic example is the act of releasing a jar full of butterflies "composed" by La Monte Young. Imagination plays a crucial part in the appreciation of INAUDIBLE MUSIC. An interviewer on a broadcast of the British Broadcasting Corporation was sent a defective copy of John and Yoko's Wedding Album (John Lennon was a member of a Liverpudlian vocal quartet, since fallen into innocuous desuetude, known as The Beatles) in which two sides were blank except for an engineer's line-up tone. The broadcaster gave it a warmly favorable review, noting that the pitches differed only by microtones, and that "this oscillation produces an almost subliminal uneven beat which maintains interest on a more basic level," and further observing that the listener could improvise an Indian raga, plainsong or Gaelic mouth music against the drone. John and his Japanese bride Yoko sent him a congratulatory telegram, announcing their intention to release the blank sides for their next album. "Heard melodies are sweet, but those unheard are sweeter."

Indeterminacy. In nuclear physics, the principle of INDETERMINACY states that it is inherently impossible to determine both the position and velocity of any subatomic particle beyond the liminal degree of accuracy. This notion has impressed some modern composers and moved them to apply the INDETERMINACY principle to composition with aleatory or stochastic elements. If the position of a note is indicated precisely, then the rhythm must be optional, and vice-versa. The performing musicians are free to improvise either the actual notes in the nucleus considered indeterminate, or its rhythm, but not both.

Induction and Deduction. In new music, which flaunts its affinity with exact sciences and mathematical logic, the terms INDUCTION and DEDUCTION may be applied with some profit. In serial composition, in particular, the method allows completion of a series by the process of INDUCTION. The Bach theme, B-flat, A, C, B, for instance, can be an inductive clue to a 12-tone series, to be completed by using the intervallic content of the subject in transposition by inversion and retrograde. The process of DEDUCTION also possesses a certain validity in composition. With the aid of thematic INDUCTION and DEDUCTION, it is easy to construct logical sequences of tones. Suppose we have a dodecaphonic series designated by the first 12 integers, 1, 2, 3 . . . 12; in its second appearance it assumes the succession 2, 3, 4 . . . 12, 1. By inductive reasoning the third series should be 3, 4, 5, 6 . . . 12, 1, 2, etc. This type of DODECAPHONIC COMPOSITION is known as ROTATION. Conversely, it is possible to derive identical serial rows by DEDUCTION from the principle of rotation, while other morphological variants can be obtained by omitting parts of the series.

Inertial Guidance. Borrowed from navigation, the term INERTIAL GUIDANCE denotes an automatic sequence which depends entirely on previously accumulated data. At its most elementary level, INERTIAL GUIDANCE is a signal of repeat, as in the recapitulation section of sonata form. In the original manuscript of Schubert's *Unfinished Symphony*, the initial 64 bars of the first movement are repeated in the recapitulation, but rather than writing them out, Schubert simply marked them numerically, 1–64. A conversion formula could be devised to take care of INERTIAL GUIDANCE for transpositions to another key, augmentations of a theme, diminutions and even fugal stretti, with symbolical directions according to a set code. For instance, S(I), where S stands for Subject and I denotes Tonic Harmony, would indicate that the second subject is to be transposed to the tonic from its original appearance in the dominant. In dodecaphonic techniques, a symbolic system for INERTIAL GUIDANCE would save the drudgery of writing out the basic forms of the tone-row. It would be possible, for instance, to program the composition of a tone-row consisting of three groups of identical intervallic conformations, the first of which spells BACH. In order to complete the 12-tone series, BACH would have to be transposed 4 semitones higher and 4 semitones lower. The formula would then appear as follows: BACH, (BACH + 4), (BACH = 4). If the second or the third group is to be inverted or reversed, it can be indicated by the subscripts i and r. In addition to INERTIAL GUIDANCE, a set of formulas can also be devised for a Command Guidance, which would interrupt the automatic processes of INERTIAL GUIDANCE, and dictate a new set of directives. It must be kept in mind, however, that the formula must not be allowed to be more complex than ordinary notation.

Infantiloquy. Onomatopoeia, whether tonal or electronically produced, is the most effective means of instrumental INFANTILOQUY. Borborygmic rumbles and oral ejaculations of sonic particles in an asymmetric pattern are infantiloquacious by nature, and they can be easily imitated by an instrumental ensemble. An infantiloquent modern piece may include fragments from nursery rhymes. An example of successful INFANTILOQUY is Karlheinz Stockhausen's *Gesang der Jünglinge,* in which a child's voice is combined with electronic sounds.

Information Theory. In relevant application to modern music, INFORMATION THEORY touches on the problems of GRAPHIC NOTATION, semantics of certain melorhythmic figures, dynamic levels of various parts of a musical work and instrumental color, etc. A composer must be able to convey a maximum amount of information with optimum efficiency. Composers of complicated music have without exception insisted that the knowledge of their modus operandi is unnecessary for the complete comprehension of the musical message. The quality of performance cannot elevate a poorly constructed musical composition to a higher degree of excellence; nor can an indifferent execution of a great masterpiece impair its inherent validity. Musical information can be conveyed with considerable impact by playing a four-hand arrangement of a Beethoven symphony, but would fail to register even in a virtuoso performance of work lacking in power of communication.

Infra-Modern Music. If Ultra-Modern Music transcends the outer limits of modernism, INFRA-MODERN MUSIC fails to reach even its lowest boundaries, and dwells in the penumbra of pretentious self-inflation. Composers of INFRA-MODERN MUSIC make frequent incursions into the alluring land of dissonant harmonies, but they seldom succeed in manufacturing even a similitudinarian counterfeit. Their attempts to inject atonal or polytonal elements in the effete body of their productions remain as sterile as their imaginations are impotent.

Integration. Harmonic INTEGRATION of a linear progression in dodecaphonic works is an essential factor in Schoenberg's method of composition with 12 tones related only to one another. Melody and harmony become two dimensions of dodecaphonic space, thus contributing to a higher unity of the compositional design. True, melody and harmony are intimately associated in classical music theory in conformity with the laws of chordal relationship, but the great difference between the two concepts lies in the fact that in classical harmony the chordal accompaniment performs the function of melodic tonality, while in serial music it is an integral part of the entire meloharmonic scheme.

Interpoint. INTERPOINT, or PUNCTUS INTER PUNCTUM, is a term devised by the Russian composer Alexander Tcherepnin to describe a special kind of contrapuntal technique, in which pairs of conjugated contrapuntal voices enter a vacancy between another pair of contrapuntal parts without overlapping. The resulting four-part counterpoint becomes in turn the intussusception between a still more dehiscent coupling. In order to achieve interpuntal polyphony, it is obviously necessary to plan in advance the upper and lower limits of the range of each air, recalling to mind Swift's verses: "So, naturalists observe, a flea/Hath smaller fleas that on him prey/ And these have smaller still to bite 'em/And so proceed *ad infinitum.*"

Intervallic Symbolism. Symbolical associations between intervals and ideas are rooted in scholastic theories. An anonymous medieval tract explains the acoustical perfection of the octave by the circumstance that "octavo die Abraha circumcisus erat." The tritone was "diabolus in musica." Bach had correlated certain intervals to specific subjects with considerable precision. Since words could not always be heard, an intervallic equation contributed to the clarity of the meaning. The ascent to heaven was depicted by a rising diatonic scale. Torment was expressed by involuted chromatic passages. The descent into hell was intervallically related to the falling diminished-seventh. Essentially, Wagner's system of leading motives is a species of INTERVALIAC SYMBOLISM. Some modern composers have revived a medieval symbolism of intervals. In Luigi Nono's spectacle for MIXED MEDIA, *Introlleranza,* the characters are associated with specific intervals: the woman with minor seconds and their inversions, major sevenths; the refugee with the tritone and perfect fourths; and his friend with perfect fourths and major seconds. As in Bach's day such associations help to follow the leading motives of the score.

Invariants. With the growing fascination shown by modern composers for the theory of sets, the term INVARIANTS has acquired a certain practical validity. Its relevance is obvious. The 12 tones of the dodecaphonic series are INVARIANTS within a certain set; the derivatives of the tone-row are variables. Number 4 is the INVARIANT in a set of instruments of a string quartet. A flute part interchangeable with that of the piccolo is a variable. Besides the advantage of scientific jargon, the system of musical INVARIANTS clarifies some processes of serial composition. Particularly frequent is the use of the term for segments of different forms of a tone-row, for instance, the basic series and its retrograde, transposed, which happen to have several notes in common, by accident or structural serendipity.

Jazz. The word JAZZ appeared for the first time in print in the sports column in *The Bulletin* of San Francisco in its issue of 6 March 1913. Describing the arrival of a baseball team, the writer "Scoop" Gleeson reported: "Everybody has come back to the old town, full of the old 'jazz' and they promise to knock the fans off their feet with their playing." Gleeson then asks himself a rhetorical question: "What is this jazz? Why, it's a little of that 'old life,' the 'gin-i-ker,' the 'pep,' otherwise known as the enthusiasalum." Reminiscing about the occasion in an article published in the same San Francisco newspaper in its issue of 3 September 1938, "Scoop" Gleeson volunteered the information that the expression "jazz" had been picked up by the Sports editor during a crap game. According to Gleeson, it was first applied to music when a bandleader named Art Hickman launched his dance band, but there is no evidence of such use in any published source. The next verified appearance of the word JAZZ was in *Variety* of 27 October 1916 in a brief communication from Chicago, reporting a concert of JAZZ music, with the word spelled *jass*. Another item in *Variety* followed on 5 January 1917 when it was spelled *Jaz*. An engagement of the Dixie Jass Band of New Orleans in a Chicago cabaret was noted in *Variety* of 16 January 1917. A week later JAZZ reached New York, and it was spelled with two z's in a report in Variety. An item in the Victor Record Review of 7 March 1917 reads: "Spell it *Jass, Jas, Jab* or JAZZ—nothing can spoil a Jass band . . . It has sufficient power and penetration to inject new life into a mummy, and will keep ordinary human dancers on their feet till breakfast time . . ." It was about the same time that the Victor Co. issued the first recording bearing the word *Jass—Dixieland Jass One-Step*.

A number of writers have attempted to connect the word JAZZ with old slang. The word *Jasm* is found in an American novel published in 1860, and a claim has been made without support that its colloquial meaning was male sperm. Other equally unfounded guesses were that the word came from the French slang expression current in New Orleans in the 19th century, and that its verbal form meant to copulate. The determination to track the word down to some kind of sexual meaning has been the motivation of many imaginative but unsupported etymologies. Some have tried to trace it to native African languages. However, considering the specific, clear and plausible description of the word JAZZ as it appeared in print for the first time in 1913, there is no reason to doubt that it was a spontaneous colloquialism generated around San Francisco. The entire history of the word JAZZ is thoroughly covered in the pioneer article by Peter Tamony in an ephemeral periodical *Jazz*, a quarterly of American music, in its issue of October 1958. Analytically, JAZZ may be described as a modern development of the counterpoint of the fourth species. Its rhythmic formula is related to the medieval *Hocketus*, in which the singing line is freely transferred from one voice to another in syncopated singultation. (The word *hocketus* itself is an etymological cognate of hiccups.) Another historical antecedent of JAZZ is the *Quodlibet*, a freely improvised interlude within a definite metrical framework. As practiced by untutored performers, JAZZ produces the collective impact of glossolalia, tonolalia or rhythmolalia.

The paradoxical nature of JAZZ is its combination of unlimited variety of rhythmic patterns with a metric and modal uniformity. JAZZ melodies, almost without exception, are set in major keys, in 4/4 time. But the major tonality is modified by the use of "blue" notes, the lowered seventh and the lowered third in the melody. Some theorists speculate that the systematic incidence of the "blue" seventh is an approximation of the seventh overtone, and is therefore a natural consonance. The lowered third, however, cannot be explained on acoustical grounds. It may well represent a true case of harmonic equivocation, in which the melodic minor third is projected on the major complex in some sort of polytriadic superfetation. It is significant that this major-minor SUPERFETATION is the constant resource of Stravinsky's tonal harmonies.

The basic characteristics of JAZZ are the symmetrical divisions of binary meters and the strong tonality in major keys. Within this framework, the melody, of a syncopated nature, often departs widely from its harmonic connotations.

Historically JAZZ evolved from RAGTIME, a syncopated type of American music that flourished in the last decade of the 19th century and during the first years of the new century. A parallel development is BLUES, a distinctively American ballad form, suffused with nostalgia and redolent of the remembered sufferings of the Negro race, as expressed in the Negro spirituals. Semantically, the term is connected with the colloquialism "to have the blues." The "blue note," that is the flatted seventh in a major key, remains a paramount feature in the BLUES. The acknowledged creator of the genre was W.C. Handy whose song *The Memphis Blues*, published in 1911, was the first of its type.

In the meantime, the temperature of JAZZ music kept rising, and soon acquired the sobriquet HOT JAZZ, as contrasted with the more leisurely type of SWEET JAZZ. HOT JAZZ gave way to COOL JAZZ, which was actually a hotter product, as though the hot water and cold water faucets became switched around in the process of transition.

A new era of JAZZ music dawned in 1935 with a riotous explosion of SWING, which signalized a certain rhythmic manner of performance rather than a definable structural form.

JAZZ, SWING and other types of popular American music of the 1930s coalesced into a general category of JIVE, a generic form that describes the playing style in the 1940s. SWING and JIVE were largely improvisatory in nature; a novel way of organizing popular forms emerged in 1938 with BOOGIE-WOOGIE, based on an orderly harmonic progression in the bass, relating it to the classical formulas of the passacaglia and the chaconne.

A lateral form, BEBOP, Rebop or simply Bop, appeared in the 1940s; in it the main emphasis was on the strong off-beat. With its raucous sound and crude assault on the musical sensorium, SWING music had no room for such poetic refinements as the "blue notes" which vanished from the Swing horizon.

For more than half a century, JAZZ in its various forms was separated from folk music. JAZZ was an urban product; folk music or country music, remained stagnant in its rural recesses. The instrumentation of JAZZ was based on the trumpet, the saxophone, the banjo, the piano and the drums, with the clarinet emerging as its flamboyant chanticleer in SWING. Country music replaced the piano by the guitar and the trumpet by the rustic fiddle. When country music invaded the radio airwaves, the television channels and the sound movies, it gradually developed into a horrendously successful creation that became known as ROCK 'N' ROLL. Marked by an unrelenting, unremitting beat, ROCK 'N' ROLL reduced the rhythmic wealth of early syncopated music to a two-dimensional construction of bland uniformity. Its cumulative impact is apt to be as powerful as the rhythmic tramp of a regiment of soldiers which can bring down a suspension bridge by generating pendulum-like vibrations of increasing amplitude.

Throughout the history of American popular music, systematic incursions were made into the stylistically distant territory of classical and romantic music, carrying away loot and booty from the uncopyrighted remains of Chopin, Tchaikovsky and Rachmaninoff. Some products of these predatory forays, such as *Russian Rag* fashioned from Rachmaninoff's defenseless C-sharp minor *Prelude*, are not devoid of inventive cleverness. Indignant outcries arose from the classical-minded musicians against such barbarous practices, but eventually this musical cannibalism subsided of its own accord.

A reconciliation between popular and serious music was effected with taste and vitality in a movement known as the THIRD STREAM, making it possible to introduce JAZZ into serious music.

Jive. JIVE is a collective noun that describes the action of JAZZ. A JIVE session is a display of coordinated glossolalia or tonolalia, spontaneous and self-conscious in their manifestation. A jam session is conducted in the language of JIVE. The semantic distinctions and confluences of these terms are illustrated by the jazzy glossolalia in a song recorded by Columbia in 1940: "Romp it, stomp it, ride it too. Jam it, Jump it, Jive it through."

Kaleidophonia. By analogy with kaleidoscopic images, the term KALEIDOPHONIA may be used to describe a musical composition derived from multiple mirror-like reflections of a central subject. By selecting a code of parameters determining intervals and durations, a Kaleidophonic structure can be designed as a harmonic complex composed of contrapuntal lines in quaquaversal rhythmic dispersion. Joseph Schillinger published in 1940 a volume of musical patterns which he entitled *Kaleidophone.*

Kinetic Energy. When applied to music, KINETIC ENERGY during a given interval of time connects the velocity (number of notes per time unit), amplitude (degree of loudness in decibels) and the height of pitch expressed in semitones counting from the lowest note in the audible range. KINETIC ENERGY is the product of all these parameters. From this it follows that the auditory impact is directly proportional to velocity, loudness and frequency of vibrations per second. There is also a psychological factor that affects the subjective measurement of KINETIC ENERGY. The off-beat chord in Haydn's *Surprise Symphony*, though in itself possessing a modest impact, carries a relatively greater charge of psycho-kinetic energy because it is unexpected. Generally

speaking, a greater impression is produced by detonations of sonic quanta in asymmetrical rhythms than much stronger discharges occurring at regular intervals of time.

Kitsch. The German patois word KITSCH denotes a pretentiously manufactured object, an unimaginative arrangement of artifacts or a heterogeneous collection which is more tasteless than artless. Christmas cards with rhymed doggerel and tinctured flowers, religious gypsum figurines with a clock in the center of the torso, a motion picture representing muscular men lifting rubber weights, chrome gargoyles, dinner plates with reproductions of members of the presidential family and all sorts of tinsel and fustian, are examples of middle-class KITSCH. In music, KITSCH is represented by so-called semi-classical compositions made up of harmonic detritus and melodic debris from the mutilated remains of Rachmaninoff's *Second Piano Concerto*, or Beethoven's *Moonlight Sonata*, or from a mixture of both. KITSCH products are usually given colorful titles such as "Purple Piano" or "Sentimental Violin," and favor for some unfathomable reason the keys of D-flat major or C minor. KITSCH is the degenerate descendant of the German Biedermeier movement. At the distance of a century, the Biedermeier products possess a certain charm of old-fashioned sentiment and the musical compositions of the period were invariably correct from the technical standpoint. Modern KITSCH is usually devoid of the most elementary type of technical proficiency and appeals to the lowest classes of commercially conditioned eyes, noses and ears.

Klangfarbe. In its present semantical usage, KLANG-FARBE is a special dimension of the musical sound. "It must be possible," Schoenberg states in his *Harmonielehre*, "to form a succession of KLANGFARBEN possessing a mutual relationship of a logical type equivalent to that of the melody formed by a succession of different tones." This melody of tone colors is exemplified in Schoenberg's movement originally entitled *The Changing Chord* in his *Five Orchestral Pieces*. Anton von Webern developed the idea in the direction of serialism of KLANGFARBEN, almost reaching the ultimate dodecaphonic order, in which the fundamental KLANGFARBE series is formed by the successive sounding of 12 different notes by 12 different instruments.

Lehrstück. The problems of writing music in a modern idiom adaptable for educational purposes among workers and young people preoccupied a number of German composers in the 1920s. The idea of a LEHRSTÜCK for accompanied chorus with the liberal application of inflected voice, SPRECHSTIMME, arose in Germany about that time. Paul Hindemith, Ernst Toch and Kurt Weill wrote several such works. Often the "teaching" element in a LEHRSTÜCK was political, as exemplified in the "instruction pieces" of Hanns Eisler.

Lipograms. An omission of an essential member of a melodic series, be it a simple diatonic tune or a dodecaphonic tone-row, a musical apocopation or an APOSIOPE-SIS, or any other similar rhetoric device that interrupts the normal progress of a musical sentence, may be described as a LIPOGRAM, a vocable derived from

Greek nomenclature, that denotes a deficiency of a letter. A LIPOGRAM in a dodecaphonic series results in the formation of a Hendecaphonic row. When the last note of a series is omitted, a melodic apocope results; when an interruption occurs dramatically in the middle of a melorhythmic paragraph, the effect is similar to that of an APOSIOPESIS. Lipogrammatic techniques provide ample resources for novel melodic, rhythmic, harmonic and instrumental patterns.

Machine Music. The modern machine became an object of artistic inspiration early in the 20th century. The Italian Futurists made a cult of automobiles and airplanes. George Antheil's *Ballet mécanique* shocked concert audiences by its bruitism. Max Brand produced the first machine opera in *Machinist Hopkins*. Honegger made a declaration of love for powerful American locomotives in his symphonic movement *Pacific 231*. Frederick S. Converse glorified the Ford car in his automobilistic musicorama *Flivver 10,000,000*. But locomotives, automobiles and airplanes soon lost their glamor and became public nuisances. By mid-century the machine as an artistic object became obsolete. It is ironic that no composer was moved to extol in lofty tones the greatest machine adventure of all ages, the landing on the moon.

Major-Minor Syndrome. It was a traditional convention in Baroque music to end a work in a minor key on a major triad; a major third that replaced a minor third in the final triad acquired the name *Tierce de Picardie*. The preference for the major third in final chords is explained by its privileged position as the fifth partial note of the harmonic series, whereas a minor third of the fundamental tone does not occur acoustically. In the practice of modern composers, a major third is often superimposed on a minor third. Scriabin employed such a MAJOR-MINOR SYNDROME in his last opus numbers, but he spread the harmony widely, so that the frictional dissonance of a semitone was avoided. It was Stravinsky who cultivated a true MAJOR-MINOR SYNDROME in placing both the minor and the major third within a triad. He made use of it as a motto in his early choral work *Zvezdoliky*. It occurs also in *Le Sacre du Printemps*. Most importantly, Stravinsky uses it as a melodic palimpsest, breaking up the combined chord, with both the major and the minor third assuming a thematic significance.

Meloharmony. In a triadically constructed melody, the harmonic arrangement is clearly outlined. In such instances, it is proper to speak of MELOHARMONY as a two-dimensional entity. In DODECAPHONIC MUSIC, MELOHARMONY acquires a particular significance, because the fundamental series can be distributed horizontally, i.e., melodically, and vertically, i.e., harmonically, and still preserve its continuity. It is also possible to speak of melocontrapuntal structures, arranged vertically, horizontally, or diagonally. A cognate term is MELORHYTHM, in which melody and rhythm are combined into a dual entity.

Melorhythm. The term *Meloritmo*, frequently used by Spanish and Latin American writers on music, and signifying a synthetic two dimensional entity possessing both melodic and rhythmic attributes is sufficiently useful to

be adopted in other languages. It is also a convenient substitute for the definition of a musical phrase, which must necessarily have the dual MELORHYTHMIC consistency. In serial music, MELORHYTHMS may be regarded as the integrals of the melodic and rhythmic differential series.

Melosomatic Effect. The neologism MELOSOMATIC suggests an interaction between Melos and the physical Soma. It may be traumatic when loud music is played without relief. But a more insidious psychological lesion is produced by personal associations. In his short story, *The Black Monk*, Anton Chekhov, who was a professional physician, describes the deadly effect produced on a young intellectual by the playing of *Angel's Serenade* by Gaetano Braga, resulting in a fatal cerebral hemorrhage when the piece is played again after a long interval of time. Autosuggestion may have been responsible for the death of the Hungarian composer Rezsö Seress, author of the pessimistic popular song *Gloomy Sunday* (it was banned in various localities after numerous suicides were purportedly engendered by it). By a delayed reaction, forty years after writing this song, the composer himself jumped out of a window. The Russian pianist Alexander Kelberine took a lethal dose of barbiturates after his last concert on January 27, 1940 in Town Hall in New York, for which he arranged a funeral program, consisting entirely of works in minor keys, the last number being Liszt's *Totentanz*. Sexual stimulation is highly melosomatic, as amply demonstrated by the reactions of the young to concerts of popular music, particularly ROCK 'N' ROLL. Tolstoy, who turned against sex after a lifetime of indulgence and sixteen illegitimate children, presented a philosophical study of musical sexuality in his novel *The Kreutzer Sonata*, wherein he tells how the last movement of Beethoven's work, with its propulsive syncopation, overwhelms the natural restraints of the performers, a middle-class married Russian woman pianist and a male violinist, hurling them into a frenzy of illicit passion. It may be questioned that amateurs could ever master the technical difficulties of that diabolically intricate last movement, let alone create enough excitement to carry them away. (There is a famous painting illustrating the climactic scene of the novel, showing the mustachioed violinist implanting a passionate kiss on the lips of a lady pianist while holding both the violin and the bow in his left hand, suggesting that he had the presence of mind to switch the bow from the right hand to the left, but leaving it unexplained as to why he did not deposit the instrument on the lid of the piano in that crucial moment. The painting is widely used as an advertisement for a brand of perfume with a sexy name.)

Melosomatic associations were responsible for the extraordinary vogue of the piano piece *A Maiden's Prayer* by a Polish composeress named Thekla Badarzewska, a wishfulfilling favorite of several generations of unmarried females. In 1937 Stravinsky instituted in Paris a suit against Warner Bros. for the production of a film entitled *The Firebird*, in which a submissive young girl is so unnerved by the phonograph playing of the *Pagan Dance* from Stravinsky's *Firebird* that she wanders into the flat of a professional seducer, who had the piece played continually with malice aforethought, and yields to his infamous desires. The judge failed to appreciate Stravinsky's attitude, since the seductive power of music is supposed to be the composer's greatest pride, and adjudicated the case by granting Stravinsky a token sum of one French franc in compensation for the offense.

Metamusic. Metaphysical visions have obsessed composers through the ages. They dreamed of a METAMUSICAL symphony in which all mankind would participate as a responsive reverberating assembly of congenial souls. Shortly before he died, Scriabin wrote an outline of a METAMUSICAL Mysterium that would embrace all senses in a pantheistic mystical action. Much more earthbound, but musically fascinating, was the project of a *Universe Symphony* by Charles Ives, a work that he hoped to see performed by several orchestras stationed on hilltops overlooking a valley. The Russian mystical composer Nicolas Obouhov envisioned a METAMUSICAL union of all religions. He completed a major part of this work which bore the title *Le Livre de Vie.* He kept the manuscript on a self-made altar under an ikon, in a corner of his small room in Paris. Since this was to be the book of his own life, body and soul, he made all annotations in the original scores in his own blood. He tried to interest American music lovers to have this work produced in a specially built temple in Hollywood, but died with his dream unfulfilled.

Composers of the AVANT-GARDE have at their disposal the means of producing METAMUSICAL scores with the aid of electronic synthesizers. They may even plan to hitch their METAMUSICAL chariot if not to the stars then at least to the planets. There is nothing mystical in the term METAMUSIC. It simply means an art transcending traditional music, by analogy with Aristotle's Metaphysics, which indicates the position of a chapter dealing with philosophy, directly after a discussion of physics in his *Organon.*

Metempsychosis. A recurrence of a theme in an altered melorhythmic shape, suggesting the effect of *déjà entendu* without literal resemblance, may be called musical METEMPSYCHOSIS. The *idée fixe* in the *Symphonie Fantastique* of Berlioz does not fall into this category because here it was deliberately implanted and reproduced in a clearly recognizable form. The discovery of melorhythmic revenants may give a clue to the composer's inner impulses, and it is particularly fruitful in serial compositions, where METEMPSYCHOSIS may appear subliminally, despite the composer's efforts to guard himself against unintentional thematic references.

Metric Modulation. In a general sense of the word, METRIC MODULATION is a change of time signature. In special modern usage, proleptically applied by Charles Ives and systematically cultivated by Elliott Carter, METRIC MODULATION is a technique in which a rhythmic pattern is superposed on another, heterometrically, and then supersedes it and becomes the basic meter. Usually, such time signatures are mutually prime, e.g., 4/4 and 3/8, and so have no common divisors. Thus the change of the basic meter decisively alters the numerical content of the beat, but the minimal denominator (1/8 when 4/4 changes to 3/8; 1/16 when, e.g., 5/8 changes to 7/16, etc.) remains constant in duration.

Microtonality. Intervals smaller than semitones were used in ancient Greece, but were abandoned in western music with the establishment of the ecclesiastical modes. When greater sensitivity towards tonal elements developed in modern times, composers and theorists began investigating the acoustical, coloristic and affective aspects of intervals smaller than a semitone, particularly quarter-tones. The Mexican composer Julián Carrillo experimented with microtonal intervals as early as 1895, when he published his *Sonido 13 (13th Sound);* the title referred to the tonal resources beyond the 12 notes of the chromatic scale. Later he organized an international society for the exploration of MICROTONALITY under the grandiose name "Cruzada Intercontinental Sonido 13." He devised special instruments for performance of microtonal intervals and proposed a numerical notation of 96 divisions of the octave, which enabled him to designate precise intervallic values for 1/2-tones, 1/4-tones, 1/6-tones, 1/8-tones and 1/16-tones. As an exercise in MICROTONALITY he arranged Beethoven's *Fifth Symphony* in quarter-tones by dividing each interval into two, so that the octave became a tritone, and the entire range of the work shrank to about three octaves, like some monstrous simulacrum of a physical universe in which the sensorium of auditory frequencies undergoes an extraction of the square root.

The English musician John Foulds experimented with quarter-tones in 1898. He writes in his book *From Music Today* (1934): "In the year 1898 I had tentatively experimented in a string quartet with smaller divisions than usual of the intervals of our scale, quarter-tones. Having proved in performance their practicability and their capability of expressing certain psychological states in a manner incommunicable by any other means known to musicians, I definitely adopted them as an item in my composing technique. . . . Facetious friends may assert roundly that they have heard quarter-tones all their lives, from the fiddle strings and larynxes of their mutual friends, who produced them without any difficulty."

The most systematic investigation of the theory and practice of quarter-tones was undertaken by Alois Hába in Czechoslovakia. "As a boy of 12," he writes, "I played with my three older brothers in my father's village band. We were poor; there were ten children in the family, and I had to contribute to household expenses. When we played for village festivals it often happened that folk singers used intervals different from the tempered scale, and they were annoyed that we could not accompany them properly. This gave me the idea to practice at home playing non-tempered scales on my violin in intervals smaller than a semitone. This was my first 'conservatory' for music in quarter-tones and in sixth-notes."

Probably the first entirely self-consistent work in quarter-tones was the string quartet written by Hába in 1919. He also compiled the first manual containing detailed instructions on composing in quarter-tones, third-tones and sixth-tones, which he published under the fitting title *Neue Harmonielehre* in 1928. Under Hába's supervision the August Foerster piano manufacturing company of Czechoslovakia constructed the first model of a quarter-tone piano which was patented on 18 March 1924. At the same time Hába established the first seminars of MICROTONAL MUSIC at the Prague Conservatory. He and his students published a number of works in quarter-tones, in Hába's special notation containing symbols for half a sharp, a sharp and a half, half a flat, and a flat and a half. A quarter-tone upright piano was constructed by Willi Möllendorf even before Foerster's, but it was only an ordinary piano tuned in quarter-tones and not a specially built instrument. It is now placed in the Deutsches Museum in Munich as a historical relic. The same museum also possesses a quarter-tone Harmonium built by Foerster and a harmonium of 19 divisions of the octave designed by Melchior Sachs.

In 1917 the Russian composer Ivan Wyschnegradsky devised a system of quarter-tones with a motto, inspired by Heraclitus, "Everything flows." In 1924, then living in Paris, he formulated the concept of "pansonority," which in his nomenclature meant a discrete continuum of quarter-tones. To produce fairly accurate quarter-tones he used two pianos or two pairs of pianos tuned a quarter-tone apart. On 10 November 1945 he conducted in Paris an entire program of his works, including a symphonic poem for four pianos entitled *Cosmos*.

In Russia itself quarter-tone music had a brief period of success in the early 1920s, cultivated by the Quarter-Tone Society of Leningrad, founded by Rimsky-Korsakov's grandson Georg.

Charles Ives, whose universal genius touched on many aspects of modern composition, contributed some pieces written in quarter-tones. He tells us that he became aware of the new resources of MICROTONAL MUSIC when his father, a band leader in the Union Army during the Civil War, experimented in tuning band instruments a quarter-tone apart.

Probably the earliest published composition containing quarter-tones was a group of two pieces for cello and piano by Richard H. Stein, composed in 1906, but quarter-tone passages in them were used only as occasional ultra-chromatic interludes. Ernest Bloch inserted quarter-tones in his first piano quintet mainly for their affective value in coloristic appoggiaturas.

American composers David Zeikel and William Harold Halberstadt investigated the potentialities of quarter-tones in the 1940s and wrote special works, mostly for the violin, in quarter-tones. For the sake of completeness it may be mentioned that Nicolas Slonimsky composed an overture for strings, trumpet and percussion in the Phrygian Greek mode using as his theme an extant version of an ancient Greek tune from the accompaniment to the tragedy *Orestes* produced in Athens in 400 B.C.; he conducted this arrangement at the Hollywood Bowl on 13 July 1933. In order to produce the needed two quarter-tones, the open strings of the violins, violas and cellos were tuned a quarter-tone up, with the rest of the string instruments preserving the ordinary pitch.

The first quarter-tone piano manufactured in the United States was patented by Hans Barth on 21 July 1931. His instrument had two keyboards of 88 notes each. The upper keyboard was tuned at the regular international pitch and had the usual five black keys and seven white keys. The lower keyboard was tuned a quarter-tone down, and its keys were blue and red.

James Paul White, a Boston musician, constructed in 1883 a microtonal keyboard which he called *Harmon*, and used a notation in which deviations from regular pitch were indicated by plus and minus signs. He theorized that 612 equal divisions of an octave would provide the most practical approximation to pure intonation. His instrument is preserved at the New England Conservatory of Music.

Perhaps the most ambitious project in MICROTONAL MUSIC has been undertaken by the American composer Harry Partch who devised a scale of 43 intervals in an octave, and constructed a number of special instruments, among them a microtonal cello, a reed organ with 43 registrations, and a modern version of the Greek kithara.

Musicologists have made numerous attempts to reconcile the tempered scale with Pythagorean intonation. Perhaps the most complete research in this direction was done by Joseph Yasser in his book *A Theory of Evolving Tonality*, published in New York in 1932, in which he proposed a system of "supra-tonality," with accidentals designated by special symbols for supra-sharp, supra-flat and supra-natural of the synthetic scale.

Quarter-tones were used by composers to suggest the Greek enharmonic mode through the centuries. Halévy incorporated a few quarter-tones in his symphonic poem *Promethée enchaîné*, and Berlioz wrote an interesting account of its first performance in *Revue et Gazette Musicale de Paris* of 25 March 1849: "The employment of quarter-tones in Halévy's work is episodic and very short, and produces a species of groaning sound in the strings, but its strangeness seems perfectly justified here and enhances considerably the wistful prosody of the music."

The Rumanian composer Georges Enesco inserted a transitional passage in quarter-tones in his opera *Oedipe* produced in Paris in 1936. In this case, too, the composer's intention was to evoke the effect of the ancient Greek enharmonic scale.

It must be said that in actual performance on instruments manipulated by humans, quarter-tones and other microtonal divisions are only rough approximations of their true acoustical value. With the advent of electronic instruments, it became possible to reproduce microtonal intervals with absolute precision. Ernst Krenek experimented with a scale of 13 equal intervals in an octave. But despite the extraordinary resources offered by electronic instruments, composers of the Avant-Garde remained singularly indifferent to microtones. The Polish modernist Krzysztof Penderecki has used quarter-tones in massive multi-octave tone-clusters, creating sonorous complexes in icositetraphonic harmony.

A curious disquisition on quarter-tones and other fractional intervals as a logical extension of Chopin's sensitive use of chromatic harmony is contained in a pamphlet by Johanna Kinkel, *Acht Briefe an eine Freundin über Clavier-Unterricht*, published in Stuttgart in 1852: "As we wonder what it is that grips us and fills us with foreboding and delight in Chopin's music, we are apt to find a solution that might appear to many as pure fantasy, namely that Chopin's intention was to release upon us a cloud of quarter-tones, which now appear only as phantom doppelgänger in the shadowy realm within the intervals produced by enharmonic change. Once the quarter-tones are emancipated, an entirely new world of tones will open to us, But since we have been accustomed to the long established divisions into semitones, these new sounds will seem weird, suggesting a splash of discordant waves. Yet the children of the next generation, or the one after next, will suck in these strange sounds with mother's milk, and may find in them a more stimulating and doubly rich art. Chopin seems to push at these mysterious portals; his melodies stream in colliding currents through the semitones as if groping for finer and more spiritual nuances than those that were available for his purposes. And when this door is finally sprung open, we will stand a step nearer to the eternal domain of natural sounds. As it is, we can only give a weak imitation of the Aeolian harp, of the rustle of the forest, of the magical ripple of the waters, unable to render them in their true impressions, because our so-called scales made up of whole tones and semitones are too coarse and have too many gaps, while Nature possesses not only quarter-tones and eighth-tones but an infinite scale of split atoms of sound!"

Migratory Tonics. When tonalities are in a state of constant flux, the laws of probability will still lead to the accidental formation of tonal centers, notes that occur more frequently than others, much in the line of the well-known paradox that if only three dozen individuals are assembled at a party, the odds are even that two of them will have the same day and month for a birthday. Such statistically established keynotes in an otherwise free modulatory environment may be called MIGRATORY TONICS, a term particularly suitable for works in which tonality is not renounced unequivocally.

Millimetrization. This is a term introduced by Villa-Lobos to describe the transfer of mathematical curves or outlines of photographs onto graph paper, precise to a millimeter. His best-known piece arranged according to MILLIMETRIZATION is *New York Skyline.*

Minimalism. Little is big and less is more, and either adage aptly applies to musical MINIMALISM, a 1960s reductionist compositional movement that produced a significant body of works notable for its maximal effect out of remarkably minimal means. The movement sprang up on the opposite coasts of the United States, San Francisco and New York especially, and, in its early years, was closely associated with the visual arts; indeed many early works were performed in alternative spaces, including galleries. The shared interest among its early proponents in radically reduced means led to a set of shared compositional tendencies: an unwavering pulse, established at the onset; highly repetitive melodies that function like motivic cells and sub-cells, slowly metamorphosing into other, closely-related motifs; in electronic works, the use of tape loops; incessant and complex rhythms, often with two or more patterns coexisting; subtle phase-shifting in both melodic and rhythmic treatment; single-movement forms, frequently quite simple and cyclic; and very little harmonic movement, resulting in MINIMALISM'S characteristic stasis.

The concerns of minimalist composers represented a clear departure from the prevailing SERIALISM of their time and thus from the prevailing practices of the princi-pal AVANT-GARDE. The aesthetic owes much to John Cage and other American experimental composers, however, but with one notable difference: the minimalist composer's desire for strict control over both compositional processes and performance, thus minimizing the potentials of aleatoric and indeterminate processes. The main proponents of early MINIMALISM were La Monte Young, Terry Riley, Steve Reich, and Philip Glass, although each has expressed himself in other, more maximal ways, including MIXED MEDIA works. MINIMALISM has been used with great effect in the theater and in dance works. MINIMALISM is also referred to as process music; see MONOTHEMATICISM and ADDITIVE COMPOSITION.

Mixed Media. Musicians of the AVANT-GARDE are increasingly laboring towards the coordination and unification of modern musical productions with those of other arts—painting, sculpture, phonograph recording, theater, radio, television, electronics—activities that are often generalized under the category of MIXED MEDIA. The practice represents in fact a return to the ancient ideal of unity of liberal arts, with music occupying the honorable position as *ancilla artis.* This tendency has generated a number of novel developments of catalytic artistic powers.

Mobile. In modern sculpture, a MOBILE is a delicately balanced construction of metal or wood, which can easily be swayed by gentle flow of air. Modern composers have adopted this term to describe a similarly flexible melorhythmic structure, usually scored or a small number of instruments, and characterized by a fine intervallic equilibrium, most often maintained by serial arrangements.

Modern Music. In the card catalogue of the British Museum, works written after 1800 are included in a section marked MODERN MUSIC. In American usage, MODERN MUSIC is a colloquialism for dance tunes, and popular songs. Medieval manuscripts dealing with musical theory often open with the phrase, "Brevitate gaudent modemi." The moderns that relished brevity were, in the opinion of the anonymous authors of these treatises, the adherents to Ars Nova. In present usage, MODERN MUSIC refers to that written since 1900. The variants are 20th-century music, New Music, Music of Our Time, Music of Today and Contemporary Music.

Modernistic Music. The flexion "istic" denotes a depreciation in the purity of the original product. Hellenistic art is inferior to that of the Golden Age of Greece; PRIMITIVISTIC paintings or compositions suggest a less virile version of the artistic qualities of primitive man; IMPRESSIONISTIC idioms are dissipated derivatives of IMPRESSIONISM. To describe a piece of music as MODERNISTIC has an aura of indulgent condescension, suggesting an adoption of models of modern music and a facile pastiche "à la manière de. . . ."

Monism. MONISM is a philosophical doctrine postulating the existence of a basic element that is the prime constituent of all material objects. In music MONISM denotes an analogous primacy of a concept or a function. The dodecaphonic series is a MONISTIC factor which determines the development of an entire work. A set of variations is intrinsically MONISTIC since it is derived from a primary source, but it is pluralistic if the variations are regarded as mutually independent entities.

Monodrama.

MONODRAMA is a stage work in which only one actor, speaker, or singer acts, recites or sings. Schoenberg introduced a type of singing recitation, SPRECHSTIMME, in which the actor enunciates his lines in an inflected manner following the melorhythmic design of the music, a technique that came to its full fruition in his *Pierrot Lunaire*. The classical example of a staged MONODRAMA is Schoenberg's *Erwartung*. The Russian composer Vladimir Rebikov evolved a novel type of MONODRAMA which he described as Psychodrama; in it an actor recites his state of mind with a musical accompaniment. In Schoenberg's *Die glückliche Hand*, the central character sings and mimes the story, and a chorus comments on the action in SPRECHSTIMME.

Monothematism and Polythematism.

"Brevitate gaudent moderni," medieval theorists said of the moderns of their own time. In the 20th century, this "joy of brevity" assumed the form of MONOTHEMATISM, in which a single subject governs the entire composition. MONOTHEMATISM is basic to the structure of a theme with variations; but if variations depart too widely from the theme, the result may be POLYTHEMATIC. Rigid MONOTHEMATISM carries an intrinsic danger of monotony; on the other hand, extreme POLYTHEMATISM courts the opposite danger of discontinuity. In MONOTHEMATISM the single theme must recur a sufficient number of times to produce an impression of uniformity; in POLYTHEMATIC constructions, similarities among successive themes must be avoided.

Monte Carlo Method.

Statistical laws govern games of chance as well as the parameters of ALEATORY MUSIC. The MONTE CARLO METHOD is the most convenient of all gambling devices for easy musical application. The numbers from 1 to 36 of roulette, of the type used in the casino of Monte Carlo, can be equalized to the 36 chromatic tones of three octaves and notated accordingly as the roulette ball finds its niche, with zero corresponding to the lowest note of an arbitrarily selected progression. Rhythmic figures can be derived from a similar process by equalizing the 36 numbers to 36 different note values; if a smaller number of different rhythms is needed, then a dozen or a half-dozen sets on the roulette table can be selected as primary units. In the MONTE CARLO METHOD the probability of occurrence of a certain number depends on the frequency of previous incidences; thus certain notes may accumulate greater statistical probability of incidence and determine the tonal tropism. Harmonization and contrapuntal lines can be obtained by combining the single melorhythmic lines determined by individual Monte Carlo runs. Normally, atonal melodies and dissonant harmonies would result, but a spontaneous appearance of a dodecaphonic series is as unlikely as picking 12 different cards from a pack a random.

Morphology.

The emergence of a great variety of new forms of composition makes it difficult to classify them according to traditional categories. It may be desirable therefore to substitute the term MORPHOLOGY for the formal analysis, with the nomenclature of botany replacing that of traditional historic terminology. The geometrical rubrics of botanical classification would add imaginative metaphors suitable to modern musical usages. It would be possible, for instance, to speak of radial symmetry in neo-classical music, of a chromatic inflorescence in an atonal melody, or even of agamogenetic axes in dodecaphonic cross-pollination. The advantage of such botanical similes lies in precision and specificity of the terms and in their easy applicability to intervallic structures.

Musicorama.

This is a telescoped word descriptive of a continuously variegated panorama of connected musical episodes.

Musique Concrète.

MUSIQUE CONCRÈTE was discovered and named on 15 April 1948 in Paris by Pierre Schaeffer, a French radio engineer. Experimenting with the newly invented magnetic tape, he found that a heterogeneous collection of songs, noises, conversations, radio commercials, etc. recorded on tape, presented a realistic phonomontage which may serve for actual composition by superimposing fragments of tape recordings in a polyphony of random sounds, splicing the tape in various ways, running it at different speeds, or backwards, etc. The raw materials of "concrete music" are susceptible to all kinds of treatment and are therefore capable of unlimited transformations. The technique of double and triple recording on the same length of tape makes it possible to create a polyphony of concrete music of great complexity. In fact it is possible to recompose a classical symphony from a recording of a single note, which can subsequently be changed in pitch and arranged in the requisite rhythmic order, superimposed on other tones derived from the original note, altered in tone color by additional electronic manipulation, until a whole work is reconstructed from these constituent tonal dynamic and instrumental elements. The Polish composer Wlodzimierz Kotoński composed an *Etude concrète* for orchestra using as his material a single stroke of the cymbal electronically altered and transposed. The American experimenter Richard Maxfield collected 30 seconds of coughs at a modern ballet recital and expanded these bronchial sonorities into a five-minute orchestral work entitled *Cough Music*.

Mutations.

In search for synonyms or paronyms to replace the ambiguous nomenclature of academic musicology, some modern composers have begun using the scientific sounding words VARIANTS or MUTATIONS for Variations. MUTATIONS may be beneficial, musically speaking, when the mutant genes add to the brilliance of thematic adornment, as in some variations in the diaphanous music of Ravel; or they may be detrimental to the bio-musical organism, as in the cluttered polyphony of Max Reger. Recessive MUTATIONS, such as Stravinsky's neo-Baroque ornamentation, may become dominant characteristics, with uncertain benefits. In human terms, MUTATIONS are found in large musical families, in which the embryo develops fully conditioned by the genetic complex of his parents. A striking example is that of Siegfried Wagner, a musical mutant who fully absorbed the musical genes of his father but acquired MUTATIONS that made him sterile. Some MUTATIONS are products of defective genes of the theme itself, a condition that may lead to melodic dyscrasia, harmonic dyslogia and contrapuntal dyskinesia. There is no relief in such cases but to destroy the theme *in statu nascendi* in order to eliminate mutagenic elements and build afresh an untainted homunculus.

Mystic Chord. In conformity with his mystical beliefs, Scriabin described the basic chord of *Prometheus*, C, F-sharp, B-flat, E, A, D, as the MYSTIC CHORD. Ex post facto, he regarded these components, seriatim, as 8th, 9th, 10th, 11th, 13th, and 14th overtones. Analytically, the MYSTIC CHORD belongs to the category of the dominant-ninth in a major key with two suspensions, as is made clear by resolving F-sharp to G and A to B-flat.

Narcolepsy. Symphony concerts are notoriously conducive to NARCOLEPSY, and their attendance is sometimes recommended by psychologists as an effective cure of insomnia. Statistical surveys indicate that the narcogenic factors are mainly the pendulum-like rhythmic beats in classical music, particularly when there is no change in dynamics. An unexpected sforzando will wake up even the most inveterate narcoleptic, as illustrated by the story of Haydn's *Surprise Symphony* with its famous chord in the slow movement that was supposed to arouse the somnolent London concert goers from their middle-aged slumber. On the other hand, modern works rarely put people to sleep because of the constant changes in rhythm and dynamics. NARCOLEPSY is also an inevitable outcome of lectures on musicology; according to observations conducted by a trained psychologist at a session of the International Musicological Congress in New York, a deep coma overtook practically the entire audience during the first twenty seconds of a reading from manuscript of a paper by an eminent Dutch musicologist. At the same occasion, attention was suddenly increased by the appearance on the podium of the inventor of a double-bass flute and an ultra-sonic piccolo. He could never succeed in blowing through the long tube of the big flute, which met with sympathy in the audience. The hyper-piccolo could not be heard by humans, but a terrier dog who strayed into the hall showed agitation at the ultra-sonics that canines can hear easily. Both the dog and the inventor were rewarded by hearty applause.

Naturalism. In musical usage, NATURALISM appears as an extreme case of VERISMO. Naturalistic opera emphasizes the negative phenomena of life without the redeeming quality of romance. In Soviet parlance NATURALISM has acquired a pejorative meaning; the word was used as a verbal missile in the attacks on Shostakovich's opera *Lady Macbeth of the District of Mzensk*, particularly with reference to the scene of adultery illustrated in an orchestral interlude by sliding trombones.

Negative Music. NEGATIVE MUSIC is synonymous with ANTI-MUSIC, but there is a scintilla of a difference between the two terms. ANTI-MUSIC stresses its opposition to any musical actions, whereas NEGATIVE MUSIC operates on the supposition that there may exist negative frequencies as mathematical abstractions, related to audible music as a negative to the positive in photography. NEGATIVE MUSIC would reverse dynamic values; a vocal text containing tender sentiments would be harmonized by loud dissonant noises; conversely, a symphonic

poem on the subject of the nuclear war would be depicted by the minutest distillation of monodically concentrated tones. The field for experimentation in NEGATIVE MUSIC is limitless, precisely because it is impossible to speculate about its nature.

Neo-classicism. When the luxuriance of IMPRESSIONISM reached its point of saturation, it became clear to many composers that further amplification of coloristic devices was no longer stimulating or novel. The Weber-Fechner law postulates that the force of physical impact must be increased exponentially in order to produce an arithmetical increase in the sensory impression, so that a hundredfold magnification of sound is needed to provide a tenfold increase in the physiological effect. It was to be expected that composers and audiences alike would rebound from such sonic inundation. This reaction coincided with the economic collapse following World War I so that it became financially impossible to engage large orchestras or grandiose operatic companies. The cry went all over Europe, "Back to Bach!" To this was added the slogan of NEW SIMPLICITY. Since it was no longer feasible to move forward, musical tastes with the aid of intellectual rationalization made a 180° turn towards the past. But the past could not be recaptured in its literal form, and the new retrograde movement was launched under the name of NEO-CLASSICISM. It was characterized by the following traits: (1) Rehabilitation of diatonicism as the dominant idiom, enhanced pandiatonic constructions, in which all seven degrees of the diatonic scale are functionally equal. (2) Elimination of all programmatic and romantic associations either in the titles or the tonal content of individual works. (3) A demonstrative revival of the Baroque forms of Sonata, Serenade, Scherzo, Passacaglia, Toccata and the florid type of variations. (4) Demotion of chromatic elements of the scale to their traditional role as passing notes. (5) Restrained use of massive sonorities and renunciation of all external and purely decorative effects, such as non-thematic melismas and non-essential harmonic figurations. (6) Cultivation of compact forms, such as symphonies and sonatas having a single movement and operas without a chorus and with a reduced orchestral contingent (usually containing 13 instruments), with an important piano part performing the function of the cembalo in Baroque music (7) Reconstruction of old Baroque instruments, particularly the harpsichord and their employment in modernized classical techniques. (8) Exploration of canonic and fugal writing without adherence to strict rules of classical polyphony. (9) Radical curtailment of the development section in Baroque forms with a purely nominal recapitulation, and a concise coda free from redundant repetition of final tonic chords.

Neo-Medievalism. NEO-CLASSICISM resuscitated Baroque music in a new guise of pandiatonic harmonies and asymmetrical rhythms. Retreating still further into the past, some modern composers discovered a world of surprisingly modernistic devices such as hocketus, heterophony and quodlibet, and the techniques of inversion and retrograde composition which are basic to SERIAL MUSIC. Modernization of these resources resulted in the stylized idiom of NEO-MEDIEVALISM, which adopted not only the old musical modalities, but the verbal usages of ecclesiastical Latin for texts. The most remarkable example of this trend is Stravinsky's oratorio *Oedipus Rex* with a specially written text in medieval Latin. Carl Orff produced a number of successful works in a NEO-MEDIEVAL style, notably *Carmina Burana,* to texts in Latin and German dialects. A significant trait of these works is their imaginative repetitive technique. The liberating power of literal repetition has a particular attraction for composers of the AVANT-GARDE who follow oriental religious practices, exemplified by the interminable turning of the Tibetan prayer wheel.

Neo-Modality. The system of modes, so potent for centuries, nearly lost all its binding power under the impact of ATONALITY and DODECAPHONY. Dormant strains have achieved a new Renaissance in the ethnically deep-rooted works of Béla Bartók. A surprising revival of modality was its adoption by the purveyors of ROCK 'N' ROLL. Roy Harris has built a sui generis *ethos* of modes by assigning specific emotions to each, according to the intervallic magnitude of the opening tetrachord, ranging from the most spacious, Lydian mode, expressing optimism, to the least spacious, Locrian mode, expressing pessimism. Avenir H. Monfred has developed a practical method of modern modal composition, diatonic NEO-MODALITY, in which a modal change is effected by altering the key signature. Thus the Dorian mode on D can be transformed, either during the process of composition or by spontaneous improvisation, into any other mode by adding sharps or flats to the key signature; it would be transmuted into D major by placing two sharps in the key signature, into the Phrygian mode by two flats, etc.

Neo-Mysticism. The words "Laus Deo" which Haydn used to append to every manuscript upon its completion were simply the expression of his piety and did not imply a claim of direct communication with the Deity. Mystical composers of the 20th century, on the other hand, believed that they were oracles of higher powers. Mahler thought he was possessed by Beelzebub. He scrawled appeals to Satan in the manuscript of his unfinished *Tenth Symphony;* he believed in the mystical magic of all of his music. But it was left to Scriabin to formalize his mystical consciousness in musical terms. His symphony *Prometheus* is based on a six-note chord which he called MYSTIC CHORD. Shortly before his death he sketched out the text for a Mysterium, which he envisioned as a synaesthetic action which would comprise all human senses as receiving organs. A large ensemble of bells was an instrumental feature of this eschatological creation, to be performed high over the Himalayan Mountains.

Neophobia. Musical NEOPHOBIA is a neurotic fear of radical innovations. Professional music critics are particularly prone to suffer from it, a condition that they attempt to disguise as profound devotion to the immutable laws of music. Like mental patients, they regard themselves as the only rational human beings in a mad world. The more enlightened among them often correct their former misapprehensions. At the first American performance of *Don Juan* by Richard Strauss, Philip Hale described it as "a good deal of a bore." Eleven years later he called it a work of "fascinating, irresistible insolence and glowing passion." Heinrich Strobel, who became the great pan-

jandrum of the AVANT-GARDE, had contributed some choice invectives against the American moderns in his report of a concert in Berlin in 1932: "For two hours Nicolas Slonimsky bore down on the musicians of the Berlin Philharmonic, until finally they could no longer refrain from openly showing their disgust. For an hour and three quarters the public tolerated the noise, but by the cacophonous melee of *Arcana* by Varèse the audience lost their patience. A scandal broke loose. It was understandable. No ear can endure this sort of noise for any length of time. It has nothing to do with music. It does not shock and it does not amuse. It is simply senseless."

Neo-Primitivism. An art saturated with culture is invariably tempted to return to its simple origins, chronologically to the cave paintings of primitive man and to the haunting drum rhythms of Homo Protomusicus, and biologically to Infantiloquy. Supreme mastery of design is used by abstract expressionist painters to emulate prehistoric color drawings, and a sophisticated instrumental technique is utilized by modern composers for children's pieces in asymmetrical rhythms.

From these dual resources, intuitively developed by primitive man and by a human child, grew the language of NEO-PRIMITIVISM. Discarding the civilized garments of romantic images and impressionistic colors, it seeks to attain the crude power of massively arrayed sonorities, asymmetrical rhythms and percussive instrumentation. In NEO-PRIMITIVISM, melodies are brief refrains, often limited to the range of a major tetrachord. Reiteration of single notes in unchanged speed is cultivated to the point of stupefaction. Vacuous progressions of naked fifths and fourths are used to form an impression of inarticulate eloquence. Heterophony, in which a mobile voice elaborates on the principal subject ignoring the niceties of counterpoint, is encountered in numerous scores of NEO-PRIMITIVISTIC music, as a curious recessive characteristic.

NEO-PRIMITIVISM is almost invariably nationalistic in character. The greatest masterpiece of NEO-PRIMITIVISM, Stravinsky's *Le Sacre du Printemps*, bears the subtitle *Scenes of Pagan Russia.* Béla Bartók's music evokes the Neo-Primitivistic landscape of immemorial Pannonia. Villa-Lobos recreates the inchoate sound of the Brazilian jungle in his symphonies. NEO-PRIMITIVISM is nurtured on the essential character of the race, but the composer himself need not be an archeologist; he derives his inspiration from the art of his own time. The French painter Henri Rousseau copied the subjects and color patterns of his exotic paintings from illustrations in a French children's book. Paul Gauguin painted his Tahitian women from photographs, preferring them to living models. Nonetheless, both created a genuinely novel type of pictorial NEO-PRIMITIVISM. In music, however, NEO-PRIMITIVISTIC representation cannot be effected without a complete mastery of modern techniques of composition. The theory that an analphabetic musician can write primitivistically authentic works by simply disregarding the civilized rules of harmony and counterpoint is false.

Neo-Romanticism. NEO-ROMANTICISM represents a secondary phase of the modern stylistic upheaval, following the repudiation of programmatic music as a valid medium. The frustrations of World War I sharpened a general disenchantment among poets, artists and musicians, but the purely negative intellectual movements, such as DADAISM, soon exhausted their shock power and gave way to a mitigated type of romantic music in the form of NEO-ROMANTICISM. Coloristic elements, so ingratiatingly used in the symphonies of Sibelius, in the tone poems of Richard Strauss and in the early ballet scores of Stravinsky were applied with apprehensive circumspection by Neo-Romantic composers. Representational onomatopoeia and literal reproduction of natural sounds replaced the subjective effusions of modern pictorialism. Benjamin Britten's sea gulls in the interludes of his opera *Peter Grimes,* Olivier Messiaen's bird-songs in his score *Chronochromie* and the phonograph record of the song of a real nightingale in Ottorino Respighi's *Pines of Rome* are modern instances of NEO-ROMANTICISM.

New Music. Newness is a recurring motive in musical nomenclature. The emergence of rhythmic modalities in the 14th century became historically known as Ars Nova. The monodic type of composition used by the Florentine initiators of opera was published under the name *Nuove musiche.* In painting, *Art Nouveau* was the description given the French art that flourished in the 1890s. The term NEW MUSIC became current about 1920; it denoted a type of modern music marked by a dissonant counterpoint, ATONALITY and brevity of expression. Later, NEW MUSIC became synonymous with ULTRA-MODERN MUSIC.

New Simplicity. During the NEO-CLASSICAL flowering of the 1920s, the slogan NEW SIMPLICITY was raised among composers eager to divest themselves of an enforced sophistication of the period. In practice, NEW SIMPLICITY meant a return to elementary and sometimes ABECEDARIAN melodic and harmonic practices, barely covered with a patina of NON-TOXIC DISSONANCES.

Non-Toxic Dissonances. DISSONANCES can be said to be NON-TOXIC or non-corrosive if they are embanked within a tonal sequence, or if their candential illation corresponds to traditional modalities. It is the harmonic context that determines the toxicity of a dissonance for an untutored ear. Among the most corrosive dissonances are atonal combinations in which intervals of a high degree of discordance, such as major sevenths, minor seconds and the tritone, are combined with acoustically euphonious intervals of a perfect fifth and a perfect fourth. The absence of thirds, whether major or minor, is the distinctive feature of corrosive harmony, but toxic sonic effects result also from the simultaneous use of two homonymous major and minor triads on account of the interference between the major and minor thirds. Changes in bio-chemical balance and nervous reactions to the impact of toxic dissonances can be measured on a neurograph, providing a scientific clue to the apperception of modern music.

Numbers. The Latin word *Numeri* had a second meaning, music, for it was governed by the law of proportions between two different sounds. In Shakespearean English, NUMBERS refer to musical composition. St. Augustine drew a distinction between *Numeri sonantes,* the actual musical tone that is perceived by the senses, and

Numeri recordabiles, music that is remembered. In St. Augustine's concept, a melody was formed by a single sound instantaneously perceived and memorably associated with several preceding sounds. Long before St. Augustine, Aristoxenus likened the musical tones of a melody to letters in a language. So intimate was the connection felt between NUMBERS and music that in medieval universities music was taught as part of the Quadrivium of exact sciences, along with arithmetic, geometry and astronomy. This association with NUMBERS was lost in classical and romantic music. Not until the 20th century did the numerical element in music regain its status. Mathematical parameters lie at the foundation of serial music. The calculus of sets is an important tool in rhythmic serialization. Some composers have applied the Fibonacci NUMBERS, in which each term is the sum of its two predecessors, to metrical, rhythmic and intervallic parameters. Simple arithmetical progressions also yield material for rhythmic arrangements. The application of NUMBERS to composition is limitless; the difficulty is to select numerical sets that would provide material for purely musical structures.

Objets Trouvés. Ready-made objects are often incorporated by modern artists as part of a sculpture or a montage. Ultra-modern composers sometimes insert passages from works by other composers as a token of homage and partly as an experiment in construction. Such OBJETS TROUVÉS need not harmonize with their environment which may be completely alien to the nature of the implant. An early example is the sudden appearance of the tune *Ach du lieber Augustin* in Schoenberg's *Second String Quertet.*

Omnitonality. In search of terms signifying various degrees of modulatory freedom, modern musicologists have chanced upon OMNITONALITY, to indicate a totality of tonalities entailing frequent collisions of different keys. OMNITONALITY enjoyed a certain vogue as a compromise definition for modern techniques that retained the basic sense of tonality but expanded it to the entire cycle of major and minor scales. It is almost synonymous with PANTONALITY.

Open Form Composition. Works based on CONTROLLED IMPROVISATION, in which materials are selected from available resources, have a venerable ancestry; classical composers supplied alternative versions for transitions and endings as a matter of course. In its modern avatar, OPEN FORM COMPOSITION often delegates the ordering of component parts to the performer. Chronological priority in developing such techniques belongs to the American composer Earle Brown whose *Folio,* written in 1952, affords great latitude in the arranging of given materials. Karlheinz Stockhausen further developed this technique in his *Klavierstücke,* consisting of separate sections which can be performed in any order.

Organized Sound. Sound is an acoustical phenomenon, which all by itself does not make music. Composition begins at the point when two sounds are connected in linear succession or vertical superposition. But the nature of these links is not circumscribed by any rules of melody and harmony. With the emancipation of dissonances in the 20th century, the vertical combinations became free from restraints imposed on them by tradition. Linear progressions, once bound within the framework of modes and scales, are developed in atonal designs. Schoenberg replaced diatonic melody and consonant harmony by the new dodecaphonic discipline. Edgar Varèse advanced the concept of ORGANIZED SOUND, as a complex of successive acoustical phenomena unrelated to one another except by considerations of sonic equilibrium. Dissonant combinations are preferred because they constitute a probabilistic majority and therefore are entitled to greater representation in ORGANIZED SOUND. For the same statistical reasons, successions of melodic notes are apt to generate atonal configurations. The form of works written according to the doctrine of ORGANIZED SOUND is athematic, and the rhythms are usually asymmetric. The valence between successive units, in melody, harmony and rhythm, under such conditions, is an idempotent.

Palimpsest. In musical semantics, the term PALIMPSEST may be used as a substitution for an intentionally erased composition. This erasure may be complete or partial, with some elements of the original idea left under the sonic surface. The hidden design may be discovered by intervallic analysis, comparable to the use of ultra-violet rays in detecting the old text in a parchment covered by a newer piece of writing.

Palindrome. Palindromic words and sentences do not change when they are read backwards. Max Reger, whose last name is a PALINDROME, replied wittily to an admirer who complained that he could see only his back while he conducted a concert: "I am no different front or back." Musical PALINDROMES are synonymous with retrograde movements. In a PALINDROMIC section in Alban Berg's opera *Lulu*, the music revolves backwards to depict the story of Lulu's incarceration and escape. Samplers of PALINDROMIC canons are found in Nicolas Slonimsky's *Thesaurus of Scales and Melodic Patterns*.

Palingenesis. The meaning of the word PALINGENESIS is rebirth, and it is parasynonymous with METEMPSYCHOSIS. In modern musical usage PALINGENESIS corresponds to a reprise, with the important difference that the original material is not recapitulated literally but appears metempsychotically in a form as dissimilar from its progenitor as a reincarnated cat is from its former human avatar. PALINGENESIS is a particularly convenient term to designate an electronically altered sonic substance, or a topologically metamorphosed thematic idea.

Pandiatessaron. This is a vertical column consisting of perfect fourths (from *Diatessaron*, the interval of a fourth in ancient Greek music). The PANDIATESSARON contains all 12 notes of the tempered scale and represents a dodecaphonic integration of quartal melodies.

Pandiatonicism. The term PANDIATONICISM was coined by Nicolas Slonimsky and was first used in the first edition of his book *Music Since 1900* published in 1937. It is a technique in which all seven degrees of the diatonic scale are used freely in democratic equality. The functional importance of the primary triads, however,

remains undiminished in PANDIATONIC harmony. PANDIATONICISM possesses both tonal and modal aspects, with the distinct preference for major keys. The earliest PANDIATONIC extension was the added major sixth over the tonic major triad. A cadential chord of the tonic major seventh is also of frequent occurrence. Independently from the development of PANDIATONICISM in serious music, American JAZZ players adopted it as a practical device. Concluding chords in piano improvisations in Jazz are usually PANDIATONIC, containing the tonic, dominant, mediant, submediant and supertonic, with the triad in open harmony in the bass topped by a series of perfect fourths. In C major, such chords would be, from the bass up, C, G, E, A, D, G. It is significant that all the components of this Pandiatonic complex are members of the natural harmonic series. With C as the fundamental generator, G is the third partial, E the fifth partial, D the 9th, B the 15th and A the 27th. The perfect fourth is excluded both theoretically and practically, for it is not a member of the harmonic series, an interesting concordance of actual practice and acoustical considerations. With the dominant in the bass, a complete succession of fourths, one of them an augmented fourth, can be built: G, C, F, B, E, A, D, G, producing a satisfying Pandiatonic complex. When the subdominant is in the bass, the most euphonious result is obtained by a major triad in open harmony, F, C, A, in the low register, and E, B, D, G in the upper register. Polytriadic combinations are natural resources of Pandiatonicism, with the dominant combined with the tonic, e.g., C, G, E, D, G, B, making allowance for a common tone; dominant over the subdominant, as in the complex, F, C, A, D, G, B, etc. True Polytonality cannot be used in Pandiatonicism, since all the notes are in the same mode. Pedal points are particularly congenial to the spirit of Pandiatonicism, always following the natural spacing of the component notes, using large intervals in the bass register and smaller intervals in the treble. The esthetic function of Pandiatonicism is to enhance the resources of triadic harmony; that is the reason why the superposition of triads, including those in minor, are always productive of a resonant diatonic bitonality. Although Pandiatonicism has evolved from tertian foundations, it lends itself to quartal and quintal constructions with satisfactory results. Pandiatonicism is a logical medium for the techniques of NEOCLASSICISM. Many sonorous usages of PANDIATONICISM can be found in the works of Debussy, Ravel, Stravinsky, Casella, Malipiero, Vaughan Williams, Aaron Copland and Roy Harris. The key of C major is particularly favored in piano music, thanks to the "white" quality of the keyboard. Indeed, Pandiatonic piano music developed empirically from free improvisation on the white keys. Small children promenading their little fingers over the piano keyboard at the head level produce Pandiatonic melodies and Pandiatonic harmonies of excellent quality and quite at random.

Panpentatonicism. By analogy with PANDIATONICISM, which denotes a free use of the seven diatonic degrees, PANPENTATONICISM grants a similar dispensation to the five notes of the pentatonic scale. Consecutive fourths and fifths are frequent contrapuntal resources. Since the leading tone is missing in the pentatonic scale, plagal cadences are the only available endings. PANPENTATONIC tone-clusters are more euphonious than the pandiatonic ones; when projected against a perfect fifth in the bass, they create an attractive sonority of a modernistic PANPENTATONIC chinoiserie.

Pantonality. The term PANTONALITY denotes the use of all major and minor keys with complete freedom and without preference for any particular tonality. PANTONALITY is almost synonymous with OMNITONALITY, the only difference being that PANTONALITY includes atonal melodic progressions and uninhibited dissonant textures, while OMNITONALITY tends to enhance the basic sense of tonality.

Parerga & Paralipomena. Like Schopenhauer, who published fragments of his philosophical writings under the high-sounding name PARERGA & PARALIPOMENA, Richard Strauss gathered some residual materials from his *Symphonia domestica*, and incorporated them in a work commissioned by the amputated pianist Paul Wittgenstein, denominated *Parergon zur Symphonia domestica*, and scored for piano left-hand and orchestra. While such creative thrift is justified when Schopenhauer or Strauss practice it, collections and arrangements of *disjecta membra* put together by composers of lesser endowment, and particularly those whose technical progress was arrested at the Abecedarian or Analphabetic niveau, are clearly objectionable.

Permeability. PERMEABILITY is a factor that determines the degree of interpenetrability of thematic, nonthematic and bruitistic elements, reinforcing the structure of a given tonal complex, and occasionally coming to a mutually annihilating collision, in which the resulting GESTALT becomes a terraced and tesselated ziggurat. The term PERMEABILITY is also used to describe the process of mutual osmosis among parameters of ORGANIZED SOUND.

Pernicious Interference. The law of contrasts is basic to every piece of modern music, but supererogatory acervation and ornamental promiscuity of melodic and harmonic elements constitute PERNICIOUS INTERFERENCE. Taste and technical skill are the sole means to avoid this danger.

Planarianism. A musical composition which can be dissected into two or more parts, with each growing out into a separate independent body may be called PLANARIAN, by analogy with the flatworm of that name that possesses a trifid intestine and is capable of regenerating each of its severed parts into new flatworms. The structure of a work in the style of PLANARIANISM may reach great complexity. Karlheinz Stockhausen has written autogenetic works that can be cut up, with each musical PLANARIAN becoming a self-sufficient sonic organism. This process of vermiculation and its concomitant divisibility has been further advanced by John Cage; at his hands each musical platyhelminth becomes a unique and irreproducible species.

Plastic, Elastic and Spastic Variations. Plasticity of texture is essential in modern Variations, securing a malleability of tonal materials. Tonal Elasticity adds intervallic flexibility to a Plastic theme. A rhythmic effect can be achieved by Spastic convulsions of the

melodic line, producing implosions which impart a stimulating sense of disquiet to the music.

Pluralistic Structures. Pluralism is an epistemological concept connoting a multiplicity of causes and events. Developments of modern music support the pluralistic view in such styles as NEO-CLASSICAL, IMPRESSIONISTIC or EXPRESSIONISTIC, in which the factors of melody, rhythm, and intervallic values are of different formulation. But the same type of structure becomes monistic if it is derived from a uniform set, as for instance in Variations. Pluralism and Monism are mutually specular, but they are reconciled in serial music. Analogies with the visible spectrum invite themselves. White light is monistic in its sensory perception, but pluralistic when it is analyzed into the prismatic constituents of the rainbow. WHITE SOUND is a monistic aggregation of sonic particles, which can be separated into a pluralistic collection of its tonal components.

Pointillism. In the nomenclature of modern art, POINTILLISM is a method of applying colored dots to the canvas, forming a cumulative design. In modern music, the term is descriptive of atonal and athematic idioms, in which separate notes are distributed individually rather than as parts of an integral melorhythmic curve. The maximal dispersion of members of a dodecaphonic series in different octave positions is an example of serial POINTILLISM.

Political Symbolism. In the affective usages of the Renaissance, major keys symbolized joy and minor keys sadness. Such correspondence of emotional states and sounds has an acoustical foundation, for the major third is the fifth overtone of the fundamental tone, while the minor third is not a member of the harmonic series and produces interference. This natural preference for major keys as acoustically superior to minor tonalities was the subject of an interesting philosophical exposition of POLITICAL SYMBOLISM given by Anatoly Lunacharsky, Soviet Commissar of Education in an introductory speech at a Moscow concert on 10 December 1919: "Major keys lift the sound; they raise it a semitone up, and its power grows. By analogy with laughter, with its exultant feeling of joy, major keys elevate the mood and cheer us up. Minor keys, on the other hand, droop, leading to a compromise, to a surrender of positions; the sound is lowered, and its power diminishes. Allow me, as an old Bolshevik, to put it this way: major tonality is Bolshevik music; but a minor key is a deeply rooted inner Menshevik. Cultural history chose to call major and minor two different species of modes in the world of sound. Bolsheviks and Mensheviks are the two parties which have not only determined the fate of Russia in the greatest years of her life, but became a world phenomenon, and brought out, along with reactionary and bourgeois slogans, the two most important banners around which all humanity gathers."

Pollution. Harmonic POLLUTION is characterized by indiscriminate disposal of chromatic refuse in a diatonic landscape. The process is vividly illustrated by a fetid organ arrangement of Chopin's *Nocturne* in E-flat major, in which the initial ascending interval of a major sixth, from B-flat to G, is infested by noxious chromatic runs. A polluted version of Prokofiev's *Peter and the Wolf* has been published in America in the absence of a copyright agreement with the Soviet Union; it is characterized by vulgar insertion of auxiliary material in every available melodic or harmonic vacancy. Orchestral POLLUTION manifests itself in a general sonic flatulence and an infarction of supernumerary thirds and sixths. The rhythmic line, too, is an easy victim of POLLUTION. In the remarkable compound rhythmic design in Gershwin's song *I Got Rhythm*, the original asymmetric line is often grossly mutilated, reducing it to Abecedarian syncopation. Erudite arrangements of works of Bach and other classics, made by musicians of intelligence and taste, cannot be cited as examples of musical POLLUTION. Even hyperchromatic pullulation found in some transcriptions by Max Reger possesses validity, though they should be labelled "artificially flavored with chromatic additives." Some morphological transformations and homeological modifications are legitimate means of modernization. Examples of such artistic enhancement are *Symphonic Metamorphoses on Themes of Carl Maria von Weber* by Hindemith and the ballet *Le Baiser de la Fée* by Stravinsky, imaginatively deformed from themes of Tchaikovsky.

Polymetry. In a linear application, POLYMETRY is a succession of changing meters; polyphonically, POLYMETRY is the simultaneous use of several different meters. POLYMETRY dates back to the Renaissance, exemplified in the double time signature of Spanish dance music, 3/4 against 6/8. In operatic usage, POLYMETRY is encountered in scenes descriptive of simultaneous uncoordinated action, known under the name Imbroglio (literally, entanglement). The concluding section of Stravinsky's *Le Sacre du Printemps*, with its constantly changing time signatures, represents linear POLYMETRY at its greatest complexity. (It is characteristic of changing fashions that in 1940 Stravinsky rearranged this section in more uniform time signatures.) The unequal division of binary and ternary meters, which is a species of linear POLYMETRY, is found in Rimsky-Korsakov's opera *The Legend of the City of Kitezh*, in which the invading Mongols are characterized by the irregularly divided measures of 2/8 + 2/8 + 2/8 + 3/8 = 9/8 and 3/8 + 2/8 + 3/8 = 8/8. Linear POLYMETRY of this type is also characteristic of Balkan popular dances. Modern composers, fascinated by purely numerical properties of fractions representing traditional time signatures, often follow a predetermined arithmetical formula to establish a desired metrical progression. Boris Blacher makes use of the series of numerators 1, 2, 3, 4, 5, 4, 3, 2, 1, in his orchestral *Ornaments*. Elliott Carter employs "metric modulation" by changing meter and tempo in polyphonic writing. The Welsh composer Daniel Jones has developed a system of complex time signatures based on repeated numerical patterns, some of them of extraordinary length, e.g., 32322322-2322323323332332/4 and 9864323468/8, both used in his *Sonata for Three Kettledrums*. He also has elaborated the techniques of augmentation, diminution and retrograde in changing time signatures, designated by such arithmetical ALGORITHMS as 6432/8 and 3464/8. The numerators in all these examples represent the succession of repeated or changing numbers of beats in a bar.

Perhaps the most remarkable instance of contrapuntal POLYMETRY is found in the second movement of *Three*

Places in New England by Charles Ives, illustrating the meeting of two marching bands, with similar marching tunes played simultaneously at different tempi, in the ratio 4/3, so that four bars of the faster march equal three bars of the slower tempo. In his original manuscript Ives coordinated these different tempi within the uniform measures in 4/4 time, marking cross-accents wherever they occurred. At the suggestion made by Nicolas Slonimsky, Ives agreed to incorporate in the published score an alternative arrangement with non-coincidental barlines, in clear polymetric notation. In his performances of the work, Nicolas Slonimsky conducted three bars in 4/4 time with his right hand and four bars in *alla breve* time with his left hand. In this polymetric coordination, the downbeat of the left hand coincides successively with the downbeat of the right hand, then with the fourth beat of the right hand, with the third beat, with the second beat and again with the downbeat of the right hand. In the first bar the upbeat of the left hand falls between the second and the third beats of the right hand; in the next bar the upbeat of the left hand occurs between the downbeat and the second beat of the right hand, and so on. Those in the orchestra who had parts with the faster march were to follow the conductor's left hand and the rest his right hand. (A critic remarked that Slonimsky's performance was evangelical, for his right hand knew not what his left hand was doing.)

Polymodality. POLYMODALITY is a special case of POLYTONALITY in which the principal melodic lines are modal rather than explicitly major or minor. Polymodal harmonies are disposed with the best effect by the use of a triple pedal point in open harmony in a minor key, suggesting Dorian, Phrygian or Aeolian constructions.

Polyrhythmy. As the etymology of the word indicates, POLYRHYTHMY is the simultaneous occurrence of several different rhythms. POLYRHYTHMY differs from POLYMETRY in that the former indicates a combination of two rhythmic groups, usually consisting of mutually prime numbers of notes or irregular groups of non-coincident patterns, while the latter merely indicates the superposition, or a palimpsest, of two different meters usually having the same note values as their common denominator. If two measures of different time signatures are isochronous, then the effect is both polymetric and polyrhythmic. The problems of the polyrhythmic notation have been solved by composers of the AVANT-GARDE who prefer to indicate the duration of individual notes or rhythmic groups in seconds rather than note values. Another possible solution of polyrhythmic notation would be to introduce time signatures with denominators not limited to the powers of two. A time signature of 2/3 or 4/7 would replace triplets or septuplets in binary meters, but attempts to introduce such numerical innovations have been unsuccessful.

Polytetrachord. A term introduced by Nicolas Slonimsky in his *Thesaurus of Scales and Melodic Patterns*, POLYTETRACHORD is omnitonal. A major POLYTETRACHORD consists of 12 conjunct major tetrachords, traversing all 12 keys of the cycle of major scales. A minor POLYTETRACHORD consists of 12 keys of the cycle of minor scales. A partial use of the POLYTETRACHORD affords a rapid linear modulation into any major or minor key.

Polytonality. POLYTONALITY is the simultaneous use of several keys. In actual practice, it is difficult to sustain the acoustical separation of more than two different keys, thus reducing POLYTONALITY to BITONALITY. Four mutually exclusive triads are workable in linear arpeggios (e.g., C major, F-sharp major, D minor, G-sharp minor, distributed in ascending quadritonal passages), but the same four keys in columnar superposition could be made effective only by careful differentiation of instrumental groups (e.g., C major in the strings, F-sharp major in muted horns, D minor in clarinets and oboes and G-sharp minor in flutes and piccolos, with optional support of the strings by the bassoons and double-bassoons).

Simultaneous linear progressions of two or more different tonalities are in the category of POLYTONALITY. Bitonal scales with their tonics at a distance of major or minor thirds or sixths are entirely consonant, even though they run along different tonalities. But even scales in parallel major sevenths, if played at sufficiently large distances, become technically consonant. Theoretically, C major played in the lowest available register of the piano and B major scale at a distance of four, five or six octaves, minus a semitone, will form consonant harmony, because B in relation to the low C at such distances constitutes the 15th, 30th and 60th partial of the harmonic series. The coda of *Also sprach Zarathustra* of Richard Strauss contains a B major triad in the high treble with a doublebass playing a low C, an instance often referred to as the first explicit use of POLYTONALITY. Actually, the members of the B major triad in the treble represent the 60th, 75th and 90th partials of the harmonic series, generated by the low C, and are therefore consonant combinations. Genuine, acoustically pure polytonal combinations can be provided by playing the triads of D major, E major, G major and others against C major in the deep bass without falling into dissonance. Beyond the audible range, even F-sharp major, the farthest key in the cycle of scales from C major, can be brought into the harmonic series. Most polytonal combinations, however, are not even theoretically consonant. An amusing example of POLYTONALITY is Mozart's *Ein musikalischer Spass*, where he makes the horns play in different keys from the rest of the orchestra. But Mozart's professed intention in this "musical joke" was to ridicule the ignorance of village musicians. He could not have anticipated the time when such musical jokes would become a new technique.

Polytriads. POLYTRIADIC harmony may be regarded as a special case of POLYTONALITY, with mobile parts containing complete triads. If the triads move along a single scale or a mode, the resulting technique is POLYMODALITY. Homonymous triads, major and minor, encased within the compass of a perfect fifth (e.g., C, E-flat, E-natural, G), are often found in modern works. Such POLYTRIADS are *e duobus unum*, giving rise to modes possessing the characteristics of both major and minor keys.

Pop Music. The colloquial abbreviation of the term Popular Music into POP MUSIC corresponds to the depreciation and devaluation of materials and resources of the original product. POP MUSIC is a counterpart of Pop Art, with its appeal directed mainly towards the heterogeneous musical, unmusical and antimusical masses.

Its effects are achieved by the application of raucous and blatant sound amplified by electronics. POP MUSIC annexes numerous forms from the vast arsenal of sentimental ballads and country music and it manages to instill a tremendous amount of kinetic energy into its public manifestations. While POP MUSIC belongs in the category of DEMOTIC MUSIC, it tends to be more cosmopolitan in its appeal and capable of attracting miscellaneous groups of people without requiring special adaptation to the changing tastes of the audiences.

Pornographic Music. It was Eduard Hanslick who said that the last movement of Tchaikovsky's *Violin Concerto* suggested to him the hideous notion that music can actually stink to the ear. The literal depiction of an episode in *Symphonia Domestica* by Richard Strauss, which illustrates his retirement to the bed chamber with Frau Strauss, to the suggestive accompaniment of two conjugated trumpets, impressed some listeners at its first performance as indecent. In a symphonic interlude in Shostakovich's opera *Lady Macbeth of the District of Mzensk*, with the marital bed occupying the center of the stage, the trombone glissandi seem to give an onomatopoeic representation of sexual intercourse. Graphic notation offers excellent opportunities for suggestive pictorial pornography. The tetraphallic score *Mooga Pook* by the American composer Charles Amirkhanian is a fine example.

Potential Techniques. The number of POTENTIAL TECHNIQUES of musical composition is unlimited, as is the number of mathematical sets or matrices. The best-known numerical set in music is the method of composition with 12 tones, or DODECAPHONIC MUSIC. But it is possible to devise a hendecaphonic method, or decaphonic method, generated respectively by eleven or ten tones in a series. Any technique of composition is valid provided it is self-consistent. It is entirely justified to postulate a system in which only dissonant intervals are used. It is also conceivable to devise a method of composing only with nominal consonances (such a system was applied by Nicolas Slonimsky in his piano suite *Studies in Black and White*, in which only consonant intervals are used in a scheme of mutually exclusive counterpoint of pandiatonic sets in the right hand played on the white keys and panpentatonic figurations in the left hand played on the black keys). Any number of deficient or lipogrammatic systems of composition can be constructed by stipulating the omission of a note or a group of notes. Some modern poets experimented with omitting certain vowels or consonants in order to achieve a special effect. An American writer tied down the E key on his typewriter and wrote a whole novel without ever using that most frequent letter of the English alphabet, thus dispensing with the definite article, most personal pronouns, etc. The following techniques may be tabulated as possessing a workable rationale and some attractive coloristic features which might give them statistical chances of survival:

(1) Exclusive use of a limited number of notes in a scale, exemplified by the five-note scale, or Pentatonic scale and the Whole-Tone scale of six notes, the so-called Rimsky-Korsakov scale of alternating whole tones and semitones, a scale of nine notes consisting of three dis-

junct minor thirds with passing notes within the interval of each minor third, etc. (2) Various lipogrammatic lipographic scales, including the hendecaphonic scale and decaphonic scale, often used by serial composers who do not wish to be restricted to the orthodox dodecaphonic method. (3) Residual scales, in which the notes left over in a lipogrammatic composition are used as a matrix in a coda or a cadential codicil. In a hendecaphonic composition, such a codicil would contain a single note repeated in unison, in octave duplications, or in triplicate, quadruplicate, quintuplicate, sextuplicate and septuplicate, using all available octave points. Residual scales are legitimate devices in the building of dodecaphonic series. Thus the seven notes of the C major scale joined by the five notes of the pentatonic scale of the black keys would form a 12-tone matrix. Such a complex may also be called a conjugated diatonic-pentatonic complex. (4) Intervallic lipographs, in which certain intervals are deliberately avoided in a serial set. Thirds and sixths, being most intimately associated with classical harmony, may be peremptorily excluded in favor of the seconds and sevenths in order to secure a prevalence of dissonant intervals. Emphatic use of naked fourths and fifths, to the exclusion of all other intervals, is a lipographic device to conjure up an archaic effect. A growing fashion in modern music is the selective assignment of a certain interval to a specific instrument. Béla Bartók made such a selective distribution of intervals in the second movement, *Game of the Couples*, of his *Concerto for Orchestra*, in which five pairs of wind instruments are each given a distinct interval to cultivate. Several modern composers apply such intervallic lipographs to instruments in chamber music. (5) Derivative sets, made available as functions of a certain melodic figure differentiated by a given intervallic modulus. Let us differentiate a descending whole-tone scale in the bass by an ascending set of the following intervals: octave, major tenth, perfect 12th, two octaves, etc. Its derivative function will be the ascending melodic line of the following intervals: whole tone, semitone, sesquitone, whole tone, etc. This is a very important progression governing the harmonization in major triads in root position in contrary motion, which is found in Liszt's symphonic poem *Divine Comedy* and in the second act of Puccini's opera *Tosca*, announcing the entrance of the Chief of Police. Let us now harmonize the ascending whole-tone scale in the melody using the same function, that is harmonization by major triads in root position in contrary motion following the intervallic distances between the melody and the bass at a perfect octave, a major tenth, a perfect 12th, a double octave, etc. The function in the bass will be a descending pattern of the following intervals: whole tone, semitone, sesquitone, whole tone, whole tone. This is the inversion of the melodic function obtained by differentiating by the same modulus the descending whole-tone scale in the bass. We find then that the whole-tone scale differentiated either in a descending bass or in an ascending melodic line will result in an identical function, inverted, and will thus constitute a reciprocal function, or an idempotent. Most interesting of all such reciprocal sets are those in which the principal equation is tonal and the derivative is atonal. A good example is an ascending diatonic scale in the melody arranged in two-part counterpoint with the stipulation that the derivative function should be a descending

set seeking the nearest available nominal consonance. Under such conditions the differentiated ascending C major scale in the melody will result in a quasi-chromatic descending derivative set in the bass: C, B, A, A-flat, G, F-sharp, E and E-flat. But an ascending C major scale in the bass, under similar conditions, will produce a different descending derivative in the melody, C, B, G-sharp, F, E, C-sharp, B, A. The different results are explained by the fact that while a perfect fifth is a consonance, its inversion, a perfect fourth, is not. Using consonant intervals as the functional operator is of interest because of the possibility of arranging atonally shaped melodies in triadic harmonies. There is a fertile field for experimentation along these lines, for instance harmonizing the ascending chromatic scale in the melody using only members of a single major triad in the bass. (Beginning with C in the melody, it is possible to harmonize the ascending chromatic scale up to A by using only members of the F major triad in the bass, descending and ascending without producing any dissonant intervals, e.g., C, A, F, C, A, F, A, C, F, A.) Such exercises in consonant counterpoint provide unexpected illumination on the nature of diatonic and chromatic scales in their relationship to triadic tonality. (6) Intervallic progressions using only consonant intervals with certain specifications can provide a fresh resource for new contrapuntal techniques. A very fertile set of conditions is this: select two consonant intervals and use them in an unbroken series of alternations, with this proviso, that one of the voices must move by degrees, that is a major or a minor second up or down, the other voice adjusting itself accordingly to form the next interval. Let us take the octave E-E and the fifth as the next interval. We now move the upper E to F; since the next interval must be a perfect fifth, the lower voice must move to B-flat. Now let us move the upper note back to E, and since the next interval is again an octave, then the lower voice must go down to E as well. It is now the turn of the lower voice to move up and down gradually. It moves up to F; since the next interval must be a perfect fifth, the upper voice must come down from E to C. The F in the lower voice now returns to E, and since the next interval must be an octave, then the upper voice ascends from C to E. Now the lower voice goes down to D; the next interval is a perfect fifth, so the upper voice comes down from E to A. Trying again, while observing the same conditions of gradual progression vs. free intervallic leaps, the upper voice may go a major second up to F-sharp; in this case the lower voice must respond by moving up to B, forming a perfect fifth with F-sharp; after a return to the octave on E, the upper voice may descend to D-sharp, which will be seconded by the lower voice going up to G-sharp. Then both voices return to their respective E's, and the lower voice will take over the role of the *cantus firmus*. It will move, as the upper voice did before, to F-sharp, forcing the upper voice to move to C-sharp, and after passing through the octave, will descend to D-sharp, necessitating the lowering of the upper voice to A-sharp. The final interval will again be the octave. What is remarkable in this little exercise is that every note of the chromatic scale will be covered, and nine minor triads will be outlined by their tonics and dominants. By adding the missing mediants for each one of these chords in different octaves, one would obtain a third voice of surprising melodiousness. The next experiment may be conducted with a dissonant interval alternating with a consonant interval and finally with two dissonant intervals. The addition of supplemental contrapuntal voices will supply a further resource. (7) Homeological variations, obtained by extensions or compressions of thematic intervals provide a novel method of structural variations. The simplest case is exemplified by a uniform duplication of all intervals. Such an operation would convert Bach's *Chromatic Fugue* into an impressionistic piece of music, because all its semitones would be replaced by progressions of exotic-sounding whole-tone scales. If the intervals of the same fugue are halved, the outcome will be a complex of icositetraphonic harmony.

Prepared Piano. PREPARED PIANO is an instrumental technique, which alters the sound by placing various small objects, such as bolts, nuts, metal clips, coins, on the piano strings. The idea may be traced to the old schoolboy trick of putting a piece of paper on the piano strings to produce a tinkling, harpsichord-like sound. The first modern composer to experiment scientifically with such devices was Henry Cowell, who initiated the technique of playing directly on the piano strings, mostly glissando, and developed an extraordinary skill in stopping the strings so as to change their pitch, enabling him to play an ascending scale on the keyboard which, because of the alteration of the length of strings, resulted in a descending scale in actual sound. His disciple John Cage explored further possibilities along these lines, and gave the name to the altered instrument of PREPARED PIANO.

Prepense Music. This is music aforethought; it is the antonym of UNPREMEDITATED MUSIC.

Probability. The PROBABILITY of incidence of certain intervals, notes and rhythms in a given piece of music depends on its predetermined melorhythmic idiom. The PROBABILITY of occurrence of an unresolved major seventh in a composition written before 1900 is virtually nil, while the PROBABILITY of such incidence in DODECAPHONIC MUSIC is very high. Similarly, the PROBABILITY of a concluding chord being a dissonance is zero for the 19th century, but it increases exponentially after 1900. The commanding importance of the tritone in ATONAL and DODECAPHONIC MUSIC makes its appearance a probable event in compositions in which the key signature is absent. The PROBABILITY of incidence of all 12 different notes and 12 different intervals in relation to the starting tone in a full chromatic scale is obviously 100%. Some problems of PROBABILITY lead to paradoxical solutions. Here is an example. How many tone-rows of 12 different notes and 11 different intervals is it possible to build within the range of the octave that would form an increasing or a decreasing arithmetical progression if only the absolute value of each interval is taken into consideration irrespective of its direction, whether ascending or descending? The surprising answer is 2. Taking C as the point of departure, the rows will be: C, B, D-flat, B-flat, D, A, E-flat, A-flat, E, G, F, F-sharp, and its retrograde, each one changing intervallic direction in alternation, pendulum-like.

Progressive Jazz. In the first half of the century JAZZ was principally a spontaneous product of mass improvisa-

tion with untutored instrumentalists achieving fantastic virtuosity simply because they were not told by any teacher that the technical tricks they performed were unplayable. In 1950 a natural desire arose among the second generation of JAZZ players to acquire gloss, polish and even theoretical knowledge. They studied with eminent European composers resident in the United States and they listened to records of modern music. They became conversant with such terms as ATONALITY and POLYTONALITY and even DODECAPHONY. They discarded the lowly banjo of the early jazz period as though ashamed to confess their plebeian social origin; they annexed a full complement of the Baroque ensemble in their orchestras. With full credentials, a movement was launched, grandly described as PROGRESSIVE JAZZ. Technical resources kept pace with the dignity of the orchestral presentation. The WHOLE-TONE SCALE was rediscovered as an ultra-modern device and played in unison by the violins. Two different keys were used simultaneously in a daring display of POLYTONALITY. The square time was diversified occasionally by asymmetric rhythms; sometimes compound meters were inserted. But despite these adornments and borrowings from respectable sources, PROGRESSIVE JAZZ could never attain distinction and soon gave way to a more homely but less pretentious style of jazzification.

Prolepsis. Schlegel said: "Der Historiker ist ein rückwärts gekehrter Prophet." The notion that a historian might be a prophet of the past is most provocative. The modern cultivation of some of the recessive traits of the musical past represents such a prophecy turned backwards. Consecutive fifths were the rule before the advent of tertian counterpoint; they were strictly forbidden in classical music, but returned early in the 20th century in the guise of neoarchaic usages, and were further reinforced in the practice of consecutive triadic harmonies. The dissonant heterophony of ancient modalities was incorporated as a novelty in NEO-PRIMITIVISM. The "Wicked Bible" became a collector's item because of a negative particle inadvertently omitted from the commandment forbidding adultery. Erik Satie drew a table of anti-commandments in his *Catéchisme du Conse-vatoire* in which he ridiculed the elevation of once forbidden practices to the status of harmonic laws: "Avec grand soin tu violeras/ Des règles du vieux rudiment./ Quintes de suite tu feras/ Et octaves pareillement./ Au grand jamais ne résoudras/ De dissonance aucunement. / Aucun morceau ne finiras/ Jamais par accord consonnant." The exclusion of major triads in the Schoenbergian table of commandments is the most striking instance of PROLEPSIS. Indeed, every determined violation of the academic rules becomes a case for PROLEPSIS if such a violation becomes itself a rule.

Proletarian Music. The ideological upheaval that accompanied the Soviet revolution of 1917 posed an immediate problem of creating arts that would be consonant with the aims and ideals of socialist society. Since the political structure of the Soviet government was that of the dictatorship of the proletariat, it was imperative to postulate a special type of literature, drama, art and music that would be proletarian in substance and therefore accessible to the popular masses. Some Soviet theoreticians proposed to wipe off the slate of the arts the entire cultural structure that preceded the revolution and to create a *tabula rasa* on which to build a new proletarian edifice. Among suggestions seriously offered by some musicians in the early days of the Soviet revolution was the confiscation of all musical instruments in order to abolish the tempered scale and to construct new instruments based on the acoustically pure intervals. A more appropriate suggestion was made to compose music which included sounds familiar to a proletarian worker. A symphony of the factory was actually staged in an experimental demonstration, with singers and players placed on roof-tops. Shostakovich included a factory whistle in the score of his *May First Symphony*. Alexander Mossolov wrote a ballet called *Iron Foundry,* in which a large sheet of steel was shaken to imitate the sound of the forge. Unsuccessful attempts were made to proletarianize the librettos of old operas. In one production, Puccini's opera *Tosca* was advanced from the Napoleonic times to those of the Paris Commune. Tosca kills not the chief of the Roman police but the anti-Communard general Gallifet, disregarding the fact that the actual general Gallifet died in bed long after the fall of the Commune. Meyerbeer's opera *The Huguenots* was renamed *The Decembrists* and the action transferred to December 1825 to celebrate the rebellion of a group of progressive-minded aristocrats against the accession to the throne of the Czar Nicholas I. The notorious Russian Association of Proletarian Musicians (RAPM) was founded in 1924 to pass judgment on the fitness and unfitness of all music for proletarian consumption. It stipulated an arbitrary code of desirable musical attributes, among them unrelenting optimism, militant socialism, proletarian class consciousness, representational programmaticism and the preferential use of major keys. Beethoven was commended by the RAPM for his rebellious spirit; among Russian composers Mussorgsky was singled out as a creator of realistic art. A difficult problem was posed by Tchaikovsky. His profound pessimism and fatalism, his reactionary political views and particularly his homosexuality seemed an insurmountable barrier for the RAPM theoreticians to overcome. But Tchaikovsky was a favorite composer not only of the popular masses but also of the entire Presidium of the Soviet of People's Commissars. Even from the purely musical standpoint Tchaikovsky was theoretically unacceptable. His preference for minor keys and for melancholy moods in his operas and symphonies were the very antinomy of all that the new society of Soviet Russia stood for. In their attempt to rationalize the popularity of the *Pathétique Symphony,* the RAPM reached the acme of casuistry. In this work, so the argument went, Tchaikovsky delivered a magnificent funeral oration on the tomb of the bourgeoisie, and the superb artistic quality of this lamentation could not fail to please proletarian listeners. But soon the dialectical self-contradictions became evident even to the most obdurate members of the RAPM and factional strife pulled their ideology apart. There were also signs of repugnance against the vicious attacks led by the RAPM against the surviving composers of the pre-revolutionary times, greatly esteemed Conservatory professors and any others who dared to oppose its untenable ideology. The entire controversy was suddenly resolved when the Soviet government summarily disbanded the RAPM. As one composer expressed the nearly unanimous satisfaction at this action, "We could once again dare to write music in 3/4 time," alluding to the RAPM's ridiculous insistence that proletarian music ought to be written in march time.

The valid residue of PROLETARIAN MUSIC found its way to Germany and to America assuming special national idioms. Simplicity of form, utilization of popular dance rhythms and, in theatrical music, a selection of subjects from Revolutionary history or class warfare, were the main characteristics of music for the Proletariat. In America, Proletarian opera flourished briefly in the 1930s with Marc Blitzstein as its chief proponent. In Germany, Kurt Weill, working in close collaboration with the dramatist Bertolt Brecht, created a type of music drama that in its social consciousness had a strong affinity with PROLETARIAN MUSIC. In Russia itself, after the disbandment of the RAPM, viable ideas of PROLETARIAN MUSIC were absorbed in the doctrine of SOCIALIST REALISM.

Prolixity. Brevity is not necessarily an ideal; PROLIXITY is not always a fault. In classical music, PROLIXITY was ingrained in the forms of sonata and court dances, with the required repetitions of complete sections. Only the impatience of modern performers impels them to disregard such redundancies. "Brevitate gaudent moderni," to quote a recurring *incipit* of medieval musical treatises. Beethoven's *Eroica* concludes with the tonic chord repeated 28 times. By contrast, Prokofiev's *March* from *Love for Three Oranges,* ends abruptly on a single C major triad. The natural aversion of modern musicians to restatement and overstatement extends also to tonal sequences with their predictable turns. This homologophobia led finally to the collapse of the tonal system itself, and inspired Schoenberg to promulgate the principle of non-repetition of thematic notes and the formulation of his method of composition with twelve tones related only to one another.

Proportional Representation. Among thousands of conflicting musical theories, each claiming superiority over the others, no attempt has yet been made to conduct a statistical survey of the frequency of occurrence of every note of the scale in a given composition. Yet such a computation might well provide an illuminating insight into PROPORTIONAL REPRESENTATION of diatonic and chromatic notes, and the role of tonal centers. In serial composition, in particular, a statistical analysis can measure the strength of the gravitational force that attracts atonal and serial groups to a putative keynote. The duration of each note will have to be considered as a multiplying factor. Thus, if the least common denominator is an eighth-note, then a half-note would carry the same specific weight as four eighth-notes. It would also be possible to evaluate the relative hierarchy of the members of a tone-row. A serial composer may plan in advance a PROPORTIONAL REPRESENTATION of specific notes, intervals and durations. If desired, an artificial tonic can be posited by assigning to it the greatest frequency of incidence. This technique is applicable to all serial sets, even those containing only three or four notes. Rhythmic sets can be similarly arranged according to a predetermined formula of PROPORTIONAL REPRESENTATION. The method is particularly fruitful in building melodies and rhythms of a primitivistic type, in which the repetition is of the essence.

Pseudo-Exoticism. To an imaginative composer, the attraction of exotic lands is in inverse ratio to available information about such lands and in direct ratio to the square of the distance from the non-beholder. "Turkish" music, which had nothing in common with real Turkish modalities, enjoyed a great vogue in the 18th century and was used as a PSEUDO-EXOTIC resource by Mozart. When dancers from Indochina came to perform at the Paris Exposition of 1889, French musicians were fascinated by the unfamiliar sounds of resonant bells and muffled drums in the percussion group that accompanied the dancers. The emergence of IMPRESSIONISM in France owes much to this dance music from the Orient as refracted through the "auricular sites" of a European. The legends of the East provided poetic materials for song texts and operatic librettos. These tenuous impressions were transmuted into a *musique nouvelle,* vibrant with voluptuous *frissons.* Oriental scales were represented in the works of Debussy, Ravel and their imitators by the pentatonic scale which could be conveniently played on the black keys of the piano keyboard. Great composers were able to create a new art derived, however inaccurately, from Oriental sonorities; in fact, several composers, natives of Asia, who studied music in Paris, began to mold their own authentic modes in the Impressionistic manner. When the novelty began to fade, the pentatonic scale, the tinkling bells and other paraphernalia of Oriental music, found their way into the commercial factories of vulgar musicians plying their trade with much profit in the semi-classical division of "modern" music, in Broadway shows and on the soundtrack of exotic movie spectaculars. The proliferation of this PSEUDO-EXOTICISM resulted in the contamination of the genuine product, so that Orientalistic music eventually disappeared from decent practice.

Pseudo-Music. PSEUDO-MUSIC differs from ANTI-MUSIC in that the latter is a rebellious inversion of all musical values, while PSEUDO-MUSIC is an imitative product of specious validity. PSEUDO-MUSIC of the modern type is manufactured by semi-professionals who possess a modicum of Abecedarian talent for sentimental melody and hymn-book harmony. Feminine PSEUDO-MUSIC, usually produced by women pianists and singing teachers, has some documentary value as an illustration of neo-Biedermeier culture. Some such pieces of salon music have achieved tremendous popularity, among them, the romances of Carrie Jacobs Bond, the pianistic trivialities of Cécile Chaminade, and, the greatest of them all, *Prière d'une vierge* by Thekla Badarzewska.

Punitive Music. Relentless playing of a trivial tune arranged in repellent harmonies may well be used, and possibly has been used by dictatorial regimes, to extract confessions from suspected music lovers. A similar practice is pursued in the form of a musical massage in democratic countries, by means of juke boxes or other instruments of torture, in public restaurants, in jet planes waiting for a chance to make a scheduled departure, at bus terminals and railroad stations, with the ultimate intention of weakening sales resistance to a commercial prod-

uct among captive listeners. For an entirely different purpose, Erik Satie, who detested audiences, directed to have his piano piece, pointedly titled *Vexations,* to be performed 840 times in succession. His punitive design, however, was circumvented by a group of sado-masochists who carried Satie's instructions to the letter and had, on 9–10 September 1963, arranged in New York 840 performances of Satie's piece, played without interruption by a relay of willing pianists who obtained thereby not only a measure of secret gratification but also a great deal of publicity.

Quaquaversal Dispersion. Macropolysyllables are not necessarily frivolous when they define a phenomenon in a memorable or picturesque phrase. QUAQUAVERSAL DISPERSION is a convenient macropolysyllable to describe a radial expansion of the central cumulus of sonic matter, similar to the process of gradual sliding of geological layers, to which the term QUAQUAVERSAL (literally, turning in different directions) is applied in science.

Quarter-Tones. QUARTER-TONES are not modern inventions; they are found in the ancient Greek enharmonic scale. Many romantic composers of the 19th century thought of reviving QUARTER-TONES as a unit of an icositetraphonic scale. George Ives, father of Charles Ives, who was Army band leader during the Civil War, experimented with tuning his instruments a quarter-tone apart. A systematic investigation of QUARTER-TONES began about 1900; among its pioneers were the Mexican composer Julián Carrillo and Alois Hába of Czechoslovakia. Further details are found in the entry on MICRO-TONALITY.

Radial Distribution. RADIAL DISTRIBUTION of a linear series is a maximum dispersion of the constituent tones, such as occurs in a technique commonly described by a term borrowed from art, POINTILLISM. The visual impression from an actual score is a picture of tonal particles appearing and disappearing in the outer registers of orchestral instruments, or extreme octaves on the piano keyboard. The geometry of this image is particularly striking in the appearance of the instrumental works by Anton von Webern.

Ragtime. RAGTIME is the earliest manifestation of American syncopated music, which was soon to rise to glory, in JAZZ. It was RAGTIME that gave prominence to the piano in popular music. Its rhythmic formula approximates that of the Toccata, with rapid motion and cross-accents. Henry F. Gilbert and Charles Ives cultivated RAGTIME rhythms early in the century. Debussy made use of RAGTIME rhythms in his *Golliwog's Cake Walk* in the piano suite *Children's Corner.* The proliferation of RAGTIME must have been pervasive, considering the outcries of shock and indignation in the music periodicals in the dying days of the old century. An editorial writer fulminated in an article entitled "Degenerate Music," published in *The Musical Courier* of 13 September 1899: "A wave of vulgar, filthy, and suggestive music has inundated the land. The pabulum of theater and summer hotel orchestras is 'coon music.' Nothing but RAGTIME prevails, and the cake-walk with its obscene posturings, its lewd gestures.... One reads with amazement and disgust of the historical and aristocratic name joining in this sex dance. Our children, our young men and women, are continually exposed to the contiguity, to the monotonous attrition of this vulgarizing music. It is artistically and morally depressing, and should be suppressed by press and pulpit." In 1901 the American Federation of Musicians adopted a resolution that its members "shall henceforth make every effort to suppress and discourage the playing and publishing of such musical trash by substituting the works of recognized and competent composers, thereby teaching the general public to appreciate a wholesome, decent, and intellectual class of music." When the famous prima donna Nordica included a song by the American composer Ethelbert Nevin in her Chicago recital in 1901, the Chicago *Tribune* deplored her "sense of the fitness of things" in singing a "coon song" alongside a group of German lieder. The monthly *Journal of the International Music Society,* in its issue of June 1905, described RAGTIME in the following words: "It suggests the gait of a hurried mule among anthills; there is a cross-rhythm, with a kind of halting contrapuntal ornamentation in the accompaniment which sometimes brings a stress onto the fourth beat of the bar. The phrases being no longer presented with regular and recurrent pulsations, give rise to a sense of disorder, which, combined with the emotional expression of the music, suggests an irresponsibility and a sense of careless jollity agreeable to the tired or vacuous brain."

As late as 1916, RAGTIME was still a phenomenon to be abhorred, to judge by a letter to the editor from the writer Ivan Narodny published in the New York *Evening Sun:* "The rhythm of RAGTIME suggests the odor of the saloon, the smell of backyards and subways. Its style is decadent. It is music meant for the tired and materially bored minds. It is essentially obvious, vulgar, and yet shockingly strong for the reason that it ends fortissimo." But there were also some philosophically analytic voices in the press. Rupert Hughes wrote soberly in the *Musical Record* of Boston of 1 April 1899: "If RAGTIME were called *tempo di raga* or *rague-temps,* it might win honors more speedily. If the word could be allied to the harmonic rage of the East Indians, it would be more acceptable. The Negroes call their clog-dancing 'ragging' and the dance a 'rag'. There is a Spanish verb *raer* (to scrape), and a French naval term, *ragué* (scraped), both doubtless from the Latin *rado.* RAGTIME will find its way gradually into the works of some great genius and will thereafter be canonized, and the day will come when the decadents of the next, the 20th century, will revolt against it and will call it 'a hidebound, sapless, scholastic form, dead as its contemporaries, canon and fugue.' Meanwhile, it is young and unhackneyed, and throbbing with life. And it is racial."

Realism. Generally speaking, the term REALISM as applied to music describes a type of programmatic romanticism, which is intended to picture a landscape or represent a psychological state. REALISM has acquired a special meaning in the nomenclature of Soviet music, usually appearing in the dual formula of SOCIALIST REALIASM whose function is to give a realistic reflection of contemporary life from the standpoint of Socialist society. Soviet composers are constantly urged to cultivate musical REALISM, to write music of concrete

images rather than abstract formalism, to preserve the national tradition of each of the constituent members of the Soviet Union, using the melodic and harmonic language accessible to the masses and contributing to the realistic understanding of life itself.

Redundancy. In electronics guidance systems, REDUNDANCY is a safety factor in the proper functioning of the machine. If a part fails, its redundant replacement immediately goes into action; and if that one fails, still another part is activated to perform the same function. In music, REDUNDANCY is represented by an ostentatious repetition of a thematic motive. It has its application in serial complexes of intervallic, rhythmic and coloristic parameters. By assigning a certain interval for a redundant use by an instrument, an associative equation is established, so that the interval becomes the identifying motto of the instrument itself. Some serial composers assign a single note to an instrument, so that the instrument and the note become inalienably bound. This evokes the memories and practices of serf orchestras in Tsarist Russia, consisting of wind instruments, of which each could produce but a single note, so that each serf playing that instrument often became known under the nickname of E-flat, F-sharp, etc. (When several serfs escaped from the estate of a music-loving Russian landlord, he put out an official notice asking the police to be on the lookout for the fugitives, giving their musical names as identification.)

Replication. In their search for effective and direct musical formulas, modern composers have increasingly turned back to the primitivistic pattern of simple repetition, a sort of bio-musical REPLICATION of a subject keeping its identity as unalterable as the design on an ancient Peruvian poncho. The most celebrated instance of such REPLICATION is Ravel's *Boléro* in which the variations are limited to changes from one instrumental color to another. A less literal type of REPLICATION is MONOTHEMATISM, of which Debussy's *String Quartet* is a perfect example. Still another variant is the thematic REPLICATION of a musical monogram, which spells out a name or a common word in letter-notes, usually in German notation. A modern example is the *Eighth String Quartet* by Shostakovich, which is built on his initials in German spelling, D. S. C. H. the letter S representing E-flat (Es). Shostakovich uses the same personal monogram in his *Tenth Symphony.* Some members of the AVANT-GARDE have carried the principle of REPLICATION to the ultimate limit of a single note recorded on tape without any change in dynamics and without a rhythmic interruption.

Rescue and Escape Terms. Many new musicological terms ambiguously descriptive of a modern style, idiom or technique are RESCUE AND ESCAPE TERMS, words and phrases used as nebulous definitions of uncertain musical events. The term OMNITONALITY belongs to this category; others may be found by industrious perusal of music magazines beginning in 1910.

Retardation. The device of RETARDATION, melodic, harmonic or contrapuntal, consists of holding over a certain note or a harmonic complex while other parts of the musical fabric are shifted. In modern music RETARDA-

TION is not developed in accord with the moving elements but continues indefinitely in order to create a sustained discord. In pandiatonic techniques, this procedure results in a chain of superpositions of the principal triadic harmonies.

Rock 'n' Roll. American popular music has evolved from the dual resources of urban and rural folksongs. Urban popular music found its primary inspiration in the unique modalities of the Negro Spirituals, with their lowered third and seventh, which constitute the foundation of the BLUES. RAGTIME, JAZZ, SWING, and such lateral developments as BE-BOP and BOOGIE-WOOGIE, all preserve the character of city music. Quite different was the type of popular music cultivated in the rural regions of the country, which represented mostly the tradition of European, and particularly English, folksongs. This country music was marked by a leisurely pace devoid of the nervous excitement and syncopated beat peculiar to the popular productions of city life. With the advent of the electronic age, the barriers between urban and rural music were brought down. In the ensuing implosion and fusion of both genres, a new art was born, which found its fullest expression in the phenomenon of ROCK 'N' ROLL.

The combination of the words ROCK and ROLL appears for the first time on a Columbia phonograph record issued in the early 1930s; the rhythm of this specimen was that of a barcarolle, and the words Rock and Roll obviously referred to the gentle swaying of a boat on the river. This rural serenade was gradually transformed into a much more aggressive type of popular music, ROCK 'N' ROLL. or simply ROCK. Its cradle was in the radio broadcasting studios of Tennessee in about 1950. In it, the weaker rhythms of country music overflowed the syncopation of classical JAZZ and reduced the aggressive asymmetry of the urban product to the monotony of an even beat in square time. In ROCK 'N' ROLL the pendulum-like rhythmic motion produces a tremendous accumulation of KINETIC ENERGY, leading to a state of catatonic stupefaction among the listeners and the players themselves. The effect of this constant rhythmic drive is similar to that of the sinusoid wave with a steadily increasing amplitude created by the march of a regiment of soldiers across a suspension bridge, which can break the strongest steel. Thanks to the electronic amplification, ROCK 'N' ROLL became the loudest music ever heard. Otologists have warned that its addicts may lose the sensitivity to the higher harmonics of the human voice and become partially deaf. Ralph Nader, the American Cassandra of urban civilization, has cautioned the public against the danger of sonic pollution by ROCK 'N' ROLL in a letter addressed to a member of the Congress of the United States.

The protagonist of ROCK 'N' ROLL was Elvis Presley, who developed the pelvic technique of rhythmic swing. (He became known as Elvis the Pelvis.) Four Liverpudlians, who became celebrated under the cognomen The Beatles (a palimpsest of Beat and Beetles), joined the ROCK 'N' ROLL movement but evolved a distinctive style of their own, with some characteristics of the English ballad.

The remarkable feature of ROCK 'N' ROLL is the revival of archaic modality with its characteristic plagal cadences, the Dorian mode being a favorite. In harmony, the submediant is lowered in major keys and becomes the minor third of the minor subdominant triad. Parallel triadic progressions, adopted by Rock 'n' Roll, also impart an archaic modal quality to the music. It may well be that the fusion of old modes and modern rhythms will create a new type of SYNCRETISM of musical folkways.

Time magazine commented on ROCK 'N' ROLL in its issue of 18 June 1956: "An unrelenting, socking syncopation that sounds like a bull whip; a choleric saxophone honking mating-call sounds; an electric guitar turned up so loud that its sound shatters and splits; a vocal group that shudders and exercises violently to the beat while roughly chanting either a near-nonsense phrase or a moronic lyric in hillbilly idiom."

The Canadian underground newspaper, grandly named *Logos*, gave in 1969 this description of ROCK 'N' ROLL as a social force: "Rock is mysticism, revolution, communion, salvation, poetry, catharsis, eroticism, satori, total communication, the most vibrant art form in the world today. Rock is a global link, as young people everywhere plug into it and add to the form. What this new music suggested was raising your level of consciousness away from the fragmented, intellectual, goal-oriented time and material world to a unified sensual direction in a timeless spiritual environment."

The greatest mass demonstration of ROCK 'N' ROLL, and perhaps the greatest manifestation of the attractive power of music in all history, was the Woodstock, New York, Festival in August 1969, when an enormous crowd of young people, estimated at quarter of a million heads, congregated in a farmland to hear their favorite Rock groups. The happening had a profound sociological significance as well, for the audience consisting of youthful non-conformists, popularly known as hippies, seemed to be infused with the spirit of mutual accommodation, altruism and love of peace. ROCK 'N' ROLL music, at least on that occasion, proved that it has indeed the power to soothe a savage breast.

Rotation. In post-Schoenbergian developments of DODECAPHONIC MUSIC the 12-tone series is often modified by ROTATION. As the term implies, the series is shifted a space, so that at its next occurrence, it begins with the second note, and ends with the first; in the subsequent incidence, it starts on the third note, and ends on the second, etc. ROTATION in its various further developments is a fertile device of dodecaphonic techniques.

Scales. The American pedagogue Percy Goetschius used to play the C major scale for his students and ask them a rhetorical question, "Who invented this scale?" and answer it himself, "God!" Then he would play the WHOLE-TONE SCALE and ask again, "Who invented this scale?" And he would announce disdainfully, "Monsieur Debussy!"

Debussy did not invent the WHOLE-TONE SCALE, but he made ample use of it. Other scales, built on quaquaversal intervallic progressions, engaged the attention of composers: the so-called Hungarian Gypsy scale, the pentatonic scale suitable for orientalistic melismas, and the scale of alternating whole tones and semitones, which is classified in Russian encyclopedias as Rimsky-Korsakov's Scale. The modern Dutch composer Willem Pijper made prolix use of it, and his disciples, believing that it was his own invention called it Pijper's Scale. In fact, this scale, formed by the insertion of passing notes in the melodically spaced diminished seventh chord, was used by Liszt, Tchaikovsky and many other composers. Scriabin derived a scale of six notes from his MYSTIC CHORD, composed of three whole tones, a minor third, a semitone and a whole tone. Alexander Tcherepnin has devised a scale of nine notes consisting of a whole tone, a semitone, a semitone, a whole tone, a semitone, a semitone, a whole tone, a semitone, a semitone. The Spanish composer Oscar Esplá wrote music based on the scale of the following intervals: semitone, whole tone, semitone, semitone, semitone, whole tone, whole tone, whole tone.

Verdi was impressed by an exotic scale which he found in an Italian music journal, where it was described as "Scala enigmatica." It consists of a semitone, a minor third, three consecutive whole tones, and two consecutive semitones. At the age of 85 Verdi wrote a choral piece based on this "enigmatic" scale.

Ferruccio Busoni experimented with possible scales of seven notes and stated that he had invented 113 different scales of various intervallic structures. The first theorist to examine and classify scales based on the symmetrical division of the octave was Alois Hába in his book *Neue Harmonielehre*. Joseph Schillinger undertook a thorough codification of all possible scales having any number of notes from two to twelve, working on the problem mathematically. In his *Thesaurus of Scales and Melodic Patterns*, Nicolas Slonimsky has tabulated some two thousand scales within the multiple octave range, including such progressions as the Polytetrachord, bitonal scales of eight notes, scales of three disjunct major or minor pentachords aggregating to two octaves, etc.

Progressions of large intervals, thirds, fourths or fifths, cannot be properly described as scales, without contradicting the etymology of the word derived from scala, a ladder. But helix-like constructions, involving spiraling chromatics may well be called scales. Quarter-tone scales and other microtonal progressions also belong in this category.

Scotophilia. In biology, SCOTOPHILIA denotes the receptive phase of circadian rhythm in which the chief activity is performed in the dark; vampire bats, usually nocturnal, are outstanding examples of Scotophiliac animals. As applied to musical composition, SCOTOPHILIA is the love of dark and somber sonorities marked by a statistically certifiable prevalence of low registers and slow tempi, as in the symphonies of Sibelius. Interestingly enough, avant-garde composers, whose chosen self-appellation connotes a rapid movement forward, betray a curious addiction to static, somber and darksome moods and compositorial habits. Such composers may well be called Scotophiliacs.

Secundal and Septimal Harmonies. A distinct shift in harmonic structures occurred early in the 20th century as the tertian harmonies of triadic derivation began to give way to the more acute progressions in SECUNDAL HARMONIES and their SEPTIMAL inversions. Debussy wrote special studies in consecutive major seconds, treating them as concords requiring no resolution. SECUNDAL HARMONIES are also represented in Impressionistic works in the form of consecutive last inversions of

seventh chords. SEPTIMAL HARMONIES are the familiar devices in early JAZZ cadences, in which the seventh was the "blue note." Composers of the later generation used tonic major sevenths as cadential chords. SECUNDAL and SEPTIMAL HARMONIES are commonly used in PANDIATONIC structures.

Sensory Impact. The quantitative expansion of technical devices in modern music led to a corresponding SENSORY IMPACT on the listeners, often reaching the threshold of physical pain. Incessant playing of modern dance music, electronically amplified beyond the endurance of an average person, may well produce a positive conditioned reflex among the young. Professional music critics have for a century complained about the loudness of modern music, beginning with that of Wagner, but in their case the SENSORY IMPACT is measured not so much by the overwhelming volume of sound as by the unfamiliarity of the idiom. The epithets such as "barbaric" were applied with a fine impartiality to Wagner, Tchaikovsky, Berlioz and Prokofiev, while Debussy, Strauss and Mahler were often described as "cacophonous." It is the relative modernity that makes the SENSORY IMPACT intolerable to a music critic. "This elaborate work is as difficult for popular comprehension as the name of the composer," wrote the Boston *Evening Transcript* in its review of Tchaikovsky's *First Piano Concerto*. An index of vituperative, pejorative and deprecatory words and phrases, the Invecticon appended to Nicolas Slonimsky's *Lexicon of Musical Invective*, demonstrates the extraordinary consistency of the critical reaction to unfamiliar music. Even the gentle Chopin did not escape contumely; he was described in a daily London newspaper as a purveyor of "ranting hyperbole and excruciating cacophony."

Serendipity. SERENDIPITY is a nonce word, coined by Horace Walpole in 1754, and derived from the Arabian tale of the princes of Serendip who made important discoveries and found fortune by opportune accident and sagacious surmise. In music, SERENDIPITY is almost equivalent to intuition or inspiration, but it is applicable particularly to the realization of melodic, harmonic and intervallic relationships seemingly unconnected with the primary aim of a composer or theorist. Examples of SERENDIPITY are tabulated in the article on POTENTIAL TECHNIQUES.

Serialism. SERIALISM is a method of composition in which thematic units are arranged in an ordered set. Tonal SERIALISM was promulgated by Schoenberg in 1924, as the culmination of a long period of experiments with atonal chromatic patterns; in retrospect, Schoenberg's method may be regarded as a special case of integral SERIALISM, much as the special theory of relativity is a subset of general relativity. Schoenberg's method deals with the 12 different notes of the chromatic scale; integral SERIALISM organizes different intervals, different rhythmic values, dynamics, etc. in autonomous sets. Fritz Klein expanded the serial concept of dodecaphonic sets to different rhythmic and intervallic values. In his score, *Die Maschine*, published in 1921, he employs sets of 12 identical notes in irregular rhythms, "Pyramid Chords" consisting of intervals arranged in a decreasing arithmetical progression of semitones, and a harmonic complex consisting of 12 different notes and 11 different intervals, the *Mutterakkord*. The mathematical term "set," for a tone-row, was introduced by the American composer Milton Babbitt in 1946. He experimented with techniques of tonal, rhythmic and intervallic sets. George Perle proposed the term "set-complex" to designate 48 different forms generated by a fundamental dodecaphonic series. In all these sets the magic number 12 plays a preponderant role. In the general concept of SERIALISM, sets may contain any number of pitches, in any scale, including non-tempered intervals.

A summary of serial parameters comprises the following: (1) Twelve different pitches as developed by using the method of composition with 12 tones, including apocopated sets, hendecaphonic, decaphonic, enneaphonic, octophonic, heptaphonic, hexaphonic, pentaphonic, tetraphonic, triphonic, diphonic, monophonic and zerophonic. (2) Organization of melody containing 12 different intervals, from a semitone to the octave and the concomitant chords containing 12 different notes and 11 different intervals. (3) Twelve different rhythmic values, which may contain a simple additive set of consecutive integers, a geometrical progression, a set of Fibonacci numbers, etc. (4) Twelve different KLANGFARBEN, in which a melody consists of a succession of disparate notes played by 12 different instruments either in succession, in contrapuntal conjugation, or harmonic coagulation. (5) Spatial SERIALISM, in which 12 different instruments are placed in quaquaversal positions, with no instruments in close proximity. (6) Vectorial SERIALISM, in which the sound generators are distributed at 12 different points of the compass, according to 12 hour marks on the face of a clock, or else arranged spatially on the ceiling, on the floor, in the corners of the auditorium. (7) Dynamic SERIALISM, with 12 different dynamic values ranging from pianississississimo to fortississississimo, including the intermediate shadings of mezzo-piano and mezzo-forte. (8) Ambulatory SERIALISM, in which 12 musicians make their entrances and exits one by one, in contrapuntal groups, in stretto, or in the fugue, the latter being understood in the literal sense of running. (9) Expressionistic SERIALISM, in which actors and singers assume definite facial expressions marking their psychological identity. (10) SERIALISM of 12 different sound generators, including steamrollers, motor lawn mowers, steam pipes, radiators, ambulance sirens, etc. (11) SERIALISM of 12 visually different mobiles, each producing a distinctive noise. (12) SERIALISM of 12 teratological borborygmuses and sonic simulacra of various physiological functions.

Sesquipedalian Macropolysyllabification. Quaquaversal lucubration about pervicacious torosity and diverticular prosiliency in diatonic formication and chromatic papulation, engendering carotic carmination and decubital nyctalopia, causing borborygmic susurration, teratological urticulation, macroptic dysmimia, bregmatic obstipation, crassamental quisquiliousness, hircinous olophonia and unflexanimous luxation, often produce volmerine cacumination and mitotic ramuliferousness leading to operculate onagerosity and testaceous favillousness, as well as faucal obsonation, parallelepipedal psellismus, pigritudinous mysophia, cimicidal conspurca-

tion, mollitious deglutition and cephalotripsical stultitiousness, resulting despite Hesychastic omphaloskepsis, in epenetic opistography, boustrophedonic malacology, lampadodromic evagination, chartulary cadastration, merognostic heautotimerousness, favaginous moliminosity, fatiscent operosity, temulencious libration and otological oscininity, aggravated by tardigrade inturgescence, nucamentacious oliguria, emunctory sternutation, veneficial pediculation, fremescent dyskinesia, hispidinous cynanthropy, torminal opitulation, crapulous vellication, hippuric rhinodynia, dyspneic nimiety and favillous erethism, and culminating in opisthographic inconcinnity, scotophiliac lipothimia, banaustic rhinorrhea, dehiscent fasciculation, oncological vomiturition, nevoid paludality, exomphalic invultuation, mysophiliac excrementatiousness, flagitious dysphoria, lipogrammatic bradygraphy, orectic aprosexia, parataxic parorexia, lucubicidal nutation, permutational paranomasia, rhoncial fremitus, specular subsaltation, crapulous crepitation, ithyphallic acervation, procephalic dyscrasia, volitional volitation, piscine dermatology, proleptic pistology, verrucous alopecia, hendecaphonic combinatoriality, microaerophilic pandiculation and quasihemidemisemibreviate illation.

Sesquitone Scales. Sesquitone is an interval of three semitones. The SESQUITONE SCALE is a progression of minor thirds, or augmented seconds, depending on notation, and is identical with the arpeggiated diminished-seventh chord. Attractive ornamental effects can be obtained by infrapolation, interpolation and ultrapolation, or a combination of these processes. An infra-inter-ultrapolation of the SESQUITONE SCALE produces a chromatically inflected melodic pattern of an orientalistic type. The interpolation of a single note between the successive degrees of the SESQUITONE SCALE forms a scale of alternating whole tones and semitones, widely used by many composers, beginning with Liszt and Tchaikovsky. In Russian reference books it is described as Rimsky-Korsakov's Scale.

Silence. Poets often spoke of the eloquent and the harmonious quality of SILENCE. The lines in Félicien David's *Symphonic Ode* are appropriate: "Ineffables accords de l'éternel silence! / Chaque grain de sable/ a sa voix/ Dans l'ether onduleux le/ concert se balance: / Je le sens, je le vois!" The longest SILENCE explicitly written out is the five-bar rest in the score of *L'apprenti Sorcier* by Paul Dukas. György Ligeti composed a work consisting of a quarter-note rest. The most ambitious composition utilizing the effect of total silence is *4' 33"* by John Cage, scored for any combination of instruments, *tacet*, and subdivided into three movements during which no intentional sounds are produced. It was unheard for the first time at Woodstock, New York, on 29 August 1952, with David Tudor at the silent piano.

Singultation. The modern practice of onomatopoeic SINGULTATION is derived from the medieval hocketus in which the singing line is interrupted by a syncopated translocation of thematic components, producing hocketus or a singultus (both words mean hiccups). Brief detonations of kinetic energy in modern works are forms of SINGULTATION.

Socialist Realism. The Soviet Union was the first modern state that has attempted to regulate its art, literature, drama and music according to explicitly defined ideological principles. Since the structure of the Soviet government was derived from the doctrine of the dictatorship of the proletariat, a Russian Association of Proletarian Musicians (RAPM) arrogated to itself the right to dictate the proper musical forms suitable for the consumption of proletarian masses. It was disbanded by the Soviet government in 1932 after its failure to help in the creative formulation of mass music became evident. With the rise of the national consciousness in the component republics of the Soviet Union, it was realized by Soviet authorities that proletarian internationalism was no longer sufficient to serve as an enduring ideology. Surviving masters of old Russian music had to be accepted as representatives of the Russian masses; their classical precursors were glorified as exponents of progressive ideals consonant with the new Socialist reality of the Soviet era. Soviet composers were urged to create an art national in form and Socialist in content, a method which eventually became known as SOCIALIST REALISM. Stylistically, SOCIALIST REALISM requires the retention of the tonal system of composition, broadly based on the folk modalities of Russian songs and the native chants of other Republics of the Soviet Union. The doctrine of SOCIALIST REALISM concentrates on the national development of operas and secular oratorios, in which revolutionary ideals can be expressed verbally as well as musically. The Aristotelian formula of catharsis through pity and terror underlies the librettos of most Soviet operas and the scenarios of most Soviet ballets. Patriotic subjects are particularly recommended; they lend themselves readily to the triune formula which opens with a scene of happiness, goes through a period of sudden horror and concludes in a victory over adverse circumstances. The so-called "Leningrad Symphony" of Shostakovich is a remarkable example of this Aristotelian construction, particularly so because it was written during continued retreats of the Soviet armies before the Nazis, and yet its finale predicts Victory. The classical tradition of the *Tierce de Picardie,* with its major cadence, suits perfectly the Soviet preference for major keys. Anatoly Lunacharsky, first Commissar of Education of Soviet Russia explained the political advantage of major keys by comparing them with the convictions of the Bolshevik party, while minor keys were reflecting the introvert pessimism of the Mensheviks.

The doctrine of SOCIALIST REALISM does not preclude lyrical expression or individual allusions. Shostakovich uses the monogram D.S.C.H., corresponding, in German notation, to the notes D, E-flat, C and B as the main subject of his *Tenth Symphony.* However, many among Soviet composers, even as eminent as Miaskovsky, were often criticized by the exponents of SOCIALIST REALISM for their musical morbidity, anxiety and solipsistic introspection. In the domain of rhythm, marching time is a natural medium for the optimistic attributes of SOCIALIST REALISM, but it is reserved for its proper position in the finale of a symphony or the final chorus of an opera. In this respect, SOCIALIST REALISM merely continues the old tradition of Russian music. Even such melancholy composers as

Tchaikovsky and Rachmaninoff excelled in triumphant march-time movements.

In authoritative Soviet declarations, SOCIALIST REALISM is opposed to FORMALISM, which is described as an artificial separation of form from content and the excessive cultivation of purely external technical devices, particularly ATONALITY, POLYTONALITY and DODECAPHONY. The statutes of the Union of Soviet Composers provide a specific guidance to Soviet composers for their ideological concepts: "The greatest attention of Soviet composers must be given to the victorious progressive foundations of reality, to the heroic and luminous beauty that distinguishes the spiritual world of Soviet man, which must be incarnated in musical images full of life-asserting force. SOCIALIST REALISM demands an implacable opposition against anti-social modernistic movements, expressive of the decadence and corruption of contemporary bourgeois art, against genuflection and slavish obsequiousness before the culture of the bourgeoisie."

Sonic Exuviation. The effectiveness of a modernistic climax depends on an astute interplay of contrasts. One of the most effective dynamic devices is SONIC EXUVIATION, the shedding of old skin of instrumental sonority, a return to a state of primordial nakedness and a new dressing-up of musical materials and a gradual building of another climax, a cut-off of sonic matter, leaving a soft exposed bodily shape. Such a dramatic EXUVIATION occurs at the end of the last movement of *Three Places in New England* by Charles Ives, where a tremendously powerful heterogeneous complex of sound suddenly crumbles, and a residual gentle chord is heard in the quiet air.

Sonic Organization. Varèse defines music as ORGANIZED SOUND. It is logical to describe any musical composition, especially of the modern constructivist type, as a Sonic Organism which follows bio-musical laws. It is autogenetic, capable of natural replication induced by contrapuntal interpenetration of contrasting melorhythmic entities. SONIC ORGANIZATION presupposes an engineering plan, which takes into consideration an appropriate cross-pollination of musical themes.

Spatial Distribution. The placement of musicians on the stage, long a matter of tradition, has assumed an unexpected significance in modern times in the guise of musical vectorialism. Elliott Carter specifies the exact position of the players in his string quartets. Lukas Foss, in his *Elytres* for 12 instruments, places the musicians at maximum distances available on the stage. The use of directional loudspeakers in performances of ultra-modern works is an electronic counterpart of SPATIAL DISTRIBUTION. In German broadcasting studios experiments have been made in distributing a 12-tone row in serial works among 12 electronic amplifiers placed in a clock-like circle, with each amplifier being assigned an individual note of the series. Empirical applications of the principle of SPATIAL DISTRIBUTION have been made by various composers early in the century, notably by Erik Satie in his *Musique d' ameublement.*

Spectrum. By analogy with the prismatic SPECTRUM of primary colors, a totality of KLANGFARBEN can be described as a tonal SPECTRUM. Before the era of ELECTRONIC MUSIC, the colors of the auditory SPECTRUM were limited to the available instruments of actual manufacture. With the aid of electronic generators it is possible to build a SPECTRUM possessing an infinite capacity of instrumental colors, and the style and idiom of an entire work can be programmed by the proportional strength of such instrumental colors. The metaphor of a musical SPECTRUM is therefore justified by the actuality of its realization.

Specular Reflection. The mirror image in Baroque counterpoint is applied to mutually conjugated melodic inversions, in which the ascending intervals are reflected by descending intervals, and vice versa. It is theoretically possible to construct an infinite SPECULAR REFLECTION, in which the intervallic distance between the two mirrors recedes, so that intervals are inverted in the outer regions of the instrumental range, extending even into the inaudible spectrum of ultra-sonic and infra-sonic sounds. In some modern works written specially for dog audiences, ultra-sonics can achieve considerable effectiveness. Beyond the canine auditory range, a gap occurs until the frequency of light waves is reached. Mystically inclined composers may find pantheistic inspiration in these notions of passing from men through dogs to infinity.

Sprechstimme. SPRECHSTIMME—literally a speech-voice—is a term popularized in its expressive use by Schoenberg in *Pierrot Lunaire* and later works. It is an inflected speech, notated on the regular music staff by special symbols indicating the approximate height of the note. The method was used systematically for the first time in 1897 in the operatic melodrama *Königskinder* by Engelbert Humperdinck.

Static Music. Although the general trend of music since 1900 has been towards greater complexity of texture and greater variety of dynamics, an opposite movement has manifested itself in some circles of the Avant-Garde, aimed at total tonal immobility and static means of expression. STATIC MUSIC finds its logical culmination in works that are limited to a single note in unchanging dynamics, usually in pianissimo. The melosomatic impact of such a production may be considerable if the listener is forced to hear a single note played by an instrumentalist for a long time. The expectation of some change, constantly deceived, may cause an emotional perturbation of great psychological interest.

Stochastic Composition. The term STOCHASTIC was introduced into music by the Greek engineer and composer Iannis Xenakis, to designate an aleatory projection in which the sonic trajectory is circumscribed by the structural parameters of the initial thematic statement. (The word itself comes from the Greek root meaning "the aim of an arrow.") STOCHASTIC procedures are in actual practice equivalent to controlled improvisation.

Strategy and Tactics. Modern composers are forever seeking metaphors from other fields to enrich the rapidly obsolescent musical nomenclature derived from vague Italian words indicating form, speed, dynamic force or expression. Among such new metaphors are STRATEGY AND TACTICS. The general scheme of a modern symphony or a sonata is Strategical, while variations, cadenzas and contrapuntal elaborations are Tactical devices. Iannis Xenakis, the originator of the STOCHASTIC method of composition, extended the concept of STRATEGY AND TACTICS into an actual tournament between two orchestras and two conductors, exemplified in his antiphonal symphony entitled *Stratégie*. According to the composer's specifications, two orchestras perform simultaneously two different compositions, following the uncoordinated pair of conductors, and stopping at climactic points to survey the mutual gains and losses. At the end of the maneuver the audience votes to nominate the winner of this instrumental encounter.

Superfetation. When several viable musical ideas occur simultaneously and are contrapuntally conjugated without a preliminary statement, a melorhythmic SUPERFETATION is the result. The thematic embryos may then be separated to pursue their different courses; or else, the non-identical germinal subjects may remain unified like Siamese twins, treated collectively as bipartite entities which subsequently may enter into a secondary SUPERFETATION. Given a complete freedom of dissonant counterpoint, SUPERFETATION can be extended to thematic triplets, quadruplets, quintuplets, sextuplets, septuplets, octuplets, etc., interpenetrating and disengaging themselves in a multiplicity of instrumental or vocal lines.

Surrealism. The word SURREALIASM was coined in 1903 by the French poet Guillaume Apollinaire in his fantastic play *Les Mamelles de Tirésias*, in which he treated the problem of a transsexual transplantation of mammary glands, and which he subtitled "drame surréaliste." SURREALISM became a fashionable movement when André Breton published a surrealist manifesto in 1924. In it, he described SURREALISM as "psychic automatism," anti-rationalistic in essence and completely spontaneous in its creative process. Fantasy and free association were the normative factors of Surrealistic literature and art. Apollinaire described SURREALISM as the rational technique of the improbable. Jean Cocteau equated it with the essence of poetry; in his film *Le Sang du Poéte* he proposed to give a "realistic account of unreal phenomena." The famous French handbook, *Nouveau Petit Larousse*, defines SURREALISM tersely as "tendance d'une école à négliger toute préoccupation logique." Surrealism is oxymoronic in essence, thriving on the incompatibility of the opposites, exemplified by such images as cold flame, thunderous silence, painstaking idleness, quiet desperation. Names of persons often have a surrealistic ring. A Boston dentist, Dr. Toothacher, a Chicago gangster Alturo Indelicato, a Canadian insurance salesman John Death, were living examples of SURREALISM. The furlined cup and saucer, created by the 23-year-old artist Megret Oppenheim in 1936, is a typical surrealistic artifact. Surrealistic incongruity was exemplified also in a piece called *Bagel Jewelry*, a composition by a New York artist, in which a real bagel was encased in a jewelry box, with a pricetag of $100.

In a modern production of *Hamlet*, the King's line, "We shall call up our friends," acquired a surrealistic twist because of a telephone receiver placed on the table. The Renaissance paintings representing Biblical scenes in which musicians perform on the lute and the theorbo, are both anachronistic and surrealistic in their effect. SURRE-ALISM possesses an oneiristic quality, in which dreams become more real than life. The etymology of the word implies a higher degree of realism, penetrating into the subliminal human psyche.

Surrealist artists are fascinated by musical subjects. Salvador Dali humanized musical instruments. In one of his paintings, a faceless cellist plays on the spinal column of a human cello mounted on a pin. On its buttocks there are the familiar resonators in the forms of symmetric gothic F's. (Life imitates art. At an avant-garde concert in New York a lady cellist performed a solo on the spine of a fellow musician, using a regular bow and applying occasional pizzicatti to his epidermis.) Another musical painting by Dali, bearing the surrealistic title *Six Apparitions of Lenin on a Piano*, represents several heads of Lenin crowned with aureoles strewn across the keyboard. The Belgian surrealist René Magritte painted a burning bass tuba. In the art work *Object for Destruction* by the American surrealist Man Ray, a print of a human eye was attached to the pendulum of a metronome. Real metronomes are the instruments in the score by the Hungarian modernist György Ligeti, containing 100 metronomes all ticking at different speeds. In his vision of Socialist music of the future, the Soviet poet Vladimir Mayakovsky conjured up a symphony with rain conduits for flutes. The American band leader Spike Jones introduced a latrinophone, a surrealistic lyre made of a toilet seat strung with violin strings.

Apollinaire urged artists, poets and musicians to cultivate "the insane verities of art." No one has followed his advice more ardently than Erik Satie. He incarnated the spirit of inversion. He entitled his utterly surrealistic score *Parade* "ballet réaliste." Jean Cocteau wrote: "Satie's *Parade* removes the sauce. The result is a completely naked object which scandalizes by its very nakedness. In the theater everything must be false in order to appear true." Satie was very much in earnest when he wrote, "J'emmerde l'art—c'est un métier de con." The titles of his piano pieces are typical of surrealistic self-contradiction: *Crépuscule matinal de midi, Heures séculaires et instantanées, Tyrolienne turque, Sonatine bureaucratique, Fantaisie musculaire, Trois morceaux en forme de poire* (the latter, printed under a cover representing a pear, was a defiant response to criticism that his music was formless).

Swing. Among the many ephemeral terms descriptive of varieties of JAZZ, SWING has gained a permanent historical position. It is not a new slang expression. The word SWING appears in the titles of old American dance tunes: *Society Swing* of 1908, *Foxtrot Swing* of 1923, *Charleston Swing* of 1925. In 1932 Duke Ellington wrote a song with the incipit, *It Don't Mean a Thing if It Ain't Got That Swing*. SWING music achieved its first great boom in 1935, largely through the agency of the jazz clarinet player Benny Goodman, introduced to the public as the King of Swing. The American magazine *Downbeat* described SWING in its issue of January 1935 as "a musician's term for perfect rhythm." The November 1935 issue of the magazine carried a glossary of "Swing terms that cats use," in which SWING was defined as "laying it in the

groove." This metaphor, borrowed from the phonograph industry, gave rise to the once popular adjective "groovy," in the sense of neat, perk and pert.

SWING music must have exercised a hypnotic effect on the youth of the 1930s. The New York *Times* of 30 May 1938 ran the banner headline, "Swing Band Puts 23,400 in Frenzy. . . . Jitterbugs Cavort as 25 Orchestras Blare in Carnival." Self-appointed guardians of public morals lamented the new craze: "Pastor Scores Swing as Debasing Youth, Declares it Shows an Obvious Degeneracy in our Culture and Frothiness of Age," the New York *Times* headlined. Stravinsky, then a recent American citizen, endorsed Swing. *Time* Magazine quoted him as saying in January, 1941: "I love swings. It is to the Harlem I go. It is so sympathetic to watch the Negro boys and girls dancing and to watch them eating the long, what is it you call them, frankfurters, no—hot dogs—in the long rolls. It is so sympathetic. I love all kinds of swings."

Symbolic Analysis. An overwhelming compulsion on the part of many modern composers to return the art of music to its source, mathematics, is behind many manifestations of the Avant-Garde. Yet no attempt has been made to apply symbolic logic to the stylistic and technical analysis of modern music. A simple statistical survey can determine the ratio between unresolved dissonances and consonant structures in modern works as compared to those of the past. Such an analysis would indicate in mathematical terms the process of the emancipation of dissonances. The next step would be to tabulate certain characteristics of a given modern school of composition and note their presence in another category, which would help to measure the extent of its influence. The Whole-Tone Scale, for instance, was cultivated particularly by the French Impressionists, but it can be found in works of composers who do not subscribe to Impressionist esthetics. Progressions of second inversions of major triads in parallel formation, moving by sesquitones, are typical of IMPRESSIONISM. But the same formations can be encountered in the music of non-impressionists. Ravel concludes his string quartet with such triadic progression, and so does Gustav Holst in his suite *The Planets*, but they are never found in the works of Hindemith, a paragon of Neo-Classicism, or in those of Prokofiev. The index of tonality is very strong, amidst dissonances, in Stravinsky, but is totally absent in Schoenberg. All these styles, idioms and techniques can be designated by a system of symbols; intervals would be numbered in semitones; upward motion would he symbolized by the plus sign, and downward motion by the minus sign. In this scheme the whole-tone scale would be shown by the formula 6 (2), denoting six degrees of two semitones each, with a plus or minus sign indicating the direction of the movement. A bitonal chord such as formed by C major and F-sharp major, can be indicated by the symbol MT for major triad and the number 6 for the tritone. The synchronization of these triads can be indicated by brackets: (MT) (MT + 6). More importantly, symbolic formulas can describe a style. The music of Hindemith, which lacks the Impressionistic element entirely, can be formulated as 50% NC (for Neo-Classical) + 50% NR (Neo-Romantic), with dissonant content and strength of tonal centers indicated by additional symbols or subscripts.

Stravinsky's early music could be circumscribed by symbols ED for Ethnic Dissonance. Dodecaphonic method could be indicated by the coefficient 12. Other symbols would denominate metric and rhythmic symmetry or asymmetry. In the SYMBOLIC ANALYSIS of an eclectic composer such as Delius, with basic romanticism modified by a considerable influx of impressionistic harmonies and colors, the following formula would be satisfactory, with R for Romanticism, C for Classicism, E for Ethnic quality and I for Impressionism: 40% R + 20% C + 30% E + 10% I. A table of styles, idioms and techniques may be drawn in the manner of the periodical table of elements. Just as vacant spaces in Mendeleyev's schematic representation indicated unknown elements which were actually discovered at a later time, so new techniques of modern composition may well come into being by searching application of SYMBOLIC ANALYSIS.

Synaesthesia. Color associations with certain sounds or tonalities are common subjective phenomena. It is said that Newton chose to divide the visible spectrum into seven distinct colors by analogy with the seven degrees of the diatonic scale. Individual musicians differed greatly in associating a sound with a certain color. The most ambitious attempt to incorporate light into a musical composition was the inclusion of a projected color organ in Scriabin's score *Prometheus*, in which the changes of instrumental coloration were to be accompanied by changing lighting in the concert hall. The most common association between tonality and color is that of C major and whiteness. It is particularly strong for pianists for the obvious reason that the C major scale is played on white keys. However, Scriabin who had a very strong feeling for color associations correlated C major with red. By all conjecture F-sharp major should be associated with black, for it comprises all five different black keys of the piano keyboard, but Scriabin associated it with bright blue and Rimsky-Korsakov with dull green. Any attempt to objectivize color associations is doomed to failure if for no other reason than the arbitrary assignment of a certain frequency to a given note. The height of pitch rose nearly a semitone in the last century, so that the color of C would now be associated with C-sharp in relation to the old standards. Some composers dreamed of a total SYNAESTHESIA in which not only audio-visual but tactile, gustatory and olfactory associations would be brought into a sensual synthesis. Baudelaire said: "Les parfums, les couleurs et les sons se répondent." J. K. Huysmans conjured up an organ of liqueurs. He describes it in Chapter IV of his book *A Rebours:* "Interior symphonies were played as one drank a drop of this or that liqueur creating the sensations in the throat analogous to those that music pours into the ear. In this organ of liqueurs, Curaçao sec corresponded to the clarinet with its somewhat astringent but velvety sound; Kummel suggested the oboe with its nasal quality; menthe and anisette were like the flute, with its combination of sugar and pepper, petulance and sweetness; kirsch recalled the fury of the trumpet; gin and whiskey struck the palate with the strident explosions of cornets and trombones; vodka fulminated with deafening noise of tubas, while raki and mastic hurled thunderclaps of the cymbal and of the bass drum with full force." Huysmans continued by suggesting a string ensemble functioning

in the mouth cavity, with the violin representing vodka, the viola tasting like rum, the cello caressing the gustatory rods with exotic liqueurs, and the doublebass contributing its share of bitters.

Composers in mixed media, anxious to embrace an entire universe of senses, are seeking ultimate SYNAESTHESIA by intuitive approximation, subjective objectivization and mystical adumbrations. Schoenberg was extremely sensitive to the correspondences between light and sound. In the score of his monodrama *Die glückliche Hand* he indicates a "crescendo of illumination" with the dark violet light in one of the two grottos quickly turning to brownish red, blue green and then to orange yellow.

Synchrony. Metric or rhythmic SYNCHRONY is an inclusive term of which POLYMETRY and POLYRHYTHMY are specific instances. Synchronization demands absolutely precise simultaneity of sets of mutually primary numbers of notes within a given unit of time, e.g., 3:2, 5:3, 11:4, etc. Triplets and quintuplets are of course common in free cadenzas since Chopin's time. (There is a consistent use of 4 beats against 3 in Chopin's *Fantaisie-Impromptu.*) But arithmetical precision in synchronizing larger mutually primary numbers of notes cannot be obtained by a human performer no matter how skillful, or by several performers playing different rhythms at once. Such SYNCHRONY becomes feasible with the aid of electronic machines. In 1931, Henry Cowell, working in collaboration with the Russian electric engineer, Leon Theremin, constructed a device, in the form of concentric wheels, which he called Rhythmicon. By manipulating a rheostat with a rudimentary crank, the performer automatically produced precise synchronization of the harmonic series, the number of beats per time unit being equal to the position in the series, so that the fundamental tone had one beat per second, or any other time unit, the second partial note had 2 beats, the third, 3 beats, etc. up to 32 beats produced by the rim of the Rhythmicon. The result was an arithmetically accurate SYNCHRONY score of 32 different time pulses. Since only the mutually non-primary numbers of beats coincided in the process, the collateral effect of rotating the machine was the production of an eerie scale of upper overtones, slower in its initial notes, faster as the position of the overtone was higher. The speed of rotation of the Rhythmicon wheel could be regulated at will, so as to create any desired alteration in tempo or pitch. The initial chord of each main division contains, necessarily so, the entire spectrum of overtones, and their simultaneous impact is of tremendous power, a perfect concord of multitonal consistency in non-tempered intonation.

An entirely novel idea of producing SYNCHRONY with mathematical precision was initiated by Conlon Nancarrow, an American composer living in Mexico City. He worked with a player-piano roll, punching holes at distances proportional to the desired rhythms. He wrote a series of etudes and canons, which could be performed only on the player piano, and which achieved the synchronization of different tempi that could not be attained by living instrumentalists. In his works he was free to select numbers with a fairly low common denominator, in which case there were occasional coincidences between the constituent parts. But the majority of his chosen proportions of the pulse tempi are such that the common denominator was not attained until the end of the piece, if at all. He also wrote a composition in which the relationship of the tempi was 2 to 2, and since the latter is an irrational number (which Nancarrow approximated to 3 decimal points) the contrapuntal parts could, at least theoretically, never meet.

Syncretism. In history and theology, SYNCRETISM denotes the coalescence of incompatible elements or concepts. Etymologically, the word is derived from the union of ancient Greece with Crete. SYNCRETISM is a useful term in music as well, applied to describe the affinity between autogenetic ethnic melodies and cultivated triadic harmonies. A typical example of SYNCRETISM is the arrangement of pentatonic tunes in tonal harmonies, often resulting in the alteration of the intervallic content, as for instance in *Londonderry Air,* a pentatonic melody which has been altered by its arranger by changing the opening interval of a minor third to a semitone in order to provide the leading tone and to convert the modality of the song into a familiar major key. In modern music, SYNCRETISM assumes a polytechnical character through the application of widely incompatible techniques in a single work. An example is Alban Berg's opera *Lulu,* a serial work, which contains also triadic progressions, as well as harmonic figurations and tonal sequences.

Synergy. SYNERGY is defined by the American architect Buckminster Fuller, the discoverer of new principles of spherical stability in designing structures, as the "behavior of a whole system unpredicted by the behavior of any of its separate parts, or the subassemblies of its parts." SYNERGY in music is a technique whereby the last note of a segment of several thematic notes is the first note of the second segment. These segments can be separated, in which case the conjunctive note is repeated. The method is of considerable value in building serial chains, in which the concatenations of adjacent links may be freely dissolved. With this separation of links, the function of the connecting tone becomes ambiguous, serving as the imaginary tonic of the first segment or an imaginary dominant of the second segment. The specification "imaginary" is important because of the esthetic differences created by such a split of the chain.

Temporal Parameters. The conjectural duration of a musical composition is a factor of importance per se, a TEMPORAL PARAMETER which has a decisive bearing on the cohesion and relative stability of the constituent parts of the entire work. The 20th century cultivated a type of Brobdingnagian grandiosity which seemed to equate quantity with quality. Among relatively well-known symphonic works, the *Alpine* by Richard Strauss held the record for absolute length, but it was eclipsed by the *Gothic Symphony* of the English composer Havergal Brian, containing 529 pages of full score. The longest piano work of the century is *Opus Clavicembalisticum* by the English-born Parsi composer Kaikhosru Sorabji, which he played for the first and last time in Glasgow on 1 December 1930. The work consists of 12 movements in the form of a theme with 44 variations and a passacaglia with 81 variations. Characteristically, it is dedicated "to the everlasting glory of those few men blessed and sanctified in the curses and execrations of those many whose praise is eternal damnation."

While some composers kept expanding the duration of their individual works, their contemporaries followed the opposite trend towards extreme brevity of musical utterance. The pioneer of this modern concision was Anton von Webern; one of his pieces written in 1911 for several instruments lasts only 19 seconds. The Hungarian composer György Ligeti wrote a movement consisting of a single quarter-tone rest. The ultimate in the infinitesimally small musical forms was achieved by John Cage in his *0' 00"*, "to be performed in any way by anyone," and first presented in this ambiguous form in Tokyo on 24 October 1962.

Teratological Borborygmus. Modern works of the first quarter of the 20th century systematically increased the amount of massive sonorities as though their intention was to produce an otological ACOUSMA, or some other tonitruant Brobdingnagian TERATOLOGICAL BORBORYGMUS, a huge and monstrous intestinal rumbling issuing from the mouthpieces of brass instruments, shrill flageolets of the piccolos and high harmonics in the strings. It was inevitable that a reaction against this loss of all moderation should have set in among composers of the avant-garde. This reaction was made necessary because of the catastrophe of World War I, when it was no longer feasible to place huge orchestral apparatus at the service of composers of macrosonic works. The era of TERATOLOGICAL BORBORYGMUS seemed to end without a hope of recurrence, but the emergence of electrically amplified popular music of the ROCK 'N' ROLL type generated an electronic circus that promised to eclipse the deafening potentialities of the past.

Third Stream. THIRD STREAM denominates a combined art of popular music and modern techniques of composition. The term itself was used first by Gunther Schuller at his lecture at the Berkshire Music Center in Tanglewood, given on 17 August 1957. If the first stream is classical, and the second stream is Jazz, THIRD STREAM is their Hegelian synthesis, which unites and reconciles the classical thesis with the popular antithesis. Instances of such synthetic usages are found in a number of modern works. The Third Stream flows in *Golliwog's Cake Walk* from Debussy's *Children's Corner,* where bits of syncopated ragtime animate the music. Gershwin's *Rhapsody in Blue* is the most important precursor of THIRD STREAM. In constructive application of THIRD STREAM, ultra-modern techniques, including serialistic procedures, can be amalgamated with popular rhythmic resources.

Tinnitus. A sustained pressure on the auditory nerve causes a condition known as TINNITUS, a persistent tintinnabulation in the cochlea in the inner ear. Schumann experienced it during the final stages of his mental illness; he heard a relentless drone on high A-flat. Smetana suffered a similar aural disturbance, but the note he heard was a high E, and he too eventually went insane. He introduced this high E in the violin part at the end of his string quartet, significantly entitled *From My Life.*

Some clinically sane composers active in the last third of the 20th century, who never suffered from a pathologic TINNITUS, experimentally created an artificial one. Morton Feldman wrote a violin part with an interminable F-sharp calculated to generate a psychic TINNITUS in the outer and inner ears of performers and listeners alike. La Monte Young devised a TINNITUS of a perfect fifth with a notation, "to be held for a long time." Other ways of affecting the listener is a tape recording of a dripping faucet, or a simulacrum of "white noise" prolonged without a prospect of ever ending. Physical action may be added to a TINNITUS, such as measured drops of luke-warm water on the occipital bone of the head held down by clamps, a device helpful to keep in subjection a particularly recalcitrant listener to a piece of avant-garde music. This method was widely practiced to subdue difficult patients in the 18th-century insane asylums.

Tonal Aura. Aura is a medical term used to describe a premonitive sensation before an epileptic seizure. TONAL AURA is a useful metaphor for a coloristic hypertension created in modern technical innovations, such as playing below the bridge of stringed instruments, flutter-tongue on the flute, glissando in the French horn, or a particularly unsettling borborygmus in the bass trombone. Schoenberg's score *Begleitungsmusik zu einer Lichtspielscene*, written for an unrealized abstract motion picture, contains striking instances of Musical Aura, beginning with the sections marked *Threatening Danger* and *Fear* and culminating in the finale, *Catastrophe*.

Tonal Tropism. By computing the frequency of recurrence of each particular note in an an atonal work and finding which of the 12 notes of the chromatic scale has a marked preponderance over the others, it may be asserted that such a frequently recurrent note represents a tonal focus, and that other members of an atonal melody have a TONAL TROPISM towards such a putative tonic. Other aspects of TONAL TROPISM are: the approach to the most frequently occurring tone by a semitone from below, suggesting a leading tone; a preferential placement of a note in the bass; an extended duration of a certain tone; its appearance at the end of a musical fascicle; a simulated cadence or some other kind of privileged position at strategic points, at a strong beat of the measure, etc. In verbal description of a composition containing such features, the term TONAL TROPISM may be used with justification.

Tone Clusters. The technique of TONE CLUSTERS was demonstrated for the first time in public by Henry Cowell at the San Francisco Music Club on 12 March 1912, on the day after his fifteenth birthday. It consists of striking a pandiatonic complex of two octaves on white keys using one's forearm or a panpentatonic set of black keys, as well as groups of 3 or 4 notes struck with the fists or the elbow. Cowell notated the TONE CLUSTERS by a thick black line on a stem for rapid notes or a white-note rod attached to a stem for half-notes. By a remarkable coincidence, the Russian composer Vladimir Rebikov made use of the same device, with an identical notation, at about the same time, in a piano piece entitled *Hymn to Inca*. Still earlier, Charles Ives made use of tone clusters in his *Concord Sonata*, to be played with a wood plank to

depress the keys. Béla Bartók used TONE CLUSTERS to be played by the palm of the hand in his *Second Piano Concerto*, a device that he borrowed expressly from Cowell, by permission.

Tonolalia. Glossolalia is a preternaturally inspired manifestation of spontaneous and simultaneous multilingual intercourse. TONOLALIA is an analogous verbal neologism, in that different instruments and voices disport themselves in a modernistic quodlibet. Particularly effective are antiphonal uses of TONOLALIA in which an improvised interlude is echoed by another instrument or a group of instruments.

Tonotripsical Impact. A cephalotripsical blow crushes the skull. A TONOTRIPSICAL IMPACT is produced by an implosion of sonic matter calculated to stun into submission and psychically incapacitate the listeners to an ultra-modern concert. At a "happening" in New York, the complete Sunday edition of the New York *Times* was thrown on the floor of a chamber music hall, and a power lawn mower was wheeled in and proceeded to chew up the newspaper with cephalotripsical effect. A literal example of Tonocephalotripsical music is the *Concerto for the Hammer and the Skull*, by a French composer who performed it himself by striking different parts of the bones of his head producing different tones, and opening his mouth as a resonator.

Total Music. In ancient Greece music was an inalienable part of drama and literature. In medieval universities, it formed a division of the quadrivium, which included also arithmetic, geometry and astronomy. In modern times, music lost this intimate connection with sciences and liberal arts. It maintained its proud independence until the middle of the 20th century when the AVANT-GARDE brought music out of its isolation into the condominium of MIXED MEDIA. The slogan of TOTAL MUSIC was launched, and the once exclusive art became at various HAPPENINGS an action to be performed on equal terms with conversation, consumption of food, sexual intercourse and sleep. Performing musicians willingly surrendered even their physical separation from the audience, and invited the collaboration of the public on the stage. Formal attire that placed musicians on a higher plane was abandoned. Since nudity became admissible in the theater, musicians followed suit. A topless female violoncellist gained notoriety by exposing her upper half to sophisticated music lovers. TOTAL MUSIC, which embraces all aspects of human behavior, is a counterpart of the French "roman total," a fictional form which combines factual reportage with unbridled fantasy.

Translocations. By altering the intervallic structure of a given musical subject and by translocating its tonal constituents, it is possible to bring any melorhythmic figure into topological congruity with any other. The number of such changes, in which the intervallic unit is a semitone and the rhythmic unit is the smallest note value occurring in the subjects, will indicate the degree of affinity existing between such two subjects. In isometric melodies, the index of rhythmic exchangeability will obviously be zero, so that only the index of the necessary intervallic changes measured by the number of semitones need be considered. In isotonal pairs only the rhythmic changes remain to be computed. The smaller the number of alterations required to transform the melorhythmic outline of one subject into that of another, the greater is the intrinsic similarity between the two. A cursive statistical survey indicates that virtually all principal leading motives in Wagner's music dramas are closely related. Thus we find that it requires but a few changes of intervals and rhythms to transmute the motive of erotic love in *Tristan und Isolde* to that of faith in *Parsifal*. The main motives of most tone poems of Richard Strauss are also topologically similar, no matter what the programmatic design is. On the other hand, the index of interchangeability of dodecaphonic tone rows is extremely high, characteristic of the numerical diversity of dodecaphonic themes. This result should not be surprising, for the works of Wagner and Richard Strauss (to take only these two composers as examples) are based on triadic formations with auxiliary chromatic notes, whereas serial music does not depend on tonality and the intervallic structure in the serial idiom is free of all restrictions. A composer, writing in any modern style, whether serial or non-serial, is in a position of selecting any desired table of approximations of main subjects, in relation to inervallic, melodic, metric and rhythmic parameters, planning in advance such incidental factors as repetition of thematic notes, lipogrammatic omissions, and thus achieving any degree of variety. ALEATORY methods can be limited in advance by numerical parameters, thus imparting to the music an individual physiognomy. Intuition, being an aleatory mental state, may also enter this preliminary outline of substantive parameters. Ernst Krenek has pointed out that the German word *Einfall*, inspiration, connotes in its etymology a falling in as though by chance. The word inspiration itself has aleatory connotations, which is drawing in of breath. Once such a tabulation is set up, the composer can proceed to operate the field of desirable TRANSLOCATIONS, the topology of form, the degree of thematic cohesion or dispersion, etc. Thus the techniques of TRANSLOCATION and its cognate, that of computation of similarities, possess practical validity from both the analytical and synthetical viewpoints. A study of translocations may eventually become an integral branch of musical didactics in perfecting the skill of manipulating and coordinating a multiplicity of technical factors.

Tritone.

The medieval theorists described the TRITONE as "diabolus in musica" and ejected melodic progressions involving the TRITONE from the body of church music as the work of the devil, encompassing as it did the discordant interval of the augmented fourth unfit for a proper tetrachord. In German schools in Bach's time a music student who inadvertently made use of the augmented fourth was punished in class by a rattan blow on the knuckles of the hand.

The earliest suggestion that the use of the TRITONE may not be a *peccatum mortale* was made by Ramos de Pareja in *Musica Practica* published in 1482, but his leniency received little approbation. It was in the natural course of events that the stone rejected by the medieval builders should become the cornerstone of modern music, in all its principal aspects, POLYTONALITY, ATONALITY, DODECAPHONY. The importance of the TRITONE is derived from the very quality that disenfranchised it before, namely its incompatibility with the tonic-dominant complex. Two major triads at the distance of a tritone formed the bitonal "Parisian chord" so popular in the first quarter of the century; complementary, hexachords in major keys with tonics distanced by a tritone redound to the formation of a symmetrical 12-tone row; a series of intervals diminishing by a semitone beginning with a major sixth and ending with its inversion, the minor third, forms a bitonal major chord with tonics at a tritone's distance; a chord containing all eleven different intervals is encompassed by five octaves and a tritone from the lowest to the highest note.

Ultra-Modern Music.

In the early 1920s it became evident to composers using advanced techniques that the term MODERN MUSIC was no longer sufficiently strong to describe the new trends. In search of further emphasis, they chose the term ULTRA-MODERN MUSIC, that is music beyond the limits of traditional modernism. In announcing the publication of *New Music* magazine, Henry Cowell, its founder and editor, declared that only works in the Ultra-Modern idiom would be acceptable for publication. Some decades later, it was realized that ULTRA-MODERN MUSIC, too, began to show unmistakable signs of obsolescence. Still, certain attributes of ULTRA-MODERN MUSIC have retained their validity: dissonant counterpoint, atonal melodic designs, polymetric and polyrhythmic combinations and novel instrumental sonorities.

Unpremeditated Music.

Strictly speaking, no piece of music can be composed with an absolute lack of premeditation. Great improvisers of the past always had a proleptic image, in definite sounds, of what they were going to play. However, the composers of ALEATORY MUSIC in the second half of the 20th century have made serious attempts to create music without a shadow of melody aforethought, or harmony prepense. The absence of premeditation in such cases becomes as essential as in capital crime.

Unwasity.

UNWASITY is an etymological transliteration of the Russian word *nebylitsa*, a fairy tale. This English neoterism may be used as an imaginative figure to describe a modernistic fairy tale, or a palingenetic form so dissimilar from its original that it becomes a literal UNWASITY, something that never was.

Urbanism.

URBANISM is the music of the modern city. It derives its inspiration from urban phenomena, governed by the cult of the machine, and comprising the art of the motion pictures, automobile traffic, newspapers and magazines. Inter-urban machines (locomotives, airplanes) also enter the general concept of URBANISM. Among the most durable works of Urbanist music was Honegger's symphonic movement, *Pacific 231*, glorifying the locomotive. Luigi Russolo wrote a suite for noise instruments, subtitled "a demonstration of automobiles and airplanes," in 1913; it was the first work which contains a reference to airplanes in the title. The American composer Emerson Whithorne composed the earliest piece of airplane music for orchestra, entitled *The Aero-*

plane, in 1926. Sports (prize fights, football, rugby) also attracted composers by their new urbanistic romanticism. "Machine" music received its greatest expansion in the 1920s; its typical products were the opera *Jonny Spielt Auf* by Ernst Krenek, *Machinist Hopkins* by Max Brand, and *Lindbergh's Flight* by Kurt Weill. In Russia musical URBANISM coalesced with the development of PROLETARIAN MUSIC, in which the machine was the hero of the production; an example is *The Iron Foundry* by Alexander Mossolov. *Technical Symphony* by the Hungarian composer Eugen Zador and *Poderes de Caballo*, ballet by Carlos Chávez are examples of urbanist symphonic and ballet music. Prokofiev's ballet *Le Pas d'acier*, representing the life in a Soviet factory, is also urbanist in its subject matter. The ostentatious realism of urbanist music fell out of fashion after World War II, but as late as 1964 Aaron Copland wrote a symphonic suite, entitled *Music for a Great City*, descriptive of the sounds of New York City.

Vectorialism. The modern preoccupation with mathematical factors in music has resulted in the formation of novel concepts and techniques, among them VECTORIALISM, which specifies the angular value of the vector-radius from the center of the concert hall to musical instruments or electronic transmitters, so that each ingredient of a melodic or harmonic pattern receives its identifying index. VECTORIALISM of sonic sources is an aspect of SPATIAL DISTRIBUTION.

Verbalization. Karlheinz Stockhausen was the first to introduce the concept of VERBALIZATION in lieu of musical notation. One of his pieces represents a parabolic curve with the following inscription: "Sound a note. Continue sounding it as long as you please. It is your prerogative." John Cage has elevated VERBALIZATION to the degree of eloquent diction. Earle Brown and Morton Feldman are inventive verbalizationists. La Monte Young tells the player: "Push the piano to the wall. Push it through the wall. Keep pushing." Nam June Paik dictates: "Cut your left arm very slowly with a razor (more than 10 centimeters)." Philip Corner limits himself to a simple command: "One anti-personnel type CBU (Cluster Bomb Unit) will be thrown into the audience."

Verismo. The term VERISMO became popular in the 1890s when it was used to describe the type of operatic naturalism exemplified by Mascagni's opera *Cavalleria Rusticana* and Leoncavallo's *Pagliacci*. The obvious etymological derivation of VERISMO is from vero, true, with reference to the realistic quality of the libretto. Soon the vogue spread into France with the production of *Louise*, a "musical romance" by Gustave Charpentier. In Germany VERISMO assumed satirical and sociological rather than naturalistic forms; in England, Benjamin Britten's *Peter Grimes* may be described as veristic in its subject and execution. VERISMO had no followers in Russia, where nationalistic themes preoccupied the interests of opera composers.

Vigesimosecular Music. A Latinized form of a common word often imparts precision lacking in its vernacular counterpart. The neologism VIGESIMOSECULAR compounds the Latin ordinal numeral 20 with the word for century. By the very ponderosity of its

SESQUIPEDALIAN MACROPOLYSYLLABIFICATION, the term evokes deep erudition and concentrated anfractuosity of elucubrarion. It is therefore reserved for advanced theories and practices of 20th-century music.

Wagneromorphism. An obsessive idolatry of Wagner, common among composers around the turn of the century, a mass genuflection and humicubation before the unquestionable genius of Wagner, produced the phenomenon of WAGNEROMORPHISM. It is characterized by a total absorption of all familiar traits of Wagner's melody and harmony, particularly chromatic suspensions, triadic fanfares, modulatory sequences and dynamic explosions followed by protracted recessions.

Wagneromanticism. This is a telescoped word to describe a style of composition much in vogue late in the 19th century, in which romantic program music is invested in Wagnerian harmonies.

White Sound. By analogy with the complementary colors of the visual spectrum, WHITE SOUND can be described as a sonic continuum containing all available tones within a certain auditory range, or a complex consisting of prescribed intervals, a pandiatonic or panpentatonic TONE CLUSTER, a dodecaphonic or icositetraphonic cumulus, etc. WHITE SOUND can be prismatically analyzed into a linear progression forming a scale of discrete tones.

Whole-Tone Scales. The WHOLE-TONE SCALE gained ephemeral popularity early in the 20th century as an exotic resource cultivated by the IMPRESSIONIST school of composers. If major tonality is masculine, and minor is feminine, then the WHOLE-TONE SCALE is of the neuter gender. It lacks modality; the intervallic progression in the WHOLE-TONE SCALE remains the same in melodic rotation. The perfect fifth and the perfect fourth, the cornerstones of tonality, are absent in the WHOLE-TONE SCALE; there is no dominant or subdominant, and no leading tone. Analytically, the WHOLE-TONE SCALE is atonal. It can also be regarded as the linear function of two mutually exclusive augmented triads. The TRITONE, the "diabolus in musica" of the medieval scholiasts is fundamental to the WHOLE-TONE SCALE, which can be built as the intussusception of three mutually exclusive tritones at the distance of a whole-tone from one another. Because of this association, the WHOLE-TONE SCALE itself became a favorite device of early modernism to portray diabolical forces, menacing apparitions and ineffable mysteries.

The earliest mention of an intentional employment of the WHOLE-TONE SCALE occurs in Mozart's comical divertimento *Die Dorfmusikanten*, subtitled "a musical joke." But Mozart used the WHOLE-TONE SCALE here not to illustrate a malevolent agency, but to ridicule the incompetence of village musicians and their inability to play in tune. The WHOLE-TONE SCALE came into its own as an ominous symbol in Glinka's opera *Ruslan and Ludmila*, in which it is used as a motto of the magician Chernomor. Rossini made use of the WHOLE-TONE SCALE in a song written in 1864 entitled *L'Amour à Pékin*, in which it was described as "gamme chinoise." The possible reason for this reference is that an ancient

Chinese panpipe contains two mutually exclusive WHOLE-TONE SCALES in symmetrically disposed tubes. Liszt was fascinated with the WHOLE-TONE SCALE, and was greatly impressed by the *Fantastic Overture* which the Russian amateur composer Baron Vietinghoff-Scheel sent him, and in which WHOLE-TONE SCALES were profusely employed. In his comment on the work, Liszt described the effect as "terrifying to all long and protruding ears." Liszt himself made use of the WHOLE-TONE SCALE in his symphonic poem *Divina Commedia*, illustrating the Inferno; and he used it systematically in his posthumously published organ pieces.

The problem of harmonizing the WHOLE-TONE SCALE tonally was solved by Glinka in a sequence of modulations. Liszt harmonized a descending WHOLE-TONE SCALE which occurs in the bass, by a series of divergent major triads in root positions. It is doubtful whether Puccini was aware of Liszt's application of this harmony, but he used a precisely identical triadic harmonization of the descending WHOLE-TONE SCALE in his opera *Tosca*, as an introduction to the appearance of the sinister Roman Chief of Police.

The Russian composer Vladimir Rebikov was probably the first to have written an entire composition derived exclusively from the WHOLE-TONE SCALE and its concomitant series of augmented triads, in his *Les Démons s'amusent* for piano; its title suggests that Rebikov was fully aware of the demoniac association of the WHOLE-TONE SCALE. But it was Debussy who elevated the WHOLE-TONE SCALE from a mere exotic device to a poetic and expressive medium. Its Protean capacity for change and adaptability greatly attracted Debussy and his followers, as an alternative variation of a diatonic scale. A very interesting application of the WHOLE-TONE SCALE occurs in *La Mer*; the principal theme of the first movement is in the Aeolian mode; in the third movement it appears isorhythmically as a progression of whole-tones. The first and the last sections of Debussy's *Voiles* for piano consist of whole tones with the middle section providing a contrast in the pentatonic scale.

A whole catalogue can be compiled of incidental usages of the WHOLE-TONE SCALE. Even Tchaikovsky, not usually given to modern inventions, made use of the WHOLE-TONE SCALE in a modulatory sequence illustrating the appearance of the ghost of the old Countess in his opera *The Queen of Spades*. Rimsky-Korsakov filled the second act of his opera *Le Coq d'or* with WHOLE-TONE SCALES and augmented triads to convey the impression of death and devastation of the battlefield. The entrance of Herod in *Salomé* of Richard Strauss is announced by a leading motive composed of whole-tones. Gustav Holst characterized Saturn in his symphonic suite *The Planets* by a series of whole-tone passages to evoke the mystery of Saturn's rings. Apart from astronomy, the whole-tone scale serves pure fantasy. In his symphonic fairy tale *Kikimora* Liadov paints the mischievous sprite in whole-tones. Paul Dukas introduces the hapless amateur magician in his *L'Apprenti Sorcier* in a series of whole-tones. The English composer Edward Maryon assigns the

WHOLE-TONE SCALE to the changelings in his opera *Werewolf*, reserving the diatonic scale for normal children. Another English composer, Havergal Brian, has a chorus singing in WHOLE-TONE SCALES in his opera *The Tigers*, to illustrate the aerial bombardment of London by the Zeppelins during World War I. There are bits of whole-tone figures in Gian Carlo Menotti's children's opera *Help, Help, the Globolinks!* to describe the creatures from outer space. The earthlings in the opera overcome the invading globolinks in victorious C major.

The symbolism of the WHOLE-TONE SCALE is strong in Soviet music. In the opera *Battleship Potemkin* by Oles Tchisko, the Tsarist officers proclaim their authority in whole-tones. In the *Anti-Fascist Symphony* by Boris Mokrousov, the Fascists march in whole-tone steps.

A remarkable demonstration of the perdurability of the whole-tone scale as a symbol of evil is provided by Stravinsky's *Elegy for J. F. K.*, which contains within a 12-tone row two intervallically congruous groups of whole tones, each embanked in a tritone, itself a symbol of deviltry.

With the gradual decline of pictorial and sensorial programmaticism in contemporary music, the WHOLE-TONE SCALE sank into innocuous desuetude. It found its temporary outlet and a stylistic rehabilitation in dodecaphonic usages in the form of two mutually exclusive hexachords. Eventually it joined the subculture of film music. The Nazis advance on the screen to the sound of WHOLE-TONE SCALES in the trombones. Mad scientists hatch their murderous schemes to blow up the world in mighty progressions of whole-tones. Mentally disturbed maidens pluck WHOLE-TONE SCALES on the harp. When Jean Harlow, in her screen biography, climbs up the ladder in the studio before her final collapse, she is accompanied by delicate whole-tone pizzicati. The WHOLE-TONE SCALE is also used, wittily so, in satirical comment on pompous personages in animated cartoons.

Zen. The philosophy of ZEN is at once an infinitely complex and fantastically simple doctrine that accepts irrelevance of response as a legitimate and even elevating part of human discourse. This paradoxical liberating trait exercises a compelling attraction for composers of the Avant-Garde, eager to achieve a total freedom of self-expression combined with the precision of indeterminacy. The verbal and psychological techniques of ZEN can be translated into music through a variety of means which may range from white noise of (theoretically) infinite duration to (theoretically) instantaneous silences. In the field of MIXED MEDIA, in particular, ZEN provides a rich vocabulary of gestures, facial expressions, inarticulate verbalization, ambulatory exercises, performance of physiological functions etc. In the composition of instrumental music, ZEN expands perception of the minutest quantities of sonic material and imparts eloquence to moments of total impassivity, in which the audible tones become interlopers between areas of inaudibility. Imagination and fantasy in the mind of a practitioner of ZEN may subjectively become more expressive than the realization of the creative impulse in written musical symbols.

INDEX

first concert of NBC Symphony, 325–6; conducts first concert of Palestine Symphony Orchestra, 313; conducts La Scala reopening, 172, 378, 400; death, 499; dedicatee of Kodály, *Szimfónia*, 548; last appearance, 476; medal for courage under fire, 135; protests anti-Semitism, 277–8; refuses to conduct *Giovinezza*, 261; reply, 357; South American tour, 351; stamp, 607; televised concert, 416; U.S. debut, 66; U.S. tour with La Scala, 165; Verdi memorial, 443; Works conducted: Barber, *Adagio for Strings*, 334; idem, *First Essay for Orchestra*, 334; Boito, *Nerone*, 192; Castelnuovo-Tedesco, cello concerto, 295; idem, *Variazioni sinfoniche*, 250; idem, violin concerto #2, 357; Chasins, *Three Chinese Pieces*, 260; Giordano, Madame Sans-Gêne, 124; Gnecchi, *Cassandra*, 43; Leoncavallo, *Zazà*, 8; Pizzetti, *Concerto dell'Estate*, 241; idem, *Fra Gherardo*, 233; idem, *Rondo veneziano*, 248; Puccini, *La Fanciulla del West*, 87; idem, *Turandot*, 213; Respighi, *Feste Romane*, 240; idem, *Fontane di Roma*, 139; Siegmeister, *Western Suite*, 395; Sinigaglia, *Danze piemontesi*, 40; Tommasini, *Il Carnevale di Venezia*, 245

Toselli, Enrico, 210

Tosti, Paolo, 82

Total music (term), 1099

Toumela, Tapio. Works: *Puls*, 886

Tournemire, Charles. *Les Dieux sont morts*, 191; #5 *(Dans les Alpes)*, 161; symphony #3 *(Moscou)*, 114

Tovey, Donald Francis. death, 352; Judges Schubert centennial contest, 236; Works: *The Bride of Dionysius*, 270; concerto, cello, 293

Towarnicka, Elzbieta. 1992 ISCM festival, 787

Tower, Joan. *Breakfast Rhythms*, 667, 732; *Concerto*, 775; *Petroushskates*, 702; *Sequoia*, 708; *Third Fanfare for the Uncommon Woman*, 775

Tower, Joan Peabody. Works: concerto, violin, 786; *Last Dance*, orchestra, 892

Toyama, Michigo, 319

T.P.O.K., 765

Tracz, Aleksander. 1992 ISCM festival, 787

Traditional Korean Music Society. 1997 ISCM festival, 860

Trainer, Fraser. 1998 ISCM festival, 872

Traject Chamber Ensemble. 1999 ISCM festival, 887

Trampler, Walter. death, 860

Translocations (term), 1099–100

Trapp, Maria Augusta, 526

Trapp, Max, 198

Trautwein, Friedrich, 1060

Travis, Roy, 627

Travlos, Michael. *Prisma* 739

Tredici, David Del. Works: *Cabbages and Kings*, soprano, chorus, violins, clarinet, and orchestra, 847

Tremain, Ronald, 460

Tremblay, Gilles. *Dzei*, 732; *Fleuves*, 686; *Katadrone: Contreci*, 756; *...le sifflement des vents porteurs de lamour...*, 682; *Oralleluiants*, 704; *Solstices (ou Les Jours et les saisons tournent)*, 653

A Tribute to Paul Bowles, 900

Trif, Flavius. 1999 ISCM festival, 886–87

Trifunović, Vitomir, 712

Trimble, Lester, 620; Works: *Symphony No. 3*, 746

Trimpin. Works: *Music*, extended woodwinds, 807

Trinidad and Tobago. National anthem, 560

Trio Contraste. 1999 ISCM festival, 886, 888

Trio des Lyres. 1994 ISCM festival, 823

Trio Recherche, Freiburg. 1995 ISCM festival, 832

Tritone (term), 1100

Trojahn, Manfred. *Trakl-Fragmente*, 779; Works: symphony, tenor and orchestra, 793

Trouhanova, Natacha, 100

Troyanos, Tatiana. death, 804

Trudić, Božidar, 499

Truman, Harry S, 335, 441, 457

Truman, Margaret, 441

Trümpy, Balz. *Kanons, Motetten un Hymnen*, 752

Trunk, Richard, 283

Tsang, Richard. Works: *Echo-Mime*, clarinets, 823; *Images of bells*, 809; *Little Chamber Music*, 886; *Silk Music*, 741; *Three Meditations*, 757

Tseng Shing-kewi. *Reincarnation*, 758

Tsepkolenko, Karmella. Works: *Parallels*, 886

Tsoupaki, Calliope. Works: *Compulsive Caress*, guitar, 829

Tsuji, Mifune. 1998 Festival Nieuwe Muziek, 874

Tuba, centennial of, 300

Tubi, Angelo. *Benvenuto Cellini*, 46

Tubin, Eduard, 649

Tucker, Richard. Death, 673

Tudor, David. Works: *Mesa*, 600; *Rainforest*, 618; Works played or unplayed: Brown, Earle, *25 Pages*, 476; Cage, concert, 513; idem, *4'33*,*" 461, 1093; idem, *Music for Amplified Toy Pianos*, 528; idem, *Water Music*, 457; Ichiyanagi, 570

Tudor, David Eugene. death, 847; Works: *Soundings: Ocean Diary*, 817

Tull, Fisher, 661

Tully, Alice, 793; death, 812

Tuong, N'Guyen Van, 566

Turchi, Guido, 650; Works: concerto, strings, 421; *Il Buon soldato Svejk*, 554; *Piccolo Concerto Notturno*, 451

Turcotte, Roxanne. Works: *MiniSérie*, 833

Turel, Bor. Works: *Four Seasons*, two-channel tape, 848

Turetsky, Bertram. *That Dada-Strain*, 750

Turina, Joaquín. performed by Sociedad Nacional de Música, 125, 425; Works: *Canto a Sevilla*, 222; *El Castillo de Almodovar*, 286; *Evangelio*, 126; *Jardín de Oriente*, 182; *Margot*, 123; *Por el Río Guadalquivir*, 308; *La Procesión del Rocío*, 109; *Rapsodia sinfónica*, 277; *Rítmos*, 236; *Sinfonia sevillana*, 163, 582; trio, piano and strings, 226

Turnage, Mark-Anthony. Works: *Barries Deviant Fantasy*, string quartet, 836; *The Country of the Blind*, chamber opera, 856–57; *A Deviant Fantasy*, clarinets, 807; *Four-Horned Fandango*, horns and orchestra, 857; *Greek*, 755; *Her Anxiety*, soprano and ensemble, 793; *The Silver*

Tassie, opera, 892; *Still Sleeping*, 871; *Twice Through the Heart*, mezzo-soprano, 856–57; *Your Rockaby*, soprano saxophone and orchestra, 814

Turner, Godfrey, 372, 423

Turner, Robert Comri. Works: *4 Last Songs*, mezzo-soprano, violin, and piano, 839; *Diverti-memento*, orchestra, 890; *Group of 7*, reciter, viola, and orchestra, 795

Turski, Zbigniew, 497, 623

Tutankhamen, 341

Tutev, Georgi, 623; Works: *Meditations*, chamber ensemble, 847

Tuthill, Burnet, 383

Tuxen-Bang, Carlos, 597

Tveitt, Geirr, 599

Twardowski, Romuald. Works: concerto breve, strings, 882; *Plejady*, violin and piano, 807; *Symfonie dzwonów I - III*, piano, 795

Twelve-tone music. *See* dodecaphonic music

Twining, Toby. Works: *Eleanor Rigby*, toy piano, 881; *Nightmare Rag*, piano and toy piano, 881; *Satie Blues*, piano and toy piano, 881

Twist forbidden, 565

2 Live Crew. obscenity controversy, 768–69; Works: *As Nasty as They Wanna Be* (album), 768–69

Tyranny, Blue Gene. Works: *The Decertified Highway of Dreams*, 900

Tzara, Tristan, 132, 154

Ugarte, Floro, 163

Uhl, Alfred. *Concerto à ballo*, 612; death, 791; *Der mysteriöse Herr X*, 599

Uitti, Frances Marie. 1998 Festival Nieuwe Muziek, 874

UK Conservatories Enxemble. 1998 ISCM festival, 870

Ullman, Viktor, 677; Works: *Der Sturz des Antichrist* (opera), 827; *Die Weise von Liebe und Tod des Cornets Christoph Rilke*, speaker and orchestra, 831; *Don Quizote tanzt Fandango* (overture), 837; *Five Variations and a Double Fugue on a Theme by Schoenberg*, 242; sonata, piano, 360; string quartet, 331; *Symphony*, 765

Ulrich, Boris, 702

Ulsen, Toon van. 1997 ISCM festival, 860

Ultra-modern music (term), 1100

Underwood, James, 714; Works: *Grendel's Mother*, orchestra, 807

Ung, Chinary. *Spiral*, 757; Works: *Grand Spiral ("Desert Flowers Bloom")*, orchestra, 791; *Inner Voices*, large orchestra, 833–34

Ungureanu, Marius. 2000 ISCM festival, 895

Ungvary, Tamas. Works: *GRATTIS mit Epilog*, 834

Union, musicians, first, 171

Union of Soviet Composers, 237, 423; Charter, 954–57

U.S. House of Representatives. Committee on Un-American Activities, 416, 961–66

U.S. Senate. Debate on folk music, 977–80

Universal edition, 11

Unpremeditated music (term), 1100

Unwasity (term), 1100